THE ● NEW
COMPACT
KEY
REFERENCE
CONCORDANCE

THE ⊕ NEW

COMPACT

KEY REFERENCE CONCORDANCE

A Time-Saving Guide to
KEY SCRIPTURE
REFERENCES
for Personal Bible Study

RONALD F. YOUNGBLOOD

THOMAS NELSON PUBLISHERS
Nashville

Published in Nashville, Tennessee, by Thomas Nelson, Inc., Publishers, and distributed in Canada by Lawson Falle, Ltd., Cambridge, Ontario.

Printed in the United States of America

Library of Congress Cataloging-in-Publication Data

Youngblood, Ronald F.
   New compact key reference concordance / Ronald F. Youngblood.
   ISBN 0-8407-6726-9
   1. Bible—Concordances, English—New King James. I. Title.
BS425.Y75 1992
220.5′2033—dc20   92–9182
                                       CIP

1 2 3 4 5 6 7 8 — 97 96 95 94 93 92

PREFACE

A biblical concordance is an alphabetical index of the words found in one or more versions of the Bible, a text-finder that enables the reader to locate a particular verse by looking up a key word contained in it. An *exhaustive* concordance lists every occurrence of every word in every verse, including "and," "the," and the like; a *complete* concordance lists every occurrence of every significant word in every verse, excluding what the compiler considers to be nonessential words; a *compact* concordance restricts itself to the most important occurrences of every significant word in the most commonly read verses where each appears.

The *New Compact Key Reference Concordance* here introduced has the following features:

• Based on the *New King James Version,* it will also prove helpful to users of other versions in the Authorized Version tradition (for example *King James Version, American Standard Version, Revised Standard Version*).

• Accompanying each word are the most important Scripture references where it is found, as well as the surrounding context in the verse where the word is used.

• The verses under each entry are listed in canonical order (from Genesis to Revelation).

• Care has been taken to include most New Testament quotations of Old Testament verses by repeating the identical surrounding context in each reference.

• Choice of references to be included has focused on key doctrines, familiar verses, and passages that the average Bible reader is most likely to want to look up.

• Crucial verses in the careers of important Bible characters have been listed, making it possible to follow the basic biographical details of that person's life by checking the verses in sequence.

• A dagger (†) following an entry heading means that every occurrence of that entry is listed.

The *New Compact Key Reference Concordance* goes forth to its readers with the sincere prayers of the compiler and publisher that it will prove to be a comprehensive and effective tool for individual Bible study, group discussion, and lesson and sermon preparation.

RONALD YOUNGBLOOD

A

AARON (see AARONITES, AARON'S)
Ex	4:14	Is not A the Levite your
Ex	4:27	And the LORD said to A, "Go
Ex	4:28	So Moses told A all the words
Ex	5: 1	A went in and told Pharaoh,
Ex	5: 4	Moses and A, why do you take
Ex	6:13	the LORD spoke to Moses and A
Ex	6:20	and she bore him A and Moses
Ex	6:23	A took to himself Elisheba,
Ex	6:26	These are the same A and Moses
Ex	7: 1	A your brother shall be your
Ex	7: 2	A your brother shall speak to
Ex	7: 7	A eighty-three years old when
Ex	7:10	A cast down his rod before
Ex	7:20	A did so, just as the LORD
Ex	8: 5	Say to A, 'Stretch out your
Ex	11:10	and A did all these wonders
Ex	12:31	Moses and A by night, and said,
Ex	15:20	prophetess, the sister of A
Ex	16:33	And Moses said to A, "Take a
Ex	16:34	so A laid it up before the
Ex	17:10	And Moses, A, and Hur went up
Ex	17:12	And A and Hur supported His
Ex	18:12	A came with all the elders of
Ex	19:24	come up, you and A with you
Ex	24: 1	Come up to the LORD, you and A
Ex	28: 1	Now take A your brother, and
Ex	28: 2	garments for A your brother
Ex	28:12	So A shall bear their names
Ex	28:38	that A may bear the iniquity
Ex	29: 4	And A and his sons you shall
Ex	29: 5	garments, put the tunic on A
Ex	29: 9	So you shall consecrate A
Ex	29:20	the tip of the right ear of A
Ex	29:21	oil, and sprinkle it on A and
Ex	29:32	Then A and his sons shall eat
Ex	29:35	Thus you shall do to A and his
Ex	29:44	I will also consecrate both A
Ex	30: 8	when A lights the lamps at
Ex	30:10	A shall make atonement upon
Ex	30:19	for A and his sons shall wash
Ex	30:30	And you shall anoint A and his
Ex	32: 1	people gathered together to A
Ex	32: 2	And A said to them,
Ex	32: 3	ears, and brought them to A
Ex	32: 5	So when A saw it, he built an
Ex	32:21	And Moses said to A, "What
Ex	32:25	were unrestrained (for A had
Ex	32:35	with the calf which A made
Ex	40:12	Then you shall bring A and his
Ex	40:31	and Moses, A, and his sons
Lev	1: 7	The sons of A the priest
Lev	6:16	And the remainder of it A
Lev	6:18	the children of A may eat it
Lev	7:35	the consecrated portion for A
Lev	8: 2	Take A and his sons with him,
Lev	8:14	Then A and his sons laid their
Lev	8:30	and he consecrated A, his
Lev	9:21	the right thigh A waved as a
Lev	9:23	A went into the tabernacle of
Lev	10: 1	Nadab and Abihu, the sons of A
Lev	16: 1	death of the two sons of A
Lev	16: 6	A shall offer the bull as a
Lev	16: 8	Then A shall cast lots for
Lev	16: 9	A shall bring the goat on
Lev	16:11	A shall bring the bull of the
Lev	16:21	A shall lay both his hands on
Lev	16:23	Then A shall come into the
Lev	24: 3	A shall be in charge of it
Num	1: 3	A shall number them by their
Num	3: 1	these are the records of A
Num	3: 9	shall give the Levites to A
Num	3:32	And Eleazar the son of A the
Num	3:48	of them is redeemed, to A
Num	3:51	their redemption money to A
Num	4:27	A and his sons shall assign
Num	8:11	A shall offer the Levites
Num	8:13	stand the Levites before A
Num	8:19	the Levites as a gift to A
Num	8:21	A made atonement for them to
Num	12: 1	A spoke against Moses because
Num	12: 5	the tabernacle, and called A
Num	12:10	Then A turned toward Miriam,
Num	12:11	So A said to Moses, "Oh, my
Num	13:26	and came back to Moses and A
Num	14: 2	complained against Moses and A
Num	14: 5	A fell on their faces before
Num	16:40	who is not a descendant of A
Num	17: 6	the rod of A was among their
Num	20:23	A in Mount Hor by the border
Num	20:24	A shall be gathered to his
Num	20:25	Take A and Eleazar his son, and
Num	20:26	strip A of his garments and
Num	20:28	A died there on the top of
Num	20:29	mourned for A thirty days
Num	26:59	and to Amram she bore A and
Num	26:60	To A were born Nadab and
Num	33:39	A was one hundred and
Deut	9:20	LORD was very angry with A
Deut	9:20	so I prayed for A also at the
Josh	21: 4	the children of A the priest
Josh	24:33	And Eleazar the son of A died
Judg	20:28	son of Eleazar, the son of A
1Sa	12: 6	who raised up Moses and A
1Ch	6:50	Now these are the sons of A
Ezra	7: 5	the son of the chief priest
Ps	77:20	By the hand of Moses and A
Ps	99: 6	A were among His priests, And
Ps	105:26	And A whom He had chosen
Ps	106:16	And A the saint of the LORD,
Ps	115:10	O house of A, trust in the
Ps	133: 2	on the beard, The beard of A
Ps	135:19	Bless the LORD, O house of A
Mic	6: 4	and I sent before you Moses, A
Luke	1: 5	was of the daughters of A
Acts	7:40	saying to A, 'Make us gods to
Heb	5: 4	called by God, just as A was
Heb	7:11	according to the order of A

AARONITES† (see AARON)
1Ch	12:27	Jehoiada, the leader of the A
1Ch	27:17	over the A, Zadok

AARON'S (see AARON)
Ex	6:25	A son, took for himself one
Ex	7:12	But A rod swallowed up their
Ex	28:30	they shall be over A heart
Ex	28:38	So it shall be on A forehead
Lev	1: 5	A sons, shall bring the blood
Num	17: 3	you shall write A name on the
Heb	9: 4	A rod that budded, and the

ABADDON†
Rev	9:11	whose name in Hebrew is A

ABANAH†
2Ki	5:12	Are not the A and the Pharpar,

ABANDON† (see ABANDONED)
Prov	19: 7	with words, yet they a him

ABANDONED† (see ABANDON)
Lam	2: 7	altar, He has a His sanctuary

ABARIM
Num	27:12	Go up into this Mount A, and

ABASE (see ABASED, ABASING, HUMBLE, PUT DOWN)

ABASED† (*see* ABASE, BROUGHT LOW, HUMBLED)
Phil   4:12 I know how to be **a**, and I know

ABASHED†
Mic   3: 7 be ashamed, and the diviners **a**

ABASING (*see* ABASE, HUMBLING)

ABATED (*see* DIMINISHED, RECEDED, SUBSIDED)

ABBA†
Mark 14:36 **A**, Father, all things are
Rom   8:15 whom we cry out, "**A**, Father"
Gal   4: 6 crying out, "**A**, Father

ABDON
Judg 12:13 him, **A** the son of Hillel the

ABED-NEGO
Dan   1: 7 and to Azariah, **A**
Dan 2:49 **A** over the affairs of the
Dan 3:12 Shadrach, Meshach, and **A**

ABEL
Gen   4: 2 this time his brother **A**
Gen   4: 4 **A** also brought of the
Gen   4: 8 rose against **A** his brother
Gen   4: 9 Where is **A** your brother
Gen   4:25 seed for me instead of **A**,
2Sa 20:14 all the tribes of Israel to **A**
Matt 23:35 **A** to the blood of Zechariah
Luke 11:51 from the blood of **A** to the
Heb 11: 4 By faith **A** offered to God a
Heb 12:24 better things than that of **A**

ABEL BETH MAACHAH†
1Ki 15:20 He attacked Ijon, Dan, **A**, and
2Ki 15:29 Assyria came and took Ijon, **A**

ABEL MIZRAIM† (*see* MIZRAIM)
Gen 50:11 its name was called **A**, which

ABHOR (*see* ABHORRED, ABHORRENCE, ABHORRENT, ABHORS)
Lev 20:23 things, and therefore I **a** them
Lev 26:11 and My soul shall not **a** you
Deut 23: 7 You shall not **a** an Edomite
Job   9:31 and my own clothes with **a** me
Job 19:19 All my close friends **a** me
Job 42: 6 Therefore I **a** myself, and
Ps   36: 4 He does not **a** evil
Ps 119:163 **a** lying, But I love Your law
Jer 14:21 Do not **a** us, for Your name's
Mic   3: 9 who **a** justice and pervert all
Rom 2:22 You who **a** idols, do you rob
Rom 12: 9 **A** what is evil

ABHORRED (*see* ABHOR)
Lev 26:43 their soul **a** My statutes
1Sa   2:17 for men **a** the offering of the
1Ki 11:25 he **a** Israel, and reigned over
Ps 22:24 nor **a** the affliction of the
Ps 107:18 Their soul **a** all manner of
Prov 22:14 he who is **a** by the LORD will

ABHORRENCE† (*see* ABHOR)
Is   66:24 shall be an **a** to all flesh

ABHORRENT† (*see* ABHOR)
Ex   5:21 us **a** in the sight of Pharaoh

ABHORS† (*see* ABHOR)
Lev 26:15 if your soul **a** My judgments
Job 33:20 So that his life **a** bread, and
Ps   5: 6 The LORD **a** the bloodthirsty
Is   49: 7 to Him whom the nation **a**

ABIATHAR
1Sa 22:20 the son of Ahitub, named **A**
1Sa 30: 7 David said to **A** the priest
2Sa 20:25 Zadok and **A** were the priests
1Ki   1: 7 with **A** the priest, and they

1Ki   2:27 So Solomon removed **A** from
Mark 2:26 the days of **A** the high priest

ABIB (*see* NISAN)
Ex   13: 4 are going out, in the month **A**
Deut 16: 1 Observe the month of **A**, and

ABIDE (*see* ABIDES, ABIDING)
Deut 12:11 chooses to make His name **a**
Deut 14:23 chooses to make His name **a**
Deut 16: 6 chooses to make His name **a**
Deut 16:11 chooses to make His name **a**
Deut 26: 2 chooses to make His name **a**
Job 24:13 its ways nor **a** in its paths
Ps 15: 1 who may **a** in Your tabernacle
Ps 61: 7 He shall **a** before God forever
Ps 91: 1 of the Most High Shall **a**
Prov 15:31 of life will **a** among the wise
Hos   3: 4 children of Israel shall **a**
Joel 3:20 But Judah shall **a** forever
Mic   5: 4 and they shall **a**, for now He
Luke 24:29 **A** with us, for it is toward
John 8:31 If you **a** in My word, you are
John 12:46 Me should not **a** in darkness
John 14:16 that He may **a** with you
John 15: 4 **A** in Me, and I in you
1Co 13:13 And now **a** faith, hope, love,
1Jn   2:24 Therefore let that **a** in you
1Jn   3:17 does the love of God **a** in him
1Jn   4:13 this we know that we **a** in Him
2Jn   9 does not **a** in the doctrine of

ABIDES (*see* ABIDE)
Ps 55:19 Even He who **a** from of old
Ps 119:90 the earth, and it **a**
Ps 125: 1 be moved, but **a** forever
John 3:36 but the wrath of God **a** on him
John 6:56 and drinks My blood **a** in Me
1Pe   1:23 God which lives and **a** forever,
1Jn   2: 6 He who says he **a** in Him ought
1Jn   3: 6 Whoever **a** in Him does not sin
1Jn   4:12 God in us, and His love has
2Jn   2 of the truth which **a** in us
2Jn   9 He who **a** in the doctrine of

ABIDING (*see* ABIDE)
John 5:38 do not have His word **a** in you

ABIEZER (*see* ABIEZRITE)
Judg 8: 2 better than the vintage of **A**

ABIEZRITE† (*see* ABIEZER, ABIEZRITES)
Judg 6:11 which belonged to Joash the **A**

ABIEZRITES (*see* ABIEZRITE)
Judg 6:24 is still in Ophrah of the **A**

ABIGAIL
1Sa 25: 3 and the name of his wife **A**
1Sa 25:39 David sent and proposed to **A**
2Sa 17:25 who had gone in to **A** the

ABIHAIL
Esth 2:15 of **A** the uncle of Mordecai
Esth 9:29 Esther, the daughter of **A**

ABIHU
Ex   6:23 and she bore him Nadab, **A**,
Ex 24: 1 you and Aaron, Nadab and **A**
Num 26:60 Aaron were born Nadab and **A**

ABIJAH (*see* ABIJAM)
1Sa   8: 2 and the name of his second, **A**
1Ki 14: 1 At that time **A** the son of
1Ch 2:24 Hezron's wife **A** bore him
1Ch 3:10 **A** was his son, Asa his son,
2Ch 11:22 Rehoboam appointed **A** the son
2Ch 12:16 Then **A** his son reigned in his
2Ch 13: 1 **A** became king over Judah
2Ch 13:22 Now the rest of the acts of **A**

2Ch   14: 1 So **A** rested with his fathers,
Matt   1: 7 Rehoboam, Rehoboam begot **A**
Luke   1: 5 of the division of **A**

ABIJAM (*see* ABIJAH)
1Ki   14:31 Then **A** his son reigned in his
1Ki   15: 1 **A** became king over Judah
1Ki   15: 7 Now the rest of the acts of **A**

ABILENE†
Luke   3: 1 and Lysanias tetrarch of **A**

ABILITY† (*see* ABLE)
Ex   35:34 in his heart the **a** to teach
Lev   27: 8 to the **a** of him who vowed
1Ch   26: 6 they were men of great **a**
Ezra   2:69 According to their **a**, they
Neh   5: 8 According to our **a** we have
Dan   1: 4 who had **a** to serve in the
Matt 25:15 each according to his own **a**
Acts 11:29 each according to his **a**,
2Co   8: 3 that according to their **a**
2Co   8: 3 yes, and beyond their **a**, they
1Pe   4:11 with the **a** which God supplies

ABIMELECH (*see* AHIMELECH)
Gen   20: 2 **A** king of Gerar sent and took
Gen   20: 3 But God came to **A** in a dream
Gen   21:22 to pass at that time that **A**
Gen   26: 1 Isaac went to **A** king of the
Judg   8:31 a son, whose name he called **A**
Judg   9: 1 **A** the son of Jerubbaal went
Judg   9: 6 and made **A** king beside the
Judg   9:55 of Israel saw that **A** was dead
2Sa   11:21 Who struck **A** the son of
1Ch   18:16 **A** the son of Abiathar were

ABINADAB
1Sa   7: 1 the house of **A** on the hill
1Sa   16: 8 So Jesse called **A**, and made
1Sa   17:13 the firstborn, next to him **A**
1Sa   31: 2 killed Jonathan, **A**, and
2Sa   6: 3 it out of the house of **A**,
1Ch   2:13 **A** the second, Shimea the

ABINOAM
Judg   4: 6 of **A** from Kedesh in Naphtali
Judg   5: 1 the son of **A** sang on that day

ABIRAM
Num   16: 1 **A** the sons of Eliab, and On
Num   16:24 tents of Korah, Dathan, and **A**
1Ki   16:34 with **A** his firstborn, and with
Ps   106:17 And covered the faction of **A**

ABISHAG
1Ki   1: 3 found **A** the Shunammite, and

ABISHAI
1Sa   26: 6 and to **A** the son of Zeruiah,
2Sa   2:18 Joab and **A** and Asahel
2Sa   3:30 **A** his brother killed Abner,
2Sa   10:10 the command of **A** his brother
2Sa   16: 9 Then **A** the son of Zeruiah
2Sa   20: 6 And David said to **A**, "Now
2Sa   23:18 Now **A** the brother of Joab,

ABISHALOM† (*see* ABSALOM)
1Ki   15: 2 the granddaughter of **A**
1Ki   15:10 the granddaughter of **A**

ABIUD
Matt   1:13 Zerubbabel begot **A**

ABLE (*see* ABILITY)
Gen   13: 6 was not **a** to support them
Gen   15: 5 if you are **a** to number them
Gen   33:14 are **a** to endure, until I come
Ex   10: 5 will be **a** to see the earth
Ex   18:18 you are not **a** to perform it
Ex   18:21 from all the people **a** men

Ex   40:35 Moses was not **a** to enter the
Lev   12: 8 if she is not **a** to bring a
Lev   14:22 such as he is **a** to afford
Lev   25:26 becomes **a** to redeem it,
Num   1: 3 all who are **a** to go to war in
Num   6:21 else his hand is **a** to provide
Num   11:14 I am not **a** to bear all these
Num   13:30 we are well **a** to overcome it
Num   13:31 We are not **a** to go up against
Num   22: 6 I shall be **a** to defeat them
Num   22:37 Am I not **a** to honor you
Num   26: 2 all who are **a** to go to war in
Deut   1: 9 I alone am not **a** to bear you
Deut 16:17 man shall give as he is **a**
Josh   1: 5 No man shall be **a** to stand
Josh 14:12 I shall be **a** to drive them
Josh 23: 9 no one has been **a** to stand
1Sa   17: 9 If he is **a** to fight with me
1Ki   3: 9 For who is **a** to judge this
2Ki   3:21 all who were **a** to bear arms
2Ch   2: 6 But who is **a** to build Him a
2Ch   20: 6 no one is **a** to withstand You
Ezra 10:13 we are not **a** to stand outside
Neh   4:10 are not **a** to build the wall
Job   41:10 Who then is **a** to stand
Ps   21:11 they are not **a** to perform
Ps   40:12 so that I am not **a** to look up
Prov 27: 4 but who is **a** to stand before
Eccl   8:17 he will not be **a** to find it
Is   36: 8 if you are **a** on your part to
Jer   10:10 the nations will not be **a** to
Jer   49:10 not be **a** to hide himself
Lam   1:14 whom I am not **a** to withstand
Ezek   7:19 their gold will not be **a** to
Ezek 33:12 be **a** to live because of his
Dan   2:26 Are you **a** to make known to me
Dan   3:17 is **a** to deliver us from the
Dan   4:18 not **a** to make known to me the
Amos   7:10 The land is not **a** to bear all
Zeph   1:18 nor their gold shall be **a** to
Matt   3: 9 is **a** to raise up children to
Matt   9:28 that I am **a** to do this
Matt 10:28 who is **a** to destroy both soul
Matt 18:25 But as he was not **a** to pay
Matt 19:12 He who is **a** to accept it, let
Matt 20:22 Are you **a** to drink the cup
Matt 22:46 no one was **a** to answer Him **a**
Matt 26:61 I am **a** to destroy the temple
Luke   1:20 not **a** to speak until the day
Luke 12:26 are not **a** to do the least
Luke 13:24 to enter and will not be **a**
Luke 14:29 is not **a** to finish it, all
Luke 21:15 be **a** to contradict or resist
John   8:43 Because you are not **a** to
John 10:29 no one is **a** to snatch them
Acts   6:10 they were not **a** to resist the
Acts 15:10 fathers nor we were **a** to bear
Acts 20:32 which is **a** to build you up and
Rom   4:21 He was also **a** to perform
Rom   8:39 shall be **a** to separate us
Rom   11:23 for God is **a** to graft them in
Rom   14: 4 for God is **a** to make him
Rom   16:25 Now to Him who is **a** to
1Co   3: 2 you were not **a** to receive it
1Co   10:13 tempted beyond what you are **a**
2Co   1: 4 that we may be **a** to comfort
2Co   9: 8 God is **a** to make all grace
Eph   3:18 may be **a** to comprehend with
Eph   3:20 who is **a** to do exceedingly
Eph   6:11 that you may be **a** to stand
1Ti   3: 2 hospitable, **a** to teach
2Ti   1:12 He is **a** to keep what I have
2Ti   2: 2 be **a** to teach others also
2Ti   2:24 to all, **a** to teach, patient,
2Ti   3: 7 and never **a** to come to the

2Ti 3:15 which are **a** to make you wise
Tit 1: 9 been taught, that he may be **a**
Heb 2:18 He is **a** to aid those who are
Heb 5: 7 tears to Him who was **a** to
Heb 7:25 Therefore He is also **a** to
Heb 11:19 God was **a** to raise him up
Jas 1:21 which is **a** to save your souls
Jas 3: 2 **a** also to bridle the whole
Jas 4:12 who is **a** to save and to
Jude 24 Now to Him who is **a** to keep
Rev 5: 3 was **a** to open the scroll, or
Rev 6:17 come, and who is **a** to stand
Rev 13: 4 Who is **a** to make war with him

ABNER
1Sa 14:50 his army was **A** the son of Ner
1Sa 17:55 the Philistine, he said to **A**
1Sa 26: 5 lay, and **A** the son of Ner, the
2Sa 2:23 Therefore **A** struck him in the
2Sa 3:30 Abishai his brother killed **A**

ABOARD†
Acts 21: 2 over to Phoenicia, we went **a**

ABOLISH† (*see* ABOLISHED)
Is 2:18 the idols He shall utterly **a**

ABOLISHED† (*see* ABOLISH)
Is 51: 6 righteousness will not be **a**
Ezek 6: 6 down, and your works may be **a**
Eph 2:15 having **a** in His flesh the
2Ti 1:10 Jesus Christ, who has **a** death

ABOMINABLE
Lev 7:21 or any **a** unclean thing, and
Lev 11:43 **a** with any creeping thing
Job 15:16 how much less man, who is **a**
Ps 14: 1 They have done **a** works,
Is 65: 4 the broth of **a** things is in
Jer 16:18 their detestable and **a** idols
Jer 44: 4 do not do this **a** thing that I
Ezek 4:14 nor has **a** flesh ever come
Ezek 8:10 **a** beasts, and all the idols of
Tit 1:16 works they deny Him, being **a**
1Pe 4: 3 parties, and **a** idolatries
Rev 21: 8 the cowardly, unbelieving, **a**

ABOMINATION (*see* ABOMINATIONS)
Gen 43:32 is an **a** to the Egyptians
Gen 46:34 is an **a** to the Egyptians
Lev 7:18 it shall be an **a**
Lev 19: 7 on the third day, it is an **a**
Lev 20:13 of them have committed an **a**
1Sa 13: 4 an **a** to the Philistines
1Ki 11: 5 Milcom the **a** of the Ammonites
Ps 88: 8 You have made me an **a** to them
Prov 3:32 person is an **a** to the LORD
Prov 6:16 yes, seven are an **a** to Him
Prov 8: 7 wickedness is an **a** to my lips
Prov 11: 1 Dishonest scales are an **a** to the LORD
Prov 11:20 heart are an **a** to the LORD
Prov 12:22 lips are an **a** to the LORD
Prov 13:19 but it is an **a** to fools to
Prov 15: 8 wicked is an **a** to the LORD
Prov 16:12 It is an **a** for kings to
Prov 20:23 weights are an **a** to the LORD
Prov 28: 9 Even his prayer is an **a**
Is 1:13 incense is an **a** to Me
Is 41:24 he who chooses you is an **a**
Is 66:17 eating swine's flesh and the **a**
Jer 2: 7 land and made My heritage an **a**
Jer 6:15 when they had committed **a**
Jer 8:12 when they had committed **a**
Ezek 16:50 and committed **a** before Me
Dan 11:31 there the **a** of desolation
Dan 12:11 the **a** of desolation is set up
Hos 9:10 They became an **a** like the
Mic 6:10 short measure that is an **a**

Mal 2:11 an **a** has been committed in
Matt 24:15 the **a** of desolation
Mark 13:14 the **a** of desolation
Luke 16:15 is an **a** in the sight of God
Rev 21:27 or causes an **a** or a lie, but

ABOMINATIONS (*see* ABOMINATION)
Lev 18:26 not commit any of these **a**
Deut 18: 9 follow the **a** of those nations
Deut 32:16 with **a** they provoked Him to
2Ki 16: 3 according to the **a** of the
2Ki 21: 2 according to the **a** of the
2Ki 21:11 of Judah has done these **a** (he
2Ki 23:24 all the **a** that were seen in
Ezra 9: 1 to the **a** of the Canaanites
Prov 26:25 are seven **a** in his heart
Jer 4: 1 away your **a** out of My sight
Jer 7:10 delivered to do all these **a**
Jer 13:27 your **a** on the hills in the
Ezek 5: 9 again, because of all your **a**
Ezek 7: 3 will repay you for all your **a**
Ezek 7: 8 will repay you for all your **a**
Ezek 7:20 from it the images of their **a**
Ezek 8: 6 the great **a** that the house of
Ezek 11:21 detestable things and their **a**
Ezek 18:13 If he has done any of these **a**
Ezek 18:24 **a** that the wicked man does
Ezek 20: 4 them the **a** of their fathers
Ezek 20:30 harlotry according to their **a**
Ezek 22: 2 Yes, show her all her **a**
Ezek 36:31 for your iniquities and your **a**
Dan 9:27 on the wing of **a** shall be one
Zech 9: 7 the **a** from between his teeth
Rev 17: 4 hand a golden cup full of **a**
Rev 17: 5 THE **A** OF THE EARTH

ABOUND (*see* ABOUNDED, ABOUNDING, ABOUNDS)
Gen 1:20 Let the waters **a** with an
Gen 8:17 that they may **a** on the earth
Deut 30: 9 you **a** in all the work of your
Matt 24:12 And because lawlessness will **a**
Rom 5:20 that the offense might **a**
Rom 6: 1 in sin that grace may **a**
Rom 15:13 that you may **a** in hope by the
2Co 1: 5 sufferings of Christ **a** in us
2Co 4:15 to **a** to the glory of God
2Co 8: 7 But as you **a** in everything
2Co 9: 8 make all grace **a** toward you
Eph 1: 8 which He made to **a** toward us
Phil 1: 9 your love may **a** still more
Phil 4:12 be abased, and I know how to **a**
1Th 3:12 **a** in love to one another and
1Th 4: 1 Jesus that you should **a** more
2Pe 1: 8 these things are yours and **a**

ABOUNDED† (*see* ABOUND)
Gen 1:21 with which the waters **a**,
Ps 105:30 Their land **a** with frogs, Even
Rom 5:15 Man, Jesus Christ, **a** to many
Rom 5:20 But where sin **a**, grace
2Co 8: 2 their deep poverty **a** in the

ABOUNDING† (*see* ABOUND)
Ex 34: 6 and **a** in goodness and truth,
Ps 103: 8 Slow to anger, and **a** in mercy
Prov 8:24 no fountains **a** with water
1Co 15:58 always **a** in the work of the
2Co 9:12 but also is **a** through many
Col 2: 7 **a** in it with thanksgiving

ABOUNDS (*see* ABOUND)
Prov 29:22 strife, and a furious man **a** in
2Th 1: 3 you all **a** toward each other

ABRAHAM (*see* ABRAHAM'S, ABRAM)
Gen 17: 5 but your name shall be **A**
Gen 17:23 So **A** took Ishmael his son,
Gen 17:24 **A** was ninety-nine years old

Gen	18: 6	So A hurried into the tent
Gen	18:17	I hide from A what I am doing
Gen	18:18	since A shall surely become a
Gen	18:22	but A still stood before the
Gen	18:33	had finished speaking with A
Gen	18:33	and A returned to his place
Gen	19:29	plain, that God remembered A
Gen	20: 1	A journeyed from there to the
Gen	20:17	So A prayed to God
Gen	21: 2	bore A a son in his old age,
Gen	21:34	A stayed in the land of
Gen	22: 1	things that God tested A, and
Gen	22: 8	A said, "My son, God will
Gen	22:11	from heaven and said, "A, A!"
Gen	22:13	So A went and took the ram, and
Gen	23: 2	A came to mourn for Sarah and
Gen	23:19	A buried Sarah his wife in
Gen	24: 1	Now A was old, well-advanced
Gen	25: 1	A again took a wife, and her
Gen	25: 6	of the concubines which A had
Gen	25: 8	Then A breathed his last and
Gen	25:10	the field which A purchased
Gen	26: 5	because A obeyed My voice and
Gen	26:24	I am the God of your father A
Gen	28: 4	and give you the blessing of A
Gen	31:53	The God of A, the God of
Gen	50:24	land of which He swore to A
Ex	2:24	His covenant with A, with
Ex	3: 6	the God of A, the God of
Ex	6: 3	I appeared to A, to Isaac, and
Ex	32:13	Remember A, Isaac, and Israel,
Lev	26:42	with A I will remember
Deut	1: 8	to A, Isaac, and Jacob
Deut	9:27	Remember Your servants, A
Josh	24: 2	Terah, the father of A and the
1Ki	18:36	LORD God of A, Isaac, and
2Ki	13:23	of His covenant with A, Isaac
1Ch	16:16	covenant which He made with A
2Ch	20: 7	of A Your friend forever
Neh	9: 7	and gave him the name A
Ps	47: 9	The people of the God of A
Ps	105: 6	O seed of A His servant, You
Is	29:22	says the LORD, who redeemed A
Is	41: 8	descendants of A My friend
Is	51: 2	Look to A your father, and to
Ezek	33:24	A was only one, and he
Mic	7:20	truth to Jacob and mercy to A
Matt	1: 1	Son of David, the Son of A
Matt	3: 9	We have A as our father
Matt	3: 9	to A from these stones
Matt	8:11	and west, and sit down with A
Matt	22:32	I am the God of A, the God
Luke	3:34	son of Isaac, the son of A
Luke	13:28	of teeth, when you see A and
Luke	16:23	saw A afar off, and Lazarus in
John	8:39	to Him, "A is our father
John	8:56	Your father A rejoiced to see
John	8:58	I say to you, before A was
Acts	3:13	The God of A, Isaac, and Jacob
Acts	7: 2	appeared to our father A when
Acts	13:26	sons of the family of A, and
Rom	4: 1	that A our father has found
Rom	4: 3	A believed God, and it was
Rom	4:16	who are of the faith of A
Rom	9: 7	they are the seed of A
Rom	11: 1	Israelite, of the seed of A
2Co	11:22	Are they the seed of A
Gal	3: 6	just as A believed God, and
Gal	3: 7	are of faith are sons of A
Gal	3: 8	the gospel to A beforehand
Gal	3: 9	are blessed with believing A
Gal	3:16	Now to A and his Seed were the
Gal	3:18	God gave it to A by promise
Gal	4:22	written that A had two sons
Heb	2:16	give aid to the seed of A

Heb	6:13	when God made a promise to A
Heb	7: 1	who met A returning from the
Heb	7: 2	to whom also A gave a tenth
Heb	11: 8	By faith A obeyed when he was
Heb	11:17	By faith A, when he was
Jas	2:21	Was not A our father
Jas	2:23	A believed God, and it was
1Pe	3: 6	as Sarah obeyed A, calling

ABRAHAM'S (see ABRAHAM)

Gen	20:18	because of Sarah, A wife
Gen	24:34	So he said, "I am A servant
Gen	25:12	A son, whom Hagar the
Gen	26:24	for My servant A sake
Luke	16:22	by the angels to A bosom
John	8:33	We are A descendants, and have
Gal	3:29	Christ's, then you are A seed

ABRAM (see ABRAHAM)

Gen	11:26	seventy years, and begot A
Gen	11:27	Terah begot A, Nahor, and
Gen	11:31	And Terah took his son A and
Gen	12: 1	Now the LORD had said to A
Gen	12: 4	A was seventy-five years old
Gen	12: 5	Then A took Sarai his wife and
Gen	12: 7	Then the LORD appeared to A
Gen	12:10	and A went down to Egypt to
Gen	13: 2	A was very rich in livestock,
Gen	13: 4	there A called on the name of
Gen	14:13	told A the Hebrew, for he
Gen	14:19	Blessed be A of God Most High
Gen	14:21	the king of Sodom said to A
Gen	15: 1	Do not be afraid, A
Gen	15:12	a deep sleep fell upon A
Gen	15:18	LORD made a covenant with A
Gen	16: 2	A heeded the voice of Sarai
Gen	16:16	A was eighty-six years old
Gen	16:16	when Hagar bore Ishmael to A
Gen	17: 1	old, the LORD appeared to A
Gen	17: 5	shall your name be called A
Neh	9: 7	are the LORD God, Who chose A

ABROAD†

Gen	11: 4	lest we be scattered **a** over
Gen	11: 8	the LORD scattered them **a**
Gen	11: 9	the LORD scattered them **a**
Gen	28:14	shall spread **a** to the west
Ex	5:12	the people were scattered **a**
Ps	112: 9	He has dispersed **a**, He has
Prov	5:16	your fountains be dispersed **a**
Is	24: 1	scatters **a** its inhabitants
Is	44:24	Who spreads the earth by
Ezek	34:21	horns, and scattered them **a**
Zech	2: 6	for I have spread you **a** like
Matt	12:30	not gather with Me scatters **a**
John	11:52	of God who were scattered **a**
2Co	9: 9	He has dispersed **a**, He has
Jas	1: 1	tribes which are scattered **a**

ABSALOM (see ABISHALOM, ABSALOM'S)

2Sa	3: 3	A the son of Maacah, the
2Sa	13: 1	this A the son of David had a
2Sa	13:22	A spoke to his brother Amnon
2Sa	13:29	So the servants of A did to
2Sa	13:29	to Amnon as A had commanded
2Sa	13:39	King David longed to go to A
2Sa	14:25	much as A for his good looks
2Sa	14:27	To A were born three sons, and
2Sa	15: 6	So A stole the hearts of the
2Sa	15:10	say, A reigns in Hebron
2Sa	17:15	and so Ahithophel advised A
2Sa	17:25	A made Amasa captain of the
2Sa	18: 9	A rode on a mule
2Sa	18:10	I just saw A hanging in a
2Sa	18:29	Is the young man A safe
2Sa	18:32	Is the young man A safe
2Sa	18:33	O my son A—my son

2Sa 18:33 O **A** my son, my son
2Sa 19: 1 is weeping and mourning for **A**
2Sa 19: 4 O my son **A**!
2Sa 19: 4 O **A**, my son, my son
1Ch 3: 2 **A** the son of Maachah, the
2Ch 11:20 Maachah the granddaughter of **A**
2Ch 11:21 of **A** more than all his wives

ABSALOM'S (*see* ABSALOM)

2Sa 14:30 **A** servants set the field on
2Sa 18:14 thrust them through **A** heart
2Sa 18:18 day it is called **A** Monument

ABSENCE† (*see* ABSENT)

Luke 22: 6 in the **a** of the multitude
Phil 2:12 but now much more in my **a**

ABSENT (*see* ABSENCE)

Gen 31:49 me when we are **a** one from
1Co 5: 3 as **a** in body but present in
2Co 5: 6 body we are **a** from the Lord
2Co 10:11 word by letters when we are **a**
2Co 13: 2 now being a I write to those
Phil 1:27 I come and see you or am **a**
Col 2: 5 though I am **a** in the flesh

ABSTAIN (*see* ABSTINENCE)

Deut 23:22 But if you **a** from vowing, it
Josh 6:18 **a** from the accursed things
Acts 15:20 to **a** from things polluted by
1Th 4: 3 that you should **a** from sexual
1Th 5:22 **A** from every form of evil
1Ti 4: 3 commanding to **a** from foods
1Pe 2:11 **a** from fleshly lusts which

ABSTINENCE† (*see* ABSTAIN)

Acts 27:21 But after long **a** from food

ABUNDANCE (*see* ABUNDANT)

Gen 1:20 with an **a** of living creatures
Deut 33:19 partake of the **a** of the seas
1Sa 1:16 woman, for out of the **a** of my
1Ki 1:19 fattened cattle and sheep in **a**
1Ki 1:25 fattened cattle and sheep in **a**
1Ki 18:41 is the sound of **a** of rain
1Ch 20: 2 spoil of the city in great **a**
2Ch 2: 9 to prepare timber for me in **a**
Neh 5:18 an **a** of all kinds of wine
Neh 9:25 groves, and fruit trees in **a**
Esth 1: 7 other, with royal wine in **a**
Job 22:11 and an **a** of water covers you
Job 36:31 He gives food in **a**
Job 38:34 that an **a** of water may cover
Ps 18:14 the foe, Lightnings in **a**, and
Ps 52: 7 in the **a** of his riches, And
Ps 65:11 And Your paths drip with **a**
Ps 72:16 There will be an **a** of grain
Ps 73: 7 Their eyes bulge with **a**
Ps 78:15 drink in **a** like the depths
Eccl 5:10 nor he who loves **a**, with
Is 7:22 from the **a** of milk they give,
Is 55: 2 your soul delight itself in **a**
Is 60: 5 because the **a** of the sea
Jer 33: 6 reveal to them the **a** of peace
Ezek 28:16 By the **a** of your trading you
Matt 12:34 For out of the **a** of the heart
Matt 13:12 given, and he will have **a**
Matt 25:29 given, and he will have **a**
Mark 12:44 all put in out of their **a**
Luke 12:15 does not consist in the **a** of
Rom 5:17 those who receive **a** of grace
2Co 8: 2 affliction the **a** of their joy
2Co 8:14 your **a** may supply their lack
2Co 9: 8 have an **a** for every good work
2Co 12: 7 by the **a** of the revelations
Rev 18: 3 through the **a** of her luxury

ABUNDANT (*see* ABUNDANCE, ABUNDANTLY)

Num 14:18 and **a** in mercy, forgiving
1Ki 10:27 he made cedars as **a** as the
1Ch 22: 5 So David made **a**
Neh 9:17 **a** in kindness, and did not
Neh 9:27 according to Your **a** mercies
Ps 86: 5 **a** in mercy to all those who
Ps 130: 7 And with Him is **a** redemption
Is 56:12 be as today, and much more **a**
Jer 51:13 **a** in treasures, your end has
Dan 4:12 were lovely, its fruit **a**, and
Jon 4: 2 **a** in lovingkindness, One who
2Co 11:23 in labors more **a**, in stripes
Phil 1:26 for me may be more **a** in Jesus
1Ti 1:14 of our Lord was exceedingly **a**
1Pe 1: 3 who according to His **a** mercy

ABUNDANTLY (*see* ABUNDANT)

Gen 9: 7 brings forth **a** in the earth and
Ex 1: 7 were fruitful and increased **a**
Ex 8: 3 shall bring forth frogs **a**
Num 20:11 and water came out **a**, and the
2Ch 31: 5 they brought in **a** the tithe
Job 36:28 drop down and pour **a** on man
Ps 65:10 You water its ridges **a**, You
Ps 132:15 I will **a** bless her provision
Is 35: 2 It shall blossom **a** and rejoice
Is 55: 7 our God, for He will **a** pardon
John 10:10 that they may have it more **a**
1Co 15:10 labored more **a** than they all
2Co 1:12 of God, and more **a** toward you
2Co 2: 4 which I have so **a** for you
2Co 12:15 though the more **a** I love you
Eph 3:20 **a** above all that we ask or
Tit 3: 6 us **a** through Jesus Christ our
Heb 6:17 determining to show more **a** to
2Pe 1:11 to you **a** into the everlasting

ABUSE (*see* ABUSED)

1Sa 31: 4 and thrust me through and **a** me
Jer 38:19 into their hand, and they **a** me
Acts 14: 5 Jews, with their rulers, to **a**
1Co 9:18 that I may not **a** my authority

ABUSED† (*see* ABUSE)

Num 22:29 Because you have **a** me
Judg 19:25 **a** her all night until morning

ABYSS†

Luke 8:31 them to go out into the **a**
Rom 10: 7 Who will descend into the **a**

ACACIA (*see* ACACIAS)

Ex 25: 5 red, badger skins, and **a** wood
Ex 26:32 of **a** wood overlaid with gold
Ex 27: 1 shall make an altar of **a** wood
Num 25: 1 Israel remained in **A** Grove
Is 41:19 the **a** tree, the myrtle and the

ACACIAS† (*see* ACACIA)

Joel 3:18 LORD and water the Valley of **A**

ACCAD†

Gen 10:10 kingdom was Babel, Erech, **A**

ACCEPT (*see* ACCEPTABLE, ACCEPTANCE, ACCEPTED, ACCEPTING, ACCEPTS)

Gen 32:20 perhaps he will **a** me
Lev 26:41 and they **a** their guilt
Deut 33:11 and **a** the work of his hands
1Sa 26:19 me, let Him **a** an offering
2Sa 24:23 May the LORD your God **a** you
Job 2:10 we indeed **a** good from God
Job 2:10 and shall we not **a** adversity
Job 42: 8 For I will **a** him, lest I deal
Ps 119:108 **A**, I pray, the freewill
Jer 14:10 the LORD does not **a** them
Jer 14:12 offering, I will not **a** them
Ezek 43:27 and I will **a** you,' says the

Mal 1: 8 Would he a you favorably
Mal 1: 9 will He a you favorably
Matt 19:11 All cannot a this saying, but
Matt 19:12 He who is able to a it, let
Mark 4:20 the word, a it, and bear fruit
Acts 24: 3 we a it always and in all
1Co   6: 7 Why do you not rather a wrong

ACCEPTABLE (see ACCEPT, ACCEPTABLY)
Ps   19:14 my heart Be a in Your sight
Ps   69:13 to You, O LORD, in the a time
Prov 10:32 the righteous know what is a
Prov 21: 3 justice is more a to the LORD
Eccl 12:10 sought to find a words
Is   49: 8 In an a time I have heard You
Is   61: 2 to proclaim the a year of the
Jer   6:20 burnt offerings are not a
Jer 42: 2 let our petition be a to you
Luke 4:19 to proclaim the a year of the
Rom 12: 1 holy, a to God, which is your
Rom 12: 2 prove what is that good and a
2Co   6: 2 In an a time I have heard you
Eph   5:10 finding out what is a to the Lord
Phil 4:18 an a sacrifice, well pleasing
1Ti   2: 3 a in the sight of God our
1Pe   2: 5 up spiritual sacrifices a to

ACCEPTABLY† (see ACCEPTABLE)
Heb 12:28 serve God a with reverence

ACCEPTANCE† (see ACCEPT)
Is   60: 7 ascend with a on My altar
Rom 11:15 what will their a be but life
1Ti   1:15 saying and worthy of all a
1Ti   4: 9 saying and worthy of all a

ACCEPTED (see ACCEPT)
Gen   4: 7 do well, will you not be a
Ex   28:38 they may be a before the LORD
Lev   1: 4 it will be a on his behalf to
Lev 22:21 it must be perfect to be a
1Sa 18: 5 he was a in the sight of all
Esth 9:23 So the Jews a the custom
Job 42: 9 for the LORD had a Job
Eccl 9: 7 God has already a your works
Is   56: 7 will be a on My altar
Luke 4:24 no prophet is a in his own
Acts 10:35 righteousness is a by Him
2Co   6: 2 Behold, now is the a time
2Co   8:12 it is a according to what one
2Co 11: 4 gospel which you have not a
Eph   1: 6 has made us a in the Beloved

ACCEPTING† (see ACCEPT)
Heb 11:35 not a deliverance, that they

ACCEPTS† (see ACCEPT)
Prov 17:23 A wicked man a a bribe behind

ACCESS†
Esth 1:14 who had a to the king's
Rom   5: 2 through whom also we have a
Eph   2:18 through Him we both have a by
Eph   3:12 a with confidence through

ACCIDENTALLY
Num 35:11 any person a may flee there

ACCO†
Judg 1:31 out the inhabitants of A or

ACCOMPANIED (see ACCOMPANY)
1Sa 25:15 anything as long as we a them
1Ch 15:16 a by instruments of music
Acts 1:21 of these men who have a us
Acts 10:23 brethren from Joppa a him
1Pe   3: 2 your chaste conduct a by fear

ACCOMPANY† (see ACCOMPANIED, ACCOMPANYING)
Heb   6: 9 yes, things that a salvation

ACCOMPANYING† (see ACCOMPANY)
2Sa   6: 4 on the hill, a the ark of God
Mark 16:20 the word through the a signs

ACCOMPLISH† (see ACCOMPLISHED, ACCOMPLISHING, ACCOMPLISHMENT)
Ex   14:13 which He will a for you today
2Ch   2:14 to a any plan which may be
Job 35: 6 what do you a against Him
Eccl 2: 2 What does it a
Is   55:11 but it shall a what I please,
Ezek 13:15 Thus will I a My wrath on the
Dan   9: 2 that He would a seventy years
Luke 9:31 was about to a at Jerusalem

ACCOMPLISHED (see ACCOMPLISH)
1Sa 11:13 has a salvation in Israel
2Ch   7:11 Solomon successfully a all
Prov 13:19 A desire a is sweet to the
Dan 11:36 till the wrath has been a
Luke 12:50 distressed I am till it is a
Luke 18:31 the Son of Man will be a
Luke 22:37 written must still be a in Me
John 19:28 that all things were now a
Rom 15:18 Christ has not a through me
Eph   3:11 He a in Christ Jesus our Lord

ACCOMPLISHING† (see ACCOMPLISH)
John 12:19 see that you are a nothing

ACCOMPLISHMENT† (see ACCOMPLISH)
2Co 10:16 in another man's sphere of a

ACCORD (see ACCORDANCE)
Lev 25: 5 What grows of its own a of
Josh 9: 2 Joshua and Israel with one a
1Ki 22:13 with one a encourage the king
Zeph 3: 9 LORD, to serve Him with one a
Luke 14:18 one a began to make excuses
Acts 1:14 with one a in prayer and
Acts 2: 1 all with one a in one place
Acts 12:10 opened to them of its own a
2Co   6:15 what a has Christ with Belial
2Co   8:17 he went to you of his own a
Phil 2: 2 the same love, being of one a

ACCORDANCE† (see ACCORD)
Judg 8:35 Gideon) in a with the good he
Esth 1: 8 In a with the law, the
Rom   2: 5 But in a with your hardness

ACCOUNT (see ACCOUNTED, ACCOUNTING, ACCOUNTS)
Gen 20:11 will kill me on a of my wife
Gen 26: 9 said, Lest I die on a of her
Josh 22:23 the LORD Himself require an a
1Ch 27:24 a of the chronicles of King
Esth 10: 2 the a of the greatness of
Ps   10:13 You will not require an a
Is   2:22 for of what a is he
Dan   7:28 This is the end of the a
Matt 12:36 they will give a of it in the
Luke 1: 3 to write to you an orderly a
Luke 16: 2 Give an a of your stewardship
Acts 1: 1 The former a I made, O
Rom 14:12 give a of himself to God
Phil 4:17 fruit that abounds to your a
Phm   18 anything, put that on my a
Heb   4:13 of Him to whom we must give a
Heb 13:17 as those who must give a
1Pe   4: 5 They will give an a to Him

ACCOUNTED (see ACCOUNT)
Gen 15: 6 LORD, and He a it to him for
Ps   44:22 We are a as sheep for the
Ps 106:31 And that was a to him for
Rom   4: 3 God, and it was a to him for
Rom   8:36 we are a as sheep for the
Gal   3: 6 God, and it was a to him for
Jas   2:23 God, and it was a to him for

ACCOUNTING† (*see* ACCOUNT, CONCLUDING)
2Ki 22: 7 However there need be no a
Job 33:13 give an a of any of His words

ACCOUNTS (*see* ACCOUNT)
Matt 18:23 to settle a with his servants

ACCUMULATED†
2Ki 20:17 fathers have a until this day
Is 39: 6 fathers have a until this day

ACCURATE† (*see* ACCURATELY)
Acts 24:22 having more a knowledge of

ACCURATELY (*see* ACCURATE)
Acts 18:25 taught a the things of the

ACCURSED
Deut 7:26 it, for it is an a thing
Deut 21:23 he who is hanged is a of God
Josh 6:18 abstain from the a things
John 7:49 does not know the law is a
Rom 9: 3 wish that I myself were a
1Co 12: 3 Spirit of God calls Jesus a
1Co 16:22 Jesus Christ, let him be a
Gal 1: 8 preached to you, let him be a
2Pe 2:14 practices, and are a children

ACCUSATION (*see* ACCUSE)
Ezra 4: 6 they wrote an a against the
Mark 15:26 of His a was written above
Luke 6: 7 might find an a against Him
Luke 16: 1 an a was brought to him that
Luke 19: 8 from anyone by false a, I
John 18:29 What a do you bring against
Acts 24: 2 upon, Tertullus began his a
Jude 9 against him a reviling a, but

ACCUSE (*see* ACCUSATION, ACCUSED, ACCUSER, ACCUSES, ACCUSING)
Matt 12:10 that they might a Him
Luke 3:14 anyone or a falsely, and be
Luke 23: 2 And they began to a Him,
Luke 23:14 things of which you a Him
John 5:45 I shall a you to the Father
Acts 24: 8 things of which we a him
Acts 25: 5 a this man, to see if there

ACCUSED
Dan 3: 8 came forward and a the Jews
Dan 6:24 those men who had a Daniel
Matt 27:12 while He was being a by the
Mark 15: 3 the chief priests a Him of
Acts 22:30 why he was a by the Jews, he
Acts 23:28 to know the reason they a him
Acts 26: 7 Agrippa, I am a by the Jews
Rev 12:10 who a them before our God day

ACCUSER† (*see* ACCUSE, ACCUSERS)
Ps 109: 6 let an a stand at his right
Rev 12:10 for the a of our brethren,

ACCUSERS (*see* ACCUSER)
Ps 109:20 be the LORD's reward to my a
John 8:10 where are those a of yours
Acts 23:30 also commanded his a to state
Acts 25:16 meets the a face to face, and

ACCUSES† (*see* ACCUSE)
John 5:45 there is one who a you

ACCUSING† (*see* ACCUSE)
Rom 2:15 a or else excusing them)

ACCUSTOMED
Jer 13:23 do good who are a to do evil
Matt 27:15 was a to releasing to the
Mark 10: 1 to Him again, and as He was a
Luke 22:39 Mount of Olives, as He was a

ACHAIA
Acts 18:12 Gallio was proconsul of A

Acts 19:21 through Macedonia and A
2Co 11:10 boasting in the regions of A

ACHAICUS†
1Co 16:17 Stephanas, Fortunatus, and A

ACHAN
Josh 7: 1 for A the son of Carmi, the

ACHBOR
2Ki 22:14 Hilkiah the priest, Ahikam, A

ACHIM†
Matt 1:14 begot Zadok, Zadok begot A
Matt 1:14 and A begot Eliud.

ACHISH
1Sa 27: 3 So David dwelt with A at Gath

ACHMETHA†
Ezra 6: 2 And at A, in the place that

ACHOR
Josh 7:24 them to the Valley of A
Hos 2:15 the Valley of A as a door of

ACHSAH
Judg 1:12 give my daughter A as wife

ACHSHAPH
Josh 11: 1 of Shimron, to the king of A

ACHZIB
Josh 19:29 at the sea by the region of A
Judg 1:31 of Sidon, or of Ahlab, A,

ACKNOWLEDGE (*see* ACKNOWLEDGED, ACKNOWLEDGES, ACKNOWLEDGMENT)
Deut 33: 9 nor did he a his brothers, or
Ps 51: 3 For I a my transgressions, And
Prov 3: 6 in all your ways a Him, and He
Jer 14:20 We a, O LORD, our wickedness
Dan 11:39 foreign god, which he shall a
Hos 8: 4 princes, but I did not a them.
1Co 16:18 therefore a such men

ACKNOWLEDGED† (*see* ACKNOWLEDGE)
Gen 38:26 So Judah a them and said
Ex 2:25 of Israel, and God a them
Ps 32: 5 I a my sin to You, And my
Acts 15: 8 a them, by giving them the

ACKNOWLEDGES† (*see* ACKNOWLEDGE)
1Ki 2:44 You know, as your heart a
Ps 142: 4 For there is no one who a me
1Jn 2:23 he who a the Son has the

ACKNOWLEDGMENT† (*see* ACKNOWLEDGE)
Tit 1: 1 the a of the truth which
Phm 6 a of every good thing which

ACQUAINT† (*see* ACQUAINTANCE, ACQUAINTED)
Job 22:21 Now a yourself with Him, and

ACQUAINTANCE† (*see* ACQUAINT, ACQUAINTANCES)
Ps 55:13 equal, My companion and my a

ACQUAINTANCES (*see* ACQUAINTANCE)
2Ki 10:11 his great men and his close a
Job 42:11 who had been his a before
Jer 20:10 All my a watched for my
Luke 2:44 among their relatives and a
Luke 23:49 But all His a, and the women

ACQUAINTED† (*see* ACQUAINT)
Ps 139: 3 And are a with all my ways
Is 53: 3 of sorrows and a with grief

ACQUIRE† (*see* ACQUIRED, ACQUIRES)
Gen 34:10 a possessions for yourselves

ACQUIRED (*see* ACQUIRE)
Gen 12: 5 whom they had a in Haran, and
Gen 31: 1 he has a all this wealth
Ruth 4:10 I have a as my wife,

Ps 78:54 which His right hand had a

ACQUIRES† (*see* ACQUIRE)
Prov 18:15 of the prudent a knowledge

ACQUIT (*see* ACQUITTED)
Job 10:14 will not a me of my iniquity
Nah 1: 3 will not at all a the wicked

ACQUITTED (*see* ACQUIT)
Ex 21:19 he who struck him shall be a
Ex 21:28 owner of the ox shall be a
Is 43:26 your case, that you may be a

ACT (*see* ACTED, ACTING, ACTS)
Deut 4: 5 that you should a according
Deut 17:13 no longer a presumptuously
Judg 19:23 beg you, do not a so wickedly
1Ki 8:32 then hear in heaven, and a
2Ch 19: 9 Thus you shall a in the fear
Neh 6:13 a that way and sin, so that
Ps 119:126 It is time for You to a, O
Is 28:16 believes will not a hastily
Dan 11:23 him he shall a deceitfully
John 8: 4 in adultery, in the very a
Rom 5:18 a the free gift came to all

ACTED (*see* ACT)
Gen 42: 7 but he a as a stranger to
Deut 9:12 out of Egypt have a corruptly
Judg 9:16 you have a in truth
Judg 9:19 you have a in truth
2Ki 10:19 But Jehu a deceptively,
2Ki 21:11 a more wickedly than all the
Job 36: 9 that they have a defiantly
Ezek 20: 9 But I a for My name's sake,
Ezek 20:14 But I a for My name's sake,

ACTING (*see* ACT)
Gen 19: 9 and he keeps a as a judge

ACTIONS†
1Sa 2: 3 and by Him a are weighed

ACTIVE (*see* ACTIVITY)
Lev 13:51 the plague is an a leprosy

ACTIVITIES† (*see* ACTIVITY)
1Co 12: 6 And there are diversities of a

ACTIVITY† (*see* ACTIVE, ACTIVITIES)
Eccl 5: 3 a dream comes through much a

ACTS (*see* ACT)
Ex 21:14 But if a man a with
Deut 11: 3 His a which He did in the
Deut 17:12 the man who a presumptuously
Judg 5:11 the righteous a of the LORD
1Ki 11:41 the rest of the a of Solomon
Esth 10: 2 Now all the a of his power and
Job 15:25 and a defiantly against the
Ps 103: 7 His a to the children of
Ps 145: 6 the might of Your awesome a
Ps 150: 2 Praise Him for His mighty a
Prov 13:16 prudent man a with knowledge
Prov 21:24 he a with arrogant pride
Is 64: 4 Who a for the one who waits
Ezek 16:20 Were your a of harlotry a
Rev 19: 8 the righteous a of the saints

ACTUALLY†
Gen 50:15 may a repay us for all the
2Ki 4:14 A, she has no son, and her
1Co 5: 1 It is a reported that there
Phil 1:12 me have a turned out for the
2Pe 2:18 the ones who have a escaped

ADAH
Gen 4:23 A and Zillah, hear my voice

ADAM
Gen 2:20 So A gave names to all cattle
Gen 3: 9 Then the LORD God called to A
Gen 3:20 A called his wife's name Eve,
Gen 4: 1 Now A knew Eve his wife, and
Gen 5: 1 book of the genealogy of A
Deut 32: 8 He separated the sons of A
1Ch 1: 1 A, Seth, Enosh,
Job 31:33 my transgressions as A, by
Luke 3:38 the son of Seth, the son of A
Rom 5:14 death reigned from A to Moses
Rom 5:14 of the transgression of A
1Co 15:22 For as in A all die, even so
1Co 15:45 The last A became a
1Ti 2:13 For A was formed first, then
1Ti 2:14 A was not deceived, but the
Jude 14 Now Enoch, the seventh from A

ADAMANT†
Ezek 3: 9 Like a stone, harder than

ADAR
Esth 9: 1 that is, the month of A, on

ADD (*see* ADDED, ADDITION, ADDS)
Gen 30:24 The LORD shall a to me
Lev 5:16 shall a one-fifth to it and
Deut 4: 2 You shall not a to the word
Deut 12:32 you shall not a to it nor
1Ki 12:11 on you, I will a to your yoke
2Ki 20: 6 I will a to your days fifteen
2Ch 28:13 You intend to a to our sins
Ps 69:27 A iniquity to their iniquity,
Prov 3: 2 and peace they will a to you
Prov 30: 6 Do not a to His words, lest
Is 5: 8 who a field to field, till
Is 29: 1 A year to year
Is 30: 1 that they may a sin to sin
Jer 7:21 A your burnt offerings to
Luke 12:25 of you by worrying can a one
Phil 1:16 supposing to a affliction to
2Pe 1: 5 a to your faith virtue, to
Rev 22:18 God will a to him the plagues

ADDED (*see* ADD)
Num 36: 4 a to the inheritance of the
Deut 5:22 and He a no more
1Sa 12:19 for we have a to all our sins
Prov 9:11 of life will be a to you
Eccl 3:14 Nothing can be a to it, and
Dan 4:36 excellent majesty was a to me
Matt 6:33 things shall be a to you
Luke 12:31 things shall be a to you
Acts 2:41 thousand souls were a to them
Acts 2:47 And the Lord a to the church

ADDITION (*see* ADD)
Gen 28: 9 to be his wife in a to the

ADDS (*see* ADD)
Prov 10:22 and He a no sorrow with it
Gal 3:15 no one annuls or a to it
Heb 10:17 then He a, "Their sins and
Rev 22:18 If anyone a to these things,

ADHERE† (*see* ADHERES)
Dan 2:43 will not a to one another

ADHERES† (*see* ADHERE)
Job 31: 7 or if any spot a to my hands

ADJACENT
Ezek 45: 6 a to the district of the holy

ADJOIN† (*see* ADJOINED, ADJOINING)
Gen 49:13 and his border shall a Sidon

ADJOINED† (*see* ADJOIN)
Josh 19:34 it a Zebulun on the south

ADJOINING† (*see* ADJOIN)
Josh   17:10 was **a** Asher on the north and
Acts   2:10 the parts of Libya **a** Cyrene

ADJOURNED†
Acts   24:22 he **a** the proceedings and said,

ADJURE (*see* EXORCISE, OATH)

ADMAH
Gen   10:19 go toward Sodom, Gomorrah, A
Hos   11: 8 How can I make you like A

ADMINISTER† (*see* ADMINISTERED, ADMINISTRATION,
   ADMINISTRATOR)
1Ki   3:28 God was in him to **a** justice
Ps   9: 8 He shall **a** judgment for the

ADMINISTERED (*see* ADMINISTER)
Deut 33:21 He **a** the justice of the LORD,
2Sa   8:15 David **a** judgment and justice
2Co   8:19 which is **a** by us to the glory

ADMINISTRATION† (*see* ADMINISTER,
   ADMINISTRATIONS)
2Co   9:12 For the **a** of this service not

ADMINISTRATIONS† (*see* ADMINISTRATION)
1Co   12:28 gifts of healings, helps, **a**

ADMINISTRATOR† (*see* ADMINISTER,
   ADMINISTRATORS)
Dan   2:48 chief **a** over all the wise men

ADMINISTRATORS (*see* ADMINISTRATOR)
Dan   3: 2 together the satraps, the **a**

ADMIRED†
2Th   1:10 to be **a** among all those who

ADMONISH† (*see* ADMONISHED, ADMONISHING,
   ADMONITION)
Ps   81: 8 O My people, and I will **a** you
Rom   15:14 able also to **a** one another
1Th   5:12 you in the Lord and **a** you,
2Th   3:15 enemy, but **a** him as a brother
Tit   2: 4 that they **a** the young women

ADMONISHED (*see* ADMONISH)
Eccl   4:13 king who will be **a** no more
Eccl   12:12 my son, be **a** by these

ADMONISHING† (*see* ADMONISH)
Col   3:16 **a** one another in psalms and

ADMONITION† (*see* ADMONISH)
1Co   10:11 they were written for our **a**
Eph   6: 4 the training and **a** of the Lord
Tit   3:10 after the first and second **a**

ADONI-BEZEK
Judg   1: 5 And they found A in Bezek, and

ADONIJAH
2Sa   3: 4 fourth, A the son of Haggith
1Ki   1:25 they say, Long live King A

ADONIRAM (*see* ADORAM)
1Ki   5:14 A was in charge of the labor

ADONI-ZEDEK
Josh   10: 1 A king of Jerusalem

ADOPTION†
Rom   8:15 of **a** by whom we cry out
Rom   8:23 eagerly waiting for the **a**
Rom   9: 4 to whom pertain the **a**, the
Gal   4: 5 might receive the **a** as sons
Eph   1: 5 having predestined us to **a** as

ADORAM (*see* ADONIRAM)
1Ki   12:18 Then King Rehoboam sent A

ADORN (*see* ADORNED, ADORNING, ADORNS)
Job   40:10 Then **a** yourself with majesty
Matt 23:29 and **a** the monuments of the

1Ti   2: 9 that the women **a** themselves
Tit   2:10 that they may **a** the doctrine

ADORNED (*see* ADORN)
Ezek 16:11 I **a** you with ornaments, put
1Pe   3: 5 in God also **a** themselves,
Rev   17: 4 and **a** with gold and precious
Rev   18:16 and **a** with gold and precious
Rev   21: 2 as a bride **a** for her husband
Rev   21:19 the wall of the city were **a**

ADORNING (*see* ADORN, ADORNMENT)

ADORNMENT (*see* ADORN)
1Pe   3: 3 Do not let your **a** be merely

ADORNS† (*see* ADORN)
Ps   93: 5 Holiness **a** Your house, O LORD
Is   61:10 as a bride **a** herself with her

ADRAMMELECH
2Ki   17:31 their children in fire to A

ADRAMYTTIUM†
Acts   27: 2 So, entering a ship of A, we

ADRIATIC†
Acts   27:27 up and down in the A Sea,

ADRIFT†
Ps   88: 5 A among the dead, Like the

ADULLAM (*see* ADULLAMITE)
2Sa   23:13 to David at the cave of A

ADULLAMITE (*see* ADULLAM)
Gen   38: 1 visited a certain A whose

ADULTERER† (*see* ADULTERERS, ADULTERY)
Lev   20:10 his neighbor's wife, the **a**
Job   24:15 The eye of the **a** waits for
Is   57: 3 you offspring of the **a** and

ADULTERERS† (*see* ADULTERER)
Ps   50:18 have been a partaker with **a**
Jer   9: 2 For they are all **a**, an
Jer   23:10 For the land is full of **a**
Hos   7: 4 They are all **a**
Mal   3: 5 against sorcerers, against **a**
Luke 18:11 extortioners, unjust, **a**, or
1Co   6: 9 nor idolaters, nor **a**, nor
Heb   13: 4 and **a** God will judge
Jas   4: 4 A and adulteresses

ADULTERESS (*see* ADULTERESSES, ADULTERY)
Lev   20:10 wife, the adulterer and the **a**
Rom   7: 3 man, she will be called an **a**

ADULTERESSES (*see* ADULTERESS)
Ezek 23:45 them after the manner of **a**

ADULTERIES (*see* ADULTERY)
Jer   13:27 I have seen your **a** and your
Hos   2: 2 and her **a** from between her
Matt 15:19 evil thoughts, murders, **a**

ADULTEROUS† (*see* ADULTERY)
Prov 30:20 This is the way of an **a** woman
Ezek   6: 9 I was crushed by their **a**
Ezek 16:32 You are an **a** wife, who takes
Matt 12:39 **a** generation seeks after a
Matt 16: 4 **a** generation seeks after a
Mark   8:38 of Me and My words in this **a**

ADULTERY (*see* ADULTERER, ADULTERESS, ADULTERIES,
   ADULTEROUS)
Ex   20:14 You shall not commit **a**
Deut   5:18 You shall not commit **a**
Jer   3: 8 Israel had committed **a**, I had
Jer   7: 9 you steal, murder, commit **a**
Ezek 23:37 committed **a** with their idols
Hos   3: 1 by a lover and is committing **a**
Hos   4:13 and your brides commit **a**
Matt   5:28 **a** with her in his heart

Matt 5:32 who is divorced commits **a**
Matt 19: 9 and marries another, commits **a**
John 8: 3 to Him a woman caught in **a**
Gal   5:19 **a**, fornication, uncleanness,
2Pe   2:14 having eyes full of **a** and that
Rev   2:22 those who commit **a** with her

ADVANCE (see ADVANCED, WELL ADVANCED)
Num 10: 5 When you sound the **a**, the
Josh 6: 7 let him who is armed **a** before
Prov 30:27 king, yet they all **a** in ranks

ADVANCED (see ADVANCE)
Josh 13: 1 Joshua was old, **a** in years
Judg 11:32 So Jephthah **a** toward the
Esth 3: 1 **a** him and set his seat above
Gal   1:14 I **a** in Judaism beyond many of

ADVANTAGE (see PROFIT)
Eccl 3:19 man has no **a** over animals, for
John 16: 7 It is to your **a** that I go
Rom   3: 1 What **a** then has the Jew, or
2Co   2:11 Satan should take **a** of us
2Co   8:10 It is to your **a** not only to
Jude   16 flattering people to gain **a**

ADVERSARIES (see ADVERSARY)
Deut 32:43 and render vengeance to His **a**
Josh 5:13 Are You for us or for our **a**
1Sa   2:10 The **a** of the LORD shall be
Job 22:20 Surely our **a** are cut down,
Ps   27:12 me to the will of my **a**
Ps   69:19 My **a** are all before You
Ps   71:13 consumed Who are **a** of my life
Ps   89:42 the right hand of his **a**
Is   59:18 He will repay, fury to His **a**
Jer 46:10 may avenge Himself on His **a**
Lam   1: 5 Her **a** have become the master,
Luke 13:17 all His **a** were put to shame
1Co 16: 9 to me, and there are many **a**
Heb 10:27 which will devour the **a**

ADVERSARY (see ADVERSARIES)
Ex   23:22 and an **a** to your adversaries
Esth 7: 6 The **a** and enemy is this wicked
Job 16: 9 my **a** sharpens His gaze on me
Is   50:8 stand together. Who is My **a**
Matt 5:25 Agree with your **a** quickly
1Pe   5: 8 because your **a** the devil

ADVERSITIES (see ADVERSITY)
1Sa 10:19 saved you out of all your **a**
Ps   31: 7 You have known my soul in **a**

ADVERSITY (see ADVERSITIES)
2Sa   4: 9 redeemed my life from all **a**
2Sa 12:11 I will raise up **a** against you
2Ch 15: 6 troubled them with every **a**
Job   2:10 God, and shall we not accept **a**
Job 42:11 **a** that the LORD had brought
Ps   10: 6 I shall never be in **a**
Ps   35:15 But in my **a** they rejoiced And
Prov 17:17 and a brother is born for **a**
Prov 24:10 If you faint in the day of **a**
Is   30:20 Lord gives you the bread of **a**
Jer 15:11 with you in the time of **a**
Jer 45: 5 I will bring **a** on all flesh

ADVICE (see ADVISE)
Gen 41:37 So the **a** was good in the eyes
Judg 20: 7 give your **a** and counsel here
2Sa 17:14 the good **a** of Ahithophel, to
1Ki 12: 8 But he rejected the **a** which
1Ki 12:14 to the **a** of the young men
Ezra 10: 3 to the **a** of my master and of
Job 26: 3 you declared sound **a** to many
Is   30: 2 Egypt, and have not asked My **a**
2Co   8:10 And in this I give my **a**

ADVISE (see ADVICE, ADVISED, ADVISORS, WELL-ADVISED)
2Sa 17:11 Therefore I **a** that all Israel
2Sa 19:43 to **a** bringing back our king
1Ki 12: 6 How do you **a** me to answer

ADVISED (see ADVISE, COUNSELED)
2Sa 17:15 and so Ahithophel **a**
2Ki   5: 6 Now be **a**, when this letter
Acts 27: 9 was already over, Paul **a** them

ADVISORS† (see ADVISE)
Dan   6: 7 satraps, the counselors and **a**

ADVOCATE†
1Jn   2: 1 we have an **A** with the Father,

AENEAS
Acts 9:33 found a certain man named **A**

AENON†
John 3:23 was baptizing in **A** near Salim

AFFAIRS (see EVENTS)
Ps 112: 5 guide his **a** with discretion
Dan   2:49 Abed-Nego over the **a** of the
Dan   3:12 **a** of the province of Babylon
2Ti   2: 4 with the **a** of this life, that

AFFECTED† (see AFFECTS)
Dan   3:27 nor were their garments **a**

AFFECTION† (see AFFECTIONATE, AFFECTIONS)
1Ch 29: 3 because I have set my **a** on
1Co   7: 3 to his wife the **a** due her
Phil 1: 8 with the **a** of Jesus Christ
Phil 2: 1 of the Spirit, if any **a** and

AFFECTIONATE† (see AFFECTION, AFFECTIONATELY)
Rom 12:10 Be kindly **a** to one another

AFFECTIONATELY† (see AFFECTIONATE)
1Th   2: 8 **a** longing for you, we were

AFFECTIONS† (see AFFECTION)
2Co   6:12 are restricted by your own **a**
2Co   7:15 his **a** are greater for you as

AFFECTS† (see AFFECTED)
Job 35: 8 Your wickedness **a** a man such

AFFIRM (see AFFIRMED)
Rom   3: 8 and as some **a** that we say
1Ti   1: 7 nor the things which they **a**

AFFIRMED (see AFFIRM)
Acts 25:19 died, whom Paul **a** to be alive

AFFLICT (see AFFLICTED, AFFLICTING, AFFLICTION)
Gen 15:13 they will **a** them four hundred
Ex   1:11 to **a** them with their burdens
Ex   22:22 You shall not **a** any widow or
Lev 16:29 you shall **a** your souls, and do
Judg 16: 5 that we may bind him to **a** him
Ps   55:19 **a** them, Even He who abides
Ps   94: 5 O LORD, And **a** Your heritage

AFFLICTED (see AFFLICT)
Ex   1:12 But the more they **a** them, the
Lev 23:29 **a** in soul on that same day
Num 11:11 Why have You **a** Your servant
Deut 26: 6 **a** us, and laid hard bondage on
Ruth 1:21 me, and the Almighty has **a** me
Job 34:28 for He hears the cry of the **a**
Ps   22:24 the affliction of the **a**
Ps   82: 3 Do justice to the **a** and needy
Ps   88: 7 You have **a** me with all Your
Ps 116:10 I am greatly **a**
Ps 119:67 Before I was **a** I went astray,
Ps 140:12 maintain The cause of the **a**
Prov 15:15 the days of the **a** are evil
Prov 22:22 nor oppress the **a** at the gate
Prov 31: 5 the justice of all the **a**

Is	49:13	and will have mercy on His **a**
Is	53: 4	smitten by God, and **a**
Is	53: 7	He was oppressed and He was **a**
Is	63: 9	all their affliction He was **a**
Matt	4:24	were **a** with various diseases
2Co	1: 6	Now if we are **a**, it is for
Heb	11:37	goatskins, being destitute, **a**

AFFLICTING (see AFFLICT)

Amos	5:12	**A** the just and taking bribes

AFFLICTION (see AFFLICT, AFFLICTIONS)

Gen	16:11	the LORD has heard your **a**
Gen	29:32	has surely looked on my **a**
Gen	31:42	God has seen my **a** and the
Gen	41:52	fruitful in the land of my **a**
Deut	16: 3	the bread of **a** for you came
1Sa	1:11	on the **a** of your maidservant
2Ch	20: 9	and cry out to You in our **a**
Job	5: 6	For **a** does not come from the
Job	30:16	the days of **a** take hold of me
Job	36: 8	held in the cords of **a**,
Ps	22:24	the **a** of the afflicted
Ps	25:18	Look on my **a** and my pain, And
Ps	66:11	You laid **a** on our backs
Ps	88: 9	eye wastes away because of **a**
Ps	106:44	He regarded their **a**, When He
Ps	119:153	Consider my **a** and deliver me,
Eccl	6: 2	is vanity, and it is an evil **a**
Is	48:10	you in the furnace of **a**
Is	63: 9	In all their **a** He was
Jer	30:12	Your **a** is incurable, your
Lam	3: 1	**a** by the rod of His wrath
Amos	6: 6	grieved for the **a** of Joseph
Mark	5:29	that she was healed of the **a**
2Co	2: 4	For out of much **a** and anguish
2Co	4:17	For our light **a**, which is but
2Co	8: 2	that in a great trial of **a**
Phil	1:16	to add **a** to my chains
1Th	1: 6	received the word in much **a**
1Th	3: 7	brethren, in all our **a** and
Heb	11:25	choosing rather to suffer **a**

AFFLICTIONS (see AFFLICTION)

Ps	34:19	Many are the **a** of the
Ps	132: 1	remember David And all his **a**
Mark	3:10	so that as many as had **a**
Luke	7:21	of their infirmities, **a**, and
Col	1:24	is lacking in the **a** of Christ
2Ti	4: 5	in all things, endure **a**, do

AFFORD

Lev	14:21	if he is poor and cannot **a** it

AFRAID

Gen	3:10	I was **a** because I was naked
Gen	15: 1	Do not be **a**, Abram
Gen	18:15	not laugh," for she was **a**
Gen	50:19	Do not be **a**, for am I in the
Ex	3: 6	for he was **a** to look upon God
Lev	26: 6	down, and none will make you **a**
Deut	1:29	be terrified, or be **a** of them
Deut	20: 3	your heart faint, do not be **a**
Deut	28:60	of Egypt, of which you were **a**
Josh	1: 9	do not be **a**, nor be dismayed,
1Sa	18:12	Now Saul was **a** of David,
2Sa	12:18	**a** to tell him that the child
1Ki	1:51	Adonijah is **a** of King Solomon
2Ki	19: 6	Do not be **a** of the words
Neh	2: 2	So I became dreadfully **a**
Neh	6: 9	all were trying to make us **a**
Job	9:28	I am **a** of all my sufferings
Job	15:24	Trouble and anguish make him **a**
Job	19:29	be **a** of the sword for
Job	23:15	consider this, I am **a** of Him
Ps	3: 6	I will not be **a** of ten
Ps	27: 1	Of whom shall I be **a**

Ps	56: 3	Whenever I am **a**, I will trust
Ps	56:11	I will not be **a**
Ps	77:16	waters saw You, they were **a**
Ps	119:120	And I am **a** of Your judgments
Prov	3:24	lie down, you will not be **a**
Prov	3:25	Do not be **a** of sudden terror,
Prov	31:21	She is not **a** of snow for her
Eccl	12: 5	when they are **a** of height
Is	8:12	nor be **a** of their threats,
Is	12: 2	I will trust and not be **a**
Is	17: 2	and no one will make them **a**
Is	41: 5	the ends of the earth were **a**
Is	51:12	be **a** of a man who will die
Jer	2:12	at this, and be horribly **a**
Jer	30:10	and no one shall make him **a**
Jer	36:24	Yet they were not **a**, nor did
Jer	42:11	Do not be **a** of the king of
Jer	42:11	of Babylon, of whom you are **a**
Ezek	2: 6	do not be **a** of them nor be
Dan	4: 5	I saw a dream which made me **a**
Dan	8:17	and when he came I was **a** and
Joel	2:22	Do not be **a**, you beasts of
Jon	1: 5	Then the mariners were **a**
Mic	7:17	They shall be **a** of the LORD
Hab	3: 2	heard your speech and was **a**
Matt	1:20	do not be **a** to take to you
Matt	2:22	Herod, he was **a** to go there
Matt	25:25	And I was **a**, and went and hid
Matt	28:10	Do not be **a**. Go and tell my
Mark	5:36	Do not be **a**; only believe.
Mark	9:32	saying, and were **a** to ask Him
Mark	16: 8	to anyone, for they were **a**
Luke	1:13	Do not be **a**, Zacharias, for
Luke	1:30	Do not be **a**, Mary, for you
Luke	5:10	Do not be **a**. From now on you
Luke	8:25	And they were **a**, and marveled
Luke	12: 4	do not be **a** of those who kill
John	6:20	"It is I; do not be **a**
John	14:27	troubled, neither let it be **a**
Acts	18: 9	Do not be **a**, but speak, and do
Acts	22: 9	saw the light and were **a**, but
Acts	22:29	and the commander was also **a**
Acts	24:25	judgment to come, Felix was **a**
Acts	27:24	saying, "Do not be **a**, Paul
Rom	13: 4	But if you do evil, be **a**
Gal	4:11	I am **a** for you, lest I have
Heb	11:23	they were not **a** of the king's
Heb	12:21	I am exceedingly **a** and
1Pe	3:14	do not be **a** of their threats,
2Pe	2:10	they are not **a** to speak evil
Rev	1:17	Do not be **a**; I am the First

AFRESH†

Job	7: 5	is cracked and breaks out **a**

AFTERNOON†

Judg	19: 8	So they delayed until **a**

AGABUS

Acts	11:28	Then one of them, named **A**

AGAG (see AGAGITE)

1Sa	15: 8	He also took **A** king of the
1Sa	15:33	Samuel hacked **A** in pieces

AGAGITE (see AGAG)

Esth	3: 1	the son of Hammedatha the **A**
Esth	8: 3	the evil of Haman the **A**

AGATE†

Ex	28:19	third row, a jacinth, an **a**
Ex	39:12	third row, a jacinth, an **a**

AGE (see AGED, AGES)

Gen	15:15	be buried at a good old **a**
Gen	18:11	passed the **a** of childbearing
Gen	21: 7	borne him a son in his old **a**
Gen	48:10	of Israel were dim with **a**

Ruth 4:15 and a nourisher of your old **a**
1Sa 2:33 die in the flower of their **a**
Job 5:26 come to the grave at a full **a**
Job 32: 7 **A** should speak, and multitude
Ps 92:14 still bear fruit in old **a**
Is 46: 4 even to your old **a**, I am He,
Dan 1:10 the young men who are your **a**
Zech 8: 4 his hand because of great **a**
Matt 12:32 this **a** or in the **a** to come
Matt 13:39 harvest is the end of the **a**
Mark 10:30 in the **a** to come, eternal
Luke 1:36 conceived a son in her old **a**
Luke 3:23 at about thirty years of **a**
Luke 8:42 about twelve years of **a**, and
Luke 20:34 The sons of this **a** marry and
John 9:21 He is of **a**; ask him.
1Co 1:20 is the disputer of this **a**
1Co 2: 6 yet not the wisdom of this **a**
1Co 2: 8 of the rulers of this **a** knew
1Co 3:18 seems to be wise in this **a**
2Co 4: 4 the god of this **a** has blinded
Gal 1: 4 us from this present evil **a**
Eph 1:21 not only in this **a** but also
Eph 6:12 of the darkness of this **a**
1Ti 6:17 present **a** not to be haughty
Heb 6: 5 the powers of the **a** to come

AGED (see AGE)
2Sa 19:32 Barzillai was a very **a** man
Job 12:12 Wisdom is with **a** men, and with
Lam 3: 4 He has **a** my flesh and my skin,
Phm 9 such a one as Paul, the **a**

AGENTS
1Ki 10:29 and thus, through their **a**,

AGES † (see AGE)
1Co 2: 7 before the **a** for our glory
1Co 10:11 the ends of the **a** have come
Eph 2: 7 that in the **a** to come He
Eph 3: 5 which in other **a** was not made
Eph 3: 9 from the beginning of the **a**
Col 1:26 which has been hidden from **a**
Heb 9:26 now, once at the end of the **a**

AGITATED †
Ezek 16:43 but a Me with all these

AGONY †
Is 23: 5 they also will be in **a** at the
Luke 22:44 And being in **a**, He prayed more

AGREE (see AGREEABLE, AGREED, AGREEMENT)
Matt 5:25 **A** with your adversary quickly
Matt 18:19 of you **a** on earth concerning
Matt 20:13 Did you not **a** with me for a
Mark 14:56 their testimonies did not **a**
Acts 15:15 the words of the prophets **a**
Rom 7:16 I **a** with the law that it is
1Jn 5: 8 and these three **a** as one

AGREEABLE † (see AGREE)
Zech 11:12 If it is **a** to you, give me my

AGREED (see AGREE)
Dan 2: 9 For you have **a** to speak lying
Amos 3: 3 together, unless they are **a**
Matt 20: 2 Now when he had **a** with the
Luke 22: 5 glad, and **a** to give him money
John 9:22 for the Jews had **a** already

AGREEMENT (see AGREE)
Num 30: 2 to bind himself by some **a**
Num 30:10 herself by an **a** with an oath
Dan 11: 6 of the North to make an **a**
2Co 6:16 what **a** has the temple of God

AGRIPPA
Acts 25:13 And after some days King **A**
Acts 26: 1 Then **A** said to Paul, "You

AGROUND
Acts 27:17 run **a** on the Syrtis Sands

AGUR †
Prov 30: 1 The words of **A** the son of

AHAB (see AHAB'S)
1Ki 16:29 **A** the son of Omri became king
1Ki 18:16 and **A** went to meet Elijah
1Ki 19: 1 And **A** told Jezebel all that
1Ki 20:13 approached **A** king of Israel
1Ki 21: 1 palace of **A** king of Samaria
1Ki 21: 2 So **A** spoke to Naboth, saying,
1Ki 22:39 Now the rest of the acts of **A**
1Ki 22:49 son of **A** said to Jehoshaphat
1Ki 22:51 Ahaziah the son of **A** became
2Ki 1: 1 Israel after the death of **A**
2Ki 3: 1 Now Jehoram the son of **A**
2Ki 8:18 as the house of **A** had done
2Ki 8:18 daughter of **A** was his wife
2Ki 10:11 of the house of **A** in Jezreel
2Ki 21:13 the plummet of the house of **A**
Jer 29:22 make you like Zedekiah and **A**

AHAB'S (see AHAB)
Mic 6:16 the works of **A** house are done

AHASUERUS
Ezra 4: 6 Now in the reign of **A**, in the
Esth 1: 1 **A** (this was the **A** who
Esth 1: 2 in those days when King **A** sat
Esth 3: 1 things King **A** promoted Haman
Esth 10: 3 the Jew was second to King **A**
Dan 9: 1 year of Darius the son of **A**

AHAZ
2Ki 15:38 Then **A** his son reigned in his
2Ki 16: 1 **A** the son of Jotham, king of
2Ki 16:10 Now King **A** went to Damascus
2Ki 16:20 So **A** rested with his fathers,
2Ki 18: 1 that Hezekiah the son of **A**
2Ki 20:11 gone down on the sundial of **A**
Is 1: 1 the days of Uzziah, Jotham, **A**
Is 7: 3 Go out now to meet **A**, you and
Is 7:10 the LORD spoke again to **A**
Is 7:12 But **A** said, "I will not ask,
Is 14:28 in the year that King **A** died
Hos 1: 1 the days of Uzziah, Jotham, **A**
Mic 1: 1 in the days of Jotham, **A**, and
Matt 1: 9 begot Jotham, Jotham begot **A**
Matt 1: 9 **A**, and **A** begot Hezekiah

AHAZIAH (see JEHOAHAZ)
1Ki 22:40 Then **A** his son reigned in his
1Ki 22:51 **A** the son of Ahab became king
2Ki 1: 2 Now **A** fell through the
2Ki 8:24 The **A** his son reigned in his
2Ki 8:25 **A** the son of Jehoram, king of
2Ki 11: 2 took Joash the son of **A**, and
2Ki 13: 1 year of Joash the son of **A**
2Ki 14:13 son of Jehoash, the son of **A**

AHIJAH (see AHIMELECH)
1Ki 11:29 that the prophet **A** the
1Ki 12:15 the Lord had spoken by **A** the
1Ki 14: 4 But **A** could not see, for his
1Ki 14:18 His servant **A** the prophet
1Ki 15:27 Then Baasha the son of **A**, of
1Ki 15:29 His servant **A** the Shilonite
1Ki 15:33 Baasha the son of **A** became
2Ch 9:29 prophecy of **A** the Shilonite

AHIKAM
2Ki 22:12 **A** the son of Shaphan, Achbor
2Ki 22:14 So Hilkiah the priest, **A**,
2Ki 25:22 he made Gedaliah the son of **A**
Jer 40: 7 son of **A** governor in the land
Jer 41: 2 struck Gedaliah the son of **A**

AHIMAAZ

2Sa	18:19	Then A the son of Zadok said,
2Sa	18:23	Then A ran by way of the

AHIMAN

Num	13:22	A, Sheshai, and Talmai, the

AHIMELECH (see ABIMELECH, AHIJAH, AHIMELECH'S)

1Sa	21: 1	came to Nob, to A the priest
1Sa	21: 2	So David said to A the priest
1Sa	22:16	You shall surely die, A, you
1Sa	23: 6	of A fled to David at Keilah
2Sa	8:17	A the son of Abiathar were
1Ch	24:31	of King David, Zadok, A, and

AHIMELECH'S (see AHIMELECH)

1Sa	30: 7	Abiathar the priest, A son,

AHINOAM

1Sa	25:43	David also took A of Jezreel
2Sa	3: 2	Amnon by A the Jezreelitess

AHIO

2Sa	6: 3	and Uzzah and A, the sons of
2Sa	6: 4	and A went before the ark

AHITHOPHEL

2Sa	15:12	sent for A the Gilonite,
2Sa	15:31	A is among the conspirators
2Sa	15:31	counsel of A into foolishness
2Sa	16:20	Then Absalom said to A
2Sa	16:23	advice of A both with David
2Sa	17:14	defeat the good advice of A
1Ch	27:33	A was the king's counselor,

AHOLIAB

Ex	31: 6	him A the son of Ahisamach
Ex	36: 2	Moses called Bezalel and A

AI (see AIATH, AIJA)

Gen	12: 8	on the west and A on the east
Gen	13: 3	between Bethel and A,
Josh	7: 2	sent men from Jericho to A
Josh	7: 2	men went up and spied out A
Josh	7: 3	men go up and attack A
Josh	7: 4	they fled before the men of A
Josh	7: 5	And the men of A struck down
Josh	8:28	So Joshua burned A and made it
Jer	49: 3	O Heshbon, for A is plundered

AIATH† (see AI)

Is	10:28	He has come to A, he has

AID (see AIDED, AIDES)

2Sa	21:17	son of Zeruiah came to his a
Phil	4:16	Thessalonica you sent a once
Heb	2:16	He does not give a to angels

AIDED† (see AID)

Judg	9:24	who a him in the killing of
Dan	11:34	they shall be a with a little

AIDES† (see AID)

2Ki	5:15	man of God, he and all his a

AIJA† (see AI)

Neh	11:31	Geba dwelt in Michmash, A

AIJALON

Josh	10:12	and Moon, in the Valley of A
Judg	12:12	and was buried at A in the

AILS

Gen	21:17	What a you, Hagar
Ps	114: 5	What a you, O sea, that you

AIM† (see AIMLESS)

Rom	15:20	it my a to preach the gospel
2Co	5: 9	Therefore we make it our a

AIMLESS† (see AIM)

1Pe	1:18	from your a conduct received

AIR

Gen	1:26	sea, over the birds of the a
Ps	8: 8	The birds of the a, And the
Prov	30:19	the way of an eagle in the a
Matt	6:26	Look at the birds of the a
Matt	8:20	and birds of the a have nests
Mark	4: 4	and the birds of the a came
Mark	4:32	a may nest under its shade
Acts	22:23	and threw dust into the a,
1Co	9:26	not as one who beats the a
1Co	14: 9	will be speaking into the a
Eph	2: 2	prince of the power of the a
1Th	4:17	to meet the Lord in the a
Rev	16:17	out his bowl into the a, and a

AKEL DAMA

Acts	1:19	in their own language, A,

AKRABBIM

Num	34: 4	side of the Ascent of A,

ALABASTER†

Esth	1: 6	on a mosaic pavement of a
Matt	26: 7	an a flask of very costly
Mark	14: 3	a woman came having an a
Luke	7:37	house, brought an a flask of

ALAMOTH

1Ch	15:20	with strings according to A

ALARM (see ALARMED)

Num	10: 9	sound an a with the trumpets
Jer	4:19	of the trumpet, the a of war

ALARMED (see ALARM)

Mark	16: 5	and they were a

ALEXANDER

Mark	15:21	a Cyrenian, the father of A
Acts	4: 6	priest, Caiaphas, John, and A
Acts	19:33	And they drew A out of the
1Ti	1:20	of whom are Hymenaeus and A
2Ti	4:14	A the coppersmith did me much

ALEXANDRIA† (see ALEXANDRIAN)

Acts	18:24	Jew named Apollos, born at A

ALEXANDRIAN† (see ALEXANDRIA, ALEXANDRIANS)

Acts	27: 6	an A ship sailing to Italy
Acts	28:11	months we sailed in an A ship

ALEXANDRIANS† (see ALEXANDRIAN)

Acts	6: 9	of the Freedmen (Cyrenians, A

ALGUM (see ALMUG)

2Ch	9:10	from Ophir, brought a wood

ALIEN (see ALIENS)

2Sa	1:13	I am the son of an a, an
Ps	69: 8	an a to my mother's children
Jer	2:21	degenerate plant of an a vine
Mal	3: 5	those who turn away an a

ALIENATE† (see ALIENATED)

Ezek	48:14	they may not a this best part

ALIENATED (see ALIENATE)

Ezek	23:17	them, and a herself from them
Eph	4:18	being a from the life of God,
Col	1:21	And you, who once were a and

ALIENS (see ALIEN)

Deut	24:14	a who is in your land within
1Ch	29:15	For we are a and pilgrims
Hos	7: 9	A have devoured his strength,
Eph	2:12	being a from the commonwealth
Heb	11:34	to flight the armies of the a

ALIGHT† (see ALIGHTED, ALIGHTING)

Prov	26: 2	without cause shall not a

ALIGHTED† (see ALIGHT)

Judg	4:15	Sisera a from his chariot and

ALIGHTING† (*see* ALIGHT)
Matt 3:16 like a dove and a upon Him

ALIVE
Gen 6:19 ark, to keep them a with you
Gen 45:28 Joseph my son is still a
Gen 50:20 day, to save many people a
Ex 1:17 but saved the male children a
Ex 1:22 daughter you shall save a
Num 16:30 they go down a into the pit
Num 31:15 Have you kept all the women a
Deut 5: 3 today, all of us who are a
Deut 6:24 that He might preserve us a
Deut 32:39 I kill and I make a
Josh 8:23 the king of Ai they took a
1Sa 27: 9 left neither man nor woman a
2Sa 12:18 while the child was a
2Sa 18:14 while he was still a in the
1Ki 20:18 out for peace, take them a
Ps 22:29 he who cannot keep himself a
Ps 30: 3 You have kept me a, that I
Ps 55:15 Let them go down a into hell
Ps 124: 3 would have swallowed us a
Prov 1:12 us swallow them a like Sheol
Eccl 4: 2 the living who are still a
Matt 27:63 while He was still a, how
Luke 15:24 my son was dead and is a again
Luke 15:32 your brother was dead and is a
Luke 24:23 of angels who said He was a
Acts 1: 3 He also presented Himself a
Acts 20:12 brought the young man in a
Acts 25:19 whom Paul affirmed to be a
Rom 6:11 but a to God in Christ Jesus
Rom 6:13 God as being a from the dead
Rom 7: 9 I was a once without the law,
1Co 15:22 in Christ all shall be made a
Eph 2: 1 And you He made a, who were
1Th 4:17 Then we who are a and remain
1Pe 3:18 but made a by the Spirit,
Rev 1:18 and behold, I am a forevermore
Rev 3: 1 I have a name that you are a
Rev 19:20 These two were cast into

ALLAYS†
Prov 15:18 is slow to anger a contention

ALLELUIA
Rev 19: 1 A! Salvation and glory and

ALLIED (*see* ALLIES)
2Ch 18: 1 by marriage he a himself with
Neh 13: 4 of our God, was a with Tobiah

ALLIES (*see* ALLIED)
Gen 14:13 and they were a with Abram
Jer 2:37 has rejected your trusted a

ALLON BACHUTH†
Gen 35: 8 the name of it was called A

ALLOTMENT (*see* ALLOTTED)
Job 31: 2 For what is the a of God from
Ps 105:11 As the a of your inheritance
Acts 13:19 their land to them by a

ALLOTTED (*see* ALLOTMENT)
Gen 47:22 rations a to them by Pharaoh
Judg 1: 3 up with me to my a territory
Job 7: 3 so I have been a months of
Ps 78:55 A them an inheritance by
Ps 125: 3 the land a to the righteous

ALLOW (*see* ALLOWANCE, ALLOWED)
Gen 31: 7 God did not a him to hurt me
Gen 31:28 you did not a me to kiss my
Ex 12:23 not a the destroyer to come
1Sa 24: 7 and did not a them to rise
Ps 16:10 Nor will You a Your Holy One
Ps 66: 9 does not a our feet to be

Ps 89:33 Nor a My faithfulness to fail
Ps 121: 3 He will not a your foot to be
Matt 23:13 nor do you a those who are
Mark 1:34 He did not a the demons to
Mark 11:16 And He would not a anyone to
Luke 4:41 did not a them to speak, for
Acts 2:27 nor will You a Your Holy One
Acts 13:35 You will not a Your Holy One
1Co 10:13 who will not a you to be
Rev 2:20 you, because you a that woman
Rev 11: 9 not a their dead bodies to be

ALLOWANCE† (*see* ALLOW)
Esth 2: 9 to her, besides her a

ALLOWED† (*see* ALLOW)
Deut 8: 3 a you to hunger, and fed you
Job 31:30 Indeed I have not a my mouth
Matt 3:15 Then he a Him
Matt 24:43 not a his house to be broken
Luke 12:39 not a his house to be broken
Acts 14:16 a all nations to walk in

ALLOY†
Is 1:25 and take away all your a

ALLURE†
Prov 6:25 nor let her a you with her
Hos 2:14 behold, I will a her, will
2Pe 2:18 they a through the lusts of

ALMIGHTY
Gen 17: 1 I am A God; walk before Me
Gen 35:11 said to him: I am God A
Ex 6: 3 Isaac, and to Jacob, as God A
Num 24: 4 who sees the vision of the A
Ruth 1:21 me, and the A has afflicted me
Job 5:17 the chastening of the A
Job 6: 4 arrows of the A are within me
Job 11: 7 find out the limits of the A
Job 13: 3 But I would speak to the A
Job 22:25 the A will be your gold and
Job 23:16 weak, and the A terrifies me
Job 24: 1 are not hidden from the A
Job 31: 2 of the A from on high
Job 31:35 that the A would answer me,
Job 33: 4 breath of the A gives me life
Ps 68:14 When the A scattered kings in
Ps 91: 1 under the shadow of the A
Is 13: 6 as destruction from the A
Ezek 1:24 like the voice of the A, a
Ezek 10: 5 like the voice of A God when
2Co 6:18 and daughters, says the LORD A
Rev 1: 8 was and who is to come, the A
Rev 4: 8 Holy, holy, holy, Lord God A
Rev 16:14 of that great day of God A
Rev 19:15 fierceness and wrath of A God

ALMOND (*see* ALMONDS)
Gen 30:37 of green poplar and of the a
Ex 25:33 like a blossoms on one branch
Eccl 12: 5 when the a tree blossoms, the
Jer 1:11 I see a branch of an a tree

ALMONDS† (*see* ALMOND)
Gen 43:11 and myrrh, pistachio nuts and a
Num 17: 8 blossoms and yielded ripe a

ALMS
Luke 12:33 Sell what you have and give a
Acts 3: 3 into the temple, asked for a
Acts 10: 2 who gave a generously to the
Acts 10: 4 your a have come up for a

ALMUG (*see* ALGUM)
1Ki 10:11 great quantities of a wood

ALOES
Prov 7:17 perfumed my bed with myrrh, a
Song 4:14 of frankincense, myrrh and a

John   19:39 a mixture of myrrh and **a**,

ALOOF†
Ps   38:11 stand **a** from my plague, And my

ALOUD
Gen   45: 2 And he wept **a**, and the
1Ki   18:27 Cry **a**, for he is a god
1Ch   16:42 to sound **a** with trumpets and
Ezra   3:12 yet many shouted **a** for joy
Ps   51:14 my tongue shall sing **a** of
Prov   1:20 Wisdom calls **a** outside
Is   58: 1 Cry **a**, spare not
Mark   15: 8 Then the multitude, crying **a**

ALPHA†
Rev   1: 8 I am the **A** and the Omega
Rev   1:11 I am the **A** and the Omega
Rev   21: 6 I am the **A** and the Omega
Rev   22:13 I am the **A** and the Omega

ALPHAEUS (*see* CLEOPAS)
Matt   10: 3 James the son of **A**, and
Mark   2:14 by, He saw Levi the son of **A**

ALTAR (*see* ALTARS, CENSER)
Gen   8:20 Noah built an **a** to the LORD
Gen   8:20 burnt offerings on the **a**
Gen   22: 9 And Abraham built an **a** there
Gen   22: 9 his son and laid him on the **a**
Gen   35: 1 make an **a** there to God, who
Ex   17:15 And Moses built an **a** and called
Ex   20:24 An **a** of earth you shall make
Ex   20:25 if you make Me an **a** of stone
Ex   24: 6 blood he sprinkled on the **a**
Ex   27: 1 make an **a** of acacia wood,
Ex   29:37 make atonement for the **a** and
Ex   29:37 And the **a** shall be most holy
Ex   30:20 come near the **a** to minister
Ex   37:25 the incense **a** of acacia wood
Ex   38: 3 all the utensils for the **a**
Ex   38: 4 of bronze network for the **a**
Ex   39:38 the gold **a**, the anointing oil
Ex   40:10 You shall anoint the **a** of the
Lev   1: 7 shall put fire on the **a**, and
Lev   1:16 beside the **a** on the east side
Lev   3:11 burn them on the **a** as food
Lev   4: 7 blood on the horns of the **a**
Lev   4:18 **a** which is before the LORD
Lev   9: 7 Go to the **a**, offer your sin
Num   4:13 away the ashes from the **a**
Num   16:38 as a covering for the **a**
Deut   12:27 on the **a** of the LORD your God
Deut   27: 5 LORD your God, an **a** of stones
Josh   8:30 Now Joshua built an **a** to the
Josh   22:10 a great, impressive **a**
Judg   6:25 tear down the **a** of Baal that
Judg   13:20 in the flame of the **a**
1Sa   14:35 Saul built an **a** to the LORD
1Ki   1:50 hold of the horns of the **a**
1Ki   8:22 Solomon stood before the **a** of
1Ki   13: 2 and said, "O **a**, altar!
1Ki   13: 5 The **a** also was split apart,
1Ki   13: 5 ashes poured out from the **a**
1Ki   13:32 LORD against the **a** in Bethel
1Ki   18:30 he repaired the **a** of the LORD
1Ki   18:32 an **a** in the name of the LORD
1Ki   18:32 **a** large enough to hold two
1Ki   18:35 water ran all around the **a**
2Ki   16:10 saw an **a** that was at Damascus
2Ki   23:16 tombs and burned them on the **a**
2Ch   15: 8 he restored the **a** of the LORD
2Ch   32:12 shall worship before one **a**
Ps   26: 6 So I will go about Your **a**
Ps   43: 4 I will go to the **a** of God
Ps   51:19 shall offer bulls on Your **a**
Ps   118:27 cords to the horns of the **a**

Is   6: 6 with the tongs from the **a**
Is   19:19 that day there will be an **a**
Is   27: 9 a like chalkstones that are
Is   56: 7 will be accepted on My **a**
Lam   2: 7 The Lord has spurned His **a**
Ezek   8: 5 and there, north of the **a** gate
Ezek   8:16 between the porch and the **a**
Ezek   40:46 who have charge of the **a**
Ezek   43:15 The **a** hearth is four cubits
Ezek   43:20 it on the four horns of the **a**
Ezek   43:26 make atonement for the **a** and
Ezek   45:19 corners of the ledge of the **a**
Amos   2: 8 They lie down by every **a** on
Amos   3:14 of the **a** shall be cut off
Amos   9: 1 the Lord standing by the **a**
Zech   14:20 like the bowls before the **a**
Mal   1: 7 offer defiled food on My **a**
Matt   5:23 you bring your gift to the **a**
Matt   23:18 And, 'Whoever swears by the **a**
Luke   1:11 side of the **a** of incense
Luke   11:51 who perished between the **a**
Acts   17:23 I even found an **a** with this
1Co   10:18 sacrifices partakers of the **a**
Heb   13:10 We have an **a** from which those
Jas   2:21 Isaac his son on the **a**
Rev   6: 9 I saw under the **a** the souls
Rev   8: 3 the saints upon the golden **a**
Rev   8: 5 it with fire from the **a**, and
Rev   14:18 angel came out from the **a**

ALTARS (*see* ALTAR)
Ex   34:13 But you shall destroy their **a**
Lev   26:30 cut down your incense **a**, and
Num   3:31 table, the lampstand, the **a**
Num   23: 1 Build seven **a** for me here
1Ki   19:10 covenant, torn down Your **a**
2Ki   11:18 priest of Baal before the **a**
2Ki   18:22 whose **a** Hezekiah has taken
2Ki   21: 3 he raised up **a** for Baal, and
2Ki   21: 4 He also built **a** in the house
2Ki   23:12 The **a** that were on the roof,
2Ki   23:12 the **a** which Manasseh had made
2Ch   31: 1 down the high places and the **a**
Ps   84: 3 Even your **a**, O LORD of hosts,
Is   17: 8 He will not look to the **a**
Is   65: 3 and burn incense on **a** of brick
Jer   11:13 up **a** to that shameful thing
Jer   11:13 **a** to burn incense to Baal
Rom   11: 3 prophets and torn down Your **a**

ALTER (*see* ALTERED, ALTERS)
Ezra   6:12 who put their hand to **a** it
Ps   89:34 Nor **a** the word that has gone

ALTERED† (*see* ALTER)
Esth   1:19 so that it will not be **a**
Luke   9:29 appearance of His face was **a**

ALTERS† (*see* ALTER)
Ezra   6:11 that whoever **a** this edict

ALWAYS (*see* FOREVER)
Ex   25:30 on the table before Me **a**
Ex   28:38 it shall **a** be on his forehead
Deut   5:29 **a** keep all My commandments,
Deut   14:23 to fear the LORD your God **a**
2Sa   9:10 shall eat bread at my table **a**
1Ki   11:36 **a** have a lamp before Me in
Ps   9:18 shall not **a** be forgotten
Ps   10: 5 His ways are **a** prospering
Ps   16: 8 have set the LORD **a** before me
Ps   73:12 ungodly, Who are **a** at ease
Ps   103: 9 He will not **a** strive with us,
Prov   5:19 **a** be enraptured with her love
Prov   8:30 rejoicing **a** before Him,
Prov   28:14 is the man who is **a** reverent
Eccl   9: 8 Let your garments **a** be white

Is	57:16	nor will I **a** be angry
Jer	20:17	her womb **a** enlarged with me
Matt	26:11	you have the poor with you **a**
Matt	28:20	and lo, I am with you **a**, even
Luke	15:31	him, 'Son, you are a with me
Luke	18: 1	that men **a** ought to pray and
John	6:34	Lord, give us this bread **a**
John	18:20	I **a** taught in synagogues and
John	18:20	temple, where the Jews **a** meet
Acts	2:25	the LORD **a** before my face
Acts	7:51	You **a** resist the Holy Spirit
Acts	10: 2	people, and prayed to God **a**
Acts	20:18	manner I **a** lived among you
Rom	1: 9	of you **a** in my prayers,
1Co	1: 4	I thank my God **a** concerning
1Co	15:58	**a** abounding in the work of
2Co	2:14	who **a** leads us in triumph in
2Co	4:10	**a** carrying about in the body
2Co	5: 6	Therefore we are **a** confident
2Co	10:0	as sorrowful, yet **a** rejoicing
2Co	9: 8	**a** having all sufficiency in
Eph	5:20	giving thanks **a** for all
Eph	6:18	praying **a** with all prayer and
Phil	1: 4	**a** in every prayer of mine
Phil	4: 4	Rejoice in the Lord **a**
Col	1: 3	Christ, praying **a** for you
Col	4: 6	your speech **a** be with grace
1Th	1: 2	thanks to God **a** for you all
1Th	4:17	thus we shall **a** be with the
1Th	5:16	Rejoice **a**,
2Th	1: 3	bound to thank God **a** for you
2Th	1:11	Therefore we also pray **a** for
2Ti	3: 7	**a** learning and never able to
Heb	3:10	They **a** go astray in their
Heb	9: 6	the priests **a** went into the
1Pe	3:15	**a** be ready to give a defense
2Pe	1:12	remind you **a** of these things

AM

Gen	4: 9	**A** I my brother's keeper
Gen	6: 7	for I **a** sorry that I have
Gen	15: 1	I **a** your shield, your
Gen	15: 7	I **a** the LORD, who brought you
Gen	17: 1	to him, "I **a** Almighty God
Gen	18:17	from Abraham what I **a** doing
Gen	18:27	I who **a** but dust and ashes
Gen	22: 1	And he said, "Here I **a**."
Gen	22:11	And he said, "Here I **a**."
Gen	26:24	I **a** the God of your father
Gen	26:24	do not fear, for I **a** with you
Gen	28:13	I **a** the LORD God of Abraham
Gen	28:15	I **a** with you and will keep you
Gen	30: 2	**A** I in the place of God, who
Gen	31:13	I **a** the God of Bethel, where
Gen	32:10	I **a** not worthy of the least
Gen	35:11	I **a** God Almighty
Gen	45: 3	to his brothers, "I **a** Joseph
Gen	45: 4	I **a** Joseph your brother, whom
Gen	46: 3	I **a** God, the God of your
Gen	50:19	for a I in the place of God
Ex	3: 4	And he said, "Here I **a**."
Ex	3: 6	I **a** the God of your father
Ex	3:11	Who **a** I that I should go to
Ex	3:14	said to Moses, "I **A** WHO I A
Ex	3:14	I **A** has sent me to you
Ex	4:10	I **a** not eloquent, neither
Ex	6: 2	I **a** the LORD
Ex	6: 6	I **a** the LORD
Ex	6: 7	I **a** the LORD
Ex	6: 8	I **a** the LORD
Ex	6:12	for I **a** of uncircumcised lips
Ex	7: 5	shall know that I **a** the LORD
Ex	7:17	shall know that I **a** the LORD
Ex	15:26	For I **a** the LORD who heals
Ex	20: 2	I **a** the LORD your God, who

Ex	20: 5	**a** a jealous God, visiting the
Lev	11:45	be holy, for I **a** holy
Num	11:14	I **a** not able to bear all
Num	18:20	I **a** your portion and your
Deut	5: 9	**a** a jealous God, visiting the
Deut	32:39	I, **a** He, and there is no God
Josh	23:14	this day I **a** going the way of
Ruth	2:10	of me, since I **a** a foreigner
Ruth	3: 9	I **a** Ruth, your maidservant
Ruth	3:12	that I **a** a close relative;
1Sa	1: 8	**A** I not better to you than
1Sa	3: 5	Here I **a**, for you called me
1Sa	3: 6	Here I **a**, for you called me
1Sa	9:19	Saul and said, "I **a** the seer
2Sa	7:18	Who **a** I, O Lord GOD
2Sa	11: 5	and said, "I **a** with child
1Ki	18:22	I alone **a** left a prophet of
1Ki	19:10	I alone **a** left
1Ki	19:14	I alone **a** left
2Ki	2:10	me when I **a** taken from you
2Ki	5: 7	**A** I God, to kill and make
Neh	6: 3	I **a** doing a great work, so
Job	10:15	If I **a** wicked, woe to me
Job	10:15	even if I **a** righteous, I
Job	10:15	I **a** full of disgrace
Job	12: 3	I **a** not inferior to you
Job	13: 2	I **a** not inferior to you
Job	40: 4	Behold, I **a** vile
Ps	6: 6	I **a** weary with my groaning
Ps	22: 6	But I **a** a worm, and no man
Ps	22:14	I **a** poured out like water, And
Ps	25:16	For I **a** desolate and afflicted
Ps	31: 9	O LORD, for I **a** in trouble
Ps	37:25	have been young, and now **a** old
Ps	40:17	But I **a** poor and needy
Ps	46:10	still, and know that I **a** God
Ps	116:16	I **a** Your servant, the son of
Ps	119:19	I **a** a stranger in the earth
Ps	120: 7	I **a** for peace
Ps	139:14	You, for I **a** fearfully and
Prov	20: 9	clean, I **a** pure from my sin"
Song	1: 5	I **a** dark, but lovely, O
Song	2: 1	I **a** the rose of Sharon, and
Song	2:16	beloved is mine, and I **a** his
Song	6: 3	I **a** my beloved's, and my
Is	1:14	I **a** weary of bearing them
Is	6: 5	Woe is me, for I **a** undone
Is	6: 5	Because I **a** a man of unclean
Is	6: 8	Here **a** I! Send me.
Is	8:18	Here **a** I and the children whom
Is	41: 4	I, the LORD, **a** the first
Is	41:10	Fear not, for I **a** with you
Is	41:10	dismayed, for I **a** your God
Is	42: 8	I **a** the LORD, that is My name
Is	43:11	I **a** the LORD, and besides Me
Is	44: 6	**a** the First and I am the Last
Is	45: 5	I **a** the LORD, and there is no
Is	45: 6	I **a** the LORD, and there is no
Is	45:18	I **a** the LORD, and there is no
Is	45:22	For I **a** God, and there is no
Is	48:12	I **a** He, I am the First, I am
Is	49:26	LORD, **a** your Savior, and your
Is	51:12	even I, **a** He who comforts you
Jer	1: 6	cannot speak, for I **a** a youth
Jer	1: 8	for I **a** with you to deliver
Jer	6:11	I **a** weary of holding it in
Jer	8:21	I **a** mourning
Jer	15:16	for I **a** called by Your name,
Jer	15:20	for I **a** with you to save you
Jer	31: 9	for I **a** a Father to Israel,
Lam	3: 1	I **a** the man who has seen
Ezek	2: 4	I **a** sending you to them, and
Ezek	6: 7	shall know that I **a** the LORD
Ezek	6:10	shall know that I **a** the LORD
Ezek	6:13	shall know that I **a** the LORD

Ezek	6:14	shall know that I a the LORD
Ezek	12:11	Say, 'I a a sign to you
Ezek	26: 3	I a against you, O Tyre, and
Ezek	27: 3	said, 'I a perfect in beauty
Ezek	28: 2	I a a god, I sit in the seat
Ezek	28:22	I a against you, O Sidon
Ezek	38: 3	I a against you, O Gog,
Ezek	39: 1	I a against you, O Gog,
Ezek	44:28	that I a their inheritance
Hos	2: 2	My wife, nor a I her Husband
Hos	11: 9	For I a God, and not man, the
Amos	7: 8	I a setting a plumb line in
Mic	3: 8	But truly I a full of power
Mal	1: 6	If then I a the Father, where
Matt	3:11	whose sandals I a not worthy
Matt	3:17	Son, in whom I a well pleased
Matt	8: 8	Lord, I a not worthy that You
Matt	8: 9	For I also a a man under
Matt	11:29	for I a gentle and lowly in
Matt	16:13	say that I, the Son of Man, a
Matt	16:15	But who do you say that I a
Matt	20:22	that I a baptized with
Matt	20:23	that I a baptized with
Matt	22:32	I a the God of Abraham, the
Matt	24: 5	I a the Christ,' and will
Matt	27:24	I a innocent of the blood of
Matt	27:43	He said, "I a the Son of God
Matt	28:20	I a with you always, even to
Mark	13: 6	in My name, saying, 'I a He
Luke	5: 8	for I a a sinful man, O Lord
Luke	15:19	a no longer worthy to be
Luke	15:21	a no longer worthy to be
Luke	18:11	that I a not like other men
Luke	22:58	Peter said, "Man, I a not
John	1:20	I a not the Christ
John	1:23	I 'The voice of one crying
John	4:26	I who speak to you a He
John	5: 7	but while I a coming, another
John	6:35	them, "I a the bread of life
John	6:51	I a the living bread which
John	7:28	and you know where I a from
John	7:34	where I a you cannot come
John	7:36	where I a you cannot come
John	8:12	I a the light of the world
John	8:14	came from and where I a going
John	8:23	I a from above
John	8:23	I a not of this world
John	8:24	do not believe that I a He
John	8:58	you, before Abraham was, I A
John	9: 5	As long as I a in the world
John	9: 9	He said, "I a he
John	10: 7	I a the door of the sheep
John	10:11	I a the good shepherd
John	10:14	I a the good shepherd
John	10:36	I said, 'I a the Son of God'
John	11:25	I a the resurrection and the
John	12:26	and where I a, there My
John	12:32	if I a lifted up from the
John	13:19	you may believe that I a He
John	14: 3	that where I a, there you may
John	14: 6	I a the way, the truth, and
John	14:10	that I a in the Father, and
John	14:28	I a going to the Father,'
John	15: 1	I a the true vine, and My
John	17:14	just as I a not of the world
John	17:16	just as I a not of the world
John	17:24	Me may be with Me where I a
John	18: 5	Jesus said to them, "I a He
John	18:37	say rightly that I a a king
John	19:21	I the King of the Jews
John	20:17	I a ascending to My Father
Acts	7:32	I a the God of your fathers
Acts	9: 5	I a Jesus, whom you are
Acts	10:21	Yes, I a he whom you seek
Acts	10:26	I myself a also a man

Acts	21:39	I a a Jew from Tarsus, in
Acts	22: 8	I a Jesus of Nazareth, whom
Acts	23: 6	I a a Pharisee, the son of a
Acts	26:15	I a Jesus, whom you are
Acts	26:25	I a not mad, most noble
Rom	1:14	I a a debt both to Greeks
Rom	1:15	me, I a ready to preach the
Rom	1:16	For I a not ashamed of the
Rom	7:14	but I a carnal, sold under
Rom	7:24	O wretched man that I a
Rom	8:38	For I a persuaded that
Rom	9: 1	I a not lying, my conscience
Rom	11:13	inasmuch as I a an apostle to
1Co	1:12	you says, "I a of Paul," or
1Co	9: 1	A I not an apostle
1Co	9: 1	A I not free? Have I not
1Co	10:30	why a I evil spoken of for
1Co	12:15	Because I a not a hand
1Co	13: 2	have not love, I a nothing
1Co	13:12	know just as I also a known
1Co	15: 9	For I a the least of the
1Co	15: 9	who a not worthy to be called
1Co	15:10	grace of God I a what I am
2Co	11:22	Hebrews? So a I.
2Co	11:23	I speak as a fool—I a more:
2Co	11:29	Who is weak, and I a not weak
2Co	11:31	knows that I a not lying
2Co	12:10	I a weak, then I a strong
2Co	12:11	apostles, though I a nothing
Eph	3: 8	who a less than the least of
Eph	6:20	for which I a an ambassador
Phil	3:12	or a already perfected
Phil	4:11	learned in whatever state I a
Col	2: 5	For though I a absent in the
Col	2: 5	yet I a with you in spirit,
Col	4: 3	for which I a also in chains,
1Ti	1:15	sinners, of whom I a chief
Phm	12	I a sending him back
Phm	19	a writing with my own hand
Jas	1:13	I a tempted by God"
2Pe	1:13	as long as I a in this tent
Rev	1: 8	I a the Alpha and the Omega,
Rev	1:11	I a the Alpha and the Omega,
Rev	1:17	I a the First and the Last
Rev	1:18	I a He who lives, and was dead
Rev	1:18	behold, I a alive forevermore
Rev	2:23	I a He who searches the minds
Rev	3:17	say, 'I a rich, have become
Rev	16:15	Behold, I a coming as a thief
Rev	22: 7	I a coming quickly
Rev	22:12	I a coming quickly
Rev	22:16	I a the Root and the Offspring

AMALEK (see AMALEKITE)

Gen	36:12	son, and she bore A to Eliphaz
Ex	17:13	So Joshua defeated A, and his
1Sa	15:20	brought back Agag king of A

AMALEKITE (see AMALEK, AMALEKITES)

1Sa	30:13	from Egypt, servant of an A
2Sa	1: 8	So I answered him, I am an A

AMALEKITES (see AMALEKITE)

Gen	14: 7	all the country of the A, and
Num	13:29	The A dwell in the land of
Num	14:25	Now the A and the Canaanites
Judg	6:33	Then all the Midianites and A
Judg	10:12	Also the Sidonians and A
1Sa	15: 8	took Agag king of the A alive
1Sa	15:20	have utterly destroyed the A

AMASA

2Sa	17:25	Absalom made A captain of the
2Sa	20: 9	Joab took A by the beard with
1Ch	2:17	Abigail bore A

AMAZED (*see* AMAZEMENT, ASTONISHED)
Is   13: 8 they will be **a** at one another
Matt 12:23 And all the multitudes were **a**
Mark   6:51 And they were greatly **a** in
Mark 16: 8 for they trembled and were **a**
Luke   2:48 they saw Him, they were **a**
Acts   9:21 Then all who heard were **a**

AMAZEMENT† (*see* AMAZED)
Mark   5:42 were overcome with great **a**
Acts   3:10 **a** at what had happened to him
Rev   17: 6 her, I marveled with great **a**

AMAZIAH
2Ki   12:21 Then **A** his son reigned in his
2Ki   13:12 against **A** king of Judah, are
2Ki   14: 1 **A** the son of Joash, king of
2Ki   14:17 **A** the son of Joash, king of
2Ki   14:18 Now the rest of the acts of **A**
2Ki   14:21 king instead of his father **A**
2Ki   15: 1 Israel, Azariah the son of **A**
Amos   7:10 Then **A** the priest of Bethel
Amos   7:12 **A** said to Amos
Amos   7:14 Amos answered, and said to **A**

AMBASSADOR† (*see* AMBASSADORS)
Prov 13:17 a faithful **a** brings health
Jer   49:14 an **a** has been sent to the
Eph   6:20 for which I am an **a** in chains

AMBASSADORS (*see* AMBASSADOR)
Josh   9: 4 and went and pretended to be **a**
Is   18: 2 which sends **a** by sea, even in
Is   33: 7 the **a** of peace shall weep
2Co   5:20 Therefore we are **a** for Christ

AMBER
Ezek   1: 4 its midst like the color of **a**

AMBITION† (*see* AMBITIONS)
Phil   1:16 preach Christ from selfish **a**
Phil   2: 3 through selfish **a** or conceit

AMBITIONS† (*see* AMBITION)
2Co   12:20 wrath, selfish **a**
Gal   5:20 wrath, selfish **a**

AMBUSH (*see* AMBUSHES)
Josh   8: 2 Lay an **a** for the city behind
Lam   3:10 in wait, like a lion in **a**
Acts 23:16 sister's son heard of their **a**
Acts 25: 3 while they lay in **a** along the

AMBUSHES† (*see* AMBUSH)
2Ch   20:22 the LORD set **a** against the
Jer   51:12 the watchmen, prepare the **a**

AMEN
Num   5:22 woman shall say, "A, so be it
Deut 27:15 shall answer and say, 'A
Deut 27:16 all the people shall say, 'A
1Ki   1:36 A! May the LORD God of my
1Ch   16:36 all the people said, "A!"
Neh   5:13 the congregation said, "A!"
Neh   8: 6 the people answered, "A, A!"
Ps   41:13 everlasting! A and Amen.
Ps   72:19 His glory. A and Amen.
Ps   89:52 forevermore! A and Amen.
Ps   106:48 let all the people say, "A!"
Jer   28: 6 A! The LORD do so
Matt   6:13 and the glory forever. A.
Matt 28:20 to the end of the age." A.
Mark 16:20 the accompanying signs. A.
Luke 24:53 praising and blessing God. A.
John 21:25 that would be written. A.
Rom   1:25 who is blessed forever. A.
Rom   11:36 to whom be glory forever. A.
Rom   15:33 peace be with you all. A.
Rom   16:20 Jesus Christ be with you. A.
1Co   14:16 A" at your giving of thanks,

1Co   16:24 you all in Christ Jesus. A.
2Co   1:20 in Him are Yes, and in Him A
2Co   13:14 Spirit be with you all. A.
Gal   1: 5 glory forever and ever. A.
Gal   6:18 Christ be with your spirit. A
Eph   3:21 world without end. A.
Col   4:18 Grace be with you. A.
Heb   13:21 be glory forever and ever. A
1Pe   4:11 dominion forever and ever. A.
1Pe   5:11 dominion forever and ever. A.
2Pe   3:18 both now and forever. A.
1Jn   5:21 keep yourselves from idols. A.
Rev   1: 7 of Him. Even so, A.
Rev   1:18 I am alive forevermore. A.
Rev   3:14 These things says the A.
Rev   5:14 living creatures said, "A!"
Rev   19: 4 saying, "A! Alleluia!"
Rev   22:20 I am coming quickly." A.
Rev   22:21 Christ be with you all. A.

AMEND
Jer   7: 3 A your ways and your doings,

AMETHYST†
Ex   28:19 a jacinth, an agate, and a **a**
Ex   39:12 a jacinth, an agate, and a **a**
Rev   21:20 jacinth, and the twelfth **a**

AMID†
Ezek 19:11 height **a** the dense foliage
Amos   1:14 **a** shouting in the day of

AMISS†
Job   5:24 habitation and find nothing **a**
Dan   3:29 which speaks anything **a**
Jas   4: 3 receive, because you ask **a**

AMITTAI†
2Ki   14:25 Jonah the son of **A**
Jon   1: 1 Jonah the son of **A**

AMMINADAB
Num   1: 7 Judah, Nahshon the son of **A**
Ruth   4:19 begot Ram, and Ram begot **A**
Matt   1: 4 Ram begot **A**, A begot Nahshon
Luke   3:33 the son of **A**, the son of Ram,

AMMON (*see* AMMONITE)
Gen   19:38 the people of **A** to this day
Deut   3:11 in Rabbah of the people of **A**
Dan   11:41 and the prominent people of **A**

AMMONITE (*see* AMMON, AMMONITES)
Deut 23: 3 An **A** or Moabite shall not
Neh   13: 1 was found written that no **A**

AMMONITES (*see* AMMONITE)
Josh 13:25 land of the **A** as far as Aroer
1Ki   11: 1 women of the Moabites, **A**,
Jer   49: 2 of war in Rabbah of the **A**

AMNON
2Sa   3: 2 His firstborn was **A** by
2Sa   13: 1 **A** the son of David loved her
2Sa   13: 6 Then **A** lay down and pretended
2Sa   13:15 Then **A** hated her exceedingly,
2Sa   13:22 For Absalom hated **A**, because

AMON
1Ki   22:26 return him to **A** the governor
2Ki   21:18 Then his son **A** reigned in his
2Ki   21:24 had conspired against King **A**
Jer   1: 2 days of Josiah the son of **A**
Nah   3: 8 Are you better than No **A** that
Zeph   1: 1 days of Josiah the son of **A**
Matt   1:10 and **A** begot Josiah

AMORITE (*see* AMORITES)
Gen   10:16 the Jebusite, the **A**, and the
Gen   14:13 trees of Mamre the **A**, brother
Ex   33: 2 out the Canaanite and the **A**

Deut 2:24 into your hand Sihon the A
Ezek 16: 3 your father was an A and your
Ezek 16:45 a Hittite and your father an A

AMORITES (see AMORITE)
Gen 14: 7 and also the A who dwelt in
Gen 15:16 of the A is not yet complete
Gen 15:21 the A, the Canaanites, the
Ex 3: 8 and the Hittites and the A and
Ex 3:17 and the Hittites and the A and
Num 13:29 the A dwell in the mountains
Num 21:21 to Sihon king of the A,
Deut 1: 4 killed Sihon king of the A
Deut 31: 4 and Og, the kings of the A
Josh 5: 1 A who were on the west side
Josh 9:10 A who were beyond the Jordan
Josh 10: 5 the five kings of the A, the
Judg 6:10 do not fear the gods of the A
Judg 10: 8 Jordan in the land of the A
1Sa 7:14 peace between Israel and the A
Ps 135:11 Sihon king of the A, Og king
Ps 136:19 Sihon king of the A, For His

AMOS
Amos 1: 1 The words of A, who was among
Amos 7: 8 A, what do you see
Amos 7:10 A has conspired against you
Amos 7:12 Then Amaziah said to A
Amos 7:14 Then A answered, and said to

AMOUNT (see AMOUNTS)
Gen 30:30 is now increased to a great a
2Sa 8: 8 took a large a of bronze

AMOUNTS† (see AMOUNT)
Ex 30:34 shall be equal a of each

AMOZ
2Ch 26:22 Isaiah the son of A wrote
2Ch 32:20 prophet Isaiah, the son of A
Is 1: 1 vision of Isaiah the son of A

AMPHIPOLIS†
Acts 17: 1 they had passed through A

AMRAM
Ex 6:18 And the sons of Kohath were A
Ex 6:20 life of A were one hundred
Num 26:59 to A she bore Aaron and Moses

AMRAPHEL†
Gen 14: 1 A king of Shinar
Gen 14: 9 A king of Shinar

ANAK (see ANAKIM)
Num 13:22 Talmai, the descendants of A
Num 13:33 of A came from the giants)
Josh 15:13 (Arba was the father of A)
Josh 15:14 three sons of A from there

ANAKIM (see ANAK)
Deut 1:28 seen the sons of the A there
Deut 2:10 and numerous and tall as the A
Deut 2:11 as giants, like the A, but
Josh 11:22 None of the A were left in
Josh 14:15 the greatest man among the A

ANANIAS
Acts 5: 3 A, why has Satan filled your
Acts 5: 5 Then A, hearing these words,
Acts 9:10 disciple at Damascus named A
Acts 9:10 Lord said in a vision, "A."
Acts 9:13 Then A answered, "Lord, I
Acts 9:17 A went his way and entered the
Acts 22:12 Then a certain A, a devout man
Acts 23: 2 the high priest A commanded

ANATH
Judg 3:31 him was Shamgar the son of A
Judg 5: 6 the days of Shamgar, son of A

ANATHOTH
Is 10:30 O poor A!
Jer 1: 1 in A in the land of Benjamin
Jer 11:21 men of A who seek your life
Jer 11:23 catastrophe on the men of A
Jer 29:27 not reproved Jeremiah of A
Jer 32: 7 Buy my field which is in A
Jer 32: 9 son of my uncle who was in A

ANCESTORS† (see ANCESTRY)
Gen 49:26 the blessings of my a, up to
Lev 26:45 the covenant of their a, whom

ANCESTRY† (see ANCESTORS)
Num 1:18 recited their a by families

ANCHOR† (see ANCHORED, ANCHORS)
Heb 6:19 we have as an a of the soul

ANCHORED† (see ANCHOR)
Mark 6:53 land of Gennesaret and a there

ANCHORS† (see ANCHOR)
Acts 27:29 dropped four a from the stern
Acts 27:30 putting out a from the prow
Acts 27:40 And they let go the a and left

ANCIENT (see ANCIENTS)
Deut 33:15 things of the a mountains
Ps 77: 5 of old, The years of a times
Prov 22:28 Do not remove the a landmark
Prov 23:10 Do not remove the a landmark
Eccl 1:10 been in a times before us
Is 19:11 the wise, the son of a kings
Is 23: 7 antiquity is from a days,
Jer 5:15 nation, it is an a nation
Dan 7: 9 and the A of Days was seated
2Pe 2: 5 and did not spare the a world

ANCIENTS† (see ANCIENT)
1Sa 24:13 As the proverb of the a says
Ps 119:100 I understand more than the a

ANDREW
Matt 10: 2 Peter, and A his brother
Mark 1:16 A his brother casting a net
Mark 1:29 the house of Simon and A, with
Mark 3:18 A, Philip, Bartholomew,
Mark 13: 3 and A asked Him privately,
John 1:44 from Bethsaida, the city of A
John 6: 8 One of His disciples, A,
John 12:22 Philip came and told A
John 12:22 and in turn A and Philip told
Acts 1:13 Peter, James, John, and A

ANER
Gen 14:13 of Eshcol and brother of A
Gen 14:24 A, Eshcol, and Mamre

ANGEL (see ANGEL'S, ANGELS)
Gen 16: 7 Now the A of the LORD found
Gen 16:11 the A of the LORD said to her
Gen 21:17 Then the a of God called to
Gen 24: 7 He will send His a before you
Gen 48:16 the A who has redeemed me
Ex 3: 2 the A of the LORD appeared to
Num 22:23 Now the donkey saw the A of
Judg 13: 6 countenance of the A of God
1Sa 29: 9 in my sight as an a of God
2Sa 14:17 for as the a of God, so is my
2Sa 14:20 to the wisdom of the a of God
2Sa 24:16 when the a stretched out His
2Sa 24:17 a who was striking the people
Ps 34: 7 The a of the LORD encamps all
Ps 35: 5 let the a of the LORD chase
Is 63: 9 the A of His Presence saved
Dan 3:28 and Abed-Nego, who sent His A
Dan 6:22 My God sent His a and shut the
Hos 12: 4 Yes, he struggled with the A
Zech 1: 9 So the a who talked with me

Zech 1:11 answered the **A** of the LORD
Matt 1:20 an **a** of the Lord appeared to
Luke 1:18 And Zacharias said to the **a**
Luke 1:26 **a** Gabriel was sent by God to
Luke 1:34 Then Mary said to the **a**
Luke 2:10 Then the **a** said to them, "Do
Luke 2:13 **a** a multitude of the heavenly
Luke 2:21 the name given by the **a**
Acts 5:19 But at night an **a** of the Lord
Acts 10:22 instructed by a holy **a** to
Acts 11:13 an **a** standing in his house
Acts 12: 7 an **a** of the Lord stood by him
Acts 23: 8 and no **a** nor spirit
2Co 11:14 himself into an **a** of light
Gal 1: 8 or an **a** from heaven, preach
Gal 4:14 received me as an **a** of God
Rev 1: 1 by His **a** to His servant John
Rev 2: 1 To the **a** of the church of
Rev 5: 2 Then I saw a strong **a**
Rev 8: 5 Then the **a** took the censer,
Rev 8: 7 The first **a** sounded
Rev 9:11 the **a** of the bottomless pit
Rev 10: 1 a coming down from heaven
Rev 10: 8 the **a** who stands on the sea
Rev 14:19 So the **a** thrust his sickle
Rev 16: 3 Then the second **a** poured out
Rev 18:21 Then a mighty **a** took up a
Rev 21:17 of a man, that is, of an **a**
Rev 22:16 have sent My **a** to testify to

ANGEL'S† (*see* ANGEL)
Rev 8: 4 before God from the **a** hand
Rev 10:10 little book out of the **a** hand

ANGELS (*see* ANGEL, ANGELS')
Gen 19: 1 Now the two **a** came to Sodom
Gen 28:12 and there the **a** of God were
Ps 8: 5 him a little lower than the **a**
Ps 78:49 By sending **a** of destruction
Ps 91:11 give His **a** charge over you
Ps 103:20 Bless the LORD, you His **a**
Ps 104: 4 Who makes His **a** spirits, His
Ps 148: 2 Praise Him, all His **a**
Matt 4: 6 He shall give His **a** charge
Matt 4:11 **a** came and ministered to Him
Matt 13:39 age, and the reapers are the **a**
Matt 16:27 of His Father with His **a**, and
Matt 18:10 always see the face of My
Matt 22:30 but are like **a** of God in
Matt 24:31 He will send His **a** with a
Matt 25:31 and all the holy **a** with Him
Matt 26:53 more than twelve legions of **a**
Mark 12:25 but are like **a** in heaven
Luke 2:15 when the **a** had gone away from
Luke 12: 8 confess before the **a** of God
Luke 15:10 **a** of God over one sinner who
Luke 16:22 by the **a** to Abraham's bosom
Luke 24:23 of **a** who said He was alive
John 1:51 the **a** of God ascending and
John 20:12 And she saw two **a** in white
Acts 7:53 the law by the direction of **a**
Rom 8:38 nor **a** nor principalities nor
1Co 6: 3 know that we shall judge **a**
1Co 11:10 on her head, because of the **a**
1Co 13: 1 the tongues of men and of **a**
2Th 1: 7 from heaven with His mighty **a**
1Ti 3:16 in the Spirit, seen by **a**,
Heb 1: 4 so much better than the **a**
Heb 2: 7 a little lower than the **a**
Heb 2: 9 a little lower than the **a**
Heb 2:16 He does not give aid to **a**
Heb 12:22 an innumerable company of **a**
Heb 13: 2 unwittingly entertained **a**
1Pe 1:12 things which **a** desire to look
1Pe 3:22 at the right hand of God, **a**
2Pe 2: 4 not spare the **a** who sinned

Jude 6 the **a** who did not keep their
Rev 1:20 the **a** of the seven churches
Rev 3: 5 My Father and before His **a**
Rev 5:11 of many **a** around the throne
Rev 8: 2 I saw the seven **a** who stand
Rev 12: 7 the dragon and his **a** fought,
Rev 14:10 in the presence of the holy **a**
Rev 21:12 twelve **a** at the gates, and

ANGELS'† (*see* ANGELS)
Ps 78:25 Men ate **a** food

ANGER (*see* ANGERED, ANGRY)
Gen 27:45 **a** turns away from you, and he
Gen 30: 2 Jacob's **a** was aroused against
Gen 44:18 and do not let your **a** burn
Gen 49: 6 for in their **a** they slew a
Ex 4:14 So the **a** of the LORD was
Ex 32:19 So Moses' **a** became hot, and he
Num 22:22 Then God's **a** was aroused
Num 22:27 so Balaam's **a** was aroused
Num 24:10 Then Balak's **a** was aroused
Num 25: 3 the **a** of the LORD was aroused
Num 25: 4 that the fierce **a** of the LORD
Deut 4:25 your God to provoke Him to **a**
Deut 9:19 For I was afraid of the **a**
Deut 13:17 from the fierceness of His **a**
Deut 19: 6 of blood, while his **a** is hot
Deut 29:23 the LORD overthrew in His **a**
Deut 32:22 For a fire is kindled in My **a**
Josh 7: 1 so the **a** of the LORD burned
1Sa 20:30 Then Saul's **a** was aroused
1Sa 20:34 from the table in fierce **a**
2Sa 12: 5 So David's **a** was greatly
Neh 9:17 and merciful, slow to **a**,
Job 4: 9 of His **a** they are consumed
Job 9: 5 He overturns them in His **a**
Job 18: 4 You who tear yourself in **a**
Job 21:17 God distributes in His **a**
Job 35:15 He has not punished in His **a**
Ps 6: 1 do not rebuke me in Your **a**
Ps 7: 6 Arise, O LORD, in Your **a**
Ps 21: 9 oven in the time of Your **a**
Ps 30: 5 For His **a** is but for a moment
Ps 37: 8 Cease from **a**, and forsake
Ps 56: 7 In **a** cast down the peoples, O
Ps 69:24 wrathful **a** take hold of them
Ps 74: 1 Why does Your **a** smoke against
Ps 78:50 He made a path for His **a**
Ps 85: 5 Your **a** to all generations
Ps 90:11 Who knows the power of Your **a**
Ps 103: 8 and gracious, Slow to **a**, and
Ps 103: 9 will He keep His **a** forever
Prov 15: 1 but a harsh word stirs up **a**
Prov 27: 4 **a** a torrent, but who is able
Eccl 5:17 much sorrow and sickness and **a**
Eccl 7: 9 for **a** rests in the bosom of
Is 10: 5 to Assyria, the rod of My **a**
Is 48: 9 name's sake I will defer My **a**
Is 63: 3 I have trodden them in My **a**
Jer 17: 4 My **a** which shall burn forever
Lam 2: 1 footstool in the day of His **a**
Ezek 5:13 Thus shall My **a** be spent
Ezek 20: 8 fulfill My **a** against them in
Ezek 20:21 fulfill My **a** against them in
Ezek 22:20 so I will gather you in My **a**
Dan 11:20 but not in **a** or in battle
Hos 12:14 Him to **a** most bitterly
Hos 13:11 I gave you a king in My **a**
Hos 14: 4 for My **a** has turned away from
Joel 2:13 and merciful, slow to **a**, and of
Amos 1:11 his **a** tore perpetually, and he
Jon 4: 2 and merciful God, slow to **a**
Mic 5:15 I will execute vengeance in **a**
Mic 7:18 does not retain His **a** forever
Nah 1: 3 the LORD is slow to **a** and

Zeph 2: 3 in the day of the LORD's **a**
Eph 4:31 Let all bitterness, wrath, **a**
Col 3: 8 **a**, wrath, malice, blasphemy,

ANGERED† (*see* ANGER)
Ps 106:32 They **a** Him also at the waters

ANGRY (*see* ANGER)
Gen 4: 5 And Cain was very **a**, and his
Gen 18:30 Let not the Lord be **a**, and I
Gen 18:32 Let not the Lord be **a**, and I
Gen 31:36 Then Jacob was **a** and rebuked
Gen 34: 7 men were grieved and very **a**
Judg 18:25 lest **a** men fall upon you, and
1Sa 18: 8 Then Saul was very **a**, and the
2Sa 6: 8 David became **a** because of the
Ps 2:12 Kiss the Son, lest He be **a**
Ps 4: 4 Be **a**, and do not sin
Ps 7:11 And God is **a** with the wicked
Ps 79: 5 Will You be **a** forever
Prov 21:19 with a contentious and **a** woman
Prov 22:24 no friendship with an **a** man
Prov 25:23 tongue an **a** countenance
Prov 29:22 An **a** man stirs up strife, and
Eccl 7: 9 hasten in your spirit to be **a**
Jer 3: 5 Will He remain **a** forever
Jer 3:12 I will not remain **a** forever
Ezek 16:42 be quiet, and be **a** no more
Dan 2:12 this reason the king was **a**
Jon 4: 1 exceedingly, and he became **a**
Jon 4: 4 Is it right for you to be **a**
Zech 1:15 for I was a little **a**, and they
Matt 2:16 wise men, was exceedingly **a**
Matt 5:22 **a** with his brother without a
Matt 18:34 And his master was **a**, and
Eph 4:26 Be **a**, and do not sin"
Heb 3:10 Therefore I was **a** with that
Heb 3:17 whom was He **a** forty years
Rev 11:18 The nations were **a**, and Your

ANGUISH
Gen 42:21 for we saw the **a** of his soul
Ex 6: 9 Moses, because of **a** of spirit
Job 15:24 Trouble and **a** make him afraid
Ps 77:10 This is my **a**; but I will
Ps 119:143 **a** have overtaken me, Yet Your
Prov 1:27 distress and **a** come upon you
Is 30: 6 **a** land of trouble and **a**, from
Jer 6:24 **A** has taken hold of us, pain
Jer 15: 8 I will cause **a** and terror to
Jer 49:24 **A** and sorrows have taken her
Ezek 30: 9 great **a** shall come upon them,
John 16:21 she no longer remembers the **a**
Rom 2: 9 tribulation and **a**, on every
2Co 2: 4 **a** of heart I wrote to you,

ANIMAL (*see* ANIMALS, BEAST)
Gen 7: 2 seven each of every clean **a**
Gen 8:19 Every **a**, every creeping thing
Ex 22: 5 grazed, and lets loose his **a**
Lev 18:23 Nor shall you mate with any **a**
Lev 24:18 make it good, **a** for a
Deut 4:17 the likeness of any **a** that is
Deut 14: 6 And you may eat every **a** with
Deut 27:21 who lies with any kind of **a**
Eccl 3:21 and the spirit of the **a**
Luke 10:34 and he set him on his own **a**

ANIMALS (*see* ANIMAL, BEASTS)
Gen 7: 2 two each of **a** that are
Gen 7: 8 Of clean **a**, of animals that
Gen 7: 8 of **a** that are unclean, of
Gen 36: 6 his cattle and all his **a**, and
Gen 45:17 Lord your **a** and depart;
Ex 11: 5 and all the firstborn of the **a**
Lev 11: 2 These are the **a** which you
Lev 20:25 distinguish between clean **a**

Num 18:15 of unclean **a** you shall redeem
Deut 14: 6 chews the cud, among the **a**
1Ki 4:33 he spoke also of **a**, of birds,
2Ch 35:11 the Levites skinned the **a**
Ps 66:15 You burnt sacrifices of fat **a**
Eccl 3:18 they themselves are like **a**
Eccl 3:19 man has no advantage over **a**
Ezek 32:13 the hooves of a muddy them
Acts 7:42 you offer Me slaughtered **a**
Acts 10:12 four-footed **a** of the earth
Acts 11: 6 four-footed **a** of the earth
Rom 1:23 and birds and four-footed **a**
1Cor 15:39 of men, another flesh of **a**

ANISE†
Matt 23:23 you pay tithe of mint and **a**

ANKLE† (*see* ANKLES, ANKLETS)
Acts 3: 7 **a** bones received strength

ANKLES† (*see* ANKLE)
Ezek 47: 3 the water came up to my **a**

ANKLETS† (*see* ANKLE)
Is 3:18 the jingling **a**, the scarves,

ANNA†
Luke 2:36 Now there was one, A, a

ANNALS†
2Ch 13:22 in the **a** of the prophet Iddo
2Ch 24:27 they are written in the **a** of

ANNAS†
Luke 3: 2 A and Caiaphas being high
John 18:13 they led Him away to A first
John 18:24 Then A sent Him bound to
Acts 4: 6 as well as A the high priest,

ANNIHILATE
Esth 3:13 to **a** all the Jews, both young
Dan 11:44 fury to destroy and **a** many

ANNOUNCE (*see* ANNOUNCED)
Deut 30:18 I **a** to you today that you
Amos 4: 5 and **a** the freewill offerings
Acts 21:26 entered the temple to **a** the

ANNOUNCED (*see* ANNOUNCE)
Judg 21:13 of Rimmon, and **a** peace to them

ANNOYED†
Acts 16:18 But Paul, greatly **a**, turned

ANNUL† (*see* ANNULLED, ANNULLING, ANNULS)
Job 40: 8 you indeed **a** My judgment
Is 14:27 purposed, and who will **a** it
Gal 3:17 cannot **a** the covenant that

ANNULLED† (*see* ANNUL)
Is 28:18 covenant with death will be **a**

ANNULLING† (*see* ANNUL)
Heb 7:18 **a** of the former commandment

ANNULS† (*see* ANNUL)
Gal 3:15 no one **a** or adds to it

ANOINT (*see* ANOINTED, ANOINTING)
Ex 28:41 You shall **a** them, consecrate
Ex 29: 7 pour it on his head, and **a** him
Ex 30:30 And you shall **a** Aaron and his
Ex 40: 9 **a** the tabernacle and all that
Deut 28:40 but you shall not **a** yourself
Judg 9: 8 forth to **a** a king over them
Ruth 3: 3 **a** yourself, put on your best
1Sa 9:16 you shall **a** him commander
1Sa 15: 1 The LORD sent me to **a** you
1Sa 15:17 did not the LORD **a** you king
1Sa 16: 3 you shall **a** for Me the one I
1Sa 16:12 the LORD said, Arise, **a** him
1Ki 1:34 Nathan the prophet **a** him king

1Ki 19:16 **a** as prophet in your place
Ps 23: 5 You **a** my head with oil
Is 21: 5 you princes, **a** the shield
Dan 9:24 and to a the Most Holy
Matt 6:17 **a** your head and wash your face
Mark 14: 8 to **a** My body for burial
Mark 16: 1 that they might come and **a** Him
Luke 7:46 You did not **a** My head with
Rev 3:18 **a** your eyes with eye salve,

ANOINTED (*see* ANOINT)
Gen 31:13 where you **a** the pillar and
Ex 29: 2 unleavened wafers **a** with oil
Lev 4: 3 if the **a** priest sins,
Lev 16:32 And the priest, who is **a** and
Num 35:25 who was **a** with the holy oil
1Sa 2:10 and exalt the horn of His **a**
1Sa 2:35 walk before My **a** forever
1Sa 10: 1 has **a** you commander over His
1Sa 12: 3 the LORD and before His **a**
1Sa 16:13 **a** him in the midst of his
2Sa 1:21 of Saul, not **a** with oil
2Sa 2: 4 there they **a** David king over
2Sa 19:10 Absalom, whom we **a** over us
2Sa 22:51 king, and shows mercy to His **a**
2Sa 23: 1 the **a** of the God of Jacob, and
1Ki 1:39 the tabernacle and **a** Solomon
1Ch 16:22 Do not touch My **a** ones, and do
2Ch 23:11 Jehoiada and his sons **a** him
Ps 2: 2 the LORD and against His **A**
Ps 18:50 king, And shows mercy to His **a**
Ps 20: 6 that the LORD saves His **a**
Ps 45: 7 has **a** You With the oil of
Ps 84: 9 look upon the face of Your **a**
Ps 105:15 Do not touch My **a** ones, And do
Ps 132:10 turn away the face of Your **A**
Ps 132:17 will prepare a lamp for My **A**
Is 61: 1 because the LORD has **a** Me to
Ezek 28:14 You were the **a** cherub who
Hab 3:13 for salvation with Your **A**
Zech 4:14 These are the two **a** ones, who
Mark 6:13 **a** with oil many who were sick
Luke 4:18 because He has **a** Me to preach
Luke 7:38 **a** them with the fragrant oil
Luke 7:46 but this woman has **a** My feet
John 9: 6 He **a** the eyes of the blind
John 11: 2 It was that Mary who **a** the
John 12: 3 **a** the feet of Jesus, and wiped
Acts 4:27 Servant Jesus, whom You **a**
Acts 10:38 how God **a** Jesus of Nazareth
2Co 1:21 in Christ and has **a** us is God,
Heb 1: 9 has **a** You with the oil of

ANOINTING (*see* ANOINT)
Ex 25: 6 and spices for the **a** oil and
Ex 40:15 for their **a** shall surely be
Lev 8:12 of the **a** oil on Aaron's head
Num 4:16 grain offering, the **a** oil
Jas 5:14 **a** him with oil in the name of
1Jn 2:20 But you have an **a** from the
1Jn 2:27 But the **a** which you have

ANT† (*see* ANTS)
Prov 6: 6 Go to the **a**, you sluggard

ANTELOPE†
Deut 14: 5 the mountain goat, the **a**
Is 51:20 streets, like an **a** in a net

ANTICHRIST† (*see* ANTICHRISTS)
1Jn 2:18 heard that the **A** is coming
1Jn 2:22 He is **a** who denies the Father
1Jn 4: 3 this is the spirit of the **A**
2Jn 7 This is a deceiver and an **a**

ANTICHRISTS† (*see* ANTICHRIST)
1Jn 2:18 even now many **a** have come

ANTICIPATED†
Matt 17:25 into the house, Jesus **a** him

ANTIOCH
Acts 6: 5 Nicolas, a proselyte from **A**
Acts 11:19 as Phoenicia, Cyprus, and **A**
Acts 11:26 first called Christians in **A**
Acts 13: 1 in the church that was at **A**
Acts 13:14 they came to **A** in Pisidia

ANTIPAS†
Rev 2:13 **A** was My faithful martyr, who

ANTIPATRIS†
Acts 23:31 and brought him by night to **A**

ANTIQUITY†
Is 23: 7 whose **a** is from ancient days,
Ezek 26:20 in places desolate from **a**

ANTITYPE†
1Pe 3:21 There is also an **a** which now

ANTS† (*see* ANT)
Prov 30:25 the **a** are a people not strong

ANVIL†
Is 41: 7 him who strikes the **a**, saying

ANXIETIES† (*see* ANXIETY)
Ps 94:19 multitude of my **a** within me
Ps 139:23 Try me, and know my **a**

ANXIETY (*see* ANXIETIES, ANXIOUS)
Prov 12:25 **A** in the heart of man causes
Ezek 4:16 eat bread by weight and with **a**
Ezek 12:18 water with trembling and **a**

ANXIOUS† (*see* ANXIETY, ANXIOUSLY)
1Sa 9:20 do not be **a** about them, for
Job 20: 2 Therefore my **a** thoughts make
Jer 17: 8 will not be **a** in the year of
Dan 2: 3 my spirit is **a** to know the
Luke 12:26 why are you **a** for the rest
Luke 12:29 drink, nor have an **a** mind
Phil 4: 6 Be **a** for nothing, but in

ANXIOUSLY† (*see* ANXIOUS)
Luke 2:48 father and I have sought You **a**

APES†
1Ki 10:22 gold, silver, ivory, **a**, and
2Ch 9:21 gold, silver, ivory, **a**, and

APHEK (*see* APHIK)
Josh 12:18 the king of **A**, one

APHIK† (*see* APHEK)
Judg 1:31 of Ahlab, Achzib, Helbah, **A**

APOLLONIA†
Acts 17: 1 through Amphipolis and **A**, they

APOLLOS
Acts 18:24 Now a certain Jew named **A**
1Co 1:12 I am of **A**," or "I am of
1Co 3: 6 **A** watered, but God gave the
1Co 3:22 whether Paul or **A** or Cephas

APOLLYON†
Rev 9:11 in Greek he has the name **A**

APOSTLE (*see* APOSTLES, APOSTLESHIP)
Rom 1: 1 Christ, called to be an **a**
Rom 11:13 as I am an **a** to the Gentiles
1Co 1: 1 called to be an **a** of Jesus
1Co 9: 1 Am I not an **a**?
1Co 15: 9 not worthy to be called an **a**
2Co 1: 1 an **a** of Jesus Christ by the
Gal 1: 1 Paul, an **a** (not from men nor
1Ti 2: 7 appointed a preacher and an **a**
Heb 3: 1 calling, consider the **A** and

APOSTLES (*see* APOSTLE, APOSTLES')
Matt 10: 2 of the twelve **a** are these

Luke 6:13 twelve whom He also named a
Luke 11:49 will send them prophets and a
Acts 1: 2 to the a whom He had chosen
Acts 1:26 numbered with the eleven a
Acts 2:37 to Peter and the rest of the a
Acts 2:43 signs were done through the a
Acts 4:33 the a gave witness to the
Acts 5:18 and laid their hands on the a
Acts 11: 1 Now the a and brethren who
Acts 15: 4 by the church and the a and the
Acts 15: 6 Now the a and elders came
Rom 16: 7 who are of note among the a
1Co 9: 5 wife, as do also the other a
1Co 12:28 first a, second prophets,
1Co 12:29 Are all a? Are all prophets?
1Co 15: 7 by James, then by all the a
1Co 15: 9 For I am the least of the a
2Co 11: 5 to the most eminent a
2Co 11:13 For such are false a,
Eph 2:20 on the foundation of the a
Eph 3: 5 by the Spirit to His holy a
Eph 4:11 He Himself gave some to be a
1Th 2: 6 made demands as a of Christ
2Pe 3: 2 of us the a of the Lord and
Jude 17 a of our Lord Jesus Christ
Rev 2: 2 those who say they are a and
Rev 18:20 her, O heaven, and you holy a
Rev 21:14 of the twelve a of the Lamb

APOSTLES' (see APOSTLES)
Acts 2:42 steadfastly in the a doctrine
Acts 4:35 and laid them at the a feet
Acts 8:18 the laying on of the a hands

APOSTLESHIP† (see APOSTLE)
Acts 1:25 and a from which Judas by
Rom 1: 5 a for obedience to the faith
1Co 9: 2 the seal of my a in the Lord
Gal 2: 8 in Peter for the a to the

APPALLED (see CONFOUNDED)

APPAREL (see APPARELED)
Judg 14:19 of their men, took their a
2Sa 13:18 virgin daughters wore such a
2Ch 9: 4 his cupbearers and their a
Is 63: 1 One who is glorious in His a
Is 63: 2 Why is Your a red, and Your
Zeph 1: 8 as are clothed with foreign a
Acts 1:10 men stood by them in white a
Acts 20:33 no one's silver or gold or a
1Ti 2: 9 adorn themselves in modest a
Jas 2: 2 with gold rings, in fine a

APPARELED † (see APPAREL)
Luke 7:25 those who are gorgeously a

APPEAL (see APPEALED, APPEALING)
2Ki 8: 3 she went to make an a to the
Acts 25:11 I a to Caesar
Phm 9 love's sake I rather a to you
Phm 10 I a to you for my son
Heb 13:22 I a to you, brethren, bear

APPEALED (see APPEAL)
Acts 25:12 You have a to Caesar
Acts 25:25 he himself had a to Augustus

APPEALING† (see APPEAL)
2Ki 8: 5 a to the king for her house
Is 4: 2 a for those of Israel who

APPEAR (see APPEARANCE, APPEARED, APPEARING, APPEARS)
Gen 1: 9 and let the dry land a"
Ex 23:15 none shall a before Me empty)
Ex 23:17 shall a before the Lord GOD
Ps 90:16 Let Your work a to Your
Ps 102:16 He shall a in His glory

Song 2:12 The flowers a on the earth
Matt 6:16 may a to men to be fasting
Matt 23:27 tombs which indeed a
Matt 23:28 outwardly a righteous to men
Matt 24:30 Son of Man will a in heaven
Luke 19:11 of God would a immediately
Acts 22:30 and all their council to a
Rom 7:13 But sin, that it might a sin
2Co 5:10 For we must all a before the
2Co 13: 7 not that we should a approved
Col 3: 4 also will a with Him in glory
Heb 9:24 now to a in the presence of
Heb 9:28 Him He will a a second time
1Pe 4:18 the ungodly and the sinner a

APPEARANCE (see APPEAR)
Gen 29:17 was beautiful of form and a
Gen 39: 6 was handsome in form and a
Lev 13:43 as the a of leprosy on the
Num 9:15 tabernacle like the a of fire
1Sa 16: 7 man looks at the outward a
Job 4:16 but I could not discern its a
Ezek 1:16 The a of the wheels and their
Ezek 1:26 the a of a man high above it
Ezek 10:22 by the River Chebar, their a
Ezek 40: 3 there was a man whose a was
Dan 1:13 Then let our a be
Dan 8:15 me one having the a of a man
Dan 10: 6 face like the a of lightning
Luke 9:29 the a of His face was altered
John 7:24 Do not judge according to a
2Co 5:12 answer those who boast in a
2Co 10: 7 according to the outward a
Phil 2: 8 And being found in a as a man
Col 2:23 a of wisdom in self-imposed
Rev 4: 3 throne, in a like an emerald

APPEARED (see APPEAR)
Gen 12: 7 Then the LORD a to Abram and
Gen 35: 9 Then God a to Jacob again,
Gen 48: 3 God Almighty a to me at Luz
Ex 3: 2 the Angel of the LORD a to
Ex 3:16 and of Jacob, a to me, saying,
Ex 4: 1 The LORD has not a to you
Ex 6: 3 I a to Abraham, to Isaac, and
Ex 16:10 of the LORD a in the cloud
Num 16:42 and the glory of the LORD a
Judg 13:10 has just now a to me
2Ki 2:11 of fire a with horses of fire
Ezek 10: 1 there a something like a
Ezek 10: 8 The cherubim a to have the
Dan 1:15 their features a better
Dan 5: 5 the fingers of a man's hand a
Dan 8: 1 Belshazzar a vision a to me
Matt 1:20 the Lord a to him in a dream
Matt 2: 7 them what time the star a
Matt 13:26 a crop, then the tares also a
Matt 17: 3 Elijah a to them, talking
Matt 27:53 the holy city and a to many
Mark 16: 9 He a first to Mary Magdalene,
Mark 16:12 He a in another form to two
Mark 16:14 Later He a to the eleven
Luke 9: 8 and by some that Elijah had a
Luke 9:31 who a in glory and spoke of
Luke 22:43 Then an angel a to Him from
Luke 24:34 indeed, and has a to Simon
Acts 2: 3 Then there a to them divided
Acts 7: 2 The God of glory a to our
Acts 7:35 who a to him in the bush
Acts 9:17 who a to you on the road as
Acts 16: 9 a vision a to Paul in the
Acts 26:16 for I have a to you for this
Acts 27:20 sun nor stars a for many days
Tit 2:11 salvation has a to all men
Tit 3: 4 God our Savior toward man a
Rev 12: 1 Now a great sign a in heaven

APPEARING† (*see* APPEAR)

1Ti	6:14	our Lord Jesus Christ's **a**
2Ti	1:10	now been revealed by the **a** of
2Ti	4: 1	living and the dead at His **a**
2Ti	4: 8	to all who have loved His **a**
Tit	2:13	glorious **a** of our great God

APPEARS (*see* APPEAR)

Ps	84: 7	Each one of them **a** before
Mal	3: 2	And who can stand when He **a**
Col	3: 4	When Christ who is our life **a**
Jas	4:14	that **a** for a little time and
1Pe	5: 4	and when the Chief Shepherd **a**
1Jn	2:28	abide in Him, that when He **a**

APPEASE† (*see* APPEASED)

Gen	32:20	I will **a** him with the present
Prov	16:14	but a wise man will **a** it
Matt	28:14	ears, we will **a** him and make

APPEASED† (*see* APPEASE)

Prov	6:35	nor will he be **a** though you

APPETITE†

Job	38:39	or satisfy the **a** of the young
Prov	23: 2	if you are a man given to **a**

APPII†

Acts	28:15	to meet us as far as **A** Forum

APPLE (*see* APPLES)

Deut	32:10	kept him as the **a** of His eye
Song	2: 3	Like an **a** tree among the

APPLES† (*see* APPLE)

Prov	25:11	like **a** of gold in settings of
Song	2: 5	of raisins, refresh me with **a**
Song	7: 8	of your breath like **a**,

APPLIED (*see* APPLY)

1Ki	6:35	overlaid them with gold **a**
Eccl	7:25	I **a** my heart to know, to

APPLY† (*see* APPLIED)

Prov	2: 2	**a** your heart to understanding
Prov	22:17	**a** your heart to my knowledge
Prov	23:12	**A** your heart to instruction,
Is	38:21	**a** it as a poultice on the

APPOINT (*see* APPOINTED, APPOINTMENT, APPOINTS)

Gen	41:34	let him **a** officers over the
Ex	21:13	then I will **a** for you a place
Num	3:10	So you shall **a** Aaron and his
Num	35: 6	shall **a** six cities of refuge
Deut	16:18	You shall **a** judges and
2Sa	6:21	to **a** me ruler over the people
Job	9:19	who will **a** my day in court
Job	14:13	You would **a** me a set time
Is	26: 1	God will **a** salvation for
Jer	49:19	man that I may **a** over her
Jer	50:44	man that I may **a** over her
Hos	1:11	**a** for themselves one head
Zeph	3:19	I will **a** them for praise and
Matt	24:51	**a** him his portion with the
1Th	5: 9	For God did not **a** us to wrath
Tit	1: 5	**a** elders in every city as I

APPOINTED (*see* APPOINT)

Gen	4:25	For God has **a** another seed
Gen	18:14	At the **a** time I will return
Gen	24:14	have **a** for Your servant Isaac
Ex	9: 5	Then the LORD **a** a set time
Num	10:10	gladness, in your **a** feasts
Deut	18:14	God has not **a** such for you
Josh	4: 4	the twelve men whom he had **a**
Josh	8:14	at an **a** place before the
Judg	20:38	Now the **a** signal between the
1Sa	25:30	has **a** you ruler over Israel,
1Ki	20:42	whom I **a** to utter destruction
2Ch	8:13	the three **a** yearly feasts

Neh	5:14	from the time that I was **a** to
Neh	6: 7	you have also **a** prophets to
Job	1: 4	houses, each on his **a** day
Job	7: 3	nights have been **a** to me
Job	14: 5	You have **a** his limits, so
Job	20:29	the heritage **a** to him by God
Job	30:23	to the house **a** for all living
Job	34:13	Or who **a** Him over the whole
Ps	78: 5	**a** a law in Israel, Which He
Ps	79:11	those who are **a** to die
Ps	104:19	He **a** the moon for seasons
Is	1:14	your **a** feasts my soul hates
Jer	43:11	to death those **a** for death
Ezek	45:17	at all the **a** seasons of the
Dan	8:19	for at the **a** time the end
Hos	9: 5	What will you do in the **a** day
Hab	1:12	You have **a** them for judgment
Zeph	3:18	sorrow over the **a** assembly
Matt	28:16	which Jesus had **a** for them
Mark	3:14	Then He **a** twelve, that they
Luke	3:13	more than what is **a** for you
Luke	10: 1	Lord **a** seventy others also
John	15:16	**a** you that you should go and
Acts	13:48	And as many as had been **a** to
Acts	14:23	So when they had **a** elders in
Acts	17:31	because He has **a** a day on
Rom	13: 1	that exist are **a** by God
1Co	12:28	God has **a** these in the church
2Co	10:13	of the sphere which God **a** us
Gal	3:19	it was **a** through angels by
Gal	4: 2	the time **a** by the father
Phil	1:17	knowing that I am **a** for the
1Ti	2: 7	for which I was **a** a preacher
Heb	1: 2	whom He has **a** heir of all
Heb	3: 2	was faithful to Him who **a** Him
Heb	9:27	as it is **a** for men to die
1Pe	2: 8	to which they also were **a**

APPOINTMENT† (*see* APPOINT)

Job	2:11	made an **a** together to come

APPOINTS† (*see* APPOINT)

Dan	5:21	**a** over it whomever He chooses
Heb	7:28	For the law **a** as high priests
Heb	7:28	law, **a** the Son who has been

APPORTION (*see* APPORTIONED)

Job	41: 6	Will they **a** him among the

APPORTIONED† (*see* APPORTION)

1Ki	11:18	**a** food for him, and gave him
2Ki	12:11	the money, which had been **a**
Esth	2:12	days of their preparation **a**

APPREHEND (*see* APPREHENDED, ARREST)

APPREHENDED† (*see* APPREHEND, ARRESTED)

Phil	3:13	do not count myself to have **a**

APPROACH (*see* APPROACHED, APPROACHES, APPROACHING)

Lev	18:14	You shall not **a** his wife
Lev	18:19	Also you shall not **a** a woman
Deut	31:14	the days **a** when you must die
Job	31:37	like a prince I would **a** Him
Job	41:13	Who can **a** him with a double
Ps	65: 4	You choose, And cause to **a** You
Ezek	43:19	who **a** Me to minister to Me,'
Luke	8:19	could not **a** Him because of
Heb	10: 1	make those who **a** perfect

APPROACHED† (*see* APPROACH)

Judg	20:24	So the children of Israel **a**
1Ki	20:13	Suddenly a prophet **a** Ahab
2Ki	16:12	the king **a** the altar and made
Ezek	18: 6	nor **a** a woman during her
Dan	6:15	Then these men **a** the king
Luke	10:40	much serving, and she **a** Him

APPROACHES† (*see* APPROACH)
Lev   20:16 If a woman **a** any beast and
Luke 12:33 where no thief **a** nor moth

APPROACHING† (*see* APPROACH)
Is   58: 2 they take delight in **a** God
Heb   10:25 the more as you see the Day **a**

APPROVE (*see* APPROVED, APPROVES)
Ps   49:13 posterity who **a** their sayings
Lam   3:36 the Lord does not **a**
Luke 11:48 **a** the deeds of your fathers
Rom   2:18 and **a** the things that are

APPROVED (*see* APPROVE)
Rom   14:18 acceptable to God and **a** by men
Rom   16:10 Greet Apelles, **a** in Christ
1Co   10:18 that those who are **a** may be
2Co   10:18 he who commends himself is **a**
2Co   13: 7 not that we should appear **a**
1Th   2: 4 But as we have been **a** by God
2Ti   2:15 to present yourself **a** to God

APPROVES† (*see* APPROVE)
Rom   14:22 condemn himself in what he **a**

APRONS†
Acts 19:12 **a** were brought from his body

AQUEDUCT
2Ki   18:17 stood by the **a** from the upper

AQUILA
Acts 18: 2 found a certain Jew named **A**
Acts 18:18 Priscilla and **A** were with him
Acts 18:26 When **A** and Priscilla heard him
2Ti   4:19 Greet Prisca and **A**, and the

ARAB (*see* ARABIA, ARABS)
Neh   2:19 Geshem the **A** heard of it,

ARABAH
Deut   3:17 Sea of the **A** (the Salt Sea)

ARABIA (*see* ARAB, ARABIAN, ARABS)
1Ki   10:15 from all the kings of **A**, and
Is   21:13 forest in **A** you will lodge
Ezek 27:21 **A** and all the princes of Kedar
Gal   1:17 but I went to **A**, and returned
Gal   4:25 Hagar is Mount Sinai in **A**

ARABIAN† (*see* ARABIA, ARABIANS)
Is   13:20 nor will the **A** pitch tents
Jer   3: 2 like an **A** in the wilderness

ARABIANS (*see* ARABIAN)
2Ch   17:11 the **A** brought him flocks,

ARABS† (*see* ARAB, ARABIA)
Neh   4: 7 when Sanballat, Tobiah, the **A**
Acts   2:11 Cretans and **A**—we hear them

ARAD
Num   21: 1 When the king of **A**, the
Judg   1:16 lies in the South near **A**

ARAM (*see* ARAMAIC, MESOPOTAMIA, SYRIA)
Num   23: 7 of Moab has brought me from **A**

ARAMAIC (*see* ARAM)
2Ki   18:26 speak to your servants in **A**
Ezra   4: 7 was written in **A** script, and
Dan   2: 4 spoke to the king in **A**, "O

ARARAT
Gen   8: 4 month, on the mountains of **A**
2Ki   19:37 escaped into the land of **A**

ARAUNAH (*see* ORNAN)
2Sa   24:16 floor of **A** the Jebusite

ARBA
Josh 14:15 (**A** was the greatest man
Josh 15:13 which is Hebron (**A** was the
Josh 21:11 gave them Kirjath **A** (**A**

ARBITRATE† (*see* ARBITRATOR)
Is   47: 3 and I will not **a** with a man

ARBITRATOR† (*see* ARBITRATE)
Luke 12:14 Me a judge or an **a** over you

ARCHANGEL†
1Th   4:16 shout, with the voice of an **a**
Jude   9 Yet Michael the **a**, in

ARCHELAUS†
Matt   2:22 But when he heard that **A** was

ARCHER† (*see* ARCHERS)
Gen   21:20 wilderness, and became an **a**
Jer   51: 3 her let the **a** bend his bow

ARCHERS (*see* ARCHER)
Judg   5:11 Far from the noise of the **a**
1Sa   31: 3 and the **a** hit him, and he was
2Ch   35:23 And the **a** shot King Josiah

ARCHIPPUS†
Col   4:17 And say to **A**, "Take heed to
Phm   2 **A** our fellow soldier, and to

ARCHIVES†
Ezra   6: 1 and a search was made in the **a**

ARCHWAY† (*see* ARCHWAYS)
Ezek 40:22 its **a** was in front of
Ezek 40:26 its **a** was in front of

ARCHWAYS (*see* ARCHWAY)
Ezek 40:16 **a** on the inside of the

AREA (*see* AREAS)
1Sa   27:10 the southern **a** of Judah, or
Ezek 43:12 The whole **a** surrounding the

AREAS (*see* AREA)
Josh 13:32 These are the **a** which Moses
Ezek 42:20 the holy **a** from the common

AREOPAGITE† (*see* AREOPAGUS)
Acts 17:34 among them Dionysius the **A**

AREOPAGUS† (*see* AREOPAGITE)
Acts 17:19 him and brought him to the **A**
Acts 17:22 stood in the midst of the **A**

ARETAS†
2Co   11:32 under **A** the king, was

ARGUING† (*see* ARGUMENTS)
Job   6:25 But what does your **a** prove

ARGUMENTS† (*see* ARGUING)
Job   23: 4 Him, and fill my mouth with **a**
2Co   10: 5 casting down **a** and every high
1Ti   6: 4 **a** over words, from which come

ARIEL (*see* JERUSALEM)
Is   29: 1 Woe to **A**, to Ariel, the city

ARIGHT†
Ps   50:23 **a** I will show the salvation
Ps   78: 8 that did not set its heart **a**
Prov 11: 5 will direct his way **a**, but
Jer   8: 6 but they do not speak **a**

ARIMATHEA
Matt 27:57 there came a rich man from **A**
Mark 15:43 Joseph of **A**, a prominent
Luke 23:51 He was from **A**, a city of the

ARIOCH
Gen   14: 1 of Shinar, **A** king of Ellasar,
Dan   2:14 and wisdom Daniel answered **A**
Dan   2:15 said to **A** the king's captain,

ARISE (*see* ARISEN, ARISES, AROSE)
Gen   13:17 **A**, walk in the land through
Gen   19:15 **A**, take your wife and your two
Gen   21:18 **A**, lift up the lad and hold
Gen   27:19 please **a**, sit and eat of my

Gen	41:30	seven years of famine will **a**
Josh	1: 2	Now therefore, **a**, go over
Judg	5:12	A, Barak, and lead your
1Sa	16:12	A, anoint him; for this
2Ki	1: 3	A, go up to meet the
2Ki	23:25	after him did any a like him
2Ch	6:41	Now therefore, **a**, O LORD God,
Neh	2:20	we His servants will **a** and
Esth	4:14	deliverance will **a** for the
Job	7: 4	down, I say, 'When shall I **a**
Ps	3: 7	A, O LORD; Save me
Ps	7: 6	A, O LORD, in Your anger
Ps	44:23	Why do You sleep, O Lord? A!
Ps	44:26	A for our help, And redeem us
Ps	82: 8	A, O God, judge the earth
Ps	88:10	Shall the dead **a** and praise
Is	26:19	my dead body they shall **a**
Is	52: 2	yourself from the dust, **a**
Is	60: 1	A, shine; For your light
Jer	2:28	Let them **a**, if they can save
Jer	18: 2	A and go down to the potter's
Dan	2:39	But after you shall **a** another
Dan	11: 3	Then a mighty king shall **a**
Dan	11: 7	one shall **a** in his place, who
Dan	11:21	place shall **a** a vile person
Jon	1: 2	A, go to Nineveh, that great
Jon	3: 2	A, go to Nineveh, that great
Mal	4: 2	**a** with healing in His wings
Matt	2:13	A, take the young Child and
Matt	9: 5	forgiven you,' or to say, 'A
Matt	9: 6	A, take up your bed, and go to
Luke	15:18	I will **a** and go to my father,
Luke	24:38	And why do doubts **a** in your
John	14:31	A, let us go from here
Acts	9:34	A and make your bed
Acts	9:40	body he said, "Tabitha, **a**.
Acts	22:10	And the Lord said to me, 'A
Acts	22:16	A and be baptized, and wash
Eph	5:14	**a** from the dead, and Christ

ARISEN† (*see* ARISE)

Deut	34:10	**a** in Israel a prophet like
Dan	11: 4	And when he has **a**, his kingdom
John	7:52	prophet has **a** out of Galilee

ARISES (*see* ARISE)

Deut	17: 8	If a matter **a** which is too
Ps	112: 4	there **a** light in the darkness
Is	2:19	when He **a** to shake the earth
Matt	13:21	a because of the word,
Heb	7:15	there **a** another priest

ARISTARCHUS†

Acts	19:29	having seized Gaius and A
Acts	20: 4	also A and Secundus of the
Acts	27: 2	A, a Macedonian of
Col	4:10	A my fellow prisoner greets
Phm	24	as do Mark, A, Demas, Luke,

ARK

Gen	6:14	yourself an **a** of gopherwood
Gen	7: 1	Come into the **a**, you and all
Gen	8:16	Go out of the **a**, you and your
Ex	2: 3	she took an **a** of bulrushes
Ex	25:10	make an **a** of acacia wood
Ex	25:21	mercy seat on top of the **a**
Ex	25:22	are on the **a** of the Testimony
Num	10:33	the **a** of the covenant of the
Num	10:35	was, whenever the **a** set out
Deut	10: 8	tribe of Levi to bear the **a**
Josh	3:15	bore the **a** came to the Jordan
Josh	4: 5	Cross over before the **a** of
Judg	20:27	inquired of the LORD (the **a**
1Sa	3: 3	LORD where the **a** of God was
1Sa	4:13	trembled for the **a** of God
1Sa	4:19	the **a** of God was captured
1Sa	5: 1	Philistines took the **a** of God

1Sa	5: 2	Philistines took the **a** of God
1Sa	5: 7	**a** of the God of Israel
1Sa	5: 8	**a** of the God of Israel
2Sa	6: 7	he died there by the **a** of God
1Ki	8: 7	cherubim overshadowed the **a**
1Ki	8:21	I have made a place for the **a**
1Ch	15:23	were doorkeepers for the **a**
1Ch	15:24	trumpets before the **a** of God
1Ch	28: 2	a house of rest for the **a** of
2Ch	6:41	You and the **a** of Your strength
2Ch	35: 3	Put the holy **a** in the house
Matt	24:38	day that Noah entered the **a**
Luke	17:27	day that Noah entered the **a**
Heb	9: 4	and the **a** of the covenant
Heb	11: 7	prepared an **a** for the saving
1Pe	3:20	Noah, while the **a** was being
Rev	11:19	the **a** of His covenant was

ARM (*see* ARMED, ARMLETS, ARMPITS, ARMRESTS, ARMS)

Ex	6: 6	you with an outstretched **a**
Ex	15:16	by the greatness of Your **a**
Num	11:23	the LORD's **a** been shortened
Num	31: 3	A some of yourselves for the
Deut	4:34	hand and an outstretched **a**
Deut	33:20	as a lion, and tears the **a**
1Sa	2:31	that I will cut off your **a**
1Sa	2:31	the **a** of your father's house,
2Sa	1:10	bracelet that was on his **a**
2Ki	17:36	power and an outstretched **a**
2Ch	32: 8	With him is an **a** of flesh
Job	26: 2	the **a** that has no strength
Job	31:22	Then let my **a** fall from my
Job	35: 9	of the **a** of the mighty
Job	38:15	and the upraised **a** is broken
Job	40: 9	Have you an **a** like God
Ps	10:15	Break the **a** of the wicked and
Ps	44: 3	Nor did their own **a** save them
Ps	44: 3	was Your right hand, Your **a**
Ps	77:15	You have with Your **a** redeemed
Ps	89:21	Also My **a** shall strengthen
Ps	98: 1	His holy **a** have gained Him
Song	8: 6	heart, as a seal upon your **a**
Is	40:10	and His **a** shall rule for Him
Is	40:11	gather the lambs with His **a**
Is	51: 5	and on My **a** they will trust
Is	51: 9	on strength, O **a** of the LORD
Is	52:10	holy **a** in the eyes of all the
Is	53: 1	to whom has the **a** of the LORD
Is	63:12	of Moses, with His glorious **a**
Jer	48:25	his **a** is broken," says the
Zech	11:17	his **a** shall completely wither
John	12:38	to whom has the **a** of the LORD
Acts	13:17	with an uplifted **a** He brought
1Pe	4: 1	**a** yourselves also with the

ARMAGEDDON†

Rev	16:16	the place called in Hebrew, A

ARMED (*see* ARM)

Gen	14:14	he **a** his three hundred and
Judg	18:11	**a** with weapons of war
1Sa	17: 5	he was **a** with a coat of mail,
1Ch	20: 1	Joab led out the **a** forces
Prov	6:11	and your need like an **a** man
Prov	24:34	and your need like an **a** man
Luke	11:21	When a strong man, fully **a**

ARMIES (*see* ARMY)

Ex	6:26	of Egypt according to their **a**
Ex	7: 4	hand on Egypt and bring My **a**
Ex	12:17	**a** out of the land of Egypt
Ex	12:41	**a** of the LORD went out from
Num	1: 3	shall number them by their **a**
Num	33: 1	**a** under the hand of Moses
Deut	20: 9	of the **a** to lead the people
Josh	10: 5	went up, they and all their **a**
1Sa	17:10	I defy the **a** of Israel this

1Sa 17:23 from the **a** of the Philistines
1Sa 17:26 the **a** of the living God
1Sa 17:36 the **a** of the living God
1Ki 2: 5 commanders of the **a** of Israel
2Ki 25:23 the captains of the **a**
2Ki 25:26 the captains of the **a**
Job 25: 3 Is there any number to His **a**
Ps 44: 9 not go out with our **a**
Ps 60:10 not go out with our **a**
Ps 68:12 Kings of **a** flee, they flee,
Is 34: 2 His fury against all their **a**
Jer 40: 7 the **a** who were in the fields
Matt 22: 7 And he sent out his **a**,
Luke 21:20 see Jerusalem surrounded by **a**
Heb 11:34 to flight the **a** of the aliens
Rev 19:14 the **a** in heaven, clothed in

ARMLETS† (see ARM)
Num 31:50 **a** and bracelets and signet

ARMOR (see ARMORBEARER, ARMORY)
1Sa 14: 1 the young man who bore his **a**
1Sa 14: 6 the young man who bore his **a**
1Sa 17:38 Saul clothed David with his **a**
1Sa 17:39 fastened his sword to his **a**
1Sa 17:54 but he put his **a** in his tent
1Sa 31: 9 head and stripped off his **a**
2Sa 18:15 Joab's **a** surrounded Absalom
2Sa 20: 8 Joab was dressed in battle **a**
1Ki 10:25 silver and gold, garments, **a**
1Ki 20:11 his **a** boast like the one who
1Ki 22:34 between the joints of his **a**
2Ch 26:14 spears, helmets, body **a**,
Neh 4:16 shields, the bows, and wore **a**
Is 22: 8 looked in that day to the **a**
Is 45: 1 him and loose the **a** of kings
Jer 46: 4 the spears, put on the **a**
Luke 11:22 all his **a** in which he trusted
Rom 13:12 let us put on the **a** of light
2Co 6: 7 by the **a** of righteousness on
Eph 6:11 the whole **a** of God
Eph 6:13 the whole **a** of God

ARMORBEARER (see ARMOR)
Judg 9:54 to the young man, his **a**, and
1Sa 14:12 called to Jonathan and his **a**
1Sa 31: 4 Then Saul said to his **a**

ARMORY (see ARMOR)
2Ki 20:13 ointment, and all his **a**
Neh 3:19 to the **A** at the buttress
Song 4: 4 of David, built on an **a**, on
Jer 50:25 The LORD has opened His **a**

ARMPITS† (see ARM)
Jer 38:12 clothes and rags under your **a**

ARMRESTS (see ARM)
1Ki 10:19 there were **a** on either side
1Ki 10:19 two lions stood beside the **a**

ARMS (see ARM)
Gen 49:24 the **a** of his hands were made
Deut 33:27 are the everlasting **a**
Judg 15:14 **a** became like flax that is
Judg 16:12 them off his **a** like a thread
Ps 18:32 It is God who **a** me with
Ps 18:34 So that my **a** can bend a bow
Ps 37:17 For the **a** of the wicked shall
Prov 5:20 in the **a** of a seductress
Prov 31:17 and strengthens her **a**
Is 51: 5 My **a** will judge the peoples
Ezek 13:20 I will tear them from your **a**
Dan 2:32 of silver, its belly and
Dan 10: 6 like torches of fire, his **a**
Hos 7:15 and strengthened their **a**, yet
Hos 11: 3 walk, taking them by their **a**
Mark 9:36 He had taken him in His **a**

ARMY (see ARMIES, TROOPS)
Gen 21:22 the commander of his **a**,
Ex 14: 4 Pharaoh and over all his **a**
Ex 15: 4 his **a** He has cast into the
Num 2: 4 And his **a** was numbered at
Num 31:14 with the officers of the **a**
Josh 5:14 but as Commander of the **a** of
Judg 4:15 all his **a** with the edge of
Judg 8: 6 should give bread to your **a**
1Sa 4: 2 men of the **a** in the field
1Sa 14:48 and he gathered an **a** and
1Sa 17:21 battle array, **a** against **a**
2Sa 8:16 son of Zeruiah was over the **a**
2Sa 10: 7 all the **a** of the mighty men
1Ki 11:15 the **a** had gone up to bury the
1Ki 20:25 you shall muster an **a** like
1Ki 22:36 **a** shout went throughout the **a**
2Ki 3: 9 there was no water for the **a**
2Ki 6:14 chariots and a great **a** there
2Ki 7: 6 the noise of a great **a**
2Ki 25: 5 All his **a** was scattered from
1Ch 7:40 among the **a** fit for battle
1Ch 12:22 a great **a**, like the **a** of God
1Ch 27:34 of the king's **a** was Joab
2Ch 13: 3 with an **a** of valiant warriors
2Ch 14:13 before the LORD and His **a**
2Ch 16: 8 the Lubim not a huge **a** with
2Ch 24:24 very great **a** into their hand
2Ch 26:14 for them, for the entire **a**
Job 29:25 so I dwelt as a king in the **a**
Ps 27: 3 Though an **a** may encamp
Ps 33:16 by the multitude of an **a**
Ps 136:15 his **a** in the Red Sea, For His
Song 6: 4 awesome as an **a** with banners
Is 43:17 the chariot and horse, the **a**
Jer 32: 2 a besieged Jerusalem, and
Jer 34: 7 a fought against Jerusalem
Jer 39: 5 the Chaldean **a** pursued them
Ezek 1:24 tumult like the noise of an **a**
Ezek 26: 7 and an **a** with many people
Ezek 27:10 were in your **a** as men of war
Ezek 27:11 your **a** were on your walls all
Ezek 29:18 his **a** to labor strenuously
Ezek 29:19 will be the wages for his **a**
Ezek 37:10 feet, an exceedingly great **a**
Ezek 38:13 gathered your **a** to take booty
Ezek 38:15 a great company and a mighty **a**
Dan 4:35 His will in the **a** of heaven
Dan 11:25 with a very great and mighty **a**
Dan 11:26 his **a** shall be swept away, and
Joel 2:11 LORD gives voice before His **a**
Joel 2:20 far from you the northern **a**
Rev 9:16 Now the number of the **a** of
Rev 19:19 on the horse and against His **a**

ARNON
Num 21:13 on the other side of the **A**
Num 21:13 for the **A** is the border of
Num 21:14 Suphah, the brooks of the **A**
Num 21:24 land from the **A** to the Jabbok
Num 21:26 from his hand as far as the **A**
Num 21:28 lords of the heights of the **A**
Deut 2:24 and cross over the River **A**
Deut 2:36 is on the bank of the River **A**
Is 16: 2 of Moab at the fords of the **A**
Jer 48:20 Tell it in **A**, that Moab is

AROER
Num 32:34 built Dibon and Ataroth and **A**
Deut 2:36 From **A**, which is on the bank
Josh 12: 2 ruled half of Gilead, from **A**
Judg 11:26 Heshbon and its villages, in **A**
2Sa 24: 5 the Jordan and camped in **A**
Is 17: 2 The cities of **A** are forsaken
Jer 48:19 O inhabitant of **A**, stand by

AROMA (see AROMAS)
Gen 8:21 the LORD smelled a soothing **a**
Ex 29:18 it is a sweet **a**, an offering
Ex 29:25 as a sweet **a** before the LORD
Lev 1: 9 fire, a sweet **a** to the LORD
Lev 1:13 fire, a sweet **a** to the LORD
Lev 1:17 fire, a sweet **a** to the LORD
Lev 2: 2 fire, a sweet **a** to the LORD
Lev 2: 9 fire, a sweet **a** to the LORD
Ps 66:15 With the sweet **a** of rams
Ezek 20:41 **a** when I bring you out from
2Co 2:16 are the **a** of death leading to death
Phil 4:18 from you, a sweet-smelling **a**

AROMAS† (see AROMA)
Lev 26:31 the fragrance of your sweet **a**

AROSE (see ARISE)
Gen 19:33 she lay down or when she **a**
Gen 22: 3 for the burnt offering, and **a**
Gen 24:54 Then they **a** in the morning,
Gen 25:34 then he ate and drank, **a**, and
Gen 26:31 Then they **a** early in the
Gen 32:22 he **a** that night and took his
Gen 37: 7 Then behold, my sheaf **a** and
Gen 37:35 daughters **a** to comfort him
Ex 1: 8 Now there **a** a new king over
Ex 24:13 So Moses **a** with his assistant
Judg 2:10 another generation **a** after
Judg 4: 9 Then Deborah **a** and went with
Judg 5: 7 **a** a mother in Israel
Judg 10: 1 After Abimelech there **a** to
Judg 16: 3 then he **a** at midnight, took
Judg 20: 8 all the people **a** as one man
Ruth 3:14 and she **a** before one could
1Sa 3: 6 So Samuel **a** and went to Eli,
1Sa 20:34 So Jonathan **a** from the table
1Sa 21:10 Then David **a** and fled that day
1Sa 26: 2 Then Saul **a** and went down to
2Sa 11: 2 that David **a** from his bed
2Sa 12:17 So the elders of his house **a**
2Sa 12:20 So David **a** from the ground,
2Sa 12:21 when the child died, you **a**
2Sa 19: 8 Then the king **a** and sat in the
2Sa 23:10 He **a** and attacked the
1Ki 19: 8 So he **a**, and ate and drank
2Ki 6:15 of the man of God **a** early
2Ki 7:12 So the king **a** in the night
2Ki 10:12 And he **a** and departed and went
2Ki 11: 1 that her son was dead, she **a**
2Ki 12:20 And his servants **a** and formed a
2Ch 36:16 the LORD **a** against His people
Ezra 1: 5 **a** to go up and build the house
Ezra 3: 9 **a** as one to oversee those
Ezra 9: 5 sacrifice I **a** from my fasting
Esth 7: 7 Then the king **a** in his wrath
Esth 8: 4 So Esther **a** and stood before
Job 1:20 Then Job **a**, tore his robe
Job 29: 8 saw me and hid, and the aged **a**
Ps 76: 9 When God **a** to judgment, To
Song 5: 5 I **a** to open for my beloved,
Dan 6:19 Then the king **a** very early in
Dan 8:27 afterward I **a** and went about
Jon 1: 3 But Jonah **a** to flee to
Jon 3: 3 So Jonah **a** and went to Nineveh
Jon 3: 6 he **a** from his throne and laid
Jon 4: 8 it happened, when the sun **a**
Matt 8:15 And she **a** and served them
Matt 8:24 a great tempest **a** on the sea
Matt 8:26 Then He **a** and rebuked the
Matt 9:25 by the hand, and the girl **a**
Matt 25: 7 Then all those virgins **a** and
Matt 26:62 And the high priest **a** and said
Luke 1:39 Now Mary **a** in those days and
Luke 4:38 Now He **a** from the synagogue
Luke 6:48 And when the flood **a**, the

Luke 9:46 Then a dispute **a** among them
Luke 15:14 there **a** a severe famine in
Luke 15:20 And he **a** and came to his father
Luke 24:12 But Peter **a** and ran to the
John 3:25 Then there **a** a dispute
Acts 5: 6 young men **a** and wrapped
Acts 6: 1 there **a** a complaint against
Acts 8: 1 **a** against the church which
Acts 9: 8 Then Saul **a** from the ground,
Acts 10:41 Him after He **a** from the dead
Acts 23: 7 a dissension **a** between the
Acts 23: 9 Then there **a** a loud outcry
Acts 23: 9 of the Pharisees' party **a**
Acts 23:10 Now when there **a** a great
Acts 27:14 a tempestuous head wind **a**
Heb 7:14 that our Lord **a** from Judah
Rev 9: 2 smoke **a** out of the pit like

AROUSE† (see AROUSED)
Job 3: 8 who are ready to **a** Leviathan

AROUSED (see AROUSE)
Gen 30: 2 anger was **a** against Rachel
Num 11: 1 heard it, and His anger was **a**
Deut 6:15 your God be **a** against you
Job 42: 7 My wrath is **a** against you
Matt 1:24 being **a** from sleep, did as

ARPAD
2Ki 19:13 king of Hamath, the king of **A**

ARPHAXAD
Gen 10:22 of Shem were Elam, Asshur, **A**
Luke 3:36 son of Cainan, the son of **A**

ARRAIGN†
Jer 49:19 Who will **a** Me
Jer 50:44 Who will **a** Me

ARRANGE (see ARRANGED, ARRANGEMENT, ARRANGING)
Ex 25:37 they shall **a** its lamps so

ARRANGED† (see ARRANGE)
Num 8: 3 he **a** the lamps to face toward
Matt 22: 2 who **a** a marriage for his son

ARRANGEMENT† (see ARRANGE)
Judg 6:26 of this rock in the proper **a**
Ezek 43:11 design of the temple and its **a**

ARRANGING† (see ARRANGE)
1Pe 3: 3 **a** the hair, wearing gold, or

ARRAY (see ARRAYED)
Judg 20:20 **a** to fight against them at
Esth 6: 9 that he may **a** the man whom
Job 40:10 and **a** yourself with glory and
Is 22: 7 themselves in **a** at the gate
Jer 50:14 Put yourselves in **a** against

ARRAYED† (see ARRAY)
Esth 6:11 **a** Mordecai and led him on
Job 6: 4 of God are **a** against me
Matt 6:29 was not **a** like one of these
Luke 12:27 was not **a** like one of these
Luke 23:11 **a** Him in a gorgeous robe, and
Acts 12:21 **a** in royal apparel, sat on
Rev 7:13 Who are these **a** in white
Rev 17: 4 The woman was **a** in purple
Rev 19: 8 granted to be **a** in fine linen

ARREST (see ARRESTED)
Judg 15:10 We have come up to **a** Samson
1Ki 13: 4 the altar, saying, "A him
Mark 13:11 But when they **a** you and
2Co 11:32 garrison, desiring to **a** me;

ARRESTED† (see ARREST)
2Sa 4:10 I **a** him and had him executed
Luke 22:54 Then, having **a** Him, they led
John 18:12 officers of the Jews **a** Jesus

Acts 1:16 a guide to those who a Jesus
Acts 12: 4 when he had a him

ARRIVAL† (*see* ARRIVALS, ARRIVE)
Num 10:21 would be prepared for their **a**

ARRIVALS† (*see* ARRIVAL)
Deut 32:17 new a that your fathers did

ARRIVE (*see* ARRIVAL, ARRIVED)
Gen 19:22 do anything until you a there

ARRIVED (*see* ARRIVE)
Luke 24:22 who a at the tomb early,
2Ti 1:17 but when he a in Rome, he

ARROGANCE (*see* ARROGANT)
1Sa 2: 3 let no a come from your mouth
Prov 8:13 pride and a and the evil way and
Is 13:11 will halt the a of the proud
Jas 4:16 But now you boast in your a

ARROGANT (*see* ARROGANCE)
Prov 21:24 he acts with a pride
Is 10:12 of the a heart of the king of
Ezek 24:21 your a boast, the desire of
Ezek 30:18 her a strength shall cease in
Zeph 2: 8 made a threats against their

ARROW (*see* ARROWS)
Ex 19:13 be stoned or shot with an a
1Sa 20:36 ran, he shot an a beyond him
Job 41:28 The a cannot make him flee
Ps 11: 2 ready their a on the string
Ps 91: 5 Nor of the a that flies by
Prov 7:23 till an a struck his liver
Prov 25:18 a club, a sword, and a sharp a
Is 34:15 There the a snake shall make
Jer 9: 8 Their tongue is an a shot out
Lam 3:12 me up as a target for the a
Zech 9:14 and His a will go forth like
Heb 12:20 or shot with an a

ARROWS (*see* ARROW)
Num 24: 8 and pierce them with his a
Deut 32:23 I will spend My a upon them
Deut 32:42 I will make My a drunk with
1Sa 20:20 three a to the side of it
2Sa 22:15 He sent out a and scattered
Job 6: 4 For the a of the Almighty are
Ps 7:13 He makes His a into fiery
Ps 18:14 He sent out His a and
Ps 21:12 You will make ready Your a on
Ps 38: 2 For Your a pierce me deeply,
Ps 45: 5 Your a are sharp in the heart
Ps 57: 4 Whose teeth are spears and a
Ps 58: 7 Let his a be as if cut in
Ps 77:17 Your a also flashed about
Ps 120: 4 Sharp a of the warrior, With
Ps 127: 4 Like a in the hand of a
Ps 144: 6 Shoot out Your a and destroy
Prov 26:18 who throws firebrands, a, and
Jer 51:11 Make the a bright
Lam 3:13 He has caused the a of His
Ezek 5:16 a of famine which shall be
Ezek 21:21 he shakes the a, he consults
Ezek 39: 3 cause the a to fall out of
Hab 3: 9 oaths were sworn over Your a
Hab 3:11 the light of Your a they went
Hab 3:14 a the head of his villages

ART (*see* ARTISTIC)
Ex 30:25 to the a of the perfumer
Acts 17:29 stone, something shaped by a

ARTAXERXES
Ezra 4: 7 wrote to A king of Persia
Ezra 7:12 A, king of kings, To Ezra the
Neh 13: 6 of A king of Babylon I had

ARTICLES
Ex 3:22 a of silver, a of gold
Ex 12:35 a of gold, and clothing
Ex 22: 7 neighbor money or a to keep
Num 18: 3 near the a of the sanctuary
Num 31: 6 the priest, with the holy a
2Sa 8:10 a of gold, and a of bronze
1Ki 7:45 All these a which Hiram made
2Ki 14:14 all the a that were found in
2Ki 23: 4 the a that were made for Baal
2Ki 24:13 he cut in pieces all the a of
2Ki 25:16 these a was beyond measure
2Ch 36:10 with the costly a from the
Ezra 1: 7 a of the house of the LORD
Ezra 1:10 kind, and one thousand other a
Ezra 8:28 the a are holy also
Ezra 8:30 the a by weight, to bring
Neh 10:39 the a of the sanctuary are
Neh 13: 5 the frankincense, the a, the

ARTISAN† (*see* ARTISANS)
Ex 36: 1 every gifted a in whom the
Ex 36: 2 every gifted a in whose heart
Is 3: 3 counselor and the skillful a

ARTISANS (*see* ARTISAN)
Ex 28: 3 speak to all who are gifted a

ARTISTIC (*see* ART, ARTISTICALLY)
Ex 26: 1 with a designs of cherubim
Ex 31: 4 to design a works, to work in
Ex 35:33 all manner of a workmanship

ARTISTICALLY (*see* ARTISTIC)
Ex 28: 6 and fine linen thread, a woven
Ex 28:15 A woven according to the
Ex 39: 8 a woven like the workmanship

ARVAD†
Ezek 27: 8 Sidon and A were your oarsmen
Ezek 27:11 Men of A with your army were

ASA
1Ki 15: 8 Then A his son reigned in his
1Ki 15: 9 A became king over Judah
1Ki 15:11 A did what was right in the
1Ki 15:13 A cut down her obscene image
1Ki 15:18 King A sent them to Ben-Hadad
1Ki 15:23 The rest of all the acts of A
1Ki 15:24 So A rested with his fathers,
1Ki 22:43 all the ways of his father A
2Ch 14:11 A cried out to the LORD his
2Ch 16:12 A became diseased in his feet
Jer 41: 9 was the same one A the king
Matt 1: 7 Abijah, and Abijah begot A
Matt 1: 8 A begot Jehoshaphat,

ASAHEL
2Sa 2:18 Joab and Abishai and A
2Sa 2:18 A was as fleet of foot as a
2Sa 2:19 So A pursued Abner, and in
2Sa 2:23 the place where A fell down
2Sa 2:32 Then they took up A and buried
2Sa 23:24 A the brother of Joab was one

ASAPH
1Ch 15:19 the singers, Herman, A, and
1Ch 16: 5 A the chief, and next to him
1Ch 16: 5 but A made music with cymbals
1Ch 16: 7 this psalm into the hand of A
1Ch 25: 1 the sons of A, of Heman,
1Ch 25: 2 the sons of A: Zaccur
1Ch 25: 2 were under the direction of A
1Ch 25: 6 A, Jeduthun, and Herman were
2Ch 29:30 of David and of A the seer
Ezra 3:10 and the Levites, the sons of A

ASCEND (*see* ASCENDED, ASCENDING, ASCENDS, ASCENT)
Deut 30:12 Who will **a** into heaven for
Deut 32:50 on the mountain which you **a**
Ps 24: 3 Who may **a** into the hill of
Ps 135: 7 He causes the vapors to **a**
Ps 139: 8 If I **a** into heaven, You are
Is 14:13 I will **a** into heaven, I will
Is 34:10 its smoke shall **a** forever
Ezek 38: 9 You will **a**, coming like a
John 6:62 of Man **a** where He was before
Acts 2:34 did not **a** into the heavens
Rom 10: 6 Who will **a** into heaven
Rev 17: 8 will **a** out of the bottomless

ASCENDED (*see* ASCEND)
Josh 8:20 smoke of the city **a**
Josh 8:21 smoke of the city **a**
Judg 13:20 **a** in the flame of the altar
Ps 68:18 You have **a** on high, You have
Prov 30: 4 Who has **a** into heaven, or
John 3:13 No one has **a** to heaven but He
John 20:17 I have not yet **a** to My Father
Eph 4: 8 When He **a** on high, He led
Rev 8: 4 **a** before God from the angel's
Rev 11:12 they **a** to heaven in a cloud,

ASCENDING (*see* ASCEND)
Gen 28:12 the angels of God were **a** and
1Sa 28:13 I saw a spirit **a** out of the
John 1:51 open, and the angels of God **a**
John 20:17 I am **a** to My Father and your

ASCENDS† (*see* ASCEND)
Rev 11: 7 the beast that **a** out of the
Rev 14:11 of their torment **a** forever

ASCENT (*see* ASCEND)
Num 34: 4 side of the **A** of Akrabbim
Josh 11:17 the **a** to Seir, even as far as
2Sa 15:30 the **a** of the Mount of Olives

ASCERTAIN
Acts 21:34 when he could not **a** the truth
Acts 24: 8 him yourself you may **a** all

ASCRIBE† (*see* ASCRIBED)
Deut 32: 3 **a** greatness to our God
Job 36: 3 I will **a** righteousness to my
Ps 68:34 **A** strength to God

ASCRIBED (*see* ASCRIBE)
1Sa 18: 8 They have **a** to David ten

ASENATH
Gen 41:45 And he gave him as a wife **A**
Gen 46:20 and Ephraim, whom **A**

ASH (*see* ASHES)
1Sa 2: 8 the beggar from the **a** heap
Ps 113: 7 the needy out of the **a** heap

ASHAMED
Gen 2:25 and his wife, and were not **a**
Ps 6:10 Let all my enemies be **a** and
Ps 22: 5 trusted in You, and were not **a**
Ps 25: 3 no one who waits on You be **a**
Ps 31:17 Do not let me be **a**, O LORD,
Ps 34: 5 And their faces were not **a**
Ps 37:19 not be **a** in the evil time
Ps 69: 6 of hosts, be **a** because of me
Ps 70: 2 Let them be **a** and confounded
Is 41:11 against you shall be **a** and
Is 49:23 not be **a** who wait for Me
Mark 8:38 For whoever is **a** of Me and My
Mark 8:38 **a** when He comes in the glory
Rom 1:16 for I am not **a** of the gospel
Phil 1:20 that in nothing I shall be **a**
2Th 3:14 with him, that he may be **a**
2Ti 1: 8 Therefore do not be **a** of the

2Ti 1:12 nevertheless I am not **a**, for
2Ti 1:16 me, and was not **a** of my chain
Heb 2:11 not **a** to call them brethren
Heb 11:16 Therefore God is not **a** to be
1Pe 4:16 a Christian, let him not be **a**
1Jn 2:28 not be **a** before Him at His

ASHDOD (*see* ASHDODITES)
Josh 11:22 in Gaza, in Gath, and in **A**
Josh 15:47 **A** with its towns and villages
1Sa 5: 5 of Dagon in **A** to this day
Neh 13:24 spoke the language of **A**, and
Is 20: 1 him, and he fought against **A**

ASHDODITES (*see* ASHDOD)
Josh 13: 3 the Gazites, the **A**, the

ASHER
Gen 30:13 So she called his name **A**
Gen 35:26 maidservant, were Gad and **A**
Ex 1: 4 Dan, Naphtali, Gad, and **A**
Num 2:27 him shall be the tribe of **A**
Luke 2:36 of Phanuel, of the tribe of **A**
Rev 7: 6 of the tribe of **A** twelve

ASHERAH (*see* ASHERAHS)
1Ki 15:13 made an obscene image of **A**
1Ki 18:19 four hundred prophets of **A**
2Ki 23: 4 were made for Baal, for **A**

ASHERAHS† (*see* ASHERAH)
Judg 3: 7 God, and served the Baals and **A**

ASHES (*see* ASH)
Ex 9: 8 handfuls of **a** from a furnace
Ex 27: 3 its pans to receive its **a**
Lev 6:11 carry the **a** outside the camp
Num 19: 9 gather up the **a** of the heifer
2Sa 13:19 Then Tamar put **a** on her head
Esth 4: 1 and put on sackcloth and **a**, and
Job 2: 8 he sat in the midst of the **a**
Job 13:12 platitudes are proverbs of **a**
Job 42: 6 and repent in dust and **a**
Is 61: 3 to give them beauty for **a**
Dan 9: 3 with fasting, sackcloth, and **a**
Heb 9:13 the **a** of a heifer, sprinkling
2Pe 2: 6 of Sodom and Gomorrah into **a**

ASHKELON (*see* ASHKELONITES)
Judg 1:18 **A** with its territory, and
1Sa 6:17 one for Gaza, one for **A**, one
2Sa 1:20 it is not in the streets of **A**

ASHKELONITES† (*see* ASHKELON)
Josh 13: 3 the Ashdodites, the **A**, the

ASHKENAZ
Gen 10: 3 The sons of Gomer were **A**,

ASHTAROTH (*see* ASHTEROTH, ASHTORETH)
Josh 9:10 king of Bashan, who was at **A**

ASHTEROTH† (*see* ASHTAROTH, KARNAIM)
Gen 14: 5 the Rephaim in **A** Karnaim, the

ASHTORETH (*see* ASHTAROTH, ASHTORETHS)
1Ki 11:33 worshiped **A** the goddess of
2Ki 23:13 for **A** the abomination of the

ASHTORETHS (*see* ASHTORETH)
Judg 2:13 LORD and served Baal and the **A**
1Sa 12:10 and served the Baals and **A**

ASIA
Acts 2: 9 and Cappadocia, Pontus and **A**
Acts 16: 6 to preach the word in **A**
Acts 19:22 stayed in **A** for a time
Acts 21:27 almost ended, the Jews from **A**
1Co 16:19 The churches of **A** greet you
2Co 1: 8 trouble which came to us in **A**
Rev 1: 4 seven churches which are in **A**
Rev 1:11 seven churches which are in **A**

ASLEEP
Jon   1: 5 had lain down, and was fast **a**
Matt 8:24 the waves. But He was **a**
Matt 26:40 the disciples and found them **a**
Matt 27:52 who had fallen **a** were raised
Acts 7:60 he had said this, he fell **a**
1Co 15: 6 but some have fallen **a**
1Co 15:18 **a** in Christ have perished
1Th 4:15 means precede those who are **a**

ASPHALT†
Gen 11: 3 and they had **a** for mortar
Gen 14:10 of Siddim was full of **a** pits
Ex   2: 3 for him, daubed it with **a**

ASPIRE†
1Th 4:11 that you also **a** to lead a

ASPS†
Ps 140: 3 The poison of **a** is under
Rom 3:13 The poison of **a** is under

ASSAIL†
Luke 11:53 began to **a** Him vehemently

ASSASSINS†
Acts 21:38 led the four thousand **a** out

ASSAULT†
Deut 21: 5 and every **a** shall be settled
Esth 7: 8 Will he also **a** the queen
Esth 8:11 or province that would **a** them

ASSAYER†
Jer 6:27 I have set you as an **a** and a

ASSEMBLE (see ASSEMBLED, ASSEMBLING, ASSEMBLY)
2Sa 20: 4 A the men of Judah for me
Dan 11:10 **a** a multitude of great forces

ASSEMBLED (see ASSEMBLE, GATHERED)
Ex 38: 8 who **a** at the door of the
Num 1:18 they **a** all the congregation
Josh 18: 1 Israel **a** together at Shiloh
1Ki 8: 1 Now Solomon **a** the elders of
John 20:19 where the disciples were **a**
Acts 1: 4 being **a** together with them,
Acts 4:31 were **a** together was shaken
Acts 15:25 being **a** with one accord, to

ASSEMBLIES† (see ASSEMBLY)
Is   1:13 Sabbaths, and the calling of **a**
Is   4: 5 of Mount Zion, and above her **a**
Amos 5:21 I do not savor your sacred **a**

ASSEMBLING† (see ASSEMBLE)
Heb 10:25 not forsaking the **a** of

ASSEMBLY (see ASSEMBLE, ASSEMBLIES, COMPANY, CONGREGATION)
Gen 28: 3 you may be an **a** of peoples
Ex 12: 6 Then the whole **a** of the
Ex 16: 3 kill this whole **a** with hunger
Lev 4:21 is a sin offering for the **a**
Lev 23:36 It is a sacred **a**, and you
Num 14: 5 **a** of the congregation of the
2Ki 10:20 Proclaim a solemn **a** for Baal
2Ch 29:28 So all the **a** worshipped, the
2Ch 30:17 the **a** who had not sanctified
Ezra 10:14 leaders of our entire **a** stand
Neh 5:13 And all the **a** said, "Amen
Neh 8:18 day there was a sacred **a**,
Ps 22:22 of the **a** I will praise You.
Ps 35:18 You thanks in the great **a**
Ps 89: 5 also in the **a** of the saints.
Ps 89: 7 feared in the **a** of the saints
Ps 107:32 also in the **a** of the people
Ps 111: 1 In the **a** of the upright and in
Prov 21:16 rest in the **a** of the dead
Jer 15:17 sit in the **a** of the mockers
Lam 1:10 commanded Not to enter Your **a**

Joel 1:14 a fast, call a sacred **a**
Joel 2:15 a fast, call a sacred **a**
Acts 19:39 be determined in the lawful **a**
Heb 2:12 in the midst of the **a** I will
Heb 12:23 to the general **a** and church of
Jas 2: 2 your **a** a man with gold rings

ASSENTED†
Acts 24: 9 And the Jews also **a**,

ASSESSED† (see ASSESSMENT)
2Ki 18:14 And the king of Assyria **a**

ASSESSMENT† (see ASSESSED)
2Ki 12: 4 money, each man's **a** money
2Ki 23:35 every one according to his **a**

ASSIGN† (see ASSIGNED, ASSIGNMENT)
Num 4:27 and his sons shall **a** all the
Num 4:32 you shall **a** to each man by

ASSIGNED (see ASSIGN, GIVEN)
2Sa 11:16 that he **a** Uriah to a place
Job 36:23 Who has **a** Him His way, or who
Prov 8:29 When He **a** to the sea its

ASSIGNMENT† (see ASSIGN)
1Ch 9:23 house of the tabernacle, by **a**

ASSIST† (see ASSISTANT)
2Ch 28:20 him, and did not **a** him
Rom 16: 2 **a** her in whatever business

ASSISTANT (see ASSIST, ASSISTANTS)
Ex 24:13 Moses arose with his **a** Joshua
Acts 13: 5 They also had John as their **a**

ASSISTANTS† (see ASSISTANT)
2Ch 31:15 his faithful **a** in the cities

ASSOCIATE (see ASSOCIATED, ASSOCIATES)
Prov 20:19 therefore do not **a** with one
Rom 12:16 things, but **a** with the humble

ASSOCIATED† (see ASSOCIATE)
Num 18: 1 **a** with your priesthood

ASSOCIATES† (see ASSOCIATE)
2Ki 9: 2 him rise up from among his **a**
2Ki 25:19 men of the king's close **a** who
Jer 52:25 men of the king's close **a** who

ASSUME†
2Ch 22: 9 to a power over the kingdom

ASSURANCE† (see ASSURE)
Deut 28:66 night, and have no **a** of life
Is   32:17 quietness and **a** forever
Acts 17:31 He has given **a** of this to all
Col 2: 2 the full **a** of understanding
1Th 1: 5 the Holy Spirit and in much **a**
Heb 6:11 full **a** of hope until the end
Heb 10:22 true heart in full **a** of faith

ASSURE† (see ASSURANCE, ASSURED, ASSUREDLY)
1Jn 3:19 shall **a** our hearts before Him

ASSURED† (see ASSURE)
Jer 14:13 you **a** peace in this place
Dan 4:26 kingdom shall be **a** to you
2Ti 3:14 you have learned and been **a** of
Heb 11:13 them afar off were **a** of them

ASSUREDLY (see ASSURE)
Matt 5:18 For **a**, I say to you, till
Matt 5:26 A, I say to you, you will by
Matt 6: 2 A, I say to you, they have
John 1:51 Most **a**, I say to you,
John 3: 3 Most **a**, I say to you, unless
Acts 2:36 know a that God has made this

ASSYRIA (see ASSYRIAN)
Gen 2:14 goes toward the east of A
Gen 10:11 From that land he went to A

2Ki	15:19	Pul king of A came against
2Ki	16: 7	to Tiglath-Pileser king of A
2Ki	18: 9	of A came up against Samaria
2Ki	18:19	the great king, the king of A
Ezra	4: 2	days of Esarhaddon king of A
Is	7:18	bee that is in the land of A
Is	10: 5	Woe to A, the rod of My anger
Is	19:23	be a highway from Egypt to A
Is	19:24	one of three with Egypt and A
Is	19:25	A the work of My hands, and
Is	20: 1	Sargon the king of A sent him
Hos	7:11	call to Egypt, they go to A
Hos	14: 3	A shall not save us, we will
Zeph	2:13	against the north, destroy A
Zech	10:11	Then the pride of A shall be

ASSYRIAN (see ASSYRIA, ASSYRIANS)

Is	10:24	do not be afraid of the A
Is	14:25	I will break the A in My land
Is	19:23	the A will come into Egypt and
Is	52: 4	then the A oppressed them
Mic	5: 6	shall deliver us from the A

ASSYRIANS (see ASSYRIAN)

2Ki	19:35	the camp of the A one hundred
Ezek	16:28	played the harlot with the A
Hos	12: 1	make a covenant with the A

ASTONISHED (see AMAZED, ASTONISHING, ASTONISHMENT)

Lev	26:32	dwell in it shall be a at it
1Ki	9: 8	who passes by it will be a
Ezra	9: 3	head and beard, and sat down a
Job	21: 5	Look at me and be a
Job	26:11	and are a at His rebuke
Is	52:14	Just as many were a at you
Jer	2:12	Be a, O heavens, at this, and
Dan	3:24	King Nebuchadnezzar was a
Dan	8:27	I was a by the vision, but no
Matt	7:28	people were a at His teaching
Matt	19:25	they were greatly a
Mark	6: 2	And many hearing Him were a
Mark	7:37	they were a beyond measure,
Mark	10:24	disciples were a at His words
Luke	5: 9	a at the catch of fish which
Luke	24:22	at the tomb early, a us
Acts	10:45	who believed were a, as many

ASTONISHING† (see ASTONISHED)

Jer	5:30	An a and horrible thing has

ASTONISHMENT (see ASTONISHED, DESOLATION)

Gen	43:33	looked in a at one another
Deut	28:37	Ad you shall become an a, a
Jer	8:21	a has taken hold of me
Jer	49:17	Edom also shall be an a

ASTOUNDED†

Hab	1: 5	be utterly a! For I will

ASTRAY

Ex	23: 4	ox or his donkey going a, you
Ps	58: 3	They go a as soon as they are
Ps	95:10	who go a in their hearts, And
Ps	119:176	I have gone a like a lost
Prov	5:23	of his folly he shall go a
Prov	10:17	he who refuses correction goes a
Prov	12:26	of the wicked leads them a
Prov	28:10	to go a in an evil way, he
Is	53: 6	All we like sheep have gone a
Jer	50: 6	shepherds have led them a
Amos	2: 4	their lies lead them a, lies
Matt	18:12	sheep, and one of them goes a
Matt	18:13	ninety-nine that did not go a
Heb	3:10	always go a in their heart
Heb	5: 2	who are ignorant and going a
1Pe	2:25	you were like sheep going a

ASTROLOGER† (see ASTROLOGERS)

Dan	2:10	things of any magician, a

ASTROLOGERS (see ASTROLOGER)

Is	47:13	let now the a, the stargazers
Dan	1:20	a who were in all his realm
Dan	2: 2	to call the magicians, the a
Dan	2: 27	demanded, the wise men, the a

ATE (see EAT)

Gen	3: 6	she took of its fruit and a
Gen	3: 13	serpent deceived me, and I a
Gen	19: 3	unleavened bread, and they a
Gen	25:28	Esau because he a of his game
Gen	40:17	the birds a them out of the
Gen	41: 4	gaunt cows a up the seven
Gen	41:20	and ugly cows a up the first
Ex	16: 3	when we a bread to the full
Ex	16:35	of Israel a manna forty years
Ex	24:11	So they saw God, and they a
Josh	5:11	they a of the produce of the
Judg	19:21	they washed their feet, and a
Ruth	2:14	and she a and was satisfied, and
1Sa	1:18	the woman went her way and a
1Sa	9:24	So Saul a with Samuel that
2Sa	9:13	for he a continually at the
2Sa	12:20	set food before him, and he a
1Ki	13:22	a bread, and drank water in
2Ki	6:29	So we boiled my son, and a him
2Ki	23: 9	but they a unleavened bread
2Ki	25:29	he a bread regularly before
2Ch	30:18	yet they a the Passover
Job	42:11	a food with him in his house
Ps	41: 9	Who a my bread, Has lifted up
Ps	78:25	Men a angels' food
Ps	78:29	So they a and were well filled
Ps	106:28	a sacrifices made to the dead
Jer	15:16	I a them, and Your word was to
Ezek	3: 3	So I a it, and it was in my
Dan	1:15	a the portion of the king's
Dan	4:33	from men and a grass like oxen
Matt	12: 4	a the showbread which was not
Matt	14:20	So they all a and were filled,
Mark	1: 6	he a locusts and wild honey
Mark	14:18	Now as they sat and a, Jesus
Luke	6: 1	a them, rubbing them in their
Luke	15:16	the pods that the swine a
Luke	24:43	it and a in their presence
John	6:31	Our fathers a the manna in
Acts	9: 9	sight, and neither a nor drank
1Co	10: 3	all a the same spiritual food
Rev	10:10	a it, and it was as sweet as

ATHALIAH

2Ki	11: 1	When A the mother of Ahaziah
2Ch	22:11	hid him from A so that she

ATHENIANS† (see ATHENS)

Acts	17:21	For all the A and the

ATHENS† (see ATHENIANS)

Acts	17:15	Paul brought him to A
Acts	17:16	Paul waited for them at A
Acts	17:22	Men of A, I perceive that in
Acts	18: 1	things Paul departed from A
1Th	3: 1	it good to be left in A alone

ATHLETICS†

2Ti	2: 5	also if anyone competes in a

ATONED (see ATONEMENT, ATONING)

1Sa	3:14	not be a for by sacrifice or

ATONEMENT (see ATONED)

Ex	29:33	with which the a was made
Ex	29:36	day as a sin offering for a
Ex	29:37	shall make a for the altar
Ex	30:10	Aaron shall make a upon its
Ex	30:15	to make a for yourselves

Ex 30:16 you shall take the **a** money of
Ex 32:30 I can make **a** for your sin
Lev 1: 4 his behalf to make **a** for him
Lev 4:20 priest shall make **a** for them
Lev 6: 7 **a** for him before the LORD
Lev 6:30 to make **a** in the holy place,
Lev 14:21 be waved, to make **a** for him
Lev 14:53 make **a** for the house, and it
Lev 16:17 to make **a** in the Holy Place
Lev 17:11 that makes **a** for the soul
Lev 23:27 **a** month shall be the Day of **A**
Num 8:12 to make **a** for the Levites
Deut 21: 8 Provide **a**, O LORD, for Your
Is 22:14 there will be no **a** for you
Ezek 43:20 cleanse it and make **a** for it
Ezek 43:26 shall make **a** for the altar
Ezek 45:15 to make **a** for them," says
Ezek 45:17 **a** for the house of Israel
Ezek 45:20 shall make **a** for the temple

ATONING† (*see* ATONED)
Lev 16:20 end of **a** for the Holy Place

ATTACHED
Gen 29:34 husband will become **a** to me
Ex 29:13 the fatty lobe **a** to the liver
1Ki 6:10 they were **a** to the temple

ATTACK (*see* ATTACKED, ATTACKERS, ATTACKING, ATTACKS)
Gen 32:11 **a** me and the mother with the
Num 25:17 the Midianites, and **a** them
Josh 7: 3 thousand men go up and **a** Ai
Ps 62: 3 How long will you **a** a man
Jer 18:18 let us **a** him with the tongue,
Dan 11:40 king of the South shall **a** him
Acts 18:10 no one will **a** you to hurt you

ATTACKED (*see* ATTACK)
Gen 14:15 and he and his servants **a** them
Gen 36:35 who **a** Midian in the field of
Judg 15: 8 So he **a** them hip and thigh
1Sa 15: 7 Saul **a** the Amalekites, from
1Sa 27: 9 Whenever David **a** the land
1Ki 20:21 **a** the horses and chariots, and
2Ki 3:24 **a** the Moabites, so that they
2Ki 3:25 slingers surrounded and **a** it
2Ki 8:21 and **a** the Edomites who had
Jer 47: 1 before Pharaoh **a** Gaza
Dan 8: 7 **a** the ram, and broke his two
Acts 17: 5 and **a** the house of Jason, and

ATTACKERS† (*see* ATTACK)
Ps 35:15 **A** gathered against me, And I

ATTACKING† (*see* ATTACK)
Deut 25:11 the hand of the one **a** him
2Ch 11: 4 turned back from **a** Jeroboam

ATTACKS (*see* ATTACK)
Gen 32: 8 **a** it, then the other company

ATTAIN (*see* ATTAINED, ATTAINING)
2Sa 23:19 he did not **a** to the first
Ps 139: 6 It is high, I cannot **a** it
Prov 1: 5 will **a** wise counsel,
Hos 8: 5 be until they **a** to innocence
Luke 20:35 counted worthy to **a** that age
Phil 3:11 I may **a** to the resurrection

ATTAINED (*see* ATTAIN)
Rom 9:30 have **a** to righteousness, even
Rom 9:31 has not **a** to the law of
Phil 3:12 Not that I have already **a**

ATTAINING† (*see* ATTAIN)
Col 2: 2 **a** to all riches of the full

ATTEMPT† (*see* ATTEMPTED, ATTEMPTING, ATTEMPTS)
Acts 14: 5 when a violent **a** was made by

Gal 5: 4 you who **a** to be justified by

ATTEMPTED† (*see* ATTEMPT)
Acts 9:29 but they **a** to kill him

ATTEMPTING† (*see* ATTEMPT)
Heb 11:29 **a** to do so, were drowned

ATTEMPTS† (*see* ATTEMPT)
Job 4: 2 If one **a** a word with you,
Eccl 8:17 a wise man **a** to know it, he

ATTEND (*see* ATTENDANT, ATTENDED, ATTENDING)
Num 1:50 they shall **a** to it and camp
Ps 17: 1 cause, O LORD, **A** to my cry
Prov 27:23 flocks, and **a** to your herds
Jer 23: 2 I will **a** to you for the evil

ATTENDANT† (*see* ATTEND)
Luke 4:20 and gave it back to the **a**

ATTENDED (*see* ATTEND)
Judg 3:19 all who **a** him went out from
Ps 66:19 He has **a** to the voice of my
Is 10:28 he has **a** to his equipment

ATTENDING† (*see* ATTEND)
Judg 3:24 He is probably **a** to his needs
Rom 13: 6 **a** continually to this very

ATTENTION (*see* ATTENTIVE)
1Ki 18:29 one answered, no one paid **a**
Prov 4: 1 I give **a** to know understanding
Prov 4:20 My son, give **a** to my words
Prov 5: 1 My son, pay **a** to my wisdom
Acts 26:26 of these things escapes his **a**
1Ti 4:13 I come, give **a** to reading, to
Jas 2: 3 you pay **a** to the one wearing

ATTENTIVE (*see* ATTENTION, ATTENTIVELY)
2Ki 20:13 And Hezekiah was **a** to them
2Ch 6:40 let Your ears be **a** to the
Neh 1:11 be **a** to the prayer of Your
Neh 8: 3 were **a** to the Book of the Law
Luke 19:48 were very **a** to hear Him

ATTENTIVELY† (*see* ATTENTIVE)
Job 37: 2 Hear **a** the thunder of His

ATTESTATION (*see* ATTESTED, CONFIRMATION)

ATTESTED†
Acts 2:22 a Man **a** by God to you by

ATTIRE† (*see* ATTIRED)
Judg 5:10 donkeys, who sit in judges' **a**
Prov 7:10 with the **a** of a harlot, and **a**
Jer 2:32 ornaments, or a bride her **a**

ATTIRED† (*see* ATTIRE)
Lev 16: 4 linen turban he shall be **a**

ATTRACTED†
Gen 34: 3 His soul was strongly **a** to

ATTRIBUTES†
Rom 1:20 invisible **a** are clearly seen

AUDITORIUM†
Acts 25:23 had entered the **a** with the

AUGUSTUS† (*see* CAESAR)
Luke 2: 1 **A** that all the world should
Acts 25:21 for the decision of **A**, I
Acts 25:25 he himself had appealed to **A**

AUNT†
Lev 18:14 his wife; she is your **a**

AUSTERE
Luke 19:21 you, because you are an **a** man

AUTHOR† (*see* CAPTAIN)
1Co 14:33 For God is not the **a** of
Heb 5: 9 He became the **a** of eternal
Heb 12: 2 looking unto Jesus, the **a**

AUTHORITIES† (*see* AUTHORITY)
Luke 12:11 and magistrates and **a**, do not
Acts 16:19 into the marketplace to the **a**
Rom   13: 1 be subject to the governing **a**
Rom   13: 1 God, and the **a** that exist are
Tit   3: 1 to be subject to rulers and **a**
1Pe   3:22 hand of God, angels and **a** and

AUTHORITY (*see* AUTHORITIES)
Gen   41:35 grain under the **a** of Pharaoh
Num   5:19 while under your husband's **a**
Num   27:20 give some of your **a** to him
Dan   11: 6 not retain the power of her **a**
Dan   11: 6 he nor his **a** shall stand
Matt   7:29 taught them as one having **a**
Matt   8: 9 For I also am a man under **a**
Matt 20:25 great exercise **a** over them
Matt 21:23 By what **a** are You doing these
Matt 28:18 All **a** has been given to Me in
Luke   4:32 for His word was with **a**
Luke   4:36 For with **a** and power He
Luke   9: 1 **a** over all demons, and to cure
Luke 10:19 I give you the **a** to trample
Luke 19:17 have **a** over ten cities
John   5:27 has given Him **a** to execute
John   7:17 whether I speak on My own **a**
John 12:49 I have not spoken on My own **a**
John 17: 2 given Him **a** over all flesh
Acts   1: 7 Father has put in His own **a**
Acts   8:27 a eunuch of great **a** under
Acts 26:12 journeyed to Damascus with **a**
Rom   13: 1 there is no **a** except from God
Rom   13: 2 whoever resists the **a** resists
1Co   7: 4 not have **a** over her own body
1Co   9:18 not abuse my **a** in the gospel
1Co   11:10 a symbol of **a** on her head
1Co   15:24 an end to all rule and all **a**
2Co   13:10 according to the **a** which the
2Th   3: 9 not because we do not have **a**
1Ti   2: 2 for kings and all who are in **a**
1Ti   2:12 teach or to have **a** over a man
Tit   2:15 exhort, and rebuke with all **a**
2Pe   2:10 of uncleanness and despise **a**
Jude   8 defile the flesh, reject **a**
Rev   9: 5 were not given **a** to kill them
Rev   13: 4 who gave **a** to the beast
Rev   18: 1 from heaven, having great **a**

AUTUMN†
Jude   12 late **a** trees without fruit,

AVAIL† (*see* AVAILS)
Job   41:26 reaches him, it cannot **a**

AVAILS† (*see* AVAIL)
Esth   5:13 Yet all this **a** me nothing
Gal   5: 6 nor uncircumcision **a** anything
Gal   6:15 nor uncircumcision **a** anything
Jas   5:16 of a righteous man **a** much

AVENGE (*see* AVENGED, AVENGER, AVENGES, AVENGING,
    GET JUSTICE)
Deut 32:43 for He will **a** the blood of
Hos   1: 4 in a little while I will **a**
Luke 18: 7 shall God not **a** His own elect
Luke 18: 8 that He will **a** them speedily
Rom   12:19 do not **a** yourselves, but
Rev   6:10 and **a** our blood on those who

AVENGED (*see* AVENGE)
Gen   4:24 If Cain shall be **a** sevenfold
2Sa   18:19 who the LORD has **a** him of his
Rev   19: 2 He has **a** on her the blood of

AVENGER (*see* AVENGE)
Num   35:12 of refuge for you from the **a**
Num   35:19 The **a** of blood himself shall
Ps   8: 2 silence the enemy and the **a**

Rom   13: 4 an **a** to execute wrath on him
1Th   4: 6 the Lord is the **a** of all such

AVENGES (*see* AVENGE)
Ps   9:12 When He **a** blood, He
Nah   1: 2 God is jealous, and the LORD **a**
Nah   1: 2 the LORD **a** and is furious

AVENGING (*see* AVENGE)
1Sa   25:26 from **a** yourself with your own
Ps   79:10 The **a** of the blood of Your
Ezek 25:12 offended by **a** itself on them

AVOID (*see* AVOIDING, TURN AWAY)
Job   36:18 would not help you **a** it
Prov   4:15 A it, do not travel on it
2Ti   2:23 But **a** foolish and ignorant

AVOIDING† (*see* AVOID)
2Co   8:20 **a** this: that anyone should
1Ti   6:20 trust, **a** the profane and vain

AWAIT† (*see* AWAITING)
Acts 20:23 chains and tribulations **a** me

AWAITING† (*see* AWAIT)
Ps   65: 1 Praise is **a** You, O God, in

AWAKE (*see* AWAKEN, AWAKES, AWAKING, AWOKE, RISE
    UP)
Judg   5:12 A, awake, Deborah!
Job   8: 6 surely now He would **a** for you
Ps   17:15 when I **a** in Your likeness
Ps   35:23 **a** to my vindication, To my
Ps   57: 8 A, lute and harp
Ps   59: 4 A to help me, and behold
Ps   59: 5 A to punish all the nations
Ps   102: 7 I lie **a**, And am like a sparrow
Ps   127: 1 The watchman stays **a** in vain
Ps   139:18 When I **a**, I am still with You
Prov   6:22 and when you **a**, they will
Song   5: 2 I sleep, but my heart is **a**
Is   51: 9 A, awake, put on strength, O
Is   51:17 A, awake! Stand up, O
Dan   12: 2 the dust of the earth shall **a**
Hab   2:19 to him who says to wood, 'A
Mal   2:12 man who does this, being **a**
Luke   9:32 and when they were fully **a**
Rom   13:11 high time to **a** out of sleep
1Co   15:34 A to righteousness, and do not
Eph   5:14 A, you who sleep, arise from

AWAKEN (*see* AWAKE, AWAKENED, AWAKENS)
Ps   57: 8 I will **a** the dawn
Song   2: 7 do not stir up nor **a** love

AWAKENED (*see* AWAKEN)
1Ki   18:27 he is sleeping and must be **a**
Song   8: 5 I **a** you under the apple tree

AWAKENS (*see* AWAKEN)
Is   50: 4 He **a** Me morning by morning,

AWAKES (*see* AWAKE)
Ps   73:20 As a dream when no one **a**, So,
Is   29: 8 but he **a**, and his soul is

AWAKING† (*see* AWAKE)
Acts 16:27 **a** from sleep and seeing the

AWARE
Song   6:12 Before I was even **a**, my soul
Jer   50:24 O Babylon, and you were not **a**
Obad   7 No one is **a** of it
Mal   2:12 does this, being awake and **a**
Matt 24:50 an hour that he is not **a** of
Matt 26:10 But when Jesus was **a** of it
Luke 11:44 over them are not **a** of them
Acts   5: 2 his wife also being **a** of it

AWE† (*see* AWESOME)
Ps   33: 8 the world stand in **a** of Him

Ps 119:161 stands in a of Your word

AWESOME (see AWE)
Gen 28:17 said, "How a is this place
Deut 7:21 great and a God, is among you
Deut 28:58 a name, THE LORD YOUR
Job 37:22 with God is a majesty
Ps 45: 4 hand shall teach You a things
Ps 47: 2 For the LORD Most High is a
Ps 65: 5 By a deeds in righteousness
Ps 66: 3 God, "How a are Your works
Ps 99: 3 praise Your great and a name
Ps 111: 9 Holy and a is His name
Ps 145: 6 of the might of Your a acts
Song 6: 4 a as an army with banners
Is 28:21 His a work, and bring to pass
Lam 1: 9 therefore her collapse was a
Ezek 1:18 they were so high they were a
Ezek 1:22 the color of an a crystal
Dan 2:31 and its form was a
Dan 9: 4 a God, who keeps His covenant

AWL†
Ex 21: 6 pierce his ear with an a
Deut 15:17 then you shall take an a and

AWOKE (see AWAKE)
Gen 9:24 So Noah a from his wine, and
Ps 3: 5 I a, for the LORD sustained
Ps 78:65 Then the Lord a as one out of
Matt 8:25 came to Him and a Him, saying,

AWRY†
Prov 15:22 Without counsel, plans go a

AX (see AXES)
Deut 19: 5 the a to cut down the tree
1Sa 13:20 plowshare, his mattock, his a
2Ki 6: 5 the iron a head fell into the
Eccl 10:10 If the a is dull, and one does
Is 10:15 Shall the a boast itself
Matt 3:10 even now the a is laid to the

AXES (see AX)
1Sa 13:21 mattocks, the forks, and the a
2Sa 12:31 saws and iron picks and iron a
Ps 74: 5 up A among the thick trees

AXLE† (see AXLES)
1Ki 7:33 their a pins, their rims,

AXLES† (see AXLE)
1Ki 7:30 a of bronze, and its four feet
1Ki 7:32 and the a of the wheels were

AZARIAH (see AHAZIAH, EZRA, UZZIAH)
2Ki 14:21 the people of Judah took A
2Ki 15: 1 A the son of Amaziah, king of
2Ki 15: 6 Now the rest of the acts of A
2Ki 15: 7 So A rested with his fathers,
2Ki 15: 8 year of A king of Judah,
2Ch 22: 6 A the son of Jehoram, king of
2Ch 31:10 A the chief priest, from the
Dan 1: 6 Hananiah, Mishael, and A
Dan 1: 7 and to A, Abed-Nego

AZEKAH
Jer 34: 7 left, against Lachish and A

AZOTUS†
Acts 8:40 But Philip was found at A

B

BAAL (see BAALE JUDAH, BAAL'S, BAALS, BEL)
Num 22:41 up to the high places of B
Num 25: 3 was joined to B of Peor, and
Judg 2:13 forsook the LORD and served B

Judg 6:28 there was the altar of B
Judg 6:31 Would you plead for B
Judg 6:32 Let B plead against him,
1Ki 16:31 he went and served B and
1Ki 16:32 for B in the temple of B
1Ki 18:19 and fifty prophets of B, and
1Ki 18:21 but if B, then follow him
1Ki 19:18 knees have not bowed to B
2Ki 3: 2 of B that his father had made
2Ki 10:18 Ahab served B a little, but
2Ki 10:19 the worshipers of B
2Ki 10:28 Jehu destroyed B from Israel
Ps 106:28 themselves also to B of Peor
Jer 2: 8 the prophets prophesied by B
Jer 7: 9 falsely, burn incense to B
Jer 12:16 My people to swear by B, then
Hos 2: 8 which they prepared for B
Rom 11: 4 have not bowed the knee to B

BAAL-BERITH† (see BERITH)
Judg 8:33 Baals, and made B their god
Judg 9: 4 silver from the temple of B

BAALE JUDAH† (see BAAL)
2Sa 6: 2 who were with him from B to

BAAL PERAZIM
2Sa 5:20 So David went to B, and David

BAAL'S† (see BAAL)
1Ki 18:22 but B prophets are four

BAALS (see BAAL)
Judg 2:11 of the LORD, and served the B
Judg 8:33 played the harlot with the B
1Sa 7: 4 of Israel put away the B and
1Ki 18:18 and you have followed the B
2Ch 17: 3 he did not seek the B,
2Ch 28: 2 made molded images for the B
2Ch 33: 3 he raised up altars for the B
Hos 2:13 her for the days of the B to
Hos 2:17 her mouth the names of the B
Hos 11: 2 They sacrificed to the B

BAAL-ZEBUB (see BEELZEBUB)
2Ki 1: 2 Go, inquire of B, the god of

BAASHA
1Ki 15:16 B king of Israel all their
1Ki 16: 5 Now the rest of the acts of B
1Ki 16: 6 So B rested with his fathers

BABBLE† (see BABBLER, BABBLINGS)
2Ki 9:11 You know the man and his b

BABBLER† (see BABBLE, BABBLERS)
Eccl 10:11 the b is no different
Acts 17:18 What does this b want to say

BABBLERS† (see BABBLER)
Is 44:25 frustrates the signs of the b

BABBLINGS† (see BABBLE)
1Ti 6:20 the profane and vain b and
2Ti 2:16 But shun profane and vain b

BABE (see BABES, BABY)
Luke 1:41 that the b leaped in her womb
Luke 2:12 You will find a B wrapped in
Luke 2:16 and the B lying in a manger
Heb 5:13 righteousness, for he is a b

BABEL† (see BABYLON)
Gen 10:10 of his kingdom was B, Erech,
Gen 11: 9 its name is called B, because

BABES (see BABE)
Ps 8: 2 Out of the mouth of b and
Is 3: 4 and b shall rule over them
Matt 11:25 and have revealed them to b
Matt 21:16 read, 'Out of the mouth of b
Rom 2:20 the foolish, a teacher of b

1Co 3: 1 to carnal, as to **b** in Christ
1Pe 2: 2 as newborn **b**, desire the pure

BABIES (*see* BABY)
Matt 24:19 with nursing **b** in those days
Acts 7:19 making them expose their **b**

BABY† (*see* BABE, BABIES)
Ex 2: 6 child, and behold, the **b** wept

BABYLON (*see* BABEL, BABYLONIAN, BABYLON'S, CHALDEA, SHESHACH)
2Ki 17:24 Assyria brought people from **B**
2Ki 20:14 from a far country, from **B**
2Ki 20:17 day, shall be carried to **B**
2Ki 25: 1 that Nebuchadnezzar king of **B**
2Ki 25:27 that Evil-Merodach king of **B**
Ezra 1:11 brought from **B** to Jerusalem
Ezra 5:13 first year of Cyrus king of **B**
Ezra 5:14 carried into the temple of **B**
Ezra 7: 6 this Ezra came up from **B**
Ezra 7:16 find in all the province of **B**
Neh 13: 6 **B** I had returned to the king
Esth 2: 6 king of **B** had carried away
Ps 137: 1 By the rivers of **B**, There we
Ps 137: 8 O daughter of **B**, who are to
Is 13: 1 The burden against **B** which
Is 13:19 And **B**, the glory of kingdoms,
Is 14: 4 proverb against the king of **B**
Is 21: 9 **B** is fallen, is fallen
Is 47: 1 dust, O virgin daughter of **B**
Is 48:14 he shall do His pleasure on **B**
Is 48:20 Go forth from **B**
Jer 21: 7 Nebuchadnezzar king of **B**
Jer 25:11 the king of **B** seventy years
Jer 27: 8 the yoke of the king of **B**
Jer 29:10 years are completed at **B**, I
Jer 39: 9 carried away captive to **B** the
Jer 50: 2 **B** is taken, Bel is shamed
Jer 50:42 against you, O daughter of **B**
Jer 51: 7 **B** has a golden cup in the
Jer 51: 8 **B** was suddenly fallen and been
Jer 51:34 the king of **B** has devoured me
Jer 51:37 **B** shall become a heap, a
Jer 51:41 How **B** has become desolate
Jer 51:42 The sea has come up over **B**
Jer 51:44 I will punish Bel in **B**, and I
Jer 51:64 Thus **B** shall sink and not
Ezek 12:13 I will bring him to **B**, to the
Ezek 17:12 king of **B** went to Jerusalem
Dan 1: 1 king of **B** came to Jerusalem
Dan 2:12 destroy all the wise men of **B**
Dan 2:48 over the whole province of **B**
Dan 2:48 over all the wise men of **B**
Dan 3: 1 of Dura, in the province of **B**
Dan 4:30 Is not this great **B**, that I
Dan 7: 1 year of Belshazzar king of **B**
Mic 4:10 and you shall go even to **B**
Zech 2: 7 dwell with the daughter of **B**
Matt 1:11 they were carried away to **B**
Matt 1:17 until the captivity in **B** are
Acts 7:43 will carry you away beyond **B**
1Pe 5:13 She who is in **B**, elect
Rev 14: 8 **B** is fallen, is fallen, that
Rev 16:19 great **B** was remembered before
Rev 17: 5 **B** THE GREAT, THE
Rev 18: 2 **B** the great is fallen, is

BABYLONIAN† (*see* BABYLON, BABYLONIANS)
Josh 7:21 spoils a beautiful **B** garment

BABYLONIANS (*see* BABYLONIAN)
Ezek 23:15 manner of the **B** of Chaldea

BABYLON'S (*see* BABYLON)
Jer 32: 2 For then the king of **B** army

BACA†
Ps 84: 6 pass through the Valley of **B**

BACKBITE† (*see* BACKBITERS, BACKBITING)
Ps 15: 3 does not **b** with his tongue

BACKBITERS† (*see* BACKBITE)
Rom 1:30 **b**, haters of God, violent,

BACKBITING† (*see* BACKBITE, BACKBITINGS)
Prov 25:23 rain, and a **b** tongue an angry

BACKBITINGS† (*see* BACKBITING)
2Co 12:20 wrath, selfish ambitions, **b**

BACKBONE†
Lev 3: 9 shall remove close to the **b**

BACKS
Ex 23:27 enemies turn their **b** to you
Neh 9:26 cast Your law behind their **b**
Prov 19:29 beatings for the **b** of fools

BACKSLIDER† (*see* BACKSLIDING)
Prov 14:14 The **b** in heart will be filled

BACKSLIDING (*see* BACKSLIDER, BACKSLIDINGS)
Is 57:17 he went on **b** in the way of
Jer 3: 6 seen what **b** Israel has done
Jer 3:14 O **b** children," says the LORD
Jer 31:22 gad about, O you **b** daughter
Hos 11: 7 people are bent on **b** from Me
Hos 14: 4 I will heal their **b**, I will

BACKSLIDINGS† (*see* BACKSLIDING)
Jer 2:19 and your **b** will reprove you
Jer 3:22 and I will heal your **b**
Jer 5: 6 their **b** have increased
Jer 14: 7 for our **b** are many, we have

BACKWARD
Gen 9:23 their shoulders, and went **b**
2Ki 20: 9 degrees or go **b** ten degrees
Is 1: 4 they have turned away **b**
Is 44:25 Who turns wise men **b**, and
Jer 7:24 their evil heart, and went **b**

BAD
Gen 24:50 speak to you either **b** or good
Gen 37: 2 Joseph brought a **b** report of
Num 13:32 a **b** report of the land which
2Ki 2:19 but the water is **b**, and the
Prov 25:19 of trouble is like a **b** tooth
Jer 24: 2 **b** figs which could not be
Jer 49:23 for they have heard **b** news
Amos 8: 6 even sell the **b** wheat
Matt 6:23 But if your eye is **b**, your
Matt 7:17 but a **b** tree bears **b** fruit
Matt 13:48 vessels, but threw the **b** away
Matt 22:10 all whom they found, both **b**
2Co 5:10 has done, whether good or **b**

BADGER (*see* BADGERS)
Ex 25: 5 red, **b** skins, and acacia wood
Ezek 16:10 and gave you sandals of **b** skin

BADGERS† (*see* BADGER)
Ps 104:18 are a refuge for the rock **b**
Prov 30:26 the rock **b** are a feeble folk,

BAG (*see* BAGS)
Deut 25:13 in your **b** differing weights
1Sa 17:40 and put them in a shepherd's **b**
Prov 7:20 He has taken a **b** of money
Hag 1: 6 to put into a **b** with holes
Matt 10:10 nor **b** for your journey, nor
Mark 6: 8 no **b**, no bread, no copper in
Luke 9: 3 neither staffs nor **b** nor
Luke 10: 4 Carry neither money **b**, sack,

BAGS (*see* BAG)
2Ki 5:23 talents of silver in two **b**
2Ki 12:10 priest came up and put it in **b**

Luke 12:33 money **b** which do not grow old

BAKE† (see BAKED, BAKER, BAKES)
Gen 11: 3 bricks and **b** them thoroughly
Ex 16:23 **B** what you will **b** today,
Lev 24: 5 and **b** twelve cakes with it
Lev 26:26 ten women shall **b** your bread
Ezek 4:12 and **b** it using fuel of human
Ezek 46:20 where they shall **b** the grain

BAKED (see BAKE)
Gen 19: 3 **b** unleavened bread, and they
Gen 40:17 kinds of **b** goods for Pharaoh
Ex 12:39 they **b** unleavened cakes of
Lev 2: 4 grain offering **b** in the oven
Lev 6:17 It shall not be **b** with leaven
Is 44:19 I have also **b** bread on its

BAKER (see BAKE, BAKERS)
Gen 40: 1 the **b** of the king of Egypt
Gen 40: 2 chief butler and the chief **b**
Hos 7: 4 like an oven heated by a **b**
Hos 7: 6 their **b** sleeps all night

BAKERS† (see BAKER, BAKERS')
1Sa 8:13 to be perfumers, cooks, and **b**

BAKERS'† (see BAKERS)
Jer 37:21 of bread from the **b** street

BAKES† (see BAKE)
Is 44:15 yes, he kindles it and **b** bread

BALAAM (see BALAAM'S)
Num 22: 5 **B** the son of Beor at Pethor
Num 22:30 So the donkey said to **B**, "Am
Josh 24:10 But I would not listen to **B**
Neh 13: 2 but hired **B** against them to
2Pe 2:15 the way of **B** the son of Beor
Jude 11 in the error of **B** for profit
Rev 2:14 who hold the doctrine of **B**

BALAAM'S (see BALAAM)
Num 22:31 Then the LORD opened **B** eyes
Num 23: 5 LORD put a word in **B** mouth

BALAK (see BALAK'S)
Num 22: 2 Now **B** the son of Zippor saw
Josh 24: 9 Then **B** the son of Zippor,
Mic 6: 5 remember now what **B** king of
Rev 2:14 Balaam, who taught **B** to put a

BALAK'S† (see BALAK)
Num 24:10 Then **B** anger was aroused

BALANCE (see BALANCES, SCALES)
Is 40:12 in scales and the hills in a **b**

BALANCES (see BALANCE, SCALES)
Dan 5:27 have been weighed in the **b**

BALD (see BALDHEAD, BALDNESS)
Lev 13:40 fallen from his head, he is **b**
Jer 16: 6 make themselves **b** for them
Jer 48:37 For every head shall be **b**

BALDHEAD† (see BALD)
2Ki 2:23 said to him, "Go up, you **b**

BALDNESS (see BALD)
Is 3:24 instead of well-set hair, **b**
Is 22:12 and for mourning, for **b** and for
Mic 1:16 enlarge your **b** like an eagle,

BALL†
Is 22:18 and toss you like a **b** into a

BALM
Gen 37:25 camels, bearing spices, **b**
Jer 8:22 is there no **b** in Gilead, is
Jer 51: 8 Take **b** for her pain
Ezek 27:17 millet, honey, oil, and **b**

BAN†
Lev 27:29 No person under the **b**, who

BAND (see BANDED, BANDS)
Gen 49:15 and became a **b** of slaves
Ex 28: 8 woven **b** of the ephod, which
Job 38: 9 darkness its swaddling **b**
Dan 4:15 earth, bound with a **b** of iron
Rev 1:13 the chest with a golden **b**

BANDAGE (see BANDAGED)
1Ki 20:38 with a **b** over his eyes

BANDAGED† (see BANDAGE)
Ezek 30:21 it has not been **b** for healing
Luke 10:34 **b** his wounds, pouring on oil

BANDED† (see BAND)
Judg 11: 3 worthless men **b** together with
Acts 23:12 some of the Jews **b** together

BANDS (see BAND)
Ex 27:10 their **b** shall be of silver
Hos 11: 4 with **b** of love, and I was to
Rev 15: 6 chests girded with golden **b**

BANISHED (see BANISHMENT)
2Sa 14:13 bring his **b** one home again
1Ki 15:12 he the perverted persons
Prov 14:32 The wicked is **b** in his

BANISHMENT† (see BANISHED)
Ezra 7:26 whether it be death, or **b**

BANK (see BANKERS, BANKS)
Gen 41: 3 cows on the **b** of the river
Ex 2: 3 in the reeds by the river's **b**
Luke 19:23 you not put my money in the **b**

BANKERS† (see BANK)
Matt 25:27 deposited my money with the **b**

BANKS (see BANK)
Num 13:29 along the **b** of the Jordan
Is 8: 7 channels and go over all his **b**

BANNER (see BANNERS)
Ps 60: 4 You have given a **b** to those
Song 2: 4 and his **b** over me was love
Is 5:26 He will lift up a **b** to the
Is 11:10 stand as a **b** to the people
Zech 9:16 lifted like a **b** over His land

BANNERS (see BANNER)
Ps 20: 5 our God we will set up our **b**
Ps 74: 4 They set up their **b** for signs
Song 6: 4 awesome as an army with **b**

BANQUET (see BANQUETING, BANQUETS)
Esth 5: 4 Haman come today to the **b**
Dan 5:10 his lords, came to the **b** hall

BANQUETING† (see BANQUET)
Song 2: 4 He brought me to the **b** house

BANQUETS† (see BANQUET)
Amos 6: 7 recline at **b** shall be removed

BAPTISM (see BAPTISMS, BAPTIZE)
Matt 3: 7 and Sadducees coming to his **b**
Matt 20:22 be baptized with the **b** that I
Matt 21:25 The **b** of John, where was it
Mark 1: 4 preaching a **b** of repentance
Luke 3: 3 preaching a **b** of repentance
Acts 10:37 the **b** which John preached
Rom 6: 4 with Him through **b** into death
Eph 4: 5 one Lord, one faith, one **b**
Col 2:12 buried with Him in **b**, in
1Pe 3:21 which now saves us—**b**

BAPTISMS† (see BAPTISM)
Heb 6: 2 of the doctrine of **b**, of

BAPTIST (see BAPTIST'S, BAPTIZE, JOHN)
Matt 3: 1 the **B** came preaching in the
Matt 11:11 one greater than John the **B**
Mark 6:24 The head of John the **B**
Mark 6:25 of John the **B** on a platter
Luke 7:33 For John the **B** came neither

BAPTIST'S † (see BAPTIST)
Matt 14: 8 Give me John the **B** head here

BAPTIZE (see BAPTISM, BAPTIST, BAPTIZED, BAPTIZES, BAPTIZING)
Matt 3:11 I indeed **b** you with water
Matt 3:11 He will **b** you with the Holy
John 4: 2 Jesus Himself did not **b**, but
1Co 1:17 Christ did not send me to **b**

BAPTIZED (see BAPTIZE)
Matt 3: 6 were **b** by him in the Jordan,
Matt 3:14 I have need to be **b** by You
Matt 3:16 Jesus, when He had been **b**
Matt 20:22 be **b** with the baptism that I
Mark 1: 8 I indeed **b** you with water,
Mark 1: 9 was **b** by John in the Jordan
Luke 3: 7 that came out to be **b** by him
Luke 12:50 I have a baptism to be **b** with
John 3:23 And they came and were **b**
John 4: 1 **b** more disciples than John
Acts 1: 5 for John truly **b** with water
Acts 1: 5 but you shall be **b** with the
Acts 2:38 let every one of you be **b** in
Acts 2:41 received his word were **b**
Acts 8:12 both men and women were **b**
Acts 8:36 What hinders me from being **b**
Acts 8:38 into the water, and he **b** him
Acts 16:15 she and her household were **b**
Acts 16:33 he and all his family were **b**
Acts 18: 8 hearing, believed and were **b**
Acts 19: 3 Into what then were you **b**
Acts 22:16 Arise and be **b**, and wash away
Rom 6: 3 were **b** into Christ Jesus were
Rom 6: 3 Jesus were **b** into His death
1Co 1:14 I thank God that I **b** none of
1Co 1:15 that I had **b** in my own name
1Co 10: 2 all were **b** into Moses in the
1Co 12:13 we were all **b** into one body
1Co 15:29 do who are **b** for the dead
Gal 3:27 **b** into Christ have put on

BAPTIZES † (see BAPTIZE)
John 1:33 this is He who **b** with the

BAPTIZING (see BAPTIZE)
Matt 28:19 **b** them in the name of the
Mark 1: 4 John came **b** in the wilderness
John 1:28 the Jordan, where John was **b**
John 1:31 therefore I came to **b** with water
John 3:23 Now John also was **b** in Aenon

BAR (see BARS)
Judg 16: 3 gateposts, pulled them up, **b**
Neh 7: 3 them shut and **b** the doors
Amos 1: 5 break the gate **b** of Damascus

BARABBAS
Matt 27:16 a notorious prisoner called **B**
Matt 27:17 **B**, or Jesus who is called
Matt 27:20 that they should ask for **B**
Matt 27:26 Then he released **B** to them
John 18:40 Not this Man, but **B**
John 18:40 Now **B** was a robber

BARAK
Judg 4:12 reported to Sisera that **B** the
Judg 4:14 Then Deborah said to **B**, "Up
Judg 4:22 as **B** pursued Sisera, Jael
Judg 5: 1 **B** the son of Abinoam sang on
Judg 5:12 Arise, **B**, and lead your
Heb 11:32 me to tell of Gideon and **B**

BARBARIAN † (see BARBARIANS)
Col 3:11 nor uncircumcised, **b**,

BARBARIANS † (see BARBARIAN)
Rom 1:14 debtor both to Greeks and to **b**

BARBER'S †
Ezek 5: 1 sword, take it as a **b** razor

BARE (see BAREFOOT)
Lev 13:45 shall be torn and his head **b**
Ps 29: 9 And strips the forests **b**
Is 32:11 yourselves, make yourselves **b**
Is 52:10 The LORD has made **b** His holy
Jer 49:10 But I have made Esau **b**
Ezek 16: 7 grew, but you were naked and **b**
Hab 3:13 by laying **b** from foundation
Zeph 2:14 He will lay **b** the cedar work

BAREFOOT (see BARE)
2Sa 15:30 his head covered and went **b**
Is 20: 2 he did so, walking naked and **b**

BAR-JESUS †
Acts 13: 6 a Jew whose name was **B**,

BAR-JONAH † (see SIMON)
Matt 16:17 Blessed are you, Simon **B**, for

BARK †
Is 56:10 all dumb dogs, they cannot **b**

BARLEY
Ex 9:31 the **b** were struck, for the
Judg 7:13 a loaf of **b** bread tumbled
Ruth 1:22 at the beginning of **b** harvest
Ruth 3: 2 he is winnowing **b** tonight at
John 6: 9 here who has five **b** loaves
John 6:13 the fragments of the five **b**
Rev 6: 6 quarts of **b** for a denarius

BARN † (see BARNS)
Hag 2:19 Is the seed still in the **b**
Matt 3:12 gather His wheat into the **b**
Matt 13:30 gather the wheat into my **b**
Luke 3:17 gather the wheat into His **b**
Luke 12:24 have neither storehouse nor **b**

BARNABAS (see JOSES)
Acts 4:36 who was also named **B** by the
Acts 9:27 But **B** took him and brought him
Acts 11:30 the elders by the hands of **B**
Acts 12:25 And **B** and Saul returned from
Acts 13: 1 **B**, Simeon who was called
Acts 13: 2 Now separate to Me **B** and Saul
Acts 14:12 they called Zeus, and Paul,
Acts 15: 2 **B** had no small dissension and
Gal 2: 9 me and **B** the right hand of
Col 4:10 with Mark the cousin of **B**

BARNS (see BARN)
Ps 144:13 That our **b** may be full,
Joel 1:17 **b** are broken down, for the
Matt 6:26 nor reap nor gather into **b**
Luke 12:18 I will pull down my **b** and

BARRACKS
Acts 21:34 to be taken into the **b**

BARREN (see BARRENNESS)
Gen 11:30 But Sarai was **b**
Gen 25:21 his wife, because she was **b**
Gen 29:31 but Rachel was **b**
Ex 23:26 or be **b** in your land
Judg 13: 2 and his wife was **b** and had no
1Sa 2: 5 Even the **b** has borne seven,
2Ki 2:19 water is bad, and the ground **b**
Job 3: 7 Oh, may that night be **b**
Ps 113: 9 He grants the **b** woman a home
Prov 30:16 the **b** womb, the earth that is
Is 54: 1 Sing, O **b**, you who have not
Luke 1: 7 because Elizabeth was **b**, and

Luke 1:36 for her who was called **b**
Luke 23:29 will say, 'Blessed are the **b**
Gal 4:27 Rejoice, O **b**, you who do not
2Pe 1: 8 you will be neither **b** nor

BARRENNESS† (*see* BARREN)
2Ki 2:21 shall be no more death or **b**
Ps 107:34 A fruitful land into to **b**, For

BARS (*see* BAR)
Ex 26:26 shall make **b** of acacia wood
Ex 35:11 it clasps, it boards, its **b**
Num 3:36 of the tabernacle, its **b**, its
Deut 3: 5 with high walls, gates, and **b**
1Sa 23: 7 a town that has gates and **b**
Neh 3: 3 its doors with its bolts and **b**
Job 38:10 My limit for it, and set **b**
Job 40:18 his ribs like for **b** of iron
Ps 107:16 And cut the **b** of iron in two
Prov 18:19 are like the **b** of a castle
Lam 2: 9 has destroyed and broken her **b**
Jon 2: 6 the earth with its **b** closed

BARSABAS† (*see* JOSEPH, JUDAS, JUSTUS)
Acts 1:23 Joseph called **B**, who was
Acts 15:22 Judas who was also named **B**

BARTERED†
Ezek 27:13 They **b** human lives and vessels

BARTHOLOMEW (*see* NATHANAEL)
Mark 3:18 Andrew, Philip, **B**, Matthew,

BARTIMAEUS† (*see* TIMAEUS)
Mark 10:46 and a great multitude, blind **B**

BARUCH
Jer 32:12 deed to **B** the son of Neriah
Jer 36: 4 **B** wrote on a scroll of a book
Jer 45: 1 spoke to **B** the son of Neriah

BARZILLAI
2Sa 17:27 **B** the Gileadite from Rogelim,

BASE (*see* BASES)
Ex 19:12 the mountain or touch its **b**
Ex 29:12 beside the **b** of the altar
Ex 30:18 with its **b** also of bronze,
Ex 30:28 and the laver and its **b**
Lev 4: 7 blood of the bull at the **b** of
Lev 4:18 the **b** of the altar of burnt
2Sa 6:20 as one of the **b** fellows
Is 3: 5 the **b** toward the honorable
Mal 2: 9 and **b** before all the people,
1Co 1:28 and **b** things of the world and

BASES (*see* BASE)
Ex 38:31 the **b** for the court gate, all
Ezra 3: 3 they set the altar on its **b**
Song 5:15 marble set on **b** of fine gold

BASHAN
Num 21:33 and went up by the way to **B**
Num 32:33 the kingdom of Og king of **B**
Josh 21: 6 half-tribe of Manasseh in **B**
Ps 22:12 Strong bulls of **B** have
Ps 68:15 of God is the mountain of **B**
Is 2:13 up, and upon all the oaks of **B**
Ezek 39:18 all of them fatlings of **B**
Amos 4: 1 Hear this word, you cows of **B**
Nah 1: 4 **B** and Carmel wither, and the
Zech 11: 2 Wail, O oaks of **B**, for the

BASIC†
Col 2: 8 according to the **b** principles
Col 2:20 the **b** principles of the world

BASIN (*see* BASINS)
Ex 12:22 in the blood that is in the **b**
John 13: 5 He poured water into a **b**

BASINS (*see* BASIN)
Ex 24: 6 half the blood and put it in **b**
Ex 38: 3 the pans, the shovels, the **b**

BASKET (*see* BASKETS)
Gen 40:17 In the uppermost **b** were
Gen 40:17 them out of the **b** on my head
Ex 29: 3 You shall put them in one **b**
Ex 29:23 one wafer from the **b** of the
Ex 29:32 and the bread that is in the **b**
Lev 8: 2 and a **b** of unleavened bread
Deut 28: 5 Blessed shall be your **b** and
Deut 28:17 Cursed shall be your **b** and
Judg 6:19 The meat he put in a **b**, and he
Jer 24: 2 One **b** had very good figs,
Amos 8: 1 Behold, a **b** of summer fruit
Zech 5: 6 It is a **b** that is going forth
Zech 5: 7 woman sitting inside the **b**"
Matt 5:15 a lamp and put it under a **b**
Mark 4:21 put under a **b** or under a bed
Luke 11:33 a secret place or under a **b**
Acts 9:25 through the wall in a large **b**
2Co 11:33 a **b** through a window in the

BASKETS (*see* BASKET)
Gen 40:16 had three white **b** on my head
Gen 40:18 The three **b** are three days
2Ki 10: 7 persons, put their heads in **b**
Ps 81: 6 hands were freed from the **b**
Jer 24: 1 there were two **b** of figs set
Matt 14:20 they took up twelve **b** full of
Matt 15:37 they took up seven large **b**
Mark 8: 8 large **b** of leftover fragments

BAT† (*see* BATS)
Lev 11:19 kind, the hoopoe, and the **b**
Deut 14:18 kind, and the hoopoe and the **b**

BATH (*see* BATHS)
Is 5:10 of vineyard shall yield one **b**
Ezek 45:10 an honest ephah, and an honest **b**

BATHE (*see* BATHED, BATHING)
Lev 15: 5 **b** in water, and be unclean
Lev 15:13 **b** his body in running water
Lev 15:18 they both shall **b** in water

BATHED† (*see* BATHE)
1Ki 22:38 his blood while the harlots **b**
Job 29: 6 my steps were **b** with cream
Is 34: 5 My sword shall be **b** in heaven
John 13:10 He who is **b** needs only to

BATHING† (*see* BATHE)
2Sa 11: 2 the roof he saw a woman **b**

BATHS (*see* BATH)
1Ki 7:26 It contained two thousand **b**
1Ki 7:38 each layer contained forty **b**
2Ch 2:10 twenty thousand **b** of wine
2Ch 2:10 and twenty thousand **b** of oil
Ezek 45:14 A kor is a homer or ten **b**

BATHSHEBA
2Sa 11: 3 Is this not **B**, the daughter
2Sa 12:24 David comforted **B** his wife
1Ki 1:11 So Nathan spoke to **B** the
1Ki 1:16 **B** bowed and did homage to the
1Ki 2:13 to **B** the mother of Solomon

BATS† (*see* BAT)
Is 2:20 to worship, to the moles and **b**

BATTEN
Judg 16:14 with the **b** of the loom, and

BATTER† (*see* BATTERED, BATTERING)
Num 24:17 and **b** the brow of Moab, and

BATTERED† (*see* BATTER)
2Sa 20:15 **b** the wall to throw it down

BATTERING (see BATTER)
Ezek 4: 2 place **b** rams against it all

BATTLE (see BATTLEFIELD, BATTLEMENT, BATTLES)
Gen   14: 8 joined together in **b** in the
Num 31:28 men of war who went out to **b**
Num 32:27 for war, before the LORD to **b**
Num 32:29 armed for **b** before the LORD
Deut   2:24 it, and engage him in **b**
Josh   8:14 went out against Israel to **b**
Josh 11:19 All the others they took in **b**
Judg 20:20 **b** array to fight against them
Judg 20:22 again formed the **b** line at
Judg 20:34 Gibeah, and the **b** was fierce
1Sa   4:16 I fled today from the **b** line
1Sa   17:47 for the **b** is the LORD's, and
1Sa   31: 3 Now the **b** became fierce
2Sa   1:25 fallen in the midst of the **b**
2Sa   2:17 was a very fierce **b** that day
2Sa   11: 1 time when kings go out to **b**
2Sa   17:11 and that you go to **b** in person
2Sa   18: 6 the field of **b** against Israel
1Ki   20:29 seventh day the **b** was joined
1Ki   22:30 disguise myself and go into **b**
2Ch   20:15 for the **b** is not yours, but
2Ch   25: 8 Be strong in **b**
Job   15:24 him, like a king ready for **b**
Job   38:23 of trouble, for the day of **b**
Job   41: 8 remember the **b**
Ps   18:39 me with strength for the **b**
Ps   24: 8 mighty, The LORD mighty in **b**
Ps   78: 9 Turned back in the day of **b**
Ps   144: 1 for war, And my fingers for **b**
Prov 21:31 is prepared for the day of **b**
Eccl   9:11 nor the **b** to the strong, nor
Is   9: 5 sandal from the noisy **b**, and
Is   13: 4 hosts musters the army for **b**
Is   16: 9 for **b** cries have fallen over
Is   28: 6 turn back the **b** at the gate
Is   42:25 anger and the strength of **b**
Jer   8: 6 the horse rushes into the **b**
Jer   18:21 be slain by the sword in **b**
Jer   50:22 A sound of **b** is in the land,
Ezek 13: 5 in **b** on the day of the LORD
Hos   1: 7 by bow, nor by sword or **b**
Zech   9:10 the **b** bow shall be cut off
Zech 14: 3 as He fights in the day of **b**
1Co   14: 8 will prepare himself for **b**
Heb   11:34 strong, became valiant in **b**
Rev   9: 7 like horses prepared for **b**
Rev   16:14 to gather them to the **b** of
Rev   20: 8 to gather them together to **b**

BATTLE-AX†
Jer   51:20 You are My **b** and weapons of
Ezek   9: 2 each with his **b** in his hand

BATTLEFIELD† (see BATTLE)
Judg   5:18 also, on the heights of the **b**

BATTLEMENT† (see BATTLE)
Song   8: 9 build upon her a **b** of silver

BATTLES (see BATTLE)
1Sa   8:20 out before us and fight our **b**
1Sa   18:17 for me, and fight the LORD's **b**

BAY†
Josh 15: 2 Sea, from the **b** that faces
Josh 15: 5 quarter began at the **b** of the
Josh 18:19 the north **b** at the Salt Sea
Acts 27:39 observed a **b** with a beach

BDELLIUM†
Gen   2:12 **B** and the onyx stone are there
Num   11: 7 its color like the color of **b**

BEACH†
Acts 27:39 they observed a bay with a **b**

BEAM (see BEAMS)
Num   4:10 and put it on a carrying **b**
1Sa   17: 7 spear was like a weaver's **b**
2Ki   6: 2 every man take a **b** from there
Hab   2:11 the **b** from the timbers will

BEAMS (see BEAM)
1Ki   6: 6 so that the support **b** would
Job   40:18 bones are like **b** of bronze
Ps   104: 3 He lays the **b** of His upper

BEANS†
2Sa   17:28 and flour, parched grain and **b**
Ezek   4: 9 for yourself wheat, barley, **b**

BEAR (see BEARERS, BEARING, BEARS, BORE, BORNE)
Gen   4:13 is greater than I can **b**
Gen   16:11 child, and you shall **b** a son
Gen   17:17 ninety years old, **b** a child
Gen   17:21 whom Sarah shall **b** to you at
Gen   43: 9 you, then let me **b** the blame
Gen   49:15 his shoulder to **b** a burden
Ex   20:16 You shall not **b** false witness
Ex   25:27 for the poles to **b** the table
Ex   27: 7 sides of the altar to **b** it
Ex   28:12 So Aaron shall **b** their names
Ex   28:30 So Aaron shall **b** the judgment
Ex   28:38 that Aaron may **b** the iniquity
Lev   5:17 and shall **b** his iniquity
Lev   7:18 who eats of it shall **b** guilt
Lev   16:22 The goat shall **b** on itself
Lev   19:17 and not **b** sin because of him
Lev   19:18 nor **b** any grudge against the
Lev   24:15 his God shall **b** his sin
Num   11:14 I am not able to **b** all these
Num   11:17 they shall **b** the burden of
Num   14:27 How long shall I **b** with this
Num   14:33 years, and **b** the brunt of your
Deut   1:12 can I alone **b** your problems
Deut   5:20 You shall not **b** false
Deut 10: 8 the tribe of Levi to **b** the
Deut 29:23 it is not sown, nor does it **b**
Josh   3: 8 who **b** the ark of the covenant
Judg   5:14 who **b** the recruiter's staff
Judg 13: 3 you shall conceive and **b** a son
Ruth   1:12 tonight and should also **b** sons
1Sa   17:36 has killed both lion and **b**
2Sa   17: 8 like a **b** robbed of her cubs
2Ki   19:30 downward, and **b** fruit upward
Job   9: 9 He made the **B**, Orion, and
Job   38:32 the Great **B** with its cubs
Ps   28: 9 also, And **b** them up forever
Ps   55:12 Then I could **b** it
Ps   89:50 How I **b** in my bosom the
Ps   91:12 They shall **b** you up in their
Ps   92:14 still **b** fruit in old age
Prov 18:14 but who can **b** a broken spirit
Prov 28:15 and a charging **b** is a wicked
Is   7:14 **b** a Son, and shall call His
Is   11: 7 The cow and the **b** shall graze
Is   53:11 many, for He shall **b** their
Jer   17:21 **b** no burden on the Sabbath
Lam   3:10 to me like a **b** lying in wait
Lam   3:27 to **b** the yoke in his youth
Ezek 16:52 **b** your own shame also,
Ezek 18:19 not **b** the guilt of the father
Dan   7: 5 beast, a second, like a **b**
Amos   5:19 from a lion, and a **b** met him
Amos   7:10 not able to **b** all his words
Mic   7: 9 I will **b** the indignation of
Zech   6:13 He shall **b** the glory, and
Matt   1:23 **b** a Son, and they shall call
Matt   3: 8 Therefore **b** fruits worthy of
Matt   3:10 not **b** good fruit is cut down
Matt   4: 6 hands they shall **b** you up
Matt   7:18 good tree cannot **b** bad fruit

Matt 17:17 How long shall I **b** with you
Matt 19:18 You shall not **b** false witness
Matt 23: 4 bind heavy burdens, hard to **b**
Matt 27:32 they compelled to **b** His cross
Mark   4:20 word, accept it, and **b** fruit
Luke   1:13 Elizabeth will **b** you a son
Luke   8:15 it and **b** fruit with patience
Luke 14:27 whoever does not **b** his cross
John   1: 7 to **b** witness of the Light,
John 10:25 name, they **b** witness of Me
John 15: 2 not **b** fruit He takes away
John 15: 2 that it may **b** more fruit
John 15: 4 cannot **b** fruit of itself,
John 15: 8 that you **b** much fruit
John 16:12 but you cannot **b** them now
Acts   9:15 to **b** My name before Gentiles
Rom   7: 4 that we should **b** fruit to God
Rom   7: 5 members to **b** fruit to death
Rom   10: 2 For I **b** them witness that
Rom   13: 4 for he does not **b** the sword
Rom   15: 1 who are strong ought to **b**
1Co   10:13 that you may be able to **b** it
1Co   15:49 we shall also **b** the image of
Gal   5:10 you shall **b** his judgment,
Gal   6: 2 **B** one another's burdens, and
Gal   6: 5 each one shall **b** his own load
Gal   6:17 for I **b** in my body the marks
Heb   9:28 once to **b** the sins of many
1Jn   5: 7 three who **b** witness in heaven
1Jn   5: 8 three that **b** witness on earth
Rev   13: 2 were like the feet of a **b**

BEARD (*see* BEARDS)
Lev   13:29 a sore on the head or the **b**
Lev   13:30 a leprosy of the head or **b**
Lev   19:27 disfigure the edges of your **b**
1Sa   17:35 me, I caught it by its **b**, and
1Sa   21:13 his saliva fall down on his **b**
2Sa   20: 9 Joab took Amasa by the **b** with
Ps   133: 2 head, Running down on the **b**
Jer   48:37 be shaved, and every **b** clipped

BEARDS (*see* BEARD)
Lev   21: 5 **b** nor make any cuttings in
2Sa   10: 4 shaved off half of their **b**
2Sa   10: 5 until your **b** have grown, and

BEARERS† (*see* BEAR)
2Ch   2:18 thousand of them **b** of burdens
2Ch   34:13 were over the burden **b** and

BEARING (*see* BEAR)
Gen   16: 2 restrained me from **b** children
Gen   29:35 Then she stopped **b**
Gen   37:25 **b** spices, balm, and myrrh, on
Num   4:47 the work of **b** burdens in the
Deut 29:18 root **b** bitterness or wormwood
Josh   3:14 with the priests **b** the ark of
2Sa   21:16 who was **b** a new sword,
1Ch   12:24 sons of Judah **b** shield
Ps   126: 6 **B** seed for sowing, Shall
Is   1:14 to Me, I am weary of **b** them
Matt 21:43 a nation the fruits of it
John 19:17 **b** His cross, went out to a
Acts 14: 3 who was **b** witness to the word
Rom   2:15 conscience also **b** witness
Eph   4: 2 **b** with one another in love,
Heb   13:13 the camp, **b** His reproach

BEARS (*see* BEAR)
Lev   5: 1 does not tell it, he **b** guilt
Lev   12: 5 But if she **b** a female child,
2Ki   2:24 two female **b** came out of the
Job   16: 8 me and **b** witness to my face
Prov 25:18 A man who **b** false witness
Is   59:11 We all growl like **b**, and moan
Matt   7:17 every good tree **b** good fruit

Luke 18: 7 though He **b** long with them
John   5:32 another who **b** witness of Me
John   8:18 I am One who **b** witness of
John   8:18 who sent Me **b** witness of Me
John 15: 2 branch that **b** fruit He prunes
John 15: 5 Me, and I in him, **b** much fruit
Acts 22: 5 the high priest **b** me witness
Rom   8:16 The Spirit Himself **b** witness
1Co   13: 7 **b** all things, believes all
Heb   6: 8 but if it **b** thorns and briars,

BEAST (*see* ANIMAL, BEASTS)
Gen   1:25 God made the **b** of the earth
Gen   3: 1 was more cunning than any **b**
Gen   6: 7 of the earth, both man and **b**
Gen   7:14 every **b** after its kind, all
Gen   9: 5 of every **b** I will require it
Gen   9:10 the ark, every **b** of the earth
Gen   37:20 Some wild **b** has devoured him
Ex   8:17 and it became lice on man and **b**
Ex   13: 2 both of man and **b**; it
Lev   5: 2 the carcass of an unclean **b**
Num   8:17 are Mine, both man and **b**
Num   18:15 to the LORD, whether man or **b**
2Ki   14: 9 a wild **b** that was in Lebanon
Ps   36: 6 LORD, You preserve man and **b**
Ps   50:10 For every **b** of the forest is
Ps   73:22 I was like a **b** before You
Ps   147: 9 He gives to the **b** its food
Is   46: 1 a burden to the weary **b**
Ezek 44:31 not eat anything, bird or **b**
Dan   4:16 Let him be given the heart of a **b**
Dan   7: 5 And suddenly another **b**, a
Dan   7: 6 The **b** also had four heads, and
Rev   11: 7 the **b** that ascends out of the
Rev   13: 3 marveled and followed the **b**
Rev   13: 4 who gave authority to the **b**
Rev   13: 4 and they worshiped the **b**,
Rev   13:11 Then I saw another **b** coming
Rev   13:12 in it to worship the first **b**
Rev   13:15 breath to the image of the **b**
Rev   13:17 the mark or the name of the **b**
Rev   13:18 calculate the number of the **b**
Rev   16: 2 men who had the mark of the **b**
Rev   17: 3 **b** which was full of names of
Rev   17: 7 of the **b** that carries her,
Rev   17:16 horns which you saw on the **b**
Rev   17:17 gave their kingdom to the **b**
Rev   19:20 Then the **b** was captured, and
Rev   20: 4 worshiped the **b** or his image
Rev   20:10 fire and brimstone where the **b**

BEASTS (*see* ANIMALS, BEAST)
Gen   7:21 birds and cattle and **b** and every
Ex   22:31 is torn by **b** in the field
Lev   7:24 torn by wild **b**, may be
1Sa   17:44 the air and the **b** of the field
Job   37: 8 The **b** go into dens, And remain
Job   40:20 all the **b** of the field play
Ps   49:12 He is like the **b** that perish
Ps   68:30 Rebuke the **b** of the reeds,
Prov 30:30 lion, which is mighty among **b**
Ezek 44:31 or was torn by wild **b**
Dan   4:15 let him graze with the **b** on
Dan   4:23 graze with the **b** of the field
Dan   5:21 his heart was made like the **b**
Dan   7: 3 four great **b** came up from the
Zeph   2:15 a place for **b** to lie down
Mark   1:13 Satan, and was with the wild **b**
1Co   15:32 have fought with **b** at Ephesus
Tit   1:12 are always liars, evil **b**,
Jude   10 know naturally, like brute **b**

BEAT (*see* BEATEN, BEATING, BEATINGS, BEATS)
Ex   39: 3 they **b** the gold into thin
Deut 25: 3 **b** him with many blows above

Ruth	2:17	**b** out what she had gleaned,
Ps	78:66	And He **b** back His enemies
Ps	89:23	I will **b** down his foes before
Prov	23:13	for if you **b** him with a rod,
Is	2: 4	they shall **b** their swords
Ezek	21:17	I also will **b** My fists
Joel	3:10	**B** your plowshares into swords
Jon	4: 8	the sun **b** on Jonah's head, so
Mic	4: 3	they shall **b** their swords
Matt	7:25	winds blew and **b** on that house
Matt	21:35	**b** one, killed one, and stoned
Matt	26:67	spat in His face and **b** Him
Mark	4:37	the waves **b** into the boat, so
Luke	6:48	the stream **b** vehemently
Luke	12:45	begins to **b** the male and female
Luke	18:13	but **b** his breast, saying
Acts	18:17	**b** him before the judgment
Acts	22:19	**b** those who believe on You
Acts	27:20	and no small tempest **b** on us

BEATEN (see BEAT)

Ex	5:14	had set over them, were **b**
Ex	37: 7	made two cherubim of **b** gold
Luke	12:47	shall be **b** with many stripes
Acts	5:40	**b** them, they commanded that
Acts	16:22	them to be **b** with rods
1Co	4:11	we are poorly clothed, and **b**
2Co	11:25	Three times I was **b** with rods
1Pe	2:20	if, when you are **b** for your

BEATING† (see BEAT)

Ex	2:11	he saw an Egyptian **b** a Hebrew
Nah	2: 7	of doves, **b** their breasts
Mark	12: 5	**b** some and killing some
Acts	21:32	soldiers, they stopped **b** Paul

BEATINGS† (see BEAT)

Prov	19:29	and **b** for the backs of fools

BEATS† (see BEAT)

Ex	21:20	if a man **b** his male or female
1Co	9:26	not as one who **b** the air

BEAUTIES (see BEAUTIFY)

Ps	110: 3	In the **b** of holiness, from

BEAUTIFUL (see BEAUTY)

Gen	6: 2	of men, that they were **b**
Gen	12:11	are a woman of **b** countenance
Gen	24:16	woman was very **b** to behold
Gen	29:17	but Rachel was **b** of form
Ex	2: 2	she saw that he was a **b** child
Lev	23:40	day the fruit of **b** trees,
Deut	6:10	cities which you did not
Josh	7:21	spoils a **b** Babylonian garment
Job	42:15	so **b** as the daughters of Job
Ps	33: 1	praise from the upright is **b**
Ps	48: 2	**B** in elevation, The joy of
Eccl	3:11	made everything **b** in its time
Song	7: 1	How **b** are your feet in
Is	4: 2	Branch of the LORD shall be **b**
Is	52: 7	How **b** upon the mountains are
Is	64:11	**b** temple, where our fathers
Jer	3:19	a **b** heritage of the hosts of
Jer	13:20	given to you, your **b** sheep
Jer	48:17	staff is broken, the **b** rod
Ezek	31: 7	Thus it was **b** in greatness
Matt	13:45	a merchant seeking **b** pearls
Matt	23:27	indeed appear **b** outwardly
Luke	21: 5	it was adorned with **b** stones
Acts	3: 2	the temple which is called **B**
Acts	3:10	at the **B** Gate of the temple
Rom	10:15	How **b** are the feet of those
Heb	11:23	they saw he was a **b** child

BEAUTIFY (see BEAUTIES, BEAUTIFYING, BEAUTY)

Ezra	7:27	to **b** the house of the LORD
Ps	149: 4	He will **b** the humble with

Jer	2:33	Why do you **b** your way to seek

BEAUTIFYING† (see BEAUTIFY)

Esth	2:12	and preparations for **b** women

BEAUTY (see BEAUTIFUL, BEAUTIFY)

Ex	28: 2	brother, for glory and for **b**
2Sa	1:19	The **b** of Israel is slain on
1Ch	16:29	the LORD in the **b** of holiness
2Ch	3: 6	with precious stones for **b**
Esth	1:11	to show her **b** to the people
Esth	2: 3	let **b** preparations be given
Ps	27: 4	To behold the **b** of the LORD
Ps	29: 2	the LORD in the **b** of holiness
Ps	45:11	will greatly desire your **b**
Ps	50: 2	of Zion, the perfection of **b**
Ps	90:17	let the **b** of the LORD our God
Ps	96: 6	and **b** are in His sanctuary
Prov	6:25	after her **b** in your heart
Prov	31:30	**b** is passing, but a woman who
Is	3:24	and branding instead of **b**
Is	33:17	will see the King in His **b**
Is	53: 2	there is no **b** that we should
Is	61: 3	to give them **b** for ashes
Ezek	16:25	made your **b** to be abhorred
Ezek	27: 3	have said, 'I am perfect in **b**
Ezek	28:17	lifted up because of your **b**
Zech	11: 7	the one I called **B**, and the

BECKONED†

Luke	1:22	for he **b** to them and remained

BED (see BEDRIDDEN, BEDROOM, BEDS, BEDSTEAD)

Gen	47:31	himself on the head of the **b**
Gen	48: 2	himself and sat up on the **b**
Gen	49: 4	went up to your father's **b**
Gen	49:33	drew his feet up into the **b**
Ex	8: 3	your bedroom, on your **b**
2Ki	4:32	child, lying dead on his **b**
Job	7:13	My **b** will comfort me, my
Ps	4: 4	within your heart on your **b**
Ps	6: 6	All night I make my **b** swim
Ps	36: 4	devises wickedness on his **b**
Ps	41: 3	him on his **b** of illness
Ps	63: 6	When I remember You on my **b**
Ps	132: 3	go up to the comfort of my **b**
Ps	139: 8	If I make my **b** in hell,
Prov	7:17	have perfumed my **b** with myrrh
Prov	26:14	the lazy man on his **b**
Song	3: 1	By night on my **b** I sought the
Song	5:13	cheeks are like a **b** of spices
Ezek	23:17	to her, into the **b** of love
Dan	2:28	of your head upon your **b**,
Amos	3:12	in the corner of a **b** and on
Matt	9: 2	Him a paralytic lying on a **b**
Matt	9: 6	Arise, take up your **b**, and go
Mark	2: 4	they let down the **b** on which
Mark	4:21	under a basket or under a **b**
Mark	7:30	her daughter lying on the **b**
Luke	11: 7	my children are with me in **b**
Luke	17:34	will be two men in one **b**
Heb	13: 4	among all, and the **b** undefiled

BEDCHAMBER (see BED, BEDROOM)

BEDRIDDEN† (see BED)

Acts	9:33	who had been **b** eight years

BEDROOM (see BED)

Ex	8: 3	your **b**, on your bed
2Sa	4: 7	was lying on his bed in his **b**
2Sa	13:10	Bring the food into the **b**
2Ki	11: 2	hid him and his nurse in the **b**

BEDS (see BED)

Ps	149: 5	them sing aloud on their **b**
Song	6: 2	to the **b** of spices, to feed
Hos	7:14	when they wailed upon their **b**
Amos	6: 4	who lie on **b** of ivory,

Mic 2: 1 And work out evil on their **b**
Mark 6:55 on **b** those who were sick to
Acts 5:15 the streets and laid them on **b**

BEDSTEAD† (*see* BED)
Deut 3:11 his **b** was an iron **b**

BEE† (*see* BEES)
Is 7:18 for the **b** that is in the land

BEELZEBUB (*see* BAAL-ZEBUB)
Matt 10:25 the master of the house **B**
Matt 12:24 cast out demons except by **B**
Mark 3:22 he has **B**," and, "By the

BEER LAHAI ROI (*see* LAHAI ROI)
Gen 16:14 the well was called **B**
Gen 25:11 And Isaac dwelt at **B**

BEERSHEBA
Gen 21:14 in the Wilderness of **B**
Gen 22:19 and Abraham dwelt at **B**
Gen 26:33 of the city is **B** to this day
Gen 28:10 Now Jacob went out from **B**
1Sa 3:20 all Israel from Dan to **B** knew
2Ki 23: 8 incense, from Geba to **B**
Amos 8:14 and, 'As the way of **B** lives

BEES† (*see* BEE)
Deut 1:44 you and chased you as **b** do
Judg 14: 8 And behold, a swarm of **b** and
Ps 118:12 They surrounded me like **b**

BEFALL (*see* BEFALLEN, BEFALLS)
Gen 42:38 If any calamity should **b** him
Gen 49: 1 shall **b** you in the last days
Ps 91:10 No evil shall **b** you, Nor

BEFALLEN (*see* BEFALL)
Lev 10:19 and such things have **b** me
Num 20:14 the hardship that has **b** us

BEFALLS† (*see* BEFALL)
Gen 44:29 from me, and calamity **b** him
Eccl 3:19 one thing **b** them

BEFITTING†
Acts 26:20 God, and do works **b** repentance

BEG (*see* BEGGAR, BEGGED, BEGGING)
Job 9:15 I would **b** mercy of my Judge
Luke 8:28 I **b** You, do not torment me
Luke 16: 3 I am ashamed to **b**

BEGET (*see* BEGETS, BEGETTING, BEGOT, BEGOTTEN)
Deut 28:41 You shall **b** sons and daughters

BEGETS (*see* BEGET)
Prov 17:21 He who **b** a scoffer does so to
Prov 23:24 he who **b** a wise child will

BEGETTING† (*see* BEGET)
Is 45:10 his father, 'What are you **b**

BEGGAR (*see* BEG)
1Sa 2: 8 lifts the **b** from the ash heap
Luke 16:20 was a certain **b** named Lazarus

BEGGARLY†
Gal 4: 9 and **b** elements, to which you

BEGGED (*see* BEG)
Matt 8:31 So the demons **b** Him, saying,
Matt 8:34 they **b** Him to depart from
Matt 18:32 that debt because you **b** me
Mark 5:12 And all the demons **b** Him,
Mark 7:32 they **b** Him to put His hand on
Mark 8:22 to Him, and **b** Him to touch him
Luke 8:41 **b** Him to come to his house,
John 9: 8 Is not this he who sat and **b**
Acts 13:42 the Gentiles **b** that these
Acts 16:15 were baptized, she **b** us,
Heb 12:19 so that those who heard it **b**

BEGGING (*see* BEG)
Ps 37:25 Nor his descendants **b** bread
Mark 10:46 of Timaeus, sat by the road **b**
Acts 3:10 **b** alms at the Beautiful Gate

BEGINNING (*see* BEGINNINGS)
Gen 1: 1 In the **b** God created the
Gen 10:10 And the **b** of his kingdom was
Ex 12: 2 shall be your **b** of months
Ruth 1:22 at the **b** of barley harvest
Ruth 3:10 at the end than at the **b**, in
Job 42:12 days of Job more than his **b**
Ps 111:10 the LORD is the **b** of wisdom
Prov 1: 7 LORD is the **b** of knowledge
Prov 8:22 me at the **b** of His way,
Prov 8:23 from everlasting, from the **b**
Prov 9:10 the LORD is the **b** of wisdom
Eccl 3:11 that God does from **b** to end
Eccl 7: 8 a thing is better than its **b**
Is 41:26 Who has declared from the **b**
Is 46:10 Declaring the end from the **b**
Is 48: 3 the former things from the **b**
Is 48: 5 even from the **b** I have
Is 48:16 spoken in secret from the **b**
Is 64: 4 For since the **b** of the world
Dan 9:21 seen in the vision at the **b**
Matt 14:30 and **b** to sink he cried out,
Matt 19: 4 them at the **b** 'made them male
Matt 19: 8 but from the **b** it was not so
Matt 24: 8 these are the **b** of sorrows
Matt 24:21 the **b** of the world until this
Mark 1: 1 The **b** of the gospel of Jesus
Luke 1: 2 from the **b** were eyewitnesses
Luke 23: 5 **b** from Galilee to this place
Luke 24:27 And **b** at Moses and all the
Luke 24:47 all nations, **b** at Jerusalem
John 1: 1 In the **b** was the Word, and the
John 1: 2 He was in the **b** with God
John 2:11 This **b** of signs Jesus did in
John 8:44 He was a murderer from the **b**
John 15:27 have been with Me from the **b**
Acts 1:22 **b** from the baptism of John to
Acts 8:35 **b** at this Scripture, preached
Eph 3: 9 which from the **b** of the ages
Phil 4:15 that in the **b** of the gospel
Col 1:18 the church, who is the **b**
2Th 2:13 because God from the **b** chose
Heb 1:10 in the **b** laid the foundation
Heb 7: 3 having neither **b** of days nor
2Pe 2:20 is worse for them than the **b**
2Pe 3: 4 were from the **b** of creation
1Jn 1: 1 That which was from the **b**
1Jn 2:13 known Him who is from the **b**
1Jn 2:14 known Him who is from the **b**
1Jn 3: 8 devil has sinned from the **b**
Rev 1: 8 the Alpha and the Omega, the **B**
Rev 3:14 the **B** of the creation of God

BEGINNINGS† (*see* BEGINNING)
Num 28:11 At the **b** of your months you
Ezek 36:11 better for you than at your **b**
Mark 13: 8 These are the **b** of sorrows

BEGOT (*see* BEGET)
Gen 4:18 Irad **b** Mehujael, and Mehujael
Gen 5: 4 After he **b** Seth, the days of
Gen 6:10 And Noah **b** three sons
Gen 10: 8 Cush **b** Nimrod
Gen 11:10 **b** Arphaxad two years after
Gen 11:27 Terah **b** Abram, Nahor, and
Gen 11:27 Haran **b** Lot
Gen 22:23 And Bethuel **b** Rebekah
Gen 25:19 Abraham **b** Isaac
Deut 32:18 Of the Rock who **b** you, you
Ruth 4:18 Perez **b** Hezron
Ruth 4:22 and Jesse **b** David

1Ch   1:10 Cush **b** Nimrod
Prov 23:22 to your father who **b** you, and
Matt   1: 2 Abraham **b** Isaac
Matt   1: 6 and Jesse **b** David the king
Matt 1:16 Jacob **b** Joseph the husband of
Acts   7: 8 and so Abraham **b** Isaac
Acts   7: 8 Jacob **b** the twelve patriarchs
1Jn   5: 1 who **b** also loves him who is

BEGOTTEN (see BEGET)
Lev 18:11 daughter, **b** by your father
Job 38:28 or who has **b** the drops of dew
Ps   2: 7 My Son, Today I have **b** You
John 1:14 of the only **b** of the Father
John 1:18 The only **b** Son, who is in the
John 3:16 that He gave His only **b** Son
John 3:18 name of the only **b** Son of God
Acts 13:33 My Son, today I have **b** You
1Co 4:15 have **b** you through the gospel
Phm   10 whom I have **b** while in my
Heb   1: 5 My Son, today I have **b** You"
Heb   5: 5 My Son, today I have **b** You
Heb 11:17 offered up his only **b** son
1Pe   1: 3 **b** us again to a living hope
1Jn   4: 9 His only **b** Son into the world
1Jn   5: 1 loves him who is **b** of Him

BEGUILE (see SEDUCE)

BEGUILING (see ENTICING)

BEHALF
Esth   7: 9 spoke good on the king's **b**
Job 36: 2 yet words to speak on God's **b**
Is   8:19 the dead on **b** of the living
Ezek 22:30 before Me on **b** of the land
Rom 16:19 Therefore I am glad on your **b**
2Co   1:11 by many persons on our **b** for
2Co   5:12 opportunity to boast on our **b**
2Co   5:20 we implore you on Christ's **b**
2Co   7: 4 is my boasting on your **b**
Phil   1:29 been granted on **b** of Christ
Col   1: 7 minister of Christ on your **b**
Phm   13 me, that on your **b** he might

BEHAVE (see BEHAVED, BEHAVES, BEHAVING, BEHAVIOR)
Deut 25:16 all who **b** unrighteously, are
2Ch 19:11 **B** courageously, and the LORD
Ps 101: 2 I will **b** wisely in a perfect
1Co 13: 5 does not **b** rudely, does not

BEHAVED (see BEHAVE)
Ex 18:11 thing in which they **b** proudly
Num   5:27 **b** unfaithfully toward her
Judg   2:19 **b** more corruptly than their
1Sa 18: 5 Saul sent him, and **b** wisely
1Ki 21:26 And he **b** very abominably in
1Th   2:10 blamelessly we **b** ourselves

BEHAVES† (see BEHAVE)
Num   5:12 **b** unfaithfully toward him,

BEHAVING (see BEHAVE)
1Co   3: 3 not carnal and **b** like mere men
1Co   7:36 he is **b** improperly toward his

BEHAVIOR (see BEHAVE)
1Sa   8: 9 show them the **b** of the king
Ezek 16:27 were ashamed of your lewd **b**
1Ti   3: 2 sober-minded, of good **b**,
Tit   2: 3 that they be reverent in **b**

BEHEADED
2Sa   4: 7 **b** him and took his head, and
Matt 14:10 sent and had John **b** in prison
Rev 20: 4 **b** for their witness to Jesus

BEHELD (see BEHOLD)
Jer   4:23 I **b** the earth, and indeed it
John   1:14 we **b** His glory, the glory as

BEHEMOTH
Job 40:15 Look now at the **b**, which I

BEHOLD (see BEHELD, BEHOLDING, BEHOLDS)
Gen   3:22 **B**, the man has become like
Gen 28:13 And **b**, the LORD stood above it
Gen 37: 7 Then **b**, my sheaf arose and
Ex   8:21 will not let My people go, **b**
Ex 23:20 **B**, I send an Angel before you
Deut 11:26 **B**, I set before you today a
Josh 24:27 **B**, this stone shall be a
Judg 13: 5 For **b**, you shall conceive and
1Sa 15:22 **B**, to obey is better than
1Ki   8:27 **B**, heaven and the heaven of
1Ki 19:11 And **b**, the LORD passed by,
Job   1:12 **B**, all that he has is in your
Job   2: 6 **B**, he is in your hand, but
Job 19:27 myself, and my eyes shall **b**
Ps 27: 4 To **b** the beauty of the LORD,
Ps 33:18 **B**, the eye of the LORD is on
Ps 40: 7 Then I said, "**B**, I come
Ps 51: 5 **B**, I was brought forth in
Ps 51: 6 **B**, You desire truth in the
Ps 92: 9 For **b**, Your enemies, O LORD,
Ps 121: 4 **B**, He who keeps Israel Shall
Ps 127: 3 **B**, children are a heritage
Ps 133: 1 **B**, how good and how pleasant
Ps 139: 8 If I make my bed in hell, **b**
Eccl 11: 7 for the eyes to **b** the sun
Song 1:15 **B**, you are fair, my love
Song 1:16 **B**, you are handsome, my
Is   5: 7 He looked for justice, but **b**
Is   5: 7 for righteousness, but **b**,
Is   6: 7 **B**, this has touched your lips
Is   7:14 **B**, the virgin shall conceive
Is 28:16 **B**, I lay in Zion a stone for
Is 40: 9 cities of Judah, "**B** your God
Is 40:10 **B**, the Lord GOD shall come
Is 40:10 **b**, His reward is with Him, and
Is 42: 1 **B**! My Servant whom I uphold
Is 42: 9 **B**, the former things have
Is 43:19 **B**, I will do a new thing, now
Is 52:13 **B**, My Servant shall deal
Is 59: 1 **B**, the LORD's hand is not
Is 60: 2 For **b**, the darkness shall
Is 65: 6 **B**, it is written before Me
Is 65:17 For **b**, I create new heavens
Is 65:18 for **b**, I create Jerusalem as
Is 66:15 For **b**, the LORD will come
Jer   1: 6 **B**, I cannot speak, for I am a
Jer 23:31 **B**, I am against the prophets,
Jer 45: 5 for **b**, I will bring adversity
Jer 46:25 **B**, I will bring punishment on
Lam   1: 9 **b** my affliction, for the
Ezek   1: 4 Then I looked, and **b**, a
Ezek   2: 9 and **b**, a scroll of a book was
Ezek 26: 3 **B**, I am against you, O Tyre,
Ezek 38: 3 **B**, I am against you, O Gog,
Dan   2:31 and **b**, a great image
Dan   4:10 I was looking, and **b**, A tree
Dan   7: 2 in my vision by night, and **b**
Hos   2:14 Therefore, **b**, I will allure
Joel   2:19 **B**, I will send you grain and
Amos 7: 8 **B**, I am setting a plumb line
Amos 8: 1 **B**, a basket of summer fruit
Nah   1:15 **B**, on the mountains the feet
Zech 1: 8 I saw by night, and **b**, a man
Zech 6:12 **B**, the Man whose name is the
Zech 9: 9 **B**, your King is coming to you
Mal   3: 1 **B**, I send My messenger, and he
Mal   3: 1 **B**, He is coming," says the
Mal   4: 5 **B**, I will send you Elijah the
Matt   1:23 **B**, a virgin shall be with
Matt   2: 1 the days of Herod the king, **b**
Matt   2: 9 and **b**, the star which they had

Matt	3:16	and **b**, the heavens were opened
Matt	4:11	Then the devil left Him, and **b**
Matt	10:16	**B**, I send you out as sheep in
Matt	11:10	**B**, I send My messenger
Matt	12:18	**B**, My Servant whom I have
Matt	13: 3	**B**, a sower went out to sow
Matt	17: 3	And **b**, Moses and Elijah
Matt	25: 6	**B**, the bridegroom is coming
Matt	26:45	**B**, the hour is at hand, and
Matt	27:51	And **b**, the veil of the temple
Matt	28: 7	**B**, I have told you
Luke	1:38	**B** the maidservant of the Lord
Luke	2: 9	And **b**, an angel of the Lord
Luke	2:10	Do not be afraid, for **b**, I
Luke	10: 3	**b**, I send you out as lambs
Luke	10:19	**B**, I give you the authority
Luke	24:39	**B** My hands and My feet, that
Luke	24:49	**B**, I send the Promise of My
John	1:29	**B**! The Lamb of God
John	1:36	he said, "**B** the Lamb of God
John	1:47	**B**, an Israelite indeed, in
John	12:15	**b**, your King is coming,
John	17:24	am, that they may **b** My glory
John	19: 5	said to them, "**B** the Man
John	19:14	to the Jews, "**B** your King
John	19:26	mother, "Woman, **b** your son
John	19:27	the disciple, **B** your mother
Rom	9:33	**B**, I lay in Zion a stumbling
1Co	15:51	**B**, I tell you a mystery
2Co	5:17	**b**, all things have become new
2Co	6: 2	**B**, now is the accepted time
2Co	6: 2	**b**, now is the day of
Heb	10: 7	Then I said, 'B, I have come
1Pe	2: 6	**B**, I lay in Zion a chief
1Jn	3: 1	**B** what manner of love the
Jude	14	**B**, the Lord comes with ten
Rev	1: 7	**B**, He is coming with clouds,
Rev	3:11	**B**, I come quickly
Rev	3:20	**B**, I stand at the door and
Rev	5: 5	**B**, the Lion of the tribe of
Rev	14: 1	Then I looked, and **b**, a Lamb
Rev	16:15	**B**, I am coming as a thief
Rev	21: 3	**B**, the tabernacle of God is
Rev	21: 5	**B**, I make all things new
Rev	22: 7	**B**, I am coming quickly

BEHOLDING† (*see* BEHOLD)
2Co	3:18	**b** as in a mirror the glory of

BEHOLDS† (*see* BEHOLD)
Job	41:34	He **b** every high thing
Ps	11: 7	His countenance **b** the upright

BEKAH†
Ex	38:26	a **b** for each man (that is,

BEL† (*see* BAAL)
Is	46: 1	**B** bows down, Nebo stoops
Jer	50: 2	Babylon is taken, **B** is shamed
Jer	51:44	I will punish **B** in Babylon

BELCH†
Ps	59: 7	they **b** out with their mouth

BELIAL†
2Co	6:15	what accord has Christ with **B**

BELIEF† (*see* BELIEVE, UNBELIEF)
2Th	2:13	the Spirit and **b** in the truth,

BELIEVE (*see* BELIEF, BELIEVED, BELIEVER, BELIEVES, BELIEVING)
Ex	4: 8	will be, if they do not **b** you
Ps	106:24	They did not **b** His word,
Ps	119:66	For I **b** Your commandments
Is	7: 9	If you will not **b**, surely you
Is	43:10	Me, and understand that I am
Matt	9:28	Do you **b** that I am able to do
Matt	27:42	the cross, and we will **b** Him

Mark	1:15	Repent, and **b** in the gospel
Mark	5:36	Do not be afraid; only **b**
Mark	9:23	If you can **b**, all things are
Mark	9:24	Lord, I **b**; help my unbelief
Mark	9:42	ones who **b** in Me to stumble
Luke	8:12	hearts, lest they should **b**
Luke	8:13	who **b** for a while and in time
Luke	8:50	only **b**, and she will be made
Luke	22:67	you, you will by no means **b**
Luke	24:25	slow of heart to **b** in all
Luke	24:41	they still did not **b** for joy
John	1: 7	that all through him might **b**
John	1:12	to those who **b** in His name
John	1:50	under the fig tree,' do you **b**
John	3:12	things and you do not **b**, how
John	3:12	how will you **b** if I tell you
John	3:36	he who does not **b** the Son
John	4:21	Me, the hour is coming when
John	5:46	Moses, you would **b** Me
John	5:47	if you do not **b** his writings
John	5:47	how will you **b** My words
John	6:29	that you **b** in Him whom He
John	6:30	that we may see it and **b** You
John	6:36	have seen Me and yet do not **b**
John	7: 5	His brothers did not **b** in Him
John	8:24	if you do not **b** that I am He
John	8:45	the truth, you do not **b** Me
John	9:35	Do you **b** in the Son of God
John	9:38	Then he said, "Lord, I **b**!"
John	10:38	**b** the works, that you may
John	10:38	**b** that the Father is in Me,
John	11:26	never die. Do you **b** this
John	11:27	I **b** that You are the Christ,
John	11:48	this, everyone will **b** in Him
John	12:36	**b** in the light, that you may
John	12:47	hears My words and does not **b**
John	14: 1	you **b** in God, **b** also in Me
John	14:11	or else **b** Me for the sake of
John	17:21	world may **b** that You sent Me
John	19:35	the truth, so that you may **b**
John	20:25	into His side, I will not **b**
John	20:31	**b** that Jesus is the Christ
Acts	8:37	If you **b** with all your heart,
Acts	8:37	I **b** that Jesus Christ is the
Acts	16:31	**B** on the Lord Jesus Christ,
Rom	3:22	Christ to all and on all who **b**
Rom	4:11	the father of all those who **b**
Rom	4:24	**b** in Him who raised up Jesus
Rom	6: 8	we **b** that we shall also live
Rom	10: 9	**b** in your heart that God has
Rom	10:14	how shall they **b** in Him of
1Co	7:12	has a wife who does not **b**
1Co	10:27	not **b** invites you to dinner
2Co	4: 4	age has blinded, who do not **b**
Eph	1:19	of His power toward us who **b**
Phil	1:29	Christ, not only to **b** in Him
1Th	1: 7	in Macedonia and Achaia who **b**
1Th	2:10	ourselves among you who **b**
1Th	2:13	works in you who **b**
1Th	4:14	For if we **b** that Jesus died
2Th	1:10	admired among all those who **b**
2Th	2:11	that they should **b** the lie
1Ti	4:10	especially of those who **b**
Heb	11: 6	to God must **b** that He is, and
Jas	2:19	You **b** that there is one God
Jas	2:19	Even the demons **b**
1Jn	3:23	that we should **b** on the name
1Jn	4: 1	do not **b** every spirit, but
1Jn	5:10	he who does not **b** God has
1Jn	5:13	**b** in the name of the Son of

BELIEVED (*see* BELIEVE, FULFILLED)
Gen	15: 6	And he **b** in the LORD, and He
Ex	4:31	So the people **b**
Ex	14:31	**b** the LORD and His servant

Ps   116:10 I **b**, therefore I spoke, 'I
Is   53: 1 Who has **b** our report
Dan   6:23 him, because he **b** in his God
Jon   3: 5 the people of Nineveh **b** God
Matt   8:13 and as you have **b**, so let it
Luke   1:45 Blessed is she who **b**, for
John   2:11 and His disciples **b** in Him
John   2:22 they **b** the Scripture and the
John   2:23 many **b** in His name when they
John   3:18 because he has not **b** in the
John   4:39 **b** in Him because of the word
John   5:46 For if you **b** Moses, you would
John   7:48 or the Pharisees **b** in Him
John   12:38 Lord, who has **b** our report
John   16:27 have **b** that I came forth from
John   17: 8 they have **b** that You sent Me
John   20: 8 and he saw and **b**
John   20:29 you have seen Me, you have **b**
John   20:29 have not seen and yet have **b**
Acts   2:44 Now all who **b** were together,
Acts   4: 4 of those who heard the word **b**
Acts   4:32 those who **b** were of one heart
Acts   10:45 who **b** were astonished, as
Acts   11:17 we **b** on the Lord Jesus Christ
Acts   11:21 them, and a great number **b**
Acts   13:12 Then the proconsul **b**, when he
Acts   13:48 appointed to enternal life **b**
Acts   15: 5 the Pharisees who **b** rose up
Acts   16:34 having **b** in God with all his
Acts   17:34 some men joined him and **b**
Acts   18:27 those who had **b** through grace
Acts   19: 2 the Holy Spirit when you **b**
Rom   4: 3 Abraham **b** God, and it was
Rom   4:18 contrary to hope, in hope **b**
Rom   10:14 Him in whom they have not **b**
Rom   10:16 Lord, who has **b** our report
Rom   13:11 nearer than when we first **b**
1Co   3: 5 ministers through whom you **b**
1Co   15:11 so we preach and so you **b**
Gal   3: 6 **b** God, and it was accounted to
Eph   1:13 in whom also, having **b**, you
2Th   1:10 our testimony among you was **b**
1Ti   3:16 **b** on in the world, received
2Ti   1:12 for I know whom I have **b**
Jas   2:23 Abraham **b** God, and it was
1Jn   4:16 **b** the love that God has for
1Jn   5:10 because he has not **b** the

BELIEVER† (*see* BELIEVE, BELIEVERS, UNBELIEVER)
2Co   6:15 has a **b** with an unbeliever

BELIEVERS† (*see* BELIEVER)
Acts   5:14 **b** were increasingly added to
1Ti   4:12 an example to the **b** in word
1Ti   6: 2 those who are benefited are **b**

BELIEVES (*see* BELIEVE)
Mark   9:23 are possible to him who **b**
John   3:15 that whoever **b** in Him should
John   3:16 that whoever **b** in Him should
John   3:18 He who **b** in Him is not
John   3:36 He who **b** in the Son has
John   5:24 and **b** in Him who sent Me has
John   6:35 he who **b** in Me shall never
John   6:40 **b** in Him may have everlasting
John   11:26 and **b** in Me shall never die
Rom   1:16 salvation for everyone who **b**
Rom   4: 5 **b** on Him who justifies the
Rom   9:33 whoever **b** on Him will not be
Rom   10: 4 to everyone who **b**
Rom   10:10 heart one **b** unto righteousness
Rom   10:11 Whoever **b** on Him will not be
Rom   14: 2 For one **b** he may eat all
1Co   13: 7 **b** all things, hopes all
1Pe   2: 6 he who **b** on Him will by no
1Jn   5: 1 Whoever **b** that Jesus is the

1Jn   5:10 He who **b** in the Son of God

BELIEVING (*see* BELIEVE)
Matt   21:22 whatever you ask in prayer, **b**
John   20:27 Do not be unbelieving, but **b**
John   20:31 that **b** you may have life in
Rom   15:13 with all joy and peace in **b**
1Co   9: 5 right to take along a **b** wife
Gal   3: 9 are blessed with **b** Abraham
1Ti   5:16 If any **b** man or woman has
1Ti   6: 2 And those who have **b** masters
1Pe   1: 8 now you do not see Him, yet **b**

BELL (*see* BELLS)
Ex   28:34 a golden **b** and a pomegranate,

BELLOW† (*see* BELLOWS)
Jer   50:11 grain, and you **b** like bulls,

BELLOWS† (*see* BELLOW)
Jer   6:29 the **b** blow fiercely, the lead

BELLS (*see* BELL)
Ex   28:33 **b** of gold between them all
Zech   14:20 on the **b** of the horses

BELLY
Gen   3:14 on your **b** you shall go, and
Ps   17:14 whose **b** You fill with Your
Dan   2:32 and arms of silver, its **b** and
Jon   1:17 Jonah was in the **b** of the
Jon   2: 1 his God from the fish's **b**
Jon   2: 2 out of the **b** of Sheol I cried
Matt   12:40 in the **b** of the great fish
Rom   16:18 Jesus Christ, but their own **b**
Phil   3:19 whose god is their **b**, and

BELONG (*see* BELONGED, BELONGING, BELONGS)
Gen   40: 8 not interpretations **b** to God
Deut   29:29 The secret things **b** to the
Ps   47: 9 shields of the earth **b** to God
Prov   24:23 things also **b** to the wise
Dan   9: 9 To the Lord our God **b** mercy
Mark   9:41 name, because you **b** to Christ
Acts   27:23 angel of the God to whom I **b**
1Pe   4:11 to whom **b** the glory and the

BELONGED (*see* BELONG)
1Ki   1: 8 the mighty men who **b** to David
Esth   1: 9 which **b** to King Ahasuerus
Luke   23: 7 He **b** to Herod's jurisdiction

BELONGING (*see* BELONG, BELONGINGS)
Ruth   2: 3 part of the field **b** to Boaz
Ezek   45: 4 land, **b** to the priests, the
Luke   9:10 place **b** to the city called

BELONGINGS (*see* BELONGING)
Ezek   12: 3 prepare your **b** for captivity,

BELONGS (*see* BELONG)
Lev   6: 5 and give it to whomever it **b**
Lev   7:20 offering that **b** to the LORD
Lev   7:21 offering that **b** to the LORD
Ps   3: 8 Salvation **b** to the LORD
Ps   62:11 That power **b** to God
Ps   62:12 Also to You, O Lord, **b** mercy
Ps   94: 1 God, to whom vengeance **b**
Dan   9: 8 to us **b** shame of face, to our
Heb   5:14 But solid food **b** to those who
Rev   7:10 Salvation **b** to our God who

BELOVED (*see* BELOVED'S, WELL-BELOVED)
Deut   33:12 The **b** of the LORD shall dwell
2Sa   1:23 Saul and Jonathan were **b** and
Neh   13:26 him, who was **b** of his God
Ps   60: 5 That Your **b** may be delivered,
Ps   127: 2 For so He gives His **b** sleep
Song   1:13 bundle of myrrh is my **b** to me
Song   1:16 you are handsome, my **b**
Song   2: 8 The voice of my **b**

Song   7:11 Come, my **b**, let us go forth
Is   5: 1 my **B** regarding His vineyard
Jer   12: 7 I have given the dearly **b** of
Dan   10:11 O Daniel, man greatly **b**,
Matt   3:17 This is My **b** Son, in whom I
Mark   12: 6 still having one son, his **b**
Acts   15:25 to you with our **b** Barnabas
Rom   1: 7 **b** of God, called to be saints
Rom   9:25 were not My people, and her **b**
Rom   11:28 the election they are **b** for
Rom   12:19 **B**, do not avenge yourselves,
1Co   4:14 but as my **b** children I warn
1Co   4:17 Timothy to you, who is my **b**
1Co   10:14 Therefore, my **b**, flee from
1Co   15:58 my **b** brethren, be steadfast,
Eph   1: 6 has made us accepted in the **B**
Eph   6:21 a **b** brother and faithful
Phil   4: 1 Therefore, my **b** and longed-for
Phil   4: 1 so stand fast in the Lord, **b**
Col   3:12 the elect of God, holy and **b**
Col   4:14 Luke the **b** physician and Demas
1Th   1: 4 **b** brethren, your election by
2Th   2:13 you, brethren **b** by the Lord,
1Ti   6: 2 benefited are believers and **b**
2Ti   1: 2 To Timothy, a **b** son
Phm   1 To Philemon our **b** friend
Phm   16 as a **b** brother, especially to
2Pe   1:17 This is My **b** Son, in whom I
2Pe   3:15 as also our **b** brother Paul,
1Jn   3: 2 **B**, now we are children of God
1Jn   4: 7 **B**, let us love one another,
1Jn   4:11 **B**, if God so loved us, we
Rev   20: 9 of the saints and the **b** city

BELOVED'S† (*see* BELOVED)
Song   6: 3 I am my **b**, and my beloved is
Song   7:10 I am my **b**, and his desire is

BELSHAZZAR
Dan   5: 1 **B** the king made a great feast

BELT (*see* BELTS)
Ex   12:11 with a **b** on your waist, your
Matt   3: 4 with a leather **b** around his
Acts   21:11 come to us, he took Paul's **b**

BELTESHAZZAR (*see* DANIEL)
Dan   1: 7 he gave Daniel the name **B**
Dan   4: 9 **B**, chief of the magicians,

BELTS (*see* BELT)
Ezek   23:15 girded with **b** around their
Mark   6: 8 no copper in their money **b**

BEMOAN (*see* BEMOANING)
Jer   15: 5 Or who will **b** you
Jer   16: 5 nor go to lament or **b** them
Jer   22:10 not for the dead, nor **b** him
Nah   3: 7 Who will **b** her

BEMOANING† (*see* BEMOAN)
Jer   31:18 heard Ephraim **b** himself

BEN-AMMI†
Gen   19:38 a son and called his name **B**

BEN-HADAD
1Ki   15:18 to **B** the son of Tabrimmon
1Ki   15:20 So **B** heeded King Asa, and sent
1Ki   20: 1 Now **B** the king of Syria
Jer   49:27 consume the palaces of **B**
Amos   1: 4 shall devour the palaces of **B**

BEN-ONI†
Gen   35:18 that she called his name **B**

BENAIAH
2Sa   8:18 **B** the son of Jehoiada was
1Ki   1:10 invite Nathan the prophet, **B**

BEND (*see* BENDS, BENT)
2Sa   22:35 my arms can **b** a bow of bronze
Ps   11: 2 The wicked **b** their bow, They

BENDS (*see* BEND)
Ps   7:12 He **b** His bow and makes it

BENEFACTORS†
Luke   22:25 over them are called **b**

BENEFIT (*see* BENEFITED, BENEFITS)
Ps   106: 5 That I may see the **b** of Your
2Co   1:15 you might have a second **b**

BENEFITED† (*see* BENEFIT)
1Ti   6: 2 those who are **b** are believers

BENEFITS† (*see* BENEFIT)
Ps   68:19 Who daily loads us with **b**
Ps   103: 2 soul, And forget not all His **b**
Ps   116:12 LORD For all His **b** toward me

BENJAMIN (*see* BENJAMIN'S, BENJAMITE)
Gen   35:18 but his father called him **B**
Gen   35:24 of Rachel were Joseph and **B**
Gen   45:14 wept, and **B** wept on his neck
Gen   45:22 but to **B** he gave three
Gen   49:27 **B** is a ravenous wolf
Num   1:36 From the children of **B**, their
Num   1:37 numbered of the tribe of **B**
Judg   19:14 Gibeah, which belongs to **B**
Judg   20:35 LORD defeated **B** before Israel
Judg   21:15 And the people grieved for **B**
1Sa   9: 1 There was a man of **B** whose
1Sa   13: 2 with Jonathan in Gibeah of **B**
1Sa   14:16 of Saul in Gibeah of **B** looked
Ps   68:27 There is little **B**, their
Ps   80: 2 before Ephraim, **B**, and
Jer   1: 1 in Anathoth in the land of **B**
Acts   13:21 Kish, a man of the tribe of **B**
Rom   11: 1 of Abraham, of the tribe of **B**
Phil   3: 5 of Israel, of the tribe of **B**

BENJAMIN'S† (*see* BENJAMIN)
Gen   43:34 but **B** serving was five times
Gen   44:12 the cup found in **B** sack
Gen   45:14 he fell on his brother **B** neck
Zech   14:10 **B** Gate to the place of the

BENJAMITE (*see* BENJAMIN, BENJAMITES)
Judg   3:15 Ehud the son of Gera, the **B**

BENJAMITES (*see* BENJAMITE)
Judg   19:16 the men of the place were **B**

BENT (*see* BEND)
Ps   37:14 have **b** their bow, To cast
Jer   9: 3 have **b** their tongues for lies
Ezek   17: 7 this vine **b** its roots toward
Dan   11:27 hearts shall be **b** on evil
Hos   11: 7 My people are **b** on
Zech   9:13 For I have **b** Judah, My bow,
Luke   13:11 was **b** over and could in no way

BEOR
Num   22: 5 Balaam the son of **B** at Pethor
2Pe   2:15 way of Balaam the son of **B**

BEQUEATHS†
Deut   21:16 shall be, on the day he **b** his

BERACHAH
2Ch   20:26 assembled in the Valley of **B**

BEREA†
Acts   17:10 and Silas away by night to **B**
Acts   17:13 God was preached by Paul at **B**
Acts   20: 4 Sopater of **B** accompanied him

BEREAVE (*see* BEREAVED, BEREAVES)
Jer   15: 7 I will **b** them of children
Ezek   36:13 **b** your nation of children,'
Hos   9:12 yet I will **b** them to the last

BEREAVED (*see* BEREAVE)
Gen 27:45 Why should I be **b** also of you
Gen 42:36 You have **b** me of my children

BEREAVES† (*see* BEREAVE)
Lam 1:20 Outside the sword **b**, at home

BERECHIAH
Zech 1: 1 to Zechariah the son of **B**
Matt 23:35 blood of Zechariah, son of **B**

BERITH† (*see* BAAL-BERITH)
Judg 9:46 of the temple of the god **B**

BERNICE
Acts 25:13 **B** came to Caesarea to greet

BERYL
Ex 28:20 and the fourth row, a **b**, an
Ezek 1:16 works was like the color of **b**
Ezek 28:13 sardius, topaz, and diamond, **b**
Dan 10: 6 His body was like **b**, his face
Rev 21:20 chrysolite, the eighth **b**, the

BESEECH†
Ps 80:14 we **b** You, O God of hosts
Rom 12: 1 I **b** you therefore, brethren,
Eph 4: 1 **b** you to have a walk worthy

BESET (*see* SUBJECT)

BESIEGE (*see* BESIEGED, BESIEGES, BESIEGING)
Deut 20:19 When you **b** a city for a long
1Sa 23: 8 go down to Keilah to **b** David

BESIEGED (*see* BESIEGE)
2Sa 11:16 while Joab **b** the city, that
1Ki 20: 1 up and **b** Samaria, and made war
Jer 32: 2 of Babylon's army **b** Jerusalem
Lam 3: 5 He has **b** me and surrounded me
Dan 1: 1 came to Jerusalem and **b** it

BESIEGES† (*see* BESIEGE)
1Ki 8:37 when their enemy **b** them in

BESIEGING† (*see* BESIEGE)
2Ki 24:11 as his servants were **b** it
Jer 37: 5 **b** Jerusalem heard news of

BEST
Gen 43:11 Take some of the **b** fruits of
Gen 45:20 for the **b** of all the land of
Ex 22: 5 from the **b** of his own field
Num 18:12 All the **b** of the oil, all the
Num 36: 6 them marry whom they think **b**
Judg 14:20 who had been his **b** man
Prov 16:28 separates the **b** of friends
Matt 23: 6 They love the **b** places at
Matt 23: 6 the **b** seats in the synagogues
Mark 12:39 and the **b** places at feasts,
Luke 15:22 Bring out the **b** robe and put
1Co 12:31 earnestly desire the **b** gifts
Heb 12:10 us as seemed **b** to them, but

BESTOW (*see* BESTOWED)
Luke 22:29 I **b** upon you a kingdom, just
1Co 12:23 on these we **b** greater honor
1Co 13: 3 though I **b** all my goods to

BESTOWED (*see* BESTOW)
Ezek 16:14 splendor which I had **b** on you
Luke 22:29 as My Father **b** one upon Me
2Co 8: 1 of God **b** on the churches of
1Jn 3: 1 love the Father has **b** on us

BETH AVEN
Hos 4:15 up to Gilgal, nor go up to **B**

BETH BARAH† (*see* BETHABARA)
Judg 7:24 watering places as far as **B**

BETH HORON
Josh 10:10 along the road that goes to **B**
1Ki 9:17 Solomon built Gezer, Lower **B**

1Ch 7:24 who built Lower and Upper **B**

BETH PEOR
Deut 3:29 in the valley opposite **B**
Deut 34: 6 the land of Moab, opposite **B**
Josh 13:20 **B**, the slopes of Pisgah, and

BETH SHAN
1Sa 31:10 his body to the wall of **B**

BETH SHEAN
1Ki 4:12 in Taanach, Megiddo, and all **B**

BETH SHEMESH
1Sa 6: 9 to its own territory, to **B**
1Sa 6:12 straight for the road to **B**
2Ki 14:11 Judah faced one another at **B**

BETHABARA† (*see* BETH BARAH)
John 1:28 done in **B** beyond the Jordan

BETHANY
Matt 21:17 and went out of the city to **B**
Matt 26: 6 when Jesus was in **B** at the
John 11: 1 man was sick, Lazarus of **B**
John 11:18 Now **B** was near Jerusalem,

BETHEL (*see* EL BETHEL)
Gen 12: 8 to the mountain east of **B**
Gen 13: 3 at the beginning, between **B**
Gen 28:19 the name of that place **B**
Gen 31:13 I am the God of **B**, where you
Gen 35: 8 she was buried below **B** under
Josh 12: 9 king of Ai, which is beside **B**
Josh 18:13 of Luz (which is **B**) southward
Judg 21:19 Shiloh, which is north of **B**
1Sa 7:16 to year on a circuit to **B**
1Ki 12:29 And he set up one in **B**, and the
1Ki 13: 1 to **B** by the word of the LORD
1Ki 13:11 Now an old prophet dwelt in **B**
1Ki 16:34 days Hiel of **B** built Jericho
2Ki 10:29 golden calves that were at **B**
Jer 48:13 of Israel was ashamed of **B**
Hos 10:15 it shall be done to you, O **B**
Hos 12: 4 He found Him in **B**, and there
Amos 4: 4 Come to **B** and transgress, at
Amos 5: 5 and **B** shall come to nothing
Amos 7:10 of **B** sent to Jeroboam king of
Amos 7:13 But never again prophesy at **B**

BETHESDA†
John 5: 2 which is called in Hebrew, **B**

BETHLEHEM (*see* BETHLEHEMITE)
Gen 35:19 way to Ephrath (that is, **B**)
Judg 17: 7 a young man from **B** in Judah
Ruth 1: 1 And a certain man of **B**, Judah,
Ruth 2: 4 Now behold, Boaz came from **B**
Ruth 4:11 Ephrathah and be famous in **B**
1Sa 16: 4 the LORD said, and went to **B**
1Sa 17:15 feed his father's sheep at **B**
2Sa 23:15 the water from the well of **B**
Mic 5: 2 **B** Ephrathah, though you are
Matt 2: 1 in **B** of Judea in the days of
Matt 2: 6 But you, **B**, in the land of
Matt 2: 8 And he sent them to **B** and said,
Matt 2:16 male children who were in **B**
Luke 2: 4 of David, which is called **B**
Luke 2:15 Let us now go to **B** and see
John 7:42 David and from the town of **B**

BETHLEHEMITE (*see* BETHLEHEM)
1Sa 16:18 seen a son of Jesse the **B**

BETHPHAGE
Mark 11: 1 came near Jerusalem, to **B**

BETHSAIDA
Matt 11:21 Woe to you, **B**! For if the
John 1:44 Now Philip was from **B**, the
John 12:21 who was from **B** of Galilee

BETHUEL
Gen 22:23 And B begot Rebekah
Gen 28: 5 Laban the son of **B** the Syrian

BETRAY (*see* BETRAYED, BETRAYER, BETRAYING, BETRAYS)
Matt 24:10 will **b** one another, and will
Matt 26:16 sought opportunity to **b** Him
Matt 26:21 to you, one of you will **b** Me
Matt 26:23 with Me in the dish will **b** Me
Mark 14:10 priests to **b** Him to them
John 12: 4 Simon's son, who would **b** Him

BETRAYED (*see* BETRAY)
Matt 10: 4 Iscariot, who also **b** Him
Matt 17:22 to be **b** into the hands of men
Matt 20:18 be **b** to the chief priests
Matt 26:24 by whom the Son of Man is **b**
Luke 21:16 You will be **b** even by parents
Luke 22:22 to that man by whom He is **b**
John 18: 2 And Judas, who **b** Him, also
1Co 11:23 in which He was **b** took bread

BETRAYER (*see* BETRAY, BETRAYERS)
Matt 26:46 See, My **b** is at hand
Matt 27: 3 Then Judas, His **b**, seeing
Mark 14:42 See, My **b** is at hand

BETRAYERS† (*see* BETRAYER)
Acts 7:52 you now have become the **b**

BETRAYING† (*see* BETRAY)
Matt 26:25 Then Judas, who as **b** Him
Matt 27: 4 sinned by **b** innocent blood
Luke 22:48 are you **b** the Son of Man with

BETRAYS† (*see* BETRAY)
Matt 26:73 because your speech **b** you
John 21:20 who is the one who **b** You

BETROTH† (*see* BETROTHAL, BETROTHED)
Deut 28:30 You shall **b** a wife, but
Hos 2:19 I will **b** you to Me forever
Hos 2:19 I will **b** you to Me in
Hos 2:20 I will **b** you to Me in

BETROTHAL† (*see* BETROTH)
Jer 2: 2 youth, the love of your **b**

BETROTHED (*see* BETROTH)
Ex 22:16 entices a virgin who is not **b**
Matt 1:18 mother Mary was **b** to Joseph
Luke 1:27 to a virgin **b** to a man whose
Luke 2: 5 his **b** wife, who was with
2Co 11: 2 For I have **b** you to one

BEULAH†
Is 62: 4 Hephzibah, and your land **B**

BEVELED
1Ki 6: 4 house windows with **b** frames

BEVERAGE†
Song 7: 2 which lacks no blended **b**

BEWAIL† (*see* BEWAILED, BEWAILING)
Lev 10: 6 **b** the burning with the LORD
Judg 11:37 **b** my virginity, my friends and
Is 16: 9 Therefore I will **b** the vine

BEWAILED† (*see* BEWAIL)
Judg 11:38 and **b** her virginity on the

BEWAILING† (*see* BEWAIL)
Jer 4:31 daughter of Zion **b** herself

BEWARE
Gen 24: 6 **B** that you do not take my son
Job 36:18 **b** lest He take you away with
Is 36:18 **B** lest Hezekiah persuade you
Matt 7:15 **B** of false prophets, who come
Matt 10:17 But **b** of men, for they will
Matt 16: 6 and **b** of the leaven of the
Mark 12:38 **B** of the scribes, who desire

Luke 12:15 **b** of covetousness, for one's
Phil 3: 2 **B** of dogs, **b** of evil workers
Phil 3: 2 **b** of the mutilation
Col 2: 8 **B** lest anyone cheat you
2Ti 4:15 You also must **b** of him, for
2Pe 3:17 **b** lest you also fall from

BEWILDERED†
Ex 14: 3 They are **b** by the land

BEWITCHED†
Gal 3: 1 Who has **b** you that you should

BEZALEL
Ex 31: 2 by name **B** the son of Uri, the
Ex 36: 1 And **B** and Aholiab, and every

BID† (*see* BIDDING)
Luke 9:61 **b** them farewell who are at my

BIDDING† (*see* BID)
1Sa 22:14 who goes at your **b**, and is

BILDAD
Job 2:11 **B** the Shuhite, and Zophar the

BILE†
Lam 2:11 my **b** is poured on the ground

BILHAH
Gen 29:29 Laban gave his maid **B** to his
Gen 35:22 and lay with **B** his father's

BILL†
Luke 16: 6 he said to him, 'Take your **b**
Luke 16: 7 he said to him, 'Take your **b**

BILLOWS†
Ps 42: 7 waves and **b** have gone over me
Jon 2: 3 all Your **b** and Your waves

BIN
1Ki 17:12 a handful of flour in a **b**

BIND (*see* BINDING, BINDS, BOUND)
Ex 28:28 They shall **b** the breastplate
Deut 6: 8 You shall **b** them as a sign on
Josh 2:18 you **b** this line of scarlet
Judg 16: 7 If they **b** me with seven fresh
Ps 118:27 **B** the sacrifice with cords to
Ps 149: 8 To **b** their kings with chains,
Prov 3: 3 **b** them around your neck,
Is 8:16 **B** up the testimony, Seal the
Is 49:18 **b** them on you as a bride does
Ezek 34:16 **b** up the broken and strengthen
Hos 6: 1 stricken, but He will **b** us up
Matt 13:30 **b** them in bundles to burn
Matt 16:19 whatever you **b** on earth will
Matt 22:13 **B** him hand and foot, take him
Matt 23: 4 For they **b** heavy burdens,
Mark 5: 3 and no one could **b** him, not
Acts 9:14 **b** all who call on Your name

BINDING (*see* BIND)
Gen 37: 7 were, **b** sheaves in the field
Gen 49:11 **B** his donkey to the vine, and
Num 30:12 the agreement **b** her, it shall
Num 30:13 every **b** oath to afflict her
Ps 56:12 made to You are **b** upon me

BINDS (*see* BIND)
Num 30: 3 **b** herself by some agreement
Job 5:18 For He bruises, but He **b** up
Job 12:18 **b** their waist with a belt
Job 26: 8 He **b** up the water in His
Job 36:13 cry for help when He **b** them
Ps 129: 7 hand, Nor he who **b** sheaves
Ps 147: 3 And **b** up their wounds
Prov 26: 8 Like one who **b** a stone in a
Matt 12:29 he first **b** the strong man

BIRD (*see* BIRD'S, BIRDS)
Gen 1:21 every winged **b** according to

Gen 7:14 every **b** after its kind, every
Gen 8:20 animal and of every clean **b**
Job 28: 7 That path no **b** knows, nor has
Job 41: 5 you play with him as with a **b**
Ps 11: 1 Flee as a **b** to your mountain
Ps 124: 7 as a **b** from the snare of the
Eccl 12: 4 rises up at the sound of a **b**
Dan 7: 6 on its back four wings of a **b**
Hos 9:11 glory shall fly away like a **b**
Rev 18: 2 for every unclean and hated **b**

BIRD'S† (see BIRD)
Deut 22: 6 If a **b** nest happens to be

BIRDS (see BIRD, BIRDS')
Gen 1:20 let **b** fly above the earth
Gen 1:26 over the **b** of the air, and
Gen 6:20 Of the **b** after their kind, of
Gen 7: 8 beasts that are unclean, of **b**
Gen 15:10 he did not cut the **b** in two
Deut 14:11 All clean **b** you may eat
1Ki 4:33 spoke also of animals, of **b**
Job 35:11 us wiser than the **b** of heaven
Ps 50:11 I know all the **b** of the
Ps 104:17 Where the **b** make their nests
Is 18: 6 for the mountain **b** of prey
Is 31: 5 Like **b** flying about, so will
Jer 5:27 As a cage is full of **b**, so
Dan 4:12 the **b** of the heavens dwelt in
Matt 6:26 Look at the **b** of the air, for
Matt 8:20 **b** of the air have nests, but
Matt 13: 4 the **b** came and devoured them
Luke 12:24 more value are you than the **b**
Luke 13:19 the **b** of the air nested in
Acts 10:12 things, and **b** of the air
Acts 11: 6 things, and **b** of the air
Rom 1:23 and **b** and four-footed beasts
1Co 15:39 of fish, and another of **b**

BIRDS'† (see BIRDS)
Dan 4:33 and his nails like **b** claws

BIRTH (see BIRTHDAY, BIRTHRIGHT, BIRTHSTOOLS, BORN, CHILDBIRTH)
Gen 25:24 fulfilled for her to give **b**
Ex 1:19 give **b** before the midwives
Ruth 2:11 mother and the land of your **b**
1Sa 4:19 she bowed herself and gave **b**
1Ki 3:17 I gave **b** while she was in the
Job 3: 1 and cursed the day of his **b**
Job 3:11 Why did I not die at **b**
Ps 22:10 I was cast upon You from **b**
Ps 29: 9 LORD makes the deer give **b**
Ps 71: 6 I have been upheld from my **b**
Eccl 7: 1 death than the day of one's **b**
Is 66: 7 she travailed, she gave **b**
Is 66: 8 be made to give **b** in one day
Jer 2:27 to a stone, 'You gave **b** to me
Jer 48:41 heart of a woman in **b** pangs
Ezek 16: 3 Your **b** and your nativity are
Hos 9:11 no **b**, no pregnancy, and no
Matt 1:18 Now the **b** of Jesus Christ was
Luke 1:14 and many will rejoice at his **b**
John 9: 1 a man who was blind from **b**
Rom 8:22 labors with **b** pangs together
Gal 4:19 for whom I labor in **b** again
Gal 4:24 which gives **b** to bondage,
Jas 1:15 conceived, it gives **b** to sin
Rev 12: 2 in labor and in pain to give **b**
Rev 12:13 who gave **b** to the male Child

BIRTHDAY (see BIRTH)
Gen 40:20 day, which was Pharaoh's **b**
Matt 14: 6 when Herod's **b** was celebrated

BIRTHRIGHT (see BIRTH)
Gen 25:33 him, and sold his **b** to Jacob
Gen 25:34 Thus Esau despised his **b**

Gen 27:36 He took away my **b**, and now
Gen 43:33 firstborn according to his **b**
1Ch 5: 1 his **b** was given to the sons
1Ch 5: 1 not listed according to the **b**
1Ch 5: 2 although the **b** was Joseph's
Heb 12:16 one morsel of food sold his **b**

BIRTHSTOOLS† (see BIRTH)
Ex 1:16 women, and see them on the **b**

BISHOP (see BISHOPS)
1Ti 3: 1 desires the position of a **b**
1Ti 3: 2 A **b** then must be blameless,

BISHOPS† (see BISHOP)
Phil 1: 1 are in Philippi, with the **b**

BIT† (see BITE, BITS)
Num 21: 6 people, and they **b** the people
Ps 32: 9 must be harnessed with **b** and
Amos 5:19 the wall, and a serpent **b** him

BITE (see BIT, BITES, BITTEN)
Eccl 10:11 A serpent may **b** when it is
Gal 5:15 But if you **b** and devour one

BITES† (see BITE)
Gen 49:17 that **b** the horse's heels so
Prov 23:32 the last it **b** like a serpent

BITHYNIA†
Acts 16: 7 they tried to go into **B**, but
1Pe 1: 1 Cappadocia, Asia, and **B**,

BITS† (see BIT)
Amos 6:11 break the great house into **b**
Jas 3: 3 we put **b** in horses' mouths

BITTEN (see BITE)
Num 21: 8 be that everyone who is **b**
Num 21: 9 if a serpent had **b** anyone

BITTER (see BITTERLY, BITTERNESS)
Gen 27:34 **b** cry, and said to his father,
Ex 1:14 lives **b** with hard bondage
Ex 12: 8 with **b** herbs they shall eat
Ex 15:23 of Marah, for they were **b**
Num 5:18 **b** water that brings a curse
Job 3:20 and life to the **b** of soul
Ps 64: 3 shoot their arrows—**b** words
Prov 5: 4 the end she is **b** as wormwood
Prov 27: 7 soul every **b** thing is sweet
Prov 31: 6 to those who are **b** of heart
Eccl 7:26 I find more **b** than death the
Is 5:20 who put **b** for sweet, and sweet
Is 24: 9 strong drink is **b** to those
Jer 31:15 **b** weeping, Rachel weeping for
Zeph 1:14 of the day of the LORD is **b**
Col 3:19 and do not be **b** toward them
Jas 3:14 But if you have **b** envy and
Rev 8:11 water, because it was made **b**
Rev 10: 9 it will make your stomach **b**

BITTERLY (see BITTER)
Gen 49:23 archers have **b** grieved him
Ruth 1:20 has dealt very **b** with me
Hos 12:14 provoked Him to anger most **b**
Luke 22:62 Then Peter went out and wept **b**

BITTERN†
Zeph 2:14 and the **b** shall lodge on the

BITTERNESS (see BITTER)
1Sa 1:10 And she was in **b** of soul, and
1Sa 15:32 Surely the **b** of death is past
Prov 14:10 The heart knows its own **b**
Prov 17:25 and **b** to her who bore him
Is 38:17 own peace that I had great **b**
Lam 3: 5 me and surrounded me with **b**
Lam 3:15 He has filled me with **b**, He
Ezek 3:14 took me away, and I went in **b**
Ezek 27:31 weep for you with **b** of heart

Acts 8:23 that you are poisoned by **b**
Rom 3:14 mouth is full of cursing and **b**
Eph 4:31 Let all **b**, wrath, anger,
Heb 12:15 lest any root of **b** springing

BLACK (*see* BLACKER, BLACKNESS)
Lev 13:31 and there is no **b** hair in it
1Ki 18:45 the sky became **b** with clouds
Job 30:30 My skin grows **b** and falls from
Song 5:11 are wavy, and **b** as a raven
Zech 6: 2 the second chariot **b** horses
Matt 5:36 make one hair white or **b**
Rev 6: 5 a **b** horse, and he who sat on
Rev 6:12 the sun became **b** as sackcloth

BLACKER† (*see* BLACK)
Lam 4: 8 appearance is **b** than soot

BLACKNESS (*see* BLACK)
Job 3: 5 may the **b** of the day terrify
Is 50: 3 I clothe the heavens with **b**
Is 59: 9 brightness, but we walk in **b**
Heb 12:18 burned with fire, and to **b**
Jude 13 the **b** of darkness forever

BLACKSMITH†
1Sa 13:19 Now there was no **b** to be
Is 44:12 The **b** with the tongs works
Is 54:16 I have created the **b** who

BLADE
Judg 3:22 the hilt went in after the **b**
Mark 4:28 first the **b**, then the head,

BLAME (*see* BLAMED, BLAMELESS)
Gen 43: 9 let me bear the **b** forever
2Co 8:20 that anyone should **b** us in
Eph 1: 4 without **b** before Him in love,

BLAMED† (*see* BLAME)
2Co 6: 3 our ministry may not be **b**
Gal 2:11 face, because he was to be **b**

BLAMELESS (*see* BLAME, BLAMELESSLY)
Gen 17: 1 walk before Me and be **b**
Gen 44:10 my slave, and you shall be **b**
Num 32:22 and be **b** before the LORD and
Josh 2:17 We will be **b** of this oath of
Job 1: 1 and that man was **b** and upright,
Job 9:21 I am **b**, yet I do not know
Job 9:22 I say, 'He destroys the **b**
Ps 19:13 Then I shall be **b**, And I shall
Ps 51: 4 speak, And **b** when You judge
Prov 13: 6 keeps him whose way is **b**, but
Matt 12: 5 profane the Sabbath, and are **b**
1Co 1: 8 that you may be **b** in the day
Phil 3: 6 which is in the law, **b**
Col 1:22 to present you holy, and **b**
1Th 5:23 body be preserved **b** at the
1Ti 3: 2 A bishop then must be **b**, the
1Ti 3:10 as deacons, being found **b**
1Ti 6:14 spot, **b** until our Lord Jesus
Tit 1: 6 if a man is **b**, the husband of
2Pe 3:14 in peace, without spot and **b**

BLAMELESSLY† (*see* BLAMELESS)
Prov 28:18 Whoever walks **b** will be saved
1Th 2:10 **b** we behaved ourselves among

BLANKET†
Judg 4:18 she covered him with a **b**

BLASPHEME† (*see* BLASPHEMED, BLASPHEMER,
BLASPHEMES, BLASPHEMING, BLASPHEMOUS,
BLASPHEMY)
2Sa 12:14 the enemies of the LORD to **b**
Ps 74:10 Will the enemy **b** Your name
Acts 26:11 and compelled them to **b**
1Ti 1:20 that they may learn not to **b**
Jas 2: 7 Do they not **b** that noble name

Rev 13: 6 to **b** His name, His tabernacle

BLASPHEMED (*see* BLASPHEME)
1Ki 21:13 Naboth has **b** God and the king
Is 52: 5 And My name is **b** continually
Matt 27:39 And those who passed by **b** Him
Luke 23:39 who were hanged **b** Him, saying
Acts 18: 6 when they opposed him and **b**
Rom 2:24 The name of God is **b** among
1Ti 6: 1 and His doctrine may not be **b**
Tit 2: 5 the word of God may not be **b**
2Pe 2: 2 the way of truth will be **b**
Rev 16: 9 they **b** the name of God who
Rev 16:11 And they **b** the God of heaven

BLASPHEMER† (*see* BLASPHEME, BLASPHEMERS)
1Ti 1:13 although I was formerly a **b**

BLASPHEMERS† (*see* BLASPHEMER)
Acts 19:37 temples nor **b** of your goddess
2Ti 3: 2 of money, boasters, proud, **b**

BLASPHEMES (*see* BLASPHEME)
Lev 24:16 whoever **b** the name of the
Matt 9: 3 themselves, "This Man **b**!"
Mark 3:29 but he who **b** against the Holy

BLASPHEMIES (*see* BLASPHEMY)
Ezek 35:12 your **b** which you have spoken
Dan 11:36 shall speak **b** against the God
Matt 15:19 thefts, false witness, **b**
Mark 2: 7 this Man speaks **b** like this
Rev 13: 5 speaking great things and **b**

BLASPHEMING† (*see* BLASPHEME)
John 10:36 into the world, 'You are **b**
Acts 13:45 and contradicting and **b**, they

BLASPHEMOUS† (*see* BLASPHEME, BLASPHEMOUSLY)
Acts 6:11 speak **b** words against Moses
Acts 6:13 **b** words against this holy
Rev 13: 1 and on his heads a **b** name

BLASPHEMOUSLY† (*see* BLASPHEMOUS)
Luke 22:65 they **b** spoke against Him

BLASPHEMY (*see* BLASPHEME, BLASPHEMIES)
2Ki 19: 3 of trouble, and rebuke, and **b**
Matt 12:31 **b** will be forgiven men, but
Matt 12:31 but the **b** against the Spirit
Matt 26:65 He has spoken **b**
Mark 7:22 an evil eye, pride,
John 10:33 do not stone You, but for **b**
Col 3: 8 anger, wrath, malice, **b**,
Rev 17: 3 which was full of names of **b**

BLAST (*see* BLASTED, BLASTS)
Ex 15: 8 with the **b** of Your nostrils
Ex 19:19 when the **b** of the trumpet
2Sa 22:16 at the **b** of the breath of His

BLASTED† (*see* BLAST)
Amos 4: 9 I **b** you with blight and mildew

BLASTS† (*see* BLAST)
Rev 8:13 because of the remaining **b** of

BLAZE† (*see* BLAZED, BLAZING)
Num 16:37 up the censers out of the **b**

BLAZED† (*see* BLAZE)
Lam 2: 3 He has **b** against Jacob like a

BLAZING† (*see* BLAZE)
Ezek 20:47 the **b** flame shall not be

BLEAT† (*see* BLEATING)
Is 34:14 goat shall **b** to its companion

BLEATING† (*see* BLEAT)
1Sa 15:14 What then is this **b** of the

BLEMISH (*see* BLEMISHED, BLEMISHES)
Ex 12: 5 Your lamb shall be without **b**

Num 19: 2 you a red heifer without **b**
Deut 17: 1 which has any **b** or defect
2Sa 14:25 head there was no **b** in him
Dan 1: 4 men in whom there was no **b**
Eph 5:27 should be holy and without **b**
1Pe 1:19 as of a lamb without **b** and

BLEMISHED† (*see* BLEMISH)
Mal 1:14 to the Lord what is **b**

BLEMISHES† (*see* BLEMISH)
2Pe 2:13 They are spots and **b**,

BLENDED†
Lev 7:12 or cakes of finely **b** flour
Song 7: 2 which lacks no **b** beverage

BLESS (*see* BLESSED, BLESSEDNESS, BLESSES, BLESSING)
Gen 12: 2 I will **b** you and make your
Gen 12: 3 I will **b** those who **b** you,
Gen 17:16 And I will **b** her and also give
Gen 26:24 I will **b** you and multiply your
Gen 27:19 game, that your soul may **b** me
Gen 27:34 **B** me, even me also, O my
Gen 32:26 let You go unless You **b** me
Gen 48:16 me from all evil, **b** the lads
Ex 12:32 and **b** me also
Num 6:24 The LORD **b** you and keep you
Deut 1:11 **b** you as He has promised you
Deut 7:13 He will also **b** the fruit of
Deut 27:12 Mount Gerizim to **b** the people
Judg 5: 9 with the people. **B** the LORD!
Ruth 2: 4 The LORD **b** you
1Sa 2:20 And Eli would **b** Elkanah and
Ps 16: 7 I will **b** the LORD who has
Ps 34: 1 I will **b** the LORD at all
Ps 62: 4 They **b** with their mouth, But
Ps 67: 1 **b** us, And cause His face to
Ps 67: 6 God, our own God, shall **b** us
Ps 96: 2 Sing to the LORD, **b** His name
Ps 100: 4 to Him, and **b** His name
Ps 103: 1 **B** the LORD, O my soul
Ps 103: 1 is within me, **b** His holy name
Ps 103:20 **B** the LORD, you His angels,
Ps 103:21 **B** the LORD, all you His hosts
Ps 103:22 **B** the LORD, all His works, In
Ps 115:12 He will **b** the house of Israel
Ps 115:13 He will **b** those who fear the
Ps 135:19 **B** the LORD, O house of Israel
Ps 135:20 who fear the LORD, **b** the LORD
Ps 145: 1 I will **b** Your name forever and
Matt 5:44 **b** those who curse you, do
Acts 3:26 Jesus, sent Him to **b** you, in
Rom 12:14 **B** those who persecute you
Rom 12:14 **b** and do not curse
1Co 4:12 Being reviled, we **b**
1Co 10:16 cup of blessing which we **b**
1Co 14:16 if you **b** with the spirit, how
Heb 6:14 Surely blessing I will **b** you
Jas 3: 9 With it we **b** our God and

BLESSED (*see* BLESS)
Gen 1:22 And God **b** them, saying,
Gen 2: 3 Then God **b** the seventh day and
Gen 5: 2 **b** them and called them
Gen 9: 1 So God **b** Noah and his sons, and
Gen 9:26 **B** be the LORD, the God of
Gen 12: 3 of the earth shall be **b**
Gen 14:19 **B** be Abram of God Most High,
Gen 14:20 **b** be God Most High, Who has
Gen 17:20 Behold, I have **b** him, and will
Gen 24: 1 the LORD had **b** Abraham in all
Gen 24:60 they **b** Rebekah and said to her
Gen 27:33 and indeed he shall be **b**
Gen 30:27 LORD has **b** me for your sake
Gen 47: 7 and Jacob **b** Pharaoh
Gen 49:28 he **b** each one according to

Ex 18:10 **B** be the LORD, who has
Ex 20:11 the LORD **b** the Sabbath day
Num 23:20 He has **b**, and I cannot reverse
Deut 28: 3 **B** shall you be in the city,
Deut 28: 4 **B** shall be the fruit of your
Josh 17:14 the LORD has **b** us until now
Judg 5:24 Most **b** among women is Jael,
Judg 13:24 child grew, and the LORD **b** him
Ruth 2:19 **B** be the one who took notice
Ruth 4:14 **B** be the LORD, who has not
2Sa 7:29 of Your servant be **b** forever
2Sa 22:47 **B** be my Rock! Let God be
Neh 9: 5 **B** be Your glorious name,
Job 1:10 You have **b** the work of his
Job 1:21 **b** be the name of the LORD
Job 42:12 Now the LORD **b** the latter
Ps 1: 1 **B** is the man Who walks not in
Ps 2:12 **B** are all those who put their
Ps 28: 6 **B** be the LORD, Because He has
Ps 32: 1 **B** is he whose transgression
Ps 32: 2 **B** is the man to whom the LORD
Ps 33:12 **B** is the nation whose God is
Ps 34: 8 **B** is the man who trusts in
Ps 65: 4 **B** is the man whom You choose,
Ps 68:35 to His people. **B** be God!
Ps 84:12 **B** is the man who trusts in
Ps 89:15 **B** are the people who know the
Ps 89:52 **B** be the LORD forevermore
Ps 118:26 **B** is he who comes in the name
Prov 10: 7 memory of the righteous is **b**
Prov 31:28 rise up and call her **b**
Is 19:25 **B** is Egypt My people, and
Jer 20:14 Let the day not be **b** in which
Dan 2:19 So Daniel **b** the God of heaven
Dan 2:20 **B** be the name of God forever
Dan 4:34 I **b** the Most High and praised
Dan 12:12 **B** is he who waits, and comes
Mal 3:12 all nations will call you **b**
Matt 5: 3 **B** are the poor in spirit, for
Matt 11: 6 **b** is he who is not offended
Matt 14:19 and looking up to heaven, He **b**
Matt 16:17 **B** are you, Simon Bar-Jonah,
Matt 21: 9 **B** is He who comes in the
Matt 25:34 you **b** of My Father, inherit
Matt 26:26 **b** it and broke it, and gave it
Mark 10:16 His hands on them, and **b** them
Mark 11:10 **B** is the kingdom of our
Mark 14:61 the Christ, the Son of the **B**
Luke 1:42 **B** are you among women, and
Luke 1:42 **b** is the fruit of your womb
Luke 1:48 generations will call me **b**
Luke 6:20 **B** are you poor, for yours is
Luke 7:23 **b** is he who is not offended
Luke 11:27 **B** is the womb that bore You,
Luke 13:35 **B** is He who Comes in the
Luke 19:38 **B** is the King who comes in
Luke 24:30 them, that He took bread, **b**
Luke 24:50 lifted up His hands and **b** them
John 12:13 **B** is He who comes in the
Acts 20:35 It is more **b** to give than to
Rom 1:25 the Creator, who is **b** forever
Rom 4: 8 **b** is the man to whom the LORD
Rom 9: 5 over all, the eternally **b** God
2Co 1: 3 **B** be the God and Father of our
Gal 3: 8 all the nations shall be **b**
Gal 3: 9 are **b** with believing Abraham
Eph 1: 3 who has **b** us with every
Tit 2:13 looking for the **b** hope and
Heb 7: 6 **b** him who had the promises
Heb 7: 7 the lesser is **b** by the better
Heb 11:21 **b** each of the sons of Joseph,
Jas 1:12 **B** is the man who endures
Rev 1: 3 **B** is he who reads and those
Rev 14:13 **B** are the dead who die in
Rev 22: 7 **B** is he who keeps the words

Rev 22:14 **B** are those who do His

BLESSEDNESS† (see BLESS)
Rom 4: 6 the **b** of the man to whom God
Rom 4: 9 Does this **b** then come upon

BLESSES (see BLESS)
Num 24: 9 Blessed is he who **b** you, and
Ps 10: 3 He **b** the greedy and renounces
Is 65:16 So that he who **b** himself in
Is 66: 3 incense, as if he **b** an idol

BLESSING (see BLESS, BLESSINGS)
Gen 12: 2 and you shall be a **b**
Gen 22:17 in **b** I will bless you, and in
Gen 27:12 a curse on myself and not a **b**
Gen 27:35 and has taken away your **b**
Gen 27:38 Have you only one **b**, my
Gen 28: 4 and give you the **b** of Abraham
Ex 32:29 bestow on you a **b** this day
Deut 11:26 I set before you today a **b**
Deut 11:29 put the **b** on Mount Gerizim
Deut 30:19 before you life and death, **b**
2Sa 7:29 with Your **b** let the house of
Neh 9: 5 which is exalted above all **b**
Neh 13: 2 God turned the curse into a **b**
Ps 24: 5 shall receive **b** from the LORD
Ps 133: 3 the LORD commanded the **b**
Is 44: 3 and My **b** on your offspring
Ezek 34:26 there shall be showers of **b**
Mal 3:10 pour out for you such **b** That
Luke 24:53 the temple praising and **b** God
Rom 15:29 the **b** of the gospel of Christ
1Co 10:16 The cup of **b** which we bless,
Gal 3:14 that the **b** of Abraham might
Eph 1: 3 us with every spiritual **b** in
Heb 6: 7 receives **b** from God
Heb 6:14 Surely **b** I will bless you, and
Heb 12:17 he wanted to inherit the **b**
Jas 3:10 of the same mouth proceed **b**
Rev 5:12 and honor and glory and **b**
Rev 7:12 **B** and glory and wisdom,

BLESSINGS (see BLESSING)
Gen 49:25 you with **b** of heaven above
Deut 28: 2 all these **b** shall come upon
Josh 8:34 the words of the law, the **b**
Ps 21: 3 him with the **b** of goodness
Prov 10: 6 **B** are on the head of the
Mal 2: 2 you, and I will curse your **b**

BLEW (see BLOW)
Ex 10:19 and **b** them into the Red Sea
Ex 15:10 You **b** with Your wind, the sea
Josh 6: 8 **b** the trumpets, and the ark of
Judg 7:19 they **b** the trumpets and broke
1Sa 13: 3 Then Saul **b** the trumpet
Matt 7:25 floods came, and the winds **b**
Acts 27:13 When the south wind **b** softly

BLIGHT (see BLIGHTED)
1Ki 8:37 **b** or mildew, locusts or
Amos 4: 9 I blasted you with **b** and

BLIGHTED (see BLIGHT)
Gen 41: 6 **b** by the east wind, sprang up
Gen 41:27 the seven empty heads **b** by
2Ki 19:26 grain **b** before it is grown

BLIND (see BLINDED, BLINDFOLD, BLINDNESS, BLINDS)
Ex 4:11 deaf, the seeing, or the **b**
Lev 21:18 a man **b** or lame, who has a
2Sa 5: 8 Jebusites (the lame and the **b**
Ps 146: 8 LORD opens the eyes of the **b**
Is 29:18 the eyes of the **b** shall see
Is 42: 7 To open **b** eyes, to bring out
Is 42:19 Who is **b** but My servant, or
Mal 1: 8 offer the **b** as a sacrifice
Matt 9:27 two **b** men followed Him,

Matt 11: 5 The **b** see and the lame
Matt 12:22 He healed him, so that the **b**
Matt 15:14 are **b** leaders of the **b**
Matt 15:14 And if the **b** leads the **b**
Matt 15:31 lame walking, and the **b** seeing
Matt 23:16 **b** guides, who say, "Whoever
Matt 23:17 Fools and **b**! For which is
Matt 23:19 Fools and **b**! For which is
Matt 23:24 **B** guides, who strain out a
Matt 23:26 **B** Pharisee, first cleanse the
Mark 10:46 **b** Bartimaeus, the son of
Luke 4:18 and recovery of sight to the **b**
John 9: 1 a man who was **b** from birth
John 9: 6 of the **b** man with the clay
John 9:25 that though I was **b**, now I
John 9:39 those who see may be made **b**
John 9:40 Are we **b** also
Rom 2:19 yourself are a guide to the **b**
Rev 3:17 wretched, miserable, poor, **b**

BLINDED (see BLIND)
John 12:40 He has **b** their eyes and
2Co 4: 4 the god of this age has **b**
1Jn 2:11 the darkness has **b** his eyes

BLINDFOLD† (see BLIND, BLINDFOLDED)
Mark 14:65 to **b** Him, and to beat Him, and

BLINDFOLDED† (see BLINDFOLD)
Luke 22:64 And having **b** Him, they struck

BLINDNESS (see BLIND)
Gen 19:11 doorway of the house with **b**
2Pe 1: 9 is shortsighted, even to **b**

BLINDS (see BLIND)
Deut 16:19 for a bribe **b** the eyes of the

BLOCK (see BLOCKED, BLOCKS)
Is 44:19 fall down before a **b** of wood
Ezek 3:20 lay a stumbling **b** before him
Rom 11: 9 and a trap, a stumbling **b** and a
1Co 1:23 to the Jews a stumbling **b**
1Co 8: 9 **b** to those who are weak

BLOCKED† (see BLOCK)
Jer 51:32 The passages are **b**, the reeds
Lam 3: 9 He has **b** my ways with hewn

BLOCKS† (see BLOCK)
Jer 6:21 **b** before this people, And the
Zeph 1: 3 the stumbling **b** along with

BLOOD (see BLOODGUILT, BLOODLINE, BLOODSHED, BLOODTHIRSTY, BLOODY, LIFEBLOOD)
Gen 4:10 **b** cries out to Me from the
Gen 4:11 brother's **b** from your hand
Gen 9: 4 with its life, that is, its **b**
Gen 9: 6 Whoever sheds man's **b**, by man
Gen 37:26 our brother and conceal his **b**
Gen 37:31 and dipped the tunic in the **b**
Gen 42:22 his **b** is now required of us
Ex 4: 9 will become **b** on the dry land
Ex 4:25 you are a husband of **b** to me
Ex 7:19 water, that they may become **b**
Ex 12: 7 they shall take some of the **b**
Ex 12:13 Now the **b** shall be a sign
Ex 12:13 And when I see the **b**, I will
Ex 12:22 dip it in the **b** that is in
Ex 12:23 He sees the **b** on the lintel
Ex 24: 6 half the **b** he sprinkled on
Ex 24: 8 the **b** of the covenant which
Lev 1:15 its **b** shall be drained out at
Lev 3:17 shall eat neither fat nor **b**
Lev 4: 6 shall dip his finger in the **b**
Lev 12: 4 in the **b** of her purification
Lev 12: 5 in the **b** of her purification
Lev 12: 7 clean from the flow of her **b**
Lev 16:15 bring its **b** inside the veil,

Lev	17:11	life of the flesh is in the **b**
Lev	17:11	the **b** that makes atonement
Lev	17:14	Its **b** sustains its life
Lev	19:26	not eat anything with the **b**
Lev	20: 9	His **b** shall be upon him
Num	23:24	drinks the **b** of the slain
Num	35:27	the avenger of **b** kills the
Deut	19:10	lest innocent **b** be shed in
Deut	32:42	make My arrows drunk with **b**
Josh	2:19	his **b** shall be on our head if
Josh	20: 3	refuge from the avenger of **b**
1Sa	25:31	you have shed **b** without cause
1Ki	2: 5	And he shed the **b** of war in
1Ki	2: 5	put the **b** of war on his belt
1Ki	18:28	until the **b** gushed out on
1Ki	21:19	dogs shall lick your **b**, even
1Ki	22:35	The **b** ran out from the wound
2Ki	3:22	on the other side as red as **b**
2Ki	9:33	some of her **b** spattered on
1Ch	11:19	Shall I drink the **b** of these
1Ch	28: 3	a man of war and have shed **b**
Job	16:18	O earth, do not cover my **b**
Job	39:30	Its young ones suck up **b**
Ps	16: 4	of **b** I will not offer, Nor
Ps	30: 9	What profit is there in my **b**
Ps	50:13	Or drink the **b** of goats
Ps	72:14	shall be their **b** in His sight
Ps	106:38	the land was polluted with **b**
Prov	6:17	hands that shed innocent **b**
Is	1:15	Your hands are full of **b**
Is	9: 5	And garments rolled in **b**,
Is	66: 3	as if he offers swine's **b**
Jer	46:10	and made drunk with their **b**
Ezek	3:18	but his **b** I will require at
Ezek	3:20	but his **b** I will require at
Ezek	16: 9	thoroughly washed off your **b**
Ezek	33: 6	but his **b** I will require at
Ezek	33: 8	but his **b** I will require at
Joel	2:30	**b** and fire and pillars of smoke
Joel	2:31	darkness, and the moon into **b**
Matt	9:20	a woman who had a flow of **b**
Matt	16:17	**b** has not revealed this to
Matt	23:35	from the **b** of righteous Abel
Matt	23:35	Abel to the **b** of Zechariah
Matt	26:28	For this is My **b** of the new
Matt	27: 8	the Field of **B** to this day
Matt	27:24	of the **b** of this just Person
Matt	27:25	His **b** be on us and on our
Luke	13: 1	**b** Pilate had mingled with
Luke	22:20	is the new covenant in My **b**
John	1:13	who were born, not of **b**, nor
John	6:53	the Son of Man and drink His **b**
John	6:54	drinks My **b** has eternal life,
John	6:56	drinks My **b** abides in Me, and
John	19:34	a spear, and immediately **b**
Acts	1:19	Dama, that is, Field of **B**
Acts	2:19	**b** and fire and vapor of smoke
Acts	2:20	darkness, and the moon into **b**
Acts	15:20	things strangled, and from **b**
Acts	15:29	offered to idols, from **b**,
Acts	17:26	He has made from one **b** every
Acts	18: 6	Your **b** be upon your own heads
Acts	20:28	He purchased with His own **b**
Acts	22:20	when the **b** of Your martyr
Rom	3:15	feet are swift to shed **b**
Rom	3:25	to be a propitiation of His **b**
Rom	5: 9	now being justified by His **b**
1Co	10:16	communion of the **b** of Christ
1Co	11:25	is the new covenant in My **b**
1Co	11:27	of the body and **b** of the Lord
1Co	15:50	**b** cannot inherit the kingdom
Gal	1:16	confer with flesh and **b**,
Eph	1: 7	have redemption through His **b**
Eph	2:13	brought near by the **b** of Christ
Eph	6:12	wrestle against flesh and **b**

Col	1:20	through the **b** of His cross
Heb	9: 7	once a year, not without **b**
Heb	9:12	Not with the **b** of goats and
Heb	9:12	but with His own **b** He entered
Heb	9:13	For if the **b** of bulls and
Heb	9:14	more shall the **b** of Christ
Heb	9:22	all things are purified with **b**
Heb	9:22	without shedding of **b** there
Heb	10: 4	possible that the **b** of bulls
Heb	10:19	the Holiest by the **b** of Jesus
Heb	10:29	counted the **b** of the covenant
Heb	13:12	the people with His own **b**
Heb	13:20	sheep, through the **b** of the
1Pe	1: 2	of the **b** of Jesus Christ
1Pe	1:19	with the precious **b** of Christ
1Jn	1: 7	the **b** of Jesus Christ His Son
1Jn	5: 6	is He who came by water and **b**
1Jn	5: 8	Spirit, the water, and the **b**
Rev	1: 5	us from our sins in His own **b**
Rev	5: 9	by Your **b** out of every tribe
Rev	6:12	and the moon became like **b**
Rev	7:14	white in the **b** of the Lamb
Rev	8: 8	a third of the sea became **b**
Rev	12:11	him by the **b** of the Lamb and
Rev	14:20	**b** came out of the winepress,
Rev	17: 6	with the **b** of the saints and
Rev	17: 6	with the **b** of the martyrs of
Rev	18:24	was found the **b** of prophets
Rev	19:13	with a robe dipped in **b**, and

BLOODGUILT (see BLOOD, BLOODSHED)

BLOODGUILTINESS (see BLOODSHED)

BLOODLINE† (see BLOOD)
Ezek	19:10	was like a vine in your **b**

BLOODSHED (see BLOOD)
Ex	22: 3	shall be guilt for his **b**
Lev	17: 4	**b** shall be imputed to that
Deut	17: 8	degrees of guilt for **b**
Deut	19:10	thus the guilt of **b** be upon
Ps	51:14	Deliver me from the guilt of **b**
Hos	1: 4	while I will avenge the **b** of
Hos	4: 2	with **b** after **b**
Hos	12:14	Lord will leave the guilt of his **b**
Joel	3:21	acquit them of the guilt of **b**
Heb	12: 4	have not yet resisted to **b**

BLOODTHIRSTY (see BLOOD)
2Sa	16: 7	You **b** man, you rogue
Ps	5: 6	The LORD abhors the **b** and
Ps	55:23	**B** and deceitful men shall not
Ps	59: 2	And save me from **b** men
Prov	29:10	The **b** hate the blameless, but

BLOODY (see BLOOD)
Ezek	24: 6	Woe to the **b** city, to the pot

BLOOM † (see BLOOMS)
Song	7:12	and the pomegranates are in **b**

BLOOMS (see BLOOM)
Song	1:14	**b** in the vineyards of En Gedi

BLOSSOM (see BLOSSOMED, BLOSSOMS)
Num	17: 5	the man whom I choose will **b**
Is	35: 1	rejoice and **b** as the rose
Hab	3:17	Though the fig tree may not **b**

BLOSSOMED† (see BLOSSOM)
Ezek	7:10	the rod has **b**, pride has

BLOSSOMS (see BLOSSOM, BLOSSOMS)
Gen	40:10	its **b** shot forth, and its
Ex	25:33	like almond **b** on one branch
Num	17: 8	forth buds, had produced **b**
Eccl	12: 5	when the almond tree **b**, the

BLOT (see BLOTS, BLOTTED)
Ex	17:14	that I will utterly **b** out the

Ex   32:32 **b** me out of Your book which
Deut   9:14 **b** out their name from under
Ps   51: 1 **B** out my transgressions
Ps   51: 9 And **b** out all my iniquities
Rev   3: 5 I will not **b** out his name

BLOTS† (*see* BLOT)
Is   43:25 even I, am He who **b** out your

BLOTTED (*see* BLOT)
Deut   25: 6 may not be **b** out of Israel
Neh   4: 5 sin be **b** out from before You
Ps   9: 5 You have **b** out their name
Ps   69:28 Let them be **b** out of the book
Is   44:22 I have **b** out, like a thick
Acts   3:19 that your sins may be **b** out

BLOW (*see* BLEW, BLOWING, BLOWN, BLOWS)
Num   10: 8 priests, shall **b** the trumpets
Judg   7:18 When I **b** the trumpet, I and
Ps   39:10 by the **b** of Your hand
Ps   78:26 east wind to **b** in the heavens
Jer   6: 1 **B** the trumpet in Tekoa, and
Jer   6:29 the bellows **b** fiercely, the
Ezek   22:21 **b** on you with the fire of My
Joel   2: 1 **B** the trumpet in Zion,
Joel   2:15 **B** the trumpet in Zion,
Luke   12:55 when you see the south wind **b**
Rev   7: 1 should not **b** on the earth

BLOWING (*see* BLOW)
Num   29: 1 it is a day of **b** the trumpets
John   6:18 because a great wind was **b**

BLOWN (*see* BLOW)
Hos   13: 3 away, like chaff **b** off from a
Amos   3: 6 If a trumpet is **b** in a city

BLOWS (*see* BLOW)
Deut   25: 3 Forty **b** he may give him and no
Prov   17:10 than a hundred **b** on a fool
Is   18: 3 when he **b** a trumpet, you hear
Is   40: 7 breath of the LORD **b** upon it
John   3: 8 The wind **b** where it wishes,

BLUE
Ex   25: 4 **b** and purple and scarlet yarn,
Esth   8:15 king in royal apparel of **b**
Rev   9:17 of fiery red, hyacinth **b**, and

BLUNT†
2Sa   2:23 with the **b** end of the spear

BLUSH†
Jer   6:15 nor did they know how to **b**
Jer   8:12 nor did they know how to **b**

BOANERGES†
Mark   3:17 to whom He gave the name **B**

BOAR†
Ps   80:13 The **b** out of the woods

BOARD (*see* BOARDED, BOARDS)
Ex   26:16 shall be the length of a **b**
Acts   20:13 intending to take Paul on **b**

BOARDED† (*see* BOARD)
Acts   21: 6 we **b** the ship, and they

BOARDS (*see* BOARD)
Ex   26:15 make the **b** of acacia wood
Song   8: 9 enclose her with **b** of cedar

BOAST (*see* BOASTED, BOASTERS, BOASTFUL, BOASTING, BOASTS)
1Ki   20:11 **b** like the one who takes it
2Ch   25:19 your heart is lifted up to **b**
Ps   34: 2 shall make its **b** in the LORD
Ps   49: 6 **b** in the multitude of their
Ps   52: 1 Why do you **b** in evil, O
Ps   97: 7 carved images, Who **b** of idols
Prov   27: 1 Do not **b** about tomorrow, for

Ezek   24:21 My sanctuary, your arrogant **b**
Rom   2:17 law, and make your **b** in God
Rom   2:23 who make your **b** in the law
1Co   9:16 I have nothing to **b** of, for
2Co   1:14 that we are your **b** as you
2Co   10:13 will not **b** beyond measure,
2Co   10:16 not to **b** in another man's
2Co   11:16 that I also may **b** a little
2Co   11:30 If I must **b**, I will **b** in
2Co   12: 1 not profitable for me to **b**
2Co   12: 5 yet of myself I will not **b**
2Co   12: 6 though I might desire to **b**
2Co   12: 9 rather **b** in my infirmities
Eph   2: 9 works, lest anyone should **b**
2Th   1: 4 so that we ourselves **b** of you
Jas   3:14 in your hearts, do not **b** and

BOASTED† (*see* BOAST)
Ezek   35:13 mouth you have **b** against Me
2Co   7:14 I have **b** to him about you

BOASTERS† (*see* BOAST)
Rom   1:30 of God, violent, proud, **b**
2Ti   3: 2 lovers of money, **b**, proud,

BOASTFUL (*see* BOAST, BOASTFULLY)
Ps   5: 5 The **b** shall not stand in Your
Ps   73: 3 For I was envious of the **b**

BOASTFULLY† (*see* BOASTFUL)
Ps   75: 4 the boastful, 'Do not deal **b**

BOASTING (*see* BOAST)
Rom   3:27 Where is **b** then
1Co   9:15 anyone should make my **b** void
2Co   1:12 For our **b** is this
2Co   7: 4 great is my **b** on your behalf
2Co   9: 4 ashamed of this confident **b**
2Co   10:15 not **b** of things beyond
2Co   12:11 I have become a fool in **b**
Jas   4:16 All such **b** is evil

BOASTS (*see* BOAST)
Ps   10: 3 For the wicked **b** of his
Prov   25:14 Whoever falsely **b** of giving
Jas   3: 5 member and **b** great things

BOAT (*see* BOATS)
Matt   4:21 in the **b** with Zebedee their
Matt   9: 1 So He got into a **b**, crossed
Matt   14:22 His disciples get into the **b**
Mark   1:19 in the **b** mending their nets
Mark   3: 9 **b** should be kept ready for
Mark   4:37 and the waves beat into the **b**
Mark   6:47 the **b** was in the middle of
Mark   8:10 into the **b** with His disciples
John   6:21 immediately the **b** was at the
John   21: 6 on the right side of the **b**

BOATS (*see* BOAT)
Mark   4:36 other little **b** were also with
Luke   5: 2 saw two **b** standing by the
Luke   5: 7 came and filled both the **b**
John   6:23 other **b** came from Tiberias,

BOAZ
Ruth   2: 3 of the field belonging to **B**
Ruth   2: 4 **B** came from Bethlehem, and
Ruth   4: 8 the close relative said to **B**
Ruth   4:13 So **B** took Ruth and she became
Ruth   4:21 and **B** begot Obed
Matt   1: 5 **B** begot Obed by Ruth, Obed
Luke   3:32 the son of Obed, the son of **B**

BODIES (*see* BODY)
1Ch   10:12 of Saul and the **b** of his sons
Ps   79: 2 The dead **b** of Your servants
Ps   110: 6 fill the places with dead **b**
Dan   3:27 whose **b** the fire had no power
Matt   27:52 many **b** of the saints who had

John   19:31 that the **b** should not remain
Rom   8:11 **b** through His Spirit who
Rom   12: 1 your **b** a living sacrifice
1Co   6:15 your **b** are members of Christ
1Co   15:40 celestial **b** and terrestrial **b**
Eph   5:28 own wives as their own **b**
Heb   10:22 our **b** washed with pure water
Rev   11: 9 not allow their dead **b** to be

BODILY (*see* BODY)
Luke   3:22 Holy Spirit descended in **b**
Col   2: 9 the fullness of the Godhead **b**
1Ti   4: 8 For **b** exercise profits a

BODY (*see* BODIES, BODILY, BODYGUARDS)
Gen   15: 4 your own **b** shall be your heir
Gen   35:11 kings shall come from your **b**
Lev   13: 2 the skin of his **b** a swelling
Lev   15: 2 has a discharge from his **b**
Lev   15:19 discharge from her **b** is blood
Lev   21:11 shall he go near any dead **b**
2Ki   23:30 **b** in a chariot from Megiddo
Job   4:15 the hair on my **b** stood up
Ps   31: 9 grief, Yes, my soul and my **b**
Prov   14:30 sound heart is life to the **b**
Prov   18: 8 go down into the inmost **b**
Is   26:19 my dead **b** they shall arise
Dan   4:33 his **b** was wet with the dew of
Dan   7:15 in my spirit within my **b**, and
Mic   6: 7 the fruit of my **b** for the sin
Matt   5:29 than for your whole **b** to be
Matt   6:22 The lamp of the **b** is the eye
Matt   6:22 your whole **b** will be full of
Matt   6:25 nor about your **b**, what you
Matt   6:25 and the **b** more than clothing
Matt   10:28 both soul and **b** in hell
Matt   14:12 came and took away the **b** and
Matt   26:12 this fragrant oil on My **b**
Matt   26:26 Take, eat; this is My **b**
Matt   27:58 and asked for the **b** of Jesus
Matt   27:59 when Joseph had taken the **b**
Mark   14: 8 to anoint My **b** for burial
Luke   24:23 When they did not find His **b**
John   2:21 of the temple of His **b**
John   19:40 Then they took the **b** of Jesus
John   20:12 where the **b** of Jesus had lain
Rom   4:19 he did not consider his own **b**
Rom   6:6 that the **b** of sin might be
Rom   6:12 sin reign in your mortal **b**
Rom   7: 4 law through the **b** of Christ
Rom   7:24 me from this **b** of death
Rom   8:10 the **b** is dead because of sin,
Rom   8:13 to death the deeds of the **b**
Rom   8:23 the redemption of our **b**
Rom   12: 4 we have many members in one **b**
Rom   12: 5 many, are one **b** in Christ, and
1Co   5: 3 as absent in **b** but present in
1Co   6:13 Now the **b** is not for sexual
1Co   6:13 Lord, and the Lord for the **b**
1Co   6:16 to a harlot is one **b** with her
1Co   6:18 sins against his own **b**
1Co   6:19 **b** is the temple of the Holy
1Co   6:20 glorify God in your **b** and in
1Co   7: 4 have authority over her own **b**
1Co   9:27 But I discipline my **b** and
1Co   10:16 communion of the **b** of Christ
1Co   10:17 many, are one bread and one **b**
1Co   11:24 this is My **b** which is broken
1Co   11:27 will be guilty of the **b** and
1Co   11:29 not discerning the Lord's **b**
1Co   12:12 For as the **b** is one and has
1Co   12:12 being many, are one **b**
1Co   12:13 were all baptized into one **b**
1Co   12:15 not a hand, I am not of the **b**
1Co   12:25 should be no schism in the **b**
1Co   12:27 Now you are the **b** of Christ

1Co   13: 3 I give my **b** to be burned, but
1Co   15:35 And with what **b** do they come
1Co   15:42 The **b** is sown in corruption,
1Co   15:44 It is sown a natural **b**, it is
1Co   15:44 it is raised a spiritual **b**
2Co   4:10 carrying about in the **b** the
2Co   5: 8 to be absent from the **b** and to
2Co   5:10 the things done in the **b**,
2Co   12: 2 in the **b** I do not know, or
2Co   12: 2 out of the **b** I do not know
Gal   6:17 for I bear in my **b** the marks
Eph   1:23 which is His **b**, the fullness
Eph   2:16 in one **b** through the cross
Eph   3: 6 fellow heirs, of the same **b**
Eph   4: 4 There is one **b** and one Spirit,
Eph   4:12 edifying of the **b** of Christ
Eph   4:16 from whom the whole **b**, joined
Eph   5:23 and He is the Savior of the **b**
Phil   1:20 will be magnified in my **b**
Phil   3:21 will transform our lowly **b**
Phil   3:21 conformed to His glorious **b**
Col   1:18 And He is the head of the **b**
Col   3:15 also you were called in one **b**
1Th   5:23 **b** be preserved blameless at
Heb   10: 5 but a **b** You have prepared for
Heb   10:10 **b** of Jesus Christ once for
Jas   2:26 For as the **b** without the
Jas   3: 2 also to bridle the whole **b**
1Pe   2:24 sins in His own **b** on the tree
Jude   9 disputed about the **b** of Moses

BODYGUARDS (*see* BODY)
2Ki   11: 4 of hundreds, of the **b** and the

BOIL (*see* BOILED, BOILING, BOILS)
Ex   23:19 You shall not **b** a young goat
Lev   13:18 body develops a **b** in the skin

BOILED (*see* BOIL)
2Ki   6:29 So we **b** my son, and ate him
2Ch   35:13 holy offerings they **b** in pots

BOILING (*see* BOIL)
1Sa   2:13 his hand while the meat was **b**
Jer   1:13 I see a **b** pot, and it is

BOILS (*see* BOIL)
Ex   9:10 they caused **b** that break out
Deut   28:27 you with the **b** of Egypt, with
Job   2: 7 struck Job with painful **b**

BOISTEROUS†
Matt   14:30 he saw that the wine was **b**

BOLD (*see* BOLDLY, BOLDNESS)
Prov   28: 1 the righteous are **b** as a lion
Acts   13:46 Then Paul and Barnabas grew **b**
Rom   10:20 But Isaiah is very **b** and says
2Co   10: 2 be **b** with that confidence by
2Co   11:21 I am **b** also
Phil   1:14 are much more **b** to speak the
1Th   2: 2 we were **b** in our God to speak
Phm   8 though I might be very **b** in

BOLDLY (*see* BOLD)
Gen   34:25 and came **b** upon the city and
Acts   9:27 and how he had preached **b** at
Acts   14: 3 speaking **b** in the Lord, who
Acts   18:26 to speak **b** in the synagogue
Heb   4:16 Let us therefore come **b** to

BOLDNESS (*see* BOLD)
Ex   14: 8 of Israel went out with **b**
Acts   4:13 when they saw the **b** of Peter
Acts   4:31 spoke the word of God with **b**
2Co   3:12 we use great **b** of speech
Eph   3:12 in whom we have **b** and access
Heb   10:19 having **b** to enter the Holiest
1Jn   4:17 that we may have **b** in the day

BOLT† (*see* BOLTS)
2Sa 13:17 me, and **b** the door behind her

BOLTS (*see* BOLT)
2Sa 22:15 lightning **b**, and He vanquished
Neh 3: 3 and hung its doors with its **b**

BOND (*see* BONDAGE, BONDS, BONDWOMAN)
Deut 32:36 no one remaining, **b** or free
Luke 13:16 from this **b** on the Sabbath
Eph 4: 3 the Spirit in the **b** of peace
Col 3:14 which is the **b** of perfection

BONDAGE (*see* BOND)
Ex 1:14 lives bitter with hard **b**
Ex 6: 9 anguish of spirit and cruel **b**
Ex 13: 3 Egypt, out of the house of **b**
Neh 5:18 because the **b** was heavy on
Jer 34: 9 keep a Jewish brother in **b**
John 8:33 never been in **b** to anyone
Rom 8:15 the spirit of **b** again to fear
Rom 8:21 the **b** of corruption into the
1Co 7:15 is not under **b** in such cases
Gal 4:24 Sinai which gives birth to **b**
Gal 5: 1 again with a yoke of **b**
Heb 2:15 their lifetime subject to **b**

BONDS (*see* BOND)
Judg 15:14 his **b** broke loose from his
Ps 2: 3 us break Their **b** in pieces
Is 58: 6 to loose the **b** of wickedness,
Zech 11:14 cut in two my other staff, **B**
Luke 8:29 and he broke the **b** and was
Acts 22:30 he released him from his **b**

BONDWOMAN (*see* BOND)
Gen 21:10 Cast out this **b** and her son
Gal 4:22 the one by a **b**, the other by

BONE (*see* BONES)
Gen 2:23 This is now **b** of my bones
Gen 29:14 Surely you are my **b** and my
Judg 9: 2 that I am your own flesh and **b**
Job 2: 5 Your hand now, and touch his **b**
Job 19:20 My **b** clings to my skin and to
Prov 25:15 and a gentle tongue breaks a **b**
Ezek 37: 7 came together, **b** to **b**

BONES (*see* BONE)
Gen 2:23 This is now bone of my **b** and
Gen 50:25 shall carry up my **b** from here
Ex 12:46 shall you break one of its **b**
Ex 13:19 Moses took the **b** of Joseph
1Ki 13: 2 men's **b** shall be burned on
2Ki 13:21 and touched the **b** of Elisha
Job 4:14 which made all my **b** shake
Job 10:11 and knit me together with **b**
Job 30:17 My **b** are pierced in me at
Job 30:30 my **b** burn with fever
Job 33:21 his **b** stick out which once
Ps 22:14 all My **b** are out of joint
Ps 22:17 I can count all My **b**
Ps 32: 3 my **b** grew old Through my
Ps 51: 8 That the **b** which You have
Ps 102: 5 My **b** cling to my skin
Prov 12: 4 is like rottenness in his **b**
Prov 15:30 report makes the **b** healthy
Prov 16:24 the soul and health to the **b**
Eccl 11: 5 or how the **b** grow in the womb
Is 66:14 your **b** shall flourish like
Jer 20: 9 burning fire shut up in my **b**
Jer 50:17 of Babylon has broken his **b**
Lam 1:13 He has sent fire into my **b**
Ezek 24: 5 also pile fuel **b** under it
Ezek 37: 3 Son of man, can these **b** live
Ezek 37: 4 and say to them, 'O dry **b**
Ezek 37: 7 the **b** came together, bone to
Ezek 37:11 these **b** are the whole house

Dan 6:24 broke all their **b** in pieces
Amos 2: 1 because he burned the **b** of
Hab 3:16 rottenness entered my **b**
Matt 23:27 are full of dead men's **b** and
Luke 24:39 flesh and **b** as you see I have
John 19:36 Not one of His **b** shall be
Eph 5:30 of His flesh and of His **b**
Heb 11:22 instructions concerning his **b**

BOOK (*see* BOOKS)
Gen 5: 1 This is the **b** of the
Ex 17:14 this for a memorial in the **b**
Ex 24: 7 he took the **B** of the Covenant
Ex 32:32 blot me out of Your **b** which
Num 21:14 the **B** of the Wars of the LORD
Deut 17:18 a copy of this law in a **b**
Deut 28:61 written in this **B** of this law
Deut 29:21 written in this **B** of the Law
Josh 8:31 in the **B** of the Law of Moses
Josh 10:13 written in the **B** of Jasher
Josh 24:26 in the **B** of the Law of God
2Sa 1:18 is written in the **B** of Jasher
1Ki 11:41 the **b** of the acts of Solomon
1Ki 14:19 they are written in the **B** of
1Ki 14:29 **b** of the chronicles of the
2Ki 22:13 obeyed the words of this **b**
2Ki 23:21 in this **B** of the Covenant
2Ch 24:27 annals of the **b** of the kings
2Ch 35:12 is written in the **B** of Moses
Neh 8: 3 attentive to the **B** of the Law
Neh 8: 5 And Ezra opened the **b** in the
Neh 8: 8 read distinctly from the **b**
Job 19:23 they were inscribed in a **b**
Job 31:35 my Prosecutor had written a **b**
Ps 40: 7 of the **B** it is written of me
Ps 69:28 out of the **b** of the living
Is 29:11 words of a **b** that is sealed
Is 34:16 Search from the **b** of the LORD
Jer 36: 2 Take a scroll of a **b** and write
Jer 36:10 the words of Jeremiah in
Jer 36:18 wrote them with ink in the **b**
Dan 12: 1 who is found written in the **b**
Dan 12: 4 seal the **b** until the time of
Nah 1: 1 The **b** of the vision of Nahum
Mal 3:16 so a **b** of remembrance was
Matt 1: 1 The **b** of the genealogy of
Mark 12:26 not read in the **b** of Moses
Luke 4:17 He was handed the **b** of the
Luke 4:20 Then He closed the **b**, and gave
Luke 20:42 said in the **B** of Psalms, 'The
John 20:30 are not written in this **b**
Acts 7:42 in the **b** of the Prophets
Gal 3:10 written in the **b** of the law
Phil 4: 3 names are in the **B** of Life
Heb 9:19 sprinkled both the **b** itself
Heb 10: 7 of the **b** it is written of Me
Rev 1:11 What you see, write in a **b**
Rev 3: 5 his name from the **B** of Life
Rev 10: 2 he had a little **b** open in his
Rev 20:12 another **b** was opened, which
Rev 22: 9 who keep the words of this **b**

BOOKS (*see* BOOK)
Eccl 12:12 Of making many **b** there is no
Dan 7:10 seated, and the **b** were opened
Dan 9: 2 understood by the **b** the
John 21:25 the **b** that would be written
2Ti 4:13 and the **b**, especially the
Rev 20:12 before God, and **b** were opened
Rev 20:12 which were written in the **b**

BOOTH† (*see* BOOTHS)
Job 27:18 like a **b** which a watchman
Is 1: 8 is left as a **b** in a vineyard

BOOTHS (*see* BOOTH)
Lev 23:42 dwell in **b** for seven days

2Ki 23: 7 he tore down the ritual **b** of
Neh 8:14 in **b** during the feast of the
Neh 8:15 of leafy trees, to make **b**

BOOTY
Num 31:11 all the spoil and all the **b**
Deut 3: 7 we took as **b** for ourselves
Ezek 38:12 to take plunder and to take **b**

BORDER (see BORDERING, BORDERS, HEM)
Gen 10:19 the **b** of the Canaanites was
Josh 15: 5 The east **b** was the Salt Sea
Josh 15:12 The west **b** was the coastline
1Ki 4:21 as far as the **b** of Egypt
Ps 78:54 He brought them to His holy **b**
Is 19:19 a pillar to the LORD at its **b**
Ezek 29:10 as far as the **b** of Ethiopia
Obad 7 shall force you to the **b**
Mal 1: 5 beyond the **b** of Israel

BORDERING† (see BORDER)
Ezek 45: 7 **b** on the holy district and the

BORDERS (see BORDER)
Gen 23:17 within all the surrounding **b**
Ex 34:24 before you and enlarge your **b**
Ps 74:17 set all the **b** of the earth
Ps 147:14 He makes peace in your **b**, And
Is 15: 8 gone all around the **b** of Moab
Is 60:18 nor destruction within your **b**

BORE (see BEAR)
Gen 4: 1 conceived and **b** Cain, and said,
Gen 21: 2 **b** Abraham a son in his old
Gen 30: 1 that she **b** Jacob no children
Gen 30:21 Afterward she **b** a daughter
Gen 31: 8 all the flocks **b** speckled
Gen 31:39 I **b** the loss of it
Ex 2: 2 woman conceived and **b** a son
Ex 6:20 and she **b** him Aaron and Moses
Ex 19: 4 how I **b** you on eagles' wings
Deut 31: 9 who **b** the ark of the covenant
Ruth 4:12 Perez, whom Tamar **b** to Judah
1Sa 14: 1 the young man who **b** his armor
1Sa 17:41 the man who **b** the shield went
2Sa 12:15 that Uriah's wife **b** to David
1Ki 10: 2 with camels that **b** spices
Prov 17:25 bitterness to her who **b** him
Prov 23:25 and let her who **b** you rejoice
Song 6: 9 favorite of the one who **b** her
Is 8: 3 and she conceived and **b** a son
Is 51: 2 father, and to Sarah who **b** you
Is 53:12 He **b** the sin of many, and made
Is 63: 9 He **b** them and carried them all
Jer 31:19 because I **b** the reproach of
Ezek 12: 7 I **b** them on my shoulder in
Hos 1: 3 she conceived and **b** him a son
Hos 1: 6 again and **b** a daughter
Matt 8:17 and **b** our sicknesses
Mark 14:57 **b** false witness against Him,
Luke 4:22 So all **b** witness to Him, and
Luke 11:27 is the womb that **b** You, and
John 1:15 John **b** witness of Him and
1Pe 2:24 who Himself **b** our sins in His
Rev 1: 2 who **b** witness to the word of
Rev 12: 5 she **b** a male Child who was to
Rev 22: 2 which **b** twelve fruits, each

BORED†
2Ki 12: 9 **b** a hole in its lid, and set

BORN (see BIRTH, BORNE)
Gen 4:18 To Enoch was **b** Irad
Gen 6: 1 and daughters were **b** to them
Gen 10: 1 sons were **b** to them after the
Gen 15: 3 indeed one **b** in my house is
Gen 17:12 he who is **b** in your house or
Gen 17:17 Shall a child be **b** to a man

Gen 17:27 **b** in the house or bought with
Ex 1:22 Every son who is **b** you shall
Lev 19:34 be to you as one **b** among you
Lev 22:27 or a sheep or a goat is **b**
Josh 5: 5 **b** in the wilderness on the
Judg 13: 8 for the child who will be **b**
Ruth 4:17 There is a son **b** to Naomi
2Sa 3: 2 Sons were **b** to David in
2Sa 5:13 and daughters were **b** to David
2Sa 12:14 the child also who is **b** to
Job 1: 2 three daughters were **b** to him
Job 3: 3 day perish on which I was **b**
Job 5: 7 yet man is **b** to trouble, as
Job 11:12 wild donkey's colt is **b** a man
Job 14: 1 Man who is **b** of woman is of
Ps 58: 3 astray as soon as they are **b**
Prov 17:17 a brother is **b** for adversity
Eccl 3: 2 A time to be **b**, and a time to
Is 9: 6 For unto us a Child is **b**,
Jer 1: 5 before you were **b** I
Jer 20:14 be the day in which I was **b**
Matt 1:16 of whom was **b** Jesus who is
Matt 2: 1 Now after Jesus was **b** in
Matt 2: 2 has been **b** King of the Jews
Matt 2: 4 where the Christ was to be **b**
Matt 11:11 among those **b** of women there
Matt 19:12 **b** thus from their mother's
Matt 26:24 that man if he had never been **b**
Luke 1:35 **b** will be called the Son of
Luke 2:11 For there is **b** to you this
John 1:13 who were **b**, not of blood, nor
John 3: 3 to you, unless one is **b** again
John 3: 4 can a man be **b** when he is old
John 3: 4 his mother's womb and be **b**
John 3: 5 you, unless one is **b** of water
John 3: 6 That which is **b** of the flesh
John 3: 6 that which is **b** of the Spirit
John 3: 7 to you, 'You must be **b** again
John 9: 2 parents, that he was **b** blind
John 9:34 You were completely **b** in sins
John 18:37 For this cause I was **b**, and
Acts 22: 3 **b** in Tarsus of Cilicia, but
Acts 22:28 But I was **b** a citizen
Rom 1: 3 who was **b** of the seed of
Rom 9:11 the children not yet being **b**
1Co 15: 8 as by one **b** out of due time
Gal 4: 4 **b** of a woman, **b** under the law
Gal 4:23 was **b** according to the flesh
Gal 4:29 was **b** according to the Spirit
Heb 11:12 were **b** as many as the stars
Heb 11:23 By faith Moses, when he was **b**
1Pe 1:23 having been **b** again, not of
1Jn 2:29 righteousness is **b** of Him
1Jn 3: 9 Whoever has been **b** of God
1Jn 4: 7 who loves is **b** of God and
1Jn 5: 1 is the Christ is **b** of God
1Jn 5:18 is **b** of God does not sin
1Jn 5:18 but he who has been **b** of God
Rev 12: 4 her Child as soon as it was **b**

BORNE (see BEAR, BORN)
Gen 16: 1 wife, had **b** him no children
Gen 21: 9 whom she had **b** to Abraham
Ruth 4:15 than seven sons, has **b** him
1Sa 2: 5 Even the barren has **b** seven
Ps 69: 7 Your sake I have **b** reproach
Is 53: 4 Surely He has **b** our griefs
Jer 15:10 my mother, that you have **b** me
Matt 20:12 to us who have **b** the burden
1Co 15:49 as we have **b** the image of the
3Jn 6 who have **b** witness of your

BORROW (see BORROWED, BORROWER, BORROWS)
Deut 15: 6 nations, but you shall not **b**
Matt 5:42 from him who wants to **b** from

BORROWED (*see* BORROW)
Neh 5: 4 We have **b** money for the

BORROWER† (*see* BORROW)
Prov 22: 7 and the **b** is servant to the
Is 24: 2 the lender, so with the **b**

BORROWS† (*see* BORROW)
Ex 22:14 if a man **b** anything from his
Ps 37:21 The wicked **b** and does not

BOSOM
Ex 4: 6 Now put your hand in your **b**
Num 11:12 to me, 'Carry them in your **b**
Ruth 4:16 child and laid him on her **b**
2Sa 12: 3 his own cup and lay in his **b**
1Ki 3:20 laid her dead child in my **b**
Job 31:33 by hiding my iniquity in my **b**
Ps 79:12 sevenfold into their **b** Their
Ps 89:50 How I bear in my **b** the
Prov 6:27 can a man take fire to his **b**
Eccl 7: 9 anger rests in the **b** of fools
Is 40:11 arm, and carry them in His **b**
Ezek 23: 3 their virgin **b** was there
Luke 16:22 by the angels to Abraham's **b**
John 1:18 who is in the **b** of the Father
John 13:23 Jesus' **b** one of His disciples

BOTTLE (*see* BOTTLES)
Ps 56: 8 Put my tears into Your **b**
Jer 13:12 Every **b** shall be filled with

BOTTLES† (*see* BOTTLE)
Job 38:37 can pour out the **b** of heaven
Jer 48:12 his vessels and break the **b**

BOTTOM (*see* BOTTOMLESS)
Ex 15: 5 sank to the **b** like a stone
Dan 6:24 ever came to the **b** of the den
Amos 9: 3 My sight at the **b** of the sea
Matt 27:51 was torn in two from top to **b**

BOTTOMLESS (*see* BOTTOM)
Rev 9: 1 given the key to the **b** pit
Rev 9:11 them the angel of the **b** pit
Rev 20: 3 and he cast him into the **b** pit

BOUGH (*see* BOUGHS)
Gen 49:22 Joseph is a fruitful **b**
Is 17: 6 at the top of the uppermost **b**

BOUGHS (*see* BOUGH)
Lev 23:40 the **b** of leafy trees, and
Ps 80:10 the mighty cedars with its **b**
Is 27:11 When its **b** are withered, they
Ezek 31: 6 made their nests in its **b**

BOUGHT (*see* BUY)
Gen 17:27 born in the house or **b** with
Gen 49:30 which Abraham **b** with the
Lev 25:28 who **b** it until the Year of
Josh 24:32 of ground which Jacob had **b**
Ruth 4: 9 this day that I have **b** all
Jer 32: 9 So I **b** the field from
Hos 3: 2 So I **b** her for myself for
Matt 13:46 sold all that he had and **b** it
Matt 21:12 and drove out all those who **b**
Matt 27: 7 and **b** with them the potter's
Mark 15:46 Then he **b** fine linen, took
Mark 16: 1 of James, and Salome **b** spices
Luke 17:28 They ate, they drank, they **b**
Acts 7:16 in the tomb that Abraham **b**
1Co 6:20 For you were **b** at a price
2Pe 2: 1 denying the Lord who **b** them

BOUND (*see* BIND)
Gen 22: 9 he **b** Isaac his son and laid
Gen 44:30 since his life is **b** up in the
Num 30: 6 while **b** by her vows or by a
Josh 2:21 she **b** the scarlet cord in the
Judg 15:13 they **b** him with two new ropes

Ps 68: 6 who are **b** into prosperity
Ps 107:10 **B** in affliction and irons
Ps 119:61 cords of the wicked have **b** me
Prov 22:15 Foolishness is **b** up in the
Prov 30: 4 Who has **b** the waters in a
Is 1: 6 have not been closed or **b** up
Is 61: 1 the prison to those who are **b**
Ezek 34: 4 nor **b** up the broken, nor
Dan 3:24 Did we not cast three men **b**
Matt 14: 3 **b** him, and put him in prison
Matt 16:19 on earth will be **b** in heaven
Matt 27: 2 And when they had **b** Him, they
Mark 5: 4 often been **b** with shackles
Mark 6:17 **b** him in prison for the sake
Mark 15: 1 they **b** Jesus, led Him away,
Luke 13:16 of Abraham, whom Satan has **b**
John 11:44 who had died came out **b** hand
John 18:12 Jews arrested Jesus and **b** Him
John 19:40 **b** it in strips of linen with
Acts 9: 2 bring them **b** to Jerusalem
Acts 10:11 sheet **b** at the four corners
Acts 12: 6 **b** with two chains between two
Acts 20:22 now I go **b** in the spirit to
Acts 23:12 **b** themselves under an oath,
Rom 7: 2 **b** by the law to her husband
1Co 7:27 Are you **b** to a wife
1Co 7:39 A wife is **b** by law as long as
2Th 1: 3 We are **b** to thank God always
Rev 20: 2 **b** him for a thousand years

BOUNDARIES (*see* BOUNDARY)
Num 34: 2 the land of Canaan to its **b**
Deut 32: 8 He set the **b** of the peoples
Acts 17:26 the **b** of their habitation,

BOUNDARY (*see* BOUNDARIES)
Num 22:36 Arnon, the **b** of the territory
Job 26:10 at the **b** of light and darkness
Ps 104: 9 You have set a **b** that they
Prov 15:25 establish the **b** of the widow

BOUNDLESS† (*see* BOUNDS)
Nah 3: 9 her strength, and it was **b**

BOUNDS (*see* BOUNDLESS)
Ex 19:23 Set **b** around the mountain and

BOUNTIFUL† (*see* BOUNTIFULLY, BOUNTY, GENEROUS)
Is 32: 5 nor the miser said to be **b**
Jer 2: 7 brought you into a **b** country

BOUNTIFULLY (*see* BOUNTIFUL)
Num 23:11 look, you have blessed them **b**
Ps 13: 6 He has dealt **b** with me
2Co 9: 6 who sows **b** will also reap **b**

BOUNTY (*see* BOUNTIFUL, GENEROSITY)
Hos 10: 1 According to the **b** of his

BOW (*see* BOWED, BOWING, BOWMEN, BOWS, BOWSHOT, BOWSTRING)
Gen 37:10 brothers indeed come to **b**
Gen 41:43 out before him, "**B** the knee
Ex 20: 5 you shall not **b** down to them
2Sa 1:18 of Judah the Song of the **B**
1Ki 22:34 man drew a **b** at random, and
2Ki 5:18 I **b** down in the temple of
2Ki 13:15 Take a **b** and some arrows
Job 20:24 a bronze **b** will pierce him
Job 39: 3 They **b** down, they bring forth
Ps 7:12 He bends His **b** and makes it
Ps 11: 2 The wicked bend their **b**, They
Ps 44: 6 For I will not trust in my **b**
Ps 78:57 aside like a treacherous **b**
Ps 86: 1 **B** down Your ear, O LORD, hear
Ps 95: 6 let us worship and **b** down
Ps 144: 5 **B** down Your heavens, O LORD,
Eccl 12: 3 and the strong men **b** down
Is 45:23 that to Me every knee shall **b**

Is   46: 2 stoop, they **b** down together
Lam   3:12 He has bent His **b** and set me
Ezek   39: 3 the **b** out of your left hand
Hos   1: 5 day that I will break the **b**
Hos   7:16 they are like a treacherous **b**
Mic   6: 6 **b** myself before the High God
Zech   9:10 the battle **b** shall be cut off
Zech   9:13 For I have bent Judah, My **b**
Rom   11:10 and **b** down their back always
Rom   14:11 every knee shall **b** to Me
Eph   3:14 For this reason I **b** my knees
Phil   2:10 of Jesus every knee should **b**

BOWED (see BOW)
Gen   33: 3 **b** himself to the ground seven
Gen   37: 7 around and **b** down to my sheaf
Gen   37: 9 the eleven stars **b** down to me
Ex   18: 7 **b** down, and kissed him
1Sa   4:19 she **b** herself and gave birth,
2Sa   22:10 He **b** the heavens also, and
1Ki   19:18 knees have not **b** to Baal, and
2Ch   20:18 Jerusalem **b** before the LORD
Ps   38: 6 troubled, I am **b** down greatly
Ps   44:25 For our soul is **b** down to the
Ps   146: 8 raises those who are **b** down
Hab   3: 6 the perpetual hills **b**
Matt   27:29 they **b** the knee before Him and
Luke   24: 5 **b** their faces to the earth,
Rom   11: 4 have not **b** the knee to Baal

BOWING † (see BOW)
Gen   24:52 LORD, **b** himself to the earth
Ezra   10: 1 **b** down before the house of
Is   60:14 you shall come **b** to you, and
Mark   15:19 **b** the knee, they worshiped
John   19:30 **b** His head, He gave up His

BOWL (see BOWLFUL, BOWLS, BOWL-SHAPED)
Deut   28: 5 basket and your kneading **b**
Judg   5:25 out cream in a lordly **b**
2Ki   2:20 Bring me a new **b**, and put salt
1Ch   28:17 gold by weight for every **b**
1Ch   28:17 silver by weight for every **b**
Prov   19:24 man buries his hand in the **b**
Eccl   12: 6 or the golden **b** is broken
Zech   4: 2 gold with a **b** on top of it
Rev   16: 2 out his **b** upon the earth, and
Rev   16: 3 poured out his **b** on the sea

BOWLFUL (see BOWL)
Judg   6:38 of the fleece, a **b** of water

BOWLS (see BOWL)
Ex   8: 3 and into your kneading **b**
Ex   25:31 shaft, its branches, its **b**
Num   4: 7 the dishes, the pans, the **b**
Num   7:84 platters, twelve silver **b**
1Ki   7:45 pots, the shovels, and the **b**
1Ki   7:50 basins, the trimmers, the **b**
1Ch   28:17 of pure gold, and the golden **b**
Jer   35: 5 the Rechabites full of wine
Amos   6: 6 who drink wine from **b**, and
Rev   5: 8 golden **b** full of incense,
Rev   15: 7 **b** full of the wrath of God
Rev   17: 1 who had the seven **b** came and

BOWL-SHAPED (see BOWL)
1Ki   7:41 the two **b** capitals that were

BOWMEN † (see BOW)
Jer   4:29 noise of the horsemen and **b**

BOWS (see BOW)
Gen   49: 9 He **b** down, he lies down as a
Ps   37:15 And their **b** shall be broken
Is   46: 1 Bel **b** down, Nebo stoops

BOWSHOT † (see BOW)
Gen   21:16 at a distance of about a **b**

BOWSTRING † (see BOW, BOWSTRINGS)
Job   30:11 Because He has loosed my **b**

BOWSTRINGS (see BOWSTRING)
Judg   16: 7 bind me with seven fresh **b**

BOX (see BOXES)
Is   41:19 pine and the **b** tree together,
John   12: 6 a thief, and had the money **b**
John   13:29 because Judas had the money **b**

BOXES † (see BOX)
Is   3:20 the perfume **b**, the charms,

BOY (see BOY'S, BOYS)
Gen   21:15 she placed the **b** under one of
1Sa   3: 1 Then the **b** Samuel ministered
Luke   2:43 The **B** Jesus lingered behind

BOY'S † (see BOY)
Judg   3:12 will be the **b** rule of life

BOYS † (see BOY)
Gen   25:27 So the **b** grew. And Esau was
Lam   5:13 **b** staggered under loads of
Zech   8: 5 the city shall be full of **b**

BRACED †
Judg   16:29 he **b** himself against them,

BRACELET † (see BRACELETS)
2Sa   1:10 the **b** that was on his arm, and

BRACELETS (see BRACELET)
Gen   24:47 nose and the **b** on her wrists

BRAIDED
Ex   28:14 of pure gold like **b** cords
1Ti   2: 9 not with **b** hair or gold or

BRAMBLE (see BRAMBLES)
Judg   9:14 all the trees said to the **b**
Luke   6:44 gather grapes from a **b** bush

BRAMBLES † (see BRAMBLE)
Is   34:13 and **b** in its fortresses

BRANCH (see BRANCHES)
Ex   25:33 like almond blossoms on one **b**
Job   15:32 and his **b** will not be green
Job   18:16 below, and his **b** withers above
Is   4: 2 In that day the **B** of the LORD
Is   11: 1 a **B** shall grow out of his
Jer   1:11 I see a **b** of an almond tree
Jer   23: 5 to David a **B** of righteousness
Ezek   8:17 they put the **b** to their nose
Dan   11: 7 But from a **b** of her roots one
Zech   3: 8 forth My Servant the **B**
Zech   6:12 the Man whose name is the **B**
Zech   6:12 From His place He shall **b** out
Mal   4: 1 leave them neither root nor **b**
Matt   24:32 When its **b** has already become
John   15: 2 every **b** that bears fruit He

BRANCHES (see BRANCH)
Gen   40:10 and in the vine were three **b**
Gen   40:12 The three **b** are three days
Ex   25:31 Its shaft, its **b**, its bowls,
Lev   23:40 **b** of palm trees, the boughs
Neh   8:15 mountain, and bring olive **b**
Ps   80:11 Sea, And her **b** to the River
Ps   104:12 They sing among the **b**
Jer   11:16 on it, and its **b** are broken
Ezek   17:22 highest **b** of the high cedar
Ezek   36: 8 you shall shoot forth your **b**
Dan   4:12 of the heavens dwelt in its **b**
Hos   14: 6 His **b** shall spread
Zech   4:12 olive **b** that drip into the
Matt   13:32 the air come and nest in its **b**
Mark   4:32 herbs, and shoots out large **b**
John   12:13 took **b** of palm trees and went
John   15: 5 I am the vine, you are the **b**

Rom	11:16	root is holy, so are the **b**
Rom	11:21	did not spare the natural **b**
Rom	11:24	these, who are the natural **b**
Rev	7: 9	with palm **b** in their hands,

BRAND† (*see* BRANDING)
| Zech | 3: 2 | Is this not a **b** plucked from |

BRANDING† (*see* BRAND)
| Is | 3:24 | and **b** instead of beauty |

BRANDISH† (*see* BRANDISHED)
| Ezek | 32:10 | when I **b** My sword before them |

BRANDISHED† (*see* BRANDISH)
| Nah | 2: 3 | and the spears are **b** |

BRASS
1Co	13: 1	**b** or a clanging cymbal
Rev	1:15	His feet were like fine **b**
Rev	9:20	and idols of gold, silver, **b**

BRAVE†
| 1Co | 16:13 | stand fast in the faith, be **b** |

BRAWLER
| Prov | 20: 1 | Strong drink is a brawler |

BRAY† (*see* BRAYED)
| Job | 6: 5 | donkey **b** when it has grass |

BRAYED† (*see* BRAY)
| Job | 30: 7 | Among the bushes they **b**, |

BRAZEN†
| Ezek | 16:30 | the deeds of a **b** harlot |

BREACH (*see* BREACHED, BREACHES)
| Ps | 106:23 | one stood before Him in the **b** |
| Is | 58:12 | called the Repairer of the **B** |

BREACHED† (*see* BREACH)
| Ezek | 26:10 | enter a city that has been **b** |

BREACHES† (*see* BREACH)
| Ps | 60: 2 | Heal its **b**, for it is shaking |

BREAD
Gen	3:19	eat **b** till you return to the
Gen	14:18	king of Salem brought out **b**
Gen	19: 3	feast, and baked unleavened **b**
Gen	41:55	people cried to Pharaoh for **b**
Gen	47:13	was no **b** in all the land
Ex	12:15	you shall eat unleavened **b**
Ex	12:17	the Feast of Unleavened **B**
Ex	13: 3	No leavened **b** shall be eaten
Ex	16: 4	I will rain **b** from heaven for
Ex	16:4	he set the **b** in order upon it
Lev	21: 6	fire, and the **b** of their God
Lev	23:20	the **b** of the firstfruits as a
Deut	8: 3	man shall not live by **b** alone
Deut	16: 3	the **b** of affliction (for you
Judg	7:13	a loaf of barley **b** tumbled
Ruth	1: 6	His people in giving them **b**
1Sa	2: 5	hired themselves out for **b**
1Sa	21: 6	So the priest gave him holy **b**
1Sa	30:11	and they gave him **b** and he ate,
2Sa	9:10	eat **b** at my table always
1Ki	13:22	Eat no **b** and drink no water,"
1Ki	17: 6	The ravens brought him **b** and
1Ki	18:13	to a cave, and fed them with **b**
2Ki	18:32	and new wine, a land of **b** and
2Ki	25:29	he ate **b** regularly before the
1Ch	16: 3	to everyone a loaf of **b**, a
2Ch	35:17	Unleavened **B** for seven days
Neh	9:15	You gave them **b** from heaven
Job	15:23	He wanders about for **b**,
Job	22: 7	withheld **b** from the hungry
Job	28: 5	the earth, from it comes **b**
Job	33:20	So that his life abhors **b**
Ps	37:25	Nor his descendants begging **b**
Ps	41: 9	whom I trusted, Who ate my **b**

Ps	78:24	given them of the **b** of heaven
Ps	80: 5	fed them with the **b** of tears
Ps	102: 9	For I have eaten ashes like **b**
Ps	127: 2	late, To eat the **b** of sorrows
Ps	132:15	will satisfy her poor with **b**
Prov	4:17	they eat the **b** of wickedness
Prov	6:26	is reduced to a crust of **b**
Prov	9:17	**b** eaten in secret is pleasant
Prov	12:11	land will be satisfied with **b**
Prov	20:17	**B** gained by deceit is sweet
Prov	22: 9	he gives of his **b** to the poor
Prov	23: 6	Do not eat the **b** of a miser
Prov	25:21	is hungry, give him **b** to eat
Prov	31:27	not eat the **b** of idleness
Eccl	9: 7	Go, eat your **b** with joy, and
Eccl	11: 1	Cast your **b** upon the waters,
Is	30:20	gives you the **b** of adversity
Is	44:19	also baked **b** on its coals
Is	55: 2	spend money for what is not **b**
Is	55:10	the sower and **b** to the eater,
Is	58: 7	share your **b** with the hungry
Jer	16: 7	Nor shall men break **b** in
Jer	37:21	of **b** from the bakers' street
Lam	1:11	her people sigh, they seek **b**
Lam	4: 4	the young children ask for **b**
Ezek	4:13	defiled **b** among the Gentiles
Ezek	4:16	they shall eat **b** by weight
Ezek	4:17	that they may lack **b** and water
Ezek	5:16	and cut off your supply of **b**
Ezek	12:18	eat your **b** with quaking, and
Ezek	12:19	eat their **b** with anxiety, and
Ezek	44: 3	it to eat **b** before the LORD
Hos	2: 5	my lovers, who give me my **b**
Amos	7:12	There eat **b**, and there
Amos	8:11	the land, not a famine of **b**
Matt	4: 3	that these stones become **b**
Matt	4: 4	Man shall not live by **b** alone
Matt	6:11	Give us this day our daily **b**
Matt	7: 9	who, if his son asks for **b**
Matt	15: 2	their hands when they eat **b**
Matt	15:26	good to take the children's **b**
Matt	16:12	to beware of the leaven of **b**
Matt	26:26	were eating, Jesus took **b**
Mark	6: 8	no bag, no **b**, no copper in
Mark	6:36	villages and buy themselves **b**
Mark	7: 2	disciples eat **b** with defiled
Mark	7: 5	but eat **b** with unwashed hands
Mark	14: 1	and the Feast of Unleavened **B**
Mark	14:12	the first day of Unleavened **B**
Luke	7:33	eating **b** nor drinking wine
Luke	11: 3	us day by day our daily **b**
Luke	14: 1	to eat **b** on the Sabbath, that
Luke	14:15	eat **b** in the kingdom of God
Luke	15:17	hired servants have **b** enough
Luke	22: 7	came the Day of Unleavened **B**
Luke	22:19	And He took **b**, gave thanks and
Luke	24:35	to them in the breaking of **b**
John	6:31	He gave them **b** from heaven
John	6:32	you the true **b** from heaven
John	6:33	For the **b** of God is He who
John	6:34	Lord, give us this **b** always
John	6:35	I am the **b** of life
John	6:41	I am the **b** which came down
John	6:51	I am the living **b** which came
John	6:51	the **b** that I shall give is My
John	6:58	He who eats this **b** will live
John	13:18	He who eats **b** with Me has
John	13:26	of **b** when I have dipped it
John	21: 9	and fish laid on it, and **b**
Acts	2:42	in the breaking of **b**, and in
Acts	2:46	and breaking **b** from house to
Acts	27:35	said these things, he took **b**
1Co	5: 8	the unleavened **b** of sincerity
1Co	10:16	The **b** which we break, is it
1Co	10:17	For we, though many, are one **b**

1Co 10:17 we all partake of that one **b**
1Co 11:23 which He was betrayed took **b**
1Co 11:26 as often as you eat this **b**
1Co 11:27 **b** or drinks this cup of the
2Th 3: 8 eat anyone's **b** free of charge
2Th 3:12 quietness and eat their own **b**

BREADTH
Judg 20:16 sling a stone at a hair's **b**
Is 8: 8 will fill the **b** of Your land
Rev 21:16 Its length, **b**, and height are

BREAK (*see* BREAKER, BREAKING, BREAKS, BROKE, BROKEN)
Gen 19: 9 came near to **b** down the door
Ex 9: 9 that **b** out in sores on man
Ex 9:10 that **b** out in sores on man
Ex 12:46 nor shall you **b** one of its
Ex 13:13 it, then you shall **b** its neck
Ex 32: 2 **B** off the golden earrings
Ex 34:20 then you shall **b** his neck
Lev 26:15 but **b** My covenant,
Num 9:12 nor **b** one of its bones
Deut 21: 4 they shall **b** the heifer's
Deut 31:20 provoke Me and **b** My covenant
Job 19: 2 **b** me in pieces with words
Ps 2: 3 Let us **b** Their bonds in
Ps 2: 9 You shall **b** them with a rod
Ps 10:15 **B** the arm of the wicked and
Ps 58: 6 **B** their teeth in their mouth,
Ps 89:31 If they **b** My statutes And do
Ps 98: 4 **B** forth in song, rejoice, and
Eccl 3: 3 a time to **b** down, and a time
Is 42: 3 A bruised reed He will not **b**
Is 44:23 **b** forth into singing, you
Is 55:12 the hills shall **b** forth into
Is 58: 6 and that you **b** every yoke
Is 58: 8 Then your light shall **b** forth
Jer 4: 3 **B** up your fallow ground, and
Jer 19:10 Then you shall **b** the flask in
Jer 28: 4 for I will **b** the yoke of the
Jer 30: 8 That I will **b** his yoke from
Jer 31:28 to **b** down, to throw down, to
Jer 48:12 his vessels and **b** the bottles
Jer 49:35 I will **b** the bow of Elam, the
Ezek 13:13 wind to **b** forth in My fury
Ezek 16:38 **b** wedlock or shed blood are
Ezek 16:39 and **b** down your high places
Ezek 23:34 you shall **b** its shards, and
Ezek 26: 4 of Tyre and **b** down her towers
Ezek 30:18 when I **b** the yokes of Egypt
Ezek 30:22 will **b** his arms, both the
Dan 2:40 that kingdom will **b** in pieces
Hos 4: 2 they **b** all restraint, with
Hos 10:12 **b** up your fallow ground, for
Joel 2: 7 and they do not **b** ranks
Matt 6:19 destroy and where thieves **b** in
Matt 9:17 or else the wineskins **b**, the
Matt 12:20 A bruised reed He will not **b**
John 19:33 dead, they did not **b** His legs
Acts 20: 7 came together to **b** bread,
1Co 10:16 The bread which we **b**, is it
Gal 4:27 **B** forth and shout, you who do

BREAKER† (*see* BREAK)
Rom 2:25 but if you are a **b** of the law

BREAKFAST
John 21:12 Come and eat **b**

BREAKING (*see* BREAK)
Ex 22: 2 If the thief is found **b** in
Ps 42:10 As with a **b** of my bones, My
Ps 144:14 there be no **b** in or going out
Ezek 16:59 the oath by **b** the covenant
Dan 7: 7 **b** in pieces, and trampling the
Luke 5: 6 of fish, and their net was **b**

Luke 24:35 to them in the **b** of bread
Acts 21:13 mean by weeping and **b** my heart
Rom 2:23 God through **b** the law

BREAKS (*see* BREAK)
Gen 32:26 Let Me go, for the day **b**
Lev 13:12 if leprosy **b** out all over the
Job 16:14 He **b** me with wound upon
Ps 29: 5 of the LORD **b** the cedars, Yes
Ps 46: 9 He **b** the bow and cuts the
Ps 119:20 My soul **b** with longing For
Prov 25:15 and a gentle tongue **b** a bone
Jer 19:11 as one **b** a potter's vessel,
Dan 2:40 inasmuch as iron **b** in pieces

BREAKTHROUGH
2Sa 5:20 before me, like a **b** of water

BREAST (*see* BREASTPLATE, BREASTS)
Ex 29:26 the **b** of the ram of Aaron's
Lev 10:14 The **b** of the wave offering and
Luke 18:13 to heaven, but beat his **b**
John 13:25 leaning back on Jesus' **b**
John 21:20 leaned on His **b** at the supper

BREASTPLATE (*see* BREAST)
Ex 28: 4 a **b**, an ephod, a robe, a
Is 59:17 put on righteousness as a **b**
Eph 6:14 put on the **b** of righteousness
1Th 5: 8 putting on the **b** of faith

BREASTPLATES (*see* BREASTPLATE)
Rev 9: 9 they had **b** like **b** of iron

BREASTS (*see* BREAST)
Gen 49:25 beneath, blessings of the **b**
Ps 22: 9 while on My mother's **b**
Song 1:13 lies all night between my **b**
Song 4: 5 Your two **b** are like two fawns
Hos 2: 2 adulteries from between her **b**
Luke 11:27 and the **b** which nursed You

BREATH (*see* BREATHE)
Gen 2: 7 his nostrils the **b** of life
Gen 7:22 the **b** of the spirit of life
2Sa 22:16 of the **b** of His nostrils
Job 4: 9 by the **b** of His anger they
Job 7: 7 remember that my life is a **b**
Job 9:18 not allow me to catch my **b**
Job 15:30 by the **b** of His mouth he will
Job 19:17 My **b** is offensive to my wife,
Job 27: 3 as long as my **b** is in me, and
Job 32: 8 the **b** of the Almighty gives
Job 34:14 Himself His Spirit and His **b**
Job 41:21 His **b** kindles coals, and a
Ps 78:39 A **b** that passes away and does
Ps 104:29 You take away their **b**, they
Ps 144: 4 Man is like a **b**
Ps 150: 6 that has **b** praise the LORD
Song 7: 8 of your **b** like apples,
Is 33:11 your **b**, as fire, shall devour
Jer 10:14 and there is no **b** in them
Ezek 37: 6 you with skin and put **b** in you
Ezek 37: 9 Prophesy to the **b**, prophesy,
Dan 5:23 who holds your **b** in His hand
Dan 10:17 now, nor is any **b** left in me
Hab 2:19 Yet in it there is no **b** at all
Acts 17:25 since He gives to all life, **b**
2Th 2: 8 with the **b** of His mouth and
Rev 13:15 **b** to the image of the beast

BREATHE† (*see* BREATH, BREATHED, BREATHES, BREATHING)
Ps 27:12 me, And such as **b** out violence
Ezek 37: 9 on these slain, that they

BREATHED (*see* BREATHE)
Gen 2: 7 and **b** into his nostrils the
Gen 25: 8 Then Abraham **b** his last and

Mark 15:37 a loud voice, and **b** His last
John 20:22 He **b** on them, and said to them

BREATHES (*see* BREATHE)
Deut 20:16 nothing that **b** remain alive

BREATHING (*see* BREATHE)
Josh 11:11 There was none left **b**
Acts 9: 1 still **b** threats and murder

BRED† (*see* BREED)
Ex 16:20 and it **b** worms and stank
Esth 8:10 horses **b** from swift steeds

BREED† (*see* BRED, BREEDS)
Lev 19:19 livestock **b** with another kind
Deut 32:14 and rams of the **b** of Bashan

BREEDS† (*see* BREED)
Job 21:10 Their bull **b** without failure

BRETHREN (*see* BROTHER)
Gen 9:25 servants He shall be to his **b**
Gen 13: 8 your herdsmen; for we are **b**
Gen 50:24 And Joseph said to his **b**, "I
Ex 2:11 a Hebrew, one of his **b**
Ex 4:18 return to my **b** who are in
Deut 1:16 Hear the cases between your **b**
Deut 17:15 one from among your **b** you
Deut 17:20 may not be lifted above his **b**
Deut 18:15 from your midst, from your **b**
Deut 18:18 like you from among their **b**
Deut 24: 7 **b** of the children of Israel
Ruth 4:10 be cut off from among his **b**
Neh 5: 1 wives against their Jewish **b**
Ps 22:22 declare Your name to My **b**
Ps 122: 8 For the sake of my **b** and
Ps 133: 1 how pleasant it is For **b** to
Prov 6:19 one who sows discord among **b**
Is 66: 5 Your **b** who hated you, who
Hos 2: 1 Say to your **b**, 'My people,'
Hos 13:15 he is fruitful among his **b**
Matt 5:47 And if you greet your **b** only
Matt 23: 8 the Christ, and you are all **b**
Matt 25:40 of the least of these My **b**
Matt 28:10 tell My **b** to go to Galilee,
Luke 22:32 to Me, strengthen your **b**
John 20:17 but go to My **b** and say to them
Acts 1:16 Men and **b**, this Scripture had
Acts 3:22 a Prophet like me from your **b**
Acts 7: 2 Men and **b** and fathers, listen
Acts 7:37 a Prophet like me from your **b**
Acts 12:17 things to James and to the **b**
Acts 15:33 from the **b** to the apostles
Acts 15:36 visit our **b** in every city
Acts 15:40 by the **b** to the grace of God
Acts 23: 6 Men and **b**, I am a Pharisee,
Rom 1:13 not want you to be unaware, **b**
Rom 8:12 Therefore, **b**, we are debtors
Rom 8:29 be the firstborn among many **b**
Rom 9: 3 accursed from Christ for my **b**
Rom 10: 1 **B**, my heart's desire and
Rom 12: 1 I beseech you therefore, **b**
Rom 16:17 Now I urge you, **b**, note those
1Co 1:10 Now I plead with you, **b**, by
1Co 1:26 For you see your calling, **b**
1Co 2: 1 And I, **b**, when I came to you,
1Co 6: 5 able to judge between his **b**
1Co 7:24 **B**, let each one remain with
1Co 8:12 you thus sin against the **b**
1Co 12: 1 concerning spiritual gifts, **b**
1Co 15: 6 over five hundred **b** at once
1Co 15:50 Now this I say, **b**, that flesh
1Co 15:58 Therefore, my beloved **b**, be
1Co 16:20 All the **b** greet you
2Co 1: 8 want you to be ignorant, **b**
2Co 11: 9 the **b** who came from Macedonia
2Co 11:26 sea, in perils among false **b**

2Co 13:11 Finally, **b**, farewell
Gal 6: 1 **B**, if a man is overtaken in
Eph 6:10 Finally, my **b**, be strong in
Eph 6:23 Peace to the **b**, and love with
Phil 1:12 But I want you to know, **b**
Phil 3: 1 Finally, my **b**, rejoice in the
Phil 3:13 **B**, I do not count myself to
Phil 4: 8 Finally, **b**, whatever things
Phil 4:21 The **b** who are with me greet
Col 1: 2 faithful **b** in Christ who are
Col 4:15 Greet the **b** who are in
1Th 1: 4 knowing, beloved **b**, your
1Th 2:14 For you, **b**, became imitators
1Th 4:10 **b** who are in all Macedonia
1Th 4:13 want you to be ignorant, **b**
1Th 5:25 **B**, pray for us
1Th 5:26 Greet all the **b** with a holy
2Th 1: 3 thank God always for you, **b**
2Th 2: 1 Now, **b**, concerning the coming
2Th 2:13 you, **b** beloved by the Lord,
2Th 2:15 Therefore, **b**, stand fast and
2Th 3: 1 Finally, **b**, pray for us, that
Heb 2:11 is not ashamed to call them **b**
Heb 2:12 declare Your name to My **b**
Heb 2:17 He had to be made like His **b**
Heb 3: 1 Therefore, holy **b**, partakers
Heb 10:19 Therefore, **b**, having boldness
Heb 13:22 And I appeal to you, **b**, bear
Jas 1: 2 My **b**, count it all joy when
Jas 1:16 not be deceived, my beloved **b**
1Pe 1:22 in sincere love of the **b**,
1Jn 2: 7 **B**, I write no new commandment
1Jn 3:13 Do not marvel, my **b**, if the
1Jn 3:14 life, because we love the **b**
1Jn 3:16 lay down our lives for the **b**
Rev 12:10 for the accuser of our **b**
Rev 22: 9 of your **b** the prophets, and of

BRIARS (*see* BRIERS)

BRIBE (*see* BRIBERY, BRIBES)
Ex 23: 8 And you shall take no **b**, for a
Ex 23: 8 for a **b** blinds the discerning
Deut 10:17 no partiality nor takes a **b**
Mic 3:11 her heads judge for a **b**, her

BRIBERY† (*see* BRIBE)
Job 15:34 will consume the tents of **b**

BRIBES (*see* BRIBE)
1Sa 8: 3 after dishonest gain, took **b**
2Ch 19: 7 partiality, nor taking of **b**
Amos 5:12 afflicting the just and taking **b**

BRICK (*see* BRICKS)
Gen 11: 3 They had **b** for stone, and
Ex 1:14 in mortar, in **b**, and in all
Ex 5: 7 straw to make **b** as before

BRICKS (*see* BRICK)
Gen 11: 3 Come, let us make **b** and bake
Ex 5: 8 of **b** which they made before
Ex 5:18 shall deliver the quota of **b**

BRIDE (*see* BRIDEGROOM, BRIDE-PRICE, BRIDES)
Is 49:18 bind them on you as a **b** does
Is 61:10 as a **b** adorns herself with
Is 62: 5 rejoices over the **b**, so shall
Jer 2:32 ornaments, or a **b** her attire
Jer 7:34 and the voice of the **b**
Joel 2:16 the **b** from her dressing room
John 3:29 He who has the **b** is the
Rev 21: 2 prepared as a **b** adorned for
Rev 22:17 And the Spirit and the **b** say

BRIDEGROOM (*see* BRIDE, BRIDEGROOM'S)
Ps 19: 5 Which is like a **b** coming out
Is 62: 5 as the **b** rejoices over the
Jer 7:34 gladness, the voice of the **b**

Matt	9:15	Can the friends of the **b** mourn
Matt	9:15	as long as the **b** is with them
Matt	25: 1	and went out to meet the **b**
Matt	25: 6	Behold, the **b** is coming
Mark	2:19	Can the friends of the **b** fast
John	2: 9	of the feast called the **b**
John	3:29	He who has the bride is the **b**
Rev	18:23	And the voice of the **b** and bride

BRIDEGROOM'S† (*see* BRIDEGROOM)
John	3:29	because of the **b** voice

BRIDE-PRICE† (*see* BRIDE)
Ex	22:16	the **b** for her to be his wife
Ex	22:17	according to the **b** of virgins

BRIDES (*see* BRIDE)
Hos	4:13	and your **b** commit adultery

BRIDLE (*see* BRIDLES)
2Ki	19:28	My **b** in your lips, and I will
Job	41:13	approach him with a double **b**
Ps	32: 9	be harnessed with bit and **b**
Prov	26: 3	a **b** for the donkey, and a rod
Jas	1:26	does not **b** his tongue but
Jas	3: 2	able also to **b** the whole body

BRIDLES† (*see* BRIDLE)
Rev	14:20	up to the horses' **b**, for one

BRIEFLY
1Pe	5:12	him, I have written to you **b**

BRIER (*see* BRIERS)
Is	55:13	instead of the **b** shall come
Ezek	28:24	no longer be a pricking **b** or

BRIERS (*see* BRIER)
Judg	8:16	thorns of the wilderness and with **b**
Is	7:24	all the land will become **b**
Heb	6: 8	but if it bears thorns and **b**

BRIGHT (*see* BRIGHTENED, BRIGHTER, BRIGHTNESS)
Lev	13: 2	swelling, a scab, or a **b** spot
1Sa	16:12	Now he was ruddy, with **b** eyes
Job	37:11	He scatters His **b** clouds
Jer	51:11	Make the arrows **b**
Ezek	1:13	the fire was **b**, and out of the
Matt	17: 5	a **b** cloud overshadowed them
Luke	11:36	as when the **b** shining of a
Acts	10:30	stood before me in **b** clothing
Rev	15: 6	clothed in pure **b** linen, and
Rev	19: 8	in fine linen, clean and **b**
Rev	22:16	the Offspring of David, the **B**

BRIGHTENED (*see* BRIGHT)
1Sa	14:27	and his countenance **b**

BRIGHTER (*see* BRIGHT)
Job	11:17	life would be **b** than noonday
Prov	4:18	that shines ever **b** unto the
Acts	26:13	**b** than the sun, shining

BRIGHTNESS (*see* BRIGHT)
Is	62: 1	righteousness goes forth as **b**
Ezek	1: 4	and **b** was all around it and
Ezek	10: 4	of the **b** of the LORD's glory
Dan	12: 3	like the **b** of the firmament
Joel	2:10	and the stars diminish their **b**
Amos	5:20	very dark, with no **b** in it
2Th	2: 8	with the **b** of His coming
Heb	1: 3	who being the **b** of His glory

BRIM
1Ki	7:23	from one **b** to the other
John	2: 7	they filled them up to the **b**

BRIMSTONE
Gen	19:24	Then the LORD rained **b** and
Deut	29:23	The whole land is **b**, salt,
Ps	11: 6	He will rain coals, Fire and **b**
Is	30:33	the LORD, like a stream of **b**

Ezek	38:22	great hailstones, fire, and **b**
Luke	17:29	**b** from heaven and destroyed
Rev	9:17	mouths came fire, smoke, and **b**
Rev	19:20	lake of fire burning with **b**
Rev	20:10	and **b** where the beast and the
Rev	21: 8	which burns with fire and **b**

BRISTLING†
Jer	51:27	to come up like the **b** locusts

BROAD (*see* BROADER, WIDE)
2Sa	22:20	brought me out into a **b** place
1Ch	4:40	pasture, and the land was **b**
Neh	3: 8	as far as the **B** Wall
Job	30:14	They come as **b** breakers
Job	37:10	and the **b** waters are frozen
Ps	119:96	commandment is exceedingly **b**
Is	33:21	be for us a place of **b** rivers
Jer	51:58	The **b** walls of Babylon shall
Amos	8: 9	the earth in **b** daylight
Nah	2: 4	one another in the **b** roads
Matt	7:13	**b** is the way that leads to
Matt	23: 5	make their phylacteries **b**

BROADER† (*see* BROAD)
Job	11: 9	the earth and **b** than the sea

BROILED†
Luke	24:42	gave Him a piece of a **b** fish

BROKE (*see* BREAK)
Ex	9:25	**b** every tree of the field
Ex	32: 3	So all the people **b** off the
Ex	34: 1	the first tablets which you **b**
Num	2:34	standards and so they **b** camp
Deut	10: 2	first tablets, which you **b**
Judg	7:19	**b** the pitchers that were in
Judg	7:20	trumpets and **b** the pitchers
Judg	15:14	his bonds **b** loose from his
Judg	16: 9	But he **b** the bowstrings as
Judg	16:12	But he **b** them off his arms
1Sa	5: 9	and tumors **b** out on them
1Ki	19:11	**b** the rocks in pieces before
2Ki	10:27	Then they **b** down the sacred
2Ki	14:13	**b** down the wall of Jerusalem
1Ch	15:13	LORD our God **b** out against us
1Ch	20: 4	war **b** out at Gezer with the
2Ch	26:19	leprosy **b** out on his forehead
Job	29:17	I **b** the fangs of the wicked,
Ps	74:13	You **b** the heads of the sea
Ps	74:14	You **b** the heads of Leviathan
Ps	74:15	You **b** open the fountain and
Ps	76: 3	There He **b** the arrows of the
Ps	106:29	the plague **b** out among them
Jer	28:10	Jeremiah's neck and **b** it
Jer	31:32	My covenant which they **b**
Ezek	17:16	and whose covenant he **b**
Dan	2:34	and clay, and **b** them in pieces
Dan	2:45	that it **b** in pieces the iron,
Dan	7:19	**b** in pieces, and trampled the
Dan	8: 7	the ram, and **b** his two horns
Matt	14:19	up to heaven, He blessed and **b**
Matt	15:36	**b** them and gave them to His
Matt	26:26	and **b** it, and gave it to the
Mark	8:19	When I **b** the five loaves for
Mark	8:20	when I **b** the seven for the
Mark	14: 3	she **b** the flask and poured it
John	5:18	He not only **b** the Sabbath
John	19:32	**b** the legs of the first and of
1Co	11:24	He had given thanks, He **b** it
Rev	12: 7	And war **b** out in heaven

BROKEN (*see* BREAK, BROKENHEARTED, DASHED)
Gen	7:11	of the great deep were **b** up
Gen	17:14	he has **b** My covenant
Lev	13:20	which has **b** out of the boil
Num	15:31	has **b** His commandment, that

1Sa	2: 4	bows of the mighty men are **b**
1Sa	5: 4	were **b** off on the threshold
Job	4:10	of the young lions are **b**
Job	17: 1	My spirit is **b**, my days are
Job	17:11	past, my purposes are **b** off
Job	24:20	should be **b** like a tree
Ps	3: 7	You have **b** the teeth of the
Ps	31:12	I am like a **b** vessel
Ps	34:18	to those who have a **b** heart
Ps	34:20	Not one of them is **b**
Ps	38: 8	I am feeble and severely **b**
Ps	51: 8	You have **b** may rejoice
Ps	51:17	a **b** spirit, A **b** and a
Ps	55:20	He has **b** his covenant
Ps	60: 1	You have **b** us down
Ps	89:10	You have **b** Rahab in pieces,
Ps	107:16	For He has **b** the gates of
Ps	109:16	even slay the **b** in heart
Prov	6:15	he shall be **b** without remedy
Prov	17:22	but a **b** spirit dries the
Eccl	4:12	cord is not quickly **b**
Eccl	12: 6	or the golden bowl is **b**, or
Eccl	12: 6	or the wheel at the well
Is	5:27	strap of their sandals be **b**
Is	9: 4	For You have **b** the yoke of
Is	14: 5	The Lord has **b** the staff of
Is	16: 8	have **b** down its choice plants
Is	19:10	And its foundations will be **b**
Is	21: 9	gods he has **b** to the ground
Is	24: 5	**B** the everlasting covenant
Is	33:20	will any of its cords be **b**
Is	36: 6	in the staff of this **b** reed
Jer	2:13	**b** cisterns that can hold no
Jer	2:16	Tahpanhes have **b** the crown of
Jer	4:26	all its cities were **b** down at
Jer	5: 5	have altogether **b** the yoke
Jer	22:28	man Coniah a despised, **b** idol
Jer	23: 9	My heart within me is **b**
Jer	28: 2	I have **b** the yoke of the
Jer	33:21	be **b** with David My servant
Jer	48:17	How the strong staff is **b**
Jer	50: 2	Merodach is **b** in pieces
Jer	50: 2	her images are **b** in pieces
Jer	50:17	of Babylon has **b** his bones
Jer	51:30	the bars of her gate are **b**
Jer	51:56	Every one of their bows is **b**
Jer	51:58	of Babylon shall be utterly **b**
Lam	3: 4	and my skin, and **b** my bones
Lam	3:16	He has also **b** my teeth with
Ezek	6: 6	incense altars shall be **b**
Ezek	6: 6	desolate, your idols may be **b**
Ezek	30:21	I have **b** the arm of Pharaoh
Ezek	31:12	its boughs lie **b** by all the
Ezek	32:28	you shall be **b** in the midst
Dan	11: 4	his kingdom shall be **b** up
Hos	8: 6	Samaria shall be **b** to pieces
Joel	1:17	barns are **b** down, for the
Jon	1: 4	the ship was about to be **b** up
Zech	11:16	nor heal those that are **b**
Matt	21:44	falls on this stone will be **b**
Matt	24:43	his house to be **b** into
Mark	2: 4	And when they had **b** through
Mark	5: 4	and the shackles **b** in pieces
Luke	20:18	falls on that stone will be **b**
John	7:23	law of Moses should not be **b**
John	10:35	and the Scripture cannot be **b**)
John	19:31	that their legs might be **b**
John	19:36	one of His bones shall be **b**
John	21:11	so many, the net was not **b**
Rom	11:17	of the branches were **b** off
Rom	11:19	Branches were **b** off that I
1Co	11:24	is My body which is **b** for you
Eph	2:14	has **b** down the middle wall of

BROKENHEARTED† (*see* BROKEN, HEART)

Ps	147: 3	He heals the **b** And binds up
Is	61: 1	He has sent Me to heal the **b**
Luke	4:18	He has sent Me to heal the **b**

BRONZE

Gen	4:22	of every craftsman in **b** and
Ex	25: 3	gold, silver, and **b**
Num	21: 9	he looked at the **b** serpent
Judg	16:21	They bound him with **b** fetters
1Sa	17: 5	He had a **b** helmet on his head
2Sa	8: 8	took a large amount of **b**
2Sa	22:35	my arms can bend a bow of **b**
1Ki	4:13	with walls and **b** gate-bars
1Ki	7:14	was a man of Tyre, a **b** worker
1Ki	7:45	the Lord were of burnished **b**
1Ki	14:27	made **b** shields in their place
2Ki	18: 4	broke in pieces the **b** serpent
1Ch	15:19	to sound the cymbals of **b**
1Ch	29: 2	**b** for things of **b**, iron
Job	6:12	Or is my flesh **b**
Job	20:24	a **b** bow will pierce him
Job	40:18	His bones are like beams of **b**
Job	41:27	as straw, and **b** as rotten wood
Ps	18:34	my arms can bend a bow of **b**
Is	48: 4	an iron sinew, and your brow **b**
Is	60:17	Instead of **b** I will bring
Is	60:17	silver, instead of wood, **b**
Jer	1:18	**b** walls against the whole
Jer	6:28	They are **b** and iron, they are
Jer	15:12	the northern iron and the **b**
Jer	15:20	people a fortified **b** wall
Jer	39: 7	bound him with **b** fetters to
Ezek	1: 7	like the color of burnished **b**
Ezek	22:18	they are all **b**, tin, iron, and
Ezek	24:11	and its **b** may burn, that its
Dan	2:32	its belly and thighs of **b**
Dan	2:39	another, a third kingdom of **b**
Dan	5: 4	the gods of gold and silver, **b**
Dan	7:19	of iron and its nails of **b**
Dan	10: 6	like burnished **b** in color
Zech	6: 1	mountains were mountains of **b**
Rev	18:12	of most precious wood, **b**,

BROOD (*see* BROODS)

Num	32:14	place, a **b** of sinful men, to
Is	1: 4	a **b** of evildoers, children
Matt	3: 7	said to them, "**B** of vipers
Luke	13:34	gathers her **b** under her wings

BROODS† (*see* BROOD)

Jer	17:11	that **b** but does not hatch

BROOK (*see* BROOKS)

Gen	32:23	them, sent them over the **b**
Lev	23:40	trees, and willows of the **b**
Josh	15:47	as far as the **B** of Egypt and
1Sa	17:40	five smooth stones from the **b**
2Sa	15:23	crossed over the **B** Kidron
1Ki	8:65	of Hamath to the **B** of Egypt
1Ki	17: 5	and stayed by the **B** Cherith
1Ki	17: 7	a while that the **b** dried up
1Ki	18:40	them down to the **B** Kishon
2Ki	23: 6	burned it at the **B** Kidron
2Ki	24: 7	the **B** of Egypt to the River
Job	6:15	dealt deceitfully like a **b**
Job	40:22	willows by the **b** surround him
Ps	110: 7	drink of the **b** by the wayside
Prov	18: 4	of wisdom is a flowing **b**
Is	15: 7	away to the **B** of the Willows
John	18: 1	disciples over the **B** Kidron

BROOKS (*see* BROOK)

Deut	8: 7	land, a land of **b** of water
Job	6:15	of the **b** that pass away,
Job	22:24	among the stones of the **b**
Ps	42: 1	deer pants for the water **b**

Is 37:25 dried up all the **b** of defense
Joel 1:20 for the water **b** are dried up

BROOM
1Ki 19: 4 and sat down under a **b** tree
Ps 120: 4 With coals of the **b** tree
Is 14:23 it with the **b** of destruction

BROTH
Judg 6:19 and he put the **b** in a pot
Is 65: 4 the **b** of abominable things is

BROTHER (see BRETHREN, BROTHERHOOD, BROTHERLY, BROTHER'S, BROTHERS)
Gen 4: 8 Cain rose against Abel his **b**
Gen 4: 9 Where is Abel your **b**
Gen 9: 5 the hand of every man's **b** I
Gen 14:14 that his **b** was taken captive
Gen 27:11 Esau my **b** is a hairy man, and
Gen 27:40 and you shall serve your **b**
Gen 27:41 then I will kill my **b** Jacob
Gen 27:43 flee to my **b** Laban in Haran
Gen 32:13 as a present for Esau his **b**
Gen 42: 4 **b** Benjamin with his brothers
Gen 42:15 your youngest **b** comes here
Gen 42:38 with you, for his **b** is dead
Gen 43: 3 unless your **b** is with you
Gen 45: 4 I am Joseph your **b**, whom you
Gen 45:12 the eyes of my **b** Benjamin see
Gen 45:14 fell on his **b** Benjamin's neck
Ex 4:14 not Aaron the Levite your **b**
Ex 7: 1 Aaron your **b** shall be your
Ex 28: 2 garments for Aaron your **b**
Lev 18:14 nakedness of your father's **b**
Lev 19:17 not hate your **b** in your heart
Lev 25:25 he may redeem what his **b** sold
Deut 15: 2 it of his neighbor or his **b**
Deut 15: 9 be evil against your poor **b**
Deut 15:11 open your hand wide to your **b**
Deut 15:12 If your **b**, a Hebrew man, or a
Deut 17:15 over you, who is not your **b**
Deut 23: 7 an Edomite, for he is your **b**
Deut 23:19 not charge interest to your **b**
Deut 25: 5 duty of a husband's **b** to her
Deut 25: 6 to the name of his dead **b**
Deut 32:50 your **b** died on Mount Hor and
Judg 9:21 for fear of Abimelech his **b**
Judg 20:23 the children of my **b** Benjamin
Judg 21: 6 grieved for Benjamin their **b**
Ruth 4: 3 belonged to our **b** Elimelech
2Sa 1:26 for you, my **b** Jonathan
2Sa 13: 4 Tamar, my **b** Absalom's sister
2Sa 13: 7 go to your **b** Amnon's house
2Sa 13:12 No, my **b**, do not force me,
2Sa 14: 7 Deliver him who struck his **b**
2Sa 14: 7 life of his **b** whom he killed
2Sa 20: 9 Are you in health, my **b**
2Sa 21:19 the **b** of Goliath the Gittite
2Sa 21:21 the **b** of David, killed him
1Ki 2:22 for he is my older **b**
2Ch 36: 4 his **b** Eliakim king over Judah
2Ch 36: 4 And Necho took Jehoahaz his **b**
2Ch 36:10 made Zedekiah, Jehoiakim's **b**
Neh 5: 7 is exacting usury from his **b**
Job 22: 6 from your **b** for no reason
Job 30:29 I am a **b** of jackals, and a
Ps 35:14 though he were my friend or **b**
Ps 49: 7 can by any means redeem his **b**
Ps 50:20 sit and speak against your **b**
Prov 17:17 a **b** is born for adversity
Prov 18: 9 is a **b** to him who is a great
Prov 18:19 A **b** offended is harder to win
Prov 18:24 who sticks closer than a **b**
Prov 27:10 nearby than a **b** far away
Eccl 4: 8 he has neither son nor **b**
Jer 9: 4 and do not trust any **b**

Jer 9: 4 for every **b** will utterly
Jer 22:18 for him, saying 'Alas, my **b**
Jer 23:35 and every one to his **b**, 'What
Jer 31:34 neighbor, and every man his **b**
Jer 34: 9 keep a Jewish **b** in bondage
Jer 34:14 man set free his Hebrew **b**
Ezek 18:18 robbed his **b** by violence, and
Ezek 44:25 for **b** or unmarried sister may
Hos 12: 3 He took his **b** by the heel in
Amos 1:11 pursued his **b** with the sword
Obad 10 violence against your **b** Jacob
Mic 7: 2 man hunts his **b** with a net
Zech 7: 9 compassion everyone to his **b**
Zech 7:10 in his heart against his **b**
Mal 1: 2 Was not Esau Jacob's **b**
Matt 4:18 called Peter, and Andrew his **b**
Matt 4:21 son of Zebedee, and John his **b**
Matt 5:22 whoever is angry with his **b**
Matt 5:24 First be reconciled to your **b**
Matt 7: 4 Or how can you say to your **b**
Matt 10:21 Now **b** will deliver up **b**
Matt 12:50 My Father in heaven is My **b**
Matt 14: 3 Herodias, his **b** Philip's wife
Matt 17: 1 Peter, James, and John his **b**
Matt 18:15 if your **b** sins against you
Matt 22:24 his **b** shall marry his wife and
Matt 22:24 raise up offspring for his **b**
Mark 1:16 Andrew his **b** casting a net
Mark 3:17 and John the **b** of James, to
Mark 3:35 does the will of God is My **b**
Mark 6: 3 **b** of James, Joses, Judas, and
Mark 12:19 to us that if a man's **b** dies
Mark 12:19 his **b** should take his wife and
Mark 12:19 raise up offspring for his **b**
Luke 3: 1 his **b** Philip tetrarch of
Luke 12:13 tell my **b** to divide the
Luke 15:32 be glad, for your **b** was dead
Luke 17: 3 If your **b** sins against you,
John 1:41 first found his own **b** Simon
John 11: 2 whose **b** Lazarus was sick
John 11:21 my **b** would not have died
John 11:23 her, "Your **b** will rise again
Acts 9:17 **B** Saul, the Lord Jesus, who
Acts 12: 2 the **b** of John with the sword
Rom 14:10 But why do you judge your **b**
Rom 14:10 you show contempt for your **b**
1Co 6: 6 **b** goes to law against **b**
1Co 7:12 If any **b** has a wife who does
1Co 8:11 shall the weak **b** perish, for
1Co 8:13 if food makes my **b** stumble
1Co 16:12 Now concerning our **b** Apollos
2Co 1: 1 will of God, and Timothy our **b**
2Co 2:13 I did not find Titus my **b**
Gal 1:19 except James, the Lord's **b**
Eph 6:21 doing, Tychicus, a beloved **b**
Col 1: 1 will of God, and Timothy our **b**
Col 4: 9 a faithful and beloved **b**, who
1Th 4: 6 defraud his **b** in this matter,
2Th 3: 6 every **b** who walks disorderly
2Th 3:15 but admonish him as a **b**
Phm 16 than a slave, as a beloved **b**
Heb 8:11 his neighbor, and none his **b**
Jas 1: 9 Let the lowly **b** glory in his
Jas 2:15 If a **b** or sister is naked and
Jas 4:11 He who speaks evil of a **b**
1Pe 5:12 our faithful **b** as I consider
2Pe 3:15 as also our beloved **b** Paul
1Jn 2: 9 in the light, and hates his **b**
1Jn 2:10 He who loves his **b** abides in
1Jn 3:17 goods, and sees his **b** in need
1Jn 5:16 If anyone sees his **b** sinning
Jude 1 **b** of James, To those who are
Rev 1: 9 I, John, both your **b** and

BROTHERHOOD† (*see* BROTHER)
Amos 1: 9 remember the covenant of **b**
Zech 11:14 break the **b** between Judah
1Pe 2:17 Love the **b**. Fear God
1Pe 5: 9 by your **b** in the world

BROTHERLY (*see* BROTHER)
Rom 12:10 to one another with **b** love
Heb 13: 1 Let **b** love continue
2Pe 1: 7 to godliness **b** kindness, and
2Pe 1: 7 and to **b** kindness love

BROTHER'S (*see* BROTHER)
Gen 4: 9 Am I my **b** keeper
Gen 4:10 The voice of your **b** blood
Gen 38: 8 Go in to your **b** wife and marry
Lev 18:16 the nakedness of your **b** wife
Deut 25: 9 will not build up his **b** house
Job 1:13 wine in their oldest **b** house
Matt 7: 3 at the speck in your **b** eye
Mark 6:18 for you to have your **b** wife
Rom 14:13 a cause to fall in our **b** way
1Jn 3:12 were evil and his **b** righteous

BROTHERS (*see* BROTHER)
Gen 9:22 and told his two **b** outside
Gen 34:25 Simeon and Levi, Dinah's **b**
Gen 37: 2 feeding the flock with his **b**
Gen 37: 5 dream, and he told it to his **b**
Gen 37:11 his **b** envied him, but his
Gen 37:28 so the **b** pulled Joseph up and
Gen 42: 3 So Joseph's ten **b** went down
Gen 42: 4 brother Benjamin with his **b**
Gen 42: 6 And Joseph's **b** came and bowed
Gen 42:13 Your servants are twelve **b**
Gen 45: 1 made himself known to his **b**
Gen 45:15 Moreover he kissed all his **b**
Gen 49: 5 Simeon and Levi are **b**
Gen 49:26 who was separate from his **b**
Gen 50:15 When Joseph's **b** saw that
Lev 25:48 One of his **b** may redeem him
Deut 25: 5 If **b** dwell together, and one
Josh 2:13 my father, my mother, my **b**
Judg 9:56 by killing his seventy **b**
Judg 11: 3 Then Jephthah fled from his **b**
Judg 21:22 **b** come to us to complain,
1Sa 16:13 him in the midst of his **b**
1Ch 4: 9 was more honorable than his **b**
1Ch 5: 2 Judah prevailed over his **b**
Job 6:15 My **b** have dealt deceitfully
Job 19:13 has removed my **b** far from me
Job 42:15 an inheritance among their **b**
Ps 69: 8 become a stranger to my **b**
Prov 19: 7 All the **b** of the poor hate
Jer 12: 6 For even your **b**, the house of
Matt 1: 2 and Jacob begot Judah and his **b**
Matt 12:46 **b** stood outside, seeking to
Matt 12:48 is My mother and who are My **b**
Matt 20:24 greatly displeased with the two **b**
Matt 22:25 there were with us seven **b**
Mark 3:31 His **b** and His mother came
Mark 3:33 Who is My mother, or My **b**
Mark 3:34 Here are My mother and My **b**
Luke 14:26 mother, wife and children, **b**
Acts 7:13 was made known to his **b**, and
Acts 28:11 figurehead was the Twin **B**
1Co 9: 5 the **b** of the Lord, and Cephas
1Pe 3: 8 love as **b**, be tenderhearted,

BROUGHT LOW
Ezek 17:14 that the kingdom might be **b**

BROW
Luke 4:29 they led Him to the **b** of the

BROWN
Gen 30:33 **b** among the lambs, will be

BRUISE (*see* BRUISED, BRUISES, BRUISING)
Gen 3:15 He shall **b** your head, and you
Gen 3:15 head, and you shall **b** His heel
Is 53:10 it pleased the LORD to **b** Him

BRUISED† (*see* BRUISE)
Lev 22:24 the LORD what is **b** or crushed
Is 42: 3 A **b** reed He will not break,
Is 53: 5 He was **b** for our iniquities
Matt 12:20 A **b** reed He will not break,

BRUISES† (*see* BRUISE)
Job 5:18 For He **b**, but He binds up
Is 1: 6 in it, but wounds and **b** and

BRUISING† (*see* BRUISE)
Luke 9:39 **b** him, it departs from him

BRUNT†
Num 14:33 bear the **b** of your infidelity

BRUSHWOOD†
Is 64: 2 as fire burns **b**, as fire

BRUTAL† (*see* BRUTALLY, BRUTE)
Ezek 21:31 you into the hands of **b** men
2Ti 3: 3 without self-control, **b**,

BRUTALLY† (*see* BRUTAL)
Deut 21:14 you shall not treat her **b**

BRUTE (*see* BRUTAL)
2Pe 2:12 like natural **b** beasts made to

BUCKET†
Is 40:15 nations are as a drop in a **b**

BUCKLER (*see* BUCKLERS)
Ps 35: 2 Take hold of shield and **b**, And

BUCKLERS (*see* BUCKLER)
Ezek 39: 9 both the shields and **b**, the

BUD (*see* BUDDED, BUDDING, BUDS)
Is 27: 6 Israel shall blossom and **b**

BUDDED (*see* BUD)
Heb 9: 4 the manna, Aaron's rod that **b**

BUDDING (*see* BUD)
Luke 21:30 When they are already **b**, you

BUDS (*see* BUD)
Num 17: 8 had sprouted and put forth **b**
1Ki 6:18 carved with ornamental **b**
1Ki 7:24 **b** encircling it all around

BUFFET†
2Co 12: 7 a messenger of Satan to **b** me

BUILD (*see* BUILDER, BUILDING, BUILDS, BUILT)
Gen 11: 4 let us **b** ourselves a city, and
Ex 20:25 you shall not **b** it of hewn
Num 23: 1 **B** seven altars for me here,
Deut 6:10 cities which you did not **b**
Deut 20:20 to **b** siegeworks against the
Deut 22: 8 When you **b** a new house, then
Deut 25: 9 not **b** up his brother's house
Deut 28:30 you shall **b** a house, but you
Josh 22:29 day, to **b** an altar for burnt
Josh 24:13 and cities which you did not **b**
1Sa 2:35 I will **b** him a sure house, and
2Sa 7: 5 Would you **b** a house for Me to
2Sa 7:13 He shall **b** a house for My
2Sa 7:27 saying, 'I will **b** you a house
1Ki 5: 3 my father David could not **b** a
1Ki 5: 5 I propose to **b** a house for
1Ki 8:18 to **b** a house for My name, you
1Ki 9:15 to **b** the house of the LORD,
1Ki 9:19 desired to **b** in Jerusalem
2Ki 19:32 nor **b** a siege mound against
1Ch 14: 1 carpenters, to **b** him a house
1Ch 22: 2 stones to **b** the house of God
1Ch 22: 6 charged him to **b** a house for

1Ch	22: 7	me, it was in my mind to **b** a
1Ch	22:19	**b** the sanctuary of the LORD
1Ch	28: 2	I had it in my heart to **b** a
1Ch	28: 6	Solomon who shall **b** My house
1Ch	29:19	to **b** the temple for which I
2Ch	2: 3	sent him cedars to **b** himself
2Ch	36:23	He has commanded me to **b**
Ezra	1: 2	He has commanded me to **b**
Ezra	4: 2	Let us **b** with you, for we
Neh	2:17	Come and let us **b** the wall of
Neh	2:18	Let us rise up and **b**
Neh	4:10	we are not able to **b** the wall
Job	19:12	**b** up their road against me
Ps	51:18	**B** the walls of Jerusalem
Ps	69:35	**b** the cities of Judah, That
Ps	89: 4	And **b** up your throne to all
Ps	102:16	For the LORD shall **b** up Zion
Ps	127: 1	They labor in vain who **b** it
Prov	24:27	and afterward **b** your house
Eccl	3: 3	break down, and a time to **b** up
Song	8: 9	a wall, we will **b** upon her a
Is	62:10	**b** up, **b** up the highway
Is	66: 1	the house that you will **b** Me
Jer	1:10	and to throw down, to **b** and to
Jer	6: 6	**b** a mound against Jerusalem
Jer	18: 9	and concerning a kingdom, to **b**
Jer	29: 5	**B** houses and dwell in them
Jer	31: 4	Again I will **b** you, and you
Jer	31:28	I will watch over them to **b**
Ezek	21:22	a siege mound, and to **b** a wall
Ezek	26: 8	you, **b** a wall against you, and
Ezek	28:26	**b** houses, and plant vineyards
Dan	9:25	**b** Jerusalem until Messiah the
Dan	11:15	**b** a siege mound, and take a
Mic	3:10	Who **b** up Zion with bloodshed
Hag	1: 8	**b** the temple, that I may take
Zech	6:12	He shall **b** the temple of the
Zech	6:13	He shall **b** the temple of the
Mal	1: 4	**b** the desolate places," Thus
Mal	1: 4	They may **b**, but I will throw
Matt	16:18	this rock I will **b** My church
Matt	23:29	Because you **b** the tombs of
Matt	26:61	God and to **b** it in three days
Luke	12:18	**b** greater, and there I will
Luke	14:28	you, intending to **b** a tower
Luke	14:30	saying, 'This man began to **b**
John	2:20	years to **b** this temple, and
Acts	7:49	What house will you **b** for Me
Acts	20:32	which is able to **b** you up
Rom	15:20	lest I should **b** on another
Gal	2:18	For if I **b** again those things

BUILDER† (*see* BUILD, BUILDERS)

1Co	3:10	as a wise master **b** I have
Heb	11:10	has foundations, whose **b** and

BUILDERS (*see* BUILDER)

1Ki	5:18	Solomon's **b**, Hiram's **b**
2Ki	12:11	**b** who worked on the house of
2Ki	22: 6	to carpenters and **b** and masons
2Ch	34:11	**b** to buy hewn stone and timber
Ps	118:22	The stone which the **b**
Matt	21:42	The stone which the **b**
Acts	4:11	which was rejected by you **b**
1Pe	2: 7	The stone which the **b**

BUILDING (*see* BUILD, BUILDINGS)

Gen	11: 8	and they ceased **b** the city
Josh	22:19	us, by **b** yourselves an altar
1Ki	6:38	So he was seven years in **b** it
Ezra	4: 4	They troubled them in **b**,
Ezra	5: 4	**b** for the **b** of this house of
Luke	6:48	He is like a man **b** a house
1Co	3: 9	God's field, you are God's **b**
2Co	5: 1	we have a **b** from God, a
Eph	2:21	in whom the whole **b**, being

Jude	20	**b** yourselves up on your most

BUILDINGS (*see* BUILDING)

Matt	24: 1	show Him the **b** of the temple
Mark	13: 2	Do you see these great **b**

BUILDS (*see* BUILD)

Josh	6:26	up and **b** this city Jericho
Ps	127: 1	Unless the LORD **b** the house
Ps	147: 2	The LORD **b** up Jerusalem
Prov	14: 1	Every wise woman **b** her house
Jer	22:13	Woe to him who **b** his house by
Ezek	13:10	one **b** a wall, and
Hab	2:12	Woe to him who **b** a town with
1Co	3:10	one take heed how he **b** on it
1Co	3:12	Now if anyone **b** on this

BUILT (*see* BUILD)

Gen	4:17	he **b** a city, and called the
Gen	8:20	Then Noah **b** an altar to the
Gen	11: 5	which the sons of men had **b**
Gen	12: 7	there he **b** an altar to the
Gen	13:18	**b** an altar there to the LORD
Gen	22: 9	Abraham **b** an altar there and
Ex	1:11	they **b** for Pharaoh supply
Ex	17:15	Moses **b** an altar and called
Ex	24: 4	**b** an altar at the foot of the
Deut	8:12	have **b** beautiful houses and
Josh	8:30	Now Joshua **b** an altar to the
2Sa	24:25	David **b** there an altar to the
1Ki	6: 2	King Solomon **b** for the LORD
1Ki	8:20	I have **b** a temple for the name
1Ki	8:43	have **b** is called by Your name
1Ki	9:10	Solomon had **b** the two houses
1Ki	9:26	King Solomon also **b** a fleet
1Ki	16:34	days Hiel of Bethel **b** Jericho
1Ki	22:39	the ivory house which he **b**
1Ch	17: 6	Why have you not **b** Me a
Ezra	6:14	And they **b** and finished it,
Neh	4: 6	so we **b** the wall, and the
Neh	12:29	for the singers had **b**
Job	3:14	who **b** ruins for themselves,
Ps	78:69	He **b** His sanctuary like the
Ps	89: 2	Mercy shall be **b** up forever
Ps	122: 3	Jerusalem is **b** As a city that
Prov	9: 1	Wisdom has **b** her house, she
Prov	24: 3	Through wisdom a house is **b**
Eccl	2: 4	I **b** myself houses, and planted
Eccl	9:14	and **b** great snares around it
Is	5: 2	He **b** a tower in its midst, and
Is	44:26	of Judah, 'You shall be **b**
Jer	7:31	they have **b** the high places
Jer	30:18	the city shall be **b** upon its
Jer	45: 4	what I have **b** I will break
Jer	52: 4	they **b** a siege wall against
Dan	4:30	that I have **b** for a royal
Dan	9:25	the street shall be **b** again
Amos	5:11	though you have **b** houses of
Hag	1: 2	the LORD's house should be **b**
Zech	1:16	my house shall be **b** in it
Zech	8: 9	that the temple might be **b**
Matt	7:24	who **b** his house on the rock
Matt	7:26	who **b** his house on the sand
Matt	21:33	winepress in it and **b** a tower
Mark	12: 1	for the wine vat and **b** a tower
Luke	4:29	on which their city was **b**
Luke	7: 5	and has **b** us a synagogue
Luke	17:28	sold, they planted, they **b**
Acts	7:47	But Solomon **b** Him a house
Eph	2:22	**b** together for a habitation
Col	2: 7	**b** up in Him and established in
1Pe	2: 5	are being **b** up a spiritual

BUL†

1Ki	6:38	year, in the month of **B**,

BULGE†
Ps 73: 7 Their eyes **b** with abundance
Is 30:13 a **b** in a high wall, whose

BULL (see BULL'S, BULLS)
Ex 29: 1 Take one young **b** and two rams
Ex 29: 3 in the basket, with the **b**
Ex 29:10 hands on the head of the **b**
Ex 29:11 kill the **b** before the LORD
Ex 29:12 some of the blood of the **b**
Ex 29:14 But the flesh of the **b**, with
Ex 29:36 you shall offer a **b** every day
Lev 4: 3 **b** without blemish as a sin
Lev 4: 4 the **b** to the door of the
Lev 4:21 carry the **b** outside the camp
Num 7:15 one young **b**, one ram, and one
Num 8: 8 **b** with its grain offering of
Num 23: 2 Balak and Balaam offered a **b**
Num 28:12 mixed with oil, for each **b**
Num 28:14 be half a hin of wine for a **b**
Num 28:20 ephah you shall offer for a **b**
Deut 18: 3 whether it is **b** or sheep
Deut 33:17 glory is like a firstborn **b**
Judg 6:25 Take your father's young **b**
1Ki 18:23 choose one **b** for themselves
1Ki 18:23 and I will prepare the other **b**
1Ki 18:33 cut the **b** in pieces, and laid
Job 21:10 Their **b** breeds without
Ps 50: 9 not take a **b** from your house
Ps 69:31 LORD better than an ox or **b**
Is 66: 3 He who kills a **b** is as if he

BULL'S (see BULL)
Lev 4: 4 lay his hand on the **b** head

BULLS (see BULL)
Num 8:12 on the heads of the young **b**
1Sa 1:24 him up with her, with three **b**
Ps 22:12 Many **b** have surrounded Me
Ps 22:12 Strong **b** of Bashan have
Ps 50:13 Will I eat the flesh of **b**
Ps 51:19 shall offer **b** on Your altar
Ps 66:15 I will offer **b** with goats
Ps 68:30 The herd of **b** with the calves
Is 1:11 not delight in the blood of **b**
Is 34: 7 young **b** with the mighty **b**
Jer 46:21 are in her midst like fat **b**
Jer 50:11 grain, and you bellow like **b**
Jer 52:20 the twelve bronze **b** which
Hos 12:11 they sacrifice **b** in Gilgal
Heb 9:13 For if the blood of **b** and
Heb 10: 4 possible that the blood of **b**

BULRUSH (see BULRUSHES)
Is 9:14 palm branch and **b** in one day
Is 58: 5 to bow down his head like a **b**

BULRUSHES† (see BULRUSH)
Ex 2: 3 she took an ark of **b** for him

BULWARKS†
Ps 48:13 Mark well her **b**
Is 26: 1 salvation for walls and **b**

BUNCH†
Ex 12:22 you shall take a **b** of hyssop

BUNDLE† (see BUNDLES)
Gen 42:35 surprisingly each man's **b** of
1Sa 25:29 lord shall be bound in the **b**
Song 1:13 A **b** of myrrh is my beloved to
Acts 28: 3 had gathered a **b** of sticks

BUNDLES (see BUNDLE)
Gen 42:35 father saw the **b** of money
Ruth 2:16 the **b** fall purposely for her
Matt 13:30 bind them in **b** to burn them

BURDEN (see BURDENED, BURDENS, BURDENSOME)
Gen 49:15 his shoulder to bear a **b**, and

Ex 18:22 they shall bear the **b** with you
Ex 23: 5 hates you lying under its **b**
2Sa 13:25 go now, lest we be a **b** to you
2Ki 9:25 the LORD laid this **b** upon him
2Ch 6:29 when each one knows his own **b**
Job 7:20 so that I am a **b** to myself
Ps 38: 4 Like a heavy **b** they are too
Ps 55:22 Cast your **b** on the LORD, And
Ps 81: 6 his shoulder from the **b**
Eccl 12: 5 the grasshopper is a **b**, and
Is 9: 4 have broken the yoke of his **b**
Is 15: 1 The **b** against Moab
Is 30:27 His anger, and His **b** is heavy
Is 46: 1 a **b** to the weary beast
Is 46: 2 they could not deliver the **b**
Jer 17:21 bear no **b** on the Sabbath day,
Ezek 12:10 This **b** concerns the prince in
Hos 8:10 because of the **b** of the king
Nah 1: 1 The **b** against Nineveh
Hab 1: 1 The **b** which the prophet
Zeph 3:18 to whom its reproach is a **b**
Zech 9: 1 The **b** of the word of the LORD
Zech 12: 1 The **b** of the word of the LORD
Mal 1: 1 The **b** of the word of the LORD
Matt 11:30 yoke is easy and My **b** is light
Matt 20:12 to us who have borne the **b**
Acts 15:28 to lay upon you no greater **b**
2Co 11: 9 I was a **b** to no one, for what
2Co 12:16 as it may, I did not **b** you
Rev 2:24 I will put on you no other **b**

BURDENED† (see BURDEN)
Prov 28:17 A man **b** with bloodshed will
Is 43:24 but you have **b** Me with your
2Co 1: 8 that we were **b** beyond measure
2Co 5: 4 in this tent groan, being **b**
2Co 8:13 should be eased and you **b**
1Ti 5:16 and do not let the church be **b**

BURDENS (see BURDEN)
Gen 49:14 lying down between two **b**
Ex 1:11 to afflict them with their **b**
Ex 2:11 brethren and looked at their **b**
Ex 6: 6 under the **b** of the Egyptians
Deut 1:12 bear your problems and your **b**
Neh 13:15 figs, and all kinds of **b**,
Is 58: 6 to undo the heavy **b**, to let
Matt 23: 4 For they bind heavy **b**, hard
Luke 11:46 load men with **b** hard to bear
Luke 11:46 **b** with one of your fingers
Gal 6: 2 Bear one another's **b**, and so

BURDENSOME (see BURDEN)
1Ki 12: 4 lighten the **b** service of your
Is 15: 4 his life will be **b** to him
2Co 11: 9 myself from being **b** to you
1Jn 5: 3 His commandments are not **b**

BURIAL (see BURY)
Gen 23: 4 for a **b** place among you, that
Gen 23: 6 the choicest of our **b** places
Gen 47:30 and bury me in their **b** place
Gen 50:13 as property for a **b** place
Eccl 6: 3 or indeed he has no **b**, I say
Jer 22:19 buried with the **b** of a donkey
Ezek 39:11 Gog a **b** place there in Israel
Matt 26:12 My body, she did it for My **b**
Mark 14: 8 to anoint My body for **b**
John 12: 7 kept this for the day of My **b**
Acts 8: 2 men carried Stephen to his **b**

BURIED (see BURY)
Gen 15:15 you shall be **b** at a good old
Gen 23:19 Abraham **b** Sarah his wife in
Gen 25:10 Abraham was **b**, and Sarah
Gen 50:13 and **b** him in the cave of the
Judg 12:10 died and was **b** at Bethlehem

Ruth	1:17	die, and there will I be **b**
1Ki	2:10	was **b** in the City of David
1Ki	14:31	was **b** with his fathers in the
2Ki	21:18	was **b** in the garden of his
2Ch	32:33	they **b** him in the upper tombs
Job	27:15	him shall be **b** in death, and
Eccl	8:10	Then I saw the wicked **b**, who
Jer	16: 4	lamented nor shall they be **b**
Jer	22:19	He shall be **b** with the burial
Matt	14:12	**b** it, and went and told Jesus
Luke	16:22	rich man also died and was **b**
Acts	2:29	that he is both dead and **b**
Acts	5: 6	up, carried him out, and **b** him
Acts	5: 9	**b** your husband are at the
Acts	5:10	her out, **b** her by her husband
Acts	13:36	was **b** with his fathers, and
Rom	6: 4	Therefore we were **b** with Him
1Co	15: 4	and that He was **b**, and that He
Col	2:12	**b** with Him in baptism, in

BURIERS† (see BURY)

Ezek	39:15	till the **b** have buried it in

BURIES (see BURY)

Prov	19:24	A lazy man **b** his hand in
Prov	26:15	The lazy man **b** his hand

BURN (see BURNED, BURNING, BURNS, BURNT)

Gen	44:18	anger **b** against your servant
Ex	3: 3	why the bush does not **b**
Ex	12:10	morning you shall **b** with fire
Ex	21:25	**b** for **b**, wound for wound,
Ex	27:20	the lamp to **b** continually
Ex	29:13	them, and **b** them on the altar
Ex	29:14	you shall **b** with fire outside
Ex	29:18	you shall **b** the whole ram on
Ex	29:34	morning, then you shall **b** the
Ex	30: 1	make an altar to **b** incense on
Ex	30: 7	Aaron shall **b** on it sweet
Ex	30: 8	he shall **b** incense on it, a
Ex	30:20	to **b** an offering made by fire
Ex	32:10	wrath may **b** hot against them
Lev	1: 9	the priest shall **b** all on
Lev	2:11	for you shall **b** no leaven nor
Lev	2:16	shall **b** the memorial portion
Lev	3: 5	Aaron's sons shall **b** it on
Lev	4:12	and **b** it on wood with fire
Lev	4:19	from it and **b** it on the altar
Lev	4:26	he shall **b** all its fat on the
Lev	8:32	bread you shall **b** with fire
Lev	13:24	a **b** on its skin by fire, and
Lev	13:24	and the raw flesh of the **b**
Lev	13:25	leprosy broken out in the **b**
Lev	17: 6	**b** the fat for a sweet aroma
Deut	7: 5	**b** their carved images with
Deut	12: 3	**b** their wooden images with
Deut	12:31	for they **b** even their sons and
Deut	13:16	completely **b** with fire the
Deut	29:20	would **b** against that man, and
Deut	32:22	shall **b** to the lowest hell
Josh	11: 6	**b** their chariots with fire
Josh	23:16	the LORD will **b** against you
Judg	9:52	the tower to **b** it with fire
Judg	12: 1	We will **b** your house down on
Judg	14:15	to us, or else we will **b** you
2Ki	16:15	On the great new altar **b** the
2Ki	23: 5	of Judah had ordained to **b**
2Ch	4:20	to **b** in the prescribed manner
2Ch	13:11	And they **b** to the LORD every
Job	30:30	my bones **b** with fever
Ps	79: 5	Your jealousy **b** like fire
Ps	89:46	Will Your wrath **b** like fire
Is	1:31	both will **b** together, and no
Jer	4: 4	**b** so that no one can quench
Jer	7: 9	**b** incense to Baal, and walk
Jer	7:31	to **b** their sons and their

Jer	36:25	the king not to **b** the scroll
Jer	44:17	to **b** incense to the queen of
Jer	44:25	to **b** incense to the queen of
Ezek	24:11	hot and its bronze may **b**, that
Ezek	39: 9	and **b** the weapons, both the
Ezek	43:21	**b** it in the appointed place
Amos	6:10	one who will **b** the bodies
Nah	2:13	I will **b** your chariots in
Hab	1:16	**b** incense to their dragnet
Mal	4: 1	is coming shall **b** them up
Matt	3:12	but He will **b** up the chaff
Matt	13:30	them in bundles to **b** them
Luke	1: 9	his lot fell to **b** incense
Luke	3:17	but the chaff He will **b** with
Luke	24:32	Did not our heart **b** within us
1Co	7: 9	marry than to **b** with passion
2Co	11:29	I do not **b** with indignation
Rev	17:16	her flesh and **b** her with fire

BURNED (see BURN)

Gen	38:24	Bring her out and let her be **b**
Ex	32:20	**b** it in the fire, and ground
Ex	40:27	he **b** sweet incense on it, as
Lev	7:17	third day must be **b** with fire
Lev	8:16	Moses **b** them on the altar
Lev	10:16	and there it was, **b** up
Num	11: 1	fire of the LORD **b** among them
Num	19: 5	and its offal shall be **b**
Deut	4:11	the mountain **b** with fire to
Deut	9:21	**b** it with fire and crushed it
Josh	6:24	But they **b** the city and all
Josh	8:28	So Joshua **b** Ai and made it a
Josh	11: 9	**b** their chariots with fire
Josh	11:11	Then he **b** Hazor with fire
Josh	11:13	Israel **b** none of them, except
Judg	15: 5	**b** up both the shocks and the
Judg	15: 6	**b** her and her father with fire
Judg	15:14	like flax that is **b** with fire
1Ki	3: 3	**b** incense at the high places
1Ki	9:16	**b** it with fire, had killed
1Ki	13: 2	men's bones shall be **b** on you
1Ki	15:13	and **b** it by the Brook Kidron
1Ki	16:18	**b** the king's house down upon
2Ki	1:14	**b** up the first two captains
2Ki	10:26	the temple of Baal and **b** them
2Ki	23: 6	**b** it at the Brook Kidron and
2Ki	23:11	he **b** the chariots of the sun
2Ki	23:15	and **b** the wooden image
2Ki	23:20	and **b** men's bones on them
2Ki	25: 9	He **b** the house of the LORD and
2Ki	25: 9	the great men, he **b** with fire
2Ch	36:19	**b** all its palaces with fire,
Neh	1: 3	and its gates are **b** with fire
Neh	4: 2	stones that are **b**
Esth	1:12	and his anger **b** within him
Job	1:16	and **b** up the sheep and the
Ps	39: 3	I was musing, the fire **b**
Ps	74: 8	They have **b** up all the
Ps	80:16	It is **b** with fire, it is cut
Ps	102: 3	my bones are **b** like a hearth
Ps	106:18	The flame **b** up the wicked
Prov	6:27	and his clothes not be **b**
Is	5: 5	its hedge, and it shall be **b**
Is	9:19	of hosts the land is **b** up
Is	24: 6	of the earth are **b**, and few
Is	44:19	I have **b** half of it in the
Jer	19:13	on whose roofs they have **b**
Jer	36:29	You have **b** this scroll,
Jer	39: 8	the Chaldeans the king's
Jer	49: 2	villages shall be **b** with fire
Jer	51:30	they have **b** her dwelling
Jer	51:32	reeds they have **b** with fire
Hos	11: 2	**b** incense to carved images
Joel	1:19	a flame has **b** all the trees
Amos	2: 1	because he **b** the bones of the

Matt	13:40	**b** in the fire, so it will be
Matt	22: 7	murderers, and **b** up their city
John	15: 6	into the fire, and they are **b**
Rom	1:27	**b** in their lust for one
1Co	3:15	If anyone's work is **b**, he
1Co	13: 3	though I give my body to be **b**
Heb	6: 8	cursed, whose end is to be **b**
Heb	12:18	and that **b** with fire, and to
Heb	13:11	sin, the **b** outside the camp
2Pe	3:10	that are in it will be **b** up
Rev	8: 7	third of the trees were **b** up
Rev	8: 7	and all green grass was **b** up
Rev	18: 8	will be utterly **b** with fire

BURNING (*see* BURN, BURNINGS)

Gen	15:17	a **b** torch that passed between
Ex	3: 2	the bush was **b** with fire, but the
Lev	6: 9	altar shall be kept **b** on it
Num	19: 6	of the fire **b** the heifer
Deut	5:23	the mountain was **b** with fire
Ps	11: 6	Fire and brimstone and a **b** wind
Ps	58: 9	pots can feel the **b** thorns
Ps	58: 9	As in His living and **b** wrath
Ps	140:10	Let **b** coals fall upon them
Prov	16:27	is on his lips like a **b** fire
Prov	26:21	As charcoal is to **b** coals
Is	4: 4	and by the spirit of **b**,
Jer	20: 9	a **b** fire shut up in my bones
Jer	36:22	with a fire **b** on the hearth
Lam	2: 6	In His **b** indignation He has
Ezek	1:13	was like **b** coals of fire, and
Dan	3: 6	midst of a **b** fiery furnace
Dan	7: 9	flame, its wheels a **b** fire
Dan	7:11	and given to the **b** flame
Amos	4:11	firebrand plucked from the **b**
Mal	4: 1	**b** like an oven, and all the
Mark	12:26	in the **b** bush passage, how
Luke	12:35	be girded and your lamps **b**
John	5:35	He was the **b** and shining lamp,
Rev	4: 5	of fire were **b** before the throne
Rev	8: 8	like a great mountain **b** with
Rev	8:10	like a torch, and it fell on
Rev	18: 9	they see the smoke of her **b**
Rev	19:20	lake of fire **b** with brimstone

BURNINGS† (*see* BURNING)

Is	33:12	shall be like the **b** of lime
Is	33:14	dwell with everlasting **b**

BURNISHED†

1Ki	7:45	of the LORD were of **b** bronze
2Ch	4:16	master craftsman made of **b**
Ezek	1: 7	like the color of **b** bronze
Dan	10: 6	feet like **b** bronze in color,

BURNS (*see* BURN)

Lev	16:28	Then he who **b** them shall wash
Ps	46: 9	He **b** the chariot in the fire
Ps	83:14	As the fire **b** the woods, And
Ps	97: 3	**b** up His enemies round about
Is	9:18	For wickedness **b** as the fire
Is	44:16	He **b** half of it in the fire
Is	62: 1	salvation as a lamp that **b**
Is	64: 2	as fire **b** brushwood, as fire
Is	65: 5	a fire that **b** all the day
Jer	48:35	and **b** incense to his gods
Hos	7: 6	in the morning it **b** like a
Joel	2: 3	and behind them a flame **b**
Rev	21: 8	in the lake which **b** with fire

BURNT (*see* BURN)

Gen	8:20	offered **b** offerings on the
Gen	22: 2	and offer him there as a **b**
Gen	22: 3	the wood for the **b** offering
Gen	22: 7	is the lamb for a **b** offering
Gen	22:13	ram, and offered it up for a **b**
Ex	30:28	the altar of **b** offering with

Lev	1: 3	is a **b** sacrifice of the herd
Lev	1: 4	on the head of the **b** offering
Lev	6:10	take up the ashes of the **b**
Lev	6:25	the **b** offering is killed, the
Lev	9: 3	blemish, as a **b** offering,
Lev	9:24	and consumed the **b** offering
Lev	14:19	he shall kill the **b** offering
Lev	14:20	shall offer the **b** offering
Num	7:15	first year, as a **b** offering
Num	7:87	All the oxen for the **b**
Num	19:17	**b** for purification from sin
Num	28: 3	day, as a regular **b** offering
Num	28:13	as a **b** offering of sweet
Deut	12:13	**b** offerings in every place
Judg	13:23	have accepted a **b** offering
1Sa	15:22	great delight in **b** offerings
2Sa	6:17	David offered **b** offerings
1Ki	9:25	Solomon offered **b** offerings
1Ki	18:33	and pour it on the **b** sacrifice
1Ki	18:38	and consumed the **b** sacrifice
2Ki	3:27	offered him as a **b** offering
2Ki	16:15	the blood of the **b** offering
1Ch	23:31	at every presentation of a **b**
2Ch	1: 6	a thousand **b** offerings on it
2Ch	13:11	and every evening **b** sacrifices
2Ch	29:24	commanded that the **b** offering
2Ch	29:31	heart brought **b** offerings
2Ch	29:32	the number of the **b** offerings
2Ch	35:14	busy in offering **b** offerings
Ezra	3: 4	offered the daily **b** offerings
Ezra	6: 9	lambs for the **b** offerings of
Ps	20: 3	And accept your **b** sacrifice
Ps	51:16	do not delight in **b** offering
Ps	66:13	Your house with **b** offerings
Ps	66:15	I will offer You **b** sacrifices
Is	1:11	enough of **b** offerings of rams
Is	40:16	sufficient for a **b** offering
Is	61: 8	I hate robbery for **b** offering
Jer	19: 5	fire for **b** offerings to Baal
Jer	51:25	and make you a **b** mountain
Ezek	40:38	they washed the **b** offering
Ezek	46:12	prince makes a voluntary **b**
Hos	6: 6	of God more than **b** offerings
Mic	6: 6	before Him with **b** offerings
Mark	12:33	all the whole **b** offerings
Heb	10: 6	In **b** offerings and sacrifices

BURST (*see* BURSTING, BURSTS)

Judg	20:33	**b** forth from their position
Job	32:19	it is ready to **b** like new
Job	38: 8	with doors, when it **b** forth
Is	35: 6	For waters shall **b** forth in
Jer	2:20	your yoke and **b** your bonds
Luke	5:37	new wine will **b** the wineskins
Acts	1:18	he **b** open in the middle and

BURSTING† (*see* BURST)

Ezek	32: 2	seas, **b** forth in your rivers,

BURSTS† (*see* BURST)

Mark	2:22	the new wine **b** the wineskins

BURY (*see* BURIAL, BURIED, BURIERS, BURIES, BURYING)

Gen	23: 4	that I may **b** my dead out of
Gen	47:29	Please do not **b** me in Egypt
Gen	49:29	**b** me with my fathers in the
Gen	50: 5	Canaan, there you shall **b** me
Deut	21:23	shall surely **b** him that day
1Ki	2:31	**b** him, that you may take away
Ps	79: 3	And there was no one to **b** them
Jer	7:32	for they will **b** in Tophet
Jer	19:11	till there is no place to **b**
Ezek	39:11	because there they will **b** Gog
Ezek	39:14	**b** those bodies remaining on
Matt	8:21	me first go and **b** my father
Matt	8:22	let the dead **b** their own dead
Matt	27: 7	field, to **b** strangers in

John 19:40 custom of the Jews is to **b**

BURYING (see BURY)
Num 33: 4 were **b** all their firstborn
2Ki 13:21 it was, as they were **b** a man
Ezek 39:12 of Israel will be **b** them, in

BUSH (see BUSHES)
Ex 3: 2 of fire from the midst of a **b**
Ex 3: 2 the **b** was burning with fire, but
Ex 3: 2 but the **b** was not consumed
Deut 33:16 of Him who dwelt in the **b**
Mark 12:26 in the burning **b** passage
Luke 6:44 grapes from a bramble **b**
Acts 7:30 him in a flame of fire in a **b**
Acts 7:35 who appeared to him in the **b**

BUSHES† (see BUSH)
Job 30: 4 who pluck mallow by the **b**
Job 30: 7 Among the **b** they brayed,

BUSINESS
Deut 24: 5 war or be charged with any **b**
Josh 2:14 of you tell this **b** of ours
1Sa 21: 2 king has ordered me on some **b**
1Ch 26:30 for all the **b** of the LORD
Neh 11:16 had the oversight of the **b**
Job 20:18 **b** he will get no enjoyment
Ps 107:23 Who do **b** on great waters,
Dan 8:27 and went about the king's **b**
Matt 22: 5 own farm, another to his **b**
Luke 2:49 I must be about My Father's **b**
Luke 19:13 to them, 'Do **b** till I come
John 2:14 and the moneychangers doing **b**
Acts 6: 3 we may appoint over this **b**
Rom 16: 2 **b** she has need of you
1Th 4:11 life, to mind your own **b**, and

BUSTLING†
Is 32:14 the **b** city will be deserted

BUSY†
1Ki 18:27 he is meditating, or he is **b**
1Ki 20:40 while your servant was **b** here
2Ch 35:14 were **b** in offering burnt
Ps 39: 6 Surely they **b** themselves in
Eccl 5:20 because God keeps them **b** with

BUSYBODIES† (see BUSYBODY)
2Th 3:11 not working at all, but are **b**
1Ti 5:13 idle but also gossips and **b**

BUSYBODY† (see BUSYBODIES)
1Pe 4:15 or as a **b** in other people's

BUTLER (see BUTLERSHIP)
Gen 40: 1 after these things that the **b**
Gen 40: 2 his two officers, the chief **b**
Gen 41: 9 Then the chief **b** spoke to

BUTLERSHIP† (see BUTLER)
Gen 40:21 chief butler to his **b** again

BUTTED†
Ezek 34:21 **b** all the weak ones with your

BUTTER†
Gen 18: 8 So he took **b** and milk and the
Ps 55:21 mouth were smoother than **b**
Prov 30:33 churning of milk produces **b**

BUTTOCKS
2Sa 10: 4 in the middle, at their **b**
Is 20: 4 with their **b** uncovered, to

BUTTRESS
2Ch 26: 9 at the corner **b** of the wall
Neh 3:19 Ascent to the Armory at the **b**
Neh 3:25 made repairs opposite the **b**

BUY (see BOUGHT, BUYER, BUYING, BUYS)
Gen 41:57 to Joseph in Egypt to **b** grain
Gen 42: 7 the land of Canaan to **b** food

Gen 47:19 **B** us and our land for bread,
Ex 21: 2 If you **b** a Hebrew servant, he
Deut 2: 6 you shall also **b** water from
Ruth 4: 5 On the day you **b** the field
Ruth 4: 5 you must also **b** it from Ruth
Ezra 7:17 be careful to **b** with this
Prov 23:23 **B** the truth, and do not sell
Is 55: 1 who have no money, come, **b**
Is 55: 1 **b** wine and milk without money
Jer 32: 7 **B** my field which is in
Jer 32:25 **B** the field for money, and
Amos 8: 6 that we may **b** the poor for
Matt 14:15 villages and **b** themselves food
Matt 25:10 And while they went to **b**, the
Mark 6:36 and **b** themselves bread
Mark 6:37 **b** two hundred denarii worth
Luke 9:13 **b** food for all these people
Luke 22:36 him sell his garment and **b** one
John 4: 8 away into the city to **b** food
John 6: 5 Where shall we **b** bread, that
John 13:29 **B** those things we need for
1Co 7:30 those who **b** as though they
Jas 4:13 a city, spend a year there, **b**
Rev 3:18 I counsel you to **b** from Me
Rev 13:17 that no one may **b** or sell

BUYER† (see BUY)
Prov 20:14 for nothing," cries the **b**
Is 24: 2 as with the **b**, so with the
Ezek 7:12 Let not the **b** rejoice, nor

BUYING† (see BUY)
2Ki 12:12 for **b** timber and hewn stone,

BUYS† (see BUY)
Lev 22:11 But if the priest **b** a person
Prov 31:16 She considers a field and **b** it
Matt 13:44 that he has and **b** that field
Rev 18:11 over her, for no one **b** their

BUZI†
Ezek 1: 3 the priest, the son of **B**, in

BUZZARD
Lev 11:13 the eagle, the vulture, the **b**

BUZZING†
Is 18: 1 land shadowed with **b** wings

BYGONE†
Acts 14:16 who in **b** generations allowed

BYPASSED†
Judg 11:18 **b** the land of Edom and the

BYWAYS†
Judg 5: 6 travelers walked along the **b**

BYWORD
Deut 28:37 a **b** among all nations where
1Ki 9: 7 and a **b** among all peoples
Job 30: 9 yes, I am their **b**
Ps 69:11 I became a **b** to them
Jer 24: 9 harm, to be a reproach and a **b**
Ezek 16:56 a **b** in your mouth in the days
Ezek 23:10 She became a **b** among women

C

CABLES†
Acts 27:17 they used **c** to undergird the

CAESAR (see AUGUSTUS, CAESAR'S, CLAUDIUS, TIBERIUS)
Matt 22:17 it lawful to pay taxes to **C**
Mark 12:17 Render to **C** the things that
Luke 2: 1 **C** Augustus that all the world
Luke 3: 1 of the reign of Tiberius **C**
John 19:12 a king speaks against **C**

CAESAREA

John	19:15	We have no king but **C**
Acts	11:28	in the days of Claudius **C**
Acts	17: 7	contrary to the decrees of **C**
Acts	25: 8	nor against **C** have I offended
Acts	25:11	me to them. I appeal to **C**

CAESAREA

Acts	8:40	the cities till he came to **C**
Acts	10: 1	man in **C** called Cornelius
Acts	25:13	came to **C** to greet Festus

CAESAREA PHILIPPI†

Matt	16:13	came into the region of **C**
Mark	8:27	went out to the towns of **C**

CAESAR'S (*see* CAESAR)

John	19:12	Man go, you are not **C** friend
Acts	25:10	I stand at **C** judgment seat,
Phil	4:22	those who are of **C** household

CAGE†

Jer	5:27	As a **c** is full of birds, so
Ezek	19: 9	put him in a **c** with chains
Hos	13: 8	I will tear open their rib **c**
Rev	18: 2	and a **c** for every unclean and

CAIAPHAS

Matt	26:57	Him away to **C** the high priest
Luke	3: 2	**C** were high priests, the
Acts	4: 6	as Annas the high priest, **C**

CAIN

Gen	4: 1	and she conceived and bore **C**
Gen	4: 2	but **C** was a tiller of the
Gen	4: 5	but He did not respect **C** and
Gen	4: 5	And **C** was very angry, and his
Gen	4: 8	that **C** rose against Abel his
Gen	4:15	And the Lord set a mark on **C**
Heb	11: 4	excellent sacrifice than **C**
1Jn	3:12	not as **C** who was of the
Jude	11	have gone in the way of **C**

CAINAN

Gen	5:10	After he begot **C**, Enosh lived
Luke	3:37	of Mahalalel, the son of **C**

CAKE (*see* CAKED, CAKES)

Ex	29:23	one **c** made with oil, and one
Lev	8:26	LORD he took one unleavened **c**
1Sa	30:12	him a piece of a **c** of figs
Hos	7: 8	Ephraim is a **c** unturned

CAKED† (*see* CAKE)

Job	7: 5	My flesh is **c** with worms and

CAKES (*see* CAKE)

Gen	18: 6	knead it and make **c**
Ex	12:39	they baked unleavened **c** of
Lev	7:12	or **c** of blended flour
1Ki	14: 3	with you ten loaves, some **c**
1Ch	12:40	**c** of figs and cup of raisins
Jer	7:18	to make **c** for the queen of
Ezek	4:12	you shall eat it as barley **c**
Hos	3: 1	the raisin **c** of the pagans

CALAMITIES† (*see* CALAMITY)

Ps	57: 1	Until these **c** have passed by

CALAMITY (*see* CALAMITIES)

Gen	42:38	If any **c** should befall him
Deut	32:35	the day of their **c** is at hand
1Ki	9: 9	brought all this **c** on them
2Ki	21:12	such **c** upon Jerusalem and
Job	30:13	up my path, they promote my **c**
Ps	18:18	me in the day of my **c**, But
Prov	1:26	I also will laugh at your **c**
Is	45: 7	I make peace and create **c**
Jer	1:14	Out of the north **c** shall
Jer	48:16	The **c** of Moab is near at hand
Jer	49: 8	bring the **c** of Esau upon him
Amos	3: 6	If there is **c** in a city, will

CALAMUS†

Song	4:14	spikenard and saffron, **c** and

CALCULATE† (*see* CALCULATED)

Rev	13:18	**c** the number of the beast

CALCULATED† (*see* CALCULATE)

Is	40:12	**c** the dust of the earth in a

CALDRON (*see* CALDRONS)

1Sa	2:14	into the pan, or kettle, or **c**
Ezek	11: 3	this city is the **c**, and we are
Mic	3: 3	the pot, Like flesh in the **c**

CALDRONS† (*see* CALDRON)

2Ch	35:13	they boiled in pots, in **c**

CALEB

Num	13: 6	Judah, **C** the son of Jephunneh
Num	14:24	But My servant **C**, because he
Josh	14:13	gave Hebron to **C** the son of
Josh	15:14	**C** drove out the three sons of
Judg	1:15	Then **C** gave her the upper
1Sa	25: 3	And he was of the house of **C**
1Ch	2:49	the daughter of **C** was Achsah

CALF (*see* CALVES)

Gen	18: 7	herd, took a tender and good **c**
Ex	32: 4	tool, and made a molded **c**
Ex	32:35	with the **c** which Aaron made
2Ch	11:15	the **c** idols which he had made
Ps	29: 6	makes them also skip like a **c**
Prov	15:17	than a fatted **c** with hatred
Jer	34:18	when they cut the **c** in two
Jer	34:19	between the parts of the **c**
Hos	4:16	is stubborn like a stubborn **c**
Luke	15:30	killed the fatted **c** for him
Rev	4: 7	living creature like a **c**, the

CALL (*see* CALLED, CALLING, CALLS)

Gen	2:19	to see what he would **c** them
Gen	4:26	Then men began to **c** on the
Gen	16:11	You shall **c** his name Ishmael,
Gen	30:13	daughters will **c** me blessed
Ex	2: 7	**c** a nurse for you from the
Deut	4: 7	reason we may **c** upon Him
Deut	4:26	I **c** heaven and earth to
Deut	30: 1	you **c** them to mind among all
Judg	18:12	(Therefore they **c** that place
Ruth	1:20	to them, "Do not **c** me Naomi
Ruth	1:20	**c** me Mara, for the Almighty
1Sa	3: 6	I did not **c**, my son
1Sa	3: 8	Here I am, for you did **c** me
1Sa	12:17	I will **c** to the LORD, and He
1Sa	14:17	Now **c** the roll and see who has
2Sa	22: 4	I will **c** upon the LORD, who
1Ki	18:25	**c** on the name of your god,
Job	14:15	You shall **c**, and I will answer
Job	19:16	I **c** my servant, but he gives
Ps	4: 1	Hear me when I **c**, O God of my
Ps	4: 3	will hear when I **c** to Him
Ps	50: 4	He shall **c** to the heavens
Ps	50:15	**C** upon Me in the day of
Ps	72:17	nations shall **c** Him blessed
Ps	77: 6	I **c** to remembrance my song in
Ps	91:15	He shall **c** upon Me, and I will
Ps	116: 2	Therefore I will **c** upon Him
Ps	145:18	is near to all who **c** upon Him
Prov	31:28	rise up and **c** her blessed
Is	5:20	Woe to those who **c** evil good
Is	7:14	shall **c** His name Immanuel
Is	31: 2	will not **c** back His words,
Is	55: 6	**c** upon Him while He is near
Is	58: 5	Would you **c** this a fast, and
Is	58:13	**c** the Sabbath a delight, the
Is	61: 6	men shall **c** you the Servants
Jer	3:19	You shall **c** Me, 'My Father,
Jer	9:17	**c** for the mourning women,

Jer	33: 3	**C** to Me, and I will answer
Dan	2: 2	command to **c** the magicians
Hos	1: 4	**C** his name Jezreel, for in a
Hos	1: 6	**C** her name Lo-Ruhamah, for I
Hos	1: 9	**C** his name Lo-Ammi, for you
Hos	2:16	no longer **c** Me 'My Master,'
Hos	7:11	they **c** to Egypt, they go to
Joel	1:14	a fast, **c** a sacred assembly
Joel	2:15	a fast, **c** a sacred assembly
Jon	1: 6	Arise, **c** on your God
Mal	3:12	nations will **c** you blessed
Matt	1:21	you shall **c** his name JESUS,
Matt	9:13	not come to **c** the righteous
Matt	19:17	Why do you **c** Me good
Matt	20: 8	**C** the laborers and give them
Matt	22:43	in the Spirit **c** Him Lord
Mark	15:12	you **c** the King of the Jews
Luke	1:13	you shall **c** his name John
Luke	1:48	generations will **c** me blessed
Luke	6:46	But why do you **c** Me 'Lord
John	4:16	**c** your husband, and come here
John	13:13	You **c** me Teacher and Lord,
John	15:15	No longer do I **c** you servants
Acts	2:39	as the Lord our God will **c**
Acts	10:28	**c** any man common or unclean
Acts	24:14	the Way which they **c** a sect
Rom	9:25	I will **c** them My people, who
Rom	10:12	is rich to all who **c** upon Him
Rom	10:14	How then shall they **c** on Him
1Co	1: 2	**c** on the name of Jesus Christ
2Co	1:23	Moreover I **c** God as witness
1Th	4: 7	For God did not **c** us to
2Ti	1: 5	when I **c** to remembrance the
Heb	2:11	ashamed to **c** them brethren
Jas	5:14	Let him **c** for the elders of
3Jn	10	I will **c** to mind his deeds

CALLED (see CALL)

Gen	1: 5	God **c** the light Day, and the
Gen	2:19	whatever Adam **c** each living
Gen	2:23	she shall be **c** Woman, because
Gen	3: 9	Then the LORD God **c** to Adam
Gen	3:20	Adam **c** his wife's name Eve,
Gen	12: 8	**c** on the name of the LORD
Gen	19:37	bore a son and **c** his name Moab
Gen	21:12	in Isaac your seed shall be **c**
Gen	22:11	the LORD **c** to him from heaven
Gen	29:32	son, and she **c** his name Reuben
Gen	31:47	Laban **c** it Jegar Sahadutha,
Gen	32:28	shall no longer be **c** Jacob
Gen	35:10	So He **c** his name Israel
Gen	35:18	but his father **c** him Benjamin
Gen	41: 8	**c** for all the magicians of
Ex	1:18	of Egypt **c** for the midwives
Ex	2: 8	went and **c** the child's mother
Ex	2:10	So she **c** his name Moses,
Ex	7:11	Pharaoh also **c** the wise men
Ex	8: 8	Then Pharaoh **c** for Moses and
Ex	16:31	of Israel **c** its name Manna
Ex	19:20	the LORD **c** Moses to the top
Josh	5: 9	place is **c** Gilgal to this day
Judg	1:26	its name Luz, which is its
1Sa	3: 4	that the LORD **c** Samuel
1Sa	3: 5	Here I am, for you **c** me
1Sa	3:10	stood and **c** as at other times,
1Sa	9: 9	for he who is now **c** a prophet
1Sa	9: 9	prophet was formerly **c** a seer
2Sa	5: 9	and **c** it the City of David
2Sa	6: 2	whose name is **c** by the Name
2Sa	12:24	son, and he **c** his name Solomon
2Sa	12:25	so he **c** his name Jedidiah,
1Ki	7:21	**c** its name Jachin, and he set
1Ki	7:21	the left and **c** its name Boaz
1Ki	18:26	**c** on the name of Baal from
2Ch	7:14	if My people who are **c** by My

Esth	9:26	So they **c** these days Purim,
Ps	18: 6	my distress I **c** upon the LORD
Ps	81: 7	You **c** in trouble, and I
Ps	88: 9	LORD, I have **c** daily upon You
Ps	99: 6	They **c** upon the LORD, and He
Ps	118: 5	I **c** on the LORD in distress
Prov	16:21	in heart will be **c** prudent
Prov	24: 8	do evil will be **c** a schemer
Song	5: 6	I **c** him, but he gave me no
Is	4: 1	only let us be **c** by your name
Is	9: 6	His name will be **c** Wonderful
Is	42: 6	have **c** You in righteousness,
Is	43: 7	everyone who is **c** by My name
Is	48:12	Me, O Jacob, and Israel, My **c**
Is	54: 5	He is **c** the God of the whole
Is	56: 7	for My house shall be **c** a
Is	62: 2	You shall be **c** by a new name,
Is	66: 4	Because, when I **c**, no one
Jer	7:10	house which is **c** by My name
Jer	25:29	city which is **c** by My name
Lam	3:55	I **c** on Your name, O LORD,
Dan	5:12	now let Daniel be **c**, and he
Hos	11: 1	and out of Egypt I **c** My son
Amos	7: 4	the Lord God **c** for conflict
Amos	9:12	Gentiles who are **c** by My name
Hag	1:11	For I **c** for a drought on the
Zech	11: 7	the one I **c** Beauty, and the
Zech	11: 7	and the other I **c** Bonds
Matt	1:16	born Jesus who is **c** Christ
Matt	1:25	And he **c** His name JESUS
Matt	2: 7	had secretly **c** the wise men
Matt	2:15	Out of Egypt I **c** My Son
Matt	2:23	He shall be **c** a Nazarene
Matt	4:18	two brothers, Simon **c** Peter
Matt	4:21	And He **c** them,
Matt	5: 9	they shall be **c** sons of God
Matt	5:19	so, shall be **c** least in the
Matt	5:19	he shall be **c** great in the
Matt	10: 1	And when He had **c** His twelve
Matt	13:55	Is not His mother **c** Mary
Matt	15:10	Then He **c** the multitude and
Matt	15:32	Then Jesus **c** His disciples to
Matt	18: 2	Jesus **c** a little child to Him
Matt	20:16	For many are **c**, but few
Matt	20:25	But Jesus **c** them to Himself
Matt	21:13	shall be **c** a house of prayer
Matt	23: 8	But you, do not be **c** 'Rabbi'
Matt	23:10	And do not be **c** teachers
Matt	26:36	them to a place **c** Gethsemane
Matt	27:16	notorious prisoner **c** Barabbas
Matt	27:22	do with Jesus who is **c** Christ
Matt	27:33	come to a place **c** Golgotha
Mark	10:49	Then they **c** the blind man,
Mark	14:72	Peter **c** to mind the word that
Mark	15:16	into the hall **c** Praetorium
Luke	1:35	born will be **c** the Son of God
Luke	1:36	for her who was **c** barren
Luke	1:60	he shall be **c** John
Luke	2: 4	which is **c** Bethlehem, because
Luke	6:15	and Simon **c** the Zealot
Luke	8: 2	Mary **c** Magdalene, out of whom
Luke	15:19	worthy to be **c** your son
Luke	19:29	at the mountain **c** Olivet
Luke	23:33	come to the place **c** Calvary
Luke	24:13	day to a village **c** Emmaus
John	1:42	You shall be **c** Cephas"
John	1:48	Before Philip **c** you, when you
John	4:25	is coming" (who is **c** Christ)
John	9:11	A Man **c** Jesus made clay and
John	12:17	He **c** Lazarus out of his tomb
John	15:15	but I have **c** you friends, for
John	19:13	place that is **c** The Pavement
John	19:17	Skull, which is **c** in Hebrew,
Acts	3: 2	temple which is **c** Beautiful
Acts	3:11	porch which is **c** Solomon's

Acts	5:21	c the council together, with
Acts	9:11	go to the street c Straight
Acts	9:11	for one c Saul of Tarsus, for
Acts	10: 1	man in Caesarea c Cornelius
Acts	10: 1	was c the Italian Regiment
Acts	11:26	first c Christians in Antioch
Acts	13: 2	work to which I have c them
Acts	13: 9	Then Saul, who also is c Paul
Acts	14:12	And Barnabas they c Zeus, and
Acts	15:17	Gentiles who are c by My name
Acts	15:37	to take with them John c Mark
Acts	16:28	But Paul c with a loud voice,
Acts	28: 1	that the island was c Malta
Acts	28:17	c the leaders of the Jews
Rom	1: 1	c to be an apostle, separated
Rom	1: 6	are the c of Jesus Christ
Rom	1: 7	of God, c to be saints
Rom	8:28	God, to those who are the c
Rom	8:30	predestined, these He also c
Rom	9: 7	In Isaac your seed shall be c
1Co	1:24	but to those who are c, both
1Co	1:26	mighty, not many noble, are c
1Co	7:15	But God has c us to peace
1Co	7:20	calling in which he was c
1Co	7:22	For he who is c in the Lord
1Co	15: 9	not worthy to be c an apostle
Gal	1:15	and c me through His grace,
Gal	5:13	have been c to liberty
Eph	2:11	who are c Uncircumcision by
Col	3:15	also you were c in one body
2Th	2: 4	is c God or that is worshiped
1Ti	6:20	what is falsely c knowledge
2Ti	1: 9	c us with a holy calling, not
Heb	5:10	c by God as High Priest
Heb	9: 3	which is c the Holiest of All
Heb	9:15	that those who are c may
Heb	11: 8	was c to go out to the place
Heb	11:16	not ashamed to be c their God
Heb	11:18	In Isaac your seed shall be c
Heb	11:24	refused to be c the son of
Jas	2: 7	noble name by which you are c
Jas	2:23	he was c the friend of God
1Pe	1:15	but as He who c you is holy
1Pe	2: 9	the praises of Him who c you
1Pe	2:21	For to this you were c,
1Pe	5:10	who c us to His eternal glory
1Jn	3: 1	should be c children of God
Rev	1: 9	was on the island that is c
Rev	11: 8	which spiritually is c Sodom
Rev	12: 9	c the Devil and Satan, who
Rev	16:16	to the place c in Hebrew,
Rev	19: 9	c to the marriage supper of
Rev	19:11	who sat on him was c Faithful
Rev	19:13	His name is c The Word of God

CALLING (see CALL)

Num	10: 2	use them for c the assembly
Matt	27:47	This Man is c for Elijah
Mark	3:31	they sent to Him, c Him
Mark	10:49	Rise, He is c you
Luke	7:19	c two of his disciples to him
John	11:28	has come and is c for you
Acts	7:59	Stephen as he was c on God
Acts	22:16	c on the name of the Lord
Rom	11:29	the c of God are irrevocable
1Co	1:26	For you see your c, brethren,
1Co	7:20	same c in which he was called
Eph	1:18	what is the hope of His c
Eph	4: 1	you to walk worthy of the c
2Ti	1: 9	us and called us with a holy c
Heb	3: 1	partakers of the heavenly c

CALLS (see CALL)

1Sa	3: 9	and it shall be, if He c you
Ps	42: 7	Deep c unto deep at the noise
Ps	147: 4	He c them all by name

Prov	1:20	Wisdom c aloud outside
Is	59: 4	No one c for justice, nor
Is	64: 7	is no one who c on Your name
Joel	2:32	c on the name of the LORD
Joel	2:32	the remnant whom the LORD c
Amos	9: 6	who c for the waters of the
Matt	22:45	If David then c Him 'Lord
John	10: 3	he c his own sheep by name and
Acts	2:21	c on the name of the LORD
Rom	9:11	of works but of Him who c)
Rom	10:13	whoever c upon the name of
1Co	12: 3	of God c Jesus accursed, and
1Th	2:12	c you into His own kingdom
1Th	5:24	He who c you is faithful, who
Rev	2:20	who c herself a prophetess,

CALM (see CALMED, CALMS)

Prov	17:27	is of a c spirit
Jon	1:11	that the sea may be c for us
Mark	4:39	ceased and there was a great c

CALMED† (see CALM)

Ps	131: 2	Surely I have c and quieted my

CALMS† (see CALM)

Ps	107:29	He c the storm, So that its

CALVARY† (see GOLGOTHA)

Luke	23:33	come to the place called C

CALVES (see CALF, CALVES')

1Sa	14:32	and took sheep, oxen, and c
1Ki	12:28	counsel and made two c of gold
2Ki	10:29	from the golden c that were
Ps	68:30	with the c of the peoples
Hos	13: 2	men who sacrifice kiss the c
Amos	6: 4	c from the midst of the stall
Mic	6: 6	offerings, with c a year old
Mal	4: 2	and grow fat like stall-fed c
Heb	9:12	with the blood of goats and c

CALVES' (see CALVES)

Ezek	1: 7	were like the soles of c feet

CAMEL (see CAMEL-LOADS, CAMEL'S, CAMELS)

Gen	24:64	she dismounted from her c
Lev	11: 4	the c, because it chews the
1Sa	15: 3	nursing child, ox and sheep, c
Zech	14:15	horse and the mule, on the c
Matt	19:24	it is easier for a c to go
Matt	23:24	out a gnat and swallow a c

CAMEL-LOADS† (see CAMEL)

2Ki	8: 9	thing of Damascus, forty c

CAMEL'S (see CAMEL)

Gen	31:34	put them in the c saddle
Matt	3: 4	himself was clothed in c hair

CAMELS (see CAMEL, CAMELS')

Gen	12:16	female donkeys, and c
Gen	24:10	took ten of his master's c
Gen	24:11	And he made his c kneel down
Gen	32:15	thirty milk c with their
Judg	6: 5	their c were without number
Judg	7:12	their c were without number
1Ki	10: 2	with a c that bore spices, very
1Ch	5:21	fifty thousand of their c
Is	21: 7	of donkeys, and a chariot of c
Is	30: 6	treasures on the humps of c
Jer	49:32	Their c shall be for booty,
Ezek	25: 5	make Rabbah a stable for c

CAMELS' (see CAMELS)

Judg	8:21	that were on their c necks

CAMP (see CAMPED, CAMPING, CAMPS, ENCAMP)

Gen	32: 2	This is God's c
Gen	32:21	lodged that night in the c
Ex	14: 2	you shall c before it by the
Ex	14:19	went before the c of Israel

Ex	16:13	at evening and covered the c
Ex	16:13	the dew lay all around the c
Ex	19:17	out of the c to meet with God
Ex	29:14	burn with fire outside the c
Ex	32:17	is a noise of war in the c
Ex	32:26	in the entrance of the c, and
Ex	36: 6	proclaimed throughout the c
Lev	4:12	the c to a clean place, where
Lev	4:21	carry the bull outside the c
Lev	14: 3	priest shall go out of the c
Lev	17: 3	or who kills it outside the c
Lev	24:10	fought each other in the c
Num	1:50	it and c around the tabernacle
Num	2: 2	shall c by his own standard
Num	2: 3	c according to their armies
Num	4:15	when the c is set to go, then
Num	5: 2	put out of the c every leper
Num	11: 1	in the outskirts of the c
Num	11: 9	fell on the c in the night
Num	11:31	other side, all around the c
Num	12:14	shut out of the c seven days
Num	15:35	him with stones outside the c
Deut	23:14	walks in the midst of your c
Deut	23:14	your c shall be holy, that He
Deut	29:11	the stranger who is in your c
Josh	5: 8	the c till they were healed
Josh	6:18	make the c of Israel a curse,
Josh	10: 6	to Joshua at the c at Gilgal
Judg	7: 8	Now the c of Midian was below
Ps	106: 16	they envied Moses in the c
Nah	3:17	which c in the hedges on a
Zech	9: 8	I will c around My house
Heb	13:11	sin, are burned outside the c
Rev	20: 9	the c of the saints and the

CAMPED (see CAMP)

Ex	15:27	so they c there by the waters
Ex	19: 2	Sinai, and c in the wilderness
Num	33:48	c in the plains of Moab by
Josh	4:19	they c in Gilgal on the east
Josh	10: 5	c before Gibeon and made war

CAMPING† (see CAMP)

Ex	14: 9	overtook them c by the sea

CAMPS (see CAMP)

Num	2:17	in the middle of the c
Num	5: 3	c in the midst of which I
Song	6:13	the dance of the two c
Amos	4:10	I made the stench of your c

CANA

John	2: 1	was a wedding in C of Galilee
John	2:11	Jesus did in C of Galilee
John	21: 2	Nathanael of C in Galilee

CANAAN (see CANAANITE)

Gen	9:18	And Ham was the father of C
Gen	9:25	Cursed be C; A servant
Gen	9:26	Shem, and may C be his servant
Gen	10: 6	were Cush, Mizraim, Put, and C
Gen	10:15	C begot Sidon his firstborn,
Gen	13:12	Abram dwelt in the land of C
Gen	28: 1	wife from the daughters of C
Gen	42: 5	famine was in the land of C
Gen	42: 7	the land of C to buy food
Gen	50:13	carried him to the land of C
Ex	15:15	of C will melt away
Lev	18: 3	the doings of the land of C
Lev	25:38	to give you the land of C
Num	13: 2	men to spy out the land of C
Num	35:14	appoint in the land of C,
Deut	32:49	view the land of C, which I
Josh	14: 1	inherited in the land of C
Josh	24: 3	throughout all the land of C
Judg	3: 1	known any of the wars in C
Judg	5:19	kings of C fought in Taanach

1Ch	16:18	of C as the allotment of your
Ps	106:38	sacrificed to the idols of C
Ps	135:11	And all the kingdoms of C
Is	19:18	will speak the language of C
Is	23:11	C to destroy its strongholds
Zeph	2: 5	the Lord is against you, O C
Matt	15:22	a woman of C came from that
Acts	13:19	nations in the land of C, He

CANAANITE (see CANAAN, CANAANITES)

Ex	33: 2	and I will drive out the C
Num	21: 1	When the king of Arad, the C
Josh	9: 1	Hittite, the Amorite, the C
Josh	13: 3	(which is counted as C)
Hos	12: 7	A cunning C! Deceitful
Zech	14:21	there shall no longer be a C
Matt	10: 4	Simon the C, and Judas

CANAANITES (see CANAANITE)

Gen	10:19	the border of the C was from
Gen	12: 6	the C were then in the land
Gen	13: 7	The C and the Perizzites then
Gen	15:21	the Amorites, the C, the
Gen	24: 3	from the daughters of the C
Ex	3:17	of Egypt to the land of the C
Num	13:29	the C dwell by the sea and
Num	14:25	the C dwell in the valley
Num	14:43	the C are there before you,
Num	21: 3	Israel and delivered up the C
Josh	3:10	out from before you the C
Josh	12: 8	Hittites, the Amorites, the C
Josh	16:10	out the C who dwelt in Gezer
Josh	17:12	but the C were determined to
Josh	17:13	put the C to forced labor
Josh	17:18	for you shall drive out the C
Judg	1: 3	we may fight against the C
Judg	1: 4	and the Lord delivered the C
Judg	1: 5	and they defeated the C and the
Judg	1:10	the C who dwelt in Hebron
Judg	1:17	and they attacked the C who
Judg	1:28	they put the C under tribute
Judg	1:32	Asherites dwelt among the C
Ezra	9: 1	to the abominations of the C
Obad	20	of the C as far as Zarephath

CANCER†

2Ti	2:17	message will spread like c

CANDACE†

Acts	8:27	of great authority under C

CANE

Ex	30:23	shekels of sweet-smelling c
Jer	6:20	sweet c from a far country
Ezek	27:19	c were among your merchandise

CANOPIES† (see CANOPY)

2Sa	22:12	made darkness c around Him
Ezek	41:26	of the temple and on the c

CANOPY† (see CANOPIES)

1Ki	7: 6	and a c was in front of them
Job	36:29	the thunder from His c
Ps	18:11	His c around Him was dark
Ezek	41:25	A wooden c was on the front

CAPABLE†

1Ch	26:31	them c men at Jazer of Gilead

CAPERNAUM

Matt	4:13	He came and dwelt in C, which
Matt	8: 5	Now when Jesus had entered C
Matt	11:23	And you, C, who are exalted to
Luke	4:23	we have heard done in C, do
Luke	10:15	And you, C, who are exalted to
John	2:12	After this He went down to C
John	4:46	whose son was sick at C
John	6:17	and went over the sea toward C
John	6:24	got into boats and came to C

John   6:59 synagogue as He taught in C

CAPITAL (*see* CAPITALS)
1Ki   7:16 of one c was five cubits, and
2Ki   25:17 the c on it was of bronze
2Ch   3:15 the c that was on the top of
Jer   52:22 pomegranates all around the c

CAPITALS (*see* CAPITAL)
Ex   38:17 of their c was of silver
Ex   38:28 the pillars, overlaid their c
1Ki   7:16 he made two c of cast bronze
1Ki   7:18 cover the c that were on top
1Ki   7:20 The c on the two pillars also
1Ki   7:20 on each of the c all around
1Ki   7:41 the two bowl-shaped c that
Zeph   2:14 lodge on the c of her pillars

CAPPADOCIA†
Acts   2: 9 in Mesopotamia, Judea and C
1Pe   1: 1 in Pontus, Galatia, C, Asia,

CAPSTONE†
Zech   4: 7 forth the c with shouts of

CAPTAIN (*see* CAPTAINS)
Gen   39: 1 c of the guard, an Egyptian,
2Ki   1: 9 c of fifty with his fifty men
2Ki   25:11 Then Nebuzaradan the c of the
Prov   6: 7 which, having no c, overseer
Dan   2:14 the c of the king's guard,
Dan   2:15 said to Arioch the king's c
Jon   1: 6 So the c came to him, and said
John   18:12 detachment of troops and the c
Acts   4: 1 the c of the temple, and the
Acts   28:16 to the c of the guard
Heb   2:10 glory, to make the c of their

CAPTAINS (*see* CAPTAIN, GENERALS)
Ex   14: 7 with c over every one of them
Ex   15: 4 His chosen c also are drowned
Num   31:14 with the c over thousands and
1Sa   8:12 He will appoint c over his
2Sa   4: 2 two men who were c of troops
1Ki   9:22 his officers, his c,
1Ki   14:27 hands of the c of the guards
1Ki   15:20 and sent the c of his armies
1Ki   20:24 and put c in their places
1Ki   22:31 thirty-two c of his chariots
2Ki   24:14 all the c and all the mighty
1Ch   11:11 a Hachmonite, chief of the c
1Ch   12:18 and made them c of the troop
1Ch   12:21 they were c in the army
1Ch   25: 1 the c of the army separated
1Ch   27: 3 the chief of all the c of the
1Ch   28: 1 the c of the divisions who
2Ch   8: 9 c of his officers
2Ch   26:11 Hananiah, one of the king's c
2Ch   32: 6 military c over the people
Job   39:25 from afar, the thunder of c
Jer   40:13 all the c of the forces that
Ezek   23: 6 who were clothed in purple, c
Ezek   23:15 all of them looking like c
Ezek   23:23 men, governors and rulers, c
Luke   22: 4 with the chief priests and c
Luke   22:52 c of the temple, and the
Rev   19:18 of kings, the flesh of c, the

CAPTIVE (*see* CAPTIVES, CAPTIVITY, CAPTURED)
Gen   14:14 that his brother was taken c
Gen   34:29 and their wives they took c
Ex   12:29 the c who was in the dungeon
Num   24:22 Asshur carries you away c
Num   31: 9 all the women of Midian c
1Ki   8:47 where they were carried c
1Ki   8:48 enemies who led them away c
2Ki   5: 2 had brought back c a young
2Ki   15:29 he carried them c to Assyria

2Ki   25:21 away c from its own land
1Ch   9: 1 But Judah was carried away c
Ezra   4:10 and noble Osnapper took c and
Ps   68:18 You have led captivity c
Ps   137: 3 away c required of us a song
Song   7: 5 king is held c by its tresses
Is   52: 2 neck, O c daughter of Zion
Jer   20: 4 shall carry them c to Babylon
Jer   40: 1 carried away c from Jerusalem
Jer   48:46 your sons have been taken c
Jer   48:46 c, and your daughters c
Jer   48:46 Nebuchadnezzar carried away c
Ezek   39:28 none of them c any longer
Dan   11: 8 carry their gods c to Egypt
Amos   4:10 along with your c horses
Luke   21:24 and be led away c into all
Eph   4: 8 on high, He led captivity c
2Ti   2:26 having been taken c by him to

CAPTIVES (*see* CAPTIVE)
Gen   31:26 like c taken with the sword
Num   31:12 Then they brought the c, the
Deut   21:11 among the c a beautiful woman
Deut   32:42 blood of the slain and the c
Judg   5:12 Barak, and lead your c away
2Ki   24:14 men of valor, ten thousand c
2Ch   28:11 therefore, and return the c
2Ch   28:13 shall not bring the c here
Ezra   1:11 the c who were brought from
Esth   2: 6 from Jerusalem with the c who
Is   20: 4 and the Ethiopians as c, young
Is   49:24 or the c of the righteous be
Is   49:25 "Even the c of the mighty
Is   61: 1 to proclaim liberty to the c
Jer   32:44 will cause their c to return
Jer   48:47 Yet I will bring back the c
Ezek   1: 1 as I was among the c by the
Ezek   3:11 And go, get to the c, to the
Ezek   3:15 I came to the c at Tel Abib
Ezek   16:53 the c of your captivity among
Ezek   29:14 bring back the c of Egypt
Ezek   39:25 bring back the c of Jacob
Dan   2:25 found a man of the c of Judah
Hos   6:11 I return the c of My people
Joel   3: 1 I bring back the c of Judah
Obad   20 The c of Jerusalem who are in
Hab   1: 9 They gather c like sand
Zech   6:10 Receive the gift from the c
Luke   4:18 preach deliverance to the c
2Ti   3: 6 and make c of gullible women

CAPTIVITY (*see* CAPTIVE)
Num   21:29 and his daughters into c, to
Deut   21:13 put off the clothes of her c
Deut   28:41 for they shall go into c
Deut   30: 3 will bring you back from c
Judg   18:30 the day of the c of the land
2Ki   24:14 carried into c all Jerusalem
2Ki   24:15 c from Jerusalem to Babylon
2Ki   25:27 thirty-seventh year of the c
1Ch   5: 6 of Assyria carried into c
2Ch   6:37 to You in the land of their c
2Ch   29: 9 and our wives are in c
Ezra   2: 1 who came back from the c, of
Ezra   3: 8 out of the c to Jerusalem
Ezra   6:16 of the descendants of the c
Ezra   9: 7 the lands, to the sword, to c
Ezra   10: 6 the guilt of those from the c
Neh   1: 2 who had survived the c, and
Neh   1: 3 who are left from the c in
Neh   4: 4 as plunder to a land of c
Neh   8:17 from the c made booths and sat
Ps   14: 7 back the c of his people
Ps   53: 6 back the c of His people, Let
Ps   68:18 high, You have led c captive
Ps   78:61 delivered His strength into c

Ps 85: 1 brought back the **c** of Jacob
Ps 126: 1 brought back the **c** of Zion
Ps 126: 4 Bring back our **c**, O LORD, As
Is 5:13 my people have gone into **c**
Jer 22:22 your lovers shall go into **c**
Jer 29:28 saying, 'This **c** is long
Jer 29:31 Send to all those in **c**,
Jer 30: 3 back from **c** My people Israel
Jer 30:10 seed from the land of their **c**
Jer 30:18 back the **c** of Jacob's tents
Jer 31:23 when I bring back their **c**
Jer 43:11 those appointed for **c**, and to
Jer 46:19 prepare yourself to go into **c**
Jer 48: 7 Chemosh shall go forth into **c**
Jer 49: 3 go into **c** with his priests
Jer 52:31 thirty-seventh year of the **c**
Lam 1: 3 Judah has gone into **c**, under
Lam 1:18 my young men have gone into **c**
Lam 4:22 no longer send you into **c**
Ezek 1: 2 year of King Jehoiachin's **c**
Ezek 11:25 So I spoke to those in **c** of
Dan 11:33 fall by sword and flame, by **c**
Amos 5:27 you into **c** beyond Damascus
Obad 12 brother in the day of his **c**
Matt 1:17 from the **c** in Babylon until
Rom 7:23 bringing me into **c** to the law
2Co 10: 5 **c** to the obedience of Christ
Eph 4: 8 He led **c** captive, and gave

CAPTURED (see CAPTIVE)
Josh 11:17 He **c** all their kings, and
1Sa 4:11 Also the ark of God was **c**
Rev 19:20 Then the beast was **c**, and with

CARAVANS†
Job 6:19 The **c** of Tema look, the

CARCASS (see CARCASSES)
Lev 5: 2 or the **c** of unclean livestock
Lev 11:24 whoever touches the **c** of any
Lev 11:39 he who touches its **c** shall be
Judg 14: 9 out of the **c** of the lion
Ezek 32: 5 fill the valleys with your **c**
Matt 24:28 For wherever the **c** is, there

CARCASSES (see CARCASS)
Gen 15:11 vultures came down on the **c**
Lev 11: 8 their **c** you shall not touch
Lev 11:11 their **c** as an abomination
Lev 26:30 cast your **c** on the lifeless
Num 14:32 your **c** shall fall in this
Num 14:33 until your **c** are consumed in
Deut 14: 8 flesh or touch their dead **c**
Deut 28:26 Your **c** shall be food for all
1Sa 17:46 give the **c** of the camp of the
Is 5:25 Their **c** were as refuse in the
Jer 9:22 'Even the **c** of men shall fall
Jer 16:18 the **c** of their detestable
Ezek 43: 9 the **c** of their kings far away

CARCHEMISH
Jer 46: 2 by the River Euphrates in **C**

CARE (see CARED, CAREFREE, CAREFUL, CARELESS, CARES, CARING)
Deut 15: 5 to observe with **c** all these
2Sa 18: 3 they will not **c** about us
1Ki 1: 2 king, and let her **c** for him
2Ki 4:13 for us with all this **c**
2Ch 19: 7 take **c** and do it, for there is
Esth 2: 8 into the **c** of Hegai the
Job 10:12 and Your **c** has preserved my
Ps 27:10 the LORD will take **c** of me
Is 21: 7 diligently with great **c**
Luke 10:34 to an inn, and took **c** of him
Luke 10:40 do You not **c** that my sister
John 10:13 does not **c** about the sheep
Acts 27: 3 to his friends and receive **c**

1Co 7:32 I want you to be without **c**
1Co 12:25 the same **c** for one another
Phil 2:20 sincerely **c** for your state
Phil 4:10 though you surely did **c**, but
1Ti 3: 5 how will he take **c** of the
Heb 2: 6 of man that You take **c** of him
1Pe 5: 7 casting all your **c** upon Him

CARED† (see CARE)
2Sa 19:24 he had not **c** for his feet,
1Ki 1: 4 she **c** for the king, and served
John 12: 6 not that he **c** for the poor,

CAREFREE† (see CARE)
Ezek 23:42 The sound of a **c** multitude

CAREFUL (see CARE, CAREFULLY)
Gen 31:24 Be **c** that you speak to Jacob
Lev 10:16 Then Moses made **c** inquiry
Num 28: 2 you shall be **c** to offer to Me
Deut 4: 6 Therefore be **c** to observe
Deut 4:15 Take **c** heed to yourselves,
Deut 17:10 And you shall be **c** to do
Deut 17:19 be **c** to observe all the words
Deut 19:18 judges shall make **c** inquiry
Deut 32:46 children to be **c** to observe
Josh 22: 5 But take **c** heed to do the
Judg 13: 4 please be **c** not to drink wine
1Ch 28: 8 God, be **c** to seek out all the
Ezra 7:17 be **c** to buy with this money
Tit 3: 8 to maintain good works

CAREFULLY (see CAREFUL)
Deut 2: 4 Therefore watch yourselves **c**
Deut 11:22 For if you **c** keep all these
Deut 15: 5 only if you **c** obey the voice
Deut 28: 1 God, to observe **c** all His
Deut 28:15 God, to observe **c** all His
Deut 31:12 **c** observe all the words of
Job 13:17 Listen **c** to my speech
Job 21: 2 Listen **c** to my speech, and let
Prov 12:26 should choose his friends **c**
Prov 23: 1 Consider **c** what is before you
Prov 27: 5 better than love **c** concealed
Is 15: 8 Listen **c** to Me, and eat
Is 38:15 I shall walk **c** all my years
Hag 2:15 now, **c** consider from this day
Matt 2: 8 search **c** for the young Child,
Luke 15: 8 search **c** until she finds it
1Ti 4: 6 which you have **c** followed
2Ti 1:17 Rome, he sought me out very **c**
1Pe 1:10 have inquired and searched

CARELESS† (see CARE)
Prov 19:16 but he who is **c** of his ways
Ezek 30: 9 make the **c** Ethiopians afraid

CARES (see CARE)
Deut 11:12 for which the LORD your God **c**
Ps 142: 4 No one **c** for my soul
Matt 13:22 the **c** of this world and the
Luke 8:14 go out and are choked with **c**
Luke 21:34 **c** of this life, and that Day
1Co 7:32 He who is unmarried **c** for the
1Co 7:34 The unmarried woman **c** about
1Pe 5: 7 upon Him, for He **c** for you

CARGO†
Jon 1: 5 threw the **c** that was in the
Acts 21: 3 the ship was to unload her **c**
Acts 27:10 much loss, not only of the **c**

CARING (see CARE)
1Sa 9: 5 cease **c** about the donkeys

CARMEL (see CARMELITE, CARMELITESS)
1Sa 25: 5 Go up to **C**, go to Nabal, and
1Ki 18:20 prophets together on Mount **C**
Song 7: 5 head crowns you like Mount **C**

Is 35: 2 to it, the excellence of **C**
Jer 46:18 as **C** by the sea, so he shall
Amos 1: 2 and the top of **C** withers
Mic 7:14 a woodland, in the midst of **C**
Nah 1: 4 **C** wither, and the flower of

CARMELITE (see CARMEL)
2Sa 2: 2 the widow of Nabal the **C**

CARMELITESS (see CARMEL)
1Sa 27: 3 and Abigail the **C**, Nabal's

CARNAL (see CARNALLY)
Rom 7:14 law is spiritual, but I am **c**
Rom 8: 7 Because the **c** mind is enmity
1Co 3: 1 spiritual people but as to **c**
1Co 3: 3 for you are still **c**
2Co 10: 4 not **c** but mighty in God for

CARNALLY (see CARNAL)
Gen 19: 5 to us that we may know them **c**
Lev 18:20 **c** with your neighbor's wife
Lev 19:20 'Whoever lies **c** with a woman
Judg 19:22 house, that we may know him **c**
Rom 8: 6 For to be **c** minded is death,

CAROUSE† (see CAROUSING)
2Pe 2:13 pleasure to **c** in the daytime

CAROUSING† (see CAROUSE)
Luke 21:34 hearts be weighed down with **c**
2Pe 2:13 **c** in their own deceptions

CARPENTER† (see CARPENTER'S, CARPENTERS)
Mark 6: 3 Is this not the **c**, the Son of

CARPENTER'S† (see CARPENTER)
Matt 13:55 Is this not the **c** son

CARPENTERS (see CARPENTER)
2Ki 12:11 and they paid it out to the **c**
2Ki 22: 6 to **c** and builders and masons
2Ch 24:12 **c** to repair the house of the
Ezra 3: 7 money to the masons and the **c**

CARRIAGES†
Is 46: 1 Your **c** were heavily loaded, a

CARRIED (see CARRY)
Gen 31:26 and **c** away my daughters like
Gen 46: 5 Israel **c** their father Jacob
Gen 50:13 For his sons **c** him to the
Ex 25:14 that the ark may be **c** by them
Num 13:23 they **c** it between two of them
Deut 1:31 how the LORD your God **c** you
Judg 11:39 he **c** out his vow with her
1Sa 5: 8 So they **c** the ark of the
2Ki 15:29 he **c** them captive to Assyria
2Ki 17: 6 **c** Israel away to Assyria, and
2Ki 20:17 day, shall be **c** to Babylon
2Ki 24:15 he **c** Jehoiachin captive to
2Ki 25:13 **c** their bronze to Babylon
2Ki 25:21 Thus Judah was **c** away captive
2Ch 21:17 **c** away all the possessions
2Ch 28: 5 **c** away a great multitude of
2Ch 28:17 Judah, and **c** away captives
2Ch 36: 4 brother and **c** him off to Egypt
Ezra 2: 1 of those who had been **c** away
Ezra 5:14 **c** into the temple of Babylon
Neh 4:17 wall, and those who **c** burdens
Job 10:19 I would have been **c** from the
Ps 46: 2 though the mountains be **c**
Ps 137: 3 For there those who **c** us away
Is 46: 3 who have been **c** from the womb
Is 49:22 shall be **c** on their shoulders
Is 53: 4 our griefs and **c** our sorrows
Is 63: 9 **c** them all the days of old
Jer 40: 1 chains among all who were **c**
Jer 52:28 Nebuchadnezzar **c** away captive
Jer 52:30 **c** away captive of the Jews

Ezek 6: 9 where they are **c** captive,
Ezek 17: 4 and **c** it to a land of trade
Dan 2:35 the wind **c** them away so that
Hos 10: 6 The idol also shall be **c** to
Hos 12: 1 and oil is **c** to Egypt
Matt 1:11 they were **c** away to Babylon
Mark 2: 3 who was **c** by four men
Luke 7:12 a dead man was being **c** out
Luke 16:22 and was **c** by the angels to
Luke 24:51 from them and **c** up into heaven
John 20:15 Sir, if You have **c** Him away
Acts 5: 6 up, **c** him out, and buried him
Acts 8: 2 devout men **c** Stephen to his
1Co 12: 2 **c** away to these dumb idols,
Gal 2:13 **c** away with their hypocrisy
Eph 4:14 **c** about with every wind of
Heb 13: 9 Do not be **c** about with
2Pe 2:17 clouds **c** by a tempest, to
Jude 12 water, **c** about by the winds
Rev 12:15 her to be **c** away by the flood
Rev 17: 3 he **c** me away in the Spirit
Rev 21:10 he **c** me away in the Spirit

CARRIERS (see CARRY)
Josh 9:23 water **c** for the house of my
Ezek 27:25 were **c** of your merchandise

CARRIES (see CARRY)
Lev 11:28 'Whoever **c** any such carcass
Lev 15:10 He who **c** any of those things
Num 11:12 as a guardian **c** a nursing
Num 14:22 Asshur **c** you away captive
Deut 1:31 you, as a man **c** his son, in
Job 21:18 chaff that a storm **c** away
Job 27:21 The east wind **c** him away, and
Rev 17: 7 and of the beast that **c** her

CARRION
Lev 11:18 the jackdaw, and the **c** vulture

CARRY (see CARRIED, CARRIERS, CARRIES, CARRYING)
Gen 37:25 on their way to **c** them down
Gen 47:30 you shall **c** me out of Egypt
Gen 50:25 you shall **c** up my bones from
Lev 6:11 **c** the ashes outside the camp
Num 1:50 they shall **c** the tabernacle
Num 11:12 'C them in your bosom, as a
Deut 14:24 are not able to **c** the tithe
2Ch 36: 6 to **c** him off to Babylon
Ezra 5:15 **c** them to the temple site
Job 5:12 cannot **c** out their plans
Ps 49:17 dies he shall **c** nothing away
Ps 90: 5 You **c** them away like a flood
Eccl 5:15 he may **c** away in his hand
Eccl 10:20 of the air may **c** your voice
Is 30: 6 they will **c** their riches on
Is 40:11 and **c** them in His bosom, and
Is 41:16 the wind shall **c** them away
Is 46: 4 to gray hairs I will **c** you
Ezek 29:19 **c** off her spoil, and remove
Dan 11: 8 he shall also **c** their gods
Dan 11:32 and **c** out great exploits
Matt 3:11 sandals I am not worthy to **c**
Mark 6:55 and began to **c** about on beds
Mark 11:16 to **c** wares through the temple
Luke 10: 4 C neither money bag, sack,
John 5:10 lawful for you to **c** your bed
John 21:18 **c** you where you do not wish
Acts 5: 9 door, and they will **c** you out
1Ti 6: 7 certain we can **c** nothing out

CARRYING (see CARRY)
Num 4:12 and put them on a **c** beam
Num 4:24 Gershonites, in serving and **c**
Num 10:17 set out, **c** the tabernacle
Num 10:21 set out, **c** the holy things
Deut 32:11 them up, **c** them on its wings,

Jer 1: 3 until the c away of Jerusalem
Jer 17:27 such as not c a burden when
Zech 5:10 Where are they c the basket
Mark 14:13 meet you c a pitcher of water
Acts 5:10 c her out, buried her by her
2Co 4:10 always c about in the body

CART (*see* CARTS, CARTWHEEL)
1Sa 6: 7 Now therefore, make a new c
1Sa 6: 7 and hitch the cows to the c
1Sa 6:11 the ark of the LORD on the c
1Sa 6:14 they split the wood of the c
2Sa 6: 3 set the ark of God on a new c
1Ki 7:30 Every c had four bronze
1Ki 7:32 wheels were joined to the c
Is 5:18 and sin as if with a c rope
Amos 2:13 as a c is weighed down that

CARTS (*see* CART)
Gen 45:21 and Joseph gave them c,
Gen 45:27 and when he saw the c which
Num 7: 7 Two c and four oxen he gave to
1Ki 7:27 He also made ten c of bronze
1Ki 7:28 this was the design of the c
1Ki 7:38 each of the ten c was a laver
2Ki 16:17 cut off the panels of the c

CARTWHEEL (*see* CART)
Is 28:27 nor is a c rolled over the

CARVE† (*see* CARVED, CARVES, CARVING)
Hab 2:18 that its maker should c it

CARVED (*see* CARVE)
Ex 20: 4 make for yourself any c image
Deut 12: 3 the c images of their gods
Deut 27:15 makes any c or molded image
1Ki 6:18 c with ornamental buds and
1Ki 6:29 Then he c all the walls of
1Ki 6:29 with c figures of cherubim,
1Ki 6:35 applied evenly on the c work
2Ch 3: 5 he c palm trees and chainwork
Song 5:14 His body is c ivory inlaid
Is 42:17 who trust in c images, who
Is 44:17 makes into a god, his c image
Is 45:20 the wood of their c image
Jer 51:17 put to shame by the c image
Jer 51:47 on the c images of Babylon

CARVES† (*see* CARVE)
Is 22:16 who c a tomb for himself in a

CARVING (*see* CARVE)
Ex 31: 5 in c wood, and to work in all
2Ch 3:10 two cherubim, fashioned by c

CASE (*see* CASES)
Gen 30: 6 God has judged my c
Ex 18:26 every small c themselves
Deut 1:17 The c that is too hard for
1Sa 24:15 and me, and see and plead my c
2Sa 15: 3 Look, your c is good and right
2Ch 19:10 Whatever c comes to you from
Job 13:18 See now, I have prepared my c
Job 23: 4 would present my c before Him
Prov 25: 9 Debate your c with your
Is 43:26 state your c, that you may be
Lam 3:59 wronged; Judge my c
Ezek 20:35 My c with you face to face
Dan 3:17 If that is the c, our God
Matt 19:10 If such is the c of the man
Acts 19:38 have a c against anyone, the
Acts 24:22 make a decision on your c
Acts 25:14 laid Paul's c before the king

CASES† (*see* CASE)
Ex 18:26 the hard c they brought to
Deut 1:16 'Hear the c between your
1Co 7:15 not under bondage in such c

CASSIA
Ps 45: 8 with myrrh and aloes and c, Out
Ezek 27:19 Wrought iron, c, and cane were

CAST (*see* CASTING, CASTS, REJECTED)
Gen 21:10 C out this bondwoman and her
Gen 37:24 took him and c him into a pit
Gen 39: 7 wife c longing eyes on Joseph
Ex 1:22 you shall c into the river
Ex 4: 3 He said, "C it on the ground
Ex 4:25 c it at Moses' feet, and said,
Ex 7: 9 c it before Pharaoh, and let
Ex 7:10 Aaron c down his rod before
Ex 15: 4 army He has c into the sea
Ex 32:19 he c the tablets out of his
Ex 32:24 I c it into the fire, and this
Lev 16: 8 Then Aaron shall c lots for
Deut 9: 4 God has c them out before you
Josh 10:11 that the LORD c down large
Josh 10:27 c them into the cave where
1Sa 18:11 Saul c the spear, for he said
1Ki 7:15 he c two pillars of bronze,
1Ki 9: 7 name I will c out of My sight
1Ki 14: 9 have c Me behind your back
2Ki 24:20 that He finally c them out
1Ch 28: 9 He will c you off forever
2Ch 25:12 c them down from the top of
2Ch 26:14 bows, and slings to c stones
2Ch 29:19 c aside in his transgression
Neh 9:26 c Your law behind their backs
Esth 3: 7 they c Pur (that is, the lot)
Job 8:20 God will not c away the
Job 15: 4 you c off fear, and restrain
Job 18: 8 For he is c into a net by his
Job 30:11 they have c off restraint
Ps 2: 3 c away Their cords from us
Ps 17:13 Confront him, c him down
Ps 22:10 I was c upon You from birth
Ps 22:18 for My clothing they c lots
Ps 37:24 shall not be utterly c down
Ps 42: 5 Why are you c down, O my soul
Ps 44:23 Do not c us off forever
Ps 50:17 And c My words behind you
Ps 51:11 Do not c me away from Your
Ps 55:22 C your burden on the LORD,
Ps 60: 8 Over Edom I will c My shoe
Ps 71: 9 Do not c me off in the time
Ps 78:49 He c on them the fierceness
Ps 89:44 And c his throne down to the
Ps 102:10 lifted me up and c me away
Ps 140:10 Let them be c into the fire,
Prov 1:14 c in your lot among us, let
Prov 16:33 The lot is c into the lap,
Prov 29:18 the people c off restraint
Eccl 3: 5 a time to c away stones, and a
Eccl 11: 1 C your bread upon the waters,
Is 25: 7 covering c over all people
Is 26:19 earth shall c out the dead
Is 38:17 for You have c all my sins
Is 57:20 rest, whose waters c up mire
Jer 7:15 I will c you out of My sight,
Jer 38: 6 c him into the dungeon of
Ezek 23:35 Me and c Me behind your back,
Ezek 27:30 and c dust on their heads
Ezek 31:16 when I c it down to hell
Ezek 32:18 c them down to the depths of
Dan 3:20 c them into the burning fiery
Dan 3:21 were c into the midst of the
Dan 3:24 Did we not c three men bound
Dan 6:16 c him into the den of lions
Dan 8:12 he c truth down to the ground
Hos 9:17 My God will c them away,
Amos 1:11 the sword, and c off all pity
Obad 11 gates and c lots for Jerusalem
Jon 1: 7 So they c lots, and the lot

Jon	2: 3	For You c me into the deep,
Mic	7:19	You will c all our sins into
Matt	5:29	pluck it out and c it from you
Matt	5:29	whole body to be c into hell
Matt	5:30	whole body to be c into hell
Matt	7: 6	nor c your pearls before
Matt	7:22	c out demons in Your name, and
Matt	8:12	be c out into outer darkness
Matt	8:16	He c out the spirits with a
Matt	8:31	If You c us out, permit us to
Matt	10: 8	raise the dead, c out demons
Matt	13:42	will c them into the furnace
Matt	17:19	Why could we not c him out
Matt	17:27	c in a hook, and take the fish
Matt	18: 8	cut if off and c it from you
Matt	18: 8	to be c into the everlasting
Matt	18: 9	pluck it out and c it from you
Matt	18: 9	eyes, to be c into hell fire
Matt	21:21	be c into the sea,' it will
Matt	22:13	c him into outer darkness
Matt	25:30	c the unprofitable servant
Matt	27:35	for My clothing they c lots
Mark	3:23	How can Satan c out Satan
Mark	16: 9	of whom He had c seven demons
Luke	12: 5	has power to c into hell
Luke	13:32	I c out demons and perform
John	6:37	Me I will by no means c out
John	9:35	heard that they had c him out
John	12:31	of this world will be c out
John	15: 6	he is c out as a branch and is
John	21: 6	C the net on the right side
Acts	1:26	they c their lots, and the lot
Acts	26:10	I c my vote against them
Rom	11: 2	God has not c away His people
Rom	11:15	For if their being c away is
Rom	13:12	Therefore let us c off the
Gal	4:30	C out the bondwoman and her
2Pe	2: 4	but c them down to hell and
Rev	2:22	Indeed I will c her into a
Rev	4:10	c their crowns before the
Rev	12: 9	So the great dragon was c out
Rev	12: 9	angels were c out with him
Rev	19:20	These two were c alive into
Rev	20: 3	he c him into the bottomless
Rev	20:10	was c into the lake of fire

CASTING (see CAST)

Ps	89:39	crown by c it to the ground
Prov	18:18	C lots causes contentions to
Matt	4:18	brother, c a net into the sea
Matt	27:35	c lots, that it might be
Mark	1:39	all Galilee, and c out demons
2Co	10: 5	c down arguments and every
1Pe	5: 7	c all your care upon Him, for

CASTLE†

Prov	18:19	are like the bars of a c

CASTS† (see CAST)

Job	18: 7	and his own counsel c him down
Job	20:15	God c them out of his belly
Ps	147: 6	He c the wicked down to the
Ps	147:17	He c out His hail like
Prov	10: 3	but He c away the desire of
Prov	19:15	Slothfulness c one into a
Is	40:19	silversmith c silver chains
Matt	9:34	He c out demons by the ruler
Matt	12:26	If Satan c out Satan, he is
Mark	3:22	of the demons He c out demons
Luke	11:15	He c out demons by Beelzebub,
1Jn	4:18	but perfect love c out fear

CASUAL†

Jer	3: 9	pass, through her c harlotry

CATASTROPHE

Jer	19: 3	bring such a c on this place

CATCH (see CATCHES, CAUGHT)

Job	9:18	not allow me to c my breath
Ps	10: 9	He lies in wait to c the poor
Prov	12:12	covet the c of evil men, but
Song	2:15	C us the foxes, the little
Ezek	19: 3	he learned to c prey
Ezek	19: 6	he learned to c prey
Mark	12:13	to c Him in His words
Luke	5: 4	and let down your nets for a c
Luke	5: 9	the c of fish which they had
Luke	5:10	From now on you will c men

CATCHES† (see CATCH)

Ex	22: 6	c in thorns, so that stacked
Lev	17:13	c any animal or bird that may
Job	5:13	He c the wise in their own
Ps	10: 9	He c the poor when he draws
John	10:12	and the wolf c the sheep and
1Co	3:19	He c the wise in their own

CATERPILLAR†

Ps	78:46	gave their crops to the c
Is	33: 4	like the gathering of the c

CATTLE

Gen	1:24	c and creeping thing and beast
Gen	2:20	So Adam gave names to all c
Gen	3:14	are cursed more than all c
Gen	7:21	birds and c and beasts and every
Ex	9: 3	be on your c in the field
Ex	20:10	your maidservant, nor your c
Josh	8: 2	its c you shall take as booty
Neh	10:36	of our sons, and our c, as it
Ps	50:10	the c on a thousand hills
Ps	78:48	gave up their c to the hail
Ps	104:14	the grass to grow for the c
Ps	107:38	does not let their c decrease
Is	30:23	In that day your c will feed
Jer	9:10	men hear the voice of the c
Joel	1:18	The herds of c are restless
Zech	13: 5	me to keep c from my youth
Matt	22: 4	fatted c are killed, and all

CAUGHT (see CATCH, TOOK)

Gen	22:13	c in a thicket by its horns
Gen	39:12	that she c him by his garment
Ex	4: 4	c it, and it became a rod in
Judg	1: 6	c him and cut off his thumbs
Judg	15: 4	went and c three hundred foxes
Judg	21:23	those who danced, whom they c
1Sa	17:35	me, I c it by its beard, and
2Sa	16: 8	So now you are c in your own
2Sa	18: 9	his head c in the terebinth
2Ki	4:27	she c him by the feet, but
2Ch	22: 9	they c him (he was hiding in
Ps	10: 2	Let them be c in the plots
Prov	3:26	keep your foot from being c
Prov	5:22	he is c in the cords of his
Prov	7:13	So she c him and kissed him
Eccl	9:12	net, like birds c in a snare
Jer	50:24	you have been found and also c
Ezek	12:13	and he shall be c in My snare
Amos	3: 4	his den, if he has c nothing
Matt	14:31	and c him, and said to him,
Luke	5: 5	toiled all night and c nothing
Luke	5: 6	they c a great number of fish
John	8: 3	to Him a woman c in adultery
Acts	8:39	of the Lord c Philip away
Acts	27:15	So when the ship was c, and
2Co	12: 4	how he was c up into Paradise
2Co	12:16	crafty, I c you with guile
1Th	4:17	remain shall be c up together
2Pe	2:12	brute beasts made to be c
Rev	12: 5	And her Child was c up to God

CAULK† (see CAULKERS)

Ezek	27: 9	were in you to c your seams

CAULKERS† (*see* CAULK)
Ezek 27:27 mariners and pilots, your c

CAUSE (*see* CAUSED, CAUSES, CAUSING)
Gen   7: 4 seven more days I will c it
Ex   8: 5 c frogs to come up on the
Ex   9: 9 it will c boils that break
Ex   22: 9 the c of both parties shall
Ex   27:20 light, to c the lamp to burn
Num   16: 5 will c him to come near to
Judg   8: 7 For this c, when the LORD has
1Sa   19: 5 to kill David without a c
1Ki   8:59 maintain the c of His servant
1Ch   4:10 evil, that I may not c pain
1Ch   21: 3 he be a c of guilt in Israel
Neh   4:11 them and c the work to cease
Job   2: 3 him, to destroy him without c
Job   5: 8 and to God I would commit my c
Job   24:10 They c the poor to go naked,
Job   38:26 to c it to rain on a land
Ps   17: 1 Hear a just c, O LORD, Attend
Ps   35: 1 Plead my c, O LORD, with
Ps   35:27 Who favor my righteous c
Ps   67: 1 c His face to shine upon us
Ps   74:22 O God, plead Your own c
Ps   80: 3 C Your face to shine, And we
Ps   119:154 Plead my c and redeem me
Ps   140:12 The c of the afflicted, And
Ps   143: 8 C me to hear Your
Ps   143: 8 C me to know the way in which
Prov 22:23 the LORD will plead their c
Prov 29: 7 considers the c of the poor
Eccl   5: 6 mouth c your flesh to sin
Eccl 10: 1 c it to give off a foul odor
Is   1:23 nor does the c of the widow
Is   28:12 you may c the weary to rest
Is   34: 8 recompense for the c of Zion
Is   42: 2 nor c His voice to be heard
Is   66: 9 Shall I who c delivery shut
Jer   3:12 I will not c My anger to fall
Jer   11:20 to You I have revealed my c
Jer   15: 8 I will c anguish and terror to
Jer   29: 8 which you c to be dreamed
Jer   29:10 c you to return to this place
Jer   29:14 I c you to be carried away
Jer   32:37 I will c them to dwell safely
Jer   51:27 c the horses to come up like
Lam   3:36 or subvert a man in his c
Ezek   7:24 I will c the pomp of the
Ezek 13:13 I will c a stormy wind to
Ezek 23:48 Thus I will c lewdness to
Ezek 25: 7 I will c you to perish from
Ezek 30:13 c the images to cease from
Ezek 34:26 I will c showers to come down
Ezek 37: 5 Surely I will c breath to
Joel   2:23 He will c the rain to come
Jon   1: 8 For whose c is this trouble
Hab   1: 3 and c me to see trouble
John 15:25 They hated Me without a c
John 18:37 For this c I was born, and for
Acts 13:28 found no c for death in Him
Rom   16:17 note those who c divisions
2Co   4:15 may c thanksgiving to abound
1Ti   1: 4 which c disputes rather than
Heb   12:15 springing up c trouble, and by
1Jn   2:10 there is no c for stumbling

CAUSED (*see* CAUSE)
Gen   2: 5 not c it to rain on the earth
Gen   2:21 the LORD God c a deep sleep
Gen   20:13 when God c me to wander from
Ex   9:10 they c boils that break out
Ex   14:21 the LORD c the sea to go back
1Sa   20:17 Jonathan again c David to vow
2Sa   7:11 have c you to rest from all
Neh   13:26 pagan women c even him to sin

Job   29:13 I c the widow's heart to sing
Job   38:12 c the dawn to know its place,
Ps   78:13 sea and c them to pass through
Ps   78:26 He c an east wind to blow in
Ps   119:49 which You have c me to hope
Jer   29: 7 have c you to be carried away
Jer   48:33 I have c wine to fail from
Jer   51:49 As Babylon has c the slain of
Ezek   3: 2 He c me to eat that scroll
Dan   9:21 being c to fly swiftly,
Hos   4:12 harlotry has c them to stray
Jon   3: 7 he c it to be proclaimed and
Mal   2: 8 you have c many to stumble at
Acts 15: 3 they c great joy to all the
2Co   2: 5 But if anyone has c grief

CAUSES (*see* CAUSE)
Ps   37: 8 it only c harm
Ps   104:14 He c the grass to grow for
Ps   107:40 And c them to wander in the
Ps   135: 7 He c the vapors to ascend
Ps   147:18 He c His wind to blow, and the
Prov 10: 5 harvest is a son who c shame
Prov 10:10 winks with the eye c trouble
Prov 17: 2 rule over a son who c shame
Is   64: 2 as fire c water to boil
Lam   3:32 Though He c grief, yet He
Ezek 14: 3 which c them to stumble into
Ezek 26: 3 as the sea c its waves to
Matt   5:29 your right eye c you to sin
Matt   5:32 c her to commit adultery
Matt 18: 9 And if your eye c you to sin
Mark   9:42 whoever c one of these little
Mark   9:43 your hand c you to sin
Mark   9:45 your foot c you to sin
Mark   9:47 And if your eye c you to sin,
2Co   9:11 which c thanksgiving through
Eph   4:16 c growth of the body for the
Rev   21:27 or c an abomination or a lie,

CAUSING† (*see* CAUSE)
Is   30:28 of the people, c them to err
Jer   33:12 c their flocks to lie down
Ezek 16:21 by c them to pass through the

CAUTIOUSLY†
1Sa   15:32 So Agag came to him c

CAVALRY
1Ki   9:19 chariots and cities for his c
1Ki   20:20 escaped on a horse with the c
Hab   1: 8 their c comes from afar

CAVE (*see* CAVES)
Gen   19:30 two daughters dwelt in a c
Gen   23: 9 that he may give me the c of
Gen   23:11 field and the c that is in it
Gen   23:19 Sarah his wife in the c of
Gen   25: 9 him in the c of Machpelah
Josh 10:18 against the mouth of the c
Josh 10:27 cast them into the c where
1Sa   24: 7 And Saul got up from the c
2Sa   23:13 to David at the c of Adullam
John 11:38 It was a c, and a stone lay

CAVES (*see* CAVE)
Judg   6: 2 themselves the dens, the c
1Sa   13: 6 then the people hid in c
Heb   11:38 in dens and c of the earth
Rev   6:15 man, hid themselves in the c

CEASE (*see* CEASED, CEASES, CEASING)
Gen   8:22 and day and night shall not c
Ex   9:29 the thunder will c, and there
Num   8:25 must c performing this work
Deut 15:11 will never c from the land
Josh 22:25 c fearing the LORD
Judg   2:19 They did not c from their own

Judg	9: 9	Should I c giving my oil,
1Sa	7: 8	Do not c to cry out to the
1Sa	9: 5	lest my father c caring about
2Ch	25:16	C! Why should you be killed
Neh	4:11	them and cause the work to c
Neh	6: 3	the work c while I leave it
Job	3:17	the wicked c from troubling
Job	10:20	C! Leave me alone
Ps	35:15	They tore at me and did not c
Ps	37: 8	C from anger, and forsake
Ps	46: 9	He makes wars c to the end of
Ps	85: 4	Your anger toward us to c
Ps	89:44	You have made his glory c
Prov	19:27	C listening to instruction,
Eccl	12: 3	when the grinders c because
Is	1:16	My eyes. C to do evil,
Is	16:10	I have made their shouting c
Is	17: 1	Damascus c from being a
Is	33: 1	When you c plundering, you
Lam	3:49	My eyes flow and do not c,
Ezek	7:24	the pomp of the strong to c
Ezek	16:41	I will make you c playing the
Ezek	23:27	will make you c your lewdness
Ezek	30:18	strength shall c in her
Ezek	33:28	her arrogant strength shall c
Ezek	34:25	beasts to c from the land
Hos	2:11	also cause all her mirth to c
Acts	5:42	they did not c teaching and
Acts	6:13	This man does not c to speak
Acts	13:10	will you not c perverting the
Acts	20:31	not c to warn everyone night
1Co	13: 8	are tongues, they will c
Eph	1:16	do not c to give thanks for
Col	1: 9	do not c to pray for you, and
2Pe	2:14	and that cannot c from sin

CEASED (see CEASE)

Gen	11: 8	and they c building the city
Ex	9:33	the thunder and the hail c
Josh	5:12	Now the manna c on the day
Judg	5: 7	life c, it c in Israel
1Sa	2: 5	were hungry have c to hunger
2Ki	4: 6	vessel." So the oil c
Job	32: 1	three men c answering Job
Ps	77: 8	Has His mercy c forever
Is	14: 4	How the oppressor has c, the
Jer	51:30	of Babylon have c fighting
Lam	5:14	The elders have c gathering
Lam	5:15	The joy of our heart has c
Hos	4:10	they have c obeying the LORD
Jon	1:15	the sea c from its raging
Matt	14:32	got into the boat, the wind c
Luke	7:45	but this woman has not c to
Luke	9:36	And when the voice had c,
Acts	20: 1	After the uproar had c, Paul
Gal	5:11	offense of the cross has c
Heb	10: 2	they not have c to be offered
1Pe	4: 1	in the flesh has c from sin

CEASES (see CEASE)

Num	9:13	c to keep the Passover, that
Is	24: 8	The mirth of the tambourine c
Is	24: 8	ends, the joy of the harp c

CEASING (see CEASE)

1Sa	12:23	the LORD in c to pray for you
Rom	1: 9	that without c I make mention
1Th	1: 3	without c your work of faith
1Th	2:13	we also thank God without c
1Th	5:17	pray without c,
2Ti	1: 3	as without c I remember you

CEDAR (see CEDARS)

Lev	14: 4	c wood, scarlet, and hyssop
2Sa	7: 2	now, I dwell in a house of c
1Ki	4:33	from the c tree of Lebanon
1Ki	7: 3	it was paneled with c above

1Ki	10:27	he made c trees as abundant as the
1Ch	22: 4	and c trees in abundance
2Ch	2: 8	Also send me c and cypress and
Ezra	3: 7	Tyre to bring c logs from
Job	40:17	He moves his tail like a c
Song	1:17	The beams of our houses are c
Song	8: 9	enclose her with boards of c
Is	41:19	plant in the wilderness the c
Ezek	17:22	branches of the high c and set
Ezek	17:23	fruit, and be a majestic c
Zeph	2:14	He will lay bare the c work
Zech	11: 2	for the c has fallen, because

CEDARS (see CEDAR)

Judg	9:15	and devour the c of Lebanon
2Ki	19:23	I will cut down its tall c
Ps	29: 5	of the LORD breaks the c, Yes
Ps	80:10	the mighty c with its boughs
Ps	148: 9	Fruitful trees and all c
Song	5:15	Lebanon, excellent as the c
Jer	22: 7	shall cut down your choice c
Jer	22:23	making your nest in the c
Ezek	31: 8	The c in the garden of God
Zech	11: 1	that fire may devour your c

CEILING†

1Ki	6:15	the c he paneled them on the
1Ki	6:16	the temple, from floor to c
1Ki	7: 7	with cedar from floor to c

CELEBRATE (see CELEBRATED)

Lev	23:32	you shall c your sabbath
Lev	23:41	You shall c it in the seventh

CELEBRATED† (see CELEBRATE)

Ezra	6:16	c the dedication of this
Esth	9:19	c the fourteenth day of the
Matt	14: 6	when Herod's birthday was c

CELESTIAL

1Co	15:40	There are also c bodies and

CELLS†

Jer	37:16	entered the dungeon and the c

CENSER (see ALTAR, CENSERS)

Lev	10: 1	of Aaron, each took his c
Num	16:17	bring his c before the LORD
Ezek	8:11	Each man had a c in his hand
Heb	9: 4	which had the golden c
Rev	8: 3	angel, having a golden c,

CENSERS (see CENSER)

Num	16: 6	Take c, Korah and all your
Num	16:38	The c of these men who sinned
Num	16:39	the priest took the bronze c
1Ki	7:50	ladles, and the c of pure gold

CENSUS

Num	1: 2	Take a c of all the
Num	26: 4	Take a c of the people from
2Ki	12: 4	each man's c money, each
Luke	2: 2	This c first took place while
Acts	5:37	rose up in the days of the c

CENTER

Judg	9:37	down from the c of the land
Ezek	48:15	and the city shall be in the c
Ezek	48:21	the temple shall be in the c
John	19:18	side, and Jesus in the c

CENTURION (see CENTURION'S, CENTURIONS)

Matt	8: 5	a c came to Him, pleading
Luke	7: 6	the c sent friends to Him,
Acts	10:22	Cornelius the c, a just man,
Acts	24:23	commanded the c to keep Paul
Acts	27: 1	a c of the Augustan Regiment
Acts	28:16	the c delivered the prisoners

CENTURION'S† (see CENTURION)

Luke	7: 2	And a certain c servant, who

CENTURIONS (*see* CENTURION)
Acts 21:32 took soldiers and **c**, and ran

CEPHAS (*see* PETER, SIMON)
John 1:42 You shall be called **C**"
1Co 3:22 whether Paul or Apollos or **C**
1Co 15: 5 and that He was seen by **C**,
Gal 2: 9 and when James, **C**, and John,

CERAMIC†
Dan 2:41 iron mixed with **c** clay
Dan 2:43 iron mixed with **c** clay

CEREMONIALLY† (*see* CEREMONY)
Num 8: 6 of Israel and cleanse them **c**

CEREMONIES† (*see* CEREMONY)
Num 9: 3 rites and **c** you shall keep it
Jer 34: 5 as in the **c** of your fathers,

CEREMONY† (*see* CEREMONIALLY, CEREMONIES)
Num 9:14 and according to its **c**

CERTAIN (*see* CERTAINLY, CERTAINTY, UNCERTAIN)
Gen 38: 2 a **c** Canaanite whose name was
Ex 16: 4 gather a **c** quota every day,
Josh 23:13 know for **c** that the LORD your
Dan 2:45 The cream is **c**, and its
Dan 3:12 There are **c** Jews whom you
Dan 10: 5 a **c** man clothed in linen,
Matt 26:18 Go into the city to a **c** man
Mark 5:25 Now a **c** woman had a flow of
Luke 10:25 a **c** lawyer stood up and tested
Luke 10:30 A **c** man went down from
Luke 10:33 But a **c** Samaritan, as he
Luke 10:38 and a **c** woman named Martha
Luke 15:11 A **c** man had two sons
John 5: 4 at a **c** time into the pool
John 11: 1 Now a **c** man was sick, Lazarus
John 12:20 Now there were **c** Greeks among
Acts 5: 1 But a **c** man named Ananias,
Acts 10: 1 There was a **c** man in Caesarea
Acts 16:14 Now a **c** woman named Lydia
Acts 16:16 that a **c** slave girl possessed
Acts 17:18 Then **c** Epicurean and Stoic
Acts 18: 2 he found a **c** Jew named Aquila
Acts 18:24 Now a **c** Jew named Apollos,
Acts 20: 9 in a window sat a **c** young man
Acts 25:26 I have nothing **c** to write to
1Ti 6: 7 it is **c** we can carry nothing
Heb 2: 6 one testified in a **c** place
Heb 4: 7 again He designates a **c** day
Heb 10:27 but a **c** fearful expectation
Jude 4 For **c** men have crept in

CERTAINLY (*see* CERTAIN)
1Sa 14:45 deliverance in Israel? **C** not!
2Ki 8:10 to him, "You shall **c** recover
Dan 11:10 and one shall **c** come and
Dan 11:13 shall **c** come at the end of
Luke 23:47 **C** this was a righteous Man
Rom 3: 6 **C** not! For then how will God
Rom 3:31 law through faith? **C** not!
Rom 6: 2 How shall we who
Rom 6:15 law but under grace? **C** not!
Rom 7: 7 Is the law sin? **C** not!
Rom 11: 1 cast away His people? **C** not!
1Co 6:15 members of a harlot? **C** not!
Gal 2:17 a minister of sin? **C** not!
Gal 3:21 the promises of God? **C** not!

CERTAINTY (*see* CERTAIN)
1Sa 23:23 and come back to me with **c**
Prov 22:21 the **c** of the words of truth
Luke 1: 4 that you may know the **c** of

CERTIFICATE (*see* CERTIFIED)
Deut 24: 1 he writes her a **c** of divorce
Is 50: 1 Where is the **c** of your

Matt 5:31 him give her a **c** of divorce

CERTIFIED† (*see* CERTIFICATE)
John 3:33 has **c** that God is true

CHAFF
Job 21:18 like **c** that a storm carries
Ps 1: 4 But are like the **c** which the
Ps 35: 5 be like **c** before the wind
Is 5:24 and the flame consumes the **c**
Is 29: 5 be as **c** that passes away
Is 33:11 You shall conceive **c**, you
Jer 23:28 What is the **c** to the wheat
Hos 13: 3 away, like **c** blown off from a
Matt 3:12 the **c** with unquenchable fire

CHAIN (*see* CHAINED, CHAINS)
Gen 41:42 put a gold **c** around his neck
Lam 3: 7 He has made my **c** heavy
Ezek 7:23 Make a **c**, For the land is
Ezek 16:11 wrists, and a **c** on your neck
Dan 5:29 put a **c** of gold around his
Acts 28:20 Israel I am bound with this **c**
2Ti 1:16 and was not ashamed of my **c**
Rev 20: 1 pit and a great **c** in his hand

CHAINED† (*see* CHAIN)
Mark 15: 7 who was **c** with his fellow
2Ti 2: 9 but the word of God is not **c**
Heb 13: 3 prisoners as if **c** with them

CHAINS (*see* CHAIN)
Ex 28:14 you shall make two **c** of pure
Ps 107:14 And broke their **c** in pieces
Ps 149: 8 To bind their kings with **c**
Prov 1: 9 head, and **c** about your neck
Song 1:10 your neck with **c** of gold
Is 40:19 silversmith casts silver **c**
Jer 40: 1 he had taken him bound in **c**
Ezek 19: 9 They put him in a cage with **c**
Mark 5: 3 bind him, not even with **c**
Mark 5: 4 the **c** had been pulled apart
Acts 12: 6 bound with two **c** between two
Acts 12: 7 And his **c** fell off his hands
Acts 16:26 and everyone's **c** were loosed
Acts 22: 5 to Damascus to bring in **c**
Acts 23:29 him worthy of death or **c**
Acts 26:29 as I am, except for these **c**
Eph 6:20 which I am an ambassador in **c**
Phil 1: 7 inasmuch as both in my **c**
Phil 1:13 rest, that my **c** are in Christ
Phil 1:16 to add affliction to my **c**
Col 4: 3 for which I am also in **c**
Col 4:18 Remember my **c**. Grace be with
Phm 10 I have begotten while in my **c**
Phm 13 to me in my **c** for the gospel
Heb 10:34 had compassion on me in my **c**
Heb 11:36 and scourgings, yes, and of **c**
2Pe 2: 4 them into **c** of darkness, to
Jude 6 **c** under darkness for the

CHAIR†
2Ki 4:10 him there, and a table and a **c**

CHALCEDONY†
Rev 21:19 second sapphire, the third **c**

CHALDEA (*see* BABYLON, CHALDEAN, CHALDEANS)
Jer 50:10 And **C** shall become plunder
Jer 51:24 all the inhabitants of **C** for
Ezek 11:24 by the Spirit of God into **C**
Ezek 16:29 as the land of the trader, **C**
Ezek 23:15 of the Babylonians of **C**, the

CHALDEAN† (*see* CHALDEA, CHALDEANS)
Ezra 5:12 king of Babylon, the **C**, who
Jer 39: 5 But the **C** army pursued them
Dan 2:10 magician, astrologer, or **C**

CHALDEANS (see CHALDEA, CHALDEAN, CHALDEANS')
Gen 11:28 native land, in Ur of the **C**
Neh 9: 7 him out of Ur of the **C**, and
Job 1:17 The **C** formed three bands,
Is 47: 1 a throne, O daughter of the **C**
Is 48:14 arm shall be against the **C**
Is 48:20 Flee from the **C**
Jer 37:13 You are defecting to the **C**
Jer 39: 8 the **C** burned the king's house
Jer 40: 9 not be afraid to serve the **C**
Jer 50: 1 the **C** by Jeremiah the prophet
Jer 50: 8 go out of the land of the **C**
Jer 50:35 A sword is against the **C**,"
Ezek 23:14 images of **C** portrayed in
Dan 1: 4 and literature of the **C**
Dan 5:11 the magicians, astrologers, **C**
Dan 5:30 Belshazzar, king of the **C**
Dan 9: 1 king over the realm of the **C**
Hab 1: 6 indeed I am raising up the **C**
Acts 7: 4 came out of the land of the **C**

CHALDEANS'† (see CHALDEANS)
Is 13:19 the beauty of the **C** pride

CHALK† (see CHALKSTONES)
Is 44:13 rule, he marks one out with **c**

CHALKSTONES† (see CHALK)
Is 27: 9 **c** that are beaten to dust

CHAMBER (see CHAMBERS, GUARDROOM)
Gen 43:30 And he went into his **c** and wept
Judg 3:24 to his needs in the cool **c**
2Ki 23:12 the roof, the upper **c** of Ahaz
Job 37: 9 From the **c** of the south comes
Ps 19: 5 coming out of his **c**, And
Song 3: 4 and into the **c** of her who
Ezek 40: 7 Each gate **c** was one rod long
Ezek 42:14 holy **c** into the outer court
Joel 2:16 bridegroom go out from his **c**

CHAMBERLAIN (see PERSONAL AIDE)

CHAMBERS (see CHAMBER)
1Ki 6: 5 temple he built **c** all around
Job 9: 9 and the **c** of the south
Ps 104: 3 of His upper **c** in the waters
Prov 7:27 descending to the **c** of death
Song 1: 4 has brought me into his **c**
Jer 22:14 a wide house with spacious **c**
Ezek 21:14 that enters their private **c**
Ezek 40:10 were three gate **c** on one side
Ezek 40:44 the **c** for the singers in the
Ezek 42:13 are the holy **c** where the

CHAMELEON†
Lev 11:30 the sand lizard, and the **c**

CHAMPION
1Sa 17:51 saw that their **c** was dead

CHANCE
1Sa 6: 9 it was by **c** that it happened
Eccl 9:11 time and **c** happen to them all
Luke 10:31 Now by **c** a certain priest

CHANGE (see CHANGED, CHANGERS', CHANGES, UNCHANGEABLE)
Gen 35: 2 and **c** your garments
Ex 13:17 Lest perhaps the people **c**
Job 14:20 You **c** his countenance and send
Job 17:12 They **c** the night into day
Job 23:13 and who can make Him **c**
Ps 15: 4 to his own hurt and does not **c**
Ps 102:26 Like a cloak You will **c** them
Prov 24:21 with those given to **c**
Jer 2:36 about so much to **c** your way

Jer 13:23 Can the Ethiopian **c** his skin
Dan 5:10 nor let your countenance **c**
Dan 7:25 and shall intend to **c** times
Hos 4: 7 I will **c** their glory into
Mal 3: 6 For I am the LORD, I do not **c**
Acts 6:14 **c** the customs which Moses
Gal 4:20 with you now and to **c** my tone
Heb 7:12 there is also a **c** of the law

CHANGED (see CHANGE)
Gen 31: 7 **c** my wages ten times, but God
Gen 41:14 **c** his clothing, and came to
Lev 13:55 plague has not **c** its color
1Sa 21:13 So he **c** his behavior before
2Ki 23:34 and **c** his name to Jehoiakim
2Ki 24:17 and **c** his name to Zedekiah
Ps 106:20 Thus they **c** their glory Into
Eccl 8: 1 sternness of his face is **c**
Is 24: 5 **c** the ordinance, Broken the
Jer 2:11 Has a nation **c** its gods,
Jer 34:11 afterward they **c** their minds
Jer 48:11 him, and his scent has not **c**
Dan 2: 9 before me till the time has **c**
Dan 3:19 on his face **c** toward Shadrach
Dan 4:16 Let his heart be **c** from that
Dan 5: 6 Then the king's countenance **c**
Mic 2: 4 He has **c** the heritage of my
Acts 28: 6 they **c** their minds and said
Rom 1:23 and **c** the glory of the
1Co 15:51 sleep, but we shall all be **c**
Heb 1:12 them up, and they will be **c**
Heb 7:12 For the priesthood being **c**

CHANGERS'† (see CHANGE)
John 2:15 and poured out the **c** money

CHANGES (see CHANGE)
Gen 45:22 to each man, **c** of garments
Lev 13:16 Or if the raw flesh **c** and
Job 10:17 **c** and war are ever with me
Dan 2:21 He **c** the times and the seasons
Hab 1:11 Then his mind **c**, and he

CHANNEL† (see CHANNELS)
Job 38:25 Who has divided a **c** for the
Is 27:12 from the **c** of the River to

CHANNELS (see CHANNEL)
Ps 18:15 Then the **c** of waters were

CHANT† (see SING)
Mic 3: 5 who **c** "Peace" while they

CHARACTER
Rom 5: 4 and perseverance, **c**
Phil 2:22 But you know his proven **c**

CHARCOAL†
Prov 26:21 As **c** is to burning coals, and

CHARGE (see CHARGED, CHARGERS, CHARGES, CHARGING)
Gen 26: 5 obeyed My voice and kept My **c**
Gen 28: 6 blessed him he gave him a **c**
Ex 22:25 you shall not **c** him interest
Deut 23:19 You shall not **c** interest to
Deut 23:20 foreigner you may **c** interest
2Sa 3: 8 you **c** me today with a fault
Job 1:22 not sin nor **c** God with wrong
Job 34:13 Who gave Him **c** over the earth
Ps 91:11 give His angels **c** over you
Song 2: 7 I **c** you, O daughters of
Is 10: 6 of My wrath I will give him **c**
Jer 39:11 king of Babylon gave **c**
Dan 6: 4 **c** against Daniel concerning
Dan 6: 4 they could find no **c** or fault
Jon 1:14 do not **c** us without innocent
Nah 3: 3 Horsemen **c** with bright sword

Hab 1: 8 Their chargers c ahead
Luke 4:10 give His angels c over You
Acts 7:60 do not c them with this sin
Acts 8:27 who had c of all her treasury
Acts 25:16 concerning the c against him
Rom 8:33 Who shall bring a c against
1Co 9:18 gospel of Christ without c
2Co 11: 7 of God to you free of c
1Th 5:27 I c you by the Lord that this
2Th 3: 8 eat anyone's bread free of c
1Ti 1: 3 may c some that they teach no
1Ti 1:18 This c I commit to you, son
1Ti 5:21 I c you before God and the

CHARGED (see CHARGE)
1Ch 22:13 with which the LORD c Moses
Luke 5:14 And He c him to tell no one,
2Ti 4:16 May it not be c against them

CHARGERS† (see CHARGE)
Hab 1: 8 Their c charge ahead

CHARGES (see CHARGE)
Deut 22:14 c her with shameful conduct,
Job 4:18 if He c His angels with error
Jer 2: 9 will yet bring c against you
Acts 25:27 to specify the c against him

CHARGING† (see CHARGE)
Prov 28:15 a c bear is a wicked ruler
2Ti 2:14 c them before the Lord not to

CHARIOT (see CHARIOTEERS, CHARIOTS)
Gen 41:43 in the second c which he had
Gen 46:29 So Joseph made ready his c
Ex 14:25 And He took off their c wheels
2Sa 8: 4 hamstrung all the c horses
1Ki 7:33 the workmanship of a c wheel
1Ki 10:26 he stationed in the c cities
1Ki 10:29 Now a c that was imported
1Ki 22:34 said to the driver of his c
1Ki 22:35 king was propped up in his c
2Ki 2:11 that suddenly a c of fire
2Ki 2:12 the c of Israel and its
2Ki 5: 9 went with his horses and c
2Ki 9:16 So Jehu rode in a c and went
2Ki 9:21 And his c was made ready
2Ki 9:27 Shoot him also in the c
2Ki 10:16 So they had him ride in his c
2Ki 23:30 his body in a c from Megiddo
1Ch 28:18 for the construction of the c
2Ch 1:17 imported from Egypt a c for
Ps 46: 9 He burns the c in the fire
Ps 104: 3 Who makes the clouds His c
Is 21: 7 he saw a c with a pair of
Is 21: 7 a c of donkeys, and a chariot
Is 21: 7 a c of camels, and he listened
Is 21: 9 here comes a c of men with a
Jer 51:21 I will break in pieces the c
Mic 1:13 harness the c to the swift
Zech 6: 2 With the first c were red
Acts 8:28 And sitting in his c, he was
Acts 8:29 Go near and overtake this c

CHARIOTEERS† (see CHARIOT)
2Sa 10:18 David killed seven hundred c
1Ch 19:18 David killed seven thousand c

CHARIOTS (see CHARIOT)
Ex 14: 7 and all the c of Egypt with
Ex 14: 9 c of Pharaoh, his horsemen and
Ex 14:28 returned and covered the c
Josh 11: 6 and burn their c with fire
Josh 17:16 of the valley have c of iron
1Ki 4:26 stalls of horses for his c
1Ki 9:19 Solomon had, cities for his c
2Ki 6:17 c of fire all around Elisha
2Ki 7: 6 to hear the noise of c and the

2Ki 13: 7 only fifty horsemen, ten c
2Ki 13:14 the c of Israel and their
2Ki 18:24 put your trust in Egypt for c
2Ki 23:11 he burned the c of the sun
1Ch 19: 6 to hire for themselves c and
2Ch 16: 8 a huge army with very many c
Ps 20: 7 Some trust in c, and some in
Ps 68:17 The c of God are twenty
Song 1: 9 to my filly among Pharaoh's c
Is 2: 7 and there is no end to their c
Is 22:18 there your glorious c shall
Is 66:15 come with fire and with His c
Jer 4:13 and his c like a whirlwind
Jer 17:25 throne of David, riding in c
Jer 22: 4 riding on horses and in c
Jer 47: 3 at the rushing of his c, at
Dan 11:40 him like a whirlwind, with c
Joel 2: 5 With a noise like c over
Nah 2: 4 The c rage in the streets,
Nah 3: 2 horses, of clattering c
Hab 3: 8 horses, your c of salvation

CHARITABLE
Matt 6: 1 do your c deeds before men
Acts 9:36 and c deeds which she did

CHARM† (see CHARMED, CHARMERS, CHARMING, CHARMS)
Prov 31:30 C is deceitful and beauty is

CHARMED† (see CHARM)
Eccl 10:11 may bite when it is not c
Jer 8:17 you, vipers which cannot be c

CHARMERS† (see CHARM)
Ps 58: 5 will not heed the voice of c
Is 19: 3 consult the idols and the c

CHARMING† (see CHARM)
Ps 58: 5 C ever so skillfully

CHARMS† (see CHARM)
Is 3:20 the perfume boxes, the c,
Jer 3:13 and have scattered your c to
Ezek 13:18 sew magic c on their sleeves
Ezek 13:20 c by which you hunt souls

CHASE (see CHASED, CHASES, CHASING)
Lev 26: 7 You will c your enemies, and
Lev 26: 8 Five of you shall c a hundred
Ps 35: 5 the angel of the LORD c them
Hos 2: 7 She will c her lovers, but

CHASED (see CHASE)
Deut 1:44 c you as bees do, and drove
Josh 10:10 c them along the road that
Judg 20:43 c them, and easily trampled
Job 18:18 and c out of the world
Job 20: 8 Yes, he will be c away like a
Is 17:13 be c like the chaff of the

CHASES† (see CHASE)
Prov 19:26 c away his mother is a son

CHASING† (see CHASE)
1Sa 17:53 from c the Philistines, and

CHASTE†
2Co 11: 2 you as a c virgin to Christ
Tit 2: 5 to be discreet, c, homemakers
1Pe 3: 2 when they observe your c

CHASTEN (see CHASTENED, CHASTENING, CHASTENS)
2Sa 7:14 I will c him with the rod of
Ps 6: 1 anger, Nor c me in Your hot
Prov 19:18 C your son while there is
Heb 12: 7 whom a father does not c
Rev 3:19 many as I love, I rebuke and c

CHASTENED (see CHASTEN)
Job 33:19 Man is also c with pain on
Ps 69:10 c my soul with fasting, That

Ps 73:14 plagued, And **c** every morning
Ps 118:18 The LORD has **c** me severely
Heb 12:10 **c** us as seemed best to them

CHASTENING (see CHASTEN)
Deut 11: 2 the **c** of the LORD your God
Job 5:17 despise the **c** of the Almighty
Prov 3:11 not despise the **c** of the LORD
Heb 12: 5 not despise the **c** of the LORD
Heb 12: 7 If you endure **c**, God deals
Heb 12:11 Now no **c** seems to be joyful

CHASTENS† (see CHASTEN)
Deut 8: 5 heart that as a man **c** his son
Deut 8: 5 so the LORD your God **c** you
Heb 12: 6 For whom the LORD loves He **c**

CHASTISE (see CHASTISED, CHASTISEMENT)
1Ki 12:11 whips, but I will **c** you with
Luke 23:16 I will therefore **c** Him
Luke 23:22 I will therefore **c** Him and

CHASTISED (see CHASTISE)
1Ki 12:11 my father **c** you with whips,

CHASTISEMENT† (see CHASTISE)
Is 53: 5 the **c** for our peace was upon
Jer 30:14 with the **c** of a cruel one,

CHATTER† (see CHATTERED)
Prov 14:23 but idle **c** leads only to

CHATTERED† (see CHATTER)
Is 38:14 a crane or a swallow, so I **c**

CHEAT† (see CHEATED)
Lev 19:13 You shall not **c** your neighbor
1Co 6: 8 you yourselves do wrong and **c**
Col 2:18 Let no one **c** you of your
Col 2: 8 Beware lest anyone **c** you

CHEATED (see CHEAT)
1Sa 12: 3 I taken, or whom have I **c**
2Co 7: 2 no one, we have **c** no one

CHEBAR
Ezek 1: 1 the captives by the River **C**
Ezek 10:15 creature I saw by the River **C**

CHEDORLAOMER
Gen 14: 1 **C** king of Elam, and Tidal king

CHEEK (see CHEEKBONE, CHEEKS)
Matt 5:39 slaps you on your right **c**
Luke 6:29 who strikes you on the one **c**

CHEEKBONE† (see CHEEK)
Ps 3: 7 all my enemies on the **c**

CHEEKS (see CHEEK)
Deut 18: 3 priest the shoulder, the **c**
Song 1:10 Your **c** are lovely with
Lam 1: 2 night, her tears are on her **c**

CHEER (see CHEERFUL, CHEERS)
Eccl 11: 9 let your heart **c** you in the
Matt 9: 2 Son, be of good **c**
Matt 9:22 Be of good **c**, daughter
Matt 14:27 Be of good **c**! It is I
John 16:33 but be of good **c**, I have
Acts 23:11 Be of good **c**, Paul

CHEERFUL† (see CHEER, CHEERFULLY, CHEERFULNESS)
Ruth 3: 7 and drunk, and his heart was **c**
1Ki 21: 7 food, and let your heart be **c**
Prov 15:13 heart makes a **c** countenance
Zech 8:19 **c** feasts for the house of
2Co 9: 7 for God loves a **c** giver
Jas 5:13 Is anyone **c**? Let him sing

CHEERFULLY† (see CHEERFUL)
Acts 24:10 I do the more **c** answer for

CHEERFULNESS† (see CHEERFUL)
Rom 12: 8 he who shows mercy, with **c**

CHEERS† (see CHEER)
Judg 9:13 which **c** both God and men, and

CHEESE† (see CHEESES)
2Sa 17:29 **c** of the herd, for David and
Job 10:10 milk, and curdle me like **c**

CHEESES† (see CHEESE)
1Sa 17:18 And carry these ten **c** to the

CHEMOSH
1Ki 11: 7 built a high place for **C** the
1Ki 11:33 **C** the god of the Moabites, and

CHERETHITES
2Sa 20:23 of Jehoiada was over the **C**
Ezek 25:16 and I will cut off the **C** and
Zeph 2: 5 seacoast, the nation of the **C**

CHERISHES†
Eph 5:29 **c** it, just as the Lord does
1Th 2: 7 mother **c** her own children

CHERITH
1Ki 17: 3 and hide by the Brook **C**,

CHERUB (see CHERUBIM)
Ex 25:19 Make one **c** at one end, and the
2Sa 22:11 He rode upon a **c**, and flew
1Ki 6:24 wing of the **c** was five cubits
Ezek 10: 2 among the wheels, under the **c**
Ezek 28:14 the anointed **c** who covers
Ezek 41:18 a palm tree between **c** and **c**

CHERUBIM (see CHERUB)
Gen 3:24 He placed **c** at the east of
Ex 25:18 you shall make two **c** of gold
Ex 26: 1 of **c** you shall weave them
Ex 26:31 with an artistic design of **c**
Ex 37: 9 The **c** spread out their wings
Num 7:89 from between the two **c**
1Sa 4: 4 who dwells between the **c**
2Sa 6: 2 who dwells between the **c**
1Ki 6:28 he overlaid the **c** with gold
1Ki 8: 7 the **c** overshadowed the ark and
2Ch 3:10 Most Holy Place he made two **c**
2Ch 3:14 fine linen, and wove **c** into it
Ezek 10: 1 was above the head of the **c**
Ezek 41:18 And it was made with **c** and palm
Heb 9: 5 above it were the **c** of glory

CHEST (see CHESTS)
1Sa 6: 8 offering in a **c** by its side
2Ki 12: 9 Jehoiada the priest took a **c**
2Ki 12:10 there was much money in the **c**
2Ch 24: 8 commandment they made a **c**
2Ch 24:11 officer came and emptied the **c**
Dan 2:32 head was of fine gold, its **c**
Rev 1:13 girded about the **c** with a

CHESTNUT
Gen 30:37 **c** trees, peeled white strips

CHESTS† (see CHEST)
Ezek 27:24 in **c** of multicolored apparel,
Rev 15: 6 having their **c** girded with

CHEW (see CHEWED, CHEWING, CHEWS)
Lev 11: 7 yet does not **c** the cud, is
Mic 3: 5 while they **c** with their teeth

CHEWED (see CHEW)
Num 11:33 their teeth, before it was **c**

CHEWING (see CHEW)
Lev 11: 3 cloven hooves and **c** the cud
Joel 1: 4 What the **c** locust left, the

CHEWS (see CHEW)
Lev 11: 4 because it **c** the cud but does

CHICKS†
Matt 23:37 gathers her c under her wings

CHIEF (see CHIEFLY, CHIEFS, CHIEFTAINS)
Gen 36:15 were C Teman, Chief
Gen 40: 2 c butler and the c baker
Gen 40:21 Then he restored the c butler
Gen 40:22 But he hanged the c baker
Gen 47: 6 then make them c herdsmen
Lev 21: 4 being a c man among his
Num 3:32 be c over the leaders of the
Num 31:26 and the c fathers of the
Josh 22:14 the c house of every tribe of
1Sa 21: 7 the c of the herdsmen who
1Sa 28: 2 one of my c guardians forever
2Sa 8:18 David's sons were c ministers
2Sa 23: 8 c among the captains
2Sa 23:18 was c of another three
2Ki 25:18 took Seraiah the c priest
1Ch 5:15 was c of their father's house
1Ch 7:40 men of valor, c leaders
1Ch 9:17 Shallum was the c
1Ch 9:26 were four c gatekeepers
1Ch 11:15 Now three of the thirty c men
1Ch 18:17 David's sons were c ministers
Ezra 7: 5 the son of Aaron the c priest
Ps 118:22 Has become the c cornerstone
Ps 137: 6 Jerusalem Above my c joy
Song 4:14 aloes, with all the c spices
Song 5:10 ruddy, c among ten thousand
Jer 31: 7 among the c of the nations
Jer 52:24 took Seraiah the c priest
Dan 1: 7 To them the c of the eunuchs
Dan 2:48 c administrator over all the
Dan 4: 9 c of the magicians, because I
Dan 10:13 Michael, one of the c princes
Amos 6: 1 persons in the c nation, to
Hab 3:19 To the C Musician
Matt 16:21 c priests and scribes, and be
Matt 20:18 be betrayed to the c priests
Matt 21:23 the c priests and the elders
Matt 21:42 has become the c cornerstone
Matt 27: 3 of silver to the c priests
Mat 27:62 the c priests and Pharisees
Mark 10:33 be delivered to the c priests
Mark 15: 3 the c priests accused Him of
Mark 15:11 But the c priests stirred up
Luke 19: 2 who was a c tax collector
Luke 22:52 Jesus said to the c priests
Luke 23: 4 Pilate said to the c priests
John 7:32 the c priests sent officers
Acts 9:14 the c priests to bind all who
Acts 14:12 because he was the c speaker
Acts 19:14 of Sceva, a Jewish c priest
Eph 2:20 being the c cornerstone,
1Ti 1:15 save sinners, of whom I am c
1Pe 2: 6 I lay in Zion a c cornerstone
1Pe 5: 4 when the C Shepherd appears,

CHIEFLY† (see CHIEF)
Rom 3: 2 C because to them were

CHIEFS (see CHIEF)
Gen 36:43 These were the c of Edom,

CHIEFTAINS† (see CHIEF)
Jer 13:21 you have taught them to be c

CHILD (see CHILDHOOD, CHILDISH, CHILDLESS, CHILDREN, CHILD'S)
Gen 11:30 was barren; she had no c
Gen 16:11 Behold, you are with c, and
Gen 17:10 Every male c among you shall
Gen 17:14 And the uncircumcised male c
Gen 44:20 a c of his old age, who is
Ex 2: 2 saw that he was a beautiful c
Ex 2: 9 Take this c away and nurse him

Ex 21:22 fight, and hurt a woman with c
Lev 12: 2 conceived, and borne a male c
Lev 12: 5 But if she bears a female c
Lev 22:13 or divorced, and has no c, and
Num 11:12 guardian carries a nursing c
Judg 11:34 and she was his only c
Judg 13: 5 for the c shall be a Nazirite
Judg 13: 7 for the c shall be a Nazirite
Judg 13: 8 do for the c who will be born
1Sa 1:27 For this c I prayed, and the
1Sa 2:11 But the c ministered to the
1Sa 2:26 the c Samuel grew in stature,
1Sa 4:21 Then she named the c Ichabod
1Sa 15: 3 and woman, infant and nursing c
2Sa 12:15 the LORD struck the c that
2Sa 12:18 came to pass that the c died
1Ki 3:20 laid her dead c in my bosom
1Ki 3:25 Divide the living c in two
1Ki 13: 2 Behold, a c, Josiah by name,
2Ki 4:26 Is it well with the c
2Ki 4:29 my staff on the face of the c
2Ki 4:31 The c has not awakened
2Ki 4:34 And he went up and lay on the c
2Ki 4:34 flesh of the c became warm
2Ki 5:14 like the flesh of a little c
2Ki 8:12 rip open their women with c
Job 3:16 not hidden like a stillborn c
Prov 20:11 Even a c is known by his
Prov 22: 6 Train up a c in the way he
Prov 22:15 bound up in the heart of a c
Prov 23:13 withhold correction from a c
Prov 23:24 a wise c will delight in him
Prov 29:15 but a c left to himself
Eccl 10:16 O land, when your king is a c
Is 3: 5 the c will be insolent toward
Is 7:16 For before the C shall know
Is 9: 6 For unto us a C is born, unto
Is 10:19 that a c may write them
Is 11: 6 a little c shall lead them
Is 11: 8 The nursing c shall play by
Is 26:17 As a woman with c is in pain
Is 49:15 a woman forget her nursing c
Is 54: 1 who have not travailed with c
Jer 30: 6 a man is ever in labor with c
Jer 31:20 Is he a pleasant c
Hos 11: 1 When Israel was a c, I loved
Matt 1:18 with c of the Holy Spirit
Matt 1:23 a virgin shall be with c
Matt 2: 8 diligently for the young C
Matt 2: 9 over where the young C was
Matt 2:13 Arise, take the young C and
Matt 2:13 the young C to destroy Him
Matt 17:18 the c was cured from that
Matt 18: 2 called a little c to Him, set
Matt 18: 4 c is the greatest in the
Mark 5:39 The c is not dead, but
Mark 5:40 entered where the c was lying
Mark 5:41 He took the c by the hand
Mark 9:24 the father of the c cried out
Mark 10:15 c will by no means enter it
Luke 1:59 they came to circumcise the c
Luke 1:66 What kind of c will this be
Luke 1:76 and you, c, will be called the
Luke 1:80 So the c grew and became
Luke 2:21 for the circumcision of the C
Luke 2:27 brought in the C Jesus, to do
Luke 2:34 this C is destined for the
Luke 2:40 the C grew and became strong
Luke 9:42 unclean spirit, healed the c
Luke 9:48 receives this little c in My
Acts 7: 5 even when Abraham had no c
1Co 13:11 I was a c, I spoke as a c
Gal 4: 1 heir, as long as he is a c
Heb 11:11 she bore a c when she was
Heb 11:23 they saw he was a beautiful c

Rev 12: 2 Then being with c, she cried
Rev 12: 4 to devour her C as soon as it
Rev 12: 5 her C was caught up to God and

CHILDBEARING†
Gen 18:11 Sarah had passed the age of c
1Ti 2:15 she will be saved in c if

CHILDBIRTH (see BIRTH)
Gen 35:16 Rachel travailed in c, and
Is 13: 8 be in pain as a woman in c

CHILDHOOD (see CHILD)
2Ti 3:15 that from c you have known

CHILDISH† (see CHILD)
1Co 13:11 a man, I put away c things

CHILDLESS (see CHILD)
Gen 15: 2 You give me, seeing I go c
Jer 22:30 Write this man down as c
Luke 20:30 her as wife, and he died c

CHILDREN (see CHILD, CHILDREN'S, GRANDCHILDREN)
Gen 3:16 pain you shall bring forth c
Gen 6: 4 of men and they bore c to them
Gen 16: 1 wife, had borne him no c
Gen 21: 7 that Sarah would nurse c
Gen 25:22 But the c struggled together
Gen 30: 1 Give me c, or else I die
Gen 36:31 reigned over the c of Israel
Gen 37: 3 Joseph more than all his c
Gen 45:10 your children's c
Ex 1: 1 these are the names of the c
Ex 1:12 in dread of the c of Israel
Ex 1:17 but saved the male c alive
Ex 2: 6 This is one of the Hebrews' c
Ex 3: 9 the cry of the c of Israel
Ex 5:14 officers of the c of Israel
Ex 12:26 when your c say to you, "What
Ex 12:27 over the houses of the c of
Ex 12:37 men on foot, besides c
Ex 14: 8 and he pursued the c of Israel
Ex 16: 2 whole congregation of the c
Ex 16:12 murmurings of the c of Israel
Ex 16:35 the c of Israel ate manna
Ex 17: 3 of Egypt, to kill us and our c
Ex 20: 5 fathers on the c to the third
Ex 21: 4 her c shall be her master's,
Ex 21: 5 my master, my wife, and my c
Ex 22:24 widows, and your c fatherless
Ex 24: 5 young men of the c of Israel
Ex 29:43 meet with the c of Israel
Ex 29:45 dwell among the c of Israel
Ex 30:16 money of the c of Israel, and
Ex 30:16 c of Israel before the LORD
Ex 32:20 made the c of Israel drink it
Ex 33: 6 So the c of Israel stripped
Ex 34: 7 of the fathers upon the c
Lev 6:18 the c of Aaron may eat it
Lev 10:14 offerings of the c of Israel
Lev 16:21 iniquities of the c of Israel
Lev 16:34 atonement for the c of Israel
Lev 25:45 the c of the strangers who
Lev 25:46 for your c after you, to
Lev 26:22 which shall rob you of your c
Lev 26:46 and the c of Israel on Mount
Num 1: 2 of the c of Israel, by their
Num 1:20 Now the c of Reuben, Israel's
Num 1:22 From the c of Simeon, their
Num 1:24 From the c of Gad, their
Num 1:26 From the c of Judah, their
Num 1:28 From the c of Issachar, their
Num 1:30 From the c of Zebulun, their
Num 1:32 the c of Ephraim, their
Num 1:34 From the c of Manasseh, their
Num 1:36 From the c of Benjamin, their
Num 1:38 From the c of Dan, their

Num 1:40 From the c of Asher, their
Num 1:42 From the c of Naphtali, their
Num 1:45 numbered of the c of Israel
Num 2: 3 the leader of the c of Judah
Num 2: 5 leader of the c of Issachar
Num 3: 8 the needs of the c of Israel
Num 3:12 womb among the c of Israel
Num 3:40 c of Israel from a month old
Num 3:46 firstborn of the c of Israel
Num 5:28 be free and may conceive c
Num 6:23 shall bless the c of Israel
Num 6:27 My name on the c of Israel
Num 8:17 the c of Israel are Mine,
Num 8:18 firstborn of the c of Israel
Num 8:19 be no plague among the c of
Num 8:19 the c of Israel come near the
Num 9:18 the c of Israel would journey
Num 9:22 the c of Israel would remain
Num 10:12 the c of Israel set out from
Num 10:15 army of the tribe of the c of
Num 11: 4 so the c of Israel also wept
Num 13:26 c of Israel in the Wilderness
Num 14: 2 all the c of Israel murmured
Num 14: 3 and c should become victims
Num 16:38 be a sign to the c of Israel
Num 16:40 to be a memorial to the c of
Num 18: 5 more wrath on the c of Israel
Num 18: 8 holy gifts of the c of Israel
Num 18:24 the tithes of the c of Israel
Num 19: 9 c of Israel for the water of
Num 25:13 atonement for the c of Israel
Num 26: 2 c of Israel from twenty years
Num 34:14 For the tribe of the c of
Num 34:14 the tribe of the c of Gad
Num 35:15 refuge for the c of Israel
Num 36: 2 by lot to the c of Israel
Num 36: 7 So the inheritance of the c
Deut 1:39 your little ones and your c
Deut 4: 9 And teach them to your c and
Deut 4:25 When you beget c and
Deut 4:40 you and with your c after you
Deut 5: 9 upon the c to the third and
Deut 5:29 them and with their c forever
Deut 11:19 shall teach them to your c
Deut 11:21 the days of your c may be
Deut 14: 1 You are the c of the LORD
Deut 17:20 his c in the midst of Israel
Deut 21:15 and they have borne him c
Deut 23: 8 The c of the third generation
Deut 24:16 be put to death for their c
Deut 32: 5 they are not His c, because
Deut 32: 8 the number of the c of Israel
Deut 32:20 c in whom is no faith
Deut 34: 8 And the c of Israel wept for
Deut 34: 9 so the c of Israel heeded him
Josh 4:12 armed before the c of Israel
Josh 4:21 When your c ask their fathers
Josh 4:22 you shall let your c know
Josh 5:10 So the c of Israel camped in
Josh 11:14 the c of Israel took as booty
Josh 11:19 peace with the c of Israel
Josh 11:22 the land of the c of Israel
Josh 12: 1 whom the c of Israel defeated
Josh 12: 6 the c of Israel had conquered
Josh 14: 1 are the areas which the c of
Josh 14: 4 For the c of Joseph were two
Josh 15:13 portion among the c of Judah
Josh 16: 5 border of the c of Ephraim
Josh 19: 1 inheritance of the c of Judah
Josh 22:12 whole congregation of the c
Josh 22:33 thing pleased the c of Israel
Josh 22:33 the c of Israel blessed God
Josh 24: 4 and his c went down to Egypt
Judg 1:21 Jebusites dwell with the c of
Judg 1:34 the Amorites forced the c of

Judg	2:11	Then the c of Israel did evil
Judg	3: 7	So the c of Israel did evil
Judg	3: 8	and the c of Israel served
Judg	3: 9	When the c of Israel cried
Judg	3: 9	deliverer for the c of Israel
Judg	4: 3	oppressed the c of Israel
Judg	6: 8	a prophet to the c of Israel
Judg	13: 2	wife was barren and had no c
Judg	19:12	are not of the c of Israel
Judg	20:15	the c of Benjamin numbered
Judg	20:23	the c of my brother Benjamin
Judg	20:27	So the c of Israel inquired
Judg	21: 6	the c of Israel grieved for
Judg	21:10	including the women and c
1Sa	1: 2	Peninnah had c
1Sa	1: 2	but Hannah had no c
1Sa	2: 5	she who has many c has become
1Sa	7: 6	Samuel judged the c of Israel
1Sa	15: 6	showed kindness to all the c
2Sa	6:23	no c to the day of her death
2Sa	7: 6	the c of Israel up from Egypt
2Sa	12: 3	with him and with his c
2Sa	21: 2	his zeal for the c of Israel
1Ki	6: 1	eightieth year after the c of
1Ki	8: 9	covenant with the c of Israel
1Ki	8:63	all the c of Israel dedicated
1Ki	12:17	Rehoboam reigned over the c
1Ki	12:24	your brethren the c of Israel
1Ki	12:33	a feast for the c of Israel
1Ki	20: 3	loveliest wives and c are mine
1Ki	20: 5	gold, your wives and your c"
1Ki	20:27	the c of Israel were mustered
1Ki	20:27	Now the c of Israel encamped
1Ki	20:29	the c of Israel killed one
2Ki	8:12	and you will dash their c, and
2Ki	14: 6	But the c of the murderers he
2Ki	14: 6	not be put to death for the c
2Ki	14: 6	nor shall the c be put to
2Ki	17: 7	the c of Israel had sinned
2Ki	17:22	For the c of Israel walked in
2Ki	17:31	c in fire to Adrammelech and
2Ki	19: 3	for the c have come to birth,
1Ch	14: 4	c whom he had in Jerusalem
1Ch	16:13	you c of Jacob, His chosen
2Ch	5:10	covenant with the c of Israel
2Ch	10:18	but the c of Israel stoned
2Ch	13:12	O c of Israel, do not fight
2Ch	13:18	the c of Judah prevailed,
2Ch	25: 4	he did not execute their c
2Ch	25:12	the c of Judah took captive
2Ch	28: 3	burned his c in the fire,
Ezra	10:44	had wives by whom they had c
Neh	5: 5	our c as their c
Neh	9:23	c as the stars of heaven, and
Neh	13:16	the Sabbath to the c of Judah
Job	17: 5	the eyes of his c will fail
Job	19:17	to the c of my own body
Job	19:18	Even young c despise me
Job	24: 5	food for them and for their c
Job	27:14	If his c are multiplied, it
Job	29: 5	me, when my c were around me
Job	41:34	king over all the c of pride
Job	42:16	and forty years, and saw his c
Ps	14: 2	from heaven upon the c of men
Ps	17:14	They are satisfied with c
Ps	34:11	Come, you c, listen to me
Ps	53: 2	from heaven upon the c of men
Ps	69: 8	And an alien to my mother's c
Ps	72: 4	will save the c of the needy
Ps	73:15	to the generation of Your c
Ps	78: 4	not hide them from their c
Ps	78: 5	make them known to their c
Ps	78: 6	and declare them to their c
Ps	82: 6	all of you are c of the Most
Ps	83: 8	They have helped the c of Lot

Ps	89:47	You created all the c of men
Ps	90: 3	And say, "Return, O c of men
Ps	90:16	And Your glory to their c
Ps	102:28	The c of Your servants will
Ps	103: 7	His acts to the c of Israel
Ps	103:13	As a father pities his c, So
Ps	103:17	righteousness to children's c
Ps	105: 6	You c of Jacob, His chosen
Ps	107: 8	works to the c of men
Ps	109: 9	Let his c be fatherless, And
Ps	109:12	any to favor his fatherless c
Ps	113: 9	Like a joyful mother of c
Ps	115:16	He has given to the c of men
Ps	127: 3	c are a heritage from the
Ps	127: 4	So are the c of one's youth
Ps	128: 3	Your c like olive plants All
Ps	128: 6	may you see your children's c
Ps	147:13	has blessed your c within you
Ps	148:12	Old men and c
Ps	149: 2	Let the c of Zion be joyful
Prov	4: 1	Hear, my c, the instruction
Prov	13:22	to his children's c, but the
Prov	17: 6	Children's c are the crown of
Prov	17: 6	and the glory of c is their
Prov	20: 7	his c are blessed after him
Prov	31:28	Her c rise up and call her
Eccl	6: 3	If a man begets a hundred c
Is	1: 2	nourished and brought up c
Is	1: 4	c who are corrupters
Is	8:18	the c whom the LORD has given
Is	13:16	Their c also will be dashed
Is	13:18	their eye will not spare c
Is	17: 3	the glory of the c of Israel
Is	23: 4	not labor, nor bring forth c
Is	30: 1	Woe to the rebellious c,"
Is	30: 9	c who will not hear the law
Is	47: 9	the loss of c, and widowhood
Is	49:21	me, since I have lost my c
Is	49:25	you, and I will save your c
Is	54: 1	For more are the c of the
Is	54: 1	the c of the married woman
Is	54:13	All your c shall be taught by
Is	54:13	shall be the peace of your c
Is	63: 8	My people, c who will not lie
Is	65:23	nor bring forth c for trouble
Jer	2:30	vain I have chastened your c
Jer	3:14	Return, O backsliding c,"
Jer	4:22	They are silly c, and they
Jer	5: 7	Your c have forsaken Me and
Jer	6:11	pour it out on the c outside
Jer	7:18	The c gather wood, the
Jer	7:30	For the c of Judah have done
Jer	9:21	palaces, to kill off the c
Jer	10:20	my c have gone from me, and
Jer	15: 7	I will bereave them of c
Jer	17:19	gate of the c of the people
Jer	18:21	up their c to the famine, and
Jer	18:21	widows and bereaved of their c
Jer	31:15	Rachel weeping for her c
Jer	31:15	to be comforted for her c
Jer	31:17	That your c shall come back
Jer	32:32	the evil of the c of Israel
Jer	32:39	of them and their c after them
Jer	38:23	wives and your c to the Chaldeans
Jer	40: 7	to him men, women, c, and the
Jer	47: 3	not look back for their c
Jer	49:11	Leave your fatherless c, I
Lam	1:16	My c are desolate because the
Lam	2:19	for the life of your young c
Lam	4:10	women have cooked their own c
Ezek	2: 4	are impudent and stubborn c
Ezek	20:21	the c rebelled against Me
Ezek	33: 2	speak to the c of your people
Ezek	48:11	the c of Israel went astray
Dan	2:38	wherever the c of men dwell

Hos	1: 2	c of harlotry, for the land
Hos	1:10	Yet the number of the c of
Hos	2: 4	will not have mercy on her c
Hos	4: 6	I also will forget your c
Hos	10: 9	the c of iniquity did not
Hos	10:14	dashed in pieces upon her c
Joel	1: 3	Tell your c about it
Joel	2:23	you c of Zion, and rejoice in
Amos	9: 7	Ethiopia to Me, O c of Israel
Mic	1:16	because of your precious c
Nah	3:10	her young c also were dashed
Zeph	1: 8	the princes and the king's c
Zech	10: 7	their c shall see it and be
Zech	10: 9	live, together with their c
Mal	4: 6	of the fathers to the c, and
Mal	4: 6	of the c to their fathers
Matt	2:16	male c who were in Bethlehem
Matt	2:18	Rachel weeping for her c
Matt	3: 9	up to Abraham from these
Matt	7:11	to give good gifts to your c
Matt	10:21	and c will rise up against
Matt	11:16	It is like c sitting in the
Matt	11:19	wisdom is justified by her c
Matt	14:21	men, besides women and c
Matt	14:38	men, besides women and c
Matt	18: 3	and become as little c, you
Matt	18:25	be sold, with his wife and c
Matt	19:13	Then little c were brought to
Matt	19:14	Let the little c come to Me
Matt	19:29	mother or wife or c or lands
Matt	22:24	if a man dies, having no c
Matt	23:37	to gather your c together
Matt	27: 9	of the c of Israel priced
Matt	27:25	blood be on us and on our c
Mark	7:27	Let the c be filled first,
Mark	10:24	C, how hard it is for those
Mark	10:29	mother or wife or c or lands
Mark	10:30	and sisters and mothers and c
Luke	1:16	he will turn many of the c of
Luke	3: 8	up to Abraham from these
Luke	7:32	They are like c sitting in
Luke	7:35	is justified by all her c
Luke	11: 7	and my c are with me in bed
Luke	20:28	a wife, and he dies without c
John	1:12	the right to become c of God
John	8:39	If you were Abraham's c, you
John	11:52	c of God who were scattered
John	13:33	Little c, I shall be with you
John	21: 5	C, have you any food
Acts	2:39	is to you and to your c, and to
Acts	13:33	fulfilled this for us their c
Acts	21:21	not to circumcise their c nor
Rom	8:16	spirit that we are c of God
Rom	8:17	and if c, then heirs
Rom	8:21	liberty of the c of God
Rom	9: 8	who are the c of the flesh
Rom	9: 8	but the c of the promise are
Rom	9:11	(for the c not yet being born
Rom	9:27	Though the number of the c of
1Co	4:14	as my beloved c I warn you
1Co	7:14	otherwise your c would be
1Co	14:20	do not be c in understanding
2Co	6:13	the same (I speak as to c)
2Co	12:14	For the c ought not to lay up
2Co	12:14	but the parents for the c
Gal	4: 3	Even so we, when we were c
Gal	4:19	My little c, for whom I labor
Gal	4:25	and is in bondage with her c
Gal	4:27	c than she who has a husband
Gal	4:28	Isaac was, are c of promise
Gal	4:31	we are not c of the bondwoman
Eph	2: 3	and were by nature c of wrath
Eph	4:14	that we should no longer be c
Eph	5: 1	be followers of God as dear c
Eph	5: 8	Walk as c of light

Eph	6: 1	C, obey your parents in the
Eph	6: 4	not provoke your c to wrath
Phil	2:15	c of God without fault in the
Col	3:20	C, obey your parents in all
Col	3:21	do not provoke your c, lest
1Th	2: 7	mother cherishes her own c
1Th	2:11	as a father does his own c
1Ti	3: 4	having his c in submission
1Ti	3:12	of one wife, ruling their c
1Ti	5: 4	widow has c or grandchildren
1Ti	5:10	if she has brought up c, if
1Ti	5:14	younger widows marry, bear c
Tit	1: 6	having faithful c not accused
Tit	2: 4	husbands, to love their c
Heb	2:13	the c whom God has given Me
Heb	11:22	departure of the c of Israel
1Pe	1:14	as obedient c, not conforming
2Pe	2:14	practices, and are accursed c
1Jn	2: 1	My little c, these things I
1Jn	2:18	Little c, it is the last hour
1Jn	2:28	And now, little c, abide in
1Jn	3: 1	we should be called c of God
1Jn	3: 2	Beloved, now we are c of God
1Jn	3: 7	Little c, let no one deceive
1Jn	3:10	In this the c of God and the
1Jn	3:10	God and the c of the devil are
1Jn	3:18	My little c, let us not love
1Jn	5: 2	that we love the c of God
1Jn	5:21	Little c, keep yourselves
2Jn	1	To the elect lady and her c
3Jn	4	hear that my c walk in truth
Rev	2:14	block before the c of Israel
Rev	2:23	I will kill her c with death
Rev	7: 4	the c of Israel were sealed

CHILDREN'S *(see* CHILDREN)

Ex	34: 7	the c children to the third
Prov	17: 6	C children are the crown of
Jer	31:29	the c teeth are set on edge
Ezek	18: 2	the c teeth are set on edge
Matt	15:26	not good to take the c bread
Mark	7:28	table eat from the c crumbs

CHILD'S† *(see* CHILD)

Ex	2: 8	went and called the c mother
1Ki	17:21	let this c soul come back to
Job	33:25	flesh shall be young like a c
Matt	2:20	the young C life are dead

CHILION

| Ruth | 1: 2 | his two sons were Mahlon and C |

CHIMNEY†

| Hos | 13: 3 | floor and like smoke from a c |

CHINNERETH *(see* CHINNEROTH, GENNESARET)

| Num | 34:11 | eastern side of the Sea of C |

CHINNEROTH *(see* CHINNERETH)

| Josh | 12: 3 | plain from the Sea of C as |

CHISEL†

| 1Ki | 6: 7 | so that no hammer or c or any |

CHISLEV†

| Neh | 1: 1 | to pass in the month of C |
| Zech | 7: 1 | the ninth month, which is C |

CHLOE'S†

| 1Co | 1:11 | by those of C household, |

CHOICE *(see* CHOICEST, CHOOSE)

Gen	27: 9	there two c kids of the goats
1Ch	7:40	c men, mighty men of valor,
Esth	2: 9	Then seven c maidservants
Prov	8:10	knowledge rather than c gold
Prov	8:19	and my revenue than c silver
Is	25: 6	people a feast of c pieces
Ezek	24: 4	fill it with c cuts
Ezek	31:16	all the trees of Eden, the c

Dan 11:15 Even his **c** troops shall have

CHOICEST (*see* CHOICE)
Gen 23: 6 in the **c** of our burial places
Deut 32:14 and goats, with the **c** wheat
Is 5: 2 and planted it with the **c** vine
Ezek 27:22 for your wares the **c** spices

CHOIR† (*see* CHOIRS)
Neh 12:38 **c** went the opposite way, and I

CHOIRS (*see* CHOIR)
Neh 12:31 two large thanksgiving **c**, one

CHOKE† (*see* CHOKED)
Matt 13:22 of riches **c** the word, and he
Mark 4:19 things entering in **c** the word

CHOKED (*see* CHOKE)
Matt 13: 7 thorns sprang up and **c** them
Mark 4: 7 **c** it, and it yielded no crop
Luke 8:14 are **c** with cares, riches, and

CHOOSE (*see* CHOICE, CHOOSES, CHOOSING, CHOSE, CHOSEN)
Ex 17: 9 **C** us some men and go out,
Num 17: 5 the man whom I **c** will blossom
Deut 1:13 **C** wise, understanding, and
Deut 7: 7 **c** you because you were more
Deut 30:19 therefore **c** life, that both
Josh 9:27 in the place which He would **c**
Josh 24:15 **c** for yourselves this day
1Ki 18:23 and let them **c** one bull for
1Ki 18:25 **C** one bull for yourselves and
2Ki 10: 3 **c** the best qualified of your
Job 9:14 **c** my words to reason with Him
Job 34:33 You must **c**, and not I
Ps 47: 4 He will **c** our inheritance for
Ps 65: 4 Blessed is the man whom You **c**
Ps 75: 2 When I **c** the proper time, I
Ps 78:67 And did not **c** the tribe of
Prov 1:29 did not **c** the fear of the
Prov 3:31 and **c** none of his ways
Is 7:15 refuse the evil and **c** the good
Is 7:16 **c** the good, the land that you
Is 14: 1 Jacob, and will still **c** Israel
Zech 1:17 and will again **c** Jerusalem
Zech 2:12 and will again **c** Jerusalem
John 6:70 Did I not **c** you, the twelve,
John 15:16 You did not **c** Me, but I chose
Phil 1:22 what I shall **c** I cannot tell

CHOOSES (*see* CHOOSE)
Deut 12: 5 where the LORD your God **c**
Deut 12:11 God **c** to make His name abide
Job 7:15 so that my soul **c** strangling
Ps 25:12 He teach in the way He **c**
Is 40:20 for such a contribution **c** a
Dan 4:25 and gives it to whomever He **c**
Dan 4:32 and gives it to whomever He **c**

CHOOSING† (*see* CHOOSE)
Heb 11:25 **c** rather to suffer affliction

CHOP (*see* CHOPS)
Jer 46:22 axes, like those who **c** wood
Dan 4:14 **C** down the tree and cut off

CHOPS† (*see* CHOP)
Is 10:15 against him who **c** with it

CHORAZIN†
Matt 11:21 Woe to you, **C**
Luke 10:13 Woe to you, **C**

CHOSE (*see* CHOOSE)
Gen 6: 2 themselves of all whom they **c**
Gen 13:11 Then Lot **c** for himself all
Ex 18:25 Moses **c** able men out of all
Deut 10:10 the LORD **c** not to destroy you
Judg 5: 8 They **c** new gods

1Sa 13: 2 Saul **c** for himself three
1Sa 17:40 he **c** for himself five smooth
2Sa 10: 9 he **c** some of the choice? men
2Sa 21: 6 of Saul, whom the LORD **c**
1Ki 8:16 but I **c** David to be over My
Neh 9: 7 Who **c** Abram, and brought him
Ps 78:68 But **c** the tribe of Judah,
Ps 78:70 He also **c** David His servant,
Ezek 20: 5 On the day when I **c** Israel
Mark 13:20 the elect's sake, whom He **c**
Luke 6:13 from them He **c** twelve whom
Luke 14: 7 how they **c** the best places
John 15:16 not choose Me, but I **c** you
John 15:19 but I **c** you out of the world,
Acts 6: 5 they **c** Stephen, a man full of
Acts 15:40 but Paul **c** Silas and departed,
Eph 1: 4 just as He **c** us in Him before
2Th 2:13 God from the beginning **c** you

CHOSEN (*see* CHOSE)
Ex 15: 4 His **c** captains also are
Deut 7: 6 the LORD your God has **c** you
Deut 21: 5 has **c** them to minister to Him
Judg 10:14 to the gods which you have **c**
1Sa 10:20 the tribe of Benjamin was **c**
1Sa 10:21 And Saul the son of Kish was **c**
1Sa 10:24 see him whom the LORD has **c**
1Sa 12:13 is the king whom you have **c**
1Sa 16: 8 has the Lord **c** this one
1Sa 16: 9 has the LORD **c** this one
1Sa 16:10 The LORD has not **c** these
1Sa 20:30 **c** the son of Jesse to your
1Sa 26: 2 having three thousand **c** men
1Ki 3: 8 Your people whom You have **c**
1Ki 8:16 I have **c** no city from any
1Ki 8:44 the city which You have **c**
1Ki 8:48 the city which You have **c**
1Ki 11:13 of Jerusalem which I have **c**
1Ch 9:22 All those **c** as gatekeepers
1Ch 16:13 children of Jacob, His **c** ones
1Ch 28: 5 **c** my son Solomon to sit on
1Ch 28:10 for the LORD has **c** you to
2Ch 6: 6 I have **c** David to be over My
Neh 1: 9 **c** as a dwelling for My name
Ps 33:12 has **c** as His own inheritance
Ps 89: 3 made a covenant with My **c**
Ps 89:19 exalted one **c** from the people
Ps 105: 6 children of Jacob, His **c** ones
Ps 106:23 Had not Moses His **c** one stood
Ps 119:30 I have **c** the way of truth
Ps 119:173 For I have **c** Your precepts
Ps 132:13 For the LORD has **c** Zion
Ps 135: 4 For the LORD has **c** Jacob for
Prov 16:16 is to be **c** rather than silver
Prov 22: 1 A good name is to be **c** rather
Is 41: 8 servant, Jacob, whom I have **c**
Is 41: 9 are My servant, I have **c** you
Is 43:10 And My servant whom I have **c**
Is 44: 1 and Israel whom I have **c**
Is 44: 2 you, Jeshurun, whom I have **c**
Is 58: 5 Is it a fast that I have **c**
Is 66: 3 as they have **c** their own ways
Jer 8: 3 Then death shall be **c** rather
Jer 33:24 families which the LORD has **c**
Jer 49:19 who is a **c** man that I may
Jer 50:44 who is a **c** man that I may
Matt 12:18 My Servant whom I have **c**
Matt 20:16 many are called, but few **c**
Luke 10:42 Mary has **c** that good part,
Luke 23:35 is the Christ, the **c** of God
John 13:18 I know whom I have **c**
Acts 1: 2 to the apostles whom He had **c**
Acts 1:24 which of these two You have **c**
Acts 9:15 for he is a **c** vessel of Mine
Acts 15:22 to send **c** men of their own

Rom 16:13 c in the Lord, and his mother
1Co 1:27 But God has c the foolish
1Co 1:27 God has c the weak things of
1Co 1:28 which are despised God has c
2Co 8:19 but who was also c by the
Jas 2: 5 Has God not c the poor of
1Pe 2: 4 but c by God and precious,
1Pe 2: 9 But you are a c generation
Rev 17:14 are with Him are called, c

CHRIST (see CHRIST'S, CHRISTS, JESUS)
Matt 1: 1 of the genealogy of Jesus C
Matt 1:16 born Jesus who is called C
Matt 1:18 of Jesus C was as follows
Matt 2: 4 where the C was to be born
Matt 16:16 You are the C, the Son of the
Matt 16:20 one that He was Jesus the C
Matt 23: 8 One is your Teacher, the C
Matt 23:10 One is your Teacher, the C
Matt 24: 5 My name, saying, 'I am the C
Matt 24:23 to you, 'Look, here is the C
Matt 27:22 do with Jesus who is called C
Mark 1: 1 of the gospel of Jesus C, the
Mark 9:41 name, because you belong to C
Mark 12:35 the C is the Son of David
Mark 15:32 Let the C, the King of Israel
Luke 2:11 a Savior, who is C the Lord
Luke 2:26 he had seen the Lord's C
Luke 20:41 say that the C is David's Son
Luke 23:35 save Himself if He is the C
Luke 24:26 Ought not the C to have
Luke 24:46 necessary for the C to suffer
John 1:17 and truth came through Jesus C
John 1:20 I am not the C
John 1:25 baptize if you are not the C
John 7:27 but when the C comes, no one
John 9:22 confessed that He was C, he
John 11:27 I believe that You are the C
John 12:34 that the C remains forever
John 17: 3 Jesus C whom You have sent
John 20:31 believe that Jesus is the C
Acts 2:30 up the C to sit on his throne
Acts 2:31 the resurrection of the C
Acts 2:36 you crucified, both Lord and C
Acts 2:38 in the name of Jesus C for
Acts 3: 6 name of Jesus C of Nazareth
Acts 4:26 against His C
Acts 8: 5 Samaria and preached C to them
Acts 8:12 of God and the name of Jesus C
Acts 8:37 Jesus C is the Son of God
Acts 9:20 the C in the synagogues, that
Acts 10:36 peace through Jesus C
Acts 11:17 believed on the Lord Jesus C
Acts 15:11 C we shall be saved in the
Acts 15:26 the name of our Lord Jesus C
Acts 16:18 of Jesus C to come out of her
Acts 16:31 Believe on the Lord Jesus C
Acts 17: 3 that the C had to suffer and
Acts 17: 3 whom I preach to you is the C
Acts 18: 5 the Jews that Jesus is the C
Acts 20:21 faith toward our Lord Jesus C
Acts 26:23 that the C would suffer, that
Rom 1: 1 Paul, a servant of Jesus C
Rom 1: 3 His Son Jesus C our Lord, who
Rom 1: 6 are the called of Jesus C
Rom 1: 7 Father and the Lord Jesus C
Rom 1:16 ashamed of the gospel of C
Rom 2:16 the secrets of men by Jesus C
Rom 3:24 redemption that is in C Jesus
Rom 5: 1 God through our Lord Jesus C
Rom 5: 6 in due time C died for the
Rom 5: 8 still sinners, C died for us
Rom 5:15 grace of the one Man, Jesus C
Rom 5:17 life through the One, Jesus C
Rom 5:21 life through Jesus C our Lord

Rom 6: 3 C Jesus were baptized into
Rom 6: 4 that just as C was raised
Rom 6: 8 Now if we died with C, we
Rom 6:23 life in C Jesus our Lord
Rom 7: 4 the law through the body of C
Rom 8: 2 of the Spirit of life in C
Rom 8:10 if C is in you, the body is
Rom 8:11 He who raised C from the dead
Rom 8:17 of God and joint heirs with C
Rom 8:34 It is C who died, and
Rom 8:35 us from the love of C
Rom 8:39 which is in C Jesus our Lord
Rom 9: 1 I tell the truth in C, I am
Rom 9: 3 from C for my brethren, my
Rom 10: 4 For C is the end of the law
Rom 10: 6 to bring C down from above)
Rom 12: 5 being many, are one body in C
Rom 13:14 But put on the Lord Jesus C
Rom 14: 9 For to this end C died and
Rom 14:10 before the judgment seat of C
Rom 15: 6 and Father of our Lord Jesus C
Rom 15:16 of Jesus C to the Gentiles
Rom 15:19 preached the gospel of C
Rom 15:20 gospel, not where C was named
Rom 15:29 blessing of the gospel of C
Rom 16: 3 my fellow workers in C Jesus
Rom 16: 7 who also were in C before me
Rom 16:16 The churches of C greet you
Rom 16:18 do not serve our Lord Jesus C
Rom 16:20 our Lord Jesus C be with you
Rom 16:24 Lord Jesus C be with you all
Rom 16:27 glory through Jesus C forever
1Co 1: 1 C through the will of God
1Co 1: 2 who are sanctified in C Jesus
1Co 1: 6 of C was confirmed in you
1Co 1: 8 the day of our Lord Jesus C
1Co 1:12 of Cephas," or "I am of C."
1Co 1:13 Is C divided?
1Co 1:17 For C did not send me to
1Co 1:17 lest the cross of C should be
1Co 1:23 but we preach C crucified
1Co 1:24 C the power of God and the
1Co 1:30 But of Him you are in C Jesus
1Co 2:16 But we have the mind of C
1Co 3: 1 to carnal, as to babes in C
1Co 3:11 is laid, which is Jesus C
1Co 3:23 are Christ's, and C is God's
1Co 4: 1 consider us, as servants of C
1Co 4:10 sake, but you are wise in C
1Co 4:17 remind you of my ways in C
1Co 5: 4 the name of our Lord Jesus C
1Co 5: 4 the power of our Lord Jesus C
1Co 5: 7 For indeed C, our Passover,
1Co 6:15 your bodies are members of C
1Co 8: 6 and one Lord Jesus C, through
1Co 8:11 perish, for whom C died
1Co 8:12 conscience, you sin against C
1Co 9:12 we hinder the gospel of C
1Co 9:21 God, but under law toward C)
1Co 10: 4 them, and that Rock was C
1Co 10: 9 nor let us tempt C, as some
1Co 10:16 communion of the blood of C
1Co 10:16 communion of the body of C
1Co 11: 1 me, just as I also imitate C
1Co 11: 3 the head of every man is C
1Co 11: 3 man, and the head of C is God
1Co 12:12 are one body, so also is C
1Co 12:27 Now you are the body of C
1Co 15: 3 that C died for our sins
1Co 15:12 Now if C is preached that He
1Co 15:13 the dead, then C is not risen
1Co 15:15 of God that He raised up C
1Co 15:17 if C is not risen, your faith
1Co 15:18 asleep in C have perished
1Co 15:19 life only we have hope in C

1Co	15:20	But now C is risen from the
1Co	15:22	even so in C all shall be
1Co	15:23	C the firstfruits, afterward
1Co	16:22	not love the Lord Jesus C
2Co	1: 5	sufferings of C abound in us
2Co	2:14	leads us in triumph in C, and
2Co	2:15	C among those who are being
2Co	2:17	in the sight of God in C
2Co	3: 4	trust through C toward God
2Co	3:14	the veil is taken away in C
2Co	4: 4	the gospel of the glory of C
2Co	4: 6	of God in the face of Jesus C
2Co	5:10	before the judgment seat of C
2Co	5:14	the love of C constrains us
2Co	5:16	C according to the flesh, yet
2Co	5:17	Therefore, if anyone is in C
2Co	5:19	that God was in C reconciling
2Co	5:20	we are ambassadors for C, as
2Co	6:15	what accord has C with Belial
2Co	8:23	the churches, the glory of C
2Co	10: 1	meekness and gentleness of C
2Co	10: 5	to the obedience of C,
2Co	11: 2	you as a chaste virgin to C
2Co	11:10	As the truth of C is in me
2Co	11:13	themselves into apostles of C
2Co	11:23	Are they ministers of C
2Co	12: 2	I know a man in C who
2Co	12: 9	power of C may rest upon me
Gal	1: 7	to pervert the gospel of C
Gal	1:12	the revelation of Jesus C
Gal	2: 4	which we have in C Jesus,
Gal	2:16	law but by faith in Jesus C
Gal	2:16	we have believed in C Jesus
Gal	2:16	be justified by faith in C
Gal	2:17	is C therefore a minister of
Gal	2:20	I have been crucified with C
Gal	2:20	I who live, but C lives in me
Gal	3: 1	before whose eyes Jesus C was
Gal	3:13	C has redeemed us from the
Gal	3:14	upon the Gentiles in C Jesus
Gal	3:16	And to your Seed," who is C
Gal	3:24	our tutor to bring us to C
Gal	3:27	into C have put on C
Gal	3:28	you are all one in C Jesus
Gal	4: 7	then an heir of God through C
Gal	4:14	angel of God, even as C Jesus
Gal	4:19	until C is formed in you,
Gal	5: 1	by which C has made us free
Gal	5: 4	have become estranged from C
Gal	5: 6	For in C Jesus neither
Gal	6: 2	and so fulfill the law of C
Gal	6:18	Jesus C be with your spirit
Eph	1: 3	in the heavenly places in C
Eph	1:12	we who first trusted in C
Eph	1:20	which He worked in C when He
Eph	2: 5	C (by grace you have been
Eph	2: 6	heavenly places in C Jesus
Eph	2: 7	kindness toward us in C Jesus
Eph	2:10	created in C Jesus for good
Eph	2:13	made near by the blood of C
Eph	2:20	Jesus C Himself being the
Eph	3: 1	of Jesus C for you Gentiles
Eph	3: 4	in the mystery of C),
Eph	3: 8	the unsearchable riches of C
Eph	3:17	that C may dwell in your
Eph	3:19	to know the love of C which
Eph	4:12	the edifying of the body of C
Eph	4:13	stature of the fullness of C
Eph	4:15	into Him who is the head—C
Eph	4:20	But you have not so learned C
Eph	4:32	just as God in C also forgave
Eph	5: 2	as C also has loved us and
Eph	5:14	and C will give you light
Eph	5:23	as also C is head of the
Eph	5:24	as the church is subject to C
Eph	6: 5	sincerity of heart, as to C
Eph	6:24	our Lord Jesus C in sincerity
Phil	1: 1	Timothy, servants of Jesus C
Phil	1: 1	To all the saints in C Jesus
Phil	1: 8	with the affection of Jesus C
Phil	1:10	offense till the day of C
Phil	1:13	rest, that my chains are in C
Phil	1:15	preach C even from envy and
Phil	1:19	of the Spirit of Jesus C,
Phil	1:21	For to me, to live is C, and
Phil	1:23	desire to depart and be with C
Phil	1:29	been granted on behalf of C
Phil	2: 1	there is any consolation in C
Phil	2: 5	you which was also in C Jesus
Phil	2:11	confess that Jesus C is Lord
Phil	2:16	C that I have not run in vain
Phil	2:30	of C he came close to death
Phil	3: 7	I have counted loss for C
Phil	3: 8	knowledge of C Jesus my Lord
Phil	3: 8	as rubbish, that I may gain C
Phil	3:12	lay hold of that for which C
Phil	3:14	upward call of God in C Jesus
Phil	3:18	the enemies of the cross of C
Phil	4: 7	and minds through C Jesus
Phil	4:13	through C who strengthens me
Phil	4:19	riches in glory by C Jesus
Phil	4:23	Lord Jesus C be with you all
Col	1:24	in the afflictions of C, for
Col	1:27	which is C in you, the hope
Col	1:28	every man perfect in C Jesus
Col	2: 6	received C Jesus the Lord
Col	2: 8	world, and not according to C
Col	2:20	if you died with C from the
Col	3: 1	then you were raised with C
Col	3: 1	which are above, where C is
Col	3: 3	life is hidden with C in God
Col	3: 4	When C who is our life
Col	3:11	free, but C is all and in all
Col	3:13	even as C forgave you, so you
Col	3:16	Let the word of C dwell in
Col	3:24	for you serve the Lord C
Col	4: 3	to speak the mystery of C
1Th	2:19	Lord Jesus C at His coming
1Th	3: 2	laborer in the gospel of C
1Th	3:13	Jesus C with all His saints
1Th	4:16	the dead in C will rise first
1Th	5:18	of God in C Jesus for you
1Th	5:23	coming of our Lord Jesus C
2Th	1:12	C may be glorified in you
2Th	2: 2	though the day of C had come
2Th	2:14	the glory of our Lord Jesus C
1Ti	1: 1	Paul, an apostle of Jesus C
1Ti	1:14	and love which are in C Jesus
1Ti	1:15	that C Jesus came into the
1Ti	2: 5	God and men, the Man C Jesus
1Ti	2: 7	I am speaking the truth in C
1Ti	4: 6	be a good minister of Jesus C
2Ti	1: 9	in C Jesus before time began
2Ti	1:13	and love which are in C Jesus
2Ti	2: 1	the grace that is in C Jesus
2Ti	2: 3	as a good soldier of Jesus C
2Ti	2:10	in C Jesus with eternal glory
2Ti	2:19	of C depart from iniquity
2Ti	3:12	godly in C Jesus will suffer
2Ti	4:22	The Lord Jesus C be with your
Tit	1: 4	the Lord Jesus C our Savior
Tit	2:13	great God and Savior Jesus C
Phm	1	Paul, a prisoner of C Jesus
Phm	23	my fellow prisoner in C Jesus
Heb	3: 1	of our confession, C Jesus,
Heb	3: 6	but C as a Son over His own
Heb	5: 5	So also C did not glorify
Heb	6: 1	elementary principles of C
Heb	9:11	But C came as High Priest of
Heb	9:14	more shall the blood of C

Heb	9:24	For **C** has not entered the
Heb	9:28	so **C** was offered once to bear
Heb	10:10	body of Jesus **C** once for all
Heb	11:26	of **C** greater riches than the
Heb	13: 8	Jesus **C** is the same yesterday
Heb	13:21	in His sight, through Jesus **C**
Jas	2: 1	the faith of our Lord Jesus **C**
1Pe	1: 1	Peter, an apostle of Jesus **C**
1Pe	1: 2	of the blood of Jesus **C**
1Pe	1: 3	and Father of our Lord Jesus **C**
1Pe	1: 3	of Jesus **C** from the dead,
1Pe	1: 7	at the revelation of Jesus **C**
1Pe	1:11	the sufferings of **C** and the
1Pe	1:13	at the revelation of Jesus **C**
1Pe	1:19	with the precious blood of **C**
1Pe	3:18	For **C** also suffered once for
1Pe	4:14	reproached for the name of **C**
1Pe	5: 1	of the sufferings of **C**, and
1Pe	5:10	His eternal glory by **C** Jesus
2Pe	1: 1	of our God and Savior Jesus **C**
2Pe	1: 8	knowledge of our Lord Jesus **C**
1Jn	1: 3	and with His Son Jesus **C**
1Jn	1: 7	the blood of Jesus **C** His Son
1Jn	2: 1	Father, Jesus **C** the righteous
1Jn	2:22	denies that Jesus is the **C**
1Jn	3:23	the name of His Son Jesus **C**
1Jn	4: 3	**C** has come in the flesh is
1Jn	5: 1	Jesus is the **C** is born of God
1Jn	5: 6	by water and blood—Jesus **C**
2Jn	7	**C** as coming in the flesh
2Jn	9	of **C** has both the Father and
Jude	1	Jude, a servant of Jesus **C**
Jude	4	Lord God and our Lord Jesus **C**
Rev	1: 1	The Revelation of Jesus **C**
Rev	1: 2	to the testimony of Jesus **C**
Rev	1: 5	and from Jesus **C**, the faithful
Rev	1: 9	and patience of Jesus **C**, was
Rev	1: 9	for the testimony of Jesus **C**
Rev	11:15	of our Lord and of His **C**, and
Rev	12:17	have the testimony of Jesus **C**
Rev	20: 4	reigned with **C** for a thousand
Rev	20: 6	be priests of God and of **C**
Rev	22:21	Lord Jesus **C** be with you all

CHRISTIAN† (see CHRISTIANS)

Acts	26:28	persuade me to become a **C**
1Pe	4:16	Yet if anyone suffers as a **C**

CHRISTIANS† (see CHRISTIAN)

Acts	11:26	first called **C** in Antioch

CHRIST'S (see CHRIST)

1Co	3:23	And you are **C**, and Christ is
1Co	4:10	We are fools for **C** sake, but
1Co	15:23	those who are **C** at His coming
2Co	2:12	to Troas to preach **C** gospel
2Co	5:20	we implore you on **C** behalf
Eph	4: 7	to the measure of **C** gift
1Ti	6:14	our Lord Jesus **C** appearing
1Pe	4:13	you partake of **C** sufferings

CHRISTS (see CHRIST)

Matt	24:24	For false **c** and false prophets

CHRONICLES

1Ki	14:19	the **c** of the kings of Israel
1Ki	14:29	the **c** of the kings of Judah

CHRYSOLITE†

Rev	21:20	sixth sardius, the seventh **c**

CHRYSOPRASE†

Rev	21:20	the ninth topaz, the tenth **c**

CHURCH (see CHURCHES)

Matt	16:18	this rock I will build My **c**
Matt	18:17	hear them, tell it to the **c**
Acts	2:47	the Lord added to the **c** daily
Acts	5:11	fear came upon all the **c** and

Acts	8: 1	arose against the **c** which was
Acts	8: 3	Saul, he made havoc of the **c**
Acts	11:22	ears of the **c** in Jerusalem
Acts	11:26	they assembled with the **c**
Acts	12: 1	to harass some from the **c**
Acts	13: 1	Now in the **c** that was at
Acts	14:23	appointed elders in every **c**
Acts	14:27	and gathered the **c** together
Acts	15: 4	they were received by the **c**
Acts	20:28	to shepherd the **c** of God
1Co	4:17	I teach everywhere in every **c**
1Co	6: 4	esteemed by the **c** to judge
1Co	10:32	the Greeks or to the **c** of God
1Co	11:18	when you come together as a **c**
1Co	11:22	do you despise the **c** of God
1Co	14: 4	who prophesies edifies the **c**
1Co	14:12	the **c** that you seek to excel
1Co	14:19	yet in the **c** I would rather
1Co	14:28	let him keep silent in **c**
1Co	14:35	for women to speak in **c**
1Co	15: 9	I persecuted the **c** of God
1Co	16:19	with the **c** that is in their
Gal	1:13	how I persecuted the **c** of God
Eph	1:22	head over all things to the **c**
Eph	3:21	to Him be glory in the **c** by
Eph	5:23	also Christ is head of the **c**
Eph	5:24	just as the **c** is subject to
Eph	5:25	as Christ also loved the **c**
Eph	5:27	it to Himself a glorious **c**
Eph	5:32	concerning Christ and the **c**
Phil	3: 6	zeal, persecuting the **c**
Col	1:18	the head of the body, the **c**
Col	1:24	of His body, which is the **c**
1Ti	3: 5	he take care of the **c** of God
1Ti	3:15	which is the **c** of the living
1Ti	5:16	do not let the **c** be burdened
Heb	12:23	**c** of the firstborn who are
Jas	5:14	call for the elders of the **c**
3Jn	10	to, putting them out of the **c**
Rev	2: 1	of the **c** of Ephesus write

CHURCHES (see CHURCH)

Acts	9:31	Then the **c** throughout all
Acts	15:41	Cilicia, strengthening the **c**
Rom	16: 4	all the **c** of the Gentiles
Rom	16:16	The **c** of Christ greet you
1Co	11:16	custom, nor do the **c** of God
1Co	14:33	as in all the **c** of the saints
1Co	14:34	women keep silent in the **c**
2Co	8:19	who was also chosen by the **c**
2Co	8:23	they are messengers of the **c**
2Co	11: 8	I robbed other **c**, taking
2Co	11:28	my deep concern for all the **c**
2Co	12:13	you were inferior to other **c**
Rev	1:11	the seven **c** which are in Asia
Rev	1:20	are the angels of the seven **c**
Rev	2: 7	what the Spirit says to the **c**
Rev	2:23	all the **c** shall know that I
Rev	22:16	to you these things in the **c**

CHURNING† (see CHURNS)

Prov	30:33	for as the **c** of milk produces

CHURNS† (see CHURNING)

Hos	11: 8	My heart **c** within Me

CILICIA

Acts	22: 3	a Jew, born in Tarsus of **C**

CINNAMON†

Ex	30:23	sweet-smelling **c** (two hundred
Prov	7:17	bed with myrrh, aloes, and **c**
Song	4:14	and saffron, calamus and **c**,
Rev	18:13	and **c** and incense, fragrant oil

CIRCLE (see CIRCLED, CIRCULAR)

Josh	6:11	ark of the LORD **c** the city
Job	22:14	walks above the **c** of heaven

Prov 8:27 when He drew a c on the face
Is 40:22 sits above the c of the earth
Mark 3:34 He looked around in a c at

CIRCLED† (see CIRCLE)
Acts 28:13 From there we c round and

CIRCUIT†
1Sa 7:16 year to year on a c to Bethel
Ps 19: 6 And its c to the other end
Eccl 1: 6 and comes again on its c
Mark 6: 6 about the villages in a c

CIRCULAR† (see CIRCLE)
Job 26:10 He drew a c horizon on the

CIRCULATE† (see CIRCULATED)
Ex 23: 1 You shall not c a false

CIRCULATED† (see CIRCULATE)
2Ch 31: 5 soon as the commandment was c

CIRCUMCISE (see CIRCUMCISED, CIRCUMCISING,
　CIRCUMCISION, UNCIRCUMCISED)
Deut 10:16 Therefore c the foreskin of
Deut 30: 6 your God will c your heart
Jer 4: 4 C yourselves to the LORD, and
Luke 1:59 that they came to c the child
John 7:22 you c a man on the Sabbath
Acts 15: 5 It is necessary to c them
Acts 21:21 that they ought not to c

CIRCUMCISED (see CIRCUMCISE)
Gen 17:10 child among you shall be c
Gen 17:11 you shall be c in the flesh
Gen 17:26 very same day Abraham was c
Gen 21: 4 Then Abraham c his son Isaac
Jer 9:25 are c with the uncircumcised
Acts 7: 8 and c him on the eighth day
Acts 15: 1 Unless you are c according to
Acts 15:24 souls, saying, "You must be c
Acts 16: 3 c him because of the Jews who
Rom 3:30 will justify the c by faith
Gal 2: 3 Greek, was compelled to be c
Gal 2: 7 gospel for the c was to Peter
Gal 2: 9 the Gentiles and they to the c
Gal 5: 3 to every man who becomes c
Gal 6:12 try to compel you to be c
Gal 6:13 those who are c keep the law
Gal 6:13 c that they may glory in your
Phil 3: 5 c the eighth day, of the
Col 2:11 In Him you were also c with
Col 3:11 nor Jew, c nor uncircumcised,

CIRCUMCISING† (see CIRCUMCISE)
Josh 5: 8 had finished c all the people

CIRCUMCISION (see CIRCUMCISE)
Ex 4:26 because of the c
Luke 2:21 for the c of the Child, His
John 7:22 Moses therefore gave you c
John 7:23 man receives c on the Sabbath
Acts 7: 8 He gave him the covenant of c
Acts 10:45 those of the c who believed
Rom 2:25 For c is indeed profitable if
Rom 2:27 with your written code and c
Rom 2:29 c is that of the heart, in
Rom 3: 1 or what is the profit of c
Rom 4:11 And he received the sign of c
Rom 4:12 the father of c to those who
Rom 15: 8 to the c for the truth of God
1Co 7:19 C is nothing and
Gal 5: 6 c nor uncircumcision avails
Gal 5:11 brethren, if I still preach c
Eph 2:11 by what is called the C made
Phil 3: 3 For we are the c, who worship
Col 2:11 with the c made without hands
Col 2:11 flesh, by the c of Christ,
Tit 1:10 especially those of the c

CIRCUMFERENCE
1Ki 7:15 cubits measured the c of each

CIRCUMSPECT† (see CIRCUMSPECTLY)
Ex 23:13 that I have said to you, be c

CIRCUMSPECTLY† (see CIRCUMSPECT)
Eph 5:15 See then that you walk c, not

CIRCUMSTANCES†
Col 4: 8 that he may know your c and

CISTERN (see CISTERNS)
Lev 11:36 Nevertheless a spring or a c
2Ki 18:31 drink the waters of his own c
Prov 5:15 Drink water from your own c

CISTERNS† (see CISTERN)
Neh 9:25 c already dug, vineyards,
Jer 2:13 waters, and hewn themselves c
Jer 2:13 broken c that can hold no
Jer 14: 3 they went to the c and found

CITADEL (see CITADELS)
1Ki 16:18 the c of the king's house
Neh 1: 1 as I was in Shushan the c

CITADELS† (see CITADEL)
Is 13:22 hyenas will howl in their c

CITIES (see CITY)
Gen 13:12 dwelt in the c of the plain
Gen 19:25 So He overthrew those c, all
Ex 1:11 built for Pharaoh supply c
Lev 25:32 the c of the Levites, and the
Num 13:28 the c are fortified and very
Num 32:16 and c for our little ones,
Num 35: 6 shall appoint six c of refuge
Deut 1:28 the c are great and fortified
Deut 2:37 or to the c of the mountains,
Deut 3:10 c of the kingdom of Og in
Deut 6:10 beautiful c which you did not
Deut 9: 1 c great and fortified up to
Josh 10: 2 city, like one of the royal c
Josh 16: 9 all the c with their villages
Josh 20: 2 for yourselves c of refuge
Josh 20: 4 he flees to one of those c
Josh 24:13 c which you did not build, and
Judg 21:23 and they rebuilt the c and
1Sa 6:18 all the c of the Philistines
2Sa 10:12 and for the c of our God
1Ki 9:19 all the storage c that
1Ki 9:19 and c for his cavalry, and
1Ki 10:26 he stationed in the chariot c
2Ki 13:25 and recaptured the c of Israel
2Ki 17: 9 high places in all their c
2Ki 19:25 c into heaps of ruins
2Ki 23: 8 priests from the c of Judah
1Ch 10: 7 dead, they forsook their c
2Ch 8: 5 fortified c with walls, gates
2Ch 11: 5 built c for defense in Judah
2Ch 14:14 and they plundered all the c
2Ch 17:13 property in the c of Judah
2Ch 19:10 brethren who dwell in their c
2Ch 25:13 they raided the c of Judah
2Ch 28:18 invaded the c of the lowland
2Ch 31: 1 returned to their own c,
Ezra 10:14 elders and judges of their c
Neh 8:15 and proclaim in all their c
Neh 9:25 And they took strong c and a
Job 15:28 He dwells in desolate c, in
Ps 9: 6 And you have destroyed c
Is 1: 7 your c are burned with fire
Is 6:11 Until the c are laid waste and
Is 14:17 wilderness and destroyed its c
Is 33: 8 He has despised the c, He
Is 37:26 c into heaps of ruins
Is 42:11 its c lift up their voice,
Is 54: 3 make the desolate c inhabited

Is 61: 4 shall repair the ruined c
Is 64:10 Your holy c are a wilderness,
Jer 2:28 of your c are your gods, O
Jer 4:16 voice against the c of Judah
Jer 4:26 all its c were broken down at
Jer 5: 6 will watch over their c
Jer 13:19 The c of the South shall be
Jer 20:16 c which the LORD overthrew
Jer 22: 6 which are not inhabited
Jer 40: 5 governor over the c of Judah
Jer 50:32 I will kindle a fire in his c
Lam 5:11 the maidens in the c of Judah
Ezek 35: 9 your c shall be uninhabited
Ezek 36: 4 the c that have been forsaken
Ezek 36:10 the c shall be inhabited and
Hos 11: 6 sword shall slash in his c
Hos 13:10 he may save you in all your c
Amos 4: 8 So two or three c wandered to
Mic 5:11 cut off the c of your land
Zeph 1:16 alarm against the fortified c
Zech 1:17 My c shall again spread out
Zech 8:20 come, inhabitants of many c
Matt 9:35 And Jesus went about all the c
Matt 11: 1 teach and to preach in their c
Matt 11:20 He began to upbraid the c in
Luke 19:17 have authority over ten c
Acts 5:16 surrounding c to Jerusalem
Acts 8:40 he preached in all the c till
Acts 26:11 them even to foreign c
2Pe 2: 6 and turning the c of Sodom
Rev 16:19 the c of the nations fell

CITIZEN† (see CITIZENS)
Luke 15:15 to a c of that country, and he
Acts 21:39 Cilicia, a c of no mean city
Acts 22:28 But I was born a c
Acts 28: 7 the leading c of the island

CITIZENS† (see CITIZEN)
Luke 19:14 But his c hated him, and sent
Eph 2:19 but fellow c with the saints

CITIZENSHIP†
Acts 22:28 a large sum I obtained this c
Phil 3:20 For our c is in heaven, from

CITRON†
Rev 18:12 scarlet, every kind of c wood

CITY (see CITIES, CITY'S)
Gen 4:17 And he built a c, and called
Gen 11: 5 LORD came down to see the c
Gen 11: 8 and they ceased building the c
Gen 18:24 fifty righteous within the c
Gen 19:14 the LORD will destroy this c
Gen 19:20 this c is near enough to flee
Gen 19:22 name of the c was called Zoar
Gen 24:11 the c by a well of water at
Gen 33:18 safely to the c of Shechem
Gen 33:18 pitched his tent before the c
Gen 34:27 the slain, and plundered the c
Lev 14:40 unclean place outside the c
Lev 14:41 unclean place outside the c
Lev 14:53 the c in the open field, and
Num 35:26 the c of refuge where he fled
Num 35:28 c of refuge until the death
Deut 3: 6 women, and children of every c
Deut 19:12 elders of his c shall send
Deut 20:10 When you go near a c to fight
Deut 20:20 siegeworks against the c that
Deut 21: 3 c nearest to the slain man
Deut 22:15 elders of the c at the gate
Deut 28: 3 Blessed shall you be in the c
Deut 28:16 Cursed shall you be in the c
Deut 34: 3 the c of palm trees, as far
Josh 2:15 her house was on the c wall
Josh 6: 3 You shall march around the c

Josh 6: 4 around the c seven times, and
Josh 6: 5 of the c will fall down flat
Josh 6:11 ark of the LORD circle the c
Josh 6:26 up and builds this c Jericho
Josh 8: 4 lie in ambush against the c
Josh 8: 4 Do not go very far from the c
Josh 8: 6 we have drawn them from the c
Josh 8: 8 you shall set the c on fire
Josh 8:20 the smoke of the c ascended
Josh 8:21 the smoke of the c ascended
Josh 10: 2 because Gibeon was a great c
Josh 15: 8 c (which is Jerusalem)
Josh 15:62 the C of Salt, and En Gedi
Josh 19:29 and to the fortified c of Tyre
Judg 1:23 of the c was formerly Luz
Judg 9:31 fortifying the c against you
Judg 9:33 rise early and rush upon the c
Judg 9:51 was a strong tower in the c
Judg 16: 3 doors of the gate of the c
Judg 17: 8 c of Bethlehem in Judah to
Judg 19:15 in the open square of the c
Judg 19:17 in the open square of the c
Judg 20:32 from the c to the highways
Judg 20:48 from every c, men and beasts,
Ruth 1:19 that all the c was excited
1Sa 1: 3 from his c yearly to worship
1Sa 5:12 the cry of the c went up to
1Sa 8:22 Every man go to his c
1Sa 9: 6 is in this c a man of God
1Sa 9:11 went up the hill to the c
1Sa 9:25 the high place into the c
1Sa 9:27 to the outskirts of the c
1Sa 20:29 has a sacrifice in the c, and
1Sa 22:19 Nob, the c of the priests, he
1Sa 27: 5 dwell in the royal c with you
1Sa 30: 3 and his men came to the c
2Sa 5: 9 and called it the C of David
2Sa 15:14 strike the c with the edge of
2Sa 15:24 crossing over from the c
2Sa 15:25 ark of God back into the c
2Sa 15:27 Return to the c in peace, and
2Sa 17:23 home to his house, to his c
2Sa 19:37 that I may die in my own c
2Sa 20:15 a siege mound against the c
1Ki 1:41 Why is the c in such a noisy
1Ki 1:45 so that the c is in an uproar
1Ki 8:44 the c which You have chosen
1Ki 8:48 the c which You have chosen
1Ki 9:16 Canaanites who dwelt in the c
1Ki 14:12 When your feet enter the c
1Ki 22:36 Every man to his c, and every
2Ki 2:23 some youths came from the c
2Ki 7: 4 c,' the famine is in the c
2Ki 7:10 to the gatekeepers of the c
2Ki 10: 5 he who was in charge of the c
2Ki 10: 6 with the great men of the c
2Ki 11:20 the c was quiet, for they had
2Ki 17: 9 watchtower to fortified c
2Ki 18: 8 watchtower to fortified c
2Ki 19:33 he shall not come into this c
2Ki 19:34 For I will defend this c
2Ki 20: 6 defend this c for My own sake
2Ki 20:20 and brought water into the c
2Ki 23:27 and will cast off this c
2Ki 24:11 of Babylon came against the c
2Ki 25: 4 Then the c wall was broken
2Ki 25:11 people who remained in the c
2Ch 28:15 Jericho, the c of palm trees
2Ch 32: 5 the Millo in the C of David
2Ch 32: 6 the open square of the c gate
Ezra 4:12 the rebellious and evil c, and
Neh 11: 1 in Jerusalem, the holy c, and
Job 24:12 The dying groan in the c, and
Ps 46: 4 shall make glad the c of God
Ps 48: 1 praised In the c of our God

Ps	48: 2	The c of the great King
Ps	48: 8	In the c of the LORD of hosts
Ps	55: 9	violence and strife in the c
Ps	59: 6	And go all around the c
Ps	59:14	And go all around the c
Ps	60: 9	bring me into the strong c
Ps	87: 3	are spoken of you, O c of God
Ps	107: 4	They found no c to dwell in
Ps	127: 1	Unless the LORD guards the c
Prov	9: 3	the highest places of the c,
Prov	9:14	the highest places of the c,
Prov	10:15	man's wealth is his strong c
Prov	16:32	spirit than he who takes a c
Prov	18:11	man's wealth is his strong c
Prov	18:19	harder to win than a strong c
Prov	21:22	scales the c of the mighty
Prov	25:28	is like a c broken down,
Prov	29: 8	Scoffers ensnare a c, but
Eccl	9:14	a little c with few men in it
Eccl	9:15	by his wisdom delivered the c
Is	1: 8	of cucumbers, as a besieged c
Is	1:21	How the faithful c has become
Is	1:26	called the c of righteousness
Is	14: 4	ceased, the golden c ceased
Is	14:31	Wail, O gate! Cry, O c! All you of
Is	19:18	called the C of Destruction
Is	22: 2	a tumultuous c, a joyous
Is	22: 9	the damage to the c of David
Is	23: 8	against Tyre, the crowning c
Is	24:10	The c of confusion is broken
Is	25: 3	the c of the terrible nations
Is	29: 1	the c where David dwelt
Is	32:13	happy homes in the joyous c
Is	32:14	the bustling c will be
Is	33:20	the c of our appointed feasts
Is	52: 1	O Jerusalem, the holy c
Is	60:14	call you The C of the LORD
Is	62:12	Sought Out, a C Not Forsaken
Jer	1:18	you this day a fortified c
Jer	17:24	of this c on the Sabbath day
Jer	17:25	this c shall remain forever
Jer	19: 8	I will make this c desolate
Jer	19:12	and make this c like Tophet
Jer	22: 8	nations will pass by this c
Jer	25:29	to bring calamity on the c
Jer	26: 6	will make this c a curse to
Jer	26:11	has prophesied against this c
Jer	29: 7	seek the peace of the c where
Jer	30:18	the c shall be built upon its
Jer	33: 5	hidden My face from this c
Jer	37:21	the bread in the c was gone
Jer	38:17	this c shall not be burned
Jer	39: 2	month, the c was penetrated
Jer	39: 4	and went out of the c by night
Jer	39: 9	people who remained in the c
Jer	49:25	Why is the c of praise not
Jer	49:25	not deserted, the c of My joy
Jer	52: 5	So the c was besieged until
Jer	52: 7	Then the c wall was broken
Lam	1: 1	How lonely sits the c that
Lam	1:19	breathed their last in the c
Lam	2:11	faint in the streets of the c
Lam	2:15	Is this the c that is called
Lam	3:51	of all the daughters of my c
Ezek	4: 1	you, and portray on it a c
Ezek	7:23	the c is full of violence
Ezek	9: 9	and the c full of perversity
Ezek	10: 2	and scatter them over the c
Ezek	11: 2	give wicked counsel in this c
Ezek	11: 3	this c is the caldron, and we
Ezek	17: 4	he set it in a c of merchants
Ezek	21:19	the head of the road to the c
Ezek	22: 2	will you judge the bloody c
Ezek	22: 3	The c sheds blood in her own
Ezek	26:17	seafaring men, O renowned c

Ezek	27:32	you, 'What c is like Tyre,
Ezek	40: 2	like the structure of a c
Ezek	48:15	be for general use by the c
Ezek	48:15	the c shall be in the center
Ezek	48:18	food for the workers of the c
Ezek	48:30	These are the exits of the c
Hos	6: 8	Gilead is a c of evildoers,
Joel	2: 9	They run to and fro in the c
Amos	3: 6	If a trumpet is blown in a c
Amos	3: 6	If there is calamity in a c
Amos	4: 7	I made it rain on one c, I
Jon	1: 2	go to Nineveh, that great c
Jon	3: 2	go to Nineveh, that great c
Jon	3: 3	was an exceedingly great c
Nah	3: 1	Woe to the bloody c
Zeph	2:15	c that dwelt securely, that
Zech	8: 3	be called the C of Truth, the
Matt	2:23	dwelt in a c called Nazareth,
Matt	4: 5	took Him up into the holy c
Matt	5:14	A c that is set on a hill
Matt	8:34	the whole c came out to meet
Matt	9: 1	over, and came to His own c
Matt	10:11	Now whatever c or town you
Matt	10:14	depart from that house or c
Matt	12:25	and every c or house divided
Matt	21:17	went out of the c to Bethany
Matt	23:34	and persecute from c to c
Luke	1:26	was sent by God to a c of
Luke	2: 3	everyone to his own c
Luke	2:11	in the c of David a Savior
Luke	7:11	He went into a c called Nain
Luke	9:10	to the c called Bethsaida
Luke	10:11	The very dust of your c
Luke	10:12	Day for Sodom than for that c
Luke	23:19	insurrection made in the c
Luke	23:51	a c of the Jews, who himself
John	1:44	the c of Andrew and Peter
John	4: 5	So He came to a c of Samaria
John	4: 8	away into the c to buy food
John	4:30	Then they went out of the c
John	4:39	of the Samaritans of that c
John	19:20	was crucified was near the c
Acts	8: 8	there was great joy in that c
Acts	8: 9	practiced sorcery in the c
Acts	11: 5	I was in the c of Joppa
Acts	12:10	iron gate that leads to the c
Acts	14:19	and dragged him out of the c
Acts	14:21	preached the gospel to that c
Acts	16:13	out of the c to the riverside
Acts	16:14	purple from the c of Thyatira
Acts	16:39	them to depart from the c
Acts	17: 5	set all the c in an uproar and
Acts	17:16	the c was given over to idols
Acts	18:10	I have many people in this c
Acts	19:35	when the c clerk had quieted
Acts	19:35	c of the Ephesians is temple
Acts	20:23	Spirit testifies in every c
Acts	21:39	a citizen of no mean c
Acts	24:12	in the synagogues or in the c
Acts	25:23	and the prominent men of the c
Rom	16:23	the treasurer of the c,
2Co	11:26	Gentiles, in perils in the c
Tit	1: 5	in every c as I commanded you
Heb	11:10	the c which has foundations
Heb	11:16	He has prepared a c for them
Heb	12:22	to the c of the living God,
Heb	13:14	here we have no continuing c
Rev	3:12	the name of the c of My God
Rev	11: 8	in the street of the great c
Rev	11:13	and a tenth of the c fell
Rev	14: 8	is fallen, that great c,
Rev	14:20	was trampled outside the c
Rev	16:19	Now the great c was divided
Rev	18:10	c Babylon, that mighty c
Rev	20: 9	the saints and the beloved c

Rev 21: 2 Then I, John, saw the holy **c**
Rev 21:15 a good reed to measure the **c**
Rev 21:16 the **c** is laid out as a square
Rev 21:18 the **c** was pure gold, like
Rev 21:21 street of the **c** was pure gold
Rev 21:23 the **c** had no need of the sun
Rev 22:19 Book of Life, from the holy **c**

CITY'S (see CITY)
2Sa 12:27 have taken the **c** water supply
Ezek 45: 7 district and the **c** property

CLAD†
Is 59:17 was **c** with zeal as a cloak

CLAIM (see CLAIMING, CLAIMS)
Judg 7: 2 lest Israel **c** glory for
Job 3: 5 and the shadow of death **c** it
Is 40:27 my just **c** is passed over by
Jer 37:12 the land of Benjamin to **c** his

CLAIMING† (see CLAIM)
Acts 5:36 rose up, **c** to be somebody
Acts 8: 9 **c** that he was someone great,

CLAIMS† (see CLAIM)
Ex 22: 9 which another **c** to be his

CLAMOR† (see CLAMOROUS)
Eph 4:31 bitterness, wrath, anger, **c**

CLAMOROUS† (see CLAMOR)
Prov 9:13 A foolish woman is **c**

CLAN† (see CLANS)
Josh 7:17 and he brought the **c** of Judah
Judg 6:15 Indeed my **c** is the weakest in

CLANGING†
1Co 13: 1 sounding brass or a **c** cymbal

CLANS† (see CLAN)
1Sa 10:19 by your tribes and by your **c**
1Sa 23:23 throughout all the **c** of Judah

CLAP† (see CLAPPED, CLAPS)
Job 27:23 Men shall **c** their hands at
Ps 47: 1 **c** your hands, all you peoples
Ps 98: 8 Let the rivers **c** their hands
Is 55:12 the field shall **c** their hands
Lam 2:15 All who pass by **c** their hands
Nah 3:19 will **c** their hands over you

CLAPPED (see CLAP)
2Ki 11:12 they **c** their hands and said,

CLAPS† (see CLAP)
Job 34:37 he **c** his hands among us, and

CLARITY†
Ex 24:10 the very heavens in its **c**

CLASH†
Job 39:21 he gallops into the **c** of arms

CLASPED† (see CLASPS)
Ex 26: 5 loops may be **c** to one another

CLASPS (see CLASPED)
Ex 26: 6 shall make fifty **c** of gold

CLASS
1Ki 12:31 from every **c** of people, who
2Co 10:12 For we dare not **c** ourselves

CLATTER† (see CLATTERING)
Judg 5:28 tarries the **c** of his chariots

CLATTERING† (see CLATTER)
Nah 3: 2 horses, of **c** chariots

CLAUDIUS (see CAESAR)
Acts 11:28 in the days of **C** Caesar
Acts 23:26 **C** Lysias, to the most

CLAWS†
Dan 4:33 and his nails like birds' **c**

CLAY
1Ki 7:46 king had them cast in **c** molds
Job 4:19 who dwell in houses of **c**,
Job 10: 9 that You have made me like **c**
Job 27:16 and piles up clothing like **c**
Job 33: 6 have been formed out of **c**
Job 38:14 on form like **c** under a seal
Ps 40: 2 pit, Out of the miry **c**, And
Is 29:16 potter be esteemed as the **c**
Is 41:25 as the potter treads **c**
Is 45: 9 Shall the **c** say to him who
Jer 18: 4 **c** was marred in the hand of
Ezek 4: 1 son of man, takes a **c** tablet
Dan 2:33 partly of iron and partly of **c**
Dan 2:41 the iron mixed with ceramic **c**
John 9: 6 and made **c** with the saliva
John 9: 6 of the blind man with the **c**
John 9:11 A Man called Jesus made **c**
John 9:15 He put **c** on my eyes, and I
Rom 9:21 potter have power over the **c**
2Ti 2:20 silver, but also of wood and **c**

CLEAN (see CLEANNESS, CLEANSE, UNCLEAN)
Gen 7: 2 seven each of every **c** animal
Gen 7: 8 Of **c** beasts, of beasts that
Gen 8:20 animal and of every **c** bird
Lev 4:12 outside the camp to a **c** place
Lev 7:19 And as for the **c** flesh, all
Lev 10:10 and between unclean and **c**,
Lev 11:37 is to be sown, it remains **c**
Lev 12: 7 she shall be **c** from the flow
Lev 13: 6 wash his clothes and be **c**
Lev 13:13 him **c** who has the sore
Lev 13:40 head, he is bald, but he is **c**
Lev 14: 4 **c** birds, cedar wood, scarlet,
Lev 14:48 shall pronounce the house **c**
Lev 22: 7 sun goes down he shall be **c**
Num 5:28 not defiled herself, and is **c**
Num 19:12 seventh day, he will not be **c**
Num 19:18 A **c** person shall take hyssop
Num 19:19 The **c** person shall sprinkle
Num 19:19 and at evening he shall be **c**
Num 31:23 the fire, and it shall be **c**
Deut 12:15 the **c** may eat of it, of the
Deut 14:11 All **c** birds you may eat
2Ki 5:14 a little child, and he was **c**
Ezra 6:20 all of them were ritually **c**
Job 11: 4 pure, And I am **c** in your eyes
Ps 19: 9 The fear of the LORD is **c**
Ps 24: 4 He who has **c** hands and a pure
Ps 51: 7 with hyssop, and I shall be **c**
Ps 51:10 Create in me a **c** heart, O God
Prov 14: 4 no oxen are, the trough is **c**
Prov 20: 9 I have made my heart **c**, I am
Eccl 9: 2 to the good, the **c**, and the
Is 1:16 yourselves, make yourselves **c**
Is 66:20 bring an offering in a **c**
Zech 3: 5 Let them put a **c** turban on
Matt 3:12 thoroughly **c** out his threshing
Matt 8: 2 willing, You can make me **c** also
Matt 23:26 outside of them may be **c** also
Luke 3:17 thoroughly **c** out his thresing
Matt 27:59 wrapped it in a **c** linen cloth
Luke 11:39 outside of the cup and dish **c**
Luke 11:41 all things are **c** to you
John 13:10 his feet, but is completely **c**
John 13:10 and you are **c**, but not all of
John 15: 3 You are already **c** because of
Rev 19:14 in fine linen, white and **c**

CLEANNESS (see CLEAN)
2Sa 22:25 according to my **c** in His eyes
Amos 4: 6 Also I gave you **c** of teeth in

CLEANSE (see CLEAN, CLEANSED, CLEANSES, CLEANSING)

Ex	29:36	You shall c the altar when
Lev	14:49	to c the house, two birds,
Num	8: 6	Israel and c them ceremonially
Num	8:21	atonement for them to c them
Neh	13: 9	commanded them to c the rooms
Job	9:30	and c my hands with soap,
Ps	19:12	C me from secret faults
Ps	51: 2	iniquity, And c me from my sin
Ps	119: 9	How can a young man c his way
Prov	20:30	Blows that hurt c away evil
Ezek	39:12	them, in order to c the land
Ezek	45:18	blemish and c the sanctuary
Matt	10: 8	c the lepers, raise the dead,
Matt	23:25	For you c the outside of the
Matt	23:26	first c the inside of the cup
2Co	7: 1	let us c ourselves from all
Eph	5:26	and c it with the washing of
Heb	9:14	your conscience from
Jas	4: 8	C your hands, you sinners
1Jn	1: 9	our sins and to c us from all

CLEANSED (see CLEANSE)

Lev	14: 4	him who is to be c two living
Lev	14: 7	is to be c from the leprosy
Lev	14:19	to be c from his uncleanness
Lev	14:31	is to be c before the LORD
Lev	15:13	is c of his discharge, then
Josh	22:17	we are not c until this day
2Ch	34: 5	and c Judah and Jerusalem
Neh	13:30	Thus I c them of everything
Ps	73:13	Surely I have c my heart in
Ezek	22:24	c or rained on in the day of
Ezek	43:22	as they c it with the bull
Dan	8:14	then the sanctuary shall be c
Matt	8: 3	I am willing; be c."
Matt	8: 3	immediately his leprosy was c
Matt	11: 5	the lepers are c and the deaf
Luke	4:27	none of them was c except
Luke	17:17	Were there not ten c
Acts	10:15	What God has c you must not
Acts	11: 9	What God has c you must not
2Pe	1:19	he was c from his old sins

CLEANSES † (see CLEANSE)

1Ti	2:21	Therefore if anyone c himself
1Jn	1: 7	His Son c us from all sin

CLEANSING (see CLEANSE)

Lev	13: 7	seen by the priest for his c
Lev	13:35	over the skin after his c
Lev	14: 2	leper for the day of his c
Lev	14:23	on the eighth day for his c
Lev	14:32	who cannot afford the usual c
Num	6: 9	his head on the day of his c
Ezek	43:23	When you have finished c it
Mark	1:44	offer for your c those things

CLEAR (see CLEARED, CLEARING, CLEARLY, CLEARS)

Gen	24:41	You will be c from this oath
Gen	44:16	Or how shall we c ourselves
Lev	26:10	c out the old because of the
Josh	17:15	c a place for yourself there
2Sa	23: 4	by c shining after rain
1Ki	7:36	there was a c space on each
Song	6:10	c as the sun, Awesome as an
Is	18: 4	place like c heat in sunshine
Ezek	32:14	I will make their waters c
1Co	3:13	one's work will become c;
2Co	7:11	to be c in this matter
Rev	21:11	a jasper stone, c as crystal
Rev	21:18	was pure gold, like c glass

CLEARED † (see CLEAR)

Job	37:21	the wind has passed and c them
Is	5: 2	c out its stones, and planted

CLEARING † (see CLEAR)

Ex	34: 7	sin, by no means c the guilty
2Co	7:11	what c of yourselves, what

CLEARLY (see CLEAR)

Matt	7: 5	then you will see c to remove
Mark	8:25	restored and saw everyone c
Luke	6:42	then you will see c to remove
Rom	1:20	attributes are c seen, being
Gal	3: 1	was c portrayed among you as
1Ti	5:24	Some men's sins are c evident

CLEARS † (see CLEAR)

Num	14:18	He by no means c the guilty

CLEFT (see CLEFTS)

Ex	33:22	put you in the c of the rock

CLEFTS (see CLEFT)

Job	30: 6	live in the c of the valleys
Song	2:14	in the c of the rock, in the

CLEMENT †

Phil	4: 3	me in the gospel, with C also

CLEOPAS † (see ALPHAEUS)

Luke	24:18	one whose name was C

CLERK †

Acts	19:35	when the city c had quieted

CLIFF † (see CLIFFS)

Ps	141: 6	by the sides of the c, And
Song	2:14	in the secret places of the c
Luke	4:29	throw Him down over the c

CLIFFS † (see CLIFF)

Ps	104:18	The c are a refuge for the

CLIMB † (see CLIMBED, CLIMBS)

Jer	4:29	thickets and c up on the rocks
Joel	2: 7	they c the wall like men of
Joel	2: 9	they c into the houses, they
Amos	9: 2	though they c up to heaven,

CLIMBED † (see CLIMB)

1Sa	14:13	Jonathan c up on his hands and
Luke	19: 4	c up into a sycamore tree to

CLIMBS (see CLIMB)

2Sa	5: 8	Whoever c up by way of the

CLING (see CLINGS, CLUNG)

Deut	28:21	plague c to you until He has
Deut	30:20	and that you may c to Him
Job	38:38	and the clods c together
Ps	102: 5	My bones c to my skin
Ps	119:31	I c to Your testimonies
Ps	137: 6	Let my tongue c to the roof
Rom	12: 9	C to what is good

CLINGS † (see CLING)

Job	19:20	My bone c to my skin and to my
Ps	22:15	And My tongue c to My jaws
Ps	41: 8	they say, "c to him
Ps	44:25	Our body c to the ground
Ps	119:25	My soul c to the dust
Jer	13:11	For as the sash c to the
Lam	4: 4	c to the roof of its mouth
Lam	4: 8	their skin c to their bones,
Luke	10:11	dust of your city which c to

CLIPPED †

Jer	48:37	be bald, and every beard c

CLOAK

Ps	102:26	Like a c You will change them
Matt	5:40	let him have your c also
1Th	2: 5	nor a c for covetousness
2Ti	4:13	Bring the c that I left with
Heb	1:12	Like a c You will fold them
1Pe	2:16	your liberty as a c for vice

CLODS

Is 28:24 his soil and breaking the c

CLOSE (see CLOSED, CLOSELY, CLOSER)

Ruth 2: 8 but stay c by my young women
2Sa 19:42 king is a c relative of ours
2Ki 10:11 his c acquaintances and his
Job 19:14 my c friends have forgotten
Ps 63: 8 My soul follows c behind You
Luke 19:43 and c you in on every side,
Phil 2:30 of Christ he came c to death

CLOSED (see CLOSE)

Gen 2:21 c up the flesh in its place
Gen 20:18 for the LORD had c up all the
Ex 14: 3 the wilderness has c them in
Num 16:33 the earth c over them, and
Judg 3:22 the fat c over the blade, for
1Sa 1: 5 the LORD had c her womb
Is 1: 6 have not been c or bound up
Is 29:10 has c your eyes, namely, the
Dan 12: 9 for the words are c up and
Jon 2: 5 the deep c around me
Jon 2: 6 its bars c behind me forever
Luke 4:20 Then he c the book, and gave

CLOSELY (see CLOSE)

Job 13:27 and watch c all my paths
Mark 3: 2 And they watched Him c,

CLOSER

Prov 18:24 who sticks c than a brother

CLOTH (see CLOTHS)

Num 4: 8 spread over them a scarlet c
1Sa 21: 9 wrapped in a c behind the
2Ki 8:15 day that he took a thick c
Matt 9:16 unshrunk c on an old garment
Matt 27:59 wrapped it in a clean linen c
John 11:44 his face was wrapped with a c

CLOTHE (see CLOTHED, CLOTHES, UNCLOTHED)

Ex 40:14 sons and c them with tunics
Esth 4: 4 sent garments to c Mordecai
Job 10:11 c me with skin and flesh, and
Ps 132:18 will c a man with shame
Prov 23:21 will c a man with rags
Is 15: 3 c themselves with sackcloth
Is 50: 3 I c the heavens with
Ezek 34: 3 c yourselves with the wool
Zech 3: 4 I will c you with rich robes
Matt 6:30 will He not much more c you
Matt 25:38 You in, or naked and c You

CLOTHED (see CLOTHE)

Gen 3:21 tunics of skin, and c them
Gen 41:42 he c him in garments of fine
Lev 8: 7 c him with the robe, and put
1Sa 17:38 So Saul c David with his
2Sa 1:24 who c you in scarlet, with
1Ch 21:16 c in sackcloth, fell on their
2Ch 5:12 c in white linen, having
2Ch 6:41 be c with salvation, and let
Job 8:22 hate you will be c with shame
Job 29:14 on righteousness, and it c me
Is 30:11 and c me with gladness,
Ps 65: 6 strength, Being c with power
Ps 65:13 pastures are c with flocks
Ps 93: 1 reigns, He is c with majesty
Ps 93: 1 The LORD is c, He has girded
Ps 104: 1 You are c with honor and
Ps 109:18 As he c himself with cursing
Prov 31:21 household is c with scarlet
Ps 61:10 for He has c me with the
Zech 3: 3 Now Joshua was c with filthy
Matt 3: 4 himself was c in camel's hair
Matt 11: 8 A man c in soft garments
Matt 25:36 I was naked and you c Me

Mark 5:15 had the legion, sitting and c
Mark 15:17 And they c Him with purple
Mark 16: 5 man c in a long white robe
Luke 8:35 at the feet of Jesus, c and in
1Co 4:11 and thirst, and we are poorly c
2Co 5: 2 earnestly desiring to be c
1Pe 5: 5 and be c with humility, for
Rev 1:13 c with a garment down to the
Rev 3: 5 shall be c in white garments
Rev 4: 4 sitting, c in white robes
Rev 10: 1 from heaven, c with a cloud
Rev 12: 1 a woman c with the sun, with
Rev 19:13 He was c with a robe dipped

CLOTHES (see CLOTHE, CLOTHING)

Gen 27:15 c of her elder son Esau,
Gen 37:34 Then Jacob tore his c, put
Ex 19:10 and let them wash their c
Lev 10: 6 your heads nor tear your c
Lev 13: 6 scab, and he shall wash his c
Lev 15: 7 discharge shall wash his c
Lev 15:22 she sat on shall wash his c
Lev 16:26 scapegoat shall wash his c
Lev 16:32 and put on the linen c, the
Num 19: 7 the priest shall wash his c
Num 19:10 the heifer shall wash his c
Num 19:19 purify himself, wash his c
Deut 21:13 off the c of have not worn out on
Deut 29: 5 Your c have not worn out on
Judg 3:16 his c on his right thigh
Judg 17:10 silver per year, a suit of c
1Sa 19:24 And he also stripped off his c
2Sa 3:31 Tear your c, gird yourselves
2Sa 12:20 himself, and changed his c
2Ki 22:11 the Law, that he tore his c
Neh 4:23 followed me took off our c
Job 9:31 and my own c will abhor me
Prov 6:27 bosom, and his c not be burned
Jer 38:12 Please put these old c and
Jer 41: 5 beards shaved and their c torn
Ezek 27:24 in purple c, in embroidered
Amos 2: 8 altar on c taken in pledge
Matt 6:30 Now if God so c the grass of
Matt 17: 2 His c became as white as the
Matt 21: 7 colt, laid their c on them
Matt 21: 8 spread their c on the road;
Matt 24:18 not go back to get his c
Matt 26:65 the high priest tore his c
Matt 27:31 off Him, put His own c on Him
Mark 5:28 If only I may touch His c
Mark 9: 3 His c became shining,
Mark 13:16 not go back to get his c
Luke 19:35 threw their own c on the colt
Luke 19:36 spread their c on the road
Acts 7:58 witnesses laid down their c
Acts 22:20 guarding the c of those who
Jas 2: 2 in a poor man in filthy c
Jas 2: 3 to the one wearing the fine c

CLOTHING (see CLOTHES)

Gen 27:27 he smelled the smell of his c
Gen 41:14 and he shaved, changed his c
Deut 10:18 giving him food and c
Judg 14:12 and thirty changes of c
Job 22: 6 stripped the naked of their c
Job 24:10 poor to go naked, without c
Job 27:16 dust, and piles up c like clay
Job 31:19 anyone perish for lack of c
Ps 22:18 And for My c they cast lots
Ps 35:13 were sick, My c was sackcloth
Ps 45:13 Her c is woven with gold
Prov 31:22 her c is fine linen and purple
Prov 31:25 Strength and honor are her c
Is 3: 6 You have c; you be our ruler
Matt 6:25 food and the body more than c
Matt 6:28 So why do you worry about c

Matt	7:15	who come to you in sheep's c
Matt	11: 8	those who wear soft c are in
Matt	27:35	and for My c they cast lots
Matt	28: 3	and his c as white as snow
Luke	10:30	who stripped him of his c
Acts	10:30	stood before me in bright c
1Ti	2: 9	or gold or pearls or costly c

CLOTHS (see CLOTH)

Ezek	16: 4	nor swathed in swaddling c
Luke	2:12	a Babe wrapped in swaddling c
Luke	24:12	he saw the linen c lying by
John	20: 7	not lying with the linen c

CLOUD (see CLOUDS, CLOUDY)

Gen	9:13	I set My rainbow in the c
Ex	13:21	a pillar of c to lead the way
Ex	13:22	of c by day or the pillar of
Ex	14:20	Thus it was a c and darkness
Ex	14:24	the pillar of fire and c, and
Ex	16:10	of the LORD appeared in the c
Ex	19:16	a thick c on the mountain
Ex	24:16	out of the midst of the c
Ex	34: 5	the LORD descended in the c
Ex	40:35	because the c rested above it
Ex	40:36	When the c was taken up from
Lev	16: 2	in the c above the mercy seat
Lev	16:13	that the c of incense may
Num	9:15	the c covered the tabernacle,
1Ki	8:10	that the c filled the house
1Ki	8:11	ministering because of the c
1Ki	8:12	He would dwell in the dark c
1Ki	18:44	There is a c, as small as a
Job	3: 5	may a c settle on it
Job	7: 9	As the c disappears and
Job	26: 9	and spreads His c over it
Job	30:15	has passed like a c
Job	37:15	the light of His c to shine
Ps	78:14	also He led them with the c
Ps	105:39	He spread a c for a covering,
Prov	16:15	like a c of the latter rain
Is	18: 4	like a c of dew in the heat
Is	19: 1	the LORD rides on a swift c
Is	25: 5	as heat in the shadow of a c
Is	44:22	blotted out, like a thick c
Is	60: 8	are these who fly like a c
Lam	3:44	covered Yourself with a c
Ezek	1: 4	a great c with raging fire
Ezek	1:28	rainbow in a c on a rainy day
Hos	6: 4	is like a morning c, and like
Matt	17: 5	a bright c overshadowed them
Matt	17: 5	a voice came out of the c
Luke	12:54	When you see a c rising out
Luke	21:27	Man coming in a c with power
Acts	1: 9	a c received Him out of their
1Co	10: 1	our fathers were under the c
1Co	10: 2	baptized into Moses in the c
Heb	12: 1	by so great a c of witnesses
Rev	10: 1	from heaven, clothed with a c
Rev	11:12	ascended to heaven in a c
Rev	14:14	looked, and behold, a white c
Rev	14:14	on the c sat One like the Son

CLOUDS (see CLOUD)

Deut	33:26	And in His excellency on the c
Judg	5: 4	the c also poured water
2Sa	22:12	and thick c of the skies
2Sa	23: 4	rises, a morning without c
1Ki	18:45	the sky became black with c
Job	20: 6	and his head reaches to the c
Job	26: 8	yet the c are not broken
Job	35: 5	behold the c which are higher
Job	36:28	Which the c drop down and pour
Job	36:29	understand the spreading of c
Job	37:11	He saturates the thick c
Job	37:11	He scatters His bright c

Job	37:16	Do you know the balance of c
Job	38: 9	when I made the c its garment
Job	38:37	can number the c by wisdom
Ps	36: 5	faithfulness reaches to the c
Ps	57:10	And Your truth unto the c
Ps	68: 4	Extol Him who rides on the c
Ps	68:34	And His strength is in the c
Ps	77:17	The c poured out water
Ps	97: 2	C and darkness surround Him
Ps	104: 3	Who makes the c His chariot
Ps	147: 8	Who covers the heavens with c
Ps	148: 8	Fire and hail, snow and c
Prov	3:20	up, and c drop down the dew
Prov	25:14	boasts of giving is like c
Eccl	11: 4	regards the c will not reap
Is	5: 6	I will also command the c
Ezek	30: 3	it will be a day of c, the
Dan	7:13	coming with the c of heaven
Joel	2: 2	like the morning c spread
Nah	1: 3	the c are the dust of His
Zech	10: 1	the LORD will make flashing c
Matt	24:30	on the c of heaven with power
Matt	26:64	and coming on the c of heaven
1Th	4:17	together with them in the c
2Pe	2:17	c carried by a tempest, to
Jude	12	they are c without water,
Rev	1: 7	Behold, He is coming with c

CLOUDY (see CLOUD)

Neh	9:12	them by day with a c pillar

CLOVEN

Lev	11: 3	the hoof, having c hooves
Deut	14: 7	chew the cud or have c hooves

CLUB† (see CLUBS)

Prov	25:18	his neighbor is like a c, a

CLUBS (see CLUB)

Matt	26:55	with swords and c to take Me

CLUMPS†

Job	38:38	when the dust hardens in c

CLUNG† (see CLING)

Ruth	1:14	but Ruth c to her
1Ki	11: 2	Solomon c to these in love

CLUSTER (see CLUSTERS)

Num	13:23	a branch with one c of grapes
Job	38:31	bind the c of the Pleiades

CLUSTERS (see CLUSTER)

1Sa	30:12	of figs and two c of raisins
Song	7: 8	breasts be like c of the vine

COAL† (see COALS)

Is	6: 6	having in his hand a live c
Is	47:14	not be a c to be warmed by

COALS (see COAL)

Lev	16:12	c of fire from the altar
2Sa	22:13	Him c of fire were kindled
Job	41:21	His breath kindles c, and a
Ps	11: 6	the wicked He will rain c
Ps	18:12	with hailstones and c of fire
Ps	120: 4	With c of the broom tree
Ps	140:10	Let burning c fall upon them
Prov	6:28	Can one walk on hot c, and his
Prov	25:22	heap c of fire on his head
Prov	26:21	As charcoal is to burning c
Is	54:16	who blows the c in the fire
John	18:18	made a fire of c stood there
John	21: 9	they saw a fire of c there
Rom	12:20	heap c of fire on his head

COARSE†

Zech	13: 4	a robe of c hair to deceive
Eph	5: 4	nor c jesting, which are not

COASTLAND (*see* COASTLANDS)
Gen 10: 5 From these the **c** peoples of
Is 23: 2 you inhabitants of the **c**

COASTLANDS (*see* COASTLAND)
Is 24:15 of Israel in the **c** of the sea
Is 42: 4 the **c** shall wait for His law
Is 66:19 to the **c** afar off who have
Dan 11:18 shall turn his face to the **c**

COASTLINE
Josh 15:12 was the **c** of the Great Sea

COASTS
Josh 9: 1 in all the **c** of the Great Sea
Joel 3: 4 and all the **c** of Philistia
Acts 27: 2 to sail along the **c** of Asia

COAT (*see* COATS)
Ex 28:32 the opening in a **c** of mail
Job 41:13 Who can remove his outer **c**

COATS† (*see* COAT)
Dan 3:21 men were bound in their **c**

COBRA† (*see* COBRA'S, COBRAS)
Job 20:14 it becomes **c** venom within him
Ps 58: 4 the deaf **c** that stops its ear
Ps 91:13 tread upon the lion and the **c**

COBRA'S† (*see* COBRA)
Is 11:18 shall play by the **c** hole, and

COBRAS† (*see* COBRA)
Deut 32:33 and the cruel venom of **c**
Job 20:16 He will suck the poison of **c**

CODE†
Rom 2:27 who, even with your written **c**

COFFIN†
Gen 50:26 and he was put in a **c** in Egypt
2Sa 3:31 And King David followed the **c**
Luke 7:14 He came and touched the open **c**

COIN† (*see* COINS)
Matt 10:29 sparrows sold for a copper **c**
Luke 15: 8 coins, if she loses one **c**

COINS (*see* COIN)
Ps 119:72 thousands of **c** of gold
Luke 12: 6 sold for two copper **c**
Luke 15: 8 woman, having ten silver **c**

COLD
Gen 8:22 seedtime and harvest, and **c**
Ps 147:17 Who can stand before His **c**
Prov 25:13 Like the **c** of snow in time of
Prov 25:20 away a garment in **c** weather
Prov 25:25 As **c** water to a weary soul,
Matt 10:42 of **c** water in the name of a
Matt 24:12 the love of many will grow **c**
John 18:18 stood there, for it was **c**
2Co 11:27 in fastings often, in **c** and
Rev 3:15 you are neither **c** nor hot

COLLAPSE† (*see* COLLAPSED)
Jer 13:18 down, for your rule shall **c**
Lam 1: 9 therefore her **c** was awesome

COLLAPSED† (*see* COLLAPSE)
Judg 7:13 and overturned, and the tent **c**

COLLAR†
Job 30:18 me about as the **c** of my coat

COLLECT (*see* COLLECTED, COLLECTING, COLLECTION, COLLECTOR)
Gen 41:34 to **c** one-fifth of the produce
Luke 19:21 You **c** what you did not

COLLECTED† (*see* COLLECT)
Luke 19:23 might have **c** it with interest

COLLECTING† (*see* COLLECT)
Eccl 2:26 the work of gathering and **c**
Luke 19:22 **c** what I did not deposit and

COLLECTION (*see* COLLECT, COLLECTIONS)
2Ch 24: 9 to bring to the LORD the **c**
Is 57:13 let your **c** of idols deliver
1Co 16: 1 the **c** for the saints, as I

COLLECTIONS (*see* COLLECTION)
1Co 16: 2 there be no **c** when I come

COLLECTOR (*see* COLLECT, COLLECTORS)
Matt 10: 3 Thomas and Matthew the tax **c**
Luke 5:27 and saw a tax **c** named Levi,
Luke 18:10 Pharisee and the other a tax **c**
Luke 19: 2 who was a chief tax **c**, and he

COLLECTORS (*see* COLLECTOR)
Matt 5:46 even the tax **c** do the same
Matt 9:10 that behold, many tax **c** and
Matt 9:11 your Teacher eat with tax **c**
Matt 11:19 winebibber, a friend of tax **c**
Luke 7:29 even the tax **c** justified God,

COLONY†
Acts 16:12 that part of Macedonia, a **c**

COLOR (*see* COLORED, COLORFUL, COLORS)
Lev 13:55 plague has not changed its **c**
Num 11: 7 **c** like the **c** of bdellium
Ezek 1: 4 its midst like the **c** of amber
Ezek 1: 7 the **c** of burnished bronze
Ezek 1:16 works was like the **c** of beryl
Ezek 1:22 the **c** of an awesome crystal

COLORED† (*see* COLOR)
Prov 7:16 **C** coverings of Egyptian linen

COLORFUL† (*see* COLOR)
Is 54:11 lay your stones with **c** gems

COLORS (*see* COLOR)
Gen 37: 3 he made him a tunic of many **c**
2Sa 13:18 she had on a robe of many **c**
Ps 45:14 the King in robes of many **c**

COLOSSE†
Col 1: 2 in Christ who are in **C**

COLT (*see* COLTS)
Gen 49:11 his donkey's **c** to the choice
Job 11:12 wild donkey's **c** is born a man
Zech 9: 9 and riding on a donkey, a **c**
Matt 21: 2 donkey tied, and a **c** with her
Matt 21: 5 and sitting on a donkey, a **c**
Luke 19:35 their own garments on the **c**
John 12:15 sitting on a donkey's **c**

COLTS† (*see* COLT)
Gen 32:15 milk camels with their **c**,

COLUMN† (*see* COLUMNS)
Judg 20:40 from the city in a **c** of smoke
Joel 2: 8 one marches in his own **c**

COLUMNS† (*see* COLUMN)
Jer 36:23 had read three or four **c**,

COMELINESS†
Is 53: 2 He has no form or **c**

COMFORT (*see* COMFORTED, COMFORTER, COMFORTING, COMFORTS)
Gen 5:29 This one will **c** us concerning
Gen 37:35 his daughters arose to **c** him
Job 2:11 mourn with him, and to **c** him
Job 6:10 Then I would still have **c**
Job 7:13 When I say, "My bed will **c** me
Job 10:20 that I may take a little **c**
Ps 23: 4 rod and Your staff, they **c** me
Ps 71:21 And **c** me on every side
Ps 119:50 This is my **c** in my affliction

Ps	119:82 When will You c me
Is	40: 1 C, yes, c My people
Is	40: 2 Speak c to Jerusalem, and cry
Is	51: 3 For the LORD will c Zion, He
Is	61: 2 to c all who mourn,
Zech	1:17 the LORD will again c Zion
Acts	9:31 in the c of the Holy Spirit,
Rom	15: 4 c of the Scriptures might
Rom	15: 5 c grant you to be like-minded
2Co	1: 3 of mercies and God of all c
2Co	1: 4 to c those who are in any
2Co	7: 4 I am filled with c
2Co	13:11 Be of good c, be of one mind,
Eph	6:22 and that he may c your hearts
Phil	2: 1 if any c of love, if any
Col	4:11 have proved to be a c to me
1Th	4:18 Therefore c one another with
1Th	5:14 c the fainthearted, uphold

COMFORTED (see COMFORT)

Gen	24:67 So Isaac was c after his
Gen	37:35 but he refused to be c, and he
Gen	50:21 he c them and spoke kindly to
Ruth	2:13 for you have c me, and have
Job	42:11 c him for all the adversity
Ps	77: 2 My soul refused to be c
Is	49:13 For the LORD has c His people
Jer	31:15 refusing to be c for her
Matt	2:18 children, refusing to be c
Matt	5: 4 mourn, for they shall be c
Acts	20:12 and they were not a little c
2Co	1: 4 we ourselves are c by God
2Co	7:13 have been c in your comfort
1Th	3: 7 distress we were c concerning

COMFORTER (see COMFORT, COMFORTERS)

Eccl	4: 1 oppressed, but they have no c

COMFORTERS (see COMFORTER)

Job	16: 2 miserable c are you all
Ps	69:20 And for c, but I found none

COMFORTING† (see COMFORT)

2Sa	14:17 lord the king will now be c
Zech	1:13 to me, with good and c words
John	11:31 c her, when they saw that

COMFORTS (see COMFORT)

Gen	27:42 Surely your brother Esau c
Ps	94:19 me, Your c delight my soul
Is	51:12 I, even I, am He who c you
Is	66:13 As one whom his mother c, so
2Co	1: 4 who c us in all our
2Co	7: 6 who c the downcast, comforted

COMMAND (see COMMANDED, COMMANDER,
COMMANDING, COMMANDMENT, COMMANDS)

Gen	18:19 that he may c his children
Gen	42:25 Then Joseph gave a c to fill
Gen	45:21 according to the c of Pharaoh
Ex	7: 2 shall speak all that I c you
Ex	8:27 LORD our God as He will c us
Ex	27:20 you shall c the children of
Ex	34:11 Observe what I c you this day
Lev	24: 2 C the children of Israel that
Num	9: 8 LORD will c concerning you
Num	14:41 transgress the c of the LORD
Num	27:14 you rebelled against My c to
Num	31:49 of war who are under our c
Deut	4: 2 add to the word which I c you
Deut	6: 2 commandments which I c you
Deut	6: 6 these words which I c you
Deut	7:11 judgments which I c you today
Deut	12:32 Whatever I c you, be careful
Josh	1:16 All that you c us we will do,
Josh	3: 8 You shall c the priests who
1Sa	16:16 master now c your servants
1Ki	5: 6 c that they cut down cedars

1Ki	11:38 if you heed all that I c you
1Ki	20:12 were drinking at the c post
2Ch	7:13 or c the locusts to devour
2Ch	13:11 for we keep the c of the LORD
2Ch	35:10 according to the king's c
Ezra	6:14 according to the c of Cyrus
Esth	2:20 for Esther obeyed the c of
Esth	3: 3 you transgress the king's c
Job	39:27 the eagle mount up at your c
Ps	44: 4 C victories for Jacob
Ps	147:15 sends out His c to the earth
Prov	6:20 My son, keep your father's c
Is	5: 6 I will also c the clouds that
Is	45:11 work of My hands, you c Me
Jer	1: 7 send you, and whatever I c you
Jer	23:32 I did not send them or c them
Dan	2: 2 the c to call the magicians
Dan	3:22 the king's c was urgent, and
Dan	5: 2 gave the c to bring the gold
Dan	5:29 Then Belshazzar gave the c
Dan	9:25 forth of the c to restore
Amos	6:11 behold, the LORD gives a c
Amos	9: 3 there I will c the serpent
Amos	9: 4 from there I will c the sword
Matt	4: 3 c that these stones become
Matt	19: 7 Why then did Moses c to give
Matt	27:64 Therefore c that the tomb be
Mark	9:25 I c you, come out of him, and
Luke	9:54 do You want us to c fire to
John	10:18 c I have received from
John	11:57 the Pharisees had given a c
John	12:49 who sent Me gave Me a c, what
John	15:14 if you do whatever I c you
Acts	15: 5 to c them to keep the law of
Acts	16:18 I c you in the name of Jesus
1Co	7:10 Now to the married I c, yet
2Th	3: 6 But we c you, brethren, in
1Ti	4:11 These things c and teach
Heb	11:23 not afraid of the king's c
Rev	3:10 have kept My c to persevere

COMMANDED (see COMMAND)

Gen	2:16 And the LORD God c the man
Gen	3:11 from the tree of which I c
Gen	6:22 to all that God c him, so he
Gen	7: 5 to all that the LORD c him
Gen	7: 9 and female, as God had c Noah
Gen	7:16 went in as God had c him
Gen	12:20 So Pharaoh c his men
Ex	1:22 So Pharaoh c all his people,
Ex	4:28 the signs which He had c him
Ex	5: 6 c the taskmasters of the
Ex	7: 6 just as the LORD c them, so
Ex	12:50 as the LORD c Moses and Aaron,
Ex	16:24 up till morning, as Moses c
Ex	34:18 unleavened bread, as I c you
Ex	39: 1 as the LORD had c Moses
Num	34:29 c to divide the inheritance
Num	36:13 judgments which the LORD c
Deut	1:16 Then I c your judges at that
Deut	5:15 c you to keep the Sabbath day
Deut	6: 1 your God has c to teach you
Deut	6:17 statutes which He has c you
Deut	6:24 the LORD c us to observe all
Deut	9:12 from the way which I c them
Deut	13: 5 LORD your God c you to walk
Deut	31:25 that Moses c the Levites, who
Deut	33: 4 Moses c a law for us, a
Josh	1: 7 which Moses My servant c you
Josh	1: 9 Have I not c you
Josh	7:11 My covenant which I c them
Ruth	2: 9 Have I not c the young men
Ruth	2:15 Boaz c his young men, saying,
2Sa	7: 7 whom I c to shepherd My
1Ki	17: 4 I have c the ravens to feed

1Ch 21:27 Then the LORD c the angel
Neh 13:19 that I c the gates to be shut
Job 38:12 Have you c the morning since
Job 42: 9 and did as the LORD c them
Ps 33: 9 He c, and it stood fast
Ps 68:28 Your God has c your strength
Ps 78:23 Yet He had c the clouds above
Ps 105: 8 forever, The word which He c
Ps 133: 3 there the LORD c the blessing
Is 13: 3 I have c My sanctified ones
Is 34:16 For My mouth has c it, and His
Jer 36: 5 And Jeremiah c Baruch, saying,
Jer 38:27 words that the king had c
Lam 2:17 which He c in days of old
Lam 3:37 when the Lord has not c it
Ezek 12: 7 So I did as I was c
Ezek 37: 7 So I prophesied as I was c
Dan 3:19 c that they heat the furnace
Matt 1:24 the angel of the Lord c him
Matt 8: 4 offer the gift that Moses c
Matt 16:20 Then He c His disciples that
Matt 17: 9 the mountain, Jesus c them
Matt 18:25 his master c that he be sold,
Matt 21: 6 went and did as Jesus c them
Matt 27:58 Then Pilate c the body to be
Matt 28:20 all things that I have c you
Mark 1:44 those things which Moses c
Mark 5:43 But He c them strictly that
Mark 6:27 and c his head to be brought
Mark 13:34 c the doorkeeper to watch
Luke 8:29 For He had c the unclean
Luke 14:22 Master, it is done as you c
Acts 1: 4 He c them not to depart from
Acts 4:18 c them not to speak at all
Acts 8:38 So he c the chariot to stand
Acts 10:42 And He c us to preach to the
Acts 10:48 he c them to be baptized in
Acts 16:22 c them to be beaten with rods
Acts 23: 2 the high priest Ananias c
Acts 23:30 also c his accusers to state
Acts 24:23 So he c the centurion to keep
1Co 9:14 Even so the Lord has c that
2Co 4: 6 who c light to shine out of
1Th 4:11 your own hands, as we c you
Tit 1: 5 in every city as I c you
Heb 9:20 covenant which God has c you
Heb 12:20 could not endure what was c
Rev 9: 4 They were c not to harm the

COMMANDER (see COMMAND, COMMANDERS)
Gen 21:22 the c of his army, spoke to
Josh 5:15 Then the C of the LORD's army
1Sa 9:16 you shall anoint him c over
1Sa 12: 9 c of the army of Hazor, into
1Ki 16: 9 c of half his chariots,
2Ki 5: 1 c of the army of the king of
Is 55: 4 a leader and c for the people
Acts 21:37 barracks, he said to the c
Acts 23:10 a great dissension, the c

COMMANDERS (see COMMANDER)
1Ki 1:25 and the c of the army, and
1Ki 9:22 c of his chariots, and his
2Ch 32: 3 c to stop the water from the
Nah 3:17 Your c are like swarming
Rev 6:15 men, the rich men, the c, the

COMMANDING† (see COMMAND)
Gen 49:33 Jacob had finished c his sons
Matt 11: 1 when Jesus finished c His
Acts 16:23 c the jailer to keep them
Acts 24: 8 c his accusers to come to you
1Ti 4: 3 c to abstain from foods which

COMMANDMENT (see COMMAND, COMMANDMENTS)
Ex 36: 6 So Moses gave a c, and they
Num 15:31 the LORD, and has broken His c

Deut 8: 1 Every c which I command you
Josh 22: 5 diligent heed to do the c
1Sa 12:14 against the c of the LORD
2Sa 12: 9 despised the c of the LORD
2Ki 17:34 law and c which the LORD had
2Ki 17:37 the c which He wrote for you,
Job 23:12 from the c of His lips
Ps 19: 8 The c of the LORD is pure,
Prov 6:23 For the c is a lamp, and the
Prov 13:18 fears the c will be rewarded
Prov 19:16 keeps the c keeps his soul
Eccl 8: 2 Keep the king's c for the
Is 29:13 Me is taught by the c of men
Lam 1:18 for I rebelled against His c
Mal 2: 1 O priests, this c is for you
Matt 22:36 is the great c in the law
Matt 22:38 This is the first and great c
Mark 7: 8 For laying aside the c of God
Luke 23:56 Sabbath according to the c
John 13:34 A new c I give to you, that
John 14:31 and as the Father gave Me c
John 15:12 This is My c, that you love
Rom 7: 8 taking opportunity by the c
Rom 7: 9 the law, but when the c came
Rom 7:12 the c holy and just and good
Rom 7:13 so that sin through the c
1Co 7: 6 as a concession, not as a c
1Co 7:25 I have no c from the Lord
2Co 8: 8 I speak not by c, but I am
Eph 6: 2 is the first c with promise
1Ti 1: 1 by the c of God our Savior and
1Ti 1: 5 Now the purpose of the c is
1Ti 6:14 you keep this c without spot
Heb 7: 5 have a c to receive tithes
Heb 7:16 to the law of a fleshly c
Heb 7:18 c because of its weakness
2Pe 2:21 the holy c delivered to them
2Pe 3: 2 of the c of us the apostles
1Jn 2: 7 I write no new c to you, but
1Jn 3:23 And this is His c
1Jn 4:21 And this c we have from Him
2Jn 5 though I wrote a new c to you

COMMANDMENTS (see COMMANDMENT)
Gen 26: 5 voice and kept My charge, My c
Ex 15:26 His sight, give ear to His c
Ex 20: 6 who love Me and keep My c
Ex 24:12 c which I have written, that
Ex 34:28 of the covenant, the Ten C
Lev 4: 2 against any of the c of the
Lev 26: 3 in My statutes and keep My c
Lev 26:14 and do not observe all these c
Lev 26:15 you do not perform all My c
Deut 4:13 perform, that is, the Ten C
Deut 4:40 His c which I command you
Deut 10: 4 the first writing, the Ten C
Deut 11:13 c which I command you today
Deut 11:22 carefully keep all these c
Deut 11:27 if you obey the c of the LORD
Deut 13: 4 and fear Him, and keep His c
Deut 26:13 have not transgressed Your c
Deut 28:13 if you heed the c of the LORD
Judg 2:17 in obeying the c of the LORD
1Ki 14: 8 servant David, who kept My c
1Ki 18:18 forsaken the c of the LORD
1Ch 28: 7 is steadfast to observe My c
1Ch 29:19 a loyal heart to keep Your c
2Ch 7:19 My c which I have set before
2Ch 24:20 transgress the c of the LORD
Ezra 7:11 words of the c of the LORD
Ezra 9:10 For we have forsaken Your c
Ezra 9:14 should we again break Your c
Ps 103:18 who remember His c to do them
Ps 112: 1 Who delights greatly in His c
Ps 119:10 let me not wander from Your c

Ps	119:19	Do not hide Your c from me
Ps	119:21	cursed, Who stray from Your c
Ps	119:32	will run in the way of Your c
Ps	119:35	me walk in the path of Your c
Ps	119:47	will delight myself in Your c
Ps	119:66	For I believe Your c
Ps	119:73	that I may learn Your c
Ps	119:86	All Your c are faithful
Ps	119:127	I love Your c More than gold
Ps	119:131	For I longed for Your c
Ps	119:143	Yet Your c are my delights
Ps	119:151	LORD, And all Your c are truth
Ps	119:176	For I do not forget Your c
Eccl	12:13	Fear God and Keep His c, for
Dan	9: 4	and with those who keep His c
Matt	5:19	one of the least of these c
Matt	15: 9	as doctrines the c of men
Matt	19:17	enter into life, keep the c
Matt	22:40	On these two c hang all the
Mark	10:19	You know the c
Mark	12:29	The first of all the c is
John	14:15	If you love Me, keep My c
John	15:10	as I have kept My Father's c
Acts	1: 2	the Holy Spirit had given c
Rom	13: 9	For the c, "You shall not
1Co	7:19	but keeping the c of God is
Eph	2:15	the law of c contained in
1Th	4: 2	for you know what c we gave
Tit	1:14	c of men who turn from the
1Jn	2: 3	we know Him, if we keep His c
1Jn	3:24	who keeps His c abides in Him
1Jn	5: 2	we love God and keep His c
1Jn	5: 3	And His c are not burdensome

COMMANDS (see COMMAND)

Ex	18:23	this thing, and God so c you
Num	32:25	servants will do as my lord c
Num	36: 6	This is what the LORD c
Deut	26:16	God c you to observe these
2Sa	15:15	whatever my lord the king c
Job	9: 7	He c the sun, and it does not
Job	36:32	lightning, and c it to strike
Prov	2: 1	and treasure my c within you
Prov	7: 2	Keep my c and live, and my law
Prov	10: 8	wise in heart will receive c
Mark	1:27	For with authority He c even
Luke	8:25	For He c even the winds and
Acts	17:30	but now c all men everywhere

COMMEMORATE†

1Ch	16: 4	the ark of the LORD, to c

COMMEND (see COMMENDABLE, COMMENDATION, COMMENDED, COMMENDING, COMMENDS)

Acts	20:32	I c you to God and to the word
1Co	8: 8	But food does not c us to God
2Co	3: 1	we begin again to c ourselves

COMMENDABLE (see COMMEND)

1Pe	2:19	For this is c, if because of

COMMENDATION† (see COMMEND)

2Co	3: 1	epistles of c to you or
2Co	3: 1	you or letters of c from you

COMMENDED (see COMMEND)

Gen	12:15	saw her and c her to Pharaoh
Prov	12: 8	A man will be c according to
Luke	16: 8	So the master c the unjust
Acts	14:23	they c them to the Lord in
Acts	15:40	being c by the brethren to

COMMENDING† (see COMMEND)

2Co	4: 2	c ourselves to every man's

COMMENDS (see COMMEND)

2Co	10:18	For not he who c himself is

COMMISSION†

Acts	26:12	c from the chief priests,

COMMIT (see COMMITS, COMMITTED, COMMITTING)

Ex	20:14	You shall not c adultery
Lev	20: 5	him to c harlotry with Molech
Num	5: 6	commits any sin that men c in
Judg	19:23	house, do not c this outrage
Job	5: 8	and to God I would c my cause
Ps	31: 5	Into Your hand I c my spirit
Ps	37: 5	C your way to the LORD, Trust
Prov	16: 3	C your works to the LORD, and
Prov	16:12	for kings to c wickedness
Is	23:17	c fornication with all the
Jer	37:21	c Jeremiah to the court of
Ezek	16:43	you shall not c lewdness in
Ezek	33:26	you c abominations, and you
Hos	4:10	they shall c harlotry, but
Matt	5:27	You shall not c adultery
Matt	19:18	You shall not c adultery
Luke	16:11	who will c to your trust the
Luke	23:46	into Your hands I c My spirit
John	2:24	did not c Himself to them
1Co	10: 8	Nor let us c sexual
2Co	11: 7	Did I c sin in abasing myself
1Ti	1:18	This charge I c to you, son
2Ti	2: 2	c these to faithful men who
Jas	2: 9	show partiality, you c sin
1Pe	4:19	to the will of God c their
1Jn	5:16	c sin not leading to death
Rev	2:14	and to c sexual immorality

COMMITS (see COMMIT)

Lev	5:15	If a person c a trespass, and
Lev	20:10	The man who c adultery with
Num	5: 6	When a man or woman c any
Deut	19:15	iniquity or any sin that he c
Ps	10:14	The helpless c himself to You
Hab	1:11	he c offense, imputing this
Matt	5:32	who is divorced c adultery
John	8:34	whoever c sin is a slave of
1Co	6:18	the body, but he who c sexual
1Jn	3: 4	sin also c lawlessness, and

COMMITTED (see COMMIT)

Gen	39:22	c to Joseph's hand all the
Ex	32:31	have c a great sin
Lev	4:28	has c comes to his knowledge
Lev	5: 6	sin which he has c
Lev	5: 7	his trespass which he has c
Lev	5:10	sin which he has c
Lev	20:12	They have c perversion
Lev	20:13	of them have c an abomination
Num	15:24	if it is unintentionally c
Deut	17: 5	who has c that wicked thing
Judg	20: 6	because they c lewdness and
Jer	2:13	My people have c two evils
Jer	39:14	c him to Gedaliah the son of
Ezek	22:29	c robbery, and mistreated the
Hos	7: 1	For they have c fraud
Luke	12:48	and to whom much has been c
John	5:22	but has c all judgment to the
Acts	25:25	had c nothing worthy of death
Rom	3: 2	were c the oracles of God
Rom	3:25	sins that were previously c
Rom	11:32	For God has c them all to
2Co	5:19	and has c to us the word of
1Ti	1:11	God which was c to my trust
2Ti	1:12	have c to Him until that Day
2Ti	1:14	good thing which was c to you
Heb	9: 7	people's sins c in ignorance
Jas	5:15	And if he has c sins, he will
1Pe	2:22	Who c no sin, nor was guile
1Pe	2:23	but c Himself to Him who
Jude	15	they have c in an ungodly way
Rev	20: 4	and judgment was c to them

COMMITTING (see COMMIT)
Ezek 20:30 c harlotry according to their
Hos 3: 1 is c adultery, just like the
Acts 8: 3 and women, c them to prison
Rom 1:27 men with men c what is

COMMON (see COMMON-LAND, COMMONLY)
Lev 4:27 If anyone of the c people
Num 16:29 by the c fate of all men,
1Sa 21: 4 There is no c bread on hand
1Ki 10:27 as c in Jerusalem as stones
Prov 22: 2 and the poor have this in c
Prov 29:13 the oppressor have this in c
Eccl 6: 1 the sun, and it is c among men
Ezek 23:42 with men of the c sort, who
Ezek 42:20 the holy areas from the c
Mark 12:37 the c people heard Him gladly
Acts 2:44 and had all things in c,
Acts 5:18 and put them in the c prison
Acts 10:14 eaten anything c or unclean
1Co 10:13 except such as is c to man
Tit   1: 4 my true son in our c faith
Heb 10:29 he was sanctified a c thing
Jude   3 concerning our c salvation

COMMON-LAND (see COMMON, COMMON-LANDS)
Lev 25:34 But the field of the c of
Num 35: 2 Levites c around the cities

COMMON-LANDS (see COMMON-LAND)
Josh 21: 3 LORD, these cities and their c

COMMONLY† (see COMMON)
Matt 28:15 this saying is c reported

COMMONWEALTH†
Eph 2:12 aliens from the c of Israel

COMMOTION† (see COMMOTIONS)
Jer 10:22 a great c out of the north
Mark 5:39 Why make this c and weep
Acts 19:23 arose a great c about the Way

COMMOTIONS† (see COMMOTION)
Luke 21: 9 when you hear of wars and c

COMMUNED† (see COMMUNION)
Eccl 1:16 I c with my heart, saying,

COMMUNICATE† (see COMMUNICATED, COMMUNICATION)
1Sa 18:22 C with David secretly, and say

COMMUNICATED† (see COMMUNICATE)
2Sa 3:17 Now Abner had c with the
Gal 2: 2 c to them that gospel which I

COMMUNICATION (see COMMUNICATE, WORD)

COMMUNION (see COMMUNED)
1Co 10:16 is it not the c of the blood
2Co 6:14 And what c has light with
2Co 13:14 the c of the Holy Spirit be

COMMUNITIES†
Neh 10:37 tithes in all our farming c

COMPACT†
Ps 122: 3 As a city that is c together

COMPANIES (see COMPANY)
Gen 32: 7 herds and camels, in two c
2Ch 26:11 men who went out to war by c

COMPANION (see COMPANIONS)
Ex 2:13 Why are you striking your c
Ex 32:27 his brother, every man his c
Job 30:29 jackals, and a c of ostriches
Ps 55:13 was you, a man my equal, My c
Ps 119:63 I am a c of all those who
Prov 2:17 forsakes the c of her youth
Prov 13:20 but the c of fools will be
Prov 28: 7 but a c of gluttons shames

Prov 29: 3 but a c of harlots wastes his
Eccl 4:10 fall, one will lift up his c
Zech 13: 7 against the Man who is My C
Mal 2:14 yet she is your c and your
Phil 4: 3 And I urge you also, true c
Rev 1: 9 c in tribulation, and in the

COMPANIONS (see COMPANION)
Num 16:40 become like Korah and his c
Ezra 6: 6 your c the Persians who are
Job 41: 6 Will your c make a banquet of
Ps 45: 7 of gladness more than Your c
Ps 45:14 her c who follow her, shall
Ps 122: 8 the sake of my brethren and c
Song 8:13 the c listen for your voice
Is 1:23 rebellious, and c of thieves
Dan 2:13 they sought Daniel and his c
Matt 11:16 and calling to their c,
Acts 4:23 go, they went to their own c
Acts 19:29 Macedonians, Paul's travel c
Heb 1: 9 of gladness more than Your c

COMPANY (see ASSEMBLY, COMPANIES)
Gen 35:11 a c of nations shall proceed
Num 16: 5 spoke to Korah and all his c
Job 15:34 For the c of hypocrites will
Job 34: 8 who goes in c with the
Ps 68:11 Great was the c of those who
Ps 106:18 A fire was kindled in their c
Ps 107:32 Him in the c of the elders
Luke 2:44 Him to have been in the c
Luke 24:22 and certain women of our c
Rom 15:24 may enjoy your c for a while
1Co 5: 9 keep c with sexually immoral
1Co 15:33 Evil c corrupts good habits
Heb 12:22 to an innumerable c of angels

COMPARABLE (see COMPARE)
Gen 2:18 make him a helper c to him

COMPARE (see COMPARABLE, COMPARED, COMPARING, COMPARISON)
Is 40:18 likeness will you c to Him
Is 46: 5 c Me, that we should be alike
Luke 13:18 And to what shall I c it
2Co 10:12 or c ourselves with those who

COMPARED† (see COMPARE)
Ps 89: 6 heavens can be c to the LORD
Prov 8:11 desire cannot be c with her
Song 1: 9 I have c you, my love, to my
Rom 8:18 time are not worthy to be c

COMPARING† (see COMPARE)
1Co 2:13 c spiritual things with
2Co 10:12 c themselves among themselves

COMPARISON (see COMPARE)
Judg 8: 2 have I done now in c with you

COMPASS†
Is 44:13 he marks it out with the c

COMPASSION (see COMPASSIONATE, COMPASSIONS)
Ex 2: 6 So she had c on him, and said,
Ex 33:19 I will have c on whom I will
Deut 32:36 have c on His servants, when
1Sa 23:21 LORD, for you have c on me
1Ki 3:26 yearned with c for her son
1Ki 8:50 grant them c before those who
2Ch 30: 9 will be treated with c by
Ps 78:38 But He, being full of c,
Ps 86:15 O Lord, are a God full of c
Ps 111: 4 LORD is gracious and full of c
Is 49:15 not have c on the son of her
Lam 3:32 yet He will show c according
Matt 9:36 He was moved with c for them
Matt 15:32 I have c on the multitude,
Matt 20:34 So Jesus had c and touched

COMPASSIONATE (continued)
Mark	9:22	have c on us and help us
Luke	15:20	his father saw him and had c
Rom	9:15	I will have c on whomever I
1Pe	3: 8	having c for one another

COMPASSIONATE† (see COMPASSION)
Lam	4:10	The hands of the c women have
Jas	5:11	that the Lord is very c and

COMPASSIONS† (see COMPASSION)
Lam	3:22	because His c fail not

COMPEL† (see COMPELLED, COMPELS)
Lev	25:39	you shall not c him to serve
Luke	14:23	c them to come in, that my
Gal	2:14	why do you c Gentiles to live
Gal	6:12	these try to c you to be

COMPELLED (see COMPEL)
1Sa	13:12	Therefore I felt c, and
Matt	27:32	Him they c to bear His cross
Acts	26:11	and c them to blaspheme
Acts	28:19	I was c to appeal to Caesar,
Gal	2: 3	was c to be circumcised

COMPELS† (see COMPEL)
Job	32:18	the spirit within me c me
Matt	5:41	whoever c you to go one mile,
2Co	5:14	For the love of Christ c us

COMPENSATE†
Esth	7: 4	never c for the king's loss

COMPETE† (see COMPETES)
2Sa	2:14	men now arise and c before us

COMPETENT†
Gen	47: 6	you know any c men among

COMPETES† (see COMPETE)
1Co	9:25	everyone who c for the prize
2Ti	2: 5	also if anyone c in athletics
2Ti	2: 5	he c according to the rules

COMPLACENCY† (see COMPLACENT)
Prov	1:32	the c of fools will destroy
Zeph	1:12	the men who are settled in c

COMPLACENT (see COMPLACENCY)
Is	32: 9	you c daughters, give ear to

COMPLAIN (see COMPLAINED, COMPLAINERS, COMPLAINING, COMPLAINT)
Ex	16: 7	that you c against us
Num	14:27	who c against me
Judg	21:22	brothers come to us to c,
Job	7:11	I will c in the bitterness of
Lam	3:39	Why should a living man c
1Co	10:10	nor c, as some of them also

COMPLAINED (see COMPLAIN)
Ex	15:24	the people c against Moses
Num	11: 1	Now when the people c, it
Num	14:29	you who have c against Me
Job	31:13	when they c against me,
Ps	77: 3	I c, and my spirit was

COMPLAINERS† (see COMPLAIN)
Jude	16	These are murmurers, c,

COMPLAINING (see COMPLAIN)
John	7:12	was much c among the people
Phil	2:14	Do all things without c

COMPLAINT (see COMPLAIN, COMPLAINTS)
Job	7:13	me, my couch will ease my c
Job	23: 2	Even today my c is bitter
Ps	55: 2	I am restless in my c, and
Ps	142: 2	I pour out my c before Him
Mic	6: 2	has a c against his people
Acts	6: 1	arose a c against the Hebrews
Col	3:13	has a c against another

COMPLAINTS (see COMPLAINT)
Ex	16: 7	for He hears your c against
Deut	1:12	and your burdens and your c
Acts	25: 7	many serious c against Paul

COMPLETE (see COMPLETED, COMPLETELY, COMPLETION)
Gen	15:16	of the Amorites is not yet c
Job	27:12	do you behave with c nonsense
Jer	5:10	but do not make a c end
2Co	8: 6	so he would also c this grace
2Co	8:11	also must c the doing of it
2Co	13: 9	pray, that you may be made c
2Co	13:11	Become c. Be of good comfort
Phil	1: 6	a good work in you will c it
Col	2:10	and you are c in Him, who is
Col	4:12	and c in all the will of God
2Ti	3:17	that the man of God may be c
Heb	13:21	make you c in every good work
Jas	1: 4	that you may be perfect and c
Rev	15: 1	in them the wrath of God is c

COMPLETED (see COMPLETE)
Lev	23:15	seven Sabbaths shall be c
Deut	31:24	when Moses had c writing the
2Ch	8:16	the house of the LORD was c
Ezra	4:13	city is built and the walls c
Jer	25:12	when seventy years are c
Jer	29:10	years are c at Babylon, I
Luke	2:21	when eight days were c for
Rev	6:11	be killed as they were, was c

COMPLETELY (see COMPLETE)
Gen	31:15	also c consumed our money
Ex	19:18	Mount Sinai was c in smoke
Judg	1:28	but did not c drive them out
1Ki	7:23	it was c round
1Ki	9:21	not been able to destroy c
Esth	4:14	For if you remain c silent at
Job	19:13	are c estranged from me
Ezek	27:31	c bald because of you, gird
Dan	12: 7	people has been c shattered
John	7:23	a man c well on the Sabbath
John	9:34	You were c born in sins, and
John	13:10	wash his feet, but is c clean
1Th	5:23	peace Himself sanctify you c

COMPLETION† (see COMPLETE)
2Co	8:11	be a c out of what you have

COMPOSED† (see COMPOSITION)
1Co	12:24	But God c the body, having

COMPOSITION (see COMPOSED)
Ex	30:32	like it, according to its c
Ps	45: 1	I recite my c concerning the

COMPOUND†
Ex	30:35	a c according to the art of

COMPREHEND† (see COMPREHENDED)
Job	37: 5	things which we cannot c
Ps	139: 3	You c my path and my lying
Luke	24:45	they might c the Scriptures
John	1: 5	and the darkness did not c it
Eph	3:18	may be able to c with all the

COMPREHENDED† (see COMPREHEND)
Job	38:18	Have you c the breadth of the

COMPRISED
1Ki	6:34	two panels c one folding door

COMPULSION† (see COMPULSORY)
Phm	14	good deed might not be by c
1Pe	5: 2	not by c but willingly, not

COMPULSORY (see COMPULSION)
Esth	1: 8	law, the drinking was not c

CONCEAL (see CONCEALED, CONCEALS)
Gen	37:26	our brother and c his blood

Job 27:11 the Almighty I will not c
Prov 25: 2 glory of God to c a matter

CONCEALED† (see CONCEAL)
Num 5:13 it is c that she has defiled
Job 6:10 for I have not c the words of
Job 28:21 c from the birds of the air
Ps 40:10 I have not c Your
Prov 27: 5 better than love carefully c

CONCEALS† (see CONCEAL)
Prov 11:13 a faithful spirit c a matter
Prov 12:23 A prudent man c knowledge

CONCEIT† (see CONCEITED)
Phil 2: 3 through selfish ambition or c

CONCEITED† (see CONCEIT)
Gal 5:26 Let us not become c,

CONCEIVE (see CONCEIVED, CONCEIVES, CONCEIVING, CONCEPTION)
Gen 30:41 they might c among the rods
Job 15:35 They c trouble and bring forth
Is 7:14 Behold, the virgin shall c
Is 59: 4 they c evil and bring forth
Luke 1:31 you will c in your womb and

CONCEIVED (see CONCEIVE)
Gen 4: 1 knew Eve his wife, and she c
Gen 30:41 the stronger livestock c,
Ex 2: 2 So the woman c and bore a son
Job 3: 3 was said, 'A male child is c
Ps 51: 5 And in sin my mother c me
Song 3: 4 the chamber of her who c me
Is 8: 3 to the prophetess, and she c
Matt 1:20 for that which is c in her is
Luke 1:24 days his wife Elizabeth c
Luke 1:36 also c a son in her old age
Luke 2:21 before He was c in the womb
Acts 5: 4 Why have you c this thing in
Jas 1:15 Then, when desire has c, it

CONCEIVES† (see CONCEIVE)
Ps 7:14 C trouble and brings forth

CONCEIVING† (see CONCEIVE)
Is 59:13 oppression and revolt, c and

CONCEPTION† (see CONCEIVE)
Gen 3:16 your sorrow and your c
Ruth 4:13 to her, the LORD gave her c
Hos 9:11 birth, no pregnancy, and no c

CONCERN (see CONCERNED, CONCERNS)
Ps 131: 1 Neither do I c myself with
Dan 4:19 may the dream c those who
John 2: 4 what does your c have to do
2Co 11:28 my deep c for all the

CONCERNED (see CONCERN)
1Co 9: 9 Is it oxen God is c about
Heb 9:10 c only with foods and drinks,

CONCERNS† (see CONCERN)
Ex 22: 9 trespass, whether it c an ox
Ps 138: 8 will perfect that which c me
Ezek 7:13 for the vision c the whole
Ezek 12:10 This burden c the prince in

CONCESSION†
1Co 7: 6 But I say this as a c, not as

CONCILIATION†
Eccl 10: 4 for c pacifies great offenses

CONCLUDE† (see CONCLUDED, CONCLUDING, CONCLUSION)
Rom 3:28 Therefore we c that a man is

CONCLUDED† (see CONCLUDE)
Ruth 3:18 he has c the matter this day
Luke 7: 1 Now when He c all His sayings

CONCLUDING† (see CONCLUDE)
Acts 16:10 c that the Lord had called us
Heb 11:19 c that God was able to raise

CONCLUSION (see CONCLUDE)
Eccl 12:13 Let us hear the c of the

CONCOURSES†
Prov 1:21 She cries out in the chief c

CONCUBINE (see CONCUBINES)
Gen 35:22 with Bilhah his father's c
Judg 19: 2 But his c played the harlot
1Ch 1:32 born to Keturah, Abraham's c

CONCUBINES (see CONCUBINE)
Gen 25: 6 of the c which Abraham had
2Sa 5:13 And David took more c and
1Ki 11: 3 and three hundred c
Song 6: 8 are sixty queens and eighty c

CONDEMN (see CONDEMNATION, CONDEMNED, CONDEMNING, CONDEMNS, UNCONDEMNED)
Deut 25: 1 righteous and c the wicked,
Job 9:20 my own mouth would c me
Ps 94:21 And c innocent blood
Ps 109:31 save him from those who c him
Prov 12: 2 of wicked devices He will c
Is 50: 9 who is he who will c Me
Matt 12:41 c it, because they repented
Matt 20:18 they will c Him to death,
Luke 6:37 C not, and you shall not be
John 3:17 into the world to c the world
John 8:11 Neither do I c you
Rom 2: 1 judge another you c yourself
Rom 14:22 Happy is he who does not c
2Co 7: 3 I do not say this to c
1Jn 3:21 if our heart does not c us

CONDEMNATION (see CONDEMN)
Matt 23:14 you will receive greater c
Matt 23:33 can you escape the c of hell
Mark 3:29 but is subject to eternal c"
Luke 23:40 you are under the same c
John 3:19 And this is the c, that the
John 5:29 to the resurrection of c
Rom 3: 8 Their c is just
Rom 5:16 one offense resulted in c
Rom 8: 1 There is therefore now no c
2Co 3: 9 the ministry of c had glory
1Ti 3: 6 into the same c as the devil
Jude 4 were marked out for this c

CONDEMNED (see CONDEMN)
Job 9:29 If I am c, why then do I
Job 32: 3 no answer, and yet had c Job
Ps 34:21 hate the righteous shall be c
Ps 34:22 who trust in Him shall be c
Matt 12: 7 not have c the guiltless
Matt 12:37 by your words you will be c
Matt 27: 3 seeing that He had been c
Luke 24:20 Him to be c to death, and
John 3:18 who believes in Him is not c
John 3:18 does not believe is c already
Rom 8: 3 He c sin in the flesh,
Rom 14:23 he who doubts is c if he eats
1Co 4: 9 last, as men c to death
1Co 11:32 may not be c with the world
Tit 2: 8 sound speech that cannot be c
Heb 11: 7 by which he c the world and
2Pe 2: 6 c them to destruction, making

CONDEMNING† (see CONDEMN)
1Ki 8:32 c the wicked, bringing his
Acts 13:27 have fulfilled them in c Him

CONDEMNS (see CONDEMN)
Job 15: 6 Your own mouth c you, and not
Rom 8:34 Who is he who c

1Jn   3:20 For if our heart c us, God is

CONDITION (see CONDITIONS)
2Ch 24:13 of God to its original c and
John   5: 6 been in that c a long time

CONDITIONS† (see CONDITION)
Luke 14:32 delegation and asks c of peace

CONDUCT (see CONDUCTED)
Ps   37:14 those who are of upright c
Ps   50:23 And to him who orders his c
Gal   1:13 of my former c in Judaism
Phil   1:27 Only let your c be worthy of
1Ti   3:15 to c yourself in the house of
1Ti   4:12 the believers in word, in c
Heb 13: 7 the outcome of their c
Jas   3:13 Let him show by good c that
1Pe   1:15 also be holy in all your c
1Pe   1:18 from your aimless c received
1Pe   2:12 having your c honorable among
1Pe   3: 2 chaste c accompanied by fear
2Pe   2: 7 the filthy c of the wicked

CONDUCTED† (see CONDUCT)
Acts 17:15 So those who c Paul brought
2Co   1:12 c ourselves in the world in
Eph   2: 3 c ourselves in the lusts of

CONFEDERACY†
Ps   83: 5 They form a c against You
Obad   7 All the men in your c shall

CONFER† (see CONFERRED)
Judg 19:30 Consider it, c and speak up
Gal   1:16 not immediately c with flesh

CONFERRED (see CONFER)
Luke 22: 4 c with the chief priests and
Acts   4:15 they c among themselves,

CONFESS (see CONFESSED, CONFESSES, CONFESSING,
CONFESSION)
Lev   5: 5 that he shall c that he has
Lev   16:21 c over it all the iniquities
Num   5: 7 then he shall c the sin
1Ki   8:33 c Your name, and pray and
Ps   32: 5 I will c my transgressions to
Matt 10:32 him I will also c before My
Luke 12: 8 c before the angels of God
John 12:42 Pharisees they did not c Him
Rom 10: 9 that if you c with your mouth
Rom 14:11 every tongue shall c to God
Phil   2:11 that every tongue should c
Jas   5:16 C your trespasses to one
1Jn   1: 9 If we c our sins, He is
1Jn   4: 3 c that Jesus Christ has come
2Jn   7 c Jesus Christ as coming in
Rev   3: 5 but I will c his name before

CONFESSED (see CONFESS)
John   1:20 He c, and did not deny, but
John   9:22 anyone c that He was Christ
1Ti   6:12 have c the good confession in
Heb 11:13 c that they were strangers and

CONFESSES (see CONFESS)
Matt 10:32 whoever c Me before men, him
1Jn   4: 2 Every spirit that c that

CONFESSING (see CONFESS)
Ezra 10: 1 praying, and while he was c
Dan   9:20 c my sin and the sin of my
Matt   3: 6 in the Jordan, c their sins
Acts 19:18 many who had believed came c

CONFESSION (see CONFESS)
Rom 10:10 with the mouth c is made to
2Co   9:13 c to the gospel of Christ
1Ti   6:13 good c before Pontius Pilate
Heb   3: 1 and High Priest of our c,

Heb   4:14 God, let us hold fast our c
Heb 10:23 the c of our hope without

CONFIDENCE (see CONFIDENT)
Judg   9:26 of Shechem put their c in him
Ps   65: 5 You who are the c of all the
Ps   118: 8 the LORD Than to put c in man
Prov   3:26 for the LORD will be your c
Prov 25:19 C in an unfaithful man in
Is   30:15 and c shall be your strength
Mic   7: 5 not put your c in a companion
Acts 28:31 Lord Jesus Christ with all c
2Co   1:15 in this c I intended to come
2Co   2: 3 having c in you all that my
Eph   3:12 access with c through faith
Phil   3: 3 and have no c in the flesh,
2Th   3: 4 And we have c in the Lord
Phm   21 Having c in your obedience, I
Heb   3: 6 we are if we hold fast the c
Heb   3:14 of our c steadfast to the end
Heb 10:35 do not cast away your c,
1Jn   2:28 He appears, we may have c
1Jn   5:14 Now this is the c that we

CONFIDENT (see CONFIDENCE, CONFIDENTLY)
Ps   27: 3 me, In this I will be c
Rom   2:19 are c that you yourself are a
2Co   9: 4 be ashamed of this c boasting
Phil   1: 6 being c of this very thing,
Phil   1:14 having become c by my chains
Heb   6: 9 we are c of better things
Heb 13:18 for we are c that we have a

CONFIDENTLY† (see CONFIDENT)
Luke 22:59 another c affirmed, saying,

CONFINED
Gen 39:20 the king's prisoners were c
Gen 40: 3 the place where Joseph was c
Gal   3:22 Scripture has c all under sin

CONFIRM (see CONFIRMATION, CONFIRMED,
CONFIRMING, CONFIRMS)
Lev   26: 9 you and c My covenant with you
1Ki   1:14 in after you and c your words
Dan   11: 1 I, even I, stood up to c
Rom 15: 8 to c the promises made to the

CONFIRMATION† (see ATTESTATION, CONFIRM)
Ruth   4: 7 and this was a c in Israel.
Phil   1: 7 c of the gospel, you all are
Heb   6:16 an oath for c is for them an

CONFIRMED (see CONFIRM)
1Ki   2:24 the Lord lives, who has c me
Ps   68: 9 rain, Whereby You c Your
Dan   9:12 He has c His words, which He
1Co   1: 6 of Christ was c in you,
Gal   3:15 covenant, yet if it is c, no
Gal   3:17 was c before by God in Christ
Heb   2: 3 and was c to us by those who
Heb   6:17 His counsel, c it by an oath,
2Pe   1:19 prophetic word c, which

CONFIRMING† (see CONFIRM)
Mark 16:20 and c the word through the

CONFIRMS (see CONFIRM)
Num 30:14 then he c all her vows or all
Is   44:26 Who c the word of His servant

CONFISCATED† (see CONFISCATION)
Ezra 10: 8 all his property would be c

CONFISCATION (see CONFISCATED)
Ezra   7:26 banishment, or c of goods, or

CONFLICT (see CONFLICTS)
Amos   7: 4 Lord GOD called for c by fire
Phil   1:30 having the same c which you
Col   2: 1 what a great c I have for you

CONFLICTS† (see CONFLICT)
2Co 7: 5 Outside were c, inside were

CONFORMED† (see CONFORMING)
Rom 8:29 be c to the image of His Son
Rom 12: 2 do not be c to this world,
Phil 3:10 being c to His death,
Phil 3:21 may be c to His glorious body

CONFORMING† (see CONFORMED)
1Pe 1:14 not c yourselves to the

CONFOUNDED (see APPALLED)
Ps 40:15 Let them be c because of
Ps 69: 6 seek You be c because of me
Ps 70: 2 ashamed and c Who seek my life
Ps 71:13 Let them be c and consumed
Ezek 36:32 c for your own ways, O house
Acts 9:22 and c the Jews who dwelt in

CONFRONT† (see CONFRONTED, CONFRONTING)
Job 30:27 days of affliction c me
Ps 17:13 O LORD, C him, cast him down
Amos 9:10 not overtake us nor c us

CONFRONTED (see CONFRONT)
2Sa 22: 6 me, the snares of death c me
Matt 21:23 c Him as He was teaching, and

CONFRONTING† (see CONFRONT)
Dan 8: 7 And I saw him c the ram

CONFUSE† (see CONFUSED, CONFUSION)
Gen 11: 7 there c their language, that

CONFUSED (see CONFUSE)
1Sa 7:10 and so c them that they were
Job 6:20 they come there and are c
Ps 70: 2 back and c Who desire my hurt
Acts 19:32 for the assembly was c, and

CONFUSION (see CONFUSE)
Ex 23:27 I will cause c among all the
Deut 28:28 and blindness and c of heart
Neh 4: 8 attack Jerusalem and create c
Ps 35:26 and brought to mutual c Who
Ps 60: 3 made us drink the wine of c
Is 24:10 The city of c is broken down
Is 34:11 out over it the line of c
Is 41:29 molded images are wind and c
Jer 20:11 Their everlasting c will
Zech 12: 4 strike every horse with c
1Co 14:33 the author of c but of peace
Jas 3:16 envy and self-seeking exist, c

CONGEALED†
Ex 15: 8 the depths c in the heart of

CONGREGATION (see ASSEMBLY, CONGREGATIONS)
Ex 12: 3 Speak to all the c of Israel
Ex 16:22 all the rulers of the c came
Lev 4:15 the elders of the c shall lay
Num 1: 2 Take a census of all the c of
Num 8: 9 c of the chidren of Israel.
Num 10: 2 use them for calling the c
Num 16: 3 for all the c is holy, every
Num 20: 2 there was no water for the c
Deut 33: 4 a heritage of the c of Jacob
Josh 9:21 water carriers for all the c
Ps 1: 5 in the c of the righteous
Ps 22:16 The c of the wicked has
Ps 82: 1 stands in the c of the mighty
Is 14:13 sit on the mount of the c on
Acts 13:43 Now when the c had broken up,

CONGREGATIONS† (see CONGREGATION)
Ps 26:12 In the c I will bless the
Ps 68:26 Bless God in the c, The Lord,

CONJURES†
Deut 18:11 or one who c spells, or a

CONQUER† (see CONQUERED, CONQUERING, CONQUERORS)
Deut 7: 2 over to you, you shall c them
Rev 6: 2 went out conquering and to c

CONQUERED (see CONQUER)
Josh 10:40 So Joshua c all the land
2Ki 10:32 and Hazael c them in all the

CONQUERING† (see CONQUER)
Rev 6: 2 to him, and he went out c and

CONQUERORS† (see CONQUER)
Rom 8:37 things we are more than c

CONSCIENCE (see CONSCIENCE', CONSCIENCES)
John 8: 9 being convicted by their c
Acts 23: 1 I have lived in all good c
Rom 2:15 their c also bearing witness,
1Co 8: 7 and their c, being weak, is
1Co 10:29 C, I say, not your own, but
1Co 10:29 judged by another man's c
2Co 1:12 the testimony of our c that
2Co 4: 2 man's c in the sight of God
1Ti 1: 5 a pure heart, from a good c
1Ti 1:19 having faith and a good c,
1Ti 3: 9 of the faith with a pure c
1Ti 4: 2 having their own c seared
Tit 1:15 their mind and c are defiled
Heb 9:14 purge your c from dead works
Heb 10:22 sprinkled from an evil c and
1Pe 2:19 if because of c toward God

CONSCIENCE' (see CONSCIENCE)
Rom 13: 5 of wrath but also for c sake
1Co 10:25 no questions for c sake

CONSCIENCES† (see CONSCIENCE)
2Co 5:11 are well-known in your c

CONSCIOUSNESS†
1Co 8: 7 with c of the idol, until now
Heb 10: 2 have had no more c of sins

CONSECRATE (see CONSECRATED, CONSECRATES, CONSECRATION)
Ex 28:41 c them, and sanctify them,
Ex 29:33 the atonement was made, to c
Lev 25:10 you shall c the fiftieth year
Joel 1:14 C a fast, call a sacred
Mic 4:13 I will c their gain to the

CONSECRATED (see CONSECRATE)
Ex 29:29 in them and to be c in them
Lev 7:35 This is the c portion for
Lev 8:15 the alter, and c it, to make
Lev 8:30 he c Aaron, his garments,
Lev 16:32 c to minister as priest in
Lev 21:10 who is c to wear the garments
Num 6: 9 him, and he defiles his c head
Num 6:19 he has shaved his c hair,
Judg 17:12 So Micah c the Levite, and the
1Sa 16: 5 Then he c Jesse and his sons
1Ki 8:64 c the middle of the court
2Ch 29:33 The c things were six hundred
Heb 10:20 living way which He c for us

CONSECRATES† (see CONSECRATE)
Lev 27: 2 When a man c by a vow
Num 6: 2 c an offering to take the vow

CONSECRATION (see CONSECRATE, CONSECRATIONS)
Ex 29:22 thigh (for it is a ram of c)
Ex 29:26 of the ram of Aaron's c and
Ex 29:34 the flesh of the c offerings
Lev 8:33 the days of your c are ended

CONSECRATIONS† (see CONSECRATION)
Lev 7:37 the trespass offering, the c

CONSENT (see CONSENTED, CONSENTING)
Gen 34:22 the men c to dwell with us

Gen   41:44 without your **c** no man may
1Sa   11: 7 and they came out with one **c**
Prov   1:10 sinners entice you, do not **c**
Acts   18:20 time with them, he did not **c**
1Co   7: 5 except with **c** for a time,
1Ti   6: 3 does not **c** to wholesome words
Phm   14 But without your **c** I wanted

CONSENTED (*see* CONSENT)
Ps   50:18 you **c** with him, And have been
Luke   23:51 He had not **c** to their counsel

CONSENTING (*see* CONSENT)
Acts   8: 1 Now Saul was **c** to his death

CONSIDER (*see* CONSIDERED, CONSIDERING, CONSIDERS)
Deut   4:39 **c** it in your heart, that the
Judg   19:30 **C** it, take counsel, and speak
1Sa   12:24 for **c** what great things He
Job   23:15 when I **c** this, I am afraid of
Job   37:14 **c** the wondrous works of God
Ps   5: 1 O LORD, **C** my meditation
Ps   8: 3 When I **c** Your heavens, the
Ps   13: 3 **C** and hear me, O LORD my God
Ps   25:19 **C** my enemies, for they are
Ps   64: 9 they shall wisely **c** His doing
Ps   119:95 But I will **c** Your testimonies
Ps   119:128 all things I **c** to be right
Ps   119:153 **C** my affliction and deliver me
Prov   6: 6 **c** her ways and be wise,
Prov   23: 1 **C** carefully what is before
Prov   24:12 He who weighs the hearts **c** it
Prov   28:22 does not **c** that poverty will
Eccl   2:12 I turned myself to **c** wisdom
Is   1: 3 not know, My people do not **c**
Is   43:18 nor **c** the things of old
Jer   2:10 **c** diligently, and see if there
Jer   30:24 the latter days you will **c** it
Lam   1: 9 she did not **c** her destiny
Lam   1:11 See, O LORD, and **c**, for I am
Ezek   12: 3 It may be that they will **c**
Dan   9:23 therefore **c** the matter, and
Hos   7: 2 They do not **c** in their hearts
Hag   1: 5 LORD of hosts: "**C** your ways
Hag   2:15 carefully **c** from this day
Matt   6:28 **C** the lilies of the field,
Matt   7: 3 but do not **c** the plank in
Luke   12:24 **C** the ravens, for they
Luke   14:31 **c** whether he is able with ten
John   11:50 nor do you **c** that it is
Acts   15: 6 together to **c** this matter
Rom   4:19 he did not **c** his own body,
Rom   8:18 For I **c** that the sufferings
Rom   11:22 Therefore **c** the goodness and
Phil   2: 6 did not **c** it robbery to be
2Ti   2: 7 **C** what I say, and may the Lord
Heb   3: 1 **c** the Apostle and High Priest
Heb   7: 4 Now **c** how great this man was,
Heb   10:24 let us **c** one another in order
Heb   12: 3 For **c** Him who endured such
1Pe   5:12 faithful brother as I **c** him

CONSIDERED (*see* CONSIDER)
Neh   13:13 for they were **c** faithful, and
Job   1: 8 Have you **c** My servant Job,
Job   2: 3 Have you **c** My servant Job,
Ps   31: 7 For You have **c** my trouble
Ps   77: 5 I have **c** the days of old, The
Prov   17:28 his lips, he is **c** perceptive
Mark   10:42 **c** rulers over the Gentiles
Luke   1:29 **c** what manner of greeting
Luke   22:24 them should be **c** the greatest
Phil   2:25 Yet I **c** it necessary to send

CONSIDERING (*see* CONSIDER)
Dan   7: 8 I was **c** the horns, and there

Acts   17:23 **c** the objects of your worship
Heb   13: 7 **c** the outcome of their

CONSIDERS (*see* CONSIDER)
Ps   33:15 He **c** all their works
Ps   41: 1 Blessed is he who **c** the poor
Prov   14:15 prudent man **c** well his steps
Prov   31:16 She **c** a field and buys it
Is   44:19 no one in his heart, nor is
Rom   14:14 but to him who **c** anything to

CONSIST†
Luke   12:15 not **c** in the abundance of the
Col   1:17 and in Him all things **c**

CONSOLATION (*see* CONSOLE)
Job   21: 2 speech, and let this be your **c**
Is   66:11 with the **c** of her bosom, that
Jer   16: 7 men give them the cup of **c** to
Luke   2:25 waiting for the **C** of Israel
2Co   1: 5 so our **c** also abounds through
Phil   2: 1 if there is any **c** in Christ
2Th   2:16 us and given us everlasting **c**
Phm   7 **c** in your love, because the
Heb   6:18 lie, we might have strong **c**

CONSOLE† (*see* CONSOLATION, CONSOLED)
Is   61: 3 to **c** those who mourn in Zion,
Lam   2:13 How shall I **c** you

CONSOLED† (*see* CONSOLE)
Job   42:11 and they **c** him and comforted

CONSPIRACY (*see* CONSPIRE)
2Sa   15:12 the **c** grew strong, for the
Is   8:12 all that this people call a **c**
Acts   23:13 forty who had formed this **c**

CONSPIRATORS† (*see* CONSPIRE)
2Sa   15:31 is among the **c** with Absalom

CONSPIRE† (*see* CONSPIRACY, CONSPIRATORS, CONSPIRED)
Nah   1: 9 What do you **c** against the

CONSPIRED (*see* CONSPIRE)
Gen   37:18 they **c** against him to kill
1Sa   22: 8 All of you have **c** against me
2Ki   15:25 **c** against him and killed him
2Ch   24:25 his own servants **c** against
Neh   4: 8 all of them to **c** together to
Amos   7:10 Amos has **c** against you in the

CONSTANT† (*see* CONSTANTLY)
Acts   12: 5 but **c** prayer was offered to

CONSTANTLY† (*see* CONSTANT)
Tit   3: 8 things) want you to affirm **c**

CONSTELLATIONS†
2Ki   23: 5 sun, to the moon, to the **c**
Is   13:10 their **c** will not give their

CONSTITUENCY
2Ki   12: 5 themselves, each from his **c**

CONSTRAIN (*see* CONSTRAINED, CONSTRAINS, CONSTRAINT, RESTRAIN)

CONSTRAINED (*see* CONSTRAIN)
2Ki   4: 8 she **c** him to eat some food
Luke   24:29 But they **c** Him, saying
Acts   18: 5 Paul was **c** by the Spirit, and

CONSTRAINS (*see* COMPELS, CONSTRAIN)

CONSTRAINT (*see* COMPULSION, CONSTRAIN)

CONSTRUCTION
1Ch   28:18 for the **c** of the chariot,
Rev   21:18 And the **c** of its wall was of

CONSULT (*see* CONSULTATION, CONSULTED, CONSULTS)
1Ch   15:13 us, because we did not **c** Him
Ezra   2:63 priest could **c** with the Urim

Neh 6: 7 and let us c together
Ps 62: 4 They only c to cast him down
Is 19: 3 and they will c the idols

CONSULTATION† (see CONSULT)
Mark 15: 1 held a c with the elders and

CONSULTED (see CONSULT)
1Ki 12: 6 Then King Rehoboam c the
2Ki 21: 6 and c spiritists and mediums
Ps 83: 3 And c together against Your
Dan 6: 7 have c together to establish

CONSULTS† (see CONSULT)
Ezek 21:21 he c the images, he looks at

CONSUME (see CONSUMED, CONSUMES, CONSUMING, CONSUMMATION, CONSUMPTION)
Ex 32:10 against them and I may c them
Num 16:21 that I may c them in a moment
Deut 5:25 For this great fire will c us
Deut 28:38 for, the locust shall c it
Job 24:19 heat c the snow waters, so
Ps 59:13 C them in wrath
Ezek 13:13 hailstones in fury to c it
Dan 7:26 take away his dominion, to c
Luke 9:54 c them, just as Elijah did
2Th 2: 8 whom the Lord will c with the

CONSUMED (see CONSUME)
Gen 19:15 here, lest you be c in the
Gen 31:15 also completely c our money
Ex 3: 2 fire, but the bush was not c
Ex 15: 7 which c them like stubble
Lev 6:10 the fire has c on the altar
Judg 6:21 c the meat and the unleavened
Ezra 9:14 with us until You had c us
Job 4: 9 of His anger they are c
Ps 49:14 shall be c in the grave, far
Ps 73:19 are utterly c with terrors
Ps 104:35 sinners be c from the earth
Ps 119:139 My zeal has c me, Because my
Prov 5:11 your flesh and your body are c
Is 1:28 forsake the LORD shall be c
Jer 20:18 days should be c with shame
Jer 36:23 until all the scroll was c in
Lam 3:22 LORD's mercies we are not c
Amos 7: 4 and it c the great deep and
Mal 3: 6 therefore you are not c, O
Gal 5:15 lest you be c by one another

CONSUMES (see CONSUME)
Job 31:12 a fire that c to destruction
Eccl 4: 5 his hands and c his own flesh

CONSUMING (see CONSUME)
Ex 24:17 a c fire on the top of the
Deut 4:24 the LORD your God is a c fire
Ezek 21:28 polished for slaughter, for c
Joel 1: 4 left, the c locust has eaten
Heb 12:29 For our God is a c fire

CONSUMMATION† (see CONSUME)
Ps 119:96 I have seen the c of all
Dan 9:27 desolate, even until the c

CONSUMPTION† (see CONSUME)
Deut 28:22 LORD will strike you with c

CONTAIN (see CONTAINED, CONTAINER, CONTAINING, CONTAINS)
1Ki 8:27 of heavens cannot c You
John 21:25 not c the books that would be

CONTAINED (see CONTAIN)
Eph 2:15 commandments c in ordinances
1Pe 2: 6 it is also c in the Scripture

CONTAINER† (see CONTAIN)
Deut 23:24 shall not put any in your c

CONTAINING† (see CONTAIN)
John 2: 6 twenty or thirty gallons

CONTAINS (see CONTAIN)
Job 28: 6 sapphires, and it c gold dust

CONTEMPLATE†
Ps 119:15 precepts, And c Your ways

CONTEMPORARIES†
Gal 1:14 many of my c in my own nation

CONTEMPT (see CONTEMPTIBLE, CONTEMPTUOUSLY)
Deut 27:16 father or his mother with c
Esth 1:18 there will be excessive c
Job 12:21 He pours c on princes, and
Ps 119:22 from me reproach and c
Ps 123: 3 are exceedingly filled with c
Ps 123: 4 ease, With the c of the proud
Is 23: 9 and to bring into c all the
Dan 12: 2 to shame and everlasting c
Luke 23:11 of war, treated Him with c
Rom 14:10 you show c for your brother

CONTEMPTIBLE (see CONTEMPT)
Mal 1: 7 The table of the LORD is c
Mal 2: 9 I also have made you c and
2Co 10:10 is weak, and his speech c

CONTEMPTUOUSLY† (see CONTEMPT)
Ps 31:18 and c against the righteous

CONTEND (see CONTENDED, CONTENDING, CONTENDS)
Ex 17: 2 Why do you c with me
Ex 21:18 If men c with each other, and
Job 9: 3 If one wished to c with Him
Job 10: 2 show me why You c with me
Job 13: 8 Will you c for God
Prov 28: 4 as keep the law c with them
Is 43:26 let us c together
Is 57:16 For I will not c forever, nor
Jer 12: 5 how can you c with horses
Jude 3 to c earnestly for the faith

CONTENDED (see CONTEND)
Ex 17: 2 the people c with Moses, and
Num 20:13 of Israel c with the LORD
Deut 33: 8 with whom You c at the waters
Acts 11: 2 the circumcision c with him

CONTENDING† (see CONTEND)
Jude 9 in c with the devil, when he

CONTENDS (see CONTEND)
Job 40: 2 Shall the one who c with the
Prov 29: 9 If a wise man c with a

CONTENT (see CONTENTMENT)
Ex 2:21 Then Moses was c to live with
Judg 17:11 Then the Levite was c to
Luke 3:14 and be c with your wages
Phil 4:11 whatever state I am, to be c
1Ti 6: 8 with these we shall be c
Heb 13: 5 be c with such things as you

CONTENTION (see CONTENTIONS, CONTENTIOUS)
Ex 17: 7 because of the c of the
Prov 15:18 who is slow to anger allays c
Prov 17:14 therefore stops c before a
Prov 22:10 the scoffer, and c will leave
Jer 15:10 a man of c to the whole earth
Hab 1: 3 there is strife, and c arises
Acts 15:39 Then the c became so sharp

CONTENTIONS (see CONTENTION)
Prov 18:18 lots causes c to cease, and
Prov 19:13 and the c of a wife are a
Prov 23:29 Who has sorrow? who has c?
1Co 1:11 that there are c among you
2Co 12:20 lest there be c, jealousies,
Gal 5:20 idolatry, sorcery, hatred, c
Tit 3: 9 disputes, genealogies, c, and

CONTENTIOUS (see CONTENTION)
Prov 21: 9 a house shared with a **c** woman
Prov 26:21 fire, so is a **c** man to kindle
1Co 11:16 But if anyone seems to be **c**

CONTENTMENT† (see CONTENT)
1Ti 6: 6 with **c** is great gain

CONTINGENTS†
2Ki 11: 7 The two **c** of you who go off

CONTINUAL (see CONTINUALLY, CONTINUE)
Ex 29:42 This shall be a **c** burnt
2Ch 2: 4 for the **c** showbread, for the
Prov 15:15 a merry heart has a **c** feast
Prov 19:13 of a wife are a **c** dripping
Is 14: 6 in wrath with a **c** stroke, he
Jer 48: 5 they ascend with **c** weeping
Luke 18: 5 her, lest by her **c** coming she
Rom 9: 2 sorrow and **c** grief in my heart

CONTINUALLY (see CONTINUAL)
Gen 6: 5 of his heart was only evil **c**
Gen 8: 3 receded **c** from the earth
Ex 27:20 to cause the lamp to burn **c**
2Sa 9: 7 shall eat bread at my table **c**
Ps 34: 1 praise shall **c** be in my mouth
Ps 38:17 And my sorrow is **c** before me
Ps 40:11 and Your truth **c** preserve me
Ps 42: 3 night, While they **c** say to me
Ps 44:15 My dishonor is **c** before me
Ps 52: 1 The goodness of God endures **c**
Ps 58: 7 away as waters which run **c**
Ps 71: 3 To which I may resort **c**
Ps 71: 6 My praise shall be **c** of You
Ps 71:14 But I will hope **c**, And will
Ps 73:23 Nevertheless I am **c** with You
Ps 109:10 his children **c** be vagabonds
Ps 119:44 So shall I keep Your law **c**
Ps 126: 6 He who **c** goes forth weeping,
Prov 6:14 his heart, he devises evil **c**
Prov 6:21 Bind them **c** upon your heart
Eccl 1: 6 the wind whirls about **c**, and
Is 49:16 your walls are **c** before Me
Is 52: 5 is blasphemed **c** every day
Is 60:11 your gates shall be open **c**
Dan 6:16 Your God, whom you serve **c**
Hos 4:18 they commit harlotry **c**
Hos 12: 6 and wait on your God **c**
Obad 16 shall all the nations drink **c**
Luke 24:53 were **c** in the temple praising
Acts 6: 4 give ourselves **c** to prayer
Acts 10: 7 those who waited on him **c**
Heb 7: 3 of God, remains a priest **c**
Heb 10: 1 they offer **c** year by year

CONTINUANCE† (see CONTINUE)
Rom 2: 7 **c** in doing good seek for

CONTINUE (see CONTINUAL, CONTINUANCE,
CONTINUED, CONTINUES, CONTINUING)
1Sa 13:14 now your kingdom shall not **c**
2Sa 7:29 that it may **c** forever before
Ps 36:10 Oh, **c** Your lovingkindness to
Ps 72:17 His name shall **c** as long as
Mal 2: 4 My covenant with Levi may **c**
Acts 14:22 them to **c** in the faith, and
Rom 6: 1 Shall we **c** in sin that grace
Rom 11:22 if you **c** in His goodness
Rom 11:23 if they do not **c** in unbelief
Col 4: 2 **C** earnestly in prayer, being
1Ti 2:15 if they **c** in faith, love, and
1Ti 4:16 **C** in them, for in doing this
Heb 8: 9 they did not **c** in My covenant
Heb 13: 1 Let brotherly love **c**
2Pe 3: 4 all things **c** as they were
Rev 13: 5 to **c** for forty-two months
Rev 17:10 comes, he must **c** a short time

CONTINUED (see CONTINUE)
Num 9:19 Even when the cloud **c** long
Neh 5:16 I also **c** the work on this
Job 27: 1 Moreover Job **c** his discourse,
Jon 1:13 for the sea **c** to grow more
Matt 15:32 have now **c** with Me three days
Luke 6:12 **c** all night in prayer to God
John 8: 7 So when they **c** asking Him
Acts 1:14 These all **c** with one accord
Acts 2:42 they **c** steadfastly in the
Acts 12:16 Now Peter **c** knocking
Acts 18:11 And he **c** there a year and six
Acts 20: 7 **c** his message until midnight
Acts 27:33 and **c** without food, and eaten
1Jn 2:19 us, they would have **c** with us

CONTINUES (see CONTINUE)
1Ti 5: 5 **c** in supplications and prayers
Heb 7:24 But He, because He **c** forever

CONTINUING† (see CONTINUE)
Jer 30:23 with fury, a **c** whirlwind
Acts 2:46 So **c** daily with one accord in
Rom 12:12 **c** steadfastly in prayer
Heb 7:23 prevented by death from **c**
Heb 13:14 For here we have no **c** city

CONTRADICT† (see CONTRADICTING, CONTRADICTION,
CONTRADICTIONS, CONTRARY)
Luke 21:15 not be able to **c** or resist
Tit 1: 9 exhort and convict those who **c**

CONTRADICTING† (see CONTRADICT)
Acts 13:45 and **c** and blaspheming, they

CONTRADICTION† (see CONTRADICT)
Heb 7: 7 Now beyond all **c** the lesser

CONTRADICTIONS† (see CONTRADICT)
1Ti 6:20 **c** of what is falsely called

CONTRARY (see CONTRADICT)
Lev 26:21 Then, if you walk **c** to Me
Lev 26:24 I also will walk **c** to you
Matt 14:24 the waves, for the wind was **c**
Luke 22:26 on the **c**, he who is greatest
Acts 17: 7 these are all acting **c** to the
Acts 18:13 to worship God **c** to the law
Rom 4:18 **c** to hope, in hope believed,
Rom 10:21 to a disobedient and **c** people
Rom 11:24 were grafted **c** to nature into
Rom 16:17 **c** to the doctrine which you
1Ti 1:10 that is **c** to sound doctrine

CONTRIBUTE† (see CONTRIBUTION)
2Ch 31: 4 to **c** support for the priests

CONTRIBUTION† (see CONTRIBUTE, CONTRIBUTIONS)
Is 40:20 a **c** chooses a tree that will
Rom 15:26 **c** for the poor among the

CONTRIBUTIONS† (see CONTRIBUTION)
2Ch 24:10 rejoiced, brought their **c**

CONTRITE
Ps 34:18 saves such as have a **c** spirit
Ps 51:17 spirit, A broken and a **c** heart
Is 57:15 place, with him who has a **c**

CONTROL
Acts 5: 4 was it not in your own **c**

CONTROVERSY
Jer 25:31 LORD has a **c** with the nations
1Ti 3:16 And without **c** great is the

CONVENIENT (see CONVENIENTLY)
Acts 24:25 when I have a **c** time I will
1Co 16:12 come when he has a **c** time

CONVENIENTLY† (see CONVENIENT)
Mark 14:11 how he might **c** betray Him

CONVERSATION† (*see* CONVERSED)
Jer 38:27 for the c had not been heard
Luke 24:17 What kind of c is this that

CONVERSED† (*see* CONVERSATION)
Luke 24:15 So it was, while they c and
Acts 24:26 him more often and c with him

CONVERSION† (*see* CONVERTED)
Acts 15: 3 describing the c of the

CONVERTED† (*see* CONVERSION, CONVERTING)
Ps 51:13 And sinners shall be c to You
Matt 18: 3 say to you, unless you are c
Acts 3:19 Repent therefore and be c,

CONVERTING† (*see* CONVERTED)
Ps 19: 7 LORD is perfect, c the soul

CONVEYED†
Col 1:13 and c us into the kingdom

CONVICT† (*see* CONVICTED, CONVICTS)
John 16: 8 He will c the world of sin,
Tit 1: 9 and c those who contradict
Jude 15 all, to c all who are ungodly

CONVICTED† (*see* CONVICT)
John 8: 9 being c by their conscience,
1Co 14:24 convinced by all, he is c by
Jas 2: 9 sin, and are c by the law as

CONVICTS† (*see* CONVICT)
John 8:46 Which of you c Me of sin

CONVINCE† (*see* CONVINCED)
2Ti 4: 2 C, rebuke, exhort, with all

CONVINCED† (*see* CONVINCE)
Job 32:12 surely not one of you c Job
Acts 26:26 for I am c that none of these
Rom 4:21 being fully c that what He
Rom 14: 5 be fully c in his own mind
Rom 14:14 am c by the Lord Jesus that
1Co 14:24 he is c by all, he is judged
2Co 10: 7 If anyone is c in himself

CONVOCATION (*see* CONVOCATIONS)
Ex 12:16 day there shall be a holy c

CONVOCATIONS (*see* CONVOCATION)
Lev 23: 2 shall proclaim to be holy c

CONVULSED (*see* CONVULSES)
Mark 1:26 the unclean spirit had c him

CONVULSES† (*see* CONVULSED)
Luke 9:39 it c him so that he foams at

COOK (*see* COOKED, COOKING, COOKS)
Ezek 24:10 c the meat well, Mix in the

COOKED† (*see* COOK)
Gen 25:29 Now Jacob a a stew
Num 11: 8 c it in pans, and made cakes
Lam 4:10 have c their own children

COOKING† (*see* COOK)
Lev 11:35 it is an oven or c stove, it
Ezek 46:23 c hearths were made under the

COOKS† (*see* COOK)
1Sa 8:13 daughters to be perfumers, c

COOL
Gen 3: 8 garden in the c of the day
Luke 16:24 in water and c my tongue

COPIED† (*see* COPY)
Prov 25: 1 of Hezekiah king of Judah c

COPIES (*see* COPY)
Heb 9:23 the c of the things in the

COPPER (*see* COPPERSMITH)
Deut 8: 9 of whose hills you can dig c

Matt 10: 9 nor c in your money belts,
Matt 10:29 sparrows sold for a c coin

COPPERSMITH† (*see* COPPER)
2Ti 4:14 Alexander the c did me much

COPY (*see* COPIED, COPIES)
Deut 17:18 are c of this law in a book
Josh 8:32 a c of the law of Moses,
Heb 8: 5 who serve the c and shadow of

CORAL† (*see* CORALS)
Job 28:18 shall be made of c or quartz

CORALS† (*see* CORAL)
Ezek 27:16 embroidery, fine linen, c

CORBAN†
Mark 7:11 from me is C (that is,

CORD (*see* CORDS)
Gen 38:18 Your signet and c, and your
Ex 28:28 of the ephod, using a blue c
Josh 2:21 the scarlet c in the window
Eccl 4:12 a threefold c is not quickly
Eccl 12: 6 before the silver c is loosed

CORDS (*see* CORD)
Job 36: 8 held in the c of affliction,
Ps 2: 3 And cast away Their c from us
Ps 118:27 Bind the sacrifice with c to
Ps 119:61 The c of the wicked have
Ps 140: 5 hidden a snare for me, and c
Prov 5:22 is caught in the c of his sin
Is 5:18 iniquity with c of vanity
Is 54: 2 lengthen your c, and
Ezek 27:24 apparel, in strong twined c
Hos 11: 4 I drew them with gentle c
John 2:15 When He had made a whip of c

CORIANDER†
Ex 16:31 And it was like white c seed
Num 11: 7 Now the manna was like c seed

CORINTH (*see* CORINTHIANS)
Acts 18: 1 from Athens and went to C
1Co 1: 2 church of God which is at C

CORINTHIANS† (*see* CORINTH)
Acts 18: 8 And many of the C, hearing,
2Co 6:11 O C! We have spoken openly

CORNELIUS
Acts 10: 1 man in Caesarea called C, a
Acts 10:22 C the centurion, a just man,
Acts 10:31 and said, "C, your prayer has

CORNER (*see* CORNERS, CORNERSTONE)
1Sa 24: 4 cut off a c of Saul's robe
Prov 7: 8 along the street near her c
Prov 7:12 square, lurking at every c
Prov 21: 9 to dwell in a c of a housetop
Ezek 46:21 in every c of the court there
Amos 3:12 in the c of a bed and on the
Acts 26:26 thing was not done in a c

CORNERS (*see* CORNER)
Ex 25:12 it, and put them in its four c
Ex 27: 2 make its horns on its four c
Lev 19: 9 reap the c of your field, nor
Deut 22:12 make tassels on the four c of
Is 11:12 from the four c of the earth
Matt 6: 5 on the c of the streets, that
Acts 10:11 sheet bound at the four c
Rev 7: 1 at the four c of the earth

CORNERSTONE (*see* CORNER)
Job 38: 6 Or who laid its c,
Ps 118:22 Has become the chief c
Is 28:16 a tried stone, a precious c
Zech 10: 4 From him comes the c, from
Matt 21:42 has become the chief c

1Pe   2: 6 I lay in Zion a chief **c**,

CORPSE (*see* CORPSES)
Lev   22: 4 anything made unclean by a **c**
Num   5: 2 becomes defiled by a **c**
Num   9: 6 by a human **c**, so
Num   9:10 unclean because of a **c**
Josh   8:29 take his **c** down from the tree
1Ki   13:24 his **c** was thrown on the road,
1Ki   13:24 the lion also stood by the **c**
1Ki   13:25 saw the **c** thrown on the road,
1Ki   13:29 up the **c** of the man of God
1Ki   13:30 he laid the **c** in his own tomb
2Ki   9:37 the **c** of Jezebel shall be as
Is   14:19 like a **c** trodden under foot
Mark   6:29 they came and took away his **c**

CORPSES (*see* CORPSE)
2Ki   19:35 the morning, there were the **c**
Is   34: 3 shall rise from their **c**, and
Is   66:24 look upon the **c** of the men
Jer   7:33 The **c** of this people will be
Jer   16: 4 their **c** shall be meat for the
Nah   3: 3 number of bodies, countless **c**

CORRECT (*see* CORRECTED, CORRECTING, CORRECTION, CORRECTLY, CORRECTS)
Job   40: 2 with the Almighty **c** Him
Ps   39:11 You **c** man for iniquity, You
Ps   94:10 the nations, shall He not **c**
Prov   29:17 **C** your son, and he will give
Jer   2:19 own wickedness will **c** you
Jer   10:24 LORD, **c** me, but with justice

CORRECTED† (*see* CORRECT)
Prov   29:19 will not be **c** by mere words
Hab   2: 1 answer when I am **c**
Heb   12: 9 had human fathers who **c** us

CORRECTING† (*see* CORRECT)
2Ti   2:25 in humility **c** those who are

CORRECTION (*see* CORRECT)
Job   37:13 it to come, whether for **c**
Prov   3:11 of the LORD, nor detest His **c**
Prov   7:22 a fool to the **c** of the stocks
Prov   10:27 he who refuses **c** goes astray
Prov   12:1 he who hates **c** is stupid
Prov   13:18 come to him who disdains **c**
Prov   15:10 Harsh **c** is for him who
Prov   16:22 but the **c** of fools is folly
Prov   22:15 but the rod of **c** will drive
Prov   23:13 not withhold **c** from a child
Jer   2:30 they received no **c**
Hab   1:12 You have marked them for **c**
2Ti   3:16 doctrine, for reproof, for **c**

CORRECTLY† (*see* CORRECT)
Judg   14:12 If you can **c** solve and explain

CORRECTS (*see* CORRECT)
Prov   3:12 for whom the LORD loves He **c**

CORRESPONDING (*see* CORRESPONDS)
Ex   38:18 **c** to the hangings of the

CORRESPONDS† (*see* CORRESPONDING)
Gal   4:25 **c** to Jerusalem which now is,

CORRODED†
Jas   5: 3 Your gold and silver are **c**

CORRUPT (*see* CORRUPTED, CORRUPTERS, CORRUPTIBLE, CORRUPTION, CORRUPTLY, CORRUPTS)
Gen   6:11 earth also was **c** before God
1Sa   2:12 Now the sons of Eli were **c**
Ps   14: 1 They are **c**, They have done
Dan   2: 9 **c** words before me till the
Dan   11:32 he shall **c** with flattery
Eph   4:22 the old man which grows **c**
Eph   4:29 Let no **c** communication

1Ti   6: 5 wranglings of men of **c** minds
Jude   10 things they **c** themselves

CORRUPTED (*see* CORRUPT)
Gen   6:12 for all flesh had **c** their way
Ex   8:24 The land was **c** because of the
Mal   2: 8 You have **c** the covenant of
2Co   11: 3 so your minds may be **c** from
Jas   5: 2 Your riches are **c**, and your
Rev   19: 2 who **c** the earth with her

CORRUPTERS† (*see* CORRUPT)
Is   1: 4 evildoers, children who are **c**
Jer   6:28 and iron, they are all **c**

CORRUPTIBLE (*see* CORRUPT)
Rom   1:23 into an image made like **c** man
1Co   15:53 For this **c** must put on
1Pe   1:18 not redeemed with **c** things
1Pe   1:23 born again, not of **c** seed but

CORRUPTION (*see* CORRUPT)
2Ki   23:13 the south of the Mount of **C**
Job   17:14 if I say to **c**, 'You are my
Ps   16:10 allow Your Holy One to see **c**
Is   38:17 my soul from the pit of **c**
Acts   2:27 allow Your Holy One to see **c**
Acts   2:31 nor did His flesh see **c**
Rom   8:21 from the bondage of **c** into
1Co   15:42 The body is sown in **c**, it is
1Co   15:50 nor does **c** inherit
Gal   6: 8 will of the flesh reap **c**, but
2Pe   1: 4 having escaped the **c** that is
2Pe   2:12 utterly perish in their own **c**
2Pe   2:19 themselves are slaves of **c**

CORRUPTLY (*see* CORRUPT)
Judg   2:19 behaved more **c** than their

CORRUPTS† (*see* CORRUPT)
1Co   15:33 Evil company **c** good habits

COST† (*see* COSTLY, COSTS)
1Ki   10:29 **c** six hundred shekels of
Ezra   6: 8 Let the **c** be paid at the
Prov   7:23 it would **c** his life.
Luke   14:28 sit down first and count the **c**

COSTLY (*see* COST)
1Ki   5:17 **c** stones, and hewn stones, to
Ps   49: 8 of their souls is **c**, And it
Matt   26: 7 flask of very **c** fragrant oil
1Ti   2: 9 gold or pearls or **c** clothing

COSTS (*see* COST)
2Sa   24:24 with that which **c** me nothing

COUCH (*see* COUCHES)
Gen   49: 4 he went up to my **c**
Esth   7: 8 across the **c** where Esther was
Ps   6: 6 I drench my **c** with my tears
Song   3: 7 Behold, it is Solomon's **c**

COUCHES (*see* COUCH)
Esth   1: 6 the **c** were of gold and silver
Amos   6: 4 ivory, stretch out on your **c**

COUNCIL (*see* COUNCILS)
Matt   5:22 shall be in danger of the **c**
Matt   26:59 and all the **c** sought false
Mark   15: 1 and scribes and the whole **c**
Mark   15:43 a prominent **c** member, who
Luke   22:66 and led Him into their **c**,
Luke   23:50 a **c** member, a good and just
John   11:47 and the Pharisees gathered a **c**
Acts   4:15 them to go aside out of the **c**
Acts   22: 5 all the **c** of the elders, from
Acts   23: 6 he cried out in the **c**, "Men

COUNCILS (*see* COUNCIL)
Matt   10:17 they will deliver you up to **c**

COUNSEL (see ADVICE, ADVISE, CONFER, CONSULT,
COUNSELED, COUNSELOR, COUNSELS, DECISION,
INQUIRE, INSTRUCTION, PLOT, PLOTS, PLOTTED, PURPOSE,
WILL)

Ex	18:19	I will give you c, and God
Num	31:16	through the c of Balaam, to
Deut	32:28	they are a nation void of c
Josh	9:14	did not ask c of the LORD
Judg	20: 7	your advice and c here and now
2Sa	15:31	turn the c of Ahithophel into
Job	5:13	the c of the cunning comes
Job	10: 3	shine on the c of the wicked
Job	38: 2	Who is this who darkens c by
Ps	1: 1	not in the c of the ungodly
Ps	2: 2	And the rulers take c together
Ps	55:14	We took sweet c together, And
Ps	73:24	You will guide me with Your c
Ps	83: 3	crafty c against Your people
Ps	106:13	They did not wait for His c
Ps	107:11	despised the c of the Most
Prov	1: 5	will attain wise c,
Prov	1:30	they would have none of my c
Prov	12:15	but he who heeds c is wise
Prov	19:20	Listen to c and receive
Prov	20:18	by wise c wage war
Prov	21:30	or c against the LORD
Prov	27: 9	friend does so by hearty c
Is	5:19	let the c of the Holy One of
Is	11: 2	the Spirit of c and might,
Is	28:29	hosts, Who is wonderful in c
Is	30: 1	Who take c, but not of Me, and
Jer	18:18	nor c from the wise, nor the
Jer	23:18	stood in the c of the LORD
Jer	32:19	You are great in c and mighty
Dan	2:14	Then with c and wisdom Daniel
Hos	4:12	My people ask c from their
Mic	4:12	nor do they understand His c
Hab	2:10	gave shameful c to your house
Zech	6:13	and the c of peace shall be
Acts	20:27	to you the whole c of God
Eph	1:11	to the c of His will,
Heb	6:17	the immutability of His c

COUNSELED (see ADVISED, COUNSEL)

Mic	6: 5	now what Balak king of Moab c

COUNSELOR (see COUNSEL, COUNSELORS)

Is	3: 3	and the honorable man, the c
Is	9: 6	will be called wonderful, C
Is	40:13	or as His c has taught Him
Is	41:28	them, but there was no c, who
Mic	4: 9	Has your c perished
Nah	1:11	against the LORD, a wicked c
Rom	11:34	Or who has become His c

COUNSELORS (see COUNSELOR)

Ezra	4: 5	and hired c against them to
Ezra	7:28	me before the king and his c
Job	3:14	c of the earth, who built
Prov	11:14	of c there is safety
Prov	12:20	evil, but c of peace have joy
Is	1:26	your c as at the beginning
Is	19:11	Pharaoh's wise c give foolish
Dan	3: 2	the governors, the c, the

COUNSELS (see COUNSEL)

Ps	5:10	Let them fall by their own c
Ps	81:12	heart, To walk in their own c
Prov	12: 5	but the c of the wicked are
Prov	22:20	you excellent things of c
Is	25: 1	Your c of old are
Is	47:13	in the multitude of your c
1Co	4: 5	reveal the c of the hearts

COUNT (see COUNTED, COUNTING, COUNTLESS, COUNTS)

Gen	15: 5	c the stars if you are able
Lev	23:16	C fifty days to the day

Lev	25: 8	you shall c seven sabbaths of
Num	23:10	Who can c the dust of Jacob,
Deut	16: 9	begin to c the seven weeks
Job	19:15	c me as a stranger
Job	31: 4	my ways, and c all my steps
Ps	22:17	I can c all My bones
Ps	48:12	around her C her towers
Luke	14:28	c the cost, whether he has
Acts	20:24	nor do I c my life dear to
Phil	3: 8	But indeed I also c all
Phil	3: 8	c them as rubbish, that I may
Phil	3:13	I do not c myself to have
2Th	1:11	c you worthy of this calling
Phm	17	If then you c me as a partner
Jas	1: 2	c it all joy when you fall
Jas	5:11	Indeed we c them blessed who
2Pe	2:13	as those who c it pleasure to
2Pe	3: 9	as some c slackness, but is

COUNTED (see COUNT)

Gen	16:10	shall not be c for multitude
Lev	25:31	be c as the fields of the
Josh	13: 3	(which is c as Canaanite)
Judg	21: 9	For when the people were c
1Ki	1:21	will be c as offenders
1Ki	3: 8	numerous to be numbered or c
2Ki	12:10	c the money that was found in
Ps	88: 4	I am c with those who go down
Prov	17:28	Even a fool is c wise when he
Prov	27:14	it will be c a curse to him
Is	32:15	field is c as a forest
Matt	14: 5	because they c him as a
Matt	26:15	And they c out to him thirty
Mark	11:32	for all c John to have been a
Luke	20:35	But those who are c worthy to
Acts	5:41	rejoicing that they were c
Acts	19:19	they c up the value of them,
Rom	2:26	be c as circumcision
Rom	4: 4	the wages are not c as grace
Rom	9: 8	the promise are c as the seed
Phil	3: 7	me, these I have c loss for
2Th	1: 5	that you may be c worthy of
1Ti	1:12	because He c me faithful,
1Ti	5:17	be c worthy of double honor
Heb	3: 3	For this One has been c
Heb	10:29	c the blood of the covenant

COUNTENANCE (see COUNTENANCES, FACE,
FEATURES)

Gen	4: 5	was very angry, and his c fell
Gen	12:11	are a woman of beautiful c
Gen	31: 2	And Jacob saw the c of Laban
Gen	31: 5	I see your father's c, that
Num	6:26	LORD lift up His c upon you
Deut	28:50	a nation of fierce c, which
Judg	13: 6	the c of the Angel of God
1Sa	14:27	and his c brightened
2Ki	8:11	Then he set his c in a stare
Job	14:20	You change his c and send him
Ps	4: 6	the light of Your c upon us
Ps	10: 4	his proud c does not seek God
Ps	42: 5	Him For the help of His c
Ps	44: 3	arm, and the light of Your c
Ps	80:16	at the rebuke of Your c
Prov	15:13	heart makes a cheerful c, but
Prov	25:23	backbiting tongue an angry c
Prov	27:17	sharpens the c of his friend
Eccl	7: 3	for by a sad c the heart is
Dan	5: 6	Then the king's c changed
Matt	28: 3	His c was like lightning, and
2Co	3: 7	because of the glory of his c
Rev	1:16	and His c was like the sun

COUNTENANCES (see APPEARANCE, COUNTENANCE)

COUNTERACT†

Esth	8: 3	c the evil plot of Haman the

COUNTING† (*see* COUNT)
Gen 41:49 the sea, until he stopped c

COUNTLESS† (*see* COUNT)
Job 21:33 as c have gone before him
Nah 3: 3 number of bodies, c corpses

COUNTRIES (*see* COUNTRY)
Gen 41:57 So all c came to Joseph in
Ps 110: 6 execute the heads of many c
Is 8: 9 Give ear, all you from far c
Jer 23: 3 of My flock out of all c
Ezek 35:10 these two c shall be mine, and
Dan 11:41 many c shall be overthrown
Zech 10: 9 shall remember Me in a far c

COUNTRY (*see* COUNTRIES, COUNTRYSIDE)
Gen 12: 1 Get out of your c, from your
Gen 24: 4 but you shall go to my c and
Gen 29:26 must not be done so in our c
Gen 42:30 and took us for spies of the c
Gen 42:33 the man, the lord of the c
Gen 47:27 of Egypt, in the c of Goshen
Lev 17:15 of your own c or a stranger
Num 20:17 let us pass through your c
Deut 28: 3 blessed shall you be in the c
Deut 28:16 cursed shall you be in the c
Josh 2: 2 of Israel to search out the c
Josh 6:22 men who had spied out the c
Josh 9: 6 We have come from a far c
Josh 11:16 the mountain c, all the South
Josh 17:15 then go up to the forest c
Judg 8:28 the c was quiet for forty
Ruth 1: 1 to sojourn in the c of Moab
1Sa 6:18 c villages, even as far as
1Ki 8:41 a far c for Your name's sake
Prov 25:25 so is good news from a far c
Is 1: 7 Your c is desolate, your
Jer 2: 7 you into a bountiful c, to
Jer 6:22 people comes from the north c
Ezek 34:13 the inhabited places of the c
Matt 2:12 for their own c another way
Matt 9:31 news about Him in all that c
Matt 13:57 honor except in his own c
Matt 21:33 and went into a far c
Mark 5:14 it in the city and in the c
Luke 1:39 into the hill c with haste
Luke 1:65 all the hill c of Judea
Luke 2: 8 Now there were in the same c
Luke 4:24 is acceptable in his own c
John 4:44 has no honor in his own c
Acts 7: 3 to him, 'Get out of your c
Heb 11:16 better, that is, a heavenly c

COUNTRYMEN
Esth 8: 6 see the destruction of my c
Esth 10: 3 speaking peace to all his c
Rom 9: 3 my c according to the flesh '
2Co 11:26 in perils of my own c, in
1Th 2:14 same things from your own c

COUNTRYSIDE (*see* COUNTRY)
Deut 22:25 young woman in the c, and the
Neh 12:28 from the c around Jerusalem

COUNTS (*see* COUNT)
Job 19:11 He c me as one of His enemies
Ps 147: 4 He c the number of the stars

COUPLE (*see* COUPLED)
Ex 26: 9 you shall c five curtains by
1Ki 17:12 I am gathering a c of sticks

COUPLED (*see* COUPLE)
Ex 26: 3 shall be c to one another
Ex 26:24 They shall be c together at
Ex 36:10 he c five curtains to one
Ex 36:29 they were c at the bottom and
Ex 36:29 c together at the top by one

COURAGE (*see* COURAGEOUS)
Num 13:20 Be of good c
Deut 31: 6 Be strong and of good c, do
Josh 2:11 c in anyone because of you
2Ch 15: 8 Oded the prophet, he took c
Jer 47: 3 for their children, lacking c
Acts 28:15 he thanked God and took c

COURAGEOUS (*see* COURAGE, COURAGEOUSLY)
Josh 1: 7 Only be strong and very c,
2Sa 13:28 Be c and valiant
Amos 2:16 The most c men of might shall

COURAGEOUSLY† (*see* COURAGEOUS)
2Ch 19:11 Behave c, and the LORD will be

COURIERS
Esth 3:13 sent by c into all the king's
Esth 8:10 letters by c on horseback

COURSE (*see* COURSES, RUN)
2Ch 21:19 it happened in the c of time
Job 1: 5 of feasting had run their c
Is 48: 7 should say, 'Of c I knew them
Jer 8: 6 Everyone turned to his own c
Jer 23:10 Their c of life is evil, and
Acts 13:25 as John was finishing his c
Acts 16:11 a straight c to Samothrace
Eph 2: 2 to the c of this world,
Jas 3: 6 set on fire the c of nature

COURSES† (*see* COURSE)
Judg 5:20 the stars from their c fought

COURT (*see* COURTS, COURTYARD)
Ex 27: 9 make the c of the tabernacle
Ex 27: 9 shall be hangings for the c
Ex 27:12 along the width of the c on
Ex 27:16 For the gate of the c there
Ex 27:18 The length of the c shall be
Deut 25: 1 men, and they come to c, that
2Sa 17:18 who had a well in his c
1Ki 6:36 he built the inner c with
1Ki 7: 8 had another c inside the hall
1Ki 7: 9 on the outside to the great c
2Ki 20: 4 gone out into the middle c
2Ch 4: 9 he made the c of the priests
2Ch 29:16 of the house of the LORD
Neh 3:25 was by the c of the prison
Esth 1: 5 in the c of the garden of the
Esth 6: 4 c of the king's palace to
Job 9:19 who will appoint my day in c
Job 9:32 we should go to c together
Job 11:19 yes, many would c your favor
Prov 25: 8 Do not go hastily to c
Jer 32: 2 up in the c of the prison
Jer 36:10 in the upper c at the entry
Ezek 10: 3 the cloud filled the inner c
Ezek 46:22 of the c were enclosed courts
Dan 7:10 The c was seated, and the
1Co 4: 3 judged by you or by a human c
Gal 4:17 They zealously c you, but for
Rev 11: 2 But leave out the c which is

COURTEOUS† (*see* COURTEOUSLY, COURTESY)
1Pe 3: 8 be tenderhearted, be c

COURTEOUSLY† (*see* COURTEOUS)
Acts 28: 7 us c for three days

COURTESY† (*see* COURTEOUS)
Acts 24: 4 I beg you to hear, by your c

COURTS (*see* COURT)
2Ki 23:12 had made in the two c of the
Ps 65: 4 That he may dwell in Your c
Ps 84: 2 faints For the c of the LORD
Ps 84:10 For a day in Your c is better
Ps 92:13 flourish in the c of our God
Ps 100: 4 And into His c with praise

Is	1:12	your hand, to trample My c
Is	62: 9	shall drink it in My holy c
Zech	3: 7	likewise have charge of My c
Luke	7:25	in luxury are in kings' c
Acts	19:38	the c are open and there are
Jas	2: 6	you and drag you into the c

COURTYARD (see COURT, COURTYARDS)

Matt	26:58	to the high priest's c
Matt	26:69	Peter sat outside in the c
Luke	22:55	a fire in the midst of the c

COURTYARDS† (see COURTYARD)

Ex	8:13	of the houses, out of the c
Neh	8:16	or in their c or the courts

COUSIN†

Col	4:10	with Mark the c of Barnabas

COVENANT (see COVENANTED, COVENANTS)

Gen	6:18	will establish My c with you
Gen	9: 9	I establish My c with you
Gen	9:11	I establish My c with you
Gen	9:12	the c which I make between Me
Gen	9:13	the sign of the c between Me
Gen	9:15	I will remember My c which is
Gen	9:16	the everlasting c between God
Gen	15:18	the LORD made a c with Abram
Gen	17: 9	for you, you shall keep My c
Gen	17:11	be a sign of the c between Me
Gen	17:13	My c shall be in your flesh
Gen	17:14	he has broken My c
Gen	21:27	and the two of them made a c
Ex	2:24	His c with Abraham
Ex	6: 5	and I have remembered My c
Ex	19: 5	obey My voice and keep My c
Ex	23:32	You shall make no c with them
Ex	24: 7	he took the Book of the C
Ex	24: 8	the blood of the c which the
Ex	31:16	generations as a perpetual c
Ex	34:12	lest you make a c with the
Ex	34:28	tablets the words of the c
Lev	26: 9	you and confirm My c with you
Lev	26:15	commandments, but break My c
Lev	26:25	execute the vengeance of My c
Lev	26:45	the c of their ancestors,
Num	10:33	the ark of the c of the LORD
Num	18:19	it is a c of salt forever
Num	25:12	I give to him My c of peace
Deut	4:13	c which He commanded you to
Deut	5: 2	God made a c with us in Horeb
Deut	5: 3	make this c with our fathers
Deut	7: 9	the faithful God who keeps c
Deut	8:18	His c which He swore to your
Deut	9:11	stone, the tablets of the c
Deut	9:15	of the c were in my two hands
Deut	17: 2	God, in transgressing His c
Deut	29: 1	c which the LORD commanded
Deut	29: 1	besides the c which He made
Deut	29: 9	keep the words of this c, and
Deut	29:14	I make this c and this oath,
Deut	29:21	c that are written in this
Deut	29:25	they have forsaken the c of
Josh	3: 8	who bear the ark of the c
1Sa	4: 3	c of the LORD from Shiloh to
1Sa	4: 4	of the c of the LORD of hosts
1Sa	4: 4	with the ark of the c of God
1Sa	18: 3	Jonathan and David made a c
1Ki	8: 1	bring up the ark of the c of
1Ki	8: 6	of the c of the LORD to its place
1Ki	8:23	like You, who keep Your c
1Ki	19:10	Israel have forsaken Your c
1Ki	19:14	Israel have forsaken Your c
2Ki	13:23	because of His c with Abraham
2Ki	23: 2	words of the Book of the C
2Ki	23: 3	took their stand for the c
1Ch	16:15	Remember His c always, the

2Ch	13: 5	and his sons, by a c of salt
2Ch	34:30	words of the book of the c
Neh	1: 5	God, You who keep Your c and
Neh	9:32	and awesome God, Who keeps c
Neh	13:29	the c of the priesthood and
Job	31: 1	I have made a c with my eyes
Ps	25:10	truth, To such as keep His c
Ps	44:17	we dealt falsely with Your c
Ps	50: 5	made a c with Me by sacrifice
Ps	50:16	Or take My c in your mouth,
Ps	74:20	Have respect to the c
Ps	89:28	My c shall stand firm with
Ps	89:34	My c I will not break, Nor
Ps	89:39	the c of Your servant
Ps	103:18	To such as keep His c, And to
Ps	105: 8	has remembered His c forever
Ps	111: 5	will ever be mindful of His c
Ps	132:12	If your sons will keep My c
Prov	2:17	and forgets the c of her God
Is	24: 5	Broken the everlasting c
Is	28:15	We have made a c with death
Is	42: 6	give You as a c to the people
Is	49: 8	give You as a c to the people
Is	54:10	nor shall My c of peace be
Is	55: 3	an everlasting c with you
Jer	11: 2	Hear the words of this c, and
Jer	31:31	when I will make a new c with
Jer	31:32	My c which they broke, though
Jer	33:20	can break My c with the day
Jer	33:20	My c with the night, so that
Jer	50: 5	c That will not be forgotten
Ezek	34:25	I will make a c of peace with
Dan	9:27	a c with many for one week
Dan	11:22	and also the prince of the c
Dan	11:28	be moved against the holy c
Hos	2:18	In that day I will make a c
Amos	1: 9	remember the c of brotherhood
Zech	9:11	of the blood of your c, I
Mal	2: 4	you, that My c with Levi may
Mal	2:14	companion and your wife by c
Mal	3: 1	even the Messenger of the c
Matt	26:28	this is My blood of the new c
Luke	1:72	and to remember His holy c
Luke	22:20	cup is the new c in My blood
Acts	3:25	of the c which God made with
Acts	7: 8	him the c of circumcision
Rom	11:27	For this is My c with them
2Co	3: 6	as ministers of the new c
Gal	3:15	Though it is only a man's c
Gal	3:17	cannot annul the c that was
Heb	7:22	become a surety of a better c
Heb	8: 6	also Mediator of a better c
Heb	8: 7	For if that first c had been
Heb	8: 8	when I will make a new c with
Heb	9: 4	the ark of the c overlaid on
Heb	9: 4	and the tablets of the c
Heb	9:15	is the Mediator of the new c
Heb	13:20	blood of the everlasting c
Rev	11:19	the ark of His c was seen in

COVENANTED† (see COVENANT)

2Ch	7:18	as I c with David your father
Hag	2: 5	to the word that I c with you

COVENANTS† (see COVENANT)

Rom	9: 4	adoption, the glory, the c
Gal	4:24	For these are the two c
Eph	2:12	from the c of promise, having

COVER (see COVERED, COVERING, COVERINGS, COVERS, UNCOVER)

Gen	6:14	c it inside and outside with
Ex	33:22	will c you with My hand while
Lev	17:13	its blood and c it with dust
Num	4: 5	c the ark of the Testimony
Num	4: 9	c the lampstand of the light,

Deut	23:13	it and turn and c your refuse
1Sa	19:13	put a c of goats' hair for
1Sa	25:20	went down under c of the hill
1Ki	7:18	c the capitals that were on
2Ch	4:13	to c the two bowl-shaped
Neh	4: 5	Do not c their iniquity, and
Job	16:18	do not c my blood, and let my
Job	21:26	in the dust, and worms c them
Job	22:14	Thick clouds c Him, so that
Job	38:34	abundance of water may c you
Ps	91: 4	He shall c you with His
Ps	104: 2	Who c Yourself with light as
Is	11: 9	LORD as the waters c the sea
Is	26:21	and will no more c her slain
Is	58: 7	see the naked, that you c him
Is	60: 2	darkness shall c the earth
Ezek	7:18	horror will c them
Ezek	24:17	do not c your lips, and do not
Ezek	32: 7	I will c the sun with a cloud
Ezek	37: 6	c you with skin and put breath
Hos	2: 9	given to c her nakedness
Hos	10: 8	say to the mountains, "C us
Hab	2:14	LORD, as the waters c the sea
Zech	5: 8	the lead c over its mouth
Luke	23:30	and to the hills, 'C us
1Co	11: 7	ought not to c his head,
Jas	5:20	and c a multitude of sins
1Pe	4: 8	love will c a multitude of

COVERED (see COVER)

Gen	7:20	and the mountains were c
Gen	9:23	and c the nakedness of their
Gen	24:65	she took a veil and c herself
Gen	38:15	because she had c her face
Ex	14:28	c the chariots, the horsemen,
Ex	15: 5	The depths have c them
Ex	16:13	c the camp, and in the morning
Ex	24:15	and a cloud c the mountain
Ex	37: 9	c the mercy seat with their
Num	9:15	the cloud c the tabernacle,
Josh	24: 7	the sea upon them, and c them
Judg	4:18	she c him with a blanket
2Sa	15:30	and he had his head c and went
2Ki	19: 1	c himself with sackcloth, and
Job	31:33	if I have c my transgressions
Ps	32: 1	is forgiven, Whose sin is c
Ps	44:19	c us with the shadow of death
Ps	65:13	valleys also are c with grain
Ps	68:13	wings of a dove c with silver
Ps	71:13	Let them be c with reproach
Ps	80:10	The hills were c with its
Ps	85: 2	You have c all their sin
Ps	139:13	You have c me in my mother's
Prov	24:31	surface was c with nettles
Prov	26:23	c with silver dross
Prov	26:26	his hatred is c by deceit
Eccl	6: 4	its name is c with darkness
Song	5: 2	for my head is c with dew
Is	6: 2	with two he c his face, with
Is	61:10	He has c me with the robe of
Lam	3:16	gravel, and c me with ashes
Lam	3:43	You have c Yourself with
Ezek	16:10	fine linen and c you with silk
Ezek	31:15	I c the deep because of it
Ezek	37: 8	them, and the skin c them over
Ezek	41:16	the windows were c
Jon	3: 8	beast be c with sackcloth, and
Hab	3: 3	Selah His glory c the heavens
Matt	8:24	the boat was c with the waves
Matt	10:26	For there is nothing c that
Rom	4: 7	forgiven, and whose sins are c
1Co	11: 4	having his head c, dishonors
1Co	11: 6	For if a woman is not c, let

COVERING (see COVER, COVERINGS)

Gen	8:13	Noah removed the c of the ark

Ex	22:27	For that is his only c, it is
Ex	25:20	c the mercy seat with their
Num	4:15	have finished c the sanctuary
Num	16:38	plates as a c for the altar
2Sa	17:19	spread a c over the well's
1Ki	7:41	the two networks c the two
Job	24: 7	and have no c in the cold
Job	26: 6	Him, and Destruction has no c
Job	31:19	or any poor man without c
Ps	105:39	He spread a cloud for a c
Is	4: 5	the glory there will be a c
Is	25: 7	of the c cast over all people
Is	28:20	and the c so narrow that he
Is	50: 3	and I make sackcloth their c
Ezek	28:16	O c cherub, from the midst of
Ezek	38: 9	c the land like a cloud, you
1Co	11:15	hair is given to her for a c

COVERINGS† (see COVER, COVERING)

Gen	3: 7	together and made themselves c
Prov	7:16	Colored c of Egyptian linen

COVERS (see COVER)

Ex	29:13	the fat that c the entrails
Lev	13:12	the leprosy c all the skin of
1Ki	1: 1	and they put c on him, but he
Job	9:24	He c the faces of its judges
Job	22:11	an abundance of water c you
Job	26: 9	He c the face of His throne,
Job	36:30	and c the depths of the sea
Job	36:32	He c His hands with lightning
Ps	73: 6	Violence c them like a
Ps	84: 6	The rain also c it with pools
Ps	147: 8	Who c the heavens with clouds
Prov	10: 6	but violence c the mouth of
Prov	10:12	strife, but love c all sins
Prov	12:16	but a prudent man c shame
Ezek	28:14	the anointed cherub who c
Mal	2:16	for it c one's garment with
Luke	8:16	c it with a vessel or puts it

COVERT†

Job	40:21	in a c of reeds and marsh

COVET (see COVETED, COVETOUS, COVETS)

Ex	20:17	You shall not c your
Ex	34:24	neither will any man c your
Rom	7: 7	You shall not c
Jas	4: 2	You murder and c and cannot

COVETED† (see COVET)

Josh	7:21	I c them and took them
Acts	20:33	I have c no one's silver or

COVETOUS† (see COVET, COVETOUSNESS)

1Co	5:10	of this world, or with the c
1Co	5:11	who is a fornicator, or c
1Co	6:10	nor thieves, nor c, nor
Eph	5: 5	unclean person, nor c man
1Ti	3: 3	not quarrelsome, not c
2Pe	2:14	heart trained in c practices

COVETOUSNESS (see COVETOUS)

Jer	6:13	them, everyone is given to c
Mark	7:22	thefts, c, wickedness, deceit
Luke	12:15	Take heed and beware of c, for
Rom	1:29	immorality, wickedness, c
Rom	7: 7	c unless the law had said
1Th	2: 5	you know, nor a cloak for c
Heb	13: 5	Let your conduct be without c
2Pe	2: 3	By c they will exploit you

COVETS† (see COVET)

Prov	21:26	He c greedily all day long,
Hab	2: 9	Woe to him who c evil gain

COW (see COWS)

Lev	22:28	Whether it is a c or ewe, do
Is	11: 7	The c and the bear shall graze

COWARDLY†
Rev 21: 8 But the **c**, unbelieving,

COWS (see COW)
Gen 32:15 with their colts, forty **c**
Gen 41: 2 up out of the river seven **c**
1Sa 6: 7 and hitch the **c** to the cart
Amos 4: 1 you **c** of Bashan, who are on

CRACKED†
Job 7: 5 worms and dust, my skin is **c**

CRACKLING†
Eccl 7: 6 For like the **c** of thorns

CRAFT† (see CRAFTSMAN)
Rev 18:22 no craftsman of any **c** shall

CRAFTILY† (see CRAFTY)
Josh 9: 4 they worked **c**, and went and
Ps 105:25 To deal **c** with His servants

CRAFTINESS (see CRAFTY)
Job 5:13 the wise in their own **c**, and
Luke 20:23 But He perceived their **c**, and
1Co 3:19 the wise in their own **c**"
2Co 11: 3 serpent deceived Eve by his **c**
Eph 4:14 in the cunning **c** by which

CRAFTSMAN (see CRAFT, CRAFTSMEN)
Gen 4:22 of every **c** in bronze and iron
2Ch 2:13 Huram my master **c**
Prov 8:30 was beside Him, as a master **c**
Is 44:13 The **c** stretches out his rule,
Rev 18:22 no **c** of any craft shall be

CRAFTSMEN (see CRAFTSMAN)
Ex 36: 4 Then all the **c** who were doing
Neh 11:35 Lod, Ono, and the Valley of **C**
Hos 13: 2 all of it is the work of **c**
Acts 19:24 no small profit to the **c**

CRAFTY (see CRAFTILY, CRAFTINESS)
1Sa 23:22 I am told that he is very **c**
Job 5:12 the devices of the **c**, so that
Job 15: 5 choose the tongue of the **c**
Ps 83: 3 They have taken **c** counsel
Prov 7:10 of a harlot, and a **c** heart

CRAG† (see CRAGS)
Job 39:28 resides on the **c** of the rock

CRAGS† (see CRAG)
Prov 30:26 make their homes in the **c**
Is 2:21 and into the **c** of the rugged

CRANE†
Is 38:14 Like a **c** or a swallow, so I

CRASHING†
Zeph 1:10 and a loud **c** from the hills

CRAVES† (see CRAVING)
Is 29: 8 is faint, and his soul still **c**

CRAVING (see CRAVES)
Num 11: 4 them yielded to intense **c**
Ps 78:30 were not deprived of their **c**

CRAWL† (see CRAWLING, CRAWLS)
Mic 7:17 they shall **c** from their holes

CRAWLING (see CRAWL)
Joel 1: 4 left, the **c** locust has eaten

CRAWLS† (see CRAWL)
Lev 11:42 Whatever **c** on its belly,

CREAM†
Judg 5:25 she brought out **c** in a lordly
Job 20:17 flowing with honey and **c**
Job 29: 6 my steps were bathed with **c**

CREATE† (see CREATED, CREATES, CREATION, CREATOR, CREATURE)
Neh 4: 8 Jerusalem and **c** confusion
Ps 51:10 **C** in me a clean heart, O God,
Is 4: 5 then the LORD will **c** above
Is 45: 7 **c** darkness, I make peace and
Is 45: 7 I make peace and **c** calamity
Is 45:18 it, Who did not **c** it in vain
Is 57:19 I **c** the fruit of the lips
Is 65:17 I **c** new heavens and a new
Is 65:18 rejoice forever in what I **c**
Is 65:18 I **c** Jerusalem as a rejoicing,
Eph 2:15 so as to **c** in Himself one new

CREATED (see CREATE)
Gen 1: 1 beginning God **c** the heavens
Gen 1:21 So God **c** great sea creatures
Gen 1:27 So God **c** man in His own image
Gen 1:27 male and female He **c** them
Gen 2: 3 all His work which God had **c**
Gen 6: 7 destroy man whom I have **c**
Ps 89:12 and the south, You have **c** them
Ps 104:30 forth Your Spirit, they are **c**
Ps 148: 5 He commanded and they were **c**
Is 41:20 Holy One of Israel has **c** it
Is 43: 7 whom I have **c** for My glory
Is 45: 8 I, the LORD, have **c** it
Mal 2:10 Has not one God **c** us
Mark 13:19 which God **c** until this time
Rom 8:39 depth, nor any other **c** thing
1Co 11: 9 Nor was man **c** for the woman,
Eph 2:10 **c** in Christ Jesus for good
Eph 3: 9 **c** all things through Jesus
Col 1:16 All things were **c** through Him
Col 3:10 to the image of Him who **c** him
Rev 4:11 for You **c** all things, and by

CREATES† (see CREATE)
Num 16:30 But if the LORD **c** a new thing
Amos 4:13 **c** the wind, who declares to

CREATION (see CREATE)
Mark 10: 6 from the beginning of the **c**
Mark 13:19 of **c** which God created until
Rom 1:20 For since the **c** of the world
Rom 8:19 the **c** eagerly waits for the
Rom 8:20 For the **c** was subjected to
Rom 8:22 know that the whole **c** groans
2Co 5:17 is in Christ, he is a new **c**
Gal 6:15 avails anything, but a new **c**
Col 1:15 God, the firstborn over all **c**
Heb 9:11 hands, that is, not of this **c**
2Pe 3: 4 were from the beginning of **c**
Rev 3:14 the Beginning of the **c** of God

CREATOR (see CREATE)
Eccl 12: 1 Remember now your **C** in the
Is 40:28 the **C** of the ends of the
Is 43:15 the **C** of Israel, your King
Rom 1:25 creature rather than the **C**
1Pe 4:19 good, as to a faithful **C**

CREATURE (see CREATE, CREATURES)
Gen 1:24 **c** according to its kind
Gen 2:19 Adam called each living **c**
Ezek 1:15 living **c** with its four faces
Mark 16:15 preach the gospel to every **c**
Acts 28: 5 shook off the **c** into the fire
Rom 1:25 served the **c** rather than the
Col 1:23 to every **c** under heaven, of
1Ti 4: 4 For every **c** of God is good,
Jas 3: 7 **c** of the sea, is tamed and has
Rev 4: 7 living **c** was like a lion, the
Rev 5:13 every **c** of which is in heaven and
Rev 16: 3 every living **c** in the sea

CREATURES (see CREATURE)
Gen 1:21 So God created great sea **c**

Ezek 1: 5 the likeness of four living c
Ezek 1:21 living c was in the wheels
Jas 1:18 kind of firstfruits of His c
Rev 4: 6 were four living c full of

CREDIT (see CREDITOR)
Luke 6:32 you, what c is that to you

CREDITOR (see CREDIT, CREDITORS)
Luke 7:41 certain c who had two debtors

CREDITORS† (see CREDITOR)
Is 50: 1 Or which of My c is it to
Hab 2: 7 Will not your c rise up

CREEP (see CREEPING, CREEPS, CREPT)
Lev 11:20 c on all fours shall be an
Lev 11:29 things that c on the earth
Ps 104:20 beasts of the forest c about
2Ti 3: 6 those who c into households

CREEPING (see CREEP)
Gen 1:24 c thing and beast of the earth
Gen 6: 7 c thing and birds of the air,
Lev 5: 2 carcass of unclean c things
Lev 22: 5 or whoever touches any c
Acts 10:12 c things, and birds of the air
Acts 11: 6 c things, and birds of the air
Rom 1:23 beasts and c things

CREEPS (see CREEP)
Gen 1:25 and everything that c on the
Lev 11:21 insect that c on all fours
Lev 20:25 thing that c on the ground

CREPT† (see CREEP)
Jude 4 men have c in unnoticed, who

CRESCENT (see CRESCENTS)
Judg 8:21 took the c ornaments that

CRESCENTS† (see CRESCENT)
Is 3:18 the scarves, and the c

CREST†
Esth 6: 8 which has a royal c placed on

CRETANS† (see CRETE)
Acts 2:11 C and Arabs—we hear them
Tit 1:12 C are always liars, evil

CRETE (see CRETANS)
Acts 27: 7 the shelter of C off Salmone
Acts 27:12 a harbor of C opening toward
Tit 1: 5 this reason I left you in C

CRIB†
Is 1: 3 And the donkey its master's c

CRICKET†
Lev 11:22 the c after its kind, and the

CRIED (see CRY)
Gen 39:14 I c out with a loud voice
Gen 41:55 the people c to Pharaoh for
Ex 14:10 of Israel c out to the LORD
Deut 22:27 betrothed young woman c out
Judg 5:28 c out through the lattice
1Ki 13:21 he c out to the man of God
2Ki 20:11 the prophet c out to the LORD
2Ch 32:20 prayed and c out to heaven
Job 29:12 delivered the poor who c out
Ps 34: 6 This poor man c out, and the
Ps 66:17 I c to Him with my mouth, And
Ps 88: 1 I have c out day and night
Ps 107: 6 Then they c out to the LORD
Ps 130: 1 of the depths I have c to You
Is 6: 3 And one c to another and said
Dan 3: 4 Then a herald c aloud
Dan 5: 7 The king c aloud to bring in
Dan 6:20 he c out with a lamenting
Jon 1: 5 every man c out to his god,
Jon 2: 2 out of the belly of Sheol I c

Matt 14:30 and beginning to sink he c out
Matt 20:30 passing by, c out, saying,
Matt 20:31 but they c out all the more,
Matt 27:46 Jesus c out with a loud voice
Mark 6:49 it was a ghost, and c out
Mark 9:24 the father of the child c out
Mark 9:26 Then the spirit c out,
Mark 15:39 saw that He c out like this
Luke 16:24 Then he c and said, 'Father
John 19: 6 officers saw Him, they c out
John 19:12 Him, but the Jews c out,
John 19:15 But they c out, "Away with
Acts 23: 6 he c out in the council,
Rev 18: 2 he c mightily with a loud
Rev 18:19 c out, weeping and wailing, and

CRIES (see CRY)
Gen 4:10 of your brother's blood c out
Ps 72:12 deliver the needy when he c
Prov 1:21 She c out in the chief
Prov 20:14 for nothing," c the buyer
Is 26:17 c out in her pangs, when she
Mic 6: 9 LORD's voice c to the city
Heb 5: 7 with vehement c and tears to
Jas 5: 4 the c of the reapers have

CRIME† (see CRIMES, CRIMINALS)
Judg 9:24 that the c done to the

CRIMES† (see CRIME)
Ezek 7:23 is filled with c of blood
Acts 18:14 of wrongdoing or wicked c

CRIMINALS (see CRIME)
Luke 23:32 There were also two others, c

CRIMSON
Is 1:18 though they are red like c

CRIPPLE†
Acts 14: 8 a c from his mother's womb,

CRITICIZED†
Mark 14: 5 And they c her sharply

CROOKED
Deut 32: 5 a perverse and c generation
Ps 125: 5 as turn aside to their c ways
Eccl 1:15 What is c cannot be made
Eccl 7:13 straight what He has made c
Is 42:16 them, and c places straight
Is 59: 8 have made themselves c paths
Phil 2:15 fault in the midst of a c

CROP (see CROPS)
Amos 7: 1 the beginning of the late c
Mark 4: 7 choked it, and it yielded no c
Luke 8: 8 yielded a c a hundredfold

CROPS (see CROP)
Mark 4:28 the earth yields c by itself
Luke 12:17 I have no room to store my c
2Ti 2: 6 be first to partake of the c

CROSS (see CROSSED, CROSSES, CROSSING,
   CROSSROADS)
Num 35:10 When you c the Jordan into
Josh 4: 5 C over before the ark of the
Is 11:15 and make men c over dryshod
Is 51:10 for the redeemed to c over
Ezek 47: 5 a river that I could not c
Matt 16:24 himself, and take up his c
Matt 27:32 they compelled to bear His c
Matt 27:40 of God, come down from the c
Mark 4:35 Let us c over to the other
Luke 9:23 and take up his c daily, and
Luke 23:26 on him they laid the c that
John 19:17 And He, bearing His c, went
John 19:19 a title and put it on the c.
John 19:25 by the c of Jesus His mother

John 19:31 **c** on the Sabbath (for that
Acts 18:27 he desired to **c** to Achaia
1Co 1:17 lest the **c** of Christ should
1Co 1:18 For the message of the **c** is
Gal 5:11 offense of the **c** has ceased
Gal 6:14 **c** of our Lord Jesus Christ
Eph 2:16 God in one body through the **c**
Phil 2: 8 even the death of the **c**
Phil 3:18 enemies of the **c** of Christ
Col 1:20 through the blood of His **c**
Col 2:14 having nailed it to the **c**
Heb 12: 2 set before Him endured the **c**

CROSSED (see CROSS)
Josh 3:17 and all Israel **c** over on dry
Ezek 47: 5 a river that could not be **c**
Matt 9: 1 **c** over, and came to His own

CROSSES (see CROSS)
Deut 31: 3 God Himself **c** over before you

CROSS-EXAMINE†
Luke 11:53 to **c** Him about many things,

CROSSING (see CROSS)
Deut 6: 1 you are **c** over to possess

CROSSROADS† (see CROSS)
Obad 14 not have stood at the **c** to

CROUCH† (see CROUCHES, CROUCHING)
Job 38:40 when they **c** in their dens, or

CROUCHES† (see CROUCH)
Ps 10:10 So he **c**, he lies low, That

CROUCHING† (see CROUCH)
Ps 17:11 eyes, **c** down to the earth,

CROW (see CROWED, CROWING, CROWS)
Luke 22:34 the rooster will not **c** this

CROWD (see CROWDS)
Ex 23: 2 not follow a **c** to do evil
Matt 9:23 and the noisy **c** wailing,
Mark 2: 4 near Him because of the **c**
Mark 5:27 she came behind Him in the **c**
Mark 7:17 a house away from the **c**, His
Mark 15:11 priests stirred up the **c**, so
Mark 15:15 wanting to gratify the **c**
Luke 4:42 the **c** sought Him and came to
Luke 6:17 with a **c** of His disciples
Luke 7: 9 said to the **c** that followed
Luke 7:12 a large **c** from the city was
Luke 23: 4 to the chief priests and the **c**
Acts 19:35 city clerk had quieted the **c**

CROWDS† (see CROWD)
Luke 9:18 Who do the **c** say that I am
Luke 11:29 And while the **c** were thickly
Acts 17:13 also and stirred up the **c**

CROWED (see CROW)
Matt 26:74 Immediately a rooster **c**.

CROWING† (see CROW)
Mark 13:35 at the **c** of the rooster, or

CROWN (see CROWNED, CROWNING, CROWNS)
Ex 29: 6 put the holy **c** on the head of
Job 2: 7 his foot to the **c** of his head
Ps 65:11 You **c** the year with Your
Ps 132:18 Himself His **c** shall flourish
Prov 4: 9 a **c** of glory she shall deliver
Prov 12: 4 wife is the **c** of her husband
Prov 14:24 The **c** of the wise is their
Prov 16:31 head is a **c** of glory, if it
Prov 17: 6 children are the **c** of old men
Lam 5:16 The **c** has fallen from our
Zech 6:11 and gold, make an elaborate **c**
Zech 9:16 be like the jewels of a **c**
Matt 27:29 had twisted a **c** of thorns

1Co 9:25 it to obtain a perishable **c**
Phil 4: 1 brethren, my joy and **c**, so
1Th 2:19 or joy, or **c** of rejoicing
2Ti 4: 8 for me the **c** of righteousness
Jas 1:12 he will receive the **c** of life
Rev 6: 2 a **c** was given to him, and he
Rev 14:14 having on His head a golden **c**

CROWNED (see CROWN)
Ps 8: 5 You have **c** him with glory and
Heb 2: 7 You **c** him with glory and honor

CROWNING† (see CROWN)
Is 23: 8 the **c** city, whose merchants

CROWNS (see CROWN)
Ps 103: 4 Who **c** you with lovingkindness
Rev 4: 4 they had **c** of gold on their
Rev 4:10 and cast their **c** before the
Rev 19:12 and on His head were many **c**

CROWS (see CROW)
Matt 26:34 night, before the rooster **c**

CRUCIFIED (see CRUCIFY)
Matt 26: 2 will be delivered up to be **c**
Matt 27:22 Let Him be **c**
Matt 27:31 Him, and led Him away to be **c**
Matt 27:35 Then they **c** Him, and divided
Matt 27:38 two robbers were **c** with Him
Matt 27:44 **c** with Him reviled Him with
Matt 28: 5 that you seek Jesus who was **c**
Mark 15:15 he had scourged Him, to be **c**
Luke 23:23 with loud voices that He be **c**
Luke 23:33 Calvary, there they **c** Him
Luke 24: 7 hands of sinful men, and be **c**
Luke 24:20 condemned to death, and **c** Him
John 19:20 Jesus was **c** was near the city
John 19:41 He was **c** there was a garden
Acts 2:23 by lawless hands, have **c**, and
Acts 4:10 of Nazareth, whom you **c**, whom
Rom 6: 6 our old man was **c** with Him
1Co 1:13 Was Paul **c** for you
1Co 1:23 but we preach Christ **c**, to
1Co 2: 2 except Jesus Christ and Him **c**
1Co 2: 8 not have **c** the Lord of glory
2Co 13: 4 though He was **c** in weakness
Gal 2:20 I have been **c** with Christ
Gal 5:24 **c** the flesh with its passions
Gal 6:14 the world has been **c** to me
Rev 11: 8 where our Lord was **c**

CRUCIFY (see CRUCIFIED)
Matt 20:19 to mock and to scourge and to **c**
Mark 15:13 they cried out again, "C Him
Mark 15:20 Him, and led Him out to **c** Him
John 19: 6 saying, "C Him, **c** Him
John 19:10 that I have power to **c** You
John 19:15 them, "Shall I **c** your King
Heb 6: 6 since they **c** again for

CRUEL (see CRUELLY, CRUELTY)
Ex 6: 9 of spirit and **c** bondage
Ps 25:19 And they hate me with **c** hatred
Ps 71: 4 of the unrighteous and **c** man
Prov 17:11 therefore a **c** messenger will
Prov 27: 4 Wrath is **c** and anger a torrent
Song 8: 6 jealousy as **c** as the grave
Is 13: 9 the day of the LORD comes, **c**

CRUELLY† (see CRUEL)
Ezek 18:18 because he **c** oppressed,

CRUELTY† (see CRUEL)
Gen 49: 5 instruments of **c** are in their
Ps 74:20 full of the habitations of **c**
Ezek 34: 4 and **c** you have ruled them

CRUMBS
Matt 15:27 the **c** which fall from their

CRUSH (see CRUSHED, CRUSHES, CRUSHING)
Job 6: 9 it would please God to c me
Amos 4: 1 who c the needy, who say to
Mark 3: 9 lest they should c Him
Rom 16:20 will c Satan under your feet

CRUSHED (see CRUSH)
Lev 22:24 the LORD what is bruised or c
Deut 9:21 c it and ground it very small,
Deut 28:33 oppressed and c continually
Judg 9:53 head and c his skull
2Ki 23:15 c it to powder, and burned the
Job 4:19 dust, who are c before a moth
Job 5: 4 they are c in the gate, and
Ps 143: 3 He has c my life to the
Prov 26:28 hates those who are c by it
Prov 27:22 a pestle along with c grain
Jer 51:34 has devoured me, he has c me
Dan 2:35 and the gold were c together
2Co 4: 8 on every side, yet not c

CRUSHES† (see CRUSH)
Job 9:17 For He c me with a tempest,
Dan 2:40 and like iron that c, that

CRUSHING (see CRUSH)
Deut 23: 1 by c or mutilation shall not
2Ki 19:25 that you should be for c

CRUST†
Prov 6:26 is reduced to a c of bread

CRY (see CRIED, CRIES, CRYING)
Gen 27:34 exceedingly great and bitter c
Ex 2:23 and their c came up to God
Ex 12:30 there was a great c in Egypt
Deut 22:24 she did not c out in the city
2Sa 22: 7 and my c entered His ears
1Ki 18:27 C aloud, for he is a god
Neh 9: 9 heard their c by the Red Sea
Job 19: 7 If I c out concerning wrong,
Job 24:12 souls of the wounded c out
Job 34:28 hears the c of the afflicted
Job 35: 9 they c out for help because
Job 38:41 when its young ones c to God
Ps 5: 2 heed to the voice of my c
Ps 9:12 forget the c of the humble
Ps 17: 1 cause, O LORD, Attend to my c
Ps 18: 6 my c came before Him, even to
Ps 22: 2 I c in the daytime, but You
Ps 27: 7 LORD, when I c with my voice
Ps 28: 1 To You I will c, O LORD my
Ps 28: 2 supplications When I c to You
Ps 34:15 His ears are open to their c
Ps 34:17 The righteous c out, and the
Ps 39:12 O LORD, And give ear to my c
Ps 40: 1 inclined to me, And heard my c
Ps 57: 2 I will c out to God Most High
Ps 61: 1 Hear my c, O God
Ps 84: 2 my flesh c out for the living
Ps 86: 3 For I c to You all day long
Ps 119:145 I c out with my whole heart
Ps 119:169 Let my c come before You, O
Ps 142: 6 Attend to my c, For I am
Ps 147: 9 And to the young ravens that c
Prov 2: 3 if you c out for discernment,
Prov 8: 1 Does not wisdom c out, and
Prov 21:13 shuts his ears to the c of
Is 5: 7 but behold, a c for help.
Is 8: 4 knowledge to c 'My father'
Is 14:31 Wail, O gate! C, O city!
Is 24:11 There is a c for wine in the
Is 24:14 shall c aloud from the sea
Is 40: 6 The voice said, "C out
Is 40: 6 What shall I c
Is 42: 2 He will not c out, nor raise
Is 42:14 Now I will c like a woman in

Is 58: 1 C aloud, spare not
Jer 2: 2 c in the hearing of Jerusalem
Jer 14: 2 the c of Jerusalem has gone
Jer 25:34 Wail, shepherds, and c
Jer 46:12 your c has filled the land
Jer 48: 5 have heard a c of destruction
Jer 48:20 Wail and c! Tell it in
Jer 51:54 The sound of a c comes from
Lam 2:19 c out in the night, at the
Lam 3:56 sighing, from my c for help
Ezek 9: 4 c over all the abominations
Ezek 21:12 C and wail, son of man
Hos 8: 2 Israel will c to Me, 'My God,
Joel 1:19 O LORD, to You I c out
Joel 1:20 the field also c out to You
Amos 3: 4 a young lion c out of his den
Jon 1: 2 city, and c out against it
Hab 1: 2 O LORD, how long shall I c
Zeph 1:10 mournful c from the Fish Gate
Matt 12:19 He will not quarrel nor c out
Matt 25: 6 And at midnight a c was heard
Mark 10:47 Nazareth, he began to c out
Luke 18: 7 His own elect who c out day
Luke 19:40 would immediately c out
Rom 8:15 adoption by whom we c out

CRYING (see CRY)
2Sa 13:19 head and went away c bitterly
Ps 69: 3 I am weary with my c
Is 40: 3 The voice of one c in the
Mal 2:13 with tears, with weeping and c
Matt 3: 3 The voice of one c in the
Matt 21:15 the children c out in the
Mark 5: 5 c out and cutting himself with
John 1:23 of one c in the wilderness
Acts 8: 7 c with a loud voice, came out
Gal 4: 6 Son into your hearts, c out,
Rev 14:15 c with a loud voice to Him
Rev 21: 4 more death, nor sorrow, nor c

CRYSTAL†
Job 28:17 gold nor c can equal it, nor
Is 54:12 of rubies, your gates of c
Ezek 1:22 the color of an awesome c
Rev 4: 6 was a sea of glass, like c
Rev 21:11 a jasper stone, clear as c
Rev 22: 1 of water of life, clear as c

CUB† (see CUBS)
Nah 2:11 the lioness and lion's c, and

CUBIT (see CUBITS)
Gen 6:16 finish it to a c from above
Deut 3:11 according to the standard c
Matt 6:27 can add one c to his stature

CUBITS (see CUBIT)
Gen 6:15 ark shall be three hundred c
Gen 7:20 prevailed fifteen c upward
Num 11:31 about two c above the surface
1Sa 17: 4 Gath, whose height was six c
Esth 5:14 gallows be made, fifty c high
Ezek 41:14 courtyard, was one hundred c
Ezek 45: 3 twenty-five thousand c long
Ezek 45: 5 twenty-five thousand c long
Dan 3: 1 whose height was sixty c
Dan 3: 1 and its width six c
Rev 21:17 one hundred and forty-four c

CUBS (see CUB)
2Sa 17: 8 robbed of her c in the field
Job 4:11 and the c of the lioness are
Job 38:32 the Great Bear with its c
Hos 13: 8 like a bear deprived of her c
Nah 2:12 in pieces enough for his c

CUCUMBERS†
Num 11: 5 we ate freely in Egypt, the c

Is   1: 8 as a hut in a garden of c

CUD
Lev   11: 3 hooves and chewing the c
Lev   11: 4 c or those that have cloven
Lev   11: 4 because it chews the c but

CUDDLED†
Lam   2:20 the children they have c

CULTIVATE† (see CULTIVATED)
Ezek   48:19 tribes of Israel, shall c it

CULTIVATED (see CULTIVATE)
Heb   6: 7 for those by whom it is c

CUMI†
Mark   5:41 Talitha, c," which is

CUMMIN
Is   28:25 does he not sow the black c
Matt   23:23 tithe of mint and anise and c

CUNNING (see CUNNINGLY)
Gen   3: 1 Now the serpent was more c
Job   5:13 the counsel of the c comes
Dan   8:25 Through his c he shall cause
Hos   12: 7 A c Canaanite!
Eph   4:14 in the c craftiness by which

CUNNINGLY† (see CUNNING)
2Pe   1:16 For we did not follow c

CUP (see CUPBEARER, CUPS)
Gen   40:11 Pharaoh's c was in my hand
Gen   44: 2 Also put my c, the silver c
Gen   44:12 the c was found in Benjamin's
1Ki   17:10 me a little water in a c,
Ps   11: 6 be the portion of their c
Ps   16: 5 of my inheritance and my c
Ps   23: 5 My c runs over
Ps   73:10 And waters of a full c are
Ps   116:13 take up the c of salvation
Prov   23:31 when it sparkles in the c
Is   51:17 of the LORD the c of His fury
Jer   16: 7 c of consolation to drink for
Jer   25:15 Take this wine c of fury from
Zech   12: 2 I will make Jerusalem a c of
Matt   10:42 a c of cold water in the name
Matt   20:22 c that I am about to drink
Matt   23:25 cleanse the outside of the c
Matt   26:27 Then He took the c, and gave
Matt   26:39 let this c pass from Me
Mark   9:41 a c of water to drink in My
Luke   22:20 also took the c after supper
Luke   22:20 This c is the new covenant in
Luke   22:42 will, remove this c from Me
1Co   10:16 The c of blessing which we
1Co   10:21 drink the c of the Lord and
1Co   10:21 the Lord and the c of demons
1Co   11:26 this bread and drink this c
Rev   14:10 into the c of His indignation
Rev   16:19 to give her the c of the wine
Rev   17: 4 golden c full of abominations
Rev   18: 6 in the c which she has mixed,

CUPBEARER† (see CUP)
Neh   1:11 For I was the king's c

CUPS (see CUP)
Ex   37:16 its dishes, its c, its bowls,
Mark   7: 8 the washing of pitchers and c

CURDLE† (see CURDS)
Job   10:10 milk, and c me like cheese,

CURDS (see CURDLE)
Deut   32:14 c from the cattle, and milk of
2Sa   17:29 honey and c, sheep and cheese
Is   7:15 C and honey He shall eat, that

CURE (see CURED, CURES)
Hos   5:13 yet he cannot c you, nor heal
Matt   17:16 but they could not c him
Luke   9: 1 all demons, and to c diseases

CURED (see CURE)
Matt   17:18 the child was c from that
John   5:10 said to him who was c, "It

CURES† (see CURE)
Luke   13:32 out demons and perform c today

CURRENCY†
Gen   23:16 of silver, c of the merchants
Num   3:47 in the c of the shekel of the

CURRENT
1Ki   10:28 them in Keveh at the c price

CURSE (see CURSED, CURSES, CURSING)
Gen   8:21 I will never again c the
Gen   12: 3 I will c him who curses the
Num   5:18 bitter water that brings a c
Num   23: 8 How shall I c whom God has
Deut   11:26 you today a blessing and a c
Deut   11:28 and the c, if you do not obey
Deut   11:29 and the c on Mount Ebal
Deut   29:20 every c that is written in
2Ki   22:19 become a desolation and a c
Neh   13: 2 Balaam against them to c them
Job   1:11 he will surely c You to Your
Job   2: 5 he will surely c You to Your
Job   2: 9 C God and die
Job   3: 8 May those c it who c the day
Ps   62: 4 mouth, But they c inwardly
Ps   109:28 Let them c, but You bless
Prov   3:33 The c of the LORD is on the
Prov   26: 2 so a c without cause shall
Prov   27:14 it will be counted a c to him
Prov   30:10 to his master, lest he c you
Eccl   10:20 Do not c the king, even in
Eccl   10:20 do not c the rich, even in
Is   8:21 c their king and their God, and
Jer   24: 9 and a byword, a taunt and a c
Jer   25:18 a hissing, and a c, as it is
Jer   29:18 to be a c, an astonishment, a
Lam   3:65 Your c be upon them
Mal   2: 2 and I will c your blessings
Mal   4: 6 and strike the earth with a c
Matt   5:44 bless those who c you, do
Matt   26:74 Then he began to c and swear,
Gal   3:10 of the law are under the c
Gal   3:13 us from the c of the law,
Gal   3:13 having become a c for us (for
Jas   3: 9 Father, and with it we c men
Rev   22: 3 And there shall be no more c

CURSED (see CURSE)
Gen   3:14 this, you are c more than all
Gen   3:17 C is the ground for your sake
Gen   4:11 now you are c from the earth
Gen   9:25 C be Canaan
Gen   27:29 C be everyone who curses you,
Gen   49: 7 C be their anger, for it is
Lev   24:11 the name of the LORD and c
Lev   24:14 the camp him who has c
Num   23: 8 I curse whom God has not c
Deut   27:15 C is the one who makes any
Deut   27:20 C is the one who lies with
Deut   28:16 C shall you be in the city,
Deut   28:16 c shall you be in the country
Deut   28:17 C shall be your basket and
1Sa   17:43 the Philistine c David by his
2Sa   16: 7 Shimei said thus when he c
Job   1: 5 and c God in their hearts
Job   3: 1 and c the day of his birth
Ps   37:22 But those who are c by Him
Ps   119:21 the c, Who stray from Your

Eccl	7:22	that even you have c others
Jer	17: 5	C is the man who trusts in
Jer	20:14	C be the day in which I was
Jer	20:15	Let the man c who brought
Mal	3: 9	You are c with a curse, for
Matt	25:41	hand, 'Depart from Me, you c
Mark	11:21	which You c has withered away
Gal	3:10	C is everyone who does not
Gal	3:13	C is everyone who hangs on a
Heb	6: 8	rejected and near to being c

CURSES (see CURSE)

Gen	12: 3	and I will curse him who c you
Ex	21:17	he who c his father or his
Lev	24:15	Whoever c his God shall bear
Num	5:23	shall write these c in a book
Jer	15:10	every one of them c me
Matt	15: 4	He who c father or mother,
Mark	7:10	He who c father or mother,

CURSING (see CURSE, CURSINGS)

Deut	30:19	life and death, blessing and c
Ps	10: 7	His mouth is full of c and
Ps	59:12	in their pride, And for the c
Ps	109:17	As he loved c, so let it come
Ps	109:18	with c as with his garment
Rom	3:14	Whose mouth is full of c and
Jas	3:10	mouth proceed blessings and c

CURSINGS† (see CURSING)

Josh	8:34	law, the blessings and the c
Hos	7:16	for the c of their tongue

CURTAIN (see CURTAINS)

Ex	26: 2	The length of each c shall be
Ps	104: 2	out the heavens like a c
Is	40:22	out the heavens like a c, and

CURTAINS (see CURTAIN)

Ex	26: 1	the tabernacle with ten c
2Sa	7: 2	of God dwells inside tent c
Esth	1: 6	blue linen c fastened with
Song	1: 5	Kedar, like the c of Solomon
Jer	10:20	tent anymore, or set up my c

CURVES†

Song	7: 1	The c of your thighs are like

CUSH (see ETHIOPIA)

Gen	2:13	the whole land of C
Gen	10: 6	The sons of Ham were C,
Gen	10: 8	C begot Nimrod
Is	45:14	of Egypt and merchandise of C

CUSHAN

Hab	3: 7	the tents of C are in affliction

CUSHAN-RISHATHAIM

Judg	3: 8	hand of C king of Mesopotamia

CUSTODIAN (see CUSTODY)

Esth	2: 3	king's eunuch, c of the women

CUSTODY (see CUSTODIAN)

Gen	40: 3	So he put them in c in the
Gen	40: 7	in the c of his lord's house
Acts	4: 3	put them in c until the next

CUSTOM (see CUSTOMARY, CUSTOMS)

Gen	19:31	as is the c of all the earth
2Ki	11:14	by a pillar according to c
Ezra	4:13	not pay tax, tribute, or c
Ps	119:132	As Your c is toward those who
Dan	6:10	as was his c since early days
Luke	2:27	according to the c of the law
Luke	2:42	to the c of the feast
Luke	4:16	And as His c was, He went into
John	19:40	as the c of the Jews is to
Acts	15: 1	according to the c of Moses
Acts	17: 2	Then Paul, as his c was, went
Acts	25:16	It is not the c of the

CUSTOMARILY† (see CUSTOMARY)

Acts	16:13	where prayer was c made

CUSTOMARY (see CUSTOM, CUSTOMARILY)

Lev	15:25	at the time of her c impurity
Lev	23: 7	you shall do no c work on it

CUSTOMS† (see CUSTOM)

Lev	18:30	any of these abominable c
Jer	10: 3	For the c of the peoples are
Ezek	11:12	c of the Gentiles which are
Matt	17:25	of the earth take c or taxes
Acts	6:14	and change the c which Moses
Acts	16:21	they teach c which are not
Acts	21:21	to walk according to the c
Acts	26: 3	you are expert in all c and
Acts	28:17	or the c of our fathers, yet
Rom	13: 7	c to whom c, fear to

CUT (see CUTS, CUTTING, WOODCUTTERS)

Gen	9:11	be c off by the waters of the
Gen	15:10	and c them in two, down the
Gen	17:14	be c off from his people
Ex	4:25	c off the foreskin of her son
Ex	12:15	shall be c off from Israel
Ex	29:17	Then you shall c the ram in
Ex	34: 1	C two tablets of stone like
Ex	34:13	c down their wooden images
Lev	22: 3	be c off from My presence
Lev	22:24	or crushed, or torn or c
Deut	19: 5	the ax to c down the tree
Deut	25:12	then you shall c off her hand
Josh	3:13	of the Jordan shall be c off
Josh	7: 9	c off our name from the earth
Judg	1: 6	c off his thumbs and big toes
Judg	20: 6	c her in pieces, and sent her
Ruth	4:10	c off from among his brethren
1Sa	17:51	and c off his head with it
1Sa	24: 5	because he had c Saul's robe
2Sa	4:12	c off their hands and feet, and
2Sa	14:26	when he c the hair of his
1Ki	5: 6	c timber like the Sidonians
1Ki	15:13	Asa c down her obscene image
1Ki	18:28	c themselves, as was their
1Ki	18:33	c the bull in pieces, and laid
2Ki	3:19	shall c down every good tree,
2Ki	6: 4	the Jordan, they c down trees
2Ki	6: 6	So he c off a stick, and threw
2Ki	19:23	I will c down its tall cedars
2Ch	2: 8	skill to c timber in Lebanon
2Ch	32:21	c down every mighty man of
2Ch	34: 7	c down all the incense altars
Job	4: 7	were the upright ever c off
Job	8:14	confidence shall be c off
Job	14: 7	for a tree, if it is c down
Job	21:21	of his months is c in half
Job	22:16	who were c down before their
Ps	31:22	I am c off from before Your
Ps	34:16	To c off the remembrance of
Ps	37: 2	soon be c down like the grass
Ps	37: 9	For evildoers shall be c off
Ps	54: 5	C them off in Your truth
Ps	58: 7	arrows be as if c in pieces
Ps	88:16	Your terrors have c me off
Ps	90:10	For it is soon c off, and we
Ps	107:16	c the bars of iron in two
Ps	109:13	Let his posterity be c off
Ps	109:15	That He may c off the memory
Ps	143:12	In Your mercy c off my
Prov	2:22	will be c off from the earth
Prov	10:31	perverse tongue will be c out
Prov	23:18	your hope will not be c off
Prov	24:14	your hope will not be c off
Is	6:13	remains when it is c down
Is	10:34	He will c down the thickets
Is	14:22	c off from Babylon the name

Is	15: 2	and every beard c off
Is	33:12	like thorns c up they shall
Is	51: 9	the arm that c Rahab apart
Is	53: 8	For He was c off from the
Is	55:13	sign that shall not be c off
Is	56: 5	name that shall not be c off
Jer	6: 6	C down trees, And build a
Jer	16: 6	them, c themselves, nor make
Jer	22:14	and c out windows for it,
Jer	34:18	when they c the calf in two
Jer	44: 7	to c off from you man and
Jer	48:25	The horn of Moab is c off
Jer	50:16	C off the sower from Babylon,
Jer	50:23	whole earth has been c apart
Ezek	5:16	c off your supply of bread
Ezek	6: 6	incense altars may be c down
Ezek	14:13	c off man and beast from it
Ezek	16: 4	your navel cord was not c
Ezek	17: 9	c off its fruit, and leave it
Dan	2: 5	you shall be c in pieces
Dan	2:34	stone was c out without hands
Dan	9:26	weeks Messiah shall be c off
Hos	10: 7	her king is c off like a twig
Hos	10:15	Israel shall be c off utterly
Obad	9	may be c off by slaughter
Mic	1:16	c off your hair, because of
Mic	5:10	That I will c off your horses
Mic	5:12	I will c off sorceries from
Nah	2:13	I will c off your prey from
Hab	3:17	flock be c off from the fold
Zech	9:10	I will c off the chariot from
Zech	9:10	the battle bow shall be c off
Matt	3:10	not bear good fruit is c down
Matt	5:30	c it off and cast it from you
Matt	26:51	high priest, and c off his ear
Mark	9:43	hand makes you sin, c it off
Mark	11: 8	others c down leafy branches
John	18:26	of him whose ear Peter c off
Acts	2:37	they were c to the heart, and
Acts	7:54	they were c to the heart, and
Acts	18:18	his hair c off at Cenchrea
Acts	27:32	Then the soldiers c away the
Rom	9:28	c it short in righteousness,
Rom	11:22	you also will be c off

CUTS (see CUT)

Is	38:12	He c me off from the loom
Is	44:14	he c down cedars for himself
Jer	10: 3	for one c a tree from the
Ezek	24: 4	fill it with choice c

CUTTING (see CUT, CUTTINGS)

Ex	31: 5	in c jewels for setting, in
Jer	44:11	and for c off all Judah
Mark	5: 5	out and c himself with stones

CUTTINGS† (see CUTTING)

Lev	19:28	You shall not make any c in
Lev	21: 5	nor make any c in their flesh
Jer	9:22	like c after the harvester,

CYMBAL† (see CYMBALS)

1Co	13: 1	brass or a clanging c

CYMBALS (see CYMBAL)

2Sa	6: 5	on sistrums, and on c
1Ch	13: 8	on tambourines, on c, and
1Ch	15:16	instruments, harps, and c, by
Ps	150: 5	Praise Him with loud c

CYPRESS

1Ki	5: 8	the cedar and c logs
1Ki	6:15	the temple with planks of c
Is	14: 8	Indeed the c trees rejoice
Is	41:19	set in the desert the c tree
Hos	14: 8	I am like a green c tree

CYPRUS

Dan	11:30	For ships from C shall come
Acts	4:36	a Levite of the country of C
Acts	11:19	as far as Phoenicia, C, and
Acts	15:39	took Mark and sailed to C
Acts	21: 3	When we had sighted C, we

CYRENIAN (see CYRENIANS)

Mark 15:21 a certain man, Simon a C, the

CYRENIANS† (see CYRENIAN)

Acts 6: 9 Synagogue of the Freedmen (C

CYRUS

2Ch	36:22	year of C king of Persia,
2Ch	36:22	spirit of C king of Persia
2Ch	36:23	Thus says C king of Persia
Ezra	5:13	year of C king of Babylon
Ezra	5:13	King C issued a decree to
Ezra	5:17	C to build this house of God
Is	44:28	who says of C, 'He is My
Is	45: 1	LORD to His anointed, to C
Dan	6:28	in the reign of C the Persian

D

DAGGER

Judg 3:16 a d (it was double-edged and a

DAGON (see DAGON'S)

Judg	16:23	sacrifice to D their god, and
1Sa	5: 2	it into the temple of D
1Sa	5: 4	The head of D and both the
1Sa	5: 4	the torso of D was left of it
1Sa	5: 7	harsh toward us and D our god

DAGON'S (see DAGON)

1Sa 5: 5 into D temple tread on the

DAILY

Ex	5:19	any bricks from your d quota
Ex	16: 5	as much as they gather d
Lev	6:20	flour as a d grain offering
Num	28:24	made by fire d for seven days
Judg	16:16	pestered him d with her words
2Ch	8:13	according to the d rate,
Ezra	3: 4	offered the d burnt offerings
Esth	3: 4	when they spoke to him d
Ps	13: 2	Having sorrow in my heart d
Ps	61: 8	That I may d perform my vows
Ps	68:19	Who d loads us with benefits,
Ps	72:15	And d He shall be praised
Ps	74:22	foolish man reproaches You d
Ps	88: 9	I have called d upon You
Prov	8:30	and I was d His delight,
Jer	20: 7	I am in derision d
Jer	37:21	d a piece of bread from the
Dan	1: 5	a d provision of the king's
Dan	11:31	take away the d sacrifices
Hos	12: 1	He d increases lies and
Matt	6:11	Give us this day our d bread
Matt	26:55	I sat d with you, teaching in
Luke	9:23	and take up his cross d, and
Acts	2:46	So continuing d with one
Acts	2:47	Lord added to the church d
Acts	3: 2	whom they laid d at the gate
Acts	5:42	d in the temple, and in every
Acts	6: 1	in the d distribution
Acts	16: 5	and increased in number d
Acts	17:11	searched the Scriptures d to
Acts	17:17	in the marketplace d with
Acts	19: 9	reasoning d in the school of
1Co	15:31	Jesus our Lord, I die d
Heb	3:13	but exhort one another d,
Heb	7:27	who does not need d, as those
Heb	10:11	priest stands ministering d

Jas 2:15 naked and destitute of **d** food

DAINTIES†
Gen 49:20 and he shall yield royal **d**

DAMAGE (*see* DAMAGED, DAMAGES)
Dan 11:30 the holy covenant, and do **d**

DAMAGED† (*see* DAMAGE)
Ps 74: 3 The enemy has **d** everything in
Jon 4: 7 it so **d** the plant that it

DAMAGES (*see* DAMAGE)
1Ki 11:27 repaired the **d** to the City of
Amos 9:11 fallen down, and repair its **d**

DAMARIS†
Acts 17:34 Areopagite, a woman named **D**

DAMASCUS
Gen 15: 2 of my house is Eliezer of **D**
2Sa 8: 5 When the Syrians of **D** came to
2Ki 5:12 the Pharpar, the rivers of **D**
2Ki 16:10 and saw an altar that was at **D**
Is 7: 8 For the head of Syria is **D**
Is 17: 1 The burden against **D**
Jer 49:23 Against **D**. "Hamath and
Jer 49:24 **D** has grown feeble And turns
Ezek 27:18 **D** was your merchant because
Amos 1: 3 For three transgressions of **D**
Acts 9: 2 him to the synagogues of **D**
Acts 9: 3 he journeyed he came near **D**
Acts 9:10 disciple at **D** named Ananias
Acts 9:19 days with the disciples at **D**
Acts 9:22 the Jews who dwelt in **D**,
Acts 9:27 at **D** in the name of Jesus
Acts 22: 5 went to **D** to bring in chains
Acts 22: 6 came near **D** at about noon,
Acts 26:20 declared first to those in **D**
2Co 11:32 In **D** the governor, under
Gal 1:17 and returned again to **D**

DAMS†
Job 28:11 He **d** up the streams from

DAN (*see* DANITES, LAISH)
Gen 14:14 went in pursuit as far as **D**
Gen 49:16 **D** shall judge his people as
Num 1:38 From the children of **D**, their
Num 26:42 These are the sons of **D**
Deut 33:22 **D** is a lion's whelp
Deut 34: 1 land of Gilead as far as **D**
Josh 19:47 They called Leshem, **D**, after
Josh 21:23 and from the tribe of **D**,
Judg 5:17 why did **D** remain on ships
Judg 18:29 called the name of the city **D**
Judg 20: 1 from **D** to Beersheba, as well
1Sa 3:20 And all Israel from **D** to
2Sa 3:10 Judah, from **D** to Beersheba
2Ki 10:29 that were at Bethel and **D**
Amos 8:14 say, As your god lives, O **D**

DANCE (*see* DANCED, DANCES, DANCING)
Job 21:11 a flock, and their children **d**
Ps 149: 3 praise His name with the **d**
Ps 150: 4 Him with the timbrel and **d**
Eccl 3: 4 time to mourn, and a time to **d**
Lam 5:15 our **d** has turned into
Matt 11:17 for you, and you did not **d**

DANCED† (*see* DANCE)
Judg 21:23 their number from those who **d**
1Sa 18: 7 So the women sang as they **d**
2Sa 6:14 Then David **d** before the LORD
Matt 14: 6 of Herodias **d** before them
Mark 6:22 daughter herself came in and **d**

DANCES (*see* DANCE)
Ex 15:20 her with timbrels and with **d**
Judg 21:21 come out to perform their **d**

1Sa 29: 5 they sang to one another in **d**
Job 41:22 neck, and sorrow **d** before him

DANCING† (*see* DANCE)
Ex 32:19 that he saw the calf and the **d**
Judg 11:34 meet him with timbrels and **d**
1Sa 18: 6 of Israel, singing and **d**, to
1Sa 30:16 land, eating and drinking and **d**
Ps 30:11 for me my mourning into **d**
Luke 15:25 house, he heard music and **d**

DANDLED†
Is 66:12 carried, and be **d** on her knees

DANGER (*see* DANGEROUS)
Matt 5:21 will be in **d** of the judgment
Matt 5:22 shall be in **d** of hell fire

DANGEROUS† (*see* DANGER)
Acts 27: 9 sailing was now **d** because the

DANIEL (*see* BELTESHAZZAR)
Ezek 14:20 even though Noah, **D**, and Job
Ezek 28: 3 (Behold, you are wiser than **D**
Dan 1: 7 he gave **D** the name
Dan 1:17 **D** had understanding in all
Dan 1:19 all none was found like **D**
Dan 2:15 made the decision known to **D**
Dan 2:19 to **D** in a night vision
Dan 2:19 So **D** blessed the God of
Dan 2:48 Then the king promoted **D** and
Dan 5:13 Are you that **D** who is one of
Dan 5:29 and they clothed **D** with purple
Dan 6: 2 governors, of whom **D** was one
Dan 6: 3 Then this **D** distinguished
Dan 6:10 Now when **D** knew that the
Dan 6:11 found **D** praying and making
Dan 6:20 **D**, servant of the living God,
Dan 6:21 Then **D** said to the king, "O
Dan 6:23 take **D** up out of the den
Dan 6:27 Who has delivered **D** from the
Dan 6:28 So this **D** prospered in the
Dan 7: 1 **D** had a dream and visions of
Dan 8:27 And I, **D**, fainted and was sick
Dan 10: 1 a message was revealed to **D**
Dan 10: 7 And I, **D**, alone saw the vision
Dan 10:11 O **D**, man greatly beloved,
Dan 12: 4 But you, **D**, shut up the words
Matt 24:15 spoken of by **D** the prophet
Mark 13:14 spoken of by **D** the prophet

DANITES (*see* DAN)
Judg 18: 1 **D** was seeking an inheritance

DAPPLED
Zech 6: 3 the fourth chariot **d** horses

DARE (*see* DARED)
Esth 7: 5 who would **d** presume in his
Job 41:10 that he would **d** stir him up
Amos 6:10 For we **d** not mention the name
Matt 22:46 anyone **d** question Him
Rom 5: 7 someone would even **d** to die
Rom 15:18 For I will not **d** to speak of

DARED (*see* DARE)
2Sa 17:17 for they **d** not be seen coming
Job 32: 6 **d** not declare my opinion to
Mark 12:34 that no one **d** question Him
John 21:12 of the disciples **d** ask Him
Acts 5:13 none of the rest **d** join them
Acts 7:32 Moses trembled and **d** not look

DARICS†
1Ch 29: 7 and ten thousand **d** of gold

DARIUS
Ezra 4: 5 the reign of **D** king of Persia
Neh 12:22 the reign of **D** the Persian
Dan 5:31 And **D** the Mede received the

Dan 6: 6 King **D**, live forever
Dan 6: 9 Therefore King **D** signed the
Dan 6:28 prospered in the reign of **D**
Dan 9: 1 of **D** the son of Ahasuerus
Hag 1: 1 In the second year of King **D**
Zech 1: 1 month of the second year of **D**

DARK (*see* DARKEN, DARKER, DARKNESS)
Gen 15:17 the sun went down and it was **d**
Num 12: 8 plainly, and not in **d** sayings
2Sa 22:12 **d** waters and thick clouds of
1Ki 8:12 He would dwell in the **d** cloud
Job 10:22 a land as **d** as darkness
Job 11:17 Though you were **d**, you would
Job 12:25 grope in the **d** without light
Job 18: 6 The light is **d** in his tent
Ps 35: 6 Let their way be **d** and
Ps 49: 4 my **d** saying on the harp
Ps 74:20 For the **d** places of the earth
Prov 7: 9 in the black and **d** night
Song 1: 5 I am **d**, but lovely, O
Is 29:15 and their works are in the **d**
Is 45:19 in a **d** place of the earth
Ezek 8:12 house of Israel do in the **d**
Ezek 34:12 on a cloudy and **d** day
Joel 2:10 the sun and moon grow **d**, and
Amos 5: 8 and makes the day **d** as night
Matt 10:27 Whatever I tell you in the **d**
John 6:17 And it was now **d**, and Jesus had
John 20: 1 early, while it was still **d**
2Pe 1:19 that shines in a **d** place,

DARKEN† (*see* DARK, DARKENED, DARKENS)
Amos 8: 9 I will **d** the earth in broad

DARKENED (*see* DARKEN)
Ex 10:15 earth, so that the land was **d**
Ps 69:23 Let their eyes be **d**, so that
Eccl 12: 2 moon and the stars, are not **d**
Is 13:10 the sun will be **d** in its
Matt 24:29 those days the sun will be **d**
Luke 23:45 Then the sun was **d**, and the
Rom 1:21 their foolish hearts were **d**
Rom 11:10 let their eyes be **d**, that
Eph 4:18 having their understanding **d**
Rev 8:12 that a third of them were **d**

DARKENS (*see* DARKEN)
Job 38: 2 Who is this who **d** counsel by

DARKER† (*see* DARK)
Gen 49:12 His eyes are **d** than wine, and

DARKNESS (*see* DARK)
Gen 1: 2 **d** was on the face of the deep
Gen 1: 4 divided the light from the **d**
Gen 1: 5 Day, and the **d** He called Night
Gen 1:18 divide the light from the **d**
Gen 15:12 and great **d** fell upon him
Ex 10:21 **d** which may even be felt
Ex 20:21 the thick **d** where God was
Job 3: 4 May that day be **d**
Job 3: 5 May **d** and the shadow of death
Job 5:14 meet with **d** in the daytime
Job 10:21 not return, to the land of **d**
Job 19: 8 and He has set **d** in my paths
Job 22:13 He judge through the deep **d**
Job 26:10 at the boundary of light and **d**
Job 28: 3 Man puts an end to **d**, and
Job 28: 3 every recess for ore in the **d**
Job 38: 9 thick **d** its swaddling band
Ps 18:28 my God will enlighten my **d**
Ps 82: 5 They walk about in **d**
Ps 88: 6 me in the lowest pit, In **d**
Ps 91: 6 pestilence that walks in **d**
Ps 97: 2 Clouds and **d** surround Him
Ps 112: 4 there arises light in the **d**
Ps 139:12 the **d** shall not hide from You

Ps 139:12 The **d** and the light are both
Prov 2:13 to walk in the ways of **d**
Prov 4:19 way of the wicked is like **d**
Eccl 2:14 head, but the fool walks in **d**
Is 5:20 for light, and light for **d**
Is 9: 2 in **d** have seen a great light
Is 45: 3 give you the treasures of **d**
Is 45: 7 I form the light and create **d**
Is 49: 9 forth,' to those who are in **d**
Is 58:10 light shall dawn in the **d**
Dan 2:22 He knows what is in the **d**
Joel 2: 2 a day of clouds and thick **d**
Joel 2:31 sun shall be turned into **d**
Amos 4:13 is, and makes the morning **d**
Amos 5:18 It will be **d**, and not light
Amos 5:20 Is not the day of the LORD **d**
Mic 7: 8 when I sit in **d**, the LORD
Zeph 1:15 a day of clouds and thick **d**
Matt 4:16 sat in **d** saw a great light
Matt 6:23 whole body will be full of **d**
Matt 6:23 how great is that **d**
Matt 8:12 will be cast out into outer **d**
Matt 27:45 there was **d** over all the land
Luke 22:53 your hour, and the power of **d**
John 1: 5 And the light shines in the **d**
John 1: 5 the **d** did not comprehend it
John 3:19 men loved **d** rather than light
John 8:12 Me shall not walk in **d**, but
Acts 2:20 sun shall be turned into **d**
Acts 26:18 to turn them from **d** to light
Rom 2:19 a light to those who are in **d**
Rom 13:12 us cast off the works of **d**
2Co 4: 6 light to shine out of **d** who
2Co 6:14 communion has light with **d**
Eph 5: 8 For you were once **d**, but now
Eph 5:11 the unfruitful works of **d**
Eph 6:12 rulers of the **d** of this age
Col 1:13 us from the power of **d** and
Heb 12:18 fire, and to blackness and **d**
1Pe 2: 9 of **d** into His marvelous light
2Pe 2: 4 them into chains of **d**, to be
2Pe 2:17 of **d** is reserved forever
1Jn 1: 5 and in Him is no **d** at all
1Jn 1: 6 with Him, and walk in **d**, we
1Jn 2:11 who hates his brother is in **d**
1Jn 2:11 because the **d** has blinded his
Jude 13 the blackness of **d** forever
Rev 16:10 his kingdom became full of **d**

DART† (*see* DARTED, DARTS)
Job 41:26 nor does spear, **d**, or javelin

DARTED† (*see* DART)
Ex 9:23 hail, and fire **d** to the ground

DARTS (*see* DART)
Eph 6:16 the fiery **d** of the wicked one

DASH (*see* DASHED, DASHES)
2Ki 8:12 you will **d** their children, and
Ps 2: 9 You shall **d** them in pieces
Ps 91:12 Lest you **d** your foot against
Matt 4: 6 lest you **d** your foot against

DASHED (*see* DASH)
Ex 15: 6 has **d** the enemy in pieces
Hos 10:14 a mother **d** in pieces upon her
Rev 2:27 they shall be **d** to pieces

DASHES† (*see* DASH)
Ps 137: 9 **d** Your little ones against

DATHAN
Num 16: 1 the son of Levi, with **D** and
Num 16:24 from the tents of Korah, **D**

DAUBED†
Ex 2: 3 **d** it with asphalt and pitch,

DAUGHTER (see DAUGHTER-IN-LAW, DAUGHTER'S,
DAUGHTERS, GRANDDAUGHTER)

Gen	20:12	She is the **d** of my father,
Gen	29: 6	his **d** Rachel is coming with
Gen	34: 5	he had defiled Dinah his **d**
Gen	41:50	the **d** of Poti-Pherah priest
Ex	1:22	every **d** you shall save alive
Ex	2: 5	Then the **d** of Pharaoh came
Ex	2:21	gave Zipporah his **d** to Moses
Ex	20:10	you, nor your son, nor your **d**
Lev	22:12	If the priest's **d** is married
Num	26:59	was Jochebed the **d** of Levi
Num	27: 8	inheritance to pass to his **d**
Judg	11:35	"Alas, my **d**! You have brought
Judg	19:24	Look, here is my virgin **d**
Ruth	2: 2	She said to her, "Go, my **d**."
2Sa	12: 3	and it was like a **d** to him
1Ki	3: 1	Egypt, and married Pharaoh's **d**
2Ki	19:21	the **d** of Zion, has despised
Ps	45:10	Listen, O **d**, Consider and
Ps	45:13	The royal **d** is all glorious
Ps	137: 8	O **d** of Babylon, who are to be
Song	7: 1	feet in sandals, O prince's **d**
Is	10:30	up your voice, O **d** of Gallim
Is	10:32	the mount of the **d** of Zion,
Is	16: 1	the mount of the **d** of Zion,
Is	22: 4	of the **d** of my people
Is	47: 1	dust, O virgin **d** of Babylon
Jer	14:17	for the virgin **d** of my people
Lam	2:13	you, O virgin **d** of Zion
Ezek	16:44	Like mother, like **d**
Ezek	26: 6	Also her **d** villages which
Hos	1: 3	took Gomer the **d** of Diblaim
Hos	1: 6	conceived again and bore a **d**
Mic	5: 1	in troops, O **d** of troops
Mic	7: 6	**d** rises against her mother,
Zeph	3:10	the **d** of My dispersed ones,
Zech	9: 9	Rejoice greatly, O **d** of Zion
Zech	9: 9	Shout, O **d** of Jerusalem
Mal	2:11	the **d** of a foreign god
Matt	9:18	My **d** has just died, but come
Matt	9:22	Be of good cheer, **d**
Matt	10:35	a **d** against her mother, and a
Matt	10:37	he who loves son or **d** more
Matt	14: 6	the **d** of Herodias danced
Matt	15:28	her **d** was healed from that
Matt	21: 5	Tell the **d** of Zion, 'Behold,
Mark	5:34	**D**, your faith has made you
Mark	7:26	cast the demon out of her **d**
Luke	8:42	for he had an only **d** about
Luke	12:53	father, mother against **d** and
Luke	13:16	being a **d** of Abraham, whom
John	12:15	Fear not, **d** of Zion
Acts	7:21	Pharaoh's **d** took him away and
Heb	11:24	called the son of Pharaoh's **d**

DAUGHTER-IN-LAW (see DAUGHTER, DAUGHTERS-IN-
LAW)

Gen	11:31	his **d** Sarai, his son Abram's
Gen	38:11	Judah said to Tamar his **d**
Lev	20:12	If a man lies with his **d**
Ruth	2:20	Then Naomi said to her **d**
Ezek	22:11	another lewdly defiles is **d**
Mic	7: 6	**d** against her mother-in-law

DAUGHTER'S (see DAUGHTER)

Lev	18:10	daughter of your **d** daughter
Deut	22:17	evidences of my **d** virginity

DAUGHTERS (see DAUGHTER)

Gen	5: 4	and he begot sons and **d**
Gen	6: 1	and **d** were born to them,
Gen	6: 2	sons of God saw the **d** of men
Gen	19: 8	I have two **d** who have not
Gen	19:12	Son-in-law, your sons, your **d**
Gen	19:14	who had married his **d**, and

Gen	19:36	Thus both the **d** of Lot were
Gen	24: 3	from the **d** of the Canaanites
Gen	24:13	the **d** of the men of the city
Gen	28: 2	the **d** of Laban your mother's
Gen	29:16	Now Laban had two **d**
Gen	31:28	me to kiss my sons and my **d**
Gen	31:41	fourteen years for your two **d**
Gen	31:55	and kissed his sons and **d** and
Gen	37:35	all his **d** arose to comfort
Gen	46: 7	and his sons' **d**, and all his
Ex	21: 9	according to the customs of **d**
Num	27: 1	Then came the **d** of Zelophehad
Deut	12:31	**d** in the fire to their gods
Judg	3: 6	gave their **d** to their sons
Judg	14: 1	of the **d** of the Philistines
Ruth	1:12	Turn back, my **d**, go your way
1Sa	8:13	take your **d** to be perfumers
2Sa	5:13	sons and **d** were born to David
2Sa	13:18	virgin **d** wore such apparel
Ezra	9:12	do not give your **d** as wives
Neh	10:30	nor take their **d** for our sons
Job	1: 2	and three **d** were born to him
Job	42:13	had seven sons and three **d**
Job	42:15	so beautiful as the **d** of Job
Ps	45: 9	Kings' **d** are among Your
Ps	48:11	Let the **d** of Judah be glad,
Ps	106:37	sons And their **d** to demons,
Ps	106:38	the blood of their sons and **d**
Ps	144:12	That our **d** may be as pillars,
Prov	30:15	The leech has two **d**, crying,
Prov	31:29	Many **d** have done well, but
Eccl	12: 4	and all the **d** of music are
Song	1: 5	O **d** of Jerusalem, like the
Is	3:16	Because the **d** of Zion are
Is	32: 9	you complacent **d**, give ear to
Is	49:22	your **d** shall be carried on
Is	56: 5	better than that of sons and **d**
Jer	9:20	teach your **d** wailing, and
Jer	11:22	their **d** shall die by famine
Jer	16: 2	have sons or **d** in this place
Jer	19: 9	sons and the flesh of their **d**
Lam	3:51	of all the **d** of my city
Ezek	13:17	against the **d** of your people
Ezek	14:16	deliver neither sons nor **d**
Ezek	14:18	deliver neither sons nor **d**
Ezek	16:46	of you, is Sodom and her **d**
Ezek	23: 2	women, the **d** of one mother
Ezek	30:18	her **d** shall go into captivity
Ezek	32:16	the **d** of the nations shall
Hos	4:13	Therefore your **d** commit
Joel	2:28	your **d** shall prophesy, your
Luke	1: 5	wife was of the **d** of Aaron
Luke	23:28	D of Jerusalem, do not weep
Acts	2:17	your **d** shall prophesy, your
Acts	21: 9	four virgin **d** who prophesied
2Co	6:18	and you shall be My sons and **d**
1Pe	3: 6	whose **d** you are if you do

DAUGHTERS-IN-LAW (see DAUGHTER-IN-LAW)

Ruth	1: 8	And Naomi said to her two **d**

DAVID (see DAVID'S)

Ruth	4:17	of Jesse, the father of D
1Sa	16:13	upon D from that day forward
1Sa	16:23	that D would take a harp and
1Sa	17:14	D was the youngest
1Sa	17:38	Saul clothed D with his armor
1Sa	17:43	So the Philistine said to D
1Sa	17:43	cursed D by his gods
1Sa	17:50	So D prevailed over the
1Sa	17:54	And D took the head of the
1Sa	18: 1	was knit to the soul of D
1Sa	18: 3	D made a covenant, because he
1Sa	18: 7	and D his ten thousands
1Sa	18: 9	So Saul eyed D from that day
1Sa	18:10	So D played music with his

1Sa	18:11	I will pin D to the wall with
1Sa	18:11	But D escaped his presence
1Sa	18:12	Now Saul was afraid of D,
1Sa	18:14	D behaved wisely in all his
1Sa	18:16	all Israel and Judah loved D
1Sa	18:20	Saul's daughter, loved D
1Sa	18:27	D brought their foreskins, and
1Sa	18:28	knew that the LORD was with D
1Sa	19: 2	So Jonathan told D, saying
1Sa	19:12	So Michal let D down through
1Sa	20: 3	Then D took an oath again, and
1Sa	20:16	covenant with the house of D
1Sa	20:41	wept together, but D more so
1Sa	21:11	Is this not D the king of the
1Sa	22: 4	that D was in the stronghold
1Sa	23: 4	Then D inquired of the LORD
1Sa	23:15	D was in the Wilderness of
1Sa	23:28	Saul returned from pursuing D
1Sa	24: 7	So D restrained his servants
1Sa	24:16	Is this your voice, my son D
1Sa	24:22	So D swore to Saul
1Sa	25:23	Now when Abigail saw D, she
1Sa	25:39	So when D heard that Nabal
1Sa	25:40	when the servants of D had
1Sa	25:42	followed the messengers of D
1Sa	26: 4	D therefore sent out spies,
1Sa	26:12	So D took the spear and the
1Sa	26:25	May you be blessed, my son D
1Sa	27:12	So Achish believed D, saying,
1Sa	29: 2	and by thousands, but D and his
1Sa	29: 3	Is this not D, the servant of
1Sa	30:18	and D rescued his two wives
2Sa	1:17	Then D lamented with this
2Sa	2: 4	there they anointed D king
2Sa	2:10	the house of Judah followed D
2Sa	3: 1	But D grew stronger and
2Sa	3: 2	Sons were born to D in Hebron
2Sa	3:10	the throne of D over Israel
2Sa	5: 3	King D made a covenant with
2Sa	5: 3	they anointed D king over
2Sa	5: 4	D was thirty years old when
2Sa	5: 7	Zion (that is, the City of D)
2Sa	5:13	D took more concubines and
2Sa	5:17	anointed D king over Israel
2Sa	6:10	So D would not move the ark
2Sa	6:14	Then D danced before the LORD
2Sa	6:14	D was wearing a linen ephod
2Sa	6:16	window and saw King D leaping
2Sa	7: 5	Go and tell My servant D
2Sa	8: 4	Also D hamstrung all the
2Sa	8:11	King D dedicated these to the
2Sa	9: 6	Then D said, "Mephibosheth
2Sa	11: 1	But D remained at Jerusalem
2Sa	11: 2	that D arose from his bed
2Sa	11: 6	And Joab sent Uriah to D
2Sa	12: 1	the LORD sent Nathan to D
2Sa	12:16	D therefore pleaded with God
2Sa	12:16	D fasted and went in and lay
2Sa	12:24	Then D comforted Bathsheba
2Sa	13: 1	Amnon the son of D loved her
2Sa	13:37	D mourned for his son every
2Sa	13:39	And King D longed to go to
2Sa	16: 6	And he threw stones at D and at
2Sa	16:10	has said to him, "Curse D
2Sa	18: 1	D numbered the people who
2Sa	18: 9	Absalom met the servants of D
2Sa	19:11	Then King D sent to Zadok and
2Sa	20: 1	We have no part in D, nor do
2Sa	20:26	was a chief minister under D
2Sa	21:12	Then D went and took the bones
2Sa	21:15	and D grew faint
2Sa	21:17	the men of D swore to him
2Sa	21:22	and fell by the hand of D
2Sa	22:51	mercy to His anointed, to D
2Sa	23: 1	these are the last words of D

2Sa	24:24	So D bought the threshing
2Sa	24:25	D built there an altar to the
1Ki	1: 1	Now King D was old, advanced
1Ki	1:31	my lord King D live forever
1Ki	1:37	the throne of my lord King D
1Ki	2: 1	Then the days of D drew near
1Ki	2:10	So D rested with his fathers,
1Ki	2:10	was buried in the City of D
1Ki	2:33	But upon D and his descendants
1Ki	2:45	and the throne of D shall be
1Ki	3: 3	the statutes of his father D
1Ki	3: 6	to your servant D my father
1Ki	3: 7	king instead of my father D
1Ki	3:14	as your father D walked,
1Ki	5: 1	for Hiram had always loved D
1Ki	5: 7	for He has given D a wise son
1Ki	8:16	but I chose D to be over My
1Ki	8:24	Your servant D my father
1Ki	8:25	Your servant D my father
1Ki	11:21	D rested with his fathers
1Ki	12:16	What portion have we in D
1Ki	12:16	see to your own house, O D
1Ki	14: 8	have not been as My servant D
1Ki	15: 5	because D did what was right
1Ki	15:11	the LORD, as did his father D
2Ki	14: 3	yet not like his father D
1Ch	9:22	D and Samuel the seer had
1Ch	11:10	of the mighty men whom D had
1Ch	11:11	of the mighty men whom D had
1Ch	13:12	D was afraid of God that day,
1Ch	18: 3	D defeated Hadadezer king of
1Ch	19:19	they made peace with D and
1Ch	21: 1	and moved D to number Israel
1Ch	21:25	So D gave Ornan six hundred
1Ch	22: 4	brought much cedar wood to D
1Ch	22: 5	Now D said, "Solomon my son
1Ch	27:24	of the chronicles of King D
1Ch	29:29	Now the acts of King D, first
2Ch	6:42	the mercies of Your servant D
2Ch	7: 6	whenever D offered praise
2Ch	8:14	for so D the man of God had
2Ch	29:26	with the instruments of D
2Ch	32:33	upper tombs of the sons of D
Neh	3:16	in front of the tombs of D
Neh	12:24	of D the man of God
Neh	12:36	of D the man of God
Neh	12:37	the stairs of the City of D
Neh	12:37	wall, beyond the house of D
Neh	12:46	For in the days of D and Asaph
Ps	18:50	mercy to His anointed, To D
Ps	72:20	The prayers of D the son of
Ps	89:49	You swore to D in Your truth
Ps	122: 5	The thrones of the house of D
Ps	132: 1	Lord, remember D And all his
Ps	132:17	will make the horn of D grow
Prov	1: 1	of Solomon the son of D, king
Eccl	1: 1	of the Preacher, the son of D
Song	4: 4	neck is like the tower of D
Is	7:13	Hear now, O house of D
Is	9: 7	no end, upon the throne of D
Is	16: 5	truth, in the tabernacle of D
Is	22:22	The key of the house of D I
Is	29: 1	Ariel, the city where D dwelt
Is	55: 3	the sure mercies of D
Jer	21:12	O house of D!
Jer	22: 2	who sit on the throne of D
Jer	22: 4	who sit on the throne of D
Jer	23: 5	That I will raise to D a
Jer	33:15	D a Branch of righteousness
Jer	33:17	D shall never lack a man to
Ezek	34:23	shall feed them—My servant D
Hos	3: 5	D their king, and fear the
Amos	6: 5	musical instruments like D
Amos	9:11	raise up The tabernacle of D
Zech	12:10	I will pour on the house of D

Matt	1: 1	of Jesus Christ, the Son of D
Matt	1: 6	and Jesse begot D the king
Matt	1: 6	D the king begot Solomon by
Matt	1:17	to D are fourteen generations
Matt	1:20	Joseph, son of D, do not be
Matt	9:27	Son of D, have mercy on us
Matt	12: 3	what D did when he was hungry
Matt	20:30	mercy on us, O Lord, Son of D
Matt	20:31	mercy on us, O Lord, Son of D
Matt	21: 9	Hosanna to the Son of D
Matt	21:15	Hosanna to the Son of D
Matt	22:43	How then does D in the Spirit
Matt	22:45	If D then calls Him 'Lord,'
Mark	12:35	the Christ is the Son of D
Luke	1:27	was Joseph, of the house of D
Luke	1:32	the throne of His father D
Luke	2: 4	into Judea, to the city of D
Luke	2: 4	of the house and lineage of D
Luke	2:11	day in the city of D a Savior
Luke	20:41	the Christ is the Son of D?
John	7:42	comes from the seed of D and
John	7:42	of Bethlehem, where D was
Acts	1:16	mouth of D concerning Judas
Acts	2:29	to you of the patriarch D
Acts	13:34	you the sure mercies of D
Acts	15:16	of D which has fallen down
Rom	1: 3	of D according to the flesh
Rom	11: 9	And D says: "Let their table
2Ti	2: 8	Christ, of the seed of D, was
Heb	4: 7	a certain day, saying in D
Heb	11:32	Samson and Jephthah, also of D
Rev	3: 7	He who has the key of D, He
Rev	5: 5	tribe of Judah, the Root of D
Rev	22:16	Root and the Offspring of D

DAVID'S (see DAVID)

1Sa	19:11	D wife, told him, saying,
1Sa	30: 5	And D two wives, Ahinoam the
2Sa	5: 8	who are hated by D soul)
1Ki	1:38	Solomon ride on King D mule
2Ki	19:34	sake and for My servant D sake
1Ch	27:32	D uncle, was a counselor, a
Ps	132:10	For Your servant D sake, Do
Jer	13:13	the kings who sit on D throne

DAWN (see DAWNED, DAWNING, DAWNS)

Job	7: 4	had my fill of tossing till d
Job	38:12	and caused the d to know its
Ps	46: 5	her, just at the break of d
Ps	57: 8	I will awaken the d
Is	58:10	light shall d in the darkness
Matt	28: 1	day of the week began to d

DAWNED (see DAWN)

Gen	19:15	When the morning d, the
Matt	4:16	shadow of death light has d

DAWNING (see DAWN)

Josh	6:15	about the d of the day, and
Judg	19:26	woman came as the day was d
Ps	119:147	before the d of the morning
Is	24:15	the LORD in the d light, the

DAWNS† (see DAWN)

2Pe	1:19	a dark place, until the day d

DAY (see DAYBREAK, DAYLIGHT, DAY'S, DAYS, DAYSPRING, DAYTIME)

Gen	1: 5	God called the light D, and
Gen	1: 5	the morning were the first d
Gen	1:16	greater light to rule the d
Gen	2: 2	on the seventh God ended
Gen	2: 2	He rested on the seventh d
Gen	2: 3	God blessed the seventh d
Gen	2:17	for in the d that you eat of
Gen	3: 8	garden in the cool of the d
Gen	8:22	and winter and summer, and d
Gen	18: 1	door in the heat of the d

Gen	27: 2	do not know the d of my death
Gen	32:24	him until the breaking of d
Gen	35: 3	me in the d of my distress
Gen	39:10	she spoke to Joseph d by day
Ex	10:13	wind on the land all that d
Ex	10:28	For in the d you see my face
Ex	12:14	So this d shall be to you a
Ex	12:15	first d until the seventh d
Ex	12:17	you shall observe this d
Ex	13: 3	Remember this d in which you
Ex	13: 8	shall tell your son in that d
Ex	13:21	by d in a pillar of cloud to
Ex	16:29	sixth d bread for two days
Ex	20: 8	Remember the Sabbath d, to
Ex	20:11	them, and rested the seventh d
Ex	20:11	LORD blessed the Sabbath d
Ex	31:15	any work on the Sabbath d
Ex	35: 2	seventh d shall be a holy d
Lev	23:16	Count fifty days to the d
Lev	23:27	shall be the D of Atonement
Num	11:32	people stayed up all that d
Num	15:32	sticks on the Sabbath d
Deut	1:33	by night and in the cloud by d
Deut	2:18	This d you are to cross over
Deut	5:12	Observe the Sabbath d, to
Deut	6:24	us alive, as it is this d
Deut	16: 4	first d at twilight remain
Deut	28:66	you shall fear d and night, and
Deut	29: 4	ears to hear, to this very d
Deut	31:22	wrote this song the same d
Deut	32:35	for the d of their calamity
Deut	33:12	shelters him all the d long
Deut	34: 6	one knows his grave to this d
Josh	1: 8	you shall meditate in it d
Josh	7:26	the Valley of Achor to this d
Josh	10:13	go down for about a whole d
Josh	10:14	there has been no d like that
Josh	22:16	rebel this d against the LORD
Josh	24:15	this d whom you will serve
Judg	4:23	So on that d God subdued
Judg	11:27	Judge, render judgment this d
Judg	13: 7	womb to the d of his death
Judg	18:30	the d of the captivity of the
Judg	19:25	when the d began to break,
Judg	19:26	came as the d was dawning
Judg	20:26	fasted that d until evening
Ruth	3:18	concluded the matter this d
Ruth	4: 5	On the d you buy the field
Ruth	4: 9	You are witnesses this d
Ruth	4:10	You are witnesses this d
Ruth	4:14	this d without a near kinsman
1Sa	9:24	Saul ate with Samuel that d
1Sa	11:11	until the heat of the d
1Sa	12: 2	from my childhood to this d
1Sa	13:22	on the d of battle, that
1Sa	14:23	the LORD saved Israel that d
1Sa	15:35	Saul until the d of his death
1Sa	16:13	David from that d forward
1Sa	17:46	This d the LORD will deliver
1Sa	21:10	fled that d from before Saul,
1Sa	23:14	Saul sought him every d, but
1Sa	25: 8	for we come on a feast d
1Sa	28:20	no food all d or all night
2Sa	3:35	eat food while it was still d
2Sa	3:38	has fallen this d in Israel
2Sa	6:23	to the d of her death
2Sa	13:37	mourned for his son every d
2Sa	19: 2	So the victory that d was
2Sa	23:20	midst of a pit on a snowy d
1Ki	5: 7	Blessed be the LORD this d
1Ki	8:29	toward this temple night and d
1Ki	20:29	d the battle was joined
2Ki	2:22	remains healed to this d,
2Ki	4: 8	Now it happened one d that
2Ki	10:27	it a refuse dump to this d

2Ki	17:23	Assyria, as it is to this **d**
2Ki	19: 3	This **d** is a day of trouble,
1Ch	16:23	His salvation from **d** to **d**
1Ch	29:22	with great gladness on that **d**
2Ch	8:14	the duty of each **d** required
2Ch	30:21	praised the LORD **d** by **d**
Ezra	9: 7	humiliation, as it is this **d**
Neh	4: 2	Will they complete it in a **d**
Neh	8:11	Be still, for the **d** is holy
Neh	10:31	to sell on the Sabbath **d**, we
Neh	13:17	you profane the Sabbath **d**
Neh	13:22	to sanctify the Sabbath **d**
Esth	9:17	made it a **d** of feasting and
Job	3: 1	cursed the **d** of his birth
Job	3: 3	May the **d** perish on which I
Job	3: 8	curse it who curse the **d**,
Job	9:19	will appoint my **d** in court
Job	20:28	away in the **d** of His wrath
Job	21:30	reserved for the **d** of doom
Ps	1: 2	And in His law he meditates **d**
Ps	7:11	angry with the wicked every **d**
Ps	18:18	me in the **d** of my calamity
Ps	19: 2	**D** unto day utters speech
Ps	20: 1	I you in the **d** of trouble
Ps	25: 5	On You I wait all the **d**
Ps	32: 3	my groaning all the **d** long
Ps	32: 4	For **d** and night Your hand was
Ps	35:28	of Your praise all the **d** long
Ps	44:22	sake we are killed all **d** long
Ps	50:15	upon Me in the **d** of trouble
Ps	56: 5	All **d** they twist my words
Ps	59:16	refuge in the **d** of my trouble
Ps	71:15	And Your salvation all the **d**
Ps	74:16	The **d** is Yours, the night
Ps	78:42	The **d** when He redeemed them
Ps	81: 3	moon, on our solemn feast **d**
Ps	84:10	For a **d** in Your courts is
Ps	86: 7	In the **d** of my trouble I will
Ps	91: 5	of the arrow that flies by **d**
Ps	95: 8	as in the **d** of trial in the
Ps	96: 2	salvation from **d** to day
Ps	110: 3	In the **d** of Your power
Ps	118:24	This is the **d** which the LORD
Ps	119:164	Seven times a **d** I praise You
Ps	121: 6	sun shall not strike you by **d**
Ps	136: 8	The sun to rule by **d**, For His
Ps	145: 2	Every **d** I will bless You, And
Prov	4:18	brighter unto the perfect **d**
Prov	6:34	spare in the **d** of vengeance
Prov	11: 4	not profit in the **d** of wrath
Prov	16: 4	the wicked for the **d** of doom
Prov	24:10	faint in the **d** of adversity
Prov	27: 1	know what a **d** may bring forth
Prov	27:15	dripping on a very rainy **d**
Eccl	7: 1	than the **d** of one's birth
Eccl	12: 3	in the **d** when the keepers of
Song	2:17	Until the **d** breaks and the
Song	8: 8	the **d** when she is spoken for
Is	2:11	shall be exalted in that **d**
Is	2:12	For the **d** of the LORD of
Is	4: 5	a cloud and smoke by **d** and the
Is	7:18	**d** that the LORD will whistle
Is	9: 4	as in the **d** of Midian
Is	13:13	in the **d** of His fierce anger
Is	19:16	In that **d** Egypt will be like
Is	19:24	In that **d** Israel will be one
Is	28:24	keep plowing all **d** to sow
Is	29:18	In that **d** the deaf shall hear
Is	34:10	not be quenched night or **d**
Is	37: 3	This **d** is a day of trouble
Is	43:13	Indeed before the **d** was, I am
Is	49: 8	in the **d** of salvation I have
Is	58: 3	in the **d** of your fast you
Is	58: 5	an acceptable **d** to the LORD
Is	58:13	your pleasure on My holy **d**
Is	60:19	no longer be your light by **d**
Is	61: 2	the **d** of vengeance of our God
Is	65: 2	stretched out My hands all **d**
Jer	1:10	I have this **d** set you over
Jer	1:18	you this **d** a fortified city
Jer	9: 1	of tears, that I might weep **d**
Jer	16:19	refuge in the **d** of affliction
Jer	17:17	are my hope in the **d** of doom
Jer	17:22	but hallow the Sabbath **d**
Jer	17:24	but hallow the Sabbath **d**
Jer	20:14	Cursed be the **d** in which I
Jer	31:35	the sun for a light by **d**, and
Jer	33:20	break My covenant with the **d**
Jer	35:14	for to this **d** they drink none
Jer	36:30	cast out to the heat of the **d**
Jer	44: 2	this **d** they are a desolation,
Jer	46:10	a **d** of vengeance, that He may
Jer	51: 2	For in the **d** of doom they
Jer	52:34	a portion for each **d**
Lam	1:12	in the **d** of His fierce anger
Lam	1:13	desolate and faint all the **d**
Lam	2: 7	as on the **d** of a set feast
Lam	2:16	is the **d** we have waited for
Lam	2:18	tears run down like a river **d**
Ezek	1:28	in a cloud on a rainy **d**, so
Ezek	4: 6	laid on you a **d** for each year
Ezek	7:19	**d** of the wrath of the LORD
Ezek	22:24	on in the **d** of indignation
Ezek	24:27	on that **d** your mouth will be
Ezek	30: 3	even the **d** of the LORD is
Ezek	30: 3	it will be a **d** of clouds, the
Ezek	34:12	on a cloudy and dark **d**
Dan	6:10	his knees three times that **d**
Dan	6:13	his petition three times a **d**
Hos	1: 5	**d** that I will break the bow
Hos	2: 3	as in the **d** she was born, and
Hos	2:21	in that **d** that I will answer
Hos	6: 2	on the third **d** He will raise
Joel	1:15	Alas for the **d**
Joel	1:15	For the **d** of the LORD is at
Joel	2: 2	a **d** of darkness and gloominess
Joel	2: 2	a **d** of clouds and thick
Joel	2:31	and terrible **d** of the LORD
Amos	1:14	in the **d** of the whirlwind
Amos	2:16	shall flee naked in that **d**
Amos	5:18	who desire the **d** of the LORD
Amos	6: 3	who put far off the **d** of doom
Jon	4: 7	next **d** God prepared a worm
Mic	2: 4	In that **d** one shall take up a
Nah	2: 3	in the **d** of his preparation
Nah	3:17	in the hedges on a cold **d**
Zeph	1:14	The great **d** of the LORD is
Zeph	1:15	That **d** is a day of wrath,
Zeph	1:15	a **d** of trouble and distress
Zeph	1:15	a **d** of darkness and gloominess
Hag	2:15	consider from this **d** forward
Zech	3: 9	of that land in one **d**
Zech	4:10	the **d** of small things
Zech	13: 1	In that **d** a fountain shall be
Zech	14: 1	the **d** of the LORD is coming.
Zech	14: 4	in that **d** His feet will stand
Zech	14: 7	neither **d** nor night
Zech	14:20	In that **d** "HOLINESS TO THE
Mal	3: 2	endure the **d** of His coming
Mal	4: 1	the **d** is coming, burning like
Mal	4: 5	and dreadful **d** of the LORD
Matt	6:11	Give us this **d** our daily
Matt	7:22	Many will say to Me in that **d**
Matt	11:24	**d** of judgment than for you
Matt	16:21	be raised again the third **d**
Matt	20: 2	laborers for a denarius a **d**
Matt	24:36	But of that **d** and hour no one
Matt	24:38	until the **d** that Noah entered
Matt	25:13	for you know neither the **d**
Matt	26:29	**d** when I drink it new with

Matt	27:62	followed the D of Preparation
Matt	27:64	made secure until the third d
Matt	28: 1	as the first d of the week
Matt	28:15	among the Jews until this d
Mark	6:21	Then an opportune d came
Mark	6:35	when the d was now far spent,
Mark	14:25	of the vine until that d when
Luke	1:59	so it was, on the eighth d
Luke	1:80	the d of his manifestation to
Luke	2:11	this d in the city of David a
Luke	4:16	synagogue on the Sabbath d
Luke	9:12	When the d began to wear away
Luke	10:12	D for Sodom than for that
Luke	11: 3	Give us d by day our daily
Luke	14: 5	pull him out on the Sabbath d
Luke	16:19	and fared sumptuously every d
Luke	17:29	but on the d that Lot went
Luke	18: 7	His own elect who cry out d
Luke	18:33	And the third d He will rise
Luke	22: 7	Then came the D of Unleavened
Luke	23:12	That very d Pilate and Herod
Luke	24:13	were traveling that same d to
Luke	24:21	today is the third d since
Luke	24:46	from the dead the third d
John	1:29	The next d John saw Jesus
John	6:39	raise it up at the last d
John	6:40	raise him up at the last d
John	6:54	raise him up at the last d
John	8:56	Abraham rejoiced to see My d
John	9: 4	Him who sent Me while it is d
John	11:24	resurrection at the last d
John	12: 7	this for the d of My burial
John	19:31	that Sabbath was a high d)
John	20: 1	On the first d of the week
John	20:19	the same d at evening
John	20:19	being the first d of the week
Acts	1: 2	until the d in which He was
Acts	2: 1	Now when the D of Pentecost
Acts	2:15	only the third hour of the d
Acts	2:20	and notable d of the LORD
Acts	2:29	his tomb is with us to this d
Acts	2:41	that d about three thousand
Acts	4: 9	If we this d are judged for a
Acts	10: 3	d he saw clearly in a vision
Acts	10:40	God raised up on the third d
Acts	13:14	synagogue on the Sabbath d
Acts	17:31	d on which He will judge the
Acts	20: 7	on the first d of the week
Acts	20:31	night and d with tears
Acts	24:21	am being judged by you this d
Acts	26: 7	serving God night and d, hope
Rom	2: 5	wrath in the d of wrath and
Rom	2:16	in the d when God will judge
Rom	8:36	sake we are killed all d long
Rom	10:21	All d long I have stretched
Rom	13:12	far spent, the d is at hand
Rom	13:13	us walk properly, as in the d
Rom	14: 5	another esteems every d alike
1Co	1: 8	d of our Lord Jesus Christ
1Co	3:13	for the D will declare it,
1Co	16: 2	On the first d of the week
2Co	1:14	in the d of the Lord Jesus
2Co	4:16	is being renewed day by day
2Co	6: 2	now is the d of salvation
2Co	11:25	a d I have been in the deep
Eph	4:30	for the d of redemption
Eph	6:13	to withstand in the evil d
Phil	1: 5	from the first d until now
Phil	3: 5	circumcised the eighth d, of
Col	1: 6	you since the d you heard
1Th	2: 9	for laboring night and d, that
1Th	3:10	d praying exceedingly that we
1Th	5: 5	of light and sons of the d
1Th	5: 8	us who are of the d be sober
2Th	1:10	when He comes, in that D, to

2Th	3: 8	with labor and toil night and d
2Ti	1:12	committed to Him until that D
2Ti	1:18	mercy from the Lord in that D
2Ti	4: 8	will give to me on that D
Heb	3: 8	in the d of trial in the
Heb	10:25	as you see the D approaching
Jas	5: 5	hearts as in a d of slaughter
1Pe	2:12	God in the d of visitation
2Pe	1:19	dark place, until the d dawns
2Pe	3: 7	fire until the d of judgment
2Pe	3: 8	one d is as a thousand years
1Jn	4:17	boldness in the d of judgment
Jude	6	the judgment of the great d
Rev	1:10	in the Spirit on the Lord's D
Rev	4: 8	they do not rest d or night
Rev	6:17	For the great d of His wrath
Rev	7:15	throne of God, and serve Him d
Rev	8:12	third of the d did not shine
Rev	9:15	prepared for the hour and d
Rev	16:14	that great d of God Almighty
Rev	20:10	And they will be tormented d
Rev	21:25	by d (there shall be no night)

DAYBREAK (see DAY)

2Sa	2:32	and they came to Hebron at d
Neh	4:21	d until the stars appeared

DAYLIGHT† (see DAY)

Judg	16: 2	In the morning, when it is d
Amos	8: 9	darken the earth in broad d
Mark	1:35	risen a long while before d

DAY'S (see DAY)

Num	11:31	about a d journey on this
1Ch	16:37	as every d work required
Jon	3: 4	the city on the first d walk
Acts	1:12	a Sabbath d journey

DAYS (see DAY, DAYS')

Gen	1:14	signs and seasons, and for d
Gen	3:14	dust all the d of your life
Gen	6: 4	on the earth in those d, and
Gen	7: 4	For after seven more d I will
Gen	7: 4	to rain on the earth forty d
Gen	8:10	he waited yet another seven d
Gen	8:12	he waited yet another seven d
Gen	17:12	He who is eight d old among
Gen	21: 4	Isaac when he was eight d old
Gen	29:20	they seemed but a few d to
Gen	35:29	being old and full of d
Gen	37:34	and mourned for his son many d
Gen	47: 9	evil have been the d of the
Gen	49: 1	befall you in the last d
Gen	50: 3	mourned for him seventy d
Ex	12:19	For seven d no leaven shall
Ex	20: 9	Six d you shall labor and do
Ex	20:11	For in six d the LORD made
Ex	20:12	that your d may be long upon
Ex	23:15	eat unleavened bread seven d
Ex	24:18	was on the mountain forty d
Lev	12: 2	she shall be unclean seven d
Lev	12: 4	the d of her purification are
Lev	23:16	Count fifty d to the day
Lev	23:42	dwell in booths for seven d
Num	6: 4	All the d of his separation
Num	6: 5	All the d of the vow of his
Num	14:34	spied out the land, forty d
Num	24:14	your people in the latter d
Deut	4: 9	heart all the d of your life
Deut	9:25	forty d and forty nights I
Deut	16: 3	Egypt all the d of your life
Deut	16:13	Feast of Tabernacles seven d
Deut	17:19	read it all the d of his life
Deut	17:20	prolong his d in his kingdom
Deut	32: 7	Remember the d of old,
Deut	33:25	as your d, so shall your
Josh	20: 6	who is high priest in those d

Judg	17: 6	In those **d** there was no king
Judg	18: 1	In those **d** there was no king
Judg	21:25	In those **d** there was no king
Ruth	1: 1	in the **d** when the judges
1Sa	3: 1	the LORD was rare in those **d**
1Ki	4:21	Solomon all the **d** of his life
1Ki	15:14	loyal to the LORD all his **d**
1Ki	19: 8	strength of that food forty **d**
2Ki	20: 1	In those **d** Hezekiah was sick
2Ki	20: 6	add to your **d** fifteen years
2Ki	23:22	**d** of the judges who judged
1Ch	5:17	by genealogies in the **d** of
1Ch	23: 1	David was old and full of **d**
1Ch	29:15	our **d** on earth are as a
2Ch	10: 5	Come back to me after three **d**
2Ch	35:17	Unleavened Bread for seven **d**
Ezra	6:22	Bread seven **d** with joy
Ezra	10:13	this the work of one or two **d**
Neh	1: 4	wept, and mourned for many **d**
Esth	9:26	So they called these **d** Purim
Esth	9:27	these two **d** every year,
Job	2:13	him on the ground seven **d**
Job	7: 1	like the **d** of a hired man
Job	7: 6	My **d** are swifter than a
Job	7:16	for my **d** are but a breath
Job	8: 9	because our **d** on earth are a
Job	10:20	Are not my **d** few
Job	14: 1	is born of woman is of few **d**
Job	14: 5	Since his **d** are determined,
Job	14:14	All the **d** of my hard service
Job	15:20	writhes with pain all his **d**
Job	17: 1	my **d** are extinguished, the
Job	17:11	My **d** are past, my purposes
Job	29: 4	as I was in the **d** of my prime
Job	29:18	and multiply my **d** as the sand
Job	30:16	the **d** of affliction take hold
Job	33:25	return to the **d** of his youth
Job	36:11	spend their **d** in prosperity
Job	38:21	the number of your **d** is great
Job	42:12	latter **d** of Job more than his
Job	42:17	So Job died, old and full of **d**
Ps	21: 4	Length of **d** forever and ever
Ps	23: 6	me All the **d** of my life
Ps	27: 4	the LORD All the **d** of my life
Ps	34:12	desires life, And loves many **d**
Ps	37:18	knows the **d** of the upright
Ps	39: 4	what is the measure of my **d**
Ps	44: 1	What deeds You did in their **d**
Ps	44: 1	in their days, In **d** of old
Ps	49: 5	I fear in the **d** of evil, When
Ps	55:23	not live out half their **d**
Ps	72: 7	In His **d** the righteous shall
Ps	77: 5	have considered the **d** of old
Ps	90:10	The **d** of our lives are
Ps	90:12	So teach us to number our **d**
Ps	90:14	rejoice and be glad all our **d**
Ps	102: 3	For my **d** are consumed like
Ps	102:11	My **d** are like a shadow that
Ps	102:23	He shortened my **d**
Ps	102:24	me away in the midst of my **d**
Ps	103:15	for man, his **d** are like grass
Ps	139:16	The **d** fashioned for me, When
Ps	143: 5	I remember the **d** of old
Prov	3: 2	for length of **d** and long life
Prov	10:27	fear of the LORD prolongs **d**
Prov	19:20	may be wise in your latter **d**
Prov	31:12	evil all the **d** of her life
Eccl	2: 3	all the **d** of their lives
Eccl	2:16	be forgotten in the **d** to come
Eccl	5:18	**d** of his life which God gives
Eccl	6:12	all the **d** of his vain life
Eccl	7:10	former **d** better than these
Eccl	7:15	all things in my **d** of vanity
Eccl	11: 8	remember the **d** of darkness
Eccl	12: 1	in the **d** of your youth,

Eccl	12: 1	before the difficult **d** come
Is	23: 7	antiquity is from ancient **d**
Is	39: 6	the **d** are coming when all
Is	39: 8	be peace and truth in my **d**
Is	53:10	seed, He shall prolong His **d**
Is	63: 9	carried them all the **d** of old
Is	65:22	for as the **d** of a tree, so
Jer	2:32	forgotten Me **d** without number
Jer	7:32	the **d** are coming," says the
Jer	9:25	the **d** are coming," says the
Jer	23: 6	In His **d** Judah will be saved,
Jer	31:31	the **d** are coming," says the
Jer	52:33	king all the **d** of his life
Lam	5:21	renew our **d** as of old,
Ezek	3:15	astonished among them seven **d**
Ezek	16:22	remember the **d** of your youth
Ezel	16:43	remember the **d** of your youth
Ezek	16:56	mouth in the **d** of your pride
Ezek	36:38	at Jerusalem on its feast **d**
Dan	1:12	test your servants for ten **d**
Dan	2:28	what will be in the latter **d**
Dan	5:11	And in the **d** of your father,
Dan	6: 7	any god or man for thirty **d**
Dan	6:10	was his custom since early **d**
Dan	7: 9	the Ancient of **D** was seated
Dan	8:14	two thousand three hundred **d**
Dan	8:27	fainted and was sick for **d**
Dan	10: 2	In those **d** I, Daniel, was
Dan	10:14	your people in the latter **d**
Dan	10:14	refers to many **d** yet to come
Dan	12:13	at the end of the **d**
Hos	1: 1	in the **d** of Uzziah, Jotham,
Hos	2:11	mirth to cease, her feast **d**
Hos	2:13	**d** of the Baals to which she
Hos	2:15	as in the **d** of her youth, as
Hos	3: 3	You shall stay with me many **d**
Hos	3: 4	many **d** without king or prince
Hos	3: 5	His goodness in the latter **d**
Hos	6: 2	After two **d** He will revive us
Joel	1: 2	like this happened in your **d**
Joel	2:29	pour out My Spirit in those **d**
Amos	5:21	hate, I despise your feast **d**
Amos	9:11	rebuild it as in the **d** of old
Jon	1:17	the belly of the fish three **d**
Jon	3: 4	Yet forty **d**, and Nineveh shall
Hab	1: 5	I will work a work in your **d**
Matt	2: 1	in the **d** of Herod the king
Matt	3: 1	In those **d** John the Baptist
Matt	4: 2	And when He had fasted forty **d**
Matt	12:40	For as Jonah was three **d** and
Matt	12:40	the Son of Man be three **d**
Matt	24:19	nursing babies in those **d**
Matt	24:22	unless those **d** were shortened
Matt	24:29	**d** the sun will be darkened
Matt	24:37	But as the **d** of Noah were, so
Matt	26: 2	after two **d** is the Passover
Matt	26:61	God and to build it in three **d**
Matt	27:40	temple and build it in three **d**
Matt	27:63	After three **d** I will rise
Mark	2:20	they will fast in those **d**
Luke	1: 5	There was in the **d** of Herod
Luke	1:39	Now Mary arose in those **d**
Luke	2:21	when eight **d** were completed
Luke	2:46	three **d** they found Him in the
Luke	4: 2	in those **d** He ate nothing, and
Luke	4:25	in Israel in the **d** of Elijah
Luke	17:22	of the **d** of the Son of Man
Luke	17:28	it was also in the **d** of Lot
John	2:12	did not stay there many **d**
John	11:17	been in the tomb four **d**
John	11:39	for he has been dead four **d**
Acts	1: 3	seen by them during forty **d**
Acts	1: 5	Spirit not many **d** from now
Acts	1:15	in those **d** Peter stood up in
Acts	2:17	come to pass in the last **d**

Acts	2:18	pour out My Spirit in those **d**
Acts	3:24	have also foretold these **d**
Acts	5:37	up in the **d** of the census
Acts	9: 9	he was three **d** without sight,
Acts	9:19	Then Saul spent some **d** with
Acts	11:28	in the **d** of Claudius Caesar
Acts	12: 3	the **D** of Unleavened Bread
Acts	13:31	He was seen for many **d** by
Acts	13:41	for I work a work in your **d**
Acts	21:26	of the **d** of purification, at
Acts	27:20	nor stars appeared for many **d**
Gal	1:18	remained with him fifteen **d**
Gal	4:10	You observe **d** and months and
Eph	5:16	time, because the **d** are evil
2Ti	3: 1	that in the last **d** perilous
Heb	1: 2	has in these last **d** spoken to
Heb	5: 7	in the **d** of His flesh, when
Heb	7: 3	of **d** nor end of life, but
Heb	11:30	were encircled for seven **d**
Heb	12:10	For they indeed for a few **d**
Jas	5: 3	up treasure in the last **d**
1Pe	3:10	would love life and see good **d**
1Pe	3:20	God waited in the **d** of Noah
2Pe	3: 3	will come in the last **d**,
Rev	11: 3	two hundred and sixty **d**,
Rev	11: 6	in the **d** of their prophecy
Rev	11: 9	dead bodies three and a half **d**
Rev	11:11	a half **d** the breath of life

DAYS' (*see* DAYS)

Gen	30:36	Then he put three **d** journey
Ex	3:18	let us go three **d** journey
Ex	5: 3	let us go three **d** journey

DAYSPRING† (*see* DAY)

Luke	1:78	with which the **D** from on high

DAYTIME (*see* DAY)

Ps	22: 2	O My God, I cry in the **d**, but
Ps	42: 8	His lovingkindness in the **d**
Luke	21:37	in the **d** He was teaching in
2Pe	2:13	pleasure to carouse in the **d**

DEACONS

Phil	1: 1	with the bishops and **d**
1Ti	3: 8	Likewise **d** must be reverent,
1Ti	3:10	then let them serve as **d**,
1Ti	3:12	Let **d** be the husbands of one

DEAD (*see* CORPSE, DEADLY, DEADNESS, DIE)

Gen	20: 3	him, "Indeed you are a **d** man
Gen	23: 4	may bury my **d** out of my sight
Gen	50:15	saw that their father was **d**
Ex	12:33	We shall all be **d**
Ex	14:30	Egyptians **d** on the seashore
Lev	11:31	are **d** shall be unclean until
Lev	19:28	in your flesh for the **d**, nor
Num	6: 6	he shall not go near a **d** body
Num	20:29	saw that Aaron was **d**, all the
Deut	18:11	or one who calls up the **d**
Deut	25: 5	the widow of the **d** man shall
Deut	25: 6	to the name of his **d** brother
Josh	1: 2	Moses My servant is **d**
Judg	2:19	to pass, when the judge was **d**
Judg	4:22	**d** with the peg in his temple
Judg	5:27	he sank, there he fell **d**
Judg	16:30	So the **d** that he killed at
Ruth	1: 8	as you have dealt with the **d**
Ruth	2:20	to the living and the **d**
Ruth	4: 5	of the **d** on his inheritance
Ruth	4:10	of the **d** on his inheritance
Ruth	4:10	that the name of the **d** may
1Sa	24:14	Whom do you pursue? A **d** dog?
1Sa	31: 7	that Saul and his sons were **d**
2Sa	11:21	Uriah the Hittite is **d** also
2Sa	11:24	Uriah the Hittite is **d** also
2Sa	12:18	tell him that the child was **d**

2Sa	14: 5	I am a widow, my husband is **d**
2Sa	18:20	because the king's son is **d**
1Ki	3:20	laid her **d** child in my bosom
1Ki	3:22	son, and the **d** one is your son
1Ki	21:14	has been stoned and is **d**
1Ki	21:16	Ahab heard that Naboth was **d**
2Ki	4:32	the child, lying **d** on his bed
2Ki	8: 5	he had restored the **d** to life
2Ki	19:35	there were the corpses—all **d**
1Ch	5:22	for many fell **d**, because the
Job	1:19	the young men, and they are **d**
Job	26: 5	The **d** tremble, those under
Ps	31:12	I am forgotten like a **d** man
Ps	76: 6	were cast into a **d** sleep
Ps	79: 2	The **d** bodies of Your servants
Ps	88: 5	Adrift among the **d**, Like the
Ps	88:10	You work wonders for the **d**
Ps	88:10	Shall the **d** arise and praise
Ps	106:28	ate sacrifices made to the **d**
Ps	115:17	The **d** do not praise the LORD,
Prov	2:18	death, and her paths to the **d**
Prov	9:18	not know that the **d** are there
Prov	21:16	in the congregation of the **d**
Eccl	9: 3	after that they go to the **d**
Eccl	9: 4	dog is better than a **d** lion
Eccl	9: 5	but the **d** know nothing, and
Eccl	10: 1	**D** flies putrefy the
Is	14: 9	it stirs up the **d** for you
Is	26:19	Your **d** shall live
Jer	16: 7	to comfort them for the **d**
Jer	22:10	Weep not for the **d**, nor
Jer	31:40	whole valley of the **d** bodies
Lam	3: 6	places like the **d** of long ago
Ezek	24:17	make no mourning for the **d**
Matt	2:19	But when Herod was **d**, behold,
Matt	2:20	the young Child's life are **d**
Matt	8:22	let the **d** bury their own
Matt	9:24	room, for the girl is not **d**
Matt	10: 8	the lepers, raise the **d**, cast
Matt	14: 2	he is risen from the **d**, and
Matt	22:31	the resurrection of the **d**
Matt	22:32	God is not the God of the **d**
Matt	23:27	are full of **d** men's bones
Matt	28: 7	that He is risen from the **d**
Mark	5:39	The child is not **d**, but
Mark	6:14	Baptist is risen from the **d**
Mark	9:26	And he became as one **d**, so
Mark	15:44	He had been **d** for some time
Luke	7:12	a **d** man was being carried out
Luke	7:15	And he who was **d** sat up and
Luke	7:22	the **d** are raised, the poor
Luke	8:52	she is not **d**, but sleeping
Luke	15:24	for this my son was **d** and is
Luke	15:32	glad, for your brother was **d**
Luke	16:30	one goes to them from the **d**
Luke	16:31	though one rise from the **d**
Luke	24:46	rise from the **d** the third day
John	5:21	as the Father raises the **d**
John	5:25	is, when the **d** will hear the
John	6:58	ate the manna, and are **d**
John	8:52	Abraham is **d**, and the prophets
John	11:14	them plainly, "Lazarus is **d**
John	11:39	for he has been **d** four days
John	20: 9	He must rise again from the **d**
Acts	2:29	David, that he is both **d** and
Acts	3:15	whom God raised from the **d**
Acts	10:42	Judge of the living and the **d**
Acts	14:19	city, supposing him to be **d**
Acts	17:32	of the resurrection of the **d**
Acts	20: 9	third story and was taken up **d**
Acts	23: 6	of the **d** I am being judged
Rom	4:17	God, who gives life to the **d**
Rom	4:24	up Jesus our Lord from the **d**
Rom	6: 4	**d** by the glory of the Father
Rom	6:11	to be **d** indeed to sin, but

Rom   6:13 God as being alive from the **d**
Rom   7: 4 you also have become **d** to the
Rom   7: 8 apart from the law sin was **d**
Rom   8:10 the body is **d** because of sin,
Rom   8:11 from the **d** dwells in you, He
Rom 10: 9 God has raised Him from the **d**
1Co 15:16 For if the **d** do not rise,
1Co 15:20 Christ is risen from the **d**
1Co 15:29 do who are baptized for the **d**
1Co 15:52 and the **d** will be raised
Eph   2: 5 when we were **d** in trespasses
Eph   5:14 who sleep, arise from the **d**
Col   1:18 the firstborn from the **d**
1Th   4:16 the **d** in Christ will rise
1Ti   5: 6 pleasure is **d** while she lives
2Ti   4: 1 the **d** at His appearing and His
Heb   6: 1 of repentance from **d** works
Heb   9:14 **d** works to serve the living
Heb   9:17 is in force after men are **d**
Heb 11: 4 it he being **d** still speaks
Heb 11:12 one man, and him as good as **d**
Heb 11:19 raise him up, even from the **d**
Heb 11:35 their **d** raised to life again
Heb 13:20 up our Lord Jesus from the **d**
Jas   2:20 that faith without works is **d**
Jas   2:26 body without the spirit is **d**
Rev   1: 5 the firstborn from the **d**
Rev   1:17 Him, I fell at His feet as **d**
Rev   1:18 I am He who lives, and was **d**
Rev   2: 8 First and the Last, who was **d**
Rev   3: 1 you are alive, but you are **d**
Rev 14:13 Blessed are the **d** who die in
Rev 20:12 And I saw the **d**, small and
Rev 20:12 the **d** were judged according
Rev 20:13 gave up the **d** who were in it

DEADLY (*see* DEAD)
Ps   17: 9 me, From my **d** enemies who
Ps   144:10 His servant From the **d** sword
Jas   3: 8 unruly evil, full of **d** poison
Rev 13: 3 and his **d** wound was healed

DEADNESS† (*see* DEAD)
Rom   4:19 and the **d** of Sarah's womb

DEAF
Ex   4:11 Or who makes the mute, the **d**
Is   29:18 In that day the **d** shall hear
Is   42:19 or **d** as My messenger whom I
Is   43: 8 eyes, and the **d** who have ears
Mark 7:32 brought to Him one who was **d**
Mark 9:25 You **d** and dumb spirit, I
Luke 7:22 the **d** hear, the dead are

DEAL (*see* DEALING, DEALS, DEALT)
Gen 19: 9 now we will **d** worse with you
Gen 24:49 Now if you will **d** kindly and
Gen 47:29 **d** kindly and truly with me
Ex   1:10 let us **d** wisely with them,
Ex   21: 9 he shall **d** with her according
2Sa 18: 5 **D** gently for my sake with the
Ps   75: 4 Do not **d** boastfully,' And to
Ps 105:25 To **d** craftily with His
Ps 119:17 **D** bountifully with Your
Ps 119:124 **D** with Your servant according
Prov 12:22 but those who **d** truthfully
Is   33: 1 and you who **d** treacherously,
Is   52:13 My Servant shall **d** prudently
Dan   1:13 fit, so **d** with your servants

DEALING (*see* DEAL, DEALINGS)
Ex   5:15 Why are you **d** thus with your

DEALINGS (*see* DEALING)
John 4: 9 have no **d** with Samaritans

DEALS (*see* DEAL)
Ps   112: 5 A good man **d** graciously and

Heb 12: 7 God **d** with you as with sons

DEALT (*see* DEAL)
Gen 16: 6 when Sarai **d** harshly with her
Gen 33:11 because God has **d** graciously
Ex   1:20 Therefore God **d** well with the
Ruth 1: 8 as you have **d** with the dead
Ruth 1:20 for the Almighty has **d** very
Job   6:15 My brothers have **d**
Ps   13: 6 Because He has **d** bountifully
Ps 103:10 He has not **d** with us
Ps 116: 7 O my soul, For the LORD has **d**
Joel 2:26 who has **d** wondrously with you
Luke 1:25 Thus the Lord has **d** with me
Luke 16: 8 because he had **d** shrewdly
Rom 12: 3 as God has **d** to each one a

DEAR (*see* DEARLY)
Luke 7: 2 servant, who was **d** to him
Acts 20:24 I count my life **d** to myself
Eph   5: 1 of God as **d** children
Col   1: 7 our **d** fellow servant, who is

DEARLY (*see* DEAR)
Jer 12: 7 I have given the **d** beloved of

DEATH (*see* DEATHS, DIE)
Gen 21:16 me not see the **d** of the boy
Gen 25:11 after the **d** of Abraham, that
Gen 27: 2 I do not know the day of my **d**
Gen 27:10 he may bless you before his **d**
Ex   19:12 shall surely be put to **d**
Ex   21:28 gores a man or a woman to **d**
Num 35:19 shall put the murderer to **d**
Num 35:25 remain there until the **d** of
Num 35:28 the **d** of the high priest
Num 35:30 a person for the **d** penalty
Deut 17: 5 shall stone to **d** that man or
Deut 17: 6 Whoever is worthy of **d** shall
Deut 21:22 committed a sin worthy of **d**
Deut 24:16 be put to **d** for their fathers
Deut 24:16 be put to **d** for his own sin
Deut 30:19 have set before you life and **d**
Josh 1: 1 After the **d** of Moses the
Josh 2:13 and deliver our lives from **d**
Judg 1: 1 Now after the **d** of Joshua it
Judg 16:16 that his soul was vexed to **d**
Judg 16:30 his **d** were more than he had
Ruth 1:17 if anything but **d** parts you
Ruth 2:11 since the **d** of your husband
1Sa 15:32 the bitterness of **d** is past
1Sa 20: 3 is but a step between me and **d**
2Sa   6:23 children to the day of her **d**
2Sa 15:21 be, whether in **d** or life,
2Sa 22: 5 the waves of **d** encompassed me
2Sa 22: 6 the snares of **d** confronted me
1Ki   2: 8 put you to **d** with the sword
2Ki   2:21 be no more **d** or barrenness
2Ki 15: 5 leper until the day of his **d**
2Ki 20: 1 Hezekiah was sick and near **d**
2Ch 32:33 honored him at his **d**
Job   3: 5 and the shadow of **d** claim it
Job   3:21 who long for **d**, but it does
Job   5:20 He shall redeem you from **d**
Job 18:13 the firstborn of **d** devours
Job 28: 3 darkness and the shadow of **d**
Job 28:22 and **D** say, We have heard a
Job 38:17 Have the gates of **d** been
Ps   7:13 for Himself instruments of **d**
Ps   13: 3 Lest I sleep the sleep of **d**
Ps   18: 4 The pangs of **d** encompassed me
Ps   18: 5 The snares of **d** confronted me
Ps   22:15 brought Me to the dust of **d**
Ps   23: 4 the valley of the shadow of **d**
Ps   49:14 **D** shall feed on them
Ps   89:48 man can live and not see **d**
Ps 102:20 To loose those apointed to **d**

Ps	116: 8	have delivered my soul from **d**
Ps	116:15	LORD Is the **d** of His saints
Prov	2:18	for her house leads down to **d**
Prov	7:27	to the chambers of **d**
Prov	8:36	all those who hate me love **d**
Prov	10: 2	righteousness delivers from **d**
Prov	11: 4	righteousness delivers from **d**
Prov	14:12	but its end is the way of **d**
Prov	16:25	but its end is the way of **d**
Prov	21: 6	fantasy of those who seek **d**
Eccl	7: 1	the day of **d** than the day of
Song	8: 6	for love is as strong as **d**
Is	9: 2	the land of the shadow of **d**
Is	25: 8	He will swallow up **d** forever
Is	28:15	have made a covenant with **d**
Is	53: 9	but with the rich at His **d**
Is	53:12	He poured out His soul unto **d**
Jer	15: 2	Such as are for **d**, to **d**
Jer	21: 8	way of life and the way of **d**
Jer	52:11	prison till the day of his **d**
Ezek	33:11	in the **d** of the wicked, but
Hos	13:14	I will redeem them from **d**
Hos	13:14	O **D**, I will be your plagues
Jon	4: 8	Then he wished **d** for himself
Jon	4: 9	for me to be angry, even to **d**
Matt	2:15	there until the **d** of Herod
Matt	2:16	and put to **d** all the male
Matt	4:16	shadow of **d** light has dawned
Matt	10:21	will deliver up brother to **d**
Matt	16:28	**d** till they see the Son of
Matt	20:18	and they will condemn Him to **d**
Matt	26:38	sorrowful, even to **d**
Matt	26:66	He is deserving of **d**
Mark	9: 1	here who will not taste **d**
Mark	14:64	Him to be worthy of **d**
Luke	1:79	darkness and the shadow of **d**
Luke	2:26	that he would not see **d**
John	5:24	has passed from **d** into life
John	8:51	My word he shall never see **d**
John	11: 4	This sickness is not unto **d**
John	11:13	However, Jesus spoke of his **d**
John	12:33	by what **d** He would die
John	18:32	by what **d** He would die
John	21:19	signifying by what **d** he would
Acts	2:24	having loosed the pains of **d**
Acts	8: 1	Saul was consenting to his **d**
Acts	22: 4	persecuted this Way to the **d**
Rom	1:32	such things are worthy of **d**
Rom	5:10	God through the **d** of His Son
Rom	5:12	and **d** through sin
Rom	5:14	Nevertheless **d** reigned from
Rom	6: 3	were baptized into His **d**
Rom	6: 9	**D** no longer has dominion over
Rom	6:10	For the **d** that He died, He
Rom	6:16	you obey, whether of sin to **d**
Rom	6:23	For the wages of sin is **d**
Rom	7:24	me from this body of **d**
Rom	8: 2	free from the law of sin and **d**
Rom	8: 6	to be carnally minded is **d**
Rom	8:13	to **d** the deeds of the body
Rom	8:38	that neither **d** nor life, nor
1Co	11:26	the Lord's **d** till He comes
1Co	15:21	For since by man came **d**, by
1Co	15:26	that will be destroyed is **d**
1Co	15:54	**D** is swallowed up in victory
1Co	15:55	O **D**, where is your sting
2Co	2:16	are the aroma of **d** to **d**
2Co	3: 7	But if the ministry of **d**,
Eph	2:16	putting to **d** the enmity
Phil	1:20	body, whether by life or by **d**
Phil	2: 8	obedient to the point of **d**
Phil	2: 8	even the **d** of the cross
Phil	2:27	he was sick almost unto **d**
Phil	3:10	being conformed to His **d**
Col	3: 5	Therefore put to **d** your

2Ti	1:10	Christ, who has abolished **d**
Heb	2: 9	might taste **d** for everyone
Heb	2:14	him who had the power of **d**
Heb	9:16	be the **d** of the testator
Heb	11: 5	so that he did not see **d**
Jas	1:15	is full-grown, brings forth **d**
Jas	5:20	way will save a soul from **d**
1Jn	3:14	we have passed from **d** to life
1Jn	5:16	sin which does not lead to **d**
Rev	1:18	the keys of Hades and of **D**
Rev	2:10	Be faithful until **d**, and I
Rev	2:11	not be hurt by the second **d**
Rev	6: 8	of him who sat on it was **D**
Rev	20:13	the dead who were in it, and **D**
Rev	20:14	Then **D** and Hades were cast
Rev	21: 4	there shall be no more **d**, nor

DEATHS† (see DEATH)

Jer	16: 4	They shall die gruesome **d**
2Co	11:23	more frequently, in **d** often

DEBASED† (see DEBASES, DESCENDED)

Rom	1:28	gave them over to a **d** mind

DEBASES† (see DEBASED)

Eccl	7: 7	and a bribe **d** the heart

DEBATE

Prov	25: 9	**D** your case with your

DEBORAH

Gen	35: 8	Now **D**, Rebekah's nurse, died,
Judg	4: 4	Now **D**, a prophetess, the wife
Judg	5: 7	ceased in Israel, until I, **D**

DEBT (see DEBTOR, DEBTS)

Matt	18:27	him, and forgave him the **d**
Rom	4: 4	not counted as grace but as **d**

DEBTOR (see DEBT, DEBTORS)

Rom	1:14	I am a **d** both to Greeks and to
Gal	5: 3	is a **d** to keep the whole law

DEBTORS (see DEBTOR)

Matt	6:12	debts, As we forgive our **d**
Luke	7:41	creditor who had two **d**
Rom	8:12	Therefore, brethren, we are **d**

DEBTS† (see DEBT)

Deut	15: 1	shall grant a release of **d**
Prov	22:26	of those who is surety for **d**
Matt	6:12	And forgive us our **d**, As we

DECAPOLIS

Matt	4:25	from Galilee, and from **D**,

DECAYS†

Job	13:28	Man **d** like a rotten thing,
Eccl	10:18	of laziness the building **d**

DECEASE†

Luke	9:31	spoke of His **d** which He was
2Pe	1:15	of these things after my **d**

DECEIT (see DECEITFUL, DECEIVE)

Job	27: 4	nor my tongue utter **d**
Ps	10: 7	mouth is full of cursing and **d**
Ps	32: 2	in whose spirit there is no **d**
Ps	34:13	your lips from speaking **d**
Ps	50:19	evil, And your tongue frames **d**
Prov	12:20	**D** is in the heart of those
Prov	14: 8	but the folly of fools is **d**
Prov	20:17	Bread gained by **d** is sweet to
Is	53: 9	nor was any **d** in His mouth
Dan	8:25	**d** to prosper under his hand
Amos	8: 5	falsifying the balances by **d**
John	1:47	indeed, in whom is no **d**!"
Acts	13:10	O full of all **d** and all fraud,
Rom	1:29	of envy, murder, strife, **d**
Rom	3:13	they have practiced **d**"
Col	2: 8	through philosophy and empty **d**
1Pe	2: 1	aside all malice, all **d**,

1Pe   2:22 Nor was **d** found in His
1Pe   3:10 And his lips from speaking **d**.
Rev   14: 5 in their mouth was found no **d**,

DECEITFUL (*see* DECEIT, DECEITFULLY, DECEITFULNESS)
Ps   5: 6 the bloodthirsty and **d** man
Ps   17: 1 that is not from **d** lips
Ps   52: 4 devouring words, You **d** tongue
Ps   78:57 turned aside like a **d** bow
Prov 12: 5 counsels of the wicked are **d**
Prov 14:25 but a **d** witness speaks lies
Prov 31:30 Charm is **d** and beauty is vain,
Jer   17: 9 The heart is **d** above all
Hos   7:16 they are like a **d** bow.
Hos   12: 7 **d** scales are in his hand
Mic   6:11 and with the bag of **d** weights
Eph   4:14 craftiness of **d** plotting,
Eph   4:22 according to the **d** lusts,

DECEITFULLY (*see* DECEITFUL)
Ps   24: 4 soul to an idol, Nor sworn **d**
Jer   48:10 does the work of the LORD **d**
2Co   4: 2 handling the word of God **d**

DECEITFULNESS (*see* DECEITFUL)
Matt 13:22 the **d** of riches choke the
Heb   3:13 hardened through the **d** of sin

DECEIVE (*see* DECEIT, DECEIVED, DECEIVER, DECEIVES,
    DECEIVING, DECEPTION, DECEPTIVE)
2Ki   18:29 Do not let Hezekiah **d** you
2Ki   19:10 God in whom you trust **d** you
Matt 24: 5 the Christ,' and will **d** many
Matt 24:24 signs and wonders, so as to **d**
Rom   16:18 and flattering speech **d** the
1Co   3:18 Let no one **d** himself
1Jn   1: 8 we **d** ourselves, and the truth
Rev   20: 8 will go out to **d** the nations

DECEIVED (*see* DECEIVE)
Gen   3:13 The serpent **d** me, and I ate
Deut 11:16 lest your heart be **d**, and you
Josh   7:11 and have both stolen and **d**
Jer   4:10 have greatly **d** this people
Obad   3 pride of your heart has **d** you
Matt   2:16 that he was **d** by the wise men
Luke 21: 8 Take heed that you not be **d**
John   7:47 Are you also **d**
Rom   7:11 **d** me, and by it killed me
1Co   6: 9 Do not be **d**
1Co   15:33 Do not be **d**
2Co   11: 3 as the serpent **d** Eve by his
Gal   6: 7 Do not be **d**, God is not
1Ti   2:14 And Adam was not **d**, but the
Rev   18:23 all the nations were **d**
Rev   20:10 who **d** them, was cast into the

DECEIVER† (*see* DECEIVE, DECEIVERS)
Gen   27:12 I shall seem to be a **d** to him
Job   12:16 the deceived and the **d** are His
Mal   1:14 But cursed be the **d** who has
Matt 27:63 still alive, how that **d** said
2Jn   7 This is a **d** and an antichrist

DECEIVERS (*see* DECEIVER)
2Co   6: 8 as **d**, and yet true
2Jn   7 For many **d** have gone out into

DECEIVES (*see* DECEIVE)
Prov 26:19 is the man who **d** his neighbor
Matt 24: 4 Take heed that no one **d** you
John   7:12 the contrary, He **d** the people
Gal   6: 3 he is nothing, he **d** himself
Jas   1:26 tongue but **d** his own heart
Rev   12: 9 Satan, who **d** the whole world

DECEIVING (*see* DECEIVE)
1Ti   4: 1 giving heed to **d** spirits
2Ti   3:13 will grow worse and worse, **d**

Jas   1:22 hearers only, **d** yourselves

DECENTLY†
1Co   14:40 Let all things be done **d** and

DECEPTION (*see* DECEIVE)
Ps   38:12 And plan **d** all the day long
Matt 27:64 So the last **d** will be worse

DECEPTIVE (*see* DECEIVE, DECEPTIVELY)
Prov 11:18 The wicked man does **d** work
Prov 23: 3 for they are **d** food
2Pe   2: 3 will exploit you with **d** words

DECEPTIVELY† (*see* DECEPTIVE)
2Ki   10:19 But Jehu acted **d**, with the

DECIDE (*see* DECIDED, DECISION)
Is   11: 4 **d** with equity for the meek of

DECIDED (*see* DECIDE)
Acts 25:25 to Augustus, I **d** to send him
Tit   3:12 for I have **d** to spend the

DECISION (*see* DECIDE)
Prov 16:33 but its every **d** is from the
Joel   3:14 multitudes in the valley of **d**
Acts 24:22 I will make a **d** on your case

DECKED† (*see* DECKS)
Hos   2:13 She **d** herself with her

DECKS† (*see* DECKED)
Gen   6:16 lower, second, and third **d**
Is   61:10 as a bridegroom **d** himself

DECLARE (*see* DECLARED, DECLARES, DECLARING)
Deut   5: 5 to **d** to you the word of the
Deut 26: 3 I **d** today to the LORD your
1Ch   16:24 D His glory among the nations
Job   32:10 me, I also will **d** my opinion
Ps   2: 7 I will **d** the decree
Ps   9:11 D His deeds among the people
Ps   19: 1 The heavens **d** the glory of
Ps   22:22 I will **d** Your name to My
Ps   22:31 and **d** His righteousness to a
Ps   66:16 I will **d** what He has done for
Ps   78: 6 **d** them to their children,
Ps   96: 3 D His glory among the nations
Ps   145: 4 And shall **d** Your mighty acts
Is   41:22 or **d** to us things to come
Is   42: 9 to pass, and new things I **d**
Is   53: 8 who will **d** His generation
Is   66:19 they shall **d** My glory among
Jer   51:10 let us **d** in Zion the work of
Dan   4:18 its interpretation, since
Mic   3: 8 and might, to **d** to Jacob his
John 16:15 take of Mine and **d** it to you
John 17:26 them Your name, and will **d** it
Acts   8:33 who will **d** His generation
Acts 13:32 And we **d** to you glad tidings
1Co   3:13 for the Day will **d** it,
1Co   15: 1 I **d** to you the gospel which I
Heb   2:12 I will **d** Your name to My
1Jn   1: 2 **d** to you that eternal life
1Jn   1: 3 seen and heard we **d** to you
1Jn   1: 5 to you, that God is light

DECLARED (*see* DECLARE)
Ps   40:10 I have **d** Your faithfulness and
Ps   119:13 With my lips I have **d** All the
Is   41:26 Who has **d** from the beginning,
Is   45:21 Who has **d** this from ancient
Is   48: 3 I have **d** the former things
John   1:18 of the Father, He has **d** Him
John 17:26 I have **d** to them Your name,
Acts 15:14 Simon has **d** how God at the
Rom   1: 4 **d** to be the Son of God with
Rom   9:17 might be **d** in all the earth
Rev   10: 7 as He **d** to His servants the

DECLARES (*see* DECLARE)
Ps 147:19 He **d** His word to Jacob, His
Amos 4:13 who **d** to man what his thought

DECLARING (*see* DECLARE)
Is 46:10 **D** the end from the beginning,

DECORATE† (*see* DECORATED)
Jer 10: 4 They **d** it with silver and gold

DECORATED† (*see* DECORATE)
2Ch 3: 6 he **d** the house with precious

DECREASE (*see* DECREASED)
John 3:30 must increase, but I must **d**

DECREASED (*see* DECREASE)
Gen 8: 5 And the waters **d** continually

DECREE (*see* DECREED, DECREES)
Ezra 5:13 King Cyrus issued a **d** to
Esth 9:32 So the **d** of Esther confirmed
Ps 2: 7 I will declare the **d**
Is 10: 1 Woe to those who **d**
Dan 2:13 So the **d** went out, and they
Dan 4:17 is by the **d** of the watchers
Dan 4:24 this is the **d** of the Most
Dan 6: 9 Darius signed the written **d**
Jon 3: 7 Nineveh by the **d** of the king
Luke 2: 1 that a **d** went out from Caesar

DECREED (*see* DECREE)
Is 10:22 the destruction **d** shall

DECREES (*see* DECREE)
Acts 17: 7 contrary to the **d** of Caesar

DEDICATE (*see* DEDICATED, DEDICATES, DEDICATION)
Deut 20: 5 battle and another man **d** it
2Ch 2: 4 God, to **d** it to Him, to burn

DEDICATED (*see* DEDICATE)
Judg 17: 3 I had wholly **d** the silver
2Sa 8:11 King David **d** these to the
1Ki 8:63 **d** the house of the LORD
2Ki 23:11 of Judah had **d** to the sun
2Ch 31:12 the tithes, and the **d** things
Heb 9:18 covenant was **d** without blood

DEDICATES
Lev 27:17 if he **d** his field

DEDICATION (*see* DEDICATE)
Num 7:10 **d** offering for the altar when
Ezra 6:17 at the **d** of this house of God
Neh 12:27 Now at the **d** of the wall of
Dan 3: 3 the **d** of the image that King
John 10:22 the Feast of **D** in Jerusalem

DEED (*see* DEEDED, DEEDS)
Gen 44:15 What **d** is this you have done
Judg 20: 3 how did this wicked **d** happen
Jer 32:10 And I signed the **d** and sealed
Matt 6: 2 when you do a charitable **d**
Luke 23:51 to their counsel and **d**
Luke 24:19 who was a Prophet mighty in **d**
Rom 15:18 through me, in word and **d**, to
Tit 2:14 us from every lawless **d** and
Phm 14 that your good **d** might not be
1Jn 3:18 word or in tongue, but in **d**

DEEDED (*see* DEED)
Gen 23:20 **d** to Abraham by the sons of

DEEDS (*see* DEED)
Gen 20: 9 You have done **d** to me that
Deut 3:24 Your works and Your mighty **d**
1Ch 16: 8 make known His **d** among the
1Ch 17:21 a name by great and awesome **d**
Neh 13:14 do not wipe out my good **d**
Ps 9:11 Declare His **d** among the
Ps 28: 4 to them according to their **d**
Ps 44: 1 What **d** You did in their days,

Ps 105: 1 Make known His **d** among the
Prov 20:11 a child is known by his **d**
Prov 24:12 each man according to his **d**
Is 12: 4 declare His **d** among the
Jer 11:15 having done lewd **d** with many
Jer 32:44 buy fields for money, sign **d**
Ezek 9:10 their **d** on their own head
Dan 9:18 because of our righteous **d**
Hos 4: 9 and reward them for their **d**
Hos 12: 2 according to his **d** He will
Matt 6: 1 your charitable **d** before men
Luke 23:41 the due reward of our **d**
John 3:19 because their **d** were evil
John 3:20 lest his **d** should be exposed
John 8:41 You do the **d** of your father
Acts 7:22 and was mighty in words and **d**
Acts 19:18 confessing and telling their **d**
Rom 2: 6 each one according to his **d**"
Rom 3:28 apart from the **d** of the law
Rom 4: 7 whose lawless **d** are forgiven
Rom 8:13 to death the **d** of the body
2Co 12:12 signs and wonders and mighty **d**
Col 3: 9 off the old man with his **d**
Rev 2: 6 that you hate the **d** of the
Rev 2:22 unless they repent of their **d**

DEEP (*see* DEEPER, DEEPLY)
Gen 1: 2 was on the face of the **d**
Gen 2:21 a **d** sleep to fall on Adam
Gen 7:11 of the great **d** were broken up
Gen 8: 2 The fountains of the **d** and the
Gen 49:25 blessings of the **d** that lies
Job 4:13 when **d** sleep falls on men,
Job 11: 7 out the **d** things of God
Ps 2: 5 them in His **d** displeasure
Ps 33: 7 lays up the **d** in storehouses
Ps 42: 7 **D** calls unto **d** at the
Ps 69: 2 I sink in **d** mire, Where there
Ps 69:14 me, And out of the **d** waters
Ps 69:15 Nor let the **d** swallow me up
Ps 80: 9 And caused it to take **d** root
Ps 92: 5 Your thoughts are very **d**
Ps 104: 6 with the **d** as with a garment
Ps 107:24 LORD, And His wonders in the **d**
Prov 8:27 a circle on the face of the **d**
Prov 8:28 the fountains of the **d**,
Prov 18: 4 of a man's mouth are **d** waters
Prov 22:14 an immoral woman is a **d** pit
Dan 2:22 He reveals **d** and secret things
Dan 8:18 I was in a **d** sleep
Dan 10: 9 I was in a **d** sleep
Amos 7: 4 and it consumed the great **d**
Jon 2: 3 For You cast me into the **d**
Jon 2: 5 the **d** closed around me
Luke 5: 4 Launch out into the **d** and let
Luke 6:48 building a house, who dug **d**
John 4:11 draw with, and the well is **d**
1Co 2:10 yes, the **d** things of God
2Co 8: 2 their **d** poverty abounded in
2Co 11:25 and a day I have been in the **d**

DEEPER (*see* DEEP)
Lev 13: 3 the sore appears to be **d** than
Job 11: 8 **D** than Sheol—what can you

DEEPLY (*see* DEEP)
1Sa 28:15 answered, "I am **d** distressed
2Sa 18:33 Then the king was **d** moved
Neh 2:10 they were **d** disturbed that a
Ps 38: 2 For Your arrows pierce me **d**
Song 5: 1 Drink, yes, drink **d**, O
Hos 9: 9 They are **d** corrupted, as in
Matt 26:37 be sorrowful and **d** distressed
Mark 8:12 But He sighed **d** in His spirit

DEER
Gen 49:21 Naphtali is a **d** let loose

2Sa 22:34 my feet like the feet of **d**
Ps 42: 1 As the **d** pants for the water
Prov 5:19 As a loving **d** and a graceful
Is 35: 6 the lame shall leap like a **d**

DEFAME† (*see* DEFAMED)
1Pe 3:16 that when they **d** you as

DEFAMED† (*see* DEFAME)
1Co 4:13 being **d**, we entreat

DEFEAT (*see* DEFEATED)
Ex 32:18 of those who cry out in **d**
Deut 7:23 and will inflict **d** upon them
2Sa 17:14 to **d** the good counsel of

DEFEATED (*see* DEFEAT)
Josh 12: 1 whom the children of Israel **d**
Judg 1: 5 they **d** the Canaanites and the
1Sa 4: 3 Why has the LORD **d** us today
Esth 9: 5 Thus the Jews **d** all their
Ps 135:10 He **d** many nations And slew

DEFECT (*see* DEFECTED)
Lev 21:20 a man who has a **d** in his eye
Lev 21:21 Aaron the priest, who has a **d**
1Ch 12:19 He may **d** to his master Saul

DEFECTED (*see* DEFECT)
Jer 38:19 who have **d** to the Chaldeans

DEFEND (*see* DEFENDED, DEFENDER, DEFENSE)
Job 13:15 I will **d** my own ways before
Ps 5:11 for joy, because You **d** them
Ps 20: 1 of the God of Jacob **d** you
Is 1:17 **d** the fatherless, plead for
Is 31: 5 the LORD of hosts **d** Jerusalem
Is 37:35 For I will **d** this city, to

DEFENDED (*see* DEFEND)
Acts 7:24 of them suffer wrong, he **d**

DEFENDER† (*see* DEFEND)
Ps 68: 5 a **d** of widows, Is God in His

DEFENSE (*see* DEFEND, DEFENSES)
2Ch 11: 5 built cities for **d** in Judah
Ps 59: 9 For God is my **d**
Acts 19:33 to make his **d** to the people
1Pe 3:15 always be ready to give a **d**

DEFENSES† (*see* DEFENSE)
Job 13:12 your **d** are **d** of clay

DEFERRED†
Prov 13:12 Hope **d** makes the heart sick,

DEFIANTLY (*see* DEFY)
Job 15:25 acts **d** against the Almighty,

DEFIED (*see* DEFY)
1Sa 17:36 seeing he has **d** the armies of

DEFILE (*see* DEFILED, DEFILES, DEFILING, UNDEFILED)
Lev 15:31 **d** My tabernacle that is among
Lev 18:20 wife, to **d** yourself with her
Lev 18:23 beast, to **d** yourself with it
Jer 32:34 is called by My name, to **d** it
Ezek 9: 7 **D** the temple, and fill the
Dan 1: 8 **d** himself with the portion of
Dan 1: 8 that he might not **d** himself
Dan 11:31 they shall **d** the sanctuary
Amos 2: 7 same girl, to **d** My holy name
Matt 15:18 the heart, and they **d** a man
Mark 7:18 man from outside cannot **d** him
Jude 8 these dreamers **d** the flesh

DEFILED (*see* DEFILE)
Gen 34: 5 he had **d** Dinah his daughter
Num 5: 2 becomes **d** by a dead body
2Ki 23: 8 **d** the high places where the
2Ki 23:10 he **d** Topheth, which is in the
2Ch 36:14 **d** the house of the LORD which

Ezra 2:62 from the priesthood as **d**
Neh 7:64 from the priesthood as **d**
Ps 74: 7 They have **d** the dwelling
Is 24: 5 The earth is also **d** under its
Is 59: 3 your hands are **d** with blood
Ezek 4:13 of Israel eat their **d** bread
Ezek 4:14 Indeed I have never **d** myself
Ezek 20:13 and they greatly **d** My Sabbaths
Hos 6: 8 evildoers, and is **d** with blood
Amos 7:17 you shall die in a **d** land
Mal 1: 7 You offer **d** food on My altar
Mal 1: 7 In what way have we **d** You
Mal 1:12 The table of the LORD is **d**
Mark 7: 2 disciples eat bread with **d**
1Co 8: 7 conscience, being weak, is **d**
Tit 1:15 pure, but to those who are **d**
Heb 12:15 and by this many become **d**
Jude 23 the garment **d** by the flesh
Rev 3: 4 who have not **d** their garments
Rev 14: 4 who were not **d** with women

DEFILES (*see* DEFILE)
Num 19:13 **d** the tabernacle of the LORD
Num 35:33 for blood **d** the land, and no
Matt 15:11 goes into the mouth **d** a man
Jas 3: 6 that it **d** the whole body, and
Rev 21:27 enter it anything that **d**, or

DEFILING (*see* DEFILE)
Is 56: 2 who keeps from **d** the Sabbath
Is 56: 6 who keeps from **d** the Sabbath

DEFRAUD† (*see* CHEAT, DEFRAUDED)
Mark 10:19 false witness,' 'Do not **d**
1Th 4: 6 **d** his brother in this matter,

DEFRAUDED (*see* CHEATED, DEFRAUD)

DEFY (*see* DEFIANTLY, DEFIED)
1Sa 17:10 I **d** the armies of Israel this

DEGENERATE†
Jer 2:21 the **d** plant of an alien vine
Ezek 16:30 How **d** is your heart

DEGREE (*see* DEGREES)
1Ch 17:17 the estate of a man of high **d**
Phil 3:16 to the **d** that we have already

DEGREES (*see* DEGREE)
2Ki 20: 9 the shadow go forward ten **d**

DEITIES
Jer 3:13 your charms to alien **d** under

DELAY (*see* DELAYED, DELAYING)
Deut 23:21 you shall not **d** to pay it
1Sa 20:38 Make haste, hurry, do not **d**
Ps 40:17 Do not **d**, O my God
Dan 9:19 Do not **d** for Your own sake,
Acts 9:38 not to **d** in coming to them

DELAYED (*see* DELAY)
Ex 32: 1 Moses **d** coming down from the
Matt 25: 5 while the bridegroom was **d**
1Ti 3:15 but if I am **d**, I write so

DELAYING† (*see* DELAY)
Matt 24:48 My master is **d** his coming
Luke 12:45 My master is **d** his coming

DELEGATION†
Luke 14:32 a great way off, he sends a **d**
Luke 19:14 sent a **d** after him, saying

DELICACIES
Ps 141: 4 do not let me eat of their **d**
Prov 23: 3 Do not desire his **d**, for they
Dan 1: 5 provision of the king's **d**

DELICATE
Gen 29:17 Leah's eyes were **d**, but

DELIGHT (*see* DELIGHTED, DELIGHTFUL, DELIGHTS)
Deut 21:14 be, if you have no **d** in her
1Sa 15:22 as great **d** in burnt offerings
Esth 6: 6 Whom would the king **d** to
Job 22:26 have your **d** in the Almighty
Ps 1: 2 But his **d** is in the law of
Ps 16: 3 ones, in whom is all my **d**
Ps 37: 4 **D** yourself also in the LORD,
Ps 40: 8 I **d** to do Your will, O my God
Ps 51:16 You do not **d** in burnt
Ps 119:16 I will **d** myself in Your
Ps 119:77 For Your law is my **d**
Prov 7:18 let us **d** ourselves with love
Prov 8:30 and I was daily His **d**,
Prov 11: 1 but a just weight is His **d**
Prov 27: 9 perfume **d** the heart, and the
Prov 29:17 he will give **d** to your soul
Is 1:11 I do not **d** in the blood of
Is 11: 3 His **d** is in the fear of the
Is 58:13 day, and call the Sabbath a **d**
Is 65:12 that in which I do not **d**
Is 66: 4 that in which I do not **d**
Jer 9:24 For in these I **d**," says the
Ezek 24:21 your eyes, the **d** of your soul
Mal 3: 1 the covenant, in whom you **d**
Rom 7:22 For I **d** in the law of God
Col 2:18 taking **d** in false humility and

DELIGHTED (*see* DELIGHT)
1Sa 19: 1 Saul's son, **d** much in David
Neh 9:25 **d** themselves in Your great

DELIGHTFUL† (*see* DELIGHT)
Mal 3:12 for you will be a **d** land

DELIGHTS (*see* DELIGHT)
Num 14: 8 If the LORD **d** in us, then He
Esth 6: 6 man whom the king **d** to honor
Esth 6: 7 man whom the king **d** to honor
Esth 6: 9 man whom the king **d** to honor
Ps 22: 8 Him, since He **d** in Him
Ps 37:23 the LORD, And He **d** in his way
Ps 119:143 Your commandments are my **d**
Prov 3:12 a father the son in whom he **d**
Is 42: 1 Elect One in whom My soul **d**
Mic 7:18 because He **d** in mercy

DELILAH
Judg 16: 6 So **D** said to Samson, "Please

DELIVER (*see* DELIVERANCE, DELIVERED, DELIVERER, DELIVERING, DELIVERS, DELIVERY, GRANT)
Gen 32:11 **D** me, I pray, from the hand
Gen 37:22 that he might **d** him out of
Ex 3: 8 So I have come down to **d** them
Ex 5:18 yet you shall **d** the quota of
Deut 1:27 to **d** us into the hand of the
Deut 7:23 God will **d** them over to you
Deut 23:14 to **d** you and give your enemies
Deut 32:39 any who can **d** from My hand
Josh 20: 5 they shall not **d** the slayer
Judg 13: 5 he shall begin to **d** Israel
1Ki 20: 5 You shall **d** to me your silver
2Ki 12: 7 but **d** it for repairing the
2Ki 18:30 The LORD will surely **d** us
Ezra 7:19 **d** in full before the God of
Job 5:19 He shall **d** you in six
Job 39: 3 young, they **d** their offspring
Ps 6: 4 Return, O LORD, **d** me
Ps 7: 2 while there is none to **d**
Ps 17:13 **D** my life from the wicked
Ps 22: 8 Let Him **d** Him, since He
Ps 22:20 **D** Me from the sword, My
Ps 40:13 Be pleased, O LORD, to **d** me
Ps 51:14 **D** me from the guilt of
Ps 59: 1 **D** me from my enemies, O my
Ps 69:14 **D** me out of the mire, And let

Ps 70: 1 Make haste, O God, to **d** me
Ps 71: 2 **D** me in Your righteousness,
Ps 72:12 For He will **d** the needy when
Ps 119:170 **D** me according to Your word
Ps 142: 6 **D** me from my persecutors, For
Ps 144: 7 **d** me out of great waters,
Prov 2:16 to **d** you from the immoral
Prov 6: 3 this, my son, and **d** yourself
Prov 6: 5 **D** yourself like a gazelle
Prov 11: 6 of the upright will **d** them
Prov 12: 6 of the upright will **d** them
Prov 23:14 rod, and **d** his soul from hell
Is 36:14 he will not be able to **d** you
Is 44:17 **D** me, for you are my god
Is 46: 2 they could not **d** the burden
Is 50: 2 Or have I no power to **d**
Jer 1: 8 for I am with you to **d** you
Jer 18:21 Therefore **d** up their children
Jer 24: 9 I will **d** them to trouble
Jer 29:18 I will **d** them to trouble
Jer 43:11 **d** to death those appointed
Ezek 14:14 they would **d** only themselves
Ezek 14:20 they would **d** only themselves
Ezek 34:10 for I will **d** My flock from
Dan 3:17 whom we serve is able to **d** us
Dan 6:14 his heart on Daniel to **d** him
Dan 8: 7 could **d** the ram from his hand
Matt 5:25 adversary **d** you to the judge
Matt 6:13 but **d** us from the evil one
Matt 10:17 for they will **d** you up to
Matt 10:21 Now brother will **d** up brother
Matt 20:19 **d** Him to the Gentiles to mock
Matt 24: 9 Then they will **d** you up to
Matt 27:43 let Him **d** Him now if He will
Mark 10:33 and **d** Him to the Gentiles
Luke 12:58 judge, the judge **d** you to the
Acts 26:17 I will **d** you from the Jewish
Rom 7:24 Who will **d** me from this body
1Co 5: 5 **d** such a one to Satan for the
Gal 1: 4 that He might **d** us from this
2Ti 4:18 the Lord will **d** me from every
2Pe 2: 9 how to **d** the godly out of

DELIVERANCE (*see* DELIVER, LIBERTY)
Gen 45: 7 save your lives by a great **d**
2Ki 13:17 The arrow of the LORD's **d**
Esth 4:14 **d** will arise for the Jews
Ps 32: 7 surround me with songs of **d**
Prov 21:31 battle, but **d** is of the LORD
Heb 11:35 tortured, not accepting **d**

DELIVERED (*see* BETRAYED, DELIVER)
Gen 14:20 Who has **d** your enemies into
Ex 2:19 An Egyptian **d** us from the
Ex 12:27 Egyptians and **d** our households
Deut 2:33 LORD our God **d** him over to us
Deut 31: 9 **d** it to the priests, the sons
Josh 10:32 the LORD **d** Lachish into the
Judg 12: 3 the LORD **d** them into my hand
1Sa 4:19 was with child, due to be **d**
1Sa 17:35 **d** the lamb from its mouth
1Sa 17:37 who **d** me from the paw of the
2Sa 12: 7 I **d** you from the hand of Saul
2Sa 22:20 He **d** me, because He delighted
2Ki 22: 7 the money **d** into their hand
Neh 9:28 and many times You **d** them
Job 16:11 God has **d** me to the ungodly,
Ps 22: 4 They trusted, and You **d** them
Ps 22: 5 They cried to You, and were **d**
Ps 33:16 is not **d** by great strength
Ps 34: 4 me, And **d** me from all my fears
Ps 81: 7 called in trouble, and I **d** you
Ps 86:13 You have **d** my soul from the
Ps 106:43 Many times He **d** them
Prov 11: 8 righteous is **d** from trouble
Prov 11: 9 the righteous will be **d**

Prov 28:26 walks wisely will be **d**
Eccl 9:15 he by his wisdom **d** the city
Is 38:17 but You have lovingly **d** my
Is 66: 7 pain came, she **d** a male child
Jer 32:16 Now when I had **d** the purchase
Ezek 3:21 you will have **d** your soul
Ezek 31:14 they have all been **d** to death
Ezek 32:20 She is **d** to the sword,
Dan 3:28 **d** His servants who trusted in
Dan 6:27 Who has **d** Daniel from the
Dan 12: 1 time your people shall be **d**
Matt 11:27 been **d** to Me by My Father
Matt 18:34 **d** him to the torturers until
Matt 25:14 and **d** his goods to them
Matt 25:20 you **d** to me five talents
Matt 26: 2 will be **d** up to be crucified
Matt 27: 2 **d** Him to Pontius Pilate the
Luke 1: 2 of the word **d** them to us,
Luke 1:57 time came for her to be **d**
Luke 2: 6 completed for her to be **d**
Luke 10:22 been **d** to Me by My Father
Luke 19:13 **d** to them ten minas, and said
Luke 24: 7 The Son of Man must be **d**
Luke 24:20 and our rulers **d** Him to be
John 18:35 priests have **d** You to me
John 18:36 I should not be **d** to the Jews
Acts 2:23 being **d** by the determined
Acts 3:13 Servant Jesus, whom you **d** up
Acts 6:14 customs which Moses **d** to us
Acts 7:10 **d** him out of all his troubles
Acts 28:16 the centurion the prisoners
Acts 28:17 yet I was **d** as a prisoner
Rom 4:25 who was **d** up because of our
Rom 7: 6 we have been **d** from the law
Rom 8:21 will be **d** from the bondage of
Rom 8:32 but **d** Him up for us all, how
1Co 11:23 that which I also **d** to you
1Co 15: 3 For I **d** to you first of all
2Co 1:10 who **d** us from so great a
2Co 4:11 **d** to death for Jesus' sake
Col 1:13 He has **d** us from the power of
1Ti 1:20 whom I **d** to Satan that they
2Ti 3:11 out of them all the Lord **d** me
2Ti 4:17 I was **d** out of the mouth of
2Pe 2: 4 hell and **d** them into chains of
2Pe 2: 7 and **d** righteous Lot, who was
Jude 3 once for all **d** to the saints
Rev 20:13 Hades **d** up the dead who were

DELIVERER (see DELIVER, DELIVERERS)
Judg 3: 9 the LORD raised up a **d** for
2Sa 22: 2 my rock, my fortress and my **d**
Ps 40:17 You are my help and my **d**
Ps 70: 5 You are my help and my **d**
Acts 7:35 a **d** by the hand o the Angel
Rom 11:26 The **D** will come out of Zion,

DELIVERERS† (see DELIVERER)
Neh 9:27 mercies You gave them **d** who

DELIVERING (see DELIVER)
Luke 21:12 **d** you up to the synagogues and
Acts 22: 4 **d** into prisons both men and

DELIVERS (see DELIVER)
Ex 22: 7 If a man **d** to his neighbor
Ex 22:10 If a man **d** to his neighbor
Ps 34: 7 who fear Him, And **d** them
Ps 34:17 And **d** them out of all their
Prov 10: 2 righteousness **d** from death
Prov 11: 4 righteousness **d** from death
Prov 14:25 A true witness **d** souls, but a
Dan 6:27 He **d** and rescues, and He works
1Co 15:24 when He **d** the kingdom to God
1Th 1:10 even Jesus who **d** us from the

DELIVERY (see DELIVER)
Is 26:17 draws near the time of her **d**

DELUDED† (see DELUSION)
Is 19:13 they have also **d** Egypt, those

DELUSION† (see DELUDED)
Zech 10: 2 For the idols speak **d**
2Th 2:11 God will send them strong **d**

DEMAND (see DEMANDING, DEMANDS)
Gen 9: 5 I will **d** a reckoning
Dan 2:23 made known to us the king's **d**

DEMANDING† (see DEMAND)
Luke 23:23 **d** with loud voices that He be

DEMANDS† (see DEMAND)
1Sa 10: 7 that you do as the occasion **d**
1Th 2: 6 made **d** as apostles of Christ

DEMOLISH† (see DEMOLISHED)
Num 33:52 and **d** all their high places

DEMOLISHED† (see DEMOLISH)
Judg 9:45 he **d** the city and sowed it

DEMON (see DEMONIC, DEMON-POSSESSED, DEMONS)
Matt 9:33 when the **d** was cast out, the
Matt 11:18 and they say, 'He has a **d**
Matt 17:18 And Jesus rebuked the **d**, and he
Luke 4:33 had a spirit of an unclean **d**
Luke 7:33 wine, and you say, 'He has a **d**
Luke 8:29 was driven by the **d** into the
Luke 9:42 the **d** threw him down and
John 8:48 are a Samaritan and have a **d**

DEMONIC† (see DEMON)
Jas 3:15 but is earthly, sensual, **d**

DEMON-POSSESSED (see DEMON)
Matt 4:24 torments, and those who were **d**
Matt 8:28 there met Him two **d** men,
Matt 15:22 My daughter is severely **d**
Mark 1:32 were sick and those who were **d**

DEMONS (see DEMON)
Deut 32:17 They sacrificed to **d**, not to
2Ch 11:15 the high places, for the **d**
Ps 106:37 sons And their daughters to **d**
Matt 7:22 cast out **d** in Your name, and
Matt 8:31 So the **d** begged Him, saying,
Matt 9:34 by the ruler of the **d**
Matt 10: 8 raise the dead, cast out **d**
Matt 12:24 Beelzebub, the ruler of the **d**
Mark 1:34 diseases, and cast out many **d**
Luke 8:2 out of whom had come seven **d**
Luke 9: 1 power and authority over all **d**
1Co 10:20 sacrifice they sacrifice to **d**
1Co 10:21 of the Lord and the cup of **d**
1Ti 4: 1 spirits and doctrines of **d**
Jas 2:19 Even the **d** believe
Rev 9:20 they should not worship **d**

DEMONSTRATE (see DEMONSTRATES, DEMONSTRATING, DEMONSTRATION)
Rom 3:25 to **d** His righteousness,

DEMONSTRATES† (see DEMONSTRATE)
Rom 3: 5 **d** the righteousness of God
Rom 5: 8 But God **d** His own love toward

DEMONSTRATING† (see DEMONSTRATE)
Acts 17: 3 and **d** that the Christ had to

DEMONSTRATION† (see DEMONSTRATE)
1Co 2: 4 but in **d** of the Spirit and of

DEN (see DENS)
Ps 10: 9 secretly, as a lion in his **d**
Is 11: 8 put his hand in the viper's **d**
Jer 7:11 become a **d** of thieves in your
Jer 9:11 of ruins and a **d** of jackals

Dan   6: 7 be cast into the **d** of lions
Dan   6:23 take Daniel up out of the **d**
Matt   21:13 have made it a '**d** of thieves

DENARII (*see* DENARIUS)
Matt   18:28 who owed him a hundred **d**
Mark   6:37 two hundred **d** worth of bread

DENARIUS (*see* DENARII)
Matt   20: 2 the laborers for a **d** a day
Matt   20: 9 hour, they each received a **d**
Matt   22:19 So they brought Him a **d**
Rev   6: 6 A quart of wheat for a **d**, and

DENIED (*see* DENY)
Gen   18:15 But Sarah **d** it, saying, "I
Job   31:28 would have **d** God who is above
Matt   26:70 But he **d** it before them all,
Luke   8:45 When all **d** it, Peter and
Luke   12: 9 Me before men will be **d**
John   13:38 you have **d** Me three times
Acts   3:13 **d** in the presence of Pilate,
Acts   3:14 But you **d** the Holy One and the
Acts   19:36 these things cannot be **d**, you
1Ti   5: 8 he has **d** the faith and is
Rev   3: 8 word, and have not **d** My name

DENIES (*see* DENY)
Matt   10:33 But whoever **d** Me before men,
1Jn   2:22 **d** that Jesus is the Christ
1Jn   2:22 antichrist who **d** the Father
1Jn   2:23 Whoever **d** the Son does not

DENOUNCE
Num   23: 8 how shall I **d** whom the LORD

DENS (*see* DEN)
Judg   6: 2 made for themselves the **d**
Job   38:40 when they crouch in their **d**
Heb   11:38 in deserts and mountains, in **d**

DENY (*see* DENIED, DENIES, DENYING)
Matt   10:33 him I will also **d** before My
Matt   16:24 after Me, let him **d** himself
Matt   26:34 you will **d** Me three times
Matt   26:75 you will **d** Me three times
Luke   20:27 who **d** that there is a
John   1:20 He confessed, and did not **d**
Acts   4:16 Jerusalem, and we cannot **d** it
2Ti   2:12 If we **d** Him, He also will **d** us
2Ti   2:13 He cannot **d** Himself
Rev   2:13 did not **d** My faith even in

DENYING† (*see* DENY)
2Ti   3: 5 of godliness but **d** its power
Tit   2:12 **d** ungodliness and worldly
2Pe   2: 1 even **d** the Lord who bought

DEPART (*see* DEPARTED, DEPARTING, DEPARTS, DEPARTURE)
Gen   49:10 shall not **d** from Judah, nor a
Ex   8:11 And the frogs shall **d** from you
Ex   33: 1 **D** and go up from here, you and
Deut   4: 9 lest they **d** from your heart
Josh   1: 8 shall not **d** from your mouth
2Sa   7:15 My mercy shall not **d** from him
2Ki   15: 9 he did not **d** from the sins of
2Ki   15:24 he did not **d** from the sins of
Ps   6: 8 **D** from me, all you workers of
Ps   34:14 **D** from evil, and do good
Ps   37:27 **D** from evil, and do good
Prov   3: 7 fear the LORD and **d** from evil
Prov   3:21 let them not **d** from your eyes
Prov   13:19 to fools to **d** from evil
Prov   22: 6 is old he will not **d** from it
Is   52:11 **D**! **D**! Go out from there
Is   59:21 shall not **d** from your mouth,
Zech   10:11 the scepter of Egypt shall **d**
Matt   7:23 **d** from Me, you who practice

Matt   8:18 to **d** to the other side
Matt   8:34 Him to **d** from their region
Matt   10:14 when you **d** from that house or
Mark   6:11 when you **d** from there, shake
Luke   2:29 Your servant **d** in peace,
John   7: 3 **D** from here and go into Judea,
John   13: 1 **d** from this world to the
John   16: 7 but if I **d**, I will send Him
Acts   1: 4 them not to **d** from Jerusalem
1Co   7:10 is not to **d** from her husband
1Co   7:11 But even if she does **d**, let
1Co   7:15 unbeliever departs, let him **d**
2Co   12: 8 times that it might **d** from me
Phil   1:23 the two, having a desire to **d**
1Ti   4: 1 some will **d** from the faith
2Ti   2:19 of Christ **d** from iniquity
Jas   2:16 **D** in peace, be warmed and

DEPARTED (*see* DEPART)
Gen   12: 4 So Abram **d** as the LORD had
Gen   31:40 and my sleep **d** from my eyes
Num   12:10 when the cloud **d** from above
Judg   16:20 that the LORD had **d** from him
1Sa   4:21 The glory has **d** from Israel
1Sa   4:22 The glory has **d** from Israel
1Sa   16:14 of the LORD **d** from Saul, and a
Ps   18:21 not wickedly **d** from my God
Ps   44:18 our steps **d** from Your way
Ps   119:102 I have not **d** from Your
Ezek   6: 9 heart which has **d** from Me
Dan   4:31 the kingdom has **d** from you
Dan   9:11 has **d** so as not to obey Your
Matt   2:12 they **d** for their own country
Matt   2:14 by night and **d** for Egypt,
Matt   4:12 in prison, He **d** to Galilee
Matt   9: 7 And he arose and **d** to his house
Matt   14:13 He **d** from there by boat to a
Matt   27: 5 of silver in the temple and **d**
Matt   27:60 the door of the tomb, and **d**
Mark   1:35 out and **d** to a solitary place
Mark   5:20 And he **d** and began to proclaim
Mark   6:46 He **d** to the mountain to pray
Luke   1:38 And the angel **d** from her
Luke   4:13 he **d** from Him until an
Luke   8:35 from whom the demons had **d**
Luke   8:38 from whom the demons had **d**
Luke   10:30 clothing, wounded him, and **d**
Acts   11:25 Then Barnabas **d** for Tarsus to
Acts   12:10 the angel **d** from him
Acts   15:40 but Paul chose Silas and **d**
Acts   18:23 spent some time there, he **d**
Acts   20: 1 them, and **d** to go to Macedonia
Acts   28:29 said these words, the Jews **d**
Phm   15 For perhaps he **d** for a while

DEPARTING (*see* DEPART)
Gen   35:18 her soul was **d** (for she died)
Dan   9: 5 even by **d** from Your precepts
Hos   1: 2 harlotry by **d** from the LORD

DEPARTS (*see* DEPART)
Ps   146: 4 His spirit **d**, he returns to
Eccl   6: 4 **d** in darkness, and its name is
Jer   17: 5 whose heart **d** from the LORD
1Co   7:15 But if the unbeliever **d**, let

DEPARTURE (*see* DEPART)
2Ti   4: 6 the time of my **d** is at hand
Heb   11:22 1made mention of the **d** of the

DEPEND (*see* DEPENDS)
Is   10:20 but will **d** on the LORD, the

DEPENDS† (*see* DEPEND)
Rom   12:18 possible, as much as **d** on you

DEPOSED
Dan   5:20 he was **d** from his kingly

DEPOSIT (*see* DEPOSITED, GUARANTEE)
Luke 19:21 collect what you did not **d**

DEPOSITED† (*see* DEPOSIT)
Matt 25:27 **d** my money with the bankers

DEPRESSION
Prov 12:25 in the heart of man causes **d**

DEPRIVE (*see* DEPRIVED)
Eccl 4: 8 do I toil and **d** myself of good
1Co 7: 5 Do not **d** one another except

DEPRIVED (*see* DEPRIVE)
Job 39:17 because God **d** her of wisdom,
Hos 13: 8 like a bear **d** of her cubs

DEPTH (*see* DEPTHS)
Ex 14:27 sea returned to its full **d**
Prov 25: 3 for height and the earth for **d**
Is 7:11 ask it either in the **d** or in
Matt 13: 5 they had no **d** of earth
Matt 18: 6 drowned in the **d** of the sea
Rom 8:39 nor height nor **d**, nor any
Rom 11:33 the **d** of the riches both of
Eph 3:18 is the width and length and **d**

DEPTHS (*see* DEPTH)
Ex 15: 5 The **d** have covered them
Ex 15: 8 the **d** congealed in the heart
Job 36:30 and covers the **d** of the sea
Ps 71:20 again from the **d** of the earth
Ps 77:16 The **d** also trembled
Ps 86:13 my soul from the **d** of Sheol
Ps 88: 6 pit, In darkness, in the **d**
Ps 106: 9 So He led them through the **d**
Ps 130: 1 Out of the **d** I have cried to
Prov 8:24 When there were no **d** I was
Prov 9:18 guests are in the **d** of hell
Prov 20:27 all the inner **d** of his heart
Is 14:15 to the lowest **d** of the Pit
Zech 10:11 all the **d** of the River shall
Rev 2:24 have not known the **d** of Satan

DERBE
Acts 14: 6 of it and fled to Lystra and **D**
Acts 14:20 departed with Barnabas to **D**

DERIDE (*see* DERIDED, DERISION)
Ps 102: 8 those who **d** me swear an oath

DERIDED† (*see* DERIDE)
Luke 16:14 these things, and they **d** Him

DERISION (*see* DERIDE)
Ps 2: 4 The LORD shall hold them in **d**
Ps 44:13 a **d** to those all around us
Ps 59: 8 have all the nations in **d**
Ps 119:51 The proud have me in great **d**
Jer 20: 8 to me a reproach and a **d** daily
Ezek 23:32 laughed to scorn and held in **d**
Hos 7:16 This shall be their **d** in the

DESCEND (*see* DESCENDANT, DESCENDED,
DESCENDING, DESCENT)
2Ki 20:18 your sons who will **d** from you
Ezek 26:20 with those who **d** into the Pit
Ezek 31:16 with those who **d** into the Pit
Mark 15:32 **d** now from the cross, that we
Rom 10: 7 Who will **d** into the abyss
1Th 4:16 **d** from heaven with a shout
Jas 3:15 wisdom does not **d** from above

DESCENDANT (*see* DESCEND, DESCENDANTS)
Gen 17:12 stranger who is not your **d**

DESCENDANTS (*see* DESCENDANT, DESCENDANTS')
Gen 9: 9 you and with your **d** after you
Gen 12: 7 To your **d** I will give this
Gen 16:10 multiply your **d** exceedingly
Gen 22:17 your **d** shall possess the gate
Gen 32:12 make your **d** as the sand of

Num 13:22 the **d** of Anak, were there
Deut 23: 2 none of his **d** shall enter the
Deut 23: 3 none of his **d** shall enter the
Josh 24: 3 Canaan, and multiplied his **d**
2Ch 20: 7 gave it to the **d** of Abraham
Ps 18:50 To David and his **d** forevermore
Ps 37:25 Nor his **d** begging bread
Ps 37:28 But the **d** of the wicked shall
Ps 69:36 the **d** of His servants shall
Is 41: 8 the **d** of Abraham My friend
Is 43: 5 bring your **d** from the east
Is 44: 3 will pour My Spirit on your **d**
Jer 22:30 none of his **d** shall prosper
Dan 1: 3 and some of the king's **d** and
Mal 2: 3 Behold, I will rebuke your **d**
John 8:33 We are Abraham's **d**, and have
Acts 7: 5 and to his **d** after him
Acts 7: 6 that his **d** would sojourn in a
Rom 4:18 So shall your **d** be

DESCENDANTS'† (*see* DESCENDANTS)
Is 59:21 mouth of your **d** descendants

DESCENDED (*see* DESCEND)
Ex 19:18 the LORD **d** upon it in fire
Ex 33: 9 that the pillar of cloud **d**
Ex 34: 5 Then the LORD **d** in the cloud
Prov 30: 4 ascended into heaven, or **d**
Is 57: 9 and even **d** to Sheol
Matt 7:25 and the rain **d**, the floods
Matt 7:27 and the rain **d**, the floods
Matt 28: 2 of the Lord **d** from heaven
Luke 3:22 the Holy Spirit **d** in bodily
Eph 4: 9 **d** into the lower parts of the

DESCENDING (*see* DESCEND)
Gen 28:12 God were ascending and **d** on it
Ps 133: 3 **D** upon the mountains of Zion
Prov 7:27 **d** to the chambers of death
Matt 3:16 Spirit of God **d** like a dove
John 1:51 and **d** upon the Son of Man
Acts 10:11 **d** to him and let down to the
Acts 11: 5 an object **d** like a great
Rev 21:10 **d** out of heaven from God,

DESCENT (*see* DESCEND)
Esth 6:13 begun to fall, is of Jewish **d**
Luke 19:37 the **d** of the Mount of Olives

DESCRIBES† (*see* DESCRIBING)
Rom 4: 6 just as David also **d** the

DESCRIBING† (*see* DESCRIBES)
Acts 15: 3 **d** the conversion of the

DESERT (*see* DESERTED, DESERTS, WILDERNESS)
Ex 3: 1 flock to the back of the **d**
Ps 73:27 those who **d** You for harlotry
Ps 106:14 And tested God in the **d**
Is 23:13 it for wild beasts of the **d**
Is 35: 1 and the **d** shall rejoice and
Is 35: 6 and streams in the **d**
Is 40: 3 make straight in the **d** a
Is 43:19 wilderness and rivers in the **d**
Is 43:20 wilderness and rivers in the **d**
Matt 24:26 to you, 'Look, He is in the **d**
John 6:31 ate the manna in the **d**

DESERTED (*see* DESERT)
Judg 5: 6 of Jael, the highways were **d**
Matt 14:13 boat to a **d** place by Himself

DESERTS (*see* DESERT)
Is 48:21 He led them through the **d**
Luke 1:80 was in the **d** till the day of
Heb 11:38 They wandered in **d** and

DESERVE (*see* DESERVES, DESERVING)
Ezra 9:13 us less than our iniquities **d**
Ps 28: 4 Render to them what they **d**

Jer 26:16 This man does not **d** to die

DESERVES (*see* DESERVE)
Deut 25: 2 the wicked man **d** to be beaten
Jer 26:11 This man **d** to die

DESERVING (*see* DESERVE)
Deut 17: 6 Whoever is **d** of death
Matt 26:66 and said, 'He is **d** of death

DESIGN
Ex 26:31 an artistic **d** of cherubim
Ex 31: 4 to **d** artistic works, to work

DESIGNATES
Heb 4: 7 again He **d** a certain day,

DESIRABLE (*see* DESIRE)
Gen 3: 6 a tree **d** to make one wise,
Prov 21:20 There is **d** treasure, and oil
Hos 13:15 the treasury of every **d** prize
Acts 6: 2 It is not **d** that we should

DESIRE (*see* DESIRABLE, DESIRED, DESIRES, DESIRING, UNDESIRABLE)
Gen 3:16 Your **d** shall be for your
Gen 4: 7 its **d** is for you, but you
1Sa 9:20 whom is all the **d** of Israel
2Sa 23: 5 all my salvation and all my **d**
Neh 1:11 who **d** to fear Your name
Job 13: 3 and I **d** to reason with God
Job 36:20 Do not **d** the night, when
Ps 10: 3 boasts of his heart's **d**
Ps 45:11 will greatly **d** your beauty
Ps 51: 6 You **d** truth in the inward
Ps 51:16 For You do not **d** sacrifice
Ps 59:10 let me see my **d** on my enemies
Ps 70: 2 and confused Who **d** my hurt
Ps 73:25 earth that I **d** besides You
Ps 145:16 satisfy the **d** of every living
Ps 145:19 He will fulfill the **d** of
Prov 13:19 A **d** accomplished is sweet to
Prov 21:25 The **d** of the slothful kills
Prov 23: 3 Do not **d** his delicacies, for
Eccl 6: 9 eyes than the wandering of **d**
Eccl 12: 5 is a burden, and **d** fails
Song 7:10 and his **d** is toward me
Is 26: 8 the **d** of our soul is for Your
Is 53: 2 beauty that we should **d** Him
Jer 2:24 sniffs at the wind in her **d**
Ezek 24:16 the **d** of your eyes with one
Dan 11:37 fathers nor the **d** of women
Hos 6: 6 For I **d** mercy and not
Amos 5:18 Woe to you who **d** the day of
Hag 2: 7 come to the **D** of All Nations
Matt 9:13 I **d** mercy and not sacrifice
Matt 15:28 Let it be to you as you **d**
Mark 12:38 who **d** to go around in long
Luke 22:15 With fervent **d** I have desired
John 15: 7 you, you will ask what you **d**
John 17:24 I **d** that they also whom You
Acts 28:22 But we **d** to hear from you
Rom 7: 8 in me all manner of evil **d**
Rom 10: 1 Brethren, my heart's **d** and
1Co 12:31 But earnestly **d** the best
1Co 14: 1 and **d** spiritual gifts, but
2Co 7: 7 he told us of your earnest **d**
2Co 7:11 what fear, what vehement **d**
Gal 4:21 you who **d** to be under the law
Phil 1:23 having a **d** to depart and be
Col 3: 5 uncleanness, passion, evil **d**
1Ti 2: 8 Therefore I **d** that the men
1Ti 5:11 Christ, they **d** to marry,
2Ti 3:12 all who **d** to live godly in
Heb 10: 5 and offering You did not **d**
Heb 10: 8 for sin You did not **d**, nor
Heb 11:16 But now they **d** a better, that
Jas 1:15 when **d** has conceived, it

1Pe 1:12 which angels **d** to look into
1Pe 2: 2 **d** the pure milk of the word,

DESIRED (*see* DESIRE)
Ps 19:10 More to be **d** are they than
Ps 27: 4 thing I have **d** of the LORD
Ps 107:30 guides them to their **d** haven
Eccl 2:10 Whatever my eyes **d** I did not
Is 26: 9 I have **d** You in the night
Matt 13:17 righteous men **d** to see what
Luke 22:15 **d** to eat this Passover with

DESIRES (*see* DESIRE)
Deut 12:20 as much meat as your heart **d**
Job 7: 2 who earnestly **d** the shade
Job 23:13 And whatever His soul **d**, that
Ps 34:12 Who is the man who **d** life
Ps 37: 4 give you the **d** of your heart
Prov 21:10 The soul of the wicked **d** evil
Matt 16:24 If anyone **d** to come after Me,
Matt 16:25 For whoever **d** to save his
Matt 20:26 but whoever **d** to become great
Matt 20:27 whoever **d** to be first among
Mark 4:19 and the **d** for other things
Luke 5:39 old wine, immediately **d** new
John 8:44 the **d** of your father you want
Gal 5:24 flesh with its passions and **d**
Eph 2: 3 fulfilling the **d** of the flesh
1Ti 2: 4 who **d** all men to be saved and
1Ti 3: 1 If a man **d** the position of a
1Ti 3: 1 of a bishop, he **d** a good work
Jas 1:14 he is drawn away by his own **d**
Jas 3: 4 rudder wherever the pilot **d**
Rev 22:17 And whoever **d**, let him take

DESIRING (*see* DESIRE)
Luke 8:20 outside, **d** to see You
Luke 16:21 **d** to be fed with the crumbs
2Co 5: 2 earnestly **d** to be clothed
2Co 11:32 a garrison, **d** to apprehend me
1Th 3: 6 greatly **d** to see us, as we
1Ti 1: 7 **d** to be teachers of the law,

DESOLATE (*see* DESOLATION)
Ex 23:29 year, lest the land become **d**
Lev 26:34 sabbaths as long as it lies **d**
2Sa 13:20 So Tamar remained **d** in her
Job 15:28 He dwells in **d** cities, in
Job 38:27 To satisfy the **d** waste, and
Ps 25:16 have mercy on me, For I am **d**
Is 1: 7 Your country is **d**, your
Is 3:26 she being **d** shall sit on the
Is 41:18 will open rivers in **d** heights
Is 49: 8 to inherit the **d** heritages
Is 49:19 **d** places, and the land of your
Is 49:21 have lost my children and am **d**
Is 54: 3 make the **d** cities inhabited
Is 62: 4 land any more be termed **D**
Jer 9:11 make the cities of Judah **d**
Jer 10:22 make the cities of Judah **d**
Jer 51:26 but you shall be **d** forever
Lam 1: 4 All her gates are **d**
Lam 1:16 My children are **d** because the
Ezek 6: 4 Then your altars shall be **d**
Ezek 29:12 cities shall be **d** forty years
Ezek 35: 9 I will make you perpetually **d**
Dan 9:17 on Your sanctuary, which is **d**
Dan 9:27 shall be one who makes **d**,
Dan 9:27 is poured out on the **d**
Mic 1: 7 all her idols I will lay **d**
Zech 7:14 they made the pleasant land **d**
Matt 23:38 Your house is left to you **d**
Gal 4:27 for the **d** has many more
Rev 17:16 hate the harlot, make her **d**

DESOLATION (see ASTONISHMENT, DESOLATE, DESOLATIONS)

Lev	26:31	bring your sanctuaries to **d**
Lev	26:32	I will bring the land to **d**
Josh	8:28	heap forever, a **d** to this day
2Ch	29: 8	them up to trouble, to **d**
Is	24:12	In the city **d** is left, and the
Is	47:11	And **d** shall come upon you
Is	51:19	**D** and destruction, famine and
Is	64:10	a wilderness, Jerusalem a **d**
Jer	22: 5	this house shall become a **d**
Jer	25:12	I will make it a perpetual **d**
Jer	34:22	Judah a **d** without inhabitant
Ezek	7:27	prince will be clothed with **d**
Ezek	23:33	the cup of horror and **d**, The
Dan	8:13	and the transgression of **d**
Dan	11:31	there the abomination of **d**
Dan	12:11	abomination of **d** is set up
Zeph	1:15	a day of devastation and **d**
Matt	24:15	you see the 'abomination of **d**
Mark	13:14	you see the 'abomination of **d**
Luke	21:20	then know that its **d** is near

DESOLATIONS (see DESOLATION)

Jer	25: 9	a hissing, and perpetual **d**
Dan	9:18	open Your eyes and see our **d**

DESPAIR (see DESPAIRED, DESPERATE)

Jer	19: 9	lives shall drive them to **d**
2Co	4: 8	are perplexed, but not in **d**

DESPAIRED† (see DESPAIR)

Eccl	2:20	**d** of all the labor in which I
2Co	1: 8	so that we **d** even of life

DESPERATE (see DESPAIR, DESPERATELY, DESPERATION)

Is	17:11	the day of grief and **d** sorrow

DESPERATELY (see DESPERATE)

Jer	17: 9	above all things, and **d** wicked

DESPERATION† (see DESPERATE)

Jer	19: 9	in the **d** with which their

DESPISE (see DESPISED, DESPISERS, DESPISES, DESPISING)

Lev	26:15	if you **d** My statutes, or if
1Sa	2:30	and those who **d** Me shall be
Job	9:21	I **d** my life
Job	19:18	Even young children **d** me
Ps	51:17	These, O God, You will not **d**
Ps	73:20	You shall **d** their image
Ps	102:17	And shall not **d** their prayer
Prov	1: 7	knowledge, but fools **d** wisdom
Prov	3:11	do not **d** the chastening of
Prov	23: 9	for he will **d** the wisdom of
Prov	23:22	do not **d** your mother when she
Jer	23:17	say to those who **d** Me, 'The
Amos	5:21	I **d** your feast days, and I
Mal	1: 6	to you priests who **d** My name
Matt	6:24	to the one and **d** the other
Matt	18:10	**d** one of these little ones
Rom	2: 4	Or do you **d** the riches of His
Rom	14: 3	eats **d** him who does not eat
1Co	11:22	Or do you **d** the church of God
1Th	5:20	Do not **d** prophecies
1Ti	4:12	Let no one **d** your youth, but
Heb	12: 5	do not **d** the chastening of
2Pe	2:10	of uncleanness and **d** authority

DESPISED (see DESPISE)

Gen	16: 4	mistress became **d** in her eyes
Gen	25:34	Thus Esau **d** his birthright
Num	11:20	because you have **d** the LORD
2Sa	6:16	and she **d** him in her heart
Neh	2:19	us to scorn and **d** us, and said,
Neh	4: 4	Hear, O our God, for we are **d**
Job	31:13	If I have **d** the cause of my
Ps	22: 6	of men, and **d** of the people

Ps	22:24	For He has not **d** nor abhorred
Ps	53: 5	shame, Because God has **d** them
Ps	107:11	**d** the counsel of the Most
Ps	119:141	I am small and **d**, Yet I do not
Prov	1:30	counsel and **d** all my reproof,
Eccl	9:16	the poor man's wisdom is **d**
Song	8: 1	I would not be **d**
Is	5:24	**d** the word of the Holy One of
Is	53: 3	He is **d** and rejected by men, a
Is	53: 3	He was **d**, and we did not
Ezek	16:59	who **d** the oath by breaking
Ezek	22: 8	You have **d** My holy things and
Amos	2: 4	because they have **d** the law
Obad	2	you shall be greatly **d**
Zech	4:10	For who has **d** the day of
Mal	1: 6	what way have we **d** Your name
Acts	19:27	great goddess Diana may be **d**
1Co	1:28	which are **d** God has chosen

DESPISERS (see DESPISE)

2Ti	3: 3	brutal, **d** of good,

DESPISES (see DESPISE)

Prov	11:12	of wisdom **d** his neighbor, but
Prov	13:13	He who **d** the word will be
Prov	14: 2	is perverse in his ways **d** Him
Prov	14:21	He who **d** his neighbor sins
Prov	15: 5	A fool **d** his father's
Prov	15:20	a foolish man **d** his mother
Prov	15:32	instruction **d** his own soul

DESPISING† (see DESPISE)

Heb	12: 2	**d** the shame, and has sat down

DESPOILED†

Judg	2:14	of plunderers who **d** them

DESTINED† (see DESTINY)

Job	15:28	which are **d** to become ruins
Luke	2:34	this Child is **d** for the fall

DESTINY† (see DESTINED)

Lam	1: 9	she did not consider her **d**

DESTITUTE

Ps	102:17	regard the prayer of the **d**
Ps	141: 8	Do not leave my soul **d**
Prov	15:21	him who is **d** of discernment
1Ti	6: 5	**d** of the truth, who suppose
Heb	11:37	and goatskins, being **d**,
Jas	2:15	is naked and **d** of daily food,

DESTROY (see DESTROYED, DESTROYER, DESTROYING, DESTROYS, DESTRUCTION, DESTRUCTIVE)

Gen	6: 7	I will **d** man whom I have
Gen	9:11	be a flood to **d** the earth
Gen	18:28	forty-five, I will not **d** it
Gen	19:13	the LORD has sent us to **d** it
Gen	19:14	for the LORD will **d** this city
Ex	8: 9	to **d** the frogs from you and
Ex	12:13	shall not be on you to **d** you
Ex	34:13	But you shall **d** their altars
Lev	26:30	I will **d** your high places,
Deut	9: 3	**d** them quickly, as the LORD
Deut	20:19	you shall not **d** its trees by
Judg	21:11	shall utterly **d** every male
2Sa	1:14	hand to **d** the LORD's anointed
2Ki	8:19	the LORD would not **d** Judah
Esth	3: 6	Haman sought to **d** all the
Esth	4: 7	treasuries to **d** the Jews
Esth	8:11	to **d**, kill, and annihilate all
Job	2: 3	him, to **d** him without cause
Job	10: 8	yet You would **d** me
Job	14:19	so You **d** the hope of man
Ps	21:10	You shall **d** from the earth
Ps	40:14	Who seek to **d** my life
Ps	55: 9	**D**, O Lord, and divide their
Ps	101: 8	Early I will **d** all the wicked
Ps	106:23	He said that He would **d** them

Ps	144: 6	out Your arrows and **d** them
Eccl	5: 6	and **d** the work of your hands
Eccl	7:16	why should you **d** yourself
Is	10: 7	but it is in his heart to **d**
Is	11: 9	nor **d** in all My holy mountain
Is	65:25	nor **d** in all My holy mountain
Jer	1:10	out and to pull down, to **d**
Jer	11:19	Let us **d** the tree with its
Jer	17:18	doom, and **d** them with double
Jer	18: 7	up, to pull down, and to **d** it
Jer	23: 1	Woe to the shepherds who **d**
Jer	50:21	Waste and utterly **d** them,"
Jer	51:20	with you I will **d** kingdoms
Lam	2: 8	The LORD has purposed to **d**
Ezek	25:16	**d** the remnant of the seacoast
Ezek	26:12	and **d** your pleasant houses
Ezek	34:16	but I will **d** the fat and the
Ezek	43: 3	saw when I came to **d** the city
Dan	2:12	gave a command to **d** all the
Dan	2:24	to **d** the wise men of Babylon
Dan	4:23	**d** it, but leave its stump and
Dan	7:26	to consume and **d** it forever
Dan	8:24	he shall **d** fearfully, and
Dan	9:26	is to come shall **d** the city
Hos	2:12	I will **d** her vines and her fig
Hos	4: 5	and I will **d** your mother
Amos	3:15	I will **d** the winter house
Matt	2:13	seek the young Child to **d** Him
Matt	5:17	to **d** the Law or the Prophets
Matt	5:17	not come to **d** but to fulfill
Matt	6:19	earth, where moth and rust **d**
Matt	10:28	who is able to **d** both soul
Matt	12:14	Him, how they might **d** Him
Matt	27:20	ask for Barabbas and **d** Jesus
Matt	27:40	You who **d** the temple and build
Mark	9:22	and into the water to **d** him
Mark	12: 9	**d** the vinedressers, and give
Luke	6: 9	evil, to save life or to **d** it
John	2:19	**D** this temple, and in three
John	10:10	to steal, and to kill, and to **d**
Rom	14:15	Do not **d** with your food the
Rom	14:20	Do not **d** the work of God for
1Co	1:19	I will **d** the wisdom of the
1Co	3:17	temple of God, God will **d** him
1Co	6:13	foods, but God will **d** both it
2Th	2: 8	**d** with the brightness of His
Heb	2:14	**d** him who had the power of
Jas	4:12	who is able to save and to **d**
1Jn	3: 8	that He might **d** the works of
Rev	11:18	**d** those who **d** the earth

DESTROYED (see DESTROY)

Gen	7:23	So He **d** all living things
Gen	13:10	(before the LORD **d** Sodom and
Gen	19:17	the mountains, lest you be **d**
Gen	19:29	when God **d** the cities of the
Ex	10: 7	not yet know that Egypt is **d**
Ex	22:20	only, he shall be utterly **d**
Deut	2:21	But the LORD **d** them before
Deut	11: 4	LORD has **d** them to this day
Deut	28:48	your neck until He has **d** you
Josh	6:21	they utterly **d** all that was
Josh	10: 1	taken Ai and had utterly **d** it
Judg	21:17	may not be **d** from Israel
1Sa	15:21	should have been utterly **d**
2Ki	10:28	Thus Jehu **d** Baal from Israel
2Ki	11: 1	and **d** all the royal heirs
2Ch	36:19	fire, and **d** all its precious
Ezra	4:15	which cause this city was **d**
Ezra	5:12	who **d** this temple and carried
Esth	7: 4	sold, my people and I, to be **d**
Job	19:26	and after my skin is **d**, this I
Ps	11: 3	If the foundations are **d**,
Ps	78:45	them, And frogs, which **d** them
Ps	78:47	He **d** their vines with hail,

Ps	78:51	**d** all the firstborn in Egypt,
Ps	137: 8	of Babylon, who are to be **d**
Prov	13:13	despises the word will be **d**
Prov	13:20	companion of fools will be **d**
Prov	29: 1	his neck, will suddenly be **d**
Jer	22:20	for all your lovers are **d**
Lam	2: 5	He has **d** her strongholds, and
Ezek	28:16	I **d** you, O covering cherub,
Dan	2:44	which shall never be **d**
Dan	7:11	was slain, and its body **d** and
Hos	4: 6	My people are **d** for lack of
Matt	22: 7	**d** those murderers, and burned
Luke	9:25	and is himself **d** or lost
Luke	17:27	the flood came and **d** them all
Acts	13:19	when He had **d** seven nations
1Co	10: 9	and were **d** by serpents
1Co	10:10	and were **d** by the destroyer
1Co	15:26	enemy that will be **d** is death
2Co	4: 9	struck down, but not **d**
2Co	5: 1	house, this tent, is **d**, we
Heb	11:28	lest he who **d** the firstborn
Rev	8: 9	a third of the ships were **d**

DESTROYER (see DESTROY, DESTROYERS)

Ex	12:23	not allow the **d** to come into
Prov	28:24	the same is companion to a **d**
Jer	4: 7	the **d** of nations is on his
1Co	10:10	and were destroyed by the **d**

DESTROYERS (see DESTROYER)

Jer	50:11	you **d** of My heritage, because

DESTROYING (see DESTROY)

Lev	11:22	the **d** locust after its kind,
Is	28: 2	a **d** storm, like a flood of
Jer	2:30	your prophets like a **d** lion
Jer	51:25	O **d** mountain, who destroys
Lam	2: 8	not withdrawn His hand from **d**

DESTROYS (see DESTROY)

Deut	8:20	which the LORD **d** before you
Prov	6:32	he who does so **d** his own soul
Prov	11: 9	with his mouth **d** his neighbor
Eccl	9:18	but one sinner **d** much good
Matt	6:20	where neither moth nor rust **d**

DESTRUCTION (see DESTROY)

Lev	27:29	become doomed to **d** among
Deut	32:24	by pestilence and bitter **d**
Josh	6:17	be doomed by the LORD to **d**
1Sa	5: 9	the city with a very great **d**
2Sa	24:16	the LORD relented from the **d**
Esth	4: 8	written decree for their **d**
Esth	9: 5	sword, with slaughter and **d**
Job	5:21	be afraid of **d** when it comes
Job	5:22	You shall laugh at **d** and
Job	26: 6	Him, and **D** has no covering
Job	28:22	**D** and Death say, 'We have
Job	31: 3	Is it not **d** for the wicked,
Job	31:12	be a fire that consumes to **d**
Job	31:23	For **d** from God is a terror to
Ps	5: 9	Their inward part is **d**
Ps	35: 8	Let **d** come upon him
Ps	52: 2	Your tongue devises **d**, Like a
Ps	55:23	them down to the pit of **d**
Ps	78:49	angels of **d** among them
Ps	88:11	in the place of **d**
Ps	91: 6	Nor of the **d** that lays waste
Ps	103: 4	Who redeems your life from **d**
Prov	1:27	your **d** comes like a whirlwind
Prov	10:15	the **d** of the poor is their
Prov	15:11	Hell and **D** are before the LORD
Prov	16:18	Pride goes before **d**, and a
Prov	18: 7	A fool's mouth is his **d**, and
Prov	18:12	Before **d** the heart of a man
Prov	27:20	Hell and **D** are never full
Is	14:23	sweep it with the broom of **d**

Is	19:18	will be called the City of **D**
Is	28:22	a **d** determined even upon the
Is	59: 7	and **d** are in their paths
Jer	4: 6	from the north, and great **d**
Jer	4:20	**D** upon destruction is cried
Jer	17:18	and destroy them with double **d**
Lam	2:11	the **d** of the daughter of my
Lam	3:48	the **d** of the daughter of my
Dan	11:16	Land with **d** in his power
Hos	13:14	O Grave, I will be your **d**
Amos	3:14	I will also visit **d** on the
Matt	7:13	is the way that leads to **d**
Rom	3:16	**d** and misery are in their ways
Rom	9:22	of wrath prepared for **d**,
1Co	5: 5	Satan for the **d** of the flesh
2Co	10: 8	edification and not for your **d**
Phil	3:19	whose end is **d**, whose god is
1Th	5: 3	then sudden **d** comes upon
2Th	1: 9	**d** from the presence of the
1Ti	6: 9	lusts which drown men in **d**
2Pe	2: 1	bring on themselves swift **d**
2Pe	2: 6	ashes, condemned them to **d**
2Pe	3:16	unstable twist to their own **d**

DESTRUCTIVE (*see* DESTROY)

2Pe	2: 1	secretly bring in **d** heresies

DETAIL† (*see* DETAILS)

Acts	21:19	he told in **d** those things
Heb	9: 5	we cannot now speak in **d**

DETAILS† (*see* DETAIL)

1Ki	6:38	was finished in all its **d**

DETERMINE (*see* DETERMINED, DETERMINING)

Ex	21:22	he shall pay as the judges **d**
Esth	3: 7	before Haman to **d** the day
Mark	15:24	casting lots for them to **d**

DETERMINED (*see* DETERMINE)

Josh	17:12	were **d** to dwell in that land
Judg	1:27	were **d** to dwell in that land
Ruth	1:18	that she was **d** to go with her
Job	14: 5	Since his days are **d**, the
Job	38: 5	Who **d** its measurements
Dan	9:24	weeks are **d** for your people
Dan	9:26	of the war desolations are **d**
Dan	11:36	what has been **d** shall be done
Matt	2: 7	**d** from them what time the
Luke	22:22	of Man goes as it has been **d**
Acts	2:23	delivered by the **d** counsel
Acts	3:13	when he was **d** to let Him go
Acts	11:29	**d** to send relief to the
Acts	15: 2	they **d** that Paul and Barnabas
Acts	17:26	and has **d** their preappointed
1Co	2: 2	For I **d** not to know anything

DETERMINING† (*see* DETERMINE)

Heb	6:17	**d** to show more abundantly to

DETEST† (*see* DETESTABLE, DETESTS)

Deut	7:26	but you shall utterly **d** it
Prov	3:11	LORD, nor **d** His correction

DETESTABLE (*see* DETEST)

Deut	14: 3	You shall not eat any **d** thing

DETESTS (*see* DETEST)

Deut	22:13	and goes in to her, and **d** her,
Deut	24: 3	if the latter husband **d** her

DEVASTATION

Zeph	1:15	and distress, a day of **d** and

DEVICE† (*see* DEVICES)

Eccl	9:10	for there is no work or **d** or

DEVICES (*see* DEVICE)

Job	5:12	the **d** of the crafty, so that
2Co	2:11	we are not ignorant of his **d**

DEVIL

Matt	4: 1	to be tempted by the **d**
Matt	4: 5	Then the **d** took Him up into
Matt	13:39	enemy who sowed them is the **d**
Matt	25:41	fire prepared for the **d** and
Luke	4: 2	for forty days by the **d**
Luke	8:12	then the **d** comes and takes
John	6:70	twelve, and one of you is a **d**
John	8:44	You are of your father the **d**
John	13: 2	the **d** having already put it
Acts	10:38	who were oppressed by the **d**
Acts	13:10	all fraud, you son of the **d**
Eph	4:27	nor give place to the **d**
Eph	6:11	against the wiles of the **d**
1Ti	3: 6	same condemnation as the **d**
1Ti	3: 7	and the snare of the **d**,
Heb	2:14	of death, that is, the **d**,
Jas	4: 7	Resist the **d** and he will flee
1Pe	5: 8	**d** walks about like a roaring
1Jn	3: 8	He who sins is of the **d**, for
1Jn	3: 8	destroy the works of the **d**
Jude	9	in contending with the **d**
Rev	12: 9	serpent of old, called the **D**
Rev	20: 2	serpent of old, who is the **D**
Rev	20:10	And the **d**, who deceived them,

DEVIOUS (*see* DEVISE)

Prov	2:15	and who are **d** in their paths

DEVISE (*see* DEVIOUS, DEVISED, DEVISES, DEVISING)

Ps	35:20	But they **d** deceitful matters
Prov	3:29	Do not **d** evil against your
Prov	14:22	they not go astray who **d** evil
Prov	16:30	his eye to **d** perverse things
Dan	11:24	he shall **d** his plans against
Mic	2: 1	Woe to those who **d** iniquity

DEVISED (*see* DEVISE)

Esth	8: 3	he had **d** against the Jews
Ps	10: 2	the plots which they have **d**
Prov	30:32	or if you have **d** evil, put
Jer	11:19	they had **d** schemes against me
2Pe	1:16	**d** fables when we made known

DEVISES (*see* DEVISE)

Ps	36: 4	He **d** wickedness on his bed
Ps	52: 2	Your tongue **d** destruction
Prov	24: 2	for their heart **d** violence
Is	32: 8	man **d** generous things, and by

DEVISING (*see* DEVISE)

Acts	17:29	shaped by art and man's **d**

DEVOID

Prov	10:13	him who is **d** of understanding
Prov	11:12	He who is **d** of wisdom

DEVOTE (*see* DEVOTED, DEVOUT)

Lev	27:28	offering that a man may **d** to

DEVOTED (*see* DEVOTE)

Lev	27:28	every **d** offering is most holy
Ps	119:38	Who is **d** to fearing You
1Co	16:15	that they have **d** themselves

DEVOUR (*see* DEVOURED, DEVOURING, DEVOURS)

Gen	49:27	morning he shall **d** the prey
Judg	9:15	and the cedars of Lebanon
2Sa	2:26	Shall the sword **d** forever
2Ch	7:13	the locusts to **d** the land
Ps	21: 9	And the fire shall **d** them
Prov	30:14	to **d** the poor from off the
Jer	17:27	it shall **d** the palaces of
Ezek	7:15	and pestilence will **d** him
Ezek	20:47	it shall **d** every green tree
Dan	7: 5	Arise, **d** much flesh
Dan	7:23	and shall **d** the whole earth,
Amos	1: 7	which shall **d** its palaces
Amos	1:10	which shall **d** its palaces

Amos 5: 6 **d** it, with no one to quench
Matt 23:14 For you **d** widows' houses, and
Gal 5:15 **d** one another, beware lest
Heb 10:27 which will **d** the adversaries
1Pe 5: 8 lion, seeking whom he may **d**
Rev 12: 4 to **d** her Child as soon as it

DEVOURED (see DEVOUR)

Gen 37:33 A wild beast has **d** him
Gen 41: 7 thin kernels **d** the seven plump
Is 24: 6 the curse has **d** the earth
Jer 3:24 For shame has **d** the labor of
Jer 50:17 the king of Assyria **d** him
Jer 51:34 the king of Babylon has **d** me
Ezek 19:14 **d** her fruit, so that she has
Dan 7:19 its nails of bronze, which **d**
Hos 7: 7 oven, and have **d** their judges
Hos 7: 9 Aliens have **d** his strength,
Amos 4: 9 trees, The locust **d** them
Nah 1:10 They shall be **d** like stubble
Zeph 1:18 **d** by the fire of His jealousy
Matt 13: 4 and the birds came and **d** them
Luke 15:30 who has **d** your livelihood
Rev 20: 9 God out of heaven and **d** them

DEVOURING (see DEVOUR)

2Sa 22: 9 and **d** fire from His mouth
Ps 52: 4 You love all **d** words, You
Dan 7: 7 it was **d**, breaking in pieces,

DEVOURS (see DEVOUR)

Num 13:32 a land that **d** its inhabitants
Num 23:24 lie down until it **d** the prey
2Sa 11:25 for the sword **d** one as well
Job 18:13 It **d** patches of his skin
Prov 19:28 of the wicked **d** iniquity
Is 5:24 as the fire **d** the stubble
Hab 1:13 **d** one more righteous than he

DEVOUT (see DEVOTE)

Luke 2:25 and this man was just and **d**
Acts 2: 5 **d** men, from every nation
Acts 8: 2 **d** men carried Stephen to his
Acts 10: 2 a **d** man and one who feared
Acts 13:43 **d** proselytes followed Paul and
Acts 17: 4 multitude of the **d** Greeks
Acts 22:12 a **d** man according to the law,

DEW

Gen 27:28 give you of the **d** of heaven
Ex 16:13 in the morning the **d** lay all
Deut 32: 2 my speech distill as the **d**
Deut 33:28 His Heavens shall also drop **d**
Judg 6:37 if there is **d** on the fleece
2Sa 1:21 of Gilboa, let there be no **d**
1Ki 17: 1 there shall not be **d** nor rain
Ps 110: 3 You have the **d** of Your youth
Ps 133: 3 It is like the **d** of Hermon
Prov 3:20 up, and clouds drop down the **d**
Song 5: 2 for my head is covered with **d**
Dan 4:33 his body was wet with the **d**
Hos 6: 4 like the early **d** it goes away
Hag 1:10 above you withhold the **d**, and

DIADEMS†

Rev 12: 3 and seven **d** on his heads

DIAL†

Is 38: 8 **d** by which it had gone down

DIAMOND

Ex 28:18 turquoise, a sapphire, and a **d**
Jer 17: 1 with the point of a **d** it is
Ezek 28:13 the sardius, topaz, and **d**,

DIANA

Acts 19:24 who made silver shrines of **D**
Acts 19:28 Great is **D** of the Ephesians
Acts 19:35 of the great goddess **D**, and of

DICTATES

Jer 3:17 follow the **d** of their hearts

DIDYMUS (see THOMAS, TWIN)

DIE (see DEAD, DEATH, DIED, DIES, DYING)
Gen 2:17 eat of it you shall surely **d**
Gen 3: 3 you touch it, lest you **d**
Gen 3: 4 You will not surely **d**
Gen 27: 4 soul may bless you before I **d**
Gen 30: 1 Give me children, or else I **d**
Gen 45:28 will go and see him before I **d**
Ex 7:18 that are in the river shall **d**
Ex 10:28 you see my face you shall **d**
Ex 11: 5 in the land of Egypt shall **d**
Ex 14:12 we should **d** in the wilderness
Ex 20:19 God speak with us, lest we **d**
Lev 20:20 they shall **d** childless
Num 23:10 Let me **d** the death of the
Num 26:11 children of Korah did not **d**
Deut 4:22 But I must **d** in this land, I
Deut 5:25 therefore, why should we **d**
Deut 18:20 gods, that prophet shall **d**
Deut 19:12 of blood, that he may **d**
Deut 22:25 man who lay with her shall **d**
Deut 24: 7 then that kidnapper shall **d**
Judg 16:30 Let me **d** with the Philistines
Ruth 1:17 Where you **d**, I will **d**, and
1Sa 26:16 lives, you are worthy to **d**
2Sa 3:33 Should Abner **d** as a fool dies
2Sa 12:14 is born to you shall surely **d**
1Ki 17:12 son, that we may eat it, and **d**
1Ki 21:10 and stone him, that he may **d**
2Ki 13:14 illness of which he would **d**
2Ch 25: 4 shall **d** for his own sin
Job 2: 9 Curse God and **d**
Job 3:11 Why did I not **d** at birth
Job 12: 2 and wisdom will **d** with you
Job 14: 8 its stump may **d** in the ground
Job 34:20 In a moment they **d**, in the
Job 36:14 They **d** in youth, and their
Ps 79:11 those who are appointed to **d**
Ps 82: 7 But you shall **d** like men, And
Ps 104:29 away their breath, they **d**
Prov 10:21 many, but fools **d** for lack of
Prov 15:10 he who hates reproof will **d**
Prov 19:16 careless of his ways will **d**
Prov 23:13 him with a rod, he will not **d**
Eccl 3: 2 to be born, and a time to **d**
Eccl 7:17 why should you **d** before your
Is 22:13 and drink, for tomorrow we **d**
Is 22:18 there you shall **d**, and there
Is 51:14 he should not **d** in the pit
Is 66:24 For their worm does not **d**
Jer 11:22 men shall **d** by the sword,
Jer 11:22 daughters shall **d** by famine
Jer 16: 4 They shall **d** gruesome deaths
Jer 20: 6 Babylon, and there you shall **d**
Jer 26:11 This man deserves to **d**
Jer 28:16 This year you shall **d**,
Jer 31:30 But every one shall **d** for his
Jer 34: 5 But you shall **d** in peace
Jer 38: 9 he is likely to **d** from hunger
Lam 4: 9 than those who **d** of hunger
Ezek 3:18 wicked, 'You shall surely **d**
Ezek 3:18 man shall **d** in his iniquity
Ezek 18: 4 the soul who sins shall **d**
Ezek 18:31 For why should you **d**, O house
Ezek 33:11 For why should you **d**, O house
Amos 6: 9 in one house, they shall **d**
Amos 7:11 Jeroboam shall **d** by the sword
Jon 4: 3 for me to **d** than to live
Jon 4: 8 for me to **d** than to live
Hab 1:12 We shall not **d**
Matt 26:35 Even if I have to **d** with You
Mark 9:44 where 'their worm does not **d**

Luke	20:36	nor can they **d** anymore, for
John	6:50	one may eat of it and not **d**
John	8:21	Me, and will **d** in your sin
John	11:25	in Me, though he may **d**, he
John	11:26	believes in Me shall never **d**
John	11:50	man should **d** for the people
John	11:51	Jesus would **d** for the nation
John	12:33	by what death He would **d**
John	18:32	by what death He would **d**
John	19: 7	to our law He ought to **d**,
John	21:23	this disciple would not **d**
Acts	21:13	but also to **d** at Jerusalem
Rom	5: 7	a righteous man will one **d**
Rom	5: 7	someone would even dare to **d**
Rom	8:13	to the flesh you will **d**
Rom	14: 8	if we **d**, we **d** to the Lord
Rom	14: 8	whether we live or **d**, we are
1Co	9:15	to **d** than that anyone should
1Co	15:22	For as in Adam all **d**, even so
1Co	15:31	Jesus our Lord, I **d** daily
1Co	15:32	and drink, for tomorrow we **d**
Phil	1:21	is Christ, and to **d** is gain
Heb	9:27	appointed for men to **d** once
Rev	14:13	who **d** in the Lord from now on

DIED (*see* DIE)

Gen	5: 5	and he **d**
Gen	7:21	all flesh **d** that moved on the
Gen	25: 8	**d** in a good old age, an old
Gen	25:17	and he breathed his last and **d**
Gen	35:19	So Rachel **d** and was buried on
Ex	2:23	time that the king of Egypt **d**
Ex	7:21	fish that were in the river **d**
Ex	8:13	the frogs **d** out of the houses
Ex	9: 6	all the livestock of Egypt **d**
Ex	9: 6	children of Israel, not one **d**
Lev	10: 2	and they **d** before the LORD
Lev	17:15	**d** naturally or what was torn
Num	14:37	**d** by the plague before the
Num	15:36	him with stones, and he **d**
Num	19:16	slain by a sword or who has **d**
Num	20: 1	and Miriam **d** there and was
Num	20:28	Aaron **d** there on the top of
Deut	34: 5	the servant of the LORD **d**
Deut	34: 7	and twenty years old when he **d**
Judg	9:54	thrust him through, and he **d**
Ruth	1: 3	Elimelech, Naomi's husband, **d**
1Sa	4:18	his neck was broken and he **d**
1Sa	25: 1	Then Samuel **d**; and the
1Sa	25:37	that his heart **d** within him
1Sa	25:38	LORD struck Nabal, and he **d**
1Sa	31: 5	on his sword, and **d** with him
2Sa	1:15	And he struck him so that he **d**
2Sa	6: 7	he **d** there by the ark of God
2Sa	11:17	and Uriah the Hittite **d** also
2Sa	12:18	came to pass that the child **d**
2Sa	17:23	and hanged himself, and **d**
2Sa	18:33	if only I had **d** in your place
1Ki	2: 5	struck him down, and he **d**
1Ki	2:46	struck him down, and he **d**
1Ki	3:19	woman's son **d** in the night
1Ki	12:18	him with stones, and he **d**
2Ki	8:15	it over his face so that he **d**
2Ki	13:20	Then Elisha **d**, and they buried
2Ch	18:34	about the time of sunset he **d**
2Ch	21:19	so he **d** in severe pain
Job	42:17	So Job **d**, old and full of days
Is	6: 1	the year that King Uzziah **d**
Is	14:28	in the year that King Ahaz **d**
Ezek	24:18	and at evening my wife **d**
Hos	13: 1	he offended in Baal, he **d**
Matt	9:18	My daughter has just **d**, but
Matt	22:27	last of all the woman **d** also
Luke	16:22	So it was that the beggar **d**
Luke	16:22	The rich man also **d** and was

Luke	20:29	a wife, and **d** without children
John	11:21	my brother would not have **d**
John	11:32	my brother would not have **d**
John	11:44	he who had **d** came out bound
Acts	7:15	and he **d**, he and our fathers
Acts	12:23	he was eaten by worms and **d**
Rom	5: 6	time Christ **d** for the ungodly
Rom	5: 8	sinners, Christ **d** for us
Rom	5:15	the one man's offense many **d**
Rom	6: 2	How shall we who **d** to sin
Rom	6: 8	Now if we **d** with Christ, we
Rom	6:10	For the death that He **d**, He
Rom	6:10	He **d** to sin once for all
Rom	7: 9	came, sin revived and I **d**
Rom	14:15	the one for whom Christ **d**
1Co	8:11	perish, for whom Christ **d**
1Co	15: 3	that Christ **d** for our sins
2Co	5:14	One **d** for all, then all **d**
Gal	2:19	For I through the law **d** to
Gal	2:21	law, then Christ **d** in vain
Col	3: 3	For you **d**, and your life is
1Th	4:14	if we believe that Jesus **d**
Heb	11:13	These all **d** in faith, not
1Pe	2:24	having **d** to sins, might live
Rev	8: 9	living creatures in the sea **d**

DIES (*see* DIE)

Lev	7:24	of a beast that **d** naturally
Num	27: 8	If a man **d** and has no son,
Deut	13:10	him with stones until he **d**
Deut	14:21	eat anything that **d** of itself
Deut	24: 3	or if the latter husband **d**
2Sa	3:33	Should Abner die as a fool **d**
Job	14:10	But man **d** and is laid away
Job	14:14	If a man **d**, shall he live
Job	21:23	One **d** in his full strength,
Prov	11: 7	When a wicked man **d**, his
Eccl	3:19	as one **d**, so **d** the other
Matt	22:24	Moses said that if a man **d**
Mark	12:19	us that if a man's brother **d**
Luke	20:28	he **d** without children, his
John	4:49	come down before my child **d**
John	12:24	falls into the ground and **d**
John	12:24	but if it **d**, it produces much
Rom	6: 9	from the dead, **d** no more
Rom	7: 2	But if the husband **d**, she is
Rom	14: 7	and no one **d** to himself
1Co	15:36	is not made alive unless it **d**
Heb	10:28	law **d** without mercy on the

DIFFER† (*see* DIFFERENCE, DIFFERENT, DIFFERING, DIFFERS)

1Co	4: 7	who makes you **d** from another
Gal	4: 1	does not **d** at all from a

DIFFERENCE (*see* DIFFER, DIFFERENCES)

Ex	8:23	I will make a **d** between My
Ex	11: 7	a **d** between the Egyptians
Ezek	22:26	the **d** between the unclean
Rom	3:22	For there is no **d**
1Co	7:34	There is a **d** between a wife
Gal	2: 6	were, it makes no **d** to me

DIFFERENCES† (*see* DIFFERENCE)

1Co	12: 5	There are **d** of ministries,

DIFFERENT (*see* DIFFER, VARIOUS)

Num	14:24	he has a **d** spirit in him and
Deut	22: 9	vineyard with **d** kinds of seed
Deut	22:11	not wear a garment of **d** sorts
Esth	3: 8	their laws are **d** from all
Dan	7: 7	It was **d** from all the beasts
1Co	12:10	to another **d** kinds of tongues
2Co	11: 4	or if you receive a **d** spirit
Gal	1: 6	of Christ, to a **d** gospel,

DIFFERING† (*see* DIFFER)

Deut	25:13	have in your bag **d** weights

Deut 25:14 have in your house **d** measures
Rom 12: 6 Having then gifts **d** according

DIFFERS† (*see* DIFFER)
1Co 15:41 for one star **d** from another

DIFFICULT (*see* DIFFICULTY)
Eccl 12: 1 youth, before the **d** days come
Dan 2:11 It is a **d** thing that the king
Matt 7:14 **d** is the way which leads to

DIFFICULTIES† (*see* DIFFICULTY)
Ex 18:19 you may bring the **d** to God

DIFFICULTY (*see* DIFFICULT, DIFFICULTIES)
Ex 18:16 When they have a **d**, they come
Luke 9:39 departs from him with great **d**
Acts 27: 8 Passing it with **d**, we came to

DIFFUSED† (*see* DIFFUSES)
Job 38:24 By what way is light **d**, or

DIFFUSES† (*see* DIFFUSED)
2Co 2:14 through us **d** the fragrance of

DIG (*see* DIGS, DUG)
Deut 6:11 wells which you did not **d**
Deut 8: 9 whose hills you can **d** copper
Ezek 8: 8 Son of man, **d** into the wall"
Amos 9: 2 Though they **d** into hell, from
Luke 13: 8 also, until I **d** around it and

DIGNITARIES (*see* DIGNITY)
2Pe 2:10 not afraid to speak evil of **d**

DIGNITY (*see* DIGNITARIES)
Gen 49: 3 strength, the excellency of **d**

DIGS (*see* DIG)
Prov 16:27 An ungodly man **d** up evil, and
Eccl 10: 8 He who **d** a pit will fall into

DILIGENCE (*see* DILIGENT)
Prov 4:23 Keep your heart with all **d**
Rom 12: 8 he who leads, with **d**
Rom 12:11 not lagging in **d**, fervent in
2Co 7:11 What **d** it produced in you,
2Co 8: 7 in knowledge, in all **d**, and
2Pe 1: 5 very reason, giving all **d**

DILIGENT (*see* CAREFUL, DILIGENCE, DILIGENTLY)
Ps 77: 6 And my spirit makes **d** search
Prov 10: 4 hand of the **d** makes one rich
Prov 21: 5 The plans of the **d** lead
2Co 8:17 exhortation, but being more **d**
2Co 8:22 often proved **d** in many things
2Ti 4: 9 Be **d** to come to me quickly
Heb 4:11 be **d** to enter that rest, lest
2Pe 1:10 be even more **d** to make your
2Pe 3:14 be **d** to be found by Him in

DILIGENTLY (*see* CAREFUL, CAREFULLY, DILIGENT EARNESTLY, ZEALOUSLY)
Deut 4: 9 **d** keep yourself, lest you
Deut 6: 7 teach them **d** to your children
2Ch 34:33 **d** serve the LORD their God
Ps 119: 4 us To keep Your precepts **d**
Prov 1:28 they will seek me **d**, but they
Prov 8:17 who seek me **d** will find me
Heb 11: 6 of those who **d** seek Him
Heb 12:17 he sought it **d** with tears

DIM (*see* DIMLY)
Gen 27: 1 his eyes were so **d** that he
Deut 34: 7 His eyes were not **d** nor his
Eccl 12: 3 through the windows grows **d**

DIMINISH (*see* DIMINISHED, REDUCE)
Ex 21:10 wife, he shall not **d** her food
Jer 26: 2 Do not **d** a word
Joel 2:10 the stars **d** their brightness

DIMINISHED (*see* ABATED, DIMINISH, REDUCED)
Deut 34: 7 dim nor his natural vigor **d**
Prov 13:11 by dishonesty will be **d**, but

DIMLY† (*see* DIM)
1Co 13:12 For now we see in a mirror, **d**

DINAH (*see* DINAH'S)
Gen 34: 3 to **D** the daughter of Jacob
Gen 34:13 he had defiled **D** their sister

DINAH'S† (*see* DINAH)
Gen 34:25 **D** brothers, each took his

DINE (*see* DINING)
Esth 7: 1 Haman went to **d** with Queen
Luke 11:37 asked Him to **d** with him
Rev 3:20 **d** with him, and he with Me

DINING† (*see* DINE)
Mark 2:15 as He was **d** in Levi's house,

DINNER
Prov 15:17 Better is a **d** of herbs where
Matt 22: 4 See, I have prepared my **d**
Luke 11:38 had not first washed before **d**
1Co 10:27 not believe invites you to **d**

DIONYSIUS†
Acts 17:34 among them **D** the Areopagite,

DIP (*see* DIPPED, DIPS)
Ex 12:22 **d** it in the blood that is in
Lev 4: 6 The priest shall **d** his
Num 19:18 **d** it in the water, sprinkle
Luke 16:24 **d** the tip of his finger in

DIPPED (*see* DIP)
Gen 37:31 and **d** the tunic in the blood
Lev 9: 9 he **d** his finger in the blood,
2Ki 5:14 **d** seven times in the Jordan,
Matt 26:23 He who **d** his hand with Me in
John 13:26 of bread when I have **d** it
Rev 19:13 with a robe **d** in blood, and

DIPS† (*see* DIP)
Mark 14:20 who **d** with Me in the dish

DIRE†
Job 36:16 brought you out of **d** distress
Lam 1: 3 overtake her in **d** straits

DIRECT (*see* DIRECTED, DIRECTION, DIRECTS)
Ps 119:133 **D** my steps by Your word, And
Prov 3: 6 Him, and He shall **d** your paths
Is 45:13 and I will **d** all his ways
2Th 3: 5 Now may the Lord **d** your

DIRECTED (*see* DIRECT)
Ps 119: 5 that my ways were **d** To keep
Is 40:13 Who has **d** the Spirit of the
Matt 27:10 field, as the LORD **d** me

DIRECTION (*see* DIRECT, DIRECTIONS)
1Ch 25: 2 were under the **d** of Asaph
Mark 1:45 they came to Him from every **d**
Acts 7:53 the law by the **d** of angels

DIRECTIONS (*see* DIRECTION)
1Ch 9:24 were assigned to the four **d**

DIRECTS† (*see* DIRECT)
Prov 16: 9 way, but the LORD **d** his steps

DIRT
1Sa 4:12 clothes torn and **d** on his head
Is 57:20 waters cast up mire and **d**

DISAPPEAR† (*see* DISAPPEARS)
Ps 12: 1 For the faithful **d** from among

DISAPPEARS† (*see* DISAPPEAR)
Job 7: 9 As the cloud **d** and vanishes
Job 14:11 As water **d** from the sea, and a

DISAPPOINT†
Rom 5: 5 Now hope does not **d**, because

DISAPPROVED†
2Ti 3: 8 minds, **d** concerning the faith

DISARMED
Col 2:15 Having **d** principalities and

DISASTER (see DISASTERS)
Neh 13:18 God bring all this **d** on us
Job 31: 3 **d** for the workers of iniquity
Jer 4: 6 I will bring **d** from the north
Jer 18: 8 I will relent of the **d** that I
Ezek 7:26 **D** will come upon **d**
Jon 3:10 God relented from the **d** that
Acts 27:10 this voyage will end with **d**

DISASTERS† (see DISASTER)
Deut 32:23 I will heap **d** upon them

DISBELIEVED†
Acts 28:24 which were spoken, and some **d**

DISCERN (see DISCERNED, DISCERNER, DISCERNING, DISCERNMENT, UNDISCERNING)
2Sa 19:35 Can I **d** between the good and
Jon 4:11 **d** between their right hand
Matt 16: 3 but you cannot **d** the signs of
Heb 5:14 exercised to **d** both good and

DISCERNED† (see DISCERN)
1Co 2:14 they are spiritually **d**

DISCERNER† (see DISCERN)
Heb 4:12 is a **d** of the thoughts and

DISCERNING (see DISCERN)
Gen 41:33 let Pharaoh select a **d** and
Ex 23: 8 for a bribe blinds the **d**
Prov 28: 7 keeps the law is a **d** son, but
1Co 11:29 not **d** the Lord's body
1Co 12:10 to another **d** of spirits, to

DISCERNMENT (see DISCERN)
Phil 1: 9 and more in knowledge and all **d**

DISCHARGE (see RELEASE)
Lev 15: 2 any man has a **d** from his body
Lev 15:25 If a woman has a **d** of blood

DISCIPLE (see DISCIPLES, DISCIPLINE)
Matt 10:24 A **d** is not above his teacher,
Matt 10:42 cold water in the name of a **d**
Matt 27:57 had also become a **d** of Jesus
Luke 14:27 come after Me cannot be My **d**
John 19:26 the **d** whom He loved standing
John 20: 4 the other **d** outran Peter and
John 21:20 saw the **d** whom Jesus loved
John 21:23 that this **d** would not die
Acts 9:36 was a certain **d** named Tabitha

DISCIPLES (see DISCIPLE, DISCIPLES')
Is 8:16 Seal the law among my **d**
Matt 5: 1 was seated His **d** came to Him
Matt 8:23 a boat, His **d** followed Him
Matt 9:14 Then the **d** of John came to
Matt 9:14 often, but Your **d** do not fast
Matt 10: 1 called His twelve **d** to Him
Matt 19:13 pray, but the **d** rebuked them
Matt 21: 1 Olives, then Jesus sent two **d**
Matt 22:16 their **d** with the Herodians
Matt 24: 3 the **d** came to Him privately,
Matt 26:26 broke it, and gave it to the **d**
Matt 26:36 Gethsemane, and said to the **d**
Matt 26:56 Then all the **d** forsook Him
Matt 28: 7 tell His **d** that He is risen
Matt 28:13 His **d** came at night and stole
Matt 28:16 Then the eleven **d** went away
Matt 28:19 make **d** of all the nations,
Mark 10:10 in the house His **d** asked Him
Mark 10:24 the **d** were astonished at His

Mark 14:14 eat the Passover with My **d**
Luke 6: 1 His **d** plucked the heads of
Luke 9:40 Your **d** to cast it out, but
Luke 9:54 And when His **d** James and John
Luke 22:45 prayer, and had come to His **d**
John 1:35 John stood with two of his **d**
John 2:12 His brothers, and His **d**
John 2:17 Then His **d** remembered that it
John 4: 1 and baptized more **d** than John
John 6: 8 One of His **d**, Andrew, Simon
John 6:61 His **d** murmured about this
John 8:31 My word, you are My **d** indeed
John 9:27 you also want to become His **d**
John 9:28 disciple, but we are Moses' **d**
John 11: 8 The **d** said to Him, "Rabbi,
John 11:16 Didymus, said to his fellow **d**
John 12: 4 Then one of His **d**, Judas
John 13:23 on Jesus' bosom one of His **d**
John 13:35 will know that you are My **d**
John 18:17 not also one of this Man's **d**
John 20:19 where the **d** were assembled
John 20:20 Then the **d** were glad when
John 21: 1 the **d** at the Sea of Tiberias
John 21:14 **d** after He was raised from
Acts 1:15 up in the midst of the **d**
Acts 6: 1 of the **d** was multiplying,
Acts 6: 7 and the number of the **d**
Acts 9:19 days with the **d** at Damascus
Acts 9:25 Then the **d** took him by night
Acts 11:26 And the **d** were first called
Acts 14:21 to that city and made many **d**
Acts 20: 1 Paul called the **d** to him
Acts 20: 7 when the **d** came together to

DISCIPLES'† (see DISCIPLES)
John 13: 5 and began to wash the **d** feet

DISCIPLINE (see DISCIPLE, DISCIPLINES)
1Co 9:27 But I **d** my body and bring it

DISCIPLINES† (see DISCIPLINE)
Prov 13:24 who loves him **d** him promptly

DISCLOSE
Is 26:21 earth will also **d** her blood

DISCONTENTED†
1Sa 22: 2 who was **d** gathered to him

DISCORD
Prov 6:19 one who sows **d** among brethren

DISCOURAGE (see DISCOURAGED)
Ezra 4: 4 to **d** the people of Judah

DISCOURAGED (see DISCOURAGE)
Deut 1:21 do not fear or be **d**
Is 42: 4 He will not fail nor be **d**
Heb 12: 5 nor be **d** when you are rebuked

DISCOURSE
Job 27: 1 Moreover Job continued his **d**

DISCREET† (see DISCRETION)
Tit 2: 5 to be **d**, chaste, homemakers,

DISCRETION (see DISCREET)
Ps 112: 5 will guide his affairs with **d**
Prov 1: 4 the young man knowledge and **d**
Prov 3:21 keep sound wisdom and **d**
Prov 11:22 is a lovely woman who lacks **d**
Jer 10:12 out the heavens at His **d**

DISCUSSED (see DISCUSSING)
Luke 6:11 **d** with one another what they

DISCUSSING (see DISCUSSED)
Mark 9:16 What are you **d** with them

DISDAINED (see DISDAINS)
Prov 1:25 because you **d** all my counsel,

DISDAINS (*see* DISDAINED)
Prov 15:32 He who **d** instruction despises

DISEASE (*see* DISEASED, DISEASES)
Lev 26:16 terror over you, wasting **d**
2Ki 8: 8 Shall I recover from this **d**
Ps 41: 8 An evil **d**," they say
Matt 4:23 and all kinds of **d** among the
John 5: 4 well of whatever **d** he had

DISEASED (*see* DISEASE)
John 6: 2 performed on those who were **d**

DISEASES (*see* DISEASE)
Deut 28:60 on you all the **d** of Egypt
Ps 103: 3 Who heals all your **d**,
Matt 4:24 were afflicted with various **d**
Luke 6:17 Him and be healed of their **d**
Luke 9: 1 over all demons, and to cure **d**
Acts 19:12 the **d** left them and the evil

DISFIGURE
Matt 6:16 For they **d** their faces that

DISGRACE (*see* DISGRACED, DISGRACEFUL)
Job 10:15 I am full of **d**
Ps 109:29 their own **d** as with a mantle

DISGRACED (*see* DISGRACE)
Is 41:11 you shall be ashamed and **d**

DISGRACEFUL (*see* DISGRACE)
Deut 22:21 has done a **d** thing in Israel
Josh 7:15 has done a **d** thing in Israel
2Sa 13:12 Do not do this **d** thing

DISGUISE (*see* DISGUISED, DISGUISES)
1Ki 14: 2 **d** yourself, that they may not

DISGUISED (*see* DISGUISE)
1Sa 28: 8 So Saul **d** himself and put on

DISGUISES (*see* DISGUISE)
Prov 26:24 **d** it with his lips, and lays

DISGUSTED†
Ps 119:158 see the treacherous, and am **d**

DISH
2Ki 21:13 Jerusalem as one wipes a **d**
Matt 23:25 the outside of the cup and **d**
Matt 26:23 Me in the **d** will betray Me
Luke 11:39 **d** clean, but your inward part

DISHONEST (*see* DISHONESTY)
1Sa 8: 3 turned aside after **d** gain
Tit 1:11 not, for the sake of **d** gain
1Pe 5: 2 not for **d** gain but eagerly

DISHONESTY† (*see* DISHONEST)
Prov 13:11 Wealth gained by **d** will be

DISHONOR (*see* DISHONORED, DISHONORS)
Ps 35:26 and **d** Who magnify themselves
Ps 44:15 My **d** is continually before me
Ps 69:19 reproach, my shame, and my **d**
John 8:49 honor My Father, and you **d** Me
Rom 1:24 to **d** their bodies among
Rom 2:23 do you **d** God through breaking
Rom 9:21 for honor and another for **d**
1Co 11:14 long hair, it is a **d** to him
1Co 15:43 It is sown in **d**, it is raised
2Ti 2:20 some for honor and some for **d**

DISHONORED† (*see* DISHONOR)
1Co 4:10 distinguished, but we are **d**
Jas 2: 6 But you have **d** the poor man

DISHONORS† (*see* DISHONOR)
Mic 7: 6 For son **d** father, daughter
1Co 11: 4 his head covered, **d** his head
1Co 11: 5 her head uncovered, **d** her head

DISLOCATED†
Heb 12:13 what is lame may not be **d**

DISMAY (*see* DISMAYED)
Jer 1:17 lest I **d** you before them

DISMAYED (*see* DISMAY)
Deut 31: 8 do not fear nor be **d**
Josh 1: 9 do not be afraid, nor be **d**
Ps 83:17 be confounded and **d** forever
Is 41:10 be not **d**, for I am your God
Jer 1:17 Do not be **d** before their

DISMEMBERED (*see* DIVIDED)

DISMISS (*see* DISMISSED)
Mark 10: 4 of divorce, and to **d** her

DISMISSED (*see* DISMISS)
Acts 19:41 things, he **d** the assembly

DISOBEDIENCE (*see* DISOBEDIENT)
Rom 5:19 For as by one man's **d** many
Rom 11:30 mercy through their **d**,
Eph 2: 2 now works in the sons of **d**
Heb 2: 2 **d** received a just reward,
Heb 4: 6 did not enter because of **d**

DISOBEDIENT (*see* DISOBEDIENCE)
Neh 9:26 Nevertheless they were **d** and
Acts 26:19 I was not **d** to the heavenly
Rom 1:30 of evil things, **d** to parents,
Rom 10:21 stretched out My hands to a **d**
Rom 11:30 For as you were once **d** to God
1Pe 2: 8 being **d** to the word, to which
1Pe 3:20 who formerly were **d**, when

DISOBEYING†
Jer 42:13 **d** the voice of the LORD your

DISORDERLY
Acts 19:40 account for this **d** gathering
2Th 3: 7 for we were not **d** among you

DISPENSATION†
Eph 1:10 that in the **d** of the fullness
Eph 3: 2 you have heard of the **d** of

DISPERSE (*see* DISPERSED, DISPERSION)
Prov 15: 7 lips of the wise **d** knowledge
Dan 11:24 he shall **d** among them the

DISPERSED (*see* DISPERSE)
Gen 10:18 of the Canaanites were **d**
Prov 5:16 your fountains be **d** abroad
Is 11:12 and gather together the **d** of

DISPERSION† (*see* DISPERSE)
John 7:35 go to the **D** among the Greeks
1Pe 1: 1 pilgrims of the **D** in Pontus

DISPLACE†
Deut 12:29 you **d** them and dwell in their

DISPLEASE (*see* DISPLEASED, DISPLEASES, DISPLEASING, DISPLEASURE)
Prov 24:18 it **d** Him, and He turn away His

DISPLEASED (*see* DISPLEASE)
2Sa 11:27 David had done **d** the LORD
Dan 6:14 was greatly **d** with himself,
Jon 4: 1 But it **d** Jonah exceedingly,
Matt 20:24 they were greatly **d** with

DISPLEASES† (*see* DISPLEASE)
Num 22:34 Now therefore, if it **d** You

DISPLEASING (*see* DISPLEASE)
Jer 42: 6 Whether it is pleasing or **d**

DISPLEASURE (*see* DISPLEASE)
Ps 2: 5 distress them in His deep **d**
Ps 6: 1 Nor chasten me in Your hot **d**
Ps 38: 1 Nor chasten me in Your hot **d**

DISPOSSESS (see DISPOSSESSED)
Num 33:53 you shall **d** the inhabitants
Deut 9: 1 go in to **d** nations greater and
Deut 19: 1 you **d** them and dwell in their

DISPOSSESSED (see DISPOSSESS)
Num 32:39 **d** the Amorites who were in it

DISPUTE (see DISPUTED, DISPUTER, DISPUTES, DISPUTING)
Deut 25: 1 If there is a **d** between men
Mark 8:11 out and began to **d** with Him
Luke 9:46 Then a **d** arose among them as
Acts 15: 7 when there had been much **d**
Heb 6:16 is for them an end of all **d**

DISPUTED (see DISPUTE)
Acts 9:29 **d** against the Hellenists, but
Jude 9 when he **d** about the body of

DISPUTER † (see DISPUTE)
1Co 1:20 Where is the **d** of this age

DISPUTES (see DISPUTE)
Rom 14: 1 but not to **d** over doubtful
1Ti 1: 4 which cause **d** rather than
2Ti 2:23 avoid foolish and ignorant **d**

DISPUTING (see DISPUTE)
Acts 6: 9 and Asia), **d** with Stephen
Acts 24:12 found me in the temple **d** with
Phil 2:14 things without murmuring and **d**

DISQUALIFIED
1Co 9:27 I myself should become **d**
Tit 1:16 and **d** for every good work

DISQUIETED † (see DISQUIETING)
Ps 42: 5 And why are you **d** within me
Ps 42:11 And why are you **d** within me
Ps 43: 5 And why are you **d** within me

DISQUIETING † (see DISQUIETED)
Job 4:13 In **d** thoughts from the

DISSENSION (see DISSENSIONS)
Acts 15: 2 and Barnabas had no small **d**
Acts 23: 7 this, a **d** arose between the

DISSENSIONS † (see DISSENSION)
Gal 5:20 wrath, selfish ambitions, **d**

DISSIPATION
Eph 5:18 with wine, in which is **d**
1Pe 4: 4 them in the same flood of **d**

DISSOLVED
Is 34: 4 the host of heaven shall be **d**
2Pe 3:12 will be **d** being on fire, and

DISTAFF †
Prov 31:19 out her hands to the **d**, and

DISTANCE
Ezek 42: 4 wide, at a **d** of one cubit
Mark 14:54 But Peter followed Him at a **d**

DISTILL †
Deut 32: 2 my speech **d** as the dew, as
Job 36:27 which **d** as rain from the mist

DISTINCTION (see DISTINCTLY, DISTINGUISH)
Acts 15: 9 made no **d** between us and them,
Rom 10:12 For there is no **d** between Jew
1Co 14: 7 they make a **d** in the sounds

DISTINCTLY † (see DISTINCTION)
Neh 8: 8 So they read **d** from the book,

DISTINGUISH (see DISTINCTION, DISTINGUISHED)
Lev 10:10 that you may **d** between holy
Lev 11:47 To **d** between the unclean and

DISTINGUISHED (see DISTINGUISH)
Dan 6: 3 Then this Daniel **d** himself

1Co 4:10 You are **d**, but we are

DISTORTS †
Is 24: 1 **d** its surface and scatters

DISTRACTED † (see DISTRACTION)
Luke 10:40 But Martha was **d** with much

DISTRACTION † (see DISTRACTED)
1Co 7:35 may serve the Lord without **d**

DISTRESS (see DISTRESSED, DISTRESSES, DISTRESSING)
Gen 35: 3 me in the day of my **d** and has
Judg 10:14 deliver you in your time of **d**
2Sa 24:14 I am in great **d**
2Ki 4:27 for her soul is in deep **d**
Job 36:16 brought you out of dire **d**
Ps 2: 5 wrath, And **d** them in His deep
Ps 4: 1 relieved me when I was in **d**
Ps 18: 6 In my **d** I called upon the
Is 21:15 bow, and from the **d** of war
Lam 1:20 See, O LORD, that I am in **d**
Obad 12 proudly in the day of **d**
Zeph 1:15 wrath, a day of trouble and **d**
Luke 21:23 will be great **d** in the land
Rom 8:35 Shall tribulation, or **d**, or
1Co 7:26 good because of the present **d**
Phil 4:14 well that you shared in my **d**

DISTRESSED (see DISTRESS)
1Sa 28:15 I am deeply **d**
2Sa 1:26 I am **d** for you, my brother
Ps 143: 4 My heart within me is **d**
Matt 26:37 to be sorrowful and deeply **d**
Luke 12:50 and how **d** I am till it is

DISTRESSES (see DISTRESS)
Ps 25:17 Oh, bring me out of my **d**
Ps 107: 6 delivered them out of their **d**
2Co 6: 4 tribulations, in needs, in **d**

DISTRESSING (see DISTRESS)
1Sa 16:14 and a **d** spirit from the LORD
Is 21: 2 a **d** vision is declared to me

DISTRIBUTE (see DISTRIBUTED, DISTRIBUTING, DISTRIBUTION)
Neh 13:13 was to **d** to their brethren
Luke 18:22 **d** to the poor, and you will

DISTRIBUTED (see DISTRIBUTE)
Josh 13:32 **d** as an inheritance in the
John 6:11 He **d** them to the disciples
Acts 4:35 they **d** to each as anyone had
1Co 7:17 But as God has **d** to each one

DISTRIBUTING † (see DISTRIBUTE)
Rom 12:13 **d** to the needs of the saints,
1Co 12:11 **d** to each one individually as

DISTRIBUTION † (see DISTRIBUTE)
Acts 6: 1 were neglected in the daily **d**

DISTRICT (see DISTRICTS)
Neh 3:17 made repairs for his **d**
Ezek 45: 7 and bordering on the holy **d**

DISTRICTS (see DISTRICT)
Neh 9:22 and divided them into **d**
Matt 2:16 in Bethlehem and in all its **d**

DISTURBED (see DISTURBS)
1Sa 28:15 Why have you **d** me by bringing
Neh 2:10 they were deeply **d** that a man
Acts 21:30 And all the city was **d**

DISTURBS † (see DISTURBED)
Jer 31:35 Who **d** the sea, and its waves

DITCH
Ps 7:15 into the **d** which he made
Matt 15:14 both will fall into a **d**

DIVERSE† (*see* DIVERSITIES)
Prov 20:10 **D** weights and **d** measures
Prov 20:23 **D** weights are an abomination

DIVERSITIES† (*see* DIVERSE)
1Co 12: 4 Now there are **d** of gifts, but
1Co 12: 6 there are **d** of activities,

DIVIDE (*see* DIVIDED, DIVIDES, DIVIDING, DIVISION)
Gen 1: 6 let it **d** the waters from the
Gen 1:14 to **d** the day from the night
Ex 14:16 hand over the sea and **d** it
Lev 1:17 but shall not **d** it completely
Lev 5: 8 but shall not **d** it completely
Josh 13: 7 **d** this land as an inheritance
1Ki 3:25 **D** the living child in two, and
Ps 22:18 **d** My garments among them
Ps 60: 6 I will **d** Shechem And measure
Ps 108: 7 I will **d** Shechem And measure
Is 9: 3 rejoice when they **d** the spoil
Is 18: 2 down, whose land the rivers **d**
Is 18: 7 down, whose land the rivers **d**
Is 53:12 Therefore I will **d** Him a
Is 53:12 He shall **d** the spoil with the
Ezek 5: 1 to weigh and **d** the hair
Luke 12:13 tell my brother to **d** the
Luke 22:17 this and **d** it among yourselves

DIVIDED (*see* DIVIDE, SEPARATED)
Gen 1: 4 and God **d** the light from the
Gen 1: 7 **d** the waters which were under
Gen 10:25 in his days the earth was **d**
Ex 14:21 land, and the waters were **d**
Deut 32: 8 when the Most High **d** their
Judg 7:16 Then he **d** the three hundred
Judg 19:29 **d** her into twelve pieces
2Sa 1:23 their death they were not **d**
1Ki 16:21 Israel were **d** into two parts
Neh 9:11 You **d** the sea before them, so
Ps 136:13 To Him who **d** the Red Sea in
Ezek 37:22 nor shall they ever be **d** into
Dan 2:41 iron, the kingdom shall be **d**
Dan 5:28 Your kingdom has been **d**, and
Dan 11: 4 **d** toward the four winds of
Hos 10: 2 Their heart is **d**
Joel 3: 2 they have also **d** up My land
Matt 12:25 Every kingdom **d** against
Matt 12:25 every city or house **d** against
Matt 12:26 he is **d** against himself
Matt 27:35 **d** His garments, casting lots,
Mark 6:41 two fish He **d** among them all
Luke 12:52 five in one house will be **d**
Luke 12:53 Father will be **d** against son
Acts 2: 3 appeared to them **d** tongues
Acts 2:45 **d** them among all, as anyone
Acts 23: 7 and the assembly was **d**
1Co 1:13 Is Christ **d**? Was Paul
Rev 16:19 city was **d** into three parts

DIVIDES (*see* DIVIDE)
Lev 11: 3 beasts, whatever **d** the hoof
Matt 25:32 as a shepherd **d** his sheep
Luke 11:22 he trusted, and **d** his spoils

DIVIDING (*see* DIVIDE)
Judg 5:30 not finding and **d** the spoil
Is 63:12 **d** the water before them to
2Ti 2:15 rightly **d** the word of truth

DIVINATION (*see* DIVINE)
Gen 44:15 as I can certainly practice **d**
Lev 19:26 you practice **d** or soothsaying
Acts 16:16 with a spirit of **d** met us

DIVINE (*see* DIVINATION, DIVINELY, DIVINER)
Ezek 21:29 while they **d** a lie to you, to
Mic 3:11 and her prophets **d** for money
Acts 17:29 the **D** Nature is like gold or

Heb 9: 1 had ordinances of **d** service
1Pe 3:20 when once the **D** longsuffering
2Pe 1: 3 as His **d** power has given to
2Pe 1: 4 be partakers of the **d** nature

DIVINELY (*see* DIVINE)
Matt 2:12 being **d** warned in a dream
Heb 8: 5 as Moses was **d** instructed
Heb 11: 7 being **d** warned of things not

DIVINER† (*see* DIVINE, DIVINER'S, DIVINERS)
Is 3: 2 and the prophet, and the **d** and

DIVINER'S† (*see* DIVINER)
Num 22: 7 with the **d** fee in their hand

DIVINERS (*see* DIVINER)
Deut 18:14 listened to soothsayers and **d**
Jer 27: 9 to your prophets, your **d**,

DIVISION (*see* DIVIDE, DIVISIONS)
1Ch 28:13 also for the **d** of the priests
Luke 1: 5 Zacharias, of the **d** of Abijah
Luke 12:51 you, not at all, but rather **d**
John 7:43 there was a **d** among them
John 9:16 there was a **d** among them
John 10:19 was a **d** again among the Jews
Heb 4:12 even to the **d** of soul and

DIVISIONS (*see* DIVISION)
Num 1:16 heads of the **d** in Israel
1Ch 28:21 Here are the **d** of the priests
Rom 16:17 note those who cause **d** and
1Co 1:10 that there be no **d** among you
1Co 11:18 that there are **d** among you
Jude 19 sensual persons, who cause **d**

DIVORCE (*see* DIVORCED, DIVORCES)
Deut 22:19 he cannot **d** her all his days
Deut 24: 1 writes her a certificate of **d**
Deut 24: 3 writes her a certificate of **d**
Is 50: 1 of your mother's **d**, whom I
Mal 2:16 Israel says that He hates **d**
Matt 5:31 give her a certificate of **d**
Matt 19: 3 to **d** his wife for just any
Matt 19: 8 permitted you to **d** your wives
1Co 7:11 husband is not to **d** his wife
1Co 7:12 with him, let him not **d** her

DIVORCED (*see* DIVORCE)
Deut 24: 4 **d** her must not take her back
Matt 5:32 who is **d** commits adultery
Matt 19: 9 who is **d** commits adultery
Luke 16:18 is **d** from her husband commits

DIVORCES (*see* DIVORCE)
Jer 3: 1 say, 'If a man **d** his wife
Matt 5:32 **d** his wife for any reason
Matt 19: 9 whoever **d** his wife, except
Mark 10:11 Whoever **d** his wife and marries

DOCTRINE (*see* DOCTRINES)
Matt 16:12 but of the **d** of the Pharisees
Mark 1:27 What new **d** is this
John 7:16 My **d** is not Mine, but His who
John 7:17 shall know concerning the **d**
Acts 2:42 in the apostles' **d** and
Acts 5:28 filled Jerusalem with your **d**
Acts 17:19 new **d** is of which you speak
Rom 6:17 **d** to which you were delivered
Rom 16:17 contrary to the **d** which you
Eph 4:14 about with every wind of **d**
1Ti 1: 3 that they teach no other **d**
1Ti 1:10 that is contrary to sound **d**
1Ti 4:13 reading, to exhortation, to **d**
1Ti 4:16 heed to yourself and to the **d**
1Ti 5:17 who labor in the word and **d**
1Ti 6: 1 His **d** may not be blasphemed
2Ti 3:16 God, and is profitable for **d**
2Ti 4: 3 they will not endure sound **d**

Tit	2:10	that they may adorn the **d** of
Heb	6: 2	of the **d** of baptisms, of
2Jn	9	does not abide in the **d** of
Rev	2:14	who hold the **d** of Balaam, who
Rev	2:15	hold the **d** of the Nicolaitans

DOCTRINES (*see* DOCTRINE)

Matt	15: 9	worship Me, teaching as **d** the
Col	2:22	commandments and **d** of men
1Ti	4: 1	spirits and **d** of demons,
Heb	13: 9	with various and strange **d**

DOCUMENT

| Esth | 3:14 | A copy of the **d** was to be |
| Esth | 8:13 | A copy of the **d** was to be |

DOE†

| Prov | 5:19 | a loving deer and a graceful **d** |

DOER (*see* DOERS, DOINGS)

| Jas | 1:23 | hearer of the word and not a **d** |
| Jas | 4:11 | you are not a **d** of the law |

DOERS† (*see* DOER, EVILDOERS)

| Rom | 2:13 | but the **d** of the law will be |
| Jas | 1:22 | But be **d** of the word, and not |

DOG (*see* DOG'S, DOGS)

Ex	11: 7	shall a **d** move its tongue
Deut	23:18	a **d** to the house of the LORD
Judg	7: 5	with his tongue, as a **d** laps
1Sa	17:43	Am I a **d**, that you come to me
1Sa	24:14	do you pursue? A dead **d**?
Ps	22:20	life from the power of the **d**
Ps	59: 6	return, They growl like a **d**
Ps	59:14	return, They growl like a **d**
Prov	26:11	As a **d** returns to his own
Prov	26:17	one who takes a **d** by the ears
Eccl	9: 4	for a living **d** is better than
2Pe	2:22	A **d** returns to his own vomit,

DOG'S (*see* DOG)

| 2Sa | 3: 8 | Am I a **d** head that belongs to |

DOGS (*see* DOG)

Ex	22:31	you shall throw it to the **d**
1Ki	14:11	The **d** shall eat whoever
1Ki	16: 4	The **d** shall eat whoever
1Ki	21:19	**d** shall lick your blood, even
1Ki	21:23	The **d** shall eat Jezebel by
Job	30: 1	to put with the **d** of my flock
Ps	22:16	For **d** have surrounded Me
Is	56:10	they are all dumb **d**, they
Is	56:11	they are greedy **d** which never
Matt	7: 6	give what is holy to the **d**
Matt	15:26	and throw it to the **d**
Luke	16:21	Moreover the **d** came and licked
Phil	3: 2	Beware of **d**, beware of evil
Rev	22:15	But outside are **d** and

DOINGS (*see* DOER)

Deut	28:20	of the wickedness of your **d**
Judg	2:19	not cease from their own **d**
1Sa	25: 3	was harsh and evil in his **d**
Is	3: 8	their **d** Are against the LORD,
Is	3:10	eat the fruit of their **d**
Jer	7: 3	Amend your ways and your **d**
Jer	18:11	make your ways and your **d** good
Ezek	20:44	according to your corrupt **d**
Mic	2: 7	Are these His **d**

DOMAIN† (*see* DOMINION)

| Jude | 6 | did not keep their proper **d** |

DOMINION (*see* DOMAIN, DOMINIONS)

Gen	1:26	let them have **d** over the fish
Num	24:19	Out of Jacob One shall have **d**
2Ch	13: 5	the **d** over Israel to David
Job	25: 2	**D** and fear belong to Him
Ps	8: 6	have **d** over the works of Your

Ps	19:13	Let them not have **d** over me
Ps	49:14	The upright shall have **d** over
Ps	72: 8	He shall have **d** also from sea
Ps	103:22	works, In all places of His **d**
Ps	114: 2	sanctuary, And Israel His **d**
Ps	145:13	Your **d** endures throughout all
Dan	4: 3	His **d** is from generation to
Dan	4:22	and your **d** to the end of the
Dan	4:34	His **d** is an everlasting **d**
Dan	7: 6	heads, and **d** was given to it
Dan	7:12	they had their **d** taken away
Dan	7:14	Then to Him was given **d** and
Dan	7:14	**d** is an everlasting **d**
Dan	11: 5	His **d** shall be a great **d**
Zech	9:10	His **d** shall be 'from sea to
Rom	6: 9	no longer has **d** over Him
Rom	6:14	sin shall not have **d** over you
Rom	7: 1	that the law has **d** over a man
2Co	1:24	we have **d** over your faith
Eph	1:21	and power and might and **d**, and
1Pe	4:11	and the **d** forever and ever
1Pe	5:11	and the **d** forever and ever
Jude	25	wise, be glory and majesty, **d**
Rev	1: 6	be glory and **d** forever and ever

DOMINIONS† (*see* DOMINION)

| Dan | 7:27 | all **d** shall serve and obey Him |
| Col | 1:16 | whether thrones or **d** or |

DONKEY (*see* DONKEY'S, DONKEYS)

Gen	22: 3	the morning and saddled his **d**
Gen	49:14	Issachar is a strong **d**, lying
Ex	4:20	his sons and set them on a **d**
Ex	13:13	a **d** you shall redeem with a
Ex	20:17	nor his ox, nor his **d**, nor
Ex	21:33	an ox or a **d** falls in it,
Num	22:23	Now the **d** saw the Angel of
Num	22:30	So the **d** said to Balaam, "Am
Deut	5:14	nor your ox, nor your **d**, nor
Josh	15:18	she dismounted from her **d**
Judg	15:15	found a fresh jawbone of a **d**
Is	1: 3	And the **d** its master's crib
Jer	22:19	buried with the burial of a **d**
Zech	9: 9	lowly and riding on a **d**, a
Matt	21: 2	you will find a **d** tied, and a
Matt	21: 5	you, lowly, and sitting on a **d**
2Pe	2:16	a dumb **d** speaking with a

DONKEY'S (*see* DONKEY)

| 2Ki | 6:25 | a **d** head was sold for eighty |
| John | 12:15 | coming, sitting on a **d** colt |

DONKEYS (*see* DONKEY)

Gen	12:16	He had sheep, oxen, male **d**
Gen	43:18	take us as slaves with our **d**
Judg	5:10	you who ride on white **d**, who
Judg	19:19	straw and fodder for our **d**
1Sa	9: 3	Now the **d** of Kish, Saul's
Job	1:14	the **d** feeding beside them,
Job	24: 5	like wild **d** in the desert,
Ps	104:11	The wild **d** quench their
Dan	5:21	dwelling was with the wild **d**

DOOM (*see* DOOMED)

Job	21:30	are reserved for the day of **d**
Prov	16: 4	the wicked for the day of **d**
Jer	11:17	has pronounced **d** against you
Jer	26:13	the **d** that He has pronounced
Ezek	7: 7	**D** has come to you, you who
Amos	6: 3	who put far off the day of **d**

DOOMED (*see* DOOM)

| Deut | 7:26 | lest you be **d** to destruction |
| Josh | 6:17 | Now the city shall be **d** by |

DOOR (*see* DOORKEEPER, DOORPOST, DOORS, DOORWAY)

| Gen | 4: 7 | do well, sin lies at the **d** |
| Gen | 6:16 | set the **d** of the ark in its |

Gen 18: 1 tent **d** in the heat of the day
Gen 19: 9 came near to break down the **d**
Ex 12:23 the LORD will pass over the **d**
Ex 29: 4 to the **d** of the tabernacle of
Lev 14:38 to the **d** of the house, and
Deut 15:17 it through his ear to the **d**
Judg 19:22 the house and beat on the **d**
Judg 19:26 fell down at the **d** of the
2Sa 11: 9 But Uriah slept at the **d** of
2Sa 13:17 me, and bolt the **d** behind her
1Ki 6:33 So for the **d** of the sanctuary
1Ki 6:34 comprised one folding **d**, and
2Ki 12: 9 the **d** put there all the money
1Ch 9:21 was keeper of the **d** of the
Job 31: 9 lurked at my neighbor's **d**
Ps 141: 3 watch over the **d** of my lips
Prov 5: 8 go near the **d** of her house
Prov 26:14 As a **d** turns on its hinges,
Song 5: 4 hand by the latch of the **d**
Is 6: 4 And the posts of the **d** were
Ezek 8:14 So He brought me to the **d** of
Ezek 8:16 at the **d** of the temple of the
Ezek 40:13 cubits, as **d** faces **d**
Ezek 41:24 two panels for one **d** and two
Ezek 42: 2 cubits), was the north **d**
Hos 2:15 of Achor as a **d** of hope
Matt 6: 6 and when you have shut your **d**
Matt 25:10 and the **d** was shut
Matt 27:60 against the **d** of the tomb
Matt 28: 2 back the stone from the **d**
Mark 2: 2 them, not even near the **d**
Luke 13:25 outside and knock at the **d**
John 10: 1 enter the sheepfold by the **d**
John 10: 2 the **d** is the shepherd of the
John 10: 7 you, I am the **d** of the sheep
John 10: 9 I am the **d**. If anyone
Acts 5: 9 your husband are at the **d**
Acts 12:13 knocked at the **d** of the gate
Acts 18: 7 was next **d** to the synagogue
1Co 16: 9 effective **d** has opened to me,
2Co 2:12 a **d** was opened to me by the
Col 4: 3 open to us a **d** for the word
Jas 5: 9 Judge is standing at the **d**
Rev 3: 8 have set before you an open **d**
Rev 3:20 Behold, I stand at the **d** and
Rev 3:20 hears My voice and opens the **d**
Rev 4: 1 a **d** standing open in heaven

DOORKEEPER (*see* DOOR, DOORKEEPERS)
Ps 84:10 I would rather be a **d** in the
John 10: 3 To him the **d** opens, and the

DOORKEEPERS (*see* DOORKEEPER)
2Ki 25:18 second priest, and the three **d**
1Ch 15:23 and Elkanah were **d** for the ark
Esth 2:21 eunuchs, Bigthan and Teresh, **d**

DOORPOST (*see* DOOR, DOORPOSTS)
Ex 21: 6 him to the door, or to the **d**
1Sa 1: 9 **d** of the tabernacle of the

DOORPOSTS (*see* DOORPOST)
Ex 12: 7 blood and put it on the two **d**
Deut 6: 9 them on the **d** of your house
Deut 11:20 them on the **d** of your house
Amos 9: 1 Strike the **d**, that the

DOORS (*see* DOOR)
Judg 3:23 shut the **d** of the upper room
Judg 11:31 the **d** of my house to meet me
Job 3:10 up the **d** of my mother's womb
Job 31:32 opened my **d** to the traveler)
Job 38: 8 Or who shut in the sea with a **d**
Job 41:14 can open the **d** of his face
Ps 24: 7 lifted up, you everlasting **d**
Ps 78:23 And opened the **d** of heaven
Eccl 12: 4 when the **d** are shut in the

Is 45: 1 open before him the double **d**
Mic 7: 5 Guard the **d** of your mouth
Matt 24:33 it is near, at the very **d**
Mark 13:29 it is near, at the very **d**
John 20:19 when the **d** were shut where
John 20:26 the **d** being shut, and stood in
Acts 5:19 the Lord opened the prison **d**

DOORWAY (*see* DOOR)
Gen 19:11 the men who were at the **d** of
Num 27: 2 by the **d** of the tabernacle of
2Ki 4:15 her, she stood in the **d**

DOR (*see* EN DOR)
Josh 12:23 the heights of **D** on the west
Josh 17:11 towns, the inhabitants of **D**

DORCAS (*see* TABITHA)
Acts 9:36 which is translated **D**

DOTHAN
Gen 37:17 brothers and found them in **D**

DOUBLE
Gen 43:12 Take **d** money in your hand, and
Ex 22: 4 or sheep, he shall restore **d**
Ex 26: 9 you shall **d** over the sixth
Deut 21:17 firstborn by giving him a **d**
1Sa 1: 5 he would give a **d** portion
2Ki 2: 9 Please let a **d** portion of
Ps 12: 2 lips and a **d** heart they speak
Is 40: 2 hand **d** for all her sins
Is 61: 7 shame you shall have **d** honor
Jer 16:18 repay **d** for their iniquity
Jer 17:18 them with **d** destruction
1Ti 5:17 be counted worthy of **d** honor
Rev 18: 6 repay her **d** according to her

DOUBLE-EDGED†
Judg 3:16 himself a dagger (it was **d**

DOUBLE-MINDED†
Ps 119:113 I hate the **d**, But I love Your
Jas 1: 8 he is a **d** man, unstable in
Jas 4: 8 and purify your hearts, you **d**

DOUBLE-TONGUED†
1Ti 3: 8 must be reverent, not **d**, not

DOUBT (*see* DOUBTED, DOUBTFUL, DOUBTING, DOUBTLESS, DOUBTS)
Gen 37:33 Without **d** Joseph is torn to
Job 12: 2 No **d** you are the people, and
Matt 14:31 little faith, why did you **d**
Matt 21:21 if you have faith and do not **d**
Mark 11:23 does not **d** in his heart, but
John 10:24 How long do You keep us in **d**
Acts 28: 4 No **d** this man is a murderer,

DOUBTED† (*see* DOUBT)
Matt 28:17 worshiped Him: but some **d**

DOUBTFUL† (*see* DOUBT)
Rom 14: 1 not to disputes over **d** things

DOUBTING (*see* DOUBT)
Acts 10:20 and go with them, **d** nothing
1Ti 2: 8 hands, without wrath and **d**
Jas 1: 6 him ask in faith, with no **d**

DOUBTLESS (*see* DOUBT)
Ps 126: 6 Shall **d** come again with
Is 63:16 **D** You are our Father, though
2Co 12: 1 It is **d** not profitable for me

DOUBTS† (*see* DOUBT)
Luke 24:38 why do **d** arise in your hearts
Rom 14:23 But he who **d** is condemned if
Gal 4:20 for I have **d** about you
Jas 1: 6 for he who **d** is like a wave

DOUGH
Ex 12:34 **d** before it was leavened,

Jer 7:18 and the women knead their **d**

DOVE (*see* DOVE'S, DOVES)
Gen 8:10 sent the **d** out from the ark
Ps 55: 6 Oh, that I had wings like a **d**
Ps 68:13 of a **d** covered with silver
Song 5: 2 me, my sister, my love, my **d**
Is 38:14 I mourned like a **d**
Hos 7:11 also is like a silly **d**,
Luke 3:22 bodily form like a **d** upon Him

DOVE'S† (*see* DOVE)
Song 1:15 You have **d** eyes
Song 4: 1 You have **d** eyes

DOVES (*see* DOVE)
Song 5:12 His eyes are like **d** by the
Is 59:11 bears, and moan sadly like **d**
Matt 10:16 as serpents and harmless as **d**
Matt 21:12 the seats of those who sold **d**

DOWNCAST†
2Co 7: 6 God, who comforts the **d**,

DOWNFALL
Lam 1: 7 saw her and mocked at her **d**

DOWNWARD
2Ki 19:30 Judah shall again take root **d**

DOWRY
1Sa 18:25 king does not desire any **d**
1Ki 9:16 it as a **d** to his daughter

DRAG (*see* DRAGGED, DRAGGING)
Luke 12:58 lest he **d** you to the judge,
Jas 2: 6 you and **d** you into the courts

DRAGGED (*see* DRAG)
Jer 22:19 the burial of a donkey, **d**
John 21:11 **d** the net to land, full of
Acts 14:19 and **d** him out of the city,
Acts 16:19 **d** them into the marketplace

DRAGGING† (*see* DRAG)
John 21: 8 cubits), **d** the net with fish
Acts 8: 3 and **d** off men and women,

DRAGNET
Hab 1:15 and gather them in their **d**
Matt 13:47 that was cast into the sea

DRAGON
Rev 12: 3 fiery red **d** having seven
Rev 12: 4 the **d** stood before the woman
Rev 12: 7 angels fought against the **d**
Rev 12: 7 and the **d** and his angels fought
Rev 12: 9 So the great **d** was cast out
Rev 13: 4 So they worshiped the **d** who

DRAINED
Lev 1:15 its blood shall be **d** out at
Is 51:17 cup of trembling, and **d** it out
Joel 2: 6 all faces are **d** of color

DRANK (*see* DRINK)
Gen 9:21 Then he **d** of the wine and was
Gen 43:34 So they **d** and were merry with
Ex 24:11 saw God, and they ate and **d**
1Ki 17: 6 and he **d** from the brook
Jer 51: 7 The nations **d** her wine
Dan 1: 8 nor with the wine which he **d**
Dan 5: 4 and his concubines **d** from them
Mark 14:23 them, and they all **d** from it
Luke 13:26 **d** in Your presence, and You
John 4:12 **d** from it himself, as well as
Acts 9: 9 sight, and neither ate nor **d**
Acts 10:41 **d** with Him after He arose
1Co 10: 4 and all **d** the same spiritual

DRAW (*see* DRAWING, DRAWN, DRAWS, DREW)
Gen 24:11 when women go out to **d** water
Gen 24:43 virgin comes out to **d** water

Ex 15: 9 I will **d** my sword, my hand
Judg 3:22 for he did not **d** the dagger
Judg 9:54 **D** your sword and kill me, lest
1Sa 14:36 Let us **d** near to God here
Job 41: 1 Can you **d** out Leviathan with
Ps 69:18 **D** near to my soul, and redeem
Ps 73:28 good for me to **d** near to God
Eccl 12: 1 the years **d** near when you say
Is 5:18 Woe to those who **d** iniquity
Is 29:13 **d** near to Me with their
Matt 15: 8 These people **d** near to Me
John 2: 8 **D** some out now, and take it to
John 4: 7 of Samaria came to **d** water
John 4:15 thirst, nor come here to **d**
John 12:32 will **d** all peoples to Myself
John 21: 6 to **d** it in because of the
Heb 7:19 which we **d** near to God
Heb 10:22 let us **d** near with a true
Heb 10:39 those who **d** back to perdition
Jas 4: 8 **D** near to God
Jas 4: 8 and He will **d** near to you

DRAWING (*see* DRAW)
Judg 19: 9 day is now **d** toward evening

DRAWN (*see* DRAW)
Num 22:23 with His **d** sword in His hand
Num 22:31 with His **d** sword in His hand
Deut 30:17 are **d** away, and worship other
Prov 24:11 those who are **d** toward death
Jer 31: 3 lovingkindness I have **d** you
Luke 21: 8 He,' and, 'The time has **d** near
John 2: 9 who had **d** the water knew)
Jas 1:14 is **d** away by his own desires

DRAWS (*see* DRAW)
Deut 25:11 the wife of one **d** near to
Deut 29:11 to the one who **d** your water
Job 24:22 But God **d** the mighty away
Job 33:22 his soul **d** near the Pit, and
Ps 88: 3 my life **d** near to the grave
Luke 21:28 your redemption **d** near
John 6:44 the Father who sent Me **d** him

DREAD (*see* DREADED, DREADFUL)
Gen 9: 2 and the **d** of you shall be on
Ex 15:16 Fear and **d** will fall on them
Deut 11:25 God will put the **d** of you
Is 7:16 the land that you **d** will be

DREADED (*see* DREAD)
Job 3:25 what I **d** has happened to me

DREADFUL (*see* DREAD, DREADFULLY)
Dan 7: 7 and behold, a fourth beast, **d**
Dan 7:19 all the others, exceedingly **d**
Mal 4: 5 great and **d** day of the LORD

DREADFULLY (*see* DREADFUL)
1Sa 17:24 from him and were **d** afraid
Matt 8: 6 home paralyzed, and **d** tormented

DREAM (*see* DREAMED, DREAMER, DREAMS)
Gen 20: 3 to Abimelech in a **d** by night
Gen 31:10 lifted my eyes and saw in a **d**
Gen 37: 5 Now Joseph had a **d**, and
Gen 40: 5 in the prison, had a **d**
Gen 40: 9 butler told his **d** to Joseph
Gen 41: 1 years, that Pharaoh had a **d**
Gen 41:11 interpretation of his own **d**
Num 12: 6 and I speak to him in a **d**
1Ki 3: 5 to Solomon in a **d** by night
Job 20: 8 He will fly away like a **d**
Job 33:15 In a **d**, in a vision of the
Ps 73:20 As a **d** when one awakes, So,
Ps 126: 1 We were like those who **d**
Jer 23:28 has a **d**, let him tell a dream
Dan 2: 3 I have had a **d**, and my spirit
Dan 2: 5 do not make known the **d** to me

Dan	2:36	This is the **d**. Now we will
Dan	2:45	The **d** is certain, and its
Dan	4: 5	I saw a **d** which made me
Dan	4: 6	the interpretation of the **d**
Dan	4:18	This **d** I, King Nebuchadnezzar
Dan	7: 1	of Babylon, Daniel had a **d**
Dan	7: 1	Then he wrote down the **d**,
Joel	2:28	your old men shall **d** dreams
Matt	1:20	Lord appeared to him in a **d**
Matt	2:12	being divinely warned in a **d**
Matt	27:19	today in a **d** because of Him
Acts	2:17	your old men shall **d** dreams

DREAMED (see DREAM)

Gen	28:12	Then he **d**, and behold, a
Jer	23:25	I have **d**, I have **d**

DREAMER (see DREAM, DREAMERS)

Gen	37:19	Look, this **d** is coming
Deut	13: 1	a prophet or a **d** of dreams

DREAMERS† (see DREAMER)

Jer	27: 9	your diviners, your **d**, your
Jude	8	also these **d** defile the flesh

DREAMS (see DREAM)

Gen	37: 8	hated him even more for his **d**
Gen	37:20	see what will become of his **d**
Gen	41: 8	And Pharaoh told them his **d**
Gen	41:12	he interpreted our **d** for us
Gen	41:25	The **d** of Pharaoh are one
Deut	13: 1	a prophet or a dreamer of **d**
1Sa	28: 6	either by **d** or by Urim or by
Jer	23:32	those who prophesy false **d**
Dan	1:17	in all visions and **d**
Dan	2: 1	reign, Nebuchadnezzar had **d**
Dan	5:12	understanding, interpreting **d**
Joel	2:28	your old men shall dream **d**
Acts	2:17	your old men shall dream **d**

DREGS

Is	51:22	the **d** of the cup of My fury
Jer	48:11	he has settled on his **d**, and

DRENCH

Ps	6: 6	I **d** my couch with my tears

DREW (see DRAW)

Gen	8: 9	**d** her into the ark to himself
Gen	24:45	down to the well and **d** water
Gen	47:29	When the time **d** near that
Gen	49:33	he **d** his feet up into the bed
Ex	2:10	Because I **d** him out of the
Ex	4: 7	**d** it out of his bosom, and
2Sa	22:17	He **d** me out of many waters
1Ki	22:34	certain man **d** a bow at random
Job	26:10	He **d** a circular horizon on
Prov	8:27	when He **d** a circle on the
Hos	11: 4	I **d** them with gentle cords,
Matt	21:34	Now when vintage-time **d** near
Matt	26:51	and **d** his sword, struck the
Luke	15: 1	the sinners **d** near to Him to
Luke	22: 1	of Unleavened Bread **d** near
Luke	22:47	**d** near to Jesus to kiss Him
Luke	23:54	and the Sabbath **d** near
Luke	24:15	that Jesus Himself **d** near
John	18:10	**d** it and struck the high
Acts	5:37	**d** away many people after him

DRIED (see DRY)

Gen	8: 7	had **d** up from the earth
Num	11: 6	now our whole being is **d** up
Josh	2:10	we have heard how the LORD **d**
Judg	16: 7	fresh bowstrings, not yet **d**
Judg	16: 8	fresh bowstrings, not yet **d**
1Sa	17:17	an ephah of this **d** grain and
Job	18:16	His roots are **d** out below
Ps	22:15	My strength is **d** up like a
Ps	74:15	You **d** up mighty rivers

Ps	106: 9	the Red Sea also, and it **d** up
Is	51:10	not the One who **d** up the sea
Mark	5:29	of her blood was **d** up, and she
Mark	11:20	fig tree **d** up from the roots
Rev	16:12	and its water was **d** up, so

DRIES (see DRY)

Prov	17:22	a broken spirit **d** the bones

DRIFT†

Heb	2: 1	we have heard, lest we **d** away

DRINK (see DRANK, DRINKING, DRINKS, DRUNK)

Gen	19:32	let us make our father **d** wine
Gen	21:19	water, and gave the lad a **d**
Gen	24:14	also give your camels a **d**'
Gen	35:14	he poured a **d** offering on it,
Ex	7:21	not **d** the water of the river
Ex	32: 6	people sat down to eat and **d**
Lev	10: 9	Do not **d** wine
Num	5:24	woman **d** the bitter water that
Num	6: 3	from wine and similar **d**
Num	6:20	that the Nazirite may **d** wine
Deut	2: 6	with money, that you may **d**
Judg	4:19	a jug of milk, gave him a **d**
Judg	7: 6	on their knees to **d** water
Judg	13: 7	**d** no wine or similar **d**
Ruth	2: 9	**d** from what the young men
1Sa	1:15	wine nor intoxicating **d**, but
2Sa	23:16	he would not **d** it, but poured
2Ki	18:27	**d** their own waste with you
Neh	8:10	**d** the sweet, and send portions
Job	1: 4	sisters to eat and **d** with them
Job	21:20	let him **d** of the wrath of the
Job	22: 7	given the weary water to **d**
Ps	50:13	Or **d** the blood of goats
Ps	69:21	they gave me vinegar to **d**
Ps	80: 5	tears to **d** in great measure
Ps	102: 9	mingled my **d** with weeping,
Ps	110: 7	He shall **d** of the brook by
Prov	4:17	and **d** the wine of violence
Prov	5:15	D water from your own cistern
Prov	20: 1	intoxicating **d** arouses
Prov	23:35	that I may seek another **d**
Prov	25:21	thirsty, give him water to **d**
Prov	31: 4	it is not for kings to **d** wine
Prov	31: 6	Give strong **d** to him who is
Prov	31: 7	Let him **d** and forget his
Eccl	2:24	than that he should eat and **d**
Eccl	9: 7	and **d** your wine with an merry
Song	5: 1	D, yes, and deeply, O beloved
Is	22:13	Let us eat and **d**, for tomorrow
Is	24: 9	strong **d** is bitter to those
Is	28: 7	erred through intoxicating **d**
Is	60:16	You shall **d** dry the milk of
Is	62: 8	shall not **d** your new wine
Is	65:13	behold, My servants shall **d**
Jer	2:18	to **d** the waters of the River
Jer	8:14	given us water of gall to **d**
Jer	25:27	D, be drunk, and vomit
Jer	35: 6	We will **d** no wine, for
Jer	44:17	pour out **d** offerings to her,
Lam	3:15	He has made me **d** wormwood
Lam	5: 4	We pay for the water we **d**
Ezek	12:18	**d** your water with trembling
Ezek	25: 4	and they shall **d** your milk
Ezek	34:18	that you have fouled
Ezek	39:17	you may eat flesh and **d** blood
Ezek	44:21	No priest shall **d** wine when
Dan	1:10	has appointed your food and **d**
Dan	5: 2	concubines might **d** from them
Hos	2: 5	and my linen, my oil and my **d**
Hos	4:18	Their **d** is rebellion, they
Amos	2: 8	**d** the wine of the condemned
Amos	2:12	gave the Nazirites wine to **d**
Amos	6: 6	who **d** wine from bowls, and

Mic	2:11	prophesy to you of wine and **d**
Hag	1: 6	you **d**, but you are not filled
Matt	6:25	will eat or what you will **d**
Matt	20:22	Are you able to **d** the cup
Matt	24:49	eat and **d** with the drunkards,
Matt	25:35	was thirsty and you gave Me **d**
Matt	26:27	**D** from it, all of you
Matt	26:29	I will not **d** of this fruit of
Matt	26:29	I **d** it new with you in My
Matt	27:34	wine mingled with gall to **d**
Mark	9:41	cup of water to **d** in My name
Mark	14:25	I **d** it new in the kingdom of
Mark	15:23	wine mingled with myrrh to **d**
Mark	16:18	if they **d** anything deadly, it
Luke	1:15	and shall **d** neither wine nor
Luke	5:30	and **d** with tax collectors and
Luke	12:19	eat, **d**, and be merry
Luke	12:29	eat or what you should **d**, nor
John	4: 7	said to her, "Give Me a **d**."
John	4: 9	ask a **d** from me, a Samaritan
John	6:53	**d** His blood, you have no life
John	6:55	and My blood is **d** indeed
John	7:37	let him come to Me and **d**
Acts	23:12	till they had killed Paul
Rom	12:20	if he thirsts, give him a **d**
Rom	14:21	nor **d** wine nor do anything by
1Co	9: 7	does not **d** of the milk of the
1Co	10: 4	drank the same spiritual **d**
1Co	10: 7	people sat down to eat and **d**
1Co	10:21	You cannot **d** the cup of the
1Co	10:31	whether you eat or **d**, or
1Co	11:25	This do, as often as you **d** it
1Co	11:26	**d** this cup, you proclaim the
1Co	11:28	that bread and **d** of that cup
1Co	12:13	made to **d** into one Spirit
1Co	15:32	Let us eat and **d**, for tomorrow
Phil	2:17	a **d** offering on the sacrifice
Col	2:16	one judge you in food or in **d**
1Ti	5:23	No longer **d** only water, but
2Ti	4: 6	poured out as a **d** offering
Rev	14: 8	she has made all nations **d** of
Rev	16: 6	have given them blood to **d**

DRINKING (see DRINK)

Gen	24:22	the camels had finished **d**
Ruth	3: 3	he has finished eating and **d**
1Ki	4:20	sea in multitude, eating and **d**
Is	5:22	Woe to men mighty at **d** wine
Matt	11:19	Son of Man came eating and **d**
Matt	24:38	flood, they were eating and **d**
Rom	14:17	of God is not eating and **d**,
1Pe	4: 3	**d** parties, and abominable

DRINKS (see DRINK)

Gen	44: 5	the one from which my lord **d**
Num	23:24	and **d** the blood of the slain
Job	6: 4	my spirit **d** in their poison
Job	15:16	Who **d** iniquity like water
Job	34: 7	Job, who **d** scorn like water,
Ezek	31:14	that no tree which **d** water
Mark	2:16	and **d** with tax collectors and
John	4:13	Whoever **d** of this water will
John	6:54	**d** My blood has eternal life,
John	6:56	**d** My blood abides in Me, and I
1Co	11:27	**d** this cup of the Lord in an
1Co	11:29	**d** in an unworthy manner eats
1Co	11:29	**d** judgment to himself, not
Heb	9:10	only with foods and **d**, various

DRIP (see DRIPPED, DRIPPING)

Ps	65:11	Your paths **d** with abundance
Prov	5: 3	of an immoral woman **d** honey
Song	4:11	my spouse, **d** as the honeycomb
Joel	3:18	shall **d** with new wine, the
Zech	4:12	two olive branches that **d**

DRIPPED† (see DRIP)

Song	5: 5	my hands **d** with myrrh, My

DRIPPING (see DRIP)

1Sa	14:26	woods, there was the honey, **d**
Prov	19:13	of a wife are a continual **d**
Song	5:13	are lilies, **d** liquid myrrh

DRIVE (see DRIVEN, DRIVER, DRIVES, DRIVING, DROVE, WELL-DRIVEN)

Gen	33:13	should **d** them hard one day
Ex	6: 1	will **d** them out of his land
Ex	33: 2	I will **d** out the Canaanite and
Deut	4:27	where the LORD will **d** you
Deut	28:37	where the Lord will **d** you
Josh	3:10	**d** out from before you the
Josh	16:10	And they did not **d** out the
Judg	1:28	did not completely **d** them out
Judg	2: 3	I will not **d** them out before
Prov	22:15	will **d** it far from him
Is	22:19	So I will **d** you out of your
Jer	19: 9	lives shall **d** them to despair
Dan	4:25	They shall **d** you from men,
Hos	9:15	I will **d** them from My house
Mark	11:15	and began to **d** out those who
Acts	27:15	into the wind, we let her **d**

DRIVEN (see DRIVE)

Gen	4:14	Surely You have **d** me out this
Ex	12:39	they were **d** out of Egypt and
Job	6:13	And is success **d** from me
Job	13:25	Will You frighten a leaf **d** to
Job	18:18	He is **d** from light into
Ps	40:14	Let them be **d** backward and
Ps	68: 2	As smoke is **d** away, So drive
Jer	16:15	the lands where He had **d** them
Ezek	34: 4	brought back what was **d** away
Dan	4:33	he was **d** from men and ate
Dan	9: 7	to which You have **d** them,
Luke	8:29	was **d** by the demon into the
Acts	27:17	they struck sail and so were **d**
Jas	1: 6	is like a wave of the sea **d**
Jas	3: 4	are **d** by fierce winds, they

DRIVER (see DRIVE)

1Ki	22:34	said to the **d** of his chariot

DRIVES (see DRIVE)

Deut	18:12	the LORD your God **d** them out
Deut	30: 1	where the LORD your God **d** you
2Ki	9:20	of Nimshi, for he **d** furiously
Ps	1: 4	chaff which the wind **d** away

DRIVING (see DRIVE)

Deut	4:38	**d** out from before you nations
2Ki	9:20	the **d** is like the **d** of
Prov	28: 3	the poor is like a **d** rain
Acts	26:24	Much learning is **d** you mad

DROP (see DROPPED, DROPS)

Deut	28:40	for your olives shall **d** off
Deut	32: 2	Let my teaching **d** as the rain
Deut	33:28	His Heavens shall also **d** dew
Is	40:15	are as a **d** in a bucket, and

DROPPED (see DROP)

Acts	27:29	they **d** four anchors from the

DROPS (see DROP)

Luke	22:44	**d** of blood falling down to
Rev	6:13	as a fig tree **d** its late figs

DROPSY†

Luke	14: 2	man before Him who had **d**

DROSS

Ps	119:119	wicked of the earth like **d**
Prov	25: 4	Take away the **d** from silver
Is	1:25	thoroughly purge away your **d**

DROUGHT (*see* DROUGHTS)
Job   24:19 As **d** and heat consume the snow
Ps   32: 4 turned into the **d** of summer
Is   58:11 and satisfy your soul in **d**
Jer   17: 8 be anxious in the year of **d**
Hag   1:11 I called for a **d** on the land

DROUGHTS† (*see* DROUGHT)
Jer   14: 1 to Jeremiah concerning the **d**

DROVE (*see* DRIVE)
Gen   3:24 So He **d** out the man
Gen 15:11 carcasses, Abram **d** them away
Josh 24:18 the LORD **d** out from before us
Judg 4:21 **d** the peg into his temple, and
2Sa   6: 3 of Abinadab, **d** the new cart
Neh 13:28 therefore I **d** him from me
Matt 21:12 **d** out all those who bought and
Mark 1:12 immediately the Spirit **d** Him
John 2:15 He **d** them all out of the
Acts 18:16 he **d** them from the judgment

DROWN† (*see* DROWNED)
Song 8: 7 love, nor can the floods **d** it
1Ti   6: 9 which **d** men in destruction

DROWNED (*see* DROWN)
Ex   15: 4 also are **d** in the Red Sea
Matt 18: 6 he were **d** in the depth of the
Heb 11:29 attempting to do so, were **d**

DROWSINESS†
Prov 23:21 **d** will clothe a man with rags

DRUNK (*see* DRINK, DRUNKARD, DRUNKEN)
Gen 9:21 he drank of the wine and was **d**
Deut 29: 6 bread, nor have you **d** wine or
Deut 32:42 make My arrows **d** with blood
Ruth 3: 7 And after Boaz had eaten and **d**
1Sa 1:13 Eli thought she was **d**
Is   29: 9 They are **d**, but not with wine
Is   51:17 you have **d** the dregs of the
Is   63: 6 made them **d** in My fury, and
Dan 5:23 have **d** wine from them
Luke 5:39 And no one, having **d** old wine,
John 2:10 when the guests have well **d**
Acts 2:15 For these are not **d**, as you
1Co 11:21 one is hungry and another is **d**
Eph 5:18 And do not be **d** with wine, in
1Th 5: 7 who get **d** are **d** at night
Rev 17: 2 made **d** with the wine of her
Rev 17: 6 **d** with the blood of the
Rev 18: 3 For all the nations have **d** of

DRUNKARD (*see* DRUNK, DRUNKARDS)
Prov 23:21 for the **d** and the glutton will
Prov 26: 9 goes into the hand of a **d** is
Is   24:20 shall reel to and fro like a **d**
1Co 5:11 or a reviler, or a **d**, or an

DRUNKARDS (*see* DRUNKARD)
Joel 1: 5 Awake, you **d**, and weep
Matt 24:49 and to eat and drink with the **d**
1Co 6:10 thieves, nor covetous, nor **d**

DRUNKEN (*see* DRUNK, DRUNKENNESS)
Ps 107:27 fro, and stagger like a **d** man

DRUNKENNESS (*see* DRUNKEN)
Luke 21:34 down with carousing, **d**, and
Rom 13:13 the day, not in revelry and **d**
Gal 5:21 envy, murders, **d**, revelries,
1Pe 4: 3 in licentiousness, lusts, **d**

DRY (*see* DRIED, DRIES)
Gen 1: 9 and let the **d** land appear"
Gen 1:10 God called the **d** land Earth
Ex   4: 9 become blood on the **d** land
Ex 14:16 of Israel shall go on **d**
Ex 14:21 and made the sea into **d** land

Josh 3:17 crossed over on **d** ground,
Judg 6:40 It was **d** on the fleece only,
1Ki 17:16 nor did the jar of oil run **d**
Ps   63: 1 My flesh longs for You In a **d**
Ps   66: 6 He turned the sea into **d** land
Ps   69: 3 My throat is **d**
Ps   95: 5 His hands formed the **d** land
Prov 17: 1 Better is a **d** morsel with
Is   44:27 Who says to the deep, 'Be **d**
Is   53: 2 and as a root out of **d** ground
Jer 50:12 a **d** land and a desert
Lam 4: 8 it has become as **d** as wood
Ezek 37: 4 O **d** bones, hear the word of
Ezek 37:11 indeed say, 'Our bones are **d**
Hos 9:14 miscarrying womb and **d** breasts
Jon 1: 9 made the sea and the **d** land
Jon 2:10 it vomited Jonah onto **d** land
Luke 23:31 what will be done in the **d**
Heb 11:29 the Red Sea as by **d** land,

DUE
Deut 18: 3 priest's **d** from the people
Deut 32:35 foot shall slip in **d** time
Ps   29: 2 LORD the glory **d** to His name
Ps 104:27 them their food in **d** season
Ps 145:15 them their food in **d** season
Prov 3:27 from those to whom it is **d**
Dan 3:12 have not paid **d** regard to you
Dan 6:13 does not show **d** regard for
Matt 18:34 pay all that was **d** to him
Matt 24:45 to give them food in **d** season
Luke 23:41 for we receive the **d** reward
Rom 1:27 of their error which was **d**
Rom 5: 6 in **d** time Christ died for the
Rom 13: 7 taxes to whom taxes are **d**
1Co 7: 3 his wife the affection **d** her
1Co 15: 8 as by one born out of **d** time
Gal 6: 9 for in **d** season we shall reap
1Ti 2: 6 to be testified in **d** time
1Pe 5: 6 He may exalt you in **d** time

DUG (*see* DIG)
Gen 21:30 that I have **d** this well
Gen 26:18 Isaac **d** again the wells of
Ex   7:24 So all the Egyptians **d** all
Ps   57: 6 They have **d** a pit before me
Ps 94:13 the pit is **d** for the wicked
Is   5: 2 He **d** it up and cleared out its
Is   5: 6 it shall not be pruned or **d**
Is 51: 1 the pit from which you were **d**
Jer 13: 7 I went to the Euphrates and **d**
Ezek 8: 8 when I **d** into the wall, there
Matt 21:33 **d** a winepress in it and built
Matt 25:18 **d** in the ground, and hid his
Luke 6:48 house, who **d** deep and laid the

DULL
Eccl 10:10 If the ax is **d**, and one does
Is   6:10 the heart of this people **d**
Matt 13:15 of this people has grown **d**
Acts 28:27 of this people has grown **d**
Heb 5:11 you have become **d** of hearing

DUMB†
Is   35: 6 and the tongue of the **d** sing
Is   56:10 they are all **d** dogs, they
Mark 9:25 **d** spirit, I command you, come
1Co 12: 2 carried away to these **d** idols
2Pe 2:16 a **d** donkey speaking with a

DUNGEON
Gen 41:14 him hastily out of the **d**
Jer 37:16 When Jeremiah entered the **d**
Jer 38:13 and lifted him out of the **d**

DUST
Gen 2: 7 man of the **d** of the ground
Gen 3:14 you shall eat **d** all the days

Gen	3:19	for **d** you are, and to **d** you
Gen	3:19	and to **d** you shall return
Gen	13:16	as the **d** of the earth
Gen	18:27	Indeed now, I who am but **d**
Ex	8:16	strike the **d** of the land, so
Deut	9:21	until it was as fine as **d**
1Sa	2: 8	He raises the poor from the **d**
2Sa	1: 2	clothes torn and **d** on his head
1Ki	16: 2	as I lifted you out of the **d**
1Ki	18:38	wood and the stones and the **d**
Job	4:19	whose foundation is in the **d**
Job	7: 5	is caked with worms and **d**, my
Job	7:21	now I will lie down in the **d**
Job	10: 9	will You turn me into **d** again
Job	27:16	he heaps up silver like **d**
Job	28: 6	and it contains gold **d**
Job	34:15	and man would return to **d**
Job	42: 6	abhor myself, and repent in **d**
Ps	18:42	fine as the **d** before the wind
Ps	22:15	brought Me to the **d** of death
Ps	22:29	to the **d** Shall bow before Him
Ps	30: 9	Will the **d** praise You
Ps	72: 9	His enemies will lick the **d**
Ps	103:14	He remembers that we are **d**
Ps	104:29	they die and return to their **d**
Prov	8:26	the primeval **d** of the world
Eccl	3:20	all are from the **d**
Eccl	3:20	and all return to **d**
Eccl	12: 7	Then the **d** will return to the
Is	26:19	and sing, you who dwell in **d**
Is	40:15	as the small **d** on the balance
Is	65:25	**d** shall be the serpent's food
Lam	2:10	they throw **d** on their heads
Dan	12: 2	**d** of the earth shall awake
Mic	1:10	roll yourself in the **d**
Nah	1: 3	clouds are the **d** of His feet
Matt	10:14	shake off the **d** from your
Acts	22:23	and threw **d** into the air,
1Co	15:47	was of the earth, made of **d**
1Co	15:48	As was the man of **d**, so also
Rev	18:19	they threw **d** on their heads

DUTIES (*see* DUTY)
Num	8:26	the Levites regarding their **d**

DUTY (*see* DUTIES)
Num	3:31	Their **d** included the ark, the
Deut	25: 7	the **d** of my husband's brother
Ruth	3:13	**d** of a near kinsman for you
Ruth	3:13	I will perform the **d** for you
2Ki	11: 9	to be on **d** on the Sabbath
Rom	15:27	their **d** is also to minister

DWELL (*see* DWELLING, DWELLS, DWELT)
Gen	4:20	of those who **d** in tents and
Gen	9:27	may he **d** in the tents of Shem
Gen	13: 6	they could not **d** together
Gen	19:30	he was afraid to **d** in Zoar
Gen	47: 4	**d** in the land of Goshen
Ex	25: 8	that I may **d** among them
Ex	25:46	that I may **d** among them
Lev	13:46	unclean, and he shall **d** alone
Lev	23:42	Israelites shall **d** in booths
Num	13:19	land they **d** in is good or bad
Num	14:25	Canaanites **d** in the valley
Num	35:34	for I the LORD **d** among the
Deut	8:12	beautiful houses and **d** in them
Deut	25: 5	If brothers **d** together, and
Deut	33:28	Then Israel shall **d** in safety
Josh	9: 7	Perhaps you **d** among us
Judg	8:11	who **d** in tents on the east of
Judg	17:11	was content to **d** with the man
1Sa	27: 5	**d** in the royal city with you
2Sa	7: 2	I **d** in a house of cedar, but
2Sa	7: 5	build a house for Me to **d** in
1Ki	3:17	and I **d** in the same house

1Ki	8:12	He would **d** in the dark cloud
1Ki	8:13	place for You to **d** in forever
1Ki	8:27	God indeed **d** on the earth
Ezra	4:17	companions who **d** in Samaria
Neh	11: 1	out of ten to **d** in Jerusalem
Job	4:19	those who **d** in houses of clay
Job	17: 2	does not my eye **d** on their
Ps	4: 8	O LORD, make me **d** in safety
Ps	5: 4	Nor shall evil **d** with You
Ps	15: 1	Who may **d** in Your holy hill
Ps	23: 6	I will **d** in the house of the
Ps	24: 1	world and those who **d** therein
Ps	27: 4	That I may **d** in the house of
Ps	37: 3	**D** in the land, and feed on His
Ps	65: 4	That he may **d** in Your courts
Ps	68:16	which God desires to **d** in
Ps	68:16	the LORD will **d** in it forever
Ps	84:10	**d** in the tents of wickedness
Ps	85: 9	That glory may **d** in our land
Ps	98: 7	world and those who **d** in it
Ps	107: 4	They found no city to **d** in
Ps	123: 1	O You who **d** in the heavens
Ps	133: 1	to **d** together in unity
Ps	139: 9	**d** in the uttermost parts of
Ps	140:13	shall **d** in Your presence
Ps	143: 3	He has made me **d** in darkness
Prov	1:33	listens to me will **d** safely
Prov	2:21	upright will **d** in the land
Prov	21: 9	It is better to **d** in a corner
Prov	25:24	It is better to **d** in a corner
Song	8:13	You who **d** in the gardens, the
Is	6: 5	I **d** in the midst of a people
Is	10:24	who **d** in Zion, do not be
Is	11: 6	also shall **d** with the lamb
Is	26: 5	down those who **d** on high, the
Is	26:19	and sing, you who **d** in dust
Is	47: 8	who **d** securely, who say in
Is	57:15	I **d** in the high and holy place
Is	58:12	Restorer of Streets to **D** In
Jer	7: 3	cause you to **d** in this place
Jer	7: 7	cause you to **d** in this place
Jer	27:11	they shall till it and **d** in it
Jer	29: 5	Build houses and **d** in them
Jer	33:16	and Jerusalem will **d** safely
Jer	44: 1	who **d** in the land of Egypt
Jer	44:13	who **d** in the land of Egypt
Jer	49: 8	turn back, **d** in the depths, O
Jer	50:39	**d** there with the jackals, and
Ezek	37:25	Then they shall **d** in the land
Ezek	43: 9	and I will **d** in their midst
Hos	14: 7	Those who **d** under his shadow
Hag	1: 4	to **d** in your paneled houses
Zech	2:11	And I will **d** in your midst
Acts	7:48	the Most High does not **d** in
Acts	17:24	does not **d** in temples made
Acts	17:26	to **d** on all the face of the
Acts	28:16	but Paul was permitted to **d**
Eph	3:17	that Christ may **d** in your
Col	1:19	Him all the fullness should **d**
Col	3:16	Let the word of Christ **d** in
1Pe	3: 7	husbands, **d** with them with
Rev	2:13	your works, and where you **d**
Rev	3:10	test those who **d** on the earth
Rev	7:15	the throne will **d** among them
Rev	13: 6	and those who **d** in heaven
Rev	21: 3	He will **d** with them, and they

DWELLING (*see* DWELL, DWELLINGS)
Gen	25:27	was a mild man, **d** in tents
Ex	15:17	You have made for Your own **d**
1Ki	8:30	hear in heaven Your **d** place
1Ki	8:39	hear in heaven Your **d** place
1Ki	8:43	hear in heaven Your **d** place
2Ch	30:27	came up to His holy **d** place
Neh	1: 9	chosen as a **d** for My name

Job	5: 3	I cursed his **d** place.
Job	8:22	the **d** place of the wicked
Job	21:28	the **d** place of the wicked
Job	38:19	is the way to the **d** of light
Ps	33:14	the place of His **d** He looks
Ps	49:11	And their **d** places to all
Ps	76: 2	And His **d** place in Zion
Ps	79: 7	And laid waste his **d** place
Ps	90: 1	You have been our **d** place in
Ps	91: 9	the Most High, your **d** place,
Ps	91:10	any plague come near your **d**
Ps	107: 7	to a city for a **d** place.
Ps	132: 5	A **d** place for the Mighty God
Ps	132:13	desired it for His **d** place:
Jer	49:33	shall be a **d** for jackals, a
Dan	2:11	whose **d** is not with flesh
Dan	4:30	a royal **d** by my mighty power
Dan	5:21	and his **d** was with the wild
Joel	3:17	**d** in Zion My holy mountain
Hab	1: 6	to possess **d** places that are
Mark	5: 3	who had his **d** among the tombs
Acts	1:19	to all those **d** in Jerusalem
Acts	1:20	let his **d** place be desolate
Acts	7:46	asked to find a **d** for the God
Acts	11:29	to the brethren **d** in Judea
Eph	2:22	for a **d** place of God
1Ti	6:16	**d** in unapproachable light,
Heb	11: 9	**d** in tents with Isaac and
2Pe	2: 8	**d** among them, tormented his
Rev	18: 2	become a **d** place of demons,

DWELLINGS (see DWELLING)

Ex	10:23	Israel had light in their **d**
Lev	7:26	any blood in any of your **d**
Lev	23:21	**d** throughout your generations
Num	24: 5	your **d**, O Israel
Ps	55:15	For wickedness is in their **d**
Ps	87: 2	More than all the **d** of Jacob
Is	32:18	habitation, in secure **d**, and
Jer	9:19	have been cast out of our **d**
Acts	17:26	the boundaries of their **d**,

DWELLS (see DWELL)

1Sa	4: 4	who **d** between the cherubim
2Sa	6: 2	who **d** between the cherubim
Ps	9:11	to the LORD, who **d** in Zion
Ps	26: 8	the place where Your glory **d**
Ps	91: 1	He who **d** in the secret place
Ps	113: 5	LORD our God, Who **d** on high,
Jer	49:31	nation that **d** securely,"
Dan	2:22	darkness, and light **d** with Him
John	14:10	but the Father who **d** in Me
John	14:17	for He **d** with you and will be
Rom	7:17	do it, but sin that **d** in me
Rom	7:18	in my flesh) nothing good **d**
Rom	7:20	do it, but sin that **d** in me
Rom	8: 9	the Spirit of God **d** in you
Rom	8:11	Jesus from the dead **d** in you
Col	2: 9	For in Him **d** all the fullness
Jas	4: 5	The Spirit who **d** in us yearns
2Pe	3:13	in which righteousness **d**
Rev	2:13	among you, where Satan **d**

DWELT (see DWELL)

Gen	4:16	**d** in the land of Nod on the
Gen	13:12	Abram **d** in the land of Canaan
Gen	13:12	Lot **d** in the cities of the
Gen	37: 1	Now Jacob **d** in the land where
Ex	2:15	and **d** in the land of Midian
Deut	2:20	giants formerly **d** there
Deut	33:16	of Him who **d** in the bush
Josh	2:15	she **d** on the wall
Judg	3: 5	Israel **d** among the Canaanites
Ruth	1: 4	they **d** there about ten years
Ruth	2:23	she **d** with her mother-in-law
2Sa	5: 9	So David **d** in the stronghold,

2Sa	7: 6	For I have not **d** in a house
2Ki	15: 5	so he **d** in an isolated house
2Ki	17:24	of Samaria and **d** in its cities
Esth	9:19	who **d** in the unwalled towns
Job	29:25	so I **d** as a king in the army,
Ps	68:10	Your congregation **d** in it
Ps	74: 2	Mount Zion where You have **d**
Ps	120: 6	My soul has **d** too long With
Is	29: 1	Ariel, the city where David **d**
Jer	2: 6	one crossed and where no one **d**
Ezek	3:15	who **d** by the River Chebar
Dan	4:12	the heavens **d** in its branches
Dan	4:21	the beasts of the field **d**
Matt	2:23	**d** in a city called Nazareth,
Matt	4:13	**d** in Capernaum, which is by
Luke	1:65	came on all who **d** around them
John	1:14	**d** among us, and we beheld His
Acts	7: 2	before he **d** in Haran,
Acts	9:22	the Jews who **d** in Damascus
Acts	19:10	so that all who **d** in Asia
Acts	28:30	Then Paul **d** two whole years
2Ti	1: 5	in you, which **d** first in your

DYED

Ex	25: 5	rams' skins **d** red, badger
Ex	26:14	skins **d** red for the tent, and
Judg	5:30	two pieces of **d** embroidery
Is	63: 1	with **d** garments from Bozrah,

DYING (see DIE)

Gen	48:21	Behold, I am **d**, but God will
Zech	11: 9	Let what is **d** die, and what is
Mark	12:20	and **d**, he left no offspring
Luke	8:42	years of age, and she was **d**
John	11:37	have kept this man from **d**
2Co	4:10	body the **d** of the Lord Jesus
2Co	6: 9	as **d**, and behold we live
Heb	11:21	By faith Jacob, when he was **d**
Heb	11:22	faith Joseph, when he was **d**

DYSENTERY†

Acts	28: 8	lay sick of a fever and **d**

E

EAGER (see EAGERLY)

Ps	17:12	that is **e** to tear his prey
Gal	2:10	which I also was **e** to do

EAGERLY (see EAGER)

Rom	8:19	**e** waits for the revealing of
Rom	8:23	**e** waiting for the adoption,
1Co	1: 7	**e** waiting for the revelation
Gal	5: 5	Spirit **e** wait for the hope of
Phil	2:28	I sent him the more **e**, that
1Th	2:17	endeavored more **e** to see your
Heb	9:28	To those who **e** wait for Him
1Pe	5: 2	not for dishonest gain but **e**

EAGLE (see EAGLE'S, EAGLES)

Lev	11:13	the **e**, the vulture, the
Deut	32:11	As an **e** stirs ûp its nest,
Job	9:26	like an **e** swooping on its
Prov	30:19	the way of an **e** in the air
Jer	48:40	one shall fly like an **e**, and
Ezek	1:10	the four had the face of an **e**
Mic	1:16	your baldness like an **e**, for
Rev	4: 7	creature was like a flying **e**
Rev	12:14	given two wings of a great **e**

EAGLE'S† (see EAGLE)

Ps	103: 5	youth is renewed like the **e**
Dan	7: 4	like a lion, and had **e** wings

EAGLES (see EAGLE, EAGLES')

2Sa	1:23	they were swifter than **e**,

Is	40:31	mount up with wings like e
Jer	4:13	His horses are swifter than e
Matt	24:28	there the e will be gathered

EAGLES'† (see EAGLES)

Ex	19: 4	and how I bore you on e wings
Dan	4:33	had grown like e feathers

EAR (see EARS)

Ex	15:26	give e to His commandments
Ex	21: 6	pierce his e with an awl
Ex	29:20	tip of the right e of Aaron
2Ki	19:16	Incline Your e, O LORD, and
Job	4:12	my e received a whisper of it
Job	42: 5	You by the hearing of the e
Ps	5: 1	Give e to my words, O LORD,
Ps	17: 6	Incline Your e to me, and hear
Ps	31: 2	Bow down Your e to me,
Ps	58: 4	deaf cobra that stops its e
Ps	71: 2	Incline Your e to me, and save
Ps	94: 9	He who planted the e, shall
Prov	2: 2	you incline your e to wisdom
Prov	20:12	The hearing e and the seeing
Eccl	1: 8	nor the e filled with hearing
Is	1: 2	Hear, O heavens, and give e
Is	50: 4	he awakens My e to hear as
Is	50: 5	The Lord GOD has opened My e
Is	59: 1	nor His e heavy, that it
Amos	3:12	two legs or a piece of an e
Matt	10:27	and what you her in the e
Matt	26:51	high priest, and cut off his e
Luke	22:51	And He touched his e and
John	18:26	of him whose e Peter cut off
1Co	2: 9	nor e heard, nor have entered
1Co	12:16	And if the e should say,
Rev	2: 7	He who has an e, let him hear
Rev	13: 9	If anyone has an e, let him

EARLY

Gen	19:27	Abraham went e in the morning
Gen	21:14	Abraham rose e in the morning
Gen	22: 3	Abraham rose e in the morning
Deut	11:14	the e rain and the latter rain
Judg	19: 9	Tomorrow go your way e, so
Judg	21: 4	that the people rose e and
1Sa	1:19	Then they rose e in the
1Sa	5: 3	people of Ashdod arose e in
1Sa	5: 4	And when they arose e the
1Sa	9:26	They arose e; and it was
1Sa	15:12	So when Samuel rose e in the
1Sa	17:20	So David rose e in the
1Sa	29:10	rise e in the morning with
1Sa	29:10	And as soon as you are up e
1Sa	29:11	So David and his men rose e
2Sa	15: 2	Now Absalom would rise e and
2Ki	3:22	Then they rose up e in the
2Ki	6:15	of the man of God arose e
Job	1: 5	and he would rise e in the
Ps	63: 1	E will I seek You; My soul
Ps	90:14	satisfy us e with Your
Ps	101: 8	E I will destroy all the
Ps	127: 2	vain for you to rise up e,
Prov	27:14	rising e in the morning, It
Song	7:12	Let us get up e to the
Is	26: 9	within me I will seek You e;
Jer	7:13	rising up e and speaking,
Jer	7:25	daily rising up e and
Jer	35:15	rising up e and sending
Jer	44: 4	rising e and sending them,
Dan	6:10	as was his custom since e
Dan	6:19	Then the king arose very e in
Hos	6: 4	And like the e dew it goes
Hos	13: 3	cloud And like the e dew
Zeph	3: 7	But they rose e and
Matt	20: 1	a landowner who went out e
Mark	16: 2	Very e in the morning, on the

Mark	16: 9	Now when He rose e on the
Luke	21:38	Then e in the morning all the
Luke	24: 1	very e in the morning, they,
Luke	24:22	who arrived at the tomb e,
John	8: 2	Now e in the morning He came
John	18:28	and it was e morning. But
John	20: 1	Magdalene went to the tomb e,
Acts	5:21	they entered the temple e in
Acts	21:16	an e disciple, with whom we
Jas	5: 7	it until it receives the e

EARNED (see EARNS)

Luke	19:16	your mina has e ten minas.'

EARNEST (see EARNESTLY)

Rom	8:19	For the e expectation of the
2Co	7: 7	when he told us of your e
Phil	1:20	according to my e expectation
Heb	2: 1	must give the more e heed

EARNESTLY (see EARNEST)

1Sa	20: 6	David e asked permission of
1Sa	20:28	David e asked permission of
Job	7: 2	Like a servant who e desires
Job	8: 5	If you would e seek God And
Ps	78:34	and sought e for God.
Jer	11: 7	For I e exhorted your fathers
Mark	5:10	Also he begged Him e that He
Luke	22:44	in agony, He prayed more e.
Acts	23: 1	looking e at the council,
Acts	26: 7	e serving God night and
1Co	12:31	But e desire the best gifts.
1Co	14:39	desire e to prophesy, and do
2Co	5: 2	e desiring to be clothed
Col	4: 2	Continue e in prayer, being
Jas	5:17	and he prayed e that it
Jude	3	exhorting you to contend e

EARNS (see EARNED)

Hag	1: 6	E wages to put into a bag

EARRING† (see EARRINGS)

Prov	25:12	Like an e of gold and an

EARRINGS (see EARRING)

Gen	35: 4	and the e which were in
Ex	32: 2	Break off the golden e which
Ex	35:22	brought e and nose rings,
Judg	8:24	of you would give me the e
Hos	2:13	decked herself with her e

EARS (see EAR)

Ex	32: 2	which are in the e of your
Lev	8:24	on the tips of their right e,
Deut	29: 4	and eyes to see and e to
Judg	17: 2	even saying it in my e—
1Sa	3:11	in Israel at which both e
1Sa	15:14	of the sheep in my e,
2Sa	7:22	we have heard with our e.
2Sa	22: 7	And my cry entered His e.
2Ki	21:12	both his e will tingle.
2Ch	7:15	eyes will be open and My e
Neh	8: 3	and the e of all the people
Job	15:21	sounds are in his e;
Job	33:16	Then He opens the e of men,
Ps	34:15	And His e are open to
Ps	40: 6	My e You have opened.
Ps	44: 1	We have heard with our e,
Ps	78: 1	Incline your e to the words
Ps	115: 6	They have e, but they do not
Ps	135:17	They have e, but they do not
Prov	21:13	Whoever shuts his e to the
Prov	23:12	And your e to words of
Prov	26:17	one who takes a dog by the e.
Is	6:10	And their e heavy, And
Is	6:10	eyes, And hear with their e,
Is	11: 3	by the hearing of His e;
Is	42:20	not observe; Opening the e,

Is	43: 8	And the deaf who have e.
Jer	26:11	you have heard with your e.
Ezek	40: 4	eyes and hear with your e,
Matt	11:15	He who has e to hear, let him
Matt	13:15	Their e are hard of
Matt	13:15	and hear with their e,
Matt	28:14	comes to the governor's e,
Mark	7:33	and put His fingers in his e,
Mark	7:35	his e were opened,
Luke	1:44	greeting sounded in my e,
Luke	9:44	words sink down into your e,
Acts	7:51	in heart and e You always
Acts	11:22	these things came to the e
Acts	17:20	some strange things to our e.
Acts	28:27	Their e are hard of
Rom	11: 8	e that they should not
2Ti	4: 3	because they have itching e,
Jas	5: 4	reapers have reached the e
1Pe	3:12	And His e are open to

EARTH (see EARTHEN, EARTHLY, EARTHQUAKE)

Gen	1: 1	the heavens and the e.
Gen	1: 2	The e was without form, and
Gen	1:10	God called the dry land E,
Gen	1:24	thing and beast of the e,
Gen	1:28	fill the e and subdue it;
Gen	2: 5	caused it to rain on the e,
Gen	2: 6	a mist went up from the e
Gen	4:11	you are cursed from the e,
Gen	4:14	and a vagabond on the e,
Gen	6: 4	There were giants on the e in
Gen	6: 5	of man was great in the e,
Gen	6:11	The e also was corrupt
Gen	6:17	floodwaters on the e,
Gen	6:17	that is on the e shall die.
Gen	7: 4	cause it to rain on the e
Gen	7:17	and it rose high above the e.
Gen	7:24	waters prevailed on the e
Gen	8: 1	a wind to pass over the e,
Gen	8:11	had receded from the e.
Gen	8:22	While the e remains,
Gen	9: 1	and multiply, and fill the e.
Gen	9:14	I bring a cloud over the e,
Gen	9:16	all flesh that is on the e.
Gen	10:25	for in his days the e was
Gen	11: 1	Now the whole e had one
Gen	11: 9	the language of all the e;
Gen	12: 3	all the families of the e,
Gen	13:16	number the dust of the e,
Gen	14:19	Possessor of heaven and e;
Gen	18:18	and all the nations of the e
Gen	18:25	not the Judge of all the e
Gen	27:28	Of the fatness of the e,
Gen	28:12	ladder was set up on the e,
Gen	37:10	come to bow down to the e
Ex	8:17	and struck the dust of the e,
Ex	9:14	none like Me in all the e.
Ex	15:12	The e swallowed them.
Ex	19: 5	for all the e is Mine.
Ex	20: 4	or that is in the e
Ex	20: 4	is in the water under the e;
Ex	20:24	An altar of e you shall make
Lev	15:12	The vessel of e that he who
Lev	26:19	like iron and your e like
Num	14:21	all the e shall be filled
Num	16:32	and the e opened its mouth
Num	16:33	the e closed over them, and
Num	16:34	Lest the e swallow us up
Deut	4:17	animal that is on the e or
Deut	4:26	I call heaven and e to
Deut	13: 7	from one end of the e to
Deut	28: 1	above all nations of the e.
Deut	30:19	I call heaven and e as
Deut	32: 1	I will speak; And hear, O e,
Deut	32:13	ride in the heights of the e,

Deut	33:16	the precious things of the e
Deut	33:17	To the ends of the e;
Josh	2:11	God in heaven above and on e
Josh	23:14	going the way of all the e.
Judg	5: 4	The e trembled and the
1Sa	4: 5	so loudly that the e shook.
1Sa	14:15	and the e quaked, so that it
1Sa	26:20	let my blood fall to the e
1Sa	28:13	ascending out of the e.
2Sa	4:11	and remove you from the e?
2Sa	7: 9	great men who are on the e.
2Sa	18: 9	hanging between heaven and e.
2Sa	23: 4	springing out of the e,
1Ki	1:40	that the e seemed to split
1Ki	8:23	God in heaven above or on e
1Ki	8:43	that all peoples of the e
1Ki	8:53	all the peoples of the e
1Ki	17:14	LORD sends rain on the e.
2Ki	5:17	be given two mule-loads of e;
2Ki	19:15	You have made heaven and e.
1Ch	16:14	judgments are in all the e.
1Ch	16:23	to the LORD, all the e;
1Ch	16:33	He is coming to judge the e.
2Ch	20:24	dead bodies, fallen on the e.
2Ch	32:19	gods of the people of the e—
Ezra	5:11	of the God of heaven and e,
Job	1: 7	going to and fro on the e,
Job	1: 8	is none like him on the e,
Job	3:14	and counselors of the e,
Job	8: 9	Because our days on e are
Job	14: 8	root may grow old in the e,
Job	14:19	wash away the soil of the e;
Job	16:18	O e, do not cover
Job	18:17	of him perishes from the e,
Job	19:25	shall stand at last on the e;
Job	20: 4	Since man was placed on e,
Job	26: 7	He hangs the e on nothing.
Job	28: 2	Iron is taken from the e,
Job	38: 4	the foundations of the e?
Job	41:33	On e there is nothing like
Ps	2: 2	The kings of the e set
Ps	2: 8	And the ends of the e for
Ps	2:10	you judges of the e.
Ps	7: 5	him trample my life to the e,
Ps	8: 1	is Your name in all the e,
Ps	8: 9	is Your name in all the e,
Ps	12: 6	tried in a furnace of e,
Ps	16: 3	the saints who are on the e,
Ps	19: 4	gone out through all the e,
Ps	24: 1	The e is the LORD's, and
Ps	33: 5	The e is full of the
Ps	33: 8	Let all the e fear the
Ps	37:11	the meek shall inherit the e,
Ps	46: 2	Even though the e be
Ps	46: 6	His voice, the e melted.
Ps	46:10	I will be exalted in the e!
Ps	47: 2	a great King over all the e,
Ps	48: 2	The joy of the whole e,
Ps	50: 1	Has spoken and called the e
Ps	57: 5	glory be above all the e.
Ps	57:11	glory be above all the e.
Ps	63: 9	the lower parts of the e.
Ps	65: 9	You visit the e and water
Ps	66: 1	Shout to God, all the e
Ps	66: 4	All the e shall worship You
Ps	67: 7	And all the ends of the e
Ps	72: 6	showers that water the e.
Ps	72: 8	River to the ends of the e.
Ps	72:16	flourish like grass of the e.
Ps	74:20	the dark places of the e
Ps	82: 8	Arise, O God, judge the e;
Ps	83:10	became as refuse on the e.
Ps	83:18	the Most High over all the e.
Ps	89:11	the e also is Yours; The
Ps	90: 2	ever You had formed the e

Ps	94: 2	Rise up, O Judge of the e;
Ps	96:13	He is coming to judge the e.
Ps	97: 1	Let the e rejoice; Let the
Ps	98: 3	All the ends of the e have
Ps	103:11	heavens are high above the e,
Ps	104: 9	not return to cover the e.
Ps	104:13	The e is satisfied with the
Ps	104:14	bring forth food from the e,
Ps	104:30	You renew the face of the e.
Ps	109:15	memory of them from the e;
Ps	115:16	But the e He has given to
Ps	119:19	I am a stranger in the e;
Ps	121: 2	Who made heaven and e.
Ps	124: 8	Who made heaven and e.
Ps	135: 6	He does, In heaven and in e,
Ps	141: 7	plows and breaks up the e.
Prov	3:19	by wisdom founded the e;
Prov	8:23	before there was ever an e.
Prov	25: 3	for height and the e for
Eccl	1: 4	But the e abides forever.
Eccl	5: 2	is in heaven, and you on e;
Eccl	12: 7	dust will return to the e
Song	2:12	The flowers appear on the e;
Is	1: 2	O e For the LORD has
Is	6: 3	The whole e is full of His
Is	11: 4	equity for the meek of the e;
Is	11: 9	For the e shall be full of
Is	11:12	the four corners of the e.
Is	24: 4	The e mourns and fades
Is	26:19	And the e shall cast out
Is	34: 1	you people! Let the e hear,
Is	40:22	above the circle of the e,
Is	40:28	Creator of the ends of the e,
Is	42: 4	established justice in the e;
Is	45:18	Who formed the e and made
Is	45:22	All you ends of the e For
Is	52:10	And all the ends of the e
Is	54: 5	the God of the whole e.
Is	55: 9	are higher than the e,
Is	55:10	there, But water the e,
Is	60: 2	darkness shall cover the e,
Is	65:17	new heavens and a new e;
Is	66: 1	And e is My footstool.
Is	66:22	new heavens and the new e
Jer	4:23	I beheld the e,
Jer	15:10	contention to the whole e
Jer	22:29	O e, earth, earth, Hear
Jer	31:22	created a new thing in the e—
Jer	51: 7	That made all the e drunk.
Ezek	1:15	a wheel was on the e beside
Ezek	1:19	were lifted up from the e,
Ezek	8: 3	lifted me up between e and
Ezek	31:18	Eden to the depths of the e,
Ezek	32:24	to the lower parts of the e,
Dan	2:10	There is not a man on e who
Dan	2:35	and filled the whole e.
Dan	2:39	shall rule over all the e.
Dan	4:22	dominion to the end of the e.
Dan	6:27	wonders In heaven and on e,
Dan	7: 4	it was lifted up from the e
Dan	7:17	which arise out of the e.
Dan	7:23	be A fourth kingdom on e,
Dan	7:23	shall devour the whole e,
Dan	12: 2	sleep in the dust of the e
Hos	2:21	And they shall answer the e.
Joel	3:16	The heavens and e will
Amos	3: 2	of all the families of the e;
Mic	1: 2	you peoples! Listen, O e,
Mic	1: 3	on the high places of the e.
Mic	4:13	to the Lord of the whole e.
Mic	7: 2	man has perished from the e,
Mic	7:17	holes like snakes of the e,
Nah	1: 5	And the e heaves at His
Hab	2:14	For the e will be filled
Hab	2:20	Let all the e keep silence

Hab	3: 6	He stood and measured the e;
Hab	3: 9	Selah You divided the e
Zeph	2:11	all the gods of the e;
Hag	2: 6	I will shake heaven and e,
Hag	2:21	'I will shake heaven and e.
Zech	1:10	to and fro throughout the e.
Zech	1:11	all the e is resting
Zech	4:14	the Lord of the whole e.
Zech	9:10	River to the ends of the e.
Zech	14: 9	shall be King over all the e.
Mal	4: 6	I come and strike the e
Matt	5: 5	they shall inherit the e.
Matt	5:13	"You are the salt of the e;
Matt	5:18	till heaven and e pass away,
Matt	5:35	"nor by the e,
Matt	6:10	Your will be done On e as
Matt	6:19	yourselves treasures on e,
Matt	9: 6	Son of Man has power on e
Matt	10:34	I came to bring peace on e.
Matt	11:25	Father, Lord of heaven and e,
Matt	12:40	nights in the heart of the e.
Matt	13: 5	they did not have much e;
Matt	16:19	and whatever you bind on e
Matt	18:18	whatever you bind on e will
Matt	18:19	if two of you agree on e
Matt	23: 9	Do not call anyone on e your
Matt	23:35	blood shed on the e,
Matt	24:30	then all the tribes of the e
Matt	24:35	Heaven and e will pass away,
Matt	27:51	and the e quaked, and the
Matt	28:18	to Me in heaven and on e.
Mark	4:31	than all the seeds on e;
Mark	9: 3	such as no launderer on e
Luke	2:14	And on e peace, goodwill
Luke	10:21	Father, Lord of heaven and e,
Luke	11:31	came from the ends of the e
Luke	18: 8	really find faith on the e?
Luke	23:44	was darkness over all the e
Luke	24: 5	bowed their faces to the e,
John	3:31	he who is of the e is
John	12:32	if I am lifted up from the e,
John	17: 4	have glorified You on the e.
Acts	1: 8	and to the end of the e.
Acts	2:19	And signs in the e
Acts	7:49	And e is My footstool.
Acts	8:33	is taken from the e.
Acts	10:11	to him and let down to the e.
Acts	10:12	four-footed animals of the e,
Acts	11: 6	four-footed animals of the e,
Rom	9:17	declared in all the e.
Rom	10:18	gone out to all the e,
1Co	10:26	the e is the LORD's,
1Co	10:28	the e is the LORD's,
1Co	15:47	The first man was of the e,
Eph	6: 3	may live long on the e.
Phil	2:10	in heaven, and of those on e,
Col	3: 2	not on things on the e.
Col	3: 5	members which are on the e:
Heb	11:13	and pilgrims on the e.
Heb	11:38	in dens and caves of the e.
Heb	12:25	refused Him who spoke on e,
Heb	12:26	whose voice then shook the e;
Heb	12:26	I shake not only the e,
2Pe	3: 5	and the e standing out of
2Pe	3:13	for new heavens and a new e
1Jn	5: 8	three that bear witness on e:
Rev	1: 5	over the kings of the e.
Rev	1: 7	And all the tribes of the e
Rev	3:10	those who dwell on the e.
Rev	5:10	And we shall reign on the e.
Rev	5:13	on the earth and under the e
Rev	6:13	of heaven fell to the e,
Rev	7: 1	at the four corners of the e,
Rev	7: 1	the four winds of the e,
Rev	7: 3	saying, "Do not harm the e,

Rev	12: 9	world; he was cast to the e,
Rev	12:16	But the e helped the woman,
Rev	12:16	and the e opened its mouth
Rev	13:11	beast coming up out of the e,
Rev	14: 3	who were redeemed from the e.
Rev	16: 1	of the wrath of God on the e.
Rev	17: 5	ABOMINATIONS OF THE E.
Rev	21: 1	saw a new heaven and a new e,
Rev	21: 1	heaven and the first e had

EARTHEN (see EARTH, EARTHENWARE)

Lev	6:28	But the e vessel in which it
Num	5:17	take holy water in an e
Jer	19: 1	Go and get a potter's e
Jer	32:14	and put them in an e vessel,
Hab	1:10	For they heap up e mounds
2Co	4: 7	we have this treasure in e

EARTHENWARE† (see EARTHEN)

Prov	26:23	a wicked heart Are like e

EARTHLY† (see EARTH)

John	3:12	If I have told you e things
John	3:31	he who is of the earth is e
2Co	5: 1	For we know that if our e
Phil	3:19	who set their mind on e
Heb	9: 1	of divine service and the e
Jas	3:15	from above, but is e,

EARTHQUAKE (see EARTH, EARTHQUAKES)

1Ki	19:11	and after the wind an e,
1Ki	19:11	the LORD was not in the e;
Is	29: 6	of hosts With thunder and e
Ezek	38:19	there shall be a great e in
Amos	1: 1	two years before the the e.
Matt	27:54	saw the e and the things
Acts	16:26	Suddenly there was a great e,
Rev	8: 5	lightnings, and an e.
Rev	11:19	noises, thunderings, an e,

EARTHQUAKES (see EARTHQUAKE)

Matt	24: 7	and e in various places.

EASE

Job	3:26	I am not at e,
Ps	73:12	Who are always at e;
Amos	6: 1	Woe to you who are at e in
Luke	12:19	for many years; take your e;

EASIER (see EASY)

Ex	18:22	So it will be e for you, for
Matt	9: 5	"For which is e,
Matt	19:24	it is e for a camel to go
Luke	16:17	And it is e for heaven and

EASILY (see EASY)

Heb	12: 1	and the sin which so e

EAST (see EASTERN, EASTWARD)

Gen	3:24	He placed cherubim at the e
Gen	4:16	in the land of Nod on the e
Gen	13:11	Jordan, and Lot journeyed e.
Gen	28:14	abroad to the west and the e,
Gen	29: 1	land of the people of the E.
Ex	14:21	to go back by a strong e
Judg	7:12	all the people of the E,
1Ch	26:14	The lot for the E Gate fell
Job	15: 2	And fill himself with the e
Ps	103:12	As far as the e is from the
Is	41: 2	raised up one from the e?
Is	46:11	a bird of prey from the e,
Jer	49:28	devastate the men of the E!
Ezek	8:16	and their faces toward the e,
Ezek	8:16	the sun toward the e.
Ezek	10:19	stood at the door of the e
Ezek	40: 6	to the gateway which faced e;
Ezek	48: 1	for Dan from its e to its
Ezek	48:18	thousand cubits to the e
Dan	11:44	But news from the e and the

Hos	12: 1	And pursues the e wind; He
Jon	4: 5	of the city and sat on the e
Jon	4: 8	God prepared a vehement e
Zech	14: 4	faces Jerusalem on the e.
Matt	2: 1	wise men from the E came to
Matt	2: 2	have seen His star in the E
Matt	8:11	that many will come from e
Matt	24:27	lightning comes from the e
Rev	21:13	three gates on the e,

EASTERN (see EAST)

Num	32:19	has fallen to us on this e

EASTWARD (see EAST)

Gen	2: 8	God planted a garden e in
Gen	13:14	are—northward, southward, e,
Ezek	11: 1	LORD's house, which faces e;

EASY (see EASIER, EASILY)

Matt	11:30	For My yoke is e and My
1Co	14: 9	utter by the tongue words e

EAT (see ATE, EATEN, EATER, EATING, EATS)

Gen	2:16	the garden you may freely e;
Gen	2:17	and evil you shall not e,
Gen	3: 5	knows that in the day you e
Gen	3:14	And you shall e dust All
Gen	3:17	In toil you shall e of it
Gen	9: 4	But you shall not e flesh
Gen	27: 4	bring it to me that I may e,
Gen	27:10	that he may e it, and that
Gen	32:32	children of Israel do not e
Gen	40:19	and the birds will e your
Gen	45:18	and you will e the fat of
Ex	10: 5	and they shall e the residue
Ex	12: 7	of the houses where they e
Ex	12: 8	Then they shall e the flesh
Ex	12: 8	bitter herbs they shall e
Ex	12:11	So you shall e it in haste.
Ex	12:15	Seven days you shall e
Ex	12:43	No foreigner shall e it.
Ex	16:15	the LORD has given you to e.
Ex	18:12	the elders of Israel to e
Ex	23:15	Bread (you shall e
Ex	32: 6	and the people sat down to e
Lev	3:17	you shall e neither fat nor
Lev	6:16	Aaron and his sons shall e;
Lev	7:19	all who are clean may e of
Lev	10:13	You shall e it in a holy
Lev	10:14	heave offering you shall e
Lev	11: 4	these you shall not e among
Lev	11:39	any animal which you may e
Lev	17:14	You shall not e the blood of
Lev	19:25	in the fifth year you may e
Lev	22: 4	shall not e the holy
Lev	22: 6	and shall not e the holy
Lev	22: 7	and afterward he may e the
Lev	22: 8	by beasts he shall not e,
Lev	22:13	she may e her father's food;
Lev	22:16	of trespass when they e
Lev	25:19	and you will e your fill,
Lev	26:38	of your enemies shall e you
Num	6: 3	nor e fresh grapes or
Num	6: 4	of his separation he shall e
Num	11:13	'Give us meat, that we may e.
Deut	2: 6	with money, that you may e;
Deut	4:28	neither see nor hear nor e
Deut	8: 9	a land in which you will e
Deut	12:15	you may slaughter and e meat
Deut	12:16	Only you shall not e the
Deut	12:23	you may not e the life with
Deut	14: 7	hooves, you shall not e,
Deut	14: 9	you may e all that have fins
Deut	14:10	and scales you shall not e;
Deut	14:11	"All clean birds you may e.
Deut	16: 3	seven days you shall e
Deut	18: 8	have equal portions to e,

Deut 20:14 and you shall e the enemies'
Deut 23:24 you may e your fill of
Deut 28:39 for the worms shall e them.
Deut 28:51 And they shall e the increase
Deut 28:55 his children whom he will e,
Deut 28:57 for she will e them secretly
Josh 24:13 you e of the vineyards and
Judg 13: 4 and not to e anything
Judg 14:14 eater came something to e,
Ruth 2:14 and e of the bread, and dip
1Sa 1: 7 she wept and did not e.
2Sa 9: 7 and you shall e bread at my
2Sa 9:10 your master's son shall e
2Sa 13: 5 that I may see it and e it
2Sa 13: 9 him, but he refused to e.
2Sa 19:35 your servant taste what I e
1Ki 2: 7 them be among those who e
1Ki 13:22 E no bread and drink no
1Ki 14:11 The dogs shall e whoever
1Ki 16: 4 The dogs shall e whoever
1Ki 18:19 who e at Jezebel's table."
1Ki 18:42 So Ahab went up to e and
1Ki 21: 5 spirit so sullen that you e
1Ki 21:23 The dogs shall e Jezebel by
2Ki 6:28 and we will e my son
2Ki 18:27 who will e and drink their
Ezra 9:12 you may be strong and e the
Neh 8:10 e the fat, drink the sweet,
Job 20:21 is left for him to e;
Job 31: 8 let me sow, and another e;
Ps 14: 4 Who e up my people as they
Ps 22:26 The poor shall e and be
Ps 78:24 down manna on them to e,
Ps 127: 2 To e the bread of sorrows;
Prov 23: 1 When you sit down to e with
Prov 23: 6 Do not e the bread of a
Prov 25:16 E only as much as you need,
Prov 25:21 hungry, give him bread to e;
Eccl 2:24 a man than that he should e
Eccl 8:15 under the sun than to e,
Eccl 9: 7 e your bread with joy, And
Song 4:16 come to his garden And e
Is 1:19 You shall e the good of the
Is 7:15 "Curds and honey He shall e,
Is 11: 7 And the lion shall e straw
Is 22:13 Let us e and drink, for
Is 50: 9 The moth will e them up.
Is 55: 1 no money, Come, buy and e.
Is 65: 4 Who e swine's flesh, And
Is 65:25 The lion shall e straw like
Lam 2:20 Should the women e their
Ezek 3: 1 e this scroll, and go, speak
Ezek 12:18 e your bread with quaking,
Ezek 24:22 not cover your lips nor e
Dan 1:12 give us vegetables to e and
Dan 4:25 and they shall make you e
Dan 4:32 They shall make you e grass
Hos 2:12 beasts of the field shall e
Hos 4: 8 They e up the sin of My
Amos 7:12 There e bread, And there
Mic 6:14 You shall e, but not be
Hag 1: 6 and bring in little; You e,
Matt 6:25 what you will e or what you
Matt 6:31 saying, 'What shall we e?
Matt 9:11 Why does your Teacher e with
Matt 12: 1 heads of grain and to e.
Matt 12: 4 was not lawful for him to e,
Matt 15:20 but to e with unwashed hands
Matt 15:27 yet even the little dogs e
Matt 26:17 us to prepare for You to e
Matt 26:26 and said, "Take, e.
Mark 7: 2 saw some of His disciples e
Mark 7: 3 and all the Jews do not e
Mark 7:28 dogs under the table e from
Mark 11:14 Let no one e fruit from you

Luke 5:30 Why do You e and drink with
Luke 5:33 but Yours e and drink?"
Luke 6: 4 for any but the priests to e?
Luke 7:36 the Pharisees asked Him to e
Luke 12:19 years; take your ease; e,
Luke 14: 1 of the Pharisees to e bread
Luke 15:23 and let us e and be merry;
Luke 22:16 I will no longer e of it
Luke 22:30 that you may e and drink at
John 4:31 Him, saying, "Rabbi, e.
John 4:32 I have food to e of which you
John 6: 5 buy bread, that these may e?
John 6:31 bread from heaven to e.
John 6:52 Man give us His flesh to e?
John 21:12 Come and e breakfast." Yet
Acts 10:13 "Rise, Peter; kill and e.
Acts 23:12 that they would neither e
Rom 14: 2 For one believes he may e all
Rom 14: 3 let not him who does not e
Rom 14:21 It is good neither to e
Rom 14:23 because he does not e
1Co 5:11 not even to e with such a
1Co 8:10 is weak be emboldened to e
1Co 8:13 I will never again e meat,
1Co 9:13 minister the holy things e
1Co 10: 7 people sat down to e
1Co 10:27 e whatever is set before
1Co 10:31 whether you e or drink, or
1Co 11:20 it is not to e the Lord's
1Co 11:24 it and said, "Take, e;
1Co 11:26 For as often as you e this
1Co 11:28 and so let him e of the
1Co 11:33 when you come together to e,
1Co 11:34 let him e at home, lest you
Gal 2:12 he would e with the
2Th 3:10 not work, neither shall he e.
Heb 13:10 have no right to e.
Jas 5: 3 against you and will e your
Rev 2: 7 overcomes I will give to e
Rev 2:14 to e things sacrificed to
Rev 2:17 of the hidden manna to e
Rev 10: 9 Take and e it; and it will
Rev 17:16 e her flesh and burn her
Rev 19:18 that you may e the flesh of

EATEN (see EAT)
Gen 3:11 Have you e from the tree of
Gen 43: 2 when they had e up the grain
Ex 12:46 "In one house it shall be e;
Ex 13: 3 No leavened bread shall be e.
Ex 21:28 and its flesh shall not be e;
Lev 11:47 the animal that may be e
Deut 6:11 when you have e and are full—
Ruth 3: 7 And after Boaz had e and
Job 6: 6 Can flavorless food be e
Job 21:25 Never having e with
Ps 69: 9 zeal for Your house has e
Ps 102: 9 For I have e ashes like
Prov 9:17 And bread e in secret is
Is 44:19 I have roasted meat and e
Jer 10:25 For they have e up Jacob,
Jer 24: 2 figs which could not be e,
Jer 31:29 The fathers have e sour
Ezek 18: 2 The fathers have e sour
Hos 10:13 You have e the fruit of
Joel 1: 4 the swarming locust has e;
Joel 2:25 the swarming locust has e,
Matt 14:21 Now those who had e were
John 2:17 for Your house has e
John 6:13 left over by those who had e.
John 21:15 So when they had e
Acts 10:14 Lord! For I have never e
Acts 12:23 And he was e by worms and

EATER (see EAT)
Judg 14:14 Out of the e came something

Is   55:10 sower And bread to the e,

EATING (see EAT)
Job   1:13 sons and daughters were e
Is   66:17 E swine's flesh and the
Matt   11:18 For John came neither e nor
Matt   11:19 The Son of Man came e and
Matt   24:38 they were e and drinking,
Matt   26:21 Now as they were e,
Matt   26:26 And as they were e,
Mark   2:16 and Pharisees saw Him e
1Co   8: 4 Therefore concerning the e of
1Co   8:10 you who have knowledge e in
1Co   11:21 For in e, each one takes

EATS (see EAT)
Ex   12:15 For whoever e leavened bread
Lev   7:18 and the person who e of it
Lev   7:21 and who e the flesh of the
Lev   7:25 For whoever e the fat of the
Lev   7:27 Whoever e any blood, that
Lev   11:40 He who e of its carcass shall
Lev   14:47 and he who e in the house
Lev   17:15 And every person who e what
Lev   22:14 And if a man e the holy
1Sa   14:24 Cursed is the man who e any
Job   40:15 He e grass like an ox.
Prov   30:20 She e and wipes her mouth,
Eccl   5:12 Whether he e little or
Eccl   5:17 All his days he also e in
Is   44:16 With this half he e meat;
Mark   2:16 How is it that He e and
Mark   14:18 one of you who e with Me
Luke   15: 2 Man receives sinners and e
John   6:51 If anyone e of this bread,
John   6:54 Whoever e My flesh and drinks
John   6:58 He who e this bread will
Rom   14: 2 but he who is weak e only
Rom   14: 3 Let not him who e despise him
Rom   14: 6 He who e, eats to the Lord,
Rom   14:23 doubts is condemned if he e,
1Co   11:27 Therefore whoever e this
1Co   11:29 in an unworthy manner e and

EBAL
Deut   11:29 and the curse on Mount E.

EBED-MELECH
Jer   38: 7 Now E the Ethiopian, one of

EBENEZER
1Sa   4: 1 and encamped beside E;

EBER
Gen   10:21 of all the children of E,

EDEN
Gen   2: 8 a garden eastward in E,
Gen   2:10 Now a river went out of E to
Gen   2:15 put him in the garden of E
Gen   4:16 land of Nod on the east of E.
Is   51: 3 make her wilderness like E,
Ezek   28:13 You were in E,
Ezek   31: 9 So that all the trees of E
Joel   2: 3 is like the Garden of E

EDGE (see EDGES)
Gen   34:26 Shechem his son with the e
Ex   13:20 camped in Etham at the e of
Ex   17:13 and his people with the e
Ex   26: 4 the e of the curtain
Ex   28:26 on the e of it, which is on
Josh   3: 8 'When you have come to the e
Josh   13:27 as far as the e of the Sea
1Sa   15:27 Saul seized the e of his
Ps   133: 2 Running down on the e of
Eccl   10:10 one does not sharpen the e,
Jer   31:29 teeth are set on e.
Ezek   18: 2 teeth are set on e'?

Amos   3:12 of a bed and on the e of a
Luke   21:24 they will fall by the e
Heb   11:34 escaped the e of the sword,

EDGES (see EDGE)
Lev   19:27 shall you disfigure the e
Job   26:14 these are the mere e of

EDICT†
Ezra   6:11 that whoever alters this e,

EDIFICATION (see EDIFY)
Rom   15: 2 for his good, leading to e.
1Co   14: 3 he who prophesies speaks e
1Co   14: 5 the church may receive e.
1Co   14:12 let it be for the e of
1Co   14:26 Let all things be done for e.
1Ti   1: 4 rather than godly e which

EDIFIED (see EDIFY)
1Co   14:17 well, but the other is not e.

EDIFIES† (see EDIFY)
1Co   8: 1 puffs up, but love e.
1Co   14: 4 He who speaks in a tongue e
1Co   14: 4 but he who prophesies e the

EDIFY (see EDIFICATION, EDIFIED, EDIFIES, EDIFYING)
Rom   14:19 things by which one may e
1Co   10:23 for me, but not all things e.

EDIFYING (see EDIFY)
Eph   4:12 for the e of the body of

EDOM (see EDOMITE, ESAU, IDUMEA, OBED-EDOM)
Gen   25:30 his name was called E.
Gen   32: 3 of Seir, the country of E.
Gen   36: 1 genealogy of Esau, who is E.
Num   20:21 Thus E refused to give Israel
2Ch   25:20 they sought the gods of E.
Ps   60: 8 Over E I will cast My shoe;
Ps   83: 6 The tents of E and the
Ps   108: 9 Over E I will cast My shoe;
Ps   137: 7 against the sons of E The
Is   63: 1 is this who comes from E,
Lam   4:21 and be glad, O daughter of E
Ezek   25:12 Because of what E did against
Amos   1: 6 To deliver them up to E.
Amos   1:11 three transgressions of E,
Amos   2: 1 the bones of the king of E
Amos   9:12 may possess the remnant of E,
Obad   8 destroy the wise men from E,
Mal   1: 4 Even though E has said,

EDOMITE (see EDOM, EDOMITES)
Deut   23: 7 "You shall not abhor an E,

EDOMITES (see EDOMITE)
Gen   36:43 was the father of the E.
2Ch   21: 8 In his days the E revolted

EFFECT (see EFFECTIVE)
2Ch   34:22 they spoke to her to that e.
Is   32:17 And the e of righteousness,
Matt   15: 6 commandment of God of no e
Mark   7:13 the word of God of no e
Rom   3: 3 of God without e?
Rom   4:14 and the promise made of no e,
1Co   1:17 should be made of no e.
Gal   3:17 make the promise of no e.

EFFECTIVE (see EFFECT, EFFECTIVELY)
Prov   17:10 Rebuke is more e for a wise
1Co   16: 9 For a great and door has
2Co   1: 6 which is e for enduring the
Eph   3: 7 of God given to me by the e
Jas   5:16 The e, fervent prayer

EFFECTIVELY (see EFFECTIVE)
Gal   2: 8 (for He who worked e in Peter
1Th   2:13 which also e works in you

EGG† (see EGGS)
Job 6: 6 taste in the white of an e?
Luke 11:12 "Or if he asks for an e,

EGGS (see EGG)
Job 39:14 For she leaves her e on the
Is 10:14 And as one gathers that
Is 59: 5 They hatch vipers' e and

EGLON
Josh 10: 3 Lachish, and Debir king of E,
Judg 3:14 children of Israel served E
Judg 3:17 (Now E was a very fat man.)

EGYPT (see EGYPTIAN, GOSHEN, MIZRAIM)
Gen 12:10 and Abram went down to E to
Gen 12:14 was, when Abram came into E,
Gen 15:18 from the river of E to the
Gen 37:28 And they took Joseph to E.
Gen 41: 8 for all the magicians of E
Gen 41:33 set him over the land of E.
Gen 41:46 before Pharaoh king of E.
Gen 41:55 So when all the land of E was
Gen 41:56 severe in the land of E.
Gen 45: 9 has made me lord of all E;
Gen 47:15 failed in the land of E and
Gen 47:29 Please do not bury me in E,
Gen 47:30 you shall carry me out of E
Gen 50:26 he was put in a coffin in E.
Ex 1: 5 persons (for Joseph was in E
Ex 1: 8 arose a new king over E,
Ex 1:17 did not do as the king of E
Ex 2:23 of time that the king of E
Ex 3: 7 of My people who are in E,
Ex 3:10 children of Israel, out of E.
Ex 3:12 brought the people out of E,
Ex 3:20 out My hand and strike E
Ex 6:11 tell Pharaoh king of E to
Ex 7: 4 out of the land of E by
Ex 7: 5 I stretch out My hand on E
Ex 7:11 so the magicians of E
Ex 8: 7 up frogs on the land of E.
Ex 9: 6 and all the livestock of E
Ex 9: 9 dust in all the land of E,
Ex 9:18 such as has not been in E
Ex 9:22 be hail in all the land of E—
Ex 10:12 hand over the land of E for
Ex 10:13 his rod over the land of E,
Ex 10:14 on all the territory of E,
Ex 10:21 darkness over the land of E,
Ex 10:22 in all the land of E three
Ex 11: 1 plague on Pharaoh and on E.
Ex 12:12 firstborn in the land of E,
Ex 12:12 against all the gods of E I
Ex 12:13 when I strike the land of E.
Ex 12:30 there was a great cry in E,
Ex 13: 9 has brought you out of E.
Ex 13:17 see war, and return to E.
Ex 14: 7 and all the chariots of E.
Ex 20: 2 you out of the land of E,
Ex 22:21 strangers in the land of E.
Ex 32:11 out of the land of E with
Num 11: 5 which we ate freely in E,
Num 11:18 it was well with us in E.
Num 13:22 seven years before Zoan in E.
Num 14: 2 had died in the land of E!
Num 14: 3 better for us to return to E?
Num 14:22 the signs which I did in E
Num 20:15 and we dwelt in E a long
Num 34: 5 from Azmon to the Brook of E,
Deut 1:30 to all He did for you in E
Deut 4:20 the iron furnace, out of E,
Deut 4:37 and He brought you out of E
Deut 4:45 after they came out of E,
Deut 5:15 a slave in the land of E,
Deut 6:21 were slaves of Pharaoh in E,

Deut 6:21 LORD brought us out of E
Deut 9:12 whom you brought out of E
Deut 10:22 fathers went down to E
Deut 16: 1 God brought you out of E by
Deut 16: 3 came out of the land of E
Deut 17:16 the people to return to E
Deut 28:27 you with the boils of E,
Deut 28:60 on you all the diseases of E,
Deut 28:68 will take you back to E in
Josh 5: 5 way as they came out of E,
Josh 5: 9 away the reproach of E from
Josh 24: 5 and Aaron, and I plagued E,
Josh 24:14 side of the River and in E.
Judg 19:30 came up from the land of E
1Sa 2:27 father when they were in E
1Sa 30:13 "I am a young man from E,
2Sa 7:23 redeemed for Yourself from E,
1Ki 3: 1 with Pharaoh king of E,
1Ki 4:30 East and all the wisdom of E.
1Ki 10:28 had horses imported from E
1Ki 11:40 Jeroboam arose and fled to E,
1Ki 11:40 Egypt, to Shishak king of E,
2Ki 17: 4 messengers to So, king of E,
2Ki 18:21 staff of this broken reed, E,
2Ki 18:24 and put your trust in E for
2Ki 23:29 days Pharaoh Necho king of E
2Ch 1:17 and imported from E a
2Ch 26: 8 as far as the entrance of E,
Ps 68:31 Envoys will come out of E;
Ps 78:43 He worked His signs in E,
Ps 80: 8 have brought a vine out of E;
Ps 105:38 E was glad when they
Ps 106:21 had done great things in E,
Ps 114: 1 When Israel went out of E,
Ps 135: 8 destroyed the firstborn of E,
Ps 136:10 To Him who struck E in their
Is 7:18 part of the rivers of E,
Is 11:15 the tongue of the Sea of E;
Is 19: 1 The burden against E.
Is 19: 1 The idols of E will totter
Is 19:18 five cities in the land of E
Is 19:23 will be a highway from E to
Is 19:24 will be one of three with E
Is 19:25 Blessed is E My people, and
Is 20: 4 uncovered, to the shame of E.
Is 27:12 the River to the Brook of E;
Is 30: 2 to trust in the shadow of E!
Is 43: 3 I gave E for your ransom,
Jer 43:12 the houses of the gods of E,
Jer 46:11 O virgin, the daughter of E;
Jer 46:14 "Declare in E,
Ezek 17:15 sending his ambassadors to E,
Ezek 20: 7 with the idols of E.
Ezek 23: 3 committed harlotry in E,
Ezek 30: 4 The sword shall come upon E,
Ezek 30: 8 I have set a fire in E and
Ezek 30:19 will execute judgments on E,
Ezek 32:12 shall plunder the pomp of E,
Ezek 32:16 shall lament for her, for E,
Hos 7:11 sense—They call to E,
Hos 11: 1 And out of E I called My
Hos 11:11 trembling like a bird from E,
Hos 12: 1 And oil is carried to E.
Amos 4:10 plague after the manner of E;
Amos 8: 8 subside Like the River of E.
Amos 9: 5 subside like the River of E.
Nah 3: 9 Ethiopia and E were her
Zech 10:11 And the scepter of E shall
Matt 2:13 and His mother, flee to E,
Matt 2:15 Out of E I called My
Matt 2:19 in a dream to Joseph in E,
Acts 7: 9 envious, sold Joseph into E.
Acts 7:10 he made him governor over E
Acts 7:15 "So Jacob went down to E;
Heb 11:26 than the treasures in E;

Heb 11:27 By faith he forsook E,
Jude 5 people out of the land of E,
Rev 11: 8 is called Sodom and E,

EGYPTIAN (see EGYPT, EGYPTIANS)
Gen 16: 1 And she had an E maidservant
Gen 21: 9 saw the son of Hagar the E,
Gen 39: 1 captain of the guard, an E,
Ex 1:19 women are not like the E
Ex 2:11 And he saw an E beating a
Ex 2:12 he killed the E and hid him
Deut 23: 7 You shall not abhor an E,
1Sa 30:11 Then they found an E in the
2Sa 23:21 The E had a spear in his
Prov 7:16 Colored coverings of E
Is 19:23 come into Egypt and the E
Acts 7:24 and struck down the E.

EGYPTIANS (see EGYPTIAN)
Gen 12:14 that the E saw the woman,
Gen 41:55 Pharaoh said to all the E,
Gen 41:56 and sold to the E.
Gen 43:32 because the E could not eat
Gen 43:32 is an abomination to the E.
Gen 46:34 is an abomination to the E.
Gen 47:15 all the E came to Joseph and
Gen 50: 3 and the E mourned for him
Ex 1: 3 So the E made the children of
Ex 3: 8 out of the hand of the E,
Ex 3: 9 oppression with which the E
Ex 3:21 favor in the sight of the E;
Ex 3:22 So you shall plunder the E.
Ex 7: 5 And the E shall know that I
Ex 7:18 and the E will loathe to
Ex 9:11 magicians and on all the E.
Ex 10: 6 and the houses of all the E—
Ex 11: 3 favor in the sight of the E.
Ex 11: 7 a difference between the E
Ex 12:23 pass through to strike the E;
Ex 12:35 they had asked from the E
Ex 14: 9 So the E pursued them, all
Ex 14:17 harden the hearts of the E,
Ex 14:20 between the camp of the E
Ex 14:24 troubled the army of the E.
Ex 14:27 So the LORD overthrew the E
Ex 14:30 and Israel saw the E dead on
Ex 18: 9 out of the hand of the E.
Num 14:13 Then the E will hear it, for
Num 20:15 and the E afflicted us and
Is 19: 2 will set Egyptians against E;
Is 20: 4 of Assyria lead away the E
Is 31: 3 Now the E are men, and not
Acts 7:22 in all the wisdom of the E,
Heb 11:29 by dry land, whereas the E,

EHUD
Judg 3:16 Now E made himself a dagger
Judg 3:21 Then E reached with his left

EIGHT (see EIGHTH)
Gen 5: 4 the days of Adam were e
Gen 17:12 He who is e days old among
Gen 21: 4 his son Isaac when he was e
1Sa 17:12 and who had e sons. And the
2Ki 22: 1 Josiah was e years old when
Eccl 11: 2 to seven, and also to e,
Ezek 40:31 and going up to it were e
Mic 5: 5 him Seven shepherds and e
Luke 2:21 And when e days were
1Pe 3:20 e souls, were saved through
2Pe 2: 5 one of e people, a

EIGHTEEN (see EIGHTEENTH)
Luke 13:11 had a spirit of infirmity e

EIGHTEENTH (see EIGHTEEN)
2Ki 22: 3 in the e year of King
Jer 52:29 in the e year of

EIGHTH (see EIGHT)
Lev 23:39 and on the e day a
Lev 25:22 And you shall sow in the e
Num 6:10 Then on the e day he shall
1Ki 6:38 which is the e month, the
Luke 1:59 on the e day, that they came
Acts 7: 8 and circumcised him on the e
Phil 3: 5 circumcised the e day, of the

EIGHTY
Ex 7: 7 And Moses was e years old
Judg 3:30 And the land had rest for e
Ps 90:10 of strength they are e
Luke 16: 7 'Take your bill, and write e.

EIGHTY-FIVE
Josh 14:10 I am this day, e years old.

EIGHTY-FOUR
Luke 2:37 was a widow of about e

EIGHTY-SIX
Gen 16:16 Abram was e years old when

EIGHTY-THREE
Ex 7: 7 years old and Aaron e years

EKRON
Josh 13: 3 as far as the border of E
1Sa 5:10 sent the ark of God to E.
1Sa 17:52 even as far as Gath and E.
2Ki 1: 2 of Baal-Zebub, the god of E,
Jer 25:20 (namely, Ashkelon, Gaza, E,

EL BETHEL† (see BETHEL)
Gen 35: 7 there and called the place E,

EL ELOHE ISRAEL†
Gen 33:20 an altar there and called it E

ELAM (see ELAMITES, PERSIA)
Gen 10:22 The sons of Shem were E,
Gen 14: 1 Chedorlaomer king of E,
Is 11:11 From E and Shinar, From
Dan 8: 2 is in the province of E;

ELAMITES (see ELAM, PERSIAN)
Acts 2: 9 "Parthians and Medes and E,

ELATH
1Ki 9:26 which is near E on the
2Ki 14:22 He built E and restored it to
2Ki 16: 6 Then the Edomites went to E,
2Ch 8:17 went to Ezion Geber and E

ELDAD
Num 11:27 E and Medad are prophesying

ELDER (see ELDERLY, ELDERS, ELDEST)
Gen 10:21 the brother of Japheth the e.
Gen 27:15 the choice clothes of her e
Gen 29:16 the name of the e was Leah,
Is 3: 2 And the diviner and the e;
Ezek 16:46 Your e sister is Samaria,
Ezek 23: 4 Oholah the e and Oholibah
1Ti 5:19 an accusation against an e
1Pe 5: 1 I who am a fellow e and a
2Jn 1 The E, To the elect lady
3Jn 1 The E, To the beloved

ELDERLY (see ELDER)
Deut 28:50 does not respect the e nor

ELDERS (see ELDER)
Gen 50: 7 the e of his house, and all
Ex 3:16 Go and gather the e of Israel
Ex 24: 1 and seventy of the e of
Lev 4:15 And the e of the congregation
Num 11:25 same upon the seventy e;
Deut 21: 2 then your e and your judges
Josh 24:31 and all the days of the e
Judg 11: 5 that the e of Gilead went to
Ruth 4: 2 he took ten men of the e of

Ruth 4:11 were at the gate, and the e,
1Sa 30:26 some of the spoil to the e
Ezra 5: 5 of their God was upon the e
Ezra 10: 8 of the leaders and e,
Job 12:20 the discernment of the e.
Ps 105:22 And teach his e wisdom.
Ps 107:32 Him in the company of the e.
Prov 31:23 When he sits among the e of
Is 3:14 into judgment With the e
Lam 1:19 My priests and my e
Lam 2:10 The e of the daughter of
Lam 5:12 And e were not respected.
Ezek 7:26 And counsel from the e.
Ezek 8: 1 I sat in my house with the e
Ezek 8:11 them seventy men of the e
Matt 15: 2 the tradition of the e?
Matt 16:21 many things from the e and
Matt 26:47 the chief priests and e of
Matt 26:59 Now the chief priests, the e,
Matt 27: 1 all the chief priests and e
Matt 27:20 But the chief priests and e
Matt 27:41 with the scribes and e,
Mark 11:27 and the e came to Him.
Luke 7: 3 he sent e of the Jews to
Acts 4: 5 day, that their rulers, e,
Acts 14:23 appointed e in every church,
Acts 15: 2 to the apostles and e,
Acts 15: 6 Now the apostles and e came
Acts 20:17 and called for the e of the
Acts 22: 5 and all the council of the e,
Acts 23:14 to the chief priests and e,
1Ti 5:17 Let the e who rule well be
Tit 1: 5 and appoint e in every city
Heb 11: 2 For by it the e obtained a
Jas 5:14 Let him call for the e of
1Pe 5: 1 The e who are among you I
1Pe 5: 5 submit yourselves to your e.
Rev 4: 4 thrones I saw twenty-four e

ELDEST† (see ELDER, OLD)
2Ki 3:27 Then he took his e son who

ELEAZAR
Ex 6:23 she bore him Nadab, Abihu, E,
Ex 6:25 E, Aaron's son, took for
Lev 10: 6 and to E and Ithamar, his
Lev 10:16 And he was angry with E and
Num 3: 4 So E and Ithamar ministered
Num 25: 7 when Phinehas the son of E,
Deut 10: 6 and E his son ministered as
Josh 14: 1 which E the priest, Joshua
Josh 24:33 And E the son of Aaron died.
1Ch 24: 3 with Zadok of the sons of E,

ELECT (see ELECTION, ELECT'S)
Is 42: 1 My E One in whom My soul
Is 45: 4 sake, And Israel My e,
Matt 24:24 if possible, even the e.
Matt 24:31 will gather together His e
Rom 8:33 a charge against God's e?
Rom 11: 7 but the e have obtained it,
Col 3:12 as the e of God, holy and
1Ti 5:21 Lord Jesus Christ and the e
2Ti 2:10 things for the sake of the e,
Tit 1: 1 to the faith of God's e and
1Pe 1: 2 e according to the
1Pe 2: 6 A chief cornerstone, e,
2Jn 1 To the e lady and her
2Jn 13 The children of your e sister

ELECT'S (see ELECT)
Matt 24:22 but for the e sake those

ELECTION† (see ELECT)
Rom 9:11 of God according to e might
Rom 11: 5 a remnant according to the e
Rom 11:28 but concerning the e they

1Th 1: 4 your e by God.
2Pe 1:10 to make your call and e

ELEMENTARY†
Heb 6: 1 the discussion of the e

ELEMENTS†
Gal 4: 3 were in bondage under the e
Gal 4: 9 to the weak and beggarly e,
2Pe 3:10 and the e will melt with
2Pe 3:12 and the e will melt with

ELEVATION
Ps 48: 2 Beautiful in e,

ELEVEN (see ELEVENTH)
Gen 32:22 and his e sons, and crossed
Gen 37: 9 and the e stars bowed down
Ex 26: 7 You shall make e curtains.
Deut 1: 2 It is e days' journey from
2Ki 23:36 and he reigned e years in
2Ki 24:18 and he reigned e years in
Matt 28:16 Then the e disciples went
Mark 16:14 Later He appeared to the e
Luke 24: 9 all these things to the e
Luke 24:33 and found the e and those
Acts 1:26 he was numbered with the e
Acts 2:14 standing up with the e,

ELEVENTH (see ELEVEN)
2Ki 25: 2 was besieged until the e
Jer 1: 3 until the end of the e year
Matt 20: 6 And about the e hour he went

ELI (see ELOI)
1Sa 1: 3 Also the two sons of E,
1Sa 1: 9 Now E the priest was sitting
1Sa 2:12 Now the sons of E were
1Sa 2:22 Now E was very old; and he
1Sa 3: 6 Samuel arose and went to E,
1Sa 4:15 E was ninety-eight years old,
1Sa 4:18 that E fell off the seat
1Ki 2:27 concerning the house of E
Matt 27:46 "E, Eli, lama sabachthani?"

ELIAKIM (see JEHOIAKIM)
2Ki 18:18 E the son of Hilkiah, who
2Ki 23:34 Then Pharaoh Necho made E the
2Ch 36: 4 made Jehoahaz's brother E

ELIEZER
Gen 15: 2 the heir of my house is E
1Ch 23:15 of Moses were Gershon and E.

ELIHU
Job 32: 4 E had waited to speak to
Job 32: 6 So E, the son of Barachel
Job 34: 1 E further answered and said:

ELIJAH
1Ki 17: 1 And E the Tishbite, of the
1Ki 17:15 according to the word of E;
1Ki 17:23 And E took the child and
1Ki 17:23 And E said, "See, your son
1Ki 18:16 him; and Ahab went to meet E.
1Ki 18:25 Now E said to the prophets
1Ki 18:31 And E took twelve stones,
1Ki 18:46 of the LORD came upon E;
1Ki 19:20 the oxen and ran after E,
2Ki 1:13 fell on his knees before E,
2Ki 1:15 angel of the LORD said to E,
2Ki 2: 1 that E went with Elisha from
2Ki 2: 2 Then E said to Elisha, "Stay
2Ki 2: 8 Now E took his mantle, rolled
2Ki 2:11 and E went up by a whirlwind
2Ki 2:13 also took up the mantle of E
2Ki 2:14 Then he took the mantle of E
2Ki 2:14 is the LORD God of E?
2Ki 2:15 The spirit of E rests on
2Ki 9:36 He spoke by His servant E

Mal   4: 5 I will send you E the
Matt 11:14 he is E who is to come.
Matt 16:14 John the Baptist, some E,
Matt 17: 3 Moses and E appeared to
Matt 17: 4 one for Moses, and one for E.
Matt 17:10 do the scribes say that E
Matt 17:12 But I say to you that E has
Matt 27:47 This Man is calling for E!"
Mark 6:15 Others said, "It is E.
Luke   1:17 in the spirit and power of E,
Luke   4:25 in Israel in the days of E,
Luke   9:54 just as E did?"
John   1:21 him, "What then? Are you E?
John   1:25 are not the Christ, nor E,
Rom   11: 2 what the Scripture says of E,
Jas   5:17 E was a man with a nature

ELIM
Ex   15:27 Then they came to E,
Num 33: 9 from Marah and came to E.

ELIMELECH
Ruth   1: 3 Then E, Naomi's husband,
Ruth   2: 3 who was of the family of E.
Ruth   4: 3 belonged to our brother E.

ELIPHAZ
Gen   36:11 And the sons of E were Teman,
Job   4: 1 Then E the Temanite answered
Job   42: 7 that the LORD said to E the

ELISHA
1Ki   19:16 And E the son of Shaphat of
2Ki   2: 2 Then Elijah said to E,
2Ki   2:15 spirit of Elijah rests on E.
2Ki   5: 8 when E the man of God heard
2Ki   6:17 of fire all around E.
2Ki   8: 7 Then E went to Damascus, and
2Ki   13:14 E had become sick with the
2Ki   13:20 Then E died, and they buried
2Ki   13:21 and touched the bones of E,
Luke   4:27 in Israel in the time of E

ELIZABETH
Luke   1: 5 Aaron, and her name was E.
Luke   1: 7 because E was barren, and
Luke   1:13 and your wife E will bear
Luke   1:24 after those days his wife E
Luke   1:40 of Zacharias and greeted E.
Luke   1:41 and E was filled with the

ELKANAH
1Sa   2:20 And Eli would bless E and his

ELKOSHITE†
Nah   1: 1 of the vision of Nahum the E.

ELOI (see ELI)
Mark 15:34 "E, Eloi, lama sabachthani?"

ELON
Judg 12:11 E the Zebulunite judged

ELOQUENT†
Ex   4:10 "O my Lord, I am not e,
Acts 18:24 an e man and mighty in the

ELUL†
Neh   6:15 the twenty-fifth day of E,

ELYMAS†
Acts 13: 8 But E the sorcerer (for so

EMBALM† (see EMBALMED)
Gen 50: 2 the physicians to e his

EMBALMED (see EMBALM)
Gen 50: 2 So the physicians e Israel.

EMBARRASSED
Judg   3:25 they waited till they were e,

EMBER
2Sa   14: 7 they would extinguish my e

EMBOLDENED†
1Co   8:10 of him who is weak be e to

EMBRACE (see EMBRACED, EMBRACES, EMBRACING)
Gen   16: 5 I gave my maid into your e;
Eccl   3: 5 gather stones; A time to e,

EMBRACED (see EMBRACE)
Gen   29:13 and e him and kissed him,
1Ki   9: 9 and have e other gods, and
Acts 20: 1 e them, and departed to go
Heb   11:13 e them and confessed that

EMBRACES† (see EMBRACE)
Song   2: 6 And his right hand e me.
Song   8: 3 And his right hand e me.

EMBRACING† (see EMBRACE)
Eccl   3: 5 a time to refrain from e;
Acts 20:10 and e him said, "Do not

EMBROIDERED (see EMBROIDERY)
Ezek 27: 7 Fine e linen from Egypt was

EMBROIDERY (see EMBROIDERED)
Judg   5:30 Two pieces of dyed e for

EMERALD
Ex   28:17 a sardius, a topaz, and an e.
Rev   4: 3 in appearance like an e.
Rev   21:19 chalcedony, the fourth e,

EMINENT†
2Co   11: 5 all inferior to the most e
2Co   12:11 was I behind the most e

EMISSION (see EMITS)
Lev   15:16 If any man has an e of

EMITS† (see EMISSION, EMITTED)
Lev   15:32 and for him who e semen

EMITTED† (see EMITS)
Gen   38: 9 that he e on the ground,

EMMAUS†
Luke 24:13 day to a village called E,

EMPIRE†
Esth   1:20 throughout all his e (for

EMPTIED (see EMPTY)
Gen   24:20 Then she quickly e her
Gen   42:35 Then it happened as they e
Is   24: 3 land shall be entirely e

EMPTINESS (see EMPTY)
2Pe   2:18 great swelling words of e,

EMPTY (see EMPTIED, EMPTINESS, EMPTY-HANDED, EMPTY-HEADED)
Gen   37:24 a pit. And the pit was e;
Gen   41:27 and the seven e heads
Ex   23:15 shall appear before Me e);
Judg   7:16 with e pitchers, and torches
Ruth   1:21 Has brought me home again e.
Job   11: 3 Should your e talk make men
Job   21:34 can you comfort me with e
Job   22: 9 You have sent widows away e,
Job   26: 7 out the north over e space;
Is   24: 1 the LORD makes the earth e
Is   29: 8 and his soul is still e;
Matt 12:44 he comes, he finds it e,
Luke   1:53 the rich He has sent away e.
1Co   15:14 then our preaching is e and
1Co   15:14 and your faith is also e.
Eph   5: 6 no one deceive you with e
Col   2: 8 you through philosophy and e

EMPTY-HANDED (see EMPTY)
Ex   3:21 go, that you shall not go e.

Ex   34:20 shall appear before Me e.
Ruth   3:17 Do not go e to your
Mark 12: 3 him and sent him away e.

EMPTY-HEADED† *(see* EMPTY)
Job   11:12 For an e man will be wise,

EN DOR *(see* DOR)
1Sa   28: 7 a woman who is a medium a **E**

EN GEDI
1Sa   23:29 and dwelt in strongholds at **E**
2Ch   20: 2 Hazazon Tamar" (which is **E**)
Song   1:14 blooms in the vinyards of **E**

ENABLED†
1Ti   1:12 Jesus our Lord who has e me,

ENCAMP *(see* CAMP, ENCAMPED, ENCAMPMENT, ENCAMPS)
Judg   6: 4 Then they would e against
Ps   27: 3 Though an army may e against

ENCAMPED *(see* ENCAMP)
Josh 10:31 and they e against it and
Judg   6:33 and they crossed over and e
1Sa   4: 1 and the Philistines e in
1Sa   17: 2 and they e in the Valley of

ENCAMPMENT *(see* ENCAMP)
Gen   43:21 when we came to the e,

ENCAMPS† *(see* ENCAMP)
Ps   34: 7 The angel of the LORD e all
Ps   53: 5 the bones of him who e

ENCHANTER† *(see* ENCHANTMENTS)
Is   3: 3 artisan, And the expert e.

ENCHANTMENTS *(see* ENCHANTER)
Ex   7:11 in like manner with their e.
Ex   7:22 of Egypt did so with their e;

ENCIRCLED
Ps   22:12 bulls of Bashan have e Me.
Heb   11:30 fell down after they were e

ENCLOSE *(see* ENCLOSED)
Jer   22:15 you reign because you e

ENCLOSED *(see* ENCLOSE)
Ps   22:16 of the wicked has e Me.
Song   4:12 A garden e Is my sister,

ENCOMPASS†
Jer   31:22 A woman shall e a man."

ENCOUNTERED†
Acts 17:18 and Stoic philosophers e

ENCOURAGE *(see* ENCOURAGED, ENCOURAGEMENT)
Deut   3:28 and e him and strengthen
2Sa   11:25 So e him."
1Th   3: 2 to establish you and e you

ENCOURAGED *(see* ENCOURAGE)
Acts 16:40 they e them and departed.
Acts 20: 2 gone over that region and e
Acts 27:36 Then they were all e,
Rom   1:12 that I may be e together
1Co   14:31 may learn and all may be e.
Phil   2:19 that I also may be e when I
Col   2: 2 that their hearts may be e,

ENCOURAGEMENT *(see* ENCOURAGE)
2Ch   30:22 And Hezekiah gave e to all
Acts   4:36 is translated Son of E),
Acts 15:31 it, they rejoiced over its e.

END *(see* ENDED, ENDLESS, ENDS)
Gen   6:13 The e of all flesh has come
Gen   8: 6 at the e of forty days, that
Gen   41: 1 at the e of two full years,
Ex   23:16 of Ingathering at the e of
Ex   25:19 other cherub at the other e;

Ex   31:18 And when He had made an e of
Ex   34:22 Ingathering at the year's e.
Lev   17: 5 to the e that the children of
Num   34: 3 extend eastward to the e of
Deut   4:32 and ask from one e of
Deut   8:16 you, to do you good in the e—
Deut 13: 7 of the earth to the other e
Deut 15: 1 At the e of every seven
Deut 32:29 consider their latter e!
Josh   8:24 when Israel had made an e
Josh 18:19 at the south e of the
Judg 19: 9 the day is coming to an e;
Ruth   2: 3 to glean until the e of
Ruth   3: 7 he went to lie down at the e
Ruth   3:10 more kindness at the e than
1Sa   3:12 house, from beginning to e.
2Sa   2:23 stomach with the blunt e of
2Sa   2:26 be bitter in the latter e?
2Sa   20:18 and so they would e
2Ki   10:25 as soon as he had made an e
Job   6:11 hope? And what is my e,
Job   8: 7 Yet your latter e would
Job   16: 3 words of wind have an e?
Job   22: 5 And your iniquity without e?
Job   28: 3 Man puts an e to darkness,
Ps   7: 9 of the wicked come to an e,
Ps   19: 4 And their words to the e of
Ps   19: 6 its circuit to the other e;
Ps   39: 4 make me to know my e,
Ps   73:17 Then I understood their e.
Ps   102:27 Your years will have no e.
Ps   107:27 And are at their wits' e.
Ps   119:112 Forever, to the very e.
Prov   5: 4 But in the e she is bitter
Prov 14:12 But its e is the way of
Prov 14:13 And the e of mirth may be
Prov 16:25 But its e is the way of
Prov 25: 8 what will you do in the e,
Eccl   3:11 God does from beginning to e.
Eccl   4: 8 Yet there is no e to all
Eccl 12:12 many books there is no e,
Is   7: 3 at the e of the aqueduct
Is   9: 7 peace There will be no e,
Is   46:10 Declaring the e from the
Is   48:20 Utter it to the e of the
Jer   3: 5 Will He keep it to the e?
Jer   4:27 I will not make a full e.
Jer   5:31 what will you do in the e?
Jer   51:13 Your e has come, The
Ezek 22: 4 and have come to the e of
Dan   1:15 And at the e of ten days
Dan   6:26 shall endure to the e.
Dan   7:28 This is the e of the
Dan   8:17 refers to the time of the e.
Dan   8:19 at the appointed time the e
Dan   9:24 To make an e of sins, To
Dan   9:26 And till the e of the war
Dan   9:27 week He shall bring an e
Dan   11:35 until the time of the e;
Dan   11:40 At the time of the e the
Dan   12: 4 book until the time of the e;
Dan   12: 8 what shall be the e of
Dan   12: 9 till the time of the e.
Dan   12:13 go your way till the e;
Dan   12:13 to your inheritance at the e
Hos   1: 4 And bring an e to the
Matt 10:22 But he who endures to the e
Matt 13:39 the harvest is the e of the
Matt 24: 6 but the e is not yet.
Matt 24:14 and then the e will come.
Matt 24:31 from one e of heaven to the
Matt 28:20 even to the e of the age."
Mark   3:26 cannot stand, but has an e.
Luke   1:33 kingdom there will be no e.
Luke 21: 9 but the e will not come

John 13: 1 He loved them to the e.
Acts 1: 8 and to the e of the earth."
Acts 27:10 that this voyage will e
Rom 6:21 For the e of those things
Rom 10: 4 For Christ is the e of the
Rom 14: 9 For to this e Christ died and
1Co 1: 8 also confirm you to the e,
1Co 15:24 when He puts an e to all
Phil 3:19 whose e is destruction,
Col 1:29 To this e I also labor,
Heb 3: 6 of the hope firm to the e.
Heb 3:14 steadfast to the e,
Heb 6: 8 whose e is to be burned.
Heb 7: 3 beginning of days nor e of
Heb 9:26 once at the e of the ages,
1Pe 1: 9 receiving the e of your
1Pe 4: 7 But the e of all things is
1Pe 4:17 what will be the e of those
2Pe 2:20 the latter e is worse for
Rev 1: 8 the Beginning and the E,
Rev 21: 6 the Beginning and the E.
Rev 22:13 the Beginning and the E,

ENDEAVORED† (see ENDEAVORING)
1Th 2:17 e more eagerly to see your

ENDEAVORING† (see ENDEAVORED)
Eph 4: 3 e to keep the unity of the

ENDED (see END)
Gen 2: 2 And on the seventh day God e
Deut 34: 8 and mourning for Moses e.
Job 7: 4 I arise, And the night be e?
Job 31:40 The words of Job are e.
Ps 72:20 David the son of Jesse are e.
Is 40: 2 her, That her warfare is e,
Jer 8:20 is past, The summer is e,
Matt 7:28 Jesus had e these sayings,
Luke 4:13 Now when the devil had e
John 13: 2 And supper being e,

ENDLESS† (see END)
1Ti 1: 4 give heed to fables and e
Heb 7:16 to the power of an e life.

ENDS (see END)
Ex 28:23 the two rings on the two e
Ps 2: 8 And the e of the earth for
Ps 22:27 All the e of the world
Ps 48:10 is Your praise to the e of
Ps 67: 7 And all the e of the earth
Ps 72: 8 from the River to the e of
Is 40:28 The Creator of the e of the
Is 45:22 All you e of the earth!
Zech 9:10 from the River to the e of
Matt 12:42 for she came from the e of
Rom 10:18 their words to the e
1Co 10:11 upon whom the e of the ages

ENDUED†
Luke 24:49 of Jerusalem until you are e

ENDURANCE (see ENDURE)
Heb 12: 1 and let us run with e the

ENDURE (see ENDURANCE, ENDURED, ENDURES, ENDURING)
Ex 18:23 then you will be able to e,
Ps 9: 7 But the LORD shall e
Ps 30: 5 Weeping may e for a night,
Ps 72: 5 long as the sun and moon e,
Ps 72:17 His name shall e forever;
Ps 89:36 His seed shall e forever,
Ps 101: 5 heart, Him I will not e.
Ps 102:26 will perish, but You will e;
Ps 104:31 the glory of the LORD e
Prov 27:24 Nor does a crown e to all
Is 1:13 I cannot e iniquity and the
Dan 6:26 And His dominion shall e

Mal 3: 2 But who can e the day of His
Mark 4:17 and so e only for a time.
1Co 4:12 being persecuted, we e;
1Co 9:12 but e all things lest we
1Th 3: 1 when we could no longer e it,
2Th 1: 4 and tribulations that you e,
2Ti 2: 3 You therefore must e hardship
2Ti 2:10 Therefore I e all things for
2Ti 2:12 we e, We shall also reign
2Ti 4: 3 come when they will not e
2Ti 4: 5 e afflictions, do the work
Heb 12: 7 If you e chastening, God
Jas 5:11 we count them blessed who e.

ENDURED (see ENDURE)
2Ti 3:11 Lystra—what persecutions I e.
Heb 6:15 so, after he had patiently e,
Heb 10:32 you e a great struggle with
Heb 11:27 for he e as seeing Him who
Heb 12: 2 that was set before Him e
Heb 12: 3 For consider Him who e such

ENDURES (see ENDURE)
1Ch 16:34 is good! For His mercy e
Ps 52: 1 The goodness of God e
Ps 100: 5 And His truth e to all
Ps 106: 1 is good! For His mercy e
Ps 111: 3 And His righteousness e
Ps 111:10 His praise e forever.
Ps 117: 2 the truth of the LORD e
Ps 119:90 Your faithfulness e to all
Ps 119:160 Your righteous judgments e
Ps 135:13 e forever, Your fame, O
Ps 136: 1 is good! For His mercy e
Ps 145:13 And Your dominion e
Matt 10:22 But he who e to the end will
Matt 13:21 but e only for a while. For
John 6:27 but for the food which e to
1Co 3:14 which he has built on it e,
1Co 13: 7 all things, e all things.
Jas 1:12 Blessed is the man who e
1Pe 1:25 word of the LORD e
1Pe 2:19 conscience toward God one e

ENDURING (see ENDURE)
1Sa 25:28 make for my lord an e house,
Ps 19: 9 is forever; The judgments of
Prov 8:18 E riches and righteousness.
Heb 10:34 you have a better and an e

ENEMIES (see ENEMY)
Gen 14:20 Who has delivered your e
Gen 22:17 possess the gate of their e.
Lev 26: 8 your e shall fall by the
Lev 26:17 shall be defeated by your e.
Num 10: 9 will be saved from your e.
Num 10:35 O LORD! Let Your e be
Num 23:11 me? I took you to curse my e,
Deut 20: 1 out to battle against your e,
Deut 20: 4 fight for you against your e,
Deut 25:19 given you rest from your e
Deut 28:48 you shall serve your e,
Deut 30: 7 all these curses on your e
Josh 10:13 had revenge Upon their e.
Josh 21:44 LORD delivered all their e
Judg 5:31 Thus let all Your e perish, O
1Sa 2: 1 the LORD. I smile at my e,
1Sa 4: 3 us from the hand of our e.
2Sa 7:11 you to rest from all your e.
2Sa 19: 6 in that you love your e and
Neh 4:15 when our e heard that it was
Esth 8:13 avenge themselves on their e.
Esth 9:22 Jews had rest from their e,
Job 19:11 counts me as one of His e.
Ps 3: 7 You have struck all my e on
Ps 6: 7 old because of all my e.
Ps 17: 9 From my deadly e who

Ps 18: 3 shall I be saved from my e.
Ps 23: 5 me in the presence of my e;
Ps 25: 2 Let not my e triumph over
Ps 27: 2 My e and foes, They
Ps 31:11 am a reproach among all my e,
Ps 35:19 me who are wrongfully my e;
Ps 37:20 And the e of the LORD,
Ps 38:19 But my e are vigorous, and
Ps 41: 5 My e speak evil of me:
Ps 42:10 My e reproach me, While
Ps 54: 5 He will repay my e for their
Ps 54: 7 seen its desire upon my e.
Ps 56: 2 My e would hound me all
Ps 59:10 me see my desire on my e.
Ps 60:12 who shall tread down our e.
Ps 71:10 For my e speak against me;
Ps 72: 9 And His e will lick the
Ps 78:53 the sea overwhelmed their e.
Ps 78:66 And He beat back His e;
Ps 80: 6 And our e laugh among
Ps 89:10 You have scattered Your e
Ps 89:42 You have made all his e
Ps 92: 9 For behold, Your e,
Ps 92: 9 Your e shall perish; All
Ps 106:11 The waters covered their e;
Ps 110: 1 Till I make Your e Your
Ps 110: 2 in the midst of Your e!
Ps 139:20 Your e take Your name in
Ps 139:22 hatred; I count them my e.
Prov 16: 7 He makes even his e to be
Is 1:24 And take vengeance on My e.
Is 59:18 Recompense to His e;
Is 66: 6 Who fully repays His e!
Jer 15: 9 to the sword Before their e,
Jer 49:37 be dismayed before their e
Lam 1: 2 her; They have become her e.
Lam 3:52 My e without cause Hunted
Lam 3:62 The lips of my e And their
Dan 4:19 concern your e!
Amos 9: 4 captivity before their e,
Nah 1: 2 He reserves wrath for His e;
Zech 10: 5 Who tread down their e
Matt 5:44 I say to you, love your e,
Mark 12:36 Till I make Your e
Luke 1:71 should be saved from our e
Luke 6:27 to you who hear: Love your e,
Rom 5:10 For if when we were e we were
Rom 11:28 the gospel they are e for
1Co 15:25 reign till He has put all e
Heb 1:13 Till I make Your e
Rev 11: 5 mouth and devours their e.

ENEMY (see ENEMIES, ENEMY'S)
Ex 15: 6 has dashed the e in pieces.
Ex 23:22 then I will be an e to your
Lev 26:25 into the hand of the e.
Num 10: 9 in your land against the e
Deut 28:53 straits in which your e
Deut 32:27 feared the wrath of the e,
Deut 32:42 of the leaders of the e.
Deut 33:27 He will thrust out the e
Judg 16:23 our hands Samson our e!"
1Sa 18:29 So Saul became David's e
1Sa 24: 4 I will deliver your e into
2Sa 22:18 me from my strong e,
1Ki 8:33 are defeated before an e
1Ki 8:37 when their e besieges them
1Ki 21:20 "Have you found me, O my e?
2Ch 26:13 help the king against the e.
Esth 7: 6 The adversary and e is this
Esth 8: 1 the e of the Jews. And
Job 13:24 And regard me as Your e?
Job 33:10 me, He counts me as His e;
Ps 8: 2 That You may silence the e
Ps 13: 2 How long will my e be

Ps 18:17 me from my strong e,
Ps 41:11 Because my e does not
Ps 42: 9 of the oppression of the e?
Ps 43: 2 of the oppression of the e?
Ps 61: 3 A strong tower from the e.
Ps 64: 1 my life from fear of the e.
Ps 74:10 Will the e blaspheme Your
Ps 78:42 He redeemed them from the e,
Pe 89:22 The e shall not outwit him,
Prov 24:17 Do not rejoice when your e
Prov 25:21 If your e is hungry, give
Prov 27: 6 But the kisses of an e are
Lam 1: 5 into captivity before the e.
Lam 2: 5 The Lord was like an e.
Mic 7:10 Then she who is my e will
Matt 5:43 neighbor and hate your e.
Matt 13:25 his e came and sowed tares
Luke 10:19 over all the power of the e,
Acts 13:10 you e of all righteousness,
Rom 12:20 If your e is hungry,
1Co 15:26 The last e that will be
2Th 3:15 do not count him as an e,
Jas 4: 4 world makes himself an e of

ENEMY'S (see ENEMY)
Ex 23: 4 If you meet your e ox or his
Job 6:23 Deliver me from the e hand'?

ENGAGED†
2Ti 2: 4 No one e in warfare entangles

ENGRAVE (see ENGRAVED, ENGRAVER, ENGRAVING)
Ex 28: 9 take two onyx stones and e
Zech 3: 9 I will e its inscription,'

ENGRAVED (see ENGRAVE)
Ex 32:16 was the writing of God e
1Ki 7:36 and on its panels he e
Jer 17: 1 of a diamond it is e On
Zech 14:20 TO THE LORD" shall be e

ENGRAVER (see ENGRAVE)
Ex 28:11 With the work of an e in

ENGRAVING (see ENGRAVE)
Ex 32: 4 he fashioned it with an e

ENIGMA (see ENIGMAS)
Prov 1: 6 a proverb and an e,

ENIGMAS (see ENIGMA)
Dan 5:16 and explain e.

ENJOY (see ENJOYED, ENJOYMENT)
Lev 26:34 the land shall rest and e
Rom 15:24 if first I may your
2Ti 6:17 us richly all things to e.
Heb 11:25 the people of God than to e

ENJOYED (see ENJOY)
2Ch 36:21 until the land had e her

ENJOYMENT (see ENJOY)
Eccl 2:25 can eat, or who can have e,
Eccl 8:15 So I commended e,

ENLARGE (see ENLARGED, ENLARGES)
Gen 9:27 May God e Japheth, And may
Ex 34:24 the nations before you and e
Ps 119:32 For You shall e my heart.
Is 54: 2 E the place of your tent,

ENLARGED (see ENLARGE)
2Sa 22:37 You e my path under me; So
Is 5:14 Therefore Sheol has e itself
Jer 20:17 And her womb always e with

ENLARGES (see ENLARGE)
Deut 19: 8 if the LORD your God e

ENLIGHTEN (see ENLIGHTENED, ENLIGHTENING)
Ps 13: 3 E my eyes, Lest I sleep

ENLIGHTENED (*see* ENLIGHTEN)
Eph 1:18 your understanding being **e**;
Heb 6: 4 for those who were once **e**,

ENLIGHTENING† (*see* ENLIGHTEN)
Ps 19: 8 LORD is pure, **e** the eyes;

ENLISTED†
2Ti 2: 4 he may please him who **e** him

ENMITY
Gen 3:15 And I will put **e** Between
Num 35:22 him suddenly without **e**,
Luke 23:12 they had been at **e** with
Rom 8: 7 the carnal mind is **e**
Eph 2:15 abolished in His flesh the **e**,
Eph 2:16 putting to death the **e**.
Jas 4: 4 with the world is **e** with

ENOCH
Gen 5:24 And **E** walked with God; and he
1Ch 1: 3 **E**, Methuselah, Lamech,
Heb 11: 5 By faith **E** was taken away so
Jude 14 **E**, the seventh from Adam,

ENOSH
1Ch 1: 1 Adam, Seth, **E**,

ENRAGED
2Sa 17: 8 and they are **e** in their
Rev 12:17 And the dragon was **e** with the

ENRAPTURED†
Prov 5:19 And always be **e** with her
Prov 5:20 be **e** by an immoral woman,

ENRICHED
1Co 1: 5 that you were **e** in everything
2Co 9:11 while you are **e** in

ENSLAVE†
Jer 30: 8 Foreigners shall no more **e**
Hos 4:11 and new wine **e** the heart.

ENSNARED (*see* ENSNARES)
Deut 12:30 yourself that you are not **e**
Prov 12:13 The wicked is **e** by the

ENSNARES† (*see* ENSNARED)
Heb 12: 1 the sin which so easily **e**

ENTANGLE† (*see* ENTANGLED, ENTANGLES)
Matt 22:15 and plotted how they might **e**

ENTANGLED† (*see* ENTANGLE)
Gal 5: 1 and do not be **e** again with a
2Pe 2:20 they are again **e** in them and

ENTANGLES† (*see* ENTANGLE)
2Ti 2: 4 No one engaged in warfare **e**

ENTER (*see* ENTERED, ENTERING, ENTERS, ENTRY)
Ex 40:35 And Moses was not able to **e**
Num 4: 3 all who **e** the service to do
Num 20:24 for he shall not **e** the land
Deut 29:12 that you may **e** into covenant
Ps 37:15 Their sword shall **e** their
Ps 45:15 They shall **e** the King's
Ps 95:11 They shall not **e** My rest.'"
Ps 100: 4 **E** into His gates with
Ps 118:20 which the righteous shall **e**.
Ps 143: 2 Do not **e** into judgment with
Prov 4:14 Do not **e** the path of the
Is 13: 2 that they may **e** the gates of
Is 26: 2 which keeps the truth may **e**
Is 26:20 **e** your chambers, And shut
Is 57: 2 He shall **e** into peace; They
Jer 8:14 And let us **e** the fortified
Jer 42:15 wholly set your faces to **e**
Ezek 7:22 For robbers shall **e** it and
Ezek 37: 5 I will cause breath to **e**
Dan 11:40 and he shall **e** the
Dan 11:41 He shall also **e** the Glorious

Joel 2: 9 They **e** at the windows like
Jon 3: 4 And Jonah began to **e** the city
Matt 5:20 you will by no means **e** the
Matt 7:13 **E** by the narrow gate; for
Matt 7:21 shall **e** the kingdom of
Matt 10: 5 and do not **e** a city of the
Matt 12:45 and they **e** and dwell there;
Matt 18: 9 It is better for you to **e**
Matt 19:23 is hard for a rich man to **e**
Matt 19:24 than for a rich man to **e**
Matt 25:21 **E** into the joy of your
Matt 25:23 **E** into the joy of your
Matt 26:41 lest you **e** into temptation.
Mark 1:45 could no longer openly **e**
Mark 3:27 No one can **e** a strong man's
Mark 5:12 that we may **e** them."
Mark 9:43 It is better for you to **e**
Mark 10:15 child will by no means **e** it.
Mark 13:15 nor **e** to take anything out
Luke 7: 6 not worthy that You should **e**
Luke 11:52 You did not **e** in yourselves,
Luke 24:26 these things and to **e** into
John 3: 4 Can he **e** a second time into
John 3: 5 he cannot **e** the kingdom of
John 10: 1 he who does not **e** the
Heb 3:11 They shall not **e** My
Heb 3:19 we see that they could not **e**
Heb 4: 6 was first preached did not **e**
Heb 10:19 having boldness to **e** the
Rev 21:27 there shall by no means **e**
Rev 22:14 and may **e** through the gates

ENTERED (*see* ENTER)
Gen 7:13 sons with them, **e** the ark—
Gen 7:16 So those that **e**,
Gen 31:33 out of Leah's tent and **e**
Ex 33: 9 when Moses **e** the tabernacle,
Num 4:35 everyone who **e** the service
Josh 8:19 and they **e** the city and took
Josh 10:20 that those who escaped **e**
Judg 9:46 they **e** the stronghold of the
2Sa 22: 7 And my cry **e** His ears.
2Ch 15:12 Then they **e** into a covenant
Jer 34:10 who had **e** into the covenant,
Jer 37:16 When Jeremiah **e** the dungeon
Ezek 2: 2 Then the Spirit **e** me when He
Hab 3:16 Rottenness **e** my bones; And
Matt 8: 5 Now when Jesus had **e**
Matt 12: 4 how he **e** the house of God and
Matt 24:38 until the day that Noah **e**
Mark 1:21 on the Sabbath He **e** the
Mark 1:29 they **e** the house of Simon
Mark 5:13 spirits went out and **e** the
Mark 5:40 and **e** where the child was
Mark 6:56 Wherever He **e** into villages,
Luke 1:40 and **e** the house of Zacharias
Luke 4:38 from the synagogue and **e**
Luke 8:30 because many demons had **e**
Luke 9:34 they were fearful as they **e**
Luke 22: 3 Then Satan **e** Judas, surnamed
John 4:38 and you have **e** into their
John 6:22 and that Jesus had not **e** the
John 18:33 Then Pilate **e** the Praetorium
Acts 3: 2 to ask alms from those who **e**
Acts 11: 8 or unclean has at any time **e**
Acts 16:40 went out of the prison and **e**
Acts 18:19 but he himself **e** the
Acts 23:16 he went and **e** the barracks
Rom 5:12 as through one man sin **e**
Rom 5:20 Moreover the law **e** that the
1Co 2: 9 Nor have **e** into the
Heb 4:10 For he who has **e** His rest has
Heb 6:20 where the forerunner has **e**
Heb 9:12 but with His own blood He **e**
Heb 9:24 For Christ has not **e** the holy

ENTERING (see ENTER)
Deut 23:20 in the land which you are **e**
Mark 4:19 desires for other things **e**
Mark 16: 5 And **e** the tomb, they saw a
Acts 8: 3 **e** every house, and dragging
Heb 4: 1 a promise remains of **e** His

ENTERS (see ENTER)
Num 4:30 everyone who **e** the service
Job 22: 4 And **e** into judgment with
Prov 2:10 When wisdom **e** your heart,
Matt 15:17 understand that whatever **e**
Mark 7:18 perceive that whatever **e** a
John 10: 2 But he who **e** by the door is
John 10: 9 If anyone **e** by Me, he will
Heb 6:19 and which **e** the Presence
Heb 9:25 as the high priest **e** the

ENTERTAIN† (see ENTERTAINED)
Heb 13: 2 Do not forget to **e** strangers,

ENTERTAINED (see ENTERTAIN)
Heb 13: 2 some have unwittingly **e**

ENTHRONED†
Ps 22: 3 **E** in the praises of Israel.
Ps 29:10 The LORD sat **e** at the

ENTICE (see ENTICED, ENTICES, ENTICING)
Deut 13:10 because he sought to **e** you
Judg 14:15 **E** your husband, that he may
Judg 16: 5 **E** him, and find out where his
Prov 1:10 if sinners **e** you, Do not

ENTICED (see ENTICE)
Job 31: 9 If my heart has been **e** by a
Jas 1:14 by his own desires and **e**.

ENTICES (see ENTICE)
Ex 22:16 If a man **e** a virgin who is
Prov 16:29 A violent man **e** his

ENTICING (see ENTICE)
Prov 7:21 With her **e** speech she caused
2Pe 2: 4 from sin, **e** unstable souls.

ENTIRE (see ENTIRELY, ENTIRETY)
Neh 4: 6 and the **e** wall was joined

ENTIRELY (see ENTIRE)
Is 24: 3 The land shall be **e** emptied
1Ti 4:15 give yourself **e** to them,

ENTIRETY (see ENTIRE)
Ps 119:160 The **e** of Your word is

ENTRAILS
Ex 12: 9 head with its legs and its **e**.
Ex 29:13 the fat that covers the **e**,
Ex 29:17 wash its **e** and its legs, and
Judg 3:22 and his **e** came out.
Acts 1:18 in the middle and all his **e**

ENTRANCE
Ex 32:26 then Moses stood in the **e** of
Num 13:21 Rehob, near the **e** of Hamath.
Josh 8:29 cast it at the **e** of the gate
Judg 1:24 Please show us the **e** to the
1Sa 17:52 Philistines as far as the **e**
1Ki 19:13 went out and stood in the **e**
1Ki 22:10 a threshing floor at the **e**
2Ch 23:13 by his pillar at the **e**;
Ps 119:130 The **e** of Your words gives
Prov 8: 3 At the **e** of the doors:
Jer 1:15 set his throne At the **e** of
Jer 43: 9 which is at the **e** to
Ezek 8: 5 image of jealousy in the **e**.
Ezek 27: 3 who are situated at the **e**
2Pe 1:11 for so an **e** will be supplied

ENTREAT (see ENTREATED)
Ex 8: 8 **E** the LORD that He may take

Ruth 1:16 **E** me not to leave you, Or
1Ki 13: 6 Please **e** the favor of the
1Co 4:13 being defamed, we **e**.

ENTREATED (see ENTREAT)
Ex 8:30 went out from Pharaoh and **e**
Ezra 8:23 So we fasted and **e** our God
Ps 119:58 I **e** Your favor with my

ENTRUSTED†
1Co 9:17 I have been **e** with a
1Th 2: 4 been approved by God to be **e**
1Pe 5: 3 as being lords over those **e**

ENTRY (see ENTER)
Prov 8: 3 at the **e** of the city, At
1Th 1: 9 us what manner of **e** we had

ENVIED (see ENVY)
Gen 30: 1 Rachel **e** her sister, and
Gen 37:11 And his brothers **e** him, but
Ps 106:16 When they **e** Moses in the
Eccl 4: 4 skillful work a man is **e** by

ENVIOUS (see ENVY)
Ps 37: 1 Nor be **e** of the workers of
Ps 73: 3 For I was **e** of the
Prov 24: 1 Do not be **e** of evil men,
Prov 24:19 Nor be **e** of the wicked;
Acts 7: 9 the patriarchs, becoming **e**,

ENVOYS†
Ps 68:31 **E** will come out of Egypt

ENVY (see ENVIED, ENVIOUS, ENVYING)
Ps 68:16 Why do you fume with **e**,
Prov 3:31 Do not **e** the oppressor,
Prov 14:30 But **e** is rottenness to the
Prov 23:17 Do not let your heart **e**
Matt 27:18 handed Him over because of **e**.
Mark 15:10 handed Him over because of **e**.
Acts 13:45 they were filled with **e**;
Rom 1:29 maliciousness; full of **e**,
Rom 13:13 lust, not in strife and **e**.
1Co 13: 4 is kind; love does not **e**;
Gal 5:21 **e**, murders, drunkenness,
Phil 1:15 preach Christ even from **e**
Tit 3: 3 living in malice and **e**,
Jas 3:14 But if you have bitter **e** and
1Pe 2: 1 all deceit, hypocrisy, **e**,

ENVYING† (see ENVY)
Gal 5:26 **e** one another.

EPAPHRAS
Col 4:12 **E**, who is one of you,
Phm 1:23 **E**, my fellow prisoner in

EPAPHRODITUS†
Phil 2:25 necessary to send to you **E**,
Phil 4:18 having received from **E** the

EPHAH (see EPHAHS)
Ex 16:36 omer is one-tenth of an **e**.
Lev 19:36 honest weights, an honest **e**,
Ezek 45:10 honest scales, an honest **e**,
Amos 8: 5 Making the **e** small and the

EPHAHS (see EPHAH)
Ruth 3:15 he measured six **e** of

EPHESIANS (see EPHESUS)
Acts 19:28 Great is Diana of the **E**!"
Acts 19:34 Great is Diana of the **E**!"

EPHESUS (see EPHESIANS)
Acts 18:19 And he came to **E**,
Acts 18:21 And he sailed from **E**.
Acts 19:17 and Greeks dwelling in **E**;
Acts 19:35 crowd, he said: "Men of **E**,
1Co 15:32 have fought with beasts at **E**,
1Co 16: 8 But I will tarry in **E** until

Eph 1: 1 To the saints who are in E,
1Ti 1: 3 remain in E that you may
2Ti 1:18 he ministered to me at E.
Rev 1:11 which are in Asia: to E,
Rev 2: 1 the angel of the church of E

EPHOD
Ex 25: 7 stones to be set in the e
Ex 28: 4 make: a breastplate, an e,
Lev 8: 7 and with it tied the e on
Judg 8:27 Gideon made it into an e
1Sa 2:18 a child, wearing a linen e.
2Sa 6:14 David was wearing a linen e.
Hos 3: 4 without e or teraphim.

EPHPHATHA†
Mark 7:34 sighed, and said to him, "E,

EPHRAIM (see EPHRAIMITE, EPHRAIM'S)
Gen 41:52 of the second he called E:
Gen 46:20 were born Manasseh and E,
Num 1:32 of Joseph, the children of E,
Deut 34: 2 Naphtali and the land of E
Josh 17:15 since the mountains of E are
Judg 8: 2 of the grapes of E
2Sa 18: 6 battle was in the woods of E.
2Ki 14:13 from the Gate of E to the
2Ch 31: 1 all Judah, Benjamin, E,
Ps 60: 7 E also is the helmet for
Ps 108: 8 E also is the helmet for
Is 7: 5 'Because Syria, E,
Is 7: 8 Within sixty-five years E
Is 7: 9 The head of E is Samaria,
Is 28: 1 pride, to the drunkards of E,
Jer 31: 9 And E is My firstborn.
Jer 31:20 Is E My dear son? Is he
Ezek 37:16 'For Joseph, the stick of E,
Hos 4:17 E is joined to idols, Let
Hos 7: 8 E is a cake unturned.
Hos 7:11 E also is like a silly dove,
Hos 11: 8 "How can I give you up, E?
Hos 11: 9 I will not again destroy E.
Hos 12: 1 E feeds on the wind, And

EPHRAIM'S (see EPHRAIM)
Gen 48:18 hand and laid it on E head,

EPHRAIMITE (see EPHRAIM)
Judg 12: 5 say to him, "Are you an E?

EPHRATH (see EPHRATHAH, EPHRATHITE)
Gen 35:19 was buried on the way to E

EPHRATHAH (see EPHRATH)
Ruth 4:11 and may you prosper in E and
Ps 132: 6 Behold, we heard of it in E;
Mic 5: 2 "But you, Bethlehem E,

EPHRATHITE† (see EPHRATH, EPHRATHITES)
1Sa 17:12 was the son of that E of

EPHRATHITES† (see EPHRATHITE)
Ruth 1: 2 E of Bethlehem, Judah. And

EPHRON
Gen 23:10 and E the Hittite answered
Gen 23:14 And E answered Abraham,

EPICUREAN†
Acts 17:18 Then certain E and Stoic

EPILEPTIC† (see EPILEPTICS)
Matt 17:15 for he is an e and suffers

EPILEPTICS† (see EPILEPTIC)
Matt 4:24 who were demon-possessed, e,

EPISTLE (see EPISTLES)
Rom 16:22 Tertius, who wrote this e,
1Co 5: 9 I wrote to you in my e not
2Co 3: 2 You are our e written in our
2Co 3: 3 clearly you are an e of

Col 4:16 Now when this e is read
Col 4:16 that you likewise read the e
1Th 5:27 you by the Lord that this e
2Th 2:15 whether by word or our e.
2Pe 3: 1 write to you this second e

EPISTLES† (see EPISTLE)
2Co 3: 1 e of commendation to you or
2Pe 3:16 as also in all his e,

EQUAL (see EQUITY, UNEQUALLY)
Deut 18: 8 They shall have e portions to
Job 28:17 gold nor crystal can e it,
Ps 55:13 it was you, a man my e,
Is 40:25 Or to whom shall I be e?
Is 46: 5 and make Me e And compare
Luke 20:36 for they are e to the angels
John 5:18 making Himself e with God.
Phil 2: 6 consider it robbery to be e
Rev 21:16 breadth, and height are e.

EQUIPMENT (see EQUIPPED)
1Sa 8:12 his weapons of war and e
1Sa 10:22 he is, hidden among the e.
Dan 11:13 with a great army and much e.

EQUIPPED† (see EQUIPMENT, EQUIPPING)
1Ch 12:23 the divisions that were e
2Ti 3:17 thoroughly e for every good

EQUIPPING† (see EQUIPPED)
Eph 4:12 for the e of the saints for

EQUITY (see EQUAL)
Ps 98: 9 And the peoples with e.
Ps 99: 4 You have established e;
Prov 1: 3 Justice, judgment, and e;
Is 11: 4 And decide with e for the
Mal 2: 6 with Me in peace and e,

ER
Gen 38: 7 But E, Judah's firstborn,
Num 26:19 The sons of Judah were E

ERASTUS†
Acts 19:22 to him, Timothy and E,
Rom 16:23 whole church, greets you. E,
2Ti 4:20 E stayed in Corinth, but

ERECH
Gen 10:10 of his kingdom was Babel, E,

ERECTED
2Sa 6:17 tabernacle that David had e
Heb 8: 2 tabernacle which the Lord e,

ERR (see ERRED, ERROR)
Is 9:16 this people cause them to e,
Is 28: 7 They e in vision, they

ERRAND†
Gen 24:33 until I have told about my e.

ERRED (see ERR)
1Sa 26:21 I have played the fool and e
Job 19: 4 And if indeed I have e,
Is 28: 7 But they also have e
Is 28: 7 and the prophet have e
Is 29:24 These also who e in spirit

ERROR (see ERR, ERRORS)
2Sa 6: 7 struck him there for his e;
Job 4:18 He charges His angels with e,
Is 32: 6 To utter e against the
Dan 6: 4 nor was there any e or fault
Rom 1:27 the penalty of their e
Jas 5:20 turns a sinner from the e
2Pe 3:17 being led away with the e of
1Jn 4: 6 of truth and the spirit of e.
Jude 11 have run greedily in the e

ERRORS (see ERROR)
Ps 19:12 Who can understand his e?

ESARHADDON
2Ki   19:37 Then E his son reigned in
Ezra   4: 2 to Him since the days of E

ESAU (see EDOM, ESAU'S)
Gen   25:25 so they called his name E.
Gen   25:27 And E was a skillful hunter,
Gen   25:28 And Isaac loved E because he
Gen   25:34 And Jacob gave E bread and
Gen   25:34 Thus E despised his
Gen   27:11 E my brother is a hairy
Gen   27:15 clothes of her elder son E,
Gen   27:22 hands are the hands of E.
Gen   27:24 "Are you really my son E?
Gen   27:38 O my father!" And E lifted
Gen   27:41 and E said in his heart,
Gen   28: 6 E saw that Isaac had blessed
Gen   36: 1 this is the genealogy of E,
Gen   36: 8 Mount Seir. E is Edom.
Josh 24: 4 To E I gave the mountains of
Obad   8 from the mountains of E?
Obad   18 remain of the house of E,
Mal   1: 2 Was not E Jacob's
Mal   1: 3 But E I have hated, And
Rom   9:13 but E I have hated."
Heb   12:16 or profane person like E,

ESAU'S (see ESAU)
Gen   25:26 and his hand took hold of E
Gen   27:23 hairy like his brother E

ESCAPE (see ESCAPED, ESCAPES)
Gen   19:17 'E for your life! Do not look
Gen   32: 8 company which is left will e.
2Ki   19:31 And those who e from Mount
Esth   4:13 your heart that you will e
Job   32:15 Words e them.
Ps   55: 8 I would hasten my e From
Ps   56: 7 Shall they e by iniquity?
Prov 19: 5 who speaks lies will not e.
Eccl   7:18 For he who fears God will e
Matt 23:33 of vipers! How can you e
Luke 21:36 may be counted worthy to e
Acts 27:42 them should swim away and e.
Rom   2: 3 that you will e the judgment
1Co   10:13 will also make the way of e,
1Th   5: 3 woman. And they shall not e.
2Ti   2:26 to their senses and e the
Heb   2: 3 how shall we e if we neglect
Heb   12:25 more shall we not e if

ESCAPED (see ESCAPE)
Gen   14:13 Then one who had e came and
Judg   3:26 the stone images and e to
1Sa   18:11 to the wall!" But David e
Neh   1: 2 the Jews who had e,
Job   1:15 and I alone have e to tell
Job   19:20 And I have e by the skin of
Ps   124: 7 Our soul has e as a bird
Ps   124: 7 is broken, and we have e.
Is   4: 2 those of Israel who have e.
Is   37:31 And the remnant who have e
Ezek 24:27 be opened to him who has e;
Ezek 33:22 the man came who had e.
John 10:39 but He e out of their hand.
Acts 28: 4 though he has e the sea, yet
2Co   11:33 and e from his hands.
Heb   11:34 e the edge of the sword, out
2Pe   1: 4 having e the corruption
2Pe   2:20 after they have e the

ESCAPES (see ESCAPE)
Ezek 24:26 on that day one who e will
Acts 26:26 that none of these things e

ESCORT
2Sa   19:15 to e the king across the

ESH-BAAL† (see ISHBOSHETH)
1Ch   8:33 Malchishua, Abinadab, and E.
1Ch   9:39 Malchishua, Abinadab, and E.

ESHCOL
Gen   14:13 brother of E and brother of
Num   13:24 was called the Valley of E,

ESHTAOL
Judg 13:25 Dan between Zorah and E.

ESPECIALLY
Josh   2: 1 e Jericho." So they went,
Ps   31:11 But e among my neighbors,
Acts 25:26 and e before you, King
1Co   14: 1 but e that you may prophesy.
Gal   6:10 e to those who are of the
1Ti   4:10 e of those who believe.
1Ti   5:17 e those who labor in the
2Ti   4:13 e the parchments.
Tit   1:10 e those of the circumcision,
Phm   1:16 e to me but how much more to
2Pe   2:10 and e those who walk

ESTABLISH (see ESTABLISHED, ESTABLISHES)
Gen   6:18 But I will e My covenant with
Gen   9: 9 I e My covenant with you and
Gen   17: 7 And I will e My covenant
Deut 28: 9 The LORD will e you as a
1Sa   1:23 only the LORD e His
2Sa   7:12 and I will e his kingdom.
2Sa   7:13 and I will e the throne of
2Sa   7:25 e it forever and do as You
Ps   48: 8 God will e it forever.
Ps   87: 5 Most High Himself shall e
Ps   89: 4 Your seed I will e forever,
Ps   90:17 e the work of our hands.
Is   9: 7 To order it and e it with
Is   26:12 You will e peace for us,
Jer   33: 2 LORD who formed it to e it
Ezek 34:23 I will e one shepherd over
Dan   6: 8 e the decree and sign the
Amos   5:15 E justice in the gate. It
Rom   3:31 the contrary, we e the law.
Rom   10: 3 and seeking to e their own
Rom   16:25 to Him who is able to e you
1Th   3: 2 to e you and encourage you
1Th   3:13 so that He may e your hearts
2Th   2:17 comfort your hearts and e you
2Th   3: 3 who will e you and guard
Heb   10: 9 the first that He may e the
1Pe   5:10 suffered a while, perfect, e,

ESTABLISHED (see CONFIRMED, ESTABLISH)
Gen   9:17 the covenant which I have e
Gen   41:32 because the thing is e by
Ex   6: 4 I have also e My covenant
Ex   15:17 which Your hands have e.
Deut 19:15 the matter shall be e.
Deut 32: 6 Has He not made you and e
1Sa   3:20 that Samuel had been e as
1Sa   13:13 now the LORD would have e
2Sa   7:16 Your throne shall be e
2Sa   7:26 of Your servant David be e
1Ki   2:12 and his kingdom was firmly e.
1Ki   2:24 and who has e a house for
1Ch   16:30 The world also is firmly e,
1Ch   17:14 and his throne shall be e
1Ch   17:24 of Your servant David be e
2Ch   12: 1 when Rehoboam had e the
2Ch   23:18 as it was e by David.
Ps   24: 2 And e it upon the waters.
Ps   40: 2 And e my steps.
Ps   78: 5 For He e a testimony in
Ps   81: 5 This He e in Joseph as a
Ps   93: 2 Your throne is e from of
Ps   96:10 The world also is firmly e,

Ps	103:19	The LORD has e His throne
Ps	119:90	You e the earth, and it
Prov	8:23	I have been e from
Prov	8:28	When He e the clouds above,
Prov	12: 3	A man is not e by
Prov	20:18	Plans are e by counsel; By
Prov	25: 5	And his throne will be e in
Prov	30: 4	Who has e all the ends of
Is	2: 2	LORD's house Shall be e
Is	7: 9	Surely you shall not be e.
Is	42: 4	Till He has e justice in
Is	45:18	Who has e it, Who did not
Jer	10:12	He has e the world by His
Jer	30:20	congregation shall be e
Jer	51:15	He has e the world by His
Hos	6: 3	His going forth is e as the
Mic	4: 1	LORD's house Shall be e
Matt	18:16	every word may be e.
2Co	13: 1	every word shall be e.
Col	2: 7	and built up in Him and e
Heb	8: 6	which was e on better
Heb	13: 9	good that the heart be e by
2Pe	1:12	though you know and are e in

ESTABLISHES (*see* ESTABLISH)

Prov	21:29	he e his way.
Prov	29: 4	The king e the land by
Dan	6:15	or statute which the king e
Hab	2:12	Who e a city by iniquity!

ESTATE

Acts	28: 7	that region there was an e

ESTEEM (*see* ESTEEMED, ESTEEMING, ESTEEMS)

Prov	3: 4	so find favor and high e
Prov	18:11	a high wall in his own e.
Is	53: 3	and we did not e Him.
Phil	2: 3	of mind let each e others
Phil	2:29	and hold such men in e;

ESTEEMED (*see* ESTEEM)

1Sa	2:30	Me shall be lightly e.
1Sa	18:30	his name became highly e.
Is	9: 1	when at first He lightly e
Is	29:16	Shall the potter be e as
Is	53: 4	Yet we e Him stricken,
Luke	16:15	For what is highly e among
Acts	5:13	but the people e them

ESTEEMING† (*see* ESTEEM)

Heb	11:26	e the reproach of Christ

ESTEEMS† (*see* ESTEEM)

Rom	14: 5	One person e one day above
Rom	14: 5	another e every day alike.

ESTHER (*see* ESTHER'S, HADASSAH)

Esth	2: 7	up Hadassah, that is, E,
Esth	5: 3	"What do you wish, Queen E?
Esth	7: 6	And E said, "The adversary

ESTHER'S† (*see* ESTHER)

Esth	2:11	to learn of E welfare and
Esth	4: 4	So E maids and eunuchs came
Esth	4:12	So they told Mordecai E

ESTRANGED

Job	19:13	are completely e from me.
Ps	58: 3	The wicked are e from the
Gal	5: 4	You have become e from

ETERNAL (*see* ETERNALLY, ETERNITY)

Deut	33:27	The e God is your refuge,
Eccl	12: 5	For man goes to his e home,
Matt	19:16	I do that I may have e life?
Matt	25:46	but the righteous into e
Mark	3:29	but is subject to e
Mark	10:30	in the age to come, e life.
Luke	10:25	what shall I do to inherit e
Luke	18:18	what shall I do to inherit e

Luke	18:30	and in the age to come e life."
John	3:15	not perish but have e life.
John	4:36	and gathers fruit for e
John	6:54	and drinks My blood has e
John	6:68	You have the words of e
John	10:28	And I give them e life, and
John	17: 2	that He should give e life
John	17: 3	that this is e life, that they
Acts	13:48	as had been appointed to e
Rom	1:20	even His e power and
Rom	6:23	but the gift of God is e
2Co	4:17	a far more exceeding and e
2Co	4:18	which are not seen are e.
2Co	5: 1	e in the heavens.
Eph	3:11	according to the e purpose
1Ti	1:17	Now to the King e,
1Ti	6:12	lay hold on e life, to which
2Ti	2:10	is in Christ Jesus with e
Tit	1: 2	in hope of e life which God,
Heb	5: 9	He became the author of e
Heb	6: 2	and of e judgment.
Heb	9:12	having obtained e
Heb	9:14	who through the e Spirit
Heb	9:15	receive the promise of the e
1Pe	5:10	who called us to His e glory
1Jn	1: 2	and declare to you that e
1Jn	5:13	you may know that you have e
1Jn	5:20	This is the true God and e
Jude	7	the vengeance of e fire.
Jude	21	our Lord Jesus Christ unto e

ETERNALLY (*see* ETERNAL)

Rom	9: 5	the e blessed God. Amen.

ETERNITY† (*see* ETERNAL)

Eccl	3:11	Also He has put e in their
Is	57:15	Lofty One Who inhabits e,
Acts	15:18	Known to God from e are all

ETHAN

1Ki	4:31	than E the Ezrahite, and
1Ch	15:19	singers, Heman, Asaph, and E,

ETHANIM†

1Ki	8: 2	the feast in the month of E,

ETHBAAL†

1Ki	16:31	Jezebel the daughter of E,

ETHIOPIA (*see* CUSH, ETHIOPIAN)

2Ki	19: 9	Tirhakah king of E,
Esth	1: 1	provinces, from India to E),
Job	28:19	The topaz of E cannot equal
Ps	68:31	E will quickly stretch out
Is	18: 1	is beyond the rivers of E,
Acts	8:27	went. And behold, a man of E,

ETHIOPIAN (*see* ETHIOPIA, ETHIOPIANS)

Num	12: 1	for he had married an E
Jer	13:23	Can the E change his skin or
Jer	38: 7	Now Ebed-Melech the E,

ETHIOPIANS (*see* ETHIOPIAN)

2Ch	21:16	who were near the E.
Is	20: 4	as prisoners and the E as
Jer	46: 9	The E and the Libyans who
Acts	8:27	Candace the queen of the E,

EUNICE†

2Ti	1: 5	Lois and your mother E,

EUNUCH (*see* EUNUCHS)

Lev	21:20	or eczema or scab, or is a e.
Acts	8:27	a e of great authority under
Acts	8:34	So the e answered Philip and

EUNUCHS (*see* EUNUCH)

Jer	38: 7	the Ethiopian, one of the e,
Dan	1: 7	To them the chief of the e
Dan	1:10	And the chief of the e said

Matt 19:12 For there are e who were born

EUPHRATES
Gen 2:14 The fourth river is the E.
Gen 15:18 the great river, the River E—
2Ki 24: 7 of Egypt to the River E.
2Ch 35:20 against Carchemish by the E;
Rev 9:14 bound at the great river E.

EUTYCHUS†
Acts 20: 9 a certain young man named E,

EVANGELIST† (see EVANGELISTS)
Acts 21: 8 the house of Philip the e,
2Ti 4: 5 do the work of an e,

EVANGELISTS† (see EVANGELIST)
Eph 4:11 some prophets, some e,

EVE†
Gen 3:20 called his wife's name E,
Gen 4: 1 Now Adam knew E his wife, and
2Co 11: 3 as the serpent deceived E by
1Ti 2:13 was formed first, then E.

EVENING (see EVENINGS)
Gen 1: 5 So the e and the morning
Gen 19: 1 came to Sodom in the e,
Gen 24:11 city by a well of water at e
Ex 12:18 day of the month at e.
Ex 16:13 was that quails came up at e
Ex 18:13 Moses from morning until e.
Num 28: 4 you shall offer in the e,
Josh 8:29 he hanged on a tree until e.
1Sa 17:16 forty days, morning and e.
1Ki 18:29 of the offering of the e
Ps 55:17 E and morning and at noon I
Ps 90: 6 In the e it is cut down and
Ps 104:23 to his labor until the e.
Prov 7: 9 In the twilight, in the e,
Eccl 11: 6 And in the e do not
Ezek 24:18 and at e my wife died; and
Dan 9:21 me about the time of the e
Hab 1: 8 And more fierce than e
Matt 14:23 when e came, He was alone
Mark 1:32 At e, when the sun had set,
Mark 13:35 the house is coming—in the e,
John 20:19 Then, the same day at e,
Acts 28:23 from morning till e.

EVENINGS† (see EVENING)
Dan 8:26 And the vision of the e and

EVENT
Eccl 2:14 perceived That the same e

EVENTS
1Ki 12:15 for the turn of e was from

EVER (see ALWAYS)
Ex 15:18 shall reign forever and e.
Ex 22:26 If you e take your neighbor's
Josh 14:10 e since the LORD spoke this
Judg 16:17 No razor has e come upon my
Job 4: 7 where were the upright e
Ps 10:16 LORD is King forever and e;
Ps 25:15 My eyes are e toward the
Ps 37:26 He is e merciful, and
Ps 45: 6 O God, is forever and e;
Ps 90: 2 Or e You had formed the
Ps 145: 1 Your name forever and e.
Ps 145: 2 Your name forever and e.
Prov 4:18 That shines e brighter unto
Prov 8:23 before there was e an earth.
Jer 7: 7 your fathers forever and e.
Jer 25: 5 your fathers forever and e.
Ezek 37:22 nor shall they e be divided
Dan 7:18 forever, even forever and e.
Dan 12: 3 the stars forever and e.
Hos 12: 9 E since the land of Egypt;

Hos 13: 4 I am the LORD your God E
Matt 21:19 Let no fruit grow on you e
Matt 24:21 nor e shall be.
Luke 23:53 where no one had e lain
John 4:39 He told me all that I e
John 7:46 No man e spoke like this
John 10: 8 All who e came before Me are
Gal 1: 5 whom be glory forever and e.
Eph 5:29 For no one e hated his own
Heb 1: 5 of the angels did He e say:
Heb 1: 8 God, is forever and e;
Rev 4: 9 who lives forever and e,
Rev 5:13 forever and e!"
Rev 11:15 He shall reign forever and e!
Rev 14:11 ascends forever and e;
Rev 19: 3 rises up forever and e!"
Rev 22: 5 shall reign forever and e.

EVERLASTING (see ETERNAL)
Gen 9:16 look on it to remember the e
Gen 17: 7 for an e covenant, to be God
Gen 17: 8 as an e possession; and I
Gen 21:33 of the LORD, the E God.
Gen 49:26 to the utmost bound of the e
Ex 12:14 keep it as a feast by an e
Lev 16:34 This shall be an e statute
Num 25:13 after him a covenant of an e
Deut 33:27 And underneath are the e
Ps 24: 7 you e doors! And the King
Ps 90: 2 Even from e to everlasting,
Ps 90: 2 Even from everlasting to e,
Ps 93: 2 of old; You are from e.
Ps 100: 5 is good; His mercy is e,
Ps 103:17 of the LORD is from e to
Ps 103:17 is from everlasting to e
Ps 139:24 And lead me in the way e.
Ps 145:13 Your kingdom is an e
Is 9: 6 E Father, Prince of Peace.
Is 24: 5 Broken the e covenant.
Is 26: 4 the LORD, is e strength.
Is 33:14 among us shall dwell with e
Is 35:10 With e joy on their heads.
Is 40:28 The e God, the LORD, The
Is 45:17 by the LORD With an e
Is 54: 8 But with e kindness I will
Is 55:13 For an e sign that shall
Is 56: 5 I will give them an e name
Is 60:19 LORD will be to you an e
Is 61: 7 E joy shall be theirs.
Is 63:16 Our Redeemer from E is
Jer 10:10 is the living God and the e
Jer 31: 3 I have loved you with an e
Dan 4: 3 His kingdom is an e
Dan 9:24 To bring in e
Dan 12: 2 Some to e life, Some to
Dan 12: 2 Some to shame and e
Mic 5: 2 are from of old, From e.
Hab 1:12 Are You not from e,
Matt 18: 8 to be cast into the e fire.
Matt 25:41 into the e fire prepared for
Matt 25:46 these will go away into e
John 3:16 not perish but have e life.
John 3:36 believes in the Son has e
John 4:14 of water springing up into e
Rom 6:22 and the end, e life.
Rom 16:26 to the commandment of the e
2Th 1: 9 shall be punished with e
1Ti 6:16 to whom be honor and e
Heb 13:20 through the blood of the e
2Pe 1:11 to you abundantly into the e
Jude 6 He has reserved in e chains
Rev 14: 6 having the e gospel to

EVIDENCE (see EVIDENCES, EVIDENT)
Ex 22:13 then he shall bring it as e,
Heb 11: 1 the e of things not seen.

EVIDENCES (see EVIDENCE)
Deut 22:20 and e of virginity are

EVIDENT (see EVIDENCE)
1Co 15:27 it is e that He who put
Gal 5:19 the works of the flesh are e,
Phil 1:13 so that it has become e to
1Ti 5:24 men's sins are clearly e,
Heb 7:14 For it is e that our Lord

EVIL (see EVILDOER, EVILDOERS, EVILS)
Gen 2: 9 the knowledge of good and e.
Gen 6: 5 of his heart was only e
Gen 8:21 of man's heart is e from
Gen 44: 4 Why have you repaid e for
Gen 47: 9 few and e have been the days
Gen 48:16 has redeemed me from all e,
Gen 50:20 you meant e against me; but
Lev 5: 4 with his lips to do e or
Num 32:13 generation that had done e
Deut 1:39 no knowledge of good and e,
Deut 4:25 and do e in the sight of the
Deut 17: 7 So you shall put away the e
Deut 30:15 life and good, death and e,
Josh 24:15 And if it seems e to you to
Judg 3:12 because they had done e in
2Sa 14:17 in discerning good and e.
2Sa 16: 8 are caught in your own e,
1Ki 11: 6 Solomon did e in the sight of
1Ki 14:22 Now Judah did e in the sight
1Ki 16:25 Omri did e in the eyes of the
2Ki 17:13 Turn from your e ways, and
2Ki 17:17 and sold themselves to do e
Ezra 4:12 the rebellious and e city,
Ezra 9:13 has come upon us for our e
Esth 8: 6 can I endure to see the e
Job 1: 1 who feared God and shunned e.
Job 2: 3 who fears God and shuns e?
Job 7: 4 If I have repaid e to him
Job 28:28 And to depart from e is
Job 30:26 e came to me; And when I
Ps 7: 4 If I have repaid e to him
Ps 21:11 For they intended e against
Ps 23: 4 of death, I will fear no e;
Ps 34:13 Keep your tongue from e,
Ps 34:14 Depart from e and do good;
Ps 37:19 not be ashamed in the e
Ps 38:20 Those also who render e for
Ps 41: 5 My enemies speak e of me:
Ps 41: 8 An e disease," they say,
Ps 49: 5 I fear in the days of e,
Ps 51: 4 And done this e in Your
Ps 52: 3 You love e more than good,
Ps 91:10 No e shall befall you, Nor
Ps 97:10 hate e! He preserves the
Ps 119:101 my feet from every e way,
Ps 121: 7 preserve you from all e;
Prov 1:16 For their feet run to e,
Prov 6:14 He devises e continually,
Prov 6:24 To keep you from the e
Prov 8:13 and arrogance and the e way
Prov 13:21 E pursues sinners, But to
Prov 15:28 of the wicked pours forth e.
Prov 16:17 upright is to depart from e;
Prov 17:11 An e man seeks only
Prov 24: 1 Do not be envious of e men,
Prov 28:22 A man with an e eye hastens
Prov 31:12 She does him good and not e
Eccl 2:21 is vanity and a great e.
Eccl 8:12 Though a sinner does e a
Eccl 10: 5 e I have seen under the sun,
Eccl 12:14 thing, Whether good or e.
Is 1:16 My eyes. Cease to do e,
Is 5:20 call evil good, and good e;
Is 7:15 He may know to refuse the e
Is 65:12 But did e before My eyes,
Jer 9: 3 they proceed from evil to e,

Jer 13:23 who are accustomed to do e.
Jer 18:20 Shall e be repaid for good?
Jer 29:11 of peace and not of e,
Dan 11:27 hearts shall be bent on e,
Amos 5:13 For it is an e time.
Amos 5:14 Seek good and not e,
Amos 5:15 Hate e, love good;
Jon 3: 8 every one turn from his e
Hab 1:13 purer eyes than to behold e,
Matt 5:11 and say all kinds of e
Matt 5:37 than these is from the e
Matt 5:45 makes His sun rise on the e
Matt 6:13 But deliver us from the e
Matt 7:11 "If you then, being e,
Matt 9: 4 Why do you think e in your
Matt 12:35 evil treasure brings forth e
Matt 12:39 An e and adulterous
Matt 15:19 out of the heart proceed e
Matt 20:15 Or is your eye e because I
Matt 24:48 But if that e servant says in
Matt 27:23 what e has He done?" But
Mark 3: 4 to do good or to do e,
Mark 7:21 proceed e thoughts,
Mark 7:22 an e eye, blasphemy, pride,
Luke 8: 2 who had been healed of e
Luke 11:13 "If you then, being e,
John 3:19 because their deeds were e.
John 3:20 For everyone practicing e
Acts 19: 9 but spoke e of the Way
Acts 23: 9 We find no e in this man; but
Rom 3: 8 Let us do e that good may
Rom 7: 8 in me all manner of e
Rom 7:19 but the e I will not to
Rom 12: 9 hypocrisy. Abhor what is e.
Rom 12:17 Repay no one evil for e.
Rom 12:21 but overcome e with good.
1Co 5:13 yourselves the e person."
1Co 10: 6 we should not lust after e
1Co 13: 5 is not provoked, thinks no e;
1Co 15:33 E company corrupts good
2Co 6: 8 by e report and good report;
Gal 1: 4 us from this present e age,
Eph 4:31 and e speaking be put away
Eph 5:16 time, because the days are e.
Eph 6:13 able to withstand in the e
1Th 5:15 See that no one renders e for
1Th 5:15 no one renders evil for e
1Th 5:22 Abstain from every form of e.
1Ti 6:10 a root of all kinds of e,
2Ti 3:13 But e men and impostors will
Tit 3: 2 to speak e of no one, to be
Heb 3:12 there be in any of you an e
Heb 5:14 to discern both good and e.
Heb 10:22 hearts sprinkled from an e
Jas 1:13 God cannot be tempted by e,
Jas 3: 8 tongue. It is an unruly e,
Jas 4:11 speaks e of the law and
Jas 4:16 All such boasting is e.
1Pe 3: 9 not returning e for evil or
1Pe 3: 9 not returning evil for e or
1Jn 3:12 Because his works were e and
3Jn 11 but he who does e has not
Rev 2: 2 cannot bear those who are e.

EVILDOER (see EVIL, EVILDOERS)
2Sa 3:39 The LORD shall repay the e
Is 9:17 is a hypocrite and an e,
John 18:30 him, "If He were not an e,
2Ti 2: 9 I suffer trouble as an e,

EVILDOERS (see EVILDOER)
Ps 37: 1 Do not fret because of e,
Ps 37: 9 For e shall be cut off; But
Ps 119:115 Depart from me, you e,
Prov 24:19 Do not fret because of e,
Is 1: 4 with iniquity, A brood of e,

1Pe 2:12 they speak against you as e,
1Pe 3:16 when they defame you as e,

EVILS (see EVIL)
Deut 31:17 And many e and troubles
Jer 2:13 people have committed two e:
Luke 3:19 and for all the e which

EWE
Gen 21:28 And Abraham set seven e lambs
2Sa 12: 3 except one little e lamb

EXACTLY†
Eccl 5:16 Just e as he came, so shall

EXACTS†
Job 11: 6 Know therefore that God e

EXALT (see EXALTATION, EXALTED, EXALTS)
Ex 15: 2 God, and I will e Him.
1Sa 2:10 And e the horn of His
Ps 34: 3 And let us e His name
Ps 66: 7 Do not let the rebellious e
Ps 99: 5 E the LORD our God, And
Ps 99: 9 E the LORD our God, And
Ps 118:28 I will e You.
Ps 137: 6 If I do not e Jerusalem
Prov 4: 8 E her, and she will promote
Is 14:13 I will e my throne above
Dan 8:25 And he shall e himself in
Dan 11:36 he shall e and magnify
1Pe 5: 6 that He may e you in due

EXALTATION (see EXALT)
Is 13: 3 who rejoice in My e.
Jas 1: 9 lowly brother glory in his e,

EXALTED (see EXALT)
Num 24: 7 And his kingdom shall be e.
1Sa 2: 1 My horn is e in the LORD.
2Sa 22:47 be my Rock! Let God be e,
Job 10:16 If my head is e,
Ps 18:46 God of my salvation be e.
Ps 46:10 I will be e in the earth!
Ps 57: 5 Be e, O God, above the
Ps 57:11 Be e, O God, above the
Ps 97: 9 You are e far above all
Ps 118:16 right hand of the LORD is e;
Ps 148:13 For His name alone is e;
Is 2: 2 And shall be e above the
Is 2:11 the LORD alone shall be e
Is 24:21 on high the host of e ones,
Is 33: 5 The LORD is e,
Is 40: 4 Every valley shall be e And
Is 52:13 He shall be e and extolled
Dan 8:11 He even e himself as high as
Matt 23:12 humbles himself will be e.
Acts 5:31 Him God has e to His right
2Co 12: 7 lest I be e above measure.
Phil 2: 9 God also has highly e Him

EXALTS (see EXALT)
Prov 14:34 Righteousness e a nation,
Matt 23:12 And whoever e himself will be
2Th 2: 4 who opposes and exalts himself

EXAMINE (see EXAMINED, EXAMINES)
Lev 13: 3 The priest shall e the sore
Ps 26: 2 E me, O LORD, and prove me
1Co 11:28 But let a man e himself,
Gal 6: 4 But let each one e his own

EXAMINED (see EXAMINE)
Dan 1:13 let our appearance be e
Luke 23:14 having e Him in your
Acts 28:18 when they had e me, wanted

EXAMINES (see EXAMINE)
Prov 18:17 his neighbor comes and e

EXAMPLE (see EXAMPLES)
Matt 1:19 to make her a public e,
John 13:15 "For I have given you an e,
Phil 3:17 join in following my e,
1Ti 4:12 but be an e to the believers
Jas 5:10 as an e of suffering and
1Pe 2:21 for us, leaving us an e,

EXAMPLES (see EXAMPLE)
1Co 10:11 things happened to them as e,
1Th 1: 7 so that you became e to all
1Pe 5: 3 but being e to the flock;

EXCEED (see EXCEEDING, EXCEEDS)
2Ch 9: 6 You e the fame of which I

EXCEEDING† (see EXCEED, EXCEEDINGLY)
Ps 43: 4 To God my e joy; And on
2Co 4:17 working for us a far more e
2Co 9:14 for you because of the e
Eph 1:19 and what is the e greatness
Eph 2: 7 to come He might show the e
1Pe 4:13 you may also be glad with e
Jude 24 of His glory with e joy,

EXCEEDINGLY (see EXCEEDING)
Gen 7:19 And the waters prevailed e on
Gen 13:13 But the men of Sodom were e
Gen 15: 1 your e great reward."
Ex 1: 7 multiplied and grew e
Ps 21: 6 You have made him e glad
Ps 119:96 But Your commandment is e
Ps 119:167 And I love them e.
Prov 30:24 But they are e wise:
Dan 3:22 and the furnace e hot, the
Dan 7: 7 e strong. It had huge iron
Dan 7:19 e dreadful, with its teeth
Dan 8: 9 a little horn which grew e
Jon 3: 3 Now Nineveh was an e great
Jon 4: 1 But it displeased Jonah e,
Matt 2:10 they rejoiced with a great
Matt 2:16 was e angry; and he sent
Matt 5:12 Rejoice and be glad, for
Matt 26:38 My soul is e sorrowful, even
2Co 7: 4 I am e joyful in all our
Eph 3:20 to Him who is able to do e
1Th 3:10 night and day praying e that
2Th 1: 3 because your faith grows e,
Rev 16:21 since that plague was e

EXCEEDS (see EXCEED)
Matt 5:20 unless your righteousness e

EXCEL (see EXCELLED, EXCELS)
Prov 31:29 But you e them all."
1Co 14:12 church that you seek to e.

EXCELLED (see EXCEL)
1Ki 4:30 Thus Solomon's wisdom e the
Eccl 2: 9 So I became great and e more

EXCELLENCE (see EXCELLENT)
Ex 15: 7 in the greatness of Your e
Ps 47: 4 The e of Jacob whom He
1Co 2: 1 did not come with e of
2Co 4: 7 that the e of the power may
Phil 3: 8 all things loss for the e

EXCELLENT (see EXCELLENCE)
Job 37:23 He is e in power, In
Ps 8: 1 How e is Your name in all
Ps 8: 9 How e is Your name in all
Ps 150: 2 Him according to His e
Prov 12: 4 An e wife is the crown of
Is 12: 5 For He has done e things;
Dan 2:31 image, whose splendor was e,
Dan 4:36 and e majesty was added to
Dan 6: 3 because an e spirit was in
Luke 1: 3 most e Theophilus,

Acts 23:26 to the most e governor
Rom 2:18 the things that are e,
1Co 12:31 And yet I show you a more e
Phil 1:10 the things that are e,
Heb 1: 4 obtained a more e name than
Heb 8: 6 now He has obtained a more e
Heb 11: 4 Abel offered to God a more e
2Pe 1:17 voice came to Him from the E

EXCELS (see EXCEL)
Eccl 2:13 excels folly As light e
2Co 3:10 because of the glory that e.

EXCHANGE (see EXCHANGED, EXCHANGING)
Matt 16:26 Or what will a man give in e
Mark 8:37 what will a man give in e

EXCHANGED (see EXCHANGE)
Job 28:17 Nor can it be e for jewelry
Rom 1:25 who e the truth of God for
Rom 1:26 For even their women e the

EXCHANGING† (see EXCHANGE)
Ruth 4: 7 concerning redeeming and e,

EXCITED†
Ruth 1:19 that all the city was e
Is 14: 9 Hell from beneath is e about

EXCLUDE† (see EXCLUDED)
Luke 6:22 And when they e you, And
Gal 4:17 they want to e you, that you

EXCLUDED (see EXCLUDE)
Rom 3:27 is boasting then? It is e.

EXCUSE† (see EXCUSING)
Eccl 5: 6 God be angry at your e and
John 15:22 but now they have no e for
Rom 1:20 so that they are without e,
2Co 12:19 do you think that we e

EXCUSING† (see EXCUSE)
Rom 2:15 thoughts accusing or else e

EXECUTE (see EXECUTED, EXECUTES, EXECUTIONER)
Ex 12:12 the gods of Egypt I will e
Ezek 45: 9 e justice and righteousness,
Zech 7: 9 E true justice, Show mercy
John 5:27 has given Him authority to e
Rom 13: 4 an avenger to e wrath on
Jude 15 to e judgment on all, to

EXECUTED (see EXECUTE)
1Ki 18:40 to the Brook Kishon and e
Ps 99: 4 You have e justice and
Dan 5:19 Whomever he wished, he e;

EXECUTES (see EXECUTE)
Ps 103: 6 The LORD e righteousness
Ps 146: 7 Who e justice for the

EXECUTIONER† (see EXECUTE, EXECUTIONERS)
Mark 6:27 the king sent an e and

EXECUTIONERS† (see EXECUTIONER)
Job 33:22 Pit, And his life to the e.

EXERCISE (see EXERCISED, EXERCISES, EXERCISING)
1Ki 21: 7 You now e authority over
Luke 22:25 and those who e authority
1Co 7: 9 but if they cannot e
1Ti 4: 7 and e yourself toward
1Ti 4: 8 For bodily e profits a

EXERCISED (see EXERCISE)
Heb 5:14 of use have their senses e

EXERCISES† (see EXERCISE)
Rev 13:12 And he e all the authority of

EXERCISING† (see EXERCISE)
Jer 9:24 e lovingkindness, judgment,

EXHORT (see EXHORTATION, EXHORTED, EXHORTING,
EXHORTS)
1Th 4: 1 we urge and e in the Lord
1Ti 5: 1 but e him as a father,
1Ti 6: 2 Teach and e these things.
2Ti 4: 2 season. Convince, rebuke, e,
Tit 2: 6 Likewise e the young men to
Tit 2: 9 E bondservants to be
Heb 3:13 but e one another daily,
1Pe 5: 1 elders who are among you I e,

EXHORTATION (see EXHORT)
Acts 13:15 if you have any word of e
Rom 12: 8 he who exhorts, in e;
1Ti 4:13 attention to reading, to e,
Heb 13:22 bear with the word of e,

EXHORTED (see EXHORT)
Acts 15:32 e and strengthened the

EXHORTING (see EXHORT)
Acts 14:22 e them to continue in the
Heb 10:25 but e one another, and so

EXHORTS† (see EXHORT)
Rom 12: 8 he who e, in exhortation;

EXIST (see EXISTED)
Rom 4:17 those things which do not e
Rev 4:11 And by Your will they are and

EXISTED† (see EXIST)
Eccl 4: 3 both is he who has never e,
2Pe 3: 6 which the world that then e

EXORCISE (see ADJURE)
Acts 19:13 We e you by the Jesus whom

EXORCISTS
Acts 19:13 of the itinerant Jewish e

EXPECT (see EXPECTANTLY, EXPECTATION, EXPECTED,
EXPECTING, UNEXPECTEDLY)
Matt 24:44 at an hour you do not e.

EXPECTANTLY (see EXPECT)
Ps 145:15 The eyes of all look e to

EXPECTATION (see EXPECT)
Ps 62: 5 For my e is from Him.
Luke 3:15 Now as the people were in e,
Acts 12:11 of Herod and from all the e
Rom 8:19 For the earnest e of the
Phil 1:20 according to my earnest e and
Heb 10:27 but a certain fearful e of

EXPECTED (see EXPECT)
Is 5: 2 So He e it to bring forth

EXPECTING (see EXPECT)
Acts 3: 5 e to receive something from

EXPEDIENT†
John 11:50 do you consider that it is e
John 18:14 the Jews that it was e that

EXPENSE (see EXPENSES)
2Sa 19:42 ever eaten at the king's e?
1Co 9: 7 goes to war at his own e?

EXPENSES (see EXPENSE)
Acts 21:24 and pay their e so that they

EXPERIENCE† (see EXPERIENCED)
Gen 30:27 for I have learned by e
Eccl 8: 5 who keeps his command will e

EXPERIENCED† (see EXPERIENCE)
1Pe 5: 9 the same sufferings are e

EXPERT
Ezra 7:11 e in the words of the
Acts 26: 3 because you are e in all

EXPIRED
Rev 20: 7 the thousand years have e,

EXPLAIN (see EXPLAINED, EXPLAINING)
Gen 41:24 was no one who could e it
Deut 1: 5 Moses began to e this law,
Dan 4: 9 e to me the visions of my
Dan 5:16 give interpretations and e
Matt 13:36 E to us the parable of the
Heb 5:11 much to say, and hard to e,

EXPLAINED (see EXPLAIN)
Judg 14:17 Then she e the riddle to the
Acts 18:26 they took him aside and e to

EXPLAINING (see EXPLAIN)
Acts 17: 3 e and demonstrating that the

EXPLOIT (see EXPLOITS)
Mal 3: 5 Against those who e wage

EXPLOITS† (see EXPLOIT)
Dan 11:32 and carry out great e.

EXPOSE (see EXPOSED)
Hos 2: 3 I strip her naked And e
Eph 5:11 but rather e them.

EXPOSED (see EXPOSE)
Ex 20:26 your nakedness may not be e
John 3:20 lest his deeds should be e.
Eph 5:13 But all things that are e are

EXPOUNDED†
Luke 24:27 He e to them in all the

EXPRESS† (see EXPRESSION, EXPRESSLY)
Eccl 1: 8 Man cannot e it. The eye
Heb 1: 3 of His glory and the e

EXPRESSION† (see EXPRESS)
Dan 3:19 and the e on his face

EXPRESSLY (see EXPRESS)
Ezek 1: 3 word of the LORD came e to
1Ti 4: 1 Now the Spirit e says that in

EXTEND (see EXTENDED, EXTENDS, EXTENT)
Ps 109:12 Let there be none to e mercy

EXTENDED (see EXTEND)
Ezra 7:28 and has e mercy to me before

EXTENDS† (see EXTEND)
Num 21:13 is in the wilderness that e
Prov 31:20 She e her hand to the poor,

EXTENSIVE† (see EXTENT)
Neh 4:19 "The work is great and e,

EXTENT (see EXTEND, EXTENSIVE)
Jon 3: 3 a three-day journey in e.
2Co 2: 5 me, but all of you to some e—

EXTINGUISH† (see EXTINGUISHED)
2Sa 14: 7 So they would e my ember

EXTINGUISHED† (see EXTINGUISH)
Job 17: 1 is broken, My days are e,
Is 43:17 shall not rise; They are e,

EXTOL† (see EXTOLLED)
Ps 30: 1 I will e You, O LORD, for
Ps 68: 4 E Him who rides on the
Ps 145: 1 I will e You, my God, O
Dan 4:37 praise and e and honor the

EXTOLLED (see EXTOL)
Is 52:13 He shall be exalted and e

EXTORTION† (see EXTORTIONER)
Prov 28: 8 possessions by usury and e
Ezek 22:12 from your neighbors by e,
Matt 23:25 inside they are full of e

EXTORTIONER (see EXTORTION, EXTORTIONERS)
1Co 5:11 or a drunkard, or an e—

EXTORTIONERS† (see EXTORTIONER)
Luke 18:11 I am not like other men—e,
1Co 5:10 or with the covetous, or e,
1Co 6:10 nor e will inherit the

EXULT†
Job 6:10 in anguish, I would e,

EYE (see EYED, EYELIDS, EYES, EYESERVICE)
Ex 21:24 e for eye, tooth for tooth,
Deut 7:16 your e shall have no pity on
Deut 15: 9 and your e be evil against
Deut 19:21 e for eye, tooth for tooth,
Deut 32:10 him as the apple of His e.
Job 7: 8 The e of him who sees me
Job 17: 7 My e has also grown dim
Job 20: 9 The e that saw him will
Job 24:15 No e will see me'; And he
Job 42: 5 But now my e sees You.
Ps 6: 7 My e wastes away because of
Ps 32: 8 I will guide you with My e.
Ps 33:18 the e of the LORD is on
Ps 35:19 let them wink with the e
Ps 54: 7 And my e has seen its
Ps 94: 9 hear? He who formed the e,
Prov 20:12 hearing ear and the seeing e,
Prov 28:22 A man with an evil e hastens
Eccl 1: 8 The e is not satisfied with
Is 52: 8 For they shall see e to eye
Lam 1:16 these things I weep; My e,
Lam 1:16 my e overflows with water;
Ezek 5:11 My e will not spare, nor
Matt 5:29 If your right e causes you to
Matt 6:22 lamp of the body is the e.
Matt 6:22 If therefore your e is good,
Matt 7: 3 speck in your brother's e,
Matt 7: 3 the plank in your own e?
Matt 18: 9 And if your e causes you to
Matt 18: 9 enter into life with one e,
Matt 19:24 a camel to go through the e
1Co 2: 9 E has not seen, nor ear
1Co 12:16 say, "Because I am not an e,
1Co 12:17 If the whole body were an e,
1Co 15:52 in the twinkling of an e,
Rev 1: 7 and every e will see Him,
Rev 3:18 and anoint your eyes with e

EYED† (see EYE)
1Sa 18: 9 So Saul e David from that day

EYELIDS (see EYE)
Ps 132: 4 my eyes Or slumber to my e,
Prov 6:25 her allure you with her e.

EYES (see EYE)
Gen 3: 5 the day you eat of it your e
Gen 3: 6 it was pleasant to the e,
Gen 6: 8 Noah found grace in the e
Gen 13:14 Lift your e now and look from
Gen 27: 1 when Isaac was old and his e
Gen 29:17 Leah's e were delicate, but
Gen 30:27 I have found favor in your e,
Gen 39: 7 wife cast longing e on
Gen 46: 4 will put his hand on your e.
Ex 13: 9 as a memorial between your e,
Ex 13:16 as frontlets between your e,
Num 5:13 and it is hidden from the e
Num 22:31 the LORD opened Balaam's e,
Deut 3:27 east; behold it with your e,
Deut 6:22 and wonders before our e,
Deut 12: 8 is right in his own e—
Deut 28:65 a trembling heart, failing e,
Deut 34: 7 His e were not dim nor his
Josh 23:13 sides and thorns in your e,
Judg 16:21 took him and put out his e,

Judg	17: 6	was right in his own **e**.
Judg	21:25	was right in his own **e**.
Ruth	2: 9	Let your **e** be on the field
Ruth	2:10	have I found favor in your **e**,
1Sa	12: 3	with which to blind my **e**?
1Sa	15:17	were little in your own **e**,
1Sa	16:12	he was ruddy, with bright **e**,
1Sa	20: 3	I have found favor in your **e**,
1Sa	26:21	life was precious in your **e**
2Sa	12:11	your wives before your **e**
2Sa	13:34	keeping watch lifted his **e**
1Ki	14: 4	for his **e** were glazed by
1Ki	15: 5	what was right in the **e**
1Ki	16:25	Omri did evil in the **e** of the
1Ki	20:38	with a bandage over his **e**.
2Ki	4:35	and the child opened his **e**.
2Ki	7: 2	shall see it with your **e**,
2Ki	9:30	and she put paint on her **e**
2Ki	25: 7	put out the **e** of Zedekiah,
2Ch	16: 9	For the **e** of the LORD run to
2Ch	29: 8	as you see with your **e**.
Job	2:12	And when they raised their **e**
Job	4:16	A form was before my **e**;
Job	16:20	My **e** pour out tears to
Job	19:27	And my **e** shall behold, and
Job	28:21	It is hidden from the **e** of
Job	29:15	I was **e** to the blind, And
Job	31: 1	made a covenant with my **e**;
Job	32: 1	was righteous in his own **e**.
Ps	13: 3	my God; Enlighten my **e**,
Ps	19: 8	is pure, enlightening the **e**;
Ps	25:15	My **e** are ever toward the
Ps	31:22	cut off from before Your **e**'
Ps	34:15	The **e** of the LORD are on
Ps	36: 1	no fear of God before his **e**.
Ps	36: 2	himself in his own **e**,
Ps	69:23	Let their **e** be darkened, so
Ps	115: 5	E they have, but they do
Ps	116: 8	My **e** from tears, And my
Ps	118:23	It is marvelous in our **e**.
Ps	119:18	Open my **e**, that I may see
Ps	119:136	of water run down from my **e**,
Ps	121: 1	I will lift up my **e** to the
Ps	132: 4	will not give sleep to my **e**
Ps	135:16	E they have, but they do
Ps	139:16	Your **e** saw my substance,
Ps	146: 8	The LORD opens the **e** of
Prov	3: 7	not be wise in your own **e**;
Prov	6: 4	Give no sleep to your **e**,
Prov	6:13	He winks with his **e**,
Prov	12:15	fool is right in his own **e**,
Prov	17:24	But the **e** of a fool are on
Prov	20:13	to poverty; Open your **e**,
Prov	23:29	cause? Who has redness of **e**?
Prov	26: 5	he be wise in his own **e**.
Prov	28:11	man is wise in his own **e**,
Prov	29:13	LORD gives light to the **e**
Eccl	2:10	Whatever my **e** desired I did
Eccl	5:11	to see them with their **e**?
Song	1:15	fair! You have dove's **e**
Song	4: 1	fair! You have dove's **e**
Song	4: 9	With one look of your **e**,
Song	7: 4	Your **e** like the pools in
Song	8:10	Then I became in his **e** As
Is	1:15	I will hide My **e** from you;
Is	3:16	necks And wanton **e**,
Is	5:15	And the **e** of the lofty
Is	5:21	are wise in their own **e**,
Is	6: 5	For my **e** have seen the
Is	6:10	heavy, And shut their **e**;
Is	6:10	Lest they see with their **e**,
Is	11: 3	judge by the sight of His **e**,
Is	33:17	Your **e** will see the King in
Is	42: 7	To open blind **e**,
Jer	4:30	Though you enlarge your **e**
Jer	7:11	a den of thieves in your **e**?
Jer	9: 1	And my **e** a fountain of
Lam	2:11	My **e** fail with tears, My
Ezek	1:18	their rims were full of **e**,
Ezek	10:12	were full of **e** all around.
Ezek	12: 2	which has **e** to see but does
Ezek	18:12	Lifted his **e** to the idols,
Ezek	23:40	for them, painted your **e**,
Ezek	24:21	boast, the desire of your **e**,
Ezek	24:25	glory, the desire of their **e**,
Ezek	40: 4	look with your **e** and hear
Dan	4:34	lifted my **e** to heaven, and
Dan	7: 8	were eyes like the **e** of a
Dan	7:20	that horn which had **e** and a
Dan	8: 5	a notable horn between his **e**.
Dan	9:18	open Your **e** and see our
Dan	10: 6	his **e** like torches of fire,
Hos	13:14	Pity is hidden from My **e**.
Amos	9: 8	the **e** of the Lord GOD are
Hab	1:13	You are of purer **e** than to
Zech	3: 9	Upon the stone are seven **e**.
Zech	8: 6	it also be marvelous in My **e**?
Zech	9: 8	now I have seen with My **e**.
Matt	9:29	Then He touched their **e**,
Matt	9:30	And their **e** were opened. And
Matt	13:15	And their **e** they have
Matt	13:15	see with their **e** and
Matt	18: 9	rather than having two **e**,
Matt	20:34	and touched their **e**.
Matt	20:34	And immediately their **e**
Matt	21:42	is marvelous in our **e**'?
Matt	26:43	for their **e** were heavy.
Mark	8:23	when He had spit on his **e**
Luke	2:30	For my **e** have seen Your
Luke	4:20	And the **e** of all who were in
Luke	10:23	Blessed are the **e** which see
Luke	16:23	he lifted up his **e** and saw
Luke	24:16	But their **e** were restrained,
Luke	24:31	Then their **e** were opened and
John	4:35	lift up your **e** and look at
John	9: 6	and He anointed the **e** of the
John	9:10	How were your **e** opened?"
John	9:11	made clay and anointed my **e**
John	9:32	of that anyone opened the **e**
John	12:40	He has blinded their **e**
John	12:40	should see with their **e**,
John	17: 1	lifted up His **e** to heaven,
Acts	9: 8	and when his **e** were opened
Acts	9:18	there fell from his **e**
Rom	3:18	of God before their **e**."
Rom	11:10	Let their **e** be darkened,
Eph	1:18	the **e** of your understanding
Heb	4:13	naked and open to the **e** of
1Pe	3:12	For the **e** of the LORD
2Pe	2:14	having **e** full of adultery and
1Jn	1: 1	we have seen with our **e**,
1Jn	2:11	darkness has blinded his **e**.
1Jn	2:16	the flesh, the lust of the **e**,
Rev	1:14	and His **e** like a flame of
Rev	3:18	and anoint your **e** with eye
Rev	4: 6	living creatures full of **e**
Rev	5: 6	seven horns and seven **e**,
Rev	7:17	away every tear from their **e**.
Rev	21: 4	away every tear from their **e**;

EYESERVICE† (*see* EYE)

Eph	6: 6	not with **e**,
Col	3:22	to the flesh, not with **e**,

EYEWITNESSES† (*see* WITNESS)

Luke	1: 2	from the beginning were **e**
2Pe	1:16	but were **e** of His majesty.

EZEKIEL†

Ezek	1: 3	LORD came expressly to E
Ezek	24:24	Thus E is a sign to you;

EZION GEBER
Num	33:36	They moved from E and camped
Deut	2: 8	plain, away from Elath and E
1Ki	9:26	built a fleet of ships at E
2Ch	8:17	Then Solomon went to E and

EZRA
Ezra	7: 6	this E came up from Babylon;
Ezra	7: 8	And E came to Jerusalem in
Ezra	7:12	To E the priest, a scribe of
Neh	8: 5	And E opened the book in the

F

FABLES
1Ti	1: 4	nor give heed to f and
1Ti	4: 7	profane and old wives' f,
Tit	1:14	not giving heed to Jewish f
2Pe	1:16	follow cunningly devised f

FACE (*see* FACED, FACES, FACING)
Gen	1: 2	God was hovering over the f
Gen	1:29	seed which is on the f of
Gen	3:19	In the sweat of your f you
Gen	4:14	shall be hidden from Your f;
Gen	11: 4	scattered abroad over the f
Gen	17: 3	Then Abram fell on his f,
Gen	32:20	afterward I will see his f;
Gen	32:30	I have seen God face to f,
Gen	35: 1	when you fled from the f of
Gen	43: 3	You shall not see my f unless
Gen	43:31	Then he washed his f and came
Ex	2:15	But Moses fled from the f of
Ex	3: 6	Jacob." And Moses hid his f,
Ex	10: 5	And they shall cover the f of
Ex	10:29	I will never see your f
Ex	33:11	spoke to Moses face to f,
Ex	34:30	the skin of his f shone, and
Ex	34:33	them, he put a veil on his f.
Lev	21:18	who has a marred f or any
Num	6:25	The LORD make His f shine
Num	12: 8	I speak with him f to face,
Num	12:14	father had but spit in her f,
Deut	25: 9	from his foot, spit in his f,
Deut	31:17	and I will hide My f from
Deut	34:10	whom the LORD knew f to
Deut	34:10	the LORD knew face to f,
Judg	6:22	the Angel of the LORD f to
Judg	6:22	Angel of the LORD face to f.
Ruth	2:10	So she fell on her f,
1Sa	1:18	and her f was no longer
1Sa	5: 4	fallen on its f to the
1Sa	25:23	fell on her f before David,
2Sa	14:24	but did not see the king's f.
1Ki	18:42	and put his f between his
1Ki	19:13	that he wrapped his f in his
1Ki	21: 4	bed, and turned away his f,
2Ki	4:29	but lay my staff on the f of
2Ki	4:31	and laid the staff on the f
2Ki	8:15	and spread it over his f so
2Ki	12:17	then Hazael set his f to go
2Ki	20: 2	Then he turned his f toward
2Ch	7:14	and pray and seek My f,
Neh	2: 2	Why is your f sad, since you
Esth	7: 8	they covered Haman's f.
Job	1:11	surely curse You to Your f!
Job	4:15	a spirit passed before my f;
Job	9:27	I will put off my sad f and
Job	16:16	My f is flushed from
Job	17: 6	I have become one in whose f
Job	41:14	can open the doors of his f,
Ps	13: 1	long will You hide Your f
Ps	24: 6	seek Him, Who seek Your f.
Ps	27: 8	heart said to You, "Your f,

Ps	27: 9	Do not hide Your f from me;
Ps	67: 1	And cause His f to shine
Ps	69: 7	Shame has covered my f.
Ps	104:15	Oil to make his f shine,
Ps	104:30	And You renew the f of the
Ps	105: 4	Seek His f evermore!
Ps	132:10	Do not turn away the f of
Prov	7:13	With an impudent f she said
Prov	8:27	He drew a circle on the f
Prov	21:29	A wicked man hardens his f,
Prov	27:19	As in water f reflects
Prov	27:19	in water face reflects f,
Song	2:14	cliff, Let me see your f,
Song	2:14	And your f is lovely."
Is	6: 2	with two he covered his f,
Jer	2:27	back to Me, and not their f.
Jer	13:26	your skirts over your f,
Jer	32: 4	and shall speak with him f
Jer	32: 4	speak with him face to f,
Jer	33: 5	I have hidden My f from
Lam	3:35	due a man Before the f of
Lam	4:16	The f of the LORD scattered
Ezek	7:18	Shame will be on every f,
Ezek	9: 8	and I fell on my f and cried
Ezek	10:14	the first f was the face of
Ezek	10:14	the second f the face of a
Ezek	10:14	the third the f of a lion,
Ezek	10:14	and the fourth the f of an
Ezek	38:18	My fury will show in My f.
Dan	3:19	and the expression on his f
Dan	10: 9	with my f to the ground.
Hos	5:15	Then they will seek My f;
Nah	3: 5	lift your skirts over your f,
Matt	6:17	your head and wash your f,
Matt	11:10	messenger before Your f,
Matt	16: 3	know how to discern the f
Matt	17: 2	His f shone like the sun,
Matt	18:10	angels always see the f of
Matt	26:39	farther and fell on His f,
Matt	26:67	Then they spat in His f and
Luke	9:29	the appearance of His f was
Luke	17:16	and fell down on his f at
Luke	22:64	they struck Him on the f and
John	11:44	and his f was wrapped with a
Acts	6:15	saw his f as the face of an
Acts	7:45	God drove out before the f
Acts	17:26	of men to dwell on all the f
Acts	20:25	will see my f no more.
Acts	25:16	meets the accusers face to f,
1Co	13:12	but then f to face. Now I
1Co	14:25	so, falling down on his f,
2Co	3: 7	not look steadily at the f
2Co	3:18	But we all, with unveiled f,
2Co	4: 6	of the glory of God in the f
2Co	11:20	if one strikes you on the f.
Gal	2:11	I withstood him to his f,
Col	2: 1	many as have not seen my f
1Th	2:17	more eagerly to see your f
Jas	1:23	man observing his natural f
1Pe	3:12	But the f of the
2Jn	12	to come to you and speak f
Rev	4: 7	living creature had a f
Rev	6:16	on us and hide us from the f
Rev	10: 1	his f was like the sun, and
Rev	22: 4	They shall see His f,

FACED (*see* FACE)
Ex	37: 9	They f one another; the
Ezek	47: 1	the front of the temple f

FACES (*see* FACE)
Ex	25:20	the f of the cherubim shall
Judg	16: 3	the top of the hill that f
2Ch	7: 3	they bowed their f to the
Ps	34: 5	And their f were not
Ps	83:16	Fill their f with shame,

Is 3:15 people And grinding the f
Is 25: 8 wipe away tears from all f;
Is 53: 3 our f from Him; He was
Jer 1: 8 Do not be afraid of their f,
Jer 30: 6 And all f turned pale?
Ezek 1: 6 Each one had four f,
Ezek 10:22 was the same as the f
Ezek 41:18 Each cherub had two f,
Dan 1:10 For why should he see your f
Joel 2: 6 All f are drained of color.
Zech 14: 4 Which f Jerusalem on the
Matt 6:16 For they disfigure their f

FACING (see FACE)
Jer 1:13 and it is f away from the
Mark 4: 1 multitude was on the land f

FACT (see FACTS)
Gen 42:13 the land of Canaan; and in f,
Ruth 3: 2 he not our relative? In f,
1Co 4: 3 or by a human court. In f,
1Co 15:15 if in f the dead do not rise.

FACTIONS†
1Co 11:19 For there must also be f

FACTS† (see FACT)
Dan 7: 1 dream, telling the main f.

FADE (see FADES)
Is 64: 6 We all f as a leaf, And
Jer 8:13 tree, And the leaf shall f;
1Pe 1: 4 and that does not f away,
1Pe 5: 4 of glory that does not f

FADES (see FADE)
Job 14: 2 forth like a flower and f
Is 24: 4 The world languishes and f
Is 40: 7 grass withers, the flower f,
Is 40: 8 grass withers, the flower f,

FAIL (see FAILED, FAILING, FAILS, FAILURE)
Josh 3:10 and that He will without f
1Sa 17:32 Let no man's heart f because
2Sa 3:29 and let there never f to be
Job 11:20 eyes of the wicked will f,
Ps 69: 3 My eyes f while I wait for
Ps 73:26 My flesh and my heart f;
Ps 119:123 My eyes f from seeking
Prov 22: 8 the rod of his anger will f.
Is 41:17 Their tongues f for thirst.
Is 42: 4 He will not f nor be
Is 51:14 that his bread should not f.
Jer 15:18 stream, As waters that f?
Lam 3:22 Because His compassions f
Luke 16:17 one tittle of the law to f.
Luke 22:32 that your faith should not f;
1Co 13: 8 are prophecies, they will f;
Heb 1:12 Your years will not f.
Heb 11:32 For the time would f me to

FAILED (see FAIL)
Gen 42:28 sack!" Then their hearts f
Josh 21:45 Not a word f of any good
Josh 23:14 not one word of them has f.
Ps 77: 8 Has His promise f
Lam 4:17 Still our eyes f us,

FAILING† (see FAIL)
Deut 28:65 f eyes, and anguish of soul.
Neh 4:10 of the laborers is f,
Luke 21:26 men's hearts f them from fear

FAILS (see FAIL)
Ps 38:10 my strength f me; As for
Ps 40:12 Therefore my heart f me.
Ps 143: 7 My spirit f! Do not hide
Eccl 12: 5 is a burden, And desire f.
Is 15: 6 withered away; The grass f,
1Co 13: 8 Love never f.

FAILURE (see FAIL)
1Co 6: 7 it is already an utter f for

FAINT (see FAINTED, FAINTHEARTED, FAINTS)
Deut 20: 3 Do not let your heart f,
Is 40:30 Even the youths shall f and
Is 40:31 They shall walk and not f.
Jer 8:18 My heart is f in me.
Amos 8:13 strong young men Shall f
Jon 4: 8 head, so that he grew f.
Matt 15:32 lest they f on the way."

FAINTED (see FAINT)
Ps 107: 5 Their soul f in them.
Dan 8:27 f and was sick for days;
Jon 2: 7 When my soul f within me, I

FAINTHEARTED (see FAINT)
Deut 20: 8 who is fearful and f?
Josh 2: 9 of the land are f because
Is 7: 4 do not fear or be f for
1Th 5:14 are unruly, comfort the f,

FAINTS† (see FAINT)
Ps 84: 2 even f For the courts of
Ps 119:81 My soul f for Your
Is 1: 5 sick, And the whole heart f.
Is 40:28 Neither f nor is weary.

FAIR (see FAIR-MINDED, FAIRER, FAIREST)
Song 1:15 Behold, you are f,
Song 2:10 my f one, And come away.
Song 6:10 F as the moon, Clear as
Amos 8:13 In that day the f virgins
Matt 16: 2 It will be f weather, for
Acts 27: 8 we came to a place called F
Col 4: 1 what is just and f,

FAIR-MINDED† (see FAIR)
Acts 17:11 These were more f than those

FAIRER† (see FAIR)
Ps 45: 2 You are f than the sons of

FAIREST (see FAIR)
Song 1: 8 O f among women, Follow in

FAITH (see FAITHFUL, FAITHLESS)
Deut 32:20 Children in whom is no f.
Hab 2: 4 the just shall live by his f.
Matt 6:30 you, O you of little f?
Matt 8:10 have not found such great f,
Matt 9: 2 bed. When Jesus saw their f,
Matt 9:22 your f has made you well."
Matt 15:28 great is your f! Let it be
Matt 17:20 if you have f as a mustard
Matt 23:23 law: justice and mercy and f.
Mark 11:22 Have f in God.
Luke 7: 9 have not found such great f,
Luke 7:50 Your f has saved you. Go in
Luke 17: 5 the Lord, "Increase our f.
Luke 17:19 Your f has made you well."
Luke 22:32 that your f should not fail;
Acts 3:16 the f which comes through
Acts 6: 5 a man full of f and the Holy
Acts 6: 7 were obedient to the f.
Acts 11:24 of the Holy Spirit and of f.
Acts 14: 9 and seeing that he had f to
Acts 14:22 them to continue in the f,
Acts 14:27 He had opened the door of f
Acts 15: 9 purifying their hearts by f.
Acts 16: 5 were strengthened in the f,
Acts 26:18 who are sanctified by f in
Rom 1: 8 that your f is spoken of
Rom 1:12 with you by the mutual f
Rom 1:17 is revealed from faith to f;
Rom 1:17 just shall live by f.
Rom 3:25 by His blood, through f,
Rom 3:28 that a man is justified by f

Rom	3:30 the uncircumcised through f.
Rom	3:31 make void the law through f?
Rom	4:13 the righteousness of f.
Rom	4:14 f is made void and the
Rom	4:19 And not being weak in f,
Rom	10: 6 But the righteousness of f
Rom	10: 8 the word of f which we
Rom	10:17 So then f comes by hearing,
Rom	12: 3 to each one a measure of f.
Rom	12: 6 in proportion to our f;
Rom	14:23 for whatever is not from f
1Co	13: 2 and though I have all f,
1Co	13:13 And now abide f,
1Co	15:14 is empty and your f is
1Co	15:17 your f is futile; you are
1Co	16:13 Watch, stand fast in the f,
2Co	5: 7 For we walk by f,
2Co	8: 7 abound in everything—in f,
2Co	13: 5 to whether you are in the f.
Gal	2:16 we might be justified by f
Gal	2:20 in the flesh I live by f in
Gal	3: 2 law, or by the hearing of f?
Gal	3: 7 only those who are of f
Gal	3:11 just shall live by f.
Gal	3:23 kept for the f which would
Gal	3:26 all sons of God through f
Gal	5: 6 but f working through love.
Gal	6:10 are of the household of f.
Eph	2: 8 have been saved through f,
Eph	3:17 in your hearts through f;
Eph	4: 5 one Lord, one f,
Eph	4:13 come to the unity of the f
Eph	6:16 taking the shield of f with
Phil	1:27 striving together for the f
Phil	3: 9 which is from God by f;
Col	1: 4 since we heard of your f in
Col	1:23 indeed you continue in the f,
1Th	3: 6 us good news of your f and
1Th	3:10 what is lacking in your f?
1Th	5: 8 on the breastplate of f and
1Ti	1: 2 Timothy, a true son in the f:
1Ti	1: 5 and from sincere f,
1Ti	2: 7 of the Gentiles in f and
1Ti	2:15 if they continue in f,
1Ti	3:13 and great boldness in the f
1Ti	4: 1 some will depart from the f,
1Ti	5: 8 he has denied the f and is
1Ti	5:12 have cast off their first f.
1Ti	6:12 Fight the good fight of f,
2Ti	4: 7 the race, I have kept the f.
Tit	1: 4 a true son in our common f:
Tit	1:13 they may be sound in the f,
Heb	10:22 heart in full assurance of f,
Heb	10:38 just shall live by f;
Heb	11: 1 Now f is the substance of
Heb	11: 3 By f we understand that the
Heb	11: 4 By f Abel offered to God a
Heb	11: 6 But without f it is
Heb	11:33 who through f subdued
Heb	11:39 a good testimony through f,
Heb	12: 2 and finisher of our f,
Jas	1: 3 that the testing of your f
Jas	1: 6 But let him ask in f,
Jas	2:14 if someone says he has f but
Jas	2:18 will say, "You have f,
Jas	2:20 that f without works is
Jas	2:22 and by works f was made
Jas	5:15 And the prayer of f will save
1Pe	1: 5 the power of God through f
1Pe	1: 7 the genuineness of your f,
1Pe	1: 9 receiving the end of your f—
1Pe	5: 9 him, steadfast in the f,
2Pe	1: 1 obtained like precious f
2Pe	1: 5 add to your f virtue, to
1Jn	5: 4 has overcome the world—our f.

Jude	3 contend earnestly for the f
Jude	20 up on your most holy f,
Rev	2:13 and did not deny My f even
Rev	13:10 is the patience and the f
Rev	14:12 of God and the f of Jesus.

FAITHFUL (see FAITH, FAITHFULLY, FAITHFULNESS, UNFAITHFUL)

Num	12: 7 He is f in all My house.
Deut	7: 9 the f God who keeps covenant
1Sa	2:35 will raise up for Myself a f
1Sa	22:14 all your servants is as f
2Sa	20:19 the peaceable and f in
Ps	31:23 the LORD preserves the f,
Ps	78: 8 And whose spirit was not f
Ps	89:37 Even like the f witness in
Ps	119:86 Your commandments are f;
Prov	14: 5 A f witness does not lie,
Prov	20: 6 But who can find a f man?
Prov	27: 6 F are the wounds of a
Is	1:21 How the f city has become a
Is	49: 7 of the LORD who is f,
Dan	6: 4 or fault, because he was f;
Hos	11:12 with the Holy One who is f.
Matt	24:45 Who then is a f and wise
Matt	25:21 good and f servant; you were
Matt	25:21 you were f over a few
Luke	16:10 He who is f in what is
Luke	16:10 in what is least is f
1Co	1: 9 God is f, by whom you were
1Co	4: 2 stewards that one be found f.
1Co	4:17 who is my beloved and f son
1Co	10:13 common to man; but God is f,
2Co	1:18 But as God is f,
Eph	1: 1 and f in Christ Jesus:
Eph	6:21 a beloved brother and f
Col	1: 2 To the saints and f brethren
1Th	5:24 He who calls you is f,
1Ti	1:15 This is a f saying and
1Ti	3:11 f in all things.
2Ti	2: 2 commit these to f men who
2Ti	2:13 are faithless, He remains f;
Tit	1: 9 holding fast the f word as he
Heb	2:17 He might be a merciful and f
Heb	10:23 for He who promised is f.
1Pe	4:19 as to a f Creator.
1Pe	5:12 our f brother as I consider
1Jn	1: 9 He is f and just to forgive
Rev	1: 5 the f witness, the firstborn
Rev	2:10 Be f until death, and I will
Rev	2:13 in which Antipas was My f
Rev	3:14 the F and True Witness, the
Rev	17:14 are called, chosen, and f.
Rev	21: 5 these words are true and f.

FAITHFULLY (see FAITHFUL)

| 2Ch | 34:12 And the men did the work f. |
| Jer | 23:28 let him speak My word f. |

FAITHFULNESS (see FAITHFUL)

1Sa	26:23 his righteousness and his f;
Ps	5: 9 For there is no f in their
Ps	36: 5 Your f reaches to the
Ps	40:10 I have declared Your f and
Ps	71:22 will praise you—And Your f,
Ps	89: 1 will I make known Your f to
Ps	89:24 But My f and My mercy shall
Ps	92: 2 And Your f every night,
Ps	98: 3 His mercy and His f to the
Is	11: 5 And f the belt of His
Lam	3:23 morning; Great is Your f.
Hos	2:20 will betroth you to Me in f,
Hos	6: 4 For your f is like a
Rom	3: 3 their unbelief make the f
Gal	5:22 kindness, goodness, f,

FAITHLESS (*see* FAITH)
Matt 17:17 O *f* and perverse generation,
2Ti   2:13 If we are *f*, He remains

FALL (*see* FALLEN, FALLING, FALLS, FELL)
Gen   2:21 caused a deep sleep to *f* on
Ex   5: 3 lest He *f* upon us with
Ex   15:16 Fear and dread will *f* on
Josh   6: 5 the wall of the city will *f*
Ruth   2:16 grain from the bundles *f*
1Sa   3:19 and let none of his words *f*
Job   13:11 And the dread of Him *f* upon
Job   31:22 Then let my arm *f* from my
Job   37: 6 *F* on the earth'; Likewise
Ps   37:24 Though he *f*, he shall not
Ps   45: 5 The peoples *f* under You.
Ps   91: 7 A thousand may *f* at your
Ps   139:11 the darkness shall *f*
Ps   140:10 Let burning coals *f* upon
Ps   141:10 Let the wicked *f* into their
Ps   145:14 The LORD upholds all who *f*,
Prov 11:14 is no counsel, the people *f*;
Prov 11:28 trusts in his riches will *f*,
Prov 16:18 a haughty spirit before a *f*.
Prov 24:16 But the wicked shall *f* by
Eccl 10: 8 He who digs a pit will *f*
Is   10: 4 And they shall *f* among the
Is   28:13 That they might go and *f*
Is   40:30 young men shall utterly *f*,
Is   44:19 Shall I *f* down before a
Is   47:11 And trouble shall *f* upon
Jer   8: 4 Will they *f* and not rise?
Jer   8:12 shall fall among those who *f*;
Jer   9:22 carcasses of men shall *f* as
Jer   46: 6 They will stumble and *f*
Jer   51:44 the wall of Babylon shall *f*.
Dan   3: 6 and whoever does not *f* down
Dan   11:14 the vision, but they shall *f*.
Hos   10: 8 to the hills, "*F* on us!"
Amos   3: 5 Will a bird *f* into a snare
Matt   4: 9 will give You if You will *f*
Matt   7:25 that house; and it did not *f*,
Matt   7:27 it fell. And great was its *f*.
Matt 15:14 both will *f* into a ditch."
Matt 15:27 dogs eat the crumbs which *f*
Matt 24:29 the stars will *f* from
Luke   2:34 is destined for the *f* and
Luke   8:13 and in time of temptation *f*
Luke 10:18 I saw Satan *f* like lightning
Luke 23:30 *F* on us!" and to the
Acts   5:15 of Peter passing by might *f*
Rom   3:23 for all have sinned and *f*
Rom   11:12 Now if their *f* is riches for
Rom   14:13 block or a cause to *f* in
1Co   10:12 stands take heed lest he *f*.
1Ti   3: 6 puffed up with pride he *f*
1Ti   3: 7 lest he *f* into reproach and
1Ti   6: 9 who desire to be rich *f*
Heb   6: 6 if they *f* away, to renew them
Heb   10:31 It is a fearful thing to *f*
Jas   1: 2 count it all joy when you *f*
Jas   5:12 lest you *f* into judgment.
Rev   4:10 the twenty-four elders *f* down
Rev   6:16 *F* on us and hide us from the

FALLEN (*see* FALL)
Gen   4: 6 why has your countenance *f*?
Josh   2: 9 the terror of you has *f* on
Judg   3:25 *f* dead on the floor.
Judg 19:27 *f* at the door of the house
1Sa   5: 4 *f* on its face to the ground
2Sa   1:19 How the mighty have *f*!
2Sa   3:38 and a great man has *f* this
2Ki   2:13 mantle of Elijah that had *f*
Ps   7:15 And has *f* into the ditch
Ps   16: 6 The lines have *f* to me in

Ps   36:12 workers of iniquity have *f*;
Ps   55: 4 the terrors of death have *f*
Ps   69: 9 who reproach You have *f* on
Is   14:12 How you are *f* from heaven,
Is   59:14 For truth is *f* in the
Lam   2:21 and my young men Have *f* by
Lam   5:16 The crown has *f* from our
Hos   7: 7 All their kings have *f*.
Amos   5: 2 The virgin of Israel has *f*;
Amos   9:11 which has *f* down, And
Matt 27:52 of the saints who had *f*
Luke 14: 5 a donkey or an ox that has *f*
Acts   8:16 For as yet He had *f* upon none
Acts 15:16 which has *f* down; I
1Co   5:18 Then also those who have *f*
Gal   5: 4 you have *f* from grace.
Rev   2: 5 from where you have *f*;
Rev   9: 1 And I saw a star *f* from
Rev   14: 8 saying, "Babylon is *f*,
Rev   14: 8 "Babylon is *f*, is *f*,
Rev   17:10 seven kings. Five have *f*,
Rev   18: 2 "Babylon the great is *f*,
Rev   18: 2 the great is *f*, is *f*,

FALLING (*see* FALL)
Ps   116: 8 tears, And my feet from *f*.
Is   34: 4 And as fruit *f* from a fig
Luke   8:47 and *f* down before Him, she
Luke 22:44 like great drops of blood *f*
Acts   1:18 and *f* headlong, he burst
1Co   14:25 *f* down on his face, he will
2Th   2: 3 not come unless the *f*

FALLOW
Ex   23:11 shall let it rest and lie *f*,
Jer   4: 3 Break up your *f* ground, And

FALLS (*see* FALL)
Ex   21:33 and an ox or a donkey *f* in
Num   24: 4 Who *f* down, with eyes wide
Num   24:16 Who *f* down, with eyes wide
Num   33:54 shall be whatever *f* to him
Deut 22: 8 your household if anyone *f*
2Sa   3:29 who leans on a staff or *f* by
2Sa   17:12 fall on him as the dew *f* on
Job   4:13 When deep sleep *f* on men,
Job   30:30 My skin grows black and *f*
Prov 13:17 A wicked messenger *f* into
Prov 17:20 who has a perverse tongue *f*
Prov 24:17 rejoice when your enemy *f*,
Eccl   9:12 When it *f* suddenly upon
Is   44:15 and *f* down to it.
Matt 12:11 and if it *f* into a pit on
Matt 17:15 for he often *f* into the fire
Matt 21:44 And whoever *f* on this stone
Matt 21:44 broken; but on whomever it *f*,
Luke 11:17 divided against a house *f*.
Luke 15:12 the portion of goods that *f*
John 12:24 unless a grain of wheat *f*
Rom   14: 4 own master he stands or *f*.
Jas   1:11 the grass; its flower *f*,
1Pe   1:24 And its flower *f* away,
Rev   11: 6 so that no rain *f* in the

FALSE (*see* FALSEHOOD, FALSELY, FALSIFYING)
Ex   20:16 You shall not bear *f* witness
Deut   5:20 You shall not bear *f* witness
Ps   119:104 Therefore I hate every *f*
Ps   119:128 I hate every *f* way.
Prov   6:19 A *f* witness who speaks
Jer   8: 8 the *f* pen of the scribe
Jer   23:32 those who prophesy *f* dreams,
Zech   8:17 And do not love a *f* oath.
Matt   7:15 Beware of *f* prophets, who
Matt 19:18 You shall not bear *f*
Matt 24:11 Then many *f* prophets will
Matt 24:24 For false christs and *f*

Matt   26:60 But at last two **f** witnesses
Luke   19: 8 anything from anyone by **f**
Rom   13: 9 You shall not bear **f**
2Co   11:13 For such are **f** apostles,
2Co   11:26 in perils among **f** brethren;
Col   2:18 taking delight in **f**
2Pe   2: 1 But there were also **f**
2Pe   2: 1 even as there will be **f**
Rev   20:10 where the beast and the **f**

FALSEHOOD (see FALSE)
Job   31: 5 "If I have walked with **f**,
Ps   5: 6 destroy those who speak **f**;
Ps   7:14 trouble and brings forth **f**.
Ps   119:78 treated me wrongfully with **f**;
Prov   30: 8 Remove **f** and lies far from
Is   57: 4 Offspring of **f**,
Jer   8: 8 the scribe certainly works **f**.
Jer   10:14 For his molded image is **f**,

FALSELY (see FALSE)
Gen   21:23 God that you will not deal **f**
Lev   6: 3 concerning it, and swears **f**—
Lev   19:11 shall not steal, nor deal **f**,
Lev   19:12 shall not swear by My name **f**,
Deut   19:18 who has testified **f** against
Jer   5:31 The prophets prophesy **f**,
Jer   6:13 priest, Everyone deals **f**.
Jer   43: 2 You speak **f**! The LORD our
Matt   5:11 kinds of evil against you **f**
Matt   5:33 old, 'You shall not swear **f**,
1Ti   6:20 contradictions of what is **f**

FALSIFYING† (see FALSE)
Amos   8: 5 F the scales by deceit,

FALTER† (see FALTERS)
1Ki   18:21 How long will you **f** between

FALTERS† (see FALTER)
Prov   25:26 A righteous man who **f**

FAME (see FAMOUS)
Num   14:15 which have heard of Your **f**
Josh   9: 9 for we have heard of His **f**,
1Ch   14:17 Then the **f** of David went out
Ps   135:13 endures forever, Your **f**,
Is   66:19 off who have not heard My **f**
Matt   4:24 Then His **f** went throughout
Mark   1:28 And immediately His **f** spread

FAMILIAR (see UNFAMILIAR)
Lev   19:31 no regard to mediums and **f**
Ps   41: 9 Even my own **f** friend in whom

FAMILIES (see FAMILY)
Gen   8:19 earth, according to their **f**,
Gen   10:32 These were the **f** of the
Gen   12: 3 And in you all the **f** of the
Num   1:18 recited their ancestry by **f**,
Num   3:15 fathers' houses, by their **f**;
Num   33:54 an inheritance among your **f**;
Num   36: 1 of the **f** of the sons of
Num   36:12 were married into the **f** of
Josh   7:14 shall come according to **f**;
Josh   21: 5 cities by lot from the **f** of
Josh   21: 6 cities by lot from the **f** of
1Ch   2:55 And the **f** of the scribes who
1Ch   4:38 were leaders in their **f**,
1Ch   5: 7 And his brethren by their **f**,
1Ch   16:28 O of the peoples, Give to
Job   31:34 dreaded the contempt of **f**,
Ps   22:27 And all the **f** of the
Ps   68: 6 God sets the solitary in **f**;
Ps   96: 7 O of the peoples, Give to
Ps   107:41 And makes their **f** like a
Jer   1:15 I am calling All the **f** of
Jer   25: 9 send and take all the **f** of
Jer   31: 1 be the God of all the **f** of

Jer   33:24 The two **f** which the LORD has
Amos   3: 2 have I known of all the **f**
Acts   3:25 in your seed all the **f**

FAMILY (see FAMILIES)
Gen   12: 1 From your **f** And from your
Gen   24: 4 go to my country and to my **f**,
Gen   24:38 father's house and to my **f**,
Lev   25:47 a member of the stranger's **f**,
Num   2:34 camp, each one by his **f**,
Num   26:40 the **f** of the Ardites; of
Num   26:58 and the **f** of the Korathites.
Num   27: 4 be removed from among his **f**
Num   27:11 closest him in his **f**,
Num   36: 6 may marry only within the **f**
Num   36:12 tribe of their father's **f**.
Deut   25: 5 a stranger outside the **f**;
Judg   1:25 let the man and all his **f**
Judg   18:19 a priest to a tribe and a **f**
Judg   21:24 every man to his tribe and **f**;
Ruth   2: 1 of the **f** of Elimelech. His
Ruth   2: 3 who was of the **f** of
1Sa   9:21 and my **f** the least of all
1Sa   10:21 the **f** of Matri was chosen.
2Ki   25:25 of Elishama, of the royal **f**,
Esth   2:10 not revealed her people or **f**,
Jer   3:14 from a city and two from a **f**,
Jer   8: 3 who remain of this evil **f**,
Amos   3: 1 against the whole **f** which I
Zech   12:12 the **f** of the house of David
Acts   4: 6 as many as were of the **f** of
Acts   7:13 and Joseph's **f** became known
Acts   13:26 sons of the **f** of Abraham,
Acts   16:33 he and all his **f** were
Eph   3:15 from whom the whole **f** in

FAMINE (see FAMINES)
Gen   12:10 for the **f** was severe in the
Gen   26: 1 besides the first **f** that was
Gen   41:27 wind are seven years of **f**.
Gen   41:54 The **f** was in all lands, but
Gen   45:11 are still five years of **f**.
Ruth   1: 1 that there was a **f** in the
2Sa   21: 1 Now there was a **f** in the days
2Sa   24:13 Shall seven years of **f** come
2Ki   8: 1 the LORD has called for a **f**,
1Ch   21:12 'either three years of **f**
2Ch   20: 9 judgment, pestilence, or **f**—
Neh   5: 3 buy grain because of the **f**.
Job   5:22 laugh at destruction and **f**,
Job   30: 3 are gaunt from want and **f**,
Ps   33:19 And to keep them alive in **f**.
Is   51:19 **f** and sword—By whom will I
Jer   5:12 Nor shall we see sword or **f**
Jer   14:15 By sword and **f** those prophets
Jer   14:18 those sick from **f**! Yes,
Jer   15: 2 And such as are for the **f**,
Jer   15: 2 for the famine, to the **f**;
Jer   16: 4 by the sword and by **f**,
Jer   34:17 and to **f**! And I will deliver
Lam   5:10 Because of the fever of **f**.
Ezek   5:12 and be consumed with **f** in
Ezek   14:21 the sword and **f** and wild
Ezek   36:29 and bring no **f** upon you.
Ezek   36:30 again bear the reproach of **f**
Amos   8:11 That I will send a **f** on the
Amos   8:11 Not a **f** of bread, Nor a
Luke   4:25 and there was a great **f**
Rom   8:35 or persecution, or **f**,
Rev   18: 8 day—death and mourning and **f**.

FAMINES (see FAMINE)
Matt   24: 7 kingdom. And there will be **f**,

FAMOUS (see FAME)
Ruth   4:11 in Ephrathah and be **f** in
Ps   136:18 And slew **f** kings, For His

FAN (see UNFANNED)
Jer 15: 7 them with a winnowing **f** in
Matt 3:12 His winnowing **f** is in His
Luke 3:17 His winnowing **f** is in His

FANGS
Job 29:17 I broke the **f** of the wicked,
Prov 30:14 And whose **f** are like

FANTASY†
Prov 21: 6 tongue Is the fleeting **f**

FARE† (see FARED)
1Sa 17:18 and see how your brothers **f**,
Jon 1: 3 Tarshish; so he paid the **f**,

FARED† (see FARE)
Luke 16:19 purple and fine linen and **f**

FAREWELL
Luke 9:61 me first go and bid them **f**
2Co 13:11 Finally, brethren, **f**.

FARMER
Gen 9:20 And Noah began to be a **f**,
Zech 13: 5 'I am no prophet, I am a **f**;
2Ti 2: 6 The hard-working **f** must be
Jas 5: 7 See how the **f** waits for the

FARTHEST
Is 7:18 the fly That is in the **f**
Is 37:24 I will enter its **f** height,
Jer 9:26 and all who are in the **f**
Mark 13:27 part of earth to the **f** part

FASHION (see FASHIONED, FASHIONS)
Job 31:15 Did not the same One **f** us

FASHIONED (see FASHION)
Job 10: 8 hands have made me and **f** me,
Ps 119:73 hands have made me and **f** me;
Ps 139:16 The days **f** for me, When

FASHIONS (see FASHION)
Ps 33:15 He **f** their hearts

FAST (see FASTED, FASTING)
Deut 4: 4 But you who held **f** to the
Judg 4:21 for he was **f** asleep and
1Ki 21: 9 saying, Proclaim a **f**,
Esth 4:16 My maids and I will **f**
Job 2: 3 And still he holds **f** to his
Job 27: 6 My righteousness I hold **f**,
Ps 33: 9 commanded, and it stood **f**.
Ps 111: 8 They stand **f** forever and
Is 56: 4 And hold **f** My covenant,
Is 58: 4 You will not **f** as you do
Is 58: 5 Would you call this a **f**,
Joel 1:14 Consecrate a **f**,
Jon 1: 5 and was **f** asleep.
Jon 3: 5 believed God, proclaimed a **f**,
Zech 8:19 And the **f** of the tenth,
Matt 6:16 "Moreover, when you **f**,
Matt 9:14 do we and the Pharisees **f**
Matt 9:14 but Your disciples do not **f**?
Luke 18:12 I **f** twice a week; I give
Acts 27: 9 now dangerous because the F
Acts 27:41 and the prow stuck **f** and
1Co 15: 2 if you hold **f** that word
1Co 16:13 stand **f** in the faith, be
Gal 5: 1 Stand **f** therefore in the
Phil 1:27 that you stand **f** in one
Phil 2:16 holding **f** the word of life,
Phil 4: 1 so stand **f** in the Lord,
Col 2:19 and not holding **f** to the
1Th 5:21 hold **f** what is good.
2Ti 1:13 Hold **f** the pattern of sound
Tit 1: 9 holding **f** the faithful word
Heb 3: 6 house we are if we hold **f**
Heb 4:14 let us hold **f** our

Rev 2:13 And you hold **f** to My name,
Rev 3:11 I am coming quickly! Hold **f**

FASTED (see FAST)
Judg 20:26 before the LORD and **f** that
1Sa 31:13 and **f** seven days.
2Sa 12:16 and David **f** and went in and
Ezra 8:23 So we **f** and entreated our God
Is 58: 3 'Why have we **f**,
Matt 4: 2 And when He had **f** forty days
Acts 13: 3 having **f** and prayed, and

FASTENED
Judg 3:16 a cubit in length) and **f** it
1Sa 17:39 David **f** his sword to his
1Sa 31:10 and they **f** his body to the
Acts 16:24 into the inner prison and **f**
Acts 28: 3 and **f** on his hand.

FASTING (see FAST, FASTINGS)
Ezra 9: 5 sacrifice I arose from my **f**;
Neh 1: 4 I was **f** and praying before
Neh 9: 1 Israel were assembled with **f**,
Ps 35:13 I humbled myself with **f**;
Ps 69:10 chastened my soul with **f**,
Ps 109:24 My knees are weak through **f**,
Jer 36: 6 house on the day of **f**.
Dan 6:18 palace and spent the night **f**;
Dan 9: 3 and supplications, with **f**,
Matt 6:16 may appear to men to be **f**.
Matt 17:21 out except by prayer and **f**
Mark 2:18 and of the Pharisees were **f**.
Acts 14:23 church, and prayed with **f**,
1Co 7: 5 you may give yourselves to **f**

FASTINGS† (see FASTING)
Luke 2:37 but served God with **f** and
2Co 6: 5 in sleeplessness, in **f**;
2Co 11:27 in **f** often, in cold and

FAT (see FATNESS, FATTED, FATTENED, FATTER, FATTY)
Gen 4: 4 of his flock and of their **f**.
Gen 41: 2 cows, fine looking and **f**;
Ex 29:22 the **f** that covers the
Ex 29:22 the two kidneys and the **f** on
Lev 3:16 all the **f** is the LORD's.
Lev 16:25 The **f** of the sin offering he
Deut 31:20 themselves and grown **f**,
Judg 3:17 (Now Eglon was a very **f**
Judg 3:22 and the **f** closed over the
1Sa 2:15 before they burned the **f**,
1Sa 15:22 And to heed than the **f** of
Neh 8:10 "Go your way, eat the **f**,
Ps 17:10 They have closed up their **f**
Ps 66:15 You burnt sacrifices of **f**
Ps 119:70 Their heart is as **f** as
Ezek 34:16 but I will destroy the **f** and
Ezek 34:20 will judge between the **f**
Mal 4: 2 you shall go out And grow **f**

FATE
Num 16:29 are visited by the common **f**

FATHER (see FATHER-IN-LAW, FATHERED, FATHERLESS, FATHER'S, FATHERS, GRANDFATHER)
Gen 2:24 a man shall leave his **f** and
Gen 4:20 He was the **f** of those who
Gen 9:18 And Ham was the **f** of
Gen 9:22 saw the nakedness of his **f**,
Gen 11:28 And Haran died before his **f**
Gen 17: 5 for I have made you a **f** of
Gen 19:31 Our **f** is old, and there is
Gen 19:32 the lineage of our **f**.
Gen 19:33 went in and lay with her **f**,
Gen 19:36 were with child by their **f**.
Gen 20:12 She is the daughter of my **f**,
Gen 22: 7 My **f**!" And he said, "Here I
Gen 26: 3 I swore to Abraham your **f**.

Gen	26:24	I am the God of your **f**
Gen	27:12	Perhaps my **f** will feel me,
Gen	27:14	such as his **f** loved.
Gen	27:31	father, and said to his **f**,
Gen	27:31	Let my **f** arise and eat of his
Gen	27:34	O my **f**!"
Gen	27:38	O my **f**!" And Esau lifted up
Gen	28: 8	Canaan did not please his **f**
Gen	28:13	LORD God of Abraham your **f**
Gen	31: 5	but the God of my **f** has been
Gen	31:53	and the God of their **f** judge
Gen	31:53	swore by the Fear of his **f**
Gen	32: 9	Abraham and God of my **f**
Gen	35:18	but his **f** called him
Gen	37: 2	bad report of them to his **f**.
Gen	37: 4	brothers saw that their **f**
Gen	37:10	and his **f** rebuked him and
Gen	37:11	but his **f** kept the matter
Gen	42:13	the youngest is with our **f**
Gen	42:29	they went to Jacob their **f**
Gen	43: 7	Is your **f** still alive? Have
Gen	43: 8	Judah said to Israel his **f**,
Gen	43:27	Is your **f** well, the old man
Gen	44:22	if he should leave his **f**,
Gen	44:22	his **f** would die.'
Gen	44:24	went up to your servant my **f**,
Gen	44:31	hair of your servant our **f**
Gen	45: 8	and He has made me a **f** to
Gen	45:27	the spirit of Jacob their **f**
Gen	46: 1	to the God of his **f** Isaac.
Gen	47:11	And Joseph situated his **f**
Gen	48:18	his father, "Not so, my **f**,
Gen	48:19	But his **f** refused and said,
Gen	50: 2	physicians to embalm his **f**.
Gen	50: 5	let me go up and bury my **f**,
Gen	50:10	days of mourning for his **f**.
Ex	3: 6	"I am the God of your **f**—
Ex	20:12	Honor your **f** and your
Ex	21:15	And he who strikes his **f** or
Ex	21:17	And he who curses his **f** or
Lev	18: 7	The nakedness of your **f** or
Lev	21: 9	harlot, she profanes her **f**.
Lev	24:10	whose **f** was an Egyptian,
Num	27: 3	Our **f** died in the wilderness;
Num	27:11	And if his **f** has no brothers,
Deut	5:16	Honor your **f** and your
Deut	26: 5	My **f** was a Syrian, about to
Deut	32: 6	people? Is He not your **F**,
Josh	2:13	"and spare my **f**,
Josh	15:18	persuaded him to ask her **f**
Josh	24: 2	father of Abraham and the **f**
Josh	24: 3	Then I took your **f** Abraham
Judg	1:14	she urged him to ask her **f**
Judg	6:25	altar of Baal that your **f**
Judg	11:39	that she returned to her **f**,
Judg	14: 3	And Samson said to his **f**,
Judg	18:19	be a **f** and a priest to us.
Ruth	4:17	the **f** of David.
1Sa	9: 3	donkeys of Kish, Saul's **f**,
1Sa	19: 2	My **f** Saul seeks to kill you.
2Sa	7:14	"I will be his **F**,
1Ki	1: 6	(And his **f** had not rebuked
1Ki	2:12	sat on the throne of his **f**
1Ki	3: 3	in the statutes of his **f**
1Ki	3: 6	to Your servant David my **f**,
1Ki	3:14	as your **f** David walked, then
1Ki	11:27	to the City of David his **f**.
1Ki	12:11	my **f** chastised you with
1Ki	15: 3	in all the sins of his **f**,
1Ki	15:26	walked in the way of his **f**,
1Ki	20:34	as my **f** did in Samaria."
2Ki	2:12	cried out, "My father, my **f**,
2Ki	3: 2	pillar of Baal that his **f**
2Ki	13:14	his face, and said, "O my **f**,
2Ki	13:14	said, "O my father, my **f**,

2Ki	14: 3	he did everything as his **f**
2Ki	21:21	served the idols that his **f**
1Ch	22:10	son, and I will be his **F**;
1Ch	28: 4	and among the sons of my **f**,
1Ch	29:10	LORD God of Israel, our **F**,
2Ch	7:18	covenanted with David your **f**,
Esth	2: 7	for she had neither **f** nor
Job	17:14	corruption, 'You are my **f**,
Job	29:16	I was a **f** to the poor, And
Job	38:28	Has the rain a **f**?
Job	42:15	and their **f** gave them an
Ps	68: 5	A **f** of the fatherless, a
Ps	89:26	cry to Me, 'You are my **F**,
Ps	103:13	As a **f** pities his children,
Prov	1: 8	the instruction of your **f**,
Prov	3:12	Just as a **f** the son in
Prov	10: 1	A wise son makes a glad **f**,
Prov	17:21	And the **f** of a fool has no
Prov	17:25	son is a grief to his **f**,
Prov	20:20	Whoever curses his **f** or his
Prov	28:24	Whoever robs his **f** or his
Prov	29: 3	loves wisdom makes his **f**
Prov	30:17	The eye that mocks his **f**,
Is	8: 4	My **f** and 'My mother,' the
Is	9: 6	Mighty God, Everlasting **F**,
Is	22:21	He shall be a **f** to the
Is	43:27	Your first **f** sinned, And
Is	45:10	to him who says to his **f**,
Is	51: 2	Look to Abraham your **f**,
Is	58:14	the heritage of Jacob your **f**.
Is	63:16	Doubtless You are our **F**,
Is	63:16	You, O LORD, are our **F**,
Is	64: 8	O LORD, You are our **F**;
Jer	2:27	to a tree, 'You are my **f**,
Jer	3:19	'You shall call Me, "My **F**,
Jer	12: 6	the house of your **f**,
Jer	20:15	Who brought news to my **f**,
Jer	22:15	Did not your **f** eat and
Jer	31: 9	For I am a **F** to Israel,
Ezek	16: 3	your **f** was an Amorite and
Ezek	16:45	was a Hittite and your **f**
Ezek	18: 4	The soul of the **f** As well
Ezek	18:14	all the sins which his **f**
Ezek	18:17	for the iniquity of his **f**;
Ezek	18:18	"As for his **f**,
Ezek	18:19	not bear the guilt of the **f**?
Ezek	18:20	nor the **f** bear the guilt of
Dan	5:11	King Nebuchadnezzar your **f**—
Amos	2: 7	A man and his **f** go in to
Mic	7: 6	For son dishonors **f**,
Mal	1: 6	"A son honors his **f**,
Mal	1: 6	master. If then I am the **F**,
Mal	2:10	Have we not all one **F**?
Matt	2:22	over Judea instead of his **f**
Matt	3: 9	'We have Abraham as our **f**.
Matt	4:21	boat with Zebedee their **f**,
Matt	5:16	works and glorify your **F** in
Matt	6: 4	and your **F** who sees in
Matt	6: 6	and your **F** who sees in
Matt	6: 9	Our **F** in heaven, Hallowed
Matt	6:26	yet your heavenly **F** feeds
Matt	7:21	he who does the will of My **F**
Matt	8:21	me first go and bury my **f**.
Matt	10:35	a man against his **f**,
Matt	10:37	He who loves **f** or mother more
Matt	11:25	and said, "I thank You, **F**,
Matt	11:26	"Even so, **F**, for so it
Matt	11:27	knows the Son except the **F**.
Matt	13:43	in the kingdom of their **F**.
Matt	15: 4	Honor your **f** and your
Matt	15: 4	He who curses **f** or
Matt	16:17	but My **F** who is in heaven.
Matt	16:27	come in the glory of His **F**
Matt	19: 5	man shall leave his **f**
Matt	19:29	or brothers or sisters or **f**

Matt 23: 9 call anyone on earth your f;
Matt 23: 9 father; for One is your F,
Matt 25:34 'Come, you blessed of My F,
Matt 28:19 them in the name of the F
Mark 13:32 nor the Son, but only the F.
Mark 14:36 And He said, "Abba, F,
Luke 1:32 give Him the throne of His f
Luke 2:48 Your f and I have sought You
Luke 3: 8 'We have Abraham as our f.
Luke 9:59 me first go and bury my f.
Luke 15:12 them said to his father, 'F,
Luke 15:18 'I will arise and go to my f,
Luke 15:27 your f has killed the fatted
Luke 16:24 F Abraham, have mercy on me,
Luke 18:20 Honor your f and your
Luke 23:34 Then Jesus said, "F,
Luke 23:46 a loud voice, He said, "F,
Luke 24:49 I send the Promise of My F
John 1:14 the only begotten of the F,
John 1:18 who is in the bosom of the F,
John 3:35 The F loves the Son, and has
John 4:12 Are You greater than our f
John 4:23 will worship the F in
John 5:17 My F has been working until
John 5:18 also said that God was His F,
John 5:26 For as the F has life in
John 5:30 will but the will of the F
John 5:36 that the F has sent Me.
John 5:45 I shall accuse you to the F;
John 6:44 can come to Me unless the F
John 8:19 to Him, "Where is Your F?
John 8:19 you would have known My F
John 8:29 The F has not left Me alone,
John 8:38 you have seen with your f.
John 8:39 to Him, "Abraham is our f.
John 8:41 fornication; we have one F—
John 8:44 You are of your f the devil,
John 8:44 for he is a liar and the f
John 8:53 Are You greater than our f
John 8:56 Your f Abraham rejoiced to
John 10:15 Me, even so I know the F;
John 10:30 I and My F are one."
John 10:38 know and believe that the F
John 11:41 up His eyes and said, "F,
John 12:27 and what shall I say? 'F,
John 13: 1 from this world to the F,
John 13: 3 knowing that the F had given
John 14: 6 No one comes to the F except
John 14: 8 Him, "Lord, show us the F,
John 14: 9 has seen Me has seen the F;
John 14:12 do, because I go to My F.
John 14:16 "And I will pray the F,
John 14:20 will know that I am in My F,
John 14:28 for My F is greater than I.
John 14:31 and as the F gave Me
John 15: 1 and My F is the vinedresser.
John 15: 8 By this My F is glorified,
John 15:16 that whatever you ask the F
John 15:23 He who hates Me hates My F
John 15:26 who proceeds from the F
John 16:23 whatever you ask the F in My
John 16:26 you that I shall pray the F
John 16:28 I came forth from the F and
John 17: 1 to heaven, and said: "F,
John 17:11 and I come to You. Holy F,
John 17:21 all may be one, as You, F,
John 17:25 O righteous F! The world has
John 18:11 not drink the cup which My F
John 20:17 to My Father and your F,
John 20:21 Peace to you! As the F has
Acts 1: 4 for the Promise of the F,
Acts 2:33 having received from the F
Rom 1: 7 you and peace from God our F
Rom 4:11 that he might be the f of
Rom 4:12 of the faith which our f

Rom 4:16 who is the f of us all
Rom 6: 4 dead by the glory of the F,
Rom 8:15 whom we cry out, "Abba, F.
Rom 15: 6 mouth glorify the God and F
1Co 8: 6 us there is one God, the F,
2Co 1: 3 the F of mercies and God of
2Co 6:18 I will be a F to you, And
Gal 1: 1 Jesus Christ and God the F
Eph 1:17 the F of glory, may give to
Eph 2:18 by one Spirit to the F.
Eph 4: 6 one God and F of all, who is
Phil 2:11 to the glory of God the F.
Phil 4:20 Now to our God and F be
Col 2: 2 both of the F and of Christ,
Col 3:17 giving thanks to God the F
Heb 1: 5 will be to Him a F,
Heb 7: 3 without f, without mother,
Heb 12: 9 be in subjection to the F
Jas 1:17 and comes down from the F of
Jas 1:27 before God and the F is
Jas 2:21 Was not Abraham our f
Jas 3: 9 it we bless our God and F,
1Pe 1: 2 foreknowledge of God the F,
2Pe 1:17 He received from God the F
1Jn 1: 2 life which was with the F
1Jn 1: 3 fellowship is with the F
1Jn 2: 1 have an Advocate with the F,
1Jn 2:15 the love of the F is not in
1Jn 2:22 antichrist who denies the F
1Jn 3: 1 what manner of love the F
1Jn 4:14 seen and testify that the F
1Jn 5: 7 witness in heaven: the F,
2Jn 3 Christ, the Son of the F,
Rev 1: 6 and priests to His God and F,
Rev 3: 5 his name before My F and

FATHER-IN-LAW (see FATHER)
Ex 3: 1 the flock of Jethro his f,
Ex 18: 1 priest of Midian, Moses' f,
Num 10:29 the Midianite, Moses' f,
John 18:13 for he was the f of Caiaphas

FATHER'S (see FATHER)
Gen 12: 1 your family And from your f
Gen 26:15 up all the wells which his f
Gen 37:12 went to feed their f flock
Gen 50: 1 Then Joseph fell on his f
Ex 6:20 his f sister, as wife; and
Ex 15: 2 My f God, and I will exalt
Lev 18: 8 The nakedness of your f wife
Lev 18: 8 it is your f nakedness.
Num 1: 4 each one the head of his f
Deut 22:30 nor uncover his f bed.
Judg 6:15 and I am the least in my f
1Sa 22:22 of all the persons of your f
2Sa 2:32 and buried him in his f
2Sa 9: 7 for Jonathan your f sake,
2Sa 15:34 as I was your f servant
2Sa 16:21 Go in to your f concubines,
1Ki 12:10 shall be thicker than my f
2Ki 10: 3 set him on his f throne,
2Ch 21:13 those of your f household,
Ezra 2:59 could not identify their f
Esth 4:14 but you and your f house
Ps 45:10 and your f house;
Prov 4: 3 When I was my f son, Tender
Prov 6:20 keep your f command, And do
Prov 13: 1 A wise son heeds his f
Prov 15: 5 A fool despises his f
Is 7:17 and your people and your f
Matt 10:29 the ground apart from your F
Matt 26:29 it new with you in My F
Luke 2:49 that I must be about My F
Luke 15:17 How many of my f hired
John 2:16 away! Do not make My F
John 5:43 I have come in My F name, and

John   10:29 to snatch them out of My **F**
John   14: 2 In My **F** house are many
John   14:24 hear is not Mine but the **F**
John   15:10 just as I have kept My **F**
1Co   5: 1 that a man has his **f** wife!
Rev   14: 1 having His **F** name written on

FATHERED† (*see* FATHER)
Deut   32:18 forgotten the God who **f** you.

FATHERLESS (*see* FATHER)
Ex   22:22 not afflict any widow or **f**
Ex   22:24 widows, and your children **f**.
Deut   10:18 justice for the **f** and the
Deut   14:29 and the stranger and the **f**
Deut   16:14 the stranger and the **f** and
Job   6:27 Yes, you overwhelm the **f**,
Job   22: 9 And the strength of the **f**
Job   24: 9 Some snatch the **f** from the
Job   29:12 The **f** and the one who
Ps   10:14 You are the helper of the **f**.
Ps   68: 5 A father of the **f**,
Ps   109: 9 Let his children be **f**,
Prov   23:10 enter the fields of the **f**;
Is   1:17 the oppressor; Defend the **f**,
Hos   14: 3 For in You the **f** finds
Zech   7:10 oppress the widow or the **f**,

FATHERS (*see* FATHER, FATHERS', FOREFATHERS)
Gen   15:15 you shall go to your **f** in
Gen   31: 3 to the land of your **f** and
Gen   47:30 "but let me lie with my **f**;
Gen   48:16 And the name of my **f**
Gen   49:29 bury me with my **f** in the
Ex   3:13 The God of your **f** has sent me
Ex   3:15 'The LORD God of your **f**,
Ex   10: 6 fathers nor your fathers' **f**
Ex   13: 5 which He swore to your **f** to
Ex   20: 5 the iniquity of the **f** on
Ex   34: 7 the iniquity of the **f** upon
Num   20:15 how our **f** went down to Egypt,
Num   20:15 afflicted us and our **f**.
Num   26:55 of the tribes of their **f**.
Num   31:26 the priest and the chief **f**
Deut   1: 8 the LORD swore to your **f**—
Deut   4: 1 the LORD God of your **f** is
Deut   5: 3 this covenant with our **f**,
Deut   24:16 **F** shall not be put to death
Deut   28:36 neither you nor your **f** have
Deut   30: 5 you and your rest with your **f**.
Deut   31:16 you will rest with your **f**;
Josh   4:21 your children ask their **f**
Josh   24: 6 Then I brought your **f** out of
Josh   24: 6 the Egyptians pursued your **f**
Judg   2:10 had been gathered to their **f**,
Judg   2:19 more corruptly than their **f**,
1Sa   12: 8 and your **f** cried out to the
2Sa   7:12 and you rest with your **f**,
1Ki   2:10 So David rested with his **f**,
1Ki   15:12 all the idols that his **f**
1Ki   21: 3 the inheritance of my **f** to
2Ki   9:28 him in his tomb with his **f**
2Ki   14:16 So Jehoash rested with his **f**,
2Ki   17:13 law which I commanded your **f**,
2Ki   20:17 and what your **f** have
2Ki   21:22 the LORD God of his **f**,
1Ch   28:18 Isaac, and Israel, our **f**,
2Ch   14: 4 the LORD God of their **f**,
2Ch   15:12 the LORD God of their **f**
2Ch   25: 4 be put to death for their **f**;
2Ch   26:23 they buried him with his **f**
2Ch   28: 9 the LORD God of your **f** was
2Ch   29: 6 For our **f** have trespassed and
2Ch   30: 8 as your **f** were, but yield
Ezra   4:15 of the records of your **f**.
Ezra   5:12 But because our **f** provoked

Neh   9: 9 saw the affliction of our **f**
Neh   9:16 But they and our **f** acted
Job   15:18 received from their **f**,
Ps   22: 4 Our **f** trusted in You; They
Ps   39:12 as all my **f** were.
Ps   49:19 to the generation of his **f**;
Ps   78: 3 And our **f** have told us.
Ps   95: 9 When your **f** tested Me; They
Ps   106: 6 We have sinned with our **f**,
Is   49:23 shall be your Father's
Jer   7: 7 land that I gave to your **f**
Jer   7:26 They did worse than their **f**.
Jer   9:14 which their **f** taught them,"
Jer   16:11 Because your **f** have forsaken
Jer   16:12 have done worse than your **f**,
Jer   23:27 as their **f** forgot My name
Jer   25: 5 has given to you and your **f**
Jer   31:29 The **f** have eaten sour grapes,
Jer   34:14 But your **f** did not obey Me
Jer   44: 3 they nor you nor your **f**.
Jer   44: 9 the wickedness of your **f**,
Jer   50: 7 LORD, the hope of their **f**.
Lam   5: 7 Our **f** sinned and are no
Ezek   5:10 and sons shall eat their **f**;
Ezek   18: 2 The **f** have eaten sour grapes,
Ezek   20: 4 the abominations of their **f**.
Dan   2:23 praise You, O God of my **f**;
Dan   11:38 and a god which his **f** did
Amos   2: 4 Lies which their **f**
Mic   7:20 You have sworn to our **f**.
Zech   1: 2 been very angry with your **f**.
Zech   8:14 to punish you When your **f**
Mal   2:10 the covenant of the **f**?
Mal   4: 6 turn The hearts of the **f**
Matt   23:30 lived in the days of our **f**,
Luke   1:17 the hearts of the **f**
Luke   1:55 As He spoke to our **f**,
Luke   1:72 the mercy promised to our **f**
John   4:20 Our **f** worshiped on this
John   6:31 Our **f** ate the manna in the
Acts   5:30 The God of our **f** raised up
Acts   7: 2 he said, "Brethren and **f**,
Acts   7:32 am the God of your **f**—
Acts   7:44 Our **f** had the tabernacle of
Acts   15:10 which neither our **f** nor we
Acts   22: 1 "Brethren and **f**,
Acts   26: 6 promise made by God to our **f**.
Acts   28:17 or the customs of our **f**,
Rom   9: 5 of whom are the **f** and from
Rom   11:28 for the sake of the **f**.
Rom   15: 8 the promises made to the **f**,
1Co   4:15 you do not have many **f**;
1Co   10: 1 to be unaware that all our **f**
Gal   1:14 for the traditions of my **f**.
Eph   6: 4 And you, **f**, do not provoke
1Ti   1: 9 for murderers of **f** and
Heb   1: 1 spoke in time past to the **f**
Heb   3: 9 Where your **f** tested Me,
Heb   12: 9 we have had human **f** who
2Pe   3: 4 For since the **f** fell asleep,
1Jn   2:13 I write to you, **f**,

FATHERS' (*see* FATHERS)
Ex   6:14 are the heads of their **f**
Lev   26:39 also in their **f** iniquities,
Num   1:18 by their **f** houses, according
Ezra   10:16 were set apart by the **f**
Neh   2: 3 the place of my **f** tombs,
Neh   10:34 according to our **f** houses,
Ezek   20:24 eyes were fixed on their **f**
Ezek   22:10 In you men uncover their **f**
Acts   22: 3 to the strictness of our **f**

FATLING† (*see* FATLINGS)
Is   11: 6 and the young lion and the **f**

FATLINGS (*see* FATLING)
1Sa 15: 9 the sheep, the oxen, the **f**,
Ezek 34: 3 wool; you slaughter the **f**,

FATNESS (*see* FAT)
Gen 27:28 Of the **f** of the earth, And
Ps 63: 5 as with marrow and **f**,
Rom 11:17 a partaker of the root and **f**

FATTED (*see* FAT)
1Sa 28:24 Now the woman had a **f** calf in
2Sa 6:13 he sacrificed oxen and **f**
Prov 15:17 Than a **f** calf with hatred.
Luke 15:27 your father has killed the **f**

FATTENED (*see* FAT)
1Ki 1:19 has sacrificed oxen and **f**
Amos 5:22 Nor will I regard your **f**
Jas 5: 5 you have **f** your hearts as in

FATTER† (*see* FAT)
Dan 1:15 appeared better and **f** in

FATTY (*see* FAT)
Ex 29:13 the **f** lobe attached to the
Lev 9:19 and the **f** lobe attached to

FAULT (*see* FAULTLESS, FAULTS)
Ex 5:16 but the **f** is in your own
1Sa 29: 3 this day I have found no **f**
2Sa 3: 8 you charge me today with a **f**
Ps 59: 4 themselves through no **f** of
Dan 6: 4 nor was there any error or **f**
Matt 18:15 go and tell him his **f**
Mark 7: 2 unwashed hands, they found **f**.
Luke 23: 4 I find no **f** in this Man."
Acts 25: 5 to see if there is any **f** in
Rom 9:19 "Why does He still find **f**?
Phil 2:15 children of God without **f** in
Rev 14: 5 for they are without **f**

FAULTLESS† (*see* FAULT)
Heb 8: 7 first covenant had been **f**,
Jude 24 And to present you **f**

FAULTS† (*see* FAULT)
Gen 41: 9 I remember my **f** this day.
Ps 19:12 Cleanse me from secret **f**.
1Pe 2:20 you are beaten for your **f**,

FAVOR (*see* FAVORABLE, FAVORED, FAVORITE)
Gen 18: 3 if I have now found **f** in
Gen 39: 4 So Joseph found **f** in his
Deut 28:50 the elderly nor show **f** to
Deut 33:16 And the **f** of Him who dwelt
Ruth 2: 2 in whose sight I may find **f**.
1Sa 2:26 and in **f** both with the LORD
1Ki 13: 6 Please entreat the **f** of the
Esth 2:15 And Esther obtained **f** in the
Job 11:19 many would court your **f**.
Ps 5:12 With **f** You will surround
Ps 30: 5 His **f** is for life;
Ps 30: 7 by Your **f** You have made my
Ps 35:27 Who **f** my righteous cause;
Ps 89:17 And in Your **f** our horn is
Ps 102:14 And show **f** to her dust.
Ps 119:58 I entreated Your **f** with my
Prov 3: 4 And so find **f** and high
Prov 8:35 And obtains **f** from the
Prov 11:27 earnestly seeks good finds **f**,
Prov 12: 2 A good man obtains **f** from
Prov 13:15 Good understanding gains **f**,
Prov 19: 6 Many entreat the **f** of the
Prov 19:12 But his **f** is like dew on
Prov 22: 1 Loving **f** rather than silver
Prov 29:26 Many seek the ruler's **f**,
Eccl 9:11 Nor **f** to men of skill; But
Dan 1: 9 brought Daniel into the **f**
Dan 7:22 a judgment was made in **f**

Hos 12: 4 and sought **f** from Him. He
Luke 1:30 for you have found **f** with
Luke 2:52 and in **f** with God and men.
Acts 2:47 praising God and having **f**
Acts 24:27 wanting to do the Jews a **f**,
Acts 25: 9 wanting to do the Jews a **f**,

FAVORABLE (*see* FAVOR, FAVORABLY)
Ps 85: 1 You have been **f** to Your

FAVORABLY (*see* FAVORABLE)
Mal 1: 8 you? Would he accept you **f**?

FAVORED (*see* FAVOR)
Deut 33:24 Let him be **f** by his
Ps 44: 3 Because You **f** them.
Luke 1:28 highly **f** one, the Lord is

FAVORITE† (*see* FAVOR, FAVORITISM)
Song 6: 9 The **f** of the one who bore

FAVORITISM† (*see* FAVORITE)
Luke 20:21 You do not show personal **f**,
Gal 2: 6 God shows personal **f** to no

FAWNS†
Song 4: 5 two breasts are like two **f**,
Song 7: 3 two breasts are like two **f**,

FEAR (*see* FEARED, FEARFUL, FEARING, FEARS)
Gen 9: 2 And the **f** of you and the
Gen 20:11 surely the **f** of God is not
Gen 21:17 **F** not, for God has heard the
Gen 22:12 for now I know that you **f**
Gen 31:42 God of Abraham and the **F** of
Lev 19:14 but shall **f** your God: I am
Deut 2:25 to put the dread and **f** of
Deut 4:10 that they may learn to **f** Me
Deut 6:13 You shall **f** the LORD your
Deut 28:66 you shall **f** day and night,
Deut 31: 8 do not **f** nor be dismayed."
Josh 24:14 **f** the LORD, serve Him in
1Sa 11: 7 And the **f** of the LORD
1Sa 12:24 Only **f** the LORD, and serve
2Ch 17:10 And the **f** of the LORD fell
Esth 8:17 because **f** of the Jews fell
Job 1: 9 Does Job **f** God for nothing?
Job 4:14 **F** came upon me, and
Job 6:14 though he forsakes the **f** of
Job 15: 4 Yes, you cast off **f**,
Job 21: 9 houses are safe from **f**,
Job 25: 2 Dominion and **f** belong to
Job 28:28 the **f** of the Lord, that is
Job 39:22 He mocks at **f**,
Ps 2:11 Serve the LORD with **f**,
Ps 15: 4 But he honors those who **f**
Ps 19: 9 The **f** of the LORD is
Ps 22:23 And **f** Him, all you
Ps 22:25 My vows before those who **f**
Ps 23: 4 I will **f** no evil; For You
Ps 25:14 LORD is with those who **f**
Ps 27: 1 salvation; Whom shall I **f**?
Ps 27: 3 me, My heart shall not **f**;
Ps 31:13 **F** is on every side; While
Ps 33: 8 Let all the earth **f** the
Ps 34: 7 all around those who **f** Him,
Ps 34: 9 is no want to those who **f**
Ps 34:11 I will teach you the **f** of
Ps 36: 1 There is no **f** of God
Ps 40: 3 Many will see it and **f**,
Ps 46: 2 Therefore we will not **f**,
Ps 52: 6 also shall see and **f**,
Ps 53: 5 in great fear Where no **f**
Ps 55:19 Therefore they do not **f**
Ps 60: 4 a banner to those who **f** You,
Ps 64: 1 Preserve my life from **f** of
Ps 67: 7 ends of the earth shall **f**
Ps 85: 9 is near to those who **f** Him,

Ps 86:11 Unite my heart to f Your
Ps 103:11 His mercy toward those who f
Ps 111:10 The f of the LORD is the
Ps 118: 4 Let those who f the LORD
Ps 145:19 the desire of those who f
Prov 1: 7 The f of the LORD is the
Prov 1:33 without f of evil."
Prov 2: 5 you will understand the f
Prov 9:10 The f of the LORD is the
Prov 15:16 is a little with the f of
Prov 24:21 f the LORD and the king;
Song 3: 8 on his thigh Because of f
Is 7: 4 do not f or be fainthearted
Is 24:17 F and the pit and the snare
Is 29:23 And f the God of Israel.
Is 41:10 F not, for I am with you
Is 41:14 F not, you worm Jacob, You
Is 43: 1 F not, for I have redeemed
Is 43: 5 F not, for I am with you
Is 44: 2 F not, O Jacob My servant;
Is 44: 8 Do not f, nor be afraid;
Is 51: 7 Do not f the reproach of
Jer 2:19 And the f of Me is not in
Jer 6:25 F is on every side.
Jer 10: 7 Who would not f You, O King
Jer 17: 8 And will not f when heat
Jer 20:10 F on every side!"
Jer 48:43 F and the pit and the snare
Dan 1:10 I f my lord the king, who has
Dan 6:26 men must tremble and f
Dan 10:12 he said to me, "Do not f,
Dan 10:19 f not! Peace be to you; be
Hos 3: 5 They shall f the LORD and
Amos 3: 8 has roared! Who will not f?
Jon 1: 9 and I f the LORD, the God
Mal 3: 5 Because they do not f Me,"
Mal 4: 2 But to you who f My name
Matt 10:26 Therefore do not f them. For
Matt 10:28 But rather f Him who is able
Matt 21:26 we f the multitude, for all
Matt 28: 4 And the guards shook for f of
Luke 1:12 and f fell upon him.
Luke 1:50 His mercy is on those who f
Luke 1:74 Might serve Him without f,
Luke 12:32 "Do not f, little flock,
Luke 18: 2 city a judge who did not f
Luke 21:26 hearts failing them from f
Luke 23:40 Do you not even f God, seeing
John 7:13 spoke openly of Him for f
John 12:15 F not, daughter of Zion;
John 20:19 for f of the Jews, Jesus
Acts 5: 5 So great f came upon all
Acts 5:11 So great f came upon all the
Acts 9:31 And walking in the f of the
Rom 3:18 There is no f of God
Rom 8:15 spirit of bondage again to f,
Rom 11:20 Do not be haughty, but f.
Rom 13: 7 whom customs, fear to whom f,
2Co 7: 1 holiness in the f of God.
Phil 1:14 to speak the word without f.
Phil 2:12 your own salvation with f
2Ti 1: 7 not given us a spirit of f,
Heb 2:15 release those who through f
Heb 5: 7 heard because of His godly f,
Heb 11: 7 yet seen, moved with godly f,
Heb 13: 6 helper; I will not f.
1Pe 2:17 F God. Honor the king.
1Pe 2:18 to your masters with all f,
1Jn 4:18 but perfect love casts out f,
Rev 11:11 and great f fell on those
Rev 11:18 And those who f Your name,
Rev 14: 7 F God and give glory to Him,

FEARED (see FEAR)
Ex 1:17 But the midwives f God, and

Ex 14:31 so the people f the LORD,
2Ki 17: 7 and they had f other gods,
2Ki 17:33 They f the LORD, yet served
1Ch 16:25 He is also to be f above
Job 1: 1 and one who f God and
Job 3:25 For the thing I greatly f
Ps 76: 8 The earth f and was still,
Ps 76:11 to Him who ought to be f.
Ps 96: 4 He is to be f above all
Ps 130: 4 with You, That You may be f.
Is 41: 5 coastlands saw it and f,
Dan 5:19 and languages trembled and f
Jon 1:16 Then the men f the LORD
Mal 1:14 And My name is to be f
Matt 21:46 they f the multitudes,
Matt 27:54 they f greatly, saying,
Mark 6:20 for Herod f John, knowing
Luke 19:21 For I f you, because you are
John 9:22 things because they f the
Acts 10: 2 a devout man and one who f

FEARFUL (see FEAR, FEARFULLY)
Ex 15:11 F in praises, doing
Judg 7: 3 Whoever is f and afraid, let
Matt 8:26 to them, "Why are you f,
Heb 10:27 but a certain f expectation
Heb 10:31 It is a f thing to fall into

FEARFULLY (see FEARFUL)
Ps 139:14 for I am f and wonderfully

FEARING (see FEAR)
Mark 5:33 f and trembling, knowing
Col 3:22 sincerity of heart, f God.
Heb 11:27 not f the wrath of the king;

FEARS (see FEAR)
Job 1: 8 one who f God and shuns
Job 2: 3 one who f God and shuns
Ps 34: 4 delivered me from all my f.
Ps 128: 1 is every one who f the
Prov 13:13 But he who f the
Prov 14:16 A wise man f and departs
Prov 31:30 But a woman who f the
Acts 10:22 one who f God and has a good
Acts 10:35 in every nation whoever f
2Co 7: 5 conflicts, inside were f.
1Jn 4:18 But he who f has not been

FEAST (see FEASTING, FEASTS)
Gen 19: 3 house. Then he made them a f,
Ex 5: 1 that they may hold a f to Me
Ex 12:14 You shall keep it as a f by
Ex 12:17 you shall observe the F
Ex 23:16 and the F of Harvest, the
Ex 23:16 and the F of Ingathering at
Deut 16:16 and at the F of Tabernacles;
Judg 14:10 And Samson gave a f there,
Judg 14:12 the seven days of the f,
Judg 21:19 there is a yearly f of the
Esth 1: 3 of his reign he made a f
Esth 2:18 the F of Esther, for all his
Job 1: 4 his sons would go and f in
Prov 15:15 heart has a continual f.
Eccl 10:19 A f is made for laughter,
Ezek 36:38 flock at Jerusalem on its f
Ezek 46: 9 the LORD on the appointed f
Dan 5: 1 the king made a great f for
Hos 2:11 Her f days, Her New Moons,
Hos 9: 5 And in the day of the f of
Hos 12: 9 the days of the appointed f.
Amos 5:21 I despise your f days, And
Zech 14:16 and to keep the F of
Zech 14:18 do not come up to keep the F
Matt 26: 5 said, "Not during the f,
Mark 6:21 on his birthday gave a f
Mark 14: 1 the Passover and the F of

Luke   2:41   every year at the F of the
Luke   14: 8   by anyone to a wedding f,
Luke   23:17   one to them at the (f).
John   2: 8   it to the master of the f.
John   4:45   they also had gone to the f.
John   5: 1   After this there was a f of
John   7: 8   not yet going up to this f,
John   7:37   that great day of the f,
John   13: 1   Now before the f of the
Acts   18:21   means keep this coming f in
1Co   5: 8   Therefore let us keep the f,
2Pe   2:13   own deceptions while they f

FEASTING (see FEAST)
Esth   9:19   of Adar with gladness and f,
Job   1: 5   when the days of f had run
Prov   17: 1   Than a house full of f
Jer   16: 8   not go into the house of f
Hab   3:14   Their rejoicing was like f

FEASTS (see FEAST)
Lev   23: 2   The f of the LORD, which you
Lev   23: 2   these are My f.
Num   10:10   in your appointed f,
2Ch   8:13   the three appointed yearly f—
Is   1:14   Moons and your appointed f
Is   5:12   And wine are in their f;
Lam   1: 4   no one comes to the set f.
Amos   8:10   I will turn your f into
Mal   2: 3   The refuse of your solemn f;
Matt   23: 6   love the best places at f,
Jude   12   are spots in your love f,

FEATHERS
Ps   91: 4   shall cover you with His f,
Dan   4:33   had grown like eagles' f

FEATURES
Dan   1:15   of ten days their f appeared

FED (see FEED)
Gen   30:36   and Jacob f the rest of
Gen   47:17   Thus he f them with bread
Gen   48:15   The God who has f me all my
Ex   16:32   see the bread with which I f
Deut   8: 3   and f you with manna which
1Ki   18:13   and f them with bread and
1Ch   27:29   was over the herds that f
Jer   5: 7   When I had f them to the
Ezek   34: 8   but the shepherds f
Dan   5:21   They f him with grass like
Zech   11: 7   and I f the flock.
Mark   5:14   So those who f the swine
Luke   16:21   desiring to be f with the
1Co   3: 2   I f you with milk and not

FEEBLE
Gen   30:42   But when the flocks were f,
Neh   4: 2   What are these f Jews doing?
Job   4: 4   you have strengthened the f
Ps   109:24   And my flesh is f from lack
Prov   30:26   The rock badgers are a f
Is   35: 3   And make firm the f knees.
Heb   12:12   and the f knees,

FEED (see FED, FEEDING, FEEDS, WELL-FED)
Gen   24:32   and provided straw and f for
Gen   37:12   Then his brothers went to f
1Sa   17:15   and returned from Saul to f
1Ki   17: 4   commanded the ravens to f
Job   24:20   The worm should f sweetly
Ps   37: 3   and f on His faithfulness.
Ps   49:14   Death shall f on them; The
Prov   30: 8   F me with the food allotted
Song   4: 5   Which f among the lilies.
Is   27:10   There the calf will f,
Is   40:11   He will f His flock like a
Is   65:25   wolf and the lamb shall f

Jer   23:15   I will f them with wormwood,
Ezek   34: 3   but you do not f the flock.
Ezek   34:16   and f them in judgment."
Ezek   34:23   He shall f them and be their
Mic   7:14   Let them f in Bashan and
Zech   11: 4   F the flock for slaughter.
Matt   25:37   did we see You hungry and f
Luke   15:15   him into his fields to f
John   21:15   F My lambs."
John   21:17   F My sheep.
Rom   12:20   f him; If he is
1Co   13: 3   I bestow all my goods to f
Rev   12: 6   that they should f her there

FEEDING (see FEED)
Gen   37: 2   was f the flock with his
Matt   8:30   was a herd of many swine f.

FEEDS (see FEED)
Ex   22: 5   and it f in another man's
Prov   15:14   But the mouth of fools f on
Song   2:16   He f his flock among the
Is   44:20   He f on ashes; A deceived
Hos   12: 1   Ephraim f on the wind, And
Matt   6:26   yet your heavenly Father f
John   6:57   so he who f on Me will live

FEEL (see FEELING, FEELINGS, FELT)
Gen   27:12   Perhaps my father will f me,
Judg   16:26   Let me f the pillars which
Prov   23:35   but I did not f it. When
Zech   11: 5   owners slaughter them and f

FEELING† (see FEEL)
Eph   4:19   who, being past f,

FEELINGS† (see FEEL)
Prov   29:11   A fool vents all his f,

FEET (see FOOT)
Gen   18: 4   be brought, and wash your f,
Gen   49:10   lawgiver from between his f,
Gen   49:33   he drew his f up into the
Ex   3: 5   Take your sandals off your f,
Ex   4:25   and cast it at Moses' f,
Ex   12:11   your sandals on your f,
Ex   24:10   And there was under His f
Lev   8:24   big toes of their right f.
Lev   11:23   insects which have four f
Deut   29: 5   have not worn out on your f.
Josh   3:13   soon as the soles of the f
Josh   9: 5   patched sandals on their f,
Josh   10:24   drew near and put their f
Judg   5:27   At her f he sank, he fell,
Ruth   3: 8   a woman was lying at his f.
1Sa   2: 9   He will guard the f of His
2Sa   3:34   were not bound Nor your f
2Sa   4: 4   son who was lame in his f
2Sa   4:12   cut off their hands and f,
2Sa   19:24   he had not cared for his f,
2Sa   22:10   With darkness under His f.
2Sa   22:37   So my f did not slip.
1Ki   15:23   age he was diseased in his f.
2Ki   4:37   she went in, fell at his f,
2Ki   13:21   revived and stood on his f.
Neh   9:21   not wear out And their f
Job   13:27   You put my f in the stocks,
Job   29:15   And I was f to the lame.
Ps   8: 6   put all things under his f,
Ps   22:16   pierced My hands and My f;
Ps   40: 2   And set my f upon a rock,
Ps   56:13   Have You not kept my f
Ps   66: 9   And does not allow our f to
Ps   73: 2   my f had almost stumbled,
Ps   115: 7   F they have, but they do
Ps   116: 8   And my f from falling.
Ps   119:101   I have restrained my f from
Ps   119:105   word is a lamp to my f

Prov	1:16	For their f run to evil,
Prov	5: 5	Her f go down to death, Her
Prov	6:13	his eyes, He shuffles his f,
Prov	6:28	And his f not be seared?
Prov	26: 6	a fool Cuts off his own f
Prov	29: 5	Spreads a net for his f.
Song	5: 3	again? I have washed my f;
Is	3:16	a jingling with their f,
Is	6: 2	with two he covered his f,
Is	49:23	lick up the dust of your f.
Is	52: 7	the mountains Are the f of
Jer	38:22	Your f have sunk in the
Lam	1:13	has spread a net for my f
Ezek	2: 1	of man, stand on your f,
Ezek	6:11	your fists and stamp your f,
Dan	2:33	its f partly of iron and
Dan	7: 4	and made to stand on two f
Nah	1: 3	are the dust of His f.
Nah	1:15	on the mountains The f of
Hab	3:19	make my feet like deer's f,
Zech	14: 4	And in that day His f will
Matt	10:14	off the dust from your f.
Matt	15:30	laid them down at Jesus' f,
Matt	18: 8	having two hands or two f,
Matt	18:29	servant fell down at his f
Matt	28: 9	came and held Him by the f
Mark	7:25	she came and fell at His f.
Mark	9:45	rather than having two f,
Luke	1:79	To guide our f into the way
Luke	7:38	and she began to wash His f
Luke	7:38	and she kissed His f and
Luke	8:35	sitting at the f of Jesus,
Luke	24:39	"Behold My hands and My f,
John	13: 5	to wash the disciples' f,
John	13: 9	not my f only, but also my
John	13:14	to wash one another's f.
John	20:12	head and the other at the f,
Acts	4:35	them at the apostles' f;
Acts	7:58	down their clothes at the f
Acts	13:25	the sandals of whose f I am
Acts	16:24	prison and fastened their f
Acts	22: 3	up in this city at the f of
Rom	3:15	Their f are swift to
Rom	10:15	beautiful are the f
Rom	16:20	crush Satan under your f
1Co	12:21	nor again the head to the f,
1Co	15:27	all things under His f.
Eph	6:15	and having shod your f with
1Ti	5:10	she has washed the saints' f,
Heb	2: 8	subjection under his f.
Heb	12:13	straight paths for your f,
Rev	1:15	His f were like fine brass,
Rev	1:17	I fell at His f as dead. But
Rev	10: 1	and his f like pillars of
Rev	12: 1	with the moon under her f,
Rev	13: 2	his feet were like the f

FEIGNED†

| 1Sa | 21:13 | f madness in their hands, |

FELIX

Acts	23:26	most excellent governor F:
Acts	24: 3	in all places, most noble F,
Acts	24:24	when F came with his wife

FELL (see FALL)

Gen	4: 5	angry, and his countenance f.
Gen	15:12	and great darkness f upon
Gen	17: 3	Then Abram f on his face, and
Gen	33: 4	and f on his neck and kissed
Lev	16: 9	on which the LORD's lot f,
Num	11: 9	And when the dew f on the
Num	11: 9	the manna f on it.
Josh	6:20	that the wall f down flat.
Josh	17: 5	Ten shares f to Manasseh,
Judg	5:27	there he f dead.

1Sa	4:18	that Eli f off the seat
1Sa	30:13	because three days ago I f
1Sa	31: 1	and f slain on Mount Gilboa.
1Sa	31: 4	Saul took a sword and f on
1Ki	18:38	the fire of the LORD f and
2Ki	6: 5	the iron ax head f into
Ezra	9: 5	I f on my knees and spread
Esth	8:17	because fear of the Jews f
Job	1:16	The fire of God f from heaven
Ps	27: 2	foes, They stumbled and f.
Ezek	1:28	I f on my face, and I heard
Ezek	8: 1	the hand of the Lord GOD f
Ezek	11: 5	the Spirit of the LORD f
Dan	2:46	Then King Nebuchadnezzar f
Dan	3:23	f down bound into the midst
Dan	4:31	a voice f from heaven:
Jon	1: 7	and the lot f on Jonah.
Matt	2:11	and f down and worshiped
Matt	7:27	beat on that house; and it f.
Matt	13: 4	some seed f by the wayside;
Matt	13: 5	Some f on stony places, where
Matt	26:39	went a little farther and f
Mark	7:25	and she came and f at His
Luke	1: 9	his lot f to burn incense
Luke	1:12	and fear f upon him.
Luke	8:23	But as they sailed He f
Luke	10:30	and f among thieves, who
Luke	13: 4	whom the tower in Siloam f
Luke	16:21	fed with the crumbs which f
John	11:32	she f down at His feet,
Acts	1:25	Judas by transgression f,
Acts	1:26	and the lot f on Matthias.
Acts	5: 5	f down and breathed his
Acts	7:60	had said this, he f asleep.
Acts	10:10	he f into a trance
Acts	10:44	the Holy Spirit f upon all
Acts	12: 7	quickly!" And his chains f
Acts	16:29	and f down trembling before
Acts	19:17	and fear f on them all, and
Acts	19:35	and of the image which f
Acts	20: 9	he f down from the third
Rom	15: 3	who reproached You f
1Ti	2:14	f into transgression.
2Pe	3: 4	For since the fathers f
Rev	1:17	I f at His feet as dead. But
Rev	5: 8	and the twenty-four elders f
Rev	6:13	And the stars of heaven f to
Rev	8:10	And a great star f from
Rev	8:10	and it f on a third of the
Rev	16:21	And great hail from heaven f

FELLOW (see FELLOWS, FELLOWSHIP)

1Sa	21:15	Shall this f come into my
Matt	26:71	This f also was with Jesus
John	9:29	to Moses; as for this f,
John	11:16	said to his f disciples,
Rom	16: 3	my f workers in Christ
Rom	16: 7	my f countrymen and my f
1Co	3: 9	For we are God's f workers;
Eph	2:19	but f citizens with the
Phil	2:25	f worker, and fellow
Phil	2:25	and f soldier, but your
1Th	3: 2	and our f laborer in the
Phm	1: 1	our beloved friend and f
1Pe	5: 1	I who am a f elder and a

FELLOWS† (see FELLOW)

| 2Sa | 6:20 | as one of the base f |
| Dan | 7:20 | was greater than his f. |

FELLOWSHIP (see FELLOW)

Acts	2:42	the apostles' doctrine and f,
1Co	1: 9	you were called into the f
1Co	10:20	I do not want you to have f
2Co	6:14	For what f has righteousness
Gal	2: 9	Barnabas the right hand of f,

Eph	3: 9	make all see what is the **f**
Eph	5:11	And have no **f** with the
Phil	1: 5	for your **f** in the gospel from
Phil	2: 1	if any **f** of the Spirit, if
Phil	3:10	and the **f** of His sufferings,
1Jn	1: 3	and truly our **f** is with the
1Jn	1: 6	If we say that we have **f** with
1Jn	1: 7	we have **f** with one another,

FELT (*see* FEEL)

Gen	27:22	and he **f** him and said, "The
Ex	10:21	which may even be **f**.
Mark	5:29	and she **f** in her body that

FEMALE

Gen	1:27	male and **f** He created them.
Gen	7: 2	unclean, a male and his **f**;
Gen	15: 9	a three-year-old **f** goat, a
Ex	11: 5	to the firstborn of the **f**
Ex	20:10	nor your **f** servant, nor your
Ex	23:12	and the son of your **f**
Lev	12: 5	But if she bears a **f** child,
Lev	27: 5	and for a **f** ten shekels;
Deut	4:16	the likeness of male or **f**,
Deut	5:14	nor your **f** servant, nor your
Deut	5:21	his **f** servant, his ox, his
Deut	12:18	your male servant and your **f**
Deut	15:17	Also to your **f** servant you
Deut	16:11	your male servant and your **f**
Deut	16:14	your male servant and your **f**
Judg	9:18	the son of his **f** servant,
Judg	19:19	for your **f** servant, and for
1Sa	8:16	your **f** servants, your finest
2Sa	17:17	so a **f** servant would come
2Ki	2:24	And two **f** bears came out of
Job	1: 3	five hundred **f** donkeys, and
Job	31:13	the cause of my male or **f**
Job	42:12	and one thousand **f** donkeys.
Eccl	2: 8	I acquired male and **f**
Jer	34: 9	set free his male and **f**
Matt	19: 4	'made them male and **f**,
Luke	12:45	to beat the male and **f**
Gal	3:28	there is neither male nor **f**;

FENCE† (*see* FENCED)

Ps	62: 3	wall and a tottering **f**.

FENCED† (*see* FENCE)

Job	19: 8	He has **f** up my way, so that

FERTILIZE†

Luke	13: 8	until I dig around it and **f**

FERVENT (*see* FERVENTLY)

Prov	26:23	**F** lips with a wicked heart
Luke	22:15	With **f** desire I have desired
Rom	12:11	**f** in spirit, serving the
Jas	5:16	**f** prayer of a righteous man
1Pe	4: 8	And above all things have **f**
2Pe	3:10	elements will melt with **f**

FERVENTLY† (*see* FERVENT)

Col	4:12	always laboring **f** for you in
1Pe	1:22	love one another **f** with a

FESTIVAL

Col	2:16	or regarding a **f** or a new

FESTUS

Acts	24:27	after two years Porcius **F**
Acts	25:14	**F** laid Paul's case before
Acts	25:22	Then Agrippa said to **F**,

FETTERS

Judg	16:21	They bound him with bronze **f**,
Ps	105:18	They hurt his feet with **f**,
Jer	52:11	bound him in bronze **f**,

FEVER

Deut	28:22	with severe burning **f**,

Job	30:30	me; My bones burn with **f**.
Lam	5:10	Because of the **f** of famine.
Matt	8:14	mother lying sick with a **f**.
Matt	8:15	and the **f** left her. And she
John	4:52	at the seventh hour the **f**

FIELD (*see* FIELDS)

Gen	2: 5	and before any herb of the **f**
Gen	2:19	formed every beast of the **f**
Gen	4: 8	when they were in the **f**,
Gen	23:17	So the **f** of Ephron which
Gen	23:19	wife in the cave of the **f**
Gen	25:10	the **f** which Abraham purchased
Gen	25:27	hunter, a man of the **f**
Gen	25:29	and Esau came in from the **f**,
Ex	9:25	struck every herb of the **f**
Ex	9:25	broke every tree of the **f**
Ex	22:31	torn by beasts in the **f**;
Lev	19: 9	reap the corners of your **f**,
Lev	19:19	You shall not sow your **f**
Lev	25: 3	years you shall sow your **f**,
Lev	27:18	But if he dedicates his **f**
Lev	27:20	not want to redeem the **f**,
Num	22: 4	licks up the grass of the **f**.
Deut	14:22	of your grain that the **f**
Deut	20:19	for the tree of the **f** is
Josh	15:18	to ask her father for a **f**.
Judg	9:32	and lie in wait in the **f**.
Ruth	2: 3	went and gleaned in the **f**
Ruth	2: 3	to come to the part of the **f**
Ruth	4: 5	On the day you buy the **f** from
1Sa	4: 2	men of the army in the **f**.
1Sa	20:24	Then David hid in the **f**.
2Sa	2:16	that place was called the **F**
2Sa	14:30	servants set the **f** on fire.
2Ki	18:17	highway to the Fuller's **F**.
Job	5:23	And the beasts of the **f**
Ps	78:12	in the **f** of Zoan.
Ps	96:12	Let the **f** be joyful, and all
Ps	103:15	grass; As a flower of the **f**,
Prov	31:16	She considers a **f** and buys
Song	7:11	Let us go forth to the **f**;
Is	5: 8	They add **f** to field, Till
Is	29:17	And the fruitful **f** be
Is	37:27	were as the grass of the **f**
Is	40: 6	is like the flower of the **f**,
Is	55:12	And all the trees of the **f**
Jer	26:18	shall be plowed like a **f**,
Jer	32: 7	Buy my **f** which is in
Ezek	17: 5	planted it in a fertile **f**;
Ezek	34:27	Then the trees of the **f** shall
Dan	4:25	be with the beasts of the **f**,
Hos	10: 4	in the furrows of the **f**.
Mic	3:12	shall be plowed like a **f**,
Matt	6:28	Consider the lilies of the **f**,
Matt	6:30	clothes the grass of the **f**,
Matt	13:24	who sowed good seed in his **f**;
Matt	13:36	of the tares of the **f**.
Matt	13:38	The **f** is the world, the good
Matt	13:44	that he has and buys that **f**.
Matt	24:40	two men will be in the **f**:
Matt	27: 7	with them the potter's **f**.
Matt	27: 8	field has been called the **F**
Luke	15:25	his older son was in the **f**.
Acts	1:19	that is, **F** of Blood.)
1Co	3: 9	workers; you are God's **f**,
Jas	1:10	as a flower of the **f** he

FIELDS (*see* FIELD)

Deut	32:13	eat the produce of the **f**;
1Sa	8:14	will take the best of your **f**,
2Sa	1:21	Nor **f** of offerings. For
Prov	8:26	not made the earth or the **f**,
Jer	32:15	Houses and **f** and vineyards
Jer	32:43	And **f** will be bought in this
Luke	2: 8	living out in the **f**,

Luke 15:15 and he sent him into his **f**
John 4:35 your eyes and look at the **f**,

FIERCE (*see* FIERCENESS)
Gen 49: 7 their anger, for it is **f**;
Ex 32:12 Turn from Your **f** wrath, and
Num 32:14 to increase still more the **f**
Deut 28:50 a nation of **f** countenance,
Judg 20:34 Gibeah, and the battle was **f**.
1Sa 31: 3 The battle became **f** against
2Sa 2:17 So there was a very **f** battle
2Ki 3:26 that the battle was too **f**
1Ch 10: 3 The battle became **f** against
Job 10:16 You hunt me like a **f** lion,
Prov 26:13 is a lion in the road! A **f**
Is 7: 4 for the **f** anger of Rezin and
Is 13:13 And in the day of His **f**
Is 19: 4 And a **f** king will rule over
Lam 4:11 He has poured out His **f**
Dan 8:23 Having **f** features, Who
Hab 1: 8 And more **f** than evening
Jas 3: 4 so large and are driven by **f**

FIERCENESS (*see* FIERCE)
Deut 13:17 LORD may turn from the **f**
2Ki 23:26 did not turn from the **f** of
Jer 25:38 desolate Because of the **f**
Rev 16:19 cup of the wine of the **f** of

FIERY (*see* FIRE)
Num 21: 6 So the LORD sent **f** serpents
Ps 7:13 He makes His arrows into **f**
Ps 21: 9 You shall make them as a **f**
Ps 78:48 And their flocks to **f**
Dan 3: 6 the midst of a burning **f**
Eph 6:16 be able to quench all the **f**
Heb 10:27 and **f** indignation which will
1Pe 4:12 it strange concerning the **f**
Rev 6: 4 **f** red, went out. And it was
Rev 12: 3 **f** red dragon having seven

FIFTEEN (*see* FIFTEENTH)
Gen 7:20 The waters prevailed **f** cubits
Lev 27: 7 your valuation shall be **f**
2Ki 20: 6 I will add to your days **f**
Is 38: 5 I will add to your days **f**
Ezek 45:12 and **f** shekels shall be your
Gal 1:18 and remained with him **f**

FIFTEENTH (*see* FIFTEEN)
Ex 16: 1 on the **f** day of the second
Lev 23:34 The **f** day of this seventh
1Ki 12:32 ordained a feast on the **f**
1Ki 12:33 had made at Bethel on the **f**
Luke 3: 1 Now in the **f** year of the

FIFTH (*see* FIVE)
Gen 1:23 and the morning were the **f**
Lev 19:25 And in the **f** year you may eat
Jer 1: 3 Jerusalem captive in the **f**
Rev 6: 9 When He opened the **f** seal, I
Rev 9: 1 Then the **f** angel sounded: And

FIFTIES (*see* FIFTY)
Ex 18:21 of hundreds, rulers of **f**,
Deut 1:15 of hundreds, leaders of **f**,
1Sa 8:12 and captains over his **f**,
2Ki 1:14 of fifties with their **f**.

FIFTIETH (*see* FIFTY)
Lev 25:10 you shall consecrate the **f**

FIFTY (*see* FIFTIES, FIFTIETH)
Gen 6:15 its width **f** cubits, and its
Gen 18:24 Suppose there were **f**
Lev 23:16 Count **f** days to the day after
Num 4: 3 even to **f** years old, all who
2Sa 15: 1 and **f** men to run before him.
2Ki 1: 9 captain of fifty with his **f**

Esth 5:14 **f** cubits high, and in the
Esth 7: 9 **f** cubits high, which Haman
Ezek 42: 7 its length was **f** cubits.
Luke 9:14 them sit down in groups of **f**.
Luke 16: 6 sit down quickly and write **f**.
John 8:57 You are not yet **f** years old,

FIFTY-THREE
John 21:11 fish, one hundred and **f**;

FIG (*see* FIGS)
Gen 3: 7 and they sewed **f** leaves
Deut 8: 8 of vines and **f** trees and
Judg 9:10 the trees said to the **f**
Song 2:13 The **f** tree puts forth her
Mic 4: 4 his vine and under his **f**
Hab 3:17 Though the **f** tree may not
Matt 21:19 Immediately the **f** tree
Matt 21:20 How did the **f** tree wither
Matt 24:32 this parable from the **f**
Mark 11:21 look! The **f** tree which You
Luke 13: 7 come seeking fruit on this **f**
John 1:50 I saw you under the **f** tree,'
Rev 6:13 as a **f** tree drops its late

FIGHT (*see* FIGHTING, FIGHTS, FOUGHT)
Ex 1:10 also join our enemies and **f**
Ex 14:14 The LORD will **f** for you, and
Ex 17: 9 **f** with Amalek. Tomorrow I
Deut 25:11 If two men **f** together, and
Judg 20:20 in battle array to **f**
1Sa 17:32 your servant will go and **f**
1Sa 18:17 and **f** the LORD's battles."
2Ch 13:12 do not **f** against the LORD
Neh 4:20 Our God will **f** for us."
Ps 56: 2 For there are many who **f**
Is 31: 4 hosts will come down To **f**
Jer 1:19 They will **f** against you,
Jer 15:20 And they will **f** against
Jer 32:24 hand of the Chaldeans who **f**
John 18:36 world, My servants would **f**,
Acts 5:39 you even be found to **f**
1Co 9:26 with uncertainty. Thus I **f**:
1Ti 6:12 **F** the good fight of faith,
2Ti 4: 7 I have fought the good **f**,
Jas 4: 2 You **f** and war. Yet you do
Rev 2:16 to you quickly and will **f**

FIGHTING (*see* FIGHT)
Ex 2:13 two Hebrew men were **f**,
2Ch 26:11 Uzziah had an army of **f** men
Acts 7:26 two of them as they were **f**,

FIGHTS (*see* FIGHT)
Ex 14:25 for the LORD **f** for them
Josh 23:10 LORD your God is He who **f**
Jas 4: 1 Where do wars and **f** come

FIGS (*see* FIG)
2Ki 20: 7 said, "Take a lump of **f**.
Song 2:13 tree puts forth her green **f**,
Jer 24: 2 One basket had very good **f**,
Jer 24: 5 Israel: 'Like these good **f**,
Jer 29:17 will make them like rotten **f**
Matt 7:16 from thornbushes or **f** from
Mark 11:13 it was not the season for **f**.
Luke 6:44 For men do not gather **f**
Jas 3:12 or a grapevine bear **f**?
Rev 6:13 a fig tree drops its late **f**

FIGURATIVE (*see* FIGURE)
John 16:25 I have spoken to you in **f**
Heb 11:19 he also received him in a **f**

FIGURE† (*see* FIGURATIVE, FIGUREHEAD)
Deut 4:16 image in the form of any **f**:
Is 44:13 And makes it like the **f** of
John 16:29 and using no **f** of speech!

FIGUREHEAD† (*see* FIGURE)
Acts 28:11 an Alexandrian ship whose f

FILL (*see* FILLED, FILLING, FILLS, FULL)
Gen   1:22 and f the waters in the
Gen   1:28 f the earth and subdue it;
Gen   9: 1 and f the earth.
Gen 42:25 Joseph gave a command to f
Deut 23:24 you may eat your f of grapes
1Sa 16: 1 F your horn with oil, and
1Ki 18:33 F four waterpots with water,
Job   7: 4 For I have had my f of
Job 23: 4 And f my mouth with
Ps   83:16 F their faces with shame,
Prov 7:18 let us take our f of love
Jer 23:24 Do I not f heaven and
Jer 51:14 Surely I will f you with men,
Ezek 3: 3 and f your stomach with this
Ezek 30:11 And f the land with the
Matt 15:33 in the wilderness to f such
John 2: 7 F the waterpots with water."
Rom 15:13 Now may the God of hope f you
Eph   4:10 that He might f all things.)
Col   1:24 and f up in my flesh what is

FILLED (*see* FILL)
Gen   6:11 and the earth was f with
Gen 21:19 And she went and f the skin
Gen 24:16 f her pitcher, and came up.
Ex   1: 7 and the land was f with
Ex   2:16 and they f the troughs to
Ex   31: 3 And I have f him with the
Ex   35:35 He has f them with skill to
Ex   40:34 and the glory of the LORD f
Num 14:21 all the earth shall be f
Deut 11:15 that you may eat and be f.
1Ki   7:14 he was f with wisdom and
1Ki   8:10 that the cloud f the house
1Ki 18:35 and he also f the trench
Neh   9:25 So they ate and were f and
Ps   72:19 let the whole earth be f
Ps   78:29 So they ate and were well f,
Ps 126: 2 Then our mouth was f with
Prov 3:10 So your barns will be f with
Prov 14:14 in heart will be f with his
Prov 20:17 his mouth will be f with
Prov 30:22 A fool when he is f with
Eccl 1: 8 Nor the ear f with hearing.
Is   6: 1 and the train of His robe f
Is   6: 4 and the house was f with
Jer 15:17 For You have f me with
Ezek 43: 5 the glory of the LORD f the
Dan   2:35 a great mountain and f the
Hos 13: 6 They were f and their heart
Hab   2:14 For the earth will be f
Zech 9:15 They shall be f with
Matt 5: 6 For they shall be f.
Matt 14:20 So they all ate and were f,
Matt 27:48 f it with sour wine and put
Luke 1:15 He will also be f with the
Luke 1:41 and Elizabeth was f with the
Luke 1:53 He has f the hungry with
Luke 1:67 his father Zacharias was f
Luke 2:40 f with wisdom; and the grace
Luke 3: 5 valley shall be f And
Luke 5:26 glorified God and were f
Luke 6:21 now, For you shall be f.
Luke 9:17 So they all ate and were f,
Luke 15:16 And he would gladly have f
John 2: 7 And they f them up to the
John 6:13 and f twelve baskets with the
John 6:26 ate of the loaves and were f.
John 12: 3 And the house was f with the
John 16: 6 sorrow has f your heart.
Acts 2: 2 and it f the whole house
Acts 2: 4 And they were all f with the

Acts 3:10 and they were f with wonder
Acts 5: 3 why has Satan f your heart
Acts 5:17 and they were f with
Acts 5:28 you have f Jerusalem with
Acts 13: 9 f with the Holy Spirit,
Acts 13:45 they were f with envy; and
Acts 13:52 And the disciples were f with
Rom   1:29 being f with all
Rom 15:14 f with all knowledge, able
Eph   3:19 that you may be f with all
Phil 1:11 being f with the fruits of
Jas   2:16 in peace, be warmed and f,
Rev 15: 8 The temple was f with smoke

FILLING (*see* FILL)
Acts 14:17 f our hearts with food and

FILLS (*see* FILL)
Ps 107: 9 And f the hungry soul with
Ps 147:14 And f you with the finest
Eph   1:23 the fullness of Him who f

FILTH (*see* FILTHY)
1Co   4:13 We have been made as the f
1Pe   3:21 (not the removal of the f

FILTHINESS (*see* FILTHY)
2Co   7: 1 ourselves from all f of the
Jas   1:21 Therefore lay aside all f
Rev 17: 4 of abominations and the f

FILTHY (*see* FILTH, FILTHINESS)
Is   64: 6 righteousnesses are like f
Zech 3: 3 Joshua was clothed with f
Col   3: 8 f language out of your
Jas   2: 2 also come in a poor man in f
Rev 22:11 be unjust still; he who is f,
Rev 22:11 let him be f still; he who

FINAL† (*see* FINALLY)
Jer 12: 4 He will not see our f end."

FINALLY (*see* FINAL)
2Co 13:11 F, brethren, farewell.
Eph   6:10 F, my brethren, be strong
Phil 4: 8 F, brethren, whatever
2Th   3: 1 F, brethren, pray for us,
2Ti   4: 8 F, there is laid up for me

FIND (*see* FINDING, FINDS, FOUND)
Gen 18:26 If I f in Sodom fifty
Gen 19:11 became weary trying to f
Gen 33:15 Let me f favor in the sight
Gen 34:11 Let me f favor in your eyes,
Ex   5:11 straw where you can f it;
Num 32:23 and be sure your sin will f
Deut 4:29 and you will f Him if you
Judg 16: 5 and f out where his great
Ezra 4:15 And you will f in the book
Job 11: 7 Can you f out the limits of
Job 23: 3 that I knew where I might f
Job 37:23 we cannot f Him; He is
Ps 132: 5 Until I f a place for the
Prov 2: 5 And f the knowledge of God.
Prov 4:22 are life to those who f
Prov 8: 9 And right to those who f
Prov 8:17 seek me diligently will f
Prov 14: 6 wisdom and does not f it,
Prov 19: 8 keeps understanding will f
Prov 20: 6 But who can f a faithful
Prov 31:10 Who can f a virtuous wife?
Eccl 3:11 except that no one can f out
Eccl 7:26 And I f more bitter than
Eccl 7:28 still seeks but I cannot f:
Eccl 8:17 he will not be able to f
Eccl 12:10 The Preacher sought to f
Song 3: 1 but I did not f him.
Song 3: 2 but I did not f him.
Song 5: 8 If you f my beloved, That

Is 41:12 shall seek them and not f
Jer 29:13 And you will seek Me and f
Ezek 3: 1 "Son of man, eat what you f;
Dan 6: 4 but they could f no charge
Hos 5: 6 But they will not f Him;
Matt 7: 7 to you; seek, and you will f;
Matt 7:14 and there are few who f it.
Matt 10:39 his life for My sake will f
Matt 11:29 and you will f rest for your
Matt 21: 2 and immediately you will f
Matt 24:46 will f so doing.
Mark 13:36 he f you sleeping.
Luke 2:12 You will f a Babe wrapped in
Luke 2:45 So when they did not f Him,
Luke 12:43 whom his master will f so
Luke 13: 7 on this fig tree and f none.
Luke 18: 8 will He really f faith on
Luke 23: 4 I f no fault in this Man."
Luke 24:23 When they did not f His body,
John 7:34 You will seek Me and not f
John 7:36 You will seek Me and not f
John 10: 9 and will go in and out and f
John 21: 6 and you will f some." So
Acts 5:22 officers came and did not f
Acts 7:46 before God and asked to f a
Acts 17: 6 But when they did not f them,
Acts 17:11 the Scriptures daily to f
Acts 17:27 might grope for Him and f
Acts 23: 9 We f no evil in this man; but
Rom 7:18 what is good I do not f.
Rom 9:19 Why does He still f fault?
2Co 9: 4 come with me and f you
Heb 4:16 we may obtain mercy and f
Rev 9: 6 seek death and will not f

FINDING (see FIND)
Gen 4:15 lest anyone f him should
Job 9:10 He does great things past f
Rom 11:33 and His ways past f out!
Eph 5:10 f out what is acceptable to
Heb 8: 8 Because f fault with them, He

FINDS (see FIND)
Gen 4:14 happen that anyone who f
Num 35:27 and the avenger of blood f
Deut 22:23 and a man f her in the city
Job 33:10 Yet He f occasions against
Ps 36: 2 When he f out his iniquity
Ps 119:162 at Your word As one who f
Prov 3:13 Happy is the man who f
Prov 8:35 For whoever f me finds life,
Prov 8:35 For whoever finds me f life,
Prov 18:22 He who finds a wife f a
Prov 21:21 righteousness and mercy F
Eccl 9:10 Whatever your hand f to do,
Hos 14: 3 For in You the fatherless f
Matt 7: 8 receives, and he who seeks f,
Matt 10:39 He who f his life will lose
Matt 12:44 he f it empty, swept, and
Luke 15: 4 which is lost until he f it?
Luke 15: 8 carefully until she f it?

FINE (see FINEST)
Gen 18: 6 ready three measures of f
Gen 41: 2 f looking and fat; and they
Gen 41:42 him in garments of f linen
Ex 9: 9 And it will become f dust in
Ex 16:14 as f as frost on the
Lev 2: 1 his offering shall be of f
Lev 5:11 one-tenth of an ephah of f
Lev 16:12 of sweet incense beaten f,
Num 6:15 cakes of f flour mixed with
Num 28: 9 of an ephah of f flour
Deut 9:21 until it was as f as dust;
Deut 22:19 and they shall f him one
2Ch 3: 5 which he overlaid with f

Ezra 8:27 and two vessels of f
Esth 1: 6 fastened with cords of f
Ps 18:42 Then I beat them as f as the
Ps 19:10 than much f gold; Sweeter
Prov 31:22 Her clothing is f linen
Is 19: 9 those who work in f flax
Is 19: 9 flax And those who weave f
Is 23:18 and for f clothing.
Is 29: 5 your foes Shall be like f
Ezek 27: 7 F embroidered linen from
Ezek 31: 3 With f branches that shaded
Dan 2:32 image's head was of f
Luke 16:19 was clothed in purple and f
Jas 2: 2 in f apparel, and there
Jas 2: 3 to the one wearing the f
Rev 1:15 His feet were like f brass,
Rev 19:14 clothed in f linen, white

FINEST (see FINE)
1Sa 8:16 your f young men, and your
Ps 81:16 fed them also with the f of
Song 5:11 His head is like the f

FINGER (see FINGERS)
Ex 8:19 This is the f of God." But
Ex 31:18 written with the f of God.
Lev 4: 6 The priest shall dip his f in
Lev 4:17 the priest shall dip his f
Lev 14:16 some of the oil with his f
Lev 14:27 sprinkle with his right f
Lev 16:14 and sprinkle with his f
Lev 16:14 some of the blood with his f
1Ki 12:10 My little f shall be thicker
2Ch 10:10 My little f shall be thicker
Luke 11:20 I cast out demons with the f
Luke 16:24 he may dip the tip of his f
John 8: 6 on the ground with His f,
John 20:25 and put my f into the print
John 20:27 Reach your f here, and look

FINGERS (see FINGER)
2Sa 21:20 who had six f on each hand
Ps 8: 3 heavens, the work of Your f,
Prov 6:13 feet, He points with his f;
Prov 7: 3 Bind them on your f;
Song 5: 5 My f with liquid myrrh, On
Is 2: 8 That which their own f have
Dan 5: 5 In the same hour the f of a
Dan 5:24 Then the f of the hand were
Matt 23: 4 them with one of their f.
Mark 7:33 and put His f in his ears,

FINISH (see FINISHED, FINISHER, FINISHING)
Ezra 5: 3 to build this temple and f
Ps 90: 9 We f our years like a sigh.
Dan 9:24 To f the transgression, To
Zech 4: 9 His hands shall also f it.
Luke 14:30 build and was not able to f.
John 4:34 and to f His work.
Acts 20:24 so that I may f my race with
Rev 11: 7 When they f their testimony,

FINISHED (see FINISH)
Gen 2: 1 all the host of them, were f.
Ex 40:33 So Moses f the work.
Ruth 2:21 young men until they have f
1Ki 3: 1 City of David until he had f
1Ki 7:40 So Huram f doing all the
1Ki 8:54 when Solomon had f praying
1Ki 9: 1 when Solomon had f building
Ezra 5:16 and it is not f.
Ezra 10:17 of the first month they f
Job 16:22 For when a few years are f,
Jer 51:63 when you have f reading this
Ezek 5: 2 the days of the siege are f;
Dan 5:26 your kingdom, and f it;
Dan 12: 7 all these things shall be f.

Matt 11: 1 when Jesus f commanding His
Matt 13:53 when Jesus had f these
Matt 19: 1 when Jesus had f these
Matt 26: 1 when Jesus had f all these
John 17: 4 I have f the work which You
John 19:30 It is f!" And bowing His
2Ti 4: 7 I have f the race, I have
Rev 10: 7 mystery of God would be f,
Rev 20: 3 the thousand years were f.
Rev 20: 5 the thousand years were f.

FINISHER† (see FINISH)
Heb 12: 2 the author and f of our

FINISHING† (see FINISH)
Ezra 4:12 and are f its walls and
Acts 13:25 And as John was f his course,

FINS
Deut 14: 9 you may eat all that have f

FIRE (see FIERY, FIREBRAND)
Gen 19:24 rained brimstone and f on
Gen 22: 6 and he took the f in his
Gen 22: 7 the f and the wood, but
Ex 3: 2 to him in a flame of f from
Ex 3: 2 the bush was burning with f,
Ex 13:22 by day or the pillar of f
Ex 19:18 LORD descended upon it in f.
Ex 24:17 was like a consuming f on
Ex 29:18 an offering made by f to the
Ex 32:24 me, and I cast it into the f,
Ex 40:38 and f was over it by night,
Lev 1: 9 an offering made by f,
Lev 6:13 A f shall always be burning
Lev 9:24 and f came out from before
Lev 10: 1 and offered profane f before
Lev 18:21 pass through the f to
Num 9:15 like the appearance of f.
Num 11: 2 the f was quenched.
Num 16:18 put f in it, laid incense on
Num 26:10 when the f devoured two
Num 31:23 that can endure f,
Num 31:23 you shall put through the f,
Deut 4:11 the mountain burned with f
Deut 4:24 your God is a consuming f,
Deut 4:36 He showed you His great f,
Deut 5:23 mountain was burning with f,
Deut 5:25 For this great f will
Deut 7:25 images of their gods with f;
Deut 9: 3 before you as a consuming f.
Deut 12: 3 their wooden images with f;
Deut 13:16 and completely burn with f
Deut 18:10 daughter pass through the f,
Deut 32:22 For a f is kindled by my
Josh 6:24 all that was in it with f.
Josh 8: 8 you shall set the city on f.
Josh 11: 6 burn their chariots with f.
Josh 11:11 Then he burned Hazor with f.
Judg 6:21 and f rose out of the rock
Judg 9:15 let f come out of the
Judg 9:20 let f come from Abimelech
Judg 9:52 the tower to burn it with f
Judg 15: 5 he had set the torches on f,
Judg 15:14 flax that is burned with f,
Judg 16: 9 breaks when it touches f.
2Sa 14:30 servants set the field on f.
2Sa 22: 9 And devouring f from His
1Ki 18:24 and the God who answers by f,
1Ki 18:25 but put no f under it."
1Ki 18:38 Then the f of the LORD fell
1Ki 19:12 and after the earthquake a f,
1Ki 19:12 the LORD was not in the f;
1Ki 19:12 and after the f a still
2Ki 1:10 And f came down from
2Ki 1:12 And the f of God came down
2Ki 2:11 appeared with horses of f,

2Ki 6:17 of horses and chariots of f
2Ki 16: 3 his son pass through the f,
2Ki 19:18 cast their gods into the f;
2Ki 21: 6 his son pass through the f,
2Ki 23:10 daughter pass through the f
Neh 1: 3 its gates are burned with f.
Neh 2: 3 its gates are burned with f?
Job 1:16 The f of God fell from heaven
Job 20:26 An unfanned f will consume
Job 41:19 Sparks of f shoot out.
Ps 18: 8 And devouring f from His
Ps 18:12 hailstones and coals of f.
Ps 50: 3 A f shall devour before
Ps 66:12 We went through f and
Ps 68: 2 As wax melts before the f,
Ps 74: 7 They have set f to Your
Ps 79: 5 Your jealousy burn like f?
Ps 83:14 sets the mountains on f,
Ps 89:46 Will Your wrath burn like f?
Ps 104: 4 His ministers a flame of f.
Ps 148: 8 F and hail, snow and clouds
Prov 6:27 Can a man take f to his
Prov 16:27 on his lips like a burning f.
Prov 25:22 you will heap coals of f on
Prov 26:20 the f goes out; And where
Prov 30:16 And the f never says,
Song 8: 6 Its flames are flames of f,
Is 1: 7 cities are burned with f;
Is 5:24 as the f devours the
Is 9:19 shall be as fuel for the f;
Is 29: 6 the flame of devouring f.
Is 30:14 A shard to take f from the
Is 30:27 tongue like a devouring f.
Is 30:33 Its pyre is f with much
Is 33:11 stubble; Your breath, as f,
Is 33:14 dwell with the devouring f?
Is 43: 2 When you walk through the f,
Is 44:16 burns half of it in the f;
Is 44:16 am warm, I have seen the f.
Is 64: 2 As f burns brushwood, As
Is 66:15 the LORD will come with f
Is 66:24 And their f is not
Jer 4: 4 My fury come forth like f,
Jer 5:14 My words in your mouth f,
Jer 15:14 For a f is kindled in My
Jer 20: 9 in my heart like a burning f
Jer 23:29 "Is not My word like a f?
Jer 32:35 to pass through the f to
Lam 4:11 He kindled a f in Zion,
Ezek 1:27 with the appearance of f all
Ezek 8: 2 like the appearance of f—
Ezek 8: 2 of His waist and downward, f;
Ezek 16:21 them to pass through the f?
Ezek 21:32 You shall be fuel for the f,
Ezek 39: 6 And I will send f on Magog
Dan 3:22 the flame of the f killed
Dan 3:24 into the midst of the f?
Dan 3:26 came from the midst of the f.
Dan 3:27 and the smell of f was not
Dan 7: 9 Its wheels a burning f;
Dan 10: 6 his eyes like torches of f,
Hos 7: 4 ceases stirring the f
Joel 2:30 Blood and f and pillars of
Amos 1: 4 But I will send a f into the
Mic 1: 4 split Like wax before the f,
Zeph 1:18 shall be devoured By the f
Zech 2: 5 will be a wall of f all
Zech 3: 2 a brand plucked from the f?
Mal 1:10 that you would not kindle f
Mal 3: 2 He is like a refiner's f.
Matt 3:10 down and thrown into the f.
Matt 3:11 with the Holy Spirit and f.
Matt 3:12 chaff with unquenchable f.
Matt 5:22 shall be in danger of hell f.
Matt 13:42 them into the furnace of f.

Matt 13:50 them into the furnace of f.
Matt 17:15 he often falls into the f
Matt 18: 8 cast into the everlasting f.
Mark 9:44 And the f is not
Mark 9:49 will be seasoned with f,
Mark 14:54 and warmed himself at the f.
Luke 9:54 do You want us to command f
Luke 12:49 I came to send f on the
Luke 17:29 out of Sodom it rained f
John 21: 9 they saw a f of coals there,
Acts 2: 3 divided tongues, as of f,
Acts 2:19 Blood and f and vapor
Acts 7:30 to him in a flame of f in a
Acts 28: 5 off the creature into the f
Rom 12:20 will heap coals of f
1Co 3:13 it will be revealed by f;
1Co 3:13 and the f will test each
1Co 3:13 saved, yet so as through f.
2Th 1: 8 in flaming f taking vengeance
Heb 1: 7 ministers a flame of f.
Heb 12:29 our God is a consuming f.
Jas 3: 5 great a forest a little f
Jas 3: 6 and sets on f the course of
Jas 3: 6 and it is set on f by hell.
1Pe 1: 7 though it is tested by f,
2Pe 3: 7 are reserved for f until the
2Pe 3:12 be dissolved, being on f,
Jude 7 the vengeance of eternal f.
Rev 1:14 His eyes like a flame of f;
Rev 3:18 Me gold refined in the f,
Rev 8: 5 filled it with f from the
Rev 10: 1 his feet like pillars of f.
Rev 11: 5 f proceeds from their mouth
Rev 14:10 He shall be tormented with f
Rev 19:20 alive into the lake of f
Rev 20: 9 And f came down from God out
Rev 20:10 was cast into the lake of f
Rev 20:14 were cast into the lake of f.
Rev 20:15 was cast into the lake of f.

FIREBRAND† (see FIRE, FIREBRANDS)
Amos 4:11 And you were like a f plucked

FIREBRANDS (see FIREBRAND)
Is 7: 4 these two stubs of smoking f,

FIRM (see FIRMLY)
Deut 25: 8 But if he stands f and
Josh 3:17 of the LORD stood f on dry
Prov 4:13 Take f hold of instruction,
Is 35: 3 And make f the feeble
Dan 2: 8 see that my decision is f:
Dan 6: 7 statute and to make a f
Heb 3: 6 the rejoicing of the hope f

FIRMAMENT
Gen 1: 6 Let there be a f in the midst
Gen 1: 8 And God called the f Heaven.
Ps 19: 1 And the f shows His
Ps 150: 1 Praise Him in His mighty f!
Ezek 1:26 And above the f over their
Ezek 10: 1 and there in the f that was
Dan 12: 3 the brightness of the f,

FIRMLY (see FIRM)
1Ki 2:12 and his kingdom was f
Ezra 6: 3 the foundations of it be f
Ps 96:10 The world also is f

FIRST (see FIRSTBORN, FIRSTFRUIT)
Gen 1: 5 and the morning were the f
Gen 2:11 The name of the f is Pishon;
Gen 8: 5 on the f day of the month,
Gen 8:13 the f day of the month,
Gen 13: 4 which he had made there at f.
Gen 26: 1 besides the f famine that
Ex 12: 5 a male of the f year. You
Ex 12:15 leavened bread from the f

Ex 23:19 The f of the firstfruits of
Ex 34: 1 that were on the f tablets
Num 6:14 one male lamb in its f year
Num 6:14 one ewe lamb in its f year
Num 18:15 Everything that f opens the
Num 24:20 Amalek was f among the
Num 28:16 the fourteenth day of the f
Num 29:17 fourteen lambs in their f
Num 33: 3 from Rameses in the f month,
Deut 18: 4 and the f of the fleece of
Judg 1: 1 Who shall be f to go up for
2Sa 23:19 he did not attain to the f
1Ki 3:27 Give the f woman the living
1Ch 29:29 f and last, indeed they are
2Ch 35:27 and his deeds from f to last,
2Ch 36:22 Now in the f year of Cyrus
Ezra 1: 1 Now in the f year of Cyrus
Ezra 3:12 old men who had seen the f
Job 40:19 He is the f of the ways of
Ps 105:36 The f of all their
Is 1:26 your judges as at the f,
Is 41: 4 'I, the LORD, am the f;
Is 43:27 Your f father sinned, And
Is 44: 6 I am the F and I am the
Jer 4:31 her who brings forth her f
Jer 7:12 where I set My name at the f,
Jer 24: 2 like the figs that are f
Jer 50:17 F the king of Assyria
Jer 52:31 in the f year of his reign,
Ezek 10:14 the f face was the face of
Dan 7: 1 In the f year of Belshazzar
Dan 7: 4 The f was like a lion, and
Dan 7: 8 before whom three of the f
Dan 8: 1 that appeared to me the f
Dan 8:21 between its eyes is the f
Hos 2: 7 will go and return to my f
Hos 9:10 on the fig tree in its f
Matt 5:24 F be reconciled to your
Matt 6:33 But seek f the kingdom of God
Matt 7: 5 Hypocrite! F remove the plank
Matt 8:21 let me f go and bury my
Matt 12:29 unless he f binds the strong
Matt 12:45 that man is worse than the f.
Matt 13:30 F gather together the tares
Matt 17:10 say that Elijah must come f?
Matt 17:27 the fish that comes up f.
Matt 19:30 But many who are f will be
Matt 19:30 will be last, and the last f.
Matt 20:27 whoever desires to be f
Matt 22:38 This is the f and great
Matt 23:26 f cleanse the inside of the
Matt 26:17 Now on the f day of the
Matt 27:64 will be worse than the f.
Matt 28: 1 as the f day of the week
Mark 4:28 f the blade, then the head,
Mark 9:35 "If anyone desires to be f,
Mark 12:28 Which is the f commandment of
Mark 13:10 And the gospel must f be
Mark 16: 2 on the f day of the week,
Mark 16: 9 He appeared to Mary
Luke 1: 3 all things from the very f,
Luke 2: 2 This census f took place
Luke 11:38 marveled that He had not f
Luke 14:28 does not sit down f and
Luke 21: 9 things must come to pass f,
Luke 24: 1 Now on the f day of the
John 1:41 He f found his own brother
John 5: 4 then whoever stepped in f
John 8: 7 him throw a stone at her f.
John 10:40 John was baptizing at f,
John 19:39 who at f came to Jesus by
John 20: 1 Now on the f day of the week
John 20: 4 Peter and came to the tomb f.
John 20:19 being the f day of the
Acts 11:26 And the disciples were f

Acts	13:24	after John had f preached,
Rom	1: 8	F, I thank my God
Rom	1:16	for the Jew f and also for
Rom	13:11	is nearer than when we f
1Co	12:28	f apostles, second prophets,
1Co	14:30	let the f keep silent.
1Co	15:45	The f man Adam became a
1Co	16: 2	On the f day of the week let
2Co	8: 5	but they f gave themselves
2Co	8:12	For if there is f a willing
Gal	4:13	the gospel to you at the f.
Eph	1:12	that we who f trusted in
Eph	4: 9	it mean but that He also f
Eph	6: 2	which is the f commandment
1Th	4:16	dead in Christ will rise f.
2Th	2: 3	the falling away comes f,
1Ti	2:13	For Adam was formed f,
2Ti	1: 5	which dwelt f in your
2Ti	2: 6	farmer must be f to partake
2Ti	4:16	At my f defense no one stood
Heb	2: 3	which at the f began to be
Heb	5:12	to teach you again the f
Heb	7:27	f for His own sins and then
Heb	8: 7	For if that f covenant had
Heb	8:13	He has made the f
Heb	9: 8	made manifest while the f
Heb	10: 9	He takes away the f that
Jas	3:17	that is from above is f
1Pe	4:17	and if it begins with us f,
2Pe	1:20	knowing this f,
1Jn	4:19	We love Him because He f
Rev	1:11	the F and the Last," and,
Rev	1:17	I am the F and the Last.
Rev	2: 4	that you have left your f
Rev	2: 5	repent and do the f works,
Rev	20: 5	This is the f resurrection.
Rev	21: 1	for the f heaven and the
Rev	21: 1	the first heaven and the f
Rev	22:13	the F and the Last."

FIRSTBORN (see FIRST)

Gen	4: 4	Abel also brought of the f of
Gen	19:33	And the f went in and lay
Gen	27:19	father, "I am Esau your f;
Gen	29:26	the younger before the f,
Gen	35:23	Leah were Reuben, Jacob's f,
Ex	4:22	"Israel is My son, My f.
Ex	4:23	I will kill your son, your f.
Ex	11: 5	from the f of Pharaoh who
Ex	13: 2	"Consecrate to Me all the f,
Ex	13:13	But every f of a donkey you
Num	3: 2	sons of Aaron: Nadab, the f,
Num	3:13	because all the f are Mine.
Num	18:15	and the f of unclean animals
Deut	21:16	of the unloved, the true f.
Deut	21:17	the unloved wife as the f
Deut	21:17	the right of the f is his.
Job	18:13	The f of death devours his
Ps	78:51	And destroyed all the f in
Mic	6: 7	Shall I give my f for my
Matt	1:25	she had brought forth her f
Rom	8:29	that He might be the f among
Col	1:15	the f over all creation.
Col	1:18	the f from the dead, that in
Heb	1: 6	when He again brings the f
Heb	12:23	and church of the f who

FIRSTFRUIT† (see FIRST, FIRSTFRUITS)

Rom	11:16	For if the f is holy, the

FIRSTFRUITS (see FIRSTFRUIT)

Ex	23:16	the f of your labors which
Ex	23:19	The first of the f of your
Ex	34:22	of the f of wheat harvest,
Lev	2:12	for the offering of the f,
Lev	2:14	a grain offering of your f

Lev	2:14	the grain offering of your f
Neh	10:35	ordinances to bring the f
Neh	10:35	of our ground and the f of
Neh	13:31	the wood offering and the f
Jer	2: 3	The f of His increase. All
Rom	8:23	but we also who have the f
Rom	16: 5	who is the f of Achaia to
1Co	15:20	and has become the f of
1Co	15:23	his own order: Christ the f,
Jas	1:18	we might be a kind of f of

FISH (see FISHHOOKS, FISHING, FISH'S)

Gen	1:26	have dominion over the f of
Gen	1:28	have dominion over the f of
Ex	7:18	And the f that are in the
Num	11: 5	We remember the f which we
Deut	4:18	or the likeness of any f
1Ki	4:33	of creeping things, and of f.
2Ch	33:14	far as the entrance of the F
Ps	8: 8	And the f of the sea That
Ps	105:29	blood, And killed their f.
Is	50: 2	Their f stink because
Jon	1:17	had prepared a great f to
Jon	1:17	was in the belly of the f
Matt	7:10	"Or if he asks for a f,
Matt	12:40	in the belly of the great f,
Matt	14:17	only five loaves and two f.
Matt	15:34	"Seven, and a few little f.
Mark	6:41	and the two f He divided
Mark	6:43	of fragments and of the f
Mark	8: 7	They also had a few small f;
Luke	5: 6	caught a great number of f,
Luke	11:11	him a serpent instead of a f?
Luke	24:42	Him a piece of a broiled f
John	6: 9	loaves and two small f,
John	21:11	net to land, full of large f,
1Co	15:39	of animals, another of f,

FISH'S† (see FISH)

Jon	2: 1	the LORD his God from the f

FISHERMEN (see FISHERS)

Matt	4:18	the sea; for they were f.

FISHERS (see FISHERMEN)

Matt	4:19	and I will make you f of

FISHHOOKS (see FISH)

Amos	4: 2	He will take you away with f,

FISHING (see FISH)

John	21: 3	said to them, "I am going f.

FIST (see FISTS)

Is	10:32	He will shake his f at the
Zeph	2:15	Shall hiss and shake his f.

FISTS (see FIST)

Ezek	6:11	Pound your f and stamp your
Ezek	21:17	I also will beat My f

FIT (see FITLY, FITTING)

Ezek	16:50	I took them away as I saw f.
Dan	1:13	delicacies; and as you see f,
Luke	9:62	is f for the kingdom of
Acts	22:22	for he is not f to live!"

FITLY (see FIT)

Prov	25:11	A word f spoken is like

FITTING (see FIT)

Prov	19:10	Luxury is not f for a fool,
Prov	26: 1	So honor is not f for a
Matt	3:15	for thus it is f for us to
Rom	1:28	those things which are not f;
Col	3:18	as is f in the Lord.

FIVE (see FIFTH)

Gen	18:28	Suppose there were f less
Gen	43:34	but Benjamin's serving was f
Lev	27: 5	and if from f years old up to

Josh 10: 5 Therefore the **f** kings of the
Josh 13: 3 the **f** lords of the
1Sa 6: 4 **F** golden tumors and five
1Ki 4:32 were one thousand and **f**.
Is 19:18 In that day **f** cities in the
Is 30:17 At the threat of **f** you
Matt 14:17 We have here only **f** loaves
Matt 14:21 who had eaten were about **f**
Matt 25: 2 and **f** were foolish.
Matt 25:15 And to one he gave **f** talents,
Luke 1:24 and she hid herself **f**
Luke 12: 6 Are not **f** sparrows sold for
Luke 19:18 your mina has earned **f**
Luke 19:19 You also be over **f** cities.'
John 4:18 for you have had **f** husbands,
Acts 4: 4 the men came to be about **f**
1Co 14:19 I would rather speak **f**
1Co 15: 6 that He was seen by over **f**
2Co 11:24 From the Jews **f** times I

FIX (see FIXED, FIXING)
Ezek 40: 4 and **f** your mind on

FIXED (see FIX)
Prov 22:18 Let them all be **f** upon your
Luke 16:26 you there is a great gulf **f**,

FIXING† (see FIX)
Acts 3: 4 And **f** his eyes on him, with

FLAME (see FLAMES, FLAMING)
Ex 3: 2 appeared to him in a **f** of
Judg 13:20 the LORD ascended in the **f**
Job 41:21 And a **f** goes out of his
Ps 104: 4 His ministers a **f** of fire.
Song 8: 6 of fire, A most vehement **f**.
Is 43: 2 Nor shall the **f** scorch you.
Dan 3:22 the **f** of the fire killed
Dan 7: 9 His throne was a fiery **f**,
Dan 11:33 shall fall by sword and **f**,
Luke 16:24 for I am tormented in this **f**.
Acts 7:30 Lord appeared to him in a **f**
Heb 1: 7 And His ministers a **f**
Rev 1:14 and His eyes like a **f** of

FLAMES (see FLAME)
Song 8: 6 Its **f** are flames of fire,

FLAMING (see FLAME)
Gen 3:24 and a **f** sword which turned
Ps 105:32 And **f** fire in their land.
2Th 1: 8 in **f** fire taking vengeance on

FLASH (see FLASHED, FLASHES)
Ezek 1:14 in appearance like a **f** of

FLASHED† (see FLASH)
Ps 77:17 Your arrows also **f** about.

FLASHES (see FLASH)
Ex 20:18 thunderings, the lightning **f**,
Matt 24:27 comes from the east and **f**

FLASK
1Sa 10: 1 Then Samuel took a **f** of oil
Jer 19: 1 and get a potter's earthen **f**,
Mark 14: 3 Then she broke the **f** and
Luke 7:37 brought an alabaster **f** of

FLAT
Num 22:31 he bowed his head and fell **f**
Josh 6:20 that the wall fell down **f**.

FLATTER (see FLATTERED, FLATTERING, FLATTERS,
FLATTERY)
Ps 5: 9 They **f** with their tongue.

FLATTERED† (see FLATTER)
Ps 78:36 Nevertheless they **f** Him with

FLATTERING (see FLATTER)
Ps 12: 2 With **f** lips and a double

Prov 6:24 From the **f** tongue of a
Prov 26:28 And a **f** mouth works ruin.
Rom 16:18 and by smooth words and **f**
1Th 2: 5 at any time did we use **f**

FLATTERS (see FLATTER)
Prov 2:16 From the seductress who **f**
Prov 20:19 not associate with one who **f**
Prov 28:23 afterward Than he who **f**
Prov 29: 5 A man who **f** his neighbor

FLATTERY (see FLATTER)
Dan 11:32 he shall corrupt with **f**;

FLAVOR (see FLAVORLESS)
Matt 5:13 but if the salt loses its **f**,

FLAVORLESS† (see FLAVOR)
Job 6: 6 Can **f** food be eaten without

FLAX
Ex 9:31 Now the **f** and the barley were
Judg 15:14 on his arms became like **f**
Prov 31:13 She seeks wool and **f**,
Is 42: 3 And smoking **f** He will not
Matt 12:20 And smoking **f** He will

FLEA
1Sa 26:20 has come out to seek a **f**,

FLED (see FLEE)
Gen 31:22 third day that Jacob had **f**.
Ex 4: 3 and Moses **f** from it.
Ex 14: 5 Egypt that the people had **f**,
Num 35:25 of refuge where he had **f**,
1Sa 4:10 and every man **f** to his tent.
1Sa 17:51 champion was dead, they **f**.
1Sa 21:10 Then David arose and **f** that
2Sa 4: 4 his nurse took him up and **f**.
1Ki 2:28 So Joab **f** to the tabernacle
2Ki 7: 7 and they **f** for their lives.
Ps 104: 7 At Your rebuke they **f**;
Ps 114: 5 ails you, O sea, that you **f**?
Is 21:15 For they **f** from the swords,
Jer 4:25 birds of the heavens had **f**.
Jer 26:21 it, he was afraid and **f**,
Dan 10: 7 so that they **f** to hide
Amos 5:19 will be as though a man **f**
Jon 1:10 For the men knew that he **f**
Jon 4: 2 Therefore I **f** previously to
Matt 26:56 disciples forsook Him and **f**.
Mark 5:14 So those who fed the swine **f**,
Mark 14:52 left the linen cloth and **f**
Mark 16: 8 they went out quickly and **f**
Acts 16:27 the prisoners had **f**,
Rev 20:11 the earth and the heaven **f**

FLEE (see FLED, FLEEING, FLEES)
Gen 19:20 city is near enough to **f**
Gen 31:27 Why did you **f** away secretly,
Lev 26:17 and you shall **f** when no one
Num 35: 6 to which a manslayer may **f**.
Num 35:11 person accidentally may **f**
Num 35:15 a person accidentally may **f**
Deut 28: 7 against you one way and **f**
Deut 28:25 one way against them and **f**
Josh 8:20 So they had no power to **f**
2Sa 15:14 "Arise, and let us **f**;
2Sa 19: 3 steal away when they **f** in
Job 41:28 The arrow cannot make him **f**;
Ps 31:11 Those who see me outside **f**
Ps 64: 8 All who see them shall **f**
Ps 68: 1 those also who hate Him **f**
Ps 68:12 "Kings of armies **f**,
Ps 68:12 of armies flee, they **f**,
Ps 139: 7 Or where can I **f** from Your
Prov 28: 1 The wicked **f** when no one
Song 2:17 breaks And the shadows **f**
Song 4: 6 breaks And the shadows **f**

Is	10: 3	To whom will you f for
Is	30:16	for we will f on
Is	30:17	One thousand shall f at
Is	30:17	threat of five you shall f,
Is	35:10	sorrow and sighing shall f
Is	51:11	Sorrow and sighing shall f
Jer	48: 6	"F, save your lives!
Jer	51: 6	F from the midst of
Amos	2:16	men of might Shall f naked
Jon	1: 3	But Jonah arose to f to
Matt	2:13	f to Egypt, and stay there
Matt	3: 7	vipers! Who warned you to f
Matt	10:23	f to another. For assuredly,
Matt	24:16	those who are in Judea f to
Mark	13:14	those who are in Judea f to
1Co	6:18	F sexual immorality. Every
1Co	10:14	f from idolatry.
2Ti	2:22	F also youthful lusts; but
Jas	4: 7	the devil and he will f
Rev	9: 6	and death will f from them.

FLEECE

Judg	6:37	if there is dew on the f
Judg	6:40	It was dry on the f only,
Job	31:20	was not warmed with the f

FLEEING (see FLEE)

Gen	16: 8	I am f from the presence of
Ex	14:27	while the Egyptians were f
Job	26:13	His hand pierced the f
Is	27: 1	Will punish Leviathan the f

FLEES (see FLEE)

Deut	19: 4	case of the manslayer who f
Deut	19:11	and he f to one of these
John	10:12	and leaves the sheep and f;
John	10:13	The hireling f because he is

FLEET

2Sa	2:18	And Asahel was as f of
1Ki	9:26	Solomon also built a f of

FLESH (see FLESHHOOK, FLESHLY)

Gen	2:21	and closed up the f in its
Gen	2:23	my bones And flesh of my f;
Gen	2:24	and they shall become one f.
Gen	6: 3	forever, for he is indeed f;
Gen	6:12	for all f had corrupted
Gen	6:13	The end of all f has come
Gen	6:19	every living thing of all f
Gen	7:16	male and female of all f,
Gen	7:21	And all f died that moved on
Gen	9: 4	But you shall not eat f with
Gen	17:11	be circumcised in the f of
Gen	17:13	covenant shall be in your f
Gen	37:27	is our brother and our f.
Ex	4: 7	restored like his other f.
Ex	12: 8	Then they shall eat the f on
Lev	7:15	The f of the sacrifice of
Lev	7:21	and who eats the f of the
Lev	8:31	Boil the f at the door of
Lev	13:10	there is a spot of raw f
Lev	17:11	For the life of the f is in
Lev	17:14	not eat the blood of any f,
Lev	21: 5	make any cuttings in their f.
Num	16:22	God of the spirits of all f,
Num	18:15	opens the womb of all f,
Judg	9: 2	that I am your own f and
1Sa	17:44	and I will give your f to
2Sa	5: 1	we are your bone and your f.
2Ki	5:14	and his f was restored like
2Ki	9:36	dogs shall eat the f of
2Ch	32: 8	"With him is an arm of f;
Job	2: 5	and touch his bone and his f,
Job	7: 5	My f is caked with worms and
Job	10: 4	Do You have eyes of f?
Job	10:11	Clothe me with skin and f,

Job	19:26	That in my f I shall see
Job	21: 6	trembling takes hold of my f.
Job	34:15	All f would perish together,
Ps	16: 9	My f also will rest in
Ps	27: 2	against me To eat up my f,
Ps	38: 7	is no soundness in my f.
Ps	56: 4	What can f do to me?
Ps	63: 1	My f longs for You In a
Ps	65: 2	To You all f will come.
Ps	73:26	My f and my heart fail;
Ps	78:39	that they were but f,
Ps	84: 2	My heart and my f cry out
Ps	119:120	My f trembles for fear of
Ps	136:25	Who gives food to all f,
Ps	145:21	And all f shall bless His
Prov	3: 8	It will be health to your f,
Eccl	2: 3	how to gratify my f
Eccl	5: 6	let your mouth cause your f
Eccl	12:12	study is wearisome to the f.
Is	31: 3	God; And their horses are f,
Is	40: 5	And all f shall see it
Is	40: 6	All f is grass, And all its
Is	49:26	All f shall know That I,
Is	65: 4	tombs; Who eat swine's f,
Is	66:17	Eating swine's f and the
Is	66:24	be an abhorrence to all f.
Jer	17: 5	trusts in man And makes f
Jer	32:27	the LORD, the God of all f.
Ezek	11:19	stony heart out of their f,
Ezek	11:19	and give them a heart of f,
Ezek	20:48	All f shall see that I, the
Ezek	37: 6	sinews on you and bring f
Ezek	37: 8	the sinews and the f came
Ezek	44: 7	heart and uncircumcised in f,
Dan	1:15	better and fatter in f than
Dan	7: 5	devour much fl'
Joel	2:28	pour out My Spirit on all f;
Matt	16:17	for f and blood has not
Matt	19: 5	two shall become one f'
Matt	24:22	no f would be saved; but for
Matt	26:41	but the f is weak."
Luke	3: 6	And all f shall see
Luke	24:39	for a spirit does not have f
John	1:13	nor of the will of the f,
John	1:14	And the Word became f and
John	3: 6	which is born of the f
John	6:52	this Man give us His f to
John	6:53	unless you eat the f of the
John	6:55	For My f is food indeed, and
John	6:63	the f profits nothing. The
John	17: 2	Him authority over all f,
Acts	2:17	of My Spirit on all f;
Acts	2:31	nor did His f see
Rom	1: 3	of David according to the f,
Rom	3:20	by the deeds of the law no f
Rom	6:19	of the weakness of your f.
Rom	7:18	in my f) nothing good
Rom	8: 1	not walk according to the f,
Rom	8: 3	it was weak through the f,
Rom	8: 3	in the likeness of sinful f,
Rom	8: 3	He condemned sin in the f,
Rom	8: 5	minds on the things of the f,
Rom	8: 9	But you are not in the f but
Rom	8:12	to live according to the f,
Rom	13:14	make no provision for the f,
1Co	1:26	many wise according to the f,
1Co	1:29	that no f should glory in His
1Co	5: 5	for the destruction of the f,
1Co	6:16	"shall become one f.
1Co	15:39	another f of animals,
2Co	3: 3	of stone but on tablets of f,
2Co	4:11	manifested in our mortal f.
2Co	10: 3	For though we walk in the f,
2Co	12: 7	a thorn in the f was given
Gal	1:16	immediately confer with f

Gal	2:16	by the works of the law no f
Gal	2:20	which I now live in the f I
Gal	5:13	as an opportunity for the f,
Gal	5:16	fulfill the lust of the f.
Gal	5:17	and the Spirit against the f;
Gal	5:24	have crucified the f with
Gal	6: 8	For he who sows to his f will
Eph	2:15	having abolished in His f the
Eph	5:29	no one ever hated his own f,
Eph	5:30	of His f and of His bones.
Eph	5:31	two shall become one f.
Eph	6:12	we do not wrestle against f
Phil	3: 3	have no confidence in the f.
Col	1:22	in the body of His f through
Col	1:24	and fill up in my f what is
Col	2: 1	not seen my face in the f,
Col	2: 5	though I am absent in the f,
Col	2:23	the indulgence of the f.
1Ti	3:16	was manifested in the f,
Heb	5: 7	who, in the days of His f,
Heb	10:20	the veil, that is, His f,
Jas	5: 3	you and will eat your f
1Pe	1:24	All f is as grass, And
1Pe	3:18	being put to death in the f
1Pe	4: 1	he who has suffered in the f
2Pe	2:10	who walk according to the f
1Jn	2:16	the world—the lust of the f,
1Jn	4: 2	Christ has come in the f is
Jude	7	and gone after strange f,
Jude	23	the garment defiled by the f.
Rev	19:21	were filled with their f.

FLESHHOOK† (see FLESH)

1Sa	2:13	come with a three-pronged f
1Sa	2:14	for himself all that the f

FLESHLY (see FLESH)

2Co	1:12	not with f wisdom but by the
Col	2:18	vainly puffed up by his f
Heb	7:16	according to the law of a f
1Pe	2:11	abstain from f lusts which

FLEW† (see FLY)

2Sa	22:11	rode upon a cherub, and f;
Ps	18:10	He rode upon a cherub, and f;
Ps	18:10	He f upon the wings of the
Is	6: 2	his feet, and with two he f.
Is	6: 6	Then one of the seraphim f

FLIES (see FLY)

Ex	8:21	I will send swarms of f on
Deut	4:17	of any winged bird that f
Ps	91: 5	Nor of the arrow that f
Eccl	10: 1	Dead f putrefy the

FLIGHT (see FLY)

Lev	26: 8	shall put ten thousand to f;
Matt	24:20	And pray that your f may not
Heb	11:34	turned to f the armies of

FLINT (see FLINTY)

Josh	5: 2	Make f knives for yourself,
Is	50: 7	I have set My face like a f,
Zech	7:12	made their hearts like f,

FLINTY (see FLINT)

Deut	32:13	And oil from the f rock;

FLOAT†

1Ki	5: 9	I will f them in rafts by
2Ki	6: 6	and he made the iron f.

FLOCK (see FLOCKS)

Gen	4: 4	of the firstborn of his f
Gen	21:28	seven ewe lambs of the f by
Gen	30:40	not put them with Laban's f.
Ex	2:16	to water their father's f.
Ex	3: 1	Now Moses was tending the f
Lev	5:18	without blemish from the f,

Deut	15:19	the firstborn of your f.
Job	30: 1	to put with the dogs of my f.
Song	2:16	He feeds his f among the
Song	4: 1	Your hair is like a f of
Is	40:11	He will feed His f like a
Is	63:11	With the shepherd of His f?
Jer	23: 2	"You have scattered My f,
Jer	25:35	Nor the leaders of the f to
Ezek	24: 5	Take the choice of the f.
Ezek	34: 3	but you do not feed the f.
Ezek	34:10	for I will deliver My f from
Ezek	34:15	"I will feed My f,
Ezek	36:38	Like a f offered as holy
Amos	6: 4	Eat lambs from the f And
Amos	7:15	took me as I followed the f,
Mic	4: 8	And you, O tower of the f,
Hab	3:17	Though the f may be cut off
Zech	11: 4	Feed the f for slaughter,
Zech	11:17	Who leaves the f! A sword
Luke	2: 8	keeping watch over their f
Luke	12:32	"Do not fear, little f,
John	10:16	and there will be one f and
1Pe	5: 2	Shepherd the f of God which
1Pe	5: 3	but being examples to the f;

FLOCKS (see FLOCK)

Gen	24:35	and He has given him f and
Gen	30:36	fed the rest of Laban's f.
Gen	30:39	So the f conceived before the
Gen	33:13	and the f and herds which
Gen	37:16	they are feeding their f.
Lev	5:15	without blemish from the f,
2Sa	12: 2	man had exceedingly many f
2Ch	32:29	and possessions of f and
Job	24: 2	They seize f violently and
Song	1: 7	who veils herself By the f
Is	32:14	wild donkeys, a pasture of f—
Jer	3:24	Their f and their herds,
Jer	33:12	shepherds causing their f
Ezek	34: 2	not the shepherds feed the f?

FLOOD (see FLOODED, FLOODING, FLOODPLAIN, FLOODS, FLOODWATERS)

Gen	7: 7	of the waters of the f.
Gen	9:11	again shall there be a f to
Gen	9:15	never again become a f to
Job	27:20	overtake him like a f;
Ps	29:10	sat enthroned at the F,
Ps	90: 5	carry them away like a f;
Is	28: 2	Like a f of mighty waters
Is	59:19	the enemy comes in like a f,
Dan	9:26	of it shall be with a f,
Matt	24:38	as in the days before the f,
Matt	24:39	did not know until the f

FLOODED (see FLOOD)

2Pe	3: 6	being f with water.

FLOODING (see FLOOD)

Ezek	13:13	and there shall be a f rain

FLOODPLAIN (see FLOOD)

Jer	12: 5	how will you do in the f of
Jer	49:19	up like a lion from the f
Jer	50:44	up like a lion from the f

FLOODS (see FLOOD)

Ex	15: 8	The f stood upright like a
Ps	93: 3	The f have lifted up, O
Song	8: 7	Nor can the f drown it. If
Is	44: 3	And f on the dry ground; I
Jon	2: 3	And the f surrounded me;
Matt	7:25	the f came, and the winds
Matt	7:27	the f came, and the winds

FLOODWATERS (see FLOOD)

Gen	6:17	I Myself am bringing f on
Gen	7: 6	years old when the f were

FLOOR (see FLOORS)
Num   5:17 of the dust that is on the f
Num   15:20 offering of the threshing f,
Num   18:27 the grain of the threshing f
Num   18:30 produce of the threshing f
Deut   16:13 from your threshing f and
Ruth   3:14 came to the threshing f.
2Sa   24:16 was by the threshing f of
1Ki   6:16 from f to ceiling, with
1Ch   21:15 stood by the threshing f of
Mic   4:12 sheaves to the threshing f.
Matt   3:12 clean out His threshing f,

FLOORS (see FLOOR)
Dan   2:35 from the summer threshing f;
Joel   2:24 The threshing f shall be

FLOUR
Ex   29: 2 shall make them of wheat f).
Lev   2: 1 offering shall be of fine f.
Judg   6:19 bread from an ephah of f,
1Sa   1:24 three bulls, one ephah of f,
1Ki   17:12 only a handful of f in a
Is   28:28 Bread f must be ground;

FLOURISH (see FLOURISHED, FLOURISHES, FLOURISHING)
Job   8:11 Can the reeds f without
Ps   72: 7 days the righteous shall f,
Ps   72:16 those of the city shall f
Ps   92: 7 the workers of iniquity f,
Ps   92:12 The righteous shall f like a
Ps   92:13 house of the LORD Shall f
Prov   11:28 But the righteous will f
Prov   14:11 tent of the upright will f.
Is   66:14 And your bones shall f like
Ezek   17:24 tree and made the dry tree f;

FLOURISHED† (see FLOURISH)
Phil   4:10 last your care for me has f

FLOURISHES† (see FLOURISH)
Ps   90: 6 In the morning it f and
Ps   103:15 flower of the field, so he f.

FLOURISHING (see FLOURISH)
Dan   4: 4 and f in my palace.

FLOW (see FLOWED, FLOWING, FLOWS)
Lev   12: 7 shall be clean from the f
Ps   147:18 to blow, and the waters f.
Is   2: 2 And all nations shall f to
Is   8: 6 waters of Shiloah that f
Is   48:21 He caused the waters to f
Jer   14:17 Let my eyes f with tears
Lam   3:49 My eyes f and do not cease,
Joel   3:18 A fountain shall f from the
Amos   9:13 And all the hills shall f
Mic   4: 1 And peoples shall f to it.
Zech   14: 8 living waters shall f from
Mark   5:25 Now a certain woman had a f
John   7:38 out of his heart will f

FLOWED† (see FLOW)
Lam   3:54 The waters f over my head;

FLOWER (see FLOWERS)
1Sa   2:33 house shall die in the f of
Job   14: 2 He comes forth like a f and
Ps   103:15 As a f of the field, so he
Is   18: 5 grape is ripening in the f,
Is   40: 8 the f fades, But the word
1Co   7:36 if she is past the f of
Jas   1:10 because as a f of the field
1Pe   1:24 And its f falls away,

FLOWERS (see FLOWER)
Song   2:12 The f appear on the earth;

FLOWING (see FLOW)
Ex   13: 5 a land f with milk and
Prov   18: 4 of wisdom is a f brook.
Is   66:12 of the Gentiles like a f
Jer   18:14 Will the cold f waters be
Jer   49: 4 Your f valley, O
Ezek   23:15 F turbans on their heads,
Ezek   47: 1 the water was f from under

FLOWS (see FLOW)
Num   13:27 It truly f with milk and
1Ki   17: 3 which f into the Jordan.

FLUSHED†
Job   16:16 My face is f from weeping,

FLUTE (see FLUTES)
Gen   4:21 who play the harp and f.
Job   21:12 to the sound of the f.
Is   5:12 The tambourine and f,
Dan   3: 5 the sound of the horn, f,
Matt   9:23 and saw the f players and
Matt   11:17 We played the f for you, And

FLUTES (see FLUTE)
Ps   150: 4 stringed instruments and f!

FLY (see FLEW, FLIES, FLIGHT, FLYING)
Gen   1:20 and let birds f above the
Job   5: 7 As the sparks f upward.
Job   20: 8 He will f away like a dream,
Ps   55: 6 like a dove! I would f
Ps   90:10 and we f away.
Prov   23: 5 They f away like an eagle
Is   7:18 LORD will whistle for the f
Dan   9:21 being caused to f swiftly,
Hos   9:11 their glory shall f away
Rev   19:17 to all the birds that f in

FLYING (see FLY)
Lev   11:20 All f insects that creep on
Ps   148:10 Creeping things and f fowl;
Prov   26: 2 like a f swallow, So a
Is   14:29 will be a fiery f serpent.
Zech   5: 1 and saw there a f scroll.

FOAL†
Zech   9: 9 the f of a donkey.
Matt   21: 5 the f of a donkey.' "

FOAMING† (see FOAMS)
Mark   9:20 f at the mouth.
Jude   13 f up their own shame;

FOAMS (see FOAMING)
Mark   9:18 he f at the mouth, gnashes

FOE† (see FOES)
Ps   18:14 arrows and scattered the f,

FOES (see FOE)
Ps   30: 1 And have not let my f

FOLD (see FOLDED, FOLDING, FOLDS)
Neh   5:13 Then I shook out the f of my
Ezek   34:14 shall lie down in a good f
John   10:16 have which are not of this f;
Heb   1:12 a cloak You will f

FOLDED† (see FOLD)
John   20: 7 but f together in a place by

FOLDING (see FOLD)
Prov   6:10 A little f of the hands to
Prov   24:33 A little f of the hands to

FOLDS (see FOLD)
Num   32:36 and f for sheep.
Job   41:23 The f of his flesh are
Eccl   4: 5 The fool f his hands And

FOLLOW (see FOLLOWED, FOLLOWERS, FOLLOWING, FOLLOWS)

Gen	24: 8	woman is not willing to f
Gen	44: 4	f the men; and when you
Deut	8:19	and f other gods, and serve
1Sa	17:13	sons of Jesse had gone to f
2Sa	17: 9	among the people who f
1Ki	11: 6	and did not fully f the
1Ki	18:21	Him; but if Baal, follow
1Ki	18:21	f him." But the people
2Ki	6:19	F me, and I will bring you
2Ki	17:34	nor do they f their statutes
2Ki	23: 3	to f the LORD and to keep
Ps	23: 6	goodness and mercy shall f
Ps	38:20	because I f what is good.
Ps	94:15	the upright in heart will f
Jer	13:10	who f the dictates of their
Matt	4:19	F Me, and I will make you
Matt	8:19	I will f You wherever You
Matt	8:22	F Me, and let the dead bury
Matt	10:38	not take his cross and f
Matt	16:24	up his cross and f Me.
Matt	19:21	and come, f Me."
Mark	1:17	F Me, and I will make you
Mark	5:37	And He permitted no one to f
Mark	16:17	And these signs will f those
Luke	9:57	I will f You wherever You
John	1:43	said to him, F Me."
John	10: 4	and the sheep f him, for
John	10:27	and they f Me.
John	13:36	I am going you cannot f Me
John	13:36	but you shall f Me
Acts	3:24	from Samuel and those who f,
1Ti	5:24	but those of some men f
1Pe	1:11	and the glories that would f.
1Pe	2:21	that you should f His steps:
2Pe	1:16	For we did not f cunningly
Rev	14:13	and their works f them."

FOLLOWED (see FOLLOW)

Num	14:24	spirit in him and has f Me
Num	32:11	they have not wholly f Me,
Josh	6: 8	the covenant of the LORD f
Judg	2:12	and they f other gods from
2Sa	17:23	that his advice was not f,
1Ki	19:21	Then he arose and f Elijah,
2Ki	13: 2	and f the sins of Jeroboam
2Ki	17:15	they f idols, became
Amos	2: 4	Lies which their fathers f
Amos	7:15	the LORD took me as I f
Matt	4:20	left their nets and f Him.
Matt	4:22	their father, and f Him.
Matt	4:25	Great multitudes f Him—from
Matt	8:23	His disciples f Him.
Matt	9:27	two blind men f Him, crying
Matt	19:27	we have left all and f You.
Matt	26:58	But Peter f Him at a distance
Matt	27:55	And many women who f Jesus
Matt	27:62	which f the Day of
Mark	14:51	Now a certain young man f
Luke	5:11	they forsook all and f Him.
Luke	18:43	and f Him, glorifying God.
John	1:40	who f Him, was Andrew, Simon
John	18:15	And Simon Peter f Jesus, and
Acts	13:43	Jews and devout proselytes f
1Co	10: 4	that spiritual Rock that f
1Ti	5:10	if she has diligently f
2Ti	3:10	But you have carefully f my
Rev	6: 8	and Hades f with him. And
Rev	8: 7	sounded: And hail and fire f,
Rev	13: 3	all the world marveled and f

FOLLOWERS (see FOLLOW)

1Th	1: 6	And you became f of us and of
1Pe	3:13	harm you if you become f of

FOLLOWING (see FOLLOW)

Deut	7: 4	turn your sons away from f
Judg	2:19	by f other gods, to serve
Ruth	1:16	Or to turn back from f
2Sa	7: 8	from f the sheep, to be
2Ch	35: 4	the written instruction of
Ps	48:13	tell it to the generation f.
Luke	13:33	tomorrow, and the day f;
John	1:38	turned, and seeing them f,
John	20: 6	f him, and went into the
John	21:20	disciple whom Jesus loved f,
Acts	23:11	But the f night the Lord
2Pe	2:15	f the way of Balaam the son

FOLLOWS (see FOLLOW)

Ps	63: 8	My soul f close behind You;
Prov	12:11	But he who f frivolity is
Prov	15: 9	But He loves him who f
Jer	17:16	being a shepherd who f
Matt	1:18	of Jesus Christ was as f:
John	8:12	He who f Me shall not walk

FOLLY (see FOOL)

1Sa	25:25	and f is with him. But I,
Job	42: 8	you according to your f;
Prov	14: 8	But the f of fools is
Prov	14:24	foolishness of fools is f.
Prov	17:12	Rather than a fool in his f
Prov	26: 4	a fool according to his f,
Prov	26:11	So a fool repeats his f.
Eccl	1:17	and to know madness and f.
Eccl	7:25	To know the wickedness of f,
Is	9:17	And every mouth speaks f.
Jer	23:13	And I have seen f in the
2Ti	3: 9	for their f will be manifest

FOOD (see FOODS)

Gen	1:29	to you it shall be for f.
Gen	1:30	every green herb for f";
Gen	2: 9	to the sight and good for f.
Gen	3: 6	the tree was good for f,
Gen	24:33	F was set before him to eat,
Gen	27: 4	"And make me savory f,
Gen	42: 7	the land of Canaan to buy f.
Ex	21:10	he shall not diminish her f,
Lev	3:11	them on the altar as f,
Lev	3:16	burn them on the altar as f,
Lev	25: 6	of the land shall be f for
Deut	28:26	Your carcasses shall be f for
Judg	13:16	Me, I will not eat your f.
2Sa	11: 8	and a gift of f from the
2Sa	12: 3	It ate of his own f and
2Sa	13: 5	and prepare the f in my
2Sa	13:10	Bring the f into the bedroom,
1Ki	4: 7	who provided f for the king
1Ki	19: 8	in the strength of that f
1Ki	21: 5	so sullen that you eat no f?
2Ki	6:22	Set f and water before them,
Job	6: 6	Can flavorless f be eaten
Job	6: 7	They are as loathsome f to
Job	23:12	More than my necessary f.
Job	34: 3	As the palate tastes f.
Job	36:31	He gives f in abundance.
Job	38:41	Who provides f for the
Job	38:41	wander about for lack of f?
Job	42:11	came to him and ate f with
Ps	42: 3	My tears have been my f day
Ps	59:15	wander up and down for f,
Ps	69:21	also gave me gall for my f,
Ps	78:25	Men ate angels' f;
Ps	78:25	He sent them f to the full.
Ps	104:14	That he may bring forth f
Ps	104:21	And seek their f from God.
Ps	104:27	You may give them their f
Ps	107:18	abhorred all manner of f,
Ps	136:25	Who gives f to all flesh,

Ps   146: 7 Who gives **f** to the hungry.
Prov   6: 8 And gathers her **f** in the
Prov   23: 3 For they are deceptive **f**.
Prov   27:27 For the **f** of your
Prov   31:14 She brings her **f** from afar.
Prov   31:15 And provides for her
Is   65:25 shall be the serpent's **f**.
Ezek   47:12 Their fruit will be for **f**,
Dan   1:10 who has appointed your **f** and
Mal   1: 7 You offer defiled **f** on My
Mal   3:10 That there may be **f** in My
Matt   3: 4 and his **f** was locusts and
Matt   6:25 Is not life more than **f** and
Matt   10:10 a worker is worthy of his **f**.
Matt   24:45 to give them **f** in due
Matt   25:35 was hungry and you gave Me **f**;
Luke   9:13 unless we go and buy **f** for
Luke   12:23 "Life is more than **f**,
Luke   24:41 Have you any **f** here?"
John   4: 8 away into the city to buy **f**.
John   4:32 I have **f** to eat of which you
John   4:34 My **f** is to do the will of Him
John   6:27 Do not labor for the **f** which
John   6:27 but for the **f** which endures
John   6:55 For My flesh is **f** indeed, and
John   21: 5 "Children, have you any **f**?"
Acts   27:21 after long abstinence from **f**,
Rom   14:15 Do not destroy with your **f**
1Co   3: 2 milk and not with solid **f**;
1Co   8: 8 But **f** does not commend us to
1Co   8:13 if **f** makes my brother
1Co   10: 3 all ate the same spiritual **f**,
1Co   10:30 I evil spoken of for the **f**
2Co   9:10 the sower, and bread for **f**,
Col   2:16 So let no one judge you in **f**
Heb   12:16 who for one morsel of **f** sold
Jas   2:15 and destitute of daily **f**,

FOODS (see FOOD)
1Co   6:13 and the stomach for **f**,
Heb   13: 9 not with **f** which have not

FOOL (see FOLLY, FOOLISH, FOOL'S, FOOLS)
1Sa   26:21 Indeed I have played the **f**
2Sa   3:33 Should Abner die as a **f** dies?
Ps   14: 1 The **f** has said in his heart,
Ps   49:10 Likewise the **f** and the
Ps   53: 1 The **f** has said in his heart,
Prov   7:22 Or as a **f** to the correction
Prov   10:18 spreads slander is a **f**.
Prov   10:23 evil is like sport to a **f**,
Prov   11:29 And the **f** will be servant
Prov   12:15 The way of a **f** is right in
Prov   15: 5 A **f** despises his father's
Prov   17: 7 is not becoming to a **f**,
Prov   17:10 Than a hundred blows on a **f**.
Prov   19: 1 in his lips, and is a **f**.
Prov   19:10 is not fitting for a **f**,
Prov   24: 7 is too lofty for a **f**;
Prov   26: 4 Do not answer a **f** according
Prov   26: 5 Answer a **f** according to his
Prov   26:11 So a **f** repeats his folly.
Prov   26:12 is more hope for a **f** than
Prov   29:11 A **f** vents all his feelings,
Eccl   2:19 he will be wise or a **f**?
Eccl   4: 5 The **f** folds his hands And
Eccl   6: 6 is the laughter of the **f**.
Eccl   10:14 A **f** also multiplies words.
Hos   9: 7 knows! The prophet is a **f**,
Matt   5:22 You **f**!' shall be in danger of
Luke   12:20 **F**! This night your soul will
1Co   3:18 let him become a **f** that he
2Co   11:23 of Christ?—I speak as a **f**—
2Co   12: 6 to boast, I will not be a **f**;

FOOL'S (see FOOL)
Prov   12:16 A **f** wrath is known at once,
Prov   18: 7 A **f** mouth is his
Prov   26: 3 And a rod for the **f** back.
Eccl   5: 3 And a **f** voice is known by

FOOLISH (see FOOL, FOOLISHLY, FOOLISHNESS)
Deut   32:21 moved Me to anger by their **f**
Job   2:10 You speak as one of the **f**
Job   5: 2 For wrath kills a **f** man,
Ps   73:22 I was so **f** and ignorant; I
Ps   74:22 Remember how the **f** man
Prov   9:13 A **f** woman is clamorous;
Prov   10: 1 But a **f** son is the grief
Prov   19:13 A **f** son is the ruin of his
Prov   21:20 But a **f** man squanders it.
Eccl   7:17 be overly wicked, Nor be **f**:
Is   19:11 wise counselors give **f**
Jer   10: 8 dull-hearted and **f**;
Ezek   13: 3 Woe to the **f** prophets, who
Matt   7:26 will be like a **f** man who
Matt   25: 2 were wise, and five were **f**.
Luke   24:25 O **f** ones, and slow of heart
Rom   1:21 and their **f** hearts were
Rom   10:19 you to anger by a **f**
1Co   1:20 Has not God made **f** the
1Co   1:27 But God has chosen the **f**
Gal   3: 1 O **f** Galatians! Who has
2Ti   2:23 But avoid **f** and ignorant
Tit   3: 9 But avoid **f** disputes,
Jas   2:20 O **f** man, that faith without
1Pe   2:15 silence the ignorance of **f**

FOOLISHLY (see FOOLISH)
Gen   31:28 Now you have done **f** in so
2Co   11:21 anyone is bold—I speak **f**—

FOOLISHNESS (see FOOLISH)
Ps   38: 5 festering Because of my **f**.
Ps   69: 5 O God, You know my **f**;
Prov   9: 6 Forsake **f** and live, And go
Prov   12:23 heart of fools proclaims **f**.
Prov   14:24 But the **f** of fools is
Prov   15: 2 mouth of fools pours forth **f**.
Prov   19: 3 The **f** of a man twists his
Prov   22:15 **F** is bound up in the heart
Eccl   7:25 Even of **f** and madness,
Is   32: 6 foolish person will speak **f**,
Is   44:25 And makes their knowledge **f**;
Mark   7:22 eye, blasphemy, pride, **f**.
1Co   1:18 message of the cross is **f**
1Co   1:21 it pleased God through the **f**
1Co   1:23 block and to the Greeks **f**,
1Co   1:25 Because the **f** of God is wiser
1Co   2:14 for they are **f** to him; nor
1Co   3:19 wisdom of this world is **f**

FOOLS (see FOOL)
2Sa   13:13 would be like one of the **f**
Prov   1: 7 But **f** despise wisdom and
Prov   1:22 And **f** hate knowledge.
Prov   10:21 But **f** die for lack of
Prov   13:19 it is an abomination to **f**
Prov   14: 8 But the folly of **f** is
Prov   14: 9 **F** mock at sin, But among
Prov   14:24 But the foolishness of **f**
Prov   16:22 But the correction of **f** is
Prov   19:29 beatings for the backs of **f**.
Prov   26: 7 a proverb in the mouth of **f**.
Eccl   5: 4 He has no pleasure in **f**.
Eccl   7: 9 rests in the bosom of **f**.
Eccl   10:15 The labor of **f** wearies them,
Matt   23:17 **F** and blind! For which is
Matt   23:19 **F** and blind! For which is
Rom   1:22 to be wise, they became **f**,
1Co   4:10 We are **f** for Christ's sake,
2Co   11:19 For you put up with **f** gladly,

Eph   5:15 not as f but as wise,

FOOT (*see* FEET, FOOTSTEP, FOOTSTOOL, FOUR-FOOTED)
Gen   8: 9 place for the sole of her f,
Ex   12:37 hundred thousand men on f,
Ex   19:17 and they stood at the f of
Ex   21:24 hand for hand, foot for f,
Ex   29:20 the big toe of their right f,
Lev   11:26 animal which divides the f,
Lev   13:12 sore, from his head to his f,
Num   20:19 me only pass through on f,
Deut   11:10 seed and watered it by f,
Deut   32:35 Their f shall slip in due
Deut   33:24 And let him dip his f in
Josh   5:15 your sandal off your f,
2Sa   2:18 Asahel was as fleet of f
Job   2: 7 from the sole of his f to
Job   23:11 My f has held fast to His
Ps   38:16 when my f slips, they exalt
Ps   66: 6 went through the river on f.
Ps   91:12 Lest you dash your f
Ps   121: 3 He will not allow your f to
Prov   1:15 Keep your f from their
Prov   25:17 Seldom set f in your
Prov   25:19 like a bad tooth and a f
Is   1: 6 From the sole of the f even
Dan   8:13 host to be trampled under f?
Matt   4: 6 Lest you dash your f
Matt   18: 8 If your hand or f causes you
Matt   22:13 'Bind him hand and f,
Mark   6:33 knew Him and ran there on f
John   11:44 came out bound hand and f
Acts   20:13 intending himself to go on f.
1Co   12:15 If the f should say,

FOOTMEN†
Jer   12: 5 you have run with the f,

FOOTSTEP† (*see* FOOT, FOOTSTEPS)
Deut   2: 5 no, not so much as one f,

FOOTSTEPS (*see* FOOTSTEP)
Ps   17: 5 That my f may not slip.

FOOTSTOOL (*see* FOOT)
2Ch   9:18 with a f of gold, which
Ps   99: 5 God, And worship at His f—
Ps   110: 1 I make Your enemies Your f.
Is   66: 1 throne, And earth is My f.
Matt   5:35 the earth, for it is His f;
Matt   22:44 Your enemies Your f' '?
Acts   7:49 And earth is My f.
Heb   1:13 Your enemies Your f'?
Jas   2: 3 or, "Sit here at my f,

FORBEAR† (*see* FORBEARANCE)

FORBEARANCE (*see* FORBEAR)
Rom   2: 4 riches of His goodness, f,
Rom   3:25 because in His f God had

FORBID (*see* FORBIDDEN, FORBIDDING)
1Sa   24: 6 The LORD f that I should do
Matt   19:14 and do not f them; for of
Acts   10:47 Can anyone f water, that
Gal   6:14 But God f that I should boast

FORBIDDEN (*see* FORBID)
Deut   2:37 the LORD our God had f us.
Acts   16: 6 they were f by the Holy

FORBIDDING† (*see* FORBID)
Luke   23: 2 and f to pay taxes to
Acts   28:31 no one f him.
1Th   2:16 f us to speak to the Gentiles
1Ti   4: 3 f to marry, and commanding

FORCE (*see* FORCED, FORCES, FORCING)
Gen   31:31 your daughters from me by f.
2Sa   13:12 do not f me, for no such

1Ki   5:13 Solomon raised up a labor f
Matt   11:12 and the violent take it by f.
John   6:15 to come and take Him by f,
Heb   9:17 For a testament is in f

FORCED (*see* FORCE)
Ex   5:13 And the taskmasters f them
2Sa   13:14 he f her and lay with her.
1Ki   8:31 and is f to take an oath,

FORCES (*see* FORCE)
Gen   14:15 He divided his f against them
Num   2: 3 of the standard of the f,
Deut   22:25 and the man f her and lies
Prov   11:21 Though they join f,
Jer   41:11 all the captains of the f

FORCING (*see* FORCE)
2Sa   8: 2 F them down to the ground,

FORD† (*see* FORDS)
Gen   32:22 and crossed over the f of

FORDS (*see* FORD)
Judg   3:28 seized the f of the Jordan
Is   16: 2 daughters of Moab at the f

FOREFATHERS† (*see* FATHERS)
Jer   11:10 to the iniquities of their f
Dan   11:24 have not done, nor his f:
Acts   7:19 people, and oppressed our f,
2Ti   1: 3 as my f did, as without

FOREFRONT
2Sa   11:15 Set Uriah in the f of the

FOREHEAD (*see* FOREHEADS)
Ex   28:38 it shall always be on his f,
1Sa   17:49 the Philistine in his f,
Rev   14: 9 receives his mark on his f
Rev   17: 5 And on her f a name was

FOREHEADS (*see* FOREHEAD)
Ezek   9: 4 and put a mark on the f of
Rev   9: 4 the seal of God on their f.
Rev   13:16 right hand or on their f,
Rev   14: 1 name written on their f.

FOREIGN (*see* FOREIGNER)
Gen   35: 2 Put away the f gods that are
Ex   2:22 have been a stranger in a f
Ex   21: 8 no right to sell her to a f
Deut   32:12 And there was no f god
Josh   24:23 put away the f gods which
Judg   10:16 So they put away the f gods
1Ki   11: 1 King Solomon loved many f
1Ki   11: 8 did likewise for all his f
Ps   81: 9 shall you worship any f god.
Ps   137: 4 the LORD's song In a f
Jer   5:19 forsaken Me and served f
Mal   2:11 married the daughter of a f
Heb   11: 9 land of promise as in a f

FOREIGNER (*see* FOREIGN, FOREIGNERS)
Gen   17:12 with money from any f who
Ex   12:43 No f shall eat it.
Deut   17:15 you may not set a f over
Ruth   2:10 of me, since I am a f?
Ezek   44: 9 says the Lord GOD: "No f,
Luke   17:18 glory to God except this f?
1Co   14:11 I shall be a f to him who

FOREIGNERS (*see* FOREIGNER)
Deut   31:16 with the gods of the f of
Is   25: 2 A palace of f to be a city
Jer   30: 8 F shall no more enslave
Lam   5: 2 aliens, And our houses to f.
Acts   17:21 all the Athenians and the f
Eph   2:19 no longer strangers and f,

FOREKNEW† (*see* FOREKNOWLEDGE)
Rom   8:29 For whom He f,

Rom 11: 2 away His people whom He f.

FOREKNOWLEDGE† (*see* FOREKNEW)
Acts 2:23 determined purpose and f of
1Pe 1: 2 elect according to the f of

FOREMEN
2Ch 34:10 put it in the hand of the f

FOREORDAINED†
1Pe 1:20 He indeed was f before the

FORERUNNER†
Heb 6:20 where the f has entered for

FORESAW† (*see* FORESEES)
Acts 2:25 I f the LORD always

FORESEEING (*see* FORESEES)
Gal 3: 8 f that God would justify the

FORESEES† (*see* FORESAW, FORESEEING)
Prov 22: 3 A prudent man f evil and
Prov 27:12 A prudent man f evil and

FORESKIN (*see* FORESKINS)
Gen 17:14 in the flesh of his f,
Ex 4:25 stone and cut off the f of
Lev 12: 3 day the flesh of his f
Deut 10:16 Therefore circumcise the f of

FORESKINS (*see* FORESKIN)
Gen 17:11 in the flesh of your f,
1Sa 18:25 any dowry but one hundred f
Jer 4: 4 And take away the f of your

FOREST (*see* FORESTS)
1Ki 7: 2 built the House of the F of
1Ki 10:17 them in the House of the F
Neh 2: 8 the keeper of the king's f,
Ps 50:10 For every beast of the f is
Is 44:23 singing, you mountains, O f,
Jer 10: 3 one cuts a tree from the f,
Ezek 20:46 and prophesy against the f
Ezek 20:47 and say to the f of the
Amos 3: 4 Will a lion roar in the f,
Zech 11: 2 For the thick f has come
Jas 3: 5 See how great a f a little

FORESTS (*see* FOREST)
Ps 29: 9 And strips the f bare; And
Ezek 39:10 nor cut down any from the f,

FORETELL† (*see* FORETOLD)
2Co 13: 2 and f as if I were present

FORETOLD† (*see* FORETELL)
Acts 3:18 those things which God f by
Acts 3:24 have also f these days.
Acts 7:52 And they killed those who f

FOREVER (*see* FOREVERMORE)
Gen 3:22 and eat, and live f"—
Gen 6: 3 shall not strive with man f,
Gen 13:15 you and your descendants f.
Ex 3:15 to you. This is My name f,
Ex 12:24 for you and your sons f.
Ex 15:18 The LORD shall reign f and
Ex 27:21 It shall be a statute f
Num 10: 8 be to you as an ordinance f
Deut 15:17 he shall be your servant f.
Josh 4:24 fear the LORD your God f.
1Sa 2:35 walk before My anointed f.
2Sa 2:26 "Shall the sword devour f?
2Sa 7:13 the throne of his kingdom f.
2Sa 7:16 shall be established f
2Sa 7:24 Your very own people f;
2Sa 7:25 establish it f and do as
2Sa 7:26 let Your name be magnified f,
2Sa 7:29 that it may continue f
2Sa 7:29 of Your servant be blessed f.
1Ki 8:13 place for You to dwell in f.

1Ki 9: 5 your kingdom over Israel f,
1Ki 10: 9 the LORD has loved Israel f,
2Ki 8:19 lamp to him and his sons f.
1Ch 16:15 Remember His covenant f,
1Ch 16:34 For His mercy endures f.
1Ch 28: 9 Him, He will cast you off f.
Neh 2: 3 May the king live f! Why
Job 7:16 life; I would not live f.
Ps 9: 5 blotted out their name f
Ps 9: 7 the LORD shall endure f;
Ps 10:16 The LORD is King f and
Ps 19: 9 LORD is clean, enduring f;
Ps 21: 4 Length of days f and ever.
Ps 23: 6 in the house of the LORD F.
Ps 29:10 the LORD sits as King f.
Ps 30:12 I will give thanks to You f.
Ps 37:29 the land, And dwell in it f.
Ps 44:23 Do not cast us off f.
Ps 45: 6 is f and ever; A scepter
Ps 45:17 people shall praise You f
Ps 52: 8 trust in the mercy of God f
Ps 61: 4 abide in Your tabernacle f;
Ps 72:19 be His glorious name f!
Ps 73:26 of my heart and my portion f.
Ps 74: 1 why have You cast us off f?
Ps 74:10 enemy blaspheme Your name f?
Ps 79: 5 LORD? Will You be angry f?
Ps 89: 1 the mercies of the LORD f;
Ps 89:36 His seed shall endure f,
Ps 89:37 It shall be established f
Ps 89:46 Will You hide Yourself f?
Ps 105: 8 He remembers His covenant f,
Ps 106: 1 For His mercy endures f.
Ps 110: 4 You are a priest f
Ps 111: 3 His righteousness endures f.
Ps 112: 3 His righteousness endures f.
Ps 117: 2 of the LORD endures f.
Ps 119:44 continually, f and ever.
Ps 119:89 F, O LORD, Your word
Ps 125: 1 be moved, but abides f.
Ps 125: 2 From this time forth and f.
Ps 131: 3 From this time forth and f.
Ps 135:13 name, O LORD, endures f,
Ps 136: 1 For His mercy endures f.
Ps 145: 1 I will bless Your name f
Ps 145: 2 I will praise Your name f
Ps 146:10 The LORD shall reign f—
Prov 27:24 For riches are not f,
Eccl 1: 4 But the earth abides f.
Is 9: 7 that time forward, even f.
Is 25: 8 He will swallow up death f,
Is 26: 4 Trust in the LORD f,
Is 32:17 quietness and assurance f.
Is 40: 8 the word of our God stands f.
Is 51: 6 But My salvation will be f,
Is 51: 8 My righteousness will be f,
Is 64: 9 Nor remember iniquity f.
Jer 3: 5 Will He remain angry f?
Jer 32:39 way, that they may fear Me f,
Jer 35:19 a man to stand before Me f.
Lam 3:31 the Lord will not cast off f.
Lam 5:20 Why do You forget us f,
Ezek 37:25 their children's children, f;
Ezek 43: 9 shall be their prince f.
Dan 2: 4 live f! Tell your servants
Dan 2:44 and it shall stand f.
Dan 4:34 and honored Him who lives f:
Dan 6: 6 "King Darius, live f!
Dan 12: 3 Like the stars f and ever.
Dan 12: 7 and swore by Him who lives f,
Hos 2:19 will betroth you to Me f;
Matt 6:13 the power and the glory f.
Luke 1:55 Abraham and to his seed f.
John 6:58 eats this bread will live f.
John 8:35 forever, but a son abides f.

FOREVERMORE (*see* FOREVER)

John	12:34	that the Christ remains **f**;
John	14:16	that He may abide with you **f**—
Rom	1:25	Creator, who is blessed **f**.
Rom	11:36	things, to whom be glory **f**.
Rom	16:27	glory through Jesus Christ **f**.
2Co	9: 9	righteousness endures **f**.
2Co	11:31	Christ, who is blessed **f**,
Gal	1: 5	to whom be glory **f** and ever.
Eph	3:21	**f** and ever. Amen.
Phm	1:15	that you might receive him **f**,
Heb	1: 8	is **f** and ever; A
Heb	5: 6	You are a priest **f**
Heb	7:24	He, because He continues **f**,
Heb	10:12	one sacrifice for sins **f**,
Heb	10:14	offering He has perfected **f**
Heb	13: 8	same yesterday, today, and **f**.
Heb	13:21	to whom be glory **f** and
1Pe	1:25	of the LORD endures **f**.
1Pe	4:11	the glory and the dominion **f**
2Pe	2:17	the blackness of darkness **f**.
2Pe	3:18	be the glory both now and **f**.
1Jn	2:17	the will of God abides **f**.
2Jn	2	in us and will be with us **f**:
Jude	13	the blackness of darkness **f**.
Rev	1: 6	Him be glory and dominion **f**
Rev	4:10	and worship Him who lives **f**
Rev	11:15	and He shall reign **f** and
Rev	14:11	of their torment ascends **f**
Rev	19: 3	Her smoke rises up **f** and
Rev	20:10	be tormented day and night **f**
Rev	22: 5	And they shall reign **f** and

FOREVERMORE (*see* FOREVER)

Ps	16:11	right hand are pleasures **f**.
Ps	86:12	I will glorify Your name **f**.
Ps	89:52	Blessed be the LORD **f**!
Ps	106:31	To all generations **f**.
Ps	113: 2	From this time forth and **f**!
Ps	132:12	shall sit upon your throne **f**.
Ps	133: 3	the blessing—Life **f**.
Rev	1:18	and behold, I am alive **f**.

FORGAVE (*see* FORGIVE)

Ps	32: 5	And You **f** the iniquity of
Matt	18:27	and **f** him the debt.
Eph	4:32	just as God in Christ **f** you.
Col	3:13	even as Christ **f** you, so you

FORGET (*see* FORGETFULNESS, FORGETS, FORGETTING, FORGOT, FORGOTTEN)

Gen	41:51	For God has made me **f** all my
Deut	4:23	lest you **f** the covenant of
Deut	6:12	lest you **f** the LORD who
Job	8:13	are the paths of all who **f**
Ps	9:17	all the nations that **f** God.
Ps	13: 1	Will You **f** me forever? How
Ps	50:22	you who **f** God, Lest I tear
Ps	74:19	to the wild beast! Do not **f**
Ps	103: 2	And **f** not all His benefits:
Ps	119:16	I will not **f** Your word.
Ps	137: 5	If I **f** you, O Jerusalem,
Ps	137: 5	Let my right hand **f** its
Prov	3: 1	do not **f** my law, But let
Is	49:15	her womb? Surely they may **f**,
Is	49:15	Yet I will not **f** you.
Lam	5:20	Why do You **f** us forever,
Heb	13: 2	Do not **f** to entertain
Heb	13:16	But do not **f** to do good and
2Pe	3: 8	do not **f** this one thing,

FORGETFULNESS† (*see* FORGET)

Ps	88:12	in the land of **f**?

FORGETS (*see* FORGET)

Prov	2:17	And **f** the covenant of her
Jas	1:24	and immediately **f** what kind

FORGETTING† (*see* FORGET)

Phil	3:13	**f** those things which are

FORGIVE (*see* FORGAVE, FORGIVEN, FORGIVES, FORGIVING, UNFORGIVING)

Gen	50:17	please **f** the trespass of
Ex	32:32	If You will **f** their sin—but
1Ki	8:30	place; and when You hear, **f**.
1Ki	8:34	and **f** the sin of Your people
2Ch	7:14	and will **f** their sin and
Dan	9:19	**f**! O Lord, listen and act!
Matt	6:12	And **f** our debts, As we
Matt	6:14	For if you **f** men their
Matt	6:14	heavenly Father will also **f**
Matt	9: 6	Man has power on earth to **f**
Matt	18:35	does not **f** his brother his
Mark	2: 7	Who can **f** sins but God
Luke	6:37	shall not be condemned. **F**,
Luke	11: 4	And **f** us our sins, For we
Luke	23:34	**f** them, for they do not know
1Jn	1: 9	He is faithful and just to **f**

FORGIVEN (*see* FORGIVE, FORGIVENESS)

Ps	32: 1	whose transgression is **f**,
Ps	85: 2	You have **f** the iniquity of
Matt	9: 2	your sins are **f** you."
Matt	12:31	sin and blasphemy will be **f**
Matt	12:31	the Spirit will not be **f**
Luke	5:20	your sins are **f** you."
Luke	6:37	Forgive, and you will be **f**.
Luke	7:48	to her, "Your sins are **f**.
John	20:23	they are **f** them; if you
Rom	4: 7	lawless deeds are **f**,
1Jn	2:12	Because your sins are **f** you

FORGIVENESS (*see* FORGIVEN)

Ps	130: 4	But there is **f** with You,
Dan	9: 9	our God belong mercy and **f**,
Acts	5:31	repentance to Israel and **f**
Eph	1: 7	the **f** of sins, according to
Col	1:14	the **f** of sins.

FORGIVES (*see* FORGIVE)

Ps	103: 3	Who **f** all your iniquities,
Luke	7:49	Who is this who even **f**

FORGIVING (*see* FORGIVE)

Ex	34: 7	**f** iniquity and transgression
Eph	4:32	**f** one another, just as God
Col	3:13	and **f** one another, if anyone

FORGOT (*see* FORGET)

Gen	40:23	Joseph, but **f** him.
Judg	3: 7	They **f** the LORD their God,
Hos	2:13	her lovers; But Me she **f**,

FORGOTTEN (*see* FORGET)

Deut	32:18	And have **f** the God who
Job	19:14	my close friends have **f** me.
Ps	42: 9	Why have You **f** me? Why do I
Ps	77: 9	Has God **f** to be gracious?
Ps	119:61	But I have not **f** Your law.
Is	44:21	you will not be **f** by Me!
Is	65:16	the former troubles are **f**,
Hos	8:14	For Israel has **f** his Maker,
2Pe	1: 9	and has **f** that he was

FORKS

Num	4:14	there—the firepans, the **f**,
1Sa	13:21	the mattocks, the **f**,

FORM (*see* FORMED, FORMS, UNFORMED)

Gen	1: 2	The earth was without **f**,
Gen	29:17	Rachel was beautiful of **f**
Gen	39: 6	Now Joseph was handsome in **f**
Deut	4:12	of the words, but saw no **f**;
Deut	4:16	a carved image in the **f** of
Job	4:16	A **f** was before my eyes;
Is	45: 7	I **f** the light and create

Is   52:14 And His f more than the
Is   53: 2 He has no f or comeliness;
Luke   3:22 descended in bodily f like
John   5:37 at any time, nor seen His f.
Rom   6:17 from the heart that f of
1Co   7:31 For the f of this world is
Phil   2: 6 being in the f of God, did
Phil   2: 7 taking the f of a
1Th   5:22 Abstain from every f of evil.
2Ti   3: 5 having a f of godliness but

FORMED (see FORM)
Gen   2: 7 And the LORD God f man of
Gen   2:19 the ground the LORD God f
Job   33: 6 I also have been f out of
Ps   90: 2 Or ever You had f the earth
Ps   94: 9 He who the eye, shall He
Ps   95: 5 And His hands f the dry
Ps   139:13 For You f my inward parts;
Is   29:16 Or shall the thing f say of
Is   43: 1 And He who f you, O Israel:
Is   44: 2 LORD who made you And f
Is   45:18 Who f the earth and made
Is   45:18 Who f it to be inhabited:
Jer   1: 5 Before I f you in the womb I
Rom   9:20 Will the thing f say to him
Rom   9:20 formed say to him who f it,
Gal   4:19 again until Christ is f in
1Ti   2:13 For Adam was f first, then

FORMER (see FORMERLY)
Ruth   4: 7 this was the custom in f
Eccl   7:10 Why were the f days better
Is   42: 9 the f things have come to
Is   46: 9 Remember the f things of
Jer   5:24 both the f and the latter,
Jer   36:28 and write on it all the f
Dan   11:29 it shall not be like the f
Hos   6: 3 Like the latter and f rain
Hag   2: 3 who saw this temple in its f
Zech   7:12 by His Spirit through the f
Acts   1: 1 The f account I made, O
Heb   7:18 is an annulling of the f
1Pe   1:14 yourselves to the f lusts,
Rev   21: 4 for the f things have passed

FORMERLY (see FORMER)
Deut   2:20 giants f dwelt there. But
Judg   1:23 name of the city was f Luz.
Judg   18:29 the name of the city f was
1Sa   9: 9 (F in Israel, when a man went
1Sa   9: 9 now called a prophet was f
1Pe   3:20 who f were disobedient, when

FORMS (see FORM)
Lev   26:30 carcasses on the lifeless f
Is   45: 9 the clay say to him who f
Zech   12: 1 and f the spirit of man

FORNICATION (see FORNICATIONS, FORNICATOR)
Gal   5:19 which are: adultery, f,
Rev   17: 2 of the earth committed f,
Rev   17: 2 drunk with the wine of her f.
Rev   17: 4 and the filthiness of her f.

FORNICATIONS (see FORNICATION)
Matt   15:19 murders, adulteries, f,

FORNICATOR (see FORNICATION, FORNICATORS)
Eph   5: 5 For this you know, that no f,

FORNICATORS (see FORNICATOR)
1Co   6: 9 not be deceived. Neither f,
Heb   13: 4 but f and adulterers God

FORSAKE (see FORSAKEN, FORSAKES, FORSAKING,
    FORSOOK)
Deut   4:31 He will not f you nor
Deut   31: 6 He will not leave you nor f

Josh   1: 5 I will not leave you nor f
Josh   24:16 it from us that we should f
1Sa   12:22 For the LORD will not f His
1Ch   28: 9 but if you f Him, He will
Neh   9:19 mercies You did not f them
Ps   27: 9 Do not leave me nor f me,
Ps   27:10 my father and my mother f
Ps   37:28 And does not f His saints;
Ps   89:30 If his sons f My law And do
Ps   119: 8 do not f me utterly!
Ps   138: 8 Do not f the works of Your
Prov   3: 3 Let not mercy and truth f
Prov   4: 6 Do not f her, and she will
Prov   9: 6 F foolishness and live, And
Prov   27:10 Do not f your own friend or
Is   55: 7 Let the wicked f his way,
Dan   11:30 show regard for those who f
Jon   2: 8 regard worthless idols F
Luke   14:33 whoever of you does not f
Heb   13: 5 never leave you nor f

FORSAKEN (see FORSAKE)
Judg   6:13 But now the LORD has f us
Judg   10:13 Yet you have f Me and served
Ruth   2:20 who has not f His kindness
1Sa   12:10 because we have f the LORD
1Ki   19:10 children of Israel have f
2Ch   24:20 He also has f you.'"
Ezra   9:10 For we have f Your
Neh   9:10 "Why is the house of God f?
Ps   22: 1 why have You f Me? Why
Ps   37:25 not seen the righteous f,
Is   1: 4 are corrupters! They have f
Is   2: 6 For You have f Your people,
Is   54: 6 called you Like a woman f
Is   62: 4 shall no longer be termed F,
Is   62:12 Sought Out, A City Not F.
Jer   2:13 They have f Me, the
Jer   7:29 the LORD has rejected and f
Jer   9:13 Because they have f My law
Jer   16:11 and have f Me and not kept
Matt   27:46 why have You f Me?"
Mark   15:34 why have You f Me?"
2Co   4: 9 persecuted, but not f;
2Ti   4:10 for Demas has f me, having

FORSAKES (see FORSAKE)
Prov   2:17 Who f the companion of her
Prov   28:13 But whoever confesses and f

FORSAKING† (see FORSAKE)
Heb   10:25 not f the assembling of

FORSOOK (see FORSAKE)
Judg   2:13 They f the LORD and served
Matt   26:56 Then all the disciples f
2Ti   4:16 but all f me. May it not be
Heb   11:27 By faith he f Egypt, not

FORT (see FORTIFY, FORTRESS, FORTS)
Nah   2: 1 Man the f! Watch the road!

FORTIETH (see FORTY)
Num   33:38 and died there in the f year
Deut   1: 3 Now it came to pass in the f

FORTIFIED (see FORTY)
Num   13:28 the cities are f and very
Deut   28:52 gates until your high and f
Josh   19:29 to Ramah and to the f city
Neh   3: 8 and they f Jerusalem as far
Jer   1:18 have made you this day A f
Jer   15:20 make you to this people a f

FORTIFY (see FORT, FORTIFIED, FORTIFYING)
Nah   3:14 your water for the siege! F

FORTIFYING† (see FORTIFY)
Judg   9:31 f the city against you.

FORTRESS (*see* FORT, FORTRESSES)
Ps 18: 2 LORD is my rock and my f
Ps 91: 2 "He is my refuge and my f;
Ps 144: 2 My lovingkindness and my f,
Jer 6:27 you as an assayer and a f
Jer 16:19 LORD, my strength and my f,
Dan 11: 7 enter the f of the king of
Dan 11:31 shall defile the sanctuary f;

FORTRESSES (*see* FORTRESS)
2Ch 17:12 and he built f and storage
Hos 10:14 And all your f shall be
Zeph 3: 6 Their f are devastated; I

FORTS (*see* FORT)
Is 32:14 The f and towers will

FORTUNE-TELLING†
Acts 16:16 her masters much profit by f.

FORTY (*see* FORTIETH)
Gen 7: 4 the earth forty days and f
Gen 7:12 the rain was on the earth f
Gen 18:29 not do it for the sake of f."
Ex 16:35 of Israel ate manna f years,
Ex 24:18 Moses was on the mountain f
Ex 24:18 mountain forty days and f
Num 13:25 spying out the land after f
Num 14:33 in the wilderness f years,
Num 14:34 namely f years, and you
Deut 8: 4 did your foot swell these f
Deut 25: 3 F blows he may give him and
Judg 3:11 So the land had rest for f
1Sa 4:18 And he had judged Israel f
1Ki 11:42 over all Israel was f
1Ki 19: 8 the strength of that food f
Neh 9:21 F years You sustained them
Ps 95:10 For f years I was grieved
Jon 3: 4 Yet f days, and Nineveh shall
Matt 4: 2 had fasted forty days and f
Mark 1:13 there in the wilderness f
Luke 4: 2 being tempted for f days by
Acts 1: 3 being seen by them during f
2Co 11:24 Jews five times I received f
Heb 3:17 Now with whom was He angry f

FORTY-EIGHT
Num 35: 7 to the Levites shall be f;
Josh 21:41 children of Israel were f

FORTY-FIVE
Gen 18:28 He said, "If I find there f,

FORTY-FOUR
Rev 14: 1 with Him one hundred and f

FORTY-NINE†
Lev 25: 8 of years shall be to you f

FORTY-SIX
John 2:20 It has taken f years to build

FORTY-TWO
2Ki 2:24 of the woods and mauled f
Neh 7:66 the whole assembly was f
Rev 11: 2 holy city underfoot for f
Rev 13: 5 authority to continue for f

FORUM†
Acts 28:15 to meet us as far as Appii F

FORWARD
Ex 14:15 children of Israel to go f.
Num 1:51 the tabernacle is to go f,
1Sa 16:13 upon David from that day f.
2Ki 20: 9 shall the shadow go f ten
Is 9: 7 justice From that time f,
Ezek 1: 9 but each one went straight f.
Dan 3: 8 certain Chaldeans came f
Hag 2:15 consider from this day f:
Matt 26:60 two false witnesses came f

2Pe 3:14 looking f to these things,

FOUGHT (*see* FIGHT)
Ex 17:10 and f with Amalek. And
Josh 10:14 for the LORD f for Israel.
Josh 10:31 encamped against it and f
Judg 5:20 stars from their courses f
Ps 109: 3 And f against me without a
1Co 15:32 I have f with beasts at
2Ti 4: 7 I have f the good fight, I
Rev 12: 7 the dragon and his angels f,

FOUL
Ps 38: 5 My wounds are f and
Is 19: 6 The rivers will turn f;
Matt 16: 3 It will be f weather

FOUND (*see* FIND, FOUNDED, FOUNDING)
Gen 2:20 for Adam there was not f a
Gen 6: 8 But Noah f grace in the eyes
Gen 8: 9 But the dove f no resting
Gen 11: 2 that they f a plain in the
Gen 18: 3 if I have now f favor in
Gen 18:29 there should be forty f
Gen 26:32 We have f water."
Gen 37:15 Now a certain man f him, and
Gen 37:17 after his brothers and f
Gen 44: 8 Canaan the money which we f
Gen 44:12 and the cup was f in
Ex 15:22 in the wilderness and f no
Ex 22: 2 If the thief is f breaking
Lev 6: 3 or if he has f what was lost
Num 15:32 they f a man gathering
Deut 21: 1 If anyone is f slain, lying
Deut 22:14 and when I came to her I f
Deut 22:22 If a man is f lying with a
Deut 22:28 and they are f out,
Deut 24: 1 in his eyes because he has f
Deut 24: 7 If a man is f kidnapping any
Judg 15:15 He f a fresh jawbone of a
Ruth 2:10 Why have I f favor in your
1Sa 13:19 was no blacksmith to be f
1Sa 29: 3 And to this day I have f no
1Sa 29: 6 For to this day I have not f
2Sa 7:27 Your servant has f it in
1Ki 13:14 and f him sitting under an
1Ki 13:28 Then he went and f his corpse
1Ki 20:36 a lion f him and killed him.
1Ki 21:20 I have f you, because you
2Ki 12:18 and all the gold f in the
2Ki 14:14 the articles that were f in
2Ki 22: 8 I have f the Book of the Law
1Ch 26:31 and there were f among them
1Ch 28: 9 He will be f by you; but if
2Ch 15: 2 He will be f by you; but if
2Ch 29:16 all the debris that they f
2Ch 34:14 Hilkiah the priest f the
Neh 8:14 And they f written in the
Neh 9: 8 You f his heart faithful
Job 19:28 the root of the matter is f
Job 28:12 where can wisdom be f?
Job 32:13 We have f wisdom'; God will
Ps 17: 3 have tried me and have f
Ps 32: 6 In a time when You may be f;
Ps 69:20 comforters, but I f none.
Ps 84: 3 Even the sparrow has f a
Ps 89:20 I have f My servant David;
Ps 107: 4 They f no city to dwell in.
Ps 109: 7 let him be f guilty, And
Ps 116: 3 I f trouble and sorrow.
Ps 132: 6 We f it in the fields of
Prov 10:13 Wisdom is f on the lips of
Prov 30: 6 and you be f a liar.
Prov 30:10 and you be f guilty.
Song 3: 4 When I f the one I love. I
Is 51: 3 Joy and gladness will be f

Is	55: 6	the LORD while He may be f,
Is	65: 1	I was f by those who did
Jer	11: 9	A conspiracy has been f among
Jer	14: 3	went to the cisterns and f
Jer	15:16	Your words were f,
Jer	29:14	I will be f by you, says the
Jer	41:12	who dug f him by the great
Jer	48:27	Was he f among thieves?
Lam	2:16	We have f it, we have seen
Ezek	28:15	Till iniquity was f in you.
Dan	1:19	among them all none was f
Dan	1:20	he f them ten times better
Dan	5:12	explaining enigmas were f
Dan	5:27	and f wanting;
Dan	6: 4	there any error or fault f
Dan	6:11	these men assembled and f
Dan	6:22	because I was f innocent
Dan	12: 1	Every one who is f written
Hos	9:10	I f Israel Like grapes in
Jon	1: 3	and f a ship going to
Matt	1:18	she was f with child of the
Matt	2: 8	and when you have f Him,
Matt	8:10	I have not f such great
Matt	13:44	which a man f and hid; and
Matt	13:46	when he had f one pearl of
Matt	21:19	He came to it and f nothing
Matt	26:40	came to the disciples and f
Matt	27:32	they f a man of Cyrene,
Mark	7: 2	hands, they f fault.
Mark	7:30	she f the demon gone out,
Mark	11: 4	and f the colt tied by the
Luke	1:30	for you have f favor with
Luke	2:16	they came with haste and f
Luke	2:46	after three days they f Him
Luke	9:36	Jesus was f alone. But they
Luke	15: 5	And when he has f it, he
Luke	15: 6	for I have f my sheep which
Luke	15: 9	And when she has f it, she
Luke	15: 9	for I have f the piece which
Luke	15:32	again, and was lost and is f.
Luke	23: 2	We f this fellow perverting
Luke	23:14	I have f no fault in this
Luke	23:22	I have f no reason for death
Luke	24: 2	But they f the stone rolled
John	1:41	He first f his own brother
John	1:41	We have f the Messiah"
John	1:45	We have f Him of whom Moses
John	12:14	when He had f a young
Acts	5:10	the young men came in and f
Acts	5:23	we f no one inside!"
Acts	5:39	lest you even be f to fight
Acts	9:30	When the brethren f out, they
Acts	17:23	I even f an altar with this
Acts	22:29	was also afraid after he f
Acts	23:29	I f out that he was accused
Rom	7:10	I f to bring death.
1Co	4: 2	in stewards that one be f
2Co	5: 3	we shall not be f naked.
2Co	12:20	and that I shall be f by
Phil	2: 8	And being f in appearance as
Phil	3: 9	and be f in Him, not having
1Ti	3:10	being f blameless.
Heb	11: 5	death, "and was not f,
Heb	12:17	for he f no place for
1Pe	1: 7	may be f to praise, honor,
1Pe	2:22	Nor was deceit f in
Rev	3: 2	for I have not f your works
Rev	5: 4	because no one was f worthy
Rev	14: 5	And in their mouth was f no
Rev	18:24	And in her was f the blood of
Rev	20:15	And anyone not f written in

FOUNDATION (*see* FOUNDATIONS)

1Ki	5:17	to lay the f of the temple.
Ps	89:14	and justice are the f of

Ps	102:25	Of old You laid the f of the
Ps	137: 7	To its very f!"
Is	28:16	lay in Zion a stone for a f,
Is	28:16	cornerstone, a sure f;
Zech	4: 9	Zerubbabel Have laid the f
Matt	13:35	kept secret from the f
Luke	6:48	who dug deep and laid the f
Luke	14:29	after he has laid the f,
Rom	15:20	build on another man's f,
1Co	3:11	For no other f can anyone lay
1Co	3:12	if anyone builds on this f
Eph	1: 4	us in Him before the f of
Eph	2:20	having been built on the f of
2Ti	2:19	Nevertheless the solid f of
Heb	1:10	beginning laid the f
Rev	13: 8	of the Lamb slain from the f
Rev	17: 8	the Book of Life from the f
Rev	21:19	the first f was jasper, the

FOUNDATIONS (*see* FOUNDATION)

Job	38: 4	were you when I laid the f
Acts	16:26	so that the f of the prison
Heb	11:10	for the city which has f,
Rev	21:14	of the city had twelve f,

FOUNDED (*see* FOUND)

Ps	24: 2	For He has f it upon the
Prov	3:19	The LORD by wisdom f the
Is	14:32	That the LORD has f Zion,
Matt	7:25	for it was f on the rock.

FOUNDING† (*see* FOUND)

Ex	9:18	been in Egypt since its f

FOUNTAIN (*see* FOUNTAINS)

Neh	2:14	Then I went on to the F Gate
Ps	36: 9	For with You is the f of
Ps	74:15	You broke open the f and the
Ps	114: 8	The flint into a f of
Prov	13:14	law of the wise is a f of
Prov	14:27	fear of the LORD is a f
Eccl	12: 6	pitcher shattered at the f,
Song	4:12	A f sealed.
Jer	2:13	the f of living waters,
Jer	6: 7	As a f wells up with water,
Jer	9: 1	And my eyes a f of tears,
Jer	17:13	The f of living waters."
Hos	13:15	And his f shall be dried
Joel	3:18	A f shall flow from the
John	4:14	him will become in him a f
Rev	21: 6	I will give of the f of the

FOUNTAINS (*see* FOUNTAIN)

Gen	8: 2	The f of the deep and the
Prov	5:16	Should your f be dispersed
Prov	8:24	When there were no f
Rev	7:17	and lead them to living f

FOUR (*see* FOUR-FOOTED, FOURS, FOURTH)

Gen	2:10	there it parted and became f
Gen	14: 9	f kings against five.
Gen	23:16	f hundred shekels of silver,
Job	1:19	wilderness and struck the f
Job	42:16	and grandchildren for f
Prov	30:18	f which I do not
Prov	30:29	f which are stately in
Jer	36:23	Jehudi had read three or f
Jer	49:36	the four winds From the f
Ezek	1: 5	it came the likeness of f
Ezek	1: 6	Each one had f faces, and
Ezek	1: 6	and each one had f wings.
Ezek	7: 2	The end has come upon the f
Ezek	10: 9	there were f wheels by the
Ezek	10:10	all f looked alike—as it
Ezek	37: 9	Come from the f winds, O
Dan	1:17	As for these f young men,
Dan	3:25	I see f men loose, walking in
Dan	7: 3	And f great beasts came up

Dan   7: 6 The beast also had **f** heads,
Dan   7:17 are **f** kings which arise
Amos   1: 3 of Damascus, and for **f**,
Amos   2: 4 of Judah, and for **f**,
Amos   2: 6 of Israel, and for **f**,
Zech   1:18 and there were **f** horns.
Matt   24:31 His elect from the **f** winds,
Mark   2: 3 who was carried by **f** men.
John   4:35 There are still **f** months and
John   11:39 for he has been dead **f**
Acts   7: 6 bondage and oppress them **f**
Acts   10:11 a great sheet bound at the **f**
Gal   3:17 which was **f** hundred and
Rev   4: 6 were **f** living creatures
Rev   7: 2 with a loud voice to the **f**

FOUR-FIFTHS†
Gen   47:24 **F** shall be your own, as seed

FOUR-FOOTED (*see* FOOT, FOUR)
Acts   10:12 In it were all kinds of **f**
Rom   1:23 and birds and **f** animals and

FOURFOLD†
2Sa   12: 6 And he shall restore **f** for
Luke   19: 8 accusation, I restore **f**.

FOURS (*see* FOUR)
Lev   11:20 that creep on all **f** shall
Lev   11:27 of animals that go on all **f**,

FOURTEEN (*see* FOURTEENTH)
Gen   31:41 I served you **f** years for
Matt   1:17 from Abraham to David are **f**
Matt   1:17 captivity in Babylon are **f**
Matt   1:17 until the Christ are **f**

FOURTEENTH (*see* FOURTEEN)
Num   9: 5 kept the Passover on the **f**

FOURTH (*see* FOUR)
Gen   1:19 and the morning were the **f**
Gen   2:14 The **f** river is the
Gen   15:16 But in the **f** generation they
Num   14:18 children to the third and **f**
2Ki   10:30 throne of Israel to the **f**
Jer   25: 1 in the **f** year of Jehoiakim
Ezek   10:14 and the **f** the face of an
Dan   2:40 And the **f** kingdom shall be as
Dan   7: 7 a **f** beast, dreadful and
Zech   8:19 The fast of the **f** month,
Matt   14:25 Now in the **f** watch of the
Rev   4: 7 and the **f** living creature
Rev   6: 7 When He opened the **f** seal, I
Rev   6: 8 was given to them over a **f**
Rev   8:12 Then the **f** angel sounded:

FOWL (*see* FOWLER)
Ps   148:10 things and flying **f**;

FOWLER† (*see* FOWL, FOWLER'S, FOWLERS)
Ps   91: 3 you from the snare of the **f**
Prov   6: 5 bird from the hand of the **f**.

FOWLER'S† (*see* FOWLER)
Hos   9: 8 But the prophet is a **f**

FOWLERS† (*see* FOWLER)
Ps   124: 7 from the snare of the **f**;

FOX (*see* FOXES)
Luke   13:32 to them, "Go, tell that **f**,

FOXES (*see* FOX)
Judg   15: 4 turned the **f** tail to tail,
Song   2:15 The little **f** that spoil the
Matt   8:20 **F** have holes and birds of the

FRAGMENTS
Matt   14:20 baskets full of the **f** that

FRAGRANCE (*see* FRAGRANT)
Song   1:12 spikenard sends forth its **f**.

Song   7: 8 The **f** of your breath like
John   12: 3 house was filled with the **f**
2Co   2:14 through us diffuses the **f**
2Co   2:15 For we are to God the **f** of

FRAGRANT (*see* FRAGRANCE)
Song   4:13 **F** henna with spikenard,
Matt   26: 7 flask of very costly **f** oil,
Matt   26:12 For in pouring this **f** oil on
Luke   7:46 has anointed My feet with **f**
Luke   23:56 and prepared spices and **f**

FRAIL† (*see* FRAILTY)
Ps   39: 4 That I may know how **f** I

FRAILTY† (*see* FRAIL)
Dan   10: 8 my vigor was turned to **f** in

FRAME (*see* FRAMED, FRAMES)
Ps   103:14 For He knows our **f**;
Ps   139:15 My **f** was not hidden from

FRAMED† (*see* FRAME)
Heb   11: 3 that the worlds were **f** by

FRAMES (*see* FRAME)
Ps   50:19 And your tongue **f** deceit.

FRANKINCENSE
Ex   30:34 and pure **f** with these sweet
Song   3: 6 Perfumed with myrrh and **f**,
Matt   2:11 gifts to Him: gold, **f**,
Rev   18:13 incense, fragrant oil and **f**,

FRAUD†
Hos   7: 1 For they have committed **f**;
Acts   13:10 full of all deceit and all **f**,
Jas   5: 4 which you kept back by **f**,

FREE (*see* FREED, FREEDMAN, FREEDOM, FREELY,
     FREEWILL, FREEWOMAN)
Ex   21: 2 seventh he shall go out **f**
Lev   19: 5 offer it of your own **f** will.
Num   5:19 be **f** from this bitter water
Deut   32:36 no one remaining, bond or **f**.
Judg   16:20 and shake myself **f**!" But he
1Ch   9:33 and were **f** from other
Job   10: 1 I will give **f** course to my
Ps   105:20 of the people let him go **f**.
Is   45:13 city And let My exiles go **f**,
Is   58: 6 To let the oppressed go **f**,
Jer   34: 9 that every man should set **f**
John   8:32 the truth shall make you **f**.
John   8:36 you shall be **f** indeed.
Rom   5:15 But the **f** gift is not like
Rom   6:18 And having been set **f** from
Rom   6:20 you were **f** in regard to
Rom   8: 2 Christ Jesus has made me **f**
1Co   7:22 he who is called while **f**
1Co   9: 1 not an apostle? Am I not **f**?
2Co   11: 7 the gospel of God to you **f**
Gal   3:28 there is neither slave nor **f**,
Gal   4:26 but the Jerusalem above is **f**,
Gal   4:31 the bondwoman but of the **f**.
Gal   5: 1 which Christ has made us **f**,
2Th   3: 8 did we eat anyone's bread **f**
1Pe   2:16 as **f**, yet not using

FREED (*see* FREE)
Rom   6: 7 he who has died has been **f**

FREEDMAN† (*see* FREE, FREEDMEN)
1Co   7:22 Ca slave is the Lord's **f**.

FREEDMEN† (*see* FREEDMAN)
Acts   6: 9 the Synagogue of the **F**

FREEDOM (*see* FREE)
Ps   146: 7 The LORD gives **f** to the

FREELY (*see* FREE)
Gen   2:16 of the garden you may **f** eat;

Ps   54: 6 I will **f** sacrifice to You;
Hos   14: 4 I will love them **f**,
Matt   10: 8 **F** you have received, freely
Matt   10: 8 have received, **f** give.
Rom   3:24 being justified **f** by His
Rom   8:32 He not with Him also **f** give
Rev   21: 6 of the water of life **f** to
Rev   22:17 him take the water of life **f**.

FREEWILL (*see* FREE)
Ex   36: 3 continued bringing to him **f**
Ps   119:108 the **f** offerings of my mouth,

FREEWOMAN (*see* FREE)
Gal   4:30 with the son of the **f**.

FREQUENT† (*see* FREQUENTLY)
1Ti   5:23 stomach's sake and your **f**

FREQUENTLY† (*see* FREQUENT)
2Co   11:23 measure, in prisons more **f**,

FRESH (*see* FRESHLY)
Num   6: 3 nor eat **f** grapes or raisins.
Judg   15:15 He found a **f** jawbone of a
Judg   16: 7 they bind me with seven **f**
Jas   3:11 Does a spring send forth **f**

FRESHLY† (*see* FRESH)
Gen   8:11 a **f** plucked olive leaf was

FRET†
Ps   37: 1 Do not **f** because of
Ps   37: 7 Do not **f** because of him who
Ps   37: 8 and forsake wrath; Do not **f**—
Prov   24:19 Do not **f** because of

FRIEND (*see* FRIENDLY, FRIENDS, FRIENDSHIP)
Ex   33:11 as a man speaks to his **f**.
Ruth   4: 1 Boaz said, "Come aside, **f**,
1Ki   4: 5 a priest and the king's **f**;
2Ch   20: 7 of Abraham Your **f** forever?
Ps   41: 9 Even my own familiar **f** in
Prov   6: 1 you become surety for your **f**,
Prov   17:17 A **f** loves at all times, And
Prov   18:24 But there is a **f** who
Prov   27: 6 are the wounds of a **f**,
Song   5:16 beloved, And this is my **f**,
Is   41: 8 descendants of Abraham My **f**.
Mic   7: 5 Do not trust in a **f**;
Matt   11:19 a **f** of tax collectors and
Luke   11: 5 midnight and say to him, 'F,
John   3:29 but the **f** of the bridegroom,
John   11:11 Our **f** Lazarus sleeps, but I
John   19:12 go, you are not Caesar's **f**.
Phm   1: 1 To Philemon our beloved **f**
Jas   2:23 And he was called the **f** of
Jas   4: 4 therefore wants to be a **f**

FRIENDLY (*see* FRIEND)
Prov   18:24 friends must himself be **f**,

FRIENDS (*see* FRIEND)
Judg   11:37 my **f** and I."
2Sa   19: 6 your enemies and hate your **f**.
Job   2:11 Now when Job's three **f** heard
Job   16:20 My **f** scorn me; My eyes pour
Job   19:19 All my close **f** abhor me,
Job   42: 7 against you and your two **f**,
Job   42:10 when he prayed for his **f**.
Prov   14:20 But the rich has many **f**.
Prov   16:28 separates the best of **f**.
Prov   17: 9 repeats a matter separates **f**.
Prov   19: 4 Wealth makes many **f**,
Song   5: 1 (To His **F**) Eat, O
Song   5: 1 O **f**! Drink, yes, drink
Song   6:12 THE BELOVED AND HIS **F**
Zech   13: 6 wounded in the house of my **f**.
Matt   9:15 Can the **f** of the bridegroom

Mark   5:19 to him, "Go home to your **f**,
Luke   7: 6 the centurion sent **f** to Him,
Luke   15: 6 he calls together his **f** and
Luke   15: 9 she calls her **f** and
Luke   23:12 Pilate and Herod became **f**
John   15:13 down one's life for his **f**.
John   15:14 You are My **f** if you do
John   15:15 but I have called you **f**,

FRIENDSHIP† (*see* FRIEND)
Prov   22:24 Make no **f** with an angry man,
Jas   4: 4 Do you not know that **f** with

FRIGHTEN (*see* FRIGHTENED)
Job   18:11 Terrors **f** him on every side,

FRIGHTENED (*see* FRIGHTEN)
Luke   24:37 they were terrified and **f**,

FROGS
Ex   8: 2 all your territory with **f**.
Rev   16:13 three unclean spirits like **f**

FRONTLETS†
Ex   13:16 a sign on your hand and as **f**
Deut   6: 8 and they shall be as **f**
Deut   11:18 and they shall be as **f**

FROST
Ex   16:14 as fine as **f** on the ground.
Jer   36:30 heat of the day and the **f**

FRUIT (*see* FRUITFUL, FRUITS)
Ezek   47:12 They will bear **f** every
Dan   4:12 Its **f** abundant, And in it
Amos   2: 9 Yet I destroyed his **f** above
Amos   7:14 And a tender of sycamore **f**.
Amos   8: 1 Behold, a basket of summer **f**.
Mic   6: 7 The **f** of my body for the
Hab   3:17 Nor **f** be on the vines;
Hag   1:10 the earth withholds its **f**.
Matt   7:17 every good tree bears good **f**,
Matt   7:17 but a bad tree bears bad **f**.
Matt   12:33 a tree is known by its **f**.
Matt   21:19 Let no **f** grow on you ever
Matt   26:29 I will not drink of this **f**
Mark   4:20 word, accept it, and bear **f**:
Luke   1:42 and blessed is the **f** of
Luke   8:15 keep it and bear **f** with
John   4:36 and gathers **f** for eternal
John   15: 2 in Me that does not bear **f**
John   15: 2 every branch that bears **f**
John   15: 2 that it may bear more **f**.
John   15: 5 and I in him, bears much **f**;
John   15:16 and that your **f** should
Rom   1:13 that I might have some **f**
Rom   7: 4 that we should bear **f** to
Rom   7: 5 in our members to bear **f** to
1Co   9: 7 and does not eat of its **f**?
Gal   5:22 But the **f** of the Spirit is
Phil   1:22 this will mean **f** from my
Phil   4:17 but I seek the **f** that
Col   1: 6 and is bringing forth **f**,
Heb   12:11 it yields the peaceable **f**
Heb   13:15 the **f** of our lips, giving
Jas   3:18 Now the **f** of righteousness is
Jude   12 late autumn trees without **f**,
Rev   22: 2 each tree yielding its **f**

FRUITFUL (*see* FRUIT, UNFRUITFUL)
Gen   1:22 Be **f** and multiply, and fill
Gen   9: 1 Be **f** and multiply, and fill
Gen   17: 6 will make you exceedingly **f**;
Is   5: 1 has a vineyard On a very **f**
Col   1:10 being **f** in every good work

FRUITS (*see* FRUIT)
Gen   43:11 Take some of the best **f** of
Song   4:16 And eat its pleasant **f**.

Matt 3: 8 Therefore bear f worthy of
Matt 7:16 will know them by their f.
Matt 21:41 will render to him the f in
Matt 21:43 to a nation bearing the f
2Co 9:10 sown and increase the f of
Phil 1:11 being filled with the f of
Jas 3:17 full of mercy and good f,
Rev 22: 2 of life, which bore twelve f,

FRUSTRATED†
Dan 3:28 and they have f the king's

FUEL
Is 9:19 the people shall be as f

FUGITIVE
Gen 4:12 A f and a vagabond you shall

FULFILL (see FULFILLED, FULFILLING, FULFILLMENT,
    FULFILLS)
Gen 29:27 F her week, and we will give
Lev 22:21 to f his vow, or a freewill
Deut 9: 5 and that He may f the word
1Ki 5: 9 And you shall f my desire by
2Ch 36:21 to f seventy years.
Ezek 20:21 out My fury on them and f
Matt 3:15 it is fitting for us to f
Matt 5:17 not come to destroy but to f.
Rom 13:14 to f its lusts.
Gal 5:16 and you shall not f the lust
Gal 6: 2 and so f the law of Christ.
Phil 2: 2 f my joy by being
Col 1:25 to f the word of God,
2Th 1:11 and f all the good pleasure
2Ti 4: 5 f your ministry.
Jas 2: 8 If you really f the royal
Rev 17:17 it into their hearts to f

FULFILLED (see FULFILL)
Gen 25:24 So when her days were f for
Num 6:13 days of his separation are f,
2Sa 7:12 When your days are f and you
1Ki 8:20 So the LORD has f His word
2Ch 36:22 mouth of Jeremiah might be f,
Ezra 1: 1 mouth of Jeremiah might be f,
Lam 4:11 The LORD has f His fury,
Dan 4:33 very hour the word was f
Dan 10: 3 three whole weeks were f.
Matt 1:22 was done that it might be f
Matt 5:18 from the law till all is f.
Matt 13:14 the prophecy of Isaiah is f,
Matt 26:54 could the Scriptures be f,
Mark 1:15 and saying, "The time is f,
Mark 14:49 But the Scriptures must be f.
Luke 1: 1 which have been f among us,
Luke 1:20 my words which will be f in
Luke 4:21 Today this Scripture is f in
Luke 21:22 which are written may be f.
Luke 21:24 times of the Gentiles are f.
Luke 22:16 eat of it until it is f in
John 3:29 this joy of mine is f.
John 17:13 that they may have My joy f
John 18: 9 that the saying might be f
John 18:32 saying of Jesus might be f
Acts 3:18 would suffer, He has thus f.
Acts 12:25 Jerusalem when they had f
Rom 8: 4 of the law might be f in us
Rom 13: 8 he who loves another has f
Gal 5:14 For all the law is f in one
Rev 17:17 until the words of God are f.

FULFILLING (see FULFILL)
Eph 2: 3 f the desires of the flesh

FULFILLMENT (see FULFILL)
Dan 11:14 shall exalt themselves in f
Dan 12: 6 How long shall the f of these
Luke 1:45 for there will be a f of

Rom 13:10 therefore love is the f of

FULFILLS† (see FULFILL)
Rom 2:27 if he f the law, judge you

FULL (see FILL, FULL-GROWN, FULLNESS, FULLY)
Gen 25: 8 an old man and f of years,
Gen 35:29 being old and f of days.
Gen 41: 7 the seven plump and f heads.
Lev 6: 5 He shall restore its f
Deut 6:11 houses f of all good things,
Deut 6:11 you have eaten and are f—
Judg 5:31 sun When it comes out in f
Ruth 1:21 "I went out f,
Ruth 2:12 and a f reward be given you
1Sa 2: 5 Those who were f have
2Ch 24:15 Jehoiada grew old and was f
Ezra 7:19 deliver in f before the God
Job 10:15 I am f of disgrace; See
Job 14: 1 woman Is of few days and f
Job 32:18 For I am f of words; The
Job 42:17 old and f of days.
Ps 10: 7 His mouth is f of cursing
Ps 26:10 And whose right hand is f
Ps 29: 4 voice of the LORD is f of
Ps 33: 5 The earth is f of the
Ps 78:38 being f of compassion,
Ps 81: 3 At the f moon, on our
Ps 88: 3 For my soul is f of
Ps 104:24 The earth is f of Your
Ps 119:64 is f of Your mercy; Teach
Ps 127: 5 man who has his quiver f of
Ps 144:13 That our barns may be f,
Prov 17: 1 Than a house f of feasting
Prov 27:20 and Destruction are never f;
Prov 30: 9 Lest I be f and deny You,
Eccl 1: 7 sea, Yet the sea is not f;
Eccl 11: 3 If the clouds are f of rain,
Is 1:15 Your hands are f of blood.
Is 2: 8 Their land is also f of
Is 6: 3 The whole earth is f of
Is 11: 9 For the earth shall be f of
Is 51:20 They are f of the fury of
Jer 4:27 Yet I will not make a f
Jer 5: 7 I had fed them to the f,
Jer 5:27 As a cage is f of birds, So
Jer 23:10 For the land is f of
Jer 28: 3 Within two f years I will
Lam 1: 1 sits the city That was f
Ezek 1:18 and their rims were f of
Ezek 7:23 And the city is f of
Ezek 28:12 F of wisdom and perfect in
Ezek 37: 1 and it was f of bones.
Ezek 39:19 shall eat fat till you are f,
Mic 3: 8 But truly I am f of power
Mic 6:12 For her rich men are f of
Hab 3: 3 And the earth was f of His
Matt 6:22 your whole body will be f of
Matt 13:48 "which, when it was f,
Matt 14:20 took up twelve baskets f of
Matt 23:27 but inside are f of dead
Matt 23:28 but inside you are f of
Mark 6:43 took up twelve baskets f of
Mark 15:36 ran and filled a sponge f
Luke 1:57 Now Elizabeth's f time came
Luke 5:12 a man who was f of leprosy
Luke 6:25 Woe to you who are f,
Luke 11:34 your whole body also is f of
Luke 16:20 f of sores, who was laid at
John 1:14 f of grace and truth.
John 15:11 and that your joy may be f.
John 16:24 that your joy may be f.
John 21:11 f of large fish, one hundred
Acts 2:13 They are f of new wine."
Acts 2:28 You will make me f of
Acts 6: 3 f of the Holy Spirit and

Acts 6: 5 a man f of faith and the
Acts 6: 8 f of faith and power, did
Acts 9:36 This woman was f of good
Rom 1:29 f of envy, murder, strife,
Rom 3:14 Whose mouth is f of
Rom 15:14 that you also are f of
1Co 4: 8 You are already f! You are
Phil 4:12 I have learned both to be f
Heb 10:22 near with a true heart in f
Jas 3: 8 f of deadly poison.
1Pe 1: 8 joy inexpressible and f of
2Pe 2:14 having eyes f of adultery and
1Jn 1: 4 you that your joy may be f.
Rev 4: 6 four living creatures f of
Rev 5: 8 and golden bowls f of
Rev 15: 7 angels seven golden bowls f
Rev 16:10 and his kingdom became f of
Rev 17: 3 scarlet beast which was f
Rev 17: 4 in her hand a golden cup f

FULL-GROWN† (see FULL, GROW)
Jas 1:15 sin; and sin, when it is f,

FULLER'S
Is 7: 3 on the highway to the F
Is 36: 2 on the highway to the F

FULLNESS (see FULL)
Deut 33:16 of the earth and its f,
Ps 16:11 In Your presence is f of
Ps 24: 1 the LORD's, and all its f,
Ps 50:12 is Mine, and all its f.
Ps 96:11 the sea roar, and all its f;
John 1:16 And of His f we have all
Rom 11:25 to Israel until the f of
Rom 15:29 I shall come in the f of the
1Co 10:26 LORD's, and all its f.
Gal 4: 4 But when the f of the time
Eph 1:10 in the dispensation of the f
Eph 1:23 the f of Him who fills all
Eph 3:19 be filled with all the f of
Eph 4:13 of the stature of the f of
Col 1:19 that in Him all the f
Col 2: 9 For in Him dwells all the f

FULLY (see FULL)
Num 14:24 in him and has followed Me f,
Luke 9:32 and when they were f awake,
Luke 11:21 f armed, guards his own
John 7: 8 for My time has not yet f
Acts 2: 1 the Day of Pentecost had f
Acts 23:20 were going to inquire more f
Rom 4:21 and being f convinced that
Rom 15:19 about to Illyricum I have f
Col 1:10 f pleasing Him, being
1Pe 1:13 and rest your hope f upon

FUNCTION†
Rom 12: 4 do not have the same f,

FURIOUS (see FURIOUSLY, FURY)
Ps 78:21 LORD heard this and was f;
Dan 2:12 king was angry and very f,
Dan 8: 6 and ran at him with f power.

FURIOUSLY (see FURIOUS)
2Ki 9:20 for he drives f!"

FURNACE
Gen 19:28 up like the smoke of a f.
Ex 9:10 they took ashes from the f
Ex 19:18 like the smoke of a f,
Deut 4:20 you out of the iron f,
1Ki 8:51 of Egypt, out of the iron f),
Prov 17: 3 pot is for silver and the f
Is 48:10 I have tested you in the f
Jer 11: 4 of Egypt, from the iron f,
Dan 3: 6 midst of a burning fiery f.
Dan 3:19 that they heat the f seven

Matt 13:42 will cast them into the f
Matt 13:50 and cast them into the f of
Rev 1:15 brass, as if refined in a f,
Rev 9: 2 like the smoke of a great f.

FURNISHED (see FURNISHINGS)
Prov 9: 2 She has also f her table.
Mark 14:15 f and prepared; there make

FURNISHINGS (see FURNISHED, FURNITURE)
Ex 39:33 the tent and all its f:

FURNITURE† (see FURNISHINGS)
Ex 31: 7 and all the f of the

FURROWS
Ps 129: 3 They made their f long."

FURTHERANCE†
Phil 1:12 turned out for the f of the

FURY (see FURIOUS)
Gen 27:44 until your brother's f turns
Prov 6:34 jealousy is a husband's f;
Is 27: 4 F is not in Me
Is 51:13 every day Because of the f
Is 51:17 the LORD The cup of His f;
Is 59:18 F to His adversaries,
Is 63: 3 And trampled them in My f;
Is 63: 6 Made them drunk in My f,
Jer 6:11 I am full of the f of the
Jer 25:15 Take this wine cup of f from
Jer 33: 5 slay in My anger and My f,
Ezek 9: 8 in pouring out Your f on
Dan 9:16 let Your anger and Your f be
Amos 5: 9 So that f comes upon the
Mic 5:15 vengeance in anger and f
Nah 1: 6 His f is poured out like

FUTILE (see FUTILITY)
Ps 94:11 of man, That they are f.
Is 1:13 Bring no more f sacrifices;
Jer 10: 3 of the peoples are f;
Jer 10:15 They are f, a work of
Jer 51:18 They are f, a work of
Rom 1:21 but became f in their
1Co 15:17 not risen, your faith is f;

FUTILITY (see FUTILE)
Job 15:31 For f will be his reward.
Job 15:35 trouble and bring forth f;
Is 30:28 nations with the sieve of f;
Rom 8:20 creation was subjected to f,
Eph 4:17 in the f of their mind,

FUTURE†
Ps 37:37 For the f of that man is
Ps 37:38 The f of the wicked shall
Jer 29:11 to give you a f and a hope.
Jer 31:17 There is hope in your f,
Dan 8:26 to many days in the f.

G

GABBATHA†
John 19:13 Pavement, but in Hebrew, G.

GABRIEL
Dan 9:21 in prayer, the man G,
Luke 1:19 and said to him, "I am G,

GAD
Gen 30:11 So she called his name G.
Num 2:14 "Then comes the tribe of G,
Deut 27:13 Ebal to curse: Reuben, G,
1Sa 13: 7 the Jordan to the land of G
1Sa 22: 5 Now the prophet G said to
1Ch 29:29 and in the book of G the

Jer   2:36 Why do you **g** about so much
Rev   7: 5 of the tribe of G twelve

GADARENES
Mark 5: 1 sea, to the country of the G.

GADITES
Deut 3:12 to the Reubenites and the G.

GAIN (see GAINED, GAINS)
1Sa   8: 3 aside after dishonest **g**,
Job 18: 2 G understanding, and
Ps 90:12 That we may **g** a heart of
Prov 1:19 everyone who is greedy for **g**;
Eccl 3: 6 A time to **g**, And a time
Dan 2: 8 for certain that you would **g**
Dan 11: 5 and he shall **g** power over
Phil 1:21 is Christ, and to die is **g**.
Phil 3: 7 But what things were **g** to me,
Phil 3: 8 that I may **g** Christ
1Ti 6: 5 godliness is a means of **g**.
1Ti 6: 6 with contentment is great **g**.
Tit 1:11 for the sake of dishonest **g**.
Jude 16 flattering people to **g**

GAINED (see GAIN)
Ps 98: 1 and His holy arm have **g** Him
Prov 20:17 Bread **g** by deceit is sweet
Eccl 1:16 and have **g** more wisdom than
Ezek 28: 4 understanding You have **g**
Matt 18:15 you have **g** your brother.
Matt 25:17 he who had received two **g**

GAINS (see GAIN)
Prov 3:13 And the man who **g**
Mark 8:36 it profit a man if he **g** the
Luke 9:25 is it to a man if he **g** the

GALATIA (see GALATIANS)
1Co 16: 1 orders to the churches of G,
Gal 1: 2 me, To the churches of G:
1Pe 1: 1 the Dispersion in Pontus, G,

GALATIANS† (see GALATIA)
Gal 3: 1 O foolish G! Who has

GALILEAN (see GALILEANS, GALILEE)
Mark 14:70 of them; for you are a G,
Luke 23: 6 he asked if the Man were a G.

GALILEANS (see GALILEAN)
John 4:45 the G received Him, having
Acts 2: 7 not all these who speak G?

GALILEE (see GALILEAN)
Josh 20: 7 they appointed Kedesh in G,
1Ki 9:11 cities in the land of G.
Is 9: 1 In G of the Gentiles:
Matt 2:22 aside into the region of G.
Matt 4:15 G of the Gentiles:
Matt 4:23 And Jesus went about all G,
Matt 4:25 followed Him—from G,
Matt 21:11 prophet from Nazareth of G.
Matt 26:32 I will go before you to G.
Matt 28:10 tell My brethren to go to G,
Mark 1:39 synagogues throughout all G,
Mark 6:21 and the chief men of G.
Luke 1:26 sent by God to a city of G
Luke 3: 1 Herod being tetrarch of G,
Luke 4:31 to Capernaum, a city of G,
John 2: 1 was a wedding in Cana of G,
John 4:47 had come out of Judea into G,
John 7:41 the Christ come out of G?
John 7:52 prophet has arisen out of G.
Acts 1:11 who also said, "Men of G,

GALL
Ps 69:21 They also gave me **g** for my
Jer 8:14 And given us water of **g** to
Lam 3:19 The wormwood and the **g**.

Matt 27:34 sour wine mingled with **g** to

GALLIO
Acts 18:12 When G was proconsul of

GALLONS†
John 2: 6 twenty or thirty **g** apiece.

GALLOPING†
Judg 5:22 **g** of his steeds.
Nah 3: 2 Of **g** horses, Of clattering

GALLOWS
Esth 7: 9 to the king, "Look! The **g**,
Esth 9:13 ten sons be hanged on the **g**.

GAMALIEL
Acts 5:34 stood up, a Pharisee named G,
Acts 22: 3 this city at the feet of G,

GAME
Gen 25:28 because he ate of his **g**,
Gen 27: 3 out to the field and hunt **g**
Gen 27:31 arise and eat of his son's **g**,

GAP (see GAPS)
Ezek 22:30 and stand in the **g** before Me

GAPE†
Job 16:10 They **g** at me with their
Ps 22:13 They **g** at Me with their

GAPS (see GAP)
Neh 4: 7 being restored and the **g**

GARDEN (see GARDENER, GARDENS)
Gen 2: 8 The LORD God planted a **g**
Gen 2:15 man and put him in the **g** of
Gen 3: 1 eat of every tree of the **g**'?
Gen 3: 8 LORD God walking in the **g**
Gen 3:23 God sent him out of the **g**
Gen 13:10 and Gomorrah) like the **g** of
Deut 11:10 by foot, as a vegetable **g**;
Neh 3:15 of Shelah by the King's G,
Song 4:12 A **g** enclosed Is my sister,
Is 1: 8 As a hut in a **g** of
Is 1:30 And as a **g** that has no
Is 51: 3 And her desert like the **g**
Ezek 17: 7 From the **g** terrace where it
Ezek 28:13 the **g** of God; Every
Luke 13:19 a man took and put in his **g**;
John 18: 1 Kidron, where there was a **g**,
John 19:41 was crucified there was a **g**,
John 19:41 and in the **g** a new tomb in

GARDENER† (see GARDEN)
John 20:15 supposing Him to be the **g**,

GARDENS (see GARDEN)
Eccl 2: 5 I made myself **g** and orchards,
Song 4:15 A fountain of **g**,
Is 65: 3 My face; Who sacrifice in **g**,
Amos 4: 9 When your **g** increased,

GARLAND†
Rev 12: 1 and on her head a **g** of

GARLIC†
Num 11: 5 leeks, the onions, and the **g**;

GARMENT (see GARMENTS)
Gen 9:23 Shem and Japheth took a **g**,
Gen 25:25 He was like a hairy **g** all
Gen 39:12 But he left his **g** in her
Ex 22:26 ever take your neighbor's **g**
Lev 6:27 blood is sprinkled on any **g**,
Lev 13:47 if a **g** has a leprous plague
Lev 19:19 Nor shall a **g** of mixed linen
Deut 22: 5 a man put on a woman's **g**,
Josh 7:21 a beautiful Babylonian **g**,
Ruth 3: 3 put on your best **g** and go
Ps 69:11 I also made sackcloth my **g**;
Ps 73: 6 covers them like a **g**.

Ps   102:26 will all grow old like a **g**;
Prov   25:20 one who takes away a **g** in
Is   50: 9 will all grow old like a **g**;
Dan   7: 9 His **g** was white as snow,
Matt   9:16 unshrunk cloth on an old **g**;
Matt   9:16 patch pulls away from the **g**,
Matt   9:20 and touched the hem of His **g**.
Matt   22:11 did not have on a wedding **g**
Mark   10:50 And throwing aside his **g**,
Luke   22:36 let him sell his **g** and buy
John   21: 7 he put on his outer **g** (for
Heb   1:11 all grow old like a **g**;
Jude   23 hating even the **g** defiled by

GARMENTS (see GARMENT)
Gen   35: 2 and change your **g**.
Gen   38:14 she took off her widow's **g**,
Gen   45:22 silver and five changes of **g**.
Ex   28: 2 And you shall make holy **g** for
Ex   28: 3 that they may make Aaron's **g**,
Ex   31:10 the **g** of ministry, the holy
Deut   8: 4 Your **g** did not wear out on
Josh   9: 5 and old **g** on themselves; and
Judg   5:30 Sisera, plunder of dyed **g**,
2Sa   10: 4 cut off their **g** in the
2Sa   13:31 king arose and tore his **g**
Ezra   2:69 and one hundred priestly **g**,
Ps   22:18 They divide My **g** among them,
Ps   45: 8 All Your **g** are scented with
Ps   133: 2 down on the edge of his **g**.
Prov   31:24 She makes linen **g** and sells
Eccl   9: 8 Let your **g** always be white,
Song   4:11 And the fragrance of your **g**
Is   3:22 the mantles; The outer **g**,
Is   9: 5 And **g** rolled in blood,
Is   61:10 He has clothed me with the **g**
Is   63: 1 With dyed **g** from Bozrah,
Is   63: 3 blood is sprinkled upon My **g**,
Dan   3:27 not singed nor were their **g**
Joel   2:13 your heart, and not your **g**;
Zech   3: 3 was clothed with filthy **g**,
Matt   11: 8 see? A man clothed in soft **g**?
Matt   27:35 They divided My **g** among
Luke   24: 4 stood by them in shining **g**.
John   13: 4 supper and laid aside His **g**,
Acts   18: 6 he shook his **g** and said to
Jas   5: 2 and your **g** are moth-eaten.
Rev   3: 4 who have not defiled their **g**;
Rev   3: 5 shall be clothed in white **g**,

GARRISON (see GARRISONS)
1Sa   13: 3 And Jonathan attacked the **g**
Acts   21:31 to the commander of the **g**

GARRISONS (see GARRISON)
2Sa   8: 6 Then David put **g** in Syria of
2Ch   17: 2 and set **g** in the land of

GATE (see GATEKEEPER, GATEPOST, GATES)
Gen   19: 1 Lot was sitting in the **g** of
Gen   22:17 shall possess the **g** of
Num   4:26 for the door of the **g** of
Deut   22:15 elders of the city at the **g**.
Ruth   4: 1 Now Boaz went up to the **g** and
2Sa   18:24 up to the roof over the **g**,
2Sa   19: 8 the king, sitting in the **g**.
2Ki   7:17 people trampled him in the **g**,
2Ki   14:13 of Jerusalem from the **G** of
2Ki   14:13 of Ephraim to the Corner **G**—
1Ch   9:18 of Levi at the King's **G** on
2Ch   23:15 the entrance of the Horse **G**
2Ch   26: 9 Corner Gate, at the Valley **G**,
2Ch   33:14 the entrance of the Fish **G**;
Neh   2:13 Well and the Refuse **G**,
Neh   2:14 I went on to the Fountain **G**
Neh   3: 1 and built the Sheep **G**;
Neh   3:26 in front of the Water **G**

Neh   8: 3 was in front of the Water **G**
Esth   5: 9 saw Mordecai in the king's **g**,
Esth   5:13 Jew sitting at the king's **g**.
Job   5: 4 They are crushed in the **g**,
Prov   22:22 the afflicted at the **g**;
Is   28: 6 back the battle at the **g**.
Is   29:21 him who reproves in the **g**,
Jer   19: 2 the entry of the Potsherd **G**;
Jer   36:10 at the entry of the New **G**
Jer   38: 7 king was sitting at the **G**
Jer   51:30 The bars of her **g** are
Jer   52: 7 at night by way of the **g**
Ezek   8: 3 to the door of the north **g**
Ezek   40: 7 between the **g** chambers was
Ezek   44: 2 This **g** shall be shut; it
Amos   1: 5 I will also break the **g** bar
Amos   5:10 the one who rebukes in the **g**,
Matt   7:13 "Enter by the narrow **g**;
Matt   7:13 for wide is the **g** and broad
Luke   16:20 sores, who was laid at his **g**,
John   10: 2 Jerusalem by the Sheep **G** a
Acts   3:10 alms at the Beautiful **G** of
Acts   12:10 they came to the iron **g** that
Acts   12:13 knocked at the door of the **g**,
Heb   13:12 suffered outside the **g**.
Rev   21:21 each individual **g** was of one

GATEKEEPER† (see GATE, GATEKEEPERS)
2Sa   18:26 the watchman called to the **g**

GATEKEEPERS (see GATEKEEPER)
2Ki   7:10 went and called to the **g** of
1Ch   9:18 then they had been **g** for
1Ch   9:19 **g** of the tabernacle. Their
1Ch   26: 1 the divisions of the **g**:
2Ch   34:13 scribes, officers, and **g**.
Ezra   7:24 priests, Levites, singers, **g**,

GATEPOST (see GATE, GATEPOSTS)
Ezek   40:16 And on each **g** were palm

GATEPOSTS (see GATEPOST)
Judg   16: 3 of the city and the two **g**,
Ezek   40:26 it had palm trees on its **g**,

GATES (see GATE)
Ex   20:10 who is within your **g**.
Deut   3: 5 fortified with high walls, **g**,
Deut   6: 9 of your house and on your **g**.
Deut   11:20 of your house and on your **g**,
Deut   12:12 Levite who is within your **g**,
Deut   14:21 alien who is within your **g**,
Deut   28:52 besiege you at all your **g**,
2Sa   18:24 sitting between the two **g**.
2Ch   23:19 the gatekeepers at the **g** of
Neh   1: 3 and its **g** are burned with
Neh   7: 3 Do not let the **g** of Jerusalem
Neh   12:25 at the storerooms of the **g**.
Job   17:16 they go down to the **g** of
Ps   9:13 who lift me up from the **g**
Ps   9:14 of all Your praise In the **g**
Ps   24: 7 O you **g**! And be lifted up,
Ps   24: 9 O you **g**! Lift up, you
Ps   87: 2 The LORD loves the **g** of
Ps   100: 4 Enter into His **g** with
Ps   122: 2 been standing Within your **g**,
Prov   8: 3 She cries out by the **g**,
Prov   14:19 And the wicked at the **g** of
Prov   31:23 husband is known in the **g**,
Prov   31:31 works praise her in the **g**,
Is   54:12 Your **g** of crystal, And all
Is   60:18 And your **g** Praise.
Is   62:10 Go through the **g**! Prepare
Jer   17:24 no burden through the **g** of
Jer   17:27 will kindle a fire in its **g**,
Jer   49:31 Which has neither **g** nor bars,
Jer   51:58 And her high **g** shall be

Lam 1: 4 All her **g** are desolate;
Ezek 21:22 battering rams against the **g**,
Nah 2: 6 The **g** of the rivers are
Matt 16:18 and the **g** of Hades shall not
Rev 21:12 and high wall with twelve **g**,
Rev 21:12 and twelve angels at the **g**,
Rev 21:25 Its **g** shall not be shut at

GATH (*see* GITTITE)
Josh 11:22 remained only in Gaza, in **G**,
1Sa 6:17 one for Ashkelon, one for **G**,
1Sa 7:14 to Israel, from Ekron to **G**;
1Sa 17: 4 named Goliath, from **G**,
1Sa 17:23 the Philistine of **G**,
1Sa 21:10 went to Achish the king of **G**.
1Sa 27: 4 that David had fled to **G**;
2Sa 1:20 Tell it not in **G**,
2Ch 26: 6 and broke down the wall of **G**,
Amos 6: 2 Then go down to **G** of the
Mic 1:10 Tell it not in **G**,

GATH HEPHER
2Ki 14:25 the prophet who was from **G**

GATHER (*see* GATHERED, GATHERING, GATHERS)
Gen 49: 2 **G** together and hear, you sons
Ex 3:16 Go and **g** the elders of Israel
Ex 5: 7 Let them go and **g** straw for
Ex 5:12 all the land of Egypt to **g**
Ex 16: 5 be twice as much as they **g**
Lev 25: 5 nor **g** the grapes of your
Lev 25:20 we shall not sow nor **g** in
Num 10: 3 all the congregation shall **g**
Deut 4:10 **G** the people to Me, and I
Deut 31:28 **G** to me all the elders of
Ruth 2: 7 Please let me glean and **g**
2Ki 4:39 went out into the field to **g**
2Ki 22:20 I will **g** you to your
Neh 1: 9 yet I will **g** them from
Esth 4:16 **g** all the Jews who are
Ps 50: 5 **G** My saints together to Me,
Ps 59: 3 The mighty **g** against me,
Ps 140: 2 They continually **g** together
Eccl 3: 5 And a time to **g** stones; A
Song 6: 2 And to **g** lilies.
Is 11:12 And **g** together the
Is 34:15 and **g** them under her
Is 40:11 He will **g** the lambs with
Is 43: 5 And **g** you from the west;
Is 66:18 It shall be that I will **g**
Jer 6: 1 **G** yourselves to flee from
Jer 7:18 The children **g** wood, the
Jer 23: 3 But I will **g** the remnant of
Jer 31: 8 And **g** them from the ends of
Ezek 20:34 out from the peoples and **g**
Ezek 20:41 out from the peoples and **g**
Joel 2:16 **G** the people, Sanctify the
Mic 4: 6 I will **g** the outcast And
Hab 1:15 And **g** them in their
Zech 10: 8 will whistle for them and **g**
Zech 10:10 And **g** them from Assyria. I
Matt 3:12 and **g** His wheat into the
Matt 13:30 First **g** together the tares
Matt 23:37 her! How often I wanted to **g**
Matt 25:26 and **g** where I have not
Mark 13:27 and **g** together His elect
Luke 6:44 For men do not **g** figs from
Luke 6:44 nor do they **g** grapes from a
John 6:12 **G** up the fragments that
John 11:52 but also that He would **g**
John 15: 6 and they **g** them and throw
Rev 19:17 Come and **g** together for the

GATHERED (*see* GATHER)
Gen 1: 9 under the heavens be **g**
Gen 12: 5 possessions that they had **g**,
Gen 25:17 and was **g** to his people.

Ex 15: 8 nostrils The waters were **g**
Ex 16:18 he who **g** much had nothing
Ex 16:18 and he who **g** little had no
Ex 16:21 So they **g** it every morning,
Num 11:32 and the quail (he who
Josh 24: 1 Then Joshua **g** all the tribes
1Sa 13: 5 Then the Philistines **g**
2Sa 14:14 which cannot be **g** up again.
2Sa 21:13 and they **g** the bones of
2Ki 22:20 and you shall be **g** to your
2Ch 13: 7 Then worthless rogues **g** to
Ezra 3: 1 the people **g** together as one
Neh 8:13 were **g** to Ezra the scribe,
Neh 12:28 the sons of the singers **g**
Esth 2:19 When virgins were **g** together
Ps 35:15 Attackers **g** against me,
Ps 107: 3 And **g** out of the lands,
Prov 30: 4 Who has **g** the wind in His
Eccl 2: 8 I also **g** for myself silver
Is 22: 9 And you **g** together the
Is 24:22 As prisoners are **g** in the
Is 27:12 And you will be **g** one by
Is 34:16 and His Spirit has **g** them.
Is 49: 5 So that Israel is **g** to Him
Jer 8: 2 They shall not be **g** nor
Ezek 29: 5 shall not be picked up or **g**.
Matt 2: 4 And when he had **g** all the
Matt 13:40 as the tares are **g** and
Matt 18:20 where two or three are **g**
Matt 22:41 While the Pharisees were **g**
Mark 1:33 And the whole city was **g**
Mark 4: 1 And a great multitude was **g**
Mark 6:30 Then the apostles **g** to Jesus
Luke 15:13 the younger son **g** all
John 6:13 Therefore they **g** them up,
Acts 4: 6 were **g** together at
Acts 14:20 when the disciples **g** around
Acts 14:27 Now when they had come and **g**
2Co 8:15 He who **g** much had
Rev 19:19 **g** together to make war

GATHERING (*see* GATHER)
Gen 1:10 and the **g** together of the
Num 15:32 they found a man **g** sticks on
Matt 25:24 and **g** where you have not
Acts 19:40 for this disorderly **g**.
2Th 2: 1 Lord Jesus Christ and our **g**

GATHERS (*see* GATHER)
Num 19:10 And the one who **g** the ashes
Ps 33: 7 He **g** the waters of the sea
Prov 6: 8 And **g** her food in the
Is 17: 5 be as when the harvester **g**
Hab 2: 5 He **g** to himself all nations
Matt 23:37 as a hen **g** her chicks under
John 4:36 and **g** fruit for eternal

GAUNT
Gen 41: 4 And the ugly and **g** cows ate
Job 30: 3 They are **g** from want and

GAVE (*see* GIVE)
Gen 2:20 So Adam **g** names to all
Gen 3: 6 She also **g** to her husband
Gen 3:12 The woman whom You **g** to be
Gen 14:20 And he **g** him a tithe of all.
Gen 16: 5 My wrong be upon you! I **g** my
Gen 21:19 and **g** the lad a drink.
Gen 24:46 and she **g** the camels a drink
Gen 25:34 And Jacob **g** Esau bread and
Gen 27:17 Then she **g** the savory food
Gen 29:24 And Laban **g** his maid Zilpah
Gen 30: 9 took Zilpah her maid and **g**
Gen 35:12 The land which I **g** Abraham
Gen 39:21 and He **g** him favor in the
Gen 45:21 and Joseph **g** them carts,
Gen 45:21 and he **g** them provisions for

Ex   2:21 and he **g** Zipporah his
Ex   14:20 and it **g** light by night to
Ex   31:18 He **g** Moses two tablets of
Deut   3:13 I **g** to half the tribe of
Josh   14:13 and **g** Hebron to Caleb the
Josh   21:43 So the LORD **g** to Israel all
Josh   21:44 The LORD **g** them rest all
Judg   5:25 she **g** milk; She brought out
Judg   14:10 And Samson **g** a feast there,
Ruth   4:13 the LORD **g** her conception,
Ruth   4:17 Also the neighbor women **g** him
1Sa   4:19 she bowed herself and **g**
1Sa   9:23 the portion which I **g**
1Sa   27: 6 So Achish **g** him Ziklag that
2Sa   12: 8 I **g** you your master's house
1Ki   3:17 and I **g** birth while she was
1Ki   4:29 And God **g** Solomon wisdom and
2Ki   21: 8 from the land which I **g**
2Ki   22: 8 And Hilkiah **g** the book to
2Ch   15:15 and the LORD **g** them rest
2Ch   28:15 **g** them food and drink, and
2Ch   32:24 and He spoke to him and **g**
Ezra   8:36 So they **g** support to the
Neh   2: 1 that I took the wine and **g**
Neh   8: 8 and they **g** the sense, and
Neh   9: 7 And **g** him the name Abraham;
Neh   9:15 You **g** them bread from heaven
Neh   9:20 You also **g** Your good Spirit
Neh   9:20 And **g** them water for their
Job   1:21 I return there. The LORD **g**,
Job   42:10 Indeed the LORD **g** Job twice
Ps   68:11 The Lord **g** the word; Great
Ps   69:21 They also **g** me gall for my
Ps   69:21 And for my thirst they **g** me
Ps   77: 1 And He **g** ear to me.
Ps   78:29 For He **g** them their own
Ps   81:12 So I **g** them over to their
Ps   99: 7 and the ordinance He **g** them.
Eccl   12: 7 will return to God who **g** it.
Song   5: 6 but he **g** me no answer.
Is   43: 3 I **g** Egypt for your ransom,
Is   50: 6 I **g** My back to those who
Jer   11:18 Now the LORD **g** me knowledge
Jer   30: 3 return to the land that I **g**
Jer   52:32 he spoke kindly to him and **g**
Ezek   36:28 dwell in the land that I **g**
Dan   1: 7 the chief of the eunuchs **g**
Dan   1:16 and **g** them vegetables.
Dan   1:17 God **g** them knowledge and
Dan   6:10 and prayed and **g** thanks
Dan   6:16 So the king **g** the command,
Hos   2: 8 she did not know That I **g**
Hos   13:11 I **g** you a king in My anger,
Amos   2:12 But you **g** the Nazirites wine
Amos   4: 6 Also I **g** you cleanness of
Matt   10: 1 He **g** them power over
Matt   14:19 He blessed and broke and **g**
Matt   15:36 loaves and the fish and **g**
Matt   21:23 And who **g** You this
Matt   25:15 And to one he **g** five talents,
Matt   25:35 for I was hungry and you **g** Me
Matt   27:10 and **g** them for the
Matt   27:34 they **g** Him sour wine mingled
Matt   28:12 they **g** a large sum of money
Mark   3:16 to whom He **g** the name Peter;
Mark   3:17 to whom He **g** the name
Mark   6:28 and **g** it to the girl; and
Luke   2:38 coming in that instant she **g**
Luke   5:29 Then Levi **g** Him a great feast
Luke   7:21 and to many blind He **g**
Luke   7:44 you **g** Me no water for My
Luke   9: 1 disciples together and **g**
Luke   9:42 and **g** him back to his
Luke   10:35 **g** them to the innkeeper,
Luke   18:43 **g** praise to God.

Luke   22:17 and **g** thanks, and said,
Luke   22:19 **g** thanks and broke it, and
Luke   23:24 So Pilate **g** sentence that it
Luke   24:42 So they **g** Him a piece of a
John   1:12 to them He **g** the right to
John   3:16 so loved the world that He **g**
John   4:12 who **g** us the well, and drank
John   6:31 He **g** them bread from
John   13:26 He **g** it to Judas Iscariot,
John   14:31 and as the Father **g** Me
John   17:12 Those whom You **g** Me I have
John   17:22 And the glory which You **g** Me
John   19: 9 But Jesus **g** him no answer.
John   19:30 He **g** up His spirit.
Acts   2: 4 as the Spirit **g** them
Acts   7:42 Then God turned and **g** them up
Acts   8:10 to whom they all **g** heed, from
Acts   14:17 **g** us rain from heaven and
Rom   1:24 Therefore God also **g** them up
1Co   3: 5 as the Lord **g** to each one?
1Co   3: 6 but God **g** the increase.
2Co   8: 5 but they first **g** themselves
Gal   1: 4 who **g** Himself for our sins,
Gal   2:20 who loved me and **g** Himself
Eph   1:22 and **g** Him to be head over
Eph   4: 8 And **g** gifts to men."
Eph   4:11 And He Himself **g** some to be
Eph   5:25 also loved the church and **g**
1Ti   2: 6 who **g** Himself a ransom for
Heb   7: 2 to whom also Abraham **g** a
Heb   11:22 and **g** instructions
Jas   5:18 and the heaven **g** rain, and
1Jn   3:23 as He **g** us commandment.
Rev   1: 1 which God **g** Him to show His
Rev   11:13 the rest were afraid and **g**
Rev   12:13 persecuted the woman who **g**
Rev   13: 2 The dragon **g** him his power,
Rev   13: 4 worshiped the dragon who **g**
Rev   15: 7 the four living creatures **g**
Rev   20:13 The sea **g** up the dead who

GAZA
Judg   1:18 Also Judah took **G** with its
Judg   16: 1 Now Samson went to **G** and saw
Amos   1: 6 three transgressions of **G**,
Acts   8:26 down from Jerusalem to **G**.

GAZE (see GAZED, GAZING)
Ex   19:21 they break through to **g** at
Is   14:16 Those who see you will **g** at

GAZED (see GAZE)
Acts   7:55 **g** into heaven and saw the

GAZELLE (see GAZELLES)
Deut   14: 5 "the deer, the **g**,
2Sa   2:18 fleet of foot as a wild **g**.
Song   2: 9 My beloved is like a **g** or a
Song   4: 5 two fawns, Twins of a **g**,

GAZELLES (see GAZELLE)
1Ch   12: 8 and were as swift as **g** on
Song   2: 7 By the **g** or by the does of

GAZING† (see GAZE)
Song   2: 9 **G** through the lattice.
Acts   1:11 why do you stand **g** up into

GEBA (see GIBEAH, GIBEON)
2Ki   23: 8 from **G** to Beersheba; also he

GEDALIAH
2Ki   25:23 king of Babylon had made **G**
2Ki   25:25 men and struck and killed **G**,

GEHAZI
2Ki   5:21 So **G** pursued Naaman. When

GENEALOGIES (see GENEALOGY)
Num   1:20 their **g** by their families,

1Ch	5:17	these were registered by **g**
1Ch	7: 7	they were listed by their **g**,
1Ch	7:40	And they were recorded by **g**
1Ti	1: 4	heed to fables and endless **g**,
Tit	3: 9	avoid foolish disputes, **g**,

GENEALOGY (*see* GENEALOGIES)

Gen	5: 1	This is the book of the **g** of
Gen	6: 9	This is the **g** of Noah. Noah
Ruth	4:18	Now this is the **g** of Perez:
1Ch	4:33	and they maintained their **g**:
1Ch	5: 1	so that the **g** is not listed
1Ch	26:31	according to his **g** of the
2Ch	31:16	up who were written in the **g**,
2Ch	31:17	who were written in the **g**
2Ch	31:18	who were written in the **g**—
Ezra	2:62	who were registered by **g**,
Neh	7: 5	might be registered by **g**.
Matt	1: 1	The book of the **g** of Jesus
Heb	7: 3	without mother, without **g**,

GENERAL

1Ch	27:34	And the **g** of the king's army
Heb	12:23	to the **g** assembly and church

GENERALS

Nah	3:17	And your **g** like great

GENERATION (*see* GENERATIONS)

Gen	7: 1	before Me in this **g**.
Gen	15:16	But in the fourth **g** they
Gen	50:23	children to the third **g**.
Ex	1: 6	his brothers, and all that **g**.
Ex	17:16	war with Amalek from **g** to
Num	32:13	until all the **g** that had
Deut	1:35	of these men of this evil **g**
Deut	23: 2	even to the tenth **g** none of
Deut	23: 3	even to the tenth **g** none of
Deut	29:22	so that the coming **g** of your
Deut	32: 5	A perverse and crooked **g**.
Ps	14: 5	For God is with the **g** of
Ps	22:30	of the Lord to the next **g**,
Ps	24: 6	the **g** of those who seek Him,
Ps	78: 6	That the **g** to come might
Ps	78: 8	A stubborn and rebellious **g**,
Ps	95:10	I was grieved with that **g**,
Ps	102:18	will be written for the **g**
Ps	112: 2	The **g** of the upright will
Ps	145: 4	One **g** shall praise Your
Prov	30:11	There is a **g** that curses
Eccl	1: 4	One **g** passes away, and
Is	53: 8	And who will declare His **g**?
Lam	5:19	throne from generation to **g**.
Dan	4: 3	His dominion is from **g** to
Dan	4:34	And His kingdom is from **g**
Matt	11:16	to what shall I liken this **g**?
Matt	12:39	An evil and adulterous **g**
Matt	12:41	in the judgment with this **g**
Matt	12:45	also be with this wicked **g**.
Matt	17:17	"O faithless and perverse **g**,
Matt	24:34	this **g** will by no means pass
Mark	8:12	Why does this **g** seek a sign?
Mark	8:38	this adulterous and sinful **g**,
Luke	11:29	to say, "This is an evil **g**.
Luke	11:30	Son of Man will be to this **g**.
Luke	11:31	with the men of this **g** and
Luke	11:50	may be required of this **g**,
Luke	16: 8	are more shrewd in their **g**
Acts	8:33	who will declare His **g**?
Phil	2:15	of a crooked and perverse **g**,
Heb	3:10	was angry with that **g**,
1Pe	2: 9	But you are a chosen **g**,

GENERATIONS (*see* GENERATION)

Gen	6: 9	a just man, perfect in his **g**.
Gen	9:12	with you, for perpetual **g**:
Ex	3:15	is My memorial to all **g**.

Ex	12:14	the LORD throughout your **g**.
Ex	20: 5	to the third and fourth **g**
Ex	31:16	Sabbath throughout their **g**
Deut	7: 9	and mercy for a thousand **g**
1Ch	5: 7	the genealogy of their **g**
1Ch	16:15	commanded, for a thousand **g**,
Job	42:16	grandchildren for four **g**.
Ps	45:17	to be remembered in all **g**;
Ps	49:11	dwelling places to all **g**;
Ps	61: 6	life, His years as many **g**.
Ps	72: 5	endure, Throughout all **g**.
Ps	79:13	forth Your praise to all **g**.
Ps	89: 1	Your faithfulness to all **g**.
Ps	90: 1	our dwelling place in all **g**.
Ps	100: 5	His truth endures to all **g**.
Ps	102:24	years are throughout all **g**.
Ps	106:31	for righteousness To all **g**
Ps	119:90	endures to all **g**;
Is	51: 9	In the **g** of old. Are You
Is	60:15	excellence, A joy of many **g**.
Is	61: 4	The desolations of many **g**.
Joel	2: 2	Even for many successive **g**.
Matt	1:17	So all the **g** from Abraham to
Eph	3:21	by Christ Jesus to all **g**,

GENEROSITY (*see* GENEROUS)

Esth	2:18	gifts according to the **g** of
2Co	9: 5	be ready as a matter of **g**

GENEROUS (*see* GENEROSITY, GENEROUSLY)

Ps	51:12	And uphold me by Your **g**

GENEROUSLY † (*see* GENEROUS)

Acts	10: 2	who gave alms **g** to the

GENNESARET † (*see* CHINNERETH)

Matt	14:34	they came to the land of G.
Mark	6:53	they came to the land of G
Luke	5: 1	He stood by the Lake of G,

GENTILE † (*see* GENTILES)

Hag	2:22	the strength of the G
Acts	17:17	the Jews and with the G

GENTILES (*see* GENTILE)

Gen	10: 5	coastland peoples of the G
Deut	32:43	"Rejoice, O G,
1Ch	16:35	and deliver us from the G,
Ps	105:44	gave them the lands of the G,
Ps	106:35	But they mingled with the G
Ps	106:41	them into the hand of the G,
Ps	106:47	gather us from among the G,
Ps	115: 2	Why should the G say, "So
Ps	117: 1	all you G! Laud Him, all
Is	9: 1	Jordan, In Galilee of the G.
Is	11:10	For the G shall seek Him,
Is	42: 1	bring forth justice to the G.
Is	49: 6	give You as a light to the G,
Is	61: 6	eat the riches of the G,
Is	61: 9	shall be known among the G,
Is	66:12	And the glory of the G like
Is	66:19	declare My glory among the G.
Jer	9:16	them also among the G,
Jer	10: 2	not learn the way of the G;
Jer	10: 2	For the G are dismayed at
Jer	10:25	Pour out Your fury on the G,
Ezek	11:12	to the customs of the G
Ezek	20:14	not be profaned before the G,
Ezek	30: 3	of clouds, the time of the G.
Matt	4:15	Galilee of the G:
Matt	6:32	all these things the G seek.
Matt	12:18	justice to the G.
Matt	12:21	And in His name G will
Matt	20:19	and deliver Him to the G to
Matt	20:25	that the rulers of the G
Luke	2:32	bring revelation to the G,
Luke	18:32	will be delivered to the G
Luke	21:24	will be trampled by G until

Luke 21:24 until the times of the G
Acts 9:15 to bear My name before G,
Acts 10:45 had been poured out on the G
Acts 13:46 behold, we turn to the G.
Acts 13:47 as a light to the G,
Acts 14: 2 Jews stirred up the G and
Acts 14:27 the door of faith to the G.
Acts 15: 3 the conversion of the G;
Acts 18: 6 now on I will go to the G.
Acts 26:23 Jewish people and to the G.
Acts 28:28 God has been sent to the G,
Rom 1:13 just as among the other G.
Rom 2:24 blasphemed among the G
Rom 3:29 not also the God of the G?
Rom 11:11 has come to the G.
Rom 11:13 as I am an apostle to the G,
Rom 11:25 until the fullness of the G
Rom 15:11 all you G! Laud Him,
Rom 15:12 In Him the G shall
Rom 16: 4 all the churches of the G.
1Co 5: 1 not even named among the G—
Gal 1:16 might preach Him among the G,
Gal 2:12 he would eat with the G;
Gal 2:14 why do you compel G to live
Eph 2:11 once G in the flesh—who are
Col 1:27 of this mystery among the G:
1Ti 2: 7 a teacher of the G in faith
1Ti 3:16 Preached among the G,
Rev 11: 2 it has been given to the G.

GENTLE (see GENTLENESS, GENTLY)
Prov 25:15 And a **g** tongue breaks a
Hos 11: 4 I drew them with **g** cords,
Matt 11:29 for I am **g** and lowly in
1Th 2: 7 But we were **g** among you, just
1Ti 3: 3 not greedy for money, but **g**,
2Ti 2:24 must not quarrel but be **g**
Tit 3: 2 no one, to be peaceable, **g**,
Jas 3:17 pure, then peaceable, **g**,

GENTLENESS (see GENTLE)
1Co 4:21 or in love and a spirit of **g**?
2Co 10: 1 you by the meekness and **g**
Gal 5:23 **g**, self-control. Against
Gal 6: 1 such a one in a spirit of **g**,
Phil 4: 5 Let your **g** be known to all
1 Ti 6:11 faith, love, patience, **g**.

GENTLY (see GENTLE)
Is 40:11 And **g** lead those who are

GENUINE† (see GENUINENESS)
2Ti 1: 5 I call to remembrance the **g**

GENUINENESS† (see GENUINE)
1Pe 1: 7 that the **g** of your faith,

GERAHS
Ex 30:13 (a shekel is twenty **g**).

GERAR
Gen 20: 2 And Abimelech king of G
Gen 26: 1 of the Philistines, in G.

GERGESENES†
Matt 8:28 to the country of the G,

GERIZIM
Deut 11:29 put the blessing on Mount G
Judg 9: 7 and stood on top of Mount G,

GERSHOM (see GERSHON)
Ex 2:22 and he called his name G;

GERSHON (see GERSHOM)
Gen 46:11 The sons of Levi were G,

GESHEM
Neh 2:19 and G the Arab heard of

GESHUR
2Sa 13:38 Absalom fled and went to G,

2Sa 15: 8 a vow while I dwelt at G in

GESTURES†
Is 33:15 Who **g** with his hands,

GET (see GETS, GETTING, GOT)
Gen 12: 1 G out of your country, From
Judg 14: 2 **g** her for me as a wife."
Ps 119:104 Through Your precepts I **g**
Prov 4: 5 G wisdom! Get understanding!
Prov 4: 5 Get wisdom! G understanding!
Prov 16:16 How much better to **g** wisdom
Song 7:12 Let us **g** up early to the
Jer 13: 1 Go and **g** yourself a linen
Jer 19: 1 Go and **g** a potter's earthen
Ezek 18:31 and **g** yourselves a new heart
Matt 5:26 you will by no means **g** out
Matt 13:54 Where did this Man **g** this
Matt 14:22 Jesus made His disciples **g**
Matt 15:33 Where could we **g** enough bread
Matt 16:23 G behind Me, Satan! You are
Matt 24:18 the field not go back to **g**
Mark 13:16 the field not go back to **g**
John 4:11 Where then do You **g** that
John 11:12 if he sleeps he will **g**

GETHSEMANE
Matt 26:36 them to a place called G,

GETS (see GET)
Prov 19: 8 He who **g** wisdom loves his
Jer 17:11 So is he who **g** riches,

GETTING (see GET)
Prov 4: 7 wisdom. And in all your **g**,

GEZER
Josh 16:10 Canaanites who dwelt in G;
Judg 1:29 Canaanites who dwelt in G;
1Ki 9:15 Hazor, Megiddo, and G.
1Ki 9:16 had gone up and taken G and

GHOST
Mark 6:49 they supposed it was a **g**,

GIANT (see GIANTS)
2Sa 21:16 one of the sons of the **g**,
2Sa 21:22 four were born to the **g** in

GIANTS (see GIANT)
Gen 6: 4 There were **g** on the earth in
Num 13:33 There we saw the **g** (the
Deut 3:13 was called the land of the **g**.

GIBEAH (see GEBA, GIBEON)
Judg 20: 4 concubine and I went into G,
Judg 20: 5 And the men of G rose against
1Sa 10:26 And Saul also went home to G;
1Sa 13:15 went up from Gilgal to G of
Is 10:29 G of Saul has fled.
Hos 5: 8 "Blow the ram's horn in G,
Hos 10: 9 sinned from the days of G;

GIBEON (see GEBA, GIBEAH, GIBEONITES)
Josh 9: 3 when the inhabitants of G
Josh 10: 2 because G was a great city,
Josh 10:12 "Sun, stand still over G;
2Sa 2:13 met them by the pool of G.
1Ki 3: 4 Now the king went to G to
1Ch 16:39 high place that was at G,
Jer 28: 1 the prophet, who was from G,
Jer 41:12 the great pool that is in G.

GIBEONITES
2Sa 21: 3 David said to the G,

GIDEON (see JERUBBAAL)
Judg 6:11 while his son G threshed
Judg 6:24 So G built an altar there to
Judg 6:34 of the LORD came upon G;
Judg 7:20 sword of the LORD and of G!
Judg 8:27 Then G made it into an ephod

Judg 8:27 It became a snare to G and
Judg 8:32 Now G the son of Joash died
Heb 11:32 would fail me to tell of G

GIFT (*see* GIFTED, GIFTS, GIVE)
Num 8:19 given the Levites as a **g** to
2Sa 11: 8 and a **g** of food from the
Prov 21:14 A **g** in secret pacifies
Eccl 3:13 it is the **g** of God.
Matt 5:23 if you bring your **g** to the
Matt 8: 4 and offer the **g** that Moses
John 4:10 If you knew the **g** of God, and
Acts 2:38 and you shall receive the **g**
Rom 1:11 to you some spiritual **g**,
Rom 5:15 But the free **g** is not like
Rom 5:17 of grace and of the **g** of
Rom 6:23 but the **g** of God is eternal
1Co 7: 7 But each one has his own **g**
1Co 13: 2 And though I have the **g** of
1Co 16: 3 I will send to bear your **g**
2Co 1:11 on our behalf for the **g**
2Co 8: 4 that we would receive the **g**
2Co 9: 5 and prepare your generous **g**
2Co 9:15 God for His indescribable **g**!
Eph 2: 8 it is the **g** of God,
Eph 3: 7 minister according to the **g**
Eph 4: 7 to the measure of Christ's **g**.
Phil 4:17 Not that I seek the **g**,
2Ti 4:14 Do not neglect the **g** that is
Heb 6: 4 have tasted the heavenly **g**,
Jas 1:17 Every good **g** and every
1Pe 4:10 As each one has received a **g**,

GIFTED (*see* GIFT)
Ex 35:10 All who are **g** artisans
Dan 1: 4 **g** in all wisdom, possessing

GIFTS (*see* GIFT)
Ps 68:18 You have received **g** among
Dan 2: 6 you shall receive from me **g**,
Dan 2:48 and gave him many great **g**;
Dan 5:17 Let your **g** be for yourself,
Matt 2:11 they presented **g** to Him:
Matt 7:11 know how to give good **g** to
Luke 11:13 know how to give good **g** to
Rom 11:29 For the **g** and the calling of
Rom 12: 6 Having then **g** differing
1Co 12: 1 Now concerning spiritual **g**,
1Co 12: 4 There are diversities of **g**,
1Co 12: 9 to another a **g** of healings by
1Co 12:31 earnestly desire the best **g**.
Eph 4: 8 And gave **g** to men."
Heb 2: 4 and **g** of the Holy Spirit,
Heb 8: 4 are priests who offer the **g**
Heb 11: 4 God testifying of his **g**;
Rev 11:10 and send **g** to one another,

GIHON
Gen 2:13 of the second river is G;
1Ki 1:45 have anointed him king at G;
2Ch 32:30 the water outlet of Upper G,

GILBOA
1Sa 31: 8 three sons fallen on Mount G.
2Sa 1:21 "O mountains of G,
2Sa 21:12 had struck down Saul in G.

GILEAD (*see* GILEADITE, JABESH GILEAD, RAMOTH
GILEAD)
Num 26:29 and Machir begot G;
Num 32:29 give them the land of G as
Josh 17: 1 of Manasseh, the father of G,
Josh 22:13 Manasseh, into the land of G,
Judg 11: 1 and G begot Jephthah.
1Sa 13: 7 to the land of Gad and G.
2Ki 10:33 including G and Bashan.
Ps 60: 7 G is Mine, and Manasseh is
Song 6: 5 of goats Going down from G.

Jer 8:22 Is there no balm in G,
Hos 12:11 Though G has idols—Surely
Amos 1: 3 they have threshed G with
Amos 1:13 the women with child in G,
Obad 19 Benjamin shall possess G.

GILEADITE (*see* GILEAD)
Judg 11:40 daughter of Jephthah the G.
1Ki 2: 7 the sons of Barzillai the G,

GILGAL
Deut 11:30 in the plain opposite G,
Josh 4:19 and they camped in G on the
Josh 4:20 Jordan, Joshua set up in G.
Josh 5: 9 of the place is called G to
Josh 5:10 of Israel camped in G,
Josh 12:23 the king of the people of G,
Judg 3:19 stone images that were at G,
1Sa 7:16 on a circuit to Bethel, G,
1Sa 11:14 let us go to G and renew the
1Sa 15:33 pieces before the LORD in G.
Hos 12:11 they sacrifice bulls in G,
Amos 4: 4 At G multiply
Amos 5: 5 seek Bethel, Nor enter G,

GIRD (*see* GIRDED, GIRDS)
Ex 29: 9 And you shall **g** them with
1Sa 25:13 Every man **g** on his sword."
2Sa 3:31 **g** yourselves with sackcloth,
Ps 45: 3 G Your sword upon Your
Ps 76:10 of wrath You shall **g**
Joel 1:13 G yourselves and lament,
John 21:18 and another will **g** you and
1Pe 1:13 Therefore **g** up the loins of

GIRDED (*see* GIRD)
Lev 8: 7 **g** him with the sash, clothed
Deut 1:41 when everyone of you had **g**
1Sa 2: 4 those who stumbled are **g**
1Sa 25:13 and David also **g** on his
1Ki 18:46 and he **g** up his loins and
Neh 4:18 builders had his sword **g** at
Ps 93: 1 He has **g** Himself with
Luke 12:35 Let your waist be **g** and
John 13: 4 took a towel and **g** Himself.
Eph 6:14 having **g** your waist with

GIRDS (*see* GIRD)
Prov 31:17 She **g** herself with strength,

GIRGASHITE (*see* GIRGASHITES)
1Ch 1:14 the Amorite, and the G;

GIRGASHITES (*see* GIRGASHITE)
Gen 15:21 the Canaanites, the G,

GIRL (*see* GIRLS)
Judg 5:30 To every man a **g** or two;
Amos 2: 7 father go in to the same **g**,
Matt 9:24 for the **g** is not dead, but
Matt 9:25 and the **g** arose.
Matt 14:11 a platter and given to the **g**,
Matt 26:69 And a servant **g** came to him,
Mark 5:41 is translated, "Little **g**,
Acts 12:13 a **g** named Rhoda came to
Acts 16:16 that a certain slave **g**
Acts 16:17 This **g** followed Paul and us,

GIRLS (*see* GIRL)
Zech 8: 5 Shall be full of boys and **g**

GITTITE (*see* GATH, GITTITES)
2Sa 6:10 the house of Obed-Edom the G.
2Sa 15:19 the king said to Ittai the G,
2Sa 21:19 brother of Goliath the G,
1Ch 20: 5 the brother of Goliath the G,

GITTITES (*see* GITTITE)
Josh 13: 3 the Ashkelonites, the G,

GIVE (*see* GAVE, GIFT, GIVEN, GIVER, GIVES, GIVING)

Gen   1:15 of the heavens to **g** light
Gen 12: 7 your descendants I will **g**
Gen 13:15 the land which you see I **g**
Gen 15: 2 what will You **g** me, seeing I
Gen 15: 7 to **g** you this land to
Gen 23: 4 **G** me property for a burial
Gen 23: 9 that he may **g** me the cave of
Gen 23:13 I will **g** you money for the
Gen 24: 7 To your descendants I **g** this
Gen 28: 4 And **g** you the blessing of
Gen 28:13 on which you lie I will **g**
Gen 28:22 You give me I will surely **g**
Gen 29:21 **G** me my wife, for my days
Gen 29:26 to **g** the younger before the
Gen 30: 1 **G** me children, or else I
Gen 38:17 Will you **g** me a pledge till
Gen 38:26 because I did not **g** her to
Gen 41:16 God will **g** Pharaoh an answer
Gen 42:25 and to **g** them provisions for
Gen 43:14 And may God Almighty **g** you
Gen 45:18 I will **g** you the best of the
Gen 47:24 the harvest that you shall **g**
Ex   1:19 for they are lively and **g**
Ex   2: 9 and I will **g** you your
Ex   3:21 And I will **g** this people
Ex   5:10 I will not **g** you straw.
Ex   6: 4 to **g** them the land of
Ex   6: 8 the land which I swore to **g**
Ex 10:25 You must also **g** us sacrifices
Ex 13:21 in a pillar of fire to **g**
Ex 15:26 **g** ear to His commandments
Ex 17: 2 **G** us water, that we may
Ex 18:19 I will **g** you counsel, and
Ex 21:23 then you shall **g** life for
Ex 22:29 of your sons you shall **g** to
Ex 22:30 the eighth day you shall **g**
Ex 24:12 and I will **g** you tablets of
Ex 25:16 the Testimony which I will **g**
Ex 30:13 who are numbered shall **g:**
Ex 30:15 The rich shall not **g** more and
Ex 30:15 and the poor shall not **g**
Ex 33:14 and I will **g** you rest."
Lev   5:16 add one-fifth to it and **g**
Lev 19:31 **G** no regard to mediums and
Lev 26: 4 then I will **g** you rain in its
Lev 26: 6 I will **g** peace in the land,
Num 11: 4 Who will **g** us meat to eat?
Num 18: 7 I **g** your priesthood to you
Num 20:21 Thus Edom refused to **g** Israel
Num 21:16 and I will **g** them water."
Num 34:13 LORD has commanded to **g** to
Num 36: 2 my lord Moses to **g** the
Deut 1:35 land of which I swore to **g**
Deut 1:45 listen to your voice nor **g**
Deut 6:10 to **g** you large and beautiful
Deut 6:23 to **g** us the land of which He
Deut 7: 3 You shall not **g** your
Deut 11:14 then I will **g** you the rain
Deut 16:17 Every man shall **g** as he is
Deut 18: 3 they shall **g** to the priest
Deut 22:29 who lay with her shall **g** to
Deut 23:14 to deliver you and **g** your
Deut 24:15 Each day you shall **g** him his
Deut 25: 3 Forty blows he may **g** him and
Deut 26: 3 swore to our fathers to **g**
Deut 32: 1 **G** ear, O heavens, and I will
Josh 7:19 **g** glory to the LORD God of
Josh 14:12 **g** me this mountain of which
Judg 4:19 Please **g** me a little water to
Judg 5: 3 O kings! **G** ear, O princes!
Judg 21:18 we cannot **g** them wives from
Ruth 4:12 which the LORD will **g** you
1Sa 2:10 He will **g** strength to His
1Sa 6: 5 and you shall **g** glory to the

1Sa 8: 6 **G** us a king to judge us." So
2Sa 3:14 **G** me my wife Michal, whom I
2Sa 22:50 Therefore I will **g** thanks to
1Ki 3: 5 Ask! What shall I **g** you?"
1Ki 3: 9 Therefore **g** to Your servant
1Ki 3:25 and **g** half to one, and half
1Ki 3:26 **g** her the living child, and
1Ki 11:13 I will **g** one tribe to your
1Ki 17:19 **G** me your son." So he took
1Ki 21: 6 **G** me your vineyard for money;
1Ki 21: 6 I will not **g** you my
2Ki 6:28 **G** your son, that we may eat
2Ki 8:19 as He promised him to **g** a
1Ch 16: 8 **g** thanks to the LORD! Call
1Ch 16:29 **G** to the LORD the glory
1Ch 22: 9 for I will **g** peace and
1Ch 22:12 Only may the LORD **g** you
2Ch 1:10 Now **g** me wisdom and
2Ch 25:18 **G** your daughter to my son as
2Ch 30:12 of God was on Judah to **g**
2Ch 31: 2 to **g** thanks, and to praise
Ezra 9: 8 enlighten our eyes and **g** us
Ezra 9: 9 not to **g** us a wall in Judah
Ezra 9:12 do not **g** your daughters as
Neh 9:12 To **g** them light on the road
Neh 9:15 Which You had sworn to **g**
Job 2: 4 all that a man has he will **g**
Job 10: 1 I will **g** free course to my
Job 33:31 **G** ear, Job, listen to me;
Ps 2: 8 and I will **g** You The
Ps 5: 1 **G** ear to my words, O LORD,
Ps 5: 2 **G** heed to the voice of my
Ps 6: 5 In the grave who will **g** You
Ps 18:49 Therefore I will **g** thanks to
Ps 28: 4 **G** them according to the
Ps 29: 1 **G** unto the LORD glory and
Ps 29:11 The LORD will **g** strength to
Ps 30:12 I will **g** thanks to You
Ps 37: 4 And He shall **g** you the
Ps 49: 7 Nor **g** to God a ransom for
Ps 51:16 or else I would **g** it; You
Ps 84:11 The LORD will **g** grace and
Ps 91:11 For He shall **g** His angels
Ps 92: 1 It is good to **g** thanks to
Ps 96: 7 **G** to the LORD, O families
Ps 97:12 And **g** thanks at the
Ps 105: 1 **g** thanks to the LORD! Call
Ps 106:47 To **g** thanks to Your holy
Ps 108:12 **G** us help from trouble, For
Ps 109: 4 But I **g** myself to
Ps 118: 1 **g** thanks to the LORD, for
Ps 118:29 **g** thanks to the LORD, for
Ps 119:62 midnight I will rise to **g**
Ps 132: 4 I will not **g** sleep to my
Ps 136: 1 **g** thanks to the LORD, for
Ps 136: 2 **g** thanks to the God of gods!
Ps 136: 3 **g** thanks to the Lord of
Ps 143: 1 **G** ear to my supplications!
Ps 145:15 And You **g** them their food
Prov 1: 4 To **g** prudence to the simple,
Prov 4: 2 For I **g** you good doctrine:
Prov 4:20 **g** attention to my words;
Prov 5: 9 Lest you **g** your honor to
Prov 6: 4 **G** no sleep to your eyes,
Prov 9: 9 **G** instruction to a wise
Prov 23:26 **g** me your heart, And let
Prov 25:21 **g** him bread to eat; And if
Prov 29:17 he will **g** delight to your
Prov 30:15 Give and **G!** There are
Prov 31: 3 Do not **g** your strength to
Prov 31: 6 **G** strong drink to him who is
Prov 31:31 **G** her of the fruit of her
Eccl 5: 1 to hear rather than to **g**
Song 7:12 There I will **g** you my love.
Song 8: 7 If a man would **g** for love

Is	1: 2	and **g** ear, O earth! For the
Is	7:14	the Lord Himself will **g** you
Is	19:11	wise counselors **g** foolish
Is	30:23	Then He will **g** the rain for
Is	36: 8	and I will **g** you two
Is	42: 8	And My glory I will not **g**
Is	42:12	Let them **g** glory to the
Is	43: 4	Therefore I will **g** men for
Is	43: 6	**G** them up!' And to the
Is	48:11	And I will not **g** My glory
Is	49: 6	I will also **g** You as a
Is	55:10	That it may **g** seed to the
Is	61: 3	To **g** them beauty for ashes,
Jer	9:15	and **g** them water of gall to
Jer	11: 5	to **g** them 'a land flowing
Jer	24: 7	Then I will **g** them a heart to
Jer	29:11	to **g** you a future and a
Jer	32:39	then I will **g** them one heart
Jer	34:20	I will **g** them into the hand
Jer	35: 2	and **g** them wine to drink."
Lam	2:18	**G** your eyes no rest.
Lam	3:30	Let him **g** his cheek to the
Ezek	2: 8	your mouth and eat what I **g**
Ezek	3: 3	with this scroll that I **g**
Ezek	3:17	and **g** them warning from Me:
Ezek	11:19	Then I will **g** them one heart,
Ezek	11:19	and **g** them a heart of flesh,
Ezek	36:26	I will **g** you a new heart and
Ezek	36:26	out of your flesh and **g** you
Ezek	39:11	in that day that I will **g**
Dan	1:12	and let them **g** us vegetables
Dan	2: 4	and we will **g** the
Dan	5:17	and **g** your rewards to
Dan	9:22	I have now come forth to **g**
Hos	2: 5	Who **g** me my bread and my
Hos	2:15	I will **g** her her vineyards
Hos	9:14	**G** them a miscarrying womb
Hos	11: 8	How can I **g** you up, Ephraim?
Mic	6: 7	Shall I **g** my firstborn for
Zech	8:12	And the heavens shall **g**
Zech	10: 1	He will **g** them showers of
Zech	11:12	**g** me my wages; and if not,
Matt	4: 6	He shall **g** His angels
Matt	4: 9	All these things I will **g** You
Matt	5:31	let him **g** her a certificate
Matt	5:42	**G** to him who asks you, and
Matt	6:11	**G** us this day our daily
Matt	7: 6	Do not **g** what is holy to the
Matt	7: 9	will **g** him a stone?
Matt	7:11	know how to **g** good gifts to
Matt	10: 8	you have received, freely **g**.
Matt	11:28	and I will **g** you rest.
Matt	14: 8	**G** me John the Baptist's head
Matt	16:19	And I will **g** you the keys of
Matt	16:26	Or what will a man **g** in
Matt	19: 7	then did Moses command to **g**
Matt	20: 8	Call the laborers and **g** them
Matt	20:23	on My left is not Mine to **g**,
Matt	20:28	and to **g** His life a ransom
Matt	24:29	and the moon will not **g** its
Matt	24:45	to **g** them food in due
Matt	25: 8	**G** us some of your oil, for
Matt	25:28	and **g** it to him who has ten
Matt	25:37	or thirsty and **g** You drink?
Mark	10:21	whatever you have and **g** to
Mark	12: 9	and the vineyard to
Mark	13:24	and the moon will not **g** its
Luke	1:77	To **g** knowledge of salvation
Luke	1:79	To **g** light to those who sit
Luke	4: 6	and I **g** it to whomever I
Luke	4:10	He shall **g** His angels
Luke	6:30	**G** to everyone who asks of
Luke	6:38	"**G**, and it will be given
Luke	11: 3	**G** us day by day our daily
Luke	11: 8	he will rise and **g** him as
Luke	11:11	will he **g** him a serpent
Luke	11:13	know how to **g** good gifts to
Luke	11:13	your heavenly Father **g** the
Luke	12:32	Father's good pleasure to **g**
Luke	12:33	Sell what you have and **g**
Luke	12:51	suppose that I came to **g**
Luke	14: 9	**G** place to this man,' and
Luke	14:12	When you **g** a dinner or a
Luke	15:12	**g** me the portion of goods
Luke	18:12	I **g** tithes of all that I
Luke	19: 8	I **g** half of my goods to the
Luke	19:24	and **g** it to him who has ten
Luke	20:16	those vinedressers and **g**
John	1:22	that we may **g** an answer to
John	3:34	for God does not **g** the
John	4: 7	**G** Me a drink."
John	4:14	of the water that I shall **g**
John	4:15	**g** me this water, that I may
John	6:32	Moses did not **g** you the
John	6:34	**g** us this bread always."
John	6:51	the bread that I shall **g** is
John	6:51	which I shall **g** for the life
John	7:19	Did not Moses **g** you the law,
John	9:24	**G** God the glory! We know that
John	10:28	And I **g** them eternal life,
John	11:22	God will **g** You."
John	13:26	It is he to whom I shall **g** a
John	13:29	or that he should **g**
John	13:34	A new commandment I **g** to you,
John	14:16	and He will **g** you another
John	14:27	My peace I **g** to you; not as
John	15:16	Father in My name He may **g**
John	17: 2	that He should **g** eternal
Acts	3: 6	but what I do have I **g** you:
Acts	7:38	the living oracles to **g** to
Acts	8:19	**G** me this power also, that
Acts	12:23	because he did not **g** glory
Acts	13:34	I will **g** you the sure
Acts	20:35	It is more blessed to **g** than
Rom	8:32	not with Him also freely **g**
Rom	12:19	but rather **g** place to
Rom	12:20	**g** him a drink; For in
Rom	14:12	So then each of us shall **g**
Rom	16: 4	to whom not only I **g** thanks,
1Co	7: 5	that you may **g** yourselves to
1Co	10:32	**G** no offense, either to the
1Co	13: 3	and though I **g** my body to be
1Co	14:17	For you indeed **g** thanks well,
2Co	4: 6	shone in our hearts to **g**
2Co	5:12	but **g** you opportunity to
2Co	8:10	And in this I **g** advice: It is
2Co	9: 7	So let each one **g** as he
Eph	1:16	do not cease to **g** thanks for
Eph	4:27	nor **g** place to the devil.
Eph	4:28	he may have something to **g**
Eph	5:14	And Christ will **g** you
Col	1: 3	We **g** thanks to the God and
1Th	5:18	in everything **g** thanks; for
1Ti	1: 4	nor **g** heed to fables and
1Ti	4:13	**g** attention to reading, to
1Ti	5:14	**g** no opportunity to the
2Ti	4: 8	will **g** to me on that Day,
Heb	2: 1	Therefore we must **g** the more
1Pe	3:15	and always be ready to **g**
1Jn	5:16	and He will **g** him life for
Rev	2: 7	him who overcomes I will **g**
Rev	2:10	and I will **g** you the crown
Rev	2:17	And I will **g** him a white
Rev	2:28	and I will **g** him the morning
Rev	4: 9	the living creatures **g**
Rev	14: 7	Fear God and **g** glory to Him,
Rev	16: 9	they did not repent and **g**
Rev	22:12	to **g** to every one according

GIVEN (*see* GIVE)

Gen	1:30	I have **g** every green herb
Gen	9: 3	I have **g** you all things,
Gen	15: 3	You have **g** me no offspring;
Gen	15:18	your descendants I have **g**
Ex	5:16	There is no straw **g** to your
Lev	17:11	and I have **g** it to you upon
Num	8:19	And I have **g** the Levites as a
Deut	2:24	I have **g** into your hand
Deut	3:20	until the LORD has **g** rest to
Deut	28:31	your sheep shall be **g** to
Josh	1: 3	will tread upon I have **g**
Josh	1:15	until the LORD has **g** your
Josh	6: 2	See! I have **g** Jericho into
Josh	13:14	the tribe of Levi he had **g**
Josh	17:14	Why have you **g** us only one
Judg	11:35	trouble me! For I have **g** my
Judg	14:20	And Samson's wife was **g** to
1Sa	18:19	should have been **g** to David,
2Sa	7: 1	and the LORD had **g** him rest
1Ki	3: 6	and You have **g** him a son to
1Ki	3:12	I have **g** you a wise and
1Ki	5: 7	for He has **g** David a wise
1Ki	9:16	and had **g** it as a dowry to
2Ki	5:17	let your servant be **g** two
2Ki	19:10	Jerusalem shall not be **g** into
2Ki	22:10	Hilkiah the priest has **g** me a
2Ki	25:30	was a regular ration **g** him
2Ch	8: 2	cities which Hiram had **g** to
2Ch	34:14	of the Law of the LORD **g**
2Ch	36:23	LORD God of heaven has **g**
Ezra	1: 2	LORD God of heaven has **g**
Neh	2: 7	let letters be **g** to me for
Neh	10:29	which was **g** by Moses the
Esth	2: 3	let beauty preparations be **g**
Esth	2:13	and she was **g** whatever she
Esth	7: 3	let my life be **g** me at my
Job	38:36	Or who has **g** understanding
Ps	16: 7	bless the LORD who has **g**
Ps	21: 2	You have **g** him his heart's
Ps	60: 4	You have **g** a banner to those
Ps	78:24	And **g** them of the bread of
Ps	79: 2	Your servants They have **g**
Ps	80: 5	And **g** them tears to drink
Ps	89:19	I have **g** help to one who
Ps	115:16	But the earth He has **g** to
Ps	118:27	And He has **g** us light;
Ps	119:50	For Your word has **g** me
Prov	23: 2	throat If you are a man **g**
Eccl	1:13	burdensome task God has **g**
Eccl	5:19	every man to whom God has **g**
Eccl	6: 2	A man to whom God has **g**
Eccl	9: 9	vain life which He has **g**
Is	8:18	whom the LORD has **g** me!
Is	9: 6	is born, Unto us a Son is **g**;
Jer	32:24	and the city has been **g** into
Ezek	37:25	in the land that I have **g**
Dan	2:23	You have **g** me wisdom and
Dan	4:16	Let him be **g** the heart of a
Dan	5:28	and **g** to the Medes and
Dan	7: 4	and a man's heart was **g** to
Dan	7:14	Then to Him was **g** dominion
Dan	7:25	the saints shall be **g**
Hos	2: 9	**G** to cover her nakedness.
Hos	2:12	wages that my lovers have **g**
Matt	7: 7	and it will be **g** to you;
Matt	9: 8	who had **g** such power to men.
Matt	12:39	and no sign will be **g** to it
Matt	13:11	to them it has not been **g**.
Matt	13:12	has, to him more will be **g**,
Matt	21:43	be taken from you and **g** to
Matt	22:30	neither marry nor are **g** in
Matt	26: 9	been sold for much and **g** to
Matt	26:48	Now His betrayer had **g** them a
Matt	27:58	commanded the body to be **g**
Matt	28:18	All authority has been **g** to
Mark	14:23	and when He had **g** thanks He
Luke	2:21	the name **g** by the angel
Luke	6:38	and it will be **g** to you:
Luke	8:10	but to the rest it is **g**
Luke	8:55	He commanded that she be **g**
Luke	11: 9	and it will be **g** to you;
Luke	11:29	and no sign will be **g** to it
Luke	20:34	of this age marry and are **g**
Luke	22:19	This is My body which is **g**
John	1:17	For the law was **g** through
John	3:27	unless it has been **g** to him
John	3:35	and has **g** all things into
John	4:10	and He would have **g** you
John	5:27	and has **g** Him authority to
John	5:36	which the Father has **g** Me
John	6:11	and when He had **g** thanks He
John	6:39	that of all He has **g** Me I
John	7:39	Holy Spirit was not yet **g**,
John	10:29	who has **g** them to Me, is
John	11:57	and the Pharisees had **g** a
John	13: 3	that the Father had **g** all
John	13:15	For I have **g** you an example,
John	16:21	but as soon as she has **g**
John	17: 2	as You have **g** Him authority
John	17: 4	the work which You have **g**
John	17: 6	to the men whom You have **g**
John	17: 8	For I have **g** to them the
John	17: 8	the words which You have **g**
John	17: 9	for those whom You have **g**
John	17:14	I have **g** them Your word; and
John	17:22	which You gave Me I have **g**
John	17:24	My glory which You have **g**
John	18:11	cup which My Father has **g**
Acts	4:12	no other name under heaven **g**
Acts	5:32	Holy Spirit whom God has **g**
Acts	8:18	hands the Holy Spirit was **g**,
Acts	17:31	He has **g** assurance of this
Rom	5: 5	by the Holy Spirit who was **g**
Rom	11: 8	God has **g** them a spirit
Rom	12: 3	through the grace **g** to me,
Rom	12:13	**g** to hospitality.
1Co	11:15	for her hair is **g** to her
1Co	11:24	and when He had **g** thanks, He
1Co	12: 7	of the Spirit is **g** to each
1Co	12: 8	for to one is **g** the word of
1Co	12:24	having **g** greater honor to
2Co	5:18	and has **g** us the ministry of
2Co	9: 9	He has **g** to the poor;
Gal	3:22	in Jesus Christ might be **g**
Gal	4:15	out your own eyes and **g**
Eph	3: 8	the saints, this grace was **g**,
Eph	4: 7	each one of us grace was **g**
Eph	4:19	have **g** themselves over to
Eph	5: 2	also has loved us and **g**
Eph	6:19	that utterance may be **g** to
Phil	2: 9	has highly exalted Him and **g**
2Th	2:16	who has loved us and **g** us
1Ti	3: 3	not **g** to wine, not violent,
2Ti	1: 7	For God has not **g** us a spirit
2Ti	3:16	All Scripture is **g** by
Heb	2:13	whom God has **g** Me.
Heb	4: 8	For if Joshua had **g** them
Jas	1: 5	and it will be **g** to him.
2Pe	3:15	according to the wisdom **g** to
1Jn	4:13	because He has **g** us of His
1Jn	5:10	testimony that God has **g** of
1Jn	5:11	that God has **g** us eternal
Rev	6: 2	and a crown was **g** to him,
Rev	8: 2	and to them were **g** seven
Rev	9: 1	To him was **g** the key to the
Rev	9: 3	And to them was **g** power, as
Rev	11: 1	Then I was **g** a reed like a
Rev	16: 8	and power was **g** to him to

GIVER† (*see* GIVE)
2Co 9: 7 for God loves a cheerful **g**.

GIVES (*see* GIVE)
Ex 21:22 so that she **g** birth
Deut 13: 1 and he **g** a sign or a
Deut 19: 8 and **g** you the land which He
Judg 21:18 Cursed be the one who **g** a
Job 5:10 He **g** rain on the earth, And
Job 32: 8 the breath of the Almighty **g**
Job 35:10 Who **g** songs in the night,
Job 36:31 He **g** food in abundance.
Ps 68:35 God of Israel is He who **g**
Ps 119:130 entrance of Your words **g**
Ps 119:130 It **g** understanding to the
Ps 127: 2 For so He **g** His beloved
Ps 136:25 Who **g** food to all flesh,
Ps 144:10 The One who **g** salvation to
Ps 146: 7 Who **g** food to the hungry.
Prov 2: 6 For the LORD **g** wisdom;
Prov 3:34 But **g** grace to the humble.
Prov 24:26 He who **g** a right answer
Prov 26: 8 in a sling Is he who **g**
Prov 29:13 The LORD **g** light to the
Eccl 2:26 For God **g** wisdom and
Eccl 5:18 of his life which God **g** him;
Is 14: 3 pass in the day the LORD **g**
Jer 5:24 Who **g** rain, both the former
Jer 31:35 Who **g** the sun for a light
Dan 2:21 He **g** wisdom to the wise
Dan 4:25 and **g** it to whomever He
Hab 2:15 Woe to him who **g** drink to
Matt 5:15 and it **g** light to all who
Matt 10:42 And whoever **g** one of these
Mark 9:41 For whoever **g** you a cup of
Luke 11:36 bright shining of a lamp **g**
John 1: 9 was the true Light which **g**
John 5:21 even so the Son **g** life to
John 6:32 but My Father **g** you the true
John 6:63 It is the Spirit who **g** life;
John 10:11 The good shepherd **g** His life
John 14:27 not as the world **g** do I give
Acts 17:25 since He **g** to all life,
Rom 4:17 who **g** life to the dead and
Rom 12: 8 in exhortation; he who **g**,
Rom 14: 6 for he **g** God thanks; and he
1Co 3: 7 but God who **g** the increase.
1Co 15:38 But God **g** it a body as He
1Co 15:57 who **g** us the victory through
2Co 3: 6 but the Spirit **g** life.
1Ti 6:17 who **g** us richly all things
Jas 1: 5 who **g** to all liberally and
Jas 1:15 it **g** birth to sin; and sin,
Jas 4: 6 But **g** grace to the
1Pe 5: 5 But **g** grace to the
Rev 22: 5 for the Lord God **g** them

GIVING (*see* GIVE)
Deut 3:20 the LORD your God is **g**
Deut 4: 1 God of your fathers is **g**
Deut 21:17 wife as the firstborn by **g**
Josh 1: 2 to the land which I am **g** to
Ruth 1: 6 had visited His people by **g**
Dan 8:13 the **g** of both the sanctuary
Matt 24:38 marrying and **g** in marriage,
Luke 17:16 **g** Him thanks. And he was a
Acts 15: 8 acknowledged them by **g** them
Rom 4:20 glory to God,
Rom 9: 4 the **g** of the law, the
Rom 12:10 in honor **g** preference to one
Col 1:12 **g** thanks to the Father who
Col 3:17 **g** thanks to God the Father
1Ti 4: 1 **g** heed to deceiving spirits
Tit 1:14 not **g** heed to Jewish fables
Heb 13:15 **g** thanks to His name.
1Pe 3: 7 **g** honor to the wife, as to

2Pe 1: 5 **g** all diligence, add to your

GLAD (*see* GLADLY, GLADNESS)
Ps 9: 2 I will be **g** and rejoice in
Ps 14: 7 rejoice and Israel be **g**.
Ps 16: 9 Therefore my heart is **g**,
Ps 34: 2 shall hear of it and be **g**.
Ps 40:16 seek You rejoice and be **g**
Ps 45: 8 which they have made You **g**.
Ps 46: 4 whose streams shall make **g**
Ps 53: 6 rejoice and Israel be **g**.
Ps 68: 3 But let the righteous be **g**;
Ps 69:32 shall see this and be **g**;
Ps 96:11 and let the earth be **g**;
Ps 97: 8 Zion hears and is **g**,
Ps 104:15 And wine that makes **g** the
Ps 118:24 We will rejoice and be **g**
Ps 122: 1 I was **g** when they said to
Ps 126: 3 for us, And we are **g**.
Prov 10: 1 A wise son makes a **g**
Prov 27:11 be wise, and make my heart **g**,
Is 52: 7 Who brings **g** tidings of
Jer 20:15 to you!" Making him very **g**.
Matt 5:12 and be exceedingly **g**,
Mark 14:11 they heard it, they were **g**,
Luke 1:19 to you and bring you these **g**
Luke 15:32 should make merry and be **g**,
Luke 23: 8 Jesus, he was exceedingly **g**;
John 8:56 and he saw it and was **g**.
John 11:15 And I am **g** for your sakes
John 20:20 Then the disciples were **g**
Acts 2:26 and my tongue was **g**;
Rom 10:15 Who bring **g** tidings of
Phil 2:17 I am **g** and rejoice with you
1Pe 4:13 you may also be **g** with
Rev 19: 7 Let us be **g** and rejoice and

GLADLY (*see* GLAD)
Mark 12:37 common people heard Him **g**.
Luke 15:16 And he would **g** have filled
Acts 21:17 the brethren received us **g**.
2Co 11:19 For you put up with fools **g**,
2Co 12: 9 Therefore most **g** I will

GLADNESS (*see* GLAD)
Deut 28:47 your God with joy and **g** of
2Sa 6:12 to the City of David with **g**.
Esth 8:16 The Jews had light and **g**,
Esth 9:17 it a day of feasting and **g**.
Ps 4: 7 You have put **g** in my heart,
Ps 30:11 and clothed me with **g**,
Ps 45: 7 You With the oil of **g** more
Ps 45:15 With **g** and rejoicing they
Ps 51: 8 Make me hear joy and **g**,
Ps 97:11 And **g** for the upright in
Ps 100: 2 Serve the LORD with **g**;
Ps 105:43 joy, His chosen ones with **g**.
Is 30:29 And **g** of heart as when one
Is 35:10 They shall obtain joy and **g**,
Jer 7:34 of mirth and the voice of **g**,
Mark 4:16 receive it with **g**;
Luke 1:14 you will have joy and **g**,
Acts 2:46 they ate their food with **g**
Phil 2:29 in the Lord with all **g**,
Heb 1: 9 You With the oil of **g**

GLASS
Rev 4: 6 there was a sea of **g**,
Rev 21:21 gold, like transparent **g**.

GLEAN (*see* GLEANED, GLEANING)
Lev 19:10 And you shall not **g** your
Deut 24:21 you shall not **g** it
Ruth 2: 7 Please let me **g** and gather
Jer 6: 9 They shall thoroughly **g** as a
Mic 7: 1 Like those who **g** vintage

GLEANED (*see* GLEAN)
Ruth 2:17 So she **g** in the field until
Ruth 2:17 and beat out what she had **g**,
Ruth 2:19 Where have you **g** today? And

GLEANING (*see* GLEAN)
Judg 8: 2 Is not the **g** of the
Jer 49: 9 they not leave some **g**

GLISTENING
Luke 9:29 robe became white and **g**.

GLITTERING
Nah 3: 3 with bright sword and **g**
Hab 3:11 At the shining of Your **g**

GLOOM (*see* GLOOMINESS)
Is 8:22 **g** of anguish; and they
Jas 4: 9 mourning and your joy to **g**.

GLOOMINESS† (*see* GLOOM)
Joel 2: 2 A day of darkness and **g**,
Zeph 1:15 A day of darkness and **g**,

GLORIES† (*see* GLORY)
Jer 9:24 But let him who **g** glory in
1Co 1:31 it is written, "He who **g**,
2Co 10:17 But "he who **g**,
1Pe 1:11 of Christ and the **g** that

GLORIFIED (*see* GLORIFY)
Is 49: 3 Israel, In whom I will be **g**.
Is 55: 5 For He has **g** you."
Is 66: 5 said, 'Let the LORD be **g**,
Dan 5:23 your ways, you have not **g**.
Matt 9: 8 they marveled and **g** God, who
Mark 2:12 that all were amazed and **g**
John 7:39 because Jesus was not yet **g**.
John 11: 4 that the Son of God may be **g**
John 12:23 that the Son of Man should be **g**.
John 12:28 I have both **g** it and will
John 13:31 and God is **g** in Him.
John 14:13 that the Father may be **g** in
John 15: 8 "By this My Father is **g**,
John 17: 4 I have **g** You on the earth. I
John 17:10 and I am **g** in them.
Acts 3:13 **g** His Servant Jesus, whom
Rom 8:17 that we may also be **g**
Rom 8:30 justified, these He also **g**.
2Th 1:12 Lord Jesus Christ may be **g**
2Th 3: 1 may run swiftly and be **g**,
1Pe 4:14 but on your part He is **g**.

GLORIFIES† (*see* GLORIFY)
Ps 50:23 Whoever offers praise **g** Me;

GLORIFY (*see* GLORIFIED, GLORIFIES, GLORIFYING, GLORY)
Ps 22:23 **g** Him, And fear Him, all
Ps 50:15 and you shall **g** Me."
Ps 86: 9 And shall **g** Your name.
Matt 5:16 see your good works and **g**
John 12:28 **g** Your name." Then a voice
John 12:28 glorified it and will **g**
John 13:32 God will also **g** Him in
John 16:14 He will **g** Me, for He will
John 17: 1 **G** Your Son, that Your Son
John 21:19 by what death he would **g**
Rom 1:21 they did not **g** Him as God,
1Co 6:20 therefore **g** God in your body
Heb 5: 5 So also Christ did not **g**
Rev 15: 4 and **g** Your name? For You

GLORIFYING† (*see* GLORIFY)
Luke 2:20 **g** and praising God for all
Luke 5:25 own house, **g** God.
Luke 18:43 **g** God. And all the people,

GLORIOUS (*see* GLORIOUSLY, GLORY)
Ex 15: 6 has become **g** in power; Your

Neh 9: 5 Blessed be Your **g** name,
Ps 45:13 royal daughter is all **g**
Ps 66: 2 His name; Make His praise **g**.
Ps 72:19 And blessed be His **g** name
Ps 76: 4 You are more **g** and
Ps 87: 3 **G** things are spoken of you,
Ps 145: 5 I will meditate on the **g**
Ps 145:12 And the **g** majesty of His
Is 60:13 make the place of My feet **g**.
Dan 8: 9 and toward the **G** Land.
2Co 3:11 what is passing away was **g**,
2Co 3:11 what remains is much more **g**.
Eph 5:27 present her to Himself a **g**
Phil 3:21 it may be conformed to His **g**
Col 1:11 according to His **g** power,
1Ti 1:11 according to the **g** gospel of
Tit 2:13 for the blessed hope and **g**

GLORIOUSLY (*see* GLORIOUS)
Ex 15: 1 For He has triumphed **g**!
Ex 15:21 For He has triumphed **g**!

GLORY (*see* GLORIES, GLORIFY, GLORIOUS, GLORYING)
Ex 16: 7 morning you shall see the **g**
Ex 16:10 the **g** of the LORD appeared
Ex 24:16 Now the **g** of the LORD rested
Ex 29:43 shall be sanctified by My **g**.
Ex 33:18 "Please, show me Your **g**.
Ex 33:22 while My **g** passes by, that I
Ex 40:34 and the **g** of the LORD
Num 14:21 shall be filled with the **g**
Num 14:22 men who have seen My **g** and
Josh 7:19 give **g** to the LORD God of
1Sa 4:21 The **g** has departed from
1Sa 6: 5 and you shall give **g** to the
1Ch 16:10 **G** in His holy name
1Ch 16:24 Declare His **g** among the
1Ch 16:29 Give to the LORD the **g** due
1Ch 29:11 The power and the **g**,
2Ch 7: 1 and the **g** of the LORD
Job 19: 9 He has stripped me of my **g**,
Ps 4: 2 Will you turn my **g** to
Ps 8: 1 Who have set Your **g** above
Ps 8: 5 You have crowned him with **g**
Ps 16: 9 and my **g** rejoices; My flesh
Ps 19: 1 The heavens declare the **g** of
Ps 24: 7 doors! And the King of **g**
Ps 24: 8 Who is this King of **g**?
Ps 24:10 hosts, He is the King of **g**.
Ps 29: 1 Give unto the LORD **g** and
Ps 29: 3 The God of **g** thunders; The
Ps 29: 9 everyone says, "**G**!"
Ps 45: 3 With Your **g** and Your
Ps 57: 5 Let Your **g** be above all
Ps 62: 7 is my salvation and my **g**;
Ps 63: 2 see Your power and Your **g**.
Ps 64:10 the upright in heart shall **g**.
Ps 71: 8 praise And with Your **g**
Ps 72:19 earth be filled with His **g**.
Ps 73:24 afterward receive me to **g**.
Ps 79: 9 For the **g** of Your name;
Ps 84:11 LORD will give grace and **g**;
Ps 85: 9 That **g** may dwell in our
Ps 90:16 And Your **g** to their
Ps 96: 3 Declare His **g** among the
Ps 97: 6 all the peoples see His **g**.
Ps 102:16 He shall appear in His **g**.
Ps 104:31 May the **g** of the LORD
Ps 105: 3 **G** in His holy name
Ps 106:20 Thus they changed their **g**
Ps 108: 5 And Your **g** above all the
Ps 113: 4 His **g** above the heavens.
Ps 138: 5 For great is the **g** of the
Ps 145:11 They shall speak of the **g** of
Ps 148:13 His **g** is above the earth
Ps 149: 5 the saints be joyful in **g**;

Prov	3:35	The wise shall inherit **g**,
Prov	17: 6	And the **g** of children is
Prov	19:11	And his **g** is to overlook a
Prov	25: 2	It is the **g** of God to
Prov	25: 2	But the **g** of kings is to
Prov	25:27	So to seek one's own **g** is
Is	6: 3	earth is full of His **g**!"
Is	10:18	And it will consume the **g** of
Is	23: 9	dishonor the pride of all **g**,
Is	24:16	**G** to the righteous!" But I
Is	28: 5	will be For a crown of **g**
Is	40: 5	The **g** of the LORD shall be
Is	41:16	And **g** in the Holy One of
Is	42: 8	And My **g** I will not give to
Is	43: 7	I have created for My **g**;
Is	46:13	in Zion, For Israel My **g**.
Is	60: 1	light has come! And the **g**
Is	60:19	light, And your God your **g**.
Is	61: 6	And in their **g** you shall
Is	66:12	And the **g** of the Gentiles
Is	66:19	And they shall declare My **g**
Jer	2:11	people have changed their **G**
Jer	9:23	Let not the wise man **g** in
Jer	9:23	Nor let the rich man **g** in
Jer	9:24	But let him who glories **g** in
Jer	13:16	Give **g** to the LORD your God
Ezek	1:28	of the likeness of the **g** of
Ezek	3:23	the **g** of the LORD stood
Ezek	3:23	like the **g** which I saw by
Ezek	8: 4	the **g** of the God of Israel
Ezek	10: 4	brightness of the LORD's **g**.
Ezek	43: 5	the **g** of the LORD filled
Dan	2:37	power, strength, and **g**;
Dan	5:20	and they took his **g** from
Dan	7:14	Him was given dominion and **g**
Hos	10: 5	Because its **g** has departed
Mic	2: 9	You have taken away My **g**
Hag	2: 3	this temple in its former **g**?
Hag	2: 7	will fill this temple with **g**,
Hag	2: 9	The **g** of this latter temple
Zech	2: 5	and I will be the **g** in her
Zech	11: 3	shepherds! For their **g** is
Mal	2: 2	To give **g** to My name,"
Matt	4: 8	of the world and their **g**.
Matt	6: 2	that they may have **g** from
Matt	6:13	and the power and the **g**
Matt	6:29	even Solomon in all his **g**
Matt	16:27	of Man will come in the **g**
Matt	19:28	sits on the throne of His **g**,
Matt	24:30	with power and great **g**.
Matt	25:31	Son of Man comes in His **g**,
Mark	10:37	on Your left, in Your **g**.
Luke	2: 9	and the **g** of the Lord shone
Luke	2:14	**G** to God in the highest, And
Luke	2:32	And the **g** of Your people
Luke	9:26	when He comes in His own **g**,
Luke	9:32	they saw His **g** and the two
Luke	17:18	who returned to give **g** to
Luke	19:38	Peace in heaven and **g** in
Luke	24:26	and to enter into His **g**?
John	1:14	us, and we beheld His **g**,
John	1:14	the **g** as of the only
John	2:11	and manifested His **g**;
John	9:24	Give God the **g**! We know that
John	11: 4	but for the **g** of God, that
John	12:41	said when he saw His **g** and
John	17: 5	with the **g** which I had with
John	17:22	And the **g** which You gave Me I
Acts	7: 2	The God of **g** appeared to our
Rom	1:23	and changed the **g** of the
Rom	3:23	and fall short of the **g** of God
Rom	4:20	giving **g** to God,
Rom	5: 2	rejoice in hope of the **g** of
Rom	5: 3	but we also **g** in
Rom	6: 4	from the dead by the **g** of

Rom	8:18	to be compared with the **g**
Rom	9: 4	pertain the adoption, the **g**,
Rom	9:23	known the riches of His **g**
Rom	9:23	prepared beforehand for **g**,
Rom	11:36	to whom be **g** forever. Amen.
Rom	16:27	be **g** through Jesus Christ
1Co	1:29	that no flesh should **g** in His
1Co	2: 7	before the ages for our **g**,
1Co	2: 8	have crucified the Lord of **g**.
1Co	10:31	do all to the **g** of God.
1Co	11: 7	since he is the image and **g**
1Co	11: 7	but woman is the **g** of man.
1Co	11:15	it is a **g** to her; for her
1Co	15:40	but the **g** of the celestial
1Co	15:41	There is one **g** of the sun,
1Co	15:43	dishonor, it is raised in **g**.
2Co	3: 7	of Moses because of the **g**
2Co	3: 7	which **g** was passing away,
2Co	3:18	into the same image from **g**
2Co	3:18	same image from glory to **g**,
2Co	4:15	to abound to the **g** of God.
2Co	4:17	and eternal weight of **g**,
2Co	10:17	let him **g** in the
Gal	1: 5	to whom be **g** forever and
Eph	1: 6	to the praise of the **g** of His
Eph	1:17	Christ, the Father of **g**,
Eph	1:18	are the riches of the **g** of
Eph	3:16	to the riches of His **g**,
Eph	3:21	to Him be **g** in the church by
Phil	2:11	to the **g** of God the Father.
Phil	4:19	to His riches in **g** by
Phil	4:20	to our God and Father be **g**
Col	1:27	are the riches of the **g**
Col	1:27	Christ in you, the hope of **g**.
Col	3: 4	will appear with Him in **g**.
1Th	2: 6	Nor did we seek **g** from men,
1Th	2:20	For you are our **g** and joy.
1Ti	3:16	the world, Received up in **g**.
2Ti	2:10	Christ Jesus with eternal **g**.
Heb	1: 3	the brightness of His **g**
Heb	2: 7	crowned him with **g** and
Heb	2:10	in bringing many sons to **g**,
Heb	13:21	to whom be **g** forever and
Jas	2: 1	Christ, the Lord of **g**,
1Pe	1: 8	inexpressible and full of **g**,
1Pe	1:21	from the dead and gave Him **g**,
1Pe	4:13	that when His **g** is revealed,
1Pe	4:14	for the Spirit of **g** and of
1Pe	5: 1	and also a partaker of the **g**
1Pe	5: 4	will receive the crown of **g**
1Pe	5:10	called us to His eternal **g**
1Pe	5:11	To Him be the **g** and the
Jude	24	the presence of His **g** with
Rev	4: 9	the living creatures give **g**
Rev	4:11	To receive **g** and honor and
Rev	5:12	strength and honor and **g**

GLORYING† (see GLORY)

1Co	5: 6	Your **g** is not good. Do you

GLUTTON† (see GLUTTONS)

Deut	21:20	he is a **g** and a drunkard.'
Prov	23:21	For the drunkard and the **g**
Matt	11:19	a **g** and a winebibber, a
Luke	7:34	a **g** and a winebibber, a

GLUTTONS† (see GLUTTON)

Prov	28: 7	But a companion of **g** shames
Tit	1:12	liars, evil beasts, lazy **g**.

GNASH† (see GNASHED, GNASHES, GNASHING)

Ps	112:10	He will **g** his teeth and
Lam	2:16	They hiss and **g** their

GNASHED† (see GNASH)

Ps	35:16	mockers at feasts They **g**
Acts	7:54	and they **g** at him with

GNASHES† (*see* GNASH)
Job 16: 9 He **g** at me with His teeth;
Ps 37:12 And **g** at him with his
Mark 9:18 **g** his teeth, and becomes

GNASHING (*see* GNASH)
Matt 8:12 There will be weeping and **g**
Matt 13:42 There will be wailing and **g**

GNAT†
Matt 23:24 who strain out a **g** and

GOAD† (*see* GOADS)
Judg 3:31 the Philistines with an ox **g**;

GOADS† (*see* GOAD)
1Sa 13:21 to set the points of the **g**.
Eccl 12:11 words of the wise are like **g**,
Acts 9: 5 you to kick against the **g**.
Acts 26:14 you to kick against the **g**.

GOAL†
Phil 3:14 I press toward the **g** for the

GOAT (*see* GOATS, GOATSKINS)
Gen 15: 9 a three-year-old female **g**,
Ex 23:19 shall not boil a young **g** in
Lev 16:20 he shall bring the live **g**.
Lev 16:26 And he who released the **g** as
Num 28:22 also one **g** as a sin
Deut 14: 5 the roe deer, the wild **g**,
Judg 6:19 in and prepared a young **g**,
Is 11: 6 lie down with the young **g**,
Dan 8: 5 suddenly a male **g** came from
Dan 8: 5 and the **g** had a notable
Dan 8:21 And the male **g** is the

GOATS (*see* GOAT, GOATS')
Gen 27:16 skins of the kids of the **g**
Gen 30:35 removed that day the male **g**
Ex 12: 5 from the sheep or from the **g**.
Deut 32:14 the breed of Bashan, and **g**,
1Sa 24: 2 on the Rocks of the Wild **G**.
Job 39: 1 when the wild mountain **g**
Ps 50:13 Or drink the blood of **g**?
Ps 104:18 hills are for the wild **g**;
Song 4: 1 hair is like a flock of **g**,
Is 34: 6 the blood of lambs and **g**,
Matt 25:32 his sheep from the **g**.
Matt 25:33 but the **g** on the left.
Heb 9:12 Not with the blood of **g** and
Heb 9:13 if the blood of bulls and **g**
Heb 10: 4 the blood of bulls and **g**

GOATS' (*see* GOATS)
Ex 26: 7 also make curtains of **g**
Prov 27:27 You shall have enough **g**

GOATSKINS† (*see* GOAT)
Heb 11:37 about in sheepskins and **g**,

GOD (*see* GOD-GIVEN, GOD-WHO-FORGIVES, GOD'S,
GODHEAD, GODLY, ONE, YAH, YOU-ARE-THE-GOD-WHO-
SEES)
Gen 1: 1 In the beginning **G** created
Gen 1: 3 Then **G** said, "Let there be
Gen 1:10 And **G** saw that it was
Gen 1:12 And **G** saw that it was
Gen 1:21 So **G** created great sea
Gen 1:22 And **G** blessed them, saying,
Gen 1:26 Then **G** said, "Let Us make
Gen 1:27 So **G** created man in His own
Gen 2: 3 Then **G** blessed the seventh
Gen 2: 4 in the day that the LORD **G**
Gen 2: 7 And the LORD **G** formed man
Gen 3: 1 Has **G** indeed said, 'You shall
Gen 3: 8 the sound of the LORD **G**
Gen 5: 1 him in the likeness of **G**.
Gen 5:22 Enoch walked with **G** three
Gen 5:24 for **G** took him.
Gen 6: 4 when the sons of **G** came in

Gen 6: 9 Noah walked with **G**.
Gen 7: 9 as **G** had commanded Noah.
Gen 8: 1 Then **G** remembered Noah, and
Gen 9:16 covenant between **G** and
Gen 14:18 he was the priest of **G** Most
Gen 15: 2 But Abram said, "Lord **G**,
Gen 17: 1 to him, "I am Almighty **G**;
Gen 17: 8 and I will be their **G**.
Gen 17:22 and **G** went up from Abraham.
Gen 19:29 that **G** remembered Abraham,
Gen 20:11 surely the fear of **G** is not
Gen 21:17 Then the angel of **G** called
Gen 21:33 the LORD, the Everlasting **G**.
Gen 22: 1 after these things that **G**
Gen 22: 8 **G** will provide for Himself
Gen 28: 3 May **G** Almighty bless you,
Gen 28:12 and there the angels of **G**
Gen 28:13 I am the LORD **G** of Abraham
Gen 28:17 other than the house of **G**,
Gen 30:22 Then **G** remembered Rachel,
Gen 30:23 **G** has taken away my
Gen 31:11 Then the Angel of **G** spoke to
Gen 31:13 I am the **G** of Bethel, where
Gen 31:42 the **G** of Abraham and the
Gen 32:28 you have struggled with **G**
Gen 32:30 For I have seen **G** face to
Gen 33: 5 The children whom **G** has
Gen 35: 5 and the terror of **G** was upon
Gen 35: 9 Then **G** appeared to Jacob
Gen 40: 8 interpretations belong to **G**?
Gen 41:38 in whom is the Spirit of **G**?
Gen 42:18 this and live, for I fear **G**:
Gen 45: 5 for **G** sent me before you to
Gen 45: 7 And **G** sent me before you to
Gen 49:24 the hands of the Mighty **G**
Gen 50:19 for am I in the place of **G**?
Gen 50:20 but **G** meant it for good, in
Ex 2:23 and their cry came up to **G**
Ex 2:24 So **G** heard their groaning,
Ex 2:24 and **G** remembered His
Ex 3: 1 to Horeb, the mountain of **G**.
Ex 3: 4 **G** called to him from the
Ex 3:15 the **G** of Abraham, the God of
Ex 3:15 the **G** of Isaac, and the God
Ex 3:18 The LORD **G** of the Hebrews
Ex 3:18 sacrifice to the LORD our **G**.
Ex 4:16 and you shall be to him as **G**.
Ex 4:20 And Moses took the rod of **G**
Ex 6: 3 as **G** Almighty, but by My
Ex 6: 7 people, and I will be your **G**.
Ex 8:19 "This is the finger of **G**.
Ex 14:19 And the Angel of **G**,
Ex 18:12 sacrifices to offer to **G**.
Ex 18:15 come to me to inquire of **G**.
Ex 20: 2 "I am the LORD your **G**,
Ex 20: 5 your God, am a jealous **G**,
Ex 20: 7 name of the LORD your **G** in
Ex 24:11 lay His hand. So they saw **G**,
Ex 31: 3 him with the Spirit of **G**,
Ex 31:18 written with the finger of **G**.
Ex 32:16 tablets were the work of **G**,
Ex 34: 6 "The LORD, the LORD **G**,
Lev 18:21 profane the name of your **G**:
Lev 21:17 to offer the bread of his **G**.
Num 16:22 the **G** of the spirits of all
Num 21: 5 the people spoke against **G**
Num 22: 9 Then **G** came to Balaam and
Num 23: 8 How shall I curse whom **G** has
Num 23:19 **G** is not a man, that He
Num 27:16 the **G** of the spirits of all
Deut 4:24 consuming fire, a jealous **G**.
Deut 4:25 sight of the LORD your **G**,
Deut 4:29 will seek the LORD your **G**,
Deut 5:14 Sabbath of the LORD your **G**.
Deut 5:26 the voice of the living **G**

Deut 6: 3 greatly as the LORD **G** of
Deut 6: 4 O Israel: The LORD our **G**,
Deut 6: 5 shall love the LORD your **G**
Deut 6:16 not tempt the LORD your **G**
Deut 7: 9 the LORD your God, He is **G**,
Deut 7: 9 the faithful **G** who keeps
Deut 7:21 God, the great and awesome **G**,
Deut 8:14 you forget the LORD your **G**
Deut 8:18 remember the LORD your **G**,
Deut 10:12 to serve the LORD your **G**
Deut 10:17 For the LORD your **G** is God
Deut 12:11 place where the LORD your **G**
Deut 12:27 altar of the LORD your **G**;
Deut 13:18 voice of the LORD your **G**,
Deut 13:18 the eyes of the LORD your **G**.
Deut 14:23 to fear the LORD your **G**
Deut 16: 1 Passover to the LORD your **G**,
Deut 16:15 feast to the LORD your **G**
Deut 18:15 The LORD your **G** will raise
Deut 20:18 sin against the LORD your **G**.
Deut 21:23 is hanged is accursed of **G**.
Deut 23: 5 because the LORD your **G**
Deut 23:21 a vow to the LORD your **G**,
Deut 24:18 and the LORD your **G**
Deut 25:19 land which the LORD your **G**
Deut 26: 7 we cried out to the LORD **G**
Deut 28:58 name, THE LORD YOUR **G**,
Deut 29:29 belong to the LORD our **G**,
Deut 32: 3 Ascribe greatness to our **G**.
Deut 32: 4 A **G** of truth and without
Deut 32:17 to demons, not to **G**,
Deut 32:39 And there is no **G** besides
Deut 33:27 The eternal **G** is your
Josh 1: 9 for the LORD your **G** is
Josh 1:11 land which the LORD your **G**
Josh 3:10 know that the living **G** is
Josh 4:23 for the LORD your **G** dried up
Josh 4:24 may fear the LORD your **G**
Josh 7:19 give glory to the LORD **G** of
Josh 14: 8 followed the LORD my **G**.
Josh 23:13 that the LORD your **G** will
Josh 24:18 the LORD, for He is our **G**.
Josh 24:24 The LORD our **G** we will
Josh 24:26 in the Book of the Law of **G**.
Josh 24:27 to you, lest you deny your **G**.
Judg 4:23 So on that day **G** subdued
Judg 13: 5 shall be a Nazirite to **G**
Judg 13: 6 A Man of **G** came to me, and
Judg 13: 6 of the Angel of **G**,
Judg 13:22 because we have seen **G**!"
Judg 16:17 have been a Nazirite to **G**
Judg 18:31 the time that the house of **G**
Ruth 1:16 people, And your God, my **G**.
1Sa 2: 2 there any rock like our **G**.
1Sa 2:25 **G** will judge him. But if a
1Sa 2:27 Then a man of **G** came to Eli
1Sa 3: 3 and before the lamp of **G** went
1Sa 3: 3 the LORD where the ark of **G**
1Sa 3:17 **G** do so to you, and more
1Sa 4: 4 the ark of the covenant of **G**.
1Sa 4: 7 **G** has come into the camp!"
1Sa 5: 1 took the ark of **G** and
1Sa 5:11 the hand of **G** was very heavy
1Sa 6:20 before this holy LORD **G**?
1Sa 9: 9 a man went to inquire of **G**,
1Sa 10: 9 that **G** gave him another
1Sa 10:10 then the Spirit of **G** came
1Sa 16:23 whenever the spirit from **G**
1Sa 17:26 the armies of the living **G**?
1Sa 17:45 the **G** of the armies of
1Sa 17:46 may know that there is a **G**
1Sa 18:10 distressing spirit from **G**
1Sa 19:20 the Spirit of **G** came upon
1Sa 25:22 May **G** do so, and more also,
1Sa 29: 9 in my sight as an angel of **G**;

2Sa 5:10 and the LORD **G** of hosts
2Sa 6: 7 died there by the ark of **G**.
2Sa 7:18 said: "Who am I, O Lord **G**?
2Sa 7:22 You are great, O Lord **G**.
2Sa 7:22 nor is there any **G**
2Sa 7:28 now, O Lord GOD, You are **G**,
2Sa 14:17 for as the angel of **G**,
2Sa 15:32 where he worshiped **G**—
2Sa 22:30 By my **G** I can leap over a
2Sa 22:48 It is **G** who avenges me,
2Sa 24: 3 Now may the LORD your **G** add
2Sa 24:24 offerings to the LORD my **G**
1Ki 4:29 And **G** gave Solomon wisdom
1Ki 8:27 But will **G** indeed dwell on
1Ki 13: 1 a man of **G** went from Judah
1Ki 16:13 in provoking the LORD **G** of
1Ki 17: 1 As the LORD **G** of Israel
1Ki 18:21 opinions? If the LORD is **G**,
1Ki 18:24 who answers by fire, He is **G**.
1Ki 18:36 LORD **G** of Abraham, Isaac,
1Ki 18:39 He is **G**! The LORD, He is
1Ki 19: 8 as Horeb, the mountain of **G**.
1Ki 20:28 The LORD is **G** of the hills,
1Ki 21:10 You have blasphemed **G** and the
2Ki 2:14 Where is the LORD **G** of
2Ki 4: 9 this is a holy man of **G**,
2Ki 5: 7 clothes and said, "Am I **G**,
2Ki 5:20 of Elisha the man of **G**,
2Ki 18:22 'We trust in the LORD our **G**,
2Ki 19: 4 to reproach the living **G**,
2Ki 19:10 Do not let your **G** in whom you
2Ki 19:15 the cherubim, You are **G**,
1Ch 9:11 officer over the house of **G**;
1Ch 9:26 treasuries of the house of **G**.
1Ch 12:17 may the **G** of our fathers
1Ch 12:22 army, like the army of **G**.
1Ch 14:10 And David inquired of **G**,
1Ch 15: 2 them to carry the ark of **G**
1Ch 16: 6 the ark of the covenant of **G**.
1Ch 16:35 O **G** of our salvation;
1Ch 16:42 the musical instruments of **G**.
1Ch 17: 2 for **G** is with you."
1Ch 17:20 nor is there any **G**
1Ch 17:26 "And now, LORD, You are **G**,
1Ch 23:14 sons of Moses the man of **G**
1Ch 28: 2 for the footstool of our **G**,
1Ch 29:18 O LORD **G** of Abraham, Isaac,
2Ch 2: 5 for our **G** is greater than
2Ch 7: 5 dedicated the house of **G**.
2Ch 15: 1 Now the Spirit of **G** came upon
2Ch 15: 3 been without the true **G**,
2Ch 20: 6 O LORD **G** of our fathers,
2Ch 20: 6 are You not **G** in heaven,
2Ch 20:20 Believe in the LORD your **G**,
2Ch 20:29 And the fear of **G** was on all
2Ch 20:30 for his **G** gave him rest all
2Ch 30: 9 for the LORD your **G** is
2Ch 30:12 Also the hand of **G** was on
2Ch 30:16 Law of Moses the man of **G**;
2Ch 32:14 that your **G** should be able
2Ch 32:19 they spoke against the **G** of
2Ch 34:32 to the covenant of **G**,
2Ch 35:21 from meddling with **G**,
2Ch 36:13 him swear an oath by **G**;
Ezra 1: 3 God of Israel (He is **G**),
Ezra 3: 8 coming to the house of **G** at
Ezra 5: 2 and the prophets of **G** were
Ezra 6:10 of sweet aroma to the **G** of
Ezra 6:17 of this house of **G**,
Ezra 7: 9 to the good hand of his **G**
Ezra 8:21 ourselves before our **G**,
Ezra 9: 6 lift up my face to You, my **G**;
Neh 1: 5 O great and awesome **G**,
Neh 4:20 Our **G** will fight for us."
Neh 5:19 Remember me, my **G**,

Neh 8:18 the Book of the Law of G.
Neh 9:31 them; For You are G,
Neh 10:38 tithes to the house of our G,
Neh 12:36 of David the man of G.
Neh 13:29 Remember them, O my G,
Neh 13:31 times. Remember me, O my G,
Job 1: 1 and one who feared G and
Job 1: 5 have sinned and cursed G in
Job 1: 9 Does Job fear G for nothing?
Job 1:16 The fire of G fell from
Job 1:22 Job did not sin nor charge G
Job 2: 9 Curse G and die!"
Job 2:10 we indeed accept good from G,
Job 3:23 And whom G has hedged in?
Job 4: 9 By the blast of G they
Job 6: 4 The terrors of G are
Job 8: 3 Does G subvert judgment? Or
Job 9: 4 G is wise in heart and
Job 11: 7 out the deep things of G?
Job 12: 4 friends, Who called on G,
Job 13: 3 I desire to reason with G.
Job 16:20 eyes pour out tears to G.
Job 19: 6 Know then that G has wronged
Job 19:22 do you persecute me as G
Job 19:26 in my flesh I shall see G,
Job 21: 9 Neither is the rod of G
Job 21:22 Can anyone teach G
Job 22: 2 a man be profitable to G,
Job 25: 4 man be righteous before G?
Job 27: 3 And the breath of G in my
Job 29: 4 the friendly counsel of G
Job 31:23 For destruction from G is
Job 31:28 For I would have denied G
Job 33: 4 The Spirit of G has made me,
Job 33:12 For G is greater than man.
Job 35:10 Where is G my Maker, Who
Job 37: 5 G thunders marvelously with
Job 37:10 By the breath of G ice is
Job 37:14 the wondrous works of G.
Job 38: 7 And all the sons of G
Job 40:19 the first of the ways of G;
Ps 3: 7 O my G! For You have struck
Ps 4: 1 O G of my righteousness!
Ps 5: 2 of my cry, My King and my G,
Ps 5:10 O G! Let them fall by their
Ps 7: 9 For the righteous G tests
Ps 7:10 My defense is of G,
Ps 7:11 G is a just judge, And God
Ps 7:11 And G is angry with the
Ps 9:17 the nations that forget G.
Ps 10:13 do the wicked renounce G?
Ps 14: 1 heart, "There is no G.
Ps 14: 2 who understand, who seek G.
Ps 16: 1 Preserve me, O G,
Ps 18: 2 and my deliverer; My G,
Ps 18:29 By my G I can leap over a
Ps 18:46 be my Rock! Let the G of
Ps 19: 1 declare the glory of G;
Ps 20: 1 May the name of the G of
Ps 22: 1 My God, My G, why have
Ps 29: 3 The G of glory thunders;
Ps 31: 5 O LORD G of truth.
Ps 33:12 is the nation whose G is
Ps 36: 1 There is no fear of G
Ps 37:31 The law of his G is in his
Ps 38:21 forsake me, O LORD; O my G,
Ps 40: 8 to do Your will, O my G,
Ps 40:17 Do not delay, O my G.
Ps 42: 1 pants my soul for You, O G.
Ps 42: 2 My soul thirsts for G,
Ps 42: 3 to me, "Where is your G?
Ps 42: 5 within me? Hope in G,
Ps 42: 8 A prayer to the G of my
Ps 43: 4 To G my exceeding joy; And
Ps 43: 4 praise You, O God, my G.

Ps 44: 4 You are my King, O G;
Ps 44: 8 In G we boast all day long,
Ps 45: 2 Therefore G has blessed You
Ps 45: 6 Your throne, O G,
Ps 45: 7 Therefore God, Your G,
Ps 46: 1 G is our refuge and
Ps 46: 4 make glad the city of G,
Ps 46: 5 G is in the midst of her,
Ps 46: 5 G shall help her, just at
Ps 46: 7 The G of Jacob is our
Ps 46:10 still, and know that I am G;
Ps 47: 8 G reigns over the nations
Ps 47: 8 G sits on His holy throne.
Ps 48: 1 In the city of our G,
Ps 49:15 But G will redeem my soul
Ps 50:16 But to the wicked G says:
Ps 51: 1 Have mercy upon me, O G,
Ps 51:10 in me a clean heart, O G,
Ps 51:14 The G of my salvation,
Ps 51:17 The sacrifices of G are a
Ps 52: 1 The goodness of G endures
Ps 53: 1 heart, "There is no G.
Ps 53: 2 G looks down from heaven
Ps 54: 1 Save me, O G, by Your
Ps 55: 1 Give ear to my prayer, O G,
Ps 56: 4 In G I have put my trust;
Ps 57: 5 Be exalted, O G,
Ps 57: 7 My heart is steadfast, O G,
Ps 59: 9 For G is my defense;
Ps 59:10 G shall let me see my
Ps 59:13 And let them know that G
Ps 59:17 My G of mercy.
Ps 60: 6 G has spoken in His holiness
Ps 62: 1 soul silently waits for G;
Ps 62:11 That power belongs to G.
Ps 63: 1 O God, You are my G;
Ps 63:11 the king shall rejoice in G;
Ps 65: 9 The river of G is full of
Ps 66: 1 Make a joyful shout to G,
Ps 66: 5 Come and see the works of G;
Ps 66: 8 Oh, bless our G,
Ps 66:19 But certainly G has heard
Ps 67: 3 the peoples praise You, O G;
Ps 68: 5 Is G in His holy
Ps 68: 6 G sets the solitary in
Ps 68:15 A mountain of G is the
Ps 68:17 The chariots of G are
Ps 68:19 The G of our salvation!
Ps 68:26 Bless G in the
Ps 68:31 stretch out her hands to G.
Ps 68:34 Ascribe strength to G;
Ps 69: 1 O G! For the waters have
Ps 69:35 For G will save Zion And
Ps 70: 1 Make haste, O G,
Ps 70: 4 Let G be magnified!"
Ps 71: 5 You are my hope, O Lord G;
Ps 71:19 have done great things; O G,
Ps 71:22 O my G! To You I will sing
Ps 73: 1 Truly G is good to Israel,
Ps 74:12 For G is my King from of
Ps 75: 1 We give thanks to You, O G,
Ps 76:11 vows to the LORD your G,
Ps 77: 1 I cried out to G with my
Ps 77:13 is so great a God as our G?
Ps 78:18 And they tested G in their
Ps 78:56 and provoked the Most High G,
Ps 79: 9 O G of our salvation, For
Ps 79:10 say, "Where is their G?
Ps 82: 8 Arise, O G, judge
Ps 83: 1 O G! Do not hold Your
Ps 84: 2 cry out for the living G.
Ps 84: 3 of hosts, My King and my G.
Ps 84:11 For the LORD G is a sun
Ps 86:15 are a G full of compassion,
Ps 87: 3 O city of G! Selah

Ps	89:26	'You are my Father, My **G**,
Ps	90: 2	to everlasting, You are **G**.
Ps	91: 2	and my fortress; My **G**,
Ps	95: 3	the LORD is the great **G**,
Ps	98: 3	seen the salvation of our **G**.
Ps	100: 3	that the LORD, He is **G**;
Ps	106:14	And tested **G** in the desert.
Ps	106:21	They forgot **G** their Savior,
Ps	108: 7	**G** has spoken in His holiness
Ps	115: 3	But our **G** is in heaven; He
Ps	119:115	the commandments of my **G**!
Ps	136: 2	give thanks to the **G** of
Ps	139:23	Search me, O **G**,
Ps	144:15	are the people whose **G** is
Ps	145: 1	I will extol You, my **G**,
Ps	146: 2	I will sing praises to my **G**
Ps	147: 7	praises on the harp to our **G**,
Ps	150: 1	the LORD! Praise **G** in His
Prov	2: 5	And find the knowledge of **G**.
Prov	2:17	the covenant of her **G**.
Prov	30: 5	Every word of **G** is pure;
Prov	30: 9	profane the name of my **G**.
Eccl	2:24	saw, was from the hand of **G**.
Eccl	2:26	For **G** gives wisdom and
Eccl	3:13	labor—it is the gift of **G**.
Eccl	3:14	I know that whatever **G** does,
Eccl	3:15	And **G** requires an account
Eccl	3:17	**G** shall judge the righteous
Eccl	5: 2	For **G** is in heaven, and
Eccl	5: 4	When you make a vow to **G**,
Eccl	5:19	As for every man to whom **G**
Eccl	7:29	That **G** made man upright,
Eccl	8: 2	the sake of your oath to **G**.
Eccl	8:17	then I saw all the work of **G**,
Eccl	11: 5	do not know the works of **G**
Eccl	11: 9	know that for all these **G**
Eccl	12: 7	the spirit will return to **G**
Eccl	12:13	Fear **G** and keep His
Eccl	12:14	For **G** will bring every work
Is	7:13	but will you weary my **G**
Is	8:10	For **G** is with us."
Is	8:21	curse their king and their **G**,
Is	9: 6	Counselor, Mighty **G**,
Is	10:21	of Jacob, To the Mighty **G**.
Is	12: 2	**G** is my salvation, I will
Is	13:19	Will be as when **G** overthrew
Is	14:13	throne above the stars of **G**;
Is	25: 1	O LORD, You are my **G**.
Is	25: 8	And the Lord **G** will wipe
Is	31: 3	are men, and not **G**;
Is	35: 2	The excellency of our **G**.
Is	35: 4	With the recompense of **G**;
Is	37: 4	to reproach the living **G**,
Is	38: 5	the **G** of David your father:
Is	40: 1	My people!" Says your **G**.
Is	40: 3	desert A highway for our **G**.
Is	40: 8	But the word of our **G**.
Is	40: 9	Behold your **G**!"
Is	40:18	whom then will you liken **G**?
Is	40:28	heard? The everlasting **G**,
Is	41:10	dismayed, for I am your **G**.
Is	44: 6	Besides Me there is no **G**.
Is	45: 5	There is no **G** besides Me.
Is	45:14	There is no other **G**.
Is	45:18	the heavens, Who is **G**,
Is	45:21	A just **G** and a Savior;
Is	45:22	of the earth! For I am **G**,
Is	50: 5	The Lord **G** has opened My
Is	52: 7	Your **G** reigns!"
Is	52:10	see The salvation of our **G**.
Is	53: 4	Him stricken, Smitten by **G**,
Is	55: 7	mercy on him; And to our **G**,
Is	57:21	is no peace," Says my **G**,
Is	60:19	And your **G** your glory.
Is	61: 1	The Spirit of the Lord **G** is
Is	61: 2	day of vengeance of our **G**;
Is	61: 6	you the servants of our **G**.
Is	65:16	earth Shall swear by the **G**
Jer	1: 6	Lord **G**! Behold, I cannot
Jer	10:10	the LORD is the true **G**;
Jer	10:10	He is the living **G** and the
Jer	23:23	Am I a **G** near at hand,"
Jer	24: 7	and I will be their **G**,
Jer	30:22	And I will be your **G**.
Jer	32:18	them—the Great, the Mighty **G**,
Jer	32:27	the **G** of all flesh. Is there
Jer	44:26	The Lord **G** lives."
Jer	50:28	vengeance of the LORD our **G**,
Ezek	1: 1	and I saw visions of **G**.
Ezek	4:14	Lord **G**! Indeed I have never
Ezek	8: 3	brought me in visions of **G**
Ezek	8: 4	the glory of the **G** of Israel
Ezek	10:20	creature I saw under the **G**
Ezek	11:20	and I will be their **G**.
Ezek	11:24	a vision by the Spirit of **G**
Ezek	13: 9	know that I am the Lord **G**.
Ezek	13:16	peace,'" says the Lord **G**.
Ezek	14:16	I live," says the Lord **G**,
Ezek	16:23	to you!' says the Lord **G**—
Ezek	23:49	know that I am the Lord **G**.
Ezek	25: 3	the word of the Lord **G**!
Ezek	28:13	in Eden, the garden of **G**;
Ezek	28:14	on the holy mountain of **G**;
Ezek	34:24	the LORD, will be their **G**,
Ezek	36:28	people, and I will be your **G**.
Ezek	37:23	and I will be their **G**.
Ezek	40: 2	In the visions of **G** He took
Ezek	43: 2	the glory of the **G** of Israel
Dan	1: 2	articles of the house of **G**,
Dan	1: 9	Now **G** had brought Daniel into
Dan	1:17	**G** gave them knowledge and
Dan	2:19	So Daniel blessed the **G** of
Dan	2:23	O **G** of my fathers; You
Dan	2:28	But there is a **G** in heaven
Dan	2:45	the great **G** has made known to
Dan	2:47	Truly your **G** is the God of
Dan	3:17	our **G** whom we serve is able
Dan	3:25	fourth is like the Son of **G**.
Dan	3:26	servants of the Most High **G**,
Dan	4: 8	the Spirit of the Holy **G**),
Dan	5:14	that the Spirit of **G** is in
Dan	5:23	and the **G** who holds your
Dan	5:26	**G** has numbered your kingdom,
Dan	6: 5	concerning the law of his **G**.
Dan	6:10	and gave thanks before his **G**,
Dan	6:16	saying to Daniel, "Your **G**,
Dan	6:22	My **G** sent His angel and shut
Dan	6:26	and fear before the **G** of
Dan	6:26	For He is the living **G**,
Dan	9: 4	Lord, great and awesome **G**,
Dan	11:36	blasphemies against the **G**
Dan	11:37	shall regard neither the **G**
Hos	1: 9	And I will not be your **G**.
Hos	1:10	are sons of the living **G**.
Hos	3: 5	and seek the LORD their **G**
Hos	4: 1	or mercy Or knowledge of **G**
Hos	4: 6	forgotten the law of your **G**,
Hos	6: 6	And the knowledge of **G** more
Hos	7:10	return to the LORD their **G**,
Hos	12: 3	strength he struggled with **G**.
Joel	2:17	peoples, 'Where is their **G**?
Amos	3: 7	Surely the Lord **G** does
Amos	4:11	As **G** overthrew Sodom and
Amos	4:12	you, Prepare to meet your **G**,
Amos	6: 8	The Lord **G** has sworn by
Amos	9: 8	the eyes of the Lord **G** are
Jon	1: 6	Arise, call on your **G**;
Jon	3: 5	people of Nineveh believed **G**,
Jon	3: 9	Who can tell if **G** will turn
Jon	3:10	and **G** relented from the

Jon	4: 2	a gracious and merciful **G**,
Jon	4: 6	And the LORD **G** prepared a
Mic	3: 7	there is no answer from **G**.
Mic	6: 6	bow myself before the High **G**?
Mic	6: 8	to walk humbly with your **G**?
Mic	7:10	"Where is the LORD your **G**?
Mic	7:18	Who is a **G** like You,
Nah	1: 2	**G** is jealous, and the
Hab	1:12	everlasting, O LORD my **G**,
Zech	8: 8	And I will be their **G**,
Mal	2:10	Has not one **G** created us?
Mal	2:17	Where is the **G** of justice?"
Mal	3: 8	"Will a man rob **G**?
Mal	3:15	They even tempt **G** and go
Matt	1:23	translated, "**G** with us."
Matt	2:22	And being warned by **G** in a
Matt	3:16	and He saw the Spirit of **G**
Matt	4: 3	"If You are the Son of **G**,
Matt	4: 4	from the mouth of **G**.
Matt	4: 7	tempt the LORD your **G**.
Matt	5: 8	heart, For they shall see **G**.
Matt	5: 9	shall be called sons of **G**.
Matt	6:24	You cannot serve **G** and
Matt	6:30	Now if **G** so clothes the grass
Matt	6:33	seek first the kingdom of **G**
Matt	12:28	demons by the Spirit of **G**,
Matt	14:33	"Truly You are the Son of **G**.
Matt	16:16	the Son of the living **G**.
Matt	16:23	mindful of the things of **G**,
Matt	19: 6	Therefore what **G** has joined
Matt	19:17	good but One, that is, **G**.
Matt	19:24	to enter the kingdom of **G**.
Matt	19:26	but with **G** all things are
Matt	22:16	and teach the way of **G** in
Matt	22:29	nor the power of **G**.
Matt	22:30	but are like angels of **G** in
Matt	22:32	the **G** of Isaac, and
Matt	22:32	and the **G** of Jacob'?
Matt	22:32	**G** is not the God of the
Matt	22:37	love the LORD your **G**
Matt	26:63	under oath by the living **G**:
Matt	26:63	the Son of **G**!"
Matt	27:40	If You are the Son of **G**,
Matt	27:43	"He trusted in **G**;
Matt	27:46	that is, "My God, My **G**,
Matt	27:54	this was the Son of **G**!
Mark	1: 1	Jesus Christ, the Son of **G**.
Mark	1:14	gospel of the kingdom of **G**,
Mark	1:15	and the kingdom of **G** is at
Mark	3:35	whoever does the will of **G**
Mark	4:11	mystery of the kingdom of **G**;
Mark	4:26	The kingdom of **G** is as if a
Mark	7:13	making the word of **G** of no
Mark	10: 6	**G** 'made them male and
Mark	10: 9	Therefore what **G** has joined
Mark	10:14	of such is the kingdom of **G**.
Mark	10:15	receive the kingdom of **G** as
Mark	10:27	for with **G** all things are
Mark	11:22	to them, "Have faith in **G**.
Mark	12:27	but the **G** of the living. You
Mark	12:29	Israel, the LORD our **G**,
Mark	12:30	love the LORD your **G**
Mark	14:25	it new in the kingdom of **G**.
Mark	15:43	waiting for the kingdom of **G**.
Mark	16:19	down at the right hand of **G**.
Luke	1: 6	were both righteous before **G**,
Luke	1:26	angel Gabriel was sent by **G**
Luke	1:30	you have found favor with **G**.
Luke	1:32	and the Lord **G** will give Him
Luke	1:35	will be called the Son of **G**.
Luke	1:37	For with **G** nothing will be
Luke	1:47	my spirit has rejoiced in **G**
Luke	1:64	and he spoke, praising **G**.
Luke	2:13	the heavenly host praising **G**
Luke	2:14	Glory to **G** in the highest,
Luke	2:20	glorifying and praising **G**
Luke	2:28	up in his arms and blessed **G**
Luke	2:52	and in favor with **G** and men.
Luke	3: 2	the word of **G** came to John
Luke	3:38	son of Adam, the son of **G**.
Luke	4: 4	but by every word of **G**.
Luke	5:25	his own house, glorifying **G**.
Luke	6:12	all night in prayer to **G**.
Luke	6:20	yours is the kingdom of **G**.
Luke	7:16	**G** has visited His people."
Luke	8: 1	tidings of the kingdom of **G**.
Luke	8:11	The seed is the word of **G**.
Luke	9:20	and said, "The Christ of **G**.
Luke	9:62	is fit for the kingdom of **G**.
Luke	11:20	demons with the finger of **G**,
Luke	11:42	by justice and the love of **G**.
Luke	11:49	Therefore the wisdom of **G**
Luke	12:28	If then **G** so clothes the
Luke	12:31	"But seek the kingdom of **G**,
Luke	16:13	You cannot serve **G** and
Luke	17:21	the kingdom of **G** is within
Luke	18:13	beat his breast, saying, '**G**,
Luke	18:16	of such is the kingdom of **G**.
Luke	20:36	the angels and are sons of **G**,
Luke	22:69	right hand of the power of **G**.
Luke	23:35	the Christ, the chosen of **G**.
John	1: 1	and the Word was with **G**,
John	1: 1	with God, and the Word was **G**.
John	1: 2	was in the beginning with **G**.
John	1: 6	There was a man sent from **G**,
John	1:12	to become children of **G**,
John	1:13	of the will of man, but of **G**.
John	1:18	No one has seen **G** at any
John	1:29	Behold! The Lamb of **G** who
John	1:49	You are the Son of **G**! You
John	1:51	and the angels of **G**
John	3: 2	are a teacher come from **G**;
John	3: 2	signs that You do unless **G**
John	3: 3	cannot see the kingdom of **G**.
John	3:16	For **G** so loved the world that
John	3:17	For **G** did not send His Son
John	3:36	but the wrath of **G** abides on
John	4:10	"If you knew the gift of **G**,
John	4:24	**G** is Spirit, and those who
John	5:18	making Himself equal with **G**.
John	5:42	do not have the love of **G**
John	6:28	we may work the works of **G**?
John	6:29	"This is the work of **G**,
John	6:33	For the bread of **G** is He who
John	6:69	the Son of the living **G**.
John	8:41	we have one Father—**G**.
John	9:16	"This Man is not from **G**,
John	9:24	Give **G** the glory! We know
John	10:33	being a Man, make Yourself **G**.
John	11:22	that whatever You ask of **G**,
John	11:27	are the Christ, the Son of **G**,
John	13: 3	and that He had come from **G**
John	13:31	and **G** is glorified in Him.
John	14: 1	troubled; you believe in **G**,
John	17: 3	know You, the only true **G**,
John	19: 7	He made Himself the Son of **G**.
John	20:17	and to My **G** and your God.'
John	20:28	My Lord and my **G**!"
John	21:19	death he would glorify **G**.
Acts	2:11	the wonderful works of **G**.
Acts	2:23	and foreknowledge of **G**,
Acts	2:32	This Jesus **G** has raised up,
Acts	2:33	to the right hand of **G**,
Acts	3: 8	leaping, and praising **G**.
Acts	3:15	whom **G** raised from the dead,
Acts	4:24	they raised their voice to **G**
Acts	5: 4	not lied to men but to **G**.
Acts	5:29	We ought to obey **G** rather
Acts	5:39	be found to fight against **G**.
Acts	7: 2	The **G** of glory appeared to

Acts	8:37	Jesus Christ is the Son of G.
Acts	10: 2	man and one who feared G
Acts	10: 2	and prayed to G always.
Acts	10:15	What G has cleansed you must
Acts	10:28	But G has shown me that I
Acts	10:34	In truth I perceive that G
Acts	10:38	how G anointed Jesus of
Acts	12:24	But the word of G grew and
Acts	13:43	continue in the grace of G.
Acts	15:10	why do you test G by putting
Acts	15:14	Simon has declared how G at
Acts	15:18	Known to G from eternity are
Acts	15:19	who are turning to G,
Acts	16:17	servants of the Most High G,
Acts	16:25	and singing hymns to G,
Acts	17:13	learned that the word of G
Acts	17:23	TO THE UNKNOWN G.
Acts	17:29	we are the offspring of G,
Acts	17:30	these times of ignorance G
Acts	18:26	to him the way of G more
Acts	19:11	Now G worked unusual
Acts	20:24	the gospel of the grace of G.
Acts	20:27	you the whole counsel of G.
Acts	23: 9	let us not fight against G.
Acts	24:15	"I have hope in G,
Acts	26: 7	earnestly serving G night
Acts	26:18	the power of Satan to G,
Acts	26:20	should repent, turn to G,
Acts	26:29	I would to G that not only
Acts	28:31	preaching the kingdom of G
Rom	1: 1	to the gospel of G
Rom	1: 4	to be the Son of G with
Rom	1: 7	to you and peace from G our
Rom	1: 8	I thank my G through Jesus
Rom	1: 9	For G is my witness, whom I
Rom	1:16	for it is the power of G to
Rom	1:17	in it the righteousness of G
Rom	1:18	For the wrath of G is
Rom	1:21	although they knew G,
Rom	1:21	did not glorify Him as G,
Rom	1:23	of the incorruptible G into
Rom	1:24	Therefore G also gave them up
Rom	1:25	who exchanged the truth of G
Rom	2: 4	that the goodness of G
Rom	2: 5	the righteous judgment of G,
Rom	2:11	is no partiality with G.
Rom	2:16	in the day when G will judge
Rom	2:29	is not from men but from G.
Rom	3: 2	committed the oracles of G.
Rom	3: 3	make the faithfulness of G
Rom	3: 4	let G be true but every man
Rom	3:11	none who seeks after G.
Rom	3:18	There is no fear of G
Rom	3:21	now the righteousness of G
Rom	3:23	fall short of the glory of G,
Rom	3:29	Or is He the G of the Jews
Rom	3:29	Is He not also the G of
Rom	4: 3	say? "Abraham believed G,
Rom	4:20	waver at the promise of G
Rom	5: 1	we have peace with G through
Rom	5: 2	in hope of the glory of G.
Rom	5: 8	But G demonstrates His own
Rom	5:10	we were reconciled to G
Rom	5:15	much more the grace of G and
Rom	6:10	that He lives, He lives to G.
Rom	6:11	but alive to G in Christ
Rom	6:22	having become slaves of G,
Rom	6:23	but the gift of G is
Rom	7: 4	we should bear fruit to G.
Rom	7:22	I delight in the law of G
Rom	8: 7	mind is enmity against G;
Rom	8: 7	not subject to the law of G,
Rom	8: 8	in the flesh cannot please G.
Rom	8:14	are led by the Spirit of G,
Rom	8:14	of God, these are sons of G.

Rom	8:16	that we are children of G,
Rom	8:17	heirs of G and joint heirs
Rom	8:21	liberty of the children of G.
Rom	8:28	for good to those who love G,
Rom	8:31	If G is for us, who can
Rom	8:33	It is G who justifies.
Rom	8:39	us from the love of G which
Rom	9: 5	the eternally blessed G.
Rom	9:26	sons of the living G.
Rom	10: 1	desire and prayer to G for
Rom	10: 2	that they have a zeal for G,
Rom	10:17	and hearing by the word of G.
Rom	11: 1	has G cast away His people?
Rom	11:21	For if G did not spare the
Rom	11:22	goodness and severity of G:
Rom	11:23	for G is able to graft them
Rom	11:29	gifts and the calling of G
Rom	11:33	wisdom and knowledge of G!
Rom	12: 1	by the mercies of G,
Rom	12: 1	holy, acceptable to G,
Rom	12: 2	and perfect will of G.
Rom	13: 1	no authority except from G,
Rom	14: 6	and gives G thanks.
Rom	14:11	shall confess to G.
Rom	14:12	give account of himself to G.
Rom	14:17	for the kingdom of G is not
Rom	15: 5	Now may the G of patience and
Rom	15:13	Now may the G of hope fill
Rom	15:16	ministering the gospel of G,
Rom	16:20	And the G of peace will crush
Rom	16:26	of the everlasting G,
1Co	1: 4	I thank my G always
1Co	1: 9	G is faithful, by whom you
1Co	1:14	I thank G that I baptized
1Co	1:18	saved it is the power of G
1Co	1:20	Has not G made foolish the
1Co	1:21	since, in the wisdom of G,
1Co	1:21	wisdom did not know G,
1Co	1:21	it pleased G through the
1Co	1:24	Christ the power of G and
1Co	1:25	the foolishness of G is
1Co	1:25	and the weakness of G is
1Co	1:27	But G has chosen the foolish
1Co	2: 7	we speak the wisdom of G in
1Co	2:10	But G has revealed them to
1Co	2:10	yes, the deep things of G.
1Co	2:11	God except the Spirit of G.
1Co	2:12	been freely given to us by G.
1Co	2:14	things of the Spirit of G,
1Co	3: 6	but G gave the increase.
1Co	3:16	you are the temple of G and
1Co	3:19	world is foolishness with G.
1Co	4: 1	of the mysteries of G.
1Co	4:20	For the kingdom of G is not
1Co	6:19	in you, whom you have from G,
1Co	6:20	therefore glorify G in your
1Co	7: 7	one has his own gift from G,
1Co	7:15	But G has called us to
1Co	7:17	But as G has distributed to
1Co	7:40	I also have the Spirit of G.
1Co	8: 4	that there is no other G
1Co	8: 6	yet for us there is one G,
1Co	8: 8	does not commend us to G;
1Co	10:13	but G is faithful, who will
1Co	10:20	to demons and not to G,
1Co	10:31	do, do all to the glory of G.
1Co	11: 3	and the head of Christ is G.
1Co	11: 7	is the image and glory of G;
1Co	11:13	for a woman to pray to G
1Co	11:22	you despise the church of G
1Co	12: 3	speaking by the Spirit of G
1Co	14: 2	not speak to men but to G,
1Co	14:25	God and report that G is
1Co	14:33	For G is not the author of
1Co	15: 9	I persecuted the church of G.

1Co	15:10	But by the grace of G I am
1Co	15:28	that G may be all in all.
1Co	15:57	But thanks be to G,
2Co	1: 3	the Father of mercies and G
2Co	1:20	For all the promises of G in
2Co	2:15	For we are to G the fragrance
2Co	2:17	many, peddling the word of G;
2Co	3: 3	the Spirit of the living G,
2Co	3: 5	our sufficiency is from G,
2Co	4: 4	who is the image of G,
2Co	4: 6	knowledge of the glory of G
2Co	4: 7	of the power may be of G
2Co	4:15	to abound to the glory of G.
2Co	5: 1	we have a building from G,
2Co	5:19	that G was in Christ
2Co	5:20	behalf, be reconciled to G.
2Co	5:21	the righteousness of G in
2Co	6: 1	to receive the grace of G
2Co	6: 4	ourselves as ministers of G:
2Co	6:16	has the temple of G with
2Co	6:16	the temple of the living G.
2Co	6:16	I will be their G,
2Co	9:14	of the exceeding grace of G
2Co	9:15	Thanks be to G for His
2Co	10: 4	not carnal but mighty in G
2Co	12: 2	G knows—such a one was
2Co	13:11	and the G of love and peace
2Co	13:14	Christ, and the love of G,
Gal	1:15	But when it pleased G,
Gal	2:20	by faith in the Son of G,
Gal	3: 6	as Abraham "believed G,
Gal	4: 4	G sent forth His Son, born
Gal	4: 6	G has sent forth the Spirit
Gal	4: 8	when you did not know G,
Gal	4:14	received me as an angel of G,
Gal	6: 7	G is not mocked; for
Gal	6:14	But G forbid that I should
Gal	6:16	and upon the Israel of G.
Eph	2: 8	it is the gift of G,
Eph	2:10	which G prepared beforehand
Eph	2:12	no hope and without G in
Eph	2:16	reconcile them both to G in
Eph	2:19	of the household of G,
Eph	2:22	for a dwelling place of G
Eph	3: 7	the gift of the grace of G
Eph	3:19	with all the fullness of G.
Eph	4: 6	one G and Father of all, who
Eph	4:13	knowledge of the Son of G,
Eph	4:18	alienated from the life of G,
Eph	4:30	grieve the Holy Spirit of G,
Eph	4:32	just as G in Christ forgave
Eph	5: 1	Therefore be imitators of G
Eph	6:11	Put on the whole armor of G,
Phil	1: 8	For G is my witness, how
Phil	2: 6	who, being in the form of G,
Phil	2: 6	robbery to be equal with G,
Phil	2: 9	Therefore G also has highly
Phil	2:11	to the glory of G the
Phil	2:13	for it is G who works in you
Phil	3:14	of the upward call of G in
Phil	4: 6	requests be made known to G;
Phil	4: 7	and the peace of G,
Phil	4: 9	and the G of peace will be
Phil	4:19	And my G shall supply all
Col	1:15	the image of the invisible G,
Col	1:25	to the stewardship from G
Col	2: 2	of the mystery of G,
Col	2:12	faith in the working of G,
Col	3: 3	is hidden with Christ in G.
Col	3: 6	these things the wrath of G
Col	3:12	as the elect of G,
Col	3:15	And let the peace of G rule
Col	4:11	for the kingdom of G who
1Th	1: 8	Your faith toward G has gone
1Th	1: 9	and how you turned to G from

1Th	1: 9	serve the living and true G,
1Th	2: 4	but G who tests our hearts.
1Th	2: 9	to you the gospel of G.
1Th	2:13	is in truth, the word of G,
1Th	4: 3	For this is the will of G,
1Th	4: 5	Gentiles who do not know G;
1Th	4:14	even so G will bring with
1Th	4:16	and with the trumpet of G.
1Th	5: 9	For G did not appoint us to
1Th	5:18	for this is the will of G in
1Th	5:23	Now may the G of peace
1Ti	1:17	to G who alone is wise, be
1Ti	2: 5	For there is one G and one
1Ti	2: 5	and one Mediator between G
1Ti	3:15	the church of the living G,
1Ti	3:16	G was manifested in the
1Ti	4: 4	For every creature of G is
1Ti	4: 5	sanctified by the word of G
1Ti	4:10	we trust in the living G,
1Ti	5: 4	good and acceptable before G.
1Ti	6:11	But you, O man of G,
2Ti	1: 6	you to stir up the gift of G
2Ti	1: 7	For G has not given us a
2Ti	2:15	yourself approved to G,
2Ti	3: 4	rather than lovers of G,
2Ti	3:16	given by inspiration of G,
2Ti	3:17	that the man of G may be
Tit	1: 1	a bondservant of G and an
Tit	1: 7	blameless, as a steward of G,
Tit	1:16	They profess to know G,
Tit	2:13	appearing of our great G
Tit	3: 4	kindness and the love of G
Heb	1: 6	all the angels of G
Heb	1: 8	"Your throne, O G,
Heb	1: 9	Therefore God, Your G,
Heb	2:13	and the children whom G
Heb	4: 9	a rest for the people of G.
Heb	4:12	For the word of G is living
Heb	5:10	called by G as High Priest
Heb	5:12	of the oracles of G;
Heb	6: 5	tasted the good word of G
Heb	6:18	it is impossible for G to
Heb	7: 1	priest of the Most High G,
Heb	7: 3	but made like the Son of G,
Heb	7:25	those who come to G through
Heb	8:10	and I will be their G,
Heb	9:14	Himself without spot to G,
Heb	9:14	works to serve the living G?
Heb	10: 7	do Your will, O G.
Heb	10:12	down at the right hand of G,
Heb	10:21	Priest over the house of G,
Heb	10:29	has trampled the Son of G
Heb	10:31	the hands of the living G.
Heb	11: 3	were framed by the word of G,
Heb	11: 4	By faith Abel offered to G
Heb	11: 6	for he who comes to G must
Heb	11:10	builder and maker is G.
Heb	11:16	Therefore G is not ashamed
Heb	11:40	G having provided something
Heb	12: 2	hand of the throne of G.
Heb	12:15	fall short of the grace of G;
Heb	12:22	to the city of the living G,
Heb	12:29	For our G is a consuming
Heb	13: 4	and adulterers G will judge.
Heb	13:20	Now may the G of peace who
Jas	1: 5	wisdom, let him ask of G,
Jas	1:13	for G cannot be tempted by
Jas	1:27	undefiled religion before G
Jas	2:19	believe that there is one G.
Jas	2:23	"Abraham believed G,
Jas	2:23	was called the friend of G.
Jas	3: 9	With it we bless our G and
Jas	4: 4	the world is enmity with G?
Jas	4: 6	G resists the proud, But
Jas	4: 7	Therefore submit to G.

Jas	4: 8	Draw near to G and He will
1Pe	1: 2	to the foreknowledge of G
1Pe	1: 5	are kept by the power of G
1Pe	2:10	but are now the people of G,
1Pe	2:12	glorify G in the day of
1Pe	2:15	For this is the will of G,
1Pe	2:17	Love the brotherhood. Fear G.
1Pe	2:20	is commendable before G.
1Pe	3: 4	precious in the sight of G.
1Pe	3:21	a good conscience toward G),
1Pe	4:10	of the manifold grace of G.
1Pe	4:11	speak as the oracles of G.
1Pe	4:14	the Spirit of glory and of G
1Pe	4:16	but let him glorify G in
1Pe	4:17	to begin at the house of G;
1Pe	5: 2	Shepherd the flock of G which
1Pe	5: 5	G resists the proud, But
1Pe	5: 6	under the mighty hand of G,
1Pe	5:10	But may the G of all grace,
2Pe	1:21	but holy men of G spoke as
2Pe	2: 4	For if G did not spare the
1Jn	1: 5	that G is light and in Him
1Jn	2: 5	truly the love of G is
1Jn	2:14	and the word of G abides in
1Jn	2:17	he who does the will of G
1Jn	3: 2	now we are children of G;
1Jn	3: 9	Whoever has been born of G
1Jn	3:17	how does the love of G abide
1Jn	4: 2	you know the Spirit of G:
1Jn	4: 2	come in the flesh is of G,
1Jn	4: 7	another, for love is of G;
1Jn	4: 7	who loves is born of G and
1Jn	4: 8	for G is love.
1Jn	4:10	is love, not that we loved G,
1Jn	4:11	if G so loved us, we also
1Jn	4:12	No one has seen G at any
1Jn	4:16	G is love, and he who abides
1Jn	4:20	If someone says, "I love G,
1Jn	5: 1	is the Christ is born of G,
1Jn	5: 5	that Jesus is the Son of G?
1Jn	5:12	does not have the Son of G
1Jn	5:13	in the name of the Son of G,
1Jn	5:20	This is the true G and
Jude	25	To G our Savior, Who alone
Rev	1: 2	witness to the word of G,
Rev	1: 6	kings and priests to His G
Rev	2: 7	midst of the Paradise of G.
Rev	3: 1	has the seven Spirits of G
Rev	3:12	down out of heaven from My G.
Rev	4: 8	Lord G Almighty, Who was
Rev	5: 9	And have redeemed us to G
Rev	6: 9	slain for the word of G and
Rev	7: 2	the seal of the living G.
Rev	7:17	And G will wipe away every
Rev	8: 2	angels who stand before G,
Rev	11:16	elders who sat before G on
Rev	12:10	accused them before our G
Rev	13: 6	mouth in blasphemy against G,
Rev	14:10	the wine of the wrath of G,
Rev	15: 7	full of the wrath of G who
Rev	16:11	They blasphemed the G of
Rev	16:14	of that great day of G
Rev	19: 6	Alleluia! For the Lord G
Rev	19:10	Worship G! For the testimony
Rev	19:13	name is called The Word of G.
Rev	19:17	the supper of the great G,
Rev	21: 2	down out of heaven from G,
Rev	21: 3	G Himself will be with them
Rev	21: 4	And G will wipe away every
Rev	22:18	G will add to him the
Rev	22:19	G shall take away his part

GOD-GIVEN† (see GOD)

Ezra	7:25	according to your G wisdom,
Eccl	3:10	I have seen the G task with

GOD-WHO-FORGIVES† (see GOD)

Ps	99: 8	our God; You were to them G,

GOD'S (see GOD)

Mal	1: 9	But now entreat G favor,
Matt	5:34	for it is G throne;
Matt	22:21	to God the things that are G.
Acts	23: 4	Do you revile G high
Rom	8:33	bring a charge against G
Rom	10: 3	For they being ignorant of G
Rom	13: 4	For he is G minister to you
1Co	3: 9	For we are G fellow workers;
1Co	3: 9	you are G building.
1Co	3:23	Christ's, and Christ is G.
1Co	6:20	in your spirit, which are G.

GODDESS (see GOD•)

1Ki	11: 5	went after Ashtoreth the g
Acts	19:27	the temple of the great g
Acts	19:37	nor blasphemers of your g.

GODHEAD† (see GOD)

Rom	1:20	His eternal power and G,
Col	2: 9	all the fullness of the G

GODLINESS (see GODLY)

1Ti	2: 2	and peaceable life in all g
1Ti	2:10	for women professing g,
1Ti	3:16	great is the mystery of g:
1Ti	4: 8	but g is profitable for all
1Ti	6: 6	Now g with contentment is
1Ti	6:11	and pursue righteousness, g,
2Ti	3: 5	having a form of g but
2Pe	1: 3	that pertain to life and g,
2Pe	1: 7	to g brotherly kindness, and

GODLY (see GOD, GODLINESS, UNGODLY)

Mal	2:15	He seeks g offspring.
2Co	7:10	For g sorrow produces
2Co	11: 2	I am jealous for you with g
2Ti	3:12	all who desire to live g in
Tit	2:12	and g in the present age,
Heb	5: 7	was heard because of His g
Heb	11: 7	moved with g fear, prepared
Heb	12:28	with reverence and g fear.

GODS (see GOD)

Gen	31:30	but why did you steal my g?
Gen	35: 2	Put away the foreign g that
Ex	12:12	and against all the g of
Ex	15:11	You, O LORD, among the g?
Ex	18:11	is greater than all the g,
Ex	20: 3	You shall have no other g
Ex	20:23	g of silver or gods of gold
Ex	23:24	not bow down to their g,
Deut	5: 7	You shall have no other g
Deut	6:14	shall not go after other g,
Deut	8:19	your God, and follow other g,
Deut	10:17	LORD your God is God of g
Deut	31:18	they have turned to other g.
Josh	22:22	of gods, the LORD God of g,
Josh	24:14	and put away the g which
Judg	2: 3	and their g shall be a snare
Judg	5: 8	They chose new g;
Ruth	1:15	to her people and to her g;
1Sa	17:43	cursed David by his g.
1Ki	12:28	Jerusalem. Here are your g,
1Ki	20:23	Their g are gods of the
2Ki	22:17	burned incense to other g,
2Ki	23:24	the household g and idols,
2Ch	2: 5	God is greater than all g.
2Ch	13: 9	of things that are not g?
2Ch	14: 3	the altars of the foreign g
2Ch	32:13	Were the g of the nations of
Ps	82: 6	I said, "You are g,
Ps	95: 3	the great King above all g.
Ps	96: 4	is to be feared above all g.
Ps	97: 7	Worship Him, all you g.

Ps	97: 9	are exalted far above all **g**.
Ps	136: 2	give thanks to the God of **g**!
Is	42:17	images, 'You are our **g**.
Is	57: 5	yourselves with **g** under
Jer	2:11	Has a nation changed its **g**,
Jer	2:11	its gods, Which are not **g**?
Jer	2:28	But where are your **g** that
Jer	10:11	The **g** that have not made the
Jer	11:13	your cities were your **g**,
Jer	16:20	Will a man make **g** for
Ezek	28: 2	I sit in the seat of **g**,
Dan	2:11	it to the king except the **g**,
Dan	2:47	your God is the God of **g**,
Dan	5: 4	and praised the **g** of gold
Dan	5:11	like the wisdom of the **g**,
Dan	5:23	And you have praised the **g**
John	10:34	You are **g**''?
John	10:35	"If He called them **g**,
Acts	7:40	Make us **g** to go before
Acts	14:11	The **g** have come down to us in
Acts	19:26	saying that they are not **g**
1Co	8: 5	if there are so-called **g**,
Gal	4: 8	which by nature are not **g**.

GOG (*see* HAMON GOG, MAGOG)

Ezek	38: 2	man, set your face against **G**,
Ezek	38:21	call for a sword against **G**
Ezek	39:11	there they will bury **G** and
Rev	20: 8	**G** and Magog, to gather them

GOLAN

Deut	4:43	and **G** in Bashan for the

GOLD (*see* GOLDEN, GOLDSMITH)

Gen	2:12	And the **g** of that land is
Gen	13: 2	in silver, and in **g**.
Gen	24:22	weighing ten shekels of **g**,
Gen	41:42	of fine linen and put a **g**
Ex	20:23	of silver or gods of **g**
Ex	25:11	shall overlay it with pure **g**,
Ex	32:31	for themselves a god of **g**
Ex	39: 3	And they beat the **g** into thin
Num	7:14	one **g** pan of ten shekels,
Num	8: 4	lampstand was hammered **g**;
Num	22:18	house full of silver and **g**,
Deut	17:17	multiply silver and **g** for
Deut	29:17	and stone and silver and **g**);
Josh	7:21	and a wedge of **g** weighing
Judg	8:24	For they had **g** earrings,
1Sa	6:11	and the chest with the **g**
1Ki	6:28	overlaid the cherubim with **g**.
1Ki	9:11	with cedar and cypress and **g**,
1Ki	9:14	and twenty talents of **g**.
1Ki	10:11	which brought **g** from Ophir,
1Ki	10:16	large shields of hammered **g**;
1Ki	10:17	three minas of **g** went into
1Ki	10:21	drinking vessels were **g**,
1Ki	10:22	ships came bringing **g**,
1Ki	12:28	advice, made two calves of **g**,
1Ki	22:48	ships to go to Ophir for **g**;
2Ki	25:15	the things of solid **g** and
1Ch	22:14	thousand talents of **g** and
1Ch	28:14	He gave **g** by weight for
1Ch	28:18	the **g** cherubim that spread
1Ch	29: 3	my own special treasure of **g**
1Ch	29: 7	and ten thousand darics of **g**,
2Ch	2:14	skilled to work in **g** and
2Ch	16: 2	Asa brought silver and **g**
Ezra	2:69	work sixty-one thousand **g**
Ezra	8:27	twenty **g** basins worth a
Ezra	8:27	bronze, precious as **g**.
Esth	1: 6	the couches were of **g** and
Esth	8:15	with a great crown of **g** and
Job	22:24	Then you will lay your **g** in
Job	23:10	me, I shall come forth as **g**.
Job	28: 1	And a place where **g** is

Job	28: 6	And it contains **g** dust.
Job	28:15	cannot be purchased for **g**,
Job	31:24	If I have made **g** my hope, Or
Job	42:11	silver and each a ring of **g**.
Ps	19:10	be desired are they than **g**,
Ps	21: 3	You set a crown of pure **g**
Ps	45:13	clothing is woven with **g**.
Ps	72:15	And the **g** of Sheba will be
Ps	115: 4	idols are silver and **g**,
Prov	8:19	My fruit is better than **g**,
Prov	11:22	As a ring of **g** in a swine's
Prov	16:16	better to get wisdom than **g**!
Prov	17: 3	silver and the furnace for **g**,
Prov	27:21	silver and the furnace for **g**,
Song	5:11	head is like the finest **g**;
Is	2:20	silver And his idols of **g**,
Jer	10: 9	And **g** from Uphaz, The work
Lam	4: 1	How the **g** has become dim!
Ezek	7:19	And their **g** will be like
Ezek	28: 4	And gathered **g** and silver
Ezek	28:13	and emerald with **g**.
Dan	2:32	image's head was of fine **g**,
Dan	2:35	and the **g** were crushed
Dan	2:38	all—you are this head of **g**.
Dan	2:45	clay, the silver, and the **g**—
Dan	3: 5	fall down and worship the **g**
Dan	3:18	nor will we worship the **g**
Dan	5: 3	Then they brought the **g**
Dan	5: 4	and praised the gods of **g**
Dan	5: 7	and have a chain of **g**
Dan	10: 5	waist was girded with **g** of
Hos	8: 4	From their silver and **g**
Nah	2: 9	of silver! Take spoil of **g**!
Hag	2: 8	and the **g** is Mine,' says
Zech	4: 2	is a lampstand of solid **g**
Zech	4:12	the receptacles of the two **g**
Zech	13: 9	And test them as **g** is
Matt	2:11	presented gifts to Him: **g**,
Acts	3: 6	Silver and **g** I do not have,
Acts	17:29	the Divine Nature is like **g**
1Co	3:12	on this foundation with **g**,
1Ti	2: 9	not with braided hair or **g**
2Ti	2:20	are not only vessels of **g**
Heb	9: 4	overlaid on all sides with **g**,
Jas	2: 2	your assembly a man with **g**
1Pe	1: 7	much more precious than **g**
1Pe	1:18	things, like silver or **g**,
Rev	3:18	counsel you to buy from Me **g**
Rev	4: 4	and they had crowns of **g** on
Rev	21:15	who talked with me had a **g**
Rev	21:18	and the city was pure **g**,

GOLDEN (*see* GOLD)

Ex	28:34	a **g** bell and a pomegranate, a
1Sa	6: 4	Five **g** tumors and five golden
2Ki	10:29	from the **g** calves that were
Esth	4:11	the king holds out the **g**
Eccl	12: 6	Or the **g** bowl is broken,
Jer	51: 7	Babylon was a **g** cup in the
Zech	4:12	gold pipes from which the **g**
Heb	9: 4	which had the **g** censer and
Rev	1:12	having turned I saw seven **g**
Rev	5: 8	and **g** bowls full of incense,
Rev	8: 3	of all the saints upon the **g**
Rev	14:14	having on His head a **g**
Rev	17: 4	having in her hand a **g** cup

GOLDSMITH (*see* GOLD)

Is	46: 6	the scales; They hire a **g**,

GOLGOTHA† (*see* CALVARY)

Matt	27:33	had come to a place called **G**,
Mark	15:22	brought Him to the place **G**,
John	19:17	which is called in Hebrew, **G**,

GOLIATH

1Sa	17: 4	of the Philistines, named **G**,

GOMER

2Sa 21:19 killed the brother of **G**
1Ch 20: 5 Lahmi the brother of **G** the

GOMER
Ezek 38: 6 **G** and all its troops; the
Hos 1: 3 So he went and took **G** the

GOMORRAH
Gen 14: 8 king of Sodom, the king of **G**,
Gen 19:24 and fire on Sodom and **G**,
Is 1: 9 would have been made like **G**.
Jer 50:40 God overthrew Sodom and **G**
Matt 10:15 for the land of Sodom and **G**
Mark 6:11 tolerable for Sodom and **G**
Rom 9:29 have been made like **G**.
Jude 7 as Sodom and **G**,

GOOD (*see* GOOD-LOOKING, GOODNESS)
Gen 1: 4 the light, that it was **g**;
Gen 1:10 And God saw that it was **g**.
Gen 1:31 and indeed it was very **g**.
Gen 2: 9 pleasant to the sight and **g**
Gen 2: 9 tree of the knowledge of **g**
Gen 2:18 It is not **g** that man should
Gen 3: 5 knowing **g** and evil."
Gen 3: 6 saw that the tree was **g**
Gen 15:15 you shall be buried at a **g**
Gen 27:46 what **g** will my life be to
Gen 40:16 the interpretation was **g**,
Gen 41:35 all the food of those **g**
Gen 43:28 servant our father is in **g**
Gen 44: 4 have you repaid evil for **g**?
Gen 50:20 me; but God meant it for **g**,
Ex 18: 9 rejoiced for all the **g**
Ex 18:17 thing that you do is not **g**.
Ex 21:34 of the pit shall make it **g**;
Lev 27:10 **g** for bad or bad for good;
Lev 27:12 whether it is **g** or bad; as
Lev 27:14 whether it is **g** or bad; as
Num 13:20 Be of **g** courage. And bring
Num 14: 7 spy out is an exceedingly **g**
Deut 1:35 generation shall see that **g**
Deut 1:39 have no knowledge of **g** and
Deut 6:11 houses full of all **g** things,
Deut 6:18 do what is right and **g** in
Deut 6:24 for our **g** always, that He
Deut 8:16 to do you **g** in the end—
Deut 10:13 command you today for your **g**?
Deut 12:28 when you do what is **g** and
Deut 28:12 LORD will open to you His **g**
Deut 30:15 before you today life and **g**,
Deut 31:23 Be strong and of **g** courage;
Josh 1: 8 and then you will have **g**
Josh 1: 9 Be strong and of **g** courage;
Josh 9:25 do with us as it seems **g** and
Josh 24:20 you, after He has done you **g**.
Judg 9:11 cease my sweetness and my **g**
1Sa 3:18 Let Him do what seems **g** to
1Sa 24:17 you have rewarded me with **g**,
1Sa 24:19 the LORD reward you with **g**
1Sa 25:21 he has repaid me evil for **g**.
2Sa 10:12 the LORD do what is **g** in
2Sa 14:17 the king in discerning **g**
2Sa 14:25 as much as Absalom for his **g**
1Ki 8:56 failed one word of all His **g**
2Ki 3:19 and shall cut down every **g**
2Ki 3:19 and ruin every **g** piece of
2Ki 7: 9 This day is a day of **g**
1Ch 16:34 for He is **g**! For His
2Ch 5:13 saying: "For He is **g**,
2Ch 7: 3 saying: "For He is **g**,
2Ch 14: 2 Asa did what was **g** and
2Ch 18: 7 he never prophesies **g**
2Ch 30:18 May the **g** LORD provide
2Ch 30:22 the Levites who taught the **g**
Ezra 8:18 by the **g** hand of our God

Ezra 8:22 God is upon all those for **g**
Ezra 9:12 may be strong and eat the **g**
Neh 5: 9 you are doing is not **g**.
Neh 5:19 Remember me, my God, for **g**,
Neh 6:19 Also they reported his **g**
Neh 9:13 **G** statutes and
Neh 9:20 You also gave Your **g** Spirit
Neh 13:14 and do not wipe out my **g**
Esth 10: 3 seeking the **g** of his people
Job 2:10 Shall we indeed accept **g**
Job 7: 7 eye will never again see **g**.
Job 10: 3 Does it seem **g** to You that
Job 30:26 But when I looked for **g**,
Ps 14: 1 There is none who does **g**.
Ps 16: 6 I have a **g** inheritance.
Ps 25: 8 **G** and upright is the LORD
Ps 27:14 Be of **g** courage, And He
Ps 31:24 Be of **g** courage, And He
Ps 34: 8 and see that the LORD is **g**;
Ps 34:10 LORD shall not lack any **g**
Ps 34:14 Depart from evil and do **g**;
Ps 35:12 They reward me evil for **g**;
Ps 37: 3 in the LORD, and do **g**;
Ps 37:23 The steps of a **g** man are
Ps 37:27 Depart from evil, and do **g**;
Ps 38:20 also who render evil for **g**,
Ps 40: 9 I have proclaimed the **g** news
Ps 45: 1 is overflowing with a **g**
Ps 51:18 Do **g** in Your good pleasure
Ps 52: 3 You love evil more than **g**,
Ps 69:16 Your lovingkindness is **g**;
Ps 73: 1 Truly God is **g** to Israel,
Ps 84:11 No **g** thing will He
Ps 85:12 LORD will give what is **g**;
Ps 86: 5 For You, Lord, are **g**,
Ps 100: 5 For the LORD is **g**;
Ps 103: 5 satisfies your mouth with **g**
Ps 106: 1 for He is **g**! For His
Ps 109: 5 have rewarded me evil for **g**,
Ps 111:10 A **g** understanding have all
Ps 112: 5 A **g** man deals graciously and
Ps 119:39 For Your judgments are **g**.
Ps 133: 1 how **g** and how pleasant it
Ps 143:10 my God; Your Spirit is **g**.
Ps 145: 9 The LORD is **g** to all, And
Ps 147: 1 the LORD! For it is **g**
Prov 3:27 Do not withhold **g** from
Prov 4: 2 For I give you **g** doctrine:
Prov 12: 2 A **g** man obtains favor from
Prov 14:19 evil will bow before the **g**,
Prov 15: 3 watch on the evil and the **g**.
Prov 15:30 And a **g** report makes the
Prov 17:13 Whoever rewards evil for **g**,
Prov 17:20 a deceitful heart finds no **g**,
Prov 17:22 A merry heart does **g**,
Prov 18:22 who finds a wife finds a **g**
Prov 20:14 It is **g** for nothing,"
Prov 20:23 dishonest scales are not **g**.
Prov 22: 1 A **g** name is to be chosen
Prov 24:25 And a **g** blessing will come
Prov 25:25 So is **g** news from a far
Prov 28:10 the blameless will inherit **g**.
Prov 28:21 show partiality is not **g**,
Prov 31:12 She does him **g** and not evil
Prov 31:18 that her merchandise is **g**,
Eccl 2:24 his soul should enjoy **g** in
Eccl 4: 8 toil and deprive myself of **g**?
Eccl 4: 9 Because they have a **g**
Eccl 5:18 It is **g** and fitting for
Eccl 7: 1 A **g** name is better than
Eccl 7:18 It is **g** that you grasp
Is 1:17 Learn to do **g**;
Is 1:19 You shall eat the **g** of the
Is 5: 2 it to bring forth **g**
Is 7:15 the evil and choose the **g**.

Is	52: 7	the feet of him who brings **g**
Is	52: 7	brings glad tidings of the **g**
Is	61: 1	has anointed Me To preach **g**
Jer	8:15	but no **g** came; And for a
Jer	13:23	Then may you also do **g** who
Jer	17: 6	And shall not see when **g**
Jer	18:10	will relent concerning the **g**
Jer	18:20	Shall evil be repaid for **g**?
Jer	29:10	visit you and perform My **g**
Jer	39:16	for adversity and not for **g**,
Lam	3:25	The LORD is **g** to those who
Ezek	34:14	I will feed them in **g**
Hos	4:13	Because their shade is **g**.
Amos	5:14	Seek **g** and not evil, That
Amos	5:15	Hate evil, love **g**;
Amos	9: 4	them for harm and not for **g**.
Mic	3: 2	You who hate **g** and love
Mic	6: 8	shown you, O man, what is **g**;
Matt	3:10	tree which does not bear **g**
Matt	5:13	It is then **g** for nothing but
Matt	5:16	that they may see your **g**
Matt	5:44	do **g** to those who hate you,
Matt	5:45	on the evil and on the **g**,
Matt	6:22	If therefore your eye is **g**,
Matt	7:11	know how to give **g** gifts to
Matt	7:17	every **g** tree bears good
Matt	8:30	Now a **g** way off from them
Matt	9: 2	be of **g** cheer; your sins are
Matt	9:22	Be of **g** cheer, daughter; your
Matt	11:26	for so it seemed **g** in Your
Matt	12:12	it is lawful to do **g** on the
Matt	12:35	A **g** man out of the good
Matt	13: 8	But others fell on **g** ground
Matt	13:24	is like a man who sowed **g**
Matt	17: 4	it is **g** for us to be here;
Matt	19:16	**G** Teacher, what good thing
Matt	19:17	No one is **g** but One, that
Matt	25:21	**g** and faithful servant; you
Matt	25:23	**g** and faithful servant; you
Matt	26:10	For she has done a **g** work
Matt	26:24	It would have been **g** for
Mark	3: 4	on the Sabbath to do **g** or
Mark	9: 5	it is **g** for us to be here;
Luke	1: 3	it seemed **g** to me also,
Luke	2:10	I bring you **g** tidings of
Luke	6: 9	on the Sabbath to do **g** or
Luke	6:27	do **g** to those who hate you,
Luke	6:35	love your enemies, do **g**,
Luke	6:38	**g** measure, pressed down,
Luke	10:21	for so it seemed **g** in Your
Luke	10:42	and Mary has chosen that **g**
Luke	11:13	know how to give **g** gifts to
John	1:46	Can anything **g** come out of
John	2:10	You have kept the **g** wine
John	7:12	He is **g**"; others said, "No,
John	10:11	I am the **g** shepherd. The good
John	10:14	I am the **g** shepherd; and I
John	10:32	Many **g** works I have shown you
Acts	6: 3	among you seven men of **g**
Acts	9:36	This woman was full of **g**
Acts	10:38	who went about doing **g** and
Acts	11:24	For he was a **g** man, full of
Acts	15:28	For it seemed **g** to the Holy
Rom	3: 8	Let us do evil that **g** may
Rom	3:12	is none who does **g**,
Rom	5: 7	yet perhaps for a **g** man
Rom	7:12	holy and just and **g**.
Rom	7:18	in my flesh) nothing **g**
Rom	7:19	For the **g** that I will to
Rom	8:28	things work together for **g**
Rom	9:11	nor having done any **g** or
Rom	10:15	bring glad tidings of **g**
Rom	12: 2	may prove what is that **g**
Rom	12: 9	is evil. Cling to what is **g**.
Rom	12:21	but overcome evil with **g**.
Rom	13: 3	are not a terror to **g** works,
Rom	13: 4	God's minister to you for **g**.
Rom	14:21	It is **g** neither to eat meat
Rom	16:19	you to be wise in what is **g**,
1Co	5: 6	Your glorying is not **g**.
1Co	7: 1	It is **g** for a man not to
1Co	7:26	therefore that this is **g**
1Co	15:33	Evil company corrupts **g**
2Co	5:10	whether **g** or bad.
2Co	9: 8	an abundance for every **g**
2Co	13:11	Be of **g** comfort, be of one
Gal	6: 9	not grow weary while doing **g**,
Gal	6:10	let us do **g** to all,
Eph	1: 9	according to His **g** pleasure
Eph	2:10	in Christ Jesus for **g** works,
Eph	6: 8	knowing that whatever **g**
Phil	1: 6	that He who has begun a **g**
Phil	1:15	and some also from **g** will:
Phil	2:13	to will and to do for His **g**
Phil	4: 8	whatever things are of **g**
Col	1:10	being fruitful in every **g**
1Th	5:21	things; hold fast what is **g**.
2Th	2:17	and establish you in every **g**
2Th	3:13	not grow weary in doing **g**.
1Ti	1: 5	from a **g** conscience, and
1Ti	1:18	by them you may wage the **g**
1Ti	2: 3	For this is **g** and acceptable
1Ti	3: 2	of **g** behavior, hospitable,
1Ti	4: 4	every creature of God is **g**,
1Ti	4: 6	you will be a **g** minister of
1Ti	4: 6	words of faith and of the **g**
1Ti	6:12	Fight the **g** fight of faith,
2Ti	1:14	That **g** thing which was
2Ti	2: 3	must endure hardship as a **g**
2Ti	2:21	prepared for every **g** work.
2Ti	3:17	equipped for every **g** work.
2Ti	4: 7	I have fought the **g** fight, I
Tit	1:16	and disqualified for every **g**
Tit	2: 5	chaste, homemakers, **g**,
Tit	2:14	zealous for **g** works.
Heb	6: 5	and have tasted the **g** word of
Heb	10: 1	having a shadow of the **g**
Heb	11: 2	it the elders obtained a **g**
Heb	11:12	and him as **g** as dead, were
Heb	13:18	confident that we have a **g**
Heb	13:21	make you complete in every **g**
Jas	1:17	Every **g** gift and every
Jas	2: 3	You sit here in a **g** place,"
Jas	3:13	Let him show by **g** conduct
1Pe	2:20	But when you do **g** and
1Pe	3:13	followers of what is **g**?
1Pe	3:16	having a **g** conscience, that
1Pe	3:21	but the answer of a **g**
1Pe	4:10	as **g** stewards of the
1Pe	4:19	souls to Him in doing **g**,

GOOD-LOOKING (*see* GOOD)

1Sa	16:12	with bright eyes, and **g**.
1Sa	17:42	only a youth, ruddy and **g**
Dan	1: 4	was no blemish, but **g**,

GOODNESS (*see* GOOD, GOODNESS')

Ex	33:19	I will make all My **g** pass
2Sa	7:28	You have promised this **g** to
Neh	9:25	themselves in Your great **g**.
Ps	23: 6	Surely **g** and mercy shall
Ps	27:13	That I would see the **g** of
Ps	31:19	Oh, how great is Your **g**,
Ps	33: 5	The earth is full of the **g**
Ps	52: 1	The **g** of God endures
Ps	65:11	crown the year with Your **g**,
Ps	107: 8	to the LORD for His **g**,
Prov	2:20	you may walk in the way of **g**,
Eccl	6: 3	soul is not satisfied with **g**,
Hos	3: 5	fear the LORD and His **g** in
Rom	2: 4	despise the riches of His **g**,

Rom   2: 4   not knowing that the **g** of
Gal   5:22   longsuffering, kindness, **g,**

GOODNESS'† (*see* GOODNESS)
Ps   25: 7   For Your **g** sake, O LORD.

GOODS
Gen   14:11   Then they took all the **g** of
Gen   14:16   his brother Lot and his **g,**
Gen   14:21   and take the **g** for
Ex   22:11   hand into his neighbor's **g;**
Eccl   5:11   When **g** increase, They
Matt   12:29   house and plunder his **g,**
Luke   12:19   you have many **g** laid up for
Luke   15:12   give me the portion of **g**
Luke   19: 8   I give half of my **g** to the
Acts   2:45   sold their possessions and **g,**
1Co   13: 3   though I bestow all my **g** to
1Jn   3:17   whoever has this world's **g,**

GOODWILL
Luke   2:14   **g** toward men!"

GOPHERWOOD†
Gen   6:14   "Make yourself an ark of **g;**

GORES
Ex   21:28   If an ox **g** a man or a woman

GORGEOUS† (*see* GORGEOUSLY)
Luke   23:11   arrayed Him in a **g** robe, and

GORGEOUSLY (*see* GORGEOUS)
Luke   7:25   Indeed those who are **g**

GOSHEN (*see* EGYPT)
Gen   45:10   shall dwell in the land of **G,**
Gen   47:27   Egypt, in the country of **G;**

GOSPEL (*see* GOSPEL'S)
Matt   4:23   preaching the **g** of the
Matt   11: 5   up and the poor have the **g**
Matt   24:14   And this **g** of the kingdom
Matt   26:13   wherever this **g** is preached
Mark   1: 1   The beginning of the **g** of
Mark   1:15   Repent, and believe in the **g.**
Mark   13:10   And the **g** must first be
Mark   16:15   the world and preach the **g**
Luke   4:18   Me To preach the **g**
Acts   15: 7   hear the word of the **g** and
Acts   20:24   to testify to the **g** of the
Rom   1: 1   separated to the **g** of God
Rom   1: 9   with my spirit in the **g** of
Rom   1:15   I am ready to preach the **g**
Rom   1:16   I am not ashamed of the **g**
Rom   10:15   those who preach the **g**
Rom   10:16   have not all obeyed the **g.**
Rom   15:16   ministering the **g** of God,
Rom   15:20   it my aim to preach the **g,**
1Co   1:17   baptize, but to preach the **g,**
1Co   4:15   begotten you through the **g.**
1Co   9:12   things lest we hinder the **g**
1Co   9:14   that those who preach the **g**
1Co   9:14   should live from the **g.**
1Co   9:16   For if I preach the **g,**
1Co   9:16   me if I do not preach the **g!**
1Co   9:18   abuse my authority in the **g.**
2Co   4: 3   But even if our **g** is veiled,
2Co   4: 4   lest the light of the **g** of
2Co   11: 4   or a different **g** which you
2Co   11: 7   because I preached the **g** of
Gal   1: 6   of Christ, to a different **g,**
Gal   1: 7   and want to pervert the **g**
Gal   1: 8   preach any other **g** to you
Gal   2: 5   that the truth of the **g**
Gal   2:14   about the truth of the **g,**
Gal   3: 8   preached the **g** to Abraham
Gal   4:13   infirmity I preached the **g**
Eph   1:13   the **g** of your salvation; in

Eph   6:15   the preparation of the **g** of
Eph   6:19   known the mystery of the **g,**
Phil   1: 5   for your fellowship in the **g**
Phil   1: 7   and confirmation of the **g,**
Phil   1:12   for the furtherance of the **g,**
Phil   1:17   for the defense of the **g.**
Phil   1:27   conduct be worthy of the **g**
Phil   1:27   for the faith of the **g,**
Phil   2:22   he served with me in the **g.**
Phil   4:15   in the beginning of the **g,**
Col   1:23   away from the hope of the **g**
1Th   1: 5   For our **g** did not come to you
1Th   2: 2   God to speak to you the **g**
1Th   2: 4   to be entrusted with the **g,**
1Ti   1:11   according to the glorious **g**
2Ti   1:10   to light through the **g,**
Phm   1:13   to me in my chains for the **g.**
Heb   4: 2   For indeed the **g** was preached
1Pe   4:17   those who do not obey the **g**
Rev   14: 6   having the everlasting **g** to

GOSPEL'S (*see* GOSPEL)
Mark   8:35   life for My sake and the **g**
1Co   9:23   Now this I do for the **g** sake,

GOSSIPS†
2Ti   5:13   and not only idle but also **g**

GOT (*see* GET)
Judg   7: 6   all the rest of the people **g**
Matt   8:23   Now when He **g** into a boat,

GOVERNING (*see* GOVERNMENT, GOVERNOR)
Luke   2: 2   place while Quirinius was **g**
Rom   13: 1   soul be subject to the **g**

GOVERNMENT† (*see* GOVERNING, GOVERNOR)
Is   9: 6   And the **g** will be upon His
Is   9: 7   Of the increase of His **g**

GOVERNOR (*see* GOVERNOR'S, GOVERNORS)
Gen   42: 6   Now Joseph was **g** over the
Mal   1: 8   Offer it then to your **g!**
Matt   27:11   Jesus stood before the **g.**
Acts   7:10   and he made him **g** over Egypt
Acts   23:26   to the most excellent **g**

GOVERNOR'S (*see* GOVERNOR)
Matt   28:14   And if this comes to the **g**

GOVERNORS (*see* GOVERNOR)
Ezra   8:36   the king's satraps and the **g**
Matt   10:18   will be brought before **g**
1Pe   2:14   or to **g,** as to those

GRACE (*see* GRACEFUL, GRACIOUS)
Gen   6: 8   But Noah found **g** in the eyes
Ps   45: 2   **G** is poured upon Your lips;
Prov   3:34   But gives **g** to the humble.
Prov   22:11   of heart And has **g** on
Is   26:10   Let **g** be shown to the
Zech   4: 7   capstone With shouts of "**G,**
Luke   2:40   and the **g** of God was upon
John   1:14   full of **g** and truth.
John   1:16   received, and grace for **g.**
John   1:17   but **g** and truth came
Acts   4:33   And great **g** was upon them
Acts   14: 3   witness to the word of His **g,**
Acts   20:24   to the gospel of the **g** of
Rom   1: 5   Him we have received **g** and
Rom   1: 7   **G** to you and peace from God
Rom   3:24   justified freely by His **g**
Rom   4: 4   wages are not counted as **g**
Rom   5: 2   access by faith into this **g**
Rom   5:15   of God and the gift by the **g**
Rom   5:20   **g** abounded much more,
Rom   5:21   even so **g** might reign
Rom   6: 1   we continue in sin that **g**
Rom   6:14   not under law but under **g.**

Rom 12: 3 through the **g** given to me,
Rom 16:20 The **g** of our Lord Jesus
1Co 1: 3 **G** to you and peace from God
1Co 15:10 But by the **g** of God I am what
2Co 4:15 are for your sakes, that **g**,
2Co 6: 1 you not to receive the **g**
2Co 8: 1 we make known to you the **g**
2Co 8: 9 For you know the **g** of our
2Co 9:14 because of the exceeding **g**
2Co 12: 9 My **g** is sufficient for you,
Gal 1:15 and called me through His **g**,
Gal 2:21 I do not set aside the **g**
Gal 5: 4 law; you have fallen from **g**.
Eph 1: 6 praise of the glory of His **g**,
Eph 1: 7 to the riches of His **g**
Eph 2: 5 together with Christ (by **g**
Eph 2: 7 exceeding riches of His **g**
Eph 2: 8 For by **g** you have been saved
Eph 3: 7 to the gift of the **g** of God
Eph 4: 7 But to each one of us **g** was
Eph 4:29 that it may impart **g** to the
Phil 1: 7 are partakers with me of **g**.
Col 1: 6 you heard and knew the **g** of
Col 3:16 singing with **g** in your
Col 4: 6 speech always be with **g**,
1Ti 1: 2 a true son in the faith: **G**,
Tit 3: 7 been justified by His **g** we
Heb 2: 9 by the **g** of God, might taste
Heb 4:16 boldly to the throne of **g**,
Heb 4:16 may obtain mercy and find **g**
Heb 10:29 and insulted the Spirit of **g**?
Heb 12:15 anyone fall short of the **g**
Jas 4: 6 But He gives more **g**.
Jas 4: 6 But gives **g** to the
1Pe 1:10 who prophesied of the **g**
1Pe 1:13 your hope fully upon the **g**
1Pe 3: 7 heirs together of the **g** of
1Pe 4:10 stewards of the manifold **g**
1Pe 5: 5 But gives **g** to the
1Pe 5:10 But may the God of all **g**,
1Pe 5:12 that this is the true **g** of
Rev 1: 4 **G** to you and peace from Him
Rev 22:21 The **g** of our Lord Jesus

GRACEFUL (see GRACE)
Prov 1: 9 For they will be a **g**
Prov 5:19 As a loving deer and a **g**

GRACIOUS (see GRACE, GRACIOUSLY)
Gen 43:29 God be **g** to you, my son."
Ex 33:19 I will be **g** to whom I will
Ex 34: 6 LORD God, merciful and **g**,
Num 6:25 And be **g** to you;
Neh 9:17 **G** and merciful, Slow to
Ps 86:15 full of compassion, and **g**,
Ps 103: 8 LORD is merciful and **g**,
Ps 111: 4 The LORD is **g** and full of
Ps 116: 5 **G** is the LORD, and
Ps 145:17 **G** in all His works.
Amos 5:15 God of hosts Will be **g** to
Jon 4: 2 for I know that You are a **g**
1Pe 2: 3 tasted that the Lord is **g**.

GRACIOUSLY (see GRACIOUS)
Gen 33:11 because God has dealt **g** with
Ps 112: 5 A good man deals **g** and

GRAFT† (see GRAFTED)
Rom 11:23 for God is able to **g** them in

GRAFTED (see GRAFT)
Rom 11:17 were **g** in among them, and
Rom 11:24 and were **g** contrary to
Rom 11:24 be **g** into their own olive

GRAIN (see GRAINFIELDS, GRAINS)
Gen 41: 5 suddenly seven heads of **g**
Gen 41:49 Joseph gathered very much **g**,

Gen 41:57 to Joseph in Egypt to buy **g**,
Gen 42:25 to fill their sacks with **g**,
Ex 22: 6 stacked grain, standing **g**,
Ex 29:41 shall offer with it the **g**
Ex 30: 9 or a **g** offering; nor shall
Num 4:16 the daily **g** offering, the
Deut 7:13 your **g** and your new wine and
Deut 12:17 gates the tithe of your **g**
Deut 16: 9 to put the sickle to the **g**.
Deut 18: 4 The firstfruits of your **g** and
Deut 25: 4 while it treads out the **g**.
Josh 5:11 bread and parched **g**,
Ruth 2: 2 and glean heads of **g** after
Ruth 3: 7 at the end of the heap of **g**;
2Ch 32:28 for the harvest of **g**,
Neh 10:31 land brought wares or any **g**
Job 5:26 As a sheaf of **g** ripens in
Ps 65:13 also are covered with **g**;
Ps 72:16 will be an abundance of **g**
Prov 11:26 curse him who withholds **g**,
Is 17: 5 the harvester gathers the **g**
Lam 2:12 Where is **g** and wine?" As
Hos 2: 8 not know That I gave her **g**,
Hos 2: 9 return and take away My **g**
Hos 2:22 earth shall answer With **g**,
Hos 10:11 That loves to thresh **g**;
Joel 1:17 For the **g** has withered.
Amos 8: 5 be past, That we may sell **g**?
Amos 9: 9 As **g** is sifted in a sieve;
Matt 12: 1 began to pluck heads of **g**
Matt 13:26 But when the **g** had sprouted
John 12:24 unless a **g** of wheat falls
John 12:24 it dies, it produces much **g**.
Acts 7:12 heard that there was **g** in
1Co 9: 9 it treads out the **g**.
1Ti 5:18 it treads out the **g**,

GRAINFIELDS (see GRAIN)
Matt 12: 1 Jesus went through the **g** on
Mark 2:23 that He went through the **g**

GRAINS† (see GRAIN)
Is 48:19 of your body like the **g** of

GRANDCHILDREN (see CHILDREN)
Deut 4: 9 to your children and your **g**,
Job 42:16 and saw his children and **g**

GRANDDAUGHTER (see DAUGHTER)
2Ki 8:26 name was Athaliah the **g** of
2Ch 22: 2 name was Athaliah the **g** of

GRANDFATHER† (see FATHER)
2Sa 9: 7 all the land of Saul your **g**;

GRANDMOTHER (see MOTHER)
2Ti 1: 5 which dwelt first in your **g**

GRANDSON (see SON)
Gen 11:31 his son Abram and his **g** Lot,
Deut 6: 2 you and your son and your **g**,

GRANT (see GRANTED)
Gen 42:34 I will **g** your brother to
Deut 15: 1 seven years you shall **g** a
Ruth 1: 9 The LORD **g** that you may find
1Sa 1:17 and the God of Israel **g** your
1Ki 8:50 and **g** them compassion before
Neh 1:11 and **g** him mercy in the sight
Esth 5: 8 if it pleases the king to **g**
Ps 85: 7 And **g** us Your salvation.
Mark 10:37 **G** us that we may sit, one on
2Ti 1:16 The Lord **g** mercy to the
2Ti 2:25 if God perhaps will **g** them

GRANTED (see GRANT)
1Sa 1:27 and the LORD has **g** me my
Neh 2: 8 And the king **g** them to me
Esth 5: 6 It shall be **g** you. What is

Esth 7: 2 It shall be **g** you. And what
Job 10:12 You have **g** me life and
Mark 15:45 he **g** the body to Joseph.
John 6:65 to Me unless it has been **g**
Phil 1:29 For to you it has been **g** on
Phm 1:22 your prayers I shall be **g**

GRAPE (*see* GRAPES, GRAPEVINE)
Lev 19:10 shall you gather every **g**
Num 6: 3 shall he drink any **g** juice,
Is 18: 5 is perfect And the sour **g**

GRAPES (*see* GRAPE)
Gen 49:11 clothes in the blood of **g**.
Num 6: 3 nor eat fresh **g** or raisins.
Num 13:23 branch with one cluster of **g**;
Deut 23:24 you may eat your fill of **g**
Deut 32:14 wine, the blood of the **g**.
Song 2:15 our vines have tender **g**.
Is 5: 2 But it brought forth wild **g**.
Jer 8:13 No **g** shall be on the vine,
Jer 25:30 as those who tread the **g**,
Jer 31:29 fathers have eaten sour **g**,
Ezek 18: 2 fathers have eaten sour **g**,
Amos 9:13 And the treader of **g** him

GRAPEVINE† (*see* GRAPE, VINE)
Num 6: 4 that is produced by the **g**,
Jas 3:12 or a **g** bear figs? Thus no

GRASPED (*see* GRASPING)
2Sa 2:16 And each one **g** his opponent

GRASPING (*see* GRASPED)
Eccl 1:14 all is vanity and **g** for the
Eccl 1:17 that this also is **g** for the

GRASS (*see* GRASSHOPPER)
Gen 1:11 the earth bring forth **g**,
2Sa 23: 4 Like the tender **g**
Job 40:15 He eats **g** like an ox.
Ps 37: 2 soon be cut down like the **g**,
Ps 72: 6 down like rain upon the **g**
Ps 72:16 city shall flourish like **g**
Ps 90: 5 the morning they are like **g**
Ps 92: 7 the wicked spring up like **g**,
Ps 103:15 man, his days are like **g**;
Prov 19:12 favor is like dew on the **g**.
Prov 27:25 and the tender **g** shows
Is 15: 6 For the green **g** has
Is 15: 6 The **g** fails, there is
Is 40: 6 I cry?" "All flesh is **g**,
Is 40: 7 The **g** withers, the flower
Is 40: 7 Surely the people are **g**.
Dan 4:25 they shall make you eat **g**
Dan 4:32 They shall make you eat **g**
Matt 6:30 if God so clothes the **g**
Mark 6:39 in groups on the green **g**.
John 6:10 Now there was much **g** in
Jas 1:11 heat than it withers the **g**;
1Pe 1:24 "All flesh is as **g**,

GRASSHOPPER (*see* GRASS, GRASSHOPPERS)
Eccl 12: 5 The **g** is a burden, And

GRASSHOPPERS (*see* GRASSHOPPER)
Num 13:33 and we were like **g** in our
Is 40:22 its inhabitants are like **g**,

GRATEFUL†
Jon 4: 6 So Jonah was very **g** for the

GRATIFY†
Eccl 2: 3 in my heart how to **g** my
Mark 15:15 wanting to **g** the crowd,

GRAVE (*see* GRAVECLOTHES, GRAVES)
Gen 18:20 because their sin is very **g**,
Gen 37:35 I shall go down into the **g**
Gen 42:38 hair with sorrow to the **g**.

Deut 34: 6 but no one knows his **g** to
1Sa 2: 6 He brings down to the **g** and
2Sa 19:37 near the **g** of my father and
1Ki 2: 6 gray hair go down to the **g**
2Ki 22:20 shall be gathered to your **g**
Job 5:26 You shall come to the **g** at a
Job 7: 9 he who goes down to the **g**
Job 10:19 from the womb to the **g**
Job 21:13 in a moment go down to the **g**.
Ps 30: 3 my soul up from the **g**;
Ps 31:17 Let them be silent in the **g**.
Ps 88: 5 the slain who lie in the **g**,
Ps 141: 7 at the mouth of the **g**,
Eccl 4: 8 also is vanity and a **g**
Eccl 9:10 or wisdom in the **g** where
Song 8: 6 Jealousy as cruel as the **g**;
Is 14:19 you are cast out of your **g**
Is 53: 9 And they made His **g** with the
Jer 20:17 mother might have been my **g**,
Hos 13:14 I will be your plagues! O **G**,

GRAVECLOTHES† (*see* GRAVE)
John 11:44 bound hand and foot with **g**,

GRAVEL†
Prov 20:17 mouth will be filled with **g**.
Lam 3:16 also broken my teeth with **g**,

GRAVELY
Lam 1: 8 Jerusalem has sinned **g**,

GRAVEN (*see* IMAGE)
Is 30:22 the covering of your **g**
Is 40:19 The workman molds a **g** image
Is 44: 9 Those who make a **g** image
Jer 10:14 put to shame by the **g** image

GRAVES (*see* GRAVE)
2Ki 23: 6 threw its ashes on the **g** of
Jer 8: 1 of Jerusalem, out of their **g**.
Ezek 37:12 I will open your **g** and cause
Ezek 37:12 you to come up from your **g**,
Matt 27:52 and the **g** were opened; and
Matt 27:53 and coming out of the **g** after
John 5:28 which all who are in the **g**

GRAY (*see* GRAYHEADED)
Gen 42:38 you would bring down my **g**
Lev 19:32 shall rise before the **g**
Prov 20:29 of old men is their **g** head.

GRAYHEADED (*see* GRAY)
1Sa 12: 2 you; and I am old and **g**,
Ps 71:18 also when I am old and **g**,

GRAZE
Is 11: 7 cow and the bear shall **g**;
Dan 4:15 And let him **g** with the

GREASE†
Ps 119:70 Their heart is as fat as **g**,

GREAT (*see* GREATER, GREATEST, GREATLY, GREATNESS)
Gen 1:16 Then God made two **g** lights:
Gen 1:21 So God created **g** sea
Gen 6: 5 wickedness of man was **g** in
Gen 7:11 all the fountains of the **g**
Gen 12: 2 I will make you a **g** nation;
Gen 12: 2 you And make your name **g**;
Gen 15: 1 your exceedingly **g** reward."
Gen 21: 8 And Abraham made a **g** feast
Ex 3: 3 turn aside and see this **g**
Ex 6: 6 outstretched arm and with **g**
Ex 14:31 Thus Israel saw the **g** work
Ex 32:11 of the land of Egypt with **g**
Ex 32:30 You have committed a **g** sin.
Num 34: 6 you shall have the **G** Sea for
Deut 1:17 the small as well as the **g**;
Deut 1:28 the cities are **g** and
Deut 4: 7 For what **g** nation is there

Deut	5:25	For this **g** fire will consume
Deut	9: 2	a people **g** and tall, the
Deut	10:17	the **g** God, mighty and
Deut	29: 3	and those **g** wonders.
Deut	29:28	and in **g** indignation, and
Josh	10: 2	because Gibeon was a **g**
Josh	24:17	who did those **g** signs in our
Judg	2: 7	who had seen all the **g** works
Judg	5:16	divisions of Reuben have **g**
Judg	16: 6	tell me where your **g**
Judg	16:15	not told me where your **g**
Ruth	2: 1	a man of **g** wealth, of the
1Sa	12:22	for His **g** name's sake,
1Sa	12:24	for consider what **g** things
1Sa	14:45	who has accomplished this **g**
1Sa	15:22	Has the LORD as **g** delight
2Sa	3:38	know that a prince and a **g**
2Sa	5:10	David went on and became **g**,
2Sa	7: 9	and have made you a **g** name,
2Sa	7:22	"Therefore You are **g**,
2Sa	7:23	and to do for Youself **g** and
2Sa	23:10	The LORD brought about a **g**
2Sa	24:14	for His mercies are **g**;
1Ki	3: 6	You have shown **g** mercy to
1Ki	7:12	The **g** court was enclosed
2Ki	6:25	And there was a **g** famine in
2Ki	7: 6	the noise of a **g** army; so
2Ki	17:21	and made them commit a **g**
2Ki	23:26	from the fierceness of His **g**
1Ch	16:25	For the LORD is **g** and
1Ch	26: 6	because they were men of **g**
2Ch	1: 8	You have shown **g** mercy to
2Ch	6:32	for the sake of Your **g** name
2Ch	28:13	guilt; for our guilt is **g**,
2Ch	30:26	So there was **g** joy in
2Ch	32:27	Hezekiah had very **g** riches
Ezra	5: 8	to the temple of the **g** God,
Ezra	5:11	which a **g** king of Israel
Neh	1: 3	the province are there in **g**
Neh	1:10	You have redeemed by Your **g**
Neh	6: 3	I am doing a **g** work, so that
Neh	8: 6	the **g** God. Then all the
Neh	9:25	themselves in Your **g**
Esth	1:20	all his empire (for it is **g**)
Esth	9: 4	For Mordecai was **g** in the
Job	1:19	and suddenly a **g** wind came
Job	9:10	He does **g** things past
Job	32: 9	men are not always wise,
Job	36:26	"Behold, God is **g**,
Job	38:32	Or can you guide the **G** Bear
Ps	18:35	gentleness has made me **g**.
Ps	19:11	in keeping them there is **g**
Ps	19:13	I shall be innocent of **g**
Ps	22:25	shall be of You in the **g**
Ps	25:11	my iniquity, for it is **g**.
Ps	31:19	how **g** is Your goodness,
Ps	47: 2	He is a **g** King over all
Ps	48: 1	**G** is the LORD, and greatly
Ps	48: 2	The city of the **g** King.
Ps	68:11	**G** was the company of those
Ps	71:19	You who have done **g** things;
Ps	77:13	Who is so **g** a God as our
Ps	86:13	For **g** is Your mercy toward
Ps	92: 5	how **g** are Your works! Your
Ps	95: 3	For the LORD is the **g** God,
Ps	95: 3	And the **g** King above all
Ps	96: 4	For the LORD is **g** and
Ps	104: 1	LORD my God, You are very **g**:
Ps	108: 4	For Your mercy is **g** above
Ps	111: 2	works of the LORD are **g**,
Ps	119:156	**G** are Your tender mercies,
Ps	119:162	word As one who finds **g**
Ps	119:165	**G** peace have those who love
Ps	126: 3	The LORD has done **g** things
Ps	136: 4	To Him who alone does **g**
Ps	139:17	O God! How **g** is the sum of
Ps	145: 3	**G** is the LORD, and greatly
Ps	145: 8	Slow to anger and **g** in
Prov	22: 1	to be chosen rather than **g**
Prov	26:10	The **g** God who formed
Eccl	2: 9	So I became **g** and excelled
Is	9: 2	in darkness Have seen a **g**
Is	12: 6	For **g** is the Holy One of
Is	32: 2	As the shadow of a **g** rock
Is	53:12	Him a portion with the **g**,
Is	54: 7	But with **g** mercies I will
Jer	32:42	as I have brought all this **g**
Jer	33: 3	and show you **g** and mighty
Jer	44:26	I have sworn by My **g** name,'
Jer	45: 5	And do you seek **g** things for
Lam	1: 1	Who was **g** among the
Lam	3:23	**G** is Your faithfulness.
Ezek	1: 4	a **g** cloud with raging fire
Ezek	8: 6	the **g** abominations that the
Ezek	28: 5	By your **g** wisdom in trade
Ezek	30: 9	And **g** anguish shall come
Ezek	36:23	And I will sanctify My **g**
Dan	2: 6	and **g** honor. Therefore tell
Dan	2:31	a **g** image! This great image,
Dan	2:35	struck the image became a **g**
Dan	2:45	the **g** God has made known to
Dan	4: 3	How **g** are His signs, And
Dan	4:30	Is not this **g** Babylon, that I
Dan	5: 1	the king made a **g** feast for
Dan	7: 3	And four **g** beasts came up
Dan	8: 8	the male goat grew very **g**;
Dan	9: 4	**g** and awesome God, who keeps
Dan	9:18	but because of Your **g**
Dan	10: 8	left alone when I saw this **g**
Dan	11: 3	who shall rule with **g**
Dan	12: 1	The **g** prince who stands
Hos	1: 2	the land has committed **g**
Hos	13: 5	In the land of **g** drought.
Joel	2:11	the day of the LORD is **g**.
Joel	2:13	and of **g** kindness; And He
Jon	1: 2	that **g** city, and cry out
Jon	1: 4	But the LORD sent out a **g**
Jon	1:17	the LORD had prepared a **g**
Nah	3: 3	A **g** number of bodies,
Zeph	1:14	The **g** day of the LORD is
Zech	4: 7	O **g** mountain? Before
Zech	7:12	Thus **g** wrath came from the
Mal	1:11	For My name shall be **g**
Mal	1:14	For I am a **g** King," Says
Mal	4: 5	Before the coming of the **g**
Matt	2:10	rejoiced with exceedingly **g**
Matt	2:18	and **g** mourning, Rachel
Matt	4:16	darkness have seen a **g**
Matt	4:25	**G** multitudes followed
Matt	5:12	for **g** is your reward in
Matt	5:19	he shall be called **g** in the
Matt	5:35	for it is the city of the **g**
Matt	6:23	how **g** is that darkness!
Matt	7:27	And **g** was its fall."
Matt	8:10	I have not found such **g**
Matt	8:24	And suddenly a **g** tempest
Matt	8:26	and there was a **g** calm.
Matt	12:40	in the belly of the **g** fish,
Matt	13:46	he had found one pearl of **g**
Matt	15:28	**g** is your faith! Let it be
Matt	19:22	for he had **g** possessions.
Matt	20:26	whoever desires to become **g**
Matt	22:38	This is the first and **g**
Matt	24:21	For then there will be **g**
Matt	24:24	will rise and show **g** signs
Matt	24:30	of heaven with power and **g**
Matt	24:31	send His angels with a **g**
Matt	28: 2	there was a **g** earthquake;
Mark	5:19	and tell them what **g** things
Mark	13: 2	Do you see these **g** buildings?

Luke 1:32 "He will be **g**,
Luke 1:49 He who is mighty has done **g**
Luke 1:58 how the Lord had shown **g**
Luke 2:10 bring you good tidings of **g**
Luke 5:29 Then Levi gave Him a **g** feast
Luke 7:16 A **g** prophet has risen up
Luke 8:39 and tell what **g** things God —
Luke 9:48 among you all will be **g**. ⌐
Luke 10: 2 "The harvest truly is **g**,
Luke 15:20 But when he was still a **g**
Luke 16:26 us and you there is a **g**
Luke 21:11 And there will be **g** —
Luke 21:11 will be fearful sights and **g**
Luke 21:27 in a cloud with power and **g**
John 7:37 that **g** day of the feast,
Acts 4:33 And with **g** power the apostles
Acts 4:33 And **g** grace was upon them
Acts 5: 5 So **g** fear came upon all
Acts 6: 8 did **g** wonders and signs ⌐
Acts 8: 1 At that time a **g** persecution
Acts 11:21 and a **g** number believed and
Acts 19:28 G is Diana of the
Acts 22: 6 suddenly a **g** light from
Acts 26:22 both to small and **g**,
Rom 9: 2 that I have **g** sorrow and
1Co 16: 9 For a **g** and effective door
2Co 1:10 who delivered us from so **g** a
2Co 3:12 we use **g** boldness of speech—
Eph 2: 4 because of His **g** love with
Eph 5:32 This is a **g** mystery, but I
Col 4:13 him witness that he has a **g**
1Th 2:17 to see your face with **g**
1Ti 3:13 a good standing and **g**
1Ti 3:16 And without controversy **g** is
1Ti 6: 6 with contentment is **g** gain.
2Ti 2:20 But in a **g** house there are
Tit 2:13 glorious appearing of our **g**
Heb 2: 3 escape if we neglect so **g** a
Heb 4:14 then that we have a **g** High
Heb 7: 4 Now consider how **g** this man
Heb 12: 1 we are surrounded by so **g** a
Heb 13:20 that **g** Shepherd of the
Jas 3: 5 a little member and boasts **g**
Jas 3: 5 See how **g** a forest a little
2Pe 3:10 will pass away with a **g**
Jude 6 for the judgment of the **g**
Rev 6:12 there was a **g** earthquake;
Rev 6:17 For the **g** day of His wrath
Rev 7: 9 a **g** multitude which no one
Rev 8:10 And a **g** star fell from
Rev 9:14 who are bound at the **g**
Rev 12: 1 Now a **g** sign appeared in
Rev 12: 9 So the **g** dragon was cast out,
Rev 12:12 having **g** wrath, because he
Rev 13: 2 and **g** authority.
Rev 13: 5 was given a mouth speaking **g**
Rev 14: 8 that **g** city, because she has
Rev 16:14 to the battle of that **g** day
Rev 17: 5 MYSTERY, BABYLON THE G,
Rev 18:10 that **g** city Babylon, that
Rev 19:17 for the supper of the **g** God,
Rev 20:11 Then I saw a **g** white throne
Rev 20:12 I saw the dead, small and **g**,
Rev 21:10 and showed me the **g** city,

GREATER (see GREAT)
Gen 1:16 the **g** light to rule the day,
Gen 4:13 My punishment is **g** than I
Ex 18:11 I know that the LORD is **g**
Num 14:12 will make of you a nation **g**
Deut 1:28 The people are **g** and taller
Josh 11: 8 them and chased them to G
2Sa 13:15 which he hated her was **g**
2Ch 2: 5 for our God is **g** than all
Job 33:12 For God is **g** than man.

Ezek 8: 6 you will see **g**
Ezek 8:15 you will see **g** abominations
Matt 11:11 there has not risen one **g**
Matt 12:41 and indeed a **g** than Jonah
Matt 12:42 and indeed a **g** than Solomon
Matt 13:32 but when it is grown it is **g**
Matt 23:14 Therefore you will receive **g**
Mark 12:31 is no other commandment **g**
Mark 12:40 These will receive **g**
Luke 12:18 down my barns and build **g**,
John 1:50 You will see **g** things than ⌐
John 4:12 Are You **g** than our father
John 5:20 and He will show Him **g** works
John 5:36 But I have a **g** witness than
John 8:53 Are You **g** than our father
John 10:29 is **g** than all; and no one is
John 13:16 a servant is not **g** than his
John 14:12 and **g** works than these he ⌐
John 14:28 for My Father is **g** than I.
John 15:13 G love has no one than this,
1Co 12:23 on these we bestow **g** honor;
Heb 6:13 He could swear by no one **g**,
Heb 11:26 the reproach of Christ **g**
1Jn 4: 4 He who is in you is **g** than

GREATEST (see GREAT)
Jer 42: 1 from the least to the **g**,
Jon 3: 5 from the **g** to the least of
Matt 18: 4 this little child is the **g**
Matt 23:11 But he who is **g** among you
Mark 9:34 who would be the **g**.
1Co 13:13 but the **g** of these is love.

GREATLY (see GREAT)
Gen 3:16 I will **g** multiply your sorrow
Gen 7:18 The waters prevailed and **g**
Gen 24:35 has blessed my master **g**,
Ex 19:18 the whole mountain quaked **g**.
Deut 15: 4 for the LORD will **g** bless
Judg 2:15 And they were **g** distressed.
1Sa 15:11 I **g** regret that I have set up
1Sa 16:21 him. And he loved him **g**,
2Sa 24:10 I have sinned **g** in what I
1Ch 16:25 the LORD is great and **g**
Neh 8:12 send portions and rejoice **g**,
Job 3:25 For the thing I **g** feared has
Ps 6: 3 My soul also is **g** troubled;
Ps 28: 7 Therefore my heart **g**
Ps 45:11 So the King will **g** desire
Ps 47: 9 He is **g** exalted.
Ps 48: 1 and **g** to be praised In the
Ps 62: 2 I shall not be **g** moved.
Ps 89: 7 God is **g** to be feared in the
Ps 96: 4 the LORD is great and **g**
Ps 145: 3 and **g** to be praised; And
Is 61:10 I will **g** rejoice in the
Dan 7:28 my thoughts **g** troubled me,
Mark 9:15 all the people were **g**
Mark 9:26 cried out, convulsed him **g**,
Luke 2: 9 and they were **g** afraid.
Luke 24: 4 as they were **g** perplexed
2Co 10:15 we shall be **g** enlarged by
Phil 1: 8 how **g** I long for you all
2Ti 1: 4 **g** desiring to see you, being
2Ti 4:15 for he has **g** resisted our
1Pe 1: 6 In this you **g** rejoice, though

GREATNESS (see GREAT)
Ex 15:16 By the **g** of Your arm They
Num 14:19 according to the **g** of Your
Deut 5:24 shown us His glory and His **g**,
Deut 9:26 have redeemed through Your **g**,
Deut 32: 3 Ascribe **g** to our God.
1Ch 29:11 Yours, O LORD, is the **g**,
Ps 145: 3 And His **g** is unsearchable.
Ps 145: 6 And I will declare Your **g**.

Ps 150: 2 to His excellent **g**!
Prov 5:23 And in the **g** of his folly
Ezek 31: 2 are you like in your **g**?
Eph 1:19 what is the exceeding **g** of

GREECE (see GREEK)
Dan 8:21 goat is the kingdom of G.
Acts 20: 2 many words, he came to G

GREED† (see GREEDILY, GREEDY)
Luke 11:39 inward part is full of **g**

GREEDILY (see GREED)
Jude 11 have run **g** in the error of

GREEDINESS (see GREEDY)
Eph 4:19 work all uncleanness with **g**.
1Ti 6:10 from the faith in their **g**,

GREEDY (see GREED, GREEDINESS)
Prov 1:19 ways of everyone who is **g**
Is 56:11 they are **g** dogs Which
1Ti 3: 3 not **g** for money, but gentle,

GREEK (see GREECE, GREEKS)
Luke 23:38 over Him in letters of G,
Acts 16: 1 but his father was G.
Rom 1:16 Jew first and also for the G.
Rom 10:12 between Jew and G,
Gal 3:28 There is neither Jew nor G,

GREEKS (see GREEK)
John 12:20 Now there were certain G
Acts 14: 1 of the Jews and of the G
Acts 17: 4 multitude of the devout G,
Acts 18: 4 persuaded both Jews and G.
Rom 1:14 I am a debtor both to G and
1Co 1:22 and G seek after wisdom;
1Co 1:23 stumbling block and to the G
1Co 1:24 are called, both Jews and G,

GREEN
Gen 1:30 I have given every **g** herb
Gen 9: 3 even as the **g** herbs.
Ps 23: 2 makes me to lie down in **g**
Ps 37: 2 And wither as the **g** herb.
Ps 52: 8 But I am like a **g** olive
Song 2:13 fig tree puts forth her **g**
Jer 17: 8 But its leaf will be **g**,
Mark 6:39 sit down in groups on the **g**
Luke 23:31 do these things in the **g**

GREET (see GREETED, GREETING, GREETS)
1Sa 10: 4 And they will **g** you and give
2Sa 8:10 to **g** him and bless him,
Matt 5:47 And if you **g** your brethren
Rom 16: 3 G Priscilla and Aquila, my
Rom 16:16 G one another with a holy
Rom 16:16 The churches of Christ **g**
Rom 16:22 **g** you in the Lord.
Phil 4:21 G every saint in Christ
Heb 13:24 G all those who rule over
1Pe 5:14 G one another with a kiss of

GREETED (see GREET)
1Sa 17:22 and came and **g** his brothers.
Mark 9:15 running to Him, **g** Him.
Acts 21: 7 **g** the brethren, and stayed

GREETING (see GREET, GREETINGS)
Luke 1:29 considered what manner of **g**
Luke 1:44 soon as the voice of your **g**

GREETINGS (see GREETING)
Matt 23: 7 **g** in the marketplaces, and to
Matt 26:49 up to Jesus and said, "G,
Acts 15:33 they were sent back with **g**

GREETS (see GREET)
2Ki 4:29 and if anyone **g** you, do not
Rom 16:23 **g** you. Erastus, the
2Jn 11 for he who **g** him shares in

GREW (see GROW)
Gen 21: 8 So the child **g** and was
Ex 1: 7 multiplied and **g** exceedingly
Ex 1:12 more they multiplied and **g**.
Ex 2:10 And the child **g**,
Ex 7:13 And Pharaoh's heart **g** hard,
2Sa 3: 1 But David **g** stronger and
2Sa 12: 3 and it **g** up together with
Ps 32: 3 my bones **g** old Through my
Dan 4:11 The tree **g** and became
Dan 8: 8 Therefore the male goat **g**
Dan 8:10 And it **g** up to the host of
Jon 4: 8 so that he **g** faint. Then he
Mark 4: 7 and the thorns **g** up and
Luke 1:80 So the child **g** and became
Luke 2:40 And the Child **g** and became
Acts 12:24 But the word of God **g** and
Acts 13:46 Then Paul and Barnabas **g** bold

GRIEF (see GRIEFS, GRIEVE)
Job 2:13 for they saw that his **g** was
Ps 6: 7 eye wastes away because of **g**;
Ps 10:14 You observe trouble and **g**,
Ps 31:10 For my life is spent with **g**,
Prov 10: 1 a foolish son is the **g** of
Eccl 1:18 in much wisdom is much **g**,
Is 53: 3 and acquainted with **g**.
Is 53:10 Him; He has put Him to **g**.
Rom 9: 2 sorrow and continual **g** in
Heb 13:17 so with joy and not with **g**,
1Pe 2:19 toward God one endures **g**,

GRIEFS† (see GRIEF)
Is 53: 4 Surely He has borne our **g**

GRIEVE (see GRIEF, GRIEVED, GRIEVES)
1Sa 2:33 consume your eyes and **g**
Zech 12:10 and **g** for Him as one grieves
Eph 4:30 And do not **g** the Holy Spirit

GRIEVED (see GRIEVE)
Gen 6: 6 and He was **g** in His heart.
Judg 21:15 And the people **g** for
1Sa 1: 8 eat? And why is your heart **g**?
2Sa 19: 2 The king is **g** for his son."
Neh 8:11 day is holy; do not be **g**.
Ps 73:21 Thus my heart was **g**,
Ps 78:40 And **g** Him in the desert!
Ps 95:10 For forty years I was **g** with
Is 63:10 But they rebelled and **g** His
Dan 7:15 was **g** in my spirit within
John 21:17 Peter was **g** because He

GRIEVES† (see GRIEVE)
Ruth 1:13 for it **g** me very much for
Zech 12:10 and grieve for Him as one **g**

GRIND (see GRINDER, GRINDING)
Is 47: 2 Take the millstones and **g**
Matt 21:44 it will **g** him to powder."
Luke 20:18 it will **g** him to powder."

GRINDER† (see GRIND, GRINDERS)
Judg 16:21 and he became a **g** in the

GRINDERS† (see GRINDER)
Eccl 12: 3 When the **g** cease because

GRINDING (see GRIND)
Eccl 12: 4 And the sound of **g** is low;
Matt 24:41 Two women will be **g** at the

GROAN (see GROANED, GROANING, GROANS)
Ps 38: 8 I **g** because of the turmoil
Joel 1:18 How the animals **g**! The
Rom 8:23 even we ourselves **g** within
2Co 5: 2 For in this we **g**,

GROANED† (see GROAN)
Ex 2:23 the children of Israel **g**

John   11:33 He **g** in the spirit and was

GROANING (*see* GROAN, GROANINGS)
Ex   2:24 So God heard their **g**,
Judg   2:18 was moved to pity by their **g**
Ps   6: 6 I am weary with my **g**;
Ps   22: 1 from the words of My **g**?
Ps   32: 3 grew old Through my **g** all
John   11:38 again **g** in Himself, came to
Acts   7:34 I have heard their **g**

GROANINGS (*see* GROANING)
Ezek   30:24 groan before him with the **g**
Rom   8:26 intercession for us with **g**

GROANS† (*see* GROAN)
Rom   8:22 that the whole creation **g**

GROPE
Job   5:14 And **g** at noontime as in the
Job   12:25 They **g** in the dark without
Is   59:10 And we **g** as if we had no
Acts   17:27 the hope that they might **g**

GROUND (*see* GROUNDED)
Gen   2: 5 was no man to till the **g**;
Gen   2: 7 man of the dust of the **g**,
Gen   2: 9 And out of the **g** the LORD
Gen   3:17 Cursed is the **g** for your
Gen   3:19 Till you return to the **g**,
Gen   3:23 of Eden to till the **g** from
Gen   4: 2 Cain was a tiller of the **g**.
Gen   4:10 cries out to Me from the **g**.
Gen   8:21 never again curse the **g** for
Gen   18: 2 and bowed himself to the **g**,
Ex   3: 5 where you stand is holy **g**.
Ex   4: 3 He said, "Cast it on the **g**.
Ex   14:22 of the sea on the dry **g**,
Ex   32:20 and **g** it to powder; and he
Num   11:31 above the surface of the **g**.
Num   16:31 that the **g** split apart under
Deut   26: 2 of all the produce of the **g**,
Josh   24:32 in the plot of **g** which Jacob
Judg   6:40 there was dew on all the **g**.
2Sa   8: 2 Forcing them down to the **g**,
2Sa   17:12 as the dew falls on the **g**.
2Ki   2: 8 them crossed over on dry **g**.
Job   1:20 and he fell to the **g** and
Job   2:13 sat down with him on the **g**
Job   5: 6 trouble spring from the **g**;
Job   14: 8 its stump may die in the **g**,
Job   39:14 she leaves her eggs on the **g**,
Is   14:12 you are cut down to the **g**,
Is   29: 4 a medium's, out of the **g**;
Is   35: 7 The parched **g** shall become a
Is   44: 3 And floods on the dry **g**;
Is   53: 2 And as a root out of dry **g**.
Jer   4: 3 "Break up your fallow **g**,
Lam   5:13 Young men **g** at the
Dan   8: 5 without touching the **g**;
Dan   8: 7 he cast him down to the **g**
Hos   10:12 Break up your fallow **g**,
Amos   9: 9 grain shall fall to the **g**.
Hag   1:11 on whatever the **g** brings
Matt   13: 8 But others fell on good **g** and
Matt   15:35 to sit down on the **g**.
Matt   25:25 and hid your talent in the **g**.
Mark   4: 8 other seed fell on good **g**
Luke   12:16 The **g** of a certain rich man
Luke   14:18 'I have bought a piece of **g**,
Luke   22:44 blood falling down to the **g**.
John   4: 5 near the plot of **g** that
John   8: 6 down and wrote on the **g**
John   9: 6 He spat on the **g** and made
John   12:24 of wheat falls into the **g**
Acts   7:33 you stand is holy **g**.
Acts   9: 8 Then Saul arose from the **g**,

Acts   22: 7 And I fell to the **g** and heard
Acts   26:14 we all had fallen to the **g**,
1Ti   3:15 the pillar and **g** of the

GROUNDED† (*see* GROUND)
Eph   3:17 being rooted and **g** in love,
Col   1:23 **g** and steadfast, and are not

GROUP (*see* GROUPS)
1Sa   10:10 there was a **g** of prophets to

GROUPS† (*see* GROUP)
Mark   6:39 make them all sit down in **g**
Luke   9:14 Make them sit down in **g** of

GROVE (*see* GROVES)
Ex   23:11 vineyard and your olive **g**.

GROVES (*see* GROVE)
Josh   24:13 of the vineyards and olive **g**

GROW (*see* FULL-GROWN, GREW, GROWING, GROWN, GROWS, GROWTH)
Gen   2: 9 LORD God made every tree **g**
Num   6: 5 of the hair of his head **g**.
Judg   16:22 hair of his head began to **g**
Ps   102:26 they will all **g** old like a
Eccl   11: 5 Or how the bones **g** in the
Is   11: 1 And a Branch shall **g** out of
Is   51: 6 The earth will **g** old like a
Is   53: 2 For He shall **g** up before Him
Joel   3:15 The sun and moon will **g**
Jon   4:10 not labored, nor made it **g**,
Matt   6:28 of the field, how they **g**:
Matt   13:30 Let both **g** together until the
Matt   21:19 Let no fruit **g** on you ever
Matt   24:12 the love of many will **g**
Luke   12:33 money bags which do not **g**
Gal   6: 9 And let us not **g** weary while
Eph   4:15 may **g** up in all things into
2Th   3:13 do not **g** weary in doing
2Ti   3:13 men and impostors will **g**
Heb   1:11 And they will all **g**
1Pe   2: 2 that you may **g** thereby,
2Pe   3:18 but **g** in the grace and

GROWING (*see* GROW)
Jon   1:11 for the sea was **g** more
Heb   8:13 is becoming obsolete and **g**

GROWL
Ps   59: 6 They **g** like a dog, And go
Is   59:11 We all **g** like bears, And
Jer   51:38 They shall **g** like lions'

GROWN (*see* GROW)
Gen   2: 5 any herb of the field had **g**.
Gen   18:12 After I have **g** old, shall I
Ruth   1:13 for them till they were **g**?
2Sa   10: 5 until your beards have **g**,
Job   17: 7 My eye has also **g** dim
Is   37:27 blighted before it is **g**.
Dan   4:22 who have **g** and become
Dan   4:22 for your greatness has **g** and
Dan   4:33 heaven till his hair had **g**
Matt   13:15 of this people have **g**
Acts   28:27 of this people have **g**

GROWS (*see* GROW)
Lev   25:11 neither sow nor reap what **g**
Job   30:30 My skin **g** black and falls
Ps   90: 5 are like grass which **g** up
Ps   90: 6 morning it flourishes and **g**
Mark   4:32 it **g** up and becomes greater
Eph   2:21 **g** into a holy temple in the
2Th   1: 3 because your faith **g**

GROWTH (*see* GROW)
Ps   65:10 showers, You bless its **g**.
Eph   4:16 causes **g** of the body for the

GRUDGE† (*see* GRUDGING, GRUDGINGLY)
Lev 19:18 nor bear any **g** against the

GRUDGING† (*see* GRUDGE, GRUDGINGLY)
2Co 9: 5 generosity and not as a **g**

GRUDGINGLY† (*see* GRUDGE, GRUDGING)
2Co 9: 7 not **g** or of necessity; for

GRUMBLE† (*see* GRUMBLING)
Jas 5: 9 Do not **g** against one another,

GRUMBLING† (*see* GRUMBLE)
1Pe 4: 9 to one another without **g**.

GUARANTEE†
2Co 1:22 Spirit in our hearts as a **g**.
2Co 5: 5 given us the Spirit as a **g**.
Eph 1:14 who is the **g** of our

GUARD (*see* GUARDED, GUARDIAN, GUARDING, GUARDROOM, GUARDS)
Gen 3:24 to **g** the way to the tree of
Gen 37:36 and captain of the **g**.
Num 10:25 children of Dan (the rear **g**
1Sa 2: 9 He will **g** the feet of His
Job 7:12 That You set a **g** over me?
Ps 39: 1 I will **g** my ways, Lest I sin
Ps 141: 3 Set a **g**, O LORD, over
Mic 7: 5 G the doors of your mouth
Matt 27:66 the stone and setting the **g**.
Matt 28:11 some of the **g** came into the
Gal 3:23 we were kept under **g** by the
Phil 1:13 to the whole palace **g**,
Phil 4: 7 will **g** your hearts and minds
2Th 3: 3 who will establish you and **g**
1Ti 6:20 O Timothy! G what was

GUARDED (*see* GUARD)
Acts 28:16 with the soldier who **g** him.

GUARDIAN† (*see* GUARD, GUARDIANS)
Num 11:12 as a **g** carries a nursing
Acts 19:35 of the Ephesians is temple **g**

GUARDIANS (*see* GUARDIAN)
Gal 4: 2 but is under **g** and stewards

GUARDING (*see* GUARD)
Matt 27:54 who were **g** Jesus, saw the

GUARDROOM (*see* GUARD)
1Ki 14:28 brought them back into the **g**.

GUARDS (*see* GUARD)
Ps 34:20 He **g** all his bones; Not one
Ps 127: 1 Unless the LORD **g** the
Prov 13: 3 He who **g** his mouth preserves
Prov 22: 5 He who **g** his soul will be
Matt 28: 4 And the **g** shook for fear of
Acts 12: 6 and the **g** before the door

GUEST (*see* GUESTS)
Mark 14:14 Where is the **g** room in which
Phm 1:22 also prepare a **g** room for

GUESTS (*see* GUEST)
John 2:10 and when the **g** have well

GUIDANCE (*see* GUIDE)
1Ch 10:13 he consulted a medium for **g**.

GUIDE (*see* GUIDANCE, GUIDED, GUIDES, GUIDING)
Ps 31: 3 Lead me and **g** me.
Ps 32: 8 I will **g** you with My eye.
Ps 48:14 He will be our **g** Even to
Prov 23:19 And **g** your heart in the
Luke 1:79 To **g** our feet into the way
John 16:13 He will **g** you into all
Rom 2:19 that you yourself are a **g**

GUIDED (*see* GUIDE)
Ex 15:13 You have **g** them in Your

GUIDES (*see* GUIDE)
Ps 25: 9 The humble He **g** in justice,
Ps 107:30 So He **g** them to their
Matt 23:16 "Woe to you, blind **g**,
Acts 8:31 unless someone **g** me?" And

GUIDING (*see* GUIDE)
Eccl 2: 3 while **g** my heart with

GUILT (*see* GUILTLESS, GUILTY)
Lev 5: 1 not tell it, he bears **g**.
Deut 19:13 you shall put away the **g**
2Ch 28:13 for our **g** is great, and
Ezra 9:13 deeds and for our great **g**,
Ezek 18:19 the son not bear the **g** of
Ezek 18:20 nor the father bear the **g** of
Matt 23:32 measure of your fathers' **g**.

GUILTLESS (*see* GUILT)
Ex 20: 7 LORD will not hold him **g**
Deut 5:11 LORD will not hold him **g**
1Sa 26: 9 LORD's anointed, and be **g**?
Matt 12: 7 not have condemned the **g**.

GUILTY (*see* GUILT)
Ex 34: 7 by no means clearing the **g**,
Lev 6: 4 he has sinned and is **g**,
Num 14:18 by no means clears the **g**,
Num 35:27 he shall not be **g** of blood,
Ps 5:10 Pronounce them **g**,
Ps 109: 7 judged, let him be found **g**,
Prov 21: 8 The way of a **g** man is
Rom 3:19 all the world may become **g**
1Co 11:27 an unworthy manner will be **g**
Jas 2:10 he is **g** of all.

GULF†
Luke 16:26 and you there is a great **g**

GULLIBLE†
2Ti 3: 6 and make captives of **g**

GUSH† (*see* GUSHED)
Jer 9:18 And our eyelids **g** with

GUSHED (*see* GUSH)
Judg 5: 5 The mountains **g** before the
1Ki 18:28 until the blood **g** out on
Ps 105:41 and water **g** out; It ran in
Acts 1:18 and all his entrails **g** out.

H

HABAKKUK†
Hab 1: 1 burden which the prophet H
Hab 3: 1 A prayer of H the prophet, on

HABITATION (*see* HOME)
Ex 15:13 strength To Your holy **h**.
Ps 68: 5 Is God in His holy **h**.
Is 32:18 will dwell in a peaceful **h**,
Is 34:13 It shall be a **h** of jackals,
Is 63:15 heaven, And see from Your **h**,
Hab 3:11 moon stood still in their **h**;
2Co 5: 2 to be clothed with our **h**

HABITS†
1Co 15:33 company corrupts good **h**.

HACKED†
1Sa 15:33 And Samuel **h** Agag in

HADAD RIMMON†
Zech 12:11 like the mourning at H in the

HADADEZER
2Sa 8: 3 David also defeated H the
2Sa 8: 5 of Damascus came to help H
1Ch 18: 3 And David defeated H king of

HADASSAH† (see ESTHER)
Esth 2: 7 Mordecai had brought up H,

HADES
Matt 11:23 will be brought down to H;
Matt 16:18 and the gates of H shall not
Luke 16:23 "And being in torments in H,
Acts 2:27 not leave my soul in H,
1Co 15:55 is your sting? O H,
Rev 1:18 And I have the keys of H and
Rev 6: 8 and H followed with him. And
Rev 20:13 and Death and H delivered up
Rev 20:14 Then Death and H were cast

HAGAR
Gen 16: 3 took H her maid, the
Gen 16:15 So H bore Abram a son; and
Gen 21:17 the angel of God called to H
Gal 4:25 for this H is Mount Sinai in

HAGGAI
Ezra 5: 1 Then the prophet H and
Ezra 6:14 the prophesying of H the
Hag 1: 1 word of the LORD came by H

HAIL (see HAILSTONE)
Ex 9:18 I will cause very heavy h
Ex 9:23 the LORD sent thunder and h,
Ps 78:47 destroyed their vines with h,
Ps 148: 8 Fire and h, snow and clouds;
Matt 27:29 and mocked Him, saying, "H,
Mark 15:18 and began to salute Him, "H,
John 19: 3 Then they said, "H,
Rev 16:21 And great h from heaven fell
Rev 16:21 of the plague of the h,

HAILSTONE† (see HAIL, HAILSTONES)
Rev 16:21 each h about the weight of

HAILSTONES (see HAILSTONE)
Josh 10:11 the LORD cast down large h
Ps 18:13 H and coals of fire.
Is 30:30 scattering, tempest, and h.

HAIR (see HAIR'S, HAIRS, HAIRY)
Gen 42:38 would bring down my gray h
Ex 25: 4 fine linen, and goats' h;
Lev 13: 4 and its h has not turned
Lev 14: 9 day he shall shave all the h
Num 6: 5 let the locks of the h of
Num 6:19 shaved his consecrated h,
Judg 16:22 the h of his head began to
1Sa 14:45 not one h of his head shall
2Sa 14:26 he weighed the h of his head
Neh 13:25 them and pulled out their h,
Job 4:15 The h on my body stood up.
Song 4: 1 Your h is like a flock of
Is 7:20 The head and the h of the
Ezek 5: 1 to weigh and divide the h.
Ezek 8: 3 took me by a lock of my h;
Dan 3:27 the h of their head was not
Dan 4:33 the dew of heaven till his h
Dan 7: 9 And the h of His head was
Zech 13: 4 not wear a robe of coarse h
Matt 3: 4 was clothed in camel's h,
Matt 5:36 you cannot make one h white
Luke 7:38 and wiped them with the h
Luke 21:18 But not a h of your head
John 11: 2 wiped His feet with her h,
Acts 18:18 He had his h cut off at
Acts 27:34 since not a h will fall from
1Co 11:14 you that if a man has long h,
1Co 11:15 But if a woman has long h,
1Co 11:15 for her h is given to her
1Ti 2: 9 not with braided h or gold
1Pe 3: 3 outward—arranging the h,
Rev 1:14 His head and h were white

HAIR'S† (see HAIR)
Judg 20:16 could sling a stone at a h

HAIRS (see HAIR)
Lev 13:21 there are no white h in
Ps 40:12 They are more than the h of
Ps 69: 4 a cause Are more than the h
Matt 10:30 But the very h of your head

HAIRY (see HAIR)
Gen 25:25 He was like a h garment
Gen 27:11 Esau my brother is a h man,
Gen 27:23 because his hands were h
2Ki 1: 8 A h man wearing a leather

HALF
Gen 24:22 golden nose ring weighing h
Ex 24: 6 and h the blood he sprinkled
Ex 30:15 shall not give less than h
Num 12:12 whose flesh is h consumed
Num 32:33 and to h the tribe of
Josh 8:33 of Mount Gerizim and h of
2Sa 10: 4 shaved off h of their
1Ki 3:25 and give h to one, and half
1Ki 10: 7 and indeed the h was not
1Ki 16:21 h of the people followed
1Ki 16:21 and h followed Omri.
Neh 3: 9 leader of h the district of
Neh 4:16 that h of my servants
Neh 4:16 while the other h held the
Esth 5: 6 up to h the kingdom? It
Ps 55:23 men shall not live out h
Is 44:16 He burns h of it in the
Is 44:16 With this h he eats meat;
Dan 7:25 For a time and times and h
Dan 12: 7 and h a time; and when the
Zech 14: 2 H of the city shall go into
Zech 14: 4 H of the mountain shall
Mark 6:23 up to h of my kingdom."
Luke 10:30 leaving him h dead.
Luke 19: 8 I give h of my goods to the
Rev 8: 1 in heaven for about h an

HALF-SHEKEL†
Ex 30:13 The h shall be an offering

HALF-TRIBE
Num 34:13 the nine tribes and to the h.
Num 34:14 and the h of Manasseh has

HALL
1Ki 7: 6 He also made the H of
1Ki 7: 7 the H of Judgment, where he
1Ki 7:50 for the doors of the main h
Dan 5:10 lords, came to the banquet h.
Matt 22:10 And the wedding h was
Mark 15:16 led Him away into the h

HALLOW (see HALLOWED)
Num 20:12 to h Me in the eyes of the
Is 8:13 of hosts, Him you shall h;
Is 29:23 They will h My name, And
Jer 17:22 but h the Sabbath day, as I

HALLOWED (see HALLOW)
Ex 20:11 the Sabbath day and h it.
Ex 29:21 and his garments, shall be h,
Lev 12: 4 She shall not touch any h
Lev 19: 8 he has profaned the h
Lev 22:32 but I will be h among the
Is 5:16 God who is holy shall be h
Ezek 38:16 when I am h in you, O Gog,
Matt 6: 9 H be Your name.
Luke 11: 2 H be Your name. Your

HAM
Gen 5:32 old, and Noah begot Shem, H,
Gen 6:10 begot three sons: Shem, H,
Gen 9:18 And H was the father of

1Ch 1: 4 Noah, Shem, **H**,
Ps 78:51 strength in the tents of **H**.
Ps 105:23 Jacob dwelt in the land of **H**.
Ps 105:27 wonders in the land of **H**.

HAMAN (*see* HAMAN'S)
Esth 3: 1 King Ahasuerus promoted **H**,
Esth 3: 5 When **H** saw that Mordecai did
Esth 6:13 When **H** told his wife Zeresh
Esth 7: 6 this wicked Haman!" So **H**
Esth 7:10 So they hanged **H** on the
Esth 9:10 the ten sons of **H** the son of

HAMAN'S (*see* HAMAN)
Esth 9:13 and let **H** ten sons be hanged

HAMATH
Num 34: 8 border to the entrance of **H**;
2Ki 14:28 Israel, from Damascus and **H**,
2Ki 18:34 Where are the gods of **H** and
2Ki 19:13 'Where is the king of **H**,
Amos 6: 2 And from there go to **H** the

HAMMEDATHA
Esth 9:10 sons of Haman the son of **H**,

HAMMER (*see* HAMMERED, HAMMERS)
Judg 4:21 a tent peg and took a **h** in
Judg 5:26 hand to the workmen's **h**;
Jer 23:29 And like a **h** that breaks the
Jer 50:23 How the **h** of the whole earth

HAMMERED (*see* HAMMER)
Ex 25:18 of **h** work you shall make
Num 8: 4 of the lampstand was **h**
1Ki 10:17 three hundred shields of **h**
2Ch 9:15 six hundred shekels of **h**

HAMMERS (*see* HAMMER)
Is 44:12 coals, Fashions it with **h**,
Jer 10: 4 fasten it with nails and **h**

HAMON GOG (*see* GOG)
Ezek 39:11 will call it the Valley of **H**

HAMOR
Gen 34: 4 spoke to his father **H**,
Gen 34:26 And they killed **H** and Shechem

HAMSTRING† (*see* HAMSTRUNG)
Josh 11: 6 You shall **h** their horses and

HAMSTRUNG (*see* HAMSTRING)
Gen 49: 6 in their self-will they **h**
Josh 11: 9 he **h** their horses and burned
2Sa 8: 4 Also David **h** all the chariot

HANANIAH (*see* SHADRACH)
Jer 28: 5 spoke to the prophet **H** in
Jer 28:17 So **H** the prophet died the
Dan 1: 6 sons of Judah were Daniel, **H**,
Dan 1: 7 name Belteshazzar; to **H**,

HAND (*see* HANDED, HANDFUL, HANDIWORK, HANDS, MEANS)
Gen 3:22 lest he put out his **h** and
Gen 4:11 brother's blood from your **h**.
Gen 9: 2 They are given into your **h**.
Gen 9: 5 and from the **h** of man. From
Gen 14:20 your enemies into your **h**.
Gen 14:22 I have raised my **h** to the
Gen 22: 6 he took the fire in his **h**,
Gen 22:10 Abraham stretched out his **h**
Gen 22:12 Do not lay your **h** on the lad,
Gen 24: 2 put your **h** under my thigh,
Gen 24:49 I may turn to the right **h**
Gen 31:39 You required it from my **h**,
Gen 32:11 from the **h** of Esau; for I
Gen 38:18 staff that is in your **h**.
Gen 38:29 as he drew back his **h**,
Gen 38:30 the scarlet thread on his **h**.
Gen 39: 3 he did to prosper in his **h**.

Gen 39: 6 that he had in Joseph's **h**,
Gen 39:12 he left his garment in her **h**,
Gen 40:11 Pharaoh's cup was in my **h**;
Gen 41:42 his signet ring off his **h**
Gen 44:17 the man in whose **h** the cup
Gen 46: 4 and Joseph will put his **h** on
Gen 48:13 Ephraim with his right **h**
Gen 49: 8 Your **h** shall be on the
Ex 3: 8 to deliver them out of the **h**
Ex 3:19 no, not even by a mighty **h**.
Ex 3:20 So I will stretch out My **h**
Ex 4: 2 "What is that in your **h**?
Ex 4: 4 Reach out your **h** and take it
Ex 4: 4 it became a rod in his **h**),
Ex 4: 6 Now put your **h** in your
Ex 4: 6 his **h** was leprous, like
Ex 5:21 to put a sword in their **h** to
Ex 6: 1 and with a strong **h** he will
Ex 7: 5 when I stretch out My **h** on
Ex 8: 6 So Aaron stretched out his **h**
Ex 9: 3 the **h** of the LORD will be
Ex 13: 3 for by strength of **h** the
Ex 13: 9 as a sign to you on your **h**
Ex 14:16 and stretch out your **h** over
Ex 14:22 to them on their right **h**
Ex 15: 6 "Your right **h**,
Ex 15: 6 in power; Your right **h**,
Ex 15:20 took the timbrel in her **h**;
Ex 16: 3 that we had died by the **h** of
Ex 17:11 when Moses held up his **h**,
Ex 18: 9 had delivered out of the **h**
Ex 19:13 Not a **h** shall touch him, but
Ex 21:24 tooth for tooth, hand for **h**,
Ex 29:20 the thumb of their right **h**
Ex 32:11 power and with a mighty **h**?
Ex 33:22 and will cover you with My **h**
Lev 4: 4 lay his **h** on the bull's
Lev 21:19 a broken foot or broken **h**,
Num 5:25 jealousy from the woman's **h**,
Num 27:18 and lay your **h** on him;
Num 35:21 he strikes him with his **h**
Deut 2: 7 in all the work of your **h**.
Deut 2:15 For indeed the **h** of the LORD
Deut 3:24 greatness and Your mighty **h**,
Deut 5:15 out from there by a mighty **h**
Deut 6: 8 them as a sign on your **h**,
Deut 10: 3 the two tablets in my **h**.
Deut 11:18 them as a sign on your **h**,
Deut 14:25 take the money in your **h**,
Deut 15: 9 the year of release, is at **h**,
Deut 15:10 all to which you put your **h**.
Deut 19:21 **h** for hand, foot for foot.
Deut 19:21 tooth for tooth, hand for **h**,
Deut 25:12 you shall cut off her **h**;
Deut 28:12 bless all the work of your **h**.
Deut 32:35 of their calamity is at **h**,
Deut 32:39 who can deliver from My **h**.
Deut 32:40 For I raise My **h** to heaven,
Deut 33: 3 His saints are in Your **h**;
Josh 5:13 His sword drawn in His **h**.
Josh 6: 2 given Jericho into your **h**,
Josh 10:32 Lachish into the **h** of
Josh 14: 2 had commanded by the **h** of
Josh 20: 5 the slayer into his **h**,
Judg 2:15 the **h** of the LORD was
Judg 2:16 delivered them out of the **h**
Judg 2:23 deliver them into the **h**
Judg 3: 8 and He sold them into the **h**
Judg 3:21 Ehud reached with his left **h**,
Judg 4: 9 will sell Sisera into the **h**
Judg 4:21 and took a hammer in her **h**,
Judg 5:26 She stretched her **h** to the
Judg 7: 2 My own **h** has saved me.'
Judg 7:16 a trumpet into every man's **h**,
Judg 9:48 took an ax in his **h** and cut

Judg	14: 6	he had nothing in his **h**.
Judg	15:12	may deliver you into the **h**
Judg	15:18	thirst and fall into the **h**
Judg	16:26	lad who held him by the **h**,
Judg	18:19	put your **h** over your mouth,
1Sa	5: 7	for His **h** is harsh toward us
1Sa	5:11	the **h** of God was very heavy
1Sa	12: 3	or from whose **h** have I
1Sa	12: 4	anything from any man's **h**.
1Sa	14:19	priest, "Withdraw your **h**.
1Sa	14:26	but no one put his **h** to his
1Sa	16:23	harp and play it with his **h**.
1Sa	17:40	and his sling was in his **h**.
1Sa	17:49	Then David put his **h** in his
1Sa	17:50	was no sword in the **h** of
1Sa	18:10	was a spear in Saul's **h**.
1Sa	23:16	and strengthened his **h** in
1Sa	24: 6	to stretch out my **h** against
1Sa	24:18	delivered me into your **h**,
1Sa	25:33	myself with my own **h**.
1Sa	26: 9	who can stretch out his **h**
1Sa	27: 1	I shall escape out of his **h**.
2Sa	3:18	By the **h** of My servant David,
2Sa	4:11	require his blood at your **h**
2Sa	6: 6	Uzzah put out his **h** to the
2Sa	13: 6	that I may eat from her **h**.
2Sa	13:19	and laid her **h** on her head
2Sa	14:19	Is the **h** of Joab with you in
2Sa	18:14	took three spears in his **h**
2Sa	20:10	sword that was in Joab's **h**.
2Sa	21:20	had six fingers on each **h**
2Sa	24:14	let us fall into the **h** of
2Sa	24:14	not let me fall into the **h**
2Sa	24:16	enough; now restrain your **h**.
1Ki	2:19	so she sat at his right **h**.
1Ki	8:15	and with His **h** has fulfilled
1Ki	8:42	name and Your strong **h** and
1Ki	13: 6	and the king's **h** was
1Ki	18:44	cloud, as small as a man's **h**,
2Ki	4:29	and take my staff in your **h**,
2Ki	5:11	and wave his **h** over the
2Ki	9: 1	this flask of oil in your **h**,
2Ki	14: 5	was established in his **h**,
2Ki	18:21	it will go into his **h** and
2Ki	18:34	delivered Samaria from my **h**?
2Ki	18:35	deliver Jerusalem from my **h**?
2Ki	22: 5	them deliver it into the **h**
2Ki	22: 7	money delivered into their **h**,
1Ch	13: 9	Uzza put out his **h** to hold
1Ch	21:16	having in his **h** a drawn
1Ch	29:12	In Your **h** is power and
2Ch	3:17	of the one on the right **h**
2Ch	6:32	name and Your mighty **h** and
Ezra	7: 9	according to the good **h** of
Neh	1:10	power, and by Your strong **h**
Neh	2: 8	me according to the good **h**
Esth	3:10	his signet ring from his **h**
Esth	8: 7	he tried to lay his **h** on
Job	1:11	stretch out Your **h** and touch
Job	1:12	only do not lay a **h** on his
Job	6: 9	That He would loose His **h**
Job	9:33	Who may lay his **h** on us
Job	13:21	Withdraw Your **h** far from me,
Job	21: 5	Put your **h** over your
Job	26:13	His **h** pierced the fleeing
Job	28: 9	He puts his **h** on the flint;
Job	30:21	the strength of Your **h** You
Job	31:27	my mouth has kissed my **h**;
Job	33: 7	Nor will my **h** be heavy on
Job	35: 7	does He receive from your **h**?
Ps	10:12	lift up Your **h**! Do not
Ps	16: 8	He is at my right **h** I
Ps	16:11	At Your right **h** are
Ps	31: 5	Into Your **h** I commit my
Ps	31: 8	not shut me up into the **h**

Ps	31:15	My times are in Your **h**;
Ps	32: 4	For day and night Your **h** was
Ps	37:24	upholds him with His **h**.
Ps	45: 4	And Your right **h** shall
Ps	63: 8	Your right **h** upholds me.
Ps	71: 4	out of the **h** of the wicked,
Ps	77:10	the years of the right **h** of
Ps	78:54	mountain which His right **h**
Ps	80:17	upon the man of Your right **h**,
Ps	89:25	Also I will set his **h** over
Ps	89:42	have exalted the right **h** of
Ps	91: 7	ten thousand at your right **h**;
Ps	95: 7	And the sheep of His **h**.
Ps	98: 1	His right **h** and His holy
Ps	108: 6	Save with Your right **h**,
Ps	110: 1	Lord, "Sit at My right **h**,
Ps	110: 5	Lord is at Your right **h**;
Ps	121: 5	your shade at your right **h**.
Ps	127: 4	Like arrows in the **h** of a
Ps	136:12	With a strong **h**,
Ps	137: 5	Let my right **h** forget its
Ps	138: 7	And Your right **h** will save
Ps	139: 5	And laid Your **h** upon me.
Ps	139:10	Even there Your **h** shall lead
Ps	139:10	And Your right **h** shall hold
Prov	3:16	of days is in her right **h**,
Prov	3:27	it is in the power of your **h**
Prov	6: 3	you have come into the **h** of
Prov	12:24	The **h** of the diligent will
Prov	19:24	A lazy man buries his **h** in
Prov	21: 1	king's heart is in the **h**
Prov	26: 9	thorn that goes into the **h**
Prov	26:15	The lazy man buries his **h**
Prov	31:19	And her **h** holds the
Prov	31:20	She extends her **h** to the
Eccl	2:24	was from the **h** of God.
Eccl	9: 1	their works are in the **h**
Eccl	9:10	Whatever your **h** finds to do,
Eccl	11: 6	do not withhold your **h**;
Song	2: 6	And his right **h** embraces
Song	8: 3	And his right **h** embraces
Is	1:12	required this from your **h**,
Is	6: 6	having in his **h** a live coal
Is	9:12	But His **h** is stretched out
Is	11: 8	child shall put his **h** in
Is	13: 6	day of the LORD is at **h**!
Is	40: 2	received from the LORD's **h**
Is	40:12	in the hollow of His **h**,
Is	41:10	with My righteous right **h**.
Is	41:13	God, will hold your right **h**,
Is	45: 1	whose right **h** I have
Is	49:22	I will lift My **h** in an oath
Is	50: 2	is My **h** shortened at all
Is	51:16	you with the shadow of My **h**,
Is	53:10	LORD shall prosper in His **h**.
Is	59: 1	the LORD's **h** is not
Is	62: 8	has sworn by His right **h**
Is	64: 8	we are the work of Your **h**.
Jer	1: 9	the LORD put forth His **h**
Jer	15:17	sat alone because of Your **h**,
Jer	18: 4	of clay was marred in the **h**
Jer	18: 6	clay is in the potter's **h**,
Jer	18: 6	hand, so are you in My **h**,
Jer	22:24	the signet on My right **h**,
Jer	25:15	wine cup of fury from My **h**,
Jer	36:14	Take in your **h** the scroll
Jer	40: 4	chains that were on your **h**.
Jer	43: 9	large stones in your **h**,
Jer	44:30	his enemies and into the **h**
Lam	1: 7	her people fell into the **h**
Lam	4: 6	With no **h** to help her!
Ezek	1: 3	and the **h** of the LORD was
Ezek	3:18	I will require at your **h**.
Ezek	10: 8	have the form of a man's **h**
Ezek	20: 5	Israel and raised My **h** in

Ezek 20:34 scattered, with a mighty **h**,
Ezek 33: 8 I will require at your **h**.
Ezek 37:17 will become one in your **h**.
Dan 3:17 will deliver us from your **h**,
Dan 4:35 No one can restrain His **h**
Dan 5: 5 the fingers of a man's **h**
Dan 7:25 shall be given into his **h**
Hos 11: 8 How can I **h** you over,
Hos 12: 7 scales are in his **h**;
Joel 1:15 day of the LORD is at **h**;
Amos 5:19 Leaned his **h** on the wall,
Amos 7: 7 with a plumb line in His **h**.
Jon 4:11 between their right **h** and
Mic 2: 1 is in the power of their **h**.
Mic 4:10 will redeem you From the **h**
Zeph 1: 7 day of the LORD is at **h**,
Zech 2: 1 a measuring line in his **h**.
Zech 4:10 The plumb line in the **h** of
Zech 13: 7 Then I will turn My **h**
Mal 1:13 I accept this from your **h**?
Matt 3: 2 kingdom of heaven is at **h**!
Matt 3:12 winnowing fan is in His **h**,
Matt 5:25 the judge **h** you over to the
Matt 5:30 And if your right **h** causes
Matt 6: 3 do not let your left **h** know
Matt 8: 3 Then Jesus put out His **h** and
Matt 8:15 So He touched her **h**,
Matt 12:10 a man who had a withered **h**.
Matt 20:21 one on Your right **h** and the
Matt 22:44 "Sit at My right **h**,
Matt 25:33 set the sheep on His right **h**,
Matt 26:18 says, "My time is at **h**;
Matt 26:23 He who dipped his **h** with Me
Matt 26:45 Behold, the hour is at **h**,
Mark 1:15 the kingdom of God is at **h**.
Mark 3: 5 and his **h** was restored as
Mark 5:41 He took the child by the **h**,
Mark 8:23 took the blind man by the **h**
Mark 16:19 and sat down at the right **h**
Luke 1: 1 as many have taken in **h** to
Luke 1:66 And the **h** of the Lord was
Luke 9:62 having put his **h** to the
Luke 15:22 and put a ring on his **h** and
Luke 23:33 one on the right **h** and the
John 3:35 given all things into His **h**.
John 7: 2 of Tabernacles was at **h**.
John 7:30 but no one laid a **h** on Him,
John 10:28 snatch them out of My **h**.
John 10:29 them out of My Father's **h**.
John 20:25 and put my **h** into His side,
Acts 2:33 exalted to the right **h** of
Acts 7:50 Has My **h** not made all
Acts 9:12 in and putting his **h** on
Acts 26: 1 So Paul stretched out his **h**
Acts 28: 3 heat, and fastened on his **h**.
Rom 13:12 far spent, the day is at **h**.
1Co 12:15 say, "Because I am not a **h**,
1Co 16:21 The salutation with my own **h**—
Gal 2: 9 me and Barnabas the right **h**
Gal 3:19 through angels by the **h** of
Gal 6:11 to you with my own **h**!
Phil 4: 5 all men. The Lord is at **h**.
2Ti 4: 6 time of my departure is at **h**.
Phm 1:19 am writing with my own **h**.
Heb 1: 3 sat down at the right **h** of
Heb 1:13 "Sit at My right **h**,
Jas 5: 8 coming of the Lord is at **h**.
1Pe 4: 7 end of all things is at **h**;
1Pe 5: 6 under the mighty **h** of God,
Rev 1:16 He had in His right **h** seven
Rev 1:17 But He laid His right **h** on
Rev 6: 5 a pair of scales in his **h**.
Rev 10: 2 a little book open in his **h**.
Rev 10: 5 on the land raised up his **h**
Rev 13:16 a mark on their right **h** or

HANDBREADTH (see HANDBREADTHS)
Ex 25:25 make for it a frame of a **h**

HANDBREADTHS† (see HANDBREADTH)
Ps 39: 5 You have made my days as **h**,

HANDED (see HAND)
Mark 7:13 tradition which you have **h**
Mark 15:10 the chief priests had **h** Him

HANDFUL (see HAND)
Lev 2: 2 shall take from it his **h** of
Eccl 4: 6 Better a **h** with quietness

HANDIWORK† (see HAND)
Ps 19: 1 the firmament shows His **h**.
Is 45: 9 Or shall your **h** say, 'He

HANDKERCHIEF† (see HANDKERCHIEFS)
Luke 19:20 I have kept put away in a **h**.
John 20: 7 and the **h** that had been

HANDKERCHIEFS† (see HANDKERCHIEF)
Acts 19:12 so that even **h** or aprons were

HANDLE (see HANDLED)
Deut 19: 5 the head slips from the **h**
1Ch 12: 8 who could **h** shield and
Ps 115: 7 hands, but they do not **h**;
Jer 2: 8 And those who **h** the law
Luke 24:39 **H** Me and see, for a spirit

HANDLED (see HANDLE)
1Jn 1: 1 upon, and our hands have **h**,

HANDMILL†
Ex 11: 5 servant who is behind the **h**,

HANDS (see ARMS, HAND)
Gen 5:29 work and the toil of our **h**,
Gen 20: 5 heart and innocence of my **h**
Gen 27:16 kids of the goats on his **h**
Gen 27:22 but the hands are the **h** of
Gen 27:23 because his **h** were hairy
Ex 9:29 I will spread out my **h** to
Ex 17:12 But Moses' **h** became heavy;
Ex 17:12 and Hur supported his **h**,
Ex 29:10 his sons shall put their **h**
Ex 32:19 the tablets out of his **h**
Lev 8:24 the thumbs of their right **h**,
Lev 16:21 Aaron shall lay both his **h** on
Deut 1:25 of the land in their **h** and
Deut 4:28 gods, the work of men's **h**,
Deut 21: 7 Our **h** have not shed His **h**
Deut 34: 9 for Moses had laid his **h** on
Josh 2:24 all the land into our **h**,
Judg 2:14 He delivered them into the **h**
Judg 2:14 and He sold them into the **h**
Judg 12: 3 I took my life in my **h** and
Judg 15:14 bonds broke loose from his **h**.
Judg 16:23 god has delivered into our **h**
1Sa 21:13 feigned madness in their **h**,
2Sa 4:12 cut off their **h** and feet,
2Sa 22:35 He teaches my **h** to make war,
1Ki 8:54 on his knees with his **h**
2Ki 4:34 and his **h** on his hands; and
2Ki 11:12 and they clapped their **h** and
Ezra 5: 8 and prospers in their **h**.
Ezra 9: 5 my knees and spread out my **h**
Neh 2:18 Then they set their **h** to
Neh 6: 9 O God, strengthen my **h**.
Esth 2:21 furious and sought to lay **h**
Job 1:10 blessed the work of his **h**,
Job 9:30 And cleanse my **h** with soap,
Job 10: 3 despise the work of Your **h**,
Job 10: 8 Your **h** have made me and
Job 16:17 no violence is in my **h**,
Job 27:23 Men shall clap their **h** at
Ps 7: 3 there is iniquity in my **h**,
Ps 8: 6 over the works of Your **h**;

Ps 18:34 He teaches my **h** to make war,
Ps 22:16 They pierced My **h** and My
Ps 24: 4 He who has clean **h** and a
Ps 26: 6 I will wash my **h** in
Ps 28: 2 When I lift up my **h** toward
Ps 44:20 Or stretched out our **h** to a
Ps 47: 1 Oh, clap your **h**,
Ps 63: 4 I will lift up my **h** in Your
Ps 68:31 quickly stretch out her **h**
Ps 73:13 And washed my **h** in
Ps 90:17 establish the work of our **h**.
Ps 91:12 In their **h** they shall bear
Ps 95: 5 And His **h** formed the dry
Ps 98: 8 the rivers clap their **h**;
Ps 115: 4 gold, The work of men's **h**.
Ps 138: 8 forsake the works of Your **h**.
Prov 6:10 A little folding of the **h**
Prov 6:17 **H** that shed innocent blood,
Prov 17:18 of understanding shakes **h**
Prov 31:13 willingly works with her **h**.
Prov 31:19 She stretches out her **h** to
Prov 31:20 she reaches out her **h** to the
Prov 31:31 her of the fruit of her **h**,
Eccl 2:11 on all the works that my **h**
Song 5: 5 And my **h** dripped with
Is 1:15 Your **h** are full of blood.
Is 19:25 and Assyria the work of My **h**,
Is 35: 3 Strengthen the weak **h**,
Is 37:19 but the work of men's **h**—
Is 45: 9 say, 'He has no **h**'?
Is 45:12 created man on it. I—My **h**—
Is 55:12 field shall clap their **h**.
Is 59: 6 of violence is in their **h**.
Is 65: 2 I have stretched out My **h**
Jer 2:37 forth from him With your **h**
Jer 6:24 Our **h** grow feeble. Anguish
Lam 2:15 who pass by clap their **h**
Lam 3:41 us lift our hearts and **h**
Ezek 1: 8 The **h** of a man were under
Ezek 21: 7 all **h** will be feeble, every
Ezek 21:14 And strike your **h**
Ezek 23:37 and blood is on their **h**.
Ezek 23:45 and blood is on their **h**.
Dan 2:34 stone was cut out without **h**,
Dan 3:15 will deliver you from my **h**?
Hos 14: 3 anymore to the work of our **h**,
Hag 1:11 on all the labor of your **h**.
Zech 4: 9 The **h** of Zerubbabel Have
Zech 4: 9 His **h** shall also finish
Matt 4: 6 In their **h** they shall
Matt 15:20 but to eat with unwashed **h**
Matt 17:12 about to suffer at their **h**.
Matt 17:22 to be betrayed into the **h**
Matt 18:28 and he laid **h** on him and
Matt 26:45 is being betrayed into the **h**
Matt 26:50 Then they came and laid **h**
Matt 26:67 with the palms of their **h**,
Matt 27:24 took water and washed his **h**
Mark 5:23 Come and lay Your **h** on her,
Mark 7: 5 eat bread with unwashed **h**?
Mark 8:25 Then He put His **h** on his
Mark 14:58 this temple made with **h**,
Mark 16:18 they will lay **h** on the sick,
Luke 6: 1 rubbing them in their **h**.
Luke 23:46 into Your **h** I commit My
Luke 24:39 Behold My **h** and My feet, that
Luke 24:40 He showed them His **h** and His
John 7:44 but no one laid **h** on Him.
John 13: 3 given all things into His **h**,
John 13: 9 but also my **h** and my
John 19: 3 they struck Him with their **h**.
John 20:20 He showed them His **h** and
John 20:25 Unless I see in His **h** the
Acts 2:23 you have taken by lawless **h**,
Acts 5:18 and laid their **h** on the

Acts 7:48 dwell in temples made with **h**,
Acts 12: 7 his chains fell off his **h**.
Acts 17:25 is He worshiped with men's **h**,
Acts 19:26 gods which are made with **h**.
Rom 10:21 stretched out My **h** To
1Co 4:12 working with our own **h**.
2Co 5: 1 God, a house not made with **h**,
2Co 11:33 wall, and escaped from his **h**.
Col 2:11 circumcision made without **h**,
1Th 4:11 and to work with your own **h**,
1Ti 2: 8 lifting up holy **h**,
Heb 1:10 are the work of Your **h**.
Heb 6: 2 baptisms, of laying on of **h**,
Heb 9:11 tabernacle not made with **h**,
Heb 10:31 thing to fall into the **h** of
Heb 12:12 Therefore strengthen the **h**
Jas 4: 8 near to you. Cleanse your **h**,
1Jn 1: 1 and our **h** have handled,
Rev 7: 9 palm branches in their **h**,
Rev 20: 4 foreheads or on their **h**.

HANDSOME
Gen 39: 6 Now Joseph was **h** in form and
1Sa 16:18 and a **h** person; and the
Song 1:16 Behold, you are **h**,

HANDWRITING†
Col 2:14 having wiped out the **h** of

HANG (*see* HANGED, HANGING, HANGS, HUNG)
Gen 40:19 off your head from you and **h**
Matt 22:40 these two commandments **h**
Heb 12:12 the hands which **h** down,

HANGED (*see* HANG)
Gen 40:22 But he **h** the chief baker, as
Deut 21:23 for he who is **h** is accursed
2Sa 17:23 and **h** himself, and died; and
Esth 7:10 So they **h** Haman on the
Matt 27: 5 and went and **h** himself.
Luke 23:39 of the criminals who were **h**

HANGING (*see* HANG, HANGINGS)
2Sa 18: 9 so he was left **h** between
2Sa 18:10 I just saw Absalom **h** in a

HANGINGS (*see* HANGING)
Ex 35:17 the **h** of the court, its

HANGS† (*see* HANG)
Job 26: 7 He **h** the earth on nothing.
Gal 3:13 is everyone who **h** on

HANNAH
1Sa 1: 2 but **H** had no children.
1Sa 1: 5 portion, for he loved **H**,
1Sa 1:19 And Elkanah knew **H** his wife,

HAPPIER† (*see* HAPPY)
1Co 7:40 But she is **h** if she remains

HAPPINESS† (*see* HAPPY)
Deut 24: 5 and bring **h** to his wife whom

HAPPY (*see* BLESSED, HAPPIER, HAPPINESS)
1Ki 10: 8 **H** are your men and happy
Job 5:17 **h** is the man whom God
Ps 127: 5 **H** is the man who has his
Ps 137: 8 **H** the one who repays you as
Ps 144:15 **H** are the people whose God
Rom 14:22 **H** is he who does not

HARAN (*see* BETH HARAN)
Gen 11:26 begot Abram, Nahor, and **H**.
Gen 11:27 **H** begot Lot.
Gen 11:32 years, and Terah died in **H**.
Acts 7: 2 before he dwelt in **H**,

HARASS (*see* HARASSED)
Acts 12: 1 out his hand to **h** some

HARASSED (*see* HARASS)
Judg 2:18 who oppressed them and **h**

HARBOR (*see* HARBORED)
Acts 27:12 a **h** of Crete opening toward

HARBORED† (*see* HARBOR)
Acts 17: 7 Jason has **h** them, and these

HARD (*see* HARDEN, HARDER, HARDNESS, HARDSHIP)
Gen 18:14 Is anything too **h** for the
Gen 35:16 and she had **h** labor.
Ex 1:14 their lives bitter with **h**
Ex 7:13 And Pharaoh's heart grew **h**,
Ex 18:26 the **h** cases they brought to
2Sa 1: 6 and horsemen followed **h**
1Ki 10: 1 she came to test him with **h**
2Ki 2:10 You have asked a **h** thing.
1Ch 10: 2 the Philistines followed **h**
Job 14:14 All the days of my **h**
Job 41:24 His heart is as **h** as stone,
Jer 32:17 There is nothing too **h** for
Jon 1:13 the men rowed **h** to return
Matt 13:15 Their ears are **h** of
Matt 19:23 I say to you that it is **h**
Matt 23: 4 **h** to bear, and lay them on
Matt 25:24 I knew you to be a **h** man,
Acts 9: 5 It is **h** for you to kick
Acts 26:14 It is **h** for you to kick
2Co 4: 8 We are **h** pressed on every
Heb 5:11 and **h** to explain, since you
2Pe 3:16 in which are some things **h**

HARD-HEARTED†
Ezek 3: 7 Israel are impudent and **h**.

HARD-WORKING†
2Ti 2: 6 The **h** farmer must be first to

HARDEN (*see* HARD, HARDENED, HARDENS)
Ex 7: 3 And I will **h** Pharaoh's heart,
Ps 95: 8 Do not **h** your hearts, as in
Heb 3: 8 Do not **h** your hearts

HARDENED (*see* BLINDED, HARDEN)
Ex 10:20 But the LORD **h** Pharaoh's
Neh 9:16 **H** their necks, And did not
Dan 5:20 and his spirit was **h** in
Mark 6:52 because their heart was **h**.
Heb 3:13 lest any of you be **h**

HARDENS (*see* HARDEN)
Prov 28:14 But he who **h** his heart will
Prov 29: 1 and **h** his neck, Will
Rom 9:18 and whom He wills He **h**.

HARDER (*see* HARD)
Jer 5: 3 have made their faces **h**
Ezek 3: 9 **h** than flint, I have made

HARDNESS (*see* HARD)
Matt 19: 8 because of the **h** of your

HARDSHIP (*see* HARD)
Ex 18: 8 all the **h** that had come upon
2Ti 2: 3 You therefore must endure **h**

HARLOT (*see* HARLOTRY, HARLOTS)
Gen 34:31 he treat our sister like a **h**?
Gen 38:15 her, he thought she was a **h**,
Ex 34:16 and his daughters play the **h**
Lev 21: 7 take a wife who is a **h** or
Deut 23:17 shall be no ritual **h** of
Josh 2: 1 and came to the house of a **h**
Judg 11: 1 but he was the son of a **h**;
Judg 16: 1 went to Gaza and saw a **h**
Prov 7:10 With the attire of a **h**,
Prov 23:27 For a **h** is a deep pit, And
Is 1:21 city has become a **h**! It
Ezek 16:30 the deeds of a brazen **h**.
Ezek 16:34 one solicited you to be a **h**.

Hos 2: 5 mother has played the **h**;
Amos 7:17 Your wife shall be a **h** in the
1Co 6:15 make them members of a **h**?
1Co 6:16 he who is joined to a **h** is
Heb 11:31 By faith the **h** Rahab did not
Jas 2:25 was not Rahab the **h** also
Rev 17: 1 the judgment of the great **h**

HARLOTRIES (*see* HARLOTRY)
Jer 3: 2 the land With your **h** and

HARLOTRY (*see* HARLOT, HARLOTRIES)
Gen 38:24 she is with child by **h**.
Num 25: 1 the people began to commit **h**
Ezek 16:25 multiplied your acts of **h**.
Hos 1: 2 take yourself a wife of **h**
Hos 1: 2 land has committed great **h**
Hos 5: 4 For the spirit of **h** is in

HARLOTS (*see* HARLOT)
1Ki 3:16 Now two women who were **h**
1Ki 22:38 up his blood while the **h**
Matt 21:31 that tax collectors and **h**
Matt 21:32 but tax collectors and **h**
Luke 15:30 your livelihood with **h**,
Rev 17: 5 THE MOTHER OF H

HARM (*see* HARMFUL, HARMLESS)
Gen 26:29 'that you will do us no **h**,
Gen 31:29 is in my power to do you **h**,
Ex 21:23 But if any **h** follows, then
Lev 5:16 make restitution for the **h**
Num 35:23 his enemy or seeking his **h**,
Josh 24:20 He will turn and do you **h**
1Sa 24: 9 'Indeed David seeks your **h**'?
2Sa 12:18 He may do some **h**!"
2Sa 20: 6 of Bichri will do us more **h**
1Ch 16:22 And do My prophets no **h**.
Neh 6: 2 But they thought to do me **h**.
Joel 2:13 And He relents from doing **h**.
Amos 9: 4 set My eyes on them for **h**
Mic 3:11 No **h** can come upon us."
Acts 9:13 how much he has done to
Acts 16:28 saying, "Do yourself no **h**,
Acts 28: 5 the fire and suffered no **h**.
Rom 13:10 Love does no **h** to a neighbor;

HARMFUL (*see* HARM)
Eccl 8: 5 will experience nothing **h**;
1Ti 6: 9 and into many foolish and **h**

HARMLESS† (*see* HARM)
Matt 10:16 be wise as serpents and **h**
Phil 2:15 may become blameless and **h**,
Heb 7:26 for us, who is holy, **h**,

HARP (*see* HARPS)
Gen 4:21 of all those who play the **h**
1Sa 16:16 a skillful player on the **h**;
1Sa 16:23 that David would take a **h**
Job 21:12 sing to the tambourine and **h**
Ps 33: 2 Praise the LORD with the **h**;
Ps 57: 8 lute and **h**! I will awaken
Ps 98: 5 to the LORD with the **h**,
Ps 144: 9 On a **h** of ten strings I
Is 24: 8 The joy of the **h** ceases.
Dan 3: 5 sound of the horn, flute, **h**,
1Co 14: 7 life, whether flute or **h**,
Rev 5: 8 the Lamb, each having a **h**,

HARPS (*see* HARP)
1Ch 13: 8 might, with singing, on **h**,
1Ch 15:28 stringed instruments and **h**.
1Ch 25: 1 who should prophesy with **h**,
Ps 137: 2 We hung our **h** Upon the
Rev 15: 2 having **h** of God.

HARSH (*see* HARSHLY)
1Sa 5: 7 for His hand is **h** toward us

1Sa   25: 3 but the man was **h** and evil
Prov 15: 1 But a **h** word stirs up
Mal   3:13 Your words have been **h**

HARSHLY (see HARSH)
Gen   16: 6 And when Sarai dealt **h**
Job   39:16 She treats her young **h**,

HARVEST
Gen   8:22 remains, Seedtime and **h**,
Gen   30:14 went in the days of wheat **h**
Ex   23:16 "and the Feast of H,
Ex   34:21 in plowing time and in **h** you
Ex   34:22 the firstfruits of wheat **h**,
Lev   19: 9 the gleanings of your **h**.
Lev   25:22 you shall eat of the old **h**.
Ruth   1:22 at the beginning of barley **h**.
Ruth   2:23 barley harvest and wheat **h**;
Ps   107:37 they may yield a fruitful **h**.
Prov   6: 8 gathers her food in the **h**.
Prov 20: 4 He will beg during **h** and
Prov 26: 1 snow in summer and rain in **h**,
Jer   5:17 they shall eat up your **h**
Jer   5:24 the appointed weeks of the **h**.
Jer   8:20 The **h** is past, The summer is
Jer   50:16 who handles the sickle at **h**
Jer   51:33 And the time of her **h** will
Amos   4: 7 still three months to the **h**.
Matt   9:37 The **h** truly is plentiful,
Matt   9:38 pray the Lord of the **h** to
Matt   9:38 send out laborers into His **h**.
Matt 13:30 grow together until the **h**,
Matt 13:39 the **h** is the end of the age,
Luke 10: 2 The **h** truly is great, but
Luke 10: 2 send out laborers into His **h**.
John   4:35 and then comes the **h**'?
John   4:35 are already white for **h**!

HASTE (see HASTEN, HASTILY, HASTY)
Gen   24:46 And she made **h** and let her
Ex   12:11 So you shall eat it in **h**.
Ps   31:22 For I said in my **h**,
Ps   38:22 Make **h** to help me, O Lord,
Prov   1:16 And they make **h** to shed
Song   8:14 Make **h**, my beloved,
Is   59: 7 And they make **h** to shed
Dan   6:19 in the morning and went in **h**
Luke 19: 5 make **h** and come down, for

HASTEN (see HASTE, HASTENED, HASTENING, HASTENS, HURRY)
Deut 32:35 And the things to come **h**
Ps   16: 4 shall be multiplied who **h**
Ps   22:19 **h** to help Me!

HASTENED (see HASTEN, HURRIED, QUICKLY)
Gen   18: 7 and he **h** to prepare it.
1Sa   28:24 and she **h** to kill it. And
Esth   6:14 and **h** to bring Haman to the
Job   31: 5 Or if my foot has **h** to

HASTENING (see HASTEN)
2Pe   3:12 looking for and **h** the coming

HASTENS (see HASTEN)
Prov   7:23 As a bird **h** to the snare,
Prov 19: 2 And he sins who **h** with his
Prov 28:22 A man with an evil eye **h**
Eccl   1: 5 And **h** to the place where it
Zeph   1:14 It is near and **h** quickly.

HASTILY (see HASTE, QUICKLY)
Prov 25: 8 Do not go **h** to court; For
Eccl   5: 2 your heart utter anything **h**
1Ti   5:22 Do not lay hands on anyone **h**,

HASTY (see HASTE)
Prov 29:20 Do you see a man **h** in his

HATCH
Is   59: 5 They **h** vipers' eggs and
Jer   17:11 that broods but does not **h**,

HATE (see HATED, HATEFUL, HATERS, HATES, HATING, HATRED)
Gen   24:60 The gates of those who **h**
Gen   50:15 Perhaps Joseph will **h** us, and
Ex   20: 5 generations of those who **h**
Lev   19:17 You shall not **h** your brother
Deut 32:41 And repay those who **h** Me.
Judg 14:16 You only **h** me! You do not
Ps   5: 5 You **h** all workers of
Ps   25:19 And they **h** me with cruel
Ps   35:19 wink with the eye who **h** me
Ps   38:19 And those who **h** me
Ps   41: 7 All who **h** me whisper
Ps   45: 7 love righteousness and **h**
Ps   50:17 Seeing you **h** instruction
Ps   97:10 **h** evil! He preserves the
Ps   118: 7 my desire on those who **h**
Ps   119:104 Therefore I **h** every false
Ps   119:113 I **h** the double-minded, But
Ps   119:163 I **h** and abhor lying, But I
Ps   139:22 I **h** them with perfect
Prov   1:22 And fools **h** knowledge.
Prov   8:13 fear of the LORD is to **h**
Prov   8:36 All those who **h** me love
Eccl   3: 8 to love, And a time to **h**;
Jer   44: 4 abominable thing that I **h**!
Amos   5:15 **H** evil, love good
Mic   3: 2 You who **h** good and love
Matt   5:43 love your neighbor and **h**
Matt   5:44 do good to those who **h** you,
Matt   6:24 for either he will **h** the one
Luke   6:22 Blessed are you when men **h**
Luke   6:27 do good to those who **h** you,
Luke 14:26 comes to Me and does not **h**
John   7: 7 The world cannot **h** you, but
Rom   7:15 not practice; but what I **h**,
Rev   2: 6 that you **h** the deeds of the
Rev   2: 6 Nicolaitans, which I also **h**.

HATED (see HATE)
Gen   27:41 So Esau **h** Jacob because of
Gen   37: 4 they **h** him and could not
2Sa   13:15 the hatred with which he **h**
Esth   9: 1 overpowered those who **h**
Ps   44: 7 put to shame those who **h** us.
Prov   1:29 Because they **h** knowledge
Prov   5:12 How I have **h** instruction,
Prov 14:20 The poor man is **h** even by
Eccl   2:17 Therefore I **h** life because
Mal   1: 3 But Esau I have **h**,
Matt 10:22 And you will be **h** by all for
John 15:18 it hated Me before it **h**
John 15:24 they have seen and also **h**
John 15:25 They **h** Me without a
John 17:14 and the world has **h** them
Rom   9:13 but Esau I have **h**.
Eph   5:29 For no one ever **h** his own
Heb   1: 9 righteousness and **h**

HATEFUL (see HATE)
Tit   3: 3 **h** and hating one another.

HATERS (see HATE)
Rom   1:30 **h** of God, violent, proud,

HATES (see HATE)
Deut 19:11 But if anyone **h** his
Job   16: 9 and **h** me; He gnashes at me
Prov   6:16 six things the LORD **h**,
Prov 12: 1 But he who **h** correction is
Prov 13: 5 A righteous man **h** lying,
Prov 13:24 He who spares his rod **h** his
Prov 15:27 But he who **h** bribes will

Prov	28:16	But he who **h** covetousness
Is	1:14	appointed feasts My soul **h**;
Mal	2:16	of Israel says That He **h**
John	3:20	everyone practicing evil **h**
John	7: 7	but it **h** Me because I
John	12:25	and who **h** his life in
John	15:18	If the world **h** you, you know
John	15:23	He who **h** Me hates My Father
1Jn	2: 9	and **h** his brother, is in
1Jn	3:13	if the world **h** you.

HATING (see HATE)

Ex	18:21	**h** covetousness; and place
Jude	23	**h** even the garment defiled

HATRED (see HATE)

2Sa	13:15	so that the **h** with which he
Ps	25:19	they hate me with cruel **h**.
Ps	109: 3	me with words of **h**,
Ps	109: 5	And **h** for my love.
Ps	139:22	I hate them with perfect **h**;
Prov	10:12	**H** stirs up strife, But love
Prov	15:17	Than a fatted calf with **h**.
Ezek	35: 5	you have had an ancient **h**,
Gal	5:20	idolatry, sorcery, **h**,

HATS

Ex	39:28	exquisite **h** of fine linen,

HAUGHTINESS (see HAUGHTY)

Is	2:11	The **h** of men shall be bowed
Is	16: 6	Of his **h** and his pride and

HAUGHTY (see HAUGHTINESS)

Ps	101: 5	The one who has a **h** look
Ps	131: 1	LORD, my heart is not **h**,
Prov	16:18	And a **h** spirit before a
Prov	18:12	the heart of a man is **h**,
Prov	21: 4	A **h** look, a proud heart,
Rom	11:20	stand by faith. Do not be **h**,
1Ti	6:17	this present age not to be **h**,
2Ti	3: 4	traitors, headstrong, **h**,

HAVEN (see HAVENS)

Ps	107:30	them to their desired **h**.

HAVENS† (see HAVEN)

Acts	27: 8	to a place called Fair **H**,

HAVOC†

Acts	8: 3	he made **h** of the church,

HAY

1Co	3:12	precious stones, wood, **h**,

HAZAEL

2Ki	8:28	son of Ahab to war against **H**
2Ki	13: 3	of Ben-Hadad the son of **H**,
2Ki	13:24	Now **H** king of Syria died.
Amos	1: 4	a fire into the house of **H**,

HAZOR

Josh	11: 1	when Jabin king of **H** heard
Josh	11:11	Then he burned **H** with fire.

HEAD (see HEADED, HEADS)

Gen	3:15	He shall bruise your **h**,
Gen	24:26	the man bowed down his **h**
Gen	40:13	Pharaoh will lift up your **h**
Gen	40:16	three white baskets on my **h**.
Gen	40:19	will lift off your **h** from
Gen	48:14	left hand on Manasseh's **h**,
Ex	9:31	for the barley was in the **h**
Ex	29: 6	put the turban on his **h**,
Ex	29: 7	oil, pour it on his **h**,
Ex	29:10	put their hands on the **h** of
Lev	13:12	from his **h** to his foot,
Lev	13:42	if there is on the bald **h**
Lev	16:21	lay both his hands on the **h**
Num	1: 4	each one the **h** of his
Num	6: 5	razor shall come upon his **h**;

Num	6: 5	locks of the hair of his **h**
Num	6: 7	to God is on his **h**.
Num	6: 9	he defiles his consecrated **h**,
Deut	21:12	and she shall shave her **h**
Deut	28:35	foot to the top of your **h**.
Deut	33:20	arm and the crown of his **h**.
Josh	11:10	Hazor was formerly the **h** of
Judg	5:26	Sisera, she pierced his **h**,
Judg	9:53	millstone on Abimelech's **h**
Judg	13: 5	razor shall come upon his **h**,
Judg	16:19	off the seven locks of his **h**.
Judg	16:22	the hair of his **h** began to
1Sa	1:11	razor shall come upon his **h**.
1Sa	5: 4	The **h** of Dagon and both the
1Sa	14:45	not one hair of his **h** shall
1Sa	17:38	put a bronze helmet on his **h**;
1Sa	17:51	and cut off his **h** with it.
1Sa	26: 7	stuck in the ground by his **h**.
2Sa	1: 2	torn and dust on his **h**.
2Sa	3: 8	Am I a dog's **h** that belongs
2Sa	3:29	Let it rest on the **h** of Joab
2Sa	4: 7	beheaded him and took his **h**,
2Sa	12:30	king's crown from his **h**.
2Sa	12:30	And it was set on David's **h**.
2Sa	13:19	Tamar put ashes on her **h**,
2Sa	14:25	foot to the crown of his **h**
2Sa	14:26	he cut the hair of his **h**—
2Sa	18: 9	and his **h** caught in the
2Ki	4:19	said to his father, "My **h**,
2Ki	6: 5	the iron ax **h** fell into
2Ki	9:30	her eyes and adorned her **h**,
Esth	2:17	the royal crown upon her **h**
Esth	6:12	mourning and having his **h**
Esth	9:25	should return on his own **h**,
Job	1:20	his robe, and shaved his **h**;
Job	2: 7	foot to the crown of his **h**.
Job	2:12	and sprinkled dust on his **h**
Job	10:15	I cannot lift up my **h**.
Job	20: 6	And his **h** reaches to the
Job	29: 3	His lamp shone upon my **h**,
Ps	3: 3	the One who lifts up my **h**.
Ps	7:16	shall return upon his own **h**,
Ps	21: 3	of pure gold upon his **h**.
Ps	22: 7	the lip, they shake the **h**,
Ps	23: 5	You anoint my **h** with oil;
Ps	38: 4	have gone over my **h**;
Ps	40:12	more than the hairs of my **h**;
Ps	110: 7	He shall lift up the **h**.
Ps	133: 2	the precious oil upon the **h**,
Prov	1: 9	graceful ornament on your **h**,
Prov	16:31	The silver-haired **h** is a
Prov	20:29	of old men is their gray **h**.
Prov	25:22	heap coals of fire on his **h**,
Eccl	9: 8	And let your **h** lack no
Song	2: 6	left hand is under my **h**,
Is	1: 5	The whole **h** is sick, And
Is	3:17	a scab The crown of the **h**
Is	7: 8	For the **h** of Syria is
Is	9:14	the LORD will cut off **h**
Is	19:15	Which the **h** or tail, Palm
Is	59:17	helmet of salvation on His **h**;
Jer	9: 1	that my **h** were waters, And
Jer	18:16	astonished And shake his **h**.
Jer	23:19	fall violently on the **h** of
Jer	48:37	For every **h** shall be bald,
Jer	52:31	lifted up the **h** of
Ezek	5: 1	and pass it over your **h** and
Ezek	10: 1	that was above the **h** of the
Ezek	17:19	will recompense on his own **h**.
Ezek	24:17	bind your turban on your **h**,
Ezek	33: 4	blood shall be on his own **h**.
Dan	2:28	and the visions of your **h**
Dan	2:38	you are this **h** of gold.
Dan	4: 5	bed and the visions of my **h**
Dan	7: 9	And the hair of His **h** was

Dan 7:20 horns that were on its **h**,
Jon 2: 5 were wrapped around my **h**.
Jon 4: 8 the sun beat on Jonah's **h**,
Zech 3: 5 put a clean turban on his **h**.
Matt 5:36 shall you swear by your **h**,
Matt 6:17 anoint your **h** and wash your
Matt 8:20 has nowhere to lay His **h**.
Matt 10:30 the very hairs of your **h**
Matt 14: 8 me John the Baptist's **h**
Matt 26: 7 and she poured it on His **h**
Matt 27:30 reed and struck Him on the **h**.
Matt 27:37 And they put up over His **h**
Mark 4:28 first the blade, then the **h**,
Luke 7:38 them with the hair of her **h**;
John 13: 9 also my hands and my **h**!"
John 19:30 finished!" And bowing His **h**,
Rom 12:20 coals of fire on his **h**.
1Co 11: 3 want you to know that the **h**
1Co 11: 3 the **h** of woman is man, and
1Co 11: 3 and the **h** of Christ is God.
1Co 11: 4 having his **h** covered,
1Co 11: 4 covered, dishonors his **h**.
1Co 11:10 of authority on her **h**,
1Co 12:21 nor again the **h** to the feet,
Eph 1:22 and gave Him to be **h** over
Eph 4:15 things into Him who is the **h**—
Eph 5:23 For the husband is **h** of the
Eph 5:23 as also Christ is **h** of the
Col 1:18 And He is the **h** of the body,
Col 2:10 who is the **h** of all
Col 2:19 not holding fast to the **H**,
Rev 1:14 His **h** and hair were white
Rev 14:14 having on His **h** a golden

HEADED (see HEAD)
1Sa 6:12 Then the cows **h** straight for

HEADLONG
Acts 1:18 of iniquity; and falling **h**,

HEADS (see HEAD)
Gen 41: 5 and suddenly seven **h** of
Gen 43:28 And they bowed their **h**
Ex 18:25 and made them **h** over the
Deut 23:25 you may pluck the **h** with
Josh 7: 6 and they put dust on their **h**.
Ruth 2: 2 and glean **h** of grain after
Neh 9: 1 and with dust on their **h**.
Neh 11:16 of the **h** of the Levites,
Ps 24: 7 Lift up your **h**,
Ps 66:12 men to ride over our **h**;
Ps 74:14 You broke the **h** of Leviathan
Ps 109:25 at me, they shake their **h**.
Ps 110: 6 He shall execute the **h** of
Is 35:10 everlasting joy on their **h**.
Jer 14: 3 And covered their **h**.
Ezek 11:21 their deeds on their own **h**,
Ezek 23:15 Flowing turbans on their **h**,
Ezek 23:42 beautiful crowns on their **h**.
Dan 7: 6 The beast also had four **h**,
Mic 3: 9 You **h** of the house of Jacob
Mic 3:11 Her **h** judge for a bribe,
Matt 12: 1 and began to pluck **h** of
Matt 27:39 wagging their **h**
Luke 21:28 look up and lift up your **h**,
Acts 18: 6 blood be upon your own **h**;
Rev 12: 3 red dragon having seven **h**
Rev 13: 1 and on his **h** a blasphemous
Rev 13: 3 And I saw one of his **h** as
Rev 17: 3 having seven **h** and ten

HEAL (see HEALED, HEALING, HEALS)
2Ch 7:14 will forgive their sin and **h**
Ps 41: 4 **H** my soul, for I have
Eccl 3: 3 to kill, And a time to **h**;
Is 61: 1 He has sent Me to **h** the
Jer 3:22 And I will **h** your

Jer 17:14 **H** me, O LORD, and I shall
Hos 6: 1 but He will **h** us; He has
Hos 14: 4 I will **h** their backsliding,
Matt 8: 7 I will come and **h** him."
Matt 10: 1 and to **h** all kinds of
Matt 10: 8 **H** the sick, cleanse the
Matt 12:10 Is it lawful to **h** on the
Luke 4:18 He has sent Me to **h**
Luke 4:23 **h** yourself! Whatever we have
John 12:40 So that I should **h**
Acts 28:27 So that I should **h**

HEALED (see HEAL)
Gen 20:17 and God **h** Abimelech, his
Deut 28:35 boils which cannot be **h**,
2Ki 2:21 I have **h** this water; from it
Ps 30: 2 And You **h** me.
Ps 107:20 He sent His word and **h** them,
Is 6:10 heart, And return and be **h**.
Is 53: 5 And by His stripes we are **h**.
Jer 15:18 Which refuses to be **h**?
Ezek 47: 8 the sea, its waters are **h**.
Hos 11: 3 they did not know that I **h**
Matt 8: 8 and my servant will be **h**.
Matt 8:13 And his servant was **h** that
Matt 8:16 and **h** all who were sick,
Matt 12:22 and He **h** him, so that the
Matt 15:28 And her daughter was **h**
Matt 15:30 and He **h** them.
Matt 21:14 and He **h** them.
Mark 5:29 in her body that she was **h**
Luke 8: 2 women who had been **h** of
Luke 8:36 been demon-possessed was **h**.
Luke 8:43 and could not be **h** by any,
Luke 9:42 **h** the child, and gave him
Luke 22:51 And He touched his ear and **h**
John 5:13 But the one who was **h** did not
Acts 3:11 as the lame man who was **h**
Acts 5:16 spirits, and they were all **h**.
Acts 14: 9 that he had faith to be **h**,
Acts 28: 8 laid his hands on him and **h**
Heb 12:13 dislocated, but rather be **h**.
1Pe 2:24 whose stripes you were **h**.
Rev 13: 3 and his deadly wound was **h**.

HEALING (see HEAL, HEALINGS)
Is 58: 8 Your **h** shall spring forth
Jer 14:19 us so that there is no **h**
Jer 14:19 good; And for the time of **h**,
Mal 4: 2 shall arise With **h** in His
Matt 4:23 and **h** all kinds of sickness
Luke 9: 6 preaching the gospel and **h**
Luke 9:11 those who had need of **h**.
Acts 10:38 went about doing good and **h**
Rev 22: 2 of the tree were for the **h**

HEALINGS (see HEALING)
1Co 12: 9 to another gifts of **h** by the

HEALS (see HEAL)
Ex 15:26 For I am the LORD who **h**
Ps 103: 3 Who **h** all your diseases,
Ps 147: 3 He **h** the brokenhearted And
Acts 9:34 Jesus the Christ **h** you.

HEALTH (see HEALTHY)
Gen 43:28 our father is in good **h**;
Ps 38: 3 Nor any **h** in my bones
Prov 3: 8 It will be **h** to your flesh,
Prov 12:18 of the wise promotes **h**.
Prov 13:17 ambassador brings **h**.
Prov 16:24 to the soul and **h** to the
Jer 8:22 no recovery For the **h** of

HEALTHY (see HEALTH)
Prov 15:30 report makes the bones **h**.

HEAP (*see* HEAPED, HEAPS)
Gen 31:46 took stones and made a **h**,
Gen 31:48 This **h** is a witness between
Ex   15: 8 stood upright like a **h**;
Josh 7:26 raised over him a great **h**
1Sa   2: 8 the beggar from the ash **h**,
Prov 25:22 For so you will **h** coals of
Song 7: 2 Your waist is a **h** of wheat
Jer   9:11 I will make Jerusalem a **h** of
Ezek 24:10 **H** on the wood, Kindle the
Rom 12:20 in so doing you will **h**
2Ti   4: 3 they will **h** up for

HEAPED† (*see* HEAP)
Zech 9: 3 **H** up silver like the dust,
Jas   5: 3 You have **h** up treasure in

HEAPS (*see* HEAP)
Ex   8:14 gathered them together in **h**,
Judg 15:16 of a donkey, Heaps upon **h**,
Job 27:16 Though he **h** up silver like

HEAR (*see* HEARD, HEARER, HEARING, HEARS, UNHEARD)
Gen   4:23 **h** my voice; Wives of
Gen 21: 6 and all who **h** will laugh
Gen 37: 6 Please **h** this dream which I
Ex   7:16 until now you would not **h**!
Ex   19: 9 that the people may **h** when I
Ex   22:27 he cries to Me, I will **h**,
Deut 1:16 **H** the cases between your
Deut 1:17 you shall **h** the small as
Deut 4: 6 of the peoples who will **h**
Deut 4:10 and I will let them **h** My
Deut 4:28 which neither see nor **h** nor
Deut 4:33 Did any people ever **h** the
Deut 5: 1 and said to them: "**H**,
Deut 6: 4 "**H**, O Israel: The LORD
Deut 13:11 So all Israel shall **h** and
Deut 18:15 brethren. Him you shall **h**,
Deut 18:16 Let me not **h** again the voice
Deut 29: 4 eyes to see and ears to **h**,
Deut 32: 1 and I will speak; And **h**,
Josh 7: 9 of the land will **h** it,
Judg 14:13 that we may **h** it."
1Sa 15:14 lowing of the oxen which I **h**?
2Sa 22:45 to me; As soon as they **h**,
1Ki   4:34 came to **h** the wisdom of
1Ki   8:29 that You may **h** the prayer
1Ki   8:30 **H** in heaven Your dwelling
1Ki   8:30 place; and when You **h**,
1Ki 10:24 the presence of Solomon to **h**
1Ki 18:26 **h** us!" But there was no
1Ki 18:37 **H** me, O LORD, hear me, that
2Ki   7: 1 **H** the word of the LORD. Thus
2Ki   7: 6 the army of the Syrians to **h**
2Ki 17:14 they would not **h**,
2Ki 19: 7 and he shall **h** a rumor and
2Ki 19:25 Did you not **h** long ago How
Job 13: 6 Now **h** my reasoning, And
Job 22:27 He will **h** you, And you
Job 26:14 how small a whisper we **h** of
Job 31:35 that I had one to **h** me!
Ps   4: 1 **H** me when I call, O God of
Ps   4: 1 and **h** my prayer.
Ps   5: 3 My voice You shall **h** in the
Ps   10:17 will cause Your ear to **h**,
Ps   13: 3 Consider and **h** me, O LORD
Ps   17: 1 **H** a just cause, O LORD,
Ps   27: 7 **H**, O LORD, when I
Ps   28: 2 **H** the voice of my
Ps   34: 2 The humble shall **h** of it
Ps   39:12 **H** my prayer, O LORD, And
Ps   49: 1 **H** this, all peoples
Ps   51: 8 Make me **h** joy and gladness,
Ps   60: 5 Your right hand, and **h** me.
Ps   61: 1 **H** my cry, O God

Ps   65: 2 O You who **h** prayer, To You
Ps   66:16 Come and **h**, all you who
Ps   69:17 **H** me speedily.
Ps   84: 8 **h** my prayer; Give ear, O
Ps   92:11 My ears **h** my desire on
Ps   94: 9 the ear, shall He not **h**?
Ps   95: 7 if you will **h** His voice:
Ps 115: 6 have ears, but they do not **h**;
Ps 135:17 have ears, but they do not **h**;
Ps 143: 1 **H** my prayer, O LORD, Give
Prov 13: 8 But the poor does not **h**
Prov 22:17 Incline your ear and **h** the
Eccl 7: 5 It is better to **h** the
Eccl 12:13 Let us **h** the conclusion of
Is   1:10 **H** the word of the LORD,
Is   1:15 many prayers, I will not **h**.
Is   6:10 And **h** with their ears, And
Is   29:18 that day the deaf shall **h**
Is   30: 9 Children who will not **h**
Is   34: 1 near, you nations, to **h**;
Is   34: 1 you people! Let the earth **h**,
Is   37:26 Did you not **h** long ago How
Is   42:20 the ears, but he does not **h**.
Is   44: 1 Yet **h** now, O Jacob My
Is   48: 6 I have made you **h** new
Is   55: 3 your ear, and come to Me. **H**,
Is   59: 1 ear heavy, That it cannot **h**.
Jer   5:21 And who have ears and **h**
Jer 11: 2 **H** the words of this covenant,
Jer 11:10 who refused to **h** My words,
Jer 13:15 **H** and give ear: Do not be
Jer 14:12 I will not **h** their cry; and
Jer 20:16 Let him **h** the cry in the
Jer 22:29 **H** the word of the LORD!
Jer 25: 4 nor inclined your ear to **h**.
Jer 49:20 Therefore **h** the counsel of
Lam   1:18 **H** now, all peoples, And
Ezek 2: 5 whether they **h** or whether
Ezek 2: 7 whether they **h** or whether
Ezek 2: 8 **h** what I say to you. Do not
Ezek 3:27 He who hears, let him **h**;
Ezek 8:18 I will not **h** them."
Ezek 12: 2 and ears to **h** but does not
Ezek 24:26 come to you to let you **h**
Ezek 37: 4 **h** the word of the LORD!
Dan   3:15 are ready at the time you **h**
Dan   5:23 which do not see or **h** or
Dan   9:17 **h** the prayer of Your
Hos   5: 1 **H** this, O priests! Take
Joel 1: 2 **H** this, you elders, And
Amos 4: 1 **H** this word, you cows of
Amos 7:16 **h** the word of the LORD:
Mic   3: 9 Now **h** this, You heads of
Mic   6: 1 And let the hills **h** your
Zech 7:12 refusing to **h** the law and
Mal   2: 2 If you will not **h**,
Matt 10:14 will not receive you nor **h**
Matt 10:27 and what you **h** in the ear,
Matt 11: 4 John the things which you **h**
Matt 11: 5 are cleansed and the deaf **h**;
Matt 11:15 "He who has ears to **h**,
Matt 12:19 Nor will anyone **h** His
Matt 12:42 the ends of the earth to **h**
Matt 13:13 and hearing they do not **h**,
Matt 13:15 with their eyes and **h**
Matt 13:18 Therefore **h** the parable of
Matt 17: 5 well pleased. "**H** Him!"
Matt 18:17 But if he refuses even to **h**
Matt 24: 6 And you will **h** of wars and
Mark 4:15 word is sown. When they **h**,
Mark 4:24 them, "Take heed what you **h**.
Mark 4:24 to you; and to you who **h**,
Mark 7:37 He makes both the deaf to **h**
Mark 12:29 the commandments is: '**H**,
Luke 5:15 came together to **h**,

Luke	6:17	who came to **h** Him and be
Luke	7:22	are cleansed, the deaf **h**,
Luke	8:12	wayside are the ones who **h**;
Luke	8:18	take heed how you **h**.
Luke	15: 1	drew near to Him to **h** Him.
Luke	16: 2	What is this I **h** about you?
Luke	16:31	If they do not **h** Moses and
Luke	18: 6	**H** what the unjust judge said.
John	3: 8	and you **h** the sound of it,
John	5:25	when the dead will **h** the
John	5:25	and those who **h** will live.
John	5:28	who are in the graves will **h**
John	9:31	we know that God does not **h**
John	10: 3	and the sheep **h** his voice;
Acts	2:11	we **h** them speaking in our own
Acts	2:22	**h** these words: Jesus of
Acts	7:37	Him you shall **h**.
Acts	13: 7	and Saul and sought to **h**
Acts	15: 7	mouth the Gentiles should **h**
Acts	17:21	but either to tell or to **h**
Acts	17:32	We will **h** you again on this
Acts	22: 1	**h** my defense before you
Acts	26: 3	Therefore I beg you to **h** me
Acts	26:29	but also all who **h** me today,
Acts	28:26	"Hearing you will **h**,
Acts	28:27	with their eyes and **h**
Rom	10:14	And how shall they **h** without
Rom	11: 8	that they should not **h**,
1Co	11:18	I **h** that there are divisions
Gal	4:21	do you not **h** the law?
Phil	1:30	you saw in me and now **h** is
Heb	3: 7	if you will **h** His
1Jn	4: 6	is not of God does not **h** us.
Rev	1: 3	he who reads and those who **h**
Rev	2: 7	let him **h** what the Spirit
Rev	9:20	which can neither see nor **h**
Rev	13: 9	anyone has an ear, let him **h**.

HEARD (*see* HEAR)

Gen	3: 8	And they **h** the sound of the
Gen	3:10	I **h** Your voice in the garden,
Ex	2:24	So God **h** their groaning, and
Ex	3: 7	and have **h** their cry because
Ex	6: 5	And I have also **h** the
Ex	16: 9	for He has **h** your
Ex	18: 1	**h** of all that God had done
Deut	4:12	You **h** the sound of the
Deut	4:12	you only **h** a voice.
Deut	4:32	anything like it has been **h**.
Deut	4:36	and you **h** His words out of
Ruth	1: 6	for she had **h** in the country
1Sa	1:13	but her voice was not **h**.
1Sa	22: 6	When Saul **h** that David and
2Sa	7:22	to all that we have **h** with
2Sa	22: 7	He **h** my voice from His
1Ki	2:42	The word I have **h** is good.'
1Ki	10: 1	when the queen of Sheba **h**
1Ki	10: 6	was a true report which I **h**
1Ki	10: 7	exceed the fame of which I **h**.
1Ki	21:15	when Jezebel **h** that Naboth
2Ki	9:30	Jezebel **h** of it; and she
2Ki	11:13	Now when Athaliah **h** the
2Ki	20: 5	I have **h** your prayer, I have
2Ki	20:12	for he **h** that Hezekiah had
2Ki	22:11	when the king **h** the words of
Ezra	9: 3	So when I **h** this thing, I
Neh	4: 1	when Sanballat **h** that we
Neh	4:15	when our enemies **h** that it
Neh	6:16	when all our enemies **h** of
Neh	9:27	You **h** from heaven; And
Neh	9:28	You **h** from heaven; And
Neh	13: 3	when they had **h** the Law,
Job	2:11	when Job's three friends **h**
Job	4:16	Then I **h** a voice saying:
Job	42: 5	I have **h** of You by the

Ps	3: 4	And He **h** me from His holy
Ps	6: 8	For the LORD has **h** the
Ps	10:17	You have **h** the desire of the
Ps	18: 6	He **h** my voice from His
Ps	19: 3	Where their voice is not **h**.
Ps	22:24	when He cried to Him, He **h**.
Ps	34: 4	and He **h** me, And delivered
Ps	34: 6	and the LORD **h** him, And
Ps	40: 1	And **h** my cry.
Ps	44: 1	We have **h** with our ears, O
Ps	48: 8	As we have **h**,
Ps	81: 5	Where I **h** a language I did
Ps	106:44	When He **h** their cry;
Ps	120: 1	And He **h** me.
Ps	132: 6	we **h** of it in Ephrathah; We
Song	2:12	of the turtledove Is **h** in
Is	6: 8	Also I **h** the voice of the
Is	21: 3	I was distressed when I **h**
Is	40:21	not known? Have you not **h**?
Is	40:28	not known? Have you not **h**?
Is	49: 8	an acceptable time I have **h**
Is	52:15	And what they had not **h**
Jer	18:13	Who has **h** such things? The
Jer	18:22	Let a cry be **h** from their
Jer	20: 1	**h** that Jeremiah prophesied
Jer	23:18	And has perceived and **h** His
Jer	23:25	I have **h** what the prophets
Jer	26:11	as you have **h** with your
Jer	31:15	A voice was **h** in Ramah,
Jer	36:16	when they had **h** all the
Jer	46:12	The nations have **h** of your
Ezek	1:24	I **h** the noise of their
Ezek	1:28	and I **h** a voice of One
Ezek	2: 2	and I **h** Him who spoke to me.
Ezek	43: 6	Then I **h** Him speaking to me
Dan	8:13	Then I **h** a holy one
Dan	12: 8	Although I **h**, I did not
Zech	8:23	for we have **h** that God is
Mal	3:16	the LORD listened and **h**
Matt	2: 3	When Herod the king **h** this,
Matt	2:18	A voice was **h** in Ramah,
Matt	4:12	Now when Jesus **h** that John
Matt	5:21	You have **h** that it was said
Matt	5:27	You have **h** that it was said
Matt	6: 7	think that they will be **h**
Matt	8:10	When Jesus **h** it, He
Matt	20:24	And when the ten **h** it, they
Matt	21:45	priests and Pharisees **h** His
Matt	25: 6	at midnight a cry was **h**:
Mark	2: 1	and it was **h** that He was in
Mark	5:27	When she **h** about Jesus, she
Mark	7:25	had an unclean spirit **h**
Mark	11:18	scribes and chief priests **h**
Mark	12:37	And the common people **h**
Mark	14:58	We **h** Him say, 'I will destroy
Mark	16:11	And when they **h** that He was
Luke	1:13	for your prayer is **h**;
Luke	1:41	when Elizabeth **h** the
Luke	1:58	neighbors and relatives **h**
Luke	2:18	And all those who **h** it
Luke	2:20	the things that they had **h**
Luke	2:47	and all who **h** Him were
Luke	6:49	But he who **h** and did nothing
Luke	7:22	things you have seen and **h**:
Luke	12: 3	in the dark will be **h** in
Luke	15:25	he **h** music and dancing.
Luke	22:71	For we have **h** it ourselves
John	1:37	The two disciples **h** him
John	3:32	"And what He has seen and **h**,
John	4:42	for we ourselves have **h** Him
John	8:26	those things which I **h** from
John	8:40	told you the truth which I **h**
John	11: 6	when He **h** that he was sick,
John	11:41	I thank You that You have **h**
John	12:34	We have **h** from the law that

John   21: 7 Now when Simon Peter **h** that
Acts   1: 4 you have **h** from Me;
Acts   2: 6 because everyone **h** them
Acts   4: 4 many of those who **h** the word
Acts   4:20 which we have seen and **h**.
Acts   7:34 I have **h** their groaning
Acts   8:30 and **h** him reading the
Acts   9: 4 and **h** a voice saying to him,
Acts   9:21 Then all who **h** were amazed,
Acts   11: 1 who were in Judea that
Acts   11: 7 And I **h** a voice saying to me,
Acts   14:14 Barnabas and Paul **h** this,
Acts   15:24 Since we have **h** that some who
Acts   18:26 When Aquila and Priscilla **h**
Acts   19: 2 We have not so much as **h**
Acts   19:10 all who dwelt in Asia **h** the
Acts   22: 7 I fell to the ground and **h**
Acts   22:15 of what you have seen and **h**.
Acts   24:22 But when Felix **h** these
Rom   10:14 Him of whom they have not **h**?
Rom   10:18 But I say, have they not **h**?
Rom   15:21 those who have not **h**
1Co   2: 9 not seen, nor ear **h**,
2Co   6: 2 time I have **h** you,
2Co   12: 4 up into Paradise and **h**
Eph   1:13 after you **h** the word of
Eph   1:15 after I **h** of your faith in
Phil   4: 9 learned and received and **h**
Col   1: 4 since we **h** of your faith in
Col   1: 9 since the day we **h** it, do
2Ti   1:13 words which you have **h** from
2Ti   2: 2 the things that you have **h**
Heb   2: 1 heed to the things we have **h**,
Jas   5:11 You have **h** of the
2Pe   1:18 And we **h** this voice which
1Jn   1: 1 beginning, which we have **h**,
1Jn   1: 3 which we have seen and **h** we
1Jn   1: 5 the message which we have **h**
Rev   1:10 and I **h** behind me a loud
Rev   3: 3 how you have received and **h**;
Rev   5:11 and I **h** the voice of many
Rev   6: 1 and I **h** one of the four
Rev   10: 4 but I **h** a voice from heaven
Rev   12:10 Then I **h** a loud voice saying
Rev   18:22 trumpeters shall not be **h**
Rev   18:23 and bride shall not be **h** in
Rev   22: 8 saw and **h** these things. And

HEARER (see HEAR, HEARERS)
Jas   1:23 For if anyone is a **h** of the

HEARERS† (see HEARER)
Rom   2:13 (for not the **h** of the law
Eph   4:29 it may impart grace to the **h**.
2Ti   2:14 profit, to the ruin of the **h**.
Jas   1:22 and not **h** only, deceiving

HEARING (see HEAR)
Gen   20: 8 all these things in their **h**;
Ex   24: 7 Covenant and read in the **h**
Lev   5: 1 If a person sins in **h** the
2Ki   18:26 to us in Hebrew in the **h** of
Job   42: 5 have heard of You by the **h**
Prov 20:12 The **h** ear and the seeing
Eccl   1: 8 Nor the ear filled with **h**.
Is   6: 9 this people: 'Keep on **h**,
Is   11: 3 Nor decide by the **h** of His
Is   33:15 Who stops his ears from **h**
Jer   36:13 read the book in the **h** of
Jer   36:15 Baruch read it in their **h**.
Amos   8:11 But of **h** the words of the
Matt 13:13 and **h** they do not hear, nor
Matt 13:14 **H** you will hear and
Matt 13:15 ears are hard of **h**,
Mark   6: 2 And many **h** Him were
Luke   4:21 is fulfilled in your **h**.

Luke   7: 1 all His sayings in the **h** of
Acts   5: 5 **h** these words, fell down and
Acts   9: 7 **h** a voice but seeing no one.
Acts   28:26 **H** you will hear, and
Acts   28:27 ears are hard of **h**,
Rom   10:17 So then faith comes by **h**,
Rom   10:17 and **h** by the word of God.
1Co   12:17 eye, where would be the **h**?
Gal   3: 2 or by the **h** of faith?
Gal   3: 5 or by the **h** of faith?—
Phm   1: 5 **h** of your love and faith
Heb   5:11 you have become dull of **h**
2Pe   2: 8 day to day by seeing and **h**

HEARS (see HEAR)
Ex   16: 7 for He **h** your complaints
Num   24: 4 The utterance of him who **h**
Num   24:16 The utterance of him who **h**
Num   30: 4 and her father **h** her vow and
1Sa   3:10 "Speak, for Your servant **h**.
1Sa   3:11 both ears of everyone who **h**
1Sa   16: 2 If Saul **h** it, he will kill
Ps   34:17 cry out, and the LORD **h**,
Ps   69:33 For the LORD **h** the poor,
Ps   97: 8 Zion **h** and is glad, And the
Prov 15:29 But He **h** the prayer of the
Prov 25:10 Lest he who **h** it expose
Is   30:19 When He **h** it, He will
Ezek   3:27 the Lord GOD.' He who **h**,
Dan   3:10 a decree that everyone who **h**
Matt   7:24 Therefore whoever **h** these
Matt 13:19 When anyone **h** the word of the
Matt 13:20 this is he who **h** the word
Matt 13:23 the good ground is he who **h**
Matt 18:15 If he **h** you, you have gained
Luke   6:47 and **h** My sayings and does
Luke 10:16 He who **h** you hears Me, he who
John   3:29 who stands and **h** him,
John   5:24 he who **h** My word and
John   8:47 He who is of God **h** God's
John   9:31 His will, He **h** him.
John 12:47 And if anyone **h** My words and
John 16:13 but whatever He **h** He will
John 18:37 who is of the truth **h** My
1Jn   4: 5 and the world **h** them.
1Jn   4: 6 He who knows God **h** us; he
1Jn   5:14 His will, He **h** us.
Rev   3:20 If anyone **h** My voice and
Rev   22:17 Come!" And let him who **h**
Rev   22:18 I testify to everyone who **h**

HEART (see BROKEN-HEARTED, HEART'S, HEARTS, WHOLE-HEARTED)
Gen   6: 5 of the thoughts of his **h**
Gen   6: 6 and He was grieved in His **h**.
Gen   8:21 the imagination of man's **h**
Gen   17:17 laughed, and said in his **h**,
Gen   20: 5 In the integrity of my **h**
Gen   43:30 Now his **h** yearned for his
Gen   45:26 And Jacob's **h** stood still,
Ex   4:14 he will be glad in his **h**.
Ex   7: 3 I will harden Pharaoh's **h**,
Ex   7:13 And Pharaoh's **h** grew hard,
Ex   10:20 LORD hardened Pharaoh's **h**,
Ex   11:10 LORD hardened Pharaoh's **h**,
Ex   15: 8 depths congealed in the **h**
Ex   35: 5 Whoever is of a willing **h**,
Ex   35:21 Then everyone came whose **h**
Ex   35:22 as many as had a willing **h**,
Lev   19:17 hate your brother in your **h**.
Lev   26:16 eyes and cause sorrow of **h**.
Num   32: 9 they discouraged the **h** of
Deut   4:29 you seek Him with all your **h**
Deut   6: 5 your God with all your **h**,
Deut   6: 6 you today shall be in your **h**.
Deut   8: 2 to know what was in your **h**,

Deut 8:14 when your **h** is lifted up, and
Deut 10:12 your God with all your **h**
Deut 10:16 the foreskin of your **h**,
Deut 11:13 serve Him with all your **h**
Deut 12:15 whatever your **h** desires,
Deut 15: 9 a wicked thought in your **h**,
Deut 17:17 lest his **h** turn away; nor
Deut 20: 3 Do not let your **h** faint, do
Deut 26:16 them with all your **h** and
Deut 28:28 blindness and confusion of **h**.
Deut 28:65 will give you a trembling **h**,
Deut 28:67 fear which terrifies your **h**,
Deut 29:19 follow the dictates of my **h**'
Deut 30:14 in your mouth and in your **h**,
Josh 5: 1 that their **h** melted; and
Josh 24:23 and incline your **h** to the
Judg 5:16 have great searchings of **h**.
Judg 16:17 that he told her all his **h**,
Judg 19: 6 and let your **h** be merry."
1Sa 2: 1 My **h** rejoices in the LORD;
1Sa 10: 9 that God gave him another **h**;
1Sa 13:14 a man after His own **h**,
1Sa 16: 7 but the LORD looks at the **h**.
1Sa 21:12 David took these words to **h**,
2Sa 4: 1 died in Hebron, he lost **h**,
2Sa 6:16 she despised him in her **h**.
2Sa 7: 3 do all that is in your **h**,
2Sa 17:10 whose heart is like the **h**
2Sa 24:10 And David's **h** condemned him
1Ki 3: 6 and in uprightness of **h** with
1Ki 3:12 a wise and understanding **h**,
1Ki 4:29 and largeness of **h** like the
1Ki 9: 3 and My eyes and My **h** will be
1Ki 9: 4 in integrity of **h** and in
1Ki 11: 3 his wives turned away his **h**.
1Ki 14: 8 followed Me with all his **h**,
2Ki 9:24 the arrow came out at his **h**,
2Ki 10:15 Is your **h** right, as my heart
1Ch 12:17 my **h** will be united with
1Ch 22:19 Now set your **h** and your soul
1Ch 29:17 that You test the **h** and have
2Ch 32:26 for the pride of his **h**,
2Ch 36:13 his neck and hardened his **h**
Ezra 6:22 and turned the **h** of the king
Neh 9: 8 You found his **h** faithful
Job 7:17 You should set Your **h** on
Job 9: 4 God is wise in **h** and mighty
Job 16:13 He pierces my **h** and does
Job 19:27 How my **h** yearns within me!
Job 22:22 lay up His words in your **h**.
Job 23:16 For God made my **h** weak, And
Job 30:27 My **h** is in turmoil and
Job 31: 9 If my **h** has been enticed by a
Job 37: 1 At this also my **h** trembles,
Job 41:24 His **h** is as hard as stone,
Ps 4: 7 have put gladness in my **h**,
Ps 7:10 Who saves the upright in **h**.
Ps 9: 1 O LORD, with my whole **h**;
Ps 12: 2 lips and a double **h** they
Ps 13: 2 Having sorrow in my **h**
Ps 13: 5 My **h** shall rejoice in Your
Ps 14: 1 The fool has said in his **h**,
Ps 15: 2 speaks the truth in his **h**;
Ps 16: 9 Therefore my **h** is glad, and
Ps 17: 3 You have tested my **h**;
Ps 19: 8 are right, rejoicing the **h**;
Ps 19:14 and the meditation of my **h**
Ps 22:14 My **h** is like wax; It has
Ps 24: 4 has clean hands and a pure **h**,
Ps 26: 2 me; Try my mind and my **h**.
Ps 27: 3 My **h** shall not fear;
Ps 27:13 I would have lost **h**,
Ps 28: 7 My **h** trusted in Him, and I
Ps 34:18 to those who have a broken **h**,
Ps 37:15 shall enter their own **h**,

Ps 37:31 law of his God is in his **h**;
Ps 38:10 My **h** pants, my strength
Ps 40: 8 Your law is within my **h**.
Ps 40:12 Therefore my **h** fails me.
Ps 44:21 knows the secrets of the **h**.
Ps 45: 1 My **h** is overflowing with a
Ps 51:10 Create in me a clean **h**,
Ps 51:17 A broken and a contrite **h**—
Ps 53: 1 The fool has said in his **h**,
Ps 57: 7 My **h** is steadfast, O God, my
Ps 61: 2 When my **h** is overwhelmed;
Ps 62: 8 Pour out your **h** before Him;
Ps 66:18 I regard iniquity in my **h**,
Ps 73: 1 To such as are pure in **h**.
Ps 73: 7 They have more than **h** could
Ps 73:13 I have cleansed my **h** in
Ps 73:26 My flesh and my **h** fail;
Ps 73:26 God is the strength of my **h**
Ps 81:12 over to their own stubborn **h**,
Ps 84: 2 My **h** and my flesh cry out
Ps 84: 5 Whose **h** is set on
Ps 86:11 Unite my **h** to fear Your
Ps 90:12 That we may gain a **h** of
Ps 101: 2 my house with a perfect **h**.
Ps 101: 4 A perverse **h** shall depart
Ps 101: 5 a haughty look and a proud **h**,
Ps 109:22 And my **h** is wounded within
Ps 119:11 word I have hidden in my **h**,
Ps 119:70 Their **h** is as fat as grease,
Ps 119:80 Let my **h** be blameless
Ps 139:23 me, O God, and know my **h**;
Prov 2: 2 And apply your **h** to
Prov 2:10 When wisdom enters your **h**,
Prov 3: 3 them on the tablet of your **h**,
Prov 3: 5 in the LORD with all your **h**,
Prov 4:23 Keep your **h** with all
Prov 6:14 Perversity is in his **h**,
Prov 6:18 A **h** that devises wicked
Prov 6:21 them continually upon your **h**;
Prov 6:25 after her beauty in your **h**,
Prov 7: 3 them on the tablet of your **h**.
Prov 7:10 of a harlot, and a crafty **h**.
Prov 12: 8 he who is of a perverse **h**
Prov 12:25 Anxiety in the **h** of man
Prov 13:12 Hope deferred makes the **h**
Prov 14:10 The **h** knows its own
Prov 14:14 The backslider in **h** will be
Prov 14:30 A sound **h** is life to the
Prov 14:33 But what is in the **h** of
Prov 15:15 But he who is of a merry **h**
Prov 16: 9 A man's **h** plans his way,
Prov 17:16 Since he has no **h** for
Prov 17:20 He who has a deceitful **h**
Prov 20: 5 Counsel in the **h** of man is
Prov 20: 9 I have made my **h** clean, I am
Prov 20:27 the inner depths of his **h**.
Prov 21: 1 The king's **h** is in the hand
Prov 21: 4 A haughty look, a proud **h**,
Prov 22:15 is bound up in the **h** of a
Prov 22:17 And apply your **h** to my
Prov 23: 7 For as he thinks in his **h**,
Prov 23:17 Do not let your **h** envy
Prov 23:19 And guide your **h** in the
Prov 23:26 My son, give me your **h**,
Prov 25:20 who sings songs to a heavy **h**.
Prov 26:25 seven abominations in his **h**;
Prov 27:19 So a man's **h** reveals the
Prov 28:14 But he who hardens his **h**
Prov 28:25 He who is of a proud **h** stirs
Prov 28:26 He who trusts in his own **h**
Eccl 1:16 I communed with my **h**,
Eccl 1:17 And I set my **h** to know wisdom
Eccl 5:20 busy with the joy of his **h**.
Eccl 8: 9 and applied my **h** to every
Eccl 8:16 When I applied my **h** to know

Eccl	9: 7	your wine with a merry **h**;
Song	4: 9	You have ravished my **h**,
Song	5: 4	And my **h** yearned for him.
Song	8: 6	me as a seal upon your **h**,
Is	1: 5	And the whole **h** faints.
Is	6:10	Make the **h** of this people
Is	6:10	And understand with their **h**,
Is	13: 7	Every man's **h** will melt,
Is	44:19	no one considers in his **h**,
Is	44:20	A deceived **h** has turned him
Is	57:15	And to revive the **h** of the
Is	63: 4	day of vengeance is in My **h**,
Is	63:17	And hardened our **h** from
Jer	4:10	the sword reaches to the **h**.
Jer	4:14	wash your **h** from wickedness,
Jer	4:19	I am pained in my very **h!**
Jer	5:23	a defiant and rebellious **h**;
Jer	8:18	My **h** is faint in me.
Jer	9:26	are uncircumcised in the **h**.
Jer	11:20	Testing the mind and the **h**,
Jer	15:16	joy and rejoicing of my **h**;
Jer	17: 1	On the tablet of their **h**,
Jer	17: 9	The **h** is deceitful above
Jer	17:10	I, the LORD, search the **h**,
Jer	23: 9	My **h** within me is broken
Jer	23:16	a vision of their own **h**,
Jer	29:13	for Me with all your **h**.
Jer	48:41	day shall be Like the **h** of
Lam	1:20	My **h** is overturned within
Lam	2:11	My **h** is troubled; My bile
Ezek	11:19	I will give them one **h**,
Ezek	11:19	and take the stony **h** out of
Ezek	11:19	and give them a **h** of flesh,
Ezek	13: 2	prophesy out of their own **h**,
Ezek	16:30	How degenerate is your **h!**"
Ezek	18:31	and get yourselves a new **h**
Ezek	25:15	vengeance with a spiteful **h**,
Ezek	28: 2	Though you set your **h** as
Ezek	36:26	I will give you a new **h** and
Ezek	36:26	I will take the **h** of stone
Ezek	36:26	your flesh and give you a **h**
Ezek	44: 7	uncircumcised in **h** and
Dan	1: 8	Daniel purposed in his **h**
Dan	4:16	Let his **h** be changed from
Dan	4:16	Let him be given the **h** of a
Dan	7: 4	and a man's **h** was given to
Dan	7:28	I kept the matter in my **h**.
Dan	8:25	exalt himself in his **h**.
Hos	4:11	and new wine enslave the **h**.
Hos	11: 8	My **h** churns within Me; My
Joel	2:13	So rend your **h**,
Jon	2: 3	Into the **h** of the seas,
Matt	5: 8	Blessed are the pure in **h**,
Matt	5:28	adultery with her in his **h**.
Matt	6:21	there your **h** will be also.
Matt	11:29	I am gentle and lowly in **h**,
Matt	12:34	of the abundance of the **h**
Matt	12:35	the good treasure of his **h**
Matt	15: 8	But their **h** is far
Matt	15:19	For out of the **h** proceed evil
Matt	22:37	God with all your **h**,
Mark	6:52	because their **h** was
Mark	7:19	it does not enter his **h** but
Mark	11:23	and does not doubt in his **h**,
Luke	2:19	and pondered them in her **h**.
Luke	2:51	all these things in her **h**.
Luke	6:45	the good treasure of his **h**
Luke	18: 1	ought to pray and not lose **h**,
Luke	24:25	and slow of **h** to believe in
Luke	24:32	Did not our **h** burn within us
John	7:38	out of his **h** will flow
John	13: 2	already put it into the **h**
John	14: 1	Let not your **h** be troubled;
Acts	2:37	they were cut to the **h**,
Acts	2:46	gladness and simplicity of **h**,

Acts	4:32	who believed were of one **h**
Acts	5: 3	why has Satan filled your **h**
Acts	7:51	and uncircumcised in **h** and
Acts	8:37	you believe with all your **h**,
Acts	13:22	a man after My own **h**,
Acts	15: 8	"So God, who knows the **h**,
Rom	2: 5	and your impenitent **h** you
Rom	2:29	is that of the **h**,
Rom	6:17	yet you obeyed from the **h**
Rom	10: 6	"Do not say in your **h**,
Rom	10: 9	Jesus and believe in your **h**
Rom	10:10	For with the **h** one believes
1Co	2: 9	entered into the **h** of
1Co	14:25	thus the secrets of his **h**
2Co	2: 4	affliction and anguish of **h**
2Co	3: 3	flesh, that is, of the **h**.
2Co	3:15	read, a veil lies on their **h**.
2Co	6:11	our **h** is wide open.
2Co	9: 7	as he purposes in his **h**,
Gal	6: 9	reap if we do not lose **h**.
Eph	5:19	and making melody in your **h**
Eph	6: 5	trembling, in sincerity of **h**,
Eph	6: 6	the will of God from the **h**,
Phil	1: 7	because I have you in my **h**,
1Ti	1: 5	is love from a pure **h**,
Phm	1:12	him, that is, my own **h**,
Phm	1:20	refresh my **h** in the Lord.
Heb	3:12	be in any of you an evil **h**
Heb	4:12	and intents of the **h**.
Heb	10:22	us draw near with a true **h**
Jas	1:26	but deceives his own **h**,
1Pe	1:22	fervently with a pure **h**,
1Pe	3: 4	the hidden person of the **h**,
1Jn	3:17	and shuts up his **h** from him,
1Jn	3:20	For if our **h** condemns us, God
1Jn	3:20	God is greater than our **h**,

HEART'S (*see* HEART)

Ps	10: 3	the wicked boasts of his **h**
Rom	10: 1	my **h** desire and prayer to

HEARTH

Ps	102: 3	my bones are burned like a **h**.
Jer	36:23	the fire that was on the **h**,

HEARTILY†

1Co	16:19	and Priscilla greet you **h**
Col	3:23	And whatever you do, do it **h**,

HEARTS (*see* HEART)

Gen	18: 5	that you may refresh your **h**.
Gen	42:28	in my sack!" Then their **h**
Ex	14:17	I indeed will harden the **h**
Ex	31: 6	I have put wisdom in the **h**
Ex	35:29	the men and women whose **h**
Lev	26:41	if their uncircumcised **h** are
Deut	1:28	have discouraged our **h**,
Deut	32:46	Set your **h** on all the words
Josh	2:11	our **h** melted; neither did
Judg	16:25	when their **h** were merry,
1Sa	6: 6	then do you harden your **h**
1Sa	10:26	whose **h** God had touched.
1Ki	8:58	that He may incline our **h** to
1Ch	28: 9	for the LORD searches all **h**
Job	1: 5	and cursed God in their **h**.
Ps	7: 9	righteous God tests the **h**
Ps	28: 3	But evil is in their **h**.
Ps	95: 8	"Do not harden your **h**,
Prov	15:11	So how much more the **h** of
Prov	17: 3	But the LORD tests the **h**.
Prov	21: 2	But the LORD weighs the **h**.
Eccl	3:11	has put eternity in their **h**,
Jer	3:17	the dictates of their evil **h**.
Jer	4: 4	away the foreskins of your **h**,
Jer	7:24	the dictates of their evil **h**,
Jer	31:33	and write it on their **h**;
Lam	3:41	Let us lift our **h** and hands

Zech	7:12	they made their **h** like
Mal	4: 6	And he will turn The **h** of
Matt	9: 4	do you think evil in your **h**?
Matt	13:15	understand with their **h**
Matt	19: 8	of the hardness of your **h**,
Mark	4:15	that was sown in their **h**.
Luke	1:17	to turn the **h** of the
Luke	1:51	the imagination of their **h**.
Luke	2:35	that the thoughts of many **h**
Luke	8:12	away the word out of their **h**,
Luke	16:15	men, but God knows your **h**.
Luke	21:26	men's **h** failing them from
Luke	24:38	do doubts arise in your **h**?
Acts	1:24	who know the **h** of all, show
Acts	15: 9	purifying their **h** by faith.
Rom	1:21	and their foolish **h** were
Rom	1:24	in the lusts of their **h**,
Rom	2:15	the law written in their **h**,
Rom	8:27	Now He who searches the **h**
Rom	16:18	speech deceive the **h** of the
1Co	4: 5	reveal the counsels of the **h**.
2Co	1:22	us the Spirit in our **h** as a
2Co	3: 2	our epistle written in our **h**,
2Co	4: 6	who has shone in our **h** to
2Co	7: 2	Open your **h** to us. We have
Gal	4: 6	of His Son into your **h**,
Eph	3:17	Christ may dwell in your **h**
Eph	6:22	that he may comfort your **h**.
Phil	4: 7	will guard your **h** and minds
Col	3:15	peace of God rule in your **h**,
Col	3:16	with grace in your **h** to the
Col	4: 8	and comfort your **h**,
1Th	2: 4	men, but God who tests our **h**.
1Th	3:13	that He may establish your **h**
Heb	3: 8	Do not harden your **h**
Heb	3:15	Do not harden your **h**
Heb	8:10	write them on their **h**;
Heb	10:16	My laws into their **h**,
Heb	10:22	having our **h** sprinkled from
Jas	3:14	and self-seeking in your **h**,
Jas	4: 8	sinners; and purify your **h**,
2Pe	1:19	morning star rises in your **h**;
1Jn	3:19	and shall assure our **h**
Rev	2:23	who searches the minds and **h**.
Rev	17:17	God has put it into their **h**

HEAT (*see* HEATED)

Gen	8:22	and harvest, Cold and **h**,
Gen	18: 1	in the tent door in the **h**
Ps	19: 6	is nothing hidden from its **h**.
Is	25: 5	As **h** in the shadow of a
Is	49:10	Neither **h** nor sun shall
Ezek	3:14	in the **h** of my spirit; but
Dan	3:19	and commanded that they **h**
Matt	20:12	borne the burden and the **h**
Acts	28: 3	came out because of the **h**,
2Pe	3:10	will melt with fervent **h**;
Rev	7:16	not strike them, nor any **h**;
Rev	16: 9	were scorched with great **h**,

HEATED† (*see* HEAT)

Dan	3:19	more than it was usually **h**.
Hos	7: 4	Like an oven **h** by a

HEATHEN†

Matt	6: 7	vain repetitions as the **h**
Matt	18:17	let him be to you like a **h**

HEAVE

Ex	29:27	and the thigh of the **h**
Ex	29:28	their **h** offering to the
Num	15:20	of your ground meal as a **h**

HEAVEN (*see* HEAVEN'S, HEAVENLY, HEAVENS)

Gen	1: 8	God called the firmament H.
Gen	6:17	to destroy from under **h** all
Gen	7:11	and the windows of **h** were

Gen	8: 2	and the rain from **h** was
Gen	14:19	Possessor of **h** and earth;
Gen	15: 5	said, "Look now toward **h**,
Gen	22:11	LORD called to him from **h**
Gen	22:17	as the stars of the **h** and
Gen	24: 3	the God of **h** and the God of
Gen	27:28	give you Of the dew of **h**,
Gen	28:12	and its top reached to **h**;
Gen	28:17	and this is the gate of **h**!
Gen	49:25	you With blessings of **h**
Ex	9:22	out your hand toward **h**,
Ex	9:23	out his rod toward **h**;
Ex	16: 4	I will rain bread from **h** for
Ex	20: 4	of anything that is in **h**
Ex	20:22	have talked with you from **h**.
Deut	1:28	great and fortified up to **h**;
Deut	2:25	nations under the whole **h**,
Deut	3:24	what god is there in **h** or
Deut	4:19	lest you lift your eyes to **h**,
Deut	4:19	the stars, all the host of **h**,
Deut	4:26	I call **h** and earth to witness
Deut	10:14	Indeed **h** and the highest
Deut	30:12	Who will ascend into **h** for us
Deut	32:40	For I raise My hand to **h**,
Josh	2:11	He is God in **h** above and on
Josh	10:13	still in the midst of **h**,
1Sa	2:10	From **h** He will thunder
2Sa	18: 9	was left hanging between **h**
1Ki	8:22	out his hands toward **h**;
1Ki	8:27	**h** and the heaven of heavens
1Ki	8:27	heaven and the **h** of heavens
1Ki	8:30	Hear in **h** Your dwelling
2Ki	1:10	let fire come down from **h**
2Ki	2: 1	to take up Elijah into **h** by
2Ki	7: 2	would make windows in **h**,
2Ki	17:16	worshiped all the host of **h**,
2Ki	19:15	You have made **h** and earth.
2Ch	2:12	who made **h** and earth, for He
2Ch	7:14	then I will hear from **h**,
2Ch	32:20	prayed and cried out to **h**.
Ezra	5:11	the servants of the God of **h**
Ezra	7:12	of the Law of the God of **h**:
Neh	9: 6	The host of **h** worships You.
Job	1:16	fire of God fell from **h**
Job	2:12	dust on his head toward **h**.
Job	11: 8	They are higher than **h**—
Job	16:19	even now my witness is in **h**,
Job	22:14	walks above the circle of **h**.
Job	26:11	The pillars of **h** tremble,
Job	35:11	us wiser than the birds of **h**?
Job	38:37	pour out the bottles of **h**,
Job	41:11	Everything under **h** is Mine.
Ps	11: 4	The LORD's throne is in **h**;
Ps	19: 6	rising is from one end of **h**,
Ps	20: 6	answer him from His holy **h**
Ps	33:13	The LORD looks from **h**;
Ps	68:33	To Him who rides on the **h** of
Ps	69:34	Let **h** and earth praise Him,
Ps	73:25	Whom have I in **h** but You?
Ps	78:23	And opened the doors of **h**,
Ps	78:24	given them of the bread of **h**.
Ps	103:19	established His throne in **h**,
Ps	115: 3	But our God is in **h**;
Ps	119:89	Your word is settled in **h**.
Ps	135: 6	In **h** and in earth, In the
Ps	136:26	give thanks to the God of **h**!
Ps	139: 8	If I ascend into **h**,
Prov	30: 4	Who has ascended into **h**,
Eccl	1:13	all that is done under **h**;
Eccl	5: 2	God. For God is in **h**,
Is	14:12	you are fallen from **h**,
Is	14:13	'I will ascend into **h**,
Is	40:12	Measured **h** with a span And
Is	63:15	Look down from **h**,
Is	66: 1	H is My throne, And earth

Jer	7:18	cakes for the queen of **h**;
Jer	10: 2	dismayed at the signs of **h**,
Jer	23:24	Do I not fill **h** and earth?"
Jer	31:37	If **h** above can be measured,
Jer	44:17	incense to the queen of **h**
Jer	49:36	From the four quarters of **h**,
Jer	51:53	were to mount up to **h**,
Lam	3:41	and hands To God in **h**.
Ezek	8: 3	me up between earth and **h**,
Dan	2:19	Daniel blessed the God of **h**.
Dan	2:28	But there is a God in **h** who
Dan	4:13	holy one, coming down from **h**.
Dan	4:15	it be wet with the dew of **h**,
Dan	4:26	you come to know that **H**
Dan	4:37	and honor the King of **h**,
Dan	7: 2	the four winds of **h** were
Dan	7:13	with the clouds of **h**! He
Dan	8:10	it grew up to the host of **h**;
Amos	9: 2	Though they climb up to **h**,
Jon	1: 9	fear the LORD, the God of **h**,
Hag	2:21	I will shake **h** and earth.
Zech	6: 5	are four spirits of **h**,
Mal	3:10	for you the windows of **h**
Matt	3: 2	for the kingdom of **h** is at
Matt	3:17	a voice came from **h**,
Matt	5: 3	theirs is the kingdom of **h**.
Matt	5:12	great is your reward in **h**,
Matt	5:16	and glorify your Father in **h**.
Matt	5:18	till **h** and earth pass away,
Matt	5:19	least in the kingdom of **h**;
Matt	5:20	means enter the kingdom of **h**.
Matt	5:34	swear at all: neither by **h**,
Matt	5:45	be sons of your Father in **h**;
Matt	5:48	just as your Father in **h** is
Matt	6: 1	reward from your Father in **h**.
Matt	6: 9	pray: Our Father in **h**,
Matt	6:10	On earth as it is in **h**.
Matt	6:20	yourselves treasures in **h**,
Matt	7:11	will your Father who is in **h**
Matt	7:21	the will of My Father in **h**.
Matt	8:11	Jacob in the kingdom of **h**.
Matt	10:32	before My Father who is in **h**.
Matt	11:11	is least in the kingdom of **h**
Matt	11:25	Lord of **h** and earth, that
Matt	12:50	the will of My Father in **h**
Matt	13:11	of the kingdom of **h**,
Matt	13:24	The kingdom of **h** is like a
Matt	16: 1	show them a sign from **h**.
Matt	16:19	the keys of the kingdom of **h**,
Matt	16:19	on earth will be bound in **h**,
Matt	16:19	on earth will be loosed in **h**.
Matt	18: 1	greatest in the kingdom of **h**?
Matt	18:10	of My Father who is in **h**.
Matt	18:14	of your Father who is in **h**
Matt	19:14	of such is the kingdom of **h**.
Matt	19:21	you will have treasure in **h**;
Matt	22:30	are like angels of God in **h**.
Matt	24:29	"And he who swears by **h**,
Matt	24:30	Son of Man will appear in **h**,
Matt	24:30	coming on the clouds of **h**
Matt	24:35	**H** and earth will pass away,
Matt	24:36	not even the angels of **h**,
Matt	28: 2	of the Lord descended from **h**,
Matt	28:18	has been given to Me in **h**
Mark	10:21	you will have treasure in **h**;
Mark	11:26	will your Father in **h**
Mark	16:19	He was received up into **h**,
Luke	2:15	gone away from them into **h**,
Luke	4:25	when the **h** was shut up three
Luke	10:18	fall like lightning from **h**.
Luke	10:20	your names are written in **h**.
Luke	10:21	Lord of **h** and earth, that
Luke	15: 7	there will be more joy in **h**
Luke	15:18	I have sinned against **h** and
Luke	16:17	And it is easier for **h** and
Luke	17:29	fire and brimstone from **h**
Luke	18:13	much as raise his eyes to **h**,
Luke	18:22	you will have treasure in **h**;
Luke	19:38	the LORD!' Peace in **h**
Luke	24:51	them and carried up into **h**.
John	1:32	the Spirit descending from **h**
John	1:51	hereafter you shall see **h**
John	3:13	No one has ascended to **h** but
John	3:13	the Son of Man who is in **h**.
John	3:27	has been given to him from **h**.
John	3:31	He who comes from **h** is above
John	6:31	gave them bread from **h**
John	12:28	Then a voice came from **h**,
John	17: 1	lifted up His eyes to **h**,
Acts	1:10	looked steadfastly toward **h**
Acts	1:11	you stand gazing up into **h**?
Acts	1:11	was taken up from you into **h**,
Acts	2: 2	there came a sound from **h**,
Acts	2: 5	from every nation under **h**.
Acts	2:19	will show wonders in **h**
Acts	3:21	whom **h** must receive until the
Acts	4:12	is no other name under **h**
Acts	7:55	gazed into **h** and saw the
Acts	9: 3	shone around him from **h**.
Acts	10:11	and saw **h** opened and an
Acts	14:17	gave us rain from **h** and
Acts	17:24	since He is Lord of **h** and
Rom	1:18	of God is revealed from **h**
Rom	10: 6	'Who will ascend into **h**?
1Co	8: 5	whether in **h** or on earth (as
1Co	15:47	Man is the Lord from **h**.
2Co	5: 2	habitation which is from **h**,
2Co	12: 2	was caught up to the third **h**.
Gal	1: 8	if we, or an angel from **h**,
Eph	3:15	whom the whole family in **h**,
Eph	6: 9	your own Master also is in **h**,
Phil	2:10	should bow, of those in **h**,
Phil	3:20	For our citizenship is in **h**,
Col	1: 5	is laid up for you in **h**,
Col	1:16	were created that are in **h**
Col	1:20	on earth or things in **h**,
Col	1:23	to every creature under **h**,
Col	4: 1	you also have a Master in **h**.
1Th	1:10	to wait for His Son from **h**,
1Th	4:16	Himself will descend from **h**
2Th	1: 7	Jesus is revealed from **h**
Heb	9:24	but into **h** itself, now to
Heb	12:23	who are registered in **h**,
Heb	12:26	the earth, but also **h**.
Jas	5:18	and the **h** gave rain, and the
1Pe	1: 4	reserved in **h** for you,
1Pe	1:12	the Holy Spirit sent from **h**—
1Pe	3:22	who has gone into **h** and is at
2Pe	1:18	this voice which came from **h**
1Jn	5: 7	three that bear witness in **h**,
Rev	3:12	which comes down out of **h**.
Rev	4: 1	a door standing open in **h**.
Rev	4: 2	behold, a throne set in **h**,
Rev	9: 1	I saw a star fallen from **h**
Rev	10: 1	angel coming down from **h**,
Rev	10: 4	but I heard a voice from **h**
Rev	11:19	of God was opened in **h**,
Rev	12: 1	a great sign appeared in **h**:
Rev	14: 7	and worship Him who made **h**
Rev	15: 5	of the testimony in **h** was
Rev	16:21	And great hail from **h** fell
Rev	18: 5	her sins have reached to **h**,
Rev	19: 1	of a great multitude in **h**,
Rev	19:11	Now I saw **h** opened, and
Rev	20: 9	came down from God out of **h**
Rev	20:11	face the earth and the **h**
Rev	21: 1	Now I saw a new **h** and a new
Rev	21: 1	for the first **h** and the
Rev	21: 2	coming down out of **h** from

HEAVEN'S† (*see* HEAVEN)
Matt 19:12 for the kingdom of **h** sake.

HEAVENLY (*see* HEAVEN)
Matt	6:14	your **h** Father will also
Matt	6:26	yet your **h** Father feeds
Matt	6:32	For your **h** Father knows that
Matt	18:35	So My **h** Father also will do
Luke	2:13	angel a multitude of the **h**
Luke	11:13	how much more will your **h**
John	3:12	you believe if I tell you **h**
Acts	26:19	was not disobedient to the **h**
1Co	15:48	and as is the **h** Man, so
Eph	1: 3	spiritual blessing in the **h**
2Ti	4:18	and preserve me for His **h**
Heb	3: 1	partakers of the **h** calling,
Heb	6: 4	and have tasted the **h** gift,
Heb	8: 5	the copy and shadow of the **h**
Heb	11:16	a **h** country. Therefore God
Heb	12:22	the **h** Jerusalem, to an

HEAVENS (*see* HEAVEN)
Gen	1: 1	beginning God created the **h**
Gen	1: 9	Let the waters under the **h** be
Gen	2: 1	Thus the **h** and the earth, and
Gen	2: 4	is the history of the **h**
Gen	2: 4	God made the earth and the **h**,
Gen	11: 4	tower whose top is in the **h**;
Gen	19:24	from the LORD out of the **h**.
Ex	20:11	days the LORD made the **h**
Deut	10:14	heaven and the highest **h**
Deut	32: 1	"Give ear, O **h**,
Deut	33:26	Who rides the **h** to help
Judg	5:20	They fought from the **h**;
1Ki	8:27	heaven and the heaven of **h**
Job	9: 8	He alone spreads out the **h**,
Job	26:13	His Spirit He adorned the **h**;
Ps	2: 4	He who sits in the **h** shall
Ps	8: 1	set Your glory above the **h**!
Ps	8: 3	When I consider Your **h**,
Ps	19: 1	The **h** declare the glory of
Ps	33: 6	the word of the LORD the **h**
Ps	68:33	who rides on the heaven of **h**,
Ps	78:26	east wind to blow in the **h**;
Ps	89:11	The **h** are Yours, the earth
Ps	96:11	Let the **h** rejoice, and let
Ps	103:11	For as the **h** are high above
Ps	104: 2	Who stretch out the **h** like
Ps	115:16	The heaven, even the **h**,
Ps	136: 5	Him who by wisdom made the **h**,
Ps	144: 5	Bow down Your **h**,
Ps	148: 4	you **h** of heavens, And you
Ps	148: 4	Him, you heavens of **h**,
Ps	148: 4	And you waters above the **h**!
Prov	8:27	When He prepared the **h**,
Prov	25: 3	As the **h** for height and the
Is	34: 4	And the **h** shall be rolled
Is	40:22	Who stretches out the **h**
Is	49:13	O **h**! Be joyful, O earth!
Is	51: 6	For the **h** will vanish away
Is	51:16	That I may plant the **h**,
Is	55: 9	For as the **h** are higher than
Is	64: 1	that You would rend the **h**!
Is	65:17	I create new **h** and a new
Is	66:22	For as the new **h** and the new
Jer	4:23	form, and void; And the **h**,
Jer	4:25	And all the birds of the **h**
Jer	8: 7	Even the stork in the **h**
Jer	10:11	that have not made the **h**
Ezek	1: 1	that the **h** were opened and
Ezek	32: 8	the bright lights of the **h**
Dan	4:11	Its height reached to the **h**,
Dan	4:12	The birds of the **h** dwelt in
Hos	2:21	"I will answer the **h**,
Joel	2:30	I will show wonders in the **h**
Joel	3:16	The **h** and earth will shake;

Zech	8:12	And the **h** shall give their
Matt	3:16	the **h** were opened to Him,
Matt	24:29	and the powers of the **h** will
Mark	1:10	He saw the **h** parting and the
Luke	12:33	a treasure in the **h** that
Acts	2:34	did not ascend into the **h**,
Acts	7:56	Look! I see the **h** opened and
2Co	5: 1	with hands, eternal in the **h**.
Eph	4:10	ascended far above all the **h**,
Heb	1:10	And the **h** are the
Heb	4:14	who has passed through the **h**,
Heb	7:26	has become higher than the **h**;
Heb	8: 1	of the Majesty in the **h**,
2Pe	3:10	in which the **h** will pass
2Pe	3:13	look for new **h** and a new
Rev	12:12	"Therefore rejoice, O **h**,

HEAVINESS (*see* HEAVY)
Ps	119:28	My soul melts from **h**;
Is	29: 2	There shall be **h** and
Is	61: 3	praise for the spirit of **h**;

HEAVY (*see* HEAVINESS)
Ex	9:18	time I will cause very **h**
Ex	17:12	But Moses' hands became **h**;
Num	11:14	the burden is too **h** for me.
Deut	25:13	a **h** and a light.
1Sa	4:18	for the man was old and **h**.
1Sa	5:11	the hand of God was very **h**
1Ki	12: 4	father made our yoke **h**;
1Ki	12:10	'Your father made our yoke **h**,
1Ki	18:45	and there was a **h** rain. So
Ps	38: 4	Like a **h** burden they are
Ps	88: 7	Your wrath lies **h** upon me,
Prov	25:20	one who sings songs to a **h**
Is	6:10	dull, And their ears **h**,
Is	30:27	And His burden is **h**;
Is	59: 1	cannot save; Nor His ear **h**,
Lam	3: 7	out; He has made my chain **h**.
Matt	11:28	all you who labor and are **h**
Matt	23: 4	For they bind **h** burdens, hard
Matt	26:43	again, for their eyes were **h**.
Luke	9:32	and those with him were **h**

HEBER (*see* HEBER'S)
Judg 4:17 the wife of **H** the Kenite;

HEBER'S† (*see* HEBER)
Judg 4:21 **H** wife, took a tent peg and

HEBREW (*see* HEBREWS)
Gen	14:13	came and told Abram the **H**,
Gen	39:17	The **H** servant whom you
Ex	1:15	king of Egypt spoke to the **H**
Ex	1:16	of a midwife for the **H**
Ex	2:11	saw an Egyptian beating a **H**,
Ex	2:13	two **H** men were fighting, and
Ex	21: 2	If you buy a **H** servant, he
2Ki	18:26	and do not speak to us in **H**
Jon	1: 9	he said to them, "I am a **H**;
Luke	23:38	of Greek, Latin, and **H**:
John	5: 2	a pool, which is called in **H**,
John	19:13	The Pavement, but in **H**,
John	19:17	Skull, which is called in **H**,
Acts	21:40	he spoke to them in the **H**
Phil	3: 5	a **H** of the Hebrews;
Rev	9:11	whose name in **H** is Abaddon,
Rev	16:16	to the place called in **H**,

HEBREWS (*see* HEBREW)
Gen	43:32	not eat food with the **H**,
Ex	3:18	The LORD God of the **H** has
Ex	9: 1	says the LORD God of the **H**:
1Sa	13:19	Lest the **H** make swords or
Phil	3: 5	a Hebrew of the **H**;

HEBRON (*see* KIRJATH ARBA)
Gen 13:18 of Mamre, which are in **H**,

Gen 23: 2 H) in the land of Canaan,
Num 13:22 (Now H was built seven years
Josh 14:13 and gave H to Caleb the son
Josh 15:13 which is H (Arba was the
Josh 15:54 Kirjath Arba (which is H),
Judg 16: 3 top of the hill that faces H.
2Sa 2:11 that David was king in H
2Sa 5: 5 In H he reigned over Judah
2Sa 15:10 Absalom reigns in H!' "

HEDGE (see HEDGED, HEDGES)
Job 1:10 Have You not made a h around
Prov 15:19 the lazy man is like a h
Is 5: 5 I will take away its h,
Hos 2: 6 I will h up your way with
Matt 21:33 a vineyard and set a h

HEDGED† (see HEDGE)
Job 3:23 hidden, and whom God has h in
Ps 139: 5 You have h me behind and
Lam 3: 7 He has h me in so that I

HEDGES (see HEDGE)
Ps 80:12 have You broken down her h,
Luke 14:23 out into the highways and h,

HEED (see HEEDED, HEEDING, HEEDS)
Gen 39:10 that he did not h her, to
Ex 3:18 Then they will h your voice;
Ex 6: 9 but they did not h Moses,
Ex 6:12 How then shall Pharaoh h me,
Ex 7:13 and he did not h them, as
Ex 10:28 Get away from me! Take h to
Ex 15:26 If you diligently h the voice
Deut 4:23 Take h to yourselves, lest
Deut 28:13 if you h the commandments of
Josh 22: 5 But take careful h to do the
1Sa 2:25 Nevertheless they did not h
1Sa 15:22 And to h than the fat of
2Ch 18:27 Take h, all you people
Neh 9:16 And did not h Your
Job 13: 6 And h the pleadings of my
Ps 5: 2 Give h to the voice of my cry
Ps 119: 9 By taking h according to
Prov 17: 4 An evildoer gives h to false
Jer 17:24 if you h Me carefully,"
Jer 18:19 Give h to me, O LORD, And
Mal 2:15 Therefore take h to your
Matt 6: 1 Take h that you do not do
Matt 24: 4 Take h that no one deceives
Mark 8:15 them, saying, "Take h,
Mark 13: 5 Take h that no one deceives
Luke 8:18 Therefore take h how you
Acts 8:10 to whom they all gave h,
Acts 16:14 Lord opened her heart to h
Acts 20:28 Therefore take h to
1Co 3:10 But let each one take h how
1Co 10:12 who thinks he stands take h
Col 4:17 Take h to the ministry which
1Ti 1: 4 nor give h to fables and
1Ti 4: 1 giving h to deceiving
1Ti 4:16 Take h to yourself and to the
Tit 1:14 not giving h to Jewish fables
Heb 2: 1 give the more earnest h to
2Pe 1:19 which you do well to h as a

HEEDED (see HEED)
Gen 3:17 Because you have h the voice
Gen 16: 2 And Abram h the voice of
Ex 6:12 of Israel have not h me.
Ex 18:24 So Moses h the voice of his
Josh 10:14 that the LORD h the voice
Judg 2:20 and has not h My voice,
2Ch 25:16 done this and have not h my
Neh 9:34 Nor h Your commandments and
Is 48:18 that you had h My
Dan 9: 6 Neither have we h Your

Acts 8: 6 with one accord h the

HEEDING† (see HEED)
Ps 103:20 H the voice of His word.

HEEDS† (see HEED)
Prov 12:15 But he who h counsel is
Prov 13: 1 A wise son h his father's
Prov 15:32 But he who h rebuke gets
Prov 16:20 He who h the word wisely

HEEL (see HEELS)
Gen 3:15 And you shall bruise His h.
Gen 25:26 hand took hold of Esau's h;
Ps 41: 9 Has lifted up his h
Hos 12: 3 took his brother by the h
John 13:18 Me has lifted up his h

HEELS (see HEEL)
Lam 5: 5 They pursue at our h;
Dan 11:43 shall follow at his h.

HEIFER (see HEIFER'S)
Gen 15: 9 Me a three-year-old h,
Num 19: 2 that they bring you a red h
Num 19: 9 gather up the ashes of the h
Judg 14:18 you had not plowed with my h,
Jer 46:20 is a very pretty h,
Hos 10:11 Ephraim is a trained h
Heb 9:13 goats and the ashes of a h,

HEIFER'S† (see HEIFER)
Deut 21: 4 and they shall break the h

HEIGHT (see HEIGHTS)
Gen 6:15 and its h thirty cubits.
Ex 25:10 and a cubit and a half its h.
1Sa 16: 7 his appearance or at the h
1Ch 11:23 Egyptian, a man of GREAT h
Ps 102:19 He looked down from the h
Prov 25: 3 As the heavens for h and
Eccl 12: 5 Also they are afraid of h,
Is 7:11 in the depth or in the h
Is 37:24 I will enter its farthest h,
Jer 31:12 come and sing in the h of
Jer 49:16 Who hold the h of the hill!
Ezek 31:10 heart was lifted up in its h,
Dan 3: 1 whose h was sixty cubits
Dan 4:10 And its h was great.
Dan 4:11 Its h reached to the
Rom 8:39 nor h nor depth, nor any
Eph 3:18 and length and depth and h—
Rev 21:16 and h are equal.

HEIGHTS (see HEIGHT)
Deut 32:13 ride in the h of the earth
Ps 95: 4 The h of the hills are His
Ps 148: 1 Praise Him in the h!
Is 14:14 I will ascend above the h of
Is 41:18 open rivers in desolate h,
Ezek 36: 2 Aha! The ancient h have

HEIR (see HEIRS)
Gen 15: 2 and the h of my house is
Gen 15: 3 born in my house is my h!"
Gen 15: 4 one shall not be your h,
Gen 21:10 bondwoman shall not be h
2Sa 14: 7 and we will destroy the h
Matt 21:38 themselves, 'This is the h.
Rom 4:13 that he would be the h of
Gal 4: 1 Now I say that the h,
Gal 4: 7 then an h of God through
Gal 4:30 shall not be h with
Heb 1: 2 whom He has appointed h of
Heb 11: 7 the world and became h of

HEIRS (see HEIR)
2Ki 11: 1 destroyed all the royal h.
Rom 4:14 who are of the law are h,
Rom 8:17 and if children, then h—

Rom   8:17 **h** of God and joint
Rom   8:17 and joint **h** with Christ,
Gal   3:29 and **h** according to the
Eph   3: 6 Gentiles should be fellow **h**,
Tit   3: 7 His grace we should become **h**
Heb   6:17 more abundantly to the **h** of
Heb   11: 9 the **h** with him of the same
Jas   2: 5 to be rich in faith and **h**
1Pe   3: 7 and as being **h** together of

HELD (*see* HOLD)
Gen   34: 5 so Jacob **h** his peace until
Ex   17:11 when Moses **h** up his hand,
Deut   4: 4 But you who **h** fast to the
Judg   7:20 they **h** the torches in their
2Ki   18: 6 For he **h** fast to the LORD;
Job   36: 8 **H** in the cords of
Ps   18:35 Your right hand has **h** me
Ps   89: 7 And to be **h** in reverence by
Song   3: 4 I **h** him and would not let
Is   45: 1 whose right hand I have **h**—
Matt   28: 9 So they came and **h** Him by
Mark   6:19 Therefore Herodias **h** it
Luke 22:63 Now the men who **h** Jesus
Acts   2:24 that He should be **h** by it.
Acts   5:34 a teacher of the law **h** in
Rom   7: 6 died to what we were **h** by,
Rev   6: 9 the testimony which they **h**.

HELL
Deut   32:22 shall burn to the lowest **h**;
Ps   55:15 them go down alive into **h**,
Ps   139: 8 If I make my bed in **h**,
Prov   5: 5 Her steps lay hold of **h**.
Prov   7:27 Her house is the way to **h**,
Prov   9:18 are in the depths of **h**.
Prov   15:11 **H** and Destruction are
Prov   15:24 he may turn away from **h**
Prov   23:14 And deliver his soul from **h**.
Is   14: 9 **H** from beneath is excited
Amos   9: 2 "Though they dig into **h**,
Hab   2: 5 he enlarges his desire as **h**,
Matt   5:22 shall be in danger of **h**
Matt   5:29 whole body to be cast into **h**.
Matt   10:28 both soul and body in **h**.
Matt   18: 9 to be cast into **h** fire.
Matt   23:15 twice as much a son of **h** as
Matt   23:33 escape the condemnation of **h**?
Mark   9:43 having two hands, to go to **h**,
Luke   12: 5 has power to cast into **h**;
Jas   3: 6 and it is set on fire by **h**.
2Pe   2: 4 but cast them down to **h** and

HELLENISTS
Acts   9:29 and disputed against the **H**,

HELMET
1Sa   17: 5 He had a bronze **h** on his
Ps   60: 7 Ephraim also is the **h** for
Is   59:17 And a **h** of salvation on His
Eph   6:17 And take the **h** of salvation,
1Th   5: 8 and as a **h** the hope of

HELP (*see* HELPED, HELPER, HELPFUL, HELPING,
  HELPLESS, HELPS)
Ex   18: 4 God of my father was my **h**,
Deut   33:29 The shield of your **h** And
Josh   10: 4 Come up to me and **h** me, that
Josh   10:33 king of Gezer came up to **h**
Judg   5:23 they did not come to the **h**
2Sa   10:11 then you shall **h** me; but if
2Sa   10:11 then I will come and **h** you.
2Sa   14: 4 herself, and said, "**H**,
2Ki   6:27 If the LORD does not **h** you,
2Ch   14:11 it is nothing for You to **h**,
2Ch   14:11 **h** us, O LORD our God, for
2Ch   25: 8 for God has power to **h** and

Job   6:13 Is my **h** not within me? And
Job   30:28 assembly and cry out for **h**.
Ps   3: 2 There is no **h** for him in
Ps   20: 2 May He send you **h** from the
Ps   22:11 For there is none to **h**.
Ps   22:19 hasten to **h** Me!
Ps   33:20 He is our **h** and our
Ps   38:22 Make haste to **h** me, O Lord,
Ps   40:17 You are my **h** and my
Ps   42: 5 yet praise Him For the **h**
Ps   42:11 The **h** of my countenance and
Ps   46: 1 A very present **h** in
Ps   46: 5 God shall **h** her, just at
Ps   60:11 For the **h** of man is
Ps   70: 5 O God! You are my **h** and my
Ps   94:17 the LORD had been my **h**,
Ps   115: 9 He is their **h** and their
Ps   121: 1 whence comes my **h**?
Ps   121: 2 My **h** comes from the LORD,
Ps   124: 8 Our **h** is in the name of the
Ps   146: 5 the God of Jacob for his **h**,
Eccl   4:10 For he has no one to **h**
Is   30: 7 For the Egyptians shall **h** in
Is   31: 1 who go down to Egypt for **h**,
Is   41:13 you, 'Fear not, I will **h** you
Is   50: 7 For the Lord God will **h** Me
Is   63: 5 but there was no one to **h**,
Jer   37: 7 army which has come up to **h**
Lam   1: 7 With no one to **h** her, The
Lam   4:17 Watching vainly for our **h**;
Dan   11:34 be aided with a little **h**;
Mark   9:24 **h** my unbelief!"
Luke   5: 7 the other boat to come and **h**
Acts   16: 9 over to Macedonia and **h** us.
Acts   26:22 having obtained **h** from God,
Phil   4: 3 **h** these women who labored
Heb   4:16 mercy and find grace to **h**

HELPED (*see* HELP)
1Sa   7:12 Thus far the LORD has **h**
2Ch   18:31 cried out, and the LORD **h** him
Neh   8: 7 **h** the people to understand
Ps   86:17 have **h** me and comforted me.
Is   49: 8 day of salvation I have **h**
Luke   1:54 He has **h** His servant Israel,
2Co   6: 2 of salvation I have **h**

HELPER (*see* HELP)
Gen   2:18 I will make him a **h**
John   14:16 He will give you another **H**,
John   14: 7 the **H** will not come to you;
Rom   16: 2 for indeed she has been a **h**
Heb   13: 6 "The LORD is my **h**;

HELPFUL (*see* HELP)
1Co   6:12 me, but all things are not **h**.
1Co   10:23 me, but not all things are **h**;

HELPING (*see* HELP)
Ps   22: 1 are You so far from **h** Me,
2Co   1:11 you also **h** together in prayer

HELPLESS (*see* HELP)
Ps   10:14 The **h** commits himself to
Acts   4: 9 for a good deed done to a **h**

HELPS (*see* HELP)
Rom   8:26 Likewise the Spirit also **h** in
1Co   12:28 then gifts of healings, **h**,

HEM
Ex   28:34 upon the **h** of the robe all
Matt   9:20 behind and touched the **h** of
Matt   14:36 they might only touch the **h**

HEMAN
1Ch   6:33 of the Kohathites were **H**

HEN
Matt 23:37 as a **h** gathers her chicks

HENCEFORTH†
Luke 1:48 **h** all generations will call

HENNA
Song 4:13 Fragrant **h** with spikenard,

HEPHZIBAH†
2Ki 21: 1 His mother's name was **H**.
Is 62: 4 But you shall be called **H**,

HERALD†
Dan 3: 4 Then a **h** cried aloud: "To

HERB (see HERBS)
Gen 1:11 the **h** that yields seed,
Gen 1:30 have given every green **h**
Gen 2: 5 the earth and before any **h**
Gen 3:18 And you shall eat the **h** of
Ex 9:25 and the hail struck every **h**
Ps 37: 2 And wither as the green **h**.

HERBS (see HERB)
Gen 9: 3 things, even as the green **h**.
Num 9:11 bread and bitter **h**.
Prov 15:17 Better is a dinner of **h**
Matt 13:32 it is greater than the **h**
Mark 4:32 becomes greater than all **h**,

HERD (see HERDS, HERDSMEN)
Gen 18: 7 And Abraham ran to the **h**,
2Sa 17:29 sheep and cheese of the **h**,
Hab 3:17 And there be no **h** in the
Matt 8:31 us to go away into the **h** of
Mark 5:13 and the **h** ran violently down
Luke 8:33 and the **h** ran violently down

HERDS (see HERD)
Gen 13: 5 had flocks and **h** and tents.
Ex 12:32 take your flocks and your **h**,
Deut 12: 6 and the firstborn of your **h**
Joel 1:18 the animals groan! The **h**

HERDSMEN (see SHEEPBREEDERS)
Gen 13: 7 was strife between the **h** of
Gen 13: 7 Abram's livestock and the **h**
Gen 26:20 quarreled with Isaac's **h**,

HERESIES†
Gal 5:20 ambitions, dissensions, **h**,
2Pe 2: 1 bring in destructive **h**,

HERITAGE
Ex 6: 8 will give it to you as a **h**:
Job 27:13 And the **h** of oppressors,
Ps 94: 5 O LORD, And afflict Your **h**.
Ps 111: 6 In giving them the **h** of the
Ps 119:111 I have taken as a **h** forever,
Ps 127: 3 children are a **h** from the
Eccl 2:21 yet he must leave his **h** to a
Jer 2: 7 My land And made My **h** an
Jer 50:11 You destroyers of My **h**,
Joel 3: 2 My **h** Israel, Whom they have

HERMES
Acts 14:12 called Zeus, and Paul, **H**,

HERMOGENES†
2Ti 1:15 whom are Phygellus and **H**.

HERMON (see SENIR, SIRION)
Deut 3: 8 the River Arnon to Mount **H**
Deut 3: 9 (the Sidonians call **H** Sirion,
Deut 4:48 to Mount Sion (that is, **H**),
Judg 3: 3 from Mount Baal **H** to the
1Ch 5:23 is, to Senir, or Mount **H**.
Ps 42: 6 And from the heights of **H**,
Ps 133: 3 It is like the dew of **H**,
Song 4: 8 From the top of Senir and **H**,

HEROD (see HEROD'S, HERODIANS)
Matt 2: 1 of Judea in the days of **H**
Matt 2:12 they should not return to **H**,
Matt 2:13 for **H** will seek the young
Matt 2:15 there until the death of **H**,
Matt 14: 1 At that time **H** the tetrarch
Matt 14: 3 For **H** had laid hold of John
Mark 6:20 for **H** feared John, knowing
Mark 6:21 an opportune day came when **H**
Mark 6:22 and pleased **H** and those who
Mark 8:15 and the leaven of **H**.
Luke 1: 5 There was in the days of **H**,
Luke 3: 1 **H** being tetrarch of Galilee,
Luke 3:19 for all the evils which **H**
Luke 23: 8 Now when **H** saw Jesus, he was
Luke 23:12 That very day Pilate and **H**
Acts 12: 1 Now about that time **H** the
Acts 12:19 But when **H** had searched for
Acts 13: 1 had been brought up with **H**

HEROD'S (see HEROD)
Matt 14: 6 But when **H** birthday was
Luke 23: 7 knew that He belonged to **H**
Acts 23:35 him to be kept in **H**

HERODIANS† (see HEROD)
Matt 22:16 their disciples with the **H**,
Mark 3: 6 plotted with the **H** against
Mark 12:13 of the Pharisees and the **H**,

HERODIAS
Matt 14: 6 the daughter of **H** danced

HESHBON
Num 21:26 For **H** was the city of Sihon
Num 21:34 the Amorites, who dwelt at **H**.
Num 32:37 children of Reuben built **H**
Deut 2:24 Sihon the Amorite, king of **H**,
Deut 2:30 But Sihon king of **H** would not

HESITATE
Job 30:10 They do not **h** to spit in my

HETH
Gen 23:16 the hearing of the sons of **H**
Gen 23:20 to Abraham by the sons of **H**

HEW† (see HEWED, HEWN, HEWS)
Deut 10: 1 **H** for yourself two tablets of

HEWED† (see HEW)
Deut 10: 3 **h** two tablets of stone like

HEWN (see HEW)
Ex 20:25 you shall not build it of **h**
2Ki 22: 6 and to buy timber and **h** stone
Prov 9: 1 She has **h** out her seven
Is 51: 1 rock from which you were **h**,
Amos 5:11 you have built houses of **h**
Matt 27:60 his new tomb which he had **h**

HEWS† (see HEW)
Is 22:16 As he who **h** himself a

HEZEKIAH
2Ki 18: 1 that **H** the son of Ahaz,
2Ki 18:14 king of Assyria assessed **H**
2Ki 18:15 So **H** gave him all the silver
2Ki 19: 5 So the servants of King **H**
2Ki 19:15 Then **H** prayed before the
2Ki 20: 1 In those days **H** was sick and
2Ki 20:20 the rest of the acts of **H**—
2Ki 20:21 So **H** rested with his fathers.
2Ki 21: 3 the high places which **H** his
1Ch 3:13 **H** his son, Manasseh his son,
2Ch 30:22 And **H** gave encouragement to
2Ch 31: 9 Then **H** questioned the priests
2Ch 32: 2 And when **H** saw that
2Ch 32:26 Then **H** humbled himself for
2Ch 32:27 **H** had very great riches and

2Ch	32:30	This same **H** also stopped the
2Ch	32:30	**H** prospered in all his
2Ch	32:33	So **H** rested with his fathers,
2Ch	33: 3	the high places which **H** his
Prov	25: 1	Solomon which the men of **H**
Is	1: 1	Uzziah, Jotham, Ahaz, and **H**,
Hos	1: 1	Uzziah, Jotham, Ahaz, and **H**,
Mic	1: 1	days of Jotham, Ahaz, and **H**,
Zeph	1: 1	son of Amariah, the son of **H**,
Matt	1: 9	begot Ahaz, and Ahaz begot **H**.
Matt	1:10	**H** begot Manasseh, Manasseh

HID (*see* HIDE)

Gen	3: 8	and Adam and his wife **h**
Gen	3:10	and I **h** myself."
Gen	35: 4	and Jacob **h** them under the
Ex	2: 2	she **h** him three months.
Ex	2:12	he killed the Egyptian and **h**
Ex	3: 6	And Moses **h** his face, for
Josh	2: 4	took the two men and **h** them.
1Sa	3:18	and nothing from him. And
1Sa	13: 6	then the people **h** in caves,
1Sa	20:24	Then David **h** in the field.
2Ki	11: 2	and they **h** him and his nurse
2Ch	22:11	**h** him from Athaliah so that
Ps	30: 7	You **h** Your face, and I was
Is	53: 3	with grief. And we **h**,
Jer	13: 5	So I went and **h** it by the
Matt	13:33	which a woman took and **h** in
Matt	13:44	which a man found and **h**;
Matt	25:25	and went and **h** your talent
Luke	1:24	and she herself five

HIDDEKEL†

Gen	2:14	of the third river is **H**;

HIDDEN (*see* HIDE)

Gen	4:14	I shall be **h** from Your face;
Deut	33:19	seas And of treasures **h**
Josh	7:22	**h** in his tent, with the
1Sa	10:22	**h** among the equipment."
1Sa	14:11	the holes where they have **h**.
2Sa	18:13	For there is nothing **h** from
1Ki	18: 4	one hundred prophets and **h**
Job	3:16	Or why was I not **h** like a
Job	3:21	search for it more than **h**
Job	28:21	It is **h** from the eyes of all
Ps	17:14	belly You fill with Your **h**
Ps	19: 6	And there is nothing **h** from
Ps	22:24	Nor has He **h** His face from
Ps	32: 5	my iniquity I have not **h**.
Ps	51: 6	And in the **h** part You will
Ps	69: 5	And my sins are not **h** from
Ps	119:11	Your word I have **h** in my
Ps	139:15	My frame was not **h** from You,
Ps	140: 5	The proud have **h** a snare for
Prov	2: 4	search for her as for **h**
Is	40:27	My way is **h** from the LORD,
Is	45: 3	of darkness And **h** riches
Is	64: 7	For You have **h** Your face,
Jer	13: 7	the place where I had **h** it;
Jer	16:17	they are not **h** from My face,
Ezek	28: 3	is no secret that can be **h**
Hos	13:14	your destruction! Pity is **h**
Matt	5:14	is set on a hill cannot be **h**.
Matt	10:26	and **h** that will not be
Matt	11:25	that You have **h** these things
Matt	13:44	of heaven is like treasure **h**
Mark	7:24	it, but He could not be **h**.
Luke	19:42	peace! But now they are **h**
1Co	2: 7	the **h** wisdom which God
1Co	4: 5	both bring to light the **h**
Eph	3: 9	of the ages has been **h** in
Col	1:26	the mystery which has been **h**
Col	2: 3	in whom are **h** all the
Col	3: 3	and your life is **h** with

Heb	4:13	And there is no creature **h**
Heb	11:23	was **h** three months by his
1Pe	3: 4	rather let it be the **h**
Rev	2:17	I will give some of the **h**

HIDE (*see* HID, HIDDEN, HIDEOUT, HIDES, HIDING)

Gen	18:17	Shall I **h** from Abraham what I
Ex	2: 3	when she could no longer **h**
Lev	4:11	But the bull's **h** and all its
Deut	31:17	I will **h** My face from them,
Deut	32:20	I will **h** My face from them,
Judg	6:11	in order to **h** it from the
1Sa	3:17	Please do not **h** it from me.
Job	3:10	Nor **h** sorrow from my eyes.
Job	13:20	Then I will not **h** myself
Job	13:24	Why do You **h** Your face, And
Ps	10: 1	Why do You **h** in times of
Ps	13: 1	How long will You **h** Your
Ps	17: 8	**H** me under the shadow of
Ps	27: 5	time of trouble He shall **h**
Ps	27: 5	His tabernacle He shall **h**
Ps	55:12	Then I could **h** from him.
Ps	64: 2	**H** me from the secret plots
Ps	89:46	Will You **h** Yourself
Ps	119:19	Do not **h** Your commandments
Ps	139:12	the darkness shall not **h**
Is	1:15	I will **h** My eyes from you;
Is	45:15	who **h** Yourself, O God of
Jer	36:19	said to Baruch, "Go and **h**,
Jer	38:14	**H** nothing from me."
Lam	3:56	Do not **h** Your ear From my
Rev	6:16	Fall on us and **h** us from the

HIDEOUT† (*see* HIDE)

1Sa	23:22	see the place where his **h**

HIDES (*see* HIDE)

Job	34:29	And when He **h** His face,
Job	42: 3	Who is this who **h** counsel
Prov	28:27	But he who **h** his eyes will

HIDING (*see* HIDE)

Job	31:33	By **h** my iniquity in my
Ps	119:114	You are my **h** place and my

HIGH (*see* HIGHER, HIGHEST, HIGHLY, LOUD)

Gen	7:17	and it rose **h** above the
Gen	7:19	and all the **h** hills under
Gen	14:18	the priest of God Most **H**.
Lev	21:10	He who is the **h** priest
Lev	26:30	I will destroy your **h** places,
Num	35:28	until the death of the **h**
Deut	3: 5	were fortified with **h**
Deut	12: 2	on the **h** mountains and on
Deut	32: 8	When the Most **H** divided
Josh	20: 6	death of the one who is **h**
2Sa	22:14	And the Most **H** uttered His
1Ki	6:10	temple, each five cubits **h**;
1Ki	11: 7	Then Solomon built a **h** place
1Ki	14:23	and wooden images on every **h**
1Ki	21:12	and seated Naboth with **h**
2Ki	18: 4	He removed the **h** places and
2Ki	22: 4	Go up to Hilkiah the **h**
2Ki	23:15	and the **h** place which
1Ch	17:17	to the rank of a man of **h**
2Ch	31: 1	and threw down the **h** places
2Ch	33: 3	For he rebuilt the **h** places
2Ch	33:17	still sacrificed on the **h**
Esth	7: 9	The gallows, fifty cubits **h**,
Job	16:19	And my evidence is on **h**.
Ps	7:17	the name of the LORD Most **H**.
Ps	9: 2	to Your name, O Most **H**.
Ps	18:13	And the Most **H** uttered His
Ps	18:33	And sets me on my **h** places.
Ps	21: 7	the mercy of the Most **H** he
Ps	27: 5	He shall set me **h** upon a
Ps	46: 4	the tabernacle of the Most **H**.

Ps	47: 2	For the LORD Most **H** is
Ps	49: 2	Both low and **h**,
Ps	57: 2	will cry out to God Most **H**,
Ps	62: 9	Men of **h** degree are a lie;
Ps	68:18	You have ascended on **h**,
Ps	75: 5	not lift up your horn on **h**;
Ps	77:10	the right hand of the Most **H**.
Ps	82: 6	are children of the Most **H**
Ps	91: 1	secret place of the Most **H**
Ps	92: 1	to Your name, O Most **H**;
Ps	103:11	For as the heavens are **h**
Ps	107:11	the counsel of the Most **H**,
Ps	107:41	Yet He sets the poor on **h**,
Ps	139: 6	wonderful for me; It is **h**,
Is	2:13	of Lebanon that are **h** and
Is	6: 1	**h** and lifted up, and the
Is	14:14	I will be like the Most **H**.
Is	22:16	himself a sepulcher on **h**,
Is	32:15	is poured upon us from on **h**,
Is	40: 9	Get up into the **h** mountain;
Is	52:13	and extolled and be very **h**.
Is	57:15	For thus says the **H** and
Is	57:15	I dwell in the **h** and holy
Jer	7:31	And they have built the **h**
Jer	17: 2	By the green trees on the **h**
Jer	17:12	A glorious **h** throne from the
Jer	25:30	LORD will roar from on **h**,
Ezek	1:26	the appearance of a man **h**
Dan	3:26	servants of the Most **H** God,
Dan	4:24	is the decree of the Most **H**,
Dan	4:25	you know that the Most **H**
Dan	4:34	and I blessed the Most **H** and
Dan	7:22	of the saints of the Most **H**,
Dan	8: 3	and the two horns were **h**;
Amos	4:13	Who treads the **h** places of
Mic	6: 6	bow myself before the **H** God?
Hag	1: 1	the **h** priest, saying,
Zech	3: 1	he showed me Joshua the **h**
Matt	4: 8	Him up on an exceedingly **h**
Matt	17: 1	led them up on a **h** mountain
Matt	26: 3	at the palace of the **h**
Matt	26:51	struck the servant of the **h**
Mark	2:26	the days of Abiathar the **h**
Mark	5: 7	Son of the Most **H** God? I
Luke	1:78	the Dayspring from on **h** has
Luke	3: 2	Annas and Caiaphas were **h**
Luke	4:38	was sick with a **h** fever, and
Luke	6:35	will be sons of the Most **H**.
Luke	8:28	Son of the Most **H** God? I beg
Luke	24:49	endued with power from on **h**.
John	11:49	being **h** priest that year,
John	18:10	drew it and struck the **h**
John	19:31	(for that Sabbath was a **h**
Acts	4: 6	as well as Annas the **h**
Acts	7:48	the Most **H** does not dwell in
Acts	16:17	the servants of the Most **H**
Acts	23: 2	And the **h** priest Ananias
Acts	23: 4	Do you revile God's **h**
Rom	12:16	Do not set your mind on **h**
Rom	13:11	that now it is **h** time to
2Co	10: 5	down arguments and every **h**
Eph	4: 8	He ascended on **h**,
Heb	1: 3	hand of the Majesty on **h**,
Heb	2:17	be a merciful and faithful **H**
Heb	3: 1	consider the Apostle and **H**
Heb	4:14	then that we have a great **H**
Heb	6:20	having become **H** Priest
Heb	7: 1	priest of the Most **H** God,
Heb	7:27	as those **h** priests, to offer
Heb	9: 7	into the second part the **h**
Heb	9:11	But Christ came as **H** Priest
Rev	21:10	the Spirit to a great and **h**
Rev	21:12	Also she had a great and **h**

HIGHER (*see* HIGH)

Job	35: 5	They are **h** than you.
Ps	61: 2	me to the rock that is **h**
Is	55: 9	For as the heavens are **h**
Is	55: 9	So are My ways **h** than your
Dan	8: 3	but one was **h** than the
Luke	14:10	say to you, 'Friend, go up **h**.
Heb	7:26	and has become **h** than the

HIGHEST (*see* HIGH)

Deut	10:14	Indeed heaven and the **h**
Prov	9: 3	She cries out from the **h**
Matt	21: 9	LORD!' Hosanna in the **h**!
Mark	11:10	the Lord! Hosanna in the **h**!
Luke	1:32	be called the Son of the **H**,
Luke	1:35	and the power of the **H** will
Luke	2:14	"Glory to God in the **h**,
Luke	19:38	in heaven and glory in the **h**!

HIGHLY† (*see* HIGH)

1Sa	18:30	so that his name became **h**
1Ch	14: 2	for his kingdom was **h**
Luke	1:28	**h** favored one, the Lord is
Luke	16:15	For what is **h** esteemed among
Acts	5:13	the people esteemed them **h**.
Rom	12: 3	to think of himself more **h**
Phil	2: 9	Therefore God also has **h**
1Th	5:13	and to esteem them very **h** in

HIGHWAY (*see* HIGHWAYS)

Num	20:17	will go along the King's **H**;
Is	7: 3	on the **h** to the Fuller's
Is	19:23	that day there will be a **h**
Is	35: 8	it shall be called the **H** of
Is	36: 2	on the **h** to the Fuller's
Is	40: 3	straight in the desert A **h**

HIGHWAYS (*see* HIGHWAY)

Judg	5: 6	The **h** were deserted, And
Matt	22: 9	Therefore go into the **h**, and

HILKIAH

2Ki	22: 4	Go up to **H** the high priest,
2Ch	34:14	**H** the priest found the Book
Jer	1: 1	of Jeremiah the son of **H**,

HILL (*see* HILLS, HILLSIDE)

Ex	17: 9	stand on the top of the **h**
1Sa	7: 1	house of Abinadab on the **h**,
1Ki	14:23	images on every high **h** and
Ps	2: 6	set My King On My holy **h**
Ps	3: 4	He heard me from His holy **h**.
Ps	15: 1	may dwell in Your holy **h**?
Ps	24: 3	Who may ascend into the **h** of
Song	4: 6	of myrrh And to the **h** of
Is	5: 1	On a very fruitful **h**.
Is	10:32	The **h** of Jerusalem.
Is	30:17	And as a banner on a **h**.
Is	40: 4	And every mountain and **h**
Jer	2:20	When on every high **h** and
Matt	5:14	A city that is set on a **h**
Luke	1:65	throughout all the **h**
Luke	3: 5	every mountain and **h**
Luke	4:29	Him to the brow of the **h** on

HILLS (*see* HILL)

Gen	7:19	and all the high **h** under the
Gen	49:26	bound of the everlasting **h**.
Deut	8: 7	flow out of valleys and **h**;
Deut	8: 9	iron and out of whose **h** you
Deut	33:15	things of the everlasting **h**,
1Ki	20:23	gods are gods of the **h**.
1Ki	20:28	"The LORD is God of the **h**,
Ps	50:10	the cattle on a thousand **h**.
Ps	65:12	And the little **h** rejoice on
Ps	95: 4	The heights of the **h** are
Ps	98: 8	Let the **h** be joyful
Ps	114: 4	The little **h** like lambs.

Ps　　121: 1 lift up my eyes to the **h**—
Prov　　8:25 were settled, Before the **h**,
Is　　　2: 2 shall be exalted above the **h**;
Is　　55:12 The mountains and the **h**
Jer　　4:24 And all the **h** moved back
Jer　　17: 2 green trees on the high **h**.
Jer　　26:18 the temple Like the bare **h**
Hos　　10: 8 "Cover us!" And to the **h**,
Mic　　4: 1 shall be exalted above the **h**;
Nah　　1: 5 The **h** melt, And the earth
Zeph　1:10 a loud crashing from the **h**.
Luke　23:30 on us!" and to the **h**,

HILLSIDE† (see HILL)
2Sa　　13:34 from the road on the **h**
2Sa　　16:13 Shimei went along the **h**

HILT†
Judg　　3:22 Even the **h** went in after the

HIN
Ex　　29:40 of a **h** of pressed oil, and
Ex　　29:40 one-fourth of a **h** of wine as
Ex　　30:24 and a **h** of olive oil.
Lev　　19:36 ephah, and an honest **h**:
Num　15:10 the drink offering half a **h**
Num　28: 7 be one-fourth of a **h** for

HINDER (see HINDERED, HINDERS)
Gen　24:56 Do not **h** me, since the LORD
Job　　9:12 who can **h** Him? Who can say
Job　11:10 Then who can **h** Him?
1Co　　9:12 endure all things lest we **h**

HINDERED (see HINDER)
Rom　　1:13 to come to you (but was **h**
Rom　15:22 I also have been much **h**
Gal　　5: 7 Who **h** you from obeying the
1Th　　2:18 but Satan **h** us.
1Pe　　3: 7 your prayers may not be **h**.

HINDERS (see HINDER)
Acts　　8:36 What **h** me from being

HINGES†
1Ki　　7:50 and the **h** of gold, both for
Prov　26:14 As a door turns on its **h**,

HINNOM
Josh　15: 8 the Valley of the Son of H
Josh　18:16 the Valley of the Son of H
Neh　11:30 Beersheba to the Valley of H.
Jer　　7:31 the Valley of the Son of H,

HIP (see HIPS)
Gen　32:25 and the socket of Jacob's **h**
Judg　15: 8 So he attacked them **h** and

HIPS (see HIP)
2Sa　　20: 8 in its sheath at his **h**;

HIRAM (see HURAM)
2Sa　　5:11 Then **H** king of Tyre sent
1Ki　　5: 1 for **H** had always loved
1Ki　　5:11 And Solomon gave **H** twenty
1Ki　10:11 Also, the ships of **H**,

HIRE (see HIRED, HIRELING)
Prov　26:10 Gives the fool his **h** and
Matt　20: 1 early in the morning to **h**

HIRED (see HIRE)
Gen　30:16 for I have surely **h** you with
Ex　12:45 A sojourner and a **h** servant
Deut　15:18 he has been worth a double **h**
1Sa　　2: 5 who were full have **h**
2Ch　24:12 and they **h** masons and
Neh　13: 2 but **h** Balaam against them to
Job　　7: 1 also like the days of a **h**
Is　20: 7 the Lord will shave with a **h**
Hos　　8: 9 Ephraim has **h** lovers.
Matt　20: 7 Because no one **h** us.' He said

Matt　20: 9 when those came who were **h**
Mark　1:20 in the boat with the **h**
Luke　15:19 Make me like one of your **h**

HIRELING (see HIRE)
John　10:13 The **h** flees because he is a

HISS (see HISSING)
1Ki　　9: 8 be astonished and will **h**,
Jer　19: 8 it will be astonished and **h**
Lam　　2:15 They **h** and shake their
Ezek　27:36 among the peoples will **h** at

HISSING (see HISS)
Jer　18:16 desolate and a perpetual **h**;
Jer　25: 9 them an astonishment, a **h**,

HISTORY
Gen　　2: 4 This is the **h** of the

HITCH† (see HITCHED)
1Sa　　6: 7 and **h** the cows to the cart;

HITCHED† (see HITCH)
1Sa　　6:10 took two milk cows and **h**

HITTITE (see HITTITES)
Gen　23:10 and Ephron the **H** answered
Gen　49:29 in the field of Ephron the **H**,
Josh　　9: 1 Sea toward Lebanon—the **H**,
2Sa　11: 3 the wife of Uriah the **H**?
2Sa　11:17 and Uriah the **H** died also.
Ezek　16: 3 Amorite and your mother a **H**.
Ezek　16:45 your mother was a **H** and

HITTITES (see HITTITE)
Gen　15:20 "the **H**, the Perizzites, the
Ex　3: 8 of the Canaanites and the **H**
Ex　23:23 in to the Amorites and the **H**
Num　13:29 the land of the South; the **H**,

HIVITE (see HIVITES)
Ex　23:28 which shall drive out the **H**,
Ex　33: 2 and the Perizzite and the **H**

HIVITES (see HIVITE)
Ex　3: 8 and the Perizzites and the **H**
Josh　　3:10 and the Hittites and the **H**

HO†
Is　55: 1 **H**! Everyone who thirsts,

HOBAB† (see JETHRO)
Num　10:29 Now Moses said to **H** the son
Judg　　4:11 of the children of **H** the

HOLD (see HELD, HOLDERS, HOLDING, HOLDS)
Gen　19:16 the men took **h** of his hand,
Ex　5: 1 that they may **h** a feast to
Ex　20: 7 for the LORD will not **h**
Deut　5:11 for the LORD will not **h**
Deut　10:20 and to Him you shall **h** fast,
Judg　16: 3 took **h** of the doors of the
Judg　16:29 And Samson took **h** of the two
1Ki　　2: 9 do not **h** him guiltless, for
1Ch　13: 9 Uzza put out his hand to **h**
Job　　2: 9 Do you still **h** fast to your
Job　　6:24 and I will **h** my tongue;
Job　　9:28 I know that You will not **h**
Job　21: 6 And trembling takes **h** of my
Job　27: 6 My righteousness I **h** fast,
Ps　　2: 4 The LORD shall **h** them in
Ps　73:23 You **h** me by my right hand.
Ps　94:18 O LORD, will **h** me up.
Ps　116: 3 the pangs of Sheol laid **h**
Ps　119:53 Indignation has taken **h** of
Ps　139:10 Your right hand shall **h** me.
Prov　3:18 of life to those who take **h**
Prov　4:13 Take firm **h** of instruction,
Prov　5: 5 Her steps lay **h** of hell.
Prov　24:11 And **h** back those stumbling
Is　4: 1 seven women shall take **h** of

Is	21: 3 Pangs have taken **h** of me,
Is	41:13 will **h** your right hand,
Is	56: 4 And **h** fast My covenant,
Jer	2:13 broken cisterns that can **h** no
Jer	6:24 Anguish has taken **h** of us,
Ezek	24:14 I will not **h** back, Nor
Matt	14: 3 For Herod had laid **h** of John
Matt	26:57 And those who had laid **h** of
Mark	7: 8 You **h** the tradition of
1Co	15: 2 if you **h** fast that word
Phil	2:29 and **h** such men in esteem;
Phil	3:12 that I may lay **h** of that for
Phil	3:12 Jesus has also laid **h** of me.
1Th	5:21 **h** fast what is good.
2Th	2:15 stand fast and **h** the
1Ti	6:12 lay **h** on eternal life, to
2Ti	1:13 **H** fast the pattern of sound
Heb	3: 6 whose house we are if we **h**
Heb	3:14 partakers of Christ if we **h**
Heb	4:14 let us **h** fast our
Jas	2: 1 do not **h** the faith of our
Rev	2:13 And you **h** fast to My name,
Rev	2:14 you have there those who **h**
Rev	20: 2 He laid **h** of the dragon, that

HOLDERS (*see* HOLD)

Ex	25:27 as **h** for the poles to bear

HOLDING (*see* HOLD)

1Sa	25:36 **h** a feast in his house, like
Jer	6:11 I am weary of **h** it in.
Mark	7: 3 **h** the tradition of the
Phil	2:16 **h** fast the word of life, so
Col	2:19 and not **h** fast to the Head,
1Ti	3: 9 **h** the mystery of the faith
Tit	1: 9 **h** fast the faithful word as

HOLDS (*see* HOLD)

Job	2: 3 And still he **h** fast to his
Prov	31:19 And her hand **h** the spindle.
Is	56: 6 And **h** fast My covenant—
Dan	5:23 and the God who **h** your
Rev	2: 1 'These things says He who **h**

HOLE (*see* HOLES)

Is	11: 8 shall play by the cobra's **h**,
Is	51: 1 And to the **h** of the pit
Jer	13: 4 and hide it there in a **h** in
Ezek	8: 7 there was a **h** in the wall.

HOLES (*see* HOLE)

1Sa	13:12 in thickets, in rocks, in **h**,
Hag	1: 6 to put into a bag with **h**.
Matt	8:20 Foxes have **h** and birds of the

HOLIDAY

Esth	2:18 and he proclaimed a **h** in the
Esth	8:17 gladness, a feast and a **h**.

HOLIER† (*see* HOLY)

Is	65: 5 For I am **h** than you!'

HOLIEST† (*see* HOLY)

Heb	9: 3 which is called the **H** of
Heb	9: 8 that the way into the **H** of
Heb	10:19 boldness to enter the **H** by

HOLINESS (*see* HOLY)

Ex	15:11 is like You, glorious in **h**,
Ex	28:36 **H TO THE LORD**.
1Ch	16:29 LORD in the beauty of **h**!
Ps	60: 6 God has spoken in His **h**:
Ps	89:35 Once I have sworn by My **h**;
Ps	93: 5 **H** adorns Your house, O
Is	35: 8 be called the Highway of **H**.
Amos	4: 2 Lord GOD has sworn by His **h**:
Zech	14:20 **H TO THE LORD**" shall be
Luke	1:75 In **h** and righteousness
Rom	1: 4 according to the Spirit of **h**,

Rom	6:19 of righteousness for **h**.
Rom	6:22 you have your fruit to **h**,
2Co	7: 1 perfecting **h** in the fear of
Eph	4:24 in true righteousness and **h**.
1Ti	2:15 in faith, love, and **h**,
Heb	12:10 may be partakers of His **h**.
Heb	12:14 with all people, and **h**,

HOLLOW

Ex	38: 7 He made the altar **h** with
Judg	15:19 So God split the **h** place that
Is	40:12 the waters in the **h** of His

HOLY (*see* HOLIER, HOLIEST, HOLINESS, SPIRIT, UNHOLY)

Ex	3: 5 place where you stand is **h**
Ex	15:13 in Your strength To Your **h**
Ex	16:23 a **h** Sabbath to the LORD.
Ex	19: 6 a kingdom of priests and a **h**
Ex	20: 8 Sabbath day, to keep it **h**.
Ex	22:31 And you shall be **h** men to
Ex	26:33 the **h** place and the
Ex	28:38 hallow in all their **h** gifts;
Ex	29: 6 and put the **h** crown on the
Ex	29:37 the altar shall be most **h**.
Ex	30:10 It is most **h** to the
Ex	30:25 shall make from these a **h**
Ex	30:35 salted, pure, and **h**.
Ex	31:15 **h** to the LORD. Whoever does
Ex	35: 2 the seventh day shall be a **h**
Lev	2: 3 It is most **h** of the
Lev	5:15 in regard to the **h** things
Lev	6:16 it shall be eaten in a **h**
Lev	10: 3 Me I must be regarded as **h**;
Lev	10:10 may distinguish between **h**
Lev	11:44 shall be holy; for I am **h**.
Lev	16: 2 at just any time into the **H**
Lev	16: 3 Aaron shall come into the **H**
Lev	16: 4 He shall put the **h** linen
Lev	16:17 to make atonement in the **H**
Lev	20: 3 sanctuary and profane My **h**
Lev	21: 8 who sanctify you, am **h**.
Lev	22: 2 themselves from the **h**
Lev	22:10 shall not eat the **h** thing.
Lev	22:15 shall not profane the **h**
Lev	23: 2 you shall proclaim to be **h**
Lev	27:14 his house to be **h** to the
Num	4:15 they shall not touch any **h**
Num	4:19 they approach the most **h**
Num	7: 9 was the service of the **h**
Num	16: 5 who is His and who is **h**,
Num	31: 6 with the **h** articles and the
Num	35:25 who was anointed with the **h**
Deut	5:12 Sabbath day, to keep it **h**,
Deut	7: 6 For you are a **h** people to
Deut	26:13 I have removed the **h** tithe
Deut	26:15 Look down from Your **h**
Josh	5:15 place where you stand is **h**.
Josh	24:19 for He is a **h** God. He is a
1Sa	2: 2 No one is **h** like the LORD,
1Sa	21: 6 So the priest gave him **h**
1Ki	7:50 the inner room (the Most **H**
1Ki	8: 4 and all the **h** furnishings
2Ki	4: 9 I know that this is a **h** man
2Ki	19:22 Against the **H** One of
1Ch	16:10 Glory in His **h** name; Let
1Ch	29: 3 I have prepared for the **h**
2Ch	23: 6 may go in, for they are **h**;
2Ch	30:27 prayer came up to His **h**
2Ch	35: 3 Put the **h** ark in the house
Ezra	9: 2 sons, so that the **h** seed is
Neh	8: 9 This day is **h** to the LORD
Neh	9:14 made known to them Your **h**
Neh	10:31 or on a **h** day; and we would
Neh	11: 1 the **h** city, and nine-tenths
Ps	2: 6 My King On My **h** hill of Zion
Ps	3: 4 He heard me from His **h** hill.

Ps	11: 4	The LORD is in His **h**
Ps	15: 1	Who may dwell in Your **h**
Ps	16:10	Nor will You allow Your **H**
Ps	20: 6	will answer him from His **h**
Ps	24: 3	Or who may stand in His **h**
Ps	28: 2	up my hands toward Your **h**
Ps	33:21	we have trusted in His **h**
Ps	46: 4	The **h** place of the
Ps	47: 8	God sits on His **h** throne.
Ps	48: 1	In His **h** mountain.
Ps	51:11	And do not take Your **H**
Ps	68: 5	Is God in His **h**
Ps	68:17	in the **H** Place.
Ps	71:22	O H One of Israel.
Ps	78:54	He brought them to His **h**
Ps	86: 2	my life, for I am **h**;
Ps	98: 1	His right hand and His **h**
Ps	99: 3	and awesome name—He is **h**.
Ps	103: 1	bless His **h** name!
Ps	105:42	For He remembered His **h**
Ps	111: 9	**H** and awesome is His name.
Ps	145:21	all flesh shall bless His **h**
Prov	9:10	And the knowledge of the **H**
Prov	30: 3	have knowledge of the **H** One.
Is	1: 4	provoked to anger The **H**
Is	4: 3	Jerusalem will be called **h**—
Is	6: 3	and said: "Holy, **h**,
Is	6:13	So the **h** seed shall be
Is	10:17	And his **H** One for a flame;
Is	11: 9	hurt nor destroy in all My **h**
Is	12: 6	For great is the **H** One of
Is	52: 1	the **h** city! For the
Is	52:10	LORD has made bare His **h**
Is	57:15	eternity, whose name is **H**:
Is	57:15	I dwell in the high and **h**
Is	58:13	doing your pleasure on My **h**
Is	62: 9	shall drink it in My **h**
Is	62:12	they shall call them The **H**
Is	63:10	rebelled and grieved His **H**
Is	63:11	Where is He who put His **H**
Is	65:25	hurt nor destroy in all My **h**
Jer	50:29	Against the **H** One of
Jer	51: 5	with sin against the **H** One
Ezek	20:39	but profane My **h** name no
Ezek	36:20	they profaned My **h** name—when
Ezek	39: 7	the **H** One in Israel.
Ezek	42:20	to separate the **h** areas from
Ezek	44:23	difference between the **h**
Dan	4: 9	that the Spirit of the **H**
Dan	4:13	a **h** one, coming down from
Dan	4:17	by the word of the **h** ones,
Dan	4:18	for the Spirit of the **H** God
Dan	9:24	And to anoint the Most **H**.
Dan	11:28	be moved against the **h**
Hos	11: 9	The **H** One in your midst;
Joel	3:17	Dwelling in Zion My **h**
Joel	3:17	Then Jerusalem shall be **h**,
Amos	2: 7	To defile My **h** name.
Jon	2: 4	look again toward Your **h**
Mic	1: 2	The Lord from His **h** temple.
Hab	1:12	my **H** One? We shall not die.
Hab	2:20	But the LORD is in His **h**
Hab	3: 3	The **H** One from Mount Paran.
Zech	2:12	as His inheritance in the **H**
Matt	1:18	found with child of the **H**
Matt	3:11	will baptize you with the **H**
Matt	4: 5	took Him up into the **h** city,
Matt	7: 6	Do not give what is **h** to the
Matt	12:32	speaks against the **H** Spirit,
Matt	24:15	standing in the **h** place"
Matt	25:31	and all the **h** angels with
Matt	27:53	they went into the **h** city
Matt	28:19	and of the Son and of the **H**
Mark	1:24	the **H** One of God!"
Mark	13:11	but the **H** Spirit.

Luke	1:15	also be filled with the **H**
Luke	1:35	The **H** Spirit will come upon
Luke	1:35	that **H** One who is to be born
Luke	1:49	And **h** is His name.
Luke	1:70	spoke by the mouth of His **h**
Luke	1:72	And to remember His **h**
Luke	2:23	womb shall be called **h**
Luke	2:26	revealed to him by the **H**
Luke	3:16	will baptize you with the **H**
Luke	3:22	And the **H** Spirit descended in
Luke	4: 1	being filled with the **H**
John	1:33	He who baptizes with the **H**
John	7:39	for the **H** Spirit was not yet
John	14:26	the **H** Spirit, whom the
John	17:11	**H** Father, keep through Your
John	20:22	Receive the **H** Spirit.
Acts	1: 2	after He through the **H**
Acts	1: 5	shall be baptized with the **H**
Acts	1: 8	receive power when the **H**
Acts	2: 4	were all filled with the **H**
Acts	2:27	will You allow Your **H**
Acts	2:33	Father the promise of the **H**
Acts	2:38	receive the gift of the **H**
Acts	3:14	But you denied the **H** One and
Acts	4:27	For truly against Your **h**
Acts	5: 3	your heart to lie to the **H**
Acts	6: 3	full of the **H** Spirit and
Acts	7:33	where you stand is **h**.
Acts	7:51	You always resist the **H**
Acts	8:15	they might receive the **H**
Acts	8:18	of the apostles' hands the **H**
Acts	9:17	and be filled with the **H**
Acts	9:31	and in the comfort of the **H**
Acts	11:16	shall be baptized with the **H**
Acts	13: 4	being sent out by the **H**
Acts	13:35	will not allow Your **H**
Acts	13:52	with joy and with the **H**
Acts	15:28	For it seemed good to the **H**
Acts	19: 2	heard whether there is a **H**
Rom	1: 2	His prophets in the **H**
Rom	5: 5	out in our hearts by the **H**
Rom	7:12	Therefore the law is **h**,
Rom	7:12	and the commandment **h** and
Rom	9: 1	bearing me witness in the **H**
Rom	12: 1	bodies a living sacrifice, **h**,
Rom	14:17	and peace and joy in the **H**
Rom	15:13	hope by the power of the **H**
Rom	15:16	sanctified by the **H** Spirit.
Rom	16:16	Greet one another with a **h**
1Co	3:17	For the temple of God is **h**,
1Co	6:19	body is the temple of the **H**
1Co	7:14	unclean, but now they are **h**.
1Co	12: 3	is Lord except by the **H**
2Co	13:14	and the communion of the **H**
Eph	1:13	you were sealed with the **H**
Eph	2:21	grows into a **h** temple in the
Eph	4:30	And do not grieve the **H**
Col	1:22	death, to present you **h**,
Col	3:12	**h** and beloved, put on tender
1Th	1: 5	and in the **H** Spirit and in
1Th	1: 6	with joy of the **H** Spirit,
1Th	4: 8	who has also given us His **H**
1Ti	2: 8	lifting up **h** hands, without
2Ti	1:14	keep by the **H** Spirit who
2Ti	3:15	you have known the **H**
Tit	1: 8	good, sober-minded, just, **h**,
Tit	3: 5	and renewing of the **H**
Heb	6: 4	become partakers of the **H**
Heb	9:12	blood He entered the Most **H**
Heb	9:24	Christ has not entered the **h**
Heb	9:25	priest enters the Most **H**
Heb	10:15	But the **H** Spirit also
1Pe	1:12	the gospel to you by the **H**
1Pe	1:15	as He who called you is **h**,
1Pe	1:16	"Be holy, for I am **h**.

1Pe	2: 5	a **h** priesthood, to offer up
1Pe	2: 9	a **h** nation, His own special
2Pe	1:21	but **h** men of God spoke as
2Pe	1:21	they were moved by the **H**
1Jn	2:20	an anointing from the **H** One,
1Jn	5: 7	and the **H** Spirit; and these
Jude	20	on your most **h** faith,
Jude	20	praying in the **H** Spirit,
Rev	3: 7	things says He who is **h**,
Rev	4: 8	saying: "Holy, holy, **h**,
Rev	6:10	**h** and true, until You judge
Rev	11: 2	And they will tread the **h**
Rev	14:10	in the presence of the **h**
Rev	15: 4	name? For You alone are **h**.
Rev	18:20	and you **h** apostles and
Rev	20: 6	Blessed and **h** is he who has
Rev	21:10	the **h** Jerusalem, descending
Rev	22:11	righteous still; he who is **h**,
Rev	22:11	let him be **h** still."

HOMAGE

1Ki	1:16	Bathsheba bowed and did **h**
Esth	3: 2	gate bowed and paid **h** to

HOME (see HOMELAND, HOMELESS, HOMEMAKERS, HOMES)

Ruth	1:21	the LORD has brought me **h**
1Ki	13:15	Come **h** with me and eat bread
Ps	84: 3	the sparrow has found a **h**,
Ps	104:12	of the heavens have their **h**
Ps	113: 9	grants the barren woman a **h**.
Prov	3:33	But He blesses the **h** of the
Prov	7:11	feet would not stay at **h**.
Prov	7:19	For my husband is not at **h**;
Eccl	12: 5	man goes to his eternal **h**,
Dan	6:10	was signed, he went **h**.
Matt	8: 6	my servant is lying at **h**
Mark	5:19	Go **h** to your friends, and
Luke	15: 6	"And when he comes **h**,
John	14:23	come to him and make Our **h**
John	19:27	took her to his own **h**.
1Co	11:34	is hungry, let him eat at **h**,
1Co	14:35	ask their own husbands at **h**;
2Co	5: 6	that while we are at **h** in
1Ti	5: 4	learn to show piety at **h**

HOMELAND† (see HOME)

Heb	11:14	plainly that they seek a **h**.

HOMELESS† (see HOME)

1Co	4:11	clothed, and beaten, and **h**.

HOMEMAKERS† (see HOME)

Tit	2: 5	to be discreet, chaste, **h**,

HOMER

Lev	27:16	A **h** of barley seed shall
Ezek	45:11	the ephah one-tenth of a **h**;
Ezek	45:14	A kor is a **h** or ten baths,

HOMES (see HOME)

Prov	30:26	Yet they make their **h** in
John	20:10	away again to their own **h**.

HOMOSEXUALS†

1Co	6: 9	nor adulterers, nor **h**,

HONEST

Gen	42:11	we are **h** men; your
Gen	42:34	but that you are **h** men. I
Lev	19:36	You shall have **h** scales,
Job	31: 6	Let me be weighed on **h**

HONEY (see HONEYCOMB)

Gen	43:11	little balm and a little **h**,
Ex	3: 8	land flowing with milk and **h**,
Ex	16:31	like wafers made with **h**.
Lev	2:11	burn no leaven nor any **h** in
Deut	8: 8	a land of olive oil and **h**;
Judg	14: 8	a swarm of bees and **h** were

Judg	14:18	"What is sweeter than **h**?
1Sa	14:25	and there was **h** on the
2Ki	18:32	a land of olive groves and **h**,
2Ch	31: 5	of grain and wine, oil and **h**,
Job	20:17	The rivers flowing with **h**
Ps	19:10	Sweeter also than **h** and the
Ps	81:16	And with **h** from the rock I
Ps	119:103	Sweeter than **h** to my
Prov	5: 3	of an immoral woman drip **h**,
Song	4:11	**H** and milk are under your
Is	7:15	Curds and **h** He shall eat,
Ezek	3: 3	it was in my mouth like **h**
Matt	3: 4	food was locusts and wild **h**.
Rev	10: 9	it will be as sweet as **h** in

HONEYCOMB (see HONEY)

Ps	19:10	also than honey and the **h**.
Prov	16:24	words are like a **h**,
Luke	24:42	of a broiled fish and some **h**.

HONOR (see HONORABLE, HONORED, HONORS)

Ex	14: 4	and I will gain **h** over
Ex	20:12	**H** your father and your
Deut	5:16	**H** your father and your
Judg	9: 9	With which they **h** God and
1Ki	3:13	not asked: both riches and **h**,
1Ch	16:27	H and majesty are before
Esth	1:20	all wives will **h** their
Esth	6: 6	whom the king delights to **h**?
Job	30:15	They pursue my **h** as the
Ps	7: 5	And lay my **h** in the dust.
Ps	8: 5	crowned him with glory and **h**.
Ps	21: 5	**H** and majesty You have
Ps	104: 1	You are clothed with **h** and
Prov	3: 9	**H** the LORD with your
Prov	3:16	her left hand riches and **h**.
Prov	11:16	A gracious woman retains **h**,
Prov	15:33	And before **h** is humility.
Prov	21:21	life, righteousness and **h**.
Prov	26: 8	a sling Is he who gives **h**
Prov	31:25	Strength and **h** are her
Eccl	10: 1	respected for wisdom and **h**.
Is	29:13	with their mouths And Me
Is	61: 7	you shall have double **h**,
Dan	4:37	praise and extol and **h** the
Dan	5:18	and majesty, glory and **h**.
Mal	1: 6	the Father, Where is My **h**?
Matt	13:57	A prophet is not without **h**
Matt	15: 4	**H** your father and your
Matt	15: 6	then he need not **h** his father
Matt	15: 8	And **h** Me with their
John	4:44	that a prophet has no **h** in
John	5:23	that all should **h** the Son
John	5:23	the Son just as they **h** the
John	8:49	but I **h** My Father, and you
John	8:54	If I **h** Myself, My honor is
John	12:26	Me, him My Father will **h**.
Rom	9:21	to make one vessel for **h**
Rom	12:10	in **h** giving preference to
Rom	13: 7	whom fear, honor to whom **h**.
1Co	12:23	on these we bestow greater **h**;
1Ti	1:17	be **h** and glory forever and
1Ti	5: 3	**H** widows who are really
1Ti	5:17	counted worthy of double **h**,
2Ti	2:20	some for **h** and some for
2Ti	2:21	he will be a vessel for **h**,
Heb	2: 7	him with glory and **h**,
1Pe	1: 7	may be found to praise, **h**,
1Pe	2:17	**H** all people. Love the
1Pe	2:17	Fear God. **H** the king.
1Pe	3: 7	giving **h** to the wife, as to
Rev	19: 1	Salvation and glory and **h**

HONORABLE (see HONOR, HONORABLY)

1Sa	9: 6	and he is an **h** man; all
Ps	45: 9	daughters are among Your **h**

Ps   111: 3 His work is **h** and glorious,
Is   42:21 exalt the law and make it **h**.
Is   58:13 holy day of the LORD **h**,
Luke   14: 8 lest one more **h** than you be
2Co   13: 7 that you should do what is **h**,
Heb   13: 4 Marriage is **h** among all, and
1Pe   2:12 having your conduct **h** among

HONORABLY † (see HONORABLE)
Heb   13:18 things desiring to live **h**.

HONORED (see HONOR)
2Sa   23:23 He was more **h** than the
2Ch   32:33 inhabitants of Jerusalem **h**
Is   43: 4 My sight, You have been **h**,
Is   43:23 Nor have you **h** Me with your
Lam   1: 8 All who **h** her despise her
Dan   4:34 Most High and praised and **h**
1Co   12:26 it; or if one member is **h**,

HONORS (see HONOR)
Ps   15: 4 But he **h** those who fear the
Mal   1: 6 A son **h** his father, And a
Mark   7: 6 This people **h** Me with
John   8:54 It is My Father who **h** Me, of

HOOF (see HOOVES)
Lev   11: 3 whatever divides the **h**,

HOOK (see HOOKS)
2Ki   19:28 Therefore I will put My **h**
Job   41: 1 draw out Leviathan with a **h**,
Matt   17:27 go to the sea, cast in a **h**,

HOOKS (see HOOK)
Is   2: 4 their spears into pruning **h**;
Ezek   38: 4 put **h** into your jaws, and
Joel   3:10 swords And your pruning **h**
Mic   4: 3 their spears into pruning **h**;

HOOVES (see HOOF)
Lev   11: 3 having cloven **h** and chewing
Lev   11: 4 but does not have cloven **h**,
Deut   14: 7 the cud or have cloven **h**,

HOPE (see HOPED, HOPES, HOPING)
Ruth   1:12 If I should say I have **h**,
Job   4: 6 of your ways your **h**?
Job   5:16 So the poor have **h**,
Job   8:13 And the **h** of the hypocrite
Job   11:18 secure, because there is **h**;
Job   14: 7 For there is **h** for a tree,
Job   14:19 So You destroy the **h** of
Job   17:15 Where then is my **h**?
Job   31:24 "If I have made gold my **h**,
Ps   16: 9 flesh also will rest in **h**.
Ps   31:24 All you who **h** in the LORD.
Ps   33:17 A horse is a vain **h** for
Ps   33:18 On those who **h** in His
Ps   38:15 For in You, O LORD, I **h**;
Ps   42: 5 **H** in God, for I shall yet
Ps   62:10 Nor vainly **h** in robbery;
Ps   71: 5 For You are my **h**,
Ps   119:81 But I **h** in Your word.
Ps   119:166 I **h** for Your salvation, And
Ps   130: 7 **h** in the LORD; For with
Prov   11: 7 And the **h** of the unjust
Prov   13:12 **H** deferred makes the heart
Prov   19:18 your son while there is **h**,
Prov   26:12 There is more **h** for a
Eccl   9: 4 to all the living there is **h**,
Is   8:17 And I will **h** in Him.
Jer   14: 8 O the **H** of Israel, his
Jer   29:11 to give you a future and a **h**.
Jer   31:17 There is **h** in your future,
Lam   3:21 my mind, Therefore I have **h**.
Lam   3:24 Therefore I **h** in Him!"
Lam   3:29 the dust—There may yet be **h**.
Ezek   37:11 our **h** is lost, and we

Hos   2:15 of Achor as a door of **h**;
Acts   16:19 masters saw that their **h** of
Acts   17:27 in the **h** that they might
Rom   4:18 who, contrary to **h**,
Rom   5: 2 and rejoice in **h** of the
Rom   5: 4 character; and character, **h**.
Rom   5: 5 Now **h** does not disappoint,
Rom   8:20 Him who subjected it in **h**;
Rom   8:24 but **h** that is seen is not
Rom   12:12 rejoicing in **h**,
Rom   15: 4 the Scriptures might have **h**.
Rom   15:12 the Gentiles shall **h**.
Rom   15:13 Now may the God of **h** fill you
1Co   9:10 who plows should plow in **h**,
1Co   13:13 And now abide faith, **h**,
1Co   15:19 in this life only we have **h**,
1Co   16: 7 but I **h** to stay a while with
Gal   5: 5 eagerly wait for the **h** of
Eph   1:18 you may know what is the **h**
Eph   2:12 having no **h** and without God
Eph   4: 4 as you were called in one **h**
Col   1:23 not moved away from the **h**
Col   1:27 the **h** of glory.
1Th   2:19 For what is our **h**,
1Th   4:13 as others who have no **h**.
1Th   5: 8 and as a helmet the **h** of
1Ti   1: 1 the Lord Jesus Christ, our **h**,
Tit   1: 2 in **h** of eternal life which
Tit   2:13 looking for the blessed **h** and
Heb   3: 6 and the rejoicing of the **h**
Heb   6:19 This **h** we have as an anchor
Heb   7:19 bringing in of a better **h**,
Heb   10:23 the confession of our **h**
1Pe   1: 3 us again to a living **h**
1Pe   1:21 so that your faith and **h** are
1Pe   3:15 asks you a reason for the **h**
1Jn   3: 3 And everyone who has this **h**

HOPED (see HOPE)
Ps   119:74 Because I have **h** in Your
Luke   23: 8 and he **h** to see some miracle
Heb   11: 1 is the substance of things **h**

HOPES † (see HOPE)
1Co   13: 7 **h** all things, endures all

HOPHNI
1Sa   1: 3 **H** and Phinehas, the priests

HOPHRA † (see PHARAOH)
Jer   44:30 I will give Pharaoh **H** king

HOPING (see HOPE)
Luke   24:21 But we were **h** that it was He

HOR
Num   20:23 Moses and Aaron in Mount **H**

HOREB (see SINAI)
Ex   3: 1 of the desert, and came to **H**,
Ex   33: 6 their ornaments by Mount **H**.
Deut   5: 2 made a covenant with us in **H**
Ps   106:19 They made a calf in **H**,

HORITES
Deut   2:12 The **H** formerly dwelt in Seir,

HORIZON †
Job   26:10 He drew a circular **h** on the

HORMAH
Num   14:45 drove them back as far as **H**.
Judg   1:17 of the city was called **H**.

HORN (see HORNS)
Josh   6: 5 long blast with the ram's **h**,
1Sa   2: 1 My **h** is exalted in the
1Sa   2:10 And exalt the **h** of His
1Sa   16: 1 Fill your **h** with oil, and
Ps   75: 5 Do not lift up your **h** on

Ps 89:17 And in Your favor our **h** is
Ps 132:17 There I will make the **h** of
Dan 3: 5 you hear the sound of the **h**,
Dan 7: 8 and there was another **h**,
Dan 7:20 and the other **h** which came
Dan 8: 5 the goat had a notable **h**
Dan 8: 8 the large **h** was broken, and
Dan 8: 9 one of them came a little **h**
Luke 1:69 And has raised up a **h** of

HORNET† (see HORNETS)
Deut 7:20 your God will send the **h**
Josh 24:12 I sent the **h** before you which

HORNETS† (see HORNET)
Ex 23:28 And I will send **h** before you,

HORNS (see HORN)
Gen 22:13 caught in a thicket by its **h**.
Ex 29:12 bull and put it on the **h**
Ex 30:10 make atonement upon its **h**
Josh 6: 4 seven trumpets of rams' **h**
1Ki 1:51 he has taken hold of the **h**
Ps 22:21 mouth And from the **h** of
Ezek 43:15 with four **h** extending upward
Dan 7: 7 before it, and it had ten **h**.
Dan 7:24 The ten **h** are ten kings
Dan 8: 3 was a ram which had two **h**,
Zech 1:18 and there were four **h**.
Rev 5: 6 having seven **h** and seven
Rev 9:13 a voice from the four **h** of
Rev 12: 3 having seven heads and ten **h**,
Rev 13: 1 having seven heads and ten **h**,
Rev 13: 1 and on his **h** ten crowns, and

HORRIBLE (see HORROR)
Ps 40: 2 brought me up out of a **h**
Jer 5:30 An astonishing and **h** thing

HORROR (see HORRIBLE)
Gen 15:12 **h** and great darkness fell
Ps 55: 5 And **h** has overwhelmed me.

HORSE (see HORSEBACK, HORSEMEN, HORSES)
Ex 15: 1 gloriously! The **h** and its
Ex 15:21 gloriously! The **h** and its
Job 39:19 Have you given the **h**
Ps 32: 9 Do not be like the **h** or
Ps 33:17 A **h** is a vain hope for
Prov 26: 3 A whip for the **h**,
Zech 1: 8 a man riding on a red **h**,
Rev 6: 2 and behold, a white **h**.
Rev 19:19 Him who sat on the **h** and

HORSEBACK (see HORSE)
Esth 6: 9 Then parade him on **h** through
Esth 8:10 letters by couriers on **h**,

HORSEMEN
Ex 14: 9 his **h** and his army, and
Ex 15:19 with his chariots and his **h**
2Ki 2:12 chariot of Israel and its **h**!
2Ki 13: 7 of Jehoahaz only fifty **h**,
2Ki 13:14 of Israel and their **h**!"
Is 28:28 Or crush it with his **h**.
Is 31: 1 And in **h** because they are
Rev 9:16 number of the army of the **h**

HORSES (see HORSE, HORSES')
Ex 14: 9 all the **h** and chariots of
Ex 14:23 of the sea, all Pharaoh's **h**,
Deut 17:16 he shall not multiply **h**
Deut 17:16 to Egypt to multiply **h**,
Josh 11: 4 with very many **h** and
Josh 11: 6 You shall hamstring their **h**
2Sa 8: 4 hamstrung all the chariot **h**,
1Ki 10:28 Also Solomon had **h** imported
2Ki 2:11 of fire appeared with **h** of
Esth 8:10 riding on royal **h** bred from

Is 30:16 for we will flee on **h**"—
Is 31: 1 for help, And rely on **h**,
Is 31: 3 And their **h** are flesh, and
Jer 4:13 His **h** are swifter than
Jer 12: 5 how can you contend with **h**?
Ezek 23: 6 men, Horsemen riding on **h**.
Ezek 23:20 is like the issue of **h**.
Hos 1: 7 By **h** or horsemen."
Joel 2: 4 is like the appearance of **h**;
Amos 6:12 Do **h** run on rocks? Does
Nah 3: 2 wheels, Of galloping **h**,
Hab 1: 8 Their **h** also are swifter
Zech 6: 2 first chariot were red **h**,
Zech 6: 2 the second chariot black **h**,
Zech 6: 3 the third chariot white **h**,
Zech 6: 3 the fourth chariot dappled **h**—
Zech 14:20 on the bells of the **h**.
Rev 19:14 followed Him on white **h**.

HORSES'
James 3: 3 we put bits in **h** mouths that

HOSANNA
Matt 21: 9 **H** to the Son of David!
Matt 21: 9 name of the LORD!' **H**
Mark 11: 9 **H**! 'Blessed is He who

HOSEA (see HOSHEA, JOSHUA)
Hos 1: 1 of the LORD that came to **H**
Rom 9:25 As He says also in **H**:

HOSHEA (see HOSEA, JOSHUA)
Num 13:16 And Moses called **H** the son
2Ki 18:10 year of **H** king of Israel,

HOSPITABLE† (see HOSPITALITY)
1Ti 3: 2 of good behavior, **h**,
Tit 1: 8 but **h**, a lover of what is
1Pe 4: 9 Be **h** to one another without

HOSPITALITY† (see HOSPITABLE)
Rom 12:13 of the saints, given to **h**.

HOST (see HOSTS)
Gen 2: 1 and all the **h** of them, were
Deut 4:19 all the **h** of heaven, you
2Ki 17:16 and worshiped all the **h** of
2Ki 21: 5 built altars for all the **h**
Neh 9: 6 The **h** of heaven worships
Ps 33: 6 And all the **h** of them by
Is 40:26 Who brings out their **h** by
Dan 8:10 it cast down some of the **h**
Luke 2:13 multitude of the heavenly **h**

HOSTILITY†
Heb 12: 3 Him who endured such **h** from

HOSTS (see HOST)
1Sa 1: 3 sacrifice to the LORD of **h**
1Sa 4: 4 covenant of the LORD of **h**,
1Sa 15: 2 "Thus says the LORD of **h**:
1Sa 17:45 the name of the LORD of **h**,
2Sa 6: 2 by the Name, the LORD of **H**,
1Ki 19:10 for the LORD God of **h**;
Ps 24:10 of glory? The LORD of **h**,
Ps 46: 7 The LORD of **h** is with us;
Ps 48: 8 the city of the LORD of **h**,
Ps 80: 4 O LORD God of **h**,
Ps 80: 7 Restore us, O God of **h**;
Ps 84: 3 Your altars, O LORD of **h**,
Ps 103:21 the LORD, all you His **h**,
Ps 148: 2 Praise Him, all His **h**!
Is 1: 9 Unless the LORD of **h** Had
Is 5:24 the law of the LORD of **h**,
Is 6: 3 holy is the LORD of **h**;
Is 6: 5 the King, The LORD of **h**.
Is 8:13 The LORD of **h**,
Is 13:13 the wrath of the LORD of **h**
Is 14:24 The LORD of **h** has sworn,

Is	14:27	For the LORD of **h** has
Is	19:16	the hand of the LORD of **h**,
Is	19:18	and swear by the LORD of **h**;
Is	24:23	For the LORD of **h** will
Is	25: 6	mountain The LORD of **h**
Is	44: 6	his Redeemer, the LORD of **h**:
Is	47: 4	the LORD of **h** is His name,
Jer	3:19	beautiful heritage of the **h**
Jer	23:36	living God, the LORD of **h**,
Jer	51:14	The LORD of **h** has sworn by
Amos	5:14	So the LORD God of **h** will
Amos	5:15	be that the LORD God of **h**.
Zeph	2:10	the people of the LORD of **h**.
Hag	1:14	the house of the LORD of **h**,
Zech	1:12	and said, "O LORD of **h**,
Zech	7:12	words which the LORD of **h**
Zech	7:12	came from the LORD of **h**.
Zech	8: 3	Mountain of the LORD of **h**,
Zech	8:21	And seek the LORD of **h**.
Zech	8:22	come to seek the LORD of **h**
Zech	9:15	The LORD of **h** will defend
Zech	10: 3	For the LORD of **h** will
Zech	14:21	holiness to the LORD of **h**.
Mal	2: 7	messenger of the LORD of **h**.
Mal	2:12	offering to the LORD of **h**!
Eph	6:12	against spiritual **h** of

HOT (see HOTTEST)

Ex	16:21	And when the sun became **h**,
Ex	22:24	"and My wrath will become **h**,
Ex	32:19	So Moses' anger became **h**,
Deut	9:19	afraid of the anger and **h**
Judg	2:14	the anger of the LORD was **h**
1Sa	11: 9	by the time the sun is **h**,
1Sa	21: 6	in order to put **h** bread in
Ps	6: 1	Nor chasten me in Your **h**
Ps	39: 3	My heart was **h** within me;
Prov	6:28	Can one walk on **h** coals,
Lam	5:10	Our skin is **h** as an oven,
Dan	3:22	the furnace exceedingly **h**,
Hos	7: 7	They are all **h**,
Luke	12:55	There will be **h** weather'; and
1Ti	4: 2	conscience seared with a **h**
Rev	3:15	you are neither cold nor **h**.

HOTTEST† (see HOT)

2Sa	11:15	in the forefront of the **h**

HOUND†

Ps	56: 2	My enemies would **h** me all

HOUR (see HOURS)

Dan	4:33	That very **h** the word was
Dan	5: 5	In the same **h** the fingers of
Matt	8:13	was healed that same **h**.
Matt	10:19	be given to you in that **h**
Matt	14:15	and the **h** is already late.
Matt	20: 3	went out about the third **h**
Matt	20: 5	the sixth and the ninth **h**,
Matt	20: 6	And about the eleventh **h** he
Matt	20:12	men have worked only one **h**,
Matt	24:36	But of that day and **h** no one
Matt	24:42	for you do not know what **h**
Matt	24:43	the house had known what **h**
Matt	24:44	Son of Man is coming at an **h**
Matt	24:50	for him and at an **h** that
Matt	25:13	neither the day nor the **h**
Matt	26:40	you not watch with Me one **h**?
Matt	26:45	the **h** is at hand, and the
Matt	27:45	sixth hour until the ninth **h**
Mark	13:11	is given you in that **h**,
Mark	14:35	the **h** might pass from Him.
Luke	1:10	praying outside at the **h** of
Luke	20:19	and the scribes that very **h**
Luke	24:33	So they rose up that very **h**
John	1:39	it was about the tenth **h**).
John	2: 4	My **h** has not yet come."

John	4:21	the **h** is coming when you
John	4:52	Yesterday at the seventh **h**
John	5:25	the **h** is coming, and now is,
John	12:27	save Me from this **h**'?
John	12:27	purpose I came to this **h**.
John	13: 1	when Jesus knew that His **h**
John	16:32	Indeed the **h** is coming, yes,
John	17: 1	the **h** has come. Glorify Your
John	19:27	mother!" And from that **h**
Acts	2:15	it is only the third **h** of
Acts	3: 1	to the temple at the **h** of
Acts	3: 1	hour of prayer, the ninth **h**.
Acts	10: 9	to pray, about the sixth **h**
Acts	23:23	to Caesarea at the third **h**
1Co	4:11	To the present **h** we both
1Co	15:30	we stand in jeopardy every **h**?
1Jn	2:18	children, it is the last **h**;
Rev	3: 3	you will not know what **h** I
Rev	3:10	will keep you from the **h** of
Rev	14: 7	for the **h** of His judgment
Rev	18:10	mighty city! For in one **h**

HOURS (see HOUR)

John	11: 9	Are there not twelve **h** in the

HOUSE (see HOUSEHOLD, HOUSES, HOUSETOP)

Gen	12: 1	And from your father's **h**,
Gen	12:15	was taken to Pharaoh's **h**.
Gen	14:14	who were born in his own **h**,
Gen	15: 2	and the heir of my **h** is
Gen	15: 3	indeed one born in my **h** is
Gen	17:12	he who is born in your **h** or
Gen	19: 3	in to him and entered his **h**.
Gen	19: 4	quarter, surrounded the **h**.
Gen	19:10	and pulled Lot into the **h**
Gen	24: 2	the oldest servant of his **h**,
Gen	24: 7	took me from my father's **h**
Gen	28:22	as a pillar shall be God's **h**,
Gen	39: 4	made him overseer of his **h**,
Gen	39: 5	on all that he had in the **h**
Gen	39: 9	is no one greater in this **h**
Gen	40: 3	them in custody in the **h** of
Gen	41:40	"You shall be over my **h**,
Gen	43:18	were brought into Joseph's **h**;
Gen	44: 1	the steward of his **h**,
Ex	2: 1	And a man of the **h** of Levi
Ex	8:24	of flies came into the **h**
Ex	12:22	go out of the door of his **h**
Ex	12:30	for there was not a **h**
Ex	12:46	In one **h** it shall be eaten;
Ex	12:46	of the flesh outside the **h**,
Ex	13: 3	out of the **h** of bondage; for
Ex	16:31	And the **h** of Israel called
Ex	19: 3	you shall say to the **h**
Ex	20: 2	out of the **h** of bondage.
Ex	20:17	not covet your neighbor's **h**;
Ex	23:19	you shall bring into the **h**
Lev	14:35	is some plague in the **h**,
Lev	14:36	that they empty the **h**,
Lev	14:39	spread on the walls of the **h**,
Lev	14:47	he who lies down in the **h**
Lev	14:47	and he who eats in the **h**
Lev	14:48	shall pronounce the **h** clean,
Lev	14:53	and make atonement for the **h**,
Lev	22:13	returned to her father's **h**
Num	1: 4	the head of his father's **h**.
Num	1:20	by their fathers' **h**,
Num	3:30	leader of the fathers' **h** of
Num	12: 7	He is faithful in all My **h**.
Num	30: 3	while in her father's **h** in
Num	30:10	she vowed in her husband's **h**,
Deut	5: 6	out of the **h** of bondage.
Deut	5:21	not desire your neighbor's **h**,
Deut	6: 7	them when you sit in your **h**,
Deut	6: 9	on the doorposts of your **h**
Deut	20: 5	who has built a new **h** and

Deut	20: 5	him go and return to his **h**,
Deut	21:12	bring her home to your **h**,
Deut	22:21	the door of her father's **h**,
Deut	22:21	the harlot in her father's **h**.
Deut	23:18	the price of a dog to the **h**
Deut	24: 1	and sends her out of his **h**,
Deut	25: 9	not build up his brother's **h**.
Deut	25:14	shall not have in your **h**
Deut	26:13	the holy tithe from my **h**,
Deut	28:30	her; you shall build a **h**,
Josh	2: 1	and came to the **h** of a
Josh	2:15	for her **h** was on the city
Josh	2:19	whoever is with you in the **h**,
Josh	6:24	into the treasury of the **h**
Josh	9:23	water carriers for the **h** of
Josh	17:17	And Joshua spoke to the **h** of
Josh	22:14	ruler each from the chief **h**
Josh	24:15	But as for me and my **h**,
Judg	6:15	the least in my father's **h**.
Judg	9: 1	all the family of the **h** of
Judg	11: 7	expel me from my father's **h**?
Judg	11:31	out of the doors of my **h** to
Judg	12: 1	We will burn your **h** down on
Judg	18:31	all the time that the **h** of
Judg	19:15	would take them into his **h**
Judg	19:18	now I am going to the **h** of
Judg	19:22	surrounded the **h** and beat
Judg	20:18	arose and went up to the **h**
Ruth	1: 8	each to her mother's **h**.
Ruth	1: 9	each in the **h** of her
Ruth	4:11	the two who built the **h** of
Ruth	4:12	May your **h** be like the house
1Sa	1: 7	when she went up to the **h**
1Sa	2:35	I will build him a sure **h**,
1Sa	3:15	opened the doors of the **h**
1Sa	9:18	me, where is the seer's **h**?
1Sa	20:16	a covenant with the **h** of
1Sa	25: 6	be to you, peace to your **h**,
1Sa	25:28	for my lord an enduring **h**,
2Sa	2: 4	David king over the **h** of
2Sa	2:11	king in Hebron over the **h**
2Sa	3:10	the kingdom from the **h** of
2Sa	5: 8	shall not come into the **h**.
2Sa	5:11	And they built David a **h**.
2Sa	6:11	the LORD remained in the **h**
2Sa	7: 2	I dwell in a **h** of cedar, but
2Sa	7: 5	Would you build a **h** for Me to
2Sa	7: 7	have you not built Me a **h**
2Sa	7:13	He shall build a **h** for My
2Sa	7:16	And your **h** and your kingdom
2Sa	7:27	'I will build you a **h**.
2Sa	7:29	it please You to bless the **h**
2Sa	9: 1	anyone who is left of the **h**
2Sa	11: 2	on the roof of the king's **h**.
2Sa	11: 8	Go down to your **h** and wash
2Sa	12: 8	I gave you your master's **h**
2Sa	12: 8	and gave you the **h** of Israel
2Sa	12:10	never depart from your **h**,
2Sa	12:15	Nathan departed to his **h**.
2Sa	13: 7	go to your brother Amnon's **h**,
2Sa	13:20	in her brother Absalom's **h**.
2Sa	16: 8	you all the blood of the **h**
2Sa	16:22	Absalom on the top of the **h**,
2Sa	24:17	me and against my father's **h**.
1Ki	2:24	and who has established a **h**
1Ki	2:27	He spoke concerning the **h**
1Ki	2:36	Build yourself a **h** in
1Ki	3: 1	finished building his own **h**,
1Ki	3:17	and I dwell in the same **h**;
1Ki	3:17	while she was in the **h**.
1Ki	3:18	the two of us in the **h**.
1Ki	5: 3	David could not build a **h**
1Ki	5: 5	he shall build the **h** for My
1Ki	6:37	the foundation of the **h** of
1Ki	6:38	the **h** was finished in all

1Ki	7: 1	years to build his own **h**;
1Ki	7:12	the inner court of the **h** of
1Ki	8:11	of the LORD filled the **h**
1Ki	8:63	of Israel dedicated the **h**
1Ki	9: 3	I have consecrated this **h**
1Ki	9: 8	"And as for this **h**,
1Ki	11:38	build for you an enduring **h**,
1Ki	12:16	Now, see to your own **h**,
1Ki	12:24	every man return to his **h**,
1Ki	13:34	thing was the sin of the **h**
1Ki	14:10	bring disaster on the **h** of
1Ki	14:17	to the threshold of the **h**
1Ki	14:26	treasures of the king's **h**;
1Ki	15:29	that he killed all the **h** of
1Ki	16:18	the citadel of the king's **h**
1Ki	16:18	and burned the king's **h**
1Ki	18: 3	who was in charge of his **h**.
1Ki	21: 2	it is near, next to my **h**
1Ki	21: 4	So Ahab went into his **h**
1Ki	22:39	the ivory **h** which he built
2Ki	4: 2	what do you have in the **h**?
2Ki	4: 2	has nothing in the **h** but a
2Ki	10: 5	who was in charge of the **h**,
2Ki	10:11	all who remained of the **h**
2Ki	11: 5	watch over the king's **h**,
2Ki	11:15	let her be killed in the **h**
2Ki	12:10	that was found in the **h** of
2Ki	12:11	who worked on the **h** of the
2Ki	12:12	repair the damage of the **h**
2Ki	12:14	and they repaired the **h** of
2Ki	12:20	and killed Joash in the **h** of
2Ki	15: 5	so he dwelt in an isolated **h**.
2Ki	20: 1	Set your **h** in order, for you
2Ki	20:15	have they seen in your **h**?
2Ki	20:15	seen all that is in my **h**;
2Ki	21:13	and the plummet of the **h** of
2Ki	21:18	in the garden of his own **h**,
2Ki	21:23	killed the king in his own **h**.
2Ki	22: 5	to those who are in the **h**
2Ki	22: 5	repair the damages of the **h**—
2Ki	22: 8	Book of the Law in the **h** of
2Ki	22: 9	that was found in the **h**,
2Ki	22: 9	who oversee the **h** of the
2Ki	23: 6	the wooden image from the **h**
2Ki	25: 9	He burned the **h** of the LORD
1Ch	6:48	of the tabernacle of the **h**
1Ch	7:23	tragedy had come upon his **h**.
1Ch	14: 1	carpenters, to build him a **h**.
1Ch	25: 6	for the music in the **h** of
1Ch	25: 6	for the service of the **h** of
1Ch	29: 3	have prepared for the holy **h**,
2Ch	3: 1	began to build the **h** of the
2Ch	5:14	of the LORD filled the **h**
2Ch	7: 5	the people dedicated the **h**
2Ch	7:11	Thus Solomon finished the **h**
2Ch	10:19	in rebellion against the **h**
2Ch	21:13	like the harlotry of the **h**
2Ch	22:12	hidden with them in the **h**
2Ch	23:14	Do not kill her in the **h** of
2Ch	24: 7	dedicated things of the **h**
2Ch	29:15	to cleanse the **h** of the
2Ch	31:10	from the **h** of Zadok,
2Ch	33:15	and the idol from the **h** of
2Ch	33:15	built in the mount of the **h**
2Ch	35: 3	Put the holy ark in the **h**
2Ch	36:14	and defiled the **h** of the
2Ch	36:23	me to build Him a **h** at
Ezra	1: 2	me to build Him a **h** at
Ezra	1: 3	and build the **h** of the LORD
Ezra	3: 8	to oversee the work of the **h**
Ezra	5:13	a decree to build this **h** of
Ezra	5:15	and let the **h** of God be
Ezra	6: 7	of the Jews build this **h** of
Ezra	6:17	at the dedication of this **h**
Ezra	7:27	to beautify the **h** of the

Ezra	9: 9	to repair the **h** of our God,
Ezra	10: 9	in the open square of the **h**
Neh	3:23	repairs opposite their **h**.
Neh	6:10	us meet together in the **h**
Neh	10:36	who minister in the **h** of
Neh	10:38	of the tithes to the **h** of
Neh	10:39	we will not neglect the **h**
Neh	12:40	choirs stood in the **h** of
Esth	1:22	be master in his own **h**,
Esth	2: 9	to the best place in the **h**
Esth	4:14	but you and your father's **h**
Esth	7: 8	queen while I am in the **h**?
Esth	8: 2	Mordecai over the **h** of
Esth	8: 7	I have given Esther the **h** of
Job	1:13	in their oldest brother's **h**;
Job	1:19	the four corners of the **h**,
Job	17:13	wait for the grave as my **h**,
Job	20:19	He has violently seized a **h**
Job	27:18	He builds his **h** like a moth,
Job	30:23	And to the **h** appointed for
Job	42:11	ate food with him in his **h**;
Ps	23: 6	And I will dwell in the **h**
Ps	26: 8	the habitation of Your **h**,
Ps	27: 4	That I may dwell in the **h**
Ps	42: 4	I went with them to the **h**
Ps	50: 9	not take a bull from your **h**,
Ps	69: 9	Because zeal for Your **h** has
Ps	84: 4	those who dwell in Your **h**;
Ps	84:10	be a doorkeeper in the **h** of
Ps	93: 5	Holiness adorns Your **h**,
Ps	112: 3	riches will be in his **h**,
Ps	114: 1	The **h** of Jacob from a
Ps	115:10	O **h** of Aaron, trust in the
Ps	115:12	He will bless the **h** of
Ps	116:19	the courts of the LORD's **h**,
Ps	118: 3	Let the **h** of Aaron now say,
Ps	119:54	been my songs In the **h** of
Ps	122: 1	Let us go into the **h** of the
Ps	127: 1	the LORD builds the **h**,
Ps	132: 3	go into the chamber of my **h**,
Ps	134: 1	by night stand in the **h** of
Ps	135: 2	You who stand in the **h** of
Ps	135:19	O **h** of Israel! Bless the
Prov	2:18	For her **h** leads down to
Prov	5: 8	go near the door of her **h**,
Prov	6:31	all the substance of his **h**.
Prov	7: 6	For at the window of my **h**
Prov	7:27	Her **h** is the way to hell,
Prov	9: 1	Wisdom has built her **h**,
Prov	9:14	sits at the door of her **h**,
Prov	11:29	He who troubles his own **h**
Prov	12: 7	But the **h** of the righteous
Prov	14: 1	The wise woman builds her **h**,
Prov	14:11	The **h** of the wicked will be
Prov	17: 1	Than a **h** full of feasting
Prov	21: 9	Than in a **h** shared with a
Prov	24: 3	Through wisdom a **h** is built,
Prov	25:17	foot in your neighbor's **h**,
Prov	25:24	Than in a **h** shared with a
Prov	27:10	Nor go to your brother's **h**
Eccl	2: 7	had servants born in my **h**.
Eccl	5: 1	when you go to the **h** of God;
Eccl	10:18	idleness of hands the **h**
Eccl	12: 3	when the keepers of the **h**
Song	3: 4	I had brought him to the **h**
Song	8: 7	All the wealth of his **h**,
Is	2: 2	mountain of the LORD's **h**
Is	2: 3	To the **h** of the God of
Is	5: 7	LORD of hosts is the **h** of
Is	5: 8	to those who join house to **h**;
Is	6: 4	and the **h** was filled with
Is	7: 2	And it was told to the **h** of
Is	7:17	people and your father's **h**—
Is	22:15	Shebna, who is over the **h**,
Is	22:22	The key of the **h** of David I
Is	38: 1	Set your **h** in order, for you
Is	42: 7	darkness from the prison **h**.
Is	46: 3	all the remnant of the **h** of
Is	48: 1	O **h** of Jacob, Who are
Is	56: 7	My house shall be called a **h**
Is	60: 7	And I will glorify the **h** of
Jer	3:18	In those days the **h** of Judah
Jer	7: 2	in the gate of the LORD's **h**,
Jer	7:10	stand before Me in this **h**
Jer	9:26	and all the **h** of Israel are
Jer	16: 5	Do not enter the **h** of
Jer	16: 8	you shall not go into the **h**
Jer	18: 2	go down to the potter's **h**,
Jer	18: 6	O **h** of Israel, can I not do
Jer	22:13	to him who builds his **h** by
Jer	22:14	will build myself a wide **h**
Jer	26:12	to prophesy against this **h**
Jer	27:16	the vessels of the LORD's **h**
Jer	31:31	a new covenant with the **h**
Jer	36: 6	the people in the LORD's **h**
Jer	36:10	New Gate of the LORD's **h**,
Jer	36:22	was sitting in the winter **h**
Jer	39: 8	burned the king's **h** and the
Jer	43: 9	the entrance to Pharaoh's **h**
Ezek	2: 5	they are a rebellious **h**—
Ezek	3: 4	go to the **h** of Israel and
Ezek	3:17	you a watchman for the **h** of
Ezek	3:24	shut yourself inside your **h**.
Ezek	4: 3	will be a sign to the **h**
Ezek	4: 5	bear the iniquity of the **h**
Ezek	8: 1	as I sat in my **h** with the
Ezek	10: 4	and the **h** was filled with
Ezek	12: 6	made you a sign to the **h** of
Ezek	17: 2	speak a parable to the **h** of
Ezek	18: 6	eyes to the idols of the **h**
Ezek	18:31	O **h** of Israel?
Ezek	29: 6	a staff of reed to the **h** of
Ezek	29:16	be the confidence of the **h**
Ezek	33: 7	you a watchman for the **h** of
Ezek	39:29	out My Spirit on the **h** of
Ezek	44: 4	of the LORD filled the **h**
Ezek	44:11	as gatekeepers of the **h** and
Ezek	44:11	house and ministers of the **h**;
Ezek	45:17	to make atonement for the **h**
Dan	1: 2	of the articles of the **h** of
Dan	1: 2	into the treasure **h** of his
Dan	2:17	Then Daniel went to his **h**,
Dan	5: 3	from the temple of the **h** of
Dan	5:23	the vessels of His **h** before
Hos	1: 4	of Jezreel on the **h** of Jehu,
Hos	1: 6	longer have mercy on the **h**
Hos	1: 7	I will have mercy on the **h**
Hos	5: 1	O **h** of the king! For yours
Hos	9:15	I will drive them from My **h**;
Joel	3:18	shall flow from the **h** of
Amos	2: 8	of the condemned in the **h**
Amos	3:15	I will destroy the winter **h**
Amos	3:15	along with the summer **h**;
Amos	5: 3	have ten left to the **h** of
Amos	6: 1	To whom the **h** of Israel
Amos	7: 9	the sword against the **h** of
Amos	7:10	you in the midst of the **h**
Obad	18	But the **h** of Esau shall
Mic	4: 1	mountain of the LORD's **h**
Mic	4: 2	To the **h** of the God of
Hag	1: 2	the time that the LORD's **h**
Hag	1:14	came and worked on the **h** of
Zech	1:16	My **h** shall be built in
Zech	13: 6	I was wounded in the **h** of
Zech	14:20	The pots in the LORD's **h**
Mal	3:10	there may be food in My **h**,
Matt	2:11	they had come into the **h**,
Matt	5:15	to all who are in the **h**.
Matt	7:24	a wise man who built his **h**
Matt	7:25	blew and beat on that **h**;

Matt	7:26	foolish man who built his **h**.
Matt	8:14	had come into Peter's **h**,
Matt	9: 6	your bed, and go to your **h**.
Matt	10: 6	to the lost sheep of the **h**
Matt	10:14	when you depart from that **h**
Matt	10:25	called the master of the **h**
Matt	12:25	and every city or **h** divided
Matt	12:29	one enter a strong man's **h**
Matt	12:29	then he will plunder his **h**.
Matt	13:57	own country and in his own **h**.
Matt	21:13	My **h** shall be called a
Matt	23:38	Your **h** is left to you
Matt	24:43	the **h** had known what hour the
Matt	26: 6	was in Bethany at the **h** of
Matt	26:18	keep the Passover at your **h**
Mark	1:29	they entered the **h** of Simon
Mark	2:11	your bed, and go to your **h**.
Mark	2:15	He was dining in Levi's **h**,
Mark	3:25	And if a **h** is divided against
Mark	3:25	that **h** cannot stand.
Mark	6:10	whatever place you enter a **h**,
Mark	7:17	When He had entered a **h** away
Mark	13:34	who left his **h** and gave
Mark	13:35	when the master of the **h** is
Luke	1:23	he departed to his own **h**.
Luke	1:27	of the **h** of David. The
Luke	1:40	and entered the **h** of
Luke	1:69	salvation for us In the **h**
Luke	2: 4	because he was of the **h** and
Luke	6:48	is like a man building a **h**
Luke	6:48	vehemently against that **h**,
Luke	6:49	And the ruin of that **h** was
Luke	7:36	He went to the Pharisee's **h**,
Luke	8:27	nor did he live in a **h** but
Luke	10: 5	first say, 'Peace to this **h**.
Luke	11:17	a house divided against a **h**
Luke	12:52	from now on five in one **h**
Luke	13:25	once the Master of the **h**
Luke	13:35	See! Your **h** is left to you
Luke	15: 8	light a lamp, sweep the **h**,
Luke	18:29	is no one who has left **h** or
Luke	19: 5	today I must stay at your **h**.
Luke	19: 9	salvation has come to this **h**,
Luke	22:54	Him into the high priest's **h**.
John	2:16	make My Father's house a **h**
John	2:17	Zeal for Your **h** has
John	8:35	does not abide in the **h**
John	11:20	Mary was sitting in the **h**.
John	12: 3	And the **h** was filled with
John	14: 2	In My Father's **h** are many
Acts	2: 2	and it filled the whole **h**
Acts	2:46	bread from house to **h**,
Acts	5:42	the temple, and in every **h**,
Acts	8: 3	the church, entering every **h**,
Acts	10: 6	whose **h** is by the sea. He
Acts	10:30	ninth hour I prayed in my **h**,
Acts	16:32	and to all who were in his **h**.
Acts	19:16	that they fled out of that **h**
Acts	20:20	publicly and from house to **h**,
Acts	28:30	years in his own rented **h**,
Rom	16: 5	church that is in their **h**.
1Co	16:19	church that is in their **h**.
2Co	5: 1	know that if our earthly **h**,
2Co	5: 1	a **h** not made with hands,
1Ti	3: 4	one who rules his own **h** well,
1Ti	3:15	to conduct yourself in the **h**
Heb	3: 2	was faithful in all His **h**.
Heb	3: 6	as a Son over His own **h**,
Heb	3: 6	whose **h** we are if we hold
Heb	8: 8	covenant with the **h** of
Heb	8: 8	Israel and with the **h**
Heb	10:21	a High Priest over the **h** of
1Pe	2: 5	being built up a spiritual **h**,
1Pe	4:17	judgment to begin at the **h**

HOUSEHOLD (*see* HOUSE, HOUSEHOLDER, HOUSEHOLDS)

Gen	7: 1	the ark, you and all your **h**,
Gen	46:31	and to his father's **h**,
Deut	22: 8	of bloodshed on your **h** if
Judg	18:14	**h** idols, a carved image, and
2Sa	6:20	returned to bless his **h**.
2Sa	17:23	Then he put his **h** in order,
2Ki	18:18	Hilkiah, who was over the **h**,
Prov	31:15	And provides food for her **h**,
Prov	31:21	not afraid of snow for her **h**,
Matt	10:36	be those of his own **h**.
John	4:53	believed, and his whole **h**.
Acts	10: 2	feared God with all his **h**,
Acts	16:31	be saved, you and your **h**.
Gal	6:10	to those who are of the **h**
Eph	2:19	saints and members of the **h**
Phil	4:22	those who are of Caesar's **h**.
Heb	11: 7	ark for the saving of his **h**,

HOUSEHOLDER† (*see* HOUSEHOLD)

Matt	13:52	of heaven is like a **h** who

HOUSEHOLDS (*see* HOUSEHOLD)

Ex	1:21	that He provided **h** for them.
Ezra	10:16	heads of the fathers' **h**,
2Ti	3: 6	are those who creep into **h**
Tit	1:11	stopped, who subvert whole **h**,

HOUSES (*see* HOUSE)

Ex	6:14	heads of their fathers' **h**:
Ex	12: 7	and on the lintel of the **h**
Ex	12:15	remove leaven from your **h**.
Ex	12:27	who passed over the **h** of the
Deut	8:12	and have built beautiful **h**
1Ki	9:10	Solomon had built the two **h**,
1Ch	15: 1	David built **h** for himself in
Neh	5: 3	lands and vineyards and **h**,
Job	1: 4	go and feast in their **h**,
Job	21: 9	Their **h** are safe from fear,
Eccl	2: 4	great, I built myself **h**,
Song	1:17	The beams of our **h** are
Is	5: 9	many **h** shall be desolate,
Is	42:22	they are hidden in prison **h**;
Jer	29: 5	Build **h** and dwell in them;
Jer	43:12	will kindle a fire in the **h**
Amos	3:15	The **h** of ivory shall
Zeph	1:13	They shall build **h**, but not
Hag	1: 4	to dwell in your paneled **h**,
Matt	11: 8	clothing are in kings' **h**.
Matt	23:14	For you devour widows' **h**,
Mark	10:30	**h** and brothers and sisters
Acts	4:34	possessors of lands or **h**

HOUSETOP (*see* HOUSE, HOUSETOPS)

Prov	21: 9	to dwell in a corner of a **h**,
Matt	24:17	Let him who is on the **h** not
Acts	10: 9	Peter went up on the **h** to

HOUSETOPS (*see* HOUSETOP)

Ps	129: 6	be as the grass on the **h**,
Zeph	1: 5	the host of heaven on the **h**;
Matt	10:27	in the ear, preach on the **h**.
Luke	12: 3	will be proclaimed on the **h**.

HOVERING† (*see* HOVERS)

Gen	1: 2	And the Spirit of God was **h**

HOVERS† (*see* HOVERING)

Deut	32:11	**H** over its young,

HOWL (*see* HOWLING)

Is	13:22	The hyenas will **h** in their
Mic	1: 8	I will wail and **h**,
Jas	5: 1	weep and **h** for your miseries

HOWLING† (*see* HOWL)

Deut	32:10	a **h** wilderness; He

HUGE
Dan   7: 7 It had **h** iron teeth; it was

HULDAH†
2Ki   22:14 and Asaiah went to H the
2Ch   34:22 had appointed went to H

HUMAN
Lev   5: 3 Or if he touches **h**
2Ki   7:10 not a **h** sound—only horses
Dan   8:25 shall be broken without **h**
John   16:21 for joy that a **h** being has
Rom   6:19 I speak in **h** terms because
1Co   2: 4 with persuasive words of **h**
1Co   4: 3 be judged by you or by a **h**
Heb   12: 9 we have had **h** fathers who

HUMBLE (see HUMBLED, HUMBLES, HUMBLING, HUMBLY)
Ex   10: 3 long will you refuse to **h**
Num   12: 3 the man Moses was very **h**,
Deut   8: 2 to **h** you and test you, to
2Ch   7:14 are called by My name will **h**
Job   22:29 Then He will save the **h**
Ps   9:12 not forget the cry of the **h**.
Ps   10:12 hand! Do not forget the **h**.
Ps   10:17 heard the desire of the **h**;
Ps   25: 9 And the **h** He teaches His
Ps   34: 2 The **h** shall hear of it
Ps   147: 6 The LORD lifts up the **h**;
Prov   3:34 But gives grace to the **h**.
Prov   16:19 Better to be of a **h** spirit
Is   57:15 revive the spirit of the **h**,
Ezek   21:26 humble, and **h** the exalted.
Dan   10:12 and to **h** yourself before
Jas   4: 6 gives grace to the **h**.
Jas   4:10 H yourselves in the sight of
1Pe   5: 5 gives grace to the **h**.
1Pe   5: 6 Therefore **h** yourselves under

HUMBLED (see HUMBLE)
Deut   8: 3 So He **h** you, allowed you to
Deut   21:14 because you have **h** her.
Deut   22:29 be his wife because he has **h**
2Ch   33:23 as his father Manasseh had **h**
Ps   35:13 I **h** myself with fasting;
Is   2:11 looks of man shall be **h**,
Dan   5:22 have not **h** your heart,
Matt   23:12 exalts himself will be **h**
Luke   14:11 exalts himself will be **h**
Luke   18:14 exalts himself will be **h**
Phil   2: 8 He **h** Himself and became

HUMBLES (see HUMBLE)
Ps   113: 6 Who **h** Himself to behold
Matt   23:12 and he who **h** himself will be

HUMBLING
2Co   11: 7 Did I commit sin in **h** myself

HUMBLY† (see HUMBLE)
2Sa   16: 4 I **h** bow before you, that I
Mic   6: 8 And to walk **h** with your

HUMILIATED (see HUMILIATION, HUMILITY)
Ezra   9: 6 I am too ashamed and **h** to
Jer   50: 2 in pieces; Her idols are **h**,

HUMILIATION (see HUMILIATED)
Acts   8:33 In His **h** His justice
Jas   1:10 but the rich in his **h**,

HUMILITY (see HUMILIATED)
Prov   15:33 And before honor is **h**.
Prov   22: 4 By **h** and the fear of the
Zeph   2: 3 Seek righteousness, seek **h**.
Acts   20:19 the Lord with all **h**,
Col   2:18 taking delight in false **h**
Col   3:12 tender mercies, kindness, **h**,
Tit   3: 2 showing all **h** to all men.
1Pe   5: 5 and be clothed with **h**,

HUNDRED (see HUNDREDFOLD, HUNDREDS, HUNDREDTH)
Gen   5: 3 And Adam lived one **h** and
Gen   5: 4 days of Adam were eight **h**
Gen   5:22 walked with God three **h**
Gen   6: 3 yet his days shall be one **h**
Gen   17:17 born to a man who is one **h**
Gen   21: 5 Now Abraham was one **h** years
Gen   33:19 for one **h** pieces of money.
Gen   50:22 And Joseph lived one **h** and
Ex   27: 9 one **h** cubits long for one
Deut   34: 7 Moses was one **h** and twenty
Josh   24:32 father of Shechem for one **h**
Judg   3:31 who killed six **h** men of the
Judg   7: 7 By the three **h** men who lapped
Judg   11:26 for three **h** years, why did
1Sa   14: 2 with him were about six **h**
1Sa   18:25 desire any dowry but one **h**
1Sa   22: 2 And there were about four **h**
1Sa   23:13 and his men, about six **h**,
1Ki   6: 1 came to pass in the four **h**
1Ki   7: 2 its length was one **h**
1Ki   11: 3 And he had seven **h** wives,
1Ki   11: 3 and three **h** concubines; and
1Ki   18: 4 that Obadiah had taken one **h**
1Ki   18:22 Baal's prophets are four **h**
Neh   3: 1 as far as the Tower of the H,
Esth   9: 6 killed and destroyed five **h**
Job   42:16 After this Job lived one **h**
Prov   17:10 for a wise man Than a **h**
Eccl   6: 3 If a man begets a **h**
Eccl   8:12 a sinner does evil a **h**
Is   65:20 the child shall die one **h**
Ezek   4: 9 three **h** and ninety days, you
Ezek   40:19 one **h** cubits toward the east
Dan   8:14 For two thousand three **h**
Dan   12:11 be one thousand two **h** and
Amos   5: 3 a thousand Shall have a **h**
Matt   18:12 If a man has a **h** sheep, and
Matt   18:28 servants who owed him a **h**
Mark   4: 8 some sixty, and some a **h**.
Mark   4:20 some sixty, and some a **h**.
Luke   16: 6 A **h** measures of oil.' So he
John   19:39 about a **h** pounds.
Acts   7: 6 and oppress them four **h**
Acts   13:20 judges for about four **h** and
1Co   15: 6 He was seen by over five **h**
Rev   7: 4 One **h** and forty-four
Rev   11: 3 prophesy one thousand two **h**
Rev   21:17 one **h** and forty-four

HUNDREDFOLD (see HUNDRED)
Gen   26:12 reaped in the same year a **h**;
Matt   13: 8 and yielded a crop: some a **h**,
Matt   13:23 fruit and produces: some a **h**,
Mark   10:30 who shall not receive a **h** now

HUNDREDS (see HUNDRED)
Ex   18:21 of thousands, rulers of **h**,
Num   31:48 thousands and captains of **h**,
Mark   6:40 they sat down in ranks, in **h**

HUNDREDTH (see HUNDRED)
Gen   7:11 In the six **h** year of Noah's

HUNG (see HANG)
Ex   40:21 **h** up the veil of the
Ex   40:33 and **h** up the screen of the
2Sa   21:12 where the Philistines had **h**
Neh   3: 1 they consecrated it and **h**
Ps   137: 2 We **h** our harps Upon the
Lam   5:12 Princes were **h** up by their
Matt   18: 6 him if a millstone were **h**

HUNGER (see HUNGRY)
Deut   8: 3 you, allowed you to **h**,
Deut   32:24 shall be wasted with **h**,

1Sa 2: 5 hungry have ceased to **h**.
Neh 9:15 from heaven for their **h**,
Ps 34:10 lions lack and suffer **h**;
Prov 19:15 an idle person will suffer **h**.
Is 49:10 They shall neither **h** nor
Lam 4: 9 Than those who die of **h**;
Mic 6:14 **H** shall be in your midst.
Matt 5: 6 Blessed are those who **h** and
John 6:35 comes to Me shall never **h**,
1Co 4:11 the present hour we both **h**
2Co 11:27 in **h** and thirst, in fastings
Rev 6: 8 to kill with sword, with **h**,

HUNGRY (see HUNGER)
1Sa 2: 5 And the **h** have ceased to
Job 22: 7 withheld bread from the **h**.
Ps 107: 5 **H** and thirsty, Their soul
Ps 107: 9 And fills the **h** soul with
Ps 146: 7 Who gives food to the **h**.
Prov 25:21 If your enemy is **h**,
Prov 27: 7 But to a **h** soul every
Is 29: 8 shall even be as when a **h**
Is 32: 6 To keep the **h** unsatisfied,
Is 58: 7 share your bread with the **h**,
Is 65:13 eat, But you shall be **h**;
Ezek 18: 7 has given his bread to the **h**
Matt 4: 2 nights, afterward He was **h**.
Matt 12: 1 And His disciples were **h**,
Matt 12: 3 what David did when he was **h**,
Matt 15:32 not want to send them away **h**,
Matt 25:35 for I was **h** and you gave Me
Mark 11:12 out from Bethany, He was **h**.
Acts 10:10 Then he became very **h** and
Rom 12:20 "If your enemy is **h**,
1Co 11:34 But if anyone is **h**,
Phil 4:12 both to be full and to be **h**,

HUNT (see HUNTED, HUNTER, HUNTING)
Gen 27: 3 go out to the field and **h**
1Sa 24:11 Yet you **h** my life to take

HUNTED (see HUNT)
Lam 3:52 enemies without cause **H** me

HUNTER (see HUNT)
Gen 10: 9 He was a mighty **h** before the
Gen 25:27 And Esau was a skillful **h**,
Prov 6: 5 from the hand of the **h**,

HUNTING (see HUNT)
Gen 27:30 brother came in from his **h**.

HUR
Ex 17:12 And Aaron and **H** supported

HURAM (see HIRAM)
2Ch 2:13 **H** my master craftsman
2Ch 4:11 So **H** finished doing the work

HURRIED
Josh 4:10 and the people **h** and crossed

HURRY
Gen 19:15 the angels urged Lot to **h**,
Gen 45: 9 "**H** and go up to my father,

HURT (see HURTING, HURTS)
Ex 21:22 and **h** a woman with child, so
Ps 15: 4 He who swears to his own **h**
Ps 35: 4 to confusion Who plot my **h**.
Ps 38:12 Those who seek my **h** speak
Ps 105:18 They **h** his feet with
Prov 23:35 struck me, but I was not **h**;
Eccl 10: 9 quarries stones may be **h** by
Is 11: 9 They shall not **h** nor destroy
Is 65:25 They shall not **h** nor
Jer 8:11 For they have healed the **h**
Dan 3:25 the fire; and they are not **h**,
Dan 6:22 so that they have not **h** me,
Rev 2:11 overcomes shall not be **h** by

HURTING† (see HURT)
Gen 4:23 Even a young man for **h** me.
1Sa 25:34 who has kept me back from **h**

HURTS† (see HURT)
Ex 21:35 If one man's ox **h** another's,

HUSBAND (see HUSBAND'S, HUSBANDS)
Gen 3: 6 She also gave to her **h** with
Gen 3:16 desire shall be for your **h**,
Gen 16: 3 and gave her to her **h** Abram
Ex 4:25 Surely you are a **h** of blood
Lev 21: 7 a woman divorced from her **h**;
Num 5:27 unfaithfully toward her **h**,
Deut 21:13 go in to her and be her **h**,
Deut 22:22 with a woman married to a **h**,
Deut 22:23 a virgin is betrothed to a **h**,
Deut 24: 3 if the latter **h** detests her
Deut 24: 3 or if the latter **h** dies who
Judg 13: 9 but Manoah her **h** was not
Ruth 1: 3 Then Elimelech, Naomi's **h**,
Ruth 1: 9 each in the house of her **h**.
Ruth 1:12 I am too old to have a **h**.
Ruth 2: 1 was a relative of Naomi's **h**,
1Sa 1: 8 Then Elkanah her **h** said to
1Sa 25:19 But she did not tell her **h**
2Sa 11:26 heard that Uriah her **h** was
2Sa 14: 5 a widow, my **h** is dead.
Prov 12: 4 wife is the crown of her **h**,
Prov 31:23 Her **h** is known in the gates,
Is 54: 5 For your Maker is your **h**,
Jer 31:32 though I was a **h** to them,
Hos 2: 2 nor am I her **H**! Let her
Hos 2: 7 go and return to my first **h**,
Hos 2:16 you will call Me 'My **H**,
Matt 1:16 Jacob begot Joseph the **h** of
Mark 10:12 if a woman divorces her **h**
Luke 2:36 and had lived with a **h** seven
Luke 16:18 who is divorced from her **h**
John 4:16 to her, "Go, call your **h**,
Acts 5: 9 who have buried your **h**
Rom 7: 2 For the woman who has a **h** is
Rom 7: 2 bound by the law to her **h**
Rom 7: 2 But if the **h** dies, she is
1Co 7: 2 each woman have her own **h**.
1Co 7: 3 Let the **h** render to his wife
1Co 7: 4 but the **h** does. And
1Co 7:10 is not to depart from her **h**.
1Co 7:11 or be reconciled to her **h**.
1Co 7:11 And a **h** is not to divorce
1Co 7:14 wife is sanctified by the **h**;
1Co 7:16 you will save your **h**?
1Co 7:34 she may please her **h**.
Gal 4:27 Than she who has a **h**.
Eph 5:23 For the **h** is head of the
Eph 5:33 that she respects her **h**.
1Ti 3: 2 the **h** of one wife,
Tit 1: 6 the **h** of one wife, having
Rev 21: 2 as a bride adorned for her **h**.

HUSBAND'S (see HUSBAND)
Num 5:19 while under your **h**
Deut 25: 5 and perform the duty of a **h**

HUSBANDS (see HUSBAND)
Esth 1:20 all wives will honor their **h**,
Amos 4: 1 needy, Who say to your **h**,
John 4:18 "for you have had five **h**,
1Co 14:35 let them ask their own **h** at
Eph 5:22 Wives, submit to your own **h**,
Col 3:18 Wives, submit to your own **h**,
1Ti 3:12 Let deacons be the **h** of one
Tit 2: 4 young women to love their **h**,
Tit 2: 5 obedient to their own **h**,
1Pe 3: 1 be submissive to your own **h**,

HUSHAI
2Sa 15:37 So H, David's friend, went
2Sa 16:16 when H the Archite, David's

HUT
Is   1: 8 As a **h** in a garden of

HYENAS†
Is   13:22 The **h** will howl in their

HYMENAEUS
1Ti   1:20 of whom are H and Alexander,

HYMN† (see** HYMNS)**
Matt 26:30 And when they had sung a **h**,
Mark 14:26 And when they had sung a **h**,

HYMNS† (see** HYMN)**
Acts 16:25 were praying and singing **h**
Eph   5:19 one another in psalms and **h**
Col   3:16 one another in psalms and **h**

HYPOCRISY (see** HYPOCRITE)**
Matt 23:28 but inside you are full of **h**
Luke 12: 1 of the Pharisees, which is **h**.
Rom   12: 9 Let love be without **h**.
1Ti   4: 2 speaking lies in **h**,
Jas   3:17 partiality and without **h**.
1Pe   2: 1 all malice, all deceit, **h**,

HYPOCRITE (see** HYPOCRISY, HYPOCRITES)**
Job   8:13 And the hope of the **h** shall
Job   20: 5 And the joy of the **h** is
Is   9:17 For everyone is a **h** and an
Matt 7: 5 H! First remove the plank
Gal   2:13 the Jews also played the **h**

HYPOCRITES (see** HYPOCRITE)**
Jer   42:20 For you were **h** in your hearts
Matt 6: 2 trumpet before you as the **h**
Matt 6: 5 shall not be like the **h**.
Matt 16: 3 H! You know how to discern
Matt 23:13 **h**! For you shut up the
Matt 23:14 **h**! For you devour widows'
Matt 24:51 him his portion with the **h**.

HYSSOP
Ex   12:22 you shall take a bunch of **h**,
Lev   14: 4 cedar wood, scarlet, and **h**.
1Ki   4:33 of Lebanon even to the **h**
Ps   51: 7 Purge me with **h**,
John 19:29 with sour wine, put it on **h**,
Heb   9:19 water, scarlet wool, and **h**,

I

ICHABOD†
1Sa   4:21 Then she named the child I,

ICONIUM
Acts 14:19 Jews from Antioch and I
Acts 14:21 they returned to Lystra, I,

IDDO
2Ch   9:29 and in the visions of I the
2Ch   13:22 the annals of the prophet I.
Ezra 5: 1 and Zechariah the son of I,

IDENTIFY
Gen   31:32 **i** what I have of yours and

IDLE (see** IDLENESS)**
Ex   5:17 You are idle! I! Therefore
Prov 14:23 But **i** chatter leads only
Prov 19:15 And an **i** person will suffer
Matt 12:36 say to you that for every **i**
Matt 20: 3 and saw others standing **i**
Luke 24:11 words seemed to them like **i**
1Ti   5:13 and not only **i** but also

1Ti   6:20 the profane and **i** babblings
Tit   1:10 both **i** talkers and
2Pe   2: 3 judgment has not been **i**,

IDLENESS (see** IDLE)**
Prov 31:27 does not eat the bread of **i**.
Eccl 10:18 And through **i** of hands the

IDOL (see** IDOL'S, IDOLATER, IDOLATRY, IDOLS)**
2Ch   33: 7 the **i** which he had made, in
Ps   24: 4 lifted up his soul to an **i**,
Jer   10: 8 A wooden **i** is a worthless
Acts 7:41 offered sacrifices to the **i**,
1Co   8: 4 we know that an **i** is
1Co   8: 7 with consciousness of the **i**,
1Co   8: 7 as a thing offered to an **i**;
1Co   10:19 That an **i** is anything, or

IDOL'S† (see** IDOL)**
1Co   8:10 knowledge eating in an **i**

IDOLATER† (see** IDOL, IDOLATERS)**
1Co   5:11 or covetous, or an **i**,
Eph   5: 5 covetous man, who is an **i**,

IDOLATERS (see** IDOLATER)**
2Ki   17:15 followed idols, became **i**,
1Co   5:10 or extortioners, or **i**,
1Co   6: 9 Neither fornicators, nor **i**,
1Co   10: 7 And do not become **i** as were
Rev   21: 8 immoral, sorcerers, **i**,

IDOLATRIES† (see** IDOLATRY)**
1Pe   4: 3 parties, and abominable **i**.

IDOLATROUS (see** IDOLATRY)**
Zeph 1: 4 The names of the **i** priests

IDOLATRY† (see** IDOL, IDOLATRIES, IDOLATROUS)**
1Sa   15:23 is as iniquity and **i**.
1Co   10:14 my beloved, flee from **i**.
Gal   5:20 **i**, sorcery, hatred,
Col   3: 5 and covetousness, which is **i**.

IDOLS (see** IDOL)**
Gen   31:19 had stolen the household **i**
Lev   26:30 the lifeless forms of your **i**;
Judg 17: 5 an ephod and household **i**;
1Ki   16:13 Israel to anger with their **i**.
2Ki   21:11 made Judah sin with his **i**),
1Ch   16:26 gods of the peoples are **i**,
2Ch   11:15 and the calf **i** which he had
Ps   31: 6 those who regard useless **i**;
Ps   115: 4 Their **i** are silver and
Is   10:10 found the kingdoms of the **i**,
Is   19: 1 The **i** of Egypt will totter
Is   19: 3 they will consult the **i** and
Jer   8:19 images—With foreign **i**?
Ezek 6: 6 your **i** may be broken and
Ezek 14: 4 to the multitude of his **i**,
Ezek 14: 5 estranged from Me by their **i**.
Ezek 23: 7 lusted, With all their **i**,
Ezek 23:37 adultery with their **i**,
Hos   4:12 counsel from their wooden **i**,
Jon   2: 8 who regard worthless **i**
Zech 10: 2 For the **i** speak delusion;
Acts 15:20 from things polluted by **i**,
Acts 15:29 from things offered to **i**,
Acts 17:16 the city was given over to **i**.
Rom   2:22 adultery? You who abhor **i**,
1Co   8: 4 of things offered to **i**,
1Co   12: 2 carried away to these dumb **i**,
2Co   6:16 has the temple of God with **i**?
1Th   1: 9 you turned to God from **i** to
1Jn   5:21 keep yourselves from **i**.
Rev   2:14 eat things sacrificed to **i**,
Rev   9:20 and **i** of gold, silver,

IDUMEA† (see** EDOM)**
Mark 3: 8 and Jerusalem and I and

IGNORANCE (*see* IGNORANT)
Ezek 45:20 unintentionally or in i.
Acts 3:17 I know that you did it in i,
Acts 17:30 these times of i God
Heb 9: 7 sins committed in i;
1Pe 1:14 former lusts, as in your i;
1Pe 2:15 may put to silence the i of

IGNORANT (*see* IGNORANCE, IGNORANTLY)
Ps 73:22 I was so foolish and i;
Is 63:16 Though Abraham was i of us,
Rom 10: 3 For they being i of God's
Rom 11:25 that you should be i of this
1Co 12: 1 I do not want you to be i:
2Co 2:11 for we are not i of his
2Ti 2:23 But avoid foolish and i
Heb 5: 2 on those who are i and

IGNORANTLY† (*see* IGNORANT)
1Ti 1:13 mercy because I did it i

ILL (*see* ILLNESS, ILLS)
Judg 9:23 God sent a spirit of i will
2Sa 13: 5 your bed and pretend to be i.

ILLEGITIMATE†
Deut 23: 2 One of i birth shall not
Heb 12: 8 then you are i and not sons.

ILLNESS† (*see* ILL)
2Ki 13:14 had become sick with the i
Ps 41: 3 him on his bed of i;

ILLS† (*see* ILL)
Is 3: 7 "I cannot cure your i,

ILLUMINATED
Heb 10:32 in which, after you were i,
Rev 21:23 for the glory of God i it.

ILLUSTRATION†
John 10: 6 Jesus used this i,

IMAGE (*see* IMAGE'S, IMAGES)
Gen 1:26 "Let Us make man in Our i,
Gen 1:27 created man in His own i;
Gen 5: 3 own likeness, after his i,
Gen 9: 6 For in the i of God He
Ex 20: 4 make for yourself a carved i,
Deut 9:12 made themselves a molded i.
Deut 16:21 any tree, as a wooden i,
1Ki 15:13 she had made an obscene i
2Ki 17:16 made a wooden i and
Ps 73:20 You shall despise their i.
Ps 106:20 their glory Into the i of
Is 40:19 The workman molds an i,
Is 44:17 into a god, His carved i.
Jer 10:14 For his molded i is
Ezek 8: 3 where the seat of the i of
Dan 2:31 a great i! This great image,
Dan 3: 1 the king made an i of gold,
Dan 3: 3 for the dedication of the i
Dan 3: 5 down and worship the gold i
Hab 2:18 "What profit is the i,
Matt 22:20 Whose i and inscription is
Rom 1:23 incorruptible God into an i
Rom 8:29 to be conformed to the i
1Co 11: 7 since he is the i and glory
1Co 15:49 And as we have borne the i of
1Co 15:49 we shall also bear the i of
2Co 3:18 transformed into the same i
2Co 4: 4 who is the i of God, should
Col 1:15 He is the i of the invisible
Col 3:10 according to the i of Him
Heb 1: 3 glory and the express i of
Heb 10: 1 and not the very i of the
Rev 13:14 on the earth to make an i
Rev 13:15 as would not worship the i
Rev 14:11 worship the beast and his i,

IMAGE'S† (*see* IMAGE)
Dan 2:32 This i head was of fine

IMAGES (*see* IMAGE)
Ex 34:13 cut down their wooden i
Num 33:52 destroy all their molded i,
Deut 7: 5 and burn their carved i with
Judg 3:19 back from the stone i that
1Sa 6: 5 images of your tumors and i
2Ch 34: 7 had beaten the carved i into
Ezek 21:21 arrows, he consults the i,
Acts 7:43 I which you made to

IMAGINATION
Gen 8:21 although the i of man's
Luke 1:51 the proud in the i of

IMITATE† (*see* IMITATORS)
1Co 4:16 i me.
1Co 11: 1 just as I also i Christ.
Heb 6:12 but i those who through
3Jn 11 do not i what is evil, but

IMITATORS (*see* IMITATE)
1Th 2:14 became i of the churches of

IMMANUEL†
Is 7:14 and shall call His name I.
Is 8: 8 breadth of Your land, O I.
Matt 1:23 shall call His name I,

IMMEDIATELY
Judg 2:23 without driving them out i;
Dan 3: 6 and worship shall be cast i
Matt 3:16 Jesus came up i from the
Matt 4:20 They i left their nets and
Matt 8: 3 I his leprosy was
Matt 13:20 he who hears the word and i
Matt 13:21 i he stumbles.
Matt 14:22 I Jesus made His disciples
Matt 20:34 And i their eyes received
Matt 21: 2 and i you will find a donkey
Matt 21:19 I the fig tree withered
Matt 24:29 I after the tribulation of
Matt 26:49 I he went up to Jesus and
Matt 26:74 I do not know the Man!" I a
Mark 1:12 I the Spirit drove Him into
Mark 1:21 and i on the Sabbath He
Mark 1:28 And i His fame spread
Mark 1:31 and i the fever left her.
Mark 1:42 i the leprosy left him, and
Mark 2: 2 I many gathered together, so
Mark 2: 8 But i, when Jesus
Mark 2:12 I he arose, took up the bed,
Mark 3: 6 the Pharisees went out and i
Mark 4: 5 and i it sprang up because
Mark 4:15 Satan comes i and takes away
Mark 4:16 i receive it with gladness;
Mark 4:17 i they stumble.
Mark 4:29 i he puts in the sickle,
Mark 5: 2 i there met Him out of the
Mark 5:29 i the fountain of her blood
Mark 5:30 i knowing in Himself that
Mark 5:42 I the girl arose and walked,
Mark 6:25 i she came in with haste to
Mark 6:27 I the king sent an
Mark 6:45 I He made His disciples get
Mark 6:50 But i He talked with them
Mark 6:54 i the people recognized Him,
Mark 7:35 i his ears were opened, and
Mark 8:10 i got into the boat with His
Mark 9:15 I, when they saw Him
Mark 9:20 i the spirit convulsed him,
Mark 9:24 I the father of the child
Mark 10:52 And i he received his
Mark 11: 3 and i he will send it
Mark 14:43 And i, while He was still
Mark 14:45 i he went up to Him and said

Mark 15: 1 I, in the morning,
Luke 19:11 of God would appear i.
Luke 19:40 the stones would i cry
John 5: 9 And i the man was made well,
John 6:21 and i the boat was at the
John 19:34 and i blood and water came
John 21: 3 They went out and i got
Acts 3: 7 and i his feet and ankle
Acts 9:18 I there fell from his eyes
Acts 9:20 I he preached the Christ in
Acts 9:34 your bed." Then he arose i.
Acts 16:26 and i all the doors were
Gal 1:16 I did not i confer with
Jas 1:24 and i forgets what kind of
Rev 4: 2 I I was in the Spirit; and

IMMORAL (see IMMORALITY)
Prov 2:16 To deliver you from the i
Prov 5: 3 For the lips of an i woman
Prov 7: 5 they may keep you from the i
Prov 22:14 The mouth of an i woman is
1Co 5: 9 keep company with sexually i
Rev 21: 8 murderers, sexually i,
Rev 22:15 and sorcerers and sexually i

IMMORALITY (see IMMORAL)
Ezek 23: 8 And poured out their i upon
Matt 5:32 any reason except sexual i
Matt 19: 9 wife, except for sexual i,
Acts 15:20 by idols, from sexual i,
Acts 15:29 strangled, and from sexual i.
Rom 1:29 unrighteousness, sexual i,
1Co 5: 1 and such sexual i as is not
1Co 6:13 body is not for sexual i
1Co 6:18 Flee sexual i
1Th 4: 3 should abstain from sexual i;
Rev 2:14 and to commit sexual i.
Rev 2:21 to repent of her sexual i,

IMMORTAL† (see IMMORTALITY)
1Ti 1:17 Now to the King eternal, i,

IMMORTALITY (see IMMORTAL)
Rom 2: 7 seek for glory, honor, and i;
1Co 15:53 this mortal must put on i.
1Ti 6:16 who alone has i,
2Ti 1:10 and brought life and i to

IMMOVABLE†
Acts 27:41 stuck fast and remained i,
1Co 15:58 brethren, be steadfast, i,

IMMUTABILITY† (see IMMUTABLE)
Heb 6:17 the heirs of promise the i

IMMUTABLE† (see IMMUTABILITY)
Heb 6:18 that by two i things, in

IMPART
Rom 1:11 that I may i to you some
Eph 4:29 that it may i grace to the

IMPATIENT†
Job 21: 4 were, why should I not be i?

IMPEDIMENT
Mark 7:32 who was deaf and had an i

IMPENITENT†
Rom 2: 5 your hardness and your i

IMPERISHABLE†
1Co 9:25 but we for an i crown.

IMPLANTED†
Jas 1:21 receive with meekness the i

IMPLEMENTS
Amos 1: 3 have threshed Gilead with i

IMPLORE (see IMPLORED, IMPLORING)
Ps 116: 4 I I You, deliver my soul!"
Mark 5: 7 I i You by God that You do

2Co 5:20 we i you on Christ's

IMPLORED (see IMPLORE)
Luke 5:12 he fell on his face and i
Luke 9:40 So I i Your disciples to cast
John 4:47 he went to Him and i Him to
Acts 27:33 Paul i them all to take

IMPLORING† (see IMPLORE)
Mark 1:40 i Him, kneeling down to Him
Acts 9:38 i him not to delay in
2Co 8: 4 i us with much urgency that

IMPORTED
1Ki 10:28 Also Solomon had horses i

IMPOSSIBLE
Matt 17:20 and nothing will be i for
Matt 19:26 men, "With men this is i,
Luke 1:37 with God nothing will be i.
Heb 6: 4 For it is i for those who
Heb 6:18 in which it is i for God to
Heb 11: 6 But without faith it is i

IMPOSTORS†
2Ti 3:13 But evil men and i will grow

IMPRISONED† (see IMPRISONMENT)
Acts 22:19 that in every synagogue I i

IMPRISONMENT (see IMPRISONED, IMPRISONMENTS)
Heb 11:36 yes, and of chains and i.

IMPRISONMENTS† (see IMPRISONMENT)
2Co 6: 5 in stripes, in i,

IMPROPER† (see IMPROPERLY)
2Sa 13: 2 And it was i for Amnon to do

IMPROPERLY† (see IMPROPER)
1Co 7:36 man thinks he is behaving i

IMPUDENT
Prov 7:13 With an i face she said to
Ezek 3: 7 the house of Israel are i

IMPULSIVE†
Prov 14:29 But he who is i exalts

IMPURITY
Lev 12: 2 the days of her customary i
2Sa 11: 4 she was cleansed from her i;

IMPUTE† (see IMPUTED, IMPUTES, IMPUTING)
1Sa 22:15 from me! Let not the king i
2Sa 19:19 Do not let my lord i iniquity
Ps 32: 2 to whom the LORD does not i
Rom 4: 8 the LORD shall not i

IMPUTED (see IMPUTE)
Lev 17: 4 of bloodshed shall be i to
Rom 4:23 sake alone that it was i to
Rom 4:24 It shall be i to us who
Rom 5:13 but sin is not i when there

IMPUTES† (see IMPUTE)
Rom 4: 6 of the man to whom God i

IMPUTING (see IMPUTE)
2Co 5:19 not i their trespasses to

IMRI
1Ch 9: 4 son of Omri, the son of I,

INCENSE
Ex 30: 1 make an altar to burn i on;
Ex 30: 7 shall burn on it sweet i
Ex 30: 8 a perpetual i before the
Ex 30: 9 shall not offer strange i
Ex 30:27 utensils, and the altar of i;.
Ex 37:29 oil and the pure i of sweet
Lev 16:13 that the cloud of i may
Ps 141: 2 be set before You as i,
Is 1:13 I is an abomination to Me.
Is 43:23 Nor wearied you with i.

Is 60: 6 They shall bring gold and i,
Jer 44:18 since we stopped burning i
Ezek 6: 6 your i altars may be cut
Ezek 8:11 and a thick cloud of i went
Ezek 16:18 and you set My oil and My i
Dan 2:46 present an offering and i
Hos 11: 2 And burned i to carved
Hab 1:16 And burn i to their
Luke 1: 9 his lot fell to burn i when
Luke 1:10 outside at the hour of i.
Luke 1:11 right side of the altar of i.
Rev 5: 8 and golden bowls full of i,
Rev 18:13 "and cinnamon and i,

INCENSED
Is 45:24 shall be ashamed Who are i

INCITED (*see* INCITING)
Job 2: 3 although you i Me against

INCITING† (*see* INCITED)
Acts 24:12 disputing with anyone nor i

INCLINATION† (*see* INCLINE)
Deut 31:21 for I know the i of their

INCLINE (*see* INCLINATION, INCLINED)
Josh 24:23 and i your heart to the
1Ki 8:58 that He may i our hearts to
2Ki 19:16 I Your ear, O LORD, and
Ps 17: 6 I Your ear to me, and hear
Ps 49: 4 I will i my ear to a
Ps 119:36 I my heart to Your
Ps 141: 4 Do not i my heart to any
Prov 22:17 I your ear and hear the
Jer 7:26 they did not obey Me or i
Dan 9:18 i Your ear and hear; open

INCLINED (*see* INCLINE)
Judg 9: 3 and their heart was i to
Ps 40: 1 And heard
Ps 116: 2 Because He has i His ear to
Ps 119:112 I have i my heart to perform
Prov 5:13 Nor i my ear to those who

INCLUDED (*see* INCLUDING)
Job 3: 6 may it not be i among the

INCLUDING (*see* INCLUDED)
Eccl 12:14 I every secret thing,

INCORRUPTIBILITY† (*see* INCORRUPTIBLE)
Tit 2: 7 integrity, reverence, i,

INCORRUPTIBLE (*see* INCORRUPTIBILITY, INCORRUPTION)
Rom 1:23 changed the glory of the i
1Co 15:52 the dead will be raised i,
1Pe 1: 4 to an inheritance i and
1Pe 1:23 of corruptible seed but i,

INCORRUPTION (*see* INCORRUPTIBLE)
1Co 15:42 it is raised in i.
1Co 15:53 corruptible must put on i,

INCREASE (*see* INCREASED, INCREASES, INCREASING)
Lev 19:25 it may yield to you its i:
Job 10:17 And i Your indignation
Ps 62:10 in robbery; If riches i,
Ps 67: 6 the earth shall yield her i;
Ps 71:21 You shall i my greatness,
Ps 85:12 our land will yield its i.
Prov 1: 5 A wise man will hear and i
Prov 3: 9 firstfruits of all your i;
Prov 28:28 they perish, the righteous i.
Eccl 6:11 there are many things that i
Is 9: 7 Of the i of His government
Is 29:19 The humble also shall i
Jer 2: 3 The firstfruits of His i.
Dan 12: 4 fro, and knowledge shall i.
Luke 17: 5 I our faith."

John 3:30 "He must i,
1Co 3: 6 watered, but God gave the i.
1Th 3:12 And may the Lord make you i
1Th 4:10 that you i more and more;

INCREASED (*see* INCREASE)
Gen 7:17 The waters i and lifted up
Gen 19:19 and you have i your mercy
Ex 1: 7 Israel were fruitful and i
Job 1:10 and his possessions have i
Ps 105:24 He i His people greatly,
Is 9: 3 the nation And i its joy;
Is 26:15 You have i the nation; You
Jer 5: 6 Their backslidings have i.
Jer 30:14 Because your sins have i.
Ezek 23:14 But she i her harlotry; She
Ezek 28: 5 wisdom in trade you have i
Hos 4: 7 "The more they i,
Mark 4: 8 i and produced: some
Luke 2:52 And Jesus i in wisdom and
Acts 9:22 But Saul i all the more in
Acts 16: 5 and i in number daily.
2Co 10:15 that as your faith is i,

INCREASES (*see* INCREASE)
Prov 16:21 And sweetness of the lips i
Prov 23:28 And i the unfaithful among
Prov 29:16 multiplied, transgression i;
Eccl 1:18 he who increases knowledge i
Eccl 8: 6 Though the misery of man i
Is 40:29 who have no might He i
Hab 2: 6 Woe to him who i What is

INCREASING† (*see* INCREASE, INCREASINGLY)
Col 1:10 in every good work and i in

INCREASINGLY (*see* INCREASING)
Acts 5:14 And believers were i added to

INCREDIBLE†
Acts 26: 8 Why should it be thought i by

INCURABLE
Job 34: 6 my right? My wound is i,
Jer 15:18 perpetual And my wound i,
Jer 30:15 Your sorrow is i.

INCURRED†
Acts 27:21 have sailed from Crete and i

INDEBTED†
Luke 11: 4 forgive everyone who is i

INDEPENDENT
1Co 11:11 nor woman i of man, in the

INDESCRIBABLE†
2Co 9:15 Thanks be to God for His i

INDIA
Esth 1: 1 from I to Ethiopia),

INDICATES† (*see* INDICATING)
Heb 12:27 i the removal of those

INDICATING† (*see* INDICATES)
Heb 9: 8 the Holy Spirit i this, that
1Pe 1:11 who was in them was i when

INDIGNANT (*see* INDIGNATION)
Matt 26: 8 saw it, they were i,

INDIGNATION (*see* INDIGNANT)
Deut 29:28 in wrath, and in great i,
2Ki 3:27 and there was great i
Job 10:17 And increase Your i toward
Ps 69:24 Pour out Your i upon them,
Ps 78:49 of His anger, Wrath, i,
Is 13: 5 LORD and His weapons of i,
Is 30:27 His lips are full of i,
Is 66:14 And His i to His enemies.
Jer 10:10 not be able to endure His i.
Jer 15:17 You have filled me with i.

Dan   8:19 in the latter time of the i;
Mic   7: 9 I will bear the i of the
Nah   1: 6 Who can stand before His i?
Acts   5:17 and they were filled with i,
Rom   2: 8 i and wrath,
Heb   10:27 and fiery i which will
Rev   14:10 into the cup of His i.

INDIVIDUALLY
Rom   12: 5 and i members of one
1Co   12:11 distributing to each one i
1Co   12:27 of Christ, and members i.

INDULGENCE†
Col   2:23 of no value against the i

INEXCUSABLE†
Rom   2: 1 Therefore you are i,

INEXPRESSIBLE†
2Co   12: 4 up into Paradise and heard i
1Pe   1: 8 you rejoice with joy i and

INFALLIBLE†
Acts   1: 3 His suffering by many i

INFANT (see INFANTS)
Jer   44: 7 man and woman, child and i,
Lam   4: 4 The tongue of the i clings

INFANTS (see INFANT)
Job   3:16 Like i who never saw light?
Ps   8: 2 of babes and nursing i You
Lam   2:11 the children and the i
Hos   13:16 Their i shall be dashed in
Matt 21:16 of babes and nursing i
Luke 18:15 Then they also brought i to

INFERIOR
Job   12: 3 I am not i to you.
Job   13: 2 I am not i to you.
Dan   2:39 arise another kingdom i to
John   2:10 have well drunk, then the i.

INFINITE†
Ps   147: 5 His understanding is i.

INFIRMITIES (see INFIRMITY)
Matt   8:17 He Himself took our i
Luke   5:15 be healed by Him of their i.
2Co   12: 5 not boast, except in my i.
1Ti   5:23 sake and your frequent i.

INFIRMITY (see INFIRMITIES)
Jer   10:19 I say, "Truly this is an i,
Luke 13:11 woman who had a spirit of i
John   5: 5 man was there who had an i
2Co   11:30 things which concern my i.
Gal   4:13 that because of physical i

INFLICTS
Rom   3: 5 Is God unjust who i wrath?

INFORM (see INFORMED)
Ruth   4: 4 And I thought to i you,

INFORMED (see INFORM)
Dan   9:22 And he i me, and talked with
Acts 21:24 things of which they were i
Acts 25: 2 the chief men of the Jews i

INGATHERING
Ex   34:22 and the Feast of I at the

INHABIT (see ENTHRONED, INHABITANT, INHABITED,
    INHABITING, INHABITS, UNINHABITED)
Num   15: 2 into the land you are to i,
Prov 10:30 But the wicked will not i
Is   65:21 shall build houses and i
Zeph   1:13 but not i them; They shall

INHABITANT (see INHABIT, INHABITANTS)
Is   6:11 are laid waste and without i,
Is   12: 6 O i of Zion, For great is

Jer   2:15 cities are burned, without i.
Jer   26: 9 be desolate, without an i'?
Jer   33:10 without man and without i

INHABITANTS (see INHABITANT)
Gen   19:25 all the i of the cities, and
Gen   34:30 me obnoxious among the i of
Ex   15:15 All the i of Canaan will
Ex   34:12 make a covenant with the i
Lev   18:25 the land vomits out its i.
Josh 13: 6 all the i of the mountains
Judg   5:23 Curse its i bitterly,
1Ch   11: 5 Then the i of Jebus said to
2Ch   34:27 this place and against its i,
Ps   33: 8 Let all the i of the world
Ps   75: 3 The earth and all its i are
Is   23: 6 you i of the coastland!
Is   24: 1 And scatters abroad its i.
Jer   23:14 And her i like Gomorrah.
Ezek 27:35 All the i of the isles will
Rev   8:13 woe to the i of the earth,

INHABITED (see INHABIT)
Ex   16:35 until they came to an i
Judg   1:21 out the Jebusites who i
Judg 11:21 who i that country.
Prov   8:31 Rejoicing in His i world,
Is   13:20 It will never be i,
Is   44:26 Jerusalem, 'You shall be i,
Is   45:18 vain, Who formed it to be i:
Is   54: 3 make the desolate cities i.
Jer   17: 6 a salt land which is not i.
Jer   46:26 Afterward it shall be i as
Jer   50:39 It shall be i no more
Ezek 26:17 O one i by seafaring men,
Zech 14:11 Jerusalem shall be safely i.

INHABITING (see INHABIT)
Job   26: 5 the waters and those i them.
Ps   74:14 him as food to the people i

INHABITS (see INHABIT)
Is   57:15 High and Lofty One Who i

INHERIT (see INHERITANCE, INHERITED)
Gen   15: 7 to give you this land to i
Gen   15: 8 shall I know that I will i
Ex   32:13 and they shall i it
Lev   25:46 to i them as a possession;
Num   14:24 and his descendants shall i
Num   32:19 For we will not i with them
Num   34:13 the land which you shall i
Deut   1:38 he shall cause Israel to i
Ps   25:13 his descendants shall i the
Ps   37:11 But the meek shall i the
Ps   37:29 The righteous shall i the
Ps   82: 8 For You shall i all
Prov   8:21 cause those who love me to i
Prov 11:29 his own house will i the
Prov 14:18 The simple i folly, But the
Prov 28:10 But the blameless will i
Is   57:13 And shall i My holy
Is   65: 9 My elect shall i it, And
Matt   5: 5 For they shall i the earth.
Matt 19:29 and i eternal life.
Matt 25:34 i the kingdom prepared for
Mark 10:17 what shall I do that I may i
1Co   6: 9 the unrighteous will not i
1Co   6:10 nor extortioners will i the
1Co   15:50 flesh and blood cannot i
1Co   15:50 nor does corruption i
Heb   1:14 for those who will i
Heb   6:12 faith and patience i the
Heb   12:17 when he wanted to i the
Rev   21: 7 He who overcomes shall i all

INHERITANCE (see INHERIT)
Gen   31:14 still any portion or i for

Ex 15:17 In the mountain of Your i,
Ex 34: 9 sin, and take us as Your i.
Num 18:20 You shall have no i in their
Num 36: 3 it will be added to the i
Num 36: 3 taken from the lot of our i.
Deut 4:20 to be His people, an i,
Deut 10: 9 the LORD is his i,
Josh 1: 6 you shall divide as an i
Josh 11:23 and Joshua gave it as an i
Josh 13:14 of Levi he had given no i;
Josh 13:33 God of Israel was their i,
Josh 24:28 depart, each to his own i.
Ruth 4: 5 of the dead through his i.
Ruth 4: 6 myself, lest I ruin my own i.
Ruth 4:10 of the dead through his i,
1Sa 10: 1 you commander over His i?
2Ki 21:14 forsake the remnant of My i
Job 42:15 their father gave them an i
Ps 2: 8 The nations for Your i,
Ps 16: 5 are the portion of my i
Ps 16: 6 Yes, I have a good i.
Ps 28: 9 people, And bless Your i;
Ps 33:12 He has chosen as His own i.
Ps 37:18 And their i shall be
Ps 78:62 And was furious with His i.
Ps 78:71 people, And Israel His i.
Ps 79: 1 have come into Your i;
Ps 94:14 Nor will He forsake His i.
Ps 106:40 that He abhorred His own i.
Prov 13:22 A good man leaves an i to
Prov 20:21 An i gained hastily at the
Eccl 7:11 Wisdom is good with an i,
Is 19:25 of My hands, and Israel My i.
Is 47: 6 I have profaned My i,
Jer 10:16 is the tribe of His i;
Ezek 47:13 divide the land as an i
Dan 12:13 and will arise to your i at
Zech 2:12 of Judah as His i in the
Matt 21:38 us kill him and seize his i.
Luke 12:13 my brother to divide the i
Acts 7: 5 And God gave him no i in it,
Gal 3:18 For if the i is of the law,
Eph 1:11 also we have obtained an i,
Eph 1:14 is the guarantee of our i
Eph 1:18 of the glory of His i in
Eph 5: 5 has any i in the kingdom of
Col 1:12 us to be partakers of the i
Col 3:24 receive the reward of the i;
Heb 1: 4 as He has by i obtained a
Heb 9:15 the promise of the eternal i.
Heb 11: 8 he would receive as an i.
1Pe 1: 4 to an i incorruptible and

INHERITED (see INHERIT)
Josh 14: 1 the children of Israel i in
Ezek 33:24 and he i the land. But we

INIQUITIES (see INIQUITY)
Lev 16:21 confess over it all the i of
Lev 16:22 bear on itself all their i
Lev 26:39 also in their fathers' i,
Ezra 9:13 punished us less than our i
Job 13:23 How many are my i and sins?
Job 13:26 And make me inherit the i
Ps 38: 4 For my i have gone over my
Ps 40:12 My i have overtaken me, so
Ps 51: 9 sins, And blot out all my i.
Ps 64: 6 They devise i;
Ps 65: 3 I prevail against me
Ps 79:8 do not remember former i
Ps 90: 8 You have set our i before
Ps 103: 3 Who forgives all your i,
Ps 103:10 us according to our i.
Ps 130: 3 You, LORD, should mark i,
Ps 130: 8 Israel From all his i.
Prov 5:22 His own i entrap the wicked

Is 43:24 have wearied Me with your i.
Is 50: 1 For your i you have sold
Is 53: 5 He was bruised for our i;
Is 53:11 For He shall bear their i.
Is 64: 6 fade as a leaf, And our i,
Jer 33: 8 I will pardon all their i
Ezek 36:33 cleanse you from all your i,
Dan 4:27 and your i by showing mercy
Dan 9:13 we might turn from our i
Dan 9:16 and for the i of our
Amos 3: 2 punish you for all your i.
Acts 3:26 one of you from your i.
Rev 18: 5 and God has remembered her i.

INIQUITY (see INIQUITIES)
Gen 15:16 for the i of the Amorites
Ex 20: 5 visiting the i of the
Ex 28:38 that Aaron may bear the i of
Ex 34: 7 forgiving i and
Ex 34: 9 and pardon our i and our
Lev 5:17 guilty and shall bear his i.
Lev 18:25 the punishment of its i
Lev 26:40 if they confess their i and
Num 5:15 for bringing i to
Num 5:31 the man shall be free from i,
Josh 22:17 Is the i of Peor not enough
Josh 22:20 not perish alone in his i.
1Sa 15:23 And stubbornness as i
1Sa 25:24 on me let this i be! And
2Sa 7:14 be My son. If he commits i,
2Sa 14: 9 let the i be on me and on
2Sa 14:32 but if there is i in me, let
2Sa 19:19 not let my lord impute i
Neh 4: 5 Do not cover their i,
Job 4: 8 Those who plow i And sow
Job 7:21 And take away my i?
Job 10:14 will not acquit me of my i.
Job 11: 6 from you Less than your i
Job 15:16 Who drinks i like water!
Job 22:23 You will remove i far from
Job 31: 3 for the workers of i?
Job 31:11 it would be i deserving
Job 31:33 By hiding my i in my bosom,
Job 33: 9 and there is no i in me.
Job 34:10 the Almighty to commit i.
Ps 7: 3 If there is i in my hands,
Ps 7:14 the wicked brings forth i;
Ps 10: 7 his tongue is trouble and i.
Ps 18:23 And I kept myself from my i.
Ps 25:11 sake, O LORD, Pardon my i,
Ps 32: 2 the LORD does not impute i,
Ps 32: 5 And You forgave the i of
Ps 38:18 For I will declare my i;
Ps 51: 2 me thoroughly from my i,
Ps 51: 5 I was brought forth in i,
Ps 53: 1 and have done abominable i;
Ps 66:18 If I regard i in my heart,
Ps 69:27 Add i to their iniquity,
Ps 85: 2 You have forgiven the i of
Ps 92: 7 when all the workers of i
Ps 109:14 Let the i of his fathers be
Ps 119:133 And let no i have dominion
Ps 125: 3 reach out their hands to i.
Prov 16: 6 Atonement is provided for i;
Prov 19:28 of the wicked devours i.
Prov 22: 8 He who sows i will reap
Is 1: 4 A people laden with i,
Is 1:13 I cannot endure i and the
Is 6: 7 Your i is taken away, And
Is 40: 2 That her i is pardoned;
Is 53: 6 LORD has laid on Him the i
Is 59: 7 thoughts are thoughts of i;
Is 64: 9 Nor remember i forever;
Jer 9: 5 weary themselves to commit i.
Jer 16:17 nor is their i hidden from

Jer 16:18 repay double for their i
Jer 31:30 one shall die for his own i;
Jer 31:34 For I will forgive their i.
Jer 36: 3 that I may forgive their i
Ezek 3:18 man shall die in his i;
Ezek 4: i it, you shall bear their i.
Ezek 14: 3 them to stumble into i.
Ezek 18:17 shall not die for the i
Ezek 18:18 he shall die for his i.
Ezek 28:18 By the i of your trading;
Ezek 33: 8 man shall die in his i;
Dan 9: 5 have sinned and committed i,
Dan 9:24 make reconciliation for i,
Hos 4: 8 set their heart on their i.
Hos 8:13 He will remember their i
Hos 10:13 You have reaped i.
Hos 13:12 The i of Ephraim is bound
Mic 2: 1 Woe to those who devise i,
Mic 7:18 Pardoning i And passing
Hab 2:12 establishes a city by i!
Mal 2: 6 And turned many away from i.
Luke 13:27 Me, all you workers of i.
Acts 1:18 a field with the wages of i;
Acts 8:23 by bitterness and bound by i.
1Co 13: 6 does not rejoice in i,
2Ti 2:19 name of Christ depart from i.
Jas 3: 6 is a fire, a world of i.
2Pe 2:16 but he was rebuked for his i:

INJURED (*see* INJURY)
Ex 22:14 and it becomes i or dies,

INJURY† (*see* INJURED)
2Ki 1: 2 I shall recover from this i.
Dan 6:23 and no i whatever was found
Nah 3:19 Your i has no healing,

INJUSTICE
Deut 32: 4 God of truth and without i;
Job 6:30 Is there i on my tongue?
Jer 2: 5 What i have your fathers
Jer 22:13 And his chambers by i,
Mal 2: 6 And i was not found on his

INK†
Jer 36:18 and I wrote them with i in
2Co 3: 3 written not with i but by
2Jn 12 to do so with paper and i;
3Jn 13 write to you with pen and i;

INN (see INNKEEPER)
Luke 2: 7 was no room for them in the i
Luke 10:34 animal, brought them to an i

INMOST†
Prov 18: 8 And they go down into the i
Prov 23:16 my i being will rejoice
Prov 26:22 And they go down into the i

INN (*see* INNKEEPER)
Luke 2: 7 was no room for them in the i
Luke 10:34 animal, brought them to an i

INNER
1Ki 6: 5 the sanctuary and the i
1Ki 6:27 the cherubim inside the i
1Ki 6:36 And he built the i court
Ps 49:11 Their i thought is that
Prov 20:27 Searching all the i depths
Matt 24:26 He is in the i rooms!' do
Luke 12: 3 have spoken in the ear in i
Acts 16:24 he put them into the i
Eph 3:16 through His Spirit in the i

INNKEEPER† (*see* INN)
Luke 10:35 denarii, gave them to the i,

INNOCENCE (*see* INNOCENT)
Gen 20: 5 integrity of my heart and i
Ps 26: 6 I will wash my hands in i;

INNOCENT (*see* INNOCENCE, INNOCENTS)
Ex 23: 7 do not kill the i and
Deut 19:10 lest i blood be shed in the
Deut 27:25 takes a bribe to slay an i
Job 4: 7 who ever perished being i?
Job 9:23 at the plight of the i.
Job 9:28 that You will not hold me i.
Job 22:30 deliver one who is not i;
Job 33: 9 transgression; I am i,
Ps 15: 5 take a bribe against the i.
Ps 19:13 And I shall be i of great
Ps 94:21 And condemn i blood.
Ps 106:38 And shed i blood, The blood
Prov 1:11 us lurk secretly for the i
Prov 6:17 Hands that shed i blood,
Prov 6:29 touches her shall not be i.
Is 59: 7 they make haste to shed i
Jer 2:35 you say, 'Because I am i,
Dan 6:22 because I was found i before
Jon 1:14 and do not charge us with i
Matt 27: 4 have sinned by betraying i
Matt 27:24 I am i of the blood of this
Acts 20:26 to you this day that I am i

INNOCENTS (*see* INNOCENT)
Jer 19: 4 with the blood of the i

INNUMERABLE
Ps 104:25 In which are i teeming
Jer 46:23 Because they are i,
Luke 12: 1 when an i multitude of
Heb 11:12 is the sand which is by the
Heb 12:22 to an i company of angels,

INQUIRE (*see* INQUIRED, INQUIRY)
Ex 18:15 the people come to me to i
Deut 17: 4 then you shall i diligently.
1Sa 9: 9 when a man went to i of God,
2Ki 1: 2 i of Baal-Zebub, the god of
Ps 27: 4 And to i in His temple.
Ezek 20: 1 elders of Israel came to i
Acts 23:20 though they were going to i

INQUIRED (*see* INQUIRE)
1Sa 23: 2 Therefore David i of the
1Sa 28: 6 And when Saul i of the LORD,
Ezek 14: 3 Should I let Myself be i of
Ezek 20: 3 I will not be i of by you."
Matt 2: 4 he i of them where the
John 4:52 Then he i of them the hour
1Pe 1:10 the prophets have i and

INQUIRY (*see* INQUIRE)
Deut 19:18 judges shall make careful i,
Acts 10:17 from Cornelius had made i
Acts 19:39 if you have any other i

INSANE
1Sa 21:14 "Look, you see the man is i.
Jer 50:38 And they are i with their

INSCRIBED† (*see* INSCRIPTION)
1Ch 9: 1 they were i in the book of
Job 19:23 that they were i in a book!
Is 49:16 I have i you on the palms

INSCRIPTION (*see* INSCRIBED)
Ex 39:30 and wrote on it an i like
Dan 5:25 And this is the i that was
Matt 22:20 Whose image and i is this?"
Mark 15:26 And the i of His accusation
Luke 23:38 And an i also was written
Acts 17:23 found an altar with this i:

INSECT†
Lev 11:21 may eat of every flying i

INSISTED
Gen 19: 3 But he i strongly; so they

INSOLENT
Ps 31:18 Which speak i things

INSPIRATION† (*see* INSPIRED)
2Ti 3:16 Scripture is given by i of

INSPIRED† (*see* INSPIRATION)
Is 41: 7 smooths with the hammer i

INSTANT
Is 30:13 comes suddenly, in an i.

INSTRUCT (*see* INSTRUCTED, INSTRUCTION, INSTRUCTOR, INSTRUCTS)
Deut 17:11 of the law in which they i
Neh 9:20 gave Your good Spirit to i
Ps 32: 8 I will i you and teach you
Dan 11:33 who understand shall i many;
1Co 2:16 LORD that he may i

INSTRUCTED (*see* INSTRUCT)
Ruth 3: 6 all that her mother-in-law i
Job 4: 3 Surely you have i many, And
Ps 2:10 be wise, O kings; Be i,
Prov 21:11 But when the wise is i,
Is 40:14 and who i Him, And taught
Luke 1: 4 things in which you were i.
Acts 18:25 This man had been i in the
Rom 2:18 being i out of the law,
Heb 8: 5 as Moses was divinely i when

INSTRUCTION (*see* INSTRUCT, INSTRUCTIONS)
Job 36:10 also opens their ear to i,
Ps 50:17 Seeing you hate i And cast
Prov 1: 2 To know wisdom and i,
Prov 1: 7 fools despise wisdom and i.
Prov 1: 8 hear the i of your father,
Prov 4:13 Take firm hold of i,
Prov 5:23 He shall die for lack of i,
Prov 8:33 Hear i and be wise, And do
Prov 9: 9 Give i to a wise man, and
Prov 12: 1 Whoever loves i loves
Prov 13: 1 son heeds his father's i,
Prov 15: 5 fool despises his father's i,
Prov 15:33 fear of the LORD is the i
Prov 23:12 Apply your heart to i,
Jer 35:13 Will you not receive i to
Jer 36:27 Baruch had written at the i
2Ti 3:16 for i in righteousness,

INSTRUCTIONS (*see* INSTRUCTION)
Heb 11:22 and gave i concerning his

INSTRUCTOR† (*see* INSTRUCT)
Gen 4:22 an i of every craftsman in
1Ch 15:22 was i in charge of the
Rom 2:20 an i of the foolish, a

INSTRUCTS (*see* INSTRUCT)
Ps 16: 7 My heart also i me in the
Ps 94:10 He who i the nations, shall

INSTRUMENT (*see* INSTRUMENTS)
1Sa 10: 5 high place with a stringed i,
Ps 33: 2 melody to Him with an i of

INSTRUMENTS (*see* INSTRUMENT)
1Sa 18: 6 with joy, and with musical i.
2Sa 6: 5 on harps, on stringed i,
2Ch 29:27 the trumpets and with the i
Ps 7:13 also prepares for Himself i
Ps 150: 4 Praise Him with stringed i
Amos 6: 5 to the sound of stringed i,
Hab 3:19 Musician. With my stringed i.
Rom 6:13 present your members as i
Rom 6:13 and your members as i of

INSUBORDINATE
1Ti 1: 9 but for the lawless and i,

INSULTED†
Luke 18:32 and will be mocked and i
Heb 10:29 and i the Spirit of grace?

INTEGRITY
Gen 20: 5 In the i of my heart and
Job 2: 3 still he holds fast to his i,
Job 31: 6 That God may know my i.
Ps 7: 8 And according to my i
Ps 26: 1 For I have walked in my i.
Prov 10: 9 He who walks with i walks
Prov 11: 3 The i of the upright will
Tit 2: 7 in doctrine showing i,

INTEND (*see* INTENDED, INTENDING, UNINTENDED)
Ex 2:14 Do you i to kill me as you
Acts 5:28 and i to bring this Man's
Acts 5:35 to yourselves what you i to

INTENDED (*see* INTEND)
Ps 21:11 For they i evil against You;
2Co 1:15 And in this confidence I i

INTENDING (*see* INTEND)
Acts 12: 4 i to bring him before the

INTENT (*see* INTENTLY, INTENTS)
Gen 6: 5 and that every i of the
Prov 21:27 he brings it with wicked i!
Eph 3:10 to the i that now the

INTENTLY (*see* INTENT)
Luke 22:56 looked i at him and said,

INTENTS (*see* INTENT)
Heb 4:12 of the thoughts and i of

INTERCEDE (*see* INTERCESSION)
Ex 8:28 I for me."

INTERCESSION (*see* INTERCEDE, INTERCESSIONS)
Is 53:12 And made i for the
Jer 7:16 nor make i to Me; for I will
Rom 8:26 the Spirit Himself makes i
Heb 7:25 He always lives to make i

INTERCESSIONS† (*see* INTERCESSION)
1Ti 2: 1 supplications, prayers, i,

INTEREST (*see* INTERESTS)
Lev 25:36 Take no usury or i from him;
Deut 23:19 You shall not charge i to
Deut 23:20 a foreigner you may charge i,
Matt 25:27 received back my own with i.

INTERESTS (*see* INTEREST)
Phil 2: 4 but also for the i of

INTERMARRY†
1Ki 11: 2 You shall not i with them,

INTERPRET (*see* INTERPRETATION, INTERPRETED, INTERPRETER, INTERPRETING, INTERPRETS)
Gen 41:15 there is no one who can i
1Co 12:30 speak with tongues? Do all i?
1Co 14:13 a tongue pray that he may i.

INTERPRETATION (*see* INTERPRET, INTERPRETATIONS)
Dan 2: 6 you tell the dream and its i,
Dan 4: 6 make known to me the i of
Dan 5: 7 writing, and tells me its i,
Dan 5:26 This is the i of each word.
1Co 12:10 to another the i of tongues.
1Co 14:26 has a revelation, has an i.
2Pe 1:20 is of any private i,

INTERPRETATIONS† (*see* INTERPRETATION)
Gen 40: 8 Do not i belong to God? Tell
Dan 5:16 that you can give i and

INTERPRETED (*see* INTERPRET)
Gen 40:22 as Joseph had i to them.
Gen 41:12 and he i our dreams for us;

INTERPRETER (*see* INTERPRET)
Gen 42:23 spoke to them through an i.
1Co 14:28 But if there is no i,

INTERPRETING† (*see* INTERPRET)
Dan   5:12 i dreams, solving riddles,

INTERPRETS† (*see* INTERPRET)
Deut 18:10 or one who i omens, or a
1Co   14: 5 tongues, unless indeed he i,

INTERVIEWED†
Dan   1:19 Then the king i them, and

INTOXICATING
Lev   10: 9 Do not drink wine or i drink,

INTRUDING
Col   2:18 i into those things which he

INVENT (*see* INVENTORS)
Amos   6: 5 And i for yourselves

INVENTORS (*see* INVENT)
Rom   1:30 i of evil things,

INVISIBLE†
Rom   1:20 creation of the world His i
Col   1:15 He is the image of the i God,
Col   1:16 are on earth, visible and i,
1Ti   1:17 King eternal, immortal, i,
Heb   11:27 as seeing Him who is i.

INVITE (*see* INVITED, INVITES)
1Sa   16: 3 Then i Jesse to the
Job   1: 4 and would send and i their
Matt   22: 9 i to the wedding.'
Luke   14:13 i the poor, the maimed,

INVITED (*see* INVITE)
1Sa   16: 5 and i them to the sacrifice.
Esth   5:12 Queen Esther i no one but me
Matt   22: 3 to call those who were i to
Luke   14: 8 When you are i by anyone to a
Luke   14:10 "But when you are i,
John   2: 2 and His disciples were i to

INVITES† (*see* INVITE)
Ex   34:15 and one of them i you and
1Co   10:27 those who do not believe i

INWARD (*see* INWARDLY)
Ps   51: 6 You desire truth in the i
Ps   64: 6 Both the i thought and
Ps   139:13 For You formed my i parts;
Rom   7:22 of God according to the i
2Co   4:16 yet the i man is being

INWARDLY† (*see* INWARD)
Ps   62: 4 mouth, But they curse i.
Matt   7:15 but i they are ravenous
Rom   2:29 he is a Jew who is one i;

IRON
Gen   4:22 craftsman in bronze and i.
Lev   26:19 make your heavens like i
Deut   3:11 his bedstead was an i
Deut   4:20 and brought you out of the i
Deut   8: 9 a land whose stones are i
Deut   28:48 and He will put a yoke of i
Josh   17:16 valley have chariots of i,
1Ki   8:51 out of the i furnace),
2Ki   6: 6 and he made the i float.
Job   19:24 on a rock With an i pen
Job   28: 2 I is taken from the earth,
Job   40:18 His ribs like bars of i.
Ps   2: 9 break them with a rod of i;
Ps   107:16 And cut the bars of i in
Prov   27:17 As i sharpens iron, So a
Jer   1:18 A fortified city and an i
Jer   11: 4 from the i furnace, saying,
Jer   17: 1 is written with a pen of i;
Jer   28:13 in their place yokes of i.
Dan   2:33 "its legs of i.
Dan   2:33 its feet partly of i and
Dan   2:41 just as you saw the i mixed

Dan   7: 7 It had huge i teeth; it was
Amos   1: 3 Gilead with implements of i.
1Ti   4: 2 seared with a hot i,
Rev   2:27 them with a rod of i;
Rev   19:15 rule them with a rod of i.

IRREPROACHABLE (*see* REPROACH)

IRREVOCABLE†
Rom   11:29 the calling of God are i.

ISAAC (*see* ISAAC'S)
Gen   17:19 you shall call his name I;
Gen   21: 3 whom Sarah bore to him—I.
Gen   21: 4 circumcised his son I when
Gen   21:12 for in I your seed shall be
Gen   22: 2 your son, your only son I,
Gen   22: 6 offering and laid it on I
Gen   22: 9 and he bound I his son and
Gen   24: 4 and take a wife for my son I.
Gen   24:67 So I was comforted after his
Gen   25: 9 And his sons I and Ishmael
Gen   25:28 And I loved Esau because he
Gen   26:18 And I dug again the wells of
Gen   27: 1 when I was old and his eyes
Gen   27:33 Then I trembled exceedingly,
Gen   28:13 your father and the God of I;
Gen   31:42 of Abraham and the Fear of I,
Gen   32: 9 and God of my father I,
Gen   48:16 of my fathers Abraham and I;
Ex   2:24 with Abraham, with I,
Ex   3: 6 God of Abraham, the God of I,
Ex   6: 8 swore to give to Abraham, I,
Deut   1: 8 your fathers—to Abraham, I,
Deut   9:27 Your servants, Abraham, I,
Josh   24: 4 To I I gave Jacob and Esau.
1Ki   18:36 "LORD God of Abraham, I,
2Ki   13:23 His covenant with Abraham, I,
1Ch   16:16 Abraham, And His oath to I,
Jer   33:26 descendants of Abraham, I,
Amos   7:16 spout against the house of I.
Matt   8:11 and sit down with Abraham, I,
Matt   22:32 Abraham, the God of I,
Luke   13:28 when you see Abraham and I
Rom   9: 7 In I your seed shall be
Rom   9:10 even by our father I
Gal   4:28 as I was, are children of
Heb   11:17 he was tested, offered up I,
Heb   11:20 By faith I blessed Jacob and
Jas   2:21 by works when he offered I

ISAAC'S (*see* ISAAC)
Gen   26:19 Also I servants dug in the
Gen   26:20 of Gerar quarreled with I

ISAIAH
2Ki   19: 2 to I the prophet, the son of
2Ki   19: 5 of King Hezekiah came to I.
2Ch   32:20 Hezekiah and the prophet I,
2Ch   32:32 written in the vision of I
Is   1: 1 The vision of I the son of
Is   20: 3 Just as My servant I has
Matt   4:14 which was spoken by I the
Matt   13:14 in them the prophecy of I
Matt   15: 7 Hypocrites! Well did I
Luke   4:17 the book of the prophet I.
John   12:41 These things I said when he
Acts   8:28 he was reading I the
Acts   28:25 spoke rightly through I the
Rom   10:16 For I says, "Lord, who
Rom   10:20 But I is very bold and says:

ISCARIOT (*see* JUDAS)
Matt   26:14 the twelve, called Judas I,
John   13: 2 it into the heart of Judas I,
John   14:22 Judas (not I) said to Him,

ISHBOSHETH (*see* ESH-BAAL)
2Sa 2: 8 took I the son of Saul and

ISHMAEL (*see* ISHMAELITES)
Gen 16:16 years old when Hagar bore I
Gen 17:26 circumcised, and his son I;
Gen 25: 9 And his sons Isaac and I
Jer 40:15 and I will kill I the son of
Jer 41: 3 I also struck down all the
Jer 41:10 Then I carried away captive

ISHMAELITES (*see* ISHMAEL)
Gen 37:28 and sold him to the I for
Gen 39: 1 bought him from the I who
Judg 8:24 because they were I.

ISLAND (*see* ISLANDS)
Acts 27:26 run aground on a certain i.
Rev 1: 9 was on the i that is called
Rev 16:20 Then every i fled away, and

ISLANDS† (*see* ISLAND)
Esth 10: 1 on the land and on the i
Is 11:11 From Hamath and the i of

ISOLATE (*see* ISOLATED)
Lev 13:21 priest shall i him seven days
Lev 13:50 i that which has the plague

ISOLATED (*see* ISOLATE)
2Ki 15: 5 so he dwelt in an i house.

ISRAEL (*see* ISRAEL'S, ISRAELITE, JACOB)
Gen 32:28 be called Jacob, but I;
Gen 32:32 this day the children of I
Gen 35:10 but I shall be your name."
Gen 36:31 over the children of I:
Gen 37: 3 Now I loved Joseph more than
Gen 42: 5 And the sons of I went to buy
Gen 43: 8 Then Judah said to I his
Gen 46: 8 names of the children of I,
Gen 46:29 Goshen to meet his father I;
Gen 46:30 And I said to Joseph, "Now
Gen 47:29 the time drew near that I
Gen 48: 2 Then I saw Joseph's sons,
Gen 48:10 Now the eyes of I were dim
Gen 49: 2 And listen to I your
Gen 49: 7 Jacob And scatter them in I.
Gen 49:24 Shepherd, the Stone of I),
Gen 49:28 are the twelve tribes of I,
Gen 50: 2 So the physicians embalmed I.
Ex 1: 1 names of the children of I
Ex 1: 7 But the children of I were
Ex 3:10 My people, the children of I,
Ex 3:11 bring the children of I out
Ex 3:16 and gather the elders of I,
Ex 4:22 I is My son, My firstborn.
Ex 5: 1 says the LORD God of I:
Ex 5: 2 obey His voice to let I go?
Ex 6:14 Reuben, the firstborn of I,
Ex 10:23 But all the children of I
Ex 11: 7 between the Egyptians and I.
Ex 12: 3 to all the congregation of I,
Ex 12:15 shall be cut off from I.
Ex 14: 8 he pursued the children of I;
Ex 14:10 and the children of I cried
Ex 14:19 went before the camp of I,
Ex 14:30 So the LORD saved I that
Ex 15: 1 Moses and the children of I
Ex 15:22 So Moses brought I from the
Ex 16: 2 of the children of I
Ex 16:31 And the house of I called its
Ex 16:35 And the children of I ate
Ex 17:11 that I prevailed; and when
Ex 19: 2 So I camped there before the
Ex 24: 1 seventy of the elders of I,
Ex 24: 9 seventy of the elders of I,
Ex 24:10 and they saw the God of I.

Ex 28: 9 the names of the sons of I:
Ex 32: 4 "This is your god, O I,
Ex 32:13 Abraham, Isaac, and I,
Ex 34:27 covenant with you and with I.
Ex 39: 7 stones for the sons of I,
Lev 4:13 the whole congregation of I
Lev 10: 6 the whole house of I,
Lev 20: 2 the strangers who dwell in I,
Lev 24:10 woman's son and a man of I
Lev 27:34 Moses for the children of I
Num 1: 3 able to go to war in I.
Num 1:16 heads of the divisions in I.
Num 1:44 with the leaders of I,
Num 1:45 of the children of I,
Num 2:32 of the children of I by
Num 3:13 all the firstborn in I,
Num 3:40 males of the children of I
Num 4:46 and the leaders of I
Num 6:23 bless the children of I.
Num 8: 9 of the children of I.
Num 8:17 among the children of I
Num 9:17 after that the children of I
Num 9:18 the LORD the children of I
Num 10: 4 heads of the divisions of I,
Num 10:12 And the children of I set out
Num 10:29 promised good things to I.
Num 10:36 To the many thousands of I.
Num 13:32 they gave the children of I
Num 14:27 which the children of I
Num 15:32 Now while the children of I
Num 16:25 and the elders of I followed
Num 16:38 a sign to the children of I.
Num 16:41 of the children of I
Num 18: 5 wrath on the children of I.
Num 18:21 of Levi all the tithes in I
Num 18:22 the children of I
Num 18:32 gifts of the children of I,
Num 19:13 shall be cut off from I.
Num 20:13 because the children of I
Num 20:14 "Thus says your brother I:
Num 20:21 Thus Edom refused to give I
Num 21: 1 then he fought against I and
Num 21: 2 So I made a vow to the LORD,
Num 21: 6 and many of the people of I
Num 21:23 But Sihon would not allow I
Num 21:25 So I took all these cities,
Num 23:21 has He seen wickedness in I.
Num 24:17 Scepter shall rise out of I,
Num 24:18 While I does valiantly.
Num 25: 3 So I was joined to Baal of
Num 25: 3 LORD was aroused against I.
Num 25: 5 said to the judges of I,
Num 26: 2 are able to go to war in I.
Num 26:63 numbered the children of I
Num 31: 5 from the divisions of I one
Num 32:14 anger of the LORD against I.
Num 35:15 refuge for the children of I
Num 36: 8 so that the children of I
Deut 1:38 for he shall cause I to
Deut 2:12 just as I did to the land of
Deut 4:46 Moses and the children of I
Deut 5: 1 And Moses called all I,
Deut 5: 1 said to them: "Hear, O I,
Deut 6: 4 "Hear, O I: The LORD
Deut 9: 1 "Hear, O I: You are to
Deut 10:12 "And now, I, what does
Deut 13:11 So all I shall hear and fear,
Deut 18: 1 part nor inheritance with I;
Deut 21: 8 O LORD, for Your people I,
Deut 21:21 and all I shall hear and
Deut 23:17 harlot of the daughters of I,
Deut 23:17 one of the sons of I.
Deut 25: 6 may not be blotted out of I.
Deut 25: 7 a name to his brother in I;
Deut 31:11 when all I comes to appear

Deut	33:28	Then I shall dwell in
Deut	34:10	there has not arisen in I a
Deut	34:12	in the sight of all I.
Josh	3:17	and all I crossed over on
Josh	4:22	I crossed over this Jordan on
Josh	5:10	Now the children of I camped
Josh	6:25	So she dwells in I to this
Josh	7:11	I has sinned, and they have
Josh	7:15	a disgraceful thing in I.
Josh	7:19	glory to the LORD God of I,
Josh	7:25	So all I stoned him with
Josh	8:14	and went out against I to
Josh	8:27	and the spoil of that city I
Josh	8:30	altar to the LORD God of I
Josh	9: 6	to him and to the men of I,
Josh	9:18	them by the LORD God of I.
Josh	10: 1	had made peace with I and
Josh	10:10	LORD routed them before I,
Josh	10:14	for the LORD fought for I.
Josh	10:42	God of Israel fought for I.
Josh	11:13	I burned none of them,
Josh	11:16	the mountains of I and its
Josh	11:19	peace with the children of I
Josh	12: 6	LORD and the children of I
Josh	13: 6	only divide it by lot to I
Josh	14: 1	tribes of the children of I
Josh	17:13	when the children of I grew
Josh	19:51	tribes of the children of I
Josh	22:33	and the children of I
Josh	24: 1	all the tribes of I to
Josh	24:23	heart to the LORD God of I.
Josh	24:31	I served the LORD all the
Judg	2:14	the LORD was hot against I.
Judg	2:22	through them I may test I,
Judg	3:10	upon him, and he judged I.
Judg	3:31	and he also delivered I.
Judg	4: 4	was judging I at that time.
Judg	5: 3	praise to the LORD God of I.
Judg	5: 7	arose, Arose a mother in I.
Judg	6: 1	Then the children of I did
Judg	6: 2	Midian prevailed against I.
Judg	6: 6	So I was greatly impoverished
Judg	6:14	and you shall save I from
Judg	8:27	And all I played the harlot
Judg	9:22	had reigned over I three
Judg	11: 4	of Ammon made war against I.
Judg	11:39	And it became a custom in I
Judg	11:40	that the daughters of I went
Judg	17: 6	there was no king in I;
Judg	18: 1	there was no king in I.
Judg	20: 6	lewdness and outrage in I.
Judg	20:13	and remove the evil from I!
Judg	20:29	Then I set men in ambush all
Judg	20:34	select men from all I came
Judg	20:35	defeated Benjamin before I.
Judg	21: 3	be one tribe missing in I?
Judg	21:15	a void in the tribes of I,
Judg	21:25	there was no king in I;
Ruth	4: 7	was a confirmation in I.
Ruth	4:11	two who built the house of I;
Ruth	4:14	may his name be famous in I!
1Sa	1:17	and the God of I grant your
1Sa	3:20	And all I from Dan to
1Sa	4: 1	word of Samuel came to all I.
1Sa	4: 1	Now I went out to battle
1Sa	4: 2	I was defeated by the
1Sa	4:18	And he had judged I forty
1Sa	4:21	glory has departed from I!
1Sa	4:22	glory has departed from I,
1Sa	5: 7	The ark of the God of I must
1Sa	6: 5	give glory to the God of I;
1Sa	7: 2	And all the house of I
1Sa	7:10	near to battle against I.
1Sa	7:10	they were overcome before I.
1Sa	7:15	And Samuel judged I all the
1Sa	8: 1	made his sons judges over I.
1Sa	8:22	Samuel said to the men of I,
1Sa	9: 9	(Formerly in I, when a man
1Sa	9:21	smallest of the tribes of I,
1Sa	13:13	your kingdom over I forever.
1Sa	14:23	So the LORD saved I that
1Sa	15:17	LORD anoint you king over I?
1Sa	15:26	you from being king over I.
1Sa	15:29	And also the Strength of I
1Sa	17: 8	cried out to the armies of I,
1Sa	17:10	I defy the armies of I this
1Sa	17:45	the God of the armies of I,
1Sa	17:46	that there is a God in I.
1Sa	23:17	You shall be king over I,
1Sa	24: 2	chosen men from all I,
1Sa	25:30	appointed you ruler over I,
1Sa	25:32	is the LORD God of I,
1Sa	31: 1	Philistines fought against I;
1Sa	31: 1	and the men of I fled from
2Sa	1:19	The beauty of I is slain on
2Sa	1:24	"O daughters of I,
2Sa	3:10	the throne of David over I
2Sa	3:38	man has fallen this day in I?
2Sa	5: 2	shall shepherd My people I,
2Sa	5: 3	anointed David king over I.
2Sa	7: 6	I brought the children of I
2Sa	7: 7	to shepherd My people I,
2Sa	7: 8	ruler over My people, over I.
2Sa	7:11	to be over My people I,
2Sa	7:24	You have made Your people I
2Sa	7:27	O LORD of hosts, God of I,
2Sa	10:18	the Syrians fled before I;
2Sa	10:19	they made peace with I and
2Sa	11:11	The ark and I and Judah are
2Sa	12: 7	'I anointed you king over I,
2Sa	12: 8	and gave you the house of I
2Sa	13:13	like one of the fools in I.
2Sa	14:25	Now in all I there was no
2Sa	15: 6	the hearts of the men of I.
2Sa	17:15	Absalom and the elders of I,
2Sa	19:22	be put to death today in I?
2Sa	19:22	that today I am king over I?
2Sa	20:19	a city and a mother in I.
2Sa	21: 5	any of the territories of I,
2Sa	21:17	you quench the lamp of I.
2Sa	23: 1	And the sweet psalmist of I:
2Sa	23: 3	The God of I said, The Rock
2Sa	23: 3	The Rock of I spoke to me:
2Sa	24: 1	LORD was aroused against I,
2Sa	24: 1	number I and Judah."
2Sa	24:25	plague was withdrawn from I.
1Ki	1:20	the eyes of all I are on
1Ki	2: 4	a man on the throne of I.
1Ki	2:11	that David reigned over I
1Ki	4: 1	Solomon was king over all I.
1Ki	4: 7	twelve governors over all I,
1Ki	4:25	And Judah and I dwelt safely,
1Ki	6:13	will not forsake My people I.
1Ki	8:16	no city from any tribe of I
1Ki	8:16	David to be over My people I.
1Ki	8:20	and sit on the throne of I,
1Ki	8:23	he said: "LORD God of I,
1Ki	8:34	the sin of Your people I,
1Ki	8:52	of Your people I,
1Ki	9: 5	of your kingdom over I
1Ki	9: 7	I will be a proverb and a
1Ki	11:25	He was an adversary of I all
1Ki	11:42	in Jerusalem over all I
1Ki	12: 1	for all I had gone to
1Ki	12:16	O I! Now, see to your own
1Ki	12:19	So I has been in rebellion
1Ki	12:28	Here are your gods, O I,
1Ki	14: 7	you ruler over My people I,
1Ki	14:15	He will uproot I from this
1Ki	14:16	who sinned and who made I

1Ki	14:19	chronicles of the kings of I.
1Ki	15:30	provoked the LORD God of I
1Ki	15:31	chronicles of the kings of I?
1Ki	15:33	became king over all I in
1Ki	16:13	the LORD God of I to anger
1Ki	16:19	he had committed to make I
1Ki	16:33	provoke the LORD God of I
1Ki	17: 1	As the LORD God of I lives,
1Ki	18:17	that you, O troubler of I?
1Ki	18:19	send and gather all I to me
1Ki	18:36	God of Abraham, Isaac, and I,
1Ki	18:36	day that You are God in I
1Ki	19:18	reserved seven thousand in I,
1Ki	21:21	from Ahab every male in I,
1Ki	22: 1	war between Syria and I.
1Ki	22:17	I saw all I scattered on the
1Ki	22:30	So the king of I disguised
1Ki	22:52	who had made I sin;
2Ki	1: 1	Moab rebelled against I
2Ki	2:12	the chariot of I and its
2Ki	3: 1	of Ahab became king over I
2Ki	3:13	Elisha said to the king of I,
2Ki	3:27	great indignation against I.
2Ki	5: 8	that there is a prophet in I.
2Ki	5:12	than all the waters of I?
2Ki	10:28	Jehu destroyed Baal from I.
2Ki	10:31	law of the LORD God of I
2Ki	13:14	the chariots of I and their
2Ki	14:26	there was no helper for I.
2Ki	14:27	blot out the name of I from
2Ki	15:12	sit on the throne of I to
2Ki	16: 3	in the way of the kings of I;
2Ki	17: 6	took Samaria and carried I
2Ki	17:13	LORD testified against I
2Ki	17:18	LORD was very angry with I,
2Ki	17:23	until the LORD removed I out
2Ki	17:34	of Jacob, whom He named I,
2Ki	19:22	Against the Holy One of I.
1Ch	6:49	and to make atonement for I,
1Ch	9: 1	the book of the kings of I.
1Ch	13: 8	Then David and all I played
1Ch	16:13	O seed of I His servant,
1Ch	16:36	be the LORD God of I
1Ch	18:14	So David reigned over all I,
1Ch	21: 1	Now Satan stood up against I,
1Ch	21: 1	and moved David to number I.
1Ch	21:14	LORD sent a plague upon I,
1Ch	21:14	seventy thousand men of I
1Ch	22: 6	house for the LORD God of I.
1Ch	22:10	throne of his kingdom over I
1Ch	27:23	had said He would multiply I
1Ch	29:10	are You, LORD God of I,
2Ch	17: 4	according to the acts of I.
2Ch	18:16	I saw all I scattered on the
2Ch	18:29	So the king of I disguised
2Ch	18:34	and the king of I propped
2Ch	19: 8	of the chief fathers of I,
2Ch	21: 6	in the way of the kings of I,
2Ch	24: 5	and gather from all I money
2Ch	25: 6	mighty men of valor from I
2Ch	25: 7	for the LORD is not with I—
2Ch	28:27	the tombs of the kings of I.
2Ch	29: 7	holy place to the God of I.
2Ch	29:24	make an atonement for all I,
2Ch	30: 5	throughout all I,
2Ch	30: 6	went throughout all I and
2Ch	30: 6	God of Abraham, Isaac, and I;
2Ch	33: 8	again remove the foot of I
2Ch	34: 9	from all the remnant of I,
2Ch	35: 3	the Levites who taught all I,
2Ch	35: 3	your God and His people I.
2Ch	35:18	been no Passover kept in I
2Ch	35:25	They made it a custom in I;
Ezra	1: 3	house of the LORD God of I
Ezra	2:70	and all I in their cities.
Ezra	3: 2	the altar of the God of I,
Ezra	3:10	ordinance of David king of I.
Ezra	4: 1	temple of the LORD God of I,
Ezra	6:22	house of God, the God of I.
Ezra	7:10	statutes and ordinances in I.
Ezra	10: 5	and all I swear an oath that
Ezra	10:10	adding to the guilt of I.
Neh	1: 6	sins of the children of I
Neh	10:33	to make atonement for I,
Neh	13: 3	the mixed multitude from I.
Neh	13:26	God made him king over all I.
Ps	14: 7	Let Jacob rejoice and I be
Ps	22: 3	in the praises of I.
Ps	22:23	all you offspring of I!
Ps	25:22	Redeem I, O God
Ps	41:13	be the LORD God of I
Ps	59: 5	God of hosts, the God of I,
Ps	68:26	Lord, from the fountain of I.
Ps	68:34	His excellence is over I,
Ps	71:22	the harp, O Holy One of I.
Ps	73: 1	Truly God is good to I,
Ps	76: 1	His name is great in I.
Ps	78: 5	And appointed a law in I,
Ps	78:41	limited the Holy One of I.
Ps	78:71	And I His inheritance.
Ps	80: 1	Give ear, O Shepherd of I,
Ps	81: 4	this is a statute for I,
Ps	81:11	And I would have none of
Ps	81:13	That I would walk in My
Ps	103: 7	acts to the children of I.
Ps	105:10	To I as an everlasting
Ps	106:48	be the LORD God of I
Ps	114: 1	When I went out of Egypt,
Ps	114: 2	And His dominion.
Ps	115: 9	O I, trust in the LORD;
Ps	118: 2	Let I now say, "His mercy
Ps	121: 4	He who keeps I Shall
Ps	122: 4	To the Testimony of I,
Ps	124: 1	Let I now say—
Ps	125: 5	Peace be upon I!
Ps	128: 6	Peace be upon I!
Ps	130: 8	And He shall redeem I From
Ps	135: 4	I for His special treasure.
Ps	136:22	A heritage to I His servant,
Ps	149: 2	Let I rejoice in their
Prov	1: 1	the son of David, king of I:
Eccl	1:12	was king over I in
Is	1: 3	But I does not know, My
Is	1: 4	to anger The Holy One of I,
Is	1:24	hosts, the Mighty One of I,
Is	5: 7	of hosts is the house of I,
Is	9:14	cut off head and tail from I,
Is	10:17	So the Light of I will be
Is	10:20	day That the remnant of I,
Is	12: 6	great is the Holy One of I
Is	19:25	and I My inheritance."
Is	27: 6	I shall blossom and bud,
Is	29:23	And fear the God of I.
Is	40:27	O Jacob, And speak, O I:
Is	41:14	You men of I! I will help
Is	41:14	Redeemer, the Holy One of I.
Is	43: 1	And He who formed you, O I:
Is	43:15	Holy One, The Creator of I.
Is	43:22	have been weary of Me, O I.
Is	44: 1	And I whom I have chosen.
Is	44:23	And glorified Himself in I.
Is	45: 4	And I My elect, I have
Is	46: 3	remnant of the house of I,
Is	46:13	For I My glory.
Is	48: 2	And lean on the God of I;
Is	49: 3	'You are My servant, O I,
Jer	2: 3	I was holiness to the
Jer	2:14	Is I a servant? Is he a
Jer	3: 6	you seen what backsliding I
Jer	3:23	God Is the salvation of I.

Jer	4: 1	"If you will return, O I,
Jer	5:15	you from afar, O house of I,
Jer	6: 9	as a vine the remnant of I;
Jer	14: 8	O the Hope of I,
Jer	16:14	up the children of I from
Jer	18:13	The virgin of I has done a
Jer	23: 2	thus says the LORD God of I
Jer	23: 6	And I will dwell safely;
Jer	29:23	done disgraceful things in I,
Jer	31: 4	O virgin of I! You shall
Jer	31: 9	For I am a Father to I,
Jer	32:32	evil of the children of I
Jer	33: 7	Judah and the captives of I
Jer	33:17	the throne of the house of I;
Jer	46:27	O I! For behold, I will
Jer	48:27	For was not I a derision to
Jer	49: 1	Has I no sons? Has he no
Jer	50:17	I is like scattered sheep;
Jer	51: 5	For I is not forsaken, nor
Jer	51: 5	against the Holy One of I.
Jer	51:19	And I is the tribe of His
Lam	2: 1	the earth The beauty of I,
Lam	2: 5	He has swallowed up I,
Ezek	3: 4	go to the house of I and
Ezek	3: 7	for all the house of I are
Ezek	3:17	watchman for the house of I;
Ezek	4: 3	be a sign to the house of I.
Ezek	6: 2	toward the mountains of I,
Ezek	8:11	the elders of the house of I,
Ezek	9: 8	all the remnant of I by
Ezek	10:20	I saw under the God of I by
Ezek	11:22	the glory of the God of I
Ezek	12:23	use it as a proverb in I
Ezek	13: 2	against the prophets of I
Ezek	14: 1	Now some of the elders of I
Ezek	14: 9	him from among My people I.
Ezek	17: 2	a parable to the house of I,
Ezek	18: 3	longer use this proverb in I.
Ezek	18:25	Hear now, O house of I,
Ezek	18:31	should you die, O house of I?
Ezek	20: 5	On the day when I chose I and
Ezek	20:13	Yet the house of I rebelled
Ezek	20:40	on the mountain height of I,
Ezek	21:12	all the princes of I.
Ezek	21:25	profane, wicked prince of I,
Ezek	33: 7	watchman for the house of I;
Ezek	33:11	should you die, O house of I?
Ezek	33:20	is not fair.' O house of I,
Ezek	34: 2	against the shepherds of I,
Ezek	37:19	Ephraim, and the tribes of I,
Ezek	37:28	I, the LORD, sanctify I,
Ezek	38:17	servants the prophets of I,
Ezek	38:19	earthquake in the land of I,
Ezek	39: 4	fall upon the mountains of I,
Ezek	39:11	a burial place there in I,
Ezek	39:29	My Spirit on the house of I,
Ezek	43: 2	the glory of the God of I
Ezek	45: 9	O princes of I! Remove
Ezek	45:17	atonement for the house of I.
Ezek	47:13	among the twelve tribes of I.
Ezek	48:31	named after the tribes of I)
Dan	9:11	all I has transgressed Your
Dan	9:20	and the sin of my people I,
Hos	1: 5	I will break the bow of I
Hos	1: 6	have mercy on the house of I,
Hos	3: 5	Afterward the children of I
Hos	4:16	For I is stubborn Like a
Hos	5: 1	O house of I! Give ear, O
Hos	5: 3	I is defiled.
Hos	5: 5	The pride of I testifies to
Hos	5: 5	Therefore I and Ephraim
Hos	7: 1	I would have healed I,
Hos	8: 8	I is swallowed up
Hos	8:14	For I has forgotten his
Hos	9:10	I found I Like grapes in

Hos	10:15	At dawn the king of I
Hos	11: 1	When I was a child, I loved
Hos	11: 8	How can I hand you over, I?
Hos	13: 1	He exalted himself in I,
Hos	13: 9	"O I, you are destroyed,
Hos	14: 5	I will be like the dew to I;
Joel	3: 2	of My people, My heritage I,
Amos	2: 6	three transgressions of I,
Amos	5: 2	The virgin of I has fallen;
Amos	5: 3	ten left to the house of I.
Amos	6: 1	To whom the house of I
Amos	7: 9	And the sanctuaries of I
Amos	7:10	sent to Jeroboam king of I,
Amos	7:11	And I shall surely be led
Amos	7:15	prophesy to My people I.
Amos	7:16	'Do not prophesy against I,
Amos	7:17	And I shall surely be led
Amos	8: 2	has come upon My people I;
Amos	9:14	the captives of My people I;
Mic	2:12	gather the remnant of I;
Mic	3: 8	his transgression And to I
Mic	5: 2	Me The One to be Ruler in I,
Nah	2: 2	Like the excellence of I,
Zeph	3:15	your enemy. The King of I,
Matt	2: 6	shepherd My people I.
Matt	8:10	not even in I!
Matt	10: 6	lost sheep of the house of I.
Matt	10:23	gone through the cities of I
Matt	15:24	lost sheep of the house of I.
Matt	19:28	the twelve tribes of I.
Matt	27:42	save. If He is the King of I,
Mark	12:29	is: 'Hear, O I,
Mark	15:32	the Christ, the King of I,
Luke	1:54	He has helped His servant I,
Luke	1:68	is the Lord God of I,
Luke	1:80	of his manifestation to I.
Luke	2:25	for the Consolation of I,
Luke	2:32	the glory of Your people I.
Luke	2:34	fall and rising of many in I,
Luke	24:21	He who was going to redeem I.
John	1:31	He should be revealed to I,
John	1:49	God! You are the King of I!
John	3:10	"Are you the teacher of I,
John	12:13	LORD!' The King of I!"
Acts	1: 6	restore the kingdom to I?
Acts	2:22	"Men of I, hear these
Acts	3:12	to the people: "Men of I,
Acts	4:27	Gentiles and the people of I,
Acts	5:31	to give repentance to I and
Acts	13:16	his hand said, "Men of I,
Acts	13:23	God raised up for I a
Rom	9: 6	For they are not all I who
Rom	9:27	of the children of I
Rom	10: 1	and prayer to God for I is
Rom	10:21	But to I he says: "All
Rom	11: 7	I has not obtained what it
Rom	11:25	in part has happened to I
Rom	11:26	And so all I will be saved,
1Co	10:18	Observe I after the flesh:
Gal	6:16	and upon the I of God.
Eph	2:12	from the commonwealth of I
Phil	3: 5	day, of the stock of I,
Heb	8: 8	with the house of I
Rev	21:12	tribes of the children of I:

ISRAEL'S (see ISRAEL)

| Josh | 22:11 | on the children of I side." |
| 1Ch | 17:24 | is I God.' And let the |

ISRAELITE (see ISRAEL, ISRAELITES)

| John | 1:47 | an I indeed, in whom is no |
| Rom | 11: 1 | not! For I also am an I, |

ISRAELITES (see ISRAELITE)

| Rom | 9: 4 | who are I, to whom pertain |
| 2Co | 11:22 | So am I. Are they I? |

ISSACHAR
Gen	35:23	and Simeon, Levi, Judah, I,
Gen	49:14	I is a strong donkey, Lying
Judg	5:15	And the princes of I were
Judg	10: 1	the son of Dodo, a man of I;
Rev	7: 7	of the tribe of I twelve

ISSUE (see ISSUED, ISSUES, POSTERITY)
Ezra	6:12	I Darius i a decree; let it
Is	22:24	house, the offspring and the i

ISSUED (see ISSUE)
Ezra	5:13	King Cyrus i a decree to
Ezra	6: 1	Then King Darius i a decree,
Esth	9:14	the decree was i in Shushan,
Job	38: 8	When it burst forth and i
Dan	4: 6	Therefore I i a decree to

ISSUES† (see ISSUE)
Prov	4:23	out of it spring the i of

ITALIAN† (see ITALY)
Acts	10: 1	of what was called the I

ITALY (see ITALIAN)
Acts	18: 2	who had recently come from I
Acts	27: 1	that we should sail to I,
Heb	13:24	Those from I greet you.

ITCHING†
2Ti	4: 3	because they have i ears,

ITHAMAR
Ex	6:23	Nadab, Abihu, Eleazar, and I.
Ex	28: 1	Nadab, Abihu, Eleazar, and I.
Lev	10:16	was angry with Eleazar and I,

ITTAI
2Sa	15:19	Then the king said to I the
2Sa	15:22	So David said to I,

ITUREA†
Luke	3: 1	Philip tetrarch of I and

IVORY
1Ki	10:18	made a great throne of i,
1Ki	22:39	the i house which he built
Ps	45: 8	Out of the i palaces, by
Song	7: 4	Your neck is like an i
Ezek	27:15	They brought you i tusks and
Amos	3:15	The houses of i shall
Amos	6: 4	Who lie on beds of i,
Rev	18:12	every kind of object of i,

J

JABAL†
Gen	4:20	And Adah bore J.

JABBOK
Gen	32:22	crossed over the ford of J.
Num	21:24	land from the Arnon to the J,
Deut	2:37	along the River J,

JABESH (see JABESH GILEAD)
1Sa	11: 1	up and encamped against J
1Sa	31:12	and they came to J and

JABESH GILEAD (see GILEAD, JABESH)
Judg	21:10	strike the inhabitants of J
Judg	21:14	saved alive of the women of J
1Sa	11: 1	came up and encamped against J
1Sa	31:11	when the inhabitants of J
2Sa	2: 4	The men of J were the ones

JABIN (see JABIN'S)
Josh	11: 1	when J king of Hazor heard
Judg	4: 2	sold them into the hand of J
Judg	4:24	until they had destroyed J
Ps	83: 9	As with J at the Brook

JABIN'S† (see JABIN)
Judg	4: 7	the commander of J army,

JACHIN
1Ki	7:21	right and called its name J,
2Ch	3:17	the one on the right hand J,

JACINTH
Ex	39:12	the third row, a j,
Rev	21:20	chrysoprase, the eleventh j,

JACKALS
Job	30:29	I am a brother of j,
Is	34:13	shall be a habitation of j,
Jer	10:22	Judah desolate, a den of j.
Jer	51:37	A dwelling place for j,

JACOB (see ISRAEL, JACOB'S, JAMES)
Gen	25:27	but J was a mild man,
Gen	25:28	game, but Rebekah loved J.
Gen	25:29	Now J cooked a stew; and
Gen	25:33	and sold his birthright to J.
Gen	25:34	And J gave Esau bread and
Gen	27:30	and J had scarcely gone out
Gen	27:36	"Is he not rightly named J?
Gen	27:41	So Esau hated J because of
Gen	27:41	I will kill my brother J.
Gen	28:16	Then J awoke from his sleep
Gen	28:20	Then J made a vow, saying,
Gen	29:11	Then J kissed Rachel, and
Gen	29:15	Then Laban said to J,
Gen	29:18	Now J loved Rachel; so he
Gen	29:20	So J served seven years for
Gen	30:40	Then J separated the lambs,
Gen	30:41	that J placed the rods
Gen	31: 1	J has taken away all that was
Gen	31:25	So Laban overtook J.
Gen	31:45	So J took a stone and set it
Gen	31:47	but J called it Galeed.
Gen	31:53	And J swore by the Fear of
Gen	32: 7	So J was greatly afraid and
Gen	32:24	Then J was left alone; and a
Gen	32:28	shall no longer be called J,
Gen	34: 3	to Dinah the daughter of J,
Gen	35: 4	and J hid them under the
Gen	35:10	name shall not be called J
Gen	35:14	So J set up a pillar in the
Gen	35:20	And J set a pillar on her
Gen	35:22	Now the sons of J were
Gen	37: 2	This is the history of J.
Gen	37:34	Then J tore his clothes, put
Gen	46: 5	Then J arose from Beersheba;
Gen	46:26	the persons who went with J
Gen	47: 7	and J blessed Pharaoh.
Gen	47: 8	Pharaoh said to J,
Gen	49: 2	and hear, you sons of J,
Gen	50:24	Abraham, to Isaac, and to J.
Ex	3: 6	of Isaac, and the God of J.
Ex	3:16	Abraham, of Isaac, and of J,
Lev	26:42	remember My covenant with J,
Num	23: 7	curse J for me, And come,
Num	24: 5	O J! Your dwellings, O
Num	24:17	A Star shall come out of J;
Deut	33: 4	of the congregation of J.
Deut	33:28	The fountain of J alone,
Josh	24: 4	To Isaac I gave J and Esau.
2Sa	23: 1	anointed of the God of J,
1Ki	18:31	the tribes of the sons of J,
Ps	14: 7	Let J rejoice and Israel
Ps	20: 1	the name of the God of J
Ps	24: 6	This is J, the generation
Ps	44: 4	Command victories for J.
Ps	46: 7	The God of J is our
Ps	46:11	The God of J is our
Ps	47: 4	The excellence of J whom He
Ps	75: 9	sing praises to the God of J.
Ps	76: 6	At Your rebuke, O God of J,

Ps 77:15 The sons of **J** and Joseph.
Ps 78: 5 established a testimony in **J**,
Ps 78:21 a fire was kindled against **J**,
Ps 78:71 To shepherd **J** His people,
Ps 81: 1 joyful shout to the God of **J**.
Ps 84: 8 O God of **J**! Selah
Ps 85: 1 back the captivity of **J**.
Ps 94: 7 Nor does the God of **J**
Ps 105:10 And confirmed it to **J** for a
Ps 105:23 And **J** dwelt in the land of
Ps 114: 7 the presence of the God of **J**,
Ps 132: 2 vowed to the Mighty One of **J**:
Ps 135: 4 For the LORD has chosen **J**
Ps 147:19 He declares His word to **J**,
Is 2: 3 the house of the God of **J**;
Is 10:21 return, the remnant of **J**,
Is 17: 4 pass That the glory of **J**
Is 29:23 hallow the Holy One of **J**,
Is 41: 8 **J** whom I have chosen, The
Is 41:14 "Fear not, you worm **J**,
Is 41:21 says the King of **J**.
Is 43: 1 LORD, who created you, O **J**,
Is 44: 1 O **J** My servant, And Israel
Is 45:19 did not say to the seed of **J**,
Is 46: 3 to Me, O house of **J**,
Is 49: 5 To bring **J** back to Him, So
Is 49:26 the Mighty One of **J**.
Is 58: 1 And the house of **J** their
Is 58:14 you with the heritage of **J**
Jer 10:16 The Portion of **J** is not
Jer 10:25 For they have eaten up **J**,
Jer 31: 7 "Sing with gladness for **J**,
Jer 31:11 the LORD has redeemed **J**,
Lam 2: 3 He has blazed against **J**
Ezek 39:25 bring back the captives of **J**,
Hos 12: 2 And will punish **J** according
Amos 6: 8 "I abhor the pride of **J**,
Amos 7: 2 that **J** may stand, For he
Amos 8: 7 has sworn by the pride of **J**:
Obad 10 against your brother **J**,
Mic 1: 5 for the transgression of **J**
Mic 3: 1 "Hear now, O heads of **J**,
Mic 3: 8 To declare to **J** his
Mal 1: 2 Yet **J** I have loved;
Mal 3: 6 not consumed, O sons of **J**.
Matt 8:11 and **J** in the kingdom of
Matt 22:32 and the God of **J**'?
Luke 1:33 reign over the house of **J**
Luke 13:28 see Abraham and Isaac and **J**
Luke 20:37 and the God of **J**.
John 4:12 greater than our father **J**,
Acts 3:13 God of Abraham, Isaac, and **J**,
Acts 7: 8 and **J** begot the twelve
Rom 9:13 **J** I have loved, but Esau
Rom 11:26 away ungodliness from **J**;
Heb 11: 9 in tents with Isaac and **J**,
Heb 11:20 By faith Isaac blessed **J** and

JACOB'S (*see* JACOB)
Gen 27:22 The voice is **J** voice, but
Gen 31:33 And Laban went into **J** tent,
Gen 32:25 and the socket of **J** hip was
Gen 45:26 And **J** heart stood still,
Gen 46: 8 Reuben was **J** firstborn.
Gen 47:28 So the length of **J** life was
Jer 30: 7 And it is the time of **J**
Mal 1: 2 Was not Esau **J** brother?"
John 4: 6 Now **J** well was there. Jesus

JAEL
Judg 4:17 on foot to the tent of **J**,
Judg 5:24 blessed among women is **J**,

JAILER†
Acts 16:23 commanding the **j** to keep

JAIR
Num 32:41 Also **J** the son of Manasseh
Josh 13:30 and all the towns of **J** which
Judg 10: 3 After him arose **J**,

JAIRUS
Mark 5:22 **J** by name. And when he saw

JAMBRES†
2Ti 3: 8 Now as Jannes and **J** resisted

JAMES (*see* JACOB)
Matt 4:21 **J** the son of Zebedee, and
Matt 10: 3 **J** the son of Alphaeus, and
Matt 13:55 Mary? And His brothers **J**,
Matt 17: 1 six days Jesus took Peter, **J**,
Matt 27:56 Mary the mother of **J** and
Mark 1:29 with **J** and John.
Mark 14:33 And He took Peter, **J**,
1Co 15: 7 After that He was seen by **J**,
Gal 1:19 the other apostles except **J**,
Jude 1 Christ, and brother of **J**,

JANNES†
2Ti 3: 8 Now as **J** and Jambres resisted

JAPHETH
Gen 7:13 sons, Shem, Ham, and **J**,
Gen 9:27 May God enlarge **J**,

JAR
1Ki 14: 3 and a **j** of honey, and go to
1Ki 17:16 nor did the **j** of oil run

JARED
Gen 5:20 So all the days of **J** were

JARMUTH (*see* RAMOTH)
Josh 10: 5 of Hebron, the king of **J**,
Josh 21:29 **J** with its common-land, and

JASHER†
Josh 10:13 not written in the Book of **J**?
2Sa 1:18 is written in the Book of **J**:

JASON
Acts 17: 5 and attacked the house of **J**,
Rom 16:21 fellow worker, and Lucius, **J**,

JASPER
Ex 28:20 a beryl, an onyx, and a **j**.
Rev 4: 3 who sat there was like a **j**
Rev 21:18 of its wall was of **j**;

JAVAN
Gen 10: 2 were Gomer, Magog, Madai, **J**,
Ezek 27:19 Dan and **J** paid for your

JAVELIN
Num 25: 7 congregation and took a **j**
1Sa 17: 6 on his legs and a bronze **j**

JAW† (*see* JAWBONE, JAWS)
Job 41: 2 Or pierce his **j** with a

JAWBONE (*see* JAW)
Judg 15:15 He found a fresh **j** of a

JAWS (*see* JAW)
Ps 22:15 My tongue clings to My **j**;
Ezek 29: 4 I will put hooks in your **j**,

JEALOUS (*see* JEALOUSY)
Ex 20: 5 am a **j** God, visiting the
Ex 34:14 the LORD, whose name is **J**,
Num 5:14 upon him and he becomes **j**
Deut 5: 9 am a **j** God, visiting the
Ezek 39:25 and I will be **j** for My holy
2Co 11: 2 For I am **j** for you with godly

JEALOUSIES† (*see* JEALOUSY)
2Co 12:20 there be contentions, **j**,
Gal 5:20 hatred, contentions, **j**,

JEALOUSY (*see* JEALOUS, JEALOUSIES)
Num   5:14 if the spirit of **j** comes upon
Num   5:15 it is a grain offering of **j**,
Deut 29:20 anger of the LORD and His **j**
Deut 32:16 They provoked Him to **j** with
Ps   78:58 And moved Him to **j** with
Ps   79: 5 Will Your **j** burn like fire?
Prov   6:34 For **j** is a husband's fury;
Song   8: 6 as cruel as the grave;
Ezek   8: 3 the seat of the image of **j**
Ezek 23:25 I will set My **j** against you,
Zeph   1:18 By the fire of His **j**,
Rom 10:19 will provoke you to **j**
1Co 10:22 do we provoke the Lord to **j**?
2Co 11: 2 jealous for you with godly **j**.

JEBUS (*see* JEBUSITE, JERUSALEM)
Josh 18:28 **J** (which is Jerusalem),
1Ch 11: 5 Then the inhabitants of **J**

JEBUSITE (*see* JEBUS, JEBUSITES)
Gen 10:16 the **J**, the Amorite
Ex   33: 2 and the Hivite and the **J**.
Josh 11: 3 the **J** in the mountains, and
Josh 15: 8 the southern slope of the **J**
2Sa 24:16 floor of Araunah the **J**.
1Ch 21:15 floor of Ornan the **J**.

JEBUSITES (*see* JEBUSITE)
Gen 15:21 the Girgashites, and the **J**.
Judg   1:21 did not drive out the **J** who
2Sa   5: 8 shaft and defeats the **J**

JECONIAH (*see* JEHOIACHIN)
1Ch   3:16 sons of Jehoiakim were **J**
Esth   2: 6 who had been captured with **J**
Matt   1:11 Josiah begot **J** and his

JEDIDIAH† (*see* SOLOMON)
2Sa 12:25 So he called his name **J**,

JEDUTHUN
1Ch 25: 1 of Asaph, of Heman, and of **J**,
1Ch 25: 3 Of Jeduthun, the sons of **J**:
2Ch 35:15 and **J** the king's seer. Also

JEGAR SAHADUTHA†
Gen 31:47 Laban called it **J**, but Jacob

JEHOAHAZ (*see* AHAZIAH, SHALLUM)
2Ki 13: 1 **J** the son of Jehu became
2Ki 13: 4 So **J** pleaded with the LORD,
2Ki 13: 7 For He left of the army of **J**
2Ki 13: 8 the rest of the acts of **J**,
2Ki 13: 9 So **J** rested with his fathers,
2Ki 14: 1 year of Joash the son of **J**,
2Ki 23:30 people of the land took **J**
2Ki 23:34 And Pharaoh took **J** and went
2Ch 36: 4 And Necho took **J** his brother

JEHOASH (*see* JOASH)
2Ki 11:21 **J** was seven years old when
2Ki 12: 1 **J** became king, and he
2Ki 12: 2 **J** did what was right in the
2Ki 12: 7 So King **J** called Jehoiada the
2Ki 12:18 And **J** king of Judah took all
2Ki 13:10 **J** the son of Jehoahaz became
2Ki 14: 9 And **J** king of Israel sent to
2Ki 14:15 the rest of the acts of **J**
2Ki 14:16 So **J** rested with his fathers,

JEHOIACHIN (*see* JECONIAH, JEHOIACHIN'S)
2Ki 24: 8 **J** was eighteen years old
2Ki 24:15 And he carried **J** captive to
2Ki 25:27 released **J** king of Judah
2Ch 36: 9 **J** was eight years old when

JEHOIACHIN'S† (*see* JEHOIACHIN)
2Ki 24:17 **J** uncle, king in his place,
Ezek 1: 2 in the fifth year of King **J**

JEHOIADA
2Sa 20:23 Benaiah the son of **J** was
2Ki 11: 9 did according to all that **J**
2Ki 11:17 Then **J** made a covenant
2Ki 12: 2 all the days in which **J** the
2Ki 12: 7 So King Jehoash called **J** the
2Ch 23:11 Then **J** and his sons anointed
2Ch 24: 6 So the king called **J**

JEHOIAKIM (*see* ELIAKIM, JEHOIAKIM'S)
2Ki 23:34 and changed his name to **J**.
2Ki 24: 1 **J** became his vassal for
2Ki 24: 5 the rest of the acts of **J**,
2Ki 24: 6 So **J** rested with his fathers.
Jer 24: 1 Jeconiah the son of **J**,
Jer 26:23 Egypt and brought him to **J**
Jer 36:32 words of the book which **J**
Dan   1: 1 year of the reign of **J** king

JEHOIAKIM'S† (*see* JEHOIAKIM)
2Ch 36:10 **J** brother, king over Judah

JEHONADAB (*see* JONADAB)
2Ki 10:15 he met **J** the son of Rechab,

JEHORAM (*see* JORAM)
1Ki 22:50 Then **J** his son reigned in
2Ki   3: 1 Now **J** the son of Ahab became
2Ki   3: 6 So King **J** went out of
2Ki   8:16 **J** the son of Jehoshaphat
2Ki   8:25 Israel, Ahaziah the son of **J**,
2Ki   9:24 full strength and shot **J**
2Ch 22: 6 And Azariah the son of **J**,

JEHOSHAPHAT
2Sa   8:16 **J** the son of Ahilud was
1Ki 15:24 Then **J** his son reigned in
1Ki 22: 2 that **J** the king of Judah
1Ki 22:41 **J** the son of Asa had become
1Ki 22:45 the rest of the acts of **J**,
1Ki 22:50 And **J** rested with his
2Ki   9: 2 there for Jehu the son of **J**,
2Ch 18: 1 **J** had riches and honor in
2Ch 18: 7 the king of Israel said to **J**,
2Ch 19: 4 So **J** dwelt at Jerusalem; and
2Ch 20: 1 came to battle against **J**.
2Ch 20: 3 And **J** feared, and set himself
2Ch 20:18 And **J** bowed his head with
2Ch 20:30 Then the realm of **J** was
2Ch 20:34 the rest of the acts of **J**,
2Ch 20:37 prophesied against **J**,
2Ch 21:12 not walked in the ways of **J**
Joel   3: 2 them down to the Valley of **J**;
Matt   1: 8 **J** begot Joram, and Joram

JEHOZADAK (*see* JOZADAK)
Hag   1: 1 and to Joshua the son of **J**,
Zech   6:11 head of Joshua the son of **J**,

JEHU
1Ki 16: 1 word of the LORD came to **J**
1Ki 16: 7 LORD came by the prophet **J**
1Ki 19:17 **J** will kill; and whoever
2Ki   9:14 So **J** the son of Jehoshaphat,
2Ki   9:16 So **J** rode in a chariot and
2Ki   9:20 is like the driving of **J**
2Ki   9:22 happened, when Joram saw **J**,
2Ki   9:22 he said, "Is it peace, **J**?
2Ki   9:27 So **J** pursued him, and said,
2Ki   9:30 Now when **J** had come to
2Ki 10: 1 And **J** wrote and sent letters
2Ki 10:11 So **J** killed all who remained
2Ki 10:19 But **J** acted deceptively,
2Ki 10:28 Thus **J** destroyed Baal from
2Ki 10:31 But **J** took no heed to walk in
2Ki 10:34 the rest of the acts of **J**,
2Ki 10:35 So **J** rested with his fathers,
2Ki 13: 1 Jehoahaz the son of **J** became

2Ch 22: 8 when **J** was executing
Hos 1: 4 of Jezreel on the house of **J**,

JEHUDI
Jer 36:21 And **J** read it in the hearing
Jer 36:23 when **J** had read three or

JEMIMAH†
Job 42:14 the name of the first **J**,

JEOPARDY†
2Sa 23:17 of the men who went in **j**
1Ch 11:19 put their lives in **j**?
Luke 8:23 with water, and were in **j**.
1Co 15:30 And why do we stand in **j**

JEPHTHAH
Judg 11: 1 Now **J** the Gileadite was a
Judg 11: 3 Then **J** fled from his brothers
Judg 11: 3 men banded together with **J**
Judg 11: 8 elders of Gilead said to **J**,
Judg 11:12 Now **J** sent messengers to the
Judg 11:29 of the LORD came upon **J**,
Judg 11:30 And **J** made a vow to the
Judg 11:34 When **J** came to his house at
Judg 11:40 to lament the daughter of **J**
Judg 12: 7 And **J** judged Israel six
1Sa 12:11 sent Jerubbaal, Bedan, **J**,
Heb 11:32 and Barak and Samson and **J**,

JEPHUNNEH
Num 14:30 for Caleb the son of **J** and
Josh 14:13 to Caleb the son of **J** as an
Josh 21:12 gave to Caleb the son of **J**

JERAHMEEL
Jer 36:26 And the king commanded **J** the

JEREMIAH (*see* JEREMIAH'S)
2Ch 35:25 **J** also lamented for Josiah.
2Ch 36:12 not humble himself before **J**
2Ch 36:22 the LORD by the mouth of **J**
Ezra 1: 1 the LORD by the mouth of **J**
Jer 1: 1 The words of **J** the son of
Jer 1:11 came to me, saying, "**J**,
Jer 7: 1 The word that came to **J** from
Jer 11: 1 The word that came to **J** from
Jer 18:18 us devise plans against **J**;
Jer 20: 2 Then Pashhur struck **J** the
Jer 20: 3 day that Pashhur brought **J**
Jer 26: 9 were gathered against **J** in
Jer 29:30 word of the LORD came to **J**,
Jer 33: 1 word of the LORD came to **J**
Jer 36: 4 Then **J** called Baruch the son
Jer 36: 5 And **J** commanded Baruch,
Jer 36:19 "Go and hide, you and **J**;
Jer 36:27 at the instruction of **J**,
Jer 36:27 word of the LORD came to **J**,
Jer 36:32 Then **J** took another scroll
Jer 36:32 it at the instruction of **J**
Jer 37:12 that **J** went out of Jerusalem
Jer 37:13 and he seized **J** the prophet,
Jer 37:15 princes were angry with **J**,
Jer 37:16 When **J** entered the dungeon
Jer 37:21 Thus **J** remained in the court
Jer 38: 6 and they let **J** down with
Jer 38: 6 So **J** sank in the mire.
Jer 38:10 and lift **J** the prophet out
Jer 38:11 ropes into the dungeon to **J**.
Jer 38:12 the Ethiopian said to **J**,
Jer 38:15 **J** said to Zedekiah, "If I
Jer 38:16 the king swore secretly to **J**,
Jer 38:19 Zedekiah the king said to **J**,
Jer 39:14 they sent someone to take **J**
Jer 40: 2 captain of the guard took **J**
Jer 40: 6 Then **J** went to Gedaliah the
Jer 43: 8 word of the LORD came to **J**
Jer 45: 1 book at the instruction of **J**,

Jer 51:60 So **J** wrote in a book all the
Jer 51:64 Thus far are the words of **J**.
Dan 9: 2 word of the LORD through **J**
Matt 2:17 what was spoken by **J** the
Matt 16:14 and others **J** or one of the
Matt 27: 9 what was spoken by **J** the

JEREMIAH'S† (*see* JEREMIAH)
Jer 28:10 the yoke off the prophet **J**

JERICHO
Num 22: 1 the Jordan across from **J**.
Num 34:15 across from **J** eastward,
Deut 32:49 land of Moab, across from **J**;
Deut 34: 3 the plain of the Valley of **J**,
Josh 2: 1 view the land, especially **J**.
Josh 2: 3 So the king of **J** sent to
Josh 4:13 battle, to the plains of **J**.
Josh 6: 1 Now **J** was securely shut up
Josh 6: 2 See! I have given **J** into your
Josh 7: 2 Now Joshua sent men from **J**
2Sa 10: 5 Wait at **J** until your beards
1Ki 16:34 days Hiel of Bethel built **J**.
2Ki 2: 5 the prophets who were at **J**
Matt 20:29 Now as they went out of **J**,
Luke 10:30 down from Jerusalem to **J**,
Luke 18:35 as He was coming near **J**,
Luke 19: 1 entered and passed through **J**.
Heb 11:30 By faith the walls of **J** fell

JEROBOAM
1Ki 11:26 **J** the son of Nebat, an
1Ki 11:28 The man **J** was a mighty man
1Ki 12: 2 when **J** the son of Nebat
1Ki 12:25 Then **J** built Shechem in the
1Ki 13: 1 and **J** stood by the altar to
1Ki 13: 4 it came to pass when King **J**
1Ki 13:34 the sin of the house of **J**,
1Ki 14:16 up because of the sins of **J**,
1Ki 14:19 the rest of the acts of **J**,
1Ki 15:25 Now Nadab the son of **J**
1Ki 16:26 walked in all the ways of **J**
1Ki 21:22 house like the house of **J**
2Ki 14:28 the rest of the acts of **J**,
2Ki 14:29 So **J** rested with his fathers,
2Ch 13: 2 was war between Abijah and **J**.
2Ch 13:15 happened that God struck **J**
2Ch 13:20 So **J** did not recover strength
Hos 1: 1 and in the days of **J** the son
Amos 1: 1 and in the days of **J** the son
Amos 7: 9 sword against the house of **J**
Amos 7:10 priest of Bethel sent to **J**
Amos 7:11 **J** shall die by the sword,

JERUBBAAL (*see* GIDEON, JERUBBESHETH)
Judg 7: 1 Then **J** (that is, Gideon) and
Judg 8:29 Then **J** the son of Joash went
Judg 9: 1 Then Abimelech the son of **J**
Judg 9: 2 all seventy of the sons of **J**
Judg 9: 5 the seventy sons of **J**,
Judg 9:57 curse of Jotham the son of **J**.
1Sa 12:11 "And the LORD sent **J**,

JERUBBESHETH† (*see* JERUBBAAL)
2Sa 11:21 Abimelech the son of **J**?

JERUSALEM (*see* ARIEL, JEBUS, SALEM)
Josh 10: 1 when Adoni-Zedek king of **J**
Josh 15: 8 Jebusite city (which is **J**)
Josh 18:28 Eleph, Jebus (which is **J**),
2Sa 9:13 So Mephibosheth dwelt in **J**,
2Sa 11: 1 But David remained at **J**.
2Sa 14:23 and brought Absalom to **J**.
2Sa 15:29 the ark of God back to **J**.
2Sa 20: 3 David came to his house at **J**.
2Sa 24:16 out His hand over **J** to
1Ki 2:36 yourself a house in **J**
1Ki 8: 1 Israel, to King Solomon in **J**,

1Ki	9:15	the Millo, the wall of J,
1Ki	10:27	silver as common in J as
1Ki	11: 7	the hill that is east of J,
1Ki	11:36	have a lamp before Me in J,
1Ki	12:27	the house of the LORD at J,
1Ki	14:25	of Egypt came up against J.
2Ki	12:17	set his face to go up to J.
2Ki	14:13	and broke down the wall of J
2Ki	16: 5	came up to J to make war;
2Ki	18:17	with a great army against J,
2Ki	18:22	and said to Judah and J,
2Ki	18:35	the LORD should deliver J
2Ki	21: 4	In J I will put My name."
2Ki	21:12	such calamity upon J and
2Ki	21:13	I will wipe J as one wipes
2Ki	23: 4	he burned them outside J in
2Ki	23: 6	the Brook Kidron outside J,
2Ki	23: 9	the altar of the LORD in J,
2Ki	23:27	will cast off this city J
2Ki	24:10	of Babylon came up against J.
2Ki	24:15	into captivity from J to
1Ch	21:15	And God sent an angel to J to
1Ch	21:16	sword stretched out over J.
2Ch	1:15	and gold as common in J as
2Ch	2:16	you will carry it up to J.
2Ch	3: 1	the house of the LORD at J
2Ch	9: 1	she came to J to test
2Ch	11: 5	So Rehoboam dwelt in J,
2Ch	12: 2	of Egypt came up against J,
2Ch	20: 5	the assembly of Judah and J,
2Ch	20:15	and you inhabitants of J,
2Ch	20:27	every man of Judah and J,
2Ch	21:11	caused the inhabitants of J
2Ch	24:18	wrath came upon Judah and J
2Ch	25:23	and broke down the wall of J
2Ch	25:27	conspiracy against him in J,
2Ch	26: 9	Uzziah built towers in J at
2Ch	28:24	altars in every corner of J.
2Ch	28:27	buried him in the city, in J;
2Ch	29: 8	LORD fell upon Judah and J,
2Ch	30: 3	gathered together at J
2Ch	30: 5	the LORD God of Israel at J,
2Ch	30:26	been nothing like this in J
2Ch	32:10	you remain under siege in J?
2Ch	32:18	in Hebrew to the people of J
2Ch	33: 4	In J shall My name be
2Ch	34: 3	began to purge Judah and J
2Ch	34: 5	and cleansed Judah and J.
2Ch	35: 1	a Passover to the LORD in J,
2Ch	35:18	and the inhabitants of J.
2Ch	35:24	And all Judah and J mourned
2Ch	36:19	broke down the wall of J,
2Ch	36:23	me to build Him a house at J
Ezra	1: 2	me to build Him a house at J
Ezra	1: 3	and let him go up to J which
Ezra	1: 4	house of God which is in J
Ezra	1:11	brought from Babylon to J.
Ezra	3: 8	out of the captivity to J,
Ezra	4: 6	inhabitants of Judah and J.
Ezra	4: 8	wrote a letter against J to
Ezra	4:20	been mighty kings over J,
Ezra	4:23	they went up in haste to J
Ezra	5:15	temple site that is in J,
Ezra	5:17	build this house of God at J,
Ezra	6: 9	of the priests who are in J—
Ezra	6:18	over the service of God in J,
Ezra	7: 8	And Ezra came to J in the
Ezra	9: 9	us a wall in Judah and J.
Neh	1: 3	The wall of J is also
Neh	2:12	put in my heart to do at J;
Neh	2:13	and viewed the walls of J
Neh	2:17	how J lies waste, and its
Neh	2:17	let us build the wall of J,
Neh	11: 1	one out of ten to dwell in J,
Neh	12:27	dedication of the wall of J

Neh	12:43	so that the joy of J was
Ps	51:18	Zion; Build the walls of J.
Ps	79: 1	They have laid J in heaps.
Ps	79: 3	shed like water all around J,
Ps	102:21	Zion, And His praise in J,
Ps	116:19	In the midst of you, O J.
Ps	122: 2	Within your gates, O J!
Ps	122: 3	J is built As a city that
Ps	122: 6	Pray for the peace of J:
Ps	125: 2	As the mountains surround J,
Ps	128: 5	may you see the good of J
Ps	135:21	Who dwells in J! Praise
Ps	137: 5	If I forget you, O J,
Ps	137: 6	If I do not exalt J Above
Ps	147: 2	The LORD builds up J;
Ps	147:12	O J! Praise your God, O
Eccl	1: 1	the son of David, king in J.
Eccl	1:12	was king over Israel in J.
Eccl	1:16	all who were before me in J.
Song	5: 8	charge you, O daughters of J,
Song	6: 4	as Tirzah, Lovely as J,
Is	1: 1	saw concerning Judah and J
Is	3: 8	For J stumbled, And Judah
Is	4: 4	and purged the blood of J
Is	10:12	work on Mount Zion and on J,
Is	10:32	of Zion, The hill of J.
Is	27:13	LORD in the holy mount at J.
Is	40: 2	"Speak comfort to J,
Is	44:26	messengers; Who says to J,
Is	51:17	awake! Stand up, O J,
Is	52: 1	beautiful garments, O J,
Is	52: 9	You waste places of J! For
Is	52: 9	people, He has redeemed J.
Is	62: 6	watchmen on your walls, O J;
Is	62: 7	And till He makes J a
Is	64:10	J a desolation.
Is	65:18	I create J as a rejoicing,
Jer	1: 3	until the carrying away of J
Jer	1:15	entrance of the gates of J,
Jer	2: 2	and cry in the hearing of J,
Jer	4: 4	Judah and inhabitants of J,
Jer	4:16	Yes, proclaim against J,
Jer	5: 1	fro through the streets of J;
Jer	6: 1	to flee from the midst of J!
Jer	6: 6	And build a mound against J.
Jer	7:34	and from the streets of J
Jer	8: 1	of the inhabitants of J,
Jer	9:11	I will make J a heap of
Jer	11: 6	and in the streets of J,
Jer	13: 9	and the great pride of J.
Jer	14:16	cast out in the streets of J
Jer	15: 5	will have pity on you, O J?
Jer	17:27	entering the gates of J on
Jer	17:27	devour the palaces of J.
Jer	19: 7	the counsel of Judah and J
Jer	23:14	thing in the prophets of J:
Jer	24: 8	the residue of J who remain
Jer	27:20	the nobles of Judah and J—
Jer	29: 1	carried away captive from J
Jer	32: 2	of Babylon's army besieged J,
Jer	33:16	And J will dwell safely.
Jer	35:17	on all the inhabitants of J
Jer	37:11	left the siege of J for
Jer	38:28	prison until the day that J
Jer	39: 8	broke down the walls of J
Jer	40: 1	carried away captive from J
Jer	44: 6	and in the streets of J;
Jer	44: 9	and in the streets of J?
Jer	44:13	Egypt, as I have punished J,
Jer	52:29	carried away captive from J
Lam	1: 8	J has sinned gravely,
Lam	1:17	J has become an unclean
Lam	2:10	The virgins of J Bow their
Lam	2:13	liken you, O daughter of J?
Lam	4:12	Could enter the gates of J—

Ezek 4: 1 and portray on it a city, J.
Ezek 4: 7 face toward the siege of J;
Ezek 4:16 off the supply of bread in J;
Ezek 8: 3 me in visions of God to J,
Ezek 9: 8 pouring out Your fury on J?
Ezek 12:10 concerns the prince in J
Ezek 13:16 who prophesy concerning J,
Ezek 14:21 four severe judgments on J—
Ezek 17:12 king of Babylon went to J
Ezek 21: 2 man, set your face toward J,
Ezek 23: 4 and J is Oholibah.
Ezek 24: 2 started his siege against J
Ezek 33:21 one who had escaped from J
Dan 1: 1 king of Babylon came to J
Dan 5: 2 temple which had been in J,
Dan 6:10 his windows open toward J,
Dan 9: 2 in the desolations of J.
Dan 9:25 To restore and build J
Joel 3:16 And utter His voice from J;
Joel 3:17 Then J shall be holy, And
Amos 1: 2 And utters His voice from J;
Obad 20 The captives of J who are
Mic 1: 1 saw concerning Samaria and J.
Mic 4: 8 kingdom of the daughter of J.
Zeph 1:12 time That I will search J
Zech 1:12 You not have mercy on J and
Zech 1:14 I am zealous for J And for
Zech 2: 2 said to me, "To measure J,
Zech 7: 7 the former prophets when J
Zech 8: 3 J shall be called the City
Zech 9: 9 O daughter of J! Behold,
Zech 12: 2 I will make J a cup of
Zech 12:11 be a great mourning in J,
Zech 14: 4 Which faces J on the east.
Zech 14: 8 waters shall flow from J,
Zech 14:21 every pot in J and Judah
Mal 2:11 committed in Israel and in J,
Matt 2: 1 men from the East came to J,
Matt 2: 3 and all J with him.
Matt 4:25 and from Decapolis, J,
Matt 5:35 is His footstool; nor by J,
Matt 16:21 that He must go to J,
Matt 20:17 Now Jesus, going up to J,
Matt 23:37 "O Jerusalem, J,
Mark 3: 8 and J and Idumea and beyond
Luke 2:25 there was a man in J whose
Luke 2:38 looked for redemption in J.
Luke 2:41 His parents went to J every
Luke 2:43 Jesus lingered behind in J.
Luke 2:45 find Him, they returned to J,
Luke 4: 9 Then he brought Him to J,
Luke 9:31 was about to accomplish at J.
Luke 9:51 set His face to go to J,
Luke 10:30 man went down from J to
Luke 13:33 should perish outside of J.
Luke 21:20 But when you see J
Luke 21:24 And J will be trampled by
Luke 23:28 them, said, "Daughters of J,
Luke 24:47 all nations, beginning at J.
Luke 24:49 but tarry in the city of J
Luke 24:52 and returned to J with great
John 1:19 priests and Levites from J
John 2:23 Now when He was in J at the
John 4:20 and you Jews say that in J
John 4:21 on this mountain, nor in J,
John 5: 1 Jews, and Jesus went up to J.
John 10:22 the Feast of Dedication in J,
John 11:18 Now Bethany was near J,
Acts 1: 4 them not to depart from J,
Acts 1: 8 be witnesses to Me in J,
Acts 1:12 Olivet, which is near J,
Acts 2: 5 there were dwelling in J
Acts 5:28 you have filled J with your
Acts 6: 7 multiplied greatly in J,
Acts 8: 1 the church which was at J;

Acts 8:26 road which goes down from J
Acts 8:27 and had come to J to
Acts 9: 2 might bring them bound to J.
Acts 9:13 has done to Your saints in J.
Acts 9:21 who called on this name in J,
Acts 11:27 days prophets came from J
Acts 16: 4 the apostles and elders at J.
Acts 20:16 he was hurrying to be at J,
Acts 20:22 go bound in the spirit to J,
Acts 21: 4 the Spirit not to go up to J.
Acts 21:13 but also to die at J for the
Acts 21:31 of the garrison that all J
Acts 24:11 days since I went up to J
Acts 25: 1 went up from Caesarea to J.
Acts 26:20 those in Damascus and in J,
Acts 28:17 as a prisoner from J into
Rom 15:25 But now I am going to J to
Rom 15:26 the saints who are in J.
Gal 1:17 nor did I go up to J to those
Gal 1:18 three years I went up to J
Gal 2: 1 years I went up again to J
Gal 4:25 and corresponds to J which
Gal 4:26 but the J above is free,
Heb 12:22 living God, the heavenly J,
Rev 3:12 city of My God, the New J,
Rev 21: 2 saw the holy city, New J,
Rev 21:10 the great city, the holy J,

JESHUA (see JOSHUA)
Ezra 2: 2 came with Zerubbabel were J,
Ezra 3: 2 Then J the son of Jozadak and
Ezra 5: 2 the son of Shealtiel and J

JESHURUN
Deut 32:15 But J grew fat and kicked;
Deut 33:26 is no one like the God of J,
Is 44: 2 My servant; And you, J,

JESSE
Ruth 4:22 Obed begot J,
Ruth 4:22 and J begot David.
1Sa 16: 1 I am sending you to J the
1Sa 16:10 Thus J made seven of his sons
1Sa 17:17 Then J said to his son David,
1Sa 22: 8 a covenant with the son of J;
2Sa 20: 1 inheritance in the son of J;
Ps 72:20 of David the son of J are
Is 11: 1 a Rod from the stem of J,
Is 11:10 there shall be a Root of J,
Matt 1: 6 and J begot David the king.
Acts 13:22 found David the son of J,
Rom 15:12 shall be a root of J;

JESTING†
Eph 5: 4 talking, nor coarse j,

JESUS (see CHRIST, JESUS', JUSTUS)
Matt 1: 1 book of the genealogy of J
Matt 1:16 of whom was born J who is
Matt 1:18 Now the birth of J Christ
Matt 1:21 you shall call His name J,
Matt 2: 1 Now after J was born in
Matt 3:13 Then J came from Galilee to
Matt 4: 1 Then J was led up by the
Matt 4:12 Now when J heard that John
Matt 7:28 when J had ended these
Matt 8: 3 Then J put out His hand and
Matt 8:13 Then J said to the centurion,
Matt 8:20 And J said to him, "Foxes
Matt 8:22 But J said to him, "Follow
Matt 8:29 have we to do with You, J,
Matt 8:34 city came out to meet J.
Matt 9: 2 When J saw their faith, He
Matt 9:35 Then J went about all the
Matt 10: 5 These twelve J sent out and
Matt 11: 1 when J finished commanding
Matt 12:25 But J knew their thoughts,

Matt	13:36	Then J sent the multitude
Matt	13:53	when J had finished these
Matt	13:57	But J said to them, "A
Matt	14:12	it, and went and told J.
Matt	14:29	on the water to go to J.
Matt	14:31	And immediately J stretched
Matt	15:32	Now J called His disciples
Matt	16:20	tell no one that He was J
Matt	16:21	From that time J began to
Matt	17: 1	Now after six days J took
Matt	17: 8	they saw no one but J only.
Matt	17:18	And J rebuked the demon, and
Matt	17:19	Then the disciples came to J
Matt	18: 2	Then J called a little child
Matt	19: 1	when J had finished these
Matt	19:14	But J said, "Let the little
Matt	20:34	So J had compassion and
Matt	21: 1	then J sent two disciples,
Matt	21:11	multitudes said, "This is J,
Matt	21:12	Then J went into the temple
Matt	26: 1	when J had finished all
Matt	26: 4	and plotted to take J by
Matt	26: 6	And when J was in Bethany at
Matt	26:26	J took bread, blessed and
Matt	26:50	came and laid hands on J
Matt	26:57	who had laid hold of J led
Matt	26:59	false testimony against J
Matt	26:63	But J kept silent. And the
Matt	26:69	You also were with J of
Matt	26:71	fellow also was with J of
Matt	27:17	or J who is called Christ?"
Matt	27:20	for Barabbas and destroy J
Matt	27:26	and when he had scourged J,
Matt	27:27	of the governor took J into
Matt	27:37	THIS IS J THE KING OF THE
Matt	27:46	And about the ninth hour J
Matt	27:57	also become a disciple of J.
Matt	27:58	and asked for the body of J.
Matt	28: 5	for I know that you seek J
Matt	28: 9	J met them, saying,
Matt	28:16	to the mountain which J had
Mark	1: 1	of the gospel of J Christ,
Mark	1: 9	pass in those days that J
Mark	1:14	J came to Galilee, preaching
Mark	1:24	J of Nazareth? Did You come
Mark	5: 6	When he saw J from afar, he
Mark	5: 7	have I to do with You, J,
Mark	5:27	When she heard about J,
Mark	6:30	the apostles gathered to J
Mark	8: 1	J called His disciples to
Mark	9: 2	Now after six days J took
Mark	9: 4	and they were talking with J.
Mark	9:39	But J said, "Do not forbid
Mark	10:42	But J called them to Himself
Mark	10:47	when he heard that it was J
Mark	10:47	to cry out and say, "J,
Mark	11: 7	they brought the colt to J
Mark	11:15	Then J went into the temple
Mark	14: 6	But J said, "Let her alone.
Mark	14:22	J took bread, blessed and
Mark	14:53	And they led J away to the
Mark	14:55	sought testimony against J
Mark	14:62	J said, "I am. And you will
Mark	15: 1	council; and they bound J,
Mark	15: 5	But J still answered nothing,
Mark	15:34	And at the ninth hour J cried
Mark	15:37	And J cried out with a loud
Mark	15:43	and asked for the body of J.
Mark	16: 6	You seek J of Nazareth, who
Luke	1:31	and shall call His name J.
Luke	2:21	His name was called J,
Luke	2:43	the Boy J lingered behind in
Luke	2:52	And J increased in wisdom and
Luke	4:14	Then J returned in the power
Luke	4:34	J of Nazareth? Did You come

Luke	5:10	And J said to Simon, "Do
Luke	5:12	was full of leprosy saw J;
Luke	8:35	sitting at the feet of J,
Luke	8:45	And J said, "Who touched
Luke	9:42	Then J rebuked the unclean
Luke	9:58	And J said to him, "Foxes
Luke	9:60	J said to him, "Let the dead
Luke	10:21	In that hour J rejoiced in
Luke	13:14	because J had healed on the
Luke	17:13	their voices and said, "J,
Luke	18:38	he cried out, saying, "J,
Luke	19: 9	And J said to him, "Today
Luke	19:35	and they set J on him.
Luke	22:47	them and drew near to J to
Luke	22:52	Then J said to the chief
Luke	22:63	Now the men who held J
Luke	23: 8	Now when Herod saw J,
Luke	23:20	wishing to release J,
Luke	23:25	but he delivered J to their
Luke	23:26	he might bear it after J.
Luke	23:34	Then J said, "Father,
Luke	23:46	And when J had cried out with
Luke	23:52	and asked for the body of J.
Luke	24:19	The things concerning J of
Luke	24:36	J Himself stood in the midst
John	1:17	and truth came through J.
John	1:37	speak, and they followed J.
John	1:45	J of Nazareth, the son of
John	1:47	J saw Nathanael coming toward
John	2: 2	Now both J and His disciples
John	2: 4	J said to her, "Woman, what
John	2: 7	J said to them, "Fill the
John	2:11	This beginning of signs J did
John	2:13	and J went up to Jerusalem.
John	3: 2	This man came to J by night
John	4:26	J said to her, "I who speak
John	4:34	J said to them, "My food is
John	4:46	So J came again to Cana of
John	4:50	J said to him, "Go your way;
John	4:54	again is the second sign J
John	5: 6	When J saw him lying there,
John	5:16	reason the Jews persecuted J,
John	6: 3	And J went up on the
John	6: 5	Then J lifted up His eyes,
John	6:11	And J took the loaves, and
John	6:14	had seen the sign that J
John	6:24	came to Capernaum, seeking J.
John	6:42	they said, "Is not this J,
John	6:67	Then J said to the twelve,
John	7: 1	After these things J walked
John	7:14	the middle of the feast J
John	7:39	because J was not yet
John	7:50	Nicodemus (he who came to J
John	8: 1	But J went to the Mount of
John	8: 6	But J stooped down and wrote
John	8:59	but J hid Himself and went
John	9:11	A Man called J made clay and
John	9:14	Now it was a Sabbath when J
John	9:35	J heard that they had cast
John	9:39	And J said, "For judgment I
John	10: 6	J used this illustration, but
John	10:23	And J walked in the temple,
John	11: 5	Now J loved Martha and her
John	11:13	J spoke of his death, but
John	11:21	Then Martha said to J,
John	11:23	J said to her, "Your brother
John	11:25	J said to her, "I am the
John	11:33	when J saw her weeping, and
John	11:35	J wept.
John	11:39	J said, "Take away the
John	11:44	J said to them, "Loose him,
John	11:51	year he prophesied that J
John	12: 1	J came to Bethany, where
John	12: 3	anointed the feet of J,
John	12: 7	But J said, "Let her alone;

John	12:11	went away and believed in J.
John	12:16	but when J was glorified,
John	12:21	"Sir, we wish to see J.
John	12:22	Andrew and Philip told J.
John	13: 1	when J knew that His hour
John	13:23	whom J loved.
John	17: 3	and J Christ whom You have
John	18: 5	J of Nazareth." Jesus said
John	18:11	So J said to Peter, "Put
John	18:12	of the Jews arrested J and
John	18:15	And Simon Peter followed J,
John	18:22	who stood by struck J with
John	18:32	that the saying of J might be
John	18:36	J answered, "My kingdom is
John	19: 1	So then Pilate took J and
John	19: 5	Then J came out, wearing the
John	19: 9	But J gave him no answer.
John	19:18	and J in the center.
John	19:19	J OF NAZARETH, THE KING
John	19:23	when they had crucified J,
John	19:25	stood by the cross of J His
John	19:38	being a disciple of J,
John	19:38	take away the body of J;
John	19:39	who at first came to J by
John	19:40	Then they took the body of J,
John	19:42	So there they laid J,
John	20: 2	whom J loved, and said to
John	20:14	did not know that it was J.
John	20:15	J said to her, "Woman, why
John	20:16	J said to her, "Mary!" She
John	20:17	J said to her, "Do not cling
John	20:19	J came and stood in the
John	20:26	J came, the doors being
John	20:29	J said to him, "Thomas,
John	20:30	And truly J did many other
John	20:31	that you may believe that J
John	21: 4	J stood on the shore; yet
John	21: 7	that disciple whom J loved
John	21:14	is now the third time J
John	21:17	J said to him, "Feed My
John	21:20	saw the disciple whom J
John	21:25	many other things that J
Acts	1: 1	of all that J began both to
Acts	1:11	up into heaven? This same J,
Acts	1:14	and Mary the mother of J,
Acts	1:16	to those who arrested J;
Acts	2:22	J of Nazareth, a Man
Acts	2:32	This J God has raised up, of
Acts	2:36	that God has made this J,
Acts	2:38	be baptized in the name of J
Acts	3:13	glorified His Servant J,
Acts	3:26	raised up His Servant J,
Acts	4:10	that by the name of J Christ
Acts	4:13	that they had been with J.
Acts	4:18	nor teach in the name of J.
Acts	4:27	against Your holy Servant J,
Acts	4:33	resurrection of the Lord J.
Acts	5:30	of our fathers raised up J
Acts	5:40	not speak in the name of J,
Acts	5:42	teaching and preaching J
Acts	7:55	and J standing at the right
Acts	8:35	preached J to him.
Acts	8:37	I believe that J Christ is
Acts	9: 5	Then the Lord said, "I am J,
Acts	9:17	"Brother Saul, the Lord J,
Acts	9:27	at Damascus in the name of J.
Acts	9:34	J the Christ heals you.
Acts	10:36	preaching peace through J
Acts	10:38	how God anointed J of
Acts	11:17	we believed on the Lord J
Acts	11:20	preaching the Lord J.
Acts	13:23	up for Israel a Savior—J—
Acts	15:11	the grace of the Lord J
Acts	15:26	for the name of our Lord J
Acts	16:18	you in the name of J Christ
Acts	16:31	Believe on the Lord J Christ,
Acts	17: 7	there is another king—J.
Acts	19:13	call the name of the Lord J
Acts	19:15	J I know, and Paul I know;
Acts	20:24	I received from the Lord J,
Acts	22: 8	I am J of Nazareth, whom you
Acts	26:15	Lord?' And He said, 'I am J,
Acts	28:23	them concerning J from both
Rom	1: 1	a bondservant of J Christ,
Rom	1: 3	concerning His Son J Christ
Rom	1: 6	you also are the called of J
Rom	1: 7	our Father and the Lord J
Rom	2:16	the secrets of men by J
Rom	3:22	through faith in J Christ,
Rom	3:26	the one who has faith in J.
Rom	4:24	in Him who raised up J our
Rom	6: 3	were baptized into Christ J
Rom	6:23	is eternal life in Christ J
Rom	8: 1	to those who are in Christ J,
Rom	8: 2	Spirit of life in Christ J
Rom	8:11	Spirit of Him who raised J
Rom	8:39	of God which is in Christ J
Rom	10: 9	with your mouth the Lord J
Rom	13:14	But put on the Lord J Christ,
Rom	15:16	I might be a minister of J
Rom	15:17	reason to glory in Christ J
Rom	16: 3	fellow workers in Christ J,
1Co	1: 1	to be an apostle of J
1Co	1: 2	are sanctified in Christ J,
1Co	1: 8	in the day of our Lord J
1Co	2: 2	anything among you except J
1Co	5: 4	with the power of our Lord J
1Co	8: 6	and one Lord J Christ,
1Co	9: 1	Have I not seen J Christ our
1Co	11:23	that the Lord J on the same
1Co	12: 3	by the Spirit of God calls J
1Co	12: 3	and no one can say that J is
1Co	15:57	victory through our Lord J
2Co	1: 2	our Father and the Lord J
2Co	4: 5	but Christ J the Lord, and
2Co	4: 6	of God in the face of J
2Co	4:10	body the dying of the Lord J,
2Co	4:10	that the life of J also may
2Co	4:14	will also raise us up with J,
Gal	1:12	through the revelation of J
Gal	2:16	of the law but by faith in J
Gal	3:14	the Gentiles in Christ J,
Gal	3:28	you are all one in Christ J.
Gal	5: 6	For in Christ J neither
Gal	6:14	in the cross of our Lord J
Gal	6:17	body the marks of the Lord J.
Eph	1: 1	and faithful in Christ J:
Eph	2: 6	heavenly places in Christ J,
Eph	2:10	created in Christ J for good
Eph	2:20	J Christ Himself being the
Eph	3: 1	the prisoner of Christ J for
Eph	4:21	by Him, as the truth is in J:
Eph	6:24	those who love our Lord J
Phil	1: 1	bondservants of J Christ,
Phil	1: 8	all with the affection of J
Phil	1:19	supply of the Spirit of J
Phil	2: 5	which was also in Christ J,
Phil	2:10	that at the name of J every
Phil	2:11	tongue should confess that J
Phil	2:19	But I trust in the Lord J to
Phil	3: 8	of the knowledge of Christ J
Phil	3:14	call of God in Christ J.
Phil	4: 7	and minds through Christ J.
Phil	4:19	riches in glory by Christ J.
Phil	4:21	every saint in Christ J.
Col	1:28	man perfect in Christ J.
Col	4:11	and J who is called Justus.
1Th	1:10	even J who delivers us from
1Th	3:13	at the coming of our Lord J
1Th	4:14	For if we believe that J died

1Th	4:14	Him those who sleep in J.
1Th	5:23	at the coming of our Lord J
2Th	1: 8	the gospel of our Lord J
2Th	2: 1	the coming of our Lord J
2Th	2:14	of the glory of our Lord J
1Ti	1:12	And I thank Christ J our
1Ti	1:15	that Christ J came into the
1Ti	2: 5	and men, the Man Christ J,
1Ti	4: 6	will be a good minister of J
1Ti	6:14	blameless until our Lord J
2Ti	1: 1	of life which is in Christ J,
2Ti	1:13	love which are in Christ J.
2Ti	2: 3	as a good soldier of J
2Ti	3:12	to live godly in Christ J
Tit	1: 4	the Father and the Lord J
Tit	2:13	our great God and Savior J
Phm	1: 1	a prisoner of Christ J,
Phm	1: 9	and now also a prisoner of J
Phm	1:23	fellow prisoner in Christ J,
Heb	2: 9	But we see J,who was made
Heb	3: 1	of our confession, Christ J,
Heb	4:14	J the Son of God, let us
Heb	6:20	has entered for us, even J,
Heb	7:22	by so much more J has become
Heb	10:10	offering of the body of J
Heb	10:19	Holiest by the blood of J,
Heb	12: 2	looking unto J,
Heb	12:24	to J the Mediator of the new
Heb	13: 8	J Christ is the same
Heb	13:20	who brought up our Lord J
Heb	13:21	through J Christ, to whom
1Pe	1: 1	an apostle of J Christ, To
1Pe	1: 7	glory at the revelation of J
1Pe	5:10	eternal glory by Christ J,
2Pe	1: 1	and apostle of J Christ,
1Jn	1: 7	and the blood of J Christ
1Jn	2: 1	J Christ the righteous.
1Jn	2:22	but he who denies that J is
1Jn	4: 2	spirit that confesses that J
1Jn	4:15	Whoever confesses that J is
1Jn	5: 5	but he who believes that J
1Jn	5: 6	J Christ; not only by water,
Jude	1	and preserved in J Christ
Rev	1: 1	The Revelation of J Christ,
Rev	1: 2	and to the testimony of J
Rev	1: 9	kingdom and patience of J
Rev	17: 6	blood of the martyrs of J.
Rev	22:21	The grace of our Lord J

JESUS' (see JESUS)

Matt	15:30	and they laid them down at J
Luke	5: 8	he fell down at J knees,
Luke	10:39	who also sat at J feet and
John	12: 9	not for J sake only, but
John	13:25	leaning back on J breast, he
2Co	4: 5	your bondservants for J
2Co	4:11	delivered to death for J

JETHRO (see HOBAB, REUEL)

| Ex | 3: 1 | was tending the flock of J |
| Ex | 18: 6 | "I, your father-in-law J, |

JEW (see JEWISH, JEWS, JUDAISM)

Esth	8: 7	Esther and Mordecai the J,
John	4: 9	is it that You, being a J,
Acts	13: 6	a J whose name was
Acts	18: 2	And he found a certain J
Acts	18:24	Now a certain J named
Acts	21:39	I am a J from Tarsus, in
Acts	22: 3	"I am indeed a J,
Rom	1:16	for the J first and also for
Rom	2: 9	of the J first and also of
Rom	2:10	to the J first and also to
Rom	2:28	For he is not a J who is
Rom	3: 1	advantage then has the J,
Rom	10:12	is no distinction between J

1Co	9:20	to the Jews I became as a J,
Gal	2:14	all, "If you, being a J,
Gal	3:28	There is neither J nor Greek,

JEWEL† (see JEWELRY, JEWELS)

| Prov | 20:15 | knowledge are a precious j. |
| Ezek | 16:12 | And I put a j in your nose, |

JEWELRY (see JEWEL)

| Gen | 24:53 | the servant brought out j |
| Job | 28:17 | can it be exchanged for j |

JEWELS (see JEWEL)

Song	7: 1	of your thighs are like j,
Is	3:21	and the rings; The nose j,
Mal	3:17	day that I make them My j.

JEWISH (see JEW)

Esth	6:13	is of J descent, you will
Jer	34: 9	no one should keep a J
Zech	8:23	grasp the sleeve of a J man,
Acts	10:28	how unlawful it is for a J
Acts	19:13	Then some of the itinerant J
Acts	19:14	a J chief priest, who did
Acts	24:24	his wife Drusilla, who was J,
Acts	26:23	proclaim light to the J
Tit	1:14	not giving heed to J fables

JEWS (see JEW, JEWS')

Ezra	5: 5	was upon the elders of the J,
Ezra	6: 7	let the governor of the J
Neh	1: 2	asked them concerning the J
Neh	4: 1	indignant, and mocked the J.
Neh	4: 2	What are these feeble J
Neh	6: 6	that you and the J plan to
Neh	13:23	In those days I also saw J
Esth	3:13	and to annihilate all the J,
Esth	4: 3	great mourning among the J,
Esth	4: 7	treasuries to destroy the J.
Esth	4:13	more than all the other J
Esth	4:14	will arise for the J from
Esth	8: 1	of Haman, the enemy of the J.
Esth	8: 3	he had devised against the J.
Esth	8:16	The J had light and gladness,
Esth	8:17	because fear of the J fell
Esth	9: 5	Thus the J defeated all their
Esth	9:15	And the J who were in
Esth	9:23	So the J accepted the custom
Esth	10: 3	and was great among the J
Jer	38:19	I am afraid of the J who have
Jer	40:12	then all the J returned out
Dan	3: 8	forward and accused the J
Dan	3:12	There are certain J whom you
Matt	2: 2	has been born King of the J?
Matt	27:11	"Are You the King of the J?
Matt	27:29	King of the J!"
Matt	27:37	JESUS THE KING OF THE J.
Matt	28:15	reported among the J until
Mark	7: 3	the Pharisees and all the J
Luke	7: 3	he sent elders of the J to
Luke	23:51	Arimathea, a city of the J,
John	2: 6	of purification of the J,
John	2:13	Now the Passover of the J
John	3: 1	Nicodemus, a ruler of the J.
John	4: 9	For I have no dealings
John	4:20	and you J say that in
John	4:22	for salvation is of the J.
John	5: 1	there was a feast of the J,
John	5:16	For this reason the J
John	7: 1	because the J sought to kill
John	7:11	the J sought Him at the
John	7:13	of Him for fear of the J.
John	8:31	Then Jesus said to those J
John	9:22	because they feared the J,
John	10:24	Then the J surrounded Him and
John	10:31	Then the J took up stones
John	11:55	And the Passover of the J was

John   18:12 and the officers of the **J**
John   18:33 "Are You the King of the **J**?
John   18:36 not be delivered to the **J**;
John   19:19 THE KING OF THE **J**.
John   19:20 Then many of the **J** read this
John   19:21 write, 'The King of the **J**,
John   19:38 secretly, for fear of the **J**,
John   19:40 as the custom of the **J** is to
John   20:19 assembled, for fear of the **J**,
Acts   2: 5 were dwelling in Jerusalem **J**,
Acts   2:10 both **J** and proselytes,
Acts   9:23 them **J** plotted to kill him.
Acts   13: 5 in the synagogues of the **J**.
Acts   14: 2 But the unbelieving **J** stirred
Acts   14: 5 by both the Gentiles and **J**,
Acts   18: 4 and persuaded both **J** and
Acts   18: 5 and testified to the **J** that
Acts   18:14 mouth, Gallio said to the **J**,
Acts   18:19 and reasoned with the **J**.
Acts   18:28 he vigorously refuted the **J**
Acts   20: 3 And when the **J** plotted
Acts   20:19 me by the plotting of the **J**;
Acts   20:21 "testifying to **J**,
Acts   21:20 how many myriads of **J** there
Acts   21:21 you that you teach all the **J**
Acts   24: 5 dissension among all the **J**
Acts   24: 9 And the **J** also assented,
Acts   24:27 wanting to do the **J** a favor,
Acts   25: 2 and the chief men of the **J**
Acts   25: 8 against the law of the **J**,
Acts   26: 2 which I am accused by the **J**,
Rom   3: 9 previously charged both **J**
Rom   3:29 Or is He the God of the **J**
Rom   9:24 not of the **J** only, but also
1Co   1:22 For **J** request a sign, and
1Co   1:23 to the **J** a stumbling block
1Co   1:24 both **J** and Greeks, Christ
1Co   9:20 and to the **J** I became as a
1Co   10:32 either to the **J** or to the
2Co   11:24 From the **J** five times I
Gal   2:14 compel Gentiles to live as **J**?
Gal   2:15 We who are **J** by nature, and
Rev   2: 9 of those who say they are **J**
Rev   3: 9 who say they are **J** and are

JEWS' † (see JEWS)
John   7: 2 Now the **J** Feast of

JEZEBEL (see JEZEBEL'S)
1Ki   16:31 that he took as wife **J** the
1Ki   18: 4 while **J** massacred the
1Ki   19: 1 And Ahab told **J** all that
1Ki   21:15 when **J** heard that Naboth had
1Ki   21:23 The dogs shall eat **J** by the
Rev   2:20 you allow that woman **J**,

JEZEBEL'S † (see JEZEBEL)
1Ki   18:19 who eat at **J** table."

JEZREEL (see JEZREELITE)
Josh   17:16 who are of the Valley of **J**.
1Ki   21: 1 a vineyard which was in **J**,
1Ki   21:23 eat Jezebel by the wall of **J**.
2Ki   9:30 Now when Jehu had come to **J**,
Hos   1: 4 to him: "Call his name **J**,
Hos   1: 5 of Israel in the Valley of **J**.
Hos   1:11 will be the day of **J**!
Hos   2:22 oil; They shall answer **J**.
1Ki   21: 6 I spoke to Naboth the **J**,
1Ki   21: 7 the vineyard of Naboth the **J**.

JEZREELITE (see JEZREEL)
1Ki   21: 7 the vineyard of Naboth the **J**
1Ki   21:15 the vineyard of Naboth the **J**
1Ki   21:16 the vineyard of Naboth the **J**
2Ki   9:21 the property of Naboth the **J**
2Ki   9:25 of the field of Naboth the **J**

JINGLING †
Is   3:16 Making a **j** with their feet,
Is   3:18 The **j** anklets, the scarves,

JOAB (see JOAB'S)
1Sa   26: 6 son of Zeruiah, brother of **J**,
2Sa   2:14 Then Abner said to **J**,
2Sa   2:18 **J** and Abishai and Asahel.
2Sa   3:22 the servants of David and **J**
2Sa   3:29 it rest on the head of **J**
2Sa   11: 6 And **J** sent Uriah to David.
2Sa   11:14 David wrote a letter to **J**
2Sa   14: 2 And **J** sent to Tekoa and
2Sa   14:19 Is the hand of **J** with you in
2Sa   14:29 Therefore Absalom sent for **J**,
2Sa   18:16 For **J** held back the people.
2Sa   20: 8 Now **J** was dressed in battle
2Sa   20: 9 And **J** took Amasa by the
2Sa   20:17 the woman said, "Are you **J**?
2Sa   23:24 Asahel the brother of **J** was
1Ki   2:28 for **J** had defected to
1Ki   2:31 the innocent blood which **J**
1Ch   11:20 Abishai the brother of **J** was

JOAB'S (see JOAB)
2Sa   14:30 **J** field is near mine, and he

JOANNA †
Luke   8: 3 and **J** the wife of Chuza,
Luke   24:10 It was Mary Magdalene, **J**,

JOASH (see JEHOASH)
Judg   7:14 sword of Gideon the son of **J**,
Judg   8:29 Jerubbaal the son of **J** went
2Ki   12:19 the rest of the acts of **J**,
2Ki   13:10 the thirty-seventh year of **J**
2Ki   13:12 the rest of the acts of **J**,
2Ki   13:14 Then **J** the king of Israel
2Ki   14: 1 In the second year of **J** the
2Ki   14:17 Amaziah the son of **J**,
2Ki   14:27 of Jeroboam the son of **J**.
2Ch   24: 1 **J** was seven years old when
2Ch   24: 2 **J** did what was right in the
Hos   1: 1 of Jeroboam the son of **J**,
Amos   1: 1 of Jeroboam the son of **J**,

JOB (see JOB'S)
Job   1: 1 of Uz, whose name was **J**;
Job   1: 5 For **J** said, "It may be that
Job   1: 5 Thus **J** did regularly.
Job   1: 8 you considered My servant **J**,
Job   1: 9 Does **J** fear God for nothing?
Job   1:20 Then **J** arose, tore his robe,
Job   1:22 In all this **J** did not sin
Job   2: 7 and struck **J** with painful
Job   3: 1 After this **J** opened his mouth
Job   31:40 The words of **J** are ended.
Job   32: 1 three men ceased answering **J**,
Job   32:12 not one of you convinced **J**,
Job   34: 7 What man is like **J**,
Job   34:35 **J** speaks without knowledge,
Job   34:36 that **J** were tried to the
Job   37:14 "Listen to this, O **J**;
Job   40: 3 Then **J** answered the LORD
Job   42: 7 as My servant **J** has.
Job   42: 8 and My servant **J** shall pray
Job   42: 9 for the LORD had accepted **J**.
Job   42:10 Indeed the LORD gave **J**
Job   42:15 as the daughters of **J**;
Job   42:17 So **J** died, old and full of
Ezek   14:14 men, Noah, Daniel, and **J**,
Ezek   14:20 and **J** were in it, as I
Jas   5:11 of the perseverance of **J**

JOB'S † (see JOB)
Job   2:11 Now when **J** three friends
Job   42:10 And the LORD restored **J**

JOCHEBED†
Ex	6:20	Amram took for himself J,
Num	26:59	name of Amram's wife was J

JOEL
Joel	1: 1	of the LORD that came to J
Acts	2:16	was spoken by the prophet J:

JOHANAN
Jer	40:13	Moreover J the son of Kareah

JOHN (*see* BAPTIST, JOHN'S, MARK•)
Matt	3: 1	In those days J the Baptist
Matt	3:13	came from Galilee to J at
Matt	4:21	and J his brother, in the
Matt	9:14	Then the disciples of J came
Matt	11:11	not risen one greater than J
Matt	11:12	And from the days of J the
Matt	11:13	the law prophesied until J.
Matt	11:18	For J came neither eating nor
Matt	14: 3	For Herod had laid hold of J
Matt	14: 8	Give me J the Baptist's head
Matt	14:10	So he sent and had J beheaded
Matt	16:14	Some say J the Baptist, some
Matt	21:25	"The baptism of J—
Mark	1: 9	and was baptized by J in the
Mark	1:19	and J his brother, who also
Mark	1:29	and Andrew, with James and J.
Mark	3:17	the son of Zebedee and J
Mark	6:14	J the Baptist is risen from
Mark	6:25	me at once the head of J
Mark	9: 2	took Peter, James, and J,
Luke	1:13	you shall call his name J.
Luke	5:33	Why do the disciples of J
Luke	7:24	When the messengers of J had
Luke	16:16	the prophets were until J.
Luke	20: 6	they are persuaded that J
Luke	22: 8	And He sent Peter and J,
John	1: 6	from God, whose name was J.
John	1:15	J bore witness of Him and
John	1:19	this is the testimony of J,
John	1:32	And J bore witness, saying,
John	3:24	For J had not yet been thrown
John	4: 1	more disciples than J
John	5:33	"You have sent to J,
John	10:41	J performed no sign, but all
Acts	1: 5	for J truly baptized with
Acts	1:13	staying: Peter, James, J,
Acts	3:11	held on to Peter and J,
Acts	4:13	the boldness of Peter and J,
Acts	12:12	the mother of J whose
Acts	12:25	they also took with them J
Acts	15:37	to take with them J called
Acts	18:25	knew only the baptism of J.
Gal	2: 9	when James, Cephas, and J,
Rev	1: 1	His angel to His servant J,

JOHN'S (*see* JOHN)
John	3:25	a dispute between some of J
Acts	19: 3	Into J baptism."

JOIN (*see* JOINED)
Ex	1:10	that they also j our enemies
Ezra	9:14	and j in marriage with the
Is	5: 8	Woe to those who j house to
Is	56: 6	sons of the foreigner Who j
Ezek	37:17	Then j them one to another
Acts	5:13	Yet none of the rest dared j
Acts	9:26	he tried to j the disciples;
Phil	3:17	j in following my example,

JOINED (*see* JOIN)
Gen	2:24	father and mother and be j
Gen	14: 8	Zoar) went out and j
Num	25: 5	you kill his men who were j
1Sa	4: 2	And when they j battle,
1Ki	20:29	seventh day the battle was j;
1Ch	12: 8	Some Gadites j David at the

Neh	4: 6	and the entire wall was j
Hos	4:17	Ephraim is j to idols, Let
Matt	19: 5	and mother and be j
Matt	19: 6	Therefore what God has j
Luke	9:18	that His disciples j Him,
Luke	15:15	Then he went and j himself to
John	11:19	And many of the Jews had j
Acts	17:34	some men j him and believed,
Acts	20: 6	and in five days j them at
1Co	1:10	but that you be perfectly j
1Co	6:16	not know that he who is j
1Co	6:17	But he who is j to the Lord
Eph	2:21	being j together, grows into
Eph	4:16	j and knit together by what
Eph	5:31	and mother and be j

JOINT (*see* JOINTS)
Gen	32:25	of Jacob's hip was out of j
Ps	22:14	all My bones are out of j;
Rom	8:17	heirs of God and j heirs with
Eph	4:16	together by what every j

JOINTS (*see* JOINT)
1Ki	22:34	of Israel between the j of
Dan	5: 6	so that the j of his hips
Col	2:19	and knit together by j and
Heb	4:12	and of j and marrow, and is

JOKING†
Gen	19:14	he seemed to be j.
Prov	26:19	I was only j!"

JONADAB (*see* JEHONADAB)
2Sa	13: 3	Now J was a very crafty
Jer	35: 6	for J the son of Rechab, our
Jer	35:10	according to all that J our

JONAH (*see* JONAH'S)
2Ki	14:25	through His servant J the
Jon	1: 1	word of the LORD came to J
Jon	1: 3	But J arose to flee to
Jon	1: 7	lots, and the lot fell on J.
Jon	1:17	a great fish to swallow J.
Jon	1:17	And J was in the belly of
Jon	2: 1	Then J prayed to the LORD
Jon	2:10	and it vomited J onto dry
Jon	3: 1	word of the LORD came to J
Jon	3: 3	So J arose and went to
Jon	4: 1	But it displeased J
Jon	4: 5	So J went out of the city
Matt	12:39	the sign of the prophet J.
Matt	12:40	For as J was three days and
Matt	12:41	at the preaching of J;
Matt	12:41	and indeed a greater than J
Luke	11:30	For as J became a sign to
John	1:42	"You are Simon the son of J.
John	21:16	time, "Simon, son of J,

JONAH'S† (*see* JONAH)
Jon	4: 8	and the sun beat on J head,

JONATHAN (*see* JONATHAN'S)
1Sa	13:22	who were with Saul and J.
1Sa	14:12	J said to his armorbearer,
1Sa	14:42	lots between my son J
1Sa	18: 1	the soul of J was knit to
1Sa	18: 1	and J loved him as his own
1Sa	18: 3	Then J and David made a
1Sa	19: 4	Thus J spoke well of David
1Sa	20:16	So J made a covenant with
1Sa	20:40	Then J gave his weapons to
1Sa	31: 2	And the Philistines killed J,
2Sa	1: 5	do you know that Saul and J
2Sa	1:17	over Saul and over J his
2Sa	1:25	the midst of the battle! J
2Sa	1:26	for you, my brother J;
2Sa	9: 3	There is still a son of J
2Sa	9: 6	Mephibosheth the son of J,

2Sa 21:12 and the bones of J his son,
1Ch   8:34 The son of J was Merib-Baal,

JONATHAN'S (*see* JONATHAN)
2Sa   9: 1 may show him kindness for J

JOPPA
2Ch   2:16 to you in rafts by sea to J,
Ezra 3: 7 Lebanon to the sea, to J,
Jon   1: 3 the LORD. He went down to J,
Acts 9:38 And since Lydda was near J,
Acts 9:43 he stayed many days in J
Acts 11: 5 I was in the city of J
Acts 11:13 said to him, 'Send men to J,

JORAM (*see* JEHORAM)
2Ki   8:16 Now in the fifth year of J
2Ki   8:23 the rest of the acts of J,
2Ki   8:24 So J rested with his fathers,
2Ki   9:21 Then J king of Israel and
Matt 1: 8 Jehoshaphat begot J,
Matt 1: 8 and J begot Uzziah.

JORDAN
Gen   13:11 himself all the plain of J,
Num   13:29 and along the banks of the J.
Num   22: 1 of Moab on the side of the J
Num   26: 3 the plains of Moab by the J,
Num   32: 5 Do not take us over the J.
Num   32:19 this eastern side of the J.
Num   33:49 They camped by the J,
Num   33:51 'When you have crossed the J
Deut 1: 1 on this side of the J in
Deut 1: 5 On this side of the J in the
Deut 3:17 with the J as the border,
Deut 3:20 is giving them beyond the J.
Deut 3:25 the good land beyond the J,
Deut 4:21 I would not cross over the J,
Josh 1: 2 arise, go over this J,
Josh 1:15 you on this side of the J
Josh 3: 8 edge of the water of the J,
Josh 3: 8 you shall stand in the J.
Josh 3:13 that the waters of the J
Josh 3:15 bore the ark came to the J,
Josh 3:15 edge of the water (for the J
Josh 3:17 ground in the midst of the J;
Josh 3:17 completely over the J.
Josh 4: 7 the waters of the J were cut
Josh 4: 9 stones in the midst of the J,
Josh 5: 1 up the waters of the J from
Josh 12: 1 and all the eastern J plainJ
Josh 12: 3 and the eastern J plain from
Josh 13:23 Reuben was the bank of the J.
Josh 15: 5 sea at the mouth of the J.
Josh 22:10 an altar there by the J—
Josh 24:11 Then you went over the J and
Judg 5:17 Gilead stayed beyond the J,
Judg 10: 9 of Ammon crossed over the J
Judg 11:13 as the Jabbok, and to the J.
Judg 12: 6 him at the fords of the J.
2Sa   17:24 Absalom crossed over the J,
2Sa   19:15 escort the king across the J.
1Ki   17: 3 which flows into the J.
2Ki   2: 7 two of them stood by the J.
2Ki   5:10 Go and wash in the J seven
2Ki   5:14 dipped seven times in the J,
Ps   42: 6 You from the land of the J,
Ps   114: 5 O sea, that you fled? O J,
Is   9: 1 way of the sea, beyond the J,
Jer   12: 5 in the floodplain of the J?
Zech 11: 3 For the pride of the J is
Matt 3: 5 all the region around the J
Matt 3: 6 baptized by him in the J,
Matt 3:13 Galilee to John at the J to
Matt 4:15 the sea, beyond the J,
Matt 4:25 Judea, and beyond the J.
Mark 1: 9 baptized by John in the J.

Luke 4: 1 returned from the J and was

JOSEPH (*see* BARSABAS, JOSEPH'S)
Gen   30:24 So she called his name J,
Gen   30:25 when Rachel had borne J,
Gen   33: 2 and Rachel and J last.
Gen   37: 2 is the history of Jacob. J,
Gen   37: 2 and J brought a bad report
Gen   37: 3 Now Israel loved J more than
Gen   37: 5 Now J had a dream, and he
Gen   37:23 when J had come to his
Gen   37:23 that they stripped J of his
Gen   37:28 so the brothers pulled J
Gen   37:28 And they took J to Egypt.
Gen   37:29 and indeed J was not in the
Gen   37:33 Without doubt J is torn to
Gen   39: 2 The LORD was with J,
Gen   39: 4 So J found favor in his
Gen   39: 6 Now J was handsome in form
Gen   39: 7 wife cast longing eyes on J,
Gen   39:10 as she spoke to J day by
Gen   40: 3 the place where J was
Gen   40: 4 of the guard charged J with
Gen   40: 9 butler told his dream to J,
Gen   40:22 as J had interpreted to
Gen   40:23 butler did not remember J,
Gen   41:14 Pharaoh sent and called J,
Gen   41:46 J was thirty years old when
Gen   41:50 And to J were born two sons
Gen   42: 6 Now J was governor over the
Gen   42: 8 So J recognized his brothers,
Gen   42: 9 Then J remembered the dreams
Gen   43:16 When J saw Benjamin with
Gen   45: 1 Then I could not restrain
Gen   45: 3 Then J said to his brothers,
Gen   45: 3 to his brothers, "I am J;
Gen   45: 4 I am J your brother, whom
Gen   45:26 J is still alive, and he is
Gen   45:28 J my son is still alive. I
Gen   47: 7 Then J brought in his father
Gen   47:17 and J gave them bread in
Gen   47:20 Then J bought all the land
Gen   47:26 And J made it a law over the
Gen   48:13 And J took them both, Ephraim
Gen   48:15 And he blessed J,
Gen   49:22 J is a fruitful bough, A
Gen   49:26 shall be on the head of J,
Gen   50: 7 So J went up to bury his
Gen   50:15 Perhaps J will hate us, and
Gen   50:17 And J wept when they spoke
Gen   50:22 And J lived one hundred and
Gen   50:23 J saw Ephraim's children to
Ex   1: 8 Egypt, who did not know J.
Ex   13:19 Moses took the bones of J
Num   13:11 from the tribe of J,
Num   27: 1 of Manasseh the son of J;
Josh 14: 4 For the children of J were
Josh 24:32 The bones of J,
Judg 1:22 And the house of J also went
Ps   77:15 The sons of Jacob and J.
Ps   78:67 He rejected the tent of J,
Ps   80: 1 You who lead J like a
Ps   81: 5 This He established in J as
Ps   105:17 sent a man before them—J—
Ezek 37:16 and write on it, 'For J,
Amos 5: 6 like fire in the house of J,
Amos 5:15 gracious to the remnant of J.
Amos 6: 6 for the affliction of J.
Obad 18 And the house of J a flame;
Matt 1:18 Mary was betrothed to J,
Matt 1:19 Then J her husband, being a
Matt 1:20 him in a dream, saying, "J,
Matt 2:13 of the Lord appeared to J
Matt 2:19 appeared in a dream to J in
Matt 27:59 When J had taken the body, he

Mark 15:43 J of Arimathea, a prominent
Mark 15:45 he granted the body to J.
Luke 1:27 to a man whose name was J,
Luke 2: 4 J also went up from Galilee,
Luke 2:16 haste and found Mary and J,
Luke 2:33 And J and His mother marveled
Luke 3:23 was supposed) the son of J,
John 1:45 of Nazareth, the son of J.
Acts 1:23 called Barsabas, who was
Acts 7: 9 sold J into Egypt. But God
Heb 11:21 each of the sons of J,
Heb 11:22 By faith J, when he was
Rev 7: 8 of the tribe of J twelve

JOSEPH'S (see JOSEPH)
Gen 37:31 So they took J tunic, killed
Gen 39:20 Then J master took him and
Gen 39:22 of the prison committed to J
Gen 42: 3 So J ten brothers went down
Gen 48: 8 Then Israel saw J sons, and
Gen 50:23 were also brought up on J
1Ch 5: 2 the birthright was J—
Luke 4:22 Is this not J son?"

JOSES (see BARNABAS)
Matt 13:55 And His brothers James, J,
Matt 27:56 the mother of James and J,
Mark 6: 3 and brother of James, J,
Mark 15:40 of James the Less and of J,

JOSHUA (see HOSEA, HOSHEA, JESHUA)
Ex 17:10 So J did as Moses said to
Ex 17:13 So J defeated Amalek and his
Ex 24:13 arose with his assistant J,
Ex 33:11 but his servant J the son of
Num 11:28 So J the son of Nun, Moses'
Num 13:16 Hoshea the son of Nun, J
Deut 31:23 Then He inaugurated J the son
Josh 4: 4 Then J called the twelve men
Josh 4: 9 Then J set up twelve stones
Josh 4:20 J set up in Gilgal.
Josh 5: 3 So J made flint knives for
Josh 5: 7 Then J circumcised their sons
Josh 5:15 the LORD's army said to J,
Josh 6:25 And J spared Rahab the
Josh 6:25 hid the messengers whom J
Josh 7: 6 Then J tore his clothes, and
Josh 7:20 And Achan answered J and
Josh 8:28 So J burned Ai and made it a
Josh 8:30 Now J built an altar to the
Josh 9: 3 of Gibeon heard what J had
Josh 9:15 So J made peace with them,
Josh 10: 6 the men of Gibeon sent to J
Josh 10:18 So J said, "Roll large
Josh 10:24 brought out those kings to J,
Josh 10:27 down of the sun that J
Josh 10:40 So J conquered all the landJ
Josh 11:13 which J burned.
Josh 11:18 J made war a long time with
Josh 11:21 J utterly destroyed them
Josh 12: 7 which J gave to the tribes
Josh 13: 1 Now J was old, advanced in
Josh 14:13 And J blessed him, and gave
Josh 18:10 and there J divided the land
Josh 23: 1 that J was old, advanced in
Josh 24:25 So J made a covenant with the
Josh 24:26 Then J wrote these words in
Josh 24:31 of the elders who outlived J,
Judg 1: 1 Now after the death of J it
Judg 2:21 any of the nations which J
Hag 1: 1 and to J the son of
Zech 3: 1 Then he showed me J the high
Zech 3: 3 Now J was clothed with filthy
Zech 3: 8 'Hear, O J, the high priest
Acts 7:45 also brought with J into the
Heb 4: 8 For if J had given them rest,

JOSIAH
1Ki 13: 2 J by name, shall be born to
2Ki 22: 1 J was eight years old when
2Ki 22: 3 eighteenth year of King J,
2Ki 23:28 the rest of the acts of J,
2Ki 23:30 took Jehoahaz the son of J,
2Ki 23:34 made Eliakim the son of J
1Ch 3:15 The sons of J were Johanan
2Ch 34: 1 J was eight years old when
2Ch 35: 7 Then J gave the lay people
2Ch 35:23 And the archers shot King J;
2Ch 35:24 and Jerusalem mourned for J.
2Ch 35:25 Jeremiah also lamented for J.
2Ch 35:26 the rest of the acts of J
2Ch 36: 1 took Jehoahaz the son of J,
Jer 1: 2 LORD came in the days of J
Jer 3: 6 also to me in the days of J
Jer 22:11 who reigned instead of J his
Jer 22:18 Jehoiakim the son of J,
Jer 37: 1 King Zedekiah the son of J
Zeph 1: 1 in the days of J the son of
Matt 1:10 begot Amon, and Amon begot J.
Matt 1:11 J begot Jeconiah and his

JOT†
Matt 5:18 one j or one tittle will by

JOTHAM
Judg 9: 5 But J the youngest son of
Judg 9:21 And J ran away and fled; and
Judg 9:57 on them came the curse of J
2Ki 15:36 the rest of the acts of J,
2Ki 15:38 So J rested with his fathers,
2Ki 16: 1 Remaliah, Ahaz the son of J,
Is 1: 1 in the days of Uzziah, J,
Is 7: 1 days of Ahaz the son of J,
Hos 1: 1 in the days of Uzziah, J,
Mic 1: 1 Moresheth in the days of J,
Matt 1: 9 Uzziah begot J,

JOURNEY (see JOURNEYED, JOURNEYING, JOURNEYS)
Gen 24:21 the LORD had made his j
Gen 29: 1 So Jacob went on his j and
Gen 30:36 Then he put three days' j
Gen 31:23 him for seven days' j
Gen 42:25 them provisions for the j.
Gen 45:23 for his father for the j.
Ex 5: 3 let us go three days' j into
Ex 13:20 So they took their j from
Ex 40:37 then they did not j till the
Num 4: 5 the camp prepares to j,
Num 9:10 or is far away on a j,
Num 9:13 is clean and is not on a j,
Num 9:17 children of Israel would j;
Num 9:19 of the LORD and did not j.
Num 9:21 morning, then they would j;
Num 9:21 was taken up, they would j.
Num 11:31 about a day's j on this side
Deut 1: 2 It is eleven days' j from
Josh 9:13 because of the very long j.
2Sa 11:10 "Did you not come from a j?
1Ki 18:27 he is busy, or he is on a j,
Ezra 7: 9 first month he began his j
Prov 7:19 He has gone on a long j;
Jon 3: 3 a three-day j in extent.
Matt 10:10 "nor bag for your j,
Mark 6: 8 to take nothing for the j
Luke 2:44 company, they went a day's j,
Luke 9: 3 "Take nothing for the j,
John 4: 6 being wearied from His j,
Acts 1:12 Jerusalem, a Sabbath day's j.
Rom 15:24 whenever I j to Spain, I
1Co 16:11 But send him on his j in

JOURNEYED (see JOURNEY)
Gen 11: 2 as they j from the east,
Gen 12: 9 So Abram j, going on still

Gen 13:11 and Lot j east. And they
Gen 35:21 Then Israel j and pitched
Ex 12:37 the children of Israel j
Num 9:23 command of the LORD they j;
Luke 9:57 Now it happened as they j on
Luke 10:33 a certain Samaritan, as he j,
Luke 15:13 j to a far country, and
Acts 9: 3 As he j he came near

JOURNEYING† (see JOURNEY)
Luke 13:22 and j toward Jerusalem.

JOURNEYS (see JOURNEY)
Ex 40:38 throughout all their j.
Num 10: 6 for them to begin their j.
Num 33: 2 starting points of their j
2Co 11:26 in j often, in perils of

JOY (see JOYFUL)
Gen 31:27 have sent you away with j
1Sa 18: 6 with tambourines, with j,
1Ki 1:40 and rejoiced with great j,
Neh 8:10 for the j of the LORD is
Esth 8:17 the Jews had j and gladness,
Job 20: 5 And the j of the hypocrite
Job 29:13 widow's heart to sing for j.
Job 38: 7 sons of God shouted for j?
Ps 16:11 presence is fullness of j;
Ps 21: 1 The king shall have j in
Ps 27: 6 I will offer sacrifices of j
Ps 30: 5 But j comes in the
Ps 32:11 righteous; And shout for j,
Ps 43: 4 God, To God my exceeding j;
Ps 48: 2 The j of the whole earth,
Ps 51: 8 Make me hear j and gladness,
Ps 51:12 Restore to me the j of Your
Ps 67: 4 be glad and sing for j!
Ps 126: 5 in tears Shall reap in j.
Ps 137: 6 Jerusalem Above my chief j.
Prov 14:10 does not share its j.
Prov 15:21 Folly is j to him who
Prov 17:21 father of a fool has no j.
Eccl 5:20 keeps him busy with the j
Eccl 9: 7 Go, eat your bread with j,
Is 12: 3 Therefore with j you will
Is 22:13 j and gladness, Slaying
Is 24: 8 The j of the harp ceases.
Is 24:11 All j is darkened, The
Is 35:10 With everlasting j on their
Is 51: 3 J and gladness will be
Is 51:11 With everlasting j on their
Is 52: 9 Break forth into j,
Is 55:12 you shall go out with j,
Is 60: 5 heart shall swell with j;
Is 61: 3 The oil of j for mourning,
Jer 15:16 Your word was to me the j
Jer 31:13 turn their mourning to j,
Jer 48:33 J and gladness are taken
Jer 49:25 deserted, the city of My j?
Lam 5:15 The j of our heart has
Ezek 36: 5 with whole-hearted j and
Joel 1:12 Surely j has withered away
Zech 8:19 Shall be j and gladness and
Matt 2:10 with exceedingly great j.
Matt 13:20 receives it with j;
Matt 25:21 Enter into the j of your
Matt 28: 8 tomb with fear and great j,
Luke 1:14 And you will have j and
Luke 1:44 babe leaped in my womb for j.
Luke 2:10 you good tidings of great j
Luke 6:23 in that day and leap for j!
Luke 8:13 receive the word with j;
Luke 10:17 the seventy returned with j,
Luke 15: 7 there will be more j in
Luke 15:10 there is j in the presence
Luke 24:41 still did not believe for j,

Luke 24:52 to Jerusalem with great j,
John 15:11 that My j may remain in you,
John 15:11 and that your j may be
John 16:20 sorrow will be turned into j.
John 16:22 and your j no one will take
John 16:24 that your j may be full.
John 17:13 that they may have My j
Acts 2:28 make me full of j in
Acts 8: 8 And there was great j in that
Acts 13:52 were filled with j and with
Acts 20:24 I may finish my race with j,
Rom 14:17 and peace and j in the Holy
Rom 15:13 of hope fill you with all j
Rom 15:32 I may come to you with j by
2Co 1:24 fellow workers for your j;
2Co 2: 3 in you all that my j is
2Co 8: 2 the abundance of their j
Gal 5:22 of the Spirit is love, j,
Phil 1: 4 request for you all with j,
Phil 1:25 all for your progress and j
Phil 2: 2 fulfill my j by being
Phil 4: 1 my j and crown, so stand
Col 1:11 and longsuffering with j;
1Th 1: 6 with j of the Holy Spirit,
1Th 2:19 For what is our hope, or j,
1Th 2:20 For you are our glory and j.
Heb 12: 2 who for the j that was set
Jas 1: 2 count it all j when you fall
1Pe 1: 8 you rejoice with j
1Pe 4:13 be glad with exceeding j.
1Jn 1: 4 we write to you that your j
3Jn 4 I have no greater j than to
Jude 24 His glory with exceeding j,

JOYFUL (see JOY, JOYFULLY)
Job 3: 7 night be barren! May no j
Ps 35: 9 And my soul shall be j in
Ps 63: 5 shall praise You with j
Ps 66: 1 Make a j shout to God, all
Ps 89:15 the people who know the j
Ps 96:12 Let the field be j,
Ps 98: 8 Let the hills be j together
Ps 100: 1 Make a j shout to the LORD,
Ps 113: 9 Like a j mother of
Ps 149: 5 Let the saints be j in
Eccl 7:14 the day of prosperity be j,
Is 49:13 Sing, O heavens! Be j,
Is 56: 7 And make them j in My house
Is 61:10 My soul shall be j in my
2Co 7: 4 I am exceedingly j in all
Heb 12:11 no chastening seems to be j

JOYFULLY (see JOYFUL)
Ps 95: 1 the LORD! Let us shout j
Ps 98: 4 Shout j to the LORD, all
Eccl 9: 9 Live j with the wife whom
Luke 19: 6 down, and received Him j.

JOZADAK (see JEHOZADAK)
Ezra 3: 2 Then Jeshua the son of J and

JUBAL†
Gen 4:21 His brother's name was J.

JUBILEE
Lev 25:11 fiftieth year shall be a J
Lev 25:28 it until the Year of J;
Lev 25:28 and in the J it shall be
Lev 25:40 you until the Year of J.
Lev 27:17 his field from the Year of J,

JUDAH (see JUDAH'S, JUDEA)
Gen 35:23 and Simeon, Levi, J,
Gen 37:26 So J said to his brothers,
Gen 38: 6 Then J took a wife for Er his
Gen 38:11 Then J said to Tamar his
Gen 49: 9 J is a lion's whelp
Gen 49:10 shall not depart from J,

Ex	1: 2	Reuben, Simeon, Levi, and J;
Ex	31: 2	of Hur, of the tribe of J.
Num	1:27	numbered of the tribe of J
Deut	34: 2	all the land of J as far as
Josh	11:21	from all the mountains of J,
Josh	19:34	and ended at J by the Jordan
Josh	21:11	in the mountains of J,
Judg	1: 2	J shall go up. Indeed I have
Judg	1:16	into the Wilderness of J,
Judg	17: 7	man from Bethlehem in J,
Judg	20:18	The LORD said, "J first!"
Ruth	1: 1	certain man of Bethlehem, J,
Ruth	1: 7	to return to the land of J.
Ruth	4:12	Perez, whom Tamar bore to J,
1Sa	27: 6	belonged to the kings of J
2Sa	2: 1	up to any of the cities of J?
2Sa	2: 4	king over the house of J.
2Sa	3:10	David over Israel and over J,
2Sa	5: 5	In Hebron he reigned over J
2Sa	19:14	hearts of all the men of J,
2Sa	19:16	came down with the men of J
2Sa	24: 1	"Go, number Israel and J
2Sa	24: 7	they went out to South J
1Ki	2:32	commander of the army of J—
1Ki	4:20	J and Israel were as
1Ki	4:25	And J and Israel dwelt
1Ki	12:21	all the house of J with the
1Ki	12:23	son of Solomon, king of J,
1Ki	12:27	lord, Rehoboam king of J,
1Ki	14:22	Now J did evil in the sight
1Ki	14:29	chronicles of the kings of J?
1Ki	15:22	throughout all J;
1Ki	19: 3	which belongs to J,
2Ki	8:19	LORD would not destroy J,
2Ki	14:12	And J was defeated by Israel,
2Ki	14:22	Elath and restored it to J,
2Ki	16: 6	and drove the men of J from
2Ki	17:18	none left but the tribe of J
2Ki	17:19	Also J did not keep the
2Ki	18:13	the fortified cities of J
2Ki	19:30	escaped of the house of J
2Ki	21:12	upon Jerusalem and J,
2Ki	23: 1	gather all the elders of J
2Ki	23: 8	priests from the cities of J,
2Ki	23:26	anger was aroused against J,
2Ki	23:27	I will also remove J from My
2Ki	24: 2	He sent them against J to
2Ki	25:21	Thus J was carried away
2Ki	25:27	Jehoiachin king of J from
2Ch	11:17	the kingdom of J,
2Ch	12:12	things also went well in J.
2Ch	13:15	Then the men of J gave a
2Ch	15: 8	from all the land of J and
2Ch	16:11	the book of the kings of J
2Ch	20: 3	a fast throughout all J.
2Ch	20:17	O J and Jerusalem!' Do not
2Ch	20:20	O J and you inhabitants of
2Ch	25:13	they raided the cities of J
2Ch	25:28	his fathers in the City of J.
2Ch	28:18	and of the South of J,
2Ch	28:19	For the LORD brought J low
2Ch	28:19	moral decline in J and had
2Ch	32: 1	Assyria came and entered J;
2Ch	32:25	looming over him and over J
2Ch	33: 9	So Manasseh seduced J and the
2Ch	34: 3	year he began to purge J
2Ch	34: 9	from all J and Benjamin, and
2Ch	36:23	at Jerusalem which is in J.
Ezra	1: 2	at Jerusalem which is in J.
Ezra	1: 8	Sheshbazzar the prince of J.
Ezra	2: 1	returned to Jerusalem and J,
Ezra	4: 1	when the adversaries of J
Ezra	9: 9	and to give us a wall in J
Neh	2: 5	I ask that you send me to J,
Neh	5:14	governor in the land of J,
Neh	13:12	Then all J brought the tithe
Neh	13:24	not speak the language of J,
Ps	48:11	Let the daughters of J be
Ps	60: 7	J is My lawgiver.
Ps	69:35	And build the cities of J,
Ps	76: 1	In J God is known; His
Ps	97: 8	And the daughters of J
Ps	114: 2	J became His sanctuary,
Prov	25: 1	men of Hezekiah king of J
Is	1: 1	which he saw concerning J
Is	2: 1	son of Amoz saw concerning J
Is	5: 7	And the men of J are His
Is	7:17	that Ephraim departed from J.
Is	11:13	Ephraim shall not envy J,
Is	26: 1	be sung in the land of J:
Is	36: 1	the fortified cities of J
Is	40: 9	Say to the cities of J,
Is	48: 1	from the wellsprings of J;
Jer	1: 3	the son of Josiah, king of J,
Jer	1:15	against all the cities of J.
Jer	1:18	land—Against the kings of J,
Jer	2:28	cities Are your gods, O J.
Jer	3: 7	And her treacherous sister J
Jer	4: 5	Declare in J and proclaim in
Jer	8: 1	the bones of the kings of J,
Jer	9:11	I will make the cities of J
Jer	10:22	To make the cities of J
Jer	11:13	cities were your gods, O J;
Jer	13: 9	I will ruin the pride of J
Jer	13:19	J shall be carried away
Jer	14: 2	J mourns, And her gates
Jer	14:19	You utterly rejected J?
Jer	17: 1	The sin of J is written with
Jer	19: 7	make void the counsel of J
Jer	19:13	the houses of the kings of J
Jer	23: 6	In His days J will be saved,
Jer	28: 4	with all the captives of J
Jer	29: 2	the princes of J and
Jer	29:22	up by all the captivity of J
Jer	30: 3	My people Israel and J,
Jer	32:35	to cause J to sin.'
Jer	33: 7	cause the captives of J and
Jer	33:16	In those days J will be
Jer	34: 7	and all the cities of J
Jer	36:31	and on the men of J all the
Jer	39: 6	killed all the nobles of J.
Jer	39:10	guard left in the land of J
Jer	40: 5	over the cities of J,
Jer	40:11	had left a remnant of J,
Jer	44: 6	kindled in the cities of J,
Jer	44: 9	wickedness of the kings of J,
Jer	44:26	in the mouth of any man of J
Jer	51: 5	is not forsaken, nor J,
Jer	51:59	with Zedekiah the king of J
Lam	1: 3	J has gone into captivity,
Lam	1:15	The virgin daughter of J.
Ezek	8: 1	house with the elders of J
Ezek	37:19	with it, with the stick of J,
Dan	1: 2	gave Jehoiakim king of J
Dan	1: 6	those of the sons of J were
Dan	5:13	one of the captives from J,
Hos	1: 1	and Hezekiah, kings of J,
Hos	1: 7	have mercy on the house of J
Hos	5: 5	J also stumbles with them.
Hos	5:12	And to the house of J like
Hos	5:13	And J saw his wound, Then
Hos	5:14	young lion to the house of J.
Hos	6: 4	what shall I do to you? O J,
Hos	11:12	But J still walks with God,
Hos	12: 2	brings a charge against J,
Joel	3: 1	back the captives of J and
Joel	3:20	But J shall abide forever,
Amos	1: 1	the days of Uzziah king of J,
Amos	2: 4	three transgressions of J,
Amos	2: 5	I will send a fire upon J,

Amos	7:12	seer! Flee to the land of **J**.
Mic	1: 1	and Hezekiah, kings of **J**,
Mic	1: 5	are the high places of **J**?
Mic	5: 2	among the thousands of **J**,
Zeph	1: 1	the son of Amon, king of **J**.
Zeph	2: 7	remnant of the house of **J**;
Hag	1: 1	of Shealtiel, governor of **J**,
Hag	2:21	to Zerubbabel, governor of **J**,
Zech	1:19	horns that have scattered **J**,
Zech	8:19	feasts For the house of **J**.
Zech	9:13	For I have bent **J**,
Zech	12: 2	they lay siege against **J**
Zech	12: 5	And the governors of **J** shall
Zech	14:21	every pot in Jerusalem and **J**
Mal	2:11	**J** has dealt treacherously,
Mal	2:11	For **J** has profaned The
Mal	3: 4	Then the offering of **J** and
Matt	1: 2	and Jacob begot **J** and his
Matt	2: 6	in the land of **J**,
Matt	2: 6	among the rulers of **J**;
Luke	1:39	with haste, to a city of **J**,
Heb	7:14	that our Lord arose from **J**,
Heb	8: 8	with the house of **J**—
Rev	5: 5	the Lion of the tribe of **J**,
Rev	7: 5	of the tribe of **J** twelve

JUDAH'S (*see* JUDAH)

Gen	38: 7	**J** firstborn, was wicked in
Jer	32: 2	which was in the king of **J**

JUDAISM † (*see* JEW)

Gal	1:13	of my former conduct in **J**,
Gal	1:14	And I advanced in **J** beyond

JUDAS (*see* BARSABAS, ISCARIOT, JUDE, THADDAEUS)

Matt	10: 4	and **J** Iscariot, who also
Matt	26:47	still speaking, behold, **J**,
Luke	22: 3	Then Satan entered **J**,
John	12: 4	**J** Iscariot, Simon's son,
John	13: 2	put it into the heart of **J**
John	13:29	because **J** had the money box,
John	14:22	**J** (not Iscariot) said to Him,
Acts	1:13	and **J** the son of James.
Acts	1:16	mouth of David concerning **J**,
Acts	1:25	apostleship from which **J** by
Acts	5:37	**J** of Galilee rose up in the
Acts	15:22	**J** who was also named

JUDE † (*see* JUDAS)

Jude	1	**J**, a bondservant of Jesus

JUDEA (*see* JUDAH)

Matt	2: 1	was born in Bethlehem of **J**
Matt	3: 1	in the wilderness of **J**,
Matt	4:25	Decapolis, Jerusalem, **J**,
Matt	19: 1	and came to the region of **J**
Mark	1: 5	Then all the land of **J**,
Luke	1:65	all the hill country of **J**.
Luke	2: 4	the city of Nazareth, into **J**,
Luke	3: 1	Pilate being governor of **J**,
Luke	5:17	of every town of Galilee, **J**,
John	4:47	that Jesus had come out of **J**
Acts	1: 8	and in all **J** and Samaria,
Acts	2: 9	**J** and Cappadocia, Pontus and
Rom	15:31	be delivered from those in **J**
2Co	1:16	helped by you on my way to **J**.
Gal	1:22	by face to the churches of **J**
1Th	2:14	of God which are in **J** in

JUDGE (*see* JUDGED, JUDGES, JUDGING, JUDGMENT)

Gen	15:14	whom they serve I will **j**;
Gen	18:25	it from You! Shall not the **J**
Ex	2:14	made you a prince and a **j**
Ex	18:13	that Moses sat to **j** the
Deut	1:16	and **j** righteously between a
Deut	17: 8	is too hard for you to **j**,
Deut	17:12	the LORD your God, or the **j**,
Deut	25: 1	that the judges may **j**

Deut	32:36	For the LORD will **j** His
Judg	2:18	the LORD was with the **j** and
Judg	2:19	when the **j** was dead, that
Judg	11:27	me. May the LORD, the **J**,
1Sa	2:10	The LORD will **j** the ends
1Sa	8: 6	Give us a king to **j** us." So
1Sa	24:12	Let the LORD **j** between you
2Sa	15: 4	that I were made **j** in the
1Ki	3: 9	an understanding heart to **j**
1Ch	16:33	For He is coming to **j** the
Ezra	7:25	and judges who may **j** all
Job	9:15	I would beg mercy of my **J**.
Job	23: 7	delivered forever from my **J**.
Ps	7: 8	The LORD shall **j** the
Ps	7: 8	**J** me, O LORD, according to
Ps	7:11	God is a just **j**,
Ps	9: 8	He shall **j** the world in
Ps	50: 6	For God Himself is **J**.
Ps	51: 4	And blameless when You **j**.
Ps	58: 1	Do you **j** uprightly, you
Ps	72: 2	He will **j** Your people with
Ps	75: 2	I will **j** uprightly.
Ps	75: 7	But God is the **J**:
Ps	82: 2	How long will you **j**
Ps	82: 8	**j** the earth; For You shall
Ps	96:13	for He is coming to **j** the
Ps	96:13	He shall **j** the world with
Prov	31: 9	**j** righteously, And plead
Eccl	3:17	God shall **j** the righteous and
Is	2: 4	He shall **j** between the
Is	11: 3	And He shall not **j** by the
Is	11: 4	righteousness He shall **j**
Is	33:22	(For the LORD is our **J**,
Jer	11:20	You who **j** righteously,
Lam	3:59	**J** my case.
Ezek	20: 4	Will you **j** them, son of man,
Ezek	34:17	I shall **j** between sheep and
Ezek	34:20	I Myself will **j** between the
Amos	2: 3	And I will cut off the **j**
Mic	3:11	Her heads **j** for a bribe,
Mic	4: 3	He shall **j** between many
Matt	5:25	deliver you to the **j**,
Matt	7: 1	**J** not, that you be not
Matt	7: 2	with what judgment you **j**,
Luke	12:14	who made Me a **j** or an
Luke	12:58	lest he drag you to the **j**,
Luke	18: 6	Hear what the unjust **j** said.
Luke	19:22	of your own mouth I will **j**
John	5:30	do nothing. As I hear, I **j**;
John	7:24	but **j** with righteous
John	7:51	Does our law **j** a man before
John	8:15	You **j** according to the flesh;
John	8:15	I **j** no one.
John	8:16	"And yet if I do **j**,
John	12:47	for I did not come to **j** the
John	12:48	that I have spoken will **j**
John	18:31	You take Him and **j** Him
Acts	7:27	you a ruler and a **j**
Acts	10:42	ordained by God to be **J**
Acts	13:46	and **j** yourselves unworthy of
Acts	17:31	a day on which He will **j**
Acts	18:15	for I do not want to be a **j**
Acts	23: 3	wall! For you sit to **j** me
Rom	2: 1	O man, whoever you are who **j**,
Rom	2: 1	for in whatever you **j**
Rom	2:16	in the day when God will **j**
Rom	3: 6	For then how will God **j** the
Rom	14: 3	not him who does not eat **j**
Rom	14: 4	Who are you to **j** another's
Rom	14:10	But why do you **j** your
Rom	14:13	Therefore let us not **j** one
1Co	6: 2	know that the saints will **j**
1Co	6: 3	you not know that we shall **j**
1Co	10:15	**j** for yourselves what I say.
1Co	11:31	For if we would **j** ourselves,

Col	2:16	So let no one j you in food
2Ti	4: 1	who will j the living and
2Ti	4: 8	the Lord, the righteous J,
Heb	10:30	The LORD will j His
Heb	12:23	to God the J of all, to the
Heb	13: 4	and adulterers God will j.
Jas	4:11	But if you j the law, you
Jas	4:12	Who are you to j another?
Jas	5: 9	the J is standing at the
1Pe	4: 5	to Him who is ready to j
Rev	6:10	until You j and avenge our

JUDGED (see JUDGE)

Ex	18:26	but they j every small case
Judg	3:10	and he j Israel. He went out
1Sa	7: 6	And Samuel j the children
Ps	37:33	condemn him when he is j.
Jer	22:16	He j the cause of the poor
Dan	9:12	against our judges who j us,
Matt	7: 1	not, that you be not j.
Luke	7:43	to him, "You have rightly j.
John	16:11	the ruler of this world is j.
Acts	23: 6	of the dead I am being j!"
Rom	2:12	sinned in the law will be j
Rom	3: 4	overcome when You are j.
1Co	6: 2	And if the world will be j
1Co	10:29	For why is my liberty j by
1Co	11:31	ourselves, we would not be j.
Heb	11:11	because she j Him faithful
Jas	2:12	so do as those who will be j
Rev	11:18	dead, that they should be j,
Rev	19: 2	because He has j the great
Rev	20:12	And the dead were j
Rev	20:13	in them. And they were j,

JUDGES (see JUDGE)

Ex	21: 6	shall bring him to the j.
Ex	21:22	and he shall pay as the j
Deut	16:18	You shall appoint j and
Deut	19:17	the priests and the j who
Deut	25: 1	that the j may judge them,
Josh	8:33	elders and officers and j,
Judg	2:16	the LORD raised up j who
Judg	2:17	would not listen to their j,
Ruth	1: 1	in the days when the j
1Sa	8: 1	old that he made his sons j
Job	9:24	covers the faces of its j.
Job	12:17	And makes fools of the j.
Job	36:31	For by these He j the
Ps	2:10	you j of the earth.
Ps	58:11	Surely He is God who j in
Ps	82: 1	He j among the gods.
Ps	148:11	Princes and all j of the
Prov	29:14	The king who j the poor with
Is	1:26	I will restore your j as at
Dan	9:12	us and against our j who
Hos	7: 7	And have devoured their j;
Zeph	3: 3	Her j are evening wolves
John	5:22	For the Father j no one, but
John	8:50	there is One who seeks and j.
Acts	13:20	After that He gave them j
1Co	2:15	But he who is spiritual j all
1Co	4: 4	but He who j me is the Lord.
Jas	2: 4	and become j with evil
Jas	4:11	evil of a brother and j his
Jas	4:11	evil of the law and j the
1Pe	1:17	who without partiality j
1Pe	2:23	Himself to Him who j
Rev	18: 8	is the Lord God who j her.
Rev	19:11	and in righteousness He j

JUDGING (see JUDGE)

Judg	4: 4	was j Israel at that time.
Matt	19:28	j the twelve tribes of
1Co	5:12	what have I to do with j

JUDGMENT (see JUDGE, JUDGMENTS)

Ex	12:12	of Egypt I will execute j:
Ex	23: 6	shall not pervert the j of
Ex	28:15	make the breastplate of j.
Lev	19:15	shall do no injustice in j.
Deut	1:17	not show partiality in j;
Deut	1:17	for the j is God's. The
Deut	16:18	judge the people with just j.
Deut	17: 9	upon you the sentence of j.
Judg	4: 5	Israel came up to her for j.
Judg	11:27	render j this day between
2Sa	8:15	and David administered j and
1Ki	7: 7	the throne, the Hall of J,
2Ki	25: 6	and they pronounced j on
1Ch	18:14	and administered j and
2Ch	22: 8	when Jehu was executing j on
Job	8: 3	Does God subvert j?
Job	14: 3	And bring me to j with
Job	22: 4	And enters into j with you?
Job	34:23	he should go before God in j.
Job	36:17	you are filled with the j
Job	40: 8	you indeed annul My j?
Ps	1: 5	shall not stand in the j,
Ps	9: 7	prepared His throne for j.
Ps	9: 8	And He shall administer j
Ps	9:16	LORD is known by the j He
Ps	76: 9	When God arose to j,
Ps	119:66	Teach me good j and
Ps	122: 5	thrones are set there for j,
Ps	143: 2	Do not enter into j with
Ps	149: 9	on them the written j—
Prov	1: 3	of wisdom, Justice, j,
Prov	16:10	must not transgress in j.
Prov	18: 1	He rages against all wise j.
Prov	20: 8	who sits on the throne of j
Prov	24:23	good to show partiality in j.
Eccl	8: 5	discerns both time and j,
Eccl	11: 9	God will bring you into j.
Eccl	12:14	will bring every work into j,
Is	4: 4	by the spirit of j and by
Is	9: 7	it and establish it with j
Is	16: 3	"Take counsel, execute j;
Is	28: 6	justice to him who sits in j,
Is	28:26	He instructs him in right j,
Is	41: 1	us come near together for j.
Is	53: 8	taken from prison and from j,
Jer	5: 1	is anyone who executes j,
Jer	5: 4	The j of their God.
Jer	8: 7	My people do not know the j
Jer	39: 5	where He pronounced j on
Jer	51: 9	For her j reaches to heaven
Jer	51:47	coming That I will bring j
Ezek	23:24	I will delegate j to them,
Ezek	34:16	strong, and feed them in j.
Dan	7:22	and a j was made in favor
Hos	10: 4	Thus j springs up like
Joel	3: 2	And I will enter into j
Hab	1: 4	Therefore perverse j
Hab	1:12	have appointed them for j;
Zech	8:16	Give j in your gates for
Matt	5:21	will be in danger of the j.
Matt	7: 2	For with what j you judge,
Matt	10:15	and Gomorrah in the day of j
Matt	12:41	will rise up in the j with
Matt	12:42	South will rise up in the j
Matt	27:19	he was sitting on the j
Luke	10:14	for Tyre and Sidon at the j
John	5:22	but has committed all j to
John	5:24	and shall not come into j,
John	5:27	Him authority to execute j
John	5:30	and My j is righteous,
John	8:16	My j is true; for I am not
John	9:39	For j I have come into this
John	12:31	Now is the j of this world;
John	16: 8	of righteousness, and of j:

John 19:13 out and sat down in the j
Acts 24:25 and the j to come, Felix was
Acts 25:10 I stand at Caesar's j seat,
Rom 1:32 knowing the righteous j of
Rom 5:18 one man's offense j came
Rom 13: 2 who resist will bring j on
Rom 14:10 all stand before the j seat
1Co 1:10 same mind and in the same j.
1Co 7:25 yet I give j as one whom the
1Co 11:29 manner eats and drinks j to
1Co 11:34 lest you come together for j.
Gal 5:10 you shall bear his j,
2Th 1: 5 evidence of the righteous j
Heb 6: 2 the dead, and of eternal j.
Heb 9:27 once, but after this the j,
Heb 10:27 fearful expectation of j,
Jas 2:13 For j is without mercy to the
Jas 2:13 mercy. Mercy triumphs over j.
Jas 3: 1 shall receive a stricter j.
Jas 5:12 "No," lest you fall into j.
1Pe 4:17 the time has come for j
2Pe 2: 4 to be reserved for j;
2Pe 2: 9 punishment for the day of j,
2Pe 3: 7 for fire until the day of j
1Jn 4:17 boldness in the day of j;
Jude 6 under darkness for the j of
Jude 15 to execute j on all, to
Rev 14: 7 for the hour of His j has
Rev 17: 1 I will show you the j of the
Rev 20: 4 and j was committed to them.

JUDGMENTS (*see* JUDGMENT)
Ex 6: 6 arm and with great j.
Ex 7: 4 the land of Egypt by great j.
Lev 18: 4 You shall observe My j and
Lev 18: 5 keep My statutes and My j,
Lev 26:15 or if your soul abhors My j,
Lev 26:43 because they despised My j
Num 33: 4 the LORD had executed j.
Deut 8:11 His commandments, His j,
1Ch 16:12 and the j of His mouth,
1Ch 16:14 His j are in all the
Neh 9:29 But sinned against Your j,
Ps 10: 5 Your j are far above, out
Ps 18:22 For all His j were before
Ps 19: 9 The j of the LORD are
Ps 36: 6 Your j are a great deep;
Ps 72: 1 Give the king Your j,
Ps 89:30 law And do not walk in My j,
Ps 119:30 Your j I have laid before
Ps 119:39 For Your j are good.
Ps 119:52 I remembered Your j of old,
Ps 119:120 And I am afraid of Your j.
Ps 119:156 me according to Your j.
Ps 119:160 one of Your righteous j
Ezek 5: 6 for they have refused My j,
Ezek 5: 8 you and will execute j in
Ezek 14:21 I send My four severe j on
Ezek 20:18 fathers, nor observe their j,
Ezek 25:11 And I will execute j upon
Ezek 36:27 and you will keep My j and
Ezek 37:24 shall also walk in My j and
Dan 9: 5 Your precepts and Your j.
Hos 6: 5 And your j are like light
Rom 11:33 How unsearchable are His j
Rev 16: 7 and righteous are Your j.

JUG
Judg 4:19 So she opened a j of milk,
1Sa 26:12 took the spear and the j of

JUICE
Num 6: 3 shall he drink any grape j,

JURISDICTION†
Luke 23: 7 He belonged to Herod's j,

JUST (*see* HONEST, JUSTICE, JUSTIFY, JUSTLY, UNJUST)
Gen 6: 9 Noah was a j man, perfect in
Gen 27:19 I have done j as you told
Ex 7: 6 j as the LORD commanded
Deut 16:18 judge the people with j
Deut 16:20 follow what is altogether j,
Judg 6:39 but let me speak j once
2Sa 23: 3 rules over men must be j,
Neh 9:13 And gave them j ordinances
Ps 7:11 God is a j judge, And God
Ps 17: 1 Hear a j cause, O LORD,
Ps 51: 4 That You may be found j when
Prov 3:12 J as a father the son in
Prov 4:18 But the path of the j is
Prov 11: 1 But a j weight is His
Eccl 7:15 There is a j man who
Eccl 7:20 For there is not a j man
Is 26: 7 The way of the j is
Is 26: 7 You weigh the path of the j.
Is 29:21 And turn aside the j by
Is 40:27 And my j claim is passed
Is 45:21 A j God and a Savior;
Is 49: 4 Yet surely my j reward is
Is 52:14 J as many were astonished at
Lam 4:13 midst The blood of the j.
Ezek 18: 5 But if a man is j And does
Amos 5:12 Afflicting the j and
Hab 2: 4 But the j shall live by his
Zech 9: 9 He is j and having
Matt 1:19 being a j man, and not
Matt 5:45 and sends rain on the j and
Matt 13:49 the wicked from among the j,
Matt 27:19 nothing to do with that j
Matt 27:24 of the blood of this j
Mark 6:56 Him that they might j touch
Mark 14:16 and found it j as He had
Mark 14:21 Son of Man indeed goes j as
Luke 1: 2 j as those who from the
Luke 2:25 and this man was j and
Luke 6:31 And j as you want men to do
Luke 14:14 at the resurrection of the j.
Luke 15: 7 than over ninety-nine j
Luke 19:32 their way and found it j
John 5:23 all should honor the Son j
Acts 10:22 a j man, one who fears God
Acts 22:14 and see the J One, and hear
Acts 24:15 both of the j and the
Rom 1:17 The j shall live by
Rom 2:13 hearers of the law are j
Rom 3: 8 say. Their condemnation is j.
Rom 3:26 that He might be j and the
Rom 5:12 j as through one man sin
Rom 6: 4 that j as Christ was raised
Rom 7:12 the commandment holy and j
1Co 13:12 but then I shall know j as I
Gal 3:11 the j shall live by
Eph 2: 3 j as the others.
Eph 4: 4 j as you were called in one
Eph 4:32 j as God in Christ forgave
Eph 5:25 j as Christ also loved the
Phil 4: 8 whatever things are j,
Col 4: 1 your bondservants what is j
1Th 5:11 j as you also are doing.
Tit 1: 8 is good, sober-minded, j,
Heb 2: 2 disobedience received a j
Heb 10:38 Now the j shall live
Heb 12:23 to the spirits of j men made
Jas 5: 6 you have murdered the j;
1Pe 3:18 the j for the unjust, that
1Jn 1: 9 He is faithful and j to
1Jn 2: 6 himself also to walk j as
1Jn 3: 3 j as He is pure.
1Jn 3: 7 j as He is righteous.
Rev 15: 3 Lord God Almighty! J and
Rev 16: 6 For it is their j due."

JUSTICE (*see* JUST)
Gen 18:19 to do righteousness and j,
Ex 23: 2 after many to pervert j.
Deut 10:18 He administers j for the
Deut 32: 4 For all His ways are j,
1Ki 3:11 understanding to discern j,
Esth 1:13 all who knew law and j,
Job 8: 3 does the Almighty pervert j?
Job 19: 7 I cry aloud, there is no j.
Job 27: 2 who has taken away my j,
Job 29:14 My j was like a robe and a
Job 34: 4 Let us choose j for
Ps 10:18 To do j to the fatherless
Ps 25: 9 The humble He guides in j,
Ps 33: 5 loves righteousness and j;
Ps 37: 6 And your j as the noonday.
Ps 37:30 And his tongue talks of j.
Ps 72: 4 He will bring j to the poor
Ps 82: 3 Do j to the afflicted and
Ps 89:14 Righteousness and j are the
Ps 101: 1 I will sing of mercy and j;
Ps 119:149 me according to Your j.
Prov 2: 8 He guards the paths of j,
Prov 13:23 And for lack of j there is
Prov 19:28 witness scorns j,
Prov 21:15 a joy for the just to do j,
Is 1:17 Learn to do good; Seek j,
Is 5: 7 plant. He looked for j,
Is 9: 7 it with judgment and j
Is 10: 2 To rob the needy of j,
Is 30:18 the LORD is a God of j;
Is 42: 1 He will bring forth j to
Is 42: 4 Till He has established j
Is 59: 4 No one calls for j,
Is 59: 9 Therefore j is far from us,
Is 59:11 like doves; We look for j,
Jer 31:23 LORD bless you, O home of j,
Dan 4:37 are truth, and His ways j.
Hos 2:19 Me In righteousness and j,
Amos 5: 7 You who turn j to wormwood,
Amos 5:12 the poor from j at the
Amos 5:15 Establish j in the gate.
Amos 5:24 But let j run down like
Amos 6:12 Yet you have turned j into
Hab 1: 4 And j never goes forth.
Zech 7: 9 of hosts: 'Execute true j,
Mal 2:17 "Where is the God of j?
Matt 12:18 And He will declare j
Matt 12:20 Till He sends forth j
Matt 23:23 j and mercy and faith. These
Luke 11:42 and pass by j and the love
Luke 18: 3 Get j for me from my
Acts 8:33 His humiliation His j

JUSTIFICATION (*see* JUSTIFY)
Rom 4:25 was raised because of our j.
Rom 5:16 many offenses resulted in j.

JUSTIFIED (*see* JUSTIFY)
Job 40: 8 condemn Me that you may be j?
Is 43: 9 that they may be j;
Matt 11:19 sinners!' But wisdom is j
Matt 12:37 by your words you will be j,
Luke 7:29 even the tax collectors j
Luke 18:14 man went down to his house j
Acts 13:39 everyone who believes in j
Acts 13:39 which you could not be j by
Rom 2:13 doers of the law will be j;
Rom 3: 4 That You may be j in
Rom 3:20 the law no flesh will be j
Rom 3:24 being j freely by His grace
Rom 3:28 we conclude that a man is j
Rom 4: 2 For if Abraham was j by
Rom 5: 1 having been j by faith, we
Rom 5: 9 having now been j by His
Rom 8:30 He called, these He also j;

1Co 6:11 but you were j in the name
Gal 2:16 that a man is not j
Gal 2:16 that we might be j by faith
Gal 2:16 the law no flesh shall be j.
Gal 3:11 But that no one is j by the
Gal 3:24 that we might be j by faith.
Gal 5: 4 you who attempt to be j by
1Ti 3:16 **J** in the Spirit, Seen by
Jas 2:21 not Abraham our father j by
Jas 2:24 see then that a man is j by
Jas 2:25 not Rahab the harlot also j

JUSTIFIER† (*see* JUSTIFY)
Rom 3:26 He might be just and the j

JUSTIFIES (*see* JUSTIFY)
Prov 17:15 He who j the wicked, and he
Rom 4: 5 but believes on Him who j
Rom 8:33 elect? It is God who j.

JUSTIFY (*see* JUST, JUSTIFICATION, JUSTIFIED, JUSTIFIER, JUSTIFIES)
Ex 23: 7 For I will not j the wicked.
Is 53:11 My righteous Servant shall j
Rom 3:30 is one God who will j the
Gal 3: 8 foreseeing that God would j

JUSTLY† (*see* JUST)
Mic 6: 8 require of you But to do j,
Luke 23:41 "And we indeed j,
1Th 2:10 how devoutly and j and

JUSTUS (*see* BARSABAS, JESUS)
Acts 1:23 Barsabas, who was surnamed **J**,
Col 4:11 and Jesus who is called **J**.

K

KAB†
2Ki 6:25 one-fourth of a **k** of dove

KADESH (*see* KADESH BARNEA, KEDESH)
Num 13:26 Wilderness of Paran, at **K**;
Num 20: 1 and the people stayed in **K**;
Ps 29: 8 shakes the Wilderness of **K**.

KADESH BARNEA (*see* KADESH)
Num 32: 8 away from **K** to see the land
Deut 1: 2 by way of Mount Seir to **K**
Deut 1:19 Then we came to **K**
Deut 2:14 **K** until we crossed over
Josh 14: 7 me from **K** to spy out the land

KARNAIM (*see* ASHTEROTH)
Gen 14: 5 the Rephaim in Ashteroth **K**,

KEDAR
Song 1: 5 Like the tents of **K**,
Is 21:17 men of the people of **K**,
Is 60: 7 All the flocks of **K** shall be
Ezek 27:21 and all the princes of **K**

KEDESH (*see* KADESH)
Josh 20: 7 So they appointed **K** in
Judg 4: 6 the son of Abinoam from **K**

KEEP (*see* KEEPER, KEEPING, KEEPS, KEPT)
Gen 2:15 of Eden to tend and **k** it.
Gen 6:19 to **k** them alive with you;
Gen 17: 9 you shall **k** My covenant, you
Gen 18:19 that they **k** the way of the
Gen 28:15 I am with you and will **k**
Gen 30:31 I will again feed and **k** your
Gen 41:35 and let them **k** food in the
Ex 6: 5 Israel whom the Egyptians **k**
Ex 12:14 and you shall **k** it as a
Ex 12:48 with you and wants to **k**
Ex 15:26 to His commandments and **k**

Ex	16:28	long do you refuse to **k**
Ex	19: 5	indeed obey My voice and **k**
Ex	20: 6	to those who love Me and **k**
Ex	20: 8	Sabbath day, to **k** it holy.
Ex	23:14	Three times you shall **k** a
Ex	31:13	My Sabbaths you shall **k,**
Lev	8:35	and the charge of the
Lev	18: 4	observe My judgments and **k**
Num	6:24	The LORD bless you and **k**
Num	31:18	But **k** alive for yourselves
Deut	4: 9	and diligently **k** yourself,
Deut	5:10	to those who love Me and **k**
Deut	5:12	to **k** it holy, as the LORD
Deut	5:15	your God commanded you to **k**
Deut	7: 8	and because He would **k** the
Deut	8: 2	whether you would **k** His
Deut	23: 9	then **k** yourself from every
Deut	24:12	you shall not **k** his pledge
Judg	2:22	whether they will **k** the ways
1Sa	17:34	Your servant used to **k** his
2Sa	18:18	I have no son to **k** my name in
1Ki	8:25	now **k** what You promised Your
2Ki	2: 3	Yes, I know, **k** silent!"
2Ki	23:21	**K** the Passover to the LORD
1Ch	4:10	and that You would **k** me
Esth	3: 8	and they do not **k** the king's
Job	22:15	Will you **k** to the old way
Ps	17: 8	**K** me as the apple of Your
Ps	19:13	**K** back Your servant also
Ps	22:29	Even he who cannot **k**
Ps	25:10	To such as **k** His covenant
Ps	33:19	And to **k** them alive in
Ps	34:13	**K** your tongue from evil,
Ps	50: 3	and shall not **k** silent; A
Ps	78:10	They did not **k** the covenant
Ps	78:56	And did not **k** His
Ps	91:11	To **k** you in all your ways.
Ps	103: 9	Nor will He **k** His anger
Ps	103:18	To such as **k** His covenant,
Ps	119:17	That I may live and **k** Your
Ps	119:33	And I shall **k** it to the
Ps	119:34	and I shall **k** Your law;
Ps	119:69	But I will **k** Your precepts
Ps	119:146	and I will **k** Your
Ps	141: 3	**K** watch over the door
Ps	140: 4	**K** me, O LORD, from the
Prov	1:15	**K** your foot from their
Prov	3:26	And will **k** your foot from
Prov	4: 4	**K** my commands, and live.
Prov	4:13	**K** her, for she is your
Prov	4:23	**K** your heart with all
Prov	6:24	To **k** you from the evil
Prov	22:18	a pleasant thing if you **k**
Eccl	2:10	my eyes desired I did not **k**
Eccl	3: 7	A time to **k** silence, And a
Eccl	4:11	they will **k** warm; But how
Eccl	8: 2	**K** the king's commandment for
Eccl	12:13	Fear God and **k** His
Is	6: 9	**K** on hearing, but do not
Is	26: 3	You will **k** him in perfect
Is	32: 6	To **k** the hungry
Is	41: 1	**K** silence before Me, O
Jer	3: 5	Will He **k** it to the end?'
Jer	34: 9	that no one should **k** a Jewish
Jer	42: 4	I will **k** nothing back from
Ezek	11:20	walk in My statutes and **k**
Dan	9: 4	and with those who **k** His
Amos	5:13	Therefore the prudent **k**
Hab	2:20	Let all the earth **k** silence
Matt	19:17	**k** the commandments."
Matt	26:18	I will **k** the Passover at
Luke	4:10	over you, To **k** you,'
Luke	11:28	hear the word of God and **k**
Luke	19:40	you that if these should **k**
John	8:55	but I do know Him and **k** His

John	9:16	because He does not **k** the
John	12:25	life in this world will **k**
John	14:15	**k** My commandments.
John	14:23	he will **k** My word; and My
John	17:11	**k** through Your name those
Acts	5: 3	lie to the Holy Spirit and **k**
Acts	10:28	it is for a Jewish man to **k**
Acts	15: 5	and to command them to **k**
Acts	15:24	must be circumcised and **k**
Acts	15:29	If you **k** yourselves from
Acts	16:23	commanding the jailer to **k**
Acts	18: 9	and do not **k** silent;
1Co	5: 8	Therefore let us **k** the feast,
1Co	11: 2	me in all things and **k** the
1Co	14:28	let him **k** silent in church,
1Co	14:34	Let your women **k** silent in
Gal	5: 3	that he is a debtor to **k**
Gal	6:13	those who are circumcised **k**
Eph	4: 3	endeavoring to **k** the unity of
2Th	3:14	that person and do not **k**
1Ti	5:22	**k** yourself pure.
2Ti	1:12	that He is able to **k** what I
2Ti	1:14	**k** by the Holy Spirit who
Phm	1:13	whom I wished to **k** with me,
Jas	1:27	and to **k** oneself unspotted
Jas	2:10	For whoever shall **k** the whole
1Jn	2: 3	if we **k** His commandments.
1Jn	5:21	**k** yourselves from idols.
Jude	6	And the angels who did not **k**
Jude	24	to Him who is able to **k** you
Rev	1: 3	and **k** those things which are
Rev	3:10	I also will **k** you from the
Rev	22: 9	and of those who **k** the words

KEEPER (see KEEP, KEEPERS)

Gen	4: 2	Now Abel was a **k** of sheep,
Gen	4: 9	know. Am I my brother's **k?**
Ps	121: 5	The LORD is your **k;**
Luke	13: 7	Then he said to the **k** of his
Acts	16:27	And the **k** of the prison,

KEEPERS (see KEEPER)

Eccl	12: 3	In the day when the **k** of the
Jer	4:17	Like **k** of a field they are

KEEPING (see KEEP)

Ex	34: 7	**k** mercy for thousands,
Deut	8:11	the LORD your God by not **k**
2Ch	23: 4	shall be in **k** watch over the
Ps	19:11	And in **k** them there is
Prov	15: 3	**K** watch on the evil and the
Ezek	13:19	and **k** people alive who
Ezek	17:14	but that by **k** his covenant
Luke	2: 8	**k** watch over their flock by
Acts	12: 6	before the door were **k** the
1Co	7:19	but **k** the commandments of

KEEPS (see KEEP)

Gen	19: 9	and he **k** acting as a judge;
Deut	7: 9	the faithful God who **k**
Job	33:18	He **k** back his soul from the
Ps	119:167	My soul **k** Your testimonies,
Ps	121: 3	He who **k** you will not
Ps	121: 4	He who **k** Israel Shall
Ps	146: 6	Who **k** truth forever,
Prov	16:17	He who **k** his way preserves
Prov	28: 7	Whoever **k** the law is a
Prov	29:18	But happy is he who **k** the
Eccl	5:20	because God **k** him busy with
Is	56: 2	And **k** his hand from doing
Dan	9: 4	who **k** His covenant and mercy
John	7:19	yet none of you **k** the law?
John	8:51	if anyone **k** My word he shall
John	14:21	has My commandments and **k**
Rom	2:26	if an uncircumcised man **k**
1Jn	2: 5	But whoever **k** His word, truly
1Jn	5:18	who has been born of God **k**

Rev 2:26 and **k** My works until the
Rev 16:15 and **k** his garments, lest he
Rev 22: 7 Blessed is he who **k** the

KEILAH
1Sa 23: 2 the Philistines, and save **K**.
1Sa 23: 5 David and his men went to **K**

KENITE (*see* KENITES)
Judg 4:17 the wife of Heber the **K**;

KENITES (*see* KENITE, MIDIANITES)
1Sa 15: 6 Then Saul said to the **K**,
1Sa 27:10 the southern area of the **K**.

KEPT (*see* KEEP, TENDING)
Gen 37:11 but his father **k** the matter
Num 9: 5 And they **k** the Passover on
Deut 32:10 He **k** him as the apple of
Josh 14:10 the LORD has **k** me alive, as
2Ch 35: 1 Now Josiah **k** a Passover to
Esth 9:28 should be remembered and **k**
Job 21:32 And a vigil **k** over the
Job 31:16 If I have **k** the poor from
Ps 17: 4 I have **k** away from the
Ps 18:23 And I **k** myself from my
Ps 30: 3 You have **k** me alive, that I
Ps 32: 3 When I **k** silent, my bones
Ps 42: 4 With a multitude that **k** a
Song 1: 6 my own vineyard I have not **k**.
Dan 5:19 he **k** alive; whomever he
Dan 7:28 but I **k** the matter in my
Amos 1:11 And he **k** his wrath forever.
Mic 6:16 the statutes of Omri are **k**;
Mal 2: 9 Because you have not **k** My
Matt 19:20 All these things I have **k**
Matt 26:63 But Jesus **k** silent. And the
Matt 27:36 they **k** watch over Him there.
Mark 10:20 all these things I have **k**
Luke 1:66 all those who heard them **k**
Luke 2:19 But Mary **k** all these things
Luke 2:51 but His mother **k** all these
Luke 8:29 and he was **k** under guard,
Luke 18:21 All these things I have **k**
Luke 20:26 at His answer and **k** silent.
John 2:10 You have **k** the good wine
John 11:37 also have **k** this man from
John 12: 7 she has **k** this for the day
John 15:10 just as I have **k** My Father's
John 18:17 Then the servant girl who **k**
Acts 5: 2 And he **k** back part of the
Acts 12: 5 Peter was therefore **k** in
Acts 25: 4 that Paul should be **k** at
Rom 16:25 revelation of the mystery **k**
2Co 11: 9 And in everything I **k** myself
Gal 3:23 we were **k** under guard by the
Gal 3:23 **k** for the faith which would
2Ti 4: 7 I have **k** the faith.
Heb 11:28 By faith he **k** the Passover
1Pe 1: 5 who are **k** by the power of God
Rev 3: 8 have **k** My word, and have not
Rev 3:10 Because you have **k** My command

KEREN-HAPPUCH†
Job 42:14 and the name of the third **K**.

KETURAH
Gen 25: 1 a wife, and her name was **K**.

KEY (*see* KEYS)
Is 22:22 The **k** of the house of David
Luke 11:52 you have taken away the **k**
Rev 3: 7 He who has the **k** of
Rev 9: 1 To him was given the **k** to
Rev 20: 1 having the **k** to the

KEYS† (*see* KEY)
Matt 16:19 And I will give you the **k** of
Rev 1:18 And I have the **k** of Hades

KEZIAH†
Job 42:14 the name of the second **K**,

KICK† (*see* KICKED)
1Sa 2:29 Why do you **k** at My sacrifice
Acts 9: 5 It is hard for you to **k**
Acts 26:14 It is hard for you to **k**

KICKED† (*see* KICK)
Deut 32:15 Jeshurun grew fat and **k**;
2Sa 16:13 threw stones at him and **k** up

KID (*see* KIDS)
Lev 4:23 bring as his offering a **k**
Lev 5: 6 a lamb or a **k** of the goats

KIDNAPS†
Ex 21:16 He who **k** a man and sells

KIDNEYS
Ex 29:13 and the two **k** and the fat
Is 34: 6 With the fat of the **k** of

KIDRON
2Sa 15:23 crossed over the Brook **K**,
John 18: 1 disciples over the Brook **K**,

KIDS (*see* KID)
Gen 27:16 she put the skins of the **k**
Lev 16: 5 children of Israel two **k** of

KILL (*see* KILLED, KILLING, KILLS)
Gen 4:14 anyone who finds me will **k**
Gen 12:12 and they will **k** me, but they
Gen 37:18 conspired against him to **k**
Ex 1:16 then you shall **k** him; but if
Ex 2:14 Do you intend to **k** me as you
Ex 2:15 he sought to **k** Moses. But
Ex 4:24 met him and sought to **k** him.
Ex 12: 6 of Israel shall **k** it at
Ex 12:21 and **k** the Passover lamb.
Ex 17: 3 to **k** us and our children and
Ex 29:11 Then you shall **k** the bull
Lev 1: 5 He shall **k** the bull before
Lev 4:24 it at the place where they **k**
Lev 16:11 and shall **k** the bull as the
Lev 16:15 Then he shall **k** the goat of
Lev 20:16 you shall **k** the woman and
Num 11:15 please **k** me here and now—if
Num 31:17 **k** every male among the
Num 31:17 and **k** every woman who has
Deut 32:39 I **k** and I make alive; I
Judg 9:54 Draw your sword and **k** me,
Judg 16: 2 we will **k** him."
1Sa 2:25 the LORD desired to **k** them.
1Sa 16: 2 he will **k** me." And the
1Sa 17: 9 able to fight with me and **k**
1Sa 19: 1 that they should **k** David;
1Sa 19: 2 My father Saul seeks to **k**
1Sa 20:33 cast a spear at him to **k**
1Sa 22:17 Turn and **k** the priests of the
1Sa 24:11 and did not **k** you, know and
2Sa 13:28 Strike Amnon!' then **k** him. Do
1Ki 3:26 and by no means **k** him!" But
2Ki 5: 7 to **k** and make alive, that
Eccl 3: 3 A time to **k**, And a time
Jer 20:17 Because he did not **k** me from
Jer 40:15 and I will **k** Ishmael the son
Matt 10:28 do not fear those who **k**
Matt 10:28 kill the body but cannot **k**
Matt 17:23 and they will **k** Him, and the
Matt 21:38 let us **k** him and seize his
Matt 24: 9 you up to tribulation and **k**
Mark 3: 4 evil, to save life or to **k**?
Mark 9:31 and they will **k** Him. And
Mark 10:34 and **k** Him. And the third day
Luke 13:31 for Herod wants to **k** You."
Luke 15:23 the fatted calf here and **k**
Luke 22: 2 sought how they might **k** Him,

John   5:16 and sought to **k** Him, because
John   7: 1 the Jews sought to **k** Him.
John   10:10 except to steal, and to **k,**
Acts   5:33 furious and plotted to **k**
Acts   9:23 the Jews plotted to **k** him.
Acts   10:13 "Rise, Peter; **k** and eat."
Acts   27:42 the soldiers' plan was to **k**
Rev   2:23 I will **k** her children with

KILLED (see KILL)
Gen   4: 8 Abel his brother and **k** him.
Gen   4:23 to my speech! For I have **k**
Gen   34:25 boldly upon the city and **k**
Gen   37:31 **k** a kid of the goats, and
Gen   38: 7 and the LORD **k** him.
Ex   2:12 he **k** the Egyptian and hid
Lev   6:25 the burnt offering is **k,**
Num   22:33 surely I would also have **k**
Deut   1: 4 after he had **k** Sihon king of
Deut   21: 1 and it is not known who **k**
Josh   10:10 **k** them with a great
Josh   10:11 the children of Israel **k**
Josh   13:22 children of Israel also **k**
Judg   9: 5 house at Ophrah and **k** his
Judg   9:54 a woman **k** him.'" So his
Judg   16:30 So the dead that he **k** at his
Judg   16:30 were more than he had **k** in
1Sa   17:36 Your servant has **k** both lion
1Sa   17:50 struck the Philistine and **k**
1Sa   22:21 told David that Saul had **k**
1Sa   31: 2 And the Philistines **k**
2Sa   1:16 I have **k** the LORD's
2Sa   4: 7 then they struck him and **k**
2Sa   12: 9 You have **k** Uriah the Hittite
2Sa   14: 6 one struck the other and **k**
1Ki   18:13 what I did when Jezebel **k**
1Ki   19:10 and **k** Your prophets with the
2Ki   10:11 So Jehu **k** all who remained of
2Ki   10:17 he **k** all who remained to
2Ki   23:29 And Pharaoh Necho **k** him at
2Ki   25:25 ten men and struck and **k**
Job   1:15 indeed they have **k** the
Job   1:17 and **k** the servants with the
Ps   44:22 Yet for Your sake we are **k**
Jer   39: 6 Then the king of Babylon **k**
Dan   3:22 the flame of the fire **k**
Amos   4:10 Your young men I **k** with a
Matt   16:21 and scribes, and be **k,**
Mark   9:31 kill Him. And after He is **k,**
Mark   12: 5 sent another, and him they **k;**
Luke   9:22 and scribes, and be **k,**
Luke   11:48 for they indeed **k** them, and
Luke   12: 5 Fear Him who, after He has **k,**
Luke   15:27 your father has **k** the fatted
Luke   22: 7 when the Passover must be **k.**
Acts   3:15 and **k** the Prince of life,
Acts   10:39 whom they **k** by hanging on a
Acts   12: 2 Then he **k** James the brother
Rom   7:11 and by it **k** me.
Rom   8:36 Your sake we are **k**
Rom   11: 3 they have **k** Your
2Co   6: 9 as chastened, and yet not **k;**
1Th   2:15 who **k** both the Lord Jesus and
Rev   2:13 who was **k** among you, where
Rev   9:18 a third of mankind was **k—**
Rev   13:15 image of the beast to be **k.**
Rev   19:21 And the rest were **k** with the

KILLING (see KILL)
Judg   9:56 had done to his father by **k**
Dan   2:13 and they began to **k** the wise
Hos   4: 2 **K** and stealing and
Mark   12: 5 beating some and **k** some.

KILLS (see KILL)
Gen   4:15 whoever **k** Cain, vengeance

Lev   17: 3 or who **k** it outside the
Lev   24:17 Whoever **k** any man shall
Deut   19: 4 Whoever **k** his neighbor
1Sa   2: 6 The LORD **k** and makes alive;
1Sa   17:26 be done for the man who **k**
Matt   23:37 the one who **k** the prophets
John   16: 2 is coming that whoever **k**
2Co   3: 6 the Spirit; for the letter **k,**

KILN†
Nah   3:14 Make strong the brick **k!**

KIN
Lev   18: 6 anyone who is near of **k** to
Prov   7: 4 your nearest **k,**

KIND (see KINDLY, KINDNESS, KINDS)
Gen   1:11 fruit according to its **k,**
Gen   6:20 "Of the birds after their **k,**
Judg   21:22 Be **k** to them for our sakes,
Matt   13:47 and gathered some of every **k,**
Matt   17:21 this **k** does not go out
Luke   1:66 What **k** of child will this
Luke   24:17 What **k** of conversation is
1Co   13: 4 Love suffers long and is **k;**
1Co   15:39 but there is one **k** of
Eph   4:32 And be **k** to one another,
1Th   1: 5 as you know what **k** of men we
Jas   1:18 that we might be a **k** of
Jas   1:24 immediately forgets what **k**

KINDLE (see KINDLED, KINDLES)
Ex   35: 3 You shall **k** no fire
Prov   26:21 is a contentious man to **k**
Jer   7:18 the fathers **k** the fire, and

KINDLED (see KINDLE)
Ex   4:14 the anger of the LORD was **k**
Deut   32:22 For a fire is **k** by my anger,
Job   19:11 He has also **k** His wrath
Ps   2:12 When His wrath is **k** but a
Ps   78:21 So a fire was **k** against
Ps   106:18 A fire was **k** in their
Ps   106:40 the wrath of the LORD was **k**
Jer   15:14 For a fire is **k** in My
Jer   44: 6 anger were poured out and **k**
Lam   4:11 He **k** a fire in Zion, And
Zech   10: 3 My anger is **k** against the
Luke   12:49 I wish it were already **k!**
Luke   22:55 Now when they had **k** a fire in

KINDLES (see KINDLE)
Is   44:15 he **k** it and bakes bread;
Jas   3: 5 a forest a little fire **k!**

KINDLY (see KIND)
Gen   24:49 Now if you will deal **k** and
Gen   34: 3 the young woman and spoke **k**
Gen   50:21 comforted them and spoke **k**
Ruth   1: 8 The LORD deal **k** with you,
Ruth   2:13 and have spoken **k** to your
Prov   26:25 When he speaks **k,**
Acts   27: 3 And Julius treated Paul **k**
Rom   12:10 Be **k** affectionate to one

KINDNESS (see KIND)
Gen   21:23 but that according to the **k**
Gen   24:12 and show **k** to my master
Josh   2:12 that you also will show **k** to
Ruth   2:20 who has not forsaken His **k**
Ruth   3:10 For you have shown more **k**
1Sa   20:14 not only show me the **k** of
2Sa   2: 6 now may the LORD show **k**
2Sa   2: 6 I also will repay you this **k,**
2Sa   9: 1 that I may show him **k** for
2Sa   9: 3 to whom I may show the **k** of
2Sa   10: 2 as his father showed **k** to
Neh   9:17 to anger, Abundant in **k,**
Ps   117: 2 For His merciful **k** is great

Prov	19:22	is desired in a man is **k**,
Is	54: 8	But with everlasting **k** I
Is	54:10	But My **k** shall not depart
Joel	2:13	to anger, and of great **k**;
Gal	5:22	joy, peace, longsuffering, **k**,
Eph	2: 7	of His grace in His **k**
Col	3:12	put on tender mercies, **k**,
Tit	3: 4	But when the **k** and the love
2Pe	1: 7	to godliness brotherly **k**,

KINDS (see KIND)

Lev	11:27	among all **k** of animals that
Lev	19:23	and have planted all **k** of
Deut	22: 9	vineyard with different **k**
Eccl	2: 5	and I planted all **k** of
Ezek	27:22	all **k** of precious stones,
Ezek	47:10	fish will be of the same **k**
Ezek	47:12	will grow all **k** of trees
Dan	3: 5	in symphony with all **k** of
Matt	4:23	and healing all **k** of
Matt	5:11	and say all **k** of evil
1Co	12:10	to another different **k** of
1Co	14:10	so many **k** of languages in
1Ti	6:10	of money is a root of all **k**
Rev	21:19	were adorned with all **k** of

KING (see KING'S, KINGLY, KINGS)

Gen	14: 1	in the days of Amraphel **k**
Gen	14: 8	And the **k** of Sodom, the king
Gen	14:18	Then Melchizedek **k** of Salem
Gen	20: 2	And Abimelech **k** of Gerar
Gen	40: 1	and the baker of the **k**
Gen	41:46	he stood before Pharaoh **k**
Ex	1: 8	Now there arose a new **k** over
Ex	2:23	process of time that the **k**
Ex	6:11	tell Pharaoh **k** of Egypt to
Ex	14: 8	the heart of Pharaoh **k** of
Num	21:21	sent messengers to Sihon **k**
Num	21:26	was the city of Sihon **k** of
Num	21:33	So Og **k** of Bashan went out
Num	23: 7	Balak the **k** of Moab has
Deut	2:26	of Kedemoth to Sihon **k** of
Deut	17:15	you shall surely set a **k** over
Deut	28:36	will bring you and the **k**
Josh	2: 2	And it was told the **k** of
Josh	8: 1	given into your hand the **k**
Josh	10: 1	to pass when Adoni-Zedek **k**
Judg	3:15	sent tribute to Eglon **k** of
Judg	4: 2	into the hand of Jabin **k** of
Judg	9: 6	went and made Abimelech **k**
Judg	9: 8	went forth to anoint a **k**
Judg	11:12	sent messengers to the **k** of
Judg	11:13	And the **k** of the people of
Judg	11:14	sent messengers to the **k** of
Judg	17: 6	those days there was no **k**
Judg	18: 1	those days there was no **k**
1Sa	2:10	will give strength to His **k**,
1Sa	8: 5	Now make us a **k** to judge us
1Sa	8:10	people who asked him for a **k**.
1Sa	10:24	Long live the **k**!"
1Sa	11:15	and there they made Saul **k**.
1Sa	12:12	LORD your God was your **k**.
1Sa	15: 1	sent me to anoint you **k**
1Sa	15:23	rejected you from being **k**.
1Sa	18: 6	to meet **K** Saul, with
1Sa	18:18	be son-in-law to the **k**?
1Sa	21:10	and went to Achish the **k** of
1Sa	24: 8	My lord the **k**!" And when
1Sa	26:15	not guarded your lord the **k**?
2Sa	2: 4	there they anointed David **k**
2Sa	2: 7	of Judah has anointed me **k**
2Sa	3:33	And the **k** sang a lament
2Sa	5: 3	and **K** David made a covenant
2Sa	5: 3	And they anointed David **k**
2Sa	6:16	through a window and saw **K**
2Sa	12: 7	I anointed you **k** over Israel,

2Sa	13:24	Then Absalom came to the **k**
2Sa	13:39	And **K** David longed to go to
2Sa	14:21	And the **k** said to Joab, "All
2Sa	14:33	to the ground before the **k**.
2Sa	14:33	Then the **k** kissed Absalom.
2Sa	15: 2	had a lawsuit came to the **k**
2Sa	15:16	But the **k** left ten women,
2Sa	15:19	Return and remain with the **k**.
2Sa	15:21	and as my lord the **k** lives,
2Sa	15:25	Then the **k** said to Zadok,
2Sa	16: 9	dead dog curse my lord the **k**?
2Sa	16:16	Long live the **k**! Long live
2Sa	18:13	is nothing hidden from the **k**,
2Sa	18:27	And the **k** said, "He is a
2Sa	18:31	my lord the **k**! For the LORD
2Sa	18:32	And the **k** said to the
2Sa	18:33	Then the **k** was deeply moved,
2Sa	19: 1	the **k** is weeping and
2Sa	19: 2	The **k** is grieved for his
2Sa	19: 4	But the **k** covered his face,
2Sa	19:12	the last to bring back the **k**?
2Sa	19:15	to escort the **k** across the
2Sa	19:16	the men of Judah to meet **K**
2Sa	19:22	not know that today I am **k**
2Sa	19:23	And the **k** swore to him.
2Sa	19:30	Mephibosheth said to the **k**,
2Sa	19:36	And why should the **k** repay
2Sa	19:43	have ten shares in the **k**;
2Sa	20: 2	remained loyal to their **k**.
2Sa	20: 3	And the **k** took the ten
1Ki	1: 1	Now **K** David was old,
1Ki	1: 4	and she cared for the **k**,
1Ki	1: 5	I will be **k**"; and he
1Ki	1:13	then has Adonijah become **k**?
1Ki	1:15	Shunammite was serving the **k**.
1Ki	1:16	and did homage to the **k**.
1Ki	1:18	look! Adonijah has become **k**;
1Ki	1:19	all the sons of the **k**,
1Ki	1:25	Long live the **k** Adonijah!'
1Ki	1:29	And the **k** took an oath and
1Ki	1:30	Solomon your son shall be **k**
1Ki	1:31	Let my lord **k** David live
1Ki	1:34	the prophet anoint him **k**
1Ki	1:34	Long live **k** Solomon!'
1Ki	1:37	than the throne of my lord **K**
1Ki	1:43	David has made Solomon **k**.
1Ki	1:45	prophet have anointed him **k**
1Ki	1:51	Adonijah is afraid of **K**
1Ki	1:53	So **K** Solomon sent them to
1Ki	2:26	to Abiathar the priest the **k**
1Ki	3: 4	Now the **k** went to Gibeon to
1Ki	3: 7	You have made Your servant **k**
1Ki	3:16	were harlots came to the **k**,
1Ki	3:24	brought a sword before the **k**.
1Ki	3:25	And the **k** said, "Divide the
1Ki	3:28	of the judgment which the **k**
1Ki	3:28	and they feared the **k**,
1Ki	4: 7	who provided food for the **k**
1Ki	4:27	and for all who came to **K**
1Ki	5: 1	Now Hiram **k** of Tyre sent his
1Ki	7:45	which Huram made for **K**
1Ki	9:15	for the labor force which **K**
1Ki	9:26	**K** Solomon also built a fleet
1Ki	10: 3	so difficult for the **k** that
1Ki	10: 6	Then she said to the **k**:
1Ki	10:10	the queen of Sheba gave to **K**
1Ki	10:22	For the **k** had merchant ships
1Ki	10:23	So **K** Solomon surpassed all
1Ki	10:27	The **k** made silver as common
1Ki	11: 1	But **K** Solomon loved many
1Ki	12: 6	Then **K** Rehoboam consulted
1Ki	12:15	So the **k** did not listen to
1Ki	12:28	Therefore the **k** asked advice,
1Ki	14:25	in the fifth year of **K**
1Ki	14:25	Rehoboam that Shishak **k** of

1Ki	15: 1	In the eighteenth year of **K**
1Ki	15: 1	Abijam became **k** over Judah.
1Ki	15: 9	Asa became **k** over Judah.
1Ki	15:16	between Asa and Baasha **k** of
1Ki	16:23	Omri became **k** over Israel,
1Ki	16:31	**k** of the Sidonians; and he
1Ki	19:15	anoint Hazael as **k** over
1Ki	20: 1	Now Ben-Hadad the **k** of Syria
1Ki	20: 2	into the city to Ahab **k** of
1Ki	21: 1	to the palace of Ahab **k** of
1Ki	21:10	blasphemed God and the **k**.
1Ki	22:10	and Jehoshaphat the **k** of
1Ki	22:34	and struck the **k** of Israel
1Ki	22:35	and the **k** was propped up in
1Ki	22:37	So the **k** died, and was
1Ki	22:44	made peace with the **k** of
2Ki	1:17	Jehoram became **k** in his
2Ki	3: 4	Now Mesha **k** of Moab was a
2Ki	3: 5	that the **k** of Moab rebelled
2Ki	3: 6	So **K** Jehoram went out of
2Ki	3: 7	The **k** of Moab has rebelled
2Ki	5: 1	of the army of the **k** of
2Ki	5: 5	will send a letter to the **k**
2Ki	6:26	"Help, my lord, O **k**!"
2Ki	8: 4	Then the **k** talked with
2Ki	8:29	Then **K** Joram went back to
2Ki	8:29	he fought against Hazael **k**
2Ki	9: 3	I have anointed you **k** over
2Ki	9:13	Jehu is **k**!"
2Ki	9:16	and Ahaziah **k** of Judah had
2Ki	9:18	and said, "Thus says the **k**:
2Ki	9:19	and said, "Thus says the **k**:
2Ki	9:21	Then Joram **k** of Israel and
2Ki	11: 8	you shall surround the **k** on
2Ki	11:12	Long live the **k**!"
2Ki	11:14	there was the **k** standing by
2Ki	12: 7	So **K** Jehoash called Jehoiada
2Ki	12:18	And Jehoash **k** of Judah took
2Ki	13:12	he fought against Amaziah **k**
2Ki	13:14	Then Joash the **k** of Israel
2Ki	14: 5	murdered his father the **k**.
2Ki	14:11	Therefore Jehoash **k** of
2Ki	14:17	Jehoahaz, **k** of Israel.
2Ki	15: 5	Then the LORD struck the **k**,
2Ki	15: 8	year of Azariah **k** of Judah,
2Ki	15:13	year of Uzziah **k** of Judah;
2Ki	15:19	Pul **k** of Assyria came against
2Ki	15:29	In the days of Pekah **k** of
2Ki	15:37	LORD began to send Rezin **k**
2Ki	16: 7	to Tiglath-Pileser **k** of
2Ki	16:10	Now **K** Ahaz went to Damascus
2Ki	16:10	to meet Tiglath-Pileser **k**
2Ki	16:12	the **k** saw the altar; and the
2Ki	16:17	And **K** Ahaz cut off the
2Ki	17: 4	brought no tribute to the **k**
2Ki	17: 6	the **k** of Assyria took
2Ki	18:10	the ninth year of Hoshea **k**
2Ki	18:13	Sennacherib **k** of Assyria
2Ki	18:14	Then Hezekiah **k** of Judah sent
2Ki	19: 9	heard concerning Tirhakah **k**
2Ki	19:10	shall speak to Hezekiah **k**
2Ki	20:12	**k** of Babylon, sent letters
2Ki	21:11	Because Manasseh **k** of Judah
2Ki	21:24	land made his son Josiah **k**
2Ki	22: 3	that the **k** sent Shaphan the
2Ki	22:10	Shaphan read it before the **k**.
2Ki	22:11	when the **k** heard the words
2Ki	23: 3	Then the **k** stood by a pillar
2Ki	23:13	Then the **k** defiled the high
2Ki	23:25	before him there was no **k**
2Ki	23:29	In his days Pharaoh Necho **k**
2Ki	23:29	went to the aid of the **k** of
2Ki	23:29	and **K** Josiah went against
2Ki	24:11	And Nebuchadnezzar **k** of
2Ki	24:12	Then Jehoiachin **k** of Judah,
2Ki	25: 2	until the eleventh year of **K**
2Ki	25: 5	the Chaldeans pursued the **k**,
2Ki	25: 6	So they took the **k** and
2Ki	25: 6	and brought him up to the **k**
2Ki	25:21	Then the **k** of Babylon struck
2Ki	25:22	whom Nebuchadnezzar **k** of
2Ki	25:24	in the land and serve the **k**
2Ki	25:27	captivity of Jehoiachin **k**
2Ki	25:27	that Evil-Merodach **k** of
2Ki	25:27	released Jehoiachin **k** of
2Ki	25:30	ration given him by the **k**,
1Ch	11: 3	Then they anointed David **k**
1Ch	15:29	through a window and saw **K**
1Ch	18: 3	David defeated Hadadezer **k**
1Ch	21:24	Then **K** David said to Ornan,
1Ch	23: 1	he made his son Solomon **k**
1Ch	25: 6	under the authority of the **k**.
1Ch	26:32	whom **K** David made officials
1Ch	27:24	of the chronicles of **K**
1Ch	27:31	were the officials over **K**
1Ch	28: 2	Then **K** David rose to his feet
1Ch	29:24	and also all the sons of **K**
1Ch	29:29	Now the acts of **K** David,
2Ch	1: 8	and have made me **k** in his
2Ch	1:15	Also the **k** made silver and
2Ch	2:12	for He has given **K** David a
2Ch	7: 5	**K** Solomon offered a sacrifice
2Ch	13: 1	Abijah became **k** over Judah.
2Ch	16: 1	Baasha **k** of Israel came up
2Ch	18: 3	So Ahab **k** of Israel said to
2Ch	18: 3	said to Jehoshaphat **k** of
2Ch	18:12	one accord encourage the **k**.
2Ch	21: 2	the sons of Jehoshaphat **k**
2Ch	23:11	Testimony, and made him **k**.
2Ch	23:12	running and praising the **k**,
2Ch	23:20	and set the **k** on the throne
2Ch	24:23	all their spoil to the **k** of
2Ch	25: 3	murdered his father the **k**.
2Ch	25:17	Now Amaziah **k** of Judah asked
2Ch	25:17	**k** of Israel, saying, "Come,
2Ch	25:18	And Joash **k** of Israel sent to
2Ch	26:18	And they withstood **K** Uzziah,
2Ch	26:21	**K** Uzziah was a leper until
2Ch	28:19	Judah low because of Ahaz **k**
2Ch	28:20	Also Tiglath-Pileser **k** of
2Ch	28:22	This is that **K** Ahaz.
2Ch	30: 4	And the matter pleased the **k**
2Ch	30: 6	with the letters from the **k**
2Ch	30: 6	to the command of the **k**:
2Ch	30:24	For Hezekiah **k** of Judah gave
2Ch	32: 1	Sennacherib **k** of Assyria
2Ch	33:25	who had conspired against **K**
2Ch	33:25	land made his son Josiah **k**
2Ch	34:16	carried the book to the **k**,
2Ch	34:18	the scribe told the **k**,
2Ch	34:18	Shaphan read it before the **k**.
2Ch	34:19	when the **k** heard the words
2Ch	34:31	Then the **k** stood in his place
2Ch	35:20	Necho **k** of Egypt came up to
2Ch	35:23	And the archers shot **K**
2Ch	35:23	and the **k** said to his
2Ch	36: 3	Now the **k** of Egypt deposed
2Ch	36: 4	brother Eliakim **k** over
2Ch	36: 6	Nebuchadnezzar **k** of Babylon
2Ch	36: 6	brought against them the **k**
2Ch	36:18	and the treasures of the **k**
2Ch	36:22	in the first year of Cyrus **k**
Ezra	1: 2	Thus says Cyrus **k** of Persia:
Ezra	4: 2	the days of Esarhaddon **k** of
Ezra	4: 5	until the reign of Darius **k**
Ezra	4: 7	wrote to Artaxerxes **k** of
Ezra	4:12	Let it be known to the **k** that
Ezra	4:17	The **k** sent an answer: To
Ezra	5:13	in the first year of Cyrus **k**
Ezra	5:13	**K** Cyrus issued a decree to

Ezra	5:17	a decree was issued by **K**
Ezra	5:17	and let the **k** send us his
Ezra	6:10	pray for the life of the **k**
Ezra	7:11	a copy of the letter that **K**
Ezra	7:12	**k** of kings, To Ezra the
Ezra	7:26	God and the law of the **k**,
Neh	2: 3	May the **k** live forever! Why
Neh	2: 8	And the **k** granted them to
Neh	6: 7	There is a **k** in Judah!' Now
Neh	13: 6	I had returned to the **k**.
Neh	13: 6	I obtained leave from the **k**,
Esth	1: 5	the **k** made a feast lasting
Esth	1: 7	to the generosity of the **k**
Esth	1:10	when the heart of the **k** was
Esth	1:11	Queen Vashti before the **k**,
Esth	1:12	therefore the **k** was furious,
Esth	2: 2	virgins be sought for the **k**;
Esth	2:13	young woman went to the **k**,
Esth	2:17	The **k** loved Esther more than
Esth	2:21	and sought to lay hands on **K**
Esth	3: 8	Then Haman said to **K**
Esth	3:10	So the **k** took his signet ring
Esth	4: 8	her to go in to the **k** to
Esth	4:11	the one to whom the **k** holds
Esth	5: 2	when the **k** saw Queen Esther
Esth	5: 2	and the **k** held out to Esther
Esth	5: 8	and if it pleases the **k** to
Esth	5: 8	then let the **k** and Haman
Esth	6: 1	That night the **k** could not
Esth	6: 1	they were read before the **k**.
Esth	6: 2	had sought to lay hands on **K**
Esth	6: 3	Then the **k** said, "What honor
Esth	6: 6	done for the man whom the **k**
Esth	6: 6	Whom would the **k** delight to
Esth	7: 7	Then the **k** arose in his
Esth	7: 9	Then the **k** said, "Hang
Esth	8: 2	So the **k** took off his signet
Esth	8: 4	And the **k** held out the golden
Esth	8:12	in all the provinces of **K**
Esth	8:15	from the presence of the **k**
Esth	10: 1	And **K** Ahasuerus imposed
Esth	10: 3	the Jew was second to **K**
Job	18:14	parade him before the **k** of
Ps	2: 6	Yet I have set My **K** On My
Ps	5: 2	My **K** and my God, For to
Ps	10:16	The LORD is **K** forever and
Ps	18:50	He gives to His **k**,
Ps	20: 9	LORD! May the **K** answer us
Ps	21: 7	For the **k** trusts in the
Ps	24: 7	doors! And the **K** of glory
Ps	24: 8	Who is this **K** of glory?
Ps	24:10	He is the **K** of glory.
Ps	29:10	And the LORD sits as **K**
Ps	33:16	No **k** is saved by the
Ps	44: 4	You are my **K**, O God;
Ps	45: 1	composition concerning the **K**;
Ps	45:14	shall be brought to the **K**
Ps	47: 2	He is a great **K** over all
Ps	47: 6	Sing praises to our **K**,
Ps	47: 7	For God is the **K** of all the
Ps	48: 2	The city of the great **K**.
Ps	63:11	But the **k** shall rejoice in
Ps	68:24	procession of my God, my **K**,
Ps	74:12	For God is my **K** from of
Ps	84: 3	My **K** and my God.
Ps	95: 3	And the great **K** above all
Ps	98: 6	before the LORD, the **K**.
Ps	145: 1	I will extol You, my God, O **K**;
Ps	149: 2	of Zion be joyful in their **K**.
Prov	1: 1	son of David, **k** of Israel:
Prov	20: 2	The wrath of a **k** is like
Prov	20:26	A wise **k** sifts out the
Prov	20:28	and truth preserve the **k**,
Prov	22:11	The **k** will be his friend.
Prov	24:21	fear the LORD and the **k**;
Prov	25: 1	which the men of Hezekiah **k**
Prov	29: 4	The **k** establishes the land
Prov	29:14	The **k** who judges the poor
Prov	30:27	The locusts have no **k**,
Prov	30:31	And a **k** whose troops are
Prov	31: 1	The words of **K** Lemuel, the
Eccl	1: 1	**k** in Jerusalem.
Eccl	1:12	was **k** over Israel in
Eccl	4:13	Than an old and foolish **k**
Eccl	4:14	comes out of prison to be **k**,
Eccl	10:16	when your **k** is a child,
Eccl	10:20	Do not curse the **k**,
Song	1: 4	THE SHULAMITE The **k** has
Song	3: 9	of Lebanon Solomon the **K**
Song	3:11	And see **K** Solomon with the
Is	6: 1	In the year that **K** Uzziah
Is	6: 5	For my eyes have seen the **K**,
Is	7: 6	and set a **k** over them, the
Is	7:17	The LORD will bring the **k** of
Is	20: 1	when Sargon the **k** of Assyria
Is	32: 1	a **k** will reign in
Is	33:17	Your eyes will see the **K** in
Is	33:22	The LORD is our **K**;
Is	39: 3	Isaiah the prophet went to **K**
Is	41:21	says the **K** of Jacob.
Is	43:15	Creator of Israel, your **K**.
Is	44: 6	the **K** of Israel, And his
Jer	8:19	Is not her **K** in her?"
Jer	10: 7	O **K** of the nations? For
Jer	10:10	God and the everlasting **K**.
Jer	25: 9	and Nebuchadnezzar the **k** of
Jer	25:26	Also the **k** of Sheshach shall
Jer	27: 3	the **k** of Moab, the king of
Jer	27: 3	the **k** of the Ammonites, the
Jer	27: 3	the **k** of Tyre, and the king
Jer	27: 3	and the **k** of Sidon, by the
Jer	27: 8	under the yoke of the **k** of
Jer	30: 9	God, And David their **k**,
Jer	34: 7	when the **k** of Babylon's army
Jer	36:21	So the **k** sent Jehudi to bring
Jer	36:22	Now the **k** was sitting in the
Jer	36:23	that the **k** cut it with
Jer	36:27	Now after the **k** had burned
Jer	37:18	Moreover Jeremiah said to **K**
Jer	37:20	hear now, O my lord the **k**.
Jer	39: 6	Then the **k** of Babylon killed
Jer	44:30	I will give Pharaoh Hophra **k**
Jer	46:17	**k** of Egypt, is but a
Jer	50:17	First the **k** of Assyria
Jer	50:17	last this Nebuchadnezzar **k**
Jer	52:10	Then the **k** of Babylon killed
Jer	52:11	Then the **k** of Babylon struck
Ezek	26: 7	**k** of kings, with horses,
Ezek	28:12	up a lamentation for the **k**
Ezek	29: 2	your face against Pharaoh **k**
Ezek	37:22	and one **k** shall be king over
Dan	1: 1	of the reign of Jehoiakim **k**
Dan	1: 1	Nebuchadnezzar **k** of Babylon
Dan	1: 5	And he appointed for them
Dan	1: 5	might serve before the **k**.
Dan	1:19	Then the **k** interviewed them,
Dan	1:20	about which the **k** examined
Dan	1:21	until the first year of **K**
Dan	2: 2	the Chaldeans to tell the **k**
Dan	2: 4	Chaldeans spoke to the **k** in
Dan	2: 4	the king in Aramaic, "O **k**,
Dan	2:12	For this reason the **k** was
Dan	2:15	is the decree from the **k** so
Dan	2:16	went in and asked the **k** to
Dan	2:16	that he might tell the **k** the
Dan	2:25	brought Daniel before the **k**,
Dan	2:25	who will make known to the **k**
Dan	2:28	and He has made known to **K**
Dan	2:29	"As for you, O **k**,
Dan	2:37	are a **k** of kings. For the

Dan	2:45	God has made known to the **k**
Dan	2:48	Then the **k** promoted Daniel
Dan	3: 1	Nebuchadnezzar the **k** made an
Dan	3: 2	And **K** Nebuchadnezzar sent
Dan	3: 7	the gold image which **K**
Dan	3:17	us from your hand, O **k**.
Dan	3:18	let it be known to you, O **k**,
Dan	3:30	Then the **k** promoted Shadrach,
Dan	4:37	and extol and honor the **K**
Dan	5: 1	Belshazzar the **k** made a great
Dan	5: 8	or make known to the **k** its
Dan	5: 9	Then **K** Belshazzar was greatly
Dan	5:11	and **K** Nebuchadnezzar your
Dan	5:17	read the writing to the **k**,
Dan	5:30	**k** of the Chaldeans, was
Dan	6: 6	**K** Darius, live forever!
Dan	6: 7	thirty days, except you, O **k**,
Dan	6: 9	Therefore **K** Darius signed the
Dan	6:17	and the **k** sealed it with his
Dan	6:19	Then the **k** arose very early
Dan	6:20	The **k** spoke, saying to
Dan	6:21	Then Daniel said to the **k**,
Dan	8:23	A **k** shall arise, Having
Dan	11: 3	Then a mighty **k** shall arise,
Dan	11: 5	Also the **k** of the South
Dan	11: 6	the South shall go to the **k**
Hos	1: 1	son of Joash, **k** of Israel.
Hos	3: 4	abide many days without **k**
Hos	3: 5	their God and David their **k**.
Hos	10: 3	they say, "We have no **k**,
Hos	13:11	I gave you a **k** in My anger,
Amos	1: 1	in the days of Uzziah **k** of
Amos	1: 1	**k** of Israel, two years
Amos	2: 1	he burned the bones of the **k**
Amos	7:10	of Bethel sent to Jeroboam **k**
Jon	3: 6	Then word came to the **k** of
Mic	6: 5	remember now What Balak **k**
Zeph	3:15	The **K** of Israel, the LORD,
Hag	1: 1	In the second year of **K**
Zech	9: 9	your **K** is coming to you; He
Zech	14: 5	In the days of Uzziah **k** of
Zech	14: 9	And the LORD shall be **K**
Zech	14:17	Jerusalem to worship the **K**,
Mal	1:14	I am a great **K**,
Matt	2: 1	in the days of Herod the **k**,
Matt	2: 2	is He who has been born **K**
Matt	5:35	is the city of the great **K**.
Matt	21: 5	your **K** is coming to
Matt	25:34	Then the **K** will say to those
Matt	27:11	Are You the **K** of the Jews?"
Matt	27:29	**K** of the Jews!"
Matt	27:37	THIS IS JESUS THE **K** OF THE
Matt	27:42	If He is the **K** of Israel,
Mark	15:32	the **K** of Israel, descend now
Luke	1: 5	the **k** of Judea, a certain
Luke	14:31	"Or what **k**, going to make
Luke	19:38	Blessed is the **K** who
Luke	23: 2	He Himself is Christ, a **K**.
John	1:49	Son of God! You are the **K**
John	6:15	Him by force to make Him **k**,
John	12:15	your **K** is coming,
John	18:37	Are You a **k** then?" Jesus
John	18:37	say rightly that I am a **k**.
John	19:12	Whoever makes himself a **k**
John	19:14	Behold your **K**!"
John	19:15	"Shall I crucify your **K**?
John	19:15	We have no **k** but Caesar!"
John	19:19	THE **K** OF THE JEWS.
John	19:21	The **K** of the Jews,' but, 'He
Acts	13:22	up for them David as **k**,
Acts	25:13	And after some days **K**
Acts	26: 7	**K** Agrippa, I am accused by
Acts	26:13	"at midday, O **k**,
Acts	26:19	**K** Agrippa, I was not
Acts	26:27	**K** Agrippa, do you believe the

1Ti	1:17	Now to the **K** eternal,
1Ti	6:15	the **K** of kings and Lord of
Heb	7: 1	**k** of Salem, priest of the
Heb	7: 2	**k** of righteousness," and
Heb	7: 2	meaning "**k** of peace,"
Heb	11:27	fearing the wrath of the **k**;
1Pe	2:13	whether to the **k** as supreme,
1Pe	2:17	Fear God. Honor the **k**.
Rev	15: 3	O **K** of the saints!
Rev	17:14	He is Lord of lords and **K**
Rev	19:16	**K** OF KINGS AND LORD OF

KING'S (*see* KING)

Gen	14:17	the **K** Valley), after his
Gen	39:20	a place where the **k**
Num	20:17	we will go along the **K**
1Sa	18:22	become the **k** son-in-law.' "
1Sa	18:25	to take vengeance on the **k**
1Sa	20:29	he has not come to the **k**
1Sa	21: 8	because the **k** business
2Sa	9:13	he ate continually at the **k**
2Sa	11: 9	slept at the door of the **k**
2Sa	12:30	Then he took their **k** crown
2Sa	13: 4	the **k** son, becoming thinner
2Sa	13:18	for the **k** virgin daughters
2Sa	13:23	so Absalom invited all the **k**
2Sa	14: 1	perceived that the **k** heart
2Sa	14:24	but did not see the **k** face.
2Sa	18:18	which is in the **K** Valley.
2Sa	18:20	because the **k** son is dead."
1Ki	1: 9	the **k** sons, and all the men
1Ki	4: 5	a priest and the **k** friend;
1Ki	22:26	the city and to Joash the **k**
2Ki	9:34	for she was a **k** daughter."
2Ki	12:10	that the **k** scribe and the
2Ki	24:15	The **k** mother, the king's
2Ki	25: 4	which was by the **k** garden,
1Ch	9:18	children of Levi at the **K**
1Ch	18:17	chief ministers at the **k**
1Ch	27:33	Ahithophel was the **k**
1Ch	27:33	the Archite was the **k**
2Ch	1:16	the **k** merchants bought them
2Ch	9:21	For the **k** ships went to
2Ch	24:11	that the **k** scribe and the
2Ch	26:11	one of the **k** captains.
2Ch	29:25	of Gad the **k** seer, and of
2Ch	35:10	according to the **k** command.
Ezra	6: 4	expenses be paid from the **k**
Ezra	8:36	And they delivered the **k**
Ezra	8:36	the king's orders to the **k**
Neh	1:11	For I was the **k** cupbearer.
Neh	2: 8	to Asaph the keeper of the **k**
Neh	2:14	Fountain Gate and to the **K**
Neh	3:15	the Pool of Shelah by the **K**
Neh	5: 4	borrowed money for the **k**
Esth	1: 5	court of the garden of the **k**
Esth	1:14	who had access to the **k**
Esth	2: 3	the custody of Hegai the **k**
Esth	2:19	Mordecai sat within the **k**
Esth	3: 3	do you transgress the **k**
Esth	3:12	and sealed with the **k** signet
Esth	7: 4	never compensate for the **k**
Esth	7: 8	As the word left the **k**
Esth	7: 9	who spoke good on the **k**
Esth	7:10	Then the **k** wrath subsided.
Esth	8:14	and pressed on by the **k**
Ps	45: 5	sharp in the heart of the **K**
Ps	45:15	They shall enter the **K**
Ps	61: 6	You will prolong the **k** life,
Ps	72: 1	Your righteousness to the **k**
Prov	16:15	In the light of the **k** face
Prov	19:12	The **k** wrath is like the
Jer	39: 4	by way of the **k** garden, by
Jer	39: 8	the Chaldeans burned the **k**
Jer	41:10	the **k** daughters and all the

Dan   1: 3 of Israel and some of the k
Dan   1: 4 ability to serve in the k
Dan   1: 5 a daily provision of the k
Dan   2:14 the captain of the k guard,
Dan   2:15 and said to Arioch the k
Dan   2:23 have made known to us the k
Dan   3:28 they have frustrated the k
Dan   4:31 word was still in the k
Dan   5: 5 of the wall of the k palace;
Dan   5: 6 Then the k countenance
Dan   5: 8 Now all the k wise men came,
Dan   6:12 and spoke concerning the k
Dan   8:27 I arose and went about the k
Amos   7: 1 the late crop after the k
Amos   7:13 For it is the k sanctuary,
Heb   11:23 were not afraid of the k

KINGDOM (see KINGDOMS)
Gen   10:10 And the beginning of his k
Gen   20: 9 brought on me and on my k a
Ex   19: 6 And you shall be to Me a k of
Num   24: 7 And his k shall be exalted.
Num   32:33 the k of Sihon king of the
Num   32:33 of the Amorites and the k
Deut 17:18 sits on the throne of his k,
Deut 17:20 prolong his days in his k,
1Sa   10:16 about the matter of the k,
1Sa   11:14 go to Gilgal and renew the k
1Sa   13:13 have established your k
1Sa   15:28 The LORD has torn the k of
1Sa   18: 8 more can he have but the k?
1Sa   24:20 and that the k of Israel
2Sa   5:12 that He had exalted His k
2Sa   7:12 and I will establish his k.
2Sa   7:13 the throne of his k forever.
1Ki   1:46 sits on the throne of the k.
1Ki   2:46 Thus the k was established
1Ki   11:11 I will surely tear the k
1Ki   12:21 that he might restore the k
1Ch   28: 5 sit on the throne of the k
1Ch   29:11 is Yours; Yours is the k,
2Ch   1: 1 was strengthened in his k,
2Ch   22: 9 to assume power over the k.
2Ch   29:21 for a sin offering for the k,
2Ch   33:13 back to Jerusalem into his k
2Ch   36:22 throughout all his k,
Ezra   1: 1 throughout all his k,
Esth   2: 3 all the provinces of his k,
Esth   4:14 you have come to the k for
Esth   5: 3 up to half the k!"
Ps   22:28 For the k is the LORD's,
Ps   45: 6 is the scepter of Your k.
Ps   103:19 And His k rules over all.
Ps   105:13 From one k to another
Ps   145:12 glorious majesty of His k.
Ps   145:13 Your k is an everlasting
Is   9: 7 of David and over His k,
Is   19: 2 k against kingdom.
Jer   18: 7 a nation and concerning a k,
Lam   2: 2 He has profaned the k and
Dan   2:37 of heaven has given you a k,
Dan   2:39 you shall arise another k
Dan   2:39 a third of bronze, which
Dan   2:40 And the fourth k shall be as
Dan   2:40 that k will break in
Dan   2:41 the k shall be divided; yet
Dan   2:44 of heaven will set up a k
Dan   4: 3 mighty His wonders! His k
Dan   4:25 Most High rules in the k of
Dan   4:31 the k has departed from you!
Dan   4:34 And His k is from
Dan   4:36 me, I was restored to my k,
Dan   5: 7 be the third ruler in the k.
Dan   5:11 There is a man in your k in
Dan   5:16 be the third ruler in the k.

Dan   5:18 your father a k and majesty,
Dan   5:21 High God rules in the k of
Dan   5:26 God has numbered your k,
Dan   5:28 Your k has been divided, and
Dan   5:31 the Mede received the k,
Dan   7:14 dominion and glory and a k,
Dan   7:18 High shall receive the k,
Dan   7:22 the saints to possess the k.
Dan   7:23 beast shall be A fourth k
Dan   7:24 shall arise from this k.
Dan   7:27 His k is an everlasting
Dan   8:21 the male goat is the k
Dan   8:23 the latter time of their k,
Dan   11: 4 his k shall be broken up and
Dan   11: 9 North shall come to the k
Dan   11:21 and seize the k by intrigue.
Hos   1: 4 And bring an end to the k
Obad   21 And the k shall be the
Matt   3: 2 for the k of heaven is at
Matt   4:17 for the k of heaven is at
Matt   4:23 the gospel of the k,
Matt   5: 3 For theirs is the k of
Matt   5:19 be called least in the k of
Matt   5:19 be called great in the k of
Matt   5:20 by no means enter the k of
Matt   6:10 Your k come. Your will be
Matt   6:13 For Yours is the k and the
Matt   6:33 But seek first the k of God
Matt   8:11 and Jacob in the k of
Matt   8:12 But the sons of the k will be
Matt 10: 7 The k of heaven is at hand.'
Matt 12:28 surely the k of God has come
Matt 13:11 know the mysteries of the k
Matt 13:24 The k of heaven is like a man
Matt 13:38 seeds are the sons of the k,
Matt 13:41 will gather out of His k
Matt 13:43 forth as the sun in the k
Matt 16:19 give you the keys of the k
Matt 16:28 Son of Man coming in His k.
Matt 18: 1 then is greatest in the k
Matt 18: 3 by no means enter the k of
Matt 18: 4 is the greatest in the k of
Matt 19:12 eunuchs for the k of
Matt 19:14 for of such is the k of
Matt 19:23 a rich man to enter the k
Matt 19:24 a rich man to enter the k
Matt 20:21 other on the left, in Your k.
Matt 24: 7 and k against kingdom. And
Matt 24:14 And this gospel of the k will
Matt 25:34 inherit the k prepared for
Matt 26:29 with you in My Father's k.
Mark   1:14 the gospel of the k of God,
Mark   1:15 and the k of God is at hand.
Mark   3:24 that k cannot stand.
Mark   4:11 to know the mystery of the k
Mark   4:26 The k of God is as if a man
Mark   4:30 what shall we liken the k
Mark   6:23 give you, up to half of my k.
Mark   9: 1 death till they see the k
Mark   9:47 for you to enter the k of
Mark 10:14 for of such is the k of God.
Mark 10:23 have riches to enter the k
Mark 10:24 in riches to enter the k of
Mark 12:34 You are not far from the k of
Mark 14:25 I drink it new in the k of
Mark 15:43 himself waiting for the k
Luke   1:33 and of His k there will be
Luke   8: 1 the glad tidings of the k
Luke   9:62 is fit for the k of God."
Luke 10: 9 The k of God has come near to
Luke 12:32 pleasure to give you the k.
Luke 13:18 What is the k of God like?
Luke 13:29 and sit down in the k of
Luke 14:15 shall eat bread in the k of
Luke 17:21 the k of God is within

Luke 18:24 have riches to enter the **k**
Luke 19:11 because they thought the **k**
Luke 19:12 to receive for himself a **k**
Luke 22:18 of the vine until the **k** of
Luke 22:30 drink at My table in My **k**,
Luke 23:42 me when You come into Your **k**.
Luke 23:51 was also waiting for the **k**
John 3: 3 he cannot see the **k** of
John 3: 5 he cannot enter the **k** of
John 18:36 My **k** is not of this world. If
Acts 1: 6 at this time restore the **k**
Acts 20:25 I have gone preaching the **k**
Acts 28:23 solemnly testified of the **k**
Rom 14:17 for the **k** of God is not
1Co 6: 9 will not inherit the **k** of
1Co 15:24 when He delivers the **k** to
Eph 5: 5 any inheritance in the **k** of
Col 1:13 and conveyed us into the **k**
Col 4:11 fellow workers for the **k** of
1Th 2:12 who calls you into His own **k**
2Th 1: 5 be counted worthy of the **k**
2Ti 4: 1 at His appearing and His **k**:
2Ti 4:18 me for His heavenly **k**.
Heb 1: 8 the scepter of Your **K**.
Heb 12:28 since we are receiving a **k**
Jas 2: 5 in faith and heirs of the **k**
2Pe 1:11 into the everlasting **k** of
Rev 1: 9 in the tribulation and **k**
Rev 17:17 and to give their **k** to the

KINGDOMS (see KINGDOM)
Deut 3:21 the LORD do to all the **k**
Josh 11:10 the head of all those **k**.
1Ki 4:21 Solomon reigned over all **k**
2Ki 19:15 of all the **k** of the earth.
2Ch 12: 8 from the service of the **k**
2Ch 36:23 All the **k** of the earth the
Ezra 1: 2 All the **k** of the earth the
Ps 46: 6 the **k** were moved; He
Ps 68:32 you **k** of the earth; Oh,
Ps 79: 6 And on the **k** that do not
Ps 135:11 And all the **k** of Canaan—
Is 10:10 As my hand has found the **k**
Is 13: 4 A tumultuous noise of the **k**
Is 13:19 And Babylon, the glory of **k**,
Is 14:16 earth tremble, Who shook **k**,
Is 23:17 fornication with all the **k**
Jer 1:10 the nations and over the **k**,
Jer 51:20 With you I will destroy **k**;
Ezek 37:22 ever be divided into two **k**
Dan 2:44 and consume all these **k**,
Dan 8:22 four **k** shall arise out of
Amos 6: 2 you better than these **k**?
Hag 2:22 strength of the Gentile **k**.
Luke 4: 5 showed Him all the **k** of the
Heb 11:33 who through faith subdued **k**,
Rev 11:15 The **k** of this world have
Rev 11:15 world have become the **k**

KINGLY † (see KING)
Dan 5:20 he was deposed from his **k**

KINGS (see KING, KINGS')
Gen 14: 9 four **k** against five.
Gen 14:10 and the **k** of Sodom and
Gen 17:16 **k** of peoples shall be from
Deut 31: 4 the **k** of the Amorites and
Josh 10: 5 Therefore the five **k** of the
Josh 10:24 feet on the necks of these **k**.
Judg 1: 7 Seventy **k** with their thumbs
Judg 5: 3 O **k**! Give ear, O princes!
Judg 5:19 The **k** came and fought, Then
2Sa 11: 1 at the time when **k** go out
1Ki 4:34 from all the **k** of the earth
1Ki 14:19 of the chronicles of the **k**
2Ki 19:17 the **k** of Assyria have laid

1Ch 9: 1 in the book of the **k** of
2Ch 21: 6 walked in the way of the **k**
2Ch 21:20 not in the tombs of the **k**.
2Ch 24:27 annals of the book of the **k**.
Ezra 7:12 Artaxerxes, king of **k**,
Esth 10: 2 of the chronicles of the **k**
Job 3:14 With **k** and counselors of the
Job 12:18 He loosens the bonds of **k**,
Ps 2: 2 The **k** of the earth set
Ps 2:10 Now therefore, be wise, O **k**;
Ps 48: 4 the **k** assembled, They
Ps 68:12 **K** of armies flee, they flee,
Ps 68:29 **K** will bring presents to
Ps 72:11 all **k** shall fall down before
Ps 89:27 The highest of the **k** of the
Ps 105:14 He rebuked **k** for their
Ps 110: 5 He shall execute **k** in the
Ps 119:46 testimonies also before **k**,
Ps 135:10 nations And slew mighty **k**—
Ps 136:17 Him who struck down great **k**,
Ps 138: 4 All the **k** of the earth shall
Prov 8:15 By me **k** reign, And rulers
Prov 22:29 He will stand before **k**;
Prov 25: 2 But the glory of **k** is to
Prov 25: 3 So the heart of **k** is
Prov 31: 4 It is not for **k** to drink
Is 1: 1 Hezekiah, **k** of Judah.
Is 19:11 wise, The son of ancient **k**?
Is 52:15 **K** shall shut their mouths
Is 60:16 And milk the breast of **k**;
Jer 1:18 Against the **k** of Judah,
Jer 13:13 even the **k** who sit on David's
Jer 22: 4 **k** who sit on the throne of
Jer 25:22 all the **k** of Tyre, all the
Jer 25:25 and all the **k** of the Medes;
Jer 25:26 all the **k** of the north, far
Jer 44: 9 the wickedness of the **k** of
Lam 4:12 The **k** of the earth, And all
Dan 2:21 He removes **k** and raises up
Dan 2:37 O king, are a king of **k**.
Dan 2:47 God of gods, the Lord of **k**,
Dan 7:17 are four **k** which arise out
Dan 7:24 The ten horns are ten **k**
Dan 7:24 And shall subdue three **k**.
Dan 8:20 they are the **k** of Media and
Dan 10:13 left alone there with the **k**
Dan 11: 2 three more **k** will arise in
Hos 7: 7 All their **k** have fallen.
Hos 8: 4 "They set up **k**,
Matt 10:18 before governors and **k** for
Luke 10:24 you that many prophets and **k**
Luke 21:12 You will be brought before **k**
Luke 22:25 The **k** of the Gentiles
Acts 4:26 The **k** of the earth
1Ti 2: 2 for **k** and all who are in
1Ti 6:15 the King of **k** and Lord of
Rev 1: 5 and the ruler over the **k** of
Rev 1: 6 and has made us **k** and priests
Rev 10:11 nations, tongues, and **k**.
Rev 16:12 so that the way of the **k**
Rev 17:10 "There are also seven **k**.
Rev 17:12 which you saw are ten **k** who
Rev 17:14 Lord of lords and King of **k**;
Rev 19:16 KING OF **K** AND LORD OF

KINGS' (see KINGS)
Ps 45: 9 **K** daughters are among Your
Prov 30:28 And it is in **k** palaces.
Matt 11: 8 wear soft clothing are in **k**

KIR
Amos 1: 5 Syria shall go captive to **K**,
Amos 9: 7 And the Syrians from **K**?

KIRJATH ARBA (see HEBRON)
Gen 35:27 or **K** (that is, Hebron), where

Josh 14:15 name of Hebron formerly was K

KIRJATH JEARIM
1Sa   7: 2 ark remained in K a long time
2Ch   1: 4 from K to the place David had

KIRJATH SEPHER
Josh 15:16 He who attacks K and takes it,
Judg 1:12 whoever attacks K and takes it,

KISH
1Sa   9: 3 Now the donkeys of K,
1Sa   9: 3 And K said to his son Saul,
1Sa 10:21 And Saul the son of K was
2Sa 21:14 in the tomb of K his father.
Acts 13:21 gave them Saul the son of K,

KISHON
Judg 4: 7 his multitude at the River K;
Judg 5:21 The torrent of K swept them
1Ki 18:40 them down to the Brook K
Ps   83: 9 with Jabin at the Brook K,

KISS (*see* KISSED, KISSES)
Gen 27:26 Come near now and k me, my
Gen 31:28 you did not allow me to k
Ps   2:12 K the Son, lest He be angry,
Song 1: 2 Let him k me with the kisses
Hos 13: 2 the men who sacrifice k
Matt 26:48 sign, saying, "Whomever I k,
Mark 14:44 saying, "Whomever I k,
Luke 7:45 woman has not ceased to k
Luke 22:47 and drew near to Jesus to k
Luke 22:48 the Son of Man with a k?
Rom 16:16 one another with a holy k.
1Th   5:26 the brethren with a holy k.
1Pe   5:14 Greet one another with a k of

KISSED (*see* KISS)
Gen 29:11 Then Jacob k Rachel, and
Gen 31:55 and k his sons and daughters
Gen 45:15 Moreover he k all his
Ruth 1: 9 Then she k them, and they
Ps   85:10 and peace have k.
Prov 7:13 So she caught him and k him;
Matt 26:49 Rabbi!" and k Him.
Luke 7:38 and she k His feet and
Luke 15:20 and fell on his neck and k
Acts 20:37 fell on Paul's neck and k

KISSES (*see* KISS)
Prov 27: 6 But the k of an enemy are
Song 1: 2 Let him kiss me with the k

KNEAD† (*see* KNEADED, KNEADING)
Gen 18: 6 k it and make cakes."
Jer   7:18 and the women k dough, to

KNEADED (*see* KNEAD)
2Sa 13: 8 Then she took flour and k

KNEADING (*see* KNEAD)
Ex   12:34 having their k bowls bound
Hos   7: 4 stirring the fire after k

KNEE (*see* KNEES)
Gen 41:43 Bow the k!" So he set him
Matt 27:29 And they bowed the k before
Rom 11: 4 have not bowed the k
Rom 14:11 Every k shall bow to
Phil 2:10 at the name of Jesus every k

KNEEL† (*see* KNEELING, KNELT)
Gen 24:11 And he made his camels k down
Ps   95: 6 Let us k before the LORD

KNEELING (*see* KNEEL)
Matt 17:14 k down to Him and saying,
Matt 20:20 k down and asking something

KNEES (*see* KNEE)
Gen 30: 3 will bear a child on my k,

Deut 28:35 will strike you in the k
Judg 7: 5 who gets down on his k to
Judg 16:19 lulled him to sleep on her k,
1Ki 18:42 put his face between his k,
Job   3:12 Why did the k receive me?
Job   4: 4 strengthened the feeble k;
Ps 109:24 My k are weak through
Is   35: 3 And make firm the feeble k.
Is   66:12 And be dandled on her k.
Dan   5: 6 hips were loosened and his k
Dan   6:10 he knelt down on his k three
Dan 10:10 made me tremble on my k and
Luke 5: 8 he fell down at Jesus' k,
Eph   3:14 For this reason I bow my k
Heb 12:12 hang down, and the feeble k,

KNELT (*see* KNEEL)
Dan   6:10 he k down on his knees three
Mark 10:17 k before Him, and asked Him,
Luke 22:41 and He k down and prayed,

KNEW (*see* KNOW)
Gen   3: 7 and they k that they were
Gen   4: 1 Now Adam k Eve his wife, and
Deut 34:10 whom the LORD k face to
Judg 19:25 And they k her and abused
Job 23: 3 that I k where I might find
Jer   1: 5 I formed you in the womb I k
Dan   5:21 till he k that the Most High
Dan   6:10 Now when Daniel k that the
Hos 13: 5 I k you in the wilderness,
Matt 7:23 I never k you; depart from
Matt 12:25 But Jesus k their thoughts,
Matt 25:24 I k you to be a hard man,
Matt 25:26 you k that I reap where I
Luke 19:22 You k that I was an austere
Luke 24:31 eyes were opened and they k
John 2: 9 who had drawn the water k),
John 2:25 for He k what was in man.
John 4:10 If you k the gift of God, and
John 13: 1 when Jesus k that His hour
John 13:11 For He k who would betray
John 13:28 But no one at the table k for
Acts 3:10 Then they k that it was he
Acts 18:25 though he k only the baptism
Rom   1:21 although they k God, they
1Co   2: 8 of the rulers of this age k;
2Co   5:21 For He made Him who k no sin

KNIFE (*see* KNIVES)
Gen 22: 6 fire in his hand, and a k,
Gen 22:10 out his hand and took the k
Prov 23: 2 And put a k to your throat
Jer 36:23 cut it with the scribe's k

KNIT
1Sa 18: 1 the soul of Jonathan was k
Job 10:11 And k me together with
Eph   4:16 joined and k together by
Col   2: 2 being k together in love,
Col   2:19 nourished and k together by

KNIVES (*see* KNIFE)
Josh 5: 2 Make flint k for yourself,

KNOCK (*see* KNOCKED, KNOCKING, KNOCKS)
Matt 7: 7 seek, and you will find; k,
Luke 11: 9 seek, and you will find; k,
Luke 13:25 to stand outside and k at
Rev   3:20 I stand at the door and k.

KNOCKED† (*see* KNOCK)
Dan   5: 6 loosened and his knees k
Acts 12:13 And as Peter k at the door of

KNOCKING† (*see* KNOCK)
Acts 12:16 Now Peter continued k;

KNOCKS (*see* KNOCK)

Song	5: 2	voice of my beloved! He **k**,
Matt	7: 8	and to him who **k** it will be
Luke	11:10	and to him who **k** it will be
Luke	12:36	that when he comes and **k**

KNOW (*see* KNEW, KNOWING, KNOWLEDGE, KNOWN, KNOWS, UNKNOWN)

Gen	3:22	to **k** good and evil. And now,
Gen	4: 9	He said, "I do not **k**.
Gen	19: 5	them out to us that we may **k**
Gen	19:33	and he did not **k** when she
Gen	22:12	for now I **k** that you fear
Gen	27: 2	I do not **k** the day of my
Gen	28:16	and I did not **k** it."
Gen	31:32	For Jacob did not **k** that
Gen	39: 8	my master does not **k** what
Gen	43:22	We do not **k** who put our
Ex	1: 8	who did not **k** Joseph.
Ex	2: 4	to **k** what would be done to
Ex	3: 7	for I **k** their sorrows.
Ex	4:14	I **k** that he can speak well.
Ex	5: 2	I do not **k** the LORD, nor
Ex	32: 1	we do not **k** what has become
Ex	32:22	You **k** the people, that they
Ex	33:12	I **k** you by name, and you have
Num	14:31	and they shall **k** the land
Num	20:14	You **k** all the hardship that
Deut	4:39	Therefore **k** this day, and
Deut	8: 2	to **k** what was in your
Deut	8: 3	manna which you did not **k**
Deut	13: 3	your God is testing you to **k**
Deut	29:26	gods that they did not **k** and
Deut	31:21	for I **k** the inclination of
Deut	31:27	for I **k** your rebellion and
Josh	2: 5	the men went I do not **k**;
Josh	23:13	**k** for certain that the LORD
Judg	3: 2	Israel might be taught to **k**
Judg	3: 4	to **k** whether they would obey
Judg	19:22	that we may **k** him
Ruth	3:11	all the people of my town **k**
1Sa	2:12	they did not **k** the LORD.
1Sa	3: 7	(Now Samuel did not yet **k** the
1Sa	17:46	that all the earth may **k**
2Sa	3:25	to **k** your going out and your
2Sa	14:20	to **k** everything that is in
2Sa	15:20	since I go I **k** not where?
2Sa	24: 2	that I may **k** the number of
1Ki	2:32	my father David did not **k**
1Ki	5: 3	You **k** how my father David
1Ki	8:39	whose heart You **k** (for You
1Ki	8:39	You know (for You alone **k**
1Ki	8:43	peoples of the earth may **k**
1Ki	17:24	Now by this I **k** that you are
2Ki	4: 9	I **k** that this is a holy man
2Ch	25:16	I **k** that God has determined
Ezra	7:25	all such as **k** the laws of
Ezra	7:25	and teach those who do not **k**
Neh	4:11	They will neither **k** nor see
Job	7:10	Nor shall his place **k** him
Job	9:21	yet I do not **k** myself; I
Job	11: 6	**K** therefore that God exacts
Job	13: 2	What you know, I also **k**;
Job	13:23	Make me **k** my transgression
Job	18:21	of him who does not **k** God.
Job	19:25	For I **k** that my Redeemer
Job	19:26	is destroyed, this I **k**,
Job	21:27	I **k** your thoughts, And the
Job	22:13	you say, 'What does God **k**?
Job	28:13	Man does not **k** its value,
Job	31: 6	That God may **k** my
Job	37:15	Do you **k** when God dispatches
Job	37:16	Do you **k** how the clouds are
Job	38: 5	Surely you **k**! Or who
Job	38:21	Do you **k** it, because you

Job	38:33	Do you **k** the ordinances of
Job	39: 1	Do you **k** the time when the
Job	42: 2	I **k** that You can do
Ps	4: 3	But **k** that the LORD has set
Ps	9:10	And those who **k** Your name
Ps	9:20	That the nations may **k**
Ps	20: 6	Now I **k** that the LORD saves
Ps	35:11	me things that I do not **k**.
Ps	39: 4	make me to **k** my end, And
Ps	39: 4	That I may **k** how frail I
Ps	46:10	and **k** that I am God; I
Ps	51: 6	part You will make me to **k**
Ps	59:13	And let them **k** that God
Ps	69: 5	You **k** my foolishness; And
Ps	69:19	You **k** my reproach, my shame,
Ps	73:11	they say, "How does God **k**?
Ps	79: 6	on the nations that do not **k**
Ps	83:18	That they may **k** that You,
Ps	89:15	are the people who **k** the
Ps	92: 6	A senseless man does not **k**,
Ps	95:10	And they do not **k** My ways.'
Ps	100: 3	**K** that the LORD, He is God
Ps	119:79	Those who **k** Your
Ps	139: 2	You **k** my sitting down and my
Ps	139: 4	You **k** it altogether.
Ps	139:23	and **k** my heart; Try me, and
Ps	139:23	and **k** my anxieties;
Prov	1: 2	To **k** wisdom and instruction,
Prov	7:23	He did not **k** it would
Prov	24:12	Surely we did not **k** this,"
Prov	27: 1	For you do not **k** what a day
Prov	30: 4	His Son's name, If you **k**?
Eccl	1:17	And I set my heart to **k**
Eccl	1:17	to know wisdom and to **k**
Eccl	7:25	I applied my heart to **k**,
Eccl	7:25	To **k** the wickedness of
Eccl	8: 7	For he does not **k** what will
Eccl	9: 5	But the dead **k** nothing,
Eccl	10:15	For they do not even **k** how
Eccl	11: 9	But **k** that for all these
Is	1: 3	But Israel does not **k**,
Is	7:15	that He may **k** to refuse the
Is	9: 9	All the people will **k**—
Is	19:21	and the Egyptians will **k** the
Is	41:20	That they may see and **k**,
Is	41:22	And **k** the latter end of
Is	44: 9	They neither see nor **k**,
Is	48: 8	hear, Surely you did not **k**;
Is	49:26	All flesh shall **k** That I,
Is	51: 7	you who **k** righteousness,
Is	52: 6	My people shall **k** My name;
Is	55: 5	call a nation you do not **k**,
Is	58: 2	And delight to **k** My ways,
Jer	2:19	**K** therefore and see that
Jer	5:15	whose language you do not **k**,
Jer	7: 9	other gods whom you do not **k**,
Jer	9: 3	And they do not **k** Me,"
Jer	10:23	I **k** the way of man is not
Jer	10:25	who do not **k** You, And on
Jer	14:18	in a land they do not **k**.
Jer	15:15	O LORD, You **k**;
Jer	15:15	**K** that for Your sake I have
Jer	17: 9	Who can **k** it?
Jer	31:34	**K** the LORD,' for they all
Jer	31:34	for they all shall **k** Me,
Jer	44: 3	gods whom they did not **k**,
Jer	48:17	And all you who **k** his name,
Ezek	2: 5	yet they will **k** that a
Ezek	6: 7	and you shall **k** that I am
Ezek	21: 5	that all flesh may **k** that I,
Ezek	25:14	and they shall **k** My
Ezek	37: 3	"O Lord GOD, You **k**.
Ezek	37:28	The nations also will **k** that
Ezek	38:16	so that the nations may **k**
Ezek	39:23	The Gentiles shall **k** that the

Dan	2: 3	my spirit is anxious to **k**
Dan	4: 9	because I **k** that the Spirit
Dan	4:25	till you **k** that the Most
Dan	4:26	after you come to **k** that
Dan	5:23	do not see or hear or **k**;
Dan	6:15	and said to the king, "**K**,
Dan	7:19	Then I wished to **k** the truth
Dan	9:25	**K** therefore and understand,
Hos	2: 8	For she did not **k** That I
Hos	2:20	And you shall **k** the LORD.
Hos	6: 3	Let us **k**, Let us pursue
Hos	7: 9	Yet he does not **k** it.
Hos	11: 3	But they did not **k** that I
Hos	13: 4	And you shall **k** no God but
Jon	1: 7	that we may **k** for whose
Jon	4: 2	for I **k** that You are a
Zech	2: 9	Then you will **k** that the
Matt	1:25	and did not **k** her till she
Matt	6: 3	do not let your left hand **k**
Matt	7:11	**k** how to give good gifts to
Matt	7:16	You will **k** them by their
Matt	7:20	by their fruits you will **k**
Matt	9: 6	But that you may **k** that the
Matt	11:27	Nor does anyone **k** the Father
Matt	13:11	has been given to you to **k**
Matt	16: 3	Hypocrites! You **k** how to
Matt	20:22	You do not **k** what you ask.
Matt	24:32	you **k** that summer is near.
Matt	24:39	and did not **k** until the flood
Matt	24:42	for you do not **k** what hour
Matt	25:12	I do not **k** you.'
Matt	25:13	for you **k** neither the day
Matt	26:72	I do not **k** the Man!"
Matt	28: 5	for I **k** that you seek Jesus
Mark	1:24	I **k** who You are—the Holy One
Mark	4:11	you it has been given to **k**
Mark	10:19	You **k** the commandments: 'Do
Mark	12:14	we **k** that You are true, and
Mark	14:40	and they did not **k** what to
Luke	1: 4	that you may **k** the certainty
Luke	1:18	How shall I **k** this? For I am
Luke	1:34	since I do not **k** a man?"
Luke	2:49	Did you not **k** that I must be
Luke	9:55	You do not **k** what manner of
Luke	21:20	then **k** that its desolation
Luke	21:31	**k** that the kingdom of God is
Luke	22:34	deny three times that you **k**
Luke	22:57	I do not **k** Him."
Luke	23:34	for they do not **k** what they
Luke	24:16	so that they did not **k** Him.
John	1:10	and the world did not **k** Him.
John	2: 9	and did not **k** where it came
John	3: 2	we **k** that You are a teacher
John	3:10	and do not **k** these things?
John	3:11	We speak what We **k** and
John	4:22	worship what you do not **k**;
John	4:22	we **k** what we worship, for
John	4:25	I **k** that Messiah is coming"
John	4:32	to eat of which you do not **k**.
John	4:42	have heard Him and we **k**
John	6:42	whose father and mother we **k**?
John	6:69	have come to believe and **k**
John	7:15	How does this Man **k** letters,
John	7:28	You both **k** Me, and you know
John	7:29	But I **k** Him, for I am from
John	8:28	then you will **k** that I am
John	8:32	And you shall **k** the truth,
John	8:37	I **k** that you are Abraham's
John	8:55	but I **k** Him. And if I say,
John	8:55	but I do **k** Him and keep His
John	9:20	We **k** that this is our son,
John	9:21	he now sees we do not **k**,
John	9:21	opened his eyes we do not **k**.
John	9:25	a sinner or not I do not **k**.
John	9:25	I do not know. One thing I **k**:
John	9:29	we do not **k** where He is
John	10: 4	for they **k** his voice.
John	10:14	and I **k** My sheep, and am
John	10:15	even so I **k** the Father; and
John	10:27	and I **k** them, and they
John	11:22	But even now I **k** that
John	11:24	I **k** that he will rise again
John	11:42	And I **k** that You always hear
John	13:12	Do you **k** what I have done to
John	13:17	If you **k** these things,
John	13:18	I **k** whom I have chosen; but
John	14: 4	"And where I go you **k**,
John	14: 4	you know, and the way you **k**.
John	14: 5	we do not **k** where You are
John	14: 5	and how can we **k** the way?"
John	14: 7	and from now on you **k** Him
John	14:17	but you **k** Him, for He dwells
John	14:31	But that the world may **k** that
John	15:18	you **k** that it hated Me
John	16:30	Now we are sure that You **k**
John	17: 3	that they may **k** You, the
John	17:23	and that the world may **k**
John	20: 9	For as yet they did not **k** the
John	20:14	and did not **k** that it was
John	21: 4	yet the disciples did not **k**
John	21:15	You **k** that I love You." He
John	21:17	You **k** all things; You know
John	21:24	and we **k** that his testimony
Acts	1: 7	It is not for you to **k** times
Acts	1:24	who **k** the hearts of all,
Acts	2:36	all the house of Israel **k**
Acts	7:18	king arose who did not **k**
Acts	13:27	because they did not **k** Him,
Acts	17:19	May we **k** what this new
Acts	19:15	and said, "Jesus I **k**,
Rom	2:18	and **k** His will, and approve
Rom	6: 3	Or do you not **k** that as many
Rom	6:16	Do you not **k** that to whom you
Rom	7:14	For we **k** that the law is
Rom	7:18	For I **k** that in me (that is,
Rom	8:28	And we **k** that all things work
Rom	10:19	But I say, did Israel not **k**?
1Co	1:21	through wisdom did not **k**
1Co	2: 2	For I determined not to **k**
1Co	2:14	nor can he **k** them, because
1Co	3:16	Do you not **k** that you are the
1Co	6:15	Do you not **k** that your bodies
1Co	7:16	husband? Or how do you **k**,
1Co	8: 4	we **k** that an idol is
1Co	9:13	Do you not **k** that those who
1Co	13: 9	For we **k** in part and we
1Co	13:12	Now I **k** in part, but then I
1Co	13:12	but then I shall **k** just as I
2Co	5: 1	For we **k** that if our earthly
2Co	8: 9	For you **k** the grace of our
2Co	12: 2	I **k** a man in Christ who
2Co	12: 2	in the body I do not **k**,
2Co	12: 3	out of the body I do not **k**,
Gal	4: 8	when you did not **k** God, you
Eph	1:18	that you may **k** what is the
Eph	3:19	to **k** the love of Christ which
Phil	3:10	that I may **k** Him and the
Phil	4:12	I **k** how to be abased, and I
Phil	4:12	and I **k** how to abound.
1Th	1: 5	as you **k** what kind of men we
1Th	4: 2	for you **k** what commandments
1Th	4: 5	the Gentiles who do not **k**
2Th	1: 8	on those who do not **k** God,
1Ti	1: 8	But we **k** that the law is
2Ti	1:12	for I **k** whom I have believed
2Ti	3: 1	But **k** this, that in the last
Tit	1:16	They profess to **k** God, but in
Heb	8:11	**K** the LORD,' for all
Heb	8:11	for all shall **k** Me,
Jas	4: 4	adulteresses! Do you not **k**

1Jn	2: 3	by this we know that we **k**
1Jn	2: 4	I **k** Him," and does not keep
1Jn	2: 5	By this we **k** that we are in
1Jn	3: 1	the world does not **k** us,
1Jn	3: 1	because it did not **k** Him.
1Jn	3: 2	but we **k** that when He is
1Jn	3:14	We **k** that we have passed from
1Jn	3:15	and you **k** that no murderer
1Jn	3:16	By this we **k** love, because
1Jn	3:24	And by this we **k** that He
1Jn	4: 2	By this you **k** the Spirit of
1Jn	4: 8	who does not love does not **k**
1Jn	4:13	By this we **k** that we abide in
1Jn	5: 2	By this we **k** that we love the
1Jn	5:13	that you may **k** that you have
1Jn	5:18	We **k** that whoever is born of
1Jn	5:19	We **k** that we are of God, and
1Jn	5:20	And we **k** that the Son of God
1Jn	5:20	that we may **k** Him who is
Rev	2: 2	I **k** your works, your labor,
Rev	2: 9	I **k** your works, tribulation,
Rev	2: 9	and I **k** the blasphemy of
Rev	2:13	I **k** your works, and where you
Rev	3: 3	and you will not **k** what hour
Rev	3:15	I **k** your works, that you are

KNOWING (see KNOW)

Gen	3: 5	**k** good and evil."
Jer	22:16	Was not this **k** Me?" says
Matt	9: 4	**k** their thoughts, said,
Matt	22:29	not **k** the Scriptures nor the
Mark	12:15	**k** their hypocrisy, said to
Luke	8:53	**k** that she was dead.
John	13: 3	**k** that the Father had given
John	19:28	**k** that all things were now
John	21:12	**k** that it was the Lord.
Acts	17:23	whom you worship without **k**,
Acts	20:22	not **k** the things that will
Rom	1:32	**k** the righteous judgment of
Rom	2: 4	not **k** that the goodness of
Rom	5: 3	**k** that tribulation produces
Rom	6: 6	**k** this, that our old man was
Rom	13:11	the time, that now it is
1Co	15:58	**k** that your labor is not in
2Co	4:14	**k** that He who raised up the
2Co	5: 6	**k** that while we are at home
Gal	2:16	**k** that a man is not justified
Eph	6: 9	**k** that your own Master also
Col	3:24	**k** that from the Lord you will
Col	4: 1	**k** that you also have a
2Ti	3:14	**k** from whom you have learned
Heb	10:34	**k** that you have a better and
Heb	11: 8	not **k** where he was going.
Jas	1: 3	**k** that the testing of your
Jas	3: 1	**k** that we shall receive a
1Pe	1:18	**k** that you were not redeemed
1Pe	5: 9	**k** that the same sufferings
2Pe	1:14	**k** that shortly I must put
2Pe	1:20	**k** this first, that no
2Pe	3: 3	**k** this first: that scoffers

KNOWLEDGE (see KNOW)

Gen	2: 9	and the tree of the **k** of
Ex	35:31	in **k** and all manner of
Num	24:16	And has the **k** of the Most
2Ch	1:10	"Now give me wisdom and **k**,
Job	21:22	"Can anyone teach God **k**,
Job	34:35	'Job speaks without **k**,
Job	35:16	multiplies words without **k**.
Job	37:16	of Him who is perfect in **k**?
Job	38: 2	counsel By words without **k**?
Job	42: 3	who hides counsel without **k**?
Ps	19: 2	night unto night reveals **k**.
Ps	73:11	And is there **k** in the Most
Ps	94:10	He who teaches man **k**?
Ps	119:66	me good judgment and **k**,

Ps	139: 6	Such **k** is too wonderful
Ps	144: 3	that You take **k** of him? Or
Prov	1: 7	LORD is the beginning of **k**,
Prov	1:22	scorning, And fools hate **k**.
Prov	2: 5	And find the **k** of God.
Prov	2: 6	From His mouth come **k** and
Prov	2:10	And **k** is pleasant to your
Prov	5: 2	And your lips may keep **k**.
Prov	8: 9	right to those who find **k**.
Prov	8:10	And **k** rather than choice
Prov	9:10	And the **k** of the Holy One
Prov	10:14	Wise people store up **k**,
Prov	12: 1	loves instruction loves **k**,
Prov	12:23	A prudent man conceals **k**,
Prov	15: 2	tongue of the wise uses **k**
Prov	15: 7	lips of the wise disperse **k**,
Prov	18:15	the ear of the wise seeks **k**.
Prov	19:25	and he will discern **k**.
Prov	22:12	eyes of the LORD preserve **k**,
Prov	22:17	apply your heart to my **k**;
Prov	22:20	things Of counsels and **k**,
Prov	24: 5	a man of **k** increases
Prov	29: 7	does not understand such **k**.
Prov	30: 3	learned wisdom Nor have **k**
Eccl	1:16	great wisdom and **k**.
Eccl	1:18	And he who increases **k**
Eccl	9:10	is no work or device or **k**
Eccl	12: 9	he still taught the people **k**;
Is	11: 2	The Spirit of **k** and of the
Is	11: 9	shall be full of the **k** of
Is	53:11	By His **k** My righteous
Jer	10:14	is dull-hearted, without **k**;
Dan	1: 4	possessing **k** and quick to
Dan	1:17	God gave them **k** and skill in
Dan	12: 4	and **k** shall increase."
Hos	4: 1	is no truth or mercy Or **k**
Hos	4: 6	are destroyed for lack of **k**.
Hos	4: 6	Because you have rejected **k**,
Hos	6: 3	Let us pursue the **k** of the
Hos	6: 6	And the **k** of God more than
Hab	2:14	will be filled With the **k**
Luke	11:52	have taken away the key of **k**.
Acts	24:22	having more accurate **k** of
Rom	1:28	to retain God in their **k**,
Rom	2:20	having the form of **k** and
Rom	3:20	for by the law is the **k** of
Rom	10: 2	God, but not according to **k**.
Rom	11:33	both of the wisdom and **k** of
Rom	15:14	goodness, filled with all **k**,
1Co	1: 5	in all utterance and all **k**,
1Co	8: 1	We know that we all have **k**.
1Co	8: 1	**K** puffs up, but love
1Co	12: 8	to another the word of **k**
1Co	13: 2	all mysteries and all **k**,
1Co	13: 8	cease; whether there is **k**,
1Co	15:34	for some do not have the **k**
2Co	2:14	the fragrance of His **k** in
2Co	4: 6	to give the light of the **k** of
2Co	6: 6	by purity, by **k**,
2Co	8: 7	faith, in speech, in **k**,
Eph	1:17	and revelation in the **k** of
Eph	3:19	of Christ which passes **k**;
Eph	4:13	of the faith and of the **k**
Phil	1: 9	still more and more in **k**
Phil	3: 8	for the excellence of the **k**
Col	1: 9	may be filled with the **k** of
Col	1:10	and increasing in the **k** of
Col	2: 2	to the **k** of the mystery of
Col	2: 3	treasures of wisdom and **k**.
Col	3:10	new man who is renewed in **k**
1Ti	2: 4	saved and to come to the **k**
1Ti	6:20	of what is falsely called **k**—
2Ti	3: 7	never able to come to the **k**
2Pe	1: 3	through the **k** of Him who
2Pe	1: 5	faith virtue, to virtue **k**,

2Pe 1: 6 to **k** self-control, to
2Pe 3:18 but grow in the grace and **k**

KNOWN (*see* KNOW)
Gen 18:19 For I have **k** him, in order
Gen 19: 8 daughters who have not **k** a
Gen 24:16 no man had **k** her. And she
Gen 45: 1 while Joseph made himself **k**
Ex 2:14 Surely this thing is **k**!"
Ex 6: 3 My name LORD I was not **k**
Ex 21:36 Or if it was **k** that the ox
Num 12: 6 make Myself **k** to him in a
Num 31:17 kill every woman who has **k**
Deut 7:15 of Egypt which you have **k**,
Deut 11: 2 who have not **k** and who have
Deut 11:28 gods which you have not **k**.
Deut 28:33 nation whom you have not **k**
Deut 28:36 you nor your fathers have **k**,
Josh 24:31 who had **k** all the works of
Judg 16: 9 of his strength was not **k**.
Ruth 3: 3 but do not make yourself **k**
Ruth 3:14 Do not let it be **k** that the
2Sa 17:19 it; and the thing was not **k**.
1Ch 16: 8 Make **k** His deeds among the
Neh 9:14 made **k** to them Your holy
Ps 18:43 A people I have not **k** shall
Ps 31: 7 You have **k** my soul in
Ps 76: 1 In Judah God is **k**;
Ps 78: 3 Which we have heard and **k**,
Ps 78: 5 they should make them **k** to
Ps 88:12 Shall Your wonders be **k** in
Ps 89: 1 my mouth will I make **k** Your
Ps 91:14 because he has **k** My name.
Ps 98: 2 The LORD has made His
Ps 103: 7 He made **k** His ways to Moses,
Ps 105: 1 Make **k** His deeds among the
Ps 106: 8 make His mighty power **k**.
Ps 139: 1 You have searched me and **k**
Ps 145:12 To make **k** to the sons of men
Prov 20:11 Even a child is **k** by his
Prov 31:23 Her husband is **k** in the
Is 12: 5 This is **k** in all the
Is 40:21 Have you not **k**?
Is 42:16 in paths they have not **k**.
Is 45: 4 though you have not **k** Me.
Is 59: 8 way of peace they have not **k**,
Is 61: 9 descendants shall be **k**
Is 64: 2 To make Your name **k** to Your
Is 66:14 of the LORD shall be **k** to
Jer 9:16 nor their fathers have **k**.
Jer 28: 9 the prophet will be **k** as
Ezek 20: 5 and made Myself **k** to them in
Ezek 32: 9 which you have not **k**.
Dan 2: 5 if you do not make **k** the
Dan 2:28 and He has made **k** to King
Dan 2:45 the great God has made **k** to
Dan 5:15 this writing and make **k** to
Amos 3: 2 You only have I **k** of all the
Hab 3: 2 of the years make it **k**;
Zech 7:14 nations which they had not **k**.
Zech 14: 7 be one day Which is **k** to
Matt 10:26 hidden that will not be **k**.
Matt 12: 7 But if you had **k** what this
Matt 12:16 them not to make Him **k**,
Matt 12:33 for a tree is **k** by its
Matt 24:43 master of the house had **k**
Luke 2:15 which the Lord has made **k** to
Luke 2:17 they made widely **k** the
Luke 8:17 hidden that will not be **k**
Luke 24:35 and how He was **k** to them in
John 8:19 If you had **k** Me, you would
John 8:19 you would have **k** My Father
John 8:55 Yet you have not **k** Him, but I
John 10:14 and am **k** by My own.
John 14: 7 If you had **k** Me, you would

John 14: 7 you would have **k** My Father
John 17:25 Father! The world has not **k**
John 17:25 but I have **k** You; and these
John 17:25 and these have **k** that You
Acts 7:13 time Joseph was made **k** to
Acts 15:18 **K** to God from eternity are
Rom 1:19 because what may be **k** of God
Rom 3:17 peace they have not **k**.
Rom 7: 7 I would not have **k** sin
Rom 9:22 and to made His power **k**,
Rom 9:23 and that He might make **k** the
Rom 11:34 For who has **k** the mind
Rom 16:19 your obedience has become **k**
Rom 16:26 Scriptures has been made **k**
1Co 2: 8 age knew; for had they **k**,
1Co 2:16 who has the mind of
1Co 8: 3 this one is **k** by Him.
1Co 13:12 know just as I also am **k**.
2Co 3: 2 **k** and read by all men;
2Co 5:16 Even though we have **k** Christ
Gal 4: 9 or rather are **k** by God, how
Eph 1: 9 having made **k** to us the
Eph 3: 3 by revelation He made **k** to
Eph 3:10 of God might be made **k** by
Eph 6:19 my mouth boldly to make **k**
Phil 4: 5 Let your gentleness be **k** to
Phil 4: 6 let your requests be made **k** to
Col 1:27 To them God willed to make **k**
2Ti 3:15 from childhood you have **k**
Heb 3:10 And they have not **k**
2Pe 1:16 fables when we made **k** to
2Pe 2:21 than having **k** it, to turn
1Jn 2:13 Because you have **k** Him who
1Jn 2:14 Because you have **k** Him who
1Jn 3: 6 has neither seen Him nor **k**
1Jn 4:16 And we have **k** and believed
Rev 2:24 who have not **k** the depths of

KNOWS (*see* KNOW, KNOWLEDGE)
Gen 3: 5 For God **k** that in the day you
Deut 34: 6 but no one **k** his grave to
Esth 4:14 Yet who **k** whether you have
Job 11:11 For He **k** deceitful men; He
Job 15:23 He **k** that a day of
Job 20:20 Because he **k** no quietness in
Job 23:10 But He **k** the way that I
Job 28: 7 That path no bird **k**,
Ps 1: 6 For the LORD **k** the way of
Ps 37:18 The LORD **k** the days of the
Ps 44:21 For He **k** the secrets of the
Ps 74: 9 there any among us who **k**
Ps 90:11 Who **k** the power of Your
Ps 94:11 The LORD **k** the thoughts of
Ps 103:14 For He **k** our frame; He
Ps 104:19 The sun **k** its going down.
Ps 138: 6 But the proud He **k** from
Ps 139:14 And that my soul **k** very
Prov 14:10 The heart **k** its own
Eccl 2:19 And who **k** whether he will be
Eccl 10:14 No man **k** what is to be;
Is 1: 3 The ox **k** its owner And the
Jer 9:24 That he understands and **k**
Dan 2:22 He **k** what is in the
Matt 6: 8 For your Father **k** the things
Matt 6:32 For your heavenly Father **k**
Matt 11:27 and no one **k** the Son except
Matt 24:36 that day and hour no one **k**,
Luke 16:15 but God **k** your hearts. For
John 7:27 no one **k** where He is from."
John 10:15 As the Father **k** Me, even so I
John 14:17 it neither sees Him nor **k**
Acts 15: 8 who **k** the heart,
Rom 8:27 He who searches the hearts **k**
1Co 2:11 For what man **k** the things of
1Co 3:20 The LORD **k** the thoughts

1Co 8: 2 if anyone thinks that he **k**
1Co 8: 2 he **k** nothing yet as he ought
2Co 12: 2 body I do not know, God **k**—
2Ti 2:19 The Lord **k** those who are
Jas 4:17 to him who **k** to do good and
1Jn 3:20 and **k** all things.
1Jn 4: 6 He who **k** God hears us; he
1Jn 4: 7 loves is born of God and **k**
Rev 2:17 name written which no one **k**

KOHATH (*see* KOHATHITES)
Gen 46:11 of Levi were Gershon, K,
Ex 6:18 And the sons of K were
Num 4: 4 service of the sons of K in
Num 4:15 meeting which the sons of K

KOHATHITES (*see* KOHATH)
Num 3:27 were the families of the K.
Num 10:21 Then the K set out, carrying

KOR
Ezek 45:14 A **k** is a homer or ten

KORAH
Ex 6:21 The sons of Izhar were K,
Num 16: 6 K and all your company;
Jude 11 in the rebellion of K.

L

LABAN (*see* LABAN'S)
Gen 24:29 a brother whose name was L,
Gen 25:20 the sister of L the Syrian.
Gen 28: 5 to L the son of Bethuel the
Gen 29:15 Then L said to Jacob,
Gen 29:16 Now L had two daughters; the
Gen 31:19 Now L had gone to shear his
Gen 31:25 So L overtook Jacob. Now
Gen 31:36 was angry and rebuked L,
Gen 31:47 L called it Jegar Sahadutha,
Gen 31:48 And L said, "This heap is a
Gen 46:18 whom L gave to Leah his
Gen 46:25 whom L gave to Rachel his

LABAN'S (*see* LABAN)
Gen 30:36 and Jacob fed the rest of L
Gen 30:42 so the feebler were L and

LABOR (*see* LABORED, LABORER, LABORING, LABORS)
Gen 35:16 and she had hard l.
Ex 5: 4 work? Get back to your l.
Ex 5: 5 make them rest from their l!
Ex 20: 9 Six days you shall l and do
Deut 5:13 Six days you shall l and do
Josh 17:13 the Canaanites to forced l,
Josh 24:13 land for which you did not l,
1Sa 4:19 for her l pains came upon
1Ki 9:21 Solomon raised forced l,
Job 9:29 Why then do I l in vain?
Job 39:11 Or will you leave your l to
Ps 90:10 Yet their boast is only l
Is 21: 3 the pangs of a woman in l.
Is 23: 4 sea, saying, "I do not l,
Is 42:14 I will cry like a woman in l,
Is 65:23 They shall not l in vain,
Jer 20:18 from the womb to see l and
Jer 30: 6 Whether a man is ever in l
Jer 30: 6 his loins Like a woman in l,
Jer 51:58 The people will l in vain,
Lam 5: 5 We l and have no rest.
Hag 1:11 and on all the l of your
Matt 11:28 all you who l and are heavy
John 6:27 Do not l for the food which
1Co 3: 8 according to his own l.
1Co 4:12 And we l, working with
1Co 15:58 knowing that your l is not

Eph 4:28 longer, but rather let him l,
Phil 1:22 will mean fruit from my l;
Col 1:29 To this end I also l,
1Th 1: 3 of love, and patience of
1Th 2: 9 our l and toil; for laboring
1Th 3: 5 and our l might be in vain.
1Th 5:12 to recognize those who l
2Th 3: 8 but worked with l and toil
1Ti 4:10 For to this end we both l
1Ti 5:17 especially those who l in
Heb 6:10 to forget your work and l
Rev 2: 2 "I know your works, your l,
Rev 12: 2 she cried out in l and to

LABORED (*see* LABOR)
Eccl 2:21 to a man who has not l for
Is 49: 4 I have l in vain, I have
Dan 6:14 and he l till the going down
Jon 4:10 for which you have not l,
John 4:38 for which you have not l;
John 4:38 not labored; others have l,
Rom 16:12 who have l in the Lord.
1Co 15:10 but I l more abundantly than
Gal 4:11 lest I have l for you in
Phil 2:16 I have not run in vain or l
Phil 4: 3 help these women who l with
Rev 2: 3 and have l for My name's

LABORER† (*see* LABOR, LABORERS)
Luke 10: 7 for the l is worthy of his
1Th 3: 2 and our fellow l in the
1Ti 5:18 The l is worthy of his
Phm 1: 1 beloved friend and fellow l,

LABORERS (*see* LABORER)
Matt 9:37 but the l are few.
Matt 9:38 of the harvest to send out l
Matt 20: 1 in the morning to hire l
Phm 1:24 Demas, Luke, my fellow l.

LABORING (*see* LABOR)
Eccl 5:12 The sleep of a l man is
Col 4:12 always l fervently for you
1Th 2: 9 for l night and day, that we

LABORS (*see* LABOR)
Ex 23:16 the firstfruits of your l
Eccl 4: 8 is no end to all his l,
Jer 31: 8 child And the one who l
John 4:38 have entered into their l.
Rom 8:22 whole creation groans and l
2Co 6: 5 in tumults, in l,
2Co 10:15 that is, in other men's l,
2Co 11:23 in l more abundant, in
Rev 14:13 they may rest from their l,

LACHISH
2Ch 32: 9 him laid siege against L),
Is 36: 2 with a great army from L to
Jer 34: 7 against L and Azekah; for

LACK (*see* LACKED, LACKING, LACKS)
Gen 18:28 all of the city for l of
Ex 16:18 who gathered little had no l.
Deut 8: 9 in which you will l nothing;
Job 31:19 seen anyone perish for l of
Ps 34:10 seek the LORD shall not l
Prov 10:21 But fools die for l of
Prov 28:27 gives to the poor will not l,
Prov 31:11 So he will have no l of
Jer 33:17 David shall never l a man to
Jer 35:19 son of Rechab shall not l a
Hos 4: 6 people are destroyed for l
Amos 4: 6 And l of bread in all your
Matt 19:20 my youth. What do I still l?
Mark 10:21 to him, "One thing you l:
Luke 22:35 did you l anything?" So
1Co 7: 5 tempt you because of your l

2Co 8:14 may supply their l,
2Co 8:15 little had no l.
1Th 4:12 and that you may l nothing.

LACKED (see LACK)
Deut 2: 7 you have l nothing." '
Luke 8: 6 withered away because it l
Acts 4:34 anyone among them who l;
Phil 4:10 but you l opportunity.

LACKING (see LACK)
Eccl 1:15 And what is l cannot be
1Co 16:17 for what was l on your part
Phil 2:30 to supply what was l in your
Col 1:24 up in my flesh what is l in
1Th 3:10 face and perfect what is l
Jas 1: 4 complete, l nothing.

LACKS (see LACK)
2Sa 3:29 or who l bread."
Eccl 6: 2 so that he l nothing for
Eccl 10: 3 He l wisdom, And he shows
1Co 12:24 honor to that part which l
Jas 1: 5 If any of you l wisdom, let
2Pe 1: 9 For he who l these things is

LAD (see LAD'S, LADS)
Gen 21:17 God heard the voice of the l.
Gen 22: 5 the l and I will go yonder
Judg 16:26 Then Samson said to the l who
John 6: 9 There is a l here who has

LAD'S† (see LAD)
Gen 44:30 life is bound up in the l

LADDER†
Gen 28:12 a l was set up on the

LADEN†
Is 1: 4 A people l with iniquity,
Matt 11:28 who labor and are heavy l,

LADIES (see LADY)
Judg 5:29 Her wisest l answered her,

LADS (see LAD)
Gen 48:16 from all evil, Bless the l;

LADY (see LADIES)
2Jn 1 To the elect l and her

LAGGING†
Rom 12:11 not l in diligence, fervent

LAHAI
Gen 16:14 the well was called Beer L

LAHAI ROI (see BEER LAHAI ROI)
Gen 16:14 the well was called Beer L

LAID (see LAY)
Gen 9:23 l it on both their
Gen 22: 6 of the burnt offering and l
Gen 22: 9 he bound Isaac his son and l
Gen 41:48 and l up the food in the
Gen 48:17 saw that his father l his
Ex 2: 3 and l it in the reeds by
Ex 16:24 So they l it up till morning,
Ex 19: 7 and l before them all these
Lev 8:14 Then Aaron and his sons l
Num 27:23 And he l his hands on him and
Deut 34: 9 for Moses had l his hands on
Judg 9:24 and their blood be l on
Judg 9:48 and took it and l it on his
Judg 19:29 l hold of his concubine, and
Ruth 3:15 and l it on her. Then she
1Ki 3:20 and l her dead child in my
1Ki 16:34 He l its foundation with
2Ki 9:25 that the LORD l this burden
2Ch 3: 3 foundation which Solomon l
Job 14:10 But man dies and is l away;
Job 16:15 And l my head in the dust.

Job 38: 4 Where were you when I l the
Ps 66:11 You l affliction on our
Ps 79: 7 And l waste his dwelling
Ps 88: 6 You have l me in the lowest
Ps 102:25 Of old You l the foundation
Ps 116: 3 And the pangs of Sheol l
Ps 119:110 The wicked have l a snare
Ps 136: 6 To Him who l out the earth
Ps 139: 5 And l Your hand upon me.
Is 6:11 Until the cities are l waste
Is 44:28 "Your foundation shall be l.
Is 51:13 out the heavens And l the
Is 53: 6 And the LORD has l on Him
Lam 3:28 Because God has l it on
Ezek 12:20 are inhabited shall be l
Dan 6:17 a stone was brought and l
Jon 3: 6 arose from his throne and l
Nah 3: 7 Nineveh is l waste! Who will
Hag 2:18 of the LORD's temple was l—
Zech 4: 9 hands of Zerubbabel Have l
Matt 3:10 And even now the ax is l to
Matt 14: 3 For Herod had l hold of John
Matt 15:30 and they l them down at
Matt 18:28 and he l hands on him and
Matt 19:15 And He l His hands on them
Matt 21: 7 l their clothes on them, and
Matt 26:50 Then they came and l hands
Matt 27:60 and l it in his new tomb
Mark 6:17 himself had sent and l hold
Mark 15:47 observed where He was l.
Mark 16: 6 See the place where they l
Luke 2: 7 and l Him in a manger,
Luke 6:48 who dug deep and l the
Luke 12:19 you have many goods l up for
Luke 13:13 And He l His hands on her,
Luke 23:26 and on him they l the cross
Luke 23:53 and l it in a tomb that
John 7:30 but no one l a hand on Him,
John 13: 4 rose from supper and l aside
John 20: 2 not know where they have l
Acts 4: 3 And they l hands on them, and
Acts 4:35 and l them at the apostles'
Acts 7:58 And the witnesses l down
Acts 16:23 And when they had l many
Acts 19: 6 And when Paul had l hands on
1Co 3:10 master builder I have l the
1Co 3:11 lay than that which is l,
1Co 9:16 for necessity is l upon me;
Phil 3:12 Christ Jesus has also l
Col 1: 5 of the hope which is l up
2Ti 4: 8 there is l up for me the
Heb 1:10 in the beginning l the
1Jn 3:16 because He l down His life
Rev 1:17 But He l His right hand on
Rev 21:16 The city is l out as a

LAIN (see LIE)
Num 5:19 If no man has l with you, and
Jon 1: 5 had l down, and was fast
Luke 23:53 where no one had ever l
John 20:12 the body of Jesus had l.

LAISH (see DAN, LESHEM)
Judg 18:29 of the city formerly was L.

LAKE
Luke 5: 1 that He stood by the L of
Luke 8:22 to the other side of the l.
Luke 8:23 windstorm came down on the l,
Luke 8:33 the steep place into the l
Rev 20:10 was cast into the l of fire
Rev 20:15 of Life was cast into the l

LAMA
Matt 27:46 l sabachthani?" that is,
Mark 15:34 l sabachthani?" which is

LAMB (see LAMB'S, LAMBS)

Gen	22: 7	but where is the l for a
Gen	22: 8	provide for Himself the l
Ex	12: 3	a l for a household.
Ex	12:21	and kill the Passover l.
Ex	13:13	you shall redeem with a l;
Lev	3: 7	If he offers a l as his
Lev	5: 6	a l or a kid of the goats as
Lev	12: 6	bring to the priest a l of
Lev	14:12	shall take one male l and
Num	15:11	or for each l or young goat.
2Sa	12: 3	except one little ewe l
2Sa	12: 4	but he took the poor man's l
Is	11: 6	also shall dwell with the l,
Is	53: 7	He was led as a l to the
Is	65:25	The wolf and the l shall
Mark	14:12	they killed the Passover l,
John	1:29	Behold! The L of God who
John	1:36	Behold the L of God!"
Acts	8:32	And as a l before its
1Pe	1:19	as of a l without blemish
Rev	5: 6	stood a L as though it had
Rev	5: 8	fell down before the L,
Rev	5:12	Worthy is the L who was slain
Rev	5:13	on the throne, And to the L,
Rev	6:16	and from the wrath of the L!
Rev	7:14	white in the blood of the L.
Rev	13: 8	in the Book of Life of the L
Rev	15: 3	God, and the song of the L,
Rev	17:14	will make war with the L,
Rev	19: 9	marriage supper of the L!'
Rev	21:14	the twelve apostles of the L.
Rev	21:23	The L is its light.

LAMB'S† (see LAMB)

Rev	21: 9	the bride, the L wife."
Rev	21:27	who are written in the L

LAMBS (see LAMB)

Gen	30:40	Then Jacob separated the l,
Ex	29:38	two l of the first year, day
Lev	14:10	day he shall take two male l
Ezra	6:20	slaughtered the Passover l
Ps	114: 4	The little hills like l.
Is	34: 6	With the blood of l and
Is	40:11	He will gather the l with
Amos	6: 4	Eat l from the flock And
Luke	10: 3	I send you out as l among
John	21:15	He said to him, "Feed My l.

LAME

Lev	21:18	approach: a man blind or l,
2Sa	4: 4	had a son who was l in
2Sa	5: 6	but the blind and the l will
Is	35: 6	Then the l shall leap like a
Jer	31: 8	them the blind and the l
Mal	1: 8	And when you offer the l
Matt	11: 5	The blind see and the l
Matt	18: 8	you to enter into life l or
Luke	7:22	the l walk, the lepers are
John	5: 3	of sick people, blind, l,
Acts	3: 2	And a certain man l from his
Acts	8: 7	who were paralyzed and l
Heb	12:13	so that what is l may not be

LAMECH

Gen	4:23	Then L said to his wives:
Gen	5:30	L lived five hundred and

LAMENT (see LAMENTATION, LAMENTED, LAMENTING, LAMENTS)

Judg	11:40	four days each year to l
2Sa	3:33	And the king sang a L over
Jer	4: 8	L and wail. For the fierce
Jer	22:18	They shall not l for him,
Lam	2: 8	the rampart and wall to l;
Joel	1:13	Gird yourselves and l,

Mic	2: 4	And l with a bitter
Matt	11:17	to you, And you did not l.

LAMENTATION (see LAMENT, LAMENTATIONS)

Gen	50:10	a great and very solemn l.
2Sa	1:17	David lamented with this l
Jer	31:15	L and bitter weeping,
Lam	2: 5	has increased mourning and l
Ezek	19: 1	Moreover take up a l for the
Ezek	27: 2	take up a l for Tyre,
Amos	8:10	And all your songs into l;
Mic	2: 4	And lament with a bitter l,
Matt	2:18	was heard in Ramah, L,
Acts	8: 2	and made great l over him.

LAMENTATIONS† (see LAMENTATION)

2Ch	35:25	speak of Josiah in their l.
Ezek	2:10	and written on it were l

LAMENTED (see LAMENT)

1Sa	6:19	and the people l because the
1Sa	28: 3	and all Israel had l for him
2Sa	1:17	Then David l with this
2Ch	35:25	Jeremiah also l for Josiah.
Luke	23:27	who also mourned and l Him.

LAMENTING† (see LAMENT)

Esth	9:31	of their fasting and l.
Dan	6:20	he cried out with a l voice

LAMENTS† (see LAMENT)

2Ch	35:25	they are written in the L.

LAMP (see LAMPS, LAMPSTAND)

Ex	27:20	to cause the l to burn
1Sa	3: 3	and before the l of God went
2Sa	21:17	lest you quench the l of
2Sa	22:29	"For You are my l,
1Ki	11:36	David may always have a l
Job	18: 6	And his l beside him is put
Job	29: 3	When His l shone upon my
Ps	18:28	For You will light my l;
Ps	119:105	Your word is a l to my
Ps	132:17	I will prepare a l for My
Prov	6:23	For the commandment is a l,
Prov	13: 9	But the l of the wicked
Prov	31:18	And her l does not go out
Is	62: 1	And her salvation as a l
Matt	5:15	Nor do they light a l and put
Matt	6:22	The l of the body is the
Mark	4:21	Is a l brought to be put
Luke	8:16	one, when he has lit a l,
Luke	11:33	one, when he has lit a l,
Luke	11:36	the bright shining of a l
Luke	15: 8	one coin, does not light a l,
John	5:35	the burning and shining l,
Rev	22: 5	They need no l nor light of

LAMPS (see LAMP)

Ex	25:37	You shall make seven l for
Ex	30: 8	when Aaron lights the l
Ex	40: 4	lampstand and light its l.
Zeph	1:12	will search Jerusalem with l,
Zech	4: 2	seven pipes to the seven l.
Matt	25: 1	ten virgins who took their l
Matt	25: 8	for our l are going out.'
Rev	4: 5	Seven l of fire were

LAMPSTAND (see LAMP, LAMPSTANDS)

Ex	25:31	You shall also make a l of
Ex	37:19	branches coming out of the l.
Num	8: 2	give light in front of the l.
Dan	5: 5	and wrote opposite the l on
Matt	5:15	under a basket, but on a l,
Mark	4:21	Is it not to be set on a l?
Luke	8:16	a bed, but sets it on a l,
Heb	9: 2	part, in which was the l,
Rev	2: 5	quickly and remove your l

LAMPSTANDS (see LAMPSTAND)
1Ki	7:49	the l of pure gold, five on
Rev	1:12	turned I saw seven golden l,
Rev	1:13	in the midst of the seven l
Rev	11: 4	olive trees and the two l

LAND (see LANDMARK, LANDOWNER, LANDS)
Gen	1: 9	and let the dry l appear";
Gen	1:10	And God called the dry l
Gen	11: 2	they found a plain in the l
Gen	12: 1	To a l that I will show
Gen	12: 6	were then in the l.
Gen	12: 7	I will give this l.
Gen	12:10	there was a famine in the l,
Gen	13: 9	Is not the whole l before
Gen	13:10	like the l of Egypt as you
Gen	13:17	walk in the l through its
Gen	15: 7	to give you this l to
Gen	15:13	will be strangers in a l
Gen	21:21	a wife for him from the l
Gen	21:32	and they returned to the l
Gen	22: 2	and go to the l of Moriah,
Gen	24: 7	house and from the l of my
Gen	24: 7	descendants I give this l,
Gen	26: 1	There was a famine in the l,
Gen	27:46	are the daughters of the l,
Gen	28: 4	That you may inherit the l
Gen	28:13	the l on which you lie I
Gen	28:15	bring you back to this l;
Gen	33:19	he bought the parcel of l,
Gen	35:12	The l which I gave Abraham
Gen	37: 1	in the l of Canaan.
Gen	40:15	I was stolen away from the l
Gen	41:29	come throughout all the l
Gen	41:30	famine will deplete the l.
Gen	41:33	and set him over the l of
Gen	41:52	me to be fruitful in the l
Gen	41:56	became severe in the l of
Gen	42: 5	for the famine was in the l
Gen	42: 6	was governor over the l;
Gen	42:30	man who is lord of the l
Gen	45:10	You shall dwell in the l of
Gen	45:18	give you the best of the l
Gen	45:18	will eat the fat of the l.
Gen	47: 6	dwell in the best of the l;
Gen	47:11	in the l of Rameses, as
Gen	47:13	was no bread in all the l;
Gen	47:15	the money failed in the l
Gen	47:20	So the l became Pharaoh's.
Gen	47:22	Only the l of the priests he
Gen	47:28	And Jacob lived in the l of
Gen	48:21	and bring you back to the l
Gen	49:15	And that the l was
Gen	50:24	and bring you out of this l
Gen	50:24	out of this land to the l
Ex	1: 7	and the l was filled with
Ex	2:15	Pharaoh and dwelt in the l
Ex	2:22	a stranger in a foreign l.
Ex	3: 8	to bring them up from that l
Ex	3: 8	land to a good and large l,
Ex	3:17	to a l flowing with milk and
Ex	4: 9	and pour it on the dry l.
Ex	4: 9	become blood on the dry l.
Ex	6: 4	the l of their pilgrimage,
Ex	6: 8	I will bring you into the l
Ex	6:13	of Israel out of the l of
Ex	7: 3	and My wonders in the l of
Ex	8: 7	brought up frogs on the l
Ex	8:16	and strike the dust of the l,
Ex	8:22	day I will set apart the l
Ex	8:24	The l was corrupted because
Ex	9:23	LORD rained hail on the l
Ex	10:13	out his rod over the l of
Ex	10:15	so that the l was darkened;
Ex	12:12	all the firstborn in the l

Ex	12:13	you when I strike the l of
Ex	12:33	send them out of the l in
Ex	13: 5	LORD brings you into the l
Ex	14:21	and made the sea into dry l,
Ex	14:29	Israel had walked on dry l
Ex	15:19	of Israel went on dry l in
Ex	16: 1	they departed from the l of
Ex	16:35	came to the border of the l
Ex	18: 3	a stranger in a foreign l'
Ex	20: 2	brought you out of the l of
Ex	20:12	days may be long upon the l
Ex	22:21	you were strangers in the l
Ex	23:30	and you inherit the l.
Ex	32: 1	brought us up out of the l
Ex	32:11	have brought out of the l
Ex	34:15	the inhabitants of the l,
Ex	34:24	will any man covet your l
Lev	18:25	For the l is defiled;
Lev	18:25	and the l vomits out its
Lev	19: 9	reap the harvest of your l,
Lev	19:29	lest the l fall into
Lev	24:16	as him who is born in the l.
Lev	25: 2	When you come into the l
Lev	25: 4	of solemn rest for the l,
Lev	25: 5	is a year of rest for the l.
Lev	25:18	and you will dwell in the l
Lev	25:19	Then the l will yield its
Lev	25:23	The l shall not be sold
Lev	25:23	for the l is Mine; for you
Lev	25:24	grant redemption of the l.
Lev	26: 4	the l shall yield its
Lev	26: 5	and dwell in your l safely.
Lev	26: 6	I will give peace in the l,
Lev	26: 6	I will rid the l of evil
Lev	27:30	'And all the tithe of the l,
Num	9:14	and the native of the l.
Num	13: 2	Send men to spy out the l of
Num	13:20	whether the l is rich or
Num	13:20	some of the fruit of the l.
Num	14: 2	only we had died in the l
Num	14: 3	LORD brought us to this l
Num	14: 7	is an exceedingly good l.
Num	14:36	a bad report of the l,
Num	15:19	eat of the bread of the l,
Num	18:20	no inheritance in their l,
Num	20:18	shall not pass through my l,
Num	20:23	Hor by the border of the l
Num	21: 4	to go around the l of Edom;
Num	32: 8	Kadesh Barnea to see the l.
Num	32:22	and the l is subdued before
Num	33:53	for I have given you the l
Num	33:54	And you shall divide the l by
Num	35:14	you shall appoint in the l
Num	35:33	you shall not pollute the l
Num	35:33	for blood defiles the l,
Deut	1: 8	I have set the l before you;
Deut	1: 8	go in and possess the l
Deut	1:22	let them search out the l
Deut	1:25	It is a good l which the
Deut	2:20	was also regarded as a l of
Deut	2:27	'Let me pass through your l;
Deut	3:18	God has given you this l to
Deut	3:25	over and see the good l
Deut	4:22	"But I must die in this l,
Deut	4:40	prolong your days in the l
Deut	5:15	you were a slave in the l
Deut	6:18	go in and possess the good l
Deut	6:23	to give us the l of which He
Deut	8: 7	bringing you into a good l,
Deut	8: 7	a l of brooks of water, of
Deut	8: 8	a l of wheat and barley, of
Deut	8: 8	a l of olive oil and honey;
Deut	8: 9	a l whose stones are iron
Deut	9:28	able to bring them to the l
Deut	10: 7	a l of rivers of water.

Deut 10:19 you were strangers in the l
Deut 11:11 over to possess is a l of
Deut 11:14 you the rain for your l in
Deut 11:25 fear of you upon all the l
Deut 12: 1 careful to observe in the l
Deut 15: 4 greatly bless you in the l
Deut 16:20 may live and inherit the l
Deut 23: 7 you were an alien in his l.
Deut 24:22 you were a slave in the l
Deut 26:15 Your people Israel and the l
Deut 28: 8 He will bless you in the l
Deut 28:12 to give the rain to your l
Deut 28:33 eat the fruit of your l and
Deut 28:42 and the produce of your l.
Deut 29:22 who comes from a far l,
Deut 29:28 uprooted them from their l
Deut 29:28 and cast them into another l,
Deut 30: 5 God will bring you to the l
Deut 31:21 I have brought them to the l
Deut 32:10 He found him in a desert l
Deut 32:43 provide atonement for His l
Deut 33:28 In a l of grain and new
Deut 34: 5 LORD died there in the l
Josh 1: 4 all the l of the Hittites,
Josh 1:14 shall remain in the l which
Josh 2: 1 saying, "Go, view the l,
Josh 4:18 feet touched the dry l,
Josh 5:12 eaten the produce of the l;
Josh 10:40 Joshua conquered all the l:
Josh 11:23 So Joshua took the whole l,
Josh 11:23 Then the l rested from war.
Josh 14: 4 part to the Levites in the l,
Josh 14: 5 did; and they divided the l.
Josh 14: 7 Barnea to spy out the l,
Josh 14: 9 Surely the l where your foot
Josh 14:15 Then the l had rest from
Josh 18: 1 And the l was subdued before
Josh 18: 6 therefore survey the l in
Josh 18: 8 "Go, walk through the l,
Josh 18:10 there Joshua divided the l
Josh 22:11 on the frontier of the l of
Josh 22:13 into the l of Gilead,
Josh 22:33 to destroy the l where the
Josh 23:13 you perish from this good l
Josh 24:15 in whose l you dwell. But as
Judg 1:32 the inhabitants of the l;
Judg 2: 1 and brought you to the l of
Judg 3:11 So the l had rest for forty
Judg 9:37 from the center of the l,
Judg 16:24 The destroyer of our l,
Judg 18: 2 to spy out the l and search
Judg 18:30 of the captivity of the l.
Ruth 1: 1 there was a famine in the l.
Ruth 1: 7 the way to return to the l
Ruth 2:11 and your mother and the l
Ruth 4: 3 sold the piece of l which
1Sa 6: 5 your rats that ravage the l,
1Sa 9:16 send you a man from the l
1Sa 14:29 father has troubled the l.
1Sa 21:11 not David the king of the l?
1Sa 27: 9 David attacked the l,
1Sa 28: 3 the spiritists out of the l.
2Sa 3:12 saying, "Whose is the l?
2Sa 7:23 and awesome deeds for Your l—
2Sa 9:10 shall work the l for him,
2Sa 15: 4 I were made judge in the l,
2Sa 21:14 heeded the prayer for the l
2Sa 24:13 three days' plague in your l?
1Ki 8:36 and send rain on Your l
1Ki 8:37 there is famine in the l,
1Ki 9:11 twenty cities in the l of
1Ki 9:21 who were left in the l
1Ki 12:28 brought you up from the l
1Ki 14:15 Israel from this good l
1Ki 15:20 with all the l of Naphtali.

1Ki 17: 7 had been no rain in the l.
2Ki 4:38 was a famine in the l.
2Ki 5: 2 a young girl from the l of
2Ki 8: 1 it will come upon the l for
2Ki 8: 3 for her house and for her l.
2Ki 11: 3 Athaliah reigned over the l.
2Ki 11:20 So all the people of the l
2Ki 13:20 from Moab invaded the l in
2Ki 15:19 Assyria came against the l;
2Ki 17:26 rituals of the God of the l;
2Ki 18:32 a l of grain and new wine, a
2Ki 18:32 a l of bread and vineyards,
2Ki 18:32 a l of olive groves and
2Ki 19: 7 and return to his own l;
2Ki 23:33 and he imposed on the l a
2Ki 23:35 but he taxed the l to give
2Ki 24:14 the poorest people of the l.
2Ki 25: 3 food for the people of the l.
2Ki 25:21 away captive from its own l.
2Ki 25:22 who remained in the l of
2Ki 25:24 Dwell in the l and serve the
1Ch 5:25 gods of the peoples of the l,
1Ch 28: 8 you may possess this good l,
2Ch 6:27 and send rain on Your l
2Ch 6:36 take them captive to a l
2Ch 6:38 all their soul in the l of
2Ch 6:38 and pray toward their l
2Ch 7:13 the locusts to devour the l,
2Ch 7:14 their sin and heal their l.
2Ch 15: 8 idols from all the l of
2Ch 32: 4 brook that ran through the l,
2Ch 34: 8 when he had purged the l and
2Ch 36: 3 and he imposed on the l a
Ezra 9:11 The l which you are entering
Ezra 9:11 to possess is an unclean l,
Ezra 9:12 and eat the good of the l,
Neh 5:14 be their governor in the l
Neh 9:25 strong cities and a rich l,
Esth 10: 1 imposed tribute on the l
Job 1: 1 There was a man in the l of
Job 1:10 have increased in the l.
Job 10:21 To the l of darkness and
Job 39: 6 And the barren l his
Job 42:15 In all the l were found no
Ps 10:16 have perished out of His l.
Ps 27:13 of the LORD In the l of
Ps 37: 3 and do good; Dwell in the l,
Ps 37:29 shall inherit the l,
Ps 42: 6 remember You from the l of
Ps 52: 5 And uproot you from the l
Ps 63: 1 You In a dry and thirsty l
Ps 66: 6 turned the sea into dry l;
Ps 74: 8 places of God in the l.
Ps 85: 1 been favorable to Your l;
Ps 85: 9 glory may dwell in our l.
Ps 85:12 And our l will yield its
Ps 88:12 Your righteousness in the l
Ps 95: 5 His hands formed the dry l.
Ps 101: 6 be on the faithful of the l,
Ps 101: 8 all the wicked of the l,
Ps 105:23 And Jacob dwelt in the l of
Ps 105:36 all the firstborn in their l,
Ps 106:24 they despised the pleasant l;
Ps 106:38 And the l was polluted with
Ps 107:34 A fruitful l into
Ps 107:35 And dry l into
Ps 116: 9 before the LORD In the l
Ps 135:12 And gave their l as a
Ps 137: 4 LORD's song In a foreign l?
Ps 143: 6 for You like a thirsty l.
Ps 143:10 Lead me in the l of
Prov 2:21 upright will dwell in the l,
Prov 29: 4 The king establishes the l
Prov 31:23 among the elders of the l.
Song 2:12 Is heard in our l.

LAND

343

LAND

Is	1:19	shall eat the good of the l;
Is	2: 8	Their l is also full of
Is	6:11	The l is utterly desolate,
Is	7:16	the l that you dread will be
Is	7:18	the bee that is in the l
Is	8: 8	fill the breadth of Your l,
Is	9: 1	He lightly esteemed The l
Is	9: 1	land of Zebulun and the l
Is	9: 2	Those who dwelt in the l of
Is	13:14	will flee to his own l.
Is	14: 1	settle them in their own l.
Is	14:20	you have destroyed your l
Is	14:25	break the Assyrian in My l,
Is	15: 9	And on the remnant of the l.
Is	18: 2	Whose l the rivers
Is	24:11	The mirth of the l is gone.
Is	27:13	about to perish in the l of
Is	27:13	who are outcasts in the l
Is	32: 2	of a great rock in a weary l.
Is	35: 7	And the thirsty l springs
Is	38:11	The LORD in the l of the
Is	41:18	And the dry l springs of
Is	60:18	no longer be heard in your l,
Is	60:21	They shall inherit the l
Is	62: 4	and your l Beulah; For the
Jer	1: 1	were in Anathoth in the l
Jer	1:18	walls against the whole l—
Jer	2: 2	In a l not sown.
Jer	2: 7	you defiled My l And made
Jer	3: 9	that she defiled the l and
Jer	3:18	come together out of the l
Jer	3:18	land of the north to the l
Jer	3:19	And give you a pleasant l,
Jer	4: 5	the trumpet in the l;
Jer	4: 7	his place To make your l
Jer	5:19	foreign gods in your l,
Jer	5:19	shall serve aliens in a l
Jer	8:16	The whole l trembled at the
Jer	8:16	come and devoured the l and
Jer	9:19	we have forsaken the l,
Jer	12: 4	How long will the l mourn,
Jer	12: 5	And if in the l of peace,
Jer	12:14	pluck them out of their l
Jer	14: 4	there was no rain in the l,
Jer	14: 8	be like a stranger in the l,
Jer	16:15	of Israel from the l of the
Jer	17: 6	In a salt l which is not
Jer	22:12	and shall see this l no
Jer	23:10	because of a curse the l
Jer	24: 5	into the l of the Chaldeans.
Jer	24: 6	bring them back to this l;
Jer	24: 8	who remain in this l,
Jer	27: 7	until the time of his l
Jer	27:10	remove you far from your l;
Jer	30:10	And your seed from the l of
Jer	31:16	shall come back from the l
Jer	32:20	signs and wonders in the l
Jer	32:41	plant them in this l,
Jer	40: 4	all the l is before you;
Jer	40: 6	who were left in the l.
Jer	40: 7	and the poorest of the l who
Jer	41: 2	had made governor over the l.
Jer	42:13	'We will not dwell in this l,
Jer	44: 1	the Jews who dwell in the l
Jer	44: 8	to other gods in the l of
Jer	46:12	your cry has filled the l;
Jer	47: 2	They shall overflow the l
Jer	47: 2	all the inhabitants of the l
Jer	50:12	A dry l and a desert.
Jer	50:22	sound of battle is in the l,
Jer	51:27	Set up a banner in the l,
Jer	51:28	All the l of his dominion.
Jer	51:29	And the l will tremble and
Jer	51:43	A l where no one dwells,
Jer	51:46	And violence in the l,
Jer	51:47	Her whole l shall be
Jer	52:16	some of the poor of the l
Jer	52:25	mustered the people of the l,
Jer	52:27	away captive from its own l.
Ezek	7: 2	the four corners of the l.
Ezek	8:12	the LORD has forsaken the l.
Ezek	8:17	For they have filled the l
Ezek	9: 9	and the l is full of
Ezek	12:19	so that her l may be emptied
Ezek	14:13	when a l sins against Me by
Ezek	14:17	I bring a sword on that l,
Ezek	14:19	a pestilence into that l
Ezek	17:13	away the mighty of the l,
Ezek	19:13	In a dry and thirsty l.
Ezek	20:46	against the forest l,
Ezek	21:30	In the l of your nativity.
Ezek	23:19	played the harlot in the l
Ezek	23:48	lewdness to cease from the l,
Ezek	26:20	establish glory in the l of
Ezek	29:14	to the l of their origin,
Ezek	32: 8	bring darkness upon your l,
Ezek	32:23	Who caused terror in the l
Ezek	33: 2	I bring the sword upon a l,
Ezek	33:24	the l has been given to us
Ezek	34:27	shall be safe in their l;
Ezek	36:18	blood they had shed on the l,
Ezek	37:14	will place you in your own l.
Ezek	38: 2	of the l of Magog, the
Ezek	38: 9	covering the l like a cloud,
Ezek	38:16	like a cloud, to cover the l.
Ezek	38:19	a great earthquake in the l
Ezek	39:12	in order to cleanse the l.
Ezek	45: 1	when you divide the l by lot
Ezek	48:14	this best part of the l,
Dan	8: 9	and toward the Glorious L.
Dan	11:39	and divide the l for gain.
Dan	11:41	also enter the Glorious L,
Hos	1: 2	For the iniquity has committed
Hos	2: 3	And set her like a dry l,
Hos	4: 1	knowledge of God in the l.
Hos	4: 3	Therefore the l will mourn;
Hos	7:16	be their derision in the l
Hos	9: 3	not dwell in the LORD's l,
Hos	12: 9	Ever since the l of Egypt;
Joel	1:10	The l mourns; For the
Joel	2:18	will be zealous for His l,
Joel	3:19	innocent blood in their l.
Amos	7: 2	eating the grass of the l,
Amos	7:10	The l is not able to bear
Amos	7:11	captive From their own l.
Amos	7:12	you seer! Flee to the l of
Amos	7:17	away captive From his own l.
Amos	8: 4	And make the poor of the l
Jon	1: 9	made the sea and the dry l.
Jon	1:13	rowed hard to return to l,
Jon	2:10	it vomited Jonah onto dry l.
Mic	5: 5	Assyrian comes into our l,
Mic	5: 6	And the l of Nimrod at its
Hab	2: 8	And the violence of the l
Hab	3: 7	The curtains of the l of
Hag	1:11	for a drought on the l and
Hag	2: 6	and earth, the sea and dry l;
Zech	2:12	inheritance in the Holy L,
Zech	3: 9	the iniquity of that l in
Zech	7:14	for they made the pleasant l
Zech	8: 7	save My people from the l
Zech	8: 7	of the east And from the l
Zech	9:16	like a banner over His l—
Zech	11: 6	the inhabitants of the l,
Zech	11:16	up a shepherd in the l who
Zech	12:12	And the l shall mourn, every
Mal	3:12	you will be a delightful l,
Matt	2: 6	in the l of Judah,
Matt	2:20	and go to the l of Israel,
Matt	4:15	The l of Zebulun and the

Matt 4:15 of Zebulun and the l
Matt 10:15 be more tolerable for the l
Matt 14:34 they came to the l of
Matt 23:15 For you travel l and sea to
Matt 27:45 was darkness over all the l.
Mark 1: 5 Then all the l of Judea, and
Mark 15:33 darkness over the whole l
Luke 4:25 famine throughout all the l;
Luke 5: 3 put out a little from the l.
Luke 5:11 had brought their boats to l,
Luke 15:14 a severe famine in that l,
Luke 21:23 be great distress in the l
John 3:22 disciples came into the l
John 6:21 the boat was at the l where
John 21: 9 soon as they had come to l,
John 21:11 up and dragged the net to l,
Acts 4:37 having l, sold it, and
Acts 5: 8 me whether you sold the l
Acts 7:45 with Joshua into the l
Acts 27:44 they all escaped safely to l.
Heb 11: 9 By faith he dwelt in the l of
Heb 11:29 the Red Sea as by dry l,
Jas 5:17 and it did not rain on the l
Jude 5 the people out of the l of
Rev 10: 2 and his left foot on the l,

LANDMARK (see LAND, LANDMARKS)
Deut 19:14 not remove your neighbor's l,
Prov 22:28 Do not remove the ancient l

LANDMARKS (see LANDMARK)
Job 24: 2 "Some remove l;

LANDOWNER (see LAND)
Matt 20: 1 of heaven is like a l who
Matt 21:33 There was a certain l who

LANDS (see LAND)
Gen 10:20 in their l and in their
Gen 10:31 their languages, in their l,
Gen 41:57 famine was severe in all l.
Neh 5: 3 We have mortgaged our l and
Neh 5: 4 for the king's tax on our l
Ps 100: 1 to the LORD, all you l!
Ps 105:44 He gave them the l of the
Ps 106:27 to scatter them in the l.
Ps 107: 3 And gathered out of the l,
Jer 16:15 the north and from all the l
Matt 19:29 or wife or children or l,
Mark 10:30 mothers and children and l,
Acts 4:34 who were possessors of l or

LANGUAGE (see LANGUAGES)
Gen 10: 5 everyone according to his l,
Gen 11: 1 the whole earth had one l
Gen 11: 7 and there confuse their l,
Ezra 4: 7 into the Aramaic l.
Esth 1:22 every people in their own l,
Esth 8: 9 in their own script and l.
Ps 19: 3 There is no speech nor l
Ps 114: 1 from a people of strange l,
Is 19:18 of Egypt will speak the l
Dan 1: 4 whom they might teach the l
Zeph 3: 9 to the peoples a pure l,
Zech 8:23 days ten men from every l
John 16:25 to you in figurative l;
Acts 1:19 is called in their own l,
Acts 2: 6 them speak in his own l.
Acts 21:40 to them in the Hebrew l,
1Co 14:11 know the meaning of the l,
Col 3: 8 filthy l out of your mouth.

LANGUAGES (see LANGUAGE)
Gen 10:20 according to their l,
Dan 3: 4 O peoples, nations, and l,
1Co 14:10 so many kinds of l in the

LANGUISH (see LANGUISHED, LANGUISHES)
Is 24: 4 people of the earth l.
Jer 14: 2 mourns, And her gates l;

LANGUISHED† (see LANGUISH)
Gen 47:13 and the land of Canaan l
Lam 2: 8 They l together.

LANGUISHES (see LANGUISH)
Is 24: 7 new wine fails, the vine l,
Jer 15: 9 She l who has borne seven;

LANTERNS†
John 18: 3 Pharisees, came there with l,

LAODICEA (see LAODICEANS)
Col 2: 1 have for you and those in L,
Col 4:15 the brethren who are in L,
Col 4:16 read the epistle from L.
Rev 1:11 to Philadelphia, and to L.

LAODICEANS† (see LAODICEA)
Col 4:16 also in the church of the L,
Rev 3:14 angel of the church of the L

LAP (see LAPPED, LAPS)
Prov 16:33 The lot is cast into the l,

LAPPED (see LAP)
Judg 7: 6 the number of those who l,

LAPS† (see LAP)
Judg 7: 5 Everyone who l from the water
Judg 7: 5 with his tongue, as a dog l,

LAST
Gen 19:34 I lay with my father l
Gen 25: 8 Then Abraham breathed his l
Gen 33: 2 and Rachel and Joseph l.
Gen 49: 1 shall befall you in the l
Gen 49:19 But he shall triumph at l.
2Sa 23: 1 Now these are the l words of
2Ch 9:29 acts of Solomon, first and l,
2Ch 28:26 his ways, from first to l,
2Ch 35:27 his deeds from first to l,
Neh 8:18 the first day until the l
Job 19:25 And He shall stand at l on
Prov 23:32 At the l it bites like a
Is 41: 4 And with the l I am He.'
Is 44: 6 the First and I am the L;
Jer 32:14 that they may l many days."
Lam 1:19 my elders Breathed their l
Dan 8: 3 the higher one came up l.
Hos 9:12 I will bereave them to the l
Matt 5:26 till you have paid the l
Matt 12:45 and the l state of that man
Matt 19:30 who are first will be l,
Matt 19:30 and the l first.
Matt 20:12 These l men have worked
Matt 21:37 Then l of all he sent his son
Matt 22:27 L of all the woman died also.
Matt 27:64 So the l deception will be
Mark 15:37 voice, and breathed His l.
Luke 12:59 you have paid the very l
John 6:39 should raise it up at the l
John 6:40 I will raise him up at the l
John 7:37 On the l day, that great
John 11:24 in the resurrection at the l
John 12:48 will judge him in the l day.
Acts 2:17 come to pass in the l
Acts 5: 5 fell down and breathed his l.
Acts 5:10 his feet and breathed her l.
1Co 4: 9 us, the apostles, l,
1Co 15: 8 Then l of all He was seen by
1Co 15:26 The l enemy that will be
1Co 15:45 The l Adam became a
1Co 15:52 at the l trumpet. For the
2Ti 3: 1 that in the l days perilous
Heb 1: 2 has in these l days spoken to

Jas 5: 3 heaped up treasure in the l
1Pe 1: 5 to be revealed in the l
1Pe 1:20 but was manifest in these l
2Pe 3: 3 scoffers will come in the l
1Jn 2:18 it is the l hour; and as you
Rev 1:11 Omega, the First and the L,
Rev 1:17 I am the First and the L.
Rev 2: 8 says the First and the L,
Rev 2:19 the l are more than the
Rev 15: 1 angels having the seven l
Rev 21: 9 filled with the seven l
Rev 22:13 End, the First and the L.

LATCH†
Song 5: 4 put his hand By the l of

LATE (see LATER)
Ps 127: 2 rise up early, To sit up l,
Amos 7: 1 at the beginning of the l
Matt 14:15 and the hour is already l.
Rev 6:13 as a fig tree drops its l

LATER (see LATE)
Mark 14:70 And a little l those who
Acts 5: 7 it was about three hours l
1Ti 5:24 those of some men follow l.

LATIN†
Luke 23:38 Him in letters of Greek, L,
John 19:20 in Hebrew, Greek, and L.

LATTER
Deut 4:30 come upon you in the l days,
Deut 11:14 the early rain and the l
Deut 32:29 they would consider their l
Job 42:12 Now the LORD blessed the l
Is 2: 2 shall come to pass in the l
Is 41:22 And know the l end of them;
Jer 5:24 both the former and the l,
Jer 49:39 shall come to pass in the l
Ezek 38: 8 In the l years you will come
Dan 2:28 what will be in the l days.
Dan 8:19 what shall happen in the l
Dan 8:23 And in the l time of their
Dan 10:14 to your people in the l
Dan 11:29 be like the former or the l.
Hos 3: 5 and His goodness in the l
Hos 6: 3 Like the l and former rain
Joel 2:23 And the l rain in the first
Mic 4: 1 shall come to pass in the l
Hag 2: 9 The glory of this l temple
Phil 1:17 but the l out of love,
1Ti 4: 1 expressly says that in l
Jas 5: 7 it receives the early and l
2Pe 2:20 the l end is worse for them

LATTICE
Judg 5:28 And cried out through the l,
2Ki 1: 2 Ahaziah fell through the l
Prov 7: 6 house I looked through my l,
Song 2: 9 Gazing through the l.

LAUD†
Ps 117: 1 all you Gentiles! L Him,
Rom 15:11 all you Gentiles! L

LAUGH (see LAUGHED, LAUGHS, LAUGHTER, RIDICULE)
Gen 18:13 Abraham, "Why did Sarah l,
Gen 18:15 but you did l!"
Gen 21: 6 said, "God has made me l,
Gen 21: 6 and all who hear will l
Job 5:22 You shall l at destruction
Ps 2: 4 sits in the heavens shall l;
Ps 59: 8 shall l at them; You shall
Ps 80: 6 And our enemies l among
Eccl 3: 4 to weep, And a time to l;
Luke 6:21 weep now, For you shall l.
Luke 6:25 Woe to you who l now, For

LAUGHED (see LAUGH, RIDICULED)
Gen 17:17 fell on his face and l,
Gen 18:12 Therefore Sarah l within

LAUGHS (see LAUGH)
Job 41:29 He l at the threat of
Ps 37:13 The Lord l at him, For He

LAUGHTER (see LAUGH)
Ps 126: 2 our mouth was filled with l,
Eccl 2: 2 I said of l—
Eccl 7: 3 Sorrow is better than l,
Jas 4: 9 mourn and weep! Let your l

LAUNCH† (see LAUNCHED)
Luke 5: 4 L out into the deep and let

LAUNCHED† (see LAUNCH)
Luke 8:22 And they l out.

LAUNDERER†
Mark 9: 3 such as no l on earth can

LAUNDERER'S
Mal 3: 2 a refiner's fire And like l

LAVER (see LAVERS)
Ex 30:18 You shall also make a l of

LAVERS (see LAVER)
1Ki 7:38 Then he made ten l of

LAW (see LAWFUL, LAWGIVER, LAWLESS, LAWS, LAWYER)
Gen 47:26 And Joseph made it a l over
Ex 12:49 One l shall be for the
Ex 16: 4 they will walk in My l or
Ex 24:12 and the l and commandments
Num 5:29 This is the l of jealousy,
Num 15:16 One l and one custom shall be
Num 31:21 is the ordinance of the l
Deut 1: 5 began to explain this l,
Deut 17:18 himself a copy of this l in
Deut 17:19 all the words of this l and
Deut 29:21 in this Book of the L,
Deut 29:29 do all the words of this l.
Deut 31: 9 So Moses wrote this l and
Deut 31:11 you shall read this l before
Josh 1: 7 to do according to all the l
Josh 1: 8 This Book of the L shall not
Josh 8:32 the stones a copy of the l
Josh 24:26 words in the Book of the L
2Ki 10:31 no heed to walk in the l of
2Ki 22: 8 found the Book of the L in
2Ki 23:24 perform the words of the l
2Ki 23:25 according to all the L of
1Ch 16:40 that is written in the L of
1Ch 22:12 that you may keep the l of
2Ch 6:16 that they walk in My l as
2Ch 12: 1 that he forsook the l of the
2Ch 14: 4 and to observe the l and the
2Ch 15: 3 priest, and without l;
2Ch 19:10 or offenses against l or
2Ch 25: 4 as it is written in the L
2Ch 33: 8 according to the whole l and
2Ch 34:19 heard the words of the L,
Ezra 7: 6 a skilled scribe in the L
Ezra 7:10 his heart to seek the L of
Ezra 7:12 a scribe of the L of the God
Ezra 7:26 will not observe the l of
Ezra 7:26 law of your God and the l
Neh 8: 7 people to understand the L;
Neh 8: 8 in the L of God; and they
Neh 9:26 Cast Your l behind their
Neh 9:29 bring them back to Your l.
Neh 10:29 an oath to walk in God's L,
Esth 3:14 was to be issued as l in
Esth 4:16 which is against the l,
Job 28:26 When He made a l for the
Ps 1: 2 his delight is in the l of

Ps	1: 2	And in His l he meditates
Ps	19: 7	The l of the LORD is
Ps	37:31	The l of his God is in his
Ps	40: 8	And Your l is within my
Ps	78: 1	ear, O my people, to my l;
Ps	78: 5	And appointed a l in
Ps	78:10	refused to walk in His l,
Ps	81: 4	A l of the God of Jacob.
Ps	89:30	If his sons forsake My l And
Ps	94:12	And teach out of Your l,
Ps	119:18	Wondrous things from Your l.
Ps	119:44	So shall I keep Your l
Ps	119:51	not turn aside from Your l.
Ps	119:53	wicked, who forsake Your l.
Ps	119:61	I have not forgotten Your l.
Ps	119:70	But I delight in Your l.
Ps	119:72	The l of Your mouth is
Ps	119:77	For Your l is my delight.
Ps	119:97	how I love Your l! It is
Ps	119:142	And Your l is truth.
Prov	1: 8	And do not forsake the l of
Prov	3: 1	My son, do not forget my l,
Prov	6:20	And do not forsake the l of
Prov	6:23	And the l a light;
Prov	7: 2	And my l as the apple of
Prov	29:18	happy is he who keeps the l.
Prov	31:26	on her tongue is the l of
Is	1:10	Give ear to the l of our
Is	2: 3	of Zion shall go forth the l,
Is	5:24	they have rejected the l of
Is	8:16	Seal the l among my
Is	8:20	To the l and to the
Is	42: 4	shall wait for His l.
Is	51: 7	in whose heart is My l:
Jer	2: 8	And those who handle the l
Jer	6:19	heeded My words, Nor My l,
Jer	9:13	they have forsaken My l
Jer	31:33	I will put My l in their
Ezek	7:26	But the l will perish from
Ezek	22:26	priests have violated My l
Dan	6: 5	him concerning the l of his
Dan	6: 8	according to the l of the
Dan	7:25	intend to change times and l.
Dan	9:11	has transgressed Your l,
Mic	4: 2	For out of Zion the l
Mal	2: 6	The l of truth was in his
Mal	2: 9	shown partiality in the l.
Mal	4: 4	Remember the L of Moses, My
Matt	5:17	I came to destroy the L or
Matt	5:18	by no means pass from the l
Matt	7:12	for this is the L and the
Matt	11:13	all the prophets and the l
Matt	22:36	great commandment in the l?
Matt	22:40	commandments hang all the L
Matt	23:23	weightier matters of the l:
Luke	2:22	according to the l of Moses
Luke	2:23	(as it is written in the l of
Luke	2:27	to the custom of the l,
Luke	5:17	and teachers of the l
Luke	16:16	The l and the prophets were
Luke	16:17	for one tittle of the l to
Luke	24:44	which were written in the L
John	1:17	For the l was given through
John	1:45	Him of whom Moses in the l,
John	7:19	not Moses give you the l,
John	7:49	that does not know the l is
John	7:51	Does our l judge a man before
John	8:17	is also written in your l
John	19: 7	and according to our l He
Acts	5:34	a teacher of the l held in
Acts	13:15	after the reading of the L
Acts	13:39	not be justified by the l
Acts	15:24	circumcised and keep the l'
Acts	18:13	God contrary to the l.
Acts	22:12	man according to the l,

Acts	23:29	questions of their l,
Acts	25: 8	Neither against the l of the
Rom	2:12	as have sinned without l
Rom	2:12	many as have sinned in the l
Rom	2:13	but the doers of the l will
Rom	2:14	who do not have the l,
Rom	2:14	are a l to themselves,
Rom	2:15	who show the work of the l
Rom	2:23	who make your boast in the l,
Rom	2:25	you are a breaker of the l,
Rom	2:27	are a transgressor of the l?
Rom	3:19	we know that whatever the l
Rom	3:19	to those who are under the l,
Rom	3:20	by the deeds of the l no
Rom	3:20	for by the l is the
Rom	3:21	of God apart from the l is
Rom	3:27	It is excluded. By what l?
Rom	3:27	but by the l of faith.
Rom	3:28	from the deeds of the l.
Rom	3:31	Do we then make void the l
Rom	3:31	contrary, we establish the l.
Rom	4:14	if those who are of the l
Rom	4:15	for where there is no l
Rom	5:13	(For until the l sin was in
Rom	5:13	imputed when there is no l.
Rom	6:14	for you are not under l but
Rom	6:15	because we are not under l but
Rom	7: 1	that the l has dominion over
Rom	7: 2	a husband is bound by the l
Rom	7: 3	she is free from that l,
Rom	7: 4	have become dead to the l
Rom	7: 6	been delivered from the l,
Rom	7: 7	sin except through the l.
Rom	7: 7	covetousness unless the l
Rom	7: 8	For apart from the l sin
Rom	7:12	Therefore the l is holy, and
Rom	7:14	For we know that the l is
Rom	7:22	For I delight in the l of God
Rom	7:23	But I see another l in my
Rom	7:23	warring against the l of my
Rom	7:23	me into captivity to the l
Rom	8: 2	For the l of the Spirit of
Rom	8: 2	has made me free from the l
Rom	8: 3	For what the l could not do
Rom	9: 4	the giving of the l,
Rom	9:31	has not attained to the l of
Rom	9:32	were, by the works of the l.
Rom	10: 4	Christ is the end of the l
Rom	13:10	is the fulfillment of the l.
1Co	6: 6	But brother goes to l against
1Co	7:39	A wife is bound by l as long
1Co	9:20	those who are under the l;
1Co	9:21	to those who are without l,
1Co	15:56	strength of sin is the l.
Gal	2:16	not by the works of the l,
Gal	2:19	For I through the l died to
Gal	3:10	as are of the works of the l
Gal	3:12	Yet the l is not of faith,
Gal	3:13	us from the curse of the l,
Gal	3:18	the inheritance is of the l,
Gal	3:19	purpose then does the l
Gal	3:23	kept under guard by the l,
Gal	3:24	Therefore the l was our tutor
Gal	4: 4	of a woman, born under the l,
Gal	4:21	law, do you not hear the l?
Gal	5: 3	a debtor to keep the whole l.
Gal	5: 4	to be justified by l;
Gal	5:14	For all the l is fulfilled in
Gal	5:23	Against such there is no l.
Gal	6: 2	and so fulfill the l of
Gal	6:13	are circumcised keep the l,
Phil	3: 5	Hebrews; concerning the l,
1Ti	1: 7	to be teachers of the l,
1Ti	1: 9	that the l is not made for a
Tit	3: 9	and strivings about the l;

Heb 7:12 is also a change of the l.
Heb 7:19 for the l made nothing
Heb 7:28 For the l appoints as high
Heb 7:28 oath, which came after the l,
Heb 9:22 And according to the l almost
Heb 10:28 who has rejected Moses' l
Jas 1:25 looks into the perfect l of
Jas 2: 8 really fulfill the royal l
Jas 2:10 shall keep the whole l,
Jas 2:11 a transgressor of the l.
Jas 4:11 law. But if you judge the l,

LAWFUL (see LAW, LAWFULLY, UNLAWFUL)
Matt 12: 2 are doing what is not l to
Matt 12: 4 showbread which was not l
Matt 12:10 Is it l to heal on the
Matt 12:12 Therefore it is l to do good
Matt 14: 4 It is not l for you to have
Matt 19: 3 Is it l for a man to divorce
Matt 22:17 Is it l to pay taxes to
John 5:10 it is not l for you to carry
John 18:31 It is not l for us to put
Acts 16:21 customs which are not l for
Acts 19:39 shall be determined in the l
Acts 22:25 Is it l for you to scourge a
1Co 6:12 All things are l for me, but
2Co 12: 4 which it is not l for a man

LAWFULLY† (see LAWFUL)
1Ti 1: 8 is good if one uses it l,

LAWGIVER (see LAW)
Gen 49:10 Nor a l from between his
Ps 60: 7 My head; Judah is My l.
Jas 4:12 There is one L,

LAWLESS (see LAW, LAWLESSNESS)
Acts 2:23 you have taken by l hands,
Rom 4: 7 are those whose l
2Th 2: 9 The coming of the l one is
Tit 2:14 redeem us from every l deed
Heb 8:12 their sins and their l

LAWLESSNESS (see LAWLESS)
Matt 7:23 you who practice l!'
Matt 23:28 are full of hypocrisy and l.
Matt 24:12 And because l will abound,
Rom 6:19 and of l leading to more
2Th 2: 7 For the mystery of l is
Heb 1: 9 and hated l;
1Jn 3: 4 commits sin also commits l,

LAWS (see LAW)
Gen 26: 5 My statutes, and My l.
Neh 9:13 just ordinances and true l,
Esth 3: 8 their l are different from
Ps 105:45 His statutes And keep His l.
Is 24: 5 they have transgressed the l,
Dan 9:10 our God, to walk in His l,
Heb 8:10 I will put My l in
Heb 10:16 I will put My l into

LAWYER (see LAW, LAWYERS)
Matt 22:35 Then one of them, a l,

LAWYERS (see LAWYER)
Luke 11:46 l! For you load men with

LAY (see LAID, LAYING, LAYS, LIE)
Gen 19:33 the firstborn went in and l
Gen 22:12 Do not l your hand on the
Gen 28:11 and he l down in that place
Gen 37:22 and do not l a hand on
Ex 5: 8 And you shall l on them the
Ex 7: 4 so that I may l My hand on
Ex 16:13 and in the morning the dew l
Ex 24:11 of Israel He did not l His
Lev 1: 7 and l the wood in order on
Lev 1: 8 shall l the parts, the head,

Lev 2:15 and l frankincense on it. It
Lev 3: 2 And he shall l his hand on
Lev 4: 4 l his hand on the bull's
Num 22:27 she l down under Balaam; so
Deut 21: 8 and do not l innocent blood
Josh 6:26 he shall l its foundation
Josh 8: 2 L an ambush for the city
Judg 4:22 there l Sisera, dead with
Judg 5:27 he l still; At her feet he
Ruth 3:14 So she l at his feet until
1Sa 2:22 and how they l with the
1Sa 3:15 So Samuel l down until
1Sa 19:24 and l down naked all that
2Sa 11: 4 and he l with her, for she
2Sa 13: 6 Then Amnon l down and
2Sa 13:14 he forced her and l with
1Ki 5:17 to l the foundation of the
1Ki 13:31 l my bones beside his bones.
1Ki 18:23 and l it on the wood, but
1Ki 21:27 and fasted and l in
2Ki 4:11 in to the upper room and l
2Ki 4:29 but l my staff on the face
2Ki 4:34 And he went up and l on the
2Ch 35: 5 of your brethren the l
Esth 2:21 furious and sought to l
Esth 4: 3 and many l in sackcloth and
Esth 8: 7 because he tried to l his
Job 1:12 only do not l a hand on his
Job 9:33 Who may l his hand on us
Job 22:22 And l up His words in your
Job 40: 4 I l my hand over my mouth.
Ps 3: 5 I l down and slept; I
Ps 7: 5 And l my honor in the dust.
Ps 38:12 also who seek my life l
Ps 84: 3 Where she may l her
Prov 5: 5 Her steps l hold of hell.
Eccl 2: 3 and how to l hold on folly,
Is 13:11 And will l low the
Is 28:16 l l in Zion a stone for a
Is 29: 3 I will l siege against you
Is 29:21 And l a snare for him who
Is 34:15 shall make her nest and l
Is 54:11 I will l your stones with
Is 54:11 And l your foundations with
Jer 2:20 every green tree You l
Jer 6:21 I will l stumbling blocks
Ezek 4: 2 L siege against it, build a
Ezek 12:23 I will l this proverb to
Ezek 16:42 So I will l to rest My fury
Ezek 35: 4 I shall l your cities waste,
Matt 6:19 Do not l up for yourselves
Matt 8:20 Son of Man has nowhere to l
Matt 9:18 but come and l Your hand on
Matt 21:46 But when they sought to l
Matt 23: 4 and l them on men's
Matt 28: 6 the place where the Lord l.
Mark 1:30 But Simon's wife's mother l
Mark 3:21 they went out to l hold of
Mark 12:12 And they sought to l hands on
Mark 16:18 they will l hands on the
John 10:15 and I l down My life for the
John 10:18 I have power to l it down,
John 11:38 and a stone l against it.
John 13:38 Will you l down your life for
John 15:13 than to l down one's life
Acts 8:19 that anyone on whom I l
Rom 9:33 "Behold, I l in Zion a
1Co 3:11 foundation can anyone l
1Co 16: 2 week let each one of you l
Phil 3:12 that I may l hold of that
1Ti 5:22 Do not l hands on anyone
1Ti 6:12 l hold on eternal life, to
Heb 6:18 have fled for refuge to l
Heb 12: 1 let us l aside every weight,
Jas 1:21 Therefore l aside all

1Pe	2: 6	I l in Zion A chief
1Jn	3:16	And we also ought to l down

LAYING (see LAY)

Ps	64: 5	They talk of l snares
Mark	7: 8	For l aside the commandment
Acts	8:18	saw that through the l on
Acts	9:17	and l his hands on him he
1Ti	4:14	you by prophecy with the l
2Ti	1: 6	is in you through the l on
Heb	6: 1	not l again the foundation
Heb	6: 2	of l on of hands, of
1Pe	2: 1	l aside all malice, all

LAYS (see LAY)

Job	18: 9	And a snare l hold of him.
Ps	33: 7	He l up the deep in
Ps	91: 6	of the destruction that l
Ps	104: 3	He l the beams of His upper
Is	30:32	Which the LORD l on him,
Zech	12: 1	l the foundation of the
Luke	12:21	So is he who l up treasure
Luke	15: 5	he l it on his shoulders,

LAZARUS

Luke	16:20	was a certain beggar named L,
Luke	16:23	and L in his bosom.
John	11: 1	L of Bethany, the town of
John	11: 2	whose brother L was sick.
John	11: 5	Martha and her sister and L.
John	11:14	L is dead.
John	11:43	cried with a loud voice, "L,

LAZY

Prov	19:24	A l man buries his hand in
Prov	26:14	So does the l man on his
Prov	26:16	The l man is wiser in his
Matt	25:26	You wicked and l servant, you
Tit	1:12	evil beasts, l gluttons."

LEAD (see LEADER, LEADING, LEADS, LED)

Ex	13:17	that God did not l them by
Ex	13:21	in a pillar of cloud to l
Ex	15:10	They sank like l in the
Job	19:24	rock With an iron pen and l,
Ps	5: 8	L me, O LORD, in Your
Ps	25: 5	L me in Your truth and teach
Ps	27:11	And l me in a smooth path,
Ps	43: 3	and Your truth! Let them l
Ps	61: 2	L me to the rock that is
Ps	80: 1	You who l Joseph like a
Ps	125: 5	The LORD shall l them away
Ps	139:10	there Your hand shall l me,
Ps	139:24	And l me in the way
Ps	143:10	L me in the land of
Is	11: 6	And a little child shall l
Is	40:11	And gently l those who are
Is	42:16	I will l them in paths they
Is	63:14	So You l Your people, To
Jer	32: 5	then he shall l Zedekiah to
Amos	2: 4	Their lies l them astray,
Matt	6:13	And do not l us into
Mark	14:44	seize Him and l Him away
Luke	6:39	Can the blind l the blind?
Luke	11: 4	And do not l us into
Acts	13:11	around seeking someone to l
1Th	4:11	that you also aspire to l a
1Jn	5:16	a sin which does not l
Rev	7:17	will shepherd them and l

LEADER (see LEAD, LEADERS)

Num	14: 4	Let us select a l and return
2Ch	32:21	every mighty man of valor, l,
Ps	68:27	is little Benjamin, their l,
Is	55: 4	A l and commander for the
Zech	9: 7	And shall be like a l in

LEADERS (see LEADER)

Num	1:16	l of their fathers' tribes,
Num	1:44	with the l of Israel, twelve
Num	3:32	to be chief over the l of
Num	16: 2	two hundred and fifty l of
Num	25: 4	Take all the l of the people
Deut	1:15	l of thousands, leaders of
Judg	5: 2	When l lead in Israel, When
1Ki	20:15	he mustered the young l of
1Ch	7:40	mighty men of valor, chief l.
1Ch	15:16	Then David spoke to the l of
1Ch	24: 4	There were more l found of
1Ch	29:24	All the l and the mighty men,
2Ch	12: 6	So the l of Israel and the
2Ch	29:30	King Hezekiah and the l
2Ch	30: 2	For the king and his l and
2Ch	32: 3	he consulted with his l and
2Ch	35: 8	And his l gave willingly to
2Ch	36:14	Moreover all the l of the
Jer	25:34	You l of the flock! For
Matt	15:14	They are blind l of the
Luke	19:47	and the l of the people
Acts	28:17	days that Paul called the l

LEADING (see LEAD)

Acts	15:22	l men among the brethren.
Acts	17: 4	and not a few of the l
Acts	28: 7	there was an estate of the l
Rom	6:19	and of lawlessness l to
Rom	15: 2	l to edification.
1Jn	5:16	those who commit sin not l

LEADS (see LEAD)

Ps	23: 2	He l me beside the still
Ps	23: 3	He l me in the paths of
Prov	2:18	For her house l down to
Prov	11:24	But it l to poverty.
Prov	19:23	The fear of the LORD l to
Matt	7:13	broad is the way that l to
Matt	7:14	is the way which l to life,
Matt	15:14	And if the blind l the
John	10: 3	his own sheep by name and l
Rom	2: 4	that the goodness of God l
Rom	12: 8	with liberality; he who l,
2Co	2:14	be to God who always l us

LEAF (see LEAVES)

Gen	8:11	a freshly plucked olive l
Ps	1: 3	Whose l also shall not
Is	34: 4	shall fall down As the l
Is	64: 6	rags; We all fade as a l,
Jer	17: 8	But its l will be green,

LEAFY

Mark	11: 8	and others cut down l

LEAH (see LEAH'S)

Gen	29:16	the name of the elder was L,
Gen	29:23	that he took L his daughter
Gen	29:30	loved Rachel more than L.
Gen	34: 1	Now Dinah the daughter of L,
Ruth	4:11	your house like Rachel and L,

LEAH'S (see LEAH)

Gen	29:17	L eyes were delicate, but
Gen	31:33	into L tent, and into the

LEAN (see LEANED, LEANING, LEANNESS, LEANS)

Judg	16:26	so that I can l on them."
Prov	3: 5	And l not on your own
Is	48: 2	And l on the God of Israel;
Ezek	34:20	between the fat and the l

LEANED (see LEAN)

Amos	5:19	l his hand on the wall,
John	21:20	who also had l on His breast

LEANING (see LEAN)

2Sa	1: 6	l on his spear; and indeed

Ps 62: 3 Like a l wall and a
John 13:23 Now there was l on Jesus'
Heb 11:21 l on the top of his staff.

LEANNESS (*see* LEAN)
Ps 106:15 But sent l into their soul.

LEANS (*see* LEAN)
2Sa 3:29 who l on a staff or falls by
2Ki 18:21 Egypt, on which if a man l,

LEAP (*see* LEAPED, LEAPING)
Ps 18:29 By my God I can l over a
Is 35: 6 Then the lame shall l like a
Zeph 1: 9 will punish All those who l
Luke 6:23 Rejoice in that day and l

LEAPED (*see* LEAP)
1Ki 18:26 Then they l about the altar
Luke 1:41 that the babe l in her womb;
Acts 14:10 on your feet!" And he l

LEAPING (*see* LEAP)
2Sa 6:16 window and saw King David l
Acts 3: 8 temple with them—walking, l,

LEARN (*see* LEARNED, LEARNING)
Deut 4:10 that they may l to fear Me
Deut 5: 1 that you may l them and be
Esth 2:11 to l of Esther's welfare and
Ps 119:71 That I may l Your statutes.
Prov 22:25 Lest you l his ways And set
Is 1:17 L to do good; Seek justice
Is 2: 4 Neither shall they l war
Is 29:24 those who complained will l
Mic 4: 3 Neither shall they l war
Matt 9:13 But go and l what this
Matt 11:29 My yoke upon you and l
Matt 24:32 Now l this parable from the
1Co 4: 6 that you may l in us not to
1Ti 1:20 to Satan that they may l
1Ti 2:11 Let a woman l in silence with
1Ti 5:13 And besides they l to be
Rev 14: 3 and no one could l that song

LEARNED (*see* LEARN)
John 6:45 who has heard and l from
Acts 7:22 And Moses was l in all the
Acts 17:13 the Jews from Thessalonica l
Acts 23:27 having l that he was a
Rom 16:17 to the doctrine which you l,
Eph 4:20 But you have not so l Christ,
Phil 4: 9 The things which you l and
Phil 4:11 for I have l in whatever
Phil 4:12 and in all things I have l
2Ti 3:14 the things which you have l
2Ti 3:14 from whom you have l them,
Heb 5: 8 yet He l obedience by the

LEARNING (*see* LEARN)
Prov 1: 5 will hear and increase l,
Acts 26:24 are beside yourself! Much l
Rom 15: 4 were written for our l,
2Ti 3: 7 always l and never able to

LEASE† (*see* LEASED)
Matt 21:41 and l his vineyard to other

LEASED (*see* LEASE)
Song 8:11 He l the vineyard to
Mark 12: 1 And he l it to vinedressers

LEASH†
Job 41: 5 Or will you l him for your
1Co 7:35 not that I may put a l on

LEATHER
Lev 13:48 or in anything made of l,
Lev 13:49 in the garment or in the l,
2Ki 1: 8 A hairy man wearing a l belt

LEAVEN (*see* LEAVENED, LEAVENS, UNLEAVENED)
Ex 12:15 day you shall remove l from
Ex 12:19 For seven days no l shall be
Lev 2:11 for you shall burn no l nor
Lev 6:17 shall not be baked with l.
Matt 13:33 kingdom of heaven is like l,
Matt 16:11 but to beware of the l of
Mark 8:15 of the Pharisees and the l
1Co 5: 6 you not know that a little l
1Co 5: 7 purge out the old l,
1Co 5: 8 nor with the l of malice and

LEAVENED (*see* LEAVEN)
Ex 12:15 For whoever eats l bread
Ex 13: 3 No l bread shall be eaten.
Hos 7: 4 the dough, Until it is l.
Matt 13:33 of meal till it was all l.

LEAVENS† (*see* LEAVEN)
1Co 5: 6 know that a little leaven l
Gal 5: 9 A little leaven l the whole

LEAVES (*see* LEAF)
Gen 3: 7 and they sewed fig l
Ezek 47:12 their l will not wither, and
Ezek 47:12 and their l for medicine."
Dan 4:12 Its l were lovely, Its
Matt 21:19 found nothing on it but l,
Matt 24:32 tender and puts forth l,
Mark 11:13 afar a fig tree having l,
Rev 22: 2 The l of the tree were for

LEBANON
Josh 11:17 Baal Gad in the Valley of L
1Ki 5: 6 down cedars for me from L;
1Ki 5: 9 bring them down from L to
1Ki 7: 2 the House of the Forest of L;
Ezra 3: 7 to bring cedar logs from L
Ps 29: 5 splinters the cedars of L.
Ps 29: 6 L and Sirion like a young
Song 4:11 Is like the fragrance of L.
Song 4:15 waters, and streams from L.
Song 7: 4 nose is like the tower of L
Is 2:13 Upon all the cedars of L
Is 35: 2 The glory of L shall be
Jer 18:14 leave the snow water of L,
Ezek 27: 5 They took a cedar from L to
Ezek 31: 3 Assyria was a cedar in L,
Hos 14: 7 be like the wine of L.

LED (*see* LEAD)
Gen 24:48 who had l me in the way of
Ex 3: 1 And he l the flock to the
Ex 13:18 So God l the people around
Ex 15:13 You in Your mercy have l
Deut 8: 2 that the LORD your God l
Deut 8:15 who l you through that great
Deut 29: 5 And I have l you forty years
Judg 2: 1 I l you up from Egypt and
1Ki 8:48 land of their enemies who l
2Ki 15:30 Hoshea the son of Elah l a
2Ch 21:11 and l Judah astray.
2Ch 23:13 and those who l in praise.
Ps 68:18 You have l captivity
Ps 77:20 You l Your people like a
Ps 78:14 In the daytime also He l
Ps 107: 7 And He l them forth by the
Ps 136:16 To Him who l His people
Prov 20: 1 And whoever is l astray by
Is 48:21 did not thirst When He l
Is 53: 7 He was l as a lamb to the
Is 55:12 And be l out with peace;
Is 63:12 Who l them by the right
Ezek 40:26 Seven steps l up to it, and
Matt 4: 1 Then Jesus was l up by the
Matt 26:57 who had laid hold of Jesus l
Matt 27:31 and l Him away to be

Mark   8:23 blind man by the hand and l
Mark   9: 2 and l them up on a high
Luke   4:29 and they l Him to the brow
Luke   23: 1 of them arose and l Him to
Luke   24:50 And He l them out as far as
John   18:13 And they l Him away to Annas
Acts   8:32 He was l as a sheep to
Acts   9: 8 But they l him by the hand
Rom   8:14 For as many as are l by the
2Co   7: 9 but that your sorrow l to
Gal   5:18 But if you are l by the
Eph   4: 8 He l captivity captive,
2Ti   3: 6 l away by various lusts,
2Pe   3:17 being l away with the error

LEECH†
Prov   30:15 The l has two

LEEKS†
Num   11: 5 cucumbers, the melons, the l,

LEFT (*see* LEFT-HANDED)
Gen   13: 9 from me. If you take the l,
Gen   48:13 hand toward Israel's l hand,
Ex   14:22 right hand and on their l.
Judg   3:21 Then Ehud reached with his l
Judg   7:20 held the torches in their l
Judg   16:29 right and the other on his l.
2Ch   3:17 the name of the one on the l
Prov   3:16 In her l hand riches and
Prov   4:27 turn to the right or the l;
Song   2: 6 His l hand is under my
Ezek   1:10 the face of an ox on the l
Ezek   4: 4 Lie also on your l side, and
Matt   6: 3 do not let your l hand know
Matt   20:21 hand and the other on the l,
Matt   20:23 on My right hand and on My l
Matt   25:33 hand, but the goats on the l.
Matt   25:41 also say to those on the l
Matt   27:38 right and another on the l.
2Co   6: 7 the right hand and on the l,

LEFT-HANDED† (*see* LEFT)
Judg   3:15 a l man. By him the children
Judg   20:16 select men who were l;

LEFTOVER†
Mark   8: 8 up seven large baskets of l
Luke   9:17 and twelve baskets of the l

LEGION (*see* LEGIONS)
Mark   5: 9 saying, "My name is L;
Mark   5:15 and had the l,

LEGIONS† (*see* LEGION)
Matt   26:53 Me with more than twelve l

LEGS
Ex   12: 9 its head with its l and its
Ps   147:10 takes no pleasure in the l
Prov   26: 7 Like the l of the lame that
Is   7:20 head and the hair of the l,
Dan   2:33 its l of iron, its feet
Amos   3:12 the mouth of a lion Two l
John   19:33 they did not break His l.

LEMUEL†
Prov   31: 1 The words of King L,
Prov   31: 4 It is not for kings, O L,

LEND (*see* LENDER, LENDS, LENT)
Ex   22:25 If you l money to any of
Lev   25:37 nor l him your food at a
Deut   24:10 When you l your brother
Prov   5: 1 L your ear to my
Luke   6:34 And if you l to those from
Luke   6:34 For even sinners l to
Luke   6:35 your enemies, do good, and l,
Luke   11: 5 l me three loaves;

LENDER (*see* LEND)
Prov   22: 7 is servant to the l.

LENDS† (*see* LEND)
Ps   37:26 is ever merciful, and l;
Ps   112: 5 man deals graciously and l;
Prov   19:17 who has pity on the poor l

LENGTH (*see* LENGTHEN)
Gen   6:15 The l of the ark shall be
Gen   13:17 in the land through its l
Gen   47:28 So the l of Jacob's life was
Deut   30:20 He is your life and the l
1Sa   28:20 Saul fell full l on the
Job   12:12 And with l of days,
Ps   21: 4 L of days forever and ever.
Prov   3: 2 For l of days and long life
Prov   3:16 L of days is in her right
Eph   3:18 what is the width and l

LENGTHEN (*see* LENGTH, LENGTHENED, LENGTHENING, LENGTHENS)
1Ki   3:14 then I will l your days."
Is   54: 2 L your cords, And

LENGTHENED† (*see* LENGTHEN)
Deut   25:15 that your days may be l in

LENGTHENING (*see* LENGTHEN)
Jer   6: 4 shadows of the evening are l.

LENGTHENS† (*see* LENGTHEN)
Ps   102:11 are like a shadow that l,
Ps   109:23 gone like a shadow when it l;

LENT (*see* LEND)
1Sa   1:28 Therefore I also have l him
Jer   15:10 Nor have men l to me for

LENTILS
Gen   25:34 Esau bread and stew of l;

LEOPARD (*see* LEOPARDS)
Is   11: 6 The l shall lie down with
Jer   13:23 change his skin or the l
Dan   7: 6 there was another, like a l,
Rev   13: 2 which I saw was like a l,

LEOPARDS (*see* LEOPARD)
Hab   1: 8 also are swifter than l,

LEPER (*see* LEPERS, LEPROSY)
Lev   13:45 Now the l on whom the sore
Num   5: 2 put out of the camp every l,
Num   12:10 and there she was, a l.
2Ki   5: 1 man of valor, but a l.
2Ch   26:21 King Uzziah was a l until the
Matt   8: 2 a l came and worshiped Him,
Matt   26: 6 at the house of Simon the l,

LEPERS (*see* LEPER)
Matt   10: 8 the sick, cleanse the l,
Luke   17:12 met Him ten men who were l,

LEPROSY (*see* LEPER, LEPROUS)
Lev   13:12 And if l breaks out all over
Lev   13:51 the plague is an active l.
Lev   14: 3 if the l is healed in the
Lev   14: 7 is to be cleansed from the l,
Lev   14:57 clean. This is the law of l.
Deut   24: 8 heed in an outbreak of l,
2Ki   5: 3 he would heal him of his l.
2Ki   5:27 Therefore the l of Naaman
2Ch   26:19 l broke out on his forehead,
Matt   8: 3 Immediately his l was
Luke   5:12 a man who was full of l saw

LEPROUS (*see* LEPROSY)
Ex   4: 6 out, behold, his hand was l,
Lev   13: 2 skin of his body like a l
Lev   13:44 he is a l man. He is
Lev   13:47 if a garment has a l plague

Lev   13:59 This is the law of the l
Num 12:10 suddenly Miriam became l,
2Ki   5:27 went out from his presence l,
2Ki   7: 3 Now there were four l men at
2Ch 26:20 on his forehead, he was l;

LESHEM (see LAISH)
Josh 19:47 dwelt in it. They called L,

LETTER (see LETTERS)
2Sa   11:14 that David wrote a l to
Ezra   7:11 This is a copy of the l
Neh   6: 5 with an open l in his hand.
Esth   9:29 to confirm this second l
Jer   29: 1 are the words of the l
Jer   29:29 the priest read this l in
Acts 23:33 and had delivered the l to
Rom   2:29 in the Spirit, not in the l;
Rom   7: 6 not in the oldness of the l.
2Co   3: 6 for the l kills, but the
2Co   7: 8 I made you sorry with my l,
2Th   2: 2 by spirit or by word or by l,

LETTERS (see LETTER)
1Ki   21: 8 And she wrote l in Ahab's
Neh   2: 7 let l be given to me for the
Neh   2: 9 and gave them the king's l.
Esth   9:20 these things and sent l to
Luke 23:38 was written over Him in l
John   7:15 "How does this Man know l,
Acts   9: 2 and asked l from him to the
2Co   3: 1 of commendation to you or l
Gal   6:11 See with what large l I have

LEVI (see LEVI'S, LEVITE, MATTHEW)
Gen 29:34 his name was called L.
Gen 34:25 sons of Jacob, Simeon and L,
Gen 35:23 firstborn, and Simeon, L,
Gen 46:11 The sons of L were Gershon,
Ex   2: 1 And a man of the house of L
Ex   2: 1 as wife a daughter of L.
Num 17: 8 of Aaron, of the house of L,
Num 26:59 Jochebed the daughter of L,
Deut 10: 9 Therefore L has no portion
1Ch   21: 6 But he did not count L and
Ps   135:20 O house of L! You who fear
Ezek 40:46 of Zadok, from the sons of L,
Mal   2: 4 That My covenant with L may
Mark   2:14 He saw L the son of
Luke   5:27 saw a tax collector named L,
Luke   5:29 Then L gave Him a great feast
Heb   7: 5 who are of the sons of L,
Heb   7: 9 Even L, who receives
Rev   7: 7 of the tribe of L twelve

LEVI'S† (see LEVI)
Mark   2:15 as He was dining in L

LEVIATHAN
Job   3: 8 who are ready to arouse L.
Job   41: 1 Can you draw out L with a
Ps   74:14 You broke the heads of L in
Is   27: 1 L that twisted serpent;

LEVITE (see LEVI, LEVITES, LEVITICAL)
Ex   4:14 Is not Aaron the L your
Deut 12:12 and the L who is within
Judg 17: 7 family of Judah; he was a L,
Judg 17: 9 I am a L from Bethlehem in
Judg 17:12 So Micah consecrated the L,
Luke 10:32 "Likewise a L,
Acts   4:36 a L of the country of

LEVITES (see LEVITE)
Ex   6:25 the fathers' houses of the L
Ex   38:21 for the service of the L,
Lev   25:32 the cities of the L,
Num   1:47 But the L were not numbered
Num   1:50 you shall appoint the L

Num   1:51 the L shall take it down;
Num   1:53 and the L shall keep charge
Num   3:32 over the leaders of the L,
Num   3:49 who were redeemed by the L.
Num   4:18 Kohathites from among the L;
Num   8:10 lay their hands on the L;
Num   8:11 Aaron shall offer the L
Num   8:12 to make atonement for the L.
Num   35: 8 some of its cities to the L,
Deut 17: 9 come to the priests, the L,
Josh 14: 4 they gave no part to the L
Josh 21:41 All the cities of the L
1Sa   6:15 The L took down the ark of
1Ch   9:33 fathers' houses of the L,
1Ch   15:14 So the priests and the L
1Ch   15:26 when God helped the L who
2Ch   5:12 and the L who were the
2Ch   8:14 the L for their duties (to
2Ch   13:10 and the L attend to their
2Ch   23: 7 And the L shall surround the
2Ch   29: 5 L! Now sanctify yourselves,
2Ch   29:34 their brethren the L helped
2Ch   29:34 for the L were more diligent
2Ch   30:15 The priests and the L were
2Ch   31:17 and to the L from twenty
2Ch   31:19 by genealogies among the L.
2Ch   34:13 And some of the L were
2Ch   35:10 and the L in their
2Ch   35:11 while the L skinned the
2Ch   35:14 therefore the L prepared
Ezra   6:20 For the priests and the L had
Ezra   8:30 So the priests and the L
Neh   8: 9 and the L who taught the
Neh   8:11 So the L quieted all the
Neh   9: 4 on the stairs of the L and
Neh   10:37 tithes of our land to the L,
Neh   10:38 and the L shall bring up a
Neh   11:22 Also the overseer of the L
Neh   12:44 over the priests and L who
Neh   12:47 and the L consecrated them
Neh   13:29 of the priesthood and the L.
Jer   33:22 David My servant and the L
Ezek 48:13 the L shall have an area
John   1:19 the Jews sent priests and L

LEVITICAL† (see LEVITE)
Heb   7:11 were through the L

LEWD (see LEWDNESS)
Ezek 16:27 who were ashamed of your l
Ezek 23:44 Oholibah, the l women.

LEWDNESS (see LEWD)
Judg 20: 6 because they committed l and
Ezek 23:21 called to remembrance the l
Hos   2:10 Now I will uncover her l in
Hos   6: 9 Surely they commit l.
Rom   13:13 not in l and lust, not in

LIAR (see LIARS, LIE)
Job   24:25 so, who will prove me a l,
Prov 19:22 poor man is better than a l.
Prov 30: 6 you, and you be found a l.
John   8:44 for he is a l and the father
Rom   3: 4 be true but every man a l.
1Jn   1:10 not sinned, we make Him a l,
1Jn   2: 4 His commandments, is a l,
1Jn   2:22 Who is a l but he who denies
1Jn   4:20 hates his brother, he is a l;
1Jn   5:10 believe God has made Him a l,

LIARS (see LIAR)
Ps   116:11 my haste, "All men are l.
Tit   1:12 "Cretans are always l,
Rev   2: 2 not, and have found them l;
Rev   21: 8 and all l shall have their

LIBERALITY† (*see* LIBERALLY)
Rom	12: 8	he who gives, with l;
2Co	8: 2	in the riches of their l.
2Co	9:11	in everything for all l,

LIBERALLY (*see* LIBERALITY)
| Jas | 1: 5 | who gives to all l and |

LIBERTY
Lev	25:10	and proclaim l throughout
Ps	119:45	And I will walk at l,
Is	61: 1	To proclaim l to the
Jer	34:16	slaves, whom he had set at l,
Luke	4:18	To proclaim l to the
Acts	27: 3	Paul kindly and gave him l
Rom	8:21	into the glorious l of the
1Co	7:39	she is at l to be married to
1Co	8: 9	beware lest somehow this l
1Co	10:29	For why is my l judged by
2Co	3:17	of the Lord is, there is l.
Gal	2: 4	by stealth to spy out our l
Gal	5: 1	fast therefore in the l by
Gal	5:13	only do not use l as an
Jas	1:25	into the perfect law of l
Jas	2:12	be judged by the law of l.
1Pe	2:16	yet not using l as a cloak
2Pe	2:19	While they promise them l,

LIBYA
| Ezek | 30: 5 | "Ethiopia, L, Lydia, |
| Acts | 2:10 | Egypt and the parts of L |

LICE
| Ex | 8:17 | and it became l on man and |
| Ps | 105:31 | And l in all their |

LICK (*see* LICKED)
1Ki	21:19	dogs shall l your blood,
Ps	72: 9	And His enemies will l the
Mic	7:17	They shall l the dust like a

LICKED (*see* LICK)
1Ki	18:38	and it l up the water that
1Ki	21:19	In the place where dogs l the
Luke	16:21	the dogs came and l his

LIE (*see* LAIN, LAY, LIAR, LIED, LIES, LYING)
Gen	19:32	and we will l with him, that
Gen	39: 7	she said, "L with me."
Gen	47:30	but let me l with my fathers;
Lev	19:11	nor l to one another.
Num	23:19	not a man, that He should l,
Deut	6: 7	when you l down, and when
Deut	28:30	but another man shall l with
Judg	21:20	l in wait in the vineyards,
Ruth	3: 4	and l down; and he will tell
2Sa	11:11	and to l with my wife? As
2Sa	12:11	and he shall l with your
2Sa	13:11	l with me, my sister."
1Ki	1: 2	and let her l in your bosom,
2Ki	9:12	A l! Tell us now." So he
Job	7:21	For now I will l down in
Ps	4: 8	I will both l down in peace,
Ps	23: 2	He makes me to l down in
Ps	56: 6	When they l in wait for my
Ps	68:13	Though you l down among the
Ps	88: 5	Like the slain who l in the
Ps	89:35	I will not l to David:
Prov	1:11	Let us l in wait to shed
Eccl	4:11	if two l down together, they
Eccl	11: 3	tree falls, there it shall l.
Is	11: 6	The leopard shall l down
Is	14:30	And the needy will l down
Is	50:11	You shall l down in
Is	65:10	a place for herds to l down,
Jer	27:10	For they prophesy a l to you,
Jer	28:15	this people trust in a l.
Jer	33:12	causing their flocks to l

Ezek	4: 4	L also on your left side,
Ezek	4: 6	l again on your right side;
Ezek	34:14	There they shall l down in a
Ezek	34:15	and I will make them l
Hos	2:18	To make them l down safely.
Hos	6: 9	As bands of robbers l in
Amos	2: 8	They l down by every altar
Amos	6: 4	Who l on beds of ivory,
Mic	2:11	false spirit And speak a l,
Mic	7: 2	They all l in wait for
Hag	1: 4	and this temple to l in
John	8:44	in him. When he speaks a l,
Acts	5: 3	filled your heart to l to
Rom	1:25	the truth of God for the l,
Gal	1:20	before God, I do not l.
Col	3: 9	Do not l to one another,
2Th	2:11	they should believe the l,
Tit	1: 2	life which God, who cannot l,
Heb	6:18	is impossible for God to l,
Jas	3:14	do not boast and l against
1Jn	1: 6	we l and do not practice the
1Jn	2:21	and that no l is of the
1Jn	2:27	and is true, and is not a l,
Rev	3: 9	are Jews and are not, but l—
Rev	22:15	loves and practices a l.

LIED (*see* LIE)
| Ps | 78:36 | And they l to Him with |
| Acts | 5: 4 | You have not l to men but to |

LIES (*see* LIE)
Gen	4: 7	sin l at the door. And its
Ex	22:16	and l with her, he shall
Ex	22:19	Whoever l with an animal
Lev	15:18	when a woman l with a man,
Lev	15:20	Everything that she l on
Lev	15:24	and every bed on which he l
Num	24: 9	he l down as a lion; And as
Deut	22:23	finds her in the city and l
Judg	16: 5	where his great strength l,
Judg	16:10	have mocked me and told me l.
Ruth	3: 4	notice the place where he l;
2Ki	9:37	Here l Jezebel.' ' "
Job	14:12	So man l down and does not
Ps	10: 9	He l in wait secretly, as a
Ps	40: 4	nor such as turn aside to l.
Ps	62: 4	position; They delight in l;
Ps	88: 7	Your wrath l heavy upon me,
Ps	101: 7	He who tells l shall not
Prov	6:19	false witness who speaks l,
Prov	19: 9	And he who speaks l shall
Prov	30: 8	Remove falsehood and l far
Is	9:15	The prophet who teaches l,
Is	59: 3	Your lips have spoken l,
Is	59: 4	in empty words and speak l;
Jer	9: 3	bent their tongues for l.
Jer	14:14	The prophets prophesy l in My
Jer	23:14	adultery and walk in l;
Ezek	29: 3	O great monster who l in
Dan	11:27	and they shall speak l at
Hos	10:13	have eaten the fruit of l,
Amos	2: 4	Their l lead them astray,
Hab	2:18	molded image, a teacher of l,
2Co	3:15	a veil l on their heart.
1Ti	4: 2	speaking l in hypocrisy,
1Jn	5:19	and the whole world l under

LIFE (*see* LIFE-GIVING, LIFEBLOOD, LIFELESS, LIFETIME, LIVE)
Gen	1:30	earth, in which there is l,
Gen	2: 7	his nostrils the breath of l;
Gen	2: 9	The tree of l was also in
Gen	3:14	dust All the days of your l.
Gen	3:24	the way to the tree of l.
Gen	6:17	in which is the breath of l;
Gen	7:22	breath of the spirit of l,

Gen	9: 4	not eat flesh with its l,
Gen	9: 5	I will require the l of man.
Gen	27:46	I am weary of my l because of
Gen	27:46	what good will my l be to
Gen	32:30	and my l is preserved."
Gen	42:15	By the l of Pharaoh, you
Gen	44:30	is bound up in the lad's l,
Gen	45: 5	me before you to preserve l.
Gen	47: 9	days of the years of my l,
Ex	4:19	the men who sought your l
Ex	21:23	you shall give life for l,
Ex	21:30	he shall pay to redeem his l,
Lev	17:11	For the l of the flesh is in
Lev	17:14	Its blood sustains its l.
Num	35:31	take no ransom for the l of
Deut	4: 9	heart all the days of your l.
Deut	12:23	you may not eat the l with
Deut	17:19	it all the days of his l,
Deut	19:21	l shall be for life, eye
Deut	30:15	have set before you today l
Deut	30:19	cursing; therefore choose l,
Deut	30:20	for He is your l and the
Judg	12: 3	I took my l in my hands and
Judg	16:30	than he had killed in his l.
Judg	18:25	you, and you lose your l,
Ruth	4:15	he be to you a restorer of l
1Sa	20: 1	father, that he seeks my l?
1Sa	26:21	because my l was precious in
1Sa	28: 9	do you lay a snare for my l,
2Sa	14:14	God does not take away a l;
2Sa	15:21	be, whether in death or l,
1Ki	1:29	who has redeemed my l from
1Ki	3:11	and have not asked long l
1Ki	19: 3	he arose and ran for his l,
1Ki	19: 4	Now, LORD, take my l,
1Ki	19:10	and they seek to take my l.
1Ki	20:31	perhaps he will spare your l.
2Ki	8: 5	had restored the dead to l,
2Ki	8: 5	whom Elisha restored to l.
Neh	6:11	the temple to save his l?
Esth	7: 7	Esther, pleading for his l,
Job	2: 4	has he will give for his l.
Job	2: 6	your hand, but spare his l.
Job	3:20	And l to the bitter of
Job	6:11	that I should prolong my l?
Job	7: 7	remember that my l is a
Job	7:16	I loathe my l;
Job	9:21	know myself; I despise my l.
Job	24:22	up, but no man is sure of l.
Job	27: 8	If God takes away his l?
Job	33: 4	of the Almighty gives me l.
Job	33:30	with the light of l.
Job	36: 6	He does not preserve the l
Ps	7: 5	let him trample my l to the
Ps	16:11	will show me the path of l;
Ps	17:13	Deliver my l from the
Ps	17:14	their portion in this l,
Ps	21: 4	He asked l from You, and
Ps	22:20	My precious l from the
Ps	23: 6	me All the days of my l;
Ps	27: 1	is the strength of my l;
Ps	27: 4	LORD All the days of my l,
Ps	30: 5	His favor is for l;
Ps	31:13	scheme to take away my l.
Ps	34:12	is the man who desires l,
Ps	35:17	My precious l from the
Ps	36: 9	You is the fountain of l;
Ps	38:12	Those also who seek my l lay
Ps	40:14	Who seek to destroy my l;
Ps	42: 8	prayer to the God of my l.
Ps	61: 6	will prolong the king's l,
Ps	63: 3	is better than l,
Ps	64: 1	Preserve my l from fear of
Ps	74:19	beast! Do not forget the l
Ps	78:50	But gave their l over to

Ps	86: 2	Preserve my l,
Ps	88: 3	And my l draws near to the
Ps	91:16	With long l I will satisfy
Ps	119:50	Your word has given me l.
Ps	128: 5	All the days of your l.
Ps	133: 3	L forevermore.
Prov	2:19	they regain the paths of l—
Prov	3: 2	length of days and long l
Prov	3:18	She is a tree of l to those
Prov	3:22	So they will be l to your
Prov	4:13	her, for she is your l.
Prov	4:22	For they are l to those who
Prov	4:23	it spring the issues of l.
Prov	5: 6	you ponder her path of l—
Prov	6:26	prey upon his precious l.
Prov	7:23	know it would cost his l.
Prov	8:35	whoever finds me finds l,
Prov	10:11	righteous is a well of l,
Prov	10:16	of the righteous leads to l,
Prov	10:17	is in the way of l,
Prov	11:30	righteous is a tree of l,
Prov	13:14	the wise is a fountain of l,
Prov	14:27	LORD is a fountain of l,
Prov	15:24	The way of l winds upward
Prov	16:15	of the king's face is l,
Prov	16:22	is a wellspring of l to
Prov	19:23	of the LORD leads to l,
Prov	20: 2	sins against his own l.
Prov	21:21	and mercy Finds l,
Prov	22: 4	Are riches and honor and l.
Prov	31:12	evil All the days of her l.
Eccl	6:12	all the days of his vain l
Eccl	8:15	labor all the days of his l
Eccl	9: 9	that is your portion in l,
Is	38:10	In the prime of my l I shall
Is	38:12	My l span is gone, Taken
Is	38:20	All the days of our l.
Jer	18:20	they have dug a pit for my l.
Jer	23:10	Their course of l is evil,
Lam	2:12	As their l is poured out
Lam	3:58	You have redeemed my l.
Ezek	3:18	wicked way, to save his l,
Ezek	33:15	walks in the statutes of l
Dan	12: 2	Some to everlasting l,
Jon	2: 6	You have brought up my l
Jon	4: 3	please take my l from me,
Matt	2:20	sought the young Child's l
Matt	6:25	do not worry about your l,
Matt	6:25	Is not l more than food and
Matt	7:14	is the way which leads to l,
Matt	10:39	He who finds his l will lose
Matt	10:39	and he who loses his l for
Matt	16:25	desires to save his l will
Matt	18: 8	for you to enter into l
Matt	19:16	do that I may have eternal l?
Matt	20:28	and to give His l a ransom
Matt	25:46	the righteous into eternal l.
Mark	3: 4	to save l or to kill?" But
Mark	10:30	the age to come, eternal l.
Mark	10:45	and to give His l a ransom
Luke	1:75	Him all the days of our l.
Luke	6: 9	to save l or to destroy?"
Luke	8:14	riches, and pleasures of l,
Luke	12:15	for one's l does not consist
Luke	12:22	do not worry about your l,
Luke	12:23	L is more than food, and the
Luke	18:30	in the age to come eternal l.
Luke	21:34	and cares of this l,
John	1: 4	In Him was l,
John	1: 4	and the l was the light of
John	3:15	perish but have eternal l.
John	3:16	but have everlasting l.
John	3:36	in the Son has everlasting l;
John	3:36	the Son shall not see l,
John	4:14	up into everlasting l.

John 4:36 gathers fruit for eternal l,
John 5:21 even so the Son gives l to
John 5:24 sent Me has everlasting l,
John 5:24 has passed from death into l.
John 5:26 For as the Father has l in
John 5:26 granted the Son to have l
John 5:29 to the resurrection of l,
John 5:39 you think you have eternal l;
John 5:40 to Me that you may have l.
John 6:27 endures to everlasting l,
John 6:33 from heaven and gives l to
John 6:35 them, "I am the bread of l.
John 6:51 I shall give for the l of
John 6:53 you have no l in you.
John 6:54 My blood has eternal l,
John 6:63 is the Spirit who gives l;
John 6:63 are spirit, and they are l.
John 6:68 have the words of eternal l.
John 8:12 but have the light of l.
John 10:10 come that they may have l,
John 10:11 good shepherd gives His l
John 10:15 and I lay down My l for the
John 10:28 "And I give them eternal l,
John 11:25 the resurrection and the l.
John 12:25 He who loves his l will lose
John 12:25 and he who hates his l in
John 12:25 will keep it for eternal l.
John 12:50 His command is everlasting l.
John 13:37 I will lay down my l for
John 14: 6 way, the truth, and the l.
John 15:13 than to lay down one's l for
John 17: 2 He should give eternal l to
John 17: 3 "And this is eternal l,
John 20:31 believing you may have l in
Acts 2:28 to me the ways of l;
Acts 3:15 "and killed the Prince of l,
Acts 11:18 the Gentiles repentance to l.
Acts 13:46 unworthy of everlasting l,
Acts 13:48 been appointed to eternal l
Acts 17:25 since He gives to all l,
Act 20:24 nor do I count my l dear to
Acts 26: 4 My manner of l from my youth,
Rom 2: 7 eternal l to those who by
Rom 4:17 who gives l to the dead and
Rom 5:10 we shall be saved by His l.
Rom 5:17 will reign in l through the
Rom 5:18 in justification of l.
Rom 5:21 righteousness to eternal l
Rom 6: 4 should walk in newness of l.
Rom 6:10 but the l that He lives,
Rom 6:22 and the end, everlasting l.
Rom 6:23 gift of God is eternal l
Rom 7:10 which was to bring l,
Rom 8: 2 the law of the Spirit of l
Rom 8: 6 be spiritually minded is l
Rom 8:11 the dead will also give l
Rom 8:38 that neither death nor l,
Rom 11: 3 and they seek my l"?
Rom 11:15 their acceptance be but l
1Co 3:22 or the world or l or death,
1Co 6: 3 that pertain to this l?
1Co 15:19 If in this l only we have
2Co 1: 8 that we despaired even of l.
2Co 2:16 to the other the aroma of l
2Co 3: 6 but the Spirit gives l.
2Co 4:10 that the l of Jesus also may
2Co 5: 4 may be swallowed up by l.
Gal 2:20 and the l which I now live
Gal 3:21 which could have given l,
Gal 6: 8 Spirit reap everlasting l.
Phil 1:20 whether by l or by death.
Phil 2:16 holding fast the word of l,
Phil 2:30 death, not regarding his l,
Phil 4: 3 names are in the Book of L.
Col 3: 3 and your l is hidden with

Col 3: 4 When Christ who is our l
1Th 4:11 aspire to lead a quiet l,
1Ti 4: 8 having promise of the l that
1Ti 6:12 faith, lay hold on eternal l,
1Ti 6:13 sight of God who gives l to
1Ti 6:19 may lay hold on eternal l.
2Ti 1: 1 to the promise of l which
2Ti 1:10 death and brought l and
2Ti 2: 4 with the affairs of this l,
2Ti 3:10 my doctrine, manner of l,
Tit 1: 2 in hope of eternal l which
Heb 7: 3 of days nor end of l,
Heb 7:16 to the power of an endless l.
Heb 11:35 their dead raised to l
Jas 1:12 will receive the crown of l
Jas 4:14 For what is your l?
1Pe 3: 7 together of the grace of l,
1Pe 3:10 He who would love l And
2Pe 1: 3 things that pertain to l
1Jn 1: 1 concerning the Word of l—
1Jn 1: 2 the l was manifested, and we
1Jn 1: 2 to you that eternal l which
1Jn 2:16 the eyes, and the pride of l—
1Jn 2:25 He has promised us—eternal l.
1Jn 3:14 have passed from death to l,
1Jn 3:15 no murderer has eternal l
1Jn 3:16 because He laid down His l
1Jn 5:11 God has given us eternal l,
1Jn 5:11 and this l is in His Son.
1Jn 5:12 He who has the Son has l;
1Jn 5:13 know that you have eternal l,
1Jn 5:20 the true God and eternal l.
Jude 21 Jesus Christ unto eternal l.
Rev 2: 7 to eat from the tree of l,
Rev 2: 8 who was dead, and came to l:
Rev 2:10 will give you the crown of l.
Rev 3: 5 his name from the Book of L;
Rev 13: 8 written in the Book of L of
Rev 17: 8 not written in the Book of L
Rev 20:15 written in the Book of L
Rev 21: 6 fountain of the water of l
Rev 21:27 in the Lamb's Book of L.
Rev 22: 1 a pure river of water of l,
Rev 22: 2 river, was the tree of l,
Rev 22:17 let him take the water of l
Rev 22:19 his part from the Book of L,

LIFE-GIVING† (*see* LIFE)
1Co 15:45 The last Adam became a l

LIFEBLOOD† (*see* BLOOD, LIFE)
Gen 9: 5 Surely for your l I will

LIFELESS† (*see* LIFE)
Lev 26:30 cast your carcasses on the l

LIFETIME (*see* LIFE)
Heb 2:15 of death were all their l

LIFT (*see* LIFTED, LIFTING, LIFTS, RAISE, UNLIFTED, UPLIFTED)
Gen 13:14 L your eyes now and look from
Ex 14:16 But l up your rod, and
Num 6:26 the LORD l up His
2Ki 19: 4 Therefore l up your prayer
Job 22:26 And l up your face to God.
Job 38:34 Can you l up your voice to
Ps 4: 6 l up the light of Your
Ps 10:12 l up Your hand! Do not
Ps 24: 7 L up your heads, O you
Ps 25: 1 I l up my soul.
Ps 93: 3 The floods l up their
Ps 110: 7 Therefore He shall l up the
Ps 121: 1 I will l up my eyes to the
Ps 123: 1 Unto You I l up my eyes, O
Is 2: 4 Nation shall not l up sword
Is 5:26 He will l up a banner to

Is	10:30	L up your voice, O daughter
Is	49:18	L up your eyes, look around
Is	49:22	I will l My hand in an oath
Is	51: 6	L up your eyes to the
Is	62:10	L up a banner for the
Lam	3:41	Let us l our hearts and
Mic	4: 3	Nation shall not l up sword
Nah	3: 5	I will l your skirts over
Luke	21:28	look up and l up your heads,
John	8:28	When you l up the Son of Man,
Jas	4:10	and He will l you up.

LIFTED (see LIFT, RAISED)

Gen	7:17	The waters increased and l
Gen	13:10	And Lot l his eyes and saw
Gen	22:13	Then Abraham l his eyes and
Gen	37:28	pulled Joseph up and l him
Gen	40:20	and he l up the head of the
Ex	7:20	So he l up the rod and
Deut	8:14	when your heart is l up, and
Deut	17:20	his heart may not be l
2Ch	25:19	and your heart is l up to
Job	2:12	they l their voices and
Ps	24: 4	Who has not l up his soul
Ps	24: 7	O you gates! And be l up,
Ps	27: 6	And now my head shall be l
Ps	30: 1	for You have l me up, And
Ps	41: 9	Has l up his heel against
Ps	93: 3	The floods have l up their
Ps	102:10	For You have l me up and
Is	6: 1	high and l up, and the train
Jer	38:13	up with ropes and l him out
Jer	52:31	l up the head of Jehoiachin
Ezek	1:19	the living creatures were l
Ezek	1:19	the wheels were l up.
Ezek	3:14	So the Spirit l me up and
Ezek	28: 2	Because your heart is l up,
Dan	4:34	l my eyes to heaven, and my
Dan	5:20	But when his heart was l up,
Dan	7: 4	and it was l up from the
Zech	1:21	horns of the nations that l
Mark	1:31	took her by the hand and l
John	3:14	And as Moses l up the serpent
John	3:14	so must the Son of Man be l
John	12:32	if I am l up from the earth,
John	12:34	The Son of Man must be l up'?
John	13:18	bread with Me has l
Acts	3: 7	him by the right hand and l
Acts	9:41	he gave her his hand and l
Acts	10:26	But Peter l him up, saying,

LIFTING (see LIFT)

1Ti	2: 8	l up holy hands, without

LIFTS (see LIFT)

1Sa	2: 7	He brings low and l up.
Ps	3: 3	My glory and the One who l
Ps	147: 6	The LORD l up the humble;
Is	18: 3	When he l up a banner on

LIGAMENTS†

Col	2:19	together by joints and l,

LIGHT (see LIGHTEN, LIGHTER, LIGHTLY, LIGHTS, LIT)

Gen	1: 3	Let there be l"; and there
Gen	1: 4	And God saw the l,
Gen	1: 4	and God divided the l from
Gen	1: 5	God called the l Day, and the
Gen	1:15	of the heavens to give l on
Gen	1:16	the greater l to rule the
Gen	1:18	and to divide the l from the
Ex	10:23	children of Israel had l in
Ex	13:21	of fire to give them l,
Ex	25: 6	"oil for the l,
Ex	35:14	the lampstand for the l,
Deut	25:13	weights, a heavy and a l.
Judg	19:26	master was, till it was l.

Esth	8:16	The Jews had l and gladness,
Job	3: 4	Nor the l shine upon it.
Job	3: 9	be dark; May it look for l,
Job	3:16	infants who never saw l?
Job	3:23	Why is l given to a man
Job	12:22	the shadow of death to l.
Job	12:25	grope in the dark without l,
Job	18: 6	The l is dark in his tent,
Job	22:28	So l will shine on your
Job	24:13	who rebel against the l;
Job	24:14	murderer rises with the l;
Job	24:16	They do not know the l.
Job	25: 3	Upon whom does His l not
Job	26:10	At the boundary of l and
Job	33:30	be enlightened with the l
Job	37:15	And causes the l of His
Job	38:19	way to the dwelling of l?
Ps	4: 6	lift up the l of Your
Ps	18:28	For You will l my lamp; The
Ps	27: 1	The LORD is my l and my
Ps	36: 9	In Your l we see light.
Ps	37: 6	your righteousness as the l,
Ps	43: 3	send out Your l and Your
Ps	44: 3	and the l of Your
Ps	49:19	They shall never see l.
Ps	56:13	walk before God In the l
Ps	89:15	in the l of Your
Ps	90: 8	Our secret sins in the l
Ps	104: 2	Who cover Yourself with l
Ps	119:105	a lamp to my feet And a l
Ps	119:130	of Your words gives l;
Ps	139:11	Even the night shall be l
Ps	139:12	The darkness and the l are
Ps	148: 3	all your stars of l!
Prov	6:23	is a lamp, And the law a l;
Prov	13: 9	The l of the righteous
Prov	15:30	The l of the eyes rejoices
Prov	16:15	In the l of the king's face
Prov	29:13	The LORD gives l to the
Eccl	11: 7	Truly the l is sweet, And
Is	2: 5	and let us walk In the l
Is	5:20	Who put darkness for l,
Is	8:20	is because there is no l
Is	9: 2	Have seen a great l;
Is	9: 2	Upon them a l has shined.
Is	10:17	So the L of Israel will be
Is	42: 6	As a l to the Gentiles,
Is	45: 7	I form the l and create
Is	49: 6	I will also give You as a l
Is	58: 8	Then your l shall break
Is	59: 9	overtake us; We look for l,
Is	60: 1	For your l has come! And
Is	60: 3	shall come to your l,
Is	60:19	be to you an everlasting l,
Dan	2:22	And l dwells with Him.
Amos	5:18	be darkness, and not l.
Amos	5:20	LORD darkness, and not l?
Matt	4:16	have seen a great l,
Matt	4:16	and shadow of death L
Matt	5:14	You are the l of the world. A
Matt	5:15	Nor do they l a lamp and put
Matt	5:15	and it gives l to all who
Matt	5:16	Let your l so shine before
Matt	6:22	whole body will be full of l.
Matt	6:23	If therefore the l that is
Matt	11:30	is easy and My burden is l.
Matt	22: 5	But they made l of it and
Matt	24:29	the moon will not give its l;
Luke	1:79	To give l to those who sit
Luke	2:32	A l to bring revelation to
Luke	8:16	who enter may see the l.
Luke	8:17	not be known and come to l.
Luke	12: 3	dark will be heard in the l,
Luke	15: 8	does not l a lamp, sweep the
Luke	16: 8	than the sons of l.

John	1: 4	and the life was the l of
John	1: 5	And the l shines in the
John	1: 7	to bear witness of the L,
John	1: 8	He was not that L,
John	1: 9	That was the true L which
John	3:19	that the l has come into the
John	3:19	loved darkness rather than l,
John	3:20	practicing evil hates the l
John	3:20	and does not come to the l,
John	3:21	the truth comes to the l,
John	5:35	a time to rejoice in his l.
John	8:12	I am the l of the world. He
John	8:12	but have the l of life."
John	9: 5	I am the l of the world."
John	11:10	because the l is not in
John	12:35	little while longer the l
John	12:35	Walk while you have the l,
John	12:36	"While you have the l,
John	12:36	the light, believe in the l,
John	12:36	you may become sons of l.
John	12:46	I have come as a l into the
Acts	9: 3	and suddenly a l shone
Acts	12: 7	and a l shone in the prison;
Acts	22: 6	suddenly a great l from
Rom	2:19	a l to those who are in
Rom	13:12	let us put on the armor of l.
1Co	4: 5	who will both bring to l the
2Co	4: 4	lest the l of the gospel of
2Co	4: 6	is the God who commanded l
2Co	4: 6	in our hearts to give the l
2Co	6:14	And what communion has l
2Co	11:14	himself into an angel of l.
Eph	5: 8	but now you are l in the
Eph	5: 8	Walk as children of l
Eph	5:13	are made manifest by the l,
Eph	5:14	And Christ will give you l.
Col	1:12	of the saints in the l.
1Th	5: 5	You are all sons of l and
2Ti	1:10	life and immortality to l
1Pe	2: 9	into His marvelous l;
2Pe	1:19	you do well to heed as a l
1Jn	1: 5	that God is l and in Him is
1Jn	1: 7	But if we walk in the l as He
1Jn	2: 8	and the true l is already
1Jn	2: 9	He who says he is in the l,
1Jn	2:10	his brother abides in the l,
Rev	21:23	it. The Lamb is its l.
Rev	21:24	saved shall walk in its l,
Rev	22: 5	They need no lamp nor l of
Rev	22: 5	the Lord God gives them l.

LIGHTEN (see LIGHT, LIGHTENED)

Jon	1: 5	to l the load. But Jonah had

LIGHTENED (see LIGHTEN)

Acts	27:38	they l the ship and threw

LIGHTER (see LIGHT)

Ps	62: 9	They are altogether l

LIGHTLY (see LIGHT)

1Sa	2:30	who despise Me shall be l

LIGHTNING (see LIGHTNINGS)

Ex	20:18	the l flashes, the sound of
Job	37: 3	His l to the ends of the
Ps	135: 7	He makes l for the rain;
Ps	144: 6	Flash forth l and scatter
Dan	10: 6	like the appearance of l,
Matt	24:27	For as the l comes from the
Matt	28: 3	His countenance was like l,
Luke	10:18	I saw Satan fall like l from

LIGHTNINGS (see LIGHTNING)

Ex	19:16	there were thunderings and l,
Ps	77:18	The l lit up the world;
Rev	4: 5	from the throne proceeded l,
Rev	16:18	noises and thunderings and l;

LIGHTS (see LIGHT)

Gen	1:14	Let there be l in the
Gen	1:16	Then God made two great l:
Ps	136: 7	To Him who made great l,
Phil	2:15	among whom you shine as l in
Jas	1:17	down from the Father of l,

LIKE-MINDED

Rom	15: 5	comfort grant you to be l
Phil	2: 2	fulfill my joy by being l,

LIKEN (see LIKENED, LIKENESS)

Is	40:18	To whom then will you l
Matt	7:24	I will l him to a wise man
Matt	11:16	But to what shall I l this
Luke	13:20	To what shall I l the kingdom

LIKENED (see LIKEN)

Matt	25: 1	of heaven shall be l to ten

LIKENESS (see LIKEN)

Gen	1:26	image, according to Our l;
Gen	5: 1	He made him in the l of God.
Gen	5: 3	begot a son in his own l,
Ex	20: 4	or any l of anything that
Deut	4:16	the l of male or female,
Ps	17:15	when I awake in Your l.
Is	40:18	Or what l will you compare
Ezek	1: 5	from within it came the l
Ezek	1: 5	they had the l of a man.
Ezek	1:28	the appearance of the l of
Dan	10:16	one having the l of the
Rom	6: 5	united together in the l of
Rom	6: 5	we also shall be in the l
Rom	8: 3	His own Son in the l of
Phil	2: 7	and coming in the l of men.
Heb	7:15	in the l of Melchizedek,

LILIES (see LILY)

Song	2:16	his flock among the l.
Matt	6:28	Consider the l of the field,

LILY (see LILIES)

Song	2: 1	And the l of the valleys.
Hos	14: 5	He shall grow like the l,

LIMB

Judg	19:29	l by limb, and sent her

LIME

Deut	27: 2	and whitewash them with l.
Amos	2: 1	of the king of Edom to l.

LIMIT (see LIMITS)

Job	15: 8	Do you l wisdom to
Prov	8:29	He assigned to the sea its l,

LIMITS (see LIMIT)

Job	11: 7	Can you find out the l of

LIMP (see LIMPED)

Is	13: 7	all hands will be l,

LIMPED† (see LIMP)

Gen	32:31	and he l on his hip.

LINE (see LINEAGE, LINES)

Josh	2:18	you bind this l of scarlet
Job	38: 5	Or who stretched the l
Ps	19: 4	Their l has gone out through
Is	28:10	L upon line, line upon
Amos	7: 7	a wall made with a plumb l,
Zech	2: 1	a man with a measuring l in
Zech	4:10	rejoice to see The plumb l

LINEAGE (see LINE)

Gen	19:32	that we may preserve the l
Luke	2: 4	he was of the house and l

LINEN

Gen	41:42	him in garments of fine l
Ex	28:42	you shall make for them l
Ex	39:29	and a sash of fine woven l

Lev	6:10	priest shall put on his l
Lev	13:47	is a woolen garment or a l
Lev	16: 4	He shall put the holy l tunic
Lev	16:32	and put on the l clothes,
Deut	22:11	such as wool and l mixed
1Sa	2:18	wearing a l ephod.
Prov	7:16	coverings of Egyptian l.
Prov	31:22	Her clothing is fine l and
Prov	31:24	She makes l garments and
Is	3:23	and the mirrors; The fine l,
Jer	13: 1	Go and get yourself a l sash,
Ezek	16:10	I clothed you with fine l
Ezek	27: 7	Fine embroidered l from
Dan	10: 5	a certain man clothed in l,
Hos	2: 5	my water, My wool and my l,
Hos	2: 9	take back My wool and My l,
Matt	27:59	he wrapped it in a clean l
Mark	14:52	and he left the l cloth and
Mark	15:46	Then he bought fine l,
Luke	16:19	in purple and fine l and
Luke	24:12	he saw the l cloths lying by
John	19:40	and bound it in strips of l
Rev	15: 6	clothed in pure bright l,
Rev	18:12	fine l and purple, silk and

LINES† (see LINE)

2Sa	8: 2	With two l he measured off
Ps	16: 6	The l have fallen to me in

LINGER (see LINGERED)

Prov	23:30	Those who l long at the
Is	46:13	My salvation shall not l.

LINGERED (see LINGER)

Luke	1:21	marveled that he l so long
Luke	2:43	the Boy Jesus l behind

LINTEL

Ex	12: 7	two doorposts and on the l
Ex	12:23	He sees the blood on the l

LION (see LION'S, LIONESS, LIONS)

Gen	49: 9	down, he lies down as a l;
Deut	33:20	Gad; He dwells as a l,
Judg	14: 6	and he tore the l apart as
Judg	14: 9	out of the carcass of the l.
Judg	14:18	what is stronger than a l?
1Sa	17:34	and when a l or a bear came
1Sa	17:36	servant has killed both l
1Ki	13:24	a l met him on the road and
1Ki	20:36	a l found him and killed
Job	10:16	You hunt me like a fierce l,
Ps	7: 2	Lest they tear me like a l,
Ps	10: 9	as a l in his den; He lies
Ps	22:13	a raging and roaring l.
Ps	91:13	You shall tread upon the l
Prov	22:13	There is a l outside! I
Prov	26:13	in the road! A fierce l
Prov	28: 1	righteous are bold as a l.
Eccl	9: 4	dog is better than a dead l.
Is	11: 6	The calf and the young l
Is	11: 7	And the l shall eat straw
Is	38:13	until morning—Like a l,
Is	65:25	The l shall eat straw like
Jer	2:30	Like a destroying l.
Lam	3:10	Like a l in ambush.
Ezek	1:10	four had the face of a l on
Ezek	10:14	the third the face of a l,
Dan	7: 4	"The first was like a l,
Hos	5:14	For I will be like a l to
Joel	1: 6	teeth are the teeth of a l,
Amos	3: 4	Will a l roar in the forest,
Amos	3: 8	A l has roared! Who will
Amos	3:12	takes from the mouth of a l
Amos	5:19	though a man fled from a l,
2Ti	4:17	out of the mouth of the l.
1Pe	5: 8	walks about like a roaring l,

Rev	4: 7	creature was like a l,
Rev	5: 5	the L of the tribe of Judah,

LION'S (see LION)

Gen	49: 9	Judah is a l whelp; From
Deut	33:22	Dan is a l whelp; He shall
Ps	22:21	Save Me from the l mouth

LIONESS (see LION)

Nah	2:11	the l and lion's cub, And

LIONS (see LION, LIONS')

2Sa	1:23	They were stronger than l.
1Ki	7:36	he engraved cherubim, l,
2Ki	17:25	therefore the LORD sent l
Ps	34:10	The young l lack and suffer
Ps	35:17	precious life from the l.
Ps	58: 6	out the fangs of the young l,
Dan	6: 7	be cast into the den of l.
Dan	6:20	to deliver you from the l?
Dan	6:24	and the l overpowered them,
Heb	11:33	stopped the mouths of l,
Rev	9:17	were like the heads of l;

LIONS' (see LIONS)

Dan	6:22	His angel and shut the l
Rev	9: 8	and their teeth were like l

LIP (see LIPS)

Ps	22: 7	Me; They shoot out the l,

LIPS (see LIP)

Ex	6:12	for I am of uncircumcised l?
1Sa	1:13	only her l moved, but her
Job	2:10	Job did not sin with his l.
Job	15: 6	your own l testify against
Job	23:12	the commandment of His l;
Job	33: 3	My l utter pure knowledge.
Ps	12: 2	With flattering l and a
Ps	16: 4	take up their names on my l.
Ps	17: 1	is not from deceitful l.
Ps	31:18	Let the lying l be put to
Ps	34:13	And your l from speaking
Ps	40: 9	I do not restrain my l,
Ps	45: 2	Grace is poured upon Your l;
Ps	63: 3	My l shall praise You.
Ps	66:14	Which my l have uttered And
Ps	71:23	My l shall greatly rejoice
Ps	106:33	he spoke rashly with his l.
Ps	141: 3	watch over the door of my l.
Prov	4:24	And put perverse l far from
Prov	5: 3	For the l of an immoral
Prov	7:21	With her flattering l she
Prov	10:18	hides hatred has lying l,
Prov	10:19	But he who restrains his l
Prov	10:32	The l of the righteous know
Prov	12:22	Lying l are an abomination
Prov	14: 3	But the l of the wise will
Prov	14: 7	not perceive in him the l
Prov	16:10	Divination is on the l of
Prov	16:30	He purses his l and brings
Prov	17: 4	gives heed to false l;
Prov	19: 1	who is perverse in his l,
Prov	23:16	will rejoice When your l
Prov	24: 2	And their l talk of
Prov	24:26	a right answer kisses the l.
Prov	26:23	Fervent l with a wicked
Eccl	10:12	But the l of a fool shall
Song	5:13	His l are lilies,
Is	6: 5	I am a man of unclean l,
Is	6: 5	of a people of unclean l;
Is	6: 7	this has touched your l;
Is	11: 4	with the breath of His l He
Is	29:13	And honor Me with their l,
Is	37:29	And My bridle in your l,
Jer	17:16	know what came out of my l;
Ezek	24:17	feet; do not cover your l,
Dan	10:16	the sons of men touched my l;

Hos	14: 2	the sacrifices of our l.
Hab	3:16	My l quivered at the
Mal	2: 7	For the l of a priest should
Matt	15: 8	honor Me with their l,
Rom	3:13	asps is under their l'
1Co	14:21	tongues and other l l
Heb	13:15	that is, the fruit of our l,
1Pe	3:10	And his l from

LIQUID

Ex	30:23	five hundred shekels of l
Song	5:13	Dripping l myrrh.

LISTEN (*see* LISTENED, LISTENING, LISTENS)

Gen	4:23	l to my speech! For I have
Ex	4: 1	will not believe me or l to
Deut	1:43	to you; yet you would not l,
Deut	1:45	but the LORD would not l to
Deut	27: 9	saying, "Take heed and l,
Judg	2:17	Yet they would not l to their
Ruth	2: 8	said to Ruth, "You will l,
1Ki	8:28	and l to the cry and the
2Ki	18:31	Do not l to Hezekiah; for
Job	13:17	L carefully to my speech,
Job	33:31	l to me; Hold your peace,
Job	35:13	Surely God will not l to
Job	42: 4	L, please, and let me
Ps	34:11	l to me; I will teach you
Ps	45:10	L, O daughter,
Ps	81: 8	if you will l to Me!
Prov	7:24	l to me, my children; Pay
Prov	13: 1	But a scoffer does not l to
Prov	19:20	L to counsel and receive
Prov	23:22	L to your father who begot
Is	46: 3	L to Me, O house of Jacob,
Is	55: 2	L carefully to Me, and eat
Jer	29: 8	nor l to your dreams which
Ezek	3: 7	house of Israel will not l
Dan	9:19	l and act! Do not delay for
Mark	4: 3	L! Behold, a sower went out
John	8:43	you are not able to l to My
John	9:27	already, and you did not l.
John	10:20	Why do you l to Him?"
Acts	7: 2	"Brethren and fathers, l:
Acts	13:16	and you who fear God, l:
Jas	2: 5	L, my beloved brethren:

LISTENED (*see* LISTEN)

Gen	23:16	And Abraham l to Ephron; and
Gen	37:27	flesh." And his brothers l.
Job	32:11	I l to your reasonings,
Jer	25: 7	Yet you have not l to Me,"

LISTENING (*see* LISTEN)

Gen	18:10	(Sarah was l in the tent
Gen	27: 5	Now Rebekah was l when Isaac
Luke	2:46	both l to them and asking
Acts	16:25	and the prisoners were l to

LISTENS (*see* LISTEN)

Prov	1:33	But whoever l to me will
Prov	8:34	Blessed is the man who l to
Jer	16:12	so that no one l to Me.

LIT (*see* LIGHT)

Ex	40:25	and he l the lamps before the
Luke	8:16	when he has l a lamp, covers
Luke	11:33	when he has l a lamp, puts

LITERATURE†

Dan	1: 4	teach the language and l of
Dan	1:17	and skill in all l and

LITTLE

Gen	19:20	and it is a l one; please
Gen	24:17	Please let me drink a l water
Gen	43: 2	buy us a l food."
Gen	45:19	the land of Egypt for your l
Ex	16:18	and he who gathered l had no

Ex	23:30	L by little I will drive them
Ruth	2: 7	though she rested a l in the
1Sa	2:19	mother used to make him a l
2Sa	12: 3	except one l ewe lamb which
2Sa	12: 8	if that had been too l,
1Ki	3: 7	but I am a l child; I do
1Ki	12:10	My l finger shall be thicker
1Ki	17:10	Please bring me a l water in
1Ki	17:12	and a l oil in a jar; and
2Ki	5:14	like the flesh of a l child,
Ps	2:12	His wrath is kindled but a l.
Ps	8: 5	For You have made him a l
Ps	37:10	For yet a l while and the
Ps	37:16	A l that a righteous man has
Ps	65:12	And the l hills rejoice on
Ps	68:27	There is l Benjamin, their
Ps	114: 4	The l hills like lambs.
Ps	137: 9	who takes and dashes Your l
Prov	6:10	A l sleep, a little slumber,
Prov	6:10	a l slumber, A little
Prov	24:33	A l folding of the hands to
Prov	30:24	four things which are l
Eccl	5:12	Whether he eats l or much;
Song	2:15	The l foxes that spoil the
Song	8: 8	We have a l sister, And
Is	11: 6	And a l child shall lead
Is	28:10	Here a little, there a l.
Is	60:22	A l one shall become a
Jer	51:33	Yet a l while And the time
Ezek	34:18	Is it too l for you to have
Dan	7: 8	a l one, coming up among
Dan	8: 9	out of one of them came a l
Dan	11:34	they shall be aided with a l
Hos	1: 4	For in a l while I will
Mic	5: 2	Though you are l among the
Hag	1: 6	sown much, and bring in l;
Matt	6:30	O you of l faith?
Matt	10:42	gives one of these l ones
Matt	14:31	O you of l faith, why did you
Matt	18: 2	Then Jesus called a l child
Matt	18: 3	converted and become as l
Matt	18: 4	humbles himself as this l
Matt	18: 5	Whoever receives one l child
Matt	19:14	Let the l children come to
Matt	26:39	He went a l farther and fell
Mark	4:36	And other l boats were also
Mark	5:23	My l daughter lies at the
Mark	5:41	L girl, I say to you,
Mark	10:15	the kingdom of God as a l
Luke	5: 3	and asked him to put out a l
Luke	7:47	But to whom l is forgiven,
Luke	12:28	O you of l faith?
Luke	12:32	l flock, for it is your
Luke	17: 2	offend one of these l ones.
Luke	19:17	were faithful in a very l,
John	7:33	I shall be with you a l while
John	13:33	L children, I shall be with
John	16:16	A l while, and you will not
1Co	5: 6	Do you not know that a l
2Co	8:15	and he who gathered l
2Co	11:16	that I also may boast a l.
Gal	4:19	My l children, for whom I
Gal	5: 9	A l leaven leavens the whole
1Ti	4: 8	bodily exercise profits a l,
1Ti	5:23	but use a l wine for your
Heb	2: 7	You have made him a l
Heb	10:37	For yet a l while, And
Jas	3: 5	Even so the tongue is a l
Jas	3: 5	See how great a forest a l
Jas	4:14	a vapor that appears for a l
1Pe	1: 6	though now for a l while, if
1Jn	2: 1	My l children, these things I
1Jn	5:21	L children, keep yourselves
Rev	3: 8	for you have a l strength,
Rev	10: 2	He had a l book open in his

Rev 20: 3 he must be released for a l

LIVE (*see* LIFE, LIVED, LIVES, LIVING)
Gen 3:22 and l forever"—
Gen 12:12 me, but they will let you l.
Gen 17:18 that Ishmael might l before
Gen 42:18 third day, "Do this and l,
Gen 43: 8 that we may l and not die,
Gen 45: 3 does my father still l?
Ex 1:16 a daughter, then she shall l.
Ex 2:21 Then Moses was content to l
Ex 19:13 man or beast, he shall not l.
Ex 33:20 no man shall see Me, and l.
Lev 16:20 he shall bring the l goat.
Lev 16:21 hands on the head of the l
Lev 18: 5 he shall l by them: I am
Num 21: 8 when he looks at it, shall l.
Deut 5:33 that you may l and that it
Deut 8: 3 know that man shall not l
Deut 19: 4 flees there, that he may l:
Deut 32:40 As I l forever,
Josh 6:17 Rahab the harlot shall l,
1Sa 10:24 Long l the king!"
2Sa 11:11 lie with my wife? As you l,
2Sa 12:22 to me, that the child may l?
2Ki 20: 1 for you shall die, and not l.
Neh 2: 3 May the king l forever! Why
Job 7:16 I would not l forever. Let
Job 14:14 shall he l again? All the
Job 21: 7 Why do the wicked l and
Ps 55:23 deceitful men shall not l
Ps 63: 4 I will bless You while I l;
Ps 69:32 God, your hearts shall l.
Ps 104:33 to the LORD as long as I l;
Ps 116: 2 upon Him as long as I l.
Ps 119:116 to Your word, that I may l;
Ps 146: 2 While I l I will praise the
Prov 4: 4 Keep my commands, and l.
Is 6: 6 having in his hand a l coal
Is 26:19 Your dead shall l;
Is 38:16 by these things men l;
Is 55: 3 Hear, and your soul shall l;
Ezek 18:23 turn from his ways and l?
Ezek 20:11 he shall l by them.'
Ezek 33:10 in them, how can we then l?
Ezek 33:11 turn from his way and l.
Ezek 33:15 iniquity, he shall surely l;
Ezek 37: 3 of man, can these bones l?
Ezek 37: 5 into you, and you shall l.
Ezek 37: 9 these slain, that they may l.
Ezek 37:14 in you, and you shall l,
Dan 2: 4 forever! Tell your
Dan 6: 6 King Darius, l forever!
Hos 6: 2 That we may l in His sight.
Amos 5: 4 of Israel: "Seek Me and l;
Amos 5: 6 Seek the LORD and l,
Amos 5:14 not evil, That you may l;
Jon 4: 3 for me to die than to l!"
Hab 2: 4 But the just shall l by his
Matt 4: 4 Man shall not l by bread
Matt 9:18 hand on her and she will l.
Luke 10:28 do this and you will l.
Luke 20:38 for all l to Him."
John 5:25 and those who hear will l.
John 6:51 he will l forever; and the
John 6:57 and I l because of the
John 6:57 so he who feeds on Me will l
John 11:25 he may die, he shall l.
John 14:19 you will l also.
Acts 17:28 for in Him we l and move and
Acts 22:22 for he is not fit to l!"
Rom 1:17 The just shall l by
Rom 6: 2 shall we who died to sin l
Rom 6: 8 that we shall also l with
Rom 8: 5 For those who l according to

Rom 8:12 to l according to the flesh.
Rom 8:13 of the body, you will l.
Rom 12:18 l peaceably with all men.
Rom 14: 8 For if we l, we live to
Rom 14: 8 we l to the Lord; and if we
1Co 7:12 and she is willing to l with
1Co 7:13 if he is willing to l with
1Co 8: 6 and through whom we l.
1Co 9:14 preach the gospel should l
2Co 5:15 that those who l should live
2Co 6: 9 as dying, and behold we l;
2Co 7: 3 to die together and to l
2Co 13: 4 but we shall l with Him by
Gal 2:14 do you compel Gentiles to l
Gal 2:19 to the law that I might l
Gal 2:20 it is no longer I who l,
Gal 2:20 and the life which I now l
Gal 3:11 the just shall l by
Gal 3:12 who does them shall l
Gal 5:25 If we l in the Spirit, let us
Eph 6: 3 with you and you may l
Phil 1:21 to l is Christ, and to die
Phil 1:22 But if I l on in the flesh,
1Th 5:10 we should l together with
2Ti 2:11 We shall also l with Him.
2Ti 3:12 and all who desire to l
Tit 2:12 we should l soberly,
Heb 10:38 Now the just shall l
Heb 13:18 in all things desiring to l
Jas 4:15 we shall l and do this or
1Pe 2:24 might l for righteousness—by
1Pe 4: 2 that he no longer should l
1Pe 4: 6 but l according to God in
2Pe 2: 6 those who afterward would l
2Pe 2:18 escaped from those who l in
1Jn 4: 9 that we might l through Him.
Rev 20: 5 rest of the dead did not l

LIVED (*see* LIVE)
Gen 5: 3 And Adam l one hundred and
Gen 9:28 And Noah l after the flood
Gen 25: 7 of Abraham's life which he l:
Gen 50:22 And Joseph l one hundred and
Ex 12:40 children of Israel who l in
Num 21: 9 at the bronze serpent, he l.
Deut 5:26 the fire, as we have, and l?
2Ki 14:17 l fifteen years after the
Job 42:16 After this Job l one hundred
Luke 2:36 and had l with a husband
Acts 20:18 in what manner I always l
Rom 14: 9 Christ died and rose and l
Col 3: 7 once walked when you l in
Rev 20: 4 And they l and reigned with

LIVELIHOOD
Luke 8:43 who had spent all her l on
Luke 15:12 So he divided to them his l.
Luke 15:30 who has devoured your l with

LIVELY†
Ex 1:19 for they are l and give

LIVER
Ex 29:13 lobe attached to the l,
Prov 7:23 Till an arrow struck his l.
Ezek 21:21 images, he looks at the l.

LIVES (*see* LIVE)
Gen 9: 3 Every moving thing that l
Gen 45: 7 and to save your l by a
Ex 1:14 And they made their l bitter
Deut 8: 3 but man l by every word
Josh 2:13 and deliver our l from
Judg 5:18 who jeopardized their l to
Judg 8:19 my mother. As the LORD l,
Ruth 3:13 as the LORD l! Lie down
1Sa 1:26 "O my lord! As your soul l,

1Sa	1:28	as long as he l he shall be
1Sa	25: 6	you shall say to him who l
1Sa	25:26	lives and as your soul l,
1Sa	25:34	the LORD God of Israel l,
2Sa	22:47	The LORD l! Blessed be my
2Sa	23:17	in jeopardy of their l?
1Ki	17:23	your son l!"
2Ki	7: 7	they fled for their l.
Esth	9:16	and protected their l,
Job	19:25	I know that my Redeemer l,
Ps	18:46	The LORD l! Blessed be my
Ps	90:10	The days of our l are
Eccl	6: 6	even if he l a thousand years
Jer	19: 7	of those who seek their l;
Jer	48: 6	save your l! And be like
Lam	5: 9	at the risk of our l,
Ezek	27:13	They bartered human l and
Dan	4:34	and honored Him who l
Dan	12: 7	and swore by Him who l
Amos	8:14	Who say, 'As your god l,
Amos	8:14	As the way of Beersheba l!'
Luke	9:56	not come to destroy men's l
John	4:50	"Go your way; your son l.
John	11:26	And whoever l and believes in
Rom	6:10	He l to God.
Rom	7: 1	over a man as long as he l?
Rom	7: 2	her husband as long as he l.
Rom	14: 7	For none of us l to himself,
1Co	7:39	law as long as her husband l;
2Co	13: 4	yet He l by the power of
Gal	2:20	but Christ l in me; and the
1Th	2: 8	of God, but also our own l,
1Ti	5: 6	But she who l in pleasure is
Heb	7: 8	it is witnessed that he l.
Heb	7:25	since He always l to make
Heb	9:17	at all while the testator l.
1Pe	1:23	the word of God which l and
1Jn	3:16	ought to lay down our l
Rev	1:18	"I am He who l,
Rev	4: 9	who l forever and ever,
Rev	4:10	throne and worship Him who l
Rev	12:11	they did not love their l

LIVESTOCK

Gen	4:20	dwell in tents and have l.
Gen	13: 2	Abram was very rich in l,
Ex	9: 6	and all the l of Egypt died;
Ex	10:26	Our l also shall go with us;
Ex	12:29	and all the firstborn of l.
Ex	17: 3	and our children and our l
Ex	34:19	male firstborn among your l,
Lev	5: 2	or the carcass of unclean l,
Deut	2:35	We took only the l as plunder
Deut	28:51	eat the increase of your l
Jon	4:11	and their left—and much l?

LIVING (see LIVE)

Gen	1:20	with an abundance of l
Gen	1:21	sea creatures and every l
Gen	2: 7	and man became a l being.
Gen	2:19	whatever Adam called each l
Gen	3:20	she was the mother of all l.
Gen	6:19	And of every l thing of all
Gen	7:23	So He destroyed all l things
Gen	8:17	Bring out with you every l
Gen	8:21	will I again destroy every l
Gen	9:16	between God and every l
Lev	14: 6	As for the l bird, he shall
Num	16:48	between the dead and the l;
Ruth	2:20	His kindness to the l and
1Sa	17:26	defy the armies of the l
1Ki	3:25	Divide the l child in two,
2Ki	19: 4	has sent to reproach the l
Job	28:13	found in the land of the l.
Job	28:21	from the eyes of all l,
Job	30:23	house appointed for all l.

Ps	27:13	LORD In the land of the l.
Ps	42: 2	for the l God. When shall I
Ps	66: 9	keeps our soul among the l,
Ps	69:28	out of the book of the l,
Ps	84: 2	my flesh cry out for the l
Ps	104:25	L things both small and
Ps	145:16	the desire of every l thing.
Eccl	4: 2	More than the l who are
Eccl	9: 4	for a l dog is better than a
Song	4:15	A well of l waters, And
Is	4: 3	who is recorded among the l
Is	8:19	the dead on behalf of the l?
Is	53: 8	off from the land of the l;
Jer	2:13	the fountain of l waters,
Jer	10:10	He is the l God and the
Jer	17:13	The fountain of l waters."
Jer	23:36	the words of the l God,
Ezek	1: 5	came the likeness of four l
Ezek	1:20	for the spirit of the l
Ezek	10:15	This was the l creature I
Ezek	26:20	glory in the land of the l.
Dan	2:30	more wisdom than anyone l,
Dan	6:20	servant of the l God, has
Hos	1:10	You are sons of the l God.'
Matt	16:16	the Son of the l God."
Matt	22:32	of the dead, but of the l.
Matt	26:63	put You under oath by the l
Luke	2: 8	the same country shepherds l
Luke	15:13	possessions with prodigal l.
Luke	24: 5	Why do you seek the l among
John	4:10	He would have given you l
John	6:51	I am the l bread which came
John	6:57	As the l Father sent Me, and
John	7:38	heart will flow rivers of l
Acts	7:38	the one who received the l
Acts	10:42	God to be Judge of the l
Rom	9:26	called sons of the l
Rom	12: 1	you present your bodies a l
Rom	14: 9	of both the dead and the l.
1Co	15:45	man Adam became a l
2Co	3: 3	but by the Spirit of the l
2Co	6:16	you are the temple of the l
Col	2:20	as though l in the world,
1Th	1: 9	from idols to serve the l
1Ti	3:15	is the church of the l God,
1Ti	4:10	because we trust in the l
2Ti	4: 1	who will judge the l and the
Tit	3: 3	l in malice and envy,
Heb	3:12	in departing from the l God;
Heb	4:12	For the word of God is l and
Heb	9:14	dead works to serve the l
Heb	10:20	by a new and l way which He
Heb	10:31	into the hands of the l God.
Heb	12:22	and to the city of the l
1Pe	1: 3	has begotten us again to a l
1Pe	2: 4	Coming to Him as to a l
1Pe	4: 5	who is ready to judge the l
Rev	4: 6	were four l creatures full
Rev	7: 2	having the seal of the l
Rev	7:17	them and lead them to l

LO

Song	2:11	For l, the winter is
Matt	28:20	I have commanded you; and l,

LO-AMMI†

Hos	1: 9	said: "Call his name L,

LOAD (see LOADED, LOADS, UNLOAD)

Jon	1: 5	the sea, to lighten the l.
Luke	11:46	lawyers! For you l men with
Gal	6: 5	one shall bear his own l.

LOADED (see LOAD)

Gen	42:26	So they l their donkeys with
2Ti	3: 6	of gullible women l down

LOADS (*see* LOAD)
Ps 68:19 Who daily l us with

LOAF (*see* LOAVES)
Judg 7:13 a l of barley bread tumbled
Mark 8:14 did not have more than one l

LOATHE (*see* LOATHED, LOATHES, LOATHSOME)
Job 7:16 I l my life; I would not
Ps 139:21 And do I not l those who

LOATHED (*see* LOATHE)
Zech 11: 8 My soul l them, and their

LOATHES (*see* LOATHE)
Num 21: 5 and our soul l this
Job 10: 1 My soul l my life; I will

LOATHSOME (*see* LOATHE)
Job 6: 7 They are as l food to me.
Prov 13: 5 But a wicked man is l and
Rev 16: 2 and a foul and l sore came

LOAVES (*see* LOAF)
1Sa 17:17 dried grain and these ten l,
Matt 16: 9 or remember the five l of
Matt 16:10 Nor the seven l of the four
Mark 6:41 blessed and broke the l,
John 6: 9 here who has five barley l
John 6:26 but because you ate of the l

LOCK† (*see* LOCKED, LOCKS)
Song 5: 5 On the handles of the l.
Ezek 8: 3 and took me by a l of my

LOCKED (*see* LOCK)
Judg 3:23 upper room behind him and l

LOCKS (*see* LOCK)
Judg 16:13 If you weave the seven l of
Judg 16:19 him shave off the seven l
Song 5:11 His l are wavy, And

LOCUST (*see* LOCUSTS)
Ex 10:19 There remained not one l in
Ps 78:46 And their labor to the l.
Ps 109:23 I am shaken off like a l.
Joel 1: 4 What the chewing l left,
Amos 7: 1 He formed l swarms at the

LOCUSTS (*see* LOCUST)
Ps 105:34 Young l without number,
Prov 30:27 The l have no king, Yet
Matt 3: 4 and his food was l and wild
Mark 1: 6 and he ate l and wild honey.
Rev 9: 3 Then out of the smoke l came

LODGE (*see* LODGED, LODGING)
Ruth 1:16 wherever you lodge, I will l;
1Ki 17:20 on the widow with whom I l,

LODGED (*see* LODGE)
Josh 2: 1 named Rahab, and l there.
Is 1:21 Righteousness l in it, But
Matt 21:17 and He l there.

LODGING (*see* LODGE)
Acts 10: 6 He is l with Simon, a tanner,

LOFTINESS
Is 2:17 The l of man shall be bowed

LOFTY (*see* LOFTINESS)
Ps 131: 1 not haughty, Nor my eyes l.
Prov 24: 7 Wisdom is too l for a fool;
Is 2:11 The l looks of man shall be
Is 2:12 upon everything proud and l,
Is 5:15 And the eyes of the l shall
Is 26: 5 The l city; He lays it
Is 57:15 thus says the High and L

LOGS
1Ki 5: 8 the cedar and cypress l.

LOINS
1Ki 18:46 and he girded up his l and
Is 5:27 will the belt on their l be
Is 11: 5 shall be the belt of His l,
Jer 30: 6 man with his hands on his l
Jer 48:37 and on the l sackcloth—
Heb 7: 5 they have come from the l
Heb 7:10 for he was still in the l of
1Pe 1:13 Therefore gird up the l of

LOIS†
2Ti 1: 5 first in your grandmother L

LONELY†
Lam 1: 1 How l sits the city That

LONG (*see* LONGED, LONGED-FOR, LONGER, LONGING, LONGS)
Gen 26: 8 when he had been there a l
Gen 31:30 gone because you greatly l
Gen 48:15 has fed me all my life l to
Ex 10: 3 How l will you refuse to
Ex 20:12 that your days may be l upon
Ex 27: 1 five cubits l and five
Lev 26:34 enjoy its sabbaths as l as
Num 9:18 as l as the cloud stayed
Num 14:11 And how l will they not
Num 14:27 How l shall I bear with
Num 20:15 and we dwelt in Egypt a l
Deut 5:16 you, that your days may be l,
Deut 12:20 because you l to eat meat,
Deut 19: 6 him, because the way is l,
Josh 6: 5 when they make a l blast
Josh 11:18 Joshua made war a l time with
1Sa 1:14 How l will you be drunk? Put
1Sa 7: 2 in Kirjath Jearim a l time;
1Sa 10:24 L live the king!"
1Ki 3:11 and have not asked l life
1Ki 18:21 How l will you falter between
Job 3:21 Who l for death, but it does
Job 6: 8 me the thing that I l for!
Job 7:19 How l? Will You not look
Job 18: 2 How l till you put an end to
Job 27: 3 As l as my breath is in me,
Job 27: 6 shall not reproach me as l
Ps 6: 3 But You, O LORD—HOW l?
Ps 13: 1 How l will You hide Your
Ps 32: 3 my groaning all the day l.
Ps 35:28 of Your praise all the day l.
Ps 44:22 sake we are killed all day l;
Ps 62: 3 How l will you attack a man?
Ps 72: 5 They shall fear You As l as
Ps 73:14 For all day l I have been
Ps 80: 4 How l will You be angry
Ps 89:16 name they rejoice all day l,
Ps 90:13 Return, O LORD! How l?
Ps 91:16 With l life I will satisfy
Ps 94: 3 How l will the wicked
Ps 104:33 will sing to the LORD as l
Ps 116: 2 I will call upon Him as l
Ps 119:40 I l for Your precepts;
Ps 129: 3 They made their furrows l.
Ps 143: 3 Like those who have l been
Prov 3: 2 For length of days and l
Prov 6: 9 How l will you slumber, O
Prov 7:19 He has gone on a l journey;
Prov 23:30 Those who linger l at the
Is 6:11 Then I said, "Lord, how l?
Is 22:11 for Him who fashioned it l
Is 65: 2 out My hands all day l to a
Jer 12: 4 How l will the land mourn,
Jer 47: 6 How l until you are quiet?
Ezek 44:20 nor let their hair grow l;
Dan 8:13 How l will the vision be,
Dan 10: 1 the appointed time was l;
Dan 12: 6 How l shall the fulfillment

Hos	8: 5	How l until they attain to
Hab	1: 2	how l shall I cry, And You
Matt	9:15	of the bridegroom mourn as l
Matt	17:17	How l shall I bear with you?
Matt	23:14	and for a pretense make l
Matt	25:19	After a l time the lord of
Mark	1:35	having risen a l while
Mark	12:38	who desire to go around in l
Mark	12:40	and for a pretense make l
Mark	16: 5	a young man clothed in a l
Luke	1:21	that he lingered so l in
Luke	8:27	city who had demons for a l
Luke	20: 9	into a far country for a l
John	5: 6	in that condition a l
John	9: 5	As l as I am in the world, I
John	14: 9	"Have I been with you so l,
Rom	1:11	For I l to see you, that I
Rom	7: 2	law to her husband as l as
Rom	8:36	are killed all day l;
Rom	10:21	All day l I have
1Co	7:39	A wife is bound by law as l
1Co	11:14	you that if a man has l
1Co	11:15	But if a woman has l hair, it
1Co	13: 4	Love suffers l and is kind;
2Co	9:14	who l for you because of the
Gal	4: 1	as l as he is a child, does
Eph	6: 3	and you may live l on
Phil	1: 8	how greatly I l for you all
Heb	4: 7	after such a l time, as it
2Pe	1:13	as l as I am in this tent,
Jude	4	who l ago were marked out
Rev	6:10	loud voice, saying, "How l,

LONGED (see LONG)

2Sa	13:39	And King David l to go to
Ps	119:131	For I l for Your

LONGED-FOR† (see LONG)

Phil	4: 1	my beloved and l brethren,

LONGER (see LONG)

Gen	4:12	it shall no l yield its
Gen	17: 5	No l shall your name be
Gen	32:28	Your name shall no l be
Ex	2: 3	But when she could no l hide
Ex	9:28	go, and you shall stay no l.
Deut	31: 2	I can no l go out and come
Josh	5: 1	was no spirit in them any l
Josh	5:12	the children of Israel no l
Ps	74: 9	There is no l any
Is	47: 5	For you shall no l be
Is	51:22	You shall no l drink it.
Is	60:19	The sun shall no l be your
Ezek	24:27	you shall speak and no l be
Ezek	33:22	and I was no l mute.
Hos	1: 6	For I will no l have mercy
Hos	2:16	And no l call Me 'My
Matt	19: 6	they are no l two but one
Mark	14:25	I will no l drink of the
Luke	15:19	and I am no l worthy to be
Luke	22:16	I will no l eat of it until
John	7:33	be with you a little while l,
John	11:54	Therefore Jesus no l walked
John	12:35	A little while l the light is
John	14:19	A little while l and the
John	15:15	No l do I call you servants,
John	16:25	is coming when I will no l
John	17:11	Now I am no l in the world,
Rom	6: 2	who died to sin live any l
Rom	6: 6	that we should no l be
Rom	6: 9	Death no l has dominion over
Rom	7:17	it is no l I who do it,
Rom	11: 6	then it is no l of works;
Rom	11: 6	otherwise grace is no l
Rom	14:15	you are no l walking in
2Co	5:15	who live should live no l

2Co	5:16	now we know Him thus no l.
Gal	2:20	it is no l I who live, but
Gal	3:18	it is no l of promise; but
Gal	3:25	we are no l under a tutor.
Gal	4: 7	Therefore you are no l a
Eph	2:19	you are no l strangers and
Eph	4:14	that we should no l be
Eph	4:17	that you should no l walk as
Eph	4:28	Let him who stole steal no l,
1Th	3: 1	when we could no l endure
1Ti	5:23	No l drink only water, but
Phm	1:16	no l as a slave but more than
Heb	10:18	there is no l an offering
Heb	10:26	there no l remains a
1Pe	4: 2	that he no l should live the
Rev	6:11	should rest a little while l,

LONGING (see LONG)

Gen	39: 7	his master's wife cast l
2Sa	23:15	And David said with l,
1Ch	11:17	And David said with l,
Ps	107: 9	For He satisfies the l soul,
Phil	2:26	since he was l for you all,
1Th	2: 8	affectionately l for you, we

LONGS (see LONG)

Ps	63: 1	My flesh l for You In a
Ps	84: 2	My soul l, yes, even
Ps	143: 6	My soul l for You like a

LONGSUFFERING

Ex	34: 6	merciful and gracious, l,
Num	14:18	The LORD is l and abundant
Ps	86:15	L and abundant in mercy and
Rom	2: 4	goodness, forbearance, and l,
Rom	9:22	endured with much l the
2Co	6: 6	purity, by knowledge, by l,
Gal	5:22	is love, joy, peace, l,
Eph	4: 2	and gentleness, with l,
Col	1:11	for all patience and l with
Col	3:12	humility, meekness, l;
2Ti	4: 2	with all l and teaching.
1Pe	3:20	when once the Divine l
2Pe	3: 9	but is l toward us, not
2Pe	3:15	and consider that the l of

LOOK (see EXAMINE, LOOKED, LOOKING, LOOKS)

Gen	9:16	and I will l on it to
Gen	13:14	Lift your eyes now and l from
Gen	15: 5	L now toward heaven, and
Gen	19:17	for your life! Do not l
Gen	22: 7	my son." Then he said, "L,
Gen	39:23	of the prison did not l
Gen	40: 7	Why do you l so sad today?"
Gen	42: 1	Why do you l at one
Gen	48: 2	And Jacob was told, "L,
Ex	3: 4	that he turned aside to l,
Ex	3: 6	for he was afraid to l upon
Num	15:39	that you may l upon it and
Deut	9:27	do not l on the stubbornness
Deut	26:15	L down from Your holy
Judg	7:17	L at me and do likewise;
1Sa	1:11	if You will indeed l on the
1Sa	9: 3	go and l for the donkeys."
1Sa	16: 7	Do not l at his appearance or
2Sa	16:12	be that the LORD will l on
Job	6:28	be pleased to l at me; For
Job	7:19	Will You not l away from
Job	21: 5	L at me and be astonished
Job	35: 5	L to the heavens and see
Ps	17: 2	Let Your eyes l on the
Ps	22:17	They l and stare at Me.
Ps	25:18	L on my affliction and my
Ps	35:17	how long will You l on?
Ps	80:14	L down from heaven and see,
Ps	84: 9	And l upon the face of Your
Ps	101: 5	one who has a haughty l and

Ps 109:25 When they l at me, they
Ps 123: 2 So our eyes l to the LORD
Ps 142: 4 L on my right hand and see,
Ps 145:15 The eyes of all l
Prov 4:25 Let your eyes l straight
Prov 6:17 A proud l, A lying tongue
Prov 21: 4 A haughty l, a proud heart,
Prov 23:31 Do not l on the wine when it
Eccl 12: 3 And those that l through
Song 1: 6 Do not l upon me, because I
Song 4: 9 my heart With one l of
Is 17: 7 In that day a man will l to
Is 33:20 L upon Zion, the city of our
Is 45:22 L to Me, and be saved, All
Is 51: 1 L to the rock from which
Is 51: 2 L to Abraham your father,
Is 56:11 They all l to their own
Is 59: 9 We l for light, but there
Is 59:11 We l for justice, but
Is 63:15 L down from heaven, And
Ezek 40: 4 l with your eyes and hear
Hos 3: 1 who l to other gods and love
Jon 2: 4 Yet I will l again toward
Mic 4:11 And let our eye l upon
Hab 1:13 And cannot l on wickedness.
Hab 1:13 Why do You l on those who
Zech 12:10 then they will l on Me whom
Matt 6:26 L at the birds of the air,
Matt 7: 3 And why do you l at the speck
Matt 11: 3 or do we l for another?"
Matt 24:26 if they say to you, 'L,
Luke 17:23 L here!' or 'Look there!' Do
Luke 21:28 l up and lift up your heads,
Luke 21:29 L at the fig tree, and all
John 4:35 lift up your eyes and l at
John 7:52 from Galilee? Search and l,
John 19:37 They shall l on Him whom
John 20:27 and l at My hands; and reach
Acts 3:12 Or why l so intently at us,
Acts 18:15 l to it yourselves; for I
2Co 10: 7 Do you l at things according
Phil 2: 4 Let each of you l out not
1Pe 1:12 which angels desire to l
2Pe 3:13 l for new heavens and a new
2Jn 8 L to yourselves, that we do
Rev 5: 3 or to l at it.

LOOKED (see LOOK)
Gen 6:12 So God l upon the earth, and
Gen 18: 2 So he lifted his eyes and l,
Gen 18:16 men rose from there and l
Gen 19:26 But his wife l back behind
Gen 29:32 The LORD has surely l on my
Ex 2:11 out to his brethren and l
Ex 2:12 So he l this way and that
Ex 2:25 And God l upon the children
Ex 3: 2 the midst of a bush. So he l,
1Sa 9:16 for I have l upon My people,
1Sa 16: 6 that he l at Eliab and said,
2Sa 6:16 l through a window and saw
2Ki 9:30 and l through a window.
Job 30:26 But when I l for good, evil
Ps 34: 5 They l to Him and were
Ps 63: 2 So I have l for You in the
Ps 69:20 I l for someone to take
Ps 102:19 For He l down from the
Prov 7: 6 the window of my house I l
Eccl 2:11 Then I l on all the works
Is 5: 7 He l for justice, but
Jer 8:15 We l for peace, but no good
Dan 10: 5 I lifted my eyes and l,
Dan 12: 5 Then I, Daniel, l;
Hab 3: 6 He l and startled the
Zech 1:18 Then I raised my eyes and l,
Matt 19:26 But Jesus l at them and said

Mark 6:41 He l up to heaven, blessed
Mark 8:33 He had turned around and l
Mark 14:67 she l at him and said, "You
Luke 1:25 in the days when He l on
Luke 2:38 of Him to all those who l
Luke 21: 1 And He l up and saw the rich
Luke 22:56 l intently at him and said,
Luke 22:61 And the Lord turned and l at
John 1:42 Now when Jesus l at him, He
John 20:11 she stooped down and l
Acts 1:10 And while they l steadfastly
Acts 13: 9 l intently at him
Heb 11:26 for he l to the reward.
1Jn 1: 1 which we have l upon, and
Rev 4: 1 After these things I l,

LOOKING (see LOOK)
Gen 41: 2 fine l and fat; and they fed
Ps 119:37 Turn away my eyes from l at
Song 2: 9 He is l through the
Dan 1:10 should he see your faces l
Matt 24:50 on a day when he is not l
Matt 27:55 were there l on from afar,
Mark 1:37 Everyone is l for You."
Mark 10:21 l at him, loved him, and
Luke 9:62 and l back, is fit for the
Luke 12:46 on a day when he is not l
John 1:36 And l at Jesus as He walked,
John 20: 5 stooping down and l in, saw
Acts 6:15 l steadfastly at him, saw
Tit 2:13 l for the blessed hope and
Heb 12: 2 l unto Jesus, the author and
Heb 12:15 l carefully lest anyone fall
2Pe 3:12 l for and hastening the

LOOKS (see LOOK)
1Sa 16: 7 for man l at the outward
1Sa 16: 7 but the LORD l at the
2Sa 14:25 as Absalom for his good l.
Ps 14: 2 The LORD l down from heaven
Ps 18:27 will bring down haughty l.
Ps 33:14 place of His dwelling He l
Ps 53: 2 God l down from heaven upon
Is 2:11 The lofty l of man shall be
Is 10:12 the glory of his haughty l.
Lam 3:50 the LORD from heaven L
Matt 5:28 I say to you that whoever l
Jas 1:25 But he who l into the perfect

LOOSE (see LOOSED, LOOSING, RELEASE)
Gen 49:21 "Naphtali is a deer let l;
Ex 22: 5 and lets l his animal, and
Judg 15:14 and his bonds broke l from
Job 38:31 Or l the belt of Orion?
Dan 3:25 answered, "I see four men l,
Matt 16:19 and whatever you l on earth
Matt 21: 2 L them and bring them to
Mark 1: 7 worthy to stoop down and l.
Rev 5: 2 to open the scroll and to l

LOOSED (see LOOSE)
Ps 116:16 You have l my bonds.
Eccl 12: 6 before the silver cord is l,
Matt 18:18 loose on earth will be l in
Mark 7:35 of his tongue was l,
Acts 2:24 having l the pains of death,
Acts 16:26 and everyone's chains were l,
1Co 7:27 Are you l from a wife? Do

LOOSING (see LOOSE)
Mark 11: 5 are you doing, l the colt?"

LORD (see LORD'S, LORDLY, LORDS, LORDSHIP, THE-LORD-
IS-MY-BANNER, THE-LORD-WILL-PROVIDE)
Gen 2: 4 in the day that the L God
Gen 2: 7 And the L God formed man of
Gen 2: 8 The L God planted a garden
Gen 2: 9 And out of the ground the L

Gen	2:15	Then the L God took the man
Gen	2:21	And the L God caused a deep
Gen	2:22	Then the rib which the L God
Gen	3: 8	heard the sound of the L
Gen	3: 9	Then the L God called to
Gen	3:13	And the L God said to the
Gen	3:21	for Adam and his wife the L
Gen	3:23	therefore the L God sent him
Gen	4: 1	acquired a man from the L.
Gen	4: 3	of the ground to the L.
Gen	4: 4	And the L respected Abel
Gen	4: 6	So the L said to Cain, "Why
Gen	4:15	And the L set a mark on
Gen	4:16	from the presence of the L
Gen	4:26	call on the name of the L.
Gen	5:29	of the ground which the L
Gen	6: 3	And the L said, "My Spirit
Gen	6: 6	And the L was sorry that He
Gen	6: 8	grace in the eyes of the L.
Gen	7:16	and the L shut him in.
Gen	8:20	built an altar to the L,
Gen	8:21	And the L smelled a soothing
Gen	9:26	said: "Blessed be the L,
Gen	10: 9	mighty hunter before the L;
Gen	11: 5	But the L came down to see
Gen	11: 8	So the L scattered them
Gen	11: 9	because there the L
Gen	12: 1	Now the L had said to Abram:
Gen	12: 7	Then the L appeared to Abram
Gen	12: 7	he built an altar to the L,
Gen	12:17	But the L plagued Pharaoh
Gen	13:10	everywhere (before the L
Gen	13:10	like the garden of the L,
Gen	14:22	raised my hand to the L,
Gen	15: 2	L GOD, what will You give
Gen	15: 6	And he believed in the L,
Gen	15: 7	said to him, "I am the L,
Gen	15: 8	L GOD, how shall I know that
Gen	15:18	On the same day the L made a
Gen	16: 2	the L has restrained me
Gen	16: 5	The L judge between you and
Gen	16: 7	Now the Angel of the L
Gen	18:12	my l being old also?"
Gen	18:14	anything too hard for the L?
Gen	18:17	And the L said, "Shall I
Gen	18:22	still stood before the L.
Gen	18:27	myself to speak to the L:
Gen	18:30	Let not the L be angry, and I
Gen	18:33	So the L went His way as
Gen	19:13	and the L has sent us to
Gen	19:16	the L being merciful to
Gen	19:24	Then the L rained brimstone
Gen	20:18	for the L had closed up all
Gen	21: 1	And the L visited Sarah as
Gen	22:14	In the Mount of The L it
Gen	24: 7	The L God of heaven, who
Gen	24:12	O L God of my master
Gen	24:26	head and worshiped the L.
Gen	25:21	and the L granted his plea,
Gen	28:13	the L stood above it and
Gen	28:13	I am the L God of Abraham
Gen	28:16	Surely the L is in this
Gen	28:21	then the L shall be my God.
Gen	31:49	May the L watch between you
Gen	33:14	Please let my l go on ahead
Gen	38: 7	in the sight of the L,
Gen	38: 7	and the L killed him.
Gen	39: 2	The L was with Joseph, and
Gen	39:23	the L made it prosper.
Gen	40: 1	of Egypt offended their l,
Gen	42:30	The man who is l of the
Gen	45: 9	God has made me l of all
Ex	3: 2	And the Angel of the L
Ex	3:15	The L God of your fathers,
Ex	3:18	The L God of the Hebrews has

Ex	3:18	we may sacrifice to the L
Ex	4: 4	Then the L said to Moses,
Ex	4: 6	Furthermore the L said to
Ex	4:10	said to the LORD, "O my L,
Ex	4:27	And the L said to Aaron,
Ex	4:28	all the words of the L who
Ex	5: 2	said, "Who is the L,
Ex	5: 2	go? I do not know the L,
Ex	5:22	to the LORD and said, "L,
Ex	6: 2	said to him: "I am the L.
Ex	6: 3	but by My name L I was not
Ex	6: 6	of Israel: 'I am the L;
Ex	6: 7	know that I am the L your
Ex	6: 8	as a heritage: I am the L.
Ex	7:16	The L God of the Hebrews has
Ex	8: 8	Entreat the L that He may
Ex	8:10	is no one like the L our
Ex	9: 3	the hand of the L will be
Ex	9:12	But the L hardened the heart
Ex	9:23	and the L sent thunder and
Ex	9:29	out my hands to the L;
Ex	9:30	you will not yet fear the L
Ex	10: 7	that they may serve the L
Ex	10: 9	must hold a feast to the L.
Ex	10:13	and the L brought an east
Ex	10:16	have sinned against the L
Ex	12:23	For the L will pass through
Ex	12:23	the L will pass over the
Ex	12:27	Passover sacrifice of the L,
Ex	12:29	pass at midnight that the L
Ex	12:42	solemn observance to the L
Ex	13:12	shall set apart to the L
Ex	13:14	By strength of hand the L
Ex	13:21	And the L went before them
Ex	14:13	see the salvation of the L,
Ex	14:14	The L will fight for you,
Ex	14:21	and the L caused the sea to
Ex	14:27	So the L overthrew the
Ex	14:30	So the L saved Israel that
Ex	14:31	so the people feared the L,
Ex	14:31	and believed the L and His
Ex	15: 1	sang this song to the L,
Ex	15: 1	"I will sing to the L,
Ex	15: 2	The L is my strength and
Ex	15: 3	The L is a man of war;
Ex	15: 3	The L is His name.
Ex	15: 6	"Your right hand, O L,
Ex	15:11	"Who is like You, O L,
Ex	15:16	Your people pass over, O L,
Ex	15:18	The L shall reign forever
Ex	15:19	and the L brought back the
Ex	15:26	For I am the L who heals
Ex	16: 7	see the glory of the L;
Ex	16: 7	complaints against the L.
Ex	16:23	a holy Sabbath to the L.
Ex	16:33	and lay it up before the L,
Ex	17: 2	me? Why do you tempt the L?
Ex	17: 4	So Moses cried out to the L,
Ex	18: 9	all the good which the L
Ex	18:10	said, "Blessed be the L,
Ex	19:18	because the L descended
Ex	19:20	Then the L came down upon
Ex	19:21	through to gaze at the L,
Ex	19:22	priests who come near the L
Ex	19:22	lest the L break out
Ex	20: 5	the L your God, am a
Ex	20: 7	not take the name of the L
Ex	20:10	is the Sabbath of the L
Ex	20:11	For in six days the L made
Ex	20:11	Therefore the L blessed the
Ex	22:11	then an oath of the L shall
Ex	22:20	except to the L only, he
Ex	24: 1	Moses, "Come up to the L,
Ex	24: 2	alone shall come near the L,
Ex	24: 5	offerings of oxen to the L.

Ex 24: 7 All that the L has said we
Ex 24: 8 of the covenant which the L
Ex 24:16 Now the glory of the L
Ex 24:17 of the glory of the L was
Ex 27:21 until morning before the L.
Ex 28:12 their names before the L
Ex 28:29 as a memorial before the L
Ex 28:30 he goes in before the L.
Ex 28:35 holy place before the L
Ex 28:36 signet: HOLINESS TO THE L.
Ex 29:11 kill the bull before the L,
Ex 29:18 a burnt offering to the L;
Ex 29:18 made by fire to the L.
Ex 29:23 bread that is before the L;
Ex 29:24 wave offering before the L.
Ex 29:25 a sweet aroma before the L.
Ex 29:28 heave offering to the L.
Ex 30: 8 incense before the L
Ex 30:10 It is most holy to the L.
Ex 30:12 ransom for himself to the L,
Ex 31:13 may know that I am the L
Ex 31:15 of rest, holy to the L.
Ex 31:17 for in six days the L made
Ex 32: 5 is a feast to the L.
Ex 32:14 So the L relented from the
Ex 32:35 So the L plagued the people
Ex 33: 7 everyone who sought the L
Ex 33: 9 and the L talked with
Ex 33:11 So the L spoke to Moses face
Ex 34: 5 the name of the L.
Ex 34: 6 And the L passed before him
Ex 34: 6 him and proclaimed, "The L,
Ex 34:14 no other god, for the L,
Ex 34:23 shall appear before the L,
Ex 34:28 So he was there with the L
Ex 35: 2 a Sabbath of rest to the L.
Ex 35:22 offering of gold to the L.
Ex 35:29 freewill offering to the L,
Ex 36: 1 artisan in whom the L has
Ex 39: 1 as the L had commanded
Ex 40:25 lit the lamps before the L,
Ex 40:34 and the glory of the L
Ex 40:38 For the cloud of the L was
Lev 1: 2 brings an offering to the L,
Lev 1: 5 kill the bull before the L;
Lev 1: 9 a sweet aroma to the L.
Lev 1:11 of the altar before the L;
Lev 2:14 your firstfruits to the L,
Lev 3: 1 blemish before the L.
Lev 4: 6 seven times before the L,
Lev 5:15 to the holy things of the L,
Lev 5:15 he shall bring to the L as
Lev 6:15 as a memorial to the L.
Lev 6:22 a statute forever to the L.
Lev 6:25 be killed before the L.
Lev 7:20 that belongs to the L,
Lev 7:35 them to minister to the L
Lev 8:26 that was before the L he
Lev 8:35 keep the charge of the L,
Lev 9: 4 for today the L will appear
Lev 9: 5 near and stood before the L.
Lev 10: 1 profane fire before the L,
Lev 10: 2 and they died before the L.
Lev 10: 7 the anointing oil of the L
Lev 10:19 in the sight of the L?
Lev 14:31 to be cleansed before the L.
Lev 16: 8 one lot for the L and the
Lev 16:10 alive before the L,
Lev 16:30 all your sins before the L.
Lev 17: 4 offer an offering to the L
Lev 18: 2 I am the L your God.
Lev 18: 5 live by them: I am the L.
Lev 18: 6 his nakedness: I am the L.
Lev 18:21 of your God: I am the L.
Lev 19: 8 hallowed offering of the L;

Lev 19:24 be holy, a praise to the L.
Lev 20: 8 I am the L who sanctifies
Lev 22:24 shall not offer to the L
Lev 22:29 of thanksgiving to the L,
Lev 23: 3 it is the Sabbath of the L
Lev 23: 4 are the feasts of the L,
Lev 23: 6 Unleavened Bread to the L;
Lev 23:20 shall be holy to the L for
Lev 23:38 the Sabbaths of the L,
Lev 24: 3 until morning before the L
Lev 24: 4 lampstand before the L
Lev 24: 6 gold table before the L.
Lev 25: 1 And the L spoke to Moses on
Lev 25: 2 keep a sabbath to the L.
Lev 26:46 and laws which the L made
Lev 27: 2 certain persons to the L,
Lev 27:28 is most holy to the L.
Num 3: 4 profane fire before the L
Num 4:49 to the commandment of the L
Num 5: 6 against the L,
Num 5: 8 wrong must go to the L
Num 5:16 and set her before the L.
Num 5:21 the L make you a curse and
Num 5:21 when the L makes your thigh
Num 6: 2 separate himself to the L,
Num 6: 6 separates himself to the L
Num 6: 8 he shall be holy to the L.
Num 6:12 shall consecrate to the L
Num 6:24 The L bless you and keep
Num 6:25 The L make His face shine
Num 6:26 The L lift up His
Num 8: 4 to the pattern which the L
Num 8:10 the Levites before the L,
Num 8:11 perform the work of the L.
Num 9: 8 that I may hear what the L
Num 9:13 the offering of the L at
Num 9:18 and at the command of the L
Num 9:19 kept the charge of the L
Num 9:20 to the command of the L
Num 10:29 the place of which the L
Num 10:29 for the L has promised good
Num 10:32 that whatever good the L
Num 10:33 from the mountain of the L
Num 10:33 of the covenant of the L
Num 10:34 And the cloud of the L was
Num 10:35 O L! Let Your enemies be
Num 11: 1 it displeased the L;
Num 11: 1 So the fire of the L burned
Num 11: 2 when Moses prayed to the L,
Num 11:18 in the hearing of the L,
Num 11:28 and said, "Moses my l,
Num 11:31 a wind went out from the L,
Num 11:33 and the L struck the people
Num 12: 2 Has the L indeed spoken only
Num 12: 2 And the L heard it.
Num 12: 6 among you, I, the L,
Num 12: 8 he sees the form of the L.
Num 12: 9 So the anger of the L was
Num 12:11 my l! Please do not lay
Num 14: 3 Why has the L brought us to
Num 14: 8 If the L delights in us,
Num 14: 9 do not rebel against the L,
Num 14:14 these people; that You, L,
Num 14:17 let the power of my L be
Num 14:18 The L is longsuffering and
Num 14:42 for the L is not among
Num 14:43 have turned away from the L,
Num 14:44 of the covenant of the L
Num 15:15 stranger be before the L.
Num 15:30 brings reproach on the L,
Num 15:31 despised the word of the L,
Num 16: 5 Tomorrow morning the L will
Num 16:17 his censer before the L,
Num 16:30 But if the L creates a new
Num 16:30 men have rejected the L.

Num 16:35 a fire came out from the L
Num 16:41 killed the people of the L
Num 18: 6 gift to you, given by the L,
Num 18:19 salt forever before the L
Num 19:13 the tabernacle of the L.
Num 19:20 the sanctuary of the L.
Num 20: 3 brethren died before the L!
Num 20: 4 up the assembly of the L
Num 20:13 Israel contended with the L,
Num 20:16 'When we cried out to the L,
Num 21: 2 Israel made a vow to the L,
Num 21: 6 So the L sent fiery serpents
Num 21:14 Book of the Wars of the L:
Num 22:22 and the Angel of the L took
Num 22:28 Then the L opened the mouth
Num 22:31 Then the L opened Balaam's
Num 23: 5 Then the L put a word in
Num 23: 8 I denounce whom the L has
Num 23:26 All that the L speaks, that
Num 24: 1 saw that it pleased the L
Num 25: 4 the offenders before the L,
Num 26: 9 contended against the L;
Num 27: 5 their case before the L.
Num 28: 7 out the drink to the L as
Num 28:16 is the Passover of the L.
Num 28:26 grain offering to the L at
Num 30: 2 a man makes a vow to the L,
Num 30: 3 woman makes a vow to the L,
Num 30: 8 and the L will release her.
Num 31: 3 to take vengeance for the L
Num 31:16 to trespass against the L
Num 31:28 levy a tribute for the L
Num 32:21 the Jordan before the L
Num 32:22 is subdued before the L,
Num 32:22 be blameless before the L
Num 32:22 possession before the L.
Num 32:25 servants will do as my l
Num 32:29 for battle before the L,
Num 32:32 over armed before the L
Num 33: 2 at the command of the L.
Num 33: 4 Also on their gods the L
Num 35:34 for I the L dwell among the
Deut 1: 8 the land which the L swore
Deut 1:27 Because the L hates us, He
Deut 1:31 where you saw how the L
Deut 1:32 you did not believe the L
Deut 1:34 And the L heard the sound
Deut 1:36 he wholly followed the L.
Deut 1:37 The L was also angry with me
Deut 1:41 have sinned against the L;
Deut 1:45 and wept before the L,
Deut 2: 7 These forty years the L
Deut 2:14 just as the L had sworn to
Deut 2:21 But the L destroyed them
Deut 3:20 until the L has given rest
Deut 3:26 But the L was angry with me
Deut 4: 3 eyes have seen what the L
Deut 4:10 day you stood before the L
Deut 4:12 And the L spoke to you out
Deut 4:15 you saw no form when the L
Deut 4:23 the covenant of the L your
Deut 4:25 evil in the sight of the L
Deut 4:29 there you will seek the L
Deut 5: 2 The L our God made a
Deut 5: 9 the L your God, am a
Deut 5:11 not take the name of the L
Deut 5:14 is the Sabbath of the L
Deut 6: 2 that you may fear the L your
Deut 6: 4 The L our God, the LORD
Deut 6: 5 You shall love the L your
Deut 6:16 shall not tempt the L
Deut 6:22 and the L showed signs and
Deut 7: 6 are a holy people to the L
Deut 7: 6 the L your God has chosen
Deut 7: 7 The L did not set His love

Deut 7: 8 but because the L loves you,
Deut 7: 9 Therefore know that the L
Deut 7:25 is an abomination to the L
Deut 8: 2 shall remember that the L
Deut 8: 3 from the mouth of the L.
Deut 8:10 then you shall bless the L
Deut 8:11 you do not forget the L
Deut 8:18 you shall remember the L
Deut 9: 7 rebellious against the L
Deut 9: 8 in Horeb you provoked the L
Deut 9:26 I prayed to the L,
Deut 10: 8 of the covenant of the L,
Deut 10: 9 the L is his inheritance,
Deut 10:12 but to fear the L your God,
Deut 10:12 to serve the L your God
Deut 10:17 God is God of gods and L
Deut 10:20 You shall fear the L your
Deut 12: 5 seek the place where the L
Deut 12:11 which you vow to the L
Deut 12:21 If the place where the L
Deut 12:29 When the L your God cuts
Deut 13: 3 know whether you love the L
Deut 14: 1 are the children of the L
Deut 14: 2 are a holy people to the L
Deut 14: 2 and the L has chosen you to
Deut 14:23 you may learn to fear the L
Deut 15: 9 and he cry out to the L
Deut 15:15 and the L your God redeemed
Deut 15:19 you shall sanctify to the L
Deut 16: 1 keep the Passover to the L
Deut 16:15 a sacred feast to the L
Deut 16:16 not appear before the L
Deut 17: 1 is an abomination to the L
Deut 18: 2 the L is their inheritance,
Deut 18: 7 stand there before the L.
Deut 18:15 The L your God will raise
Deut 18:21 know the word which the L
Deut 18:22 speaks in the name of the L,
Deut 18:22 is the thing which the L
Deut 20:18 and you sin against the L
Deut 23: 1 enter the assembly of the L.
Deut 23:21 you make a vow to the L
Deut 26: 3 to the country which the L
Deut 26: 4 before the altar of the L
Deut 28: 7 The L will cause your
Deut 28:11 And the L will grant you
Deut 28:21 The L will make the plague
Deut 28:22 The L will strike you with
Deut 28:58 THE L YOUR GOD,
Deut 28:64 Then the L will scatter you
Deut 29:20 and the L would blot out
Deut 29:28 And the L uprooted them from
Deut 30: 6 to love the L your God with
Deut 31:11 to appear before the L
Deut 31:12 may learn to fear the L
Deut 31:27 rebellious against the L,
Deut 31:29 evil in the sight of the L,
Deut 32: 3 proclaim the name of the L:
Deut 33: 2 The L came from Sinai, And
Deut 33:12 The beloved of the L shall
Deut 33:29 a people saved by the L,
Deut 34: 1 And the L showed him all
Deut 34:10 whom the L knew face to
Deut 34:11 and wonders which the L
Josh 1: 1 Moses the servant of the L,
Josh 2:10 we have heard how the L
Josh 2:12 you, swear to me by the L,
Josh 3:11 of the covenant of the L of
Josh 4:23 for the L your God dried up
Josh 5:14 of the army of the L I
Josh 6:11 So he had the ark of the L
Josh 6:19 are consecrated to the L;
Josh 6:19 into the treasury of the L.
Josh 6:27 So the L was with Joshua,
Josh 7: 1 so the anger of the L

Josh	7:19	give glory to the L God of
Josh	7:20	I have sinned against the L
Josh	7:25	The L will trouble you this
Josh	9:14	not ask counsel of the L.
Josh	10:10	So the L routed them before
Josh	10:11	that the L cast down large
Josh	10:14	that the L heeded the voice
Josh	10:14	for the L fought for
Josh	14: 8	I wholly followed the L my
Josh	14: 9	have wholly followed the L
Josh	14:10	the L has kept me alive, as
Josh	18: 7	for the priesthood of the L
Josh	19:51	lot in Shiloh before the L,
Josh	21:44	The L gave them rest all
Josh	21:44	the L delivered all their
Josh	22: 5	to love the L your God, to
Josh	22:16	this day against the L?
Josh	22:22	The L God of gods, the LORD
Josh	22:22	the L God of gods, He
Josh	22:25	You have no part in the L.
Josh	23:15	come upon you which the L
Josh	24:14	therefore, fear the L,
Josh	24:15	house, we will serve the L.
Josh	24:16	we should forsake the L to
Josh	24:18	We also will serve the L,
Josh	24:24	The L our God we will serve,
Josh	24:29	Nun, the servant of the L,
Judg	2: 1	Then the Angel of the L came
Judg	2:11	evil in the sight of the L,
Judg	2:12	and they provoked the L to
Judg	2:13	They forsook the L and
Judg	2:14	And the anger of the L was
Judg	2:15	the hand of the L was
Judg	2:16	the L raised up judges who
Judg	2:18	the L was with the judge
Judg	2:18	for the L was moved to pity
Judg	3: 7	They forgot the L their
Judg	3: 9	the L raised up a deliverer
Judg	3:10	The Spirit of the L came
Judg	4: 2	So the L sold them into the
Judg	4:15	And the L routed Sisera and
Judg	5: 3	even I, will sing to the L;
Judg	5:11	the righteous acts of the L,
Judg	5:31	O L! But let those who
Judg	6: 8	that the L sent a prophet to
Judg	6:22	O L GOD! For I have seen
Judg	6:22	seen the Angel of the L
Judg	6:34	But the Spirit of the L came
Judg	7:20	The sword of the L and of
Judg	8:19	As the L lives, if you had
Judg	8:23	the L shall rule over
Judg	11:10	The L will be a witness
Judg	11:30	made a vow to the L,
Judg	11:35	have given my word to the L,
Judg	13: 3	And the Angel of the L
Judg	13: 8	Manoah prayed to the L,
Judg	13: 8	LORD, and said, "O my L,
Judg	13:24	and the L blessed him.
Judg	13:25	And the Spirit of the L
Judg	16:20	he did not know that the L
Judg	16:28	Samson called to the L,
Judg	20:35	The L defeated Benjamin
Ruth	1: 8	The L deal kindly with you,
Ruth	1:13	that the hand of the L has
Ruth	1:17	The L do so to me, and
Ruth	2: 4	The L be with you!" And
Ruth	2: 4	The L bless you!"
Ruth	4:11	The L make the woman who is
Ruth	4:13	the L gave her conception,
Ruth	4:14	Naomi, "Blessed be the L,
1Sa	1: 3	and sacrifice to the L of
1Sa	1: 5	although the L had closed
1Sa	1: 7	up to the house of the L,
1Sa	1: 9	of the tabernacle of the L.
1Sa	1:11	I will give him to the L
1Sa	1:19	and the L remembered her.
1Sa	1:21	went up to offer to the L
1Sa	1:28	also have lent him to the L;
1Sa	2: 1	heart rejoices in the L;
1Sa	2: 1	horn is exalted in the L,
1Sa	2: 2	one is holy like the L,
1Sa	2: 6	The L kills and makes alive;
1Sa	2:21	Samuel grew before the L.
1Sa	2:26	in favor both with the L
1Sa	3: 4	that the L called Samuel.
1Sa	3: 7	did not yet know the L,
1Sa	3: 9	you must say, 'Speak, L,
1Sa	3:15	doors of the house of the L.
1Sa	4: 6	that the ark of the L had
1Sa	5: 6	But the hand of the L was
1Sa	7: 2	Israel lamented after the L.
1Sa	7:10	But the L thundered with a
1Sa	7:12	Thus far the L has helped
1Sa	8: 6	So Samuel prayed to the L.
1Sa	10:24	Do you see him whom the L
1Sa	11: 7	And the fear of the L
1Sa	11:15	Saul king before the L in
1Sa	12:13	the L has set a king over
1Sa	12:14	If you fear the L and serve
1Sa	12:18	and the L sent thunder and
1Sa	12:18	greatly feared the L and
1Sa	12:24	"Only fear the L,
1Sa	13:12	made supplication to the L.
1Sa	14: 6	For nothing restrains the L
1Sa	14:35	built an altar to the L.
1Sa	15: 1	The L sent me to anoint you
1Sa	15:10	Now the word of the L came
1Sa	15:15	to sacrifice to the L your
1Sa	15:19	not obey the voice of the L?
1Sa	15:22	Has the L as great delight
1Sa	15:22	obeying the voice of the L?
1Sa	15:23	rejected the word of the L,
1Sa	15:26	and the L has rejected you
1Sa	15:28	The L has torn the kingdom
1Sa	15:33	in pieces before the L in
1Sa	15:35	and the L regretted that He
1Sa	16: 7	For the L does not see
1Sa	16: 7	but the L looks at the
1Sa	16: 8	Neither has the L chosen
1Sa	16:13	and the Spirit of the L
1Sa	16:14	spirit from the L troubled
1Sa	16:18	and the L is with him."
1Sa	20:42	May the L be between you and
1Sa	22:10	And he inquired of the L for
1Sa	22:17	kill the priests of the L,
1Sa	24:12	Let the L judge between you
1Sa	24:12	and let the L avenge me on
1Sa	25:28	fights the battles of the L,
1Sa	25:38	that the L struck Nabal,
1Sa	26:19	be cursed before the L,
1Sa	26:23	May the L repay every man
1Sa	28: 6	when Saul inquired of the L,
1Sa	28: 6	the L did not answer him,
1Sa	28:18	not obey the voice of the L
2Sa	2: 6	And now may the L show
2Sa	3:39	The L shall repay the
2Sa	4: 8	and the L has avenged my
2Sa	6: 2	the L of Hosts, who dwells
2Sa	6: 5	played music before the L
2Sa	6: 9	How can the ark of the L
2Sa	6:11	And the L blessed Obed-Edom
2Sa	6:14	David danced before the L,
2Sa	7:18	O L GOD? And what is my
2Sa	8: 6	The L preserved David
2Sa	12: 1	Then the L sent Nathan to
2Sa	12:13	have sinned against the L.
2Sa	12:14	to the enemies of the L to
2Sa	12:15	And the L struck the child
2Sa	14:11	As the L lives, not one
2Sa	15: 7	vow which I made to the L.

2Sa	16: 9	this dead dog curse my l
2Sa	16:12	and that the L will repay
2Sa	19: 7	For I swear by the L,
2Sa	19:37	let him cross over with my l
2Sa	22: 1	Then David spoke to the L
2Sa	22: 2	The L is my rock and my
2Sa	22: 4	I will call upon the L,
2Sa	22: 7	I called upon the L,
2Sa	22:14	The L thundered from heaven,
2Sa	22:19	But the L was my support.
2Sa	22:21	The L rewarded me according
2Sa	22:22	have kept the ways of the L,
2Sa	22:29	You are my lamp, O L;
2Sa	22:32	who is God, except the L?
2Sa	22:50	give thanks to You, O L,
2Sa	23: 2	The Spirit of the L spoke by
2Sa	23:16	but poured it out to the L.
2Sa	24: 1	Again the anger of the L was
2Sa	24:14	fall into the hand of the L,
2Sa	24:15	So the L sent a plague upon
2Sa	24:16	the L relented from the
2Sa	24:16	And the angel of the L
2Sa	24:18	erect an altar to the L on
2Sa	24:25	So the L heeded the prayers
1Ki	1:31	Let my l King David live
1Ki	1:37	As the L has been with my
1Ki	2:23	King Solomon swore by the L,
1Ki	2:27	from being priest to the L,
1Ki	2:33	be peace forever from the L.
1Ki	3: 3	And Solomon loved the L,
1Ki	3: 5	At Gibeon the L appeared to
1Ki	3:17	And one woman said, "O my l,
1Ki	3:26	son; and she said, "O my l,
1Ki	5: 3	for the name of the L his
1Ki	5:12	So the L gave Solomon
1Ki	6: 1	to build the house of the L.
1Ki	7:51	for the house of the L was
1Ki	8:11	for the glory of the L
1Ki	8:56	"Blessed be the L,
1Ki	8:57	May the L our God be with
1Ki	8:61	be loyal to the L our God,
1Ki	10:12	for the house of the L and
1Ki	11: 4	was not loyal to the L his
1Ki	11: 6	evil in the sight of the L,
1Ki	11: 9	So the L became angry with
1Ki	13: 6	man of God entreated the L,
1Ki	13:21	disobeyed the word of the L,
1Ki	14: 5	Now the L had said to
1Ki	14:15	For the L will strike
1Ki	14:15	provoking the L to anger.
1Ki	15: 3	was not loyal to the L his
1Ki	15: 4	for David's sake the L his
1Ki	15: 5	right in the eyes of the L,
1Ki	15:14	heart was loyal to the L
1Ki	15:26	evil in the sight of the L,
1Ki	18: 1	days that the word of the L
1Ki	18: 7	that you, my l Elijah?"
1Ki	18:12	servant have feared the L
1Ki	18:13	the prophets of the L,
1Ki	18:21	If the L is God, follow
1Ki	18:22	am left a prophet of the L;
1Ki	18:36	L God of Abraham, Isaac, and
1Ki	18:38	Then the fire of the L fell
1Ki	18:39	and they said, "The L,
1Ki	19: 4	"It is enough! Now, L,
1Ki	19: 7	And the angel of the L came
1Ki	19:11	the mountain before the L.
1Ki	19:11	the L passed by, and a
1Ki	19:11	in pieces before the L,
1Ki	19:11	but the L was not in the
1Ki	20:28	The L is God of the hills,
1Ki	22: 7	still a prophet of the L
1Ki	22:19	I saw the L sitting on His
1Ki	22:28	the L has not spoken by
2Ki	1:15	And the angel of the L said

2Ki	2:14	Where is the L God of
2Ki	2:16	the Spirit of the L has
2Ki	3:15	that the hand of the L came
2Ki	4: 1	your servant feared the L.
2Ki	5:18	in this thing may the L
2Ki	6:18	him, Elisha prayed to the L,
2Ki	6:33	calamity is from the L;
2Ki	10:16	and see my zeal for the L.
2Ki	10:30	And the L said to Jehu,
2Ki	10:31	to walk in the law of the L
2Ki	11:15	in the house of the L.
2Ki	11:17	a covenant between the L,
2Ki	13:23	But the L was gracious to
2Ki	15: 3	right in the sight of the L,
2Ki	15: 5	Then the L struck the king,
2Ki	17: 9	secretly did against the L
2Ki	17:11	things to provoke the L to
2Ki	17:20	And the L rejected all the
2Ki	17:23	until the L removed Israel
2Ki	17:25	they did not fear the L,
2Ki	17:25	therefore the L sent lions
2Ki	17:41	these nations feared the L,
2Ki	18: 6	For he held fast to the L;
2Ki	18:22	We trust in the L our God,'
2Ki	19:14	and spread it before the L.
2Ki	19:15	prayed before the L,
2Ki	19:16	"Incline Your ear, O L,
2Ki	19:16	hear; open Your eyes, O L,
2Ki	19:19	O L our God, I pray, save
2Ki	19:31	The zeal of the L of hosts
2Ki	20: 2	wall, and prayed to the L,
2Ki	20: 3	"Remember now, O L,
2Ki	21:22	He forsook the L God of his
2Ki	22: 8	Law in the house of the L.
2Ki	22: 9	oversee the house of the L.
2Ki	22:13	is the wrath of the L
2Ki	23: 3	a covenant before the L,
2Ki	23:21	the Passover to the L
2Ki	24: 4	which the L would not
2Ki	25: 9	burned the house of the L
1Ch	15:29	of the covenant of the L
1Ch	16: 8	give thanks to the L! Call
1Ch	16:11	Seek the L and His
1Ch	16:23	Sing to the L,
1Ch	16:25	For the L is great and
1Ch	16:26	But the L made the
1Ch	16:28	Give to the L,
1Ch	16:29	Give to the L the glory
1Ch	16:29	worship the L in the beauty
1Ch	16:31	The L reigns."
1Ch	17:16	O L God? And what is my
1Ch	18: 6	So the L preserved David
1Ch	19:13	And may the L do what is
1Ch	21:12	days the sword of the L—
1Ch	21:14	So the L sent a plague upon
1Ch	21:15	the L looked and relented
1Ch	21:15	And the angel of the L
1Ch	21:18	erect an altar to the L on
1Ch	23: 5	four thousand praised the L
1Ch	23:13	burn incense before the L,
1Ch	25: 6	in the house of the L,
1Ch	25: 7	in the songs of the L,
1Ch	26:27	maintain the house of the L.
1Ch	28: 9	for the L searches all
1Ch	29: 1	not for man but for the L
1Ch	29: 9	offered willingly to the L;
1Ch	29:10	L God of Israel, our
1Ch	29:11	Yours is the kingdom, O L,
1Ch	29:22	ate and drank before the L
1Ch	29:25	So the L exalted Solomon
2Ch	1: 1	and the L his God was with
2Ch	1: 6	bronze altar before the L,
2Ch	5: 1	for the house of the L was
2Ch	5:13	praising and thanking the L,
2Ch	5:13	of music, and praised the L,

2Ch	5:14	for the glory of the L
2Ch	6:41	O L God, be clothed with
2Ch	6:42	O L God, do not turn away
2Ch	8:16	So the house of the L was
2Ch	11:16	their heart to seek the L
2Ch	12: 1	he forsook the law of the L,
2Ch	12:14	his heart to seek the L.
2Ch	13: 9	out the priests of the L,
2Ch	13:20	and the L struck him, and
2Ch	14:11	against this multitude. O L,
2Ch	14:14	for the fear of the L came
2Ch	16: 9	For the eyes of the L run to
2Ch	18: 6	still a prophet of the L
2Ch	18:18	I saw the L sitting on His
2Ch	18:22	Therefore look! The L has
2Ch	19: 9	act in the fear of the L,
2Ch	19:10	trespass against the L and
2Ch	20:17	see the salvation of the L,
2Ch	20:20	Believe in the L your God,
2Ch	21: 7	Yet the L would not destroy
2Ch	22: 7	whom the L had anointed to
2Ch	22: 9	who sought the L with all
2Ch	24:12	restore the house of the L.
2Ch	24:22	The L look on it, and
2Ch	26:16	transgressed against the L
2Ch	26:18	to burn incense to the L,
2Ch	26:20	because the L had struck
2Ch	28: 9	But a prophet of the L was
2Ch	28:10	also guilty before the L
2Ch	28:19	For the L brought Judah low
2Ch	28:19	unfaithful to the L.
2Ch	29:11	for the L has chosen you to
2Ch	29:15	cleanse the house of the L.
2Ch	29:25	in the house of the L with
2Ch	29:30	to sing praise to the L
2Ch	30: 8	yield yourselves to the L;
2Ch	30: 9	if you return to the L,
2Ch	30:17	to sanctify them to the L.
2Ch	30:18	May the good L provide
2Ch	31: 3	written in the Law of the L.
2Ch	31:20	and true before the L his
2Ch	32: 8	but with us is the L our
2Ch	32:22	Thus the L saved Hezekiah
2Ch	32:23	brought gifts to the L at
2Ch	32:24	and he prayed to the L;
2Ch	33:10	And the L spoke to Manasseh
2Ch	33:16	repaired the altar of the L,
2Ch	33:23	humble himself before the L,
2Ch	36: 7	from the house of the L to
2Ch	36:21	fulfill the word of the L
2Ch	36:22	the L stirred up the spirit
Ezra	1: 1	the L stirred up the spirit
Ezra	1: 3	build the house of the L
Ezra	2:68	came to the house of the L
Ezra	3: 5	freewill offering to the L,
Ezra	6:21	in order to seek the L God
Ezra	6:22	for the L made them joyful,
Neh	1: 5	L God of heaven, O great
Neh	8: 9	day is holy to the L
Neh	8:10	for the joy of the L is
Neh	9: 3	Book of the Law of the L
Neh	9: 6	You alone are the L;
Job	1: 7	And the L said to Satan,
Job	1:21	The L gave, and the LORD
Job	1:21	and the L has taken away;
Job	1:21	be the name of the L.
Job	28:28	'Behold, the fear of the L,
Job	38: 1	Then the L answered Job out
Job	42: 9	for the L had accepted Job.
Job	42:10	Indeed the L gave Job twice
Job	42:12	Now the L blessed the latter
Ps	1: 2	is in the law of the L,
Ps	1: 6	For the L knows the way of
Ps	2: 2	Against the L and against
Ps	2: 7	The L has said to Me,

Ps	2:11	Serve the L with fear, And
Ps	3: 8	belongs to the L.
Ps	4: 3	But know that the L has set
Ps	4: 3	The L will hear when I
Ps	5: 6	The L abhors the
Ps	5: 8	Lead me, O L,
Ps	6: 2	LORD, for I am weak; O L,
Ps	6: 3	troubled; But You, O L—
Ps	9: 1	I will praise You, O L,
Ps	9:11	Sing praises to the L,
Ps	9:13	O L! Consider my trouble
Ps	10: 1	do You stand afar off, O L?
Ps	10:16	The L is King forever and
Ps	11: 4	The L is in His holy
Ps	11: 5	The L tests the righteous,
Ps	12: 6	The words of the L are
Ps	13: 6	I will sing to the L,
Ps	14: 2	The L looks down from
Ps	14: 7	out of Zion! When the L
Ps	16: 7	I will bless the L who has
Ps	16: 8	I have set the L always
Ps	18: 1	I will love You, O L,
Ps	18: 2	The L is my rock and my
Ps	18:28	The L my God will
Ps	18:46	The L lives! Blessed be
Ps	19: 7	The law of the L is
Ps	19: 7	The testimony of the L is
Ps	19: 8	The statutes of the L are
Ps	19: 8	The commandment of the L
Ps	19: 9	The fear of the L is
Ps	19: 9	The judgments of the L
Ps	19:14	in Your sight, O L,
Ps	21: 7	the king trusts in the L,
Ps	21: 9	The L shall swallow them
Ps	22: 8	"He trusted in the L,
Ps	22:27	remember and turn to the L,
Ps	22:30	will be recounted of the L
Ps	23: 1	The L is my shepherd; I
Ps	23: 6	dwell in the house of the L
Ps	24: 3	into the hill of the L?
Ps	24: 5	receive blessing from the L,
Ps	24: 8	The L strong and mighty,
Ps	24: 8	The L mighty in battle.
Ps	24:10	The L of hosts, He is
Ps	25: 4	Show me Your ways, O L;
Ps	25:12	the man that fears the L?
Ps	26: 1	Vindicate me, O L,
Ps	26: 2	Examine me, O L,
Ps	26: 6	go about Your altar, O L,
Ps	27: 1	The L is my light and my
Ps	27: 1	The L is the strength of
Ps	27: 4	I have desired of the L,
Ps	27: 4	behold the beauty of the L,
Ps	27: 8	said to You, "Your face, L,
Ps	27:11	Teach me Your way, O L,
Ps	27:13	see the goodness of the L
Ps	28: 7	The L is my strength and
Ps	29: 2	Give unto the L the glory
Ps	29: 2	Worship the L in the
Ps	29: 3	The voice of the L is over
Ps	29:10	The L sat enthroned at the
Ps	29:10	And the L sits as King
Ps	29:11	The L will bless His
Ps	30: 1	I will extol You, O L,
Ps	30:10	Hear, O L, and have mercy
Ps	30:10	and have mercy on me; L,
Ps	31:24	All you who hope in the L.
Ps	32: 2	is the man to whom the L
Ps	32: 5	my transgressions to the L,
Ps	33: 2	Praise the L with the harp;
Ps	33: 5	of the goodness of the L.
Ps	33:12	nation whose God is the L,
Ps	33:13	The L looks from heaven;
Ps	33:18	the eye of the L is on
Ps	33:20	Our soul waits for the L;

Ps	34: 1	I will bless the L at all
Ps	34: 2	make its boast in the L;
Ps	34: 3	magnify the L with me, And
Ps	34: 4	I sought the L,
Ps	34: 6	and the L heard him, And
Ps	34: 7	The angel of the L encamps
Ps	34: 8	taste and see that the L
Ps	34:17	and the L hears, And
Ps	34:18	The L is near to those who
Ps	35:10	my bones shall say, "L,
Ps	37: 3	Trust in the L,
Ps	37: 4	yourself also in the L,
Ps	37: 5	Commit your way to the L,
Ps	37: 7	Rest in the L,
Ps	37:23	man are ordered by the L,
Ps	38:22	Make haste to help me, O L,
Ps	40: 1	waited patiently for the L;
Ps	44:23	Why do You sleep, O L?
Ps	46: 7	The L of hosts is with us;
Ps	48: 1	Great is the L,
Ps	50: 1	The Mighty One, God the L,
Ps	55:22	Cast your burden on the L,
Ps	59:11	O L our shield.
Ps	68:11	The L gave the word; Great
Ps	68:32	Oh, sing praises to the L,
Ps	69:33	For the L hears the poor,
Ps	70: 5	help and my deliverer; O L,
Ps	76:11	Make vows to the L your
Ps	77: 7	Will the L cast off forever?
Ps	80:19	O L God of hosts; Cause
Ps	84: 2	For the courts of the L;
Ps	84: 3	O L of hosts, My King and
Ps	84:11	For the L God is a sun and
Ps	84:11	The L will give grace and
Ps	86: 1	Bow down Your ear, O L,
Ps	86: 3	Be merciful to me, O L,
Ps	86:11	Teach me Your way, O L;
Ps	89: 1	of the mercies of the L
Ps	89: 6	can be compared to the L?
Ps	89: 8	is mighty like You, O L?
Ps	90:17	let the beauty of the L
Ps	92: 9	behold, Your enemies, O L,
Ps	93: 1	The L reigns, He is clothed
Ps	94: 1	O L God, to whom vengeance
Ps	94:17	Unless the L had been my
Ps	94:22	But the L has been my
Ps	95: 1	let us sing to the L! Let
Ps	95: 3	For the L is the great
Ps	95: 6	Let us kneel before the L
Ps	96: 1	sing to the L a new song!
Ps	96: 1	a new song! Sing to the L,
Ps	96: 4	For the L is great and
Ps	96: 5	But the L made the
Ps	96: 7	Give to the L glory and
Ps	96: 9	worship the L in the beauty
Ps	96:10	The L reigns; The world
Ps	98: 1	sing to the L a new song!
Ps	98: 4	Shout joyfully to the L,
Ps	100: 1	a joyful shout to the L,
Ps	100: 2	Serve the L with gladness;
Ps	100: 3	Know that the L,
Ps	100: 5	For the L is good; His
Ps	102:19	From heaven the L viewed
Ps	103: 1	Bless the L, O my soul;
Ps	103:13	So the L pities those who
Ps	103:17	But the mercy of the L is
Ps	104: 1	O my soul! O L my God, You
Ps	105: 1	give thanks to the L! Call
Ps	105:45	Praise the L!
Ps	106: 1	Praise the L! Oh, give
Ps	106: 1	Oh, give thanks to the L,
Ps	106: 2	the mighty acts of the L?
Ps	107: 2	Let the redeemed of the L
Ps	107: 6	they cried out to the L in
Ps	107: 8	would give thanks to the L
Ps	109:27	is Your hand—That You, L,
Ps	110: 1	The L said to my Lord,
Ps	110: 2	The L shall send the rod of
Ps	110: 4	The L has sworn And will
Ps	110: 5	The L is at Your right
Ps	111: 4	The L is gracious and
Ps	111:10	The fear of the L is the
Ps	113: 2	be the name of the L From
Ps	113: 4	The L is high above all
Ps	115: 1	Not unto us, O L,
Ps	115:17	dead do not praise the L,
Ps	115:18	But we will bless the L
Ps	116: 1	I love the L,
Ps	116: 5	Gracious is the L,
Ps	116: 6	The L preserves the simple;
Ps	116: 9	I will walk before the L
Ps	116:12	shall I render to the L
Ps	116:14	will pay my vows to the L
Ps	117: 1	Praise the L,
Ps	118: 5	I called on the L in
Ps	118: 8	better to trust in the L
Ps	118:14	The L is my strength and
Ps	118:15	The right hand of the L
Ps	118:24	This is the day the L has
Ps	118:26	comes in the name of the L!
Ps	118:26	you from the house of the L.
Ps	119:33	Teach me, O L,
Ps	119:89	Forever, O L, Your word is
Ps	119:107	very much; Revive me, O L,
Ps	119:156	Your tender mercies, O L;
Ps	120: 1	distress I cried to the L,
Ps	121: 2	My help comes from the L,
Ps	121: 5	The L is your keeper; The
Ps	121: 5	The L is your shade at
Ps	121: 7	The L shall preserve you
Ps	122: 1	go into the house of the L.
Ps	124: 1	If it had not been the L who
Ps	125: 1	Those who trust in the L
Ps	125: 2	So the L surrounds His
Ps	125: 4	Do good, O L,
Ps	126: 1	When the L brought back the
Ps	126: 2	The L has done great things
Ps	127: 1	Unless the L builds the
Ps	127: 1	Unless the L guards the
Ps	127: 3	are a heritage from the L,
Ps	130: 3	should mark iniquities, O L,
Ps	130: 6	My soul waits for the L
Ps	130: 7	O Israel, hope in the L;
Ps	130: 7	For with the L there is
Ps	135: 1	Praise the name of the L;
Ps	135: 1	O you servants of the L!
Ps	135: 5	And our L is above all
Ps	135: 6	Whatever the L pleases He
Ps	135:19	of Israel! Bless the L,
Ps	136: 1	Oh, give thanks to the L,
Ps	136: 3	give thanks to the L of
Ps	137: 7	Remember, O L,
Ps	138: 5	is the glory of the L.
Ps	139: 4	tongue, But behold, O L,
Ps	139:21	Do I not hate them, O L,
Ps	141: 3	Set a guard, O L,
Ps	144: 1	Blessed be the L my Rock,
Ps	144: 5	Bow down Your heavens, O L,
Ps	144:15	people whose God is the L!
Ps	145: 3	Great is the L,
Ps	145: 9	The L is good to all, And
Ps	145:10	works shall praise You, O L,
Ps	145:17	The L is righteous in all
Ps	146: 7	The L gives freedom to the
Ps	146: 8	The L opens the eyes of
Ps	147: 2	The L builds up Jerusalem;
Prov	1: 7	The fear of the L is the
Prov	2: 6	For the L gives wisdom;
Prov	3: 5	Trust in the L with all
Prov	3: 9	Honor the L with your

Prov	3:11	the chastening of the L,
Prov	3:12	For whom the L loves He
Prov	3:19	The L by wisdom founded
Prov	3:32	is an abomination to the L,
Prov	6:16	These six things the L
Prov	8:13	The fear of the L is to
Prov	8:22	The L possessed me at the
Prov	8:35	obtains favor from the L;
Prov	9:10	The fear of the L is the
Prov	15: 3	The eyes of the L are in
Prov	15:16	with the fear of the L,
Prov	16: 2	But the L weighs the
Prov	16: 7	a man's ways please the L,
Prov	16: 9	But the L directs his
Prov	16:33	decision is from the L.
Prov	17: 3	But the L tests the
Prov	19:14	prudent wife is from the L.
Prov	19:23	The fear of the L leads to
Prov	20:12	The L has made them both.
Prov	20:24	man's steps are of the L;
Prov	21: 2	But the L weighs the
Prov	22:23	For the L will plead their
Prov	29:13	The L gives light to the
Prov	31:30	a woman who fears the L,
Is	1: 2	O earth! For the L has
Is	1: 4	They have forsaken the L,
Is	1: 9	Unless the L of hosts Had
Is	1:20	For the mouth of the L has
Is	2: 3	up to the mountain of the L,
Is	2: 3	And the word of the L from
Is	2: 5	walk In the light of the L.
Is	2:11	And the L alone shall be
Is	3:13	The L stands up to plead,
Is	5: 7	For the vineyard of the L
Is	6: 1	I saw the L sitting on a
Is	6: 3	holy is the L of hosts;
Is	7:12	nor will I test the L!"
Is	7:14	Therefore the L Himself will
Is	7:17	The L will bring the king of
Is	8:18	and the children whom the L
Is	8:18	in Israel From the L of
Is	9: 7	The zeal of the L of hosts
Is	11: 2	The Spirit of the L shall
Is	11: 2	and of the fear of the L.
Is	11: 9	of the knowledge of the L
Is	12: 2	afraid; 'For YAH, the L,
Is	12: 5	Sing to the L,
Is	14: 5	The L has broken the staff
Is	19: 1	the L rides on a swift
Is	19:19	will be an altar to the L
Is	19:19	and a pillar to the L at
Is	23:17	that the L will visit Tyre.
Is	24: 1	the L makes the earth empty
Is	24:15	Therefore glorify the L in
Is	25: 8	And the L GOD will wipe
Is	26: 4	Trust in the L forever,
Is	26: 4	For in YAH, the L,
Is	26:15	increased the nation, O L,
Is	29:15	counsel far from the L,
Is	29:19	their joy in the L,
Is	30:18	For the L is a God of
Is	30:29	into the mountain of the L,
Is	30:30	The L will cause His
Is	30:33	wood; The breath of the L,
Is	31: 3	When the L stretches out
Is	32: 6	utter error against the L,
Is	33: 6	The fear of the L is His
Is	33:21	But there the majestic L
Is	33:22	(For the L is our Judge,
Is	33:22	The L is our King; He
Is	34: 6	For the L has a sacrifice
Is	37:36	Then the angel of the L
Is	38: 2	wall, and prayed to the L,
Is	40: 3	"Prepare the way of the L;
Is	40: 5	The glory of the L shall be
Is	40: 7	the breath of the L blows
Is	40:13	the Spirit of the L,
Is	40:27	way is hidden from the L,
Is	40:28	The everlasting God, the L,
Is	40:31	those who wait on the L
Is	41: 4	the beginning? 'I, the L,
Is	42: 8	I am the L, that is My
Is	42:10	Sing to the L a new song,
Is	43:11	I, even I, am the L,
Is	44:23	for the L has done it!
Is	44:23	tree in it! For the L has
Is	45: 6	besides Me. I am the L,
Is	45: 8	up together. I, the L,
Is	48: 1	swear by the name of the L,
Is	48:20	The L has redeemed His
Is	48:22	is no peace," says the L,
Is	49: 1	peoples from afar! The L
Is	49:13	O mountains! For the L has
Is	49:14	And my L has forgotten
Is	50: 5	The L GOD has opened My
Is	51: 3	For the L will comfort
Is	51: 3	like the garden of the L;
Is	51:13	And you forget the L your
Is	51:17	drunk at the hand of the L
Is	52: 8	see eye to eye When the L
Is	52: 9	of Jerusalem! For the L
Is	52:10	The L has made bare His
Is	53: 1	whom has the arm of the L
Is	53: 6	And the L has laid on Him
Is	53:10	Yet it pleased the L to
Is	53:10	And the pleasure of the L
Is	55: 6	Seek the L while He may be
Is	55: 7	Let him return to the L,
Is	58: 5	an acceptable day to the L?
Is	58: 9	and the L will answer; You
Is	58:13	The holy day of the L
Is	58:14	delight yourself in the L;
Is	59:19	fear The name of the L
Is	60: 1	And the glory of the L is
Is	60:14	call you The City of the L,
Is	61: 1	The Spirit of the L GOD is
Is	61: 1	Because the L has anointed
Is	61: 2	acceptable year of the L,
Is	61: 3	The planting of the L,
Is	61: 6	named the priests of the L,
Is	62: 8	The L has sworn by His
Is	62:12	The Redeemed of the L;
Is	63: 7	lovingkindnesses of the L
Is	63:16	acknowledge us. You, O L,
Is	66: 5	Let the L be glorified,
Is	66:15	the L will come with fire
Is	66:16	and by His sword The L
Jer	1: 4	Then the word of the L came
Jer	1: 6	L GOD! Behold, I cannot
Jer	1: 8	deliver you," says the L.
Jer	1: 9	Then the L put forth His
Jer	1:19	am with you," says the L,
Jer	2: 3	was holiness to the L,
Jer	2:19	you have forsaken the L
Jer	3: 1	return to Me," says the L.
Jer	3:17	called The Throne of the L,
Jer	3:25	have sinned against the L
Jer	4: 8	the fierce anger of the L
Jer	4:10	L GOD! Surely You have
Jer	5:12	They have lied about the L,
Jer	5:22	not fear Me?' says the L.
Jer	6:11	full of the fury of the L.
Jer	7: 4	LORD, the temple of the L,
Jer	7:29	for the L has rejected and
Jer	7:32	are coming," says the L,
Jer	8:12	be cast down," says the L.
Jer	8:14	have sinned against the L.
Jer	9: 3	not know Me," says the L.
Jer	9:24	knows Me, That I am the L,
Jer	9:24	I delight," says the L.

Jer	10:10	But the L is the true God;
Jer	11:18	Now the L gave me knowledge
Jer	11:20	O L of hosts, You who
Jer	12: 1	Righteous are You, O L,
Jer	13:16	Give glory to the L your
Jer	14:13	L GOD! Behold, the prophets
Jer	15:20	deliver you," says the L.
Jer	17: 5	heart departs from the L.
Jer	17: 7	the man who trusts in the L,
Jer	17: 7	And whose hope is the L.
Jer	17:14	Heal me, O L,
Jer	18: 6	this potter?" says the L.
Jer	20:12	O L of hosts, You who test
Jer	20:16	the cities Which the L
Jer	22: 5	by Myself," says the L,
Jer	22: 9	the covenant of the L
Jer	22:16	knowing Me?" says the L.
Jer	22:29	Hear the word of the L!
Jer	23: 1	of My pasture!" says the L.
Jer	23: 6	L OUR RIGHTEOUSNESS.
Jer	23:18	in the counsel of the L,
Jer	23:19	a whirlwind of the L has
Jer	23:28	to the wheat?" says the L.
Jer	23:32	false dreams," says the L,
Jer	23:34	The oracle of the L!' I will
Jer	25:30	The L will roar from on
Jer	25:31	For the L has a controversy
Jer	25:33	that day the slain of the L
Jer	25:36	For the L has plundered
Jer	25:37	the fierce anger of the L.
Jer	26:12	The L sent me to prophesy
Jer	26:13	then the L will relent
Jer	28: 6	Amen! The L do so; the LORD
Jer	28: 6	the L perform your words
Jer	28: 9	be known as one whom the L
Jer	28:15	the L has not sent you, but
Jer	29: 9	not sent them, says the L.
Jer	29:14	be found by you, says the L,
Jer	29:15	The L has raised up prophets
Jer	29:22	The L make you like Zedekiah
Jer	29:26	The L has made you priest
Jer	29:32	rebellion against the L.
Jer	30: 9	But they shall serve the L
Jer	30:10	servant Jacob,' says the L,
Jer	30:23	the whirlwind of the L
Jer	31: 3	The L has appeared of old
Jer	31:15	Thus says the L:
Jer	31:31	days are coming, says the L,
Jer	31:32	husband to them, says the L.
Jer	31:33	those days, says the L:
Jer	31:34	saying, 'Know the L,
Jer	33: 2	Thus says the L who made it,
Jer	33: 2	the L who formed it to
Jer	33: 2	it to establish it (the L
Jer	33:16	L OUR RIGHTEOUSNESS.'
Jer	34:17	liberty to you,' says the L—
Jer	36: 9	a fast before the L to all
Jer	36:11	all the words of the L
Jer	37:17	there any word from the L?
Jer	37:20	O my l the king. Please, let
Jer	42: 2	and pray for us to the L
Jer	42: 5	Let the L be a true and
Jer	42:20	Pray for us to the L our
Jer	44:22	So the L could no longer
Jer	44:23	have sinned against the L,
Jer	44:29	a sign to you,' says the L,
Jer	45: 5	on all flesh," says the L.
Jer	47: 6	"O you sword of the L,
Jer	48:25	arm is broken," says the L.
Jer	48:47	latter days," says the L.
Jer	49:31	securely," says the L,
Jer	50: 5	us join ourselves to the L
Jer	50: 7	of justice, The L,
Jer	50:13	of the wrath of the L She
Jer	50:21	destroy them," says the L,
Jer	50:25	The L has opened His
Jer	50:28	the vengeance of the L our
Jer	50:35	the Chaldeans," says the L,
Jer	51:39	not awake," says the L.
Jer	51:45	the fierce anger of the L.
Jer	51:48	the north," says the L.
Jer	52:13	burned the house of the L
Jer	52:17	were in the house of the L,
Lam	1: 9	had no comforter. "O L,
Lam	1:15	The L has trampled underfoot
Lam	2: 7	The L has spurned His altar,
Lam	2: 9	find no vision from the L.
Lam	3:18	Have perished from the L.
Lam	3:25	The L is good to those who
Lam	3:31	For the L will not cast off
Lam	3:40	And turn back to the L;
Lam	3:50	Till the L from heaven
Lam	4:11	The L has fulfilled His
Lam	5:21	Turn us back to You, O L,
Ezek	1: 3	and the hand of the L was
Ezek	1:28	of the glory of the L.
Ezek	3:14	but the hand of the L was
Ezek	6: 7	shall know that I am the L.
Ezek	6:10	shall know that I am the L;
Ezek	7: 9	know that I am the L who
Ezek	7:19	day of the wrath of the L;
Ezek	8:12	The L does not see us, the
Ezek	8:12	the L has forsaken the
Ezek	8:16	toward the temple of the L
Ezek	9: 9	The L has forsaken the land,
Ezek	10: 4	Then the glory of the L went
Ezek	11: 5	Then the Spirit of the L
Ezek	11:23	And the glory of the L went
Ezek	13: 5	battle on the day of the L.
Ezek	16:23	woe to you!' says the L
Ezek	16:58	abominations," says the L.
Ezek	18:25	The way of the L is not
Ezek	18:29	The way of the L is not
Ezek	20:12	know that I am the L who
Ezek	20:42	shall know that I am the L,
Ezek	20:44	shall know that I am the L,
Ezek	20:48	shall see that I, the L,
Ezek	20:49	L GOD! They say of me,
Ezek	25: 5	shall know that I am the L.
Ezek	30: 3	Even the day of the L is
Ezek	33:17	The way of the L is not
Ezek	37: 1	The hand of the L came upon
Ezek	37: 1	out in the Spirit of the L,
Ezek	37: 3	O L GOD, You know."
Ezek	37: 4	hear the word of the L!
Ezek	37:14	performed it," says the L.
Ezek	38:14	Thus says the L GOD: "On
Ezek	39: 6	shall know that I am the L.
Ezek	39: 7	know that I am the L,
Ezek	39:20	says the L GOD.
Ezek	43: 5	the glory of the L filled
Ezek	43:24	a burnt offering to the L.
Ezek	44: 4	the glory of the L filled
Ezek	44:15	says the L GOD.
Ezek	44:27	says the L GOD.
Ezek	46: 3	this gateway before the L
Ezek	46: 4	the prince offers to the L
Ezek	46: 9	the land come before the L
Ezek	46:14	be made regularly to the L.
Ezek	48:14	for it is holy to the L.
Ezek	48:35	THE L IS THERE."
Dan	2:47	the L of kings, and a
Dan	5:23	yourself up against the L
Dan	9: 2	by the word of the L
Dan	9: 4	And I prayed to the L my
Dan	9: 4	confession, and said, "O L,
Dan	9:19	"O Lord, hear! O L,
Dan	12: 8	Then I said, "My l,
Hos	1: 2	When the L began to speak
Hos	1: 7	Will save them by the L

Hos	2:13	Me she forgot," says the L.
Hos	2:20	And you shall know the L.
Hos	2:21	I will answer," says the L;
Hos	3: 1	Then the L said to me, "Go
Hos	3: 5	shall return and seek the L
Hos	3: 5	They shall fear the L and
Hos	4: 1	Hear the word of the L,
Hos	4: 1	For the L brings a charge
Hos	5: 4	And they do not know the L.
Hos	6: 1	and let us return to the L;
Hos	6: 3	the knowledge of the L.
Hos	9:14	Give them, O L—
Hos	10: 3	we did not fear the L.
Hos	10:12	it is time to seek the L,
Hos	12: 5	The L is His memorable
Hos	12: 9	But I am the L your God,
Hos	12:13	By a prophet the L brought
Hos	13: 4	Yet I am the L your God
Hos	14: 1	return to the L your God,
Hos	14: 9	For the ways of the L are
Joel	1:15	day! For the day of the L
Joel	2: 1	For the day of the L is
Joel	2:17	who minister to the L,
Joel	2:17	"Spare Your people, O L,
Joel	2:21	For the L has done
Joel	2:31	and awesome day of the L.
Joel	2:32	calls on the name of the L
Joel	2:32	the remnant whom the L
Joel	3:16	The L also will roar from
Joel	3:16	But the L will be a
Joel	3:18	from the house of the L
Amos	1: 2	The L roars from Zion, And
Amos	1: 3	Thus says the L:
Amos	3: 6	will not the L have done
Amos	3: 7	Surely the L GOD does
Amos	3:10	to do right,' Says the L,
Amos	4: 2	The L GOD has sworn by His
Amos	4: 6	to Me," Says the L.
Amos	5: 6	Seek the L and live, Lest
Amos	5:15	It may be that the L God
Amos	5:18	desire the day of the L!
Amos	5:20	Is not the day of the L
Amos	5:27	Damascus," Says the L,
Amos	6:10	mention the name of the L.
Amos	7: 2	O L GOD, forgive, I pray!
Amos	7: 3	So the L relented
Amos	7: 3	shall not be," said the L.
Amos	7: 5	O L GOD, cease, I pray! Oh,
Amos	7: 6	So the L relented
Amos	7: 7	the L stood on a wall made
Amos	8: 7	The L has sworn by the
Jon	1: 3	from the presence of the L.
Jon	1: 4	But the L sent out a great
Jon	1: 9	a Hebrew; and I fear the L,
Jon	1:16	Then the men feared the L
Jon	1:16	a sacrifice to the L and
Jon	1:17	Now the L had prepared a
Jon	2: 1	Then Jonah prayed to the L
Jon	2: 6	my life from the pit, O L,
Jon	2: 9	Salvation is of the L.
Jon	2:10	So the L spoke to the fish,
Jon	4: 6	And the L God prepared a
Mic	1: 2	The L from His holy temple.
Mic	2: 7	Is the Spirit of the L
Mic	3: 8	by the Spirit of the L,
Mic	3:11	Yet they lean on the L,
Mic	4: 2	up to the mountain of the L,
Mic	4: 2	And the word of the L from
Mic	4: 7	So the L will reign over
Mic	4:12	know the thoughts of the L,
Mic	4:13	their substance to the L of
Mic	6: 2	For the L has a complaint
Mic	6: 6	shall I come before the L,
Mic	6: 7	Will the L be pleased with
Mic	6: 8	And what does the L

Mic	7: 8	The L will be a light to
Nah	1: 2	and the L avenges; The
Nah	1: 3	The L is slow to anger and
Hab	1:12	O L my God, my Holy One?
Hab	2:20	But the L is in His holy
Hab	3:18	I will rejoice in the L,
Hab	3:19	The L God is my strength;
Zeph	1:12	The L will not do good, Nor
Zeph	1:14	The great day of the L is
Zeph	1:14	noise of the day of the L
Zeph	2: 3	Seek the L, all you meek
Zeph	3:17	The L your God in your
Hag	1:14	So the L stirred up the
Zech	1: 2	The L has been very angry
Zech	1:12	Then the Angel of the L
Zech	1:13	And the L answered the angel
Zech	1:17	The L will again comfort
Zech	1:20	Then the L showed me four
Zech	2:11	you will know that the L
Zech	2:13	all flesh, before the L,
Zech	3: 2	And the L said to Satan,
Zech	3: 2	The L rebuke you, Satan! The
Zech	4:10	They are the eyes of the L,
Zech	4:14	who stand beside the L of
Zech	6:12	build the temple of the L;
Zech	8:17	that I hate,' Says the L.
Zech	9: 1	burden of the word of the L
Zech	10: 1	Ask the L for rain In the
Zech	10: 6	For I am the L their God,
Zech	10: 7	shall rejoice in the L.
Zech	10:12	strengthen them in the L,
Zech	11:13	into the house of the L
Zech	12: 8	In that day the L will
Zech	14: 1	the day of the L is coming,
Zech	14: 7	Which is known to the L—
Zech	14: 9	And the L shall be King
Zech	14: 9	The L is one," And His
Zech	14:20	HOLINESS TO THE L" shall
Mal	1: 2	loved you," says the L.
Mal	1: 2	brother?" Says the L.
Mal	1: 7	The table of the L is
Mal	2: 7	is the messenger of the L
Mal	2:17	You have wearied the L
Mal	3: 1	way before Me. And the L,
Mal	3: 4	Will be pleasant to the L,
Mal	4: 5	and dreadful day of the L.
Matt	1:20	an angel of the L appeared
Matt	1:22	which was spoken by the L
Matt	3: 3	the way of the L;
Matt	4: 7	shall not tempt the L
Matt	4:10	shall worship the L
Matt	7:21	everyone who says to Me, 'L,
Matt	8: 2	worshiped Him, saying, "L,
Matt	8: 8	answered and said, "L,
Matt	8:21	disciples said to Him, "L,
Matt	8:25	and awoke Him, saying, "L,
Matt	11:25	L of heaven and earth, that
Matt	12: 8	For the Son of Man is L even
Matt	14:28	answered Him and said, "L,
Matt	15:27	And she said, "Yes, L,
Matt	16:22	"Far be it from You, L;
Matt	17: 4	and said to Jesus, "L,
Matt	18:21	came to Him and said, "L,
Matt	20:25	rulers of the Gentiles I it
Matt	21: 3	The L has need of them,' and
Matt	21: 9	in the name of the L!
Matt	22:37	You shall love the L
Matt	22:44	The L said to my Lord,
Matt	22:45	David then calls Him 'L,
Matt	24:42	do not know what hour your L
Matt	25:21	His l said to him, 'Well
Matt	25:21	Enter into the joy of your l.
Matt	26:22	began to say to Him, "L,
Matt	27:10	as the L directed
Matt	28: 2	for an angel of the L

Matt	28: 6	see the place where the L
Mark	9:24	out and said with tears, "L,
Mark	12:29	the L is one.
Mark	12:30	you shall love the L
Mark	13:20	And unless the L had
Luke	1: 6	and ordinances of the L
Luke	1: 9	into the temple of the L.
Luke	1:15	great in the sight of the L,
Luke	1:28	the L is with you; blessed
Luke	1:32	and the L God will give Him
Luke	1:38	the maidservant of the L!
Luke	1:43	that the mother of my L
Luke	1:45	were told her from the L.
Luke	1:46	"My soul magnifies the L,
Luke	1:58	relatives heard how the L
Luke	2: 9	an angel of the L stood
Luke	2: 9	and the glory of the L shone
Luke	2:11	Savior, who is Christ the L.
Luke	2:15	which the L has made known
Luke	2:22	to present Him to the L
Luke	4:18	The Spirit of the L is
Luke	4:19	year of the L.
Luke	5:12	implored Him, saying, "L,
Luke	5:17	And the power of the L was
Luke	7: 6	to Him, saying to Him, "L,
Luke	9:57	someone said to Him, "L,
Luke	10:27	You shall love the L
Luke	12:41	Then Peter said to Him, "L,
Luke	19: 8	said to the Lord, "Look, L,
Luke	22:31	And the L said, "Simon,
Luke	22:61	And the L turned and looked
Luke	22:61	remembered the word of the L,
Luke	23:42	Then he said to Jesus, "L,
Luke	24:34	The L is risen indeed, and
John	6:23	they ate bread after the L
John	6:68	Peter answered Him, "L,
John	8:11	She said, "No one, L.
John	9:36	and said, "Who is He, L,
John	11:21	Martha said to Jesus, "L,
John	11:27	She said to Him, "Yes, L,
John	11:32	His feet, saying to Him, "L,
John	12:38	which he spoke: "L,
John	12:38	has the arm of the L
John	13: 6	And Peter said to Him, "L,
John	13:13	"You call me Teacher and L,
John	13:14	your L and Teacher, have
John	13:36	Peter said to Him, "L,
John	14: 5	Thomas said to Him, "L,
John	14: 8	Philip said to Him, "L,
John	20: 2	They have taken away the L
John	20:18	that she had seen the L,
John	20:20	glad when they saw the L.
John	20:28	My L and my God!"
John	21: 7	It is the L!" Now when Simon
John	21: 7	heard that it was the L,
John	21:15	He said to Him, "Yes, L;
John	21:20	at the supper, and said, "L,
Acts	1:24	prayed and said, "You, O L,
Acts	2:20	awesome day of the L.
Acts	2:21	on the name of the L
Acts	2:36	both L and Christ."
Acts	2:39	as many as the L our God
Acts	2:47	And the L added to the
Acts	3:22	The L your God will
Acts	5: 9	to test the Spirit of the L?
Acts	5:14	increasingly added to the L,
Acts	5:19	at night an angel of the L
Acts	7:30	an Angel of the L appeared
Acts	7:59	L Jesus, receive my spirit."
Acts	7:60	out with a loud voice, "L,
Acts	8:25	preached the word of the L,
Acts	8:26	Now an angel of the L spoke
Acts	8:39	the Spirit of the L caught
Acts	9: 5	he said, "Who are You, L?
Acts	9: 5	Then the L said, "I am

Acts	9: 6	and astonished, said, "L,
Acts	9:27	them how he had seen the L
Acts	9:42	and many believed on the L.
Acts	10:14	L! For I have never eaten
Acts	10:48	in the name of the L.
Acts	11:24	people were added to the L.
Acts	12: 7	an angel of the L stood by
Acts	14: 3	speaking boldly in the L,
Acts	15:35	preaching the word of the L,
Acts	16:31	Believe on the L Jesus
Acts	17:24	since He is L of heaven and
Acts	17:27	that they should seek the L,
Acts	18: 9	Now the L spoke to Paul in
Acts	18:25	the things of the L,
Acts	19:20	So the word of the L grew
Acts	21:14	The will of the L be done."
Acts	22: 8	I answered, 'Who are You, L?
Acts	22:10	I said, 'What shall I do, L?
Rom	4: 8	the man to whom the L
Rom	4:24	who raised up Jesus our L
Rom	6:23	life in Christ Jesus our L.
Rom	9:29	Unless the L of Sabaoth
Rom	10: 9	with your mouth the L Jesus
Rom	10:12	for the same L over all is
Rom	10:13	on the name of the L
Rom	10:16	For Isaiah says, "L,
Rom	11:34	the mind of the L?
Rom	12:11	in spirit, serving the L;
Rom	12:19	will repay," says the L.
Rom	13:14	But put on the L Jesus
Rom	14: 6	day, observes it to the L;
Rom	14: 6	He who eats, eats to the L,
Rom	14: 8	if we live, we live to the L;
Rom	14: 8	if we die, we die to the L.
Rom	14: 9	that He might be L of both
Rom	16:12	who have labored in the L.
Rom	16:20	The grace of our L Jesus
1Co	1: 9	His Son, Jesus Christ our L.
1Co	1:31	him glory in the L.
1Co	2: 8	not have crucified the L of
1Co	2:16	the mind of the L
1Co	4: 4	He who judges me is the L.
1Co	5: 4	In the name of our L Jesus
1Co	5: 4	with the power of our L
1Co	6:13	and the L for the body.
1Co	7:10	yet not I but the L:
1Co	7:12	But to the rest I, not the L,
1Co	7:25	no commandment from the L;
1Co	7:32	Lord—how he may please the L.
1Co	7:35	and that you may serve the L
1Co	8: 6	and one L Jesus Christ,
1Co	9: 1	not seen Jesus Christ our L?
1Co	9: 1	Are you not my work in the L?
1Co	9: 2	of my apostleship in the L.
1Co	10:21	drink the cup of the L and
1Co	10:22	Or do we provoke the L to
1Co	11:23	For I received from the L
1Co	11:23	that the L Jesus on the
1Co	11:27	or drinks this cup of the L
1Co	11:27	the body and blood of the L.
1Co	12: 3	one can say that Jesus is L
1Co	12: 5	ministries, but the same L.
1Co	15:47	the second Man is the L
1Co	15:58	in the work of the L,
1Co	15:58	is not in vain in the L.
1Co	16:10	he does the work of the L,
1Co	16:22	let him be accursed. O L,
2Co	3:16	when one turns to the L,
2Co	3:17	where the Spirit of the L
2Co	3:18	a mirror the glory of the L,
2Co	4:10	the body the dying of the L
2Co	5: 6	we are absent from the L.
2Co	5: 8	and to be present with the L.
2Co	6:17	be separate, says the L.
2Co	10:17	him glory in the L.

2Co	10:18	but whom the L commends.
2Co	12: 8	thing I pleaded with the L
Gal	6:14	in the cross of our L Jesus
Gal	6:17	my body the marks of the L
Eph	1:15	heard of your faith in the L
Eph	2:21	into a holy temple in the L,
Eph	4: 1	the prisoner of the L,
Eph	4: 5	one L, one faith, one
Eph	5: 8	now you are light in the L.
Eph	5:10	what is acceptable to the L.
Eph	5:17	what the will of the L is.
Eph	5:19	in your heart to the L,
Eph	5:22	own husbands, as to the L.
Eph	5:29	just as the L does the
Eph	6: 1	obey your parents in the L,
Eph	6: 7	doing service, as to the L,
Phil	2:11	that Jesus Christ is L,
Phil	4: 1	so stand fast in the L,
Phil	4: 2	be of the same mind in the L.
Phil	4: 4	Rejoice in the L always.
Phil	4: 5	The L is at hand.
Col	1:10	you may walk worthy of the L,
Col	3:16	in your hearts to the L.
Col	3:23	as to the L and not to men,
Col	3:24	for you serve the L Christ.
Col	4: 7	and fellow servant in the L,
1Th	1: 3	patience of hope in our L
1Th	1: 6	followers of us and of the L,
1Th	2:15	who killed both the L Jesus
1Th	2:19	you in the presence of our L
1Th	3: 8	if you stand fast in the L.
1Th	4:17	in the clouds to meet the L
1Th	4:17	shall always be with the L.
2Th	2: 8	whom the L will consume with
2Th	3: 3	But the L is faithful, who
2Th	3:16	Now may the L of peace
1Ti	1: 1	of God our Savior and the L
1Ti	1:12	I thank Christ Jesus our L
1Ti	6:14	blameless until our L Jesus
1Ti	6:15	the King of kings and L of
2Ti	1: 8	of the testimony of our L,
2Ti	2:19	The L knows those who are
2Ti	2:22	those who call on the L out
2Ti	2:24	And a servant of the L must
Phm	1:20	refresh my heart in the L.
Heb	7:14	it is evident that our L
Heb	7:21	The L has sworn And
Heb	8:11	saying, 'Know the L,
Heb	10:30	will repay," says the L.
Heb	10:30	The L will judge His
Heb	12: 5	chastening of the L,
Heb	12: 6	For whom the L loves
Heb	13:20	peace who brought up our L
Jas	1:12	crown of life which the L
Jas	2: 1	the L of glory, with
Jas	5: 4	reached the ears of the L
Jas	5: 8	for the coming of the L is
Jas	5:11	the end intended by the L—
Jas	5:14	oil in the name of the L.
Jas	5:15	and the L will raise him up.
1Pe	2: 3	you have tasted that the L
1Pe	3: 6	Abraham, calling him l,
1Pe	3:15	But sanctify the L God in
2Pe	1:11	kingdom of our L and Savior
2Pe	2: 1	even denying the L who
2Pe	3: 2	the apostles of the L and
2Pe	3: 8	that with the L one day is
2Pe	3: 9	The L is not slack concerning
2Pe	3:10	But the day of the L will
Jude	4	and deny the only L God and
Jude	9	The L rebuke you!"
Jude	14	the L comes with ten
Rev	1: 8	and the End," says the L,
Rev	4: 8	L God Almighty, Who was
Rev	4:11	"You are worthy, O L,

Rev	6:10	saying, "How long, O L,
Rev	11:15	the kingdoms of our L and
Rev	14:13	the dead who die in the L
Rev	17:14	for He is L of lords and
Rev	19: 6	Alleluia! For the L God
Rev	19:16	KING OF KINGS AND L OF
Rev	22:21	The grace of our L Jesus

LORD'S (see LORD)

Ex	9:29	that the earth is the L.
Ex	12:11	It is the L Passover.
Ex	13: 9	that the L law may be in
Ex	13:12	the males shall be the L.
Ex	32:26	Whoever is on the L
Lev	3:16	all the fat is the L.
Lev	23: 5	month at twilight is the L
Num	11:23	Has the L arm been
Num	11:29	that all the L people were
Num	32:10	So the L anger was aroused
Deut	32: 9	For the L portion is His
Josh	1:15	which Moses the L servant
Josh	5:15	Then the Commander of the L
Josh	22:19	where the L tabernacle
1Sa	2: 8	of the earth are the L,
1Sa	14: 3	the L priest in Shiloh, was
1Sa	16: 6	Surely the L anointed is
1Sa	17:47	for the battle is the L,
Ps	11: 4	The L throne is in
Ps	22:28	For the kingdom is the L,
Ps	24: 1	The earth is the L,
Ps	113: 3	to its going down The L
Ps	115:16	the heavens, are the L;
Ps	116:19	In the courts of the L
Ps	118:23	This was the L doing; It
Ps	137: 4	How shall we sing the L
Prov	16:11	and scales are the L;
Is	2: 2	the mountain of the L
Is	34: 8	it is the day of the L
Is	40: 2	she has received from the L
Is	42:19	And blind as the L
Is	59: 1	the L hand is not
Jer	19:14	stood in the court of the L
Jer	27:16	the vessels of the L house
Lam	2:22	In the day of the L anger
Lam	3:22	Through the L mercies we
Ezek	10: 4	of the brightness of the L
Dan	9:17	and for the L sake cause
Hos	9: 3	shall not dwell in the L
Mic	4: 1	the mountain of the L
Zeph	2: 2	Before the L fierce anger
Hag	1: 2	the time that the L house
Hag	1:13	the L messenger, spoke the
Hag	2:18	the foundation of the L
Zech	14:20	The pots in the L house
Matt	21:42	This was the L doing,
Matt	25:18	and hid his l money.
Luke	2:26	before he had seen the L
Rom	14: 8	we live or die, we are the L.
1Co	7:22	Lord while a slave is the L
1Co	10:21	you cannot partake of the L
1Co	10:26	"the earth is the L,
1Co	11:20	it is not to eat the L
1Co	11:26	you proclaim the L death
1Co	11:29	not discerning the L body.
Gal	1:19	the L brother.
1Pe	2:13	ordinance of man for the L
Rev	1:10	I was in the Spirit on the L

LORDLY † (see LORD)

Judg	5:25	brought out cream in a l

LORDS (see LORD)

Gen	19: 2	he said, "Here now, my l,
Deut	10:17	God of gods and Lord of l,
Josh	13: 3	the five l of the
Ps	136: 3	thanks to the Lord of l!

Is 16: 8 The l of the nations have
Dan 5: 1 for a thousand of his l,
1Co 8: 5 are many gods and many l),
1Ti 6:15 King of kings and Lord of l,
1Pe 5: 3 nor as being l over those
Rev 17:14 for He is Lord of l and King
Rev 19:16 OF KINGS AND LORD OF L.

LORDSHIP† (see LORD)
Luke 22:25 of the Gentiles exercise l

LOSE (see LOSES, LOSS, LOST)
Judg 18:25 and you l your life, with
Eccl 3: 6 to gain, And a time to l;
Matt 10:39 who finds his life will l
Matt 10:42 he shall by no means l his
Matt 16:25 to save his life will l it,
Luke 18: 1 ought to pray and not l
John 12:25 who loves his life will l
Gal 6: 9 we shall reap if we do not l
Eph 3:13 I ask that you do not l

LOSES (see LOSE)
Matt 5:13 but if the salt l its
Matt 10:39 and he who l his life for My
Matt 16:26 and l his own soul? Or what
Luke 15: 4 if he l one of them, does
Luke 15: 8 if she l one coin, does not

LOSS (see LOSE)
Job 11:20 And their hope—l of life!"
Dan 6: 2 the king would suffer no l.
Acts 27:10 end with disaster and much l,
1Co 3:15 is burned, he will suffer l;
Phil 3: 7 these I have counted l for
Phil 3: 8 I also count all things l
Phil 3: 8 whom I have suffered the l

LOST (see LOSE)
Lev 6: 3 if he has found what was l
Num 6:12 the former days shall be l,
Ps 27:13 I would have l heart,
Ps 119:176 I have gone astray like a l
Is 49:21 Since I have l my children
Jer 50: 6 My people have been l sheep.
Ezek 34:16 I will seek what was l and
Ezek 37:11 bones are dry, our hope is l,
Matt 10: 6 But go rather to the l sheep
Matt 15:24 was not sent except to the l
Matt 18:11 to save that which was l.
Luke 9:25 is himself destroyed or l?
Luke 14:34 but if the salt has l its
Luke 15: 4 go after the one which is l
Luke 15: 6 found my sheep which was l!'
Luke 15: 9 found the piece which I l!'
Luke 15:24 he was l and is found.' And
Luke 15:32 and was l and is found.'"
Luke 21:18 hair of your head shall be l.
John 6:12 remain, so that nothing is l.
John 17:12 and none of them is l except
John 18: 9 whom You gave Me I have l

LOT (see LOTS)
Lev 16: 8 one l for the LORD and the
Lev 16: 8 the LORD and the other l
Num 26:55 land shall be divided by l;
Num 33:54 whatever falls to him by l.
Josh 16: 1 The l fell to the children of
Esth 3: 7 cast Pur (that is, the l),
Ps 16: 5 my cup; You maintain my l.
Prov 1:14 Cast in your l among us,
Prov 16:33 The l is cast into the lap,
Is 17:14 And the l of those who rob
Jer 13:25 This is your l,
Jon 1: 7 and the l fell on Jonah.
Luke 1: 9 his l fell to burn incense
Acts 1:26 and the l fell on Matthias.

LOT* (see LOT'S)
Gen 11:27 and Haran. Haran begot L.
Gen 11:31 son Abram and his grandson L,
Gen 13:10 And L lifted his eyes and saw
Gen 13:11 Then L chose for himself all
Gen 13:12 and L dwelt in the cities of
Gen 19: 1 and L was sitting in the
Gen 19:10 out their hands and pulled L
Gen 19:15 the angels urged L to hurry,
Gen 19:29 and sent L out of the midst
Gen 19:36 both the daughters of L
Luke 17:28 it was also in the days of L:
Luke 17:29 but on the day that L went
2Pe 2: 7 and delivered righteous L,

LOT'S† (see LOT·)
Gen 13: 7 and the herdsmen of L
Luke 17:32 Remember L wife.

LOTS (see LOT)
Lev 16: 8 Then Aaron shall cast l for
Josh 18:10 Then Joshua cast l for them
Ps 22:18 for My clothing they cast l.
Jon 1: 7 upon us." So they cast l,
Matt 27:35 My clothing they cast l.
Acts 1:26 And they cast their l,

LOUD (see LOUDER, LOUDLY)
Gen 39:14 and I cried out with a l
Ex 19:16 of the trumpet was very l,
Deut 5:22 with a l voice; and He added
1Sa 28:12 she cried out with a l
2Ki 18:28 and called out with a l
2Ch 30:21 accompanied by l
Ps 150: 5 Praise Him with l cymbals;
Prov 7:11 She was l and rebellious,
Zeph 1:10 And a l crashing from the
Matt 27:46 Jesus cried out with a l
Luke 1:42 Then she spoke out with a l
John 11:43 He cried with a l voice,
Acts 16:28 But Paul called with a l
Acts 23: 9 Then there arose a l outcry.
Rev 1:10 and I heard behind me a l
Rev 8:13 saying with a l voice,
Rev 11:15 And there were l voices in
Rev 14: 2 and like the voice of l
Rev 14: 7 saying with a l voice, "Fear
Rev 14:18 and he cried with a l cry to
Rev 21: 3 And I heard a l voice from

LOUDER (see LOUD)
Ex 19:19 sounded long and became l

LOUDLY (see LOUD)
Mark 5:38 those who wept and wailed l.

LOVE (see LOVED, LOVER, LOVES, LOVESICK, LOVING,
LOVINGKINDNESS, UNLOVED)
Gen 22: 2 only son Isaac, whom you l,
Gen 27: 4 me savory food, such as I l,
Ex 20: 6 to those who l Me and keep
Lev 19:18 but you shall l your
Lev 19:34 and you shall l him as
Deut 6: 5 You shall l the LORD your
Deut 7: 7 LORD did not set His l
Deut 7: 9 with those who l Him and
Deut 10:19 Therefore l the stranger, for
Judg 16:15 I l you,' when your heart is
2Sa 1:26 Your l to me was wonderful,
2Sa 1:26 Surpassing the l of women.
Ps 4: 2 How long will you l
Ps 5:11 Let those also who l Your
Ps 18: 1 I will l You, O LORD, my
Ps 31:23 l the LORD, all you His
Ps 40:16 Let such as l Your
Ps 45: 7 You l righteousness and hate
Ps 52: 3 You l evil more than good,
Ps 69:36 And those who l His name

Ps	91:14	Because he has set his l upon
Ps	97:10	You who l the LORD, hate
Ps	109: 5	good, And hatred for my l.
Ps	116: 1	I l the LORD, because He
Ps	119:47	commandments, Which I l.
Ps	119:97	how I l Your law! It is my
Ps	119:119	Therefore I l Your
Ps	119:159	Consider how I l Your
Ps	122: 6	May they prosper who l you.
Ps	145:20	LORD preserves all who l
Prov	4: 6	L her, and she will keep
Prov	5:19	be enraptured with her l.
Prov	7:18	let us take our fill of l
Prov	8:17	I l those who love me, And
Prov	8:36	All those who hate me l
Prov	10:12	But l covers all sins.
Prov	15:17	a dinner of herbs where l
Prov	20:13	Do not l sleep, lest you
Eccl	3: 8	A time to l, And a time
Eccl	9: 1	People know neither l nor
Eccl	9: 9	with the wife whom you l
Song	1: 2	For your l is better than
Song	1: 7	Tell me, O you whom I l,
Song	1:15	my l! Behold, you are
Song	2: 4	his banner over me was l.
Song	2: 7	Do not stir up nor awaken l
Song	2:10	said to me: "Rise up, my l,
Song	3: 1	my bed I sought the one I l;
Song	3: 3	"Have you seen the one I l?
Song	3: 4	When I found the one I l.
Song	4:10	How fair is your l,
Song	7:12	There I will give you my l.
Song	8: 6	For l is as strong as
Song	8: 7	Many waters cannot quench l,
Song	8: 7	If a man would give for l
Is	61: 8	I justice; I hate robbery
Jer	31: 3	you with an everlasting l;
Dan	9: 4	and mercy with those who l
Hos	3: 1	l a woman who is loved by
Hos	3: 1	just like the l of the LORD
Hos	3: 1	who look to other gods and l
Hos	9:15	I will l them no more. All
Hos	11: 4	cords, With bands of l,
Hos	14: 4	I will l them freely, For
Amos	5:15	l good; Establish justice
Mic	3: 2	You who hate good and l
Mic	6: 8	To l mercy, And to walk
Matt	5:43	You shall l your neighbor
Matt	5:44	l your enemies, bless those
Matt	5:46	For if you l those who love
Matt	5:46	if you love those who l
Matt	6: 5	For they l to pray standing
Matt	6:24	he will hate the one and l
Matt	19:19	You shall l your neighbor
Matt	22:37	You shall l the LORD
Matt	23: 6	They l the best places at
Matt	24:12	the l of many will grow
Mark	12:31	You shall l your neighbor
Mark	12:33	And to l Him with all the
Mark	12:33	and to l one's neighbor as
Luke	11:43	to you Pharisees! For you l
Luke	16:13	he will hate the one and l
John	8:42	you would l Me, for I
John	11: 3	he whom You l is sick."
John	13:34	that you l one another; as I
John	14:15	If you l Me, keep My
John	14:23	and My Father will l him,
John	14:24	He who does not l Me does not
John	14:31	the world may know that I l
John	15: 9	loved you; abide in My l.
John	15:13	Greater l has no one than
John	15:19	the world would l its own.
John	21:15	do you l Me more than
John	21:15	You know that I l You." He
Rom	5: 5	because the l of God has

Rom	5: 8	God demonstrates His own l
Rom	8:28	for good to those who l God,
Rom	8:35	separate us from the l of
Rom	12: 9	Let l be without
Rom	12:10	one another with brotherly l,
Rom	13:10	L does no harm to a neighbor;
Rom	13:10	therefore l is the
Rom	14:15	are no longer walking in l.
1Co	2: 9	for those who l Him.
1Co	8: 1	but l edifies.
1Co	13: 1	of angels, but have not l,
1Co	13: 2	mountains, but have not l,
1Co	13: 3	to be burned, but have not l,
1Co	13: 4	L suffers long and is kind;
1Co	13: 4	l does not envy; love does
1Co	13: 4	l does not parade itself, is
1Co	13: 8	L never fails. But whether
1Co	13:13	And now abide faith, hope, l,
1Co	13:13	the greatest of these is l.
1Co	14: 1	Pursue l, and desire
2Co	8:24	the proof of your l and of
2Co	13:11	and the God of l and peace
2Co	13:14	and the l of God, and the
Gal	5: 6	but faith working through l.
Gal	5:22	the fruit of the Spirit is l,
Eph	1: 4	blame before Him in l,
Eph	2: 4	because of His great l with
Eph	3:17	rooted and grounded in l,
Eph	3:19	to know the l of Christ which
Eph	4: 2	with one another in l,
Eph	4:15	but, speaking the truth in l,
Eph	4:16	the edifying of itself in l.
Eph	5: 2	And walk in l,
Eph	5:25	l your wives, just as Christ
Eph	5:28	So husbands ought to l their
Eph	5:33	of you in particular so l
Phil	1: 9	that your l may abound still
Phil	1:17	but the latter out of l,
Phil	2: 1	Christ, if any comfort of l,
Phil	2: 2	having the same l,
Col	1:13	kingdom of the Son of His l,
Col	2: 2	being knit together in l,
Col	3:14	all these things put on l,
1Th	1: 3	work of faith, labor of l,
1Th	3: 6	news of your faith and l,
1Th	3:12	increase and abound in l to
1Th	5: 8	breastplate of faith and l,
1Ti	1: 5	of the commandment is l
1Ti	4:12	in word, in conduct, in l,
1Ti	6:10	For the l of money is a root
1Ti	6:11	godliness, faith, l,
2Ti	1: 7	but of power and of l and of
Tit	2: 2	sound in faith, in l,
Tit	2: 4	the young women to l their
Phm	1: 5	hearing of your l and faith
Heb	6:10	your work and labor of l
Heb	10:24	in order to stir up l and
Heb	13: 1	Let brotherly l continue.
Jas	1:12	has promised to those who l
1Pe	1: 8	whom having not seen you l.
1Pe	1:22	the Spirit in sincere l of
1Pe	2:17	L the brotherhood. Fear God.
1Pe	4: 8	all things have fervent l
1Pe	4: 8	l will cover a multitude
1Pe	5:14	one another with a kiss of l.
2Pe	1: 7	and to brotherly kindness l.
1Jn	2:15	Do not l the world or the
1Jn	2:15	the l of the Father is not
1Jn	3: 1	Behold what manner of l the
1Jn	3:10	nor is he who does not l
1Jn	3:11	that we should l one
1Jn	3:16	By this we know l,
1Jn	3:17	how does the l of God abide
1Jn	3:18	let us not l in word or in
1Jn	3:23	His Son Jesus Christ and l

1Jn	4: 7	for l is of God; and
1Jn	4: 8	He who does not l does not
1Jn	4: 8	not know God, for God is l.
1Jn	4: 9	In this the l of God was
1Jn	4:10	In this is l, not that we
1Jn	4:11	we also ought to l one
1Jn	4:12	If we l one another, God
1Jn	4:12	and His l has been perfected
1Jn	4:16	God has for us. God is l,
1Jn	4:16	and he who abides in l
1Jn	4:18	There is no fear in l;
1Jn	4:19	We l Him because He first
1Jn	4:20	I l God," and hates his
1Jn	4:20	for he who does not l his
1Jn	4:20	how can he l God whom he has
1Jn	5: 2	By this we know that we l the
1Jn	5: 2	when we l God and keep His
1Jn	5: 3	For this is the l of God,
2Jn	6	This is l, that we walk
Rev	2: 4	you have left your first l.
Rev	2:19	"I know your works, l,

LOVED (see LOVE)

Gen	25:28	And Isaac l Esau because he
Gen	25:28	but Rebekah l Jacob.
Gen	27:14	food, such as his father l.
Gen	29:18	Now Jacob l Rachel; so he
Gen	37: 3	Now Israel l Joseph more than
1Sa	1: 5	for he l Hannah, although
1Sa	18: 1	and Jonathan l him as his
1Ki	3: 3	And Solomon l the LORD,
1Ki	11: 1	But King Solomon l many
Ps	38:11	My l ones and my friends
Ps	78:68	Mount Zion which He l.
Jer	31: 3	I have l you with an
Hos	3: 1	love a woman who is l by a
Hos	11: 1	I l him, And out of Egypt I
Mal	1: 2	I have l you," says the
Luke	7:47	for she l much. But to whom
John	3:16	For God so l the world that
John	3:19	and men l darkness rather
John	11: 5	Now Jesus l Martha and her
John	11:36	See how He l him!"
John	12:43	for they l the praise of men
John	13: 1	having l His own who were in
John	13: 1	He l them to the end.
John	13:23	His disciples, whom Jesus l.
John	14:28	If you l Me, you would
John	15: 9	I also have l you; abide in
John	15:12	one another as I have l you.
John	20: 2	other disciple, whom Jesus l,
Rom	8:37	through Him who l us.
Rom	9:13	"Jacob I have l,
Gal	2:20	who l me and gave Himself
Eph	2: 4	great love with which He l
Eph	5: 2	as Christ also has l us and
Eph	5:25	just as Christ also l the
2Ti	4: 8	but also to all who have l
2Ti	4:10	having l this present world,
Heb	1: 9	You have l righteousness
1Jn	4:10	not that we l God, but that
1Jn	4:10	but that He l us and sent
1Jn	4:11	if God so l us, we also
1Jn	4:19	love Him because He first l
Rev	1: 5	To Him who l us and washed
Rev	3: 9	and to know that I have l

LOVELINESS† (see LOVELY)

Is	40: 6	And all its l is like the

LOVELY (see LOVELINESS)

Ps	84: 1	How l is Your tabernacle,
Song	1: 5	I am dark, but l,
Song	4: 3	And your mouth is l.
Song	5:16	Yes, he is altogether l.
Phil	4: 8	pure, whatever things are l,

LOVER† (see LOVE, LOVERS)

Hos	3: 1	woman who is loved by a l
Tit	1: 8	a l of what is good,

LOVERS (see LOVER)

Hos	2: 5	said, 'I will go after my l,
Hos	8: 9	itself; Ephraim has hired l.
Luke	16:14	who were l of money, also
2Ti	3: 2	For men will be l of
2Ti	3: 2	l of money, boasters, proud,
2Ti	3: 4	l of pleasure rather than
2Ti	3: 4	of pleasure rather than l

LOVES (see LOVE)

Gen	27: 9	your father, such as he l.
Deut	7: 8	but because the LORD l you,
Deut	10:18	and l the stranger, giving
Ruth	4:15	who l you, who is better to
Ps	33: 5	He l righteousness and
Ps	34:12	And l many days, that he
Ps	37:28	For the LORD l justice,
Ps	47: 4	of Jacob whom He l.
Ps	87: 2	The LORD l the gates of
Prov	3:12	For whom the LORD l He
Prov	12: 1	Whoever l instruction loves
Prov	17:17	A friend l at all times,
Prov	29: 3	Whoever l wisdom makes his
Is	1:23	Everyone l bribes, And
Matt	10:37	He who l father or mother
Matt	10:37	And he who l son or daughter
Luke	7: 5	for he l our nation, And
John	3:35	The Father l the Son, and has
John	12:25	He who l his life will lose
John	14:21	it is he who l Me. And he
John	16:27	for the Father Himself l you,
1Co	8: 3	But if anyone l God, this one
2Co	9: 7	for God l a cheerful giver.
Eph	5:28	he who loves his wife l
Heb	12: 6	For whom the LORD l
1Jn	2:10	He who l his brother abides
1Jn	2:15	If anyone l the world, the
1Jn	4: 7	and everyone who l is born
1Jn	4:21	that he who l God must love

LOVESICK† (see LOVE)

Song	2: 5	me with apples, For I am l.
Song	5: 8	That you tell him I am l!

LOVING (see LOVE)

Prov	5:19	As a l deer and a graceful

LOVINGKINDNESS (see LOVE, LOVINGKINDNESSES)

Ps	36: 7	How precious is Your l,
Ps	36:10	continue Your l to those who
Ps	40:10	I have not concealed Your l
Ps	40:11	Let Your l and Your truth
Ps	51: 1	O God, According to Your l;
Ps	63: 3	Because Your l is better
Ps	92: 2	To declare Your l in the
Ps	103: 4	Who crowns you with l and
Ps	107:43	they will understand the l
Jer	31: 3	Therefore with l I have
Jer	32:18	You show l to thousands, and
Hos	2:19	In l and mercy;
Jon	4: 2	to anger and abundant in l,

LOVINGKINDNESSES (see LOVINGKINDNESS)

Ps	25: 6	tender mercies and Your l,
Is	63: 7	to the multitude of His l.

LOWING†

1Sa	6:12	l as they went, and did not
1Sa	15:14	and the l of the oxen which

LOWLAND (see LOWLANDS)

Deut	1: 7	the mountains and in the l,

LOWLANDS (see LOWLAND)

Josh	11:16	of Israel and its l,

LOWLINESS† (see LOWLY)
Eph 4: 2 with all l and gentleness,
Phil 2: 3 but in l of mind let each

LOWLY (see LOWLINESS)
Ps 136:23 Who remembered us in our l
Ps 138: 6 high, Yet He regards the l;
Prov 16:19 a humble spirit with the l,
Zech 9: 9 L and riding on a donkey,
Matt 11:29 for I am gentle and l in
Matt 21: 5 is coming to you, L,
Luke 1:48 For He has regarded the l
Luke 1:52 thrones, And exalted the l.

LOYAL (see LOYALTY)
1Ki 8:61 your heart therefore be l
Matt 6:24 or else he will be l to the

LOYALTY (see LOYAL)
2Sa 3: 8 Today I show l to the house

LUCIFER†
Is 14:12 are fallen from heaven, O L,

LUKE†
Col 4:14 L the beloved physician and
2Ti 4:11 Only L is with me. Get Mark
Phm 1:24 Mark, Aristarchus, Demas, L,

LUKEWARM†
Rev 3:16 "So then, because you are l,

LULLED†
Judg 16:19 Then she l him to sleep on

LUMP
2Ki 20: 7 Take a l of figs." So they
Rom 9:21 from the same l to make one
Rom 11:16 the l is also holy; and if
1Co 5: 6 leaven leavens the whole l?
1Co 5: 7 that you may be a new l,

LURKING
Prov 7:12 L at every corner.

LUST (see LUSTED, LUSTFUL, LUSTS, LUSTY)
Prov 6:25 Do not l after her beauty in
Matt 5:28 looks at a woman to l for
Rom 1:27 burned in their l for one
Rom 13:13 not in lewdness and l,
1Co 10: 6 intent that we should not l
Gal 5:16 you shall not fulfill the l
1Th 4: 5 not in passion of l,
Jas 4: 2 You l and do not have. You
2Pe 1: 4 is in the world through l.
1Jn 2:16 the l of the eyes, and the
1Jn 2:17 and the l of it; but he who

LUSTED (see LUST)
1Co 10: 6 evil things as they also l.

LUSTFUL† (see LUST)
Jer 13:27 your adulteries And your l

LUSTS (see LUST)
Rom 1:24 in the l of their hearts, to
Rom 6:12 you should obey it in its l.
Rom 13:14 flesh, to fulfill its l.
Gal 5:17 For the flesh l against the
Eph 4:22 according to the deceitful l
1Ti 6: 9 many foolish and harmful l
2Ti 2:22 Flee also youthful l;
2Ti 3: 6 sins, led away by various l,
Tit 2:12 ungodliness and worldly l,
1Pe 1:14 yourselves to the former l,
1Pe 2:11 abstain from fleshly l which

LUSTY† (see LUST)
Jer 5: 8 They were like well-fed l

LUTE†
Ps 57: 8 l and harp! I will awaken
Ps 71:22 Also with the l I will

Ps 81: 2 pleasant harp with the l.
Ps 92: 3 of ten strings, On the l,
Ps 108: 2 l and harp! I will awaken
Ps 150: 3 Praise Him with the l and

LUXURY
Prov 19:10 L is not fitting for a fool,
Luke 7:25 appareled and live in l are
Jas 5: 5 the earth in pleasure and l;
Rev 18: 3 the abundance of her l.

LUZ
Gen 28:19 name of that city had been L

LYDDA
Acts 9:38 And since L was near Joppa,

LYDIA
Ezek 27:10 "Those from Persia, L,
Acts 16:14 Now a certain woman named L

LYE†
Jer 2:22 you wash yourself with l,

LYING (see LIE)
Deut 33:13 And the deep l beneath,
Ruth 3: 8 a woman was l at his feet.
Ps 31:18 Let the l lips be put to
Ps 59:12 And for the cursing and l
Ps 119:163 I hate and abhor l,
Prov 6:17 A l tongue, Hands that
Prov 12:22 L lips are an abomination
Matt 8: 6 my servant is l at home
Matt 8:14 He saw his wife's mother l
Matt 9: 2 to Him a paralytic l on a
Mark 5:40 where the child was l.
Mark 7:30 and her daughter l on the
Luke 2:12 l in a manger."
Luke 2:16 and the Babe l in a manger.
Luke 5:25 took up what he had been l
Luke 11:54 l in wait for Him, and
Luke 24:12 he saw the linen cloths l by
John 5: 6 When Jesus saw him l there,
John 11:41 where the dead man was l.
John 20: 5 saw the linen cloths l
John 20: 6 he saw the linen cloths l
Rom 9: 1 truth in Christ, I am not l,
Eph 4:25 Therefore, putting away l,
2Th 2: 9 and l wonders,
1Ti 2: 7 truth in Christ and not l—

LYSTRA
Acts 16: 1 Then he came to Derbe and L.
2Ti 3:11 at Antioch, at Iconium, at L—

M

MACEDONIA
Acts 16: 9 A man of M stood and pleaded
Acts 16: 9 Come over to M and help us."
2Co 8: 1 on the churches of M:
1Th 1: 7 became examples to all in M
1Th 1: 8 not only in M and Achaia,

MACHIR
Num 32:40 So Moses gave Gilead to M the

MACHPELAH
Gen 23: 9 he may give me the cave of M
Gen 23:17 of Ephron which was in M,
Gen 25: 9 buried him in the cave of M,
Gen 50:13 the cave of the field of M,

MAD (see MADMAN, MADNESS)
Deut 28:34 So you shall be driven m
John 10:20 "He has a demon and is m.
Acts 26:24 learning is driving you m!
Acts 26:25 But he said, "I am not m,

MADE (*see* ESTABLISHED, MAKE, TOOK)

Gen	1: 7	Thus God **m** the firmament, and
Gen	1:16	Then God **m** two great lights:
Gen	1:16	He **m** the stars also.
Gen	1:31	saw everything that He had **m**,
Gen	2: 3	which God had created and **m**.
Gen	3: 7	fig leaves together and **m**
Gen	5: 1	He **m** him in the likeness of
Gen	6: 7	for I am sorry that I have **m**
Gen	8: 1	And God **m** a wind to pass
Gen	9: 6	in the image of God He **m**
Gen	14:23	I have **m** Abram rich'—
Gen	15:18	On the same day the LORD **m**
Gen	19: 3	Then he **m** them a feast, and
Gen	19:33	So they **m** their father drink
Gen	21: 6	God has **m** me laugh, and all
Gen	24:37	Now my master **m** me swear,
Gen	24:46	And she **m** haste and let her
Gen	26:22	For now the LORD has **m** room
Gen	27:14	and his mother **m** savory
Gen	28:20	Then Jacob **m** a vow, saying,
Gen	30:40	and **m** the flocks face toward
Gen	33:17	and **m** booths for his
Gen	37: 3	Also he **m** him a tunic of
Gen	39: 4	Then he **m** him overseer of
Gen	41:51	For God has **m** me forget all
Gen	45: 8	and He has **m** me a father to
Gen	45: 9	God has **m** me lord of all
Gen	46:29	So Joseph **m** ready his chariot
Gen	47:26	And Joseph **m** it a law over
Gen	50: 5	My father **m** me swear, saying,
Ex	1:14	And they **m** their lives bitter
Ex	1:14	service in which they **m**
Ex	2:14	Who **m** you a prince and a
Ex	4:11	Who has **m** man's mouth? Or who
Ex	5: 8	quota of bricks which they **m**
Ex	7: 1	I have **m** you as God to
Ex	15:25	the waters were **m** sweet.
Ex	15:25	There He **m** a statute and an
Ex	18:25	and **m** them heads over the
Ex	20:11	For in six days the LORD **m**
Ex	29:18	an offering **m** by fire to the
Ex	31:18	And when He had **m** an end of
Ex	32: 4	and **m** a molded calf. Then
Ex	32:31	and have **m** for themselves a
Ex	32:35	with the calf which Aaron **m**.
Ex	37: 1	Then Bezalel **m** the ark of
Ex	39: 1	and **m** the holy garments for
Lev	1: 9	an offering **m** by fire, a
Lev	2:11	to the LORD shall be **m**
Lev	13:48	in leather or in anything **m**
Lev	13:49	or in anything **m** of leather,
Lev	22: 4	whoever touches anything **m**
Num	5: 8	with which atonement is **m**
Num	5:27	When he has **m** her drink the
Num	6: 3	made from wine nor vinegar **m**
Num	8:21	and Aaron **m** atonement for
Num	14:36	who returned and **m** all the
Num	21: 2	So Israel **m** a vow to the
Num	21: 9	So Moses **m** a bronze serpent,
Num	30:11	and **m** no response to her
Num	30:12	her husband has **m** them void,
Num	32:13	and He **m** them wander in the
Deut	1:15	and **m** them heads over you,
Deut	2:30	hardened his spirit and **m**
Deut	5: 2	The LORD our God **m** a
Deut	9:21	the calf which you had **m**,
Deut	29: 1	the covenant which He **m**
Deut	32:13	He **m** him ride in the heights
Deut	32:13	He **m** him draw honey from
Deut	32:15	Then he forsook God who **m**
Josh	2:20	from your oath which you **m**
Josh	5: 3	So Joshua **m** flint knives for
Josh	8:28	So Joshua burned Ai and **m** it
Josh	9:15	So Joshua **m** peace with them,

Josh	9:15	and **m** a covenant with them
Josh	10: 5	camped before Gibeon and **m**
Josh	11:18	Joshua **m** war a long time with
Josh	24:25	So Joshua **m** a covenant with
Josh	24:25	and **m** for them a statute and
Judg	3:16	Now Ehud **m** himself a dagger
Judg	9: 6	and they went and **m**
Judg	9:27	and **m** merry. And they went
Judg	11:30	And Jephthah **m** a vow to the
Judg	17: 4	and he **m** it into a carved
1Sa	1:11	Then she **m** a vow and said,
1Sa	3:13	because his sons **m**
1Sa	8: 1	Samuel was old that he **m**
1Sa	11:15	and there they **m** Saul king
1Sa	15:35	regretted that He had **m**
1Sa	16: 8	and **m** him pass before
1Sa	16:10	Thus Jesse **m** seven of his
1Sa	18: 3	Then Jonathan and David **m** a
1Sa	20:16	So Jonathan **m** a covenant
2Sa	5: 3	and King David **m** a covenant
2Sa	7: 9	and have **m** you a great name,
2Sa	8:13	And David **m** himself a name
1Ki	1:43	Our lord King David has **m**
1Ki	1:44	and they have **m** him ride on
1Ki	3: 1	Now Solomon **m** a treaty with
1Ki	3: 7	You have **m** Your servant king
1Ki	4: 7	each one **m** provision for one
1Ki	5:12	and the two of them **m** a
1Ki	6: 4	And he **m** for the house
1Ki	10: 9	therefore He **m** you king, to
1Ki	12: 4	Your father **m** our yoke heavy;
1Ki	12:20	and **m** him king over all
1Ki	12:28	**m** two calves of gold, and
1Ki	12:31	He **m** shrines on the high
1Ki	12:31	and **m** priests from every
1Ki	14: 7	and **m** you ruler over My
1Ki	14: 9	for you have gone and **m** for
1Ki	14:16	who sinned and who **m** Israel
1Ki	14:26	shields which Solomon had **m**.
1Ki	15:26	in his sin by which he had **m**
1Ki	15:30	sinned and by which he had **m**
1Ki	15:34	in his sin by which he had **m**
1Ki	18:26	the altar which they had **m**.
1Ki	18:32	and he **m** a trench around the
1Ki	22:44	Also Jehoshaphat **m** peace with
1Ki	22:45	and how he **m** war, are they
1Ki	22:48	Jehoshaphat **m** merchant ships
1Ki	22:52	who had **m** Israel sin;
2Ki	6: 6	and he **m** the iron float.
2Ki	9:21	And his chariot was **m**
2Ki	11:17	Then Jehoiada **m** a covenant
2Ki	14:21	and **m** him king instead of
2Ki	16: 3	indeed he **m** his son pass
2Ki	17:21	and they **m** Jeroboam the son
2Ki	17:30	the men of Cuth **m** Nergal,
2Ki	18: 4	serpent that Moses had **m**;
2Ki	19:15	You have **m** heaven and earth.
2Ki	20:20	and how he **m** a pool and a
2Ki	21: 7	of Asherah that he had **m**,
2Ki	21:11	and has also **m** Judah sin
2Ki	21:24	the people of the land **m**
2Ki	23: 3	stood by a pillar and **m** a
2Ki	23:34	Then Pharaoh Necho **m** Eliakim
1Ch	16: 5	but Asaph **m** music with
1Ch	22: 8	shed much blood and have **m**
1Ch	28: 2	and had **m** preparations to
2Ch	6:29	whatever supplication is **m**
2Ch	6:40	attentive to the prayer **m**
2Ch	12: 9	shields which Solomon had **m**.
2Ch	12:10	Then King Rehoboam **m** bronze
2Ch	25:27	they **m** a conspiracy against
2Ch	26: 5	God **m** him prosper.
2Ch	33:25	the people of the land **m**
2Ch	34:31	stood in his place and **m** a
2Ch	35:25	They **m** it a custom in

2Ch	36:22	so that he **m** a proclamation
Ezra	1: 1	so that he **m** a proclamation
Ezra	5:14	whom he had **m** governor.
Neh	3: 9	Jerusalem, and **m** repairs.
Neh	4: 9	Nevertheless we **m** our prayer
Neh	9:10	So You **m** a name for
Esth	1: 5	the king **m** a feast lasting
Esth	1: 9	Queen Vashti also **m** a feast
Esth	2:17	crown upon her head and **m**
Esth	5:14	to him, "Let a gallows be **m**,
Esth	9:17	month they rested and **m** it
Esth	9:18	and **m** it a day of feasting
Job	1:10	Have You not **m** a hedge around
Job	4:14	Which **m** all my bones shake.
Job	10: 9	that You have **m** me like
Job	17: 6	But He has **m** me a byword of
Job	23:16	For God **m** my heart weak,
Job	27: 2	who has **m** my soul bitter,
Job	28:26	When He **m** a law for the
Job	31: 1	I have **m** a covenant with my
Job	31:15	Did not He who **m** me in the
Job	33: 4	The Spirit of God has **m** me,
Ps	8: 5	For You have **m** him a little
Ps	8: 6	You have **m** him to have
Ps	18: 4	the floods of ungodliness **m**
Ps	18:35	Your gentleness has **m** me
Ps	18:43	You have **m** me the head of
Ps	22: 9	You **m** Me trust while on My
Ps	33: 6	the LORD the heavens were **m**,
Ps	39: 5	You have **m** my days as
Ps	72:15	Prayer also will be **m** for
Ps	74:17	You have **m** summer and
Ps	78:13	And He **m** the waters stand
Ps	80:15	And the branch that You **m**
Ps	80:17	the son of man whom You **m**
Ps	89:44	You have **m** his glory cease,
Ps	92: 4	have **m** me glad through Your
Ps	95: 5	for He **m** it; And His hands
Ps	98: 2	The LORD has **m** known His
Ps	100: 3	It is He who has **m** us,
Ps	103: 7	He **m** known His ways to
Ps	104:24	In wisdom You have **m** them
Ps	104:26	Leviathan Which You have **m**
Ps	106:19	They **m** a calf in Horeb, And
Ps	115:15	Who **m** heaven and earth.
Ps	118:24	is the day the LORD has **m**;
Ps	136: 5	To Him who by wisdom **m** the
Ps	136: 7	To Him who **m** great lights,
Ps	139:14	fearfully and wonderfully **m**;
Ps	139:15	When I was **m** in secret,
Prov	13: 4	of the diligent shall be **m**
Prov	20: 9	I have **m** my heart clean, I
Prov	20:12	The LORD has **m** them both.
Eccl	1:15	is crooked cannot be **m**
Eccl	2: 4	I **m** my works great, I built
Eccl	2: 5	I **m** myself gardens and
Eccl	3:11	He has **m** everything beautiful
Eccl	7:29	That God **m** man upright,
Is	1: 9	We would have been **m** like
Is	2: 8	their own fingers have **m**.
Is	2:20	idols of gold, Which they **m**,
Is	5: 2	And also **m** a winepress in
Is	22:11	You also **m** a reservoir
Is	27:11	Therefore He who **m** them
Is	28:15	We have **m** a covenant with
Is	28:15	for we have **m** lies our
Is	29:16	For shall the thing **m** say
Is	31: 7	which your own hands have **m**
Is	40: 4	crooked places shall be **m**
Is	43: 7	I have **m** him."
Is	45:18	Who formed the earth and **m**
Is	49: 1	matrix of My mother He has **m**
Is	51:12	son of a man who will be **m**
Is	52:10	The LORD has **m** bare His
Is	53: 9	And they **m** His grave with
Is	53:12	And **m** intercession for the
Is	63: 6	**M** them drunk in My fury,
Is	66: 2	those things My hand has **m**,
Jer	1:18	I have **m** you this day A
Jer	2: 7	you defiled My land And **m**
Jer	10:11	The gods that have not **m** the
Jer	17:23	but **m** their neck stiff, that
Jer	18: 4	And the vessel that he **m** of
Jer	18: 4	so he **m** it again into
Jer	19:11	which cannot be **m** whole
Jer	25:17	and **m** all the nations drink,
Jer	29:26	The LORD has **m** you priest
Jer	31:32	to the covenant that I **m**
Jer	34:11	changed their minds and **m**
Jer	34:15	and you **m** a covenant before
Jer	46:16	He **m** many fall; Yes, one
Lam	1:13	He has **m** me desolate And
Lam	1:14	He **m** my strength fail; The
Lam	3: 2	He has led me and **m** me walk
Lam	3: 7	He has **m** my chain heavy.
Lam	3:15	He has **m** me drink wormwood.
Ezek	3: 8	I have **m** your face strong
Ezek	3: 9	I have **m** your forehead; do
Ezek	3:17	I have **m** you a watchman for
Ezek	12: 6	for I have **m** you a sign to
Ezek	16:25	and **m** your beauty to be
Ezek	20: 5	and **m** Myself known to them
Ezek	22:12	you have **m** profit from your
Ezek	27:11	They **m** your beauty
Ezek	27:16	the abundance of goods you **m**.
Ezek	29: 9	and I have **m** it.'
Ezek	31: 9	I **m** it beautiful with a
Ezek	33: 7	I have **m** you a watchman for
Dan	2:28	and He has **m** known to King
Dan	2:29	He who reveals secrets has **m**
Dan	3: 1	Nebuchadnezzar the king **m** an
Dan	4: 5	I saw a dream which **m** me
Dan	5: 1	Belshazzar the king **m** a great
Dan	9: 4	and confession, and said,
Dan	10:10	which **m** me tremble on my
Hos	8: 4	silver and gold They **m**
Hos	8: 6	A workman **m** it, and it is
Amos	5: 8	He **m** the Pleiades and Orion;
Jon	1: 9	who **m** the sea and the dry
Jon	4: 5	There he **m** himself a shelter
Jon	4: 6	God prepared a plant and **m**
Jon	4:10	nor **m** it grow, which came up
Zeph	2: 8	And **m** arrogant threats
Mal	2: 9	Therefore I also have **m** you
Matt	9:16	and the tear is **m** worse.
Matt	9:22	your faith has **m** you well."
Matt	15:31	the maimed **m** whole, the
Matt	18:25	had, and that payment be **m**.
Matt	19:12	there are eunuchs who were **m**
Matt	21:13	but you have **m** it a 'den.
Matt	24:45	whom his master **m** ruler over
Matt	25:16	and **m** another five talents.
Matt	26:33	Even if all are **m** to stumble
Matt	27:64	command that the tomb be **m**
Matt	27:66	So they went and **m** the tomb
Mark	2:27	The Sabbath was **m** for man,
Mark	10: 6	**m** them male and female.'
Mark	14:58	will destroy this temple **m**
Luke	1:62	So they **m** signs to his
Luke	2:15	which the Lord has **m** known
Luke	2:17	they **m** widely known the
Luke	3: 5	places shall be **m**
Luke	4:38	and they **m** request of Him
Luke	9:15	and **m** them all sit down.
Luke	12:14	who **m** Me a judge or an
Luke	23:19	for a certain rebellion **m**
John	1: 3	All things were **m** through
John	1: 3	nothing was made that was **m**.
John	1:10	and the world was **m** through
John	2: 9	tasted the water that was **m**

John 2:15 When He had **m** a whip of
John 5: 4 was **m** well of whatever
John 5: 6 Do you want to be **m** well?"
John 8:33 You will be **m** free'?"
John 9: 6 He spat on the ground and **m**
John 9:11 A Man called Jesus **m** clay and
John 15:15 from My Father I have **m**
John 17:23 that they may be **m** perfect
John 19: 7 because He **m** Himself the Son
John 19:23 took His garments and **m** four
Acts 1: 1 The former account I **m**,
Acts 2:36 assuredly that God has **m**
Acts 3:12 power or godliness we had **m**
Acts 7:48 does not dwell in temples **m**
Acts 8: 3 he **m** havoc of the church,
Acts 15: 9 and **m** no distinction between
Acts 16:13 prayer was customarily **m**;
Acts 17:24 who **m** the world and
Acts 17:24 does not dwell in temples **m**
Acts 17:26 And He has **m** from one blood
Acts 19:26 are not gods which are **m**
Rom 1:20 by the things that are **m**,
Rom 1:23 God into an image **m** like
Rom 4:14 made void and the promise **m**
Rom 4:17 I have **m** you a father
Rom 5:19 disobedience many were **m**
Rom 5:19 obedience many will be **m**
Rom 9:20 Why have you **m** me like
Rom 9:29 we would have been **m**
Rom 10:10 the mouth confession is **m**
Rom 15: 8 to confirm the promises **m**
Rom 15:20 And so I have **m** it my aim to
Rom 16:26 but now has been **m** manifest,
Rom 16:26 Scriptures has been **m** known
1Co 1:17 cross of Christ should be **m**
1Co 1:20 Has not God **m** foolish the
1Co 4:13 We have been **m** as the filth
1Co 9:19 I have **m** myself a servant to
1Co 12:13 and have all been **m** to drink
1Co 15:22 so in Christ all shall be **m**
1Co 15:28 Now when all things are **m**
1Co 15:36 what you sow is not **m** alive
1Co 15:47 **m** of dust; the second Man
2Co 5: 1 a house not **m** with hands,
2Co 5:21 For He **m** Him who knew no sin
2Co 12: 9 for My strength is **m** perfect
2Co 13: 9 that you may be **m** complete.
Gal 3: 3 are you now being **m** perfect
Gal 3:19 to whom the promise was **m**;
Gal 5: 1 by which Christ has **m** us
Eph 1: 6 by which He has **m** us
Eph 1: 8 which He **m** to abound toward
Eph 1: 9 having **m** known to us the
Eph 2: 1 And you He **m** alive, who
Eph 2: 5 **m** us alive together with
Eph 2: 6 and **m** us sit together in
Eph 2:14 who has **m** both one, and has
Phil 2: 7 but **m** Himself of no
Phil 4: 6 let your requests be **m** known
Col 1:20 having **m** peace through the
Col 2:11 with the circumcision **m**
Col 2:13 He has **m** alive together with
Col 2:15 He **m** a public spectacle of
Heb 1: 2 through whom also He **m** the
Heb 2: 7 You have **m** him a
Heb 6:13 For when God **m** a promise to
Heb 7: 3 but **m** like the Son of God,
Heb 7:19 for the law **m** nothing
Heb 8: 9 the covenant that I **m**
Heb 8:13 He has **m** the first
Heb 9:11 perfect tabernacle not **m**
Heb 9:24 entered the holy places **m**
Heb 10:13 till His enemies are **m** His
Heb 11: 3 which are seen were not **m**
Heb 11:22 **m** mention of the departure

Heb 11:34 out of weakness were **m**
Heb 12:23 to the spirits of just men **m**
Heb 12:27 as of things that are **m**,
Jas 2:22 and by works faith was **m**
1Pe 3:18 to death in the flesh but **m**
1Pe 3:22 and powers having been **m**
2Pe 1:16 devised fables when we **m**
1Jn 5:10 does not believe God has **m**
Rev 1: 6 and has **m** us kings and

MADMAN (*see* MAD, MADMEN)
1Sa 21:15 this fellow to play the **m**

MADMEN (*see* MADMAN)
1Sa 21:15 "Have I need of **m**,

MADNESS (*see* MAD)
Deut 28:28 will strike you with **m** and
1Sa 21:13 feigned **m** in their hands,
Eccl 1:17 to know wisdom and to know **m**
2Pe 2:16 voice restrained the **m** of

MAGDALA† (*see* MAGDALENE)
Matt 15:39 and came to the region of **M**.

MAGDALENE (*see* MAGDALA)
Mark 16: 9 He appeared first to Mary **M**,
Luke 8: 2 infirmities—Mary called **M**,
John 20:18 Mary **M** came and told the

MAGGOT†
Job 25: 6 much less man, who is a **m**,
Is 14:11 The **m** is spread under you,

MAGIC (*see* MAGICIAN)
Acts 19:19 of those who had practiced **m**

MAGICIAN (*see* MAGIC, MAGICIANS)
Dan 2:10 asked such things of any **m**,

MAGICIANS (*see* MAGICIAN)
Gen 41: 8 and called for all the **m** of
Ex 7:22 Then the **m** of Egypt did so
Dan 2: 2 the command to call the **m**,

MAGISTRATE† (*see* MAGISTRATES)
Luke 12:58 with your adversary to the **m**,

MAGISTRATES (*see* MAGISTRATE)
Luke 12:11 you to the synagogues and **m**
Acts 16:20 they brought them to the **m**,

MAGNIFIED (*see* EXALTED, MAGNIFY)
2Sa 7:26 So let Your name be **m**
Ps 35:27 "Let the LORD be **m**,
Ps 138: 2 For You have **m** Your word
Acts 19:17 name of the Lord Jesus was **m**.
Phil 1:20 so now also Christ will be **m**

MAGNIFIES† (*see* MAGNIFY)
Luke 1:46 My soul **m** the Lord,

MAGNIFY (*see* EXALT, MAGNIFIED, MAGNIFIES)
Ps 34: 3 **m** the LORD with me, And
Dan 11:36 he shall exalt and **m** himself
Acts 10:46 speak with tongues and **m**
Rom 11:13 I **m** my ministry,

MAGOG† (*see* GOG)
Gen 10: 2 of Japheth were Gomer, **M**,
1Ch 1: 5 of Japheth were Gomer, **M**,
Ezek 38: 2 Gog, of the land of **M**,
Ezek 39: 6 And I will send fire on **M** and
Rev 20: 8 of the earth, Gog and **M**,

MAHANAIM
2Sa 17:24 Then David went to **M**.

MAHER-SHALAL-HASH-BAZ
Is 8: 3 to me, "Call his name **M**;

MAHLON
Ruth 4:10 Moabitess, the widow of **M**,

MAID (*see* MAIDEN, MAIDS)
Gen   16: 2   Please, go in to my **m**;
Gen   16: 8   He said, "Hagar, Sarai's **m**,
Gen   29:24   And Laban gave his **m** Zilpah
Ex   2: 5   she sent her **m** to get it.

MAIDEN† (*see* MAID, MAIDENS)
Ex   2: 8   So the **m** went and called
Jer   51:22   the young man and the **m**;

MAIDENS (*see* MAIDEN)
Ex   2: 5   And her **m** walked along the
Ps   68:25   Among them were the the **m**
Ps   148:12   Both young men and **m**;
Prov   9: 3   She has sent out her **m**,

MAIDS (*see* MAID)
Gen   24:61   Then Rebekah and her **m**
Esth   4:16   My **m** and I will fast

MAIDSERVANT (*see* FEMALE, MAIDSERVANTS, SERVANT)
Gen   16: 1   And she had an Egyptian **m**
Gen   25:12   the Egyptian, Sarah's **m**,
Gen   35:25   sons of Bilhah, Rachel's **m**,
Gen   35:26   the sons of Zilpah, Leah's **m**,
Ruth   2:13   have spoken kindly to your **m**,
Ruth   3: 9   "I am Ruth, your **m**.
Ruth   3: 9   Take your **m** under your wing,
1Sa   1:11   on the affliction of Your **m**
Ps   86:16   And save the son of Your **m**.
Prov   30:23   And a **m** who succeeds her
Luke   1:38   Behold the **m** of the Lord! Let
Luke   1:48   the lowly state of His **m**;

MAIDSERVANTS (*see* FEMALE, MAIDSERVANT)
Gen   33: 1   Leah, Rachel, and the two **m**.
Ruth   2:13   I am not like one of your **m**.
Prov   31:15   And a portion for her **m**.
Joel   2:29   menservants and on My **m** I
Acts   2:18   and on My **m** I will

MAIL
1Sa   17: 5   was armed with a coat of **m**,
1Sa   17:38   clothed him with a coat of **m**.

MAIMED
Lev   22:22   are blind or broken or **m**,
Matt   15:30   the lame, blind, mute, **m**,
Matt   15:31   the **m** made whole, the lame
Matt   18: 8   to enter into life lame or **m**,
Luke   14:13   invite the poor, the **m**,

MAIN
1Ki   7:50   and for the doors of the **m**
Heb   8: 1   Now this is the **m** point of

MAINTAIN (*see* MAINTAINED)
1Ki   8:45   and their cause.
1Ch   26:27   battles they dedicated to **m**
Ps   16: 5   You **m** my lot.
Tit   3: 8   God should be careful to **m**

MAINTAINED (*see* MAINTAIN)
Ps   9: 4   For You have **m** my right and

MAJESTIC (*see* MAJESTY)
Job   37: 4   He thunders with His **m**
Is   33:21   But there the **m** LORD will

MAJESTY (*see* MAJESTIC)
1Ch   16:27   Honor and **m** are before Him;
Job   37:22   With God is awesome **m**.
Ps   29: 4   of the LORD is full of **m**.
Ps   45: 3   With Your glory and Your **m**.
Ps   45: 4   And in Your **m** ride
Ps   93: 1   reigns, He is clothed with **m**;
Ps   96: 6   Honor and **m** are before Him;
Ps   145: 5   glorious splendor of Your **m**,
Ps   145:12   And the glorious **m** of His
Is   2:10   And the glory of His **m**.

Is   26:10   And will not behold the **m**
Dan   4:30   and for the honor of my **m**?
Mic   5: 4   In the **m** of the name of the
Luke   9:43   were all amazed at the **m** of
Heb   1: 3   at the right hand of the **M**
Heb   8: 1   hand of the throne of the **M**
2Pe   1:16   were eyewitnesses of His **m**.
Jude   25   is wise, Be glory and **m**,

MAKE (*see* MADE, MAKER, MAKES, MAKING)
Gen   1:26   Let Us **m** man in Our image,
Gen   2:18   I will **m** him a helper
Gen   3: 6   and a tree desirable to **m**
Gen   6:14   **M** yourself an ark of
Gen   9:12   of the covenant which I **m**
Gen   11: 3   let us **m** bricks and bake
Gen   11: 4   let us **m** a name for
Gen   12: 2   I will **m** you a great nation;
Gen   12: 2   I will bless you And **m**
Gen   13:16   And I will **m** your descendants
Gen   17: 2   And I will **m** My covenant
Gen   17: 6   and I will **m** nations of you,
Gen   19:34   let us **m** him drink wine
Gen   27: 4   And me savory food, such as
Gen   35: 1   and **m** an altar there to God,
Gen   40:14   **m** mention of me to Pharaoh,
Ex   5: 7   give the people straw to **m**
Ex   9: 4   And the LORD will **m** a
Ex   20: 4   You shall not **m** for yourself
Ex   20:23   You shall not **m** anything to
Ex   22: 3   He should **m** full
Ex   23:13   be circumspect and **m** no
Ex   23:32   You shall **m** no covenant with
Ex   25:10   And they shall **m** an ark of
Ex   28: 2   And you shall **m** holy garments
Ex   29:36   cleanse the altar when you **m**
Ex   32: 1   **m** us gods that shall go
Ex   33:19   I will **m** all My goodness pass
Lev   4:35   So the priest shall **m**
Lev   22:22   nor **m** an offering by fire of
Lev   26: 1   You shall not **m** idols for
Lev   26: 6   and none will **m** you afraid;
Lev   26:22   and **m** you few in number; and
Num   5:21   the LORD **m** you a curse and
Num   5:22   and **m** your belly swell and
Num   5:24   And he shall **m** the woman
Num   6:25   The LORD **m** His face shine
Num   12: 6   **m** Myself known to him in a
Num   15:38   Tell them to **m** tassels on
Num   21: 8   **M** a fiery serpent, and set
Deut   4:25   and act corruptly and **m** a
Deut   12:11   LORD your God chooses to **m**
Deut   20:12   if the city will not **m**
Deut   22: 8   then you shall **m** a parapet
Deut   23:21   When you **m** a vow to the
Deut   32:39   I kill and I **m** alive; I
Josh   1: 8   For then you will **m** your way
Josh   9: 7   so how can we **m** a covenant
Judg   8:24   I would like to **m** a request
Judg   9:48   **m** haste and do as I have
Ruth   3: 3   but do not **m** yourself known
Ruth   4:11   The LORD **m** the woman who is
1Sa   1: 6   to **m** her miserable, because
1Sa   2:19   his mother used to **m** him a
1Sa   6: 7   **m** a new cart, take two milk
1Sa   8: 5   Now **m** us a king to judge us
1Sa   13:19   Lest the Hebrews **m** swords or
1Sa   20:38   **M** haste, hurry, do not
2Sa   7:11   tells you that He will **m**
2Sa   7:23   to **m** for Himself a name—and
1Ki   1:37   and **m** his throne greater
1Ki   8:33   and pray and **m** supplication
1Ki   12:10   but you **m** it lighter on
2Ki   4:10   let us **m** a small upper room
2Ki   8: 3   and she went to **m** an appeal

2Ki	16: 5	came up to Jerusalem to **m**
2Ki	18:30	nor let Hezekiah **m** you trust
1Ch	12:31	by name to come and **m** David
1Ch	16: 8	**M** known His deeds among the
2Ch	7:20	and will **m** it a proverb and
Ezra	10:11	**m** confession to the LORD
Neh	2: 8	he must give me timber to **m**
Neh	8:15	to **m** booths, as it is
Job	5:18	but His hands **m** whole.
Job	11:19	and no one would **m** you
Job	13:23	**M** me know my transgression
Job	22:27	You will **m** your prayer to
Job	34:29	who then can **m** trouble? And
Ps	4: 8	**m** me dwell in safety.
Ps	5: 8	**M** Your way straight before
Ps	18:34	He teaches my hands to **m**
Ps	31:16	**M** Your face shine upon Your
Ps	33: 2	**M** melody to Him with an
Ps	34: 2	My soul shall **m** its boast in
Ps	38:22	**M** haste to help me, O Lord,
Ps	39: 4	**m** me to know my end, And
Ps	40:13	**m** haste to help me!
Ps	46: 4	river whose streams shall **m**
Ps	51: 6	the hidden part You will **m**
Ps	51: 8	**M** me hear joy and gladness,
Ps	57: 1	of Your wings I will **m** my
Ps	66: 1	**M** a joyful shout to God, all
Ps	66: 2	**M** His praise glorious.
Ps	76:11	**M** vows to the LORD your
Ps	89: 1	With my mouth will I **m**
Ps	100: 1	**M** a joyful shout to the
Ps	104:17	Where the birds **m** their
Ps	105: 1	**M** known His deeds among the
Ps	110: 1	Till I **m** Your enemies Your
Ps	115: 8	Those who **m** them are like
Ps	119:27	**M** me understand the way of
Ps	135:18	Those who **m** them are like
Ps	139: 8	If I **m** my bed in hell,
Prov	1:16	And they **m** haste to shed
Prov	27:11	and **m** my heart glad, That I
Prov	30:26	Yet they **m** their homes in
Eccl	5: 4	When you **m** a vow to God, do
Eccl	7:13	For who can **m** straight what
Song	8:14	**M** haste, my beloved, And be
Is	1:15	Even though you **m** many
Is	1:16	**m** yourselves clean; Put
Is	6:10	**M** the heart of this people
Is	7: 1	went up to Jerusalem to **m**
Is	11:15	And **m** men cross over
Is	17: 2	and no one will **m** them
Is	23:16	**M** sweet melody, sing many
Is	28:17	Also I will **m** justice the
Is	35: 3	And **m** firm the feeble
Is	40: 3	**M** straight in the desert A
Is	41:15	I will **m** you into a new
Is	41:18	I will **m** the wilderness a
Is	42:16	I will **m** darkness light
Is	43:19	I will even **m** a road in the
Is	44: 9	Those who **m** an image, all
Is	45: 2	will go before you And **m**
Is	45: 7	I **m** peace and create
Is	46: 5	and **m** Me equal And compare
Is	53:10	When You **m** His soul an
Is	55: 3	And I will **m** an everlasting
Is	59: 7	And they **m** haste to shed
Is	60:13	And I will **m** the place of
Is	64: 2	To **m** Your name known to Your
Jer	7:16	nor **m** intercession to Me;
Jer	7:18	to **m** cakes for the queen of
Jer	9:11	I will **m** Jerusalem a heap of
Jer	16:20	Will a man **m** gods for
Jer	18: 4	good to the potter to **m**.
Jer	19:12	and **m** this city like Tophet.
Jer	20: 9	I will not **m** mention of Him,
Jer	31:31	when I will **m** a new covenant

Jer	32:40	And I will **m** an everlasting
Jer	46:27	No one shall **m** him afraid.
Ezek	3:26	I will **m** your tongue cling to
Ezek	15: 3	Or can men **m** a peg from it
Ezek	24:17	**m** no mourning for the dead;
Ezek	30:12	I will **m** the rivers dry,
Ezek	30:12	I will **m** the land waste,
Ezek	34:25	I will **m** a covenant of peace
Ezek	35:11	and I will **m** Myself known
Ezek	37:19	and **m** them one stick, and
Ezek	37:22	and I will **m** them one nation
Ezek	37:26	Moreover I will **m** a covenant
Ezek	45:15	to **m** atonement for them,"
Dan	4:25	and they shall **m** you eat
Dan	5:15	read this writing and **m**
Dan	6: 7	a royal statute and to **m** a
Dan	9:24	To **m** an end of sins, To
Dan	9:24	To **m** reconciliation for
Dan	11:35	and **m** them white, until
Hos	2:18	To **m** them lie down safely.
Hos	11: 8	How can I **m** you like Admah?
Amos	8: 9	That I will **m** the sun go down
Mic	1:16	**M** yourself bald and cut off
Mic	4: 4	And no one shall **m** them
Hab	1:14	Why do You **m** men like fish
Hab	2: 2	Write the vision And **m** it
Hab	3: 2	In the midst of the years **m**
Hab	3:19	He will **m** my feet like
Hab	3:19	And He will **m** me walk on my
Zeph	3:13	And no one shall **m** them
Hag	2:23	and will **m** you like a signet
Mal	3:17	On the day that I **m** them My
Matt	1:19	and not wanting to **m** her a
Matt	3: 3	**M** His paths straight.'
Matt	4:19	and I will **m** you fishers of
Matt	5:36	because you cannot **m** one
Matt	8: 2	You can **m** me clean."
Matt	12:16	Yet He warned them not to **m**
Matt	12:33	Either **m** the tree good and
Matt	17: 4	let us **m** here three
Matt	22:44	Till I **m** Your enemies
Matt	23: 5	They **m** their phylacteries
Matt	23:14	and for a pretense **m** long
Matt	23:15	you **m** him twice as much a
Matt	24:47	I say to you that he will **m**
Matt	25:21	I will **m** you ruler over many
Matt	28:19	Go therefore and **m** disciples
Mark	14:15	there **m** ready for us."
Luke	1:17	to **m** ready a people prepared
Luke	9:14	**M** them sit down in groups of
Luke	11:39	Now you Pharisees **m** the
Luke	11:40	He who made the outside **m**
Luke	14:18	with one accord began to **m**
Luke	15:19	**M** me like one of your hired
Luke	15:29	that I might **m** merry with my
Luke	16: 9	**m** friends for yourselves by
Luke	19: 5	**m** haste and come down, for
Luke	19:42	the things that **m** for your
Luke	22:12	there **m** ready."
John	2:16	these things away! Do not **m**
John	6:15	and take Him by force to **m**
John	8:32	and the truth shall **m** you
John	8:53	Whom do You Yourself out
John	10:33	**m** Yourself God."
John	14:23	We will come to him and **m**
Acts	2:28	You will **m** me full of
Rom	1: 9	that without ceasing I **m**
Rom	2:17	and **m** your boast in God,
Rom	3: 3	Will their unbelief **m** the
Rom	3:31	Do we then **m** void the law
Rom	9:21	from the same lump to **m** a
Rom	9:22	to show His wrath and to **m**
Rom	13:14	and **m** no provision for the
Rom	14: 4	for God is able to **m** him
Rom	14:19	pursue the things which **m**

Rom	15:18	to **m** the Gentiles obedient--
1Co	8:13	lest I **m** my brother stumble.
1Co	10:13	the temptation will also **m**
1Co	14: 7	when they **m** a sound, unless
1Co	14: 7	unless they **m** a distinction
2Co	8: 1	we **m** known to you the grace
2Co	9: 8	And God is able to **m** all
Gal	2:18	I **m** myself a transgressor.
Gal	3:17	that it should **m** the promise
Gal	6:12	As many as desire to **m** a good
Eph	3: 9	and to **m** all see what is the
Eph	6:19	open my mouth boldly to **m**
Col	4: 4	that I may **m** it manifest, as
1Th	3:12	And may the Lord **m** you
2Th	3: 9	but to **m** ourselves an
2Ti	3: 6	creep into households and **m**
2Ti	3:15	which are able to **m** you wise
Heb	1:13	Till I **m** Your enemies
Heb	2:17	to **m** propitiation for the
Heb	7:25	since He always lives to **m**
Heb	8: 8	when I will **m** a new
Heb	13:21	**m** you complete in every good
Jas	3:18	sown in peace by those who **m**
Jas	4:13	and **m** a profit'';
2Pe	1:10	be even more diligent to **m**
1Jn	1:10	we **m** Him a liar, and His
Rev	11: 7	of the bottomless pit will **m**
Rev	13: 7	It was granted to him to **m**
Rev	21: 5	I **m** all things new.'' And He

MAKER (see MAKE)

Job	4:17	man be more pure than his **M**?
Ps	95: 6	kneel before the LORD our **M**.
Ps	149: 2	Israel rejoice in their **M**;
Prov	22: 2	The LORD is the **m** of them
Is	45: 9	him who strives with his **M**!
Is	51:13	you forget the LORD your **M**,
Is	54: 5	For your **M** is your husband,
Hos	8:14	Israel has forgotten his **M**,
Heb	11:10	whose builder and **m** is God.

MAKES (see MAKE)

Lev	7: 7	the priest who **m** atonement
Num	30: 2	If a man **m** a vow to the
Deut	20:12	but **m** war against you, then
1Sa	2: 6	The LORD kills and **m** alive;
1Sa	2: 7	The LORD **m** poor and makes
2Sa	22:34	He **m** my feet like the feet
Ps	18:32	And **m** my way perfect.
Ps	18:33	He **m** my feet like the feet
Ps	23: 2	He **m** me to lie down in green
Ps	29: 6	He **m** them also skip like a
Ps	46: 9	He **m** wars cease to the end
Ps	104: 3	Who **m** the clouds His
Ps	104: 4	Who **m** His angels spirits,
Ps	104:15	And wine that **m** glad the
Ps	107:41	And **m** their families like
Ps	135: 7	He **m** lightning for the
Ps	147: 8	Who **m** grass to grow on the
Ps	147:14	He **m** peace in your borders,
Prov	10: 1	A wise son **m** a glad father,
Prov	13:12	Hope deferred **m** the heart
Prov	15:13	A merry heart **m** a cheerful
Prov	16: 7	He **m** even his enemies to be
Prov	19: 4	Wealth **m** many friends, But
Prov	31:24	She **m** linen garments and
Eccl	10:19	And wine **m** merry; But
Is	44:15	Indeed he **m** a god and
Is	44:15	He **m** it a carved image, and
Jer	10:13	He **m** lightning for the
Dan	6:13	but **m** his petition three
Dan	9:27	shall be one who **m** desolate,
Matt	5:45	for He **m** His sun rise on the
Mark	7:37	He **m** both the deaf to hear
John	8:36	Therefore if the Son **m** you
Rom	8:26	but the Spirit Himself **m**

Rom	8:27	because He **m** intercession
1Co	4: 7	For who **m** you differ from
1Co	8:13	if food **m** my brother
1Co	14: 8	For if the trumpet **m** an
Heb	1: 7	Who **m** His angels spirits
Jas	4: 4	be a friend of the world **m**

MAKING (see MAKE)

1Ch	15:28	**m** music with stringed
Ps	19: 7	**m** wise the simple;
Eccl	12:12	Of **m** many books there is
Is	45: 9	forms it, 'What are you **m**?
Jer	18: 3	**m** something at the wheel.
Dan	6:11	found Daniel praying and **m**
Amos	8: 5	**M** the ephah small and the
Mark	7:13	**m** the word of God of no
John	5:18	**m** Himself equal with God.
Rom	1:10	**m** request if, by some means,
2Co	6:10	yet **m** many rich; as having
Eph	1:16	**m** mention of you in my
Eph	2:15	thus **m** peace,
Eph	5:19	singing and **m** melody in your
1Th	1: 2	**m** mention of you in our
2Pe	2: 6	**m** them an example to those

MALCHUS†

John	18:10	The servant's name was **M**.

MALE (see MALES)

Gen	1:27	**m** and female He created
Gen	5: 2	He created them **m** and female,
Gen	6:19	they shall be **m** and female.
Gen	7: 2	a **m** and his female; two each
Gen	17:10	Every **m** child among you
Gen	17:14	And the uncircumcised **m**
Gen	34:24	every **m** was circumcised, all
Ex	1:18	and saved the **m** children
Ex	12: 5	a **m** of the first year. You
Ex	20:10	nor your **m** servant, nor your
Ex	34:19	and every **m** firstborn among
Lev	3: 1	whether **m** or female, he
Lev	18:22	You shall not lie with a **m** as
Lev	27: 5	then your valuation for a **m**
Num	3:15	you shall number every **m**
Deut	4:16	the likeness of **m** or female,
Deut	5:14	nor your **m** servant, nor your
Judg	21:11	utterly destroy every **m**,
1Sa	1:11	give Your maidservant a **m**
1Sa	8:16	And he will take your **m**
1Ki	11:15	after he had killed every **m**
Job	3: 3	A **m** child is conceived.'
Jer	20:15	A **m** child has been born to
Jer	34: 9	man should set free his **m**
Dan	8: 5	suddenly a **m** goat came from
Dan	8:21	And the **m** goat is the
Matt	2:16	and put to death all the **m**
Matt	19: 4	made them **m** and female,'
Luke	2:23	Every **m** who opens the
Gal	3:28	there is neither **m** nor
Rev	12: 5	She bore a **m** Child who was to

MALES (see MALE)

Gen	34:25	city and killed all the **m**.
Ex	23:17	times in the year all your **m**
Num	3:40	Number all the firstborn **m** of

MALICE

1Co	5: 8	nor with the leaven of **m** and
1Co	14:20	in **m** be babes, but in
Eph	4:31	away from you, with all **m**.
Col	3: 8	all these: anger, wrath, **m**,
1Pe	2: 1	laying aside all **m**,

MALTA†

Acts	28: 1	that the island was called **M**.

MAMMON

Matt	6:24	You cannot serve God and **m**.

Luke 16: 9 yourselves by unrighteous **m**,

MAMRE
Gen 23:19 before **M** (that is, Hebron)

MAN (*see* MAN'S, MANKIND, MEN, SON)
Gen 1:26 Let Us make **m** in Our image,
Gen 1:27 So God created **m** in His own
Gen 2: 5 and there was no **m** to till
Gen 2: 7 And the LORD God formed **m**
Gen 2: 7 and **m** became a living being.
Gen 2: 8 and there He put the **m** whom
Gen 2:18 It is not good that **m**
Gen 2:22 LORD God had taken from **m**
Gen 2:22 and He brought her to the **m**.
Gen 2:23 she was taken out of **M**.
Gen 2:24 Therefore a **m** shall leave his
Gen 2:25 the **m** and his wife, and were
Gen 3:22 the **m** has become like one of
Gen 3:24 So He drove out the **m**;
Gen 4: 1 I have acquired a **m** from the
Gen 4:23 For I have killed a **m** for
Gen 6: 3 shall not strive with **m**
Gen 6: 5 saw that the wickedness of **m**
Gen 6: 7 I will destroy **m** whom I have
Gen 6: 9 of Noah. Noah was a just **m**,
Gen 9: 5 I will require the life of **m**.
Gen 9: 6 By **m** his blood shall be
Gen 9: 6 the image of God He made **m**.
Gen 13:16 so that if a **m** could number
Gen 19: 8 who have not known a **m**;
Gen 25: 8 an old **m** and full of
Gen 25:27 a **m** of the field; but Jacob
Gen 25:27 but Jacob was a mild **m**,
Gen 27:11 my brother is a hairy **m**,
Gen 32:24 and a **M** wrestled with him
Gen 41:12 there was a young Hebrew **m**
Gen 41:38 a **m** in whom is the Spirit
Gen 44:20 'We have a father, an old **m**,
Ex 8:18 So there were lice on **m** and
Ex 9: 9 break out in sores on **m** and
Ex 11: 3 Moreover the **m** Moses was
Ex 13:13 And all the firstborn of **m**
Ex 15: 3 The LORD is a **m** of war;
Ex 21:12 He who strikes a **m** so that
Ex 21:16 He who kidnaps a **m** and sells
Ex 21:20 And if a **m** beats his male or
Ex 21:26 If a **m** strikes the eye of his
Ex 21:28 If an ox gores a **m** or a
Ex 22:14 And if a **m** borrows anything
Ex 22:16 If a **m** entices a virgin who
Ex 33:11 as a **m** speaks to his friend.
Ex 33:20 for no **m** shall see Me, and
Lev 13: 2 When a **m** has on the skin of
Lev 16:21 by the hand of a suitable **m**.
Lev 20:10 The **m** who commits adultery
Lev 20:13 If a **m** lies with a male as he
Lev 20:15 If a **m** mates with an animal,
Lev 20:17 If a **m** takes his sister, his
Lev 21:18 For any **m** who has a defect
Lev 22:14 And if a **m** eats the holy
Num 5: 8 But if the **m** has no relative
Num 5:13 and a **m** lies with her
Num 6: 2 When either a **m** or woman
Num 8:17 both **m** and beast; on the
Num 9:13 that **m** shall bear his sin.
Num 12: 3 (Now the **m** Moses was very
Num 15:32 they found a **m** gathering
Num 23:19 "God is not a **m**,
Num 23:19 should lie, Nor a son of **m**,
Num 27: 8 If a **m** dies and has no son,
Num 27:18 a **m** in whom is the Spirit,
Num 30: 2 If a **m** makes a vow to the
Num 32:27 every **m** armed for war,
Deut 8: 3 but **m** lives by every word
Deut 15:12 your brother, a Hebrew **m**,

Deut 16:17 Every **m** shall give as he is
Deut 21:15 If a **m** has two wives, one
Deut 21:22 If a **m** has committed a sin
Deut 22:13 If any **m** takes a wife, and
Deut 22:16 gave my daughter to this **m**
Deut 22:25 But if a **m** finds a betrothed
Deut 22:25 and the **m** forces her and
Deut 24: 5 When a **m** has taken a new
Deut 24: 7 If a **m** is found kidnapping
Deut 25: 5 the widow of the dead **m**
Deut 33: 1 with which Moses the **m** of
Josh 3:12 one **m** from every tribe.
Josh 5:13 a **M** stood opposite him with
Josh 8:17 There was not a **m** left in Ai
Josh 10:14 heeded the voice of a **m**;
Josh 23:10 One **m** of you shall chase a
Judg 3:17 (Now Eglon was a very fat **m**.
Judg 5:30 To every **m** a girl or two;
Judg 6:12 you mighty **m** of valor!"
Judg 11:39 he had vowed. She knew no **m**.
Judg 13: 6 A **M** of God came to me, and
Judg 16: 7 and be like any other **m**.
Judg 17: 5 The **m** Micah had a shrine, and
Judg 17:11 content to dwell with the **m**;
Judg 17:12 and the young **m** became his
Judg 18:15 house of the young Levite **m**—
Judg 19:22 Bring out the **m** who came to
Judg 19:25 So the **m** took his concubine
Judg 20: 1 gathered together as one **m**
Judg 21:11 woman who has known a **m**
Ruth 2: 1 a **m** of great wealth, of the
Ruth 2:20 This **m** is a relation of
Ruth 3:18 for the **m** will not rest
Ruth 4: 7 one **m** took off his sandal
1Sa 2:27 Then a **m** of God came to Eli
1Sa 9: 1 There was a **m** of Benjamin
1Sa 9: 6 there is in this city a **m**
1Sa 9: 9 when a **m** went to inquire of
1Sa 9:10 to the city where the **m** of
1Sa 10: 6 and be turned into another **m**.
1Sa 13:14 has sought for Himself a **m**
1Sa 14: 1 of Saul said to the young **m**
1Sa 14: 6 said to the young **m** who
1Sa 15:29 relent. For He is not a **m**,
1Sa 16: 7 LORD does not see as **m**
1Sa 16: 7 for **m** looks at the outward
1Sa 16:16 to seek out a **m** who is a
1Sa 16:18 a mighty **m** of valor, a man
1Sa 16:18 a **m** of war, prudent in
1Sa 17:26 shall be done for the **m** who
1Sa 17:58 son are you, young **m**?
1Sa 21:14 you see the **m** is insane. Why
1Sa 27: 9 he left neither **m** nor woman
1Sa 27:11 David would save neither **m**
1Sa 28:14 An old **m** is coming up, and he
2Sa 3:38 that a prince and a great **m**
2Sa 7:19 Is this the manner of **m**,
2Sa 12: 2 The rich **m** had exceedingly
2Sa 12: 3 But the poor **m** had nothing,
2Sa 12: 7 You are the **m**! Thus says the
2Sa 14:21 bring back the young **m**
2Sa 16: 7 Come out! You bloodthirsty **m**,
2Sa 18:12 anyone touch the young **m**
2Sa 19:22 Shall any **m** be put to death
2Sa 20: 1 Every **m** to his tents, O
2Sa 21:20 where there was a **m** of
2Sa 22:49 me from the violent **m**.
2Sa 24:14 me fall into the hand of **m**.
1Ki 1:42 for you are a prominent **m**
1Ki 1:52 he proves himself a worthy **m**,
1Ki 4:25 each **m** under his vine and
1Ki 8:25 shall not fail to have a **m**
1Ki 13: 1 a **m** of God went from Judah
1Ki 13:29 took up the corpse of the **m**
1Ki 17:18 O **m** of God? Have you come to

1Ki	22:34	Now a certain m drew a bow
2Ki	1: 8	A hairy m wearing a leather
2Ki	1: 9	M of God, the king has said,
2Ki	4: 9	know that this is a holy m
2Ki	4:42	Then a m came from Baal
2Ki	4:42	and brought the m of God
2Ki	5: 8	when Elisha the m of God
2Ki	8:11	and the m of God wept.
2Ki	13:19	And the m of God was angry
2Ki	13:21	as they were burying a m,
2Ki	14:12	and every m fled to his
2Ki	18:21	on which if a m leans, it
1Ch	12: 4	a mighty m among the thirty,
2Ch	8:14	for so David the m of God
2Ch	30:16	to the Law of Moses the m
Ezra	3: 1	gathered together as one m
Neh	6:11	Should such a m as I flee?
Neh	7: 2	for he was a faithful m and
Neh	9:29	Which if a m does, he shall
Esth	9: 4	for this m Mordecai became
Job	1: 1	There was a m in the land of
Job	1: 8	a blameless and upright m,
Job	2: 4	all that a m has he will
Job	4:17	Can a m be more pure than
Job	5: 7	Yet m is born to trouble,
Job	7: 1	a time of hard service for m
Job	7: 1	like the days of a hired m?
Job	7:17	"What is m, that You
Job	9: 2	But how can a m be
Job	9:32	"For He is not a m,
Job	10: 4	Or do You see as m sees?
Job	10: 5	like the days of a mortal m?
Job	11:12	For an empty-headed m will
Job	12:25	stagger like a drunken m.
Job	13:28	M decays like a rotten
Job	14: 1	M who is born of woman Is
Job	14:10	But m dies and is laid away;
Job	14:19	You destroy the hope of m.
Job	15: 7	Are you the first m who was
Job	15:16	How much less m,
Job	16:21	that one might plead for a m
Job	20: 4	Since m was placed on
Job	24:22	but no m is sure of life.
Job	25: 4	How then can m be righteous
Job	25: 6	a maggot, And a son of m,
Job	28: 3	M puts an end to darkness,
Job	32: 8	there is a spirit in m,
Job	33:12	For God is greater than m.
Job	34: 7	What m is like Job, Who
Job	34:15	And m would return to dust.
Job	34:21	eyes are on the ways of m,
Job	38: 3	prepare yourself like a m;
Ps	1: 1	Blessed is the m Who walks
Ps	8: 4	What is m that You are
Ps	8: 4	And the son of m that You
Ps	10:15	the wicked and the evil m;
Ps	18:25	With a blameless m You will
Ps	18:48	me from the violent m.
Ps	19: 5	rejoices like a strong m to
Ps	22: 6	But I am a worm, and no m;
Ps	32: 2	Blessed is the m to whom
Ps	34: 6	This poor m cried out, and
Ps	34: 8	Blessed is the m who
Ps	36: 6	You preserve m and beast.
Ps	37:23	The steps of a good m are
Ps	37:37	For the future of that m
Ps	39:11	Surely every m is vapor.
Ps	52: 1	boast in evil, O mighty m?
Ps	55:13	a m my equal, My companion
Ps	56:11	What can m do to me?
Ps	60:11	For the help of m is
Ps	62: 3	long will you attack a m?
Ps	64: 6	thought and the heart of m
Ps	76:10	Surely the wrath of m shall
Ps	80:17	Your hand be upon the m of

Ps	80:17	Upon the son of m whom You
Ps	84: 5	Blessed is the m whose
Ps	94:11	knows the thoughts of m,
Ps	104:15	makes glad the heart of m,
Ps	104:23	M goes out to his work And
Ps	107:27	and stagger like a drunken m,
Ps	108:12	For the help of m is
Ps	118: 6	What can m do to me?
Ps	118: 8	Than to put confidence in m.
Ps	119: 9	How can a young m cleanse
Ps	144: 3	LORD, what is m,
Ps	144: 3	of him? Or the son of m,
Ps	144: 4	M is like a breath
Ps	147:10	pleasure in the legs of a m.
Prov	1: 4	To the young m knowledge
Prov	1: 5	A wise m will hear and
Prov	1: 5	And a m of understanding
Prov	3: 4	In the sight of God and m.
Prov	3:13	Happy is the m who finds
Prov	3:13	And the m who gains
Prov	6:11	your need like an armed m.
Prov	6:27	Can a m take fire to his
Prov	9: 8	hate you; Rebuke a wise m,
Prov	12: 2	A good m obtains favor from
Prov	12: 3	A m is not established by
Prov	12:25	Anxiety in the heart of m
Prov	14:12	that seems right to a m,
Prov	14:20	The poor m is hated even by
Prov	15:18	A wrathful m stirs up
Prov	15:19	The way of the lazy m is
Prov	16:25	that seems right to a m,
Prov	17:10	more effective for a wise m
Prov	17:12	Let a m meet a bear robbed
Prov	17:18	A m devoid of understanding
Prov	17:23	A wicked m accepts a bribe
Prov	18:12	the heart of a m is haughty,
Prov	19: 6	And every m is a friend to
Prov	19:24	A lazy m buries his hand in
Prov	20: 5	Counsel in the heart of m
Prov	20: 6	who can find a faithful m?
Prov	20:27	The spirit of a m is the
Prov	21: 2	Every way of a m is right
Prov	21:20	But a foolish m squanders
Prov	21:29	A wicked m hardens his face,
Prov	24: 5	a m of knowledge increases
Prov	24:12	He not render to each m
Prov	24:34	your need like an armed m.
Prov	25:18	A m who bears false witness
Prov	26:13	The lazy m says, "There
Prov	26:15	The lazy m buries his hand
Prov	26:21	So is a contentious m to
Prov	27: 2	Let another m praise you,
Prov	27:17	So a m sharpens the
Prov	27:19	a man's heart reveals the m.
Prov	28:11	The rich m is wise in his
Prov	29:20	Do you see a m hasty in his
Prov	29:22	An angry m stirs up strife,
Prov	30: 2	am more stupid than any m,
Eccl	1: 3	What profit has a m from all
Eccl	2:21	leave his heritage to a m
Eccl	2:22	For what has m for all his
Eccl	2:24	Nothing is better for a m
Eccl	5:19	As for every m to whom God
Eccl	6: 2	A m to whom God has given
Eccl	6: 8	what more has the wise m
Eccl	7:14	So that m can find out
Eccl	7:28	One m among a thousand I
Eccl	7:29	That God made m upright,
Eccl	8:17	that a m cannot find out the
Eccl	8:17	For though a m labors to
Eccl	9:12	For m also does not know his
Eccl	11: 8	But if a m lives many years
Eccl	11: 9	Rejoice, O young m,
Eccl	12: 5	For m goes to his eternal
Song	8: 7	If a m would give for love

Is	2: 9	And each **m** humbles himself;
Is	2:17	The loftiness of **m** shall be
Is	5:15	Each **m** shall be humbled,
Is	6: 5	undone! Because I am a **m**
Is	6:11	The houses are without a **m**,
Is	9:20	Every **m** shall eat the flesh
Is	13:14	Every **m** will turn to his
Is	14:16	Is this the **m** who made the
Is	16:14	as the years of a hired **m**,
Is	19:14	As a drunken **m** staggers in
Is	33: 8	The traveling **m** ceases. He
Is	36: 6	on which if a **m** leans, it
Is	44:13	it like the figure of a **m**,
Is	50: 2	I came, was there no **m**?
Is	52:14	was marred more than any **m**,
Is	53: 3	A **M** of sorrows and
Is	55: 7	And the unrighteous **m** his
Jer	3: 1	If a **m** divorces his wife,
Jer	9:23	Let not the wise **m** glory in
Jer	9:23	Let not the mighty **m** glory
Jer	9:23	Nor let the rich **m** glory
Jer	10:23	I know the way of **m** is not
Jer	10:23	It is not in **m** who walks
Jer	15:10	A **m** of strife and a man of
Jer	15:10	A man of strife and a **m** of
Jer	17: 5	is the man who trusts in **m**
Jer	17: 7	Blessed is the **m** who trusts
Jer	20:15	Let the **m** be cursed Who
Jer	22:30	Write this **m** down as
Jer	26:11	This **m** deserves to die! For
Jer	26:16	This **m** does not deserve to
Jer	30: 6	Whether a **m** is ever in
Jer	31:22	woman shall encompass a **m**.
Jer	31:34	No more shall every **m** teach
Jer	31:34	and every **m** his brother,
Jer	33:17	David shall never lack a **m** to
Jer	34: 9	that every **m** should set free
Jer	34: 9	a Hebrew **m** or woman—that no
Jer	38: 4	let this **m** be put to death,
Jer	44: 7	to cut off from you **m** and
Jer	51:22	I will break in pieces **m**
Lam	3: 1	I am the **m** who has seen
Ezek	1: 5	they had the likeness of a **m**.
Ezek	1:10	each had the face of a **m**;
Ezek	2: 1	He said to me, "Son of **m**,
Ezek	3:18	that same wicked **m** shall
Ezek	10:14	second face the face of a **m**,
Ezek	14:21	to cut off **m** and beast from
Ezek	18:21	But if a wicked **m** turns from
Ezek	18:26	When a righteous **m** turns
Ezek	20:11	if a **m** does, he shall live
Ezek	22:30	So I sought for a **m** among
Ezek	28: 2	the seas,' Yet you are a **m**,
Ezek	28: 9	But you shall be a **m**,
Ezek	33: 8	that wicked **m** shall die in
Dan	2:10	There is not a **m** on earth who
Dan	4:16	changed from that of a **m**,
Dan	5:11	There is a **m** in your kingdom
Dan	6: 7	petitions any god or **m** for
Dan	7: 8	eyes like the eyes of a **m**,
Dan	7:13	One like the Son of **M**,
Dan	8:17	me, "Understand, son of **m**,
Dan	9:21	the **m** Gabriel, whom I had
Dan	10: 5	a certain **m** clothed in
Dan	10:11	**m** greatly beloved,
Hos	11: 9	For I am God, and not **m**,
Amos	2: 7	A **m** and his father go in to
Amos	4:13	Who declares to **m** what his
Jon	1: 5	and every **m** cried out to his
Mic	6: 8	He has shown you, O **m**,
Nah	2: 1	**M** the fort! Watch the
Zech	2: 1	a **m** with a measuring line in
Zech	13: 7	Against the **M** who is My
Mal	3: 8	Will a **m** rob God? Yet you
Matt	1:19	her husband, being a just **m**,

Matt	4: 4	**M** shall not live by
Matt	7: 9	Or what **m** is there among you
Matt	7:24	I will liken him to a wise **m**
Matt	7:26	will be like a foolish **m** who
Matt	8: 9	For I also am a **m** under
Matt	8:20	but the Son of **M** has nowhere
Matt	9: 6	may know that the Son of **M**
Matt	11:19	The Son of **M** came eating and
Matt	12: 8	For the Son of **M** is Lord even
Matt	12:29	he first binds the strong **m**?
Matt	12:35	A good **m** out of the good
Matt	12:35	and an evil **m** out of the
Matt	12:40	so will the Son of **M** be
Matt	12:45	the last state of that **m**
Matt	13:31	which a **m** took and sowed in
Matt	15:11	into the mouth defiles a **m**;
Matt	16:13	men say that I, the Son of **M**,
Matt	18: 7	but woe to that **m** by whom
Matt	19: 6	let not **m** separate."
Matt	19:20	The young **m** said to Him,
Matt	19:24	a needle than for a rich **m**
Matt	20:18	and the Son of **M** will be
Matt	24:30	the sign of the Son of **M**
Matt	24:30	they will see the Son of **M**
Matt	24:37	the coming of the Son of **M**
Matt	25:14	of heaven is like a **m**
Matt	25:24	I knew you to be a hard **m**,
Matt	26:72	I do not know the **M**!"
Matt	27:57	there came a rich **m** from
Mark	2: 7	Why does this **M** speak
Mark	5: 2	met Him out of the tombs a **m**
Mark	8:22	and they brought a blind **m**
Mark	12: 1	A **m** planted a vineyard and
Mark	14:51	Now a certain young **m**
Mark	15:39	Truly this **M** was the Son of
Luke	1:18	know this? For I am an old **m**,
Luke	1:27	to a virgin betrothed to a **m**
Luke	1:34	be, since I do not know a **m**?
Luke	2:25	there was a **m** in Jerusalem
Luke	2:25	and this **m** was just and
Luke	5:12	a **m** who was full of leprosy
Luke	5:18	men brought on a bed a **m** who
Luke	6:48	He is like a **m** building a
Luke	7: 8	For I also am a **m** placed
Luke	7:12	a dead **m** was being carried
Luke	7:14	And He said, "Young **m**,
Luke	8:33	the demons went out of the **m**
Luke	8:41	there came a **m** named Jairus,
Luke	13: 6	A certain **m** had a fig tree
Luke	13:19	which a **m** took and put in
Luke	15: 2	This **M** receives sinners and
Luke	15:11	A certain **m** had two sons.
Luke	16:22	The rich **m** also died and was
Luke	18: 2	not fear God nor regard **m**.
Luke	18:25	a needle than for a rich **m**
Luke	19: 2	there was a **m** named
Luke	19:21	because you are an austere **m**.
Luke	22:48	you betraying the Son of **M**
Luke	22:58	them." But Peter said, "**M**,
Luke	23: 4	"I find no fault in this **M**."
Luke	23:18	saying, "Away with this **M**,
Luke	23:41	but this **M** has done nothing
Luke	23:47	this was a righteous **M**!"
John	1: 6	There was a **m** sent from God,
John	1: 7	This **m** came for a witness, to
John	1: 9	which gives light to every **m**
John	1:13	flesh, nor of the will of **m**,
John	1:30	After me comes a **M** who is
John	1:51	descending upon the Son of **M**.
John	2:10	Every **m** at the beginning sets
John	2:25	for He knew what was in **m**.
John	3: 2	This **m** came to Jesus by night
John	3: 4	How can a **m** be born when he
John	3:14	even so must the Son of **M** be
John	4:29	see a **M** who told me all

John	6:53	the flesh of the Son of M
John	7:15	How does this M know letters,
John	7:46	No m ever spoke like this
John	9: 2	this m or his parents, that
John	9:11	A M called Jesus made clay
John	12:23	has come that the Son of M
John	12:34	The Son of M must be lifted
John	18:40	again, saying, "Not this M,
John	19: 5	Behold the M!"
Acts	6: 5	a m full of faith and the
Acts	7:56	opened and the Son of M
Acts	10:22	the centurion, a just m,
Acts	13:22	a m after My own
Acts	16: 9	A m of Macedonia stood and
Acts	17:31	in righteousness by the M
Acts	22:26	for this m is a Roman."
Acts	23: 9	"We find no evil in this m;
Rom	1:23	made like corruptible m—
Rom	2: 1	you are inexcusable, O m,
Rom	3: 4	let God be true but every m
Rom	3: 5	wrath? (I speak as a m.
Rom	4: 6	the blessedness of the m to
Rom	5: 7	scarcely for a righteous m
Rom	5: 7	yet perhaps for a good m
Rom	5:12	just as through one m sin
Rom	5:15	by the grace of the one M,
Rom	6: 6	that our old m was crucified
Rom	7:22	according to the inward m.
Rom	9:10	also had conceived by one m,
1Co	2: 9	into the heart of m
1Co	2:11	For what m knows the things
1Co	2:14	But the natural m does not
1Co	7: 1	It is good for a m not to
1Co	7:26	that it is good for a m to
1Co	9: 8	these things as a mere m?
1Co	10:13	such as is common to m;
1Co	11: 3	that the head of every m is
1Co	11: 3	the head of woman is m,
1Co	11: 7	but woman is the glory of m.
1Co	11: 8	For m is not from woman, but
1Co	11:28	But let a m examine himself,
1Co	13:11	child; but when I became a m,
1Co	15:21	For since by m came death,
1Co	15:45	The first m Adam became
1Co	15:47	the second M is the Lord
2Co	4:16	Even though our outward m is
2Co	4:16	yet the inward m is being
2Co	12: 2	I know a m in Christ who
Gal	1: 1	(not from men nor through m,
Eph	2:15	create in Himself one new m
Eph	3:16	His Spirit in the inner m,
Eph	4:22	the old m which grows
Eph	4:24	that you put on the new m
Eph	5:31	For this reason a m
Phil	2: 8	found in appearance as a m,
Col	1:28	warning every m and teaching
Col	1:28	that we may present every m
Col	3: 9	you have put off the old m
Col	3:10	and have put on the new m
2Th	2: 3	and the m of sin is
1Ti	2: 5	the M Christ Jesus,
1Ti	3: 1	If a m desires the position
1Ti	6:11	O m of God, flee these
1Ti	6:16	whom no m has seen or can
2Ti	3:17	that the m of God may be
Heb	2: 6	What is m that You are
Heb	2: 6	Or the son of m that
Heb	7: 4	consider how great this m
Heb	11:12	Therefore from one m,
Heb	13: 6	What can m do to
Jas	1: 8	he is a double-minded m,
Jas	1:11	So the rich m also will fade
Jas	1:23	he is like a m observing his
Jas	1:24	forgets what kind of m he
Jas	3: 8	But no m can tame the tongue.

Jas	5:16	prayer of a righteous m
1Pe	1:24	all the glory of m as
2Pe	1:21	never came by the will of m,
Rev	1:13	One like the Son of M,
Rev	4: 7	creature had a face like a m,
Rev	13:18	for it is the number of a m:
Rev	21:17	to the measure of a m,

MAN'S (*see* MAN)

Gen	8:21	curse the ground for m sake,
Gen	8:21	the imagination of m heart
Gen	9: 6	Whoever sheds m blood, By
Gen	44: 1	and put each m money in the
Lev	20:10	adultery with another m
Num	5:12	If any m wife goes astray and
Ruth	2:19	The m name with whom I worked
2Sa	12: 4	but he took the poor m lamb
1Ki	18:44	as small as a m hand, rising
Ps	104:15	bread which strengthens m
Prov	13: 8	The ransom of a m life is
Prov	16: 7	When a m ways please the
Prov	20:24	A m steps are of the LORD;
Prov	27:19	So a m heart reveals the
Ezek	10: 8	to have the form of a m
Ezek	38:21	Every m sword will be against
Dan	5: 5	same hour the fingers of a m
Dan	7: 4	and a m heart was given to
Dan	8:16	And I heard a m voice between
Jon	1:14	not let us perish for this m
Mic	7: 6	A m enemies are the men of
Matt	10:36	a m enemies will be
Matt	10:41	shall receive a righteous m
Matt	12:29	how can one enter a strong m
Luke	16:21	which fell from the rich m
Acts	13:23	From this m seed, according
Acts	17:29	shaped by art and m
Rom	5:15	For if by the one m offense
Rom	5:19	For as by one m disobedience
Rom	15:20	I should build on another m
1Co	2:13	not in words which m wisdom

MANAGE†

1Ti	5:14	m the house, give no

MANASSEH (*see* MANASSEH'S)

Gen	41:51	the name of the firstborn M:
Gen	48: 5	your two sons, Ephraim and M,
Deut	3:13	gave to half the tribe of M.
Josh	21: 5	and from the half-tribe of M.
2Ki	10:33	of Gilead—Gad, Reuben, and M—
2Ki	20:21	Then M his son reigned in
2Ki	21: 9	and M seduced them to do
2Ki	21:11	Because M king of Judah has
2Ki	24: 3	because of the sins of M,
1Ch	3:13	his son, M his son,
2Ch	33:11	who took M with hooks, bound
Matt	1:10	Hezekiah begot M,
Rev	7: 6	of the tribe of M twelve

MANASSEH'S (*see* MANASSEH)

Gen	48:14	and his left hand on M head,

MANDRAKES

Gen	30:14	me some of your son's m.
Song	7:13	The m give off a fragrance,

MANGER

Luke	2: 7	cloths, and laid Him in a m,
Luke	2:16	and the Babe lying in a m.

MANIFEST (*see* MANIFESTATION, MANIFESTED)

John	14:21	and I will love him and m
Rom	1:19	may be known of God is m in
Eph	5:13	that are exposed are made m
2Ti	3: 9	for their folly will be m to
1Pe	1:20	but was m in these last
1Jn	3:10	children of the devil are m:

MANIFESTATION (*see* MANIFEST)
Luke 1:80 till the day of his **m** to
1Co 12: 7 But the **m** of the Spirit is

MANIFESTED (*see* MANIFEST)
John 2:11 and **m** His glory; and His
John 17: 6 I have **m** Your name to the
2Co 4:10 life of Jesus also may be **m**
1Ti 3:16 God made **m** in the flesh,
1Jn 1: 2 the life was **m**,
1Jn 4: 9 this the love of God was **m**

MANIFOLD
Ps 104:24 how **m** are Your works! In
Amos 5:12 For I know your **m**
1Pe 4:10 as good stewards of the **m**

MANKIND (*see* MAN)
Gen 5: 2 them and called them **M** in
Acts 15:17 So that the rest of **m**

MANNA
Ex 16:31 of Israel called its name **M**.
Ex 16:33 a pot and put an omer of **m**
Ex 16:35 the children of Israel ate **m**
Num 11: 7 Now the **m** was like coriander
Num 11: 9 the **m** fell on it.
Josh 5:12 Then the **m** ceased on the day
Ps 78:24 Had rained down **m** on them to
John 6:31 Our fathers ate the **m** in the
Heb 9: 4 golden pot that had the **m**,
Rev 2:17 give some of the hidden **m**

MANNER
Gen 31:35 for the **m** of women is with
Gen 32:19 In this **m** you shall speak to
Ex 1:14 and in all **m** of service in
Lev 5:10 to the prescribed **m**.
2Sa 7:19 Is this the **m** of man, O
Ps 107:18 Their soul abhorred all **m** of
Matt 6: 9 "In this **m**, therefore, pray:
Mark 13: 1 see what **m** of stones and
Luke 1:29 and considered what **m** of
Acts 1:11 will so come in like **m** as
Acts 26: 4 My **m** of life from my youth,
1Co 11:25 In the same **m** He also took
1Co 11:29 and drinks in an unworthy **m**
Gal 2:14 live in the **m** of Gentiles
Gal 3:15 I speak in the **m** of men:
2Th 3:11 among you in a disorderly **m**,
Heb 10:25 as is the **m** of some, but
1Pe 1:11 or what **m** of time, the
2Pe 3:11 what **m** of persons ought
1Jn 3: 1 Behold what **m** of love the

MANOAH
Judg 13: 8 Then **M** prayed to the LORD,
Judg 13: 9 but **M** her husband was not

MANSIONS†
John 14: 2 My Father's house are many **m**;

MANSLAYER
Num 35: 6 to which a **m** may flee. And
Num 35:24 shall judge between the **m**
Num 35:27 avenger of blood kills the **m**,
Num 35:28 of the high priest the **m**

MANTLE
1Ki 19:13 he wrapped his face in his **m**
2Ki 2: 8 Now Elijah took his **m**,

MARA†
Ruth 1:20 not call me Naomi; call me **M**,

MARAH
Ex 15:23 not drink the waters of **M**,

MARBLE
Song 5:15 His legs are pillars of **m**

MARCH (*see* MARCHED, MARCHING)
Num 10:28 Thus was the order of **m** of
Josh 6: 3 You shall **m** around the city,

MARCHED (*see* MARCH)
Ex 14:10 the Egyptians **m** after them.
Josh 6:15 and **m** around the city seven

MARCHING (*see* MARCH)
2Sa 5:24 you hear the sound of **m** in

MARINERS
Jon 1: 5 Then the **m** were afraid; and

MARK (*see* MARKED, MARKS)
Gen 4:15 And the LORD set a **m** on
Ps 48:13 **M** well her bulwarks
Ps 130: 3 should **m** iniquities, O
Ezek 9: 4 and put a **m** on the foreheads
Rev 13:16 to receive a **m** on their
Rev 16: 2 upon the men who had the **m**

MARK* (*see* JOHN)
Acts 12:12 of John whose surname was **M**,
Acts 15:39 And so Barnabas took **M** and
2Ti 4:11 Get **M** and bring him with
1Pe 5:13 and so does **M** my son.

MARKED (*see* MARK)
Prov 8:29 When He **m** out the

MARKET (*see* MARKETPLACE)
1Co 10:25 is sold in the meat **m**,

MARKETPLACE (*see* MARKET, MARKETPLACES)
Luke 7:32 children sitting in the **m**
Acts 17:17 and in the **m** daily with

MARKETPLACES (*see* MARKETPLACE)
Matt 11:16 children sitting in the **m**
Matt 23: 7 "greetings in the **m**,
Mark 12:38 love greetings in the **m**,

MARKS (*see* MARK)
Gal 6:17 for I bear in my body the **m**

MARRED
Is 52:14 So His visage was **m** more
Jer 18: 4 that he made of clay was **m**

MARRIAGE (*see* MARRIAGES, MARRY)
Ezra 9:14 and join in **m** with the
Matt 22:30 marry nor are given in **m**,
Matt 24:38 marrying and giving in **m**,
1Co 7:38 then he who gives her in **m**
1Co 7:38 who does not give her in **m**
Heb 13: 4 **M** is honorable among all,
Rev 19: 9 who are called to the **m**

MARRIAGES (*see* MARRIAGE)
Gen 34: 9 And make **m** with us; give your

MARRIED (*see* MARRY)
Gen 19:14 who had his daughters, and
Num 12: 1 for he had **m** an Ethiopian
1Ki 3: 1 and **m** Pharaoh's daughter;
Is 62: 4 And your land shall be **m**.
Matt 22:25 first died after he had **m**,
Luke 14:20 I have **m** a wife, and
Rom 7: 3 though she has **m** another
1Co 7:10 Now to the **m** I command, yet
1Co 7:33 But he who is **m** cares about

MARRIES (*see* MARRY)
Matt 5:32 and whoever **m** a woman who is
Matt 19: 9 and **m** another, commits
Luke 16:18 and whoever **m** her who is
Rom 7: 3 she **m** another man, she will
1Co 7:28 sinned; and if a virgin **m**,

MARROW
Ps 63: 5 be satisfied as with **m** and
Heb 4:12 spirit, and of joints and **m**,

MARRY (*see* MARRIAGE, MARRIED, MARRIES, MARRYING, UNMARRIED)
Deut 20: 7 the battle and another man **m**
Is 62: 5 So shall your sons **m** you;
Matt 19:10 wife, it is better not to **m.**
Matt 22:24 his brother shall **m** his wife
Matt 22:30 resurrection they neither **m**
Luke 20:34 The sons of this age **m** and
1Co 7: 9 self-control, let them **m.**
1Co 7: 9 For it is better to **m** than
1Co 7:36 He does not sin; let them **m.**
1Ti 4: 3 forbidding to **m,**
1Ti 5:14 that the younger widows **m,**

MARRYING (*see* MARRY)
Matt 24:38 **m** and giving in marriage,

MARTHA
Luke 10:40 But **M** was distracted with
John 11: 1 of Mary and her sister **M.**
John 11: 5 Now Jesus loved **M** and her
John 12: 2 and **M** served, but Lazarus

MARTYR† (*see* MARTYRS)
Acts 22:20 when the blood of Your **m**
Rev 2:13 Antipas was My faithful **m,**

MARTYRS† (*see* MARTYR)
Rev 17: 6 and with the blood of the **m**

MARVEL (*see* MARVELED, MARVELOUS, MARVELS)
John 3: 7 Do not **m** that I said to you,
John 5:20 than these, that you may **m.**
Rev 17: 8 dwell on the earth will **m,**

MARVELED (*see* MARVEL)
Matt 8:10 When Jesus heard it, He **m,**
Matt 9: 8 they **m** and glorified God,
Mark 15: 5 nothing, so that Pilate **m.**
Luke 2:33 And Joseph and His mother **m**
Luke 20:26 And they **m** at His answer and
John 4:27 and they **m** that He talked
Acts 2: 7 they were all amazed and **m,**

MARVELOUS (*see* MARVEL)
Ps 9: 1 I will tell of all Your **m**
Ps 17: 7 Show Your **m** lovingkindness
Ps 78:12 **M** things He did in the sight
Ps 98: 1 new song! For He has done **m**
Ps 118:23 It is **m** in our eyes.
Ps 139:14 **M** are Your works, And
Is 29:14 A **m** work and a wonder; For
Joel 2:21 For the LORD has done **m**
Matt 21:42 And it is **m** in our
John 9:30 this is a **m** thing, that you
1Pe 2: 9 out of darkness into His **m**
Rev 15: 3 Great and **m** are Your works,

MARVELS† (*see* MARVEL)
Ex 34:10 all your people I will do **m**

MARY
Matt 1:16 Joseph the husband of **M,**
Matt 1:18 After His mother **M** was
Matt 2:11 saw the young Child with **M**
Matt 27:56 among whom were **M** Magdalene,
Matt 27:56 **M** the mother of James and
Mark 6: 3 the carpenter, the Son of **M,**
Mark 16: 9 He appeared first to **M**
Luke 1:27 The virgin's name was **M.**
Luke 1:30 her, "Do not be afraid, **M,**
Luke 2: 5 to be registered with **M,**
Luke 2:19 But **M** kept all these things
John 11: 2 It was that **M** who anointed
John 11:19 women around Martha and **M,**
John 12: 3 Then **M** took a pound of very
John 19:25 **M** the wife of Clopas, and
John 20:16 **M!**" She turned and said to
Acts 1:14 with the women and **M** the

MASONS
2Sa 5:11 trees, and carpenters and **m.**
2Ki 12:12 and to **m** and stonecutters,

MASSACRED†
1Ki 18: 4 while Jezebel **m** the prophets

MASSAH (*see* MERIBAH)
Deut 6:16 God as you tempted Him in **M.**
Deut 33: 8 one, Whom You tested at **M,**

MAST
Prov 23:34 who lies at the top of the **m.**

MASTER (*see* MASTER'S, MASTERS)
Gen 24:12 O LORD God of my **m** Abraham,
Gen 27:29 Be **m** over your brethren,
Ex 21: 6 and his **m** shall pierce his
Judg 19:22 They spoke to the **m** of the
2Sa 2: 7 for your **m** Saul is dead, and
2Ch 2:13 Huram my **m** craftsman
Job 3:19 servant is free from his **m.**
Prov 8:30 I was beside Him as a **m**
Prov 30:10 malign a servant to his **m,**
Is 19: 4 Into the hand of a cruel **m,**
Dan 1: 3 the **m** of his eunuchs, to
Hos 2:16 And no longer call Me 'My **M,**
Mal 1: 6 My honor? And if I am a **M,**
Matt 10:24 nor a servant above his **m.**
Matt 24:45 whom his **m** made ruler over
Matt 24:46 is that servant whom his **m,**
Matt 24:48 My **m** is delaying his coming,'
Mark 14:14 say to the **m** of the house,
Luke 5: 5 and said to Him, "**M,**
Luke 8:24 Him, saying, "Master, **M,**
Luke 8:45 and those with him said, "**M,**
Luke 9:33 Peter said to Jesus, "**M,**
Luke 13:25 When once the **M** of the house
Luke 14:21 Then the **m** of the house,
Luke 16: 5 'How much do you owe my **m?**
Luke 16: 8 So the **m** commended the unjust
Luke 17:13 voices and said, "Jesus, **M,**
John 2: 8 and take it to the **m** of the
John 13:16 is not greater than his **m;**
John 15:20 is not greater than his **m.**
1Co 3:10 as a wise **m** builder I have
Gal 4: 1 though he is **m** of all,
Eph 6: 9 knowing that your own **M** also
2Ti 2:21 and useful for the **M,**

MASTER'S (*see* MASTER)
Gen 24:36 And Sarah my **m** wife bore a
2Sa 12: 8 I gave you your **m** house and
2Sa 12: 8 master's house and your **m**
Is 1: 3 owner And the donkey its **m**
Luke 16: 5 he called every one of his **m**

MASTERS (*see* MASTER, MASTERS', TASKMASTERS)
Matt 6:24 "No one can serve two **m;**
Acts 16:16 who brought her **m** much
Eph 6: 9 And you, **m,**
Col 3:22 obey in all things your **m**
Col 4: 1 **M,** give your bondservants
1Ti 6: 2 those who have believing **m,**

MASTERS' (*see* MASTERS)
Matt 15:27 which fall from their **m**

MATCH†
Luke 5:36 out of the new does not **m**

MATERIAL
Rom 15:27 to minister to them in **m**
1Co 9:11 thing if we reap your **m**

MATTANIAH (*see* ZEDEKIAH)
2Ki 24:17 the king of Babylon made **M,**

MATTHEW (*see* LEVI)
Matt 9: 9 He saw a man named **M** sitting

Matt 10: 3 Thomas and **M** the tax
Mark 3:18 Philip, Bartholomew, **M**,

MATTHIAS
Acts 1:26 lots, and the lot fell on **M**.

MATTOCK†
1Sa 13:20 each man's plowshare, his **m**,

MATURE† (*see* MATURITY)
1Co 2: 6 wisdom among those who are **m**,
1Co 14:20 but in understanding be **m**.
Phil 3:15 let us, as many as are **m**,

MATURITY† (*see* MATURE)
Luke 8:14 and bring no fruit to **m**.

MAULED†
2Ki 2:24 came out of the woods and **m**

MEAL (*see* GRAIN, MEALTIME)
Gen 18: 6 three measures of fine **m**;
Gen 37:25 And they sat down to eat a **m**.
Ezek 39:17 A great sacrificial **m** on
Matt 13:33 hid in three measures of **m**

MEALTIME† (*see* MEAL)
Ruth 2:14 Now Boaz said to her at **m**,

MEAN (*see* MEANING, MEANS, MEANT)
Josh 4: 6 What do these stones **m** to
Jon 1: 6 said to him, "What do you **m**,
Luke 8: 9 "What does this parable **m**?
Acts 21:39 a citizen of no **m** city; and
Eph 4: 9 what does it **m** but that He
Phil 1:22 this will **m** fruit from my

MEANING (*see* MEAN)
Dan 8:15 vision and was seeking the **m**,
1Co 14:11 if I do not know the **m** of

MEANS (*see* MEAN)
Ps 49: 7 None of them can by any **m**
Dan 8:25 be broken without human **m**.
Matt 5:18 or one tittle will by no **m**
Matt 5:20 you will by no **m** enter the
Matt 9:13 go and learn what this **m**:
Matt 12: 7 you had known what this **m**,
Matt 24:35 but My words will by no **m**
John 6:37 comes to Me I will by no **m**
John 9:21 but by what **m** he now sees we
Acts 13:41 which you will by no **m**
Rom 1:10 making request if, by some **m**,
Rom 11:14 if by any **m** I may provoke to
1Co 9:22 that I might by all **m** save
Gal 2: 2 lest by any **m** I might run,
Phil 3:11 if, by any **m**, I may attain
1Th 4:15 of the Lord will by no **m**
2Th 2: 3 no one deceive you by any **m**;
1Ti 6: 5 that godliness is a **m** of
Heb 9:15 by **m** of death, for the
1Pe 2: 6 on Him will by no **m**
Rev 21:27 But there shall by no **m** enter

MEANT (*see* MEAN)
Gen 50:20 you **m** evil against me; but
Gen 50:20 but God **m** it for good, in

MEASURE (*see* MEASURED, MEASURES, MEASURING)
Deut 25:15 weight, a perfect and just **m**,
Ps 39: 4 And what is the **m** of my
Ps 60: 6 will divide Shechem And **m**
Ps 108: 7 will divide Shechem And **m**
Is 40:12 the dust of the earth in a **m**?
Zech 2: 2 To **m** Jerusalem, to see what
Matt 7: 2 and with the **m** you use, it
Matt 23:32 the **m** of your fathers'
Mark 7:37 were astonished beyond **m**,
Luke 6:38 will be given to you: good **m**,
John 3:34 not give the Spirit by **m**.
Rom 12: 3 has dealt to each one a **m**

2Co 1: 8 we were burdened beyond **m**,
2Co 10:13 will not boast beyond **m**,
Eph 4: 7 given according to the **m** of
Eph 4:13 to the **m** of the stature of
1Th 2:16 as always to fill up the **m**
Rev 11: 1 Rise and **m** the temple of God,
Rev 21:17 according to the **m** of a

MEASURED (*see* MEASURE)
2Sa 8: 2 he **m** them off with a line.
Is 40:12 Who has **m** the waters in the
Jer 31:37 "If heaven above can be **m**,
Jer 33:22 nor the sand of the sea **m**,
Ezek 40: 5 and he **m** the width of the
Hos 1:10 Which cannot be **m** or
Matt 7: 2 it will be **m** back to you.
Rev 21:16 And he **m** the city with the
Rev 21:17 Then he **m** its wall: one

MEASURES (*see* MEASURE)
Gen 18: 6 make ready three **m** of fine
Deut 25:14 in your house differing **m**,
Prov 20:10 weights and diverse **m**,
Matt 13:33 took and hid in three **m** of

MEASURING (*see* MEASURE)
Is 28:17 I will make justice the **m**
Zech 2: 1 a man with a **m** line in his
2Co 10:12 **m** themselves by themselves,
Rev 11: 1 I was given a reed like a **m**

MEAT
Ex 16: 8 when the LORD gives you **m**
Num 11:13 over me, saying, 'Give us **m**,
Num 11:18 and you shall eat **m**;
Ps 78:20 Can He provide **m** for His
Ps 78:27 He also rained **m** on them
Is 44:16 With this half he eats **m**;
Dan 10: 3 no **m** or wine came into my
Rom 14:21 is good neither to eat **m**
1Co 8:13 I will never again eat **m**,
1Co 10:25 whatever is sold in the **m**

MEDAD
Num 11:27 Eldad and **M** are prophesying

MEDDLES†
Prov 26:17 He who passes by and **m** in

MEDE† (*see* MEDES, MEDIA)
Dan 5:31 And Darius the **M** received the
Dan 11: 1 first year of Darius the **M**,

MEDEBA
Josh 13: 9 and all the plain of **M** as
Is 15: 2 wail over Nebo and over **M**;

MEDES (*see* MEDE)
Esth 1:19 of the Persians and the **M**,
Is 13:17 I will stir up the **M** against
Dan 5:28 and given to the **M** and
Dan 6: 8 to the law of the **M** and
Acts 2: 9 Parthians and **M** and Elamites,

MEDIA (*see* MEDE)
Ezra 6: 2 is in the province of **M**,
Esth 1:14 princes of Persia and **M**,
Dan 8:20 they are the kings of **M** and

MEDIATOR†
Job 9:33 Nor is there any **m** between
Job 33:23 is a messenger for him, A **m**,
Gal 3:19 angels by the hand of a **m**.
Gal 3:20 Now a **m** does not mediate for
1Ti 2: 5 there is one God and one **M**
Heb 8: 6 inasmuch as He is also **M** of
Heb 9:15 for this reason He is the **M**
Heb 12:24 to Jesus the **M** of the new

MEDICINE†
Prov 17:22 heart does good, like **m**,

Ezek 47:12 food, and their leaves for **m**.

MEDITATE (*see* MEDITATES, MEDITATING, MEDITATION)
Gen 24:63 And Isaac went out to **m** in
Josh 1: 8 but you shall **m** in it day
Ps 63: 6 I **m** on You in the night
Ps 77: 6 I **m** within my heart, And
Ps 119:15 I will **m** on Your precepts,
Ps 119:27 So shall I **m** on Your
Ps 119:48 And I will **m** on Your
Ps 119:148 That I may **m** on Your word.
Ps 143: 5 I **m** on all Your works; I
Phil 4: 8 **m** on these things.
1Ti 4:15 **M** on these things; give

MEDITATES (*see* MEDITATE)
Ps 1: 2 And in His law he **m** day and

MEDITATING† (*see* MEDITATE)
1Ki 18:27 he is a god; either he is **m**,

MEDITATION (*see* MEDITATE)
Ps 5: 1 O LORD, Consider my **m**.
Ps 19:14 words of my mouth and the **m**
Ps 119:97 love Your law! It is my **m**
Ps 119:99 Your testimonies are my **m**.

MEDIUM (*see* MEDIUMS)
1Sa 28: 7 is a woman who is a **m** at
1Ch 10:13 because he consulted a **m**

MEDIUMS (*see* MEDIUM)
1Sa 28: 9 how he has cut off the **m** and

MEEK (*see* MEEKNESS)
Ps 37:11 But the **m** shall inherit the
Is 11: 4 with equity for the **m** of
Matt 5: 5 Blessed are the **m**,

MEEKNESS (*see* MEEK)
Col 3:12 kindness, humility, **m**,
Jas 1:21 and receive with **m** the
1Pe 3:15 with **m** and fear;

MEET (*see* MEETING, MEETS, MET)
Gen 18: 2 ran from the tent door to **m**
Ex 18: 7 So Moses went out to **m** his
Ex 25:22 And there I will **m** with you,
Num 23: 3 the LORD will come to **m** me,
Num 23:15 burnt offering while I **m**
Judg 11:31 the doors of my house to **m**
Judg 11:34 coming out to **m** him with
Neh 6: 2 let us **m** together among the
Ps 59:10 of mercy shall come to **m** me;
Prov 17:12 Let a man **m** a bear robbed of
Is 7: 3 Go out now to **m** Ahaz, you and
Hos 13: 8 I will **m** them like a bear
Amos 4:12 Prepare to **m** your God, O
Matt 8:34 the whole city came out to **m**
Matt 25: 1 lamps and went out to **m** the
Mark 14:13 and a man will **m** you
John 18:20 where the Jews always **m**,
1Th 4:17 them in the clouds to **m** the
Tit 3:14 to **m** urgent needs, that

MEETING (*see* MEET)
Ex 27:21 "In the tabernacle of **m**,
Ex 39:40 for the tent of **m**;
Ex 40: 2 tabernacle of the tent of **m**.
Ps 74: 4 roar in the midst of Your **m**
Ps 74: 8 have burned up all the **m**
Is 1:13 iniquity and the sacred **m**.

MEETS (*see* MEET)
Gen 32:17 When Esau my brother **m** you

MEGIDDO
Judg 5:19 Taanach, by the waters of **M**;
1Ki 9:15 wall of Jerusalem, Hazor, **M**,
2Ki 23:30 his body in a chariot from **M**,
2Ch 35:22 to fight in the Valley of **M**.

Zech 12:11 Rimmon in the plain of **M**.

MELCHIZEDEK
Gen 14:18 Then **M** king of Salem brought
Ps 110: 4 According to the order of **M**.
Heb 5: 6 to the order of **M**";
Heb 7: 1 For this **M**, king of Salem,
Heb 7:15 if, in the likeness of **M**,

MELODY
Ps 33: 2 Make **m** to Him with an
Eph 5:19 singing and making **m** in your

MELONS†
Num 11: 5 Egypt, the cucumbers, the **m**,

MELT (*see* MELTED, MELTS)
Josh 14: 8 the heart of the people **m**,
Ps 39:11 You make his beauty **m** away
Ps 97: 5 The mountains **m** like wax at
Ps 112:10 will gnash his teeth and **m**
2Pe 3:10 and the elements will **m** with

MELTED (*see* MELT)
Ex 16:21 the sun became hot, it **m**.
Josh 2:11 these things, our hearts **m**;
Ps 22:14 It has **m** within Me.
Ps 46: 6 His voice, the earth **m**.

MELTS (*see* MELT)
Ps 68: 2 As wax **m** before the fire,
Ps 107:26 Their soul **m** because of
Amos 9: 5 touches the earth and it **m**,

MEMBER (*see* MEMBERS)
Luke 23:50 named Joseph, a council **m**,
1Co 12:14 fact the body is not one **m**
1Co 12:26 And if one **m** suffers, all the
1Co 12:26 or if one **m** is honored, all
Jas 3: 5 so the tongue is a little **m**

MEMBERS (*see* MEMBER)
Matt 5:29 for you that one of your **m**
Rom 6:13 And do not present your **m** as
Rom 7: 5 law were at work in our **m**
Rom 7:23 law of sin which is in my **m**
Rom 12: 4 For as we have many **m** in one
Rom 12: 4 but all the **m** do not have
Rom 12: 5 and individually of one
1Co 6:15 know that your bodies are **m**
1Co 6:15 of Christ and make them **m**
1Co 12:12 body is one and has many **m**,
1Co 12:20 indeed there are many **m**,
1Co 12:22 those **m** of the body which
Eph 2:19 with the saints and **m** of
Eph 4:25 for we are **m** of one
Eph 5:30 For we are **m** of His body, of
Jas 3: 6 is so set among our **m** that
Jas 4: 1 pleasure that war in your **m**?

MEMORIAL (*see* MEMORY)
Ex 12:14 this day shall be to you a **m**;
Ex 13: 9 you on your hand and as a **m**
Ex 17:14 Write this for a **m** in the
Ex 28:12 of the ephod as **m** stones
Lev 2: 9 from the grain offering a **m**
Num 31:54 of meeting as a **m** for the
Josh 4: 7 stones shall be for a **m** to
Matt 26:13 will also be told as a **m** to
Acts 10: 4 alms have come up for a **m**

MEMORY (*see* MEMORIAL)
Job 18:17 The **m** of him perishes from
Prov 10: 7 The **m** of the righteous is
Eccl 9: 5 For the **m** of them is
Is 26:14 And made all their **m** to

MEMPHIS† (*see* NOPH)
Hos 9: 6 **M** shall bury them. Nettles

MEN (*see* MAN, MEN-PLEASERS, MEN'S, PEOPLE)

Gen	4:26	Then **m** began to call on the
Gen	6: 1	when **m** began to multiply on
Gen	6: 2	God saw the daughters of **m**,
Gen	6: 4	Those were the mighty **m** who
Gen	6: 4	were of old, **m** of renown.
Gen	11: 5	tower which the sons of **m**
Gen	13:13	But the **m** of Sodom were
Gen	18: 2	three **m** were standing by
Gen	32:28	with God and with **m**,
Gen	41: 8	of Egypt and all its wise **m**.
Gen	42:11	sons; we are honest **m**;
Gen	43:18	Now the **m** were afraid because
Ex	2:13	two Hebrew **m** were fighting,
Ex	4:19	for all the **m** who sought
Ex	5: 9	more work be laid on the **m**,
Ex	7:11	also called the wise **m** and
Ex	10: 7	Let the **m** go, that they may
Ex	18:25	And Moses chose able **m** out of
Ex	21:22	If **m** fight, and hurt a woman
Num	11:16	Gather to Me seventy **m** of the
Num	13: 2	Send **m** to spy out the land of
Num	16:14	put out the eyes of these **m**?
Num	16:29	men die naturally like all **m**,
Num	32:14	place, a brood of sinful **m**,
Num	32:21	and all your armed **m** cross
Deut	1:15	wise and knowledgeable **m**,
Deut	2:34	we utterly destroyed the **m**,
Deut	3:18	All you **m** of valor shall
Deut	27:14	voice and say to all the **m**
Josh	1:14	all your mighty **m** of valor,
Josh	2: 4	the woman took the two **m**
Josh	10: 6	And the **m** of Gibeon sent to
Judg	6:27	So Gideon took ten **m** from
Judg	7: 6	mouth, was three hundred **m**;
Judg	7:16	divided the three hundred **m**
Judg	9: 4	worthless and reckless **m**;
Judg	9: 9	which they honor God and **m**,
Judg	9:13	cheers both God and **m**,
Judg	9:18	king over the **m** of Shechem,
Judg	9:54	lest **m** say of me, 'A woman
Judg	15:16	I have slain a thousand **m**!
Judg	16:27	Now the temple was full of **m**
Judg	20: 5	And the **m** of Gibeah rose
Judg	20:13	the perverted **m** who are in
Judg	20:16	seven hundred select **m** who
Judg	20:37	the **m** in ambush spread out
Judg	20:41	the **m** of Benjamin panicked,
Ruth	2: 9	I not commanded the young **m**
Ruth	2:21	stay close by my young **m**
Ruth	4: 2	And he took ten **m** of the
1Sa	2:17	the sin of the young **m** was
1Sa	2:26	both with the LORD and **m**.
1Sa	24: 4	Then the **m** of David said to
1Sa	30:22	the wicked and worthless **m**
1Sa	31: 4	lest these uncircumcised **m**,
2Sa	3:34	a man falls before wicked **m**,
2Sa	7:14	him with the rod of **m** and
2Sa	7:14	the blows of the sons of **m**.
2Sa	10: 7	all the army of the mighty **m**.
2Sa	11:16	knew there were valiant **m**.
2Sa	15: 6	stole the hearts of the **m**
2Sa	23: 9	one of the three mighty **m**
2Sa	23:17	not the blood of the **m** who
1Ki	1: 5	and fifty **m** to run before
1Ki	4:30	the wisdom of all the **m** of
1Ki	4:31	For he was wiser than all **m**—
1Ki	9:22	because they were **m** of war
1Ki	10: 8	Happy are your **m** and happy
2Ki	23:14	places with the bones of **m**.
1Ch	9:13	They were very able **m** for
1Ch	10: 4	lest these uncircumcised **m**
1Ch	11:10	the heads of the mighty **m**
1Ch	12:33	stouthearted **m** who could
1Ch	22:15	and all types of skillful **m**
1Ch	26:31	found among them capable **m**
2Ch	6:18	God indeed dwell with **m** on
2Ch	14: 9	with an army of a million **m**
2Ch	35:25	this day all the singing **m**
Ezra	5: 4	them the names of the **m** who
Neh	2:12	I and a few with me; I
Neh	4:21	and half of the **m** held the
Neh	8: 3	before the **m** and women and
Neh	11: 2	the people blessed all the **m**
Esth	1:13	the king said to the wise **m**
Job	4:13	When deep sleep falls on **m**,
Job	7:20	done to You, O watcher of **m**?
Job	12:12	Wisdom is with aged **m**,
Job	17: 6	become one in whose face **m**
Job	27:23	**M** shall clap their hands at
Job	30: 8	fools, Yes, sons of vile **m**;
Job	32: 9	Great **m** are not always
Job	33:15	deep sleep falls upon **m**,
Job	33:16	Then He opens the ears of **m**,
Job	34:34	**M** of understanding say to me,
Job	35:12	of the pride of evil **m**.
Job	37:24	Therefore **m** fear Him; He
Ps	4: 2	How long, O you sons of **m**,
Ps	9:20	themselves to be but **m**.
Ps	11: 4	eyelids test the sons of **m**.
Ps	12: 1	from among the sons of **m**.
Ps	12: 8	exalted among the sons of **m**.
Ps	14: 2	upon the children of **m**,
Ps	22: 6	and no man; A reproach of **m**,
Ps	45: 2	fairer than the sons of **m**;
Ps	53: 2	upon the children of **m**,
Ps	62: 9	Surely **m** of low degree are
Ps	62: 9	**M** of high degree are a
Ps	64: 9	All **m** shall fear, And shall
Ps	68:18	have received gifts among **m**,
Ps	78:25	**M** ate angels' food
Ps	78:63	fire consumed their young **m**,
Ps	82: 7	But you shall die like **m**,
Ps	90: 3	"Return, O children of **m**.
Ps	107: 8	that **m** would give thanks to
Ps	107: 8	works to the children of **m**!
Ps	116:11	All **m** are liars."
Ps	140: 1	me, O LORD, from evil **m**;
Ps	140: 1	Preserve me from violent **m**,
Ps	141: 4	wicked works With **m** who
Ps	148:12	Both young **m** and maidens;
Ps	148:12	Old **m** and children.
Prov	8:31	was with the sons of **m**.
Prov	17: 6	are the crown of old **m**,
Prov	20:29	The glory of young **m** is
Prov	20:29	And the splendor of old **m**
Prov	24: 1	Do not be envious of evil **m**,
Prov	28: 5	Evil **m** do not understand
Prov	29: 8	But wise **m** turn away
Prov	30:14	And the needy from among **m**.
Eccl	2: 3	was good for the sons of **m**
Eccl	3:14	that **m** should fear before
Eccl	3:21	the spirit of the sons of **m**,
Eccl	7: 2	that is the end of all **m**;
Eccl	9:11	Nor riches to **m** of
Eccl	9:14	a little city with few **m** in
Is	2:11	The haughtiness of **m** shall
Is	5:22	Woe to **m** mighty at drinking
Is	6:12	The LORD has removed **m** far
Is	7:13	thing for you to weary **m**,
Is	9: 3	As **m** rejoice when they
Is	19:12	they? Where are your wise **m**?
Is	29:13	by the commandment of **m**,
Is	31: 3	Now the Egyptians are **m**,
Is	38:16	by these things **m** live;
Is	40:30	And the young **m** shall
Is	41:14	You **m** of Israel! I will
Is	45:24	To Him **m** shall come, And
Is	52:14	form more than the sons of **m**;
Is	53: 3	despised and rejected by **m**,

Is	66:24	Upon the corpses of the **m**
Jer	9: 2	assembly of treacherous **m**.
Jer	11:22	The young **m** shall die by the
Jer	11:23	bring catastrophe on the **m**
Jer	32:44	**M** will buy fields for money,
Jer	33: 5	with the dead bodies of **m**
Jer	49:15	nations, Despised among **m**.
Jer	52: 7	and all the **m** of war fled
Lam	1:15	me To crush my young **m**;
Lam	2:21	My virgins and my young **m**
Ezek	9: 4	on the foreheads of the **m**
Ezek	14:14	"Even if these three **m**,
Ezek	26:17	one inhabited by seafaring **m**,
Ezek	27: 8	your oarsmen; Your wise **m**,
Ezek	34:31	of My pasture; you are **m**,
Dan	1:15	flesh than all the young **m**
Dan	1:17	As for these four young **m**,
Dan	2:12	to destroy all the wise **m**
Dan	3:21	Then these **m** were bound in
Dan	3:23	And these three **m**,
Dan.	3:25	I see four **m** loose, walking
Dan	4:17	rules in the kingdom of **m**,
Dan	4:33	he was driven from **m** and ate
Dan	5: 8	Now all the king's wise **m**
Hos	6: 7	But like **m** they transgressed
Hos	13: 2	Let the **m** who sacrifice kiss
Joel	2:28	Your old **m** shall dream
Joel	2:28	Your young **m** shall see
Amos	6: 9	that if ten **m** remain in one
Amos	8:13	virgins And strong young **m**
Jon	1:13	Nevertheless the **m** rowed hard
Jon	1:16	Then the **m** feared the LORD
Mic	5: 5	and eight princely **m**.
Zeph	1:17	they shall walk like blind **m**,
Matt	2: 1	wise **m** from the East came to
Matt	4:19	I will make you fishers of **m**.
Matt	5:13	and trampled underfoot by **m**.
Matt	5:16	your light so shine before **m**,
Matt	5:19	and teaches **m** so, shall be
Matt	6: 1	charitable deeds before **m**,
Matt	6: 2	they may have glory from **m**.
Matt	6: 5	that they may be seen by **m**.
Matt	6:14	For if you forgive their
Matt	6:15	if you do not forgive **m**,
Matt	6:16	that they may appear to **m**
Matt	7:12	whatever you want **m** to do to
Matt	7:16	Do **m** gather grapes from
Matt	8:28	Him two demon-possessed **m**,
Matt	9: 8	had given such power to **m**.
Matt	10:32	confesses Me before **m**,
Matt	12:31	blasphemy will be forgiven **m**,
Matt	12:31	will not be forgiven **m**.
Matt	12:36	that for every idle word **m**
Matt	12:41	The **m** of Nineveh will rise up
Matt	14:21	were about five thousand **m**,
Matt	15:38	who ate were four thousand **m**,
Matt	16:13	Who do **m** say that I, the Son
Matt	17:22	betrayed into the hands of **m**,
Matt	19:26	With **m** this is impossible,
Matt	21:25	from? From heaven or from **m**?
Matt	24:40	Then two **m** will be in the
Matt	28: 4	him, and became like dead **m**.
Mark	2: 3	who was carried by four **m**.
Mark	7: 7	the commandments of **m**.
Mark	7: 8	you hold the tradition of **m**—
Mark	7:21	out of the heart of **m**,
Luke	2:14	goodwill toward **m**!"
Luke	2:52	and in favor with God and **m**.
Luke	6:44	For **m** do not gather figs
Luke	11:46	lawyers! For you load **m** with
Luke	16:15	justify yourselves before **m**,
Luke	17:12	there met Him ten **m** who were
Luke	18: 1	that **m** always ought to pray
Luke	18:11	that I am not like other **m**—
John	1: 4	the life was the light of **m**.
John	2:24	them, because He knew all **m**,
John	3:19	and **m** loved darkness rather
John	5:41	do not receive honor from **m**.
Acts	1:10	two **m** stood by them in white
Acts	1:11	**M** of Galilee, why do you
Acts	1:16	**M** and brethren, this
Acts	2: 5	in Jerusalem Jews, devout **m**,
Acts	2:17	Your young **m** shall see
Acts	2:17	Your old **m** shall dream
Acts	2:22	**M** of Israel, hear these
Acts	4:12	under heaven given among **m**
Acts	4:13	uneducated and untrained **m**,
Acts	5: 4	You have not lied to **m** but
Acts	5:29	to obey God rather than **m**.
Acts	6: 3	out from among you seven **m**
Acts	11: 3	went in to uncircumcised **m**
Acts	13:50	women and the chief **m** of
Acts	14:15	We also are **m** with the same
Acts	17: 5	took some of the evil **m** from
Acts	17:12	prominent women as well as **m**.
Acts	17:22	**M** of Athens, I perceive that
Acts	17:26	one blood every nation of **m**
Acts	17:30	but now commands all **m**
Rom	1:18	and unrighteousness of **m**,
Rom	1:27	**m** with men committing what
Rom	2:29	whose praise is not from **m**
Rom	5:12	thus death spread to all **m**,
Rom	5:18	judgment came to all **m**,
Rom	5:18	free gift came to all **m**,
Rom	12:17	things in the sight of all **m**.
Rom	12:18	live peaceably with all **m**.
1Co	1:25	of God is wiser than **m**,
1Co	2: 5	not be in the wisdom of **m**
1Co	3: 3	and behaving like mere **m**?
1Co	7: 7	For I wish that all **m** were
1Co	9:19	though I am free from all **m**,
1Co	9:22	become all things to all **m**,
1Co	13: 1	speak with the tongues of **m**
1Co	14: 2	a tongue does not speak to **m**
1Co	14:21	With **m** of other tongues
1Co	15:19	we are of all **m** the most
1Co	15:39	is one kind of flesh of **m**,
2Co	3: 2	known and read by all **m**;
2Co	5:11	of the Lord, we persuade **m**;
Gal	1: 1	an apostle (not from **m** nor
Gal	1:10	For do I now persuade **m**,
Eph	4: 8	And gave gifts to **m**.
Eph	6: 7	as to the Lord, and not to **m**,
Phil	2: 7	coming in the likeness of **m**.
Phil	4: 5	gentleness be known to all **m**.
Col	3:23	as to the Lord and not to **m**,
1Th	1: 5	as you know what kind of **m**
1Th	2: 4	we speak, not as pleasing **m**,
1Th	2:13	it not as the word of **m**,
1Ti	2: 4	who desires all **m** to be saved
1Ti	2: 5	Mediator between God and **m**,
1Ti	2: 8	desire therefore that the **m**
1Ti	4:10	who is the Savior of all **m**,
1Ti	6: 9	harmful lusts which drown **m**
2Ti	2: 2	commit these to faithful **m**
2Ti	3:13	But evil **m** and impostors will
Tit	2: 2	that the older **m** be sober,
Tit	2:11	has appeared to all **m**,
Heb	9:27	as it is appointed for **m** to
Heb	12:23	to the spirits of just **m**
Jas	3: 9	and with it we curse **m**,
1Pe	2:15	the ignorance of foolish **m**—
2Pe	1:21	but holy **m** of God spoke as
2Pe	3: 7	and perdition of ungodly **m**.
1Jn	2:13	I write to you, young **m**,
Jude	4	For certain **m** have crept in
Rev	9: 7	were like the faces of **m**.
Rev	16:21	**M** blasphemed God because of
Rev	18:13	and bodies and souls of **m**,
Rev	21: 3	tabernacle of God is with **m**,

MEN-PLEASERS† (*see* MEN)
Eph 6: 6 not with eyeservice, as **m**,
Col 3:22 not with eyeservice, as **m**,

MEN'S (*see* MEN)
Deut 4:28 the work of **m** hands, wood
Matt 23: 4 and lay them on **m**
Matt 23:27 inside are full of dead **m**
Luke 21:26 **m** hearts failing them from
Acts 17:25 Nor is He worshiped with **m**
2Co 10:15 in other **m** labors, but
1Ti 5:24 Some **m** sins are clearly

MENAHEM
2Ki 15:20 And **M** exacted the money from

MENDING†
Matt 4:21 **m** their nets. He called
Mark 1:19 who also were in the boat **m**

MENE†
Dan 5:25 that was written: MENE, **M**,
Dan 5:26 of each word. **M**:

MENTION (*see* MENTIONED)
Gen 40:14 make **m** of me to Pharaoh, and
Rom 1: 9 without ceasing I make **m** of
Eph 1:16 making **m** of you in my
Phm 1:19 not to **m** to you that you owe
Heb 11:22 made **m** of the departure of

MENTIONED (*see* MENTION)
2Ch 20:34 which is **m** in the book of

MEPHIBOSHETH (*see* MERIB-BAAL)
2Sa 9: 6 Then David said, "**M**?
2Sa 19:24 Now **M** the son of Saul came
2Sa 21: 7 But the king spared **M** the

MERARI
Gen 46:11 were Gershon, Kohath, and **M**.

MERCHANDISE
Prov 31:18 She perceives that her **m** is
Ezek 27:33 many luxury goods and your **m**.
John 2:16 Father's house a house of **m**!

MERCHANT (*see* MERCHANTS)
1Ki 10:22 For the king had **m** ships at
Prov 31:14 She is like the **m** ships,
Matt 13:45 of heaven is like a **m**

MERCHANTS (*see* MERCHANT)
Gen 23:16 of silver, currency of the **m**.
1Ki 10:28 the king's **m** bought them in
Prov 31:24 supplies sashes for the **m**.
Rev 18:11 And the **m** of the earth will

MERCIES (*see* MERCIES', MERCY)
Gen 32:10 of the least of all the **m**
2Sa 24:14 for His **m** are great; but do
Neh 9:27 to Your abundant **m** You
Ps 25: 6 Your tender **m** and Your
Ps 51: 1 multitude of Your tender **m**,
Ps 89: 1 I will sing of the **m** of the
Is 55: 3 The sure **m** of David.
Lam 3:22 Through the LORD's **m** we
Dan 9:18 but because of Your great **m**.
Acts 13:34 give you the sure **m**
Rom 12: 1 by the **m** of God, that you
2Co 1: 3 the Father of **m** and God of
Col 3:12 and beloved, put on tender **m**,

MERCIES' (*see* MERCIES, MERCY)
Ps 6: 4 save me for Your **m** sake!

MERCIFUL (*see* MERCY, UNMERCIFUL)
Gen 19:16 the LORD being **m** to him,
Ex 34: 6 **m** and gracious,
Ps 18:25 With the **m** You will show
Ps 41: 4 be **m** to me; Heal my soul,
Ps 56: 1 Be **m** to me, O God, for man

Ps 67: 1 God be **m** to us and bless us,
Ps 103: 8 The LORD is **m** and
Ps 116: 5 Yes, our God is **m**.
Joel 2:13 For He is gracious and **m**,
Jon 4: 2 You are a gracious and **m**
Matt 5: 7 Blessed are the **m**,
Luke 6:36 "Therefore be **m**,
Luke 18:13 be **m** to me a sinner!'
Heb 2:17 that He might be a **m** and
Jas 5:11 is very compassionate and **m**.

MERCY (*see* MERCIES, MERCIES', MERCIFUL)
Gen 19:19 you have increased your **m**
Ex 15:13 You in Your **m** have led forth
Ex 20: 6 but showing **m** to thousands,
Ex 25:17 You shall make a **m** seat of
Lev 16:15 and sprinkle it on the **m**
Num 14:18 and abundant in **m**,
Deut 5:10 but showing **m** to thousands,
Deut 7: 9 God who keeps covenant and **m**
1Ch 16:34 for He is good! For His **m**
Neh 9:32 Who keeps covenant and **m**:
Ps 4: 1 Have **m** on me, and hear my
Ps 5: 7 in the multitude of Your **m**;
Ps 6: 2 Have **m** on me, O LORD, for I
Ps 13: 5 I have trusted in Your **m**;
Ps 18:50 And shows **m** to His
Ps 23: 6 Surely goodness and **m** shall
Ps 25: 7 According to Your **m**
Ps 31: 7 glad and rejoice in Your **m**,
Ps 32:10 **m** shall surround him.
Ps 33:18 On those who hope in His **m**,
Ps 51: 1 Have **m** upon me, O God,
Ps 57: 3 God shall send forth His **m**
Ps 59:16 I will sing aloud of Your **m**
Ps 59:17 is my defense, My God of **m**.
Ps 62:12 to You, O Lord, belongs **m**;
Ps 85:10 **M** and truth have met
Ps 86:13 For great is Your **m** toward
Ps 90:14 satisfy us early with Your **m**,
Ps 98: 3 He has remembered His **m** and
Ps 100: 5 His **m** is everlasting, And
Ps 101: 1 I will sing of **m** and
Ps 103: 8 to anger, and abounding in **m**.
Ps 103:11 So great is His **m** toward
Ps 103:17 But the **m** of the LORD is
Ps 106: 1 for He is good! For His **m**
Ps 119:64 O LORD, is full of Your **m**;
Ps 130: 7 with the LORD there is **m**,
Ps 136: 1 for He is good! For His **m**
Ps 136: 2 the God of gods! For His **m**
Ps 136: 3 Lord of lords! For His **m**
Ps 136: 4 For His **m** endures forever;
Ps 145: 8 to anger and great in **m**.
Prov 3: 3 Let not **m** and truth forsake
Prov 28:13 forsakes them will have **m**.
Is 14: 1 For the LORD will have **m** on
Is 47: 6 hand. You showed them no **m**;
Is 55: 7 And He will have **m** on him;
Dan 9: 4 who keeps His covenant and **m**
Dan 9: 9 the Lord our God belong **m**
Hos 1: 6 I will no longer have **m** on
Hos 2:19 In lovingkindness and **m**;
Hos 2:23 who had not obtained **m**,
Hos 4: 1 There is no truth or **m** Or
Hos 6: 6 For I desire **m** and not
Hos 14: 3 You the fatherless finds **m**.
Mic 6: 8 to do justly, To love **m**,
Mic 7:18 Because He delights in **m**.
Mic 7:20 give truth to Jacob And **m**
Hab 3: 2 known; In wrath remember **m**.
Matt 5: 7 For they shall obtain **m**.
Matt 9:13 I desire **m** and not
Matt 9:27 have **m** on us!"
Matt 15:22 Have **m** on me, O Lord, Son of

Matt 23:23 justice and **m** and faith.
Luke 1:50 And His **m** is on those who
Luke 1:58 the Lord had shown great **m**
Luke 1:78 Through the tender **m** of our
Luke 16:24 have **m** on me, and send
Rom 9:15 I will have **m** on
Rom 9:16 runs, but of God who shows **m**.
Rom 9:23 glory on the vessels of **m**,
Rom 11:30 yet have now obtained **m**
2Co 4: 1 as we have received **m**,
Gal 6:16 peace and **m** be upon them,
Eph 2: 4 But God, who is rich in **m**,
Phil 2: 1 if any affection and **m**,
Phil 2:27 but God had **m** on him, and
1Ti 1: 2 son in the faith: Grace, **m**,
1Ti 1:13 but I obtained **m** because I
Tit 3: 5 but according to His **m** He
Heb 4:16 that we may obtain **m** and
Heb 9: 5 of glory overshadowing the **m**
Heb 10:28 Moses' law dies without **m**
Jas 2:13 For judgment is without **m** to
1Pe 1: 3 according to His abundant **m**
1Pe 2:10 who had not obtained **m** but

MERIB-BAAL (*see* MEPHIBOSHETH)
1Ch 8:34 The son of Jonathan was **M**,

MERIBAH (*see* MASSAH)
Ex 17: 7 of the place Massah and **M**,
Ps 81: 7 you at the waters of **M**.

MERODACH†
Jer 50: 2 **M** is broken in pieces; Her

MERODACH-BALADAN†
Is 39: 1 At that time **M** the son of

MEROM
Josh 11: 7 suddenly by the waters of **M**,

MERRY
Gen 43:34 So they drank and were **m**
Esth 1:10 the heart of the king was **m**
Prov 15:13 A **m** heart makes a cheerful
Eccl 8:15 than to eat, drink, and be **m**;
Eccl 10:19 laughter, And wine makes **m**;
Luke 12:19 ease; eat, drink, and be **m**.
Rev 11:10 rejoice over them, make **m**,

MESHA
2Ki 3: 4 Now **M** king of Moab was a

MESHACH (*see* MISHAEL)
Dan 1: 7 Shadrach; to Mishael, **M**;
Dan 3:12 of Babylon: Shadrach, **M**,

MESHECH
Ezek 32:26 There are **M** and Tubal and
Ezek 38: 3 O Gog, the prince of Rosh, **M**,

MESOPOTAMIA (*see* ARAM)
Gen 24:10 And he arose and went to **M**,
Judg 3: 8 Cushan-Rishathaim king of **M**;
Acts 2: 9 those dwelling in **M**,
Acts 7: 2 Abraham when he was in **M**,

MESSAGE (*see* MESSENGER)
Judg 3:19 I have a secret **m** for you, O
1Co 1:18 For the **m** of the cross is
1Co 1:21 the foolishness of the **m**
2Ti 2:17 And their **m** will spread like
1Jn 1: 5 This is the **m** which we have

MESSENGER (*see* MESSAGE, MESSENGERS)
Job 1:14 and a **m** came to Job and said,
Prov 25:13 of harvest Is a faithful **m**
Is 42:19 Or deaf as My **m** whom I
Mal 2: 7 For he is the **m** of the
Mal 3: 1 "Behold, I send My **m**,
Mal 3: 1 Even the **M** of the covenant,
Matt 11:10 I send My **m** before

2Co 12: 7 a **m** of Satan to buffet me,
Phil 2:25 but your **m** and the one who

MESSENGERS (*see* MESSENGER)
2Sa 11: 4 Then David sent **m**,
Is 18: 2 saying, "Go, swift **m**,
Luke 7:24 When the **m** of John had
2Co 8:23 they are **m** of the
Jas 2:25 when she received the **m** and

MESSIAH†
Dan 9:25 and build Jerusalem Until **M**
Dan 9:26 after the sixty-two weeks **M**
John 1:41 We have found the **M**" (which
John 4:25 I know that **M** is coming"

MET (*see* MEET)
Ps 85:10 Mercy and truth have **m**
Amos 5:19 And a bear **m** him! Or as
Matt 8:28 there **m** Him two
Luke 17:12 there **m** Him ten men who were
John 11:30 in the place where Martha **m**
John 18: 2 for Jesus often **m** there with
Acts 10:25 Cornelius **m** him and fell
Heb 7: 1 who **m** Abraham returning from
Heb 7:10 father when Melchizedek **m**

METHUSELAH
Gen 5:27 So all the days of **M** were

MICAH (*see* MICAIAH)
Judg 17: 1 Ephraim, whose name was **M**.
Judg 17:12 So **M** consecrated the Levite,
Jer 26:18 **M** of Moresheth prophesied in
Mic 1: 1 of the LORD that came to **M**

MICAIAH (*see* MICAH)
1Ki 22: 8 **M** the son of Imlah, by whom

MICHAEL
Dan 10:21 except **M** your prince.
Dan 12: 1 At that time **M** shall stand
Jude 9 Yet **M** the archangel, in
Rev 12: 7 **M** and his angels fought with

MICHAL
2Sa 3:14 saying, "Give me my wife **M**,

MICHMASH
1Sa 13: 2 were with Saul in **M** and in
1Sa 13:16 Philistines encamped in **M**.
1Sa 13:23 went out to the pass of **M**.

MIDDAY
Neh 8: 3 Gate from morning until **m**,
Acts 26:13 "at **m**, O king, along

MIDDLE
Gen 15:10 cut them in two, down the **m**,
2Sa 10: 4 off their garments in the **m**,
1Ki 3:20 So she arose in the **m** of the
Job 34:20 in the **m** of the night; The
Is 16: 3 like the night in the **m** of
Ezek 1:16 a wheel in the **m** of a wheel.
Ezek 10:10 a wheel in the **m** of a wheel.
Dan 9:27 But in the **m** of the week
Mark 6:47 the boat was in the **m** of the
Acts 1:18 he burst open in the **m** and
Eph 2:14 and has broken down the **m**
Rev 22: 2 In the **m** of its street, and

MIDIAN (*see* MIDIANITE)
Ex 2:15 and dwelt in the land of **M**;
Ex 18: 1 And Jethro, the priest of **M**,
Judg 7: 8 Now the camp of **M** was below
Judg 8:12 he took the two kings of **M**,
Is 9: 4 As in the day of **M**.

MIDIANITE (*see* MIDIAN, MIDIANITES)
Gen 37:28 Then **M** traders passed by; so
Num 25:14 who was killed with the **M**

MIDIANITES (*see* KENITES, MIDIANITE)
Gen 37:36 Now the **M** had sold him in
Judg 6:14 from the hand of the **M**.
Judg 6:33 Then all the **M** and

MIDNIGHT
Ex 12:29 And it came to pass at **m**
Ruth 3: 8 Now it happened at **m** that
Matt 25: 6 And at **m** a cry was heard:
Luke 11: 5 and go to him at **m** and say
Acts 16:25 But at **m** Paul and Silas were

MIDWIFE† (*see* MIDWIVES)
Gen 35:17 that the **m** said to her, "Do
Gen 38:28 and the **m** took a scarlet
Ex 1:16 you do the duties of a **m**

MIDWIVES (*see* MIDWIFE)
Ex 1:17 But the **m** feared God, and did

MIGDOL
Ex 14: 2 between **M** and the sea,
Ezek 29:10 from **M** to Syene, as far as

MIGHT (*see* STRENGTH)
Gen 49: 3 My **m** and the beginning of
1Ch 29:12 Your hand is power and **m**;
Eccl 9:10 to do, do it with your **m**;
Is 11: 2 The Spirit of counsel and **m**,
Is 40:26 By the greatness of His **m**
Jer 9:23 mighty man glory in his **m**,
Dan 2:20 For wisdom and **m** are His.
Dan 2:23 have given me wisdom and **m**,
Zech 4: 6 Not by **m** nor by power, but by
Eph 1:21 and power and **m** and
Eph 3:16 to be strengthened with **m**
Eph 6:10 and in the power of His **m**.
Rev 7:12 and honor and power and **m**,

MIGHTIER (*see* MIGHT, MIGHTY)
Ex 1: 9 of Israel are more and **m**
Ps 93: 4 The LORD on high is **m**
Matt 3:11 who is coming after me is **m**

MIGHTILY (*see* MIGHT)
Judg 14: 6 Spirit of the LORD came **m**
Acts 19:20 the word of the Lord grew **m**
Col 1:29 working which works in me **m**.

MIGHTY (*see* MIGHT, MIGHTIER)
Gen 6: 4 Those were the **m** men who
Gen 10: 9 Like Nimrod the **m** hunter
Gen 49:24 By the hands of the **M** God
Ex 1:20 multiplied and grew very **m**.
Ex 32:11 great power and with a **m**
Num 22: 6 for they are too **m** for me.
Deut 9:29 You brought out by Your **m**
Deut 26: 5 he became a nation, great, **m**,
Josh 1:14 all your **m** men of valor, and
2Sa 23: 9 one of the three **m** men with
Ezra 4:20 There have also been **m** kings
Job 36: 5 "Behold, God is **m**,
Ps 24: 8 The LORD strong and **m**,
Ps 24: 8 The LORD **m** in battle.
Ps 29: 1 O you **m** ones, Give unto the
Ps 33:16 A **m** man is not delivered by
Ps 50: 1 The **M** One, God the LORD,
Ps 59: 3 The **m** gather against me,
Ps 68:33 out His voice, a **m** voice.
Ps 74:15 You dried up **m** rivers.
Ps 82: 1 in the congregation of the **m**;
Ps 89: 6 among the sons of the **m** can
Ps 89: 8 Who is **m** like You, O
Ps 89:10 Your enemies with Your **m**
Ps 106: 2 Who can utter the **m** acts of
Ps 106: 8 That He might make His **m**
Ps 132: 2 And vowed to the **m** One of
Ps 150: 1 Praise Him in His **m**
Prov 16:32 anger is better than the **m**,

Is 1:24 the **M** One of Israel, "Ah,
Is 5:22 Woe to men **m** at drinking
Is 9: 6 **M** God, Everlasting Father,
Is 10:21 To the **M** God.
Is 10:34 Lebanon will fall by the **M**
Is 17:12 like the rushing of **m**
Is 43:16 And a path through the **m**
Is 49:26 the **M** One of Jacob."
Is 63: 1 righteousness, **m** to save."
Jer 9:23 Let not the **m** man glory in
Jer 32:18 the **M** God, whose name is
Jer 33: 3 and show you great and **m**
Jer 51:30 The **m** men of Babylon have
Dan 4:30 for a royal dwelling by my **m**
Dan 8:24 His power shall be **m**,
Dan 11: 3 Then a **m** king shall arise,
Amos 5:24 And righteousness like a **m**
Jon 1: 4 and there was a **m** tempest on
Zeph 3:17 The **M** One, will save; He
Matt 11:20 in which most of His **m**
Mark 6: 5 Now He could do no **m** work
Luke 1:49 For He who is **m** has done
Luke 1:52 He has put down the **m** from
Luke 24:19 who was a Prophet **m** in deed
Acts 2: 2 as of a rushing **m** wind, and
Acts 7:22 and was **m** in words and
Acts 18:24 an eloquent man and **m** in
1Co 1:26 to the flesh, not many **m**,
1Co 1:27 shame the things which are **m**;
2Co 10: 4 are not carnal but **m** in
2Co 13: 3 but **m** in you.
Eph 1:19 to the working of His **m**
2Th 1: 7 from heaven with His **m**
1Pe 5: 6 yourselves under the **m** hand
Rev 18:10 that **m** city! For in one hour

MILCOM (*see* MOLECH, MOLOCH)
1Ki 11: 5 and after **M** the abomination
1Ki 11:33 and **M** the god of the people
Zeph 1: 5 But who also swear by **M**;

MILD†
Gen 25:27 but Jacob was a **m** man,

MILDEW
Deut 28:22 with scorching, and with **m**;
1Ki 8:37 pestilence or blight or **m**,

MILE† (*see* MILES)
Matt 5:41 compels you to go one **m**,

MILES (*see* MILE)
Luke 24:13 which was seven **m** from
John 11:18 about two **m** away.

MILETUS
Acts 20:17 From **M** he sent to Ephesus
2Ti 4:20 Trophimus I have left in **M**

MILK
Ex 3: 8 to a land flowing with **m** and
Ex 23:19 young goat in its mother's **m**.
Judg 5:25 asked for water, she gave **m**;
Is 55: 1 buy wine and **m** Without
1Co 3: 2 I fed you with **m** and not with
Heb 5:12 and you have come to need **m**
Heb 5:13 who partakes only of **m** is
1Pe 2: 2 desire the pure **m** of the

MILL†
Matt 24:41 will be grinding at the **m**:

MILLO
1Ki 11:27 Solomon had built the **M** and
2Ch 32: 5 also he repaired the **M** in

MILLSTONE (*see* MILLSTONES)
Judg 9:53 woman dropped an upper **m** on
Matt 18: 6 be better for him if a **m**
Rev 18:22 and the sound of a **m** shall

MILLSTONES (see MILLSTONE)
Is   47: 2 Take the **m** and grind meal.
Jer   25:10 the sound of the **m** and the

MINA
Luke   19:16 your **m** has earned ten

MINCING†
Is   3:16 Walking and **m** as they go,

MIND (see MINDED, MINDFUL, MINDS, UNMINDFUL)
Gen   37:11 kept the matter in **m**.
Lev   24:12 that the **m** of the LORD
1Ch   12:38 of Israel were of one **m** to
1Ch   28: 9 heart and with a willing **m**;
Neh   4: 6 for the people had a **m** to
Ps   26: 2 Try my **m** and my heart.
Ps   73:21 And I was vexed in my **m**.
Is   26: 3 Whose **m** is stayed on
Is   65:17 be remembered or come to **m**.
Jer   12: 2 mouth But far from their **m**.
Jer   17:10 the heart, I test the **m**,
Lam   3:21 This I recall to my **m**,
Dan   2:29 thoughts came to your **m**
Hab   1:11 Then his **m** changes, and he
Matt   22:37 and with all your **m**.
Mark   3:21 said, "He is out of His **m**.
Mark   5:15 clothed and in his right **m**.
Luke   12:29 drink, nor have an anxious **m**.
Rom   1:28 them over to a debased **m**,
Rom   7:23 against the law of my **m**,
Rom   8: 7 Because the carnal **m** is
Rom   8:27 the hearts knows what the **m**
Rom   11:34 who has known the **m**
Rom   12: 2 by the renewing of your **m**,
Rom   12:16 Do not set your **m** on high
Rom   14: 5 fully convinced in his own **m**.
1Co   1:10 together in the same **m** and
1Co   2:16 who has known the **m** of
1Co   2:16 But we have the **m** of
2Co   8:12 there is first a willing **m**,
2Co   8:19 and to show your ready **m**,
Eph   4:17 in the futility of their **m**,
Eph   4:23 in the spirit of your **m**,
Phil   1:27 with one **m** striving together
Phil   2: 3 but in lowliness of **m** let
Phil   2: 5 Let this **m** be in you which
Phil   3:19 who set their **m** on earthly
Phil   4: 2 to be of the same **m** in the
Col   2:18 puffed up by his fleshly **m**,
Col   3: 2 Set your **m** on things above,
1Th   4:11 to **m** your own business, and
2Ti   1: 7 and of love and of a sound **m**.
Heb   8:10 put My laws in their **m**
1Pe   3: 8 all of you be of one **m**,

MINDED (see MIND)
Matt   1:19 was **m** to put her away
Rom   8: 6 For to be carnally **m** is
Rom   8: 6 but to be spiritually **m** is

MINDFUL (see MIND)
Ps   8: 4 What is man that You are **m**
Ps   111: 5 He will ever be **m** of His
Ps   115:12 The LORD has been **m** of us;
2Ti   1: 4 being **m** of your tears, that
Heb   2: 6 is man that You are **m**

MINDS (see MIND)
Ps   7: 9 God tests the hearts and **m**.
Jer   31:33 I will put My law in their **m**,
Jer   34:11 they changed their **m** and
Rom   8: 5 to the flesh set their **m** on
2Co   3:14 But their **m** were blinded. For
2Co   4: 4 whose **m** the god of this age
2Co   11: 3 so your **m** may be corrupted
Phil   4: 7 will guard your hearts and **m**
1Ti   6: 5 of men of corrupt **m** and

Heb   10:16 and in their **m** I will
Rev   2:23 I am He who searches the **m**

MINGLED
Matt   27:34 they gave Him sour wine **m**
Luke   13: 1 whose blood Pilate had **m**

MINISTER (see MINISTERED, MINISTERING, MINISTERS, MINISTRY)
Ex   28: 1 that he may **m** to Me as
Lev   16:32 and consecrated to **m** as
1Ch   16: 4 some of the Levites to **m**
Matt   25:44 and did not **m** to You?'
Acts   26:16 to make you a **m** and a
Rom   13: 4 For he is God's **m** to you for
Rom   15:16 that I might be a **m** of Jesus
Rom   15:25 I am going to Jerusalem to **m**
1Co   9:13 not know that those who **m**
Eph   3: 7 of which I became a **m**
Eph   6:21 brother and faithful **m** in
Col   1:23 of which I, Paul, became a **m**.
1Ti   4: 6 you will be a good **m** of
Heb   1:14 spirits sent forth to **m** for
Heb   8: 2 a **M** of the sanctuary and of
1Pe   4:10 **m** it to one another, as good

MINISTERED (see MINISTER)
1Sa   2:18 But Samuel **m** before the
Matt   4:11 angels came and **m** to Him.
Acts   13: 2 As they **m** to the Lord and
Phil   2:25 messenger and the one who **m**
Heb   6:10 in that you have **m** to the

MINISTERING (see MINISTER)
1Ch   6:32 They were **m** with music before
Rom   1:16 the gospel of God, that
2Co   8: 4 and the fellowship of the **m**
Heb   1:14 Are they not all **m** spirits
Heb   10:11 And every priest stands **m**
1Pe   1:12 but to us they were **m** the

MINISTERS (see MINISTER)
Ex   28:35 be upon Aaron when he **m**,
Ps   103:21 You **m** of His, who do His
Ps   104: 4 His **m** a flame of fire.
Luke   1: 2 were eyewitnesses and **m** of
Rom   13: 6 for they are God's **m**
2Co   3: 6 made us sufficient as **m** of
2Co   6: 4 we commend ourselves as **m**
2Co   11:15 transform themselves into **m**
2Co   11:23 Are they **m** of Christ?—I speak
Heb   1: 7 spirits And His **m** a
1Pe   4:11 oracles of God. If anyone **m**,

MINISTRIES† (see MINISTRY)
1Co   12: 5 There are differences of **m**,

MINISTRY (see MINISTER, MINISTRIES)
Luke   3:23 Jesus Himself began His **m**
Acts   1:17 obtained a part in this **m**.
Acts   6: 4 to prayer and to the **m** of
Acts   12:25 they had fulfilled their **m**,
Rom   11:13 the Gentiles, I magnify my **m**,
1Co   16:15 devoted themselves to the **m**
2Co   3: 7 But if the **m** of death,
2Co   3: 8 how will the **m** of the Spirit
2Co   3: 9 For if the **m** of condemnation
2Co   3: 9 the **m** of righteousness
Eph   4:12 the saints for the work of **m**,
Col   4:17 Take heed to the **m** which you
1Ti   1:12 putting me into the **m**,
2Ti   4: 5 evangelist, fulfill your **m**.
2Ti   4:11 for he is useful to me for **m**.
Heb   8: 6 obtained a more excellent **m**,
Heb   9:21 and all the vessels of the **m**.

MINT
Matt   23:23 For you pay tithe of **m** and

MINUS†
2Co 11:24 I received forty stripes **m**

MIRACLE (see MIRACLES)
Ex 7: 9 Show a **m** for yourselves,'
Mark 9:39 for no one who works a **m** in
Luke 23: 8 and he hoped to see some **m**
Acts 4:22 years old on whom this **m** of

MIRACLES (see MIRACLE, SIGNS)
Judg 6:13 And where are all His **m**
Acts 2:22 attested by God to you by **m**,
Acts 19:11 Now God worked unusual **m** by
1Co 12:10 to another the working of **m**,
1Co 12:28 third teachers, after that **m**,
1Co 12:29 Are all workers of **m**?
Heb 2: 4 and wonders, with various **m**,

MIRE (see MIRY)
Ps 69:14 Deliver me out of the **m**,
Is 57:20 Whose waters cast up **m** and
Jer 38: 6 So Jeremiah sank in the **m**.
2Pe 2:22 to her wallowing in the **m**.

MIRIAM
Ex 15:20 Then **M** the prophetess, the
Num 12:10 suddenly **M** became leprous,
Num 26:59 and Moses and their sister **M**.

MIRROR† (see MIRRORS)
Job 37:18 Strong as a cast metal **m**?
1Co 13:12 For now we see in a **m**,
2Co 3:18 beholding as in a **m** the
Jas 1:23 his natural face in a **m**;

MIRRORS (see MIRROR)
Ex 38: 8 from the bronze **m** of the

MIRTH
Ps 137: 3 plundered us requested **m**,
Jer 7:34 of Jerusalem the voice of **m**

MIRY† (see MIRE)
Ps 40: 2 Out of the **m** clay, And set

MISCARRIAGE (see MISCARRYING)
Ex 23:26 No one shall suffer **m** or be

MISCARRYING† (see MISCARRIAGE)
Hos 9:14 Give them a **m** womb And dry

MISERABLE (see MISERY)
Job 16: 2 **M** comforters are you all!
Rev 3:17 that you are wretched, **m**,

MISERY (see MISERABLE)
Job 11:16 you would forget your **m**,
Prov 31: 7 And remember his **m** no more.
Jon 4: 6 to deliver him from his **m**.
Rom 3:16 Destruction and **m** are

MISHAEL (see MESHACH)
Dan 1: 6 were Daniel, Hananiah, **M**,
Dan 1: 7 to Hananiah, Shadrach; to **M**,

MISS (see MISSED, MISSING)
Judg 20:16 a hair's breadth and not **m**.

MISSED (see MISS)
1Sa 25:21 so that nothing was **m** of all

MISSING (see MISS)
Num 31:49 and not a man of us is **m**.

MIST
Gen 2: 6 but a **m** went up from the
Job 36:27 distill as rain from the **m**,

MISTAKEN
Matt 22:29 said to them, "You are **m**,

MISTREAT† (see MISTREATED)
Ex 22:21 You shall neither **m** a

MISTREATED (see MISTREAT)
Deut 26: 6 But the Egyptians **m** us,
Heb 13: 3 with them—those who are **m**—

MISTRESS
Gen 16: 4 her **m** became despised in her

MITE† (see MITES)
Luke 12:59 have paid the very last **m**.

MITES (see MITE)
Mark 12:42 came and threw in two **m**,

MIX (see MIXED)
Dan 2:43 just as iron does not **m** with

MIXED (see MIX)
Ex 12:38 A **m** multitude went up with
Ex 29: 2 unleavened cakes **m** with oil,
Lev 19:19 Nor shall a garment of **m**
Dan 2:41 just as you saw the iron **m**
Hos 7: 8 Ephraim has **m** himself among
Zech 9: 6 A **m** race shall settle in
Heb 4: 2 not being **m** with faith in

MIZPAH
Gen 31:49 also **M**, because he said,
Judg 11:29 and passed through **M** of
1Sa 7: 5 "Gather all Israel to **M**,
1Sa 7:16 to Bethel, Gilgal, and **M**,
Jer 40: 8 they came to Gedaliah at **M**—

MIZRAIM (see ABEL MIZRAIM, EGYPT)
Gen 10: 6 sons of Ham were Cush, **M**,

MOAB (see MOABITE, MOABITESS)
Gen 19:37 a son and called his name **M**;
Ex 15:15 The mighty men of **M**,
Num 22: 3 And **M** was exceedingly afraid
Num 23: 7 Balak the king of **M** has
Num 25: 1 harlotry with the women of **M**.
Num 26:63 of Israel in the plains of **M**
Num 31:12 the camp in the plains of **M**
Deut 2: 8 way of the Wilderness of **M**.
Deut 34: 5 died there in the land of **M**,
Judg 3:15 tribute to Eglon king of **M**.
Ruth 1: 1 to dwell in the country of **M**,
Ruth 1: 4 took wives of the women of **M**:
1Ki 11: 7 Chemosh the abomination of **M**,
2Ki 1: 1 **M** rebelled against Israel
2Ki 3: 4 Now Mesha king of **M** was a
Ps 60: 8 **M** is My washpot
Is 15: 1 The burden against **M**.
Jer 48: 1 Against **M**. Thus says the
Jer 48:42 And **M** shall be destroyed as
Amos 2: 1 three transgressions of **M**,
Zeph 2: 9 Surely **M** shall be like Sodom,

MOABITE (see MOAB, MOABITES)
Deut 23: 3 An Ammonite or **M** shall not
Ruth 2: 6 It is the young **M** woman who

MOABITES (see MOABITE)
Gen 19:37 he is the father of the **M**
1Ki 11:33 Chemosh the god of the **M**,
2Ki 3:18 He will also deliver the **M**
2Ki 23:13 the abomination of the **M**,

MOABITESS (see MOAB)
Ruth 1:22 and Ruth the **M** her

MOAN
Is 59:11 And **m** sadly like doves; We

MOB
Acts 17: 5 and gathering a **m**,
Acts 21:35 of the violence of the **m**.

MOCK (see MOCKED, MOCKER, MOCKING, MOCKS)
Gen 39:14 in to us a Hebrew to **m** us.
Job 30: 1 But now they **m** at me, men
Matt 20:19 Him to the Gentiles to **m**

Luke 14:29 all who see it begin to **m**

MOCKED (see MOCK)
Judg 16:15 You have **m** me these three
1Ki 18:27 that Elijah **m** them and said,
Neh 4: 1 and **m** the Jews.
Job 12: 4 I am one **m** by his friends,
Lam 1: 7 adversaries saw her And **m**
Matt 27:29 the knee before Him and **m**
Luke 18:32 the Gentiles and will be **m**
Luke 22:63 the men who held Jesus **m**
Luke 23:36 The soldiers also **m** Him,
Acts 17:32 of the dead, some **m**,
Gal 6: 7 be deceived, God is not **m**;

MOCKER† (see MOCK, MOCKERS)
Prov 20: 1 Wine is a **m**,

MOCKERS (see MOCKER)
Jer 15:17 sit in the assembly of the **m**,
Jude 18 you that there would be **m**

MOCKING (see MOCK)
Matt 27:41 **m** with the scribes and
Acts 2:13 Others **m** said, "They are

MOCKS (see MOCK)
Jer 20: 7 Everyone **m** me.

MODEST† (see MODESTY)
1Ti 2: 9 women adorn themselves in **m**

MODESTY† (see MODEST)
1Co 12:23 parts have greater **m**,

MOIST† (see MOISTURE)
Job 21:24 the marrow of his bones is **m**.

MOISTURE (see MOIST)
Luke 8: 6 away because it lacked **m**.

MOLDED (see MOLDS)
Ex 32: 4 and made a **m** calf. Then they
Ex 34:17 You shall make no **m** gods for
Num 33:52 destroy all their **m** images,
Judg 17: 3 make a carved image and a **m**
Judg 17: 4 into a carved image and a **m**
2Ch 28: 2 and made **m** images for the
Ps 106:19 And worshiped the **m** image.
Is 41:29 Their **m** images are wind
Jer 10:14 For his **m** image is

MOLDS (see MOLDED)
Is 40:19 The workman **m** an image, The

MOLDY
Josh 9: 5 provision was dry and **m**.

MOLECH (see MILCOM, MOLOCH)
Lev 18:21 pass through the fire to **M**,
1Ki 11: 7 and for **M** the abomination of

MOLOCH† (see MILCOM, MOLECH)
Acts 7:43 up the tabernacle of **M**,

MOMENT
Num 16:21 I may consume them in a **m**.
Job 7:18 And test him every **m**?
Job 20: 5 hypocrite is but for a **m**?
Job 34:20 In a **m** they die, in the
Ps 30: 5 His anger is but for a **m**,
Prov 12:19 lying tongue is but for a **m**.
Luke 4: 5 of the world in a **m** of time.
1Co 15:52 in a **m**, in the twinkling of
2Co 4:17 which is but for a **m**,

MONEY (see MONEY BELTS, MONEY CHANGERS)
Gen 17:23 who were bought with his **m**,
Ex 21:11 out free, without paying **m**.
Ex 22:25 If you lend **m** to any of My
Ex 30:16 shall take the atonement **m**
Num 3:51 gave their redemption **m** to
Deut 21:14 shall not sell her for **m**;

Deut 23:19 interest on **m** or food or
Judg 16:18 up to her and brought the **m**
1Ki 21: 6 'Give me your vineyard for **m**;
2Ki 12: 4 each man's assessment **m**—
2Ki 12:15 hand they delivered the **m**
2Ki 17: 3 and paid him tribute **m**.
Ezra 3: 7 They also gave **m** to the
Neh 5: 4 We have borrowed **m** for the
Neh 5:10 am lending them **m** and grain.
Eccl 10:19 But **m** answers everything.
Is 52: 3 shall be redeemed without **m**.
Is 55: 1 And you who have no **m**,
Is 55: 1 buy wine and milk Without **m**
Is 55: 2 Why do you spend **m** for what
Jer 32:10 and weighed the **m** on the
Jer 32:25 GOD, "Buy the field for **m**,
Mic 3:11 her prophets divine for **m**.
Matt 10: 9 silver nor copper in your **m**
Matt 17:27 you will find a piece of **m**;
Matt 22:19 "Show Me the tax **m**.
Matt 25:18 ground, and hid his lord's **m**.
Matt 28:12 they gave a large sum of **m**
Luke 9: 3 nor bag nor bread nor **m**;
Luke 16:14 who were lovers of **m**,
Luke 19:23 then did you not put my **m**
John 2:15 poured out the changers' **m**
John 13:29 because Judas had the **m** box,
Acts 4:37 and brought the **m** and laid
Acts 8:20 Your **m** perish with you,
1Ti 3: 3 violent, not greedy for **m**,
1Ti 3: 8 much wine, not greedy for **m**,
1Ti 6:10 For the love of **m** is a root
2Ti 3: 2 of themselves, lovers of **m**,

MONEY BELTS (see MONEY)
Matt 10: 9 copper in your **M**, "nor bag

MONEY CHANGERS† (see MONEY)
Matt 21:12 overturned the tables of the **m**
John 2:14 and the **m** doing business.

MONSTER
Ezek 32: 2 And you are like a **m** in

MONTH (see MONTHS)
Gen 8: 4 ark rested in the seventh **m**,
Gen 8:13 first year, in the first **m**,
Ex 12: 2 it shall be the first **m** of
Ex 12: 6 fourteenth day of the same **m**.
Ex 13: 4 in the **m** Abib.
Ex 19: 1 In the third **m** after the
Lev 27: 6 and if from a **m** old up to
Num 11:21 they may eat for a whole **m**.
1Ki 6: 1 in the **m** of Ziv, which is
1Ki 6:38 in the **m** of Bul, which is
1Ki 8: 2 at the feast in the **m** of
1Ch 27: 1 in and went out month by **m**
1Ch 27: 2 division for the first **m**
Ezra 6:15 on the third day of the **m**
Neh 1: 1 It came to pass in the **m** of
Esth 2:16 which is the **m** of Tebeth,
Esth 8: 9 which is the **m** of Sivan, on
Jer 1: 3 captive in the fifth **m**.
Dan 10: 4 day of the first **m**,
Joel 2:23 latter rain in the first **m**.
Zech 1: 7 which is the **m** Shebat, in
Zech 8:19 The fast of the fourth **m**,
Luke 1:26 Now in the sixth **m** the angel
Rev 9:15 for the hour and day and **m**
Rev 22: 2 yielding its fruit every **m**.

MONTHS (see MONTH)
Ex 2: 2 child, she hid him three **m**.
Ex 12: 2 be your beginning of **m**;
Judg 11:37 me: let me alone for two **m**,
Job 3: 6 into the number of the **m**.
Amos 4: 7 there were still three **m**

Luke 1:24 and she hid herself five **m**,
Luke 1:56 with her about three **m**,
Luke 4:25 up three years and six **m**,
John 4:35 There are still four **m** and
Acts 18:11 there a year and six **m**,
Acts 19: 8 and spoke boldly for three **m**,
Acts 20: 3 and stayed three **m**.
Heb 11:23 was hidden three **m** by his
Jas 5:17 for three years and six **m**.
Rev 11: 2 underfoot for forty-two **m**.
Rev 13: 5 to continue for forty-two **m**.

MONUMENT
2Sa 18:18 day it is called Absalom's **M**.

MOON (see MOONS)
Gen 37: 9 this time, the sun, the **m**,
Num 29: 6 grain offering for the New **M**,
Deut 17: 3 either the sun or **m** or any
Josh 10:12 still over Gibeon; And **M**,
Josh 10:13 And the **m** stopped, Till
2Ki 23: 5 Baal, to the sun, to the **m**,
Job 31:26 Or the **m** moving in
Ps 8: 3 The **m** and the stars, which
Ps 72: 5 As long as the sun and **m**
Ps 72: 7 Until the **m** is no more.
Ps 121: 6 Nor the **m** by night.
Ps 136: 9 The **m** and stars to rule by
Ps 148: 3 Praise Him, sun and **m**;
Song 6:10 the morning, Fair as the **m**,
Jer 31:35 The ordinances of the **m** and
Joel 2:10 The sun and **m** grow dark,
Joel 2:31 And the **m** into blood,
Joel 3:15 The sun and **m** will grow
Amos 8: 5 When will the New **M** be past,
Hab 3:11 The sun and **m** stood still in
Matt 24:29 and the **m** will not give its
Luke 21:25 signs in the sun, in the **m**,
Acts 2:20 And the **m** into blood,
1Co 15:41 sun, another glory of the **m**,
Rev 6:12 and the **m** became like blood.

MOONS (see MOON)
1Ch 23:31 Sabbaths and on the New **M**
Is 1:13 to Me. The New **M**,
Hos 2:11 Her feast days, Her New **M**,

MORDECAI (see MORDECAI'S)
Esth 2: 5 Jew whose name was **M** the
Esth 2: 7 **M** took her as his own
Esth 5:13 so long as I see **M** the Jew
Esth 10: 2 of the greatness of **M**,

MORDECAI'S (see MORDECAI)
Esth 2:22 informed the king in **M** name.

MOREH
Gen 12: 6 as the terebinth tree of **M**.

MORESHETH
Jer 26:18 Micah of **M** prophesied in the
Mic 1: 1 that came to Micah of **M** in

MORIAH†
Gen 22: 2 and go to the land of **M**,
2Ch 3: 1 at Jerusalem on Mount **M**,

MORNING
Gen 1: 5 So the evening and the **m**
Gen 21:14 Abraham rose early in the **m**,
Gen 22: 3 Abraham rose early in the **m**
Ex 7:15 "Go to Pharaoh in the **m**,
Ex 12:10 none of it remain until **m**,
Ex 14:24 in the **m** watch, that the
Ex 16: 8 and in the **m** bread to the
Ex 16:13 and in the **m** the dew lay all
Ex 16:19 one leave any of it till **m**.
Ex 18:13 stood before Moses from **m**
Ex 29:39 you shall offer in the **m**,

Ex 34: 2 and come up in the **m** to
Ex 36: 3 freewill offerings every **m**.
Lev 22:30 leave none of it until **m**:
Num 9:21 cloud was taken up in the **m**,
Num 28: 8 as the **m** grain offering and
Deut 28:67 that it were **m**!' because of
Judg 6:31 him be put to death by **m**!
Judg 19:25 abused her all night until **m**;
Ruth 3:14 she lay at his feet until **m**,
1Sa 3:15 So Samuel lay down until **m**,
1Sa 11:11 midst of the camp in the **m**
1Sa 14:36 and plunder them until the **m**
1Sa 19:11 him and to kill him in the **m**.
2Sa 23: 4 A **m** without clouds, Like
1Ki 3:21 And when I rose in the **m** to
1Ki 18:26 on the name of Baal from **m**
Neh 8: 3 of the Water Gate from **m**
Job 1: 5 he would rise early in the **m**
Job 24:17 For the **m** is the same to
Job 38: 7 When the **m** stars sang
Job 38:12 Have you commanded the **m**
Ps 30: 5 But joy comes in the **m**.
Ps 55:17 Evening and **m** and at noon I
Ps 59:16 aloud of Your mercy in the **m**;
Ps 88:13 And in the **m** my prayer
Ps 90: 5 In the **m** they are like
Ps 90: 6 In the **m** it flourishes and
Ps 92: 2 Your lovingkindness in the **m**,
Ps 110: 3 from the womb of the **m**,
Ps 130: 6 those who watch for the **m**—
Ps 139: 9 I take the wings of the **m**,
Prov 7:18 our fill of love until **m**;
Eccl 11: 6 In the **m** sow your seed, And
Is 5:11 who rise early in the **m**,
Is 14:12 son of the **m**! How you are
Is 58: 8 shall break forth like the **m**,
Jer 20:16 him hear the cry in the **m**
Lam 3:23 They are new every **m**;
Ezek 24:18 and the next **m** I did as I
Dan 6:19 arose very early in the **m**
Hos 6: 4 faithfulness is like a **m**
Amos 4: 4 your sacrifices every **m**,
Amos 4:13 And makes the **m** darkness,
Jon 4: 7 But as **m** dawned the next day
Matt 16: 3 "and in the **m**,
Matt 20: 1 who went out early in the **m**
Mark 13:35 of the rooster, or in the **m**—
Mark 16: 2 Very early in the **m**,
Acts 5:21 the temple early in the **m**
2Pe 1:19 the day dawns and the **m**
Rev 2:28 and I will give him the **m**
Rev 22:16 the Bright and **M** Star."

MORSEL
Prov 17: 1 Better is a dry **m** with
Heb 12:16 who for one **m** of food sold

MORTAL (see MORTALITY, MORTALLY)
Job 4:17 Can a **m** be more righteous
Rom 6:12 not let sin reign in your **m**
Rom 8:11 also give life to your **m**
1Co 15:53 and this **m** must put on
2Co 4:11 may be manifested in our **m**

MORTALITY (see MORTAL)
2Co 5: 4 that **m** may be swallowed up

MORTALLY (see MORTAL)
Ezek 30:24 with the groanings of a **m**
Rev 13: 3 heads as if it had been **m**

MORTAR
Gen 11: 3 and they had asphalt for **m**.
Ex 1:14 with hard bondage—in **m**,
Prov 27:22 you grind a fool in a **m**

MOSES (see MOSES')
Ex 2:10 So she called his name **M**,

Ex	2:15	matter, he sought to kill M.
Ex	2:21	Zipporah his daughter to M.
Ex	3: 1	Now M was tending the flock
Ex	3: 4	of the bush and said, "M,
Ex	4:20	And M took the rod of God in
Ex	5:20	they met M and Aaron who
Ex	6:20	and she bore him Aaron and M.
Ex	7: 7	And M was eighty years old
Ex	8: 8	Then Pharaoh called for M
Ex	8:12	And M cried out to the LORD
Ex	9:23	And M stretched out his rod
Ex	10:22	So M stretched out his hand
Ex	11: 3	Moreover the man M was very
Ex	13:19	And M took the bones of
Ex	14:31	the LORD and His servant M.
Ex	15:24	people complained against M,
Ex	16:20	And M was angry with them.
Ex	17:10	fought with Amalek. And M,
Ex	17:15	And M built an altar and
Ex	18: 1	all that God had done for M
Ex	18: 8	And M told his father-in-law
Ex	18:13	that M sat to judge the
Ex	18:25	And M chose able men out of
Ex	18:26	hard cases they brought to M,
Ex	24: 2	And M alone shall come near
Ex	24: 4	And M wrote all the words of
Ex	24: 8	And M took the blood,
Ex	24:18	And M was on the mountain
Ex	31:18	He gave M two tablets of the
Ex	32:11	Then M pleaded with the
Ex	32:15	And M turned and went down
Ex	32:26	then M stood in the entrance
Ex	33: 7	M took his tent and pitched
Ex	33:11	So the LORD spoke to M face
Ex	34:35	then M would put the veil on
Ex	36: 2	Then M called Bezalel and
Ex	39: 1	as the LORD had commanded M.
Ex	39:43	Then M looked over all the
Ex	40:18	So M raised up the
Ex	40:33	So M finished the work.
Lev	8:10	Also M took the anointing
Lev	8:13	Then M brought Aaron's sons
Lev	8:16	and M burned them on the
Lev	11: 1	Now the LORD spoke to M and
Num	3:16	So M numbered them according
Num	3:51	And M gave their redemption
Num	11: 2	and when M prayed to the
Num	11:10	M also was displeased.
Num	12: 1	and Aaron spoke against M
Num	12: 2	indeed spoken only through M?
Num	12: 3	(Now the man M was very
Num	12: 7	Not so with My servant M;
Num	13:16	And M called Hoshea the son
Num	16: 3	gathered together against M
Num	16: 8	Then M said to Korah, "Hear
Num	20: 3	the people contended with M
Num	20:28	M stripped Aaron of his
Num	20:28	Then M and Eleazar came down
Num	21: 7	So M prayed for the
Num	21: 9	So M made a bronze serpent,
Num	26:63	who were numbered by M and
Num	30: 1	Then M spoke to the heads of
Num	31: 6	Then M sent them to the war,
Num	31:41	And M gave the tribute which
Num	33: 1	armies under the hand of M
Num	36:13	of Israel by the hand of M
Deut	1: 1	are the words which M
Deut	1: 5	M began to explain this law,
Deut	4:41	Then M set apart three
Deut	4:45	and the judgments which M
Deut	31: 9	So M wrote this law and
Deut	31:22	Therefore M wrote this song
Deut	31:24	when M had completed writing
Deut	33: 1	the blessing with which M
Deut	33: 4	M commanded a law for us, A
Deut	34: 5	So M the servant of the
Deut	34: 7	M was one hundred and twenty
Deut	34: 8	weeping and mourning for M
Deut	34: 9	for M had laid his hands on
Deut	34:10	in Israel a prophet like M
Deut	34:12	all the great terror which M
Josh	1: 1	After the death of M the
Josh	1: 2	M My servant is dead. Now
Josh	1: 5	your life; as I was with M,
Josh	1:17	with you, as He was with M.
Josh	8:31	in the Book of the Law of M:
Josh	8:32	a copy of the law of M,
Josh	20: 2	I spoke to you through M,
Josh	23: 6	in the Book of the Law of M,
Judg	4:11	Hobab the father-in-law of M,
1Ki	2: 3	is written in the Law of M,
1Ki	8: 9	two tablets of stone which M
2Ki	14: 6	in the Book of the Law of M,
2Ki	18: 4	the bronze serpent that M
2Ki	23:25	to all the Law of M;
1Ch	23:15	The sons of M were Gershon
2Ch	8:13	to the commandment of M,
2Ch	25: 4	in the Law in the Book of M,
2Ch	30:16	according to the Law of M
2Ch	33: 8	ordinances by the hand of M.
Ezra	7: 6	scribe in the Law of M,
Ps	77:20	a flock By the hand of M
Ps	99: 6	M and Aaron were among His
Ps	103: 7	He made known His ways to M,
Ps	106:23	Had not M His chosen one
Is	63:12	them by the right hand of M,
Jer	15: 1	Even if M and Samuel stood
Matt	8: 4	and offer the gift that M
Matt	17: 3	M and Elijah appeared to
Matt	17: 4	one for You, one for M,
Matt	19: 7	Why then did M command to
Matt	22:24	M said that if a man dies,
Mark	7:10	For M said, 'Honor your
Mark	10: 4	M permitted a man to write
Mark	12:19	M wrote to us that if a
Mark	12:26	not read in the book of M,
Luke	2:22	according to the law of M
Luke	16:31	If they do not hear M and the
Luke	24:27	And beginning at M and all
Luke	24:44	written in the Law of M and
John	1:17	the law was given through M,
John	1:45	have found Him of whom M
John	3:14	And as M lifted up the
John	5:45	is one who accuses you—M,
John	5:46	"For if you believed M,
John	6:32	M did not give you the bread
John	7:19	Did not M give you the law,
John	9:29	know that God spoke to M;
Acts	6:11	blasphemous words against M
Acts	7:22	And M was learned in all the
Acts	13:39	be justified by the law of M.
Acts	15: 1	according to the custom of M,
Acts	15:21	For M has had throughout many
Acts	21:21	the Gentiles to forsake M,
Acts	26:22	which the prophets and M
Acts	28:23	from both the Law of M and
Rom	5:14	death reigned from Adam to M,
Rom	9:15	For He says to M,
Rom	10: 5	For M writes about the
Rom	10:19	First M says: "I will
1Co	9: 9	is written in the law of M,
1Co	10: 2	all were baptized into M in
2Co	3:15	when M is read, a veil lies
2Ti	3: 8	and Jambres resisted M,
Heb	3: 2	as M also was faithful in
Heb	8: 5	as M was divinely instructed
Heb	11:23	By faith M, when he was
Jude	9	disputed about the body of M,
Rev	15: 3	They sing the song of M,

MOSES' (see MOSES)
Ex   4:25   her son and cast it at **M**
Ex   17:12   But **M** hands became heavy; so
Ex   34:35   that the skin of **M** face
Matt   23: 2   and the Pharisees sit in **M**
John   9:28   but we are **M** disciples.
Heb   10:28   Anyone who has rejected **M** law

MOTH (see MOTH-EATEN)
Job   4:19   Who are crushed before a **m**?
Is   51: 8   For the **m** will eat them up
Matt   6:20   where neither **m** nor rust
Luke   12:33   no thief approaches nor **m**

MOTH-EATEN† (see MOTH)
Job   13:28   Like a garment that is **m**.
Jas   5: 2   and your garments are **m**.

MOTHER (see GRANDMOTHER, MOTHER-IN-LAW, MOTHER'S, MOTHERS)
Gen   2:24   leave his father and **m** and
Gen   3:20   because she was the **m** of all
Gen   20:12   but not the daughter of my **m**;
Gen   27:14   and his **m** made savory food,
Ex   2: 8   and called the child's **m**.
Ex   20:12   your father and your **m**,
Ex   21:15   strikes his father or his **m**
Ex   21:17   curses his father or his **m**
Josh   2:13   "and spare my father, my **m**,
Josh   6:23   out Rahab, her father, her **m**,
Judg   5: 7   Arose a **m** in Israel.
Judg   5:28   The **m** of Sisera looked
Ruth   2:11   left your father and your **m**
1Sa   2:19   Moreover his **m** used to make
2Sa   20:19   to destroy a city and a **m**
1Ki   1:11   spoke to Bathsheba the **m** of
1Ki   2:19   throne set for the king's **m**;
1Ki   3:27   kill him; she is his **m**.
1Ki   15:13   from being queen **m**,
1Ki   17:23   house, and gave him to his **m**.
2Ki   4:30   And the **m** of the child said,
2Ki   9:22   as the harlotries of your **m**
Job   17:14   You are my **m** and my sister,'
Ps   35:14   one who mourns for his **m**.
Ps   51: 5   And in sin my **m** conceived
Ps   113: 9   Like a joyful **m** of
Ps   131: 2   a weaned child with his **m**;
Prov   1: 8   forsake the law of your **m**;
Prov   10: 1   son is the grief of his **m**.
Prov   15:20   a foolish man despises his **m**.
Prov   31: 1   the utterance which his **m**
Song   3: 4   him to the house of my **m**,
Song   6: 9   one, The only one of her **m**,
Is   8: 4   to cry 'My father' and 'My **m**,
Jer   15:10   Woe is me, my **m**,
Jer   20:14   not be blessed in which my **m**
Jer   20:17   That my **m** might have been
Ezek   16: 3   was an Amorite and your **m**
Ezek   16:44   proverb against you: 'Like **m**,
Hos   2: 5   For their **m** has played the
Hos   4: 5   And I will destroy your **m**.
Matt   2:13   the young Child and His **m**,
Matt   2:20   the young Child and His **m**,
Matt   8:14   He saw his wife's **m** lying
Matt   10:37   He who loves father or **m** more
Matt   12:47   Your **m** and Your brothers are
Matt   12:48   Who is My **m** and who are My
Matt   14: 8   been prompted by her **m**,
Matt   14:11   and she brought it to her **m**.
Matt   15: 4   your father and your **m**'
Matt   19: 5   leave his father and **m**
Matt   19:29   or sisters or father or **m**
Mark   1:30   But Simon's wife's **m** lay sick
Luke   1:43   that the **m** of my Lord should
Luke   2:51   but His **m** kept all these
Luke   12:53   **m** against daughter and

John   2: 1   and the **m** of Jesus was
John   19:25   by the cross of Jesus His **m**,
John   19:27   Behold your **m**!" And from
Acts   1:14   the women and Mary the **m** of
Gal   4:26   which is the **m** of us all.
Eph   5:31   leave his father and **m**
Eph   6: 2   your father and **m**,
1Th   2: 7   just as a nursing **m**
2Ti   1: 5   grandmother Lois and your **m**
Heb   7: 3   without father, without **m**,
Rev   17: 5   THE **M** OF HARLOTS AND OF

MOTHER-IN-LAW (see MOTHER)
Deut   27:23   the one who lies with his **m**.
Ruth   1:14   and Orpah kissed her **m**,
Ruth   3: 1   Then Naomi her **m** said to her,
Mic   7: 6   against her **m**;
Matt   10:35   against her **m**';
Luke   12:53   against her **m**.

MOTHER'S (see MOTHER)
Gen   24:67   was comforted after his **m**
Ex   23:19   boil a young goat in its **m**
Lev   20:19   the nakedness of your **m**
Judg   16:17   a Nazirite to God from my **m**
Ruth   1: 8   return each to her **m** house.
Job   1:21   Naked I came from my **m** womb,
Ps   22: 9   made Me trust while on My **m**
Ps   50:20   You slander your own **m** son.
Ps   69: 8   And an alien to my **m**
Ps   139:13   You covered me in my **m**
Song   8: 1   Who nursed at my **m** breasts!
Is   50: 1   the certificate of your **m**
John   3: 4   a second time into his **m**
John   19:25   and His **m** sister, Mary the
Acts   14: 8   a cripple from his **m** womb,
Gal   1:15   who separated me from my **m**

MOTHERS (see MOTHER)
Jer   16: 3   and concerning their **m** who
Mark   10:30   brothers and sisters and **m**
1Ti   1: 9   fathers and murderers of **m**,
1Ti   5: 2   older women as **m**,

MOUND (see MOUNDS)
2Sa   20:15   and they cast up a siege **m**
Jer   30:18   be built upon its own **m**,
Jer   49: 2   It shall be a desolate **m**,

MOUNDS (see MOUND)
Josh   11:13   cities that stood on their **m**,
Hab   1:10   they heap up earthen **m** and

MOUNT (see MOUNTAIN)
Gen   22:14   In the **M** of The LORD it
Gen   36: 8   So Esau dwelt in **M** Seir. Esau
Ex   19:18   Now **M** Sinai was completely
Num   20:23   to Moses and Aaron in **M** Hor
Num   28: 6   which was ordained at **M**
Num   33:39   years old when he died on **M**
Deut   2: 1   and we skirted **M** Seir for
Deut   11:29   shall put the blessing on **M**
Deut   11:29   Gerizim and the curse on **M**
Josh   19:26   it reached to **M** Carmel
1Sa   31: 1   and fell slain on **M** Gilboa.
2Ch   33:15   that he had built in the **m**
Job   39:27   Does the eagle **m** up at your
Ps   48: 2   Is **M** Zion on the sides of
Ps   107:26   They **m** up to the heavens,
Ps   125: 1   in the LORD Are like **M**
Song   4: 1   Going down from **M** Gilead.
Is   8:18   Who dwells in **M** Zion.
Is   14:13   I will also sit on the **m** of
Is   24:23   of hosts will reign On **M**
Is   27:13   the LORD in the holy **m** at
Is   40:31   They shall **m** up with wings
Jer   4:15   proclaims affliction from **M**
Jer   51:53   Though Babylon were to **m** up

Ezek	10:16	lifted their wings to **m** up
Hab	3: 3	The Holy One from **M** Paran.
Zech	14: 4	feet will stand on the **M** of
Matt	24: 3	Now as He sat on the **M** of
Acts	1:12	to Jerusalem from the **m**
Gal	4:25	for this Hagar is **M** Sinai in
Heb	12:22	But you have come to **M** Zion
Rev	14: 1	a Lamb standing on **M** Zion,

MOUNTAIN (*see* MOUNT, MOUNTAINS)

Ex	3: 1	the **m** of God.
Ex	3:12	shall serve God on this **m**.
Ex	18: 5	he was encamped at the **m** of
Ex	19: 3	called to him from the **m**,
Ex	19:12	Whoever touches the **m** shall
Ex	19:16	and a thick cloud on the **m**;
Ex	19:18	and the whole **m** quaked
Ex	19:20	Sinai, on the top of the **m**.
Ex	19:20	Moses to the top of the **m**,
Ex	20:18	and the **m** smoking; and when
Ex	24:18	And Moses was on the **m** forty
Ex	25:40	which was shown you on the **m**.
Deut	1: 6	dwelt long enough at this **m**.
Deut	4:11	and the **m** burned with fire
Deut	9: 9	then I stayed on the **m** forty
Deut	9:10	had spoken to you on the **m**
Deut	10: 1	and come up to Me on the **m**
Deut	32:50	and die on the **m** which you
Josh	10:40	the **m** country and the South
1Sa	17: 3	Philistines stood on a **m** on
1Sa	17: 3	and Israel stood on a **m** on
Ps	48: 1	of our God, In His holy **m**.
Is	2: 2	latter days That the **m** of
Is	2: 3	and let us go up to the **m** of
Is	11: 9	nor destroy in all My holy **m**,
Is	30:25	will be on every high **m**
Is	40: 4	be exalted And every **m** and
Is	56: 7	I will bring to My holy **m**,
Is	65:25	nor destroy in all My holy **m**,
Is	66:20	to My holy **m** Jerusalem,"
Jer	26:18	And the **m** of the temple
Jer	51:25	against you, O destroying **m**,
Ezek	28:14	You were on the holy **m** of
Dan	2:35	the image became a great **m**
Dan	2:45	stone was cut out of the **m**
Dan	9:16	city Jerusalem, Your holy **m**;
Dan	11:45	seas and the glorious holy **m**;
Joel	3:17	Dwelling in Zion My holy **m**.
Amos	4: 1	who are on the **m** of
Mic	3:12	And the **m** of the temple
Mic	4: 1	latter days That the **m** of
Mic	4: 2	and let us go up to the **m** of
Zech	8: 3	The **M** of the LORD of
Matt	4: 8	up on an exceedingly high **m**,
Matt	5: 1	He went up on a **m**,
Matt	8: 1	He had come down from the **m**,
Matt	17: 1	led them up on a high **m** by
Matt	17: 9	as they came down from the **m**,
Matt	17:20	seed, you will say to this **m**,
Matt	28:16	to the **m** which Jesus had
Mark	6:46	He departed to the **m** to
Luke	3: 5	be filled And every **m**
Luke	19:29	at the **m** called Olivet,
John	4:20	fathers worshiped on this **m**,
Heb	8: 5	shown you on the **m**.
Heb	12:18	you have not come to the **m**
2Pe	1:18	were with Him on the holy **m**.
Rev	6:14	and every **m** and island was

MOUNTAINS (*see* MOUNTAIN)

Gen	7:20	and the **m** were covered.
Gen	8: 4	on the **m** of Ararat.
Gen	8: 5	the tops of the **m** were seen.
Gen	19:17	the plain. Escape to the **m**,
Gen	22: 2	offering on one of the **m** of
Josh	17:15	since the **m** of Ephraim are

Josh	20: 7	(which is Hebron) in the **m**
Judg	11:37	I may go and wander on the **m**
Judg	11:38	her virginity on the **m**.
2Sa	1:21	O **m** of Gilboa, Let there
1Ki	5:15	who quarried stone in the **m**,
Ps	46: 2	And though the **m** be carried
Ps	50:11	know all the birds of the **m**,
Ps	87: 1	foundation is in the holy **m**.
Ps	90: 2	Before the **m** were brought
Ps	97: 5	The **m** melt like wax at the
Ps	104: 6	waters stood above the **m**.
Ps	114: 4	The **m** skipped like rams,
Ps	148: 9	**M** and all hills
Prov	8:25	Before the **m** were settled,
Song	8:14	Or a young stag On the **m**
Is	2: 2	on the top of the **m**,
Is	18: 3	lifts up a banner on the **m**,
Is	34: 3	And the **m** shall be melted
Is	40:12	Weighed the **m** in scales
Is	52: 7	How beautiful upon the **m**
Is	54:10	For the **m** shall depart And
Is	55:12	The **m** and the hills Shall
Is	64: 3	The **m** shook at Your
Jer	31: 5	yet plant vines on the **m** of
Lam	4:19	They pursued us on the **m**
Ezek	6: 3	O **m** of Israel, hear the word
Ezek	34:13	I will feed them on the **m** of
Ezek	34:14	in rich pasture on the **m**
Ezek	36: 1	prophesy to the **m** of Israel,
Ezek	38:20	The **m** shall be thrown down,
Ezek	38:21	Gog throughout all My **m**,
Hos	10: 8	They shall say to the **m**,
Joel	3:18	in that day That the **m**
Obad	21	Mount Zion To judge the **m**
Mic	6: 2	Hear, O you **m**,
Nah	1:15	on the **m** The feet of him
Hab	3: 6	And the everlasting **m** were
Zech	6: 1	coming from between two **m**,
Matt	24:16	are in Judea flee to the **m**.
Mark	13:14	are in Judea flee to the **m**.
1Co	13: 2	so that I could remove **m**,
Heb	11:38	wandered in deserts and **m**,
Rev	17: 9	The seven heads are seven **m**

MOURN (*see* MOURNED, MOURNER, MOURNING, MOURNS)

Gen	23: 2	and Abraham came to **m** for
Job	2:11	together to come and **m** with
Eccl	3: 4	time to laugh; A time to **m**,
Is	61: 2	God; To comfort all who **m**,
Is	61: 3	To console those who **m** in
Lam	1: 4	The roads to Zion **m** Because
Ezek	24:16	yet you shall neither **m** nor
Ezek	24:23	you shall neither **m** nor
Hos	4: 3	Therefore the land will **m**;
Amos	1: 2	pastures of the shepherds **m**,
Zech	12:10	they will **m** for Him as one
Matt	5: 4	Blessed are those who **m**,
Matt	9:15	friends of the bridegroom **m**
Matt	24:30	tribes of the earth will **m**,
Luke	6:25	For you shall **m** and weep.
Rev	1: 7	tribes of the earth will **m**
Rev	18:11	of the earth will weep and **m**

MOURNED (*see* MOURN)

Gen	37:34	and **m** for his son many days.
Gen	50: 3	and the Egyptians **m** for him
1Sa	15:35	Nevertheless Samuel **m** for
2Sa	1:12	And they **m** and wept and
2Sa	11:26	she **m** for her husband.
2Sa	13:37	And David **m** for his son
Is	38:14	I **m** like a dove; My eyes
Luke	23:27	and women who also **m** and

MOURNER† (*see* MOURN, MOURNERS)

2Sa	14: 2	"Please pretend to be a **m**,

MOURNERS (*see* MOURNER)
Eccl 12: 5 And the **m** go about the
Hos 9: 4 shall be like bread of **m**

MOURNING (*see* MOURN)
Gen 37:35 the grave to my son in **m**.
Gen 50:10 He observed seven days of **m**
2Sa 14: 2 and put on **m** apparel; do not
Ps 30:11 You have turned for me my **m**
Ps 38: 6 I go **m** all the day long.
Ps 42: 9 Why do I go **m** because of
Eccl 7: 2 to go to the house of **m**
Is 61: 3 ashes, The oil of joy for **m**,
Jer 6:26 about in ashes! Make **m** as
Jer 16: 5 not enter the house of **m**,
Jer 31:13 For I will turn their **m** to
Lam 5:15 Our dance has turned into **m**.
Ezek 24:17 make no **m** for the dead; bind
Amos 8:10 will turn your feasts into **m**,
Matt 2:18 weeping, and great **m**,
Jas 4: 9 laughter be turned to **m** and
Rev 18: 8 death and **m** and famine. And

MOURNS (*see* MOURN)
Is 24: 4 The earth **m** and fades away,
Zech 12:10 will mourn for Him as one **m**

MOUTH (*see* MOUTHS)
Gen 4:11 which has opened its **m** to
Gen 8:11 olive leaf was in her **m**;
Gen 29: 2 stone was on the well's **m**.
Gen 44: 1 each man's money in the **m**
Ex 4:11 him, "Who has made man's **m**?
Ex 4:12 and I will be with your **m**
Ex 4:15 and put the words in his **m**.
Ex 13: 9 LORD's law may be in your **m**;
Num 16:32 and the earth opened its **m**
Num 22:28 Then the LORD opened the **m**
Num 23: 5 put a word in Balaam's **m**,
Num 30: 2 that proceeds out of his **m**.
Deut 8: 3 that proceeds from the **m** of
Deut 18:18 will put My words in His **m**,
Deut 19:15 by the **m** of two or three
Deut 30:14 in your **m** and in your heart,
Josh 1: 8 shall not depart from your **m**,
1Sa 1:12 that Eli watched her **m**.
2Sa 1:16 for your own **m** has testified
2Sa 22: 9 devouring fire from His **m**;
2Ki 4:34 and put his **m** on his mouth,
2Ch 18:22 put a lying spirit in the **m**
2Ch 36:22 word of the LORD by the **m**
Ezra 1: 1 word of the LORD by the **m**
Job 3: 1 After this Job opened his **m**
Job 7:11 I will not restrain my **m**;
Job 9:20 my own **m** would condemn me;
Job 16:10 gape at me with their **m**,
Job 23:12 the words of His **m** More
Job 29:10 stuck to the roof of their **m**.
Job 35:16 Therefore Job opens his **m** in
Ps 8: 2 Out of the **m** of babes and
Ps 10: 7 His **m** is full of cursing and
Ps 18: 8 devouring fire from His **m**;
Ps 19:14 Let the words of my **m** and
Ps 22:21 Save Me from the lion's **m**
Ps 33: 6 them by the breath of His **m**.
Ps 34: 1 continually be in my **m**.
Ps 35:21 They also opened their **m**
Ps 40: 3 has put a new song in my **m**—
Ps 51:15 And my **m** shall show forth
Ps 54: 2 ear to the words of my **m**.
Ps 58: 6 their teeth in their **m**,
Ps 62: 4 They bless with their **m**,
Ps 63: 5 And my **m** shall praise You
Ps 69:15 let not the pit shut its **m**
Ps 71:15 My **m** shall tell of Your
Ps 78: 2 I will open my **m** in a

Ps 89: 1 With my **m** will I make known
Ps 109:30 praise the LORD with my **m**;
Ps 119:103 than honey to my **m**!
Ps 137: 6 cling to the roof of my **m**—
Ps 144: 8 Whose **m** speaks vain words,
Ps 144:11 Whose **m** speaks lying words,
Prov 5: 3 And her **m** is smoother than
Prov 6:12 Walks with a perverse **m**;
Prov 10:11 The **m** of the righteous is a
Prov 10:14 But the **m** of the foolish
Prov 12:14 good by the fruit of his **m**,
Prov 16:26 For his hungry **m** drives
Prov 19:24 so much as bring it to his **m**
Prov 22:14 The **m** of an immoral woman
Prov 26: 7 Is a proverb in the **m** of
Prov 27: 2 you, and not your own **m**;
Prov 30:20 She eats and wipes her **m**,
Prov 31:26 She opens her **m** with wisdom,
Eccl 5: 2 Do not be rash with your **m**,
Song 1: 2 me with the kisses of his **m**—
Song 4: 3 And your **m** is lovely. Your
Song 5:16 His **m** is most sweet, Yes,
Is 1:20 For the **m** of the LORD has
Is 6: 7 And he touched my **m** with
Is 11: 4 earth with the rod of His **m**,
Is 45:23 word has gone out of My **m**
Is 49: 2 And He has made My **m** like a
Is 51:16 have put My words in your **m**;
Is 53: 7 So He opened not His **m**.
Is 53: 9 was any deceit in His **m**.
Is 55:11 be that goes forth from My **m**;
Is 58:14 The **m** of the LORD has
Jer 1: 9 His hand and touched my **m**,
Jer 1: 9 have put My words in your **m**.
Jer 12: 2 You are near in their **m**
Ezek 2: 8 open your **m** and eat what I
Ezek 3: 2 So I opened my **m**,
Dan 3:26 went near the **m** of the
Dan 4:31 was still in the king's **m**,
Dan 6:17 brought and laid on the **m**
Dan 7: 5 and had three ribs in its **m**
Dan 7: 8 and a **m** speaking pompous
Dan 10: 3 meat or wine came into my **m**,
Hos 6: 5 them by the words of My **m**;
Amos 3:12 a shepherd takes from the **m**
Mic 4: 4 For the **m** of the LORD of
Zech 5: 8 the lead cover over its **m**.
Matt 4: 4 proceeds from the **m** of
Matt 5: 2 Then He opened His **m** and
Matt 12:34 of the heart the **m** speaks.
Matt 13:35 I will open My **m** in
Matt 15: 8 to Me with their **m**,
Matt 15:11 Not what goes into the **m**
Matt 18:16 by the **m** of two or
Matt 21:16 Out of the **m** of babes
Mark 9:18 him down; he foams at the **m**,
Mark 9:20 wallowed, foaming at the **m**.
Luke 1:64 Immediately his **m** was opened
Luke 1:70 As He spoke by the **m** of His
Luke 19:22 Out of your own **m** I will
Luke 22:71 it ourselves from His own **m**.
John 19:29 hyssop, and put it to His **m**.
Acts 4:25 who by the **m** of Your servant
Acts 8:32 He opened not His **m**.
Acts 23: 2 him to strike him on the **m**.
Rom 3:14 Whose **m** is full of
Rom 3:19 that every **m** may be stopped,
Rom 10: 8 in your **m** and in your
Rom 10: 9 if you confess with your **m**
Eph 6:19 that I may open my **m** boldly
Col 3: 8 language out of your **m**.
2Th 2: 8 with the breath of His **m**
2Ti 4:17 I was delivered out of the **m**
Jas 3:10 Out of the same **m** proceed
1Pe 2:22 deceit found in His **m**'

Rev	1:16	out of His **m** went a sharp
Rev	3:16	I will vomit you out of My **m**.
Rev	10: 9	as sweet as honey in your **m**.
Rev	12:16	and the earth opened its **m**
Rev	13: 5	And he was given a **m** speaking
Rev	16:13	out of the **m** of the beast,
Rev	16:13	and out of the **m** of the

MOUTHS (see MOUTH)

Ps	17:10	With their **m** they speak
Ps	22:13	gape at Me with their **m**,
Ps	115: 5	They have **m**,
Ps	135:17	there any breath in their **m**.
Is	29:13	draw near with their **m** And
Is	52:15	Kings shall shut their **m** at
Dan	6:22	angel and shut the lions' **m**,
Heb	11:33	stopped the **m** of lions,

MOVE (see MOVED, MOVES, MOVING)

Gen	9: 2	on all that **m** on the earth,
Jer	50: 8	**M** from the midst of Babylon,
Matt	17:20	to there,' and it will **m**;
Acts	17:28	for in Him we live and **m** and

MOVED (see MOVE)

Gen	12: 8	And he **m** from there to the
Gen	13:18	Then Abram **m** his tent, and
Num	21:12	From there they **m** and camped
Deut	32:21	They have **m** Me to anger by
1Sa	1:13	her heart; only her lips **m**,
2Sa	7: 6	but have **m** about in a tent
Ezra	1: 5	all whose spirits God had **m**,
Ps	10: 6	heart, "I shall not be **m**;
Ps	62: 6	defense; I shall not be **m**.
Ps	66: 9	not allow our feet to be **m**.
Ps	125: 1	Zion, Which cannot be **m**,
Is	7: 2	heart of his people were **m**
Matt	9:36	He was **m** with compassion for
Heb	11: 7	**m** with godly fear, prepared
2Pe	1:21	God spoke as they were **m**
Rev	6:14	mountain and island was **m**

MOVES (see MOVE)

| Gen | 1:21 | every living thing that **m**, |

MOVING (see MOVE)

| Gen | 9: 3 | Every **m** thing that lives |
| John | 5: 3 | waiting for the **m** of the |

MOWINGS†

| Amos | 7: 1 | late crop after the king's **m**. |

MULBERRY

| 2Sa | 5:24 | in the tops of the **m** trees, |
| Luke | 17: 6 | you can say to this **m** tree, |

MULE (see MULE-LOADS, MULES)

| 1Ki | 1:38 | ride on King David's **m**, |
| Ps | 32: 9 | the horse or like the **m**, |

MULE-LOADS† (see MULE)

| 2Ki | 5:17 | your servant be given two **m** |

MULES (see MULE)

| 1Ki | 18: 5 | to keep the horses and **m** |

MULTIPLIED (see MULTIPLY)

Ex	1: 7	**m** and grew exceedingly
Ex	11: 9	so that My wonders may be **m**
Ps	16: 4	Their sorrows shall be **m** who
Is	9: 3	You have **m** the nation And
Dan	4: 1	Peace be **m** to you.
Acts	6: 7	number of the disciples **m**
Acts	12:24	the word of God grew and **m**.
1Pe	1: 2	Grace to you and peace be **m**.

MULTIPLIES (see MULTIPLY)

| Job | 9:17 | And **m** my wounds without |
| Job | 35:16 | He **m** words without |

MULTIPLY (see MULTIPLIED, MULTIPLIES, MULTIPLYING)

| Gen | 1:22 | saying, "Be fruitful and **m**, |

Gen	3:16	I will greatly **m** your sorrow
Gen	6: 1	when men began to **m** on the
Gen	9: 1	to them: "Be fruitful and **m**,
Gen	17: 2	and will **m** you
Ex	1:10	with them, lest they **m**,
Ex	7: 3	and **m** My signs and My
Deut	17:16	But he shall not **m** horses for
Deut	17:17	Neither shall he **m** wives for
Amos	4: 4	At Gilgal **m** transgression;

MULTIPLYING† (see MULTIPLY)

Gen	22:17	and **m** I will multiply your
Acts	6: 1	of the disciples was **m**,
Heb	6:14	and **m** I will multiply

MULTITUDE (see MULTITUDES)

Gen	16:10	shall not be counted for **m**.
Gen	48:19	shall become a **m** of nations.
Ex	12:38	A mixed **m** went up with them
Deut	1:10	as the stars of heaven in **m**.
Judg	7:12	sand by the seashore in **m**.
2Sa	6:19	among the whole **m** of Israel,
1Ki	4:20	as the sand by the sea in **m**,
2Ch	1: 9	the dust of the earth in **m**.
Ps	42: 4	For I used to go with the **m**;
Ps	51: 1	According to the **m** of Your
Ps	109:30	will praise Him among the **m**.
Prov	11:14	But in the **m** of counselors
Is	1:11	To what purpose is the **m** of
Is	63: 7	According to the **m** of His
Ezek	39:11	will bury Gog and all his **m**.
Matt	13: 2	and the whole **m** stood on the
Matt	13:34	things Jesus spoke to the **m**
Matt	15:32	"I have compassion on the **m**,
Matt	15:35	So He commanded the **m** to sit
Matt	20:29	a great **m** followed Him.
Mark	3: 9	for Him because of the **m**,
Mark	9:14	He saw a great **m** around
Mark	12:12	on Him, but feared the **m**,
Luke	2:13	was with the angel a **m** of
Luke	6:19	And the whole **m** sought to
Luke	12: 1	when an innumerable **m** of
Luke	19:37	the whole **m** of the disciples
John	5: 3	In these lay a great **m** of
John	21: 6	draw it in because of the **m**
Acts	2: 6	the **m** came together, and
Heb	11:12	as the stars of the sky in **m**—
Jas	5:20	from death and cover a **m** of
1Pe	4: 8	love will cover a **m** of
Rev	7: 9	a great **m** which no one could

MULTITUDES (see MULTITUDE)

Joel	3:14	**m** in the valley of decision!
Matt	4:25	Great **m** followed Him—from
Matt	5: 1	And seeing the **m**,
Matt	9:33	And the **m** marveled, saying,
Matt	23: 1	Then Jesus spoke to the **m** and
Luke	8:42	the **m** thronged Him.
Acts	5:14	**m** of both men and women,

MURDER (see MURDERED, MURDERER, MURDERS)

Ex	20:13	"You shall not **m**.
Deut	5:17	'You shall not **m**.
Jer	7: 9	"Will you steal, **m**,
Matt	5:21	of old, 'You shall not **m**,
Luke	23:25	who for rebellion and **m** had
Acts	9: 1	breathing threats and **m**
Rom	1:29	full of envy, **m**,
Rom	13: 9	"You shall not **m**,

MURDERED (see MURDER)

| Matt | 23:31 | you are sons of those who **m** |
| Acts | 5:30 | raised up Jesus whom you **m** |

MURDERER (see MURDER, MURDERERS)

Num	35:16	the **m** shall surely be put to
2Ki	9:31	**m** of your master?"
John	8:44	He was a **m** from the

Acts 28: 4 "No doubt this man is a **m**,
1Pe 4:15 none of you suffer as a **m**,
1Jn 3:15 hates his brother is a **m**,

MURDERERS (see MURDERER)
1Ti 1: 9 murderers of fathers and **m**
Rev 21: 8 unbelieving, abominable, **m**,

MURDERS (see MURDER)
Matt 5:21 and whoever **m** will be in
Matt 15:19 proceed evil thoughts, **m**,
Mark 7:21 adulteries, fornications, **m**,
Gal 5:21 envy, **m**, drunkenness,

MURMUR
John 6:43 Do not **m** among yourselves.

MUSCLE
Gen 32:32 of Jacob's hip in the **m**

MUSIC (see MUSICAL, MUSICIAN)
1Sa 18:10 So David played **m** with his
1Ch 15:16 by instruments of **m**,
1Ch 15:22 in charge of the **m**,
1Ch 16: 5 but Asaph made **m** with
Eccl 12: 4 And all the daughters of **m**
Dan 3: 5 symphony with all kinds of **m**,
Luke 15:25 he heard **m** and dancing.

MUSICAL (see MUSIC)
1Sa 18: 6 and with **m** instruments.
Amos 6: 5 invent for yourselves **m**

MUSICIAN (see MUSIC, MUSICIANS)
Hab 3:19 high hills. To the Chief **M**.

MUSICIANS (see MUSICIAN)
Dan 6:18 and no **m** were brought before

MUST
Ruth 4: 5 you **m** also buy it from Ruth
Jer 10:19 And I **m** bear it."
Matt 16:21 to His disciples that He **m**
Matt 17:10 scribes say that Elijah **m**
Matt 18: 7 of offenses! For offenses **m**
Matt 24: 6 for all these things **m**
Mark 8:31 them that the Son of Man **m**
Mark 13:10 And the gospel **m** first be
Mark 14:49 But the Scriptures **m** be
Luke 2:49 Did you not know that I **m** be
Luke 19: 5 for today I **m** stay at your
John 3: 7 You **m** be born again.'
John 3:14 even so **m** the Son of Man be
John 3:30 He **m** increase, but I must
John 3:30 but I **m** decrease.
John 9: 4 I **m** work the works of Him who
John 10:16 them also I **m** bring, and
Acts 3:21 whom heaven **m** receive until
Acts 4:12 among men by which we **m** be
Acts 9: 6 you will be told what you **m**
Acts 10:15 God has cleansed you **m**
Acts 11: 9 'What God has cleansed you **m**
Acts 16:30 what **m** I do to be saved?"
Acts 23:11 so you **m** also bear witness
Rom 13: 5 Therefore you **m** be subject,
1Co 15:25 For He **m** reign till He has
1Co 15:53 For this corruptible **m** put on
2Co 5:10 For we **m** all appear before
1Ti 3: 2 A bishop then **m** be blameless,
1Ti 3: 8 Likewise deacons **m** be
1Ti 3:11 Likewise their wives **m** be
Heb 4:13 eyes of Him to whom we **m**
Heb 11: 6 for he who comes to God **m**
Rev 1: 1 things which **m** shortly take

MUSTARD
Matt 13:31 of heaven is like a **m** seed,
Matt 17:20 if you have faith as a **m**

MUTE
Ex 4:11 mouth? Or who makes the **m**,
Ezek 24:27 speak and no longer be **m**.
Matt 9:33 the **m** spoke. And the
Matt 12:22 demon-possessed, blind and **m**;

MUTILATION
Phil 3: 2 beware of the **m**!

MUTTER
Is 8:19 wizards, who whisper and **m**,

MUTUAL
Rom 1:12 together with you by the **m**

MUZZLE
Deut 25: 4 You shall not **m** an ox while
1Co 9: 9 You shall not **m** an ox
1Ti 5:18 You shall not **m** an ox

MYRRH
Gen 37:25 bearing spices, balm, and **m**,
Prov 7:17 have perfumed my bed With **m**,
Song 1:13 A bundle of **m** is my beloved
Song 5:13 lilies, Dripping liquid **m**.
Matt 2:11 gold, frankincense, and **m**.
Mark 15:23 Him wine mingled with **m** to

MYRTLE
Neh 8:15 **m** branches, palm branches,
Zech 1: 8 and it stood among the **m**

MYSTERIES (see MYSTERY)
Matt 13:11 given to you to know the **m**
Luke 8:10 been given to know the **m** of
1Co 13: 2 and understand all **m** and all

MYSTERY (see MYSTERIES)
Mark 4:11 been given to know the **m** of
Rom 11:25 should be ignorant of this **m**,
Rom 16:25 to the revelation of the **m**
1Co 2: 7 the wisdom of God in a **m**,
1Co 15:51 Behold, I tell you a **m**:
Eph 1: 9 made known to us the **m** of
Eph 3: 4 my knowledge in the **m** of
Eph 3: 9 is the fellowship of the **m**,
Eph 5:32 This is a great **m**,
Eph 6:19 boldly to make known the **m**
Col 1:26 the **m** which has been hidden
Col 1:27 of the glory of this **m**
Col 2: 2 to the knowledge of the **m** of
2Th 2: 7 For the **m** of lawlessness is
1Ti 3: 9 holding the **m** of the faith
1Ti 3:16 controversy great is the **m**
Rev 1:20 The **m** of the seven stars
Rev 17: 5 a name was written: **M**,

N

NAAMAN
2Ki 5:20 my master has spared **N** this
Luke 4:27 them was cleansed except **N**

NAAMATHITE
Job 2:11 Shuhite, and Zophar the **N**.

NABAL (see NABAL'S)
1Sa 25: 4 in the wilderness that **N**
1Sa 25:19 did not tell her husband **N**.
1Sa 25:25 lord regard this scoundrel **N**.
1Sa 25:25 **N** is his name, and folly

NABAL'S (see NABAL)
1Sa 25:14 **N** wife, saying, "Look,

NABOTH
1Ki 21: 2 So Ahab spoke to **N**,
1Ki 21: 7 give you the vineyard of **N**
1Ki 21:14 **N** has been stoned and is

1Ki 21:19 dogs licked the blood of N,

NADAB
Ex 24: 9 Moses went up, also Aaron, N,
Ex 28: 1 Aaron and Aaron's sons: N,
Num 3: 4 N and Abihu had died before
1Ki 15:25 Now N the son of Jeroboam

NAHASH
1Sa 11: 1 Then N the Ammonite came up

NAHOR
Gen 11:27 Terah: Terah begot Abram, N,
Gen 11:29 Then Abram and N took wives:
Gen 24:10 to the city of N.
Gen 29: 5 you know Laban the son of N?
Gen 31:53 God of Abraham, the God of N,

NAHSHON
Num 1: 7 N the son of Amminadab;
Matt 1: 4 Amminadab, Amminadab begot N,

NAHUM
Nah 1: 1 The book of the vision of N

NAILED† (see NAILS)
Col 2:14 having **n** it to the cross.

NAILS (see NAILED)
Eccl 12:11 are like well-driven **n**,
Dan 4:33 eagles' feathers and his **n**
Dan 7:19 its teeth of iron and its **n**
John 20:25 His hands the print of the **n**,

NAIN†
Luke 7:11 He went into a city called N;

NAKED (see NAKEDNESS)
Gen 2:25 And they were both **n**,
Gen 3: 7 they knew that they were **n**;
Gen 3:10 I was afraid because I was **n**;
1Sa 19:24 and lay down **n** all that day
Job 1:21 N I came from my mother's
Job 26: 6 Sheol is **n** before Him, And
Eccl 5:15 **n** shall he return, To go as
Is 20: 3 servant Isaiah has walked **n**
Is 20: 4 **n** and barefoot, with their
Mic 1: 8 I will go stripped and **n**;
Matt 25:36 I was **n** and you clothed Me;
Mark 14:52 cloth and fled from them **n**.
2Co 5: 3 we shall not be found **n**.
Heb 4:13 but all things are **n** and
Jas 2:15 If a brother or sister is **n**
Rev 3:17 poor, blind, and **n**—

NAKEDNESS (see NAKED)
Gen 9:23 backward and covered the **n**
Ex 28:42 trousers to cover their **n**;
Lev 18: 7 The **n** of your father or the
Deut 28:48 in hunger, in thirst, in **n**,
Lam 1: 8 they have seen her **n**;
Rom 8:35 persecution, or famine, or **n**,
2Co 11:27 often, in cold and **n**—

NAME (see NAMED, NAME'S, NAMES)
Gen 2:13 The **n** of the second river is
Gen 2:19 creature, that was its **n**.
Gen 3:20 Adam called his wife's **n**
Gen 4:26 men began to call on the **n**
Gen 11: 4 let us make a **n** for
Gen 12: 2 bless you And make your **n**
Gen 17: 5 No longer shall your **n** be
Gen 17: 5 but your **n** shall be Abraham;
Gen 17:15 but Sarah shall be her **n**.
Gen 30:28 N me your wages, and I will
Gen 32:27 to him, "What is your **n**?
Gen 35:10 Your **n** is Jacob; your name
Gen 35:10 your **n** shall not be called
Gen 35:10 but Israel shall be your **n**.
Gen 41:45 Pharaoh called Joseph's **n**

Ex 3:13 say to me, 'What is His **n**?
Ex 3:15 This is My **n** forever, and
Ex 5:23 Pharaoh to speak in Your **n**,
Ex 6: 3 but by My **n** LORD I was not
Ex 15: 3 of war; The LORD is His **n**.
Ex 20: 7 You shall not take the **n** of
Ex 20: 7 guiltless who takes His **n**
Ex 33:12 have said, 'I know you by **n**,
Ex 34: 5 and proclaimed the **n** of the
Ex 34:14 whose **n** is Jealous, is a
Lev 18:21 nor shall you profane the **n**
Lev 19:12 you shall not swear by My **n**
Lev 24:11 son blasphemed the **n** of
Deut 3:14 Bashan after his own **n**,
Deut 5:11 You shall not take the **n** of
Deut 5:11 guiltless who takes His **n**
Deut 10: 8 to Him and to bless in His **n**,
Deut 12:11 God chooses to make His **n**
Deut 14:23 He chooses to make His **n**
Deut 16: 2 LORD chooses to put His **n**.
Deut 18:22 a prophet speaks in the **n**
Deut 25: 6 bears will succeed to the **n**
Deut 25: 6 that his **n** may not be
Deut 28:58 this glorious and awesome **n**,
Josh 7: 9 and cut off our **n** from the
Josh 15:15 of Debir (formerly the **n** of
Judg 13:18 him, "Why do you ask My **n**,
Ruth 4: 5 to perpetuate the **n** of the
Ruth 4:14 and may his **n** be famous in
1Sa 17:23 of Gath, Goliath by **n**,
1Sa 17:45 But I come to you in the **n**
1Sa 25:25 For as his **n** is, so is he:
1Sa 25:25 so is he: Nabal is his **n**,
2Sa 7:13 shall build a house for My **n**,
2Sa 8:13 And David made himself a **n**
2Sa 12:24 and he called his **n** Solomon.
2Sa 12:25 So he called his **n** Jedidiah,
2Sa 18:18 the pillar after his own **n**.
2Sa 22:50 And sing praises to Your **n**.
1Ki 7:21 the right and called its **n**
1Ki 7:21 on the left and called its **n**
1Ki 8:33 to You and confess Your **n**,
1Ki 9: 3 you have built to put My **n**
1Ki 18:24 and I will call on the **n** of
1Ki 18:26 and called on the **n** of Baal
2Ki 14:27 He would blot out the **n** of
1Ch 16:10 Glory in His holy **n**;
1Ch 16:29 LORD the glory due His **n**;
1Ch 16:35 give thanks to Your holy **n**,
2Ch 6:32 for the sake of Your great **n**
2Ch 7:14 who are called by My **n** will
2Ch 36: 4 and changed his **n** to
Neh 9: 5 be Your glorious **n**
Job 1: 1 whose **n** was Job; and that
Job 1:21 Blessed be the **n** of the
Ps 8: 1 How excellent is Your **n** in
Ps 9: 2 will sing praise to Your **n**,
Ps 9: 5 have blotted out their **n**
Ps 20: 5 And in the **n** of our God we
Ps 22:22 I will declare Your **n** to My
Ps 29: 2 LORD the glory due to His **n**;
Ps 34: 3 And let us exalt His **n**
Ps 44: 8 And praise Your **n** forever.
Ps 63: 4 lift up my hands in Your **n**.
Ps 68: 4 By His **n** YAH, And rejoice
Ps 83:18 whose **n** alone is the LORD,
Ps 86:11 my heart to fear Your **n**.
Ps 86:12 And I will glorify Your **n**
Ps 96: 2 to the LORD, bless His **n**;
Ps 99: 3 Your great and awesome **n**—
Ps 100: 4 to Him, and bless His **n**.
Ps 103: 1 bless His holy **n**!
Ps 105: 3 Glory in His holy **n**;
Ps 109:13 following let their **n** be
Ps 113: 2 Blessed be the **n** of the

Ps   118:10 But in the **n** of the LORD
Ps   118:26 is he who comes in the **n**
Ps   138: 2 Your word above all Your **n**.
Ps   139:20 Your enemies take Your **n**
Ps   147: 4 He calls them all by **n**.
Prov   18:10 The **n** of the LORD is a
Prov   22: 1 A good **n** is to be chosen
Prov   30: 4 the earth? What is His **n**,
Prov   30: 4 and what is His Son's **n**,
Is   7:14 and shall call His **n**
Is   8: 3 **n** Maher-Shalal-Hash-Baz
Is   9: 6 And His **n** will be called
Is   29:23 They will hallow My **n**,
Is   40:26 He calls them all by **n**,
Is   42: 8 am the LORD, that is My **n**;
Is   43: 1 have called you by your **n**;
Is   47: 4 the LORD of hosts is His **n**,
Is   57:15 whose **n** is Holy: "I dwell
Is   62: 2 shall be called by a new **n**,
Is   62: 2 mouth of the LORD will **n**.
Is   63:16 from Everlasting is Your **n**.
Jer   7:10 which is called by My **n**,
Jer   14: 9 And we are called by Your **n**;
Jer   14:14 prophesy lies in My **n**.
Jer   20: 9 Nor speak anymore in His **n**.
Ezek   24: 2 write down the **n** of the day,
Dan   1: 7 he gave Daniel the **n**
Dan   9:15 hand, and made Yourself a **n**,
Hos   1: 4 Call his **n** Jezreel, For in a
Hos   1: 6 Call her **n** Lo-Ruhamah, For I
Hos   1: 9 Call his **n** Lo-Ammi, For you
Joel   2:32 whoever calls on the **n** of
Amos   2: 7 girl, To defile My holy **n**.
Zech   14: 9 is one," And His **n** one.
Mal   1: 6 you priests who despise My **n**.
Matt   1:21 and you shall call His **n**
Matt   1:23 they shall call His **n**
Matt   6: 9 heaven, Hallowed be Your **n**.
Matt   7:22 we not prophesied in Your **n**,
Matt   7:22 cast out demons in Your **n**,
Matt   7:22 done many wonders in Your **n**?
Matt   10:42 cup of cold water in the **n**
Matt   12:21 And in His **n** Gentiles
Matt   18:20 gathered together in My **n**,
Matt   21: 9 He who comes in the **n**
Matt   23:39 He who comes in the **n**
Matt   28:19 baptizing them in the **n** of
Mark   3:16 to whom He gave the **n** Peter;
Mark   3:17 to whom He gave the **n**
Mark   5: 9 My **n** is Legion; for we are
Luke   1:13 and you shall call his **n**
Luke   1:27 The virgin's **n** was Mary.
Luke   1:49 for me, And holy is His **n**.
Luke   10:17 are subject to us in Your **n**.
Luke   24:47 should be preached in His **n**
John   1: 6 whose **n** was John.
John   1:12 those who believe in His **n**:
John   3:18 he has not believed in the **n**
John   5:43 have come in My Father's **n**,
John   10: 3 he calls his own sheep by **n**
John   12:28 "Father, glorify Your **n**.
John   14:13 whatever you ask in My **n**,
John   17: 6 I have manifested Your **n** to
John   17:12 world, I kept them in Your **n**.
John   20:31 you may have life in His **n**.
Acts   2:21 whoever calls on the **n**
Acts   2:38 of you be baptized in the **n**
Acts   4: 7 By what power or by what **n**
Acts   4:12 for there is no other **n**
Acts   4:18 at all nor teach in the **n**
Acts   5:41 to suffer shame for His **n**.
Acts   9:15 vessel of Mine to bear My **n**
Acts   10:48 to be baptized in the **n** of
Acts   16:18 I command you in the **n** of
Rom   2:24 the **n** of God is blasphemed

Rom   10:13 whoever calls on the **n**
1Co   1:13 were you baptized in the **n**
Eph   1:21 and every **n** that is named,
Phil   2: 9 name which is above every **n**,
Phil   2:10 that at the **n** of Jesus every
Col   3:17 do all in the **n** of the Lord
Heb   1: 4 obtained a more excellent **n**
Heb   2:12 I will declare Your **n** to
Jas   5:14 him with oil in the **n** of
1Pe   4:14 are reproached for the **n** of
1Jn   5:13 to you who believe in the **n**
Rev   2:13 And you hold fast to My **n**,
Rev   2:17 and on the stone a new **n**
Rev   3: 5 I will not blot out his **n**
Rev   3:12 name of My God and the **n** of
Rev   6: 8 And the **n** of him who sat on
Rev   8:11 The **n** of the star is
Rev   13:17 who has the mark or the **n**
Rev   13:17 or the number of his **n**.
Rev   15: 4 O Lord, and glorify Your **n**?
Rev   16: 9 and they blasphemed the **n** of
Rev   17: 5 And on her forehead a **n** was
Rev   19:13 and His **n** is called The Word

NAMED (*see* NAME)
Gen   27:36 Is he not rightly **n** Jacob?
2Ki   17:34 whom He **n** Israel,
Matt   9: 9 He saw a man **n** Matthew
Luke   5:27 and saw a tax collector **n**
Luke   6:14 whom He also **n** Peter, and
John   3: 1 was a man of the Pharisees **n**
Rom   15:20 not where Christ was **n**,
1Co   5: 1 immorality as is not even **n**
Eph   1:21 and every name that is **n**,
Eph   3:15 in heaven and earth is **n**,
Eph   5: 3 let it not even be **n** among

NAME'S (*see* NAME)
Ps   23: 3 of righteousness For His **n**
Ps   25:11 For Your **n** sake, O LORD,
Jer   14: 7 Do it for Your **n** sake; For
Matt   10:22 be hated by all for My **n**
Matt   19:29 for My **n** sake, shall receive
Matt   24: 9 by all nations for My **n**
Acts   9:16 he must suffer for My **n**

NAMES (*see* NAME)
Gen   2:20 So Adam gave **n** to all cattle,
Ex   28:10 six of their **n** on one stone,
Ps   16: 4 Nor take up their **n** on my
Dan   1: 7 chief of the eunuchs gave **n**:
Matt   10: 2 Now the **n** of the twelve
Luke   10:20 rejoice because your **n** are
Phil   4: 3 whose **n** are in the Book of
2Ti   2:19 Let everyone who **n** the name
Rev   3: 4 You have a few **n** even in
Rev   17: 8 whose **n** are not written in

NAOMI (*see* NAOMI'S)
Ruth   1: 2 the name of his wife was **N**,
Ruth   1:22 So **N** returned, and Ruth the
Ruth   3: 1 Then **N** her mother-in-law said

NAOMI'S (*see* NAOMI)
Ruth   1: 3 **N** husband, died; and she was

NAPHTALI
Gen   35:25 maidservant, were Dan and **N**;
2Ki   1:29 Galilee, all the land of **N**;
Is   9: 1 of Zebulun and the land of **N**,
Matt   4:15 and the land of **N**,
Rev   7: 6 of the tribe of **N** twelve

NARRATIVE†
Luke   1: 1 in hand to set in order a **n**

NARROW
Matt   7:14 Because **n** is the gate and

NATHAN
2Sa	7: 2	that the king said to N the
1Ki	1:11	So N spoke to Bathsheba the
2Ch	9:29	not written in the book of N

NATHANAEL (*see* BARTHOLOMEW)
John	1:45	Philip found N and said to
John	21: 2	N of Cana in Galilee, the

NATION (*see* NATIONS)
Gen	12: 2	I will make you a great n;
Gen	15:14	And also the n whom they
Ex	19: 6	of priests and a holy n.
Ex	32:10	I will make of you a great n.
Ex	33:13	And consider that this n is
Deut	4: 7	For what great n is there
Deut	4: 8	And what great n is there
Deut	28:33	A n whom you have not known
Deut	28:50	a n of fierce countenance,
Deut	32:21	by those who are not a n;
2Sa	7:23	the one n on the earth whom
Ps	33:12	Blessed is the n whose God
Ps	83: 4	cut them off from being a n,
Ps	147:20	not dealt thus with any n;
Prov	14:34	Righteousness exalts a n,
Is	1: 4	Alas, sinful n, A people
Is	2: 4	not lift up sword against n,
Is	9: 3	You have multiplied the n
Is	18: 2	to a n tall and smooth of
Is	26:15	You have increased the n,
Jer	2:11	Has a n changed its gods,
Jer	12:17	pluck up and destroy that n,
Jer	18: 7	I speak concerning a n and
Jer	18: 8	if that n against whom I have
Jer	49:31	go up to the wealthy n that
Jer	50:41	And a great n and many
Lam	4:17	we watched For a n that
Ezek	2: 3	to a rebellious n that has
Dan	3:29	a decree that any people, n,
Dan	8:22	shall arise out of that n,
Dan	12: 1	was since there was a n,
Amos	6: 1	persons in the chief n,
Mic	4: 3	not lift up sword against n,
Hab	1: 6	A bitter and hasty n Which
Mal	3: 9	Me, Even this whole n.
Matt	21:43	from you and given to a n
Matt	24: 7	nation will rise against n,
Luke	7: 5	"for he loves our n,
Luke	23: 2	fellow perverting the n,
John	11:50	and not that the whole n
John	11:51	Jesus would die for the n,
John	11:52	and not for that n only, but
Acts	2: 5	from every n under heaven.
Acts	10:35	But in every n whoever fears
Acts	17:26	made from one blood every n
Rom	10:19	those who are not a n,
1Pe	2: 9	a royal priesthood, a holy n,
Rev	5: 9	and tongue and people and n,
Rev	13: 7	every tribe, tongue, and n.
Rev	14: 6	on the earth—to every n,

NATIONS (*see* NATION)
Gen	10: 5	their families, into their n.
Gen	10:31	lands, according to their n.
Gen	17: 4	shall be a father of many n.
Gen	17:16	shall be a mother of n,
Gen	18:18	and all the n of the earth
Gen	25:23	Two n are in your womb, Two
Lev	26:33	scatter you among the n and
Num	24:20	was first among the n,
Deut	7: 1	seven n greater and mightier
Deut	7:22	God will drive out those n
Deut	18: 9	the abominations of those n.
Deut	28:37	and a byword among all n
1Sa	8: 5	to judge us like all the n,
1Sa	8:20	also may be like all the n,

2Ki	17: 8	in the statutes of the n
2Ki	19:12	Have the gods of the n
1Ch	16:24	His glory among the n,
2Ch	32:17	As the gods of the n of
Neh	1: 8	will scatter you among the n;
Neh	5: 8	who were sold to the n.
Ps	2: 1	Why do the n rage, And the
Ps	2: 8	and I will give You The n
Ps	9: 5	You have rebuked the n,
Ps	18:43	made me the head of the n;
Ps	22:27	all the families of the n
Ps	22:28	And He rules over the n.
Ps	46:10	will be exalted among the n,
Ps	47: 3	And the n under our feet.
Ps	47: 8	God reigns over the n;
Ps	67: 2	Your salvation among all n.
Ps	67: 4	let the n be glad and sing
Ps	72:11	All n shall serve Him.
Ps	72:17	All n shall call Him
Ps	79:10	there be known among the n
Ps	96: 3	His glory among the n,
Ps	96:10	Say among the n,
Ps	98: 2	in the sight of the n.
Ps	110: 6	He shall judge among the n,
Ps	113: 4	LORD is high above all n,
Ps	135:15	The idols of the n are
Ps	149: 7	execute vengeance on the n,
Is	2: 2	And all n shall flow to it.
Is	2: 4	shall judge between the n,
Is	5:26	lift up a banner to the n
Is	14:12	You who weakened the n!
Is	30:28	To sift the n with the
Is	40:15	the n are as a drop in a
Is	45: 1	To subdue n before him And
Is	52:15	So shall He sprinkle many n.
Is	56: 7	a house of prayer for all n.
Is	64: 2	That the n may tremble at
Jer	1: 5	you a prophet to the n.
Jer	1:10	this day set you over the n
Jer	4: 7	And the destroyer of n is
Jer	10: 7	fear You, O King of the n?
Jer	14:22	any among the idols of the n
Jer	25:17	and made all the n drink, to
Jer	25:31	has a controversy with the n;
Jer	28:14	on the neck of all these n,
Jer	30:11	I make a full end of all n
Jer	46: 1	the prophet against the n.
Jer	50:23	a desolation among the n!
Jer	51:27	the trumpet among the n!
Lam	1: 1	Who was great among the n!
Ezek	5: 5	her in the midst of the n
Ezek	5:14	and a reproach among the n
Ezek	5:15	and an astonishment to the n
Ezek	25: 7	give you as plunder to the n;
Ezek	36:15	you hear the taunts of the n
Ezek	36:23	been profaned among the n,
Ezek	36:23	and the n shall know that I
Ezek	37:22	shall no longer be two n,
Ezek	39:21	set My glory among the n;
Ezek	39:28	into captivity among the n,
Dan	4: 1	the king, To all peoples, n,
Hos	9:17	be wanderers among the n.
Mic	4: 2	Many n shall come and say,
Mic	4: 3	And rebuke strong n afar
Hab	1: 5	Look among the n and
Hag	2: 7	'and I will shake all n,
Hag	2: 7	come to the Desire of All N,
Zech	9:10	shall speak peace to the n;
Mal	1:11	shall be great among the n,
Mal	1:14	to be feared among the n.
Mal	3:12	And all n will call you
Matt	24: 9	you will be hated by all n
Matt	24:14	as a witness to all the n,
Matt	28:19	make disciples of all the n,
Mark	11:17	of prayer for all n"?

Mark 13:10 be preached to all the **n**.
Luke 12:30 For all these things the **n** of
Acts 4:25 Why did the **n** rage, And
Acts 13:19 He had destroyed seven **n** in
Gal 3: 8 In you all the **n** shall
Rev 7: 9 one could number, of all **n**,
Rev 12: 5 Child who was to rule all **n**
Rev 17:15 are peoples, multitudes, **n**,
Rev 18: 3 For all the **n** have drunk of

NATIVE (*see* NATIVE-BORN)
Jer 22:10 Nor see his **n** country.

NATIVE-BORN (*see* NATIVE)
Ex 12:49 One law shall be for the **n**

NATURAL (*see* NATURALLY, NATURE)
Deut 34: 7 eyes were not dim nor his **n**
Rom 1:27 leaving the **n** use of the
Rom 11:24 who are **n** branches, be
1Co 2:14 But the **n** man does not
1Co 15:44 It is sown a **n** body, it is
Jas 1:23 like a man observing his **n**

NATURALLY (*see* NATURAL)
Lev 17:15 who eats what died **n** or

NATURE (*see* NATURAL)
Acts 17:29 to think that the Divine **N**
Rom 1:26 use for what is against **n**.
Rom 2:14 by **n** do the things in the
Rom 11:24 tree which is wild by **n**,
1Co 11:14 Does not even **n** itself teach
Gal 2:15 "We who are Jews by **n**,
Eph 2: 3 and were by **n** children of
Jas 3: 6 sets on fire the course of **n**;
Jas 5:17 Elijah was a man with a **n**
2Pe 1: 4 be partakers of the divine **n**,

NAZARENE† (*see* NAZARENES, NAZARETH)
Matt 2:23 "He shall be called a **N**.

NAZARENES† (*see* NAZARENE)
Acts 24: 5 of the sect of the **N**.

NAZARETH (*see* NAZARENE)
Matt 2:23 and dwelt in a city called **N**,
Matt 21:11 the prophet from **N** of
Matt 26:71 also was with Jesus of **N**.
John 1:46 anything good come out of **N**?
John 19:19 the writing was: JESUS OF **N**,
Acts 3: 6 name of Jesus Christ of **N**,

NAZIRITE (*see* NAZIRITES)
Num 6: 2 to take the vow of a **N**,
Num 6:18 Then the **N** shall shave his
Num 6:20 After that the **N** may drink
Judg 13: 5 for the child shall be a **N**

NAZIRITES (*see* NAZIRITE)
Amos 2:12 But you gave the **N** wine to

NEAPOLIS†
Acts 16:11 and the next day came to **N**,

NEBAT
1Ki 15: 1 King Jeroboam the son of **N**,

NEBO (*see* PISGAH)
Deut 34: 1 plains of Moab to Mount **N**,
Is 46: 1 **N** stoops; Their idols were

NEBUCHADNEZZAR
2Ki 24:10 that time the servants of **N**
Dan 2: 1 **N** had dreams; and his spirit
Dan 2:46 Then King **N** fell on his
Dan 3: 1 **N** the king made an image of
Dan 3:19 Then **N** was full of fury, and
Dan 4:28 All this came upon King **N**.
Dan 5: 2 vessels which his father **N**

NEBUZARADAN
2Ki 25: 8 **N** the captain of the guard,

Jer 39:11 concerning Jeremiah to **N**

NECESSARY
Job 23:12 of His mouth More than my **n**
Luke 24:46 and thus it was **n** for the
Acts 15: 5 It is **n** to circumcise them,
1Co 12:22 seem to be like our weaker are **n**.
Jude 3 I found it **n** to write to you

NECESSITIES† (*see* NECESSITY)
Acts 20:34 hands have provided for my **n**,
Phil 4:16 aid once and again for my **n**.

NECESSITY (*see* NECESSITIES)
1Co 9:16 for **n** is laid upon me; yes,
2Co 9: 7 not grudgingly or of **n**;
Heb 7:12 of **n** there is also a change
Heb 9:16 there must also of **n** be the

NECHO (*see* PHARAOH)
2Ki 23:29 And Pharaoh **N** killed him

NECK (*see* NECKS)
Gen 41:42 a gold chain around his **n**.
Gen 45:14 and Benjamin wept on his **n**.
Ex 13:13 then you shall break its **n**.
Deut 31:27 rebellion and your stiff **n**.
1Sa 4:18 and his **n** was broken and he
Ps 69: 1 waters have come up to my **n**.
Prov 3: 3 Bind them around your **n**,
Prov 3:22 soul And grace to your **n**.
Prov 29: 1 rebuked, and hardens his **n**,
Song 7: 4 Your **n** is like an ivory
Is 8: 8 He will reach up to the **n**;
Jer 27: 2 and put them on your **n**,
Jer 28:10 off the prophet Jeremiah's **n**
Jer 28:14 put a yoke of iron on the **n**
Jer 30: 8 break his yoke from your **n**,
Dan 5: 7 a chain of gold around his **n**;
Matt 18: 6 were hung around his **n**,
Luke 15:20 and ran and fell on his **n**

NECKS (*see* NECK)
Josh 10:24 put their feet on their **n**.
2Sa 22:41 have also given me the **n** of
2Ki 17:14 hear, but stiffened their **n**,
Neh 9:16 proudly, Hardened their **n**,
Is 3:16 walk with outstretched **n**
Jer 27:12 Bring your **n** under the yoke
Rom 16: 4 who risked their own **n** for my

NEED (*see* NEEDED, NEEDFUL, NEEDS, NEEDY)
Ezra 6: 9 And whatever they **n**—
Prov 6:11 And your **n** like an armed
Dan 3:16 we have no **n** to answer you
Matt 3:14 I **n** to be baptized by You,
Matt 6: 8 knows the things you have **n**
Matt 6:32 Father knows that you **n** all
Matt 9:12 who are well have no **n** of a
Matt 21: 3 The Lord has **n** of them,' and
Mark 2:17 who are well have no **n** of a
Mark 2:25 David did when he was in **n**
Luke 15: 7 just persons who **n** no
Luke 22:71 further testimony do we **n**?
Acts 2:45 among all, as anyone had **n**.
1Co 12:21 I have no **n** of you."
Eph 4:28 to give him who has **n**.
Phil 2:25 one who ministered to my **n**;
Phil 4:12 to abound and to suffer **n**.
Phil 4:19 God shall supply all your **n**
1Th 1: 8 so that we do not **n** to say
2Ti 2:15 a worker who does not **n** to
Heb 4:16 grace to help in time of **n**.
Heb 5:12 you **n** someone to teach you
1Jn 3:17 and sees his brother in **n**,
Rev 3:17 and have **n** of nothing'—and
Rev 21:23 The city had no **n** of the sun
Rev 22: 5 They **n** no lamp nor light of

NEEDED (see NEED)
Luke 10:42 "But one thing is **n**,
John 4: 4 But He **n** to go through
Acts 17:25 as though He **n** anything,
Jas 2:16 them the things which are **n**

NEEDFUL† (see NEED)
Phil 1:24 in the flesh is more **n** for

NEEDLE
Matt 19:24 to go through the eye of a **n**
Mark 10:25 to go through the eye of a **n**

NEEDS (see NEED)
Luke 11: 8 and give him as many as he **n**.
John 13:10 He who is bathed **n** only to
Rom 12:13 distributing to the **n** of the

NEEDY (see NEED)
Deut 15:11 to your poor and your **n**,
Ps 9:18 For the **n** shall not always
Ps 37:14 To cast down the poor and **n**,
Ps 40:17 But I am poor and **n**;
Ps 72:13 will save the souls of the **n**.
Is 10: 2 To rob the **n** of justice,
Ezek 18:12 has oppressed the poor and **n**,
Amos 4: 1 the poor, Who crush the **n**,
Amos 8: 4 you who swallow up the **n**,
Amos 8: 6 And the **n** for a pair of

NEGLECT (see NEGLECTED)
Col 2:23 and **n** of the body, but are
1Ti 4:14 Do not **n** the gift that is in
Heb 2: 3 how shall we escape if we **n**

NEGLECTED† (see NEGLECT)
Matt 23:23 and have **n** the weightier
Acts 6: 1 because their widows were **n**

NEHEMIAH
Ezra 2: 2 Zerubbabel were Jeshua, N,

NEHUSHTAN†
2Ki 18: 4 to it, and called it N.

NEIGHBOR (see NEIGHBOR'S, NEIGHBORS)
Ex 3:22 woman shall ask of her **n**,
Ex 20:16 false witness against your **n**.
Ex 21:14 premeditation against his **n**,
Ex 22:14 borrows anything from his **n**,
Lev 19:13 'You shall not cheat your **n**,
Lev 19:18 but you shall love your **n** as
Deut 4:42 flee there, who kills his **n**
Deut 5:20 false witness against your **n**.
1Sa 15:28 and has given it to a **n** of
Ps 101: 5 secretly slanders his **n**,
Prov 14:20 is hated even by his own **n**,
Prov 24:28 be a witness against your **n**
Prov 27:10 Better is a **n** nearby than
Jer 31:34 shall every man teach his **n**,
Jer 34:15 proclaiming liberty to his **n**;
Zech 8:16 each man the truth to his **n**;
Matt 5:43 You shall love your **n** and
Luke 10:29 to Jesus, "And who is my **n**?
Rom 13: 9 You shall love your **n** as
Rom 13:10 Love does no harm to a **n**;
Eph 4:25 speak truth with his **n**,
Heb 8:11 them shall teach his **n**,

NEIGHBOR'S (see NEIGHBOR)
Ex 20:17 shall not covet your **n**
Ex 20:17 nor anything that is your **n**.
Ex 22:26 If you ever take your **n**
Lev 20:10 commits adultery with his **n**
Deut 5:21 'You shall not covet your **n**
Deut 5:21 you shall not desire your **n**
Deut 19:14 shall not remove your **n**
Jer 5: 8 one neighed after his **n**

NEIGHBORS (see NEIGHBOR)
Ps 28: 3 Who speak peace to their **n**,
Ps 44:13 make us a reproach to our **n**,
Jer 12:14 Against all My evil **n** who
Luke 14:12 your relatives, nor rich **n**,
Luke 15: 6 together his friends and **n**,
John 9: 8 Therefore the **n** and those who

NEIGHED†
Jer 5: 8 Every one **n** after his

NER
1Sa 14:50 army was Abner the son of N,
2Sa 3:37 to kill Abner the son of N.

NERGAL†
2Ki 17:30 the men of Cuth made N,

NERIAH
Jer 32:12 deed to Baruch the son of N,
Jer 36:32 the scribe, the son of N,

NEST (see NESTED, NESTS)
Deut 32:11 As an eagle stirs up its **n**,
Ps 84: 3 And the swallow a **n** for
Jer 48:28 the dove which makes her **n**
Jer 49:16 Though you make your **n** as
Matt 13:32 birds of the air come and **n**

NESTED† (see NEST)
Luke 13:19 and the birds of the air **n**

NESTS (see NEST)
Ps 104:17 the birds make their **n**;
Matt 8:20 and birds of the air have **n**,

NET (see NETS)
Job 19: 6 has surrounded me with His **n**.
Ps 25:15 pluck my feet out of the **n**.
Ps 57: 6 They have prepared a **n** for
Prov 1:17 in vain the **n** is spread In
Eccl 9:12 fish taken in a cruel **n**,
Lam 1:13 He has spread a **n** for my
Mic 7: 2 hunts his brother with a **n**.
Hab 1:16 they sacrifice to their **n**,
Matt 4:18 casting a **n** into the sea;
Mark 1:16 his brother casting a **n**
Luke 5: 5 word I will let down the **n**.
John 21: 6 Cast the **n** on the right side
John 21:11 the **n** was not broken.

NETHANIAH
2Ki 25:23 Mizpah—Ishmael the son of N,
Jer 41:18 Ishmael the son of N had

NETHINIM
1Ch 9: 2 priests, Levites, and the N.
Ezra 7:24 singers, gatekeepers, N,

NETS (see NET)
Ps 141:10 wicked fall into their own **n**,
Is 19: 8 will languish who spread **n**
Ezek 26:14 a place for spreading **n**,
Matt 4:20 immediately left their **n**
Matt 4:21 father, mending their **n**.
Luke 5: 2 and were washing their **n**.
Luke 5: 4 the deep and let down your **n**

NEW (see NEWBORN, NEWNESS, NEWS)
Ex 1: 8 Now there arose a **n** king
Num 18:12 all the best of the **n** wine
Deut 22: 8 When you build a **n** house,
Judg 5: 8 They chose **n** gods; Then
Judg 16:12 Therefore Delilah took **n**
1Sa 6: 7 make a **n** cart, take two milk
2Ki 16:14 from between the **n** altar and
Job 32:19 It is ready to burst like a
Ps 33: 3 Sing to Him a **n** song; Play
Ps 40: 3 He has put a **n** song in my
Ps 96: 1 sing to the LORD a **n** song!
Eccl 1: 9 And there is nothing **n**

Is	1:13	The N Moons, the Sabbaths,
Is	42: 9	And n things I declare;
Is	42:10	Sing to the LORD a n song,
Is	43:19	I will do a n thing, Now it
Is	65:17	I create n heavens and a new
Jer	36:10	court at the entry of the N
Lam	3:23	They are n every morning;
Ezek	11:19	and I will put a n spirit
Ezek	18:31	and get yourselves a n heart
Ezek	18:31	a new heart and a n spirit.
Hos	2: 8	n wine, and oil, And
Joel	2:24	vats shall overflow with n
Amos	8: 5	When will the N Moon be past,
Matt	9:17	But they put new wine into n
Matt	13:52	of his treasure things n
Matt	26:28	this is My blood of the n
Matt	26:29	that day when I drink it n
Matt	27:60	and laid it in his n tomb
Mark	1:27	What n doctrine is this?
Mark	2:21	or else the n piece pulls
Mark	16:17	they will speak with n
John	13:34	A n commandment I give to
John	19:41	and in the garden a n tomb
Acts	2:13	They are full of n wine."
Acts	17:21	to tell or to hear some n
1Co	5: 7	that you may be a n lump,
1Co	11:25	This cup is the n covenant in
2Co	3: 6	as ministers of the n
2Co	5:17	he is a n creation; old
2Co	5:17	all things have become n.
Gal	6:15	anything, but a n creation.
Eph	2:15	to create in Himself one n
Eph	4:24	and that you put on the n man
Col	3:10	and have put on the n man
Heb	8: 8	when I will make a n
Heb	9:15	He is the Mediator of the n
Heb	10:20	by a n and living way which
2Pe	3:13	look for n heavens and a new
1Jn	2: 7	I write no n commandment to
Rev	2:17	and on the stone a n name
Rev	3:12	the N Jerusalem, which comes
Rev	5: 9	And they sang a n song,
Rev	21: 1	I saw a new heaven and a n
Rev	21: 2	N Jerusalem, coming down out
Rev	21: 5	I make all things n.

NEWBORN† (see NEW)

1Pe	2: 2	as n babes, desire the pure

NEWNESS (see NEW)

Rom	6: 4	so we also should walk in n

NEWS (see NEW)

2Sa	18:27	man, and comes with good n.
1Ki	14: 6	sent to you with bad n.
Prov	25:25	So is good n from a far
Is	52: 7	of him who brings good n,
Jer	20:15	be cursed Who brought n
1Th	3: 6	and brought us good n of

NICODEMUS

John	3: 1	man of the Pharisees named N,
John	7:50	N (he who came to Jesus by

NICOLAITANS

Rev	2:15	hold the doctrine of the N,

NIGER† (see SIMEON, SIMON)

Acts	13: 1	Simeon who was called N,

NIGHT (see NIGHTS)

Gen	1: 5	and the darkness He called N.
Gen	1:14	to divide the day from the n;
Gen	1:16	lesser light to rule the n.
Gen	19:33	father drink wine that n.
Josh	1: 8	meditate in it day and n,
Judg	19: 9	evening; please spend the n.
1Sa	28: 8	they came to the woman by n.

Neh	1: 6	before You now, day and n,
Esth	6: 1	That n the king could not
Job	3: 3	And the n in which it was
Job	4:13	from the visions of the n,
Job	5:14	at noontime as in the n.
Job	33:15	dream, in a vision of the n,
Job	35:10	Who gives songs in the n,
Ps	1: 2	law he meditates day and n.
Ps	6: 6	All n I make my bed swim;
Ps	16: 7	also instructs me in the n
Ps	19: 2	And night unto n reveals
Ps	22: 2	And in the n season, and am
Ps	30: 5	Weeping may endure for a n,
Ps	32: 4	For day and n Your hand was
Ps	42: 3	have been my food day and n,
Ps	63: 6	I meditate on You in the n
Ps	74:16	the n also is Yours; You
Ps	77: 6	remembrance my song in the n;
Ps	90: 4	And like a watch in the n.
Ps	91: 5	be afraid of the terror by n,
Ps	92: 2	Your faithfulness every n,
Ps	121: 6	by day, Nor the moon by n.
Ps	136: 9	moon and stars to rule by n,
Ps	139:11	Even the n shall be light
Prov	31:15	also rises while it is yet n,
Prov	31:18	lamp does not go out by n.
Song	3: 1	By n on my bed I sought the
Is	21:11	"Watchman, what of the n?
Is	26: 9	I have desired You in the n,
Is	34:14	Also the n creature shall
Jer	9: 1	I might weep day and n For
Jer	33:20	and My covenant with the n,
Dan	2:19	revealed to Daniel in a n
Dan	5:30	That very n Belshazzar, king
Dan	7: 2	"I saw in my vision by n,
Amos	5: 8	And makes the day dark as n;
Jon	4:10	which came up in a n and
Zech	14: 7	the LORD—Neither day nor n.
Matt	2:14	Child and His mother by n
Matt	28:13	His disciples came at n and
Luke	2: 8	watch over their flock by n.
Luke	5: 5	we have toiled all n and
Luke	6:12	and continued all n in
Luke	12:20	Fool! This n your soul will
John	3: 2	This man came to Jesus by n
John	9: 4	the n is coming when no one
John	13:30	immediately. And it was n.
John	21: 3	and that n they caught
Acts	5:19	But at n an angel of the Lord
Acts	12: 6	that n Peter was sleeping,
Acts	20:31	not cease to warn everyone n
Rom	13:12	The n is far spent, the day
1Co	11:23	Lord Jesus on the same n
1Th	5: 2	so comes as a thief in the n.
1Th	5: 5	We are not of the n nor of
1Th	5: 7	those who sleep, sleep at n,
2Ti	1: 3	you in my prayers n and day,
2Pe	3:10	come as a thief in the n,
Rev	14:11	they have no rest day or n,
Rev	20:10	will be tormented day and n
Rev	21:25	by day (there shall be no n

NIGHTS (see NIGHT)

Gen	7: 4	earth forty days and forty n,
Ex	24:18	forty days and forty n.
1Ki	19: 8	food forty days and forty n
Job	2:13	seven days and seven n,
Jon	1:17	fish three days and three n.
Matt	4: 2	forty days and forty n,
Matt	12:40	was three days and three n

NIMROD

Gen	10: 9	Like N the mighty hunter

NINE (see NINTH)

Josh	13: 7	as an inheritance to the n

Luke 17:17 But where are the **n**?

NINETY
Gen 5: 9 Enosh lived **n** years, and

NINETY-NINE
Gen 17:24 Abraham was **n** years old when
Matt 18:12 does he not leave the **n** and
Luke 15: 7 who repents than over **n**

NINEVEH
Gen 10:11 went to Assyria and built N,
Jon 1: 2 "Arise, go to N,
Jon 3: 2 "Arise, go to N,
Jon 3: 4 and N shall be overthrown!"
Jon 4:11 "And should I not pity N,
Nah 3: 7 N is laid waste! Who will
Luke 11:32 The men of N will rise up in

NINTH (see NINE)
Matt 20: 5 about the sixth and the **n**
Matt 27:46 And about the **n** hour Jesus
Acts 3: 1 of prayer, the **n** hour.

NISAN (see ABIB)
Esth 3: 7 which is the month of N,

NOAH
Gen 5:32 and N begot Shem, Ham, and
Gen 6: 8 But N found grace in the eyes
Gen 6: 9 N was a just man, perfect in
Gen 6: 9 N walked with God.
Gen 8: 1 Then God remembered N,
Gen 8:20 Then N built an altar to the
Gen 9: 1 So God blessed N and his
Is 54: 9 is like the waters of N to
Ezek 14:20 "even though N,
Luke 17:26 as it was in the days of N,
Heb 11: 7 By faith N, being divinely
1Pe 3:20 waited in the days of N,
2Pe 2: 5 ancient world, but saved N,

NOB
1Sa 22:11 the priests who were in N.

NOBLE (see NOBLEMAN, NOBLES)
Acts 24: 3 most **n** Felix, with all
Acts 26:25 most **n** Festus, but speak the
1Co 1:26 not many mighty, not many **n**,
Phil 4: 8 true, whatever things are **n**,
Jas 2: 7 Do they not blaspheme that **n**

NOBLEMAN (see NOBLE)
Luke 19:12 A certain **n** went into a far
John 4:46 And there was a certain **n**

NOBLES (see NOBLE)
Prov 8:16 By me princes rule, and **n**,
Dan 1: 3 and some of the **n**,
Jon 3: 7 decree of the king and his **n**,

NOD†
Gen 4:16 and dwelt in the land of N

NOISE (see NOISES)
Ex 32:17 There is a **n** of war in the
Ex 32:18 It is not the **n** of the
2Ki 7: 6 the **n** of a great army; so
Ps 42: 7 calls unto deep at the **n** of
Ps 93: 4 is mightier Than the **n** of
Is 29: 6 and earthquake and great **n**,
Is 66: 6 The sound of **n** from the
Jer 4:19 heart! My heart makes a **n**
Jer 49:21 The earth shakes at the **n** of
Ezek 1:24 I heard the **n** of their
Ezek 3:13 and the **n** of the wheels
Ezek 37: 7 I prophesied, there was a **n**,
Amos 5:23 Take away from Me the **n** of
Zeph 1:14 The **n** of the day of the
2Pe 3:10 pass away with a great **n**,

NOISES (see NOISE)
Rev 8: 5 the earth. And there were **n**,

NOON (see NOONDAY)
1Ki 18:26 from morning even till **n**,
Ps 55:17 and morning and at **n** I
Jer 20:16 And the shouting at **n**,
Amos 8: 9 make the sun go down at **n**,
Acts 22: 6 near Damascus at about **n**,

NOONDAY (see NOON)
Deut 28:29 "And you shall grope at **n**,
Ps 37: 6 And your justice as the **n**.
Ps 91: 6 that lays waste at **n**.
Is 58:10 darkness shall be as the **n**.

NOPH (see MEMPHIS)
Is 19:13 The princes of N are
Jer 44: 1 Migdol, at Tahpanhes, at N,

NORTH (see NORTHERN, NORTHWARD)
Job 26: 7 He stretches out the **n** over
Ps 48: 2 Zion on the sides of the **n**,
Ps 89:12 The **n** and the south, You
Ps 107: 3 From the **n** and from the
Eccl 1: 6 And turns around to the **n**;
Is 14:13 the farthest sides of the **n**;
Jer 1:13 it is facing away from the **n**.
Jer 1:14 Out of the **n** calamity shall
Jer 46:10 has a sacrifice In the **n**
Ezek 26: 7 against Tyre from the **n**
Dan 11: 7 of the king of the N,
Zech 6: 8 rest to My Spirit in the **n**
Luke 13:29 from the **n** and the south,

NORTHERN (see NORTH)
Num 34: 7 And this shall be your **n**

NORTHWARD (see NORTH)
Gen 13:14 the place where you are—**n**,
1Sa 14: 5 The front of one faced **n**
Dan 8: 4 the ram pushing westward, **n**,

NOSE (see NOSES)
Gen 24:30 when he saw the **n** ring, and
2Ki 19:28 I will put My hook in your **n**
Song 7: 4 Your **n** is like the tower
Ezek 8:17 put the branch to their **n**.

NOSES† (see NOSE)
Ps 115: 6 N they have, but they do

NOSTRILS
Gen 2: 7 and breathed into his **n** the
Gen 7:22 All in whose **n** was the
Ex 15: 8 with the blast of Your **n**
Num 11:20 it comes out of your **n** and
2Sa 22: 9 Smoke went up from His **n**,
Ps 18:15 of the breath of Your **n**.
Lam 4:20 The breath of our **n**,

NOTABLE (see NOTE)
Dan 8: 5 and the goat had a **n** horn
Amos 6: 1 N persons in the chief

NOTE (see NOTABLE, NOTICE)
1Sa 24: 1 Take **n**! David is in the
2Sa 3:36 Now all the people took **n** of
Job 23: 6 No! But He would take **n** of
Is 30: 8 And **n** it on a scroll, That

NOTICE (see NOTE, UNNOTICED)
Ruth 2:10 that you should take **n** of
Ruth 3: 4 that you shall **n** the place
Is 58: 3 our souls, and You take no **n**?
Acts 18:17 But Gallio took no **n** of

NOTORIOUS†
Matt 27:16 at that time they had a **n**

NOURISHED (see NOURISHES)
2Sa 12: 3 which he had bought and **n**;

Is   1: 2 I have **n** and brought up
Col   2:19 **n** and knit together by
1Ti   4: 6 **n** in the words of faith and

NOURISHER† (*see* NOURISHES)
Ruth   4:15 a restorer of life and a **n**

NOURISHES (*see* NOURISHED, NOURISHER)
Eph   5:29 but **n** and cherishes it, just

NOVICE†
1Ti   3: 6 not a **n**, lest being puffed

NUMBER (*see* NUMBERED, NUMEROUS)
Gen   13:16 so that if a man could **n** the
Gen   15: 5 stars if you are able to **n**
Num   1: 3 You and Aaron shall **n** them
Num   3:15 you shall **n** every male from
Num   3:48 with which the excess **n** of
Deut   4:27 you will be left few in **n**
Deut   7: 7 because you were more in **n**
Judg   6: 5 their camels were without **n**;
2Sa   24: 1 **n** Israel and Judah."
1Ch   21: 1 and moved David to **n** Israel.
Job   3: 6 May it not come into the **n**
Job   5: 9 Marvelous things without **n**.
Job   14:16 For now You **n** my steps, But
Job   38:37 Who can **n** the clouds by
Ps   90:12 So teach us to **n** our days,
Ps   105:12 When they were few in **n**,
Ps   139:18 they would be more in **n** than
Ps   147: 4 He counts the **n** of the
Dan   9: 2 by the books the **n** of the
Luke   5: 6 they caught a great **n** of
John   6:10 in **n** about five thousand.
Acts   6: 1 when the **n** of the
Acts   11:21 and a great **n** believed and
Acts   16: 5 and increased in **n** daily.
Rom   9:27 Though the **n** of the
Rev   7: 9 which no one could **n**,
Rev   13:17 or the **n** of his name.
Rev   13:18 for it is the **n** of a man:
Rev   13:18 of a man: His **n** is 666.
Rev   20: 8 whose **n** is as the sand of

NUMBERED (*see* NUMBER)
Gen   13:16 descendants also could be **n**.
Gen   32:12 which cannot be **n** for
2Sa   24:10 him after he had **n** the
1Ki   3: 8 too numerous to be **n** or
Ps   40: 5 They are more than can be **n**.
Eccl   1:15 what is lacking cannot be **n**.
Is   53:12 And He was **n** with the
Dan   5:26 God has **n** your kingdom, and
Hos   1:10 cannot be measured or **n**.
Matt   10:30 hairs of your head are all **n**.
Mark   15:28 And He was **n** with the
Luke   22: 3 who was **n** among the twelve.
Acts   1:26 And he was **n** with the eleven

NUMEROUS (*see* NUMBER)
Deut   2:10 a people as great and **n** and
Judg   6: 5 coming in as **n** as locusts;
1Ki   4:20 and Israel were as **n** as
Jer   46:23 And more **n** than

NUN
Ex   33:11 servant Joshua the son of **N**,
Num   13: 8 Ephraim, Hoshea the son of **N**;

NURSE (*see* NURSED, NURSING)
Gen   21: 7 Abraham that Sarah would **n**
Gen   24:59 their sister and their **n**,
Gen   35: 8 Now Deborah, Rebekah's **n**,
Ex   2: 7 that she may **n** the child for
Ruth   4:16 and became a **n** to him.
2Sa   4: 4 and his **n** took him up and
1Ki   3:21 I rose in the morning to **n**
Lam   4: 3 present their breasts To **n**

NURSED (*see* NURSE)
Ex   2: 9 woman took the child and **n**
Song   8: 1 Who **n** at my mother's
Luke   11:27 and the breasts which **n**
Luke   23:29 and breasts which never **n**!'

NURSING (*see* NURSE)
Is   11: 8 The **n** child shall play by
Is   49:15 Can a woman forget her **n**
Matt   21:16 mouth of babes and **n**
Matt   24:19 and to those who are **n**
1Th   2: 7 just as a **n** mother

O

OAK (*see* OAKS)
Josh   24:26 set it up there under the **o**
Is   6:13 a terebinth tree or as an **o**,

OAKS (*see* OAK)
Amos   2: 9 he was as strong as the **o**;
Zech   11: 2 O **o** of Bashan, For the

OATH (*see* OATHS)
Gen   21:31 the two of them swore an **o**
Num   5:19 priest shall put her under **o**,
Num   32:10 that day, and He swore an **o**,
Deut   7: 8 because He would keep the **o**
Deut   29:14 this covenant and this **o**,
Josh   2:20 we will be free from your **o**
1Ch   16:16 And His **o** to Isaac,
Neh   10:29 into a curse and an **o** to
Ps   105: 9 And His **o** to Isaac,
Ps   106:26 up His hand in an **o**
Eccl   9: 2 He who takes an **o** as he
Matt   26:63 I put you under **o** by the

OATHS (*see* OATH)
Deut   10:20 and take **o** in His name.
Matt   5:33 but shall perform your **o** to

OBADIAH
1Ki   18: 3 And Ahab had called **O**,
1Ki   18: 4 that **O** had taken one hundred
Obad   1 The vision of **O**.

OBED (*see* OBED-EDOM)
Ruth   4:21 begot Boaz, and Boaz begot **O**;
Matt   1: 5 Boaz begot **O** by Ruth, Obed

OBED-EDOM (*see* EDOM, OBED)
2Sa   6:11 remained in the house of **O**
2Sa   6:11 And the LORD blessed **O** and

OBEDIENCE (*see* OBEDIENT)
Gen   49:10 to Him shall be the **o** of
Rom   1: 5 grace and apostleship for **o**
Rom   5:19 so also by one Man's **o** many
Rom   6:16 or of **o** leading to
Rom   16:19 For your **o** has become known
Rom   16:26 for **o** to the faith—
2Co   10: 5 into captivity to the **o** of
Heb   5: 8 yet He learned **o** by the
1Pe   1: 2 for **o** and sprinkling of the

OBEDIENT (*see* OBEDIENCE, OBEY)
Ex   24: 7 said we will do, and be **o**.
Is   1:19 If you are willing and **o**,
Acts   6: 7 many of the priests were **o**
Rom   15:18 deed, to make the Gentiles **o**—
Eph   6: 5 be **o** to those who are your
Phil   2: 8 Himself and became **o** to
Tit   2: 5 **o** to their own husbands,
Tit   2: 9 bondservants to be **o** to
1Pe   1:14 as **o** children, not conforming

OBEY (*see* OBEDIENT, OBEYED, OBEYING)
Gen   27:43 **o** my voice: arise, flee to

Ex   5: 2 that I should **o** His voice to
Ex   19: 5 if you will indeed **o** My
Deut 4:30 to the LORD your God and **o**
Deut 11:13 be that if you earnestly **o**
Deut 15: 5 only if you carefully **o** the
Josh 24:24 and His voice we will **o**!"
1Sa 8:19 the people refused to **o**
1Sa 12:14 LORD and serve Him and **o**
1Sa 15:22 to **o** is better than
1Sa 28:18 Because you did not **o** the
Jer 7:28 is a nation that does not **o**
Jer 11: 3 is the man who does not **o**
Jer 18:10 sight so that it does not **o**
Dan 7:27 dominions shall serve and **o**
Matt 8:27 the winds and the sea **o** Him?
Mark 1:27 and they **o** Him."
Acts 5:29 We ought to **o** God rather than
Acts 5:32 God has given to those who **o**
Acts 7:39 our fathers would not **o**,
Rom 2: 8 self-seeking and do not **o**
Rom 6:12 that you should **o** it in its
Rom 6:16 yourselves slaves to **o**,
Eph 6: 1 **o** your parents in the Lord,
Col 3:20 **o** your parents in all
Col 3:22 **o** in all things your masters
2Th 1: 8 and on those who do not **o**
2Th 3:14 And if anyone does not **o** our
Tit   3: 1 rulers and authorities, to **o**,
Heb 3:18 but to those who did not **o**?
Heb 5: 9 salvation to all who **o** Him,
Heb 13:17 **O** those who rule over you,
1Pe 3: 1 that even if some do not **o**
1Pe 4:17 end of those who do not **o**

OBEYED (see OBEY)
Gen 22:18 because you have **o** My
Gen 26: 5 because Abraham **o** My voice
Dan 9:10 We have not **o** the voice of
Dan 9:14 though we have not **o** His
Rom 6:17 yet you **o** from the heart
Rom 10:16 But they have not all **o** the
Heb 11: 8 By faith Abraham **o** when he
1Pe 3: 6 as Sarah **o** Abraham, calling

OBEYING (see OBEY)
Judg 2:17 in **o** the commandments of the
1Sa 15:22 As in **o** the voice of the
Gal 5: 7 Who hindered you from **o** the

OBIL
1Ch 27:30 **O** the Ishmaelite was over

OBJECT (see OBJECTS)
Acts 10:11 saw heaven opened and an **o**

OBJECTS† (see OBJECT)
Acts 17:23 and considering the **o** of

OBLIGATION†
2Co 9: 5 and not as a grudging **o**.

OBNOXIOUS†
Gen 34:30 troubled me by making me **o**

OBSCENE
1Ki 15:13 because she had made an **o**

OBSERVANCE (see OBSERVE)
Ex 12:42 It is a night of solemn **o** to

OBSERVATION† (see OBSERVE)
Luke 17:20 of God does not come with **o**;

OBSERVE (see OBSERVANCE, OBSERVATION, OBSERVED,
   OBSERVES, OBSERVING)
Ex 12:17 So you shall **o** the Feast
Ex 31:16 to **o** the Sabbath throughout
Lev 18: 4 You shall **o** My judgments and
Deut 4: 1 which I teach you to **o**,
Deut 5:12 **O** the Sabbath day, to keep

Deut 12:28 **O** and obey all these words
Deut 16: 1 **O** the month of Abib, and keep
Deut 24: 8 that you carefully **o** and do
2Ch 14: 4 and to **o** the law and the
Ps   10:14 for You **o** trouble and grief,
Ps   66: 7 His eyes **o** the nations; Do
Ps 119:34 I shall **o** it with my whole
Ezek 45:21 you shall **o** the Passover, a
Hos 12: 6 **O** mercy and justice, And
Matt 28:20 teaching them to **o** all things
Acts 7:31 and as he drew near to **o**,
Rom 14: 6 and he who does not **o** the
1Co 10:18 **O** Israel after the flesh: Are
Gal 4:10 You **o** days and months and
1Pe 3: 2 when they **o** your chaste

OBSERVED (see KEPT, OBSERVE)
Gen 50:10 He **o** seven days of mourning
Deut 33: 9 For they have **o** Your word
Mark 15:47 Mary the mother of Joses **o**

OBSERVES (see OBSERVE)
Rom 14: 6 He who **o** the day, observes
Jas   1:24 for he **o** himself, goes away,

OBSERVING (see OBSERVE)
Jas   1:23 he is like a man **o** his

OBSOLETE
Heb 8:13 He has made the first **o**.

OBTAIN (see OBTAINED, OBTAINS)
Gen 16: 2 perhaps I shall **o** children
Is   35:10 They shall **o** joy and
Matt 5: 7 For they shall **o** mercy.
Rom 11:31 shown you they also may **o**
1Co 9:25 Now they do it to **o** a
1Th 5: 9 but to **o** salvation through
Heb 4:16 that we may **o** mercy and find
Heb 11:35 that they might **o** a better
Jas   4: 2 and covet and cannot **o**.

OBTAINED (see OBTAIN)
Hos 2:23 on her who had not **o**
Rom 11: 7 but the elect have **o** it, and
Rom 11:30 yet have now **o** mercy through
Eph 1:11 In Him also we have **o** an
1Ti   1:16 for this reason I **o** mercy,
Heb 1: 4 as He has by inheritance **o**
Heb 6:15 he **o** the promise.
Heb 8: 6 But now He has **o** a more
Heb 9:12 having **o** eternal redemption.
Heb 11: 2 For by it the elders **o** a
Heb 11: 4 through which he **o** witness
Heb 11:33 **o** promises, stopped the
Heb 11:39 having **o** a good testimony
1Pe 2:10 who had not **o** mercy but now

OBTAINS† (see OBTAIN)
Prov 8:35 And **o** favor from the LORD;
Prov 12: 2 A good man **o** favor from the
Prov 18:22 And **o** favor from the LORD.

OCCASION
Rom 7:11 taking **o** by the commandment,

OCCUPATION
Gen 46:34 Your servants' **o** has been
Gen 47: 3 brothers, "What is your **o**?
Jon 1: 8 upon us? What is your **o**?
Acts 18: 3 for by **o** they were

OCCURRED
Rev 16:18 earthquake as had not **o**

OFFAL
Lev 4:11 and legs, its entrails and **o**—
Num 19: 5 and its **o** shall be burned.

OFFEND (see OFFENDED, OFFENSE, OFFENSIVE)
Matt 13:41 kingdom all things that **o**,

Luke 17: 2 than that he should o one of
John 6:61 Does this o you?

OFFENDED (*see* OFFEND)
Prov 18:19 A brother o is harder to
Hos 13: 1 But when he o through Baal
Matt 11: 6 blessed is he who is not o
Matt 13:57 So they were o at Him. But
Matt 15:12 that the Pharisees were o
Matt 24:10 "And then many will be o,

OFFENSE (*see* OFFEND, OFFENSES)
Is   8:14 of stumbling and a rock of o
Jer 37:18 What o have I committed
Matt 16:23 Satan! You are an o to Me,
Matt 18: 7 to that man by whom the o
Acts 24:16 have a conscience without o
Rom 5:15 free gift is not like the o.
Rom 5:15 For if by the one man's o
Rom 9:33 stone and rock of o,
1Co 10:32 Give no o, either to the
Gal   5:11 Then the o of the cross has
Phil 1:10 may be sincere and without o
1Pe   2: 8 And a rock of o.

OFFENSES (*see* OFFENSE)
Matt 18: 7 to the world because of o!
Rom   4:25 up because of our o,
Rom   5:16 which came from many o

OFFENSIVE† (*see* OFFEND)
Job 19:17 My breath is o to my wife,

OFFER (*see* OFFERED, OFFERING, OFFERS)
Gen 22: 2 and o him there as a burnt
Ex   23:18 You shall not o the blood of
Ex   29:36 And you shall o a bull every
Ex   29:39 One lamb you shall o in the
Ex   30: 9 You shall not o strange
Lev   1: 3 let him o a male without
Lev   6:14 The sons of Aaron shall o it
Lev 10:15 to o as a wave offering
Lev 16: 6 Aaron shall o the bull as a
Lev 17: 5 and o them as peace
Lev 22:20 a defect, you shall not o,
Lev 22:23 long or too short you may o
Lev 23:27 and o an offering made by
Num   8:11 and Aaron shall o the Levites
Num 15: 7 a drink offering you shall o
Num 16:40 should come near to o
Num 18:19 the children of Israel o to
Num 28: 3 by fire which you shall o
Deut 18: 3 from those who o a
Judg 5: 2 When the people willingly o
1Sa   1:21 all his house went up to o
2Sa 24:12 I o you three things; choose
2Ki 17:36 and to Him you shall o
1Ch 29:17 who are present here to o
Job   1: 5 early in the morning and o
Job 42: 8 and o up for yourselves a
Ps   16: 4 of blood I will not o,
Ps   50:14 O to God thanksgiving, And
Ps   51:19 Then they shall o bulls on
Jer 11:12 to the gods to whom they o
Jer 33:18 lack a man to o burnt
Ezek 43:22 the second day you shall o
Ezek 44:27 he must o his sin offering
Hos   9: 4 They shall not o wine
Amos 4: 5 O a sacrifice of
Amos 5:22 Though you o Me burnt
Amos 5:25 Did you o Me sacrifices and
Hag   2:14 and what they o there is
Mal   1: 7 You o defiled food on My
Mal   1: 8 And when you o the blind as
Luke 6:29 o the other also. And from
Luke 11:12 will he o him a scorpion?
Heb   5: 3 to o sacrifices for sins.

Heb   7:27 to o up sacrifices, first
Heb   8: 3 One also have something to o.
Heb   9:25 not that He should o Himself
Heb 10: 1 which they o continually
Heb 13:15 by Him let us continually o
1Pe   2: 5 to o up spiritual sacrifices

OFFERED (*see* OFFER)
Gen   8:20 and o burnt offerings on the
Gen 22:13 and o it up for a burnt
Gen 31:54 Then Jacob o a sacrifice on
Lev   7:15 eaten the same day it is o.
Lev 10: 1 and o profane fire before
Num 26:61 and Abihu died when they o
Judg 13:19 and o it upon the rock to
1Sa   6:14 the wood of the cart and o
2Sa   6:17 Then David o burnt offerings
1Ki   3: 4 Solomon o a thousand burnt
Neh 12:43 Also that day they o great
Is   57: 6 have you o a grain
Jer 32:29 on whose roofs they have o
Ezek 6:13 wherever they o sweet
Ezek 16:25 You o yourself to everyone
Jon   1:16 and o a sacrifice to the
Mark 15:36 and o it to Him to drink,
Acts 7:41 o sacrifices to the idol,
Acts 15:29 you abstain from things o
Acts 21:25 themselves from things o
1Co   8: 4 the eating of things o to
1Co 10:19 or what is o to idols is
Heb   5: 7 when He had o up prayers and
Heb   7:27 did once for all when He o
Heb   9: 7 which he o for himself and
Heb   9:14 through the eternal Spirit o
Heb   9:28 so Christ was o once to bear
Heb 10:12 after He had o one sacrifice
Heb 11: 4 By faith Abel o to God a
Heb 11:17 o up Isaac, and he who had
Heb 11:17 had received the promises o
Jas   2:21 by works when he o Isaac

OFFERING (*see* OFFER, OFFERINGS)
Gen   4: 4 respected Abel and his o,
Gen   4: 5 not respect Cain and his o.
Gen 22: 2 him there as a burnt o on
Gen 22: 3 the wood for the burnt o,
Gen 22: 7 is the lamb for a burnt o?
Gen 22:13 offered it up for a burnt o
Gen 35:14 and he poured a drink o on
Ex   25: 2 that they bring Me an o.
Ex   29:14 the camp. It is a sin o.
Ex   29:18 an o made by fire to the
Ex   29:24 shall wave them as a wave o
Ex   29:27 and the thigh of the heave o
Ex   29:36 a bull every day as a sin o
Ex   29:40 a hin of wine as a drink o.
Ex   29:41 offer with it the grain o
Ex   29:42 be a continual burnt o
Ex   30: 9 incense on it, or a burnt o,
Ex   30:10 with the blood of the sin o
Ex   30:28 the altar of burnt o with all
Ex   35:22 every man who made an o of
Ex   35:29 Israel brought a freewill o
Lev   1: 2 you shall bring your o of
Lev   1:14 then he shall bring his o of
Lev   2: 1 his o shall be of fine
Lev   3: 2 hand on the head of his o,
Lev   3:12 And if his o is a goat,
Lev   4: 3 without blemish as a sin o.
Lev   4: 8 fat of the bull as the sin o.
Lev   4:25 of the blood of the sin o
Lev   4:25 of the altar of burnt o,
Lev   5: 6 kid of the goats as a sin o.
Lev   5:10 the second as a burnt o
Lev   5:15 sanctuary, as a trespass o.
Lev   6:10 up the ashes of the burnt o

Lev	6:14	is the law of the grain o:
Lev	7:13	thanksgiving of his peace o.
Lev	7:16	is a vow or a voluntary o,
Lev	7:20	the sacrifice of the peace o
Lev	9:15	he brought the people's o,
Lev	10:14	The breast of the wave o and
Lev	10:15	The thigh of the heave o and
Lev	14:10	mixed with oil as a grain o,
Lev	14:14	the blood of the trespass o,
Lev	16: 3	of a young bull as a sin o,
Lev	16: 3	and of a ram as a burnt o.
Lev	16: 5	kids of the goats as a sin o,
Lev	16:15	kill the goat of the sin o,
Lev	19: 8	profaned the hallowed o of
Lev	22:10	shall eat the holy o;
Lev	23:13	and its drink o shall be
Lev	27:28	'Nevertheless no devoted o
Num	5:15	He shall bring the o
Num	5:15	an o for remembering, for
Num	6: 2	or woman consecrates an o
Num	6:14	without blemish as a burnt o,
Num	6:21	who vows to the LORD the o
Num	7:10	offered the dedication o
Num	7:16	kid of the goats as a sin o;
Num	7:17	This was the o of Nahshon
Num	7:18	Issachar, presented an o.
Num	7:88	This was the dedication o
Num	16:15	"Do not respect their o.
Num	16:35	and fifty men who were o
Num	28:10	this is the burnt o
Num	28:13	as a grain o for each lamb,
Num	28:23	is for a regular burnt o.
Num	28:24	offer the food of the o
Num	28:26	you bring a new grain o to
Num	29: 6	offering with its grain o
Num	29:11	besides the sin o for
Num	31:52	And all the gold of the o
Deut	23:18	your God for any vowed o,
Judg	11:31	offer it up as a burnt o.
1Sa	2:17	for men abhorred the o of
1Sa	3:14	atoned for by sacrifice or o
1Sa	6:14	the cows as a burnt o to
1Sa	7:10	Now as Samuel was o up the
1Ki	18:29	until the time of the o of
2Ki	3:27	offered him as a burnt o
Ezra	8:35	male goats as a sin o.
Neh	10:33	for the regular burnt o of
Neh	10:34	for bringing the wood o
Job	42: 8	up for yourselves a burnt o;
Ps	40: 6	Sacrifice and o You did not
Ps	40: 6	Burnt o and sin offering
Ps	51:16	do not delight in burnt o.
Ps	51:19	offering and whole burnt o;
Ps	96: 8	due His name; Bring an o,
Is	53:10	You make His soul an o for
Is	57: 6	you have poured a drink o,
Jer	11:17	to provoke Me to anger in o
Ezek	40:42	slaughtered the burnt o and
Ezek	43:22	without blemish for a sin o;
Ezek	45:16	the land shall give this o
Ezek	45:19	of the blood of the sin o
Ezek	45:23	of the goats daily for a sin o.
Ezek	46:14	This grain o is a perpetual
Dan	2:46	they should present an o.
Dan	9:21	the time of the evening o.
Dan	9:27	an end to sacrifice and o.
Mal	1:10	Nor will I accept an o from
Mal	2:13	So He does not regard the o
Mal	3: 3	offer to the LORD An o in
Luke	5:14	and make an o for your
Luke	23:36	coming and o Him sour wine,
Rom	15:16	that the o of the Gentiles
Eph	5: 2	an o and a sacrifice to God
2Ti	4: 6	poured out as a drink o,
Heb	10: 5	Sacrifice and o You did

Heb	10: 8	saying, "Sacrifice and o,
Heb	10:10	sanctified through the o of
Heb	10:11	ministering daily and o
Heb	10:14	For by one o He has perfected
Heb	10:18	there is no longer an o

OFFERINGS (*see* OFFERING)

Gen	8:20	and offered burnt o on the
Ex	20:24	on it your burnt o and your
Ex	24: 5	who offered burnt o and
Lev	2: 3	It is most holy of the o
Lev	6:12	on it the fat of the peace o.
Lev	7:38	of Israel to offer their o
Lev	8:28	They were consecration o
Lev	8:31	the basket of consecration o,
Lev	10:15	they shall bring with the o
Lev	22:18	or for any of his freewill o,
Lev	23:37	a sacrifice and drink o,
Num	10:10	trumpets over your burnt o
Num	18: 8	you charge of My heave o,
Num	18:11	with all the wave o of the
Num	29:39	(besides your vowed o and
Num	29:39	and your freewill o) as
Deut	12:11	and all your choice o which
1Sa	6:15	Shemesh offered burnt o and
1Sa	15:22	great delight in burnt o
2Sa	1:21	upon you, Nor fields of o.
2Ki	12:16	money from the trespass o
2Ch	1: 6	offered a thousand burnt o
2Ch	29:34	not skin all the burnt o;
2Ch	31: 3	the burnt o for the Sabbaths
2Ch	35: 6	slaughter the Passover o,
Ezra	3: 3	morning and evening burnt o
Ezra	8:35	offered burnt o to the God
Neh	12:44	of the storehouse for the o,
Job	1: 5	morning and offer burnt o
Ps	16: 4	Their drink o of blood I
Ps	20: 3	May He remember all your o,
Ps	66:13	into Your house with burnt o;
Ps	119:108	the freewill o of my mouth,
Prov	7:14	I have peace o with me;
Is	1:11	have had enough of burnt o
Jer	7:18	and they pour out drink o
Jer	19: 5	sons with fire for burnt o
Jer	33:18	before Me, to kindle grain o,
Jer	41: 5	with o and incense in their
Ezek	20:28	and provoked Me with their o.
Ezek	42:13	shall eat the most holy o.
Ezek	45:17	and the peace o to make
Hos	6: 6	of God more than burnt o.
Amos	5:22	regard your fattened peace o.
Amos	5:25	offer Me sacrifices and o
Mic	6: 6	come before Him with burnt o,
Mal	3: 8	You?' In tithes and o.
Mark	12:33	than all the whole burnt o
1Co	9:13	the altar partake of the o
Heb	10: 6	In burnt o and sacrifices
Heb	10: 8	and o for sin You did

OFFERS (*see* OFFER)

Lev	2: 1	When anyone o a grain
Ps	50:23	Whoever o praise glorifies
Is	66: 3	as if he o swine's
Ezek	46: 4	offering that the prince o
John	16: 2	you will think that he o

OFFICE (*see* OFFICER)

Gen	41:13	He restored me to my o,
1Ch	9:22	them to their trusted o.
Ps	109: 8	And let another take his o.
Matt	9: 9	Matthew sitting at the tax o.
Mark	2:14	sitting at the tax o.
Luke	5:27	Levi, sitting at the tax o.
Acts	1:20	another take his o.

OFFICER (*see* OFFICE, OFFICERS)

Gen	37:36	an o of Pharaoh and captain

2Ki	7:17	king had appointed the **o** on
2Ki	15:25	an **o** of his, conspired
1Ch	9:11	the **o** over the house of God;
2Ch	24:11	and the high priest's **o**
Matt	5:25	judge hand you over to the **o**,
Luke	12:58	and the **o** throw you into

OFFICERS (see OFFICER)

Gen	41:34	and let him appoint **o** over
Ex	5:10	of the people and their **o**
Num	31:14	Moses was angry with the **o**
Deut	1:15	and **o** for your tribes.
Deut	16:18	shall appoint judges and **o**
Josh	1:10	Joshua commanded the **o** of
Josh	8:33	with their elders and **o** and
Josh	23: 2	judges, and for their **o**,
Josh	24: 1	judges, and for their **o**;
2Ki	11:15	the **o** of the army, and said
2Ch	26:12	The total number of chief **o**
2Ch	34:13	the Levites were scribes, **o**,
Jer	39:13	king of Babylon's chief **o**;
Mark	14:65	Prophesy!" And the **o** struck
John	7:32	the chief priests sent **o** to
John	7:46	The **o** answered, "No man ever
John	18:12	and the captain and the **o**
Acts	16:35	the magistrates sent the **o**,

OFFICIALS

Esth	1:18	will say to all the king's **o**
Eccl	5: 8	and higher **o** are over them.
Dan	3: 2	and all the **o** of the
Acts	19:31	Then some of the **o** of Asia,

OFFICIATED†

Heb	7:13	from which no man has **o** at

OFFSCOURING†

Lam	3:45	You have made us an **o** and
1Co	4:13	the **o** of all things until

OFFSPRING

Gen	15: 3	You have given me no **o**;
Deut	7:13	of your cattle and the **o** of
Judg	8:30	sons who were his own **o**,
Ruth	4:12	because of the **o** which the
Job	39: 3	young, They deliver their **o**.
Ps	21:10	Their **o** You shall destroy
Ps	22:23	all you **o** of Israel!
Is	44: 3	And My blessing on your **o**;
Is	48:19	And the **o** of your body like
Is	57: 1	**O** of falsehood,
Lam	2:20	the women eat their **o**,
Mal	2:15	why one? He seeks godly **o**.
Matt	22:24	his wife and raise up **o** for
Matt	22:25	had married, and having no **o**,
Mark	12:20	and dying, he left no **o**.
Acts	17:28	said, 'For we are also His **o**.
Acts	17:29	since we are the **o** of God,
Rev	22:16	I am the Root and the **O** of

OG

Num	21:33	So **O** king of Bashan went out
Deut	3:10	cities of the kingdom of **O**
Deut	31: 4	as He did to Sihon and **O**,
Ps	135:11	**O** king of Bashan, And all
Ps	136:20	And **O** king of Bashan, For

OHOLAH

Ezek	23: 4	**O** the elder and Oholibah her
Ezek	23: 4	their names, Samaria is **O**,

OHOLIBAH

Ezek	23: 4	Oholah the elder and **O** her
Ezek	23: 4	Oholah, and Jerusalem is **O**.

OIL (see OILS)

Gen	28:18	and poured **o** on top of it.
Ex	25: 6	**o** for the light, and spices
Ex	25: 6	spices for the anointing **o**

Ex	29: 2	cakes mixed with **o**,
Ex	30:24	and a hin of olive **o**.
Ex	37:29	made the holy anointing **o**
Lev	6:21	be made in a pan with **o**.
Lev	14:16	sprinkle some of the **o** with
Num	4: 9	and all its **o** vessels, with
Num	11: 8	of pastry prepared with **o**.
Num	35:25	was anointed with the holy **o**.
Deut	7:13	and your new wine and your **o**,
Deut	32:13	And **o** from the flinty rock;
Deut	33:24	let him dip his foot in **o**.
Judg	9: 9	'Should I cease giving my **o**,
1Sa	10: 1	Samuel took a flask of **o**
1Sa	16: 1	Fill your horn with **o**,
2Sa	1:21	of Saul, not anointed with **o**.
1Ki	17:12	and a little **o** in a jar; and
2Ki	4: 6	So the **o** ceased.
2Ki	4: 7	sell the **o** and pay your
2Ki	9: 6	And he poured the **o** on his
2Ch	2:15	the wheat, the barley, the **o**,
Ezra	3: 7	and **o** to the people of Sidon
Neh	5:11	the new wine and the **o**,
Neh	8:15	branches of **o** trees, myrtle
Esth	2:12	six months with **o** of myrrh,
Job	29: 6	rock poured out rivers of **o**
Ps	23: 5	You anoint my head with **o**;
Ps	45: 7	anointed You With the **o** of
Ps	55:21	words were softer than **o**,
Ps	104:15	**O** to make his face shine,
Ps	109:18	And like **o** into his bones.
Ps	133: 2	It is like the precious **o**
Ps	141: 5	shall be as excellent **o**;
Prov	5: 3	mouth is smoother than **o**;
Prov	27:16	And grasps **o** with his right
Eccl	9: 8	And let your head lack no **o**.
Is	61: 3	The **o** of joy for mourning,
Jer	31:12	wheat and new wine and **o**,
Ezek	32:14	make their rivers run like **o**,
Ezek	45:25	grain offering, and the **o**.
Hos	2: 5	My **o** and my drink.'
Hos	2: 8	her grain, new wine, and **o**,
Hos	12: 1	And **o** is carried to Egypt.
Joel	1:10	dried up, The **o** fails.
Mic	6: 7	Ten thousand rivers of **o**?
Zech	4:12	from which the golden **o**
Matt	25: 4	but the wise took **o** in their
Matt	26: 7	of very costly fragrant **o**,
Matt	26:12	in pouring this fragrant **o**
Mark	6:13	and anointed with **o** many who
Mark	14: 4	Why was this fragrant **o**
Luke	7:37	flask of fragrant **o**,
Luke	10:34	pouring on **o** and wine; and
Heb	1: 9	You With the **o** of
Jas	5:14	anointing him with **o** in the

OILS† (see OIL)

Luke	23:56	spices and fragrant **o**.

OINTMENT (see OINTMENTS)

Ex	30:25	an **o** compounded according to
Prov	27: 9	**O** and perfume delight the
Eccl	7: 1	is better than precious **o**,
Is	1: 6	bound up, Or soothed with **o**.

OINTMENTS (see OINTMENT)

Song	1: 3	the fragrance of your good **o**,
Amos	6: 6	yourselves with the best **o**,

OLD (see ELDEST, OLDER, OLDEST, OLDNESS)

Gen	6: 4	mighty men who were of **o**,
Gen	15:15	shall be buried at a good **o**
Gen	17: 1	was ninety-nine years **o**,
Gen	18:11	Now Abraham and Sarah were **o**,
Gen	19:31	younger, "Our father is **o**,
Gen	21: 2	bore Abraham a son in his **o**
Gen	21: 4	when he was eight days **o**,
Gen	25: 8	last and died in a good **o**

Gen	25: 8	an **o** man and full of
Gen	37: 2	being seventeen years **o**,
Gen	50:26	one hundred and ten years **o**;
Ex	7: 7	Moses was eighty years **o**
Ex	30:14	from twenty years **o** and
Lev	27: 3	old up to sixty years **o**,
Lev	27: 5	old up to twenty years **o**,
Lev	27: 6	month old up to five years **o**,
Num	3:15	every male from a month **o**
Num	4: 3	from thirty years **o** and
Num	4: 3	above, even to fifty years **o**,
Num	8:24	From twenty-five years **o** and
Deut	4:25	and have grown **o** in the
Deut	32: 7	"Remember the days of **o**,
Deut	34: 7	hundred and twenty years **o**
Josh	9: 5	**o** and patched sandals on
Josh	9: 5	and **o** garments on
Josh	24:29	one hundred and ten years **o**.
Ruth	1:12	for I am too **o** to have a
Ruth	4:15	and a nourisher of your **o**
1Sa	2:22	Now Eli was very **o**;
1Sa	8: 5	to him, "Look, you are **o**,
1Sa	28:14	An **o** man is coming up, and he
2Sa	2:10	was forty years **o** when he
1Ki	1: 1	Now King David was **o**,
1Ki	11: 4	was so, when Solomon was **o**,
1Ki	13:11	Now an **o** prophet dwelt in
1Ch	23: 1	So when David was **o** and full
1Ch	29:28	So he died in a good **o** age,
2Ch	31:17	Levites from twenty years **o**
Job	4:11	The **o** lion perishes for lack
Job	14: 8	Though its root may grow **o**
Job	22:15	Will you keep to the **o** way
Job	42:17	**o** and full of days.
Ps	25: 6	For they are from of **o**.
Ps	32: 3	my bones grew **o** Through my
Ps	37:25	been young, and now am **o**;
Ps	55:19	He who abides from of **o**.
Ps	71:18	Now also when I am **o** and
Ps	74:12	God is my King from of **o**,
Ps	77: 5	considered the days of **o**,
Ps	77:11	remember Your wonders of **o**.
Ps	78: 2	will utter dark sayings of **o**,
Ps	92:14	shall still bear fruit in **o**
Ps	102:25	Of **o** You laid the foundation
Ps	102:26	they will all grow **o** like a
Ps	148:12	**O** men and children.
Prov	8:22	way, Before His works of **o**.
Prov	17: 6	are the crown of **o** men,
Prov	22: 6	And when he is **o** he will
Prov	23:22	your mother when she is **o**.
Is	20: 4	as captives, young and **o**,
Is	25: 1	Your counsels of **o** are
Is	43:18	consider the things of **o**.
Is	46: 4	Even to your **o** age, I am
Is	46: 9	the former things of **o**,
Is	50: 9	they will all grow **o** like a
Is	63: 9	them All the days of **o**.
Is	65:20	die one hundred years **o**,
Jer	31: 3	LORD has appeared of **o** to
Lam	5:21	Renew our days as of **o**,
Joel	2:28	Your **o** men shall dream
Amos	9:11	it as in the days of **o**;
Mic	5: 2	goings forth are from of **o**,
Mic	6: 6	With calves a year **o**?
Mic	7:20	our fathers From days of **o**.
Matt	2:16	from two years **o** and under,
Matt	5:21	it was said to those of **o**,
Matt	9:16	of unshrunk cloth on an **o**
Matt	9:17	do they put new wine into **o**
Matt	13:52	treasure things new and **o**.
Luke	1:18	For I am an **o** man, and my
Luke	1:36	conceived a son in her **o**
Luke	2:42	when He was twelve years **o**,
Luke	9: 8	by others that one of the **o**

Luke	9:19	say that one of the **o**
John	3: 4	a man be born when he is **o**?
John	8:57	are not yet fifty years **o**,
John	21:18	wished; but when you are **o**,
Acts	2:17	Your **o** men shall dream
Rom	6: 6	that our **o** man was crucified
1Co	5: 7	Therefore purge out the **o**
2Co	3:14	in the reading of the **O**
2Co	5:17	**o** things have passed away;
Eph	4:22	the **o** man which grows
Col	3: 9	you have put off the **o** man
1Ti	4: 7	But reject profane and **o**
Heb	1:11	they will all grow **o**
Heb	8:13	obsolete and growing **o** is
2Pe	1: 9	he was cleansed from his **o**
1Jn	2: 7	but an **o** commandment which
Rev	12: 9	cast out, that serpent of **o**,
Rev	20: 2	dragon, that serpent of **o**,

OLDER (see OLD)

Gen	25:23	And the **o** shall serve the
Luke	15:25	Now his **o** son was in the
Rom	9:12	The **o** shall serve the
1Ti	5: 1	Do not rebuke an **o** man, but
1Ti	5: 2	**o** women as mothers, younger
Tit	2: 2	that the **o** men be sober,

OLDEST (see OLD)

Gen	24: 2	So Abraham said to the **o**
Gen	44:12	He began with the **o** and left
Num	1:20	Israel's **o** son, their
1Sa	17:13	The three **o** sons of Jesse had
Job	1:13	and drinking wine in their **o**

OLDNESS† (see OLD)

Rom	7: 6	Spirit and not in the **o** of

OLIVE (see OLIVES)

Gen	8:11	a freshly plucked **o** leaf
Ex	23:11	your vineyard and your **o**
Deut	6:11	vineyards and **o** trees which
Deut	24:20	When you beat your **o** trees,
Judg	9: 8	And they said to the **o**
1Ki	6:23	he made two cherubim of **o**
Neh	8:15	and bring **o** branches,
Ps	52: 8	But I am like a green **o**
Is	17: 6	Like the shaking of an **o**
Is	24:13	be like the shaking of an **o**
Zech	4: 3	Two **o** trees are by it, one
Rom	11:17	being a wild **o** tree, were
Rom	11:24	be grafted into their own **o**
Rev	11: 4	These are the two **o** trees and

OLIVES (see OLIVE)

Ex	27:20	you pure oil of pressed **o**
2Sa	15:30	Ascent of the Mount of **O**,
Mic	6:15	reap; You shall tread the **o**,
Zech	14: 4	will stand on the Mount of **O**,
Matt	21: 1	Bethphage, at the Mount of **O**,
Matt	26:30	went out to the Mount of **O**.
Mark	13: 3	as He sat on the Mount of **O**
Jas	3:12	tree, my brethren, bear **o**,

OLIVET

Luke	19:29	at the mountain called **O**,

OMEGA†

Rev	1: 8	"I am the Alpha and the **O**,
Rev	1:11	"I am the Alpha and the **O**,
Rev	21: 6	I am the Alpha and the **O**,
Rev	22:13	"I am the Alpha and the **O**,

OMENS†

Deut	18:10	or one who interprets **o**,

OMER

Ex	16:16	one **o** for each person,
Ex	16:33	Take a pot and put an **o** of

OMNIPOTENT†

Rev 19: 6 For the Lord God **O** reigns!

OMRI

1Ki 16:23 **O** became king over Israel,
1Ki 16:25 **O** did evil in the eyes of the
1Ki 16:29 Ahab the son of **O** became
Mic 6:16 For the statutes of **O** are

ONAN

Gen 38: 9 But **O** knew that the heir
Gen 46:12 sons of Judah were Er, **O**,
Gen 46:12 and Zerah (but Er and **O** died

ONCE (see ONE)

Gen 18:32 and I will speak but **o** more:
Lev 16:34 **o** a year." And he did as
Josh 6:14 marched around the city **o**
Judg 6:39 just **o** more with the fleece;
Job 40: 5 **O** I have spoken, but I will
Rom 6:10 He died to sin **o** for all;
1Co 15: 6 five hundred brethren at **o**,
Gal 1:23 the faith which he **o** tried
Eph 2: 2 in which you **o** walked
Eph 2:13 in Christ Jesus you who **o**
Eph 5: 8 For you were **o** darkness, but
Col 1:21 who **o** were alienated and
Col 3: 7 in which you yourselves **o**
Heb 6: 4 for those who were **o**
Heb 7:27 for this He did **o** for all
Heb 9: 7 high priest went alone **o** a
Heb 9:12 the Most Holy Place **o** for
Heb 9:27 appointed for men to die **o**,
Heb 9:28 so Christ was offered **o** to
Heb 12:26 Yet **o** more I shake not
1Pe 2:10 who **o** were not a people but
1Pe 3:18 For Christ also suffered **o**
Jude 3 for the faith which was **o**

ONE (see ONCE)

Gen 1: 9 be gathered together into **o**
Gen 2:21 and He took **o** of his ribs,
Gen 2:24 and they shall become **o**
Gen 3:22 the man has become like **o** of
Gen 10: 8 he began to be a mighty **o** on
Gen 11: 1 earth had one language and **o**
Gen 15: 3 indeed **o** born in my house is
Gen 15: 4 This **o** shall not be your
Gen 19:20 to, and it is a little **o**;
Gen 22: 2 as a burnt offering on **o** of
Gen 27:38 Have you only **o** blessing, my
Gen 31:49 and me when we are absent **o**
Gen 41:25 dreams of Pharaoh are **o**;
Ex 8:31 Not **o** remained.
Ex 9: 6 of Israel, not **o** died.
Ex 12:46 nor shall you break **o** of its
Ex 28:10 six of their names on **o**
Lev 26:17 and you shall flee when no **o**
Num 7:89 he heard the voice of **O**
Num 9:12 nor break **o** of its bones.
Deut 4: 4 today, every **o** of you.
Deut 6: 4 our God, the LORD is **o**!
Deut 19:11 and he flees to **o** of these
Deut 21:15 **o** loved and the other
Deut 27:15 Cursed is the **o** who makes a
Deut 28:31 and you shall have no **o** to
Deut 28:64 from **o** end of the earth to
Deut 31: 2 I am **o** hundred and twenty
Deut 33:26 There is no **o** like the God
Judg 20: 8 all the people arose as **o**
Judg 21: 3 that today there should be **o**
Ruth 2:13 though I am not like **o** of
Ruth 2:20 **o** of our close relatives."
1Sa 13: 1 Saul reigned **o** year; and when
1Sa 16: 8 has the LORD chosen this **o**.
1Sa 16:12 for this is the **o**!"
2Sa 7:23 the **o** nation on the earth

2Sa 12: 3 except **o** little ewe lamb
1Ki 3:22 No! But the living **o** is my
1Ki 3:22 and the dead **o** is your
1Ki 3:25 in two, and give half to **o**,
1Ki 11:13 I will give **o** tribe to your
1Ki 18:26 no **o** answered. Then they
1Ki 18:29 no **o** paid attention.
2Ki 18:31 his own vine and every **o**
2Ki 19:22 Against the Holy **O** of
Neh 2:12 I told no **o** what my God had
Neh 4:17 themselves so that with **o**
Esth 9:19 for sending presents to **o**
Job 1: 8 **o** who fears God and shuns
Job 2:10 You speak as **o** of the foolish
Job 2:13 and no **o** spoke a word to
Job 16:21 that **o** might plead for a man
Job 19:11 And He counts me as **o** of
Job 31:35 that I had **o** to hear me!
Ps 3: 3 My glory and the **O** who
Ps 14: 3 who does good, No, not **o**.
Ps 16:10 will You allow Your Holy **O**
Ps 19: 6 Its rising is from **o** end of
Ps 27: 4 **O** thing I have desired of
Ps 34:20 Not **o** of them is broken.
Ps 50: 1 The Mighty **O**, God the
Ps 53: 3 Every **o** of them has turned
Ps 53: 3 who does good, No, not **o**.
Ps 71:22 O Holy **O** of Israel.
Ps 83: 5 consulted together with **o**
Ps 105:13 When they went from **o** nation
Ps 132: 2 And vowed to the Mighty **O**
Ps 132: 5 place for the Mighty **O** of
Ps 137: 3 Sing us **o** of the songs of
Ps 142: 4 For there is no **o** who
Ps 144: 2 My shield and the **O** in
Prov 9:10 the knowledge of the Holy **O**
Prov 12: 9 Better is the **o** who is
Prov 26:17 not his own Is like **o**
Prov 28: 1 The wicked flee when no **o**
Prov 30: 3 have knowledge of the Holy **O**.
Eccl 3:11 except that no **o** can find
Eccl 3:19 as **o** dies, so dies the
Eccl 4: 9 Two are better than **o**,
Eccl 7:14 God has appointed the **o** as
Eccl 12:11 given by **o** Shepherd.
Song 2:10 up, my love, my fair **o**,
Song 3: 2 squares I will seek the **o**
Song 5: 2 love, My dove, my perfect **o**;
Is 1: 4 to anger The Holy **O** of
Is 1:24 the Mighty **O** of Israel,
Is 4: 1 women shall take hold of **o**
Is 6: 2 each **o** had six wings: with
Is 6: 6 Then **o** of the seraphim flew
Is 12: 6 For great is the Holy **O** of
Is 17: 2 and no **o** will make them
Is 22:22 and no **o** shall shut; And he
Is 29:23 And hallow the Holy **O** of
Is 30:17 **O** thousand shall flee at
Is 37:16 the **O** who dwells between
Is 40: 3 The voice of **o** crying in
Is 42: 1 My Elect **O** in whom My
Is 47: 8 and there is no **o** else
Is 53: 6 We have turned, every **o**,
Is 57:15 says the High and Lofty **O**
Is 63: 1 This **O** who is glorious
Jer 24: 2 **O** basket had very good figs,
Jer 32:39 then I will give them **o** heart
Ezek 1: 6 Each **o** had four faces, and
Ezek 1:28 and I heard a voice of **O**
Ezek 10:14 Each **o** had four faces: the
Ezek 11:19 Then I will give them **o**
Ezek 23: 2 The daughters of **o** mother.
Ezek 34:23 I will establish **o** shepherd
Ezek 37:24 and they shall all have **o**
Dan 2: 9 there is only **o** decree

Dan	4:13	was a watcher, a holy o,
Dan	7: 5	It was raised up on o side,
Dan	7: 8	was another horn, a little o,
Dan	7:13	O like the Son of Man,
Dan	8: 3	but o was higher than the
Dan	9:27	a covenant with many for o
Dan	12: 1	Every o who is found
Hos	11: 9	The Holy O in your midst;
Amos	6: 9	that if ten men remain in o
Amos	6:12	Does o plow there with
Jon	4: 2	O who relents from doing
Mic	4: 4	And no o shall make them
Mic	5: 2	come forth to Me The O to
Zech	3: 9	iniquity of that land in o
Zech	12:10	they will mourn for Him as o
Zech	12:10	and grieve for Him as o
Zech	14: 9	is one," And His name o.
Mal	2:10	Have we not all o Father?
Mal	2:10	Has not o God created us?
Matt	3: 3	The voice of o crying in
Matt	5:18	one jot or o tittle will by
Matt	5:19	Whoever therefore breaks o of
Matt	5:29	profitable for you that o
Matt	5:36	because you cannot make o
Matt	5:41	whoever compels you to go o
Matt	6:13	deliver us from the evil o.
Matt	6:24	No o can serve two masters;
Matt	6:27	of you by worrying can add o
Matt	6:29	was not arrayed like o of
Matt	7:29	for He taught them as o
Matt	8: 4	"See that you tell no o;
Matt	8: 9	me. And I say to this o,
Matt	11: 3	Him, "Are You the Coming O,
Matt	11:11	women there has not risen o
Matt	11:27	and no o knows the Son
Matt	12:11	is there among you who has o
Matt	13:46	when he had found o pearl of
Matt	16:14	and others Jeremiah or o of
Matt	17: 4	o for You, one for Moses,
Matt	17: 8	they saw no o but Jesus
Matt	17: 9	Tell the vision to no o until
Matt	18: 6	But whoever causes o of
Matt	18: 9	to enter into life with o
Matt	19: 5	the two shall become o
Matt	19:17	No o is good but One, that
Matt	20:12	men have worked only o
Matt	20:21	o on Your right hand and the
Matt	23: 8	for O is your Teacher, the
Matt	23: 9	for O is your Father, He who
Matt	23:15	travel land and sea to win o
Matt	24: 2	not o stone shall be left
Matt	24:36	of that day and hour no o
Matt	24:40	o will be taken and the
Matt	25:15	And to o he gave five
Matt	25:40	as you did it to o of the
Matt	26:21	of you will betray Me."
Matt	26:40	you not watch with Me o
Matt	27:38	o on the right and another
Mark	2:22	And no o puts new wine into
Mark	7:32	Then they brought to Him o
Mark	7:36	that they should tell no o;
Mark	9:26	And he became as o dead, so
Mark	9:47	the kingdom of God with o
Mark	10:21	O thing you lack: Go your
Mark	11: 2	on which no o has sat. Loose
Mark	12:29	God, the LORD is o.
Mark	14:70	Surely you are o of them;
Luke	1:28	"Rejoice, highly favored o,
Luke	1:35	that Holy O who is to be
Luke	2:15	that the shepherds said to o
Luke	7: 8	under me. And I say to o,
Luke	9:62	Jesus said to him, "No o,
Luke	10:42	But o thing is needed, and
Luke	12:25	of you by worrying can add o
Luke	12:27	was not arrayed like o of

Luke	15: 4	and go after the o which is
Luke	15: 7	be more joy in heaven over o
Luke	15:19	Make me like o of your hired
Luke	16:13	either he will hate the o
Luke	16:31	they be persuaded though o
Luke	17: 2	that he should offend o of
Luke	18:22	You still lack o thing. Sell
1Co	11:21	and o is hungry and another
1Co	12: 3	and no o can say that Jesus
1Co	12:11	But o and the same Spirit
1Co	12:12	For as the body is o and has
1Co	12:13	For by o Spirit we were all
1Co	12:13	we were all baptized into o
1Co	12:26	And if o member suffers, all
1Co	15: 8	as by o born out of due
1Co	15:23	But each o in his own order:
2Co	2:16	To the o we are the aroma
2Co	3:16	Nevertheless when o turns to
2Co	5:14	that if O died for all, then
2Co	9: 7	So let each o give as he
2Co	11:24	forty stripes minus o.
Gal	3:11	But that no o is justified by
Gal	3:28	for you are all o in Christ
Gal	6: 1	spiritual restore such a o
Gal	6: 2	Bear o another's burdens, and
Eph	2:14	peace, who has made both o,
Eph	2:15	so as to create in Himself o
Eph	2:18	Him we both have access by o
Eph	4: 4	just as you were called in o
Eph	4: 5	o Lord, one faith, one
Eph	4: 6	o God and Father of all, who
Eph	4:32	And be kind to o another,
Eph	4:32	forgiving o another, just as
Eph	5:21	submitting to o another in
Eph	5:29	For no o ever hated his own
Eph	6:16	fiery darts of the wicked o.
Phil	2: 2	being of o accord, of one
Phil	3:13	but o thing I do,
Col	2:16	So let no o judge you in food
Col	3: 9	Do not lie to o another,
Col	3:13	bearing with o another, and
Col	3:13	and forgiving o another, if
Col	3:15	also you were called in o
Col	3:16	teaching and admonishing o
1Th	5:11	each other and edify o
1Th	5:15	See that no o renders evil
2Th	2: 8	And then the lawless o will
1Ti	2: 5	For there is o God and one
1Ti	3: 2	the husband of o wife,
1Ti	3: 4	o who rules his own house
1Ti	4:12	Let no o despise your youth,
Heb	6:13	He could swear by no o
Heb	10:14	For by o offering He has
Heb	10:25	but exhorting o another,
Heb	11:12	Therefore from o man, and him
Heb	12:14	without which no o will see
Jas	2:10	and yet stumble in o point,
1Pe	3: 8	all of you be of o mind,
2Pe	3: 8	and a thousand years as o
1Jn	1: 7	we have fellowship with o
1Jn	2:13	have overcome the wicked o.
1Jn	3:11	that we should love o
1Jn	4:12	No o has seen God at any
1Jn	5: 7	and these three are o.
1Jn	5: 8	and these three agree as o.
Rev	1:13	of the seven lampstands O
Rev	3: 7	and shuts and no o
Rev	7: 4	O hundred and forty-four
Rev	7: 9	a great multitude which no o
Rev	14:14	and on the cloud sat O like
Rev	16: 5	The O who is and who was
Rev	22:12	to give to every o according

ONE-FIFTH

Gen	47:24	that you shall give o to

Lev 5:16 and shall add o to it and
Lev 27:31 he shall add o to it.

ONE-TENTH
Ex 16:36 Now an omer is o of an
Ezek 45:11 so that the bath contains o
Ezek 45:11 and the ephah o of a homer;

ONE-THIRD
Ezek 5:12 O of you shall die of the

ONESIMUS†
Col 4: 9 with O, a faithful and
Phm 1:10 I appeal to you for my son O,

ONESIPHORUS
2Ti 1:16 mercy to the household of O,

ONIONS†
Num 11: 5 the melons, the leeks, the o,

ONYX
Gen 2:12 Bdellium and the o stone
Ex 25: 7 o stones, and stones to be
Job 28:16 In precious o or sapphire.
Ezek 28:13 and diamond, Beryl, o,

OPEN (see OPENED, OPENING, OPENLY, OPENS)
Gen 19: 2 spend the night in the o
Ex 34:19 All that o the womb are
Judg 19:20 not spend the night in the o
2Ki 8:12 and rip o their women with
Neh 8:16 and in the o square of the
Ps 5: 9 Their throat is an o tomb;
Ps 34:15 And His ears are o to
Ps 51:15 o my lips, And my mouth
Ps 104:28 You o Your hand, they are
Ps 118:19 O to me the gates of
Ps 119:18 O my eyes, that I may see
Song 5: 2 O for me, my sister, my love,
Is 22:22 shut, and no one shall o.
Is 37:17 o Your eyes, O LORD, and
Is 42: 7 To o blind eyes, To bring
Jer 13:19 And no one shall o them;
Ezek 2: 8 o your mouth and eat what I
Ezek 3:27 I will o your mouth, and you
Ezek 37:12 I will o your graves and
Dan 6:10 with his windows o toward
Dan 9:18 o Your eyes and see our
Amos 1:13 Because they ripped o the
Matt 13:35 I will o My mouth in
Matt 25:11 'Lord, Lord, o to us!'
Luke 12:36 comes and knocks they may o
John 1:51 you shall see heaven o,
John 9:26 How did He o your eyes?"
Acts 1:18 he burst o in the middle and
Acts 16:27 seeing the prison doors o,
Rom 3:13 Their throat is an o
2Co 7: 2 O your hearts to us
Eph 6:19 that I may o my mouth boldly
Col 4: 3 that God would o to us a
Heb 4:13 all things are naked and o
Heb 6: 6 and put Him to an o shame.
1Pe 3:12 And His ears are o to
Rev 3: 8 I have set before you an o
Rev 5: 2 Who is worthy to o the scroll
Rev 10: 2 He had a little book o in his

OPENED (see OPEN)
Gen 3: 5 of it your eyes will be o,
Gen 7:11 the windows of heaven were o.
Gen 29:31 He o her womb; but Rachel
Num 16:32 and the earth o its mouth and
2Ki 4:35 and the child o his eyes.
Ps 40: 6 desire; My ears You have o.
Ps 105:41 He o the rock, and water
Ps 106:17 The earth o up and swallowed
Is 35: 5 eyes of the blind shall be o,
Is 53: 7 Yet He o not His mouth; He

Ezek 1: 1 that the heavens were o and
Ezek 3: 2 So I o my mouth, and He
Ezek 37:13 when I have o your graves, O
Dan 7:10 And the books were o.
Matt 3:16 the heavens were o to Him,
Matt 5: 2 Then He o His mouth and
Matt 7: 7 and it will be o to you.
Matt 27:52 and the graves were o;
Mark 7:34 that is, "Be o.
Mark 7:35 Immediately his ears were o,
Luke 1:64 Immediately his mouth was o
Luke 4:17 And when He had o the book,
Luke 24:32 and while He o the
Luke 24:45 And He o their understanding,
John 9:14 Jesus made the clay and o
Acts 5:19 an angel of the Lord o the
Acts 7:56 Look! I see the heavens o and
Acts 8:32 So He o not His mouth.
Acts 8:35 Then Philip o his mouth, and
1Co 16: 9 and effective door has o to
Rev 6: 1 Now I saw when the Lamb o one
Rev 9: 2 And he o the bottomless pit,
Rev 19:11 Now I saw heaven o,
Rev 20:12 before God, and books were o.

OPENING (see OPEN)
Is 42:20 O the ears, but he does not
Is 61: 1 And the o of the prison to

OPENLY (see OPEN)
Matt 6: 6 in secret will reward you o.
John 11:54 Jesus no longer walked o

OPENS (see OPEN)
Ex 13: 2 whatever o the womb among
Num 16:30 and the earth o its mouth
Ps 146: 8 The LORD o the eyes of
Luke 2:23 Every male who o the
John 10: 3 "To him the doorkeeper o,
Rev 3: 7 shuts and no one o":
Rev 3:20 anyone hears My voice and o

OPHEL
2Ch 27: 3 extensively on the wall of O.

OPHIR
1Ki 10:11 which brought gold from O,
1Ki 22:48 merchant ships to go to O
2Ch 8:18 the servants of Solomon to O,

OPHRAH
Judg 9: 5 to his father's house at O

OPINION (see OPINIONS)
Job 32:10 I also will declare my o.
Rom 11:25 should be wise in your own o,
Rom 12:16 Do not be wise in your own o.

OPINIONS† (see OPINION)
1Ki 18:21 you falter between two o?

OPPORTUNE† (see OPPORTUNITY)
Mark 6:21 Then an o day came when Herod
Luke 4:13 from Him until an o time.

OPPORTUNITY (see OPPORTUNE)
Matt 26:16 from that time he sought o
Luke 22: 6 So he promised and sought o
Rom 7: 8 taking o by the commandment,
Gal 5:13 do not use liberty as an o
Gal 6:10 Therefore, as we have o,
Phil 4:10 did care, but you lacked o.
1Ti 5:14 give no o to the adversary

OPPOSE (see OPPOSES)
Dan 8:12 over to the horn to o

OPPOSES† (see OPPOSE)
2Th 2: 4 who o and exalts himself

OPPOSITE
Matt 21: 2 Go into the village o you,

Mark 13: 3 sat on the Mount of Olives o

OPPRESS (*see* OPPRESSED, OPPRESSES, OPPRESSION, OPPRESSOR)
Ex 3: 9 with which the Egyptians o
Lev 25:14 you shall not o one another.
Ps 17: 9 From the wicked who o me,
Amos 4: 1 Who o the poor, Who crush
Zech 7:10 Do not o the widow or the
Acts 7: 6 them into bondage and o

OPPRESSED (*see* OPPRESS)
1Sa 12: 4 have not cheated us or o us,
Ps 9: 9 will be a refuge for the o,
Ps 10:18 to the fatherless and the o,
Ps 76: 9 To deliver all the o of the
Ps 103: 6 justice for all who are o.
Is 53: 7 He was o and He was
Is 58: 6 To let the o go free, And
Amos 3: 9 And the o within her.
Luke 4:18 liberty those who are o;
Acts 10:38 and healing all who were o

OPPRESSES (*see* OPPRESS)
Ps 56: 1 Fighting all day he o me.
Prov 28: 3 A poor man who o the poor

OPPRESSION (*see* OPPRESS)
Ex 3: 7 I have surely seen the o of
Ps 12: 5 For the o of the poor, for
Ps 42: 9 go mourning because of the o
Ps 55: 3 Because of the o of the
Ps 72:14 redeem their life from o
Is 5: 7 for justice, but behold, o;
Jer 6: 6 She is full of o in her
Acts 7:34 have surely seen the o

OPPRESSOR (*see* OPPRESS, OPPRESSORS)
Ps 72: 4 will break in pieces the o.
Prov 3:31 Do not envy the o,
Is 1:17 Seek justice, Rebuke the o;
Is 9: 4 shoulder, The rod of his o,
Is 14: 4 How the o has ceased, The

OPPRESSORS (*see* OPPRESSOR)
Ps 54: 3 And o have sought after my
Ps 119:121 Do not leave me to my o.

ORACLE (*see* ORACLES)
Num 23: 7 And he took up his o and
Ps 36: 1 A within my heart
Jer 23:33 What is the o of the LORD?'

ORACLES (*see* ORACLE)
Acts 7:38 who received the living o
Rom 3: 2 to them were committed the o
Heb 5:12 first principles of the o
1Pe 4:11 let him speak as the o of

ORCHARDS†
Eccl 2: 5 I made myself gardens and o,

ORDAIN† (*see* ORDAINED)
1Co 7:17 And so I o in all the

ORDAINED (*see* ORDAIN)
Ps 8: 3 the stars, which You have o,
Jer 1: 5 I o you a prophet to the
Acts 17:31 by the Man whom He has o.
1Co 2: 7 hidden wisdom which God o

ORDER (*see* ORDERED, ORDERLY, ORDERS)
Gen 22: 9 And placed the wood in o;
Num 10:28 Thus was the o of march of
2Ki 23: 4 the priests of the second o,
Ps 110: 4 forever According to the o
Eccl 12: 9 and sought out and set in o
Is 9: 7 To o it and establish it
Matt 12:44 empty, swept, and put in o.
Luke 1: 1 taken in hand to set in o a
Luke 1: 8 priest before God in the o

1Co 14:40 be done decently and in o.
1Co 15:23 But each one in his own o:
Heb 5: 6 According to the o of
Heb 6:20 forever according to the o
Heb 7:11 be called according to the o

ORDERED (*see* ORDER)
Gen 43:17 Then the man did as Joseph o,
Ps 37:23 steps of a good man are o

ORDERLY (*see* ORDER)
Luke 1: 3 to write to you an o
Acts 21:24 you yourself also walk o

ORDERS (*see* ORDER)
2Sa 14: 8 and I will give o concerning
Ps 50:23 And to him who o his
1Co 16: 1 as I have given o to the

ORDINANCE (*see* ORDINANCES)
Ex 12:14 a feast by an everlasting o.
Ex 15:25 He made a statute and an o
Ezra 3:10 according to the o of David
Ps 99: 7 His testimonies and the o
Rom 13: 2 the authority resists the o
1Pe 2:13 yourselves to every o of

ORDINANCES (*see* ORDINANCE)
Lev 18: 3 shall you walk in their o.
Ps 119:43 For I have hoped in Your o.
Jer 31:35 The o of the moon and the
Luke 1: 6 all the commandments and o
Eph 2:15 commandments contained in o,
Heb 9: 1 the first covenant had o
Heb 9:10 and fleshly o imposed until

OREB
Judg 7:25 O and Zeeb. They killed Oreb
Judg 7:25 They killed O at the rock of

ORIGIN†
Ezek 29:14 to the land of their o,

ORIGINALLY†
1Co 14:36 did the word of God come o

ORION†
Job 9: 9 He made the Bear, O,
Job 38:31 Or loose the belt of O?
Amos 5: 8 He made the Pleiades and O;

ORNAMENT (*see* ORNAMENTS)
Prov 1: 9 they will be a graceful o
Prov 4: 9 place on your head an o of

ORNAMENTS (*see* ORNAMENT)
Judg 8:21 and took the crescent o that
Song 1:10 cheeks are lovely with o,
Jer 2:32 Can a virgin forget her o,

ORNAN (*see* ARAUNAH)
1Ch 21:15 by the threshing floor of O
1Ch 21:22 Then David said to O,

ORPAH
Ruth 1:14 and O kissed her

ORPHANS
Lam 5: 3 We have become o and waifs,
John 14:18 "I will not leave you o;
Jas 1:27 to visit o and widows in

OTHNIEL
Judg 3: 9 O the son of Kenaz, Caleb's

OUTBREAK
Deut 24: 8 Take heed in an o of
2Sa 6: 8 because of the LORD's o

OUTCAST (*see* OUTCASTS)
Mic 4: 6 I will gather the o And

OUTCASTS (*see* OUTCAST)
Is 11:12 And will assemble the o of

OUTCOME†
Acts 5:24 they wondered what the **o**
Heb 13: 7 considering the **o** of their

OUTCRY
Gen 18:20 Because the **o** against Sodom
Acts 23: 9 Then there arose a loud **o**.

OUTER
Job 41:13 Who can remove his **o** coat?
Matt 8:12 will be cast out into **o**
John 21: 7 he put on his **o** garment

OUTLIVED†
Josh 24:31 the days of the elders who **o**
Judg 2: 7 the days of the elders who **o**

OUTRAGE†
Judg 19:23 house, do not commit this **o**.
Judg 20: 6 committed lewdness and **o** in

OUTRAN†
2Sa 18:23 and **o** the Cushite.
John 20: 4 and the other disciple **o**

OUTSIDER (see FOREIGNER)
Lev 22:12 daughter is married to an **o**,

OUTSKIRTS
Num 11: 1 and consumed some in the **o**

OUTSTRETCHED
Ex 6: 6 I will redeem you with an **o**
Deut 5:15 by a mighty hand and by an **o**
Is 3:16 And walk with **o** necks And

OUTWARD (see OUTWARDLY)
1Sa 16: 7 for man looks at the **o**
2Co 4:16 Even though our **o** man is
2Co 10: 7 at things according to the **o**
1Pe 3: 3 your adornment be merely **o**—

OUTWARDLY (see OUTWARD)
Matt 23:27 indeed appear beautiful **o**,
Rom 2:28 is not a Jew who is one **o**,

OVEN
Gen 15:17 there appeared a smoking **o**
Hos 7: 4 Like an **o** heated by a
Mal 4: 1 coming, Burning like an **o**,
Matt 6:30 is thrown into the **o**,

OVERCAME† (see OVERCOME)
Rev 3:21 as I also **o** and sat down
Rev 12:11 And they **o** him by the blood

OVERCOME (see OVERCAME, OVERCOMES)
John 16:33 I have **o** the world."
Rom 3: 4 And may **o** when You
Rom 12:21 Do not be **o** by evil, but
1Jn 2:13 Because you have **o** the
1Jn 2:14 And you have **o** the wicked
1Jn 5: 4 is the victory that has **o**
Rev 17:14 and the Lamb will **o** them,

OVERCOMES (see OVERCOME)
1Jn 5: 4 whatever is born of God **o**
Rev 2: 7 To him who **o** I will give to

OVERFLOW (see OVERFLOWED, OVERFLOWING, OVERFLOWS)
Is 8: 8 He will **o** and pass over,

OVERFLOWED
Josh 4:18 to their place and **o** all

OVERFLOWING (see OVERFLOW)
Ps 45: 1 My heart is **o** with a good
Jer 47: 2 And shall be an **o** flood;

OVERFLOWS† (see OVERFLOW)
Josh 3:15 the water (for the Jordan **o**
Lam 1:16 my eye **o** with water;

OVERLOOK† (see OVERLOOKED)
Prov 19:11 And his glory is to **o** a

OVERLOOKED† (see OVERLOOK)
Acts 17:30 times of ignorance God **o**,

OVERLY†
Eccl 7:16 Do not be **o** righteous, Nor
Eccl 7:16 Nor be **o** wise: Why should
Eccl 7:17 Do not be **o** wicked, Nor be

OVERNIGHT
Deut 21:23 body shall not remain **o**

OVERPOWER (see OVERPOWERED)
Judg 16: 5 and by what means we may **o**

OVERPOWERED (see OVERPOWER)
Dan 6:24 and the lions **o** them, and

OVERSEE (see OVERSEER, OVERSIGHT)
2Ki 22: 9 who **o** the house of the

OVERSEER (see OVERSEE)
Gen 39: 4 Then he made him **o** of his
1Pe 2:25 to the Shepherd and **O** of

OVERSEERS
Acts 20:28 Holy Spirit has made you **o**,
1Pe 5: 2 is among you, serving as **o**,

OVERSHADOW† (see OVERSHADOWED, OVERSHADOWING)
Luke 1:35 power of the Highest will **o**

OVERSHADOWED (see OVERSHADOW)
1Ki 8: 7 and the cherubim **o** the ark
Matt 17: 5 a bright cloud **o** them; and

OVERSHADOWING† (see OVERSHADOW)
Heb 9: 5 the cherubim of glory **o** the

OVERSIGHT (see OVERSEE)
Gen 43:12 sacks; perhaps it was an **o**.

OVERTAKE (see OVERTAKEN, OVERTOOK)
Gen 19:19 lest some evil **o** me and I
Hos 2: 7 But not **o** them; Yes, she
Amos 9:13 When the plowman shall **o** the
Acts 8:29 Go near and **o** this chariot."
1Th 5: 4 so that this Day should **o**

OVERTAKEN (see OVERTAKE)
Ps 40:12 My iniquities have **o** me, so
1Co 10:13 No temptation has **o** you
Gal 6: 1 if a man is **o** in any

OVERTHREW (see OVERTHROW)
Gen 19:25 So He **o** those cities, all the
Ex 14:27 So the LORD **o** the Egyptians
Jer 50:40 As God **o** Sodom and Gomorrah

OVERTHROW (see OVERTHREW, OVERTHROWN, OVERTHROWS)
Gen 19:29 out of the midst of the **o**,
Deut 29:23 like the **o** of Sodom and
Acts 5:39 you cannot **o** it—lest you
2Ti 2:18 and they **o** the faith of

OVERTHROWN (see OVERTHROW)
Prov 12: 7 The wicked are **o** and are no
Lam 4: 6 Which was **o** in a moment,
Jon 3: 4 and Nineveh shall be **o**!"

OVERTHROWS (see OVERTHROW)
Prov 22:12 But He **o** the words of the

OVERTOOK (see OVERTAKE)
Gen 31:25 So Laban **o** Jacob. Now Jacob
Jer 52: 8 and they **o** Zedekiah in the

OVERTURNED (see OVERTURNS)
Lam 1:20 My heart is **o** within me,
Matt 21:12 and **o** the tables of the
John 2:15 the changers' money and **o**

OVERTURNS (see OVERTURNED)
Job 9: 5 they do not know When He **o**

OVERWHELMED
Ps 55: 5 And horror has o me.
Ps 61: 2 to You, When my heart is o;
Ps 78:53 But the sea o their
Ps 142: 3 When my spirit was o within
Dan 10:16 vision my sorrows have o me,

OWE (see OWED, OWES)
Matt 18:28 Pay me what you o!'
Luke 16: 5 How much do you o my master?'
Rom 13: 8 O no one anything except the
Phm 1:19 to mention to you that you o

OWED (see OWE)
Deut 15: 3 up your claim to what is o
Matt 18:24 one was brought to him who o

OWES† (see OWE)
Phm 1:18 if he has wronged you or o

OWL
Ps 102: 6 I am like an o of the

OWN (see OWNER)
Gen 1:27 So God created man in His o
Gen 5: 3 and begot a son in his o
Gen 15: 4 who will come from your o
Ex 32:13 to whom You swore by Your o
Lev 22:29 offer it of your o free
Lev 25: 5 What grows of its o accord of
Deut 12: 8 whatever is right in his o
Deut 24:16 be put to death for his o
Deut 28:53 eat the fruit of your o
Josh 2:19 blood shall be on his o
Josh 24:28 each to his o inheritance.
Judg 7: 2 My o hand has saved me.'
Judg 17: 6 what was right in his o
Ruth 4: 6 lest I ruin my o
1Sa 13:14 Himself a man after His o
1Sa 18: 3 he loved him as his o soul.
2Sa 7:24 people Israel Your very o
1Ki 7: 1 years to build his o house;
1Ki 10: 7 I came and saw with my o
1Ki 12:16 see to your o house, O
2Ki 18:31 drink the waters of his o
1Ch 17:22 people Israel Your very o
2Ch 25: 4 a person shall die for his o
Ezra 2: 1 everyone to his o city.
Esth 2: 7 Mordecai took her as his o
Job 9:20 my o mouth would condemn me;
Job 9:31 And my o clothes will abhor
Job 40:14 confess to you That your o
Ps 5:10 Let them fall by their o
Ps 9:16 snared in the work of his o
Ps 15: 4 He who swears to his o
Ps 36: 2 he flatters himself in his o
Ps 41: 9 Even my o familiar friend in
Ps 44: 3 Nor did their o arm save
Ps 50:20 You slander your o mother's
Ps 106:40 So that He abhorred His o
Ps 141:10 the wicked fall into their o
Prov 1:18 lie in wait for their o
Prov 3: 5 And lean not on your o
Prov 3: 7 Do not be wise in your o
Prov 5:15 running water from your o
Prov 6:32 who does so destroys his o
Prov 12:15 of a fool is right in his o
Prov 14:10 The heart knows its o
Prov 14:20 man is hated even by his o
Prov 16: 2 of a man are pure in his o
Prov 20: 2 to anger sins against his o
Prov 20:24 can a man understand his o
Prov 26: 5 Lest he be wise in his o
Prov 26:11 As a dog returns to his o
Prov 26:17 in a quarrel not his o Is
Prov 27: 2 and not your o mouth; A
Prov 27:10 Do not forsake your o friend

Prov 31:31 And let her o works praise
Is 2: 8 That which their o fingers
Is 31: 7 which your o hands have made
Is 37:35 to save it For My o sake
Is 53: 6 to his o way; And the LORD
Is 59:16 Therefore His o arm brought
Is 66: 3 as they have chosen their o
Jer 1:16 the works of their o hands.
Jer 9:14 to the dictates of their o
Jer 31:30 one shall die for his o
Lam 4:10 women Have cooked their o
Ezek 13: 3 who follow their o spirit
Ezek 37:21 and bring them into their o
Dan 3:28 any god except their o God!
Dan 6:17 king sealed it with his o
Dan 9:19 act! Do not delay for Your o
Joel 3: 4 your retaliation upon your o
Jon 2: 8 idols Forsake their o
Matt 2:12 they departed for their o
Matt 6:34 for the day is its o
Matt 7: 3 the plank in your o eye?
Matt 8:22 let the dead bury their o
Matt 10:36 will be those of his o
Matt 16:26 and loses his o soul? Or
Matt 25:27 have received back my o
Matt 27:31 put His o clothes on Him,
Mark 6: 4 honor except in his o
Luke 2: 3 everyone to his o city.
Luke 2:35 will pierce through your o
Luke 6:44 every tree is known by its o
John 1:11 He came to His o,
John 1:41 He first found his o brother
John 4:44 has no honor in his o
John 5:30 because I do not seek My o
John 5:43 if another comes in his o
John 7:17 or whether I speak on My o
John 10: 3 and he calls his o sheep by
John 10:12 one who does not the
John 11:51 this he did not say on his o
John 13: 1 having loved His o who were
John 19:27 disciple took her to his o
Acts 1: 7 the Father has put in His o
Acts 1:19 field is called in their o
Acts 1:25 that he might go to his o
Acts 2: 8 each in our o language in
Acts 5: 4 remained, was it not your o?
Acts 13:22 a man after My o
Acts 17:28 as also some of your o poets
Acts 20:28 He purchased with His o
Acts 28:30 two whole years in his o
Rom 4:19 he did not consider his o
Rom 5: 8 But God demonstrates His o
Rom 8: 3 God did by sending His o
Rom 8:32 He who did not spare His o
Rom 10: 3 seeking to establish their o
Rom 11:25 you should be wise in your o
Rom 16:18 but their o belly, and by
1Co 1:15 that I had baptized in my o
1Co 3: 8 reward according to his o
1Co 3:19 the wise in their o
1Co 4:12 working with our o hands.
1Co 6:18 sins against his o body.
1Co 6:19 God, and you are not your o?
1Co 7: 2 let each man have his o
1Co 7: 4 have authority over her o
1Co 10:33 not seeking my o profit, but
1Co 11:21 each one takes his o supper
1Co 13: 5 rudely, does not seek its o,
1Co 14:35 let them ask their o
1Co 15:23 But each one in his o order:
1Co 16:21 The salutation with my o
Gal 6: 4 let each one examine his o
Gal 6: 5 each one shall bear his o
Eph 5:22 submit to your o husbands,
Eph 5:28 ought to love their o wives

Eph	5:29	For no one ever hated his **o**
Phil	2: 4	look out not only for his **o**
Phil	2:12	work out your **o** salvation
Phil	2:21	For all seek their **o**,
Col	4:18	This salutation by my **o**
1Th	4:11	to mind your **o** business, and
2Th	2: 6	he may be revealed in his **o**
2Th	3:17	of Paul with my **o** hand,
1Ti	3: 5	not know how to rule his **o**
1Ti	5: 8	does not provide for his **o**,
2Ti	1: 9	but according to His **o**
Tit	2:14	purify for Himself His **o**
Heb	3: 6	Christ as a Son over His **o**
Heb	7:27	first for His **o** sins and
Heb	9:12	but with His **o** blood He
Jas	1:14	he is drawn away by his **o**
1Pe	2: 9	His **o** special people, that
1Pe	2:24	bore our sins in His **o** body
2Pe	2:22	dog returns to his **o**
2Pe	3:16	people twist to their **o**
Jude	6	but left their **o** abode, He
Rev	1: 5	us from our sins in His **o**

OWNER (*see* OWN)

Ex	21:28	but the **o** of the ox shall
Ex	22:12	make restitution to the **o**
Is	1: 3	The ox knows its **o** And the
Matt	13:27	So the servants of the **o** came
Matt	20: 8	the **o** of the vineyard said

OX (*see* OXEN)

Gen	49: 6	they hamstrung an **o**.
Ex	20:17	female servant, nor his **o**,
Ex	21:28	If an **o** gores a man or a
Ex	22: 1	If a man steals an **o** or a
Deut	25: 4	You shall not muzzle an **o**
1Sa	12: 3	Whose **o** have I taken, or
Ps	29: 6	Sirion like a young wild **o**.
Prov	7:22	as an **o** goes to the
Is	1: 3	The **o** knows its owner And
Is	11: 7	shall eat straw like the **o**.
Is	65:25	shall eat straw like the **o**,
Ezek	1:10	four had the face of an **o**
1Co	9: 9	shall not muzzle an **o**
1Ti	5:18	shall not muzzle an **o**

OXEN (*see* OX)

Gen	12:16	her sake. He had sheep, **o**,
Ex	20:24	your sheep and your **o**.
Ex	22: 1	he shall restore five **o** for
Ex	24: 5	peace offerings of **o** to the
1Sa	11: 7	So he took a yoke of **o** and
1Sa	15:14	and the lowing of the **o**
2Sa	6: 6	for the **o** stumbled.
2Sa	24:22	here are **o** for burnt
1Ki	7:44	and twelve **o** under the Sea;
2Ch	5: 6	were sacrificing sheep and **o**
Job	1:14	The **o** were plowing and the
Job	42:12	one thousand yoke of **o**,
Ps	8: 7	All sheep and **o**—
Ps	22:21	the horns of the wild **o**!
Dan	4:25	make you eat grass like **o**.
Amos	6:12	one plow there with **o**?
John	2:14	the temple those who sold **o**
1Co	9: 9	Is it **o** God is concerned

P

PADAN ARAM

Gen	25:20	of Bethuel the Syrian of **P**
Gen	28: 5	Jacob away, and he went to **P**

PAGAN

Ezra	10: 2	and have taken **p** wives from
Neh	13:27	our God by marrying **p** women?

Zeph	1: 4	priests with the **p** priests—

PAID (*see* PAY)

1Ki	18:29	no one **p** attention.
Esth	3: 2	the king's gate bowed and **p**
Prov	7:14	Today I have **p** my vows.
Jon	1: 3	so he **p** the fare, and went
Matt	5:26	out of there till you have **p**
Heb	7: 9	**p** tithes through Abraham, so

PAIN (*see* PAINED, PAINFUL, PAINS)

Gen	3:16	In **p** you shall bring forth
Ps	25:18	on my affliction and my **p**,
Is	26:17	a woman with child Is in **p**
Jer	6:24	**P** as of a woman in labor.
Jer	15:18	Why is my **p** perpetual And
Rev	21: 4	There shall be no more **p**,

PAINED† (*see* PAIN)

Ps	55: 4	My heart is severely **p**
Jer	4:19	my soul! I am **p** in my very

PAINFUL (*see* PAIN)

Job	2: 7	and struck Job with **p** boils
Ps	73:16	It was too **p** for me—
Heb	12:11	for the present, but **p**;

PAINS (*see* PAIN)

1Sa	4:19	for her labor **p** came upon
Ps	116: 3	The **p** of death surrounded
Acts	2:24	having loosed the **p** of

PAINT

2Ki	9:30	and she put **p** on her eyes

PAIR

Judg	15: 4	put a torch between each **p**
Amos	2: 6	And the poor for a **p** of
Amos	8: 6	And the needy for a **p** of
Luke	2:24	A **p** of turtledoves or

PALACE (*see* PALACES)

1Ki	21: 1	next to the **p** of Ahab king
Ps	45:13	all glorious within the **p**;
Dan	1: 4	to serve in the king's **p**,
Dan	5: 5	of the wall of the king's **p**;
Matt	26: 3	people assembled at the **p**
Phil	1:13	evident to the whole **p**

PALACES (*see* PALACE)

Ps	45: 8	cassia, Out of the ivory **p**,
Ps	48: 3	God is in her **p**;
Prov	30:28	And it is in kings' **p**.
Lam	2: 7	given up the walls of her **p**
Amos	1: 7	Which shall devour its **p**.

PALATE†

Job	34: 3	ear tests words As the **p**

PALE

Rev	6: 8	a **p** horse. And the name of

PALM (*see* PALMS)

Ex	15:27	wells of water and seventy **p**
Deut	34: 3	the city of **p** trees, as far
Judg	4: 5	she would sit under the **p**
Neh	8:15	**p** branches, and branches of
Ps	92:12	shall flourish like a **p**
Song	7: 7	of yours is like a **p** tree,
Jer	10: 5	like a **p** tree, And they
John	12:13	took branches of **p** trees and
John	18:22	by struck Jesus with the **p**
Rev	7: 9	with **p** branches in their

PALMS (*see* PALM)

Judg	1:16	went up from the City of **P**
Is	49:16	have inscribed you on the **p**
Matt	26:67	struck Him with the **p** of

PAMPHYLIA

Acts	13:13	they came to Perga in **P**;
Acts	27: 5	which is off Cilicia and **P**,

PAN
Lev 2: 5 grain offering baked in a **p**,
1Sa 2:14 would thrust it into the **p**,

PANELED (see PANELING)
1Ki 6: 9 and he **p** the temple with
1Ki 7: 3 And it was **p** with cedar
Hag 1: 4 to dwell in your **p** houses,

PANELING† (see PANELED)
Jer 22:14 **P** it with cedar And

PANGS
Ps 18: 4 The **p** of death surrounded
Ps 116: 3 And the **p** of Sheol laid
Is 21: 3 like the **p** of a woman in
Jer 48:41 heart of a woman in birth **p**.
Mic 4: 9 For **p** have seized you like
Rom 8:22 and labors with birth **p**

PANTS
Ps 38:10 My heart **p**, my strength
Ps 42: 1 As the deer **p** for the water
Ps 42: 1 So **p** my soul for You, O

PAPYRUS†
Job 8:11 Can the **p** grow up without a
Is 19: 7 The **p** reeds by the River, by

PARABLE (see PARABLES)
Ps 78: 2 I will open my mouth in a **p**;
Ezek 17: 2 and speak a **p** to the house
Matt 13:18 Therefore hear the **p** of the
Matt 13:24 Another **p** He put forth to
Matt 13:34 and without a **p** He did not
Matt 13:36 Explain to us the **p** of the
Mark 4:13 you not understand this **p**?
Luke 8: 9 What does this **p** mean?"

PARABLES (see PARABLE)
Ezek 20:49 of me, 'Does he not speak **p**?
Matt 13:10 do You speak to them in **p**?
Matt 21:45 and Pharisees heard His **p**,
Mark 4: 2 taught them many things by **p**,
Luke 8:10 the rest it is given in **p**,

PARADE
1Co 13: 4 love does not **p** itself, is

PARADISE†
Luke 23:43 you will be with Me in **P**.
2Co 12: 4 how he was caught up into **P**
Rev 2: 7 is in the midst of the **P** of

PARALYTIC (see PARALYTICS, PARALYZED)
Matt 9: 2 they brought to Him a **p**
Mark 2: 9 is easier, to say to the **p**,

PARALYTICS† (see PARALYTIC)
Matt 4:24 epileptics, and **p**;

PARALYZED (see PARALYTIC)
Matt 8: 6 servant is lying at home **p**,
John 5: 3 sick people, blind, lame, **p**,
Acts 8: 7 and many who were **p** and lame

PARAN
Gen 21:21 dwelt in the Wilderness of **P**;
Hab 3: 3 The Holy One from Mount **P**.

PARAPET†
Deut 22: 8 then you shall make a **p** for

PARCHED
Ruth 2:14 and he passed **p** grain to
Is 35: 7 The **p** ground shall become a

PARCHMENTS†
2Ti 4:13 the books, especially the **p**.

PARDON (see PARDONED, PARDONING)
Ex 34: 9 and **p** our iniquity and our
1Sa 15:25 please **p** my sin, and return
Neh 9:17 You are God, Ready to **p**,

Is 55: 7 For He will abundantly **p**.

PARDONED (see PARDON)
Is 40: 2 That her iniquity is **p**;
Lam 3:42 rebelled; You have not **p**.

PARDONING† (see PARDON)
Mic 7:18 **P** iniquity And passing

PARENTS
Matt 10:21 will rise up against **p** and
Luke 2:41 His **p** went to Jerusalem
Luke 18:29 one who has left house or **p**
John 9: 2 sinned, this man or his **p**,
Rom 1:30 things, disobedient to **p**,
2Co 12:14 not to lay up for the **p**,
2Co 12:14 but the **p** for the children.
Eph 6: 1 obey your **p** in the Lord, for
2Ti 3: 2 disobedient to **p**,
Heb 11:23 hidden three months by his **p**,

PART (see PARTED, PARTING, PARTLY, PARTS, SHARE)
Josh 22:27 You have no **p** in the LORD."
Ps 5: 9 Their inward **p** is
Ps 51: 6 in the hidden **p** You
Mark 13:27 of earth to the farthest **p**
Luke 10:42 Mary has chosen that good **p**,
Luke 11:39 but your inward **p** is full of
John 13: 8 you have no **p** with Me."
Acts 1:17 with us and obtained a **p** in
Acts 5: 3 Spirit and keep back **p** of
Rom 11:25 that blindness in **p** has
1Co 13: 9 in part and we prophesy in **p**.
1Co 13:10 then that which is in **p** will
1Co 13:12 to face. Now I know in **p**,
1Co 15: 6 of whom the greater **p** remain
2Co 6:15 Or what **p** has a believer
Eph 4:16 working by which every **p**
Heb 7: 2 also Abraham gave a tenth **p**
1Pe 4:14 On their **p** He is blasphemed,
1Pe 4:14 but on your **p** He is
Rev 20: 6 and holy is he who has **p**
Rev 21: 8 liars shall have their **p** in
Rev 22:19 God shall take away his **p**

PARTAKE (see PARTAKER)
1Co 9:13 who serve at the altar **p** of
1Co 10:17 for we all **p** of that one
2Ti 2: 6 farmer must be first to **p**
1Pe 4:13 to the extent that you **p** of

PARTAKER (see PARTAKERS, PARTAKES)
Rom 11:17 and with them became a **p** of
1Pe 5: 1 and also a **p** of the glory

PARTAKERS (see PARTAKER)
Rom 15:27 if the Gentiles have been **p**
1Co 10:18 who eat of the sacrifices **p**
2Co 1: 7 we know that as you are **p**
Eph 3: 6 and **p** of His promise in
Eph 5: 7 Therefore do not be **p** with
Phil 1: 7 you all are **p** with me of
Col 1:12 has qualified us to be **p** of
Heb 3: 1 **p** of the heavenly calling,
Heb 6: 4 and have become **p** of the
Heb 12:10 that we may be **p** of His
2Pe 1: 4 through these you may be **p**

PARTED (see PART)
Gen 2:10 and from there it **p** and
Luke 24:51 that He was **p** from them and

PARTHIANS†
Acts 2: 9 **P** and Medes and Elamites,

PARTIALITY
Ex 23: 3 You shall not show **p** to a
Prov 28:21 To show **p** is not good,
Mal 2: 9 My ways But have shown **p**
Acts 10:34 perceive that God shows no **p**.

Rom 2:11 For there is no **p** with God.
1Ti 5:21 doing nothing with **p**.
Jas 2: 9 but if you show **p**,
1Pe 1:17 who without **p** judges

PARTING (*see* PART)
Mark 1:10 He saw the heavens **p** and the
Luke 9:33 as they were **p** from Him,

PARTLY (*see* PART)
Dan 2:33 feet partly of iron and **p**
Dan 2:42 shall be partly strong and **p**

PARTNER
Prov 29:24 Whoever is a **p** with a thief
Phm 1:17 If then you count me as a **p**,

PARTS (*see* PART)
Deut 14: 6 the hoof split into two **p**,
Ruth 1:17 If anything but death **p**
Ps 51: 6 desire truth in the inward **p**,
Ps 63: 9 Shall go into the lower **p**
Ps 139: 9 dwell in the uttermost **p** of
Ps 139:13 For You formed my inward **p**;
Is 3:17 will uncover their secret **p**.
Jer 34:18 and passed between the **p** of
Jon 1: 5 gone down into the lowest **p**
John 19:23 His garments and made four **p**,
1Co 12:23 and our unpresentable **p**
Rev 16:19 was divided into three **p**,

PARTY
Acts 23: 9 scribes of the Pharisees' **p**

PASHHUR
Jer 20: 2 Then **P** struck Jeremiah the

PASS (*see* PASSED, PASSES, PASSING)
Gen 8: 1 And God made a wind to **p**
Gen 31:52 that I will not **p** beyond
Gen 41:32 will shortly bring it to **p**.
Ex 12:12 For I will **p** through the land
Ex 12:13 I will **p** over you; and the
Ex 15:16 Till Your people **p** over, O
Ex 33:19 will make all My goodness **p**
Num 20:17 Please let us **p** through your
Deut 18:10 his son or his daughter **p**
1Sa 13:23 went out to the **p** of
1Sa 16:10 made seven of his sons **p**
Ps 8: 8 the fish of the sea That **p**
Ps 37: 5 And He shall bring it to **p**.
Ps 78:13 the sea and caused them to **p**
Ps 104: 9 that they may not **p** over,
Ps 129: 8 Neither let those who **p** by
Ps 148: 6 a decree which shall not **p**
Prov 9:15 To call to those who **p** by,
Prov 22: 3 But the simple **p** on and are
Is 2: 2 Now it shall come to **p** in
Is 42: 9 former things have come to **p**,
Lam 1:12 all you who **p** by? Behold
Lam 2:15 All who **p** by clap their
Ezek 12:25 which I speak will come to **p**;
Dan 4:16 And let seven times **p** over
Dan 7:14 Which shall not **p** away,
Amos 7: 8 I will not **p** by them
Matt 5:18 till heaven and earth **p**
Matt 5:18 tittle will by no means **p**
Matt 26:39 let this cup **p** from Me;
Mark 14:35 the hour might **p** from Him.
Luke 21: 9 these things must come to **p**
John 13:19 that when it does come to **p**,
1Co 15:54 then shall be brought to **p**
Jas 1:10 of the field he will **p** away.
2Pe 3:10 in which the heavens will **p**

PASSAGE
Num 20:21 refused to give Israel **p**
Mark 12:26 in the burning bush **p**,

PASSED (*see* PASS)
Gen 18:11 and Sarah had **p** the age of
Ex 12:27 who **p** over the houses of the
Ex 34: 6 And the LORD **p** before him
Num 14: 7 The land we **p** through to spy
1Ki 19:11 the LORD **p** by, and a great
Job 4:15 Then a spirit **p** before my
Ps 90: 9 For all our days have **p** away
Matt 27:39 And those who **p** by blasphemed
Mark 2:14 As He **p** by, He saw Levi the
Mark 9:30 departed from there and **p**
Luke 10:31 he **p** by on the other side.
John 5:24 but has **p** from death into
Rom 3:25 in His forbearance God had **p**
1Co 10: 1 all **p** through the sea,
2Co 5:17 old things have **p** away;
Heb 4:14 great High Priest who has **p**
1Jn 3:14 We know that we have **p** from
Rev 21: 1 and the first earth had **p**
Rev 21: 4 for the former things have **p**

PASSES (*see* PASS)
Ex 33:22 while My glory **p** by, that I
Lev 27:32 of whatever **p** under the rod,
Ps 78:39 A breath that **p** away and
Ps 103:16 For the wind **p** over it, and
Eccl 1: 4 One generation **p** away, and
Hos 13: 3 like the early dew that **p**
Eph 3:19 the love of Christ which **p**

PASSING (*see* PASS)
Ps 144: 4 His days are like a **p**
Prov 31:30 deceitful and beauty is **p**,
Luke 18:37 Jesus of Nazareth was **p** by.
1Co 7:31 the form of this world is **p**
2Co 3: 7 which glory was **p** away,
Heb 11:25 of God than to enjoy the **p**
1Jn 2: 8 because the darkness is **p**
1Jn 2:17 And the world is **p** away, and

PASSION (*see* PASSIONS)
1Co 7: 9 marry than to burn with **p**.
1Th 4: 5 not in **p** of lust, like the

PASSIONS (*see* PASSION)
Rom 1:26 God gave them up to vile **p**.
Gal 5:24 the flesh with its **p** and

PASSOVER
Ex 12:11 haste. It is the LORD's **P**.
Ex 12:21 and kill the **P** lamb.
Ex 12:27 It is the **P** sacrifice of the
Ex 34:25 of the Feast of the **P** be
Josh 5:10 and kept the **P** on the
2Ki 23:22 Such a **P** surely had never
Matt 26:17 prepare for You to eat the **P**?
Mark 14:12 when they killed the **P**
Mark 14:14 in which I may eat the **P**
Luke 22:15 I have desired to eat this **P**
John 2:13 Now the **P** of the Jews was at
John 12: 1 Then, six days before the **P**,
John 19:14 the Preparation Day of the **P**,
1Co 5: 7 For indeed Christ, our **P**,
Heb 11:28 By faith he kept the **P** and

PAST
Job 9:10 He does great things **p**
Song 2:11 For lo, the winter is **p**,
Jer 8:20 "The harvest is **p**,
Amos 8: 5 will the New Moon be **p**,
Rom 11:33 His judgments and His ways **p**
1Co 7:36 if she is **p** the flower of
2Ti 2:18 resurrection is already **p**;
Heb 1: 1 ways spoke in time **p** to the
Heb 11:11 bore a child when she was **p**

PASTORS†
Eph 4:11 and some **p** and teachers,

PASTURE (see PASTURES)
Ps   74: 1 against the sheep of Your **p**?
Ps   95: 7 we are the people of His **p**,
Ps   100: 3 and the sheep of His **p**.
Jer   23: 1 scatter the sheep of My **p**!
Ezek 34:14 "I will feed them in good **p**,
John   10: 9 go in and out and find **p**.

PASTURES (see PASTURE)
Ps   23: 2 me to lie down in green **p**;
Is   30:23 cattle will feed In large **p**.
Ezek 45:15 from the rich **p** of Israel.
Joel   1:20 fire has devoured the open **p**.
Amos   1: 2 The **p** of the shepherds

PATCH† (see PATCHED)
Matt   9:16 for the **p** pulls away from

PATCHED† (see PATCH)
Josh   9: 5 old and **p** sandals on their

PATH (see PATHS, PATHWAY)
Job   28: 7 That **p** no bird knows, Nor
Job   38:25 Or a **p** for the thunderbolt,
Ps   1: 1 Nor stands in the **p** of
Ps   16:11 You will show me the **p** of
Ps   18:36 You enlarged my **p** under me,
Ps   27:11 And lead me in a smooth **p**,
Ps   77:19 Your **p** in the great waters,
Ps   78:50 He made a **p** for His anger;
Ps   119:35 Make me walk in the **p** of
Ps   119:105 my feet And a light to my **p**.
Ps   139: 3 You comprehend my **p** and my
Ps   142: 3 me, Then You knew my **p**.
Prov   1:15 Keep your foot from their **p**;
Prov   2: 9 Equity and every good **p**.
Prov   4:18 But the **p** of the just is
Prov   4:26 Ponder the **p** of your feet,
Prov   5: 6 Lest you ponder her **p** of
Prov   7: 8 And he took the **p** to her
Is   40:14 And taught Him in the **p** of

PATHS (see PATH)
Ps   8: 8 That pass through the **p** of
Ps   17: 4 I have kept away from the **p**
Ps   23: 3 He leads me in the **p** of
Ps   25: 4 O LORD; Teach me Your **p**.
Prov   2: 8 He guards the **p** of justice,
Prov   2:18 And her **p** to the dead;
Prov   2:19 Nor do they regain the **p** of
Prov   3: 6 And He shall direct your **p**.
Prov   3:17 And all her **p** are peace.
Is   2: 3 And we shall walk in His **p**.
Is   42:16 I will lead them in **p** they
Jer   6:16 see, And ask for the old **p**,
Matt   3: 3 Make His **p** straight.'
Heb   12:13 and make straight **p** for your

PATHWAY† (see PATH, PATHWAYS)
Ps   85:13 make His footsteps our **p**.
Prov   12:28 And in its **p** there is no

PATHWAYS† (see PATHWAY)
Jer   18:15 To walk in **p** and not on a

PATIENCE (see PATIENT)
Matt   18:26 have **p** with me, and I will
Luke   21:19 By your **p** possess your souls.
Rom   15: 4 that we through the **p** and
Rom   15: 5 Now may the God of **p** and
2Co   6: 4 ministers of God: in much **p**,
Col   1:11 for all **p** and longsuffering
1Th   1: 3 and **p** of hope in our Lord
2Th   3: 5 love of God and into the **p**
1Ti   6:11 godliness, faith, love, **p**,
Heb   6:12 who through faith and **p**
Jas   1: 3 of your faith produces **p**.
Jas   1: 4 But let **p** have its perfect
Jas   5:10 example of suffering and **p**.

Rev   2: 2 works, your labor, your **p**,
Rev   14:12 Here is the **p** of the saints;

PATIENT (see PATIENCE, PATIENTLY)
Rom   2: 7 life to those who by **p**
Rom   12:12 **p** in tribulation, continuing
1Th   5:14 the weak, be **p** with all.
2Ti   2:24 to all, able to teach, **p**,
Jas   5: 7 Therefore be **p**, brethren,

PATIENTLY (see PATIENT)
Ps   37: 7 and wait **p** for Him; Do not
Ps   40: 1 I waited **p** for the LORD;
Heb   6:15 after he had **p** endured, he
Jas   5: 7 waiting **p** for it until it
1Pe   2:20 your faults, you take it **p**?

PATMOS†
Rev   1: 9 the island that is called **P**

PATRIARCH† (see PATRIARCHS)
Acts   2:29 speak freely to you of the **p**
Heb   7: 4 to whom even the **p** Abraham

PATRIARCHS (see PATRIARCH)
Acts   7: 8 Jacob begot the twelve **p**.

PATTERN
Ex   25: 9 the **p** of the tabernacle and
Ex   25:40 them according to the **p**
2Ti   1:13 Hold fast the **p** of sound
Heb   8: 5 according to the **p**

PAUL (see PAUL'S, SAUL)
Acts   13: 9 Saul, who also is called **P**,
Acts   13:46 Then **P** and Barnabas grew bold
Acts   14:19 they stoned **P** and dragged
Acts   15:40 but **P** chose Silas and
Acts   16:25 But at midnight **P** and Silas
Acts   17:13 of God was preached by **P** at
Acts   17:15 So those who conducted **P**
Acts   18: 9 Now the Lord spoke to **P** in
Acts   19: 1 was at Corinth, that **P**,
Acts   19: 6 And when **P** had laid hands on
Acts   19:11 miracles by the hands of **P**,
Acts   19:13 you by the Jesus whom **P**
Acts   19:15 and **P** I know; but who are
Acts   24: 1 to the governor against **P**.
Acts   25: 4 But Festus answered that **P**
Acts   26: 1 Then Agrippa said to **P**,
Acts   28:30 Then **P** dwelt two whole years
1Co   1:12 of you says, "I am of **P**,
1Co   1:13 Was **P** crucified for you? Or
1Co   1:13 baptized in the name of **P**?
1Co   3:22 whether **P** or Apollos or
Phil   1: 1 **P** and Timothy, bondservants
2Pe   3:15 also our beloved brother **P**,

PAUL'S
1Co   16:21 with my own hand—**P**.

PAVEMENT
Esth   1: 6 and silver on a mosaic **p**
John   19:13 place that is called The **P**,

PAVILION
Ps   27: 5 He shall hide me in His **p**;

PAW†
1Sa   17:37 who delivered me from the **p**
1Sa   17:37 of the lion and from the **p**

PAY (see PAID)
Ex   21:19 He shall only **p** for the
Ex   22: 7 he shall **p** double.
2Ki   4: 7 sell the oil and your
Ezra   4:13 they will not **p** tax,
Esth   3: 2 Mordecai would not bow or **p**
Ps   22:25 I will **p** My vows before
Prov   5: 1 **p** attention to my wisdom;
Eccl   5: 4 **P** what you have vowed—

Jon	2: 9	I will **p** what I have vowed.
Mic	3:11	Her priests teach for **p**,
Matt	17:24	Does your Teacher not **p** the
Matt	18:30	prison till he should **p** the
Matt	22:17	Is it lawful to **p** taxes to
Matt	23:23	hypocrites! For you **p** tithe
Rom	13: 6	because of this you also **p**
Jas	2: 3	and you **p** attention to the

PEACE (see PEACEABLE, PEACEMAKERS, PEACETIME)
Gen	15:15	go to your fathers in **p**;
Gen	26:29	and have sent you away in **p**.
Gen	34: 5	so Jacob held his **p** until
Gen	43:23	**P** be with you, do not be
Ex	4:18	said to Moses, "Go in **p**.
Ex	14:14	and you shall hold your **p**.
Num	6:26	upon you, And give you **p**.
Num	25:12	give to him My covenant of **p**;
Josh	10: 1	of Gibeon had made **p** with
Judg	6:23	**P** be with you; do not fear,
1Sa	7:14	Also there was **p** between
1Sa	25: 6	**P** be to you, peace to your
1Ki	2: 6	go down to the grave in **p**.
2Ki	9:17	and let him say, 'Is it **p**?
2Ch	34:28	gathered to your grave in **p**;
Ezra	5: 7	Darius the king: All **p**.
Esth	9:30	with words of **p** and truth,
Ps	4: 8	I will both lie down in **p**,
Ps	28: 3	Who speak **p** to their
Ps	29:11	will bless His people with **p**.
Ps	34:14	Seek **p** and pursue it.
Ps	37:11	in the abundance of **p**.
Ps	37:37	future of that man is **p**.
Ps	72: 3	The mountains will bring **p**
Ps	85: 8	For He will speak **p** To His
Ps	85:10	Righteousness and **p** have
Ps	119:165	Great **p** have those who love
Ps	120: 7	I am for **p**; But when I
Ps	122: 6	Pray for the **p** of Jerusalem:
Ps	122: 7	**P** be within your walls,
Ps	125: 5	**P** be upon Israel!
Prov	3:17	And all her paths are **p**.
Prov	16: 7	even his enemies to be at **p**
Prov	29: 9	or laughs, there is no **p**.
Eccl	3: 8	of war, And a time of **p**.
Is	9: 6	Father, Prince of **P**.
Is	9: 7	of His government and **p**
Is	26: 3	will keep him in perfect **p**,
Is	45: 7	I make and create
Is	48:22	"There is no **p**," says the
Is	52: 7	good news, Who proclaims **p**,
Is	53: 5	The chastisement for our **p**
Is	54:10	Nor shall My covenant of **p**
Is	57:21	"There is no **p**," Says my
Is	59: 8	The way of **p** they have not
Is	66:12	I will extend **p** to her like
Jer	6:14	people slightly, Saying, '**P**,
Jer	6:14	**p**!' When there is no
Jer	8:11	people slightly, Saying, '**P**,
Jer	8:11	When there is no **p**.
Jer	8:15	"We looked for **p**,
Jer	28: 9	prophet who prophesies of **p**,
Jer	29: 7	And seek the **p** of the city
Jer	29: 7	in its peace you will have **p**.
Jer	43:12	shall go out from there in **p**.
Ezek	13:10	**P**!' when there is no
Ezek	13:16	and who see visions of **p** for
Ezek	34:25	will make a covenant of **p**
Ezek	37:26	I will make a covenant of **p**
Dan	4: 1	**P** be multiplied to you.
Nah	1:15	Who proclaims **p**! O Judah,
Zech	8:16	for truth, justice, and **p**;
Zech	8:19	Therefore love truth and **p**.
Zech	9:10	He shall speak **p** to the
Mal	2: 5	with him, one of life and **p**,

Matt	10:13	let your **p** come upon it. But
Matt	10:13	let your **p** return to you.
Matt	10:34	that I came to bring **p** on
Matt	10:34	I did not come to bring **p**
Mark	4:39	and said to the sea, "**P**,
Mark	5:34	has made you well. Go in **p**,
Luke	1:79	our feet into the way of **p**.
Luke	2:14	the highest, And on earth **p**,
Luke	2:29	Your servant depart in **p**,
Luke	10: 5	**P** to this house.'
Luke	10: 6	And if a son of **p** is there,
Luke	12:51	that I came to give **p** on
Luke	14:32	and asks conditions of **p**.
Luke	19:38	name of the LORD!' **P**
Luke	19:42	that make for your **p**! But
John	14:27	**P** I leave with you, My peace
John	16:33	that in Me you may have **p**.
Acts	10:36	preaching **p** through Jesus
Rom	1: 7	Grace to you and **p** from God
Rom	3:17	And the way of **p** they
Rom	5: 1	we have **p** with God through
Rom	8: 6	minded is life and **p**.
Rom	10:15	preach the gospel of **p**,
Rom	14:17	but righteousness and **p** and
Rom	14:19	things which make for **p**
Rom	15:33	Now the God of **p** be with you
Rom	16:20	And the God of **p** will crush
1Co	7:15	But God has called us to **p**.
1Co	14:33	of confusion but of **p**,
Gal	5:22	the Spirit is love, joy, **p**,
Gal	6:16	**p** and mercy be upon them,
Eph	2:14	For He Himself is our **p**,
Eph	2:15	the two, thus making **p**,
Eph	2:17	And He came and preached **p** to
Eph	4: 3	the Spirit in the bond of **p**.
Eph	6:15	of the gospel of **p**;
Phil	4: 7	and the **p** of God, which
Phil	4: 9	and the God of **p** will be
Col	1:20	having made **p** through the
Col	3:15	And let the **p** of God rule in
1Th	5: 3	**P** and safety!" then sudden
2Ti	2:22	**p** with those who call on the
Heb	7: 2	Salem, meaning "king of **p**,
Heb	12:14	Pursue **p** with all people,
Heb	13:20	Now may the God of **p** who
Jas	2:16	says to them, "Depart in **p**,
1Pe	1: 2	Grace to you and **p** be
1Pe	3:11	Let him seek **p** and
Rev	1: 4	Grace to you and **p** from Him
Rev	6: 4	one who sat on it to take **p**

PEACEABLE (see PEACE, PEACEABLY)
1Ti	2: 2	we may lead a quiet and **p**
Heb	12:11	afterward it yields the **p**
Jas	3:17	above is first pure, then **p**,

PEACEABLY (see PEACEABLE)
Gen	37: 4	him and could not speak **p**
Rom	12:18	live **p** with all men.

PEACEMAKERS† (see PEACE)
Matt	5: 9	Blessed are the **p**,

PEACETIME† (see PEACE)
1Ki	2: 5	shed the blood of war in **p**,

PEARL† (see PEARLS)
Matt	13:46	when he had found one **p** of
Rev	21:21	individual gate was of one **p**.

PEARLS (see PEARL)
Matt	7: 6	nor cast your **p** before
1Ti	2: 9	braided hair or gold or **p**
Rev	21:21	twelve gates were twelve **p**:

PEDDLING†
2Co	2:17	**p** the word of God; but as of

PEELED
Gen 30:37 **p** white strips in them, and

PEG
Judg 4:21 to him and drove the **p** into
Judg 5:26 her hand to the tent **p**,
Is 22:23 I will fasten him as a **p** in
Ezek 15: 3 Or can men make a **p** from it

PEKAH
2Ki 15:29 In the days of **P** king of
Is 7: 1 Rezin king of Syria and **P**

PEKAHIAH
2Ki 15:22 Then **P** his son reigned in

PELEG
Gen 10:25 sons: the name of one was **P**,

PELETHITES
2Sa 8:18 the Cherethites and the **P**;

PEN
Job 19:24 on a rock With an iron **p**
Ps 45: 1 My tongue is the **p** of a
Jer 8: 8 the false **p** of the scribe
Jer 17: 1 Judah is written with a **p**
3Jn 13 wish to write to you with **p**

PENALTY
Rom 1:27 in themselves the **p** of

PENIEL† (see PENUEL)
Gen 32:30 the name of the place **P**:

PENINNAH
1Sa 1: 2 **P** had children, but Hannah

PENNY†
Matt 5:26 you have paid the last **p**.

PENTECOST†
Acts 2: 1 When the Day of **P** had fully
Acts 20:16 if possible, on the Day of **P**.
1Co 16: 8 tarry in Ephesus until **P**.

PENUEL (see PENIEL)
Gen 32:31 Just as he crossed over **P** the

PEOPLE (see PEOPLE'S, PEOPLES)
Gen 11: 6 Indeed the **p** are one and
Gen 17:14 shall be cut off from his **p**;
Gen 25: 8 and was gathered to his **p**.
Gen 25:23 One **p** shall be stronger
Gen 49:10 be the obedience of the **p**.
Gen 50:20 to save many **p** alive.
Ex 1:20 and the **p** multiplied and
Ex 4:21 that he will not let the **p**
Ex 4:31 So the **p** believed; and when
Ex 5: 1 Let My **p** go, that they may
Ex 7:14 he refuses to let the **p** go.
Ex 8:23 a difference between My **p**
Ex 13:17 when Pharaoh had let the **p**
Ex 14:31 so the **p** feared the LORD,
Ex 15:16 Till Your **p** pass over, O
Ex 15:24 And the **p** complained against
Ex 17: 1 was no water for the **p** to
Ex 17: 4 shall I do with this **p**?
Ex 18:13 Moses sat to judge the **p**;
Ex 19: 5 treasure to Me above all **p**;
Ex 19: 7 for the elders of the **p**,
Ex 19:10 Go to the **p** and consecrate
Ex 19:21 "Go down and warn the **p**,
Ex 24: 8 sprinkled it on the **p**,
Ex 30:33 shall be cut off from his **p**.
Ex 32: 6 and the **p** sat down to eat
Ex 32: 9 it is a stiff-necked **p**!
Ex 32:31 these **p** have committed a
Ex 32:35 So the LORD plagued the **p**
Lev 4: 3 bringing guilt on the **p**,
Lev 4:27 If anyone of the common **p**
Lev 7:20 shall be cut off from his **p**.

Lev 9:15 the sin offering for the **p**,
Lev 9:23 came out and blessed the **p**.
Lev 10: 6 wrath come upon all the **p**.
Lev 19:16 a talebearer among your **p**;
Lev 26:12 God, and you shall be My **p**.
Num 11: 1 Now when the **p** complained,
Num 11: 2 Then the **p** cried out to
Num 11:29 that all the LORD's **p** were
Num 12:15 and the **p** did not journey
Num 13:32 and all the **p** whom we saw in
Num 14: 1 and the **p** wept that night.
Num 14:19 the iniquity of this **p**,
Num 16:47 plague had begun among the **p**.
Num 16:47 and made atonement for the **p**
Num 20: 1 and the **p** stayed in Kadesh;
Num 21: 6 fiery serpents among the **p**,
Num 21: 6 and many of the **p** of Israel
Num 22: 6 curse this **p** for me, for
Num 26: 4 a census of the **p** from
Num 33:14 was no water for the **p** to
Deut 1:28 The **p** are greater and taller
Deut 4: 6 a wise and understanding **p**.
Deut 4:10 Gather the **p** to Me, and I
Deut 4:33 Did any **p** ever hear the
Deut 7: 6 For you are a holy **p** to the
Deut 7: 6 God has chosen you to be a **p**
Deut 7: 7 in number than any other **p**,
Deut 9:26 do not destroy Your **p** and
Deut 14: 2 For you are a holy **p** to the
Deut 14: 2 has chosen you to be a **p**
Deut 20: 1 horses and chariots and **p**
Deut 26:15 and bless Your **p** Israel and
Deut 26:18 you to be His special **p**,
Deut 27:12 Mount Gerizim to bless the **p**,
Deut 27:16 And all the **p** shall say,
Deut 28: 9 establish you as a holy **p**
Deut 32:36 the LORD will judge His **p**
Deut 33:29 a **p** saved by the LORD, The
Josh 3:17 until all the **p** had crossed
Josh 5: 8 circumcising all the **p**,
Josh 6:20 and the **p** shouted with a
Josh 7: 5 the hearts of the **p** melted
Josh 8:11 And all the **p** of war who
Josh 11: 4 as many **p** as the sand that
Josh 17:17 You are a great **p** and have
Josh 24:25 made a covenant with the **p**
Judg 2: 7 So the **p** served the LORD
Judg 7: 4 The **p** are still too many;
Judg 10: 6 the gods of the **p** of Ammon,
Judg 11: 6 we may fight against the **p**
Judg 14:16 a riddle to the sons of my **p**,
Judg 18:10 you will come to a secure **p**
Judg 21:15 And the **p** grieved for
Ruth 1: 6 the LORD had visited His **p**
Ruth 1:16 Your **p** shall be my
Ruth 4: 4 and the elders of my **p**.
1Sa 5: 6 LORD was heavy on the **p** of
1Sa 9: 2 taller than any of the **p**.
1Sa 9:17 one shall reign over My **p**.
1Sa 13: 6 then the **p** hid in caves, in
1Sa 15: 1 anoint you king over His **p**,
2Sa 3:18 I will save My **p** Israel from
2Sa 3:36 king did pleased all the **p**.
2Sa 5: 2 You shall shepherd My **p**
2Sa 7: 8 sheep, to be ruler over My **p**,
2Sa 7:23 "And who is like Your **p**,
2Sa 7:23 to redeem for Himself as a **p**,
2Sa 7:24 Israel Your very own **p**
2Sa 14:13 such a thing against the **p**
2Sa 17: 9 is a slaughter among the **p**
2Sa 17:29 The **p** are hungry and weary
2Sa 18: 8 the woods devoured more **p**
2Sa 19:40 And all the **p** of Judah
2Sa 22:28 You will save the humble **p**;
2Sa 24: 2 may know the number of the **p**.

2Sa	24:15	thousand men of the **p** died.
2Sa	24:17	angel who was striking the **p**,
1Ki	3: 8	is in the midst of Your **p**
1Ki	3: 8	You have chosen, a great **p**,
1Ki	5: 7	wise son over this great **p**!
1Ki	8:52	the supplication of Your **p**
1Ki	8:56	who has given rest to His **p**
1Ki	9:23	who ruled over the **p** who did
1Ki	12:13	Then the king answered the **p**
1Ki	12:31	from every class of **p**,
1Ki	16: 2	and have made My **p** Israel
1Ki	21: 9	with high honor among the **p**;
2Ki	4:13	"I dwell among my own **p**.
2Ki	7:17	But the **p** trampled him in
2Ki	11:17	LORD, the king, and the **p**,
2Ki	12: 8	more money from the **p**,
2Ki	24:14	except the poorest **p** of the
1Ch	29:14	who am I, and who are my **p**,
2Ch	7:14	if My **p** who are called by My
2Ch	30:20	to Hezekiah and healed the **p**.
2Ch	32:19	as against the gods of the **p**
2Ch	35: 7	Then Josiah gave the lay **p**
2Ch	36:23	is among you of all His **p**?
Ezra	1: 3	is among you of all His **p**?
Ezra	3:13	of the weeping of the **p**,
Ezra	4: 4	tried to discourage the **p**
Ezra	10: 9	and all the **p** sat in the
Neh	4: 6	for the **p** had a mind to
Neh	5:15	me laid burdens on the **p**,
Neh	7: 5	the rulers, and the **p**,
Neh	8: 5	standing above all the **p**;
Neh	8: 5	all the **p** stood up.
Neh	8: 7	helped the **p** to understand
Neh	8: 9	For all the **p** wept, when
Neh	11: 1	Now the leaders of the **p**
Neh	11: 1	the rest of the **p** cast lots
Esth	3: 8	There is a certain **p**
Esth	3: 8	and dispersed among the **p**
Esth	4: 8	plead before him for her **p**
Esth	9: 2	fear of them fell upon all **p**.
Job	1:19	and it fell on the young **p**,
Job	12: 2	"No doubt you are the **p**,
Job	17: 6	made me a byword of the **p**,
Ps	2: 1	And the **p** plot a vain
Ps	9:11	His deeds among the **p**.
Ps	14: 4	Who eat up my **p** as they
Ps	14: 7	back the captivity of His **p**,
Ps	22: 6	men, and despised by the **p**.
Ps	29:11	will give strength to His **p**;
Ps	29:11	the LORD will bless His **p**
Ps	47: 9	The princes of the **p** have
Ps	47: 9	The **p** of the God of
Ps	62: 8	in Him at all times, you **p**;
Ps	67: 4	For You shall judge the **p**
Ps	72: 2	He will judge Your **p** with
Ps	77:15	Your arm redeemed Your **p**,
Ps	77:20	You led Your **p** like a flock
Ps	78:52	But He made His own **p** go
Ps	79:13	Your **p** and sheep of Your
Ps	85: 8	will speak peace To His **p**
Ps	95: 7	And we are the **p** of His
Ps	100: 3	We are His **p** and the
Ps	106:48	And let all the **p** say,
Ps	114: 1	house of Jacob from a **p** of
Ps	135:12	A heritage to Israel His **p**.
Ps	136:16	To Him who led His **p** through
Ps	144:15	Happy are the **p** whose God
Ps	148:14	exalted the horn of His **p**,
Prov	14:34	sin is a reproach to any **p**.
Prov	29: 2	man rules, the **p** groan.
Prov	29:18	the **p** cast off restraint;
Prov	30:25	The ants are a **p** not
Eccl	12: 9	he still taught the **p**
Is	1: 3	My **p** do not consider."
Is	1: 4	A **p** laden with iniquity, A

Is	6: 5	I dwell in the midst of a **p**
Is	6: 9	said, "Go, and tell this **p**:
Is	6:10	Make the heart of this **p**
Is	8:19	should not a **p** seek their
Is	9: 2	The **p** who walked in darkness
Is	10:24	Lord GOD of hosts: "O My **p**,
Is	11:10	stand as a banner to the **p**;
Is	14: 6	He who struck the **p** in wrath
Is	18: 7	the LORD of hosts From a **p**
Is	19:25	"Blessed is Egypt My **p**,
Is	24: 4	The haughty **p** of the earth
Is	25: 7	the covering cast over all **p**,
Is	28: 5	To the remnant of His **p**,
Is	29:13	Inasmuch as these **p** draw near
Is	30:26	up the bruise of His **p** And
Is	30:28	bridle in the jaws of the **p**,
Is	33:19	A **p** of obscure speech,
Is	40: 1	comfort My **p**!" Says your
Is	40: 7	Surely the **p** are grass.
Is	42: 6	You as a covenant to the **p**,
Is	49: 8	You As a covenant to the **p**,
Is	52: 5	That My **p** are taken away for
Is	53: 8	the transgressions of My **p**
Is	55: 4	him as a witness to the **p**,
Is	55: 4	and commander for the **p**.
Is	62:10	Prepare the way for the **p**;
Is	65: 2	day long to a rebellious **p**,
Is	65: 3	A **p** who provoke Me to anger
Jer	2:11	But My **p** have changed their
Jer	2:13	For My **p** have committed two
Jer	2:32	Yet My **p** have forgotten Me
Jer	4:11	Toward the daughter of My **p**—
Jer	5:31	And My **p** love to have it
Jer	6:14	also healed the hurt of My **p**
Jer	6:22	a **p** comes from the north
Jer	7:16	do not pray for this **p**,
Jer	7:23	God, and you shall be My **p**.
Jer	8: 7	But My **p** do not know the
Jer	8:19	cry of the daughter of my **p**
Jer	26: 8	the prophets and all the **p**
Jer	26:23	the graves of the common **p**.
Jer	31:33	God, and they shall be My **p**.
Jer	32:38	'They shall be My **p**,
Jer	34: 8	a covenant with all the **p**
Jer	38: 4	seek the welfare of this **p**,
Jer	52:15	captive some of the poor **p**,
Lam	1: 1	city That was full of **p**!
Ezek	21:12	sword will be against My **p**;
Ezek	33: 3	the trumpet and warns the **p**,
Ezek	37:13	opened your graves, O My **p**,
Ezek	37:23	Then they shall be My **p**,
Ezek	38:14	On that day when My **p** Israel
Dan	3:29	I make a decree that any **p**,
Dan	9:16	Jerusalem and Your **p** are a
Dan	9:19	for Your city and Your **p** are
Dan	9:26	And the **p** of the prince who
Dan	10:14	what will happen to your **p**
Hos	1: 9	For you are not My **p**,
Hos	2: 1	Say to your brethren, 'My **p**,
Hos	4: 6	My **p** are destroyed for lack
Hos	4: 9	And it shall be: like **p**,
Amos	7:15	prophesy to My **p** Israel.'
Jon	3: 5	So the **p** of Nineveh believed
Mic	3: 2	strip the skin from My **p**,
Mic	3: 3	also eat the flesh of My **p**,
Mic	7:14	Shepherd Your **p** with Your
Zeph	3:12	midst A meek and humble **p**,
Hag	1: 2	This **p** says, "The time has
Matt	1:21	for He will save His **p** from
Matt	2: 6	Who will shepherd My **p**
Matt	4:16	The **p** who sat in
Matt	9:35	every disease among the **p**.
Matt	13:15	the hearts of this **p**
Matt	15: 8	These **p** draw near to Me
Mark	6: 5	His hands on a few sick **p**

Mark   6:12 out and preached that **p**
Mark   7: 6 This **p** honors Me with
Mark 12:37 And the common **p** heard Him
Luke   1:17 to make ready a **p** prepared
Luke   1:25 away my reproach among **p**.
Luke   2:10 joy which will be to all **p**.
Luke   2:32 And the glory of Your **p**
Luke   3:21 When all the **p** were
Luke   9:13 and buy food for all these **p**.
Luke 23: 5 saying, "He stirs up the **p**,
Luke 23:35 And the **p** stood looking on.
John   7:31 And many of the **p** believed in
John 11:50 one man should die for the **p**,
John 12:29 Therefore the **p** who stood by
John 18:14 one man should die for the **p**.
Acts   2:47 having favor with all the **p**.
Acts   4:25 And the **p** plot vain
Acts   5:16 bringing sick **p** and those
Acts   5:26 for they feared the **p**,
Acts   5:37 and drew away many **p** after
Acts   6: 8 and signs among the **p**.
Acts 10: 2 alms generously to the **p**,
Acts 15:14 to take out of them a **p** for
Acts 18:10 for I have many **p** in this
Acts 21:39 permit me to speak to the **p**.
Acts 26:23 light to the Jewish **p** and
Acts 28:27 the hearts of this **p**
Rom   9:25 will call them My **p**,
Rom 10:21 and contrary **p**.
Rom 11: 1 has God cast away His **p**?
Rom 11: 2 God has not cast away His **p**
1Co 10: 7 The **p** sat down to eat
2Co   6:16 they shall be My **p**.
Tit   2:14 Himself His own special **p**,
Heb   2:17 for the sins of the **p**
Heb   4: 9 therefore a rest for the **p**
Heb   8:10 and they shall be My **p**.
Heb   9:19 book itself and all the **p**,
Heb 10:30 LORD will judge His **p**.
Heb 11:25 affliction with the **p** of
Heb 13:12 that He might sanctify the **p**
1Pe   2: 9 nation, His own special **p**,
1Pe   2:10 a people but are now the **p**
2Pe   2: 5 Noah, one of eight **p**,
Rev   5: 9 tribe and tongue and **p** and
Rev 14: 6 nation, tribe, tongue, and **p**—

PEOPLE'S (see PEOPLE)
Heb   7:27 own sins and then for the **p**,
1Pe   4:15 or as a busybody in other **p**

PEOPLES (see PEOPLE)
Gen 17:16 kings of **p** shall be from
Gen 25:23 Two **p** shall be separated
Deut   7: 6 treasure above all the **p** on
Deut   7: 7 you were the least of all **p**;
Deut 32: 8 set the boundaries of the **p**
1Ch 16: 8 known His deeds among the **p**!
Ps   7: 8 The LORD shall judge the **p**;
Ps   33:10 makes the plans of the **p** of
Ps   47: 1 all you **p**! Shout to God
Ps   49: 1 Hear this, all **p**;
Ps   65: 7 And the tumult of the **p**.
Ps   67: 3 Let the **p** praise You, O God;
Ps   67: 3 Let all the **p** praise You.
Ps   87: 6 When He registers the **p**:
Ps   96:13 And the **p** with His truth.
Ps   98: 9 And the **p** with equity.
Ps   99: 2 He is high above all the **p**.
Ps 105: 1 known His deeds among the **p**!
Is   12: 4 His deeds among the **p**,
Is   49:22 set up My standard for the **p**;
Is   51: 4 rest As a light of the **p**.
Is   62:10 Lift up a banner for the **p**!
Ezek 32:10 I will make many **p**
Dan   3: 4 you it is commanded, O **p**,

Dan   4: 1 the king, To all **p**,
Hos   7: 8 mixed himself among the **p**;
Mic   4: 1 And **p** shall flow to it.
Mic   4: 3 shall judge between many **p**,
Zeph   3: 9 I will restore to the **p** a
Zech 10: 9 will sow them among the **p**,
John 12:32 will draw all **p** to
Rev   7: 9 of all nations, tribes, **p**,
Rev 11: 9 Then those from the **p**,

PEOR
Num 23:28 took Balaam to the top of P,
Num 25: 3 was joined to Baal of P,
Deut   4: 3 what the LORD did at Baal P;

PERCEIVE (see PERCEIVED, PERCEIVES)
Deut 29: 4 not given you a heart to **p**
Prov   1: 2 To **p** the words of
Is   6: 9 on seeing, but do not **p**.
Matt 13:14 you will see and not **p**;
Luke   6:41 but do not **p** the plank in
John   4:19 I **p** that You are a prophet.
Acts 10:34 In truth I **p** that God shows
Acts 17:22 I **p** that in all things you

PERCEIVED (see PERCEIVE)
2Sa   12:19 David **p** that the child was
Luke   5:22 But when Jesus **p** their
Luke   8:46 for I **p** power going out from
Gal   2: 9 **p** the grace that had been

PERCEIVES† (see PERCEIVE)
Prov 31:18 She **p** that her merchandise

PERDITION
John 17:12 is lost except the son of **p**,
2Th   2: 3 is revealed, the son of **p**,
2Pe   3: 7 the day of judgment and **p**
Rev 17: 8 bottomless pit and go to **p**.

PERES† (see UPHARSIN)
Dan   5:28 "P: Your kingdom has

PEREZ
Gen 46:12 were Er, Onan, Shelah, P,
1Ch   4: 1 The sons of Judah were P,
Matt   1: 3 Judah begot P and Zerah by

PERFECT (see PERFECTED, PERFECTING, PERFECTION, PERFECTLY)
Gen   6: 9 **p** in his generations. Noah
Deut 25:15 a **p** and just measure, that
Deut 32: 4 is the Rock, His work is **p**;
2Sa   22:33 And He makes my way **p**.
Ps   19: 7 The law of the LORD is **p**,
Ps 138: 8 The LORD will **p** that
Ps 139:22 I hate them with **p** hatred;
Prov   4:18 ever brighter unto the **p**
Is   26: 3 You will keep him in **p**
Ezek 27: 3 I am **p** in beauty.'
Ezek 28:12 Full of wisdom and **p** in
Matt   5:48 "Therefore you shall be **p**,
Matt   5:48 your Father in heaven is **p**.
Luke   1: 3 having had **p** understanding
John 17:23 that they may be made **p** in
Rom 12: 2 good and acceptable and **p**
1Co 13:10 But when that which is **p** has
2Co 12: 9 for My strength is made **p** in
Eph   4:13 to a **p** man, to the measure
Col   1:28 we may present every man **p**
Col   4:12 that you may stand **p** and
1Th   3:10 we may see your face and **p**
Heb   2:10 captain of their salvation **p**
Heb   7:19 for the law made nothing **p**;
Heb 12:23 spirits of just men made **p**,
Jas   1: 4 But let patience have its **p**
Jas   1:17 Every good gift and every **p**
Jas   1:25 But he who looks into the **p**
Jas   2:22 by works faith was made **p**?

Jas 3: 2 he is a **p** man, able also to
1Pe 5:10 you have suffered a while, **p**,
1Jn 4:18 but **p** love casts out fear,
Rev 3: 2 have not found your works **p**

PERFECTED (*see* PERFECT)
Matt 21:16 infants You have **p**
Luke 13:32 the third day I shall be **p**.
Phil 3:12 attained, or am already **p**;
Heb 7:28 the Son who has been **p**
Heb 10:14 For by one offering He has **p**
1Jn 2: 5 truly the love of God is **p**

PERFECTING† (*see* PERFECT)
2Co 7: 1 **p** holiness in the fear of

PERFECTION (*see* PERFECT)
Col 3:14 love, which is the bond of **p**.
Heb 6: 1 of Christ, let us go on to **p**,
Heb 7:11 if **p** were through the

PERFECTLY (*see* PERFECT)
1Co 1:10 but that you be **p** joined

PERFORM (*see* PERFORMED)
Gen 26: 3 and I will **p** the oath which
Num 8:11 that they may **p** the work of
Deut 25: 5 and **p** the duty of a
Judg 16:25 that he may **p** for us." So
Ruth 3:13 shall be that if he will **p**
Ps 61: 8 That I may daily **p** my vows.
Is 9: 7 of the LORD of hosts will **p**
Is 44:28 And he shall **p** all My
Matt 5:33 but shall **p** your oaths to
Matt 23:16 he is obliged to **p** it.'
Luke 13:32 I cast out demons and **p**
John 6:30 What sign will You **p** then,
Rom 4:21 He was also able to **p**.
Rom 7:18 but how to **p** what is good I

PERFORMED (*see* PERFORM)
Judg 16:27 roof watching while Samson **p**.
Is 10:12 when the LORD has **p** all His
Is 41: 4 Who has **p** and done it,
Luke 2:39 So when they had **p** all
John 6: 2 saw His signs which He **p** on
John 10:41 John **p** no sign, but all the

PERFUMED† (*see* PERFUMES)
Prov 7:17 I have **p** my bed With myrrh,
Song 3: 6 **P** with myrrh and

PERFUMER'S† (*see* PERFUMERS)
Eccl 10: 1 Dead flies putrefy the **p**

PERFUMERS (*see* PERFUMER'S, PERFUMES)
1Sa 8:13 your daughters to be **p**,

PERFUMES (*see* PERFUMED)
Song 4:10 And the scent of your **p**

PERGA
Acts 13:13 they came to **P** in Pamphylia;

PERGAMOS†
Rev 1:11 to Ephesus, to Smyrna, to **P**,
Rev 2:12 the angel of the church in **P**

PERIL† (*see* PERILOUS, PERILS)
Rom 8:35 famine, or nakedness, or **p**,

PERILOUS (*see* PERIL)
2Ti 3: 1 that in the last days **p**

PERILS (*see* PERIL)
2Co 11:26 in **p** of waters, in perils
2Co 11:26 in **p** of robbers, in perils
2Co 11:26 in **p** of my own

PERISH (*see* PERISHABLE, PERISHED, PERISHES,
  PERISHING)
Gen 41:36 that the land may not **p**
Deut 4:26 that you will soon utterly **p**

Esth 4:16 against the law; and if I **p**,
Job 3: 3 May the day **p** on which I was
Job 3:11 Why did I not **p** when I
Job 4:20 They **p** forever, with no one
Job 34:15 All flesh would **p** together,
Ps 1: 6 way of the ungodly shall **p**.
Ps 2:12 And you **p** in the way,
Ps 37:20 But the wicked shall **p**;
Ps 41: 5 will he die, and his name **p**?
Ps 49:12 is like the beasts that **p**
Ps 80:16 They **p** at the rebuke of
Ps 92: 9 behold, Your enemies shall **p**;
Ps 102:26 They will **p**, but You will
Is 31: 3 They all will **p** together.
Jer 18:18 for the law shall not **p** from
Ezek 7:26 But the law will **p** from the
Dan 2:18 his companions might not **p**
Jon 1: 6 us, so that we may not **p**.
Jon 1:14 please do not let us **p** for
Jon 3: 9 anger, so that we may not **p**?
Matt 5:29 that one of your members **p**,
Matt 18:14 these little ones should **p**.
Matt 26:52 who take the sword will **p**
Luke 13: 3 you will all likewise **p**.
Luke 15:17 and I **p** with hunger!
John 3:16 in Him should not **p** but
John 10:28 life, and they shall never **p**;
John 11:50 the whole nation should **p**.
Acts 8:20 Your money **p** with you,
Rom 2:12 without law will also **p**
1Co 8:11 shall the weak brother **p**,
Heb 1:11 They will **p**, but You

PERISHABLE† (*see* PERISH)
1Co 9:25 they do it to obtain a **p**

PERISHED (*see* PERISH)
Job 4: 7 who ever **p** being innocent?
Ps 9: 6 Even their memory has **p**.
Jer 49: 7 Has counsel **p** from the
Jon 4:10 came up in a night and **p** in
Mic 7: 2 The faithful man has **p** from
Luke 11:51 the blood of Zechariah who **p**
1Co 15:18 asleep in Christ have **p**.
2Pe 3: 6 world that then existed **p**,
Jude 11 and **p** in the rebellion of

PERISHES (*see* PERISH)
Is 57: 1 The righteous **p**,
John 6:27 labor for the food which **p**,
1Pe 1: 7 precious than gold that **p**,

PERISHING (*see* PERISH)
Prov 31: 6 strong drink to him who is **p**,
Matt 8:25 save us! We are **p**!"

PERIZZITE (*see* PERIZZITES)
Ex 33: 2 and the Hittite and the **P**
Josh 9: 1 the Canaanite, the **P**,

PERIZZITES (*see* PERIZZITE)
Gen 13: 7 The Canaanites and the **P**
Josh 17:15 there in the land of the **P**
Judg 3: 5 the Amorites, the **P**,

PERMISSION (*see* PERMIT)
1Sa 20:28 David earnestly asked **p** of
Mark 5:13 at once Jesus gave them **p**.
John 19:38 and Pilate gave him **p**.

PERMIT (*see* PERMISSION, PERMITS, PERMITTED)
Matt 8:31 **p** us to go away into the
Acts 16: 7 but the Spirit did not **p**
1Ti 2:12 And I do not **p** a woman to

PERMITS† (*see* PERMIT)
1Co 16: 7 with you, if the Lord **p**.
Heb 6: 3 And this we will do if God **p**.

PERMITTED (see PERMIT)
Deut 22:29 he shall not be **p** to divorce
Matt 19: 8 **p** you to divorce your wives,
Mark 5:37 And He **p** no one to follow Him
Acts 28:16 but Paul was **p** to dwell by

PERPETUAL (see PERPETUALLY)
Gen 9:12 for **p** generations:
Ex 29: 9 shall be theirs for a **p**
Ex 30: 8 a **p** incense before the LORD
Ex 31:16 their generations as a **p**
Lev 25:34 for it is their **p**
Jer 8: 5 in a **p** backsliding? They
Jer 15:18 Why is my pain **p** And my
Jer 23:40 and a **p** shame, which shall
Jer 49:13 all its cities shall be **p**
Jer 50: 5 to the LORD In a **p**

PERPETUALLY (see PERPETUAL)
Amos 1:11 all pity; His anger tore **p**,

PERPETUATE
Ruth 4: 5 to **p** the name of the dead

PERPLEXED
2Co 4: 8 yet not crushed; we are **p**,

PERSECUTE (see PERSECUTED, PERSECUTING,
PERSECUTION, PERSECUTOR)
Ps 31:15 And from those who **p** me.
Ps 119:86 They **p** me wrongfully; Help
Jer 17:18 Let them be ashamed who **p**
Dan 7:25 Shall **p** the saints of the
Matt 5:11 you when they revile and **p**
Matt 5:44 who spitefully use you and **p**
Matt 23:34 in your synagogues and
Luke 11:49 of them they will kill and **p**,
John 15:20 they will also **p** you. If
Rom 12:14 Bless those who **p** you; bless

PERSECUTED (see PERSECUTE)
Ps 109:16 But **p** the poor and needy
Ps 143: 3 For the enemy has **p** my soul;
Matt 5:10 are those who are **p** for
Matt 5:12 for so they **p** the prophets
John 15:20 If they **p** Me, they will
Acts 22: 4 I **p** this Way to the death,
1Co 15: 9 because I **p** the church of
2Co 4: 9 **p**, but not forsaken;

PERSECUTING (see PERSECUTE)
Acts 9: 5 "I am Jesus, whom you are **p**.
Phil 3: 6 **p** the church; concerning the

PERSECUTION (see PERSECUTE, PERSECUTIONS)
Matt 13:21 For when tribulation or **p**
Acts 8: 1 At that time a great **p** arose
Acts 11:19 were scattered after the **p**
Rom 8:35 or distress, or **p**,
Gal 6:12 that they may not suffer **p**
2Ti 3:12 Christ Jesus will suffer **p**.

PERSECUTIONS (see PERSECUTION)
Mark 10:30 children and lands, with **p**—
2Ti 3:11 what **p** I endured. And out of

PERSECUTOR† (see PERSECUTE, PERSECUTORS)
1Ti 1:13 formerly a blasphemer, a **p**,

PERSECUTORS (see PERSECUTOR)
Jer 15:15 vengeance for me on my **p**.

PERSEVERANCE (see PERSEVERE)
Rom 5: 3 that tribulation produces **p**;
2Co 12:12 among you with all **p**,
2Ti 3:10 longsuffering, love, **p**,
Jas 5:11 You have heard of the **p** of
2Pe 1: 6 to **p** godliness,

PERSEVERE† (see PERSEVERANCE, PERSEVERED)
Rev 3:10 have kept My command to **p**,

PERSEVERED† (see PERSEVERE)
Rev 2: 3 and you have **p** and have

PERSIA (see ELAM, PERSIAN)
2Ch 36:22 year of Cyrus king of P,
Ezra 4: 7 to Artaxerxes king of P;
Ezra 4:24 reign of Darius king of P.
Esth 1: 3 the powers of P and Media,
Dan 10:13 prince of the kingdom of P
Dan 10:20 fight with the prince of P;

PERSIAN† (see ELAMITES, PERSIA, PERSIANS)
Neh 12:22 the reign of Darius the P,
Dan 6:28 in the reign of Cyrus the P.

PERSIANS (see PERSIAN)
Dan 5:28 and given to the Medes and P.
Dan 6: 8 the law of the Medes and P,

PERSISTENCE†
Luke 11: 8 yet because of his **p** he will

PERSON (see PERSONAL, PERSONS)
Gen 17:14 that **p** shall be cut off from
Lev 20: 6 set My face against that **p**
Lev 22:11 But if the priest buys a **p**
Num 5: 6 and that **p** is guilty,
Num 15:28 make atonement for the **p**
Num 19:17 And for an unclean **p** they
Deut 27:25 bribe to slay an innocent **p**
1Sa 9: 2 was not a more handsome **p**
1Ki 14: 6 pretend to be another **p**?
Job 1:12 do not lay a hand on his **p**.
Ezek 44:25 by coming near a dead **p**.
Dan 11:21 place shall arise a vile **p**,
Matt 5:39 you not to resist an evil **p**.
Matt 22:16 for You do not regard the **p**
Matt 27:24 of the blood of this just P.
Rom 14: 5 One **p** esteems one day above
1Co 5:11 even to eat with such a **p**.
1Ti 1: 9 not made for a righteous **p**,
Heb 1: 3 the express image of His **p**,
Heb 12:16 any fornicator or profane **p**
1Pe 3: 4 let it be the hidden **p**

PERSONAL† (see PERSON)
Luke 20:21 and You do not show **p**
Acts 12:20 made Blastus the king's **p**
Gal 2: 6 God shows **p** favoritism to no

PERSONAL AIDE
Acts 12:20 the king's **p** their friend,

PERSONS (see PERSON)
Gen 14:21 to Abram, "Give me the **p**,
Luke 15: 7 over ninety-nine just **p** who
2Pe 3:11 what manner of **p** ought you

PERSUADE (see PERSUADED, PERSUASIVE)
1Ki 22:21 and said, 'I will **p** him.'
Acts 26:28 You almost **p** me to become a
2Co 5:11 we **p** men; but we are well
Gal 1:10 For do I now **p** men, or God?

PERSUADED (see PERSUADE)
Jer 20: 7 You induced me, and I was **p**;
Luke 16:31 neither will they be **p**
Acts 17: 5 But the Jews who were not **p**,
Acts 18: 4 and **p** both Jews and Greeks.
Rom 8:38 For I am **p** that neither death
2Ti 1: 5 and I am **p** is in you also.
2Ti 1:12 I have believed and am **p**

PERSUASIVE (see PERSUADE)
1Co 2: 4 preaching were not with **p**

PERTAIN† (see PERTAINING)
Rom 9: 4 to whom **p** the adoption, the
Rom 15:17 in the things which **p** to
1Co 6: 3 things that **p** to this life?
2Pe 1: 3 to us all things that **p** to

PERTAINING (*see* PERTAIN)
Acts	1: 3	speaking of the things **p** to
1Co	6: 4	concerning things **p** to this
Heb	2:17	High Priest in things **p** to
Heb	5: 1	for men in things **p** to God,

PERTURBED†
Prov	30:21	three things the earth is **p**,

PERVERSE (*see* PERVERT)
Deut	32: 5	A **p** and crooked generation.
1Sa	20:30	to him, "You son of a **p**,
Prov	4:24	And put **p** lips far from
Prov	10:31	But the **p** tongue will be
Prov	11:20	Those who are of a **p** heart
Is	19:14	The LORD has mingled a **p**
Matt	17:17	O faithless and **p** generation,
Phil	2:15	the midst of a crooked and **p**

PERVERT (*see* PERVERSE, PERVERTED, PERVERTING, PERVERTS)
Ex	23: 2	turn aside after many to **p**
Job	8: 3	Or does the Almighty **p**
Amos	2: 7	And **p** the way of the
Gal	1: 7	trouble you and want to **p**

PERVERTED (*see* PERVERT)
Judg	19:22	**p** men, surrounded the house
Jer	3:21	For they have **p** their way;

PERVERTING† (*see* PERVERT)
Luke	23: 2	We found this fellow **p** the
Acts	13:10	will you not cease **p** the

PERVERTS (*see* PERVERT)
Deut	27:19	Cursed is the one who **p** the
Prov	10: 9	But he who **p** his ways will

PESTERED†
Judg	16:16	when she **p** him daily with

PESTILENCE (*see* PESTILENCES)
Ex	5: 3	lest He fall upon us with **p**
Ex	9: 3	on the sheep—a very severe **p**.
Num	14:12	will strike them with the **p**
2Ch	6:28	**p** or blight or mildew,
Ps	91: 3	And from the perilous **p**.
Ps	91: 6	Nor of the **p** that walks in
Jer	27: 8	sword, the famine, and the **p**,
Ezek	6:11	sword, by famine, and by **p**.
Hab	3: 5	Before Him went **p**,

PESTILENCES (*see* PESTILENCE)
Matt	24: 7	And there will be famines, **p**,

PETER (*see* CEPHAS, PETER'S, SIMON)
Matt	4:18	two brothers, Simon called **P**,
Matt	26:69	Now **P** sat outside in the
Matt	26:75	And **P** remembered the word of
Mark	3:16	to whom He gave the name **P**;
Mark	8:33	His disciples, He rebuked **P**,
Mark	14:33	And He took **P**, James, and
Mark	14:67	And when she saw **P** warming
Mark	16: 7	go, tell His disciples—and **P**—
Luke	22:34	He said, "I tell you, **P**,
Luke	22:58	But **P** said, "Man, I am
Luke	22:61	Lord turned and looked at **P**.
Luke	22:62	So **P** went out and wept
John	1:44	the city of Andrew and **P**.
John	18:10	Then Simon **P**, having a
John	18:18	And **P** stood with them and
John	18:26	of him whose ear **P** cut
John	18:27	**P** then denied again; and
John	20: 4	the other disciple outran **P**
Acts	1:13	where they were staying; **P**,
Acts	1:15	those days **P** stood up
Acts	2:38	Then **P** said to them,
Acts	3: 1	Now **P** and John went up
Acts	3: 6	Then **P** said, "Silver and
Acts	4: 8	Then **P**, filled with the

Acts	4:13	they saw the boldness of **P**
Acts	5:29	But **P** and the other apostles
Acts	10: 5	for Simon whose surname is **P**.
Acts	10:13	voice came to him, "Rise, **P**;
Acts	10:14	But **P** said, "Not so, Lord!
Acts	10:25	As **P** was coming in, Cornelius
Acts	12: 6	that night **P** was sleeping,
Acts	12: 7	and he struck **P** on the side
Acts	12:13	And as **P** knocked at the door
Gal	1:18	up to Jerusalem to see **P**,
1Pe	1: 1	**P**, an apostle of Jesus
2Pe	1: 1	Simon **P**, a bondservant

PETER'S (*see* PETER)
Matt	8:14	when Jesus had come into **P**
John	1:40	Simon **P** brother.

PETITION (*see* PETITIONED, PETITIONS)
1Sa	1:17	God of Israel grant your **p**
Esth	5: 7	My **p** and request is this:
Dan	6:13	but makes his **p** three times

PETITIONED (*see* PETITION)
Dan	2:49	Also Daniel **p** the king, and

PETITIONS (*see* PETITION)
Ps	20: 5	the LORD fulfill all your **p**.
Dan	6: 7	that whoever **p** any god or
1Jn	5:15	we know that we have the **p**

PHARAOH (*see* NECHO, PHARAOH'S)
Gen	12:15	The princes of **P** also saw her
Gen	37:36	an officer of **P** and captain
Gen	41: 1	that **P** had a dream; and
Gen	41:25	The dreams of **P** are one; God
Gen	47:24	shall give one-fifth to **P**.
Ex	1:11	And they built for **P** supply
Ex	1:19	And the midwives said to **P**,
Ex	2: 5	Then the daughter of **P** came
Ex	2:15	fled from the face of **P** and
Ex	6:11	tell **P** king of Egypt to let
Ex	7: 1	I have made you as God to **P**,
Ex	7: 9	rod and cast it before **P**,
Ex	7:15	Go to **P** in the morning, when
Ex	8:32	But **P** hardened his heart at
Ex	9: 7	But the heart of **P** became
Ex	9:12	hardened the heart of **P**;
Ex	9:35	So the heart of **P** was hard;
Ex	11: 1	yet one more plague on **P**
Ex	11: 5	from the firstborn of **P** who
Ex	12:30	So **P** rose in the night, he,
Ex	13:15	when **P** was stubborn about
Ex	13:17	when **P** had let the people
Ex	14: 4	and I will gain honor over **P**
Ex	14: 9	horses and chariots of **P**,
Deut	6:21	We were slaves of **P** in Egypt,
1Sa	6: 6	as the Egyptians and **P**
1Ki	3: 1	made a treaty with **P** king
1Ki	11: 1	as well as the daughter of **P**:
2Ki	23:29	In his days **P** Necho king of
2Ki	23:29	And **P** Necho killed him at
2Ki	23:34	Then **P** Necho made Eliakim the
Neh	9:10	signs and wonders against **P**,
Ps	136:15	But overthrew **P** and his army
Jer	44:30	I will give **P** Hophra king of
Jer	46:25	**P** and those who trust in him.
Ezek	30:25	but the arms of **P** shall fall
Acts	7:10	wisdom in the presence of **P**,
Rom	9:17	For the Scripture says to **P**,

PHARAOH'S (*see* PHARAOH)
Gen	12:15	And the woman was taken to **P**
Gen	40: 7	So he asked **P** officers who
Gen	40:11	Then **P** cup was in my hand;
Gen	40:20	which was **P** birthday, that
Gen	45:16	report of it was heard in **P**
Gen	47:25	and we will be **P** servants."
Ex	2: 7	Then his sister said to **P**

Ex   5:14 whom P taskmasters had set
Ex   7: 3 And I will harden P heart,
Ex   10:11 they were driven out from P
Ex   10:20 But the LORD hardened P
Ex   10:27 But the LORD hardened P
Ex   15: 4 P chariots and his army He
Song   1: 9 To my filly among P
Jer   37: 5 Then P army came up from
Ezek   30:24 but I will break P arms, and
Acts   7:21 P daughter took him away and
Heb   11:24 to be called the son of P

PHARISEE (see PHARISEES)
Matt   23:26 "Blind P, first cleanse the
Luke   11:37 a certain P asked Him to
Luke   18:10 one a P and the other a tax
Acts   5:34 a P named Gamaliel, a
Acts   23: 6 a Pharisee, the son of a P;
Acts   26: 5 of our religion I lived a P.
Phil   3: 5 concerning the law, a P;

PHARISEES (see PHARISEE, PHARISEES')
Matt   5:20 of the scribes and P,
Matt   9:14 Why do we and the P fast
Matt   16: 1 Then the P and Sadducees
Matt   16: 6 of the leaven of the P and
Matt   16:12 but of the doctrine of the P
Matt   21:45 when the chief priests and P
Matt   22:15 Then the P went and plotted
Matt   23: 2 The scribes and the P sit in
Matt   23:14 "Woe to you, scribes and P,
Mark   2:18 of John and of the P fast,
Luke   5:30 And their scribes and P
Luke   6: 7 So the scribes and P watched
Luke   7:30 But the P and lawyers
Luke   16:14 Now the P, who were
John   3: 1 There was a man of the P
John   7:45 to the chief priests and P,
John   9:13 formerly was blind to the P.
John   11:47 the chief priests and the P
Acts   23: 7 arose between the P and the

PHARISEES'†
Acts   23: 9 And the scribes of the P

PHARPAR†
2Ki   5:12 not the Abanah and the P,

PHICHOL
Gen   21:22 time that Abimelech and P,
Gen   26:26 and P the commander of his

PHILADELPHIA†
Rev   1:11 to Thyatira, to Sardis, to P,
Rev   3: 7 the angel of the church in P

PHILIP (see PHILIP'S)
Mark   3:18 Andrew, P, Bartholomew,
Luke   3: 1 his brother P tetrarch of
John   1:44 Now P was from Bethsaida, the
John   1:45 P found Nathanael and said to
John   12:22 P came and told Andrew, and
Acts   6: 5 and the Holy Spirit, and P,
Acts   8:26 angel of the Lord spoke to P,
Acts   8:29 Then the Spirit said to P,
Acts   8:38 And both P and the eunuch
Acts   21: 8 and entered the house of P

PHILIP'S† (see PHILIP)
Matt   14: 3 his brother P wife.
Mark   6:17 his brother P wife; for he
Luke   3:19 his brother P wife, and for

PHILIPPI (see PHILIPPIANS)
Acts   16:12 and from there to P,
Phil   1: 1 in Christ Jesus who are in P,
1Th   2: 2 were spitefully treated at P,

PHILIPPIANS† (see PHILIPPI)
Phil   4:15 Now you P know also that in

PHILISTIA (see PHILISTINE)
Ps   60: 8 Edom I will cast My shoe; P,
Ps   87: 4 O P and Tyre, with Ethiopia:
Ps   108: 9 Over P I will triumph."
Joel   3: 4 and all the coasts of P?

PHILISTINE (see PHILISTIA, PHILISTINES)
1Sa   17: 8 up for battle? Am I not a P,
1Sa   17:23 the P of Gath, Goliath by
1Sa   17:26 who is this uncircumcised P,
1Sa   17:43 And the P cursed David by
1Sa   17:49 slung it and struck the P
1Sa   17:50 David prevailed over the P
1Sa   17:54 took the head of the P and
1Sa   21: 9 "The sword of Goliath the P,

PHILISTINES (see PHILISTINE)
Gen   21:32 to the land of the P.
Gen   26: 1 to Abimelech king of the P,
Ex   13:17 by way of the land of the P,
Josh   13: 3 the five lords of the P—
Judg   3:31 six hundred men of the P
Judg   10: 6 Ammon, and the gods of the P;
Judg   13: 1 them into the hand of the P
Judg   14: 1 of the daughters of the P.
Judg   14: 3 from the uncircumcised P?
Judg   15: 5 the standing grain of the P,
Judg   16: 9 The P are upon you,
Judg   16:28 take vengeance on the P for
Judg   16:30 Let me die with the P!" And
1Sa   4: 2 Israel was defeated by the P,
1Sa   5: 1 Then the P took the ark of
1Sa   13: 4 an abomination to the P.
1Sa   18:25 hundred foreskins of the P,
2Sa   1:20 the daughters of the P
2Sa   3:14 a hundred foreskins of the P.
2Sa   5:25 and he drove back the P from
2Sa   8: 1 that David attacked the P
1Ki   4:21 River to the land of the P,
2Ch   26: 6 Ashdod and among the P.
Is   11:14 upon the shoulder of the P
Amos   1: 8 And the remnant of the P
Amos   6: 2 go down to Gath of the P,
Amos   9: 7 The P from Caphtor, And
Zeph   2: 5 O Canaan, land of the P:
Zech   9: 6 cut off the pride of the P.

PHILOSOPHERS† (see PHILOSOPHY)
Acts   17:18 Epicurean and Stoic p

PHILOSOPHY† (see PHILOSOPHERS)
Col   2: 8 anyone cheat you through p

PHINEHAS
Num   25: 7 Now when P the son of
Josh   22:30 Now when P the priest and
1Sa   1: 3 sons of Eli, Hophni and P,
Ps   106:30 Then P stood up and

PHOEBE†
Rom   16: 1 I commend to you P our

PHOENICIA
Acts   21: 2 a ship sailing over to P,

PHRYGIA
Acts   16: 6 they had gone through P and

PHYLACTERIES†
Matt   23: 5 They make their p broad and

PHYSICAL†
Gal   4:13 You know that because of p

PHYSICIAN (see PHYSICIANS)
Jer   8:22 Is there no p there? Why
Matt   9:12 are well have no need of a p,
Luke   4:23 say this proverb to Me, 'P,
Col   4:14 Luke the beloved p and Demas

PHYSICIANS (see PHYSICIAN)
Gen 50: 2 his servants the **p** to
Job 13: 4 You are all worthless **p**.
Mark 5:26 many things from many **p**.
Luke 8:43 all her livelihood on **p** and

PICK (see PICKED)
2Ki 4:36 **P** up your son."
Jon 1:12 **P** me up and throw me into the

PICKED (see PICK)
2Ki 4:37 then she **p** up her son and
Jon 1:15 So they **p** up Jonah and threw

PIECE (see PIECES)
Ruth 2:14 and dip your **p** of bread in
Job 42:11 Each one gave him a **p** of
Amos 3:12 of a lion Two legs or a **p**
Matt 9:16 No one puts a **p** of unshrunk
Matt 17:27 you will find a **p** of money;
Luke 15: 9 for I have found the **p** which
Luke 24:42 So they gave Him a **p** of a
John 13:30 Having received the **p** of
John 19:23 woven from the top in one **p**.

PIECES (see PIECE)
Gen 15:17 that passed between those **p**.
Gen 37:33 doubt Joseph is torn to **p**.
Josh 24:32 of Shechem for one hundred **p**
Judg 19:29 divided her into twelve **p**,
1Sa 11: 7 of oxen and cut them in **p**,
1Sa 15:33 And Samuel hacked Agag in **p**
1Ki 11:30 and tore it into twelve **p**.
Ps 2: 3 us break Their bonds in **p**
Ps 2: 9 You shall dash them to **p**
Ps 72: 4 And will break in **p** the
Ps 74:14 the heads of Leviathan in **p**,
Ps 89:10 You have broken Rahab in **p**,
Is 13:16 also will be dashed to **p**
Jer 23:29 that breaks the rock in **p**?
Jer 50: 2 Merodach is broken in **p**;
Jer 51:20 I will break the nation in **p**;
Jer 51:21 With you I will break in **p**
Lam 3:11 my ways and torn me in **p**;
Ezek 24: 4 Gather **p** of meat in it,
Dan 2: 5 you shall be cut in **p**,
Dan 2:40 as iron breaks in **p** and
Dan 2:40 kingdom will break in **p**
Dan 3:29 Abed-Nego shall be cut in **p**,
Dan 6:24 broke all their bones in **p**
Hos 13:16 infants shall be dashed in **p**,
Amos 6:11 And the little house into **p**.
Zech 11:12 out for my wages thirty **p**
Matt 26:15 counted out to him thirty **p**
Matt 27: 5 Then he threw down the **p** of
Rev 2:27 shall be dashed to **p**

PIERCE (see PIERCED, PIERCING)
Ex 21: 6 and his master shall **p** his
2Ki 18:21 will go into his hand and **p**
Job 41: 2 Or **p** his jaw with a hook?
Luke 2:35 a sword will **p** through your

PIERCED (see PIERCE)
Judg 5:26 she **p** his head, She split
Ps 22:16 They **p** My hands and My
Zech 12:10 will look on Me whom they **p**.
John 19:34 But one of the soldiers **p** His
John 19:37 on Him whom they **p**.
1Ti 6:10 and **p** themselves through
Rev 1: 7 even they who **p** Him. And all

PIERCING† (see PIERCE)
Heb 4:12 **p** even to the division of

PIGEON† (see PIGEONS)
Gen 15: 9 a turtledove, and a young **p**.
Lev 12: 6 and a young **p** or a

PIGEONS (see PIGEON)
Lev 5: 7 turtledoves or two young **p**,
Luke 2:24 or two young **p**.

PILATE (see PONTIUS)
Matt 27: 2 delivered Him to Pontius **P**
Luke 3: 1 Pontius **P** being governor of
Luke 13: 1 the Galileans whose blood **P**
Luke 23: 1 them arose and led Him to **P**.
Luke 23:12 That very day **P** and Herod
John 18:33 Then **P** entered the Praetorium
1Ti 6:13 confession before Pontius **P**,

PILGRIMAGE (see PILGRIMS)
Gen 47: 9 days of the years of my **p**
Ps 84: 5 Whose heart is set on **p**.

PILGRIMS (see PILGRIMAGE)
Heb 11:13 they were strangers and **p**
1Pe 1: 1 To the **p** of the Dispersion

PILLAR (see PILLARS)
Gen 19:26 and she became a **p** of salt.
Gen 28:18 his head, set it up as a **p**,
Gen 31:52 and this **p** is a witness,
Ex 13:21 and by night in a **p** of fire
2Sa 18:18 had taken and set up a **p**
1Ki 7:21 he set up the **p** on the right
2Ki 23: 3 Then the king stood by a **p**
Jer 1:18 fortified city and an iron **p**,
1Ti 3:15 the **p** and ground of the

PILLARS (see PILLAR)
Ex 23:24 break down their sacred **p**.
Ex 24: 4 and twelve **p** according to
Judg 16:26 Let me feel the **p** which
1Ki 7: 6 He also made the Hall of **P**:
Job 26:11 The **p** of heaven tremble,
Ps 144:12 our daughters may be as **p**,
Prov 9: 1 has hewn out her seven **p**;
Song 5:15 His legs are **p** of marble
Joel 2:30 Blood and fire and **p** of
Gal 2: 9 and John, who seemed to be **p**,
Rev 10: 1 and his feet like **p** of fire.

PIM
1Sa 13:21 for a sharpening was a **p**

PIN
1Sa 18:11 I will **p** David to the wall!"

PINNACLE†
Matt 4: 5 set Him on the **p** of the
Luke 4: 9 set Him on the **p** of the

PIPES
Zech 4: 2 seven lamps with seven **p** to

PISGAH (see NEBO)
Deut 34: 1 Mount Nebo, to the top of **P**,

PISHON†
Gen 2:11 The name of the first is **P**;

PISIDIA
Acts 13:14 they came to Antioch in **P**,

PIT (see PITS)
Gen 37:22 but cast him into this **p**
Job 33:18 back his soul from the **P**,
Ps 7:15 He made a **p** and dug it out,
Ps 28: 1 those who go down to the **p**.
Ps 40: 2 me up out of a horrible **p**,
Ps 49: 9 And not see the **P**.
Ps 88: 6 have laid me in the lowest **p**,
Prov 23:27 For a harlot is a deep **p**,
Is 14:15 the lowest depths of the **P**.
Is 24:17 Fear and the **p** and the snare
Is 38:17 my soul from the **p** of
Jer 18:20 For they have dug a **p** for
Jer 48:43 Fear and the **p** and the snare
Ezek 28: 8 throw you down into the **P**,

Jon 2: 6 up my life from the **p**,
Matt 12:11 and if it falls into a **p** on
Rev 9:11 angel of the bottomless **p**,

PITCH (see PITCHED)
Gen 6:14 it inside and outside with **p**.
Ex 2: 3 daubed it with asphalt and **p**,
Jer 10:20 There is no one to **p** my

PITCHED (see PITCH)
Gen 13:12 cities of the plain and **p**
Ex 33: 7 Moses took his tent and **p** it

PITCHER (see PITCHERS)
Gen 24:15 came out with her **p** on her
Eccl 12: 6 Or the **p** shattered at the
Mark 14:13 will meet you carrying a **p**

PITCHERS (see PITCHER)
Ex 7:19 in buckets of wood and **p**
Judg 7:16 and torches inside the **p**.
Mark 7: 4 like the washing of cups, **p**,

PITHOM†
Ex 1:11 cities, **P** and Raamses.

PITIABLE† (see PITY)
1Co 15:19 we are of all men the most **p**.

PITIES (see PITY)
Ps 103:13 As a father **p** his children,

PITS (see PIT)
Gen 14:10 was full of asphalt **p**;

PITY (see PITIABLE, PITIES)
Deut 13: 8 nor shall your eye **p** him,
Judg 2:18 the LORD was moved to **p** by
2Sa 12: 6 and because he had no **p**.
Ezek 7: 9 spare, Nor will I have **p**;
Amos 1:11 sword, And cast off all **p**;
Jon 4:11 And should I not **p** Nineveh,
Matt 18:33 just as I had **p** on you?'

PLAGUE (see PLAGUES)
Ex 11: 1 will bring yet one more **p**
Lev 13:47 if a garment has a leprous **p**
Deut 28:61 every sickness and every **p**,
1Ch 21:14 So the LORD sent a **p** upon
Ps 91:10 Nor shall any **p** come near
Acts 24: 5 we have found this man a **p**,

PLAGUES (see PLAGUE)
Gen 12:17 and his house with great **p**
Hos 13:14 I will be your **p**! O Grave,
Rev 9:18 By these three **p** a third of
Rev 15: 1 having the seven last **p**,
Rev 22:18 God will add to him the **p**

PLAIN (see PLAINLY, PLAINS)
Gen 19:29 the cities of the **p**,
Ezek 8: 4 vision that I saw in the **p**.
Hab 2: 2 the vision And make it **p**

PLAINLY (see PLAIN)
Num 12: 8 him face to face, Even **p**,
Mark 7:35 was loosed, and he spoke **p**.
John 10:24 are the Christ, tell us **p**.

PLAINS (see PLAIN)
Num 26: 3 spoke with them in the **p** of
Josh 4:13 to the **p** of Jericho.

PLAN (see PLANNED, PLANS)
Ps 140: 2 Who **p** evil things in their
Acts 5:38 for if this **p** or this work

PLANK
Matt 7: 5 First remove the **p** from

PLANNED (see PLAN)
Rom 1:13 that I often **p** to come to

PLANS (see PLAN)
Prov 6:18 heart that devises wicked **p**,
Prov 16: 9 A man's heart **p** his way,
Jer 18:18 Come and let us devise **p**

PLANT (see PLANTED, PLANTS)
Gen 2: 5 before any **p** of the field was
Deut 6:11 trees which you did not **p**—
Eccl 3: 2 a time to die; A time to **p**,
Is 5: 7 of Judah are His pleasant **p**.
Is 53: 2 up before Him as a tender **p**,
Jer 1:10 down, To build and to **p**.
Jer 18: 9 to build and to **p** it,
Amos 9:15 I will **p** them in their land,
Jon 4: 6 the LORD God prepared a **p**

PLANTED (see PLANT)
Gen 2: 8 The LORD God **p** a garden
Gen 9:20 and he **p** a vineyard.
Ps 1: 3 He shall be like a tree **P**
Ps 80:15 which Your right hand has **p**,
Ps 94: 9 He who the ear, shall He
Eccl 3: 2 a time to pluck what is **p**;
Is 5: 2 And **p** it with the choicest
Is 40:24 Scarcely shall they be **p**,
Jer 17: 8 he shall be like a tree **p**
Matt 21:33 a certain landowner who **p** a
Luke 17: 6 up by the roots and be **p** in
Luke 17:28 bought, they sold, they **p**,
1Co 3: 6 I **p**, Apollos watered, but

PLANTS (see PLANT)
Prov 31:16 From her profits she **p** a
1Co 3: 7 So then neither he who **p** is

PLASTER
Dan 5: 5 the lampstand on the **p** of

PLATFORM
Neh 8: 4 the scribe stood on a **p** of

PLATTER
Matt 14: 8 Baptist's head here on a **p**.

PLAY (see PLAYED, PLAYING)
Gen 4:21 father of all those who **p**
Ex 32: 6 and drink, and rose up to **p**
Ex 34:15 and they **p** the harlot with
1Sa 16:17 me now a man who can **p** well,
1Co 10: 7 and rose up to **p**.

PLAYED (see PLAY)
1Sa 26:21 Indeed I have **p** the fool and
Matt 11:17 We **p** the flute for you, And
Gal 2:13 the rest of the Jews also **p**

PLAYER†
1Sa 16:16 a man who is a skillful **p**

PLAYING (see PLAY)
1Sa 16:18 who is skillful in **p**,
Rev 14: 2 the sound of harpists **p**

PLEAD (see PLEADED, PLEADING, PLEADS)
Judg 6:31 let him **p** for himself,
Ps 35: 1 **P** my cause, O LORD, with
Is 1:17 **P** for the widow.
1Co 1:10 Now I **p** with you, brethren,

PLEADED (see PLEAD)
Ex 32:11 Then Moses **p** with the LORD
Luke 15:28 his father came out and **p**
2Co 12: 8 Concerning this thing I **p**

PLEADING (see PLEAD)
Luke 7: 3 **p** with Him to come and heal
2Co 5:20 as though God were **p** through

PLEADS (see PLEAD)
Is 51:22 Who **p** the cause of His
Rom 11: 2 how he **p** with God against

PLEASANT (*see* PLEASANTNESS)
Gen   3: 6 that it was **p** to the eyes,
2Sa   1:26 You have been very **p** to me;
Ps   16: 6 lines have fallen to me in **p**
Ps   133: 1 how good and how **p** it is
Prov   9:17 bread eaten in secret is **p**.
Song   7: 6 How fair and how **p** you are,
Is   5: 7 the men of Judah are His **p**
Mal   3: 4 and Jerusalem Will be **p** to

PLEASANTNESS† (*see* PLEASANT)
Prov   3:17 Her ways are ways of **p**,

PLEASE (*see* PLEASED, PLEASES, PLEASING)
Gen   12:13 **P** say you are my sister,
Gen   16: 6 hand; do to her as you **p**.
Gen   28: 8 of Canaan did not **p** his
Ruth   2: 7 **P** let me glean and gather
1Sa   25:24 this iniquity be! And **p**
Prov   16: 7 When a man's ways **p** the
Is   55:11 it shall accomplish what I **p**,
Jon   4: 3 **p** take my life from me, for
John   8:29 do those things that **p** Him.
Rom   8: 8 are in the flesh cannot **p**
Rom   15: 2 Let each of us **p** his
Rom   15: 3 For even Christ did not **p**
1Co   7:32 how he may **p** the Lord.
1Co   7:33 how he may **p** his wife.
1Co   7:34 how she may **p** her husband.
Gal   1:10 Or do I seek to **p** men? For
1Th   4: 1 you ought to walk and to **p**
2Ti   2: 4 that he may **p** him who
Heb   11: 6 it is impossible to **p**

PLEASED (*see* PLEASE)
Num   24: 1 when Balaam saw that it **p**
Judg   14: 7 and she **p** Samson well.
2Sa   3:36 whatever the king did **p** all
Neh   2: 6 So it **p** the king to send
Ps   40:13 Be **p**, O LORD, to
Ps   51:19 Then You shall be **p** with the
Is   53:10 Yet it **p** the LORD to
Dan   6: 1 It **p** Darius to set over the
Jon   1:14 have done as it **p** You."
Mic   6: 7 Will the LORD be **p** with
Mal   1: 8 governor! Would he be **p**
Matt   3:17 Son, in whom I am well **p**.
Matt   14: 6 danced before them and **p**
1Co   1:21 it **p** God through the
1Co   10: 5 of them God was not well **p**,
Gal   1:10 For if I still **p** men, I
Gal   1:15 But when it **p** God, who
Col   1:19 For it **p** the Father that
Heb   11: 5 testimony, that he **p** God.
Heb   13:16 sacrifices God is well **p**.
2Pe   1:17 Son, in whom I am well **p**.

PLEASES (*see* PLEASE)
Judg   14: 3 for she **p** me well."
Ps   115: 3 He does whatever He **p**.
Ps   135: 6 Whatever the LORD **p** He
Eccl   8: 3 for he does whatever **p**
Song   2: 7 nor awaken love Until it **p**.

PLEASING (*see* PLEASE)
Acts   7:20 and was well **p** to God; and
Phil   4:18 sacrifice, well **p** to God.
Col   1:10 fully **p** Him, being fruitful
1Th   2: 4 not as **p** men, but God who
Heb   13:21 in you what is well **p** in
1Jn   3:22 do those things that are **p**

PLEASURE (*see* PLEASURES)
Gen   18:12 grown old, shall I have **p**,
Ps   5: 4 are not a God who takes **p**
Ps   35:27 Who has **p** in the prosperity
Ps   51:18 Do good in Your good **p** to
Ps   103:21 of His, who do His **p**.

Ps   111: 2 Studied by all who have **p**
Ps   147:11 The LORD takes **p** in those
Ps   149: 4 For the LORD takes **p** in His
Eccl   12: 1 I have no **p** in them":
Is   53:10 And the **p** of the LORD
Is   58:13 From doing your **p** on My
Mal   1:10 I have no **p** in you," Says
Luke   12:32 it is your Father's good **p**
2Co   12:10 Therefore I take **p** in
Eph   1: 5 according to the good **p** of
Phil   2:13 and to do for His good **p**.
1Ti   5: 6 But she who lives in **p** is
2Ti   3: 4 lovers of **p** rather than
Heb   10: 8 nor had **p** in them"
Heb   10:38 My soul has no **p** in
Jas   4: 1 from your desires for **p**

PLEASURES (*see* PLEASURE)
Ps   16:11 At Your right hand are **p**
Luke   8:14 and **p** of life, and bring no
Tit   3: 3 serving various lusts and **p**,
Heb   11:25 than to enjoy the passing **p**
Jas   4: 3 you may spend it on your **p**.

PLEDGE
Ex   22:26 neighbor's garment as a **p**,
Deut   24:17 a widow's garment as a **p**.
Prov   17:18 shakes hands in a **p**
Amos   2: 8 altar on clothes taken in **p**,

PLEIADES
Job   9: 9 the Bear, Orion, and the **P**,
Amos   5: 8 He made the **P** and Orion; He

PLENTIFUL (*see* PLENTY)
Gen   41:34 land of Egypt in the seven **p**
Matt   9:37 "The harvest truly is **p**,

PLENTY (*see* PLENTIFUL)
Gen   41:53 Then the seven years of **p**
Jer   44:17 For then we had **p** of food,

PLOT (*see* PLOTS, PLOTTED)
Josh   24:32 in the **p** of ground which
Neh   4:15 God had brought their **p** to
Ps   2: 1 And the people **p** a vain
Ps   35: 4 brought to confusion Who **p**
John   4: 5 near the **p** of ground that
Acts   4:25 And the people **p** vain

PLOTS (*see* PLOT)
Ps   64: 2 Hide me from the secret **p** of

PLOTTED (*see* PLOT)
Matt   12:14 the Pharisees went out and **p**
John   11:53 they **p** to put Him to death.
Acts   5:33 they were furious and **p** to

PLOW (*see* PLOWED, PLOWING, PLOWMAN, PLOWSHARE)
Deut   22:10 You shall not **p** with an ox
Job   4: 8 Those who **p** iniquity And
Amos   6:12 Does one **p** there with
Luke   9:62 having put his hand to the **p**,
1Co   9:10 that he who plows should **p**

PLOWED (*see* PLOW)
Judg   14:18 If you had not **p** with my
Jer   26:18 Zion shall be **p** like a
Mic   3:12 of you Zion shall be **p**

PLOWING (*see* PLOW)
1Ki   19:19 who was **p** with twelve yoke

PLOWMAN (*see* PLOW)
Amos   9:13 When the **p** shall overtake the

PLOWSHARE† (*see* PLOW, PLOWSHARES)
1Sa   13:20 to sharpen each man's **p**,

PLOWSHARES (*see* PLOWSHARE)
Is   2: 4 beat their swords into **p**,
Joel   3:10 Beat your **p** into swords And

Mic   4: 3 beat their swords into **p**,

PLUCK (*see* PLUCKED)
Deut 23:25 you may **p** the heads with
Eccl   3: 2 And a time to **p** what is
Jer   18: 7 to **p** up, to pull down, and
Matt   5:29 **p** it out and cast it from
Matt 12: 1 and began to **p** heads of
Mark   9:47 **p** it out. It is better for

PLUCKED (*see* PLUCK)
Gen   8:11 a freshly **p** olive leaf was
Dan   7: 8 of the first horns were **p**
Amos   4:11 you were like a firebrand **p**
Luke   6: 1 And His disciples **p** the

PLUMB
Amos   7: 7 on a wall made with a **p**
Zech   4:10 seven rejoice to see The **p**

PLUMMET
Is   28:17 And righteousness the **p**;

PLUNDER (*see* PLUNDERED, PLUNDERERS, PLUNDERING)
Ex   3:22 So you shall **p** the
Ezra   9: 7 sword, to captivity, to **p**,
Esth   3:13 and to **p** their possessions.
Esth   9:10 did not lay a hand on the **p**.
Ps   109:11 And let strangers **p** his
Jer   20: 8 Violence and **p**!" Because
Matt 12:29 a strong man's house and **p**
Matt 12:29 And then he will **p** his

PLUNDERED (*see* PLUNDER)
Ex   12:36 Thus they **p** the Egyptians.
Ps   137: 3 And those who **p** us
Jer   4:20 For the whole land is **p**.
Ezek 39:10 will plunder those who **p**
Hab   2: 8 Because you have **p** many

PLUNDERERS (*see* PLUNDER)
Judg   2:14 them into the hands of **p**

PLUNDERING (*see* PLUNDER)
Is   22: 4 me Because of the **p** of the
Jer   48: 3 **P** and great destruction!'

PODS†
Luke   15:16 his stomach with the **p** that

POETS†
Acts   17:28 as also some of your own **p**

POINT (*see* POINTS)
Judg   5:18 their lives to the **p** of
Jer   17: 1 With the **p** of a diamond it
Mark   5:23 daughter lies at the **p** of
Phil   2: 8 became obedient to the **p**
Jas   2:10 and yet stumble in one **p**,

POINTS (*see* POINT)
1Sa   13:21 and to set the **p** of the
Prov   6:13 He **p** with his fingers;
Heb   4:15 but was in all **p** tempted as

POISON
Ps   140: 3 The **p** of asps is under
Rom   3:13 The **p** of asps is under
Jas   3: 8 evil, full of deadly **p**.

POLE
Num   13:23 between two of them on a **p**.
Num   21: 8 serpent, and set it on a **p**;

POLLUTED
Ps   106:38 And the land was **p** with
Prov   25:26 a murky spring and a **p** well.
Jer   3: 1 not that land be greatly **p**?
Acts   15:20 to abstain from things **p** by

POMEGRANATE (*see* POMEGRANATES)
Ex   28:34 "a golden bell and a **p**,
Song   6: 7 Like a piece of **p** Are your

POMEGRANATES (*see* POMEGRANATE)
Ex   39:24 on the hem of the robe **p** of
Ex   39:25 put the bells between the **p**
Num   20: 5 grain or figs or vines or **p**;
Song   4:13 plants are an orchard of **p**

POMP (*see* POMPOUS)
Is   14:11 Your **p** is brought down to
Acts   25:23 had come with great **p**,

POMPOUS (*see* POMP)
Dan   7: 8 and a mouth speaking **p**

PONDER† (*see* PONDERED)
Prov   4:26 **P** the path of your feet,
Prov   5: 6 Lest you **p** her path of

PONDERED (*see* PONDER)
Luke   2:19 kept all these things and **p**

PONTIUS (*see* PILATE)
Matt 27: 2 away and delivered Him to **P**
1Ti   6:13 the good confession before **P**

PONTUS
Acts   18: 2 Jew named Aquila, born in **P**,
1Pe   1: 1 of the Dispersion in **P**,

POOL (*see* POOLS)
2Ki   18:17 aqueduct from the upper **p**,
2Ki   20:20 and how he made a **p** and a
Is   22: 9 the waters of the lower **p**.
John   5: 7 no man to put me into the **p**
John   9: 7 wash in the **p** of Siloam"

POOLS (*see* POOL)
Ps   107:35 turns a wilderness into **p**
Song   7: 4 Your eyes like the **p** in
Is   42:15 And I will dry up the **p**.

POOR (*see* POOREST)
Gen   41:19 **p** and very ugly and gaunt,
Deut   15: 4 when there may be no **p**
Deut   15:11 For the **p** will never cease
Ruth   3:10 whether **p** or rich.
2Sa   12: 4 but he took the **p** man's lamb
Job   5:16 So the **p** have hope, And
Job   24:10 They cause the **p** to go
Job   24:14 He kills the **p** and needy;
Job   29:16 I was a father to the **p**,
Job   34:28 caused the cry of the **p** to
Ps   34: 6 This **p** man cried out, and
Ps   40:17 But I am **p** and needy; Yet
Ps   69:29 But I am **p** and sorrowful;
Ps   82: 3 Defend the **p** and fatherless;
Ps   113: 7 He raises the **p** out of the
Ps   132:15 I will satisfy her **p** with
Prov   14:20 The **p** man is hated even by
Prov   14:31 He who oppresses the **p**
Prov   19:22 And a **p** man is better than
Prov   22: 9 gives of his bread to the **p**
Prov   22:16 He who oppresses the **p** to
Prov   22:22 Do not rob the **p** because he
Prov   29:14 The king who judges the **p**
Prov   31:20 extends her hand to the **p**,
Is   3:15 grinding the faces of the **p**?
Is   41:17 The **p** and needy seek water,
Is   61: 1 preach good tidings to the **p**;
Amos   2: 6 And the **p** for a pair of
Amos   8: 6 That we may buy the **p** for
Matt   5: 3 Blessed are the **p** in spirit,
Matt 11: 5 are raised up and the **p**
Matt 19:21 you have and give to the **p**,
Matt 26:11 For you have the **p** with you
Mark 12:42 Then one **p** widow came and
Mark 14: 5 denarii and given to the **p**.
Luke   4:18 the gospel to the **p**;
Luke   6:20 "Blessed are you **p**,
Luke 14:13 give a feast, invite the **p**,

Luke 19: 8 half of my goods to the **p**;
Rom 15:26 contribution for the **p**
1Co 13: 3 all my goods to feed the **p**,
2Co 6:10 yet always rejoicing; as **p**,
2Co 8: 9 for your sakes He became **p**,
Jas 2: 2 should also come in a **p** man
Rev 3:17 are wretched, miserable, **p**,
Rev 13:16 small and great, rich and **p**,

POOREST (see POOR)
2Ki 24:14 None remained except the **p**

POPULATED
Gen 9:19 these the whole earth was **p**.

PORCH (see PORCHES)
John 10:23 the temple, in Solomon's **p**.

PORCHES (see PORCH)
John 5: 2 Bethesda, having five **p**.

PORTION (see PORTIONS, SHARE)
Gen 14:24 Mamre; let them take their **p**.
Lev 2: 9 grain offering a memorial **p**,
Deut 10: 9 Therefore Levi has no **p** nor
Deut 21:17 by giving him a double **p** of
1Sa 1: 5 he would give a double **p**,
2Ki 2: 9 Please let a double **p** of your
Ps 11: 6 wind Shall be the **p** of
Ps 16: 5 You are the **p** of my
Ps 73:26 of my heart and my **p**
Ps 119:57 You are my **p**, O LORD;
Prov 31:15 And a **p** for her
Eccl 9: 9 for that is your **p** in life,
Is 53:12 I will divide Him a **p** with
Jer 10:16 The **P** of Jacob is not like
Jer 51:19 The **P** of Jacob is not like
Dan 1: 8 defile himself with the **p**
Dan 1:13 the young men who eat the **p**
Matt 24:51 two and appoint him his **p**
Luke 15:12 give me the **p** of goods that

PORTIONS (see PORTION)
Neh 8:10 and send **p** to those for whom
Neh 8:12 to send **p** and rejoice
Ezek 47:13 Joseph shall have two **p**.

PORTRAYED
Gal 3: 1 Jesus Christ was clearly **p**

POSITION
Ps 62: 4 him down from his high **p**;
1Ti 3: 1 If a man desires the **p** of a

POSSESS (see POSSESSED, POSSESSES, POSSESSING, POSSESSION, POSSESSOR)
Gen 22:17 and your descendants shall **p**
Deut 4: 5 the land which you go to **p**.
Deut 4:22 you shall cross over and **p**
Deut 19: 2 your God is giving you to **p**.
Josh 1:11 to go in to **p** the land which
Dan 7:18 and **p** the kingdom forever,
Dan 7:22 came for the saints to **p**
Amos 9:12 That they may **p** the remnant
Luke 18:12 give tithes of all that I **p**.
Luke 21:19 By your patience **p** your
1Co 7:30 buy as though they did not **p**,
1Th 4: 4 of you should know how to **p**

POSSESSED (see POSSESS)
Josh 13: 1 very much land yet to be **p**.
Neh 9:24 the people went in And **p**
Prov 8:22 The LORD **p** me at the
Acts 16:16 that a certain slave girl **p**

POSSESSES (see POSSESS)
Luke 12:15 abundance of the things he **p**.

POSSESSING (see POSSESS)
2Co 6:10 and yet **p** all things.

POSSESSION (see POSSESS, POSSESSIONS)
Gen 17: 8 Canaan, as an everlasting **p**;
Gen 36:43 in the land of their **p**.
Gen 49:30 of Ephron the Hittite as a **p**
Lev 25:10 of you shall return to his **p**,
Lev 25:34 for it is their perpetual **p**.
2Ki 17:24 and they took **p** of Samaria
Ps 2: 8 of the earth for Your **p**.
Acts 5: 1 Sapphira his wife, sold a **p**.
Acts 7: 5 to give it to him for a **p**,
Eph 1:14 of the purchased **p**,
Heb 10:34 a better and an enduring **p**

POSSESSIONS (see POSSESSION)
Gen 15:14 shall come out with great **p**.
Gen 26:14 possessions of flocks and **p**
Deut 21:16 the day he bequeaths his **p**
Job 1:10 and his **p** have increased in
Ps 104:24 The earth is full of Your **p**—
Prov 3: 9 Honor the LORD with your **p**,
Prov 28: 8 One who increases his **p** by
Matt 19:22 for he had great **p**.
Luke 15:13 and there wasted his **p** with
Acts 2:45 and sold their **p** and goods,

POSSESSOR (see POSSESS)
Gen 14:19 **P** of heaven and earth;

POSSIBLE
Matt 19:26 with God all things are **p**.
Matt 24:24 and wonders to deceive, if **p**,
Matt 26:39 "O My Father, if it is **p**,
Mark 9:23 all things are **p** to him who
Luke 18:27 impossible with men are **p**
Rom 12:18 If it is **p**, as much as
Heb 10: 4 For it is not **p** that the

POSTERITY
Gen 45: 7 before you to preserve a **p**
Ps 22:30 A **p** shall serve Him. It
Ps 109:13 Let his **p** be cut off, And
Is 14:22 And offspring and **p**,

POSTPONED
Ezek 12:28 None of My words will be **p**

POSTS
Is 6: 4 And the **p** of the door were

POT (see POTS, POTSHERD, WASHPOT, WATERPOT)
Ex 16:33 Take a **p** and put an omer of
Eccl 7: 6 of thorns under a **p**,
Jer 1:13 I said, "I see a boiling **p**,
Zech 14:21 every **p** in Jerusalem and
Heb 9: 4 in which were the golden **p**

POTENTATE†
1Ti 6:15 is the blessed and only **P**,

POTIPHAR†
Gen 37:36 had sold him in Egypt to **P**,
Gen 39: 1 taken down to Egypt. And **P**,

POTS (see POT)
Zech 14:20 The **p** in the LORD's house

POTSHERD (see POT)
Job 2: 8 And he took for himself a **p**
Ps 22:15 is dried up like a **p**,
Jer 19: 2 is by the entry of the **P**

POTTER (see POTTER'S)
Is 29:16 turned around! Shall the **p**
Is 41:25 As the **p** treads clay.
Is 64: 8 are the clay, and You our **p**;
Jer 18: 4 marred in the hand of the **p**;
Zech 11:13 Throw it to the **p**"—that
Rom 9:21 Does not the **p** have power

POTTER'S (see POTTER)
Ps 2: 9 dash them to pieces like a **p**
Jer 18: 6 as the clay is in the **p**

Dan 2:41 partly of **p** clay and partly
Matt 27: 7 and bought with them the **p**

POUCH†
1Sa 17:40 in a **p** which he had, and his

POULTICE†
Is 38:21 and apply it as a **p** on the

POUND (see POUNDS)
John 12: 3 Then Mary took a **p** of very

POUNDS† (see POUND)
John 19:39 and aloes, about a hundred **p**.

POUR (see POURED, POURING)
Ex 4: 9 water from the river and **p**
Ex 29:12 and **p** all the blood beside
Lev 2: 1 And he shall **p** oil on it,
Lev 4:25 and **p** its blood at the base
Lev 17:13 he shall **p** out its blood and
Job 3:24 And my groanings **p** out like
Job 16:20 My eyes **p** out tears to
Ps 42: 4 I **p** out my soul within me.
Ps 62: 8 **P** out your heart before
Ps 79: 6 **P** out Your wrath on the
Is 44: 3 I will **p** My Spirit on your
Is 45: 8 And let the skies **p** down
Jer 44:25 to the queen of heaven and **p**
Joel 2:28 afterward That I will **p**
Joel 2:29 My maidservants I will **p**
Mal 3:10 the windows of heaven And **p**
Rev 16: 1 Go and **p** out the bowls of the

POURED (see POUR)
Gen 28:18 and **p** oil on top of it.
Lev 4:12 where the ashes are **p** out,
Lev 8:15 And he **p** the blood at the
Lev 21:10 the anointing oil was **p** and
Judg 5: 4 trembled and the heavens **p**,
1Sa 1:15 but have **p** out my soul
Ps 22:14 I am **p** out like water, And
Song 1: 3 Your name is ointment **p**
Is 32:15 Until the Spirit is **p** upon
Is 53:12 Because He **p** out His soul
Jer 7:20 anger and My fury will be **p**
Matt 26: 7 and she **p** it on His head as
John 2:15 and **p** out the changers'
John 13: 5 He **p** water into a basin and
Acts 2:33 He **p** out this which you now
Rom 5: 5 the love of God has been **p**
Phil 2:17 and if I am being **p** out as
Rev 16: 2 So the first went and **p** out

POURING (see POUR)
Matt 26:12 For in **p** this fragrant oil on
Luke 10:34 **p** on oil and wine; and he

POVERTY
Prov 6:11 So shall your **p** come on you
Prov 11:24 right, But it leads to **p**.
Prov 14:23 chatter leads only to **p**.
Prov 20:13 sleep, lest you come to **p**;
Prov 23:21 the glutton will come to **p**,
Prov 31: 7 him drink and forget his **p**,
Mark 12:44 but she out of her **p** put in
2Co 8: 2 their joy and their deep **p**
2Co 8: 9 that you through His **p** might
Rev 2: 9 and **p** (but you are rich);

POWDER
Ex 32:20 fire, and ground it to **p**;
Matt 21:44 it will grind him to **p**.

POWER (see POWERFUL, POWERLESS, POWERS)
Gen 31:29 It is in my **p** to do you harm,
Ex 9:16 that I may show My **p** in
1Ch 29:11 The **p** and the glory, The
Ps 21:13 will sing and praise Your **p**.
Ps 22:20 precious life from the **p**

Ps 49:15 redeem my soul from the **p**
Ps 65: 6 Being clothed with **p**;
Ps 66: 3 the greatness of Your **p**
Ps 68:35 He who gives strength and **p**
Ps 78:42 They did not remember His **p**:
Ps 89:48 deliver his life from the **p**
Ps 90:11 Who knows the **p** of Your
Prov 3:27 When it is in the **p** of your
Is 40:29 He gives **p** to the weak, And
Jer 10:12 has made the earth by His **p**,
Dan 2:37 has given you a kingdom, **p**,
Dan 3:27 bodies the fire had no **p**;
Dan 4:30 dwelling by my mighty **p** and
Dan 6:27 delivered Daniel from the **p**
Mic 2: 1 Because it is in the **p** of
Mic 3: 8 But truly I am full of **p** by
Nah 1: 3 slow to anger and great in **p**,
Zech 4: 6 'Not by might nor by **p**,
Matt 6:13 is the kingdom and the **p**
Matt 9: 6 that the Son of Man has **p**
Matt 9: 8 who had given such **p** to men.
Matt 10: 1 He gave them **p** over unclean
Matt 22:29 the Scriptures nor the **p** of
Matt 24:30 the clouds of heaven with **p**
Matt 26:64 at the right hand of the **P**,
Mark 3:15 and to have **p** to heal
Mark 5:30 knowing in Himself that **p**
Mark 9: 1 of God present with **p**.
Luke 1:17 Him in the spirit and **p** of
Luke 1:35 and the **p** of the Highest
Luke 4:14 Jesus returned in the **p** of
Luke 6:19 for **p** went out from Him and
Luke 8:46 for I perceived **p** going out
Luke 12: 5 has **p** to cast into hell;
Luke 22:53 and the **p** of darkness."
Luke 22:69 on the right hand of the **p**
Luke 24:49 until you are endued with **p**
John 10:18 I have **p** to lay it down, and
John 19:10 You not know that I have **p**
John 19:11 You could have no **p** at all
Acts 1: 8 But you shall receive **p** when
Acts 4: 7 By what **p** or by what name
Acts 6: 8 Stephen, full of faith and **p**,
Acts 10:38 the Holy Spirit and with **p**,
Acts 26:18 and from the **p** of Satan to
Rom 1: 4 be the Son of God with **p**
Rom 1:16 for it is the **p** of God to
Rom 1:20 even His eternal **p** and
Rom 9:17 that I may show My **p**
Rom 9:21 Does not the potter have **p**
Rom 9:22 His wrath and to make His **p**
Rom 15:13 may abound in hope by the **p**
1Co 1:18 are being saved it is the **p**
1Co 1:24 Christ the **p** of God and the
1Co 4:20 God is not in word but in **p**.
1Co 15:43 weakness, it is raised in **p**.
2Co 4: 7 the excellence of the **p** may
2Co 12: 9 that the **p** of Christ may
Eph 1:19 greatness of His **p** toward
Eph 1:19 the working of His mighty **p**
Eph 1:21 all principality and **p** and
Eph 2: 2 to the prince of the **p** of
Eph 3: 7 effective working of His **p**.
Eph 3:20 according to the **p** that
Eph 6:10 in the Lord and in the **p** of
Phil 3:10 I may know Him and the **p** of
Col 1:11 according to His glorious **p**,
Col 1:13 has delivered us from the **p**
Col 2:10 of all principality and **p**.
1Th 1: 5 in word only, but also in **p**,
2Th 1: 9 and from the glory of His **p**,
2Ti 1: 7 but of **p** and of love and of
2Ti 3: 5 godliness but denying its **p**.
Heb 1: 3 things by the word of His **p**,
Heb 2:14 destroy him who had the **p**

Heb   7:16 but according to the **p** of an
1Pe   1: 5 who are kept by the **p** of God
Jude   25 and majesty, Dominion and **p**,
Rev   4:11 glory and honor and **p**;
Rev   9: 3 And to them was given **p**,
Rev   9:19 For their **p** is in their mouth
Rev   12:10 and the **p** of His Christ have
Rev   20: 6 the second death has no **p**,

POWERFUL (see POWER)
Ps   29: 4 voice of the LORD is **p**;
Heb   4:12 word of God is living and **p**,

POWERLESS† (see POWER)
Hab   1: 4 Therefore the law is **p**,

POWERS (see POWER)
Esth   1: 3 the **p** of Persia and Media,
Rom   8:38 nor principalities nor **p**,
Eph   3:10 to the principalities and **p**
Heb   6: 5 good word of God and the **p**
1Pe   3:22 angels and authorities and **p**

PRACTICE (see PRACTICED, PRACTICES, PRACTICING)
Matt   7:23 you who **p** lawlessness!'
Rom   1:32 that those who **p** such things
Gal   5:21 that those who **p** such things
1Jn   1: 6 we lie and do not **p** the

PRACTICED (see PRACTICE)
Rom   3:13 tongues they have **p**

PRACTICES (see PRACTICE)
Deut   18:10 or one who **p** witchcraft,
Rom   13: 4 execute wrath on him who **p**

PRACTICING (see PRACTICE)
Rom   2: 3 you who judge those who **p** such

PRAETORIUM
Mark   15:16 away into the hall called **P**,

PRAISE (see PRAISED, PRAISES, PRAISEWORTHY, PRAISING, THANK)
Ex   15: 2 and I will **p** Him; My
2Ch   20:21 **P** the LORD, For His mercy
Neh   9: 5 above all blessing and **p**!
Ps   9: 1 I will **p** You, O LORD, with
Ps   22:23 **p** Him! All you descendants
Ps   33: 2 **P** the LORD with the harp
Ps   34: 1 His **p** shall continually
Ps   42: 5 for I shall yet **p** Him For
Ps   66: 2 Make His **p** glorious.
Ps   67: 3 Let the peoples **p** You, O
Ps   69:34 Let heaven and earth **p** Him,
Ps   88:10 the dead arise and **p** You?
Ps   100: 4 And into His courts with **p**.
Ps   104:33 I will sing **p** to my God
Ps   104:35 O my soul! **P** the LORD!
Ps   119:164 Seven times a day I **p** You,
Ps   135: 1 **P** the LORD! Praise the
Ps   145: 2 And I will **p** Your name
Ps   145: 4 One generation shall **p** Your
Ps   148: 1 **P** Him in the heights!
Ps   150: 1 Praise the LORD! **P** God in
Ps   150: 2 **P** Him for His mighty acts
Prov   31:31 And let her own works **p** her
Is   38:18 Death cannot **p** You; Those
Is   60:18 Salvation, And your gates **P**.
Jer   20:13 Sing to the LORD! **P** the
Jer   51:41 how the **p** of the whole earth
Dan   4:37 **p** and extol and honor the
Matt   21:16 You have perfected **p**'?
John   12:43 for they loved the **p** of men
John   12:43 of men more than the **p** of
Rom   2:29 whose **p** is not from men but
1Co   11:22 I do not **p** you.
Eph   1: 6 to the **p** of the glory of His
Phil   1:11 to the glory and **p** of God.

Heb   2:12 assembly I will sing **p**
Heb   13:15 offer the sacrifice of **p** to
1Pe   1: 7 by fire, may be found to **p**,
Rev   19: 5 **P** our God, all you His

PRAISED (see PRAISE)
1Ch   16:25 great and greatly to be **p**;
Ps   18: 3 who is worthy to be **p**;
Ps   48: 1 and greatly to be **p** In the
Prov   31:30 the LORD, she shall be **p**.
Dan   5: 4 and **p** the gods of gold and

PRAISES (see PRAISE)
Ex   15:11 in holiness, Fearful in **p**,
Ps   9:11 Sing **p** to the LORD, who
Ps   22: 3 Enthroned in the **p** of
Ps   47: 6 Sing **p** to God, sing praises!
Prov   31:28 and he **p** her:
1Pe   2: 9 that you may proclaim the **p**

PRAISEWORTHY† (see PRAISE)
Phil   4: 8 and if there is anything **p**—

PRAISING (see PRAISE)
Luke   1:64 and he spoke, **p** God.
Luke   2:13 of the heavenly host **p** God
Luke   2:20 glorifying and **p** God for all
Luke   24:53 continually in the temple **p**
Acts   2:47 **p** God and having favor with

PRAY (see PRAYED, PRAYER, PRAYING, PRAYS)
Gen   20: 7 and he will **p** for you and
Ex   32:32 their sin—but if not, I **p**,
2Ch   7:14 and **p** and seek My face, and
Job   42: 8 and My servant Job shall **p**
Ps   55:17 and at noon I will **p**,
Ps   122: 6 **P** for the peace of Jerusalem
Is   16:12 come to his sanctuary to **p**;
Is   45:20 And **p** to a god that cannot
Jer   7:16 Therefore do not **p** for this
Jon   1:14 the LORD and said, "We **p**,
Matt   5:44 and **p** for those who
Matt   6: 5 "And when you **p**,
Matt   6: 5 For they love to **p** standing
Matt   6: 6 **p** to your Father who is in
Matt   6: 9 this manner, therefore, **p**:
Matt   9:38 Therefore **p** the Lord of the
Matt   14:23 the mountain by Himself to **p**.
Matt   26:41 "Watch and **p**, lest you
Luke   6:28 and **p** for those who
Luke   11: 1 Him, "Lord, teach us to **p**,
Luke   11: 2 said to them, "When you **p**,
John   14:16 And I will **p** the Father, and
John   17: 9 I **p** for them. I do not pray
John   17: 9 I do not **p** for the world but
John   17:20 I do not **p** for these alone,
Acts   10: 9 went up on the housetop to **p**,
Rom   8:26 do not know what we should **p**
1Co   11:13 it proper for a woman to **p**
1Co   14:13 him who speaks in a tongue **p**
1Co   14:14 For if I **p** in a tongue, my
1Co   14:15 I will **p** with the spirit,
Col   1: 9 do not cease to **p** for you,
1Th   5:17 **p** without ceasing,
1Th   5:25 Brethren, **p** for us.
Jas   5:13 you suffering? Let him **p**.
Jas   5:14 and let them **p** over him,

PRAYED (see PRAY)
Gen   20:17 So Abraham **p** to God; and God
Num   11: 2 and when Moses **p** to the
1Sa   1:27 "For this child I **p**,
Neh   2: 4 So I **p** to the God of
Job   42:10 Job's losses when he **p** for
Dan   6:10 and **p** and gave thanks before
Jon   2: 1 Then Jonah **p** to the LORD his
Jon   4: 2 So he **p** to the LORD, and
Matt   26:39 and fell on His face, and **p**,

Mark 14:35 and **p** that if it were
Luke 22:41 And He knelt down and **p**,
Acts 4:31 And when they had **p**,
Acts 6: 6 and when they had **p**,
Acts 10: 2 and **p** to God always.
Jas 5:17 and he **p** earnestly that it
Jas 5:18 And he **p** again, and the

PRAYER (see PRAY, PRAYERS)
Ezra 8:23 this, and He answered our **p**.
Neh 1: 6 that You may hear the **p** of
Ps 4: 1 mercy on me, and hear my **p**.
Ps 17: 1 Give ear to my **p** which is
Ps 35:13 And my **p** would return to my
Ps 39:12 "Hear my **p**, O LORD, And
Ps 42: 8 A **p** to the God of my life.
Ps 66:19 to the voice of my **p**.
Ps 84: 8 God of hosts, hear my **p**;
Ps 102:17 He shall regard the **p** of the
Prov 15: 8 But the **p** of the upright
Prov 15:29 But He hears the **p** of the
Is 56: 7 be called a house of **p** for
Jer 11:14 or lift up a cry or **p** for
Lam 3: 8 shout, He shuts out my **p**.
Dan 9:17 hear the **p** of Your servant,
Jon 2: 7 And my **p** went up to You,
Hab 3: 1 A **p** of Habakkuk the prophet,
Matt 17:21 does not go out except by **p**
Matt 21:13 be called a house of **p**,
Matt 21:22 whatever things you ask in **p**,
Acts 1:14 with one accord in **p** and
Acts 3: 1 the temple at the hour of **p**,
Rom 10: 1 my heart's desire and **p** to
Rom 12:12 continuing steadfastly in **p**;
1Co 7: 5 yourselves to fasting and **p**;
Eph 6:18 praying always with all **p** and
Phil 1: 4 always in every **p** of mine
Phil 4: 6 but in everything by **p** and
Col 4: 2 Continue earnestly in **p**,
1Ti 4: 5 by the word of God and **p**.
Jas 5:15 And the **p** of faith will save
Jas 5:16 fervent **p** of a righteous man

PRAYERS (see PRAYER)
Ps 72:20 The **p** of David the son of
Matt 23:14 for a pretense make long **p**.
Luke 2:37 God with fastings and **p**
Luke 5:33 John fast often and make **p**,
Luke 20:47 for a pretense make long **p**.
Acts 2:42 breaking of bread, and in **p**.
Acts 10: 4 Your **p** and your alms have
Rom 1: 9 of you always in my **p**,
Rom 15:30 together with me in **p** to
Col 4:12 fervently for you in **p**,
2Ti 1: 3 I remember you in my **p**
Heb 5: 7 when He had offered up **p** and
1Pe 3: 7 that your **p** may not be
1Pe 3:12 are open to their **p**;
Rev 5: 8 which are the **p** of the

PRAYING (see PRAY)
Dan 6:11 and found Daniel **p** and
Mark 11:25 "And whenever you stand **p**,
Luke 1:10 of the people was **p** outside
Luke 9:18 happened, as He was alone **p**,
Luke 11: 1 as He was **p** in a certain
Acts 11: 5 was in the city of Joppa **p**;
Acts 16:25 Paul and Silas were **p** and
1Co 11: 4 Every man **p** or prophesying,
Eph 6:18 praying with all prayer and
Col 1: 3 **p** always for you,
Col 4: 3 meanwhile **p** also for us, that
Jude 20 **p** in the Holy Spirit,

PRAYS (see PRAY)
1Ki 8:42 when he comes and **p** toward
1Co 11: 5 But every woman who **p** or

1Co 14:14 in a tongue, my spirit **p**,

PREACH (see PREACHED, PREACHER, PREACHES, PREACHING, PROCLAIM)
Is 61: 1 LORD has anointed Me To **p**
Matt 4:17 that time Jesus began to **p**
Matt 10: 7 "And as you go, **p**,
Matt 10:27 **p** on the housetops.
Mark 3:14 He might send them out to **p**,
Mark 16:15 into all the world and **p**
Luke 4:43 I must **p** the kingdom of God
Acts 15:21 generations those who **p** him
Acts 16: 6 by the Holy Spirit to **p** the
Acts 16:10 the Lord had called us to **p**
Acts 17: 3 This Jesus whom I **p** to you is
Rom 1:15 I am ready to **p** the gospel
Rom 10: 8 word of faith which we **p**):
Rom 10:15 And how shall they **p** unless
Rom 15:20 I have made it my aim to **p**
1Co 1:17 but to **p** the gospel, not
1Co 1:23 but we **p** Christ crucified, to
1Co 9:14 commanded that those who **p**
1Co 9:16 For if I **p** the gospel, I have
1Co 9:16 woe is me if I do not **p** the
2Co 4: 5 For we do not **p** ourselves,
Gal 1: 8 **p** any other gospel to you
Gal 2: 2 them that gospel which I **p**
Phil 1:15 Some indeed **p** Christ even
Col 1:28 Him we **p**, warning every
2Ti 4: 2 **P** the word! Be ready in
Rev 14: 6 the everlasting gospel to **p**

PREACHED (see PREACH)
Zech 1: 4 whom the former prophets **p**,
Matt 11: 5 the poor have the gospel **p**
Matt 24:14 of the kingdom will be **p** in
Mark 6:12 So they went out and **p** that
Mark 13:10 the gospel must first be **p**
Mark 14: 9 wherever this gospel is **p** in
Luke 16:16 kingdom of God has been **p**,
Acts 8:35 **p** Jesus to him.
Acts 10:37 the baptism which John **p**:
Rom 15:19 to Illyricum I have fully **p**
1Co 1:21 of the message **p** to save
1Co 9:27 when I have **p** to others, I
1Co 15: 1 to you the gospel which I **p**
1Co 15:12 Now if Christ is **p** that He
2Co 1:19 who was **p** among you by us—by
2Co 11: 7 because I **p** the gospel of
Gal 3: 8 **p** the gospel to Abraham
Eph 2:17 And He came and **p** peace to
Phil 1:18 or in truth, Christ is **p**;
Col 1:23 which was **p** to every
2Ti 4:17 that the message might be **p**
Heb 4: 2 For indeed the gospel was **p**
1Pe 3:19 by whom also He went and **p** to
1Pe 4: 6 this reason the gospel was **p**

PREACHER (see PREACH)
Eccl 1: 2 of vanities," says the **P**;
Rom 10:14 shall they hear without a **p**?
1Ti 2: 7 which I was appointed a **p**
2Pe 2: 5 a **p** of righteousness,

PREACHES† (see PREACH)
Acts 19:13 you by the Jesus whom Paul **p**.
2Co 11: 4 For if he who comes **p** another
Gal 1: 9 if anyone **p** any other gospel
Gal 1:23 persecuted us now **p** the

PREACHING (see PREACH)
Matt 3: 1 John the Baptist came **p** in
Matt 4:23 **p** the gospel of the kingdom,
Matt 12:41 they repented at the **p** of
Mark 1: 4 in the wilderness and **p** a
Luke 9: 6 **p** the gospel and healing
Acts 5:42 did not cease teaching and **p**

Acts 10:36 **p** peace through Jesus
Acts 11:20 **p** the Lord Jesus.
Rom 16:25 to my gospel and the **p** of
1Co 2: 4 And my speech and my **p** were
1Co 15:14 then our **p** is empty and
Tit 1: 3 His word through **p**,

PRECEDE†
1Th 4:15 the Lord will by no means **p**

PRECEPT (see PRECEPTS)
Is 28:10 precept must be upon **p**,

PRECEPTS (see PRECEPT)
Ps 119: 4 us To keep Your **p**
Ps 119:15 I will meditate on Your **p**,
Dan 9: 5 by departing from Your **p**

PRECIOUS
Ps 22:20 My **p** life from the power
Ps 35:17 My **p** life from the lions.
Ps 36: 7 How **p** is Your
Ps 116:15 **P** in the sight of the LORD
Ps 133: 2 It is like the **p** oil upon
Ps 139:17 How **p** also are Your thoughts
Prov 3:15 She is more **p** than rubies,
Is 28:16 a **p** cornerstone, a sure
1Co 3:12 **p** stones, wood, hay, straw,
1Pe 1: 7 being much more **p** than gold
1Pe 1:19 but with the **p** blood of
1Pe 2: 4 but chosen by God and **p**,
1Pe 2: 6 cornerstone, elect, **p**,
1Pe 2: 7 you who believe, He is **p**;
1Pe 3: 4 which is very **p** in the sight
2Pe 1: 4 us exceedingly great and **p**

PREDESTINED
Rom 8:29 He also **p** to be conformed
Eph 1: 5 having **p** us to adoption as

PREEMINENCE
Col 1:18 all things He may have the **p**.

PREFERENCE (see PREFERRED)
Rom 12:10 in honor giving **p** to one

PREFERRED (see PREFERENCE)
John 1:15 He who comes after me is **p**

PREMATURELY†
Ex 21:22 so that she gives birth **p**,

PREPARATION (see PREPARE)
Matt 27:62 which followed the Day of P,
Eph 6:15 shod your feet with the **p**

PREPARE (see PREPARATION, PREPARED)
Is 40: 3 **P** the way of the LORD; Make
Amos 4:12 **P** to meet your God, O
Mal 3: 1 And he will **p** the way
Matt 3: 3 **P** the way of the LORD;
Matt 11:10 Who will **p** Your way
Matt 26:17 Where do You want us to **p** for
John 14: 2 I go to **p** a place for you.
1Co 14: 8 who will **p** himself for

PREPARED (see PREPARE)
Ezra 7:10 For Ezra had **p** his heart to
Neh 8:10 those for whom nothing is **p**;
Job 13:18 I have **p** my case, I know
Ps 31:19 Which You have **p** for those
Ps 57: 6 They have **p** a net for my
Hos 2: 8 Which they **p** for Baal.
Jon 1:17 Now the LORD had **p** a great
Jon 4: 6 And the LORD God **p** a plant
Jon 4: 7 dawned the next day God **p** a
Jon 4: 8 that God **p** a vehement east
Matt 25:34 inherit the kingdom **p** for
Matt 25:41 into the everlasting fire **p**
Matt 26:19 and they **p** the Passover.
Mark 14:15 upper room, furnished and **p**;

Luke 1:17 to make ready a people **p** for
Rom 9:23 which He had **p** beforehand
1Co 2: 9 things which God has **p**
Eph 2:10 which God **p** beforehand that
2Ti 2:21 **p** for every good work.
Heb 9: 2 For a tabernacle was **p**:
Heb 10: 5 a body You have **p** for
Heb 11: 7 **p** an ark for the saving of
Heb 11:16 for He has **p** a city for
Rev 21: 2 **p** as a bride adorned for her

PRESCRIBED
Lev 5:10 offering according to the **p**

PRESENCE (see PRESENT)
Gen 3: 8 hid themselves from the **p**
Gen 16: 6 her, she fled from her **p**.
Ex 33:14 My **P** will go with you, and
2Ki 24:20 cast them out from His **p**.
Job 1:12 So Satan went out from the **p**
Job 2: 7 Satan went out from the **p**
Job 23:15 I am terrified at His **p**;
Ps 16:11 In Your **p** is fullness of
Ps 23: 5 a table before me in the **p**
Ps 51:11 not cast me away from Your **p**,
Ps 52: 9 And in the **p** of Your saints
Ps 76: 7 And who may stand in Your **p**
Ps 95: 2 Let us come before His **p**
Ps 100: 2 Come before His **p** with
Ps 114: 7 At the **p** of the God of
Ps 116:14 to the LORD Now in the **p**
Ps 116:18 to the LORD Now in the **p**
Ps 139: 7 where can I flee from Your **p**?
Is 63: 9 And the Angel of His **P**
Is 64: 3 mountains shook at Your **p**.
Jon 1:10 that he fled from the **p** of
Luke 13:26 'We ate and drank in Your **p**,
Luke 15:10 there is joy in the **p** of the
1Co 1:29 flesh should glory in His **p**.
2Co 2:10 one for your sakes in the **p**
Phil 2:12 not as in my **p** only, but now
2Th 1: 9 destruction from the **p** of
1Ti 6:12 good confession in the **p** of
Heb 6:19 and which enters the **P**
Jude 24 faultless Before the **p** of

PRESENT (see PRESENCE, PRESENTABLE, PRESENTED, PRESENTS, UNPRESENTABLE)
Num 6:14 And he shall **p** his offering
Job 1: 6 the sons of God came to **p**
Job 23: 4 I would **p** my case before
Ps 46: 1 A very **p** help in trouble.
Mark 9: 1 see the kingdom of God **p**
Luke 2:22 Him to Jerusalem to **p** Him
John 14:25 spoken to you while being **p**
Rom 6:13 And do not **p** your members as
Rom 6:16 not know that to whom you **p**
Rom 7:18 for to will is **p** with me,
Rom 8:18 the sufferings of this **p**
Rom 8:38 nor things **p** nor things to
Rom 11: 5 at this **p** time there is a
Rom 12: 1 that you **p** your bodies a
1Co 3:22 or things **p** or things to
1Co 5: 3 as absent in body but **p** in
1Co 5: 3 judged (as though I were **p**)
1Co 7:26 is good because of the **p**
1Co 9:18 I may **p** the gospel of Christ
1Co 15: 6 greater part remain to the **p**,
2Co 5: 8 from the body and to be **p**
2Co 5: 9 whether **p** or absent, to be
2Co 11: 2 that I may **p** you as a
Gal 1: 4 deliver us from this **p** evil
Eph 5:27 that He might **p** her to
Col 1:22 to **p** you holy, and
Col 1:28 that we may **p** every man
2Ti 4:10 having loved this **p** world,

Tit   2:12 and godly in the **p** age,
Heb   12:11 seems to be joyful for the **p**,
Jude   24 And to **p** you faultless
PRESENTABLE† (*see* PRESENT)
1Co   12:24 but our **p** parts have no
PRESENTED (*see* PRESENT)
Gen   47: 2 among his brothers and **p**
Num   7:18 **p** an offering.
Josh   24: 1 and they **p** themselves before
Matt   2:11 they **p** gifts to Him: gold,
Luke   7:15 And He **p** him to his mother.
Acts   1: 3 to whom He also **p** Himself
PRESENTS (*see* PRESENT)
Num   15: 4 then he who **p** his offering to
2Ch   32:23 and **p** to Hezekiah king of
Ps   68:29 Kings will bring **p** to You.
PRESERVE (*see* PRESERVED, PRESERVES)
Gen   19:32 that we may **p** the lineage of
Ps   16: 1 **P** me, O God, for in You I
Ps   32: 7 You shall **p** me from
Ps   41: 2 The LORD will **p** him and
Ps   64: 1 **P** my life from fear of the
Ps   121: 7 The LORD shall **p** you from
Ps   121: 7 He shall **p** your soul.
Ps   121: 8 The LORD shall **p** your going
Ps   140: 1 **P** me from violent men,
Prov   4: 6 and she will **p** you; Love
Prov   22:12 The eyes of the LORD **p**
Luke   17:33 loses his life will **p** it.
2Ti   4:18 from every evil work and **p**
PRESERVED (*see* PRESERVE)
Gen   32:30 to face, and my life is **p**.
Matt   9:17 wineskins, and both are **p**.
1Th   5:23 and body be **p** blameless at
2Pe   3: 7 the earth which are now **p**
PRESERVES (*see* PRESERVE)
Ps   31:23 saints! For the LORD **p**
Ps   145:20 The LORD **p** all who love
Prov   13: 3 He who guards his mouth **p**
Prov   16:17 He who keeps his way **p** his
PRESS (*see* PRESSED, PRESSES, PRESSING)
Phil   3:12 but I **p** on, that I may lay
Phil   3:14 I **p** toward the goal for the
PRESSED (*see* PRESS)
Gen   19: 9 So they **p** hard against the
Mark   3:10 as many as had afflictions **p**
Luke   6:38 **p** down, shaken together, and
2Co   4: 8 We are hard **p** on every
Phil   1:23 For I am hard **p** between the
PRESSES (*see* PRESS)
Ps   38: 2 And Your hand **p** me down.
PRESSING (*see* PRESS)
Luke   16:16 and everyone is **p** into it.
PRESUMPTUOUS† (*see* PRESUMPTUOUSLY)
Ps   19:13 Your servant also from **p**
2Pe   2:10 authority. They are **p**,
PRESUMPTUOUSLY (*see* PRESUMPTUOUS)
Deut   18:22 the prophet has spoken it **p**;
PRETEND
2Sa   13: 5 Lie down on your bed and **p** to
PRETENSE
Matt   23:14 and for a **p** make long
Phil   1:18 whether in **p** or in truth,
PREVAIL (*see* PREVAILED)
Is   7: 1 but could not **p** against it.
Jer   1:19 But they shall not **p**
Jer   15:20 But they shall not **p**
Matt   16:18 gates of Hades shall not **p**

PREVAILED (*see* PREVAIL)
Gen   7:24 And the waters **p** on the earth
Gen   32:28 God and with men, and have **p**.
Ex   17:11 let down his hand, Amalek **p**.
Ps   129: 2 Yet they have not **p** against
Jer   20: 7 stronger than I, and have **p**.
Hos   12: 4 with the Angel and **p**;
PREVENT† (*see* PREVENTED)
Matt   3:14 And John tried to **p** Him,
PREVENTED† (*see* PREVENT)
Heb   7:23 because they were **p** by death
PREVIOUSLY
Rom   3:25 over the sins that were **p**
PREY
Job   4:11 lion perishes for lack of **p**,
Job   9:26 an eagle swooping on its **p**.
Ps   124: 6 Who has not given us as **p**
Prov   6:26 And an adulteress will **p**
PRICE (*see* PRICED)
Gen   23: 9 give it to me at the full **p**,
Job   28:18 For the **p** of wisdom is
Is   45:13 Not for **p** nor reward,"
Is   55: 1 Without money and without **p**.
Matt   13:46 found one pearl of great **p**,
Matt   27: 6 because they are the **p** of
Acts   5: 3 keep back part of the **p** of
1Co   6:20 For you were bought at a **p**;
1Co   7:23 You were bought at a **p**;
PRICED (*see* PRICE)
Matt   27: 9 value of Him who was **p**,
PRIDE (*see* PROUD)
1Sa   17:28 I know your **p** and the
Ps   10: 2 The wicked in his **p**
Ps   59:12 even be taken in their **p**,
Prov   11: 2 When **p** comes, then comes
Prov   13:10 By **p** comes nothing but
Prov   16:18 **P** goes before destruction,
Is   9: 9 Who say in **p** and arrogance
Jer   13: 9 manner I will ruin the **p** of
Dan   4:37 And those who walk in **p** He
Amos   8: 7 LORD has sworn by the **p** of
1Ti   3: 6 lest being puffed up with **p**
1Jn   2:16 and the **p** of life—is not of
PRIEST (*see* PRIEST'S, PRIESTHOOD, PRIESTS)
Gen   14:18 he was the **p** of God Most
Ex   18: 1 the **p** of Midian, Moses'
Ex   31:10 garments for Aaron the **p**
Lev   1: 9 And the **p** shall burn all on
Lev   4: 6 The **p** shall dip his finger in
Lev   4:16 The anointed **p** shall bring
Lev   6: 6 trespass offering, to the **p**.
Lev   13: 3 The **p** shall examine the sore
Lev   13: 6 then the **p** shall pronounce
Lev   14:27 Then the **p** shall sprinkle
Lev   21: 7 for the **p** is holy to his
Lev   21: 9 'The daughter of any **p**,
Lev   21:10 He who is the high **p**
Lev   27: 8 and the **p** shall set a value
Num   5:17 The **p** shall take holy water
Num   5:23 Then the **p** shall write these
Num   16:39 So Eleazar the **p** took the
Num   35:28 the death of the high **p**.
Josh   22:30 Now when Phinehas the **p** and
Judg   17:13 since I have a Levite as **p**!
Judg   18:19 be a father and a **p** to us.
1Sa   1: 9 Now Eli the **p** was sitting on
1Sa   2:35 up for Myself a faithful **p**
1Sa   21: 6 So the **p** gave him holy
1Sa   30: 7 David said to Abiathar the **p**,
2Sa   15:27 also said to Zadok the **p**,
2Ki   11: 9 to all that Jehoiada the **p**

2Ch 15: 3 God, without a teaching **p**,
2Ch 19:11 Amariah the chief **p** is over
2Ch 34:14 Hilkiah the **p** found the Book
Ezra 2:63 most holy things till a **p**
Ezra 7:11 Artaxerxes gave Ezra the **p**,
Ezra 10:10 Then Ezra the **p** stood up and
Neh 8: 2 So Ezra the **p** brought the Law
Neh 8: 9 Ezra the **p** and scribe, and
Ps 110: 4 You are a **p** forever
Is 24: 2 the people, so with the **p**;
Is 28: 7 The **p** and the prophet have
Jer 23:11 For both prophet and **p** are
Ezek 1: 3 expressly to Ezekiel the **p**,
Ezek 7:26 law will perish from the **p**,
Hos 4: 9 be: like people, like **p**.
Amos 7:10 Then Amaziah the **p** of Bethel
Mal 2: 7 For the lips of a **p** should
Matt 8: 4 way, show yourself to the **p**,
Matt 26:51 the servant of the high **p**,
Matt 26:57 away to Caiaphas the high **p**,
Mark 2:26 days of Abiathar the high **p**,
Luke 1: 5 a certain **p** named Zacharias,
Luke 10:31 Now by chance a certain **p**
John 11:49 being high **p** that year, said
Acts 4: 6 as well as Annas the high **p**,
Acts 14:13 Then the **p** of Zeus, whose
Acts 23: 4 "Do you revile God's high **p**?
Heb 2:17 and faithful High **P** in
Heb 3: 1 the Apostle and High **P** of
Heb 4:14 that we have a great High **P**
Heb 5: 6 You are a **p** forever
Heb 7: 1 **p** of the Most High God, who
Heb 7: 3 remains a **p** continually.
Heb 7:20 as He was not made **p**
Heb 8: 1 We have such a High **P**,
Heb 9: 7 the second part the high **p**
Heb 9:11 But Christ came as High **P**
Heb 9:25 as the high **p** enters the

PRIEST'S (*see* PRIEST)
Lev 14:18 of the oil that is in the **p**
Lev 22:12 If the **p** daughter is married
Matt 26:58 at a distance to the high **p**
Luke 22:54 brought Him into the high **p**

PRIESTHOOD (*see* PRIEST)
Ex 29: 9 The **p** shall be theirs for a
Num 25:13 covenant of an everlasting **p**,
Heb 7:12 For the **p** being changed, of
Heb 7:24 has an unchangeable **p**.
1Pe 2: 5 a spiritual house, a holy **p**,
1Pe 2: 9 chosen generation, a royal **p**,

PRIESTS (*see* PRIEST)
Ex 19: 6 be to Me a kingdom of **p** and
Ex 28:41 they may minister to Me as **p**.
Lev 16:33 make atonement for the **p**
Num 3: 3 of Aaron, the anointed **p**,
Josh 3:13 soles of the feet of the **p**
Josh 6: 4 And seven **p** shall bear seven
1Sa 22:11 the **p** who were in Nob. And
2Sa 15:35 to Zadok and Abiathar the **p**,
1Ki 12:31 and made **p** from every class
1Ki 12:32 at Bethel he installed the **p**
2Ki 23: 4 the **p** of the second order,
2Ki 23: 5 he removed the idolatrous **p**
2Ki 23:20 He executed all the **p** of the
1Ch 24: 6 fathers' houses of the **p**
1Ch 28:21 are the divisions of the **p**
2Ch 4: 9 he made the court of the **p**,
2Ch 11:15 he appointed for himself **p**
2Ch 30:16 the **p** sprinkled the blood
2Ch 31: 4 support for the **p** and the
Ezra 3: 2 and his brethren the **p**,
Ezra 6:18 They assigned the **p** to their
Ezra 8:24 of the leaders of the **p**—

Neh 3:28 the Horse Gate the **p** made
Neh 10:34 We cast lots among the **p**,
Ps 99: 6 and Aaron were among His **p**,
Ps 132:16 I will also clothe her **p**
Is 61: 6 you shall be named the **p** of
Jer 1: 1 of the **p** who were in
Jer 1:18 its princes, Against its **p**,
Jer 26:16 all the people said to the **p**
Jer 49: 3 into captivity With his **p**
Ezek 22:26 Her **p** have violated My law
Ezek 46: 2 The **p** shall prepare his
Hos 5: 1 O **p**! Take heed, O house of
Mic 3:11 Her **p** teach for pay, And
Zeph 1: 4 names of the idolatrous **p**
Mal 1: 6 the LORD of hosts To you **p**
Matt 16:21 from the elders and chief **p**
Matt 20:18 be betrayed to the chief **p**
Matt 26: 3 Then the chief **p**,
Matt 27: 3 of silver to the chief **p**
Mark 2:26 to eat, except for the **p**,
Mark 15: 3 And the chief **p** accused Him
Luke 6: 4 lawful for any but the **p** to
Luke 17:14 show yourselves to the **p**.
Luke 23: 4 Pilate said to the chief **p**
Acts 9:21 them bound to the chief **p**?
Acts 26:10 authority from the chief **p**;
Rev 1: 6 and has made us kings and **p**
Rev 5:10 have made us kings and **p** to

PRIME
Is 38:10 In the **p** of my life I shall

PRINCE (*see* PRINCELY, PRINCES)
Gen 23: 6 You are a mighty **p** among
Ex 2:14 Who made you a **p** and a judge
Ezra 1: 8 out to Sheshbazzar the **p** of
Is 9: 6 Father, **P** of Peace.
Ezek 28: 2 say to the **p** of Tyre, 'Thus
Ezek 38: 2 the **p** of Rosh, Meshech, and
Ezek 38: 3 the **p** of Rosh, Meshech, and
Dan 8:11 himself as the **P**
Dan 8:25 even rise against the **P** of
Dan 9:25 Until Messiah the **P**,
Dan 9:26 And the people of the **p** who
Dan 10:20 return to fight with the **p**
Dan 10:20 indeed the **p** of Greece will
Dan 10:21 these, except Michael your **p**.
Dan 11:22 and also the **p** of the
Hos 3: 4 many days without king or **p**,
Acts 3:15 and killed the **P** of life,
Acts 5:31 to His right hand to be **P**
Eph 2: 2 according to the **p** of the

PRINCELY (*see* PRINCE)
Zech 11:13 that **p** price they set on me.

PRINCES (*see* PRINCE)
Gen 12:15 The **p** of Pharaoh also saw her
Gen 17:20 He shall beget twelve **p**,
Judg 5: 3 O **p**! I, even I, will sing
1Sa 18:30 Then the **p** of the Philistines
Job 12:21 He pours contempt on **p**,
Ps 45:16 Whom You shall make **p** in
Ps 105:22 To bind his **p** at his
Ps 107:40 He pours contempt on **p**,
Ps 113: 8 He may seat him with **p**—
Ps 118: 9 Than to put confidence in **p**.
Ps 146: 3 Do not put your trust in **p**,
Ps 148:11 **P** and all judges of the
Prov 8:16 By me **p** rule, and nobles,
Is 1:23 Your **p** are rebellious, And
Jer 1:18 of Judah, Against its **p**,
Jer 48: 7 His priests and his **p**
Lam 5:12 **P** were hung up by their
Dan 8:25 rise against the Prince of **p**;
Dan 10:13 Michael, one of the chief **p**,
Hos 7: 3 And **p** with their lies.

Hos   8: 4 but not by Me; They made **p**,
Hos   9:15 All their **p** are
Zeph   3: 3 Her **p** in her midst are

PRINCESS† (*see* PRINCESSES)
Lam   1: 1 among the nations! The **p**

PRINCESSES† (*see* PRINCESS)
1Ki   11: 3 had seven hundred wives, **p**,

PRINCIPAL (*see* PRINCIPALITY)
Prov   4: 7 Wisdom is the **p** thing;

PRINCIPALITIES (*see* PRINCIPALITY)
Rom   8:38 nor angels nor **p** nor powers,
Eph   6:12 and blood, but against **p**,
Col   2:15 Having disarmed **p** and powers,

PRINCIPALITY (*see* PRINCIPAL, PRINCIPALITIES)
Eph   1:21 far above all **p** and power and

PRINCIPLES†
Col   2: 8 according to the basic **p** of
Col   2:20 Christ from the basic **p** of
Heb   5:12 teach you again the first **p**
Heb   6: 1 of the elementary **p** of

PRINT
John   20:25 I see in His hands the **p** of

PRISCA† (*see* PRISCILLA)
2Ti   4:19 Greet **P** and Aquila, and the

PRISCILLA (*see* PRISCA)
Acts   18: 2 from Italy with his wife **P**
Rom   16: 3 Greet **P** and Aquila, my

PRISON (*see* PRISONER, PRISONS)
Gen   39:20 him and put him into the **p**,
Gen   39:21 sight of the keeper of the **p**.
Judg   16:21 he became a grinder in the **p**.
2Ki   25:29 changed from his **p** garments,
Neh   12:39 stopped by the Gate of the **P**.
Is   53: 8 He was taken from **p** and from
Is   61: 1 And the opening of the **p** to
Jer   38:13 in the court of the **p**.
Matt   4:12 that John had been put in **p**,
Matt   14:10 and had John beheaded in **p**.
Matt   25:36 I was in **p** and you came to
Matt   25:39 did we see You sick, or in **p**,
Luke   12:58 the officer throw you into **p**.
Acts   5:18 and put them in the common **p**.
Acts   5:19 of the Lord opened the **p**
Acts   12: 5 was therefore kept in **p**,
Acts   12: 7 and a light shone in the **p**;
Acts   16:27 And the keeper of the **p**,
Acts   16:27 from sleep and seeing the **p**
1Pe   3:19 preached to the spirits in **p**,

PRISONER (*see* PRISON, PRISONERS)
Ps   102:20 hear the groaning of the **p**,
Matt   27:16 time they had a notorious **p**
Acts   23:18 Paul the **p** called me to him
Col   4:10 Aristarchus my fellow **p**
2Ti   1: 8 of our Lord, nor of me His **p**,
Phm   1: 1 a **p** of Christ Jesus, and
Phm   1:23 my fellow **p** in Christ Jesus,

PRISONERS (*see* PRISONER)
Gen   39:20 a place where the king's **p**
Ps   146: 7 LORD gives freedom to the **p**.
Is   20: 4 away the Egyptians as **p** and
Is   42: 7 To bring out **p** from the
Acts   16:27 supposing the **p** had fled,
Rom   16: 7 countrymen and my fellow **p**,
Heb   13: 3 Remember the **p** as if chained

PRISONS (*see* PRISON)
Acts   22: 4 and delivering into **p** both
2Co   11:23 in **p** more frequently, in

PRIVATE (*see* PRIVATELY)
2Pe   1:20 of Scripture is of any **p**

PRIVATELY (*see* PRIVATE)
Matt   17:19 disciples came to Jesus **p**
Luke   9:10 took them and went aside **p**

PRIZE
1Co   9:24 run, but one receives the **p**?
Phil   3:14 toward the goal for the **p**

PROCEED (*see* PROCEEDED, PROCEEDS)
Is   51: 4 For law will **p** from Me,
Matt   15:19 For out of the heart **p** evil
Eph   4:29 Let no corrupt word **p** out of
Jas   3:10 Out of the same mouth **p**

PROCEEDED (*see* PROCEED)
John   8:42 for I **p** forth and came from
Rev   19:21 with the sword which **p** from

PROCEEDS (*see* PROCEED)
Deut   8: 3 lives by every word that **p**
Matt   4: 4 by every word that **p**
John   15:26 the Spirit of truth who **p**

PROCLAIM (*see* PROCLAIMED, PROCLAIMER, PROCLAIMS, PROCLAMATION)
Ex   33:19 and I will **p** the name of the
Lev   25:10 and **p** liberty throughout
2Sa   1:20 **P** it not in the streets of
Ps   26: 7 That I may **p** with the voice
Ps   96: 2 **P** the good news of His
Is   61: 1 To **p** liberty to the
Is   61: 2 To **p** the acceptable year of
Mark   1:45 he went out and began to **p**
Luke   4:19 To **p** the acceptable
1Co   11:26 you **p** the Lord's death till
1Pe   2: 9 that you may **p** the praises

PROCLAIMED (*see* PROCLAIM)
Ex   34: 5 and **p** the name of the LORD.
Ps   68:11 the company of those who **p**
Jon   3: 5 **p** a fast, and put on
Mark   7:36 the more widely they **p** it.
Luke   12: 3 in inner rooms will be **p** on

PROCLAIMER† (*see* PROCLAIM)
Acts   17:18 He seems to be a **p** of foreign

PROCLAIMS (*see* PROCLAIM)
Is   52: 7 Who **p** peace, Who brings
Nah   1:15 Who **p** peace! O Judah, keep

PROCLAMATION (*see* PROCLAIM)
Dan   5:29 and made a **p** concerning him

PROCONSUL
Acts   18:12 When Gallio was **p** of Achaia,

PRODIGAL†
Luke   15:13 his possessions with **p**

PRODUCE (*see* PRODUCED, PRODUCES, PRODUCING)
Gen   41:34 one-fifth of the **p** of
Ex   22:29 the first of your ripe **p**
Deut   14:28 out the tithe of your **p** of
Jas   1:20 the wrath of man does not **p**

PRODUCED (*see* PRODUCE)
Matt   13:26 grain had sprouted and **p** a
Rom   7: 8 **p** in me all manner of
Jas   5:18 and the earth **p** its fruit.

PRODUCES (*see* PRODUCE)
Prov   30:33 as the churning of milk **p**
John   12:24 it **p** much grain.
Rom   5: 3 knowing that tribulation **p**
2Co   7:10 For godly sorrow **p** repentance
Jas   1: 3 the testing of your faith **p**

PRODUCING† (*see* PRODUCE)
Rom   7:13 was **p** death in me through

PROFANE (see PROFANED, PROFANING)

Lev 10: 1 and offered **p** fire before
Lev 18:21 nor shall you **p** the name of
Lev 20: 3 to defile My sanctuary and **p**
Neh 13:17 by which you **p** the Sabbath
Mal 1:12 But you **p** it, In that you
Matt 12: 5 the priests in the temple **p**
1Ti 1: 9 for the unholy and **p**,
1Ti 4: 7 But reject **p** and old wives'
2Ti 2:16 But shun **p** and idle
Heb 12:16 be any fornicator or **p**

PROFANED (see PROFANE)

Ex 20:25 on it, you have **p** it.

PROFANING (see PROFANE)

Neh 13:18 added wrath on Israel by **p**

PROFESS† (see PROFESSING)

Tit 1:16 They **p** to know God, but in

PROFESSING (see PROFESS)

Rom 1:22 **P** to be wise, they became
1Ti 6:21 by **p** it some have strayed

PROFIT (see PROFITABLE, PROFITED, PROFITS)

Gen 37:26 What **p** is there if we kill
Lev 25:37 lend him your food at a **p**.
Prov 10: 2 Treasures of wickedness **p**
Prov 11: 4 Riches do not **p** in the day
Prov 14:23 In all labor there is **p**,
Eccl 1: 3 What **p** has a man from all
Is 57:12 For they will not **p** you.
Jer 2: 8 after things that do not **p**.
Ezek 22:12 you have made **p** from your
Mark 8:36 For what will it **p** a man if
Luke 9:25 For what **p** is it to a man
Acts 16:16 brought her masters much **p**
Rom 3: 1 or what is the **p** of
1Co 7:35 this I say for your own **p**,
1Co 14: 6 what shall I **p** you unless I
2Ti 2:14 strive about words to no **p**,
Heb 12:10 to them, but He for our **p**,
Jas 2:14 What does it **p**, my brethren,
Jas 4:13 and sell, and make a **p**";
Jude 11 in the error of Balaam for **p**,

PROFITABLE (see PROFIT, UNPROFITABLE)

Jer 13: 7 It was **p** for nothing.
Matt 5:29 for it is more **p** for you
2Co 12: 1 It is doubtless not **p** for me
1Ti 4: 8 but godliness is **p** for all
2Ti 3:16 and is **p** for doctrine, for
Tit 3: 8 These things are good and **p**
Phm 1:11 but now is **p** to you and to

PROFITED (see PROFIT)

Heb 13: 9 with foods which have not **p**

PROFITS (see PROFIT)

Prov 31:16 From her **p** she plants a
John 6:63 the flesh **p** nothing. The
1Co 13: 3 it **p** me nothing.
1Ti 4: 8 For bodily exercise **p** a

PROJECTS

Neh 3:25 and on the tower which **p**

PROLONG (see PROLONGED)

Deut 5:33 and that you may **p** your
Ps 85: 5 Will You **p** Your anger to
Is 53:10 He shall **p** His days, And

PROLONGED (see PROLONG)

Deut 6: 2 and that your days may be **p**.
Dan 7:12 yet their lives were **p** for a

PROMINENT

Ezek 17:22 plant it on a high and **p**
Acts 17:12 **p** women as well as men.

PROMISE (see PROMISED, PROMISES)

1Ki 8:56 one word of all His good **p**,
2Ch 1: 9 let Your **p** to David my
Neh 5:13 who does not perform this **p**.
Ps 77: 8 Has His **p** failed
Ps 105:42 He remembered His holy **p**,
Luke 24:49 I send the **P** of My Father
Acts 1: 4 but to wait for the **P** of the
Acts 2:33 from the Father the **p** of
Acts 2:39 For the **p** is to you and to
Acts 13:23 seed, according to the **p**,
Rom 4:13 For the **p** that he would be
Rom 4:14 is made void and the **p** made
Rom 4:20 He did not waver at the **p** of
Rom 9: 9 For this is the word of **p**:
Gal 3:14 that we might receive the **p**
Gal 3:18 law, it is no longer of **p**;
Gal 3:18 God gave it to Abraham by **p**.
Gal 3:19 should come to whom the **p**
Gal 3:22 that the **p** by faith in Jesus
Gal 3:29 and heirs according to the **p**.
Gal 4:23 of the freewoman through **p**,
Gal 4:28 was, are children of **p**.
Eph 1:13 with the Holy Spirit of **p**,
Eph 2:12 from the covenants of **p**,
Eph 3: 6 and partakers of His **p** in
Eph 6: 2 the first commandment with **p**:
1Ti 4: 8 having **p** of the life that
Heb 4: 1 since a **p** remains of
Heb 6:15 endured, he obtained the **p**.
Heb 6:17 to the heirs of **p** the
Heb 9:15 called may receive the **p** of
Heb 11: 9 heirs with him of the same **p**;
Heb 11:39 faith, did not receive the **p**,
2Pe 3: 4 Where is the **p** of His coming?
2Pe 3: 9 not slack concerning His **p**,
2Pe 3:13 we, according to His **p**,
1Jn 2:25 And this is the **p** that He has

PROMISED (see PROMISE)

Deut 9:28 them to the land which He **p**
2Sa 7:28 and You have **p** this goodness
1Ki 9: 5 as I **p** David your father,
Matt 14: 7 Therefore he **p** with an oath
Luke 1:72 To perform the mercy to
Rom 1: 2 which He **p** before through His
Rom 4:21 that what He had **p** He was
Tit 1: 2 **p** before time began,
Heb 10:23 for He who **p** is faithful.
Heb 11:11 Him faithful who had **p**.
Jas 1:12 of life which the Lord has **p**

PROMISES (see PROMISE)

Rom 9: 4 service of God, and the **p**;
Rom 15: 8 to confirm the **p** made to
2Co 1:20 For all the **p** of God in Him
2Co 7: 1 Therefore, having these **p**,
Gal 3:21 the law then against the **p**
Heb 6:12 and patience inherit the **p**.
Heb 7: 6 blessed him who had the **p**.
Heb 8: 6 was established on better **p**.
Heb 11:13 not having received the **p**,
Heb 11:17 he who had received the **p**
Heb 11:33 righteousness, obtained **p**,
2Pe 1: 4 great and precious **p**,

PROMOTED

Dan 2:48 Then the king **p** Daniel and
Dan 3:30 Then the king **p** Shadrach,

PRONOUNCE (see PRONOUNCED)

Judg 12: 6 for he could not **p** it

PRONOUNCED (see PRONOUNCE)

Jer 11:17 has **p** doom against you for
Ezek 20:26 and I **p** them unclean because

PROOF (*see* PROOFS)
2Co	8:24	before the churches the **p**
Phil	1:28	which is to them a **p** of

PROOFS† (*see* PROOF)
Acts	1: 3	by many infallible **p**,

PROPER (*see* PROPERLY)
Jer	26:14	with me as seems good and **p**
1Co	11:13	Is it **p** for a woman to pray
1Ti	2:10	which is **p** for women
Tit	2: 1	the things which are **p** for
Jude	6	who did not keep their **p**

PROPERLY† (*see* PROPER)
Rom	13:13	Let us walk **p**, as in the
1Th	4:12	that you may walk **p** toward

PROPERTY
Gen	23: 4	Give me **p** for a burial place

PROPHECIES (*see* PROPHECY)
Lam	2:14	envisioned for you false **p**
1Co	13: 8	But whether there are **p**,

PROPHECY (*see* PROPHECIES, PROPHESY, PROPHETIC)
Dan	9:24	To seal up vision and **p**,
Matt	13:14	And in them the **p** of Isaiah
Rom	12: 6	let us use them: if **p**,
1Co	13: 2	I have the gift of **p**,
1Ti	4:14	which was given to you by **p**
2Pe	1:20	that no **p** of Scripture is of
2Pe	1:21	for **p** never came by the will
Rev	1: 3	who hear the words of this **p**,
Rev	22: 7	keeps the words of the **p** of
Rev	19:10	of Jesus is the spirit of **p**.
Rev	22:10	not seal the words of the **p**
Rev	22:18	hears the words of the **p** of
Rev	22:19	words of the book of this **p**,

PROPHESIED (*see* PROPHESY)
Num	11:25	upon them, that they **p**,
1Sa	10:10	and he **p** among them.
1Ch	25: 3	who **p** with a harp to give
Ezra	5: 1	**p** to the Jews who were in
Jer	2: 8	The prophets **p** by Baal,
Jer	20: 1	heard that Jeremiah **p** these
Jer	20: 6	to whom you have **p** lies.'"
Jer	26:18	Micah of Moresheth **p** in the
Jer	26:20	there was also a man who **p**
Ezek	37: 7	So I **p** as I was commanded;
Matt	7:22	have we not **p** in Your name,
Matt	11:13	the prophets and the law **p**
Luke	1:67	with the Holy Spirit, and **p**,
John	11:51	high priest that year he **p**
Acts	19: 6	spoke with tongues and **p**.
1Pe	1:10	who **p** of the grace that
Jude	14	**p** about these men also,

PROPHESIES (*see* PROPHESY)
Jer	28: 9	As for the prophet who **p** of
Ezek	12:27	and he **p** of times far off.'
1Co	11: 5	every woman who prays or **p**
1Co	14: 4	but he who **p** edifies the

PROPHESY (*see* PROPHECY, PROPHESIED, PROPHESIES, PROPHESYING, PROPHET, PROPHETESS)
1Ki	22:18	not tell you he would not **p**
1Ch	25: 1	who should **p** with harps,
Jer	5:31	The prophets **p** falsely, And
Jer	14:14	The prophets **p** lies in My
Jer	19:14	the LORD had sent him to **p**;
Ezek	11: 4	Therefore **p** against them,
Ezek	13:17	who **p** out of their own
Ezek	21:14	therefore, son of man, **p**,
Ezek	34: 2	**p** against the shepherds of
Ezek	37: 4	**P** to these bones, and say to
Ezek	37: 9	**P** to the breath, prophesy,
Ezek	39: 1	**p** against Gog, and say,

PROPHESYING (*see* PROPHESY)
Num	11:27	Eldad and Medad are **p** in the
Ezra	6:14	prospered through the **p** of
1Co	11: 4	Every man praying or **p**,
1Co	14:22	but **p** is not for unbelievers

PROPHET (*see* PROPHESY, PROPHET'S, PROPHETS)
Gen	20: 7	man's wife; for he is a **p**,
Ex	7: 1	your brother shall be your **p**.
Num	12: 6	If there is a **p** among you,
Deut	13: 1	there arises among you a **p**
Deut	18:15	will raise up for you a **P**
Deut	18:20	But the **p** who presumes to
Deut	18:20	other gods, that **p** shall die.'
Deut	34:10	has not arisen in Israel a **p**
1Sa	9: 9	he who is now called a **p**
1Sa	22: 5	Now the **p** Gad said to David,
2Sa	7: 2	king said to Nathan the **p**,
1Ki	13:11	Now an old **p** dwelt in
1Ki	18:22	I alone am left a **p** of the
1Ki	18:36	that Elijah the **p** came near
1Ki	19:16	you shall anoint as **p** in
2Ki	5: 3	my master were with the **p**
2Ki	5: 8	know that there is a **p** in
2Ki	9: 1	And Elisha the **p** called one
2Ki	19: 2	sackcloth, to Isaiah the **p**,
2Ch	26:22	the **p** Isaiah the son of Amoz
2Ch	29:25	seer, and of Nathan the **p**;
2Ch	32:32	the vision of Isaiah the **p**,
2Ch	36:12	before Jeremiah the **p**,
Ezra	5: 1	Then the **p** Haggai and
Ps	74: 9	There is no longer any **p**;
Is	9:15	The **p** who teaches lies, he
Jer	1: 5	I ordained you a **p** to the
Jer	6:13	And from the **p** even to the
Jer	18:18	nor the word from the **p**.
Jer	23:11	For both **p** and priest are
Jer	23:28	The **p** who has a dream, let
Jer	28:10	took the yoke off the **p**
Ezek	2: 5	they will know that a **p**
Ezek	7:26	will seek a vision from a **p**;
Ezek	14: 7	then comes to a **p** to inquire
Dan	9: 2	LORD through Jeremiah the **p**,
Hos	4: 5	The **p** also shall stumble
Hos	9: 7	Israel knows! The **p** is a
Hos	12:13	By a **p** the LORD brought
Amos	7:14	to Amaziah: "I was no **p**,
Amos	7:14	Nor was I a son of a **p**,
Hab	1: 1	The burden which the **p**
Hab	3: 1	A prayer of Habakkuk the **p**,
Hag	1: 3	LORD came by Haggai the **p**,
Mal	4: 5	I will send you Elijah the **p**
Matt	1:22	by the Lord through the **p**,
Matt	2: 5	thus it is written by the **p**:
Matt	2:17	was spoken by Jeremiah the **p**,
Matt	3: 3	who was spoken of by the **p**
Matt	10:41	He who receives a **p** in the
Matt	11: 9	did you go out to see? A **p**?
Matt	11: 9	to you, and more than a **p**.
Matt	12:39	it except the sign of the **p**
Matt	13:57	A **p** is not without honor
Matt	21:11	the **p** from Nazareth of

PROPHET (*continued from first column*)
Joel	2:28	and your daughters shall **p**,
Amos	3: 8	has spoken! Who can but **p**?
Amos	7:12	eat bread, And there **p**.
Amos	7:13	But never again **p** at Bethel,
Amos	7:15	**p** to My people Israel.'
Matt	15: 7	Well did Isaiah **p** about you,
Matt	26:68	**P** to us, Christ! Who is the
Luke	22:64	**P**! Who is the one who struck
Acts	2:17	your daughters shall **p**,
Rom	12: 6	let us **p** in proportion to
1Co	13: 9	we know in part and we **p** in
1Co	14: 1	especially that you may **p**.
1Co	14:39	desire earnestly to **p**,

Matt 21:26 for all count John as a **p**.
Matt 24:15 spoken of by Daniel the **p**,
Mark 6:15 others said, "It is the **P**,
Luke 1:76 will be called the **p** of the
Luke 4:17 was handed the book of the **p**
Luke 4:24 no **p** is accepted in his own
Luke 4:27 in the time of Elisha the **p**,
Luke 24:19 who was a **P** mighty in deed
John 6:14 This is truly the **P** who is to
Acts 2:16 is what was spoken by the **p**
Acts 3:22 raise up for you a **P**
Acts 7:37 raise up for you a **P**
Acts 8:28 he was reading Isaiah the **p**.
Acts 8:34 of whom does the **p** say this,
Acts 13: 6 certain sorcerer, a false **p**,
Acts 13:20 years, until Samuel the **p**.
Rev 20:10 the beast and the false **p**.

PROPHET'S† (see PROPHET)
Matt 10:41 a prophet shall receive a **p**

PROPHETESS (see PROPHESY)
Ex 15:20 Then Miriam the **p**,
Judg 4: 4 Now Deborah, a **p**,
2Ki 22:14 Asaiah went to Huldah the **p**,
Is 8: 3 Then I went to the **p**,
Luke 2:36 there was one, Anna, a **p**,
Rev 2:20 who calls herself a **p**,

PROPHETIC† (see PROPHECY)
Rom 16:26 and by the **p** Scriptures has
2Pe 1:19 And so we have the **p** word

PROPHETS (see PROPHET)
Num 11:29 the LORD's people were **p**
1Sa 10: 5 you will meet a group of **p**
1Sa 10:11 prophesied among the **p**,
1Sa 10:12 "Is Saul also among the **p**?
1Ki 18: 4 Jezebel massacred the **p** of
1Ki 18:19 four hundred and fifty **p** of
1Ki 19:14 and killed Your **p** with the
2Ki 2: 3 Now the sons of the **p** who
2Ki 2: 5 Now the sons of the **p** who
2Ki 6: 1 And the sons of the **p** said to
2Ki 17:13 to you by My servants the **p**.
1Ch 16:22 And do My **p** no harm."
Neh 9:30 by Your Spirit in Your **p**.
Ps 105:15 And do My **p** no harm."
Is 29:10 your eyes, namely, the **p**;
Jer 2: 8 The **p** prophesied by Baal,
Jer 23:13 I have seen folly in the **p**
Jer 23:21 "I have not sent these **p**,
Lam 2: 9 And her **p** find no vision
Lam 4:13 of the sins of her **p** And
Ezek 13: 3 GOD: "Woe to the foolish **p**,
Ezek 13: 4 your **p** are like foxes in the
Dan 9: 6 heeded Your servants the **p**,
Dan 9:10 us by His servants the **p**.
Hos 6: 5 I have hewn them by the **p**,
Amos 3: 7 secret to His servants the **p**.
Mic 3:11 And her **p** divine for money.
Zeph 3: 4 Her **p** are insolent,
Zech 7:12 Spirit through the former **p**.
Matt 2:23 which was spoken by the **p**,
Matt 5:17 to destroy the Law or the **P**.
Matt 7:15 "Beware of false **p**,
Matt 11:13 For all the **p** and the law
Matt 16:14 Jeremiah or one of the **p**.
Matt 23:30 them in the blood of the **p**.
Matt 23:31 of those who murdered the **p**.
Mark 6:15 or like one of the **p**.
Luke 1:70 by the mouth of His holy **p**,
Luke 11:50 the blood of all the **p**
Luke 16:16 The law and the **p** were until
Luke 16:29 They have Moses and the **p**
Luke 24:44 the Law of Moses and the **P**
Acts 3:21 the mouth of all His holy **p**

Acts 3:25 "You are sons of the **p**,
Acts 10:43 To Him all the **p** witness
Acts 13:27 nor even the voices of the **P**
Acts 15:15 with this the words of the **p**
Rom 1: 2 before through His **p** in the
Rom 11: 3 have killed Your **p** and
1Co 12:28 first apostles, second **p**,
1Co 12:29 all apostles? Are all **p**?
1Co 14:29 Let two or three **p** speak, and
1Co 14:32 And the spirits of the **p** are
1Co 14:32 are subject to the **p**.
Eph 2:20 of the apostles and **p**,
Eph 4:11 to be apostles, some **p**,
Heb 1: 1 past to the fathers by the **p**,
Heb 11:32 David and Samuel and the **p**:
1Pe 1:10 Of this salvation the **p** have
2Pe 2: 1 But there were also false **p**
1Jn 4: 1 because many false **p** have
Rev 10: 7 to His servants the **p**.

PROPITIATION
Rom 3:25 whom God set forth as a **p** by
Heb 2:17 to make **p** for the sins of
1Jn 4:10 sent His Son to be the **p**

PROPORTION
Rom 12: 6 let us prophesy in **p** to

PROPOSE (see PROPOSED)
Gen 11: 6 now nothing that they **p** to

PROPOSED (see PROPOSE)
Acts 1:23 And they **p** two: Joseph called

PROSECUTOR†
Job 31:35 That my **P** had written a

PROSELYTE† (see PROSELYTES)
Matt 23:15 land and sea to win one **p**,
Acts 6: 5 a **p** from Antioch,

PROSELYTES† (see PROSELYTE)
Acts 2:10 from Rome, both Jews and **p**,
Acts 13:43 of the Jews and devout **p**

PROSPER (see PROSPERED, PROSPERITY, PROSPEROUS, PROSPERS)
Gen 24:40 His angel with you and **p**
Josh 1: 7 that you may **p** wherever you
Ps 1: 3 whatever he does shall **p**.
Ps 122: 6 May they **p** who love you.
Is 53:10 of the LORD shall **p** in His
Jer 12: 1 does the way of the wicked **p**?

PROSPERED (see PROSPER)
Gen 24:56 since the LORD has **p** my
Dan 6:28 So this Daniel **p** in the

PROSPERITY (see PROSPER)
Ezra 9:12 never seek their peace or **p**,
Ps 73: 3 When I saw the **p** of the
Ps 122: 7 **P** within your palaces."

PROSPEROUS (see PROSPER)
Gen 24:21 had made his journey **p** or
Gen 26:13 until he became very **p**;
Josh 1: 8 you will make your way **p**,

PROSPERS (see PROSPER)
Ps 37: 7 fret because of him who **p**
Prov 17: 8 Wherever he turns, he **p**.

PROUD (see PRIDE, PROUDLY)
Job 40:11 Look on everyone who is **p**,
Ps 12: 3 the tongue that speaks **p**
Ps 86:14 the **p** have risen against me,
Ps 101: 5 has a haughty look and a **p**
Ps 119:85 The **p** have dug pits for me,
Ps 138: 6 But the **p** He knows from
Ps 140: 5 The **p** have hidden a snare
Prov 6:17 A **p** look, A lying tongue,
Jer 48:29 Moab (He is exceedingly **p**)

Luke 1:51 He has scattered the **p** in
Rom   1:30 haters of God, violent, **p**,
2Ti   3: 2 lovers of money, boasters, **p**,
Jas   4: 6 "God resists the **p**,
1Pe   5: 5 "God resists the **p**,

PROUDLY (*see* PROUD)
Ps   17:10 their mouths they speak **p**.

PROVE (*see* PROVED, PROVING, TEST, TRY)
Job   24:25 who will **p** me a liar, And
Ps   26: 2 and **p** me; Try my mind and
Rom   12: 2 that you may **p** what is that

PROVED (*see* PROVE, TESTED)
Heb   2: 2 word spoken through angels **p**

PROVERB (*see* PROVERBS)
Deut   28:37 become an astonishment, a **p**,
Ps   49: 4 will incline my ear to a **p**;
Prov   1: 6 To understand a **p** and an
Prov   26: 9 hand of a drunkard Is a **p**
Ezek   14: 8 and make him a sign and a **p**,
Luke   4:23 You will surely say this **p** to
2Pe   2:22 them according to the true **p**:

PROVERBS (*see* PROVERB)
1Ki   4:32 He spoke three thousand **p**,
Prov   1: 1 The **p** of Solomon the son of
Prov   10: 1 The **P** of Solomon: A wise son
Prov   25: 1 These also are **p** of Solomon
Eccl   12: 9 out and set in order many **p**.

PROVIDE (*see* PROVIDED, PROVIDES, PROVISION)
Gen   22: 8 God will **p** for Himself the
Ps   78:20 Can He **p** meat for His
Matt   26:53 and He will **p** Me with more
Luke   12:33 **p** yourselves money bags
Acts   24:23 any of his friends to **p** for
1Ti   5: 8 But if anyone does not **p** for

PROVIDED (*see* PROVIDE)
Gen   22:14 of The LORD it shall be **p**.
Heb   11:40 God having **p** something better

PROVIDES (*see* PROVIDE)
Prov   31:15 And **p** food for her

PROVINCE (*see* PROVINCES)
Ezra   5: 8 that we went into the **p** of
Dan   2:48 him ruler over the whole **p**
Acts   23:34 he asked what **p** he was from.

PROVINCES (*see* PROVINCE, REGION)
Esth   1:16 who are in all the **p** of
Dan   3: 3 all the officials of the **p**

PROVING† (*see* PROVE)
Acts   9:22 **p** that this Jesus is the

PROVISION (*see* PROVIDE)
1Ki   4:22 Now Solomon's **p** for one day
Rom   13:14 and make no **p** for the flesh,

PROVOKE (*see* PROVOKED, PROVOKING)
Ex   23:21 do not **p** Him, for He will
Deut   4:25 of the LORD your God to **p**
Jer   32:29 to **p** Me to anger;
Rom   10:19 I will **p** you to jealousy
1Co   10:22 Or do we **p** the Lord to
Eph   6: 4 do not **p** your children to

PROVOKED (*see* PROVOKE)
Deut   32:16 They **p** Him to jealousy with
1Sa   1: 6 And her rival also **p** her
Is   1: 4 They have **p** to anger The
Acts   17:16 his spirit was **p** within him
1Co   13: 5 not seek its own, is not **p**,

PROVOKING (*see* PROVOKE)
Gal   5:26 **p** one another, envying one

PROWLER
Prov   6:11 poverty come on you like a **p**,

PRUDENCE (*see* PRUDENT)
Prov   1: 4 To give **p** to the simple, To
Prov   8:12 "I, wisdom, dwell with **p**,
Eph   1: 8 us in all wisdom and **p**,

PRUDENT (*see* PRUDENCE, PRUDENTLY)
1Sa   16:18 **p** in speech, and a handsome
Prov   14: 8 The wisdom of the **p** is to
Prov   19:14 But a **p** wife is from the
Prov   22: 3 A **p** man foresees evil and
Jer   49: 7 counsel perished from the **p**?
Amos   5:13 Therefore the **p** keep silent
Matt   11:25 things from the wise and **p**
1Co   1:19 understanding of the **p**.

PRUDENTLY (*see* PRUDENT)
Is   52:13 My Servant shall deal **p**;

PRUNED† (*see* PRUNES)
Is   5: 6 It shall not be **p** or dug,

PRUNES† (*see* PRUNED, PRUNING, PRUNING HOOKS)
John   15: 2 that bears fruit He **p**,

PRUNING (*see* PRUNES, PRUNING HOOKS)
Is   2: 4 And their spears into **p**
Joel   3:10 into swords And your **p**
Mic   4: 3 And their spears into **p**

PRUNING HOOKS (*see* PRUNES, PRUNING)
Joel   3:10 And your **p** into spears;

PSALM (*see* PSALMIST, PSALMS, PSALTERY)
1Ch   16: 7 first delivered this **p**
Ps   98: 5 harp and the sound of a **p**,
Acts   13:33 also written in the second **P**:
1Co   14:26 each of you has a **p**,

PSALMIST† (*see* PSALM)
2Sa   23: 1 And the sweet **p** of Israel:

PSALMS (*see* PSALM)
Neh   12: 8 led the thanksgiving **p**,
Ps   105: 2 sing **p** to Him; Talk of all
Luke   20:42 said in the Book of **P**:
Luke   24:44 and the Prophets and the **P**
Acts   1:20 is written in the book of **P**:
Eph   5:19 to one another in **p** and
Col   3:16 one another in **p** and hymns
Jas   5:13 cheerful? Let him sing **p**.

PSALTERY† (*see* PSALM)
Dan   3: 5 flute, harp, lyre, and **p**,
Dan   3:10 flute, harp, lyre, and **p**,
Dan   3:15 flute, harp, lyre, and **p**,

PUBLIC†
Matt   1:19 not wanting to make her a **p**
Col   2:15 He made a **p** spectacle of

PUFFED (*see* PUFFS)
1Co   4: 6 that none of you may be **p** up
1Co   13: 4 is not **p** up;
1Ti   3: 6 lest being **p** up with pride

PUFFS† (*see* PUFFED)
1Co   8: 1 Knowledge **p** up, but love

PUL
2Ki   15:19 **P** king of Assyria came

PULL (*see* PULLED, PULLING, PULLS)
Ps   31: 4 **P** me out of the net which
Luke   12:18 I will **p** down my barns and

PULLED (*see* PULL)
Gen   37:28 so the brothers **p** Joseph
Judg   16: 3 **p** them up, bar and all, put
Luke   17: 6 Be **p** up by the roots and be

PULLING† (*see* PULL)
2Co 10: 4 but mighty in God for **p**
Jude 23 **p** them out of the fire,

PULLS (*see* PULL)
Mark 2:21 or else the new piece **p** away

PUNISH (*see* PUNISHED, PUNISHMENT, UNPUNISHED)
Is 13:11 I will **p** the world for its
Is 27: 1 Will **p** Leviathan the
Jer 5: 9 Shall I not **p** them for
Jer 14:10 And **p** their sins."
Hos 2:13 I will **p** her For the days

PUNISHED (*see* PUNISH)
Ps 103:10 Nor **p** us according to our
Acts 22: 5 there to Jerusalem to be **p**.
Acts 26:11 And I **p** them often in every

PUNISHMENT (*see* PUNISH)
Gen 4:13 My **p** is greater than I can
Ex 32:34 I will visit **p** upon them for
Is 10: 3 will you do in the day of **p**,
Jer 8:12 In the time of their **p**
Jer 11:23 even the year of their **p**.
Lam 4: 6 The **p** of the iniquity of the
Hos 9: 7 The days of **p** have come;
Amos 1: 3 I will not turn away its **p**,
Matt 25:46 go away into everlasting **p**,
Heb 10:29 Of how much worse **p**,
1Pe 2:14 are sent by him for the **p**
2Pe 2: 9 reserve the unjust under **p**

PUR (*see* PURIM)
Esth 3: 7 they cast **P** (that is, the
Esth 9:26 days Purim, after the name **P**.

PURCHASE (*see* PURCHASED)
Prov 17:16 in the hand of a fool the **p**
Jer 32:12 and I gave the **p** deed to

PURCHASED (*see* PURCHASE)
Job 28:15 It cannot be **p** for gold,
Acts 1:18 (Now this man **p** a field with
Acts 20:28 the church of God which He **p**
Eph 1:14 the redemption of the **p**

PURE (*see* PURER, PURIFY, PURITY)
Ex 25:17 make a mercy seat of **p** gold;
Ex 25:31 also make a lampstand of **p**
Ex 27:20 that they bring you **p** oil
Ex 30:34 and **p** frankincense with
2Sa 22:27 With the **p** You will show
Job 4:17 Can a man be more **p** than
Job 15:15 And the heavens are not **p**
Job 16:17 hands, And my prayer is **p**
Job 25: 5 And the stars are not **p** in
Job 33: 9 'I am **p**, without
Ps 12: 6 words of the LORD are **p**
Ps 18:26 With the **p** You will show
Ps 18:26 You will show Yourself **p**;
Ps 19: 8 of the LORD is **p**,
Ps 24: 4 who has clean hands and a **p**
Ps 73: 1 To such as are **p** in heart.
Prov 16: 2 the ways of a man are **p** in
Prov 20: 9 I am **p** from my sin"?
Prov 30: 5 Every word of God is **p**;
Dan 7: 9 hair of His head was like **p**
Matt 5: 8 Blessed are the **p** in heart,
Phil 4: 8 just, whatever things are **p**,
1Ti 1: 5 is love from a **p** heart,
1Ti 3: 9 of the faith with a **p**
1Ti 5:22 sins; keep yourself **p**.
Heb 10:22 and our bodies washed with **p**
Jas 1:27 **P** and undefiled religion
Jas 3:17 is from above is first **p**,
1Pe 2: 2 desire the **p** milk of the
1Jn 3: 3 himself, just as He is **p**.
Rev 15: 6 clothed in **p** bright linen,

Rev 21:21 street of the city was **p**

PURER† (*see* PURE)
Hab 1:13 You are of **p** eyes than to

PURGE (*see* PURGED)
Ps 51: 7 **P** me with hyssop, and I
1Co 5: 7 Therefore **p** out the old

PURGED (*see* PURGE, PURIFIED)
Is 6: 7 taken away, And your sin **p**.
Heb 1: 3 when He had by Himself **p** our

PURIFICATION (*see* PURIFY)
Lev 12: 4 until the days of her **p** are
Luke 2:22 Now when the days of her **p**
John 2: 6 to the manner of **p** of the

PURIFIED (*see* PURIFY)
Num 8:21 And the Levites **p** themselves
Dan 12:10 "Many shall be **p**,
Heb 9:22 law almost all things are **p**
Heb 9:23 in the heavens should be **p**
1Pe 1:22 Since you have **p** your souls

PURIFIES† (*see* PURIFY)
1Jn 3: 3 who has this hope in Him **p**

PURIFY (*see* PURE, PURIFICATION, PURIFIED, PURIFIES, PURIFYING)
Gen 35: 2 **p** yourselves, and change
Mal 3: 3 He will **p** the sons of Levi,
John 11:55 to **p** themselves.
Tit 2:14 every lawless deed and **p**
Jas 4: 8 and **p** your hearts, you

PURIFYING (*see* PURIFY)
Acts 15: 9 **p** their hearts by faith.
Heb 9:13 sanctifies for the **p** of the

PURIM (*see* PUR)
Esth 9:26 So they called these days **P**,

PURITY (*see* PURE)
1Ti 4:12 in spirit, in faith, in **p**.

PURPLE
Prov 31:22 is fine linen and **p**.
Song 7: 5 hair of your head is like **p**;
Jer 10: 9 Blue and **p** are their
Dan 5:29 they clothed Daniel with **p**
John 19: 5 crown of thorns and **p**
Acts 16:14 She was a seller of **p** from
Rev 17: 4 The woman was arrayed in **p**

PURPOSE (*see* PURPOSED, PURPOSES)
Ex 9:16 But indeed for this **p** I have
Job 42: 2 And that no **p** of Yours
Ps 20: 4 And fulfill all your **p**.
Eccl 3: 1 A time for every **p** under
Luke 4:43 because for this **p** I have
John 12:27 But for this **p** I came to
Acts 2:23 by the determined **p** and
Acts 11:23 them all that with **p** of
Rom 8:28 called according to His **p**.
Rom 9:17 For this very **p** I have
Gal 3:19 What **p** then does the law
Eph 1:11 according to the **p** of Him
Eph 3:11 according to the eternal **p**
1Ti 1: 5 Now the **p** of the commandment
2Ti 3:10 doctrine, manner of life, **p**,
1Jn 3: 8 For this **p** the Son of God
Rev 17:17 hearts to fulfill His **p**,

PURPOSED (*see* PURPOSE)
Dan 1: 8 But Daniel **p** in his heart
Acts 19:21 Paul **p** in the Spirit, when
Eph 1: 9 good pleasure which He **p** in

PURPOSES (*see* PURPOSE)
2Co 9: 7 let each one give as he **p**

PURSUE (*see* PURSUED, PURSUES, PURSUING, PURSUIT)
Ex 14: 4 so that he will **p** them; and
Deut 19: 6 **p** the manslayer and overtake
Josh 10:19 but **p** your enemies, and
Job 30:15 They **p** my honor as the
Ps 34:14 Seek peace and **p** it.
Ps 35: 3 And stop those who **p** me.
Ps 35: 6 let the angel of the LORD **p**
Jer 29:18 And I will **p** them with the
Hos 6: 3 Let us **p** the knowledge of
Rom 9:30 who did not **p** righteousness,
Rom 14:19 Therefore let us **p** the things
1Co 14: 1 **P** love, and desire spiritual
1Th 5:15 but always **p** what is good
1Ti 6:11 flee these things and **p**
Heb 12:14 **P** peace with all people, and
1Pe 3:11 him seek peace and **p**

PURSUED (*see* PURSUE)
Ps 18:37 I have **p** my enemies and
Amos 1:11 Because he **p** his brother

PURSUES (*see* PURSUE)
Lev 26:17 you shall flee when no one **p**
Prov 28: 1 wicked flee when no one **p**,
Hos 12: 1 And **p** the east wind; He

PURSUING (*see* PURSUE)
Rom 9:31 **p** the law of righteousness,

PURSUIT (*see* PURSUE)
Gen 14:14 and went in **p** as far as Dan.

PUSHED
Judg 16:30 the Philistines!" And he **p**

PUT DOWN (*see* ABASE)
Dan 4:37 walk in pride He is able to **p**

PUTREFYING†
Is 1: 6 wounds and bruises and **p**

Q

QUAIL (*see* QUAILS)
Num 11:32 and gathered the **q** (he who
Ps 105:40 asked, and He brought **q**,

QUAILS† (*see* QUAIL)
Ex 16:13 So it was that **q** came up at

QUAKED
Ex 19:18 and the whole mountain **q**
Matt 27:51 to bottom; and the earth **q**,

QUALIFIED
Col 1:12 to the Father who has **q** us

QUARREL (*see* QUARRELED, QUARRELSOME)
Matt 12:19 He will not **q** nor cry

QUARRELED (*see* QUARREL)
Gen 26:20 But the herdsmen of Gerar **q**

QUARRELSOME† (*see* QUARREL)
1Ti 3: 3 for money, but gentle, not **q**,

QUARTER (*see* QUARTERS)
2Ki 22:14 in Jerusalem in the Second **Q**.

QUARTERS (*see* QUARTER)
Jer 49:36 four winds From the four **q**

QUEEN (*see* QUEENS)
1Ki 10: 1 Now when the **q** of Sheba heard
Jer 7:18 to make cakes for the **q** of
Jer 44:17 to burn incense to the **q** of
Matt 12:42 The **q** of the South will rise
Rev 18: 7 in her heart, 'I sit as **q**,

QUEENS (*see* QUEEN)
Song 6: 8 There are sixty **q** And

QUENCH (*see* QUENCHED, UNQUENCHABLE)
Song 8: 7 Many waters cannot **q** love,
Is 42: 3 smoking flax He will not **q**;
Matt 12:20 flax He will not **q**,
1Th 5:19 Do not **q** the Spirit.

QUENCHED (*see* QUENCH)
Mark 9:43 fire that shall never be **q**—
Heb 11:34 **q** the violence of fire,

QUESTION (*see* QUESTIONED, QUESTIONS)
Job 38: 3 I will **q** you, and you shall
Matt 22:35 a lawyer, asked Him a **q**,
Matt 22:46 day on did anyone dare **q**

QUESTIONED (*see* QUESTION)
Luke 23: 9 Then he **q** Him with many

QUESTIONS (*see* QUESTION)
1Ki 10: 3 Solomon answered all her **q**;
Luke 2:46 to them and asking them **q**.

QUICK† (*see* QUICK-TEMPERED, QUICKLY)
Dan 1: 4 possessing knowledge and **q**

QUICK-TEMPERED† (*see* QUICK)
Prov 14:17 A **q** man acts foolishly,
Tit 1: 7 God, not self-willed, not **q**,

QUICKLY (*see* QUICK)
Deut 11:17 and you perish **q** from the
Eccl 4:12 a threefold cord is not **q**
Matt 5:25 with your adversary **q**,
Matt 28: 7 And go **q** and tell His
John 11:31 saw that Mary rose up **q** and
John 13:27 to him, "What you do, do **q**.
2Ti 4: 9 Be diligent to come to me **q**;
Rev 2: 5 or else I will come to you **q**
Rev 3:11 I am coming **q**! Hold fast
Rev 22:20 says, "Surely I am coming **q**.

QUIET (*see* QUIETLY, QUIETNESS)
Is 7: 4 to him: 'Take heed, and be **q**;
Jer 47: 6 How long until you are **q**?
Mark 1:25 rebuked him, saying, "Be **q**,
1Th 4:11 you also aspire to lead a **q**
1Pe 3: 4 beauty of a gentle and **q**

QUIETLY (*see* QUIET)
Zech 1:11 all the earth is resting **q**.

QUIETNESS (*see* QUIET)
Is 30:15 In **q** and confidence shall
2Th 3:12 Christ that they work in **q**

QUIRINIUS†
Luke 2: 2 first took place while **Q**

QUIVER
Ps 127: 5 is the man who has his **q**
Is 49: 2 In His **q** He has hidden

QUOTA
Ex 5: 8 you shall lay on them the **q**

R

RAAMSES† (*see* RAMESES)
Ex 1:11 supply cities, Pithom and **R**.

RABBAH
2Sa 11: 1 of Ammon and besieged **R**.
Amos 1:14 a fire in the wall of **R**,

RABBI (*see* RABBONI)
Matt 23: 7 and to be called by men, '**R**,
Matt 26:25 Him, answered and said, "**R**,
Mark 9: 5 and said to Jesus, "**R**,
John 1:49 and said to Him, "**R**,

RABBONI (*see* RABBI)
John 20:16 R!" (which is to say,

RABSHAKEH
Is 36: 2 king of Assyria sent the R

RACA†
Matt 5:22 R!' shall be in danger of the

RACE†
Ps 19: 5 a strong man to run its r.
Eccl 9:11 The r is not to the swift,
Zech 9: 6 A mixed r shall settle in
Acts 20:24 so that I may finish my r
1Co 9:24 that those who run in a r
2Ti 4: 7 fight, I have finished the r,
Heb 12: 1 us run with endurance the r

RACHEL (*see* RACHEL'S)
Gen 29:11 Then Jacob kissed R,
Gen 29:16 name of the younger was R.
Gen 29:18 Now Jacob loved R;
Gen 29:20 served seven years for R,
Gen 30:25 when R had borne Joseph,
Gen 35:19 So R died and was buried on
Ruth 4:11 coming to your house like R
Jer 31:15 R weeping for her children,
Matt 2:18 R weeping for her

RACHEL'S (*see* RACHEL)
Gen 30: 7 And R maid Bilhah conceived

RADIANT
Ps 34: 5 looked to Him and were r,

RAFTS†
1Ki 5: 9 I will float them in r by
2Ch 2:16 we will bring it to you in r

RAGE (*see* RAGING)
Ps 2: 1 Why do the nations r,
Dan 3:13 in r and fury, gave the
Acts 4:25 did the nations r,

RAGING (*see* RAGE)
Ps 22:13 Like a r and roaring lion.
Jon 1:15 the sea ceased from its r.
Luke 8:24 rebuked the wind and the r
Jude 13 r waves of the sea, foaming

RAGS
Is 64: 6 are like filthy r;
Jer 38:12 put these old clothes and r

RAHAB
Josh 2: 1 house of a harlot named R,
Ps 89:10 You have broken R in pieces,
Matt 1: 5 Salmon begot Boaz by R,
Heb 11:31 By faith the harlot R did not
Jas 2:25 was not R the harlot also

RAIDED
Job 1:15 when the Sabeans r them and

RAIN (*see* RAINED, RAINS, RAINY)
Gen 2: 5 God had not caused it to r
Gen 7: 4 days I will cause it to r
Ex 9:18 cause very heavy hail to r
Ex 16: 4 I will r bread from heaven
Lev 26: 4 then I will give you r in its
Deut 11:11 drinks water from the r of
Deut 11:14 the early r and the latter
Deut 32: 2 my teaching drop as the r,
1Sa 12:17 He will send thunder and r,
2Sa 1:21 there be no dew nor r
1Ki 17: 1 there shall not be dew nor r
1Ki 18:41 the sound of abundance of r.
Job 29:23 wide as for the spring r.
Job 36:27 Which distill as r from the
Ps 11: 6 Upon the wicked He will r
Ps 135: 7 makes lightning for the r;
Eccl 11: 3 If the clouds are full of r,

Eccl 12: 2 do not return after the r;
Song 2:11 The r is over and gone.
Is 4: 6 a shelter from storm and r.
Is 45: 8 R down, you heavens, from
Is 55:10 For as the r comes down, and
Hos 6: 3 will come to us like the r,
Amos 4: 7 I also withheld r from you,
Zech 10: 1 Ask the LORD for r In the
Matt 5:45 and sends r on the just and
Matt 7:25 and the r descended, the
Jas 5:17 and it did not r on the land
Jas 5:18 again, and the heaven gave r,

RAINBOW
Gen 9:13 I set My r in the cloud, and
Rev 10: 1 And a r was on his head,

RAINED (*see* RAIN)
Gen 19:24 Then the LORD r brimstone
Ex 9:23 And the LORD r hail on the
Ps 78:24 Had r down manna on them to
Ps 78:27 He also r meat on them like
Luke 17:29 Lot went out of Sodom it r

RAINS (*see* RAIN)
2Sa 21:10 of harvest until the late r
Hos 10:12 Till He comes and r

RAINY† (*see* RAIN)
Prov 27:15 dripping on a very r day
Ezek 1:28 a rainbow in a cloud on a r

RAISE (*see* PERPETUATE, RAISED, RAISES, RAISING)
Gen 38: 8 and r up an heir to your
Deut 18:18 I will r up for them a
Deut 32:40 For I r My hand to heaven,
Is 13: 2 R your voice to them; Wave
Is 29: 3 And I will r siegeworks
Is 49: 6 should be My Servant To r
Hos 6: 2 On the third day He will r
Amos 9:11 On that day I will r up The
Matt 3: 9 to you that God is able to r
Matt 10: 8 r the dead, cast out demons.
Matt 22:24 shall marry his wife and r
Mark 12:19 should take his wife and r
Luke 18:13 would not so much as r his
John 2:19 and in three days I will r
John 6:40 and I will r him up at the
Acts 2:30 He would r up the Christ to
Acts 3:22 LORD your God will r
1Co 6:14 up the Lord and will also r
1Co 15:15 whom He did not r up—if in
2Co 4:14 the Lord Jesus will also r
Heb 11:19 that God was able to r
Jas 5:15 and the Lord will r him up.

RAISED (*see* RAISE)
Gen 14:22 I have r my hand to the
Ex 9:16 for this purpose I have r
Judg 2:16 the LORD r up judges who
Judg 3: 9 the LORD r up a deliverer
2Sa 20:21 has r his hand against the
Job 2:12 And when they r their eyes
Is 41: 2 Who r up one from the east?
Jer 29:15 The LORD has r up prophets
Dan 7: 5 It was r up on one side, and
Matt 11: 5 the dead are r up and the
Matt 16:21 and be r the third day.
Matt 26:32 "But after I have been r,
Matt 27:52 who had fallen asleep were r;
Luke 7:22 deaf hear, the dead are r,
John 12: 1 whom He had r from the dead.
Acts 2:32 This Jesus God has r up, of
Acts 3:26 having r up His Servant
Acts 4:10 whom God r from the dead, by
Acts 4:24 they r their voice to God
Rom 4:24 us who believe in Him who r
Rom 4:25 and was r because of our

Rom   6: 4 that just as Christ was **r**
Rom   8:11 if the Spirit of Him who **r**
Rom   9:17 very purpose I have **r**
Rom   10: 9 in your heart that God has **r**
1Co   6:14 And God both **r** up the Lord
1Co   15:12 preached that He has been **r**
1Co   15:42 it is **r** in incorruption.
2Co   4:14 knowing that He who **r** up the
Eph   2: 6 and **r** us up together, and
Col   2:12 in which you also were **r**
Heb   11:35 Women received their dead **r**

RAISES (*see* RAISE)
1Sa   2: 8 He **r** the poor from the dust
Prov   1:20 She **r** her voice in the open
Dan   2:21 He removes kings and **r** up
John   5:21 For as the Father **r** the dead

RAISIN† (*see* RAISINS)
Hos   3: 1 other gods and love the **r**

RAISING (*see* RAISE)
Acts 17:31 of this to all by **r** Him

RAISINS (*see* RAISIN)
1Ch   12:40 cakes of figs and cakes of **r**,

RAM (*see* RAM'S, RAMS)
Gen   15: 9 goat, a three-year-old **r**,
Gen   22:13 Abraham went and took the **r**,
Ex   29:15 "You shall also take one **r**,
Ex   29:15 hands on the head of the **r**;
Lev   5:15 as his trespass offering a **r**
Lev   8:22 And he brought the second **r**,
Lev   8:22 the **r** of consecration. Then
Ruth   4:19 Hezron begot **R**,
Dan   8: 3 was a **r** which had two horns,
Matt   1: 4 **R** begot Amminadab, Amminadab
Luke   3:33 of Amminadab, the son of **R**,

RAM'S† (*see* RAM)
Josh   6: 5 a long blast with the **r**
Hos   5: 8 Blow the **r** horn in Gibeah,

RAMAH (*see* RAMOTH)
1Sa   8: 4 and came to Samuel at **R**,
1Sa   25: 1 buried him at his home in **R**.
Jer   31:15 "A voice was heard in **R**,
Matt   2:18 voice was heard in **R**,

RAMESES (*see* RAAMSES)
Gen   47:11 the land, in the land of **R**,
Ex   12:37 of Israel journeyed from **R**

RAMOTH (*see* JARMUTH, RAMAH)
Deut   4:43 **R** in Gilead for the Gadites,
2Ki   9: 4 went to **R** Gilead.
2Ch   22: 5 Hazael king of Syria at **R**

RAMPART
Nah   3: 8 Whose **r** was the sea,
Hab   2: 1 And set myself on the **r**,

RAMS (*see* RAM, RAMS')
Gen   31:10 the **r** which leaped upon the
Ex   29: 1 one young bull and two **r**
Lev   8: 2 as the sin offering, two **r**,
1Sa   15:22 to heed than the fat of **r**.
Ps   114: 4 mountains skipped like **r**,
Is   1:11 of burnt offerings of **r**
Ezek 21:22 to set up battering **r**,
Mic   6: 7 pleased with thousands of **r**,

RAMS' (*see* RAMS)
Josh   6: 4 bear seven trumpets of **r**

RAN (*see* RUN)
Gen   18: 2 he **r** from the tent door to
Gen   33: 4 But Esau **r** to meet him, and
1Sa   3: 5 So he **r** to Eli and said,
1Sa   17:51 Therefore David **r** and stood
1Ki   18:35 So the water **r** all around the

Jer   23:21 these prophets, yet they **r**.
Matt   8:32 the whole herd of swine **r**
Matt 28: 8 and **r** to bring His disciples
Luke 24:12 But Peter arose and **r** to the
John   2: 3 And when they **r** out of wine,
Acts 27:41 they **r** the ship aground; and
Gal   5: 7 You **r** well. Who hindered you

RANDOM†
1Ki   22:34 certain man drew a bow at **r**,
2Ch   18:33 certain man drew a bow at **r**,

RANKS
Prov 30:27 Yet they all advance in **r**;
Mark   6:40 So they sat down in **r**,

RANSOM (*see* RANSOMED)
Num   35:31 you shall take no **r** for the
Ps   49: 7 Nor give to God a **r** for
Prov 13: 8 The **r** of a man's life is
Hos   13:14 I will **r** them from the power
Matt 20:28 and to give His life a **r** for
Mark 10:45 and to give His life a **r** for
1Ti   2: 6 who gave Himself a **r** for all,

RANSOMED (*see* RANSOM)
Is   35:10 And the **r** of the LORD shall
Jer   31:11 And **r** him from the hand of

RARE
1Sa   3: 1 the word of the LORD was **r**

RASH
Num   30: 6 bound by her vows or by a **r**
Eccl   5: 2 Do not be **r** with your mouth,

RATION†
2Ki   25:30 there was a regular **r**
Jer   52:34 there was a regular **r** given

RATS
1Sa   6: 4 tumors and five golden **r**,

RATTLING
Ezek 37: 7 a noise, and suddenly a **r**;

RAVEN (*see* RAVENS)
Gen   8: 7 Then he sent out a **r**,
Song   5:11 wavy, And black as a **r**

RAVENOUS
Gen   49:27 Benjamin is a **r** wolf; In the
Matt   7:15 but inwardly they are **r**

RAVENS (*see* RAVEN)
1Ki   17: 6 The **r** brought him bread and
Luke 12:24 "Consider the **r**,

RAVISHED
Song   4: 9 You have **r** my heart, My
Zech 14: 2 rifled, And the women **r**.

RAW
Ex   12: 9 'Do not eat it **r**,

RAZE†
Ps   137: 7 **R** it, raze it, To its very

RAZOR
Num   6: 5 vow of his separation no **r**
Judg 13: 5 And no **r** shall come upon his
1Sa   1:11 and no **r** shall come upon his
Is   7:20 will shave with a hired **r**,

READ (*see* READER, READING, READS)
Ex   24: 7 Book of the Covenant and **r**
Deut 17:19 and he shall **r** it all the
Neh   8: 3 Then he **r** from it in the open
Neh   8: 8 So they **r** distinctly from the
Jer   36: 6 And you shall also **r** them in
Dan   5: 8 but they could not **r** the
Matt 12: 5 Or have you not **r** in the law
Luke   4:16 day, and stood up to **r**.
John 19:20 Then many of the Jews **r** this

Acts 8:32 in the Scripture which he **r**
Acts 13:27 of the Prophets which are **r**
Acts 15:21 being **r** in the synagogues
2Co 3: 2 known and **r** by all men;
2Co 3:15 to this day, when Moses is **r**,
Col 4:16 Now when this epistle is **r**

READER† (see READ)
Mark 13:14 it ought not" (let the **r**

READINESS† (see READY)
Acts 17:11 received the word with all **r**,
2Co 8:11 that as there was a **r** to

READING (see READ)
Neh 8: 8 them to understand the **r**.
Acts 8:28 he was **r** Isaiah the prophet.
Acts 8:30 understand what you are **r**?
2Co 3:14 remains unlifted in the **r**
1Ti 4:13 I come, give attention to **r**,

READS† (see READ)
Dan 5: 7 Whoever **r** this writing, and
Hab 2: 2 That he may run who **r** it.
Matt 24:15 the holy place" (whoever **r**,
Rev 1: 3 Blessed is he who **r** and

READY (see READINESS)
Ex 19:15 Be **r** for the third day; do
Neh 9:17 **R** to pardon, Gracious and
Ps 11: 2 They make **r** their arrow on
Ps 45: 1 tongue is the pen of a **r**
Ps 86: 5 and **r** to forgive, And
Jer 1:12 for I am **r** to perform My
Dan 3:15 Now if you are **r** at the time
Matt 22: 8 servants, 'The wedding is **r**,
Matt 24:44 "Therefore you also be **r**,
Luke 1:17 to make **r** a people prepared
Luke 7: 2 was sick and **r** to die.
Acts 21:13 For I am **r** not only to be
Rom 1:15 I am **r** to preach the
2Co 8:19 and to show your **r** mind,
2Co 12:14 for the third time I am **r**
2Ti 4: 2 Preach the word! Be **r** in
Tit 3: 1 to be **r** for every good work,
Heb 8:13 and growing old is **r** to
1Pe 1: 5 faith for salvation **r** to be
1Pe 3:15 and always be **r** to give a
1Pe 4: 5 an account to Him who is **r**
Rev 12: 4 before the woman who was **r**

REALLY
Luke 18: 8 will He **r** find faith on the

REAP (see REAPED, REAPER, REAPING, REAPS)
Lev 25:11 you shall neither sow nor **r**
Ps 126: 5 who sow in tears Shall **r**
Prov 22: 8 He who sows iniquity will **r**
Hos 8: 7 And **r** the whirlwind. The
Matt 6:26 for they neither sow nor **r**
Matt 25:26 you knew that I **r** where I
John 4:38 I sent you to **r** that for
2Co 9: 6 sows sparingly will also **r**
Gal 6: 7 sows, that he will also **r**.
Gal 6: 8 flesh will of the flesh **r**
Gal 6: 8 Spirit will of the Spirit **r**
Rev 14:15 in Your sickle and **r**,

REAPED (see REAP)
Hos 10:13 You have **r** iniquity. You

REAPER (see REAP, REAPERS)
Amos 9:13 plowman shall overtake the **r**,

REAPERS (see REAPER)
Ruth 2: 3 in the field after the **r**.
Matt 13:39 and the **r** are the angels.

REAPING (see REAP)
Matt 25:24 **r** where you have not sown,

REAPS (see REAP)
John 4:36 And he who **r** receives wages,
John 4:36 he who sows and he who **r**

REAR
Num 10:25 the children of Dan (the **r**
Is 58: 8 of the LORD shall be your **r**

REASON (see REASONABLE, REASONED, REASONING)
Ps 90:10 And if by **r** of strength
Is 1:18 and let us **r** together,"
Matt 16: 8 why do you **r** among
Luke 5:21 and the Pharisees began to **r**,
Luke 23:22 I have found no **r** for death
Acts 26:25 the words of truth and **r**.
Rom 1:26 For this **r** God gave them up
Eph 5:31 For this **r** a man shall
1Pe 3:15 to everyone who asks you a **r**

REASONABLE† (see REASON)
Rom 12: 1 which is your **r** service.

REASONED (see REASON)
Matt 16: 7 And they **r** among themselves,
Acts 18: 4 And he **r** in the synagogue

REASONING (see REASON)
Mark 12:28 and having heard them **r**
Luke 5:22 Why are you **r** in your hearts?
Acts 19: 8 **r** and persuading concerning

REBECCA† (see REBEKAH)
Rom 9:10 but when **R** also had

REBEKAH (see REBECCA, REBEKAH'S)
Gen 25:28 but **R** loved Jacob.
Gen 26:35 grief of mind to Isaac and **R**.

REBEKAH'S (see REBEKAH)
Gen 35: 8 **R** nurse, died, and she was

REBEL (see REBELLED, REBELLING, REBELLION, REBELLIOUS)
Josh 22:19 but do not **r** against the
Is 1:20 But if you refuse and **r**,
Is 36: 5 that you **r** against me?

REBELLED (see REBEL)
Gen 14: 4 the thirteenth year they **r**.
2Ki 3: 5 that the king of Moab **r**
2Ki 24:20 Then Zedekiah **r** against the
Ps 5:10 For they have **r** against
Is 1: 2 And they have **r** against Me;
Lam 3:42 We have transgressed and **r**;
Dan 9: 5 we have done wickedly and **r**,
Hos 8: 1 My covenant And **r** against

REBELLING† (see REBEL)
Ps 78:17 even more against Him By **r**

REBELLION (see REBEL)
Deut 31:27 for I know your **r** and your
1Sa 15:23 For **r** is as the sin of
Ps 95: 8 your hearts, as in the **r**,
Mark 15: 7 committed murder in the **r**.
Luke 23:19 into prison for a certain **r**
Acts 21:38 time ago stirred up a **r** and
Heb 3: 8 hearts as in the **r**,
Jude 11 and perished in the **r** of

REBELLIOUS (see REBEL)
Deut 21:20 of ours is stubborn and **r**;
1Sa 20:30 **r** woman! Do I not know that
Ps 78: 8 A stubborn and **r**
Prov 7:11 She was loud and **r**,
Is 30: 1 Woe to the **r** children," says
Is 65: 2 My hands all day long to a **r**
Jer 5:23 people has a defiant and **r**
Ezek 2: 5 for they are a **r** house—yet
Hos 9:15 All their princes are **r**.

REBUILD (see REBUILDING, REBUILT)
Ezra 9: 9 to r its ruins, and to give
Is 61: 4 And they shall r the old
Acts 15:16 return And will r the

REBUILDING (see REBUILD)
Ezra 5:11 and we are r the temple that
Neh 6: 6 you are r the wall, that you

REBUILT (see REBUILD)
Judg 18:28 So they r the city and dwelt
2Ki 21: 3 For he r the high places
Ezra 5:15 let the house of God be r

REBUKE (see REBUKED)
Ruth 2:16 and do not r her."
Ps 6: 1 do not r me in Your anger,
Ps 50: 8 I will not r you for your
Ps 50:21 But I will r you, And set
Ps 119:21 You r the proud—the cursed,
Prov 9: 8 R a wise man, and he will
Prov 27: 5 Open r is better Than love
Prov 30: 6 Lest He r you, and you be
Is 1:17 R the oppressor; Defend
Jer 15:15 Your sake I have suffered r.
Mic 4: 3 And r strong nations afar
Zech 3: 2 The LORD r you, Satan! The
Mal 3:11 And I will r the devourer for
Matt 11:20 Then He began to r the
Matt 16:22 Him aside and began to r
Luke 19:39 r Your disciples."
1Ti 5: 1 Do not r an older man, but
2Ti 4: 2 out of season. Convince, r,
Tit 2:15 and r with all authority.

REBUKED (see REBUKE)
Gen 37:10 and his father r him and
Ps 9: 5 You have r the nations, You
Ps 105:14 He r kings for their sakes,
Ps 106: 9 He r the Red Sea also, and
Prov 29: 1 He who is often r,
Matt 8:26 Then He arose and r the
Matt 17:18 And Jesus r the demon, and it
Matt 19:13 but the disciples r them.
Mark 8:33 He r Peter, saying, "Get
Mark 9:25 He r the unclean spirit,
Luke 4:39 So He stood over her and r
Heb 12: 5 when you are r by Him;
2Pe 2:16 but he was r for his

REBUKES
Prov 9: 7 And he who r a wicked man

RECALL
Lam 3:21 This I r to my mind,
Heb 10:32 But r the former days in

RECEDED
Gen 8: 3 And the waters r continually
Gen 8: 8 to see if the waters had r
Rev 6:14 Then the sky r as a scroll

RECEIVE (see RECEIVED, RECEIVES, RECEIVING)
Gen 4:11 has opened its mouth to r
Job 3:12 Why did the knees r me? Or
Ps 24: 5 He shall r blessing from the
Ps 49:15 For He shall r me. Selah
Ps 73:24 And afterward r me to
Prov 19:20 Listen to counsel and r
Dan 2: 6 you shall r from me gifts,
Mal 3:10 not be room enough to r
Matt 10:14 And whoever will not r you
Matt 10:41 name of a prophet shall r a
Matt 11:14 if you are willing to r
Matt 19:29 shall r a hundredfold, and
Matt 21:22 believing, you will r.
Mark 10:51 that I may r my sight."
Mark 11:24 believe that you r them,
Luke 9: 5 And whoever will not r you,

Luke 18:30 who shall not r many times
Luke 23:41 for we r the due reward of
John 1:11 and His own did not r Him.
John 3:11 and you do not r Our
John 5:41 I do not r honor from men.
John 12:48 and does not r My words, has
John 14: 3 I will come again and r you
John 14:17 whom the world cannot r,
John 16:24 My name. Ask, and you will r,
John 20:22 R the Holy Spirit.
Acts 1: 8 But you shall r power when
Acts 2:38 and you shall r the gift of
Acts 3:21 whom heaven must r until the
Acts 7:59 Lord Jesus, r my spirit."
Acts 20:35 blessed to give than to r.
Rom 8:15 For you did not r the spirit
Rom 14: 1 R one who is weak in the
1Co 2:14 the natural man does not r
1Co 3:14 he will r a reward.
1Co 4: 7 you have that you did not r?
Gal 3: 2 Did you r the Spirit by the
Gal 4: 5 that we might r the adoption
Heb 9:15 those who are called may r
Heb 11: 8 the place which he would r
Heb 11:39 did not r the promise,
Jas 1: 7 man suppose that he will r
Jas 1:12 he will r the crown of life
Jas 4: 3 You ask and do not r,
1Pe 5: 4 you will r the crown of
1Jn 3:22 And whatever we ask we r from
Rev 4:11 To r glory and honor and
Rev 13:16 to r a mark on their right

RECEIVED (see RECEIVE)
1Sa 12: 3 or from whose hand have I r
Job 4:12 And my ear r a whisper of
Ps 68:18 You have r gifts among men,
Is 40: 2 For she has r from the
Matt 10: 8 demons. Freely you have r,
Matt 17:24 those who r the temple tax
Mark 16:19 He was r up into heaven, and
Luke 9:51 had come for Him to be r up,
John 1:12 But as many as r Him, to them
John 1:16 His fullness we have all r,
John 9:11 and I r sight."
Acts 1: 9 and a cloud r Him out of
Acts 8:17 and they r the Holy Spirit.
Acts 15: 4 they were r by the church
Rom 1: 5 Through Him we have r grace
Rom 4:11 And he r the sign of
Rom 5:11 through whom we have now r
Rom 8:15 but you r the Spirit of
1Co 4: 7 boast as if you had not r
1Co 11:23 For I r from the Lord that
1Co 15: 3 of all that which I also r:
Gal 1:12 For I neither r it from man,
Phil 4: 9 which you learned and r and
1Th 1: 6 having r the word in much
2Th 3: 6 to the tradition which he r
1Ti 3:16 R up in glory.
1Ti 4: 3 which God created to be r
Heb 2: 2 and disobedience r a just
Heb 7: 6 is not derived from them r
Heb 7:11 (for under it the people r
Heb 10:26 willfully after we have r
Heb 11:13 not having r the promises,
1Pe 4:10 As each one has r a gift,
1Jn 2:27 anointing which you have r
Rev 2:27 as I also have r from My
Rev 19:20 he deceived those who r the

RECEIVES (see RECEIVE)
Prov 15: 5 But he who r correction is
Matt 7: 8 "For everyone who asks r,
Matt 10:40 He who r you receives Me,
Matt 10:41 He who r a prophet in the

Matt 13:20 the word and immediately **r**
Matt 18: 5 Whoever **r** one little child
Luke 15: 2 This Man **r** sinners and eats
John 3:32 and no one **r** His testimony.
John 4:36 And he who reaps **r** wages, and
1Co 9:24 but one **r** the prize? Run in
Heb 6: 7 **r** blessing from God;
Heb 12: 6 every son whom He **r**.

RECEIVING (see RECEIVE)
Rom 1:27 and **r** in themselves the
Heb 12:28 since we are **r** a kingdom
1Pe 1: 9 **r** the end of your faith—the

RECHAB (see RECHABITES)
2Ki 10:15 met Jehonadab the son of **R**,
Jer 35: 8 of Jonadab the son of **R**,

RECHABITES (see RECHAB)
Jer 35: 5 sons of the house of the **R**

RECITE†
Ps 45: 1 I **r** my composition

RECKON (see RECKONING)
Rom 6:11 **r** yourselves to be dead

RECKONING (see RECKON)
Gen 9: 5 I will demand a **r**;

RECLINE†
Amos 6: 7 And those who **r** at banquets

RECOGNIZE (see RECOGNIZED)
Gen 27:23 And he did not **r** him, because
Job 2:12 and did not **r** him, they

RECOGNIZED (see RECOGNIZE)
Gen 42: 8 So Joseph **r** his brothers, but
Acts 12:14 When she **r** Peter's voice,

RECOMPENSE
Deut 32:35 Vengeance is Mine, and **r**;
Hos 9: 7 The days of **r** have come.

RECONCILE (see RECONCILED, RECONCILIATION, RECONCILING)
Eph 2:16 and that He might **r** them both
Col 1:20 and by Him to **r** all things to

RECONCILED (see RECONCILE)
Matt 5:24 First be **r** to your brother,
Rom 5:10 we were enemies we were **r**
2Co 5:20 be **r** to God.
Col 1:21 yet now He has **r**

RECONCILIATION† (see RECONCILE)
Dan 9:24 To make **r** for iniquity, To
Rom 5:11 we have now received the **r**.
2Co 5:18 given us the ministry of **r**,
2Co 5:19 to us the word of **r**.

RECONCILING (see RECONCILE)
2Co 5:19 that God was in Christ **r** the

RECOVER (see RECOVERED, RECOVERY)
2Ki 8: 8 Shall I **r** from this disease?'
Is 38:21 on the boil, and he shall **r**.
Mark 16:18 on the sick, and they will **r**.

RECOVERED (see RECOVER)
2Ki 20: 7 it on the boil, and he **r**.

RECOVERY† (see RECOVER)
Jer 8:22 Why then is there no **r** For
Luke 4:18 to the captives And **r**

RED (see REDNESS)
Gen 25:25 And the first came out **r**.
Gen 25:30 feed me with that same **r**
Ex 10:19 and blew them into the **R**
Ex 25: 5 "ram skins dyed **r**,
Ps 106: 9 He rebuked the **R** Sea also,
Ps 136:13 To Him who divided the **R** Sea

Prov 23:31 on the wine when it is **r**,
Is 1:18 Though they are **r** like
Is 63: 2 Why is Your apparel **r**,
Zech 1: 8 a man riding on a **r** horse,
Zech 6: 2 the first chariot were **r**
Matt 16: 2 weather, for the sky is **r**';
Heb 11:29 they passed through the **R**
Rev 6: 4 Another horse, fiery **r**,
Rev 12: 3 fiery **r** dragon having seven

REDEEM (see REDEEMED, REDEEMER, REDEEMING, REDEEMS, REDEMPTION)
Ex 6: 6 and I will **r** you with an
Ex 13:13 of a donkey you shall **r**
Ex 13:15 the firstborn of my sons I **r**.
Lev 25:25 relative comes to **r** it,
Lev 27:20 if he does not want to **r**
Ruth 4: 4 If you will **r** it, redeem
Ruth 4: 6 I cannot **r** it for myself,
2Sa 7:23 the earth whom God went to **r**
Job 5:20 In famine He shall **r** you
Ps 44:26 And **r** us for Your mercies'
Ps 49:15 But God will **r** my soul from
Ps 130: 8 And He shall **r** Israel From
Hos 13:14 I will **r** them from death.
Mic 4:10 There the LORD will **r** you
Luke 24:21 it was He who was going to **r**
Gal 4: 5 to **r** those who were under the
Tit 2:14 that He might **r** us from

REDEEMED (see REDEEM)
Gen 48:16 The Angel who has **r** me from
Ex 15:13 The people whom You have **r**;
2Sa 4: 9 who has **r** my life from all
Ps 31: 5 You have **r** me, O LORD God
Ps 55:18 He has **r** my soul in peace
Ps 71:23 my soul, which You have **r**.
Ps 77:15 You have with Your arm **r**
Ps 106:10 And **r** them from the hand of
Ps 107: 2 Let the **r** of the LORD say
Is 43: 1 for I have **r** you; I have
Is 62:12 The **R** of the LORD; And
Luke 1:68 For He has visited and **r**
Gal 3:13 Christ has **r** us from the
1Pe 1:18 knowing that you were not **r**
Rev 5: 9 And have **r** us to God by

REDEEMER (see REDEEM)
Job 19:25 For I know that my **R** lives,
Ps 19:14 LORD, my strength and my **R**.
Prov 23:11 For their **R** is mighty; He
Is 41:14 says the LORD and your **R**,
Is 49: 7 The **R** of Israel, their Holy
Is 49:26 am your Savior, And your **R**,
Is 63:16 Our **R** from Everlasting is

REDEEMING (see REDEEM)
Eph 5:16 **r** the time, because the days

REDEEMING RELATIVE
Lev 25:25 if his **r** comes to redeem it,

REDEEMS† (see REDEEM)
Ps 34:22 The LORD **r** the soul of His
Ps 103: 4 Who **r** your life from

REDEMPTION (see REDEEM)
Ps 49: 8 For the **r** of their souls is
Ps 130: 7 And with Him is abundant **r**.
Luke 2:38 all those who looked for **r**
Luke 21:28 because your **r** draws near."
Rom 3:24 by His grace through the **r**
Rom 8:23 the **r** of our body.
1Co 1:30 and sanctification and **r**—
Eph 1: 7 In Him we have **r** through His
Eph 4:30 were sealed for the day of **r**.
Col 1:14 in whom we have **r** through His
Heb 9:12 having obtained eternal **r**.

REDNESS† (*see* RED)
Prov 23:29 Who has **r** of eyes?

REDUCE
Ex 5:19 You shall not **r** any bricks

REDUCED
Ex 5:11 none of your work will be **r**.

REED (*see* REEDS)
2Ki 18:21 the staff of this broken **r**,
Is 42: 3 A bruised **r** He will not
Matt 11: 7 A **r** shaken by the wind?
Matt 12:20 A bruised **r** He will
Rev 21:15 talked with me had a gold **r**

REEDS (*see* REED)
Ex 2: 5 she saw the ark among the **r**,

REFERS
Dan 8:17 that the vision **r** to the

REFINED
Job 28: 1 a place where gold is **r**.
Ps 66:10 You have **r** us as silver is
Rev 1:15 as if **r** in a furnace, and

REFORMATION†
Heb 9:10 imposed until the time of **r**.

REFRAIN
Eccl 3: 5 And a time to **r** from
1Co 9: 6 I who have no right to **r**

REFRESH (*see* REFRESHED, REFRESHING)
Song 2: 5 **R** me with apples, For I
Phm 1:20 **r** my heart in the Lord.

REFRESHED (*see* REFRESH)
Ex 23:12 and the stranger may be **r**.
Ex 31:17 day He rested and was **r**.
1Co 16:18 For they **r** my spirit and

REFRESHING (*see* REFRESH)
Acts 3:19 so that times of **r** may come

REFUGE
Num 35: 6 appoint six cities of **r**,
Deut 33:27 The eternal God is your **r**,
Ruth 2:12 wings you have come for **r**.
Ps 9: 9 A **r** in times of trouble.
Ps 14: 6 But the LORD is his **r**.
Ps 46: 1 God is our **r** and strength,
Ps 46: 7 The God of Jacob is our **r**.
Ps 91: 2 He is my **r** and my fortress;
Heb 6:18 who have fled for **r** to lay

REFUSE (*see* REFUSED, REFUSES, REFUSING)
Ex 10: 4 if you **r** to let My people
2Ki 9:37 of Jezebel shall be as **r** on
Prov 21:25 For his hands **r** to labor.
Is 1:20 But if you **r** and rebel, You
Is 7:15 that He may know to **r** the
Ezek 2: 5 they hear or whether they **r**—
1Ti 5:11 But **r** the younger widows;
Heb 12:25 See that you do not **r** Him

REFUSED (*see* REFUSE)
Gen 37:35 but he **r** to be comforted,
1Sa 16: 7 because I have **r** him. For
Ps 77: 2 My soul **r** to be comforted.
Is 8: 6 Inasmuch as these people **r**
1Ti 4: 4 and nothing is to be **r** if it
Heb 11:24 **r** to be called the son of
Heb 12:25 if they did not escape who **r**

REFUSES (*see* REFUSE)
Ex 7:14 he **r** to let the people go.
Prov 10:17 But he who **r** correction
Matt 18:17 And if he **r** to hear them,

REFUSING (*see* REFUSE)
Jer 31:15 **R** to be comforted for her

Matt 2:18 **R** to be comforted,

REGAIN
Prov 2:19 Nor do they **r** the paths of

REGARD (*see* REGARDED, REGARDING, REGARDS)
Job 13:24 And **r** me as Your enemy?
Ps 66:18 If I **r** iniquity in my heart,
Ps 102:17 He shall **r** the prayer of the
Jon 2: 8 Those who **r** worthless idols
Luke 18: 2 who did not fear God nor **r**
2Co 5:16 we **r** no one according to the

REGARDED (*see* REGARD)
Luke 1:48 For He has **r** the lowly state

REGARDING (*see* REGARD)
Luke 14: 6 they could not answer Him **r**
Col 2:16 or **r** a festival or a new

REGARDS (*see* REGARD)
Ps 138: 6 Yet He **r** the lowly; But
Prov 13:18 But he who **r** a rebuke will

REGENERATION
Tit 3: 5 through the washing of **r** and

REGIMENT
Acts 10: 1 was called the Italian **R**,

REGION (*see* REGIONS)
Ezra 4:11 the men of the **r** beyond
Matt 8:34 Him to depart from their **r**.
Luke 7:17 and all the surrounding **r**.

REGIONS (*see* REGION)
Matt 4:13 in the **r** of Zebulun and
Acts 19: 1 passed through the upper **r**,
2Co 10:16 preach the gospel in the **r**

REGISTERED
Luke 2: 1 all the world should be **r**.
Luke 2: 5 to be **r** with Mary, his
Heb 12:23 of the firstborn who are **r**

REGRETTED
1Sa 15:35 and the LORD **r** that He had
Matt 21:29 but afterward he **r** it and

REGULAR (*see* REGULARLY)
Num 28: 3 as a **r** burnt offering.
2Ki 25:30 there was a **r** ration given

REGULARLY (*see* REGULAR)
Job 1: 5 hearts." Thus Job did **r**.

REGULATIONS
Col 2:20 you subject yourselves to **r**—

REHOBOAM
1Ki 12: 1 And **R** went to Shechem, for
1Ki 12:21 restore the kingdom to **R**,
Matt 1: 7 Solomon begot **R**,

REIGN (*see* REIGNED, REIGNS)
Gen 37: 8 Shall you indeed **r** over us?
Ex 15:18 The LORD shall **r** forever and
Judg 9: 8 **R** over us!'
1Sa 8:11 of the king who will **r** over
1Ki 1:13 your son Solomon shall **r**
Ezra 4: 5 even until the **r** of Darius
Ps 146:10 The LORD shall **r**
Prov 8:15 By me kings **r**,
Is 24:23 the LORD of hosts will **r**
Jer 33:21 he shall not have a son to **r**
Dan 2: 1 year of Nebuchadnezzar's **r**,
Dan 6:28 of Darius and in the **r** of
Luke 1:33 And He will **r** over the house
Luke 3: 1 the fifteenth year of the **r**
Luke 19:27 who did not want me to **r**
Rom 5:17 of righteousness will **r** in
Rom 5:21 even so grace might **r**
Rom 6:12 Therefore do not let sin **r** in

1Co 4: 8 that we also might r with
1Co 15:25 For He must r till He has put
2Ti 2:12 We shall also r with Him.
Rev 5:10 And we shall r on the
Rev 11:15 and He shall r forever and
Rev 20: 6 and shall r with Him a
Rev 22: 5 And they shall r forever and

REIGNED (see REIGN)
Gen 36:31 of Edom before any king r
1Sa 13: 1 Saul r one year; and when he
2Sa 5: 4 and he r forty years.
2Sa 5: 5 In Hebron he r over Judah
1Ki 4:21 So Solomon r over all
1Ki 12:17 But Rehoboam r over the
Rom 5:14 Nevertheless death r from
Rom 5:17 one man's offense death r
Rom 5:21 so that as sin r in death,
Rev 20: 4 And they lived and r with

REIGNS (see REIGN)
1Sa 12:14 both you and the king who r
2Sa 15:10 Absalom r in Hebron!'"
Ps 96:10 the nations, "The LORD r;
Rev 19: 6 the Lord God Omnipotent r!

REJECT (see REJECTED, REJECTS)
Num 14:11 long will these people r Me?
Hos 4: 6 I also will r you from
1Ti 4: 7 But r profane and old wives'

REJECTED (see REJECT)
1Sa 8: 7 for they have not r you, but
1Sa 15:23 Because you have r the word
Ps 118:22 stone which the builders r
Is 5:24 Because they have r the law
Is 53: 3 He is despised and r by men,
Jer 14:19 Have You utterly r Judah?
Hos 4: 6 Because you have r
Hos 8: 3 Israel has r the good; The
Matt 21:42 which the builders r
Luke 17:25 suffer many things and be r
Acts 4:11 stone which was r by you
Heb 10:28 Anyone who has r Moses' law
Heb 12:17 the blessing, he was r,
1Pe 2: 7 which the builders r

REJECTS (see REJECT)
Luke 10:16 he who r you rejects Me, and
1Th 4: 8 Therefore he who r this does

REJOICE (see REJOICED, REJOICES, REJOICING)
Deut 12:12 And you shall r before the
1Sa 2: 1 Because I r in Your
Ps 2:11 And r with trembling.
Ps 9: 2 I will be glad and r in You;
Ps 9:14 I will r in Your salvation.
Ps 13: 5 My heart shall r in Your
Ps 14: 7 Let Jacob r and Israel be
Ps 20: 5 We will r in your salvation,
Ps 32:11 Be glad in the LORD and r,
Ps 33: 1 R in the LORD, O you
Ps 35:19 Let them not r over me who
Ps 51: 8 bones You have broken may r.
Ps 63: 7 of Your wings I will r.
Ps 85: 6 That Your people may r in
Ps 90:14 That we may r and be glad
Ps 96:11 Let the heavens r,
Ps 97: 1 reigns; Let the earth r;
Ps 97:12 R in the LORD, you
Ps 107:42 The righteous see it and r,
Ps 118:24 We will r and be glad in
Ps 119:162 I r at Your word As one who
Prov 5:18 And r with the wife of your
Prov 23:15 is wise, My heart will r—
Prov 24:17 Do not r when your enemy
Prov 31:25 She shall r in time to
Eccl 3:22 than that a man should r in

Eccl 11: 9 R, O young man,
Is 9: 3 As men r when they divide
Is 25: 9 We will be glad and r in
Is 35: 1 And the desert shall r and
Is 62: 5 So shall your God r over
Is 65:13 Behold, My servants shall r,
Jer 15:17 of the mockers, Nor did I r;
Hab 3:18 Yet I will r in the LORD,
Zech 9: 9 R greatly, O daughter of
Matt 5:12 R and be exceedingly glad,
Matt 28: 9 R!" So they came and held
Luke 1:14 and many will r at his
Luke 1:28 the angel said to her, "R,
Luke 6:23 R in that day and leap for
Luke 10:20 but rather r because your
Luke 15: 6 R with me, for I have found
Luke 15: 9 R with me, for I have found
John 4:36 sows and he who reaps may r
Rom 5: 2 and r in hope of the glory
Rom 5:11 but we also r in God through
Rom 12:15 R with those who rejoice, and
1Co 12:26 all the members r with it.
1Co 13: 6 does not r in iniquity, but
Gal 4:27 For it is written: "R,
Phil 1:18 is preached; and in this I r,
Phil 2:16 so that I may r in the day
Phil 3: 1 r in the Lord. For me to
Phil 3: 3 r in Christ Jesus, and have
Phil 4: 4 R in the Lord always. Again I
Col 1:24 I now r in my sufferings for
1Th 5:16 R always,
1Pe 1: 6 In this you greatly r,
1Pe 1: 8 you r with joy inexpressible
1Pe 4:13 but r to the extent that you
Rev 12:12 "Therefore r, O heavens,
Rev 19: 7 Let us be glad and r and give

REJOICED (see REJOICE)
1Sa 6:13 and r to see it.
Ps 119:14 I have r in the way of Your
Matt 2:10 they r with exceedingly
Luke 1:47 And my spirit has r in God
Luke 10:21 In that hour Jesus r in the
John 8:56 Your father Abraham r to see
Acts 2:26 Therefore my heart r,
Phil 4:10 But I r in the Lord greatly

REJOICES (see REJOICE)
1Sa 2: 1 My heart r in the LORD; My
Ps 19: 5 And r like a strong man to
Matt 18:13 he r more over that sheep
1Co 13: 6 but r in the truth;

REJOICING (see REJOICE)
Ps 19: 8 r the heart; The
Ps 107:22 declare His works with r.
Ps 119:111 For they are the r of my
Ps 126: 6 doubtless come again with r,
Prov 8:30 R always before Him,
Jer 15:16 was to me the joy and r of
Luke 15: 5 lays it on his shoulders, r.
Acts 5:41 r that they were counted
Acts 8:39 and he went on his way r.
Rom 12:12 r in hope, patient in
2Co 6:10 as sorrowful, yet always r;
1Th 2:19 hope, or joy, or crown of r?

RELATION
Ruth 2:20 This man is a r of ours, one

RELATIVE (see RELATION, RELATIVES)
Ruth 2: 1 There was a r of Naomi's
Ruth 3:12 is true that I am a close r;
Luke 1:36 Elizabeth your r has also

RELATIVES (see RELATIVE)
Mark 6: 4 own country, among his own r,
Luke 2:44 sought Him among their r

Luke 14:12 your brothers, your **r**,
Acts 10:24 had called together his **r**

RELEASE (*see* RELEASED, RELEASING)
Lev 16:22 and he shall **r** the goat in
Deut 15: 9 seventh year, the year of **r**,
Ps 102:20 To **r** those appointed to
Eccl 8: 8 There is no **r** from that
Matt 27:17 Whom do you want me to **r** to
Mark 15:11 so that he should rather **r**
Luke 23:17 was necessary for him to **r**

RELEASED (*see* RELEASE)
Lev 16:26 And he who **r** the goat as the
Matt 27:26 Then he **r** Barabbas to them;
Rev 20: 7 Satan will be **r** from his

RELEASING (*see* RELEASE)
Mark 15: 6 he was accustomed to **r** one

RELENT (*see* RELENTED, RELENTS)
1Sa 15:29 not a man, that He should **r**.
Ps 110: 4 has sworn And will not **r**,
Jer 18: 8 I will **r** of the disaster
Jon 3: 9 tell if God will turn and **r**,
Heb 7:21 sworn And will not **r**,

RELENTED (*see* RELENT)
Ex 32:14 So the LORD **r** from the harm
Amos 7: 3 So the LORD **r** concerning
Jon 3:10 and God **r** from the disaster

RELENTS† (*see* RELENT)
Joel 2:13 And He **r** from doing harm.
Jon 4: 2 One who **r** from doing harm.

RELIEF
Esth 4:14 **r** and deliverance will arise

RELIGION (*see* RELIGIOUS)
Jas 1:27 Pure and undefiled **r** before

RELIGIOUS† (*see* RELIGION)
Acts 17:22 in all things you are very **r**;
Jas 1:26 among you thinks he is **r**,

REMAIN (*see* REMAINED, REMAINING, REMAINS, REMNANT)
Ex 12:10 You shall let none of it **r**
Lev 27:18 to the years that **r** till
Esth 4:14 For if you **r** completely
Jer 3: 5 Will He **r** angry forever?
Jer 24: 8 residue of Jerusalem who **r**
Lam 5:19 **r** forever; Your throne from
Amos 6: 9 that if ten men **r** in one
John 6:12 up the fragments that **r**,
John 15:11 that My joy may **r** in you,
John 15:16 that your fruit should **r**,
1Co 7: 8 is good for them if they **r**
1Co 7:11 let her **r** unmarried or be
1Co 7:26 it is good for a man to **r**
Phil 1:24 Nevertheless to **r** in the
1Th 4:15 that we who are alive and **r**
Heb 1:11 will perish, but You **r**;
Heb 12:27 which cannot be shaken may **r**
Rev 3: 2 the things which **r**,

REMAINED (*see* REMAIN)
Gen 7:23 were with him in the ark **r**
2Sa 11: 1 But David **r** at Jerusalem.
2Sa 11:12 So Uriah **r** in Jerusalem
Jer 37:21 Thus Jeremiah **r** in the court
Dan 10: 8 no strength **r** in me; for
Luke 1:22 he beckoned to them and **r**
John 1:32 And He **r** upon Him.
Gal 1:18 and **r** with him fifteen days.

REMAINING (*see* REMAIN)
John 1:33 and **r** on Him, this is He who

REMAINS (*see* REMAIN)
Gen 8:22 "While the earth **r**,

Ex 12:10 and what **r** of it until
1Sa 16:11 There **r** yet the youngest, and
Is 6:13 Whose stump **r** when it is
Jer 21: 9 He who **r** in this city shall
Dan 10:17 no strength **r** in me now, nor
Hag 2: 5 so My Spirit **r** among you; do
John 9:41 see.' Therefore your sin **r**.
John 12:24 it **r** alone; but if it dies,
1Co 7:40 But she is happier if she **r**
2Co 3:14 this day the same veil **r**
2Ti 2:13 He **r** faithful; He cannot
Heb 4: 9 There **r** therefore a rest for
Heb 7: 3 **r** a priest continually.
Heb 10:26 there no longer **r** a
1Jn 3: 9 for His seed **r** in him; and

REMALIAH
2Ki 15:27 Pekah the son of **R** became

REMEDY
Prov 6:15 he shall be broken without **r**.
Prov 29: 1 and that without **r**.

REMEMBER (*see* REMEMBERED, REMEMBERING, REMEMBERS, REMEMBRANCE)
Gen 9:15 and I will **r** My covenant
Gen 40:23 the chief butler did not **r**
Gen 41: 9 I **r** my faults this day.
Ex 13: 3 **R** this day in which you went
Ex 20: 8 **R** the Sabbath day, to keep
Deut 5:15 And **r** that you were a slave
Deut 9: 7 "**R**! Do not forget how
Deut 32: 7 **R** the days of old, Consider
1Sa 1:11 of Your maidservant and **r**
1Ch 16:12 **R** His marvelous works which
Neh 4:14 **R** the Lord, great and
Neh 5:19 **R** me, my God, for good,
Neh 13:14 **R** me, O my God, concerning
Neh 13:31 **R** me, O my God, for good!
Ps 20: 7 But we will **r** the name of
Ps 25: 7 Do not **r** the sins of my
Ps 25: 7 According to Your mercy **r**
Ps 42: 4 When I **r** these things, I
Ps 42: 6 Therefore I will **r** You from
Ps 63: 6 When I **r** You on my bed, I
Ps 77:10 But I will **r** the years
Ps 79: 8 do not **r** former iniquities
Ps 105: 5 **R** His marvelous works which
Ps 119:55 I **r** Your name in the night,
Ps 137: 6 If I do not **r** you, Let my
Prov 31: 7 And **r** his misery no more.
Eccl 12: 1 **R** now your Creator in the
Is 43:18 Do not **r** the former things,
Is 43:25 And I will not **r** your sins.
Is 46: 9 **R** the former things of old,
Is 47: 7 Nor **r** the latter end of
Is 64: 9 Nor **r** iniquity forever;
Jer 15:15 **R** me and visit me, And
Jer 31:34 and their sin I will **r** no
Lam 3:19 **R** my affliction and my
Amos 1: 9 And did not **r** the covenant
Hab 3: 2 In wrath **r** mercy.
Luke 1:72 to our fathers And to **r**
Luke 17:32 **R** Lot's wife.
Luke 23:42 me when You come into Your
John 15:20 **R** the word that I said to
Acts 20:35 And **r** the words of the Lord
Gal 2:10 only that we should **r** the
Eph 2:11 Therefore **r** that you, once
Col 4:18 **R** my chains. Grace be with
2Ti 1: 3 as without ceasing I **r** you
Heb 8:12 lawless deeds I will **r**
Heb 13: 7 **R** those who rule over you,
Rev 2: 5 **R** therefore from where you

REMEMBERED (*see* REMEMBER, REMEMBERS)
Gen 8: 1 Then God **r** Noah, and every

Gen	19:29	that God r Abraham, and sent
Gen	42: 9	Then Joseph r the dreams
Ex	6: 5	and I have r My covenant.
Ps	98: 3	He has r His mercy and His
Ps	105:42	For He r His holy promise,
Ps	111: 4	His wonderful works to be r;
Ps	136:23	Who r us in our lowly state,
Ps	137: 1	we wept When we r Zion.
Is	65:17	the former shall not be r
Hos	2:17	And they shall be r by
Jon	2: 7	I r the LORD; And my
Matt	26:75	And Peter r the word of Jesus
Luke	24: 8	And they r His words.
Rev	18: 5	and God has r her

REMEMBERING (see REMEMBER)

Mark	11:21	And Peter, r, said to Him,
1Th	1: 3	r without ceasing your work

REMEMBERS (see REMEMBER)

Ps	103:14	He r that we are dust.
Ps	103:16	And its place r it no more.
Ps	105: 8	He r His covenant forever,

REMEMBRANCE (see REMEMBER)

Ex	17:14	will utterly blot out the r
Deut	25:19	you will blot out the r of
Ps	6: 5	in death there is no r of
Ps	34:16	To cut off the r of them
Ps	97:12	And give thanks at the r of
Ps	112: 6	will be in everlasting r.
Eccl	1:11	There is no r of former
Mal	3:16	So a book of r was written
Luke	1:54	In r of His mercy,
Luke	22:19	do this in r of Me."
1Co	11:24	do this in r of Me."
1Co	11:25	drink it, in r of Me."
Phil	1: 3	I thank my God upon every r
2Ti	1: 5	when I call to r the genuine

REMIND (see REMINDER)

2Ti	1: 6	Therefore I r you to stir up
Tit	3: 1	R them to be subject to

REMINDER (see REMIND)

Heb	10: 3	sacrifices there is a r

REMISSION

Matt	26:28	is shed for many for the r
Luke	1:77	to His people By the r of
Luke	24:47	and that repentance and r of
Acts	10:43	in Him will receive r of
Heb	9:22	of blood there is no r.
Heb	10:18	Now where there is r of

REMNANT (see REMAIN)

Ex	26:12	The r that remains of the
2Sa	14: 7	husband neither name nor r
2Ki	19: 4	up your prayer for the r
2Ki	19:30	And the r who have escaped
2Ki	19:31	of Jerusalem shall go a r,
2Ki	21:14	So I will forsake the r of My
2Ch	34: 9	from all the r of Israel,
Ezra	9:14	that there would be no r
Is	1: 9	left to us a very small r,
Is	10:20	in that day That the r of
Is	10:21	The r will return, the
Is	10:21	the r of Jacob, To the
Is	11:11	time To recover the r of
Is	11:16	will be a highway for the r
Is	14:22	from Babylon the name and r,
Is	37: 4	up your prayer for the r
Is	37:31	And the r who have escaped
Is	37:32	of Jerusalem shall go a r,
Jer	23: 3	But I will gather the r of My
Jer	40:15	and the r in Judah perish?"
Ezek	6: 8	"Yet I will leave a r,
Ezek	11:13	a complete end of the r of

Amos	1: 8	And the r of the
Amos	5:15	Will be gracious to the r
Amos	9:12	they may possess the r of
Mic	2:12	I will surely gather the r
Mic	5: 7	Then the r of Jacob Shall
Mic	7:18	the transgression of the r
Rom	9:27	The r will be saved.
Rom	11: 5	present time there is a r

REMOVAL (see REMOVE)

1Pe	3:21	baptism (not the r of the

REMOVE (see REMOVAL, REMOVED, REMOVES, TAKE)

Ex	12:15	On the first day you shall r
Lev	3: 4	the kidneys, he shall r;
Job	22:23	You will r iniquity far
Ps	119:22	R from me reproach and
Prov	22:28	Do not r the ancient
Is	7:20	And will also r the beard.
Jer	27:10	to r you far from your land;
Hos	5:10	Judah are like those who r
Matt	7: 4	Let me r the speck from your
Matt	7: 5	Hypocrite! First r the plank
1Co	13: 2	so that I could r mountains,
Rev	2: 5	come to you quickly and r

REMOVED (see REMOVE)

Gen	8:13	and Noah r the covering of
1Ki	15:14	the high places were not r.
2Ki	17:23	until the LORD r Israel out
2Ki	18: 4	He r the high places and
2Ch	34:33	Thus Josiah r all the
Ps	46: 2	Even though the earth be r,
Ps	103:12	So far has He r our
Prov	10:30	righteous will never be r,
Is	6:12	The LORD has r men far
Is	54:10	My covenant of peace be r,
Matt	21:21	Be r and be cast into the
John	21: 7	outer garment (for he had r

REMOVES (see REMOVE)

Dan	2:21	He r kings and raises up

REND†

Is	64: 1	that You would r the
Joel	2:13	So r your heart, and not

RENDER (see RENDERS)

Judg	11:27	r judgment this day between
Ps	28: 4	R to them what they
Ps	38:20	Those also who r evil for
Ps	62:12	For You r to each one
Ps	116:12	What shall I r to the LORD
Matt	21:41	vinedressers who will r to
Matt	22:21	R therefore to Caesar the
Rom	2: 6	will r to each one
Rom	13: 7	R therefore to all their due;
1Co	7: 3	Let the husband r to his wife
1Th	3: 9	For what thanks can we r to

RENDERS† (see RENDER)

1Th	5:15	See that no one r evil for

RENEW (see RENEWED, RENEWING)

1Sa	11:14	let us go to Gilgal and r
Ps	51:10	And r a steadfast spirit
Ps	104:30	And You r the face of the
Is	40:31	wait on the LORD Shall r
Is	41: 1	And let the people r their
Heb	6: 6	to r them again to

RENEWED (see RENEW)

Ps	103: 5	So that your youth is r
2Co	4:16	the inward man is being r
Eph	4:23	and be r in the spirit of
Col	3:10	on the new man who is r in

RENEWING† (see RENEW)

Rom	12: 2	but be transformed by the r
Tit	3: 5	of regeneration and r of

RENOWN
Gen 6: 4 who were of old, men of r.

RENTED†
Acts 28:30 two whole years in his own r

REPAID (see REPAY)
1Sa 25:21 And he has r me evil for
Ps 7: 4 If I have r evil to him who
Rom 11:35 And it shall be r to
Col 3:25 he who does wrong will be r

REPAIR (see REPAIRED, REPAIRER, REPAIRS)
2Ch 24:12 masons and carpenters to r
Amos 9:11 And r its damages; I will

REPAIRED (see REPAIR)
Neh 3: 7 r the residence of the

REPAIRER† (see REPAIR)
Is 58:12 you shall be called the R

REPAIRS (see REPAIR)
Neh 3: 4 the son of Koz, made r

REPAY (see REPAID, REPAYS)
Ruth 2:12 The LORD r your work, and a
1Sa 26:23 May the LORD r every man
Ps 37:21 borrows and does not r,
Ps 54: 5 He will r my enemies for
Is 59:18 deeds, accordingly He will r,
Jer 16:18 And first I will r double for
Jer 51:24 And I will r Babylon And
Luke 10:35 I will r you.'
Rom 12:17 R no one evil for evil. Have
Rom 12:19 is Mine, I will r,
1Ti 5: 4 show piety at home and to r
2Ti 4:14 May the Lord r him according
Phm 1:19 with my own hand. I will r—
Heb 10:30 is Mine, I will r,
Rev 18: 6 and r her double according

REPAYS (see REPAY)
Ps 137: 8 Happy the one who r you as

REPEATED (see REPEATS, REPETITIONS)
Gen 41:32 And the dream was r to

REPEATS (see REPEATED)
Prov 26:11 So a fool r his folly.

REPEL
2Sa 5: 6 blind and the lame will r

REPENT (see REPENTANCE, REPENTED, REPENTS)
Num 23:19 son of man, that He should r.
Job 42: 6 And r in dust and ashes."
Jer 25: 5 R now everyone of his evil
Ezek 14: 6 says the Lord GOD: "R,
Hos 11: 5 Because they refused to r.
Matt 3: 2 and saying, "R,
Matt 4:17 to preach and to say, "R,
Mark 1:15 kingdom of God is at hand. R,
Luke 13: 3 but unless you r you will
Acts 3:19 R therefore and be converted,
Acts 17:30 all men everywhere to r,
Acts 26:20 Gentiles, that they should r,
Rev 2: 5 r and do the first works, or
Rev 3: 3 and heard; hold fast and r.
Rev 9:20 did not r of the works of

REPENTANCE (see REPENT)
Matt 3: 8 bear fruits worthy of r,
Matt 3:11 you with water unto r,
Matt 9:13 righteous, but sinners, to r.
Mark 1: 4 and preaching a baptism of r
Luke 3: 8 bear fruits worthy of r,
Luke 15: 7 just persons who need no r.
Luke 24:47 and that r and remission of
Acts 11:18 granted to the Gentiles r
Acts 13:24 the baptism of r to all the
Acts 20:21 r toward God and faith

Acts 26:20 and do works befitting r.
Rom 2: 4 of God leads you to r?
2Co 7: 9 that your sorrow led to r.
2Co 7:10 For godly sorrow produces r
Heb 6: 1 again the foundation of r
Heb 6: 6 to renew them again to r,
Heb 12:17 for he found no place for r,
2Pe 3: 9 that all should come to r.

REPENTED (see REPENT)
Matt 11:21 they would have r long ago
Luke 11:32 for they r at the preaching
2Co 12:21 before and have not r of

REPENTS (see REPENT)
Luke 15:10 of God over one sinner who r.

REPETITIONS† (see REPEATED)
Matt 6: 7 do not use vain r as the

REPHAIM
Gen 14: 5 him came and attacked the R
Josh 15: 8 the end of the Valley of R
2Sa 5:18 in the Valley of R.

REPHIDIM
Ex 17: 1 the LORD, and camped in R;

REPORT (see REPORTED)
Gen 37: 2 and Joseph brought a bad r
Is 53: 1 Who has believed our r?
Luke 4:37 And the r about Him went out
John 12:38 who has believed our r?
Rom 10:16 who has believed our r?
Phil 4: 8 things are of good r,

REPORTED (see REPORT)
Rom 3: 8 as we are slanderously r and
1Co 5: 1 It is actually r that there

REPROACH (see REPROACHED, REPROACHES)
Gen 30:23 "God has taken away my r.
Ruth 2:15 and do not r her.
Ps 22: 6 A r of men, and despised by
Ps 31:11 I am a r among all my
Ps 44:13 You make us a r to our
Ps 69: 7 for Your sake I have borne r,
Ps 79: 4 We have become a r to our
Ps 102: 8 My enemies r me all day
Prov 14:34 But sin is a r to any
Is 51: 7 Do not fear the r of men,
Jer 23:40 will bring an everlasting r
Jer 31:19 Because I bore the r of my
Dan 9:16 and Your people are a r to
Luke 1:25 to take away my r among
Col 1:22 and above r in His sight—
1Ti 4:10 we both labor and suffer r,
Heb 11:26 esteeming the r of Christ
Heb 13:13 the camp, bearing His r.
Jas 1: 5 all liberally and without r,

REPROACHED (see REPROACH)
Job 19: 3 These ten times you have r
Ps 79:12 with which they have r You,
Rom 15: 3 of those who r You
1Pe 4:14 If you are r for the name of

REPROACHES (see REPROACH)
Ps 55:12 it is not an enemy who r
Ps 69: 9 And the r of those who
Prov 27:11 I may answer him who r me.
Rom 15: 3 The r of those who
2Co 12:10 in infirmities, in r,

REPROOF (see REBUKE)
2Ti 3:16 for doctrine, for r,

REPROVES (see REBUKES)
Is 29:21 lay a snare for him who r

REPTILE
Is 27: 1 And He will slay the r that

Jas   3: 7 of **r** and creature of the

REPULSIVE
Job   19:17 And I am **r** to the children

REPUTATION
Acts   6: 3 you seven men of good **r**,
Acts   10:22 fears God and has a good **r**
Phil   2: 7 but made Himself of no **r**,

REQUEST (see REQUESTED, REQUESTS)
Ruth   3:11 do for you all that you **r**,
Esth   5: 6 granted you. What is your **r**,
Esth   5: 7 My petition and **r** is this:
Ps   21: 2 have not withheld the **r** of
Ps   106:15 And He gave them their **r**,
Prov   30: 7 Two things I **r** of You
Rom   1:10 making **r** if, by some means,
1Co   1:22 For Jews **r** a sign, and Greeks
Phil   1: 4 prayer of mine making **r** for

REQUESTED (see REQUEST)
Ex   12:36 granted them what they **r**
Dan   1: 8 therefore he **r** of the chief

REQUESTS (see REQUEST)
Phil   4: 6 let your **r** be made known to

REQUIRE (see REQUIRED, REQUIREMENT, REQUIRES)
Gen   9: 5 of every beast I will **r** it,
Gen   9: 5 man's brother I will **r** the
Deut   15: 3 Of a foreigner you may **r** it;
Deut   18:19 I will **r** it of him.
Deut   23:21 your God will surely **r** it
Josh   22:23 let the LORD Himself **r** an
1Ki   8:59 Israel, as each day may **r**,
Ps   40: 6 sin offering You did not **r**.
Ezek   3:18 but his blood I will **r** at
Ezek   3:20 but his blood I will **r** at
Ezek   33: 6 but his blood I will **r** at
Mic   6: 8 And what does the LORD **r**

REQUIRED (see REQUIRE)
Num   5:15 shall bring the offering **r**
Is   1:12 Who has **r** this from your
Luke   11:50 of the world may be **r** of
Luke   12:20 night your soul will be **r**
Luke   12:48 from him much will be **r**;
1Co   4: 2 Moreover it is **r** in stewards

REQUIREMENT† (see REQUIRE, REQUIREMENTS)
Rom   8: 4 that the righteous **r** of the

REQUIREMENTS† (see REQUIREMENT)
Rom   2:26 man keeps the righteous **r**
Col   2:14 out the handwriting of **r**

REQUIRES (see REQUIRE)
Eccl   3:15 And God **r** an account of

RESCUE
Ex   6: 6 I will **r** you from their
Ps   22: 8 let Him **r** Him; Let Him
Ps   144: 7 **R** me and deliver me out of
Hos   5:14 away, and no one shall **r**.

RESERVE (see RESERVED)
2Pe   2: 9 out of temptations and to **r**

RESERVED (see RESERVE)
Gen   27:36 Have you not **r** a blessing for
1Ki   19:18 Yet I have **r** seven thousand
Job   21:30 For the wicked are **r** for the
1Pe   1: 4 **r** in heaven for you,
2Pe   2: 4 to be **r** for judgment;
2Pe   2:17 for whom is **r** the blackness
2Pe   3: 7 are **r** for fire until the day
Jude   6 He has **r** in everlasting
Jude   13 stars for whom is **r** the

RESERVOIR†
Is   22:11 You also made a **r** between

RESIDENCE
Amos   7:13 And it is the royal **r**.

RESIDUE
Dan   7: 7 and trampling the **r** with its
Zeph   2: 9 The **r** of My people shall

RESIST (see RESISTED, RESISTS)
Matt   5:39 But I tell you not to **r** an
Acts   6:10 And they were not able to **r**
Acts   7:51 and ears! You always **r** the
2Ti   3: 8 so do these also **r** the
Jas   4: 7 **R** the devil and he will flee
1Pe   5: 9 **R** him, steadfast in the

RESISTED (see RESIST)
Rom   9:19 For who has **r** His will?"
2Ti   3: 8 Now as Jannes and Jambres **r**
Heb   12: 4 You have not yet **r** to

RESISTS (see RESIST)
Rom   13: 2 Therefore whoever **r** the
Jas   4: 6 God **r** the proud, But
1Pe   5: 5 God **r** the proud, But

RESORT†
Ps   71: 3 To which I may **r**

RESPECT (see RESPECTED, RESPECTS)
Gen   4: 5 but He did not **r** Cain and his
Ps   40: 4 And does not **r** the proud,
Ps   74:20 Have **r** to the covenant; For
Is   22:11 Nor did you have **r** for Him
Matt   21:37 They will **r** my son.'
Mark   12: 6 They will **r** my son.'
Acts   5:34 of the law held in **r** by all
Heb   12: 9 us, and we paid them **r**

RESPECTED (see RESPECT)
Gen   4: 4 And the LORD **r** Abel and his

RESPECTS† (see RESPECT)
Eph   5:33 let the wife see that she **r**

REST (see RESTED, RESTING, RESTS)
Gen   18: 4 and **r** yourselves under the
Ex   16:23 'Tomorrow is a Sabbath **r**,
Ex   23:11 year you shall let it **r**
Ex   23:12 the seventh day you shall **r**,
Ex   33:14 you, and I will give you **r**
Deut   12: 9 you have not come to the **r**
Deut   31:16 you will **r** with your
Josh   14:15 Then the land had **r** from
Judg   3:11 So the land had **r** for forty
Ruth   1: 9 grant that you may find **r**,
Ruth   3:18 for the man will not **r** until
2Sa   7: 1 the LORD had given him **r**
1Ki   5: 4 LORD my God has given me **r**
1Ki   11:41 Now the **r** of the acts of
1Ch   22: 9 you, who shall be a man of **r**;
1Ch   28: 2 heart to build a house of **r**
Ezra   3: 8 and the **r** of their brethren
Ezra   4: 3 and Jeshua and the **r** of the
Ezra   4: 7 and the **r** of their
Neh   6:14 Noadiah and the **r** of the
Esth   9:22 days on which the Jews had **r**
Job   3:17 there the weary are at **r**.
Ps   16: 9 My flesh also will **r** in
Ps   37: 7 **R** in the LORD, and wait
Ps   55: 6 would fly away and be at **r**.
Ps   95:11 'They shall not enter My **r**.
Ps   116: 7 Return to your **r**,
Prov   24:33 folding of the hands to **r**;
Is   11: 2 Spirit of the LORD shall **r**
Is   14: 7 The whole earth is at **r** and
Is   18: 4 to me, "I will take My **r**,
Is   28:12 may cause the weary to **r**,
Is   34:14 the night creature shall **r**
Is   57:20 sea, When it cannot **r**,

Is   62: 1 sake I will not r,
Jer   6:16 Then you will find r for
Jer   41:10 away captive all the r of
Jer   45: 3 my sighing, and I find no r.
Jer   47: 6 R and be still!
Lam   5: 5 We labor and have no r.
Dan   4: 4 was at r in my house, and
Matt   11:28 laden, and I will give you r.
Matt   11:29 and you will find r for your
Luke   8:10 but to the r it is given
Luke   10: 6 your peace will r on it; if
1Co   7:12 But to the r I, not the Lord,
1Co   11:34 And the r I will set in
2Co   12: 9 the power of Christ may r
Eph   4:17 no longer walk as the r of
2Th   1: 7 you who are troubled r with
Heb   3:11 shall not enter My r.
Heb   4: 8 if Joshua had given them r,
Heb   4: 9 There remains therefore a r
1Pe   1:13 and r your hope fully upon
2Pe   3:16 as they do also the r of
Rev   4: 8 And they do not r day or
Rev   20: 5 But the r of the dead did not

RESTED (see REST)
Gen   2: 2 and He r on the seventh day
Ex   20:11 and r the seventh day.
Num   11:25 when the Spirit r upon them,
1Ki   2:10 So David r with his fathers,
Luke   23:56 And they r on the Sabbath
Heb   4: 4 And God r on the seventh

RESTING (see REST)
Gen   8: 9 But the dove found no r place
Ps   132:14 This is My r place forever;
Zech   1:11 all the earth is r
Matt   26:45 you still sleeping and r?
Mark   14:41 you still sleeping and r?

RESTITUTION
Ex   22: 3 He should make full r;

RESTORATION† (see RESTORE)
Acts   3:21 until the times of r of all

RESTORE (see RESTORATION, RESTORED, RESTORER,
   RESTORES)
Gen   20: 7 r the man's wife; for he is
Gen   40:13 lift up your head and r you
Gen   42:25 to r every man's money to
Ex   22: 4 he shall r double.
2Sa   12: 6 And he shall r fourfold for
Ps   51:12 R to me the joy of Your
Ps   60: 1 Oh, r us again!
Ps   80: 3 R us, O God
Prov   6:31 he must r sevenfold; He may
Is   1:26 I will r your judges as at
Jer   31:18 R me, and I will return,
Dan   9:25 forth of the command To r
Joel   2:25 So I will r to you the years
Matt   17:11 is coming first and will r
Luke   19: 8 I r fourfold."
Acts   1: 6 will You at this time r the
Gal   6: 1 you who are spiritual r

RESTORED (see RESTORE)
Gen   20:14 and he r Sarah his wife to
Gen   40:21 Then he r the chief butler to
Gen   42:28 "My money has been r,
Ex   4: 7 it was r like his other
2Ki   5:10 and your flesh shall be r to
2Ki   8: 5 is her son whom Elisha r
2Ki   14:25 He r the territory of Israel
Job   42:10 And the LORD r Job's losses
Lam   5:21 O LORD, and we will be r;
Dan   4:36 I was r to my kingdom, and
Mark   3: 5 and his hand was r as whole
Luke   6:10 and his hand was r as whole

RESTORER† (see RESTORE)
Ruth   4:15 And may he be to you a r of
Is   58:12 The R of Streets to Dwell

RESTORES (see RESTORE)
Ps   23: 3 He r my soul; He leads me
Mark   9:12 is coming first and r all

RESTRAIN (see RESTRAINED, RESTRAINING,
   RESTRAINS, RESTRAINT)
Gen   45: 1 Then Joseph could not r
1Sa   3:13 and he did not r them.
Ps   40: 9 I do not r my lips, O
Dan   4:35 No one can r His hand Or

RESTRAINED (see RESTRAIN)
Gen   8: 2 the rain from heaven was r.
Gen   43:31 and he r himself, and said,
Ex   32:25 (for Aaron had not r them,
Ps   119:101 I have r my feet from every
Luke   24:16 But their eyes were r,

RESTRAINING† (see RESTRAIN)
2Th   2: 6 And now you know what is r,

RESTRAINS (see RESTRAIN)
Prov   10:19 But he who r his lips is
Prov   27:16 Whoever r her restrains the
2Th   2: 7 only He who now r will do

RESTRAINT (see RESTRAIN)
Prov   29:18 the people cast off r;
Hos   4: 2 adultery, They break all r,

RESTS (see REST)
2Ki   2:15 The spirit of Elijah r on
1Pe   4:14 of glory and of God r upon

RESULTED (see RESULTING)
Rom   5:16 came from one offense r

RESULTING (see RESULTED)
Rom   5:18 r in condemnation, even so

RESURRECTION
Matt   22:23 who say there is no r,
Matt   22:31 But concerning the r of the
Matt   27:53 of the graves after His r,
Luke   14:14 shall be repaid at the r of
John   5:29 to the r of life, and those
John   5:29 to the r of condemnation.
John   11:24 he will rise again in the r
John   11:25 I am the r and the life. He
Acts   1:22 a witness with us of His r.
Acts   17:18 to them Jesus and the r.
Acts   17:32 when they heard of the r of
Acts   23: 6 concerning the hope and r of
Acts   23: 8 say that there is no r—
Rom   1: 4 by the r from the dead.
Rom   6: 5 in the likeness of His r,
1Co   15:13 But if there is no r of the
1Co   15:42 So also is the r of the
Phil   3:10 Him and the power of His r,
Phil   3:11 I may attain to the r from
2Ti   2:18 saying that the r is already
Heb   11:35 they might obtain a better r.
1Pe   1: 3 a living hope through the r
1Pe   3:21 through the r of Jesus
Rev   20: 6 who has part in the first r.

RETAIN (see RETAINED)
John   20:23 if you r the sins of any,
Rom   1:28 as they did not like to r

RETAINED (see RETAIN)
John   20:23 the sins of any, they are r.

RETINUE
1Ki   10: 2 with a very great r,

RETURN (see RETURNED, RETURNING, RETURNS)
Gen   3:19 shall eat bread Till you r

Gen   3:19 And to dust you shall r.
Gen   16: 9 R to your mistress, and
Gen   31: 3 R to the land of your fathers
Ex   4:18 Please let me go and r to my
Ex   13:17 and r to Egypt."
Num   14: 4 us select a leader and r to
Deut   5:30 R to your tents."
Deut 17:16 You shall not r that way
Deut 20: 5 Let him go and r to his
Deut 30: 2 and you r to the LORD your
Ruth   1: 8 r each to her mother's
1Sa   7: 3 If you r to the LORD with
2Sa   12:23 but he shall not r to me."
1Ki   2:33 blood shall therefore r
1Ki   8:48 and when they r to You with
1Ki   12:24 Let every man r to his
1Ki   12:26 Now the kingdom may r to the
2Ki   19: 7 he shall hear a rumor and r
2Ch   18:27 If you ever r in peace, the
Neh   2: 6 be? And when will you r?
Neh   7: 5 had come up in the first r,
Job   1:21 And naked shall I r there.
Job   10:21 from which I shall not r,
Job   16:22 I shall go the way of no r.
Job   34:15 And man would r to dust.
Ps   6: 4 R, O LORD, deliver me!
Ps   7:16 His trouble shall r upon his
Ps   59: 6 At evening they r,
Ps   90: 3 destruction, And say, "R,
Ps   116: 7 R to your rest, O my soul,
Prov   2:19 None who go to her r,
Eccl   1: 7 There they r again.
Eccl   3:20 and all r to dust.
Eccl   5:15 womb, naked shall he r,
Eccl 12: 2 And the clouds do not r
Eccl 12: 7 Then the dust will r to the
Eccl 12: 7 And the spirit will r to
Song   6:13 O Shulamite; Return, r,
Is   6:10 And r and be healed."
Is   10:21 The remnant will r,
Is   35:10 of the LORD shall r,
Is   51:11 of the LORD shall r,
Is   55: 7 Let him r to the LORD,
Is   55:10 And do not r there, But
Is   55:11 It shall not r to Me void,
Jer   3:12 the north, and say: 'R,
Jer   5: 3 They have refused to r.
Jer   15:19 says the LORD: "If you r,
Jer   15:19 But you must not r to them.
Jer   30:10 captivity. Jacob shall r,
Ezek 16:55 r to their former state, and
Dan   11:13 the king of the North will r
Hos   2: 7 I will go and r to my first
Hos   3: 5 children of Israel shall r
Hos   6: 1 and let us r to the LORD;
Hos   9: 3 But Ephraim shall r to
Hos   14: 1 r to the LORD your God,
Zeph   2: 7 And r their captives.
Zeph   3:20 When I r your captives
Zech   1: 3 R to Me," says the LORD of
Zech   1: 3 and I will r to you," says
Mal   3: 7 and I will r to you," Says
Mal   3: 7 'In what way shall we r?'
Matt   2:12 that they should not r to
Matt 10:13 let your peace r to you.
Luke   6:35 hoping for nothing in r;
1Pe   2:23 reviled, did not revile in r;

RETURNED (see RETURN)
Gen   8: 9 and she r into the ark to
Gen   18:33 and Abraham r to his place.
Gen   22:19 So Abraham r to his young
Gen   37:29 that Reuben r to the pit,
Gen   43:18 which was r in our sacks the
Gen   50:14 Joseph r to Egypt, he and

Ex   4:18 So Moses went and r to
Num   13:25 And they r from spying out
Josh   4:18 the waters of the Jordan r
Judg 11:39 of two months that she r to
Ruth   1:22 So Naomi r, and Ruth
1Sa   7:17 But he always r to Ramah, for
1Sa   17:57 as David r from the
1Ch   16:43 and David r to bless his
1Ch   21:27 and he r his sword to its
2Ch   10: 2 that Jeroboam r from Egypt.
2Ch   31: 1 the children of Israel r to
Ezra   2: 1 and who r to Jerusalem and
Neh   2:15 by the Valley Gate, and so r.
Neh   4:15 that all of us r to the
Neh   7: 6 and who r to Jerusalem and
Eccl   4: 7 Then I r, and I saw
Eccl   9:11 I r and saw under the sun
Is   38: 8 So the sun r ten degrees
Dan   4:34 and my understanding r to
Amos   4: 6 Yet you have not r to Me,"
Luke   2:20 Then the shepherds r,
Luke 10:17 Then the seventy r with joy,
Luke 24: 9 Then they r from the tomb and
Luke 24:52 and r to Jerusalem with
Acts   1:12 Then they r to Jerusalem
Acts 12:25 And Barnabas and Saul r from
Gal   1:17 and r again to Damascus.
1Pe   2:25 but have now r to the

RETURNING (see RETURN)
1Sa   18: 6 when David was r from the
Is   30:15 In r and rest you shall be
Heb   7: 1 who met Abraham r from the
1Pe   3: 9 not r evil for evil or

RETURNS (see RETURN)
Prov 26:11 As a dog r to his own vomit,
Luke 17: 4 and seven times in a day r
2Pe   2:22 A dog r to his own

REUBEN (see REUBENITES)
Gen   29:32 and she called his name R;
Gen   35:23 the sons of Leah were R,
Gen   37:29 Then R returned to the pit,
Gen   46: 8 R was Jacob's firstborn.
Ex   1: 2 R, Simeon, Levi, and
Num   13: 4 names: from the tribe of R,
Num   26: 5 R was the firstborn of
Num   32:29 of Gad and the children of R
Josh 18: 7 inheritance. And Gad, R,
2Ki   10:33 the land of Gilead—Gad, R,
Rev   7: 5 of the tribe of R twelve

REUBENITES
Deut   3:16 And to the R and the Gadites
Deut 29: 8 as an inheritance to the R,

REUEL (see JETHRO)
Ex   2:18 When they came to R their
Num   10:29 said to Hobab the son of R

REVEAL (see REVEALED, REVEALS, REVELATION)
Esth   2:10 had charged her not to r
Dan   2:47 since you could r this
Matt 11:27 to whom the Son wills to r
Luke 10:22 to whom the Son wills to r
1Co   4: 5 things of darkness and r
Gal   1:16 to r His Son in me, that I
Phil   3:15 God will r even this to you.

REVEALED (see REVEAL)
1Sa   3: 7 the word of the LORD yet r
Is   40: 5 of the LORD shall be r,
Is   53: 1 the arm of the LORD been r?
Dan   2:19 Then the secret was r to
Matt 10:26 covered that will not be r,
Matt 11:25 wise and prudent and have r
Matt 16:17 flesh and blood has not r

Luke 2:26 And it had been **r** to him by
Luke 2:35 of many hearts may be **r**.
Luke 17:30 day when the Son of Man is **r**.
John 1:31 but that He should be **r** to
John 9: 3 works of God should be **r** in
John 12:38 of the LORD been **r**?
Acts 23:22 no one that you have **r**
Rom 1:17 righteousness of God is **r**
Rom 1:18 For the wrath of God is **r**
Rom 3:21 God apart from the law is **r**,
Rom 8:18 the glory which shall be **r**
1Co 2:10 But God has **r** them to us
1Co 3:13 because it will be **r** by
1Co 14:25 secrets of his heart are **r**;
Gal 3:23 which would afterward be **r**.
Col 1:26 but now has been **r** to His
2Th 1: 7 us when the Lord Jesus is **r**
2Th 2: 3 and the man of sin is **r**,
2Th 2: 8 the lawless one will be **r**,
2Ti 1:10 but has now been **r** by the
1Pe 1: 5 for salvation ready to be **r**
1Pe 1:12 To them it was **r** that, not to
1Pe 4:13 that when His glory is **r**,
1Pe 5: 1 of the glory that will be **r**:
1Jn 3: 2 and it has not yet been **r**
1Jn 3: 2 we know that when He is **r**,

REVEALS (*see* REVEAL)
Ps 19: 2 And night unto night **r**
Dan 2:28 is a God in heaven who **r**
Amos 3: 7 Unless He **r** His secret to

REVELATION (*see* REVEAL)
1Sa 3: 1 there was no widespread **r**.
Prov 29:18 Where there is no **r**,
Luke 2:32 A light to bring **r** to the
1Co 14: 6 I speak to you either by **r**,
1Co 14:26 has a tongue, has a **r**,
Gal 1:12 but it came through the **r**
Gal 2: 2 And I went up by **r**,
Eph 1:17 the spirit of wisdom and **r**
Eph 3: 3 how that by **r** He made known
1Pe 1: 7 and glory at the **r** of Jesus
1Pe 1:13 be brought to you at the **r**
Rev 1: 1 The **R** of Jesus Christ, which

REVELRIES† (*see* REVELRY)
Gal 5:21 murders, drunkenness, **r**,
1Pe 4: 3 lusts, drunkenness, **r**,

REVELRY† (*see* REVELRIES)
Rom 13:13 not in **r** and drunkenness,

REVENUE
Prov 8:19 And my **r** than choice

REVERE (*see* REVERENCE, REVERENT)
Lev 19: 3 Every one of you shall **r** his

REVERENCE (*see* REVERENT)
1Ti 2: 2 life in all godliness and **r**.
1Ti 3: 4 in submission with all **r**
Heb 12:28 serve God acceptably with **r**

REVERENT (*see* REVERENCE)
1Ti 3: 8 deacons must be **r**,
1Ti 3:11 their wives must be **r**,
Tit 2: 2 the older men be sober, **r**,

REVERSE
Is 43:13 and who will **r** it?"

REVILE (*see* REVILED, REVILER, REVILERS, REVILING)
Ex 22:28 You shall not **r** God, nor
Matt 5:11 are you when they **r**
Acts 23: 4 Do you **r** God's high priest?"
1Pe 2:23 did not **r** in return; when He
1Pe 3:16 those who **r** your good

REVILED (*see* REVILE)
Mark 15:32 were crucified with Him **r**
1Co 4:12 with our own hands. Being **r**,
1Pe 2:23 who, when He was **r**,

REVILER† (*see* REVILE)
1Co 5:11 or an idolater, or a **r**,

REVILERS† (*see* REVILE)
1Co 6:10 nor drunkards, nor **r**,

REVILING (*see* REVILE)
1Ti 6: 4 which come envy, strife, **r**,
2Pe 2:11 do not bring a **r** accusation

REVIVE (*see* REVIVED)
Ps 71:20 Shall **r** me again, And
Ps 85: 6 Will You not **r** us again,
Ps 119:40 **R** me in Your righteousness.
Is 57:15 To **r** the spirit of the
Is 57:15 And to **r** the heart of the
Hos 6: 2 After two days He will **r** us;
Hab 3: 2 **r** Your work in the midst of

REVIVED (*see* REVIVE)
Gen 45:27 of Jacob their father **r**.
2Ki 13:21 he **r** and stood on his feet.
Rom 7: 9 sin **r** and I died.

REWARD (*see* REWARDED, REWARDER, REWARDS)
Gen 15: 1 your exceedingly great **r**.
Ps 19:11 them there is great **r**.
Ps 35:12 They **r** me evil for good,
Ps 127: 3 fruit of the womb is a **r**.
Prov 25:22 And the LORD will **r** you.
Eccl 4: 9 Because they have a good **r**
Is 49: 4 Yet surely my just **r** is
Matt 5:12 for great is your **r** in
Matt 5:46 what **r** have you? Do not even
Matt 6: 1 Otherwise you have no **r** from
Matt 6: 2 to you, they have their **r**.
Matt 6: 4 in secret will Himself **r**
Matt 10:41 shall receive a prophet's **r**.
Matt 10:42 shall by no means lose his **r**.
Matt 16:27 and then He will **r** each
Luke 23:41 for we receive the due **r** of
1Co 3: 8 one will receive his own **r**
1Co 9:18 What is my **r** then? That when
Col 3:24 Lord you will receive the **r**
Heb 2: 2 received a just **r**,
Heb 10:35 which has great **r**.
Heb 11:26 for he looked to the **r**.
Rev 22:12 and My **r** is with Me, to

REWARDED (*see* REWARD)
Ps 18:20 The LORD **r** me according to
Ps 109: 5 Thus they have **r** me evil for

REWARDER† (*see* REWARD)
Heb 11: 6 and that He is a **r** of those

REWARDS (*see* REWARD)
Dan 2: 6 receive from me gifts, **r**,
Dan 5:17 and give your **r** to another;

REZIN
2Ki 16: 5 Then **R** king of Syria and

RHODA†
Acts 12:13 a girl named **R** came to

RHODES†
Acts 21: 1 Cos, the following day to **R**,

RIB (*see* RIBS)
Gen 2:22 Then the **r** which the LORD

RIBLAH
2Ki 25:20 to the king of Babylon at **R**.
2Ki 25:21 and put them to death at **R**

RIBS (*see* RIB)
Gen 2:21 and He took one of his **r**,

RICH (*see* RICHES, RICHLY)
Gen	13: 2	Abram was very **r** in
Gen	14:23	say, 'I have made Abram **r**'—
1Sa	2: 7	LORD makes poor and makes **r**;
2Sa	12: 1	one **r** and the other poor.
Ps	49: 2	**R** and poor together.
Prov	10:22	of the LORD makes one **r**,
Prov	13: 4	the diligent shall be made **r**.
Prov	22: 2	The **r** and the poor have this
Is	53: 9	But with the **r** at His death,
Jer	9:23	Nor let the **r** man glory in
Matt	19:23	you that it is hard for a **r**
Matt	19:24	eye of a needle than for a **r**
Matt	27:57	there came a **r** man from
Luke	1:53	And the **r** He has sent away
Luke	12:16	The ground of a certain **r** man
Luke	12:21	and is not **r** toward God."
Luke	16:21	which fell from the **r** man's
Rom	10:12	the same Lord over all is **r**
1Co	4: 8	full! You are already **r**!
2Co	6:10	as poor, yet making many **r**;
2Co	8: 9	Christ, that though He was **r**,
2Co	8: 9	His poverty might become **r**.
Eph	2: 4	who is **r** in mercy, because
Jas	1:11	So the **r** man also will fade
Jas	2: 5	of this world to be **r** in
Jas	2: 6	Do not the **r** oppress you and
Jas	5: 1	Come now, you **r**,
Rev	2: 9	and poverty (but you are **r**);
Rev	3:17	"Because you say, 'I am **r**,

RICHES (*see* RICH)
1Ki	3:11	nor have asked **r** for
1Ki	3:13	both **r** and honor, so that
Ps	39: 6	in vain; He heaps up **r**,
Ps	49: 6	in the multitude of their **r**,
Ps	62:10	If **r** increase, Do not set
Ps	119:14	As much as in all **r**.
Prov	3:16	In her left hand **r** and
Prov	8:18	**R** and honor are with me,
Prov	11: 4	**R** do not profit in the day
Prov	11:28	He who trusts in his **r** will
Prov	13: 7	poor, yet has great **r**.
Prov	13: 8	of a man's life is his **r**,
Prov	19:14	Houses and **r** are an
Prov	22: 1	chosen rather than great **r**,
Prov	27:24	For **r** are not forever, Nor
Eccl	5:19	man to whom God has given **r**
Jer	9:23	the rich man glory in his **r**;
Matt	13:22	and the deceitfulness of **r**
Mark	10:24	is for those who trust in **r**
Rom	2: 4	Or do you despise the **r** of
Rom	9:23	He might make known the **r**
Rom	11:33	the depth of the **r** both of
2Co	8: 2	poverty abounded in the **r**
Eph	1: 7	according to the **r** of His
Eph	1:18	what are the **r** of the glory
Eph	2: 7	might show the exceeding **r**
Eph	3: 8	Gentiles the unsearchable **r**
Phil	4:19	need according to His **r** in
Col	1:27	to make known what are the **r**
1Ti	6:17	nor to trust in uncertain **r**
Heb	11:26	of Christ greater than
Rev	18:17	in one hour such great **r**

RICHLY† (*see* RICH)
Col	3:16	of Christ dwell in you **r** in
1Ti	6:17	who gives us **r** all things to

RIDDLE (*see* RIDDLES)
Judg	14:12	Let me pose a **r** to you. If
Ezek	17: 2	"Son of man, pose a **r**,

RIDDLES† (*see* RIDDLE)
Prov	1: 6	of the wise and their **r**.

Dan	5:12	dreams, solving **r**,

RIDE (*see* RIDER, RIDES, RIDING, RODE)
Judg	5:10	you who **r** on white donkeys,
1Ki	1:33	and have Solomon my son **r** on
Ps	45: 4	And in Your majesty **r**
Is	30:16	We will **r** on swift

RIDER (*see* RIDE, RIDERS)
Gen	49:17	heels So that its **r** shall
Ex	15: 1	The horse and its **r** He
Ex	15:21	The horse and its **r** He

RIDERS (*see* RIDER)
2Ki	18:23	able on your part to put **r**

RIDES (*see* RIDE)
Deut	33:26	Who **r** the heavens to help
Ps	68: 4	Extol Him who **r** on the
Ps	68:33	To Him who **r** on the heaven
Is	19: 1	the LORD **r** on a swift
Amos	2:15	Nor shall he who **r** a horse

RIDICULE
Ps	22: 7	All those who see Me **r** Me;

RIDICULED
Matt	9:24	And they **r** Him.
Mark	5:40	And they **r** Him. But when He

RIDING (*see* RIDE)
Zech	1: 8	a man **r** on a red horse, and
Zech	9: 9	Lowly and **r** on a donkey, A

RIGHT (*see* RIGHTLY)
Gen	13: 9	then I will go to the **r**;
Gen	18:25	Judge of all the earth do **r**?
Gen	48:13	Ephraim with his **r** hand
Gen	48:13	left hand toward Israel's **r**
Gen	48:18	put your **r** hand on his
Ex	14:22	a wall to them on their **r**
Ex	29:20	put it on the tip of the **r**
Lev	7:33	shall have the **r** thigh for
Deut	12:28	you do what is good and **r**
Deut	21:17	the **r** of the firstborn is
Judg	5:26	Her **r** hand to the workmen's
Judg	12: 6	he could not pronounce it **r**.
Judg	17: 6	everyone did what was **r** in
Judg	21:25	everyone did what was **r** in
Ruth	4: 6	You redeem my **r** of
1Ki	11:33	in My ways to do what is **r**
1Ki	15:11	Asa did what was **r** in the
2Ki	14: 3	And he did what was **r** in
2Ki	16: 2	he did not do what was **r**
2Ch	3:17	the name of the one on the **r**
Job	33:27	and perverted what was **r**,
Job	35: 2	"Do you think this is **r**?
Job	40:14	to you That your own **r**
Job	42: 7	not spoken of Me what is **r**,
Job	42: 8	not spoken of Me what is **r**,
Ps	9: 4	You have maintained my **r**
Ps	16: 8	Because He is at my **r**
Ps	16:11	At Your **r** hand are
Ps	19: 8	statutes of the LORD are **r**,
Ps	20: 6	the saving strength of His **r**
Ps	33: 4	the word of the LORD is **r**,
Ps	44: 3	But it was Your **r** hand,
Ps	63: 8	Your **r** hand upholds me.
Ps	73:23	You hold me by my **r** hand.
Ps	78:54	This mountain which His **r**
Ps	80:17	be upon the man of Your **r**
Ps	91: 7	And ten thousand at your **r**
Ps	98: 1	His **r** hand and His holy arm
Ps	107: 7	He led them forth by the **r**
Ps	110: 1	Sit at My **r** hand, Till I
Ps	110: 5	The Lord is at Your **r** hand;
Ps	121: 5	is your shade at your **r**
Ps	137: 5	Let my **r** hand forget its
Ps	138: 7	And Your **r** hand will save

Ps	139:10	And Your r hand shall hold
Prov	3:16	of days is in her r hand,
Prov	4:11	I have led you in r paths.
Prov	12:15	The way of a fool is r in
Prov	14:12	is a way that seems r to
Prov	21: 2	Every way of a man is r in
Prov	27:16	And grasps oil with his r
Song	2: 6	And his r hand embraces me.
Is	41:10	you with My righteous r
Is	45: 1	whose r hand I have held—To
Is	45:19	I declare things that are r.
Is	62: 8	LORD has sworn by His r
Jer	22:24	were the signet on My r
Jer	32: 7	for the r of redemption is
Jer	32: 8	for the r of inheritance is
Ezek	1:10	the face of a lion on the r
Ezek	4: 6	lie again on your r side;
Ezek	18: 5	does what is lawful and r;
Ezek	21:27	Until He comes whose r it
Hos	14: 9	the ways of the LORD are r;
Jon	4: 4	Is it r for you to be
Jon	4: 9	Is it r for you to be angry
Jon	4:11	discern between their r
Zech	3: 1	and Satan standing at his r
Matt	5:29	If your r eye causes you to
Matt	5:30	And if your r hand causes you
Matt	5:39	whoever slaps you on your r
Matt	20:21	one on Your r hand and the
Matt	22:44	Sit at My r hand, Till
Matt	25:33	will set the sheep on His r
Matt	26:64	Son of Man sitting at the r
Matt	27:29	and a reed in His r hand.
Matt	27:38	one on the r and another on
Mark	5:15	and clothed and in his r
Mark	16:19	and sat down at the r hand
Luke	6: 6	And a man was there whose r
Luke	15:32	It was r that we should make
Luke	22:50	priest and cut off his r
John	1:12	to them He gave the r to
John	21: 6	Cast the net on the r side of
Acts	2:25	For He is at my r
Acts	7:55	and Jesus standing at the r
Rom	8:34	who is even at the r hand of
1Co	9: 4	Do we have no r to eat and
Eph	1:20	and seated Him at His r
Eph	6: 1	in the Lord, for this is r.
Phil	1: 7	just as it is r for me to
Heb	1: 3	sat down at the r hand of
Heb	1:13	Sit at My r hand, Till
Rev	1:16	He had in His r hand seven
Rev	1:17	But He laid His r hand on
Rev	22:14	that they may have the r to

RIGHTEOUS (see RIGHTEOUSLY, RIGHTEOUSNESS, UNRIGHTEOUS)

Gen	7: 1	I have seen that you are r
Gen	18:23	You also destroy the r with
Gen	18:24	Suppose there were fifty r
Gen	38:26	She has been more r than I,
Ex	23: 8	perverts the words of the r.
Job	4:17	Can a mortal be more r than
Job	9: 2	But how can a man be r
Job	22:19	The r see it and are glad,
Job	32: 1	because he was r in his own
Job	34: 5	"For Job has said, 'I am r,
Ps	1: 5	in the congregation of the r.
Ps	1: 6	LORD knows the way of the r,
Ps	7: 9	For the r God tests the
Ps	14: 5	with the generation of the r.
Ps	19: 9	the LORD are true and r
Ps	34:15	of the LORD are on the r,
Ps	37:16	A little that a r man has
Ps	37:17	But the LORD upholds the r.
Ps	37:25	Yet I have not seen the r
Ps	37:29	The r shall inherit the

Ps	52: 6	The r also shall see and
Ps	55:22	shall never permit the r to
Ps	58:10	The r shall rejoice when he
Ps	58:11	is a reward for the r;
Ps	92:12	The r shall flourish like a
Ps	97:11	Light is sown for the r,
Ps	107:42	The r see it and rejoice,
Ps	112: 4	full of compassion, and r.
Ps	118:15	Is in the tents of the r;
Ps	119: 7	When I learn Your r
Ps	143: 2	sight no one living is r
Ps	145:17	The LORD is r in all His
Prov	10: 7	The memory of the r is
Prov	10:11	The mouth of the r is a
Prov	10:16	The labor of the r leads to
Prov	10:28	The hope of the r will be
Prov	10:30	The r will never be removed,
Prov	11:10	it goes well with the r,
Prov	11:23	The desire of the r is only
Prov	11:28	But the r will flourish
Prov	11:30	The fruit of the r is a
Prov	12: 7	But the house of the r will
Prov	12:12	But the root of the r
Prov	13:22	is stored up for the r.
Prov	15:29	He hears the prayer of the r.
Prov	18:10	The r run to it and are
Prov	24:16	For a r man may fall seven
Prov	28: 1	But the r are bold as a
Prov	28:12	When the r rejoice, there
Prov	29:27	is an abomination to the r,
Eccl	7:16	Do not be overly r,
Is	41:10	I will uphold you with My r
Is	53:11	By His knowledge My r
Is	57: 1	The r perishes, And no man
Jer	3:11	has shown herself more r
Ezek	3:21	if you warn the r man that
Ezek	18:26	When a r man turns away from
Ezek	33:12	nor shall the r be able to
Dan	9:14	for the LORD our God is r
Dan	9:18	before You because of our r
Amos	2: 6	Because they sell the r for
Matt	9:13	I did not come to call the r,
Matt	10:41	And he who receives a r man
Matt	13:43	Then the r will shine forth
Matt	23:28	you also outwardly appear r
Matt	23:35	from the blood of r Abel to
Matt	25:46	but the r into eternal
Luke	1: 6	And they were both r before
Luke	23:47	Certainly this was a r Man!"
John	5:30	judge; and My judgment is r,
John	17:25	O r Father! The world has not
Rom	1:32	knowing the r judgment of
Rom	2:26	man keeps the r
Rom	3:10	"There is none r,
Rom	5: 7	For scarcely for a r man will
Rom	5:18	even so through one Man's r
Rom	5:19	many will be made r.
Rom	8: 4	that the r requirement of the
2Ti	4: 8	the r Judge, will give to me
Heb	11: 4	witness that he was r,
Jas	5:16	fervent prayer of a r man
1Pe	3:12	the LORD are on the r,
1Pe	4:18	If the r one is scarcely
2Pe	2: 7	and delivered r Lot, who
1Jn	2: 1	Father, Jesus Christ the r.
Rev	16: 5	waters saying: "You are r,
Rev	16: 7	true and r are Your
Rev	19: 8	for the fine linen is the r
Rev	22:11	be filthy still; he who is r,

RIGHTEOUSLY (see RIGHTEOUS)

Tit	2:12	we should live soberly, r,
1Pe	2:23	Himself to Him who judges r;

RIGHTEOUSNESS (*see* RIGHTEOUS, RIGHTEOUSNESS',
RIGHTEOUSNESSES)

Gen	15: 6	He accounted it to him for **r**
Deut	9: 5	is not because of your **r**
Job	29:14	I put on **r**, and it clothed
Job	35: 2	My **r** is more than God's'?
Ps	4: 1	O God of my r! You have
Ps	7: 8	O LORD, according to my **r**,
Ps	7:17	the LORD according to His **r**,
Ps	9: 8	shall judge the world in **r**,
Ps	22:31	will come and declare His **r**
Ps	23: 3	leads me in the paths of **r**
Ps	24: 5	And **r** from the God of his
Ps	35:28	shall speak of Your **r** And
Ps	37: 6	shall bring forth your **r** as
Ps	40: 9	the good news of **r** In the
Ps	45: 6	A scepter of **r** is the
Ps	45: 7	You love **r** and hate
Ps	48:10	right hand is full of **r**.
Ps	71:15	mouth shall tell of Your **r**
Ps	72: 1	And Your **r** to the king's
Ps	85:10	**R** and peace have kissed.
Ps	96:13	shall judge the world with **r**,
Ps	97: 6	The heavens declare His **r**,
Ps	103: 6	The LORD executes **r** And
Ps	103:17	And His **r** to children's
Ps	106:31	was accounted to him for **r**
Ps	111: 3	And His **r** endures forever.
Ps	119:142	Your **r** is an everlasting
Prov	2: 9	Then you will understand **r**
Prov	2:20	And keep to the paths of **r**.
Prov	10: 2	But **r** delivers from death.
Prov	11:18	But he who sows **r** will
Prov	11:19	As **r** leads to life, So he
Prov	14:34	**R** exalts a nation, But sin
Prov	16: 8	Better is a little with **r**,
Prov	16:12	a throne is established by **r**.
Is	1:21	**R** lodged in it, But now
Is	1:26	be called the city of **r**,
Is	5: 7	behold, oppression; For **r**,
Is	11: 4	But with **r** He shall judge
Is	11: 5	**R** shall be the belt of His
Is	28:17	And **r** the plummet; The
Is	32: 1	a king will reign in **r**,
Is	45: 8	And let **r** spring up
Is	45:13	I have raised him up in **r**,
Is	45:23	gone out of My mouth in **r**,
Is	51: 7	to Me, you who know **r**,
Is	56: 1	"Keep justice, and do **r**,
Is	57:12	I will declare your **r** And
Is	59:14	And **r** stands afar off; For
Is	61:10	me with the robe of **r**,
Is	62: 2	Gentiles shall see your **r**,
Jer	22: 3	"Execute judgment and **r**,
Jer	23: 5	raise to David a Branch of **r**;
Jer	23: 6	be called: THE LORD OUR **R**.
Ezek	14:14	only themselves by their **r**,
Ezek	14:20	only themselves by their **r**.
Ezek	18:22	because of the **r** which he
Ezek	33:12	The **r** of the righteous man
Ezek	33:13	but he trusts in his own **r**
Dan	9: 7	**r** belongs to You, but to us
Dan	9:24	To bring in everlasting **r**,
Dan	12: 3	those who turn many to **r**
Hos	2:19	betroth you to Me In **r** and
Hos	10:12	Till He comes and rains **r**
Amos	5:24	And **r** like a mighty stream.
Amos	6:12	And the fruit of **r** into
Zeph	2: 3	upheld His justice. Seek **r**,
Zech	8: 8	their God, In truth and **r**
Mal	3: 3	the LORD An offering in **r**.
Mal	4: 2	fear My name The Sun of **R**
Matt	3:15	for us to fulfill all **r**.
Matt	5: 6	who hunger and thirst for **r**,
Matt	5:20	that unless your **r** exceeds
Matt	5:20	exceeds the **r** of the
Matt	6:33	the kingdom of God and His **r**,
John	16: 8	the world of sin, and of **r**,
Acts	13:10	devil, you enemy of all **r**,
Acts	17:31	He will judge the world in **r**
Acts	24:25	Now as he reasoned about **r**,
Rom	1:17	For in it the **r** of God is
Rom	3: 5	demonstrates the **r** of God,
Rom	3:21	But now the **r** of God apart
Rom	4: 3	accounted to him for **r**.
Rom	4: 5	his faith is accounted for **r**,
Rom	4: 6	man to whom God imputes **r**
Rom	4:11	a seal of the **r** of the faith
Rom	5:17	grace and of the gift of **r**
Rom	6:13	as instruments of **r** to God.
Rom	6:16	of obedience leading to **r**?
Rom	6:18	sin, you became slaves of **r**.
Rom	8:10	Spirit is life because of **r**.
Rom	9:31	pursuing the law of **r**,
Rom	10: 3	being ignorant of God's **r**,
Rom	10: 3	to establish their own **r**,
Rom	10: 4	the end of the law for **r** to
Rom	10:10	heart one believes unto **r**,
Rom	14:17	but **r** and peace and joy in
1Co	1:30	and **r** and sanctification and
2Co	5:21	that we might become the **r**
2Co	6: 7	by the armor of **r** on the
2Co	11:15	into ministers of **r**,
Gal	2:21	for if **r** comes through the
Gal	3: 6	accounted to him for **r**.
Gal	3:21	truly **r** would have been by
Eph	6:14	put on the breastplate of **r**,
Phil	3: 9	in Him, not having my own **r**,
1Ti	6:11	these things and pursue **r**,
2Ti	2:22	youthful lusts; but pursue **r**,
2Ti	3:16	for instruction in **r**,
2Ti	4: 8	up for me the crown of **r**,
Tit	3: 5	not by works of **r** which we
Heb	1: 8	A scepter of **r** is the
Heb	1: 9	You have loved **r** and
Heb	7: 2	being translated "king of **r**,
Heb	11: 7	and became heir of the **r**
Heb	11:33	subdued kingdoms, worked **r**,
Heb	12:11	the peaceable fruit of **r** to
Jas	1:20	man does not produce the **r**
Jas	2:23	accounted to him for **r**.
1Pe	2:24	to sins, might live for **r**—
2Pe	2: 5	people, a preacher of **r**,
2Pe	3:13	and a new earth in which **r**
1Jn	2:29	everyone who practices **r** is

RIGHTEOUSNESS' (*see* RIGHTEOUSNESS)

Matt	5:10	who are persecuted for **r**
1Pe	3:14	if you should suffer for **r**

RIGHTEOUSNESSES† (*see* RIGHTEOUSNESS)

Is	64: 6	And all our **r** are like

RIGHTLY (*see* RIGHT)

Gen	27:36	Is he not **r** named Jacob? For
Luke	22:70	You **r** say that I am."
John	8:48	Do we not say **r** that You are
1Co	2:15	yet he himself is **r** judged
2Ti	2:15	**r** dividing the word of

RIGOR

Ex	1:13	of Israel serve with **r**.

RIMS

Ezek	1:18	and their **r** were full of

RING (*see* RINGS)

Gen	24:22	the man took a golden nose **r**
Gen	41:42	Pharaoh took his signet **r**
Job	42:11	of silver and each a **r** of
Prov	11:22	As a **r** of gold in a swine's
Dan	6:17	it with his own signet **r**
Luke	15:22	and put a **r** on his hand and

RINGS (*see* RING)
Ex 25:14 put the poles into the **r** on
Jas 2: 2 assembly a man with gold **r**,

RIP† (*see* RIPPED)
2Ki 8:12 and **r** open their women with

RIPE (*see* RIPENS)
Num 18:13 Whatever first **r** fruit is in
Jer 24: 2 the figs that are first **r**;
Joel 3:13 sickle, for the harvest is **r**.

RIPENS (*see* RIPE)
Mark 4:29 "But when the grain **r**,

RIPPED (*see* RIP)
Amos 1:13 Because they **r** open the

RISE (*see* RISEN, RISES, RISING, ROSE)
Ex 8:20 **R** early in the morning and
Num 10:35 **R** up, O LORD! Let Your
Num 24:17 A Scepter shall **r** out of
Deut 2:13 Now **r** and cross over the
Deut 6: 7 and when you **r** up.
Deut 11:19 and when you **r** up.
Deut 29:22 of your children who **r** up
Neh 2:18 Let us **r** up and build." Then
Job 1: 5 and he would **r** early in the
Job 14:12 man lies down and does not **r**.
Ps 3: 1 me! Many are they who **r**
Ps 27: 3 Though war should **r** against
Ps 89: 9 the sea; When its waves **r**,
Ps 94: 2 **R** up, O Judge of the earth
Prov 31:28 Her children **r** up and call
Song 2:10 **R** up, my love, my fair one,
Is 5:11 Woe to those who **r** early in
Is 24:20 and not **r** again.
Dan 7:24 And another shall **r** after
Matt 5:45 for He makes His sun **r** on
Matt 12:41 The men of Nineveh will **r** up
Matt 12:42 queen of the South will **r**
Matt 20:19 And the third day He will **r**
Matt 24: 7 For nation will **r** against
Matt 24:11 many false prophets will **r**
Matt 27:63 'After three days I will **r**.
Mark 12:23 resurrection, when they **r**,
Mark 12:25 For when they **r** from the
Luke 5:23 **R** up and walk'?
Luke 11: 8 of his persistence he will **r**
Luke 16:31 be persuaded though one **r**
Luke 22:46 **R** and pray, lest you enter
John 11:23 Your brother will **r** again."
Acts 3: 6 **r** up and walk."
Acts 10:13 And a voice came to him, "**R**,
Acts 26:23 He would be the first to **r**
1Co 15:15 in fact the dead do not **r**.
1Th 4:16 the dead in Christ will **r**
Heb 7:11 that another priest should **r**

RISEN (*see* RISE)
Ps 27:12 For false witnesses have **r**
Matt 11:11 of women there has not **r**
Matt 17: 9 until the Son of Man is **r**
Matt 28: 6 is not here; for He is **r**.
Mark 1:35 having **r** a long while before
Mark 3:26 And if Satan has **r** up against
Mark 6:14 John the Baptist is **r** from
Mark 16:14 had seen Him after He had **r**.
Luke 24: 6 but is **r**! Remember how He
Luke 24:34 The Lord is **r** indeed, and has
1Co 15:13 dead, then Christ is not **r**.

RISES (*see* ARISES, RISE)
Deut 19:16 If a false witness **r** against
2Sa 23: 4 the morning when the sun **r**,
Ps 104:22 When the sun **r**, they gather
Prov 31:15 She also **r** while it is yet
Eccl 1: 5 The sun also **r**,

Eccl 12: 4 When one **r** up at the sound
Mic 7: 6 Daughter **r** against her
2Pe 1:19 and the morning star **r** in

RISING (*see* RISE)
Num 2: 3 toward the **r** of the sun,
1Ki 18:44 **r** out of the sea!" So he
2Ch 36:15 **r** up early and sending
Ps 19: 6 Its **r** is from one end of
Ps 50: 1 the earth From the **r** of
Ps 139: 2 my sitting down and my **r** up;
Is 9:18 They shall mount up like **r**
Is 41:25 From the **r** of the sun he
Is 60: 3 to the brightness of your **r**.
Jer 7:13 **r** up early and speaking, but
Lam 3:63 sitting down and their **r** up;
Mal 1:11 For from the **r** of the sun,
Luke 2:34 destined for the fall and **r**
Luke 12:54 Whenever you see a cloud **r**
Rev 13: 1 And I saw a beast **r** up out

RISKED
Rom 16: 4 who **r** their own necks for my

RIVAL
1Sa 1: 6 And her **r** also provoked her

RIVER (*see* RIVERHEADS, RIVERS, RIVERSIDE)
Gen 2:10 Now a **r** went out of Eden to
Gen 15:18 from the **r** of Egypt to the
Gen 15:18 of Egypt to the great **r**,
Ex 1:22 you shall cast into the **r**,
Ex 7:21 The fish that were in the **r**
Deut 2:24 and cross over the **R** Arnon.
Deut 2:37 anywhere along the **R** Jabbok,
Josh 24: 3 from the other side of the **R**,
1Ki 4:24 kings on this side of the **R**;
Ezra 4:11 the region beyond the **R**,
Ps 46: 4 There is a **r** whose streams
Ps 66: 6 They went through the **r** on
Ps 72: 8 And from the **R** to the ends
Is 8: 7 them The waters of the **R**,
Ezek 1: 1 among the captives by the **R**
Ezek 47: 5 a **r** that could not be
Mark 1: 5 by him in the Jordan **R**,
Rev 9:14 who are bound at the great **r**
Rev 22: 1 And he showed me a pure **r** of

RIVERHEADS† (*see* RIVER)
Gen 2:10 it parted and became four **r**.

RIVERS (*see* RIVER)
2Ki 5:12 the **r** of Damascus, better
Ps 1: 3 a tree Planted by the **r** of
Ps 74:15 You dried up mighty **r**.
Ps 78:44 Turned their **r** into blood,
Ps 137: 1 By the **r** of Babylon, There
Eccl 1: 7 All the **r** run into the sea,
Is 18: 2 Whose land the **r** divide."
Is 44:27 And I will dry up your **r**';
Mic 6: 7 Ten thousand **r** of oil?
John 7:38 of his heart will flow **r** of
Rev 8:10 it fell on a third of the **r**

RIVERSIDE (*see* RIVER)
Ex 2: 5 maidens walked along the **r**;
Acts 16:13 out of the city to the **r**,

ROAD
Matt 20:30 blind men sitting by the **r**,
Matt 21: 8 and spread them on the **r**.
Matt 21:19 seeing a fig tree by the **r**,
Mark 10:46 sat by the **r** begging.
Luke 10:31 priest came down that **r**.
Luke 24:32 He talked with us on the **r**,
Acts 26:13 along the **r** I saw a light

ROAR (*see* ROARED, ROARING, ROARS)
Ps 46: 3 Though its waters **r** and be

Ps   96:11 be glad; Let the sea r,
Jer   25:30 The LORD will r from on
Jer   31:35 And its waves r (The LORD
Amos   3: 4 Will a lion r in the forest,

ROARED (see ROAR)
Amos   3: 8 A lion has r! Who will not

ROARING (see ROAR)
Judg   14: 5 a young lion came r against
Ps   22:13 Like a raging and r lion.
1Pe   5: 8 devil walks about like a r

ROARS (see ROAR)
Amos   1: 2 The LORD r from Zion, And
Rev   10: 3 voice, as when a lion r.

ROAST (see ROASTED)
Deut   16: 7 And you shall r and eat it

ROASTED (see ROAST)
Ex   12: 8 r in fire, with unleavened

ROB (see ROBBED, ROBBER, ROBBERY)
Lev   19:13 nor r him. The wages of him
Prov   22:22 Do not r the poor because
Is   10: 2 To r the needy of justice,
Mal   3: 8 Will a man r God? Yet you
Rom   2:22 do you r temples?

ROBBED (see ROB)
2Sa   17: 8 like a bear r of her cubs in
Mal   3: 8 Yet you have r Me! But you
2Co   11: 8 I r other churches, taking

ROBBER (see PROWLER, ROB, ROBBERS)
Matt   26:55 you come out, as against a r,
John   10: 1 the same is a thief and a r.
John   18:40 Now Barabbas was a r.

ROBBERS (see ROBBER)
Matt   27:38 Then two r were crucified
John   10: 8 before Me are thieves and r,
2Co   11:26 of waters, in perils of r,

ROBBERY (see ROB)
Phil   2: 6 did not consider it r to be

ROBE (see ROBES)
Ex   28: 4 a breastplate, an ephod, a r,
Ex   29: 5 and the r of the ephod, the
1Sa   2:19 used to make him a little r,
1Sa   15:27 seized the edge of his r,
1Sa   24: 4 cut off a corner of Saul's r.
2Sa   13:18 Now she had on a r of many
2Sa   15:32 to meet him with his r torn
Esth   6: 8 let a royal r be brought
Job   1:20 Then Job arose, tore his r,
Job   2:12 and each one tore his r and
Song   5: 3 I have taken off my r;
Is   6: 1 and the train of His r
Is   61:10 has covered me with the r
Matt   27:28 Him and put a scarlet r on
Luke   15:22 Bring out the best r and put
John   19: 2 they put on Him a purple r.
Rev   6:11 Then a white r was given to
Rev   19:13 He was clothed with a r

ROBES (see ROBE)
Ps   45:14 be brought to the King in r
Is   63: 3 And I have stained all My r.
Mark   12:38 to go around in long r,
Rev   7: 9 Lamb, clothed with white r,
Rev   7:14 and washed their r and made

ROCK (see ROCKS)
Ex   17: 6 and you shall strike the r,
Ex   33:22 you in the cleft of the r,
Num   20: 8 water for them out of the r,
Num   20:11 his hand and struck the r
Deut   32: 4 He is the **R**,
Deut   32:13 him draw honey from the r,

1Sa   2: 2 Nor is there any r like
2Sa   22: 2 The LORD is my r and my
Job   19:24 they were engraved on a r
Ps   18: 2 The LORD is my r and my
Ps   27: 5 shall set me high upon a r.
Ps   28: 1 You I will cry, O LORD my **R**:
Ps   31: 3 For You are my r and my
Ps   40: 2 And set my feet upon a r,
Ps   61: 2 Lead me to the r that is
Ps   78:16 brought streams out of the r,
Ps   81:16 And with honey from the r
Ps   94:22 And my God the r of my
Ps   137: 9 little ones against the r!
Prov   30:19 The way of a serpent on a r,
Is   8:14 a stone of stumbling and a r
Is   32: 2 As the shadow of a great r
Is   51: 1 Look to the r from which
Jer   23:29 a hammer that breaks the r
Matt   7:24 who built his house on the r:
Matt   7:25 for it was founded on the r.
Matt   16:18 and on this r I will build
Matt   27:60 he had hewn out of the r;
Luke   8: 6 "Some fell on r;
Rom   9:33 a stumbling stone and r
1Co   10: 4 drank of that spiritual **R**
1Co   10: 4 and that **R** was Christ.
1Pe   2: 8 of stumbling And a r

ROCKS (see ROCK)
1Sa   13: 6 in caves, in thickets, in r,
1Ki   19:11 mountains and broke the r
Amos   6:12 Do horses run on r?
Matt   27:51 and the r were split,
Acts   27:29 should run aground on the r,

ROD (see RODS)
Ex   4: 4 and it became a r in his
Ex   4:20 And Moses took the r of God
Ex   7:12 But Aaron's r swallowed up
Ex   8:16 Aaron, 'Stretch out your r,
Lev   27:32 whatever passes under the r,
Num   20:11 the rock twice with his r;
2Sa   7:14 will chasten him with the r
Ps   2: 9 shall break them with a r
Ps   23: 4 Your r and Your staff, they
Prov   10:13 But a r is for the back of
Prov   13:24 He who spares his r hates
Prov   22: 8 And the r of his anger will
Prov   22:15 The r of correction will
Prov   23:13 if you beat him with a r,
Prov   26: 3 And a r for the fool's
Is   9: 4 The r of his oppressor, As
Is   10: 5 the r of My anger And the
Is   11: 1 There shall come forth a **R**
Lam   3: 1 seen affliction by the r of
Ezek   40: 3 of flax and a measuring r
Ezek   40: 6 which was one r wide, and
1Co   4:21 Shall I come to you with a r,
Heb   9: 4 Aaron's r that budded, and
Rev   2:27 rule them with a r of
Rev   19:15 will rule them with a r of

RODE (see RIDE)
2Sa   18: 9 Absalom r on a mule. The
2Sa   22:11 He r upon a cherub, and
2Ki   9:16 So Jehu r in a chariot and
Ps   18:10 And He r upon a cherub, and

RODS (see ROD)
Gen   30:39 conceived before the r,
Ex   7:12 rod swallowed up their r.
Ezek   42:16 five hundred r by the
Acts   16:22 them to be beaten with r.
2Co   11:25 times I was beaten with r;

ROLL (see ROLLED)
Gen   29: 3 and they would r the stone

Prov 26:27 a stone will have it **r** back
Jer 6:26 Dress in sackcloth And **r**
Mic 1:10 In Beth Aphrah **R** yourself
Mark 16: 3 Who will **r** away the stone

ROLLED (*see* ROLL)
Gen 29:10 that Jacob went near and **r**
Is 9: 5 And garments **r** in blood,
Is 34: 4 And the heavens shall be **r**
Matt 27:60 and He **r** a large stone
Rev 6:14 as a scroll when it is **r** up,

ROMAN (*see* ROMANS, ROME)
Acts 22:26 you do, for this man is a **R**.

ROMANS (*see* ROMAN)
Acts 16:21 not lawful for us, being **R**,

ROME (*see* ROMAN)
Acts 23:11 must also bear witness at **R**.
2Ti 1:17 but when he arrived in **R**,

ROOF
Gen 19: 8 under the shadow of my **r**.
Deut 22: 8 make a parapet for your **r**,
2Sa 11: 2 his bed and walked on the **r**
Ps 137: 6 my tongue cling to the **r** of
Matt 8: 8 You should come under my **r**.
Mark 2: 4 they uncovered the **r** where
Luke 7: 6 You should enter under my **r**.

ROOM (*see* ROOMS)
1Ki 7:50 for the doors of the inner **r**
1Ki 17:19 carried him to the upper **r**
Dan 6:10 home. And in his upper **r**,
Mal 3:10 there will not be **r**
Matt 6: 6 you pray, go into your **r**,
Mark 2: 2 that there was no longer **r**
Mark 14:14 Where is the guest **r** in which
Luke 2: 7 because there was no **r** for
Luke 14:22 and still there is **r**.
Acts 1:13 went up into the upper **r**
Phm 1:22 also prepare a guest **r** for

ROOMS (*see* ROOM)
Gen 6:14 make **r** in the ark, and cover

ROOSTER
Matt 26:34 before the **r** crows, you will
Mark 14:30 before the **r** crows twice,
John 18:27 and immediately a **r** crowed.

ROOT (*see* ROOTED, ROOTS)
Deut 29:18 may not be among you a **r**
Job 19:28 Since the **r** of the matter
Prov 12: 3 But the **r** of the righteous
Is 11:10 that day there shall be a **R**
Is 53: 2 And as a **r** out of dry
Jer 1:10 To **r** out and to pull down,
Mal 4: 1 will leave them neither **r**
Matt 3:10 now the ax is laid to the **r**
Matt 13: 6 and because they had no **r**
Rom 11:16 and if the **r** is holy, so
Rom 15:12 There shall be a **r** of
1Ti 6:10 the love of money is a **r** of
Heb 12:15 lest any **r** of bitterness
Rev 5: 5 the **R** of David, has
Rev 22:16 I am the **R** and the Offspring

ROOTED (*see* ROOT)
Eph 3:17 being **r** and grounded in
Col 2: 7 **r** and built up in Him and

ROOTS (*see* ROOT)
Is 11: 1 shall grow out of his **r**.
Dan 7: 8 were plucked out by the **r**.
Amos 2: 9 his fruit above And his **r**
Mark 11:20 fig tree dried up from the **r**.
Jude 12 dead, pulled up by the **r**;

ROPE (*see* ROPES)
Josh 2:15 by a **r** through the window
Is 5:18 and sin as if with a cart **r**;

ROPES (*see* ROPE)
Judg 15:13 bound him with two new **r**
Jer 38: 6 let Jeremiah down with **r**.
Jer 38:13 pulled Jeremiah up with **r**

ROSE (*see* RISE)
Gen 4: 8 that Cain **r** up against Abel
Gen 22: 3 So Abraham **r** early in the
Ex 32: 6 and **r** up to play.
Josh 6:15 the seventh day that they **r**
Ruth 2:15 And when she **r** up to glean,
1Sa 25:42 So Abigail **r** in haste and
2Ch 13: 6 **r** up and rebelled against
Ps 18:39 under me those who **r** up
Ps 124: 2 When men **r** up against us,
Song 2: 1 I am the **r** of Sharon, And
Is 35: 1 rejoice and blossom as the **r**;
John 11:31 when they saw that Mary **r** up
John 13: 4 **r** from supper and laid aside
Acts 5:36 some time ago Theudas **r**
Acts 18:12 the Jews with one accord **r**
Rom 14: 9 this end Christ died and **r**
1Co 10: 7 and **r** up to play."
1Co 15: 4 and that He **r** again the
2Co 5:15 Him who died for them and **r**
1Th 4:14 that Jesus died and **r** again,

ROSH
Ezek 38: 3 you, O Gog, the prince of **R**,

ROT (*see* ROTTEN)
Is 40:20 a tree that will not **r**;

ROTTEN (*see* ROT, ROTTENNESS)
Jer 29:17 and will make them like **r**

ROTTENNESS (*see* ROTTEN)
Prov 12: 4 who causes shame is like **r**
Prov 14:30 But envy is **r** to the

ROUGH (*see* ROUGHLY)
Is 40: 4 be made straight And the **r**
Luke 3: 5 straight And the **r**

ROUGHLY (*see* ROUGH)
Gen 42:30 lord of the land spoke **r** to

ROUND (*see* ROUNDED)
Ex 16:14 was a small **r** substance, as
Deut 12:10 rest from all your enemies **r**

ROUNDED† (*see* ROUND)
Song 7: 2 Your navel is a **r** goblet;

ROUSE
Gen 49: 9 who shall **r** him?

ROWED† (*see* ROWS)
Jon 1:13 Nevertheless the men **r** hard
John 6:19 So when they had **r** about

ROWS (*see* ROWED)
Ex 39:10 And they set in it four **r** of

ROYAL
Ps 45:13 The **r** daughter is all
Dan 4:29 he was walking about the **r**
Amos 7:13 And it is the **r**
Acts 12:21 arrayed in **r** apparel, sat on
Jas 2: 8 If you really fulfill the **r**
1Pe 2: 9 a **r** priesthood, a holy

RUBBED† (*see* RUBBING)
Ezek 16: 4 you were not **r** with salt nor
Ezek 29:18 and every shoulder **r** raw;

RUBBING† (*see* RUBBED)
Luke 6: 1 **r** them in their hands.

RUBBISH
Phil 3: 8 things, and count them as **r**,

RUBIES
Job 28:18 price of wisdom is above **r**.
Prov 3:15 is more precious than **r**,
Prov 8:11 wisdom is better than **r**,
Prov 31:10 her worth is far above **r**.

RUDDER
Jas 3: 4 are turned by a very small **r**

RUDDY
1Sa 16:12 him in. Now he was **r**,
Song 5:10 My beloved is white and **r**,

RUDELY†
1Co 13: 5 does not behave **r**,

RUE†
Luke 11:42 For you tithe mint and **r**

RUIN (*see* RUINED, RUINS)
Ruth 4: 6 lest I **r** my own inheritance.
Prov 5:14 was on the verge of total **r**,
Prov 19:13 A foolish son is the **r** of
Luke 6:49 And the **r** of that house was
2Ti 2:14 to the **r** of the hearers.

RUINED (*see* RUIN)
Is 24:16 But I said, "I am **r**,
Is 60:12 nations shall be utterly **r**.
Is 61: 4 And they shall repair the **r**
Joel 1: 7 And **r** My fig tree; He has
Matt 9:17 and the wineskins are **r**.
Luke 5:37 and the wineskins will be **r**.

RUINS (*see* RUIN)
2Ki 19:25 cities into heaps of **r**.
Is 61: 4 they shall rebuild the old **r**,
Jer 9:11 make Jerusalem a heap of **r**,
Jer 26:18 shall become heaps of **r**,
Amos 9:11 I will raise up its **r**,
Mic 3:12 shall become heaps of **r**,
Hag 1: 4 this temple to lie in **r**?
Acts 15:16 I will rebuild its **r**,

RULE (*see* RULED, RULER, RULES, RULING)
Gen 1:16 the greater light to **r** the
Gen 3:16 And he shall **r** over you."
Gen 4: 7 but you should **r** over it."
Judg 8:23 the LORD shall **r** over
Ps 110: 2 **R** in the midst of Your
Ps 136: 8 The sun to **r** by day, For
Prov 8:16 By me princes **r**,
Prov 17: 2 A wise servant will **r** over a
Is 3: 4 And babes shall **r** over
Is 3:12 And women **r** over them. O
Is 40:10 And His arm shall **r** for
Lam 5: 8 Servants **r** over us; There
Dan 2:39 which shall **r** over all the
1Co 15:24 He puts an end to all **r** and
Gal 6:16 as walk according to this **r**,
Phil 3:16 let us walk by the same **r**,
Col 3:15 And let the peace of God **r** in
1Ti 3: 5 a man does not know how to **r**
1Ti 5:17 Let the elders who **r** well be
Heb 13:17 Obey those who **r** over you,
Rev 2:27 He shall **r** them with a
Rev 12: 5 a male Child who was to **r**

RULED (*see* RULE)
Gen 24: 2 who **r** over all that he had,
Ruth 1: 1 the days when the judges **r**,
Is 14: 6 He who **r** the nations in

RULER (*see* RULE, RULER'S, RULERS)
1Sa 25:30 and has appointed you **r** over
2Sa 5: 2 and be **r** over Israel.'"
2Sa 7: 8 to be **r** over My people, over

Dan 2:38 and has made you **r** over them
Dan 5: 7 and he shall be the third **r**
Mic 5: 2 to Me The One to be **R** in
Matt 2: 6 of you shall come a **R**
Matt 9:34 casts out demons by the **r**
Matt 25:21 I will make you **r** over many
Mark 5:38 came to the house of the **r**
John 3: 1 a **r** of the Jews.
John 12:31 now the **r** of this world will
Acts 7:27 Who made you a **r** and a
Rev 1: 5 and the **r** over the kings of

RULER'S (*see* RULER)
Matt 9:23 When Jesus came into the **r**

RULERS (*see* RULER)
Ex 18:21 **r** of hundreds, rulers of
Neh 5: 7 I rebuked the nobles and **r**,
Ps 2: 2 And the **r** take counsel
Eccl 7:19 the wise More than ten **r**
Is 1:10 You **r** of Sodom; Give ear
Matt 2: 6 the least among the **r**
Mark 5:22 one of the **r** of the
Mark 13: 9 You will be brought before **r**
Luke 14: 1 the house of one of the **r**
Acts 3:17 as did also your **r**.
Acts 17: 6 and some brethren to the **r**
Rom 13: 3 For **r** are not a terror to
1Co 2: 6 nor of the **r** of this age,
Eph 6:12 against the **r** of the
Tit 3: 1 them to be subject to **r** and

RULES (*see* RULE)
Ps 22:28 And He **r** over the nations.
Ps 59:13 let them know that God **r** in
Ps 103:19 And His kingdom **r** over all.
Prov 16:32 And he who **r** his spirit
Dan 4:17 know That the Most High **r**
Dan 4:26 come to know that Heaven **r**.
1Ti 3: 4 one who **r** his own house well,
2Ti 2: 5 competes according to the **r**.

RULING (*see* RULE)
1Ti 3:12 **r** their children and their

RUMOR (*see* RUMORS)
2Ki 19: 7 and he shall hear a **r** and

RUMORS (*see* RUMOR)
Matt 24: 6 you will hear of wars and **r**

RUN (*see* RAN, RUNNING, RUNS)
Gen 49:22 His branches **r** over the
2Sa 15: 1 and fifty men to **r** before
1Ki 17:16 nor did the jar of oil **r**
2Ch 16: 9 the eyes of the LORD **r**
Ps 18:29 For by You I can **r** against a
Ps 19: 5 like a strong man to **r** its
Prov 1:16 For their feet **r** to evil,
Prov 18:10 The righteous **r** to it and
Eccl 1: 7 All the rivers **r** into the
Is 40:31 They shall **r** and not be
Jer 9:18 That our eyes may **r** with
Jer 12: 5 If you have **r** with the
Lam 2:18 Let tears **r** down like a
Dan 12: 4 many shall **r** to and fro, and
Amos 5:24 But let justice **r** down like
Hab 2: 2 That he may **r** who reads it.
1Co 9:24 not know that those who **r**
Gal 2: 2 lest by any means I might **r**,
2Th 3: 1 the word of the Lord may **r**
Heb 12: 1 and let us **r** with endurance
1Pe 4: 4 it strange that you do not **r**
Jude 11 have **r** greedily in the error

RUNNING (*see* RUN)
Ps 133: 2 **R** down on the beard, The
Prov 5:15 And **r** water from your own

RUNS (*see* RUN)
Ps   23: 5 My cup **r** over.
Rom   9:16 who wills, nor of him who **r**,

RUSHED (*see* RUSHES, RUSHING)
Acts   19:29 and **r** into the theater with

RUSHES (*see* RUSHED)
Is   19: 6 The reeds and **r** will

RUSHING (*see* RUSHED)
Acts   2: 2 as of a **r** mighty wind, and

RUST†
Matt   6:19 where moth and **r** destroy and
Matt   6:20 where neither moth nor **r**

RUTH
Ruth   1:16 But **R** said: "Entreat me
Ruth   1:22 and **R** the Moabitess her

S

SABACHTHANI†
Matt   27:46 saying, "Eli, Eli, lama **s**?
Mark   15:34 saying, "Eloi, Eloi, lama **s**?

SABAOTH†
Rom   9:29 Unless the LORD of **S**
Jas   5: 4 the ears of the Lord of **S**.

SABBATH (*see* SABBATHS)
Ex   16:23 Tomorrow is a **S** rest, a holy
Ex   20: 8 Remember the **S** day, to keep
Ex   20:11 the LORD blessed the **S** day
Ex   31:15 does any work on the **S** day,
Ex   35: 2 a **S** of rest to the LORD.
Lev   23: 3 but the seventh day is a **S**
Lev   23:16 the day after the seventh **S**;
Num   15:32 gathering sticks on the **S**
2Ki   4:23 the New Moon nor the **S**.
2Ki   11: 7 you who go off duty on the **S**
Neh   10:31 any grain to sell on the **S**
Is   58:13 And call the **S** a delight,
Amos   8: 5 may sell grain? And the **S**,
Matt   12: 1 the grainfields on the **S**.
Matt   12: 2 is not lawful to do on the **S**!
Matt   12: 8 of Man is Lord even of the **S**.
Mark   2:27 man, and not man for the **S**.
Mark   16: 1 Now when the **S** was past, Mary
Luke   4:16 into the synagogue on the **S**
John   7:22 circumcise a man on the **S**.
Acts   1:12 a **S** day's journey.
Acts   13:27 which are read every **S**,

SABBATHS (*see* SABBATH)
Ex   31:13 Surely My **S** you shall keep,
Lev   23:15 seven **S** shall be completed.
Is   1:13 to Me. The New Moons, the **S**,
Luke   4:31 was teaching them on the **S**.
Acts   17: 2 and for three **S** reasoned
Col   2:16 festival or a new moon or **s**,

SACK (*see* SACKS)
Gen   42:25 every man's money to his **s**,
Gen   44:12 was found in Benjamin's **s**.

SACKCLOTH
Gen   37:34 put **s** on his waist, and
2Ki   19: 1 covered himself with **s**,
Neh   9: 1 assembled with fasting, in **s**,
Esth   4: 3 and many lay in **s** and ashes.
Dan   9: 3 with fasting, **s**,
Jon   3: 5 a fast, and put on **s**,
Matt   11:21 have repented long ago in **s**

SACKS (*see* SACK)
Gen   42:25 a command to fill their **s**

Gen   43:22 who put our money in our **s**.
Josh   9: 4 And they took old **s** on their

SACRED
Ex   23:24 break down their **s** pillars.
Lev   23:36 It is a **s** assembly, and
Deut   16:15 days you shall keep a **s**
2Ki   12:18 king of Judah took all the **s**
Is   1:13 endure iniquity and the **s**
Hos   3: 4 without sacrifice or **s**
Joel   1:14 Call a **s** assembly; Gather

SACRIFICE (*see* SACRIFICED, SACRIFICES)
Ex   3:18 that we may **s** to the LORD
Ex   8:27 into the wilderness and **s**
Ex   12:27 It is the Passover **s** of the
Ex   23:18 nor shall the fat of My **s**
Ex   34:15 with their gods and make **s**
Lev   1: 3 his offering is a burnt **s**
Lev   3: 1 When his offering is a **s** of
Lev   7:12 with the **s** of thanksgiving,
Lev   7:20 who eats the flesh of the **s**
Lev   17: 8 offers a burnt offering or **s**,
Num   15: 8 or as a **s** to fulfill a vow,
Judg   16:23 together to offer a great **s**
1Sa   1: 3 yearly to worship and **s** to
1Sa   1:21 to the LORD the yearly **s**
1Sa   9:13 because he must bless the **s**;
1Sa   15:22 to obey is better than **s**,
2Sa   24:22 here are oxen for burnt **s**,
1Ki   3: 4 the king went to Gibeon to **s**
1Ki   8:63 And Solomon offered a **s** of
1Ki   18:29 offering of the evening **s**.
1Ki   18:36 offering of the evening **s**,
2Ki   5:17 either burnt offering or **s**
2Ki   10:19 for I have a great **s** for
2Ki   16:15 and all the blood of the **s**.
2Ch   7:12 for Myself as a house of **s**.
Ps   40: 6 **S** and offering You did not
Ps   50: 5 made a covenant with Me by **s**.
Ps   51:16 For You do not desire **s**,
Dan   9:27 He shall bring an end to **s**
Dan   12:11 the time that the daily **s**
Hos   3: 4 without **s** or sacred pillar,
Hos   6: 6 I desire mercy and not **s**,
Jon   2: 9 But I will **s** to You With
Mal   1: 8 you offer the blind as a **s**,
Matt   9:13 desire mercy and not **s**.
Matt   12: 7 desire mercy and not **s**,
Rom   12: 1 your bodies a living **s**,
1Co   10:20 things which the Gentiles **s**
Eph   5: 2 an offering and a **s** to God
Phil   4:18 aroma, an acceptable **s**,
Heb   9:26 to put away sin by the **s** of
Heb   10: 5 **S** and offering You did
Heb   10:12 after He had offered one **s**
Heb   10:26 there no longer remains a **s**
Heb   11: 4 to God a more excellent **s**
Heb   13:15 us continually offer the **s**

SACRIFICED (*see* SACRIFICE)
Ex   24: 5 burnt offerings and **s** peace
Ex   32: 8 and worshiped it and **s** to
Deut   32:17 They **s** to demons, not to
1Ki   11: 8 who burned incense and **s** to
Ps   106:37 They even **s** their sons And
Hos   11: 2 They **s** to the Baals, And
1Co   5: 7 our Passover, was **s** for us.
Rev   2:14 to eat things **s** to idols,
Rev   2:20 immorality and eat things **s**

SACRIFICES (*see* SACRIFICE)
Ex   18:12 burnt offering and other **s**
Ex   29:28 of Israel from the **s** of
Lev   10:13 of the **s** made by fire to the
Deut   12:27 and the blood of your **s**
Deut   32:38 Who ate the fat of their **s**,

Ps 4: 5 Offer the s of
Ps 51:17 The s of God are a broken
Ps 106:28 And ate s made to the dead.
Ps 107:22 Let them sacrifice the s of
Is 1:11 is the multitude of your s
Is 1:13 Bring no more futile s;
Is 43:23 you honored Me with your s.
Dan 8:11 and by him the daily s were
Hos 14: 2 For we will offer the s of
Amos 4: 4 Bring your s every morning,
Amos 5:25 Did you offer Me s and
Mal 1:14 But s to the Lord what is
Luke 13: 1 had mingled with their s.
Acts 7:41 offered s to the idol, and
1Co 10:18 not those who eat of the s
Heb 5: 1 may offer both gifts and s
Heb 5: 3 to offer s for sins.
Heb 7:27 high priests, to offer up s,
Heb 9:23 themselves with better s
Heb 10: 6 burnt offerings and s
Heb 10:11 repeatedly the same s,
Heb 13:16 for with such s God is well
1Pe 2: 5 to offer up spiritual s

SAD
1Sa 1:18 her face was no longer s.
Neh 2: 2 to me, "Why is your face s,

SADDLE (see SADDLED)
Gen 31:34 put them in the camel's s,

SADDLED (see SADDLE)
Gen 22: 3 early in the morning and s
Num 22:21 s his donkey, and went with
2Ki 4:24 Then she s a donkey, and said

SADDUCEES
Matt 3: 7 many of the Pharisees and S
Luke 20:27 Then some of the S,
Acts 5:17 (which is the sect of the S)
Acts 23: 8 For S say that there is no

SAFE (see SAFELY, SAFETY)
2Sa 18:29 "Is the young man Absalom s?
Prov 18:10 run to it and are s.
Luke 15:27 he has received him s and

SAFELY (see SAFE)
Gen 33:18 Then Jacob came s to the
1Ki 4:25 And Judah and Israel dwelt s,
Prov 1:33 listens to me will dwell s,
Acts 23:24 and bring him s to Felix
Acts 27:44 was that they all escaped s

SAFETY (see SAFE)
Ps 4: 8 O LORD, make me dwell in s.
Ps 33:17 horse is a vain hope for s;
Prov 11:14 of counselors there is s.
Is 14:30 the needy will lie down in s;
1Th 5: 3 Peace and s!" then sudden

SAILED
Luke 8:23 But as they s He fell asleep.
Acts 14:26 From there they s to Antioch,

SAINT† (see SAINTS)
Ps 106:16 And Aaron the s of the
Phil 4:21 Greet every s in Christ

SAINTS (see SAINT)
Deut 33: 2 came with ten thousands of s;
1Sa 2: 9 will guard the feet of His s,
Ps 16: 3 As for the s who are on the
Ps 30: 4 You s of His, And give
Ps 34: 9 you His s! There is no
Ps 89: 5 in the assembly of the s.
Ps 97:10 preserves the souls of His s;
Ps 116:15 Is the death of His s.
Ps 132: 9 And let Your s shout for
Ps 149: 5 Let the s be joyful in

Prov 2: 8 preserves the way of His s.
Dan 7:18 But the s of the Most High
Dan 7:21 was making war against the s,
Zech 14: 5 And all the s with You.
Matt 27:52 and many bodies of the s who
Acts 26:10 and many of the s I shut up
Rom 1: 7 of God, called to be s:
Rom 8:27 makes intercession for the s
Rom 12:13 to the needs of the s,
Rom 15:25 to minister to the s.
Rom 16: 2 in a manner worthy of the s,
1Co 1: 2 Jesus, called to be s,
1Co 6: 2 Do you not know that the s
1Co 14:33 in all the churches of the s.
1Co 16: 1 the collection for the s,
1Co 16:15 to the ministry of the s—
2Co 1: 1 with all the s who are in
Eph 1:15 and your love for all the s,
Eph 1:18 of His inheritance in the s,
Eph 2:19 fellow citizens with the s
Eph 3: 8 than the least of all the s,
Eph 3:18 to comprehend with all the s
Eph 4:12 for the equipping of the s
Eph 6:18 supplication for all the s—
Col 1:12 of the inheritance of the s
1Th 3:13 Jesus Christ with all His s.
2Th 1:10 to be glorified in His s and
Jude 3 for all delivered to the s.
Jude 14 with ten thousands of His s,
Rev 5: 8 are the prayers of the s.
Rev 13: 7 him to make war with the s
Rev 15: 3 O King of the s!
Rev 17: 6 with the blood of the s and

SAKE (see SAKES)
Gen 3:17 is the ground for your s;
Gen 8:21 curse the ground for man's s,
Gen 18:29 will not do it for the s
1Sa 12:22 for His great name's s,
2Sa 9: 1 kindness for Jonathan's s?
Ps 6: 4 save me for Your mercies' s!
Ps 23: 3 For His name's s.
Ps 25: 7 me, For Your goodness' s,
Ps 44:22 Yet for Your s we are killed
Ps 122: 8 For the s of my brethren and
Is 45: 4 For Jacob My servant's s,
Is 48:11 For My own s, for My own
Ezek 20: 9 I acted for My name's s,
Ezek 20:14 I acted for My name's s,
Ezek 36:22 but for My holy name's s,
Ezek 36:32 Not for your s do I do
Matt 5:10 for righteousness' s,
Matt 5:11 against you falsely for My s.
Matt 10:39 who loses his life for My s
Matt 16:25 loses his life for My s
Matt 19:29 or lands, for My name's s,
Matt 24:22 but for the elect's s those
Luke 6:22 For the Son of Man's s.
John 12: 9 not for Jesus' s only, but
John 13:37 lay down my life for Your s.
Acts 9:16 must suffer for My name's s.
Rom 8:36 For Your s we are killed
Rom 11:28 are beloved for the s of
Rom 13: 5 but also for conscience' s.
1Co 4:10 We are fools for Christ's s,
1Co 9:23 this I do for the gospel's s,
1Co 10:25 questions for conscience' s;
2Co 4: 5 bondservants for Jesus' s.
Phil 1:29 but also to suffer for His s,
Col 1:24 for the s of His body, which
1Ti 5:23 wine for your stomach's s
2Ti 2:10 endure all things for the s
Tit 1:11 for the s of dishonest gain.
1Pe 3:14 suffer for righteousness' s,
1Jn 2:12 you for His name's s.

Rev 2: 3 labored for My name's **s** and

SAKES (see SAKE)
Ps 105:14 He rebuked kings for their **s**,
Dan 2:30 but for our **s** who make
John 17:19 And for their **s** I sanctify
1Co 4: 6 and Apollos for your **s**,
2Co 8: 9 yet for your **s** He became

SALEM (see JERUSALEM)
Gen 14:18 Then Melchizedek king of S
Ps 76: 2 In S also is His tabernacle,
Heb 7: 1 this Melchizedek, king of S,

SALIM†
John 3:23 baptizing in Aenon near S,

SALIVA
John 9: 6 and made clay with the **s**;

SALMON
Ruth 4:20 Nahshon, and Nahshon begot S;
Matt 1: 4 Nahshon, and Nahshon begot S.

SALOME
Mark 16: 1 and S bought spices, that

SALT
Gen 14: 3 (that is, the S Sea).
Gen 19:26 and she became a pillar of **s**.
Num 18:19 it is a covenant of **s**
Judg 9:45 the city and sowed it with **s**.
2Ki 14: 7 Edomites in the Valley of S,
2Ch 13: 5 his sons, by a covenant of **s**?
Matt 5:13 You are the **s** of the earth;
Col 4: 6 with grace, seasoned with **s**,
Jas 3:12 Thus no spring yields both **s**

SALUTATION† (see SALUTE)
1Co 16:21 The **s** with my own
Col 4:18 This **s** by my own hand—Paul.
2Th 3:17 The **s** of Paul with my own

SALUTE† (see SALUTATION)
Mark 15:18 and began to **s** Him, "Hail,

SALVATION (see SAVE)
Ex 14:13 and see the **s** of the LORD,
Ex 15: 2 And He has become my **s**;
Deut 32:15 esteemed the Rock of his **s**.
1Sa 2: 1 Because I rejoice in Your **s**.
2Sa 22: 3 shield and the horn of my **s**,
Ps 3: 8 S belongs to the LORD
Ps 9:14 I will rejoice in Your **s**.
Ps 27: 1 LORD is my light and my **s**;
Ps 40:16 Let such as love Your **s** say
Ps 51:12 to me the joy of Your **s**,
Ps 51:14 O God, The God of my **s**,
Ps 62: 2 only is my rock and my **s**;
Ps 67: 2 Your **s** among all nations.
Ps 69:13 me in the truth of Your **s**
Ps 71:15 righteousness And Your **s**
Ps 89:26 God, and the rock of my **s**.
Ps 95: 1 to the Rock of our **s**.
Ps 96: 2 the good news of His **s** from
Ps 98: 2 LORD has made known His **s**;
Ps 98: 3 of the earth have seen the **s**
Ps 116:13 I will take up the cup of **s**,
Ps 118:14 And He has become my **s**.
Is 12: 3 water From the wells of **s**.
Is 45:17 LORD With an everlasting **s**;
Is 52: 7 things, Who proclaims **s**,
Is 52:10 the earth shall see The **s**
Is 59:16 His own arm brought **s** for
Is 59:17 And a helmet of **s** on His
Is 60:18 you shall call your walls S,
Jon 2: 9 S is of the LORD.
Hab 3:13 For **s** with Your Anointed.
Zech 9: 9 He is just and having **s**,
Luke 1:69 has raised up a horn of **s**

Luke 2:30 my eyes have seen Your **s**
Luke 3: 6 flesh shall see the **s**
Luke 19: 9 Today **s** has come to this
John 4:22 for **s** is of the Jews.
Acts 4:12 Nor is there **s** in any other,
Acts 16:17 proclaim to us the way of **s**.
Rom 1:16 it is the power of God to **s**
Rom 10:10 confession is made unto **s**.
Rom 11:11 **s** has come to the
Rom 13:11 for now our **s** is nearer
2Co 1: 6 for your consolation and **s**,
2Co 6: 2 behold, now is the day of **s**.
2Co 7:10 repentance leading to **s**,
Eph 1:13 truth, the gospel of your **s**;
Eph 6:17 And take the helmet of **s**,
Phil 1:28 perdition, but to you of **s**,
Phil 2:12 work out your own **s** with
1Th 5: 8 as a helmet the hope of **s**.
1Th 5: 9 but to obtain **s** through our
2Ti 2:10 they also may obtain the **s**
2Ti 3:15 able to make you wise for **s**
Tit 2:11 grace of God that brings **s**
Heb 1:14 for those who will inherit **s**?
Heb 2: 3 if we neglect so great a **s**,
Heb 2:10 make the captain of their **s**
Heb 5: 9 the author of eternal **s** to
Heb 6: 9 yes, things that accompany **s**,
1Pe 1: 5 of God through faith for **s**
1Pe 1: 9 the **s** of your souls.
1Pe 1:10 Of this **s** the prophets have
Rev 7:10 S belongs to our God who
Rev 19: 1 Alleluia! S and glory and

SALVE†
Rev 3:18 anoint your eyes with eye **s**,

SAMARIA (see SAMARITAN)
1Ki 16:24 And he bought the hill of S
1Ki 16:24 the city which he built, S,
1Ki 21: 1 the palace of Ahab king of S.
Is 7: 9 The head of Ephraim is S,
Luke 17:11 through the midst of S and
John 4: 4 He needed to go through S.
John 4: 7 A woman of S came to draw
Acts 1: 8 and in all Judea and S,

SAMARITAN† (see SAMARIA, SAMARITANS)
Luke 10:33 "But a certain S,
Luke 17:16 Him thanks. And he was a S.
John 4: 9 a S woman?" For Jews have
John 8:48 say rightly that You are a S

SAMARITANS (see SAMARITAN)
Matt 10: 5 do not enter a city of the S.
John 4: 9 Jews have no dealings with S.
Acts 8:25 in many villages of the S.

SAMSON
Judg 15: 1 it happened that S visited
Judg 16: 6 So Delilah said to S,
Judg 16:29 And S took hold of the two
Heb 11:32 of Gideon and Barak and S

SAMUEL
1Sa 1:20 a son, and called his name S,
1Sa 3: 1 Then the boy S ministered to
1Sa 3:10 S! Samuel!" And Samuel
1Sa 7:15 And S judged Israel all the
1Sa 15:34 Then S went to Ramah, and
1Sa 16:10 And S said to Jesse, "The
1Sa 16:13 Then S took the horn of oil
1Sa 19:22 Where are S and David?" And
1Sa 25: 1 Then S died; and the
1Sa 28:11 Bring up S for me."
1Sa 28:12 When the woman saw S,
1Ch 29:29 written in the book of S
Acts 3:24 from S and those who follow,
Acts 13:20 until S the prophet.

Heb 11:32 also of David and **S** and the

SANBALLAT
Neh 6:14 God, remember Tobiah and **S**,

SANCTIFICATION (see SANCTIFY)
1Co 1:30 and righteousness and **s** and
1Th 4: 3 is the will of God, your **s**:
1Th 4: 4 possess his own vessel in **s**
2Th 2:13 you for salvation through **s**

SANCTIFIED (see SANCTIFY)
Gen 2: 3 the seventh day and **s** it,
Ex 19:14 to the people and **s** the
Ex 29:43 the tabernacle shall be **s**
1Ch 15:14 priests and the Levites **s**
2Ch 7:16 now I have chosen and **s**
Jer 1: 5 Before you were born I **s**
John 10:36 say of Him whom the Father **s**
John 17:19 that they also may be **s** by
Acts 20:32 among all those who are **s**.
Acts 26:18 among those who are **s** by
Rom 15:16 **s** by the Holy Spirit.
1Co 1: 2 to those who are **s** in Christ
1Co 6:11 were washed, but you were **s**,
1Co 7:14 unbelieving husband is **s** by
2Ti 2:21 **s** and useful for the Master,
Jude 1 **s** by God the Father, and

SANCTIFIES (see SANCTIFY)
Ex 31:13 that I am the LORD who **s**
Heb 2:11 For both He who **s** and those
Heb 9:13 **s** for the purifying of the

SANCTIFY (see SANCTIFICATION, SANCTIFIED, SANCTIFIES)
Ex 29:36 you shall anoint it to **s** it.
Num 6:11 and he shall **s** his head that
Neh 13:22 to **s** the Sabbath day.
Job 1: 5 that Job would send and **s**
Ezek 36:23 And I will **s** My great name,
Ezek 38:23 I will magnify Myself and **s**
John 17:17 **S** them by Your truth. Your
John 17:19 And for their sakes I **s**
Eph 5:26 that He might **s** and cleanse
1Th 5:23 the God of peace Himself **s**
Heb 13:12 that He might **s** the people
1Pe 3:15 But **s** the Lord God in your

SANCTUARY
Ex 25: 8 "And let them make Me a **s**,
Ex 30:13 to the shekel of the **s** (a
Lev 4: 6 front of the veil of the **s**.
Lev 16:33 atonement for the Holy **S**,
Lev 21:12 nor profane the **s** of his
Num 3:28 keeping charge of the **s**.
Num 4:12 which they minister in the **s**,
Num 19:20 he has defiled the **s** of the
2Ch 30:19 to the purification of the **s**.
Ps 28: 2 my hands toward Your holy **s**.
Ps 63: 2 have looked for You in the **s**,
Ps 74: 3 damaged everything in the **s**.
Ps 74: 7 have set fire to Your **s**;
Ps 96: 6 and beauty are in His **s**.
Ps 114: 2 Judah became His **s**,
Ps 150: 1 LORD! Praise God in His **s**;
Lam 2: 7 He has abandoned His **s**;
Ezek 9: 6 the mark; and begin at My **s**.
Ezek 37:28 when My **s** is in their midst
Ezek 41: 1 he brought me into the **s**
Ezek 48: 8 with the **s** in the center.
Dan 9:17 Your face to shine on Your **s**,
Dan 9:26 destroy the city and the **s**.
Amos 7:13 For it is the king's **s**,
Heb 8: 2 a Minister of the **s** and of
Heb 9: 1 service and the earthly **s**.
Heb 13:11 blood is brought into the **s**

SAND (see SANDS)
Gen 22:17 of the heaven and as the **s**
Gen 32:12 your descendants as the **s**
Ex 2:12 and hid him in the **s**.
1Ki 4:20 were as numerous as the **s**
Ps 139:18 be more in number than the **s**;
Matt 7:26 who built his house on the **s**:
Rom 9:27 of Israel be as the **s**

SANDAL (see SANDALS)
Gen 14:23 from a thread to a **s** strap,
Ruth 4: 8 So he took off his **s**.
Mark 1: 7 whose **s** strap I am not

SANDALS (see SANDAL)
Ex 3: 5 Take your **s** off your feet,
Deut 29: 5 and your **s** have not worn out
Amos 2: 6 the poor for a pair of **s**.
Amos 8: 6 the needy for a pair of **s**—
Matt 3:11 whose **s** I am not worthy to
Acts 13:25 the **s** of whose feet I am not

SANG (see SING)
Ezra 3:11 And they **s** responsively,
Job 38: 7 When the morning stars **s**
Rev 5: 9 And they **s** a new song,

SANK (see SINK)
Judg 5:27 At her feet he **s**,
1Sa 17:49 so that the stone **s** into his
Jer 38: 6 So Jeremiah **s** in the mire.

SAPPHIRA†
Acts 5: 1 with **S** his wife, sold a

SAPPHIRE
Ex 24:10 as it were a paved work of **s**
Ex 28:18 shall be a turquoise, a **s**,
Ezek 1:26 in appearance like a **s**
Rev 21:19 was jasper, the second, **s**,

SARAH (see SARAI)
Gen 17:15 but **S** shall be her name.
Gen 17:19 **S** your wife shall bear you a
Gen 18:12 Therefore **S** laughed within
Gen 21: 1 And the LORD visited **S** as He
Gen 21: 3 whom **S** bore to him—Isaac.
Gen 23: 2 So **S** died in Kirjath Arba
Is 51: 2 And to **S** who bore you;
Heb 11:11 By faith **S** herself also
1Pe 3: 6 as **S** obeyed Abraham, calling

SARAI (see SARAH)
Gen 11:29 name of Abram's wife was **S**,
Gen 11:30 But **S** was barren; she had no
Gen 16: 6 And when **S** dealt harshly

SARDIS
Rev 1:11 Pergamos, to Thyatira, to **S**,
Rev 3: 1 the angel of the church in **S**

SARDIUS
Ex 28:17 first row shall be a **s**,
Rev 21:20 fifth sardonyx, the sixth **s**,

SARGON†
Is 20: 1 when **S** the king of Assyria

SASH
Is 3:24 be a stench; Instead of a **s**,
Jer 13: 1 and get yourself a linen **s**,

SAT (see SIT)
Gen 31:34 and **s** on them. And Laban
Ex 2:15 and he **s** down by a well.
Ex 32: 6 and the people **s** down to eat
Ruth 4: 1 went up to the gate and **s**
Ezra 10: 9 and all the people **s** in the
Neh 1: 4 that I **s** down and wept, and
Job 2: 8 to scrape himself while he **s**
Job 2:13 So they **s** down with him on
Ps 29:10 The LORD **s** enthroned at

Ps	137: 1	There we s down, yea, we
Jer	15:17	I s alone because of Your
Ezek	3:15	and I sat where they s,
Ezek	8: 1	as I is in my house with the
Jon	3: 6	with sackcloth and s in
Jon	4: 5	made himself a shelter and s
Matt	4:16	The people who s in
Matt	26:20	He s down with the twelve.
Mark	11: 2	tied, on which no one has s.
Mark	16:14	to the eleven as they s at
Mark	16:19	and s down at the right hand
Luke	4:20	back to the attendant and s
Luke	10:39	who also s at Jesus' feet
Luke	18:35	that a certain blind man s
John	4: 6	s thus by the well. It was
John	13:12	and s down again, He said to
Acts	2: 3	and one s upon each of
Acts	20: 9	And in a window s a certain
1Co	10: 7	The people s down to eat
Heb	1: 3	s down at the right hand of
Heb	10:12	s down at the right hand of
Rev	3:21	as I also overcame and s
Rev	4: 2	and One s on the throne.
Rev	14:14	and on the cloud s One like
Rev	19:19	make war against Him who s

SATAN (*see* SATAN'S)

1Ch	21: 1	Now S stood up against
Job	1: 6	and S also came among them.
Zech	3: 1	and S standing at his right
Matt	4:10	S! For it is written, 'You
Matt	12:26	If S casts out Satan, he is
Matt	16:23	S! You are an offense to Me,
Mark	1:13	forty days, tempted by S,
Mark	4:15	comes immediately and
Luke	10:18	I saw S fall like lightning
Luke	11:18	If S also is divided against
Luke	22: 3	Then S entered Judas,
Acts	5: 3	why has S filled your heart
Acts	26:18	and from the power of S to
Rom	16:20	God of peace will crush S
1Co	5: 5	deliver such a one to S for
2Co	2:11	lest S should take advantage
2Co	11:14	And no wonder! For S himself
2Co	12: 7	a messenger of S to buffet
1Th	2:18	but S hindered us.
1Ti	1:20	whom I delivered to S that
1Ti	5:15	already turned aside after S.
Rev	2: 9	but are a synagogue of S.
Rev	2:13	where S dwells.
Rev	2:24	not known the depths of S,
Rev	12: 9	old, called the Devil and S,
Rev	20: 7	S will be released from his

SATAN'S† (*see* SATAN)

Rev	2:13	where S throne is. And you

SATISFIED (*see* SATISFY)

Lev	26:26	you shall eat and not be s.
Ps	22:26	The poor shall eat and be s;
Ps	63: 5	My soul shall be s as with
Prov	27:20	the eyes of man are never s.
Prov	30:15	things that are never s,
Eccl	1: 8	The eye is not s with
Is	53:11	labor of His soul, and be s.
Mic	6:14	You shall eat, but not be s;
Hab	2: 5	like death, and cannot be s,

SATISFIES (*see* SATISFY)

Ps	103: 5	Who s your mouth with good

SATISFY (*see* SATISFIED, SATISFIES)

Ps	90:14	s us early with Your mercy,
Ps	91:16	With long life I will s him,
Ps	145:16	You open Your hand And s
Prov	5:19	Let her breasts s you at
Is	55: 2	wages for what does not s?

SATRAPS

Ezra	8:36	orders to the king's s and
Dan	3: 3	So the s, the administrators,

SAUL (*see* PAUL, SAUL'S)

1Sa	9: 3	And Kish said to his son S,
1Sa	9:17	And when Samuel saw S,
1Sa	10:11	Is S also among the
1Sa	11:15	and there they made S king
1Sa	14: 1	that Jonathan the son of S
1Sa	15:31	Samuel turned back after S,
1Sa	16:14	of the LORD departed from S,
1Sa	16:22	Then S sent to Jesse, saying,
1Sa	17:38	So S clothed David with his
1Sa	18: 7	S has slain his thousands,
1Sa	18: 9	So S eyed David from that day
1Sa	18:11	And S cast the spear, for he
1Sa	18:29	So S became David's enemy
1Sa	19:10	Then S sought to pin David to
1Sa	26: 7	and there S lay sleeping
1Sa	31:12	and took the body of S and
2Sa	1:17	this lamentation over S and
2Sa	1:23	S and Jonathan were beloved
2Sa	1:24	of Israel, weep over S,
2Sa	2: 8	Ishbosheth the son of S and
2Sa	9: 2	a servant of the house of S
Acts	7:58	feet of a young man named S.
Acts	8: 1	Now S was consenting to his
Acts	9: 4	a voice saying to him, "S,
Acts	11:30	the hands of Barnabas and S.
Acts	13:21	so God gave them S the son

SAUL'S (*see* SAUL)

1Sa	18:10	but there was a spear in S
1Sa	18:20	S daughter, loved David.
1Sa	24: 4	cut off a corner of S robe.

SAVE (*see* SALVATION, SAVED, SAVES, SAVING)

Gen	50:20	to s many people alive.
Ex	1:22	every daughter you shall s
1Sa	17:47	that the LORD does not s
2Sa	22:42	but there was none to s;
Job	40:14	your own right hand can s
Ps	3: 7	S me, O my God! For You
Ps	6: 4	s me for Your mercies' sake!
Ps	22:21	S Me from the lion's mouth
Ps	37:40	And s them, Because they
Ps	44: 3	Nor did their own arm s
Ps	57: 3	send from heaven and s me;
Ps	59: 2	And s me from bloodthirsty
Ps	69: 1	S me, O God! For the waters
Ps	72:13	And will s the souls of the
Ps	86:16	And s the son of Your
Ps	138: 7	And Your right hand will s
Is	45:20	pray to a god that cannot s.
Is	49:25	And I will s your children.
Is	59: 1	shortened, That it cannot s;
Is	63: 1	righteousness, mighty to s.
Jer	15:20	For I am with you to s you
Jer	17:14	S me, and I shall be saved,
Jer	46:27	I will s you from afar, And
Ezek	3:18	to s his life, that same
Ezek	13:22	from his wicked way to s
Ezek	34:22	therefore I will s My flock,
Hos	1: 7	Will s them by the LORD
Zeph	3:19	I will s the lame, And
Matt	1:21	for He will s His people
Matt	8:25	s us! We are perishing!"
Matt	16:25	For whoever desires to s his
Matt	18:11	the Son of Man has come to s
Matt	27:40	s Yourself! If You are the
Matt	27:42	others; Himself He cannot s.
Matt	27:49	see if Elijah will come to s
Mark	3: 4	to s life or to kill?" But
Mark	8:35	and the gospel's will s it.
Mark	15:30	s Yourself, and come down

Luke 23:37 of the Jews, s Yourself."
John 12:27 s Me from this hour'? But
John 12:47 to judge the world but to s
1Co 1:21 of the message preached to s
1Co 7:16 whether you will s your
1Co 9:22 that I might by all means s
1Ti 1:15 came into the world to s
1Ti 4:16 for in doing this you will s
Heb 5: 7 to Him who was able to s
Heb 7:25 He is also able to s to the
Jas 1:21 which is able to s your
Jas 2:14 Can faith s him?
Jas 5:15 the prayer of faith will s
Jas 5:20 the error of his way will s

SAVED (see SAVE)
Ex 1:17 but s the male children
Ex 14:30 So the LORD s Israel that
Ps 18: 3 So shall I be s from my
Ps 34: 6 And s him out of all his
Ps 80: 3 And we shall be s!
Ps 116: 6 brought low, and He s me.
Is 30:15 and rest you shall be s;
Is 45:22 "Look to Me, and be s,
Is 63: 9 the Angel of His Presence s
Jer 8:20 And we are not s!"
Jer 17:14 Save me, and I shall be s,
Joel 2:32 of the LORD Shall be s.
Matt 10:22 endures to the end will be s
Matt 19:25 saying, "Who then can be s?
Matt 24:22 no flesh would be s;
Matt 27:42 He s others; Himself He
Mark 16:16 and is baptized will be s;
Luke 7:50 Your faith has s you. Go in
John 3:17 world through Him might be s.
John 10: 9 enters by Me, he will be s,
Acts 2:21 the LORD Shall be s.
Acts 2:47 daily those who were being s.
Acts 4:12 men by which we must be s.
Acts 16:30 what must I do to be s?
Acts 16:31 Christ, and you will be s,
Acts 27:31 in the ship, you cannot be s.
Rom 5: 9 we shall be s from wrath
Rom 5:10 we shall be s by His life.
Rom 10: 1 Israel is that they may be s.
Rom 10: 9 from the dead, you will be s.
Rom 10:13 the LORD shall be s.
Rom 11:26 And so all Israel will be s,
1Co 1:18 but to us who are being s it
1Co 3:15 but he himself will be s,
1Co 5: 5 that his spirit may be s in
1Co 15: 2 by which also you are s,
2Co 2:15 among those who are being s
Eph 2: 5 (by grace you have been s),
Eph 2: 8 For by grace you have been s
1Th 2:16 Gentiles that they may be s,
1Ti 2: 4 who desires all men to be s
1Ti 2:15 Nevertheless she will be s in
2Ti 1: 9 who has s us and called us
Tit 3: 5 according to His mercy He s
1Pe 3:20 were s through water.
1Pe 4:18 one is scarcely s,
Rev 21:24 nations of those who are s

SAVES (see SAVE)
Ps 7:10 Who s the upright in heart.
Ps 34:18 And s such as have a

SAVING (see SAVE)
Ps 28: 8 And He is the s refuge of
Heb 10:39 those who believe to the s
Heb 11: 7 prepared an ark for the s of

SAVIOR
Ps 106:21 They forgot God their S,
Is 19:20 and He will send them a S
Is 43: 3 Holy One of Israel, your S;

Is 43:11 besides Me there is no s.
Is 45:21 Me, A just God and a S;
Hos 13: 4 For there is no S besides
Luke 1:47 has rejoiced in God my S.
Luke 2:11 day in the city of David a S,
John 4:42 the S of the world."
Acts 5:31 hand to be Prince and S,
Eph 5:23 and He is the S of the body.
Phil 3:20 also eagerly wait for the S,
1Ti 1: 1 the commandment of God our S
1Ti 4:10 who is the S of all men,
Tit 2:13 of our great God and S
2Pe 1: 1 of our God and S Jesus
2Pe 1:11 kingdom of our Lord and S
1Jn 4:14 has sent the Son as S of

SAVORY
Gen 27: 4 And make me s food, such as I

SCABBARD†
Jer 47: 6 Put yourself up into your s,

SCALES
Lev 11:10 that do not have fins and s,
Is 40:12 Weighed the mountains in a
Acts 9:18 his eyes something like s,
Rev 6: 5 sat on it had a pair of s

SCAPEGOAT
Lev 16:10 and to let it go as the s

SCARCELY
Rom 5: 7 For s for a righteous man
1Pe 4:18 the righteous one is s

SCARLET
Gen 38:28 and the midwife took a s
Josh 2:18 you bind this line of s cord
Prov 31:21 household is clothed with s.
Is 1:18 your sins are like s,
Matt 27:28 stripped Him and put a s
Heb 9:19 s wool, and hyssop, and
Rev 17: 3 I saw a woman sitting on a s
Rev 17: 4 was arrayed in purple and s,

SCATTER (see SCATTERED, SCATTERS)
Jer 49:32 I will s to all winds those
Mark 4:26 God is as if a man should s

SCATTERED (see SCATTER)
Gen 11: 4 lest we be s abroad over the
Gen 11: 8 So the LORD s them abroad
1Ki 22:17 I saw all Israel s on the
Ps 18:14 sent out His arrows and s
Ps 44:11 And have s us among the
Ps 92: 9 of iniquity shall be s.
Jer 23: 2 You have s My flock, driven
Jer 30:11 all nations where I have s
Ezek 34: 6 My flock was s over the
Ezek 34:12 on the day he is among his s
Zech 13: 7 And the sheep will be s;
Matt 25:24 where you have not s seed.
Mark 14:27 the sheep will be s.
Luke 1:51 He has s the proud in the
Acts 8: 4 Therefore those who were s
Jas 1: 1 twelve tribes which are s

SCATTERS (see SCATTER)
Matt 12:30 does not gather with Me s
John 10:12 wolf catches the sheep and s

SCENT (see SCENTED)
Song 4:10 And the s of your perfumes

SCENTED (see SCENT)
Ps 45: 8 All Your garments are s with

SCEPTER
Gen 49:10 The s shall not depart from
Num 24:17 A S shall rise out of
Ps 45: 6 A s of righteousness is

SCHEME   485   SEA

Ps   45: 6 of righteousness is the **s**
Ps   125: 3 For the **s** of wickedness
Heb   1: 8 A **s** of righteousness

SCHEME (*see* SCHEMES)
Ps   31:13 They **s** to take away my

SCHEMES (*see* SCHEME)
Ps   37: 7 the man who brings wicked **s**
Jer   11:19 know that they had devised **s**

SCOFFER (*see* SCOFFERS)
Prov   9: 8 Do not correct a **s**,

SCOFFERS (*see* SCOFFER)
2Pe   3: 3 that **s** will come in the last

SCORN (*see* SCORNFUL, SCORNS)
2Ki   19:21 you, laughed you to **s**;
Job   16:20 My friends **s** me; My eyes
Job   34: 7 Who drinks **s** like water,

SCORNFUL (*see* SCORN)
Ps   1: 1 sits in the seat of the **s**;

SCORNS (*see* SCORN)
Prov   30:17 And **s** obedience to his

SCORPION† (*see* SCORPIONS)
Luke   11:12 egg, will he offer him a **s**?
Rev   9: 5 was like the torment of a **s**

SCORPIONS (*see* SCORPION)
Luke   10:19 to trample on serpents and **s**,

SCOUNDREL (*see* SCOUNDRELS)
1Sa   25:25 not my lord regard this **s**

SCOUNDRELS (*see* SCOUNDREL)
1Ki   21:13 and the **s** witnessed against

SCOURGE (*see* SCOURGED, SCOURGES, SCOURGINGS)
Is   28:15 When the overflowing **s**
Matt   10:17 you up to councils and **s**
Matt   23:34 some of them you will **s** in
Mark   10:34 and **s** Him, and spit on Him,

SCOURGED (*see* SCOURGE)
John   19: 1 then Pilate took Jesus and **s**

SCOURGES (*see* SCOURGE)
1Ki   12:11 I will chastise you with **s**!
Heb   12: 6 And **s** every son whom

SCOURGINGS† (*see* SCOURGE)
Heb   11:36 had trial of mockings and **s**,

SCRAPE
Job   2: 8 a potsherd with which to **s**

SCRATCHED†
1Sa   21:13 **s** on the doors of the gate,

SCREEN
Ex   26:36 You shall make a **s** for the

SCRIBE (*see* SCRIBE'S, SCRIBES)
2Ki   18:18 the household, Shebna the **s**,
2Ki   22: 3 the king sent Shaphan the **s**,
Ezra   7: 6 and he was a skilled **s** in
Ezra   7:11 gave Ezra the priest, the **s**,
Ezra   7:12 a **s** of the Law of the God of
Is   33:18 terror: "Where is the **s**?
Jer   8: 8 the false pen of the **s**
Jer   36:32 and gave it to Baruch the **s**,
Matt   8:19 Then a certain **s** came and
1Co   1:20 the wise? Where is the **s**?

SCRIBE'S (*see* SCRIBE)
Jer   36:23 the king cut it with the **s**

SCRIBES (*see* SCRIBE)
2Ch   34:13 some of the Levites were **s**,
Matt   2: 4 all the chief priests and **s**
Matt   5:20 righteousness of the **s** and
Matt   7:29 authority, and not as the **s**.

Matt   15: 1 Then the **s** and Pharisees who
Matt   23: 2 The **s** and the Pharisees sit
Matt   23:14 **s** and Pharisees, hypocrites!
Mark   9:11 Why do the **s** say that Elijah

SCRIPT
Ezra   4: 7 was written in Aramaic **s**,
Esth   8: 9 to the Jews in their own **s**

SCRIPTURE (*see* SCRIPTURES)
Dan   10:21 you what is noted in the **S**
Mark   12:10 you not even read this **S**:
Mark   15:28 So the **S** was fulfilled which
Luke   4:21 Today this **S** is fulfilled in
John   2:22 and they believed the **S** and
John   7:38 as the **S** has said, out of
John   10:35 word of God came (and the **S**
Acts   8:32 The place in the **S** which he
Acts   8:35 and beginning at this **S**,
Rom   4: 3 For what does the **S** say?
2Ti   3:16 All **S** is given by
Jas   2: 8 royal law according to the **S**,
Jas   4: 5 Or do you think that the **S**
1Pe   2: 6 is also contained in the **S**,
2Pe   1:20 that no prophecy of **S** is of

SCRIPTURES (*see* SCRIPTURE)
Matt   21:42 you never read in the **S**:
Matt   22:29 not knowing the **S** nor the
Matt   26:54 How then could the **S** be
Luke   24:27 to them in all the **S** the
Luke   24:32 and while He opened the **S** to
Luke   24:45 they might comprehend the **S**.
John   5:39 "You search the **S**,
Acts   17: 2 with them from the **S**,
Acts   17:11 and searched the **S** daily to
Acts   18:24 man and mighty in the **S**,
Acts   18:28 showing from the **S** that
Rom   1: 2 His prophets in the Holy **S**,
Rom   16:26 and by the prophetic **S** has
1Co   15: 3 our sins according to the **S**,
1Co   15: 4 third day according to the **S**,
2Ti   3:15 you have known the Holy **S**,
2Pe   3:16 do also the rest of the **S**.

SCROLL
Ezra   6: 2 a **s** was found, and in it a
Ps   40: 7 In the **s** of the book it
Is   34: 4 shall be rolled up like a **s**;
Jer   36: 2 Take a **s** of a book and write
Jer   36: 4 and Baruch wrote on a **s** of a
Jer   36:27 the king had burned the **s**
Ezek   3: 1 what you find; eat this **s**,
Zech   5: 1 and saw there a flying **s**.
Rev   5: 2 is worthy to open the **s**
Rev   6:14 Then the sky receded as a **s**

SCYTHIAN
Col   3:11 uncircumcised, barbarian, **S**,

SEA (*see* SEAS, SEASHORE)
Gen   1:21 So God created great **s**
Gen   1:26 over the fish of the **s**,
Gen   1:28 over the fish of the **s**,
Gen   14: 3 Siddim (that is, the Salt **S**).
Gen   32:12 as the sand of the **s**,
Ex   10:19 and blew them into the Red **S**.
Ex   14:16 through the midst of the **s**.
Ex   14:21 and made the **s** into dry
Ex   15: 4 army He has cast into the **s**;
Ex   15: 4 are drowned in the Red **S**.
Ex   20:11 heavens and the earth, the **s**,
Num   11:31 it brought quail from the **s**
Num   34: 6 you shall have the Great **S**
Deut   3:17 as the east side of the **S**
Deut   11:24 even to the Western **S**,
1Ki   4:20 as the sand by the **s** in
1Ki   18:44 rising out of the **s**!" So he

1Ch 16:32 Let the **s** roar, and all its
Neh 9:11 And You divided the **s** before
Job 7:12 Am I a **s**, or a sea serpent,
Job 9: 8 treads on the waves of the **s**;
Job 26:12 He stirs up the **s** with His
Ps 8: 8 And the fish of the **s** That
Ps 33: 7 gathers the waters of the **s**
Ps 66: 6 He turned the **s** into dry
Ps 72: 8 have dominion also from **s**
Ps 74:13 You divided the **s** by Your
Ps 77:19 Your way was in the **s**,
Ps 95: 5 The **s** is His, for He made
Ps 96:11 Let the **s** roar, and all its
Ps 107:23 Those who go down to the **s**
Ps 114: 3 The **s** saw it and fled;
Ps 114: 5 What ails you, O **s**,
Ps 139: 9 the uttermost parts of the **s**,
Eccl 1: 7 the rivers run into the **s**,
Eccl 1: 7 Yet the **s** is not full;
Is 9: 1 her, By the way of the **s**,
Is 11: 9 As the waters cover the **s**.
Is 11:15 destroy the tongue of the **S**
Is 21: 1 the Wilderness of the **S**.
Is 42:10 You who go down to the **s**,
Is 43:16 who makes a way in the **s**,
Is 51:10 the One who dried up the **s**,
Is 57:20 are like the troubled **s**,
Dan 7: 3 beasts came up from the **s**,
Hos 1:10 be as the sand of the **s**,
Amos 8:12 They shall wander from **s** to
Jon 1: 4 a mighty tempest on the **s**,
Jon 1: 9 who made the **s** and the dry
Jon 1:12 up and throw me into the **s**;
Hab 2:14 As the waters cover the **s**.
Zech 9:10 from **s** to sea, And from the
Matt 4:13 Capernaum, which is by the **s**,
Matt 4:15 By the way of the **s**,
Matt 4:18 walking by the **S** of Galilee,
Matt 4:18 casting a net into the **s**;
Matt 8:24 great tempest arose on the **s**,
Matt 8:27 even the winds and the **s**
Matt 8:32 the steep place into the **s**,
Matt 14:26 saw Him walking on the **s**,
Matt 21:21 and be cast into the **s**,
Matt 23:15 For you travel land and **s**
Mark 4: 1 He began to teach by the **s**.
Mark 4: 1 and sat in it on the **s**;
John 6: 1 which is the **S** of
John 21: 7 it), and plunged into the **s**.
Acts 4:24 heaven and earth and the **s**,
Acts 10:32 of Simon, a tanner, by the **s**.
Rom 9:27 as the sand of the **s**,
1Co 10: 1 all passed through the **s**,
1Co 10: 2 in the cloud and in the **s**,
2Co 11:26 in perils in the **s**,
Heb 11:29 passed through the Red **S** as
Jas 1: 6 is like a wave of the **s**
Rev 4: 6 the throne there was a **s**
Rev 8: 8 and a third of the **s** became
Rev 10: 2 set his right foot on the **s**
Rev 13: 1 beast rising up out of the **s**,
Rev 20:13 The **s** gave up the dead who
Rev 21: 1 Also there was no more **s**.

SEAL (see SEALED, SEALING, SEALS)
Job 38:14 on form like clay under a **s**,
Song 8: 6 Set me as a **s** upon your
Is 8:16 **S** the law among my
Jer 32:44 sign deeds and **s** them, and
Dan 8:26 Therefore **s** up the vision,
Dan 12: 4 and **s** the book until the
John 6:27 the Father has set His **s** on
2Ti 2:19 of God stands, having this **s**:
Rev 6: 3 When He opened the second **s**,
Rev 10: 4 **S** up the things which the

Rev 22:10 Do not **s** the words of the

SEALED (see SEAL)
Esth 3:12 and **s** with the king's signet
Jer 32:10 I signed the deed and **s**
Dan 12: 9 words are closed up and **s**
2Co 1:22 who also has **s** us and given
Eph 1:13 you were **s** with the Holy
Eph 4:30 by whom you were **s** for the
Rev 5: 1 **s** with seven seals.
Rev 7: 5 twelve thousand were **s**;

SEALING† (see SEAL)
Matt 27:66 **s** the stone and setting the

SEALS (see SEAL)
Rev 6: 1 the Lamb opened one of the **s**;

SEAM
John 19:23 Now the tunic was without **s**,

SEANCE†
1Sa 28: 8 Please conduct a **s** for me,

SEARCH (see SEARCHED, SEARCHES, SEARCHING)
Deut 1:22 and let them **s** out the land
Ezra 4:19 and a **s** has been made, and
Job 3:21 And **s** for it more than
Job 11: 7 Can you **s** out the deep things
Ps 139:23 **S** me, O God, and know my
Prov 2: 4 And **s** for her as for
Eccl 1:13 I set my heart to seek and **s**
Jer 17:10 **s** the heart, I test the
Jer 29:13 when you **s** for Me with all
Ezek 34:11 Indeed I Myself will **s** for My
Matt 2: 8 Go and **s** carefully for the
John 5:39 You **s** the Scriptures, for in

SEARCHED (see SEARCH)
Gen 31:34 And Laban **s** all about the
Ps 139: 1 You have **s** me and known me.
Eccl 2: 3 I **s** in my heart how to
Acts 12:19 But when Herod had **s** for him
Acts 17:11 and **s** the Scriptures daily
1Pe 1:10 prophets have inquired and **s**

SEARCHES (see SEARCH)
1Ch 28: 9 for the LORD **s** all hearts
Rom 8:27 Now He who **s** the hearts knows
1Co 2:10 For the Spirit **s** all things,
Rev 2:23 know that I am He who **s** the

SEARCHING (see SEARCH, SEARCHINGS)
1Pe 1:11 **s** what, or what manner of

SEARCHINGS† (see SEARCHING)
Judg 5:16 of Reuben have great **s** of

SEARED†
Prov 6:28 And his feet not be **s**?
1Ti 4: 2 their own conscience **s** with

SEAS (see SEA)
Gen 1:10 of the waters He called **S**.
Gen 1:22 and fill the waters in the **s**,
Ps 8: 8 through the paths of the **s**.
Ps 24: 2 He has founded it upon the **s**,
Ps 69:34 The **s** and everything that
Ps 78:27 fowl like the sand of the **s**;
Ps 135: 6 In the **s** and in all deep
Jer 15: 8 more than the sand of the **s**;
Ezek 27: 4 are in the midst of the **s**.
Ezek 32: 2 are like a monster in the **s**,
Jon 2: 3 Into the heart of the **s**,

SEASHORE (see SEA)
Gen 22:17 the sand which is on the **s**;
Ex 14:30 the Egyptians dead on the **s**.
Judg 7:12 as the sand by the **s** in
1Sa 13: 5 the sand which is on the **s**
1Ki 4:29 heart like the sand on the **s**.
Heb 11:12 the sand which is by the **s**.

SEASON (*see* SEASONED, SEASONS)
Ex   13:10 keep this ordinance in its **s**
Lev   26: 4 will give you rain in its **s**,
Ps   1: 3 forth its fruit in its **s**,
Ps   22: 2 hear; And in the night **s**,
Ps   104:27 them their food in due **s**.
Prov   15:23 And a word spoken in due **s**,
Eccl   3: 1 everything there is a **s**,
Is   50: 4 how to speak A word in **s**
Dan   7:12 were prolonged for a **s** and
Matt   24:45 to give them food in due **s**?
Mark   9:50 how will you **s** it? Have salt
Mark   11:13 for it was not the **s** for
Gal   6: 9 for in due **s** we shall reap
2Ti   4: 2 the word! Be ready in **s**

SEASONED (*see* SEASON)
Matt   5:13 flavor, how shall it be **s**?
Mark   9:49 For everyone will be **s** with
Mark   9:49 every sacrifice will be **s**
Col   4: 6 **s** with salt, that you may

SEASONS (*see* SEASON)
Gen   1:14 let them be for signs and **s**,
Ps   16: 7 instructs me in the night **s**.
Dan   2:21 changes the times and the **s**;
Matt   21:41 to him the fruits in their **s**.
Acts   1: 7 for you to know times or **s**
Gal   4:10 days and months and **s** and
1Th   5: 1 the times and the **s**,

SEAT (*see* SEATED, SEATS)
Ex   25:22 you from above the mercy **s**,
Lev   16:15 sprinkle it on the mercy **s**
Job   23: 3 I might come to His **s**!
Ps   1: 1 Nor sits in the **s** of the
Ezek   28: 2 I sit in the **s** of gods,
Matt   23: 2 Pharisees sit in Moses' **s**.
Matt   27:19 sitting on the judgment **s**,
Acts   18:12 him to the judgment **s**,
Acts   25:10 stand at Caesar's judgment **s**,
Rom   14:10 stand before the judgment **s**
2Co   5:10 before the judgment **s** of
Heb   9: 5 overshadowing the mercy **s**.

SEATED (*see* SEAT)
Dan   7: 9 the Ancient of Days was **s**;
Dan   7:10 before Him. The court was **s**,
Eph   1:20 Him from the dead and **s**
Heb   8: 1 who is **s** at the right hand

SEATS (*see* SEAT)
Matt   21:12 money changers and the **s** of
Mark   12:39 the best **s** in the synagogues,

SECOND
Gen   22:15 LORD called to Abraham a **s**
2Ki   22:14 dwelt in Jerusalem in the **S**
Jon   3: 1 LORD came to Jonah the **s**
Zeph   1:10 A wailing from the **S**
John   3: 4 Can he enter a **s** time into
John   4:54 This again is the **s** sign
Acts   13:33 it is also written in the **s**
Heb   9: 3 and behind the **s** veil, the
Heb   9:28 for Him He will appear a **s**
Heb   10: 9 that He may establish the **s**.
Rev   2:11 shall not be hurt by the **s**
Rev   20:14 This is the **s** death.

SECRET (*see* SECRETLY, SECRETS)
Deut   29:29 The **s** things belong to the
Judg   16: 9 So the **s** of his strength was
Ps   18:11 He made darkness His **s**
Ps   19:12 Cleanse me from **s** faults.
Ps   27: 5 In the **s** place of His
Ps   90: 8 Our **s** sins in the light of
Ps   91: 1 He who dwells in the **s** place
Ps   139:15 You, When I was made in **s**,

Eccl   12:14 Including every **s** thing,
Dan   2:19 Then the **s** was revealed to
Amos   3: 7 Unless He reveals His **s** to
Matt   6: 4 your Father who sees in **s**
Luke   8:17 For nothing is **s** that will
Luke   11:33 puts it in a **s** place or
Rom   16:25 of the mystery kept **s** since
Eph   5:12 which are done by them in **s**.

SECRETLY (*see* SECRET)
Matt   1:19 was minded to put her away **s**.
Matt   2: 7 when he had **s** called the
John   11:28 she went her way and **s**

SECRETS (*see* SECRET)
Ps   44:21 For He knows the **s** of the
Dan   2:28 God in heaven who reveals **s**,
Rom   2:16 when God will judge the **s**
1Co   14:25 And thus the **s** of his heart

SECT
Acts   24: 5 and a ringleader of the **s** of
Acts   24:14 the Way which they call a **s**,

SECURE (*see* SECURELY)
Judg   18: 7 the Sidonians, quiet and **s**.
Prov   1:33 dwell safely, And will be **s**,
Matt   27:64 that the tomb be made **s**

SECURELY (*see* SECURE)
Judg   15:13 but we will tie you **s** and
Judg   16:11 If they bind me **s** with new
Prov   10: 9 walks with integrity walks **s**,
Acts   5:23 we found the prison shut **s**,
Acts   16:23 the jailer to keep them **s**.

SEDUCED (*see* SEDUCTRESS)
Num   25:18 schemes by which they **s** you
Prov   7:21 her flattering lips she **s**

SEDUCTRESS (*see* SEDUCED)
Prov   6:24 the flattering tongue of a **s**.
Prov   23:27 And a **s** is a narrow well.

SEED (*see* SEEDS, SEEDTIME)
Gen   1:11 the herb that yields **s**,
Gen   1:12 whose **s** is in itself
Gen   3:15 And between your **s** and her
Gen   21:12 for in Isaac your **s** shall be
Gen   22:18 In your **s** all the nations of
Ex   16:31 was like white coriander **s**,
Lev   26:16 And you shall sow your **s** in
Num   6: 4 from **s** to skin.
2Sa   7:12 I will set up your **s** after
1Ch   16:13 O **s** of Israel His servant,
Ezra   9: 2 so that the holy **s** is mixed
Ps   89:36 His **s** shall endure forever,
Ps   126: 6 Bearing **s** for sowing,
Is   6:13 So the holy **s** shall be
Is   53:10 sin, He shall see His **s**,
Is   55:10 That it may give **s** to the
Matt   13: 4 some **s** fell by the wayside;
Matt   13:24 like a man who sowed good **s**
Matt   13:31 heaven is like a mustard **s**,
Matt   17:20 have faith as a mustard **s**,
Luke   1:55 To Abraham and to his **s**
Luke   8:11 The **s** is the word of God.
John   7:42 the Christ comes from the **s**
Acts   3:25 And in your **s** all the
Acts   13:23 "From this man's **s**,
Rom   1: 3 who was born of the **s** of
Rom   9: 7 In Isaac your **s** shall be
Rom   9: 8 promise are counted as the **s**.
Rom   9:29 had left us a **s**,
Rom   11: 1 of the **s** of Abraham, of the
2Co   9:10 Now may He who supplies **s** to
Gal   3:16 of one, "And to your **S**,
Gal   3:29 then you are Abraham's **s**,
Heb   11:18 In Isaac your **s** shall be

1Pe	1:23	not of corruptible s but
1Jn	3: 9	for His s remains in him;

SEEDS (see SEED)

Matt	13:32	is the least of all the s;
Matt	13:38	the good s are the sons of
Gal	3:16	He does not say, "And to s,

SEEDTIME† (see SEED)

Gen	8:22	S and harvest, Cold and

SEEK (see SEEKING, SEEKS, SOUGHT)

Deut	4:29	But from there you will s the
Deut	4:29	you will find Him if you s
1Ki	19:10	and they s to take my
1Ch	16:11	S the LORD and His strength
2Ch	7:14	and pray and s My face, and
2Ch	15: 2	If you s Him, He will be
Ezra	7:10	had prepared his heart to s
Job	8: 5	If you would earnestly s God
Ps	9:10	not forsaken those who s
Ps	14: 2	understand, who s God.
Ps	22:26	Those who s Him will praise
Ps	24: 6	generation of those who s
Ps	27: 4	of the LORD, That will I s:
Ps	34:14	S peace and pursue it.
Ps	53: 2	understand, who s God.
Ps	63: 1	Early will I s You; My
Ps	71:13	and dishonor Who s my hurt.
Ps	104:21	And s their food from God.
Ps	105: 4	S the LORD and His strength
Ps	105: 4	S His face evermore!
Prov	2: 4	If you s her as silver, And
Prov	28: 5	But those who s the LORD
Eccl	1:13	And I set my heart to s and
Eccl	7:25	To search and s out wisdom
Song	3: 2	and then in the squares I will s
Is	1:17	S justice, Rebuke the
Is	8:19	Should they s the dead on
Is	11:10	For the Gentiles shall s
Is	41:12	You shall s them and not
Is	55: 6	S the LORD while He may be
Jer	29: 7	And s the peace of the city
Jer	29:13	And you will s Me and find
Jer	45: 5	And do you s great things for
Ezek	34:11	search for My sheep and s
Ezek	34:16	I will s what was lost and
Hos	2: 7	she will s them, but not
Hos	3: 5	of Israel shall return and s
Hos	10:12	For it is time to s the
Amos	5: 4	S Me and live;
Amos	5: 6	S the LORD and live, Lest
Amos	5:14	S good and not evil, That
Mal	3: 1	And the Lord, whom you s,
Matt	2:13	for Herod will s the young
Matt	6:32	these things the Gentiles s.
Matt	6:33	But s first the kingdom of
Matt	7: 7	it will be given to you; s
Matt	28: 5	for I know that you s Jesus
Mark	8:12	Why does this generation s a
Mark	16: 6	You s Jesus of Nazareth, who
Luke	12:29	And do not s what you should
Luke	12:30	the nations of the world s
Luke	13:24	will s to enter and will not
Luke	19:10	the Son of Man has come to s
Luke	24: 5	Why do you s the living among
John	1:38	to them, "What do you s?
John	4:27	no one said, "What do You s?
John	5:30	because I do not s My own
John	7:34	You will s Me and not find
John	8:50	And I do not s My own glory;
Acts	6: 3	s out from among you seven
Acts	10:21	"Yes, I am he whom you s.
Acts	15:17	rest of mankind may s
Acts	17:27	so that they should s the
Rom	10:20	by those who did not s

Rom	11: 3	and they s my life"?
1Co	1:22	and Greeks s after wisdom;
1Co	7:27	Do not s a wife.
1Co	13: 5	does not s its own, is not
Gal	1:10	Or do I s to please men? For
Phil	2:21	For all s their own, not the
Phil	4:17	Not that I s the gift, but I
1Th	2: 6	Nor did we s glory from men,
Heb	11: 6	of those who diligently s
Heb	11:14	declare plainly that they s
Heb	13:14	but we s the one to come.
1Pe	3:11	Let him s peace and

SEEKING (see SEEK)

Gen	37:16	I am s my brothers. Please
Dan	8:15	seen the vision and was s
Matt	12:43	s rest, and finds none.
Matt	12:46	s to speak with Him.
Mark	8:11	s from Him a sign from
Luke	11:54	and s to catch Him in
Luke	13: 7	three years I have come s
John	4:23	for the Father is s such to
John	18: 4	to them, "Whom are you s?
John	20:15	you weeping? Whom are you s?
Rom	10: 3	and s to establish their own
1Pe	5: 8	s whom he may devour.

SEEKS (see SEEK)

1Sa	19: 2	My father Saul s to kill you.
1Sa	22:23	For he who s my life seeks
Prov	15:14	him who has understanding s
Prov	18:15	And the ear of the wise s
Prov	31:13	She s wool and flax, And
Ezek	34:12	As a shepherd s out his flock
Matt	7: 8	and he who s finds, and to
Matt	12:39	and adulterous generation s
Rom	3:11	There is none who s
Rom	11: 7	has not obtained what it s;

SEEN

Gen	8: 5	tops of the mountains were s.
Gen	31:42	God has s my affliction and
Gen	32:30	For I have s God face to
Ex	19: 4	You have s what I did to the
Ex	33:23	but My face shall not be s.
Deut	4: 9	the things your eyes have s,
Judg	2: 7	who had s all the great
Judg	6:22	O Lord GOD! For I have s
Judg	13:22	because we have s God!"
Ezra	3:12	old men who had s the first
Job	4: 8	Even as I have s,
Ps	37:25	Yet I have not s the
Ps	98: 3	the ends of the earth have s
Prov	25: 7	Whom your eyes have s.
Eccl	1:14	I have s all the works that
Eccl	5:13	severe evil which I have s
Eccl	6: 1	is an evil which I have s
Song	3: 3	Have you s the one I love?"
Is	6: 5	For my eyes have s the
Is	9: 2	walked in darkness Have s
Is	64: 4	Nor has the eye s any God
Jer	1:12	You have s well, for I am
Lam	1: 8	her Because they have s
Lam	3: 1	I am the man who has s
Ezek	10:22	as the faces which I had s
Dan	8:15	had s the vision and was
Zech	9: 8	For now I have s with My
Matt	2: 2	For we have s His star in
Matt	6: 1	to be s by them. Otherwise
Mark	16:11	He was alive and had been s
Mark	16:14	not believe those who had s
Luke	1:22	perceived that he had s a
Luke	2:17	Now when they had s Him,
Luke	2:20	that they had heard and s,
Luke	2:26	see death before he had s
Luke	2:30	For my eyes have s Your

Luke 7:22 John the things you have **s**
Luke 24:37 and supposed they had **s** a
John   1:18 No one has **s** God at any time.
John   1:34 And I have **s** and testified
John   3:11 and testify what We have **s**,
John   3:21 his deeds may be clearly **s**,
John   3:32 And what He has **s** and heard,
John   5:37 nor **s** His form.
John   6:46 Not that anyone has **s** the
John   8:57 and have You **s** Abraham?"
John   9:37 You have both **s** Him and it is
John 14: 7 on you know Him and have **s**
John 14: 9 He who has **s** Me has seen the
John 19:35 And he who has **s** has
John 20:18 the disciples that she had **s**
John 20:25 We have **s** the Lord." So he
John 20:29 because you have **s** Me, you
John 20:29 are those who have not **s**
Acts   1: 3 being **s** by them during forty
Acts   7:44 to the pattern that he had **s**,
Acts   9:27 to them how he had **s** the
Acts 13:31 He was **s** for many days by
Rom   1:20 attributes are clearly **s**,
Rom   8:24 but hope that is **s** is not
1Co   2: 9 "Eye has not **s**,
1Co   9: 1 Have I not **s** Jesus Christ
1Co 15: 5 and that He was **s** by Cephas,
1Co 15: 8 Then last of all He was **s** by
2Co   4:18 at the things which are **s**,
2Co   4:18 For the things which are **s**
1Ti   3:16 **S** by angels, Preached
1Ti   6:16 whom no man has **s** or can
Heb 11: 1 the evidence of things not **s**.
Heb 11: 3 that the things which are **s**
Heb 11: 7 warned of things not yet **s**,
Heb 11:13 but having **s** them afar off
1Pe   1: 8 whom having not **s** you love.
1Jn   1: 1 which we have **s** with our
1Jn   1: 3 that which we have **s** and
1Jn   3: 6 Whoever sins has neither **s**
1Jn   4:12 No one has **s** God at any
1Jn   4:14 And we have **s** and testify
1Jn   4:20 his brother whom he has **s**,
1Jn   4:20 love God whom he has not **s**?
Rev   1:19 the things which you have **s**,

SEER
1Sa   9: 9 was formerly called a **s**.
2Sa 24:11 the prophet Gad, David's **s**,
1Ch   9:22 David and Samuel the **s** had
Amos 7:12 you **s**! Flee to the land of

SEIR
Gen 36: 8 So Esau dwelt in Mount **S**.
2Ch 25:14 the gods of the people of **S**,

SEIZE (*see* SEIZED, SEIZES)
Job   3: 6 may darkness **s** it; May it
Ps   55:15 Let death **s** them; Let them
Ps 109:11 Let the creditor **s** all that
Matt 21:38 let us kill him and **s** his
Matt 26:55 and you did not **s** Me.
Luke 20:20 that they might **s** on His
Acts 12: 3 he proceeded further to **s**

SEIZED (*see* SEIZE)
Luke   8:29 For it had often **s** him, and
Acts 16:19 they **s** Paul and Silas and

SEIZES (*see* SEIZE)
Deut 22:28 and he **s** her and lies with
Luke   9:39 a spirit **s** him, and he

SELECT
Num 14: 4 Let us **s** a leader and return

SELF-CONTROL
Acts 24:25 about righteousness, **s**,

1Co   7: 5 because of your lack of **s**.
Gal   5:23 gentleness, **s**. Against such
2Pe   1: 6 to knowledge **s**,

SELF-SEEKING
Rom   2: 8 but to those who are **s** and do

SELFISH
Gal   5:20 **s** ambitions, dissensions,
Phil   1:16 former preach Christ from **s**

SELL (*see* SELLS, SOLD)
Gen 25:31 **S** me your birthright as of
Gen 37:27 Come and let us **s** him to the
2Ki   4: 7 **s** the oil and pay your debt;
Amos 2: 6 Because they **s** the
Amos 8: 5 That we may **s** grain? And
Amos 8: 6 Even **s** the bad wheat?"
Matt 19:21 **s** what you have and give to
Jas   4:13 a year there, buy and **s**,
Rev 13:17 and that no one may buy or **s**

SELLS (*see* SELL)
Ex   21: 7 And if a man **s** his daughter
Prov 31:24 makes linen garments and **s**

SEND (*see* SENDING, SENDS, SENT)
Gen 24: 7 He will **s** His angel before
Gen 38:17 I will **s** a young goat from
Ex   3:10 and I will **s** you to Pharaoh
Ex   8:21 I will **s** swarms of flies
Ex   23:20 I **s** an Angel before you to
Neh   2: 5 I ask that you **s** me to
Neh   2: 6 So it pleased the king to **s**
Neh   8:10 and **s** portions to those for
Ps   20: 2 May He **s** you help from the
Ps   43: 3 **s** out Your light and Your
Ps   57: 3 He shall **s** from heaven and
Ps 104:30 You **s** forth Your Spirit,
Is   6: 8 saying: "Whom shall I **s**,
Is   6: 8 Here am I! **S** me."
Is   42:19 as My messenger whom I **s**?
Jer   1: 7 shall go to all to whom I **s**
Jer 14:15 in My name, whom I did not **s**,
Ezek 7: 3 And I will **s** My anger
Ezek 39: 6 And I will **s** fire on Magog
Amos 1: 7 But I will **s** a fire upon the
Mal   3: 1 I **s** My messenger, And he
Mal   4: 5 I will **s** you Elijah the
Matt 9:38 the Lord of the harvest to **s**
Matt 10:16 I **s** you out as sheep in the
Matt 11:10 I **s** My messenger before
Matt 14:15 **S** the multitudes away, that
Matt 24:31 And He will **s** His angels with
Mark 5:12 **S** us to the swine, that we
Mark 6: 7 and began to **s** them out two
Luke 12:49 I came to **s** fire on the
Luke 24:49 I **s** the Promise of My Father
John   3:17 For God did not **s** His Son
John 16: 7 I will **s** Him to you.
John 20:21 I also **s** you."
Acts 11:29 determined to **s** relief to
1Co   1:17 For Christ did not **s** me to
Phil   2:19 trust in the Lord Jesus to **s**
2Th   2:11 for this reason God will **s**
Rev   1:11 write in a book and **s** it to

SENDING (*see* SEND)
Rom   8: 3 God did by **s** His own Son in
Phm   1:12 I am **s** him back. You

SENDS (*see* SEND)
Ps   68:33 He **s** out His voice, a mighty
Ps 147:15 He **s** out His command to
Ps 147:18 He **s** out His word and melts
Matt 5:45 and **s** rain on the just and
Matt 12:20 Till He **s** forth

SENIR (*see* HERMON)
Deut   3: 9 and the Amorites call it S),

SENNACHERIB
2Ki 18:13 S king of Assyria came up
2Ch 32: 2 And when Hezekiah saw that S

SENSE†
Neh   8: 8 of God; and they gave the s,
Hos   7:11 like a silly dove, without s—
Heb 11:19 him in a figurative s.

SENSUAL
Jas   3:15 above, but is earthly, s,

SENT (*see* SEND)
Gen   8: 7 Then he s out a raven, which
Gen   8:10 and again he s the dove out
Gen 19:29 and s Lot out of the midst
Ex   3:12 a sign to you that I have s
Ex   3:14 I AM has s me to you.'"
Num 16:28 know that the LORD has s
Num 21: 6 So the LORD s fiery serpents
Num 24:12 your messengers whom you s
Deut   9:23 when the LORD s you from
Judg 11:38 And he s her away for two
1Sa 15: 1 The LORD s me to anoint you
2Sa 11: 6 And Joab s Uriah to David.
2Sa 11:14 a letter to Joab and s it
2Sa 12: 1 Then the LORD s Nathan to
2Sa 24:15 So the LORD s a plague upon
2Ki 17:25 therefore the LORD s lions
Ezra   4:18 The letter which you s to us
Job 22: 9 You have s widows away
Ps   18:14 He s out His arrows and
Ps   18:16 He s from above, He took me;
Ps 107:20 He s His word and healed
Prov   9: 3 She has s out her maidens,
Is   48:16 GOD and His Spirit Have s
Is   55:11 the thing for which I s
Is   61: 1 He has s Me to heal the
Jer 26:12 The LORD s me to prophesy
Jer 28: 9 whom the LORD has truly s.
Jer 28:15 the LORD has not s you, but
Ezek 39:28 who s them into captivity
Dan   3:28 who s His Angel and
Dan   6:22 My God s His angel and shut
Jon   1: 4 But the LORD s out a great
Zech   2:11 the LORD of hosts has s Me
Matt   2: 8 And he s them to Bethlehem
Matt 10: 5 These twelve Jesus s out and
Matt 10:40 Me receives Him who s Me.
Matt 13:36 Then Jesus s the multitude
Matt 15:24 I was not s except to the
Mark   9:37 not Me but Him who s Me.
Luke   1:26 the angel Gabriel was s by
Luke   1:53 And the rich He has s away
Luke   4:18 He has s Me to heal
Luke 10: 1 and s them two by two before
Luke 10:16 Me rejects Him who s Me.
Luke 23:11 and s Him back to Pilate.
John   1: 6 There was a man s from God,
John   1: 8 but was s to bear witness
John   4:34 to do the will of Him who s
John   4:38 I s you to reap that for
John   5:24 and believes in Him who s
John   5:37 who s Me, has testified of
John   6:39 will of the Father who s Me,
John   8:16 I am with the Father who s
John   9: 4 work the works of Him who s
John   9: 7 (which is translated, S).
John 13:16 sent greater than he who s
John 13:20 Me receives Him who s Me.
John 17: 3 Jesus Christ whom You have s.
John 20:21 to you! As the Father has s
Rom 10:15 preach unless they are s?
Gal   4: 4 God s forth His Son, born of

Heb   1:14 all ministering spirits s
1Pe   1:12 to you by the Holy Spirit s
1Jn   4: 9 that God has s His only
1Jn   4:10 but that He loved us and s
1Jn   4:14 that the Father has s the
Rev   1: 1 And He s and signified it

SENTENCE
Luke 23:24 So Pilate gave s that it
2Co   1: 9 we had the s of death in

SEPARATE (*see* SEPARATED, SEPARATES, SEPARATION)
Matt 19: 6 together, let not man s.
Acts 13: 2 Now s to Me Barnabas and Saul
Rom   8:35 Who shall s us from the love
Rom   8:39 shall be able to s us from
2Co   6:17 among them And be s,
Heb   7:26 s from sinners, and has

SEPARATED (*see* SEPARATE)
Is   59: 2 But your iniquities have s
Rom   1: 1 s to the gospel of God
Gal   1:15 who s me from my mother's

SEPARATES (*see* SEPARATE)
Num   6: 6 All the days that he s

SEPARATION (*see* SEPARATE)
Num   6: 5 days of the vow of his s no

SEPHARAD†
Obad   20 of Jerusalem who are in S

SERAPHIM†
Is   6: 2 Above it stood s;
Is   6: 6 Then one of the s flew to

SERIOUS
Neh   5: 7 After s thought, I rebuked
1Pe   4: 7 therefore be s and watchful

SERPENT (*see* SERPENT'S, SERPENTS)
Gen   3: 1 Now the s was more cunning
Gen   3: 4 Then the s said to the woman,
Gen   3:13 The s deceived me, and I
Ex   7:15 rod which was turned to a s
Num 21: 8 to Moses, "Make a fiery s,
Num 21: 9 So Moses made a bronze s,
2Ki 18: 4 in pieces the bronze s that
Job 26:13 hand pierced the fleeing s.
Prov 23:32 the last it bites like a s,
Prov 30:19 The way of a s on a rock,
Is   27: 1 Leviathan the fleeing s,
Amos   5:19 And a s bit him!
Mic   7:17 shall lick the dust like a s;
Matt   7:10 a fish, will he give him a s?
John   3:14 as Moses lifted up the s in
2Co 11: 3 as the s deceived Eve by his
Rev 12: 9 that s of old, called the
Rev 20: 2 that s of old, who is the

SERPENT'S (*see* SERPENT)
Is   65:25 And dust shall be the s

SERPENTS (*see* SERPENT)
Ex   7:12 his rod, and they became s.
Num 21: 6 So the LORD sent fiery s
Jer   8:17 I will send s among you,
Matt 10:16 Therefore be wise as s and
Matt 23:33 "S, brood of vipers!
Mark 16:18 "they will take up s;
Luke 10:19 authority to trample on s

SERVANT (*see* MAIDSERVANT, SERVANT'S, SERVANTS, SERVE)
Gen   9:25 A s of servants He shall
Gen   9:26 And may Canaan be his s.
Gen 18: 3 do not pass on by Your s.
Gen 24:34 he said, "I am Abraham's s.
Gen 26:24 your descendants for My s
Gen 39:17 The Hebrew s whom you brought

Ex	4:10	You have spoken to Your s;
Ex	14:31	the LORD and His s Moses.
Ex	21: 2	"If you buy a Hebrew s,
Lev	22:10	the priest, or a hired s,
Num	12: 7	Not so with My s Moses; He
Deut	15:18	been worth a double hired s
Deut	34: 5	So Moses the s of the LORD
Josh	1: 2	Moses My s is dead. Now
1Sa	3: 9	for Your s hears.'" So
1Sa	17:58	I am the son of your s
2Sa	3:18	By the hand of My s David, I
2Sa	7:26	And let the house of Your s
2Sa	7:29	let the house of Your s be
2Sa	11:21	Your s Uriah the Hittite is
1Ki	3: 6	shown great mercy to Your s
1Ki	8:28	regard the prayer of Your s
2Ki	5: 6	I have sent Naaman my s to
2Ki	5:15	take a gift from your s.
2Ki	9:36	which He spoke by His s
2Ki	14:25	He had spoken through His s
Neh	1:11	and let Your s prosper this
Job	1: 8	Have you considered My s Job,
Job	2: 3	Have you considered My s Job,
Job	42: 8	and My s Job shall pray for
Ps	19:11	Moreover by them Your s is
Ps	19:13	Keep back Your s also from
Ps	27: 9	Do not turn Your s away in
Ps	31:16	Your face shine upon Your s;
Ps	69:17	hide Your face from Your s,
Ps	86:16	Your strength to Your s,
Ps	89: 3	I have sworn to My s David:
Ps	116:16	O LORD, truly I am Your s;
Ps	119:17	bountifully with Your s,
Ps	119:135	Your face shine upon Your s,
Ps	136:22	A heritage to Israel His s,
Prov	11:29	And the fool will be s to
Prov	17: 2	A wise s will rule over a
Prov	22: 7	And the borrower is s to
Is	20: 3	Just as My s Isaiah has
Is	37:35	My own sake and for My s
Is	41: 8	you, Israel, are My s,
Is	41: 9	said to you, 'You are My s,
Is	42: 1	Behold! My S whom I uphold,
Is	42:19	Who is blind but My s,
Is	43:10	And My s whom I have chosen,
Is	44:21	formed you, you are My s;
Is	49: 3	said to me, 'You are My s,
Is	50:10	obeys the voice of His S?
Is	52:13	My S shall deal prudently;
Is	53:11	His knowledge My righteous S
Jer	25: 9	the king of Babylon, My s,
Ezek	34:23	My s David. He shall feed
Ezek	37:24	David My s shall be king
Dan	6:20	s of the living God, has
Dan	9:17	hear the prayer of Your s,
Hag	2:23	take you, Zerubbabel My s,
Zech	3: 8	I am bringing forth My S the
Matt	8: 6	my s is lying at home
Matt	8: 8	and my s will be healed.
Matt	10:24	nor a s above his master.
Matt	12:18	Behold! My S whom I
Matt	24:45	is a faithful and wise s,
Matt	25:21	done, good and faithful s;
Matt	25:30	'And cast the unprofitable s
Matt	26:51	struck the s of the high
Matt	26:69	And a s girl came to him,
Mark	9:35	shall be last of all and s
Luke	1:54	He has helped His s Israel,
Luke	2:29	now You are letting Your s
Luke	7: 2	And a certain centurion's s,
Luke	12:43	Blessed is that s whom his
Luke	16:13	No s can serve two masters;
John	12:26	there My s will be also. If
John	13:16	a s is not greater than his
Acts	3:13	glorified His S Jesus, whom
Acts	3:26	having raised up His S
Acts	4:30	the name of Your holy S
Rom	14: 4	are you to judge another's s?
Rom	15: 8	Jesus Christ has become a s
1Co	9:19	I have made myself a s to
Col	4: 7	and fellow s in the Lord,
Heb	3: 5	in all His house as a s,
Rev	1: 1	it by His angel to His s

SERVANT'S (*see* SERVANT)

2Sa	7:19	have also spoken of Your s
Is	45: 4	For Jacob My s sake, And
John	18:10	The s name was Malchus.

SERVANTS (*see* SERVANT, SERVANTS')

Gen	9:25	A servant of s He shall be
Gen	40:20	the chief baker among his s.
Gen	42:13	Your s are twelve brothers,
Deut	9:27	'Remember Your s,
Deut	32:36	have compassion on His s,
Deut	32:43	avenge the blood of His s,
Josh	9:11	to them, "We are your s;
1Sa	17: 9	me, then we will be your s.
2Sa	8: 2	Moabites became David's s,
2Sa	11:24	and some of the king's s
1Ki	10: 8	and happy are these your s,
2Ki	9: 7	may avenge the blood of My s
2Ki	10:19	prophets of Baal, all his s,
2Ki	17:13	which I sent to you by My s
Ezra	2:55	The sons of Solomon's s:
Neh	4:16	that half of my s worked at
Neh	7:57	The sons of Solomon's s:
Job	1:15	they have killed the s with
Job	4:18	He puts no trust in His s,
Ps	34:22	redeems the soul of His s,
Ps	90:13	have compassion on Your s.
Ps	113: 1	O s of the LORD, Praise
Ps	135:14	have compassion on His s.
Eccl	2: 7	I acquired male and female s,
Is	65:14	My s shall sing for joy of
Is	66:14	shall be known to His s,
Lam	5: 8	S rule over us
Dan	1:12	Please test your s for ten
Dan	2: 7	Let the king tell his s the
Dan	3:26	s of the Most High God, come
Dan	3:28	Angel and delivered His s
Dan	9: 6	have we heeded Your s the
Amos	3: 7	reveals His secret to His s
Matt	18:23	settle accounts with his s.
Matt	21:36	"Again he sent other s,
Mark	1:20	in the boat with the hired s,
Mark	13:34	and gave authority to his s,
Luke	12:38	so, blessed are those s.
Luke	15:17	many of my father's hired s
Luke	15:19	me like one of your hired s.
Luke	17:10	say, 'We are unprofitable s.
Luke	19:13	"So he called ten of his s,
John	2: 9	it came from (but the s who
John	15:15	"No longer do I call you s,
John	18:36	My s would fight, so that I
Acts	10: 7	two of his household s and
1Co	4: 1	as s of Christ and stewards
1Pe	2:18	S, be submissive to your
Rev	1: 1	God gave Him to show His s—
Rev	11:18	You should reward Your s
Rev	19: 5	all you His s and those who
Rev	22: 3	and His s shall serve Him.

SERVANTS' (*see* SERVANTS)

| Gen | 46:34 | Your s occupation has been |
| Is | 65: 8 | So will I do for My s |

SERVE (*see* SERVANT, SERVED, SERVES, SERVICE, SERVING)

Gen	15:14	also the nation whom they s
Gen	25:23	And the older shall s the
Gen	27:29	Let peoples s you, And

Gen	29:18	I will s you seven years for
Ex	1:14	in which they made them s
Ex	3:12	you shall s God on this
Ex	4:23	let My son go that he may s
Ex	8: 1	that they may s Me.
Ex	20: 5	not bow down to them nor s
Ex	21: 2	he shall s six years; and in
Ex	21: 6	and he shall s him forever.
Ex	23:33	For if you s their gods, it
Deut	5: 9	not bow down to them nor s
Deut	7: 4	to s other gods; so the
Josh	22: 5	and to s Him with all your
Josh	24:14	s Him in sincerity and in
Josh	24:15	this day whom you will s,
Josh	24:15	we will s the LORD."
Josh	24:21	but we will s the LORD!"
1Sa	7: 3	and s Him only; and He will
Ps	2:11	S the LORD with fear, And
Ps	72:11	All nations shall s Him.
Ps	97: 7	all be put to shame who s
Ps	100: 2	S the LORD with gladness
Jer	11:10	gone after other gods to s
Jer	25:11	and these nations shall s
Jer	27: 7	So all nations shall s him
Dan	1: 5	of that time they might s
Dan	3:17	our God whom we s is able to
Dan	3:18	that we do not s your gods,
Dan	6:16	whom you s continually, He
Matt	4:10	Him only you shall s.
Matt	6:24	No one can s two masters;
Matt	6:24	You cannot s God and mammon.
Matt	20:28	come to be served, but to s,
Mark	10:45	come to be served, but to s,
Luke	1:74	Might s Him without fear,
Acts	6: 2	leave the word of God and s
Rom	1: 9	whom I s with my spirit in
Rom	7:25	with the mind I myself s the
Rom	9:12	The older shall s the
Rom	16:18	those who are such do not s
1Co	9:13	and those who s at the altar
Gal	3:19	then does the law s?
Gal	5:13	but through love s one
Col	3:24	for you s the Lord Christ.
1Th	1: 9	to God from idols to s the
1Ti	3:10	then let them s as deacons,
2Ti	1: 3	whom I s with a pure
Heb	9:14	from dead works to s the
Heb	13:10	from which those who s the
Rev	7:15	and s Him day and night in
Rev	22: 3	and His servants shall s

SERVED (*see* SERVE)

Gen	29:20	So Jacob s seven years for
Gen	29:30	And he s with Laban still
Deut	17: 3	who has gone and s other gods
Josh	24: 2	and they s other gods.
Judg	2: 7	So the people s the LORD
Judg	2:11	and s the Baals;
Judg	2:13	They forsook the LORD and s
Judg	3: 7	and s the Baals and
Judg	10:13	you have forsaken Me and s
1Sa	7: 4	and s the LORD only.
1Ki	1: 4	and s him; but the king did
2Ki	10:18	Ahab s Baal a little, Jehu
2Ch	24:18	and s wooden images and
2Ch	33: 3	all the host of heaven and s
Jer	5:19	you have forsaken Me and s
Jer	52:12	who s the king of Babylon,
Matt	8:15	And she arose and s them.
Matt	20:28	of Man did not come to be s,
Mark	10:45	of Man did not come to be s,
John	12: 2	Him a supper; and Martha s,
Rom	1:25	and worshiped and s the
Gal	4: 8	you s those which by nature
Phil	2:22	a son with his father he s

SERVES (*see* SERVE)

Deut	15:12	is sold to you and s you six
Luke	22:27	among you as the One who s.
John	12:26	If anyone s Me, him My

SERVICE (*see* SERVE)

Ex	1:14	and in all manner of s in
Ex	12:25	that you shall keep this s.
Ex	12:26	'What do you mean by this s?
Ex	13: 5	that you shall keep this s
Ex	27:19	the tabernacle for all its s,
Ex	30:16	shall appoint it for the s
Ex	36: 1	manner of work for the s of
Num	4:12	take all the utensils of s
Num	4:35	everyone who entered the s
2Sa	9: 2	He said, "At your s!"
1Ki	12: 4	lighten the burdensome s of
1Ch	9:13	men for the work of the s
Job	7: 1	there not a time of hard s
Ps	104:14	And vegetation for the s of
Luke	1:23	as soon as the days of his s
John	16: 2	think that he offers God s.
Rom	9: 4	the s of God, and the
Rom	12: 1	which is your reasonable s.
2Co	9:12	the administration of this s
Eph	6: 7	with goodwill doing s,
Phil	2:17	on the sacrifice and s of
Heb	9: 1	had ordinances of divine
Rev	2:19	"I know your works, love, s,

SERVING (*see* SERVE)

Gen	43:34	but Benjamin's s was five
Ex	14: 5	we have let Israel go from s
Deut	15:18	a double hired servant in s
Luke	1: 8	that while he was s as
Luke	10:40	was distracted with much s,
Luke	15:29	many years I have been s
Rom	12:11	in spirit, s the Lord;
1Pe	5: 2	s as overseers, not by
Jude	12	s only themselves. They

SETH

Gen	4:25	bore a son and named him S,
1Ch	1: 1	Adam, S, Enosh,
Luke	3:38	son of Enos, the son of S,

SETTLE (*see* SETTLED)

Job	3: 5	May a cloud s on it; May
Is	14: 1	and s them in their own
Matt	18:23	certain king who wanted to s
1Pe	5:10	strengthen, and s you.

SETTLED (*see* SETTLE)

Num	10:12	then the cloud s down in the
Ezra	4:10	Osnapper took captive and s
Ps	119:89	Your word is s in heaven.
Prov	8:25	Before the mountains were s,
Jer	48:11	He has s on his dregs, And
Zeph	1:12	punish the men Who are s
Matt	25:19	of those servants came and s

SEVEN (*see* SEVENTH)

Gen	7: 2	You shall take with you s
Gen	8:10	And he waited yet another s
Gen	29:20	So Jacob served s years for
Gen	29:30	with Laban still another s
Gen	33: 3	himself to the ground s
Gen	41: 2	came up out of the river s
Gen	41: 5	and suddenly s heads of
Gen	41:53	Then the s years of plenty
Gen	41:54	and the s years of famine
Ex	12:19	For s days no leaven shall be
Ex	23:15	eat unleavened bread s days,
Ex	25:37	You shall make s lamps for
Lev	4:17	the blood and sprinkle it s
Lev	23:15	s Sabbaths shall be
Lev	23:42	shall dwell in booths for s
Num	12:14	be shut out of the camp s

Num 13:22 (Now Hebron was built **s**
Deut 7: 1 **s** nations greater and
Deut 15: 1 At the end of every **s** years
Deut 16:13 the Feast of Tabernacles **s**
Josh 6: 4 march around the city **s**
Josh 18: 6 survey the land in **s** parts
Judg 14:12 it to me within the **s** days
Judg 16: 7 If they bind me with **s** fresh
Judg 16:19 and had him shave off the **s**
Ruth 4:15 who is better to you than **s**
1Sa 2: 5 Even the barren has borne **s**,
1Sa 10:10 Thus Jesse made **s** of his sons
2Sa 5: 5 he reigned over Judah **s**
2Sa 24:13 Shall **s** years of famine come
1Ki 11: 3 And he had **s** hundred wives,
1Ki 19:18 Yet I have reserved **s**
2Ki 4:35 then the child sneezed **s**
2Ki 5:14 So he went down and dipped **s**
Job 1: 2 And **s** sons and three
Job 2:13 with him on the ground **s**
Job 42:13 He also had **s** sons and three
Ps 119:164 **S** times a day I praise You,
Prov 6:16 **s** are an abomination to
Prov 9: 1 She has hewn out her **s**
Prov 26:25 For there are **s**
Is 4: 1 And in that day **s** women
Jer 15: 9 languishes who has borne **s**;
Jer 34:14 At the end of **s** years let
Jer 52:25 **s** men of the king's close
Ezek 3:15 astonished among them **s**
Ezek 40:22 it was ascended by **s** steps,
Dan 3:19 that they heat the furnace **s**
Dan 4:16 And let **s** times pass over
Dan 9:25 There shall be **s** weeks
Zech 4: 2 and on the stand **s** lamps
Matt 12:45 he goes and takes with him **s**
Matt 15:36 And He took the **s** loaves and
Matt 15:37 and they took up **s** large
Matt 18:21 Up to **s** times?"
Matt 18:22 but up to seventy times **s**.
Matt 22:28 whose wife of the **s** will she
Luke 2:36 had lived with a husband **s**
Luke 8: 2 out of whom had come **s**
Luke 11:26 goes and takes with him **s**
Luke 24:13 which was **s** miles from
Acts 6: 3 seek out from among you **s**
Rom 11: 4 reserved for Myself **s**
Heb 11:30 they were encircled for **s**
Rev 1: 4 to the **s** churches which are
Rev 1: 4 and from the **s** Spirits who
Rev 1:12 And having turned I saw **s**
Rev 1:16 He had in His right hand **s**
Rev 5: 1 sealed with **s** seals.
Rev 8: 2 and to them were given **s**
Rev 10: 3 **s** thunders uttered their
Rev 12: 3 fiery red dragon having **s**
Rev 15: 7 gave to the seven angels **s**
Rev 15: 8 the seven plagues of the **s**
Rev 17:10 There are also **s** kings. Five
Rev 17:11 the eighth, and is of the **s**,
Rev 21: 9 bowls filled with the **s**

SEVENFOLD
Gen 4:15 shall be taken on him **s**.
Gen 4:24 If Cain shall be avenged **s**,
Prov 6:31 is found, he must restore **s**;

SEVENTEEN
Gen 37: 2 being **s** years old, was
Jer 32: 9 **s** shekels of silver.

SEVENTH (see SEVEN)
Gen 2: 2 and He rested on the **s** day
Gen 2: 3 Then God blessed the **s** day
Gen 8: 4 Then the ark rested in the **s**
Ex 12:15 the first day until the **s**

Ex 20:10 but the **s** day is the Sabbath
Ex 20:11 and rested the **s** day.
Ex 23:11 but the **s** year you shall let
Ex 31:15 but the **s** is the Sabbath of
Lev 25: 4 but in the **s** year there shall
Ezra 7: 7 up to Jerusalem in the **s**
Heb 4: 4 God rested on the **s**
Jude 14 the **s** from Adam, prophesied

SEVENTY
Gen 11:26 Now Terah lived **s** years, and
Ex 1: 5 descendants of Jacob were **s**
Ex 15:27 twelve wells of water and **s**
Ex 24: 1 and **s** of the elders of
Deut 10:22 went down to Egypt with **s**
Judg 8:30 Gideon had **s** sons who were
Ps 90:10 days of our lives are **s**
Jer 25:11 serve the king of Babylon **s**
Jer 25:12 when **s** years are completed,
Jer 29:10 After **s** years are completed
Dan 9: 2 that He would accomplish **s**
Dan 9:24 **S** weeks are determined For
Zech 1:12 which You were angry these **s**
Matt 18:22 but up to **s** times seven.
Luke 10: 1 things the Lord appointed **s**

SEVENTY-FIVE
Gen 12: 4 And Abram was **s** years old
Gen 25: 7 one hundred and **s** years.
Acts 7:14 relatives to him, **s** people.

SEVENTY-SEVEN
Gen 5:31 were seven hundred and **s**

SEVENTY-SEVENFOLD†
Gen 4:24 sevenfold, Then Lamech **s**.

SEVERE (see SEVERELY, SEVERITY)
Gen 12:10 for the famine was **s** in the
Jer 10:19 for my hurt! My wound is **s**.
Luke 15:14 there arose a **s** famine in

SEVERELY (see SEVERE)
1Sa 1: 6 rival also provoked her **s**,
1Sa 31: 3 and he was **s** wounded by the
Matt 17:15 an epileptic and suffers **s**;

SEVERITY (see SEVERE)
Rom 11:22 consider the goodness and **s**

SEW (see SEWED, SEWS)
Eccl 3: 7 to tear, And a time to **s**;

SEWED† (see SEW)
Gen 3: 7 and they **s** fig leaves

SEWS† (see SEW)
Mark 2:21 No one **s** a piece of unshrunk

SEXUAL (see SEXUALLY)
Matt 5:32 wife for any reason except **s**
Matt 19: 9 except for **s** immorality, and
Acts 15:29 and from **s** immorality. If
Acts 21:25 and from **s** immorality."
Rom 1:29 **s** immorality, wickedness,
1Co 5: 1 reported that there is **s**
1Co 6:13 Now the body is not for **s**
1Co 6:18 Flee **s** immorality. Every sin
1Co 7: 2 because of **s** immorality, let
1Th 4: 3 you should abstain from **s**
Jude 7 given themselves over to **s**
Rev 2:14 and to commit **s** immorality.
Rev 9:21 their sorceries or their **s**

SEXUALLY (see SEXUAL)
1Co 5: 9 not to keep company with **s**
Rev 22:15 dogs and sorcerers and **s**

SHACKLES
Mark 5: 4 had often been bound with **s**
Luke 8:29 bound with chains and **s**;

SHADE

Ps   121: 5 The LORD is your **s** at
Dan   4:12 beasts of the field found **s**
Jon   4: 5 and sat under it in the **s**,
Mark   4:32 the air may nest under its **s**.

SHADOW (see SHADOWS)

Gen   19: 8 they have come under the **s**
2Ki   20: 9 shall the **s** go forward ten
Job   8: 9 our days on earth are a **s**.
Ps   17: 8 Hide me under the **s** of Your
Ps   23: 4 through the valley of the **s**
Ps   36: 7 put their trust under the **s**
Ps   39: 6 man walks about like a **s**;
Ps   80:10 were covered with its **s**,
Ps   91: 1 Shall abide under the **s** of
Ps   102:11 My days are like a **s** that
Ps   107:14 out of darkness and the **s**
Ps   109:23 I am gone like a **s** when it
Ps   144: 4 days are like a passing **s**.
Eccl   6:12 which he passes like a **s**?
Eccl   8:13 days, which are as a **s**,
Is   9: 2 dwelt in the land of the **s**
Is   32: 2 As the **s** of a great rock in
Is   49: 2 In the **s** of His hand He has
Matt   4:16 in the region and **s**
Luke   1:79 sit in darkness and the **s**
Acts   5:15 that at least the **s** of Peter
Col   2:17 which are a **s** of things to
Heb   8: 5 who serve the copy and **s** of
Heb   10: 1 having a **s** of the good
Jas   1:17 there is no variation or **s**

SHADOWS (see SHADOW)

Song   2:17 the day breaks And the **s**

SHADRACH (see HANANIAH)

Dan   3:12 the province of Babylon: **S**,
Dan   3:28 "Blessed be the God of **S**,
Dan   3:30 Then the king promoted **S**,

SHAFT

Ex   37:17 he made the lampstand. Its **s**,
2Sa   5: 8 up by way of the water **s**
2Sa   21:19 the **s** of whose spear was
Job   28: 4 He breaks open a **s** away from

SHAKE (see SHAKEN, SHAKES, SHOOK)

Judg   16:20 and **s** myself free!" But he
Job   4:14 Which made all my bones **s**.
Job   16: 4 And **s** my head at you;
Job   17: 3 Who is he who will **s**
Ps   46: 3 Though the mountains **s**
Ps   109:25 they **s** their heads.
Is   2:19 When He arises to **s** the
Is   11:15 His mighty wind He will **s**
Ezek   38:20 face of the earth shall **s**
Hag   2: 6 is a little while) I will **s**
Hag   2:21 I will **s** heaven and earth.
Matt   10:14 **s** off the dust from your
Heb   12:26 Yet once more I **s** not

SHAKEN (see SHAKE)

Ps   112: 6 Surely he will never be **s**;
Matt   11: 7 A reed **s** by the wind?
Matt   24:29 of the heavens will be **s**.
Luke   6:38 **s** together, and running over
Acts   4:31 assembled together was **s**;
Acts   16:26 of the prison were **s**;
2Th   2: 2 not to be soon **s** in mind or
Heb   12:27 things that are being **s**,
Heb   12:28 a kingdom which cannot be **s**,

SHAKES (see SHAKE)

Ps   29: 8 The voice of the LORD **s** the

SHALLUM (see JEHOAHAZ)

Jer   22:11 says the LORD concerning **S**

SHALMANESER†

2Ki   17: 3 **S** king of Assyria came up
2Ki   18: 9 that **S** king of Assyria came

SHAME (see SHAMEFUL)

2Sa   13:13 I, where could I take my **s**?
Ps   4: 2 you turn my glory to **s**?
Ps   35: 4 Let those be put to **s** and
Ps   69: 7 **S** has covered my face.
Ps   69:19 You know my reproach, my **s**,
Ps   71: 1 Let me never be put to **s**.
Ps   71:24 For they are brought to **s**
Ps   119:31 do not put me to **s**!
Ps   129: 5 who hate Zion Be put to **s**
Prov   10: 5 is a son who causes **s**.
Prov   19:26 Is a son who causes **s** and
Is   20: 4 to the **s** of Egypt.
Jer   17:18 do not let me be put to **s**;
Dan   9: 8 to us belongs **s** of face, to
Dan   12: 2 Some to **s** and everlasting
Joel   2:26 shall never be put to **s**.
Nah   3: 5 And the kingdoms your **s**.
Acts   5:41 counted worthy to suffer **s**
Rom   9:33 will not be put to **s**.
Rom   10:11 will not be put to **s**.
1Co   1:27 of the world to put to **s**
1Co   6: 5 I say this to your **s**.
Heb   6: 6 and put Him to an open **s**.
Heb   12: 2 the cross, despising the **s**,
1Pe   2: 6 no means be put to **s**.

SHAMEFUL (see SHAME)

Jer   11:13 set up altars to that **s**
Rom   1:27 men committing what is **s**,
1Co   11: 6 But if it is **s** for a woman
1Co   14:35 for it is **s** for women to
Eph   5:12 For it is **s** even to speak of

SHAMGAR†

Judg   3:31 After him was **S** the son of
Judg   5: 6 "In the days of **S**,

SHAPED

Acts   17:29 something **s** by art and man's

SHAPHAN

2Ki   22: 3 that the king sent **S** the
2Ki   22: 8 Hilkiah gave the book to **S**,

SHARE (see SHARED, SHARING)

2Sa   20: 1 We have no **s** in David, Nor
1Ki   12:16 What **s** have we in David? We
Is   58: 7 Is it not to **s** your bread
Gal   6: 6 who is taught the word **s** in
Eph   4:16 which every part does its **s**,
1Ti   6:18 ready to give, willing to **s**,
2Ti   1: 8 but **s** with me in the
Heb   13:16 forget to do good and to **s**,

SHARED (see SHARE)

Prov   21: 9 Than in a house **s** with a
Phil   4:14 have done well that you **s**

SHARING (see SHARE)

Phm   1: 6 that the **s** of your faith may

SHARON

1Ch   27:29 over the herds that fed in **S**,
Song   2: 1 I am the rose of **S**,

SHARP (see SHARPER)

Ex   4:25 Then Zipporah took a **s** stone
2Sa   2:16 was called the Field of **S**
Ps   57: 4 And their tongue a **s** sword.
Ps   120: 4 **S** arrows of the warrior,
Prov   5: 4 **S** as a two-edged sword.
Is   49: 2 has made My mouth like a **s**
Rev   1:16 out of His mouth went a **s**
Rev   14:14 and in His hand a **s** sickle.
Rev   19:15 out of His mouth goes a **s**

SHARPEN (see SHARPENING, SHARPENS)
1Sa 13:20 down to the Philistines to **s**
Ps 64: 3 Who **s** their tongue like a

SHARPENING† (see SHARPEN)
1Sa 13:21 and the charge for a **s** was a

SHARPENS (see SHARPEN)
Prov 27:17 As iron **s** iron, So a man

SHARPER (see SHARP)
Heb 4:12 and **s** than any two-edged

SHATTERED (see SHATTERS)
Eccl 12: 6 Or the pitcher **s** at the
Dan 12: 7 people has been completely **s**,

SHATTERS† (see SHATTERED)
Dan 2:40 iron breaks in pieces and **s**

SHAVE (see SHAVED, SHAVEN)
Lev 21: 5 nor shall they **s** the edges
Num 6:18 Then the Nazirite shall **s** his
Judg 16:19 for a man and had him **s** off
Acts 21:24 expenses so that they may **s**

SHAVED (see SHAVE)
Num 6:19 the Nazirite after he has **s**
2Sa 10: 4 **s** off half of their beards,
Job 1:20 and **s** his head; and he fell
1Co 11: 6 for a woman to be shorn or **s**,

SHAVEN (see SHAVE)
Judg 16:17 my mother's womb. If I am **s**,

SHEAF (see SHEAVES)
Gen 37: 7 and bowed down to my **s**.

SHEALTIEL
Ezra 3: 2 and Zerubbabel the son of **S**
Matt 1:12 and **S** begot Zerubbabel.
Luke 3:27 Zerubbabel, the son of **S**,

SHEAR-JASHUB†
Is 7: 3 you and **S** your son, at the

SHEARER† (see SHEARERS, SHORN)
Acts 8:32 as a lamb before its **s**

SHEARERS (see SHEARER)
Is 53: 7 as a sheep before its **s** is

SHEATH
1Sa 17:51 and drew it out of its **s**
John 18:11 "Put your sword into the **s**.

SHEAVES (see SHEAF)
Gen 37: 7 and indeed your **s** stood all
Ps 126: 6 Bringing his **s** with him.

SHEBA
1Ki 10: 4 And when the queen of **S** had
Ps 72:15 And the gold of **S** will be
Jer 6:20 Comes frankincense from **S**,

SHEBAT†
Zech 1: 7 month, which is the month **S**,

SHEBNA
2Ki 18:18 **S** the scribe, and Joah the

SHECHEM (see SYCHAR)
Gen 33:18 came safely to the city of **S**,
Gen 34: 2 And when **S** the son of Hamor
Gen 37:12 their father's flock in **S**.
Josh 24:32 of Egypt, they buried at **S**,
Judg 9:23 Abimelech and the men of **S**;
1Ki 12: 1 And Rehoboam went to **S**,

SHED (see SHEDDING, SHEDS)
Gen 9: 6 By man his blood shall be **s**;
Prov 1:11 Let us lie in wait to **s**
Prov 6:17 Hands that **s** innocent
Matt 23:35 all the righteous blood **s**
Matt 26:28 which is **s** for many for the

Luke 11:50 all the prophets which was **s**
Luke 22:20 which is **s** for you.
Acts 22:20 of Your martyr Stephen was **s**,
Rom 3:15 feet are swift to **s**

SHEDDING (see SHED)
Heb 9:22 and without **s** of blood there

SHEDS (see SHED)
Gen 9: 6 Whoever **s** man's blood, By

SHEEP (see SHEEP'S, SHEEPFOLD, SHEEPSKINS)
Gen 4: 2 Now Abel was a keeper of **s**,
Gen 29: 6 Rachel is coming with the **s**.
Gen 30:32 the speckled and spotted **s**,
Ex 12: 5 You may take it from the **s**
Ex 22: 1 a man steals an ox or a **s**,
1Sa 8:17 will take a tenth of your **s**.
1Sa 15:14 is this bleating of the **s**
1Sa 16:19 David, who is with the **s**.
1Sa 25: 4 Nabal was shearing his **s**,
2Sa 6:13 sacrificed oxen and fatted **s**.
2Sa 7: 8 from following the **s**,
2Sa 24:17 done wickedly; but these **s**,
Neh 3: 1 the priests and built the **S**
Job 1:16 heaven and burned up the **s**
Job 42:12 he had fourteen thousand **s**,
Ps 8: 7 All **s** and oxen—Even the
Ps 74: 1 anger smoke against the **s**
Ps 78:52 own people go forth like **s**,
Ps 95: 7 And the **s** of His hand.
Ps 100: 3 are His people and the **s**
Ps 119:176 gone astray like a lost **s**;
Song 6: 6 teeth are like a flock of **s**
Is 7:21 alive a young cow and two **s**;
Is 53: 6 All we like **s** have gone
Is 53: 7 And as a **s** before its
Ezek 34:11 Myself will search for My **s**
Zech 13: 7 And the **s** will be
Matt 9:36 like having no shepherd.
Matt 10: 6 go rather to the lost **s**
Matt 10:16 I send you out as **s** in the
Matt 12:11 among you who has one **s**,
Matt 18:12 If a man has a hundred **s**,
Matt 18:13 rejoices more over that **s**
Matt 25:32 as a shepherd divides his **s**
Mark 14:27 And the **s** will be
Luke 15: 6 for I have found my **s** which
John 2:15 with the **s** and the oxen, and
John 5: 2 is in Jerusalem by the **S**
John 10: 2 is the shepherd of the **s**.
John 10: 3 and the **s** hear his voice;
John 10: 7 you, I am the door of the **s**.
John 10:11 gives His life for the **s**.
John 10:14 shepherd; and I know My **s**,
John 10:15 I lay down My life for the **s**.
John 10:16 And other **s** I have which are
John 10:27 My **s** hear My voice, and I
John 21:16 He said to him, "Tend My **s**.
John 21:17 said to him, "Feed My **s**.
Acts 8:32 He was led as a **s** to
Rom 8:36 We are accounted as **s**
Heb 13:20 that great Shepherd of the **s**,
1Pe 2:25 For you were like **s** going

SHEEP'S† (see SHEEP)
Matt 7:15 who come to you in **s**

SHEEPBREEDER
Amos 7:14 But I was a **s** And a

SHEEPBREEDERS
Amos 1: 1 who was among the **s** of

SHEEPFOLD (see SHEEP)
2Sa 7: 8 "I took you from the **s**,
John 10: 1 he who does not enter the **s**

SHEEPSKINS† (*see* SHEEP)
Heb 11:37 They wandered about in s and

SHEET
Acts 10:11 and an object like a great s

SHEKEL (*see* SHEKELS)
Gen 24:22 nose ring weighing half a s,
Ex 30:13 a shekel according to the s
Ex 30:24 according to the s of the
Amos 8: 5 the ephah small and the s

SHEKELS (*see* SHEKEL)
Gen 23:15 is worth four hundred s
Gen 37:28 Ishmaelites for twenty s
Ex 21:32 to their master thirty s of
Lev 27: 4 valuation shall be thirty s;
Lev 27: 5 for a male shall be twenty s,
Lev 27: 5 and for a female ten s;
Jer 32: 9 seventeen s of silver.
Hos 3: 2 for myself for fifteen s

SHELAH
Gen 38:11 house till my son S is
Gen 46:12 of Judah were Er, Onan, S,
Neh 3:15 the wall of the Pool of S
Luke 3:35 son of Eber, the son of S,

SHELTER
Judg 9:15 Then come and take s in
Ps 61: 4 I will trust in the s of
Is 4: 6 and for a s from storm and
Jon 4: 5 There he made himself a s

SHEM
Gen 5:32 years old, and Noah begot S,
Gen 6:10 And Noah begot three sons: S,
Gen 9:27 he dwell in the tents of S;
Luke 3:36 of Arphaxad, the son of S,

SHEMAIAH (*see* SHIMEI)
1Ki 12:22 the word of God came to S

SHEOL
2Sa 22: 6 The sorrows of S surrounded
Job 11: 8 can you do? Deeper than S—
Job 17:16 go down to the gates of S?
Job 26: 6 S is naked before Him, And
Ps 16:10 will not leave my soul in S,
Ps 86:13 my soul from the depths of S.
Ps 116: 3 And the pangs of S laid
Prov 1:12 us swallow them alive like S,
Is 5:14 Therefore S has enlarged
Is 14:15 shall be brought down to S,
Is 38:18 For S cannot thank You,
Jon 2: 2 Out of the belly of S I

SHEPHERD (*see* SHEPHERDS)
Gen 46:34 for every s is an
Gen 49:24 Jacob (From there is the S,
Num 27:17 like sheep which have no s.
2Sa 7: 7 whom I commanded to s My
Ps 23: 1 The LORD is my s;
Ps 78:71 To s Jacob His people, And
Ps 80: 1 O S of Israel, You who lead
Eccl 12:11 nails, given by one S.
Is 40:11 will feed His flock like a s;
Is 44:28 says of Cyrus, 'He is My s,
Ezek 34:12 As a s seeks out his flock on
Ezek 37:24 they shall all have one s;
Amos 3:12 As a s takes from the mouth
Mic 7:14 S Your people with Your
Zech 11:15 implements of a foolish s.
Zech 11:17 "Woe to the worthless s,
Zech 13: 7 of hosts. "Strike the S,
Matt 2: 6 a Ruler Who will s
Matt 9:36 sheep having no s.
Matt 25:32 as a s divides his sheep
Matt 26:31 'I will strike the S,

John 10: 2 enters by the door is the s
John 10:11 "I am the good s.
John 10:11 The good s gives His life
John 10:12 he who is not the s,
John 10:14 "I am the good s;
John 10:16 will be one flock and one s.
Acts 20:28 to s the church of God which
Heb 13:20 that great S of the sheep,
1Pe 2:25 have now returned to the S
1Pe 5: 2 S the flock of God which is
1Pe 5: 4 and when the Chief S appears,
Rev 7:17 midst of the throne will s

SHEPHERDS (*see* SHEPHERD)
Gen 47: 3 "Your servants are s,
Ex 2:17 Then the s came and drove
Jer 23: 1 Woe to the s who destroy and
Jer 50: 6 Their s have led them
Ezek 34: 2 Woe to the s of Israel who
Ezek 34:10 I am against the s,
Amos 1: 2 The pastures of the s
Luke 2: 8 were in the same country s

SHESHACH† (*see* BABYLON)
Jer 25:26 Also the king of S shall
Jer 51:41 how S is taken! Oh, how the

SHESHBAZZAR (*see* ZERUBBABEL)
Ezra 1: 8 and counted them out to S

SHIBBOLETH† (*see* SIBBOLETH)
Judg 12: 6 S'!" And he would say,

SHIELD (*see* SHIELDS)
Gen 15: 1 afraid, Abram. I am your s,
2Sa 1:21 For the s of the mighty is
Ps 3: 3 are a s for me, My glory
Ps 18: 2 My s and the horn of my
Ps 18:30 He is a s to all who trust
Ps 18:35 have also given me the s of
Ps 28: 7 is my strength and my s;
Ps 33:20 He is our help and our s.
Ps 84:11 LORD God is a sun and s;
Ps 115: 9 is their help and their s.
Prov 2: 7 He is a s to those who
Eph 6:16 taking the s of faith with

SHIELDS (*see* SHIELD)
1Ki 10:16 made two hundred large s
1Ki 14:27 King Rehoboam made bronze s
Neh 4:16 half held the spears, the s,
Ps 47: 9 For the s of the earth

SHILOAH† (*see* SILOAM)
Is 8: 6 refused The waters of S

SHILOH
Gen 49:10 Until S comes; And to Him
Josh 18: 9 to Joshua at the camp in S.
Judg 18:31 the house of God was in S.
1Sa 1:24 the house of the LORD in S.
1Sa 14: 3 Eli, the LORD's priest in S,
Ps 78:60 forsook the tabernacle of S,
Jer 7:12 to My place which was in S,
Jer 26: 6 will make this house like S,

SHIMEI (*see* SHEMAIAH)
2Sa 16:13 S went along the hillside
2Sa 19:21 Shall not S be put to death
1Ki 2:42 king sent and called for S,

SHINAR
Gen 10:10 and Calneh, in the land of S.
Gen 11: 2 a plain in the land of S,
Gen 14: 1 days of Amraphel king of S,
Dan 1: 2 carried into the land of S

SHINE (*see* SHINED, SHINES, SHINING, SHONE)
Num 6:25 The LORD make His face s
Job 3: 4 Nor the light s upon it.

Ps	31:16	Make Your face s upon Your
Ps	50: 2	God will s forth.
Ps	80: 3	O God; Cause Your face to s,
Ps	104:15	Oil to make his face s,
Is	60: 1	Arise, s; For your light
Dan	12: 3	Those who are wise shall s
Matt	5:16	Let your light so s before
2Co	4: 6	God who commanded light to s
Phil	2:15	among whom you s as lights
Rev	21:23	the sun or of the moon to s

SHINED† (see SHINE)

Is	9: 2	Upon them a light has s.

SHINES (see SHINE)

Ps	139:12	But the night s as the day;
Prov	4:18	That s ever brighter unto
John	1: 5	And the light s in the
2Pe	1:19	to heed as a light that s

SHINING (see SHINE)

2Ki	3:22	and the sun was s on the
Mark	9: 3	His clothes became s,
Luke	24: 4	two men stood by them in s
John	5:35	He was the burning and s
1Jn	2: 8	the true light is already s.
Rev	1:16	was like the sun s in its

SHIP (see SHIPS, SHIPWRECK)

Prov	30:19	The way of a s in the midst
Jon	1: 3	and found a s going to
Acts	27:41	they ran the s aground; and

SHIPS (see SHIP)

Deut	28:68	take you back to Egypt in s,
Judg	5:17	And why did Dan remain on s?
1Ki	9:26	also built a fleet of s at
1Ki	10:22	three years the merchant s
1Ki	22:48	for the s were wrecked at
2Ch	20:36	himself with him to make s
Ps	107:23	who go down to the sea in s,
Is	23: 1	you s of Tarshish! For it
Is	33:21	Nor majestic s pass by
Ezek	27: 9	All the s of the sea And

SHIPWRECK† (see SHIP, SHIPWRECKED)

1Ti	1:19	the faith have suffered s,

SHIPWRECKED† (see SHIPWRECK)

2Co	11:25	stoned; three times I was s;

SHISHAK

2Ch	12: 2	that S king of Egypt came

SHOD†

Eph	6:15	and having s your feet with

SHOE†

Ps	60: 8	Over Edom I will cast My s;
Ps	108: 9	Over Edom I will cast My s;

SHONE (see SHINE)

Ex	34:35	the skin of Moses' face s,
Matt	17: 2	His face s like the sun, and
Luke	2: 9	and the glory of the Lord s
Acts	9: 3	and suddenly a light s
Acts	12: 7	and a light s in the prison;
2Co	4: 6	who has s in our hearts to

SHOOK (see SHAKE)

Ps	18: 7	Then the earth s and
Matt	28: 4	And the guards s for fear of
Acts	13:51	But they s off the dust from
Acts	28: 5	But he s off the creature
Heb	12:26	whose voice then s the earth;

SHOOT (see SHOOTS, SHOT)

Ps	22: 7	They s out the lip, they

SHOOTS (see SHOOT)

Job	14: 7	And that its tender s will

SHORE

Matt	13: 2	multitude stood on the s.
John	21: 4	come, Jesus stood on the s;

SHORN (see SHEARER)

1Co	11: 6	for a woman to be s or

SHORT (see SHORTENED, SHORTLY)

Job	20: 5	of the wicked is s,
Ps	89:47	Remember how s my time is;
Luke	19: 3	for he was of s stature.
Rom	3:23	all have sinned and fall s
1Co	7:29	brethren, the time is s,
Heb	12:15	lest anyone fall s of the
Rev	12:12	he knows that he has a s

SHORTENED (see SHORT)

Num	11:23	"Has the LORD's arm been s?
Ps	102:23	He s my days.
Is	50: 2	Is My hand s at all that it
Matt	24:22	unless those days were s,

SHORTLY (see SHORT)

1Co	4:19	But I will come to you s,
2Pe	1:14	knowing that s I must put
Rev	1: 1	things which must s take
Rev	22: 6	the things which must s

SHOT (see SHOOT)

Ex	19:13	shall surely be stoned or s

SHOULDER (see SHOULDERS)

Gen	24:15	with her pitcher on her s.
Is	9: 6	will be upon His s.

SHOULDERS (see SHOULDER)

Gen	9:23	laid it on both their s,
1Sa	9: 2	From his s upward he was
Is	49:22	shall be carried on their s;
Matt	23: 4	and lay them on men's s;
Luke	15: 5	it, he lays it on his s,

SHOUT (see SHOUTED, SHOUTING, SHOUTS)

Ps	32:11	And s for joy, all you
Ps	35:27	Let them s for joy and be
Ps	47: 1	all you peoples! S to God
Ps	47: 5	God has gone up with a s,
Ps	66: 1	Make a joyful s to God, all
Ps	98: 4	S joyfully to the LORD, all
Ps	100: 1	Make a joyful s to the
Zech	9: 9	O daughter of Zion! S,
Gal	4:27	Break forth and s,
1Th	4:16	descend from heaven with a s,

SHOUTED (see SHOUT)

Job	38: 7	And all the sons of God s
Luke	23:21	But they s, saying, "Crucify

SHOUTING (see SHOUT)

Amos	1:14	Amid s in the day of

SHOUTS (see SHOUT)

Zech	4: 7	forth the capstone With s

SHOW (see SHOWED, SHOWING, SHOWN, SHOWS)

Gen	12: 1	To a land that I will s
Gen	24:12	and s kindness to my master
Ex	9:16	that I may s My power in
Ex	23: 3	You shall not s partiality to
Ex	25: 9	According to all that I s
Ex	33:18	s me Your glory."
Judg	4:22	I will s you the man whom
Judg	6:17	then s me a sign that it is
2Ki	20:13	that Hezekiah did not s
Esth	1:11	in order to s her beauty to
Job	10:16	And again You s Yourself
Ps	16:11	You will s me the path of
Ps	18:25	the merciful You will s
Ps	25: 4	S me Your ways, O LORD
Ps	50:23	conduct aright I will s
Ps	51:15	And my mouth shall s forth

Is	41:22	Let them s the former
Is	41:23	S the things that are to
Jer	32:18	You s lovingkindness to
Jer	33: 3	and s you great and mighty
Lam	3:32	Yet He will s compassion
Joel	2:30	And I will s wonders in the
Zech	7: 9	S mercy and compassion
Matt	8: 4	s yourself to the priest,
Matt	16: 1	Him asked that He would s
Matt	16:21	that time Jesus began to s
Matt	22:19	S Me the tax money." So they
Matt	24: 1	His disciples came up to s
Matt	24:24	prophets will rise and s
John	2:18	What sign do You s to us,
John	5:20	and He will s Him greater
John	7: 4	s Yourself to the world."
John	14: 9	S us the Father"?
Acts	1:24	s which of these two You
Acts	2:19	I will s wonders in
Acts	7: 3	a land that I will s
Rom	9:22	wanting to s His wrath and
1Co	12:31	And yet I s you a more
Eph	2: 7	the ages to come He might s
1Ti	5: 4	let them first learn to s
Heb	6:11	that each one of you s the
Jas	2: 9	but if you s partiality, you
Jas	2:18	S me your faith without
Rev	4: 1	and I will s you things

SHOWBREAD

Num	4: 7	On the table of s they shall
1Ch	9:32	in charge of preparing the s
Matt	12: 4	house of God and ate the s
Heb	9: 2	the table, and the s,

SHOWED (see SHOW)

Deut	6:22	and the LORD s signs and
Deut	34: 1	And the LORD s him all the
1Sa	15: 6	For you s kindness to all
2Ki	22:10	Then Shaphan the scribe s the
Jer	24: 1	The LORD s me, and there
Amos	7: 1	Thus the Lord GOD s me:
Matt	4: 8	and s Him all the kingdoms
Luke	4: 5	s Him all the kingdoms of
Luke	10:37	He who s mercy on him." Then
Luke	24:40	He s them His hands and His
John	20:20	He s them His hands and His
John	21:14	now the third time Jesus s
Rev	21:10	and s me the great city, the

SHOWERS

Ps	72: 6	Like s that water the
Ezek	34:26	there shall be s of
Zech	10: 1	He will give them s of

SHOWING (see SHOW)

Ex	20: 6	but s mercy to thousands, to
Deut	5:10	but s mercy to thousands, to
Acts	18:28	s from the Scriptures that
Tit	3: 2	s all humility to all men.

SHOWN (see SHOW)

Ex	25:40	to the pattern which was s
Ps	78:11	His wonders that He had s
Mic	6: 8	He has s you, O man, what
John	10:32	Many good works I have s you
Acts	10:28	But God has s me that I
Rom	1:19	for God has s it to them.
Heb	8: 5	to the pattern s you
Jas	2: 4	have you not s partiality

SHOWS (see SHOW)

Deut	10:17	who s no partiality nor
2Sa	22:51	And s mercy to His
Ps	19: 1	And the firmament s His
Ps	37:21	But the righteous s mercy
Mark	14:70	and your speech s it."
Acts	10:34	truth I perceive that God s

Rom	9:16	but of God who s mercy.
Rom	12: 8	he who s mercy, with

SHREWD (see SHREWDLY)

Ps	18:26	You will show Yourself s.
Luke	16: 8	of this world are more s in

SHREWDLY † (see SHREWD)

Ex	1:10	let us deal s with them,
Luke	16: 8	because he had dealt s.

SHRINE (see SHRINES)

Judg	17: 5	The man Micah had a s,

SHRINES (see SHRINE)

1Ki	12:31	He made s on the high places,
Acts	19:24	who made silver s of Diana,

SHUHITE

Job	2:11	the Temanite, Bildad the S,

SHULAMITE

Song	6:13	Return, return, O S;

SHUN † (see SHUNNED, SHUNS)

2Ti	2:16	But s profane and idle

SHUNAMMITE

1Ki	1:15	and Abishag the S was
1Ki	2:17	he may give me Abishag the S
2Ki	4:25	"Look, the S woman!

SHUNEM

2Ki	4: 8	day that Elisha went to S,

SHUNNED (see SHUN)

Job	1: 1	and one who feared God and s

SHUNS (see SHUN)

Job	1: 8	one who fears God and s
Job	2: 3	one who fears God and s

SHUR

Gen	16: 7	the spring on the way to S.
Ex	15:22	out into the Wilderness of S.

SHUSHAN

Ezra	4: 9	and Erech and Babylon and S,
Neh	1: 1	as I was in S the citadel,
Dan	8: 2	looking, that I was in S,

SHUT (see SHUTS)

Gen	7:16	and the LORD s him in.
Gen	19: 6	s the door behind him,
Num	12:15	So Miriam was s out of the
Josh	6: 1	Now Jericho was securely s up
1Ki	8:35	When the heavens are s up
Neh	13:19	commanded the gates to be s,
Ps	69:15	And let not the pit s its
Ps	88: 8	I am s up, and I cannot
Eccl	12: 4	When the doors are s in the
Is	6:10	And s their eyes; Lest
Is	22:22	open, and no one shall s;
Is	44:18	For He has s their eyes, so
Is	52:15	Kings shall s their mouths
Jer	20: 9	like a burning fire S up
Jer	32: 2	Jeremiah the prophet was s
Ezek	44: 2	me, "This gate shall be s;
Dan	6:22	God sent His angel and s
Dan	12: 4	s up the words, and seal the
Matt	6: 6	and when you have s your
Matt	25:10	wedding; and the door was s.
Luke	3:20	that he s John up in prison.
Luke	4:25	when the heaven was s up
John	20:26	came, the doors being s,
Acts	26:10	and many of the saints I s
Rev	3: 8	and no one can s it; for you
Rev	21:25	Its gates shall not be s at

SHUTS (see SHUT)

Prov	21:13	Whoever s his ears to the
Is	33:15	And s his eyes from seeing
Rev	3: 7	who opens and no one s,

SIBBOLETH† (*see* SHIBBOLETH)
Judg 12: 6 And he would say, "S,

SICK (*see* SICKNESS)
2Ki   20: 1 In those days Hezekiah was s
Neh   2: 2 sad, since you are not s?
Prov 13:12 deferred makes the heart s,
Is   1: 5 more. The whole head is s,
Dan   8:27 fainted and was s for days;
Mal   1: 8 you offer the lame and s,
Matt   4:24 they brought to Him all s
Matt   8:14 his wife's mother lying s
Matt   8:16 and healed all who were s,
Matt   9:12 but those who are s.
Matt 10: 8 "Heal the s, cleanse
Matt 25:36 I was s and you visited Me;
Mark   6:13 with oil many who were s,
Mark 16:18 they will lay hands on the s,
John 11: 2 whose brother Lazarus was s.
1Co   11:30 reason many are weak and s
Phil   2:27 For indeed he was s almost
Jas   5:14 Is anyone among you s?
Jas   5:15 of faith will save the s,

SICKLE
Deut 16: 9 you begin to put the s to
1Sa   13:20 mattock, his ax, and his s;
Joel   3:13 Put in the s, for the harvest
Mark   4:29 immediately he puts in the s,
Rev   14:14 and in His hand a sharp s.

SICKNESS (*see* SICK, SICKNESSES)
Deut 28:61 Also every s and every
Is   38: 9 and had recovered from his s:
Matt   4:23 and healing all kinds of s
John 11: 4 This s is not unto death, but

SICKNESSES (*see* SICKNESS)
Matt   8:17 And bore our s.

SIDE (*see* RIVERSIDE, SIDES)
Gen   6:16 the door of the ark in its s.
Ex   17:12 his hands, one on one s,
Ex   32:26 is on the LORD's s—
Lev   1:15 be drained out at the s of
Josh 24: 2 dwelt on the other s of the
Judg   2: 3 shall be thorns in your s,
Judg   8:34 all their enemies on every s;
1Sa   12:11 of your enemies on every s;
1Ki   3:20 and took my son from my s,
1Ki   5: 4 has given me rest on every s;
2Ki   9:32 and said, "Who is on my s?
Neh   4:18 his sword girded at his s
Job   1:10 all that he has on every s?
Ps   91: 7 thousand may fall at your s,
Ps   118: 6 The LORD is on my s;
Ps   124: 1 the LORD who was on our s,
Jer   20:10 Fear on every s!"
Ezek   4: 4 "Lie also on your left s,
Ezek   4: 6 lie again on your right s;
Dan   7: 5 It was raised up on one s,
Jon   4: 5 city and sat on the east s
Mark   4:35 us cross over to the other s.
Mark   9:40 not against us is on our s.
Mark 16: 5 robe sitting on the right s;
Luke   1:11 standing on the right s of
Luke 10:31 he passed by on the other s.
Luke 10:32 and passed by on the other s.
John 19:18 with Him, one on either s,
John 19:34 the soldiers pierced His s
John 20:20 them His hands and His s.
John 20:25 and put my hand into His s,
2Co   4: 8 are hard pressed on every s,
2Co   7: 5 we were troubled on every s.
Rev   22: 2 and on either s of the

SIDES (*see* SIDE)
Lev   19:27 not shave around the s of

Num   33:55 eyes and thorns in your s,
Ps   48: 2 Is Mount Zion on the s of
Is   14:13 On the farthest s of the
Heb   9: 4 covenant overlaid on all s

SIDON (*see* SIDONIANS)
Gen   10:15 Canaan begot S his
Josh 11: 8 and chased them to Greater S,
Judg 10: 6 gods of Syria, the gods of S,
Is   23: 2 You merchants of S,
Matt 15:21 to the region of Tyre and S.
Luke   6:17 the seacoast of Tyre and S,

SIDONIANS (*see* SIDON)
Judg   3: 3 all the Canaanites, the S,
Judg 18: 7 in the manner of the S,
1Ki   11: 5 the goddess of the S,

SIEGE
2Sa   20:15 and they cast up a s mound
2Ki   25: 1 and they built a s wall
2Ch   32: 9 the forces with him laid s
Mic   5: 1 He has laid s against us;

SIFT
Luke 22:31 that he may s you as wheat.

SIGH (*see* SIGHED, SIGHING)
Ps   90: 9 finish our years like a s.
Lam   1:11 All her people s,

SIGHED (*see* SIGH)
Mark   8:12 But He s deeply in His

SIGHING (*see* SIGH)
Ps   31:10 grief, And my years with s;
Ps   38: 9 And my s is not hidden from
Is   35:10 And sorrow and s shall flee
Is   51:11 Sorrow and s shall flee
Lam   3:56 not hide Your ear From my s,

SIGHT
Gen   2: 9 that is pleasant to the s
Gen   23: 4 may bury my dead out of my s.
Gen   39: 4 Joseph found favor in his s,
Ex   3: 3 aside and see this great s,
Ex   5:21 made us abhorrent in the s
Ex   15:26 do what is right in His s,
Ex   33:12 also found grace in My s.
Ex   40:38 in the s of all the house of
Num   13:33 grasshoppers in our own s,
Deut   4:25 and do evil in the s of the
Deut   6:18 is right and good in the s
Deut 28:34 driven mad because of the s
Deut 34:12 Moses performed in the s of
Judg   2:11 of Israel did evil in the s
Judg   6:21 LORD departed out of his s.
Ruth   2:13 me find favor in your s,
1Sa   1:18 find favor in your s.
2Sa   7:19 was a small thing in Your s,
2Sa   12:11 with your wives in the s of
2Sa   16:22 concubines in the s of all
1Ki   11: 6 Solomon did evil in the s of
1Ki   14:22 Now Judah did evil in the s
1Ki   15:26 And he did evil in the s of
2Ki   1:13 yours be precious in your s.
2Ki   14: 3 what was right in the s
2Ki   17:18 and removed them from His s;
Neh   1:11 grant him mercy in the s of
Esth   5: 2 she found favor in his s,
Job   15:15 are not pure in His s,
Job   25: 5 stars are not pure in His s,
Ps   18:24 of my hands in His s.
Ps   19:14 Be acceptable in Your s,
Ps   51: 4 done this evil in Your s—
Ps   90: 4 a thousand years in Your s
Ps   116:15 Precious in the s of the
Prov   4: 3 and the only one in the s
Eccl   6: 9 Better is the s of the eyes

Is   5:21 And prudent in their own **s**!
Is   11: 3 He shall not judge by the **s**
Is   43: 4 you were precious in My **s**,
Jer   7:15 I will cast you out of My **s**,
Jer   18:10 if it does evil in My **s** so
Jer   19:10 break the flask in the **s** of
Ezek   5:14 in the **s** of all who pass by.
Ezek   12: 5 through the wall in their **s**,
Ezek   20:43 yourselves in your own **s**
Ezek   36:34 of lying desolate in the **s**
Hos   2:10 her lewdness in the **s** of
Hos   6: 2 That we may live in His **s**.
Amos   9: 3 Though they hide from My **s**
Jon   2: 4 have been cast out of Your **s**;
Matt   11:26 so it seemed good in Your **s**.
Luke   1:15 he will be great in the **s**
Luke   4:18 And recovery of **s** to
Luke   10:21 so it seemed good in Your **s**.
Luke   15:21 against heaven and in your **s**,
Luke   16:15 is an abomination in the **s**
Luke   24:31 and He vanished from their **s**.
John   9:11 and washed, and I received **s**.
Acts   1: 9 received Him out of their **s**.
Acts   7:31 it, he marveled at the **s**;
Acts   9: 9 he was three days without **s**,
Acts   22:13 Saul, receive your **s**.
Rom   3:20 will be justified in His **s**,
Rom   12:17 for good things in the **s** of
2Co   4: 2 man's conscience in the **s**
2Co   5: 7 we walk by faith, not by **s**.
Col   1:22 and above reproach in His **s**—
Heb   4:13 creature hidden from His **s**,
Heb   13:21 is well pleasing in His **s**,
Jas   4:10 Humble yourselves in the **s** of
1Pe   3: 4 is very precious in the **s**
1Jn   3:22 that are pleasing in His **s**.

SIGN (see SIGNED, SIGNS)

Gen   9:12 This is the **s** of the
Gen   17:11 and it shall be a **s** of the
Ex   3:12 And this shall be a **s** to
Ex   12:13 Now the blood shall be a **s**
Ex   31:17 It is a **s** between Me and the
Deut   6: 8 You shall bind them as a **s** on
Deut   11:18 and bind them as a **s** on your
Judg   6:17 then show me a **s** that it is
Is   7:11 Ask a **s** for yourself from the
Is   7:14 Himself will give you a **s**:
Is   20: 3 three years for a **s** and a
Is   55:13 For an everlasting **s** that
Jer   32:44 **s** deeds and seal them, and
Ezek   24:24 Thus Ezekiel is a **s** to you;
Dan   6: 8 establish the decree and **s**
Matt   12:39 generation seeks after a **s**,
Matt   12:39 be given to it except the **s**
Matt   16: 1 that He would show them a **s**
Matt   24: 3 And what will be the **s** of
Matt   24:30 Then the **s** of the Son of Man
Matt   26:48 betrayer had given them a **s**,
Luke   2:12 And this will be the **s** to
Luke   2:34 and for a **s** which will be
John   2:18 What do You show to us,
John   4:54 This again is the second **s**
John   10:41 said, "John performed no **s**,
Rom   4:11 And he received the **s** of
1Co   1:22 For Jews request a **s**,
1Co   14:22 tongues are for a **s**,

SIGNAL
Mark   14:44 betrayer had given them a **s**,

SIGNED (see SIGN)
Jer   32:10 And I **s** the deed and sealed
Dan   6:10 knew that the writing was **s**,

SIGNET
Gen   38:18 Your **s** and cord, and your

Jer   22:24 were the **s** on My right hand,
Dan   6:17 sealed it with his own **s**
Hag   2:23 and will make you like a **s**

SIGNIFIED† (see SIGNIFYING)
Rev   1: 1 And He sent and **s** it by His

SIGNIFYING† (see SIGNIFIED)
John   12:33 **s** by what death He would
John   18:32 **s** by what death He would
John   21:19 **s** by what death he would

SIGNS (see SIGN)
Gen   1:14 and let them be for **s** and
Ex   4: 9 not believe even these two **s**,
Ex   7: 3 and multiply My **s** and My
Deut   34:11 in all the **s** and wonders
Ps   78:43 When He worked His **s** in
Ps   135: 9 He sent **s** and wonders into
Is   8:18 given me! We are for **s**
Dan   6:27 And He works **s** and wonders
Matt   16: 3 you cannot discern the **s**
Matt   24:24 will rise and show great **s**
Mark   16:20 through the accompanying **s**.
Luke   21:25 And there will be **s** in the
John   2:11 This beginning of **s** Jesus did
John   3: 2 for no one can do these **s**
John   4:48 Unless you people see **s** and
John   6:26 not because you saw the **s**,
John   7:31 will He do more **s** than these
John   9:16 who is a sinner do such **s**?
Acts   2:22 and **s** which God did through
Acts   5:12 of the apostles many **s** and
Acts   6: 8 did great wonders and **s**
Acts   8:13 seeing the miracles and **s**
Rom   15:19 in mighty **s** and wonders, by
2Co   12:12 Truly the **s** of an apostle
2Th   2: 9 of Satan, with all power, **s**,
Heb   2: 4 bearing witness both with **s**
Rev   13:13 He performs great **s**,

SIHON
Num   21:23 But **S** would not allow Israel
Deut   2:30 But **S** king of Heshbon would
Ps   135:11 **S** king of the Amorites, Og

SILAS (see SILVANUS)
Acts   15:27 therefore sent Judas and **S**,
Acts   15:40 but Paul chose **S** and
Acts   17:14 but both **S** and Timothy

SILENCE (see SILENCED, SILENT)
Ps   8: 2 That You may **s** the enemy
Ps   115:17 Nor any who go down into **s**.
Eccl   3: 7 to sew; A time to keep **s**,
Is   41: 1 Keep **s** before Me, O
Hab   2:20 Let all the earth keep **s**
1Ti   2:11 Let a woman learn in **s** with
Rev   8: 1 there was **s** in heaven for

SILENCED (see SILENCE)
Matt   22:34 heard that He had **s** the

SILENT (see SILENCE)
2Ki   2: 3 "Yes I know; keep **s**!"
Esth   4:14 if you remain completely **s**
Job   13: 5 Oh, that you would be **s**,
Ps   22: 2 night season, and am not **s**.
Ps   32: 3 When I kept **s**,
Ps   83: 1 Do not keep **s**,
Is   53: 7 before its shearers is **s**,
Matt   26:63 But Jesus kept **s**.
Mark   3: 4 to kill?" But they kept **s**.
Acts   8:32 before its shearer is **s**,
1Co   14:28 let him keep **s** in church,
1Co   14:34 Let your women keep **s** in the

SILLY
Hos   7:11 Ephraim also is like a **s**

SILOAM (*see* SHILOAH)
Luke 13: 4 on whom the tower in S fell
John 9: 7 wash in the pool of S"

SILVANUS (*see* SILAS)
1Th 1: 1 Paul, S, and Timothy,
1Pe 5:12 By S, our faithful brother

SILVER (*see* SILVERSMITH)
Gen 13: 2 very rich in livestock, in s,
Gen 23:15 four hundred shekels of s.
Gen 37:28 for twenty shekels of s.
Gen 44: 2 the s cup, in the mouth of
Ex 20:23 gods of s or gods of gold you
Ex 21:32 master thirty shekels of s,
Num 10: 2 Make two s trumpets for
Num 22:18 give me his house full of s
Deut 17:17 shall he greatly multiply s
Deut 29:17 wood and stone and s and
Judg 16: 5 eleven hundred pieces of s.
1Ki 10:22 ships came bringing gold, s,
1Ki 10:27 The king made s as common
2Ki 14:14 he took all the gold and s,
2Ki 23:35 he exacted the s and gold
1Ch 22:14 and one million talents of s,
2Ch 9:14 country brought gold and s
Ezra 2:69 five thousand minas of s,
Job 3:15 filled their houses with s;
Job 27:16 Though he heaps up s like
Job 28: 1 there is a mine for s,
Job 42:11 one gave him a piece of s
Ps 12: 6 Like s tried in a furnace
Ps 66:10 You have refined us as s is
Ps 68:13 of a dove covered with s,
Ps 115: 4 Their idols are s and gold,
Ps 135:15 idols of the nations are s
Prov 2: 4 If you seek her as s,
Prov 16:16 to be chosen rather than s.
Prov 25:11 of gold In settings of s.
Prov 26:23 earthenware covered with s
Eccl 2: 8 I also gathered for myself s
Eccl 12: 6 your Creator before the s
Is 1:22 Your s has become dross,
Is 2:20 cast away his idols of s
Is 46: 6 And weigh s on the scales;
Is 48:10 refined you, but not as s;
Jer 32: 9 money—seventeen shekels of s.
Dan 2:32 its chest and arms of s,
Dan 5: 2 to bring the gold and s
Dan 5: 4 the gods of gold and s,
Hos 2: 8 And multiplied her s and
Hos 3: 2 for fifteen shekels of s,
Amos 2: 6 sell the righteous for s,
Amos 8: 6 we may buy the poor for s,
Hag 2: 8 The s is Mine, and the gold
Zech 9: 3 Heaped up s like the dust,
Zech 11:12 my wages thirty pieces of s.
Mal 3: 3 refiner and a purifier of s;
Matt 26:15 to him thirty pieces of s.
Matt 27: 9 the thirty pieces of s,
Luke 15: 8 having ten s coins, if she
Acts 3: 6 S and gold I do not have, but
Acts 17:29 Nature is like gold or s or
Acts 19:24 who made s shrines of Diana,
1Co 3:12 foundation with gold, s,
2Ti 2:20 only vessels of gold and s,
1Pe 1:18 like s or gold, from your

SILVERSMITH (*see* SILVER)
Acts 19:24 man named Demetrius, a s,

SIMEON (*see* NIGER)
Gen 34:25 S and Levi, Dinah's
Gen 35:23 Jacob's firstborn, and S,
Num 2:12 shall be the tribe of S,
Luke 2:34 Then S blessed them, and said
Acts 13: 1 S who was called Niger,

Rev 7: 7 of the tribe of S twelve

SIMILAR
Num 6: 3 himself from wine and s
Judg 13: 4 not to drink wine or s
Jer 36:32 were added to them many s

SIMILITUDE†
Jas 3: 9 who have been made in the s

SIMON (*see* BAR-JONAH, CEPHAS, NIGER, PETER)
Matt 4:18 S called Peter, and Andrew
Matt 10: 4 S the Canaanite, and Judas
Matt 13:55 His brothers James, Joses, S,
Matt 16:16 S Peter answered and said,
Matt 16:17 S Bar-Jonah, for flesh and
Mark 15:21 S a Cyrenian, the father of
Luke 6:15 and S called the Zealot;
Luke 22:31 And the Lord said, "S,
Luke 24:34 and has appeared to S!"
John 1:41 found his own brother S.
John 1:42 You are S the son of Jonah.
John 6:71 Iscariot, the son of S,
John 18:10 Then S Peter, having a sword,
John 18:25 Now S Peter stood and warmed
John 21:15 said to Simon Peter, "S,
John 21:16 him again a second time, "S,
John 21:17 to him the third time, "S,
Acts 9:43 many days in Joppa with S,
Acts 10: 5 and send for S whose surname
Acts 15:14 S has declared how God at the
2Pe 1: 1 S Peter, a bondservant and

SIMPLE (*see* SIMPLICITY)
Ps 19: 7 is sure, making wise the s;
Ps 116: 6 The LORD preserves the s;
Ps 119:130 gives understanding to the s.
Prov 1: 4 To give prudence to the s,
Prov 8: 5 O you s ones, understand
Prov 9: 4 "Whoever is s, let him turn
Prov 27:12 The s pass on and are
Rom 16:18 deceive the hearts of the s.
Rom 16:19 and s concerning evil.

SIMPLICITY (*see* SIMPLE)
Acts 2:46 food with gladness and s of
2Co 11: 3 may be corrupted from the s

SIN (*see* SINFUL, SINNED, SINNER, SINNING, SINS)
Gen 4: 7 s lies at the door. And its
Gen 18:20 and because their s is very
Gen 39: 9 and s against God?"
Ex 10:17 please forgive my s only
Ex 20:20 you, so that you may not s.
Ex 29:36 a bull every day as a s
Ex 32:30 have committed a great s.
Ex 32:30 make atonement for your s.
Ex 34: 7 and transgression and s,
Ex 34: 9 our iniquity and our s,
Lev 4: 3 bull without blemish as a s
Lev 4:29 hand on the head of the s
Lev 5: 9 some of the blood of the s
Lev 5:10 on his behalf for his s
Lev 6:25 This is the law of the s
Lev 12: 6 or a turtledove as a s
Lev 16: 5 two kids of the goats as a s
Lev 19:22 And the s which he has
Lev 20:20 They shall bear their s;
Num 9:13 that man shall bear his s.
Num 12:11 Please do not lay this s
Num 15:22 If you s unintentionally,
Num 19:17 for purification from s,
Num 27: 3 but he died in his own s;
Num 32:23 and be sure your s will find
Num 33:11 in the Wilderness of S.
Deut 15: 9 and it become s among you.
Deut 21:22 a man has committed a s
Deut 23:21 and it would be s to you.

Deut 24:16 put to death for his own s.
1Sa 15:23 rebellion is as the s of
1Sa 15:25 please pardon my s,
2Sa 12:13 also has put away your s;
1Ki 8:46 is no one who does not s),
1Ki 14:16 sinned and who made Israel s.
1Ki 22:52 Nebat, who had made Israel s;
2Ki 21:11 and has also made Judah s
Neh 4: 5 and do not let their s be
Neh 13:26 women caused even him to s.
Job 1:22 In all this Job did not s
Ps 32: 1 Whose s is covered.
Ps 32: 5 I acknowledged my s to You,
Ps 32: 5 forgave the iniquity of my s.
Ps 40: 6 Burnt offering and s
Ps 51: 2 And cleanse me from my s.
Ps 51: 3 And my s is always before
Ps 51: 5 And in s my mother
Ps 109:14 And let not the s of his
Ps 119:11 That I might not s against
Prov 10:16 wages of the wicked to s.
Prov 14:34 But s is a reproach to
Prov 20: 9 I am pure from my s"?
Eccl 7:20 does good And does not s.
Is 5:18 And s as if with a cart
Is 6: 7 And your s purged."
Is 30: 1 That they may add s to sin;
Is 53:10 His soul an offering for s,
Is 53:12 And He bore the s of many,
Jer 31:34 and their s I will remember
Ezek 3:20 he shall die in his s,
Ezek 45:19 some of the blood of the s
Dan 9:20 and confessing my s and the
Hos 13: 2 Now they s more and more,
Mic 3: 8 And to Israel his s.
Mic 6: 7 fruit of my body for the s
Matt 5:29 right eye causes you to s,
Matt 18:21 how often shall my brother s
John 1:29 of God who takes away the s
John 5:14 S no more, lest a worse
John 8: 7 He who is without s among
John 8:11 go and s no more."
John 8:34 whoever commits s is a slave
John 8:46 of you convicts Me of s?
John 9:41 blind, you would have no s;
John 9:41 Therefore your s remains.
John 16: 8 will convict the world of s,
John 19:11 Me to you has the greater s.
Acts 7:60 not charge them with this s.
Rom 3: 9 that they are all under s.
Rom 4: 8 shall not impute s.
Rom 5:12 just as through one man s
Rom 5:12 world, and death through s,
Rom 5:20 But where s abounded, grace
Rom 5:21 so that as s reigned in
Rom 6: 1 Shall we continue in s that
Rom 6: 6 no longer be slaves of s.
Rom 6: 7 died has been freed from s.
Rom 6:10 He died to s once for all;
Rom 6:14 For s shall not have dominion
Rom 6:17 though you were slaves of s,
Rom 6:23 For the wages of s is death,
Rom 7: 7 I would not have known s
Rom 7: 9 s revived and I died.
Rom 7:14 I am carnal, sold under s.
Rom 7:17 but s that dwells in me.
Rom 7:23 captivity to the law of s
Rom 8: 2 me free from the law of s
Rom 8: 3 He condemned s in the flesh,
Rom 14:23 is not from faith is s.
1Co 8:12 you s against Christ.
1Co 15:56 The sting of death is s,
1Co 15:56 and the strength of s is
2Co 5:21 He made Him who knew no s
Gal 2:17 therefore a minister of s?

Gal 3:22 has confined all under s,
2Th 2: 3 and the man of s is
Heb 3:13 the deceitfulness of s.
Heb 4:15 as we are, yet without s.
Heb 9:26 has appeared to put away s
Heb 10: 8 and offerings for s You
Heb 10:26 For if we s willfully after
Heb 11:25 the passing pleasures of s,
Heb 12: 1 and the s which so easily
Heb 12: 4 striving against s.
Jas 1:15 it gives birth to s;
Jas 1:15 it gives birth to sin; and s,
Jas 2: 9 partiality, you commit s,
Jas 4:17 not do it, to him it is s.
1Pe 2:22 "Who committed no s,
1Pe 4: 1 the flesh has ceased from s,
1Jn 1: 7 Son cleanses us from all s.
1Jn 1: 8 If we say that we have no s,
1Jn 3: 4 and s is lawlessness.
1Jn 3: 6 abides in Him does not s.
1Jn 3: 9 been born of God does not s,
1Jn 3: 9 in him; and he cannot s,
1Jn 5:16 There is s leading to
1Jn 5:17 All unrighteousness is s,

SINAI (see HOREB)
Ex 19: 1 came to the Wilderness of S.
Ex 19:20 LORD came down upon Mount S,
Deut 33: 2 "The LORD came from S,
Gal 4:25 for this Hagar is Mount S in

SINCERE (see SINCERITY)
1Ti 1: 5 and from s faith,
1Pe 1:22 through the Spirit in s

SINCERITY (see SINCERE)
Josh 24:14 serve Him in s and in truth,
1Co 5: 8 the unleavened bread of s
Eph 6: 5 in s of heart, as to Christ;
Eph 6:24 our Lord Jesus Christ in s.
Col 3:22 but in s of heart, fearing

SINEWS
Ezek 37: 6 I will put s on you and bring

SINFUL (see SIN)
Gen 13:13 exceedingly wicked and s
Is 1: 4 s nation, A people laden
Mark 8:38 in this adulterous and s
Luke 5: 8 for I am a s man, O Lord!"
Luke 24: 7 into the hands of s men,
Rom 8: 3 own Son in the likeness of s

SING (see SANG, SINGERS, SINGING, SONG, SUNG)
Ex 15: 1 I will s to the LORD, For
Ex 15:21 S to the LORD, For He has
Judg 5: 3 I will s praise to the
Ps 9: 2 I will s praise to Your
Ps 13: 6 I will s to the LORD,
Ps 33: 3 S to Him a new song
Ps 47: 6 S praises to God, sing
Ps 51:14 And my tongue shall s
Ps 67: 4 the nations be glad and s
Ps 81: 1 S aloud to God our strength
Ps 89: 1 I will s of the mercies of
Ps 92: 1 And to s praises to Your
Ps 95: 1 let us s to the LORD! Let
Ps 96: 1 s to the LORD a new song!
Ps 104:33 I will s to the LORD as
Ps 105: 2 S to Him, sing psalms to Him
Ps 137: 4 How shall we s the LORD's
Is 5: 1 Now let me s to my
Is 12: 5 S to the LORD, For He has
Is 42:10 S to the LORD a new song,
Amos 6: 5 who s to the sound of
1Co 14:15 I will s with the spirit,
Jas 5:13 Let him s psalms.
Rev 15: 3 They s the song of Moses, the

SINGED†
Dan 3:27 of their head was not s nor

SINGERS
2Ch 23:13 also the s with musical
Neh 13:10 of the Levites and the s
Ps 68:25 The s went before, the
Eccl 2: 8 I acquired male and female s,

SINGING (see SING)
Ex 32:18 But the sound of s I
Ps 100: 2 before His presence with s.
Ps 126: 2 And our tongue with s.
Song 2:12 The time of s has come,
Is 14: 7 They break forth into s.
Is 35:10 And come to Zion with s,
Is 51:11 And come to Zion with s,
Acts 16:25 and Silas were praying and s
Eph 5:19 s and making melody in your
Col 3:16 s with grace in your hearts

SINK (see SANK, SUNK)
Ps 69: 2 I s in deep mire, Where
Matt 14:30 and beginning to s he cried
Luke 9:44 Let these words s down into

SINNED (see SIN)
Ex 10:16 I have s against the LORD
Num 6:11 because he s in regard to
1Sa 15:24 said to Samuel, "I have s,
2Sa 12:13 I have s against the LORD."
2Sa 24:10 I have s greatly in what I
1Ki 8:50 Your people who have s
1Ki 14:16 who s and who made Israel
2Ki 17: 7 the children of Israel had s
Neh 1: 6 father's house and I have s.
Job 1: 5 may be that my sons have s
Job 7:20 Have I s? What have I done
Ps 51: 4 You, You only, have I s,
Ps 78:17 But they s even more against
Is 43:27 Your first father s,
Jer 50:14 For she has s against the
Lam 1: 8 Jerusalem has s gravely,
Lam 5: 7 Our fathers s and are no
Dan 9: 8 because we have s against
Hos 4: 7 The more they s against Me;
Matt 27: 4 I have s by betraying
Luke 15:18 I have s against heaven and
John 9: 2 Him, saying, "Rabbi, who s,
John 9: 3 this man nor his parents s,
Rom 2:12 For as many as have s without
Rom 3:23 for all have s and fall short
Rom 5:12 to all men, because all s—
1Co 7:28 you do marry, you have not s;
2Pe 2: 4 not spare the angels who s,
1Jn 1:10 If we say that we have not s,
1Jn 3: 8 for the devil has s from the

SINNER (see SIN, SINNERS)
Prov 11:31 more the ungodly and the s.
Luke 7:39 touching Him, for she is a s.
Luke 15: 7 joy in heaven over one s
Luke 15:10 the angels of God over one s
Luke 18:13 be merciful to me a s!'
Luke 19: 7 guest with a man who is a s.
John 9:16 How can a man who is a s do
John 9:24 We know that this Man is a s.
Rom 3: 7 I also still judged as a s?
Jas 5:20 know that he who turns a s
1Pe 4:18 the ungodly and the s

SINNERS (see SINNER)
Ps 1: 1 Nor stands in the path of s,
Ps 1: 5 Nor s in the congregation
Ps 51:13 And s shall be converted to
Prov 1:10 if s entice you, Do not
Prov 23:17 not let your heart envy s,
Matt 9:10 many tax collectors and s

Matt 9:11 with tax collectors and s?
Matt 9:13 to call the righteous, but s,
Matt 11:19 of tax collectors and s!'
Matt 26:45 betrayed into the hands of s.
Luke 6:32 For even s love those who
John 9:31 that God does not hear s;
Rom 5: 8 that while we were still s,
Gal 2:15 and not s of the Gentiles,
1Ti 1: 9 for the ungodly and for s,
1Ti 1:15 into the world to save s,
Heb 7:26 undefiled, separate from s,
Jas 4: 8 Cleanse your hands, you s;

SINNING (see SIN)
Gen 20: 6 I also withheld you from s
1Jn 5:16 anyone sees his brother s a

SINS (see SIN)
Lev 4: 2 If a person s unintentionally
1Ki 15:30 because of the s of Jeroboam,
2Ki 13:11 not depart from all the s
Neh 9: 2 stood and confessed their s
Ps 19:13 also from presumptuous s;
Ps 25: 7 Do not remember the s of my
Ps 25:18 pain, And forgive all my s.
Ps 51: 9 Hide Your face from my s,
Ps 90: 8 Our secret s in the light
Ps 103:10 with us according to our s,
Prov 10:12 But love covers all s.
Prov 20: 2 provokes him to anger s
Is 1:18 Though your s are like
Is 38:17 For You have cast all my s
Is 40: 2 hand Double for all her s
Is 43:25 I will not remember your s.
Is 44:22 And like a cloud, your s.
Jer 14:10 now, And punish their s.
Ezek 18: 4 The soul who s shall die.
Dan 9:16 mountain; because for our s,
Dan 9:24 To make an end of s,
Amos 5:12 And your mighty s:
Mic 7:19 You will cast all our s
Matt 1:21 save His people from their s.
Matt 3: 6 Jordan, confessing their s.
Matt 9: 2 your s are forgiven you."
Matt 9: 6 power on earth to forgive s'
Matt 18:15 if your brother s
Matt 26:28 many for the remission of s.
Luke 11: 4 And forgive us our s,
Luke 17: 4 And if he s against you seven
Luke 24:47 and remission of s should
John 8:24 that you will die in your s;
John 9:34 were completely born in s,
John 20:23 If you forgive the s of any,
John 20:23 if you retain the s of any,
Acts 2:38 for the remission of s;
Acts 3:19 that your s may be blotted
Acts 22:16 and wash away your s,
Rom 4: 7 And whose s are
1Co 6:18 commits sexual immorality s
1Co 15: 3 that Christ died for our s
1Co 15:17 you are still in your s!
Gal 1: 4 who gave Himself for our s,
Eph 1: 7 blood, the forgiveness of s,
Eph 2: 1 dead in trespasses and s,
1Th 2:16 up the measure of their s;
1Ti 5:24 Some men's s are clearly
2Ti 3: 6 women loaded down with s,
Heb 1: 3 had by Himself purged our s,
Heb 2:17 make propitiation for the s
Heb 5: 3 to offer sacrifices for s.
Heb 7:27 first for His own s and then
Heb 9:28 offered once to bear the s
Heb 10: 2 no more consciousness of s.
Heb 10: 4 and goats could take away s.
Heb 10:12 offered one sacrifice for s
Jas 5:15 And if he has committed s,

Jas	5:20	and cover a multitude of s.
1Pe	2:24	who Himself bore our s in His
1Pe	2:24	that we, having died to s,
1Pe	3:18	also suffered once for s,
1Pe	4: 8	cover a multitude of s.
2Pe	1: 9	was cleansed from his old s.
1Jn	1: 9	If we confess our s,
1Jn	1: 9	just to forgive us our s
1Jn	2: 1	may not sin. And if anyone s,
1Jn	2: 2	the propitiation for our s,
1Jn	3: 8	He who s is of the devil, for
Rev	1: 5	us and washed us from our s

SIR (*see* SIRS)

John	4:15	The woman said to Him, "S,
John	20:15	gardener, said to Him, "S,

SIRION† (*see* HERMON)

Deut	3: 9	Sidonians call Hermon S,
Ps	29: 6	Lebanon and S like a young

SIRS† (*see* SIR)

Acts	16:30	them out and said, "S,

SISERA

Judg	4: 2	commander of his army was S,
Judg	4:18	And Jael went out to meet S,
Judg	5:26	hammer; She pounded S,

SISTER (*see* SISTER-IN-LAW, SISTERS)

Gen	12:13	"Please say you are my s,
Gen	20:12	indeed she is truly my s.
Gen	26: 7	She is my s"; for he was
Gen	34:13	he had defiled Dinah their s.
Ex	2: 7	Then his s said to Pharaoh's
Ex	15:20	the s of Aaron, took the
Deut	27:22	the one who lies with his s,
Song	4: 9	ravished my heart, My s,
Song	5: 2	"Open for me, my s,
Song	8: 8	We have a little s,
Matt	12:50	heaven is My brother and s
John	11: 1	the town of Mary and her s
Rom	16: 1	commend to you Phoebe our s,
Jas	2:15	If a brother or s is naked
2Jn	13	The children of your elect s

SISTER-IN-LAW (*see* SISTER)

Ruth	1:15	your s has gone back to her

SISTERS (*see* SISTER)

Job	1: 4	and invite their three s to
Job	42:11	all his brothers, all his s,
Hos	2: 1	'My people,' And to your s,
Matt	19:29	houses or brothers or s or
Mark	10:29	left house or brothers or s

SIT (*see* SAT, SITS, SITTING)

Deut	6: 7	talk of them when you s in
Deut	11:19	speaking of them when you s
1Ki	8:25	not fail to have a man s
Ps	110: 1	S at My right hand, Till I
Prov	23: 1	When you s down to eat with
Is	14:13	I will also s on the mount
Is	42: 7	Those who s in darkness
Mic	4: 4	But everyone shall s under
Matt	8:11	and s down with Abraham,
Matt	14:19	the multitudes to s down on
Matt	19:28	followed Me will also s on
Matt	20:21	these two sons of mine may s,
Matt	20:23	but to s on My right hand
Matt	22:44	S at My right hand,
Matt	23: 2	scribes and the Pharisees s
Luke	1:79	give light to those who s
Luke	13:29	and s down in the kingdom of
Luke	14:10	go and s down in the lowest
Luke	16: 6	and s down quickly and write
Acts	2:34	S at My right hand,
Eph	2: 6	and made us s together in
Heb	1:13	S at My right hand,

Jas	2: 3	You s here in a good place,"

SITS (*see* SIT)

Ex	11: 5	firstborn of Pharaoh who s
Ps	1: 1	Nor s in the seat of the
Ps	2: 4	He who s in the heavens
Ps	29:10	And the LORD s as King
Prov	9:14	For she s at the door of her
Is	40:22	It is He who s above the
Lam	1: 1	How lonely s the city
2Th	2: 4	so that he s as God in the
Rev	4: 9	and thanks to Him who s on

SITTING (*see* SIT)

Gen	18: 1	as he was s in the tent door
Gen	19: 1	and Lot was s in the gate of
1Ki	22:19	I saw the LORD s on His
Ps	139: 2	You know my s down and my
Is	6: 1	I saw the Lord s on a
Ezek	8: 1	with the elders of Judah s
Ezek	8:14	women were s there weeping
Matt	9: 9	He saw a man named Matthew s
Matt	21: 5	and s on a donkey, A
Matt	26:64	will see the Son of Man s
Mark	16: 5	in a long white robe s on
Luke	2:46	s in the midst of the
Luke	8:35	s at the feet of Jesus,
Luke	10:13	s in sackcloth and ashes.
John	11:20	but Mary was s in the house.
John	20:12	saw two angels in white s,
Acts	2: 2	house where they were s.
Acts	8:28	And s in his chariot, he was
Col	3: 1	s at the right hand of God.
Rev	4: 4	I saw twenty-four elders s,

SIVAN†

Esth	8: 9	which is the month of S,

SIX (*see* SIXTH)

Ex	20: 9	S days you shall labor and do
Ex	20:11	For in s days the LORD made
Ex	21: 2	he shall serve s years; and
Ex	28:10	s of their names on one
1Sa	30: 9	he and the s hundred men who
2Sa	2:11	Judah was seven years and s
2Sa	21:20	fingers on each hand and s
1Ki	10:19	The throne had s steps, and
Prov	6:16	These s things the LORD
Is	6: 2	each one had s wings: with
Matt	17: 1	Now after s days Jesus took
John	2: 6	Now there were set there s
Jas	5:17	land for three years and s
Rev	4: 8	each having s wings, were

SIXTH (*see* SIX)

Gen	1:31	and the morning were the s
Matt	27:45	Now from the s hour until
Luke	1:26	Now in the s month the angel
Rev	6:12	looked when He opened the s
Rev	9:13	Then the s angel sounded:

SIXTY

Gen	25:26	Isaac was s years old when
Dan	3: 1	whose height was s cubits
Matt	13: 8	some a hundredfold, some s,
Mark	4: 8	some thirtyfold, some s,
1Ti	5: 9	Do not let a widow under s

SIXTY-FIVE

Gen	5:23	were three hundred and s
Is	7: 8	Within s years Ephraim will

SIXTY-NINE†

Gen	5:27	were nine hundred and s

SIXTY-TWO

Dan	5:31	being about s years old.
Dan	9:25	be seven weeks and s weeks;
Dan	9:26	And after the s weeks

SKILL (*see* SKILLED, SKILLFUL)
Ex 35:35 He has filled them with s to
1Ki 5: 6 is none among us who has s
Ps 137: 5 right hand forget its s!
Dan 1:17 gave them knowledge and s
Dan 9:22 come forth to give you s to

SKILLED (*see* SKILL)
2Ch 2:14 s to work in gold and
Ezra 7: 6 and he was a s scribe in

SKILLFUL (*see* GIFTED, SKILL, SKILLFULLY)
Gen 25:27 And Esau was a s hunter, a
1Sa 16:16 seek out a man who is a s

SKILLFULLY (*see* SKILLFUL)
Ps 139:15 And s wrought in the

SKIN (*see* SKINS, SMOOTH-SKINNED)
Gen 3:21 LORD God made tunics of s,
Ex 34:35 that the s of Moses' face
Lev 1: 6 And he shall s the burnt
Lev 7: 8 have for himself the s of
Lev 13:11 is an old leprosy on the s
Num 6: 4 grapevine, from seed to s.
1Sa 1:24 and a s of wine, and brought
Job 2: 4 Skin for s! Yes, all that a
Job 7: 5 My s is cracked and breaks
Job 19:20 My bone clings to my s and
Job 19:20 I have escaped by the s of
Job 19:26 And after my s is destroyed,
Job 30:30 My s grows black and falls
Ps 102: 5 My bones cling to my s.
Is 18: 2 tall and smooth of s,
Jer 13:23 the Ethiopian change his s

SKINS (*see* SKIN)
Gen 27:16 And she put the s of the kids
Ex 25: 5 ram s dyed red, badger skins,
1Sa 25:18 two s of wine, five sheep

SKIP† (*see* SKIPPED, SKIPPING)
Ps 29: 6 He makes them also s like a

SKIPPED (*see* SKIP)
Ps 114: 4 The mountains s like rams,

SKIPPING† (*see* SKIP)
Song 2: 8 S upon the hills.

SKIRTS
Jer 13:26 I will uncover your s over

SKULL
Judg 9:53 head and crushed his s.
Matt 27:33 that is to say, Place of a S,

SKY
Ps 89:37 faithful witness in the s.
Matt 16: 2 for the s is red';
Matt 16: 3 to discern the face of the s,
Heb 11:12 many as the stars of the s

SLACK (*see* SLACKNESS)
2Pe 3: 9 The Lord is not s concerning

SLACKNESS† (*see* SLACK)
2Pe 3: 9 promise, as some count s,

SLAIN (*see* SLAY)
Num 31:19 whoever has touched any s,
1Sa 18: 7 Saul has s his thousands,
1Sa 21:11 Saul has s his thousands,
1Sa 29: 5 Saul has s his thousands,
2Sa 1:25 battle! Jonathan was s in
Prov 7:26 And all who were s by her
Prov 22:13 lion outside! I shall be s
Jer 9: 1 day and night For the s of
Ezek 11: 6 its streets with the s.
Ezek 16:21 that you have s My children
Ezek 31:17 with those s by the sword;
Ezek 37: 9 and breathe on these s,

Dan 5:30 king of the Chaldeans, was s.
Dan 7:11 watched till the beast was s,
Hos 6: 5 I have s them by the words
Acts 5:36 joined him. He was s,
Heb 11:37 were s with the sword. They
Rev 5: 6 Lamb as though it had been s,
Rev 5: 9 its seals; For You were s,
Rev 6: 9 of those who had been s for
Rev 13: 8 Book of Life of the Lamb s
Rev 18:24 and of all who were s on the

SLANDER (*see* SLANDERERS)
Ps 50:20 You s your own mother's
Prov 10:18 And whoever spreads s is a

SLANDERERS (*see* SLANDER)
1Ti 3:11 must be reverent, not s,
2Ti 3: 3 unloving, unforgiving, s,

SLAUGHTER (*see* SLAUGHTERED)
Josh 10:20 them with a very great s,
Judg 15: 8 hip and thigh with a great s;
1Sa 17:57 as David returned from the s
1Sa 18: 6 was returning from the s of
2Sa 1: 1 had returned from the s of
2Ch 30:17 Levites had charge of the s
Ps 44:22 accounted as sheep for the s.
Prov 7:22 her, as an ox goes to the s,
Prov 24:11 those stumbling to the s.
Is 53: 7 was led as a lamb to the s,
Jer 7:32 Hinnom, but the Valley of S;
Jer 11:19 docile lamb brought to the s;
Jer 12: 3 out like sheep for the s,
Jer 51:40 down Like lambs to the s,
Acts 8:32 as a sheep to the s;
Rom 8:36 as sheep for the s.
Jas 5: 5 your hearts as in a day of s.

SLAUGHTERED (*see* SLAUGHTER)
1Sa 1:25 Then they s a bull, and
2Ch 35: 1 and they s the Passover
Acts 7:42 Did you offer Me s

SLAVE (*see* SLAVES)
Deut 5:15 remember that you were a s
Ps 105:17 was sold as a s.
Jer 2:14 Is he a homeborn s?
Jer 34: 9 free his male and female s—
Matt 20:27 among you, let him be your s—
Mark 10:44 to be first shall be s of
John 8:34 whoever commits sin is a s
Acts 16:16 that a certain s girl
1Co 7:22 in the Lord while a s is
1Co 7:22 while free is Christ's s.
Gal 3:28 there is neither s nor free,
Gal 4: 7 you are no longer a s but a
Eph 6: 8 whether he is a s or free.
Col 3:11 s nor free, but Christ is
Phm 1:16 no longer as a s but more

SLAVES (*see* SLAVE)
Lev 25:42 they shall not be sold as s.
Lev 25:44 may buy male and female s.
Lev 25:46 shall be your permanent s.
Deut 6:21 We were s of Pharaoh in
Esth 7: 4 sold as male and female s,
Jer 34:10 free his male and female s,
Rom 6: 6 we should no longer be s of
Rom 6:16 you present yourselves to
Rom 6:17 that though you were s of
Rom 6:18 you became s of
Rom 6:19 your members as s of
Rom 6:22 and having become s of God,
1Co 7:23 do not become s of men.
1Co 12:13 whether s or free—and have

SLAY (*see* SLAIN, SLAYER, SLEW)
Gen 18:25 to s the righteous with the

Gen 22:10 and took the knife to **s** his
Job 13:15 Though He **s** me, yet will I
Ps 37:14 To **s** those who are of
Ps 94: 6 They **s** the widow and the
Ps 139:19 that You would **s** the wicked,

SLAYER (*see* SLAY)
Josh 21:13 (a city of refuge for the **s**)

SLEDGE
Is 41:15 you into a new threshing **s**

SLEEP (*see* SLEEPER, SLEEPING, SLEEPLESSNESS, SLEEPS, SLEPT)
Gen 2:21 LORD God caused a deep **s**
Gen 15:12 a deep **s** fell upon Abram;
Gen 28:11 lay down in that place to **s**.
Judg 16:19 Then she lulled him to **s** on
Esth 6: 1 night the king could not **s**.
Job 4:13 When deep **s** falls on men,
Ps 4: 8 lie down in peace, and **s**;
Ps 13: 3 Lest I **s** the sleep of
Ps 44:23 Awake! Why do You **s**,
Ps 121: 4 Shall neither slumber nor **s**.
Ps 127: 2 so He gives His beloved **s**.
Ps 132: 4 I will not give **s** to my eyes
Prov 3:24 you will lie down and your **s**
Prov 6:10 A little **s**, a little
Prov 6:10 folding of the hands to **s**—
Prov 24:33 A little **s**, a little
Eccl 5:12 will not permit him to **s**.
Jer 51:39 And **s** a perpetual sleep
Jer 51:57 And they shall **s** a
Dan 2: 1 was so troubled that his **s**
Dan 6:18 Also his **s** went from him.
Dan 12: 2 And many of those who **s** in
Matt 1:24 Joseph, being aroused from **s**,
Luke 22:46 said to them, "Why do you **s**?
Rom 13:11 high time to awake out of **s**;
1Co 11:30 sick among you, and many **s**.
1Co 15:51 mystery: We shall not all **s**,
Eph 5:14 says: "Awake, you who **s**,
1Th 4:14 bring with Him those who **s**
1Th 5: 6 Therefore let us not **s**,
1Th 5:10 that whether we wake or **s**,

SLEEPER† (*see* SLEEP)
Jon 1: 6 him, "What do you mean, **s**?

SLEEPING (*see* SLEEP)
1Ki 18:27 or perhaps he is **s** and must
Matt 9:24 the girl is not dead, but **s**.
Matt 26:45 Are you still **s** and resting?
Acts 12: 6 out, that night Peter was **s**,

SLEEPLESSNESS (*see* SLEEP)
2Co 11:27 in **s** often, in hunger and

SLEEPS (*see* SLEEP)
John 11:11 them, "Our friend Lazarus **s**,

SLEPT (*see* SLEEP)
Gen 2:21 to fall on Adam, and he **s**;
2Sa 11: 9 But Uriah **s** at the door of
Matt 25: 5 they all slumbered and **s**.
Matt 28:13 stole Him away while we **s**.

SLEW (*see* SLAY)
Ps 135:10 many nations And **s** mighty
Ps 136:18 And **s** famous kings, For His

SLING
Judg 20:16 every one could **s** a stone at
1Sa 17:40 and his **s** was in his hand.

SLIP (*see* SLIPPED, SLIPPERY, SLIPS)
Ps 17: 5 my footsteps may not **s**.
Ps 18:36 me, So my feet did not **s**.

SLIPPED (*see* SLIP)
Ps 73: 2 My steps had nearly **s**.

SLIPPERY (*see* SLIP)
Ps 73:18 Surely You set them in **s**

SLIPS (*see* SLIP)
Ps 38:16 me, Lest, when my foot **s**,

SLOTHFUL (*see* LAZY)
Prov 18: 9 He who is **s** in his work Is

SLOW
Ex 4:10 but I am **s** of speech and
Neh 9:17 **S** to anger, Abundant in
Ps 103: 8 **S** to anger, and abounding
Ps 145: 8 **S** to anger and great in
Joel 2:13 **S** to anger, and of great
Jon 4: 2 **s** to anger and abundant in
Nah 1: 3 The LORD is **s** to anger and
Luke 24:25 and **s** of heart to believe in
Jas 1:19 to speak, slow to wrath;

SLUGGARD (*see* LAZY)
Prov 6: 6 you **s**! Consider her ways

SLUMBER (*see* SLUMBERED)
Ps 121: 3 He who keeps you will not **s**.
Ps 121: 4 Israel Shall neither **s** nor
Ps 132: 4 sleep to my eyes Or **s** to
Prov 6:10 A little sleep, a little **s**,

SLUMBERED† (*see* SLUMBER)
Matt 25: 5 they all **s** and slept.

SMALL (*see* SMALLER, SMALLEST)
Ex 18:26 but they judged every **s** case
2Sa 7:19 And yet this was a **s** thing in
1Ki 18:44 as **s** as a man's hand, rising
1Ki 19:12 and after the fire a still **s**
Job 3:19 The **s** and great are there,
Ps 104:25 Living things both **s** and
Is 1: 9 Had left to us a very **s**
Is 7:13 house of David! Is it a **s**
Amos 7: 2 For he is **s**!"
Amos 8: 5 Making the ephah **s** and the
Zech 4:10 has despised the day of **s**
Mark 8: 7 They also had a few **s** fish;
Acts 12:18 there was no **s** stir among
Acts 15: 2 Paul and Barnabas had no **s**
Jas 3: 4 they are turned by a very **s**
Rev 20:12 **s** and great, standing before

SMALLER (*see* SMALL)
Mark 4:31 is **s** than all the seeds on

SMALLEST (*see* SMALL)
1Sa 9:21 of the **s** of the tribes of

SMELL (*see* SMELLED, SMELLING)
Gen 27:27 the **s** of my son Is like
Deut 4:28 see nor hear nor eat nor **s**.
Ps 115: 6 they have, but they do not **s**;
Dan 3:27 and the **s** of fire was not on

SMELLED† (*see* SMELL)
Gen 8:21 And the LORD **s** a soothing
Gen 27:27 and he **s** the smell of his

SMELLING† (*see* SMELL)
1Co 12:17 where would be the **s**?

SMITTEN†
Is 53: 4 **S** by God, and afflicted.

SMOKE (*see* SMOKING)
Gen 19:28 the **s** of the land which went
Ex 19:18 Sinai was completely in **s**,
Ps 18: 8 **S** went up from His nostrils,
Ps 102: 3 my days are consumed like **s**,
Is 6: 4 the house was filled with **s**.
Is 34:10 Its **s** shall ascend forever.
Joel 2:30 and fire and pillars of **s**.
Acts 2:19 fire and vapor of **s**.
Rev 19: 3 Alleluia! Her **s** rises up

SMOKING† (*see* SMOKE)
Gen 15:17 there appeared a **s** oven and
Ex 20:18 trumpet, and the mountain **s**;
Is 7: 4 for these two stubs of **s**
Is 42: 3 And **s** flax He will not
Matt 12:20 And **s** flax He will

SMOOTH (*see* SMOOTH-SKINNED, SMOOTHER, SMOOTHLY)
Gen 27:16 on his hands and on the **s**
1Sa 17:40 he chose for himself five **s**
Ps 27:11 And lead me in a **s** path,
Is 18: 2 to a nation tall and **s** of
Is 40: 4 the rough places **s**;
Luke 3: 5 And the rough ways **s**;
Rom 16:18 and by **s** words and

SMOOTH-SKINNED† (*see* SKIN, SMOOTH)
Gen 27:11 and I am a **s** man.

SMOOTHER (*see* SMOOTH)
Prov 5: 3 And her mouth is **s** than

SMOOTHLY (*see* SMOOTH)
Prov 23:31 When it swirls around **s**;

SMYRNA†
Rev 1:11 in Asia: to Ephesus, to **S**,
Rev 2: 8 the angel of the church in **S**

SNARE (*see* SNARED, SNARES)
Ps 91: 3 deliver you from the **s** of
Ps 119:110 The wicked have laid a **s** for
Prov 20:25 It is a **s** for a man to
Eccl 9:12 Like birds caught in a **s**,
Is 24:17 Fear and the pit and the **s**
Jer 48:43 Fear and the pit and the **s**
1Ti 3: 7 into reproach and the **s** of
1Ti 6: 9 fall into temptation and a **s**,
2Ti 2:26 senses and escape the **s**

SNARED (*see* SNARE)
Prov 6: 2 You are **s** by the words of
Eccl 9:12 So the sons of men are **s**

SNARES (*see* SNARE)
Ps 18: 5 The **s** of death confronted
Ps 38:12 also who seek my life lay **s**
Prov 14:27 turn one away from the **s**

SNATCH (*see* SNATCHES)
John 10:28 neither shall anyone **s** them

SNATCHES (*see* SNATCH)
Matt 13:19 the wicked one comes and **s**

SNEERED†
Luke 23:35 even the rulers with them **s**,

SNEEZED†
2Ki 4:35 then the child **s** seven

SNOUT†
Prov 11:22 ring of gold in a swine's **s**,

SNOW
Ex 4: 6 hand was leprous, like **s**.
Num 12:10 leprous, as white as **s**.
Ps 51: 7 and I shall be whiter than **s**.
Prov 26: 1 As **s** in summer and rain in
Prov 31:21 She is not afraid of **s** for
Is 1:18 They shall be as white as **s**;
Is 55:10 and the **s** from heaven, And
Dan 7: 9 His garment was white as **s**,
Matt 28: 3 his clothing as white as **s**.
Rev 1:14 like wool, as white as **s**,

SO-CALLED†
1Co 8: 5 For even if there are **s** gods,

SOAP
Jer 2:22 with lye, and use much **s**,
Mal 3: 2 fire And like launderer's **s**.

SOBER (*see* SOBER-MINDED, SOBERLY)
1Th 5: 6 but let us watch and be **s**.
1Th 5: 8 us who are of the day be **s**,
Tit 2: 2 that the older men be **s**,
1Pe 1:13 the loins of your mind, be **s**,
1Pe 5: 8 Be **s**, be vigilant;

SOBER-MINDED (*see* SOBER)
1Ti 3: 2 of one wife, temperate, **s**,
Tit 2: 6 exhort the young men to be **s**,

SOBERLY† (*see* SOBER)
Rom 12: 3 to think, but to think **s**,
Tit 2:12 lusts, we should live **s**,

SOCKET
Gen 32:25 He touched the **s** of his hip;
Gen 32:25 and the **s** of Jacob's hip was
Job 31:22 my arm be torn from the **s**.

SODOM (*see* SODOMITES)
Gen 13:10 the LORD destroyed **S** and
Gen 18:26 If I find in **S** fifty
Gen 19:24 brimstone and fire on **S** and
Deut 29:23 like the overthrow of **S** and
Is 1: 9 We would have become like **S**,
Is 1:10 the LORD, You rulers of **S**;
Lam 4: 6 punishment of the sin of **S**,
Ezek 16:48 neither your sister **S** nor her
Matt 10:15 tolerable for the land of **S**
Matt 11:23 you had been done in **S**,
Rom 9:29 have become like **S**,
Jude 7 as **S** and Gomorrah, and the
Rev 11: 8 spiritually is called **S** and

SODOMITES† (*see* SODOM)
1Co 6: 9 nor homosexuals, nor **s**,
1Ti 1:10 for fornicators, for **s**,

SOFT (*see* SOFTLY)
Prov 15: 1 A **s** answer turns away wrath,
Matt 11: 8 A man clothed in **s** garments?

SOFTLY (*see* SOFT)
Is 8: 6 of Shiloah that flow **s**,

SOJOURN (*see* SOJOURNER)
Ex 12:40 Now the **s** of the children of

SOJOURNER (*see* SOJOURN, SOJOURNERS)
Lev 25:35 him, like a stranger or a **s**,

SOJOURNERS (*see* SOJOURNER)
Jer 35: 7 in the land where you are **s**.
1Pe 2:11 I beg you as **s** and

SOLD (*see* SELL)
Gen 25:33 and **s** his birthright to
Gen 37:28 and **s** him to the Ishmaelites
Lev 27:28 shall be **s** or redeemed;
Ruth 4: 3 **s** the piece of land which
Neh 13:16 and **s** them on the Sabbath
Matt 13:46 went and **s** all that he had
Matt 21:12 all those who bought and **s**
Matt 21:12 and the seats of those who **s**
Matt 26: 9 oil might have been **s** for
Luke 17:28 drank, they bought, they **s**,
John 2:14 in the temple those who **s**
Acts 2:45 and **s** their possessions and
Acts 4:34 of lands or houses **s** them,
Acts 5: 4 your own? And after it was **s**,
Acts 7: 9 **s** Joseph into Egypt. But God
Rom 7:14 I am carnal, **s** under sin.
1Co 10:25 Eat whatever is **s** in the meat
Heb 12:16 who for one morsel of food **s**

SOLDIER (*see* SOLDIERS)
Acts 10: 7 servants and a devout **s**
Phil 2:25 fellow worker, and fellow **s**,
2Ti 2: 3 endure hardship as a good **s**

SOLDIERS (see SOLDIER)

1Sa	4:10	thirty thousand foot s.
Matt	8: 9	having s under me. And I say
Matt	28:12	large sum of money to the s,
Mark	15:16	Then the s led Him away into
John	19: 2	And the s twisted a crown of
John	19:34	But one of the s pierced His
Acts	12: 6	two chains between two s;

SOLE (see SOLES)

Gen	8: 9	no resting place for the s
Deut	28:35	and from the s of your foot
Job	2: 7	painful boils from the s of
Is	1: 6	From the s of the foot even

SOLEMN (see SOLEMNLY)

Lev	16:31	It is a sabbath of s rest
2Ki	10:20	Proclaim a s assembly for

SOLEMNLY (see SOLEMN)

Gen	43: 3	The man s warned us, saying,

SOLES (see SOLE)

Josh	4:18	and the s of the priests'

SOLID

2Ki	25:15	the things of s gold and
1Co	3: 2	you with milk and not with s
Heb	5:12	come to need milk and not s

SOLITARY†

Ps	68: 6	God sets the s in families;
Mark	1:35	went out and departed to a s

SOLOMON (see JEDIDIAH, SOLOMON'S)

1Ki	1:11	to Bathsheba the mother of S,
1Ki	1:43	lord King David has made S
1Ki	3: 4	S offered a thousand burnt
1Ki	3: 5	the LORD appeared to S in
1Ki	4:29	And God gave S wisdom and
1Ki	5:10	Then Hiram gave S cedar and
1Ki	6:14	So S built the temple and
1Ki	8:54	when S had finished praying
1Ki	9:26	King S also built a fleet of
1Ki	10:10	of Sheba gave to King S.
1Ki	10:23	So King S surpassed all the
1Ki	10:26	And S gathered chariots and
1Ki	10:28	Also S had horses imported
1Ki	11: 1	But King S loved many foreign
1Ki	11: 6	S did evil in the sight of
1Ki	11: 9	LORD became angry with S,
1Ki	11:31	out of the hand of S and
1Ki	11:41	the rest of the acts of S,
1Ki	11:41	in the book of the acts of S?
1Ki	11:43	Then S rested with his
1Ki	12:21	to Rehoboam the son of S.
1Ki	14:21	And Rehoboam the son of S
1Ch	22: 9	around. His name shall be S,
1Ch	29:19	And give my son S a loyal
2Ch	8:17	Then S went to Ezion Geber
2Ch	9: 1	Sheba heard of the fame of S,
2Ch	9: 1	came to Jerusalem to test S
2Ch	9: 2	nothing so difficult for S
Neh	13:26	Did not S king of Israel sin
Prov	1: 1	The proverbs of S the son of
Prov	10: 1	The Proverbs of S:
Prov	25: 1	also are proverbs of S
Song	3:11	And see King S with the
Matt	1: 6	David the king begot S by
Matt	1: 7	S begot Rehoboam, Rehoboam
Matt	6:29	I say to you that even S in
Matt	12:42	to hear the wisdom of S;
Matt	12:42	a greater than S
Acts	7:47	But S built Him a house.

SOLOMON'S (see SOLOMON)

1Ki	4:22	Now S provision for one day
1Ki	4:30	Thus S wisdom excelled the
1Ki	11:26	Then S servant, Jeroboam the

Song	1: 1	song of songs, which is S.
Song	3: 7	it is S litter, With sixty
John	10:23	in the temple, in S porch.

SOLVE† (see SOLVED, SOLVING)

Judg	14:12	If you can correctly s and

SOLVED† (see SOLVE)

Judg	14:18	You would not have s my

SOLVING† (see SOLVE)

Dan	5:12	s riddles, and explaining

SON (see GRANDSON, SON-IN-LAW, SON'S, SONS)

Gen	4:17	city after the name of his s—
Gen	4:25	and she bore a s and named
Gen	11:31	And Terah took his s Abram
Gen	16:11	And you shall bear a s.
Gen	16:15	So Hagar bore Abram a s;
Gen	17:23	Abraham took Ishmael his s,
Gen	21: 2	and bore Abraham a s in his
Gen	21: 5	years old when his s Isaac
Gen	21:10	out this bondwoman and her s;
Gen	22: 2	He said, "Take now your s,
Gen	22:16	and have not withheld your s,
Gen	22:16	your son, your only s—
Gen	27:24	Are you really my s Esau?"
Gen	29: 5	Do you know Laban the s of
Gen	29:32	Leah conceived and bore a s,
Gen	30:12	Zilpah bore Jacob a second s.
Gen	37: 3	because he was the s of his
Gen	37:34	and mourned for his s many
Gen	45:28	Joseph my s is still alive.
Ex	1:22	Every s who is born you shall
Ex	4:22	the LORD: "Israel is My s,
Ex	4:23	let My s go that he may
Ex	13:14	when your s asks you in time
Ex	33:11	his servant Joshua the s of
Num	1:20	of Reuben, Israel's oldest s,
Num	4:28	authority of Ithamar the s
Num	13:16	Moses called Hoshea the s
Num	14: 6	But Joshua the s of Nun and
Num	20:25	Aaron and Eleazar his s,
Num	23:19	Nor a s of man, that He
Num	27: 1	families of Manasseh the s
Num	27: 8	'If a man dies and has no s,
Deut	7: 3	your daughter to their s,
Deut	18:10	you anyone who makes his s
Deut	21:16	firstborn status on the s
Deut	21:16	wife in preference to the s
Deut	21:20	This s of ours is stubborn
Josh	18:16	before the Valley of the S
Josh	22:32	And Phinehas the s of
Judg	1:13	And Othniel the s of Kenaz,
Judg	3:15	Ehud the s of Gera, the
Judg	3:31	him was Shamgar the s of
Judg	5: 1	Deborah and Barak the s of
Judg	6:29	Gideon the s of Joash has
Judg	8:23	nor shall my s rule over
Judg	8:29	Then Jerubbaal the s of
Judg	9: 1	Then Abimelech the s of
Judg	13: 3	shall conceive and bear a s.
Ruth	4:13	conception, and she bore a s.
Ruth	4:17	There is a s born to Naomi."
1Sa	1:20	conceived and bore a s,
1Sa	9: 2	had a choice and handsome s
1Sa	10:21	And Saul the s of Kish was
1Sa	13:16	Saul, Jonathan his s,
1Sa	14: 3	the s of Eli, the LORD's
1Sa	17:17	Then Jesse said to his s
1Sa	17:58	Whose s are you, young
1Sa	20:30	You s of a perverse,
1Sa	26: 5	and Abner the s of Ner, the
2Sa	1: 5	Saul and Jonathan his s are
2Sa	2: 8	took Ishbosheth the s of
2Sa	2:13	And Joab the s of Zeruiah,
2Sa	13: 1	After this Absalom the s of

2Sa	14:11	not one hair of your **s** shall
2Sa	18:18	I have no **s** to keep my name
2Sa	18:19	Then Ahimaaz the **s** of Zadok
2Sa	18:33	"O my son Absalom—my **s**,
1Ki	1:17	Assuredly Solomon your **s**
1Ki	3:22	But the living one is my **s**,
1Ki	3:22	and the dead one is your **s**.
1Ki	5: 7	He has given David a wise **s**
1Ki	11:26	Jeroboam the **s** of Nebat, an
1Ki	12:21	kingdom to Rehoboam the **s**
1Ki	12:23	Speak to Rehoboam the **s** of
1Ki	16:29	Ahab the **s** of Omri became
1Ki	19:16	And Elisha the **s** of Shaphat
2Ki	1:17	year of Jehoram the **s** of
2Ki	3: 1	Now Jehoram the **s** of Ahab
2Ki	4:36	he said, "Pick up your **s**.
2Ki	6:29	"So we boiled my **s**,
2Ki	9:20	the driving of Jehu the **s**
2Ki	10:15	he met Jehonadab the **s** of
2Ki	14:25	His servant Jonah the **s** of
2Ki	19:20	Then Isaiah the **s** of Amoz
2Ki	23:10	is in the Valley of the **S**
2Ki	23:10	no man might make his **s** or
1Ch	17:13	Father, and he shall be My **s**;
1Ch	28: 5	sons) He has chosen my **s**
2Ch	22: 1	made Ahaziah his youngest **s**
Ezra	3: 2	and Zerubbabel the **s** of
Ezra	5: 1	Haggai and Zechariah the **s**
Job	25: 6	And a **s** of man, who is a
Ps	2: 7	said to Me, 'You are My **S**,
Ps	2:12	Kiss the **S**, lest He be
Ps	8: 4	And the **s** of man that You
Ps	50:20	slander your own mother's **s**.
Ps	72: 1	to the king's **S**.
Ps	72:20	The prayers of David the **s**
Ps	116:16	the **s** of Your maidservant;
Ps	144: 3	Or the **s** of man, that You
Prov	1: 1	proverbs of Solomon the **s**
Prov	1: 8	My **s**, hear the instruction
Prov	3:12	Just as a father the **s** in
Prov	4: 3	When I was my father's **s**,
Prov	4:10	Hear, my **s**, and receive
Prov	10: 1	A wise **s** makes a glad
Prov	10: 1	But a foolish **s** is the
Prov	13:24	spares his rod hates his **s**,
Prov	19:18	Chasten your **s** while there
Eccl	1: 1	the **s** of David, king in
Is	1: 1	The vision of Isaiah the **s**
Is	7:14	shall conceive and bear a **S**,
Is	9: 6	Unto us a **S** is given; And
Is	14:12	**s** of the morning! How you
Jer	1: 1	words of Jeremiah the **s** of
Jer	6:26	mourning as for an only **s**,
Jer	7:31	is in the Valley of the **S**
Jer	15: 4	because of Manasseh the **s** of
Jer	22:24	though Coniah the **s** of
Jer	24: 1	away captive Jeconiah the **s**
Jer	32:12	deed to Baruch the **s** of
Jer	35: 6	for Jonadab the **s** of Rechab,
Jer	39:14	him to Gedaliah the **s** of
Jer	40: 5	Go back to Gedaliah the **s** of
Jer	40: 6	went to Gedaliah the **s** of
Jer	40: 8	Ishmael the **s** of Nethaniah,
Ezek	2: 1	**S** of man, stand on your feet,
Ezek	2: 3	**S** of man, I am sending you to
Ezek	2: 6	**s** of man, do not be afraid
Ezek	11: 4	O **s** of man!"
Ezek	18:20	bear the guilt of the **s**.
Ezek	37: 3	**S** of man, can these bones
Dan	3:25	of the fourth is like the **S**
Dan	7:13	One like the **S** of Man,
Dan	8:17	**s** of man, that the vision
Hos	1: 1	that came to Hosea the **s** of
Hos	1: 3	conceived and bore him a **s**.
Hos	1: 8	she conceived and bore a **s**.
Hos	11: 1	out of Egypt I called My **s**.
Amos	7:14	Nor was I a **s** of a
Amos	8:10	like mourning for an only **s**,
Jon	1: 1	LORD came to Jonah the **s**
Hag	1: 1	prophet to Zerubbabel the **s**
Hag	1: 1	and to Joshua the **s** of
Zech	1: 1	came to Zechariah the **s** of
Zech	1: 7	came to Zechariah the **s** of
Mal	1: 6	A **s** honors his father, And
Matt	1: 1	the **S** of David, the Son of
Matt	1:20	**s** of David, do not be afraid
Matt	1:21	she will bring forth a **S**,
Matt	2:15	of Egypt I called My **S**.
Matt	3:17	"This is My beloved **S**,
Matt	4: 3	If You are the **S** of God,
Matt	4: 6	If You are the **S** of God,
Matt	4:21	James the **s** of Zebedee,
Matt	7: 9	if his **s** asks for bread,
Matt	8:20	but the **S** of Man has nowhere
Matt	9: 2	said to the paralytic, "**S**,
Matt	9: 6	you may know that the **S** of
Matt	9:27	**S** of David, have mercy on
Matt	10: 3	James the **s** of Alphaeus,
Matt	10:37	And he who loves **s** or
Matt	11:19	The **S** of Man came eating and
Matt	11:27	and no one knows the **S**
Matt	12: 8	For the **S** of Man is Lord even
Matt	12:32	speaks a word against the **S**
Matt	13:37	sows the good seed is the **S**
Matt	13:55	this not the carpenter's **s**?
Matt	16:13	the **S** of Man, am?"
Matt	16:16	the **S** of the living God."
Matt	20:18	and the **S** of Man will be
Matt	20:30	O Lord, **S** of David!"
Matt	21: 9	Hosanna to the **S** of David!
Matt	22:42	Whose **S** is He?" They said
Matt	23:15	make him twice as much a **s**
Matt	23:35	**s** of Berechiah, whom you
Matt	24:27	will the coming of the **S** of
Matt	24:30	Then the sign of the **S** of Man
Matt	26:63	the **S** of God!"
Matt	27:54	Truly this was the **S** of
Matt	28:19	of the Father and of the **S**
Mark	1: 1	Jesus Christ, the **S** of God.
Mark	1:19	He saw James the **s** of
Mark	2: 5	said to the paralytic, "**S**,
Mark	2:14	He saw Levi the **s** of
Mark	3:11	You are the **S** of God."
Mark	5: 7	**S** of the Most High God? I
Mark	6: 3	the **S** of Mary, and brother
Mark	14:61	the **S** of the Blessed?"
Mark	15:39	Truly this Man was the **S** of
Luke	1:13	Elizabeth will bear you a **s**,
Luke	1:31	womb and bring forth a **S**,
Luke	1:32	and will be called the **S** of
Luke	1:35	be born will be called the **S**
Luke	1:36	has also conceived a **s** in
Luke	2: 7	forth her firstborn **S**,
Luke	2:48	His mother said to Him, "**S**,
Luke	3:23	(as was supposed) the **s** of
Luke	3:38	son of Adam, the **s** of God.
Luke	6:16	Judas the **s** of James, and
Luke	10: 6	And if a **s** of peace is there,
Luke	12:53	will be divided against **s**
Luke	12:53	be divided against son and **s**
Luke	15:13	the younger **s** gathered all
Luke	15:19	worthy to be called your **s**.
Luke	15:25	Now his older **s** was in the
Luke	17:30	it be in the day when the **S**
Luke	18: 8	when the **S** of Man comes,
Luke	18:38	**S** of David, have mercy on
Luke	20:44	how is He then his **S**?
Luke	22:48	are you betraying the **S** of
John	1:18	time. The only begotten **S**,
John	1:42	You are Simon the **s** of Jonah.

John	1:49	You are the **S** of God! You
John	1:51	and descending upon the **S**
John	3:14	even so must the **S** of Man be
John	3:16	He gave His only begotten **S**,
John	3:17	For God did not send His **S**
John	3:18	name of the only begotten **S**
John	3:35	"The Father loves the **S**,
John	3:36	He who believes in the **S** has
John	3:36	who does not believe the **S**
John	4: 5	that Jacob gave to his **s**
John	4:50	your **s** lives." So the man
John	5:20	"For the Father loves the **S**,
John	6:53	you eat the flesh of the **S** of
John	6:62	if you should see the **S** of
John	8:36	Therefore if the **S** makes you
John	9:20	"We know that this is our **s**,
John	10:36	I am the **S** of God'?
John	12:23	hour has come that the **S** of
John	12:34	The **S** of Man must be lifted
John	17:12	of them is lost except the **s**
John	19:26	behold your **s**!"
John	21:15	**s** of Jonah, do you love Me
Acts	4:36	(which is translated **S** of
Acts	8:37	that Jesus Christ is the **S**
Acts	13:10	you **s** of the devil, you
Acts	13:33	Psalm: 'You are My **S**,
Acts	23: 6	the **s** of a Pharisee;
Rom	1: 4	and declared to be the **S**
Rom	1: 9	in the gospel of His **S**,
Rom	5:10	through the death of His **S**,
Rom	8: 3	did by sending His own **S**
Rom	8:29	to the image of His **S**,
Rom	8:32	who did not spare His own **S**,
Rom	9: 9	Sarah shall have a **s**.
1Co	4:17	is my beloved and faithful **s**
Gal	1:16	to reveal His **S** in me, that I
Gal	2:20	I live by faith in the **S** of
Gal	4: 4	come, God sent forth His **S**,
Gal	4: 6	forth the Spirit of His **S**
Gal	4: 7	no longer a slave but a **s**,
Gal	4: 7	slave but a son, and if a **s**,
Gal	4:30	the bondwoman and her **s**,
Col	1:13	into the kingdom of the **S**
1Th	1:10	and to wait for His **S** from
2Th	2: 3	the **s** of perdition,
1Ti	1: 2	a true **s** in the faith:
2Ti	1: 2	To Timothy, a beloved **s**:
Heb	1: 2	days spoken to us by His **S**,
Heb	1: 5	say: "You are My **S**,
Heb	1: 5	shall be to Me a **S**"?
Heb	1: 8	But to the **S** He says:
Heb	2: 6	Or the **s** of man that
Heb	5: 5	to Him: "You are My **S**,
Heb	5: 8	though He was a **S**,
Heb	7: 3	but made like the **S** of God,
Heb	10:29	who has trampled the **S** of
Heb	11:17	up his only begotten **s**,
Heb	11:24	refused to be called the **s**
Heb	12: 5	you as to sons: "My **s**,
Heb	12: 6	And scourges every **s**
Jas	2:21	when he offered Isaac his **s**
2Pe	1:17	"This is My beloved **S**,
1Jn	1: 3	the Father and with His **S**
1Jn	1: 7	blood of Jesus Christ His **S**
1Jn	4: 9	has sent His only begotten **S**
1Jn	4:14	the Father has sent the **S**
1Jn	4:15	that Jesus is the **S** of God,
1Jn	5:10	He who believes in the **S** of
1Jn	5:11	and this life is in His **S**.
1Jn	5:12	He who has the **S** has life; he
Rev	1:13	lampstands One like the **S**
Rev	21: 7	his God and he shall be My **s**.

SON-IN-LAW (*see* SON, SONS-IN-LAW)

1Sa	18:18	that I should be **s** to the

1Sa	22:14	David, who is the king's **s**,

SON'S (*see* SON)

Gen	27:25	and I will eat of my **s** game,
Prov	30: 4	and what is His **S** name, If

SONG (*see* SING, SONGS)

Ex	15: 1	of Israel sang this **s** to
Ex	15: 2	LORD is my strength and **s**,
Judg	5:12	sing a **s**! Arise, Barak, and
2Sa	1:18	children of Judah the **S**
Ps	33: 3	Sing to Him a new **s**;
Ps	40: 3	He has put a new **s** in my
Ps	42: 8	And in the night His **s**
Ps	77: 6	I call to remembrance my **s**
Ps	96: 1	sing to the LORD a new **s**!
Ps	98: 1	sing to the LORD a new **s**!
Ps	118:14	LORD is my strength and **s**,
Ps	137: 3	away captive asked of us a **s**,
Ps	137: 4	shall we sing the LORD's **s**
Song	1: 1	The **s** of songs, which is
Is	5: 1	to my Well-beloved A **s** of
Is	12: 2	LORD, is my strength and **s**;
Is	25: 5	The **s** of the terrible ones
Is	42:10	Sing to the LORD a new **s**,
Rev	5: 9	And they sang a new **s**,
Rev	14: 3	They sang as it were a new **s**
Rev	15: 3	They sing the **s** of Moses, the
Rev	15: 3	and the **s** of the Lamb,

SONGS (*see* SONG)

1Ki	4:32	and his **s** were one thousand
Neh	12:46	and **s** of praise and
Job	35:10	Who gives **s** in the night,
Ps	32: 7	shall surround me with **s** of
Ps	137: 3	Sing us one of the **s** of
Song	1: 1	The song of **s**,
Is	38:20	we will sing my **s** with
Amos	5:23	from Me the noise of your **s**,
Eph	5:19	and hymns and spiritual **s**,
Col	3:16	and hymns and spiritual **s**,

SONS (*see* SON, SONS')

Gen	5: 4	and he had **s** and daughters.
Gen	6: 2	that the **s** of God saw the
Gen	6:10	And Noah begot three **s**:
Gen	6:18	go into the ark—you, your **s**,
Gen	10: 2	The **s** of Japheth were
Gen	10: 6	The **s** of Ham were Cush,
Gen	10:22	The **s** of Shem were Elam,
Gen	11: 5	and the tower which the **s**
Gen	23: 3	and spoke to the **s** of Heth,
Gen	25: 9	And his **s** Isaac and Ishmael
Gen	31:17	Jacob rose and set his **s**
Gen	32:22	servants, and his eleven **s**,
Gen	35:22	Now the **s** of Jacob were
Gen	35:23	the **s** of Leah were Reuben,
Gen	35:24	the **s** of Rachel were Joseph
Gen	35:25	the **s** of Bilhah, Rachel's
Gen	35:26	and the **s** of Zilpah, Leah's
Gen	41:50	to Joseph were born two **s**
Gen	42:11	"We are all one man's **s**;
Gen	49:32	were purchased from the **s**
Ex	13:15	all the firstborn of my **s** I
Ex	28: 1	priest, Aaron and Aaron's **s**:
Ex	29: 9	consecrate Aaron and his **s**.
Ex	29:20	of the right ear of his **s**,
Ex	34:16	their gods and make your **s**
Lev	10: 6	Eleazar and Ithamar, his **s**,
Lev	16: 1	the death of the two **s** of
Num	3:17	These were the **s** of Levi by
Num	3:18	are the names of the **s** of
Num	3:19	And the **s** of Kohath by their
Num	3:20	And the **s** of Merari by their
Num	4: 2	Take a census of the **s**
Num	18: 9	most holy for you and your **s**.
Num	24:17	And destroy all the **s** of

Deut 28:53 the flesh of your **s** and your
Judg 1:20 from there the three **s** of
Judg 8:19 the **s** of my mother. As the
Judg 8:30 Gideon had seventy **s** who were
Judg 14:16 posed a riddle to the **s** of
Judg 14:17 the riddle to the **s** of her
Ruth 1: 5 the woman survived her two **s**
Ruth 4:15 better to you than seven **s**,
1Sa 1: 8 not better to you than ten **s**?
1Sa 2:12 Now the **s** of Eli were
1Sa 8: 1 was old that he made his **s**
1Sa 8: 3 But his **s** did not walk in his
1Sa 16: 5 consecrated Jesse and his **s**,
1Sa 17:12 Jesse, and who had eight **s**.
1Sa 31: 8 found Saul and his three **s**
1Sa 31:12 Saul and the bodies of his **s**
2Sa 7:14 and with the blows of the **s**
2Ki 2: 3 Now the **s** of the prophets who
2Ki 10: 1 Now Ahab had seventy **s** in
2Ki 10: 1 those who reared Ahab's **s**,
2Ki 10: 8 the heads of the king's **s**.
2Ki 10:13 sons of the king and the **s**
1Ch 10: 8 they found Saul and his **s**
1Ch 23: 6 into divisions among the **s**
2Ch 32:33 in the upper tombs of the **s**
Ezra 3:10 the **s** of Asaph, with
Esth 9:10 the ten **s** of Haman the son of
Job 1: 2 And seven **s** and three
Job 1: 4 And his **s** would go and feast
Job 1: 5 It may be that my **s** have
Job 1: 6 there was a day when the **s**
Job 38: 7 And all the **s** of God
Job 42:13 He also had seven **s** and three
Ps 4: 2 O you **s** of men, Will you
Ps 45:16 Your fathers shall be Your **s**,
Ps 89:30 If his **s** forsake My law And
Ps 106:37 even sacrificed their **s**
Ps 137: 7 against the **s** of Edom The
Eccl 2: 3 what was good for the **s** of
Song 1: 6 My mother's **s** were angry
Is 43: 6 keep them back!' Bring My **s**
Is 49:22 They shall bring your **s** in
Is 52:14 His form more than the **s** of
Is 62: 5 So shall your **s** marry you;
Jer 7:31 to burn their **s** and their
Jer 19: 5 to burn their **s** with fire
Jer 19: 9 to eat the flesh of their **s**
Jer 35:16 Surely the **s** of Jonadab the
Ezek 5:10 fathers shall eat their **s**
Ezek 40:46 these are the **s** of Zadok,
Ezek 40:46 from the **s** of Levi, who come
Dan 1: 6 from among those of the **s**
Dan 5:21 he was driven from the **s** of
Hos 1:10 You are **s** of the living
Joel 2:28 Your **s** and your daughters
Zech 9:13 O Zion, Against your **s**,
Mal 3: 3 He will purify the **s** of
Mal 3: 6 O **s** of Jacob.
Matt 5: 9 For they shall be called **s**
Matt 5:45 that you may be **s** of your
Matt 8:12 But the **s** of the kingdom will
Matt 13:38 but the tares are the **s** of
Matt 20:21 Grant that these two **s** of
Matt 26:37 Him Peter and the two **s** of
Mark 3:17 S of Thunder";
Mark 3:28 sins will be forgiven the **s**
Luke 6:35 and you will be **s** of the
Luke 11:19 by whom do your **s** cast them
Luke 16: 8 For the **s** of this world are
Luke 16: 8 their generation than the **s**
Luke 20:34 The **s** of this age marry and
Luke 20:36 being **s** of the resurrection.
John 12:36 that you may become **s** of
Rom 8:14 these are **s** of God.
Rom 9:26 they shall be called **s**

Gal 3: 7 who are of faith are **s** of
Gal 3:26 For you are all **s** of God
Gal 4: 5 receive the adoption as **s**.
Gal 4:22 that Abraham had two **s**:
Eph 1: 5 us to adoption as **s** by
Eph 2: 2 who now works in the **s** of
Eph 5: 6 of God comes upon the **s** of
Col 3: 6 of God is coming upon the **s**
1Th 5: 5 You are all **s** of light and
Heb 2:10 in bringing many **s** to glory,
Heb 12: 8 are illegitimate and not **s**.

SONS-IN-LAW (see SON-IN-LAW)
Gen 19:14 went out and spoke to his **s**,

SONS' (see SONS)
Gen 6:18 and your **s** wives with you.

SOON
Matt 21:20 fig tree wither away so **s**?
Mark 1:29 Now as **s** as they had come
Luke 8: 6 and as **s** as it sprang up, it
2Th 2: 2 not to be **s** shaken in mind or

SOOTHING
Gen 8:21 And the LORD smelled a **s**

SOOTHSAYER (see SOOTHSAYERS, SOOTHSAYING)
Deut 18:10 witchcraft, or a **s**,

SOOTHSAYERS (see SOOTHSAYER)
Deut 18:14 dispossess listened to **s**
Dan 2:27 and the **s** cannot declare to

SOOTHSAYING (see SOOTHSAYER)
Lev 19:26 you practice divination or **s**.

SORCERER (see SORCERERS, SORCERY)
Deut 18:10 who interprets omens, or a **s**,
Acts 13: 8 But Elymas the **s** (for so his

SORCERERS (see SORCERER)
Ex 7:11 the wise men and the **s**;
Dan 2: 2 the astrologers, the **s**,

SORCERIES (see SORCERY)
Mic 5:12 I will cut off **s** from your
Acts 8:11 astonished them with his **s**
Rev 9:21 of their murders or their **s**

SORCERY (see SORCERER, SORCERIES)
2Ch 33: 6 used witchcraft and **s**,
Acts 8: 9 who previously practiced **s**
Gal 5:20 idolatry, **s**, hatred,

SORE (see SORES)
Lev 13: 2 his body like a leprous **s**,
Rev 16: 2 and a foul and loathsome **s**

SOREK†
Judg 16: 4 a woman in the Valley of **S**,

SORES (see SORE)
Ex 9: 9 boils that break out in **s**
Is 1: 6 and bruises and putrefying **s**;
Luke 16:20 named Lazarus, full of **s**,

SORROW (see SORROWFUL, SORROWS)
Gen 3:16 greatly multiply your **s** and
Gen 42:38 down my gray hair with **s** to
Ps 13: 2 Having **s** in my heart
Ps 35:12 To the **s** of my soul.
Ps 90:10 boast is only labor and **s**;
Ps 116: 3 me; I found trouble and **s**.
Prov 10:22 And He adds no **s** with it.
Prov 22: 8 sows iniquity will reap **s**,
Prov 23:29 Who has woe? Who has **s**?
Eccl 1:18 knowledge increases **s**.
Is 35:10 And **s** and sighing shall
Is 51:11 **S** and sighing shall flee
Jer 30:15 Your **s** is incurable.
Luke 22:45 found them sleeping from **s**.
John 16: 6 **s** has filled your heart.

Rom	9: 2	that I have great s and
2Co	2: 1	not come again to you in s.
2Co	2: 3	I should have s over those
2Co	7:10	For godly s produces
1Th	4:13	lest you s as others who
Rev	21: 4	be no more death, nor s,

SORROWFUL (see SORROW)

Ps	69:29	But I am poor and s;
Matt	17:23	And they were exceedingly s.
Matt	19:22	that saying, he went away s,
Matt	26:38	"My soul is exceedingly s,

SORROWS (see SORROW)

Ex	3: 7	for I know their s.
Ps	18: 5	The s of Sheol surrounded
Ps	127: 2	late, To eat the bread of s;
Is	13: 8	Pangs and s will take hold
Is	53: 3	A Man of s and acquainted
Is	53: 4	griefs And carried our s;
Matt	24: 8	are the beginning of s.
1Ti	6:10	through with many s.

SORRY

Gen	6: 6	And the LORD was s that He
Mark	6:26	the king was exceedingly s;

SORT

Gen	6:19	shall bring two of every s
Gen	7:14	kind, every bird of every s.
1Co	3:13	of what s it is.
2Ti	3: 6	For of this s are those who

SOSTHENES†

Acts	18:17	Then all the Greeks took S,
1Co	1: 1	and S our brother,

SOUGHT (see SEEK)

Ex	2:15	he s to kill Moses. But
Ex	33: 7	to pass that everyone who s
1Sa	19:10	Then Saul s to pin David to
2Ch	14: 7	because we have s the LORD
Ps	34: 4	I s the LORD, and He heard
Ps	77: 2	the day of my trouble I s
Ps	119:10	my whole heart I have s You;
Ps	119:94	For I have s Your precepts.
Eccl	12:10	The Preacher s to find
Song	3: 1	By night on my bed I s the
Song	3: 1	I s him, but I did not find
Jer	10:21	And have not s the LORD;
Dan	6: 4	the governors and satraps s
Hos	12: 4	and s favor from Him. He
Matt	21:46	But when they s to lay hands
Luke	2:44	and s Him among their
Luke	2:48	Your father and I have s You
Luke	4:42	And the crowd s Him and came
John	7: 1	because the Jews s to kill
John	11:56	Then they s Jesus, and spoke
John	19:12	From then on Pilate s to

SOUL (see SOULS)

Gen	19:20	) and my s shall live."
Gen	27: 4	that my s may bless you
Gen	35:18	as her s was departing (for
Lev	17:11	makes atonement for the s.
Num	30:13	oath to afflict her s,
Deut	4:29	heart and with all your s.
Deut	6: 5	your heart, with all your s,
Judg	5:21	torrent of Kishon. O my s,
Judg	16:16	so that his s was vexed to
1Sa	1:10	she was in bitterness of s,
1Sa	1:15	but have poured out my s
1Sa	1:26	O my lord! As your s lives,
1Sa	18: 1	the s of Jonathan was knit
1Sa	18: 1	Jonathan was knit to the s
1Sa	18: 1	loved him as his own s.
1Sa	18: 3	he loved him as his own s.
2Sa	5: 8	are hated by David's s),

1Ki	17:21	let this child's s come back
Job	7:11	in the bitterness of my s.
Job	10: 1	My s loathes my life; I will
Job	23:13	And whatever His s
Job	30:16	And now my s is poured out
Job	33:18	He keeps back his s from the
Ps	6: 3	My s also is greatly
Ps	11: 5	one who loves violence His s
Ps	16:10	You will not leave my s in
Ps	19: 7	perfect, converting the s;
Ps	23: 3	He restores my s;
Ps	24: 4	has not lifted up his s to
Ps	25: 1	You, O LORD, I lift up my s.
Ps	30: 3	You brought my s up from the
Ps	33:19	To deliver their s from
Ps	33:20	Our s waits for the LORD;
Ps	34: 2	My s shall make its boast in
Ps	34:22	The LORD redeems the s of
Ps	42: 1	So pants my s for You, O
Ps	42: 2	My s thirsts for God, for
Ps	42: 4	I pour out my s within me.
Ps	42: 5	are you cast down, O my s?
Ps	42:11	are you cast down, O my s?
Ps	43: 5	are you cast down, O my s?
Ps	49:15	But God will redeem my s
Ps	56:13	For You have delivered my s
Ps	63: 1	My s thirsts for You; My
Ps	84: 2	My s longs, yes, even faints
Ps	86: 4	You, O Lord, I lift up my s.
Ps	103: 1	Bless the LORD, O my s;
Ps	103:22	Bless the LORD, O my s!
Ps	106:15	sent leanness into their s.
Ps	107: 9	He satisfies the longing s,
Ps	107: 9	And fills the hungry s with
Ps	116: 7	Return to your rest, O my s,
Ps	116: 8	For You have delivered my s
Ps	121: 7	He shall preserve your s.
Ps	123: 4	Our s is exceedingly filled
Ps	130: 6	My s waits for the Lord
Ps	139:14	And that my s knows very
Ps	141: 8	Do not leave my s
Ps	142: 4	me; No one cares for my s.
Prov	2:10	is pleasant to your s,
Prov	3:22	they will be life to your s
Prov	13: 4	The s of a lazy man
Prov	13:19	is sweet to the s,
Prov	16:24	Sweetness to the s and
Prov	21:23	and tongue Keeps his s
Prov	22: 5	He who guards his s will be
Prov	22:25	And set a snare for your s.
Prov	25:25	As cold water to a weary s,
Prov	29:17	will give delight to your s.
Eccl	6: 3	but his s is not satisfied
Is	1:14	your appointed feasts My s
Is	38:15	In the bitterness of my s.
Is	42: 1	My Elect One in whom My s
Is	53:10	When You make His s an
Is	53:11	shall see the labor of His s,
Is	53:12	He poured out His s unto
Is	55: 2	And let your s delight
Is	55: 3	and your s shall live; And
Is	61:10	My s shall be joyful in my
Jer	32:41	My heart and with all My s.
Jer	38:17	then your s shall live; this
Lam	3:20	My s still remembers And
Ezek	18: 4	The s of the father As
Ezek	18: 4	The s who sins shall die.
Ezek	24:21	eyes, the delight of your s;
Jon	2: 5	surrounded me, even to my s;
Jon	2: 7	When my s fainted within me,
Mic	6: 7	my body for the sin of my s?
Matt	10:28	body but cannot kill the s.
Matt	10:28	is able to destroy both s
Matt	12:18	Beloved in whom My s
Matt	16:26	world, and loses his own s?

Matt 16:26 give in exchange for his **s**?
Matt 22:37 heart, with all your **s**,
Matt 26:38 My **s** is exceedingly
Luke   1:46 My **s** magnifies the Lord,
Luke   2:35 pierce through your own **s**
Luke 12:19 I will say to my soul, "**S**,
Luke 12:20 Fool! This night your **s** will
John 12:27 Now My **s** is troubled, and
Acts   2:43 Then fear came upon every **s**,
Acts   4:32 were of one heart and one **s**;
Rom   13: 1 Let every **s** be subject to the
2Co   1:23 God as witness against my **s**,
1Th   5:23 and may your whole spirit, **s**,
Heb   4:12 even to the division of **s**
Heb   6:19 have as an anchor of the **s**,
Heb   10:38 My **s** has no pleasure
Heb   10:39 to the saving of the **s**.
Jas   5:20 of his way will save a **s**
1Pe   2:11 which war against the **s**,

SOULS (see SOUL)
Lev   17:11 to make atonement for your **s**;
Num   16:38 sinned against their own **s**,
Ps   72:13 And will save the **s** of the
Ps   97:10 evil! He preserves the **s**
Prov 11:30 And he who wins **s** is wise.
Prov 14:25 A true witness delivers **s**,
Jer   6:16 will find rest for your **s**.
Ezek 18: 4 all **s** are Mine; The soul that
Matt 11:29 will find rest for your **s**.
Luke 21:19 your patience possess your **s**.
Acts   2:41 day about three thousand **s**
Jas   1:21 which is able to save your **s**.
1Pe   1: 9 salvation of your **s**.
1Pe   2:25 and Overseer of your **s**.
1Pe   3:20 a few, that is, eight **s**,
2Pe   2:14 sin, enticing unstable **s**.
Rev   6: 9 I saw under the altar the **s**

SOUND (see SOUNDED, SOUNDING, SOUNDNESS,
   SOUNDS)
Gen   3: 8 And they heard the **s** of the
Ps   89:15 who know the joyful **s**!
Ps   98: 5 With the harp and the **s** of
Ps   150: 3 Praise Him with the **s** of the
Prov   3:21 Keep **s** wisdom and
Prov 14:30 A **s** heart is life to the
Eccl 12: 4 And the **s** of grinding is
Eccl 12: 4 When one rises up at the **s**
Dan   3: 5 at the time you hear the **s**
Amos   6: 5 Who sing idly to the **s** of
Matt 24:31 His angels with a great **s**
Luke 15:27 has received him safe and **s**,
John   3: 8 and you hear the **s** of it,
Acts   2: 2 And suddenly there came a **s**
Rom   10:18 Their **s** has gone out to
1Co   14: 8 trumpet makes an uncertain **s**,
1Co   15:52 For the trumpet will **s**,
2Co   5:13 or if we are of **s** mind, it
1Ti   1:10 thing that is contrary to **s**
2Ti   1: 7 and of love and of a **s** mind.
2Ti   1:13 Hold fast the pattern of **s**
2Ti   4: 3 when they will not endure **s**
Heb   12:19 and the **s** of a trumpet and
Rev   1:15 and His voice as the **s** of
Rev   19: 6 as the **s** of many waters and

SOUNDED (see SOUND)
Ex   19:19 the blast of the trumpet **s**
Luke   1:44 voice of your greeting **s** in
1Th   1: 8 the word of the Lord has **s**
Rev   8: 7 The first angel **s**:

SOUNDING (see SOUND)
1Co   13: 1 I have become **s** brass or a

SOUNDNESS (see SOUND)
Ps   38: 3 There is no **s** in my flesh
Is   1: 6 There is no **s** in it,

SOUNDS (see SOUND)
1Co   14: 7 make a distinction in the **s**,

SOUR
Jer   31:29 The fathers have eaten **s**
Ezek 18: 2 The fathers have eaten **s**
Matt 27:34 they gave Him **s** wine mingled

SOUTH (see SOUTHWARD)
Gen   12: 9 going on still toward the **S**.
Gen   28:14 east, to the north and the **s**;
Job   9: 9 And the chambers of the **s**;
Eccl   1: 6 The wind goes toward the **s**,
Dan   8: 9 great toward the **s**,
Dan   11: 9 kingdom of the king of the **S**,
Matt 12:42 The queen of the **S** will rise
Luke 12:55 And when you see the **s** wind

SOUTHWARD (see SOUTH)
Gen   13:14 where you are—northward, **s**,
Dan   8: 4 westward, northward, and **s**,

SOW (see SOWED, SOWER, SOWING, SOWN, SOWS)
Ex   23:10 Six years you shall **s** your
Job   4: 8 who plow iniquity And **s**
Ps   126: 5 Those who **s** in tears Shall
Jer   4: 3 And do not **s** among thorns.
Jer   31:27 that I will **s** the house of
Hos   2:23 Then I will **s** her for Myself
Hos   8: 7 They **s** the wind, And reap
Zech 10: 9 I will **s** them among the
Matt   6:26 for they neither **s** nor reap
Matt 13: 3 a sower went out to **s**.
Matt 13:27 did you not **s** good seed in
Luke 19:21 and reap what you did not **s**.

SOWED (see SOW)
Judg   9:45 he demolished the city and **s**
Matt 13: 4 "And as he **s**, some seed fell

SOWER (see SOW)
Is   55:10 it may give seed to the **s**
Matt 13: 3 a **s** went out to sow.
Matt 13:18 hear the parable of the **s**:
2Co   9:10 who supplies seed to the **s**,

SOWING (see SOW)
Ps   126: 6 weeping, Bearing seed for **s**,

SOWN (see SOW)
Deut 21: 4 is neither plowed nor **s**,
Is   40:24 Scarcely shall they be **s**,
Jer   2: 2 wilderness, In a land not **s**.
Matt 13:19 snatches away what was **s** in
Matt 25:24 reaping where you have not **s**,
Mark   4:15 wayside where the word is **s**.
1Co   9:11 If we have **s** spiritual things
1Co   15:42 The body is **s** in
Jas   3:18 fruit of righteousness is **s**

SOWS (see SOW)
Prov   6:14 He **s** discord.
Prov 22: 8 He who **s** iniquity will reap
Matt 13:37 He who **s** the good seed is the
Mark   4:14 The sower **s** the word.
John   4:37 One **s** and another reaps.'
2Co   9: 6 He who **s** sparingly will also
Gal   6: 7 mocked; for whatever a man **s**,
Gal   6: 8 For he who **s** to his flesh

SPACE
Job   26: 7 out the north over empty **s**;

SPAIN†
Rom   15:24 whenever I journey to **S**,
Rom   15:28 shall go by way of you to **S**.

SPAN
1Sa 17: 4 was six cubits and a s.
Is   40:12 Measured heaven with a s

SPARE (*see* SPARED, SPARES, SPARINGLY)
Gen 18:24 destroy the place and not s
Job   2: 6 but s his life."
Ps   72:13 He will s the poor and
Ps   78:50 He did not s their soul
Jer 51: 3 Do not s her young men;
Ezek 5:11 you; My eye will not s,
Joel 2:17 S Your people, O LORD, And
Luke 15:17 have bread enough and to s,
Rom   8:32 He who did not s His own Son,
Rom 11:21 For if God did not s the
2Pe   2: 4 For if God did not s the
2Pe   2: 5 and did not s the ancient

SPARED (*see* SPARE)
Josh 6:25 And Joshua s Rahab the
1Sa 15: 9 But Saul and the people s

SPARES (*see* SPARE)
Prov 13:24 He who s his rod hates his
Prov 17:27 He who has knowledge s his

SPARINGLY† (*see* SPARE)
2Co   9: 6 He who sows s will also reap

SPARKLES†
Prov 23:31 When it s in the cup,

SPARKS
Job   5: 7 As the s fly upward.

SPARROW (*see* SPARROWS)
Ps   84: 3 Even the s has found a home,

SPARROWS (*see* SPARROW)
Matt 10:29 Are not two s sold for a
Matt 10:31 of more value than many s.

SPAT (*see* SPIT)
Matt 26:67 Then they s in His face and
Mark 7:33 and He s and touched his
John 9: 6 He s on the ground and made

SPATTERED†
2Ki   9:33 and some of her blood s on

SPEAK (*see* SPEAKING, SPEAKS, SPEECH, SPOKE, SPOKEN)
Gen 18:27 taken it upon myself to s
Gen 37: 4 hated him and could not s
Ex   4:14 I know that he can s well.
Ex   4:15 Now you shall s to him and
Ex   19: 6 the words which you shall s
Ex   20:19 but let not God s with us,
Ex   23:22 voice and do all that I s,
Lev   1: 2 S to the children of Israel,
Num 12: 6 I s to him in a dream.
Num 12: 8 I s with him face to face,
Deut 18:18 and He shall s to them all
Deut 18:20 prophet who presumes to s a
Deut 18:20 have not commanded him to s,
Deut 32: 1 ear, O heavens, and I will s;
1Sa   3:10 And Samuel answered, "S,
1Sa 25:24 let your maidservant s in
2Sa 19: 7 go out and s comfort to your
1Ki   2:17 Please s to King Solomon, for
1Ki 22:13 and s encouragement."
2Ki 18:26 and do not s to us in Hebrew
2Ki 19:10 Thus you shall s to Hezekiah
2Ch 35:25 men and the singing women s
Neh 13:24 and could not s the language
Esth 1:22 and s in the language of his
Job   2:10 You s as one of the foolish
Job 10: 1 I will s in the bitterness
Job 11: 5 But oh, that God would s,
Job 12: 8 Or s to the earth, and it
Job 13: 3 But I would s to the

Job 13:22 I will answer; Or let me s,
Job 32: 4 Elihu had waited to s to
Job 32: 7 I said, 'Age should s,
Job 33:31 your peace, and I will s.
Job 42: 4 please, and let me s;
Ps   2: 5 Then He shall s to them in
Ps   17:10 With their mouths they s
Ps   28: 3 Who s peace to their
Ps   31:18 Which s insolent things
Ps   41: 5 My enemies s evil of me:
Ps   49: 3 My mouth shall s wisdom,
Ps   51: 4 may be found just when You s,
Ps   71:10 For my enemies s against me;
Ps   77: 4 so troubled that I cannot s.
Ps   85: 8 For He will s peace To His
Ps 115: 5 mouths, but they do not s;
Ps 119:46 I will s of Your testimonies
Ps 119:172 My tongue shall s of Your
Ps 120: 7 for peace; But when I s,
Prov 8: 6 for I will s of excellent
Eccl 3: 7 silence, And a time to s;
Is   8:10 S the word, but it will not
Is   19:18 in the land of Egypt will s
Is   30:10 S to us smooth things,
Is   40: 2 S comfort to Jerusalem, and
Is   41: 1 come near, then let them s;
Is   45:19 s righteousness, I declare
Is   50: 4 I should know how to s A
Jer   1: 6 GOD! Behold, I cannot s,
Jer   1: 7 I command you, you shall s.
Jer   1:17 And s to them all that I
Jer   8: 6 But they do not s aright.
Jer   9: 5 taught their tongue to s
Jer 12: 6 Even though they s smooth
Jer 18: 7 The instant I s concerning a
Jer 20: 9 Nor s anymore in His
Jer 23:16 They s a vision of their
Jer 34: 2 Go and s to Zedekiah king of
Jer 43: 2 You s falsely! The LORD our
Ezek 2: 7 You shall s My words to them,
Ezek 3:18 nor s to warn the wicked
Ezek 17: 2 and s a parable to the house
Ezek 20: 3 s to the elders of Israel,
Ezek 24:27 you shall s and no longer be
Dan   7:25 He shall s pompous words
Dan 11:36 shall s blasphemies against
Hos   1: 2 When the LORD began to s
Zech 9:10 He shall s peace to the
Matt 8: 8 But only s a word, and my
Matt 10:19 how or what you should s.
Matt 10:20 "for it is not you who s,
Matt 12:36 every idle word men may s,
Matt 13:34 a parable He did not s to
Mark 7:37 to hear and the mute to s.
Mark 9:39 My name can soon afterward s
Mark 16:17 they will s with new
Luke 1:20 be mute and not able to s
Luke 6:26 Woe to you when all men s
Luke 7:15 dead sat up and began to s.
John 3:11 We s what We know and
John 4:26 I who s to you am He."
John 6:63 The words that I s to you
John 7:17 is from God or whether I s
John 9:21 He will s for himself."
Acts 2: 4 Holy Spirit and began to s
Acts 2: 6 everyone heard them s in
Acts 4:20 For we cannot but s the
Acts 5:40 that they should not s in
Acts 10:46 For they heard them s with
Acts 21:37 Can you s Greek?
Acts 26: 1 You are permitted to s for
Rom   3: 5 (I s as a man.)
Rom   6:19 I s in human terms because
1Co   1:10 that you all s the same
1Co   2: 6 we s wisdom among those who

1Co 12:30 Do all **s** with tongues? Do
1Co 13: 1 Though I **s** with the tongues
1Co 14:19 the church I would rather **s**
1Co 14:23 and all **s** with tongues, and
1Co 14:35 is shameful for women to **s**
2Co 6:13 in return for the same (I **s**
2Co 12: 6 for I will **s** the truth. But
Eph 6:20 boldly, as I ought to **s**.
Phil 1:14 are much more bold to **s** the
Tit 3: 2 to **s** evil of no one, to be
Heb 9: 5 things we cannot now **s** in
Jas 1:19 be swift to hear, slow to **s**,
Jas 4:11 Do not **s** evil of one
1Pe 4:11 let him **s** as the oracles
2Jn 12 I hope to come to you and **s**

SPEAKING (see SPEAK)
Gen 18:33 as soon as He had finished **s**
Job 1:16 While he was still **s**,
Ps 34:13 And your lips from **s**
Ezek 1:28 and I heard a voice of One **s**.
Dan 7: 8 and a mouth **s** pompous words.
Matt 15:31 when they saw the mute **s**,
John 2:21 But He was **s** of the temple of
Acts 1: 3 during forty days and **s** of
Acts 2:11 we hear them **s** in our own
Acts 26:14 I heard a voice **s** to me and
1Co 14: 6 if I come to you **s** with
1Co 14: 9 For you will be **s** into the
Eph 4:15 **s** the truth in love, may
Eph 5:19 **s** to one another in psalms
1Ti 2: 7 I am **s** the truth in Christ
1Pe 3:10 And his lips from **s**

SPEAKS (see SPEAK)
Ex 33:11 as a man **s** to his friend.
Deut 18:20 or who **s** in the name of
Deut 18:22 when a prophet **s** in the name
Job 2:10 one of the foolish women **s**.
Ps 12: 3 And the tongue that **s**
Ps 15: 2 And **s** the truth in his
Matt 12:32 Anyone who **s** a word against
Matt 12:34 of the heart the mouth **s**.
Luke 5:21 Who is this who **s**
John 7:26 But look! He **s** boldly, and
Rom 10: 6 righteousness of faith **s** in
1Co 14: 2 For he who **s** in a tongue does
1Co 14:27 If anyone **s** in a tongue, let
Heb 11: 4 it he being dead still **s**.
Heb 12:24 blood of sprinkling that **s**
Heb 12:25 you do not refuse Him who **s**.
Jas 4:11 He who **s** evil of a brother
1Pe 4:11 If anyone **s**, let him speak

SPEAR (see SPEARS)
1Sa 17:47 not save with sword and **s**;
1Sa 19:10 and he drove the **s** into the
John 19:34 pierced His side with a **s**,

SPEARS (see SPEAR)
1Sa 13:19 the Hebrews make swords or **s**.
Is 2: 4 And their **s** into pruning
Joel 3:10 your pruning hooks into **s**;
Mic 4: 3 And their **s** into pruning

SPECIAL
Ex 19: 5 then you shall be a **s**
Deut 7: 6 a **s** treasure above all the
Deut 26:18 proclaimed you to be His **s**
Tit 2:14 for Himself His own **s**
1Pe 2: 9 His own **s** people, that you

SPECIES
Gen 7: 3 to keep the **s** alive on the

SPECK
Matt 7: 3 why do you look at the **s** in

SPECKLED
Gen 30:32 and the spotted and **s** among
Gen 31: 8 then all the flocks bore **s**.

SPECTACLE
1Co 4: 9 for we have been made a **s** to
Col 2:15 He made a public **s** of them,

SPEECH (see SPEAK, SPEECHLESS)
Gen 11: 1 had one language and one **s**.
Gen 11: 7 understand one another's **s**.
Ex 4:10 but I am slow of **s** and slow
Deut 32: 2 My **s** distill as the dew,
1Sa 16:18 a man of war, prudent in **s**,
Ps 19: 2 Day unto day utters **s**,
Ps 19: 3 There is no **s** nor language
Is 33:19 A people of obscure **s**,
Ezek 3: 5 to a people of unfamiliar **s**
Matt 26:73 for your **s** betrays you."
Mark 7:32 had an impediment in his **s**,
John 16:29 and using no figure of **s**!
Col 4: 6 Let your **s** always be with

SPEECHLESS (see SPEECH)
Acts 9: 7 journeyed with him stood **s**,

SPEED (see SPEEDILY)
Acts 17:15 to come to him with all **s**,

SPEEDILY (see SPEED)
Ps 31: 2 ear to me, Deliver me **s**;
Ps 102: 2 day that I call, answer me **s**.
Is 58: 8 healing shall spring forth **s**,

SPELLS†
Deut 18:11 "or one who conjures **s**,

SPEND (see SPENT)
Gen 19: 2 your servant's house and **s**
Judg 19: 9 please **s** the night. See, the
Is 55: 2 Why do you **s** money for what
Luke 10:35 him; and whatever more you **s**,
1Co 16: 6 or even **s** the winter with
2Co 12:15 And I will very gladly **s** and
Jas 4: 3 that you may **s** it on your
Jas 4:13 **s** a year there, buy and

SPENT (see SPEND)
Judg 19:11 Jebus, and the day was far **s**;
Ezek 5:13 when I have **s** My fury upon
Mark 5:26 She had **s** all that she had
Mark 6:35 When the day was now far **s**,
Luke 8:43 who had **s** all her livelihood
Luke 15:14 But when he had **s** all, there
Luke 24:29 and the day is far **s**.
Acts 17:21 foreigners who were there **s**
Rom 13:12 The night is far **s**,
2Co 12:15 very gladly spend and be **s**

SPICES
Gen 37:25 with their camels, bearing **s**,
Ex 25: 6 and **s** for the anointing oil
Song 5:13 cheeks are like a bed of **s**,
Song 8:14 stag On the mountains of **s**.
Mark 16: 1 James, and Salome bought **s**,

SPIED (see SPY)
Num 13:21 So they went up and **s** out
Josh 7: 2 So the men went up and **s**

SPIES (see SPY)
Gen 42:31 honest men; we are not **s**.
Num 13:32 which we have gone as **s** is
Josh 6:23 the young men who had been **s**

SPIKENARD
Song 1:12 My **s** sends forth its
Mark 14: 3 of very costly oil of **s**.

SPILLED
2Sa 14:14 and become like water **s** on
Mark 2:22 the wineskins, the wine is **s**,

SPIN†

Matt	6:28	they neither toil nor s;
Luke	12:27	they neither toil nor s;

SPINDLE†

Prov	31:19	And her hand holds the s.

SPIRIT (*see* HOLY, SPIRITS)

Gen	1: 2	And the S of God was
Gen	6: 3	My S shall not strive with
Gen	41:38	a man in whom is the S of
Ex	28: 3	I have filled with the s of
Ex	31: 3	I have filled him with the S
Num	5:14	if the s of jealousy comes
Num	11:29	the LORD would put His S
Num	27:18	you, a man in whom is the S,
Judg	3:10	The S of the LORD came upon
Judg	11:29	Then the S of the LORD came
Judg	15:19	and his s returned, and he
1Sa	10:10	then the S of God came upon
1Sa	11: 6	Then the S of God came upon
1Sa	16:14	and a distressing s from the
1Sa	28:13	I saw a s ascending out of
2Sa	23: 2	The S of the LORD spoke by
1Ki	22:21	Then a s came forward and
1Ki	22:22	go out and be a lying s in
2Ki	2: 9	a double portion of your s
2Ki	2:15	The s of Elijah rests on
2Ch	36:22	the LORD stirred up the s
Ezra	1: 1	the LORD stirred up the s
Neh	9:30	against them by Your S in
Job	4:15	Then a s passed before my
Job	33: 4	The S of God has made me,
Ps	31: 5	Your hand I commit my s;
Ps	32: 2	And in whose s there is
Ps	34:18	such as have a contrite s.
Ps	51:10	And renew a steadfast s
Ps	51:11	And do not take Your Holy S
Ps	51:12	me by Your generous S.
Ps	51:17	of God are a broken s,
Ps	104:30	You send forth Your S,
Ps	106:33	they rebelled against His S,
Ps	139: 7	Where can I go from Your S?
Ps	146: 4	His s departs, he returns to
Prov	1:23	I will pour out my s on you;
Prov	16:18	And a haughty s before a
Prov	16:19	to be of a humble s with
Prov	16:32	And he who rules his s than
Prov	18:14	But who can bear a broken s?
Prov	20:27	The s of a man is the lamp
Eccl	7: 8	The patient in s is better
Eccl	12: 7	And the s will return to
Is	4: 4	by the s of judgment and by
Is	11: 2	The S of the LORD shall
Is	11: 2	The S of wisdom and
Is	30: 1	plans, but not of My S,
Is	31: 3	horses are flesh, and not s.
Is	32:15	Until the S is poured upon
Is	40:13	Who has directed the S of
Is	42: 1	delights! I have put My S
Is	44: 3	I will pour My S on your
Is	48:16	now the Lord GOD and His S
Is	57:15	has a contrite and humble s,
Is	57:15	To revive the s of the
Is	61: 1	The S of the Lord GOD is
Is	63:10	and grieved His Holy S;
Is	63:11	is He who put His Holy S
Is	66: 2	is poor and of a contrite s,
Ezek	2: 2	Then the S entered me when He
Ezek	8: 3	and the S lifted me up
Ezek	11:19	and I will put a new s
Ezek	11:24	Then the S took me up and
Ezek	18:31	a new heart and a new s.
Ezek	36:26	a new heart and put a new s
Ezek	36:27	I will put My S within you
Ezek	37: 1	and brought me out in the S
Ezek	37:14	I will put My S in you, and
Dan	2: 1	and his s was so troubled
Dan	4: 8	in him is the S of the Holy
Dan	4:18	for the S of the Holy God
Joel	2:28	That I will pour out My S
Joel	2:29	I will pour out My S in
Zech	4: 6	nor by power, but by My S,
Zech	6: 8	have given rest to My S in
Zech	13: 2	prophets and the unclean s
Mal	2:15	take heed to your s,
Mal	2:16	take heed to your s,
Matt	1:18	with child of the Holy S.
Matt	3:11	baptize you with the Holy S
Matt	3:16	and He saw the S of God
Matt	4: 1	Jesus was led up by the S
Matt	5: 3	are the poor in s,
Matt	12:18	I will put My S upon
Matt	12:28	I cast out demons by the S
Matt	12:31	the blasphemy against the S
Matt	12:32	speaks against the Holy S,
Matt	26:41	The s indeed is willing,
Matt	27:50	voice, and yielded up His s.
Matt	28:19	of the Son and of the Holy S,
Mark	1:10	heavens parting and the S
Mark	1:12	Immediately the S drove Him
Mark	8:12	He sighed deeply in His s,
Mark	14:38	The s indeed is willing,
Luke	1:15	be filled with the Holy S,
Luke	1:35	The Holy S will come upon
Luke	1:41	was filled with the Holy S.
Luke	1:47	And my s has rejoiced in God
Luke	1:67	was filled with the Holy S,
Luke	2:25	and the Holy S was upon him.
Luke	2:26	to him by the Holy S that
Luke	4: 1	being filled with the Holy S,
Luke	4:18	The S of the LORD is
Luke	11:13	Father give the Holy S to
Luke	12:10	against the Holy S,
Luke	23:46	hands I commit My s.
Luke	24:39	for a s does not have flesh
John	1:32	I saw the S descending from
John	3: 5	is born of water and the S,
John	3:34	for God does not give the S
John	4:23	worship the Father in s and
John	4:24	"God is S, and those who
John	4:24	Him must worship in s and
John	6:63	It is the S who gives life;
John	6:63	that I speak to you are s,
John	7:39	for the Holy S was not yet
John	11:33	He groaned in the s and was
John	13:21	things, He was troubled in s,
John	14:17	the S of truth, whom the
John	14:26	"But the Helper, the Holy S,
John	19:30	His head, He gave up His s.
John	20:22	them, "Receive the Holy S.
Acts	1: 2	after He through the Holy S
Acts	1: 5	be baptized with the Holy S
Acts	1: 8	power when the Holy S has
Acts	1:16	which the Holy S spoke
Acts	2: 4	all filled with the Holy S
Acts	2:17	will pour out of My S
Acts	2:33	the promise of the Holy S,
Acts	2:38	the gift of the Holy S.
Acts	4: 8	filled with the Holy S,
Acts	5: 3	heart to lie to the Holy S
Acts	7:51	You always resist the Holy S;
Acts	7:59	"Lord Jesus, receive my s.
Acts	10:44	the Holy S fell upon all
Acts	11:16	be baptized with the Holy S.
Acts	11:24	full of the Holy S and of
Acts	15:28	it seemed good to the Holy S,
Acts	19: 2	Did you receive the Holy S
Acts	19: 2	whether there is a Holy S.
Rom	1: 4	power according to the S of
Rom	5: 5	in our hearts by the Holy S

Rom   7: 6 in the newness of the S and
Rom   8: 1 but according to the S,
Rom   8: 2 For the law of the S of life
Rom   8: 5 live according to the S,
Rom   8: 9 if indeed the S of God
Rom   8: 9 anyone does not have the S
Rom   8:10 but the S is life because
Rom   8:11 But if the S of Him who
Rom   8:15 you did not receive the s
Rom   8:16 The S Himself bears witness
Rom   8:16 bears witness with our s
Rom   8:23 the firstfruits of the S,
Rom   8:26 but the S Himself makes
Rom   8:27 what the mind of the S is,
Rom   12:11 in diligence, fervent in s,
Rom   14:17 peace and joy in the Holy S.
Rom   15:13 by the power of the Holy S.
1Co   2: 4 in demonstration of the S
1Co   2:10 For the S searches all
1Co   2:11 things of God except the S
1Co   4:21 or in love and a s of
1Co   5: 3 in body but present in s,
1Co   5: 5 that his s may be saved in
1Co   6:19 is the temple of the Holy S
1Co   6:20 in your body and in your s,
1Co   7:40 I think I also have the S
1Co   12: 3 no one speaking by the S of
1Co   12: 4 of gifts, but the same S.
1Co   12: 7 the manifestation of the S
1Co   12: 8 word of wisdom through the S,
1Co   14: 2 in the s he speaks
1Co   14:14 my s prays, but my
2Co   1:22 us and given us the S in
2Co   3: 3 not with ink but by the S
2Co   3: 6 of the letter but of the S;
2Co   3: 6 but the S gives life.
2Co   3:17 and where the S of the Lord
2Co   5: 5 who also has given us the S
2Co   11: 4 you receive a different s
2Co   13:14 the communion of the Holy S
Gal   3: 2 Did you receive the S by the
Gal   3: 3 Having begun in the S,
Gal   4:29 born according to the S,
Gal   5:16 I say then: Walk in the S,
Gal   5:17 flesh lusts against the S,
Gal   5:18 But if you are led by the S,
Gal   5:22 But the fruit of the S is
Gal   5:25 let us also walk in the S.
Gal   6: 8 but he who sows to the S
Eph   1:13 were sealed with the Holy S
Eph   2: 2 the s who now works in the
Eph   2:18 we both have access by one S
Eph   3: 5 now been revealed by the S
Eph   3:16 with might through His S in
Eph   4: 3 to keep the unity of the S
Eph   4: 4 is one body and one S,
Eph   4:30 do not grieve the Holy S of
Eph   5:18 but be filled with the S,
Eph   6:17 and the sword of the S,
Phil   2: 1 if any fellowship of the S,
1Th   1: 6 with joy of the Holy S,
1Th   5:19 Do not quench the S.
1Th   5:23 and may your whole s,
1Ti   3:16 flesh, Justified in the S,
1Ti   4: 1 Now the S expressly says that
2Ti   1: 7 God has not given us a s of
Tit   3: 5 and renewing of the Holy S,
Heb   2: 4 and gifts of the Holy S,
Heb   3: 7 as the Holy S says:
Heb   4:12 the division of soul and s,
Heb   6: 4 partakers of the Holy S,
Heb   10:29 and insulted the S of grace?
Jas   2:26 as the body without the s
Jas   4: 5 The S who dwells in us yearns
1Pe   1: 2 in sanctification of the S,

1Pe   3:18 but made alive by the S,
2Pe   1:21 were moved by the Holy S.
1Jn   3:24 by the S whom He has given
1Jn   4: 2 By this you know the S of
1Jn   4: 6 By this we know the s of
1Jn   5: 6 And it is the S who bears
1Jn   5: 7 the Word, and the Holy S;
1Jn   5: 8 bear witness on earth: the S,
Rev   1:10 I was in the S on the Lord's
Rev   2: 7 let him hear what the S says
Rev   22:17 And the S and the bride say,

SPIRITISTS
1Sa   28: 3 put the mediums and the s

SPIRITS (see SPIRIT)
Lev   19:31 to mediums and familiar s;
Num   16:22 the God of the s of all
Ps   104: 4 Who makes His angels s,
Prov   16: 2 But the LORD weighs the s.
Zech   6: 5 These are four s of heaven,
Matt   8:16 And He cast out the s with a
Matt   10: 1 them power over unclean s,
Luke   8: 2 had been healed of evil s
1Co   12:10 to another discerning of s,
1Co   14:32 And the s of the prophets are
Heb   1: 7 Who makes His angels s
Heb   1:14 they not all ministering s
Heb   12:23 to the s of just men made
1Pe   3:19 went and preached to the s
1Jn   4: 1 every spirit, but test the s,
Rev   1: 4 and from the seven S who are

SPIRITUAL (see SPIRITUALLY)
Rom   1:11 I may impart to you some s
Rom   7:14 we know that the law is s,
1Co   2:13 comparing s things with
1Co   3: 1 not speak to you as to s
1Co   10: 3 all ate the same s food,
1Co   10: 4 and all drank the same s
1Co   10: 4 For they drank of that s
1Co   12: 1 Now concerning s gifts,
1Co   14: 1 and desire s gifts, but
1Co   15:44 it is raised a s body. There
Gal   6: 1 you who are s restore such
Eph   1: 3 has blessed us with every s
Eph   5:19 in psalms and hymns and s
Eph   6:12 against s hosts of
Col   3:16 in psalms and hymns and s
1Pe   2: 5 are being built up a s

SPIRITUALLY (see SPIRITUAL)
Rom   8: 6 but to be s minded is life
1Co   2:14 because they are s

SPIT (see SPAT, SPITTING)
Job   17: 6 one in whose face men s.
Mark   8:23 And when He had s on his
Mark   10:34 and s on Him, and kill Him.

SPITE (see SPITEFULLY)
Ps   78:32 In s of this they still

SPITEFULLY (see SPITE)
Matt   5:44 and pray for those who s use
Luke   6:28 and pray for those who s use

SPITTING†
Is   50: 6 My face from shame and s.

SPLENDOR
Job   40:10 yourself with majesty and s,
Ps   145: 5 meditate on the glorious s
Dan   4:36 my honor and s returned to

SPLINTERS†
Ps   29: 5 the LORD s the cedars of

SPLIT
Gen   22: 3 and he s the wood for the

Num	16:31	that the ground s apart
Deut	14: 6	having the hoof s into two
Ps	78:15	He s the rocks in the
Is	24:19	The earth is s open, The
Zech	14: 4	Mount of Olives shall be s
Matt	27:51	quaked, and the rocks were s,

SPOIL (see SPOILS)

Ps	68:12	at home divides the s.
Prov	1:13	shall fill our houses with s;
Song	2:15	The little foxes that s the
Is	9: 3	when they divide the s.
Is	53:12	And He shall divide the s

SPOILS (see SPOIL)

Luke	11:22	trusted, and divides his s.
Heb	7: 4	gave a tenth of the s.

SPOKE (see SPEAK)

Gen	8:15	Then God s to Noah, saying,
Gen	16:13	the name of the LORD who s
Gen	31:11	Then the Angel of God s to me
Gen	35:15	of the place where God s
Gen	42: 7	as a stranger to them and s
Gen	43:27	the old man of whom you s?
Gen	50:21	And he comforted them and s
Ex	4:30	And Aaron s all the words
Ex	6: 2	And God s to Moses and said
Ex	33:11	So the LORD s to Moses face
Num	12: 1	Then Miriam and Aaron s
Num	21: 5	And the people s against God
Deut	1: 6	The LORD our God s to us in
Deut	32:44	Joshua the son of Nun and s
Judg	13:11	Are You the Man who s to this
1Sa	1:13	Now Hannah s in her heart;
1Sa	9:17	the man of whom I s to you.
2Sa	7:17	so Nathan s to David.
1Ki	4:32	He s three thousand proverbs,
1Ki	4:33	Also he s of trees, from the
2Ki	10:10	LORD has done what He s by
1Ch	17:15	so Nathan s to David.
Neh	9:13	And s with them from
Neh	13:24	And half of their children s
Job	2:13	and no one s a word to him,
Job	3: 2	And Job s, and said:
Ps	33: 9	For He s, and it was done;
Ps	116:10	I believed, therefore I s,
Jer	7:13	and I s to you, rising up
Jer	26:11	priests and the prophets s
Jer	26:12	Then Jeremiah s to all the
Jer	37: 2	of the LORD which He s by
Ezek	2: 2	Spirit entered me when He s
Dan	7:20	had eyes and a mouth which s
Dan	9: 6	who s in Your name to our
Jon	2:10	So the LORD s to the fish,
Matt	9:33	was cast out, the mute s.
Matt	13:33	Another parable He s to
Mark	7:35	and he s plainly.
Luke	1:55	As He s to our fathers, To
Luke	7:39	he s to himself, saying,
Luke	9:31	who appeared in glory and s
Luke	22:65	things they blasphemously s
Luke	24: 6	is risen! Remember how He s
Luke	24:44	are the words which I s to
John	7:13	no one s openly of Him for
John	7:46	No man ever s like this
John	9:29	We know that God s to Moses;
John	11:13	Jesus s of his death, but
John	18: 9	be fulfilled which He s,
Acts	1:16	which the Holy Spirit s
Acts	8:26	Now an angel of the Lord s
Acts	9:29	And he s boldly in the name
Acts	19: 6	and they s with tongues and
Acts	21:40	he s to them in the Hebrew
Acts	22: 2	when they heard that he s
1Co	13:11	I s as a child, I understood

1Co	14: 5	I wish you all s with
Heb	1: 1	times and in various ways s
2Pe	1:21	but holy men of God s as

SPOKEN (see SPEAK)

Gen	21: 1	did for Sarah as He had s.
Ex	10:29	You have s well. I will never
Ex	19: 8	All that the LORD has s we
Num	12: 2	Has the LORD indeed s only
Num	12: 2	Has He not s through us
Deut	18:17	What they have s is good.
Deut	18:21	which the LORD has not s?
Ruth	2:13	and have s kindly to your
2Sa	7:29	have s it, and with Your
2Ki	20:19	the LORD which you have s
2Ki	24: 2	of the LORD which He had s
Job	42: 7	for you have not s of Me
Ps	87: 3	Glorious things are s of
Ps	108: 7	God has s in His holiness:
Prov	15:23	And a word s in due
Prov	25:11	A word fitly s is like
Song	8: 8	In the day when she is s
Is	1: 2	earth! For the LORD has s:
Is	1:20	the mouth of the LORD has s.
Is	23: 4	O Sidon; For the sea has s,
Is	40: 5	the mouth of the LORD has s.
Is	59: 3	Your lips have s lies,
Jer	23:21	I have not s to them, yet
Jer	32:24	What You have s has
Ezek	5:13	have s it in My zeal, when
Ezek	5:15	I, the LORD, have s.
Ezek	5:17	you. I, the LORD, have s.
Ezek	36: 5	Surely I have s in My burning
Hos	12:10	I have also s by the
Matt	1:22	be fulfilled which was s by
Matt	2:15	be fulfilled which was s by
Matt	2:17	was fulfilled what was s by
Matt	2:23	be fulfilled which was s by
Matt	3: 3	For this is he who was s of
Matt	4:14	be fulfilled which was s by
Matt	8:17	be fulfilled which was s by
Matt	12:17	be fulfilled which was s by
Matt	24:15	s of by Daniel the prophet,
Matt	26:65	He has s blasphemy! What
Mark	12:32	You have s the truth, for
Luke	2:34	for a sign which will be s
Luke	12: 3	whatever you have s in the
Luke	20:39	You have s well."
Luke	24:25	that the prophets have s!
John	12:29	An angel has s to Him."
John	12:49	For I have not s on My own
John	14:25	These things I have s to you
Acts	1: 9	Now when He had s these
Acts	2:16	But this is what was s by the
Acts	16: 2	He was well s of by the
Rom	1: 8	that your faith is s of
Heb	1: 2	has in these last days s to
Heb	2: 2	For if the word s through
Heb	3: 5	things which would be s
Heb	4: 4	For He has s in a certain
Heb	13: 7	who have s the word of God

SPOKESMAN

Ex	4:16	So he shall be your s to the

SPONGE

Mark	15:36	someone ran and filled a s

SPOT (see SPOTS, SPOTTED, UNSPOTTED)

Lev	13: 2	a scab, or a bright s,
Song	4: 7	And there is no s in you.
Eph	5:27	not having s or wrinkle or
Heb	9:14	offered Himself without s
1Pe	1:19	blemish and without s.
2Pe	3:14	without s and blameless;

SPOTS (see SPOT)
Lev 13:38 man or a woman has bright s
2Pe 2:13 They are s and blemishes,

SPOTTED (see SPOT)
Gen 30:32 there all the speckled and s

SPOUSE
Song 4: 9 my heart, My sister, my s;

SPRANG (see SPRING)
Matt 13: 5 and they immediately s up
Matt 13: 7 and the thorns s up and

SPREAD (see SPREADING, SPREADS)
Ex 40:19 And he s out the tent over
Lev 13: 5 and the sore has not s on
Ps 140: 5 They have s a net by the
Prov 7:16 I have s my bed with
Is 1:15 When you s out your hands,
Is 37:14 and s it before the LORD.
Is 42: 5 Who s forth the earth and
Matt 9:31 they s the news about Him in
Matt 21: 8 from the trees and s them
Mark 11: 8 And many s their clothes on
Acts 6: 7 Then the word of God s,
Acts 13:49 word of the Lord was being s
Rom 5:12 and thus death s to all men,
2Co 4:15 having s through the many,
2Ti 2:17 And their message will s like

SPREADING (see SPREAD)
Ezek 26:14 shall be a place for s

SPREADS (see SPREAD)
2Ch 6:29 and s out his hands to this
Job 9: 8 He alone s out the heavens,
Jer 17: 8 Which s out its roots by

SPRING (see SPRANG, SPRINGING, SPRINGS, WELLSPRING)
Gen 16: 7 the LORD found her by a s
2Sa 11: 1 It happened in the s of the
Job 5: 6 Nor does trouble s from the
Job 29:23 mouth wide as for the s
Ps 84: 6 of Baca, They make it a s;
Ps 92: 7 When the wicked s up like
Prov 4:23 For out of it s the issues
Prov 25:26 wicked Is like a murky s
Song 4:12 A s shut up, A fountain
Is 42: 9 Before they s forth I tell
Is 58: 8 Your healing shall s forth
Jas 3:11 Does a s send forth fresh

SPRINGING (see SPRING)
John 4:14 in him a fountain of water s
Heb 12:15 any root of bitterness s up

SPRINGS (see SPRING)
Num 33: 9 At Elim were twelve s of
Josh 15:19 So he gave her the upper s
1Ki 4:33 even to the hyssop that s
Is 37:30 And the second year what s
Hos 10: 4 Thus judgment s up like

SPRINKLE (see SPRINKLED, SPRINKLING)
Ex 29:16 shall take its blood and s
Ex 29:21 and s it on Aaron and on
Lev 1: 5 shall bring the blood and s
Lev 14:16 and shall s some of the oil
Lev 16:14 the blood of the bull and s
Lev 16:14 the mercy seat he shall s
Num 8: 7 S water of purification on
Is 52:15 So shall He s many nations.
Ezek 36:25 Then I will s clean water on

SPRINKLED (see SPRINKLE)
Ex 24: 6 and half the blood he s on
Ex 24: 8 s it on the people, and
2Ki 16:13 his drink offering and s

Job 2:12 each one tore his robe and s
Heb 9:19 and s both the book itself
Heb 10:22 having our hearts s from an

SPRINKLING (see SPRINKLE)
Heb 12:24 and to the blood of s that
1Pe 1: 2 for obedience and s of the

SPROUT† (see SPROUTED)
Job 14: 7 that it will s again, And
Mark 4:27 and the seed should s and

SPROUTED (see SPROUT)
Matt 13:26 But when the grain had s and

SPY (see SPIED, SPIES, SPYING)
Josh 6:25 whom Joshua sent to s out
Judg 18: 2 to s out the land and search
Gal 2: 4 came in by stealth to s out

SPYING† (see SPY)
Num 13:25 they returned from s out the

SQUANDERS†
Prov 21:20 But a foolish man s it.

SQUARE (see SQUARES)
Gen 19: 2 the night in the open s.
Ex 27: 1 wide—the altar shall be s—
Judg 19:15 he sat down in the open s of
Job 29: 7 I took my seat in the open s,
Rev 21:16 The city is laid out as a s;

SQUARES (see SQUARE)
Prov 1:20 her voice in the open s.

STAFF (see STAFFS)
Gen 38:25 signet and cord, and s.
Ex 12:11 and your s in your hand. So
Ps 23: 4 me; Your rod and Your s,
Is 9: 4 of his burden And the s of
Mark 6: 8 for the journey except a s—
Heb 11:21 leaning on the top of his s.

STAFFS† (see STAFF)
Zech 11: 7 I took for myself two s:
Matt 10:10 tunics, nor sandals, nor s;
Luke 9: 3 neither s nor bag nor bread

STAG†
Song 2: 9 like a gazelle or a young s.
Song 2:17 like a gazelle Or a young s
Song 8:14 a gazelle Or a young s On

STAGGER (see STAGGERS)
Ps 107:27 and s like a drunken man,

STAGGERS† (see STAGGER)
Is 19:14 As a drunken man s in his

STAINED†
Is 63: 3 and I have s all My robes

STAIRS
Acts 21:40 Paul stood on the s and

STAKES
Is 54: 2 And strengthen your s.

STALK
Gen 41: 5 of grain came up on one s,

STALL† (see STALLS)
Amos 6: 4 from the midst of the s;
Luke 13:15 his ox or donkey from the s,

STALLIONS†
Jer 5: 8 were like well-fed lusty s;

STALLS (see STALL)
Hab 3:17 there be no herd in the s—

STAND (see STANDING, STANDS, STOOD)
Ex 3: 5 for the place where you s
Ex 9:11 the magicians could not s
Ex 14:13 S still, and see the

Ex   18:19 **S** before God for the people,
Lev   26:37 shall have no power to **s**
Num   23: 3 **S** by your burnt offering, and
Num   30: 4 then all her vows shall **s**,
Deut   5:31 **s** here by Me, and I will
Deut   7:24 no one shall be able to **s**
Deut   27:13 and these shall **s** on Mount
Josh   1: 5 man shall be able to **s**
Josh   5:15 for the place where you **s**
Josh   10:12 **s** still over Gibeon; And
1Sa   16:22 Please let David **s** before me,
2Ki   23: 3 And all the people took a **s**
2Ch   20:17 **s** still and see the
Neh   7: 3 and while they **s** guard, let
Job   19:25 And He shall **s** at last on
Ps   1: 5 the ungodly shall not **s** in
Ps   24: 3 Or who may **s** in His holy
Ps   76: 7 And who may **s** in Your
Ps   130: 3 O Lord, who could **s**?
Prov   8: 2 She takes her **s** on the top
Is   7: 7 GOD: "It shall not **s**,
Is   14:24 purposed, so it shall **s**:
Is   46:10 Saying, 'My counsel shall **s**,
Jer   15:19 You shall **s** before Me; If
Ezek   2: 1 **s** on your feet, and I will
Ezek   22:30 and **s** in the gap before Me
Dan   2:44 and it shall **s** forever.
Dan   7: 4 the earth and made to **s** on
Dan   12: 1 that time Michael shall **s**
Amos   7: 2 pray! Oh, that Jacob may **s**,
Zech   4: 2 and on the **s** seven lamps
Zech   14: 4 in that day His feet will **s**
Mal   3: 2 And who can **s** when He
Matt   12:25 against itself will not **s**.
Matt   12:26 How then will his kingdom **s**?
Mark   11:25 And whenever you **s** praying,
John   8:44 and does not **s** in the
Acts   1:11 why do you **s** gazing up into
Acts   4:26 the earth took their **s**,
Acts   25:10 I **s** at Caesar's judgment
Rom   5: 2 this grace in which we **s**,
Rom   9:11 to election might **s**,
Rom   11:20 and you **s** by faith. Do not
Rom   14:10 For we shall all **s** before
1Co   15: 1 received and in which you **s**,
1Co   15:30 And why do we **s** in jeopardy
1Co   16:13 **s** fast in the faith, be
Gal   5: 1 **S** fast therefore in the
Eph   6:11 that you may be able to **s**
Eph   6:13 and having done all, to **s**.
Eph   6:14 **S** therefore, having girded
Phil   4: 1 so **s** fast in the Lord,
Col   4:12 that you may **s** perfect and
1Th   3: 8 if you **s** fast in the Lord.
Jas   2: 3 You **s** there," or, "Sit here
1Pe   5:12 grace of God in which you **s**.
Rev   3:20 I **s** at the door and knock.

STANDARD
Num   2: 2 shall camp by his own **s**,
Deut   3:11 according to the **s** cubit.
2Sa   14:26 according to the king's **s**.

STANDING (see STAND)
Gen   18: 2 three men were **s** by him; and
Ps   122: 2 Our feet have been **s** Within
Zech   3: 1 and Satan is at his right
Matt   6: 5 For they love to pray **s** in
Matt   16:28 there are some **s** here who
Matt   24:15 **s** in the holy place"
Mark   9: 1 to you that there are some **s**
Acts   7:55 and Jesus **s** at the right
Heb   9: 8 first tabernacle was still **s**.
2Pe   3: 5 and the earth **s** out of water
Rev   20:12 **s** before God, and books were

STANDS (see STAND)
Ps   1: 1 Nor **s** in the path of
Ps   45: 9 At Your right hand **s** the
Ps   82: 1 God **s** in the congregation of
Ps   119:161 But my heart **s** in awe of
Is   40: 8 But the word of our God **s**
John   1:26 but there **s** One among you
1Co   10:12 let him who thinks he **s**

STANK (see STINK)
Ex   7:21 the river died, the river **s**,
Ex   8:14 in heaps, and the land **s**.

STAR (see STARS)
Matt   2: 2 For we have seen His **s** in
1Co   15:41 for one **s** differs from
2Pe   1:19 day dawns and the morning **s**
Rev   2:28 will give him the morning **s**.
Rev   8:10 And a great **s** fell from
Rev   22:16 the Bright and Morning **S**.

STARE
Ps   22:17 They look and **s** at Me.

STARS (see STAR)
Gen   1:16 He made the **s** also.
Gen   15: 5 and count the **s** if you are
Gen   22:17 your descendants as the **s**
Gen   37: 9 and the eleven **s** bowed down
Deut   4:19 the sun, the moon, and the **s**,
Judg   5:20 The **s** from their courses
Job   38: 7 When the morning **s** sang
Ps   8: 3 fingers, The moon and the **s**,
Ps   136: 9 The moon and **s** to rule by
Ps   147: 4 counts the number of the **s**;
Ps   148: 3 all you **s** of light!
Is   14:13 exalt my throne above the **s**
Dan   12: 3 to righteousness Like the **s**
Matt   24:29 the **s** will fall from heaven,
1Co   15:41 and another glory of the **s**;
Rev   1:16 in His right hand seven **s**,
Rev   6:13 And the **s** of heaven fell to
Rev   8:12 moon, and a third of the **s**,

START† (see STARTS)
Prov   20: 3 Since any fool can **s** a

STARTLED†
Ruth   3: 8 midnight that the man was **s**,
Hab   3: 6 He looked and **s** the

STARTS† (see START)
Prov   17:14 before a quarrel **s**.

STATE
Ps   136:23 remembered us in our lowly **s**,
Matt   12:45 and the last **s** of that man
Luke   1:48 He has regarded the lowly **s**
Phil   4:11 I have learned in whatever **s**

STATELY
Prov   30:29 four which are **s** in walk:

STATIONED
Judg   16:25 And they **s** him between the

STATURE
Num   13:32 in it are men of great **s**.
1Sa   2:26 the child Samuel grew in **s**,
2Sa   21:20 there was a man of great **s**,
Matt   6:27 can add one cubit to his **s**?
Luke   2:52 increased in wisdom and **s**,
Luke   19: 3 crowd, for he was of short **s**.
Eph   4:13 to the measure of the **s** of

STATUTE (see STATUTES)
Ex   27:21 It shall be a **s** forever
Ex   29: 9 be theirs for a perpetual **s**.
Dan   6: 7 to establish a royal **s** and
Dan   6:15 that no decree or **s** which

STATUTES (*see* STATUTE)
Gen   26: 5 My commandments, My s,
Ex   15:26 and keep all His s,
Ex   18:20 you shall teach them the s
Lev   26: 3 If you walk in My s and keep
Lev   26:43 their soul abhorred My s.
Deut   4:45 are the testimonies, the s,
Deut   5: 1 the s and judgments which I
Deut   11: 1 and keep His charge, His s,
Deut   11:32 to observe all the s and
Deut   30:10 His commandments and His s
1Ki   11:11 kept My covenant and My s,
2Ch   33: 8 to the whole law and the s
Ezra   7:10 and to teach s and
Neh   9:13 Good s and commandments.
Ps   18:22 I did not put away His s
Ps   19: 8 The s of the LORD are
Ps   119:12 O LORD! Teach me Your s!
Ps   119:71 That I may learn Your s.
Ps   119:118 those who stray from Your s,
Ezek   5: 6 they have not walked in My s.
Mic   6:16 For the s of Omri are kept;

STEADFAST (*see* STEADFASTLY)
Ps   51:10 And renew a s spirit within
Ps   57: 7 My heart is s,
Ps   78:37 For their heart was not s
1Co   15:58 my beloved brethren, be s,
Col   1:23 in the faith, grounded and s,
Heb   3:14 of our confidence s to the
Heb   6:19 of the soul, both sure and s,
1Pe   5: 9 s in the faith, knowing that

STEADFASTLY (*see* STEADFAST)
Luke   9:51 that He s set His face to go
Acts   1:10 And while they looked s
Acts   2:42 And they continued s in the
Rom   12:12 continuing s in prayer;

STEAL (*see* STEALING, STEALS, STOLE)
Gen   31:30 but why did you s my
Ex   20:15 "You shall not s.
Deut   5:19 'You shall not s.
Matt   6:19 where thieves break in and s;
Matt   19:18 'You shall not s,
John   10:10 does not come except to s,
Eph   4:28 Let him who stole s no

STEALING† (*see* STEAL)
Hos   4: 2 Killing and s and

STEALS (*see* STEAL)
Ex   22: 1 If a man s an ox or a sheep,

STEEP
Matt   8:32 ran violently down the s

STEM†
Is   11: 1 come forth a Rod from the s

STENCH
John   11:39 by this time there is a s,

STEPHEN
Acts   6: 5 multitude. And they chose S,
Acts   7:59 And they stoned S as he was

STEPPED
John   5: 4 then whoever s in first,

STEPS
1Ki   10:19 The throne had six s,
Job   23:11 foot has held fast to His s;
Ps   17: 5 Uphold my s in Your paths,
Ps   37:23 The s of a good man are
Ps   37:31 None of his s shall slide.
Prov   16: 9 But the LORD directs his s.
Prov   20:24 A man's s are of the LORD;
Ezek   40:22 it was ascended by seven s,
John   5: 7 another s down before me."

1Pe   2:21 that you should follow His s:

STEW
Gen   25:34 Jacob gave Esau bread and s

STEWARD (*see* STEWARDS, STEWARDSHIP)
Gen   44: 4 off, Joseph said to his s,
Dan   1:16 Thus the s took away their
Matt   20: 8 the vineyard said to his s,
Luke   12:42 is that faithful and wise s,
Luke   16: 8 commended the unjust s
Tit   1: 7 as a s of God, not

STEWARDS (*see* STEWARD)
1Co   4: 2 it is required in s that
1Pe   4:10 as good s of the manifold

STEWARDSHIP (*see* STEWARD)
Luke   16: 2 Give an account of your s,
1Co   9:17 have been entrusted with a s.
Col   1:25 minister according to the s

STICK (*see* STICKS)
Job   33:21 And his bones s out which
Ezek   37:16 take a s for yourself and
Ezek   37:19 Judah, and make them one s,

STICKS (*see* STICK)
Num   15:32 found a man gathering s on
1Sa   17:43 that you come to me with s?
1Ki   17:10 widow was there gathering s.
Prov   18:24 there is a friend who s
Ezek   37:20 And the s on which you write
Acts   28: 3 had gathered a bundle of s

STIFF (*see* STIFFENED)
Deut   31:27 your rebellion and your s

STIFF-NECKED (*see* STIFFENED, STIFFNECKED)
Ex   32: 9 and indeed it is a s
Deut   10:16 and be s no longer.

STIFFENED (*see* STIFF, STIFF-NECKED)
Neh   9:29 S their necks, And would

STIFFNECKED
Acts   7:51 You s and uncircumcised in

STILL
Gen   18:22 but Abraham s stood before
Gen   45:26 And Jacob's heart stood s,
Ex   14:13 "Do not be afraid. Stand s,
Josh   3:16 down from upstream stood s,
Josh   10:12 stand s over Gibeon; And
Judg   5:27 he sank, he fell, he lay s;
Judg   7: 4 The people are s too many;
1Ki   19:12 and after the fire a s small
Job   1:16 While he was s speaking,
Job   1:17 While he was s speaking,
Job   1:18 While he was s speaking,
Job   3:13 now I would have lain s and
Ps   23: 2 He leads me beside the s
Ps   46:10 Be s, and know that I am
Ps   78:32 In spite of this they s
Ps   107:29 So that its waves are s.
Ps   139:18 I am s with You.
Prov   9: 9 and he will be s wiser;
Eccl   12: 9 he s taught the people
Is   5:25 His hand is stretched out s.
Is   9:12 His hand is stretched out s.
Is   9:17 His hand is stretched out s.
Is   9:21 His hand is stretched out s.
Is   10: 4 His hand is stretched out s.
Jer   47: 6 Rest and be s!
Dan   4:31 While the word was s in
Jon   4: 2 what I said when I was s in
Hab   3:11 The sun and moon stood s in
Matt   19:20 What do I s lack?"
Mark   4:39 be s!" And the wind ceased
Mark   14:41 Are you s sleeping and

Luke 18:22 You **s** lack one thing. Sell
Luke 22:37 which is written must **s** be
Luke 24: 6 spoke to you when He was **s**
Luke 24:44 I spoke to you while I was **s**
John 4:35 There are **s** four months and
John 16:12 I **s** have many things to say
Acts 8:38 the chariot to stand **s**.
Acts 9: 1 **s** breathing threats and
Rom 4:11 which he had while **s**
Rom 5: 6 For when we were **s** without
Rom 5: 8 in that while we were **s**
1Co 3: 3 for you are **s** carnal. For
1Co 15:17 you are **s** in your sins!
Phil 1: 9 that your love may abound **s**
Heb 7:10 for he was **s** in the loins of
Heb 9: 8 the first tabernacle was **s**
Heb 11: 4 through it he being dead **s**
Rev 22:11 unjust, let him be unjust **s**;

STILLBORN
Job 3:16 was I not hidden like a **s**

STING†
1Co 15:55 Death, where is your **s**?
1Co 15:56 The **s** of death is sin, and

STINK (see STANK)
Ex 7:18 shall die, the river shall **s**,
Is 50: 2 Their fish **s** because there

STIR (see STIRRED, STIRRING, STIRS)
Ps 80: 2 **S** up Your strength, And
Song 2: 7 Do not **s** up nor awaken love
Is 13:17 I will **s** up the Medes
Dan 11:10 However his sons shall **s** up
Acts 12:18 there was no small **s** among
2Ti 1: 6 Therefore I remind you to **s**
Heb 10:24 one another in order to **s**
2Pe 1:13 to **s** you up by reminding
2Pe 3: 1 (in both of which I **s** up

STIRRED (see STIR)
Ex 35:21 came whose heart was **s**,
1Ki 21:25 because Jezebel his wife **s**
2Ch 36:22 the LORD **s** up the spirit of
Ezra 1: 1 the LORD **s** up the spirit of
Mark 15:11 But the chief priests **s** up
John 5: 4 time into the pool and **s** up
Acts 14: 2 But the unbelieving Jews **s** up
2Co 9: 2 and your zeal has **s** up the

STIRRING (see STIR)
John 5: 4 after the **s** of the water,

STIRS (see STIR)
Deut 32:11 As an eagle **s** up its nest,
Prov 10:12 Hatred **s** up strife, But
Prov 15: 1 But a harsh word **s** up
Prov 15:18 A wrathful man **s** up strife,
Prov 28:25 who is of a proud heart **s**
Luke 23: 5 He **s** up the people, teaching

STOCK (see STOCKS)
Is 40:24 Scarcely shall their **s** take
Phil 3: 5 of the **s** of Israel, of the

STOCKS (see STOCK)
Job 13:27 You put my feet in the **s**,
Acts 16:24 fastened their feet in the **s**.

STOIC†
Acts 17:18 Then certain Epicurean and **S**

STOLE (see STEAL, STOLEN)
Matt 28:13 came at night and **s** Him
Eph 4:28 Let him who **s** steal no

STOLEN (see STOLE)
Gen 31:19 and Rachel had **s** the
Ps 69: 4 Though I have **s** nothing, I
Prov 9:17 **S** water is sweet, And bread

STOMACH (see STOMACH'S)
Num 5:22 the curse go into your **s**,
2Sa 3:27 there stabbed him in the **s**,
Matt 15:17 the mouth goes into the **s**
Mark 7:19 enter his heart but his **s**,
Luke 15:16 gladly have filled his **s**
1Co 6:13 Foods for the **s** and the
1Co 6:13 for the stomach and the **s**

STOMACH'S† (see STOMACH)
1Ti 5:23 use a little wine for your **s**

STONE (see STONE'S, STONED, STONES, STONY)
Gen 2:12 Bdellium and the onyx **s** are
Gen 11: 3 They had brick for **s**,
Gen 29: 2 A large **s** was on the well's
Gen 31:45 So Jacob took a **s** and set it
Gen 35:14 with him, a pillar of **s**;
Gen 49:24 the **S** of Israel),
Ex 4:25 Zipporah took a sharp **s** and
Ex 7:19 of wood and pitchers of **s**.
Ex 15: 5 sank to the bottom like a **s**.
Ex 17: 4 They are almost ready to **s**
Ex 20:25 if you make Me an altar of **s**,
Ex 24:10 a paved work of sapphire **s**,
Ex 28:10 of their names on one **s**,
Ex 34: 1 Cut two tablets of **s** like the
Num 14:10 the congregation said to **s**
Deut 17: 5 and shall **s** to death that
Deut 28:36 serve other gods—wood and **s**.
Josh 24:27 this **s** shall be a witness to
Judg 20:16 every one could sling a **s** at
1Sa 17:50 with a sling and a **s**,
1Sa 25:37 him, and he became like a **s**.
Job 38:30 The waters harden like **s**,
Job 41:24 His heart is as hard as **s**,
Ps 91:12 dash your foot against a **s**.
Ps 118:22 The **s** which the builders
Prov 27: 3 A **s** is heavy and sand is
Is 8:14 But a **s** of stumbling and a
Is 28:16 I lay in Zion a **s** for a
Jer 2:27 are my father,' And to a **s**,
Ezek 1:26 appearance like a sapphire **s**;
Ezek 36:26 I will take the heart of **s**
Dan 2:34 You watched while a **s** was cut
Dan 2:35 And the **s** that struck the
Dan 6:17 Then a **s** was brought and laid
Amos 5:11 have built houses of hewn **s**,
Zech 3: 9 Upon the **s** are seven eyes.
Matt 4: 6 your foot against a **s**.
Matt 7: 9 for bread, will give him a **s**?
Matt 21:42 The **s** which the builders
Matt 21:44 whoever falls on this **s**
Matt 24: 2 not one **s** shall be left
Matt 27:60 and he rolled a large **s**
John 2: 6 set there six waterpots of **s**,
John 8: 7 let him throw a **s** at her
John 10:31 took up stones again to **s**
John 11:39 said, "Take away the **s**.
Acts 4:11 **s** which was rejected by
Acts 17:29 is like gold or silver or **s**,
Rom 9:33 in Zion a stumbling **s**
2Co 3: 3 not on tablets of **s** but on
1Pe 2: 4 to Him as to a living **s**,
1Pe 2: 7 The **s** which the builders
1Pe 2: 8 A **s** of stumbling And a
Rev 2:17 I will give him a white **s**,
Rev 2:17 and on the **s** a new name

STONE'S† (see STONE)
Luke 22:41 from them about a **s** throw

STONED (see STONE)
Ex 19:13 but he shall surely be **s** or
Josh 7:25 So all Israel **s** him with
1Ki 21:14 Naboth has been **s** and is
Matt 21:35 killed one, and **s** another.

John 8: 5 us that such should be s.
Acts 7:59 And they s Stephen as he was
Acts 14:19 they s Paul and dragged
2Co 11:25 with rods; once I was s;
Heb 11:37 They were s, they were sawn

STONES (see STONE)
Gen 28:11 And he took one of the s of
Ex 25: 7 "onyx s, and stones to be
Ex 39:14 There were twelve s
Num 14:10 said to stone them with s.
Deut 8: 9 a land whose s are iron and
Deut 27: 5 your God, an altar of s;
Josh 4: 3 for yourselves twelve s
Josh 4: 6 What do these s mean to
Josh 8:32 he wrote on the s a copy of
1Sa 17:40 for himself five smooth s
1Ki 10:27 common in Jerusalem as s,
1Ki 18:31 And Elijah took twelve s,
Job 14:19 As water wears away s,
Eccl 3: 5 And a time to gather s;
Is 5: 2 it up and cleared out its s,
Ezek 28:14 in the midst of fiery s.
Matt 3: 9 to Abraham from these s.
Matt 4: 3 command that these become
Mark 5: 5 and cutting himself with s.
Mark 12: 4 and at him they threw s,
Mark 13: 1 see what manner of s and
Luke 13:34 who kills the prophets and s
Luke 19:40 the s would immediately cry
John 8:59 Then they took up s to throw
John 10:31 Then the Jews took up s
1Co 3:12 gold, silver, precious s,
2Co 3: 7 written and engraved on s,
1Pe 2: 5 you also, as living s,

STONY (see STONE)
Ezek 11:19 and take the s heart out of
Matt 13: 5 Some fell on s places, where

STOOD (see STAND)
Gen 18:22 but Abraham still s before
Gen 28:13 the LORD s above it and
Gen 37: 7 my sheaf arose and also s
Gen 45:26 And Jacob's heart s still,
Ex 2: 4 And his sister s afar off, to
Ex 19:17 and they s at the foot of
Deut 31:15 and the pillar of cloud s
2Ki 18:17 they went and s by the
2Ki 23: 3 Then the king s by a pillar
1Ch 21: 1 Now Satan s up against
Ezra 10:10 Then Ezra the priest s up and
Neh 8: 4 So Ezra the scribe s on a
Neh 8: 5 all the people s up.
Job 4:15 The hair on my body s up.
Ps 33: 9 commanded, and it s fast.
Ps 104: 6 The waters s above the
Ps 106:23 not Moses His chosen one s
Is 6: 2 Above it s seraphim; each one
Jer 15: 1 if Moses and Samuel s
Ezek 1:21 these went; when those s,
Dan 8:18 and s me upright.
Dan 10:11 I s trembling.
Amos 7: 7 the Lord s on a wall made
Hab 3:11 The sun and moon s still in
Matt 2: 9 till it came and s over
Luke 4:16 and s up to read.
Luke 17:12 who s afar off.
Luke 24: 4 two men s by them in shining
Luke 24:36 Jesus Himself s in the midst
John 20:19 Jesus came and s in the
Acts 1:10 two men s by them in white
Acts 3: 8 s and walked and entered the
Acts 16: 9 A man of Macedonia s and
Acts 21:40 Paul s on the stairs and
2Ti 4:16 At my first defense no one s

2Ti 4:17 But the Lord s with me and

STOOP† (see STOOPED, STOOPING, STOOPS)
Is 46: 2 They s, they bow down
Mark 1: 7 strap I am not worthy to s

STOOPED (see STOOP)
John 8: 6 But Jesus s down and wrote

STOOPING (see STOOP)
John 20: 5 s down and looking in, saw

STOOPS† (see STOOP)
Is 46: 1 Bel bows down, Nebo s;

STOPPED
Gen 8: 2 of heaven were also s,
Gen 26:15 Now the Philistines had s up
Num 16:48 living; so the plague was s.
Josh 10:13 stood still, And the moon s,
Zech 7:11 and s their ears so that
Luke 5: 4 When He had s speaking, He
Luke 8:44 her flow of blood s.
Rom 3:19 that every mouth may be s,
Tit 1:11 whose mouths must be s,
Heb 11:33 s the mouths of lions,

STORAGE (see STORE)
1Ki 9:19 all the s cities that Solomon

STORE (see STORAGE, STORED, STOREHOUSE, STORES)
Gen 41:35 and s up grain under the
Deut 14:28 produce of that year and s
Prov 10:14 Wise people s up knowledge,
Luke 12:17 since I have no room to s my

STORED (see STORE)
Prov 13:22 wealth of the sinner is s
Jer 36:20 but they s the scroll in the

STOREHOUSE (see STORE, STOREHOUSES)
Mal 3:10 all the tithes into the s,
Luke 12:24 which have neither s nor

STOREHOUSES (see STOREHOUSE)
Gen 41:56 and Joseph opened all the s

STORES (see STORE)
Prov 2: 7 He s up sound wisdom for the

STORK
Ps 104:17 The s has her home in the
Jer 8: 7 Even the s in the heavens

STORM (see STORMY, WINDSTORM)
Is 4: 6 and for a shelter from s and
Is 25: 4 A refuge from the s,
Nah 1: 3 the whirlwind and in the s,

STORMY (see STORM)
Ps 107:25 He commands and raises the s
Ps 148: 8 S wind, fulfilling His

STORY
Acts 20: 9 fell down from the third s

STRAIGHT
Ps 5: 8 Make Your way s before my
Prov 9:15 Who go s on their way:
Eccl 1:15 is crooked cannot be made s,
Is 40: 3 Make s in the desert A
Is 40: 4 places shall be made s And
Is 45: 2 make the crooked places s;
Matt 3: 3 Make His paths s.
John 1:23 Make s the way of the
Acts 9:11 go to the street called S,
Heb 12:13 and make s paths for your

STRAIN†
Matt 23:24 who s out a gnat and swallow

STRANGE (see STRANGER)
Prov 23:33 Your eyes will see s things,
Heb 13: 9 about with various and s

1Pe 4: 4 they think it **s** that you do
Jude 7 immorality and gone after **s**

STRANGER (*see* FOREIGNER, STRANGE, STRANGERS)
Gen 17: 8 land in which you are a **s**,
Ex 2:22 I have been a **s** in a foreign
Ex 12:48 And when a **s** dwells with you
Ex 22:21 shall neither mistreat a **s**
Lev 19:10 them for the poor and the **s**:
Lev 25:35 like a **s** or a sojourner,
Num 15:30 he is native-born or a **s**,
Deut 10:18 the widow, and loves the **s**,
Deut 24:17 pervert justice due the **s**
Deut 26:12 it to the Levite, the **s**,
Ps 69: 8 I have become a **s** to my
Ps 94: 6 slay the widow and the **s**,
Ps 119:19 I am a **s** in the earth; Do
Prov 6: 1 hands in pledge for a **s**,
Prov 14:10 And a **s** does not share its
Prov 27: 2 and not your own mouth; A **s**,
Matt 25:35 I was a **s** and you took Me

STRANGERS (*see* STRANGER)
Gen 15:13 your descendants will be **s**
Ex 6: 4 in which they were **s**.
Lev 17: 8 or of the **s** who dwell among
Lev 25:23 for you are **s** and
Ps 54: 3 For **s** have risen up against
Ps 105:12 very few, and **s** in it.
Is 1: 7 **S** devour your land in your
Matt 27: 7 field, to bury **s** in.
Acts 13:17 people when they dwelt as **s**
Eph 2:12 of Israel and **s** from the
Heb 13: 2 Do not forget to entertain **s**,

STRANGLED†
Acts 15:20 immorality, from things **s**,
Acts 15:29 from blood, from things **s**,
Acts 21:25 from blood, from things **s**,

STRAP (*see* STRAPS)
Gen 14:23 from a thread to a sandal **s**,
Mark 1: 7 whose sandal **s** I am not

STRAPS (*see* STRAP)
Ex 28:25 put them on the shoulder **s**

STRAW
Gen 24:32 and provided **s** and feed for
Ex 5: 7 no longer give the people **s**
Ex 5:12 gather stubble instead of **s**.
Is 11: 7 And the lion shall eat **s**
Is 65:25 The lion shall eat **s** like
1Co 3:12 stones, wood, hay, **s**,

STRAY (*see* STRAYED, STRAYING)
Prov 7:25 Do not **s** into her paths;

STRAYED (*see* STRAY)
Ps 119:110 Yet I have not **s** from Your
1Ti 1: 6 from which some, having **s**,

STRAYING† (*see* STRAY)
Matt 18:12 to seek the one that is **s**?

STREAKED
Gen 30:39 the flocks brought forth **s**,

STREAM (*see* STREAMS)
Jer 15:18 to me like an unreliable **s**,
Dan 7:10 A fiery **s** issued And came
Amos 5:24 like a mighty **s**.
Luke 6:48 the **s** beat vehemently

STREAMS (*see* STREAM)
Ex 8: 5 with your rod over the **s**,
Ps 46: 4 There is a river whose **s**
Ps 78:16 He also brought **s** out of the
Prov 5:16 **S** of water in the streets?
Is 35: 6 And **s** in the desert.

STREET (*see* STREETS)
Is 42: 2 voice to be heard in the **s**.
Dan 9:25 The **s** shall be built again,
Acts 9:11 Arise and go to the **s** called
Rev 21:21 And the **s** of the city was

STREETS (*see* STREET)
2Sa 1:20 Proclaim it not in the **s**
Prov 5:16 Streams of water in the **s**?
Prov 22:13 I shall be slain in the **s**!
Prov 26:13 A fierce lion is in the **s**!
Eccl 12: 4 the doors are shut in the **s**,
Eccl 12: 5 the mourners go about the **s**.
Song 3: 2 In the **s** and in the squares
Is 58:12 The Restorer of **S** to Dwell
Matt 6: 5 and on the corners of the **s**,
Matt 12:19 His voice in the **s**.

STRENGTH (*see* STRENGTHEN)
Gen 4:12 shall no longer yield its **s**
Gen 49: 3 and the beginning of my **s**,
Ex 15: 2 The LORD is my **s** and song,
Lev 26:20 And your **s** shall be spent in
Num 23:22 He has **s** like a wild ox.
Deut 6: 5 soul, and with all your **s**.
Deut 33:25 so shall your **s** be.
Josh 14:11 so now is my **s** for war,
Judg 8:21 as a man is, so is his **s**.
Judg 16: 9 So the secret of his **s** was
Judg 16:19 and his **s** left him.
1Sa 2: 9 For by **s** no man shall
1Sa 2:10 He will give **s** to His king,
1Sa 15:29 And also the **S** of Israel will
1Ki 19: 8 and he went in the **s** of that
1Ch 16:11 Seek the LORD and His **s**;
2Ch 6:41 You and the ark of Your **s**.
Neh 8:10 joy of the LORD is your **s**.
Job 9:19 If it is a matter of **s**,
Job 12:13 Him are wisdom and **s**,
Ps 8: 2 infants You have ordained **s**,
Ps 18: 1 will love You, O LORD, my **s**.
Ps 18: 2 my deliverer; My God, my **s**,
Ps 18:32 is God who arms me with **s**,
Ps 18:39 You have armed me with **s**
Ps 19:14 my **s** and my Redeemer.
Ps 20: 6 heaven With the saving **s**
Ps 21: 1 shall have joy in Your **s**,
Ps 22:15 My **s** is dried up like a
Ps 22:19 not be far from Me; O My **S**,
Ps 27: 1 The LORD is the **s** of my
Ps 28: 7 The LORD is my **s** and my
Ps 29: 1 unto the LORD glory and **s**.
Ps 29:11 The LORD will give **s** to His
Ps 31:10 My **s** fails because of my
Ps 33:16 is not delivered by great **s**.
Ps 38:10 my **s** fails me; As for the
Ps 43: 2 You are the God of my **s**;
Ps 46: 1 God is our refuge and **s**,
Ps 68:34 Ascribe **s** to God; His
Ps 71:16 I will go in the **s** of the
Ps 81: 1 Sing aloud to God our **s**;
Ps 84: 7 They go from **s** to strength;
Ps 86:16 mercy on me! Give Your **s**
Ps 90:10 And if by reason of **s** they
Ps 93: 1 has girded Himself with **s**.
Ps 96: 6 **S** and beauty are in His
Ps 96: 7 to the LORD glory and **s**.
Ps 110: 2 send the rod of Your **s** out
Ps 118:14 The LORD is my **s** and song,
Ps 132: 8 You and the ark of Your **s**.
Prov 20:29 of young men is their **s**,
Prov 31: 3 Do not give your **s** to women,
Prov 31:17 She girds herself with **s**,
Prov 31:25 **S** and honor are her
Is 12: 2 is my **s** and song; He also
Is 26: 4 the LORD, is everlasting **s**.

Is 40:31 LORD Shall renew their s;
Jer 17: 5 man And makes flesh his s,
Dan 2:37 you a kingdom, power, s,
Dan 2:41 yet the s of the iron shall
Dan 10: 8 and no s remained in me; for
Hos 7: 9 Aliens have devoured his s,
Hos 12: 3 And in his s he struggled
Mark 12:30 and with all your s.
Luke 1:51 He has shown s with His arm;
Luke 10:27 soul, with all your s,
Rom 5: 6 when we were still without s,
1Co 15:56 and the s of sin is the
2Co 12: 9 for My s is made perfect in
Rev 1:16 the sun shining in its s.
Rev 3: 8 it; for you have a little s,

STRENGTHEN (see STRENGTH, STRENGTHENED,
STRENGTHENING, STRENGTHENS)
Neh 6: 9 O God, s my hands.
Ps 20: 2 And s you out of Zion;
Ps 119:28 S me according to Your
Is 35: 3 S the weak hands, And make
Is 54: 2 And s your stakes.
Ezek 34:16 bind up the broken and s
Luke 22:32 s your brethren."
Heb 12:12 Therefore s the hands which
1Pe 5:10 while, perfect, establish, s,
Rev 3: 2 and s the things which

STRENGTHENED (see STRENGTHEN)
Job 4: 4 And you have s the feeble
Acts 9:19 had received food, he was s.
Acts 16: 5 So the churches were s in the
Eph 3:16 to be s with might through
Col 1:11 s with all might, according

STRENGTHENING (see STRENGTHEN)
Acts 15:41 s the churches.

STRENGTHENS (see STRENGTHEN)
Ps 104:15 And bread which s man's
Phil 4:13 things through Christ who s

STRETCH (see STRETCHED, STRETCHES)
Ex 7: 5 when I s out My hand on
Ex 7:19 Take your rod and s out your
Ex 8:16 S out your rod, and strike
Ex 9:22 S out your hand toward
Num 24: 6 Like valleys that s out,
Job 1:11 s out Your hand and touch
Job 2: 5 But s out Your hand now, and
Job 11:13 And s out your hands toward
Ps 68:31 Ethiopia will quickly s out
Ps 104: 2 Who s out the heavens like
Ezek 14: 9 and I will s out My hand
Ezek 14:13 I will s out My hand against
Ezek 25: 7 I will s out My hand against
Amos 6: 4 S out on your couches, Eat
Matt 12:13 S out your hand." And he
John 21:18 you will s out your hands,

STRETCHED (see STRETCH)
Gen 22:10 And Abraham s out his hand
Ex 9:15 Now if I had s out My hand
Ex 9:23 And Moses s out his rod
1Ki 17:21 And he s himself out on the
2Ki 4:34 and he s himself out on the
Is 5:25 But His hand is s out
Is 9:12 But His hand is s out
Is 9:17 But His hand is s out
Is 9:21 But His hand is s out
Is 10: 4 But His hand is s out
Is 48:13 And My right hand has s out
Ezek 1:11 Their wings s upward; two

STRETCHES (see STRETCH)
Job 26: 7 He s out the north over
Prov 31:19 She s out her hands to the

Is 40:22 Who s out the heavens like

STRICKEN
Ps 102: 4 My heart is s and withered
Is 53: 4 Yet we esteemed Him s,
Is 53: 8 of My people He was s.
Hos 6: 1 He will heal us; He has s,

STRICTER†
Jas 3: 1 that we shall receive a s

STRIFE
Gen 13: 7 And there was s between the
Ps 106:32 Him also at the waters of s,
Prov 10:12 Hatred stirs up s,
Prov 17: 1 full of feasting with s.
Jer 15:10 A man of s and a man of
Hab 1: 3 are before me; There is s,
Rom 1:29 full of envy, murder, s,
Rom 13:13 not in s and envy.

STRIKE (see STRIKES, STRUCK)
Ex 3:20 stretch out My hand and s
Ex 7:17 I will s the waters which
Ex 17: 6 and you shall s the rock,
2Sa 15:14 and the city with the edge
Ps 121: 6 The sun shall not s you by
Is 10:24 He shall s you with a rod
Zech 13: 7 S the Shepherd, And the
Matt 26:31 I will s the Shepherd,
John 18:23 why do you s Me?"
Acts 23: 3 God will s you, you

STRIKES (see STRIKE)
Ex 21:15 And he who s his father or
Ex 21:26 If a man s the eye of his
Lam 3:30 his cheek to the one who s
2Co 11:20 if one s you on the face.

STRINGED (see STRINGS)
2Sa 6: 5 on s instruments, on
1Ki 10:12 also harps and s instruments
Ps 150: 4 Praise Him with s
Amos 6: 5 sing idly to the sound of s
Hab 3:19 With my s instruments.

STRINGS (see STRINGED)
Ps 33: 2 with an instrument of ten s.
Ps 144: 9 On a harp of ten s I will

STRIP (see STRIPPED, STRIPS)
Num 20:26 and s Aaron of his garments
1Sa 31: 8 the Philistines came to s
Hos 2: 3 Lest I s her naked And
Mic 3: 2 Who s the skin from My

STRIPE† (see STRIPES)
Ex 21:25 for wound, s for stripe.

STRIPES (see STRIPE)
Is 53: 5 And by His s we are healed.
Luke 12:47 shall be beaten with many s.
2Co 11:24 times I received forty s
1Pe 2:24 by whose s you were healed.

STRIPPED (see STRIP)
Gen 37:23 that they s Joseph of his
Num 20:28 Moses s Aaron of his garments
Matt 27:28 And they s Him and put a
Luke 10:30 who s him of his clothing,

STRIPS† (see STRIP)
Gen 30:37 peeled white s in them, and
Ps 29: 9 And s the forests bare;
John 19:40 and bound it in s of linen

STRIVE (see STRIVES, STRIVING)
Gen 6: 3 My Spirit shall not s with
Ps 103: 9 He will not always s with
Luke 13:24 S to enter through the narrow

STRIVES† (*see* STRIVE)
Is 45: 9 Woe to him who **s** with his

STRIVING (*see* STRIVE)
Heb 12: 4 **s** against sin.

STROKE
Ezek 24:16 of your eyes with one **s**;

STRONG (*see* STRONGER)
Ex 6: 1 and with a **s** hand he will
Num 13:28 who dwell in the land are **s**;
Deut 31: 7 Be **s** and of good courage, for
Josh 1: 6 Be **s** and of good courage, for
Josh 17:13 children of Israel grew **s**,
Judg 14:14 And out of the **s** came
1Ki 8:42 Your great name and Your **s**
2Ch 16: 9 to show Himself **s** on behalf
Neh 1:10 and by Your **s** hand.
Ps 19: 5 And rejoices like a **s** man
Ps 22:12 **S** bulls of Bashan have
Ps 24: 8 The LORD **s** and mighty,
Ps 136:12 With a **s** hand, and with an
Prov 30:25 ants are a people not **s**,
Prov 31: 6 Give **s** drink to him who is
Eccl 9:11 Nor the battle to the **s**,
Eccl 12: 3 And the **s** men bow down;
Song 8: 6 For love is as **s** as
Jer 50:34 Their Redeemer is **s**;
Ezek 34:16 destroy the fat and the **s**,
Dan 8: 8 great; but when he became **s**,
Mic 4: 3 And rebuke **s** nations afar
Hag 2: 4 says the LORD; 'and be **s**,
Matt 12:29 Or how can one enter a **s**
Matt 12:29 unless he first binds the **s**
Luke 1:15 drink neither wine nor **s**
Luke 11:21 When a **s** man, fully armed,
Rom 15: 1 We then who are **s** ought to
1Co 4:10 but you are **s**! You are
2Co 12:10 when I am weak, then I am **s**.
Eph 6:10 be **s** in the Lord and in the
2Th 2:11 reason God will send them **s**
2Ti 2: 1 be **s** in the grace that is in
Heb 11:34 out of weakness were made **s**,

STRONGER (*see* STRONG)
Num 13:31 for they are **s** than we."
Judg 14:18 And what is **s** than a
2Sa 1:23 They were **s** than lions.
1Co 1:25 and the weakness of God is **s**
1Co 10:22 Are we **s** than He?

STRONGHOLD (*see* STRONGHOLDS)
Judg 9:49 and set the **s** on fire above
1Sa 22: 4 time that David was in the **s**.
2Sa 5: 7 David took the **s** of Zion
Ps 18: 2 horn of my salvation, my **s**.

STRONGHOLDS (*see* STRONGHOLD)
1Sa 23:14 And David stayed in **s** in the
2Co 10: 4 in God for pulling down **s**,

STRUCK (*see* STRIKE)
Gen 19:11 And they **s** the men who were
Ex 7:20 he lifted up the rod and **s**
Ex 8:17 his hand with his rod and **s**
Ex 12:29 at midnight that the LORD **s**
Num 22:23 So Balaam **s** the donkey to
Josh 8:24 returned to Ai and **s** it
1Sa 5: 6 and He ravaged them and **s**
1Sa 17:50 and **s** the Philistine and
1Sa 25:38 that the LORD **s** Nabal, and
2Sa 12:15 And the LORD **s** the child
Job 2: 7 and **s** Job with painful boils
Ps 69:26 the ones You have **s**,
Ps 78:20 He **s** the rock, So that the
Is 50: 6 gave My back to those who **s**
Is 60:10 For in My wrath I **s** you,

Dan 2:35 And the stone that **s** the
Matt 26:51 **s** the servant of the high
Matt 26:67 and others **s** Him with the
2Co 4: 9 **s** down, but not destroyed—

STRUGGLED
Gen 32:28 for you have **s** with God and
Hos 12: 3 And in his strength he **s**
Hos 12: 4 he **s** with the Angel and

STUBBLE
Ex 5:12 land of Egypt to gather **s**
Ex 15: 7 It consumed them like **s**.
Mal 4: 1 who do wickedly will be **s**.

STUBBORN (*see* STUBBORNNESS)
Ex 13:15 when Pharaoh was **s** about
Deut 21:20 This son of ours is **s** and
Ezek 2: 4 they are impudent and **s**

STUBBORNNESS (*see* STUBBORN)
1Sa 15:23 And **s** is as iniquity and

STUBS†
Is 7: 4 for these two **s** of smoking

STUDIED (*see* STUDY)
John 7:15 know letters, having never **s**?

STUDY† (*see* STUDIED)
Eccl 12:12 and much **s** is wearisome to

STUMBLE (*see* STUMBLED, STUMBLES, STUMBLING)
Ps 119:165 nothing causes them to **s**.
Prov 3:23 And your foot will not **s**.
Prov 4:19 not know what makes them **s**.
Is 8:15 And many among them shall **s**;
Is 28: 7 they **s** in judgment.
Ezek 14: 4 him what causes him to **s**
Hos 14: 9 But transgressors **s** in
1Co 8:13 if food makes my brother **s**,
Jas 2:10 and yet **s** in one point, he
1Pe 2: 8 of offense." They **s**,

STUMBLED (*see* STUMBLE)
2Sa 6: 6 hold of it, for the oxen **s**.
Ps 73: 2 for me, my feet had almost **s**;

STUMBLES (*see* STUMBLE)
Rom 14:21 by which your brother **s** or

STUMBLING (*see* STUMBLE)
Prov 24:11 And hold back those **s** to
Is 8:14 But a stone of **s** and a rock
Is 57:14 Take the **s** block out of the
Rom 9:33 I lay in Zion a **s**
Rom 14:13 not to put a **s** block or a
1Co 1:23 to the Jews a **s** block and to
1Co 8: 9 liberty of yours become a **s**
1Pe 2: 8 A stone of **s** And a
1Jn 2:10 and there is no cause for **s**
Jude 24 is able to keep you from **s**,

STUMP
Job 14: 8 And its **s** may die in the
Is 6:13 Whose **s** remains when it is
Is 6:13 holy seed shall be its **s**.

STUPOR†
Rom 11: 8 them a spirit of **s**,

SUBDUE (*see* SUBDUED)
Gen 1:28 fill the earth and **s** it;
Phil 3:21 which He is able even to **s**

SUBDUED (*see* SUBDUE)
Heb 11:33 who through faith **s** kingdoms,

SUBJECT (*see* SUBJECTED, SUBJECTION)
Luke 2:51 and was **s** to them, but His
Luke 10:20 that the spirits are **s** to
1Co 14:32 of the prophets are **s** to
1Co 15:28 when all things are made **s**

SUBJECTED (see SUBJECT)
Eph 5:24 just as the church is s to
Heb 5: 2 is also s to weakness.

SUBJECTED (see SUBJECT)
Rom 8:20 For the creation was s to

SUBJECTION (see SUBJECT)
Jer 34:16 and brought them back into s,
1Co 9:27 my body and bring it into s,
Heb 2: 8 put all things in s

SUBMISSION (see SUBMIT)
1Ti 2:11 learn in silence with all s.

SUBMISSIVE (see SUBMIT)
1Pe 2:18 be s to your masters with
1Pe 3: 1 be s to your own husbands,

SUBMIT (see SUBMISSION, SUBMISSIVE)
Gen 16: 9 and s yourself under her
Eph 5:22 s to your own husbands, as
Jas 4: 7 Therefore s to God. Resist
1Pe 5: 5 s yourselves to your

SUBSIDED
Gen 8: 1 the earth, and the waters s.
Judg 8: 3 their anger toward him s

SUBSTANCE
Ps 139:16 Your eyes saw my s,
Heb 11: 1 Now faith is the s of things

SUCCESS
Gen 24:12 please give me s this day,
Josh 1: 8 then you will have good s.

SUCCOTH
Ex 12:37 journeyed from Rameses to S,
Ps 60: 6 measure out the Valley of S.

SUDDEN (see SUDDENLY)
1Th 5: 3 Peace and safety!" then s

SUDDENLY (see SUDDEN)
Prov 29: 1 Will s be destroyed, and
Mal 3: 1 Will s come to His temple,
Luke 2:13 And s there was with the
Acts 2: 2 And s there came a sound from
Acts 9: 3 and s a light shone around

SUE†
Matt 5:40 If anyone wants to s you and

SUFFER (see SUFFERED, SUFFERING, SUFFERS)
Mark 8:31 that the Son of Man must s
Luke 24:46 for the Christ to s and to
Acts 5:41 were counted worthy to s
Acts 9:16 how many things he must s
Acts 17: 3 that the Christ had to s
Rom 8:17 if indeed we s with Him,
1Co 3:15 he will s loss; but he
Phil 1:29 but also to s for His sake,
Phil 4:12 both to abound and to s
Heb 11:25 choosing rather to s
1Pe 2:20 But when you do good and s,
1Pe 4:15 But let none of you s as a

SUFFERED (see SUFFER)
Jer 15:15 that for Your sake I have s
Luke 24:26 not the Christ to have s
2Co 7:12 for the sake of him who s
Phil 3: 8 for whom I have s the loss
Heb 2:18 For in that He Himself has s,
Heb 13:12 s outside the gate.
1Pe 2:21 because Christ also s for
1Pe 5:10 after you have s a while,

SUFFERING (see SUFFER, SUFFERINGS)
Acts 1: 3 Himself alive after His s
Heb 2: 9 for the s of death crowned
Jas 5:10 as an example of s and
Jas 5:13 Is anyone among you s?
1Pe 2:19 grief, s wrongfully.

SUFFERINGS (see SUFFERING)
Rom 8:18 For I consider that the s of
2Co 1: 5 For as the s of Christ abound
2Co 1: 7 you are partakers of the s,
Phil 3:10 and the fellowship of His s,
Col 1:24 I now rejoice in my s for
2Ti 1: 8 but share with me in the s
Heb 2:10 salvation perfect through s.
1Pe 1:11 testified beforehand the s
1Pe 4:13 you partake of Christ's s,
1Pe 5: 1 and a witness of the s of
1Pe 5: 9 knowing that the same s are

SUFFERS (see SUFFER)
Matt 11:12 now the kingdom of heaven s
1Co 12:26 And if one member s,
1Co 13: 4 Love s long and is kind;
1Pe 4:16 Yet if anyone s as a

SUFFICIENCY (see SUFFICIENT)
2Co 3: 5 but our s is from God,

SUFFICIENT (see SUFFICIENCY)
Matt 6:34 S for the day is its own
John 14: 8 and it is s for us."
2Co 2:16 And who is s for these
2Co 12: 9 My grace is s for you, for My

SUITABLE
Lev 16:21 by the hand of a s man.

SUM
Ps 139:17 O God! How great is the s
Matt 28:12 they gave a large s of money

SUMMER
Gen 8:22 and heat, Winter and s,
Ps 32: 4 turned into the drought of s.
Jer 8:20 The s is ended, And we are
Amos 8: 1 a basket of s fruit.
Matt 24:32 you know that s is near.

SUMPTUOUSLY†
Luke 16:19 and fine linen and fared s

SUN (see SUNDIAL)
Gen 15:12 Now when the s was going
Deut 24:15 and not let the s go down on
Josh 10:12 the sight of Israel: "S,
2Sa 12:11 wives in the sight of this s.
2Ki 23:11 Judah had dedicated to the s,
Ps 19: 4 set a tabernacle for the s,
Ps 50: 1 From the rising of the s
Ps 84:11 For the LORD God is a s
Ps 104:19 The s knows its going down.
Ps 121: 6 The s shall not strike you
Ps 136: 8 The s to rule by day, For
Ps 148: 3 s and moon; Praise Him, all
Eccl 1: 3 which he toils under the s?
Eccl 1: 5 The s also rises, and the
Eccl 1: 9 is nothing new under the s.
Eccl 4: 7 and I saw vanity under the s:
Eccl 10: 5 evil I have seen under the s,
Dan 6:14 the going down of the s to
Joel 3:15 The s and moon will grow
Mal 4: 2 you who fear My name The S
Matt 5:45 for He makes His s rise on
Matt 17: 2 His face shone like the s,
Matt 24:29 of those days the s will be
Acts 2:20 The s shall be turned
Eph 4:26 do not let the s go down on
Rev 21:23 city had no need of the s
Rev 22: 5 no lamp nor light of the s,

SUNDIAL (see SUN)
2Ki 20:11 it had gone down on the s

SUNG (see SING)
Matt 26:30 And when they had s a hymn,

SUNK (*see* SINK)
Jer   38:22 Your feet have **s** in the

SUPPER
Luke   14:16 certain man gave a great **s**
Luke   22:20 also took the cup after **s**,
John   13: 2 And **s** being ended, the devil
John   21:20 on His breast at the **s**,
1Co   11:20 is not to eat the Lord's **S**.
1Co   11:25 also took the cup after **s**,
Rev   19: 9 called to the marriage **s** of

SUPPLANTED†
Gen   27:36 For he has **s** me these two

SUPPLICATION (*see* SUPPLICATIONS)
Ps   6: 9 The LORD has heard my **s**;
Ps   55: 1 not hide Yourself from my **s**.
Dan   6:11 Daniel praying and making **s**
Dan   9:20 and presenting my **s** before
Zech   12:10 the Spirit of grace and **s**;
Acts   1:14 one accord in prayer and **s**,
Eph   6:18 with all prayer and **s** in
Eph   6:18 with all perseverance and **s**
Phil   4: 6 everything by prayer and **s**,

SUPPLICATIONS (*see* SUPPLICATION)
Ps   28: 6 has heard the voice of my **s**!
Ps   86: 6 attend to the voice of my **s**.
Dan   9: 3 make request by prayer and **s**,
1Ti   2: 1 I exhort first of all that **s**,
Heb   5: 7 had offered up prayers and **s**,

SUPPLIED (*see* SUPPLY)
1Co   16:17 lacking on your part they **s**.

SUPPLIES (*see* SUPPLY)
Prov   31:24 And **s** sashes for the
2Co   9:10 Now may He who **s** seed to the
Eph   4:16 by what every joint **s**,
1Pe   4:11 with the ability which God **s**,

SUPPLY (*see* SUPPLIED, SUPPLIES)
Ex   1:11 And they built for Pharaoh **s**
2Co   8:14 time your abundance may **s**
Phil   2:30 to **s** what was lacking in
Phil   4:19 And my God shall **s** all your

SUPPORT (*see* SUPPORTED)
Gen   13: 6 the land was not able to **s**
Judg   16:26 me feel the pillars which **s**

SUPPORTED (*see* SUPPORT)
Ex   17:12 And Aaron and Hur **s** his
Judg   16:29 two middle pillars which **s**

SUPPOSE (*see* SUPPOSED, SUPPOSING)
Gen   18:24 **S** there were fifty righteous
John   21:25 I **s** that even the world
Acts   2:15 are not drunk, as you **s**,
Jas   1: 7 For let not that man **s** that

SUPPOSED (*see* SUPPOSE)
Mark   6:49 they **s** it was a ghost, and
Luke   3:23 being (as was **s**) the son of

SUPPOSING (*see* SUPPOSE)
Luke   2:44 but **s** Him to have been in the
John   20:15 **s** Him to be the gardener,
Acts   16:27 **s** the prisoners had fled,

SUPPRESS†
Rom   1:18 who **s** the truth in

SUPREME†
1Pe   2:13 whether to the king as **s**,

SURE (*see* SURETY)
Num   32:23 and be **s** your sin will find
Ps   19: 7 testimony of the LORD is **s**,
Is   55: 3 The **s** mercies of David.
Acts   13:34 I will give you the **s**
Heb   6:19 both **s** and steadfast, and

2Pe   1:10 your call and election **s**,

SURETY (*see* SURE)
Heb   7:22 more Jesus has become a **s**

SURFACE
Gen   7:18 ark moved about on the **s** of

SURNAME (*see* SURNAMED)
Acts   10: 5 and send for Simon whose **s**

SURNAMED (*see* SURNAME)
Luke   22: 3 **s** Iscariot, who was numbered

SURPASSES† (*see* SURPASSING)
Phil   4: 7 which **s** all understanding,

SURPASSING† (*see* SURPASSES)
2Sa   1:26 **S** the love of women.

SURROUND (*see* SURROUNDED, SURROUNDS)
Ps   17: 9 my deadly enemies who **s** me.

SURROUNDED (*see* SURROUND)
Gen   19: 4 every quarter, **s** the house.
Judg   19:22 **s** the house and beat on the
2Sa   22: 5 When the waves of death **s** me,
Ps   18: 4 The pangs of death **s** me,
Ps   18: 5 The sorrows of Sheol **s** me;
Ps   22:12 Many bulls have **s** Me;
Jon   2: 3 And the floods **s** me; All
Jon   2: 5 The waters **s** me, even to my
Luke   21:20 when you see Jerusalem **s** by
Heb   12: 1 since we are **s** by so great a

SURROUNDS (*see* SURROUND)
Ps   125: 2 So the LORD **s** His people

SUSANNA†
Luke   8: 3 Herod's steward, and **S**,

SUSPICIONS†
1Ti   6: 4 strife, reviling, evil **s**,

SUSTAINED
Neh   9:21 Forty years You **s** them in

SUSTAINS†
Lev   17:14 Its blood **s** its life.

SWADDLING
Ezek   16: 4 with salt nor wrapped in **s**
Luke   2: 7 and wrapped Him in **s** cloths,

SWALLOW (*see* SWALLOWED)
Num   16:34 Lest the earth **s** us up
Ps   84: 3 And the **s** a nest for
Is   25: 8 He will **s** up death forever,
Amos   8: 4 you who **s** up the needy, And
Jon   1:17 prepared a great fish to **s**
Matt   23:24 who strain out a gnat and **s**

SWALLOWED (*see* SWALLOW)
Ex   7:12 But Aaron's rod **s** up their
Ex   15:12 The earth **s** them.
Ps   124: 3 Then they would have **s** us
1Co   15:54 Death is **s** up in

SWARMING
Joel   1: 4 the **s** locust has eaten;
Nah   3:15 like the **s** locusts!

SWARMS
Ex   8:21 I will send **s** of flies on
Ps   105:31 and there came **s** of flies,
Amos   7: 1 He formed locust **s** at the

SWAY
Judg   9: 9 And go to **s** over trees?'

SWEAR (*see* SWEARING, SWEARS, SWORE, SWORN)
Is   19:18 language of Canaan and **s** by
Matt   5:34 do not **s** at all: neither by
Matt   26:74 Then he began to curse and **s**,
Heb   6:13 because He could **s** by no one

Heb 6:16 For men indeed s by the

SWEARING (*see* SWEAR)
Hos 4: 2 By s and lying, Killing

SWEARS (*see* SWEAR)
Num 30: 2 or s an oath to bind himself
Ps 15: 4 He who s to his own hurt
Prov 29:24 He s to tell the truth, but
Matt 23:16 Whoever s by the temple, it

SWEAT
Gen 3:19 In the s of your face you
Luke 22:44 Then His s became like great

SWEEP (*see* SWEPT)
Is 14:23 I will s it with the broom
Luke 15: 8 s the house, and search

SWEET (*see* SWEET-SMELLING, SWEETER, SWEETNESS)
Ex 15:25 the waters were made s.
Ex 25: 6 anointing oil and for the s
Ex 29:25 as a s aroma before the
Lev 1: 9 a s aroma to the LORD.
Judg 14:14 the strong came something s.
2Sa 23: 1 And the s psalmist of
Neh 8:10 eat the fat, drink the s,
Ps 104:34 May my meditation be s to
Ps 119:103 How s are Your words to my
Prov 3:24 and your sleep will be s.
Prov 9:17 "Stolen water is s,
Eccl 5:12 of a laboring man is s,
Song 2: 3 And his fruit was s to my
Song 5:16 His mouth is most s,
Is 5:20 Who put bitter for s,
Jer 31:26 and my sleep was s to me.

SWEET-SMELLING (*see* SWEET)
Eph 5: 2 a sacrifice to God for a s
Phil 4:18 a s aroma, an acceptable

SWEETER (*see* SWEET)
Judg 14:18 What is s than honey? And
Ps 19:10 S also than honey and the

SWEETNESS (*see* SWEET)
Judg 9:11 Should I cease my s and my
Prov 16:24 S to the soul and health to
Ezek 3: 3 in my mouth like honey in s.

SWELL (*see* SWELLING)
Num 5:27 bitter, and her belly will s,
Deut 8: 4 nor did your foot s these

SWELLING (*see* SWELL)
2Pe 2:18 For when they speak great s

SWEPT (*see* SWEEP)
Judg 5:21 The torrent of Kishon s them
Matt 12:44 comes, he finds it empty, s,

SWIFT (*see* SWIFTER)
1Ch 12: 8 and were as s as gazelles
Prov 6:18 Feet that are s in running
Eccl 9:11 race is not to the s,
Is 18: 2 s messengers, to a nation
Amos 2:14 shall perish from the s,
Rom 3:15 Their feet are s to shed

SWIFTER (*see* SWIFT)
2Sa 1:23 They were s than eagles,

SWIM
Ps 6: 6 All night I make my bed s;
Ezek 47: 5 water in which one must s,

SWINE (*see* SWINE'S)
Deut 14: 8 Also the s is unclean for
Matt 7: 6 cast your pearls before s,
Matt 8:32 the whole herd of s ran

SWINE'S (*see* SWINE)
Prov 11:22 As a ring of gold in a s

Is 65: 4 Who eat s flesh, And the

SWOOP†
1Sa 15:19 Why did you s down on the

SWORD (*see* SWORDS)
Gen 3:24 and a flaming s which turned
Gen 34:26 son with the edge of the s,
Lev 26: 7 and they shall fall by the s
Num 22:23 in the way with His drawn s
Josh 5:13 opposite him with His s
Judg 7:18 The s of the LORD and of
Judg 7:22 the LORD set every man's s
1Sa 17:39 David fastened his s to his
1Sa 17:47 LORD does not save with s
1Sa 31: 4 armorbearer, "Draw your s,
1Sa 31: 5 dead, he also fell on his s,
2Sa 2:26 Shall the s devour forever?
2Sa 11:25 for the s devours one as
1Ki 19: 1 all the prophets with the s.
Neh 4:18 of the builders had his s
Job 1:15 with the edge of the s;
Job 33:18 life from perishing by the s.
Ps 22:20 Deliver Me from the s,
Ps 37:15 Their s shall enter their
Ps 57: 4 And their tongue a sharp s.
Prov 5: 4 Sharp as a two-edged s.
Is 2: 4 Nation shall not lift up s
Is 27: 1 the LORD with His severe s,
Is 31: 8 Assyria shall fall by a s
Jer 5:12 Nor shall we see s or
Jer 15: 3 the s to slay, the dogs to
Jer 47: 6 O you s of the LORD, How
Ezek 5: 1 son of man, take a sharp s,
Ezek 32:22 them slain, fallen by the s.
Ezek 32:25 slain by the s;
Hos 1: 7 Nor by s or battle, By
Amos 1:11 his brother with the s,
Amos 7:11 shall die by the s,
Mic 4: 3 Nation shall not lift up s
Matt 10:34 come to bring peace but a s.
Matt 26:51 out his hand and drew his s,
Matt 26:52 Put your s in its place, for
Matt 26:52 sword will perish by the s.
Luke 2:35 a s will pierce through your
Luke 22:36 and he who has no s,
John 18:11 Put your s into the sheath.
Rom 8:35 or nakedness, or peril, or s?
Rom 13: 4 for he does not bear the s
Eph 6:17 and the s of the Spirit,
Heb 4:12 sharper than any two-edged s,
Heb 11:34 escaped the edge of the s,
Rev 1:16 went a sharp two-edged s,
Rev 2:16 against them with the s of
Rev 19:15 of His mouth goes a sharp s,

SWORDS (*see* SWORD)
1Sa 13:19 Lest the Hebrews make s or
2Sa 2:16 called the Field of Sharp S,
Prov 30:14 whose teeth are like s,
Is 2: 4 They shall beat their s
Joel 3:10 your plowshares into s And
Mic 4: 3 They shall beat their s
Matt 26:55 with s and clubs to take Me?
Luke 22:38 look, here are two s.

SWORE (*see* SWEAR)
Ex 6: 8 you into the land which I s
1Ki 1:17 you s by the LORD your God
Ps 95:11 So I s in My wrath, "They
Dan 12: 7 and s by Him who lives
Heb 3:11 So I s in My wrath,
Heb 6:13 He s by Himself,
Rev 10: 6 and s by Him who lives

SWORN (*see* SWEAR)
Gen 22:16 said: "By Myself I have s,

Ps 24: 4 Nor **s** deceitfully.
Ps 89: 3 I have **s** to My servant
Ps 89:35 Once I have **s** by My
Ps 110: 4 The LORD has **s** And will
Is 62: 8 The LORD has **s** by His right
Jer 44:26 I have **s** by My great name,'
Heb 7:21 The LORD has **s** And

SYCAMORE
Amos 7:14 And a tender of **s** fruit.
Luke 19: 4 and climbed up into a **s**

SYCHAR† (*see* SHECHEM)
John 4: 5 of Samaria which is called S,

SYMBOL† (*see* SYMBOLIC)
1Co 11:10 woman ought to have a **s**

SYMBOLIC† (*see* SYMBOL)
Gal 4:24 which things are **s**.
Heb 9: 9 It was **s** for the present

SYMPATHIZE†
Heb 4:15 a High Priest who cannot **s**

SYMPHONY†
Dan 3: 5 in **s** with all kinds of
Dan 3: 7 in **s** with all kinds of
Dan 3:10 in **s** with all kinds of
Dan 3:15 in **s** with all kinds of

SYNAGOGUE (*see* SYNAGOGUES)
Matt 13:54 He taught them in their **s**,
Mark 1:21 the Sabbath He entered the **s**
Mark 5:22 one of the rulers of the **s**
Luke 7: 5 nation, and has built us a **s**.
John 6:59 things He said in the **s** as
John 9:22 he would be put out of the **s**.
Acts 14: 1 they went together to the **s**
Rev 2: 9 but are a **s** of Satan.

SYNAGOGUES (*see* SYNAGOGUE)
Matt 23: 6 the best seats in the **s**,
Mark 1:39 He was preaching in their **s**
John 16: 2 will put you out of the **s**;
Acts 9: 2 letters from him to the **s**
Acts 15:21 being read in the **s** every

SYRIA (*see* ARAM, SYRIAN)
1Ki 19:15 Hazael as king over S.
1Ki 20:20 and Ben-Hadad the king of S
2Ki 13:24 Now Hazael king of S died.
2Ki 15:37 to send Rezin king of S and
Is 7: 4 fierce anger of Rezin and S,
Is 7: 8 For the head of S is
Luke 2: 2 Quirinius was governing S.
Gal 1:21 I went into the regions of S

SYRIAN (*see* SYRIA, SYRIANS, SYRO-PHOENICIAN)
Gen 25:20 the sister of Laban the S.
Deut 26: 5 God: 'My father was a S,
2Ki 5:20 has spared Naaman this S,
Luke 4:27 cleansed except Naaman the S.

SYRIANS (*see* SYRIAN)
2Sa 8: 5 When the S of Damascus came
2Sa 8: 6 and the S became David's
2Sa 10:18 Then the S fled before
2Ki 5: 2 And the S had gone out on
2Ki 7:16 plundered the tents of the S.
Amos 9: 7 And the S from Kir?

SYRO-PHOENICIAN† (*see* SYRIAN)
Mark 7:26 a S by birth, and she kept

T

TAANACH
Judg 5:19 kings of Canaan fought In T,

TABEL
Is 7: 6 over them, the son of T''—

TABERNACLE (*see* TABERNACLES)
Ex 25: 9 the pattern of the **t** and the
Ex 26: 7 to be a tent over the **t**.
Ex 27:21 In the **t** of meeting, outside
Ex 38:21 the **t** of the Testimony,
Ex 40:18 So Moses raised up the **t**,
Ex 40:34 of the LORD filled the **t**.
Lev 8:10 and anointed the **t** and all
Lev 26:11 I will set My **t** among you,
Num 3: 7 to do the work of the **t**.
1Sa 1: 9 by the doorpost of the **t** of
1Ch 9:19 gatekeepers of the **t**.
1Ch 23:26 shall no longer carry the **t**,
Ps 15: 1 who may abide in Your **t**?
Ps 19: 4 In them He has set a **t** for
Ps 27: 5 the secret place of His **t**
Ps 43: 3 holy hill And to Your **t**.
Ps 46: 4 The holy place of the **t** of
Ps 76: 2 In Salem also is His **t**,
Ps 78:60 So that He forsook the **t** of
Ps 84: 1 How lovely is Your **t**,
Amos 9:11 day I will raise up The **t**
Acts 15:16 will rebuild the **t** of
Heb 8: 2 sanctuary and of the true **t**
Heb 9: 8 manifest while the first **t**
Heb 9:11 greater and more perfect **t**
Rev 21: 3 the **t** of God is with men,

TABERNACLES (*see* TABERNACLE)
Deut 16:13 shall observe the Feast of T
Ezra 3: 4 also kept the Feast of T,
Zech 14:18 up to keep the Feast of T.
John 7: 2 Now the Jews' Feast of T was

TABITHA (*see* DORCAS)
Acts 9:40 to the body he said, "T,

TABLE (*see* TABLES)
Ex 25:23 You shall also make a **t** of
Num 4: 7 On the **t** of showbread they
2Sa 9: 7 you shall eat bread at my **t**
1Ki 4:27 who came to King Solomon's **t**.
1Ki 7:48 and the **t** of gold on which
1Ki 18:19 who eat at Jezebel's **t**.
Ps 23: 5 You prepare a **t** before me in
Ps 78:19 Can God prepare a **t** in the
Prov 9: 2 has also furnished her **t**.
Mal 1:12 The **t** of the LORD is
Matt 9:10 as Jesus sat at the **t** in the
Matt 15:27 fall from their masters' **t**.
Matt 26: 7 head as He sat at the **t**.
Mark 14: 3 leper, as He sat at the **t**,
Luke 7:37 that Jesus sat at the **t** in
Luke 16:21 fell from the rich man's **t**.
Luke 22:21 is with Me on the **t**.
Luke 22:30 may eat and drink at My **t**
1Co 10:21 partake of the Lord's **t** and
1Co 10:21 Lord's table and of the **t**
Heb 9: 2 was the lampstand, the **t**,

TABLES (*see* TABLE)
1Ch 28:16 he gave gold for the **t** of
Matt 21:12 and overturned the **t** of the
John 2:15 money and overturned the **t**.
Acts 6: 2 the word of God and serve **t**.

TABLET (*see* TABLETS)
Prov 3: 3 Write them on the **t** of your
Prov 7: 3 Write them on the **t** of your
Jer 17: 1 it is engraved On the **t**
Ezek 4: 1 take a clay **t** and lay it
Luke 1:63 And he asked for a writing **t**,

TABLETS (*see* TABLET)
Ex 24:12 and I will give you **t** of

Ex	31:18	He gave Moses two t of the
Ex	32:16	of God engraved on the t.
Ex	34: 1	Cut two t of stone like the
Ex	34: 1	that were on the first t
Deut	9: 9	the t of the covenant which
Deut	10: 5	and put the t in the ark
Hab	2: 2	And make it plain on t,
2Co	3: 3	not on t of stone but on
2Co	3: 3	on tablets of stone but on t
Heb	9: 4	and the t of the covenant;

TABOR

Judg	4: 6	and deploy troops at Mount T

TAHPANHES

Jer	43: 9	to Pharaoh's house in T;

TAIL (*see* TAILS)

Ex	4: 4	hand and take it by the t'
Ex	29:22	fat of the ram, the fat t,
Deut	28:13	you the head and not the t;
Judg	15: 4	turned the foxes t to

TAILS (*see* TAIL)

Judg	15: 4	torch between each pair of t.
Rev	9:10	They had t like scorpions,

TAKE (*see* TAKEN, TAKES, TAKING, TOOK)

Gen	13: 9	If you t the left, then I
Gen	22: 2	T now your son, your only
Gen	24: 4	and t a wife for my son
Ex	3: 5	T your sandals off your
Ex	19:12	T heed to yourselves that
Ex	20: 7	You shall not t the name of
Num	1: 2	T a census of all the
Num	6: 2	an offering to t the vow of
Num	26: 2	T a census of all the
Deut	5:11	You shall not t the name of
Deut	16:19	nor t a bribe, for a bribe
Josh	5:15	T your sandal off your foot,
Ruth	2:10	that you should t notice of
1Sa	8:11	He will t your sons and
1Sa	8:13	He will t your daughters to
2Sa	24:10	t away the iniquity of Your
1Ki	19: 4	t my life, for I am no
1Ki	19:10	and they seek to t my
1Ki	20:18	t them alive; and if they
2Ki	10:14	T them alive!" So they took
Job	7:21	And t away my iniquity?
Job	10:20	that I may t a little
Job	23:10	He knows the way that I t;
Job	32:22	my Maker would soon t me
Ps	2: 2	And the rulers t counsel
Ps	16: 4	Nor t up their names on my
Ps	27:10	Then the LORD will t care
Ps	28: 3	Do not t me away with the
Ps	51:11	And do not t Your Holy
Ps	91: 4	under His wings you shall t
Ps	102:24	Do not t me away in the
Ps	104:29	You t away their breath,
Ps	139: 9	If I t the wings of the
Ps	141: 8	In You I t refuge; Do not
Ps	143: 9	In You I t shelter.
Prov	4:13	T firm hold of instruction,
Prov	6:27	Can a man t fire to his
Prov	7:18	let us t our fill of love
Is	1:24	And t vengeance on My
Is	4: 1	that day seven women shall t
Is	42:25	Yet he did not t it to
Jer	16: 2	You shall not t a wife, nor
Jer	29: 6	T wives and beget sons and
Hos	1: 2	t yourself a wife of
Hos	2: 9	And will t back My wool and
Hos	14: 2	T words with you, And
Jon	4: 3	please t my life from me,
Matt	2:13	t the young Child and His
Matt	9: 6	t up your bed, and go to

Matt	10:38	And he who does not t his
Matt	11:12	and the violent t it by
Matt	11:29	T My yoke upon you and learn
Matt	16:24	and t up his cross, and
Matt	24:34	away till all these things t
Matt	25:38	we see You a stranger and t
Matt	26:26	the disciples and said, "T,
Matt	26:52	for all who t the sword will
Mark	14: 1	sought how they might t Him
Mark	14:36	T this cup away from Me;
Mark	16:18	they will t up serpents; and
Luke	9: 3	T nothing for the journey,
Luke	9:23	and t up his cross daily,
Luke	12:19	t your ease; eat, drink,
Luke	21:32	pass away till all things t
Luke	22:42	t this cup away from Me;
John	6:15	were about to come and t
John	10:17	down My life that I may t
John	16:14	for He will t of what is
Acts	1:20	Let another t his
Rom	11:27	When I t away their
1Co	10:12	him who thinks he stands t
1Co	11:24	He broke it and said, "T,
Eph	6:13	Therefore t up the whole
Eph	6:17	And t the helmet of
Heb	2: 6	son of man that You t
Heb	10: 4	of bulls and goats could t
1Pe	2:20	if you t it patiently, this
Rev	1: 1	which must shortly t
Rev	22:17	let him t the water of life
Rev	22:19	God shall t away his part

TAKEN (*see* TAKE)

Gen	2:23	Because she was t out of
Gen	3:23	ground from which he was t.
Gen	30:23	God has t away my reproach."
Num	10:11	that the cloud was t up from
Deut	24: 5	When a man has t a new wife,
2Sa	12:10	and have t the wife of Uriah
2Ki	2: 9	before I am t away from
2Ki	2:10	if you see me when I am t
2Ki	2:16	Spirit of the LORD has t
Job	1:21	and the LORD has t away;
Is	6: 6	a live coal which he had t
Is	6: 7	Your iniquity is t away,
Is	21: 3	Pangs have t hold of me,
Is	53: 8	He was t from prison and
Jer	38:28	the day that Jerusalem was t.
Dan	6:23	So Daniel was t up out of
Matt	24:40	one will be t and the other
Matt	25:29	even what he has will be t
Luke	1: 1	Inasmuch as many have t in
John	20:13	Because they have t away my
Acts	1: 2	the day in which He was t
Acts	1:11	who was t up from you into
2Co	3:14	because the veil is t away
Heb	11: 5	By faith Enoch was t away so

TAKES (*see* TAKE)

Ex	20: 7	hold him guiltless who t
Num	6:21	to the vow which he t,
Deut	5:11	hold him guiltless who t
Job	9:12	If He t away, who can hinder
Is	57: 1	And no man t it to heart;
John	1:29	The Lamb of God who t away
John	10:18	No one t it from Me, but I
John	15: 2	does not bear fruit He t

TAKING (*see* TAKE)

Ps	119: 9	By t heed according to Your
Hos	11: 3	T them by their arms; But
Luke	4: 5	t Him up on a high mountain,
Rom	7: 8	t opportunity by the
Rom	7:11	t occasion by the
Eph	6:16	t the shield of faith with
Phil	2: 7	t the form of a bondservant,

2Th   1: 8 in flaming fire t vengeance

TALENT (*see* TALENTS)
1Ki 20:39 or else you shall pay a t of
Matt 25:24 who had received the one t

TALENTS (*see* TALENT)
Ex   38:27 And from the hundred t of
Matt 18:24 who owed him ten thousand t.
Matt 25:15 "And to one he gave five t,

TALITHA†
Mark 5:41 hand, and said to her, "T,

TALL (*see* TALLER)
Deut   9: 2 "a people great and t,
Is   18: 2 to a nation t and smooth of

TALLER (*see* TALL)
Deut   1:28 people are greater and t
1Sa   9: 2 shoulders upward he was t

TAMAR
Gen 38:11 Then Judah said to T his
Gen 38:24 T your daughter-in-law has
Ruth 4:12 whom T bore to Judah,
2Sa   13: 2 over his sister T that he
2Sa 13:10 Then Amnon said to T,
2Sa 13:22 he had forced his sister T.
Matt 1: 3 begot Perez and Zerah by T,

TAME†
Mark 5: 4 neither could anyone t him.
Jas   3: 8 But no man can t the tongue.

TAMMUZ†
Ezek 8:14 sitting there weeping for T.

TANNER
Acts 9:43 in Joppa with Simon, a t.

TAPESTRY
Prov 7:16 I have spread my bed with t,

TARES
Matt 13:25 his enemy came and sowed t

TARRIES (*see* TARRY)
Hab 2: 3 will not lie. Though it t,

TARRY (*see* TARRIES)
Hab 2: 3 surely come, It will not t.
Heb 10:37 come and will not t.

TARSHISH
Gen 10: 4 of Javan were Elishah, T,
2Ch 9:21 the king's ships went to T
Ps   48: 7 You break the ships of T
Ezek 27:12 T was your merchant because
Jon 1: 3 But Jonah arose to flee to T
Jon 4: 2 I fled previously to T;

TARSUS
Acts 9:11 for one called Saul of T,
Acts 21:39 said, "I am a Jew from T,

TASKMASTERS (*see* MASTERS)
Ex   1:11 Therefore they set t over
Ex   5:14 whom Pharaoh's t had set

TASSELS
Deut 22:12 You shall make t on the four

TASTE (*see* TASTED)
Ex 16:31 and the t of it was like
Ps   34: 8 t and see that the LORD is
Ps 119:103 sweet are Your words to my t,
Song 2: 3 his fruit was sweet to my t.
Matt 16:28 here who shall not t death
Luke 14:24 who were invited shall t my
John 8:52 My word he shall never t
Col 2:21 "Do not touch, do not t,
Heb 2: 9 might t death for everyone.

TASTED (*see* TASTE)
Heb 6: 4 and have t the heavenly

TAUGHT (*see* TEACH)
Neh 8: 9 and the Levites who t the
Prov 31: 1 which his mother t him:
Eccl 12: 9 he still t the people
Hos 11: 3 I t Ephraim to walk, Taking
Matt 5: 2 He opened His mouth and t
Matt 7:29 for He t them as one having
Matt 13:54 He t them in their
Mark 9:31 For He t His disciples and
Luke 11: 1 as John also t his
John 8: 2 and He sat down and t them.
John 8:28 but as My Father t Me, I
Gal 1:12 nor was I t it, but it
2Th 2:15 traditions which you were t,

TAUNT
Jer 24: 9 a t and a curse, in all

TAX (*see* TAXES)
Matt 5:46 Do not even the t collectors
Matt 9:11 does your Teacher eat with t
Matt 10: 3 Thomas and Matthew the t
Matt 17:24 who received the temple t
Luke 19: 2 Zacchaeus who was a chief t

TAXES (*see* TAX)
Matt 22:17 Is it lawful to pay t to
Rom 13: 7 taxes to whom t are due,

TEACH (*see* TAUGHT, TEACHER, TEACHES, TEACHING)
Ex   4:12 be with your mouth and t
Ex 18:20 And you shall t them the
Deut 6: 7 You shall t them diligently
Deut 11:19 You shall t them to your
Job 21:22 Can anyone t God knowledge,
Job 32: 7 multitude of years should t
Ps 25: 4 O LORD; T me Your paths.
Ps 27:11 T me Your way, O LORD, And
Ps 51:13 Then I will t transgressors
Ps 90:12 So t us to number our days,
Is   2: 3 He will t us His ways, And
Jer 31:34 No more shall every man t his
Dan 1: 4 and whom they might t the
Matt 22:16 and t the way of God in
Luke 11: 1 t us to pray, as John also
John 14:26 He will t you all things,
Acts 1: 1 Jesus began both to do and t,
1Co 4:17 as I t everywhere in every
1Co 14:19 that I may t others also,
1Ti 1: 3 may charge some that they t
1Ti 2:12 I do not permit a woman to t
1Ti 3: 2 hospitable, able to t;
2Ti 2: 2 men who will be able to t
2Ti 2:24 be gentle to all, able to t,

TEACHER (*see* TEACH, TEACHERS)
Matt 8:19 came and said to Him, "T,
Matt 9:11 Why does your T eat with tax
Matt 10:24 disciple is not above his t,
Matt 23: 8 'Rabbi'; for One is your T,
Mark 10:17 Him, and asked Him, "Good T,
John 3: 2 we know that You are a t
John 3:10 Are you the t of Israel, and

TEACHERS (*see* TEACHER)
Ps 119:99 understanding than all my t,
Luke 2:46 in the midst of the t,
1Co 12:28 second prophets, third t,
Eph 4:11 and some pastors and t,
2Ti 4: 3 heap up for themselves t;
Jas 3: 1 let not many of you become t,
2Pe 2: 1 as there will be false t

TEACHES (*see* TEACH)
Ps 25: 8 Therefore He t sinners in
Ps 94:10 He who t man knowledge?

Matt   5:19 and t men so, shall be
Rom   12: 7 our ministering; he who t,
1Ti   6: 3 If anyone t otherwise and

TEACHING (see TEACH)
2Ch   15: 3 without a t priest, and
Matt   4:23 t in their synagogues,
Matt   7:28 were astonished at His t,
Matt 28:20 t them to observe all things
Mark   1:22 were astonished at His t,
John   9:34 and are you t us?" And they
Acts   5:42 they did not cease t and
Rom   12: 7 he who teaches, in t;
Col   1:28 warning every man and t
Col   3:16 t and admonishing one
2Ti   4: 2 with all longsuffering and t.

TEAR (see TEARS, TORE, TORN)
Eccl   3: 7 A time to t, and a time
Matt   9:16 and the t is made worse.
Rev   7:17 God will wipe away every t
Rev   21: 4 God will wipe away every t

TEARS (see TEAR)
Ps   6: 6 I drench my couch with my t.
Ps   56: 8 Put my t into Your bottle;
Ps   116: 8 from death, My eyes from t,
Ps   126: 5 Those who sow in t Shall
Is   25: 8 Lord GOD will wipe away t
Jer   9: 1 And my eyes a fountain of t,
Luke   7:38 to wash His feet with her t,
Acts   20:31 night and day with t.
Heb   12:17 sought it diligently with t.

TEBETH†
Esth   2:16 which is the month of T,

TEETH (see TOOTH)
Num   11:33 was still between their t,
Job   19:20 escaped by the skin of my t.
Ps   58: 6 Break their t in their
Song   4: 2 Your t are like a flock of
Jer   31:29 And the children's t are
Ezek   18: 2 And the children's t are
Dan   7: 7 strong. It had huge iron t;
Amos   4: 6 I gave you cleanness of t
Matt   8:12 be weeping and gnashing of t.
Matt   13:42 be wailing and gnashing of t.

TEKEL†
Dan   5:25 was written: MENE, MENE, T,
Dan   5:27 "T: You have been weighed

TEKOA
2Sa   14: 4 And when the woman of T
Jer   6: 1 Blow the trumpet in T,
Amos   1: 1 among the sheepbreeders of T,

TEL ABIB†
Ezek   3:15 I came to the captives at T

TEMA
Job   6:19 The caravans of T look, The

TEMAN (see TEMANITE)
Gen   36:11 the sons of Eliphaz were T,

TEMANITE (see TEMAN)
Job   2:11 his own place—Eliphaz the T,

TEMPERATE
1Co   9:25 for the prize is t in
1Ti   3: 2 the husband of one wife, t,

TEMPEST (see TEMPESTUOUS)
Jon   1: 4 and there was a mighty t on
Matt   8:24 And suddenly a great t arose

TEMPESTUOUS (see TEMPEST)
Jon   1:11 the sea was growing more t.

TEMPLE (see TEMPLES, THRESHOLD)
Judg   4:21 and drove the peg into his t,

Judg   16:26 pillars which support the t,
Judg   16:30 and the t fell on the lords
2Ki   10:21 So they came into the t of
2Ki   12: 5 repair the damages of the t,
1Ch   6:10 as priest in the t that
2Ch   6:32 they come and pray in this t;
2Ch   7: 1 of the LORD filled the t.
Ezra   3:12 men who had seen the first t,
Ezra   5:11 and we are rebuilding the t
Ps   11: 4 The LORD is in His holy t,
Ps   18: 6 heard my voice from His t,
Ps   27: 4 And to inquire in His t.
Is   6: 1 of His robe filled the t.
Jer   7: 4 the t of the LORD are
Dan   5: 3 had been taken from the t
Jon   2: 4 again toward Your holy t.
Mic   3:12 And the mountain of the t
Hab   2:20 the LORD is in His holy t.
Hag   2: 3 among you who saw this t in
Mal   3: 1 Will suddenly come to His t,
Matt   4: 5 Him on the pinnacle of the t,
Matt   12: 6 is One greater than the t.
Matt   27: 5 pieces of silver in the t
Matt   27:51 the veil of the t was torn
Mark   13: 3 of Olives opposite the t,
Luke   11:51 between the altar and the t
John   2:15 drove them all out of the t,
John   2:19 to them, "Destroy this t,
Acts   3: 1 went up together to the t
1Co   3:16 not know that you are the t
1Co   6:19 that your body is the t of
Eph   2:21 grows into a holy t in the
Rev   15: 8 The t was filled with smoke
Rev   21:22 But I saw no t in it, for
Rev   21:22 and the Lamb are its t.

TEMPLES (see TEMPLE)
Acts   7:48 High does not dwell in t
Acts   17:24 does not dwell in t made

TEMPORARY†
2Co   4:18 things which are seen are t,

TEMPT (see TEMPTATION, TEMPTED, TEMPTER)
Deut   6:16 You shall not t the LORD
Matt   4: 7 You shall not t the
Luke   4:12 You shall not t the
1Co   7: 5 so that Satan does not t
Jas   1:13 nor does He Himself t

TEMPTATION (see TEMPT)
Matt   6:13 And do not lead us into t,
Luke   11: 4 And do not lead us into t,
1Co   10:13 No t has overtaken you except
1Co   10:13 but with the t will also

TEMPTED (see TEMPT)
Deut   6:16 the LORD your God as you t
Ps   78:41 again and again they t God,
Matt   4: 1 into the wilderness to be t
Mark   1:13 t by Satan, and was with the
Luke   4: 2 being t for forty days by the
Gal   6: 1 yourself lest you also be t.
Heb   2:18 has suffered, being t,
Heb   11:37 were sawn in two, were t,
Jas   1:13 I am t by God"; for God

TEMPTER (see TEMPT)
Matt   4: 3 Now when the t came to Him,

TEN (see TENS, TENTH)
Gen   18:32 Suppose t should be found
Gen   31: 7 me and changed my wages t
Gen   50:22 lived one hundred and t
Ex   34:28 the T Commandments.
Lev   27: 5 and for a female t shekels;
Num   14:22 Me to the test now these t
Josh   24:29 being one hundred and t

1Sa	1: 8	I not better to you than t
2Sa	15:16	But the king left t women,
2Ki	20:10	for the shadow to go down t
Ps	33: 2	Him with an instrument of t
Ps	91: 7	And t thousand at your
Ps	144: 9	On a harp of t strings I
Song	5:10	Chief among t thousand.
Is	38: 8	t degrees backward." So the
Dan	1:12	test your servants for t
Dan	1:20	he found them t times better
Dan	7: 7	and it had t horns.
Dan	7:10	T thousand times ten
Dan	7:24	The t horns are ten kings
Mic	6: 7	T thousand rivers of oil?
Matt	25: 1	heaven shall be likened to t
Matt	25:28	give it to him who has t
Luke	15: 8	having t silver coins, if
Luke	17:12	there met Him t men who were
Jude	14	the Lord comes with t
Rev	13: 1	having seven heads and t

TEND (*see* TENDER)

Gen	2:15	in the garden of Eden to t
Deut	28:39	shall plant vineyards and t
Song	8:12	And those who t its fruit
John	21:16	to him, "T My sheep."

TENDER (*see* TEND, TENDERHEARTED)

Gen	18: 7	took a t and good calf, gave
Job	14: 7	And that its t shoots will
Job	38:27	forth the growth of t grass?
Ps	51: 1	to the multitude of Your t
Is	53: 2	grow up before Him as a t
Matt	24:32	branch has already become t

TENDERHEARTED† (*see* TENDER)

Eph	4:32	be kind to one another, t,
1Pe	3: 8	love as brothers, be t,

TENS (*see* TEN)

Ex	18:21	of fifties, and rulers of t.

TENT (*see* TENTMAKERS, TENTS)

Gen	9:21	became uncovered in his t.
Gen	12: 8	and he pitched his t with
Ex	40: 6	of the tabernacle of the t
Num	9:15	the t of the Testimony; from
Josh	7:22	it was, hidden in his t,
Judg	4:21	took a t peg and took a
Judg	7: 8	Israel, every man to his t,
2Co	5: 1	our earthly house, this t,
2Pe	1:14	shortly I must put off my t,

TENTH (*see* TEN)

Gen	28:22	me I will surely give a t
Num	18:26	the LORD, a t of the tithe.
Deut	23: 2	even to the t generation
Is	6:13	But yet a t will be in it,
John	1:39	day (now it was about the t
Heb	7: 2	whom also Abraham gave a t

TENTMAKERS† (*see* TENT)

Acts	18: 3	by occupation they were t.

TENTS (*see* TENT)

Gen	4:20	of those who dwell in t and
Num	24: 5	"How lovely are your t,
1Ki	12:16	the son of Jesse. To your t,
Ps	78:51	of their strength in the t
Ps	84:10	my God Than dwell in the t
Ps	118:15	and salvation Is in the t
Heb	11: 9	dwelling in t with Isaac and

TERAH

Gen	11:27	This is the genealogy of T:
Gen	11:32	and T died in Haran.
Josh	24: 2	'Your fathers, including T,
Luke	3:34	of Abraham, the son of T,

TERAPHIM†

Hos	3: 4	pillar, without ephod or t.

TEREBINTH

Gen	12: 6	as far as the t tree of
Gen	13:18	and went and dwelt by the t
Gen	35: 8	below Bethel under the t
1Sa	10: 3	from there and come to the t
2Sa	18:10	saw Absalom hanging in a t
Is	6:13	As a t tree or as an oak,

TERMS

Rom	6:19	I speak in human t because

TERRESTRIAL

1Co	15:40	also celestial bodies and t

TERRIBLE (*see* TERROR)

Deut	1:19	through all that great and t
Ezek	30:11	the most t of the nations,
Ezek	32:12	all of them the most t of
Dan	7: 7	fourth beast, dreadful and t,

TERRIFIED

Esth	7: 6	Haman!" So Haman was t
Luke	21: 9	and commotions, do not be t;

TERRITORY

Ex	10:14	and rested on all the t of
Num	20:17	have passed through your t.
Deut	19: 8	your God enlarges your t,
Judg	1: 3	up with me to my allotted t,
Judg	1:18	Judah took Gaza with its t,
Judg	19:29	her throughout all the t of
2Ki	14:25	He restored the t of Israel
Amos	1:13	they might enlarge their t.

TERROR (*see* TERRIBLE, TERRORS)

Gen	35: 5	and the t of God was upon
Ps	91: 5	not be afraid of the t by
Prov	3:25	not be afraid of sudden t,
Is	2:10	From the t of the LORD
Rom	13: 3	For rulers are not a t to

TERRORS (*see* TERROR)

Job	18:14	him before the king of t.
Job	27:20	T overtake him like a flood
Ps	55: 4	And the t of death have
Eccl	12: 5	And of t in the way; When

TEST (*see* TESTED, TESTING, TESTS)

Ex	20:20	for God has come to t you,
Num	14:22	and have put Me to the t now
Deut	8: 2	to humble you and t you, to
Deut	8:16	you and that He might t you,
Judg	2:22	that through them I may t
Judg	6:39	just once more: Let me t,
1Ki	10: 1	she came to t him with hard
1Ch	29:17	that You t the heart and
Ps	11: 4	His eyelids t the sons of
Is	7:12	nor will I t the LORD!"
Dan	1:12	Please t your servants for
Matt	22:18	Why do you t Me, you
John	6: 6	But this He said to t him,
Acts	5: 9	have agreed together to t
Acts	15:10	why do you t God by putting
1Co	3:13	and the fire will t each
2Co	2: 9	I might put you to the t,
2Co	13: 5	T yourselves. Do you not
1Th	5:21	T all things; hold fast what
1Jn	4: 1	but t the spirits, whether
Rev	3:10	to t those who dwell on the

TESTAMENT (*see* TESTATOR)

2Co	3:14	in the reading of the Old T,

TESTATOR (*see* TESTAMENT)

Heb	9:16	be the death of the t.

TESTED (*see* TEST)

Gen	22: 1	these things that God t

TESTIFIED (see TESTIFY)

Deut 33: 8 Whom You **t** at Massah, And
Ps 17: 3 You have **t** my heart; You
Ps 66:10 have **t** us; You have refined
Dan 1:14 and **t** them ten days.
Luke 10:25 lawyer stood up and **t** Him,
Heb 3: 9 Where your fathers **t**
Heb 11:17 faith Abraham, when he was **t**,
1Pe 1: 7 though it is **t** by fire, may

TESTIFIED (see TESTIFY)

John 1:34 And I have seen and **t** that
John 5:37 has **t** of Me. You have
John 19:35 And he who has seen has **t**,
Acts 18: 5 and **t** to the Jews that
1Ti 2: 6 to be **t** in due time,
Heb 2: 6 But one **t** in a certain place,
1Pe 1:11 was indicating when He **t**
1Jn 5: 9 of God which He has **t** of

TESTIFIES (see TESTIFY)

John 3:32 seen and heard, that He **t**;
John 21:24 This is the disciple who **t** of
Acts 20:23 that the Holy Spirit **t** in
Rev 22:20 He who **t** to these things

TESTIFY (see TESTIFIED, TESTIFIES, TESTIFYING)

Job 15: 6 your own lips **t** against you.
Is 59:12 And our sins **t** against us;
Matt 27:13 hear how many things they **t**
John 3:11 We speak what We know and **t**
John 5:39 and these are they which **t**
John 15:26 the Father, He will **t** of Me.
1Jn 4:14 And we have seen and **t** that
Rev 22:16 have sent My angel to **t** to

TESTIFYING (see TESTIFY)

Heb 11: 4 God **t** of his gifts; and

TESTIMONIES (see TESTIMONY)

Deut 4:45 These are the **t**, the statutes,
2Ki 23: 3 His commandments and His **t**
Ps 25:10 keep His covenant and His **t**.
Ps 93: 5 Your **t** are very sure;
Ps 119:36 Incline my heart to Your **t**,
Mark 14:56 but their **t** did not agree.

TESTIMONY (see TESTIMONIES)

Ex 16:34 laid it up before the **T**,
Ex 25:22 are on the ark of the **T**,
Ex 31:18 Moses two tablets of the **T**,
Lev 24: 3 "Outside the veil of the **T**,
Num 1:50 over the tabernacle of the **T**,
Num 35:30 be put to death on the **t** of
Ps 19: 7 The **t** of the LORD is
Ps 78: 5 For He established a **t** in
Is 8:16 Bind up the **t**, Seal the
Is 8:20 To the law and to the **t**! If
Matt 8: 4 commanded, as a **t** to them."
Matt 26:59 the council sought false **t**
Luke 22:71 What further **t** do we need?
John 1:19 Now this is the **t** of John,
John 3:33 He who has received His **t** has
John 21:24 and we know that his **t** is
1Ti 3: 7 he must have a good **t** among
2Ti 1: 8 do not be ashamed of the **t**
Heb 10:28 dies without mercy on the **t**
Heb 11: 2 elders obtained a good **t**.
Heb 11: 5 he was taken he had this **t**,
Heb 11:39 having obtained a good **t**
1Jn 5:10 he has not believed the **t**
Rev 1: 9 word of God and for the **t**
Rev 19:10 brethren who have the **t** of

TESTING (see TEST)

Deut 13: 3 for the LORD your God is **t**
Matt 19: 3 **t** Him, and saying to Him,
Jas 1: 3 knowing that the **t** of your

TESTS (see TEST)

Ps 7: 9 For the righteous God **t** the
Prov 17: 3 But the LORD **t** the hearts.
1Th 2: 4 but God who **t** our hearts.

TETRARCH

Luke 3: 1 Herod being **t** of Galilee,

THADDAEUS (see JUDAS)

Mark 3:18 the son of Alphaeus, **T**,

THANK (see THANKFUL, THANKS)

2Ch 29:31 and bring sacrifices and **t**
Is 38:18 For Sheol cannot **t** You,
Dan 2:23 I **t** You and praise You, O
Matt 11:25 I **t** You, Father, Lord of
Luke 18:11 I **t** You that I am not like
Rom 1: 8 I **t** my God through Jesus
1Co 1:14 I **t** God that I baptized none
Phil 1: 3 I **t** my God upon every
1Th 2:13 For this reason we also **t**
2Ti 1: 3 I **t** God, whom I serve with a
Phm 1: 4 I **t** my God, making mention

THANKFUL† (see THANK, UNTHANKFUL)

Ps 100: 4 Be **t** to Him, and bless His
Rom 1:21 Him as God, nor were **t**,
Col 3:15 called in one body; and be **t**.

THANKS (see THANK, THANKSGIVING)

Ps 18:49 Therefore I will give **t** to
Ps 92: 1 It is good to give **t** to
Ps 105: 1 give **t** to the LORD! Call
Ps 107: 1 give **t** to the LORD, for He
Ps 107: 8 that men would give **t** to
Ps 118: 1 give **t** to the LORD, for He
Ps 136: 1 I give **t** to the LORD, for He
Ps 136: 2 give **t** to the God of gods!
Ps 136:26 give **t** to the God of heaven!
Dan 6:10 and prayed and gave **t** before
Matt 15:36 and the fish and gave **t**,
Matt 26:27 He took the cup, and gave **t**,
Rom 14: 6 not eat, and gives God **t**.
1Co 11:24 and when He had given **t**,
1Co 15:57 But **t** be to God, who gives
2Co 9:15 **T** be to God for His
Eph 1:16 do not cease to give **t** for
Eph 5:20 giving **t** always for all
1Th 3: 9 For what **t** can we render to
1Th 5:18 in everything give **t**;

THANKSGIVING (see THANKS)

Lev 7:12 with the sacrifice of **t**,
Ps 95: 2 before His presence with **t**;
Ps 100: 4 Enter into His gates with **t**,
Jon 2: 9 to You With the voice of **t**;
2Co 4:15 may cause **t** to abound to the
Phil 4: 6 and supplication, with **t**,
1Ti 4: 4 if it is received with **t**;
Rev 7:12 **T** and honor and power and

THE-LORD-IS-MY-BANNER† (see LORD)

Ex 17:15 altar and called its name, **T**;

THE-LORD-WILL-PROVIDE† (see LORD)

Gen 22:14 the name of the place, **T**;

THEME†

Ps 45: 1 is overflowing with a good **t**;

THEOPHILUS†

Luke 1: 3 account, most excellent **T**,
Acts 1: 1 former account I made, O **T**,

THESSALONICA

Acts 17: 1 Apollonia, they came to **T**,
Acts 27: 2 a Macedonian of **T**,

THEUDAS†

Acts 5:36 For some time ago **T** rose up,

THICK (*see* THICKER)
Ex	8:24	T swarms of flies came
Ex	10:22	and there was t darkness in
Ex	19: 9	I come to you in the t
Zeph	1:15	A day of clouds and t

THICKER† (*see* THICK)
| 1Ki | 12:10 | little finger shall be t |
| 2Ch | 10:10 | little finger shall be t |

THICKET (*see* THICKETS)
| Gen | 22:13 | was a ram caught in a t by |

THICKETS (*see* THICKET)
| 1Sa | 13: 6 | people hid in caves, in t, |

THIEF (*see* THIEVES)
Ex	22: 2	If the t is found breaking
Matt	24:43	had known what hour the t
John	10: 1	the same is a t and a
John	10:10	The t does not come except to
1Th	5: 2	of the Lord so comes as a t
1Th	5: 4	should overtake you as a t.
1Pe	4:15	suffer as a murderer, a t,
2Pe	3:10	of the Lord will come as a t
Rev	3: 3	I will come upon you as a t,

THIEVES (*see* THIEF)
Is	1:23	And companions of t;
Jer	7:11	become a den of t in your
Matt	6:19	and rust destroy and where t
Matt	21:13	have made it a 'den of t.
Luke	10:30	to Jericho, and fell among t,
John	10: 8	ever came before Me are t

THIGH (*see* THIGHS)
| Gen | 24: 2 | put your hand under my t, |
| Ps | 45: 3 | Your sword upon Your t, |

THIGHS (*see* THIGH)
| Song | 7: 1 | The curves of your t are |
| Dan | 2:32 | its belly and t of bronze, |

THIN
| Gen | 41: 6 | seven t heads, blighted by |
| Gen | 41:27 | And the seven t and ugly cows |

THINK (*see* THINKS, THOUGHT)
Matt	5:17	Do not t that I came to
Matt	9: 4	Why do you t evil in your
John	5:39	for in them you t you have
Rom	12: 3	not to t of himself more
Rom	12: 3	but to t soberly, as God has
1Co	7:40	and I t I also have the
Eph	3:20	above all that we ask or t,
1Pe	4:12	do not t it strange

THINKS (*see* THINK)
Prov	23: 7	For as he t in his heart, so
1Co	7:36	But if any man t he is
1Co	10:12	Therefore let him who t he
1Co	13: 5	not provoked, t no evil;
Jas	1:26	If anyone among you t he is

THIRD (*see* THREE)
Gen	50:23	Ephraim's children to the t
Ex	19: 1	In the t month after the
Ex	20: 5	on the children to the t
1Sa	3: 8	called Samuel again the t
1Ki	18:34	Do it a t time," and they
Dan	5: 7	and he shall be the t ruler
Hos	6: 2	On the t day He will raise
Matt	16:21	and be raised the t day.
Matt	20: 3	he went out about the t
Matt	26:44	and prayed the t time,
Luke	12:38	or come in the t watch, and
Luke	24:46	to rise from the dead the t
John	21:17	He said to him the t time,
Acts	2:15	since it is only the t hour
Acts	20: 9	he fell down from the t

1Co	15: 4	and that He rose again the t
2Co	12: 2	a one was caught up to the t
Rev	9:15	were released to kill a t of

THIRST (*see* THIRSTS, THIRSTY)
Ps	69:21	And for my t they gave me
Matt	5: 6	are those who hunger and t
John	4:13	drinks of this water will t
John	6:35	believes in Me shall never t.
John	19:28	fulfilled, said, I t!"
1Co	4:11	hour we both hunger and t,
Rev	7:16	neither hunger anymore nor t

THIRSTS (*see* THIRST, THIRSTY)
Ps	42: 2	My soul t for God, for the
Is	55: 1	"Ho! Everyone who t,
John	7:37	out, saying, "If anyone t,
Rev	21: 6	of life freely to him who t.
Rev	22:17	Come!" And let him who t

THIRSTY (*see* THIRST)
Ps	63: 1	for You In a dry and t
Matt	25:35	I was t and you gave Me
Rom	12:20	feed him; If he is t,

THIRTEEN
| Gen | 17:25 | And Ishmael his son was t |
| 1Ki | 7: 1 | But Solomon took t years to |

THIRTIETH† (*see* THIRTY)
| Ezek | 1: 1 | it came to pass in the t |

THIRTY (*see* THIRTIETH)
Gen	18:30	Suppose t should be found
Ex	12:40	was four hundred and t
Num	4: 3	from t years old and above,
2Sa	5: 4	David was t years old when
2Sa	23:13	Then three of the t chief
2Sa	23:24	of Joab was one of the t;
Zech	11:12	weighed out for my wages t
Matt	26:15	they counted out to him t
Luke	3:23	His ministry at about t
John	2: 6	containing twenty or t

THIRTY-THREE
| 2Sa | 5: 5 | in Jerusalem he reigned t |

THISTLES
| Gen | 3:18 | Both thorns and t it shall |
| Matt | 7:16 | thornbushes or figs from t? |

THOMAS (*see* DIDYMUS)
| Mark | 3:18 | Bartholomew, Matthew, T, |
| John | 20:27 | Then He said to T, |

THORN (*see* THORNBUSHES, THORNS)
| 2Co | 12: 7 | a t in the flesh was given |

THORNBUSHES† (*see* THORN)
| Matt | 7:16 | Do men gather grapes from t |

THORNS (*see* THORN)
Gen	3:18	Both t and thistles it shall
Ps	58: 9	can feel the burning t,
Prov	24:31	it was, all overgrown with t;
Eccl	7: 6	For like the crackling of t
Song	2: 2	Like a lily among t,
Is	5: 6	shall come up briers and t.
Hos	2: 6	hedge up your way with t,
Matt	13: 7	"And some fell among t,
Matt	27:29	had twisted a crown of t,
Luke	6:44	do not gather figs from t,
John	19: 5	wearing the crown of t and

THOUGHT (*see* THINK, THOUGHTS)
Ps	50:21	You t that I was altogether
Ps	139: 2	You understand my t afar
Amos	4:13	declares to man what his t
Acts	26: 8	Why should it be incredible
1Co	13:11	I t as a child; but when I
2Co	10: 5	bringing every t into

THOUGHTS (see THOUGHT)

Gen   6: 5 that every intent of the t
Job   4:13 In disquieting t from the
Job 20: 2 Therefore my anxious t make
Ps   92: 5 are Your works! Your t are
Ps   94:11 The LORD knows the t of
Ps 139:17 precious also are Your t to
Prov 12: 5 The t of the righteous are
Prov 15:26 The t of the wicked are an
Is   55: 7 the unrighteous man his t;
Is   55: 8 For My t are not your
Dan   4:19 and his t troubled him. So
Matt   9: 4 But Jesus, knowing their t,
Matt 15:19 of the heart proceed evil t,
Rom   1:21 but became futile in their t,
Heb   4:12 and is a discerner of the t

THOUSAND (see THOUSANDS)

Ex   12:37 about six hundred t men on
Lev 26: 8 of you shall put ten t to
Deut   7: 9 covenant and mercy for a t
Deut 32:30 How could one chase a t,
Deut 32:30 And two put ten t to
Judg 16:27 about three t men and women
1Ki   4:26 Solomon had forty t stalls
1Ki   4:32 He spoke three t proverbs,
1Ki 19:18 I have reserved seven t
2Ki 19:35 hundred and eighty-five t;
1Ch 16:15 for a t generations,
Esth   3: 9 and I will pay ten t talents
Job   1: 3 his possessions were seven t
Job 42:12 for he had fourteen t sheep,
Ps   84:10 courts is better than a t.
Ps   90: 4 For a t years in Your sight
Ps   91: 7 A t may fall at your side,
Ps 105: 8 for a t generations,
Song   5:10 ruddy, Chief among ten t.
Is   30:17 One t shall flee at the
Ezek 48:13 shall be twenty-five t
Ezek 48:13 thousand and its width ten t.
Dan   7:10 Ten t times ten thousand
Jon   4:11 one hundred and twenty t
Mic   6: 7 Ten t rivers of oil? Shall
Matt 14:21 had eaten were about five t
Matt 15:38 those who ate were four t
Acts   2:41 and that day about three t
Acts   4: 4 men came to about five t.
Rom 11: 4 for Myself seven t men
1Co 14:19 than ten t words in a
2Pe   3: 8 the Lord one day is as a t
Rev   5:11 was ten thousand times ten t,
Rev 14: 1 hundred and forty-four t,
Rev 20: 2 and bound him for a t years;
Rev 20: 6 and shall reign with Him a t
Rev 21:16 twelve t furlongs. Its

THOUSANDS (see THOUSAND)

Ex   20: 6 but showing mercy to t,
Ex   34: 7 "keeping mercy for t,
Deut 33: 2 And He came with ten t of
1Sa 18: 7 "Saul has slain his t,
1Sa 18: 7 And David his ten t.
Ps 119:72 is better to me Than t of
Jer 32:18 show lovingkindness to t,
Mic   5: 2 you are little among the t
Mic   6: 7 the LORD be pleased with t
Jude   14 the Lord comes with ten t of
Rev   5:11 thousand, and thousands of t,

THREAD

Gen 38:28 midwife took a scarlet t
Ex   25: 4 purple, and scarlet t,
Judg 16:12 them off his arms like a t.

THREATENING (see THREATS)

Matt 16: 3 for the sky is red and t.

THREATS (see THREATENING)

Acts   9: 1 still breathing t and murder

THREE (see THIRD, THREE-AND-A-HALF, THREE-DAY, THREE-PRONGED, THREE-YEAR-OLD)

Gen   6:10 And Noah begot t sons: Shem,
Gen 18: 2 men were standing by him;
Gen 30:36 Then he put t days' journey
Ex   2: 2 she hid him t months.
Ex   3:18 let us go t days' journey
Ex   23:17 T times in the year all your
Lev 25:21 forth produce enough for t
Num 22:32 struck your donkey these t
Num 35:14 You shall appoint t cities on
Deut 17: 6 on the testimony of two or t
Deut 19:15 by the mouth of two or t
Judg 7: 8 and retained those t hundred
Judg 11:26 for t hundred years, why did
Judg 16:15 You have mocked me these t
2Sa 23:13 Then t of the thirty chief
2Sa 23:16 So the t mighty men broke
2Sa 23:19 not attain to the first t.
2Sa 24:12 I offer you t things; choose
1Ki   4:32 He spoke t thousand proverbs,
1Ki 11: 3 and t hundred concubines;
1Ki 22: 1 Now t years passed without
2Ki 17: 5 and besieged it for t years.
2Ki 23:31 and he reigned t months in
2Ki 24: 8 he reigned in Jerusalem t
Job   1: 2 And seven sons and t
Job   1: 4 send and invite their t
Job   2:11 Now when Job's t friends
Prov 30:15 and Give! There are t
Is   19:24 day Israel will be one of t
Is   20: 3 walked naked and barefoot t
Ezek 14:14 Even if these t men, Noah,
Dan   3:23 And these t men, Shadrach,
Dan   6:10 he knelt down on his knees t
Dan   7: 5 and had t ribs in its mouth
Amos 1: 3 For t transgressions of
Amos 4: 4 Your tithes every t days.
Amos 4: 7 When there were still t
Jon   1:17 of the fish three days and t
Matt 12:40 For as Jonah was t days and
Matt 13:33 a woman took and hid in t
Matt 17: 4 let us make here t
Matt 18:16 the mouth of two or t
Matt 18:20 For where two or t are
Matt 26:34 you will deny Me t times."
Matt 27:63 After t days I will rise.'
Luke 1:56 remained with her about t
Luke 4:25 the heaven was shut up t
John 2:19 and in t days I will raise
Acts   2:41 and that day about t
Acts   9: 9 And he was t days without
Acts 10:16 This was done t times. And
Acts 20:31 and remember that for t
1Co 13:13 faith, hope, love, these t;
1Co 14:27 be two or at the most t,
2Co 11:25 T times I was beaten with
Gal   1:18 Then after t years I went up
Heb 11:23 was hidden t months by his
Jas   5:17 not rain on the land for t
1Jn   5: 7 For there are t that bear
1Jn   5: 7 and these t are one.

THREE-AND-A-HALF

Rev 11:11 Now after the t days the

THREE-DAY† (see THREE)

Jon   3: 3 a t journey in extent.

THREE-PRONGED† (see THREE)

1Sa   2:13 servant would come with a t

THREE-YEAR-OLD (see THREE)

Gen 15: 9 Bring Me a t heifer, a

THREEFOLD†
Eccl   4:12 And a t cord is not quickly

THRESHED (see THRESHES, THRESHING)
Judg   6:11 while his son Gideon t wheat
Amos   1: 3 Because they have t Gilead

THRESHES† (see THRESHED)
1Co   9:10 and he who t in hope should

THRESHING (see THRESHED)
Num   18:27 it were the grain of the t
Judg   6:37 a fleece of wool on the t
Ruth   3: 6 So she went down to the t
2Sa   24:16 of the LORD was by the t
2Sa   24:24 So David bought the t
1Ch   21:18 altar to the LORD on the t
Is   28:27 is not threshed with a t
Hos   9: 2 The t floor and the
Matt   3:12 thoroughly clean out His t

THRESHOLD
Judg 19:27 with her hands on the t.
1Sa   5: 4 were broken off on the t;
1Sa   5: 5 house tread on the t of
Zeph   1: 9 those who leap over the t,

THREW (see THROW)
Ex   7:12 For every man t down his rod,
2Ki   9:33 So they t her down, and
Jon   1: 5 and t the cargo that was in
Matt 27: 5 Then he t down the pieces of
Mark 11: 7 the colt to Jesus and t
Mark 12: 4 and at him they t stones,
Luke   9:42 the demon t him down and

THROAT
Ps   5: 9 Their t is an open tomb;
Ps   69: 3 My t is dry; My eyes fail
Prov 23: 2 And put a knife to your t
Matt 18:28 him and took him by the t
Rom   3:13 Their t is an open tomb;

THRONE (see THRONES)
Gen   41:40 only in regard to the t will
Ex   11: 5 of Pharaoh who sits on his t,
Deut 17:18 when he sits on the t of his
2Sa   3:10 and set up the t of David
2Sa   7:16 Your t shall be established
1Ki   2: 4 not lack a man on the t of
1Ki   22:19 the LORD sitting on His t,
1Ch   28: 5 son Solomon to sit on the t
Ps   11: 4 The LORD's t is in
Ps   45: 6 Your t, O God, is
Ps   89:14 the foundation of Your t;
Ps   103:19 LORD has established His t
Ps   132:12 also shall sit upon your t
Is   6: 1 saw the Lord sitting on a t,
Is   9: 7 Upon the t of David and
Is   14:13 I will exalt my t above the
Is   66: 1 LORD: "Heaven is My t,
Ezek   1:26 was the likeness of a t,
Dan   5:20 deposed from his kingly t,
Zech   6:13 shall be a priest on His t,
Matt   5:34 by heaven, for it is God's t;
Matt 19:28 Son of Man sits on the t of
Luke   1:32 God will give Him the t of
Acts   2:30 the Christ to sit on his t,
Acts   7:49 'Heaven is My t, And earth
Heb   1: 8 Son He says: "Your t,
Heb   4:16 come boldly to the t of
Heb   8: 1 at the right hand of the t
Rev   1: 4 Spirits who are before His t,
Rev   2:13 where Satan's t is. And you
Rev   3:21 down with My Father on His t.
Rev   4: 3 was a rainbow around the t,
Rev   4: 9 to Him who sits on the t,

Rev   20:11 Then I saw a great white t
Rev   22: 1 proceeding from the t of God

THRONES (see THRONE)
Matt 19:28 Me will also sit on twelve t,
Luke   1:52 the mighty from their t,
Col   1:16 whether t or dominions or
Rev   4: 4 throne were twenty-four t,

THROW (see THREW, THROWN, THROWS)
Eccl   3: 6 And a time to t away;
Jer   1:10 To destroy and to t down,
Jon   1:12 Pick me up and t me into the
Zech 11:13 T it to the potter"—that
Matt   4: 6 t Yourself down. For it is
Matt 15:26 the children's bread and t
Luke   4:29 that they might t Him down
Luke 12:58 and the officer t you into
Luke 22:41 from them about a stone's t,
John   8: 7 let him t a stone at her
John   8:59 they took up stones to t at

THROWN (see THROW)
Ex   15: 1 and its rider He has t
Matt   3:10 good fruit is cut down and t
Matt   5:13 for nothing but to be t out
Matt   5:25 and you be t into prison.
Matt   6:30 and tomorrow is t into the
Matt 24: 2 that shall not be t down."
Mark   9:22 And often he has t him both
Mark 14:51 having a linen cloth t
John   3:24 For John had not yet been t

THROWS (see THROW)
Mark   9:18 it t him down; he foams at

THRUST
Deut 15:17 you shall take an awl and t
1Sa   31: 4 and t me through with it,
Rev   14:15 T in Your sickle and reap,

THUMB (see THUMBS)
Ex   29:20 on the t of their right hand

THUMBS (see THUMB)
Lev   8:24 on the t of their right
Judg   1: 6 him and cut off his t and

THUMMIM (see URIM)
Ezra   2:63 consult with the Urim and T.

THUNDER (see THUNDERED, THUNDERS)
Ex   9:23 and the LORD sent t and
Mark   3:17 that is, "Sons of T";

THUNDERED (see THUNDER)
John 12:29 heard it said that it had t.

THUNDERS (see THUNDER)
Ps   29: 3 waters; The God of glory t;

THYATIRA
Acts 16:14 of purple from the city of T,
Rev   2:18 the angel of the church in T

TIBERIAS
John   6: 1 which is the Sea of T.

TIBERIUS† (see CAESAR)
Luke   3: 1 year of the reign of T

TIDINGS (see NEWS)
Ps   112: 7 will not be afraid of evil t;
Is   40: 9 Zion, You who bring good t,
Is   52: 7 Who brings glad t of good
Is   61: 1 Me To preach good t to the
Nah   1:15 of him who brings good t,
Luke   2:10 I bring you good t of great
Rom   10:15 Who bring glad t of

TIE (see TIED)
Judg 15:13 but we will t you securely
Prov   6:21 T them around your neck.

TIED (see TIE)
Matt 21: 2 you will find a donkey t,

TIGLATH-PILESER
2Ki 15:29 T king of Assyria came and

TIGRIS†
Dan 10: 4 great river, that is, the T,

TILLER†
Gen 4: 2 but Cain was a t of the

TIMAEUS† (see BARTIMAEUS)
Mark 10:46 Bartimaeus, the son of T,

TIMBER
1Ki 5: 6 us who has skill to cut t
1Ki 5:18 and they prepared t and
2Ch 2: 8 have skill to cut t in

TIMBREL (see TIMBRELS)
Ex 15:20 took the t in her hand; and
Ps 150: 4 Praise Him with the t and

TIMBRELS (see TIMBREL)
Ex 15:20 went out after her with t
Judg 11:34 out to meet him with t and

TIME (see TIMES)
Gen 17:21 bear to you at this set t
Gen 22:15 to Abraham a second t out
Gen 24:11 a well of water at evening t,
Gen 24:11 the t when women go out to
Ex 9:18 tomorrow about this t I will
Ex 23:15 at the t appointed in the
Num 20:15 we dwelt in Egypt a long t,
Josh 6:16 And the seventh t
Judg 15: 1 in the t of wheat harvest,
1Sa 3: 8 Samuel again the third t.
1Sa 7: 2 in Kirjath Jearim a long t;
2Sa 11: 1 at the t when kings go out
1Ki 18:34 he said, "Do it a second t,
Ezra 5:16 but from that t even until
Neh 2: 6 send me; and I set him a t.
Esth 4:14 to the kingdom for such a t
Job 22:16 were cut down before their t,
Ps 27: 5 For in the t of trouble He
Ps 32: 6 shall pray to You In a t
Ps 37:19 not be ashamed in the evil t,
Ps 69:13 LORD, in the acceptable t,
Ps 71: 9 not cast me off in the t of
Ps 89:47 Remember how short my t is;
Ps 113: 2 of the LORD From this t
Prov 31:25 She shall rejoice in t to
Eccl 3: 1 A t for every purpose under
Eccl 3: 2 A t to be born, And a time
Eccl 3:11 everything beautiful in its t.
Eccl 7:17 should you die before your t?
Eccl 8: 6 every matter there is a t
Eccl 9:11 But t and chance happen to
Song 2:12 The t of singing has come,
Is 9: 7 and justice From that t
Is 45:21 declared this from ancient t?
Is 49: 8 In an acceptable t I have
Jer 46:21 The t of their punishment.
Jer 50:16 the sickle at harvest t.
Dan 3:15 if you are ready at the t
Dan 7:12 for a season and a t.
Dan 7:25 time and times and half a t.
Dan 8:17 the vision refers to the t
Dan 8:19 happen in the latter t of
Dan 11:35 until the t of the end;
Dan 12: 9 up and sealed till the t of
Hos 2: 9 take away My grain in its t
Hos 10:12 For it is t to seek the
Amos 5:13 keep silent at that t,
Amos 5:13 time, For it is an evil t.
Jon 3: 1 came to Jonah the second t,
Matt 2: 7 determined from them what t

Matt 8:29 to torment us before the t?
Matt 26:18 My t is at hand; I will keep
Mark 1:15 The t is fulfilled, and the
Luke 1:57 Now Elizabeth's full t came
Luke 12:56 you do not discern this t?
John 1:18 No one has seen God at any t.
John 3: 4 Can he enter a second t into
John 7: 6 My t has not yet come, but
John 21:17 He said to him the third t,
Acts 1: 6 will You at this t restore
Acts 17:21 were there spent their t in
Rom 5: 6 in due t Christ died for the
Rom 13:11 that now it is high t to
1Co 4: 5 judge nothing before the t,
1Co 7:29 the t is short, so that
1Co 15: 8 as by one born out of due t.
2Co 6: 2 In an acceptable t I
2Co 6: 2 now is the accepted t,
Gal 4: 4 when the fullness of the t
Eph 2:12 that at that t you were
Eph 5:16 redeeming the t, because
1Ti 2: 6 to be testified in due t,
2Ti 1: 9 us in Christ Jesus before t
2Ti 4: 6 and the t of my departure is
Heb 1: 1 in various ways spoke in t
Heb 4:16 and find grace to help in t
Heb 9:10 imposed until the t of
Heb 9:28 He will appear a second t,
Heb 11:32 For the t would fail me to
Jas 4:14 that appears for a little t
1Pe 1: 5 to be revealed in the last t.
1Pe 1:11 what, or what manner of t,
1Pe 5: 6 He may exalt you in due t,
1Jn 4:12 one has seen God at any t.
Rev 1: 3 in it; for the t is near.
Rev 12:14 time and times and half a t,
Rev 22:10 for the t is at hand.

TIMES (see TIME)
Gen 27:36 supplanted me these two t.
Gen 31: 7 and changed my wages ten t,
Gen 33: 3 to the ground seven t,
Ex 23:17 Three t in the year all your
Lev 23: 4 at their appointed t.
Lev 25: 8 seven t seven years; and the
Num 22:32 your donkey these three t?
Josh 6: 4 around the city seven t,
Judg 16:15 have mocked me these three t,
Judg 16:20 go out as before, at other t,
1Sa 3:10 and called as at other t,
2Ki 4:35 the child sneezed seven t,
2Ki 5:10 wash in the Jordan seven t,
Ps 9: 9 A refuge in t of trouble.
Ps 31:15 My t are in Your hand;
Ps 34: 1 bless the LORD at all t;
Ps 77: 5 old, The years of ancient t.
Ps 119:164 Seven t a day I praise You,
Prov 17:17 A friend loves at all t,
Is 41:26 we may know? And former t,
Is 46:10 And from ancient t things
Dan 1:20 he found them ten t better
Dan 3:19 heat the furnace seven t
Dan 4:16 And let seven t pass over
Dan 6:10 down on his knees three t
Dan 7:10 Ten thousand t ten thousand
Dan 7:25 his hand For a time and t
Dan 12: 7 it shall be for a time, t,
Matt 16: 3 discern the signs of the t.
Matt 18:22 but up to seventy t seven.
Matt 26:34 you will deny Me three t.
Luke 21:24 by Gentiles until the t of
Acts 1: 7 is not for you to know t
Acts 3:19 so that t of refreshing may
Acts 10:16 This was done three t.
Acts 17:30 these t of ignorance God

Eph 1:10 of the fullness of the **t** He
1Ti 4: 1 says that in latter **t** some
2Ti 3: 1 in the last days perilous **t**
Heb 1: 1 who at various **t** and in
1Pe 1:20 was manifest in these last **t**

TIMNAH
Judg 14: 1 Now Samson went down to T,

TIMOTHY
Acts 16: 1 disciple was there, named T,
Acts 17:14 but both Silas and T
Acts 18: 5 When Silas and T had come
2Co 1:19 by us, Silvanus, and T—
Phil 1: 1 Paul and T, bondservants
Heb 13:23 Know that our brother T has

TINGLE†
1Sa 3:11 everyone who hears it will **t**.
2Ki 21:12 of it, both his ears will **t**.
Jer 19: 3 hears of it, his ears will **t**.

TIRHAKAH†
2Ki 19: 9 the king heard concerning T
Is 37: 9 the king heard concerning T

TIRZAH
1Ki 15:33 king over all Israel in T,
Song 6: 4 you are as beautiful as T,

TISHBITE
1Ki 17: 1 And Elijah the T, of the

TITHE (*see* TITHES)
Gen 14:20 And he gave him a **t** of all.
Num 18:26 the LORD, a tenth of the **t**.
Deut 26:13 I have removed the holy **t**
Matt 23:23 hypocrites! For you pay **t** of

TITHES (*see* TITHE)
Num 18:21 children of Levi all the **t**
Deut 12: 6 your sacrifices, your **t**,
Amos 4: 4 Your **t** every three days.
Mal 3: 8 In **t** and offerings.
Mal 3:10 Bring all the **t** into the
Luke 18:12 I give **t** of all that I
Heb 7: 6 from them received **t** from
Heb 7: 9 paid **t** through Abraham, so

TITTLE
Matt 5:18 one jot or one **t** will by no

TITUS
2Co 2:13 because I did not find T my
Gal 2: 1 and also took T with me.

TOBIAH
Neh 2:10 the Horonite and T the
Neh 4: 7 happened, when Sanballat, T,
Neh 6:19 T sent letters to frighten

TODAY
Deut 5: 3 us, those who are here **t**,
Deut 11:26 I set before you **t** a
Deut 29:15 who stands here with us **t**
Deut 30:15 I have set before you **t** life
Ps 2: 7 T I have begotten You.
Ps 95: 7 the sheep of His hand. T,
Matt 6:30 which **t** is, and tomorrow is
Luke 4:21 T this Scripture is fulfilled
Acts 13:33 T I have begotten
Heb 1: 5 T I have begotten
Heb 3: 7 the Holy Spirit says: "T,
Heb 3:13 while it is called "T,
Heb 3:15 while it is said: "T,
Heb 5: 5 T I have begotten
Heb 13: 8 is the same yesterday, **t**,

TOES
Judg 1: 6 cut off his thumbs and big **t**.
Dan 2:41 you saw the feet and **t**,

TOIL (*see* TOILED, TOILS)
Gen 3:17 In **t** you shall eat of it
Matt 6:28 they neither **t** nor spin;
1Th 2: 9 brethren, our labor and **t**;

TOILED (*see* TOIL)
Eccl 2:18 my labor in which I had **t**
Luke 5: 5 we have **t** all night and

TOILS (*see* TOIL)
Eccl 1: 3 all his labor In which he **t**

TOLERABLE
Matt 10:15 it will be more **t** for the
Mark 6:11 it will be more **t** for Sodom

TOMB (*see* TOMBS)
2Sa 2:32 buried him in his father's **t**,
1Ki 13:30 laid the corpse in his own **t**;
Ps 5: 9 Their throat is an open **t**;
Matt 27:60 and laid it in his new **t**
Matt 27:60 against the door of the **t**,
Mark 16: 5 And entering the **t**,
Luke 24: 2 stone rolled away from the **t**.
John 11:17 he had already been in the **t**
John 12:17 called Lazarus out of his **t**
John 19:41 and in the garden a new **t** in
John 20: 1 Mary Magdalene went to the **t**
John 20: 4 Peter and came to the **t**
Acts 2:29 and his **t** is with us to this
Rom 3:13 throat is an open **t**;

TOMBS (*see* TOMB)
2Ch 21:20 but not in the **t** of the
Neh 3:16 place in front of the **t** of
Matt 8:28 men, coming out of the **t**,
Matt 23:27 you are like whitewashed **t**
Matt 23:29 Because you build the **t** of

TOMORROW
Ex 16:23 T is a Sabbath rest, a holy
Prov 27: 1 Do not boast about **t**,
Is 22:13 and drink, for **t** we die!"
Matt 6:30 and **t** is thrown into the
Matt 6:34 do not worry about **t**,
Luke 13:33 I must journey today, **t**,
1Co 15:32 and drink, for **t** we die!"
Jas 4:14 know what will happen **t**.

TONGS
Is 6: 6 he had taken with the **t**

TONGUE (*see* TONGUES)
Ex 4:10 slow of speech and slow of **t**.
Judg 7: 5 from the water with his **t**,
Job 29:10 And their **t** stuck to the
Ps 5: 9 They flatter with their **t**.
Ps 22:15 And My **t** clings to My jaws;
Ps 34:13 Keep your **t** from evil, And
Ps 39: 1 ways, Lest I sin with my **t**;
Ps 45: 1 My **t** is the pen of a ready
Ps 57: 4 And their **t** a sharp sword.
Ps 109: 2 against me with a lying **t**.
Ps 137: 6 Let my **t** cling to the roof
Prov 6:17 A proud look, A lying **t**,
Prov 6:24 From the flattering **t** of a
Prov 10:31 But the perverse **t** will be
Prov 25:15 And a gentle **t** breaks a
Prov 25:23 And a backbiting **t** an angry
Song 4:11 and milk are under your **t**;
Is 50: 4 GOD has given Me The **t** of
Mark 7:33 He spat and touched his **t**.
Luke 16:24 in water and cool my **t**;
Acts 2:26 and my **t** was glad;
Rom 14:11 And every **t** shall
1Co 14: 4 He who speaks in a **t** edifies
1Co 14:19 ten thousand words in a **t**.
Phil 2:11 and that every **t** should
Jas 1:26 and does not bridle his **t**

Jas   3: 6 And the t is a fire, a world
Jas   3: 8 But no man can tame the t.
Rev   5: 9 Out of every tribe and t

TONGUES (see TONGUE)
Ps   140: 3 They sharpen their t like a
Mark 16:17 they will speak with new t;
Acts   2: 3 appeared to them divided t,
Acts   2: 4 began to speak with other t,
Acts   2:11 them speaking in our own t
1Co   12:10 the interpretation of t.
1Co   13: 1 Though I speak with the t of
1Co   13: 8 fail; whether there are t,
1Co   14: 5 I wish you all spoke with t,
1Co   14:39 not forbid to speak with t.
Rev   7: 9 tribes, peoples, and t,

TONIGHT
Gen   19: 5 the men who came to you t?
Ruth   3: 2 he is winnowing barley t at

TOOK (see TAKE)
Gen   5:24 he was not, for God t him.
Gen   6: 2 and they t wives for
Gen   19:16 the men t hold of his hand,
Gen   22:10 out his hand and t the
Gen   22:13 So Abraham went and t the
Deut   4:47 And they t possession of his
Josh   7:21 I coveted them and t them.
Josh   11:16 Thus Joshua t all this land:
Judg   16:29 And Samson t hold of the two
Ruth   4: 8 So he t off his sandal.
1Sa   20: 3 Then David t an oath again,
2Sa   3:36 Now all the people t note of
1Ki   2:28 and t hold of the horns of
2Ch   36:18 all these he t to Babylon.
Ezra   6: 5 which Nebuchadnezzar t from
Ps   22: 9 But You are He who t Me out
Ps   78:70 And t him from the
Jer   52:11 t him to Babylon, and put
Ezek   3:14 Spirit lifted me up and t
Ezek   11:24 Then the Spirit t me up and
Hos   12: 3 He t his brother by the heel
Jon   1:16 to the LORD and t vows.
Matt   4: 5 Then the devil t Him up into
Matt   8:17 He Himself t our
Matt   21:39 So they t him and cast him
Matt   25:35 I was a stranger and you t
Matt   26:26 Jesus t bread, blessed and
John   19:40 Then they t the body of
Acts   4:26 kings of the earth t
1Co   11:23 in which He was betrayed t
1Co   11:25 the same manner He also t

TOOL
Deut   27: 5 shall not use an iron t on

TOOTH (see TEETH)
Ex   21:24 "eye for eye, tooth for t,
Matt   5:38 for an eye and a t

TOP (see TOPS)
Gen   11: 4 and a tower whose t is in
Gen   28:12 and its t reached to heaven;
Ex   25:21 put the mercy seat on t of
Deut   28:35 sole of your foot to the t
Matt   27:51 was torn in two from t to
Heb   11:21 leaning on the t of his

TOPAZ
Ex   28:17 shall be a sardius, a t,
Rev   21:20 eighth beryl, the ninth t,

TOPHET (see TOPHETH)
Jer   7:31 built the high places of T,
Jer   19:13 defiled like the place of T,

TOPHETH† (see TOPHET)
2Ki   23:10 And he defiled T,

TOPS (see TOP)
Gen   8: 5 the t of the mountains were
2Sa   5:24 sound of marching in the t

TORCH (see TORCHES)
Gen   15:17 oven and a burning t that
Judg   15: 4 and put a t between each

TORCHES (see TORCH)
Judg   7:16 and t inside the pitchers.
John   18: 3 came there with lanterns, t,

TORE (see TEAR)
Gen   37:34 Then Jacob t his clothes, put
1Sa   15:27 edge of his robe, and it t.
1Ki   11:30 and t it into twelve
1Ki   14: 8 and t the kingdom away from
2Ki   11:18 and t it down. They
Job   1:20 t his robe, and shaved his
Amos   1:11 His anger t perpetually,
Matt   26:65 Then the high priest t his

TORMENT (see TORMENTED)
Judg   16:19 Then she began to t him, and
Matt   8:29 Have You come here to t us
Luke   16:28 also come to this place of t.

TORMENTED (see TORMENT)
Matt   8: 6 home paralyzed, dreadfully t.
Luke   6:18 as well as those who were t
Luke   16:24 for I am t in this flame.'
Heb   11:37 destitute, afflicted, t—
2Pe   2: 8 t his righteous soul from

TORN (see TEAR)
Gen   31:39 That which was t by beasts
Gen   37:33 Without doubt Joseph is t to
Judg   6:28 t down; and the wooden image
1Sa   15:28 The LORD has t the kingdom
1Ki   19:10 t down Your altars, and
Matt   27:51 veil of the temple was t in
Rom   11: 3 Your prophets and t

TORTURED† (see TORTURERS)
Heb   11:35 again. And others were t,

TORTURERS† (see TORTURED)
Matt   18:34 and delivered him to the t

TOSSED
Matt   14:24 t by the waves, for the wind
Eph   4:14 t to and fro and carried
Jas   1: 6 of the sea driven and t by

TOTTERING†
Ps   62: 3 Like a leaning wall and a t

TOUCH (see TOUCHED, TOUCHES, TOUCHING)
Gen   3: 3 nor shall you t it, lest you
Ruth   2: 9 the young men not to t you?
Job   1:11 stretch out Your hand and t
Job   2: 5 and t his bone and his
Ps   105:15 Do not t My anointed ones,
Ps   144: 5 T the mountains, and they
Is   52:11 T no unclean thing; Go
Matt   14:36 Him that they might only t
Mark   3:10 pressed about Him to t Him.
1Co   7: 1 is good for a man not to t
Col   2:21 "Do not t, do not taste,

TOUCHED (see TOUCH)
Gen   32:25 He t the socket of his hip;
1Sa   10:26 him, whose hearts God had t.
2Ki   13:21 the man was let down and t
Is   6: 7 And he t my mouth with it,
Is   6: 7 this has t your lips; Your
Jer   1: 9 put forth His hand and t my
Matt   8:15 So He t her hand, and the
Matt   20:34 Jesus had compassion and t
Mark   5:30 Who t My clothes?"
Luke   22:51 And He t his ear and

Heb 12:18 the mountain that may be t

TOUCHES (*see* TOUCH)
Ex   19:12 Whoever t the mountain shall
Lev 11:24 whoever t the carcass of any
Ps 104:32 He t the hills, and they
Zech   2: 8 for he who touches you t the

TOUCHING (*see* TOUCH)
Dan   8: 5 without t the ground; and
Luke   7:39 of woman this is who is t

TOWEL†
John 13: 4 took a t and girded Himself.
John 13: 5 and to wipe them with the t

TOWER (*see* TOWERS)
Gen 11: 4 and a t whose top is in the
Ps   144: 2 My high t and my deliverer,
Prov 18:10 of the LORD is a strong t;
Song   4: 4 Your neck is like the t of
Mic   4: 8 O t of the flock, The
Matt 21:33 in it and built a t.
Luke 13: 4 eighteen on whom the t in

TOWERS (*see* TOWER)
Ps   48:12 all around her. Count her t;
Song 8:10 wall, And my breasts like t;

TOWN (*see* TOWNS)
Ruth   3:11 for all the people of my t
Matt 10:11 Now whatever city or t you
Luke   5:17 who had come out of every t
John   7:42 of David and from the t of

TOWNS (*see* TOWN)
Mark   1:38 "Let us go into the next t,

TRADE (*see* TRADED, TRADERS, TRADING)
Amos   8: 5 That we may t wheat?
Acts 18: 3 because he was of the same t,

TRADED (*see* TRADE)
Matt 25:16 the five talents went and t

TRADERS (*see* TRADE)
Gen 37:28 Then Midianite t passed by;

TRADING (*see* TRADE)
Luke 19:15 every man had gained by t.

TRADITION (*see* TRADITIONS)
Matt 15: 2 disciples transgress the t
Matt 15: 6 God of no effect by your t.
Mark   7: 8 you hold the t of men—the
1Pe   1:18 conduct received by t from

TRADITIONS (*see* TRADITION)
1Co 11: 2 in all things and keep the t
2Th   2:15 stand fast and hold the t

TRAIN† (*see* TRAINED, TRAINING)
Prov 22: 6 T up a child in the way he
Is   6: 1 and the t of His robe

TRAINED (*see* TRAIN)
Heb 12:11 to those who have been t by
2Pe   2:14 They have a heart t in

TRAINING† (*see* TRAIN)
Dan   1: 5 and three years of t for
Eph   6: 4 but bring them up in the t

TRAITOR† (*see* TRAITORS)
Luke   6:16 Iscariot who also became a t.

TRAITORS† (*see* TRAITOR)
2Ti   3: 4 t, headstrong, haughty,

TRAMPLE (*see* TRAMPLED)
Ps   91:13 and the serpent you shall t
Is   1:12 your hand, To t My courts?
Luke 10:19 give you the authority to t

TRAMPLED (*see* TRAMPLE)
Is   63: 3 And t them in My fury;
Matt   5:13 but to be thrown out and t
Heb 10:29 be thought worthy who has t

TRANCE
Acts 10:10 made ready, he fell into a t

TRANSFIGURED†
Matt 17: 2 and He was t before them. His
Mark   9: 2 and He was t before them.

TRANSFORM (*see* TRANSFORMED, TRANSFORMING, TRANSFORMS)
Phil   3:21 who will t our lowly body

TRANSFORMED† (*see* TRANSFORM)
Rom 12: 2 but be t by the renewing of
2Co   3:18 are being t into the same

TRANSFORMING† (*see* TRANSFORM)
2Co 11:13 t themselves into apostles

TRANSFORMS† (*see* TRANSFORM)
2Co 11:14 wonder! For Satan himself t

TRANSGRESS (*see* TRANSGRESSED, TRANSGRESSION, TRANSGRESSOR)
Ps   17: 3 that my mouth shall not t.
Amos   4: 4 "Come to Bethel and t,
Matt 15: 2 Why do Your disciples t the

TRANSGRESSED (*see* TRANSGRESS)
Lam   3:42 We have t and rebelled; You
Dan   9:11 all Israel has t Your law,

TRANSGRESSION (*see* TRANSGRESS, TRANSGRESSIONS)
Ex   34: 7 forgiving iniquity and t and
Job 14:17 My t is sealed up in a bag,
Ps   19:13 shall be innocent of great t.
Ps   32: 1 Blessed is he whose t is
Prov 17: 9 He who covers a t seeks
Prov 17:19 He who loves t loves strife,
Prov 19:11 glory is to overlook a t.
Is   57: 4 Are you not children of t,
Dan   9:24 holy city, To finish the t,
Amos   4: 4 At Gilgal multiply t;
Mic   3: 8 To declare to Jacob his t
Mic   6: 7 give my firstborn for my t,
Acts   1:25 from which Judas by t fell,
Rom   4:15 is no law there is no t.
Rom   5:14 to the likeness of the t of
1Ti   2:14 being deceived, fell into t.

TRANSGRESSIONS (*see* TRANSGRESSION)
Josh 24:19 He will not forgive your t
Job 31:33 If I have covered my t as
Ps   32: 5 I will confess my t to the
Ps   51: 1 mercies, Blot out my t.
Ps   51: 3 For I acknowledge my t,
Ps 103:12 far has He removed our t
Is   44:22 like a thick cloud, your t,
Is   53: 5 He was wounded for our t,
Is   53: 8 For the t of My people He
Amos   1: 3 For three t of Damascus, and
Amos   3:14 I punish Israel for their t,
Heb   9:15 for the redemption of the t

TRANSGRESSOR (*see* TRANSGRESS, TRANSGRESSORS)
Rom   2:27 are a t of the law?
Jas   2:11 you have become a t of the

TRANSGRESSORS (*see* TRANSGRESSOR)
Ps   51:13 Then I will teach t Your
Is   53:12 He was numbered with the t,
Is   53:12 made intercession for the t.
Hos 14: 9 But t stumble in them.
Mark 15:28 was numbered with the t.
Luke 22:37 was numbered with the t.

TRANSLATED (*see* TAKEN)
Ezra 4: 7 and t into the Aramaic
Matt 1:23 Immanuel," which is t,

TRAP (*see* TRAPS)
Rom 11: 9 become a snare and a t,

TRAPS (*see* TRAP)
Ps 140: 5 They have set t for me.

TRAVEL (*see* TRAVELER, TRAVELING)
Matt 23:15 hypocrites! For you t land

TRAVELER (*see* TRAVEL)
2Sa 12: 4 And a t came to the rich man,

TRAVELING (*see* TRAVEL)
Matt 25:14 heaven is like a man t to
Luke 24:13 two of them were t that same

TREACHEROUS (*see* TREACHEROUSLY)
Is 24:16 ruined! Woe to me! The t

TREACHEROUSLY (*see* TREACHEROUS)
Is 24:16 dealers have dealt t,
Acts 7:19 This man dealt t with our

TREAD (*see* TREADER, TREADS)
Deut 11:25 all the land where you t,
Ps 60:12 For it is He who shall t
Ps 91:13 You shall t upon the lion
Ps 108:13 For it is He who shall t
Is 16:10 No treaders will t out wine
Amos 5:11 because you t down the poor
Mic 1: 3 He will come down And t on

TREADER† (*see* TREAD)
Amos 9:13 And the t of grapes him who

TREADS (*see* TREAD)
Deut 11:24 the sole of your foot t
Deut 25: 4 not muzzle an ox while it t
1Co 9: 9 an ox while it t out
1Ti 5:18 an ox while it t out
Rev 19:15 He Himself t the winepress

TREASON
2Ki 11:14 T! Treason!"

TREASURE (*see* TREASURES, TREASURING, TREASURY)
Gen 43:23 your father has given you t
Ex 19: 5 you shall be a special t to
Ps 119:162 As one who finds great t.
Is 33: 6 fear of the LORD is His t.
Matt 6:21 For where your t is, there
Matt 12:35 good man out of the good t
Matt 13:44 kingdom of heaven is like t
Matt 13:52 who brings out of his t
Matt 19:21 and you will have t in
Luke 6:45 evil man out of the evil t
Luke 12:21 So is he who lays up t for
2Co 4: 7 But we have this t in
Jas 5: 3 You have heaped up t in the

TREASURES (*see* TREASURE)
1Ki 14:26 And he took away the t of the
Job 3:21 for it more than hidden t;
Prov 2: 4 for her as for hidden t;
Matt 2:11 when they had opened their t,
Matt 6:19 not lay up for yourselves t
Col 2: 3 in whom are hidden all the t
Heb 11:26 greater riches than the t

TREASURIES (*see* TREASURY)
1Ki 15:18 of the LORD and the t of
Jer 10:13 brings the wind out of His t.

TREASURING† (*see* TREASURE)
Rom 2: 5 impenitent heart you are t

TREASURY (*see* TREASURE, TREASURIES)
Josh 6:19 they shall come into the t
Ezra 4:13 and the king's t will be

Acts 8:27 who had charge of all her t,

TREAT (*see* TREATED)
Gen 34:31 Should he t our sister like a

TREATED (*see* TREAT)
Gen 12:16 He t Abram well for her sake.
Mark 9:12 suffer many things and be t
1Th 2: 2 and were spitefully t at
Heb 10:33 of those who were so t;

TREATY
1Ki 3: 1 Now Solomon made a t with

TREE (*see* TREES)
Gen 1:11 and the fruit t that
Gen 2: 9 The t of life was also in
Gen 2: 9 and the t of the knowledge
Gen 3: 6 the woman saw that the t
Gen 40:19 from you and hang you on a t;
Deut 12: 2 and under every green t.
Judg 4: 5 would sit under the palm t
1Ki 4:33 from the cedar t of Lebanon
Job 14: 7 "For there is hope for a t,
Ps 1: 3 He shall be like a t
Prov 3:18 She is a t of life to those
Prov 11:30 of the righteous is a t
Song 8: 5 you under the apple t.
Jer 1:11 see a branch of an almond t.
Jer 17: 8 For he shall be like a t
Dan 4:11 The t grew and became
Hos 14: 6 shall be like an olive t,
Hos 14: 8 am like a green cypress t;
Mic 4: 4 his vine and under his fig t,
Hab 3:17 Though the fig t may not
Matt 7:17 every good t bears good
Matt 12:33 for a t is known by its
Matt 21:19 Immediately the fig t
Matt 24:32 this parable from the fig t:
Luke 17: 6 can say to this mulberry t,
Luke 19: 4 up into a sycamore t to see
John 1:50 'I saw you under the fig t,
Acts 10:39 killed by hanging on a t.
Rom 11:17 you, being a wild olive t,
Gal 3:13 who hangs on a t"),
1Pe 2:24 in His own body on the t,
Rev 2: 7 will give to eat from the t
Rev 22: 2 The leaves of the t were
Rev 22:14 may have the right to the t

TREES (*see* TREE)
Ex 15:27 of water and seventy palm t;
Deut 34: 3 Jericho, the city of palm t,
Judg 9: 9 men, And go to sway over t?
2Sa 5:24 the tops of the mulberry t,
1Ch 22: 4 and cedar t in abundance; for
Ps 104:16 The t of the LORD are full
Zech 1:11 who stood among the myrtle t,
Zech 4:11 are these two olive t—
Matt 3:10 is laid to the root of the t.
Matt 21: 8 cut down branches from the t
Mark 8:24 and said, "I see men like t,
John 12:13 took branches of palm t and
Rev 11: 4 These are the two olive t and

TREMBLE (*see* TREMBLED, TREMBLES, TREMBLING)
Ps 60: 2 You have made the earth t;
Ps 96: 9 the beauty of holiness! T
Ps 99: 1 Let the peoples t! He
Eccl 12: 3 the keepers of the house t,
Dan 6:26 of my kingdom men must t
Jas 2:19 demons believe—and t!

TREMBLED (*see* TREMBLE)
Gen 27:33 Then Isaac t exceedingly, and
Ex 19:16 who were in the camp t.
Ex 20:18 they t and stood afar off.
Ps 18: 7 Then the earth shook and t;

Hab 3:16 When I heard, my body t;
Mark 16: 8 for they t and were amazed.
Acts 7:32 And Moses t and dared not

TREMBLES (see TREMBLE)
Ps 97: 4 world; The earth sees and t.

TREMBLING (see TREMBLE)
Is 51:22 of your hand The cup of t,
1Co 2: 3 in fear, and in much t.
Phil 2:12 salvation with fear and t;

TRENCH
1Ki 18:35 and he also filled the t

TRESPASS (see TRESPASSED, TRESPASSES)
Gen 50:17 forgive the t of the
Lev 14:14 some of the blood of the t
Gal 6: 1 a man is overtaken in any t,

TRESPASSED (see TRESPASS)
Deut 32:51 because you t against Me

TRESPASSES (see TRESPASS)
Matt 6:14 if you forgive men their t,
2Co 5:19 not imputing their t to
Eph 2: 1 who were dead in t and sins,
Col 2:13 being dead in your t and the

TRIAL (see TRIALS)
Gal 4:14 And my t which was in my
1Pe 4:12 concerning the fiery t
Rev 3:10 keep you from the hour of t

TRIALS (see TRIAL)
Deut 7:19 the great t which your eyes
Jas 1: 2 when you fall into various t,
1Pe 1: 6 been grieved by various t,

TRIBE (see TRIBES)
Ex 31: 2 of Hur, of the t of Judah.
Num 1: 4 shall be a man from every t,
Num 1:47 them by their fathers' t;
Num 1:49 Only the t of Levi you shall
Num 26:54 To a large t you shall give
Num 26:54 and to a small t you shall
Num 32:33 and to half the t of
Num 36: 3 to the inheritance of the t
Num 36: 7 not change hands from t to
Deut 10: 8 the LORD separated the t
Josh 3:12 Israel, one man from every t.
Judg 20:12 sent men through all the t
Judg 21: 3 today there should be one t
Judg 21: 6 One t is cut off from Israel
Ps 74: 2 The t of Your inheritance,
Jer 10:16 And Israel is the t of His
Jer 51:19 And Israel is the t of
Luke 2:36 of the t of Asher. She was
Heb 7:14 of which t Moses spoke
Rev 5: 5 the Lion of the t of Judah,
Rev 7: 5 of the t of Judah twelve
Rev 7: 5 of the t of Reuben twelve
Rev 14: 6 the earth—to every nation, t,

TRIBES (see TRIBE)
Gen 49:28 these are the twelve t of
Num 1:16 leaders of their fathers' t,
Num 34:13 to give to the nine t and
Num 34:15 The two t and the half-tribe
Deut 1:15 I took the heads of your t,
Judg 21:15 had made a void in the t of
1Sa 9:21 of the smallest of the t of
1Ki 11:35 and give it to you—ten t.
Is 49: 6 Servant To raise up the t
Is 63:17 The t of Your inheritance.
Matt 19:28 judging the twelve t of
Matt 24:30 and then all the t of the
Jas 1: 1 To the twelve t which are
Rev 7: 9 number, of all nations, t,

TRIBULATION (see TRIBULATIONS)
Matt 13:21 For when t or persecution
Matt 24: 9 will deliver you up to t
Matt 24:21 then there will be great t,
Matt 24:29 Immediately after the t of
John 16:33 In the world you will have t;
Rom 5: 3 knowing that t produces
Rom 8:35 the love of Christ? Shall t,
Rom 12:12 in hope, patient in t,
2Co 1: 4 who comforts us in all our t,
Rev 2:22 with her into great t,
Rev 7:14 who come out of the great t,

TRIBULATIONS (see TRIBULATION)
Acts 14:22 We must through many t enter
Acts 20:23 saying that chains and t
Rom 5: 3 but we also glory in t,

TRIBUTE
2Ki 17: 3 and paid him t money.

TRICKERY
Matt 26: 4 plotted to take Jesus by t
Eph 4:14 by the t of men, in the

TRIED (see TRY)
Ps 12: 6 Like silver t in a furnace
Ps 17: 3 You have t me and have

TRIMMED
Matt 25: 7 those virgins arose and t

TRIUMPH (see TRIUMPHED, TRIUMPHING, TRIUMPHS)
Ps 25: 2 Let not my enemies t over
Ps 47: 1 to God with the voice of t!
Ps 92: 4 I will t in the works of
Ps 94: 3 How long will the wicked t?
2Co 2:14 who always leads us in t in

TRIUMPHED† (see TRIUMPH)
Ex 15: 1 For He has t gloriously!
Ex 15:21 For He has t gloriously!

TRIUMPHING (see TRIUMPH)
Col 2:15 t over them in it.

TRIUMPHS† (see TRIUMPH)
Jas 2:13 Mercy t over judgment.

TROAS
Acts 20: 5 ahead, waited for us at T.
2Co 2:12 when I came to T to preach

TRODDEN
Is 63: 3 I have t the winepress

TROOPS
2Ch 14:10 and they set the t in battle

TROUBLE (see TROUBLED, TROUBLER, TROUBLES, TROUBLESOME, TROUBLING)
Josh 7:25 The LORD will t you this
2Ki 19: 3 'This day is a day of t,
Neh 9:27 And in the time of their t,
Job 3:26 no rest, for t comes."
Job 4: 8 who plow iniquity And sow t
Job 5: 7 Yet man is born to t,
Job 14: 1 of few days and full of t.
Job 38:23 reserved for the time of t,
Ps 9: 9 A refuge in times of t.
Ps 10: 1 do You hide in times of t?
Ps 20: 1 answer you in the day of t;
Ps 22:11 For t is near; For there
Ps 27: 5 For in the time of t He
Ps 46: 1 A very present help in t.
Ps 50:15 upon Me in the day of t;
Ps 54: 7 delivered me out of all t;
Ps 73: 5 They are not in t as
Ps 107: 6 out to the LORD in their t,
Ps 116: 3 I found t and sorrow.
Prov 25:19 man in time of t Is
Is 46: 7 Nor save him out of his t.

Jer　30: 7　it is the time of Jacob's t,
Dan　4:19　or its interpretation it you.
Dan　5:10　Do not let your thoughts t
Dan　12: 1　there shall be a time of t,
Jon　1: 7　know for whose cause this t
Matt　6:34　for the day is its own t.
Matt　26:10　Why do you t the woman? For
2Ti　2: 9　for which I suffer t as an
Jas　1:27　and widows in their t,

TROUBLED (*see* TROUBLE)
Gen　41: 8　that his spirit was t,
1Sa　16:14　spirit from the LORD t him.
Ps　6: 3　My soul also is greatly t;
Ps　77: 4　I am so t that I cannot
Is　57:20　the wicked are like the t
Lam　2:11　with tears, My heart is t;
Dan　2: 1　and his spirit was so t
Dan　4: 5　the visions of my head t me.
Dan　5: 9　Belshazzar was greatly t,
Matt　2: 3　king heard this, he was t,
Matt　14:26　on the sea, they were t,
Luke　1:29　she was t at his saying, and
Luke　24:38　to them, "Why are you t?
John　12:27　"Now My soul is t,
John　14: 1　"Let not your heart be t;
2Co　7: 5　but we were t on every side.

TROUBLER (*see* TROUBLE)
1Ki　18:17　that you, O t of Israel?"

TROUBLES (*see* TROUBLE)
Ps　25:22　Out of all their t!
Ps　34: 6　saved him out of all his t.
Prov　11:29　He who t his own house will
Mark　13: 8　there will be famines and t.
Acts　7:10　him out of all his t,

TROUBLESOME (*see* TROUBLE)
Dan　9:25　the wall, Even in t times.

TROUBLING (*see* TROUBLE)
1Sa　16:15　spirit from God is t you.
Job　3:17　the wicked cease from t,

TROUGHS
Gen　30:38　in the watering t where the

TRUE (*see* TRULY, TRUTH)
2Sa　7:28　God, and Your words are t,
Ps　19: 9　of the LORD are t and
Jer　10:10　But the LORD is the t God;
Zech　7: 9　Execute t justice, Show
John　1: 9　That was the t Light which
John　4:23　when the t worshipers will
John　6:32　My Father gives you the t
John　8:17　testimony of two men is t.
John　15: 1　I am the t vine, and My
John　17: 3　the only t God, and Jesus
John　21:24　know that his testimony is t.
Rom　3: 4　let God be t but every man a
2Co　6: 8　as deceivers, and yet t;
Eph　4:24　in t righteousness and
Phil　4: 8　whatever things are t,
1Th　1: 9　to serve the living and t
1Ti　1: 2　a t son in the faith:
Heb　9:24　which are copies of the t,
Heb　10:22　let us draw near with a t
1Jn　2: 8　and the t light is already
1Jn　5:20　This is the t God and
Rev　3:14　the Faithful and T Witness,
Rev　6:10　long, O Lord, holy and t,
Rev　19:11　was called Faithful and T,
Rev　22: 6　words are faithful and t.

TRULY (*see* TRUE)
Ps　73: 1　T God is good to Israel,
Matt　14:33　T You are the Son of God."
1Co　14:25　God and report that God is t

1Jn　1: 3　and t our fellowship is

TRUMPET (*see* TRUMPETS)
Judg　6:34　Gideon; then he blew the t,
Judg　7:16　and he put a t into every
Ps　150: 3　Him with the sound of the t;
1Co　14: 8　For if the t makes an
1Co　15:52　of an eye, at the last t.
1Co　15:52　For the t will sound, and
1Th　4:16　and with the t of God. And

TRUMPETS (*see* TRUMPET)
Num　10: 2　Make two silver t for
Josh　6: 4　priests shall bear seven t
Rev　8: 2　to them were given seven t.

TRUST (*see* TRUSTED, TRUSTING, TRUSTS)
Job　13:15　yet will I t Him. Even so,
Ps　2:12　all those who put their t
Ps　7: 1　my God, in You I put my t;
Ps　18: 2　strength, in whom I will t;
Ps　18:30　is a shield to all who t
Ps　20: 7　Some t in chariots, and
Ps　22: 9　You made Me t while on My
Ps　31: 1　In You, O LORD, I put my t;
Ps　37: 3　T in the LORD, and do good
Ps　37: 5　T also in Him, And He
Ps　62: 8　T in Him at all times, you
Ps　71: 5　You are my t from my
Ps　91: 2　My God, in Him I will t.
Ps　118: 8　It is better to t in the
Prov　3: 5　T in the LORD with all your
Prov　22:19　So that your t may be in the
Is　59: 4　They t in empty words and
Jer　7: 4　Do not t in these lying
Matt　12:21　name Gentiles will t.
Mark　10:24　hard it is for those who t
John　5:45　you—Moses, in whom you t.
1Ti　1:11　which was committed to my t.
1Ti　6:17　nor to t in uncertain riches
1Ti　6:20　what was committed to your t,
Heb　2:13　I will put My t in

TRUSTED (*see* TRUST)
Ps　13: 5　But I have t in Your mercy;
Ps　22: 4　Our fathers t in You; They
Ps　22: 8　He t in the LORD, let Him
Matt　27:43　He t in God; let Him deliver
Eph　1:12　that we who first t in Christ
Eph　1:13　In Him you also t,

TRUSTING (*see* TRUST)
Ps　112: 7　steadfast, t in the LORD.

TRUSTS (*see* TRUST)
Ps　57: 1　to me! For my soul t in
Ps　115: 8　So is everyone who t in
Prov　31:11　of her husband safely t her;
Is　26: 3　Because he t in You.

TRUTH (*see* TRUE)
Ex　18:21　such as fear God, men of t,
Ex　34: 6　abounding in goodness and t,
Deut　32: 4　A God of t and without
Ps　15: 2　And speaks the t in his
Ps　25: 5　Lead me in Your t and teach
Ps　43: 3　out Your light and Your t!
Ps　51: 6　You desire t in the inward
Ps　85:10　Mercy and t have met
Ps　96:13　And the peoples with His t.
Ps　100: 5　And His t endures to all
Ps　145:18　all who call upon Him in t.
Prov　8: 7　For my mouth will speak t;
Prov　29:24　He swears to tell the t,
Eccl　12:10　was upright—words of t.
Dan　10:21　noted in the Scripture of T.
Zech　8: 3　be called the City of T,
Matt　22:16　teach the way of God in t;

John   1:14 Father, full of grace and t.
John   1:17 but grace and t came
John   3:21 But he who does the t comes
John   4:23 the Father in spirit and t;
John   4:24 must worship in spirit and t.
John   8:32 "And you shall know the t,
John   8:32 and the t shall make you
John   8:44 does not stand in the t,
John   14: 6 him, "I am the way, the t,
John   16:13 when He, the Spirit of t,
John   16:13 He will guide you into all t;
John   17:17 "Sanctify them by Your t.
John   17:17 Your truth. Your word is t.
John   18:37 Everyone who is of the t
John   18:38 said to Him, "What is t?
Rom   1:18 who suppress the t in
Rom   1:25 who exchanged the t of God
Rom   9: 1 I tell the t in Christ, I am
1Co   5: 8 bread of sincerity and t.
1Co   13: 6 but rejoices in the t;
Gal   2: 5 that the t of the gospel
Eph   1:13 you heard the word of t,
Eph   4:15 speaking the t in love, may
Eph   4:21 as the t is in Jesus:
Eph   5: 9 righteousness, and t),
Eph   6:14 girded your waist with t,
Phil   1:18 whether in pretense or in t,
1Th   2:13 of men, but as it is in t,
1Ti   2: 4 to the knowledge of the t.
1Ti   2: 7 I am speaking the t in Christ
1Ti   3:15 pillar and ground of the t.
2Ti   2:15 dividing the word of t.
2Ti   2:18 strayed concerning the t,
Heb   10:26 the knowledge of the t,
Jas   5:19 among you wanders from the t,
2Pe   2: 2 of whom the way of t will
1Jn   1: 6 and do not practice the t.
1Jn   1: 8 and the t is not in us.
1Jn   2: 4 and the t is not in him.
1Jn   3:18 tongue, but in deed and in t.
1Jn   5: 6 because the Spirit is t.
2Jn   1 children, whom I love in t,
2Jn   4 your children walking in t,

TRY (see TRIED, TRYING)
Ps   26: 2 T my mind and my heart.
Ps   139:23 T me, and know my
Mal   3:10 And t Me now in this,"
1Pe   4:12 fiery trial which is to t

TRYING (see TRY)
Gen   19:11 so that they became weary t

TUBAL
Ezek   38: 2 of Rosh, Meshech, and T,

TUMORS
1Sa   5: 6 them and struck them with t,
1Sa   6: 4 Five golden t and five golden

TUMULT
Matt   27:24 but rather that a t was

TUNIC (see TUNICS)
Gen   37: 3 Also he made him a t of
Ex   29: 5 put the t on Aaron, and the
Matt   5:40 sue you and take away your t,
John   19:23 Now the t was without seam,

TUNICS (see TUNIC)
Gen   3:21 wife the LORD God made t
Matt   10:10 for your journey, nor two t,

TUNNEL†
2Ki   20:20 how he made a pool and a t
2Ch   32:30 and brought the water by t

TURBAN
Lev   8: 9 And he put the t on his head.

Zech   3: 5 So they put a clean t on

TURN (see TURNED, TURNING, TURNS, UNTURNED)
Ex   3: 3 I will now t aside and see
Deut   2:27 and I will t neither to the
Deut   4:30 when you t to the LORD your
Deut   17:17 lest his heart t away; nor
Deut   31:29 and t aside from the way
1Ki   8:35 and t from their sin because
2Ch   7:14 and t from their wicked
2Ch   36:10 At the t of the year King
Job   10: 9 And will You t me into dust
Ps   4: 2 Will you t my glory to
Ps   6:10 Let them t back and be
Ps   27: 9 Do not t Your servant away
Ps   40: 4 nor such as t aside to lies.
Ps   119:37 T away my eyes from looking
Prov   4:27 Do not t to the right or the
Prov   7:25 Do not let your heart t
Prov   9: 4 let him t in here!" As
Prov   29: 8 But wise men t away wrath.
Is   58:13 If you t away your foot from
Ezek   10:11 they did not t aside when
Ezek   14: 6 t away from your idols, and
Ezek   33: 9 if you warn the wicked to t
Ezek   33:11 t from your evil ways! For
Dan   12: 3 And those who t many to
Joel   2:12 T to Me with all your heart,
Amos   1: 3 I will not t away its
Amos   5: 7 You who t justice to
Jon   3: 9 Who can tell if God will t
Jon   3: 9 and t away from His fierce
Hag   2:17 yet you did not t to Me,'
Zech   1: 4 T now from your evil ways and
Mal   4: 6 And he will t The hearts of
Matt   5:39 t the other to him also.
Matt   5:42 to borrow from you do not t
Luke   1:16 And he will t many of the
Luke   1:17 to t the hearts of the
Acts   13:46 we t to the Gentiles.
Acts   26:20 t to God, and do works
Phil   1:19 I know that this will t out
2Ti   3: 5 And from such people t away!
Jude   4 who t the grace of our God
Rev   11: 6 have power over waters to t

TURNED (see TURN)
Gen   3:24 and a flaming sword which t
Ex   3: 4 when the LORD saw that he t
Lev   13: 3 the hair on the sore has t
Num   25:11 has t back My wrath from the
Deut   31:18 in that they have t to other
1Ki   2:15 the kingdom has been t over,
1Ki   11: 3 and his wives t away his
2Ki   23:25 who t to the LORD with all
Ps   14: 3 They have all t aside, They
Ps   53: 3 Every one of them has t
Ps   66: 6 He t the sea into dry land;
Ps   78:44 T their rivers into blood,—
Ps   114: 3 and fled; Jordan t back.
Eccl   2:12 Then I t myself to consider
Is   5:25 all this His anger is not t
Is   9:12 all this His anger is not t
Is   9:17 all this His anger is not t
Is   9:21 all this His anger is not t
Is   10: 4 all this His anger is not t
Is   12: 1 Your anger is t away, and
Is   53: 6 have gone astray; We have t,
Jer   2:27 For they have t their
Lam   3: 3 Surely He has t His hand
Lam   5: 2 Our inheritance has been t
Lam   5:15 Our dance has t into
Dan   10:15 I t my face toward the
Hos   14: 4 For My anger has t away
Joel   2:31 The sun shall be t into
Amos   6:12 Yet you have t justice into

Jon	3:10	that they **t** from their evil
Mal	2: 6	And **t** many away from
Matt	16:23	But He **t** and said to Peter,
John	16:20	but your sorrow will be **t**
John	20:14	she **t** around and saw Jesus
Acts	2:20	The sun shall be **t**
Acts	7:42	Then God **t** and gave them up
Acts	11:21	great number believed and **t**
Acts	17: 6	These who have **t** the world
1Th	1: 9	and how you **t** to God from
1Ti	5:15	For some have already **t** aside
Jas	4: 9	Let your laughter be **t** to

TURNING (*see* TURN)

John	21:20	**t** around, saw the disciple
Acts	3:26	in **t** away every one of you
Acts	15:19	the Gentiles who are **t** to
Jas	1:17	no variation or shadow of **t**.

TURNS (*see* TURN)

Deut	29:18	whose heart **t** away today
Prov	15: 1	A soft answer **t** away wrath,
Prov	26:14	As a door **t** on its hinges,
Ezek	3:20	when a righteous man **t** from
Ezek	18:21	But if a wicked man **t** from
2Co	3:16	Nevertheless when one **t** to

TURQUOISE

Ex	28:18	second row shall be a **t**,

TURTLEDOVE (*see* TURTLEDOVES)

Gen	15: 9	a three-year-old ram, a **t**,
Lev	12: 6	and a young pigeon or a **t** as
Song	2:12	And the voice of the **t** Is

TURTLEDOVES (*see* TURTLEDOVE)

Lev	5: 7	two **t** or two young pigeons:
Lev	12: 8	then she may bring two **t** or
Luke	2:24	A pair of **t** or two

TUTOR

Gal	3:24	Therefore the law was our **t**

TWELVE

Gen	35:22	the sons of Jacob were **t**:
Gen	49:28	All these are the **t** tribes
Ex	24: 4	and **t** pillars according to
Ex	39:14	There were **t** stones
Josh	4: 9	Then Joshua set up **t** stones
Judg	19:29	and divided her into **t**
1Ki	7:44	and **t** oxen under the Sea;
1Ki	10:20	T lions stood there, one on
1Ki	11:30	and tore it into **t** pieces.
1Ki	18:31	And Elijah took **t** stones,
Matt	10: 1	And when He had called His **t**
Matt	10: 2	Now the names of the **t**
Matt	19:28	Me will also sit on **t**
Matt	19:28	judging the **t** tribes of
Matt	26:53	provide Me with more than **t**
Luke	2:42	And when He was **t** years old,
Acts	7: 8	and Jacob begot the **t**
1Co	15: 5	by Cephas, then by the **t**.
Jas	1: 1	To the **t** tribes which are
Rev	7: 5	of the tribe of Judah **t**
Rev	7: 5	of the tribe of Reuben **t**
Rev	21:12	a great and high wall with **t**
Rev	22: 2	which bore **t** fruits, each

TWENTY

Gen	6: 3	shall be one hundred and **t**
Gen	18:31	it for the sake of **t**.
Gen	31:41	I have been in your house **t**
Gen	37:28	him to the Ishmaelites for **t**
Lev	27: 3	is of a male from **t** years
Lev	27: 5	for a male shall be **t**
Num	1:18	from **t** years old and above,
Deut	31: 2	I am one hundred and **t** years
Deut	34: 7	Moses was one hundred and **t**
Judg	16:31	He had judged Israel **t**

2Ch	31:17	and to the Levites from **t**

TWENTY-FIVE

Num	8:24	From **t** years old and above
Ezek	48: 8	**t** thousand cubits in width,
Ezek	48: 9	for the LORD shall be **t**

TWENTY-FOUR

1Ch	27: 1	each division having **t**
1Ch	27: 2	and in his division were **t**
Rev	4: 4	Around the throne were **t**
Rev	4:10	the **t** elders fall down before
Rev	5: 8	living creatures and the **t**

TWENTY-THREE

1Co	10: 8	and in one day **t** thousand

TWENTY-TWO

2Sa	8: 5	David killed **t** thousand of

TWICE

Ex	16:22	that they gathered **t** as
Num	20:11	hand and struck the rock **t**
Job	42:10	Indeed the LORD gave Job **t**
Matt	23:15	you make him **t** as much a son
Mark	14:30	before the rooster crows **t**,
Mark	14:72	"Before the rooster crows **t**,

TWILIGHT

Ex	12: 6	of Israel shall kill it at **t**.
Ex	29:39	lamb you shall offer at **t**.
Deut	16: 6	sacrifice the Passover at **t**,
Job	24:15	adulterer waits for the **t**,

TWINKLING†

1Co	15:52	in the **t** of an eye, at the

TWIN

John	11:16	Thomas, who is called the **t**

TWINS

Gen	25:24	indeed there were **t** in her
Gen	38:27	**t** were in her womb.
Song	7: 3	two fawns, T of a gazelle.

TWIST† (*see* TWISTED, TWISTS)

Ps	56: 5	All day they **t** my words;
2Pe	3:16	and unstable people **t** to

TWISTED (*see* TWIST)

Is	27: 1	Leviathan that **t** serpent;
Mark	15:17	and they **t** a crown of

TWISTS (*see* TWIST)

Deut	16:19	the eyes of the wise and **t**

TWO (*see* TWO-EDGED)

Gen	1:16	Then God made **t** great lights:
Gen	4:19	Lamech took for himself **t**
Gen	7:15	the ark to Noah, two by **t**,
Gen	15:10	to Him and cut them in **t**,
Gen	22: 6	and the **t** of them went
Gen	22: 8	So the **t** of them went
Gen	25:23	T nations are in your womb,
Ex	31:18	He gave Moses **t** tablets of
Ex	34: 1	Cut **t** tablets of stone like
Lev	5: 7	**t** turtledoves or two young
Num	7:89	from between the **t** cherubim;
Deut	17: 6	death on the testimony of **t**
Deut	21:15	If a man has **t** wives, one
Ruth	1: 1	he and his wife and his **t**
Ruth	1: 8	And Naomi said to her **t**
1Sa	1: 2	And he had **t** wives: the name
1Sa	4: 4	And the **t** sons of Eli,
1Sa	30: 5	And David's **t** wives, Ahinoam
1Ki	3:25	the living child in **t**,
1Ki	18:21	will you falter between **t**
Prov	30: 7	T things I request of You
Eccl	4: 9	T are better than one,
Eccl	4:11	if **t** lie down together, they
Song	4: 5	Your **t** breasts are like two
Is	6: 2	with **t** he covered his face,

Jer	2:13	My people have committed t
Jer	24: 1	and there were t baskets of
Ezek	1:11	and t covered their bodies.
Ezek	37:22	they shall no longer be t
Dan	8: 3	was a ram which had t horns,
Amos	3: 3	Can t walk together, unless
Zech	4:11	What are these t olive
Zech	4:14	These are the t anointed
Matt	2:16	from t years old and under,
Matt	5:41	go one mile, go with him t.
Matt	18:16	take with you one or t more,
Matt	18:16	by the mouth of t or
Matt	18:19	I say to you that if t of
Matt	18:20	For where t or three are
Matt	19: 5	and the t shall become
Matt	22:40	On these t commandments hang
Matt	26:37	with Him Peter and the t
Matt	27:38	Then t robbers were crucified
Matt	27:51	of the temple was torn in t
Mark	6: 7	to send them out two by t,
Luke	2:24	of turtledoves or t
Luke	21: 2	poor widow putting in t
Luke	22:38	here are t swords." And He
Luke	24:13	t of them were traveling
John	20:12	And she saw t angels in white
Acts	1:10	t men stood by them in white
2Co	13: 1	By the mouth of t or
Gal	4:24	For these are the t
Eph	2:15	one new man from the t,
Eph	5:31	and the t shall become
Phil	1:23	hard pressed between the t,
Heb	6:18	that by t immutable things,
Heb	10:28	mercy on the testimony of t
Heb	11:37	stoned, they were sawn in t,
Rev	11: 3	I will give power to my t
Rev	11: 4	These are the t olive trees

TWO-EDGED (see TWO)

Prov	5: 4	Sharp as a t sword.
Heb	4:12	and sharper than any t
Rev	1:16	of His mouth went a sharp t

TYPE†

| Rom | 5:14 | who is a t of Him who was to |

TYRE

Josh	19:29	to the fortified city of T;
2Sa	5:11	Then Hiram king of T sent
Ezra	3: 7	to the people of Sidon and T
Ezek	27: 2	take up a lamentation for T,
Amos	1: 9	three transgressions of T,
Matt	11:22	be more tolerable for T and
Mark	3: 8	and those from T and Sidon,

U

UGLY

| Gen | 41: 4 | And the u and gaunt cows ate |

UNAPPROACHABLE†

| 1Ti | 6:16 | dwelling in u light, whom no |

UNAWARE

| Rom | 1:13 | I do not want you to be u, |
| 1Co | 10: 1 | I do not want you to be u |

UNBELIEF (see BELIEF, UNBELIEVING)

Matt	13:58	there because of their u.
Mark	9:24	I believe; help my u!"
Rom	4:20	the promise of God through u,
Rom	11:23	if they do not continue in u,
1Ti	1:13	I did it ignorantly in u.
Heb	3:12	of you an evil heart of u
Heb	3:19	not enter in because of u.

UNBELIEVER (see BELIEVER, UNBELIEVERS)

1Co	7:15	But if the u departs, let him
2Co	6:15	has a believer with an u?
1Ti	5: 8	faith and is worse than an u.

UNBELIEVERS (see UNBELIEVER)

Luke	12:46	him his portion with the u.
1Co	14:22	those who believe but to u;
2Co	6:14	yoked together with u.

UNBELIEVING (see UNBELIEF)

John	20:27	into My side. Do not be u,
1Co	7:14	For the u husband is
Rev	21: 8	"But the cowardly, u,

UNCERTAIN (see CERTAIN, UNCERTAINTY)

| 1Co | 14: 8 | if the trumpet makes an u |
| 1Ti | 6:17 | nor to trust in u riches but |

UNCERTAINTY† (see UNCERTAIN)

| 1Co | 9:26 | I run thus: not with u. |

UNCHANGEABLE† (see CHANGE)

| Heb | 7:24 | has an u priesthood. |

UNCIRCUMCISED (see CIRCUMCISE, UNCIRCUMCISION)

Gen	17:14	And the u male child, who is
Ex	6:12	for I am of u lips?"
Lev	26:41	if their u hearts are
Jer	6:10	Indeed their ear is u,
Ezek	44: 7	u in heart and uncircumcised
Rom	2:27	will not the physically u,
Rom	3:30	by faith and the u through
Rom	4: 9	or upon the u also? For we
Rom	4:12	Abraham had while still u.
1Co	7:18	Let him not become u.
Gal	2: 7	that the gospel for the u
Col	3:11	nor Jew, circumcised nor u,

UNCIRCUMCISION (see UNCIRCUMCISED)

Rom	2:25	circumcision has become u.
1Co	7:19	is nothing and u is nothing,
Gal	5: 6	neither circumcision nor u
Eph	2:11	who are called U by what is
Col	2:13	in your trespasses and the u

UNCLEAN (see CLEAN, UNCLEANNESS)

Gen	7: 2	each of animals that are u,
Lev	5: 2	if a person touches any u
Lev	5: 2	it is the carcass of an u
Lev	7:21	or any abominable u thing,
Lev	10:10	and between u and clean,
Lev	11: 4	hooves, it is u to you;
Lev	11:47	distinguish between the u
Lev	12: 2	then she shall be u seven
Lev	12: 5	then she shall be u two
Lev	13: 8	priest shall pronounce him u.
Lev	13:45	and cry, 'U! Unclean!'
Lev	15:20	that she sits on shall be u.
Deut	14: 8	Also the swine is u for you,
Judg	13: 7	drink, nor eat anything u,
Job	14: 4	a clean thing out of an u?
Is	6: 5	Because I am a man of u
Is	6: 5	the midst of a people of u
Is	52:11	Touch no u thing; Go out
Is	64: 6	But we are all like an u
Zech	13: 2	cause the prophets and the u
Matt	10: 1	He gave them power over u
Luke	4:33	man who had a spirit of an u
Acts	10:14	eaten anything common or u.
Acts	10:28	not call any man common or u.
1Co	7:14	your children would be u,
2Co	6:17	not touch what is u,
Heb	9:13	a heifer, sprinkling the u,
Rev	16:13	And I saw three u spirits

UNCLEANNESS (see UNCLEAN)

| Deut | 24: 1 | because he has found some u |

Matt 23:27 dead men's bones and all **u**.
Rom 1:24 God also gave them up to **u**,
Rom 6:19 your members as slaves of **u**,
Gal 5:19 adultery, fornication, **u**,
1Th 4: 7 For God did not call us to **u**,
2Pe 2:10 the flesh in the lust of **u**

UNCLOTHED† (*see* CLOTHE)
2Co 5: 4 not because we want to be **u**,

UNCONDEMNED (*see* CONDEMN)
Acts 22:25 a man who is a Roman, and **u**?

UNCOVER (*see* COVER, UNCOVERED)
Lev 18: 6 to **u** his nakedness: I am
Ruth 3: 4 **u** his feet, and lie down;
Lam 4:22 He will **u** your sins!

UNCOVERED (*see* UNCOVER)
Gen 9:21 and became **u** in his tent.
Ruth 3: 7 **u** his feet, and lay down.
Is 20: 4 with their buttocks **u**,
Mark 2: 4 they **u** the roof where He
1Co 11: 5 prophesies with her head **u**
1Co 11:13 pray to God with her head **u**?

UNDEFILED† (*see* DEFILE)
Ps 119: 1 Blessed are the **u** in the
Heb 7:26 who is holy, harmless, **u**,
Heb 13: 4 among all, and the bed **u**;
Jas 1:27 Pure and **u** religion before
1Pe 1: 4 incorruptible and **u** and

UNDERFOOT
Heb 10:29 trampled the Son of God **u**,

UNDERSTAND (*see* UNDERSTANDING, UNDERSTANDS, UNDERSTOOD)
Gen 11: 7 that they may not **u** one
Deut 28:49 language you will not **u**,
Neh 8: 3 women and those who could **u**;
Neh 8: 7 helped the people to **u** the
Job 26:14 of His power who can **u**?
Job 42: 3 uttered what I did not **u**,
Ps 14: 2 see if there are any who **u**,
Ps 19:12 Who can **u** his errors?
Ps 53: 2 see if there are any who **u**,
Ps 82: 5 do not know, nor do they **u**;
Ps 139: 2 You **u** my thought afar off.
Prov 1: 6 To **u** a proverb and an
Prov 2: 5 Then you will **u** the fear of
Prov 30:18 Yes, four which I do not **u**:
Is 6: 9 on hearing, but do not **u**;
Is 6:10 And **u** with their heart,
Is 43:10 And **u** that I am He.
Is 44:18 They do not know nor **u**;
Dan 1: 4 knowledge and quick to **u**,
Dan 10:12 that you set your heart to **u**,
Dan 12: 8 I heard, I did not **u**.
Dan 12:10 but the wise shall **u**.
Hos 14: 9 Let him **u** these things.
Matt 13:15 Lest they should **u**
Matt 24:15 (whoever reads, let him **u**),
Mark 4:13 Do you not **u** this parable?
Mark 13:14 not" (let the reader **u**),
John 6:60 saying; who can **u** it?"
John 13: 7 I am doing you do not **u** now,
Acts 8:30 Do you **u** what you are
1Co 13: 2 and **u** all mysteries and all
1Co 14:16 since he does not **u** what you
Eph 5:17 but **u** what the will of the
Heb 11: 3 By faith we **u** that the worlds
2Pe 3:16 are some things hard to **u**,

UNDERSTANDING (*see* UNDERSTAND)
Ex 35:31 of God, in wisdom and **u**,
1Ki 3: 9 give to Your servant an **u**
1Ki 4:29 and exceedingly great **u**,
Neh 8: 2 all who could hear with **u**

Job 12:12 And with length of days, **u**.
Job 28:28 to depart from evil is **u**.
Ps 111:10 A good **u** have all those who
Ps 119:99 I have more **u** than all my
Ps 119:130 It gives **u** to the simple.
Ps 147: 5 in power; His **u** is infinite.
Prov 1: 2 To perceive the words of **u**,
Prov 2: 2 And apply your heart to **u**;
Prov 3: 5 And lean not on your own **u**;
Prov 3:19 By **u** He established the
Prov 4: 7 in all your getting, get **u**.
Prov 6:32 with a woman lacks **u**;
Prov 7: 7 A young man devoid of **u**,
Prov 9:10 of the Holy One is **u**.
Prov 16:22 **U** is a wellspring of life
Prov 18: 2 A fool has no delight in **u**,
Prov 21:30 There is no wisdom or **u**
Eccl 9:11 Nor riches to men of **u**,
Is 11: 2 The Spirit of wisdom and **u**,
Is 29:16 formed it, "He has no **u**"?
Is 40:28 His **u** is unsearchable.
Dan 1:17 and Daniel had **u** in all
Dan 4:34 and my **u** returned to me; and
Luke 2:47 Him were astonished at His **u**
Luke 24:45 And He opened their **u**,
1Co 14:15 I will also pray with the **u**.
1Co 14:19 speak five words with my **u**,
1Co 14:20 but in **u** be mature.
Eph 1:18 the eyes of your **u** being
Eph 4:18 having their **u** darkened,
Phil 4: 7 God, which surpasses all **u**,
Col 1: 9 all wisdom and spiritual **u**;
2Ti 2: 7 and may the Lord give you **u**
Jas 3:13 Who is wise and **u** among

UNDERSTANDS (*see* UNDERSTAND)
Jer 9:24 That he **u** and knows Me,
Rom 3:11 There is none who **u**;
1Co 14: 2 for no one **u** him; however,

UNDERSTOOD (*see* UNDERSTAND)
Neh 8:12 because they **u** the words
Eccl 1:16 My heart has **u** great wisdom
Is 40:21 Have you not **u** from the
Dan 8:27 vision, but no one **u** it.
Dan 9: 2 **u** by the books the number of
Mark 6:52 For they had not **u** about the
Rom 1:20 being **u** by the things that
1Co 13:11 I **u** as a child, I thought as

UNDESIRABLE† (*see* DESIRE)
Zeph 2: 1 together, O **u** nation,

UNDIGNIFIED†
2Sa 6:22 And I will be even more **u**

UNDISCERNING† (*see* DISCERN)
Rom 1:31 **u**, untrustworthy,

UNDONE
Is 6: 5 for I am **u**! Because I am a
Matt 23:23 without leaving the others **u**.

UNEQUALLY† (*see* EQUAL)
2Co 6:14 Do not be **u** yoked together

UNEXPECTEDLY (*see* EXPECT)
Ps 35: 8 destruction come upon him **u**,
Luke 21:34 and that Day come on you **u**.

UNFAITHFUL (*see* FAITHFUL, UNFAITHFULLY, UNFAITHFULNESS)
Lev 26:40 in which they were **u** to Me,
Prov 23:28 And increases the **u** among

UNFAITHFULLY (*see* UNFAITHFUL)
Ps 78:57 But turned back and acted **u**

UNFAITHFULNESS (*see* UNFAITHFUL)
1Ch 10:13 So Saul died for his **u** which

Dan 9: 7 because of the **u** which they

UNFAMILIAR (*see* FAMILIAR)
Ezek 3: 5 not sent to a people of **u**

UNFANNED† (*see* FAN)
Job 20:26 An **u** fire will consume him;

UNFORGIVING† (*see* FORGIVE)
Rom 1:31 untrustworthy, unloving, **u**,
2Ti 3: 3 unloving, **u**, slanderers,

UNFORMED† (*see* FORM)
Ps 139:16 my substance, being yet **u**.

UNFRUITFUL (*see* FRUITFUL)
Matt 13:22 the word, and he becomes **u**.
Eph 5:11 no fellowship with the **u**
2Pe 1: 8 be neither barren nor **u** in

UNGODLINESS (*see* UNGODLY)
Is 32: 6 iniquity: To practice **u**,
Rom 1:18 from heaven against all **u**
Rom 11:26 He will turn away **u**
Tit 2:12 denying **u** and worldly lusts,

UNGODLY (*see* GODLY, UNGODLINESS)
Ps 1: 1 not in the counsel of the **u**,
Ps 1: 6 But the way of the **u** shall
Rom 4: 5 on Him who justifies the **u**,
Rom 5: 6 time Christ died for the **u**.
1Pe 4:18 Where will the **u** and
2Pe 2: 5 flood on the world of the **u**;
2Pe 3: 7 judgment and perdition of **u**
Jude 4 **u** men, who turn the grace of
Jude 15 among them of all their **u**
Jude 18 according to their own **u**

UNHEARD† (*see* HEAR)
John 9:32 world began it has been **u**

UNHOLY (*see* HOLY)
Lev 10:10 between holy and **u**,
1Ti 1: 9 for the **u** and profane, for
2Ti 3: 2 to parents, unthankful, **u**,

UNINHABITED (*see* INHABIT)
Ezek 35: 9 and your cities shall be **u**;

UNINTENDED† (*see* INTEND, UNINTENTIONALLY)
Num 15:25 for their **u** sin.

UNINTENTIONALLY (*see* UNINTENDED)
Deut 19: 4 Whoever kills his neighbor **u**,

UNIQUE†
Job 23:13 "But He is **u**, and who can

UNITE† (*see* UNITED, UNITY)
Ps 86:11 U my heart to fear Your

UNITED (*see* UNITE)
Rom 6: 5 For if we have been **u**

UNITY (*see* UNITE)
Ps 133: 1 to dwell together in **u**!
Eph 4: 3 endeavoring to keep the **u** of
Eph 4:13 till we all come to the **u** of

UNJUST (*see* JUST)
Matt 5:45 on the just and on the **u**.
Luke 16: 8 the master commended the **u**
Luke 18: 6 Hear what the **u** judge said.
Acts 24:15 both of the just and the **u**.
Heb 6:10 For God is not **u** to forget
1Pe 3:18 for sins, the just for the **u**,
2Pe 2: 9 and to reserve the **u** under
Rev 22:11 "He who is **u**, let him be

UNKNOWN (*see* KNOW)
Acts 17:23 TO THE U GOD. Therefore, the

UNLAWFUL† (*see* LAWFUL)
Acts 10:28 You know how **u** it is for a

UNLEAVENED (*see* LEAVEN)
Ex 12: 8 with **u** bread and with
Ex 12:17 observe the Feast of U
Ex 29: 2 and **u** wafers anointed with
Matt 26:17 day of the Feast of the U
Acts 12: 3 it was during the Days of U
1Co 5: 7 lump, since you truly are **u**.

UNLIFTED† (*see* LIFT)
2Co 3:14 day the same veil remains **u**

UNLIKE†
2Co 3:13 **u** Moses, who put a veil over

UNLOAD† (*see* LOAD)
Acts 21: 3 for there the ship was to **u**

UNLOVED (*see* LOVE, UNLOVING)
Gen 29:31 LORD saw that Leah was **u**,
Deut 21:15 one loved and the other **u**,

UNLOVING (*see* UNLOVED)
Rom 1:31 untrustworthy, **u**,

UNMARRIED (*see* MARRY)
1Co 7: 8 But I say to the **u** and to the
1Co 7:32 He who is **u** cares for the

UNMERCIFUL† (*see* MERCIFUL)
Rom 1:31 unloving, unforgiving, **u**;

UNMINDFUL† (*see* MIND)
Deut 32:18 who begot you, you are **u**,

UNNOTICED† (*see* NOTICE)
Jude 4 certain men have crept in **u**,

UNPRESENTABLE† (*see* PRESENT)
1Co 12:23 and our **u** parts have

UNPROFITABLE (*see* PROFITABLE)
Matt 25:30 And cast the **u** servant into
Luke 17:10 We are **u** servants. We have
Rom 3:12 have together become **u**;
Phm 1:11 who once was **u** to you, but

UNPUNISHED (*see* PUNISH)
Prov 19: 5 false witness will not go **u**,

UNQUENCHABLE (*see* QUENCH)
Matt 3:12 burn up the chaff with **u**

UNRELIABLE†
Jer 15:18 surely be to me like an **u**

UNRIGHTEOUS (*see* RIGHTEOUS, UNRIGHTEOUSNESS)
Ps 71: 4 Out of the hand of the **u**
Is 55: 7 And the **u** man his thoughts;
Luke 16: 9 friends for yourselves by **u**
1Co 6: 1 go to law before the **u**,
1Co 6: 9 Do you not know that the **u**

UNRIGHTEOUSNESS (*see* UNRIGHTEOUS)
Ps 92:15 and there is no **u** in Him.
John 7:18 and no **u** is in Him.
Rom 1:18 who suppress the truth in **u**,
Rom 6:13 as instruments of **u** to sin,
Rom 9:14 Is there **u** with God?
2Th 2:12 truth but had pleasure in **u**.
2Pe 2:13 will receive the wages of **u**,
1Jn 1: 9 and to cleanse us from all **u**.
1Jn 5:17 All **u** is sin, and there is

UNSEARCHABLE
Ps 145: 3 And His greatness is **u**.
Rom 11:33 and knowledge of God! How **u**
Eph 3: 8 among the Gentiles the **u**

UNSHRUNK
Mark 2:21 No one sews a piece of **u**

UNSPOTTED† (*see* SPOT)
Jas 1:27 and to keep oneself **u** from

UNSTABLE
Prov 5: 6 path of life—Her ways are **u**;
Jas 1: 8 man, **u** in all his ways.
2Pe 2:14 enticing **u** souls. They
2Pe 3:16 which untaught and **u** people

UNTHANKFUL (*see* THANKFUL)
2Ti 3: 2 disobedient to parents, **u**,

UNTURNED† (*see* TURN)
Hos 7: 8 Ephraim is a cake **u**.

UNVEILED† (*see* VEIL)
2Co 3:18 with **u** face, beholding as in

UNWASHED (*see* WASH)
Matt 15:20 but to eat with **u** hands does

UNWISE (*see* WISE)
Hos 13:13 He is an **u** son, For he
Rom 1:14 both to wise and to **u**.
Eph 5:17 Therefore do not be **u**,

UNWITTINGLY†
Heb 13: 2 for by so doing some have **u**

UNWORTHY (*see* WORTHY)
1Co 11:27 cup of the Lord in an **u**

UPHARSIN† (*see* PERES)
Dan 5:25 MENE, MENE, TEKEL, U.

UPHOLD (*see* UPHOLDING, UPHOLDS)
Ps 51:12 And **u** me by Your generous
Ps 119:116 U me according to Your word,
Is 42: 1 My Servant whom I **u**,

UPHOLDING† (*see* UPHOLD)
Heb 1: 3 and **u** all things by the word

UPHOLDS (*see* UPHOLD)
Ps 37:17 But the LORD **u** the
Ps 63: 8 Your right hand **u** me.

UPLIFTED† (*see* LIFT)
Acts 13:17 and with an **u** arm He brought

UPPER
Judg 9:53 a certain woman dropped an **u**
2Ki 4:10 let us make a small **u** room
2Ki 18:17 by the aqueduct from the **u**
Dan 6:10 And in his **u** room, with his
Mark 14:15 he will show you a large **u**
Acts 1:13 they went up into the **u** room
Acts 19: 1 having passed through the **u**

UPRIGHT (*see* UPRIGHTLY, UPRIGHTNESS)
Gen 37: 7 sheaf arose and also stood **u**;
Deut 32: 4 Righteous and **u** is He.
Job 1: 1 that man was blameless and **u**,
Job 1: 8 a blameless and **u** man, one
Ps 25: 8 Good and **u** is the LORD;
Ps 111: 1 In the assembly of the **u**
Prov 2: 7 up sound wisdom for the **u**;
Prov 15:19 But the way of the **u** is a
Eccl 7:29 found: That God made man **u**,
Eccl 12:10 what was written was **u**—
Dan 8:18 touched me, and stood me **u**.
Hab 2: 4 His soul is not **u** in him;

UPRIGHTLY (*see* UPRIGHT)
Ps 15: 2 He who walks **u**, And works
Ps 84:11 From those who walk **u**.
Prov 2: 7 a shield to those who walk **u**;

UPRIGHTNESS (*see* UPRIGHT)
Ps 143:10 Lead me in the land of **u**.
Prov 2:13 who leave the paths of **u**

UPROAR
1Ki 1:45 so that the city is in an **u**.
Matt 26: 5 lest there be an **u** among the
Acts 17: 5 set all the city in an **u** and
Acts 21:31 all Jerusalem was in an **u**.

UPROOT (*see* UPROOTED)
Matt 13:29 up the tares you also **u** the

UPROOTED (*see* UPROOT)
Job 19:10 My hope He has **u** like a
Dan 11: 4 for his kingdom shall be **u**,

UPSIDE
Ps 146: 9 way of the wicked He turns **u**
Acts 17: 6 who have turned the world **u**

UPWARD
2Ki 19:30 downward, And bear fruit **u**.
Job 5: 7 As the sparks fly **u**.
Phil 3:14 goal for the prize of the **u**

UR
Gen 11:28 in U of the Chaldeans.
Neh 9: 7 And brought him out of U of

URGE (*see* URGED, URGENT)
1Co 16:15 I **u** you, brethren—you know
Heb 13:19 But I especially **u** you to do

URGED (*see* URGE)
Gen 19:15 the angels **u** Lot to hurry,
John 4:31 the meantime His disciples **u**

URGENT (*see* URGE)
Dan 2:15 decree from the king so **u**?

URIAH
2Sa 11: 3 the wife of U the Hittite?"
2Sa 11:17 and U the Hittite died also.
Is 8: 2 U the priest and Zechariah
Matt 1: 6 had been the wife of U.

URIM (*see* THUMMIM)
Ex 28:30 of judgment the U and the
1Sa 28: 6 either by dreams or by U or
Ezra 2:63 could consult with the U

USEFUL
2Ti 2:21 sanctified and **u** for the
2Ti 4:11 for he is **u** to me for

USELESS
Ps 31: 6 hated those who regard **u**
Ps 60:11 For the help of man is **u**.
Tit 3: 9 they are unprofitable and **u**.
Jas 1:26 this one's religion is **u**.

USUALLY†
Dan 3:19 times more than it was **u**

USURY
Lev 25:36 Take no **u** or interest from
Neh 5: 7 Each of you is exacting **u**

UTMOST (*see* UTTERMOST)
2Ti 4:21 Do your **u** to come before

UTTER (*see* UTTERANCE, UTTERED, UTTERS)
Ps 119:171 My lips shall **u** praise, For
Prov 14: 5 But a false witness will **u**
Mark 3:28 blasphemies they may **u**;
2Co 12: 4 is not lawful for a man to **u**.

UTTERANCE (*see* UTTER)
Acts 2: 4 as the Spirit gave them **u**.
Eph 6:19 that **u** may be given to me,

UTTERED (*see* UTTER)
Job 42: 3 Therefore I have **u** what I
Ps 66:14 Which my lips have **u** And my
Rom 8:26 groanings which cannot be **u**.

UTTERLY
Josh 17:13 but did not **u** drive them
Ps 119: 8 do not forsake me **u**!
Song 8: 7 It would be **u** despised.
Is 6:11 The land is **u** desolate,
2Pe 2:12 and will **u** perish in their

UTTERMOST (*see* UTMOST)
Ps 139: 9 And dwell in the **u** parts
Heb 7:25 also able to save to the **u**

UTTERS (*see* UTTER)
Ps 19: 2 Day unto day **u** speech, And

UZ
Job 1: 1 was a man in the land of U,
Jer 25:20 the kings of the land of U,
Lam 4:21 who dwell in the land of U!

UZZAH
2Sa 6: 6 U put out his hand to the

UZZIAH (*see* AZARIAH)
2Ch 26:21 King U was a leper until the
Is 6: 1 In the year that King U died,
Hos 1: 1 of Beeri, in the days of U,
Amos 1: 1 Israel in the days of U
Zech 14: 5 In the days of U king of
Matt 1: 8 Joram, and Joram begot U.

VAGABOND
Gen 4:12 A fugitive and a **v** you shall

VAIN (*see* EMPTY, USELESS)
Ex 20: 7 who takes His name in **v**.
Deut 5:11 who takes His name in **v**.
Ps 2: 1 And the people plot a **v**
Ps 127: 1 They labor in **v** who build
Ps 139:20 take Your name in **v**.
Eccl 6:12 all the days of his **v** life
Is 45:18 Who did not create it in **v**,
Matt 6: 7 do not use **v** repetitions as
Acts 4:25 And the people plot **v**
Rom 13: 4 does not bear the sword in **v**;
1Co 15: 2 you—unless you believed in **v**.
1Co 15:58 that your labor is not in **v**
Gal 2: 2 might run, or had run, in **v**.
Gal 2:21 law, then Christ died in **v**.
Gal 3: 4 vain—if indeed it was in **v**?
Phil 2:16 run in vain or labored in **v**.
1Th 2: 1 coming to you was not in **v**.

VALIANT (*see* VALIANTLY)
Heb 11:34 became **v** in battle, turned

VALIANTLY (*see* VALIANT)
Ps 60:12 Through God we will do **v**,
Ps 118:15 hand of the LORD does **v**.

VALLEY (*see* VALLEYS)
Num 13:23 Then they came to the V of
Josh 10:12 in the V of Aijalon."
Ps 23: 4 though I walk through the **v**
Is 22: 1 The burden against the V of
Is 40: 4 Every **v** shall be exalted
Jer 7:32 but the V of Slaughter; for
Hos 1: 5 the bow of Israel in the V
Joel 3: 2 bring them down to the V of
Joel 3:14 the LORD is near in the **v**
Luke 3: 5 Every **v** shall be filled

VALLEYS (*see* VALLEY)
Deut 11:11 is a land of hills and **v**,
1Ki 20:28 but He is not God of the **v**,
Song 2: 1 And the lily of the **v**.
Ezek 32: 5 And fill the **v** with your

VALOR
Josh 1:14 all your mighty men of **v**,
Judg 6:12 you mighty man of **v**!"
2Ki 5: 1 was also a mighty man of **v**,

VALUE (*see* FULL, VALUED)
Lev 6: 5 He shall restore its full **v**,
Job 28:13 Man does not know its **v**,
Matt 6:26 Are you not of more **v** than
Matt 27: 9 the **v** of Him who was
Col 2:23 but are of no **v** against

VALUED (*see* VALUE)
Prov 27:21 And a man is **v** by what

VANISH (*see* VANISHED, VANISHES)
Is 51: 6 For the heavens will **v** away
1Co 13: 8 knowledge, it will **v** away.
Heb 8:13 growing old is ready to **v**

VANISHED (*see* VANISH)
Luke 24:31 and He **v** from their sight.

VANISHES (*see* VANISH)
Jas 4:14 for a little time and then **v**

VANITIES† (*see* VANITY)
Eccl 1: 2 "Vanity of **v**," says the
Eccl 12: 8 "Vanity of **v**," says the

VANITY (*see* VANITIES)
Eccl 1: 2 V of vanities," says the
Eccl 1: 2 of vanities, all is **v**.
Eccl 2: 1 but surely, this also was **v**.
Is 5:18 iniquity with cords of **v**,
Hos 12:11 idols—Surely they are **v**—

VAPOR
Ps 39:11 Surely every man is **v**.
Acts 2:19 Blood and fire and **v**
Jas 4:14 It is even a **v** that appears

VARIATION† (*see* VARIETIES)
Jas 1:17 with whom there is no **v** or

VARIETIES† (*see* VARIATION, VARIOUS)
1Co 12:28 **v** of tongues.

VARIOUS (*see* VARIETIES)
Heb 1: 1 who at **v** times and in
Heb 13: 9 not be carried about with **v**
Jas 1: 2 all joy when you fall into **v**
1Pe 1: 6 you have been grieved by **v**

VASHTI
Esth 1:12 But Queen V refused to come
Esth 2:17 made her queen instead of V.

VATS
Prov 3:10 And your **v** will overflow

VEGETABLES
Dan 1:12 and let them give us **v** to
Rom 14: 2 he who is weak eats only **v**.

VEHEMENT (*see* VEHEMENTLY)
Song 8: 6 of fire, A most **v** flame.
Jon 4: 8 that God prepared a **v** east
Heb 5: 7 with **v** cries and tears to

VEHEMENTLY (*see* VEHEMENT)
Luke 6:48 the stream beat **v** against

VEIL (*see* UNVEILED, VEILED)
Gen 24:65 So she took a **v** and
Gen 38:14 covered herself with a **v**
Ex 26:33 The **v** shall be a divider for
Ex 34:33 he put a **v** on his face.
Lev 16:15 bring its blood inside the **v**,
Song 4: 1 dove's eyes behind your **v**.
Matt 27:51 the **v** of the temple was torn
2Co 3:13 who put a **v** over his face
2Co 3:15 a **v** lies on their heart.
Heb 6:19 the Presence behind the **v**,
Heb 10:20 for us, through the **v**,

VEILED (*see* VEIL)
2Co 4: 3 But even if our gospel is **v**,

VENGEANCE
Gen	4:15	v shall be taken on him
Deut	32:35	V is Mine, and recompense
Ps	94: 1	to whom v belongs—O God, to
Prov	6:34	not spare in the day of v.
Is	1:24	And take v on My enemies.
Is	34: 8	is the day of the LORD's v,
Is	61: 2	And the day of v of our
Jer	46:10	GOD of hosts, A day of v,
Jer	51: 6	the time of the LORD's v;
Mic	5:15	And I will execute v in
Nah	1: 2	The LORD will take v on
Luke	21:22	these are the days of v,
Rom	12:19	V is Mine, I will repay,"
2Th	1: 8	in flaming fire taking v on
Heb	10:30	V is Mine, I will repay,"
Jude	7	suffering the v of eternal

VESSEL (see VESSELS)
Lev	14: 5	be killed in an earthen v
Lev	15:12	and every v of wood shall be
Num	5:17	holy water in an earthen v,
Ps	2: 9	to pieces like a potter's v.
Jer	18: 4	made it again into another v,
Jer	19:11	as one breaks a potter's v,
Jer	32:14	and put them in an earthen v,
John	19:29	Now a v full of sour wine was
Acts	9:15	for he is a chosen v of Mine
Rom	9:21	the same lump to make one v
1Th	4: 4	how to possess his own v in
2Ti	2:21	he will be a v for honor,
1Pe	3: 7	the wife, as to the weaker v,

VESSELS (see PITCHERS, VESSEL)
Jer	28: 6	to bring back the v of the
Dan	5: 2	bring the gold and silver v
Matt	13:48	and gathered the good into v,
Matt	25: 4	the wise took oil in their v
Rom	9:22	much longsuffering the v of
Rom	9:23	of His glory on the v of
2Co	4: 7	this treasure in earthen v,
2Ti	2:20	house there are not only v

VESTIBULE
1Ki	7:12	of the LORD and the v of

VEXED
Judg	16:16	so that his soul was v to

VICE†
1Pe	2:16	liberty as a cloak for v,

VICTORIES† (see VICTORY)
Ps	44: 4	Command v for Jacob.

VICTORY (see VICTORIES)
2Sa	23:12	brought about a great v.
Ps	98: 1	arm have gained Him the v.
Matt	12:20	sends forth justice to v;
1Co	15:54	is swallowed up in v.
1Co	15:57	who gives us the v through
1Jn	5: 4	And this is the v that has
Rev	15: 2	and those who have the v

VIEW
Deut	32:49	v the land of Canaan, which

VIGILANT
1Pe	5: 8	Be sober, be v; because your

VIGOR
Deut	34: 7	not dim nor his natural v

VILE
Judg	19:24	this man do not do such a v
Rom	1:26	reason God gave them up to v

VILLAGE (see VILLAGES)
Judg	5: 7	V life ceased, it ceased in
Matt	21: 2	Go into the v opposite you,
Luke	8: 1	through every city and v,

Luke	24:13	that same day to a v called

VILLAGES (see VILLAGE)
Josh	13:23	the cities and their v.
Ezek	26: 6	Also her daughter v which
Matt	9:35	about all the cities and v,
Acts	8:25	the gospel in many v of the

VINDICATE (see VINDICATED, VINDICATES)
Ps	26: 1	V me, O LORD, For I have
Ps	54: 1	And v me by Your strength.

VINDICATED (see VINDICATE)
Job	13:18	I know that I shall be v.

VINDICATES† (see VINDICATE)
Gen	20:16	indeed this v you before all

VINE (see GRAPEVINE, VINEDRESSER, VINES, VINEYARD)
Judg	9:12	the trees said to the v,
1Ki	4:25	each man under his v and his
Ps	128: 3	be like a fruitful v In
Is	5: 2	it with the choicest v.
Mic	4: 4	shall sit under his v and
Mark	14:25	drink of the fruit of the v
John	15: 1	"I am the true v,

VINEDRESSER† (see VINE, VINEDRESSERS)
John	15: 1	vine, and My Father is the v.

VINEDRESSERS (see VINEDRESSER)
Matt	21:33	And he leased it to v and

VINEGAR
Num	6: 3	he shall drink neither v
Ps	69:21	my thirst they gave me v to

VINES (see VINE)
Song	2:15	foxes that spoil the v,
Hab	3:17	Nor fruit be on the v;

VINEYARD (see VINE, VINEYARDS)
Gen	9:20	a farmer, and planted a v.
1Ki	21: 1	the Jezreelite had a v
1Ki	21:16	to take possession of the v
Prov	31:16	her profits she plants a v
Song	1: 6	But my own v I have not
Is	1: 8	is left as a booth in a v,
Is	5: 1	my Beloved regarding His v:
Is	5: 7	For the v of the LORD of
Matt	20: 1	to hire laborers for his v.
Matt	21:28	'Son, go, work today in my v.
Luke	13: 6	a fig tree planted in his v,
1Co	9: 7	Who plants a v and does not

VINEYARDS (see VINEYARD)
Neh	5: 4	tax on our lands and v.
Eccl	2: 4	houses, and planted myself v.
Zeph	1:13	them; They shall plant v,

VINTAGE
Judg	8: 2	of Ephraim better than the v

VIOLENCE (see VIOLENT)
Gen	6:11	the earth was filled with v.
Job	16:17	Although no v is in my
Ps	27:12	And such as breathe out v.
Ps	72:14	life from oppression and v;
Prov	24: 2	For their heart devises v,
Is	53: 9	Because He had done no v,
Jer	22:17	practicing oppression and v.
Ezek	7:23	And the city is full of v.
Ezek	8:17	have filled the land with v;
Mic	2: 2	fields and take them by v,
Hab	1: 2	V!" And You will not save.
Matt	11:12	kingdom of heaven suffers v,
Acts	21:35	soldiers because of the v
Heb	11:34	quenched the v of fire,

VIOLENT (see VIOLENCE, VIOLENTLY)
Ps	140: 1	Preserve me from v men,
Matt	11:12	and the v take it by force.

Rom 1:30 backbiters, haters of God, **v**,
1Ti 3: 3 not given to wine, not **v**,
Tit 1: 7 not given to wine, not **v**,

VIOLENTLY (*see* VIOLENT)
Mark 5:13 and the herd ran **v** down the

VIPER (*see* VIPER'S, VIPERS)
Prov 23:32 And stings like a **v**.
Acts 28: 3 a **v** came out because of the

VIPER'S (*see* VIPER)
Is 11: 8 put his hand in the **v** den.

VIPERS (*see* VIPER)
Matt 12:34 Brood of **v**! How can you,

VIRGIN (*see* VIRGIN'S, VIRGINITY, VIRGINS)
Gen 24:16 beautiful to behold, a **v**;
Ex 22:16 If a man entices a **v** who is
Judg 19:24 here is my **v** daughter and
Prov 30:19 the way of a man with a **v**.
Is 7:14 the **v** shall conceive and
Is 47: 1 O **v** daughter of Babylon;
Jer 31: 4 O **v** of Israel! You shall
Matt 1:23 the **v** shall be with
Luke 1:27 to a **v** betrothed to a man
1Co 7:28 and if a **v** marries, she has
2Co 11: 2 present you as a chaste **v**

VIRGIN'S† (*see* VIRGIN)
Luke 1:27 The **v** name was Mary.

VIRGINITY (*see* VIRGIN)
Deut 22:17 of my daughter's **v**.
Judg 11:37 mountains and bewail my **v**,

VIRGINS (*see* VIRGIN)
Esth 2: 2 Let beautiful young **v** be
Song 1: 3 Therefore the **v** love you.
Matt 25: 1 shall be likened to ten **v**
1Co 7:25 Now concerning **v**:

VIRTUE (*see* VIRTUOUS)
Phil 4: 8 if there is any **v** and if
2Pe 1: 5 add to your faith **v**,

VIRTUOUS† (*see* VIRTUE)
Ruth 3:11 town know that you are a **v**
Prov 31:10 Who can find a **v** wife? For

VISAGE† (*see* VISION)
Is 52:14 So His **v** was marred more

VISIBLE (*see* VISION)
Heb 11: 3 made of things which are **v**.

VISION (*see* VISAGE, VISIBLE, VISIONS)
Gen 15: 1 LORD came to Abram in a **v**,
Num 12: 6 Myself known to him in a **v**;
1Sa 3:15 was afraid to tell Eli the **v**.
Is 1: 1 The **v** of Isaiah the son of
Is 22: 1 against the Valley of V.
Jer 14:14 prophesy to you a false **v**,
Ezek 8: 4 like the **v** that I saw in the
Ezek 11:24 me up and brought me in a **v**
Dan 2:19 to Daniel in a night **v**.
Dan 7: 2 I saw in my **v** by night, and
Dan 8: 1 reign of King Belshazzar a **v**
Dan 8:26 Therefore seal up the **v**,
Dan 10:14 for the **v** refers to many
Hab 2: 2 Write the **v** And make it
Matt 17: 9 Tell the **v** to no one until
Acts 9:10 to him the Lord said in a **v**,
Acts 11: 5 and in a trance I saw a **v**,
Acts 26:19 to the heavenly **v**,

VISIONS (*see* VISION)
Ezek 1: 1 were opened and I saw **v** of
Ezek 8: 3 and brought me in a **v** of God
Ezek 40: 2 In the **v** of God He took me
Dan 1:17 had understanding in all **v**

Dan 4: 5 on my bed and the **v** of my
Dan 7: 1 this I saw in the night **v**,
Joel 2:28 Your young men shall see **v**.
Acts 2:17 young men shall see **v**,

VISIT (*see* VISITATION, VISITED, VISITING)
Gen 50:25 God will surely **v** you, and
Ps 8: 4 the son of man that You **v**
Ps 106: 4 **v** me with Your salvation,
Matt 25:43 in prison and you did not **v**
Jas 1:27 to **v** orphans and widows in

VISITATION† (*see* VISIT)
Luke 19:44 not know the time of your **v**.
1Pe 2:12 glorify God in the day of **v**.

VISITED (*see* VISIT)
Gen 21: 1 And the LORD **v** Sarah as He
Ex 3:16 I have surely **v** you and seen
Matt 25:36 I was sick and you **v** Me; I
Luke 1:78 from on high has **v** us;
Acts 15:14 how God at the first **v** the

VISITING† (*see* VISIT)
Ex 20: 5 **v** the iniquity of the
Ex 34: 7 **v** the iniquity of the
Num 14:18 **v** the iniquity of the
Deut 5: 9 **v** the iniquity of the

VOICE (*see* SOUND, VOICES)
Gen 3:10 I heard Your **v** in the garden,
Gen 4:10 The **v** of your brother's
Gen 22:18 because you have obeyed My **v**.
Gen 27:22 The **v** is Jacob's voice, but
Ex 19: 5 if you will indeed obey My **v**
Deut 4:12 form; you only heard a **v**.
Deut 28: 1 if you diligently obey the **v**
Deut 28: 2 because you obey the **v** of
Josh 10:14 that the LORD heeded the **v**
1Sa 15:22 As in obeying the **v** of the
1Sa 28:12 she cried out with a loud **v**,
2Sa 22:14 the Most High uttered His **v**.
1Ki 19:12 the fire a still small **v**.
2Ki 18:28 called out with a loud **v** in
Job 37: 2 the thunder of His **v**,
Job 37: 4 thunders with His majestic **v**,
Ps 5: 2 Give heed to the **v** of my
Ps 19: 3 language Where their **v** is
Ps 26: 7 I may proclaim with the **v**
Ps 29: 4 The **v** of the LORD is
Ps 29: 5 The **v** of the LORD breaks
Ps 29: 7 The **v** of the LORD divides
Ps 31:22 You heard the **v** of my
Ps 46: 6 moved; He uttered His **v**,
Ps 86: 6 And attend to the **v** of my
Ps 95: 7 if you will hear His **v**:
Ps 130: 2 hear my **v**! Let Your ears be
Prov 1:20 She raises her **v** in the
Song 2: 8 The **v** of my beloved!
Song 2:12 And the **v** of the turtledove
Is 6: 4 door were shaken by the **v**
Is 6: 8 Also I heard the **v** of the
Is 40: 3 The **v** of one crying in the
Is 42: 2 cry out, nor raise His **v**,
Is 42: 2 Nor cause His **v** to be heard
Is 65:19 The **v** of weeping shall no
Is 65:19 Nor the **v** of crying.
Jer 7:34 streets of Jerusalem the **v**
Jer 7:34 the **v** of the bridegroom and
Jer 10:13 When He utters His **v**,
Jer 31:15 A **v** was heard in Ramah,
Ezek 1:24 like the **v** of the Almighty,
Ezek 1:25 A **v** came from above the
Ezek 1:28 and I heard a **v** of One
Ezek 43: 2 His **v** was like the sound of
Dan 9:14 we have not obeyed His **v**.
Joel 3:16 And utter His **v** from

Amos 1: 2 And utters His **v** from
Jon 2: 2 cried, And You heard my **v**.
Jon 2: 9 to You With the **v** of
Matt 2:18 A **v** was heard in Ramah,
Matt 3: 3 The **v** of one crying in
Matt 3:17 And suddenly a **v** came from
Matt 27:46 cried out with a loud **v**,
Luke 3:22 and a **v** came from heaven
Luke 4:33 he cried out with a loud **v**,
John 5:25 the dead will hear the **v** of
John 5:28 the graves will hear His **v**
John 10: 4 him, for they know his **v**.
John 10:27 "My sheep hear My **v**,
John 18:37 is of the truth hears My **v**.
Acts 8: 7 crying with a loud **v**,
Acts 9: 7 hearing a **v** but seeing no
Acts 22: 7 to the ground and heard a **v**
1Th 4:16 with the **v** of an archangel,
Heb 3: 7 if you will hear His **v**,
Heb 3:15 if you will hear His **v**,
Heb 4: 7 if you will hear His **v**.
Rev 1:10 I heard behind me a loud **v**,
Rev 1:15 and His **v** as the sound of
Rev 3:20 If anyone hears My **v** and
Rev 6: 1 creatures saying with a **v**
Rev 14: 2 like the **v** of many waters,
Rev 18:23 and the **v** of bridegroom and

VOICES (*see* VOICE)
Job 2:12 they lifted their **v** and

VOID
Gen 1: 2 was without form, and **v**;
Is 55:11 It shall not return to Me **v**,
Jer 4:23 it was without form, and **v**;
Rom 3:31 Do we then make **v** the law

VOLUME
Heb 10: 7 In the **v** of the book

VOLUNTARY
Phm 1:14 as it were, but **v**.

VOMIT (*see* VOMITED)
Lev 18:28 lest the land **v** you out also
Prov 26:11 a dog returns to his own **v**,
2Pe 2:22 returns to his own **v**,
Rev 3:16 I will **v** you out of My

VOMITED (*see* VOMIT)
Jon 2:10 and it **v** Jonah onto dry

VOW (*see* VOWED, VOWS)
Gen 28:20 Then Jacob made a **v**,
Num 6: 2 an offering to take the **v**
Judg 11:30 And Jephthah made a **v** to the
Judg 11:39 and he carried out his **v**
Eccl 5: 4 When you make a **v** to God,

VOWED (*see* VOW)
Eccl 5: 4 fools. Pay what you have **v**—
Jon 2: 9 I will pay what I have **v**.

VOWS (*see* MAKES, VOW)
Ps 61: 8 I may daily perform my **v**.
Prov 20:25 to reconsider his **v**.
Prov 31: 2 womb? And what, son of my **v**?
Jon 1:16 to the LORD and took **v**.
Nah 1:15 feasts, Perform your **v**.

VULTURES
Gen 15:11 And when the **v** came down on

W

WAFERS
Ex 16:31 the taste of it was like **w**

WAGE (*see* WAGES)
1Ti 1:18 that by them you may **w** the

WAGES (*see* WAGE)
Gen 31: 7 me and changed my **w** ten
Is 55: 2 And your **w** for what does
Hag 1: 6 Earns **w** to put into a bag
Zech 11:12 So they weighed out for my **w**
Matt 20: 8 and give them their **w**,
Luke 3:14 and be content with your **w**.
Luke 10: 7 laborer is worthy of his **w**.
John 4:36 he who reaps receives **w**,
Acts 1:18 a field with the **w** of
Rom 6:23 For the **w** of sin is death,
1Ti 5:18 laborer is worthy of his **w**.

WAILING
Esth 4: 3 with fasting, weeping, and **w**;
Jer 9:19 For a voice of **w** is heard
Zeph 1:10 A **w** from the Second
Matt 13:42 There will be **w** and gnashing

WAIST
Gen 37:34 put sackcloth on his **w**,
1Ki 2: 5 belt that was around his **w**,
1Ki 12:10 thicker than my father's **w**!
2Ki 1: 8 a leather belt around his **w**.
Jer 13: 1 and put it around your **w**,
Ezek 47: 4 water came up to my **w**.
Matt 3: 4 a leather belt around his **w**;
Eph 6:14 having girded your **w** with

WAIT (*see* WAITED, WAITING, WAITS)
Judg 16: 2 the place and lay in **w**
Ruth 1:13 would you **w** for them till
Ps 25: 5 On You I **w** all the day.
Ps 27:14 **W** on the LORD; Be of
Ps 37: 7 and **w** patiently for Him; Do
Ps 37: 9 But those who **w** on the
Ps 62: 5 **w** silently for God alone,
Ps 69: 6 Let not those who **w** for You,
Prov 1:11 Let us lie in **w** to shed
Is 8:17 And I will **w** on the LORD,
Is 40:31 But those who **w** on the LORD
Is 42: 4 And the coastlands shall **w**
Is 49:23 shall not be ashamed who **w**
Lam 3:10 to me a bear lying in **w**,
Hos 12: 6 And **w** on your God
Hab 2: 3 **w** for it; Because it will
Acts 1: 4 but to **w** for the Promise of
1Co 11:33 **w** for one another.
Phil 3:20 which we also eagerly **w** for
1Th 1:10 and to **w** for His Son from

WAITED (*see* WAIT)
Ps 40: 1 I **w** patiently for the LORD;
Luke 1:21 And the people **w** for
Heb 11:10 for he **w** for the city which
1Pe 3:20 the Divine longsuffering **w**

WAITING (*see* WAIT)
Luke 2:25 **w** for the Consolation of
John 5: 3 **w** for the moving of the
Acts 10:24 Now Cornelius was **w** for
Rom 8:23 eagerly **w** for the adoption,
1Co 1: 7 eagerly **w** for the revelation
Jas 5: 7 **w** patiently for it until it

WAITS (*see* WAIT)
Ps 33:20 Our soul **w** for the LORD;
Ps 130: 5 for the LORD, my soul **w**,
Dan 12:12 "Blessed is he who **w**,
Rom 8:19 of the creation eagerly **w**
Jas 5: 7 See how the farmer **w** for

WAKE
1Th 5:10 that whether we **w** or sleep,

WALK (*see* WALKED, WALKING, WALKS)
Gen	17: 1	**w** before Me and be
Lev	18: 4	to **w** in them: I am the
Deut	6: 7	when you **w** by the way, when
Deut	11:22	to **w** in all His ways, and to
Josh	18: 8	**w** through the land, survey
1Sa	2:35	and he shall **w** before My
1Sa	8: 3	But his sons did not **w** in his
2Ch	6:16	that they **w** in My law as you
Ps	23: 4	though I **w** through the
Ps	48:12	**W** about Zion, And go all
Ps	82: 5	They **w** about in darkness;
Ps	84:11	withhold From those who **w**
Ps	115: 7	they have, but they do not **w**;
Ps	138: 7	Though I **w** in the midst of
Is	2: 3	And we shall **w** in His
Is	2: 5	come and let us **w** In the
Is	30:21	**w** in it," Whenever you
Is	40:31	They shall **w** and not faint.
Is	43: 2	When you **w** through the
Jer	7: 6	or **w** after other gods to
Hos	11: 3	"I taught Ephraim to **w**,
Hos	14: 9	The righteous **w** in them,
Amos	3: 3	Can two **w** together, unless
Mic	4: 5	But we will **w** in the name
Mic	6: 8	And to **w** humbly with your
Matt	9: 5	or to say, 'Arise and **w**'?
Matt	11: 5	blind see and the lame **w**;
John	8:12	who follows Me shall not **w**
Rom	6: 4	even so we also should **w** in
Rom	8: 1	who do not **w** according to
Rom	8: 4	fulfilled in us who do not **w**
2Co	5: 7	For we **w** by faith, not by
Gal	6:16	And as many as **w** according
Eph	2:10	beforehand that we should **w**
Eph	4:17	that you should no longer **w**
Eph	4:17	the rest of the Gentiles **w**,
Eph	5: 2	And **w** in love, as Christ also
Eph	5: 8	**W** as children of light
Phil	3:16	let us **w** by the same rule,
Col	1:10	that you may **w** worthy of the
Col	2: 6	the Lord, so **w** in Him,
Col	4: 5	**W** in wisdom toward those who
1Th	4: 1	from us how you ought to **w**
1Jn	1: 6	and **w** in darkness, we lie
1Jn	1: 7	But if we **w** in the light as
1Jn	2: 6	Him ought himself also to **w**
Rev	3: 4	and they shall **w** with Me in

WALKED (*see* FOLLOWED, WALK)
Gen	5:24	And Enoch **w** with God; and he
Gen	6: 9	Noah **w** with God.
1Ki	11:33	and have not **w** in My ways to
2Ki	17:19	but **w** in the statutes of
Ps	26: 1	For I have **w** in my
Ps	55:14	And **w** to the house of God
Is	9: 2	The people who **w** in darkness
Is	20: 3	as My servant Isaiah has **w**
Matt	14:29	he **w** on the water to go to
Mark	1:16	And as He **w** by the Sea of
Mark	5:42	the girl arose and **w**,
John	5: 9	well, took up his bed, and **w**.
Acts	3: 8	stood and **w** and entered the
2Co	10: 2	who think of us as if we **w**
Eph	2: 2	in which you once **w** according
Col	3: 7	which you yourselves once **w**
1Jn	2: 6	also to walk just as He **w**.

WALKING (*see* WALK)
Gen	3: 8	sound of the LORD God **w** in
1Ki	16:19	in **w** in the way of Jeroboam,
Job	1: 7	and from **w** back and forth on
Is	20: 2	**w** naked and barefoot.
Dan	3:25	**w** in the midst of the fire;
Dan	4:29	the twelve months he was **w**
Matt	4:18	**w** by the Sea of Galilee, saw

Matt	14:25	to them, **w** on the sea.
Matt	15:31	made whole, the lame **w**,
Mark	8:24	"I see men like trees, **w**.
Acts	3: 8	the temple with them—**w**,
Acts	9:31	And **w** in the fear of the
2Co	4: 2	not **w** in craftiness nor

WALKS (*see* WALK)
Job	22:14	And He **w** above the circle
Ps	1: 1	Blessed is the man Who **w**
Ps	91: 6	of the pestilence that **w**
Ps	104: 3	Who **w** on the wings of the
Eccl	2:14	But the fool **w** in darkness.
John	11: 9	If anyone **w** in the day, he
John	11:10	But if one **w** in the night, he
2Th	3: 6	from every brother who **w**
1Pe	5: 8	your adversary the devil **w**
1Jn	2:11	is in darkness and **w** in
Rev	2: 1	who **w** in the midst of the

WALL (*see* WALLS)
Ex	14:22	and the waters were a **w** to
Ex	14:29	and the waters were a **w** to
Josh	2:15	her house was on the city **w**;
Josh	6:20	that the **w** fell down flat.
1Sa	18:11	I will pin David to the **w**!"
2Sa	22:30	my God I can leap over a **w**.
1Ki	3: 1	and the **w** all around
2Ki	9:33	her blood spattered on the **w**
2Ki	18:27	to the men who sit on the **w**,
2Ki	20: 2	turned his face toward the **w**,
Ezra	5: 3	temple and finish this **w**?
Neh	2:17	Come and let us build the **w**
Neh	4: 1	we were rebuilding the **w**,
Song	8: 9	If she is a **w**, We will build
Is	2:15	And upon every fortified **w**
Jer	15:20	people a fortified bronze **w**;
Ezek	4: 2	build a siege **w** against it,
Ezek	8: 8	dig into the **w**"; and when I
Dan	5: 5	on the plaster of the **w** of
Dan	9:25	be built again, and the **w**,
Hos	2: 6	And **w** her in, So that she
Amos	1: 7	will send a fire upon the **w**
Amos	5:19	Leaned his hand on the **w**,
Zech	2: 5	will be a **w** of fire all
Acts	23: 3	you whitewashed **w**! For you
2Co	11:33	through a window in the **w**,
Eph	2:14	broken down the middle **w** of
Rev	21:12	she had a great and high **w**

WALLOWED (*see* WALLOWING)
Mark	9:20	he fell on the ground and **w**,

WALLOWING† (*see* WALLOWED)
2Pe	2:22	to her **w** in the mire."

WALLS (*see* WALL)
Deut	3: 5	were fortified with high **w**,
Ps	51:18	Build the **w** of Jerusalem.
Ps	122: 7	Peace be within your **w**,
Is	49:16	Your **w** are continually
Is	60:18	But you shall call your **w**
Is	62: 6	have set watchmen on your **w**,
Jer	1:18	And bronze **w** against the
Zech	2: 4	as towns without **w**,
Heb	11:30	By faith the **w** of Jericho

WANDER (*see* WANDERED, WANDERING, WANDERS)
Job	12:24	And makes them **w** in a
Ps	119:10	let me not **w** from Your
Amos	8:12	They shall **w** from sea to

WANDERED (*see* WANDER)
Josh	14:10	to Moses while Israel **w** in
Ezek	34: 6	My sheep **w** through all the
Heb	11:37	They **w** about in sheepskins
Heb	11:38	They **w** in deserts and

WANDERING (*see* WANDER)
Gen   37:15 **w** in the field. And the man

WANDERS (*see* WANDER)
Jas   5:19 if anyone among you **w** from

WANT (*see* NEED, WANTED, WANTING, WANTS)
Ps   23: 1 my shepherd; I shall not **w**.
Matt   26:17 Where do You **w** us to prepare
Matt   27:17 Whom do you **w** me to release
Luke   15:14 and he began to be in **w**.
John   9:27 Why do you **w** to hear it
John   9:27 Do you also **w** to become His
Acts   7:28 Do you **w** to kill me as
Acts   9: 6 what do You **w** me to do?"
Rom   1:13 Now I do not **w** you to be
1Co   12: 1 I do not **w** you to be
Phil   1:12 But I **w** you to know,

WANTED (*see* WANT)
Ezek   1:12 went wherever the spirit **w**
Matt   23:37 sent to her! How often I **w**
Luke   13:34 sent to her! How often I **w**
1Th   2:18 Therefore we **w** to come to

WANTING (*see* WANT)
Dan   5:27 in the balances, and found **w**;
Matt   1:19 and not **w** to make her a
Acts   24:27 **w** to do the Jews a favor,
Acts   25: 9 **w** to do the Jews a favor,
Rom   9:22 **w** to show His wrath and to

WANTS (*see* WANT)
Matt   5:42 and from him who **w** to borrow
John   7:17 If anyone **w** to do His will,

WAR (*see* WARFARE, WARRING, WARS)
Ex   1:10 it happen, in the event of **w**,
Ex   15: 3 The LORD is a man of **w**;
Ex   32:17 There is a noise of **w** in
Num   1:20 who were able to go to **w**:
Num   31:21 priest said to the men of **w**
Deut   1:41 girded on his weapons of **w**,
Josh   8: 1 take all the people of **w**
Josh   11:23 Then the land rested from **w**.
Judg   3: 2 might be taught to know **w**,
Judg   5: 8 Then there was **w** in the
1Sa   16:18 man of valor, a man of **w**,
2Sa   1:27 And the weapons of **w**
2Sa   17: 8 your father is a man of **w**,
1Ki   20:18 if they have come out for **w**,
2Ki   18:20 plans and power for **w**;
Ps   27: 3 Though **w** should rise
Ps   120: 7 I speak, they are for **w**.
Prov   20:18 By wise counsel wage **w**.
Eccl   3: 8 a time to hate; A time of **w**,
Is   2: 4 Neither shall they learn **w**
Is   7: 1 up to Jerusalem to make **w**
Is   42:13 up His zeal like a man of **w**.
Dan   7:21 the same horn was making **w**
Mic   4: 3 Neither shall they learn **w**
1Co   9: 7 Who ever goes to **w** at his own
2Co   10: 3 we do not **w** according to the
Jas   4: 1 for pleasure that **w** in your
1Pe   2:11 from fleshly lusts which **w**
Rev   12: 7 And **w** broke out in heaven:
Rev   17:14 These will make **w** with the

WARFARE† (*see* WAR)
Is   40: 2 That her **w** is ended, That
2Co   10: 4 For the weapons of our **w** are
1Ti   1:18 them you may wage the good **w**,
2Ti   2: 4 No one engaged in **w** entangles

WARM (*see* WARMED, WARMING)
2Ki   4:34 flesh of the child became **w**.

WARMED (*see* WARM)
John   18:25 Now Simon Peter stood and **w**

Jas   2:16 be **w** and filled," but you

WARMING† (*see* WARM)
Mark   14:67 And when she saw Peter **w**

WARN (*see* WARNED, WARNING)
Ezek   3:19 if you **w** the wicked, and he
Ezek   33: 9 Nevertheless if you **w** the
Acts   20:31 years I did not cease to **w**

WARNED (*see* WARN)
Gen   43: 3 The man solemnly **w** us,
Ps   19:11 by them Your servant is **w**,
Matt   2:12 being divinely **w** in a dream
Matt   2:22 And being **w** by God in a
Matt   3: 7 Brood of vipers! Who **w** you to
Heb   11: 7 being divinely **w** of things

WARNING (*see* WARN)
Ezek   3:18 die,' and you give him no **w**,
Col   1:28 **w** every man and teaching

WARRING (*see* WAR)
Rom   7:23 **w** against the law of my

WARS (*see* WAR)
Num   21:14 is said in the Book of the **W**
Ps   46: 9 He makes **w** cease to the end
Matt   24: 6 hear of wars and rumors of **w**.
Jas   4: 1 Where do **w** and fights come

WASH (*see* UNWASHED, WASHED, WASHING, WASHPOT)
Gen   18: 4 and **w** your feet, and rest
Gen   19: 2 and **w** your feet; then you
Ex   29:17 **w** its entrails and its legs,
Lev   16:26 as the scapegoat shall **w**
Ruth   3: 3 Therefore **w** yourself and
1Sa   25:41 a servant to **w** the feet of
2Ki   5:10 Go and **w** in the Jordan seven
Ps   51: 2 **W** me thoroughly from my
Ps   51: 7 **W** me, and I shall be whiter
Is   1:16 **W** yourselves, make yourselves
Matt   15: 2 For they do not **w** their
Luke   7:38 and she began to **w** His feet
John   9: 7 **w** in the pool of Siloam"
John   13: 5 into a basin and began to **w**
John   13: 8 You shall never **w** my feet!"
John   13:14 you also ought to **w** one
Acts   22:16 and **w** away your sins,

WASHED (*see* WASH)
Gen   43:24 and they **w** their feet; and
Gen   43:31 Then he **w** his face and came
Ex   19:14 and they **w** their clothes.
Ps   73:13 And **w** my hands in
Song   5:12 **W** with milk, And fitly
Is   4: 4 When the Lord has **w** away the
Matt   27:24 he took water and **w** his
Luke   7:44 but she has **w** My feet with
Luke   11:38 that He had not first **w**
John   9: 7 Sent). So he went and **w**,
John   9:15 put clay on my eyes, and I **w**,
John   13:12 So when He had **w** their feet,
1Co   6:11 some of you. But you were **w**,
Heb   10:22 conscience and our bodies **w**
Rev   1: 5 To Him who loved us and **w** us
Rev   7:14 and **w** their robes and made

WASHING (*see* WASH)
Mark   7: 4 like the **w** of cups, pitchers
Luke   5: 2 gone from them and were **w**
John   13: 6 are You **w** my feet?"
Eph   5:26 and cleanse her with the **w**
Tit   3: 5 **w** of regeneration

WASHPOT† (*see* POT, WASH)
Ps   60: 8 Moab is My **w**; Over Edom
Ps   108: 9 Moab is My **w**; Over Edom

WASTE (*see* WASTED, WASTES, WASTING)
Lev   26:31 I will lay your cities **w** and
2Ki   18:27 eat and drink their own **w**
Ps   31:10 And my bones **w** away.
Ps   91: 6 destruction that lays **w** at
Matt 26: 8 saying, "Why this **w**?

WASTED (*see* WASTE)
Mark 14: 4 was this fragrant oil **w**?
Luke 15:13 and there **w** his possessions

WASTES (*see* WASTE)
Ps   31: 9 My eye **w** away with grief,

WASTING (*see* WASTE)
Luke 16: 1 to him that this man was **w**

WATCH (*see* WATCHED, WATCHER, WATCHES, WATCHFUL,
  WATCHING, WATCHMAN)
Gen   31:49 May the LORD **w** between you
Ex   14:24 to pass, in the morning **w**,
Judg   7:19 beginning of the middle **w**,
Neh   4: 9 because of them we set a **w**
Ps   90: 4 And like a **w** in the night.
Ps   130: 6 Lord More than those who **w**
Nah   2: 1 Man the fort! **W** the road!
Hab   2: 1 I will stand my **w** And set
Matt 14:25 Now in the fourth **w** of the
Matt 24:42 **W** therefore, for you do not
Matt 26:40 Could you not **w** with Me one
Matt 26:41 **W** and pray, lest you enter
Luke   2: 8 keeping **w** over their flock
Luke 12:38 should come in the second **w**,
Luke 12:38 or come in the third **w**,
Heb   13:17 for they **w** out for your
Rev   3: 3 Therefore if you will not **w**,

WATCHED (*see* WATCH)
1Sa   1:12 that Eli **w** her mouth.
Luke   6: 7 the scribes and Pharisees **w**

WATCHER (*see* WATCH, WATCHERS)
Job   7:20 O **w** of men? Why have You

WATCHERS (*see* WATCHER)
Dan   4:17 is by the decree of the **w**,

WATCHES (*see* WATCH)
Ps   63: 6 on You in the night **w**.
Prov 31:27 She **w** over the ways of her
Rev   16:15 thief. Blessed is he who **w**,

WATCHFUL (*see* WATCH)
Eph   6:18 being **w** to this end with all
1Pe   4: 7 therefore be serious and **w**
Rev   3: 2 "Be **w**, and strengthen

WATCHING (*see* WATCH)
Prov   8:34 **W** daily at my gates,
Dan   7:13 I was **w** in the night
Luke 12:37 when he comes, will find **w**.

WATCHMAN (*see* WATCH, WATCHMEN)
2Sa   18:24 And the **w** went up to the
Ps   127: 1 The **w** stays awake in vain.
Ezek   3:17 I have made you a **w** for the
Ezek 33: 7 I have made you a **w** for the

WATCHMEN (*see* WATCHMAN)
Song   3: 3 The **w** who go about the city
Is   62: 6 I have set **w** on your walls,

WATER (*see* WATERED, WATERFALLS, WATERING,
  WATERPOT, WATERS)
Gen   2:10 river went out of Eden to **w**
Gen   24:11 when women go out to draw **w**.
Gen   24:13 I stand by the well of **w**,
Gen   29: 3 **w** the sheep, and put the
Ex   2:10 I drew him out of the **w**.
Ex   15:27 were twelve wells of **w** and
Ex   17: 3 people thirsted there for **w**,
Ex   20: 4 or that is in the **w** under

Lev   11: 9 whatever in the **w** has fins
Lev   15: 5 his clothes and bathe in **w**,
Num   5:17 priest shall take holy **w** in
Num   5:18 in his hand the bitter **w**
Num   5:26 make the woman drink the **w**.
Num   8: 7 Sprinkle **w** of purification
Num   19:18 hyssop and dip it in the **w**,
Num   20:13 This was the **w** of Meribah,
Deut   4:18 any fish that is in the **w**,
Deut   8: 7 land, a land of brooks of **w**,
Deut 11:11 which drinks **w** from the rain
Josh   2:10 the LORD dried up the **w** of
Josh   9:21 them be woodcutters and **w**
Josh 15:19 give me also springs of **w**.
Judg   5:25 He asked for **w**,
Judg   6:38 the fleece, a bowlful of **w**.
Judg   7: 6 on their knees to drink **w**.
2Sa   5: 8 climbs up by way of the **w**
1Ki   18:35 filled the trench with **w**.
1Ki   18:38 and it licked up the **w** that
2Ki   2:21 LORD: 'I have healed this **w**;
2Ki   6: 5 ax head fell into the **w**;
Neh   8: 3 that was in front of the **W**
Job   14:19 As **w** wears away stones,
Job   15:16 Who drinks iniquity like **w**!
Ps   1: 3 Planted by the rivers of **w**,
Ps   22:14 I am poured out like **w**,
Ps   42: 1 As the deer pants for the **w**
Ps   63: 1 land Where there is no **w**.
Ps   72: 6 Like showers that **w** the
Ps   105:41 and **w** gushed out; It ran in
Ps   107:35 a wilderness into pools of **w**,
Prov   5:15 Drink **w** from your own
Prov   5:15 And running **w** from your own
Prov   9:17 Stolen **w** is sweet, And bread
Prov 20: 5 of man is like deep **w**,
Prov 25:21 give him **w** to drink;
Prov 25:25 As cold **w** to a weary soul,
Is   55:10 But **w** the earth, And make
Jer   2:13 cisterns that can hold no **w**.
Jer   9:18 And our eyelids gush with **w**.
Jer   13: 1 but do not put it in **w**.
Lam   1:16 eye, my eye overflows with **w**;
Lam   5: 4 We pay for the **w** we drink,
Ezek 47: 1 the **w** was flowing from under
Ezek 47: 4 the **w** came up to my
Ezek 47: 5 **w** in which one must swim, a
Dan   1:12 us vegetables to eat and **w**
Amos   5:24 let justice run down like **w**,
Amos   8:11 bread, Nor a thirst for **w**,
Matt   3:11 indeed baptize you with **w**
Matt 10:42 ones only a cup of cold **w**
Matt 14:28 me to come to You on the **w**.
Matt 17:15 fire and often into the **w**.
Mark   1: 8 indeed baptized you with **w**,
Mark   9:22 the fire and into the **w** to
Mark 14:13 you carrying a pitcher of **w**;
Luke   8:25 even the winds and **w**,
Luke 16:24 the tip of his finger in **w**
John   1:26 saying, "I baptize with **w**,
John   2: 7 "Fill the waterpots with **w**.
John   2: 9 the feast had tasted the **w**
John   3: 5 unless one is born of **w** and
John   4: 7 of Samaria came to draw **w**.
John   4:10 have given you living **w**.
John   5: 3 for the moving of the **w**.
John   7:38 will flow rivers of living **w**.
John 13: 5 He poured **w** into a basin and
John 19:34 and immediately blood and **w**
Acts   1: 5 John truly baptized with **w**,
Acts   8:38 eunuch went down into the **w**,
Acts 10:47 "Can anyone forbid **w**,
Acts 11:16 'John indeed baptized with **w**,
Eph   5:26 her with the washing of **w**
1Ti   5:23 No longer drink only **w**,

Heb	10:22	bodies washed with pure **w**.
Jas	3:11	a spring send forth fresh **w**
1Pe	3:20	souls, were saved through **w**.
2Pe	3: 5	the earth standing out of **w**
2Pe	3: 5	out of water and in the **w**,
1Jn	5: 6	This is He who came by **w** and
1Jn	5: 8	on earth: the Spirit, the **w**,
Rev	16:12	and its **w** was dried up, so
Rev	22: 1	showed me a pure river of **w**
Rev	22:17	let him take the **w** of life

WATERED (*see* WATER)

Gen	2: 6	up from the earth and **w** the
Gen	13:10	that it was well **w**
1Co	3: 6	I planted, Apollos **w**,

WATERFALLS† (*see* WATER)

Ps	42: 7	deep at the noise of Your **w**;

WATERING (*see* WATER)

Gen	30:38	in the **w** troughs where the

WATERPOT† (*see* POT, WATER, WATERPOTS)

John	4:28	The woman then left her **w**,

WATERPOTS (*see* WATERPOT)

1Ki	18:33	Fill four **w** with water, and
John	2: 7	Fill the **w** with water." And

WATERS (*see* FLOODWATERS, WATER)

Gen	1: 2	over the face of the **w**.
Gen	1: 6	divide the waters from the **w**.
Gen	7:24	And the **w** prevailed on the
Gen	8: 1	and the **w** subsided.
Gen	9:15	the **w** shall never again
Ex	14:21	and the **w** were divided.
Ex	15:25	the **w** were made sweet. There
Judg	5:19	by the **w** of Megiddo; They
Ps	23: 2	leads me beside the still **w**.
Ps	24: 2	established it upon the **w**.
Ps	29: 3	of the LORD is over the **w**;
Ps	32: 6	in a flood of great **w** They
Ps	69: 1	O God! For the **w** have come
Ps	69: 2	I have come into deep **w**,
Ps	77:19	Your path in the great **w**,
Ps	105:29	He turned their **w** into
Ps	107:23	Who do business on great **w**,
Prov	18: 4	of a man's mouth are deep **w**;
Eccl	11: 1	Cast your bread upon the **w**,
Song	8: 7	Many **w** cannot quench love,
Is	8: 6	these people refused The **w**
Is	18: 2	in vessels of reed on the **w**,
Is	40:12	Who has measured the **w** in
Is	43: 2	When you pass through the **w**,
Is	43:16	a path through the mighty **w**,
Is	55: 1	who thirsts, Come to the **w**;
Is	57:20	Whose **w** cast up mire and
Jer	2:13	Me, the fountain of living **w**,
Jer	9: 1	Oh, that my head were **w**,
Jer	15:18	stream, As **w** that fail?
Jer	17: 8	like a tree planted by the **w**,
Jer	17:13	The fountain of living **w**.
Ezek	1:24	like the noise of many **w**,
Ezek	43: 2	like the sound of many **w**;
Jon	2: 5	The **w** surrounded me, even
Hab	2:14	As the **w** cover the sea.
Rev	1:15	voice as the sound of many **w**;
Rev	7:17	to living fountains of **w**.
Rev	19: 6	as the sound of many **w** and

WAVE (*see* WAVED, WAVES)

Ex	29:24	you shall wave them as a **w**
Jas	1: 6	he who doubts is like a **w**

WAVED (*see* WAVE)

Ex	29:27	the wave offering which is **w**,

WAVER†

Rom	4:20	He did not **w** at the promise

WAVES (*see* WAVE)

Ps	42: 7	All Your **w** and billows have
Jon	2: 3	All Your billows and Your **w**
Matt	14:24	of the sea, tossed by the **w**,
Luke	21:25	the sea and the **w** roaring;
Jude	13	raging **w** of the sea, foaming

WAX

Ps	22:14	joint; My heart is like **w**;
Ps	68: 2	As **w** melts before the fire,
Ps	97: 5	The mountains melt like **w** at

WAY (*see* WAYS, WAYSIDE)

Gen	3:24	sword which turned every **w**,
Gen	24:40	with you and prosper your **w**;
Ex	2:12	looked this way and that **w**,
Ex	13:21	of cloud to lead the **w**,
Deut	1:33	to show you the **w** you should
Deut	6: 7	when you walk by the **w**,
Deut	11:28	but turn aside from the **w**
Josh	1: 8	then you will make your **w**
Josh	23:14	this day I am going the **w**
1Sa	12:23	you the good and the right **w**.
2Sa	5: 8	Whoever climbs up by **w** of the
1Ki	2: 4	sons take heed to their **w**,
1Ki	13:33	did not turn from his evil **w**,
1Ki	15:26	and walked in the **w** of his
Neh	8:10	he said to them, "Go your **w**,
Job	16:22	I shall go the **w** of no
Job	19: 8	He has fenced up my **w**,
Job	22:15	Will you keep to the old **w**
Job	23:10	But He knows the **w** that I
Ps	1: 6	For the LORD knows the **w** of
Ps	1: 6	But the **w** of the ungodly
Ps	2:12	And you perish in the **w**,
Ps	18:30	His **w** is perfect; The word
Ps	25: 9	the humble He teaches His **w**.
Ps	27:11	Teach me Your **w**, O LORD,
Ps	32: 8	you and teach you in the **w**
Ps	37: 5	Commit your **w** to the LORD,
Ps	37: 7	of him who prospers in his **w**,
Ps	119: 9	a young man cleanse his **w**?
Ps	119:104	I hate every false **w**.
Ps	139:24	if there is any wicked **w**
Ps	139:24	And lead me in the **w**
Prov	2:12	To deliver you from the **w** of
Prov	2:20	So you may walk in the **w** of
Prov	4:11	I have taught you in the **w**
Prov	7:27	Her house is the **w** to hell,
Prov	8:22	me at the beginning of His **w**,
Prov	14:12	There is a **w** that seems
Prov	14:12	But its end is the **w** of
Prov	16: 9	A man's heart plans his **w**,
Prov	16:25	There is a **w** that seems
Prov	16:25	But its end is the **w** of
Prov	22: 6	Train up a child in the **w** he
Prov	30:19	The **w** of an eagle in the
Prov	30:19	And the **w** of a man with a
Is	9: 1	By the **w** of the sea,
Is	30:21	saying, "This is the **w**,
Is	40: 3	Prepare the **w** of the LORD;
Is	40:27	My **w** is hidden from the
Is	53: 6	every one, to his own **w**;
Is	55: 7	the wicked forsake his **w**,
Is	57:14	Heap it up! Prepare the **w**,
Is	59: 8	The **w** of peace they have not
Jer	5: 4	For they do not know the **w**
Jer	10: 2	Do not learn the **w** of the
Jer	10:23	I know the **w** of man is not
Jer	21: 8	the way of life and the **w**
Jer	23:22	them from their evil **w** And
Ezek	3:18	the wicked from his wicked **w**,
Ezek	18:25	is it not My **w** which is
Ezek	33: 8	warn the wicked from his **w**,
Dan	12: 9	And he said, "Go your **w**,
Hos	2: 6	I will hedge up your **w** with

Jon	3:10	turned from their evil **w**;
Mal	1: 2	In what **w** have You loved us?'
Mal	1: 6	In what **w** have we despised
Mal	1: 7	In what **w** have we defiled
Matt	2:12	their own country another **w**.
Matt	3: 3	Prepare the **w** of the
Matt	4:15	By the **w** of the sea,
Matt	7:13	the gate and broad is the **w**
Matt	8: 4	tell no one; but go your **w**,
Matt	10: 5	Do not go into the **w** of the
Mark	10:21	thing you lack: Go your **w**,
Mark	10:52	said to him, "Go your **w**;
Luke	15:20	when he was still a great **w**
Luke	20:21	but teach the **w** of God in
John	4:50	said to him, "Go your **w**;
John	4:50	to him, and he went his **w**.
John	10: 1	but climbs up some other **w**,
John	14: 6	said to him, "I am the **w**,
Acts	9: 2	found any who were of the **W**,
Acts	16:17	who proclaim to us the **w** of
Acts	18:26	and explained to him the **w**
Acts	19:23	great commotion about the **W**.
Acts	24:22	accurate knowledge of the **W**,
Rom	3: 2	Much in every **w**! Chiefly
Rom	3:17	And the **w** of peace
1Co	10:13	will also make the **w** of
1Co	12:31	show you a more excellent **w**.
Phil	1:18	then? Only that in every **w**,
Heb	9: 8	that the **w** into the Holiest
Heb	10:20	by a new and living **w** which
Jude	11	For they have gone in the **w**

WAYS (*see* WAY)

Deut	10:12	to walk in all His **w** and to
Deut	11:22	God, to walk in all His **w**,
Deut	32: 4	For all His **w** are justice,
1Sa	8: 3	sons did not walk in his **w**;
2Ch	7:14	and turn from their wicked **w**,
Job	26:14	are the mere edges of His **w**,
Job	40:19	He is the first of the **w** of
Ps	18:21	For I have kept the **w** of the
Ps	25: 4	Show me Your **w**, O LORD;
Ps	39: 1	I said, "I will guard my **w**,
Ps	51:13	teach transgressors Your **w**,
Ps	91:11	To keep you in all your **w**.
Ps	103: 7	He made known His **w** to
Ps	145:17	is righteous in all His **w**,
Prov	3: 6	In all your **w** acknowledge
Prov	5: 6	Her **w** are unstable; You do
Prov	6: 6	sluggard! Consider her **w**
Prov	16: 7	When a man's **w** please the
Prov	31:27	She watches over the **w** of
Eccl	11: 9	Walk in the **w** of your
Is	2: 3	He will teach us His **w**,
Is	55: 8	Nor are your **w** My ways,"
Is	55: 9	My ways higher than your **w**,
Is	66: 3	they have chosen their own **w**,
Jer	7: 3	Amend your **w** and your doings,
Jer	17:10	every man according to his **w**,
Ezek	33:11	turn from your evil **w**! For
Mic	4: 2	He will teach us His **w**,
Hag	1: 5	of hosts: "Consider your **w**!
Hag	1: 7	of hosts: "Consider your **w**!
Zech	1: 4	Turn now from your evil **w** and
Luke	3: 5	And the rough **w** smooth;
Acts	2:28	known to me the **w** of
Rom	11:33	are His judgments and His **w**
Heb	1: 1	times and in various **w**
Jas	1: 8	man, unstable in all his **w**.
Rev	15: 3	Just and true are Your **w**,

WAYSIDE (*see* WAY)

Ps	110: 7	drink of the brook by the **w**;
Matt	13: 4	some seed fell by the **w**;

WEAK (*see* WEAKER, WEAKNESS)

Judg	16: 7	dried, then I shall become **w**,
Job	4: 3	And you have strengthened **w**
Ps	109:24	My knees are **w** through
Is	35: 3	Strengthen the **w** hands,
Is	40:29	He gives power to the **w**,
Matt	26:41	willing, but the flesh is **w**.
Rom	4:19	And not being **w** in faith, he
Rom	8: 3	not do in that it was **w**
Rom	15: 1	with the scruples of the **w**,
1Co	1:27	and God has chosen the **w**
1Co	4:10	wise in Christ! We are **w**,
1Co	8: 7	their conscience, being **w**,
1Co	8:11	your knowledge shall the **w**
1Co	9:22	to the weak I became as **w**,
1Co	9:22	weak, that I might win the **w**.
1Co	11:30	For this reason many are **w**
2Co	12:10	sake. For when I am **w**,

WEAKER (*see* WEAK)

1Pe	3: 7	as to the **w** vessel, and as

WEAKNESS (*see* WEAK, WEAKNESSES)

Rom	6:19	terms because of the **w** of
1Co	1:25	and the **w** of God is stronger
1Co	15:43	in glory. It is sown in **w**,
2Co	12: 9	is made perfect in **w**.
2Co	13: 4	though He was crucified in **w**,
Heb	5: 2	himself is also subject to **w**.
Heb	11:34	out of **w** were made strong,

WEAKNESSES† (*see* WEAKNESS)

Rom	8:26	Spirit also helps in our **w**.
Heb	4:15	cannot sympathize with our **w**,

WEALTH

Deut	8:17	hand have gained me this **w**.
Ruth	2: 1	husband, a man of great **w**,
2Ch	1:12	I will give you riches and **w**
Ps	49: 6	Those who trust in their **w**
Ps	49:10	And leave their **w** to
Ps	112: 3	**W** and riches will be in
Prov	13:11	**W** gained by dishonesty
Prov	19: 4	**W** makes many friends, But
Prov	29: 3	of harlots wastes his **w**.
Eccl	5:19	God has given riches and **w**,

WEANED

Gen	21: 8	same day that Isaac was **w**.
1Sa	1:22	"Not until the child is **w**;
Hos	1: 8	Now when she had **w**

WEAPON (*see* WEAPONS)

Neh	4:17	and with the other held a **w**.

WEAPONS (*see* WEAPON)

2Sa	1:27	And the **w** of war perished!"
Eccl	9:18	Wisdom is better than **w** of
John	18: 3	lanterns, torches, and **w**.
2Co	10: 4	For the **w** of our warfare are

WEAR (*see* WEARING, WORE, WORN)

Ex	18:18	are with you will surely **w**
Deut	8: 4	Your garments did not **w** out
Matt	6:31	drink?' or 'What shall we **w**?
Matt	11: 8	those who **w** soft clothing

WEARIED (*see* WEARY)

Is	43:24	You have **w** Me with your
Jer	12: 5	and they have **w** you, Then
Mal	2:17	In what way have we **w** Him?"
John	4: 6	being **w** from His journey,

WEARINESS (*see* WEARY)

2Co	11:27	in **w** and toil, in

WEARING (*see* WEAR)

1Sa	2:18	a child, **w** a linen ephod.
2Sa	6:14	and David was **w** a linen
2Ki	1: 8	A hairy man **w** a leather belt

John 19: 5 **w** the crown of thorns and
Jas 2: 3 pay attention to the one **w**

WEARISOME (*see* WEARY)
Eccl 12:12 and much study is **w** to the

WEARY (*see* WEARIED, WEARINESS, WEARISOME)
Gen 19:11 so that they became **w**
Job 3:17 And there the **w** are at
Ps 6: 6 I am **w** with my groaning;
Ps 69: 3 I am **w** with my crying; My
Prov 25:25 As cold water to a **w** soul,
Is 1:14 I am **w** of bearing them.
Is 7:13 a small thing for you to **w**
Is 32: 2 of a great rock in a **w** land.
Is 40:30 youths shall faint and be **w**,
Is 40:31 They shall run and not be **w**,
Jer 6:11 I am **w** of holding it in.
Luke 18: 5 her continual coming she **w**
Gal 6: 9 And let us not grow **w** while
2Th 3:13 do not grow **w** in doing

WEATHER
Matt 16: 2 say, 'It will be fair **w**,

WEAVE (*see* WEAVER'S, WOVE, WOVEN)
Judg 16:13 If you **w** the seven locks of

WEAVER'S (*see* WEAVE)
1Sa 17: 7 his spear was like a **w** beam,

WEB
Judg 16:13 locks of my head into the **w**
Job 8:14 whose trust is a spider's **w**.

WEDDING
Matt 22: 3 who were invited to the **w**;
John 2: 1 the third day there was a **w**

WEDGE
Josh 7:21 and a **w** of gold weighing

WEEDS
Jon 2: 5 **W** were wrapped around my

WEEK (*see* WEEKS)
Gen 29:27 "Fulfill her **w**, and we will
Dan 9:27 covenant with many for one **w**;
Mark 16: 2 on the first day of the **w**,
Luke 18:12 'I fast twice a **w**; I give
Acts 20: 7 on the first day of the **w**,
1Co 16: 2 On the first day of the **w**

WEEKS (*see* WEEK)
Ex 34:22 shall observe the Feast of **W**,
Deut 16: 9 You shall count seven **w** for
Dan 9:24 Seventy **w** are determined

WEEP (*see* WEEPING, WEPT)
1Sa 1: 8 her, "Hannah, why do you **w**?
Eccl 3: 4 A time to **w**, And a time
Jer 9: 1 That I might **w** day and
Jer 13:17 My eyes will **w** bitterly
Lam 1:16 "For these things I **w**;
Ezek 24:16 shall neither mourn nor **w**,
Luke 6:21 Blessed are you who **w**
Luke 7:13 and said to her, "Do not **w**.
Luke 23:28 do not **w** for Me, but weep
Luke 23:28 but **w** for yourselves and for
John 11:31 is going to the tomb to **w**
Rom 12:15 and **w** with those who weep.
1Co 7:30 those who **w** as though they
1Co 7:30 as though they did not **w**,
Jas 5: 1 **w** and howl for your miseries

WEEPING (*see* WEEP)
Esth 4: 3 the Jews, with fasting, **w**,
Ps 6: 8 has heard the voice of my **w**.
Ps 30: 5 **W** may endure for a night,
Ps 126: 6 who continually goes forth **w**,
Jer 31:15 Rachel **w** for her children,
Ezek 8:14 women were sitting there **w**

Matt 2:18 Rachel **w** for her children,
Matt 8:12 There will be **w** and gnashing
John 11:33 when Jesus saw her **w**,
John 20:11 stood outside by the tomb **w**,
John 20:13 her, "Woman, why are you **w**?

WEIGH (*see* WEIGHED, WEIGHS, WEIGHT)
Ps 58: 2 You **w** out the violence of
Is 26: 7 You **w** the path of the just.

WEIGHED (*see* WEIGH)
Gen 23:16 and Abraham **w** out the silver
1Sa 2: 3 And by Him actions are **w**.
Is 40:12 **W** the mountains in scales
Dan 5:27 You have been **w** in the
Zech 11:12 So they **w** out for my wages

WEIGHS (*see* WEIGH)
Prov 16: 2 But the LORD **w** the
Prov 21: 2 But the LORD **w** the hearts.

WEIGHT (*see* WEIGH, WEIGHTIER, WEIGHTS)
Deut 25:15 have a perfect and just **w**,
Prov 11: 1 But a just **w** is His
2Co 4:17 exceeding and eternal **w** of
Heb 12: 1 let us lay aside every **w**,

WEIGHTIER† (*see* WEIGHT)
Matt 23:23 and have neglected the **w**

WEIGHTS (*see* WEIGHT)
Lev 19:36 have honest scales, honest **w**,
Deut 25:13 have in your bag differing **w**,
Prov 16:11 Honest **w** and scales are the
Mic 6:11 with the bag of deceitful **w**?

WELCOME (*see* WELCOMED)
Col 4:10 **w** him),

WELCOMED† (*see* WELCOME)
Luke 8:40 that the multitude **w** Him,
Luke 10:38 woman named Martha **w** Him
1Th 2:13 you **w** it not as the word

WELL (*see* WELLS, WELLSPRING)
Gen 21:19 and she saw a **w** of water.
Ex 2:15 and he sat down by a **w**.
Prov 5:15 water from your own **w**.
Song 4:15 A **w** of living waters, And
John 4: 6 Now Jacob's **w** was there.

WELL ADVANCED (*see* ADVANCE)
Gen 24: 1 Now Abraham was old, **w** in age

WELL-ADVISED† (*see* ADVISE)
Prov 13:10 But with the **w** is wisdom.

WELL-BEING
Gen 43:27 he asked them about their **w**,
1Co 10:24 but each one the other's **w**.

WELL-BELOVED (*see* BELOVED)
Is 5: 1 My **W** has a vineyard On a

WELL-DRIVEN† (*see* DRIVE)
Eccl 12:11 words of scholars are like **w**

WELL-FED† (*see* FEED)
Jer 5: 8 They were like **w** lusty

WELLS (*see* WELL, WELLSPRING)
Gen 26:18 And Isaac dug again the **w** of
2Pe 2:17 These are **w** without water,

WELLSPRING (*see* SPRING, WELL, WELLS)
Prov 16:22 Understanding is a **w** of

WEPT (*see* WEEP)
Gen 27:38 lifted up his voice and **w**.
Gen 33: 4 and kissed him, and they **w**.
Gen 37:35 Thus his father **w** for him.
Gen 45:14 Benjamin's neck and **w**,
Ex 2: 6 and behold, the baby **w**.
Ruth 1: 9 lifted up their voices and **w**.

WEST

2Sa	12:22	was alive, I fasted and **w**;
2Ki	20: 3	And Hezekiah **w** bitterly.
Neh	1: 4	words, that I sat down and **w**,
Neh	8: 9	weep." For all the people **w**,
Job	2:12	lifted their voices and **w**;
Ps	137: 1	we **w** When we remembered
Hos	12: 4	Angel and prevailed; He **w**,
Luke	19:41	He saw the city and **w** over
Luke	22:62	So Peter went out and **w**
John	11:35	Jesus **w**.

WEST (*see* WESTERN)

Gen	12: 8	tent with Bethel on the **w**
Ex	10:19	turned a very strong **w** wind,
Josh	5: 1	Amorites who were on the **w**
Ps	103:12	as the east is from the **w**,
Is	43: 5	And gather you from the **w**;
Dan	8: 5	a male goat came from the **w**,
Zech	14: 4	in two, From east to **w**,
Matt	8:11	will come from east and **w**,

WESTERN (*see* WEST)

Deut	11:24	even to the **W** Sea, shall be

WET

Dan	4:33	his body was **w** with the dew
Dan	5:21	and his body was **w** with the

WHEAT

Deut	8: 8	a land of **w** and barley, of
Ps	81:16	also with the finest of **w**;
Song	7: 2	Your waist is a heap of **w**
Jer	23:28	What is the chaff to the **w**?
Amos	8: 5	That we may trade **w**?
Matt	3:12	and gather His **w** into the
Matt	13:25	and sowed tares among the **w**
Luke	22:31	that he may sift you as **w**.
John	12:24	unless a grain of **w** falls

WHEEL (*see* WHEELS)

Eccl	12: 6	Or the **w** broken at the
Jer	18: 3	making something at the **w**.
Ezek	1:16	a wheel in the middle of a **w**.

WHEELS (*see* WHEEL)

Ezek	1:19	the **w** were lifted up.
Ezek	1:20	creatures was in the **w**.
Dan	7: 9	Its **w** a burning fire;

WHIP (*see* WHIPS)

Prov	26: 3	A **w** for the horse, A bridle
John	2:15	When He had made a **w** of

WHIPS† (*see* WHIP)

1Ki	12:11	father chastised you with **w**,
1Ki	12:14	father chastised you with **w**,
2Ch	10:11	father chastised you with **w**,
2Ch	10:14	father chastised you with **w**,

WHIRLING

2Sa	6:16	saw King David leaping and **w**

WHIRLWIND

2Ki	2: 1	up Elijah into heaven by a **w**,
Job	38: 1	answered Job out of the **w**,
Prov	1:27	destruction comes like a **w**,
Hos	8: 7	the wind, And reap the **w**.

WHISPER (*see* WHISPERING)

Job	4:12	And my ear received a **w** of
Job	26:14	And how small a **w** we hear
Is	8:19	who **w** and mutter," should

WHISPERING (*see* WHISPER)

2Sa	12:19	saw that his servants were **w**,

WHISTLE

Is	7:18	day That the LORD will **w**

WHITE (*see* WHITEN, WHITER, WHITEWASHED)

Lev	13: 4	if the bright spot is **w** on
Num	12:10	as **w** as snow. Then Aaron

Job	6: 6	is there any taste in the **w**
Eccl	9: 8	your garments always be **w**,
Is	1:18	They shall be as **w** as snow;
Dan	7: 9	His garment was **w** as snow,
Matt	5:36	you cannot make one hair **w**
Matt	28: 3	and his clothing as **w** as
Luke	9:29	and His robe became **w** and
John	4:35	for they are already **w** for
John	20:12	And she saw two angels in **w**
Acts	1:10	two men stood by them in **w**
Rev	1:14	His head and hair were **w**
Rev	2:17	And I will give him a **w**
Rev	3: 4	they shall walk with Me in **w**,
Rev	7:14	their robes and made them **w**
Rev	19:11	a **w** horse. And He who sat on
Rev	20:11	Then I saw a great **w** throne

WHITEN† (*see* WHITE)

Mark	9: 3	no launderer on earth can **w**

WHITER (*see* WHITE)

Ps	51: 7	and I shall be **w** than snow.

WHITEWASHED† (*see* WHITE)

Matt	23:27	For you are like **w** tombs
Acts	23: 3	you **w** wall! For you sit to

WHOLE (*see* WHOLE-HEARTED, WHOLLY)

Gen	7:19	the high hills under the **w**
Gen	11: 1	Now the **w** earth had one
Gen	13: 9	Is not the **w** land before
Num	11:21	that they may eat for a **w**
Deut	2:25	upon the nations under the **w**
Josh	10:13	to go down for about a **w**
1Sa	7: 9	lamb and offered it as a **w**
2Ch	16: 9	to and fro throughout the **w**
Job	34:13	appointed Him over the **w**
Ps	9: 1	with my **w** heart; I will
Ps	48: 2	The joy of the **w** earth,
Ps	51:19	With burnt offering and **w**
Ps	72:19	name forever! And let the **w**
Eccl	12:13	hear the conclusion of the **w**
Is	1: 5	The **w** head is sick, And
Is	6: 3	The **w** earth is full of His
Jer	19:11	which cannot be made **w**
Lam	2:15	The joy of the **w** earth'?"
Dan	2:35	mountain and filled the **w**
Mic	4:13	to the Lord of the **w** earth.
Zech	4:10	to and fro throughout the **w**
Matt	5:29	than for your **w** body to be
Matt	12:13	and it was restored as **w** as
Matt	16:26	to a man if he gains the **w**
Mark	12:33	is more than all the **w** burnt
Acts	2: 2	and it filled the **w** house
Acts	4:10	man stands here before you **w**.
Acts	20:27	to declare to you the **w**
1Co	5: 6	little leaven leavens the **w**
1Co	12:17	If the **w** body were an eye,
Gal	5: 9	little leaven leavens the **w**
Eph	2:21	in whom the **w** building, being
Eph	4:16	from whom the **w** body, joined
Eph	6:11	Put on the **w** armor of God,
1Th	5:23	and may your **w** spirit, soul,
Jas	2:10	For whoever shall keep the **w**
Jas	3: 2	able also to bridle the **w**
1Jn	2: 2	ours only but also for the **w**
1Jn	5:19	and the **w** world lies under
Rev	3:10	which shall come upon the **w**

WHOLE-HEARTED† (*see* HEART, WHOLE)

Ezek	36: 5	with **w** joy and spiteful

WHOLLY (*see* WHOLE)

Lev	6:22	It shall be **w** burned.
Josh	14: 8	but I **w** followed the LORD

WICKED (*see* EVIL, WICKEDLY, WICKEDNESS)

Gen	13:13	of Sodom were exceedingly **w**

Gen	18:25	the righteous with the **w**,
2Ch	7:14	and turn from their **w** ways,
Job	3:17	There the **w** cease from
Job	36: 6	preserve the life of the **w**,
Ps	9: 5	You have destroyed the **w**;
Ps	10:15	Break the arm of the **w** and
Ps	11: 6	Upon the **w** He will rain
Ps	22:16	The congregation of the **w**
Ps	36: 1	the transgression of the **w**:
Ps	37:17	For the arms of the **w** shall
Ps	37:20	But the **w** shall perish; And
Ps	91: 8	And see the reward of the **w**.
Ps	92: 7	When the **w** spring up like
Ps	92:11	hear my desire on the **w**
Ps	112:10	The **w** will see it and be
Ps	139:19	that You would slay the **w**,
Ps	139:24	see if there is any **w**
Prov	4:14	not enter the path of the **w**,
Prov	6:18	A heart that devises **w**
Prov	11: 7	When a **w** man dies, his
Prov	13: 9	But the lamp of the **w** will
Prov	15:26	The thoughts of the **w** are
Prov	16: 4	even the **w** for the day of
Prov	18: 5	to show partiality to the **w**,
Prov	24:20	The lamp of the **w** will be
Prov	26:23	Fervent lips with a **w** heart
Prov	28: 1	The **w** flee when no one
Eccl	7:17	Do not be overly **w**,
Is	5:23	Who justify the **w** for a
Is	11: 4	His lips He shall slay the **w**.
Is	48:22	says the LORD, "for the **w**.
Is	53: 9	made His grave with the **w**—
Is	55: 7	Let the **w** forsake his way,
Is	57:20	But the **w** are like the
Is	57:21	Says my God, "for the **w**.
Jer	17: 9	things, And desperately **w**;
Ezek	3:18	nor speak to warn the **w** from
Ezek	3:18	warn the wicked from his **w**
Ezek	3:18	that same **w** man shall die
Ezek	3:19	"Yet, if you warn the **w**,
Ezek	33: 8	do not speak to warn the **w**
Ezek	33: 8	that **w** man shall die in his
Ezek	33:11	in the death of the **w**,
Matt	12:45	seven other spirits more **w**
Matt	12:45	shall it also be with this **w**
Matt	13:38	tares are the sons of the **w**
Matt	16: 4	A **w** and adulterous generation
Matt	18:32	You **w** servant! I forgave you
Eph	6:16	all the fiery darts of the **w**
2Pe	2: 7	the filthy conduct of the **w**
1Jn	2:13	you have overcome the **w** one.

WICKEDLY (see WICKED)

Gen	19: 7	brethren, do not do so **w**!
Judg	19:23	do not act so **w**! Seeing
Neh	9:33	But we have done **w**.
Ps	139:20	they speak against You **w**;
Dan	9:15	sinned, we have done **w**!

WICKEDNESS (see WICKED)

Gen	6: 5	the LORD saw that the **w** of
1Sa	25:39	LORD has returned the **w** of
1Ki	2:44	LORD will return your **w** on
Ps	5: 4	God who takes pleasure in **w**,
Ps	28: 4	And according to the **w** of
Ps	36: 4	He devises **w** on his bed; He
Ps	45: 7	righteousness and hate **w**;
Ps	84:10	dwell in the tents of **w**.
Ps	125: 3	For the scepter of **w** shall
Prov	4:17	For they eat the bread of **w**,
Prov	12: 3	man is not established by **w**,
Is	58: 6	To loose the bonds of **w**,
Jer	7:12	I did to it because of the **w**
Ezek	3:19	he does not turn from his **w**,
Ezek	18:27	man turns away from the **w**
Ezek	33:19	the wicked turns from his **w**

Hos	7: 1	And the **w** of Samaria. For
Hos	10:13	You have plowed **w**;
Jon	1: 2	for their **w** has come up
Mark	7:22	"thefts, covetousness, **w**,
Rom	1:29	sexual immorality, **w**,
1Co	5: 8	the leaven of malice and **w**,
Eph	6:12	spiritual hosts of **w** in

WIDE

Num	24: 4	down, with eyes **w** open:
2Ch	26:15	So his fame spread far and **w**,
Ps	31: 8	You have set my feet in a **w**
Mic	7:11	decree shall go far and **w**,
Matt	7:13	for **w** is the gate and broad
2Co	6:11	our heart is **w** open.

WIDOW (see WIDOW'S, WIDOWHOOD, WIDOWS)

Lev	21:14	A **w** or a divorced woman or a
Deut	10:18	for the fatherless and the **w**,
Deut	25: 5	the **w** of the dead man shall
1Sa	30: 5	and Abigail the **w** of Nabal
Is	1:17	fatherless, Plead for the **w**.
Lam	1: 1	of people! How like a **w**
Luke	2:37	and this woman was a **w** of
Luke	4:26	to a woman who was a **w**.
Luke	21: 2	He saw also a certain poor **w**
1Ti	5: 4	But if any **w** has children or

WIDOW'S (see WIDOW)

Gen	38:14	took off her **w** garments

WIDOWHOOD (see WIDOW)

Gen	38:19	put on the garments of her **w**.

WIDOWS (see WIDOW, WIDOWS')

Ps	68: 5	fatherless, a defender of **w**,
Mal	3: 5	exploit wage earners and **w**
Luke	4:25	many **w** were in Israel in the
Acts	6: 1	because their **w** were
1Co	7: 8	the unmarried and to the **w**:
1Ti	5: 3	Honor **w** who are really
Jas	1:27	to visit orphans and **w** in

WIDOWS' (see WIDOWS)

Mark	12:40	who devour **w** houses, and for

WIFE (see WIFE'S, WIVES)

Gen	2:24	and be joined to his **w**,
Gen	4: 1	Now Adam knew Eve his **w**,
Gen	7: 7	Noah, with his sons, his **w**,
Gen	18:10	Sarah your **w** shall have a
Gen	23:19	Abraham buried Sarah his **w**
Gen	24:67	Rebekah and she became his **w**,
Gen	25: 1	Abraham again took a **w**,
Ex	4:20	Then Moses took his **w** and his
Ex	18: 2	took Zipporah, Moses' **w**,
Ex	20:17	not covet your neighbor's **w**,
Lev	20:10	with another man's **w**,
Num	5:12	If any man's **w** goes astray
Deut	5:21	not covet your neighbor's **w**;
Deut	21:17	the son of the unloved **w**
Deut	25: 7	want to take his brother's **w**,
Judg	4:21	Then Jael, Heber's **w**,
Judg	14: 2	get her for me as a **w**.
Judg	21:21	and every man catch a **w** for
Ruth	1: 2	the name of his **w** was
1Sa	1:19	Elkanah knew Hannah his **w**,
1Sa	25:14	men told Abigail, Nabal's **w**,
2Sa	11: 3	the **w** of Uriah the
2Sa	12:24	comforted Bathsheba his **w**,
1Ki	16:31	that he took as **w** Jezebel
Job	2: 9	Then his **w** said to him, "Do
Job	19:17	breath is offensive to my **w**,
Prov	5:18	And rejoice with the **w** of
Prov	18:22	He who finds a **w** finds a
Prov	19:14	But a prudent **w** is from
Prov	31:10	Who can find a virtuous **w**?
Eccl	9: 9	Live joyfully with the **w**

Jer	16: 2	"You shall not take a **w**,
Ezek	24:18	and at evening my **w** died;
Hos	1: 2	take yourself a **w** of
Hos	2: 2	For she is not My **w**,
Mal	2:14	Between you and the **w** of
Matt	1: 6	her who had been the **w**
Matt	1:20	to take to you Mary your **w**,
Matt	5:31	'Whoever divorces his **w**,
Matt	19:29	or father or mother or **w** or
Matt	22:24	brother shall marry his **w**
Matt	22:28	whose **w** of the seven will
Luke	1:13	and your **w** Elizabeth will
Luke	2: 5	with Mary, his betrothed **w**,
Luke	17:32	"Remember Lot's **w**.
Acts	5: 1	Ananias, with Sapphira his **w**,
1Co	7: 1	a man has his father's **w**!
1Co	7: 2	let each man have his own **w**,
1Co	7: 4	The **w** does not have authority
1Co	7:11	is not to divorce his **w**.
1Co	7:14	and the unbelieving **w** is
1Co	7:27	Are you bound to a **w**?
1Co	7:33	he may please his **w**.
Eph	5:23	the husband is head of the **w**,
Eph	5:31	and be joined to his **w**,
1Ti	3: 2	the husband of one **w**,
Tit	1: 6	the husband of one **w**,
1Pe	3: 7	giving honor to the **w**,
Rev	21: 9	you the bride, the Lamb's **w**.

WIFE'S (*see* WIFE)

Mark	1:30	But Simon's **w** mother lay sick

WILD

Gen	16:12	He shall be a **w** man; His
Gen	37:20	Some **w** beast has devoured
Ps	22:21	And from the horns of the **w**
Is	5: 2	But it brought forth **w**
Matt	3: 4	his food was locusts and **w**
Mark	1:13	and was with the **w** beasts;
Acts	10:12	**w** beasts, creeping things,
Rom	11:17	being a **w** olive tree, were

WILDERNESS

Gen	16: 7	a spring of water in the **w**,
Ex	3:18	days' journey into the **w**,
Ex	5: 1	hold a feast to Me in the **w**.
Ex	14:11	us away to die in the **w**?
Ex	19: 2	had come to the **W** of Sinai,
Lev	16:10	as the scapegoat into the **w**.
Num	14: 2	only we had died in this **w**!
Num	32:13	He made them wander in the **w**
Deut	1:19	that great and terrible **w**
Deut	8: 2	these forty years in the **w**,
Job	1:19	wind came from across the **w**
Job	12:24	them wander in a pathless **w**.
Ps	29: 8	of the LORD shakes the **w**;
Ps	78:15	He split the rocks in the **w**,
Ps	107:35	He turns a **w** into pools of
Ps	136:16	led His people through the **w**,
Prov	21:19	Better to dwell in the **w**,
Is	21: 1	The burden against the **W** of
Is	35: 6	shall burst forth in the **w**,
Is	40: 3	voice of one crying in the **w**:
Is	41:18	I will make the **w** a pool of
Is	43:19	even make a road in the **w**
Jer	2: 6	Who led us through the **w**,
Jer	2:24	A wild donkey used to the **w**,
Jer	17: 6	the parched places in the **w**,
Hos	2: 3	born, And make her like a **w**,
Amos	2:10	forty years through the **w**,
Matt	3: 1	came preaching in the **w** of
Matt	3: 3	of one crying in the **w**:
Matt	4: 1	up by the Spirit into the **w**
Matt	11: 7	did you go out into the **w**
Mark	1: 4	came baptizing in the **w** and
Mark	1:13	And He was there in the **w**

Luke	15: 4	the ninety-nine in the **w**,
John	1:23	of one crying in the **w**:
John	3:14	up the serpent in the **w**,
John	6:49	ate the manna in the **w**,
1Co	10: 5	were scattered in the **w**.
2Co	11:26	city, in perils in the **w**,
Heb	3:17	whose corpses fell in the **w**?

WILES†

Eph	6:11	able to stand against the **w**

WILL (*see* WILLFULLY, WILLING, WILLS)

Lev	19: 5	offer it of your own free **w**.
Ps	40: 8	I delight to do Your **w**,
Ps	143:10	Teach me to do Your **w**,
Dan	4:35	He does according to His **w**
Dan	8: 4	he did according to his **w**
Matt	6:10	Your **w** be done On earth as
Matt	7:21	but he who does the **w** of My
Matt	26:42	drink it, Your **w** be done."
Luke	7:30	and lawyers rejected the **w**
Luke	22:42	"Father, if it is Your **w**,
John	1:13	nor of the **w** of the flesh,
John	4:34	My food is to do the **w** of Him
John	5:30	I do not seek My own **w** but
John	7:17	anyone wants to do His **w**,
Acts	21:14	The **w** of the Lord be done."
Rom	1:10	I may find a way in the **w**
Rom	9:19	For who has resisted His **w**?
Rom	12: 2	acceptable and perfect **w** of
1Co	1: 1	Jesus Christ through the **w**
2Co	8: 5	and then to us by the **w** of
Eph	1: 5	the good pleasure of His **w**,
Eph	1: 9	to us the mystery of His **w**,
Eph	1:11	to the counsel of His **w**,
Eph	5:17	but understand what the **w** of
1Th	4: 3	For this is the **w** of God,
Heb	10: 7	of Me—To do Your **w**,
Heb	13:21	every good work to do His **w**,
1Pe	2:15	For this is the **w** of God,
1Pe	4: 2	but for the **w** of God.
1Pe	4: 3	lifetime in doing the **w** of
2Pe	1:21	never came by the **w** of man,
1Jn	2:17	but he who does the **w** of God
1Jn	5:14	anything according to His **w**,

WILLFULLY (*see* WILL)

Heb	10:26	For if we sin **w** after we

WILLING (*see* WILL, WILLINGLY)

Gen	24: 8	And if the woman is not **w** to
Ex	35: 5	Whoever is of a **w** heart,
Ex	35:21	everyone whose spirit was **w**,
Is	1:19	If you are **w** and obedient,
Matt	8: 2	saying, "Lord, if You are **w**,
Matt	11:14	And if you are **w** to receive
Matt	26:41	The spirit indeed is **w**,
John	5:35	and you were **w** for a time to
Acts	18:21	return again to you, God **w**.
1Co	7:12	and she is **w** to live with
2Co	8: 3	they were freely **w**,
2Co	8:12	For if there is first a **w**
2Pe	3: 9	not **w** that any should perish

WILLINGLY (*see* WILLING)

Judg	5: 2	When the people **w** offer
Prov	31:13	And **w** works with her hands.
1Co	9:17	For if I do this **w**, I have
1Pe	5: 2	not by compulsion but **w**,

WILLOWS

Ps	137: 2	hung our harps Upon the **w**

WILLS (*see* WILL)

Matt	11:27	the one to whom the Son **w**

WIN (*see* WINS)

Matt	23:15	you travel land and sea to **w**
1Co	9:19	that I might **w** the more;

1Co 9:20 that I might **w** Jews; to

WIND (*see* WINDS, WINDSTORM)
Gen 8: 1 And God made a **w** to pass
Gen 41: 6 blighted by the east **w**,
Ex 10:13 the east **w** brought the
Ex 10:19 turned a very strong west **w**,
1Ki 19:11 the LORD was not in the **w**;
1Ki 19:11 and after the **w** an
Job 1:19 and suddenly a great **w** came
Ps 1: 4 like the chaff which the **w**
Ps 18:10 flew upon the wings of the **w**.
Ps 103:16 for the **w** passes over it,
Ps 135: 7 He brings the **w** out of His
Prov 11:29 own house will inherit the **w**,
Prov 25:23 The north **w** brings forth
Eccl 1: 6 The **w** goes toward the south,
Eccl 1:14 and grasping for the **w**.
Is 41:16 the **w** shall carry them away,
Is 41:29 Their molded images are **w**
Jer 2:24 That sniffs at the **w** in
Jer 5:13 And the prophets become **w**,
Ezek 5: 2 you shall scatter in the **w**.
Hos 8: 7 "They sow the **w**, And reap
Hos 12: 1 "Ephraim feeds on the **w**,
Jon 1: 4 LORD sent out a great **w** on
Jon 4: 8 prepared a vehement east **w**;
Matt 11: 7 see? A reed shaken by the **w**?
Matt 14:30 But when he saw that the **w**
Matt 14:32 the boat, the **w** ceased.
Mark 4:39 He arose and rebuked the **w**,
Mark 4:41 that even the **w** and the sea
John 3: 8 The **w** blows where it wishes,
Acts 2: 2 as of a rushing mighty **w**,
Eph 4:14 carried about with every **w**
Jas 1: 6 driven and tossed by the **w**.

WINDOW (*see* WINDOWS)
Gen 8: 6 that Noah opened the **w** of
Josh 2:15 down by a rope through the **w**,
Josh 2:21 the scarlet cord in the **w**.
1Sa 19:12 let David down through a **w**.
Acts 20: 9 And in a **w** sat a certain
2Co 11:33 in a basket through a **w** in

WINDOWS (*see* WINDOW)
Gen 7:11 and the **w** of heaven were
Eccl 12: 3 that look through the **w**
Jer 9:21 death has come through our **w**,
Dan 6:10 with his **w** open toward
Mal 3:10 will not open for you the **w**

WINDS (*see* WIND)
Ezek 37: 9 GOD: "Come from the four **w**,
Dan 7: 2 the four **w** of heaven were
Matt 7:25 and the **w** blew and beat on
Matt 8:27 that even the **w** and the sea
Matt 24:31 His elect from the four **w**,
Jas 3: 4 and are driven by fierce **w**,

WINDSTORM (*see* STORM, WIND)
Luke 8:23 And a **w** came down on the

WINE (*see* WINEBIBBER, WINEPRESS, WINESKINS)
Gen 9:24 So Noah awoke from his **w**,
Gen 14:18 brought out bread and **w**,
Gen 19:32 us make our father drink **w**,
Gen 49:11 He washed his garments in **w**,
Num 6: 3 separate himself from **w** and
Num 6:20 the Nazirite may drink **w**.
Deut 28:51 leave you grain or new **w** or
Judg 13: 7 Now drink no **w** or similar
1Sa 1:14 Put your **w** away from you!"
Neh 2: 1 when **w** was before him,
Neh 2: 1 that I took the **w** and gave
Job 1:13 were eating and drinking **w**
Ps 75: 8 And the **w** is red; It is
Ps 104:15 And **w** that makes glad the

Prov 3:10 will overflow with new **w**.
Prov 20: 1 **W** is a mocker, Strong
Prov 23:30 who linger long at the **w**,
Prov 23:31 Do not look on the **w** when it
Prov 31: 4 is not for kings to drink **w**,
Eccl 9: 7 And drink your **w** with a
Song 1: 2 your love is better than **w**.
Song 7: 9 THE SHULAMITE The **w**
Is 1:22 Your **w** mixed with water.
Is 5:22 to men mighty at drinking **w**,
Is 16:10 treaders will tread out **w**
Is 28: 1 who are overcome with **w**!
Is 28: 7 also have erred through **w**,
Is 55: 1 buy **w** and milk Without
Jer 25:15 Take this **w** cup of fury from
Jer 35: 6 said, "We will drink no **w**,
Dan 1: 8 nor with the **w** which he
Dan 5:23 have drunk **w** from them. And
Hos 2: 8 I gave her grain, new **w**,
Hos 2:22 With grain, With new **w**,
Hos 7: 5 him sick, inflamed with **w**;
Hos 7:14 together for grain and new **w**,
Amos 2:12 you gave the Nazirites **w** to
Amos 4: 1 to your husbands, "Bring **w**,
Amos 6: 6 Who drink **w** from bowls, And
Zech 9:15 drink and roar as if with **w**;
Matt 9:17 Nor do they put new **w** into
Matt 27:34 they gave Him sour **w** mingled
Luke 1:15 and shall drink neither **w**
Luke 10:34 wounds, pouring on oil and **w**;
John 2: 9 the water that was made **w**,
John 2:10 You have kept the good **w**
John 4:46 He had made the water **w**.
Acts 2:13 "They are full of new **w**.
Eph 5:18 And do not be drunk with **w**,
1Ti 3: 3 not given to **w**, not violent,
1Ti 5:23 but use a little **w** for your
Rev 14:10 shall also drink of the **w**

WINEBIBBER (*see* WINE)
Matt 11:19 'Look, a glutton and a **w**,

WINEPRESS (*see* WINE)
Judg 6:11 threshed wheat in the **w**,
Is 63: 3 I have trodden the **w** alone,
Matt 21:33 dug a **w** in it and built a

WINESKINS (*see* WINE)
Josh 9: 4 old **w** torn and mended,
Matt 9:17 they put new wine into old **w**,

WING (*see* WINGED, WINGS)
Ruth 3: 9 maidservant under your **w**,
1Ki 6:24 One **w** of the cherub was five
Ezek 16: 8 so I spread My **w** over you
Dan 9:27 And on the **w** of abominations

WINGED† (*see* WING)
Gen 1:21 and every **w** bird according
Deut 4:17 or the likeness of any **w**

WINGS (*see* WING)
Ex 19: 4 I bore you on eagles' **w** and
Deut 32:11 up, Carrying them on its **w**,
Ruth 2:12 under whose **w** you have come
Ps 17: 8 under the shadow of Your **w**,
Ps 18:10 He flew upon the **w** of the
Ps 55: 6 that I had **w** like a dove!
Ps 57: 1 in the shadow of Your **w** I
Ps 61: 4 in the shelter of Your **w**.
Ps 91: 4 And under His **w** you shall
Ps 104: 3 Who walks on the **w** of the
Ps 139: 9 If I take the **w** of the
Is 6: 2 seraphim; each one had six **w**.
Is 18: 1 land shadowed with buzzing **w**;
Is 40:31 They shall mount up with **w**
Ezek 1: 6 and each one had four **w**.
Ezek 10: 5 And the sound of the **w** of the

Dan 7: 4 a lion, and had eagle's **w**.
Mal 4: 2 arise With healing in His **w**;
Matt 23:37 her chicks under her **w**,
Rev 4: 8 creatures, each having six **w**,

WINKS
Prov 10:10 He who **w** with the eye causes

WINNOWING†
Ruth 3: 2 he is **w** barley tonight at
Jer 15: 7 I will winnow them with a **w**
Matt 3:12 His **w** fan is in His hand,
Luke 3:17 His **w** fan is in His hand,

WINS† (*see* WIN)
Prov 11:30 And he who **w** souls is

WINTER
Gen 8:22 **W** and summer, And day and
Song 2:11 the **w** is past, The rain is
Jer 36:22 king was sitting in the **w**
Amos 3:15 I will destroy the **w** house
Matt 24:20 your flight may not be in **w**
John 10:22 in Jerusalem, and it was **w**.
2Ti 4:21 your utmost to come before **w**.

WIPE (*see* WIPED, WIPES)
Is 25: 8 And the Lord GOD will **w**
John 13: 5 and to **w** them with the
Rev 21: 4 And God will **w** away every

WIPED (*see* WIPE)
John 11: 2 with fragrant oil and **w** His
Col 2:14 having **w** out the handwriting

WIPES† (*see* WIPE)
2Ki 21:13 wipe Jerusalem as one **w** a
Prov 30:20 She eats and **w** her mouth,

WISDOM (*see* WISE)
Ex 28: 3 filled with the spirit of **w**,
Ex 31: 3 with the Spirit of God, in **w**,
1Ki 4:29 And God gave Solomon **w** and
1Ki 4:34 came to hear the **w** of
1Ki 10: 4 of Sheba had seen all the **w**
Job 12: 2 And **w** will die with you!
Job 12:12 **W** is with aged men, And
Job 12:13 With Him are **w** and strength,
Job 28:18 For the price of **w** is
Job 28:28 fear of the Lord, that is **w**,
Ps 51: 6 You will make me to know **w**.
Ps 90:12 we may gain a heart of **w**.
Ps 104:24 are Your works! In **w** You
Ps 111:10 LORD is the beginning of **w**;
Ps 136: 5 To Him who by **w** made the
Prov 1: 2 To know **w** and instruction,
Prov 1: 7 But fools despise **w** and
Prov 1:20 **W** calls aloud outside; She
Prov 3:19 The LORD by **w** founded the
Prov 4: 5 Get **w**! Get understanding!
Prov 4: 7 **W** is the principal thing
Prov 8:11 For **w** is better than
Prov 8:12 "I, **w**, dwell with
Prov 9: 1 **W** has built her house, She
Prov 9:10 LORD is the beginning of **w**,
Prov 10:21 But fools die for lack of **w**.
Prov 18: 4 The wellspring of **w** is a
Prov 24: 3 Through **w** a house is built,
Prov 31:26 She opens her mouth with **w**,
Eccl 1:16 and have gained more **w** than
Eccl 1:17 And I set my heart to know **w**
Eccl 2:12 turned myself to consider **w**
Eccl 9:10 or device or knowledge or **w**
Eccl 9:16 **W** is better than strength.
Eccl 10:10 But **w** brings success.
Is 11: 2 The Spirit of **w** and
Jer 9:23 the wise man glory in his **w**,
Dan 1: 4 gifted in all **w**, possessing
Dan 1:17 in all literature and **w**;

Dan 2:21 He gives **w** to the wise And
Matt 11:19 and sinners!' But **w** is
Matt 12:42 of the earth to hear the **w**
Matt 13:54 did this Man get this **w**
Luke 1:17 the disobedient to the **w** of
Luke 2:40 in spirit, filled with **w**;
Luke 2:52 And Jesus increased in **w** and
Luke 11:49 Therefore the **w** of God also
Acts 6: 3 of the Holy Spirit and **w**,
Acts 7:22 was learned in all the **w** of
Rom 11:33 of the riches both of the **w**
1Co 1:17 not with **w** of words, lest
1Co 1:19 I will destroy the **w** of
1Co 1:20 not God made foolish the **w**
1Co 1:22 and Greeks seek after **w**;
1Co 1:24 the power of God and the **w**
1Co 1:30 who became for us **w** from
1Co 2: 4 persuasive words of human **w**,
1Co 2: 6 yet not the **w** of this age,
1Co 2: 7 the hidden **w** which God
1Co 3:19 For the **w** of this world is
1Co 12: 8 one is given the word of **w**
2Co 1:12 not with fleshly **w** but by
Eph 1: 8 to abound toward us in all **w**
Eph 1:17 give to you the spirit of **w**
Col 2: 3 all the treasures of **w** and
Col 2:23 have an appearance of **w** in
Col 3:16 dwell in you richly in all **w**,
Col 4: 5 Walk in **w** toward those who
Jas 1: 5 If any of you lacks **w**,
Jas 3:17 But the **w** that is from above
2Pe 3:15 according to the **w** given to
Rev 5:12 power and riches and **w**,
Rev 13:18 Here is **w**. Let him who

WISE (*see* UNWISE, WISDOM, WISELY, WISER)
Gen 3: 6 desirable to make one **w**,
Gen 41: 8 of Egypt and all its **w** men.
Ex 7:11 Pharaoh also called the **w**
2Sa 14: 2 and brought from there a **w**
2Sa 20:16 Then a **w** woman cried out
1Ki 3:12 I have given you a **w** and
Job 9: 4 God is **w** in heart and
Ps 2:10 Now therefore, be **w**,
Ps 19: 7 making **w** the simple;
Prov 1: 5 A **w** man will hear and
Prov 1: 6 The words of the **w** and
Prov 3: 7 Do not be **w** in your own
Prov 6: 6 Consider her ways and be **w**,
Prov 9: 8 Rebuke a **w** man, and he
Prov 10: 1 A **w** son makes a glad
Prov 11:30 And he who wins souls is **w**.
Prov 14: 1 The **w** woman builds her
Prov 15:24 life winds upward for the **w**,
Prov 17: 2 A **w** servant will rule over a
Prov 20: 1 is led astray by it is not **w**.
Prov 20:18 By **w** counsel wage war.
Prov 22:17 and hear the words of the **w**,
Prov 26: 5 Lest he be **w** in his own
Prov 30:24 But they are exceedingly **w**:
Eccl 4:13 Better a poor and **w** youth
Eccl 7:16 righteous, Nor be overly **w**:
Eccl 9:11 strong, Nor bread to the **w**,
Eccl 12: 9 because the Preacher was **w**,
Eccl 12:11 The words of the **w** are like
Jer 9:23 Let not the **w** man glory in
Jer 18:18 nor counsel from the **w**,
Dan 2:12 to destroy all the **w** men
Dan 12: 3 Those who are **w** shall shine
Hos 14: 9 Who is **w**? Let him
Matt 2: 1 **w** men from the East came to
Matt 7:24 I will liken him to a **w** man
Matt 10:16 Therefore be **w** as serpents
Matt 11:25 these things from the **w**
Matt 24:45 then is a faithful and **w**

Matt   25: 2   "Now five of them were **w**,
Rom   1:14   both to **w** and to unwise.
Rom   1:22   Professing to be **w**,
Rom   11:25   lest you should be **w** in your
Rom   16:27   to God, alone **w**, be glory
1Co   1:19   the wisdom of the **w**,
1Co   1:26   that not many **w** according to
1Co   3:10   as a **w** master builder I have
1Co   3:19   He catches the **w** in
1Co   4:10   but you are **w** in Christ! We
1Co   10:15   I speak as to **w** men; judge
Eph   5:15   not as fools but as **w**,
1Ti   1:17   to God who alone is **w**,
2Ti   3:15   are able to make you **w** for
Jas   3:13   Who is **w** and understanding
Jude   25   our Savior, Who alone is **w**,

WISELY (*see* SHREWDLY, WISE)
Mark 12:34   Jesus saw that he answered **w**,

WISER (*see* WISE)
1Ki   4:31   For he was **w** than all
Ezek 28: 3   you are **w** than Daniel!
1Co   1:25   the foolishness of God is **w**

WISH (*see* WISHED, WISHES)
Luke   4: 6   I give it to whomever I **w**.
John   12:21   we **w** to see Jesus."
John   21:18   you where you do not **w**.
Rom   9: 3   For I could **w** that I myself
1Co   7: 7   For I **w** that all men were
1Co   14: 5   I **w** you all spoke with
Gal   5:17   not do the things that you **w**.
Rev   3:15   I could **w** you were cold or

WISHED (*see* WISH)
Matt 17:12   did to him whatever they **w**.
John 21:18   and walked where you **w**;

WISHES (*see* WISH)
John   3: 8   "The wind blows where it **w**,

WITCHCRAFT
Deut 18:10   or one who practices **w**,
1Sa   15:23   is as the sin of **w**,

WITHDRAW (*see* WITHDRAWN, WITHDREW)
1Ti   6: 5   From such **w** yourself.

WITHDRAWN (*see* WITHDRAW)
2Sa   24:25   and the plague was **w** from

WITHDREW (*see* WITHDRAW)
Matt 12:15   He **w** from there. And great
Luke   5:16   So He Himself often **w** into

WITHER (*see* WITHERED, WITHERS)
Ps   1: 3   Whose leaf also shall not **w**;
Ps   37: 2   And **w** as the green herb.
Is   40:24   on them, And they will **w**,
Matt 21:20   How did the fig tree **w** away

WITHERED (*see* WITHER)
Jon   4: 7   damaged the plant that it **w**.
Matt 12:10   there was a man who had a **w**
Matt 13: 6   they had no root they **w**
Matt 21:19   Immediately the fig tree **w**
John 15: 6   out as a branch and is **w**;

WITHERS (*see* WITHER)
Ps   90: 6   evening it is cut down and **w**.
Is   40: 7   The grass **w**, the flower
1Pe   1:24   thc grass. The grass **w**,

WITHHELD (*see* WITHHOLD)
Gen   11: 6   they propose to do will be **w**
Gen   22:12   since you have not **w** your

WITHHOLD (*see* WITHHELD)
Ps   84:11   No good thing will He **w**
Luke   6:29   do not **w** your tunic either.

WITHSTAND (*see* WITHSTOOD)
Dan   8: 4   so that no animal could **w**
Acts 11:17   who was I that I could **w**

WITHSTOOD (*see* WITHSTAND)
Gal   2:11   I **w** him to his face, because

WITNESS (*see* EYEWITNESSES, WITNESSED, WITNESSES)
Gen   31:48   This heap is a **w** between you
Gen   31:50   God is **w** between you and
Ex   20:16   shall not bear false **w**
Num 17: 7   LORD in the tabernacle of **w**.
Num 35:30   but one **w** is not sufficient
Deut   4:26   call heaven and earth to **w**
Deut   5:20   'You shall not bear false **w**
Josh 24:27   this stone shall be a **w** to
Job   16:19   Surely even now my **w** is in
Ps   89:37   Even like the faithful **w**
Prov   6:19   A false **w** who speaks lies,
Prov   14:25   But a deceitful **w** speaks
Is   55: 4   I have given him as a **w** to
Matt 19:18   shall not bear false **w**,
Matt 24:14   in all the world as a **w** to
Mark 10:19   'Do not bear false **w**,
Mark 14:56   For many bore false **w** against
John   1: 7   This man came for a **w**,
John   1: 8   but was sent to bear **w** of
John   1:15   John bore **w** of Him and cried
John   5:32   is another who bears **w** of
John 12:17   him from the dead, bore **w**.
Acts 10:43   To Him all the prophets **w**
Acts 14:17   not leave Himself without **w**,
Rom   1: 9   For God is my **w**, whom
Rom   2:15   conscience also bearing **w**,
Rom   8:16   The Spirit Himself bears **w**
Rom   10: 2   For I bear them **w** that they
Phil   1: 8   For God is my **w**, how greatly
Heb   11: 4   through which he obtained **w**
1Jn   1: 2   and we have seen, and bear **w**,
1Jn   5: 6   it is the Spirit who bears **w**,
1Jn   5: 7   there are three that bear **w**
1Jn   5: 8   there are three that bear **w**
Rev   1: 2   who bore **w** to the word of
Rev   1: 5   Jesus Christ, the faithful **w**,
Rev   3:14   the Faithful and True **W**,
Rev   20: 4   been beheaded for their **w**

WITNESSED (*see* WITNESS)
Heb   7: 8   of whom it is **w** that he

WITNESSES (*see* WITNESS)
Deut 17: 6   testimony of two or three **w**;
Josh 24:22   they said, "We are **w**!"
Ruth   4:11   elders, said, "We are **w**.
Ps   27:12   For false **w** have risen
Is   43:10   "You are My **w**," says
Jer   32:12   and in the presence of the **w**
Matt 18:16   of two or three **w**
Matt 26:60   Even though many false **w**
Matt 26:65   further need do we have of **w**?
John   5:32   that the witness which He **w**
Acts   1: 8   and you shall be **w** to Me in
Acts   3:15   the dead, of which we are **w**.
Acts   7:58   And the **w** laid down their
2Co   13: 1   of two or three **w**
1Ti   5:19   except from two or three **w**.
1Ti   6:12   in the presence of many **w**.
2Ti   2: 2   heard from me among many **w**,
Heb   10:15   But the Holy Spirit also **w** to
Heb   10:28   testimony of two or three **w**.
Heb   12: 1   by so great a cloud of **w**,
Rev   11: 3   will give power to my two **w**,

WITS'†
Ps   107:27   And are at their **w** end.

WIVES (see WIFE, WIVES')

Gen	4:19	took for himself two **w**:
Gen	6: 2	and they took **w** for
Gen	6:18	and your sons' **w** with you.
Gen	30:26	Give me my **w** and my children
Deut	17:17	shall he multiply **w**
Deut	21:15	"If a man has two **w**,
Judg	21: 7	give them our daughters as **w**?
1Sa	1: 2	And he had two **w**:
1Sa	27: 3	and David with his two **w**,
2Sa	12: 8	house and your master's **w**
2Sa	12:11	he shall lie with your **w** in
1Ki	11: 3	And he had seven hundred **w**,
1Ki	11: 3	and his **w** turned away his
1Ki	11: 8	for all his foreign **w**,
Ezra	9: 2	of their daughters as **w**
Ezra	10: 3	God to put away all these **w**
Ezra	10:17	men who had taken pagan **w**.
Neh	5: 1	of the people and their **w**
Is	13:16	be plundered And their **w**
Matt	19: 8	you to divorce your **w**,
Luke	17:27	they drank, they married **w**,
1Co	7:29	now on even those who have **w**
Eph	5:22	**W**, submit to your own
Eph	5:25	Husbands, love your **w**,
Col	3:18	**W**, submit to your own
1Ti	3:11	Likewise their **w** must be
1Pe	3: 1	**W**, likewise, be submissive
1Pe	3: 1	by the conduct of their **w**,

WIVES' † (see WIVES)

1Ti	4: 7	profane and old **w** fables,

WOE

Prov	23:29	Who has **w**? Who has sorrow?
Is	5: 8	**W** to those who join house
Is	5:11	**W** to those who rise early
Is	5:18	**W** to those who draw
Is	5:20	**W** to those who call evil
Is	6: 5	**W** is me, for I am undone!
Is	29: 1	**W** to Ariel, to Ariel, the
Jer	23: 1	**W** to the shepherds who
Ezek	2:10	and mourning and **w**.
Ezek	34: 2	**W** to the shepherds of Israel
Amos	5:18	**W** to you who desire the day
Amos	6: 1	**W** to you who are at ease
Hab	2: 6	**W** to him who increases What
Hab	2: 9	**W** to him who covets evil
Hab	2:12	**W** to him who builds a town
Hab	2:15	**W** to him who gives drink to
Hab	2:19	**W** to him who says to wood,
Matt	11:21	**W** to you, Chorazin! Woe to
Matt	18: 7	but **w** to that man by whom
Matt	23:14	**W** to you, scribes and
Matt	23:16	**W** to you, blind guides, who
Matt	24:19	But **w** to those who are
Matt	26:24	but **w** to that man by whom
Luke	6:24	But **w** to you who are rich,
Luke	6:25	**W** to you who are full, For
Luke	6:25	**W** to you who laugh now,
Luke	6:26	**W** to you when all men speak
1Co	9:16	**w** is me if I do not preach
Rev	8:13	with a loud voice, "Woe, **w**,

WOLF (see WOLVES)

Gen	49:27	"Benjamin is a ravenous **w**;
Is	11: 6	The **w** also shall dwell with
Is	65:25	The **w** and the lamb shall
John	10:12	sees the **w** coming and leaves

WOLVES (see WOLF)

Zeph	3: 3	Her judges are evening **w**
Matt	7:15	inwardly they are ravenous **w**.
Matt	10:16	as sheep in the midst of **w**.

WOMAN (see WOMEN)

Gen	2:22	from man He made into a **w**,

Gen	2:23	She shall be called **W**,
Gen	3: 4	the serpent said to the **w**,
Gen	3:12	The **w** whom You gave to be
Gen	3:15	Between you and the **w**,
Lev	18:22	lie with a male as with a **w**.
Num	12: 1	had married an Ethiopian **w**.
Deut	22:27	and the betrothed young **w**
Judg	4: 9	Sisera into the hand of a **w**.
Judg	9:54	A **w** killed him.'" So his
Ruth	2: 6	It is the young Moabite **w**
Ruth	3:11	that you are a virtuous **w**.
1Sa	28: 7	Find me a **w** who is a medium,
1Sa	28:12	When the **w** saw Samuel, she
2Sa	11: 2	And from the roof he saw a **w**
2Sa	14: 2	brought from there a wise **w**,
2Sa	20:16	Then a wise **w** cried out from
1Ki	1: 2	said to him, "Let a young **w**,
1Ki	3:27	Give the first **w** the living
2Ki	4:12	"Call this Shunammite **w**.
2Ch	24: 7	of Athaliah, that wicked **w**,
Job	14: 1	Man who is born of **w** Is of
Ps	48: 6	as of a **w** in birth pangs,
Ps	58: 8	a stillborn child of a **w**,
Ps	113: 9	He grants the barren **w** a
Prov	2:16	you from the immoral **w**,
Prov	5:20	enraptured by an immoral **w**,
Prov	6:24	To keep you from the evil **w**,
Prov	14: 1	The wise **w** builds her house,
Prov	21: 9	shared with a contentious **w**.
Prov	31:30	But a **w** who fears the
Is	49:15	Can a **w** forget her nursing
Is	54: 1	children of the married **w**,
Jer	22:23	Like the pain of a **w** in
Jer	34: 9	slave—a Hebrew man or **w**—
Hos	3: 1	love a **w** who is loved by a
Mic	4:10	Like a **w** in birth pangs.
Matt	5:28	that whoever looks at a **w**
Matt	9:20	a **w** who had a flow of blood
Matt	15:28	and said to her, "O **w**,
Mark	10:12	And if a **w** divorces her
Mark	14: 3	a **w** came having an alabaster
Mark	14: 9	what this **w** has done will
Luke	2:37	and this **w** was a widow of
Luke	7:46	but this **w** has anointed My
Luke	10:38	and a certain **w** named Martha
Luke	15: 8	"Or what **w**, having ten
Luke	22:57	he denied Him, saying, "**W**,
John	2: 4	Jesus said to her, "**W**,
John	4: 7	A **w** of Samaria came to draw
John	4:21	Jesus said to her, "**W**,
John	8: 3	brought to Him a **w** caught
John	19:26	He said to His mother, "**W**,
John	20:13	Then they said to her, "**W**,
John	20:15	Jesus said to her, "**W**,
Acts	16:14	Now a certain **w** named Lydia
Acts	17:34	a **w** named Damaris, and
Rom	7: 2	For the **w** who has a husband
1Co	7: 1	for a man not to touch a **w**.
1Co	7:34	The unmarried **w** cares about
1Co	11: 3	the head of **w** is man, and
1Co	11: 7	but is the glory of man.
1Co	11: 8	For man is not from **w**,
1Co	11:15	But if a **w** has long hair, it
Gal	4: 4	forth His Son, born of a **w**,
1Ti	2:11	Let a **w** learn in silence with
1Ti	2:12	And I do not permit a **w** to
1Ti	2:14	but the **w** being deceived,
Rev	2:20	because you allow that **w**
Rev	17: 3	And I saw a **w** sitting on a
Rev	17: 4	The **w** was arrayed in purple

WOMB

Gen	25:23	nations are in your **w**,
Gen	29:31	unloved, He opened her **w**;
Gen	38:27	behold, twins were in her **w**.

Deut   7:13   bless the fruit of your **w**
Judg   13: 5   a Nazirite to God from the **w;**
Ruth   1:11   there still sons in my **w,**
1Sa   1: 5   the LORD had closed her **w.**
Job   1:21   I came from my mother's **w,**
Ps   22: 9   He who took Me out of the **w;**
Ps   110: 3   from the **w** of the morning,
Ps   127: 3   The fruit of the **w** is a
Ps   139:13   covered me in my mother's **w.**
Prov   30:16   The grave, The barren **w,**
Prov   31: 2   son? And what, son of my **w?**
Is   44: 2   And formed you from the **w,**
Jer   1: 5   I formed you in the **w** I
Jer   20:17   did not kill me from the **w,**
Hos   12: 3   brother by the heel in the **w,**
Luke   1:41   the babe leaped in her **w;**
Luke   11:27   Blessed is the **w** that bore
John   3: 4   time into his mother's **w**
Rom   4:19   the deadness of Sarah's **w.**
Gal   1:15   me from my mother's **w** and

WOMEN (*see* WOMAN)
Gen   24:11   the time when **w** go out to
Gen   31:35   for the manner of **w** is with
Ex   1:16   a midwife for the Hebrew **w,**
Judg   5:24   Most blessed among **w** is Jael,
2Sa   1:26   Surpassing the love of **w.**
1Ki   3:16   Now two **w** who were harlots
1Ki   11: 1   Solomon loved many foreign **w,**
Job   2:10   as one of the foolish **w**
Ps   45: 9   are among Your honorable **w;**
Prov   31: 3   not give your strength to **w,**
Song   5: 9   beloved, O fairest among **w?**
Is   3:12   And **w** rule over them. O My
Jer   9:17   send for skillful wailing **w,**
Lam   2:20   Should the **w** eat their
Lam   5:11   They ravished the **w** in Zion,
Ezek   8:14   **w** were sitting there weeping
Hos   13:16   And their **w** with child
Amos   1:13   they ripped open the **w** with
Matt   11:11   among those born of **w** there
Matt   14:21   besides **w** and children.
Matt   24:41   Two **w** will be grinding at
Matt   27:55   And many **w** who followed Jesus
Luke   1:28   blessed are you among **w!**"
Luke   1:42   "Blessed are you among **w,**
Acts   8: 3   and dragging off men and **w,**
Acts   8:12   both men and **w** were
Acts   22: 4   into prisons both men and **w,**
Rom   1:26   For even their **w** exchanged
1Co   14:34   Let your **w** keep silent in the
1Co   14:35   for it is shameful for **w** to
2Ti   3: 6   make captives of gullible **w**
Heb   11:35   **W** received their dead raised

WONDER (*see* WONDERFUL, WONDERS, WONDROUS)
Deut   13: 1   he gives you a sign or a **w,**
Acts   3:10   and they were filled with **w**
2Co   11:14   And no **w!** For Satan himself

WONDERFUL (*see* WONDER, WONDERFULLY)
Judg   13:18   ask My name, seeing it is **w?**
2Sa   1:26   me; Your love to me was **w,**
Job   42: 3   Things too **w** for me, which
Ps   107: 8   And for His **w** works to the
Ps   139: 6   Such knowledge is too **w**
Prov   30:18   things which are too **w**
Is   9: 6   His name will be called **W,**
Is   28:29   Who is **w** in counsel and
Acts   2:11   in our own tongues the **w**

WONDERFULLY† (*see* WONDERFUL)
Ps   139:14   for I am fearfully and **w**

WONDERS (*see* WONDER)
Ex   3:20   strike Egypt with all My **w**
Deut   4:34   by trials, by signs, by **w,**

Ps   77:14   You are the God who does **w;**
Ps   105:27   And **w** in the land of Ham.
Ps   136: 4   Him who alone does great **w,**
Dan   4: 3   And how mighty His **w!** His
Dan   6:27   And He works signs and **w**
Matt   7:22   and done many **w** in Your
Mark   13:22   rise and show signs and **w**
John   4:48   you people see signs and **w,**
Rom   15:19   in mighty signs and **w,**
2Th   2: 9   power, signs, and lying **w,**
Heb   2: 4   both with signs and **w,**

WONDROUS (*see* WONDER)
1Ch   16: 9   Talk of all His **w** works!
Ps   26: 7   And tell of all Your **w**
Ps   72:18   Who only does **w** things!
Ps   119:18   that I may see **W** things

WOOD (*see* WOODCUTTERS, WOODEN, WOODS)
Gen   22: 6   So Abraham took the **w** of the
Ex   25:10   make an ark of acacia **w;**
Lev   14: 4   and clean birds, cedar **w,**
Deut   4:28   **w** and stone, which neither
1Sa   6:14   So they split the **w** of the
1Ki   6:23   two cherubim of olive **w,**
1Ki   18:23   pieces, and lay it on the **w,**
1Ch   22: 4   Tyre brought much cedar **w**
2Ch   2:16   And we will cut **w** from
Prov   26:20   Where there is no **w,**
Is   44:19   down before a block of **w?**
Lam   5:13   staggered under loads of **w.**
Dan   5: 4   and iron, **w** and stone.
Hab   2:19   Woe to him who says to **w,**
Luke   23:31   these things in the green **w,**
1Co   3:12   silver, precious stones, **w,**

WOODCUTTERS (*see* CUT, WOOD)
Josh   9:23   **w** and water carriers for the

WOODEN (*see* WOOD)
Ex   34:13   and cut down their **w** images
Deut   12: 3   and burn their **w** images with
Judg   6:28   and the **w** image that was
Jer   10: 8   A **w** idol is a worthless

WOODS (*see* WOOD)
Deut   19: 5   when a man goes to the **w**
1Sa   23:18   And David stayed in the **w,**

WOODSMEN
1Ch   22:15   **w** and stonecutters, and all
2Ch   2:10   the **w** who cut timber, twenty

WOOL
Prov   31:13   She seeks **w** and flax, And
Is   1:18   crimson, They shall be as **w.**
Dan   7: 9   of His head was like pure **w.**
Hos   2: 5   My **w** and my linen, My oil
Rev   1:14   and hair were white like **w,**

WORD (*see* WORDS)
Gen   15: 4   the **w** of the LORD came to
Ex   8:10   it be according to your **w,**
Ex   8:13   did according to the **w** of
Ex   9:20   He who feared the **w** of the
Num   13:26   they brought back **w** to them
Num   23: 5   Then the LORD put a **w** in
Deut   8: 3   but man lives by every **w**
Deut   18:20   who presumes to speak a **w**
Deut   30:14   But the **w** is very near you,
Josh   21:45   Not a **w** failed of any good
1Sa   3: 1   And the **w** of the LORD was
1Sa   15:23   you have rejected the **w** of
1Sa   15:26   for you have rejected the **w**
2Sa   23: 2   And His **w** was on my
1Ki   2:30   And Benaiah brought back **w**
1Ki   6:12   then I will perform My **w**
1Ki   8:56   There has not failed one **w**
2Ki   18:36   and answered him not a **w;**

2Ch   6:17 let Your **w** come true, which
2Ch   10:15 LORD might fulfill His **w**,
2Ch   36:22 that the **w** of the LORD by
Job   2:13 and no one spoke a **w** to him,
Job   4:12 Now a **w** was secretly brought
Ps   17: 4 By the **w** of Your lips, I
Ps   33: 4 For the **w** of the LORD is
Ps   33: 6 By the **w** of the LORD the
Ps   56: 4 God (I will praise His **w**),
Ps   68:11 The Lord gave the **w**;
Ps   103:20 Heeding the voice of His **w**.
Ps   107:20 He sent His **w** and healed
Ps   119: 9 heed according to Your **w**.
Ps   119:11 Your **w** I have hidden in my
Ps   119:16 I will not forget Your **w**.
Ps   119:89 Your **w** is settled in
Ps   119:105 Your **w** is a lamp to my
Ps   119:114 my shield; I hope in Your **w**.
Ps   119:162 I rejoice at Your **w** As one
Ps   138: 2 You have magnified Your **w**
Ps   139: 4 For there is not a **w** on my
Prov   15: 1 But a harsh **w** stirs up
Prov   15:23 And a **w** spoken in due
Prov   25:11 A **w** fitly spoken is like
Prov   30: 5 Every **w** of God is pure;
Is   1:10 Hear the **w** of the LORD,
Is   2: 1 The **w** that Isaiah the son of
Is   40: 8 But the **w** of our God stands
Is   45:23 The **w** has gone out of My
Is   55:11 So shall My **w** be that goes
Jer   1: 4 Then the **w** of the LORD came
Jer   1:12 I am ready to perform My **w**.
Jer   7: 2 Hear the **w** of the LORD, all
Jer   8: 9 they have rejected the **w** of
Jer   18:18 nor the **w** from the prophet.
Jer   23:29 Is not My **w** like a fire?"
Jer   26: 2 to them. Do not diminish a **w**.
Lam   2:17 He has fulfilled His **w**
Dan   4:17 And the sentence by the **w**
Amos   4: 1 Hear this **w**, you cows of
Jon   1: 1 Now the **w** of the LORD came
Zech   9: 1 The burden of the **w** of the
Zech   12: 1 The burden of the **w** of the
Mal   1: 1 The burden of the **w** of the
Matt   2: 8 bring back **w** to me, that I
Matt   4: 4 but by every **w** that
Matt   8: 8 my roof. But only speak a **w**,
Matt   8:16 out the spirits with a **w**,
Matt   13:20 this is he who hears the **w**
Matt   13:22 of riches choke the **w**,
Matt   26:75 And Peter remembered the **w** of
Mark   2: 2 And He preached the **w** to
Mark   7:13 making the **w** of God of no
Mark   16:20 them and confirming the **w**
Luke   1: 2 and ministers of the **w**
Luke   1:38 be to me according to your **w**.
Luke   2:29 peace, According to Your **w**;
Luke   3: 2 the **w** of God came to John
Luke   5: 5 nevertheless at Your **w** I
Luke   7: 7 come to You. But say the **w**,
Luke   8:11 The seed is the **w** of God.
Luke   12:10 And anyone who speaks a **w**
Luke   24:19 mighty in deed and **w** before
John   1: 1 In the beginning was the **W**,
John   1: 1 and the **W** was with God, and
John   1: 1 and the **W** was God.
John   1:14 And the **W** became flesh and
John   8:31 Him, "If you abide in My **w**,
John   8:51 if anyone keeps My **w** he
John   10:35 to whom the **w** of God came
John   15: 3 clean because of the **w**
John   17: 6 and they have kept Your **w**.
John   17:17 Your **w** is truth.
John   17:20 in Me through their **w**
Acts   2:41 who gladly received his **w**

Acts   4: 4 of those who heard the **w**
Acts   6: 2 that we should leave the **w**
Acts   6: 4 and to the ministry of the **w**.
Acts   6: 7 Then the **w** of God spread, and
Acts   12:24 But the **w** of God grew and
Acts   13: 5 they preached the **w** of God
Acts   14: 3 bearing witness to the **w** of
Acts   15: 7 Gentiles should hear the **w**
Acts   15:27 report the same things by **w**
Acts   17:11 in that they received the **w**
Rom   9: 9 For this is the **w** of
Rom   10: 8 The **w** is near you, in
Rom   10:17 and hearing by the **w** of God.
1Co   4:20 kingdom of God is not in **w**
1Co   12: 8 for to one is given the **w** of
1Co   14:36 Or did the **w** of God come
1Co   15: 2 if you hold fast that **w**
2Co   1:18 our **w** to you was not Yes and
2Co   2:17 peddling the **w** of God; but
2Co   4: 2 nor handling the **w** of God
2Co   5:19 has committed to us the **w**
Gal   5:14 law is fulfilled in one **w**,
Eph   4:29 Let no corrupt **w** proceed out
Eph   5:26 washing of water by the **w**,
Eph   6:17 which is the **w** of God;
Phil   1:14 more bold to speak the **w**
Phil   2:16 holding fast the **w** of life,
Col   3:16 Let the **w** of Christ dwell in
Col   3:17 And whatever you do in **w** or
Col   4: 3 open to us a door for the **w**
1Th   1: 5 did not come to you in **w**
1Th   1: 6 having received the **w** in
1Th   1: 8 For from you the **w** of the
1Th   2:13 welcomed it not as the **w**
2Th   2: 2 either by spirit or by **w** or
2Th   2:15 whether by **w** or our epistle.
2Th   2:17 you in every good **w** and
1Ti   4: 5 it is sanctified by the **w**
1Ti   4:12 to the believers in **w**,
1Ti   5:17 those who labor in the **w**
2Ti   2: 9 but the **w** of God is not
2Ti   2:15 rightly dividing the **w** of
2Ti   4: 2 Preach the **w**! Be ready in
Heb   1: 3 all things by the **w** of His
Heb   2: 2 For if the **w** spoken through
Heb   4:12 For the **w** of God is living
Heb   5:13 milk is unskilled in the **w**
Heb   6: 5 and have tasted the good **w** of
Heb   11: 3 worlds were framed by the **w**
Jas   1:21 meekness the implanted **w**,
Jas   1:22 But be doers of the **w**,
Jas   3: 2 anyone does not stumble in **w**,
1Pe   1:25 But the **w** of the LORD
1Pe   2: 2 the pure milk of the **w**,
2Pe   1:19 so we have the prophetic **w**
2Pe   3: 5 that by the **w** of God the
2Pe   3: 7 now preserved by the same **w**,
1Jn   1: 1 concerning the **W** of life—
1Jn   1:10 and His **w** is not in us.
1Jn   2: 5 But whoever keeps His **w**,
1Jn   2:14 and the **w** of God abides in
1Jn   3:18 let us not love in **w** or in
1Jn   5: 7 in heaven: the Father, the **W**,
Rev   1: 2 who bore witness to the **w** of
Rev   1: 9 is called Patmos for the **w**
Rev   12:11 of the Lamb and by the **w** of
Rev   19:13 His name is called The **W** of
Rev   20: 4 to Jesus and for the **w** of

WORDS (*see* WORD)
Gen   37: 8 for his dreams and for his **w**.
Ex   4:15 speak to him and put the **w**
Ex   20: 1 And God spoke all these **w**,
Ex   24: 4 And Moses wrote all the **w** of
Ex   24: 8 you according to all these **w**.

Ex	34: 1	on these tablets the **w**
Ex	34:27	to Moses, "Write these **w**,
Ex	34:28	wrote on the tablets the **w**
Deut	1: 1	These are the **w** which Moses
Deut	18:18	and will put My **w** in His
Deut	18:19	whoever will not hear My **w**,
Josh	24:26	Then Joshua wrote these **w** in
1Sa	3:19	him and let none of his **w**
2Sa	7:28	and Your **w** are true, and You
2Sa	23: 1	Now these are the last **w** of
Ezra	7:11	expert in the **w** of the
Job	12:11	Does not the ear test **w** And
Job	16: 3	Shall **w** of wind have an end?
Job	19:23	that my **w** were written! Oh,
Job	31:40	The **w** of Job are ended.
Job	32:18	For I am full of **w**;
Job	34:37	And multiplies his **w**
Job	38: 2	who darkens counsel By **w**
Ps	5: 1	Give ear to my **w**,
Ps	12: 6	The **w** of the LORD are pure
Ps	12: 6	of the LORD are pure **w**,
Ps	19: 4	And their **w** to the end of
Ps	19:14	Let the **w** of my mouth and
Ps	22: 1	And from the **w** of My
Ps	50:17	instruction And cast My **w**
Ps	119:103	How sweet are Your **w** to my
Ps	119:130	The entrance of Your **w** gives
Prov	1: 6	The **w** of the wise and their
Prov	1:21	the city She speaks her **w**:
Prov	2: 1	My son, if you receive my **w**,
Prov	2:16	who flatters with her **w**,
Prov	4: 5	nor turn away from the **w** of
Prov	12: 6	The **w** of the wicked are,
Prov	15:26	But the **w** of the pure
Prov	19:27	you will stray from the **w**
Prov	22:17	your ear and hear the **w** of
Prov	30: 1	The **w** of Agur the son of
Prov	30: 6	Do not add to His **w**,
Prov	31: 1	The **w** of King Lemuel, the
Eccl	1: 1	The **w** of the Preacher, the
Eccl	9:17	**W** of the wise, spoken
Eccl	12:11	The **w** of the wise are like
Is	51:16	And I have put My **w** in your
Is	59: 4	They trust in empty **w** and
Jer	1: 9	I have put My **w** in your
Jer	7: 4	not trust in these lying **w**,
Jer	11: 2	Hear the **w** of this covenant,
Jer	15:16	Your **w** were found, and I ate
Jer	29:23	and have spoken lying **w** in
Jer	36: 2	and write on it all the **w**
Jer	36:27	the scroll with the **w** which
Jer	36:32	added to them many similar **w**.
Ezek	2: 7	You shall speak My **w** to them,
Dan	7: 8	a mouth speaking pompous **w**,
Dan	12: 4	you, Daniel, shut up the **w**,
Dan	12: 9	for the **w** are closed up and
Hos	14: 2	Take **w** with you, And return
Amos	7:10	not able to bear all his **w**.
Amos	8:11	But of hearing the **w** of the
Mal	2:17	the LORD with your **w**;
Matt	6: 7	be heard for their many **w**.
Matt	12:37	For by your **w** you will be
Mark	10:24	were astonished at His **w**.
Mark	12:13	to catch Him in His **w**.
Luke	1:20	you did not believe my **w**
Luke	3: 4	in the book of the **w** of
Luke	24:44	These are the **w** which I
John	3:34	God has sent speaks the **w**
John	5:47	how will you believe My **w**?
John	6:68	You have the **w** of eternal
John	12:47	And if anyone hears My **w** and
John	14:10	The **w** that I speak to you I
John	14:24	love Me does not keep My **w**;
John	15: 7	and My **w** abide in you, you
Acts	2:22	of Israel, hear these **w**:

Acts	6:11	him speak blasphemous **w**
Acts	7:22	and was mighty in **w** and
Rom	10:18	And their **w** to the
Rom	16:18	and by smooth **w** and
1Co	1:17	gospel, not with wisdom of **w**,
1Co	14: 9	you utter by the tongue **w**
1Co	14:19	I would rather speak five **w**
1Co	14:19	than ten thousand **w** in a
1Ti	6: 4	and arguments over **w**,
Heb	13:22	have written to you in few **w**.
Rev	1: 3	and those who hear the **w** of
Rev	22: 6	These **w** are faithful and
Rev	22: 9	and of those who keep the **w**
Rev	22:18	to everyone who hears the **w**
Rev	22:19	takes away from the **w** of

WORE (*see* WEAR, WEARING)

1Ki	20:32	So they **w** sackcloth around
1Ch	15:27	David also **w** a linen ephod.

WORK (*see* WORKED, WORKER, WORKING, WORKMAN, WORKS)

Gen	2: 2	seventh day God ended His **w**
Ex	5: 9	Let more **w** be laid on the
Ex	14:31	Thus Israel saw the great **w**
Ex	20: 9	labor and do all your **w**,
Ex	20:10	In it you shall do no **w**:
Ex	23:12	days you shall do your **w**,
Ex	31:15	**W** shall be done for six days,
Ex	34:21	"Six days you shall **w**,
Ex	40:33	So Moses finished the **w**.
Lev	23: 7	you shall do no customary **w**
Num	3: 7	to do the **w** of the
Deut	4:28	the **w** of men's hands, wood
Deut	5:13	labor and do all your **w**,
Deut	5:14	In it you shall do no **w**:
Deut	32: 4	His **w** is perfect; For all
Ruth	2:12	"The LORD repay your **w**.
Neh	4: 6	the people had a mind to **w**.
Neh	6: 3	"I am doing a great **w**,
Neh	6: 3	Why should the **w** cease while
Job	1:10	You have blessed the **w** of
Job	10: 3	You should despise the **w** of
Job	24: 5	They go out to their **w**,
Job	34:11	man according to his **w**,
Ps	8: 3	the **w** of Your fingers, The
Ps	62:12	each one according to his **w**.
Ps	74: 6	they break down its carved **w**,
Ps	77:12	also meditate on all Your **w**,
Ps	90:17	And establish the **w** of our
Ps	104:23	Man goes out to his **w** And
Ps	115: 4	The **w** of men's hands.
Ps	135:15	The **w** of men's hands.
Prov	24:29	the man according to his **w**.
Eccl	3:17	purpose and for every **w**.
Eccl	8: 9	applied my heart to every **w**
Eccl	9:10	for there is no **w** or
Eccl	12:14	For God will bring every **w**
Is	2: 8	They worship the **w** of their
Is	28:21	do His work, His awesome **w**,
Is	29:14	will again do a marvelous **w**
Is	64: 8	And all we are the **w** of
Jer	17:22	Sabbath day, nor do any **w**,
Mic	5:13	shall no more worship the **w**
Hab	1: 5	For I will work a **w** in
Hab	3: 2	revive Your **w** in the midst
Matt	21:28	**w** today in my vineyard.'
Matt	26:10	For she has done a good **w**
Mark	6: 5	Now He could do no mighty **w**
John	4:34	sent Me, and to finish His **w**.
John	6:28	that we may **w** the works of
John	6:29	This is the **w** of God, that
John	9: 4	I must **w** the works of Him who
John	9: 4	is coming when no one can **w**.
John	17: 4	I have finished the **w** which
Acts	5:38	for if this plan or this **w**

Rom 4: 5 But to him who does not **w**
Rom 7: 5 by the law were at **w** in our
Rom 8:28 we know that all things **w**
Rom 11: 6 work is no longer **w**.
Rom 14:20 Do not destroy the **w** of God
1Co 3:13 fire will test each one's **w**,
1Co 9: 1 Are you not my **w** in the
1Co 15:58 always abounding in the **w** of
2Co 9: 8 abundance for every good **w**.
Gal 6: 4 each one examine his own **w**,
Eph 4:12 of the saints for the **w** of
Phil 1: 6 He who has begun a good **w**
Phil 2:12 **w** out your own salvation
Col 1:10 fruitful in every good **w**
1Th 1: 3 without ceasing your **w** of
1Th 4:11 and to **w** with your own
2Th 2: 7 lawlessness is already at **w**;
2Th 2:17 you in every good word and **w**.
2Th 3:10 this: If anyone will not **w**,
2Th 3:12 Jesus Christ that they **w** in
1Ti 3: 1 bishop, he desires a good **w**.
2Ti 3:17 equipped for every good **w**.
2Ti 4: 5 do the **w** of an evangelist,
2Ti 4:18 me from every evil **w** and
Tit 3: 1 to be ready for every good **w**,
Heb 1:10 the heavens are the **w**
Heb 13:21 complete in every good **w** to
Jas 1: 4 patience have its perfect **w**,
Jas 1:25 hearer but a doer of the **w**,
1Pe 1:17 according to each one's **w**,
Rev 22:12 every one according to his **w**.

WORKED (see WORK)
Matt 20:12 These last men have **w** only
Gal 2: 8 (for He who **w** effectively in
Eph 1:20 which He **w** in Christ when He
Heb 11:33 **w** righteousness, obtained

WORKER (see WORK, WORKERS)
Eccl 3: 9 What profit has the **w** from
Matt 10:10 for a **w** is worthy of his
Rom 16: 9 our fellow **w** in Christ, and
Rom 16:21 Timothy, my fellow **w**,
2Ti 2:15 a **w** who does not need to be

WORKERS (see WORKER)
Ps 5: 5 You hate all **w** of iniquity.
1Co 3: 9 For we are God's fellow **w**;
1Co 12:29 Are all **w** of miracles?
2Co 6: 1 as **w** together with Him
Phil 4: 3 and the rest of my fellow **w**,
Col 4:11 are my only fellow **w** for

WORKING (see WORK)
Neh 4:22 our guard by night and a **w**
John 5:17 My Father has been **w** until
1Co 4:12 **w** with our own hands. Being
1Co 12:10 to another the **w** of miracles,
2Co 4:12 So then death is **w** in us, but
Gal 5: 6 but faith **w** through love.
Eph 1:19 according to the **w** of His
Eph 4:16 to the effective **w** by which
Eph 4:28 **w** with his hands what is
Col 2:12 Him through faith in the **w**
2Th 2: 9 one is according to the **w**
Heb 13:21 **w** in you what is well
Jas 2:22 Do you see that faith was **w**

WORKMAN (see WORK, WORKMANSHIP, WORKMEN)
Song 7: 1 of the hands of a skillful **w**.
Hos 8: 6 A **w** made it, and it is not

WORKMANSHIP (see WORKMAN)
Ex 31: 5 to work in all manner of **w**.
Eph 2:10 For we are His **w**,

WORKMEN (see WORKMAN)
2Ki 12:15 the money to be paid to **w**,

Is 44:11 would be ashamed; And the **w**,

WORKS (see WORK)
Deut 15:10 bless you in all your **w** and
1Ch 16:12 Remember His marvelous **w**
Neh 9:35 turn from their wicked **w**.
Job 37:14 and consider the wondrous **w**
Ps 8: 6 to have dominion over the **w**
Ps 9: 1 tell of all Your marvelous **w**.
Ps 66: 3 How awesome are Your **w**!
Ps 66: 5 Come and see the **w** of God;
Ps 78: 4 and His wonderful **w** that He
Ps 103:22 Bless the LORD, all His **w**,
Ps 104:24 how manifold are Your **w**! In
Ps 105: 2 Talk of all His wondrous **w**!
Ps 105: 5 Remember His marvelous **w**!
Ps 107: 8 And for His wonderful **w** to
Ps 139:14 made; Marvelous are Your **w**,
Ps 145:10 All Your **w** shall praise You,
Prov 8:22 Before His **w** of old.
Prov 31:13 And willingly with her
Prov 31:31 And let her own **w** praise
Eccl 1:14 I have seen all the **w** that
Dan 6:27 And He **w** signs and wonders
Matt 5:16 they may see your good **w**
Matt 11:21 For if the mighty **w** which
John 5:20 He will show Him greater **w**
John 6:28 that we may work the **w** of
John 9: 3 but that the **w** of God should
John 9: 4 I must work the **w** of Him who
John 11:47 For this Man **w** many signs.
John 14:11 Me for the sake of the **w**
John 14:12 the **w** that I do he will do
John 14:12 and greater **w** than these he
Acts 2:11 own tongues the wonderful **w**
Acts 26:20 to God, and do **w** befitting
Rom 4: 2 Abraham was justified by **w**,
Rom 4: 4 Now to him who **w**,
Rom 4: 6 righteousness apart from **w**:
Rom 9:11 not of **w** but of Him who
Rom 11: 6 then it is no longer of **w**;
Rom 13: 3 are not a terror to good **w**,
Rom 13:12 let us cast off the **w** of
1Co 12: 6 but it is the same God who **w**
1Co 12:11 one and the same Spirit **w**
Gal 2:16 in Christ and not by the **w**
Gal 5:19 Now the **w** of the flesh are
Eph 2: 2 the spirit who now **w** in the
Eph 2: 9 not of **w**, lest anyone
Eph 2:10 in Christ Jesus for good **w**,
Eph 3:20 to the power that **w** in us,
Eph 5:11 with the unfruitful **w** of
Phil 2:13 for it is God who **w** in you
1Ti 5:10 well reported for good **w**:
2Ti 1: 9 not according to our **w**,
2Ti 4:14 repay him according to his **w**.
Tit 2:14 people, zealous for good **w**.
Tit 3: 5 not by **w** of righteousness
Tit 3: 8 careful to maintain good **w**.
Heb 2: 7 set him over the **w** of
Heb 6: 1 of repentance from dead **w**
Heb 10:24 to stir up love and good **w**,
Jas 2:14 faith but does not have **w**?
Jas 2:18 me your faith without your **w**,
Jas 2:20 that faith without **w** is
1Jn 3: 8 that He might destroy the **w**
Rev 2: 2 "I know your **w**, your labor,
Rev 2:26 and keeps My **w** until the
Rev 15: 3 and marvelous are Your **w**,
Rev 20:13 each one according to his **w**.

WORLD (see FOREVER, WORLD'S, WORLDLY, WORLDS)
Ps 9: 8 He shall judge the **w** in
Ps 19: 4 words to the end of the **w**.
Ps 22:27 All the ends of the **w** Shall
Ps 24: 1 The **w** and those who dwell

Ps	50:12	For the **w** is Mine, and all
Ps	90: 2	formed the earth and the **w**,
Ps	96:13	He shall judge the **w** with
Ps	98: 7	The **w** and those who dwell
Is	23:17	all the kingdoms of the **w**
Matt	4: 8	all the kingdoms of the **w**
Matt	5:14	"You are the light of the **w**.
Matt	13:22	and the cares of this **w** and
Matt	13:35	the foundation of the **w**.
Matt	13:38	"The field is the **w**,
Matt	16:26	man if he gains the whole **w**,
Matt	25:34	from the foundation of the **w**:
Matt	26:13	is preached in the whole **w**,
Mark	16:15	Go into all the **w** and preach
John	1: 9	every man coming into the **w**.
John	1:10	and the **w** was made through
John	1:29	takes away the sin of the **w**!
John	3:16	For God so loved the **w** that
John	3:17	not send His Son into the **w**
John	3:17	the world to condemn the **w**,
John	3:19	light has come into the **w**,
John	4:42	Christ, the Savior of the **w**.
John	7: 7	The **w** cannot hate you, but it
John	8:12	"I am the light of the **w**.
John	9: 5	"As long as I am in the **w**,
John	12:25	who hates his life in this **w**
John	12:31	is the judgment of this **w**;
John	13: 1	His own who were in the **w**,
John	14:17	whom the **w** cannot receive,
John	14:27	not as the **w** gives do I give
John	14:30	for the ruler of this **w** is
John	15:19	therefore the **w** hates you.
John	16: 8	He will convict the **w** of
John	16:28	I leave the **w** and go to the
John	16:33	cheer, I have overcome the **w**.
John	17: 5	I had with You before the **w**
John	17:21	that the **w** may believe that
John	17:23	and that the **w** may know that
John	18:36	kingdom is not of this **w**.
John	21:25	I suppose that even then the **w**
Acts	3:21	holy prophets since the **w**
Acts	17: 6	who have turned the **w**
Acts	17:31	on which He will judge the **w**
Rom	1:20	since the creation of the **w**
Rom	5:12	one man sin entered the **w**,
Rom	10:18	to the ends of the **w**.
Rom	12: 2	not be conformed to this **w**,
Rom	16:25	kept secret since the **w**
1Co	1:20	foolish the wisdom of this **w**?
1Co	1:27	the weak things of the **w** to
1Co	2:12	not the spirit of the **w**,
1Co	3:19	For the wisdom of this **w** is
1Co	3:22	or the **w** or life or death,
1Co	6: 2	the saints will judge the **w**?
1Co	7:31	For the form of this **w** is
1Co	7:33	about the things of the **w**—
1Co	7:34	about the things of the **w**—
2Co	5:19	in Christ reconciling the **w**
Gal	6:14	to me, and I to the **w**.
Eph	2: 2	to the course of this **w**,
Eph	2:12	and without God in the **w**.
Phil	2:15	you shine as lights in the **w**,
Col	2: 8	basic principles of the **w**,
1Ti	1:15	Jesus came into the **w** to
1Ti	3:16	Believed on in the **w**,
1Ti	6: 7	brought nothing into this **w**,
2Ti	4:10	having loved this present **w**,
Heb	1: 6	the firstborn into the **w**,
Heb	9:26	the foundation of the **w**;
Heb	11: 7	by which he condemned the **w**
Heb	11:38	of whom the **w** was not worthy.
Jas	2: 5	chosen the poor of this **w**
Jas	3: 6	a **w** of iniquity. The tongue
Jas	4: 4	to be a friend of the **w**
2Pe	1: 4	that is in the **w** through

2Pe	2: 5	did not spare the ancient **w**,
1Jn	2: 2	but also for the whole **w**.
1Jn	2:15	Do not love the **w** or the
1Jn	2:17	And the **w** is passing away,
1Jn	4: 9	only begotten Son into the **w**,
1Jn	4:14	the Son as Savior of the **w**.
1Jn	5: 4	born of God overcomes the **w**.
Rev	11:15	The kingdoms of this **w** have
Rev	12: 9	who deceives the whole **w**;
Rev	13: 8	from the foundation of the **w**.

WORLD'S† (*see* WORLD)

1Jn	3:17	But whoever has this **w** goods,

WORLDLY† (*see* WORLD)

Tit	2:12	denying ungodliness and **w**

WORLDS† (*see* WORLD)

Heb	1: 2	whom also He made the **w**;
Heb	11: 3	we understand that the **w**

WORM (*see* WORMS)

Ps	22: 6	But I am a **w**, and no
Is	41:14	you **w** Jacob, You men of
Is	66:24	For their **w** does not die,
Jon	4: 7	next day God prepared a **w**,
Mark	9:44	Their **w** does not die,

WORMS (*see* WORM)

Acts	12:23	And he was eaten by **w** and

WORMWOOD

Prov	5: 4	the end she is bitter as **w**,
Lam	3:15	He has made me drink **w**.
Amos	5: 7	You who turn justice to **w**,
Amos	6:12	of righteousness into **w**,
Rev	8:11	The name of the star is **W**.

WORN (*see* WEAR)

Deut	29: 5	Your clothes have not **w** out

WORRIED (*see* WORRY)

Luke	10:41	you are **w** and troubled about

WORRY (*see* WORRIED, WORRYING)

Matt	6:25	do not **w** about your life,
Matt	6:34	for tomorrow will **w** about

WORRYING (*see* WORRY)

Matt	6:27	Which of you by **w** can add one

WORSHIP (*see* WORSHIPED, WORSHIPERS, WORSHIPS)

Gen	22: 5	and I will go yonder and **w**,
Ex	34:14	(for you shall **w** no other
Deut	11:16	and serve other gods and **w**
Ps	29: 2	**W** the LORD in the beauty
Ps	66: 4	All the earth shall **w** You
Ps	95: 6	let us **w** and bow down; Let
Ps	96: 9	**w** the LORD in the beauty of
Ps	97: 7	**W** Him, all you gods.
Ps	138: 2	I will **w** toward Your holy
Is	2: 8	They **w** the work of their
Jer	44:19	to **w** her, and pour out drink
Dan	3: 5	you shall fall down and **w**
Zeph	1: 5	Those who **w** the host of
Zech	14:16	go up from year to year to **w**
Zech	14:17	come up to Jerusalem to **w**
Matt	2: 2	the East and have come to **w**
Matt	4: 9	if You will fall down and **w**
Matt	4:10	You shall **w** the LORD
Matt	15: 9	And in vain they **w** Me,
John	4:20	place where one ought to **w**.
John	4:21	Jerusalem, **w** the Father.
John	4:22	You **w** what you do not know;
John	4:24	and those who **w** Him must
John	4:24	who worship Him must **w** in
Acts	8:27	had come to Jerusalem to **w**,
Acts	17:23	the objects of your **w**,
Acts	17:23	the One whom you **w** without
1Co	14:25	he will **w** God and report

Col 2:18 in false humility and **w** of
Heb 1: 6 the angels of God **w**
Rev 4:10 who sits on the throne and **w**
Rev 9:20 that they should not **w**
Rev 14: 7 and **w** Him who made heaven
Rev 14:11 who **w** the beast and his
Rev 22: 9 of this book. **W** God."

WORSHIPED (see WORSHIP)
1Ki 16:31 went and served Baal and **w**
2Ki 17:16 made a wooden image and **w**
Job 1:20 he fell to the ground and **w**.
Dan 3: 7 languages fell down and **w**
Matt 8: 2 a leper came and **w** Him,
Matt 9:18 a ruler came and **w** Him,
John 4:20 Our fathers **w** on this
Acts 17:25 Nor is He **w** with men's hands,
Rom 1:25 and **w** and served the
Rev 5:14 elders fell down and **w** Him
Rev 7:11 before the throne and **w** God,
Rev 13: 4 So they **w** the dragon who gave
Rev 13: 4 and they **w** the beast,

WORSHIPERS (see WORSHIP)
2Ki 10:19 intent of destroying the **w**
John 4:23 when the true **w** will worship
Acts 17:17 Jews and with the Gentile **w**,

WORSHIPS (see WORSHIP)
Is 44:15 he makes a god and **w** it;
Rev 14: 9 If anyone **w** the beast and his

WORTH (see WORTHLESS)
Prov 31:10 For her **w** is far above

WORTHLESS (see WORTH)
Job 13: 4 You are all **w** physicians.
Zech 11:17 Woe to the **w** shepherd, Who

WORTHY (see UNWORTHY)
Gen 32:10 I am not **w** of the least of
Ps 18: 3 who is **w** to be praised;
Matt 3: 8 Therefore bear fruits **w** of
Matt 3:11 whose sandals I am not **w** to
Matt 8: 8 I am not **w** that You should
Matt 10:10 for a worker is **w** of his
Matt 10:37 more than Me is not **w** of Me.
Luke 10: 7 for the laborer is **w** of his
Luke 15:19 and I am no longer **w** to be
Acts 5:41 that they were counted **w** to
Rom 8:18 this present time are not **w**
Eph 4: 1 beseech you to walk **w** of the
Col 1:10 that you may walk **w** of the
1Ti 1:15 is a faithful saying and **w**
1Ti 4: 9 is a faithful saying and **w**
1Ti 5:17 who rule well be counted **w**
1Ti 5:18 The laborer is **w** of his
Heb 11:38 of whom the world was not **w**.
Rev 3: 4 Me in white, for they are **w**.
Rev 4:11 "You are **w**, O Lord, To
Rev 5: 2 Who is **w** to open the scroll
Rev 5:12 **W** is the Lamb who was slain

WOUND (see WOUNDED, WOUNDING, WOUNDS)
Ex 21:25 **w** for wound, stripe for
Jer 15:18 my pain perpetual And my **w**
1Co 8:12 and **w** their weak conscience,

WOUNDED (see WOUND)
Is 53: 5 But He was **w** for our
Zech 13: 6 Those with which I was **w** in

WOUNDING† (see WOUND)
Gen 4:23 I have killed a man for **w**

WOUNDS (see WOUND)
Ps 147: 3 And binds up their **w**.
Prov 23:29 Who has **w** without cause?
Prov 27: 6 Faithful are the **w** of a
Is 1: 6 But **w** and bruises and

Mic 1: 9 For her **w** are incurable.
Zech 13: 6 What are these **w** between your
Luke 10:34 to him and bandaged his **w**,

WOVE (see WEAVE)
Judg 16:14 So she **w** it tightly with the

WOVEN (see WEAVE)
Ps 45:13 Her clothing is **w** with
John 19:23 **w** from the top in one piece.

WRAPPED
Jon 2: 5 Weeds were **w** around my
Matt 27:59 he **w** it in a clean linen
Luke 2: 7 and **w** Him in swaddling

WRATH (see WRATHFUL)
Deut 9: 8 you provoked the LORD to **w**,
Job 20:28 away in the day of His **w**.
Ps 2: 5 shall speak to them in His **w**,
Ps 2:12 When His **w** is kindled but a
Ps 21: 9 swallow them up in His **w**,
Ps 38: 1 do not rebuke me in Your **w**,
Ps 89:46 Will Your **w** burn like fire?
Ps 95:11 So I swore in My **w**,
Ps 124: 3 When their **w** was kindled
Prov 14:29 He who is slow to **w** has
Prov 15: 1 A soft answer turns away **w**,
Prov 29: 8 But wise men turn away **w**.
Lam 3: 1 by the rod of His **w**.
Hos 13:11 And took him away in My **w**.
Amos 1:11 And he kept his **w** forever.
Hab 3: 2 In **w** remember mercy.
Zeph 1:15 That day is a day of **w**,
Matt 3: 7 you to flee from the **w** to
John 3:36 but the **w** of God abides on
Rom 1:18 For the **w** of God is revealed
Rom 2: 5 wrath in the day of **w** and
Rom 4:15 the law brings about **w**;
Rom 5: 9 we shall be saved from **w**
Rom 9:22 the vessels of **w** prepared
Rom 12:19 but rather give place to **w**;
Rom 13: 4 an avenger to execute **w** on
2Co 12:20 jealousies, outbursts of **w**,
Gal 5:20 jealousies, outbursts of **w**,
Eph 2: 3 were by nature children of **w**,
Eph 4:26 the sun go down on your **w**,
Eph 4:31 Let all bitterness, **w**,
Eph 5: 6 of these things the **w** of
Eph 6: 4 provoke your children to **w**,
1Th 1:10 who delivers us from the **w**
1Th 2:16 but **w** has come upon them to
1Th 5: 9 God did not appoint us to **w**,
1Ti 2: 8 without **w** and doubting;
Heb 3:11 So I swore in My **w**,
Jas 1:19 slow to speak, slow to **w**;
Rev 6:16 on the throne and from the **w**
Rev 6:17 For the great day of His **w**
Rev 15: 7 golden bowls full of the **w**

WRATHFUL (see WRATH)
Prov 15:18 A **w** man stirs up strife,

WRESTLE† (see WRESTLED)
Eph 6:12 For we do not **w** against flesh

WRESTLED (see WRESTLE)
Gen 30: 8 great wrestlings I have **w**
Gen 32:25 hip was out of joint as He **w**

WRETCHED†
Rom 7:24 O **w** man that I am! Who will
Rev 3:17 do not know that you are **w**,

WRINKLE
Eph 5:27 not having spot or **w** or any

WRISTS
Gen 24:22 and two bracelets for her **w**

WRITE (see WRITER, WRITES, WRITING, WRITTEN, WROTE)
Ex   17:14 **W** this for a memorial in the
Deut   6: 9 You shall **w** them on the
Deut   11:20 And you shall **w** them on the
Deut   17:18 that he shall **w** for himself
Prov   3: 3 **W** them on the tablet of
Jer   22:30 **W** this man down as childless,
Jer   31:33 and **w** it on their hearts;
Jer   36:28 and **w** on it all the former
Ezek   24: 2 **w** down the name of the day,
Ezek   37:16 a stick for yourself and **w**
Hab   2: 2 **W** the vision And make it
Mark   10: 4 permitted a man to **w** a
Luke   1: 3 to **w** to you an orderly
Luke   16: 6 and sit down quickly and **w**
1Co   4:14 I do not **w** these things to
1Th   4: 9 no need that I should **w** to
Heb   8:10 in their mind and **w**
1Jn   1: 4 And these things we **w** to you
1Jn   2: 1 these things I **w** to you, so
1Jn   2: 8 a new commandment I **w** to
1Jn   2:12 I **w** to you, little children,
1Jn   2:13 I **w** to you, fathers,
2Jn   12 Having many things to **w** to
3Jn   13 but I do not wish to **w** to
Rev   1:11 **w** in a book and send it to
Rev   1:19 **W** the things which you have
Rev   2: 1 of the church of Ephesus **w**,
Rev   2: 8 of the church in Smyrna **w**,
Rev   3:12 And I will **w** on him My
Rev   14:13 heaven saying to me, "**W**:

WRITER (see WRITE)
Ps   45: 1 is the pen of a ready **w**.

WRITES (see WRITE)
Deut   24: 1 and he **w** her a certificate
Rom   10: 5 For Moses **w** about the

WRITING (see WRITE, WRITINGS)
2Ch   36:22 and also put it in **w**,
Ezra   1: 1 and also put it in **w**,
Dan   5: 8 they could not read the **w**,
Dan   6:10 when Daniel knew that the **w**
Luke   1:63 And he asked for a **w** tablet,
John   19:19 And the **w** was: JESUS OF
Phm   1:19 am **w** with my own hand. I

WRITINGS† (see WRITING)
John   5:47 if you do not believe his **w**,

WRITTEN (see WRITE)
Ex   31:18 **w** with the finger of God.
Ex   32:15 The tablets were **w** on both
Deut   29:21 of the covenant that are **w**
1Ki   14:29 are they not **w** in the book
Job   19:23 that my words were **w**! Oh,
Ps   40: 7 of the book it is **w** of me.
Prov   22:20 Have I not **w** to you
Eccl   12:10 and what was **w** was
Jer   36: 6 the scroll which you have **w**
Dan   5:24 Him, and this writing was **w**.
Dan   12: 1 Every one who is found **w** in
Matt   2: 5 for thus it is **w** by the
Matt   4: 4 answered and said, "It is **w**,
Matt   26:24 indeed goes just as it is **w**
Mark   15:26 of His accusation was **w**
Luke   10:20 because your names are **w** in
Luke   24:44 be fulfilled which were **w**
John   19:20 and it was **w** in Hebrew,
John   19:22 answered, "What I have **w**,
John   20:30 which are not **w** in this
John   20:31 but these are **w** that you may
John   21:25 the books that would be **w**.
Rom   1:17 faith to faith; as it is **w**,
Rom   2:15 show the work of the law **w**

Rom   2:27 even with your **w** code and
Rom   4:23 Now it was not **w** for his sake
Rom   15: 4 For whatever things were **w**
Rom   15: 4 were written before were **w**
Rom   15:15 I have **w** more boldly to you
1Co   10:11 and they were **w** for our
2Co   3: 2 You are our epistle **w** in our
2Co   3: 3 **w** not with ink but by the
Gal   6:11 what large letters I have **w**
Heb   10: 7 of the book it is **w**
Heb   13:22 for I have **w** to you in few
1Jn   2:14 I have **w** to you, fathers,
1Jn   2:14 I have **w** to you, young men,
1Jn   2:26 These things I have **w** to you
Rev   1: 3 those things which are **w** in
Rev   2:17 on the stone a new name **w**
Rev   5: 1 sat on the throne a scroll **w**
Rev   14: 1 having His Father's name **w**
Rev   20:12 by the things which were **w**
Rev   20:15 And anyone not found **w** in the
Rev   22:18 him the plagues that are **w**

WRONG (see WRONGED, WRONGFULLY)
Job   1:22 sin nor charge God with **w**.
Dan   6:22 I have done no **w** before
Luke   23:41 this Man has done nothing **w**.
1Co   6: 7 do you not rather accept **w**?

WRONGED (see WRONG)
Job   19: 6 Know then that God has **w** me,

WRONGFULLY (see WRONG)
1Pe   2:19 endures grief, suffering **w**.

WROTE (see WRITE)
Ex   24: 4 And Moses **w** all the words of
Ex   34:28 And He **w** on the tablets the
Deut   4:13 and He **w** them on two tablets
Deut   5:22 And He **w** them on two tablets
Deut   31: 9 So Moses **w** this law and
Deut   31:22 Therefore Moses **w** this song
1Sa   10:25 and **w** it in a book and laid
2Sa   11:14 it happened that David **w** a
2Ch   26:22 Isaiah the son of Amoz **w**.
Jer   36: 4 and Baruch **w** on a scroll of
Jer   36:18 and I **w** them with ink in
Dan   5: 5 the part of the hand that **w**.
Dan   6:25 Then King Darius **w**:
Luke   1:63 for a writing tablet, and **w**,
John   5:46 for he **w** about Me.
John   8: 6 Jesus stooped down and **w** on
Rom   16:22 who **w** this epistle, greet
1Co   7: 1 the things of which you **w**

WROUGHT
Ps   139:15 And skillfully **w** in the

Y

YAH (see GOD)
Ps   68: 4 the clouds, By His name **Y**,
Is   12: 2 and not be afraid; 'For **Y**,

YARN (see THREAD)
Judg   16: 9 bowstrings as a strand of **y**

YEA
Ps   19:10 are they than gold, **Y**,
Ps   23: 4 **Y**, though I walk

YEAR (see YEARLY, YEARS)
Gen   17:21 you at this set time next **y**.
Ex   12: 2 the first month of the **y** to
Ex   12: 5 a male of the first **y**.
Ex   23:17 Three times in the **y** all your
Lev   25: 5 for it is a **y** of rest for
Lev   25:10 consecrate the fiftieth **y**,

Lev	25:13	In this **Y** of Jubilee, each
Num	14:34	shall bear your guilt one **y**,
Deut	1: 3	to pass in the fortieth **y**,
Deut	15: 9	the **y** of release, is at
1Sa	2:19	bring it to him year by **y**
1Sa	13: 1	Saul reigned one **y**;
2Sa	11: 1	in the spring of the **y**,
2Ki	19:29	You shall eat this **y** such
2Ch	36:22	Now in the first **y** of Cyrus
Ezra	1: 1	Now in the first **y** of Cyrus
Ezra	7: 7	Jerusalem in the seventh **y**
Job	3: 6	among the days of the **y**,
Ps	65:11	You crown the **y** with Your
Is	6: 1	In the **y** that King Uzziah
Is	29: 1	David dwelt! Add year to **y**;
Is	61: 2	proclaim the acceptable **y**
Is	63: 4	And the **y** of My redeemed
Ezek	1: 1	to pass in the thirtieth **y**,
Ezek	4: 6	laid on you a day for each **y**.
Dan	1: 1	In the third **y** of the reign
Mic	6: 6	With calves a **y** old?
Luke	2:41	went to Jerusalem every **y**
Luke	4:19	the acceptable **y** of
John	11:49	being high priest that **y**,
Heb	9: 7	priest went alone once a **y**,

YEARLY (see YEAR)

1Sa	1: 3	man went up from his city **y**
1Sa	1:21	to offer to the LORD the **y**

YEARNED (see YEARNS)

Song	5: 4	And my heart **y** for him.

YEARNS (see YEARNED)

Job	19:27	How my heart **y** within me!

YEARS (see YEAR)

Gen	1:14	seasons, and for days and **y**;
Gen	5:27	hundred and sixty-nine **y**;
Gen	6: 3	be one hundred and twenty **y**.
Gen	12: 4	Abram was seventy-five **y**
Gen	15:13	afflict them four hundred **y**.
Gen	17:17	who is ninety **y** old, bear a
Gen	25: 8	an old man and full of **y**,
Gen	29:20	So Jacob served seven **y** for
Gen	31:41	been in your house twenty **y**;
Gen	37: 2	being seventeen **y** old, was
Gen	41:26	seven good cows are seven **y**,
Gen	41:26	good heads are seven **y**;
Gen	41:27	by the east wind are seven **y**
Gen	50:22	lived one hundred and ten **y**.
Ex	7: 7	And Moses was eighty **y** old
Ex	7: 7	old and Aaron eighty-three **y**
Ex	12:40	four hundred and thirty **y**.
Ex	16:35	of Israel ate manna forty **y**,
Ex	21: 2	he shall serve six **y**;
Ex	30:14	from twenty **y** old and above,
Lev	25: 8	seven times seven **y**;
Lev	25: 8	of the seven sabbaths of **y**
Lev	25: 8	shall be to you forty-nine **y**.
Lev	27: 3	is of a male from twenty **y**
Num	1: 3	from twenty **y** old and
Num	4: 3	from thirty **y** old and above,
Num	8:24	From twenty-five **y** old and
Num	8:25	and at the age of fifty **y**
Num	14:33	in the wilderness forty **y**,
Deut	31: 2	am one hundred and twenty **y**
Deut	31:10	the end of every seven **y**,
Josh	13: 1	was old, advanced in **y**.
Josh	24:29	one hundred and ten **y** old.
Judg	3:11	land had rest for forty **y**.
Judg	11:26	Arnon, for three hundred **y**,
Judg	16:31	had judged Israel twenty **y**.
2Sa	5: 4	David was thirty **y** old when
2Sa	5: 4	and he reigned forty **y**.
2Sa	24:13	Shall seven **y** of famine come
1Ki	1: 1	David was old, advanced in **y**;

1Ki	7: 1	But Solomon took thirteen **y**
1Ki	17: 1	not be dew nor rain these **y**,
1Ki	22: 1	Now three **y** passed without
2Ch	36:21	to fulfill seventy **y**.
Ezra	3: 8	the Levites from twenty **y**
Job	32: 6	said: "I am young in **y**,
Job	42:16	one hundred and forty **y**,
Ps	90: 4	For a thousand **y** in Your
Ps	90: 9	We finish our **y** like a
Ps	90:10	of our lives are seventy **y**;
Ps	90:10	strength they are eighty **y**,
Ps	95:10	For forty **y** I was grieved
Ps	102:27	And Your **y** will have no
Prov	4:10	And the **y** of your life will
Eccl	12: 1	And the **y** draw near when
Is	20: 3	naked and barefoot three **y**
Is	38: 5	add to your days fifteen **y**.
Jer	25:11	king of Babylon seventy **y**.
Jer	29:10	After seventy **y** are
Dan	1: 5	and three **y** of training for
Amos	1: 1	two **y** before the earthquake.
Hab	3: 2	In the midst of the **y** make
Matt	2:16	from two **y** old and under,
Mark	5:25	a flow of blood for twelve **y**,
Luke	1: 7	were both well advanced in **y**.
Luke	2:37	widow of about eighty-four **y**,
Luke	2:42	And when He was twelve **y** old,
Luke	3:23	at about thirty **y** of age,
John	2:20	It has taken forty-six **y** to
John	8:57	You are not yet fifty **y** old,
Acts	28:30	Then Paul dwelt two whole **y**
2Co	12: 2	man in Christ who fourteen **y**
Gal	1:18	Then after three **y** I went up
Heb	1:12	And Your **y** will not
Jas	5:17	on the land for three **y** and
Rev	20: 2	bound him for a thousand **y**;
Rev	20: 6	reign with Him a thousand **y**.

YESTERDAY

Ps	90: 4	in Your sight Are like **y**
Heb	13: 8	Jesus Christ is the same **y**,

YIELD (see YIELDED, YIELDING, YIELDS)

Gen	4:12	it shall no longer **y** its
Lev	25:19	Then the land will **y** its
Lev	26: 4	the land shall **y** its
2Ch	30: 8	but **y** yourselves to the
Hab	3:17	And the fields **y** no food;

YIELDED (see YIELD)

Num	11: 4	who were among them **y** to
Matt	13: 8	fell on good ground and **y** a
Matt	27:50	and **y** up His spirit.

YIELDING (see YIELD)

Rev	22: 2	each tree **y** its fruit every

YIELDS (see YIELD)

Gen	1:11	the herb that **y** seed, and
Heb	12:11	afterward it **y** the peaceable
Jas	3:12	Thus no spring **y** both salt

YOKE (see YOKED)

Num	19: 2	no defect and on which a **y**
Deut	21: 3	has not pulled with a **y**.
1Ki	12: 4	Your father made our **y** heavy;
1Ki	12:11	on you, I will add to your **y**;
1Ki	19:19	was plowing with twelve **y**
Is	9: 4	For You have broken the **y** of
Jer	27: 8	put its neck under the **y** of
Jer	28:14	I have put a **y** of iron on the
Matt	11:29	Take My **y** upon you and learn
Matt	11:30	For My **y** is easy and My
Gal	5: 1	be entangled again with a **y**

YOKED† (see YOKE)

1Sa	6: 7	cows which have never been **y**,
2Co	6:14	Do not be unequally **y**

YONDER†
Gen 22: 5 the lad and I will go **y** and

YOU-ARE-THE-GOD-WHO-SEES† (*see* GOD)
Gen 16:13 LORD who spoke to her, **Y**;

YOUNG (*see* YOUNGER, YOUNGEST, YOUTH)
Gen 4:23 Even a **y** man for hurting
Gen 15: 9 and a **y** pigeon."
2Sa 14:21 bring back the **y** man
2Sa 18:29 Is the **y** man Absalom safe?"
1Ki 12: 8 and consulted the **y** men who
1Ki 12:10 Then the **y** men who had grown
1Ki 12:14 to the advice of the **y** men,
Job 1:19 and it fell on the **y** people,
Ps 37:25 I have been **y**, and now am
Ps 84: 3 Where she may lay her **y**—
Ps 119: 9 How can a **y** man cleanse his
Ps 148:12 Both **y** men and maidens; Old
Prov 1: 4 To the **y** man knowledge and
Song 2: 9 is like a gazelle or a **y**
Is 11: 6 shall lie down with the **y**
Is 40:11 lead those who are with **y**.
Is 40:30 And the **y** men shall utterly
Ezek 23: 6 All of them desirable **y**
Dan 1: 4 **y** men in whom there was no
Joel 2:28 Your **y** men shall see
Matt 2: 9 and stood over where the **y**
Matt 2:20 for those who sought the **y**
Mark 16: 5 they saw a **y** man clothed in
Luke 2:24 of turtledoves or two **y**
Acts 2:17 Your **y** men shall see
Acts 7:58 clothes at the feet of a **y**
Acts 20: 9 in a window sat a certain **y**

YOUNGER (*see* YOUNG)
Gen 9:24 and knew what his **y** son had
Gen 19:35 And the **y** arose and lay with
Gen 25:23 the older shall serve the **y**.
Gen 29:26 to give the **y** before the
John 21:18 say to you, when you were **y**,
Rom 9:12 older shall serve the **y**.
1Ti 5: 1 **y** men as brothers,
1Pe 5: 5 Likewise you **y** people,

YOUNGEST (*see* YOUNG)
Gen 42:13 the **y** is with our father
Gen 42:15 this place unless your **y**
Gen 44: 2 mouth of the sack of the **y**,
1Sa 17:14 David was the **y**. And the

YOUTH (*see* YOUNG, YOUTHFUL, YOUTHS)
Gen 8:21 heart is evil from his **y**;
1Sa 17:42 him; for he was only a **y**,
1Ki 18:12 feared the LORD from my **y**.
Ps 25: 7 remember the sins of my **y**,
Ps 71: 5 are my trust from my **y**.
Ps 103: 5 So that your **y** is renewed
Ps 110: 3 You have the dew of Your **y**.
Prov 2:17 the companion of her **y**,
Prov 5:18 with the wife of your **y**.
Eccl 4:13 Better a poor and wise **y**
Eccl 12: 1 in the days of your **y**,
Jer 1: 6 cannot speak, for I am a **y**.
Jer 1: 7 "Do not say, 'I am a **y**,
Hos 2:15 As in the days of her **y**,
Mal 2:14 you and the wife of your **y**,
Matt 19:20 things I have kept from my **y**.
1Co 7:36 she is past the flower of **y**,
1Ti 4:12 Let no one despise your **y**,

YOUTHFUL (*see* YOUTH)
2Ti 2:22 Flee also **y** lusts; but pursue

YOUTHS (*see* YOUTH)
2Ki 2:24 mauled forty-two of the **y**.
Is 40:30 Even the **y** shall faint and

Z

ZACCHAEUS
Luke 19: 5 him, and said to him, "**Z**,

ZACHARIAS (*see* ZECHARIAH)
Luke 1: 5 a certain priest named **Z**,
Luke 3: 2 came to John the son of **Z**

ZADOK
2Sa 8:17 **Z** the son of Ahitub and
2Sa 15:29 Therefore **Z** and Abiathar
1Ki 1:39 Then **Z** the priest took a horn
Ezek 44:15 the Levites, the sons of **Z**,

ZALMUNNA
Judg 8:12 kings of Midian, Zebah and **Z**,
Ps 83:11 princes like Zebah and **Z**,

ZAPHNATH-PAANEAH†
Gen 41:45 called Joseph's name **Z**.

ZAREPHATH
1Ki 17: 9 "Arise, go to **Z**, which
Luke 4:26 was Elijah sent except to **Z**, which

ZEAL (*see* ZEALOT, ZEALOUS)
Ps 69: 9 Because **z** for Your house has
Is 59:17 And was clad with **z** as a
John 2:17 **Z** for Your house has
Rom 10: 2 witness that they have a **z**
2Co 7:11 vehement desire, what **z**,
Phil 3: 6 concerning **z**, persecuting
Col 4:13 that he has a great **z** for

ZEALOT† (*see* ZEAL)
Luke 6:15 and Simon called the **Z**;
Acts 1:13 of Alphaeus and Simon the **Z**;

ZEALOUS (*see* ZEAL, ZEALOUSLY)
1Ki 19:10 I have been very **z** for the
Acts 21:20 and they are all **z** for the
Acts 22: 3 and was **z** toward God as you
Tit 2:14 people, **z** for good works.
Rev 3:19 Therefore be **z** and repent.

ZEALOUSLY (*see* ZEALOUS)
2Ti 1:17 he sought me out very **z** and

ZEBAH
Judg 8:10 Now **Z** and Zalmunna were at
Judg 8:21 So Gideon arose and killed **Z**
Ps 83:11 all their princes like **Z** and

ZEBEDEE
Matt 4:21 James the son of **Z**,
Matt 4:21 in the boat with **Z** their
Matt 26:37 Peter and the two sons of **Z**,
Mark 10:35 and John, the sons of **Z**,

ZEBULUN
Gen 35:23 Levi, Judah, Issachar, and **Z**;
Is 9: 1 esteemed The land of **Z** and
Matt 4:15 The land of **Z** and the
Rev 7: 8 of the tribe of **Z** twelve

ZECHARIAH
2Ki 15: 8 **Z** the son of Jeroboam
Ezra 5: 1 the prophet Haggai and **Z**
Luke 11:51 of Abel to the blood of **Z**

ZEDEKIAH (*see* MATTANIAH)
2Ki 25: 7 eyes, put out the eyes of **Z**,
Jer 1: 3 of the eleventh year of **Z**
Jer 32: 5 then he shall lead **Z** to
Jer 37:18 Jeremiah said to King **Z**,
Jer 39: 5 pursued them and overtook **Z**
Jer 52: 3 Then **Z** rebelled against the

ZEEB
Judg 7:25 killed at the winepress of **Z**.

Ps 83:11 nobles like Oreb and like **Z**,

ZELOPHEHAD
Num 26:33 names of the daughters of **Z**

ZEPHANIAH
Zeph 1: 1 of the LORD which came to **Z**

ZERAH
Gen 38:30 And his name was called **Z**.
1Ch 2: 4 bore him Perez and **Z**.
2Ch 14: 9 Then **Z** the Ethiopian came
Matt 1: 3 Judah begot Perez and **Z** by

ZERUBBABEL (*see* SHESHBAZZAR)
Ezra 3: 2 and **Z** the son of Shealtiel
Hag 2: 4 'Yet now be strong, **Z**,
Hag 2:23 My servant, the son of
Zech 4:10 plumb line in the hand of **Z**.
Matt 1:12 and Shealtiel begot **Z**.

ZERUIAH
2Sa 2:13 And Joab the son of **Z**,
2Sa 2:18 Now the three sons of **Z** were
2Sa 18: 2 hand of Abishai the son of **Z**,

ZEUS
Acts 14:12 And Barnabas they called **Z**,
Acts 19:35 which fell down from **Z**?

ZIKLAG
1Sa 27: 6 So Achish gave him **Z** that
1Sa 30: 1 David and his men came to **Z**,

ZIMRI
1Ki 16:15 **Z** had reigned in Tirzah
2Ki 9:31 she said, "Is it peace, **Z**,

ZIN
Num 27:14 in the Wilderness of **Z**.

ZION
1Ki 8: 1 City of David, which is **Z**.
2Ki 19:21 virgin, the daughter of **Z**,
Ps 2: 6 King On My holy hill of **Z**.
Ps 14: 7 would come out of **Z**!
Ps 48: 2 Is Mount **Z** on the sides
Ps 50: 2 Out of **Z**, the perfection
Ps 51:18 in Your good pleasure to **Z**;
Ps 76: 2 And His dwelling place in **Z**.
Ps 97: 8 **Z** hears and is glad, And
Ps 99: 2 The LORD is great in **Z**,
Ps 125: 1 the LORD Are like Mount **Z**,
Ps 126: 1 back the captivity of **Z**,

Ps 129: 5 Let all those who hate **Z** Be
Song 3:11 Go forth, O daughters of **Z**,
Is 1: 8 So the daughter of **Z** is left
Is 2: 3 For out of **Z** shall go
Is 28:16 I lay in **Z** a stone for a
Is 37:22 virgin, the daughter of **Z**,
Is 51: 3 the LORD will comfort **Z**,
Is 51:11 And come to **Z** with singing,
Is 52: 8 the LORD brings back **Z**.
Is 59:20 Redeemer will come to **Z**,
Is 61: 3 console those who mourn in **Z**,
Jer 26:18 **Z** shall be plowed like a
Jer 51:10 and let us declare in **Z** the
Lam 5:11 ravished the women in **Z**,
Joel 2: 1 Blow the trumpet in **Z**,
Joel 3:16 LORD also will roar from **Z**,
Amos 1: 2 "The LORD roars from **Z**,
Amos 6: 1 you who are at ease in **Z**,
Mic 3:12 because of you **Z** shall be
Mic 4: 2 For out of **Z** the law
Zech 1:17 LORD will again comfort **Z**,
Zech 9: 9 O daughter of **Z**! Shout, O
Matt 21: 5 the daughter of **Z**,
Rom 9:33 I lay in **Z** a stumbling
Rom 11:26 will come out of **Z**,
Heb 12:22 But you have come to Mount **Z**
1Pe 2: 6 I lay in **Z** A chief

ZIPPOR
Num 22: 4 And Balak the son of **Z**

ZIPPORAH
Ex 4:25 Then **Z** took a sharp stone and
Ex 18: 2 Moses' father-in-law, took **Z**,

ZIV†
1Ki 6: 1 Israel, in the month of **Z**,
1Ki 6:37 was laid, in the month of **Z**.

ZOAN
Num 13:22 built seven years before **Z**
Ps 78:43 wonders in the field of **Z**;

ZOAR
Gen 19:23 the earth when Lot entered **Z**.

ZOPHAR
Job 2:11 and **Z** the Naamathite. For

ZORAH
Judg 13: 2 was a certain man from **Z**,
Judg 16:31 up and buried him between **Z**